Hoover Institution Bibliographies 53

Index Africanus

INDEX AFRICANUS

J. O. Asamani

Hoover Institution Press
Stanford University
Stanford, California

The Hoover Institution on War, Revolution and Peace, founded at Stanford University in 1919 by the late President Herbert Hoover, is a center for advanced study and research on public and international affairs in the twentieth century. The views expressed in its publications are entirely those of the authors and do not necessarily reflect the views of the staff, officers, or Board of Overseers of the Hoover Institution.

Library of Congress Cataloging in Publication Data

Asamani, J   O   1934-
   Index Africanus.

   (Hoover Institution bibliographies ; 53)
   Includes index.
   1. Africa--Bibliography. I. Title. II. Series: Stanford University. Hoover Institution on War, Revolution, and Peace. Bibliographical series ; 53.
Z3501.A73 [DT3]   016.96   76-187266
ISBN 0-8179-2531-7

Hoover Institution Bibliographies 53
International Standard Book Number 0-8179-2531-7
Library of Congress Catalog Card Number 76-187266
© 1975 by the Board of Trustees of the
   Leland Stanford Junior University
All rights reserved
Printed in the United States of America

Contents

Preface	ix
List of Sources	xi

AFRICA GENERAL

General	3
Agriculture	10
Anthropology. Folk-Lore	11
Art. Antiquities. Archaeology. Architecture. Music. Sculpture	15
Biography	20
Economics	22
Education	31
Geography. Topography. Travel	35
Government. Politics. Administration	37
History	49
Languages. Literature	55
Law	64
Religion	68
Science	73
Sociology	78

NORTH AFRICA

General	89
United Arab Republic	95
Sudan	100
Libya	120
Tunisia	122
Algeria	127

CENTRAL AFRICA

    Cameroun   243

    Chad   251

    Central African Republic   253

    Congo   254

    Gabon   256

    Zaire   257

    Rwanda. Burundi   288

    Spanish Guinea   290

EAST AFRICA

    General   295

    Ethiopia   307

    Somalia   316

    French Somaliland   319

    Kenya   319

    Tanzania   328

    Uganda   344

SOUTHERN AFRICA

    General   363

    Rhodesia   368

    Zambia   385

    Malawi   391

    Basutoland. Lesotho   397

    Bechuanaland   399

    Swaziland   400

    Republic of South Africa   401

NORTH AFRICA

    Morocco   130

    Spanish Sahara   135

    Ceuta, Melilla, Canary Islands   136

WEST AFRICA

    General   141

    French West Africa   153

    Mauritania   157

    Senegal   159

    Mali   164

    Guinea   168

    Ivory Coast   172

    Togoland   174

    Upper Volta   176

    Dahomey   178

    Niger   181

    Gambia   182

    Sierra Leone   183

    Ghana   188

    Nigeria   203

    Liberia   230

    Portuguese Guinea   233

    Cape Verde Islands   237

CENTRAL AFRICA

    General   241

    French Equatorial Africa   242

SOUTHERN AFRICA

    South West Africa   426

    Angola   427

    Mozambique   433

    Mauritius   444

    Malagassy   445

    Reunion   451

    Seychelles   451

    St. Helena   451

INDEX   453

Preface

Index Africanus is a catalogue of articles in Western languages dealing with Africa and published from 1885 to 1965 in periodicals, Festschriften or memorial volumes, symposia, and proceedings of congresses and conferences.

In a comparatively new field such as African studies, where scholars and facilities for publication are few, the periodical article is often likely to remain for many years the only authority available on a range of subjects. It is likely to contain much information which will not be incorporated in any monograph or standard reference book for many years, and much that may never see publication elsewhere at all. Some guide to published articles is therefore greatly needed. For this reason, the Library of the School of Oriental and African Studies (SOAS) at the University of London decided to compile an index to the principal periodical articles dealing with Africa.

Africa in this context includes not only Sub-Saharan Africa but the Saharan and Northern parts of the continent, with the exception, however, that Islamic culture has been excluded because it belongs to the domain of Index Islamicus.

The present Index contains articles published in journals concerned with Africa as a whole, as well as those dealing with individual regions or countries or disciplines. In addition, following Dr. Bradford's law of scattering, a large number of journals in various fields not dealing exclusively with Africa have been examined. As far as possible every article on an African topic published in these journals is listed in the present catalogue. Also included are select items of information, such as "communications," "notes," and the like. Editorial and news items are omitted, as are book reviews; however, review articles are normally included. All subjects are covered, but there is an emphasis on the humanities and the social sciences.

The compiler has included only entries that he has examined personally. In all, a little more than 200 periodical titles, some 20 Festschriften, and nearly 60 congress proceedings and other collective works were examined, yielding a total of some 23,000 articles.

There is no standard classification for Africa, and the compiler did not use any of the conventional published schemes. Classification has thus been pragmatic, following basically the subject headings in use at SOAS. The arrangement is primarily by geographical region subdivided by subject. A detailed subdivision of these subjects would have enhanced the catalogue's convenience to users, but time limitations made a more refined breakdown impossible. Each regional division may have some or all of the following subject subdivisions: General—libraries, bibliography, catalogues, congresses, societies, and institutions; agriculture; anthropology and folklore; art, antiquities, archaeology, architecture, music, and sculpture; biography; economics; education; geography, travel, and topography; government, politics, and administration; history; language and literature; religion; sciences; and sociology.

In a paper read to the Library Association's University and Research Section at Bristol in 1953, Mr. J. D. Pearson, former librarian of SOAS, declared: "I have already done a considerable amount of work on an index of Islam and I hope before I die to compile, or instigate others to compile, indexes to India, the rest of the Near East, and Africa." Index Africanus is the outcome of this instigation. Mr. Pearson's constant encouragement, more than any other factor, has been responsible for the completion of the Index. Besides, after the compiler's leave of absence from Cape Coast expired, Mr. Pearson filled many of the gaps in issues of periodicals which were not obtainable previously. (He also arranged for the publication of the work.) Mr. B. C. Bloomfield, Librarian of SOAS, and Mr. Malcolm McKee, Assistant Librarian in charge of the African section, have given useful advice and have checked some of the entries when time permitted.

Thanks are also offered to members of the academic staff of SOAS who showed interest in the work by their suggestions. They include Professor D. W. Arnott, Professor C. F. Beckingham, Professor P. H. Gulliver, Professor R. Oliver, Professor A. N. Tucker, Dr. B. W. Andrzejewski, Dr. H. J. Fisher, Dr. J. R. Gray, the late Dr. J. H. G. Lebon, Dr. Shula Marks, Dr. Joan E. M. Maw, and Dr. W. M. Warren.

Material for the work was collected mainly from the Library of SOAS, but occasional visits were made to the University of London Library and the Library of the Royal Commonwealth Society. To custodians of those libraries the compiler expresses his gratitude for granting him easy access to their collections.

Financial support for the work of compilation has come mainly from SOAS and from the Hoover Institution at Stanford University. The compiler is also grateful to his employer, the University of Cape Coast, Ghana, for granting him fifteen months' leave of absence to complete the Index.

The compiler owes a special debt of gratitude to his friend David Hall of the SOAS Library. His abundant kindness made life reasonably comfortable for the compiler during his stay in Britain.

J. O. ASAMANI

SOAS
London
November 1972

List of Sources

Periodicals

Abbia 1(1963) - 11 (1965)
Acta geogr.: Acta geographica 1(1947) - 58(1965) [Wants vols. 2, 5, 6].
Aequatoria 2 (1939) - 25 (1962)
Afr. affairs: African affairs 43 (1944) - 64 (1965); formerly Journal of the African Society
Afr. bull.: Africana bulletin 1 (1964) - 3 (1965).
Afr. ed.: Africa education 1, no. i (1963) - 2, nos. i-ii (1964)
Afr. et Asie: L'Afrique et l'Asie 1 (1948) - 72 (1965)
Afr. forum: African forum 1 (1965)
Afr. historian: The African historian 1 (1963) - 3 (1965)
Africa (Journal of the International African Institute) 1 (1928) - 34 (1965)
Africa (Rome) 10 (1955) - 20 (1965)
Afrika (Berlin) 1 (1942) - 3 (1944)
Afr. lang. stud.: African language studies 1 (1960 - (1965)
Afr. music: African music 1948 - 1964
Afr. notes: African notes 1 (1963) - 3 (1965)
Afro-Asian and w. aff.: Afro-Asian and world affairs 1 (1964) - 2 (1965)
Afr. quart.: Africa quarterly 1 (1961) - 5 (1965)
Afr. South: Africa South 1 (1956) - 6 (1961)
Afr. stud.: African studeis 1(1942) - 24 (1965); formerly Bantu studies
Afr. stud. bull.: African studies bulletin 1 (1958) - 7 (1964)
Afr. und Üb.: Afrika und Übersee see Zeitschrift für Kolonialsprachen
Afr. women: African women 1 (1954) - 5 (1963) continued as Women today 6, no.i (1963) - 6, no.v (1965)
Agricultural history 33 (1959) - 39 (1965)
Amer. anthr.: American anthropologist 1 (1899) - 67 (1965)
Amer. econ. rev.: American economic review 1 (1911) - 67 (1965)
Amer. hist. rev.: American historical review 1 (1895) - 71 (1965)
Am. j. phys. anthr.: American journal of physical anthropology 1 (1918) - 22 (1964)
Am. j. soc.: American journal of sociology 1 (1895) - 71 (1965)
Am. soc. rev.: American sociological review 1 (1936) - 30 (1965)
Annales afr.: Annales africaines 1954 - 1965
Ann. Ethiopie: Annales d'Ethiopie 3 (1959) - 6 (1965)
Ann. Univ. Abidjan: Annales de l'Université d'Abidjan 1 (1965)
Ann. Univ. Madag.: Annales de l'Université de Madagascar 1 (1963) - 4 (1965)
Anthr. quart.: Anthropological quarterly 23 (1950) - 38 (1965)
Applied statistics 1 (1952) - 14 (1965)
Arch. Inst. Est. Afr.: Archivos del Instituto de Estudios Africanos 1 (1947) - 77 (1965)
Archives 1 (1949) - 7 (1965)
Art quarterly 21 (1958) - 28 (1965)
Bantu stud.: Bantu studies 1 (1922) - 15 (1941); continued as African studies
BCGP: Boletim cultural da Guiné portuguesa 5 (1950) - 20 (1965)
BIHR: Bulletin of the Institute of Historical Research 1 (1923) - 38 (1965)
Bibliotheca afr.: Bibliotheca africana 1 (1924) - 4 (1931)
BO: Black Orpheus 1 (1957) - 18 (1965)
Bol. cult. Guiné prot.: Boletim cultural da Guiné portuguesa 5 (1950) - 20 (1965)
Bol. Inst. Angola: Boletim do Instituto de Angola 1 (1953 - 23 (1965)
Il BOLL.: Il bolletino 1 (1953) - 2 (1957)
BSEC: Bulletin de la Société d'Etudes Camerounaises 1935 - 48; continued as Etudes camerounaises 1949 - 58
BSEM: Boletim da Sociedade de Estudos de Macambique 72 (1951) - 145 (1965). [Wants nos. 33 - 40, 43]
Bull. Acad. malg.: Bulletin de l'Académie Malgache (3 (1916 - 17) - 17 (1934). [Wants 7, 16]

Bull. Afr. Stud. Assoc.: Bulletin of the African Studies Association of the United Kingdom 1 (1964) - 2 (1965)
Bull. Afr. stud. Canada: Bulletin of African studies in Canada 1 (1963) - 3 (1965)
Bulletin of the School of Oriental Studies 1 (1920) - 9 (1939); continued as Bulletin of the School of Oriental and African Studies 10 (1940) - 28 (1965)
Bul. I.E.C.: Bulletin de l'Institut d'Études Centrafricaines 1 (1945) - 19-20 (1960)
Bull. IFAN: Bulletin de l'Institut Francais d'Afrique Noire 1 (1939) - 15 (1953); superseded by its Bulletin Série B, sciences humaines 16 (1954) - 27 (1965)
Bull. Imp. Inst.: Bulletin of the Imperial Institute 1 (1903) - 46 (1948)
Bull. séances IRCB: Bulletin des séances, Institut Royal Colonial Belge 1 (1930) - 5 (1934)
Bull. SOAS: Bulletin of the School of Oriental and African Studies; see Bulletin of the School of Oriental Studies
Bull. Soc. Afr. Church Hist.: Bulletin of the Society for African Church History 1964 - 65
Bull. Soc. Hist. Maurice: Bulletin de la Société de l'Histoire de l'Ile Maurice 1 (1938) - 4 (1953)
Bull. Uganda Soc.: Bulletin of the Uganda Society 1 (1943) - 5 (1945)
Business history 1 (1958) - 7 (1965)
Business hist. rev.: Business history review 25 (1951) - 39 (1965)
Cah. et. afr.: Cahiers d'études africaines 1 (1960) - 5 (1965)
Cahiers d'histoire mondiale; see Journal of world history
Cah. int. sociol.: Cahiers internationaux de sociologie 37 (1964) - 38 (1965)
Camb. hist. j.: Cambridge historical journal 1 (1923) - 13 (1947); continued as Historical journal
Canadian hist. rev.: Canadian historical review 1 (1920) - 45 (1965)
Centre de Linguistique Appliquée de Dakar Nos. 1, 11, 13, 16, 18 - 19
Civilisations 1 (1951) - 14 (1964)
Comp. studs. soc. hist.: Comparative studies in society and history 1 (1958) - 8 (1965)
Congo 1920 - 1940
Contemp. rev.: Contemporary review 1 (1866) - 207 (1965)
Corona 1 (1949) - 14 (1962)
CT: Les cahiers de Tunisie 1 (1953) - 13 (1965)
Cuad. afr. or.: Cuadernos africanos y orientales; see Cuadernos de estudios africanos
Cuad. est. afr.: Cuadernos de estudios africanos; continued as Cuadernos africanos y orientales 1 (1946) - 40 (1957)
Current anthr.: Current anthropology 1 (1960) - 6 (1965)
E. Afr. ec. rev.: The East African economic review, NS 1 (1964-65)
EAISR: East African Institute of Social Research conference papers, 1952 - 65
Econ. bull. afr.: Economic bulletin for Africa 1 (1961) - 5 (1965)
Econ. development and cultural change: Economic development and cultural change 1 (1952-53) - 4 (1965)
Econ. j.: The economic journal 1 (1891) - 75 (1965)
Econometrica 1 (1933) - 33 (1965)
Economica NS 1 (1934) - NS 32 (1965)
Eng. hist. rey.: English history review 1 (1886) - 80 (1965)
Et. camer.: Etudes camerounaises; see Bulletin de la Société d'Etudes Camerounaises
Et. cong.: Études congolaises 1 (1961) - 8 (1965)
Et. dahom.: Études dahoméennes 1 (1948) - 22 (1959), N.S. 1 (1963) - N.S.5 (1965)
Et. eburn.: Études éburnéennes 2 (1951) - 8 (1960)
Et. guin.: Études guinéennes 1 (1947) - 13 (1955)
Ethnology 1 (1962) - 4 (1965)
Et. seneg.: Études sénégalaises 1 (1949) - 9, fascs. i-iii, v, vi, ix (1960-65)
Et. volt.: Études voltaïques 1 (1950) - 5 (1964)
Foreign affairs 1 (1922) - 44 (1965)
Foundations of language 1 (1965)

Genève-Afr.: Genève-Afrique; acta africana 1 (1962) - 4 (1965)
Geog. rev.: The geographical review 1 (1916) - 55 (1965)
Ghana bull. theorl.: Ghana bulletin of theology 2, nos. 8 - 10 (1965)
Ghana library j.: Ghana library journal 1 (1963-64)
Ghana med. j.: Ghana medical journal 1 (1962) - 4 (1965)
Ghana notes: Ghana notes and queries 1 (1961) - 7 (1965)
Gold Coast rev.: Gold Coast review 1 (1925) - 5 (1931)
Hist. educ. j.: History of education joural 1 (1949) - 9 (1958)
Hist. educ. quart.: History of education quarterly 1 (1961) - 5 (1965)
Historical j.: Historical journal 1 (1958) - 8 (1965); formerly Cambridge historical journal
History 1 (1916) - 50 (1965)
History of religions 1 (1961) - 5 (1965)
History today 1 (1951) - 15 (1965)
IMF staff papers: International Monetary Fund. Staff papers, 1950 - 1965
Internat. affairs: International affairs 1 (1922) - 41 (1965)
Internat. j. comp. sociol.: International journal of comparative sociology 1 (1960) - 6 (1965)
Int. rev. missions: International review of missions 1 (1912) - 54 (1965)
Int. soc. sc. bull.: International social science bulletin 1 (1949) - 10 (1958); continued as International social science journal
Int. soc. sc. j.: International social science journal 12 (1960) - 17 (1965); formerly International social science bulletin. [Wants 11]
J. Afr. adm.: Journal of African administration 1 (1949) - 13 (1961)
J. Afr. hist.: Journal of African history 1 (1960) - 6 (1965)
J. Afr. langs.: Journal of African languages 1(1962) - 4 (1965)
J. Afr. law: Journal of African law 1 (1957) - 9 (1965)
J. Afr. Soc.: Journal of the African Society 1 (1901) - 33 (1934)
J. Comm. Market studs.: Journal of Common Market studies 1 (1962-63) - 4 (1965)
J. Comm. pol. studs.: Journal of Commonwealth political studies 1 (1961) - 3 (1965)
J. development studs.: Journal of development studies 1 (1964) - 2 (1965)
J. econ. hist.: Journal of economic history 1 (1941) - 25 (1965)
J. Ethiop. law: Journal of Ethiopian law 1 (1964) - 2 (1965)
J. Ethiop. studs.: Journal of Ethiopian studies 1 (1963) - 3 (1965)
J. Int. Comm. Jurists: Journal of the International Commission of Jurists 1 (1957) - 6 (1965)
J. Hist. Soc. Nig.: Journal of the Historical Society of Nigeria 1 (1956) - 3 (1965)
J. ind. econ.: Journal of industrial economics 1 (1952) - 14 (1965)
J. local adm. ov.: Journal of local administration overseas 1 (1962) - 4 (1965)
J. Methodist Hist. Soc. of S. Afr.: The journal of the Methodist Historical Society of South Africa 1 (1952) - 2 (1957)
JMAS: Journal of modern African studies 1 (1963) - 3 (1965)
J. mod. Afr. studs.: Journal of modern African studies 1 (1963) - 3 (1965)
J. mod. hist.: Journal of modern history 1 (1929) - 37 (1965)
J. of gen. educ.: Journal of general education 1 (1946) - 17 (1965)
J. of Linguistics: Journal of linguistics 1 (1965)
Journal of documentation 1 (1945) - 21 (1965)
Journal of the Royal African Society; see Journal of the African Society
Journal of transport history 1 (1953) - 6 (1964)
Journal of tropical geography; see Malayan journal of tropical geography
J. polit. econ.: Journal of political economy 55 (1947) - 73 (1965)
JRAI: Journal of the Royal Anthropological Institute 1 (1871) - 95 (1965)
J. Seychelles Soc.: Journal of the Seychelles Society 1 (1961) - 4 (1965)
J. Soc. Afr.: Journal de la Société des Africanistes 1 (1931) - 35 (1965)
J. W. Afr. langs.: Journal of West African languages 1 (1964) - 2 (1965)
J. world hist.: Journal of world history; or Cahiers d'histoire mondiale 1 (1953) - 9, no. ii (1965)
Kano studies 1 (1965)
Kongo-Overzee 1 (1934) - 25 (1959)
Language 1 (1925) - 40 (1964)
Language and speech 1 (1958) - 8 (1965)
Lesotho 1 (1959) - 4 (1963-64)
Liberia bull.: Liberia bulletin 1 (1892) - 34 (1909)
Libia 1 (1953) - 4 (1956)
Libri 1 (1950) - 15 (1965)
Lingua 1 (1947) - 15 (1965)
LLJ: Liberia law journal 1 (1965)

Lloyds Bank review 1 (1946) - 78 (1965)
Makerere j.: Makerere journal 1 (1958) - 11 (1965)
Malayan j. tr. geog.: Malayan journal of tropical geography 1 (1953) - 10 (1957); continued as Journal of tropical geography 11 (1958) - 19 (1964)
Manchester School of Economic and Social Studies 1 (1930) - 33 (1965)
MISM: Mémoires de l'Institut Scientifuge de Madagascar 1 (1952) - 9 (1959)
NADA 1 (1923) - 9 (1965). [Wants 20]
Nigerian field 1 (1932) - 30 (1965)
Nigerian libs.: Nigerian libraries 1 (1964-65)
Nig. goegr. j.: Nigerian geographical journal 1 (1957) - 4(1961)
NISER: Nigerian Institute of Social and Economic Research; see West African Institute of Social and Economic Research
NJESS: Nigerian journal of economic and social studies; see West African Institute of Social and Economic Research
NLJ: Nigerian law journal 1, no. i (1964) - 1, no. ii (1965)
Numen 1 (1954) - 12 (1965)
Nyasa. j.: Nyasaland journal 1 (1948) - 18 (1965)
Odu 1 (1955) - 8 (1960), N.S. 1 (1964) - 2 (1965)
Oxford economic papers N.S. 1 (1949) - N.S. 16 (1964)
Past and present 1 (1952) - 32 (1965)
Port em Afr.: Portugal em Africa 1 (1944) - 22 (1965)
PRCI: Proceedings. Royal Colonial Institute 1 (1869-70) - 40 (1909)
Présence afr.: Présence africaine 1 (1947) - 16 (1954), N.S. 1 (1955) - N.S. 56 (1965). [Wants 5, 12]
QBSAL: Quarterly bulletin of the South African Library 1 (1946) - 20 (1965). [Wants 17 - 18]
Quarterly journal of economics 1 (1886) - 79 (1965)
Race 1 (1959) - 7 (1965)
Race relations 1 (1933) - 17 (1950); continues as Race relations journal 17 (1950) - 23 (1956)
Rass. studi etiop.: Rassegna di studi etiopici 1 (1941) - 21 (1965)
Rech. afr.: Recherches africaines 1959 - 1964
Rech. et. cam.: Recherches et études camerounaises 1 (1960) - 9 (1965)
Religious studies 1 (1965)
Res. bull. Centre Aragic Doc. Ibadan: Research bulletin. Centre of Arabic Documentation, University of Ibadan 1 (1964-65)
Rev. franc. hist. outre-mer: Revue francaise d'histoire d'Outre-mer; see Revue de l'histoire des colonies francaises (RHCF)
Rev. hist. col.: Revue de l'histoire des colonies; see Revue de l'histoire des colonies francaises (RHCF)
Review of economic statistics; continued as Review of economics and statistics 1 (1919) - 47 (1965)
Rev. juridique de Madagascar: Revue juridique de Madagascar 1 (1951)
Rev. tun. droit: Revue tunisienne de droit 1 (1953) - 6 (1958)
Rev. tun. sc. soc.: Revue tunisienne des sciences sociales 1 (1954) - 4 (1965)
RHCF: Revue de l'histoire des colonies francaises 1913 - 37; continued as Revue d'histoire des colonies 1938 - 58; continued as Revue francaise d'histoire d'Outre-mer (1959 - 1965)
Rhodesiana 1 (1956) - 13 (1965)
Rhodes - Liv. j.: Rhodes - Livingstone journal 1 (1944) - 38 (1965)
RJPUF: Revue juridique et politique de l'Union Francaise 2 (1948) - 12 (1958)
RLJ: Rhodesia law journal; see Rhodesia and Nyasaland law journal (RNLJ)
RNLJ: Rhodesia and Nyasaland law journal; continued as Rhodesia law journal 1 (1961) - 5 (1965)
Royal Col. Inst. pr.: Royal Colonial Institute proceedings 1 (1869 - 70) - 40 (1909)
Scandinavian economic history review 1 (1953) - 13 (1965)
Scottish historical review 1 (1904) - 44 (1965)
Sierra L. bull. rel.: Sierra Leone bulletin of religion 1, no. 2 (1959) - 7 (1965)
Sierra Leone Geographical Association bulletin 7 (1964) - 9 (1965)
Sierra Leone lang. rev.: Sierra Leone language review 1 (1962) - 4 (1965)
Sierra Leone stud.: Sierra Leone studies 1 (1953) - 17 (1963)
Soc. and econ. studs.: Social and economic studies 1 (1953) - 14 (1965)
Sociological review 1 (1908) - 20 (1928)
Sociologus 1 (1951) - 15 (1965)
Somaliland journal 1 (1954 - 55)
Southwestern j. anthr.: Southwestern journal of anthropology 1 (1945) - 20 (1964)
St. Antony's papers 1 (1956) - 17 (1965)
Studia linguistica 1 (1947) - 19 (1965)
Tang. notes: Tanganyika notes and records 1 (1936) - 64 (1965)
Tarikh 1, no. i (1965)
Transition 1 (1961) - 23 (1965)

Trans. Philological Soc.: Transactions of the Philological
    Society 1911 - 1965
Tr. Hist. Soc. Ghana: Transactions of the Historical Society
    of Ghana 1 (1952 - 55) - 8 (1965); formerly Transactions
    of the Gold Coast and Togoland Historical Society
TRHS: Transactions of the Royal Historical Society N.S.1
    (1883) - 5th. series 15 (1965)
Tristan da Cunha newsletter 1 (1930) - 25 (1960)
Uganda journal 1 (1934) - 29 (1965)
UGLJ: University of Ghana law journal 1 (1964) - 2 (1965)
Unesco bull. libs.: UNESCO bulletin for libraries 1 (1947) -
    19 (1965)
Univ. Birm. hist. j.: University of Birmingham history journal
    1 (1947) - 10 (1965)
Universitas 1953 - 1962
Univ. Ghana res. rev.: University of Ghana Institute of
    African Studies research review 1 - 2 (1965)
WAISER: West African Institute of Social and Economic Research.
    Proceedings of annual conference 1952 - 56 (1, i; 2, i; 3,
    i; wants 4); continued as Nigerian Institute of Social and
    Economic Research. Superseded by Nigerian journal of
    economic and social studies 1959 - 1965
WASU, the journal of the West African Students Union of Great
    Britain 1 (1926) - 5 (1927)
West Africa military medical bulletin 1 (1942) - 3 (1945)
Women today 6, no. i (1963) - 6, no. v (1965); formerly
    African women 1 (1954) - 5 (1963)
Word 1 (1945) - 19 (1963)
World politics 1 (1948) - 17 (1965)
Yearbook of world affairs 1 (1947) - 19 (1965)
Yorkshire bulletin of economic and social research 1 (1948) -
    16 (1964)
Zaire 1 (1947) - 15 (1961)
ZAOS: Zeitschrift für afrikanische und oceanische Sprachen
    1 (1895) - 5 (1900)
ZAS: Zeitschrift für afrikanische Sprachen 1 (1887 - 1888)
Zeitschrift für Kolonialsprachen 1 (1910) - 35 (1949 - 50);
    continued as Afrika und Übersee 36 (1951) - 48 (1964-65)

ERRATA

Pages vi and vii should be reversed.

The material below is to follow p. xiii.

(ii) Festschriften

The Bible and the Ancient Near East: essays in honor of William Foxwell ALBRIGHT. Ed. by G. Ernest Wright. London, 1961.
Mémorial André BASSET (1895-1956). Paris, 1957.
Mélanges René BASSET. 2 vols. Paris, 1923-25.
Das Laienapostolat in den Missionen Festschrift Prof. Dr. Johannes BECKMANN. Hrsg. Johann Specker, Walbert Bühlmann. Schöneck-Beckenried, 1961.
Homages à Joseph BIDEZ et à Franz CUMONT. Bruxelles, 1949.
Festschrift Alfred BUHLER. Hrsg. von Carl A. Schmitz und Robert Wildhaber. Basel, 1965.
Basileia Walter FREYTAG. Hrsg. von Jan Hermelink und Hans Jochen Margull. Stuttgart, 1959.
Professor GHURYE felicitation volume. Ed. K. M. Kopadia. Bombay, 1954.
Festschrift Eduard HAHN zum LX. Geburtstag dargebracht von Freunden und Schulern. Stuttgart, 1917.
Evolution und Hominisation. Festschrift zum 60. Geburtstag von Gerhard HEBERER. Hrsg. von Gottfried Kurth. Stuttgart, 1962.
Mélanges offerts á M. Nicolas IORGA par ses amis de France et des pays de langue française. Paris, 1933.
Festschrift für Ad. E. JENSEN. Hrsg. von Eike Haberland, Meinhard Schuster und Helmut Straube. 2 vols. München, 1964.
Custom is king. Essays presented to R. R. MARETT. Ed. L. H. Dudley Buxton. London, 1936.
The seed of wisdom. Essays in honor of T. J. MEEK. Ed. W. S. McCullough. Toronto, 1964.
Festschrift MEINHOF. Sprachwissenschaftliche und andere Studien. Hamburg, 1927.
Koloniale Studien. Hans MEYER zum siebzigsten Geburtstage. Berlin, 1928.
Essays in geography for Austin MILLER. Eds. J. H. Wittow and P. D. Wood. Reading, 1965.
The emerging world. Jawaharlal NEHRU memorial volume. London, 1964.
Culture in history. Essays in honor of Paul RADIN. Ed. Stanley Diamond. New York, 1960.
Essays presented to C. G. SELIGMAN. Eds. E. E. Evans-Pritchard, Raymond Firth, Bronislaw Malinowski and Isaac Schapera. London, 1934.

(iii) Congress Proceedings and Other Collective Works

Africa: the dynamics of change. Conference on representative government and national progress organized by the Congress for Cultural Freedom, held at Ibadan, 1959. Eds. H. Passin and K.A.B. Jones-Quartey. Ibadan, 1963.
African agrarian systems, Second International African Seminar, Lovanium University, Leopoldville, 1960. Ed. Daniel Biebuyck. London, 1963.
African conference on the rule of law, Lagos, 1961. Geneve, 1961.
African law: adaptation and development. Eds. Hilda Kuper and Leo Kuper. Berkeley and Los Angeles, 1965.
African literature and the universities (a conference held at Dakar University and Fourah Bay College, 1963). Ed. Gerald Moore. Ibadan, 1965.
African political systems. Eds. M. Fortes and E. E. Evans-Pritchard. London, 1940.
African primary products and international trade. Papers delivered at an international seminar in the University of Edinburgh, September 1964. Eds. I. G. Stewart and H. W. Ord. Edinburgh, 1965.
African systems of kinship and marriage. Eds. A. R. Radcliffe-Brown and Daryll Forde. London, 1950.
African systems of thought, Third International African Seminar in Salisbury, 1960. London, 1965.
Anthropology and Africa today. Conference held by the New York Academy of Sciences in May 1961 in Annals of the New York Academy of Sciences, 96 (1962), pp. 491-680.
Ashanti research project. First conference, May 1963. Legon, 1964.
Boston University papers in African history. Ed. Jeffrey Butler 1(1964).

Le Canada et les Pays Africains Francophones. Rapport de la Conférence régionale tenne à Montreal, 1965.
Catholic education in the service of Africa. Report of the Pan-African Catholic Education Conference. Leopoldville, 1965.
Changing law in developing countries. Ed J.N.D. Anderson. (Studies on modern Asia and Africa, no. 2) London, 1963.
Christian literature for the Bantu of Southern Africa. Report of the Conference on Christian literature for the Bantu of Southern Africa, Johannesburg, 1956. Johannesburg, 1957.
The Church in changing Africa. Report of the All-African Church conference held at Ibadan, 1958. New York.
Commonwealth and Empire law conference 1 (1955) - 2 (1960).
Commonwealth perspectives. Duke University Commonwealth-Studies Centre Publications, no. 8. Ed. Nicholas Mansergh and others. London, 1958.
Congrès international des sciences anthropologiques et ethnologiques 1 (1934) - 4 (1952, 6 (1960).
Congrès international d'histoire des religions 1 (1900) - 9 (1958) [Wants 6, 7]
Congress of the universities of the Empire 1 (1912) - 5 (1936) [Wants 4]; continued as Congress of the universities of the Commonwealth 6 (1948) - 9 (1963).
La cooperazione internazionale in Africa. Atti Convegno di studi tenuto a Mogadiscio dal 14 al 16 gennaio 1960. Milano, 1960.
Desert research. Proceedings, international symposium held in Jerusalem, May, 1952. Jerusalem, 1953.
Discovering Africa's past (Uganda Museum occasional paper, 4) Kampala, 1959.
East African Institute of Social Research conference, papers, 1952-1965.
Economic development for Africa South of the Sahara. Proceedings of a conference held by the International Economic Association. Ed. E. A. G. Robinson. London, 1965.
Economic development in Africa. Papers presented to the Nyasaland economic symposium held in Blantyre 18 to 28 July 1962. Ed. E. F. Jackson. Oxford, 1965.
The family estate in Africa. Studies in the role of property in family structure and lineage continuity. Eds. Robert F. Gray and P. H. Gulliver. London, 1964.
Food and society in the Sudan, being the proceedings of the 1953 annual conference of the Philosophical Society of the Sudan. Khartoum, 1955.
The future of customary law in Africa. Symposium-Colloque Amsterdam 1955. Leiden, 1956.
Geographers and the tropics: Liverpool essays. Eds. R. W. Steel and R. M. Prothero. London, 1964.
Les grandes voies maritimes dans le monde XVe-XIXe siecles. Rapports présentés au XIIe congres international des sciences historiques. VIIe colloque, Vienne, 1965. Paris, 1965.
History of the Pan-African Congress. Ed. George Padmore. London, 1947.
Human factors of productivity in Africa: absenteeism and labor turnover. Sixth inter-African labor conference, Abidjan, 1961. CCTA, 1962.
International Congress of Linguists 1 (1928) - 9 (1962) [Wants 3 (1933)].
International Congress of Phonetic Sciences 1 (1932) - 5 (1964).
Inter-university cooperation in West Africa. International seminar sponsored by the Congress for Cultural Freedom and the University College of Sierra Leone, Fourah Bay College. Freetown, 1961.
Land tenure. Eds. Kenneth H. Parsons, Raymond J. Penn, and Philip M. Raup. Proceedings of the International conference on land tenure and related problems in world agriculture held at Madison, Wisconsin, 1951.
Language in Africa. Papers of the Leverhulme Conference on universities and the language problems of Tropical Africa, held at University College, Ibadan. Ed. John Spencer. Cambridge, 1963.
Malnutrition in African mothers, infants and young children. Report of the second inter-African (CCTA) conference on nutrition, Gambia 1952. London, 1954.

Man and Africa. A Ciba Foundation symposium jointly with the Haile Sellassie I Prize Trust. Eds. Gordon Wolstenholme and Maeve O'Connor. London, 1965.

New forces in Africa (Record of a colloquium on Africa held at Georgetown University). Ed. William H. Lewis. Washington, 1962.

Pan-Africanism reconsidered (Third annual conference of the American Society of African Culture, held in Philadelphia, June, 1960). Los Angeles, 1962.

The politics of the developing areas. Eds. Gabriel A. Almond, James S. Coleman. Princeton, 1960.

Problems of economic development in East Africa. Ten papers on economic planning, manpower utilization and regional development (Contemporary African monographs series, no. 2). Nairobi, 1965.

Proceedings of the East African Academy. Second symposium, 1964. Ed. W. B. Banage. Nairobi, 1966.

The proceedings of the first International Congress of Africanists. Accra, 1962. Eds. Lalage Bown and Michael Growder. London, 1964.

Proceedings of the Graduate Academy of the University of California 1 (1963) - 3 (1965).

Proceedings of the Pan-African Congress on pre-history. 1 (1947) - 5 (1965).

Proceedings of the symposium on the granites of West Africa. Unesco, 1965.

La rédaction des coutumes dans le passe et dans le present. Colloque organisé par le Centre d'Histoire et d'Ethnologie juridiques, 1960. Bruxelles, 1962.

Les religions africaines traditionnelles. Rencontres internationales de Bouaké. Paris, 1965.

Studies in the laws of succession in Nigeria. Ed. J. D. M. Derrett. London, 1965.

Towards a literate Africa. Report of a conference held under the auspices of the International Committee on Christian literature for Africa and the Colonial Department of the University of London Institute of Education, December, 1947. Eds. L. J. Lewis, Margaret Wrong. London, 1948.

Tribes without rulers: studies in African segmentary systems. Eds. John Middleton and David Tait. London, 1958.

The United Nations and the emerging African nations. The second annual Governor's conference on the United Nations. Milwaukee, Wisconsin, 1961.

The West African intellectual community. International seminar on inter-university cooperation in West Africa, held in Freetown, 1961. Ibadan. See Inter-university cooperation in West Africa.

What are the problems of parliamentary government in West Africa? The report of a conference held by the Hansard Society for Parliamentary Government, at Oxford, 1957, under the chairmanship of Geoffrey de Freitas. London, 1958.

Africa: General

GENERAL

African Studies

1 BERTOLA, A. Per il programma di un corso di storia e istituzioni dei paesi afro-asiatici. AFRICA (Rome) 18 (1963), pp. 263-268.

2 BRASIO, A. Os Estudantes do Império em Portugal. PORT. EM AFR. 7 (1950), pp. 145-151.

3 BULCK, G. VAN. Comment faire concorder entre elles les synthèses, récentes des africanistes préhistoriens, ethnologues, linguistes et historiens? CONG. INT. SC. ANTH. ET ETHN. 6, i (1960), pp. 329-335.

4 CANHAM, P. H. Social science research. CORONA 1, no. 3 (1949), pp. 14-17.

5 COHEN, R. Afro-Asian studies in Canada. BULL. AFR. STUD. CANADA 1, no. 1 (1963), pp. 5-29.

6 COLE, T. African studies and training in West Germany. AFR. STUD. BULL. 6, no. i (1963), pp. 14-21.

7 COLEMAN, J. S. Research on Africa in European centers. AFR. STUD. BULL. 2, no. iii (1959), pp. 1-33.

8 CONSIGLIO, G. Il contributo dell'iniziativa privata ai rapporti tra l'Europa e l'Africa. [Convegno del gruppo nazionale del C.E.P.E.S., aprile, 1954.] AFRICA (Rome) 10 (1955), pp. 201-202.

9 COSTANZO-BECCARIA, G. A. New developments in African studies in Italy. BULL. AFR. STUD. ASSOC. 6 (1965), pp. 23-24.

10 COUPLAND, R. The Hailey survey. AFRICA 12 (1939), pp. 1-10.

11 DIKE, K. O. The importance of African studies. PROC. INT. CONG. AFR. 1 (1962), pp. 19-28.

12 ESSER, J. La recherche scientifique dans la Colonie. AEQUATORIA 11 (1948), p. 147.

13 FLETCHER, J. L. A note on government sponsored African programs at Boston University. AFR. STUD. BULL. 7, no. ii (1964), pp. 13-14.

14 FODERARO, S. L'Africa e gli studi universitari in Italia. AFRICA (Rome) 14 (1959), pp. 115-116.

15 FODERARO, S. La collaborazione degli enti africanisti europei negli studi e nelle ricerche sul continente africano. COOPERAZIONE INT. AFR., 1960, pp. 228-236.

16 FORDE, D. African studies in the Soviet Union. BULL. AFR. STUD. ASSOC. 4 (1965), pp. 17-18.

17 FORDE, D. Tropical African studies: a report on the conference organized by the International African Institute in conjunction with the University of Ibadan, 5-11 April, 1964. AFRICA 35 (1965), pp. 30-95.

18 FREDERICKS, W. The department of African studies, University of New Delhi. AFR. STUD. BULL. 3, no. ii (1960), pp. 16-18.

19 GIGLIO, C. Le discipline africanistiche orientalistiche e coloniali nelle Università italiane. AFRICA (Rome) 15 (1960), pp. 107-120.

20 GRIAULE, M. L'inconnue noire. PRESENCE AFR. 1 (1947), pp. 21-27.

21 HARRIS, J. Cooperation between universities in printing and publishing. INTER-UNIV. COOP. IN W. AFR., 1961, paper SL/VII.

22 HARTOG, P. J. The origins of the School of Oriental [and African] Studies. BULL. SOAS 1 (1917), pp. 5-22.

23 HATTERSLEY, A. F. Canada and South Africa: a plea for inter-Dominion historical study. CANADIAN HIST. REV. 3 (1922), pp. 114-119.

24 HERSKOVITS, M. J. The contribution of Afro-American studies to Africanist research. AMER. ANTHR. 50 (1948), pp. 1-10.

25 HERSKOVITS, M. J. The development of Africanist studies in Europe and America. PROC. INT. CONG. AFR. 1 (1962), pp. 29-45.

26 HERSKOVITS, M. J. Some thoughts on American research in Africa. AFR. STUD. BULL. 1, no. ii (1958), pp. 1-11.

27 HOLDSWORTH, M. African studies in the U.S.S.R. ST. ANTONY'S PAPERS 10 (1961), pp. 89-101. Also in: AFR. STUD. BULL. 5, no. i (1962), pp. 9-13.

28 HUNTER, G. Centre of African studies, Edinburgh. BULL. AFR. STUD. ASSOC. 5 (1965), pp. 6-8.

29 JOHNSTON, H. H. Notes on African subjects of special interest for future investigation. J. AFR. SOC. 1 (1901), pp. 17-22.

30 KILLAM, D. Fictional sources for African studies. J. HIST. SOC. NIG. 3 (1965), pp. 377-402.

31 KIRK-GREENE, A. Career and consultant: new elements in African studies. J. AFR. ADM. 13 (1961), pp. 220-234.

32 LAVROFF, D. A. G. Réflexions sur les recherches africaines dans quelques Universités des Etats-Unis d'Amérique. ANNALES AFR., 1965, pp. 121-128.

33 LEGTERS, L. H. The National Defense Education Act and African studies. AFR. STUD. BULL. 7, no. iii (1964), pp. 3-10.

34 MACDONA, B. F. The African scene. AFR. AFFAIRS 62 (1963), pp. 224-235.

35 MARTINS, D. As Ciências Sociais no Panorama Africano. BSEM 125 (1960), B 1.

36 MAUNY, R. Le Centre de Recherches africaines de la Sorbonne. BULL. IFAN 26 (1964), pp. 271-273.

37 MAZRUI, A. The scholar and his residence permit. TRANSITION 14 (1964), pp. 20-21.

38 MILDENBERGER, K. W. African studies and the National Defense Act. AFR. STUD. BULL. 3, no. iv (1960), pp. 16-23.

39 MONOD, TH. L'Afrique continent marginal. PRESENCE AFR. 8 (1950), pp. 25-30.

40 MUKHERJEE, S. N. Afro-Asian studies in India. AFRO-ASIAN AND W. AFF. 1 (1964), pp. 236-240.

41 OLBRECHTS, M. L'activité africaniste belge dans le domaine des sciences de l'homme. Année 1949. ZAIRE 4 (1950), pp. 753-766.

42 PERHAM, M. [Progress of African studies] inaugural address. AFR. AFFAIRS, Special Issue, 1965, pp. 1-14.

43 RHODES, W. Fellowship opportunities and research grants in African humanities. AFR. STUD. BULL. 5, no. iii (1962), pp. 42-44.

44 SHELTON, A. J. Essence and accident in African research: approaches in Africana. GENEVE-AFR. 3 (1964), pp. 265-268.

45 STRELCYN, S. Les études africaines à l'Université de Varsovie. AFR. BULL. 1 (1964), pp. 151-161. English revised version 2 (1965), pp. 89-96.

46 THOMAS, B. E. Middle Africa and other regional terms. AFR. STUD. BULL. 3, no. iii (1960), p. 15.

47 TUCKER, A. N. The scholar and his passport. TRANSITION 14 (1964), pp. 19-20.

48 VERMA, S. N. African studies in India. AFRO-ASIAN AND W. AFF. 2 (1965), pp. 149-152.

49 WELMERS, W. E. African studies and the National Defense Education Act. AFR. STUD. BULL. 2, no. iii (1959), pp. 34-39.

50 WICKERT, F. R. American universities and Africa. AFR. STUD. BULL. 3, no. iv (1960), pp. 24-49.

51 A propos de la recherche coloniale anglaise. ZAIRE 6 (1952), pp. 193-194.

52 Activités africanistes en Amérique. ZAIRE 7 (1953), p. 200.

53 L'Africa nelle Università italiane. AFRICA (Rome) 10 (1955), p. 172.

54 African activities at the University of Nottingham. BULL. AFR. STUD. ASSOC. 2 (1964), pp. 23-25.

55 The African Language and Area Center, Michigan State University, East Lansing, Michigan. INT. SOC. SC. BULL. 14 (1962), pp. 368-369.

56 African studies at Cambridge University. BULL. AFR. STUD. ASSOC. 2 (1964), pp. 3-6.

57 African studies at the Food Research Institute of Stanford University. BULL. AFR. STUD. ASSOC. 2 (1964), pp. 29-31.

58 African studies at the Hoover Institution, Stanford University, California. BULL. AFR. STUD. ASSOC. 3 (1964), pp. 30-32.

59 African studies at the University of California, Berkeley. BULL. AFR. STUD. ASSOC. 2 (1964), pp. 31-33.

60 African studies at the University of Leeds. BULL. AFR. STUD. ASSOC. 3 (1964), pp. 18-25.

61 African studies in Canada and Scandinavia. AFR. STUD. BULL. 6, no. ii (1963), pp. 10-13.

62 African studies in Canada and the United Kingdom. AFR. STUD. BULL. 6, no. iii (1963), pp. 19-22.

63 African studies in the United States. AFR. STUD. BULL. 4, no. ii (1961), pp. 9-20; 5, no. i (1962), pp. 19-30; 6, no. i (1963), pp. 43-56; 7, no. i (1964), pp. 12-24.

64 Colonial studies at Oxford. AFR. AFFAIRS 43 (1944), pp. 6-7.

65 Co-operation between British and African universities. BULL. AFR. STUD. ASSOC. 4 (1965), pp. 9-13.

66 Cours d'été sur l'Afrique aux Etats-Unis [à Northwestern University, à Evanston-Chicago]. ZAIRE 5 (1951), pp. 405-406.

67 Création d'un séminaire de sciences humaines. ZAIRE 10 (1956), p. 203.

68 E necessario un riordinamento degli studi africanisti in Italia. AFRICA (Rome) 14 (1959), pp. 17-20, 41.

69 Etudes africaines à l'Université de Yale. ZAIRE 4 (1950), p. 894.

70 Etudes soviétiques des langages asiatiques et africains. GENEVE-AFR. 1 (1962), p. 217.

71 A five-year plan of research (International African Institute). AFRICA 5 (1932), pp. 1-13.

72 International African Institute: an enquiry into the development and scope of African studies [Ibadan, April, 1964]. BULL. AFR. STUD. ASSOC. 1 (1964), pp. 5-11.

73 Nouveau programme d'études africaines aux Etats-Unis. ZAIRE 6 (1952), p. 292.

74 Nuffield College colonial research scheme. J. AFR. SOC. 41 (1942), p. 88.

75 Post-graduate awards for African studies. BULL. AFR. STUD. ASSOC. 4 (1965), pp. 6-7; 5 (1965), p. 4.

76 Teaching and research in African studies at Manchester University. BULL. AFR. STUD. ASSOC. 3 (1964), pp. 11-18.

77 University of Wisconsin. Program in comparative tropical history. BULL. AFR. STUD. ASSOC. 1 (1964), pp. 12-14.

See also 526, 606, 1179, 2534, 3172, 3350, 3378, 3623, 3830.

Institutions. Societies

78 BUNGENER, P. Institut Africain de Genève, premières expériences. GENEVE-AFR. 1 (1962), pp. 241-245.

79 C., J. A propos de l'Africa Bureau, de Londres. ZAIRE 8 (1954), pp. 860-861.

80 CASADIO, F. A. La Societa Italiana per l'Organizzazione Internazionale e l'Africa. COOPERAZIONE INT. AFR., 1960, pp. 218-223.

81 CEBE-HABERSKY, J. J. The work of the United Nations in Africa. COOPERAZIONE INT. AFR., 1960, pp. 61-73.

82 CHILVER, E. The Institutes of Social and Economic Research in the African Colonies. J. AFR. ADM. 3 (1951), pp. 178-186.

83 COLQUHOUN, A. R. A link of empire: the Royal Colonial Institute. ROYAL COL. INST. PR. 38 (1906-1907), pp. 119-123.

84 CORA, G. L'Afrique, objet des activités de l'Institut International des Civilisations Différentes. COOPERAZIONE INT. AFR., 1960, pp. 173-176.

85 COWAN, L. G. History of the African Studies Association. AFR. STUD. BULL. 4, no. ii (1961), pp. 32-33.

86 DEMPSTER, J. B. The Empire Article Exchange Society. J. AFR. SOC. 38 (1939), pp. 327-328.

87 DOBOSIEWICS, Z. Les recherches africaines à l'Institut Polonais des Affaires Internationales. AFR. BULL. 1 (1964), pp. 162-163.

88 DORATO, M. Attività e programmi dell'Istituto Italiano per l'Africa. COOPERAZIONE INT. AFR., 1960, pp. 209-214.

89 ENGEL, J. The African-American Institute. AFR. STUD. BULL. 6, no. iii (1963), pp. 13-18.

90 FAGE, J. D. African Studies Association of the United Kingdom: the 1964 Conference. AFR. STUD. BULL. 7, no. iii (1964), pp. 13-14.

91 FORDE, D. Statements issued by the administrative director of the International African Institute. COOPERAZIONE INT. AFR., 1960, pp. 187-190.

92 FOURMARIER, P. Rapport sur les travaux de la Commission du Ministère des Colonies, pendant l'année 1934. BULL. SEANCES IRCB 6 (1935), pp. 213-222.

93 FROIDEVAUX, H. Les morts de la Société de l'Histoire des Colonies francaises, entre 1940 et 1946. REV. HIST. COL. 33 (1940 - 1946), pp. 96 - 109.

94 GAYET, G. Le rôle de l'Academie des Sciences d'Outre Mer et ses activités récentes sur l'Afrique orientale et sur Madagascar. COOPERAZIONE INT. AFR., 1960, pp. 193-199.

95 GILLE, A. and GREVISSE, F. The social and scientific role of C.E.P.S.I. AFR. AFFAIRS 49 (1950), pp. 151-157.

96 HAILEY, W. M. The past and the future of the Institute [International African Institute]. AFRICA 17 (1947), pp. 229-234.

97 HAMILTON, Sir R. The International Institute of African Languages and Cultures. J. AFR. SOC. 31 (1932), pp. 371-374.

98 HUBERT, H. Les dix premières années du Comité d'Etudes historiques et scientifiques de l'Afrique Occidentale française (1916-1925). RHCF 21 (1928), pp. 1-32.

99 IDENBURG, P. J. Rapport sur les activités du Afrika-Studiecentrum. COOPERAZIONE INT. AFR., 1960, pp. 200-204.

100 JOHNSTON, Sir H. H. The work of the African Society. J. AFR. SOC. 2 (1903), pp. 349-358.

101 JONGHE, E. DE. L'Institut International des Langues et des Civilisations Africaines à Bruxelles. CONGO 2 (1938), pp. 1-6.

102 LEE, M. The Overseas Development Institute and its publications. J. MOD. AFR. STUD. 2 (1964), pp. 565-571.

103 LUGARD, Sir F. D. The future of the [International] Institute [of African Languages and Cultures] and its present activities. J. AFR. SOC. 41 (1942), pp. 198-204.

104 LUGARD, Sir F. D. The International Institute of African Languages and Cultures. AFRICA 1 (1928), pp. 1-12.

105 MARTINEAU, A. La Société de l'Histoire des Colonies françaises. RHCF 1 (1913), pp. 5-10.

106 MEEUSSEN, A. E. Voor meer internationale samenwerking in het International African Institute. KONGO-OVERZEE 12-13 (1946-47), pp. 129-132.

107 MONOD, TH. L'Institut Français d'Afrique Noire. AFRICA 14 (1943), pp. 194-199.

108 NOGARA, A. La Società Nazionale Dante Alighieri in Africa. COOPERAZIONE INT. AFR., 1960, pp. 224-228.

109 PELT, A. Activities of WFUNA and UNAs in Africa. COOPERAZIONE INT. AFR., 1960, pp. 183-186.

110 PERBAL, A. L'Institut scientifique missionnaire à Rome. ZAIRE 2 (1948), pp. 787-795.

111 REX, F. J. Africa Literacy and Writing Centre. INT. REV. MISSIONS 49 (1960), pp. 91-94.

112 ROCHARD-MOLARD, J. Les grandes enquêtes de l'I.F.A.N. ET. DAHOM. 1 (1948), pp. 92-95.

113 SHELFORD, F. Some notes on the history of the African Society. J. AFR. SOC. 34 (1935), pp. 223-226.

114 SILVA AMORIM. Centro de Estudos Históricos Ultramarinos. PORT. EM AFR. 12 (1955), pp. 163-168.

115 SMITH, E. W. The story of the [International] Institute [of African Languages and Cultures]. A survey of seven years. AFRICA 7 (1934), pp. 1-27.

116 SOBRAL DIAS, D. A. Report by the representative of the Junta de Investigacoes do Ultramar (Portuguese Overseas Council for Research). COOPERAZIONE INT. AFR., 1960, pp. 215-218.

117 SPEECKAERT, G. P. Les organisations internationales et l'Afrique. COOPERAZIONE INT. AFR., 1960, pp. 177-183.

118 VANDEPLAS, A. La fondation du Comité national hongrois de l'Association Internationale Africaine. ZAIRE 14 (1960), pp. 69-81.

119 VECCHI, B. V. Sintesi delle attività del Gruppo Vittorio Bottego. COOPERAZIONE INT. AFR., 1960, pp. 204-206.

120 VERONESE, V. L'Unesco e l'Africa. AFRICA (Rome) 13 (1958), pp. 141-142.

121 WERNER, A. The School of Oriental Studies. J. AFR. SOC. 16 (1917), pp. 227-233.

122 WESTERMANN, D. The work of the International Institute of African Languages and Cultures. INT. REV. MISSIONS 26 (1937), pp. 493-499.

123 WILSON, J. O. Stewart Missionary Foundation for Africa in Gammon Theological Seminary. LIBERIA BULL. 19 (1901), pp. 6-12.

124 WINGATE, Sir R. The retirement of Lord Buxton [as president of the African Society]. J. AFR. SOC. 33 (1934), pp. 113-122.

125 WYATT, B. International African Institute. CIVILISATIONS 4 (1954), pp. 213-217; French summary, pp. 217-218.

126 L'Activité du Colonial Social Service Research Council en 1947-48. ZAIRE 3 (1949), pp. 87-88.

127 Activités africaines de la Carnegie Corporation. ZAIRE 4 (1950), pp. 1020-1021.

128 Activités africaines du Phelps Stokes Fund. ZAIRE 5 (1951), pp. 1070-1071.

129 Activités du Colonial Research Council anglais en 1949-1950. ZAIRE 5 (1951), p. 294.

130 The African circle. J. AFR. SOC. 35 (1936), pp. 306-310.

131 The African Studies Association [U.S.A.]. AFR. STUD. BULL. 1, no. i (1958), pp. 3-5.

132 Associazione tecnici Oltremare. AFRICA (Rome) 10 (1955), p. 76.

133 Attività dell' Associazione Internazionale per lo studio dei Problemi d'Oltremare (A.I.P.E.P.O.). AFRICA (Rome) 10 (1955), p. 178.

134 A Bureau of Missions and Colonial Planning [University of Aberdeen]. J. AFR. SOC. 41 (1942), pp. 8-9.

135 Center of documentation and research on urbanization in Africa south of the Sahara. BULL. AFR. STUD. ASSOC. 6 (1965), p. 28.

136 Centre d'Analyse Documentaire pour l'Afrique Noire: Fiches Analytiques. BULL. AFR. STUD. ASSOC. 6 (1965), p. 27.

137 Centre de Documentation et d'Information de la Société des Africanistes (C.D.I.S.A.). BULL. AFR. STUD. ASSOC. 4 (1965), pp. 21-22.

138 Centre d'étude et de documentation pour l'Afrique et l'Outre-Mer (C.E.D.A.O.M.). BULL. AFR. STUD. ASSOC. 4 (1965), pp. 19-20.

139 Centre d'études africaines à New York. ZAIRE 6 (1952), p. 83.

140 Centre of African Studies, University of Cambridge. BULL. AFR. STUD. ASSOC. 6 (1965), pp. 16-18.

141 Centre of West African Studies, University of Birmingham. BULL. AFR. STUD. ASSOC. 2 (1964), pp. 7-12.

142 Centro de Estudos Afro-Orientais, Universidade da Bahia (Salvador, Bahia, Brasil). BULL. AFR. STUD. ASSOC. 1 (1964), p. 27.

143 Cinquantenaire de la Royal African Society. ZAIRE 6 (1952), p. 84.

144 The Committee on African Studies in Canada. BULL. AFR. STUD. CANADA 1, no. 1 (1963), pp. 31-37.

145 Committee on African Studies in Canada. BULL. AFR. STUD. ASSOC. 1 (1964), pp. 14-15.

146 Compte rendu de l'Assemblée Générale statutaire [du Comité Permanent du Congrès Colonial National]. ZAIRE 3 (1949), pp. 185-196.

147 Department of African Studies, University of Delhi. BULL. AFR. STUD. ASSOC. 3 (1964), pp. 33-34.

148 The Department of Technical Co-operation. J. AFR. ADM. 13 (1961), pp. 235-236.

149 Educational and cultural exchange with Africa: the program of the Department of State. AFR. STUD. BULL. 4, no. ii (1961), pp. 1-8.

150 The Empire Societies' War Hospitality Committee. J. AFR. SOC. 39 (1940), pp. 105-107, 200-201.

151 A Escola Superior Colonial. PORT. EM AFR. 3 (1946), pp. 371-374.

152 The Fabian Society's colonial bureau and journal Empire. J. AFR. SOC. 40 (1941), pp. 297-298.

153 Fifty years of British African Society [Royal African Society]. AFR. AFFAIRS 50 (1951), pp. 178-195.

154 Inaugural meeting [of the African Society]. J. AFR. SOC. 1 (1902), pp. i-xxxiv.

155 Un institut africain aux Etats-Unis [à Lincoln University en Pennsylvanie]. ZAIRE 5 (1951), p. 405.

156 L'Institut National de Recherches et de Documentation. RECH. AFR. 3 (1960), pp. 68-71.

157 International organizations for development in Africa. J. AFR. ADM. 11 (1959), pp. 187-192.

158 International Technical Co-operation—1. The United Nations and other organizations. 2. Sources of aid other than from the United Kingdom. J. LOCAL ADM. OV. 1 (1962), pp. 47-58, 112-123.

159 The Istituto Italiano per l'Africa. INT. SOC. SC. J. 13 (1961), pp. 316-318.

160 The Jubilee of the Imperial Institute. J. AFR. SOC. 42 (1943), pp. 127-128.

161 London School of Oriental Studies. J. AFR. SOC. 13 (1914), pp. 423-429.

162 The Netherlands' Centre of African Studies, Leiden. BULL. AFR. STUD. ASSOC. 2 (1964), pp. 25-29.

163 News from the Geneva-Africa Institute. GENEVE-AFR. 2 (1963), pp. 95-96, 231-233; 3 (1964), pp. 102, 283-287; 4 (1965) pp. 93-94, 246-248.

164 La réorganisation de l'Ecole Nationale de la France d'Outre-Mer. CIVILISATIONS 1 (ii), 1951, pp. 8-11; English summary, p. 11.

165 The Royal African Society and Belgian Africa. J. AFR. SOC. 39 (1940), pp. 293-294.

166 The Royal African Society and French Africa. J. AFR. SOC. 39 (1940), pp. 292-293.

167 The Royal African Society and the War. J. AFR. SOC. 39 (1940), pp. 97-105, 196-197.

168 Royal Colonial Institute: historical sketch, 1868-1889. ROYAL COL. INST. PR. 20 (1889-90), pp. 225-227.

169 The Royal Empire Society. CORONA 4 (1952), pp. 155-156.

170 Scandinavian Institute of African Studies, University of Uppsala. BULL. AFR. STUD. ASSOC. 1 (1964), pp. 19-20.

171 School of African and Asian Studies at the University of Sussex. BULL. AFR. STUD. ASSOC. 3 (1964), pp. 25-29.

172 Séance d'inauguration de l'Institut [Institut Royal Colonial Belge]. BULL. SEANCES IRCB 1 (1930), pp. 21-42.

173 Société des Amis de l'Institut Français d'Afrique Noire. ET. GUIN. 2 (1947), pp. 79-83.

174 La Suisse, Genève et l'Afrique: l'Institut Africain de Genève. GENEVE-AFR. 1 (1962), pp. 115-116; English translation, pp. 117-118.

175 University of Sussex, School of African and Asian Studies. BULL. AFR. STUD. ASSOC. 6 (1965), pp. 13-15.

See also 645, 718, 949, 1156, 1198, 1398, 1819, 2534, 3378, 3751, 3788.

General Conferences

176 BALANDIER, G. La participation de l'A.E.F. à la Conférence internationale des Africanistes de l'Ouest. BULL. I.E.C. N.S. 1 (1950), pp. 79-80.

177 BILSEN, J. VAN. Conferenties. ZAIRE 4 (1950), pp. 873-874.

178 BREUIL, H. Envoi du Professeur Abbé H. Breuil, président du IIIe Congrès panafricain de préhistoire tenu à Bulawayo (North Rhodesia) 1955. J. SOC. AFR. 27 (1957), pp. 7-17.

179 BULCK, G. VAN. Le deuxième congrès pan-africain de la Jeunesse Ouvrière Chrétienne (Rome, 26-27 août 1957). ZAIRE 11 (1957), pp. 739-753.

180 C., J. Séminaire africain à Washington. ZAIRE 8 (1954), pp. 861-862.

181 CHARLES, V. Rencontres internationales. Le Colloque de Brazzaville. ZAIRE 7 (1953), pp. 386-387.

182 CHARLES, V. Les travaux du premier congrès des mutualités africaines. ZAIRE 10 (1956), pp. 361-365.

183 CHITTICK, H. N. The fourth Panafrican Congress on prehistory at Lovanium. TANGANYIKA NOTES AND RECORDS 54 (1960), pp. 111-112.

184 CORREA, A. A. M. A Conferência Internacional dos Africanistas Ocidentais. PORT. EM AFR. 5 (1948), pp. 169-176.

185 COSTANZO, G. A. La coopération internationale en Afrique: Le Congrès de Mogadiscio. CIVILISATIONS 10 (1960), pp. 161-164; English summary, p. 164.

186 CRUZ, J. H. M. Doenças malignas sua actualidade. Impressões do Congresso de East London. BSEM 120 (1960), pp. 105-126.

187 DIOP, A. Il senso di un Congresso. AFRICA (Rome) 14 (1959), pp. 125-128.

188 DOUTRELOUX, A. Pérégrinations d'une science. Note sur le troisième Séminaire International Africain. ZAIRE 14 (1960), pp. 549-554.

189 F., H. A. Third Pan-African Congress on pre-history. TANGANYIKA NOTES AND RECORDS 41 (1955), pp. 67-68.

190 FILESI, T. Conferenza ad Accra. AFRICA (Rome) 14 (1959), pp. 7-10.

191 FONLON, B. The Africanist gathering in Ghana. ABBIA 2 (1963), pp. 31-47; French tr., pp. 47-63.

192 GAVIN, R. J. Seminar on current trends in the humanities and social studies. AFRICAN NOTES 1, no. 3 (1964), pp. 24-26.

193 GELDERS, V. Deux Congrès italiens d'Etudes africaines. Le système de "Trusteeship." ZAIRE 3 (1949), pp. 395-411.

194 GELDERS, V. Problèmes de rencontre des civilisations. Compte rendu abrégé de la XXVe session de l'Institut INCIDI, tenue à Bruxelles, les 28, 29 et 30 novembre 1949. ZAIRE 4 (1950), pp. 79-90.

195 GRAY, J. A. Rome Conference. AFR. AFFAIRS 58 (1959), pp. 34-36.

196 HULSTAERT, G. Conférence interafricaine de Bukavu. AEQUATORIA 18 (1955), pp. 96-97.

197 JUNOD, H.-P. Proceedings of the First International Congress of Africanists, Accra 11th-18th December 1962. GENEVE-AFR. 3 (1964), pp. 269-275.

198 LEWIS, W. H. International congress on French-speaking Africa [Washington, 1964]. AFR. STUD. BULL. 7, no. iii (1964), pp. 11-12.

199 LYNN, C. W. The Cambridge Conference: impressions of an agriculturalist. CORONA 1, no. 10 (1949), pp. 18-19.

200 M., L. C. Le Congrès de l'Abako (Thysville 25 août-4 septembre 1963). ET. CONG. 5, no. 8 (1963), pp. 34-41.

201 MCADAMS, D. Premier Congrès International des Africanistes. Accra, Ghana, 18 décembre 1962. ET. CONG. 4, no. 2 (1963), pp. 23-25, 65-72.

202 MAFFI, Q. Vitalità dell' africanismo italiano. Il Congresso per il centenario del progetto italiano per il Canale di Suez. AFRICA (Rome) 10 (1955), pp. 205-207.

203 MAQUET, E. Un séminaire anglo-belge de sciences humaines à Kampala. ZAIRE 7 (1953), pp. 291-293.

204 MAQUET, E. Un séminaire des sciences humaines à Astrida. ZAIRE 9 (1955), pp. 183-186.

205 MAUNY, R. La 2e conférence d'histoire africaine de Londres (Juillet 1957). BULL. IFAN. Série B: Sciences humaines 20 (1958), pp. 303-305.

206 MAUNY, R. La troisième conference internationale des Africanistes de l'Ouest. BULL. IFAN 12 (1950), pp. 531-535.

207 ORSINI, P. D'A. Il congresso di Bamako. AFRICA (Rome) 12 (1957), p. 162.

208 PHILIPPS, T. The twenty-fourth biennial session of the Institut Colonial International, Rome, June 1939. J. AFR. SOC. 39 (1940), pp. 17-21.

209 PHILIPPS, T. The Volta meeting in Rome. J. AFR. SOC. 38 (1939), pp. 19-32.

210 POTEKHIN, I. I. Toward the First Congress of Africanists. AFR. STUD. BULL. 5, no. iii (1962), pp. 34-35.

211 PRIESTLEY, M. A. Africanists in Salisbury. GHANA NOTES 1 (1961), pp. 12-13.

212 RIMMER, D. German Africa Society's symposium, Cologne, 18-19 June 1965. BULL. AFR. STUD. ASSOC. 6 (1965), pp. 36-38.

213 RIVIEREZ, H. Spirito di un congresso. AFRICA (Rome) 15 (1960), pp. 62-64.

214 RUSSELL, P. Letter from Europe. TRANSITION 17 (1964), pp. 47-52.

215 SCHOELL, F. L. Le Deuxième Congrès Panafricain et la Société des Nations. GENEVE-AFR. 4 (1965), pp. 175-184.

216 SEWEJE, M. A. Observations de la société africaine de culture pour le second Congrès du Rome. PRESENCE AFR. 27-28 (1959), pp. 314-320.

217 TOURE, S. Message...au Colloque d'Abidjan, Avril 1961. RECH. AFR. 2 (1962), pp. 3-6.

218 WELBOURN, F. B. What is an Africanist? The First International Congress of Africanists held at the University of Ghana, Legon, 12th-17th December, 1962. MAKERERE J. 7 (1963), pp. 90-103.

219 WOLF, J. Le Colloque international de Bergneustadt: un dialogue loyal entre l'Afrique et l'Europe (17-21 septembre 1963). CIVILISATIONS 13 (1963), pp. 325-332.

220 WOLF, J. Le Colloque de Pérouse. CIVILISATIONS 14 (1964), pp. 359-370.

221 WOLF, J. Les Colloques Méditerranéens (Florence, 22-26 juin 1963). CIVILISATIONS 13 (1963), pp. 321-324.

222 WOLF, J. Le IVème Colloque Méditerranéen. CIVILISATIONS 14 (1964), pp. 213-219.

223 L'Africa al 7° Congresso UCID. AFRICA (Rome) 10 (1955), p. 173.

224 African Studies Association of the United Kingdom. The 1964 Conference. BULL. AFR. STUD. ASSOC. 3 (1964), pp. 6-8.

225 The bulletin of the African Studies Association of the United Kingdom. BULL. AFR. STUD. ASSOC. 1 (1964), pp. 3-4.

226 La collaboration internationale en Afrique. ZAIRE 5 (1951), pp. 859-861.

227 Colloque international de Bergneustadt sur le présent et l'avenir de l'Afrique. PRESENCE AFR. N.S. 48 (1963), pp. 227-229.

228 Conférence internationale à Monrovia. ZAIRE 7 (1953), p. 79.

229 Congrès international des Africanistes. GENEVE-AFR. 2 (1963), pp. 82-84.

230 Le Congrès international des études africaines à Florence en 1951. ZAIRE 4 (1950), pp. 212-213.

231 Cycle de conférences africaines aux Etats-Unis. ZAIRE 4 (1950), pp. 895-896.

232 First International Congress of Africanists [University of Ghana, Legon, 1962]. AFR. STUD. BULL. 6, no. i (1963), pp. 38-42.

233 The first International Congress of Africanists. ABBIA 1 (1963), pp. 110-111; includes French translation.

234 International African Institute: international African seminar on the emergence of new social classes and the roles of elites in contemporary Africa [Ibadan, July, 1964]. BULL. AFR. STUD. ASSOC. 1 (1964), pp. 11-12.

235 International African seminar on the impact of Christianity in Tropical Africa. BULL. AFR. STUD. ASSOC. 3 (1964), pp. 35-37.

236 International Congress of Africanists: recommendations: 1962. PROC. INT. CONG. AFR. 1 (1962), pp. 352-356.

237 Journee d'études africaines à Paris. PRESENCE AFR. N.S. 45 (1963), pp. 227-228.

238 Liverpool conference [on African affairs, organised by Royal African Society]. AFR. AFFAIRS 54 (1955), pp. 52-56.

239 Réunion africaniste aux Etats-Unis. ZAIRE 7 (1953), pp. 729-730.

240 Routa d'Africa [conference held in Jan.-Feb. 1955, May 1955 in Rome]. AFRICA (Rome) 10 (1955), p. 34, 182.

241 Second International African Seminar [January, 1960]. J. AFR. LAW 4 (1960), pp. 6-7.

242 Slotmotie van het Italiaans Koloniaal Congres te Florentië. ZAIRE 2 (1948), pp. 305-306.

243 Statutes of the International Congress of Africanists. PROC. INT. CONG. AFR. 1 (1962), pp. 347-351.

244 Le Symposium international de Bristol. ZAIRE 4 (1950), pp. 667-672.

245 Transition conference questionnaire [African writers' conference]. TRANSITION 5 (1962), pp. 11-12.

246 Tropical African studies conference, April, 1964. AFRICAN NOTES 1, no. 3 (1964), pp. 19-22.

247 Tropical African studies conference, Ibadan, 5-11 avril 1964. BULL. IFAN 26 (1964), pp. 714-716.

248 The world YWCA All-Africa Conference. AFR. WOMEN 4 (1961), pp. 25-27.

249 Xe Congres de la Federation des Etudiants Africains en France (F.E.A.N.F.). PRESENCE AFR. N.S. 22 (1958), pp. 142-143.

250 Le XIe Congrès de la F.E.A.N.F. [et le panafricanisme]. PRESENCE AFR. N.S. 30 (1960), pp. 106-107.

251 La 32e session d'études de l'Incidi, tenue à Munich du 19 au 22 septembre 1960. CIVILISATIONS 10 (1960), pp. 385-400; English translation, pp. 519-532.

See also 8, 494, 3350.

African scholars: biographies. obituary

252 IRWIN, G. W. Africanists in Moscow. GHANA NOTES 1 (1961), pp. 5-6.

253 C., J. Africanistes Américains. ZAIRE 8 (1954), pp. 525-526.

254 Africanistes américains. ZAIRE 5 (1951), pp. 748-750.

255 FELE, B. Avec les Africanistes sovietiques. PRESENCE AFR. N.S. 16 (1957), pp. 152-154.

256 Chercheurs scientifiques Americains en Afrique. ZAIRE 4 (1950), p. 1017.

257 Liste des chercheurs dans les Etats francophones de l'Afrique Noire et Madagascar. J. SOC. AFR. 32 (1962), pp. 179-205.

258 LUKAS, J. R. C. Abraham zum Gedenken. AFR. UND UB. 47 (1964), p. 161.

259 HAIR, P. E. H. A bibliography of R. C. Abraham—linguist and lexicographer. J. W. AFR. LANG. 2 (1965), pp. 63-66.

260 MVENG, P. E. Agatharchide de Cnide. AFRICA (Rome) 20 (1965), pp. 33-39.

261 Mrs. E. O. Ashton. AFR. UND UB. 48 (1964-1965), p. 1.

262 AURIGEMMA, S. In memoriam: Renato Bartoccini libico. AFRICA (Rome) 19 (1964), p. 44.

263 In memoriam: D. H. Bate. PROC. PAN-AFR. CONGR. PRE-HIST. 2 (1952), pp. 27-28.

264 CERBELLA, G. Ricordo di Francesco Beguinot. LIBIA 1, no. 2 (1953), pp. 123-133.

265 KLINGENHEBEN, A. Francesco Beguinot zum Gedächtnis. AFR. UND UB. 38 (1953-1954), p. 92.

266 PALES, L. L'abbé Breuil (1877-1961). J. SOC. AFR. 32 (1962), pp. 7-52.

267 In memoriam: R. Broom. PROC. PAN-AFR. CONGR. PRE-HIST. 2 (1952), pp. 28-29.

268 CARTER, G. M. A political scientist in Africa. AFR. STUD. BULL. 2, no. iv (1959), pp. 1-12.

269 RICCI, L. Laurea in lettere honoris causa ad Enrico Cerulli. AFRICA (Rome) 19 (1964), pp. 3-6.

270 ZILIOTTO, G. Un africanista scomparso: Massimo Colucci. AFRICA (Rome) 11 (1956), p. 219.

271 WESTERMANN, D. Jan Cuny. AFRIKA (Berlin) 2 (1943), pp. 1-3.

272 BRAMBILLA, C. Bernard Dadie. AFRICA (Rome) 13 (1958), p. 341.

273 LABOURET, H. Maurice Delafosse. AFRICA 1 (1928), pp. 112-115.

274 MEINHOF, C. Maurice Delafosse. AFR. UND UB. 17 (1926-1927), p. 156.

275 MEINHOF, C. Otto Dempwolff [Nachruf]. AFR. UND UB. 29 (1939), p. 81.

276 DESSARRE, E. La passion du monde. AFRICA (Rome) 17 (1962), pp. 19-23.

277 In memoriam: A. Du Toit. PROC. PAN-AFR. CONGR. PRE-HIST. 2 (1952), pp. 28-29.

278 HOFFMAN, A. C. In memoriam: Thomas Frederik Dreyer. PROC. PAN-AFR. CONGR. PRE-HIST. 3 (1955), pp. xxv-xxvi.

279 MEINHOF, C. Professor Karl Endemann. AFR. UND UB. 9 (1918), p. 65.

280 BROWN, W. O. Edward Franklin Frazier (September 24, 1894-May 17, 1962). AFR. STUD. BULL. 5, no. ii (1962), pp. 1-2.

281 DIKE, K. O. In memoriam: Melville Jean Herskovits. AFR. STUD. BULL. 6, no. i (1963), pp. 1-3.

282 GREENBERG, J. H. In memoriam: Melville Jean Herskovits. AFR. STUD. BULL. 6, no. i (1963), p. 3.

283 Obituary: Melville Herskovits. CIVILISATIONS 12 (1962), p. 546.

284 Obituary: M. J. Herskovits, 1895-1963. AFRICA 33 (1963), pp. 181-182.

285 MEINHOF, C. and KLINGENHEBEN, A. Dr. phil. Richard Heydorn. AFR. UND UB. 34 (1943-1944), p. 24.

286 KAHLER-MEYER, E. Pfarrer i.R. Johannes Ittmann. AFR. UND UB. 47 (1964), pp. 1-8.

287 MORTELMANS, G. In memoriam: Jean Paul Janmart. PROC. PAN-AFR. CONGR. PRE-HIST. 3 (1955), p. xxvi.

288 In memoriam: Neville Jones. PROC. PAN-AFR. CONGR. PRE-HIST. 3 (1955), p. xxviii.

289 BRAMBILLA, C. John Samuel Mbiti. AFRICA (Rome) 13 (1958), p. 182.

290 LUKAS, J. Carl Meinhof. AFR. UND UB. 34 (1943-1944), pp. 81-93.

291 MEYER, E. Das Werk von Carl Meinhof. AFR. UND UB. 34 (1943-1944), pp. 131-172.

292 In memory of Carl Meinhof. AFR. STUD. 5 (1946), pp. 73-81.

293 MONTEIL, V. Hommage au professeur Théodore Monod. BULL. IFAN 27 (1965), p. 411.

294 KLINGENHEBEN, A. Martino Mario Moreno zum Gedächtnis. AFR. UND UB. 48 (1964-1965), p. 80.

295 In memoriam: René Neuville. PROC. PAN-AFR. CONGR. PRE-HIST. 2 (1952), p. 29.

296 DEAN, J. Obituary: Richard Offor. GHANA LIBRARY JOURNAL 1 (1964), pp. 74-75.

297 A propos d'une démission à Oxford [Margery Perham]. ZAIRE 3 (1949), pp. 213-214.

298 BECCARO, F. DEL. Ritratto di Carlo Piaggia. AFRICA (Rome) 17 (1962), pp. 27-33.

299 SKOROV, G. In memoriam: Ivan Potekhine, homme, savant et ami de l'Afrique. PRESENCE AFR. N.S. 53 (1965), pp. 215-220.

300 Obituary: Prof. A. R. Radcliffe-Brown. AFR. STUD. 15 (1956), pp. 87-88.

301 Robert Sutherland Rattray. J. AFR. SOC. 37 (1938), p. 325.

302 MEINHOF, C. Hofrat Prof. Dr. Leo Reinisch. AFR. UND UB. 10 (1919-1920), p. 1.

303 T., L. R. Obituary: Sir Edward Denison Ross. BULL. SOAS 10 (1940-42), pp. 832-836.

304 In memoriam: A. Ruhlmann. PROC. PAN-AFR. CONGR. PRE-HIST. 2 (1952), pp. 29-34.

305 Bibliographie d'Achille Salée (1883-1932). BULL. SEANCES IRCB 4 (1933), pp. 38-39.

306 BULCK, G. VAN In memoriam: ...P. J. Schumacher (22-i-1878—26-viii-1957). ZAIRE 12 (1958), pp. 293-303.

307 HADDON, A. C. [C. G. Seligman:] Appreciation. ESSAYS PRESENTED TO C. G. SELIGMAN, 1934, pp. 1-4.

308 ROEYKENS, P. A. L'oeuvre scientifique de feu Mgr. Tanghe. AEQUATORIA 11 (1948), pp. 87-97.

309 Publications du R. P. H. Vanderyst, missionnaire au Congo belge. BULL. SEANCES IRCB 6 (1935), pp. 39-46.

310 LASEBIKAN, E. L. Ida Ward. AFR. AFFAIRS 49 (1950), pp. 30-32.

311 LUKAS, J. Ida C. Ward. AFR. UND UB. 35 (1949-1950), p. 160.

312 TUCKER, A. N. Obituary: Ida Caroline Ward. BULL. SOAS 19 (1949-1951), pp. 542-544.

313 WESTERMANN, D. Professor Ida Ward: an appreciation. AFRICA 20 (1950), pp. 2-4.

314 MEINHOF, C. Alice Werner. AFR. UND UB. 26 (1935-1936), p. 1.

315 In memoriam: Alice Werner. BANTU STUD. 9 (1935), pp. 177-178.

316 LUKAS, J. In Memoriam: Diedrich Westermann. AFR. UND UB. 41 (1957), pp. 1-2.

317 G., B. D. Margaret Wrong. INT. REV. MISSIONS 37 (1948), pp. 292-294.

318 MEINHOF, C. Wilhelm Wundt. AFR. UND UB. 10 (1919-1920), pp. 241-243.

319 GORINI, E. P. Joseph Zobel: la via delle baracche negre. AFRICA (Rome) 15 (1960), pp. 29-30.

See also 3244 (Koelle), 4843 (Breuil).

Periodicals. Newspapers

320 BRAASEM, W. A. Black Orpheus. KONGO-OVERZEE 24 (1958), pp. 66-71.

321 DELAVIGNETTE, R. La Revue Française d'Histoire d'Outre-Mer. REV. FRANC. HIST. OUTRE-MER 46 (1959), pp. 5-6.

322 MAFFI, Q. Dal 1946 al 1956: dieci anni di vita di Africa [Rome]. AFRICA (Rome) 11 (1956), pp. 93-95.

323 MOORE, G. The achievement of Black Orpheus. TRANSITION 1 (1961), p. 28.

324 African newspapers microfilming project. AFR. STUD. BULL. 4, no. iii (1961), p. 12.

325 African newspapers on microfilm. AFR. STUD. BULL. 3, no. ii (1960), pp. 24-25.

326 Africana newsletter [published by the Hoover Institution of Stanford University]. BULL. AFR. STUD. ASSOC. 1 (1964), p. 19.

327 British Museum microfilms of African newspapers. AFR. STUD. ASSOC. 6 (1965), pp. 25-26.

328 Cultural events in Africa: newsletter of the Transcription Centre. BULL. AFR. STUD. ASSOC. 4 (1965), p. 16.

329 Report on reporter: the Transition profile. TRANSITION 4 (1962), pp. 15-17.

See also 3367.

Libraries
[For archives, see History]

330 BASSET, A. Pour une collecte des noms propres. BULL. IFAN 12 (1950), pp. 535-539.

331 BENNETT, N. R. Materials for African history in the Peabody Museum and Essex Institute. AFR. STUD. BULL. 5, no. iii (1962), pp. 13-22.

332 BURNS, R. Survey of Africanist periodicals in Canadian universities. BULL. AFR. STUD. CANADA 1, no. 2 (1964), pp. 21-39.

333 CONOVER, H. F. The Library of Congress holdings on Africa. AFR. STUD. BULL. 2, no. i (1959), pp. 2-8.

334 DADZIE, K.E.W. Les bibliothèques publiques au service des collectivités rurales africaines. PRESENCE AFR. N.S. 23 (1958-1959), pp. 88-96.

335 DADZIE, K.E.W. Libraries, bibliography and archives in French-speaking countries of Africa. UNESCO BULL. LIBS. 15 (1961), pp. 242-253.

336 DEAN, J. The African collection, University of Ghana Library. GHANA LIBRARY JOURNAL 1 (1964), pp. 71-74.

337 DUIGNAN, P. The Africa collections at Stanford University. AFR. STUD. BULL. 3, no. iv (1960), pp. 11-15.

338 EVANS, E. J. A. Library resources in English-speaking countries of West Africa. UNESCO BULL. LIBS. 15 (1961), pp. 227-231.

339 HERRICK, M. D. The library collection of the Boston University African program. AFR. STUD. BULL. 2, no. i (1959), pp. 13-16.

340 HERRICK, M. D. Report on Africana in American theological collections. AFR. STUD. BULL. 3, no. ii (1960), pp. 5-12.

341 HOLDSWORTH, H. University and special libraries and higher education in Africa. UNESCO BULL. LIBS. 15 (1961), pp. 254-258.

342 HORROCKS, S. H. Public and school libraries and popular education in Africa. UNESCO BULL. LIBS. 15 (1961), pp. 259-262.

343 HUTSON, J. B. African materials in the Schomburg Collection of Negro literature and history. AFR. STUD. BULL. 3, no. ii (1960), pp. 1-4.

344 JOLLY, D. Northwestern University's Africana collections. AFR. STUD. BULL. 2, no. i (1959), pp. 9-12.

345 LEE, H.-W. Africana at Duquesne University Library. AFR. STUD. BULL. 6, no. iii (1963), pp. 25-27.

346 MORROW, J. J. Africa publications in the Library of the Department of State. AFR. STUD. BULL. 2, no. ii (1959), pp. 14-15.

347 OFFOR, R. University libraries in the British colonies and the Sudan. LIBRI 5 (1954-1955), pp. 54-75.

348 PEELER, E. H. Education for librarianship in West Africa. NIGERIAN LIBS. 1 (1964), pp. 61-75.

349 PINA, J. R. DE. Construction of libraries in tropical countries. UNESCO BULL. LIBS. 15 (1961), pp. 263-270.

350 PLUMBE, W. J. Furniture and equipment in tropical libraries. UNESCO BULL. LIBS. 15 (1961), pp. 271-276.

351 PORTER, D. B. The African collection at Howard University. AFR. STUD. BULL. 2, no. i (1959), pp. 17-21.

352 REINING, C. C. Activities of the African section of Library of Congress, March 1960 to June 1962. AFR. STUD. BULL. 5, no. iii (1962), pp. 36-41.

353 RICHARDS, C. G. The mechanics of book distribution. TOWARDS A LITERATE AFRICA, 1948, pp. 66-74.

354 ROZSA, G. The international exchange of publications with Afro-Asian countries. UNESCO BULL. LIBS. 16 (1962), pp. 141-143.

355 SAWYER, C. R. Collecting Africana. AFR. AFFAIRS 54 (1955), pp. 312-316.

356 SPYER, G. The architect-client relationship. GHANA LIBRARY JOURNAL 1 (1963), pp. 15-20.

357 VARLEY, D. H. Conference of university libraries in tropical Africa. UNESCO BULL. LIBS. 19 (1965), pp. 73-76.

358 VARLEY, D. H. University library cooperation in tropical Africa. LIBRI 15(1965), pp. 64-71.

359 WILKS, I. Arabic manuscripts from West Africa in Denmark. RES. BULL. CENTRE ARABIC DOC. IBADAN 1 (1964), p. 12.

360 Bibliographia: Standing Conference on Library Materials on Africa (Scolma). J. AFR. LANG. 4 (1965), pp. 226-228.

361 Collections of Africana. UNESCO BULL. LIBS. 15 (1961), pp. 277-287.

362 Leverhulme conference on university library problems in Tropical Africa: Salisbury, Southern Rhodesia, Sept., 1964. BULL. AFR. STUD. ASSOC. 4 (1965), p. 14.

363 Library development in Africa. UNESCO BULL. LIBS. 15 (1961), pp. 225-226.

364 The library of the Royal African Society: a notable gift. J. AFR. SOC. 40 (1941), p. 104.

365 Public libraries in Africa. UNESCO BULL. LIBS. 8 (1954), item 183.

366 Regional library training centre for French-speaking Africa. NIGERIAN LIBS. 1 (1964), p. 91.

367 Regional seminar on the development of public libraries in Africa. UNESCO BULL. LIBS. 17 (1963), pp. 106-122.

368 Standing Conference on Library Materials on Africa. LIBRI 12 (1962), p. 240.

369 The Standing Conference on Library Materials on Africa. BULL. AFR. STUD. ASSOC. 1 (1964), pp. 4-5.

370 Survey of government documents pertaining to Africa held by Canadian libraries. BULL. AFR. STUD. CANADA 2, no. 2 (1965), pp. 9-104; 3, no. 1 (1965), pp. 2-86.

371 Unesco seminar on the development of public libraries in Africa. UNESCO BULL. LIBS. 6 (1952), item 562.

See also 4678, 5111, 5442, 9178, 9461, 18670, 18751, 18768.

Bibliographies

372 BEAUCHENE, G. DE and GARDE, A. Bibliographie africaniste. J. SOC. AFR. 31 (1961), pp. 273-307.

373 BEAUCHENE, G. DE, HARTWEG, R. and JEAN, S. Bibliographie africaniste. J. SOC. AFR. 27 (1957), pp. 221-278.

374 BEAUCHENE, G. DE and HUGON, M. Bibliographie africaniste. J. SOC. AFR. 34 (1964), pp. 317-344.

375 BEAUCHENE, G. DE and HUGON, M. Bibliographie africaniste. J. SOC. AFR. 35 (1965), pp. 425-449.

376 BEAUCHENE, G. DE and LECHEVALLIER-CHEVIGNARD, A. Bibliographie africaniste. J. AFR. SOC. 30 (1960), pp. 233-235.

377 BEAUCHENE, G. DE et al. Bibliographie africaniste, par G. de Beauchêne, O. Ducret, M. Hugon. J. SOC. AFR. 33 (1963), pp. 331-365.

378 BEAUCHENE, G. DE et al. Bibliographie africaniste, par G. de Beauchêne, A. Lechevallier-Chevignard, J. Capron, W. Staude. J. SOC. AFR. 29 (1959), pp. 307-387.

379 BEAUCHENE, G. DE et al. Bibliographie africaniste, par G. de Beauchêne, R. Sillans, O. Rubens-Duval. J. SOC. AFR. 32 (1962), pp. 343-345.

380 BRANNEY, L. Bibliography of recent publications on Africa. AFR. AFFAIRS 49 (1950), pp. 266-268, 354-356.

381 CORNEVIN, R. Publications sur l'ancienne Afrique française au Sud du Sahara. AFR. STUD. BULL. 6, no. iii (1963), pp. 7-12.

382 FERREIRA PAULO, Z. Organização da documentação científica ultramarina. BSEM 127 (1961), L 4.

383 FOLLEVILLE, A. DE. Bibliographie africaniste. J. SOC. AFR. 16 (1946), pp. 51-86; 17 (1947), pp. 93-136.

384 HUGHES, H. G. A. The bibliography of British Africa and the co-ordination of African studies. AFR. AFFAIRS 48 (1949), pp. 63-72.

385 HUGHES, H. G. A. Bibliography of recent publications on Africa. AFR. AFFAIRS 49 (1950), pp. 85-88, 176-178.

386 JONES, R. Africa bibliography series. TANGANYIKA NOTES AND RECORDS 58/59 (1962), p. 294.

387 KLINGBERG, F. J. A survey of recent books on British Africa, with special reference to the native problem. J. MOD. HIST. 10 (1938), pp. 77-93.

388 KUNTZ, M. Bibliographie africaniste. J. SOC. AFR. 13 (1943), pp. 219-229; 14 (1944), pp. 51-78; 15 (1945), pp. 39-106.

389 LESTER, P. Bibliographie africaniste. J. SOC. AFR. 1 (1931), pp. 315-428; 2 (1932), pp. 253-338; 3 (1933), pp. 353-429; 4 (1934), pp. 327-392; 5 (1935), pp. 277-343; 6 (1936), pp. 247-326; 7 (1937), pp. 241-333; 8 (1938), pp. 219-288; 9 (1939), pp. 227-286.

390 LEWIN, J. and ROLLNICK, J. A select bibliography on racial affairs, September 1939-July 1940. RACE RELATIONS 7 (1940), p. 52.

391 MARTI, P. Bibliographie africaniste. J. SOC. AFR. 22 (1952), pp. 161-241.

392 MARTI, P. Bibliographie africaniste. J. SOC. AFR. 23 (1953), pp. 147-212.

393 MARTI, P. Bibliographie africaniste. J. SOC. AFR. 24 (1954), pp. 147-226.

394 MARTI, P. and CHELHOD, J. Bibliographie africaniste. J. SOC. AFR. 25 (1955), pp. 101-191.

395 MARTI, P. and CHELHOD, J. Bibliographie africaniste. J. SOC. AFR. 26 (1956), pp. 291-356.

396 PASQUIER, R. L'Afrique noire d'expression française. REV. FRANC. HIST. OUTRE-MER 48 (1961), pp. 438-457; 50 (1963), pp. 382-535.

397 PATEL, K. H. Selected bibliography on Africa. AFR. QUART. 2 (1962-1963), pp. 305-307.

398 PAULME, D. Bibliographie africaniste. J. SOC. AFR. 10 (1940), pp. 201-258; 11 (1941), pp. 209-221; 12 (1942), pp. 267-272.

399 PAUVERT, C. Bibliographie africaniste. J. SOC. AFR. 18 (1948), pp. 151-194; 19 (1949), pp. 225-254; 20 (1950), pp. 309-347.

400 REINING, C. C. American doctoral dissertations concerned with Africa. AFR. STUD. BULL. 4, no. 1 (1961), pp. 1-49.

401 RELISSIER, R. L'Afrique portugaise dans les publications de la Junta de Investigações do Ultramar (Lisbonne). GENEVE-AFR. 4 (1965), pp. 249-270.

402 WITHERELL, J. W. Articles on African affairs translated by Joint Publications Research Service. AFR. STUD. BULL. 6, no. i (1963), pp. 22-37.

403 WOOLBERT, R. G. Italian colonial expansion in Africa, a bibliographical article. J. MOD. HIST. 4 (1932), pp. 430-445.

404 Bibliographie courante. Literatuuropgave. ZAIRE 1 (1947), pp. 1159-1174; 3 (1949), pp. 101-116, 221-236, 337-355, 463-479, 589-604; 3 (1949), pp. 703-716, 823-840, 941-959, 1051-1061, 1147-1162; 4 (1950), pp. 99-115, 223-238, 339-356, 451-466, 565-579, 685-702, 795-812, 909-926, 1041-1060, 1149-1166; 5 (1951), pp. 93-112, 205-223, 317-335, 428-448, 543-560, 653-671, 763-784, 875-896, 993-1008, 1095-1115; 6 (1952), pp. 93-112, 205-224, 313-336, 427-448, 543-560, 651-671, 763-784, 881-895, 989-1008, 1105-1119; 7 (1953), pp. 97-112, 209-224, 321-336, 429-448, 543-560, 659-672, 769-784, 881-896, 993-1008; 8 (1954), pp.97-111, 217-224, 329-336, 433-448, 541-559, 657-672, 765-784, 875-896, 989-1007, 1103-1120; 9 (1955), pp. 97-111, 207-224, 315-335, 431-448, 545-560, 655-672, 767-784, 877-896, 993-1007, 1101-1119; 10 (1956), pp. 105-112, 217-224, 317-335, 429-447, 545-560, 767-783, 877-895, 991-1008, 1087-1112; 11 (1957), pp. 97-112, 209-224, 317-336, 433-448, 545-559, 653-671, 765-783, 873-896, 1067-1093; 12 (1958), pp. 97-112, 205-224, 311-335, 423-447, 533-560, 659-672, 769-783, 891-904; 13 (1959), pp. 89-111, 203-224, 315-336, 425-448, 537-560, 647-671, 763-783, 871-890; 14 (1960), pp. 91-110, 261-279, 367-400, 603-622.

405 Bibliography of African books. J. AFR. SOC. 14 (1914-1915), pp. 112-115, 226-228, 341-343, 452-454.

406 Bibliography of current literature dealing with African languages and cultures. J. AFR. SOC. 40 (1941), pp. 91-96.

407 La documentazione dell'opera del governo italiano in Africa. AFRICA (Rome) 12 (1957), pp. 119-120.

408 Historical theses on African subjects completed in Great Britain. AFR. STUD. BULL. 4, no. iii (1961), pp. 1-9.

409 A select bibliography on racial affairs, January-August 1939. RACE RELATIONS 6 (1939), pp. 130-131.

See also 502, 530, 548, 550, 732, 817, 841, 874, 886, 935, 955, 959, 985, 1143, 1177, 1562, 1601, 1819, 1895, 2433, 2514, 2582, 2735, 2911, 3048, 3065, 3198, 3258, 3358, 3790, 5067, 5178, 5439, 5440, 5444, 5555, 6617, 6744, 7465, 7491, 7493, 7542, 7590, 8174, 8177, 8383, 8484, 8834, 9404, 9409, 9411, 9705, 9896, 9899, 9994, 9997, 10006, 10605, 10738, 11130, 12009, 12921, 13124, 13295, 13319, 13424, 13756, 13853, 13969, 13995, 14333, 14588, 15003, 15734, 15773, 16105, 16114, 16466, 16685, 16884, 17667, 17668, 17781, 17985, 18632, 19809, 19849, 20785, 21793, 21936, 22664, 22707, 23366, 23368, 24323, 24326, 24344, 24668, 24684.

A G R I C U L T U R E (Farming, Forestry, Fisheries, Soils)

410 A., C. Factores restrictivos en la agricultura africana. CUAD. EST. AFR. 16 (1951), pp. 33-41.

411 ACOCK, A. M. Agricultural potentialities in Africa. MAN AND AFRICA, 1965, pp. 239-257.

412 ALEGRIA, M. DE. Aspectos da formação professional agrícola em Portugal. BSEM 131 (1962), pp. 47-57.

413 ANGLADETTE, A. Lutte contre les pertes subies par les produits agricoles après récolte dans les territoires tropicaux de l'Union Française. CIVILISATIONS 4 (1954), pp. 409-417; English summary, p. 418.

414 ARMSTRONG, C. P. Land usage and land tenure in Sub-Saharan Africa: a brief review of some developments in agricultural areas. PROC. 3RD. GRAD. ACAD. UCLA, 1965, pp. 1-13.

415 BADOUIN, R. Le lancement de la croissance économique par le secteur agricole. ANNALES AFR.,1962, pp. 315-324.

416 BALLICO, P. I 50 dell'Istituto Agronomico per l'Oltremare. AFRICA (Rome) 10 (1955), pp. 227-228.

417 BEKOMBO, M. Incidences sociales de la modernisation en agriculture en Afrique Noire. PRESENCE AFR. N.S. 55 (1965), pp. 135-144.

418 BENIPARRELL, C. DE. La pesca en el Africa Subsahariana, aspectos económico-sociales. CUAD. AFR. OR. 31 (1955), pp. 47-57.

419 BERGE, G. L'aspect humain des problèmes de restauration des sols en Afrique du Nord. AFR. ET ASIE 29 (1955), pp. 29-36; 31 (1955), p. 59.

420 BIEBUYCK, D. Introduction [to African agrarian systems]. AFR. AGRARIAN SYSTEMS, 1963, pp. 1-64.

421 BRASNETT, N. V. Soil erosion. UGANDA J. 4 (1936), pp. 156-161.

422 CECCHELLA, A. Il mondo rurale africano. AFRICA (Rome) 18 (1963), pp. 271-290.

423 CLARK, J. D. The spread of food production in sub-Saharan Africa. J. AFR. HIST. 3 (1962), pp. 211-228.

424 DELEVOY, G. A propos des incendies précoces des herbes. (Réserves forestières, pâturage et contrôle des Glossines en Afrique tropicale). BULL. SEANCES IRCB 5 (1934), pp. 726-734.

425 DUCKHAM, A. N. Farmers versus famine. CORONA 4 (1952), pp. 8-11.

426 DUMONT, R. Les conditions du développement agricole de l'Asie et de l'Afrique tropicales. PRESENCE AFR. N.S. 44 (1962), pp. 60-80.

427 DUMONT, R. Quelques problèmes agricoles africains et malgaches (Madagascar, Côte d'Ivoire, Guinée). PRESENCE AFR. N.S. 31 (1960), pp. 34-44.

428 FICKENDEY, E. Tierra calcinada en los trópicos. ARCH. INST. EST. AFR. 4, no. 12 (1950), pp. 7-18.

429 FRENCH, C. N. Agriculture and development in Tropical African colonies. J. AFR. SOC. 32 (1933), pp. 48-54.

430 GOULDING, E. The present position of sisal hemp cultivation with special reference to the British empire. BULL. IMP. INST. 22 (1924), pp. 39-55.

431 GOUSSAULT, Y. Participation paysanne au développement et aux structures nouvelles. PRESENCE AFR. N.S. 44 (1962), pp. 183-189.

432 GREAT BRITAIN. COLONIAL OFFICE. Notes on some agricultural development schemes in Africa [a report]. J. AFR. ADM. 4 (1952), p. 43.

433 HERFORD, G. V. B. The more important insect pests of cacao, tobacco and dried fruit. BULL. IMP. INST. 31 (1933), pp. 39-55.

434 HUTCHINSON, J. B. The dissemination of cotton in Africa. UGANDA J. 16 (1952), pp. 1-14.

435 HUXLEY, E. The menace of soil erosion. J. AFR. SOC. 36 (1937), pp. 357-370.

436 KIRBY, R. H. Jute and its substitutes: possibilities of production in the Colonial Empire. BULL. IMP. INST. 45 (1947), pp. 97-131.

437 LETOUZEY, R. La forêt à Lophira alata Banks du littoral camerounais. Hypothèses sur ses origines possibles. BULL. I.E.C. 19-20 (1960), pp. 219-240.

438 MAIRE, L. La FAO et l'Afrique noire. Fiat Panis. GENEVE-AFR. 1 (1962), pp. 136-150; with English summary, pp. 151-155.

439 MASEFIELD, G. B. The development of African agriculture. AFR. AFFAIRS 53 (1954), pp. 41-51.

440 MOORE, H. F. Agricultural and technical education in the colonies. ROYAL COL. INST. PR. 22 (1890-1891), pp. 65-110.

441 MOUBRAY, J. M. An agricultural testament, by Sir A. Howard. J. AFR. SOC. 39 (1940), pp. 367-375.

442 OLIPHANT, J. N. The future of forestry in Tropical Africa. J. AFR. SOC. 39 (1940), pp. 248-263.

443 ORMSBY-GORE, W. Agricultural research. J. AFR. SOC. 33 (1934), pp. 18-21.

444 PATRICOLO, M. Su trattrici agricole attraverso l'Africa. AFRICA (Rome) 10 (1955), pp. 366-367.

445 PEARSON, E. O. Problems of insect pests of cotton in Tropical Africa. UGANDA J. 16 (1952), pp. 15-27.

446 PEREIRA MARTINHO, J. P. Criação e exploração racional de animais selvagens. BSEM 128 (1961), pp. 135-151.

447 PORTERES, R. Berceaux agricoles primaires sur le continent africain. J. AFR. HIST. 3 (1962), pp. 195-210.

448 ROYAL AFRICAN SOCIETY. Commission of research: Africa (and other tropical countries). Commission set up to study deforestation and erosion in tropical countries. J. AFR. SOC. 41 (1942), pp. 223-230; 42 (1943), pp. 23-28, 78-85, 125-139; 43 (1944), pp. 78-80.

449 SA, F. V. DE. Problemas basicos de la produccion lechera en los paises tropicales. BSEM 129 (1961), pp. 5-31.

450 SCHARF, J. W. A vital element in agriculture. J. AFR. SOC. 41 (1942), pp. 114-118.

451 SILVA, A. M. DA. Os Serviços e Institutos de Agricultura e a Faculdade ou Escola de Agronomia. BSEM 128 (1961), pp. 17-28.

452 SMITH, J. Livestock development. CORONA 1, no. 9 (1949), pp. 10-12.

453 SOUSA MELO, J. M. DE et al. Processos de conservação da semente de algodão e sua influência na faculdade germinativa. BSEM 124 (1960), pp. 1-14.

454 STEBBING, E. P. Forests and erosion. J. AFR. SOC. 40 (1941), pp. 27-47.

455 STEEL, R. W. Population increase and food production in Tropical Africa. AFR. AFFAIRS, Special Issue (1965), pp. 55-68.

456 TEMPANY, Sir H. Soil erosion: a commonwealth problem. CORONA 1, no. 8 (1949), pp. 3-6.

457 TODD, J. A. The war and the world's cotton crops. BULL. IMP. INST. 13 (1915), pp. 385-392.

458 W. Agrarisch beleid in overzeese gebieden (Symposion van het "Afrika-Instituut" te Amsterdam). ZAIRE 5 (1951), pp. 67-69.

459 WILSON, F. Mechanisation in colonial agriculture. CORONA 4 (1952), pp. 138-143.

460 XABREGRAS, J. Os institutos franceses de Agronomia Tropical. BOL. INST. ANGOLA 19 (1964), pp. 67-75.

461 YUDELMAN, M. Some aspects of African agricultural development. ECON. DEV. FOR AFRICA, 1965, pp. 554-587.

462 Agriculture, husbandry, and nutrition. J. AFR. SOC. 38 (1939), pp. 150-153.

463 Report of a survey of problems in the mechanisation of Native agriculture in tropical African colonies. J. AFR. ADM. 3 (1951), p. 47.

464 Les terroirs tropicaux d'Afrique. PRESENCE AFR. 15 (1953), pp. 259-282.

465 Third International Congress of Tropical Agriculture, London, 1914. BULL. IMP. INST. 12 (1914), pp. 375-407.

See also 199, 631, 699, 1162, 1279, 1503, 1706, 1924, 1934, 2738, 2875, 4158, 4251, 4252, 4354, 4613, 4748.

ANTHROPOLOGY. FOLK-LORE

466 AKANJI. Wenger: an example of Afro-European culture contact. BO 2 (1958), pp. 29-31.

467 ALBERTO, M. S. Da necessidade da efectivação dum circuito antropológica na Africa negra. BSEM 90 (1955), pp. 45-51.

468 ALBERTO, M. S. Plano para a realização dum circuito antropológico na Africa negra. BSEM 97 (1956), pp. 141-148.

469 ALLISON, A. C. Blood groups and African prehistory. PROC. PAN-AFR. CONGR. PRE-HIST. 2 (1952), pp. 307-313.

470 ALMEIDA, A. DE. O sabão e sucedâneos entre os incultos e civilizados. PORT. EM AFR. 2 (1945), pp. 155-159.

471 BA, A. H. Animisme en savane africaine. RELIGIONS AFR. TRAD., 1965, pp. 33-55.

472 BALANDIER, G. Structures sociales traditionnelles et changements économiques. CAH. ET. AFR. 1 (1960), pp. 1-14.

473 BARNES, J. A. The collection of genealogies. RHODES-LIV. J. 5 (1947), pp. 48-55.

474 BARTLETT, F. C. Psychological methods and anthropological problems. AFRICA 10 (1937), pp. 401-419.

475 BARTLETT, F. C. Psychological methods for the study of 'hard' and 'soft' features of culture. AFRICA 16 (1946), pp. 145-155.

476 BASTIDE, R. L'homme africain à travers sa religion traditionnelle. PRESENCE AFR. N.S. 40 (1962), pp. 32-43.

477 BAUMANN, H. Die Afrikanischen kulturkreise. AFRICA 7 (1934), pp. 129-139.

478 BAUMANN, H. The division of work according to sex in African hoe culture. AFRICA 1 (1928), pp. 289-319.

479 BEIER, H. U. Les anciennes religions africaines et le monde moderne. PRESENCE AFR. N.S. 41 (1962), pp. 129-136.

480 BERNARD, J. L'homme primitif a la lumière de l'ethnologie moderne. CONGO 1 (1937), pp. 34-99.

481 BIOBAKU, S. O. De l'emploi et de l'interprétation des mythes: les mythes et la tradition orale. PRESENCE AFR. N.S. 7 (1956), pp. 120-125.

482 BOELAERT, E. De "Bantoe-filosofie" volgens E. P. Tempels. ZAIRE 1 (1947), pp. 387-398.

483 BOSI, R. Costumanze bantu fattori di cultura. AFRICA (Rome) 12 (1957), pp. 121-122.

484 BOULNOIS, J. La mystique de la fécondité et la symbolique de l'arbre, du serpent, de la pierre et de la déesse-mère dans le monde des noirs. BULL. IFAN 7 (1945), pp. 115-147.

485 BRAIN, J. L. More modern witchfinding. TANG. NOTES 62 (1964), pp. 44-48.

486 BULCK, G. VAN. L'anthropologie, la paléontologie, la préhistoire en 1952. ZAIRE 7 (1953), pp. 625-641.

487 BULCK, G. VAN. Le cinquième Congrès international des Sciences anthropologiques et ethnologiques (Philadelphie, U.S.A. 1-9 september 1956). ZAIRE 10 (1956), pp. 965-983.

488 BULCK, G. VAN. Un demi-siecle d'ethnologie: le R. P. W. Schmidt, S.V.D. (16-2-1868—10-2-1954). ZAIRE 8 (1954), pp. 1029-1042.

489 BULCK, G. VAN. L'ethnologie en 1952. ZAIRE 7 (1953), pp. 395-410.

490 BULCK, G. VAN. In memoriam: deux missionnaires ethnographes: les R. P. B. Costermans (11-xi-1903—14-v-1957) et P. J. Schumacher (22-i-1878—26-viii-1957). ZAIRE 12 (1958), pp. 293-303.

491 BULCK, G. VAN. Où en est l'application des cycles culturels dans l'ethnologie africaine? ZAIRE 3 (1949), pp. 3-27.

492 BULCK, G. VAN. Phénomènes religieux et cycles culturels en Afrique. CONGO 2 (1936), pp. 1-55, 161-197.

493 BULCK, G. VAN. Les Pygmées asiatiques et les Pygmées africains constituent-ils une race unique? Nouvelle contribution du R. P. P. Schebesta. ZAIRE 7 (1953), pp. 845-850.

494 BULCK, G. VAN. Le temps et l'au-delà. Journées d'études "Ethnologie et Chrétienté" (Paris, 27 juin-1 juillet 1955). ZAIRE 10 (1956), pp. 165-179.

495 BULCK, G. VAN. Naar een indeling van de afrikaanse stammen. ZAIRE 2 (1948), pp. 15-24.

496 BULCK, G. VAN. Nederlandsche Ethnologendag. KONGO-OVERZEE 4 (1938), pp. 54-81.

497 CAMERON, Lieut. On the anthropology of Africa. JRAI 6 (1876), pp. 167-181.

498 CARRINGTON, J. F. African music in Christian worship. INT. REV. MISSIONS 37 (1948), pp. 198-205.

499 CHAPLIN, J. H. A preliminary note on the rainbow in Africa south of the Sahara. ETHNOS 24 (1959), pp. 151-171.

500 COHEN, R. "Order and Rebellion in Tribal Africa": review article. AMER. ANTHR. 67 (1965), pp. 950-957.

501 COLA ALBERICH, J. Derivaciones sociológicas de la industrialización de Africa. CUAD. EST. AFR. 27 (1954), pp. 41-49.

502 CROWLEY, D. J. African oral literature [a bibliography]. AFR. STUD. BULL. 5, no. ii (1962), pp. 43-44.

503 CULWICK, G. M. New ways for old in the treatment of adolescent African girls. AFRICA 12 (1939), pp. 425-432.

504 CUNHA, A. X. DA. A biologia e as raças humanas. BOL. INST. ANGOLA 10 (1957), pp. 5-19.

505 DADIE, B. Le rôle de la légende dans la culture populaire des Noirs d'Afrique. PRESENCE AFR. N.S. 14-15 (1957), pp. 165-174.

506 DART, R. A. The phylogenetic implications of African and Palestinian mandible profiles. AMER. J. PHY. ANTHR. 12 (1954), pp. 487-502.

507 DOKE, C. M. Bantu wisdom-lore. AFR. STUD. 6 (1947), pp. 101-120.

508 DOMINUS. Skin pigmentation. NADA 36 (1959), pp. 92-96.

509 DOTSON, F. Some reflections on Anthropology and History by E. E. Evans-Pritchard. RHODES-LIV. J. 31 (1962), pp. 55-60.

510 DOUGALL, J. W. C. Characteristics of African thought. AFRICA 5 (1932), pp. 249-265.

511 DRIBERG, J. H. The secular aspect of ancestor-worship in Africa. J. AFR. SOC. 35 (1936), supplement.

512 DU BOIS, W. E. B. La foi des ancêtres. PRESENCE AFR. N.S. 13 (1957), pp. 31-40.

513 DUCHEMIN, J. G. Comment il vit [Diversité du noir africain]. PRESENCE AFR. 8 (1950), pp. 49-60.

514 EDEL, M. On punitive and non-punitive ancestors in Africa. CONGR. INT. ANTHR. ET ETHN. 6, ii (1960), pp. 377-380.

515 EICKSTEDT, Baron VON. Los Hamitas y el paralelismo indio-africano. ARCH. INST. EST. AFR. 4, no. 11 (1950), pp. 7-25.

516 EISENSTADT, S. N. African age groups: a comparative study. AFRICA 24 (1954), pp. 100-112.

517 ESTERMANN, P. C. Missiologia e Etnologia. PORT. EM AFR. 4 (1947), pp. 20-29.

518 EVANS-PRITCHARD, E. E. Applied anthropology. AFRICA 16 (1946), pp. 92-98.

519 EVANS-PRITCHARD, E. E. Sorcery and native opinion. AFRICA 4 (1931), pp. 22-54.

520 EYKEN, A. G. M. VAN. Witchcraft and the supernatural. UGANDA J. 22 (1958), pp. 151-157.

521 FABRO, C. Controverses sur la pensée des primitifs. ZAIRE 3 (1949), pp. 915-924.

522 FARQUHAR, J. H. Bride price. NADA 9, no. 2 (1965), pp. 70-72.

523 FERNANDEZ, J. W. Folklore as an agent of nationalism. AFR. STUD. BULL. 5, no. ii (1962), pp. 3-8.

524 FISCHER, H. TH. Ethnologische beschonwing over kultuur en kulturen. ZAIRE 1 (1947), pp. 1037-1047.

525 FORAN, W. R. Lycanthropy in Africa. AFR. AFFAIRS 55 (1956), pp. 124-134.

526 FORDE, D. Social anthropology in African studies. AFR. AFFAIRS, Special Issue (1965), pp. 15-28.

527 FORTES, M. Some reflections on ancestor worship in Africa. AFRICAN SYSTEMS OF THOUGHT, 1965, pp. 122-144.

528 FORTES, M. The structure of unilineal descent groups. AMER. ANTHR. 55 (1953), pp. 17-41.

529 FRANK, B. Der Hund als Opfertier und Kulturheros in Afrika. FESTSCHRIFT FUR A. E. JENSEN, 1964, pp. 135-144.

530 GARDIN, J. C. Les Human Relations Area Files et la mécanographie dans la documentation ethnographique. CAH. ET. AFR. 1 (1960), pp. 150-152.

531 GARLICK, J. P. Blood group maps of Africa. J. AFR. HIST. 3 (1962), pp. 297-300.

532 GLUCKMAN, M. Malinowski's contribution to social anthropology. AFR. STUD. 6 (1947), pp. 41-

533 GLUCKMAN, M. The origins of social organization. RHODES-LIV. J. 12 (1951), pp. 1-11.

534 GOLDSCHMIDT, W. Theory and strategy in the study of cultural adaptability. AMER. ANTHR. 67 (1965), pp. 402-408.

535 GOSSELIN, G. Pour une anthropologie du travail rural en Afrique noire. CAH. ET. AFR. 3 (1963), pp. 511-550.

536 GRILO, V. H. V. and ALBERTO, M. S. Contribuição para a identificação dos actuais representantes da "Vanished Race" de Breuil, ou "Nordic Race" de R. Dart. BSEM 108 (1958), pp. 99-107.

537 HADDON, E. B. Whistled signals. UGANDA J. 17 (1953), pp. 189-191.

538 HAMBLY, W. D. The serpent in African belief and custom. AMER. ANTHR. 31 (1929), pp. 655-666.

539 HANDY, E. S. C. The religious significance of land. J. AFR. SOC. 38 (1939), pp. 114-123.

540 HARRIS, J. Anthropology during the war: VIII. South and British Central Africa. AMER. ANTHR. 49 (1947), pp. 530-532.

541 HARRIS, R. The political significance of double unilineal descent. JRAI 92 (1962), pp. 86-101.

542 HAWARD, L. R. C. Extra-cultural influences on drawings of the human figure by African children. ETHNOS 21 (1956), pp. 220-230.

543 HERSKOVITS, M. J. African gods and Catholic Saints in New World Negro belief. AMER. ANTHR. 39 (1937), pp. 635-643.

544 HERSKOVITS, M. J. Anthropology and Africa—a wider perspective: the Lugard memorial lecture for 1959. AFRICA 29 (1959), pp. 225-237.

545 HERSKOVITS, M. J. The culture areas of Africa. AFRICA 3 (1930), pp. 59-76.

546 HERSKOVITS, M. J. De l'humanisme en anthropologie. PRESENCE AFR. N.S. 46 (1963), pp. 14-34.

547 HERSKOVITS, M. J. A preliminary consideration of the culture areas of Africa. AMER. ANTHR. 26 (1924), pp. 50-63.

548 HERZFELD, R. F. Some recent anthropological publications on India and Africa. ANTHR. QUART. 36 (1963), pp. 71-73.

549 HEUSCH, L. DE. Les voies de l'anthropologie structurale. ZAIRE 12 (1958), pp. 787-818.

550 HEYDRICH, M. Grundsätzliche Fragen völkerkundlicher Bibliographie. AFRICA 1 (1928), pp. 381-386.

551 HIERNAUX, J. Aspects biologiques de métissage. KONGO-OVERZEE 20 (1954), pp. 181-187.

552 HIRSCHBERG, W. Der ahnencharakter des afrikanischen schwirrholzes. ETHNOS 5 (1940), pp. 112-121.

553 HOBLEY, C. W. Some reflections on native magic in relation to witchcraft. J. AFR. SOC. 33 (1934), pp. 243-249.

554 HOERNLE, R. F. A. Philosophers and anthropologists. BANTU STUD. 14 (1940), pp. 395-408.

555 HOLAS, B. Organisations socio-religieuses en Afrique noire. BULL. IFAN 26 (1964), pp. 40-70.

556 HOLAS, B. Quelques réflexions sur les méthodes et l'organisation de la recherche ethnographique. ZAIRE 8 (1954), pp. 401-413.

557 HOOKER, J. R. The anthropologists' frontier: the last phase of African exploitation. J. MOD. AFR. STUD. 1 (1963), pp. 455-459.

558 HOWLETT, J. Défense et illustration d'une ethnographie engagée. ZAIRE 5 (1951), pp. 621-624.

559 JACOBS, J. Seminarie der Wetenschappen omtrent de Mens te Astrida. KONGO-OVERZEE 20 (1954), pp. 78-83.

560 JADIN, J. Rapport sur une mission d'études anthropologiques effectuée au Congo belge (juillet 1934-février 1935). BULL. SEANCES IRCB 6 (1935), pp. 382-411.

561 JAMBEIN, S. M. and KNAPPERT, J. Utenzi wa Miiraji. The ascension of the Prophet Mohammed. AFR. UND UB. 48 (1964-1965), pp. 241-274.

562 JEFFREYS, M. D. W. African marriages and lobolo. AFR. STUD. 18 (1959), p. 215.

563 JEFFREYS, M. D. W. Democratic institutions in primitive societies. CIVILISATIONS 4 (1954), pp. 35-40; French summary, pp. 41-42.

564 JEFFREYS, M. D. W. The diffusion of cowries and Egyptian culture in Africa. AMER. ANTHR. 50 (1948), pp. 45-53.

565 JEFFREYS, M. D. W. Dual organisation in Africa. AFR. STUD. 5 (1946), pp. 82-105, 157-176.

566 JEFFREYS, M. D. W. Lobolo é o preço da criança. BSEM 132 (1962), pp. 9-81.

567 JEFFREYS, M. D. W. Lobolo is child-price. AFR. STUD. 10 (1951), pp. 145-184.

568 JEFFREYS, M. D. W. Où est le sauvage? PRESENCE AFR. 8 (1950), pp. 95-106.

569 JEFFREYS, M. D. W. Samsonic suicide or suicide of revenge among Africans. AFR. STUD. 11 (1952), pp. 118-122.

570 JEFFREYS, M. D. W. Serpents - kings. NIGERIAN FIELD 12 (1947), pp. 35-41.

571 JEFFREYS, M. D. W. The wanderers. AFR. AFFAIRS 45 (1946), pp. 37-40.

572 JOHNSON, G. B. The negro spiritual: a problem in anthropology. AMER. ANTHR. 33 (1931), pp. 157-171.

573 JOHNSTON, H. H., Sir. On the races of the Congo and the Portuguese colonies in Western Africa. JRAI 13(1884), pp. 461-479.

574 JOHNSTON, H. H., Sir. A survey of the ethnography of Africa: and the former racial and tribal migrations in that continent. JRAI 43(1913), pp. 375-421.

575 JUNOD, H. A. Le noir africain: comment faut-il le juger? AFRICA 4 (1931), pp. 330-342.

576 JUNOD, H.-P. L'Anthropologie gagnerait à se développer en profondeur. CIVILISATIONS 8 (1958), pp. 557-566; English summary, pp. 567-568.

577 KIRCHHOFF, P. Kinship organisation: a study of terminology. AFRICA 5 (1932), pp. 184-191.

578 KNAK, D. S. Einflüsse der europäischen Zivilisation auf das Familienleben der Bantu. AFRICA 4 (1931), pp. 178-200.

579 KOPYTOFF, I. The training of American anthropologists as Africanists. ANTHROPOLOGY AND AFRICA TODAY, 1962, pp. 629-633.

580 KRAUSE, F. Ethnology and the study of culture change. AFRICA 5 (1932), pp. 383-392.

581 LAGERCRANTZ, S. The chewing brush, especially in Africa. ETHNOS 11 (1946), pp. 63-70.

582 LAGERCRANTZ, S. Did bolas anciently occur in Africa? ETHNOS 1 (1936), pp. 30-34.

583 LAGERCRANTZ, S. Ethnographical reflections on "Hottentot aprons." ETHNOS 2 (1937), pp. 145-174.

584 LAGERCRANTZ, S. The milky way in Africa. ETHNOS 17 (1952), pp. 64-72.

585 LAGERCRANTZ, S. Cap.: Notizen, Ringflasche, Ausbreitung. ETHNOS 2(1937), pp. 7-15.

586 LAGERCRANTZ, S. The sacral king in Africa. ETHNOS 9 (1944), pp. 118-140.

587 LAGERCRANTZ, S. Schädeldeformationen und ihre verbreitung in Afrika. ETHNOS 6 (1941), pp. 135-173.

588 LAGERCRANTZ, S. Toe-rings. ETHNOS 10 (1945), pp. 39-43.

589 LAGERCRANTZ, S. Traditional beliefs in Africa concerning meteors, comets, and shooting stars. FESTSCHRIFT FUR A. E. JENSEN, 1964, pp. 319-329.

590 LEAKEY, L. S. B. Man's African origin. ANTHROPOLOGY AND AFRICA TODAY, 1962, pp. 495-503.

591 LEAKEY, L. S. B. A new classification of the bow and arrow in Africa. JRAI 56 (1926), pp. 259-299.

592 LEIRIS, M. Réflexions sur la statuaire religieuse de l'Afrique noire. RELIGIONS AFR. TRAD. 1965, pp. 171-197.

593 LESTRANGE, M. DE. Les crêtes papillaires digitales de 1.491 Noirs d'Afrique occidentale. BULL. IFAN 15 (1953), pp. 1278-1315.

594 LEWIS, I. M. The classification of African political systems: a review article [on Tribes Without Rulers, Studies in African Segmentary Systems]. RHODES-LIV. J. 25 (1959), pp. 59-69.

595 LINDBLOM, G. African harpoon arrows. ETHNOS 4 (1939), pp. 62-72.

596 LINDBLOM, G. Drinking-tubes, especially in Africa. ETHNOS 6 (1941), pp. 48-74.

597 LINDBLOM, G. Mosquito "nets" etc. in Africa. ETHNOS 13 (1948), pp. 124-140.

598 LOUW, A. A. The animism of the Bantu. NADA 4 (1926), pp. 57-61.

599 LUNDMAN, B. Die Blutgruppenverteilung in Afrika. ETHNOS 22 (1957), pp. 120-127.

600 LUNDMAN, B. Einige Grundzüge der jetzigen Anthropologie Afrikas. ETHNOS 15 (1950), pp. 195-200.

601 MACBEATH, A. The study of tribal ethics. RHODES-LIV. J. 24 (1959), pp. 38-50.

602 MAIR, L. P. Chieftainship in modern Africa. AFRICA 9 (1936), pp. 305-315.

603 MAIR, L. P. Witchcraft as a problem in the study of religion. CAH. ET. AFR. 4 (1964), pp. 335-348.

604 MALINOWSKI, B. The pan-African problem of culture contact. AM. J. SOC. 48 (1942-1943), pp. 649-665.

605 MALINOWSKI, B. Practical anthropology. AFRICA 2 (1929), pp. 22-38.

606 MALINOWSKI, B. The present state of studies in culture contact. Some comments on an American approach. AFRICA 12 (1939), pp. 27-47.

607 MAQUET, J. Connaissance des religions traditionnelles. RELIGIONS AFR. TRAD. 1965, pp. 57-74.

608 MARINOV, V. La sokha en Asie, Afrique et Europe. Etude d'ethnologie, d'archéologie et de préhistoire. CONG. INT. SC. ANTH. ET ETHN. 6, i (1960), pp. 569-575.

609 MARWICK, M. G. Mr. Ritchie's double hypothesis [in The African as Suckling and as Adult]. RHODES-LIV. J. 2 (1944), pp. 69-76.

610 MAUNY, R. Séminaire d'Ethno-Histoire (Dakar 11-20 décembre 1961). BULL. IFAN 24 (1962), pp. 614-619.

611 MEADE, H. M. T. The origin and universality of taboo and totemism. NADA 8 (1930), pp. 14-21.

612 MENDES CORREIA, A. A. Africa Inermis. PORT. EM AFR. 3 (1946), pp. 193-196.

613 MENNESSON-RIGAUD, O. Le rôle du Vaudou dans l'indépendance d'Haïti. PRESENCE AFR. N.S. 18-19 (1958), pp. 43-67.

614 MIGEOD, F. W. H. The basis of African religion. J. AFR. SOC. 19 (1919), pp. 20-39.

615 MIGEOD, F. W. H. Some aspects of thinking black. J. AFR. SOC. 15 (1916), pp. 343-355.

616 MISCHEL, F. African "powers" in Trinidad: the Shango cult. ANTHR. QUART. 30 (1957), pp. 45-59.

617 MITCHELL, P. E. The anthropologist and the practical man: a reply and a question. AFRICA 3 (1930), pp. 217-223.

618 MITCHELL, Sir P. The survey of African marriage and family life. AFRICA 24 (1954), pp. 149-156.

619 MOORE, G. [Wilson] Tiberio. BO 9 (1961), p. 62.

620 MOURANT, A. E. The use in anthropology of blood groups and other genetical characters. J. AFR. HIST. 3 (1962), pp. 291-296.

621 MOUSSI, E. E. Les médecines africaines, populaires et autochtones. PRESENCE AFR. N.S. 53 (1965), pp. 194-207.

622 MUMFORD, W. B. and SMITH, C. E. Racial comparisons and intelligence testing. J. AFR. SOC. 37 (1938), pp. 46-57.

623 NADEL, S. F. Experiments on culture psychology. AFRICA 10 (1937), pp. 421-435.

624 NASSAU, R. H. The philosophy of fetishism. J. AFR. SOC. 3 (1904), pp. 257-270.

625 NORBECK, E. Reply to van den Berghe. AMER. ANTHR. 67 (1965), pp. 487-489.

626 NORTON, W. A. Customs of Central and South Africa. J. AFR. SOC. 14 (1914-1915), pp. 81-87.

627 PALES, L. Comment il est fait [Diversité du noir africain]. PRESENCE AFR. 8 (1950), pp. 39-47.

628 PALES, L. Les mutilations tégumentaires en Afrique noire. De l'ethnologie à la pathologie. J. SOC. AFR. 16 (1946), pp. 1-8.

629 PAUL, E. C. Tâches et responsabilités de l'ethnologie. PRESENCE AFR. 27-28 (1959), pp. 237-243.

630 PAULME, D. Que savons-nous des religions africaines? RELIGIONS AFR. TRAD., pp. 13-32.

631 PAULME, D. Régimes fonciers traditionnels en Afrique Noire. PRESENCE AFR. N.S. 48 (1963), pp. 109-132.

632 PAULME, D. Structures sociales traditionnelles en Afrique Noire. CAH. ET. AFR. 1 (1960), pp. 15-27.

633 PELAGE, . La fin d'un mythe scientifique. PRESENCE AFR. 1 (1947), pp. 158-161.

634 PERSON, Y. Tradition orale et chronologie. CAH. ET. AFR. 2 (1962), pp. 462-476.

635 PETTERSON, O. The germ of life: outlines to a study of African cosmology. ETHNOS 21 (1956), pp. 95-104.

636 POSSOZ, E. La magie des primitifs. PRESENCE AFR. N.S. 40 (1962), pp. 88-117.

637 PREUSS, K. TH. Die Hochgottidee bei den Naturvölkern. AFRICA 4 (1931), pp. 287-300.

638 PRINS, A. H. J. Cultuurprovincies in Afrika. KONGO-OVERZEE 19 (1953), pp. 289-305.

639 RADCLIFFE-BROWN, A. R. A further note on joking relationships. AFRICA 19 (1949), pp. 133-140.

640 RADCLIFFE-BROWN, A. R. On joking relationships. AFRICA 13 (1940), pp. 195-210.

641 RATTRAY, R. S. The African child in proverb, folklore, and fact. AFRICA 6 (1933), pp. 456-471.

642 RAUM, O. F. The rolling target (hoop-and-pole) game in Africa. AFR. STUD. 12 (1953), pp. 104-121, 163-180.

643 RICHARDS, A. I. African kings and their royal relatives. JRAI 91 (1961), pp. 135-150.

644 RICHARDS, A. I. Anthropology on the scrap-heap? J. AFR. ADM. 13 (1961), pp. 3-10.

645 RICHARDS, A. I. Practical anthropology in the lifetime of the International African Institute. AFRICA 14 (1944), pp. 289-300.

646 RIPPEN, B. VAN. Practices and customs of the African natives involving dental procedure. AMER. ANTHR. 20 (1918), pp. 461-463.

647 RITCHIE, J. F. The African as grown-up nursling. RHODES-LIV. J. 1 (1944), pp. 55-60.

648 ROLLNICK, J. Problems in classifying literature on the Bantu. BANTU STUD. 15 (1941), pp. 191-195.

649 ROSE, B. W. African and European magic: a first comparative study of beliefs and practices. AFR. STUD. 23 (1964), pp. 1-9.

650 ROUMEGUERE-EBERHARDT, J. Sociologie de la connaissance et connaissance mythique chez les Bantu. CAH. INT. SOCIOL. 35 (1963), pp. 113-125.

651 SANCEAU, E. A lenda do Preste João: e a sua influência sobre os descobrimentos. PORT. EM AFR. SUPPL. (1960-1961), pp. 118-121.

652 SAREVSKAJA, B. I. La Méthode de l'Ethnographie de Marcel Griaule et les questions de méthodologie dans l'ethnographie française contemporaine. CAH. ET. AFR. 4 (1964), pp. 590-602.

653 SCHAPERA, I. Anthropology and the administrator. J. AFR. ADM. 3 (1951), pp. 128-135.

654 SCHEBESTA, P. Recent literature on Bantu tribes: some ethnological and linguistic publications. AFRICA 1 (1928), pp. 116-124.

655 SEITZ, T. Die Grundlagen der Ehe bei den Bantu. AFRICA 3 (1930), pp. 83-89.

656 SELIGMAN, B. Z. Marital gerontocracy in Africa. JRAI 54 (1924), pp. 231-250.

657 SHROPSHIRE, D. The Bantu conception of the supra-mundane world. J. AFR. SOC. 30 (1931), pp. 58-68.

658 SHROPSHIRE, D. Marriage rites and their meaning. NADA 5 (1927), pp. 85-95.

659 SHRUBSALL, F. Crania of African bush races. JRAI 27 (1898), pp. 263-292.

660 SHRUBSALL, F. A study of A-Bantu skulls and crania. JRAI 28 (1899), pp. 55-94.

661 SIMOONS, F. J. The use and rejection of hippopotamus flesh as food in Africa. TANGANYIKA NOTES AND RECORDS 51 (1958), pp. 195-197.

662 SINGER, R. and WEINER, J. S. Biological aspects of some indigeneous African populations. SOUTHWESTERN J. ANTHR. 19 (1963), pp. 168-176.

663 SITHOLE, N. African nationalism and Christianity. TRANSITION 10 (1963), pp. 37-39.

664 SMITH, E. W. Africa: what do we know of it? (Presidential address). JRAI 65 (1935), pp. 1-81.

665 SMITH, E. W. African symbolism. JRAI 82 (1952), pp. 1-81.

666 SMITH, E. W. The function of folk-tales. J. AFR. SOC. 39 (1940), pp. 64-83.

667 SMITH, M. G. On segmentary lineage systems. JRAI 86, pt. II (1956), pp. 39-80.

668 STRUBE, H. Beiträge zur Sinndeutung der wichtigsten künstlichen Körperverstümmelungen in Afrika. FESTSCHRIFT FUR A. E. JENSEN, 1964, pp. 671-722.

669 STRUCK, B. African ideas on the subject of earthquakes. J. AFR. SOC. 8 (1909), pp. 398-411.

670 TASTEVIN, P. C. A grafia etimológica dos nomes tribais africanos. PORT. EM AFR. 4 (1947), pp. 332-338.

671 THOMAS, E. S. The African throwing knife. JRAI 55 (1925), pp. 129-145.

672 THOMAS, L. V. The study of death in Negro Africa. PROC. INT. CONG. AFR. 1 (1962), pp. 146-168.

673 THOMPSON, P. E. S. Reflections upon the African idea of God. SIERRA L. BULL. REL. 7 (1965), pp. 56-61.

674 THOMSON, J. Note on the African tribes of the British Empire. JRAI 16 (1887), pp. 182-186.

675 THURNWALD, R. C. The African in transition. Some comparisons with Melanesia. AFRICA 11 (1938), pp. 174-186.

676 TOBIAS, P. V. Early members of the Genus Homo in Africa. EVOLUTION UND HOMINISATION, 1962, pp. 191-204.

677 TOBIAS, P. V. Studies on the occipital bone in Africa: 1. Pearson's occipital index and the chord-arc index in modern African crania: means, minimum values and variability. JRAI 89 (1959), pp. 233-252.

678 TOIT, B. M. DU. Some aspects of the soul-concept among the Bantu-speaking tribes of South Africa. ANTHR. QUART. 33 (1960), pp. 134-142.

679 TORDAY, E. The principles of Bantu marriage. AFRICA 2 (1929), pp. 255-290.

680 TOSCANO, F. Sôbre os indígenas portugueses ao sul do Zambeze. BSEM 44 (1941), pp. 65-147.

681 TURNER, V. W. A revival in the study of African ritual. RHODES-LIV. J. 17 (1954), pp. 51-56.

682 VAN DEN BERGHE, P. L. Institutionalized license and normative stability. CAH. ET. AFR. 3 (1963), pp. 413-423.

683 VAN DEN BERGHE, P. L. Some comments on Norbeck's "African Rituals of Conflict." AMER. ANTHR. 67 (1965), pp. 485-487.

684 VAZ, M. A Credulidade entre os africanos (Complemento ao estudo do teiticismo o profetismo africanos). PORT. EM AFR. 16 (1959), pp. 153-156.

685 VEIGA, J. Altar Missionário [poema]. PORT. EM AFR. 12 (1955), p. 216.

686 VERDIER, R. Féodalités et collectivismes africains. Etude critique. PRESENCE AFR. N.S. 39 (1961), pp. 79-99.

687 VERGER, P. Les religions traditionnelles africaines sont-elles compatibles avec les formes actuelles de l'existence? RELIGIONS AFR. TRAD. 1965, pp. 97-118.

688 VERNER, S. P. The yellow men of Central Africa. AMER. ANTHR. 5 (1903), pp. 539-544.

689 VINCKE, J. L. Systématique des termes de parenté. CAH. ET. AFR. 2 (1961), pp. 271-291.

690 WADE, Sir A. The unseen world. CORONA 4 (1952), pp. 63-64.

691 WANGER, W. Afrikanische Völkernamen in europäischen Sprachen. AFRICA 2 (1929), pp. 413-418.

692 WARNER, W. L. Methodology and field research in Africa. AFRICA 6 (1933), pp. 51-58.

693 WEISSENBORN, J. Animal-worship in Africa. J. AFR. SOC. 5 (1906), pp. 167-181, 269-289.

694 WELBOURN, F. B. An empirical approach to ghosts. PROC. INT. CONG. AFR. 1 (1962), pp. 124-133.

695 WELBOURN, F. B. The importance of ghosts. TRANSITION 6-7 (1962), pp. 46-50.

696 WERDER, P. VON. Staatstypus und Verwandtschaftssystem. AFRICA 12 (1939), pp. 217-232.

697 WERNER, A. African folk-lore. CONTEMP. REV. 70 (1896), pp. 377-390.

698 WERNER, A. Anthropology and administration. J. AFR. SOC. 6 (1907), pp. 281-285.

699 WERNER, A. The evolution of agriculture. J. AFR. SOC. 9 (1910), pp. 401-415.

700 WESTERMANN, D. The missionary as an anthropological fieldworker. AFRICA 4 (1931), pp. 164-176.

701 WIESCHHOFF, H. A. Some reflections on African cosmographies. ETHNOS 4 (1939), pp. 35-47.

702 WILLIAMS, D. Schmidt Rottluff. BO 11 (1962), pp. 16-17.

703 WILSON, G. Anthropology as a public service. AFRICA 13 (1940), pp. 43-60.

704 WISSE, J. Tot verandering drijvende krachten in primitieve culturen. ZAIRE 1 (1947), pp. 1121-1137.

705 WOLFEL, D. J. Einige afrikanische Axiome und ihre Grundlagen. BIBLIOTHECA AFR. 3 (1929), pp. 109-116.

706 XAVIER DA CUNHA, A. A Biologia e as raças humanas. PORT EM AFR. 16 (1959), pp. 116-126.

707 YOUNG, F. W. Menstrual taboos and social rigidity. ETHNOLOGY 3 (1964), pp. 225-240.

708 The African explains witchcraft. AFRICA 8 (1935), pp. 504-559.

709 Anthropologists in congress [the International Congress of Anthropological and Ethnological Sciences, London]. J. AFR. SOC. 33 (1934), pp. 398-403.

710 O casamento canónico nas colónias Portuguesas. PORT. EM AFR. 3 (1946), pp. 65-76.

711 L'ethnographie en 1952. ZAIRE 7 (1953), pp. 503-524.

712 A Filosofia Bântu. PORT. EM AFR. 4 (1947), pp. 344-356.

713 Groupements ethniques et collectivités d'Afrique Noire. PRESENCE AFR. 15 (1953), pp. 33-44.

714 Groupements ethniques et civilisations nègres d'Afrique. PRESENCE AFR. 15 (1953), pp. 13-32.

715 Le mariage indigène en Afrique française. ZAIRE 6 (1952), p. 288.

716 Myth in modern Africa. RHODES-LIV. J. 27 (1960), pp. 59-67.

717 Proposition sur le folklore. PRESENCE AFR. N.S. 1 (1955), pp. 186-188.

718 Plaidoyer pour une nouvelle paysannerie en Afrique Noire. PRESENCE AFR. 15(1953), pp. 283-291.

719 Recommendations pour l'étude de la famille. BSEC 3(1943), pp. 87-92.

720 The Royal Anthropological Institute. AFR. AFFAIRS 43(1944), p. 9.

721 Séminaire d'Anthropologie Sociale d'Afrique Orientale. ZAIRE 5 (1951), pp. 1079-1080.

See also 470, 531, 542, 830, 963, 2178, 2767, 3097, 3150, 3663, 3781, 4617.

ART. ANTIQUITIES. ARCHAEOLOGY. ARCHITECTURE. MUSIC. SCULPTURE

Archaeology. Pre-history. Proto-history

722 A., G. and A., A. J. The first Pan-African Congress on Prehistory. SUDAN NOTES 28 (1947), pp. 169-171.

723 ARAMBOURG, C. The African Pleistocene mammals. PROC. PAN-AFR. CONGR. PRE-HIST. 1 (1947), pp. 18-25.

724 ARAMBOURG, C. Observations sur la phylogénie des primates et l'origine des hominiens. PROC. PAN-AFR. CONGR. PRE-HIST. 1 (1947), pp. 116-119.

725 ARKELL, A. J. An introduction to African prehistory. AFR. AFFAIRS 49 (1950), pp. 56-67.

726 BONE, E. Le continent africain et les origines humaines. ZAIRE 8 (1954), pp. 1075-1079.

727 BONE, E. La "Pebble-Culture" africaine citée devant le Congrès de Livingstone. ZAIRE 9 (1955), pp. 863-866.

728 BOSCH-GIMPERA, P. Néo-énéolithique espagnol et africain. PROC. PAN-AFR. CONGR. PRE-HIST. 2 (1952), pp. 503-508.

729 BREUIL, H. et al. Excursion archéologique dans l'Afrique du Nord, by H. Breuil, M. Reygasse, P. Roffo. J. SOC. AFR. 6 (1936), pp. 163-166.

730 BREUIL, H. E. P. Raised marine beaches round the African continent and their relation to stone age cultures. PROC. PAN-AFR. CONGR. PRE-HIST. 1 (1947), pp. 91-93.

731 CATON-THOMPSON, G. The evidence of South Arabian Palaeoliths in the question of Pleistocene land connection with Africa. PROC. PAN-AFR. CONGR. PRE-HIST. 3 (1955), pp. 380-384.

732 CHAMPION, P. Publications de l'abbé Henri Breuil sur l'Afrique. J. SOC. AFR. 32 (1962), pp. 75-89.

733 CLARK, J. D. The atlas of African prehistory: a report on progress. PROC. PAN-AFR. CONGR. PRE-HIST. 5 (1965), pp. 311-328.

734 CLARK, J. D. Carbon 14 chronology in Africa South of the Sahara. PROC. PAN-AFR. CONGR. PRE-HIST. 4, iii (1962), pp. 303-310.

735 CLARK, J. D. Changing trends and developing values in African prehistory. AFR. AFFAIRS, Special Issue, 1965, pp. 76-98.

736 CLARK, J. D. Environment and culture-contact in prehistoric Africa South of the Sahara. PROC. PAN-AFR. CONGR. PRE-HIST. 2 (1952), pp. 359-365.

737 CLARK, J. D. The prehistoric origins of African culture. J. AFR. HIST. 5 (1964), pp. 161-183.

738 CLARK, J. D. The stone ball: its associations and use by prehistoric man in Africa. PROC. PAN-AFR. CONGR. PRE-HIST. 2 (1952), pp. 403-417.

739 DAVIDSON, B. A note on "pre-european" Africa. PRESENCE AFR. N.S. 13 (1957), pp. 146-150.

740 DAVIES, O. The neolithic revolution in Tropical Africa. TR. HIST. SOC. GHANA 4 (1960), pp. 3-13.

741 DE GRAFT-JOHNSON, J. C. African empires of the past. PRESENCE AFR. N.S. 13 (1957), pp. 58-64.

742 DIOP, CH.-A. Histoire primitive de l'humanité: évolution du monde noir. BULL. IFAN 24 (1962), pp. 449-541. Also in: PRESENCE AFR. N.S. 51 (1964), pp. 3-13.

743 EWER, R. F. Faunal evidence on the dating of the Australopithecinae. PROC. PAN-AFR. CONGR. PRE-HIST. 3 (1955), pp. 135-142.

744 FAGAN, B. M. Radiocarbon dates for sub-Saharan Africa (from c. 1000 B.C.). J. AFR. HIST. 2 (1961), pp. 137-139; 4 (1963), pp. 127-128; 6 (1965), pp. 107-116.

745 FLEURE, H. J. Drifts of mankind in Africa and Europe. BANTU STUD. 4 (1930), pp. 11-32.

746 HOWELL, F. C. Homicides, pebble tools and the African Villafranchian. AMER. ANTHR. 56 (1954), pp. 378-386.

747 JEFFREYS, M. D. W. Occam's razor: a reply. NADA 31 (1954), pp. 110-113.

748 KELLEY, H. Les collections africaines du département de préhistoire exotique du Musée d'ethnographie du Trocadéro. III. Bifaces acheuléens trouvés dans l'Adrar des Iforas. IV. Haches a gorges africaines. J. SOC. AFR. 5 (1935), pp. 153-157.

749 KIRWAN, L. P. Recent archaeology in British Africa. J. AFR. SOC. 37 (1938), pp. 494-501.

750 KWAPONG, A. A. Africa Antiqua. TR. HIST. SOC. GHANA 2 (1956), pp. 1-11.

751 LANNING, E. C. The third Pan-African Congress on prehistory. UGANDA J. 20 (1956), pp. 202-209.

752 LEAKEY, L. S. B. Capsian or Aurignacian? Which term should be used in Africa? PROC. PAN-AFR. CONGR. PRE-HIST. 1 (1947), pp. 205-206.

753 LEAKEY, L. S. B. Remains of man with Oldowan culture at Olduvai. PROC. PAN-AFR. CONGR. PRE-HIST. 4 (1962), pp. 361-364.

754 LOMBARD, J. Quelques remarques sur le quaternaire de l'Afrique tropicale et équatoriale. J. SOC. AFR. 5 (1935), pp. 175-180.

755 MALAN, B. D. The term Middle Stone Age. PROC. PAN-AFR. CONGR. PRE-HIST. 3 (1955), pp. 223-227.

756 MAUNY, R. L'Afrique tropicale de la période pharaonique à l'arrivée des Arabes. PRESENCE AFR. N.S. 52 (1964), pp. 68-93.

757 MAUNY, R. Le Congrès panafricain de Préhistoire d'Alger. BULL. IFAN 15 (1953), pp. 867-870.

758 MAUNY, R. Le IIIe congrès panafricain de préhistoire (Livingstone). BULL. IFAN 18 (1956), pp. 285-289.

759 MOUTA. F. Contribution du Continent Africain à la préhistoire humaine: les vestiges fossiles. BSEM 101 (1956), pp. 33-46.

760 NENQUIN, J. Inventaria archaeologica Africana. CURRENT ANTHR. 5 (1964), pp. 450-452.

761 NENQUIN, J., ed. Inventaria Archaeologica Africana. J. AFR. HIST. 5 (1964), pp. 449-453.

762 OAKLEY, K. P. Dating of the Australopithecinae of Africa. AMER. J. PHY. ANTHR. 12 (1954), pp. 9-28.

763 PERICOT GARCIA, L. España en el II Congreso Panafricano de Prehistoria. ARCH. INST. EST. AFR. 8, no. 35 (1955), pp. 69-80.

764 PERICOT GARCIA, L. Problemas de la prehistoria africana. ARCH. INST. EST. AFR. 6, no. 2 (1952), pp. 53-68.

765 PERICOT GARCIA, L. El III Congreso Panafricano de Prehistoria. ARCH. INST. EST. AFR. 9, no. 38 (1956), pp. 31-40.

766 PERICOT GARCIA, L. El IV Congreso Panafricano de Prehistoria. ARCH. INST. EST. AFR. 14, no. 56 (1960), pp. 31-40.

767 PERICOT GARCIA, L. El V Congreso Panafricano de Prehistoria. ARCH. INST. EST. AFR. 19, no. 75 (1965), pp. 7-18.

768 PRICE-MARS, J. La paléontologie, la prehistoire et l'archéologie; au point de vue des origines de la race humaine et du rôle joué par l'Afrique dans la genèse de l'humanité. PRESENCE AFR. N.S. 24-25 (1959), pp. 49-59.

769 RAGIR, S. The meaning of stone features in lower paleolithic habitation sites in Africa and Europe. PROC. 3RD. GRAD. ACAD. UCLA, 1965, pp. 235-237.

770 SHERWOOD, E. G. P. The Pan-African Congress on Prehistory, 1947. UGANDA J. 12 (1948), pp. 153-160.

771 SHINNIE, P. L. The teaching of African archaeology. BULL. AFR. STUD. ASSOC. 2 (1964), pp. 15-18.

772 SNOWDEN, F. M. The Negro in ancient Greece. AMER. ANTHR. 50 (1948), pp. 31-44.

773 TARRADELL, M. El problema de las relaciones prehistóricas entre España y Africa: Nuevas perspectivas. ARCH. INST. EST. AFR. 19, no. 75 (1965), pp. 19-34.

774 VANSINA, J. La deuxième conférence sur l'histoire et l'archéologie africaines (Londres, 16-18 juillet 1957). ZAIRE 11 (1957), pp. 865-872.

775 VAUFREY, R. L'âge de la pierre en Afrique. J. SOC. AFR. 23 (1953), pp. 103-138.

776 WRIGLEY, C. Speculations on the economic prehistory of Africa. J. AFR. HIST. 1 (1960), pp. 189-203.

777 African archaeology in the University of Oxford. BULL. AFR. STUD. ASSOC. 3 (1964), pp. 8-9.

778 Comunicaciones del Prof. don Luis Pericot al III Congreso Panafricano de Prehistoria, celebrado en Livingstone en Julio de 1956. Se leyeron acompañadas con proyecciones. ARCH. INST. EST. AFR. 10, no. 41 (1957), pp. 23-27.

779 Inventaria Archaeologica Africana. AFR. STUD. BULL. 7, no. ii (1964), pp. 11-12.

See also 486, 608.

Art in general. Visual arts

780 ACHILLE, L. T. L'artiste noir et son peuple. PRESENCE AFR. N.S. 16 (1957), pp. 32-52.

781 ADANDE, A. Fonction et signification sociales des masques en Afrique Noire. PRESENCE AFR. N.S. 1 (1955), pp. 24-38.

782 ADANDE, A. L'impérieuse nécessité des musées africains. PRESENCE AFR. 10 (1951), pp. 194-198.

783 ANGIOLINO, G. Francobolli d'Africa. AFRICA (Rome) 14 (1959), pp. 79-80.

784 ANTUBAM, K. La peinture en Afrique Noire. PRESENCE AFR. 27-28 (1959), pp. 275-285.

785 ATKINSON, G. A. African housing. AFR. AFFAIRS 49 (1950), pp. 228-237.

786 BAHNA, S. L'architecture et les hommes. PRESENCE AFR. N.S. 49 (1964), pp. 129-149.

787 BALANDIER, G. Les conditions sociologiques de l'art noir. PRESENCE AFR. 10 (1951), pp. 58-71.

788 BALANDIER, G. and HOWLETT, J. Avant-propos [introduction to special volume devoted to African art]. PRESENCE AFR. 10 (1951), pp. 9-11.

789 BASCOM, W. Comment: African arts and social control. AFR. STUD. BULL. 5, no. ii (1962), pp. 22-25.

790 BEIER, V. Aginaldo Dos Santos, an Afro-Brazilian artist. BLACK ORPHEUS 13 (1963), pp. 32-33.

791 BENIPARRELL, C. DE. Importancia social del arte negro africano. CUAD. AFR. OR. 33 (1956), pp. 63-73.

792 BOCHET, G. Les masques sénoufo, de la forme à la signification. BULL. IFAN 27 (1965), pp. 636-677.

793 BOSCH-GIMPERA, P. La problème de la chronologie de l'art rupestre de l'est de l'art rupestre de l'est de l'Espagne et l'Afrique. PROC. PAN-AFR. CONGR. PRE-HIST. 2 (1952), pp. 695-699.

794 BRASIO, P. A. A Iconografia do Negro na Arte Portuguesa. PORT. EM AFR. 4 (1947), pp. 152-154.

795 BRIJBHUSHAN, J. African handicrafts. AFR. QUART. 1, no. ii (1961), pp. 38-43.

796 BROOKS, D. The influence of African art on contemporary European art. AFR. AFFAIRS 55 (1956), pp. 51-59.

797 BROWNE, G. St. J. O. An African shell ornament. J. AFR. SOC. 29 (1930), pp. 285-289.

798 CAILLENS, J. Dix ans de peinture cubaine. PRESENCE AFR. N. S. 37 (1961), pp. 148-150.

799 CAILLENS, J. Prélude au IIe congrès des écrivains et artistes noirs. PRESENCE AFR. N.S. 20 (1958), pp. 130-132.

800 CHAVES, L. Monumentos Portugueses em Africa. PORT. EM AFR. 3 (1946), pp. 149-153.

801 CLAIR, A. Les Nègres, de Jean Genêt. PRESENCE AFR. N.S. 30 (1960), pp. 118-119.

802 COLEMAN, J. S. Comment: African arts and political science. AFR. STUD. BULL. 5, no. ii (1962), pp. 27-29.

803 COLIN, R. Situation de l'art nègre. PRESENCE AFR. N.S. 26 (1959), pp. 52-66.

804 CURTIN, P. D. Comment: African art and African history. AFR. STUD. BULL. 5, no. ii (1962), pp. 25-27.

805 DECAUDIN, M. Guillaume Appollinaire devant l'art nègre. PRESENCE AFR. 2 (1948), pp. 317-324.

806 DIAZ DE VILLEGAS, J. Palabras pronunciadas en el acto de la VI Exposición de Pintores de Africa el día 17 de marzo de 1955. ARCH. INST. EST. AFR. 9, no. 38 (1956), pp. 63-64.

807 DIOP, A. L'artiste n'est pas seul au monde. PRESENCE AFR. 10 (1951), pp. 5-8.

808 DIOP, A. Discours d'ouverture [1er Congrès International des Ecrivains et Artistes Noirs]. PRESENCE AFR. N.S. 8-10 (1956), pp. 9-18.

809 DIOP, A. Le sens de ce [IIe] Congrès [des écrivains et artistes noirs]. Discours d'ouverture. PRESENCE AFR. N.S. 24-25 (1959), pp. 40-48.

810 DREYFUS, J. Note sur l'utilisation du béton de terre et du béton de terre stabilisé pour la construction. BULL. IFAN 14 (1952), pp. 1111-1118.

811 DROST, D. Besondere Verhaltensweisen in Verbindung mit dem Töpferhandwerk in Afrika. FESTSCHRIFT FUR A. E. JENSEN, 1964, pp. 103-111.

812 ENWONWU, B. Problems of the African artist today. PRESENCE AFR. N.S. 8-10 (1956), pp. 174-178.

813 EPANYA, E. "Halleluyah": ou l'exploitation du genie artistique du negre. PRESENCE AFR. N.S. 5 (1955-1956), pp. 113-114.

814 FOUCHER, L. Influence de la peinture hellénistique sur la mosaïque africaine aux IIe et IIIe siècles. CT 7 (1959), pp. 263-274.

815 FRANCES, J. Apostillas a la VI Exposición de Pintores de Africa. ARCH. INST. EST. AFR. 9, no. 38 (1956), pp. 51-61.

816 FRANCES, J. Entre el sí y el no del Arte contemporáneo. ARCH. INST. EST. AFR. 13, no. 49 (1959), pp. 7-15.

817 FRASER, D. African architecture [a bibliography]. AFR. STUD. BULL. 5, no. ii (1962), pp. 47-49.

818 FURLONG, J. R. The marking of hides and skins. BULL. IMP. INST. 43 (1945), pp. 8-13.

819 FURLONG, J. R. Trials to determine the value of certain new insecticides as preventives against hide beetle [in leatherwork]. BULL. IMP. INST. 45 (1947), pp. 325-335.

820 GARLANDA, V. Ricordo i costruttori d'Africa biellesi. AFRICA (Rome) 12 (1957), pp. 129-133.

821 GIULIO, F. La prima pittura di negro. RASS. STUDI ETIOP. 3 (1943), pp. 139-147.

822 GONÇALVES, J. J. O Museu do Ultramar e a Protecção das artes plásticas negro-africanas. BCGP 12 (1957), pp. 347-353.

823 GOODWIN, A. J. H. The art of Africa: an introduction. AFR. SOUTH 2, no. 4 (1958), pp. 94-101.

824 GRIAULE, M. Les symboles des arts africains. PRESENCE AFR. 10 (1951), pp. 12-24.

825 GROTTANELLI, V. L. Sul significato della scultura Africana. AFRICA 31 (1961), pp. 324-338; English summary, pp. 338-343.

826 GUERIN, D. "Authentique célébration du culte Vaudou" au Vieux-Colombier. PRESENCE AFR. N.S. 30 (1960), pp. 119-120.

827 HARDING, J. R. Conus shell disc ornaments (Vibangwa) in Africa. JRAI 91 (1961), pp. 52-66.

828 HASELBERGER-BLAHA, H. [On African art]. PRESENCE AFR. N.S. 24-25 (1959), pp. 283-285.

829 HAWARD, L. R. C. African art: a psychological study. AFR. AFFAIRS 59 (1960), pp. 324-327.

830 HEUSCH, L. DE. Le rayonnement de l'Egypte antique dans l'art et la mythologie de l'Afrique occidentale. J. SOC. AFR. 28 (1958), pp. 91-109.

831 HILL, J. N. The idiom in African art with special emphasis on African sculpture. PAN-AFRICANISM RECONSIDERED, 1962, pp. 324-336.

832 HOWLETT, J. L'art negre? Connais pas! PRESENCE AFR. 10 (1951), pp. 85-90.

833 ITALIAANDER, R. Incontri con artisti dell'Africa nuova. AFRICA (Rome) 18 (1963), pp. 63-74.

834 ITALIAANDER, R. Introduction à l'art nouveau en Afrique. PRESENCE AFR. N.S. 20 (1958), pp. 25-43.

835 JAHN, J. Kuntu. L'impossibilité de la métamorphose du style. PRESENCE AFR. N.S. 22 (1958), pp. 10-28.

836 JEFFREYS, M. D. W. Guns. AFR. AFFAIRS 43 (1944), pp. 25-27.

837 JEFFREYS, M. D. W. Negro influences on Indonesia. AFR. MUSIC, 1961, pp. 10-16.

838 JEFFREYS, M. D. W. Snake stones. J. AFR. SOC. 41 (1942), pp. 250-253.

839 JELENSKI, K. A. Beyond the Sistine chapel, beyond a mask from the Ivory Coast. TRANSITION 18 (1965), pp. 46-50.

840 JOACHIM, P. "Le Vaudou haïtien" sur la scène du Vieux-Colombier (l'héritage africain renié à 90 pour cent). PRESENCE AFR. N.S. 30 (1960), pp. 121-122.

841 JOLLY, D. Bibliography and the arts of Africa. AFR. STUD. BULL. 3, no. i (1960), pp. 4-9.

842 KAHNWEILER, D.-H. L'Art nègre et le cubisme. PRESENCE AFR. 3 (1948), pp. 367-377.

843 KILLENS, J. D. L'héritage de Handy. PRESENCE AFR. N.S. 26 (1959), pp. 77-88.

844 KINGDON, J. Reflections. TRANSITION 6-7 (1962), pp. 36-37.

845 LABOURET, H. L'apport de l'Afrique à la civilisation planétaire. PRESENCE AFR. 8 (1950), pp. 403-408.

846 LAFUENTE FERRARI, E. Africa en la pintura. ARCH. INST. EST. AFR. 13, no. 51 (1959), pp. 7-18.

847 LAVACHERY, H. L'art des Noirs d'Afrique et son destin. PRESENCE AFR. 10 (1951), pp. 38-57.

848 LEM, F.-H. Variété et unité des traditions plastiques de l'Afrique noire. PRESENCE AFR. 10 (1951), pp. 25-37.

849 LINDBLOM, K. G. Spears with two or more heads, particularly in Africa. ESSAYS PRESENTED TO C. G. SELIGMAN, 1934, pp. 149-181.

850 MALIK, H. The art of Africa. AFR. QUART. 2, no. i (1962), pp. 27-34.

851 MANGONES, A. Architecture et civilisation négro-africaine. PRESENCE AFR. 27-28 (1959), pp. 286-290.

852 MAZZA, C. Allocution du sénateur C. Mazza, représentant du gouvernement, au cours de la séance inaugurale au Capitole. PRESENCE AFR. N.S. 24-25 (1959), pp. 27-28.

853 MONTEZ, C. Portugal na Exposição de Paris. BSEM 1 (1931), pp. 35-36.

854 MOODY, R. The background of African art. PRESENCE AFR. N.S. 14-15 (1957), pp. 175-179.

855 MURRAY, K. C. The Colonial Art Exhibition. NIGERIAN FIELD 17 (1952), pp. 41-42.

856 MVENG, E. L'art africain d'hier et l'Afrique d'aujourd'hui... PRESENCE AFR. N.S. 46 (1963), pp. 35-51.

857 MVENG, E. Structures fondamentales de l'art negro-africain. PRESENCE AFR. N.S. 49 (1964), pp. 116-128; N.S. 52 (1964), pp. 104-127.

858 NENQUIN, J. Inventaria Archaeologica Africana. AMER. ANTHR. 67 (1965), pp. 499-502.

859 NJAU, E. P. African art. PROC. INT. CONG. AFR. 1(1962), pp. 235-242.

860 NJAU, E. P. Copying puts God to sleep: some thoughts on the true African and art. TRANSITION 9(1963), pp. 15-17.

861 OBAMA, J.-B. L'art nègre dans la vie africaine. ABBIA 8 (1965), pp. 76-96.

862 OBAMA, J.-B. Propos sur les arts nègres. PRESENCE AFR. N.S. 41 (1962), pp. 58-74.

863 OVEJERO, A. La visión artística de Africa. ARCH. INST. EST. AFR. 2, no. 6 (1948), pp. 137-153.

864 PATERSON, E. Cyrene art in London, 1954. NADA 32(1955), pp. 72-76.

865 PATERSON, E. The nature of Bantu art and some suggestions for its encouragement. NADA 19(1942), pp. 41-50.

866 PAUVERT, J. C. Approche de l'art africain noir. PRESENCE AFR. 10 (1951), pp. 72-84.

867 PORTER, J. A. The American Negro artist looks at Africa. PAN-AFRICANISM RECONSIDERED, 1962, pp. 293-296.

868 POSNANSKY, M. Bantu genesis. UGANDA J. 25 (1961), pp. 86-93.

869 RIESER, H. F. African ivories. AFR. SOUTH 5, no. 4 (1961), pp. 112-116.

870 ROBINSON, A. E. Rock pictures. J. AFR. SOC. 33 (1934), pp. 353-360.

871 SEGY, L. Aspects of African art for the museums. CAH. ET. AFR. 1 (1960), pp. 125-128.

872 SEKOTO, G. La responsabilité et la solidarité dans la culture africaine. PRESENCE AFR. 27-28 (1959), pp. 263-267.

873 SHAW, T. Early smoking pipes: in Africa, Europe, and America. JRAI 90 (1960), pp. 272-305.

874 SIEBER, R. African art [a bibliography]. AFR. STUD. BULL. 5, no. ii (1962), pp. 40-42.

875 SIEBER, R. The arts and their changing social function. ANTHROPOLOGY AND AFRICA TODAY, 1962, pp. 653-659.

876 SIEBER, R. Masks as agents of social control. AFR. STUD. BULL. 5, no. ii (1962), pp. 8-13.

877 SIERRA OCHOA, A. Ausencia y presencia del Arte mayor en la VII Exposición de Pintores de Africa. ARCH. INST. EST. AFR. 9, no. 39 (1956), pp. 25-57.

878 SILONE, I. La souffrance transformée en valeur [allocution au IIe Congrès des écrivains et artistes noirs]. PRESENCE AFR. N.S. 24-25 (1959), p. 34.

879 SIMOONS, F. J. A rain cape common to South Asia and Africa. UGANDA J. 23 (1959), pp. 84-85.

880 SMITH, H. Creativity and the negro. AFR. FORUM 1 (1965), pp. 117-120.

881 SYDOW, E. VON. African sculpture. AFRICA 1 (1928), pp. 210-227.

882 SYDOW, E. VON. The image of Janus in African sculpture. AFRICA 5 (1932), pp. 14-27.

883 TAYLOR, B. Exhibition of traditional art from the colonies. CORONA 3 (1951), pp. 303-305.

884 TODA OLIVA, E. Africa en la pintura española actual (Primera Exposición de pintores de Africa). CUAD. EST. AFR. 9 (1950), pp. 119-126.

885 TROWELL, M. From Negro sculpture to modern painting. UGANDA J. 6 (1939), pp. 169-175.

886 WALTON, J. Patterned walling in African folk building. J. AFR. HIST. 1 (1960), pp. 19-30.

887 Le peintre Tiberio. PRESENCE AFR. N.S. 50 (1964), pp. 251-253.

See also 592.

Music. Dancing. Cinema. Theatre

888 ACHILLE, L. T. Chanter avec dieu, danser avec lui. PRESENCE AFR. N.S. 54 (1965), pp. 127-136.

889 BANSISA, Y. Music in Africa. UGANDA J. 4 (1936), pp. 108-114.

890 BASCOM, W. Main problems of stability and change in tradition. AFR. MUSIC, 1958, pp. 6-10.

891 BASIL, Dr. the Rev. B. Wandering from pitch. AFR. MUSIC, 1958, pp. 54-55.

892 BASSORI, T. Un cinéma mort-né? PRESENCE AFR. N.S. 49 (1964), pp. 111-115.

893 BATAILLE. Cinéma et acteurs noirs. PRESENCE AFR. 4 (1948), pp. 690-696.

894 BILSEN, J. VAN. Vlaamse toneelgroep en cultureel leven. ZAIRE 4 (1950), pp. 871-872.

895 BLACKING, J. Some notes on a theory of African rhythm advanced by Erich von Hornbostel. AFR. MUSIC, 1955, pp. 12-20.

896 BORNEMAN, E. Les racines de la musique américaine noire. PRESENCE AFR. 4 (1948), pp. 576-589.

897 CHILKOVSKY, N. African dance [a bibliography]. AFR. STUD. BULL. 5, no. ii (1962), pp. 45-47.

898 COPE, T. "African music," a lecture given at Natal University. AFR. MUSIC, 1959, pp. 33-41.

899 COYNE, A. E. Visual indication of pitch. AFR. MUSIC, 1951, pp. 19-25.

900 DIGGS, I. A note on Fernando Ortiz and Afro-Cuban music. ZAIRE 8 (1954), pp. 301-304.

901 DOR. Serengheti non deve morire. AFRICA (Rome) 15 (1960), pp. 31-32.

902 DUNBAR, R. La musique africaine et son influence dans le monde. PRESENCE AFR. 27-28 (1959), pp. 291-302.

903 FILESI, T. Con il cinema incontro agli africani. AFRICA (Rome) 11 (1956), pp. 143-146.

904 FODEBA, K. La danse africaine et la scène. PRESENCE AFR. N.S. 14-15 (1957), pp. 202-209.

905 FONDEVILLE, P. M. Langage musical négro-africain. AFR. ET ASIE 35 (1956), pp. 53-56.

906 GEORGE, Z. Note sugli spirituals negri. AFRICA (Rome) 15 (1960), pp. 81-85.

907 GRIFFITH, W. J. On the appreciation of African music. NIGERIAN FIELD 16 (1951), pp. 88-93.

908 HORNBOSTEL, E. M. VON. African negro music. AFRICA 1 (1928), pp. 30-62.

909 HORNBOSTEL, E. M. VON. The ethnology of African sound-instruments: comments on Geist und Werden der Musikinstrumente, by C. Sachs. AFRICA 6 (1933), pp. 129-157, 277-311.

910 HYSLOP, G. The need for research in African music. AFR. MUSIC, 1964, pp. 20-24.

911 JONES, A. M. African drumming. A study in the combination of rhythms in African music. BANTU STUD. 8 (1934), pp. 1-16.

912 JONES, A. M. African metrical lyrics. AFR. MUSIC, 1964, pp. 6-14.

913 JONES, A. M. African metrical lyrics. AFR. LANG. STUD. 5 (1964), pp. 52-63.

914 JONES, A. M. African music [Press report of lecture to Bulawayo Music Club, September, 1949]. AFR. MUSIC, 1963, pp. 16-18.

915 JONES, A. M. African rhythm. AFRICA 24 (1954), pp. 26-47.

916 JONES, A. M. Blue notes and hot rhythm. AFR. MUSIC, 1951, pp. 9-12.

917 JONES, A. M. Drums down the centuries. AFR. MUSIC, 1957, pp. 4-10.

918 JONES, A. M. East and West, North and South. AFR. MUSIC, 1954, pp. 57-62.

919 JONES, A. M. Experiment with a xylophone key. AFR. MUSIC, 1963, pp. 6-10.

920 JONES, A. M. Hymns for the African. AFR. MUSIC, 1950, pp. 8-12.

921 JONES, A. M. Indonesia and Africa: the xylophone as a culture-indicator. AFR. MUSIC, 1960, pp. 36-47. Also in JRAI 89 (1959), pp. 155-168.

922 JONES, A. M. Instruments de musique africains. PRESENCE AFR. N.S. 34-35 (1960-1961), pp. 132-150.

923 JONES, A. M. On transcribing African music. AFR. MUSIC, 1958, pp. 11-14.

924 JONES, A. M. What's in a smile? AFR. MUSIC, 1950, pp. 13-16.

925 KAUFFMAN, R. A. Impressions of African church music. AFR. MUSIC, 1964, pp. 109-110.

926 KING, A. V. and BOSTON, J. S. Suggestions for the organisation of an archive of recorded music. AFRICAN NOTES 1, no. 3 (1964), pp. 12-18.

927 KINGUE, M. D. L'apport de l'Afrique dans la musique de jazz. ABBIA 2 (1963), pp. 122-134; 3 (1963), pp. 133-140.

928 LE MAILLOUX, M. A música dos pretos. PORT. EM AFR. 3 (1946), pp. 274-280.

929 LESHOAI, B. Theatre and the common man in Africa. TRANSITION 19 (1965), pp. 44-47.

930 LONG, K. R. The future of African music. NADA 23 (1946), pp. 24-28.

931 LOUNG, M. Pour une rénovation de la musique négro-africaine. ABBIA 3 (1963), pp. 128-132.

932 MCHARG, J. Wild flowers of folk-song. [With additional note by Fr. F. Giorgetti.] AFR. MUSIC, 1949, pp. 7-8.

933 MACLEOD, Sir J. M. A ballad of the army of the Nile. J. AFR. SOC. 40 (1941), pp. 312-315.

934 MANERA, G. Il cinema in Africa nei suoi riflessi economici. AFRICA (Rome) 12 (1957), pp. 72-74.

935 MERRIAM, A. P. An annotated bibliography of African and African-derived music since 1936. AFRICA 21 (1951), pp. 319-329.

936 MERRIAM, A. P. Musical instruments and techniques of performance among the Bashi. ZAIRE 9 (1955), pp. 121-132.

937 MERRIAM, A. P. Songs of the Ketu cult of Bahia, Brazil. AFR. MUSIC, 1956, pp. 53-67.

938 MICKLEBURGH, R. Music on stamps. AFR. MUSIC, 1960, p. 63.

939 MORISSEAU-LEROY, F. Le théâtre dans la révolution africaine. PRESENCE AFR. N.S. 52 (1964), pp. 60-67.

940 NICOLAS, F. J. Origine et valeur du vocabulaire désignant les xylophones africains. ZAIRE 11 (1957), pp. 69-89.

941 NKETIA, J. H. African gods and music. UNIVERSITAS 4 (1959), pp. 3-7.

942 NKETIA, J. H. Unity and diversity in African music: a problem of synethesis. PROC. INT. CONG. AFR. 1 (1962), pp. 256-263.

943 OBAMA, J. B. Do folclore gregoriano ao tam-tam africano. PORT. EM AFR. 21 (1964), pp. 183-196.

944 OBAMA, J. B. Du folklore grégorien au tam-tam africain. AFRICA (Rome) 18 (1963), pp. 138-144.

945 OBAMA, J. B. Musica tradicional africana. PORT. EM AFR. 20 (1963), pp. 290-304.

946 OBAMA, J. B. Musique africaine traditionnelle. AFRICA (Rome) 17 (1962), pp. 125-132.

947 PANASSIE, H. Le mal blanc. PRESENCE AFR. 1 (1947), pp. 146-148.

948 RHODES, W. Music as an agent of political expression. AFR. STUD. BULL. 5, no. ii (1962), pp. 14-22.

949 RHODES, W. Society of Ethnomusicology. AFR. MUSIC, 1956, pp. 70-71.

950 ROUGET, G. Josephine Baker. PRESENCE AFR. N.S. 7 (1956), p. 141.

951 ROUGET, G. La musique. PRESENCE AFR. N.S. 3 (1955), pp. 71-73.

952 SCHAEFFNER, A. La découverte de la musique noire. PRESENCE AFR. 8 (1950), pp. 205-218.

953 SCHAEFFNER, A. Timbales et longues trompettes. BULL. IFAN 14 (1952), pp. 1466-1489.

954 SENGHOR, B. Pour un authentique cinéma africain. PRESENCE AFR. N.S. 49 (1964), pp. 104-110.

955 SHORE, H. L. African theatre and drama [a bibliography]. AFR. STUD. BULL. 5, no. ii (1962), pp. 49-53.

956 SMITH, H. L. George W. Cable and two sources of jazz. AFR. MUSIC, 1960, pp. 59-62.

957 SOWANDE, F. African music. AFRICA 14 (1943), pp. 340-342.

958 TEGETHOFF, W. Tendances nouvelles dans la musicologie comparative. AEQUATORIA 18 (1955), pp. 26-28.

959 THIEME, D. L. A selected bibliography of periodical articles on the music of the native peoples of sub-Saharan Africa. AFR. MUSIC, 1962, pp. 103-110.

960 TRACEY, H. African music. NYASA. J. 3, no. 2 (1950), pp. 16-18.

961 TRACEY, H. African music: a modern view. NADA 19 (1942), pp. 57-60.

962 TRACEY, H. African music within its social setting. AFR. MUSIC, 1958, pp. 56-58.

963 TRACEY, H. The arts in Africa. The visual and the aural. AFR. MUSIC, 1962, pp. 20-32.

964 TRACEY, H. Behind the lyrics. AFR. MUSIC, 1963, pp. 17-22.

965 TRACEY, H. The development of music. AFR. MUSIC, 1963, pp. 36-40.

966 TRACEY, H. The development of music in Africa. TANG. NOTES 63 (1964), pp. 213-221.

967 TRACEY, H. The importance of African music in the present day. AFR. AFFAIRS 60 (1961), pp. 155-162.

968 TRACEY, H. Música Africana. BSEM 69 (1951), pp. 61-64.

969 TRACEY, H. Recording African music in the field. AFR. MUSIC, 1955, pp. 6-11.

970 TRACEY, H. The social role of African music. AFRICA 53 (1954), pp. 234-241.

971 TRACEY, H. The state of folk music in Bantu Africa. AFR. MUSIC, 1954, pp. 8-11.

972 TRACEY, H. Tina's lullaby. NADA 40 (1963), pp. 46-49.

973 TRACEY, H. Towards an assessment of African scales. AFR. MUSIC, 1958, pp. 15-20.

974 VAUGHAN, J. K. Africa south of the Sahara and the cinema. PRESENCE AFR. N.S. 14-15 (1957), pp. 210-221.

975 VIEYRA, P. S. La cinéma et la révolution africaine. PRESENCE AFR. N.S. 34-35 (1960-1961), pp. 92-103.

976 VIEYRA, P. S. Où en sont le cinéma et le theatre africains? PRESENCE AFR. N.S. 13 (1957), pp. 143-146.

977 VIEYRA, P. S. Propos sur le cinéma africain. PRESENCE AFR. N.S. 22 (1958), pp. 106-117.

978 VIEYRA, P. S. Quand le cinéma français parle au nom de l'Afrique Noire. PRESENCE AFR. N.S. 11 (1957), pp. 142-145.

979 VIEYRA, P. S. Réflexions sur le premier concours international du film d'outre-mer. PRESENCE AFR. N.S. 17 (1957-1958), pp. 118-122.

980 VIEYRA, P. S. Responsabilités du cinéma dans la formation d'une conscience nationale africaine. PRESENCE AFR. 27-28 (1959), pp. 303-313.

981 WACHSMANN, K. P. An approach to African music. UGANDA J. 6(1939), pp. 148-163.

982 WACHSMANN, K. P. The sociology of recording in Africa south of the Sahara. AFR. MUSIC, 1959, pp. 77-79.

983 WISCHNEGRADSKY, D. Le blues. PRESENCE AFR. N.S. 37 (1961), pp. 157-188.

984 ZINEVRAKIS, E. L'Africa al festival internazionale del film della montagna a dell'esplorazione. AFRICA (Rome) 13 (1958), pp. 357-358.

985 African music [a bibliography]. AFR. STUD. BULL. 5, no. ii (1962), pp. 35-40.

986 The International Library of African Music. AFR. MUSIC, 1954, pp. 71-73; 1958, pp. 63-64.

987 Music for African schools—a discussion. AFR. MUSIC, 1951, pp. 29-31.

988 Musique africaine. PRESENCE AFR. N.S. 45 (1963), pp. 224-227.

989 A new enterprise. The Osborn awards for the best African musicians of the year. AFR. MUSIC, 1953, pp. 65-67; 1954, pp. 69-70; 1958, pp. 74-76.

990 Notes on Monsieur Herbert Pepper's address to Venice Festival 1949. AFR. MUSIC, 1950, pp. 3-7.

991 Notes on music in African schools. AFR. MUSIC, 1957, pp. 48-51.

See also 502, 608, 1084, 1549, 1762, 1767, 3906, 3990, 4376, 4378, 4407, 4733.

BIOGRAPHY

992 GLUCKMAN, M. As men are everywhere else [appreciation of Frank Debenham's The Way to Ilala: David Livingstone's Pilgrimage and Jack Simmon's Livingstone and Africa]. RHODES-LIV. J. 20 (1956), pp. 68-73.

993 BERLAND, L. In memoriam: Charles Alluaud. BULL. IFAN 12 (1950), p. 513.

994 DOKE, C. M. Mrs. E. O. Ashton—90. AFR. STUD. 23 (1964), p. 166.

995 GALWAY, Lady. The Right Hon. The Earl of Athlone; by M. E. Sara. J. AFR. SOC. 40 (1941), pp. 202-203.

996 HAILEY, Lord. Death of the Earl of Athlone. AFR. AFFAIRS 56 (1957), p. 94.

997 MEINHOF, C. Herr Heinrich Wilhelm Augustin [Nachruf]. AFR. UND UB. 29 (1939), p. 76.

998 BACON, L. W. The services of Leonard Bacon to African colonization. LIBERIA BULL. 15 (1899), pp. 1-21; 16 (1900), pp. 40-55.

999 BOVILL, E. W. Henry Barth. J. AFR. SOC. 25 (1926), pp. 311-320.

1,000 Obituary [Sir G. Orde Browne and others]. AFR. AFFAIRS 46 (1947), pp. 169-170.

1,001 Obituary: Sir David Bruce. J. AFR. SOC. 31 (1932), pp. 100-102.

1,002 PEREIRA, B. "Sir" Richard Burton: Lacerda e Almeida. BSEM 93 (1955), pp. 205-212.

1,003 WINGATE, Sir R. In memoriam. Sydney Charles, Earl Buxton. J. AFR. SOC. 34 (1935), pp. 1-6.

1,004 ARMATTOE, R. E. G. Death of Dr. George Washington Carver. AFR. AFFAIRS 43 (1944), pp. 54-55.

1,005 BARBOUR, G. In memoriam: Pierre Teilhard de Chardin. PROC. PAN-AFR. CONGR. PRE-HIST. 3 (1955), pp. xxviii-xxix.

1,006 Obituary: Dr. Cuthbert Christy. J. AFR. SOC. 31 (1932), pp. 339-341.

1,007 PINAR LOPEZ, B. Africa o muerte. Daniel Comboni, Pionero de las Misiones de Africa. ARCH. INST. EST. AFR. 19, no. 77 (1965), pp. 41-60.

1,008 Jules Cornet [obituary]. BULL. SEANCES IRCB 2 (1931), pp. 24-31.

1,009 B. Costermans. See 490

1,010 MARQUES, C. Azevedo Coutinho. PORT. EM AFR. 2 (1945), pp. 22-27.

1,011 KLINGENHEBEN, A. and LUKAS, J. Zum Tode von Wilhelm Czermak. AFR. UND UB. 37 (1952-1953), p. 97.

1,012 Luigi Del Giudice. AFRICA (Rome) 10 (1955), p. 88.

1,013 LEVA, A. E. Cheikh Anta Diop e il primato morale e civile dei negri. AFRICA (Rome) 16 (1961), pp. 63-69.

1,014 BLAIR, T. Du Bois et le siècle de la libération africaine. PRESENCE AFR. N.S. 49 (1964), pp. 184-191.

1,015 FONLON, B. The passing of a great African: a tribute [to Dr. W. E. B. DuBois]. ABBIA 4 (1963), pp. 3-15.

1,016 ISAACS, H. R. DuBois and Africa. RACE 2, no. 1 (1960-1961), pp. 3-23.

1,017 Obituary [Sir W. Egerton and others]. AFR. AFFAIRS 46 (1947), pp. 169-170.

1,018 CAETANO, M. António Enes. PORT. EM AFR. 4 (1947), pp. 12-18.

1,019 MAINBERGER, G. A la mémoire de Frantz Fanon. Mythe et réalité de l'homme noir. PRESENCE AFR. N.S. 46 (1963), pp. 78-92.

1,020 Major-General Lord Edward Gleichen—1863-1937. J. AFR. SOC. 37 (1938), p. 1.

1,021 HUSSEY, E. R. J. Obituary: Sir William Gowers. AFR. AFFAIRS 54 (1955), pp. 57-58.

1,022 PICCINNI, F. G. [Rodolfo] Graziani. AFRICA (Rome) 10 (1955), pp. 27-28.

1,023 FIGUEIREDO, P. A. R. DE. D. Henrique, o Navegador; ao serviço de Deus e de Portugal (O sentido das Conquistas e das Descobertas). BSEM 130 (1962), pp. 85-93.

1,024 WILSON, H. F. In memoriam: Sir C. L. Hill. J. AFR. SOC. 12 (1913), pp. 337-342.

1,025 Obituary [C. W. Hobley and others]. AFR. AFFAIRS 46 (1947), pp. 169-170.

1,026 GLUCKMAN, M. and SCHAPERA, I. Dr. Winifred Hoernlé: an appreciation. AFRICA 30 (1960), pp. 262-263.

1,027 KAHLER-MEYER, E. Missionar C. Hoffmann zum Gedächtnis. AFR. UND UB. 46 (1962-1963), p. 249.

1,028 TRACEY, H. A tribute to...Gustav Holst (1874-1934)... AFR. MUSIC, 1958, pp. 59-60.

1,029 GREEN, A. S. A founder of the Society [J. Holt]. J. AFR. SOC. 15 (1915), pp. 11-16.

1,030 In memoriam: Le Docteur Lucien Van Hoof. ZAIRE 3 (1949), pp. 215-216.

1,031 Obituary: Eric Hussey. AFR. AFFAIRS 57 (1958), p. 211.

1,032 DOVER, C. Dr. Charles S. Johnson. PRESENCE AFR. N.S. 11 (1957), pp. 116-118.

1,033 JOHNSTON, A. Sir Harry Johnston. J. AFR. SOC. 27 (1927), pp. 1-6.

1,034 FAUBLEE, J. Harper Kelley. J. SOC. AFR. 32 (1962), pp. 325-326.

1,035 TOMLINSON, Sir G. Death of Dr. F. P. Keppel. AFR. AFFAIRS 43 (1944), pp. 53-54.

1,036 FLINT, J. E. Mary Kingsley. AFR. AFFAIRS 64 (1965), pp. 150-161.

1,037 KIPLING, R. Mary Kingsley. J. AFR. SOC. 31 (1932), pp. 351-353.

1,038 NATHAN, Sir M. Some reminiscences of Miss Mary Kingsley. J. AFR. SOC. 7 (1907), pp. 28-31.

1,039 RATTRAY, R. S. The life of Mary Kingsley; by Stephen Gwynn. J. AFR. SOC. 31 (1932), pp. 354-365.

1,040 KRAUSE, G. A. Eine Vertheidigung des Missionars S. W. Koelle. ZAOS 2 (1896), pp. 40-41.

1,041 Major Gordon Laing. AFR. AFFAIRS 63 (1964), pp. 267-269.

1,042 MERCIER, P. In memoriam: Maurice Leenhardt. BULL. IFAN 16 (1954), pp. 416-417.

1,043 Obituary [Sir H. Leggett, Sir G. Orde Browne, C. W. Hobley, Sir W. Egerton]. AFR. AFFAIRS 46 (1947), pp. 169-170.

1,044 BERLAND, L. In memoriam: Pierre Lesne. BULL. IFAN 12 (1950), p. 513.

1,045 CHAMPION, P. Paul Lester. J. SOC. AFR. 18 (1948), pp. 145-147.

1,046 David Livingstone. The centenary commemoration in London, December 11th, 1940. J. AFR. SOC. 40 (1941), pp. 108-120.

1,047 The Livingstone centenary. J. AFR. SOC. 40 (1941), p. 8.

1,048 ALLEN, B. M. Livingstone and Gordon. J. AFR. SOC. 40 (1941), pp. 121-127.

1,049 MARAN, R. Le Professeur Alain Leroy Locke. PRESENCE AFR. 6 (1949), pp. 135-138.

1,050 NICHOLSON, R. Lord Lugard. AFR. AFFAIRS 45 (1946), pp. 41-43.

1,051 PERHAM, M. Lord Lugard: a general appreciation. AFRICA 15 (1945), pp. 114-122.

1,052 PERHAM, M. Lord Lugard: a preliminary evaluation. AFRICA 20 (1950), pp. 228-239.

1,053 TATE, H. R. et al. Lugard, by H. R. Tate, Sir J. Eaglesome and Sir S. Grier. AFR. AFFAIRS 44 (1945), pp. 101-107.

1,054 SEGONZAC, R. DE. Lyautey. The last journey. J. AFR. SOC. 35 (1936), pp. 1-3.

1,055 G., M. Davide Manes. AFRICA (Rome) 10 (1955), p. 218.

1,056 DAMAS, L.-G. René Maran n'est plus. PRESENCE AFR. N.S. 30 (1960), pp. 125-126.

1,057 General Eduardo Marques. PORT. EM AFR. 1 (1944), pp. 310-311.

1,058 BLANCO SOLER, C. El ideal africanista de Vázquez de Mella como reflejo de su patriotismo. ARCH. INST. EST. AFR. 17, no. 66 (1963), pp. 87-98.

1,059 PIERRE, F. Hommage à Alfred Métraux, un grand ami d'Haiti. PRESENCE AFR. N.S. 47 (1963), pp. 224-229.

1,060 CATROUX, Général. Hommage à Robert Montagne. AFR. ET ASIE 32 (1955), pp. 3-8.

1,061 RETIF, R. P. Un homme qui aima les hommes [Robert Montagne]. AFR. ET ASIE 32 (1955), pp. 58-60.

1,062 Obituary: R. P. Nicholson. AFR. AFFAIRS 49 (1950), pp. 252-253.

1,063 HOLAS, B. In memoriam: Frans-M. Olbrechts (1899-1958). BULL. IFAN 21 (1959), pp. 240-241.

1,064 BENNETT, G. Paramountcy to partnership: J. H. Oldham and Africa. AFRICA 30 (1960), pp. 356-360.

1,065 Georges Padmore n'est plus. PRESENCE AFR. N.S. 29 (1959-1960), p. 116.

1,066 JESMAN, C. The African ancestry of Alexander Pushkin. TRANSITION 14 (1964), pp. 28-35.

1,067 Jacques Richard-Molard, 1913-1951. AFR. ET ASIE 16 (1951), p. 8.

1,068 MONOD, TH. Jacques Richard-Molard (1913-1951). BULL. IFAN 13 (1951), pp. 953-964.

1,069 MONOD, TH. Jacques Richard-Molard. PRESENCE AFR. 15 (1953), pp. 5-10.

1,070 BOAHEN, A. A. James Richardson: the forgotten philanthropist and explorer. J. HIST. SOC. NIG. 3 (1964), pp. 61-71.

1,071 DAMMAN, E. Karl Roehl zum Gedächtnis. AFR. UND UB. 36 (1951-1952), pp. 1-2.

1,072 W. Schmidt. See 488.

1,073 V. Schoelcher. See 2947.

1,074 TRACEY, H. A tribute to...Percy Scholes (1877-1958). AFR. MUSIC, 1958, pp. 59-60.

1,075 J. Schumacher. See 490.

1,076 PYCRAFT, W. P. A great hunter. Captain Frederick Courtney Selous, D.S.O. J. AFR. SOC. 16 (1917), pp. 200-215.

1,077 GOLDIE, Sir G. T. and JOHNSTON, Sir H. H. Stanley's autobiography. J. AFR. SOC. 9 (1910), pp. 146-152.

1,078 JOHNSTON, Sir H. H. Stanley: a biographical notice. J. AFR. SOC. 3 (1904), pp. 449-463.

1,079 Obituary: C. H. Stigand. SUDAN NOTES 3 (1920), p. 83.

1,080 Mort d'un précurseur du racisme. [L. Stoddard]. ZAIRE 4 (1950), pp. 1017-1018.

1,081 Lt. Col. Sir Stewart Symes. AFR. AFFAIRS 62 (1963), p. 6.

1,082 Alberto Theodoli. AFRICA (Rome) 10 (1955), p. 215.

1,083 BAUER, G. Adriano Torelli. AFRICA (Rome) 10 (1955), p. 28.

1,084 JEFFREYS, M. D. W. Obituary: Dr. G. K. F. Wagner. AFR. STUD. 11 (1952), pp. 143-144.

1,085 WESTERMANN, D. Gunter Wagner. AFR. UND UB. 37 (1952-1953), p. 49.

1,086 HERMENT, G. Un grand musicien noir: Chick Webb. PRESENCE AFR. 3 (1948), pp. 505-512.

1,087 WINGATE, Sir R. Sir Henry Wellcome. J. AFR. SOC. 35 (1936), pp. 357-367.

1,088 KOHLER, O. Professor Diedrich Westermann. AFR. STUD. 15 (1956), pp. 217-218.

1,089 JOHNSON, J. A. William Wilberforce, 1759-1833. CONTEMP. REV. 196 (1959), pp. 105-108.

1,090 TRACEY, H. A tribute to Ralph Vaughan Williams (1872-1958), Gustav Holst (1874-1934) and Percy Scholes (1877-1958). AFR. MUSIC, 1958, pp. 59-60.

1,091 THEIS, E. Un écrivain: Richard Wright. PRESENCE AFR. 8 (1950), pp. 141-148.

1,092 THOMAS, H. B. Eugen Wolf, 1850-1912. UGANDA J. 21 (1957), pp. 221-223.

See also 93.

ECONOMICS

Economics in general. Foreign aid.
Economic relations. Markets. Industrialization

1,093 ABEL, A. Le Centre National Belge pour l'étude des problèmes du monde musulman contemporain. CIVILISATIONS 9 (1959), pp. 187-190.

1,094 ABOYADE, O. A note on external trade, capital distortion and planned development. AFR. PRIMARY PRODUCTS AND INT. TRADE, 1965, pp. 26-43.

1,095 ALBERTINI, J. M. Les problèmes du sous-développement et la reconversion de la science économique. CT 6 (1958), pp. 101-117.

1,096 AMBROSINI, G. La valorizzazione dell'Africa e la cooperazione tra l'Europa e l'Africa. COOPERAZIONE INT. AFR. 1960, pp. 239-243.

1,097 AMERY, L. S. The Imperial Economic Conference. INTERNAT. AFFAIRS 11 (1932), pp. 678-699.

1,098 ANSELME-RABINOVITCH, L. Les Accords de coopération: étape de l'intégration africaine. GENEVE-AFR. 3 (1964), pp. 243-254.

1,099 ARDANT, P. Ingénieurs et administrateurs dans les pays en voie de développement. ANNALES AFR., 1962, pp. 472-485.

1,100 ASFOUR, E. Y. International cooperation in Africa and the establishment of the United Nations Economic Commission for Africa (ECA). COOPERAZIONE INT. AFR., 1960, pp. 74-84. Also in CIVILISATIONS 10 (1960), pp. 181-188; French summary, pp. 188-189.

1,101 AYARI, C. Quelques observations sur la méthodologie de l'évaluation de l'aide en capital aux pays en voie de développement. REV. TUN. SC. SOC. 3 (1965), pp. 109-131.

1,102 AYMAT MARECA, J. M. Conmemoración del vuelo de la Atlántida. Lo que va de ayer a hoy. ARCH. INST. EST. AFR. 10, no. 42 (1957), pp. 7-22.

1,103 AZEVEDO, A. DE. Africa continente do futuro (Impressões de viagem). PORT. EM AFR. 7 (1950), pp. 257-269.

1,104 BADEN-POWELL, Sir G. The financial relations of the empire. Can they be improved? ROYAL COL. INST. PR. 28 (1896-1897), pp. 306-344.

1,105 BALANDIER, G. Le développement industriel de la prolétarisation en Afrique noire. AFR. ET ASIE 20 (1952), pp. 45-53.

1,106 BALANDIER, G. Problemas do desenvolvimento da Africa Negra. PORT. EM AFR. SUPPL. (1960-1961), pp. 327-334.

1,107 BALDAZZI, G. L'Agip in Africa. AFRICA (Rome) 10 (1955), pp. 328-330.

1,108 BALDWIN, R. E. Investment policy in underdeveloped countries. ECON. DEV. IN AFRICA, 1965, pp. 236-253.

1,109 BALOGH, T. Africa and the Common Market. J. COMMON MARKET STUD. 1 (1962-1963), pp. 79-112.

1,110 BAREL, Y. Industrialisation et artisanat dans les pays en voie de développement. GENEVE-AFR. 3 (1964), pp. 19-26.

1,111 BARTOCCI, E. L'Africa deve colpire la pubblica opinione. AFRICA (Rome) 10 (1955), pp. 181-182.

1,112 BARTOCCI, E. Uno strumento di lavoro e di propaganda ai fini degli scambi italo-africani e i suoi possibili sviluppi. AFRICA (Rome) 12 (1957), pp. 77-78.

1,113 BASCHERA, R. Lavoro italiano in piena Africa equatoriale. AFRICA (Rome) 11 (1956), pp. 27-28.

1,114 BATTISTELLA, R. I rapporti tra Europa e Africa. AFRICA (Rome) 13 (1958), pp. 170-175.

1,115 BAUER, P. T. Issues in commodity stabilization in Africa. ECON. DEV. FOR AFRICA, 1965, pp. 532-553.

1,116 BAUER, P. T. Some aspects and problems of trade in Africa. ECON. DEV. IN AFRICA, 1965, pp. 106-128.

1,117 BAYLISS, M. Africa's economic future. CONTEMP. REV. 179 (1951), pp. 234-238.

1,118 BAZIN, H. Problèmes et perspectives de la coopération économique a l'intérieur du tiers-monde. PRESENCE AFR. N.S. 55 (1965), pp. 119-134.

1,119 BEHANZIN, L. Outillage théorique pour la construction de l'Afrique Noire "Francophone" et de Madagascar. PRESENCE AFR. N.S. 11 (1957), pp. 148-151.

1,120 BEKAJAHA. Vocation africaine dans la société économique de notre temps. PRESENCE AFR. N.S. 48 (1963), pp. 202-205.

1,121 BENARD, J. Quelques réflexions sur la planification et les échanges extérieurs des pays sous-développés. ANNALES AFR., 1962, pp. 325-336.

1,122 BENSON, W. The study of African development. J. AFR. SOC. 31 (1932), pp. 148-152.

1,123 BERG, E. J. Socialism and economic development in Tropical Africa. QUART. J. ECON. 78 (1964), pp. 549-573.

1,124 BERNAL, J. D. Need there be need? AFRO-ASIAN AND W. AFF. 1 (1964), pp. 29-42.

1,125 BERNSTEIN, E. M. De l'inflation, dans ses rapports avec le développement économique. CIVILISATIONS 3 (1953), pp. 3-42; English summary, pp. 42-50.

1,126 BETTELHEIM, C. Les exigences fondamentales d'une croissance accélérée de l'économie africaine. PRESENCE AFR. N.S. 32-33 (1960), pp. 8-19.

1,127 BETTELHEIM, C. Planification et croissance économique. PRESENCE AFR. N.S. 21 (1958), pp. 23-35.

1,128 BEVILLE, A. Problèmes des pays sous-développés. PRESENCE AFR. N.S. 32-33 (1960), pp. 20-48.

1,129 BIRCHENOUGH, H. Some effects of the war on trade in Africa. J. AFR. SOC. 14 (1914-1915), pp. 229-249.

1,130 BLACK, L. D. United States economic aid to Africa. AFR. STUD. BULL. 7, no. i (1964), pp. 1-6.

1,131 BLAIR, T. L. V. Le développement économique Africain: Capital, planification et science sociale. PRESENCE AFR. N.S. 56 (1965), pp. 26-44.

1,132 BLANKENHEIMER, B. International activities of the United States Department of Commerce with particular reference to Africa. AFR. STUD. BULL. 5, no. iii (1962), pp. 3-12.

1,133 BLELLOCH, D. Some problems of aid for development. CIVILISATIONS 8 (1958), pp. 35-49.

1,134 BOIS, W. E. B. DU. The realities in Africa. European profit or Negro development? FOREIGN AFFAIRS 21 (1942-1943), pp. 721-732.

1,135 BONOMI, E. L'industrie pétrolière et le développement économique des pays nouveaux. CIVILISATIONS 14 (1964), pp. 183-188; English summary, pp. 189-191.

1,136 BRESSAN, E. Problemi della partecipazione industriale italiana in Africa. AFRICA (Rome) 12 (1957), pp. 26-36.

1,137 BRITANNICUS. Economic planning in the British Colonies. FOREIGN AFFAIRS 27 (1948-1949), pp. 58-67.

1,138 BROWN, A. J. Should African countries form economic unions? ECON. DEV. IN AFRICA, 1965, pp. 176-193.

1,139 BROWN, A. J. Wealth of colonies. CORONA 3 (1951), pp. 231-233.

1,140 BROWN, J. A. C. A brief survey of prospects for African exports of agricultural products. AFR. PRIMARY PRODUCTS AND INT. TRADE, 1965, pp. 1-7.

1,141 BRUYAS, J. La Convention de Yaoundé. Charte de l'Association conclue entre la C.E.E. et dix-huit Etats africains et malgache (20 Juillet 1963). ANNALES AFR., 1965, pp. 129-172.

1,142 BUISSERET, A. Inga c'est 150 milliards de confiance internationale. AFRICA (Rome) 13 (1958), pp. 61-63.

1,143 BUSIN, S. Transports, énergie, productions agricoles et industrielles: tour d'horizon bibliographique. GENEVE-AFR. 2 (1963), pp. 234-246.

1,144 BUTLER, W. Trade and the less developed areas. FOREIGN AFFAIRS 41 (1962-1963), pp. 372-383.

1,145 C., J. Enquête des Nations Unies sur l'économie africaine. ZAIRE 5 (1951), pp. 413-421.

1,146 CAHAN, T. Secondary industries for Tropical Africa. AFRICA 14 (1943), pp. 170-176.

1,147 CALZAVARINI, E. Alcuni aspetti dell'espansione commerciale italiana in Africa. AFRICA (Rome) 12 (1957), pp. 75-76.

1,148 CALZAVARINI, E. Gli scambi italo-africani nel quadro del l'economia africana. AFRICA (Rome) 11 (1956), pp. 100-102.

1,149 CARBON, L. B. DE. Problems of economic development of French-language countries and territories. ECON. DEV. FOR AFRICA, 1965, pp. 138-183.

1,150 CARRINGTON, C. E. Between the Commonwealth and Europe. INTERNAT. AFFAIRS 38 (1962), pp. 449-459.

1,151 CARSTAIRS, C. Y. Industrial development in the colonies. CORONA 4 (1952), pp. 339-343.

1,152 CECCHELLA, A. La disoccupazione in Africa. AFRICA (Rome) 19 (1964), pp. 141-148.

1,153 CERULLI, E. Il nuovo posto dell'Italia nel continente africano. AFRICA (Rome) 14 (1959), pp. 175-176.

1,154 CHAULEUR, P. Le nouveau visage de l'Afrique Noire. CIVILISATIONS 12 (1962), pp. 356-370; English summary, pp. 371-374.

1,155 CHESNAU, J. Les modalités d'intervention du fonds d'aide et de cooperation (FAC) aux peuples de la Communauté. COOPERAZIONE INT. AFR. 1960, pp. 375-381.

1,156 CHIDZERO, B. T. G. The United Nations Economic Commission for Africa. AFR. STUD. BULL. 6, no. ii (1963), pp. 1-5.

1,157 CHISIZA, D. K. The temper, aspirations and problems of contemporary Africa. ECON. DEV. IN AFRICA, 1965, pp. 1-18.

1,158 CHUDSON, W. A. The outlook for African exports. ECON. DEV. IN AFRICA, 1965, pp. 167-175.

1,159 CIUCCI, C. L'assistenza tecnica ai Paesi in via di industrializzazione e ammodernamento intesa quale premessa fondamentale alla creazione di nostre iniziative commerciali, finanziarie ed industriali. AFRICA (Rome) 12 (1957), pp. 59-61.

1,160 CLARK, R. Multilateral aid. TRANSITION 16 (1964), pp. 22-26.

1,161 CLAUSON, Sir G. Economic and Social Council of UNO. CORONA 4 (1952), pp. 21-23.

1,162 CLAYTON, E. Planning the development of peasant agriculture. AFR. PRIMARY PRODUCTS AND INT. TRADE, 1965, pp. 148-158.

1,163 COLA ALBERICH, J. Africa en transición. CUAD. AFR. OR. 35 (1956), pp. 75-86.

1,164 COLA ALBERICH, J. La destrucción de los suelos del Africa Negra: sus consecuencias económicosociales. CUAD. EST. AFR. 23 (1953), pp. 37-53.

1,165 COMHAIRE, J. Expériences économiques en Afrique britannique. ZAIRE 4 (1950), pp. 823-835.

1,166 CONSIGLIO, G. Aiutare gli scambi africani. AFRICA (Rome) 19 (1964), pp. 111-113.

1,167 CONSIGLIO, G. Un aspetto dell' in Africa: agenti e rapprestanti. AFRICA (Rome) 12 (1957), pp. 74-75.

1,168 CONSIGLIO, G. Il Piano Pella e l'Africa. AFRICA (Rome) 13 (1958), pp. 119-120.

1,169 CONSIGLIO, G. Trasformazione ed espansione economica africana. AFRICA (Rome) 14 (1959), pp. 185-187.

1,170 COSTANZO, G. A. The Association of overseas countries and territories with the Common Market. CIVILISATIONS 8 (1958), pp. 505-524; French summary, pp. 524-526.

1,171 COX-GEORGE, N. A. Economie politique de l'unité africaine. PRESENCE AFR. N.S. 31 (1960), pp. 7-23.

1,172 CRABTREE, W. A. Economic resources of German colonies in Africa. J. AFR. SOC. 16 (1917), pp. 125-134.

1,173 CROOKER, W. R. Faut-il accélérer ou freiner l'industrialisation de l'Afrique. PRESENCE AFR. 8 (1950), pp. 409-424.

1,174 CROUZET, E. Quelques aspects psychologiques de l'équipement économique des pays neufs. CIVILISATIONS 8 (1958), pp. 569-575; English summary, pp. 575-576.

1,175 CROUZET, E. Les solutions au sous-développement en Afrique: de l'investissement humain à l'aide étrangère? ET. CONG. 4, no. 2 (1963), pp. 1-22.

1,176 CUNHA, J. M. DA S. Problemas actuais da Africa negra. PORT. EM AFR. 21 (1964), pp. 103-114.

1,177 CUYVERS, J. B. L'opera del CIDESA per la documentazione africana. AFRICA (Rome) 17 (1962), p. 282.

1,178 DALTON, G. The development of subsistence and peasant economies in Africa. INT. SOC. SC. J. 16 (1964), pp. 378-389.

1,179 DALTON, G. Economics in African studies. AFR. STUD. BULL. 7, no. i (1964), pp. 3-6.

1,180 DALTON, G. Traditional production in primitive African economies. QUART. J. ECON. 76 (1962), pp. 360-378.

1,181 DAVIDSON, B. L'Afrique de demain. PRESENCE AFR. N.S. 45 (1963), pp. 19-34.

1,182 DAVIES, I. La Grande-Bretagne, le Commonwealth et l'Europe. PRESENCE AFR. N.S. 44 (1962), pp. 109-128.

1,183 DELVAL, J. Reconversion des plans d'investissement outremer? AFR. ET ASIE 23 (1953), pp. 35-44.

1,184 DEMONTS, R. and PERROUX, F. Grand firme—petite nation. PRESENCE AFR. N.S. 38 (1961), pp. 3-19.

1,185 DIA, M. Proposition pour l'Afrique Noire. PRESENCE AFR. N.S. 13 (1957), pp. 41-57.

1,186 DIOP, C. A. Alerte sous les Tropiques. PRESENCE AFR. N.S. 5 (1955-1956), pp. 8-33.

1,187 DISCHAMPS, J.-C. Le problème du financement du développement économique. ANNALES AFR. 1962, pp. 337-346.

1,188 DRESCH, J. Les investissements en Afrique noire. PRESENCE AFR. 13 (1952), pp. 232-241.

1,189 DUMAINE, A.-L. La signification réelle du second plan d'équipement et de modernisation des territoires d'Outre-Mer. PRESENCE AFR. N.S. 1 (1955), pp. 66-93.

1,190 DUFOUR. Sur la fiscalité du développement. ANNALES AFR., 1959, pp. 109-127.

1,191 DUPRIEZ, L. H. Commodity and trade policy in Africa: the terms of trade of African producers. ECON. DEV. FOR AFRICA, 1965, pp. 503-531.

1,192 DURAND, J. Le rôle de la ville dans la vie moderne: de la nécessité de son étude. PRESENCE AFR. N.S. 48 (1963), pp. 65-83.

1,193 DURET, J. Analyse marxiste du sous-développement. PRESENCE AFR. N.S. 21 (1958), pp. 5-13.

1,194 ECONOMIC COMMISSION FOR AFRICA. E.C.A. programme of work. AFRICA QUART. 5, no. i (1965), pp. 52-58.

1,195 ECONOMIC COMMISSION FOR AFRICA. The seventh session of E.C.A. AFRICA QUART. 4, no. iv (1965), pp. 259-274.

1,196 ENKE, S. Creating incentives for economic development. ECON. DEV. FOR AFRICA, 1965, pp. 361-381.

1,197 EVANS, S. The wealth of Africa. J. AFR. SOC. 32 (1933), pp. 12-20.

1,198 EWING, A. F. Industrialisation and the U.N. Economic Commission for Africa. J. MOD. AFR. STUD. 2 (1964), pp. 351-363.

1,199 EWING, A. F. and PATEL, S. J. Perspectives for industrialization in Africa. MAN AND AFRICA, 1965, pp. 299-328.

1,200 FAUVEL, L. L'O.N.U. et les pays insuffisamment développés. ANNALES AFR., 1956, pp. 171-211.

1,201 FEARN, H. The economist in the field: the task of the modern missionary. UNIVERSITAS 4 (1959), pp. 15-18.

1,202 FEIS, H. The future of British imperial preferences. FOREIGN AFFAIRS 24 (1945-1946), pp. 661-674.

1,203 FICKENDEY, E. La importancia de la plantación en el Africa tropical. ARCH. INST. EST. AFR. 8, no. 33 (1955), pp. 25-30.

1,204 FIERENS, P. Pour une assistance concrète aux Pays neufs. COOPERAZIONE INT. AFR., 1960, pp. 382-390.

1,205 FILESI, T. Significato di Accra. AFRICA (Rome) 13 (1958), pp. 124-127.

1,206 FILESI, T. Valorizzazione e trasformazione del Continente Africano. AFRICA (Rome) 13 (1958), pp. 51-58.

1,207 FISHER, A. G. B. The Commonwealth's place in the world economic structure. INTERNAT. AFFAIRS 20 (1944), pp. 32-42.

1,208 FODERARO, S. Africa 1964: Bilancio di un anno. AFRICA (Rome) 20 (1965), pp. 3-14.

1,209 FODERARO, S. Italia ed Africa di fronte al mercato comune. AFRICA (Rome) 14 (1959), pp. 167-171.

1,210 FODERARO, S. Per una politica africana dell'Italia. AFRICA (Rome) 18 (1963), pp. 211-222.

1,211 FODERARO, S. Le prospettive dei rapporti italo-africani. AFRICA (Rome) 17 (1962), pp. 3-12.

1,212 FRANK, I. Aid, trade and economic development: issues before the U.N. Conference [Geneva, 1964]. FOREIGN AFFAIRS 42 (1963-1964), pp. 210-226.

1,213 FRANKEL, S. H. Capital and capital supply in relation to the development of Africa. ECON. DEV. FOR AFRICA, 1965, pp. 407-443.

1,214 FRANKEL, S. H. Economic aspects of political independence in Africa. INTERNAT. AFFAIRS 36 (1960), pp. 440-446.

1,215 FRANKEL, S. H. Some aspects of investment and economic development in the continent of Africa. AFRICA 22 (1952), pp. 50-58.

1,216 GAMBELLI, E. La coopération internationale en Afrique et la C.E.E. CIVILISATIONS 10 (1960), pp. 190-199; English summary, pp. 199-200.

1,217 GAMBELLI, E. Relazione del representante della Commissione della Comunità Economica Europea. COOPERAZIONE INT. AFR., 1960, pp. 138-153.

1,218 GARDINER, R. K. A. Development problems in Africa. AFRICA QUART. 4, no. ii (1964), pp. 84-89.

1,219 GEORGES-PICOT, G. Lo sviluppo minerario e industriale dell'Africa da un punto di vista eurafricano. AFRICA (Rome) 10 (1955), pp. 3-5.

1,220 GILMER, J. H. The economic development of the Algerian Departments, the Overseas Departments, and the Overseas Territories of the French Republic. CIVILISATIONS 6 (1956), pp. 419-435.

1,221 GILMER, J. H. Economic evolution of the French Union in 1954. CIVILISATIONS 5 (1955), pp. 253-270, 424-436.

1,222 GIROLA, U. I grandi lavori italiani attualmente in corso in Africa. AFRICA (Rome) 17 (1962), pp. 62-66.

1,223 GLENDALE, Lord H. Some aspects of Commonwealth development. AFR. AFFAIRS 63 (1964), pp. 221-232.

1,224 GOLDMAN, M. I. A balance sheet of Soviet foreign aid. FOREIGN AFFAIRS 43 (1964-1965), pp. 349-360.

1,225 GOSSELIN, M. Position des pays d'Outre-Mer dans la zone franc. AFR. ET ASIE 26 (1954), pp. 54-58.

1,226 GOUROU, P. Les conditions du développement de l'Afrique tropicale. GENEVE-AFR. 1 (1962), pp. 43-50; English summary, pp. 51-52.

1,227 GOUROU, P. Espérances et diversités economiques en Afrique Noire. CIVILISATIONS 9 (1959), pp. 162-170; English summary, pp. 171-172.

1,228 GRAY, A. Aid for overseas countries. AFR. AFFAIRS 60 (1961), pp. 6-7.

1,229 GRAY, A. C.D.C. [United Kingdom Colonial Development Corporation] doing well. AFR. AFFAIRS 59 (1960), pp. 284-286; 60 (1961), pp. 492-493.

1,230 GRAY, A. Common market. AFR. AFFAIRS 60 (1961), pp. 487-488.

1,231 GRAY, A. Commonwealth investment. AFR. AFFAIRS 56 (1957), p. 252.

1,232 GRAY, A. Economic co-operation. AFR. AFFAIRS 60 (1961), pp. 377-378.

1,233 GRAY, A. Financing colonial advance. AFR. AFFAIRS 57 (1958), pp. 264-265.

1,234 GRAY, A. Record colonial aid. AFR. AFFAIRS 55 (1956), pp. 261-262.

1,235 GRAY, A. Tangier Conference. AFR. AFFAIRS 59 (1960), pp. 98-99.

1,236 GREEN, R. H. Economic development; means, mirages, mysteries. UNIVERSITAS 4 (1961), pp. 177-182.

1,237 GREEN, R. H. Four African development plans: Ghana, Kenya, Nigeria, and Tanzania. J. MOD. AFR. STUD. 3 (1965), pp. 249-279.

1,238 GREEN, R. H. Multi-purpose economic institutions in Africa. J. MOD. AFR. STUD. 1 (1963), pp. 163-184.

1,239 GUGLIELMI, J.-L. Quelques aspects monétaires des problèmes posés par le développement économique. ANNALES AFR., 1962, pp. 347-355.

1,240 GUGLIELMONE, T. Orientamenti per una nuova politica italiana in Africa. AFRICA (Rome) 14 (1959), pp. 3-5.

1,241 GUPTA, P. S. The Afro-Asian Economic Seminar at Algiers [Feb., 1965]. AFRO-ASIAN AND W. AFF. 2 (1965), pp. 103-108.

1,242 H., F. Expériences africaines de planifications économiques. ET. CONG. 1, no. 3 (1961), pp. 1-10.

1,243 HAHN, E. Zur Wirtschaftsgeschichte von Afrika. KOLONIALE STUDIEN: HANS MEYER FESTSCHRIFT, 1928, pp. 97-108.

1,244 HANCE, W. A. The economic potentials of Africa: economic development in Tropical Africa. AMER. ECON. REV. 46, no. ii (1956), pp. 441-451.

1,245 HARRIS, J. The African survey [by Lord Hailey]. CONTEMP. REV. 155 (1939), pp. 140-145.

1,246 HASSAN MOHAMED HASSAN. Cooperazione economica internazionale fra Paesi afr-asiatici. COOPERAZIONE INT. AFR. 1960, pp. 406-413.

1,247 HAWKINS, E. K. The analysis of inflation in underdeveloped economies. WAISER. EC. 2 (1953), pp. 56-71.

1,248 HAYTER, T. French aid to Africa—its scope and achievements. INTERNAT. AFFAIRS 41 (1965), pp. 236-251.

1,249 HENRY, P.-M. La commission de coopération technique en Afrique au Sud du Sahara. RJPUF 7 (1953), pp. 286-321.

1,250 HERSKOVITS, M. J. African economic development in cross-cultural perspective. AMER. ECON. REV. 46, no. ii (1956), pp. 452-461.

1,251 HILL, P. Markets in Africa. J. MOD. AFR. STUD. 1 (1963), pp. 441-453.

1,252 HOWITZ, R. White settlement in Africa. AFR. STUD. 5 (1946), pp. 63-66.

1,253 HOFFMAN, P. G. Operation breakthrough. FOREIGN AFFAIRS 38 (1959-1960), pp. 31-45.

1,254 HOLLOWAY, J. E. The influence of capital development on the Africans. AFR. AFFAIRS 56 (1957), pp. 40-48.

1,255 HOLMES, F. The Commonwealth and a free-trade area in Europe. INTERNAT. AFFAIRS 34 (1958), pp. 38-48.

1,256 HOLNESS, J. The crisis of colonial industrial technique. PRESENCE AFR. N.S. 14-15 (1957), pp. 84-106.

1,257 HOLUB, E. The past, present, and future trade of the Cape Colonies with Central Africa. PRCI 11 (1879-1880), pp. 57-87.

1,258 HOSELITZ, B. F. The development of African entrepreneurs. ECON. DEV. IN AFRICA, 1965, pp. 86-105.

1,259 HOSELITZ, B. H. Some reflections on the social and cultural conditions of economic productivity. CIVILISATIONS 12 (1962), pp. 489-498; French summary, 499-501.

1,260 HOYT, E. E. Consumer spending under the impact of technological change: some observations bearing on social policy. ZAIRE 8 (1954), pp. 115-122.

1,261 HUXLEY, E. Must Africa starve? CORONA 1, no. 10 (1949), pp. 15-17.

1,262 IANNETTONE, G. L'Africa e l'espansione economica della Communità Economica Europea. AFRICA (Rome) 15 (1960), pp. 220-222.

1,263 IANNETTONE, G. Prodomi di una nuova impostazione della politica economica africana. AFRICA (Rome) 16 (1961), pp. 188-190.

1,264 INTRONA, S. L'Africa al convegno mondiale del petrolio [Rome]. AFRICA (Rome) 10 (1955), pp. 211-212.

1,265 INTRONA, S. Alla fiera-guida di Bari il Levante e l'Africa. AFRICA (Rome) 10 (1955), pp. 301-302.

1,266 INTRONA, S. Avanguardie d'Italia sui mercati africani. AFRICA (Rome) 10 (1955), pp. 177-178.

1,267 INTRONA, S. Commercio e credito svizzero in Africa. AFRICA (Rome) 11 (1956), pp. 104-105.

1,268 INTRONA, S. Consuntivo africano dell'Expo' 1958. AFRICA (Rome) 13 (1958), pp. 353-354.

1,269 INTRONA, S. Dettagli dell'organizzazione commerciale in Africa. AFRICA (Rome) 12 (1957), p. 77.

1,270 INTRONA, S. Gli investimenti europei in Africa visti da Strasburgo. AFRICA (Rome) 11 (1956), pp. 23-24.

1,271 INTRONA, S. Più della politica, l'economia potrà unire l'Africa all' Europa. AFRICA (Rome) 17 (1962), pp. 37-38.

1,272 INTRONA, S. Scambi e comunicazioni con l'Africa. AFRICA (Rome) 13 (1958), pp. 90-92.

1,273 INTRONA, S. Troppa parte dell'Africa è assente dalla Fiera di Milano. AFRICA (Rome) 10 (1955), p. 106.

1,274 JACKSON, B. W. Foreign aid: strategy or stopgap? FOREIGN AFFAIRS 41 (1962-1963), pp. 90-104.

1,275 JACKSON, B. W. Free Africa and the Common Market. FOREIGN AFFAIRS 40 (1961-1962), pp. 419-430.

1,276 JANNUCCELLI, I. I regolamenti valutari con il continente africano. AFRICA (Rome) 12 (1957), pp. 61-67.

1,277 JOHNSTON, A. The French view of the negro labour question. J. AFR. SOC. 3 (1903), pp. 12-16.

1,278 JOHNSTON, Sir H. H. The importance of Africa. J. AFR. SOC. 17 (1918), pp. 177-198.

1,279 JONES, W. O. Increasing agricultural productivity in Tropical Africa. ECON. DEV. IN AFRICA, 1965, pp. 19-50.

1,280 JUNIOR, A. D. Considerações sobre o I Congresso dos Economistes Portugueses. BOL. INST. ANGOLA 7 (1955), pp. 57-61.

1,281 KALDOR, N. International trade and economic development. J. MOD. AFR. STUD. 2 (1964), pp. 491-511.

1,282 KARP, M. Problems of economic development. NEW FORCES IN AFRICA, 1962, pp. 95-100.

1,283 KHALY, N. Les conséquences économiques et sociales de la loi-cadre. PRESENCE AFR. N.S. 18-19 (1958), pp. 82-89.

1,284 KLEIN, W. C. Some remarks on European co-operation in tropical Africa. AFR. AFFAIRS 53 (1954), pp. 119-129.

1,285 KORDT, E. Germany's part in international cooperation in Africa. COOPERAZIONE INT. AFR., 1960, pp. 399-405.

1,286 KUIPER, F. Some aspects of the operations of marketing boards. NISER 6 (1958), pp. 43-49.

1,287 LADIKPO, R. La Conférence Mondiale du Commerce et du Développement. GENEVE-AFR. 3 (1964), pp. 255-264.

1,288 LA ROSA, C. Problemi dell'organizzazione commerciale italiana in Africa. AFRICA (Rome) 12 (1957), pp. 36-45.

1,289 LASSUDRIE-DUCHENE, M. Les techniques d'attraction des capitaux privés dans les économies en voie de développement. ANNALES AFR., 1962, pp. 356-369.

1,290 LAVIN, G. E. The African as a producer. INTERNAT. AFFAIRS 26 (1950), pp. 349-353.

1,291 LEBRET, L.-J. Le gigantesque effort à entreprendre. PRESENCE AFR. N.S. 21 (1958), pp. 42-47.

1,292 LECAILLON, J. L'intégration de l'Union française dans l'Union européenne et les enseignements de la théorie économique. ANNALES AFR., 1954, pp. 19-48.

1,293 LECLERCQ, H. Le développement des capitaux privés en Afrique. A propos des Journées internationales d'Etudes africaines de Gand. ZAIRE 13 (1959), pp. 627-642.

1,294 LEDUC, G. Prices and price formation in African economies. ECON. DEV. FOR AFRICA, 1965, pp. 382-406.

1,295 LEDUC, G. Réflexions sur les plans de développement des Territoire français d'Outre-Mer. CIVILISATIONS 6 (1956), pp. 529-552; English summary, pp. 552-576.

1,296 LEDUC, G. L'utilisation des ressources locales dans le financement du développement économique de l'Outre-mer (avec application aux territoires d'Outre-mer de l'Union Française). Communication faite au Congrès d'Achimota, 14-17 avril 1953. CIVILISATIONS 3 (1953), pp. 331-341; English summary, pp. 341-342.

1,297 LEDUC, M. Note sur les marchés communs africains. ANNALES AFR., 1962, pp. 370-382.

1,298 LEDUC, M. Le rôle anti-inflationniste des institutions de la zone franc en Afrique de l'Ouest. ANNALES AFR., 1961, pp. 7-44.

1,299 LEDUC, M. Stabilisation et revalorisation des cours des "produits de base" d'origine tropicale. ANNALES AFR., 1963, pp. 7-72.

1,300 LEFEBVRE, J. Perspectives des Territoires d'Outre-Mer dans le Marché Commun. CIVILISATIONS 8 (1958), pp. 349-359; English summary, pp. 358-360.

1,301 LEFEBVRE, J. Les territoires d'Outre-Mer dans l'intégration économique européenne. ZAIRE 8 (1954), pp. 353-363.

1,302 LEMAIGNEN, R. La Comunità Economica Europea e i Paesi in via di sviluppo. AFRICA (Rome) 15 (1960), pp. 27-28.

1,303 LEONE, E. DE. La preparazione tecnico-culturale necessaria premessa alla ripresa dei rapporti economici con l'Africa. AFRICA (Rome) 12 (1957), pp. 84-85.

1,304 LEUBUSCHER, C. Marketing schemes for native-grown produce in African territories. AFRICA 12 (1939), pp. 163-187.

1,305 LEURQUIN, P. and BAECK, L. Revenu national et économie dualiste. ZAIRE 10 (1956), pp. 339-350.

1,306 LEWIS, B. W. Notes on governmental measures to promote industrialisation. ECON. DEV. IN AFRICA, 1965, pp. 213-219.

1,307 LIGTHART, G. J. and ABBAI, B. Economic development in Africa: aims and possibilities. ECON. DEV. FOR AFRICA, 1965, pp. 3-47.

1,308 LURY, D. A. National accounts in Africa. J. MOD. AFR. STUD. 2 (1964), pp. 99-110.

1,309 M., G. La 5ème session de la Conférence Economique pour l'Afrique. Léopoldville 18 février-2 mars 1963. ET. CONG. 4, no. 4 (1963), pp. 26-31.

1,310 M., Q. Significato di un viaggio in Africa. La missione del Sottosegretario Badini-Confalonieri. AFRICA (Rome) 10 (1955), pp. 113-115.

1,311 MACGREGOR, J. J. Development of African primary products and international trade in timber. AFR. PRIMARY PRODUCTS AND INT. TRADE, 1965, pp. 181-201.

1,312 MCLEAN, W. H. Economic and social development in the colonies. J. AFR. SOC. 35 (1936), pp. 191-201.

1,313 MAFFI, Q. Il finanziamento dello sviluppo economico dell'Africa. AFRICA (Rome) 11 (1956), p. 229.

1,314 MALAVIA, H. D. International trade and the problem of the developing countries. AFRO-ASIAN AND W. AFF. 1 (1964), pp. 18-28.

1,315 MANCINI, G. Investment planning and development in Africa. MAN AND AFRICA, 1965, pp. 329-344.

1,316 MARNHAM, J. E. Technical assistance. CORONA 4 (1952), pp. 96-98.

1,317 MARTUCCI, G. Aspetti politici della collaborazione economica eurafricana. AFRICA (Rome) 12 (1957), p. 86.

1,318 MASSEI, E. L'importanza delle piccole imprese per lo sviluppo civile dell'Africa. AFRICA (Rome) 18 (1963), pp. 3-7.

1,319 MATTEOTTI, C. La storia e la situazione economica attuale dell'Africa e della Somalia in particolare. COOPERAZIONE INT. AFR., 1960, pp. 266-278.

1,320 MAY, S. Folklore and fact about underdeveloped areas. FOREIGN AFFAIRS 33 (1954-1955), pp. 212-224.

1,321 MAZRUI, A. A. African attitudes to the European Economic Community. INTERNAT. AFFAIRS 39 (1963), pp. 24-36.

1,322 MEAD, M. Food as a basis for international co-operation. AFRICA 14 (1943), pp. 258-264.

1,323 MEAD, M. The underdeveloped and the overdeveloped. FOREIGN AFFAIRS 41 (1962-1963), pp. 78-89.

1,324 MEIER, G. M. The role of an expert advisory group in a young government. ECON. DEV. IN AFRICA, 1965, pp. 194-206.

1,325 MEILLASSOUX, C. Essai d'interpretation du phénomène économique dans les sociétés traditionnelles d'auto-subsistance. CAH. ET. AFR. 1 (1960), pp. 38-67.

1,326 MELLAND, F. The natural resources of Africa. J. AFR. SOC. 31 (1932), pp. 113-132.

1,327 MENDES, M. J. F. Relatório do delegado português, elaborado em conformidade com as resoluções tomadas na reunião da commissão de 21 de Abril de 1958. BSEM 117 (1959), pp. 7-34.

1,328 MENDES-FRANCE, P. Europe and the developing countries. THE EMERGING WORLD: JAWAHARLAL NEHRU MEMORIAL VOLUME, 1964, pp. 106-118.

1,329 MERCATOR. L'Africa alla 25ª Fiera di Milano. AFRICA (Rome) 11 (1956), pp. 108-109.

1,330 MILHAUD, M. Les Nations Unies et l'assistance technique en Afrique. GENEVE-AFR. 1 (1962), pp. 20-39; English summary, pp. 40-41.

1,331 MIRACLE, M. P. Seasonal hunger: a vague concept and an unexplored problem. NISER 6 (1958), pp. 36-42.

1,332 MOFFAT, A. L. The Marshall Plan and British Africa. AFR. AFFAIRS 49 (1950), pp. 302-308.

1,333 MONOD, T. Conservation of natural resources in Africa. MAN AND AFRICA, 1965, pp. 258-280.

1,334 MONTAIGU, G. Du colonialisme mercantile au Néo-Colonialism. Les causes profondes du sous-développement. RECH. AFR. 1 (1961), pp. 3-31; 2 (1961), pp. 3-30.

1,335 MONTEIL, J. Planification indicative et développement économique. ANNALES AFR., 1962, pp. 383-386.

1,336 MORAN, W. E. Tropical Africa and the world economy. ECON. DEV. FOR AFRICA, 1965, pp. 475-502.

1,337 MORGAN, J. T. Africa's opportunities for American commerce and the American Negro. LIBERIA BULL. 6 (1895), pp. 12-39.

1,338 MORSE, D. A. The I.L.O. and Africa. CIVILISATIONS 9 (1959), pp. 3-16.

1,339 MOSHER, N. W. Information available from statistical sources in Africa under British influence. AFR. STUD. BULL. 4, no. iii (1961), pp. 13-18.

1,340 MURE, G. Qualche considerazione sul problema del finanziamento delle iniziative economiche italiane in Africa. AFRICA (Rome) 12 (1957), p. 82.

1,341 MURRAY, S. S. The African as producer. J. AFR. SOC. 38 (1939), pp. 334-346.

1,342 MYRDAL, G. Un défi. PRESENCE AFR. N.S. 21 (1958), pp. 61-66.

1,343 MYRDAL, G. Priorities in the development efforts of underdeveloped countries and their trade and financial relations with rich countries. AFRO-ASIAN AND W. AFF. 1 (1964), pp. 182-192.

1,344 NAPOLITANO, G. Comunita' Europea Africa e Medio Oriente. AFRICA (Rome) 14 (1959), pp. 59-64.

1,345 NAPOLITANO, G. Contributo alla ricerca del modo più efficace per i finanziamenti italiani in Africa. AFRICA (Rome) 12 (1957), pp. 78-80.

1,346 NDEGWA, P. Aid and trade: economic aid and the development of underdeveloped countries. TRANSITION 16 (1964), pp. 27-30.

1,347 NDEGWA, P. Preferential trade arrangements among developing countries. E. AFR. EC. REV. 1, no. 3 (1965), pp. 1-22.

1,348 NEWLYN, W. T. The present state of African economic studies. AFR. AFFAIRS, Special Issue (1965), pp. 37-49.

1,349 NEWLYN, W. T. Take-off considered in an African setting. YORKSHIRE BULL. ECON. SOC. RES. 13 (1961), pp. 19-32.

1,350 N'GOM-N'GOUDI, P. L'expérience israélienne et le développement en Afrique. PRESENCE AFR. N.S. 51 (1964), pp. 62-86.

1,351 N'GOM-N'GOUDI, P. L'industrialisation: base de l'unité africaine. PRESENCE AFR. N.S. 53 (1965), pp. 68-95.

1,352 NICHOLLS, G. H. Empire settlement in Africa in its relation to trade and the native races. J. AFR. SOC. 25 (1926), pp. 105-116.

1,353 NOSTI, J. Cultivos arbóres coloniales. ARCH. INST. EST. AFR. 2, no. 4 (1948), pp. 61-74.

1,354 OKELO-ODONGO, T. The role of economic planning in African socialism. PROBLEMS OF EC. DEVELOPMENT IN E. AFR., 1965, pp. 41-48.

1,355 ONITIRI, H. M. A. The role of international organisations in developing African primary products. AFR. PRIMARY PRODUCTS AND INT. TRADE, 1965, pp. 8-18.

1,356 ORD, H. W. Agricultural commodity projections, real growth and the gains from trade. AFR. PRIMARY PRODUCTS AND INT. TRADE, 1965, pp. 95-116.

1,357 PACHECO DE AMORIM, F. Condições de uma política de verdadeira integração. PORT. EM AFR. SUPPL. (1960-1961), pp. 269-288.

1,358 PALAMENGHI-CRISPI, F. Appunti per una cooperazione momentaria africana. COOPERAZIONE INT. AFR., 1960, pp. 278-296.

1,359 PARASASSI, M. Considerazioni sull'intervento del prof. Giuseppe Murè circa il finanziamento delle iniziative economiche italiane in Africa. AFRICA (Rome) 12 (1957), p. 86.

1,360 PARASASSI, M. Un esempio di piano di sviluppo di territorio d'oltremare associato alla C.E.E. AFRICA (Rome) 13 (1958), pp. 59-60.

1,361 PARASASSI, M. Problemi del finanziamento delle iniziative economiche italiane in Africa. AFRICA (Rome) 12 (1957), pp. 45-56.

1,362 PARENT, J. Note sur les critères d'investissement dans les pays en voie de développement. ANNALES AFR., 1962, pp. 387-405.

1,363 PATEL, S. J. Economic transition in Africa. J. MOD. AFR. STUD. 2 (1964), pp. 329-349.

1,364 PATEL, S. J. Esquisse de la transition économique en Afrique. ET. CONG. 6, no. 1 (1964), pp. 1-18.

1,365 PEACOCK, A. T. Monetary and fiscal policy in relation to African development. ECON. DEV. FOR AFRICA, 1965, pp. 654-676.

1,366 PEARSON, D. S. African advancement in commerce and industry. J. MOD. AFR. STUD. 3 (1965), pp. 231-247.

1,367 PEISER, G. L'aide américaine à l'Afrique noire. ANNALES AFR., 1965, pp. 95-120.

1,368 PELZER, K. J. Capital investment in Africa. GEOG. REV. 29 (1939), pp. 656-658.

1,369 PETERSON, V. C. Report on the U.S.A. program of the international cooperation in Africa. COOPERAZIONE INT. AFR., 1960, pp. 391-398.

1,370 PHILIP, A. Les conditions politiques de l'expansion des pays sous-développés. PRESENCE AFR. N.S. 21 (1958), pp. 36-41.

1,371 PILLAY, V. The European Economic Community and Africa. AFR. SOUTH 2, no. 4 (1958), pp. 76-81.

1,372 PIM, Sir A. Capital investment in Africa [by C. Herbert Frankel]. J. AFR. SOC. 38 (1939), pp. 239-245.

1,373 PINCUS, J. A. Aid, trade and economic development: what policy for commodities? FOREIGN AFFAIRS 42 (1963-1964), pp. 227-241.

1,374 PLANT, A. An African Survey [a review article]. ECONOMICA 6 (1939), pp. 205-212.

1,375 POBLETE, O. Economic sovereignty of nations, development of underdeveloped countries and international economic cooperation. AFRO-ASIAN AND W. AFF. 2 (1965), pp. 239-245.

1,376 POTEKHIN, I. Problems of economic independence of African countries. PROC. INT. CONG. AFR. 1 (1962), pp. 171-183.

1,377 POYNTON, Sir H. The economic picture [of the colonies]. CORONA 2 (1950), pp. 435-441.

1,378 PRE, R. Problems of the African mining economy. ECON. DEV. FOR AFRICA, 1965, pp. 588-615.

1,379 PROBYN, L. C. The money of the British empire. ROYAL COL. INST. PR. 21 (1889-1890), pp. 117-150.

1,380 PURI, G. S. Science and development of natural resources in developing nations. AFR. QUART. 5 (1965), pp. 192-202.

1,381 QUINTAVALLE, B. A. Lo sviluppo dei T.O.M. nel quadro del Mercato Comune e l'apporto dei capitali americani. AFRICA (Rome) 12 (1957), pp. 163-167.

1,382 QUIRION, J.-M. Aide économique. CANADA ET LES PAYS AFR. FRANCOPHONES, 1965, pp. 125-131.

1,383 RAJ, K. N. National budgets and their uses. ECON. DEV. IN AFRICA, 1965, pp. 207-212.

1,384 RAMANOELINA, M. Commerce extérieur et culture humaine (Quelques réflexions après la Conférence de Genève). PRESENCE AFR. N.S. 52 (1964), pp. 143-149.

1,385 RANDIER, R. L'Aménagement du territoire rural: intégrer le monde rural dans la nation (l'expérience française). PRESENCE AFR. N.S. 48 (1963), pp. 84-93.

1,386 READER, D. H. A survey of categories of economic activities among the peoples of Africa. AFRICA 34 (1964), pp. 28-44.

1,387 REUT, C. Les coopératives peuvent-elles prospérer parmi les populations d'Outre-Mer? AFR. ET ASIE 26 (1954), pp. 47-53.

1,388 RICHARD-MOLARD, J. A propos des Plans d'équipement en Afrique Noire. AFR. ET ASIE 16 (1951), pp. 9-38.

1,389 RIMMER, D. Poor countries. UNIVERSITAS 4 (1960), pp. 72-76.

1,390 RIST, L. Capital and capital supply in relation to the development of Africa. ECON. DEV. FOR AFRICA, 1965, pp. 444-474.

1,391 RIVKIN, A. Incentives in African life. J. AFR. ADM. 12 (1960), pp. 224-227.

1,392 ROBERTSON, Sir J. The challenge of the under-developed territories. AFR. AFFAIRS 62 (1963), pp. 236-248.

1,393 ROBINSON, A. Problems of African economic development. ECON. DEV. FOR AFRICA, 1965, pp. 48-70.

1,394 ROBSON, P. Monetary systems and integration: a note. E. AFR. EC. REV. N.S. 1, no. 2 (1965), pp. 107-111.

1,395 ROCHE, J. C. African attitudes to economic study. AFR. AFFAIRS 59 (1960), pp. 124-135.

1,396 ROSENSTEIN-RODAN, P. N. The international development of economically backward areas. INTERNAT. AFFAIRS 20 (1944), pp. 157-165.

1,397 ROUX, R. L'évolution de l'émission outre-mer. RJPUF 4 (1950), pp. 153-197.

1,398 RUBBENS, A. L'INCIDI et le problème des cadres dans les pays neufs. ZAIRE 14 (1960), pp. 554-570.

1,399 RUOCCO, D. Come ha esportato l'Africa nell'ultimo trentennio. AFRICA (Rome) 15 (1960), pp. 170-174.

1,400 S., E. Problemi di infrastruttura nella Afrique noire. AFRICA (Rome) 10 (1955), pp. 214-215.

1,401 SABBADINI, E. I piani per la valorizzazione dell'Africa Nera francese. AFRICA (Rome) 10 (1955), pp. 259-260.

1,402 SACHS, I. Barriers to growth. AFR. BULL. 2 (1965), pp. 29-33.

1,403 SALERNO, N. I traffici marittimi con l'Africa. AFRICA (Rome) 12 (1957), pp. 80-81.

1,404 SAMPEDRO, J. L. El nuevo enfoque del problema colonial de la cuestión colonial al derecho a las materias primas. CUAD. EST. AFR. 4 (1948), pp. 9-26.

1,405 SAMUELS, L. H. Monetary and fiscal policy in relation to African development. ECON. DEV. FOR AFRICA, 1965, pp. 677-711.

1,406 SANSUMWA, M. Foreign investment and the dilemma of African socialism. TRANSITION 18 (1965), pp. 43-44.

1,407 SANTAGATA, F. Il credito Africano e l'Italia. AFRICA (Rome) 10 (1955), pp. 35-40, 77-79, 107-110, 145-147.

1,408 SANTAGATA, F. I piani di sviluppo in Africa. AFRICA (Rome) 10 (1955), pp. 254-256.

1,409 SARDINHA, R. M. DE A. A política de desenvolvimento e a agricultura. BCGP 20 (1965), pp. 235-258.

1,410 SARMENTO RODRIGUES, M. O Plano de Fomento no Ultramar. PORT. EM AFR. 10 (1953), pp. 222-237.

1,411 SAUVY, A. Problèmes de l'emploi et de la population en économie rurale. REV. TUN. SC. SOC. 2 (1965), pp. 95-119.

1,412 SEERS, D. International aid: the next steps. J. MOD. AFR. STUD. 2 (1964), pp. 471-489.

1,413 SEERS, D. The role of industry in development: some fallacies. J. MOD. AFR. STUD. 1 (1963), pp. 461-465.

1,414 SEERS, D. International trade and development: the special interests of Africa. AFR. PRIMARY PRODUCTS AND INT. TRADE, 1965, pp. 19-25.

1,415 SERVOISE, R. La répercussion du "Marché Commun européen" sur les pays tiers. CIVILISATIONS 8 (1958), pp. 361-366; English summary, p. 367.

1,416 SIMONI, M. Economie africane ed automazione. AFRICA (Rome) 14 (1959), pp. 73-74.

1,417 SIMONI, M. Struttura e tendenze dell'economia africana moderna. AFRICA (Rome) 13 (1958), pp. 185-188.

1,418 SINGER, H. W. Small-scale industry in African economic development. ECON. DEV. FOR AFRICA, 1965, pp. 638-653.

1,419 SMITH, E. W. Africa emergent [by W. M. Macmillan]. J. AFR. SOC. 38 (1939), pp. 75-90.

1,420 SMITH, E. W. The book of the quarter: consumption and production. J. AFR. SOC. 37 (1938), pp. 298-303.

1,421 SOPER, T. The EEC and aid to Africa. INTERNAT. AFFAIRS 41 (1965), pp. 463-477.

1,422 SPADARO, S. Il controllo sulla publica gestione nelle sue forme antiche ed attuali in alcuni paesi europei, con anologie e riflessi del problema in alcuni paesi africani e del Medio Oriente. COOPERAZIONE INT. AFR., 1960, pp. 309-337.

1,423 SPILLMANN, G. Trois ans d'indépendance des Pays africains d'expression française. AFR. ET ASIE 61 (1963), pp. 3-14.

1,424 SPIRO, J.-M. La Banque africaine de développement et son environnement. GENEVE-AFR. 3 (1964), pp. 27-45.

1,425 STALEY, E. Political implications of economic development and pitfalls to be avoided. ECON. DEV. IN AFRICA, 1965, pp. 309-321.

1,426 STANOVNIK, J. Aid, trade and economic development: the changing political context. FOREIGN AFFAIRS 42 (1963-1964), pp. 242-254.

1,427 STAZYK, K. An advanced course in national economic planning. AFR. BULL. 1 (1964), pp. 166-167.

1,428 STETSON, G. R. Commercial Africa. LIBERIA BULL. 3 (1893), pp. 11-65.

1,429 STOLPER, W. Comprehensive development planning. E. AFR. EC. REV. N.S. 1, no. 1 (1964), pp. 1-21.

1,430 STOLPER, W. The contribution of economic research to African development. ECON. DEV. FOR AFRICA, 1965, pp. 712-733.

1,431 STRANGE, S. The Commonwealth and the sterling area. THE YEAR BOOK OF WORLD AFFAIRS 13 (1959), pp. 24-44.

1,432 STRICKLAND, C. F. Co-operation for Africa. AFRICA 6 (1933), pp. 15-26.

1,433 STRICKLAND, C. F. The co-operative movement in Africa. J. AFR. SOC. 34 (1935), supplement.

1,434 SUTTON, F. X. The Ford Foundation's development program in Africa. AFR. STUD. BULL. 3, no. iv (1960), pp. 1-7.

1,435 SWANZY, H. African development. AFR. AFFAIRS 46 (1947), p. 182.

1,436 SWANZY, H. United Africa Company. AFR. AFFAIRS 46 (1947), pp. 62-63.

1,437 TOURE, M. L'association des pays et territoires d'Outre-Mer au Marché Commun. PRESENCE AFR. N.S. 21 (1958), pp. 67-88.

1,438 TOURE, M. La contribution de la Communauté Economique Européenne à la solution des problèmes du sous-développement dans les pays et territoires d'outre-mer qui lui sont associés. CIVILISATIONS 9 (1959), pp. 329-340; English summary, pp. 340-342.

1,439 TOURE, M. Responsabilités de l'économiste africain. PRESENCE AFRICAINE 27-28 (1959), pp. 244-251.

1,440 USHER, A. A. Etudes des besoins de l'Afrique et des priorités à établir. CANADA ET LES PAYS AFR. FRANCOPHONES, 1965, pp. 23-39.

1,441 VALANTIN, X. A propos des "étapes de la croissance économique" de Rostow. PRESENCE AFR. N.S. 44 (1962), pp. 204-209.

1,442 VALLE FERNANDEZ, R. DEL. Las colonias inglesas en el plano de economía africana. CUAD. EST. AFR. 27 (1954), pp. 51-59.

1,443 VEDOVATO, G. Africa e Comunità Economica Europa. AFRICA (Rome) 12 (1957), pp. 108-111.

1,444 VEDOVATO, G. Cooperazione economica, finanziaria e tecnica internazionale in Africa. COOPERAZIONE INT. AFR., 1960, pp. 244-266.

1,445 VENTURA, R. O Plano de Fomento e os Transportes no Ultramar. PORT. EM AFR. 10 (1953), pp. 293-307.

1,446 VILJOEN, D. J. Problems of large-scale industry in Africa. ECON. DEV. FOR AFRICA, 1965, pp. 616-637.

1,447 W., A. A. Africa's petroleum resources. AFRICA QUART. 1, iii (1961), pp. 39-41.

1,448 WADE, A. L'effet de percussion en Economie. ANNALES AFR., 1964, pp. 177-186.

1,449 WADE, A. Que reste-t-il de la notion de "take-off." ANNALES AFR., 1961, pp. 67-84.

1,450 WAHLEN, F. T. La Suisse et la Coopération technique. GENEVE-AFR. 1 (1962), pp. 132-135.

1,451 WALIGORSKI, A. Economie paysanne dans les territoires coloniaux et postcoloniaux. AFR. BULL. 2 (1965), pp. 15-27.

1,452 WALKER, D. Problems of economic development of East Africa. ECON. DEV. FOR AFRICA, 1965, pp. 89-137.

1,453 WEILLER, J. La coopération économique internationale selon les niveaux de développement. ANNALES AFR., 1962, pp. 451-458.

1,454 WERNER, A. African economics and African administration. J. AFR. SOC. 31 (1932), pp. 245-254.

1,455 WHITE, J. West German aid to developing countries. INTERNAT. AFFAIRS 41 (1965), pp. 74-88.

1,456 WIGGLESWORTH, A. Signposts in Tropical development. J. AFR. SOC. 35 (1936), pp. 169-177.

1,457 WIGNARAJA, P. The conflict between economic rationality and cultural values: a problem in the economic development of underdeveloped areas. CIVILISATIONS 3 (1953), pp. 51-60; French summary, pp. 61-71.

1,458 WILCHER, L. C. and SOPER, T. P. Technical aid: the personnel problem. CIVILISATIONS 9 (1959), pp. 151-160; French summary, pp. 160-162.

1,459 WILSON, D. China's economic relations with Africa. RACE 5, no. 4 (1963-1964), pp. 61-71.

1,460 YEDOVATO, G. La coopération internationale en Afrique, sur les plans économique, financier et technique. CIVILISATIONS 10 (1960), pp. 165-178; English summary, pp. 179-180.

1,461 ZAREMBA, P. African problems in the work of the Szczecin Academic Centre. AFR. BULL. 1 (1964), pp. 164-165.

1,462 ZIMMERMAN, A. Trade of the German protectorates. J. AFR. SOC. 1 (1902), pp. 184-191.

1,463 A propos des plans d'équipement en Afrique Noire. PRESENCE AFR. 15 (1953), pp. 307-334.

1,464 L'Agip in Africa. AFRICA (Rome) 15 (1960), pp. 292-296.

1,465 L'aide americaine et l'Afrique. PRESENCE AFR. N.S. 49 (1964), pp. 233-235.

1,466 Airways in Africa [developments under stress of war]. J. AFR. SOC. 41 (1942), pp. 6-7.

1,467 Analysis of future production possibilities of selected African industries. ECON. BULL. AFR. 3 (1963), pp. 66-79.

1,468 Atti del III convegno sui rapporti economici e commerciali con il Continente Africano. Bari 18 e 19 settembre 1959. AFRICA (Rome) 14 (1959), pp. 221-372.

1,469 Atti del V convegno sui rapporti economici e commerciali con il Continente Africano. AFRICA (Rome) 16 (1961), pp. 221-272.

1,470 Atti dell' VIII convegno sui rapporti economici con il Continente Africano. AFRICA (Rome) 19 (1964), pp. 169-213.

1,471 Au sujet de l'assistance internationale: une mise au point. ZAIRE 7 (1953), pp. 74-75.

1,472 Bilan du programme "Point Quatre." ZAIRE 7 (1953), pp. 288-289.

1,473 Collaborazione italo-francese per l'Africa. AFRICA (Rome) 10 (1955), p. 204.

1,474 Colloque entre Musulmans et Occidentaux au sujet d'un marché commun Afro-Asiatique. CIVILISATIONS 9 (1959), pp. 185-186.

1,475 Il commercio della Germania con i paesi africani. AFRICA (Rome) 11 (1956), pp. 103-104.

1,476 Co-ordination of development plans in Africa. ECON. BULL. AFR. 4(1964), pp. 39-63.

1,477 Covegno sui rapporti economici e commerciali con il Continente Africano, Bari 18-19 settembre 1958. AFRICA (Rome) 13(1958), pp. 229-320.

1,478 Demographic factors related to social and economic development in Africa. ECON. BULL. AFR. 2, no. 2 (1962), pp. 59-81.

1,479 Documentation législative et administrative africaine, 1er Janvier-31 Décembre 1960. ANNALES AFR., 1961 (2), pp. 5-167.

1,480 Economic development in Africa: aims and possibilities (selected countries). ECON. BULL. AFR. 2, no. 2 (1962), pp. 7-28.

1,481 Economic planning in Africa. ECON. BULL. AFR. 2, no. 2 (1962), pp. 29-44.

1,482 An economic survey of the Colonial Territories [1952]. J. AFR. ADM. 4 (1952), p. 143.

1,483 Experts Américains en Afrique. ZAIRE 4 (1950), pp. 1018-1019.

1,484 Le fonds d'investissement pour le développement économique et social des territoires d'outre-mer. PRESENCE AFR. N.S. 11 (1957), pp. 47-56; N.S. 12 (1957), pp. 142-163.

1,485 French Union. Economic conditions in 1952. CIVILISATIONS 3 (1953), pp. 273-290.

1,486 Funzionari italiani presso Governi africani. AFRICA (Rome) 10 (1955), p. 204.

1,487 Gli industriali Italiani e Francesi esaminano le possibilità di collaborazione in Africa. AFRICA (Rome) 10 (1955), p. 14.

1,488 Industrialization and economic planning. ECON. BULL. AFR. 3 (1963), pp. 55-65.

1,489 Institutional changes in the field of foreign trade and payments, money and banking. ECON. BULL. AFR. 1, no. 1 (1961), pp. 56-73.

1,490 Local industries. AFR. AFFAIRS 44 (1945), p. 50.

1,491 Migrations de travailleurs africains. ZAIRE 6 (1952), pp. 192-193.

1,492 National accounts in Africa and relevant ECA activities. ECON. BULL. AFR. 1, no. 2 (1961), pp. 29-49.

1,493 Nations "riches" et pays "pauvres." PRESENCE AFR. N.S. 50 (1964), pp. 239-242.

1,494 Les Nations-Unies et les problèmes économiques posés par les pays insuffisamment développés. CIVILISATIONS 2 (1952), pp. 81-86.

1,495 Notes on a method of comprehensive planning in Tropical Africa. ECON. BULL. AFR. 2, no. 2 (1962), pp. 45-58.

1,496 Un plan de développement économique des colonies portugaises. PRESENCE AFR. N.S. 3 (1955), pp. 67-70.

1,497 Planificazione africana e politica del credito. AFRICA (Rome) 10 (1955), p. 79.

1,498 Le proces de l'assistance technique. PRESENCE AFR. N.S. 49 (1964), pp. 223-225.

1,499 Programme d'action américaine en Afrique. ZAIRE 6 (1952), p. 639.

1,500 Recent demographic levels and trends in Africa. ECON. BULL. AFR. 5 (1965), pp. 30-79.

1,501 Recent trends in African trade. ECON. BULL. AFR. 1, no. 1 (1961), pp. 10-33; 2, no. 1 (1962), pp. A9-A39; 3 (1963), pp. 5-29; 4 (1964), pp. 7-38; 5 (1965), pp. 2-29.

1,502 Réorganisation du programme "Point Quatre." ZAIRE 8 (1954), p. 199.

1,503 Revenu national et agriculture en Afrique noire. PRESENCE AFR. 13 (1952), pp. 193-201.

1,504 Social aspects of African development planning: patterns and trends. ECON. BULL. AFR. 4 (1964), pp. 64-101.

1,505 Social aspects of economic development. ECON. BULL. AFR. 2, no. 2 (1962), pp. 92-101.

1,506 Some problems of social development planning in relation to economic development. ECON. BULL. AFR. 2, no. 2 (1962), pp. 82-91.

1,507 La structure de l'industrie et du commerce. PRESENCE AFR. 13 (1952), pp. 219-231.

1,508 A survey of colonial production and trade. J. AFR. SOC. 32 (1933), pp. 187-189.

1,509 Survey of development programmes and policies in selected African countries and territories. ECON. BULL. AFR. 1, no. 1 (1961), pp. 74-89.

1,510 Sviluppi della collaborazione internazionale fra giornalisti e studiosi di problemi d'oltremare. AFRICA (Rome) 10 (1955), pp. 304-305.

1,511 Symposium on professional and labor organization in Negro Africa [Paris, January 18th, 1958]. CIVILISATIONS 8 (1958), pp. 170-252.

1,512 World economic conditions: impact on primary exporting countries. ECON. BULL. AFR. 1, no. 1 (1961), pp. 5-9.

1,513 Working party on economic and social development. ECON. BULL. AFR. 2, no. 2 (1962), pp. 1-6.

See also 1768, 3630, 3657, 4153, 4475, 4709.

Special topics: communications. transport. land tenure. labor. trade unions. mines. commodities. wages and prices. taxation

1,514 A'BECKETT, A. W. The Colonial press. ROYAL COL. INST. PR. 38 (1906-1907), pp. 54-91.

1,515 ALLPRESS, P. L. From Enugu to Bulawayo by car: a transcontinental journey. NIGERIAN FIELD 15 (1950), pp. 54-76.

1,516 BAKER, G. The place of information in developing Africa. AFR. AFFAIRS 63 (1964), pp. 209-220.

1,517 BARTOCCI, E. Ali italiane per l'Africa. AFRICA (Rome) 16 (1961), p. 10.

1,518 BARTOCCI, E. La motorizzazione in Africa. AFRICA (Rome) 16 (1961), pp. 75-81.

1,519 BARTOCCI, E. Prospettive per un ampliamento della rete aerea italiana in Africa. AFRICA (Rome) 15 (1960), pp. 179-180.

1,520 BASCOM, W. Some problems of land tenure in contemporary Africa: a comment. LAND TENURE, 1951, pp. 239-242.

1,521 BENSON, W. African labour in 1930. J. AFR. SOC. 30 (1931), pp. 142-147.

1,522 BENSON, W. Geneva and forced labour. J. AFR. SOC. 29 (1929), pp. 39-41.

1,523 BENTSI-ENCHILL, K. Do African systems of land tenure require a special terminology? J. AFR. LAW 9 (1965), pp. 114-139.

1,524 BERG, E. J. The development of a labor force in sub-Saharan Africa. ECON. DEVELOPMENT AND CULTURAL CHANGE 13 (1964-1965), pp. 394-412.

1,525 BOHANNAN, P. Land, tenure and land-tenure. AFR. AGRARIAN SYSTEMS, 1963, pp. 101-115.

1,526 BOVY, L. La nature du mouvement syndical nord-ouest africain d'après la législation. AFRICA (Rome) 18 (1963), pp. 175-183.

1,527 BRIEY, P. DE. Les rapports du travail et la sécurité sociale dans les territoires non métropolitains d'Afrique. CIVILISATIONS 9 (1959), pp. 37-57; English summary, pp. 57-59.

1,528 BROWNE, G. St. J. O. African labour and international relations. J. AFR. SOC. 31 (1932), pp. 394-401.

1,529 BRYCE, M. D. Creating a practical industrial development programme. NJESR 4 (1962), pp. 233-246.

1,530 BUNBURY, I. Broadcasting to Africans. AFR. WOMEN 4 (1961), pp. 49-61.

1,531 BURCHALL, H. Air services in Africa. J. AFR. SOC. 32 (1933), pp. 55-73.

1,532 BURDEN, E. N. Labour migration in Africa. CORONA 3 (1951), pp. 55-58, 100-102.

1,533 C., J. La production minière en Afrique. ZAIRE 9 (1955), p. 167.

1,534 CABRAL, A. Imposto indígena. BSEM 18 (1934), pp. 211-216.

1,535 CALTHROP, E. R. Light railways for the colonies. ROYAL COL. INST. PR. 29 (1897-1898), pp. 98-103.

1,536 CHANDLER, S. E. Finding a market for Empire timbers. Work of the Imperial Institute. BULL. IMP. INST. 35 (1937), pp. 428-433.

1,537 CHARLES, V. La Conférence Interafricaine du Travail. ZAIRE 4 (1950), pp. 1127-1133.

1,538 COLTART, J. M. The influence of newspaper and television in Africa. AFR. AFFAIRS 62 (1963), pp. 202-210.

1,539 CONSIGLIO, G. Il lavoro e gli africani. AFRICA (Rome) 10 (1955), pp. 285-287.

1,540 CORNEVIN, R. Information et mass media. CANADA ET LES PAYS AFR. FRANCOPHONES, 1965, pp. 135-149.

1,541 COUZENS, A. H. Colonial trade unions: some growing pains. CORONA 2 (1950), pp. 259-261.

1,542 CUMMING, Sir D. Aviation in Africa. AFR. AFFAIRS 61 (1962), pp. 29-39.

1,543 DEGUENT, R. and ALLARD, E. Quelques considérations practiques sur la navigation aérienne élémentaire. (Voyages de grand tourisme: Afrique, Asie, Europe). BULL. SEANCE IRCB 4 (1933), pp. 247-264.

1,544 DELANGE, J. La discussion parlementaire sur le code du travail en Afrique noire. PRESENCE AFR. 13 (1952), pp. 377-400.

1,545 ELKAN, W. Migrant labor in Africa: an economist's approach. AMER. ECON. REV. 49, no. ii (1959), pp. 188-197.

1,546 ERROLL, F. J. Transport in Africa: impressions from a recent journey. J. AFR. SOC. 36 (1937), pp. 50-55.

1,547 FARRAR, F. W. Africa and the drink trade. CONTEMP. REV. 52 (1887), pp. 39-54.

1,548 FAWCETT, D. Native wages in the Colonies. KONGO-OVERZEE 20 (1954), pp. 272-274.

1,549 FENICIO. L'Africa e il cinematografo: alla ricerca della realtà africana. AFRICA (Rome) 11 (1956), pp. 141-142.

1,550 FOSBROOKE, H. A. Public opinion and changes in land tenure. J. AFR. ADM. 4 (1952), supplement, pp. 28-36.

1,551 FURLONG, J. R. The market for hides and skins. CORONA 4 (1952), pp. 416-419.

1,552 GARDINI, D. L'organizzazione internazionale del lavoro e la sua importanza in Africa. AFRICA (Rome) 16 (1961), pp. 7-9.

1,553 GAYER, J. H. Telecommunications in Africa. MAN AND AFRICA, 1965, pp. 179-193.

1,554 GAYET, G. Les évolutions syndicales en Afrique noire française. CIVILISATIONS 8 (1958), pp. 204-214; English summary, pp. 215-216.

1,555 GAZZINI, M. Brusnengo in Africa: Epopea africana di un piccolo Commune italiano. AFRICA (Rome) 11 (1956), pp. 29-31.

1,556 GEISS, I. Some remarks on the development of African trade unions. J. HIST. SOC. NIG. 3 (1965), pp. 365-376.

1,557 GELPI BLANCO, J. Estudios sobre el aprovechamiento de las distintas formas de energía en las posesiones españolas de Africa. ARCH. INST. EST. AFR. 10, no. 40 (1957), pp. 19-34.

1,558 GLUCKMAN, M. Studies in African land tenure. [Native Land Tenure in Bechuanaland Protectorate by I. Schapera; Land Tenure in an Ibo Village by M. M. Green]. AFR. STUD. 3 (1944), pp. 14-21.

1,559 GONIDEC, P.-F. La Conférence africaine du travail. ANNALES AFR., 1954, pp. 7-18.

1,560 GREAT BRITAIN, LEAGUE OF NATIONS UNION. The conference on forced and contract labour. J. AFR. SOC. 28 (1929), pp. 281-287.

1,561 HAILEY, W. M. The land tenure problem in Africa. J. AFR. ADM. 4 (1952), Supplement, pp. 3-7.

1,562 HAMEL, H. Bibliographie Ferroviare. ET. CAMER. 55 (1957), pp. 34-41.

1,563 HAUSER, A. La troisième Conférence Interafricaine du travail (Bamako, 27 janvier-4 février 1953). BULL. IFAN 16 (1954), pp. 214-215.

1,564 HEGAZY, A. M. Land and air transport within the continent of Africa. MAN AND AFRICA, 1965, pp. 170-178.

1,565 HERSKOVITS, M. J. Some problems of land tenure in contemporary Africa. LAND TENURE, 1951, pp. 231-239.

1,566 HIMBURY, W. H. Empire cotton. J. AFR. SOC. 17 (1918), pp. 262-275.

1,567 HOPKINSON, T. A new age of newspapers in Africa? TRANSITION 22 (1965), pp. 38-40.

1,568 HOPKINSON, T. Why the press should be free. TRANSITION 14 (1964), pp. 15-18.

1,569 HOUGHTON, D. H. The problems of labour in African development. ECON. DEV. FOR AFRICA, 1965, pp. 312-339.

1,570 HOWARD-GOLDSMITH, R. C. The rôle of minerals in African development. MAN AND AFRICA, 1965, pp. 281-298.

1,571 JEFFREYS, M. D. W. Aggrey beads. AFR. STUD. 20 (1961), pp. 97-113.

1,572 JOHNSON, P. Some African transport problems. J. AFR. SOC. 32 (1933), pp. 270-279.

1,573 JOHNSTON, A. Fresh fields for African railways. J. AFR. SOC. 3 (1904), pp. 271-276.

1,574 JOHNSTON, Sir H. H. Recent Portuguese legislation on the negro labour question in Portuguese Africa. J. AFR. SOC. 3 (1904), pp. 166-172.

1,575 JONES, I. G. A trade unionist in the colonial service. CORONA 1, no. 7 (1949), pp. 21-23.

1,576 KALDOR, N. The choice of taxes in developing countries. ECON. DEV. IN AFRICA, 1965, pp. 156-166.

1,577 KALDOR, N. Taxation for economic development. JMAS 1 (1963), pp. 7-23.

1,578 KALDOR, N. Will underdeveloped countries learn to tax? FOREIGN AFFAIRS 41 (1962-1963), pp. 410-419.

1,579 KAMARCK, A. M. Notes on under-employment. ECON. DEV. IN AFRICA, 1965, pp. 78-85.

1,580 LATIL, M. La pénurie de main-d'oeuvre dans les pays sous-développés et sous-peuplés. ANNALES AFR., 1958, pp. 87-121.

1,581 LEUBUSCHER, C. The cocoa-processing industries. BULL. IMP. INST. 45 (1947), pp. 225-244.

1,582 LODGE, G. C. Labor's role in newly developing countries. FOREIGN AFFAIRS 37 (1958-1959), pp. 660-671.

1,583 M., Q. La valorizzazione del lavoro in Africa nelle conclusioni delle Giornate di studi internazionali africani di Gand. AFRICA (Rome) 10 (1955), pp. 295-299.

1,584 MCFARQUHAR, A. M. M. The importance of seasonal variations in the value of labour on family farms. NISER 6 (1958), pp. 26-35.

1,585 MCLOUGHLIN, P. F. M. The need to study the history of labor policy in Africa. CIVILISATIONS 12 (1962), pp. 388-391; French summary, pp. 392-393.

1,586 MCLOUGHLIN, P. F. M. The policy relationship between individual rights to land and migrant labor systems in Africa. CIVILISATIONS 14 (1964), pp. 12-18; includes French summary.

1,587 MAIR, L. P. Modern developments in African land tenure: an aspect of culture change. AFRICA 18 (1948), pp. 184-189.

1,588 MARECA, J. A. La aviación en Africa. ARCH. INST. EST. AFR. 4, no. 14 (1950), pp. 39-54.

1,589 MATHESON, H. Broadcasting in Africa. J. AFR. SOC. 34 (1935), pp. 387-390.

1,590 MAXWELL-LEFROY, H. Silk production in the empire. BULL. IMP. INST. 22 (1924), pp. 152-172.

1,591 MBOYA, T. Relations between the press and governments in Africa. TRANSITION 4 (1962), pp. 11-14.

1,592 MEEK, C. K. A note on primitive systems of land-holding and on methods of investigation. J. AFR. ADM. 3 (1951), pp. 9-13.

1,593 MEEK, C. K. Some social aspects of land tenure in Africa. J. AFR. ADM. 4 (1952), supplement, pp. 15-21.

1,594 MITCHELL, J. C. White-collar workers and supervisors in a plural society. CIVILISATIONS 10 (1960), pp. 293-304; French summary, pp. 305-306.

1,595 N., P. Note sur le syndicalisme en Afrique noire. PRESENCE AFR. 13 (1952), pp. 359-367.

1,596 NAJERA Y ANGULO, F. El abastecimiento del mercado nacional de maderas. ARCH. INST. EST. AFR. 2, no. 5 (1948), pp. 11-133.

1,597 NAVILLE, P. Données statistiques sur la structure de la main-d'oeuvre salariée et de l'industrie en Afrique noire. PRESENCE AFR. 13 (1952), pp. 279-314.

1,598 NOON, J. A. La mécanique des bas salaires en Afrique noire. PRESENCE AFR. 13 (1952), pp. 202-218.

1,599 ORDE-BROWNE, G. St. J. The African labourer. AFRICA 3 (1930), pp. 13-30.

1,600 P., D. La Conférence Syndicale Interafricaine de Dakar. ET. CONG. 2, no. 2 (1962), pp. 44-48.

1,601 PANOFSKY, H. E. Migratory labour in Africa—a bibliographical note. J. MOD. AFR. STUD. 1 (1963), pp. 521-529.

1,602 PARRY, E. Colonial trade unions. CORONA 1, no. 7 (1949), pp. 19-21.

1,603 PEDLER, F. J. Some employers' problems in Commonwealth Africa. CIVILISATIONS 10 (1960), pp. 211-215; French summary, pp. 215-216.

1,604 RASCHI, R. La partecipazione industriale italiana in Africa e i problemi del lavoro. AFRICA (Rome) 12 (1957), pp. 71-72.

1,605 RAVNDAL, G. B. The Cape to Cairo railway. LIBERIA BULL. 21 (1902), pp. 7-9.

1,606 REBELO, D. J. S. A distribuição, a pesca e o comércio da lagosta espinhosa no Continente Africano (um estudo economico). BSEM 132 (1962), pp. 93-111, including English summary.

1,607 RIDDELL, J. Trade unionism in Africa as a factor in nation building. CIVILISATIONS 12 (1962), pp. 27-40; French summary, pp. 41-45.

1,608 ROWLING, C. W. African land tenures—a plea. J. AFR. ADM. 3 (1951), pp. 4-8.

1,609 RUOFF, T. B. F. Systems of land tenure and transfer in the Commonwealth and Empire: their advantages and disadvantages. COMM. AND EMP. LAW CONF. 1 (1955), pp. 320-334.

1,610 SABBADINI, E. Collaborazione aeronautica franco-tedesca in Africa? AFRICA (Rome) 10 (1955), pp. 75-76.

1,611 SABBADINI, E. 30 anni di aviazione civile italiana in Africa. AFRICA (Rome) 14(1959), pp. 197-200.

1,612 SAINT-JACQUES. L'aluminium et la Bauxite. PRESENCE AFR. N.S. 20 (1958), pp. 122-124.

1,613 SCHMITZ, L. L'ouvrier africain. CONGO 2 (1934), pp. 332-356.

1,614 SHELFORD, F. Land tenure in the crown colonies. J. AFR. SOC. 25 (1925), pp. 23-26.

1,615 SHELFORD, F. Transport in Africa by road, rail, air and water. J. AFR. SOC. 19 (1920), pp. 165-175.

1,616 SIMPSON, S. R. Land tenure: some explanations and definitions. J. AFR. ADM. 6 (1954), pp. 50-64.

1,617 SOPER, T. Labour migration in Africa. J. AFR. ADM. 11 (1959), pp. 93-99.

1,618 SPITALERI, O. La Confederazione Internazionale dei Sindacati Liberi e l'azione sindicale democratica in Africa. COOPERAZIONE INT. AFR., 1960, pp. 167-173.

1,619 STRICKLAND, P. Need of direct steamship service to Africa. LIBERIA BULL. 20 (1902), pp. 9-18.

1,620 SURET-CANALE, J. L'économie de traite en Afrique Noire sous domination française (1900-1914). RECH. AFR. 2 (1960), pp. 3-39.

1,621 SWANZY, H. Food [shortage in Africa]. AFR. AFFAIRS 45 (1946), p. 112.

1,622 SWANZY, H. Labour [W.F.T.U. conference at Dakar, 1947]. AFR. AFFAIRS 46 (1947), pp. 121-122.

1,623 SWANZY, H. The new evangelism [the framework of African journalism]. RHODES-LIV. J. 4 (1945), pp. 85-89.

1,624 TUN WAI, U. Interest rates outside the organized money markets of underdeveloped countries. INT. MONETARY FUND STAFF PAPERS 6 (1957-1958), pp. 80-142.

1,625 WALKER, D. Taxation and taxable capacity in underdeveloped countries. ECON. DEV. IN AFRICA, 1965, pp. 129-155.

1,626 WALMSLEY, L. The recent trans-African flight and its lesson. GEOG. REV. 9 (1920), pp. 149-160.

1,627 WHITLEY, O. J. Development of colonial broadcasting. CORONA 1, no. 8 (1949), pp. 24-27.

1,628 WILLIAMS, J. G. Broadcasting in Africa. CORONA 4 (1952), pp. 92-95.

1,629 WILLIAMS, R. The Cape to Cairo railway. J. AFR. SOC. 20 (1921), pp. 241-258.

1,630 WILLIAMS, R. W. Trade unions in Africa. AFR. AFFAIRS 54 (1955), pp. 267-279.

1,631 WILLIAMS, S. Start-up of a textile industry: cost and benefits to the economy of an underdeveloped country. NJESR 4 (1962), pp. 247-256.

1,632 WILLS, J. T. The Cape to Cairo. The Bulawayo-Tanganyika and other railways. CONTEMP. REV. 75 (1899), pp. 161-168.

1,633 YAKEMTCHOUK, R. Le syndicalisme africain. ET. CONG. 8, no. 4 (1965), pp. 53-69.

1,634 African labour. AFR. AFFAIRS 45 (1946), pp. 192-196.

1,635 African land tenure. Report of the Conference on African Land Tenure in East and Central Africa held at Arusha, Tanganyika, February, 1956. J. AFR. ADM. 8 (1956), Supplement.

1,636 La course au tungstène. ZAIRE 7 (1953), p. 289.

1,637 Discriminations raciales et travail forcé dans les territoires d'outre-mer. PRESENCE AFR. 13 (1952), pp. 368-376.

1,638 The employment of African women. AFR. WOMEN 3 (1958-1960), pp. 1-4.

1,639 Le fonds d'investissement pour le développement économique et social des territoires d'outre-mer. PRESENCE AFR. 12 (1952), pp. 142-163.

1,640 La funzione della stampa europea ed africana per lo sviluppo dei rapporti di collaborazione tra i due Continenti. AFRICA (Rome) 17 (1962), pp. 223-261.

1,641 The future of transport in tropical Africa (Record of discussion at a meeting of the African Group of the Institute of International Affairs on Dec. 15th, 1926). INTERNAT. AFFAIRS 6 (1927), pp. 179-184.

1,642 The native labour question in Africa. J. AFR. SOC. 2 (1902), pp. 64-69.

1,643 Natural rubber supplies. J. AFR. SOC. 42 (1943), pp. 55-56.

1,644 Notes on railway construction. J. AFR. SOC. 12 (1913), pp. 290-295.

1,645 Notes on selected export commodities of the African region. ECON. BULL. AFR. 1, no. 1 (1961), pp. 34-55.

1,646 Notes on selected export commodities of the African region 1961-62. ECON. BULL. AFR. 3 (1963), pp. 30-54.

1,647 L'organizzazione Internazionale del Lavoro e la sua attività nei confronti dell'Africa. AFRICA (Rome) 13 (1958), pp. 349-351.

1,648 Public finance in African countries. ECON. BULL. AFR. 1, no. 2 (1961), pp. 1-28.

1,649 The recruiting of native labour. J. AFR. SOC. 34 (1935), pp. 287-295.

1,650 The study of labour migration: an open discussion. WAISER 5 (1956), pp. 31-35.

1,651 Travail, salaires et prix. PRESENCE AFR. 13 (1952), pp. 265-278.

See also 1682, 1842, 2078, 3931.

EDUCATION

Education in general. Community development

1,652 THE AFRICAN STUDIES BRANCH. Administration of education in Africa. J. AFR. ADM. 5 (1953), pp. 182-184.

1,653 AMOO-GOTTFRIED, K. A review of 'An African student in China.' RACE 5, no. 4 (1963-1964), pp. 72-74.

1,654 ANIMASHAWUN, G. K. African students in Britain. RACE 5, no. 1 (1963-1964), pp. 38-47.

1,655 ARCAIS, G. F. D'. Problemi della collaborazione educativa e della collaborazione intellettuale in Africa. COOPERAZIONE INT. AFR., 1960, pp. 349-355.

1,656 AUGER, G. A. The factual position of Catholic education in Africa and Madagascar. CATHOLIC ED. IN THE SERVICE OF AFR., 1965, pp. 43-104.

1,657 AUGER, G. A. and MOERMAN, J. Technical and agricultural education. CATHOLIC ED. IN THE SERVICE OF AFR., 1965, pp. 256-264.

1,658 AUTRA, R. Conference mondiale des enseignants (Varsovie, 20-29 août 1957). PRESENCE AFR. N.S. 16 (1957), pp. 155-161.

1,659 AZIKIWE, B. N. How shall we educate the African? J. AFR. SOC. 33 (1934), pp. 143-151.

1,660 BAUDERT, S. Thoughts and reflections on the education of Africans. INT. REV. MISSIONS 20 (1931), pp. 525-533.

1,661 BEIT, A. Educational services. RACE RELATIONS 16 (1949), pp. 26-31.

1,662 BENHAM, F. Education and economic development in the underdeveloped countries. INTERNAT. AFFAIRS 35 (1959), pp. 181-187.

1,663 BIESHEUVEL, S. The study of African ability. AFR. STUD. 11 (1952), pp. 45-57, 104-117.

1,664 BILLE, E. The activities of UNESCO in the field of education in Africa south of the Sahara and Madagascar. CATHOLIC ED. IN THE SERVICE OF AFR., 1965, pp. 211-223.

1,665 BLACKLOCK, M. Co-operation in health education. AFRICA 4 (1931), pp. 202-208.

1,666 BOADU, J. A. UNESCO workshop on programmed instruction. AFR. ED. 2, no. 1 (1964), pp. 17-20.

1,667 BOVET, P. Education as viewed by the Phelps-Stokes Commissions. INT. REV. MISSIONS 15 (1926), pp. 483-492.

1,668 BRACKETT, D. G. and WRONG, M. Notes on hygiene books used in Africa. AFRICA 3 (1930), pp. 506-515.

1,669 BRACKETT, D. G. and WRONG, M. Some notes on history and geography text-books used in Africa. AFRICA 7 (1934), pp. 199-212.

1,670 BROOKES, E. African mental ability. AFR. AFFAIRS 43 (1944), pp. 171-177.

1,671 BROWN, G. N. British educational policy in West and Central Africa. J. MOD. AFR. STUD. 2 (1964), pp. 365-377.

1,672 BULCK, G. VAN. La semaine internationale d'études sur la formation religieuse et humaine en Afrique Noire (Léopoldville, 22-27 août 1955). ZAIRE 10 (1956), pp. 181-185.

1,673 BUNBURY, I. African women in journalism. AFR. WOMEN 4 (1961), pp. 34-37.

1,674 BUXTON, T. F. V. Education of the African. J. AFR. SOC. 17 (1918), pp. 212-222.

1,675 C., J. L'enseignement en Afrique française. ZAIRE 8 (1954), pp. 521-522.

1,676 CAENEGHEM, R. VAN. Les langues indigènes dans l'enseignement. ZAIRE 4 (1950), pp. 707-720.

1,677 CAMBOURNE, F. J. C. The African diet and the health of the children. AFR. WOMEN 2 (1956-1958), pp. 61-62.

1,678 CAMERLYNCK, G.-M. L'education de base dans les territoires d'Outre-mer. RJPUF 8 (1954), pp. 1-24.

1,679 CARRINGTON, C. E. The growth of an educated class. INTERNAT. AFFAIRS 32 (1956), pp. 446-455.

1,680 CARVALHO, A. DE. Instrução e educação da mulher africana. PORT. EM AFR. 13 (1956), pp. 65-75.

1,681 CASADIO, F. Organizzazione dell'OMS e dell'UNESCO e loro attività in Africa. AFRICA (Rome) 13 (1958), pp. 193-198.

1,682 CASH, W. C. A critique of manpower planning and educational change in Africa. ECON. DEVELOPMENT AND CULTURAL CHANGE 14 (1965), pp. 33-47.

1,683 CASH, W. C. The developmental role of education in a plural society. EAISR, Jan. (1965), pp. 1-7.

1,684 CASTLE, E. B. The necessity of the useless in African education. UGANDA J. 29 (1965), pp. 55-59.

1,685 CASTRO, L. F. DE O. E. O Educador no Africa de hoje. PORT. EM AFR. 22 (1965), pp. 41-50.

1,686 CHUKWUKERE, B. I. African culture and modern African education. AFRICA 3, no. ii (1963), pp. 92-100.

1,687 CLARKE, F. The double mind in African education. AFRICA 5 (1932), pp. 158-168.

1,688 CLIFFORD, W. 'Formation des cadres.' CATHOLIC ED. IN THE SERVICE OF AFR., 1965, pp. 305-314.

1,689 COCATRE-ZILGIEN, A. Du rôle de l'enseignement secondaire et de l'enseignement technique dans la formation des cadres moyens et supérieurs des secteurs public et privé en Afrique. ANNALES AFR., 1962, pp. 486-500.

1,690 COLA ALBERICH, J. La U.N.E.S.C.O. y el mundo que se emancipa. CUAD. AFR. OR. 32 (1955), pp. 21-37.

1,691 COLLINS, S. The school teacher in his role as leader in West Indian and African societies. CIVILISATIONS 10 (1960), pp. 315-324; French summary, p. 325.

1,692 CONTON, W. F. History in the classroom. TR. HIST. SOC. GHANA 3 (1958), pp. 157-168.

1,693 COORNAERT, F. The teachers' point of view on the adaptation of school text-books. AFR. ED. 1, no. 1 (1963), pp. 3-5.

1,694 DA CRUZ, V. Des responsabilités de l'intellectuel noir. PRESENCE AFR. 27-28 (1959), pp. 321-339.

1,695 D'AETH, R. Conference on African education. CORONA 4 (1952), pp. 405-407.

1,696 DARTON, G. C. The "new method" of teaching English. AFR. STUD. 4 (1945), pp. 41-44.

1,697 DE GRAFT-JOHNSON, J. C. African traditional education. PRESENCE AFR. N.S. 7 (1956), pp. 51-55.

1,698 DEKEYSER, P. L. Education et écologie (Conférence Technique Internationale pour la Protection de la Nature, Lake Success, 1949). BULL. IFAN 12 (1950), pp. 1139-1146.

1,699 DIOP, A. Malentendus [editorial note on Présence africaine]. PRESENCE AFR. 6 (1949), pp. 3-8.

1,700 DOGBEH, R. Les difficultés intellectuelles du Noir. ET. DAHOM. N.S. 1 (1963-1964), pp. 101-104.

1,701 DOGBEH, R. Intelligence et éducation. PRESENCE AFR. N.S. 37 (1961), pp. 136-143.

1,702 DOUGALL, J. W. C. The case for and against mission schools. J. AFR. SOC. 38 (1939), pp. 91-108.

1,703 DOUGALL, J. W. C. The development of the education of the African in relation to Western contact. AFRICA 11 (1938), pp. 312-323.

1,704 DUBOIS, H. M. La pédagogie appliquée à nos noirs d'Afrique. AFRICA 2 (1929), pp. 381-403; English summary, pp. 403-404.

1,705 EKWA, M. Catholic education in the mind of the Church. CATHOLIC ED. IN THE SERVICE OF AFR., 1965, pp. 149-178.

1,706 EVANS, P. C. C. Western education and rural productivity in tropical Africa. AFRICA 32 (1962), pp. 313-323.

1,707 FELE, B. Crise de l'enseignement dans les colonies portugaises. PRESENCE AFR. N.S. 7 (1956), pp. 85-93.

1,708 FRASER, A. G. Aims of African education. INT. REV. MISSIONS 14 (1925), pp. 514-522.

1,709 GENIES, M. S. DE. Formation professionnelle dans les Territoires français d'Outre-Mer. CIVILISATIONS 8 (1958), pp. 231-250; English summary, pp. 250-252.

1,710 GREAVES, L. B. African education: a commentary on the Cambridge Conference, September 1952. INT. REV. MISSIONS 42 (1953), pp. 318-331.

1,711 GWILLIAM, F. H. The challenge of education in British overseas territories. AFR. AFFAIRS 57 (1958), pp. 99-109.

1,712 HAMMOND, S. A. Biology and African education. INT. REV. MISSIONS 17 (1928), pp. 495-504.

1,713 HARDY, G. La 'Librairie' des écoles indigènes en Afrique. AFRICA 1 (1928), pp. 145-156.

1,714 HEISLER, H. Social administration and education in Africa. J. LOCAL ADM. OV. 3 (1964), pp. 77-87.

1,715 HERVOUET, L. Préformation scolaire et professionnelle des jeunes Africaines. AFR. ET ASIE 55 (1961), pp. 35-39.

1,716 HESSEL, S. Les cadres de l'enseignement dans les Etats de la communauté francophone. CIVILISATIONS 10 (1960), pp. 307-312; English summary, pp. 313-314.

1,717 HOERNLE, A. W. An outline of the native conception of education in Africa. AFRICA 4 (1931), pp. 145-163.

1,718 HOPKINS, P. G. H. The role of adult education in economic development. ECON. DEV. IN AFRICA, 1965, pp. 51-70.

1,719 HOWMAN, R. The emotional side of African education. NADA 22 (1945), pp. 18-25.

1,720 HUNTER, G. Western culture and the advancing African: the task of adult education. CIVILISATIONS 9 (1959), pp. 313-324; French summary, pp. 325-328.

1,721 HUSSEY, E. R. J. An American's educational philosophy for Africa. Education of primitive people, by A. D. Helser. J. AFR. SOC. 39 (1940), pp. 361-366.

1,722 HUSSEY, E. R. J. Educational policy and political development in Africa. AFR. AFFAIRS 45 (1946), pp. 72-80.

1,723 HUSSEY, E. R. J. Village education in Africa. Report of the inter-territorial Jeanes Conference. J. AFR. SOC. 36 (1937), pp. 56-61.

1,724 HUSSEY, E. R. J. The year book of education, 1940, ed. F. H. Spencer. J. AFR. SOC. 40 (1941), pp. 68-78.

1,725 IBARROLA, R. Problemas educativos en las Colonias, consecuentes a las diferencias raciales. ARCH. INST. EST. AFR. 9, no. 38 (1956), pp. 7-30.

1,726 IRVINE, F. R. The teaching of agriculture in West Africa. AFRICA 5 (1932), pp. 464-473.

1,727 IRVINE, S. H. Ability testing in English-speaking Africa: an overview of predictive and comparative studies. RHODES-LIV. J. 34 (1964), pp. 44-55.

1,728 JAQUES, A. A. Teaching of hygiene in native primary schools. AFRICA 3 (1930), pp. 501-505.

1,729 K., P. Le développement de l'Enseignement dans les territoires français d'Outre-Mer. CIVILISATIONS 1, no. ii (1951), pp. 12-17; English summary, p. 18.

1,730 KINGUE, M. D. Les Conférences de Tananarive sur l'Enseignement en Afrique. ABBIA 1 (1963), pp. 72-80; English tr., pp. 81-87.

1,731 KI-ZERBO, J. Enseignement et culture africaine. PRESENCE AFR. N.S. 38 (1961), pp. 45-60.

1,732 KNAPEN, M. T. Un conférence internationale sur l'enfant africain à Yaoundé (2-7 janvier 1957). ZAIRE 11 (1957), pp. 297-309.

1,733 KOHLER, O. Massenerziehung in Afrika: ein britisches Erziehungsprogramm. AFRIKA (Berlin) 3 (1944), pp. 47-48.

1,734 LAGRAVE, R. L'Unité africaine commence à l'école. PRESENCE AFR. N.S. 53 (1965), pp. 250-253.

1,735 LANGFORD-SMITH, N. Mass education in rural Africa. INT. REV. MISSIONS 34 (1945), pp. 9-135.

1,736 LEGER, J.-M. Culture et éducation. CANADA ET LES PAYS AFR. FRANCOPHONES, 1965, pp. 93-109.

1,737 LUGARD, Lord. Education and race relations. J. AFR. SOC. 32 (1933), pp. 1-11.

1,738 MCKENNA, J. C. The sociological aspects of Catholic education in Africa. CATHOLIC ED. IN THE SERVICE OF AFR., 1965, pp. 179-190.

1,739 MACMILLAN, W. M. The importance of the educated African. J. AFR. SOC. 33 (1934), pp. 137-142.

1,740 MAGNINO, L. Considerazioni e proposte per una politica dell' insegnamento nell'Africa tropicale. AFRICA (Rome) 18 (1963), pp. 187-194.

1,741 MAGNINO, L. Necessità di una pianificazione della scuola nei paesi africani. AFRICA (Rome) 16 (1961), pp. 159-162.

1,742 MAQUET, M. Un centre international d'éducation de base en Afrique noire? ZAIRE 6 (1952), pp. 281-286.

1,743 MAYHEW, A. A comparative survey of educational aims and methods in British India and British Tropical Africa. AFRICA 6 (1933), pp. 172-186.

1,744 MERCIER, P. Textes de Blyden. PRESENCE AFR. 1 (1947), pp. 47-49.

1,745 MILLER, K. What knowledge is of most worth to the Negro at the present time. LIBERIA BULL. 20 (1902), pp. 64-74.

1,746 MILLMAN, W. Health instruction in African schools: suggestions for a curriculum. AFRICA 3 (1930), pp. 484-499.

1,747 MOERMAN, J. Catholic education and international organisations. CATHOLIC ED. IN THE SERVICE OF AFR., 1965, pp. 343-352.

1,748 MOERMAN, J. Catholic education and religious and apostolic training. CATHOLIC ED. IN THE SERVICE OF AFR., 1965, pp. 292-304.

1,749 MOERMAN, J. Catholic schools and African environment. CATHOLIC ED. IN THE SERVICE OF AFR., 1965, pp. 227-237.

1,750 MOERMAN, J. Catholic schools and other religions. CATHOLIC ED. IN THE SERVICE OF AFR., 1965, pp. 337-343.

1,751 MOERMAN, J. Catholic schools and the state. CATHOLIC ED. IN THE SERVICE OF AFR., 1965, pp. 333-337.

1,752 MOERMAN, J. The education of women. CATHOLIC ED. IN THE SERVICE OF AFR., 1965, pp. 318-328.

1,753 MOERMAN, J. and AUGER, G. A. Catholic schools and Catholic environment. CATHOLIC ED. IN THE SERVICE OF AFR., 1965, pp. 238-249.

1,754 MUMFORD, W. B. and JACKSON, R. The problem of mass education in Africa. AFRICA 11 (1938), pp. 187-206.

1,755 MUMFORD, W. B. and PARKER, B. N. Education in British African dependencies. A review of the 1935 annual reports on native education in Nyasaland, N. Rhodesia, Tanganyika, Uganda, Gold Coast, Nigeria and Sierra Leone. J. AFR. SOC. 36 (1937), pp. 17-32.

1,756 MUNANAIRI, C. Les graines vivantes. PRESENCE AFR. N.S. 54 (1965), pp. 198-202.

1,757 MURRAY, A. V. Education under indirect rule. J. AFR. SOC. 34 (1935), pp. 227-268.

1,758 MUSGROVE, F. Bias in the African secondary school. CORONA 4 (1952), pp. 298-300.

1,759 NICHOLSON, M. Training Africans for life in a modern economy. CIVILISATIONS 8 (1958), pp. 217-228; French summary, pp. 228-230.

1,760 OLDHAM, J. H. Educational policy of the British government in Africa. INT. REV. MISSIONS 14 (1925), pp. 421-427.

1,761 OLDHAM, J. H. The educational work of missionary societies. AFRICA 7 (1934), pp. 47-59.

1,762 OLIVEIRA, F. R. DE. O cinema como elemento educacional nos meios rurais Africanos. BSEM 135 (1963), pp. 39-51.

1,763 OLIVER, R. A. C. Psychological and pedagogical considerations in the making of text-books. AFRICA 3 (1930), pp. 293-304.

1,764 OPTIMIST (pseud.). Missionaries and education in pagan Africa. J. AFR. SOC. 23 (1923), pp. 44-47.

1,765 O'RIORDAN, M. C. M. The professional aspects of Catholic education in Africa. CATHOLIC ED. IN THE SERVICE OF AFR., 1965, pp. 203-209.

1,766 ORMSBY-GORE, W. Educational problems of the colonial empire. J. AFR. SOC. 36 (1937), pp. 162-169.

1,767 ORR, J. R. The use of the kinema in the guidance of backward races. J. AFR. SOC. 30 (1931), pp. 238-244.

1,768 PAGE, A. Education et développement économique. ANNALES AFR., 1962, pp. 535-559.

1,769 PARRY, S. B. Programmed instruction: from technique to technology. AFR. ED. 2, no. 1 (1964), pp. 7-10.

1,770 PAUVERT, J.-C. L'éducation et le développement accéléré: tendances et problèmes en Afrique d'expression française. CIVILISATIONS 10 (1960), pp. 457-470; English summary, pp. 471-472.

1,771 PAYE, L. Deux expériences de formation des cadres et de perfectionnement des travailleurs et employés africains. CIVILISATIONS 9 (1959), pp. 301-310; English summary, pp. 311-312.

1,772 PEILLON, P. The pastoral aspects of Catholic education in Africa. CATHOLIC ED. IN THE SERVICE OF AFR., 1965, pp. 191-202.

1,773 PESHKIN, A. Educational reform in colonial and independent Africa. AFR. AFFAIRS 64 (1965), pp. 210-216.

1,774 PHILLIPS, A. S. Selection procedures for teacher training colleges. AFR. ED. 2, no. 2 (1964), pp. 18-26.

1,775 PHILLIPS, J. H. Negro teachers for Negro schools. LIBERIA BULL. 11 (1897), pp. 24-28.

1,776 READE, H. English schools and colonial education: how can they be linked? ROYAL COL. INST. PR. 36 (1904-1905), pp. 190-208.

1,777 REED, P. Colonial students: what the British Council does. CORONA 2 (1950), pp. 228-231.

1,778 RIVENC, P. and GUBERINA, P. Projet en vue du développement de l'education des adultes en Afrique. PRESENCE AFR. N.S. 40 (1962), pp. 79-87.

1,779 ROBERT, M. African education. CORONA 1, no. 2 (1949), pp. 21-22.

1,780 SAR, A. et al. Esprit et situation de l'enseignement en Afrique Noire, by A. Sar, I. Fofana and K. Banny. PRESENCE AFR. N.S. 11 (1957), pp. 71-83.

1,781 SCHMIDT, P. W. The use of the vernacular in education in Africa. AFRICA 3 (1930), pp. 137-145.

1,782 SCIASCIA, G. L'éducation et l'instruction en Afrique éléments constitutionnels d'unité. CIVILISATIONS 14 (1964), pp. 202-206; English summary, pp. 207-208.

1,783 SCOTT, H. S. Education and nutrition in the colonies. AFRICA 10 (1937), pp. 458-471.

1,784 SCOTT, H. S. Native authorities and education. AFRICA 15 (1945), pp. 173-182.

1,785 SEQUARIS, M. Traditional teaching: programmed instruction. AFR. ED. 2, no. 1 (1964), pp. 10-17.

1,786 SHRIVER, S. Two years of the Peace Corps. FOREIGN AFFAIRS 41 (1962-1963), pp. 694-707.

1,787 SILVEY, J. Aptitude testing and educational selection in Africa. RHODES-LIV. J. 34 (1964), pp. 9-22.

1,788 SILVEY, J. Testing ability tests: issues in the measurement of ability among African schoolboys. EAISR, Jan. (1963), pp. 1-20.

1,789 SMITH, E. W. Indigenous education in Africa. ESSAYS PRESENTED TO C. G. SELIGMAN, 1934, pp. 319-334.

1,790 SMITH, R. International conference on African children. J. AFR. SOC. 30 (1931), pp. 272-276.

1,791 SMITH, R. Education in British Africa. J. AFR. SOC. 31 (1932), pp. 54-76, 133-147, 255-281.

1,792 SPENS, T. Rural home economics programmes need the support of men. AFR. WOMEN 5 (1962), pp. 10-13.

1,793 STEAD, C. The education of primitive peoples. NADA 13 (1935), pp. 84-92.

1,794 STEWART, M. Courses for overseas women in London. AFR. WOMEN 1 (1955), pp. 32-33.

1,795 SUTTON, F. X. Africa's educational needs and opportunities. MAN AND AFRICA, 1965, pp. 194-221.

1,796 SWANZY, H. Mass education. AFR. AFFAIRS 46 (1947), p. 4.

1,797 THOMPSON, E. W. The Bible in the religious education of Africa. INT. REV. MISSIONS 16 (1927), pp. 394-404.

1,798 TOWA, M. Principes de l'éducation coloniale. ABBIA 3 (1963), pp. 25-38.

1,799 TREGEAR, P. S. The primary school leaver in Africa. NADA 40 (1963), pp. 17-26.

1,800 UWECHUE, R. C. Our stay in Geneva. GENEVE-AFR. 3 (1964), pp. 103-104.

1,801 VAIZEY, J. Education in African economic growth. ECON. DEV. FOR AFRICA, 1965, pp. 340-360.

1,802 VERDIER, E. T. CCTA/CSA and interafrican cooperation in the field of education. COOPERAZIONE INT. AFR., 1960, pp. 154-166.

1,803 VERDIER, E. T. CCTA-CSA and international cooperation in the field of education. CIVILISATIONS 10 (1960), pp. 201-208; French summary, pp. 209-210.

1,804 VERHAEGEN, B. Le deuxième Congrès National de la Jeunesse (Coquilhatville, 16 au 22 janvier 1962). ET. CONG. 2, no. 3 (1962), pp. 16-19.

1,805 VERHAEGEN, P. L'orientation scolaire et les aptitudes des enfants africains à la fin de l'école primaire. ZAIRE 14 (1960), pp. 211-223.

1,806 VISCHER, H. Mass education in African society. AFRICA 14 (1944), pp. 336-339.

1,807 VISCHER, H. Native education in German Africa. J. AFR. SOC. 14 (1914-1915), pp. 123-142.

1,808 VOGHEL, R. DE. Curricular reform. CATHOLIC ED. IN THE SERVICE OF AFR., 1965, pp. 251-256.

1,809 WADE, A. Examen critique des méthodes pédagogiques. PRESENCE AFR. N.S. 7 (1956), pp. 56-73.

1,810 WANTMAN, M. J. The development of examinations. RHODES-LIV. J. 34 (1964), pp. 1-8.

1,811 WARD, W. E. The writing of history text-books for Africa. AFRICA 9 (1934), pp. 191-198.

1,812 WINTERBOTTOM, J. M. Looking back [impressions of a retired Colonial education officer]. RHODES-LIV. J. 13 (1953), pp. 30-34.

1,813 WINTERBOTTOM, J. M. Plain thoughts on African education. TANG. NOTES 27 (1949), pp. 65-68.

1,814 WRONG, M. Literacy and literature for African peoples. INT. REV. MISSIONS 33 (1944), pp. 193-199.

1,815 WRONG, M. Mass education in Africa. AFR. AFFAIRS 43 (1944), pp. 105-111.

1,816 WRONG, M. and BRACKETT, D. G. Notes on nature study and agricultural text-books used in Africa. AFRICA 5 (1932), pp. 474-486.

1,817 Supplementary notes on hygiene books used in Africa. AFRICA 5 (1932), pp. 71-74.

1,818 L'Afrique et l'information. PRESENCE AFR. N.S. 40 (1962), pp. 161-163.

1,819 Bibliography of programmed instruction. AFR. ED. 2, no. 1 (1964), pp. 21-26.

1,820 Le Centre d'initiation aux problèmes africains de Paris. ZAIRE 6 (1952), pp. 82-83.

1,821 "Classiques" Africains. PRESENCE AFR. N.S. 54 (1965), pp. 259-262.

1,822 Community development. CORONA 1, no. 2 (1949), pp. 3-5.

1,823 Co-operation with Free France. J. AFR. SOC. 40 (1941), pp. 101-102.

1,824 Courses in public administration and local government. J. AFR. ADM. 12 (1960), pp. 235-240.

1,825 Educational problems in the non self-governing Territories. [UNESCO General Conference, April, 1950]. CIVILISATIONS 1, no. i (1951), pp. 73-76; French translation, pp. 77-80.

1,826 Homecraft consultant's study tour. AFR. WOMEN 5 (1962), pp. 9-10.

1,827 Home economics education for Africa. WOMEN TODAY 6 (1964), pp. 56-57.

1,828 Impiego degli audiovisivi per l'educazione in Africa. AFRICA (Rome) 17 (1962), pp. 179-198.

1,829 L'Institut Panafricain pour le développement: a training school for African community development leaders. BULL. AFR. STUD. ASSOC. 5 (1965), p. 29.

1,830 Mass education in African society. A British Colonial Office publication. AFR. AFFAIRS 43 (1944), pp. 93-95.

1,831 Reforma do ensino primário no Ultramar. PORT. EM AFR. 21 (1964), pp. 368-383.

1,832 A study of African manpower needs and educational capabilities. BULL. AFR. STUD. ASSOC. 4 (1965), p. 19.

1,833 Teacher supply in African Territories. AFR. WOMEN 4 (1960), pp. 8-10.

1,834 The teaching of English in African schools. NADA 36 (1959), pp. 16-18.

1,835 Les techniques audio-visuelles et l'Afrique. PRESENCE AFR. N.S. 50 (1964), pp. 250-251.

1,836 Text-books for African Schools: a preliminary memorandum by the International Council. AFRICA 1 (1928), pp. 13-22.

1,837 The training of village teachers in Africa. INT. REV. MISSIONS 18 (1929), pp. 231-249.

1,838 L'U.N.E.S.C.O. fera-t-elle apporter l'éducation dans les contrées arriérées? PRESENCE AFR. 2 (1948), pp. 325-327.

1,839 Vocational training for African women. AFR. WOMEN 5 (1962), pp. 4-7; 5 (1963), pp. 35-37.

1,840 What is programmed instruction? AFR. ED. 2, no. 1 (1964), pp. 4-7.

See also 342, 622, 1886, 1925, 2018, 2562, 3075, 3095, 3274, 3787, 4509, 4641.

Higher education

1,841 ADAMS, W. Higher education. CORONA 2 (1950), pp. 86-88.

1,842 ADAMS, W. New universities of the Commonwealth. UNIVERSITAS 1, no. 1 (1953), pp. 5-8.

1,843 ALLIOT, M. Tradition universitaire et formation des cadres outre-mer. ANNALES AFR., 1962, pp. 459-471.

1,844 ASHBY, Sir E. and LOGAN, Sir D. The diversity of universities in the Commonwealth. CONGR. OF THE UNIVS. OF THE COMMONWEALTH 9 (1963), pp. 3-17.

1,845 ASHTON, K. G. Overseas service training in the United Kingdom. CIVILISATIONS 9 (1959), pp. 479-492; French summary, pp. 492-495.

1,846 BAKOLE, M. M. L'Université: signification, mesure et condition de l'Africanisation. PRESENCE AFR. N.S. 53 (1965), pp. 149-161.

1,847 BIGELOW, K. W. Higher education in Tropical Africa. PAN-AFRICANISM RECONSIDERED, 1962, pp. 205-213.

1,848 BOUAERT, J. C. Les students en Grande Bretagne. ZAIRE 10 (1956), pp. 739-754.

1,849 CHARLES, V. Les "Colonial Students" d'Afrique en Grande-Bregagne. ZAIRE 5 (1951), pp. 1059-1065.

1,850 DILLON, W. S. Universities and nation-building in Africa. JMAS 1 (1963), pp. 75-89.

1,851 FILESI, T. Gli africani vanno all'Università. AFRICA (Rome) 10 (1955), pp. 291-294.

1,852 FRAZIER, E. F. Problèmes de l'étudiant noir aux Etats-Unis. PRESENCE AFR. 14 (1953), pp. 275-283.

1,853 FRENKIEL, J. Réflexions sur l'enseignement supérieur en Afrique. GENEVE-AFR. 4 (1965), pp. 234-238.

1,854 GARIGUE, P. [L'étudiant africain en Angleterre]. PRESENCE AFR. 14 (1953), pp. 247-256.

1,855 GAY, J. H. Higher education in Tropical Africa. AFR. AFFAIRS 62 (1963), pp. 153-155.

1,856 GOMEZ ANTON, F. Un caso de assistencia técnico-universitaria al Africa: La Universidad de Navarra. ARCH. INST. EST. AFR. 19, no. 77 (1965), pp. 29-40.

1,857 GRAY, A. Commonwealth scholarships. AFR. AFFAIRS 59 (1960), pp. 9-10.

1,858 GROSHENS, J.-C. and ARDANT, P. L'enseignement supérieur et la formation des cadres supérieurs dans les Etats nouvellement indépendants. ANNALES AFR., 1962, pp. 529-534.

1,859 HARBISON, F. The African university and human resource development. JMAS 3 (1965), pp. 53-62.

1,860 IDENBURG, P. J. Problèmes de formation universitaire dans les pays tropicaux et sub-tropicaux. CIVILISATIONS 5 (1955), pp. 341-344.

1,861 JOACHIM, K. P. A travers la presse étudiante Africaine. PRESENCE AFR. N.S. 1 (1955), pp. 177-178.

1,862 KEITH, J. L. African students in Great Britain. AFR. AFFAIRS 45 (1946), pp. 65-72.

1,863 LOGAN, D. W. and MORRILL, J. L. The establishment of new universities. CONGR. OF THE UNIVS. OF THE COMMONWEALTH 8 (1958), pp. 62-75.

1,864 MAGNINO, L. Le università in Africa e la loro funzione mediatrice. AFRICA (Rome) 13 (1958), pp. 135-138.

1,865 MORGAN, D. Study group on Catholics and higher education. CATHOLIC ED. IN THE SERVICE OF AFR., 1965, pp. 353-375.

1,866 MURRAY, R. N. Training the teachers of youth and adults in an expanding educational system. Excerpts from the Camilla Wedgwood lecture, 12th May, 1964. AFR. ED. 2, no. 2 (1964), pp. 2-11.

1,867 OF SU-APPIAH, L. H. Réflexions sur les Universités Africaines. PRESENCE AFR. 36 (1961), pp. 71-78.

1,868 OTIENO, N. C. Current problems in the education of an African scientist—and the role such a scientist could play in the economic and social development of Africa. PROC. INT. CONG. AFR. 1 (1962), pp. 309-317.

1,869 PARKES, R. No ivory towers. TRANSITION 11 (1963), pp. 43-46.

1,870 PARKIN, G. R. The Rhodes scholarships. ROYAL COL. INST. PR. 36 (1904-1905), pp. 8-28.

1,871 SLOAN, R. Les étudiants africains aux Etats-Unis. PRESENCE AFR. 14 (1953), pp. 257-274.

1,872 TREVELYAN, M. The place of the African student in the international student community. AFR. AFFAIRS 62 (1963), pp. 258-261.

1,873 VERHAEGEN, B. L'Université et les Etudiants; sociologie d'une grève. PRESENCE AFR. N.S. 52 (1964), pp. 128-142.

1,874 WEBSTER, S. L'étudiant africain en Angleterre. PRESENCE AFR. 14 (1953), pp. 241-247.

1,875 WEEKS, S. G. Whither universities in Africa? [review article on They built for the future: a chronicle of Makerere University College 1922-1962, by M. MacPherson, African universities and Western tradition, by E. Ashby]. TRANSITION 18 (1965), pp. 51-53.

1,876 A propos des étudiants africains aux Etats-Unis. ZAIRE 4 (1950), p. 893; 5 (1951), pp. 1071-1072.

1,877 Un Africain sur les rives de la Tamise. PRESENCE AFR. N.S. 45 (1963), pp. 218-223.

1,878 Etudiants africains en Angleterre. ZAIRE 4 (1950), p. 1025.

1,879 Les Nations-Unies et les étudiants africains. ZAIRE 5 (1951), pp. 753-754.

1,880 Os Estudantes do Ultramar. PORT. EM AFR. 10 (1953), pp. 258-260.

1,881 Première conférence pan-Africaine des étudiants. PRESENCE AFR. N.S. 34-35 (1960-1961), pp. 214-217.

1,882 Situation des étudiants noirs dans le monde. PRESENCE AFR. 14 (1953), pp. 223-240.

1,883 Les universités de couleur aux Etats-Unis. ZAIRE 4 (1950), pp. 894-895.

GEOGRAPHY. TOPOGRAPHY. TRAVEL

1,884 ANDREW, G. Water supply. SUDAN NOTES 28 (1947), pp. 172-173.

1,885 ANDREWS, A. W. The Empire and geographical teaching. ROYAL COL. INST. PR. 31 (1899-1900), pp. 41-45.

1,886 BALCH, E. S. American explorers of Africa. GEOG. REV. 5 (1918), pp. 274-281.

1,887 BALEN, F. Cartografía náutica del Africa española. ARCH. INST. EST. AFR. 2, no. 6 (1948), pp. 99-120.

1,888 BARRADAS, L. A. Para a cronologia do Quaternário na Africa Meridional. BSEM 96 (1956), pp. 77-90.

1,889 BENEDIC, A. La navigation fluviale dans les colonies françaises. J. AFR. SOC. 31 (1932), pp. 15-37.

1,890 BERENGUER Y ELIZALDE, D. Del Abrego al Malaspina, veinticinco años de investigación oceanográfica en Africa. ARCH. INST. EST. AFR. 19, no. 76 (1965), pp. 21-36.

1,891 BOWDEN, B. N. The dry seasons of inter-tropical Africa and Madagascar. J. TROP. GEOG. 19 (1964), pp. 1-3.

1,892 CHRISTY, C. African bush and forest. J. AFR. SOC. 19 (1920), pp. 85-91.

1,893 COLA ALBERICH, J. La hidrografía como factor biodinámico y sociológico en Africa. CUAD. EST. AFR. 12 (1950), pp. 47-56.

1,894 COUNSELL, E. H. M. An African journey. NIGERIAN FIELD 7 (1938), pp. 55-56.

1,895 DAHLBERG, R. E. An analysis and bibliography of recent African atlases. AFR. STUD. BULL. 5, no. iii (1962), pp. 23-33; 6 no. ii (1963), pp. 6-9.

1,896 DAHLBERG, R. E. and THOMAS, B. E. Map resources on Africa. AFR. STUD. BULL. 5, no. i (1962), pp. 1-8.

1,897 DEBENHAM, F. The changing physical environment of Tropical Africa. CORONA 3 (1951), pp. 367-373.

1,898 DEBENHAM, F. The water resources of Africa. SUDAN NOTES AND RECORDS 35, pt. 2 (1954), pp. 69-75.

1,899 DEKKER, G. Climate and water resources in Africa. MAN AND AFRICA, 1965, pp. 30-64.

1,900 DESHLER, W. Cattle in Africa: distribution, types, and problems. GEOG. REV. 53 (1963), pp. 52-58.

1,901 DIXEY, F. African landscape. GEOG. REV. 34 (1944), pp. 457-465.

1,902 FALKNER, F. R. Quotients hydro-thermiques. BULL. IFAN 14 (1952), pp. 356-358.

1,903 FITZGERALD, W. The impact of western civilization on Negro Africa. GEOG. REV. 26 (1936), pp. 77-87.

1,904 FORBES, R. H. The black man's industries. GEOG. REV. 23 (1933), pp. 230-247.

1,905 GARCIA-BAQUERO, M. León el Africano y la cartografia. ARCH. INST. EST. AFR. 6, no. 27 (1953), pp. 31-56.

1,906 GILG, J.-P. and REMY, G. Une documentation cartographique sur l'Afrique au sud du Sahara. CAH. ET AFR. 5 (1965), pp. 635-638.

1,907 GILLILAND, H. B. Some current problems concerning the understanding of African vegetation. GEOG. REV. 40 (1950), pp. 466-468.

1,908 GILLMAN, C. Musings from the air. TANG. NOTES 11 (1941), pp. 25-31.

1,909 GOUROU, P. Conditions géographiques en Afrique tropicale. PRESENCE AFR. 13 (1952), pp. 43-57.

1,910 GRAY, J. The journey of an Arab caravan from east to west Africa and back, 1851-1854. TANGANYIKA NOTES AND RECORDS 58-59 (1962), p. 174.

1,911 GRAY, R. Eclipse maps. J. AFR. HIST. 6 (1965), pp. 251-262.

1,912 GUALCO, G. L'alpinismo in Africa. AFRICA (Rome) 14 (1959), pp. 11-16.

1,913 HAILEY, Lord. [Speech on visits to Africa and on Africa during the war]. J. AFR. SOC. 40 (1941), pp. 239-254.

1,914 HAMDAN, G. The political map of the new Africa. GEOG. REV. 53 (1963), pp. 418-439.

1,915 HANCE, W. A. et al. Source areas of export production in tropical Africa, by W. A. Hance, V. Kotschar, R. J. Peterec. GEOG. REV. 51 (1961), pp. 487-499.

1,916 HELLER, E. The geographical barriers to the distribution of big game animals in Africa. GEOG. REV. 6 (1918), pp. 297-319.

1,917 JEFFREYS, M. D. W. Feux de brousse. BULL. IFAN 13 (1951), pp. 682-710.

1,918 KAMIAN, B. La géographie de l'Afrique présentée par les Occidentaux. PRESENCE AFR. 27-28 (1959), pp. 100-107.

1,919 KIMBLE, G. H. T. Tropical Africa in transition. GEOG. REV. 42 (1952), pp. 7-15.

1,920 KIRK, W. The N.E. monsoon and some aspects of African history. J. AFR. HIST. 3 (1962), pp. 263-267.

1,921 LAST, G. C. The geographical implications of man and his future in Africa. MAN AND AFRICA, 1965, pp. 6-29.

1,922 LEE, J. B. Photography as an aid to the exploration of new countries. J. AFR. SOC. 1 (1902), pp. 302-311.

1,923 LEVA, A. E. Ibn Batûta nell'Africa Nera. AFRICA (Rome) 16 (1961), pp. 169-177.

1,924 LIGHT, R. and M. Contrasts in African farming: aerial views from Cape to Cairo. GEOG. REV. 28 (1938), pp. 529-555.

1,925 LINIGER-GOUMAZ, M. L'enseignement de la géographie en Afrique. GENEVE-AFR. 4 (1965), pp. 65-77.

1,926 LOMBARDERO, M. El servicio geográfico del Ejército en colonias. Un año más en trabajos del Mapa. ARCH. INST. EST. AFR. 3, no. 9 (1949), pp. 17-59.

1,927 LYNE, R. N. Climate the controlling factor in the tropics. J. AFR. SOC. 38 (1939), pp. 477-482.

1,928 MACLEOD, M. N. Co-ordination of African surveys. J. AFR. SOC. 35 (1936), pp. 372-380.

1,929 MONOD, TH. Autour du problème du desséchement africain. BULL. IFAN 12 (1950), pp. 514-523.

1,930 MONOD, TH. Le ciel austral et l'orientation (Autour d'un article de Louis Massignon). BULL. IFAN 25 (1963), pp. 415-426.

1,931 MONTEIL, V. L'Oeuvre d'Idrisi. BULL. IFAN 1 (1939), pp. 837-857.

1,932 MORGAN, A. E. An African night. AFR. AFFAIRS 51 (1952), pp. 158-160.

1,933 MOSS, R. P. Land use mapping in Tropical Africa. NIGERIAN GEOG. J. 3, no. 1 (1959), pp. 8-17.

1,934 MURDOCK, G. P. Staple subsistence crops of Africa. GEOG. REV. 50 (1960), pp. 523-540.

1,935 MUSSIO, G. Conscienza della nuova realtà africana. AFRICA (Rome) 13 (1958), pp. 75-89.

1,936 NICOLAS, J.-P. Les climato africains en biogéographie humaine. BULL. IFAN, Série B: Sciences humaines 20 (1958), pp. 7-67.

1,937 OGILVIE, A. G. An African survey and science in Africa. GEOG. REV. 29 (1939), pp. 653-656.

1,938 OGILVIE, A. G. Geography at the South African meeting of the British Association. GEOG. REV. 20 (1930), pp. 631-641.

1,939 ONDE, H. La géographie régionale et le monde africain. GENEVE-AFR. 2 (1963), pp. 149-162.

1,940 PROTHERO, R. M. Some contributions of geography to tropical studies: the need for integration. WAISER SOC. 2 (1953), pp. 73-88.

1,941 RAWSON, H. E. The climate of Africa. J. AFR. SOC. 11 (1912), pp. 285-289.

1,942 RICHARD-MOLARD, J. Terres de démesure. PRESENCE AFR. 8 (1950), pp. 31-38.

1,943 SHANTZ, H. L. The problem of Tropical Africa: a review of recent books. GEOG. REV. 16 (1926), pp. 597-613.

1,944 SKINNER, A. N. Pilgrimage in reverse. NIGERIAN FIELD 16 (1951), pp. 4-14.

1,945 STEBBING, E. P. Africa and its intermittent rainfall. J. AFR. SOC. 37 (1938), supplement.

1,946 STEBBING, E. P. The man-made desert in Africa. Erosion and drought. J. AFR. SOC. 37 (1938), supplement.

1,947 STEEL, R. W. Africa surveyed: a discussion of some recent books. GEOG. REV. 48 (1958), pp. 248-256.

1,948 STEEL, R. W. Geographers in Africa. AFR. AFFAIRS 53 (1954), pp. 52-55.

1,949 STEEL, R. W. The human geography of inter-tropical Africa. J. AFR. ADM. 2 (1950), pp. 39-40.

1,950 TATE, H. R. Two African explorers. 1. David Livingstone. 2. Joseph Thomson. J. AFR. SOC. 37 (1938), pp. 304-317, 449-463.

1,951 TOUPET, CH. Un congrès de géographie tropicale en Uganda. BULL. IFAN 18 (1956), pp. 514-515.

1,952 TROCHAIN, J. L. Accord interafricain sur la définition des types de végétation de l'Afrique Tropicale. BULL. I.E.C. N.S. 13-14 (1957), pp. 55-93.

1,953 WADE, E. K. Some African adventures of the chief scout [Lord Baden-Powell]. J. AFR. SOC. 40 (1941), pp. 204-222.

1,954 WALL, P. and MACDONA, B. F. News out of Africa. AFR. AFFAIRS 59 (1960), pp. 213-225.

1,955 WAYLAND, E. J. The study of past climates in Tropical Africa. PROC. PAN-AFR. CONGR. PRE-HIST. 1 (1947), pp. 59-66.

1,956 WILDEMAN, E. DE. La photographie par avion dans l'étude de la phytogéographie des régions tropicales. BULL. SEANCES IRCB 6 (1935), pp. 431-446.

1,957 WILLIAMSON, J. Across Africa by car. NYASA. J. 6, no. 2 (1953), pp. 13-34.

1,958 WINID, B. Atlases and serial maps in Africa. AFR. BULL. 1 (1964), pp. 135-148.

1,959 WRENCH, W. A round Africa tour. J. AFR. SOC. 37 (1938), pp. 72-74.

1,960 The description of Africa. TANG. NOTES 3 (1937), pp. 1-7.

1,961 Un équipage d'avion de l'Institut Géographique National péri en Afrique. BULL. IFAN 11 (1949), p. 541.

1,962 Un nouveau pas vers une organisation internationale de l'étude des déserts. BULL. IFAN 12 (1950), pp. 241-242.

1,963 Seminar on rift valley system in Africa. BULL. AFR. STUD. ASSOC. 6 (1965), pp. 34-35.

GOVERNMENT. POLITICS. ADMINISTRATION

Colonial period

1,964 A., P. En marge d'une loi. AFR. ET ASIE 34 (1956), pp. 55-59.

1,965 ABRAHAMS, P. The [Pan-African] Congress in perspective. HISTORY OF THE PAN-AFRICAN CONGRESS, 1945, pp. 11-12, 13-26.

1,966 ACHILLE, L. T. Amérique du nord. PRESENCE AFR. 8 (1950), pp. 357-381.

1,967 THE AFRICAN STUDIES BRANCH. The member system in British African Territories. J. AFR. ADM. 1 (1949), pp. 51-59.

1,968 THE AFRICAN STUDIES BRANCH. Methods of direct taxation in British Tropical Africa. J. AFR. ADM. 2 (1950), pp. 3-11; 3 (1951), pp. 30-41, 77-87.

1,969 THE AFRICAN STUDIES BRANCH. A survey of the development of Local Government in the African territories since 1947. J. AFR. ADM. 4 (1952), supplement.

1,970 AFRICANUS (pseud.). Africa and the League of Nations. J. AFR. SOC. 19 (1920), pp. 317-319.

1,971 AFRICANUS, P. Emancipations africaines: la loi-cadre au banc d'essai. AFR. ET ASIE 39 (1957), pp. 14-30.

1,972 AKPAN, N. U. Have traditional authorities a place in modern Local Government systems? J. AFR. ADM. 7 (1955), pp. 109-116.

1,973 ALTRINCHAM, Lord. The British Commonwealth and western union. FOREIGN AFFAIRS 27 (1948-1949), pp. 601-617.

1,974 AMAMOO, A. G. Africa calls again. AFR. AFFAIRS 55 (1956), pp. 43-45.

1,975 AMERY, L. S. The Crown and Africa. AFR. AFFAIRS 52 (1953), pp. 179-185.

1,976 AMERY, L. S. General von Epp's case examined. J. AFR. SOC. 36 (1937), supplement.

1,977 AMERY, L. S. The problem of the cession of Mandated Territories in relation to the world situation. INTERNAT. AFFAIRS 16 (1937), pp. 3-22.

1,978 AMERY, L. S. Some aspects of the Imperial Conference. INTERNAT. AFFAIRS 6 (1927), pp. 2-24.

1,979 ANASTASIO, E. Importancia de la Marina en una politica colonial. ARCH. INST. EST. AFR. 4, no. 15 (1950), pp. 47-85.

1,980 ANCIAN, G. L'évolution de la politique des Puissances européennes en Afrique Noire en matière rurale. AFR. ET ASIE 31 (1955), pp. 32-40.

1,981 ANDRIANTSILANIARIVO, E. Le colonialisme. PRESENCE AFR. N.S. 24-25 (1959), pp. 192-207.

1,982 ANGELL, N. The new imperialism and the old nationalism. INTERNAT. AFFAIRS 9 (1930), pp. 69-83.

1,983 APTER, D. E. Africa and the social scientist. WORLD POLITICS 6 (1953-1954), pp. 538-548.

1,984 ARNAUD, M. Le mythe nègre. PRESENCE AFR. 7 (1949), pp. 306-308.

1,985 B., R. G. Perspectivas y resultados después de la Conferencia de Bandung. CUAD. AFR. OR. 30 (1955), pp. 59-63.

1,986 BAKER, G. America discovers Africa. AFR. AFFAIRS 57 (1958), pp. 110-119.

1,987 BALANDIER, G. Contribution à l'étude des nationalismes en Afrique Noire. ZAIRE 8 (1954), pp. 379-389.

1,988 BANWELL, G. H. Local administration in Germany and its lessons for Africa. J. AFR. ADM. 1 (1949), pp. 74-76.

1,989 BEATTIE, J. H. M. Checks on the abuse of political power in some African States: a preliminary framework for analysis. SOCIOLOGUS 9 (1959), pp. 97-115.

1,990 BELOFF, M. Democracy in Africa. AFR. AFFAIRS 52 (1953), pp. 137-140.

1,991 BEN-HORIN, E. Israel and Africa. AFR. SOUTH 2, no. 1 (1957), pp. 90-96.

1,992 BENSON, W. Closer union in Africa. J. AFR. SOC. 30 (1931), pp. 337-343.

1,993 BERNARD, A. Germany's colonial aims. J. AFR. SOC. 16 (1917), pp. 306-313.

1,994 BEVIN, E. Impressions of the British Commonwealth Relations Conference, 1938. INTERNAT. AFFAIRS 18 (1939), pp. 56-76.

1,995 BILSEN, J. VAN. Politique africaine. ZAIRE 4 (1950), p. 534.

1,996 BINNS, A. L. The formation and development of local education authorities in Africa. J. AFR. ADM. 5 (1953), pp. 7-11.

1,997 BIRD, O. M. Administrative problems of elections in developing countries. J. AFR. ADM. 9 (1957), pp. 167-174.

1,998 BLANCO IZAGA, E. Política africana. CUAD. EST. AFR. 1 (1946), pp. 43-56.

1,999 BOELAERT, E. L'O.N.U. et les Territoires non autonomes. AEQUATORIA 14 (1951), pp. 74-76.

2,000 BORDEN, Sir R. The Imperial Conference [an address at, by Sir Robert Borden on June 14th, 1927]. INTERNAT. AFFAIRS 6 (1927), pp. 197-213.

2,001 BOTZARIS, A. Comunismo en Africa. ARCH. INST. EST. AFR. 6, no. 25 (1953), pp. 59-74.

2,002 BOURDILLON, Sir B. H. Colonial development and welfare. INTERNAT. AFFAIRS 20 (1944), pp. 369-380.

2,003 BOUTET, R. Oltre il comunicato di Bandoeng. AFRICA (Rome) 10 (1955), pp. 139-140.

2,004 BRADLEY, K. The passing of an epoch. AFR. AFFAIRS 50 (1951), pp. 318-321.

2,005 BRANTENAAR, A. D. J. Blanke Kolonisatie in de Afrikaanse tropen. ZAIRE 3 (1949), pp. 441-445.

2,006 BROCKWAY, F. British colonial problems. AFR. SOUTH 1, no. 1 (1956), pp. 91-95.

2,007 BROWNE, G. ST. J. O. British justice and the African. J. AFR. SOC. 32 (1933), pp. 148-159, 280-293.

2,008 BRUCE, Sir C. The Crown Colonies and places. ROYAL COL. INST. PR. 36 (1904-1905), pp. 210-265.

2,009 BULKELEY, G. V. O. Colonial policies to-day [Colonial Policies in Africa, by H. A. Wieschhoff; Labour Problems in Africa, by J. A. Noon]. AFR. STUD. 4 (1945), pp. 199-206.

2,010 BULKELEY, G. V. O. Colonies from three angles [The Future of Colonial Peoples by Lord Hailey; The Atlantic Charter and Africa from an American Standpoint]. AFR. STUD. 3 (1944), pp. 140-145.

2,011 BUXTON, Earl [SYDNEY CHARLES]. Anglo-French co-operation. [The Society's letter to The Times]. J. AFR. SOC. 32 (1933), pp. 234-235.

2,012 C., J. Liquidation des colonies italiennes. ZAIRE 5 (1951), pp. 301-302.

2,013 CABRAL, J. A Portuguese letter. AFR. SOUTH 5, no. 1 (1960), pp. 60-62.

2,014 CABRAL, J. Salazar and his empire. CONTEMP. REV. 199 (1961), pp. 304-306.

2,015 CAETANO, M. Portuguese Oversea Territories (Africa). CIVILISATIONS 1, no. 4 (1951), pp. 113-119.

2,016 CARRINGTON, C. E. A new theory of the Commonwealth. INTERNAT. AFFAIRS 31 (1955), pp. 137-148.

2,017 CARRINGTON, C. E. The New Zealand Commonwealth Conference and its predecessors. INTERNAT. AFFAIRS 35 (1959), pp. 332-340.

2,018 CARSTAIRS, C. Y. Colonial research. AFR. AFFAIRS 44 (1945), pp. 19-26.

2,019 CARSTAIRS, C. Y. Information services as an aid to administration. J. AFR. ADM. 5 (1953), pp. 2-7.

2,020 CASADIO, F. A. and PONZANO, S. A. I paesi e i territori africani nel sistema giuridico e nella attività politica delle Nazioni Unite. AFRICA (Rome) 12 (1957), pp. 123-128, 168-171.

2,021 CATRICE, P. Vers une organisation fédérale de l'Union Française. ZAIRE 3 (1949), pp. 559-563.

2,022 CEPOLLARO, A. Il fenomeno linguistico nella problematica dei nazionalismi africani. AFRICA (Rome) 14 (1959), pp. 129-131.

2,023 CHURCHILL, Sir W. S. C. The development of Africa. J. AFR. SOC. 6 (1907), pp. 291-296.

2,024 CLAIR, M. H. Politique coloniale anglaise. KONGO-OVERZEE 20 (1954), pp. 270-271.

2,025 CLAIR, M. H. Propaganda coloniale...ou silence? KONGO-OVERZEE 22 (1956), pp. 392-394.

2,026 COHEN, Sir A. The new Africa and the United Nations. INTERNAT. AFFAIRS 36 (1960), pp. 476-488. Also in AFR. AFFAIRS 60 (1961), pp. 508-517.

2,027 COLA ALBERICH, J. Antecedentes políticos del Africa Negra francesa. CUAD. AFR. OR. 36 (1956), pp. 49-60.

2,028 COLEMAN, J. S. America and Africa. WORLD POLITICS 9 (1956-1957), pp. 593-609.

2,029 COLLET, C. Internationalisation schemes for colonies: from the point of view of the colonial peoples. J. AFR. SOC. 39 (1940), pp. 316-319.

2,030 COLQUHOUN, A. R. Our future colonial policy. ROYAL COL. INST. PR. 33 (1901-1902), pp. 301-329.

2,031 CONINCK, A. DE. Après Bandoeng. PRESENCE AFR. 4 (1955), pp. 82-85.

2,032 CORDERO TORRES, J. M. Independencia colonial o evolución colonizadora? CUAD. EST. AFR. 11 (1950), pp. 21-32.

2,033 CORDERO TORRES, J. M. Panorama diplomático de Afrasia. CUAD. AFR. OR. 33 (1956), pp. 9-20.

2,034 CORDERO TORRES, J. M. Plazas y Provincias Africanas. CUAD. AFR. OR. 36 (1956), pp. 9-13.

2,035 CORDERO TORRES, J. M. Viejas y nuevas formas politicas de la colonizacion. CUAD. EST. AFR. 6 (1949), pp. 35-58.

2,036 CORNELIS, H. Developments in colonial policy. KONGO-OVERZEE 10-11 (1944-1945), pp. 115-126.

2,037 CREECH JONES, Sir A. Africa and the British political parties: Labour and the colonies. AFR. AFFAIRS 44 (1945), pp. 111-115.

2,038 CREECH JONES, Sir A. Our African territories. AFR. AFFAIRS 45 (1946), pp. 127-131.

2,039 CREECH JONES, Sir A. An African survey—revised 1956. J. AFR. ADM. 10 (1958), pp. 3-10.

2,040 CREECH JONES, Sir A. The place of African local administration in colonial policy. J. AFR. ADM. 1 (1949), pp. 3-6.

2,041 CUNLIFFE-LISTER, Sir P. Great Britain and Africa. J. AFR. SOC. 31(1932), pp. 225-233.

2,042 CURRIE, D. Thoughts upon the present and future of South Africa, and Central Eastern Africa. PRCI 8 (1876-1877), pp. 380-418.

2,043 CURRIE, Sir J. Present-day difficulties of a young officer in the Tropics. J. AFR. SOC. 32 (1933), pp. 31-36.

2,044 DELAVIGNETTE, R. Lord Lugard et la politique Africaine. AFRICA 21 (1951), pp. 177-186.

2,045 DELONCLE, P. The claim for colonies. A French view. J. AFR. SOC. 36 (1937), supplement.

2,046 DEPESTRE, R. Une expérience inoubliable: le Festival de Moscou. PRESENCE AFR. N.S. 16 (1957), p. 151.

2,047 DERNBURG, B. Germany and England in Africa. J. AFR. SOC. 9 (1910), pp. 113-119.

2,048 DEVERNOIS, G. Educational and cultural trends in the overseas and trust territories and in Algeria. CIVILISATIONS 8 (1958), pp. 88-111, 271-310, 388-410, 585-610; 9 (1959), pp. 69-78, 208-222; 12 (1962), pp. 113-127, 273-288.

2,049 DEVERNOIS, G. Institutional developments in the French community. CIVILISATIONS 9 (1959), pp. 369-384.

2,050 DILTHEY, R. German and British colonisation in Africa. J. AFR. SOC. 4 (1905), pp. 238-241.

2,051 DIOP, A. Refuges de l'amour-propre "imperial." PRESENCE AFR. N.S. 7(1956), pp. 133-137.

2,052 DIOP, M. L'unique issue: l'indépendance totale la seule voie: un large mouvement d'union anti-impérialiste. PRESENCE AFR. 14(1953), pp. 145-184.

2,053 DIOP, T. Bamako 1957. PRESENCE AFR. N.S. 16(1957), pp. 162-170.

2,054 DIOP, T. Forme traditionnelle de gouvernement en Afrique Noire. PRESENCE AFR. N.S. 23(1958-1959), pp. 16-21.

2,055 DORATO, M. Evoluzione del colonialismo. AFRICA (Rome) 14 (1959), pp. 172-174.

2,056 DRESCH, J. L'Eurafrique. PRESENCE AFR. N.S. 7 (1956), pp. 13-25.

2,057 DUBOIS, H. M. Assimilation ou adaptation? AFRICA 2 (1929), pp. 1-21.

2,058 DU BOIS, W. E. B. Africa and the American Negro intelligentsia. PRESENCE AFR. N.S. 5 (1955-1956), pp. 34-51.

2,059 DUFFY, J. Portugal in Africa. FOREIGN AFFAIRS 39 (1960-1961), pp. 481-493.

2,060 DUNN, P. W. D. The role of the police in a democratic state. J. AFR. ADM. 4 (1952), pp. 46-50.

2,061 DURIEUX, A. L'Acte Colonial portugais. Ses caractères et principes essentiels. Essai comparatif avec la Charte Coloniale belge. ZAIRE 3 (1949), pp. 719-741.

2,062 DURIEUX, A. La revision de la Constitution politique portugaise et l'Acte colonial. ZAIRE 5 (1951), pp. 1011-1040.

2,063 EKPO, L. U. A Nigerian looks at English Local Government. J. AFR. ADM. 2 (1950), pp. 12-23; 3 (1951), pp. 27-30.

2,064 ELLIOTT, H. Under-studies in West Africa? CORONA 2 (1950), pp. 365-367, 403-405.

2,065 ELLIOTT, W. Y. The riddle of the British Commonwealth. FOREIGN AFFAIRS 8 (1939), pp. 442-464.

2,066 EPP, R. VON. The question of colonies. The German standpoint. J. AFR. SOC. 36 (1937), supplement.

2,067 FALLERS, L. A. Africa: scholarship and policy. WORLD POLITICS 9 (1956-1957), pp. 287-294.

2,068 FARGUES, G. Le Portugal face aux nationalismes africains. AFR. ET ASIE 65 (1964), pp. 13-25.

2,069 FARQUHAR, J. H. Political representation of Africans. NADA 23 (1946), pp. 62-67.

2,070 FAWCETT, D. Colonial renaissance? KONGO-OVERZEE 19 (1953), pp. 132-135.

2,071 FAWCETT, D. This hated Colonialism. KONGO-OVERZEE 20 (1954), pp. 65-67.

2,072 FERREIRA MENDES, M. J. Intervenção das autoridades administrativas no estudo e execução de obras públicas. BSEM 92 (1955), pp. 37-52.

2,073 FILESI, T. Delusioni e speranze per l'Africa: a Palermo il CEPES ha guardato oltre il Mezzogiorno. AFRICA (Rome) 10 (1955), pp. 361-364.

2,074 FILESI, T. La loi cadre una tappa ardita e una grande speranza per la Francia in Africa. AFRICA (Rome) 12 (1957), pp. 155-161.

2,075 FILESI, T. Nazionalismi africani e comunismo. AFRICA (Rome) 10 (1955), pp. 141-143.

2,076 FILESI, T. Il quadro politico dell'Africa d'oggi. AFRICA (Rome) 14 (1959), pp. 177-180.

2,077 FILESI, T. Testimonianze della presenza cinese in Africa. AFRICA (Rome) 17 (1962), pp. 115-123.

2,078 FISCHER, G. Syndicats et décolonisation. PRESENCE AFR. N.S. 34-35 (1960-1961), pp. 17-60.

2,079 FRANKLIN, A. DE S. The Portuguese system of protecting native land property. J. AFR. ADM. 9 (1957), pp. 16-22.

2,080 FREYMOND, J. Colonialisme et nationalisme. ZAIRE 11 (1957), pp. 187-204.

2,081 FROELICH, J. C. Voltaire et le sous-développement. AFR. ET ASIE 68 (1964), pp. 42-45.

2,082 FROOMKIN, J. Fiscal management of municipalities and economic development. J. AFR. ADM. 8 (1956), pp. 15-26.

2,083 G., A. S. The civil service of the Dutch East Indies as compared with that of Britain in India and Africa. J. AFR. SOC. 2 (1903), pp. 433-442.

2,084 G., J. Les colonies anglaises d'Afrique en 1953. ZAIRE 8 (1954), pp. 305-307.

2,085 GARES, V. A. The French Union. UNIVERSITAS 1, no. 3 (1954), pp. 10-13.

2,086 GATHORNE-HARDY, G. M. The British Commonwealth Relations Conference, 1933; a personal impression. INTERNAT. AFFAIRS 12 (1933), pp. 763-774.

2,087 GELDERS, V. Le désisolationisme aux Etats-Unis et l'Afrique noire. KONGO-OVERZEE 12-13 (1946-1947), pp. 265-281.

2,088 GIL BENUMEYA, R. Esencia y trayectoria del bloque africano-asiático. CUAD. EST. AFR. 24 (1953), pp. 9-22.

2,089 GILMER, J. H. The French Union in 1954-55. 1. Overseas territories and territories under trusteeship. CIVILISATIONS 5 (1955), pp. 606-616.

2,090 GILMER, J. H. French Union, Negro Africa... CIVILISATIONS 6 (1956), pp. 261-281, 639-650; 7 (1957), pp. 66-74, 237-250, 389-399.

2,091 GISBORNE, W. Colonisation. ROYAL COL. INST. PR. 20 (1888-1889), pp. 53-88.

2,092 GOMEZ TELLO, J. L. El Ultramar Português. ARCH. INST. EST. AFR. 17, no. 67 (1963), pp. 31-48.

2,093 GONIDEC, P.-F. La Communauté et les relations internationales. ANNALES AFR., 1959, pp. 15-39.

2,094 GORE, D. O. [Lord Harlech]. Native Administration in the British Territories in Africa, by W. M. Hailey [Lord Hailey]. J. AFR. ADM. 6 (1954), pp. 2-5.

2,095 GOWER, R. H. Training within industry: its use in district administration. CORONA 4 (1952), pp. 304-306.

2,096 GRAY, A. Africa at UNO. AFR. AFFAIRS 56 (1957), pp. 4-5.

2,097 GRAY, A. Africa at Westminster. AFR. AFFAIRS 55 (1956), pp. 80-84, 223-229.

2,098 GRAY, A. Africa day conference. AFR. AFFAIRS 55 (1956), pp. 33-36, 285-286; 56 (1957), pp. 58-59.

2,099 GRAY, A. Afro-Asian talks. AFR. AFFAIRS 54 (1955), pp. 88-89.

2,100 GRAY, A. Aid for colonies. AFR. AFFAIRS 54 (1955), pp. 87-88.

2,101 GRAY, A. America and Africa. AFR. AFFAIRS 56 (1957), pp. 175-179.

2,102 GRAY, A. Black states confer. AFR. AFFAIRS 58 (1959), pp. 268-269.

2,103 GRAY, A. Cairo conference. AFR. AFFAIRS 57 (1958), pp. 91-92.

2,104 GRAY, A. Colonial service. AFR. AFFAIRS 55 (1956), pp. 172-173.

2,105 GRAY, A. Colonialism and nationalism. AFR. AFFAIRS 58 (1959), pp. 271-273.

2,106 GRAY, A. Labour and the colonies. AFR. AFFAIRS 54 (1955), pp. 12-13.

2,107 GREAVES, L. B. Missions and colonial administration. CORONA 3 (1951), pp. 13-16.

2,108 GRIFFITHS, J. Opening address to the 1951 Cambridge Summer Conference on African administration. J. AFR. ADM. 3 (1951), pp. 152-157.

2,109 GUTTERIDGE, W. F. Federal solutions within the Commonwealth. CONTEMP. REV. 188 (1955), pp. 115-120.

2,110 HAILEY, W. M. [Lord Hailey]. The differing faces of Africa. FOREIGN AFFAIRS 36 (1957-1958), pp. 143-153.

2,111 HAILEY, W. M. [Lord Hailey]. Local Government institutions in India and Africa. J. AFR. ADM. 4 (1952), pp. 2-6.

2,112 HAILEY, W. M. [Lord Hailey]. Nationalism in Africa. J. AFR. SOC. 36 (1937), pp. 134-147.

2,113 HAILEY, W. M. [Lord Hailey]. Native administration in Africa. INTERNAT. AFFAIRS 23 (1947), pp. 336-342.

2,114 HAILEY, W. M. [Lord Hailey]. Selection and training for locally-recruited administrative services. J. AFR. ADM. 11 (1959), pp. 115-117.

2,115 HAILEY, W. M. [Lord Hailey]. Some problems dealt with in the African Survey. INTERNAT. AFFAIRS 18 (1939), pp. 194-210.

2,116 HAILEY, W. M. [Lord Hailey]. A turning point in colonial administration. INTERNAT. AFFAIRS 28 (1952), pp. 177-183.

2,117 HAILEY, W. M. [Lord Hailey]. World thought on the colonial question. AFR. STUD. 6 (1947), pp. 51-56.

2,118 HARE, W. F. [Earl of Listowel]. The modern conception of government in British Africa. J. AFR. ADM. 1 (1949), pp. 99-105.

2,119 HART, N. DE V. British policy in Africa. CONTEMP. REV. 136 (1929), pp. 502-508.

2,120 HASTINGS, L. Democracy and the African. AFR. AFFAIRS 49 (1950), pp. 211-223.

2,121 HENRY, P. M. A functional approach to regional co-operation. AFR. AFFAIRS 52 (1953), pp. 308-316.

2,122 HERCULANO DE OLIVEIRA. Moviemento Messiânico-comunista Africano. PORT. EM AFR. 15 (1958), pp. 18-35.

2,123 HICKS, U. K. Financial responsibility and self government. J. AFR. ADM. 9 (1957), pp. 196-199.

2,124 HODGKIN, T. Teorie e miti. AFRICA (Rome) 14 (1959), pp. 117-121.

2,125 HODSON, H. V. Imperial economic policy. INTERNAT. AFFAIRS 14 (1935), pp. 531-550.

2,126 HOWE, C. H. W. An experimental classification of political systems. EAISR, June (1958), pp. 1-47.

2,127 HOWMAN, R. African leadership in transition: an outline. NADA 33 (1956), pp. 13-25.

2,128 HUDSON, G. F. How unified is the Commonwealth? FOREIGN AFFAIRS 33 (1954-1955), pp. 679-688.

2,129 HUIZINGA, J. H. Africa, the continent of tomorrow's troubles. AFR. AFFAIRS 49 (1950), pp. 120-128.

2,130 HUIZINGA, J. H. Unique experiment in French Black Africa. AFR. AFFAIRS 58 (1959), pp. 25-33.

2,131 HUXLEY, E. Africa's tomorrow. CORONA 2 (1950), pp. 442-445.

2,132 INGRAMS, H. Communism and the African. CORONA 1, no. 6 (1949), pp. 3-6; 1, no. 7 (1949), pp. 11-13.

2,133 JACKSON, B. W. Britain's imperial legacy. FOREIGN AFFAIRS 35 (1956-1957), pp. 412-421.

2,134 JACOB, E. G. Afrikanische Probleme in französischer Beleuchtung. AFRIKA (Berlin) 2 (1943), pp. 65-96.

2,135 JERNINGHAM, Sir H. E. H. Colonial administration. ROYAL COL. INST. PR. 33 (1901-1902), pp. 195-218.

2,136 JOHNSON, C. Politics and local government. CORONA 3 (1951), pp. 406-411.

2,137 JOHNSTON, A. Peaceful penetration. J. AFR. SOC. 4 (1905), pp. 190-193.

2,138 JONES, A. C. British colonial policy, with particular reference to Africa. INTERNAT. AFFAIRS 27 (1951), pp. 176-183.

2,139 JONES, A. C. The British experiment in colonial development and welfare. CIVILISATIONS 6 (1956), pp. 557-563; French summary, pp. 563-564.

2,140 JONES, A. L. German methods of developement [sic] in Africa. J. AFR. SOC. 1 (1901), pp. 23-39.

2,141 JONES, H. J. E. Recruitment for the colonial service. CORONA 3 (1951), pp. 212-214.

2,142 JONES-QUARTEY, K. A. B. Les problèmes généraux de l'intercommunication en Afrique. PRESENCE AFR. 27-28 (1959), pp. 215-229.

2,143 JULY, R. W. Nineteenth century negritude: Edward W. Blyden. J. AFR. HIST. 5 (1964), pp. 73-86.

2,144 K., P. L'Egalité des status des fonctionnaires en France d'Outre-Mer. CIVILISATIONS 1, no. ii (1951), pp. 4-6; English summary, p. 7.

2,145 K., P. and F., C. Citizenship of the French Union. CIVILISATIONS 1, no. ii (1951), pp. 1-3.

2,146 KARSTEDT, O. Zur englischen Kolonialpolitik. AFRIKA (Berlin) 3 (1944), pp. 1-8.

2,147 KEITH, A. B. The revision of the Berlin Act. J. AFR. SOC. 17 (1918), pp. 249-261.

2,148 KEITH-LUCAS, B. Electoral procedure in Africa. ZAIRE 11 (1957), pp. 475-484.

2,149 KERIS, G. LE B. L'Africa fra due civiltà. AFRICA (Rome) 13 (1958), pp. 323-329.

2,150 KHALY, N. La loi-cadre et les elections territoriales en Afrique Noire. PRESENCE AFR. N.S. 13 (1957), pp. 126-132.

2,151 KHAMA, T. Chieftainship under indirect rule. J. AFR. SOC. 35 (1936), pp. 251-261.

2,152 KILSON, M. L., Jr. The analysis of African Nationalism. WORLD POLITICS 10 (1957-1958), pp. 484-497.

2,153 KRAFT, L. Colonial policies in Africa. RACE RELATIONS 15 (1948), pp. 126-141.

2,154 LABOURET, H. France's colonial policy in Africa. J. AFR. SOC. 39 (1940), pp. 22-35.

2,155 LANGENHOVE, F. VAN. La notion de Territoires dépendants. CIVILISATIONS 1, no. i (1951), pp. 8-14; English summary, p. 14.

2,156 LAPIE, P. O. The new colonial policy of France. FOREIGN AFFAIRS 23 (1944-1945), pp. 104-111.

2,157 LEONE, E. DE. Le prospettive del prossimo futuro. AFRICA (Rome) 14 (1959), pp. 181-182.

2,158 LEWIS, H. R. J. The outlook for a devil in the Colonies or a Colonial viewpoint on witchcraft, homicide, and the supernatural. J. AFR. ADM. 11 (1959), pp. 15-21.

2,159 LEWIS, R. Commonwealth et Empire Britanniques. CIVILISATIONS 5 (1955), pp. 97-113, 241-252.

2,160 LIVIE-NOBLE, F. S. Closer union in Africa. J. AFR. SOC. 31 (1932), pp. 77-79.

2,161 LOCKHART, J. G. The Commonwealth Parliamentary Association. CORONA 4 (1952), pp. 258-260.

2,162 LONGRIGG, S. H. Disposal of Italian Africa. INTERNAT. AFFAIRS 21 (1945), pp. 363-369.

2,163 LUGARD, Lord. The basis of the claim for colonies. INTERNAT. AFFAIRS 15 (1936), pp. 3-25.

2,164 LUGARD, Lord et al. Lord Hailey's African Survey. J. AFR. SOC. 38 (1939), supplement.

2,165 LUGARD, Sir F. Problems of Equatorial Africa. INTERNAT. AFFAIRS 6 (1927), pp. 214-232.

2,166 LUKAS, J. Neue Beiträge zur Kolonialforschung. AFRIKA (Berlin) 3 (1944), pp. 9-18.

2,167 LYNE, R. N. Germany's claim to colonies: the African mandates. J. AFR. SOC. 38 (1939), pp. 273-280.

2,168 M., Q. Transformazione e fine del colonialismo. AFRICA (Rome) 10 (1955), p. 217.

2,169 MCKAY, V. Too slow or too fast? Political change in African trust territories. FOREIGN AFFAIRS 35 (1956-1957), pp. 295-310.

2,170 MACKENZIE, W. J. M. Local Government elections in towns. J. AFR. ADM. 8 (1956), pp. 61-68.

2,171 MAFFI, Q. Coscienza e cultura africana. AFRICA (Rome) 14 (1959), pp. 183-184.

2,172 MAI, E. Afrikanische Probleme in britischer Beleuchtung. AFRIKA (Berlin) 1 (1942), pp. 101-124.

2,173 MAIR, L. P. African chiefs today: the Lugard memorial lecture for 1958. AFRICA 28 (1958), pp. 195-205.

2,174 MAIR, L. P. Colonial administration as a science. J. AFR. SOC. 32 (1933), pp. 366-371.

2,175 MAIR, L. P. Representative Local Government as a problem in social change. J. AFR. ADM. 10 (1958), pp. 11-24.

2,176 MAKSOUD, C. Arab policy on Portuguese colonialism. AFRICA QUART. 1, no. iii (1961), pp. 10-12.

2,177 MALIK, H. Seminar on Portuguese colonies. AFRICA QUART. 1, no. iii (1961), pp. 45-54.

2,178 MALINOWSKI, B. The rationalization of anthropology and administration. AFRICA 3 (1930), pp. 405-429.

2,179 MALVEZZI, A. Italian colonies and colonial policy. INTERNAT. AFFAIRS 6 (1927), pp. 233-245.

2,180 MANSERGH, N. Commonwealth membership. COMMONWEALTH PERSPECTIVES, 1958, pp. 1-34.

2,181 MARCHAND, J. Il divenire dell'Africa Nera. AFRICA (Rome) 11 (1956), pp. 1-6.

2,182 MARQUES, C. As colónias Africanas a O.N.U....e a Rússia. PORT. EM AFR. 7 (1950), pp. 76-82.

2,183 MARSHALL, A. H. The adaptation of English Local Government principles to colonial territories. J. AFR. ADM. 2 (1950), pp. 34-39.

2,184 MARTELLI, G. Portugal and the United Nations. INTERNAT. AFFAIRS 40 (1964), pp. 453-465.

2,185 MARTIN DE LA ESCALERA, C. Unión Federal Francesa. CUAD. EST. AFR. 1 (1946), pp. 101-109.

2,186 MASEFIELD, G. B. Colonial aims. CORONA 1, no. 6 (1949), pp. 21-22.

2,187 MASSIGLI, R. New conceptions of French policy in Tropical Africa. INTERNAT. AFFAIRS 33 (1957), pp. 403-415.

2,188 MASSON-OURSEL, P. L'Afrique participante. PRESENCE AFR. 1 (1947), p. 30.

2,189 MATTHEWS, Z. K. An African view of indirect rule. J. AFR. SOC. 36 (1937), pp. 433-437.

2,190 MILLER, R. African development: some hard facts. CORONA 2 (1950), pp. 222-225, 250-252.

2,191 MILVERTON, Lord. The realities of African civilisation. AFR. AFFAIRS 55 (1956), pp. 178-187.

2,192 MIRANDA SANTOS, A. A Ascenção dos Povos de cor. PORT. EM AFR. 15 (1958), pp. 221-232.

2,193 MITCHELL, P. Native Administration in the British Territories in Africa by Lord Hailey. J. AFR. ADM. 3 (1951), pp. 55-65.

2,194 MOELLER DE LADDERSOUS, A. Le message de Lord Lugard et l'Afrique d'aujourd'hui. AFRICA 22 (1952), pp. 197-214.

2,195 MONTAGNE, R. L'Etat Moderne en Afrique et en Asie. AFR. ET ASIE 2, no. 1 (1949), pp. 3-25.

2,196 MOODY, R. Colonial spectator. CORONA 3 (1951), pp. 292-294.

2,197 MOREIRA, A. De Bandung ao Cairo. PORT. EM AFR. 15 (1958), pp. 133-151.

2,198 MOREIRA, A. Political unity and the status of peoples. AFR. AFFAIRS 59 (1960), pp. 249-259.

2,199 MOREIRA, E. Portuguese colonial policy. AFRICA 17 (1947), pp. 181-191.

2,200 MOREIRA DA SILVA, M. Timor, exemplo da colonização portuguesa. PORT. EM AFR. 9 (1952), pp. 219-234.

2,201 MOREL, E. D. The Belgian curse in Africa. CONTEMP. REV. 81 (1902), pp. 358-377.

2,202 MOSTAZA, B. Discurso sobre la continentalización de Eurafrica. CUAD. EST. AFR. 13 (1951), pp. 9-26.

2,203 MOUSLEY, E. Empire and foreign policy. INTERNAT. AFFAIRS 2 (1923), pp. 91-106.

2,204 N., J. Les conditions de détention du R. P. Pinto de Andrade. PRESENCE AFR. N.S. 42 (1962), pp. 206-208.

2,205 NALDONI, N. L'Unione Francese. AFRICA (Rome) 11 (1956), p. 26.

2,206 NAVILLE, P. L'Afrique. Enjeu stratégique. PRESENCE AFR. N.S. 3 (1955), pp. 20-27.

2,207 NEHRU, J. Portuguese colonialism: an anachronism. AFRICA QUART. 1, no. iii (1961), pp. 5-9.

2,208 NEUMANN, H. Portugal's policy in Africa: the four years since the beginning of the uprising in Angola. INTERNAT. AFFAIRS 41 (1965), pp. 663-675.

2,209 NICOLSON, H. The colonial problem. INTERNAT. AFFAIRS 17 (1938), pp. 32-50.

2,210 NICOLSON, T. R. Africa: Communist target for to-morrow. CONTEMP. REV. 178 (1950), pp. 149-152.

2,211 NOLDE, E. Des Colonies à l'Union Française. CIVILISATIONS 3 (1953), pp. 323-329; English summary, pp. 329-330.

2,212 NOOTEBOOM, C. Gevaren van indirect bestuur. ZAIRE 3 (1949), pp. 1011-1016.

2,213 OLIVER, S. Are we going to act justly in Africa. CONTEMP. REV. 118 (1920), pp. 198-206.

2,214 OLIVIER. The British trust in Africa. CONTEMP. REV. 135 (1929), pp. 273-281.

2,215 ORMSBY-GORE, W. The meaning of "Indirect Rule." The principles of native administration and their application; by Sir Donald Cameron. J. AFR. SOC. 34 (1935), pp. 283-286.

2,216 ORTS, M. P. The claim for colonies: a Belgian view. INTERNAT. AFFAIRS 16 (1937), pp. 201-221. Also in J. AFR. SOC., supplement.

2,217 PARKINSON, F. Bandung and the underdeveloped countries. THE YEAR BOOK OF WORLD AFFAIRS 10 (1956), pp. 65-83.

2,218 PERHAM, M. African facts and American criticisms. FOREIGN AFFAIRS 22 (1943-1944), pp. 444-457.

2,219 PERHAM, M. The British problem in Africa. FOREIGN AFFAIRS 29 (1950-1951), pp. 637-650.

2,220 PERHAM, M. A re-statement of indirect rule. AFRICA 7 (1934), pp. 321-334.

2,221 PERHAM, M. Some problems of indirect rule in Africa. J. AFR. SOC. 34 (1935), supplement.

2,222 PERHAM, M. White minorities in Africa. FOREIGN AFFAIRS 37 (1958-1959), pp. 637-648.

2,223 PERROUX, F. La coexistence hostile et l'apparition des pouvoirs mondiaux. PRESENCE AFR. N.S. 21 (1958), pp. 48-60.

2,224 PERTH, Lord et al. The future of the mandates: a symposium. AFR. AFFAIRS 43 (1944), pp. 159-171.

2,225 PHILIPPS, J. E. T. The tide of colour. J. AFR. SOC. 21 (1922), pp. 129-135, 309-314.

2,226 PONS, R. French Union. CIVILISATIONS 3 (1953), pp. 575-595.

2,227 PONS, R. French Union. 2nd half 1952 and 1953. CIVILISATIONS 4 (1954), pp. 95-122, 285-310, 457-485, 603-614.

2,228 PONSONBY, C. E. Africa and the British political parties: A Conservative view. AFR. AFFAIRS 44 (1945), pp. 115-119.

2,229 POSSOZ, E. La précision dans la politique coloniale. ZAIRE 4 (1950), pp. 989-1000.

2,230 PRADHAN, R. C. The United Nations and the Portuguese colonial question: problems and prospects. AFRO-ASIAN AND W. AFF. 1 (1964), pp. 107-115.

2,231 RABEMANJARA, J. L'Europe et nous. PRESENCE AFR. N.S. 8-10 (1956), pp. 20-28.

2,232 RAPPARD, W. E. The practical working of the Mandates system. INTERNAT. AFFAIRS 4 (1925), pp. 205-226.

2,233 RATTRAY, R. S. Anthropology and Christian Missions: their mutual bearing on the problems of colonial administration. AFRICA 1 (1928), pp. 98-106.

2,234 RAWSON, H. E. The native problem. J. AFR. SOC. 11 (1912), pp. 151-172.

2,235 READ, J. S. Constitutions on the move. Constitutional and political developments in 1958. J. AFR. LAW 3 (1959), pp. 39-64.

2,236 RENNELL, Lord [Rodd, F. J. R.]. Africa and the British political parties: a Liberal viewpoint. AFR. AFFAIRS 44 (1945), pp. 107-110.

2,237 RIVKIN, A. Israel and the Afro-Asian world. FOREIGN AFFAIRS 37 (1958-1959), pp. 486-495.

2,238 ROBINSON, K. The end of empire: another view. INTERNAT. AFFAIRS 30 (1954), pp. 186-195.

2,239 ROBINSON, R. E. The progress of Provincial Councils in the British African Territories. J. AFR. ADM. 1 (1949), pp. 59-68.

2,240 ROBINSON, R. E. The relationship of major and minor Local Government authorities. J. AFR. ADM. 1 (1949), pp. 30-33.

2,241 ROBINSON, R. E. Why Indirect Rule has been replaced by Local Government in the nomenclature of British native administration. J. AFR. ADM. 2 (1950), pp. 12-15.

2,242 ROCHE, J. La loi-cadre du 23 juin 1956. ANNALES AFR., 1957, pp. 97-133.

2,243 ROMERO MOLINER, R. Comunismo, nacionalismo y mentalidad primitiva. CUAD. EST. AFR. 11 (1950), pp. 53-60.

2,244 RONDOT, P. La place de l'Afrique noire dans les problèmes d'Outre-Mer. AFR. ET ASIE 48 (1959), pp. 5-15.

2,245 ROSS, E. The dual mandate for tomorrow. AFRICA 23 (1953), pp. 331-338.

2,246 ROUCEK, J. S. The geopolitics of Portuguese colonialism. CONTEMP. REV. 205 (1964), pp. 284-296.

2,247 ROUGEVIN-BAVILLE, M. The organization and content of training for public administration in Africa. J. LOCAL ADM. OV. 2 (1963), pp. 123-136.

2,248 RUBIO GARCIA, L. En el Africa Negra: Avances politicos y factores sociales y economicos. CUAD. EST. AFR. 26 (1954), pp. 51-67.

2,249 RYCKMANS, P. Belgian "Colonialism." FOREIGN AFFAIRS 34 (1955-1956), pp. 89-101.

2,250 SACKVILLE (DE LA WARR), H. E. D. B. [On Africa, a speech at annual dinner of Royal Africa Society, March 30, 1950]. AFR. AFFAIRS 49 (1950), pp. 250-252.

2,251 SADY, E. J. Community development and Local Government. J. AFR. ADM. 11 (1959), pp. 179-186.

2,252 SALAZAR, A. DE O. Realities and trends of Portuguese policies. INTERNAT. AFFAIRS 39 (1963), pp. 169-183.

2,253 SALVADOR, P. Consideraciones en torno al concepto de Colonia. CUAD. EST. AFR. 1 (1946), pp. 67-100.

2,254 SANDER, E. Der Gestaltwandel Afrikas. Eine geopolitische Studie. KOLONIALE STUDIEN: HANS MEYER FESTSCHRIFT, 1928, pp. 86-96.

2,255 SANTOS, M. DOS. Déclaration de principe de la Conférence des Organisations nationalites des colonies portugaises (C.O.N.C.P.)... PRESENCE AFR. N.S. 42 (1962), pp. 214-217.

2,256 SCAGLIONE, F. A. Leggendo un libro su Amedeo d'Aosta. AFRICA (Rome) 11 (1956), pp. 98-99.

2,257 SCOTT, D. J. R. The development of Local Government: Yugoslavia's experience. J. AFR. ADM. 6 (1954), pp. 129-137.

2,258 SENGAT-KUO, F. Communauté et Afrique Noire. PRESENCE AFR. N.S. 22 (1958), pp. 5-9.

2,259 SENGAT-KUO, F. De la conférence d'Accra à l'unité de l'Afrique. PRESENCE AFR. N.S. 18-19 (1958), pp. 225-229.

2,260 SENGAT-KUO, F. L'Europe à l'heure de la panique. PRESENCE AFR. N.S. 1 (1955), pp. 169-176.

2,261 SENGAT-KUO, F. La France fait son examen de conscience ou "le Fédéralisme sauvera-t-il l'Union Française"? PRESENCE AFR. N.S. 3 (1955), pp. 86-95.

2,262 SENGAT-KUO, F. La loi-cadre et les partis politiques africains. PRESENCE AFR. N.S. 18-19 (1958), pp. 103-112.

2,263 SENGHOR, L. S. L'Afrique s'interroge? Subir ou choisir? PRESENCE AFR. 8 (1950), pp. 437-443.

2,264 SENGHOR, L. S. Ciò che l'Africa attende dall' Europa. AFRICA (Rome) 10 (1955), pp. 185-188.

2,265 SEVILLA, D. Politica africana de Canalejas. ARCH. INST. EST. AFR. 11, no. 46 (1958), pp. 29-49.

2,266 SHEPHERD, G. W. The United States discovers Africa. AFR. SOUTH 1, no. 1 (1956), pp. 84-91.

2,267 SHERIDAN, L. A. The changing conception of the Commonwealth. THE YEAR BOOK OF WORLD AFFAIRS 11 (1957), pp. 236-256.

2,268 SHILS, E. The concentration and dispersion of charisma. WORLD POLITICS 11 (1958-1959), pp. 1-19.

2,269 SILVA REGO, A. DA. Alguns aspectos da colonização moderna. PORT. EM AFR. 5 (1948), pp. 208-216.

2,270 SIMEY, P. A. T. A day in the life of a district commissioner. J. AFR. SOC. 38 (1939), pp. 427-437.

2,271 SINGH, D. Portuguese colonies. AFRICA QUART. 1, no. ii (1961), pp. 8-11.

2,272 SMITH, A. Trusteeship and partnership in British Africa. THE YEAR BOOK OF WORLD AFFAIRS 7 (1953), pp. 170-203.

2,273 SMITH, R. The French colonial exhibition. J. AFR. SOC. 30 (1931), pp. 410-414.

2,274 SMUTS, J. Speech delivered by Field Marshal Smuts on October 12th 1946 in Brussels. KONGO-OVERZEE 12-13 (1946-1947), pp. 36-44.

2,275 SMUTS, J. C. The British Empire and world peace. INTERNAT. AFFAIRS 9 (1930), pp. 141-153.

2,276 SOARES BARATA, O. El Ultramar português en la presente coyuntura internacional. ARCH. INST. EST. AFR. 17, no. 65 (1963), pp. 49-60.

2,277 STANLEY, Sir H. Trends in the colonial administration in Africa. RACE RELATIONS 15 (1948), pp. 118-125.

2,278 STEVENS, R. A. The application of English Local Government principles in Africa. J. AFR. ADM. 1 (1949), pp. 68-73.

2,279 STOKES, R. R. Local Government in the Republic of Ireland. J. AFR. ADM. 7 (1955), pp. 27-33.

2,280 STOPFORD, R. W. The intangible in colonial development. CORONA 3 (1951), pp. 250-252.

2,281 SURET-CANALE, J. L'anticolonialisme en France sous la IIIe République: Paul Vigne d'Octon. RECH. AFR. 1-4 (1959), pp. 23-34.

2,282 SWANZY, H. Commonwealth et Empire britanniques. Evolution économique en 1953. CIVILISATIONS 4 (1954), pp. 269-284, 447-456.

2,283 SWANZY, H. Regions of the mind. CORONA 2 (1950), pp. 243-246.

2,284 SWANZY, H. Union Française. AFR. AFFAIRS 45 (1946), pp. 110-111; 46 (1947), pp. 122-123.

2,285 SYMES, S. Military government. AFR. AFFAIRS 47 (1948), pp. 220-222.

2,286 TAGART, E. S. B. The African Chief under European rule. AFRICA 4 (1931), pp. 63-74.

2,287 TATE, H. R. The French colonial empire. J. AFR. SOC. 39 (1940), pp. 322-330.

2,288 THOMAS, A. R. The Colonial Office. CORONA 3 (1951), pp. 449-453.

2,289 THOMAS, I.B. Commonwealth et Empire Britanniques. Changements constitutionnels 1940-1950. CIVILISATIONS 1, no. iii (1951), pp. 74-107; 1, no. 1v (1951), pp. 71-96; 2 (1952), pp. 87-106, 231-249, 369-377, 545-567.

2,290 THOMAS, I.B. Commonwealth et Empire Britanniques. Les développements economiques en 1951-1952. CIVILISATIONS 3 (1953), pp. 263-571.

2,291 THOMAS, I.B. Commonwealth et Empire Britanniques. Les Territoires Coloniaux en 1951-1953. CIVILISATIONS 3 (1953), pp 567-574.

2,292 THOMAS, I.B. Commonwealth et Empire Britanniques. Territoires Coloniaux; les changements dans l'organisation constitutionelle 1951-1952. CIVILISATIONS 3 (1953), pp. 83-103.

2,293 THOMAS, I.B. Empire Britannique. Territoires Coloniaux changements constitutionnels en 1953. CIVILISATIONS 4 (1954), pp. 81-93, 596-602.

2,294 THOMAS, I.B. Territoires britanniques d'Outre-Mer 1955-56; 1956-57; 1957-58. CIVILISATIONS 6 (1956), pp. 413-418, 631-638; 7 (1957), pp. 59-65, 223-236, 381-387; 7 (1957), pp. 591-596; 8 (1958), pp. 80-87, 254-270, 379-387, 579-584; 9 (1959), pp. 63-69; 193-207, 355-368, 497-504; 10 (1960), pp. 77-88, 239-246, 343, 349, 481-488; 11 (1961), pp. 69-78, 187-193, 318-327, 451-462; 12 (1962), pp. 128-132, 261-272, 394-403, 502-516.

2, 295 THOMAS, I.B. Territoires coloniaux britanniques 1954-1955. CIVILISATIONS 5 (1955), pp. 415-423, 601-605; 6 (1956), pp. 105-110; 6 (1956), pp. 251-260.

2,296 TOURE, M. Conséquences financières de la loi-cadre. PRESENCE AFR. N.S. 18-19 (1958), pp. 90-102.

2,297 TOUSSAINT, C. E. The colonial controversy in the United Nations. THE YEAR BOOK OF WORLD AFFAIRS 10 (1956), pp. 170-198.

2,298 TRENCHARD, Viscount. Administration of the colonial empire. J. AFR. SOC. 41 (1942), pp. 172-179.

2,299 TRUJEDA INCERA, L. La crisis del mundo colonial. CUAD. EST. AFR. 9 (1950), pp. 61-76.

2,300 USBORNE, C. V. Africa and sea power. J. AFR. SOC. 37 (1938), pp. 156-166.

2,301 V., J. El punto cuatro, rumbo a su realización (Sector Oriente Medio y Africa). CUAD. EST. AFR. 15 (1951), pp. 9-17.

2,302 VAN DER POST, L. The Africa I know. AFR. AFFAIRS 51 (1952), pp. 216-221.

2,303 VANMAELE, G. De integratie van de politieke instellingen in de Franse overzeese gebieden. KONGO-OVERZEE 23 (1957), pp. 99-112.

2,304 VINDEB. Il risveglio dei popoli afro-asiatici. AFRICA (Rome) 11 (1956), pp. 57-59.

2,305 WADE, A. Afrique noire et Union française. PRESENCE AFR. 14 (1953), pp. 118-144.

2,306 WADE, A. Imposture de fédéralisme. PRESENCE AFR. N.S. 5 (1955-1956), pp. 101-105.

2,307 WALKER, E. A. Argument of Empire [review article on Argument of Empire by W. K. Hancock]. INTERNAT. AFFAIRS 19 (1943), pp. 665-666.

2,308 WALLIS, C. A. G. The foundations of Local Government in India and Africa. J. AFR. ADM. 7 (1955), pp. 2-11.

2,309 WALLIS, C. A. G. Local Government and the maintenance of law and order. J. AFR. ADM. 5 (1953), pp. 11-15.

2,310 WARD, C. United Nations work in Africa. AFR. AFFAIRS 54 (1955), pp. 209-213.

2,311 WARREN, J. H. Associations of Local Government staffs. J. AFR. ADM. 3 (1951), pp. 171-178.

2,312 WASON, J. C. The African colonies. What is to be their future? J. AFR. SOC. 17 (1918), pp. 145-148.

2,313 WATSON, J. The official in Local Government in the colonies. J. AFR. ADM. 6 (1954), pp. 11-18.

2,314 WHITTLESEY, D. British and French colonial technique in West Africa. FOREIGN AFFAIRS 15 (1936-1937), pp. 362-373.

2,315 WILLEMS, M. L'avenir des colonies (commentaire d'un livre anglais). KONGO-OVERZEE 14 (1948), pp. 45-46.

2,316 WILLEMS, M. British literature and colonial policies. KONGO-OVERZEE 12-13 (1946-1947), pp. 113-116.

2,317 WOODROFFE, I. The relationship between Central and Local Government. J. AFR. ADM. 9 (1957), pp. 3-15.

2,318 WOODS, O. Africa's new look. AFR. AFFAIRS 56 (1957), pp. 200-208.

2,319 WOOLBERT, R. G. The future of Portugal's colonies. FOREIGN AFFAIRS 15 (1936-1937), pp. 374-380.

2,320 WRAITH, R. E. A note on Local Government training for the Colonial Service. J. AFR. ADM. 2 (1950), pp. 30-35.

2,321 WRIGHT, J. W. Reference marks in land settlement. J. AFR. ADM. 8 (1956), pp. 38-45.

2,322 WYNDHAM, H. A. The British empire, its structure and spirit. J. AFR. SOC. 42 (1943), pp. 140-144.

2,323 WYNDHAM, H. A. Survey of British commonwealth affairs: Vol. 2, by W. K. Hancock. J. AFR. SOC. 41 (1942), pp. 189-194.

2,324 YOUNG, T. C. Africa talking. AFR. AFFAIRS 47 (1948), pp. 215-220.

2,325 ZIMMERN, A. E. Is there an Empire foreign policy? INTERNAT. AFFAIRS 13 (1934), pp. 303-324.

2,326 A propos des besoins stratégiques des Etats-Unis. ZAIRE 5 (1951), pp. 973-974.

2,327 African nationalism [review of books by T. M. Uzo, J. O. Ajibola, S. D. Cudjoe, George Padmore]. AFR. AFFAIRS 49 (1950), pp. 224-228.

2,328 Agostinho Neto et la police de sécurité portugaise. PRESENCE AFR. N.S. 42 (1962), pp. 209-211.

2,329 De Bandoeng au Caire. La Conférence des peuples afro-asiatiques. PRESENCE AFR. N.S. 17 (1957-1958), pp. 113-114.

2,330 The British presence [review of four books on empire]. AFR. AFFAIRS 50 (1951), pp. 52-61.

2,331 Colonial development and welfare. AFR. AFFAIRS 44 (1945), p. 47.

2,332 Colonial international regional commissions. J. AFR. SOC. 42 (1943), p. 150.

2,333 Les colonies anglaises d'Afrique durant le premier semestre 1950. ZAIRE 4 (1950), pp. 1015-1016.

2,334 La Conférence de Bandoeng. Interventions des délégués africains. PRESENCE AFR. N.S. 3 (1955), pp. 28-38.

2,335 Conférence des Etats indépendants Africains (Accra, 22 avril 1958). PRESENCE AFR. N.S. 18-19 (1958), pp. 247-249.

2,336 Conférence des peuples africains. Accra, 13 au 15 décembre 1958. PRESENCE AFR. N.S. 22 (1958), pp. 137-138.

2,337 La conferenza afroasiatica di Bandoeng. AFRICA (Rome) 10 (1955), p. 105.

2,338 Congrès extraordinaire de la Fédération des Etudiants d'Afrique Noire en France (F.E.A.N.F.), Paris (21-22-23 juin 1958). PRESENCE AFR. N.S. 18-19 (1958), pp. 250-255.

2,339 Les colonies anglaises d'Afrique durant le premier semestre de 1951. ZAIRE 5 (1951), pp. 971-972.

2,340 Development and welfare of the colonial empire. J. AFR. SOC. 39 (1940), pp. 107-109, 197-199.

2,341 Les élus des T.O.M. et la loi-cadre. PRESENCE AFR. N.S. 18-19 (1958), pp. 121-124.

2,342 Ethics for the Local Government officer. J. AFR. ADM. 12 (1960), p. 113.

2,343 An experiment in colonial journalism, by a British Nigerian. AFR. AFFAIRS 45 (1946), pp. 80-87.

2,344 French African policy. AFR. AFFAIRS 45 (1946), pp. 35-37.

2,345 French overseas development plan. AFR. AFFAIRS 46 (1947), pp. 223-225.

2,346 The French Union. CIVILISATIONS 1, no. iii (1951), pp. 109-132; 1, no. iv (1951), pp. 97-112; 2 (1952), pp. 107-124, 250-258, 379-389, 569-584; 3 (1953), pp. 105-109, 369-387.

2,347 Mandates and trusteeship. UNO visiting missions. CORONA 1, no. 7 (1949), pp. 28-29.

2,348 Members and officers of Local Authorities. J. AFR. ADM. 6 (1954), pp. 144-146.

2,349 A Mística Portuguesa da Colonização. PORT. EM AFR. 11 (1954), pp. 6-11.

2,350 O.N.U., Africa ed U.S.A. AFRICA (Rome) 10 (1955), p. 138.

2,351 The Oxford University summer school on colonial administration, 3rd-7th July, 1937. J. AFR. SOC. 37 (1938), pp. 95-99.

2,352 Política proteccionista ao indígena. PORT. EM AFR. 2 (1945), pp. 354-360.

2,353 Le Président Truman parle du Point Quatre. ZAIRE 6 (1952), pp. 637-638.

2,354 Principles of Local Government finance in Africa. A memorandum prepared by the Colonial Local Government Advisory Panel. J. AFR. ADM. 8 (1956), supplement.

2,355 Réflexions sur les problèmes coloniaux actuels. ZAIRE 3 (1949), pp. 789-801.

2,356 Situation depuis Janvier 1961 dans les territoires administres par le Portugal. PRESENCE AFR. N.S. 45 (1963), pp. 136-157.

2,357 Slotmotie van het Italiaans Koloniaal Congres te Florentie (12-15 mei 1947). ZAIRE 2 (1948), pp. 305-306.

2,358 Témoignages des Africains sur Bandoeng. PRESENCE AFR. N.S. 3 (1955), pp. 38-44.

2,359 United States of Africa. J. AFR. SOC. 40 (1941), p. 5.

2,360 What the United States representative at the Berlin Conference, 1884, and the Brussels Conference, 1890, did in reference to the restriction and prohibition of the liquor traffic in Africa. LIBERIA BULL. 7 (1895), pp. 45-48.

Independence and after

2,361 ADIE, W. A. C. China and Africa today. RACE 5, no. 4 (1963-1964), pp. 3-25.

2,362 ADOTEVI, S. Du nationalisme à la nation. ET. DAHOM. N.S. 1 (1963-1964), pp. 105-106; N.S. 2 (1964), pp. 101-109.

2,363 AFRICANUS, P. Colonialisme, anticolonialisme, névrose, péché, dictionnaire, snobisme. AFR. ET ASIE 62 (1963), pp. 50-57.

2,364 AFRIKANUS. Da ficção à realidade. PORT. EM AFR. 18 (1961), pp. 209-216.

2,365 ALBERT, A. Notes sur la décolonisation. PRESENCE AFR. N. S. 53 (1965), pp. 47-67.

2,366 ALEXANDRE, P. Marxisme et tradition culturelle africaine. AFR. ET ASIE 67 (1964), pp. 8-25.

2,367 ANTI-TAYLOR, W. China through African eyes. RACE 5, no. 4 (1963-1964), pp. 48-51.

2,368 APTER, D. E. The role of the political opposition in new nations. AFR., THE DYNAMICS OF CHANGE, 1963, pp. 56-85.

2,369 APTER, D. E. and COLEMAN, J. S. Pan-Africanism or nationalism in Africa. PAN-AFRICANISM RECONSIDERED, 1962, pp. 81-115.

2,370 APTHORPE, R. The introduction of bureaucracy into African politics. Foreword by H. A. Fosbrooke. J. AFR. ADM. 12 (1960), pp. 125-134.

2,371 APTHORPE, R. Political change, centralization and role differentiation. CIVILISATIONS 10 (1960), pp. 217-222; French summary, pp. 222-223.

2,372 ARBOUSSIER, G. D'. Idées et forces politiques en Afrique. GENEVE-AFR. 3 (1964), pp. 167-179.

2,373 ARBOUSSIER, G. D'. L'unité africaine. CANADA ET LES PAYS AFR. FRANCOPHONES, 1965, pp. 59-77.

2,374 ARDEN-CLARKE, Sir C. The West and Africa's challenge. AFR. AFFAIRS 60 (1961), pp. 501-507.

2,375 AZIKIWE, N. L'avenir du pan-africainisme. PRESENCE AFR. N.S. 40 (1962), pp. 5-31.

2,376 AZIKIWE, N. Realities of African unity. AFR. FORUM 1 (1965), pp. 7-22.

2,377 B., J. L. Impressions sur l'Afrique d'aujourd'hui. AFR. ET ASIE 61 (1963), pp. 47-51.

2,378 BAILEY, G. The new United Nations. CONTEMP. REV. 203 (1963), pp. 77-80.

2,379 BALEWA, A. T. et al. The responsibilities of independence [from speeches by Abubakar Tafawa Balewa, Ahmadu Bello and Julius Nyerere]. J. AFR. ADM. 13 (1961), pp. 175-178.

2,380 BARTLETT, V. The awakening of the Afro-Asian nations. AFR. AFFAIRS 59 (1960), pp. 105-111.

2,381 BASTID, S. Le rôle joué par les Etats nouvellement indépendants dans les organisations internationales. ANNALES AFR., 1962, pp. 113-128.

2,382 BEN-AMOR, A. and CLAIRMONTE, F. Planning in Africa. JMAS 3 (1965), pp. 473-497.

2,383 BERUBE, L. Bilan des réalisations canadiennes en Afrique francophone. CANADA ET LES PAYS AFR. FRANCOPHONES, 1965, pp. 41-57.

2,384 BETHUNE, E. DE and WEMBI, A. Le problème de la sous-administration dans les pays d'Afrique noire indépendante. CIVILISATIONS 12 (1962), pp. 446-456; English summary, pp. 457-460.

2,385 BLAIR, T. L. V. The process of nation-building. AFRICA QUART. 4, no. iv (1965), pp. 249-252.

2,386 BOEG, P. The United Nations and the decolonization of Africa. GENEVE-AFR. 4 (1965), pp. 185-205.

2,387 BONN, M. J. The Commonwealth: parting of the continents? THE YEAR BOOK OF WORLD AFFAIRS 16 (1962), pp. 12-22.

2,388 BOSSCHERE, G. DE. La gauche révolutionnaire et le Tiers-Monde. PRESENCE AFR. N.S. 45 (1963), pp. 212-216.

2,389 BOSSCHERE, G. DE. Le néo-colonialisme. PRESENCE AFR. N.S. 38 (1961), pp. 61-71.

2,390 BOURGUIBA, H. The outlook for Africa. INTERNAT. AFFAIRS 37 (1961), pp. 425-431.

2,391 BOYD, A. The Third World. INTERNAT. AFFAIRS 39 (1963), pp. 564-569.

2,392 BRIEY, P. DE. The institutions of the new states. (Report of the discussions at the 33rd session of INCIDI held at Palermo from 23rd to 27th September 1963). CIVILISATIONS 13 (1963), pp. 227-249; includes French translation.

2,393 BROCKWAY, F. Commonwealth et pan-africanisme. PRESENCE AFR. N.S. 44 (1962), pp. 129-134.

2,394 BRUNSCHWIG, H. Colonisation-Décolonisation. Essai sur vocabulaire usuel de la politique coloniale. CAH. ET. AFR. 1 (1960), pp. 44-54.

2,395 BRUYAS, J. L'Esprit des institutions politiques. ANNALES AFR., 1964, pp. 137-175.

2,396 BUCHMANN, J. Le problème des structures politiques en Afrique Noire. ET. CONG. 1, no. 5 (1961), pp. 1-32.

2,397 BUCHMANN, J. Regimes politiques d'Afrique Noire. ZAIRE 14 (1960), pp. 283-306.

2,398 BUCHMANN, J. La tendance au présidentialisme dans les nouvelles Constitutions négro-africaines. CIVILISATIONS 12 (1962), pp. 46-68; English summary, pp. 69-74.

2,399 BUDHRAJ. V. S. Pan-African unification. AFRICA QUART. 5, no. i (1965), pp. 4-19.

2,400 BUNGENER, P. Défense de la personnalité africaine. GENEVE-AFR. 2 (1963), pp. 127-143.

2,401 BUSTIN, E. Les partis politiques africains. ET. CONG. 3, no. 7 (1962), pp. 1-80.

2,402 C., A. J. L'Union Africaine et Malgache au lendemain de la conférence de Bangui. ET. CONG. 3, no. 6 (1962), pp. 28-39.

2,403 CALVOCORESSI, P. The lure of the horizon. Aspects of British foreign policy with particular reference to Africa and Asia. AFR. AFFAIRS 64 (1965), pp. 191-201.

2,404 CAMERON, J. Africa and the British electorate. AFR. SOUTH 4, no. 2 (1960), pp. 105-109.

2,405 CAMERON, J. Portrait of Iain Macleod. AFR. SOUTH 4, no. 4 (1960), pp. 75-77.

2,406 CARRINGTON, C. E. Decolonization: the last stages. INTERNAT. AFFAIRS 38 (1962), pp. 29-40.

2,407 CARVALHO, J. V. DE. A Africa na guerra fria. PORT. EM AFR. 22 (1965), pp. 85-89.

2,408 CHADWICK, C. M. Decision-making case studies in administrative training. J. LOCAL ADM. OV. 4 (1965), pp. 232-238.

2,409 CHISIZA, D. K. Africa: what lies ahead. AFRICA QUART. 1, no. ii (1961), pp. 54-78; 1, no. iii (1961), pp. 55-71.

2,410 CHODAK, S. Single-party and socialism in the building of modern African political systems. AFRO-ASIAN AND W. AFF. 1 (1964), pp. 100-106.

2,411 CLAIRMONTE, F. F. Cuba and Africa. J. MOD. AFR. STUD. 2 (1964), pp. 419-430.

2,412 COLEMAN, J. S. The politics of sub-Saharan Africa. THE POLITICS OF THE DEVELOPING AREAS, 1960, pp. 247-368.

2,413 COMTE, P. L'Afrique à la recherche de son unité. GENEVE-AFR. 1 (1962), pp. 179-199; English summary, pp. 200-205.

2,414 COOPER, H. The process of decolonization: problems and issues. NEW FORCES IN AFRICA, 1962, pp. 88-94.

2,415 COURTNEY, W. F. Focus on Africa: the 15th U.N. General Assembly. AFR. SOUTH 5, no. 3 (1961), pp. 107-114.

2,416 COWEN, D. V. Constitution-making for a democracy. AFR. AFFAIRS 60 (1961), pp. 77-103.

2,417 CRAWLEY, A. M. Communism and African independence. AFR. AFFAIRS 64 (1965), pp. 91-102.

2,418 CRAWLEY, A. Patterns of government in Africa. AFR. AFFAIRS 60 (1961), pp. 392-399.

2,419 CROWDER, M. Indirect rule—French and British style. AFRICA 34 (1964), pp. 197-205.

2,420 CROZIER, B. The struggle for the Third World. INTERNAT. AFFAIRS 40 (1964), pp. 440-452.

2,421 CUNHA, S. Aspectos políticos da nova Africa. PORT. EM AFR. 21 (1964), pp. 215-226.

2,422 DAVIES, H. O. The new African profile. FOREIGN AFFAIRS 40 (1961-1962), pp. 293-302.

2,423 DEBRAH, E. M. The psychology of African nationalism. NEW FORCES IN AFRICA, 1962, pp. 51-66.

2,424 DECRAENE, P. L'évolution des partis politiques en Afrique au Sud du Sahara. CIVILISATIONS 12 (1962), pp. 196-206; English summary, pp. 207-210.

2,425 DECRAENE, P. Panafricanisme et grandes puissances. CIVILISATIONS 13 (1963), pp. 445-456; English summary, pp. 457-462.

2,426 DEMPSTER, R. T. Les forces qui contrecarrent la révolution africaine. PRESENCE AFR. N.S. 50 (1964), pp. 79-80.

2,427 DESCHAMPS, H. Et maintenant, Lord Lugard? AFRICA 33 (1963), pp. 293-306.

2,428 DESMARESCAUX, J. The evolution of the countries of French civilisation in Africa. CIVILISATIONS 12 (1962), pp. 407-421, 522-541; 13 (1963), pp. 171-187, 188-202, 351-361, 489-499; 14 (1964), pp. 116-133, 220-232, 383-397.

2,429 DIENG, D. From UAM to OCAM. AFR. FORUM 1 (1965), pp. 29-35.

2,430 DIOP, A. Remarks on African personality and negritude. PAN-AFRICANISM RECONSIDERED, 1962, pp. 337-345.

2,431 DIOP, T. Africa and its relations with the world. AFR., THE DYNAMICS OF CHANGE, 1963, pp. 111-123.

2,432 DROR, Y. Public-policy-making in avant-garde development states. CIVILISATIONS 13 (1963), pp. 395-405; French summary, pp. 406-410.

2,433 DUIGNAN, P. Pan-Africanism: a bibliographic essay. AFR. FORUM

2,434 DUNAYEVSKAYA, R. "Socialismes africains et problèmes nègres" vus par une militante de "l'humanisme marxiste." PRESENCE AFR. N.S. 48 (1963), pp. 49-64.

2,435 EFRAT, E. S. Pan-Africanism: problems and prospects. BULL. AFR. STUD. CANADA 2, no. 1 (1964), pp. 11-24.

2,436 EISENBERG, D. The Commonwealth Conference. AFR. SOUTH 4, no. 4 (1960), pp. 58-63.

2,437 EISENSTADT, S. N. Initial institutional patterns of political modernisation; a comparative study. CIVILISATIONS 12 (1962), pp. 461-474; 13 (1963), pp. 15-29; French summary.

2,438 EISENSTADT, S. N. Patterns of political leadership and support. AFR., THE DYNAMICS OF CHANGE, 1963, pp. 36-53.

2,439 EMERSON, R. American policy in Africa. FOREIGN AFFAIRS 40 (1961-1962), pp. 303-315.

2,440 EVANS-PRITCHARD, E. E. The Zande state. JRAI 93 (1963), pp. 134-154.

2,441 F., J. C. Réflexions sur l'Afrique Noire. AFR. ET ASIE 62 (1963), pp. 38-44.

2,442 F., T. Il cammino dell'Africa da Bandung ad Addis Ababa. AFRICA (Rome) 16 (1961), pp. 5-6.

2,443 FARMER, J. An American negro leader's view of African unity. AFR. FORUM 1 (1965), pp. 69-89.

2,444 FILESI, T. Comunità e Commonwealth. AFRICA (Rome) 15 (1960), pp. 55-61.

2,445 FILESI, T. Decolonizzazione bianca e colonizzazione rossa. AFRICA (Rome) 17 (1962), p. 178.

2,446 FILESI, T. L'evoluzione politica dell'Africa. AFRICA (Rome) 15 (1960), pp. 263-285.

2,447 FILESI, T. Orientamento e revisionismo costituzionale nei nuovi stati africani; con particolare riguardo a quelli di lingua inglese a sud del Sahara. AFRICA (Rome) 18 (1963), pp. 223-232.

2,448 FILESI, T. Gli sviluppi dell'azione del comunismo in Africa. AFRICA (Rome) 18 (1963), pp. 107-122.

2,449 FILESI, T. La via africana del socialismo. AFRICA (Rome) 18 (1963), pp. 159-172.

2,450 FLETCHER-COOKE, Sir J. The failure of the "Westminster Model" in Africa. AFR. AFFAIRS 63 (1964), pp. 197-208.

2,451 FODERARO, S. L'Africa all'inizio del 1961 e la politica africana dell'Italia. AFRICA (Rome) 16 (1961), pp. 55-62.

2,452 FODERARO, S. I principî ispiratori delle Costituzioni africane. AFRICA (Rome) 19 (1964), pp. 57-62.

2,453 FROELICH, J.-C. L'Armée au Pouvoir en Afrique. AFR. ET ASIE 72 (1965), pp. 13-21.

2,454 FURTER, P. Quelques réflexions sur le panafricanisme. GENEVE-AFR. 3 (1964), pp. 276-277.

2,455 GAZIER, F. Les problèmes spécifiques de l'administration publique en pays sous-développé. CIVILISATIONS 11 (1961), pp. 143-155; English summary, pp. 156-158.

2,456 GIGLIO, C. A proposito di colloqui sull'Africa. AFRICA (Rome) 17 (1962), pp. 13-18.

2,457 GLICKMAN, H. Introducing political Africa. J. MOD. AFR. STUD. 1 (1963), pp. 229-236.

2,458 GOMEZ TELLO, J. L. Africa y el neutralismo. AFR. INST. EST. AFR. 16, no. 63 (1962), pp. 33-52.

2,459 GONCHAROV, L. New forms of colonialism in Africa. J. MOD. AFR. STUD. 1 (1963), pp. 467-474.

2,460 GORVINE, A. The utilization of Local Government for national development. J. LOCAL ADM. OV. 4 (1965), pp. 225-231.

2,461 GORWALA, A. D. Democratic government in an under-developed country. AFR., THE DYNAMICS OF CHANGE, 1963, pp. 234-255.

2,462 GRAY, A. Accra Conference. AFR. AFFAIRS 58 (1959), pp. 97-99.

2,463 GRAY, A. Colonialism and the U.K. AFR. AFFAIRS 62 (1963), pp. 94-104.

2,464 GRAY, A. Co-operation by African states. AFR. AFFAIRS 60 (1961), pp. 128-135.

2,465 GRAY, A. Lagos conference. AFR. AFFAIRS 61 (1962), pp. 108-110.

2,466 GRAY, A. Wind of change [part of Harold Macmillan's speech to South African parliamentarians]. AFR. AFFAIRS 59 (1960), pp. 90-93.

2,467 GRAY, R. F. Political parties in new African nations: an anthropological view. COMP. STUD. SOC. HIST. 5 (1962-1963), pp. 449-465.

2,468 GRAY, R. F. Political parties in new African states: a reply to Lucy Mair. COMP. STUD. SOC. HIST. 6 (1963-1964), pp. 230-232.

2,469 GRIGG, J. E. P. Tories and the Commonwealth. AFR. SOUTH 4, no. 2 (1960), pp. 100-104.

2,470 GROSS, E. A. Adlai Stevenson, the United Nations, and Africa. AFR. FORUM 1 (1965), pp. 3-6.

2,471 HAILEY, W. M. [Lord Hailey]. The decline of the colonial system in Africa. THE YEAR BOOK OF WORLD AFFAIRS 13 (1959), pp. 1-23.

2,472 HAILU, S. L. Quel sera le nouveau taux de la neutralité? PRESENCE AFR. N.S. 49 (1964), pp. 235-237.

2,473 HAMON, L. Formes et perspectives de la démocratie en Afrique. CIVILISATIONS 11 (1961), pp. 245-261; English summary, pp. 262-264.

2,474 HAMON, L. Les groupes interetatiques à vocation panafricaine. THE YEAR BOOK OF WORLD AFFAIRS 17 (1963), pp. 96-122.

2,475 HAMON, L. Partis politiques et développement. Tendances et problèmes. ANNALES AFR., 1962, pp. 206-212.

2,476 HAZARD, J. N. Socialisme et Humanisme. ANNALES AFR., 1965, pp. 71-94.

2,477 HENRY, P.-M. Pan-Africanism: a dream come true. FOREIGN AFFAIRS 37 (1958-1959), pp. 443-452.

2,478 HERRERO TEJEDOR, F. Rusia, primera potencia colonial del mundo. ARCH. INST. EST. AFR. 16, no. 63 (1962), pp. 67-75.

2,479 HERSKOVITS, M. J. African values in the world scene. THE UN AND THE EMERGING AFRICAN NATIONS... 2 (1961), pp. 23-27.

2,480 HILAIRE, J. Nos ancêtres les Gaulois. ANNALES AFR., 1964, pp. 7-77.

2,481 HODGKIN, T. A note on the language of African nationalism. ST. ANTONY'S PAPERS 10 (1961), pp. 22-40.

2,482 HORWITZ, R. Pan-Africa without illusions. RACE RELATIONS 12 (1945), pp. 1-5.

2,483 HOSKYNS, C. The African states and the United Nations, 1958-1964. INTERNAT. AFFAIRS 40 (1964), pp. 466-480.

2,484 HOSKYNS, C. Pan-Africanism at Accra. AFR. SOUTH 3, no. 3 (1959), pp. 72-76.

2,485 HOSKYNS, C. Tunis diary. AFR. SOUTH 4, no. 4 (1960), pp. 104-111.

2,486 HOUPHOUET-BOIGNY, F. L'avenir de la communauté franco-africaine (allocution prononcée devant la XVIIIe promotion le 4 Février 1958). AFR. ET ASIE 41 (1958), pp. 3-5.

2,487 HOUPHOUET-BOIGNY, F. Black Africa and the French Union. FOREIGN AFFAIRS 35 (1956-1957), pp. 593-599.

2,488 HOWARD, L. C. Des différences entre l'impérialisme et le colonialisme. PRESENCE AFR. N.S. 37 (1961), pp. 9-26.

2,489 HUXLEY, E. The next-to-last act in Africa. FOREIGN AFFAIRS 39 (1960-1961), pp. 655-669.

2,490 HUNTER, G. Independence and development. Some comparisons between tropical Africa and South-East Asia. INTERNAT. AFFAIRS 40 (1964), pp. 47-59.

2,491 HUSSEIN, A. H. Cooperazione tra i parlamenti in Africa. COOPERAZIONE INT. AFR. 1960, pp. 303-308.

2,492 JAMESON, H. Y a-t-il une voie africaine du socialisme? PRESENCE AFR. N.S. 49 (1964), pp. 50-63.

2,493 JENNINGS, I. Is a party system possible in Africa? TRANSITION 1 (1961), pp. 11-12.

2,494 JESMAN, C. The roots of Chinese policy in Africa: [a review of Le Relazione della cina con l'Africa nel Medio-Evo by Teobaldi Filesi, Milan, 1962]. RACE 5, no. 4 (1963-1964), pp. 26-34.

2,495 JOHNSON, W. R. African-speaking Africa? Lessons from the Cameroon. AFR. FORUM 1 (1965), pp. 65-77.

2,496 JONES-QUARTEY, K. A. B. Institutions of public opinion in a rapidly changing West Africa. AFRICA, THE DYNAMICS OF CHANGE, 1963, pp. 146-176.

2,497 JULIEN, C. Les Etats-Unis, Cuba et le Tiers Monde. PRESENCE AFR. N.S. 37 (1961), pp. 35-47.

2,498 K., C. M. The civil service in Africa [review article on The civil service in new African states, by A. L. Adu]. TRANSITION 19 (1965), pp. 49-50.

2,499 KACHAMA-NKOY, S. De Karl Marx à Pierre Teilhard de Chardin dans la pensée de L. S. Senghor et Mamadou Dia. CIVILISATIONS 13 (1963), pp. 98-117; English summary, pp. 118-121.

2,500 KALONJI, B. De l'U.A.M. à l'O.C.A.M. ET. CONG. 8, no. 4 (1965), pp. 78-90.

2,501 KAMBONA, O. Colonialism and the African Liberation Committee. AFR. STUD. BULL. 6, no. iii (1963), pp. 1-6.

2,502 KAPUSCZA, A. America in Africa: image and reality. TRANSITION 6-7 (1962), pp. 25-26.

2,503 KAREFA-SMART, J. Africa in world affairs. AFR. STUD. BULL. 6, no. i (1963), pp. 4-13.

2,504 KAUNDA, K. The future of democracy in Africa. TRANSITION 15 (1964), pp. 37-39.

2,505 KAYE, I. Les crimes politiques en Afrique et la clairvoyance des masses. PRESENCE AFR. N.S. 53 (1965), pp. 253-254.

2,506 KEITA, M. Le parti unique en Afrique. PRESENCE AFR. N.S. 30 (1960), pp. 3-24.

2,507 KENADID, Y. O. Le monde libre. PRESENCE AFR. N.S. 38 (1961), pp. 98-106.

2,508 KENYATTA, J. African socialism and Africa unity. AFR. FORUM 1 (1965), pp. 23-37.

2,509 KILSON, M. African political change and the modernisation process. J. MOD. AFR. STUD. 1 (1963), pp. 425-440.

2,510 KING, P. Aspects militaires de l'unité africaine. PRESENCE AFR. N.S. 47 (1963), pp. 92-122.

2,511 KIRK-GREENE, A. H. M. and SMITH, J. H. Administrative techniques. A suggestion for administrative service training curricula. J. LOCAL ADM. OV. 1 (1962), pp. 164-172.

2,512 KI-ZERBO, J. L'Afrique violentée ou partenaire. PRESENCE AFR. N.S. 48 (1963), pp. 32-48.

2,513 KNAPPERT, J. New nations and national languages. EAISR, Jan. (1963), pp. 1-10.

2,514 KNIGHT, M. M. French colonial policy: the decline of association, a bibliographical article. J. MOD. HIST. 5 (1933), pp. 208-224.

2,515 KOUYATE, S. B. Politiques de développement et voies africaines du socialisme. PRESENCE AFR. N.S. 47 (1963), pp. 59-73.

2,516 KUMAR, M. Reactions and attitudes of African countries to Chinese aggression on India. AFRICA QUART. 2 (1962-1963), pp. 290-300.

2,517 KUMAR, M. The United Nations in Africa. AFRICA QUART. 5, no. 2 (1965), pp. 76-88.

2,518 KUMAR, S. The United Nations Committee of 24: its origins and work. AFRICA QUART. 5 (1965), pp. 174-187.

2,519 LANGER, W. L. Farewell to empire. FOREIGN AFFAIRS 41 (1962-1963), pp. 115-130.

2,520 LAQUEUR, W. Z. Communism and nationalism in tropical Africa. FOREIGN AFFAIRS 39 (1960-1961), pp. 610-621.

2,521 LARA, D.-K. Quelques réflexions sur le panafricanisme: ancêtres et nouvelles vagues. GENEVE-AFR. 2 (1963), pp. 207-214.

2,522 LAVROFF, D.-G. Les aspects actuels de l'unification de l'Afrique Noire francophone. ANNALES AFR., 1961, pp. 45-65.

2,523 LEGUM, C. The changing ideas of Pan-Africanism. AFR. FORUM 1 (1965), pp. 50-61.

2,524 LEGUM, C. Modern political ideas in Africa. AFRICA QUART. 1, no. iv (1962), pp. 28-42.

2,525 LEGUM, C. Pan-Africanism, the Communists and the West. AFR. AFFAIRS 63 (1964), pp. 186-196.

2,526 LEGUM, C. What kind of radicalism for Africa? FOREIGN AFFAIRS 43 (1964-1965), pp. 237-250.

2,527 LEGUM, C. 1960—year of decision. AFR. SOUTH 2, no. 2 (1958), pp. 68-74.

2,528 LEMOS, V. DE. Violence in Portuguese Africa. TRANSITION 22 (1965), pp. 41-43.

2,529 LEWIS, M. D. One hundred million Frenchmen: the assimilation theory in French colonial policy. COMP. STUD. SOC. HIST. 4 (1961-1962), pp. 129-153.

2,530 LEWIS, W. H. Functional elites: an emergent political force. NEW FORCES IN AFRICA, 1962, pp. 114-126.

2,531 LEYS, C. Violence in Africa. TRANSITION 21 (1965), pp. 17-20.

2,532 LEYS, C. What is the problem about corruption? J. MOD. AFR. STUD. 3 (1965), pp. 215-230.

2,533 LIPSCOMB, J. F. African image. CONTEMP. REV. 207 (1965), pp. 127-130.

2,534 LIVINGSTONE, A. S. Training in public administration for overseas government servants. A one-year course in the University of Manchester. J. AFR. ADM. 13 (1961), pp. 105-107.

2,535 LOGAN, R. W. The historical aspects of Pan-Africanism, 1900-1945. PAN-AFRICANISM RECONSIDERED, 1962, pp. 37-52.

2,536 LOGAN, R. W. The historical aspects of Pan-Africanism: a personal chronicle. AFR. FORUM 1 (1965), pp. 90-104.

2,537 LUTULI, A. L'Afrique et la liberté. (Discours prononcé à Oslo à l'occasion de la remise du Prix Nobel de la Paix.) PRESENCE AFR. N.S. 44 (1962), pp. 9-24.

2,538 M., G. Le Pafmecsa. ET. CONG. 4, no. 1 (1963), pp. 43-53.

2,539 MCAUSLAN, P. Sir Ivor Jennings' democracy (for Africa). TRANSITION 13 (1964), pp. 13-14.

2,540 MACDONA, B. F. The African scene. AFR. AFFAIRS 60 (1961), pp. 40-51.

2,541 MCHUGH, R. Masks and master races. AFRICA QUART. 2, no. iii (1962), pp. 152-154.

2,542 MACMILLAN, H. Africa. AFR. AFFAIRS 59 (1960), pp. 191-200.

2,543 MAGLITTO, N. La posizione dell'Africa nelle Nazioni Unite. AFRICA (Rome) 19 (1964), pp. 149-152.

2,544 MALCOLM X. La communauté noire américaine et la révolution africaine. PRESENCE AFR. N.S. 54 (1965), pp. 37-53.

2,545 MAQUET, J. J. Une hypothèse pour l'étude des féodalités africaines. CAH. ET. AFR. 2 (1961), pp. 292-314.

2,546 MAQUET, J. J. A research definition of African feudality. J. AFR. HIST. 3 (1962), pp. 307-310.

2,547 MARCUM, J. Pan-Africanism: present and future. PAN-AFRICANISM RECONSIDERED, 1962, pp. 53-65.

2,548 MARCUM, J. A. Pan-Africanism or fragmentation? NEW FORCES IN AFRICA, 1962, pp. 25-41.

2,549 MARGAI, M. and KASA-VUBU, J. Quelques témoignages. PRESENCE AFR. N.S. 50 (1964), pp. 76-78.

2,550 MARTIN, P. La politique du gouvernement canadien face à l'Afrique. CANADA ET LES PAYS AFR. FRANCOPHONES, 1965, pp. 79-87.

2,551 MAZRUI, A. A. Pan-Africanism in the cold war. EAISR, Jan. (1965), pp. 1-13.

2,552 MBOYA, T. J. The party system and democracy in Africa. FOREIGN AFFAIRS 41 (1962-1963), pp. 650-658.

2,553 MEYERS, B. D. The Organization of African Unity and the problems of decolonization. PROC. 3RD. GRAD. ACAD. UCLA, 1965, pp. 263-278.

2,554 MIRANDA SANTOS, A. Da Mulemba ao Arranha-céus. A transformação das relações. PORT. EM AFR. 22 (1965), pp. 311-327.

2,555 MITRA, A. Resurgent Africa. AFRICA QUART. 3, no. iii (1963), pp. 164-171.

2,556 MORAES, F. The importance of being black: an Asian looks at Africa. FOREIGN AFFAIRS 43 (1964-1965), pp. 99-111.

2,557 MORGAN, G. D. The social scientist in African politics. TRANSITION 13 (1964), pp. 33-36.

2,558 MORTIMER, M. Too many mansions in Africa. CONTEMP. REV. 197 (1960), pp. 22-24.

2,559 MOSTAZA, B. La presión del conflicto ruso-chino en Africa. ARCH. INST. EST. AFR. 19, no. 73 (1965), pp. 29-43.

2,560 NAVILLE, P. Y a-t-il un neo-colonialisme soviétique? PRESENCE AFR. N.S. 37 (1961), pp. 27-34.

2,561 NEHRU, J. The emergent Africa. AFRICA QUART. 1, no. i (1961), pp. 7-9.

2,562 NICOL, D. Politics, nationalism and universities in Africa. AFR. AFFAIRS 62 (1963), pp. 20-28.

2,563 NICULESCU, B. M. Recruitment of foreign staff for newly developing countries. CIVILISATIONS 10 (1960), pp. 13-21; French summary, pp. 22-24.

2,564 NIGER, F. Reflections on the new African myths. TRANSITION 16 (1964), pp. 14-17.

2,565 NKRUMAH, K. African prospect. FOREIGN AFFAIRS 37 (1958), pp. 45-53.

2,566 NKRUMAH, K. Le "Consciencisme." PRESENCE AFR. N.S. 49 (1964), pp. 8-34.

2,567 NOVE, A. The Soviet model and under-developed countries. INTERNAT. AFFAIRS 37 (1961), pp. 29-38.

2,568 NYERERE, J. K. African nationalism. AFRICA QUART. 3, no. ii (1963), pp. 115-121.

2,569 NYERERE, J. K. Les fondements du socialisme africain. PRESENCE AFR. N.S. 47 (1963), pp. 8-17.

2,570 NYERERE, J. K. The nature and requirements of African unity. AFR. FORUM 1 (1965), pp. 38-52.

2,571 NYERERE, J. K. On the boycott [of South African goods]. AFR. SOUTH 4, no. 1 (1959), pp. 7-8.

2,572 NYERERE, J. K. One party government. TRANSITION 2 (1961), pp. 9-11.

2,573 NYERERE, J. K. L'unité africaine. PRESENCE AFR. N.S. 39 (1961), pp. 5-11.

2,574 NYERERE, J. K. A United States of Africa. JMAS 1 (1963), pp. 1-6.

2,575 OGOT, B. From chief to president. TRANSITION 10 (1963), pp. 26-30.

2,576 OGUNSHEYE, A. Problems of federation in Africa. AFR., THE DYNAMICS OF CHANGE, 1963, pp. 89-107.

2,577 OKOYE, M. Africa and the West. AFRICA QUART. 5, no. ii (1965), pp. 89-94.

2,578 OLYMPIO, S. E. African problems and the cold war. FOREIGN AFFAIRS 40 (1961-1962), pp. 50-57.

2,579 ORGANIZATION OF AFRICAN UNITY. Charter of the organization of African unity. AFRICA QUART. 3, no. i (1963), pp. 58-65.

2,580 OTTO DE HABSBURGO. Europeos y Africanos: La entente necesaria. ARCH. INST. EST. AFR. 18, no. 70 (1964), pp. 7-22.

2,581 PADMORE, G. Extraits de l'ouvrage de Georges Padmore. "Panafricanisme ou communisme?" PRESENCE AFR. N.S. 29 (1959-1960), pp. 117-121.

2,582 PANE, H. T. Tenth anniversary celebration of the Bandung Conference and of the Afro-Asian solidarity movement. AFRO-ASIAN AND W. AFF. 2 (1965), pp. 96-98.

2,583 PANOFSKY, H. E. Pan-Africanism: a bibliographic note on organizations. AFR. FORUM 1 (1965), pp. 62-64.

2,584 PERROTT, R. The public relations of Africa. AFR. SOUTH 5, no. 2 (1961), pp. 102-106.

2,585 PFEFFER, K. H. Die Ausweitung Staatlicher Funktionen in den Entwicklungsländern—ein Beispiel für die Probleme soziologischer kategorienbildung in weltweitem Maßstab. SOCIOLOGUS 14 (1964), pp. 113-128.

2,586 PICK, H. The Brazzaville Twelve. AFR. SOUTH 5, no. 3 (1961), pp. 76-84.

2,587 PINTO, L. I. L'Afrique face à son destin. AFRICA (Rome) 17 (1962), pp. 55-61.

2,588 POSSY-BERRY, Q. Le drame de l'Afrique. AFRICA (Rome) 15 (1960), pp. 23-26.

2,589 PRADHAN, R. C. Pan-Africanism: a discussion. AFRO-ASIAN AND W. AFF. 2 (1965), pp. 385-388.

2,590 PURCELL, J. F. H. Political pluralism and political change: their consequences for the shape of the new Africa. PROC. 3RD. GRAD. ACAD. UCLA, 1965, pp. 57-67.

2,591 QUAISON-SACKEY, A. Africa and the United Nations: observations of a Ghanaian diplomat. AFR. FORUM 1 (1965), pp. 53-68.

2,592 QUAISON-SACKEY, A. The African viewpoint. THE U.N. AND THE EMERGING AFRICAN NATIONS... 2 (1961), pp. 9-15.

2,593 QUERMONNE, J.-L. Les nouvelles institutions politiques des Etats africains d'expression française. CIVILISATIONS 11 (1961), pp. 171-183; English summary, pp. 184-186.

2,594 RAI, K. B. Africa in the Indian parliament. AFRICA QUART. 5, no. i (1965), pp. 20-29.

2,595 RAI, K. B. India's stake in Africa. AFRICA QUART. 4, no. iii (1964), pp. 152-156.

2,596 RAINERO, R. L'évolution du neutralisme et ses caractéristiques africaines. GENEVE-AFR. 4 (1965), pp. 35-51.

2,597 RAKE, A. Is Pan-Africa possible? TRANSITION 4 (1962), pp. 29-30.

2,598 RAMANOELINA, M. Simples jalons pour une révolution créatrice. PRESENCE AFR. N.S. 44 (1962), pp. 25-59; N.S. 48 (1963), pp. 94-108.

2,599 RAO, U. R. Africa and the non-violent way. AFRICA QUART. 2, no. ii (1962), pp. 86-93.

2,600 REESE, T. R. Keeping calm about the Commonwealth. INTERNAT. AFFAIRS 41 (1965), pp. 451-462.

2,601 RENNIE, Sir G. Prospects of division in Africa. AFR. AFFAIRS 60 (1961), pp. 177-188.

2,602 RICHARDSON, B. The Commonwealth Conference [March, 1961]. AFR. SOUTH 5, no. 4 (1961), pp. 7-12.

2,603 RIVKIN, A. Lost goals in Africa. FOREIGN AFFAIRS 44 (1965), pp. 111-126.

2,604 RIVKIN, A. Principal elements of U.S. policy towards underdeveloped countries. INTERNAT. AFFAIRS 37 (1961), pp. 452-464.

2,605 ROBERTS, M. Summitry at Casablanca. AFR. SOUTH 5, no. 3 (1961), pp. 68-75.

2,606 ROBINSON, K. British work on government and politics in Africa. BULL. AFR. STUD. ASSOC. 4 (1965), pp. 1-5.

2,607 ROGIN, M. Rosseau in Africa. TRANSITION 10 (1963), pp. 23-25.

2,608 ROOSEVELT, E. The role of the United Nations in Africa. THE U.N. AND THE EMERGING AFRICAN NATIONS... 2 (1961), pp. 17-21.

2,609 ROSBERG, C. G., JR. Democracy and the new African states. ST. ANTONY'S PAPERS 15 (1963), pp. 23-53.

2,610 ROSTOW, W. W. Some lessons of history for Africa. PAN-AFRICANISM RECONSIDERED, 1962, pp. 155-168.

2,611 ROTHCHILD, D. Force and consent in African region-building. MAKERERE J. 11 (1965), pp. 23-38.

2,612 ROTHCHILD, D. Progress and the one-party state. TRANSITION 10 (1963), pp. 31-34.

2,613 SADY, E. J. Improvement of Local Government and administration for development purposes. J. LOCAL ADM. OV. 1 (1962), pp. 135-148.

2,614 SAMANTAR, Y. O. Le néo-impérialisme en Afrique. PRESENCE AFR. N.S. 38 (1961), pp. 210-215.

2,615 SANGER, C. Toward unity in Africa. FOREIGN AFFAIRS 42 (1963-1964), pp. 269-281.

2,616 SCALAPINO, R. A. Sino-Soviet competition in Africa. FOREIGN AFFAIRS 42 (1963-1964), pp. 640-654.

2,617 SCHOELL, F. L. Un Français considère les développements africains. GENEVE-AFR. 2 (1963), pp. 46-66; English summary, p. 67.

2,618 SEGAL, A. Africa newly divided? J. MOD. AFR. STUD. 2 (1964), pp. 73-90.

2,619 SELASSIE I, H. Towards African unity. J. MOD. AFR. STUD. 1 (1963), pp. 281-291.

2,620 SENGHOR, L. S. Negritude and African socialism. ST. ANTONY'S PAPERS 15 (1963), pp. 9-22.

2,621 SENGHOR, L. Some thoughts on Africa: a continent in development. INTERNAT. AFFAIRS 38 (1962), pp. 189-195.

2,622 SHEPHERD, G. Socialism as religion. TRANSITION 23 (1965), pp. 11-14.

2,623 SIEGEL, M. Keeper of the umbilical cord. AFR. SOUTH 5, no. 4 (1961), pp. 101-111.

2,624 SILVA CUNHA, J. M. DA. Political aspects of the new Africa. AFR. AFFAIRS 63 (1964), pp. 270-280.

2,625 SIMONI, M. La conquista dell'indipendenza: Aspetti del problema nei paesi sottosviluppati. AFRICA (Rome) 14 (1959), pp. 193-197.

2,626 SINGH, D. The African scene. AFRICA QUART. 2, no. i (1962), pp. 21-26.

2,627 SITHOLE, E. F. C. Appréhensions européennes à l'égard des nouveaux gouvernements africains. PRESENCE AFR. N.S. 44 (1962), pp. 135-145.

2,628 SLAWECKI, L. M. S. The two Chinas in Africa. FOREIGN AFFAIRS 41 (1962-1963), pp. 398-409.

2,629 SMITH, T. E. The background to census-taking and vital registration among semi-literate societies. J. AFR. ADM. 12 (1960), pp. 150-157.

2,630 SOPER, T. La Belgique et l'Aide Economique Aux Pays Sous-Développés Institut Royal Des Relations Internationales, Brussels, 1959. J. AFR. ADM. 12 (1960), pp. 164-169.

2,631 SOPER, T. Independent Africa and its links with Europe. AFR. AFFAIRS 64 (1965), pp. 25-31.

2,632 STORELLI, L. Notes sur le contrôle de la gestion financière dans certains Etats d'Afrique. CIVILISATIONS 14 (1964), pp. 371-372.

2,633 STROVY, B. The Universal Declaration of Human Rights and the Protection of Human Rights and Fundamental Freedoms in some African countries. COOPERAZIONE INT. AFR., 1960, pp. 338-349.

2,634 TELLI, D. The Organization of African Unity in historical perspective. AFR. FORUM 1 (1965), pp. 7-28.

2,635 TEVOEDJRE, A. Qu'est-ce que le néo-colonialisme? GENEVE-AFR. 3 (1964), pp. 8-18.

2,636 THOMAS, I. B. Nouveaux et futurs Etats du Commonwealth Britannique. CIVILISATIONS 13 (1963), pp. 161-170, 333-350, 500-525; 14 (1964), pp. 101-115, 233-245, 373-382.

2,637 THOMSON, G. What socialism should mean in the new countries of Africa. ECON. DEV. IN AFRICA, 1965, pp. 322-331.

2,638 TINKER, H. Local Government in Devoloping Countries-II. Democracy, decentralization and development by Henry Maddick. J. LOCAL ADM. OV. 2 (1963), pp. 170-174.

2,639 TINKER, H. The name and nature of foreign aid. INTERNAT. AFFAIRS 35 (1959), pp. 43-52.

2,640 TINKER, H. New lamps for old. Review article on Kenneth Younger's The Public Service in New States. INTERNAT. AFFAIRS 36 (1960), pp. 489-494.

2,641 TOLEN, A. Addis-Ababa: un diagnostic, deux thérapeutiques, un compromis. PRESENCE AFR. N.S. 49 (1964), pp. 35-49.

2,642 TOLEN, A. La contre-révolution en Afrique. PRESENCE AFR. N.S. 50 (1964), pp. 81-88.

2,643 TORDOFF, W. Commonwealth affairs [a review article]. UNIVERSITAS 5 (1962), pp. 15-17.

2,644 TOURE, A. S. La Révolution et l'unité populaire. RECH. AFR. 4 (1963), pp. 3-33.

2,645 TOURE, S. Africa's future and the world. FOREIGN AFFAIRS 41 (1962-1963), pp. 141-151.

2,646 V., B. La Conférence de Lagos (25 au 30 janvier 1962). ET. CONG. 2, no. 3 (1962), pp. 20-23.

2,647 VANSINA, J. A comparison of African kingdoms. AFRICA 32 (1962), pp. 324-335.

2,648 VENKATARAMAN, K. Local finance in developing countries. J. LOCAL ADM. OV. 4 (1965), pp. 194-201.

2,649 VILLORESI, M. Noi in Africa. La collaborazione culturare, come nel caso della Libia, è il più valido presuppostodei nostri rapporti con i Paesi africani. AFRICA (Rome) 16 (1961), pp. 3-5.

2,650 WACHUKU, J. A. The relation of AMSAC and the American Negro to Africa and Pan-Africanism. PAN-AFRICANISM RECONSIDERED, 1962, pp. 361-376.

2,651 WALLIS, C. A. G. Urgent Local Government problems in Africa. J. LOCAL ADM. OV. 2 (1963), pp. 61-74.

2,652 WEATHERHEAD, A. Local Government in Developing Countries—1. Democracy, decentralization and development by Henry Maddick. J. LOCAL ADM. OV. 2 (1963), pp. 167-169.

2,653 WHITAKER, P. The right of entry [into Great Britain]. TRANSITION 2 (1961), pp. 15-17.

2,654 WILLIAMS, G. M. The United States and the new Africa. AFR. STUD. BULL. 5, no. iv (1962), pp. 5-12.

2,655 WILLIAMS, G. M. United States policy toward Africa and the United Nations. THE U.N. AND THE EMERGING AFRICAN NATIONS... 2 (1961), pp. 5-8.

2,656 YAMBO, [O.]. Marx et l'étrangeté d'un socialisme africain. PRESENCE AFR. N.S. 50 (1964), pp. 20-37.

2,657 YANGUAS MESSIA, J. El clima político de ayer y de hoy en Africa. ARCH. INST. EST. AFR. 13, no. 49 (1959), pp. 81-94.

2,658 YANNAY, Y. La coopération technique d'Israël avec l'Afrique. GENEVE-AFR. 3 (1964), pp. 46-59.

2,659 ZAJACZKOWSKI, A. L'evoluzione del concetto di negritudine. Gli Africani alla ricerca di se stessi. AFRICA (Rome) 20 (1965), pp. 115-142.

2,660 China in Africa by S. K. G. AFRICA QUART. 4, no. iv (1965), pp. 224-228.

2,661 Colonialism and nationalism in Africa and Europe. PAST AND PRESENT 24 (1963), pp. 65-74.

2,662 Conditions à un haut commandement africain. PRESENCE AFR. N.S. 54 (1965), pp. 255-259.

2,663 La conférence des états africains d'expression française. PRESENCE AFR. N.S. 34-35 (1960-1961), pp. 220-222.

2,664 Conférence internationale sur les problèmes du néo-colonialisme [Leipzig 5-8 avril 1961]. RECH. AFR. 2 (1962), pp. 45-46.

2,665 Le congrès de Dakar sur le socialisme africain. GENEVE-AFR. 2 (1963), pp. 78-80.

2,666 De dures realités. PRESENCE AFR. N.S. 41 (1962), pp. 166-169.

2,667 De la Conférence de Bamako. PRESENCE AFR. N.S. 48 (1963), pp. 223-227.

2,668 Le "dollar africaniste et scientifique." PRESENCE AFR. N.S. 51 (1964), pp. 174-175.

2,669 French-speaking Africa. GENEVE-AFR. 1 (1962), p. 218.

2,670 L'Organisation de l'Unité Africaine. La conférence d'Accra (21-26 octobre 1965). ET. CONG. 8, no. 6 (1965), pp. 57-84.

2,671 Le PAFMECSA. GENEVE-AFR. 2 (1963), pp. 80-81.

2,672 A propos de la lutte des classes en Afrique Noire. PRESENCE AFR. N.S. 53 (1965), pp. 246-250.

2,673 Relationship in districts between administrative and departmental officers. J. AFR. ADM. 13 (1961), pp. 50-52.

2,674 Report of the Committee on Training in Public Administration for Overseas Countries. J. LOCAL ADM. OV. 2 (1963), pp. 175-178.

2,675 Seminar on Inter-state relations in Africa at Freiburg/Breisgau. BULL. AFR. STUD. ASSOC. 1 (1964), pp. 25-26.

2,676 La IIe session de la conference générale de l'U.N.E.S.C.O. PRESENCE AFR. N.S. 34-35 (1960-1961), pp. 224-226.

2,677 The struggle for African independence and continental unity [a note issued jointly by the African Missions in India]. AFRO-ASIAN AND W. AFF. 1 (1964), pp. 217-235.

See also 523, 594, 653, 663, 698, 802, 1211, 1212, 1284, 1480, 2684, 2694, 2972, 3682, 3846, 4163, 6149, 14682.

HISTORY

2,678 ACHUFUSI, M. Devoirs et responsabilités des historiens africains. PRESENCE AFR. 27-28 (1959), pp. 81-95.

2,679 ADAMS, C. C. The African colonies of Germany and the war. GEOG. REV. 1 (1916), pp. 452-454.

2,680 ALBRECHT-CARRIE, R. Italian colonial policy, 1914-1918. J. MOD. HIST. 18 (1946), pp. 123-147.

2,681 ALLEN, B. Professor Malvezzi's book on Italian colonial policy. J. AFR. SOC. 34 (1935), pp. 423-433.

2,682 ALMEIDA, J. L. DE. A política ultramarina de El-Rei D. Carlos. BOL. INST. ANGOLA 19 (1964), pp. 55-66.

2,683 ALSTYNE, R. W. VAN. The British right of search and the African slave trade. J. MOD. HIST. 2 (1930), pp. 37-47.

2,684 AMERY, L. S. and ORMSBY-GORE, W. Problems and development in Africa. J. AFR. SOC. 28 (1929), pp. 325-339.

2,685 ARNETT, E. J. and ALLEN, B. M. Europe in Africa. J. AFR. SOC. 38 (1939), pp. 160-165.

2,686 ARTHUR, H.R.H. Prince. The development of Africa. J. AFR. SOC. 23 (1924), pp. 169-175.

2,687 AZAM, P. Les limites de l'Islam Africain. AFR. ET ASIE 1, no. 1 (1948), pp. 16-30.

2,688 BADEN-POWELL, Sir G. The development of tropical Africa. ROYAL COL. INST. PR. 27 (1895-1896), pp. 218-255.

2,689 BASILE, K. L'Afrique Noire et son destin face à la France. Essai de critique du réformisme dans les colonies. PRESENCE AFR. N.S. 12 (1957), pp. 109-126.

2,690 BASTIDE, R. A propos d'un livre brésilien sur l'Afrique. PRESENCE AFR. N.S. 41 (1962), pp. 123-128.

2,691 BEAZLEY, C. R. The colonial empire of the Portuguese to the death of Albuquerque. TRHS N.S. 8 (1894), pp. 109-127.

2,692 BEAZLEY, C. R. Prince Henry of Portugal and the African crusade of the fifteenth century. AM. HIST. REV. 16 (1910-1911), pp. 11-23.

2,693 BEAZLEY, C. R. Prince Henry of Portugal and his political, commercial, and colonizing work. AM. HIST. REV. 17 (1911-1912), pp. 252-267.

2,694 BEHANZIN, L. S. Fondements historiques de la loi-cadre. PRESENCE AFR. N.S. 18-19 (1958), pp. 69-74.

2,695 BIOBAKU, S. Les responsabilités de l'historien africain en ce qui concerne l'histoire et l'Afrique. PRESENCE AFR. 27-28 (1959), pp. 96-99.

2,696 BIRCHENOUGH, H. Some aspects of our imperial trade. ROYAL COL. INST. PR. 29 (1897-1898), pp. 104-138.

2,697 BLYDEN, E. W. The native African: his line and his work. LIBERIA BULL. 24 (1904), pp. 61-74.

2,698 BOAHEN, A. A. The African Association, 1788-1805. TR. HIST. SOC. GHANA 5 (1961), pp. 43-64.

2,699 BOSTON, H. J. L. Fifty years hence. WASU 1 (1926), pp. 15-19.

2,700 BOUQUET, M. R. The capture of the Sunny South slaver. HISTORY TODAY 10 (1960), pp. 573-578.

2,701 BOVILL, E. W. Clapperton's letter to Denham reporting Oudney's death. J. AFR. SOC. 35 (1936), pp. 165-168.

2,702 BOXER, C. R. From Maghgreb to the Moluccas, 1415-1521. HISTORY TODAY 11 (1961), pp. 38-47.

2,703 BOXER, C. R. S. R. Welch and his history of the Portuguese in Africa, 1495-1806. J. AFR. HIST. 1 (1960), pp. 55-63.

2,704 BRASIO, P. A. Uma Empresa de Civilização Africana. PORT. EM AFR. 8 (1951), pp. 15-26.

2,705 BRASIO, P. A. Páginas de Crítica. PORT. EM AFR. 6 (1949), pp. 93-101.

2,706 BRASIO, P. A. Política do Espírito no Ultramar Português. PORT. EM AFR. 6 (1949), pp. 20-29, 75-86, 209-223.

2,707 BRASIO, P. A. Portugalliae Imperium. PORT. EM AFR. 5 (1948), pp. 193-207.

2,708 BRUCHHAUSEN, P. German colonial propaganda in Africa. CONTEMP. REV. 147 (1935), pp. 77-85.

2,709 BRUNSKILL, G. S. Studies in war-time organisation: AFLOC. AFR. AFFAIRS 44 (1945), pp. 125-130.

2,710 BUELL, R. L. The struggle in Africa. FOREIGN AFFAIRS 6 (1927-1928), pp. 22-40.

2,711 BUFFON, J. A propos de "l'avènement de l'Afrique Noire" de M. Brunschwig. PRESENCE AFR. N.S. 50 (1964), pp. 151-177.

2,712 BULCK, G. VAN. L'histoire en 1952. ZAIRE 7 (1953), pp. 707-726.

2,713 C., J. Centenaires africains. ZAIRE 8 (1954), pp. 946-947.

2,714 C., J. Les colonies anglaises d'Afrique en 1954. ZAIRE 9 (1955), pp. 163-165.

2,715 CAETANO, M. Garrett Colonialista. PORT. EM AFR. 11 (1954), pp. 361-372.

2,716 CANA, F. R. German aims in Africa. J. AFR. SOC. 14 (1914-1915), pp. 355-365.

2,717 CASARIEGO, J. E. Las grandes exploraciones maritimas del Africa en la antigüedad. ARCH. INST. EST. AFR. 4, no. 14 (1950), pp. 7-38.

2,718 CHAMBERLAIN, J. The British African colonies. LIBERIA BULL. 14 (1899), pp. 80-82.

2,719 CHARPENTIER, C. Les Anciens Combattants dans les états africains d'expression française. AFR. ET ASIE 53 (1961), pp. 16-19.

2,720 CHAVES, L. Portugal em Africa. PORT. EM AFR. 1 (1944), pp. 56-58.

2,721 CHENET, G. Haïti et l'héritage africain. RECH. AFR. 3 (1961), pp. 3-23.

2,722 CHISIZA, D. K. The outlook for contemporary Africa. JMAS 1 (1963), pp. 25-38.

2,723 COCATRE-ZILGIEN, A. Un génie méconnu du XVIIIe siècle: l'avocat Linguet (1736-1794), incendiaire, réactionnaire et visionnaire. ANNALES AFR., 1960, pp. 83-122.

2,724 COMHAIRE, J. Coup d'oeil sur l'histoire des peuples africains et Afro-Américains. ZAIRE 7 (1953), pp. 687-706, 1027-1051.

2,725 CORDERO TORRES, J. M. Balance colonial del último tercio de siglo. CUAD. EST. AFR. 20 (1952), pp. 9-29.

2,726 CORNEVIN, R. Afrique, point d'interrogation, trait d'union, terre d'espérance. CANADA ET LES PAYS AFR. FRANCOPHONES, 1965, pp. 1-22.

2,727 CORNEVIN, R. L'histoire des peuples de l'Afrique noire: branche de l'ethnologie ou science à part entière? J. AFR. HIST. 2 (1961), pp. 15-23.

2,728 CORNEVIN, R. Leo Frobenius et le réveil de l'Afrique. FESTSCHRIFT FUR A. E. JENSEN, 1964, pp. 59-62.

2,729 CORNEVIN, R. Note au sujet des origines des esclaves aux Antilles. BULL. IFAN 27 (1965), pp. 370-371.

2,730 COSTA, M. G. DA. Um célebre inédito seiscentista. O Itinerário de Jerónimo Lobo. PORT. EM AFR. 22 (1965), pp. 68-75.

2,731 COSTA, M. G. DA. O Itinerário do P. Jerónimo Lobo. PORT. EM AFR. 22 (1965), pp. 140-145.

2,732 COURTOIS, C. Les rapports entre l'Afrique et la Gaule au début du moyen-âge. C.T. 2 (1954), pp. 127-145.

2,733 CRABTREE, W. A. German colonies in Africa. J. AFR. SOC. 14 (1914-1915), pp. 1-14.

2,734 CRANBORNE, Lord. British colonial policy. AFR. AFFAIRS 43 (1944), pp. 50-51.

2,735 CRAVEN, W. F. Historical study of the British empire, a bibliographical article. J. MOD. HIST. 6 (1934), pp. 40-69.

2,736 CURTIN, P. D. The British Empire and Commonwealth in recent historiography. AM. HIST. REV. 65 (1959-1960), pp. 72-91.

2,737 CURTIN, P. D. Third Conference on African History and Archaeology [London, 1961]. AFR. STUD. BULL. 4, no. iii (1961), pp. 10-11.

2,738 DALE, I. R. The Indian origins of some African cultivated plants and African cattle. UGANDA J. 19 (1955), pp. 68-72.

2,739 DANQUAH, J. B. Is the Negro a dead letter? WASU 1 (1926), pp. 23-25.

2,740 DAVIDSON, B. The fact of African history: an introduction. AFR. SOUTH 2, no. 2 (1958), pp. 44-49.

2,741 DAVIDSON, B. History in Africa. AFR. SOUTH 5, no. 1 (1960), pp. 107-109.

2,742 DAVIDSON, B. The tents of Kedar: pre-European Africa. HISTORY TODAY 7 (1957), pp. 645-652.

2,743 DEBBASCH, Y. Poésie et traite: l'opinion française sur le commerce négrier au début XIXe siècle. REV. FRANC. HIST. OUTRE-MER 48 (1961), pp. 311-352.

2,744 DEBIEN, G. Destinées d'esclaves à la Martinique (1746-1778). BULL. IFAN 22 (1960), pp. 1-91.

2,745 DEBIEN, G. Les origines des esclaves des Antilles. BULL. IFAN 23 (1961), pp. 361-387; 25 (1963), pp. 1-38, 215-265; 26 (1964), pp. 166-211, 601-675; 27 (1965), pp. 755-799.

2,746 DEBIEN, G. and HOUDAILLE, J. Les origines des esclaves aux Antilles. BULL. IFAN 26 (1964), pp. 166-211. See also 23 (1961), pp. 361-387; 25 (1963), pp. 1-38, 215-265; 26 (1964), pp. 601-675.

2,747 DECHAMBRE, E. Projet d'enquête sur les origines de la domestication. J. SOC. AFR. 12 (1942), pp. 133-137.

2,748 DECLE, L. The development of our British African empire. ROYAL COL. INST. PR. 37 (1905-1906), pp. 311-340.

2,749 DELAFOSSE, M. and DEBIEN, G. Les origines des esclaves aux Antilles. BULL. IFAN 27 (1965), pp. 319-369.

2,750 DIAZ DE VILLEGAS, J. Africa en la postguerra. ARCH. INST. EST. AFR. 14, no. 55 (1960), pp. 7-30.

2,751 DIAZ DE VILLEGAS, J. La epopeya de Enrique el Navegante 500 años despues. ARCH. INST. EST. AFR. 15, no. 57 (1961), pp. 7-25.

2,752 DIKE, K. O. The study of African history. PROC. INT. CONG. AFR. 1 (1962), pp. 55-67.

2,753 DIOP, A. Africa's path in history. AFR. SOUTH 4, no. 3 (1960), pp. 95-98.

2,754 DJIBRIL, D. Quo vadis, Africa? PRESENCE AFR. 6 (1949), pp. 142-143.

2,755 DOUTRELOUX, A. Mythe et réalité du colonialisme. GENEVE-AFR. 4 (1965), pp. 7-34.

2,756 DU BOIS, W. E. B. Black Africa tomorrow. FOREIGN AFFAIRS 17 (1938-1939), pp. 100-110.

2,757 DUDLEY, B. J. The military in the new states of Africa. NJESS 6 (1964), pp. 351-361.

2,758 ECA, V. A. D'. The Colonial Congress at Lisbon, 1901 (translated from the Portuguese with an introductory note by J. Barrett-Lennard). J. AFR. SOC. 2 (1903), pp. 292-307.

2,759 EDEN, A. The British Empire. J. AFR. SOC. 39 (1940), pp. 194-196.

2,760 EGERTON, H. E. The system of British colonial administration of the crown colonies in the seventeenth and eighteenth centuries compared with the system prevailing in the nineteenth century. TRHS, 4th series, 1 (1918), pp. 190-217.

2,761 EHRLICH, C. African history and African historians. MAKERERE J. 1 (1958), pp. 25-34.

2,762 ELWELL-SUTTON, A. S. The importance of Africa. CONTEMP. REV. 163 (1943), pp. 87-91.

2,763 ENGHOLM, G. Independence and after: Independence and after, revolution in underdeveloped countries by R. Harris. TRANSITION 6-7 (1962), p. 53.

2,764 ENGLAND, D. Henry the Navigator (1394-1460). CONTEMP. REV. 198 (1960), pp. 635-637.

2,765 EVERAERT, J. Les fluctuations du trafic négrier nantais (1763-1792). C.T. 43 (1963), pp. 37-62.

2,766 F., T. L'Africa di Lord Hailey. AFRICA (Rome) 13 (1958), pp. 117-118.

2,767 FAGE, J. D. Anthropology, botany, and the history of Africa [G. P. Murdock's Africa; its peoples and their culture history]. J. AFR. HIST. 2 (1961), pp. 299-309.

2,768 FERRANDIS TORRES, M. La constante africana en nuestra historia. ARCH. INST. EST. AFR. 7, no. 31 (1954), pp. 51-66.

2,769 FERRANDIS TORRES, M. Mujeres españolas en la Historia de Africa. ARCH. INST. EST. AFR. 9, no. 39 (1956), pp. 59-75.

2,770 FERRANDIS TORRES, M. La política africana de Carlos V. ARCH. INST. EST. AFR. 13, no. 50 (1959), pp. 55-70.

2,771 FILESI, T. Africa d'oggi. AFRICA (Rome) 10 (1955), pp. 101-105.

2,772 FILESI, T. Storia dell'Africa coloniale e storia dell'Africa. AFRICA (Rome) 16 (1961), pp. 11-13.

2,773 FILESI, T. Ulisse: il tramonto del colonialismo. AFRICA (Rome) 13 (1958), pp. 175-178.

2,774 FILESI, T. I viaggi dei Cinesi in Africa nel Medioevo. AFRICA (Rome) 16 (1961), pp. 275-288.

2,775 FLANDRAU, G. What Africa is not. CONTEMP. REV. 138 (1930), pp. 771-776.

2,776 FRIPP, C. E. A note on medieval Chinese-African trade. NADA 17 (1940), pp. 88-96; 18 (1941), pp. 12-22.

2,777 FROIDEVAUX, H. Les études d'histoire coloniale en France et dans les pays de colonisation française. RHCF 1 (1913), pp. 11-38.

2,778 FROIDEVAUX, H. L'histoire des Colonies français à l'exposition de la bibliothèque nationale. RHCF 2 (1914), pp. 77-104.

2,779 GALLAGHER, J. Fowell Buxton and the new African policy, 1838-1842. CAMB. HIST. J. 10 (1950), pp. 36-58.

2,780 GALLAGHER, J. White settlers in Tropical Africa by L. H. Gann and P. Duignan [a review article]. HISTORICAL J. 5 (1962), pp. 198-203.

2,781 GARCIA FIGUERAS, T. Españoles en Africa en el Siglo XVI. I. Los geógrafos e historiadores. Luis del Mármol Carvajal (1520-1599). ARCH. INST. EST. AFR. 3, no. 10 (1949), pp. 69-99.

2,782 GAUSSIN, P. R. Les anciennes dominations en Afrique noire. ANN. UNIV. MADAG. 1 (1963), pp. 45-94; 3 (1964), pp. 97-150.

2,783 GIFFEN, Sir R. The relative growth of the component parts of the Empire. ROYAL COL. INST. PR. 30 (1898-1899), pp. 136-170.

2,784 GIGLIO, C. Le questioni africane nei documenti diplomatici italiani. AFRICA (Rome) 15 (1960), pp. 239-240.

2,785 GOMEZ TELLO, J. L. Defensa de Europa en Africa. ARCH. INST. EST. AFR. 19, no. 73 (1965), pp. 7-28.

2,786 GOODY, J. Feudalism in Africa? J. AFR. HIST. 4 (1963), pp. 1-18.

2,787 GOWERS, Sir W. The African elephant in warfare. AFR. AFFAIRS 46 (1947), pp. 42-49; 47 (1948), pp. 173-180.

2,788 GRAY, A. The defence of Africa [an agreement between Britain and Egypt]. AFR. AFFAIRS 54 (1955), pp. 9-10.

2,789 GREAVES, I. C. A modern colonial fallacy. FOREIGN AFFAIRS 14 (1935-1936), pp. 627-638.

2,790 GREEN, W. S. B. Colonisation, and expansion of the empire. ROYAL COL. INST. PR. 27 (1895-1896), pp. 41-44.

2,791 GREENBERG, J. Historical references from linguistic research in Sub-Saharan Africa. BOSTON UNIV. PAPERS IN AFR. HIST. 1 (1964), pp. 1-15.

2,792 GRILO, Velez. Mouzinho de Albuquerque e os problemas africanos. BSEM 94-95, no. ii (1955), pp. 397-409.

2,793 GUEDES, A. M. A Vocação Missionária na fundação do Império Português. PORT. EM AFR. 2 (1945), pp. 138-142.

2,794 GUERIN, D. Un futur pour les Antilles? PRESENCE AFR. N.S. 6 (1956), pp. 20-27.

2,795 HARDY, G. Histoire Coloniale et psychologie ethnique. RHCF 18 (1925), pp. 161-172.

2,796 HAILEY, W. M. [Lord Hailey]. Colonies and world organization. AFR. AFFAIRS 44 (1945), pp. 54-58.

2,797 HAILEY, W. M. [Lord Hailey]. Development in Africa over the past 20 years. AFRICA (Rome) 13 (1958), pp. 115-116.

2,798 HAILEY, W. M. [Lord Hailey]. The foundation of self-government in the African colonies. AFR. AFFAIRS 47 (1948), pp. 147-153.

2,799 HAILEY, W. M. [Lord Hailey] et al. International aspects of the future of Africa, by Lord Hailey, A. de Vleeschauwer, V. Mook. J. AFR. SOC. 42 (1943), pp. 108-118, 165-176, 177-182.

2,800 HAIR, P. E. H. The enslavement of Koelle's informants. J. AFR. HIST. 6 (1965), pp. 193-203.

2,801 HALLETT, R. The European approach to the interior of Africa in the eighteenth century. J. AFR. HIST. 4 (1963), pp. 191-206.

2,802 HAMIDULLAH, M. L'Afrique découvre l'Amerique avant Christophe Colomb. PRESENCE AFR. N.S. 18-19 (1958), pp. 173-183.

2,803 HARGREAVES, J. D. Biography and the debate about imperialism. J. MOD. AFR. STUD. 2 (1964), pp. 279-285.

2,804 HARGREAVES, J. D. "Educated Africans." CONTEMP. REV. 196 (1959), pp. 210-213.

2,805 HARGREAVES, J. D. Towards a history of the partition of Africa. J. AFR. HIST. 1 (1960), pp. 97-109.

2,806 HARRIS, J. H. Back to slavery? CONTEMP. REV. 120 (1921), pp. 190-197.

2,807 HARRIS, J. H. War contributions from Africa. J. AFR. SOC. 15 (1916), pp. 367-371.

2,808 HART, J. DE. Notes on the exploration of Africa among the ancients. With special reference to Hanno. J. AFR. SOC. 25 (1926), pp. 264-277.

2,809 HASAN, K. N. The scramble for Africa (1875-1914 A.D.). AFRICA QUART. 1, no. 2 (1961), pp. 12-29.

2,810 HAWKIN, R. C. A German free state in Africa. CONTEMP. REV. 140 (1931), pp. 337-340.

2,811 HEINTZEN, H. The role of Islam in the era of nationalism. NEW FORCES IN AFRICA, 1962, pp. 42-50.

2,812 HEMEDI BIN ABDULLAH. A history of Africa translated by E. C. Barker. TANG. NOTES 32 (1952), pp. 65-82.

2,813 HENDERSON, W. O. The conquest of the German colonies, 1914-18. HISTORY 27 (1942), pp. 124-139.

2,814 HERNANDEZ PACHECO, E. Panorama Histórico-Geográfico de la época de León el Africano (1485-1552). ARCH. INST. EST. AFR. 7, no. 30 (1954), pp. 13-31.

2,815 HERSKOVITS, M. J. Les Noirs du Nouveau Monde: sujet de recherches africanistes. J. SOC. AFR. 8 (1938), pp. 65-82.

2,816 HESS, R. L. Italy and Africa: colonial ambitions in the First World War. J. AFR. HIST. 4 (1963), pp. 105-126.

2,817 HEYSE, T. The Congrès de Berlin (1884-1885), d'après documents diplomatiques français. BULL. SEANCES IRCB 4 (1933), pp. 694-723.

2,818 HILZHEIMER, M. Die ättesten Beziehungen Zwischen Asien und Afrika nachgewiesen an den Haustieren. AFRICA 3 (1930), pp. 472-482; English summary, pp. 482-483.

2,819 HODGKIN, T. Islam, history, and politics. JMAS 1 (1963), pp. 91-97.

2,820 HOLT, E. Garnet Wolseley: soldier of empire. HISTORY TODAY 8 (1958), pp. 706-713.

2,821 HOSKINS, H. L. British policy in Africa 1873-1877: a study in geographical politics. GEOG. REV. 32 (1942), pp. 140-149.

2,822 HOUDAILLE, J. Origines des esclaves des Antilles. BULL. IFAN 26 (1964), pp. 601-675. See also 23 (1961), pp. 361-387; 25 (1963), pp. 1-38, 215-265; 26 (1964), pp. 166-211.

2,823 HOUDAILLE, J. et al. Les origines des esclaves des Antilles, by J. Houdaille, R. Massio, G. Debien. BULL. IFAN 25 (1963), pp. 215-265. See also 23 (1961), pp. 361-387; 25 (1963), pp. 1-38; 26 (1964), pp. 166-211, 601-675.

2,824 HRBEK, I. The project of fontes Africae Historiae. PROC. INT. CONG. AFR. 1 (1962), pp. 68-71.

2,825 HUISMAN, M. Les préliminaires de la politique coloniale belge. RHCF 25 (1932), pp. 159-174.

2,826 HUTCHISON, W. F. Tropical Africa in relation to Western civilization and the British empire. WASU 5 (1927), pp. 6-10.

2,827 HUTTON, E. T. H. A co-operative system for the defence of the empire. ROYAL COL. INST. PR. 29 (1897-1898), pp. 222-258.

2,828 ILIFFE, J. Imperialism and politics [review article on Africa and the Victorians: the Official Mind of Imperialism]. TRANSITION 2 (1961), pp. 38-39.

2,829 JAMES, C. L. The Black Jacobins. PRESENCE AFR. 6 (1949), pp. 23-25.

2,830 JEBB, R. Notes on imperial organisation. ROYAL COL. INST. PR. 38 (1906-1907), pp. 4-36.

2,831 JOHNSTON, Sir H. H. The Africa of the immediate future. J. AFR. SOC. 18 (1919), pp. 161-182.

2,832 JULLIEN, C. A. From the French Empire to the French Union. INTERNAT. AFFAIRS 26 (1950), pp. 487-502.

2,833 KAKE, I. L'histoire, une dimension de l'unité. PRESENCE AFR. N.S. 49 (1964), pp. 64-80.

2,834 KELTIE, J. S. British interests in Africa. CONTEMP. REV. 54 (1888), pp. 115-125.

2,835 KENT, R. K. Palmares: an African state in Brazil. J. AFR. HIST. 6 (1965), pp. 161-175.

2,836 KERR, P. From Empire to Commonwealth. FOREIGN AFFAIRS 1, no. ii (1922), pp. 83-98.

2,837 KIEWIET, C. W. DE. African dilemmas. FOREIGN AFFAIRS 33 (1954-1955), pp. 445-457.

2,838 KINROSS, J. The foreign Legion. HISTORY TODAY 2 (1952), pp. 558-570.

2,839 KI-ZERBO, J. L'histoire: levier fondamental. PRESENCE AFR. N.S. 37 (1961), pp. 144-147.

2,840 LANGENHOVE, F. VAN. Factors of decolonisation. CIVILISATIONS 11 (1961), pp. 401-423; French summary, pp. 424-428.

2,841 LANGTON, A. V. Limiting the area of conflict. J. AFR. SOC. 40 (1941), p. 238.

2,842 LANGTON, A. V. Progress of the world war. J. AFR. SOC. 42 (1943), pp. 21-22.

2,843 LEVA, A. E. Discorso sulla prima indagine di Erodoto in Africa. AFRICA (Rome) 20 (1965), pp. 339-344.

2,844 LEWICKI, T. L'Afrique Noire dans le Kitāb al-Masālik wa' l-mamālik d'Abu 'Ubayd al-Bakrī (xi^e s.). AFR. BULL. 2 (1965), pp. 9-14.

2,845 LEWIN, E. The black cloud in Africa. FOREIGN AFFAIRS 4 (1925-1926), pp. 637-648.

2,846 LOKKE, C. L. French dreams of colonial empire under Directory and Consulate. J. MOD. HIST. 2 (1930), pp. 237-250.

2,847 LOUIS, W. R. Great Britain and the African peace settlement of 1919. AM. HIST. REV. 71 (1965-1966), pp. 875-892.

2,848 LOUIS, W. R. The United States and the African Conference of 1919: the pilgrimage of George Louis Beer. J. AFR. HIST. 4 (1963), pp. 413-433.

2,849 LUCAS, C. P. On the teaching of Imperial history. HISTORY 1 (1916), pp. 5-11.

2,850 LUGARD, F. D. The extension of British influence (and trade) in Africa. ROYAL COL. INST. PR. 27 (1895-1896), pp. 4-40.

2,851 LUGARD, Lord. Africa and the powers. J. AFR. SOC. 35 (1936), pp. 4-17.

2,852 LUGARD, Lord. The claims to colonies. J. AFR. SOC. 35 (1936), pp. 115-122.

2,853 LUGARD, Lord. 'Slavery in all its forms.' AFRICA 6 (1933), pp. 1-14.

2,854 LUTHY, H. Fine degli Imperi d'Europa. AFRICA (Rome) 13 (1958), pp. 7-14.

2,855 LY, A. La formation de l'économie sucrière et le développement du marché d'esclaves africains dans les Îles françaises d'Amérique au XVIIe siècle. PRESENCE AFR. N.S. 13 (1957), pp. 7-22; N.S. 16 (1957), pp. 112-134.

2,856 LYAUTEY, L. H. G. Une oeuvre coloniale en Afrique. J. AFR. SOC. 28 (1929), pp. 115-121.

2,857 LYNE, R. N. The German menace to Africa; being a review of The Unfinished War by E. M. Ritchie. J. AFR. SOC. 39 (1940), pp. 216-224.

2,858 MACALUSO-ALEO, G. I primi passi del l'Italia in Africa. RHCF 25 (1932), pp. 289-378.

2,859 MALOWIST, M. Les aspects sociaux de la première phase de l'expansion coloniale. AFR. BULL. 1 (1964), pp. 11-40.

2,860 MARKOV, W. Congrès international de l'histoire des découvertes. Lisbonne, 4-11 septembre 1960. RECH. AFR. 3 (1961), pp. 79-81.

2,861 MARTINS, A. O mapa cor de rosa. BSEM 130 (1962), pp. 189-193.

2,862 MASSON, A. L'opinion française et les problèmes coloniaux à la fin du Second Empire. REV. FRANC. HIST. OUTRE-MER. 49 (1962), pp. 366-437.

2,863 MATIP, B. Dialectique du problème colonial. AFRICA (Rome) 13 (1958), pp. 65-68.

2,864 MAUNY, R. Conference on African History (Londres, juillet 1953). BULL. IFAN 16 (1954), p. 423.

2,865 MAUNY, R. Le déblocage d'un continent par les voies maritimes: le cas africain. Aperçu général: les deux afriques. LES GRANDES VOIES MARITIMES DANS LE MONDE XVe-XIXe, 1965, pp. 175-190.

2,866 MAUNY, R. Perspectives et limites de l'Ethno-Histoire en Afrique. BULL. IFAN 24 (1962), pp. 620-627.

2,867 MELLAND, F. "The great opportunity." J. AFR. SOC. 30 (1931), pp. 262-271.

2,868 MELON, A. Actual conocimiento de Africa. ARCH. INST. EST. AFR. 5, no. 17 (1951), pp. 33-48.

2,869 MELON, A. Juan Leon Africano y su Descripcion de Africa. ARCH. INST. EST. AFR. 7, no. 29 (1954), pp. 31-47.

2,870 MENDES, F. F. Portugal and her colonial empire. J. AFR. SOC. 39 (1940), pp. 225-230, 331-338.

2,871 MENENDEZ PIDAL, R. El Padre Las Casas y la leyenda negra. ARCH. INST. EST. AFR. 17, no. 65 (1963), pp. 7-17.

2,872 MERCIER, P. Contacts de civilisation en Afrique et en Océanie au XIXe siècle. J. WORLD HIST. 3 (1956-1957), pp. 625-646.

2,873 MERINO, M. M. El XXV aniversario del vuelo de la patrulla Atlantida. ARCH. INST. EST. AFR. 6, no. 21 (1952), pp. 41-61.

2,874 MILNER, Lord. The two empires. ROYAL COL. INST. PR. 39 (1907-1908), pp. 329-348.

2,875 MIRACLE, M. P. The introduction and spread of maize in Africa. J. AFR. HIST. 6 (1965), pp. 39-55.

2,876 MISIPO, D. Léo Frobenius, le Tacite de l'Afrique. PRESENCE AFR. N.S. 37 (1961), pp. 151-156.

2,877 MONIOT, H. Autour de quelques livres d'histoire africaine. CAH. ET. AFR. 3 (1962), pp. 115-138.

2,878 MONIOT, H. Histoire et tradition africaines: à propos de quelques livres récents. CAH. ET. AFR. 5 (1965), pp. 145-155.

2,879 MONOD, African states south of the Sahara [review article on Geschichte Afrikas: Staatenbildungen südlich der Sahara by D. Westermann]. INT. REV. MISSIONS 42 (1953), pp. 200-206.

2,880 MONTEIRO, A. Portugal in Africa. J. AFR. SOC. 38 (1939), pp. 259-272.

2,881 MONTERO DIAZ, S. Stanley en España. CUAD. EST. AFR. 2 (1946), pp. 45-68.

2,882 MORAL, D. Responsabilidad histórica de Europa en Africa. ARCH. INST. EST. AFR. 19, no. 76 (1965), pp. 7-20.

2,883 MORALES OLIVER, L. El testamento de la reina Isabel y su reflejo en Africa. ARCH. INST. EST. AFR. 11, no. 47 (1958), pp. 7-21.

2,884 MOREL, E. D. Two African policies. CONTEMP. REV. 124 (1923), pp. 310-320.

2,885 MORGAN, B. H. The development of empire trade and industry. ROYAL COL. INST. PR. 40 (1908-1909), pp. 198-222.

2,886 MULHALL, M. G. Our colonial empire. CONTEMP. REV. 67 (1895), pp. 632-643.

2,887 MURASHIKI, A. M. The African Past [by Basil Davidson; review article]. AFRO-ASIAN AND W. AFF. 2 (1965), pp. 369-372.

2,888 MUSSIO, G. Premessa alla conoscenza dell'Africa. AFRICA (Rome) 13 (1958), pp. 149-151.

2,889 NAGA, P. What have Europeans done for Africans? KONGO-OVERZEE 12-13 (1946-1947), pp. 234-240.

2,890 NAVILLE, P. L'abolition de l'esclavage et la Révolution française. PRESENCE AFR. 6 (1949), p. 22.

2,891 NENEKHALY-CAMARA, C. A propos des ancêtres africains de l'homme. RECH. AFR. 3 (1961), pp. 72-74.

2,892 NEWMAN, E. W. P. Italian policy in Africa. CONTEMP. REV. 147 (1935), pp. 549-556.

2,893 NEWTON, A. P. Africa and historical research. J. AFR. SOC. 22 (1923), pp. 266-277.

2,894 NKRUMAH, K. Africanisme et culture. PRESENCE AFR. N.S. 45 (1963), pp. 5-18.

2,895 NOWELL, C. E. Portugal and the partition of Africa. J. MOD. HIST. 19 (1947), pp. 1-17.

2,896 OLDHAM, J. H. Developments in the relations between white and black in Africa (1911-1931). J. AFR. SOC. 32 (1933), pp. 160-170.

2,897 OLIVER, S. The repartition of Africa. CONTEMP. REV. 115 (1919), pp. 15-22.

2,898 OLIVERA E CASTRO, L. F. DE. Política ultramarina portuguesa. ARCH. INST. EST. AFR. 19, no. 75 (1965), pp. 53-73.

2,899 OLIVIER. The European problem in Africa. CONTEMP. REV. 134 (1929), pp. 454-460.

2,900 OMER-COOPER, J. D. The question of unity in African history. J. HIST. SOC. NIG. 3 (1964), pp. 103-112.

2,901 OWEN, J. F. The military defence forces of the colonies. ROYAL COL. INST. PR. 21 (1889-1890), pp. 277-326.

2,902 PANT, A. B. Notes on certain problems of Africa. J. WORLD HIST. 5 (1959-1960), pp. 634-657.

2,903 PAULME, D. L'Afrique noire jusqu'au XIVe siècle. J. WORLD HIST. 3 (1956-1957), pp. 277-301, 561-581.

2,904 PEASE, A. E. Africa north of the equator. CONTEMP. REV. 70 (1896), pp. 37-45.

2,905 PERICOT GARCIA, L. Africa y América. El problema de sus posibles contactos precolombinos. ARCH. INST. EST. AFR. 17, no. 67 (1963), pp. 7-14.

2,906 PHATAK, D. M. A note on the German two-rupee coin and the Maria Theresa dollar. TANGANYIKA NOTES AND RECORDS 57 (1961), pp. 177-179.

2,907 PICK, F. W. Portuguese Africa. CONTEMP. REV. 164 (1943), pp. 234-239.

2,908 PRICE-MARS, J. Les survivances africaines dans la communauté haïtienne. ET. DAHOM. 6 (1951), pp. 5-10.

2,909 RAU, V. and DIFFIE, B. W. Alleged fifteenth-century Portuguese joint-stock companies and the articles of Dr. Fitzler. BULL. INST. HIST. RES. 26 (1953), pp. 181-199.

2,910 RENAUT, F.-P. Etudes sur le Pacte de Famille et la politique coloniale française. RHCF 15 (1923), pp. 33-142.

2,911 REYMOND, F. Recherches sur la politique de la France à la Conférence africaine de Berlin (1884-1885), tour d'horizon bibliographique. GENEVE-AFR. 3 (1964), pp. 107-119.

2,912 RICHARD, R. and DEBIEN, G. Les origines des esclaves des Antilles. BULL. IFAN 25 (1963), pp. 1-38. See also 23 (1961), pp. 361-387; 25 (1963), pp. 215-265; 26 (1964), pp. 166-211, 601-675.

2,913 RIVKIN, A. Arms for Africa? FOREIGN AFFAIRS 38 (1959-1960), pp. 84-94.

2,914 ROBINSON, Sir J. The colonies and the century. ROYAL COL. INST. PR. 30 (1898-1899), pp. 324-367.

2,915 ROBSON, E. British colonization in the seventeenth century. HISTORY TODAY 3 (1953), pp. 257-265.

2,916 RODRIGUES, J. H. The influence of Africa on Brazil and of Brazil on Africa. J. AFR. HIST. 3 (1962), pp. 49-67.

2,917 ROEYKENS, A. Banning et la Conférence géographique de Bruxelles en 1876. ZAIRE 8 (1954), pp. 227-271.

2,918 ROMERO MOLINER, R. R. La historia en las culturas negro-africanas. CUAD. EST. AFR. 3 (1947), pp. 43-55.

2,919 ROMULO, C. P. Asia, Africa, and the world. THE EMERGING WORLD: JAWAHARLAL NEHRU MEMORIAL VOLUME, 1964, pp. 190-196.

2,920 ROOTH, A. R. The United States African Squadron 1843-1861. BOSTON UNIV. PAPERS IN AFR. HIST. 1 (1964), pp. 77-117.

2,921 ROTBERG, R. I. The teaching of African history. AM. HIST. REV. 69 (1963-1964), pp. 47-63.

2,922 RUMEU DE ARMAS, A. Don Enrique el Navegante y sus planes politicos de integridad Afroatlantica. ARCH. INST. EST. AFR. 15, no. 57 (1961), pp. 71-83.

2,923 RUMEU DE ARMAS, A. La exploración del Atlántico por mallorquines y catalanes en el siglo XIV. ARCH. INST. EST. AFR. 18, no. 72 (1964), pp. 7-20.

2,924 RUMEU DE ARMAS, A. Los reinos hispánicos y la hegemonía de Africa. ARCH. INST. EST. AFR. 11, no. 45 (1958), pp. 17-31.

2,925 SABBEN-CLARKE, E. E. African troops in Asia. AFR. AFFAIRS 44 (1945), pp. 151-157.

2,926 SANCHO DE SOPRANIS, H. La cooperacion española a la obra Portuguesa en Africa. ARCH. INST. EST. AFR. 16, no. 61 (1962), pp. 63-80.

2,927 SANDERSON, G. N. Contributions from African sources to the history of European competition in the upper valley of the Nile. J. AFR. HIST. 3 (1962), pp. 69-90.

2,928 SANTA RITA, J. G. A Mulher na colonização Portuguesa. PORT. EM AFR. 2 (1945), pp. 337-342.

2,929 SAN VALERO APARISI, J. Datos cronologicos de las culturas primitivas africanas. CUAD. EST. AFR. 4 (1948), pp. 49-63.

2,930 SAROLEA, C. The French African empire. CONTEMP. REV. 128 (1925), pp. 33-40.

2,931 SCHNAPPER, B. La fin du régime de l'exclusif: le commerce étranger dans les possessions françaises d'Afrique tropicale (1817-1870). ANNALES AFR., 1959, pp. 149-199.

2,932 SCOTT, W. R. The constitution and finance of the Royal African Company of England from its foundation till 1720. AM. HIST. REV. 8 (1902-1903), pp. 241-259.

2,933 SECK, A. Geographie, colonisation et culture. PRESENCE AFR. N.S. 14-15 (1957), pp. 46-57.

2,934 SEME, P. K. I. The regeneration of Africa. J. AFR. SOC. 5 (1906), pp. 404-408.

2,935 SEVILLA ANDRES, D. Política española en Africa de 1931 a 1936. ARCH. INST. EST. AFR. 17, no. 68 (1963), pp. 37-58.

2,936 SHAW, F. L. Colonial expansion. ROYAL COL. INST. PR. 26 (1894-1895), pp. 3-29.

2,937 SHELTON, A. J. Historiography and New African History: a short exposition. GENEVE-AFR. 3 (1964), pp. 81-89.

2,938 SHEPPERSON, G. Abolitionism and African political thought. TRANSITION 12 (1964), pp. 22-26.

2,939 SHEPPERSON, G. Notes on Negro American influences on the emergence of African nationalism. J. AFR. HIST. 1 (1960), pp. 299-312.

2,940 SILVA, J. D. Uma reivindicação histórica. PORT. EM AFR. 3 (1946), pp. 8-11.

2,941 SILVA REGO, A. DA. Outre-mer portugais. REV. HIST. COL. 45 (1948), pp. 288-299.

2,942 SIMAR, T. L'Unité de l'histoire coloniale. CONGO 2 (1921), pp. 14-20.

2,943 SINCLAIR, W. The African Association of 1788. J. AFR. SOC. 1 (1901), pp. 145-149.

2,944 SMITH, E. W. African dilemma. [by] Frank Melland and Cullen Young. J. AFR. SOC. 37 (1938), pp. 58-65.

2,945 SOLANKE, L. Lifting the veil [that rests over African history]. WASU 1 (1926), pp. 11-15.

2,946 STENGERS, J. A propos de l'Acte de Berlin, ou comment naît une légende. ZAIRE 7 (1953), pp. 839-844.

2,947 STENGERS, J. L'impérialisme colonial de la fin du XIXe siècle: mythe ou réalité. J. AFR. HIST. 3 (1962), pp. 469-491.

2,948 STOKES, E. Great Britain and Africa: the myth of imperialism. HISTORY TODAY 10 (1960), pp. 554-563.

2,949 SUMMERSCALES, J. The war effort of the French colonies. J. AFR. SOC. 39 (1940), pp. 123-128.

2,950 SWAYNE, H. G. C. The central area of Africa and the mandate principle. CONTEMP. REV. 132 (1928), pp. 461-468.

2,951 TATE, H. R. A medieval navigator: Vasco da Gama. AFR. AFFAIRS 43 (1944), pp. 61-65.

2,952 TEMPERLEY, H. W. V. The imperial control of native races. CONTEMP. REV. 89 (1906), pp. 804-813.

2,953 TERSEN, . Victor Schoelcher. PRESENCE AFR. 6 (1949), pp. 15-21.

2,954 TRAMOND, J. Des conclusions sur la colonisation comparée. RHCF 25 (1932), pp. 527-540.

2,955 TROWELL, M. Clues to African tribal history. UGANDA J. 10 (1946), pp. 54-63.

2,956 VERLINDEN, C. Les origines coloniales de la civilisation atlantique. J. WORLD HIST. 1 (1953-1954), pp. 378-398.

2,957 VIGNES, K. Etude sur la rivalité d'influence entre les puissances européennes en Afrique équatoriale et occidentale depuis l'acte général de Berlin jusqu'au seuil du XXe siècle. REV. FRANC. HIST. OUTRE-MER 48 (1961), pp. 5-95.

2,958 VIGNES, K. Etudes sur les relations diplomatiques franco-britanniques qui conduisirent à la convention du 14 juin 1898. REV. FRANC. HIST. OUTRE-MER 52 (1965), pp. 352-403.

2,959 VINCENT, H. Inter-British trade, and its influence on the unity of the empire. ROYAL COL. INST. PR. 22 (1890-1891), pp. 265-303.

2,960 WADIYAR, J. C. Emergence of Africa. AFRICA QUART. 1, no. iv (1962), pp. 5-13.

2,961 WEBB, E. J. The alleged Phoenician circumnavigation of Africa. ENG. HIST. REV. 22 (1907), pp. 1-14.

2,962 WESTERMANN, D. Cultural history of Negro Africa. J. WORLD HIST. 3 (1956-1957), pp. 985-1004.

2,963 WESTERMANN, D. The value of the African's past. INT. REV. MISSIONS 15 (1926), pp. 418-437.

2,964 WIGGLESWORTH, A. African post-war problems. CONTEMP. REV. 165 (1944), pp. 102-105.

2,965 WINGATE, Sir R. Presentation of the gold medal of the Royal African Society to His Majesty Leopold III, King of the Belgians. On the 17th November, 1937. J. AFR. SOC. 37 (1938), pp. 3-8.

2,966 WIRTH, F. German colonial ambitions. CONTEMP. REV. 163 (1943), pp. 36-39.

2,967 WRIGLEY, C. Linguistic clues to African history. J. AFR. HIST. 3 (1962), pp. 269-272.

2,968 WRIGLEY, G. M. The military campaigns against Germany's African colonies. GEOG. REV. 5 (1918), pp. 44-65.

2,969 WYBERGH, W. Imperial organisation and the colour question. CONTEMP. REV. 91 (1907), pp. 695-705, 805-815.

2,970 ZERBO, J. K. L'économie de traite en Afrique Noire ou le pillage organisé (XVe-XXe siècle). PRESENCE AFR. N.S. 11 (1957), pp. 7-31.

2,971 ZERBO, J. K. Histoire et conscience nègre. PRESENCE AFR. N.S. 16 (1957), pp. 53-69.

2,972 ZERBO, J. K. La loi-cadre se meurt. PRESENCE AFR. N.S. 18-19 (1958), pp. 113-120.

2,973 Africa and the war. J. AFR. SOC. 39 (1940), pp. 289-292; 40 (1941), pp. 1, 97.

2,974 Le Commonwealth à l'aube d'une ère nouvelle. ZAIRE 6 (1952), pp. 185-186.

2,975 Les colonies anglaises d'Afrique durant le second semestre de 1950. ZAIRE 5 (1951), pp. 525-527.

2,976 Les colonies anglaises d'Afrique en 1952. ZAIRE 7 (1953), pp. 281-283.

2,977 Demobilisation: first moves. AFR. AFFAIRS 44 (1945), pp. 94-95; 45 (1946), pp. 2-3.

2,978 Empire opinion [an extract from a letter]. J. AFR. SOC. 39 (1940), pp. 297-298.

2,979 Formation of the French Committee of National Liberation. J. AFR. SOC. 42 (1943), pp. 147-150.

2,980 Free France and Free French Africa. J. AFR. SOC. 41 (1942), pp. 85-86.

2,981 Free France and the War. J. AFR. SOC. 40 (1941), pp. 3-4, 100-101.

2,982 The Free French Agreements. J. AFR. SOC. 40 (1941), pp. 195-197.

2,983 The German view of African colonisation. J. AFR. SOC. 14 (1914-1915), pp. 40-52.

2,984 International Conference on African history. TR. HIST. SOC. GHANA 1 (1952-1955), pp. 96-97.

2,985 Native Africans and the war [from the Daily Telegraph and The Times]. J. AFR. SOC. 41 (1942), pp. 220-221.

2,986 The next stage. AFR. AFFAIRS 47 (1948), pp. 99-106.

2,987 Portugal in Europe and overseas. J. AFR. SOC. 39 (1940), p. 203.

2,988 Le Premier Congrès International d'Histoire Coloniale (21-25 Septembre 1931 [à Paris]). RHCF 24 (1931), pp. 457-516.

2,989 Professor Coupland's epilogue. J. AFR. SOC. 38 (1939), p. 464.

2,990 The rally of the empire in Africa. J. AFR. SOC. 39 (1940), pp. 295-297.

2,991 Le rôle de soldat en Afrique indépendante. PRESENCE AFR. N.S. 48 (1963), pp. 213-217.

2,992 Second Conference on African history and archaeology. TR. HIST. SOC. GHANA 3 (1958), pp. 218-219.

2,993 Signor Mussolini and peace. J. AFR. SOC. 39 (1940), pp. 112-114.

2,994 War-time progress in the British colonial empire. J. AFR. SOC. 42 (1943), pp. 151-152.

See also 77, 205, 343, 407, 610, 634, 804, 1920, 3108.

Archives

2,995 CURTIN, P. D. The archives of Tropical Africa. J. AFR. HIST. 1 (1960), pp. 129-147.

2,996 DUBOSCQ, G. The importance of modern archives for the developing countries. UNESCO BULL. LIBS. 17 (1963), pp. 259-263.

2,997 FREEMAN-GRENVILLE, G. S. P. Archives de France (French National Archives). UNIV. GHANA RES. REV. 1 (1965), pp. 25-26.

2,998 FREEMAN-GRENVILLE, G. S. P. Portuguese archives. UNIV. GHANA RES. REV. 1 (1965), pp. 23-25.

2,999 GANN, L. H. Archives and the study of society. RHODES-LIV. J. 20 (1956), pp. 49-67.

3,000 IRWIN, G. European sources for Tropical African history. BOSTON UNIV. PAPERS IN AFR. HIST. 1 (1964), pp. 35-53.

3,001 JENKINSON, H. The records of the English African companies. TRHS, 3rd. series, 6 (1912), pp. 185-220.

3,002 MONTEIL, V. Les manuscrits historiques arabo-africains. BULL. IFAN 27 (1965), pp. 531-542.

3,003 MVENG, E. Les sources de l'histoire négro-africaine: Agatharchide de Cnide. PRESENCE AFR. N.S. 55 (1965), pp. 92-99.

3,004 RIEGER, M. Preliminary report on materials in the National Archives relating to Africa. AFR. STUD. BULL. 2, no. ii (1959), pp. 1-13.

3,005 RIEGER, M. Proposal for compilation of a guide to unpublished documentation relating to Africa in the United States. AFR. STUD. BULL. 5, no. i (1962), pp. 14-18.

3,006 THOMPSON, C. H. Colonial archives: their importance in administration. CORONA 1, no. 9 (1949), pp. 27-29.

3,007 VAUX DE FOLETIER, F. de. Les sources de l'histoire coloniale aux Archives de la Charente-Inférieure. RHCF 28 (1935), pp. 49-64.

3,008 VAUX DE FOLETIER, F. de. Sources d'histoire coloniale aux Archives de la Seine. REV. HIST. COL. 38 (1951), pp. 359-366.

3,009 VIGNOLS, L. La destruction d'Archives Coloniales. RHCF 22 (1929), pp. 45-52.

3,010 The Oxford Colonial Records project. BULL. AFR. STUD. ASSOC. 2 (1964), pp. 18-22.

LANGUAGES. LITERATURE

Language

3,011 AFRICAN SOCIETY. A catalogue of linguistic works in the library of the African Society. J. AFR. SOC. 7 (1908), pp. 284-306, 410-429.

3,012 ALEXANDRE, P. Les problèmes linguistiques africains vus de Paris. LANGUAGE IN AFRICA, 1963, pp. 53-59.

3,013 ALEXANDRE, P. Problèmes linguistiques des Etats négro-africains à l'heure de l'indépendance. CAH. ET. AFR. 2 (1961), pp. 177-195.

3,014 ALEXANDRE, P. Sur la linguistique africaine. PRESENCE AFR. N.S. 41 (1962), pp. 23-33.

3,015 ALEXANDRE, P. Sur les possibilités expressives des langues africaines en matière de terminologie politique. AFR. ET ASIE 56 (1961), pp. 13-28.

3,016 ALEXANDRE, P. Sur quelques aspects internationaux de la linguistique négro-africaine. AFR. ET ASIE 58 (1962), pp. 14-22.

3,017 AMERICO FERREIRA. A presença do Afro-negro na língua portuguesa. PORT. EM AFR. SUPPL. (1960-1961), pp. 168-178.

3,018 ANDRZEJEWSKI, B. W. Emotional bias in the translation and presentation of African oral art. SIERRA LEONE LANG. REV. 4 (1965), pp. 95-102.

3,019 ARMSTRONG, R. G. Glottochronology and African linguistics. J. AFR. HIST. 3 (1962), pp. 283-290.

3,020 ARMSTRONG, R. G. Vernacular languages and cultures in modern Africa. LANGUAGE IN AFRICA, 1963, pp. 64-72.

3,021 ASHTON, E. O. Notes on form and structure in Bantu speech. AFRICA 15 (1945), pp. 4-20.

3,022 ASHTON, E. O. The structure of a Bantu language with special reference to Swahili, or form and function through Bantu eyes. BULL. SOAS 8 (1935-1937), pp. 1111-1120.

3,023 ATKINS, G. Notes on the concords and classes of Bantu numerals. AFR. LANG. STUD. 2 (1961), pp. 42-48.

3,024 BEACH, D. M. The science of tonetics and its application to Bantu languages. BANTU STUD. 2 (1923), pp. 75-106.

3,025 BENSON, T. G. A century of Bantu lexicography. AFR. LANG. STUD. 5 (1964), pp. 64-91.

3,026 BERGER, P. Die mit B.-Île gebildeten Perfektstämme in den Bantusprachen. AFR. UND UB. 28 (1937-1938), pp. 81-122, 199-230, 255-286.

3,027 BLOK, H. P. Negro-African linguistics. LINGUA 3 (1952-1953), pp. 269-294.

3,028 BLOK, H. P. Nieuwe aanwinsten op het gebied van de geluidsopnamen van Afrikaanse talen aan de Rijks-Universiteit te Leiden. KONGO-OVERZEE 18 (1952), pp. 432-437.

3,029 BLOK, H. P. Opmerkingen naar aanlaiding van enige Bantoewerkwoordsvormen. KONGO-OVERZEE 15 (1949), pp. 251-272.

3,030 BOECK, E. DE. Vingernamen bij de Kinderen en Kinderspelen. KONGO-OVERZEE 5 (1939), pp. 36-39.

3,031 BOECK, L. B. DE. La géographie linguistique et les langues bantoues. ZAIRE 4 (1950), pp. 501-513.

3,032 BOECK, L. B. DE. KP en GP in Noord-Bantoe. ZAIRE 2 (1948), pp. 57-63.

3,033 BOURQUIN, W. Entstehung von Nasalen durch den Einfluss von i im Bantu. AFR. UND UB. 23 (1932-1933), pp. 195-202.

3,034 BOURQUIN, W. Notes on the "close vowels" in Bantu. AFR. STUD. 14 (1955), pp. 49-62.

3,035 BOURQUIN, W. Weitere Ur-Bantu-Wortstämme. AFR. UND UB. 38 (1953-1954), pp. 27-48.

3,036 BRINCKER, P. H. Andeutungen über die etymologisch-mythologische Bedeutung der verschiedenen Namen für Vater und Mutter in der Lingua Bantu. ZAOS 3 (1897), pp. 332-337.

3,037 BRINCKER, P. H. Die Bedeutung der Nominalpräformative und deren Pronominalcharaktere und der Verbalaffixe von e. g. sechs Dialekten der Lingua Bantu. ZAOS 3 (1897), pp. 318-331.

3,038 BRINCKER, P. H. Contributions towards Bantu philology. J. AFR. SOC. 3 (1904), pp. 300-305.

3,039 BRINCKER, P. H. Suppositionen über die etymologisch-mythologische Bedeutung der Nominum für Leben, Seele, Geist und Tod in der Lingua-Bantu. ZAOS 1 (1895), pp. 164-168.

3,040 BROSNAHAN, L. F. Some aspects of the linguistic situation in tropical Africa. LINGUA 12 (1963), pp. 54-65.

3,041 BROSNAHAN, L. F. Some historical cases of language imposition. LANGUAGE IN AFRICA, 1963, pp. 7-24.

3,042 BROWNE, G. ST. J. On some aspects of interpreting. J. AFR. SOC. 25 (1926), pp. 321-325.

3,043 BULCK, G. VAN. Cinq nouvelles classifications des langues bantoues. ZAIRE 2 (1948), pp. 969-987.

3,044 BULCK, G. VAN. Cinquante ans de bantouistique dans l'école de C. Meinhof. ZAIRE 5 (1951), pp. 951-958.

3,045 BULCK, G. VAN. Existe-t-il un groupe de langues soudanaises équatoriales? ZAIRE 3 (1949), pp. 607-616.

3,046 BULCK, G. VAN. La linguistique en 1952. ZAIRE 7 (1953), pp. 265-280.

3,047 BULCK, V. VAN. Classification des groupes de langues en Afrique selon Westermann. ZAIRE 4 (1950), pp. 189-201.

3,048 BULCK, V. VAN. Een paar beschouwingen bij C. Doke's Bantubibliografie. KONGO-OVERZEE 12-13 (1946-1947), pp. 151-155.

3,049 BULCK, V. VAN. International Bantu-Sudanese team. AEQUATORIA 15 (1952), pp. 81-92.

3,050 BULCK, V. VAN. Taalstudie op de Bantoetaalgrens (Jun. 1949-Jan. 1951) (International Bantu-Sudanese Team). KONGO-OVERZEE 18 (1952), pp. 35-49.

3,051 CALAME-GRIAULE, G. L'art de la parole dans la culture africaine. PRESENCE AFR. N.S. 47 (1963), pp. 73-91.

3,052 CAPELL, A. Bantu and North Australian: a study in agglutination. AFR. STUD. 10 (1951), pp. 49-57.

3,053 COLE, D. T. African linguistic studies, 1943-1960. AFR. STUD. 19 (1960), pp. 219-229.

3,054 COLE, D. T. Doke's classification of Bantu languages. AFR. STUD. 18 (1959), pp. 197-213.

3,055 COLE-BEUCHAT, P. D. Riddles in Bantu. AFR. STUD. 16 (1957), pp. 133-149.

3,056 COUPEZ, A. La linguistique et le statut des langues africaines. ZAIRE 9 (1955), pp. 705-721.

3,057 CRABTREE, W. A. Bantu speech: a philological study. J. AFR. SOC. 17 (1918), pp. 307-313; 18 (1918), pp. 32-44, 101-113, 202-214, 290-301.

3,058 CRABTREE, W. A. Consonant change in Bantu speech. J. AFR. SOC. 27 (1927), pp. 57-68.

3,059 CRABTREE, W. A. A monumental work [Comparative study of the Bantu and semi-Bantu Languages by H. H. Johnston]. J. AFR. SOC. 19 (1919), pp. 1-14.

3,060 CRABTREE, W. A. The Ntu element in Hausu. BIBLIOTHECA AFR. 2 (1926), pp. 208-228.

3,061 CRABTREE, W. A. Reminiscences and modern theories. J. AFR. SOC. 29 (1930), pp. 499-506.

3,062 CRABTREE, W. A. The systematic study of African languages. J. AFR. SOC. 12 (1913), pp. 177-189.

3,063 CRAWFORD, D. African shibboleths. A new check in phonology. J. AFR. SOC. 4 (1905), pp. 232-237.

3,064 CZERMAK, W. Die Lokalvorstellung und ihre Bedeutung für den grammatischen Aufbau afrikanischer Sprachen. FESTSCHRIFT MEINHOF, 1927, pp. 204-222.

3,065 DAMMANN, E. Afrikasprachliche Literatur in russischer Sprache. AFR. UND UB. 44 (1960), pp. 282-286.

3,066 DAMMANN, E. The influence of religion on African languages. PROC. INT. CONG. AFR. 1 (1962), pp. 115-123.

3,067 DAMMANN, E. Inversiva und repetitiva in Bantusprachen. AFR. UND UB. 43 (1959-1960), pp. 116-127.

3,068 DAMMANN, E. Kontaktiva in Bantusprachen. AFR. UND UB. 46 (1962-1963), pp. 118-126.

3,069 DAMMANN, E. Die Präformative der Demonstrativpronomina in den Bantusprachen. AFR. UND UB. 36 (1951-1952), pp. 31-44.

3,070 DAMMANN, E. Die sogenannten Kausativa auf -eka in Bantusprachen. AFR. UND UB. 42 (1958), pp. 173-178.

3,071 DAMMANN, E. Der Suffixe der Demonstrativa in Bantusprachen. AFR. UND UB. 37 (1952-1953), pp. 21-33, 81-94.

3,072 DAMMANN, E. Tierbezeichnungen in der 3/4. Nominalklasse der Bantusprachen. AFR. UND UB. 47 (1964), pp. 233-244.

3,073 DECLERCQ, A. Les préfixes en langues Bantoues. ZAOS 4 (1898), pp. 179-198.

3,074 DELAFOSSE, M. La numeration chez les nègres. AFRICA 1 (1928), pp. 387-390.

3,075 DENNY, N. Languages and education in Africa. LANGUAGE IN AFRICA, 1963, pp. 40-52.

3,076 DHLOMO, H. I. E. Nature and variety of tribal drama. BANTU STUD. 13 (1939), pp. 33-48.

3,077 DIAGUE, P. Linguistique et culture en Afrique. PRESENCE AFR. N.S. 46 (1963), pp. 52-63.

3,078 DOKE, C. M. Bantu language pioneers of the nineteenth century. AFR. STUD. 18 (1959), pp. 1-27.

3,079 DOKE, C. M. Bantu language pioneers of the nineteenth century. BANTU STUD. 14 (1940), pp. 207-246.

3,080 DOKE, C. M. Bantu languages, inflexional with a tendency towards agglutination. AFR. STUD. 9 (1950), pp. 1-19.

3,081 DOKE, C. M. The basis of Bantu literature. AFRICA 18 (1948), pp. 284-301.

3,082 DOKE, C. M. The earliest records of Bantu. AFR. STUD. 19 (1960), pp. 26-32.

3,083 DOKE, C. M. The earliest records of Bantu. BANTU STUD. 12 (1938), pp. 135-144.

3,084 DOKE, C. M. Early Bantu literature--The Age of Brusciotto. AFR. STUD. 18 (1959), pp. 49-67.

3,085 DOKE, C. M. Early Bantu literature--The Age of Brusciotto. BANTU STUD. 9 (1935), pp. 84-114.

3,086 DOKE, C. M. The growth of comparative Bantu philology. AFR. STUD. 2 (1943), pp. 41-64; 19 (1960), pp. 193-218.

3,087 DOKE, C. M. The linguistic work and manuscripts of R. D. MacMinn. AFR. STUD. 18 (1959), pp. 180-189.

3,088 DOKE, C. M. Scripture translation into Bantu languages. AFR. STUD. 17 (1958), pp. 82-99.

3,089 DOKE, C. M. The significance of Class 1a of Bantu nouns. FESTSCHRIFT MEINHOF, 1927, pp. 196-203.

3,090 DOKE, C. M. Some notes on the infinitive in Bantu. BANTU STUD. 1, no. i (1922), pp. 3-4.

3,091 DREXEL, A. Parallèles Soudanais. BIBLIOTHECA AFR. 1 (1924), pp. 56-61.

3,092 DREXEL, A. Vom Entstehungswert der grammatischen Genuswörter. BIBLIOTHECA AFR. 3 (1929), pp. 231-241.

3,093 DREXEL, A. and GAU, A. Afrikanische Glossen zum indogermanischen Probleme. BIBLIOTHECA AFR. 2 (1927), pp. 334-339.

3,094 EISELEN, W. Die Veränderung der Konsonanten durch ein vorhergehendes i in den Bantusprachen. AFR. UND UB. 14 (1923-1924), pp. 81-153.

3,095 ELLIOTT, A. V. P. The teaching of African languages in African schools; a need for improvement. AFRICA 11 (1938), pp. 73-78.

3,096 ENDEMANN, K. Uber die Wiedergabe von Fremdwörtern und -Namen in Bantusprachen. AFR. UND UB. 1 (1910), pp. 284-289.

3,097 ESTERMANN, P. C. Etnografia e Linguística. PORT. EM AFR. 5 (1948), pp. 219-225.

3,098 FORTUNE, G. The parts of speech in Bantu. NADA 31 (1954), pp. 99-109.

3,099 FORTUNE, G. Some possible contributions of linguistics to vernacular language teaching in African schools. LANGUAGE IN AFRICA, 1963, pp. 73-77.

3,100 FRAZAO, S. Velharias linguísticas. PORT. EM AFR. 2 (1945), pp. 92-97.

3,101 GONZALEZ ECHEGARAY, C. Una encuesta lingüistica en el Africa negra. ARCH. INST. EST. AFR. 14, no. 56 (1960), pp. 41-52.

3,102 GRAEVE, F. DE. Woordkunst van Zwart Afrika. ZAIRE 11 (1957), pp. 525-529.

3,103 GREENBERG, J. H. The classification of African languages. AMER. ANTHR. 50 (1948), pp. 24-30.

3,104 GREENBERG, J. H. Etude sur la classification des langues africaines. BULL. IFAN, Série B: Sciences humaines, 17 (1955), pp. 59-108.

3,105 GREENBERG, J. H. Etude sur la classification des langues africaines; traduit de l'americain par C. Tardits. BULL. IFAN 16 (1954), pp. 83-142.

3,106 GREENBERG, J. H. The history and present status of African linguistic studies. PROC. INT. CONG. AFR. 1 (1962), pp. 85-96.

3,107 GREENBERG, J. H. The labial consonants of Proto-Afro-Asiatic. WORD 14 (1958), pp. 295-302.

3,108 GREENBERG, J. H. Langues et histoire en Afrique. PRESENCE AFR. N.S. 45 (1963), pp. 35-45.

3,109 GREENBERG, J. H. Studies in African linguistic classification. SOUTHWESTERN J. ANTHR. 5 (1949), pp. 79-100, 190-198, 309-317; 6 (1950), pp. 47-63, 143-160, 223-237, 388-398; 10 (1954), pp. 405-415.

3,110 GREENBERG, J. H. The tonal system of Proto-Bantu. WORD 4 (1948), pp. 196-208.

3,111 GREENBERG, J. H. Vowel and nasal harmony in Bantu languages. ZAIRE 5 (1951), pp. 813-820.

3,112 GUTHRIE, M. Bantu origins: a tentative new hypothesis. J. AFR. LANGS. 1 (1962), pp. 9-21.

3,113 GUTHRIE, M. Comparative Bantu: a preview. J. AFR. LANGS. 4 (1965), pp. 40-45.

3,114 GUTHRIE, M. Gender, number and person in Bantu languages. BULL. SOAS 12 (1947-1948), pp. 847-856.

3,115 GUTHRIE, M. Language classification and African studies. AFR. AFFAIRS, Special Issue (1965), pp. 29-36.

3,116 GUTHRIE, M. Observations on nominal classes in Bantu languages. BULL. SOAS 18 (1956), pp. 545-560.

3,117 GUTHRIE, M. Some developments in the prehistory of the Bantu languages. J. AFR. HIST. 3 (1962), pp. 273-282.

3,118 GUTHRIE, M. The status of radical extensions in Bantu languages. J. AFR. LANGS. 1 (1962), pp. 202-220.

3,119 GUTHRIE, M. A two-stage method of comparative Bantu study. AFR. LANG. STUD. 3 (1962), pp. 1-24.

3,120 HADDON, E. The locative in Bantu. AFR. STUD. 10 (1951), pp. 97-105.

3,121 HOFFMANN, C. Zur Verbreitung der Zahlwortstämme in Bantusprachen. AFR. UND UB. 37 (1952-1953), pp. 65-80.

3,122 HOMBURGER, L. De l'origine des classes nominales dans les langues négro-africaines. LINGUA 1 (1947-1948), pp. 235-246.

3,123 HOMBURGER, L. L'Inde et L'Afrique. J. SOC. AFR. 25 (1955), pp. 13-18.

3,124 HOMBURGER, L. La linguistique et l'histoire de l'Afrique. BULL. IFAN, Série B: Sciences humaines, 20 (1958), pp. 554-561.

3,125 HOMBURGER, L. Préfix bantous et égyptiens. INT. CONG. LING. 2 (1931), pp. 236-239.

3,126 HOMBURGER, L. Du rôle des adjectifs qualificatifs dans le développement des systèmes de classes et de genres africains. INT. CONG. LING. 1 (1928), pp. 149-154.

3,127 HOMBURGER, L. Les sonantes en Sindo-africain. J. SOC. AFR. 34 (1964), pp. 281-283.

3,128 HOUIS, M. Comment écrire les langues africaines? PRESENCE AFR. N.S. 17 (1957-1958), pp. 76-92.

3,129 HULSTAERT, G. Taaleenmaking en dialektenstudie. ZAIRE 1 (1947), pp. 885-901.

3,130 HUSSEY, E. R. J. The languages of literature in Africa. AFRICA 5 (1932), pp. 169-175.

3,131 IRELE, A. Le problème des langues en Afrique (à propos de "Language in Africa," de John Spencer). PRESENCE AFR. N.S. 47 (1963), pp. 218-223.

3,132 JAMES, A. L. Phonetics and African languages. AFRICA 1 (1928), pp. 358-371.

3,133 JAMES, A. L. The practical orthography of African languages. AFRICA 1 (1928), pp. 125-129.

3,134 JEFFREYS, M. D. W. Corsali 1515 on Bantu and Sudanic languages. AFR. STUD. 11 (1952), p. 191.

3,135 JEFFREYS, M. D. W. The origin of the Portuguese word zaburro as their name for maize. BULL. IFAN 19 (1957), pp. 111-136.

3,136 JEFFREYS, M. D. W. Some historical notes on African tone languages. AFR. STUD. 4 (1945), pp. 135-145.

3,137 JOHNSTON, Sir H. H. The Bantu and the semi-Bantu languages. J. AFR. SOC. 16 (1917), pp. 97-110.

3,138 JOHNSTON, Sir H. H. The basis for a comparative grammar of the Bantu languages. J. AFR. SOC. 7 (1907), pp. 13-19.

3,139 JOHNSTON, Sir H. H. The origin of the Bantu. J. AFR. SOC. 6 (1907), pp. 329-340.

3,140 JUNOD, H. P. Langues vernaculaires et véhiculaires en Afrique. GENEVE-AFR. 2 (1963), pp. 21-44; English summary, p. 45.

3,141 KAHLER-MEYER, E. Studien zur tonalen Struktur der Bantusprachen. AFR. UND UB. 46 (1962-1963), pp. 1-42, 250-295.

3,142 KLINGENHEBEN, A. Ablaut in Afrika. AFR. UND UB. 21 (1930-1931), pp. 81-98.

3,143 KLINGENHEBEN, A. Influence of analogy in African languages. J. AFR. LANGS. 1 (1962), pp. 30-42.

3,144 KLINGENHEBEN, A. Zum Problem der Silbe in Afrikanischen Sprachen. AFR. UND UB. 37 (1952-1953), pp. 7-20.

3,145 KNAPPERT, J. Compound nouns in Bantu languages. J. AFR. LANGS. 4 (1965), part D, pp. 211-225.

3,146 KNAPPERT, J. Language problems of the new nations of Africa. AFR. QUART. 5, no. 2 (1965), pp. 95-105.

3,147 KNAPPERT, J. Languages unite and divide. EAISR, Jan. (1964), pp. 1-8.

3,148 KOHLER, O. Zur Frage der Unterscheidung der Pronomina pers. conj. ya und yu der Einzahl der Menschenklasse im Bantu. AFR. UND UB. 40 (1956), pp. 85-90.

3,149 LACROIX, P. F. Connaissance et méconnaissance des langues africaines. PRESENCE AFR. N.S. 51 (1964), pp. 87-96.

3,150 LANG, K. Eine vokabularische Skizze zur Stein- und Eisenzeitkultur in Afrika. BIBLIOTHECA AFR. 1 (1924), pp. 27-30.

3,151 LANHAM, L. W. The proliferation and extension of Bantu phonemic systems influenced by Bushman and Hottentot. INT. CONG. LING. 9 (1962), pp. 382-391.

3,152 LEBLANC, M. Evolution linguistique et relations humaines. ZAIRE 9 (1955), pp. 787-799.

3,153 LESTRADE, G. P. Bantu grammatical classification and linguistic nomenclature. BANTU STUD. 10 (1936), pp. 57-65.

3,154 LESTRADE, G. P. The classification of the Bantu languages [review of Malcolm Guthrie's book]. AFR. STUD. 7 (1948), pp. 175-184.

3,155 LONGMORE, L. The future of the Bantu languages. AFR. AFFAIRS 61 (1962), pp. 158-162.

3,156 MADAN, A. C. Early stages of speech and thought in Bantu. J. AFR. SOC. 15 (1915), pp. 24-35.

3,157 MADAN, A. C. Self expression in Bantu. J. AFR. SOC. 14 (1914-1915), pp. 60-74.

3,158 MADAN, A. C. Standards of Bantu speech. J. AFR. SOC. 17 (1917), pp. 25-37.

3,159 MADAN, A. C. The syllabic basis of Bantu. J. AFR. SOC. 13 (1914), pp. 296-306.

3,160 MARTONNE, E. DE. Les noms de lieux d'origine française aux colonies. RHCF 29 (1936), pp. 5-50.

3,161 MAYER, J. L'Université, garant de la pureté du langage dans les pays de langue française. LANGUAGE IN AFRICA, 1963, pp. 60-63.

3,162 MAYR, J. Dravidische Nominalsuffixe und ihre afrikanischen Parallelen. BIBLIOTHECA AFR. 1 (1924), pp. 44-56.

3,163 MEEUSSEN, A. E. L'information en linguistique africaine. AEQUATORIA 25 (1962), pp. 92-94.

3,164 MEEUSSEN, A. E. Klinkerlengte in het Oerbantoe. KONGO-OVERZEE 20 (1954), pp. 423-431.

3,165 MEEUSSEN, A. E. Meinhof's rule in Bantu. AFR. LANG. STUD. 3 (1962), pp. 25-29.

3,166 MEEUSSEN, A. E. Oerbantoe ny-en nj-. KONGO-OVERZEE 20 (1954), pp. 267-269.

3,167 MEEUSSEN, A. E. Le ton de l'infixe en bantou. AEQUATORIA 23 (1960), pp. 130-135.

3,168 MEEUSSEN, A. E. The tones of prefixes in common Bantu. AFRICA 24 (1954), pp. 48-53.

3,169 MEEUSSEN, A. E. La voyelle des radicaux CV en Bantou commun. AFRICA 22 (1952), pp. 367-371.

3,170 MEINHOF, C. Aus der Literatur. AFR. UND UB. 12 (1921-1922), pp. 304-306.

3,171 MEINHOF, C. The basis of Bantu philology. AFRICA 2 (1929), pp. 39-56.

3,172 MEINHOF, C. Dr. C. G. Büttner und die afrikanische Sprachforschung. ZAOS 1 (1895), pp. 329-333.

3,173 MEINHOF, C. Die Entstehung des grammatischen Geschlechts. AFR. UND UB. 27 (1936-1937), pp. 81-90.

3,174 MEINHOF, C. Entstehung und Gebrauch der Lokativendung in Bantusprachen. AFR. UND UB. 32 (1942), pp. 161-164.

3,175 MEINHOF, C. The problems of comparative philology in Africa. J. AFR. SOC. 25 (1926), pp. 326-332; 26 (1926), pp. 40-46.

3,176 MEINHOF, C. Pwani. AFR. UND UB. 32 (1942), pp. 300-302.

3,177 MEINHOF, C. The soul of an African language. INT. REV. MISSIONS 16 (1927), pp. 76-84.

3,178 MEINHOF, C. Sprache und Volkstum. AFRICA 1 (1928), pp. 23-29.

3,179 MEINHOF, C. Das Studium der Kolonialsprachen. AFR. UND UB. 1 (1910), pp. 1-4.

3,180 MEINHOF, C. Verkehrs-Sprachen, Pidgin-Sprachen, Sonder-Sprachen. AFR. UND UB. 29 (1929), pp. 312-313.

3,181 MEINHOF, C. Was Können uns die Hamitensprachen für den Bau des semitischen Verbum lehren? AFR. UND UB. 12 (1921-1922), pp. 241-275.

3,182 MEINHOF, C. and JONES, D. Principles of practical orthography for African languages.—I, II. AFRICA 1 (1928), pp. 228-236, 237-239.

3,183 MEINHOF, D. C. Recent German research in African languages. INT. REV. MISSIONS 1 (1912), pp. 312-318.

3,184 MEYER, E. Das Fragewort in den Bantusprachen. AFR. UND UB. 35 (1949-1950), pp. 81-106.

3,185 MONTEIL, V. La classification des langues de l'Afrique. BULL. IFAN 27 (1965), pp. 155-168.

3,186 MONTEIL, V. Sur l'arabisation des langues négro-africaines. GENEVE-AFR. 2 (1963), pp. 12-19; English summary, p. 20.

3,187 MONTENEGRO, J. P. Breve notícia sobre os nossos gramáticos [Portuguese]. BOL. INST. ANGOLA 3 (1954), pp. 45-48.

3,188 NORTON, W. A. Bantu place names in Africa. BIBLIOTHECA AFR. 1 (1924), pp. 31-43.

3,189 NTAHOKAJA, J. B. La place des langues bantu dans la culture Africaine. KONGO-OVERZEE 23 (1957), pp. 232-241.

3,190 OKARA, G. African speech...English words. TRANSITION 10 (1963), pp. 15-16.

3,191 OTTO, B. A plea for more method. BANTU STUD. 1, no. i (1922), pp. 2-3.

3,192 PANCONCELLI-CALZIA, G. Untersuchungen mit Röntgenstrahlen. AFR. UND UB. 9 (1918-1919), pp. 20-25.

3,193 PARNWELL, E. C. Progressive English for Africans. AFR. STUD. 2 (1943), pp. 162-166.

3,194 PAULHA. Les coloniaux doivent-ils connaître les langues africaines? PRESENCE AFR. 2 (1948), pp. 328-332.

3,195 PIENAAR, P. DE V. A few notes on the phonetic aspect of clicks and the relationship thereof to certain other classes of speech-sounds. BANTU STUD. 10 (1936), pp. 41-55.

3,196 RAUM, O. F. The African chapter in the history of writing. AFR. STUD. 2 (1943), pp. 179-192.

3,197 RICHARDSON, I. Some problems of language classification with particular reference to the northwest Bantu Borderland. AFRICA 25 (1955), pp. 161-169.

3,198 RODRIGUES, A. D. Portugiesische Literatur über afrikanische Sprachen. AFR. UND UB. 42 (1958), pp. 119-134.

3,199 ROWLING, F. The mother tongue for African readers. J. AFR. SOC. 38 (1939), pp. 133-144.

3,200 SAKILIBA, D.-F. Présent et futur des langues africaines. PRESENCE AFR. N.S. 12 (1957), pp. 127-141; N.S. 13 (1957), pp. 65-73.

3,201 SAMARIN, W. J. Intonation in tone languages. AFR. STUD. 11 (1952), pp. 80-82.

3,202 SAMARIN, W. J. Perspective on African ideophones. AFR. STUD. 24 (1965), pp. 117-121.

3,203 SANTOS, L. F. DOS. Línguas Bantas ou Bantu? PORT. EM AFR. 11 (1954), pp. 220-222.

3,204 SCHUMACHER, P. Bantu und Indonesier. Eine sprachvergleichende Studie nebst ethnologischen Bemerkungen. BIBLIOTHECA AFR. 3 (1929), pp. 215-230.

3,205 SEIDENBERG, A. On the Eastern Bantu root for six. AFR. STUD. 18 (1959), pp. 28-34.

3,206 SPENCER, J. Language and independence. LANGUAGE IN AFRICA, 1963, pp. 25-39.

3,207 STAPLETON, W. H. The terms for "right hand" and "left hand" in the Bantu languages. J. AFR. SOC. 4 (1905), pp. 431-433.

3,208 STEVICK, E. W. Two Bantu consonant systems. LANGUAGE 40 (1964), pp. 58-74.

3,209 STRUCK, B. Einige Sudan-Wortstämme. AFR. UND UB. 2 (1911-1912), pp. 233-253, 309-323.

3,210 TASTEVIN, C. Comment il parle [Diversité du Noir Africain]. PRESENCE AFR. 8 (1950), pp. 61-70.

3,211 TEMPELS, P. De studie der Bantoe-talen in het licht der Bantoe-filosofie. KONGO-OVERZEE 12-13 (1946-1947), pp. 225-233.

3,212 THOMAS, N. W. On the position of the dependent genitive. BIBLIOTHECA AFR. 1 (1925), pp. 89-98.

3,213 THOMAS, N. W. The Sudanic languages. BULL. SOAS 1, no. 4 (1920), pp. 107-114.

3,214 TROMBETTI, A. Le lingue dei Papua e gl'idiomi dell'Africa. FESTSCHRIFT MEINHOF, 1927, pp. 146-173.

3,215 TUCKER, A. N. African alphabets and the telegraph problem. BANTU STUD. 10 (1936), pp. 67-73.

3,216 TUCKER, A. N. The meaning and value of comparative Bantu philology. TRANS. PHILOLOGICAL SOC., 1938, pp. 13-24.

3,217 TUCKER, A. N. Philology and Africa. BULL. SOAS 20 (1957), pp. 541-554.

3,218 TUCKER, A. N. The spelling of African place-names on maps. BULL. SOAS 12 (1947-1948), pp. 824-830.

3,219 TUCKER, A. N. Systems of tone-marking African languages. BULL. SOAS 27 (1964), pp. 594-611.

3,220 U TAM'SI, T. Les langues sans écriture. PRESENCE AFR. N. S. 52 (1964), pp. 162-166.

3,221 VANNESTE, M. Het Begrip Kring in verschillende Afrikaansche Talen. KONGO-OVERZEE 7-8 (1941-1942), pp. 204-206.

3,222 VINAY, J. P. Phonétique et langues africaines. J. SOC. AFR. 11 (1941), pp. 95-113.

3,223 VYCICHL, W. Was sind Hamitensprachen? AFRICA 8 (1935), pp. 76-89.

3,224 WALEY, A. and ARMBRUSTER, C. H. The verb to say as an auxiliary in Africa and China. BULL. SOAS 7 (1933-1935), pp. 573-576.

3,225 WANGER, W. Affixless genitive? BIBLIOTHECA AFR. 2 (1926), pp. 232-235.

3,226 WANGER, W. Ntu instead of Bantu. Ntu proper names. BIBLIOTHECA AFR. 1 (1924), pp. 6-18.

3,227 WANGER, W. Ntu philology. J. AFR. SOC. 29 (1930), pp. 401-423.

3,228 WANGER, W. Richtlinien fur eine vergleichende Grammatik der Ntu Sprachen. BIBLIOTHECA AFR. 3 (1929), pp. 59-76, 161-189; 3 (1929-1930), pp. 265-285; 4 (1930-1931), pp. 1-30; 4, no. 2 (1930-1931), pp. 1-21.

3,229 WARD, I. C. The phonetic analysis of African languages. INT. CONG. PHONETIC SCIENCES 1 (1932), pp. 159-161.

3,230 WARD, I. C. Practical suggestions for learning an African language in the field. AFRICA 10, no. 2 (1937), supplement.

3,231 WARD, I. et al. Linguistic principles in literacy development, by I. Ward, M. M. Green, J. Williamson, C. O. Botchway. TOWARDS A LITERATE AFRICA, 1948, pp. 1-13.

3,232 Ward, I. Note on vernacular literature. J. AFR. SOC. 40 (1941), pp. 88-91.

3,233 WARMELD, N. J. V. Early Bantu ethnography: from a philological point of view. AFRICA 3 (1930), pp. 31-48.

3,234 WERNER, A. English contributions to the study of African languages. BIBLIOTHECA AFR. 3 (1929), pp. 199-214. Also in J. AFR. SOC. 29 (1930), pp. 509-528.

3,235 WERNER, A. The languages of Africa. J. AFR. SOC. 12 (1913), pp. 120-135.

3,236 WERNER, A. Note on clicks in the Bantu languages. J. AFR. SOC. 2 (1903), pp. 416-424.

3,237 WERNER, A. Note on the terms used for "right hand" and "left hand" in the Bantu languages. J. AFR. SOC. 4 (1904), pp. 112-116.

3,238 WERNER, A. Recent work in Bantu philology. J. AFR. SOC. 5 (1905), pp. 59-71.

3,239 WERNER, A. Some Bantu linguistic problems. J. AFR. SOC. 28 (1929), pp. 155-165.

3,240 WERNER, A. Some recent linguistic publications. J. AFR. SOC. 9 (1910), pp. 289-310.

3,241 WERNER, A. Zu P. H. Brincker's Aufstz: Andeutungen über die etymologisch-mythologische Bedeutung der verschieden Namen für Vater und Mutter in der Lingua Bantu. ZAOS 4 (1898), pp. 199-200.

3,242 WESCOTT, R. W. Linguistics as a tool in African studies. ANTHROPOLOGY AND AFRICA TODAY, 1962, pp. 606-609.

3,243 WESTERMANN, D. African linguistic classification. AFRICA 22 (1952), pp. 250-256.

3,244 WESTERMANN, D. Aufgaben der Kolonialen Sprachforschung. AFRIKA (Berlin) 1 (1942), pp. 1-6.

3,245 WESTERMANN, D. Charakter und Einteilung der Sudansprachen. AFRICA 8 (1935), pp. 129-148.

3,246 WESTERMANN, D. Koloniale Nachkriegspläne. AFRIKA (Berlin) 3 (1944), pp. 73-82.

3,247 WESTERMANN, D. Notes on a collection of linguistic material. AFRICA 12 (1939), pp. 350-356.

3,248 WESTERMANN, D. The place and function of the vernacular in African education. INT. REV. MISSIONS 14 (1925), pp. 25-36.

3,249 WESTERMANN, D. Sigismund Wilhelm Koelle. Ein Pionier der afrikanischen Sprachforschung. AFR. UND UB. 38 (1953-1954), pp. 49-51.

3,250 WESTERMANN, D. The study of African languages. Present results and future needs. AFRICA 12 (1939), pp. 12-25.

3,251 WILLOUGHBY, W. C. Some conclusions concerning the Bantu conception of the soul. AFRICA 1 (1928), pp. 338-347.

3,252 WILS, J. Het Bantuïde taaltype. KONGO-OVERZEE 18 (1952), pp. 273-281.

3,253 WILSON, C. E. A survey of Christian literature in African languages. INT. REV. MISSIONS 10 (1921), pp. 376-384.

3,254 WIRTH, A. Entwicklung der Bantu. ZAOS 5 (1900), pp. 270-281.

3,255 WOLFF, H. Problems in vernacular orthographies: word division. J. AFR. LANGS. 1 (1962), pp. 221-231.

3,256 ZYHLARZ, E. Das geschichtliche Fundament der hamitischen Sprachen. AFRICA 9 (1936), pp. 433-451.

3,257 ZYHLARZ, E. Das Land Pun.t. AFR. UND UB. 32 (1942), pp. 302-311.

3,258 Bibliographia: African linguistic serial publications. J. AFR. LANGS. 4 (1965), pp. 131-134.

3,259 A handbook of African languages. AFRICA 16 (1946), pp. 156-159.

3,260 Internationale Linguistische Expeditie op de Bantoe-Soedaneze grenslijn (1949-1950). AEQUATORIA 11 (1948), pp. 153-154.

3,261 Languages. AFR. AFFAIRS 44 (1945), pp. 48-49.

3,262 Les langues africaines dans l'Afrique moderne. PRESENCE AFR. N.S. 55 (1965), pp. 193-197.

3,263 The orthography of African names and languages. J. AFR. SOC. 2 (1903), pp. 456-459.

3,264 The spelling of African words. J. AFR. SOC. 5 (1905), pp. 108-109.

3,265 The spelling of names of Bantu languages and tribes in English. BANTU STUD. 11 (1937), pp. 373-375.

3,266 The voice of Africa [specimens of African poetry in English]. AFRICA 1 (1928), pp. 249-258.

See also 259, 654, 940, 2022, 2513, 2791, 2967, 3941, 3944, 4038, 4058, 4580.

Literature: general criticism. history

3,267 ACHEBE, C. The role of the writer in a new nation. NIGERIAN LIBS. 1 (1964), pp. 113-119.

3,268 ALEXIS, J. S. Débat autour des conditions d'un roman national chez les peuples noirs. Où va le roman? PRESENCE AFR. N.S. 13 (1957), pp. 81-101.

3,269 ALLEN, S. W. Negritude: agreement and disagreement. PAN-AFRICANISM RECONSIDERED, 1962, pp. 310-323.

3,270 BASTIDE, R. Naissance de la poésie nègre au Brésil. PRESENCE AFR. 7 (1949), pp. 215-225.

3,271 BEART, C. Congrès des Ecrivains et Artistes Noirs. CIVILISATIONS 6 (1956), pp. 625-628.

3,272 BEIER, U. L. S. Senghor: the theme of the ancestors in Senghor's poetry. BO 5 (1959), pp. 15-17.

3,273 BILEN, M. Le poète africain, chantre de son peuple. PRESENCE AFR. N.S. 54 (1965), pp. 137-141.

3,274 BLAIR, D. African literature in university education. AFR. LIT. AND THE UNIVERSITIES, 1963, pp. 74-79.

3,275 BRAASEM, W. A. Zwarte tam-tam met een blank snoer. Moderne negerlyriek. KONGO-OVERZEE 24 (1958), pp. 179-184.

3,276 BRAMBILLA, C. Alla Sorbona il primo Congesso degli scrittori e artisti negri. AFRICA (Rome) 11 (1956), pp. 206-210.

3,277 BRAMBILLA, C. Temi del 2^e Congresso Mondiale degli scrittori e artisti neri. AFRICA (Rome) 14 (1959), pp. 122-124.

3,278 CLARK, J. P. Poetry in Africa today. TRANSITION 18 (1965), pp. 20-26.

3,279 CREIGHTON, T. R. M. An attempt to define African literature. AFR. LIT. AND THE UNIVERSITIES, 1965, pp. 84-88.

3,280 CREIGHTON, T. R. M. The teaching of literature. AFR. LIT. AND THE UNIVERSITIES, 1965, pp. 115-123.

3,281 DADIE, B. Le conte, élément de solidarité et d'universalité. PRESENCE AFR. 27-28 (1959), pp. 69-80.

3,282 DADIE, B. B. Folklore and literature. PROC. INT. CONG. AFR. 1 (1962), pp. 199-219.

3,283 DATHORNE, O. R. African writers of the eighteenth century. BO 18 (1965), pp. 51-57.

3,284 DEI ANANG. La culture africaine comme base d'une manière d'écriture originale. PRESENCE AFR. 27-28 (1959), pp. 5-10.

3,285 DEMPSTER, R. T. L'écrivain, son travail et son profit. PRESENCE AFR. 36 (1961), pp. 79-84.

3,286 DEPESTRE, R. Reponse à Aimé Césaire (Introduction à un art poétique haïtien). PRESENCE AFR. N.S. 4 (1955), pp. 42-62.

3,287 DESPORTES, G. Points de vue sur la poésie nationale. PRESENCE AFR. N.S. 11 (1957), pp. 88-99.

3,288 DIAKHATE, L. Le Processus d'acculturation en Afrique Noire et ses rapports avec la Négritude. PRESENCE AFR. N.S. 56 (1965), pp. 68-81.

3,289 DIOP, A. The spirit of Présence Africaine. PROC. INT. CONG. AFR. 1 (1962), pp. 46-51.

3,290 DIOP, D. Contribution au débat sur la poésie nationale. PRESENCE AFR. N.S. 6 (1956), pp. 113-115.

3,291 DRAYTON, A. D. McKay's human pity: a note on his protest poetry. BLACK ORPHEUS 17 (1965), pp. 39-48.

3,292 EAST, R. and SANDILANDS, A. The preparation of African literature. TOWARDS A LITERATE AFRICA, 1948, pp. 14-29.

3,293 ELIET, E. Aimé Césaire: poète de la négritude. RECH. AFR. 4 (1962), pp. 3-32.

3,294 F., A. B. Avec Nicolas Guillen. PRESENCE AFR. N.S. 3 (1955), pp. 74-77.

3,295 FONLON, B. African writers meet in Uganda. ABBIA 1 (1963), pp. 39-54; French translation, pp. 55-71.

3,296 FONLON, B. Culture africaine et langues de diffusion. A propos de la Conférence de Kampala. PRESENCE AFR. N.S. 45 (1963), pp. 182-196.

3,297 FRANKLIN, A. Ce nouveau livre qui parle d'eux... PRESENCE AFR. 16 (1954), pp. 421-426.

3,298 FRANKLIN, A. La Négritude: réalité ou mystification? PRESENCE AFR. 14 (1953), pp. 287-303.

3,299 FULLER, H. W. Reverberations from a writers' conference. AFR. FORUM 1 (1965), pp. 78-84.

3,300 GAPPERT, G. Janheinz Jahn and the new Africa. TRANSITION 2 (1961), pp. 40-42.

3,301 GLEASON, J. Out of the irony of words [formal aspects of the new African literature]. TRANSITION 18 (1965), pp. 34-38.

3,302 GLISSANT, E. Le romancier noir et son peuple. Notes pour une conférence. PRESENCE AFR. N.S. 16 (1957), pp. 26-31.

3,303 GORE, J. L. The solitude of Cheikh Kane. Solitude as the theme of Aventure Ambigü by Cheikh Hamidou Kane. AFR. LIT. AND THE UNIVERSITIES, 1965, pp. 27-40.

3,304 GRATIANT, G. D'une poésie martiniquaise dite nationale. PRESENCE AFR. N.S. 5 (1955-1956), pp. 84-89.

3,305 GUBERINA, P. Structure de la poésie noire d'expression française. PRESENCE AFR. N.S. 5 (1955-1956), pp. 52-78.

3,306 GUNTER, H. George Lamming. BO 6 (1959), pp. 39-43.

3,307 HINDMARSH, R. Africa: the inward exploration. TRANSITION 6-7 (1962), pp. 41-45.

3,308 HINDMARSH, R. The bitter thing: The African Image by Ezekiel Mphahlele. TRANSITION 4 (1962), pp. 23-25.

3,309 HOFFMANN, L. F. L'image de la femme dans la poésie haïtienne. PRESENCE AFR. N.S. 34-35 (1960-1961), pp. 183-206.

3,310 HOWLETT, J. Le Ier congrès des écrivains et artistes noirs et la presse internationale. PRESENCE AFR. N.S. 20 (1958), pp. 111-117.

3,311 HOWLETT, J. Spectacle africain à la maison des lettres. PRESENCE AFR. 4 (1948), pp. 705-706.

3,312 IRELE, A. A defence of negritude. A propos of Black Orpheus by Jean Paul Sartre. TRANSITION 13 (1964), pp. 9-11.

3,313 IRELE, A. Négritude—literature and ideology. JMAS 3 (1965), pp. 499-526.

3,314 IRELE, A. Négritude or black cultural nationalism. JMAS 3 (1965), pp. 321-348.

3,315 IRELE, A. The tragic conflict in Achebe's novels. BLACK ORPHEUS 17 (1965), pp. 24-32.

3,316 IVY, J. W. Ecrits nègres aux Etats-Unis. PRESENCE AFR. N.S. 26 (1959), pp. 67-76.

3,317 JAHN, J. Aimé Césaire. BO 2 (1958), pp. 32-36.

3,318 JAHN, J. Rhythm and style in African poetry. AFR. LIT. AND THE UNIVERSITIES, 1965, pp. 51-56.

3,319 JAHN, J. Sur la littérature africaine. PRESENCE AFR. N.S. 48 (1963), pp. 151-162.

3,320 JAHN, J. World Congress of Black writers [September, 1956]. BO 1 (1957), pp. 39-46.

3,321 JAMESON, H. The voice of African patriots in prison. PRESENCE AFR. N.S. 37 (1961), p. 89.

3,322 JEANPIERRE, W. Négritude and its enemies. AFR. LIT. AND THE UNIVERSITIES, 1965, pp. 18-21; reply by E. Mphahlele, pp. 22-26.

3,323 JEANPIERRE, W. A. La "Négritude," vue par un Afro-Américain. PRESENCE AFR. N.S. 39 (1961), pp. 102-117.

3,324 JEANSON, F. Sartre et le monde noir. PRESENCE AFR. 7 (1949), pp. 189-214.

3,325 JONES, E. D. Academic problems and critical techniques. AFR. LIT. AND THE UNIVERSITIES, 1965, pp. 89-95.

3,326 JUIN, H. Aimé Césaire, poète de la liberté. PRESENCE AFR. 4 (1948), pp. 564-575.

3,327 JULY, R. W. African personality: African literature and the African personality. BO 14 (1964), pp. 33-45.

3,328 LAGNEAU-KESTELOOT, L. Introduction à la littérature négro-africaine de langue française. ET. CONG. 1, no. 2 (1961), pp. 32-39.

3,329 LAGNEAU-KESTELOOT, L. Problèmes du critique littéraire en Afrique. ABBIA 8 (1965), pp. 13-28; English translation, pp. 29-44.

3,330 LAMMING, G. The Negro writer and his world. PRESENCE AFR. N.S. 8-10 (1956), pp. 318-325.

3,331 LEBAR, P. Communication de M. P. Lebar, représentant de l'U.N.E.S.C.O. au IIe Congrès des écrivains et artistes noirs. PRESENCE AFR. N.S. 24-25 (1959), pp. 37-39.

3,332 LEBEUF, J. P. Système du monde et écriture en Afrique Noire. PRESENCE AFR. N.S. 53 (1965), pp. 129-135.

3,333 LUBIN, M. A. De la poésie haïtienne. PRESENCE AFR. N.S. 39 (1961), pp. 182-201.

3,334 MARTEAU, P. A propos de "cadastre" d'Aimé Césaire. PRESENCE AFR. N.S. 37 (1961), pp. 125-135.

3,335 MARTEAU, P. "La mort de l'impossible et le mot du printemps." PRESENCE AFR. N.S. 30 (1960), pp. 82-95.

3,336 MAYER, J. Le roman en Afrique noire francophone et l'aventure d'une race. ANN. UNIV. ABIDJAN 1 (1965), pp. 5-16.

3,337 MELONE, T. Le thème de la négritude et ses problèmes littéraires. PRESENCE AFR. N.S. 48 (1963), pp. 133-150.

3,338 MICHELMAN, F. Négritude in French-African literature. PROC. 3RD. GRAD. ACAD. UCLA, 1965, pp. 209-221.

3,339 MKAPA, B. W. What black is black? Thoughts on Jean Genet's The Blacks. TRANSITION 1 (1961), pp. 39-40.

3,340 MODISANE, B. African writers' summit. TRANSITION 5 (1962), pp. 5-6.

3,341 MOORE, G. The language of poetry. AFR. LIT. AND THE UNIVERSITIES, 1965, pp. 96-115.

3,342 MOORE, G. Les lettres africaines vues de Salisbury. PRESENCE AFR. N.S. 31 (1960), pp. 82-89.

3,343 MOORE, G. Macbeth and African drama. TRANSITION 4 (1962), pp. 27-28.

3,344 MOORE, G. Mots anglais, vies africaines. PRESENCE AFR. N.S. 54 (1965), pp. 116-126.

3,345 MOORE, G. Surrealism and negritude in the poetry of Tchikaya U Tam'si. BLACK ORPHEUS 13 (1963), pp. 5-12.

3,346 MOORE, G. Surrealism on the river Congo. Surrealism and négritude in the poetry of Tchicaya U Tam'si. AFR. LIT. AND THE UNIVERSITIES, 1965, pp. 41-50.

3,347 MOORE, G. and STUART, D. African literature, French and English. MAKERERE J. 8 (1963), pp. 29-34.

3,348 MOSER, G. M. African literature in the Portuguese language. J. OF GEN. EDUC. 13 (1961-1962), pp. 270-304.

3,349 MPHAHLELE, E. African literature. PROC. INT. CONG. AFR. 1 (1962), pp. 220-232.

3,350 MPHAHLELE, E. African literature and universities: a report on two conferences to discuss African literature and the university curriculum. TRANSITION 10 (1963), pp. 16-18.

3,351 MPHAHLELE, E. The Freetown Conference: a postscript on Dakar. AFR. LIT. AND THE UNIVERSITIES, 1965, pp. 80-83.

3,352 MPHAHLELE, E. Il negro come scrittore. AFRICA (Rome) 13 (1958), p. 128.

3,353 NGUGI, J. T. A Kenyan at the conference [of African writers]. TRANSITION 5 (1962), p. 7.

3,354 OLIVER, L. M. La resonancia de Africa en Cervantes. ARCH. INST. EST. AFR. 5, no. 17 (1951), pp. 7-20.

3,355 PAGEARD, R. Les grands faits de la vie littéraire dans l'Afrique noire d'expression française en 1964. GENEVE-AFR. 4 (1965), pp. 95-101.

3,356 PAGEARD, R. Soundiata keita et la tradition orale: a propos du livre de Djibril Tamsir Niane: Soundjata ou l'Epopée Mandingue. PRESENCE AFR. 36 (1961), pp. 51-70.

3,357 PIRA, G. L. [Message de Giorgio L. Pira, à l'occasion du IIe Congrès des Ecrivains et Artistes noirs]. PRESENCE AFR. N.S. 24-25 (1959), p. 30.

3,358 PORTER, D. B. Fiction by African authors: a preliminary checklist. AFR. STUD. BULL. 5, no. ii (1962), pp. 54-66.

3,359 POVEY, J. F. How do you make a course in African literature? TRANSITION 18 (1965), pp. 39-42.

3,360 PRICE-MARS, J. Discours du Capitole [au IIe Congrès des écrivains et artistes noirs]. PRESENCE AFR. N.S. 24-25 (1959), pp. 35-36.

3,361 RABEMANANJARA, J. Le poète noir et son peuple. PRESENCE AFR. N.S. 16 (1957), pp. 9-25.

3,362 REED, J. Between two worlds. Some notes on the presentation by African novelists of the individual in modern African society. MAKERERE J. 7 (1963), pp. 1-14.

3,363 ROUCH, J. Vers une littérature africaine. PRESENCE AFR. 6 (1949), pp. 144-146.

3,364 RUBADIRI, D. Why African literature? TRANSITION 15 (1964), pp. 39-42.

3,365 SADJI, A. Littérature et colonisation. PRESENCE AFR. 6 (1949), pp. 139-141.

3,366 SAINVILLE, L. A propos du "débat autour des conditions d'un roman national chez les peuples noirs." PRESENCE AFR. N.S. 18-19 (1958), pp. 217-220.

3,367 SARTRE, J. P. Black Orpheus. PRESENCE AFR. 10 (1951), pp. 219-247.

3,368 SENGHOR, L. S. The poetry of Sedar-Senghor. AFR. SOUTH 2, no. 4 (1958), pp. 111-112.

3,369 SENGHOR, L. S. Suite du débat autour des conditions d'une poésie nationale chez les peuples noirs: Réponse. PRESENCE AFR. N.S. 5 (1955-1956), pp. 79-83.

3,370 SHELTON, A. The black mystique: reactionary extremes in "Negritude." AFR. AFFAIRS 63 (1964), pp. 115-128.

3,371 TAYLOR, J. H. The development of African drama for education and evangelism. INT. REV. MISSIONS 39 (1950), pp. 292-301.

3,372 THIAM. Des contes et des fables en Afrique noire. PRESENCE AFR. 4 (1948), pp. 667-671.

3,373 THOMAS, L.-V. Senghor à la recherche de l'homme "nègre." PRESENCE AFR. N.S. 54 (1965), pp. 7-36.

3,374 TOWET, T. Le rôle d'un philosophe africain. PRESENCE AFR. 27-28 (1959), pp. 108-128.

3,375 WADE, A. M. Autour d'une poésie nationale. PRESENCE AFR. N.S. 11 (1957), pp. 84-87.

3,376 WALI, O. The dead end of African literature? TRANSITION 10 (1963), pp. 13-15.

3,377 WALI, O. The individual and the novel in Africa. TRANSITION 18 (1965), pp. 31-33.

3,378 African literature in the Department of English, University of Ibadan. BULL. AFR. STUD. ASSOC. 2 (1964), p. 22.

3,379 Chants populaires d'Afrique Noire. PRESENCE AFR. 12 (1957), pp. 86-88.

3,380 Conférence de Tachkent (1er au 7 october 1958). PRESENCE AFR. N.S. 22 (1958), pp. 135-137.

3,381 Un débat autour des conditions d'une poésie nationale chez les peuples noirs. PRESENCE AFR. N.S. 4 (1955), pp. 36-38.

3,382 Exposition de littérature noire à New York. ZAIRE 5 (1951), pp. 69-70.

3,383 L'hymne de l'Afrique unifiée. PRESENCE AFR. N.S. 47 (1963), pp. 233-235.

3,384 Justification de la Négritude. PRESENCE AFR. N.S. 49 (1964), pp. 237-240.

3,385 Literatura Africana. PORT. EM AFR. 2 (1945), pp. 98-104, 298-305.

3,386 Négritude. BO 2 (1958), pp. 22-28.

3,387 Où il est question de Négritude, de mythe et de science. PRESENCE AFR. N.S. 50 (1964), pp. 253-255.

3,388 Le séminaire inter-africain de traduction de Libamba. ABBIA 3 (1963), pp. 164-166.

See also 4386, 4684, 8672.

Literature in English

3,389 ABRAHAMS, P. Office boy. PRESENCE AFR. 6 (1949), pp. 84-93.

3,390 ACHEBE, C. Arrow of God [fiction]. TRANSITION 9 (1963), pp. 9-14.

3,391 ACHEBE, C. English and the African writer. TRANSITION 18 (1965), pp. 27-30.

3,392 ACHEBE, C. The voter. BLACK ORPHEUS 17 (1965), pp. 4-7.

3,393 ALLEN, S. W. Be not overly amused. PRESENCE AFR. 7 (1949), p. 301.

3,394 ALLEN, S. W. Little lamb, who made thee? PRESENCE AFR. 7 (1949), p. 300.

3,395 ALLEN, S. W. A moment, please. PRESENCE AFR. 6 (1949), p. 76.

3,396 ALLEN, S. W. Sonnet. PRESENCE AFR. 6 (1949), p. 77.

3,397 ALLEN, S. W. When I am done with Heaven. PRESENCE AFR. 7 (1949), p. 302.

3,398 ASALACHE, K. Metamorphosis [poem]. TRANSITION 17 (1964), p. 41.

3,399 ATTARRAH, C. Tangled web. BLACK ORPHEUS 13 (1963), pp. 27-31.

3,400 BEMBA, S. The dark room [fiction]. TRANSITION 14 (1964), pp. 9-14.

3,401 BROOKS, G. Ballad of Pearl May Lee [with French translation by M. Gautier]. PRESENCE AFR. 1 (1947), pp. 112-119.

3,402 BUCH, V. Saturday afternoon. PRESENCE AFR. 7 (1949), pp. 288-298.

3,403 CAMILLE, R. Our song [a poem]. BO 2 (1958), p. 23.

3,404 CLARK, J. P. Six poems. BLACK ORPHEUS 13 (1963), pp. 22-26.

3,405 CLARK, J. P. Thèmes de la poésie africaine d'expression anglaise. PRESENCE AFR. N.S. 54 (1965), pp. 96-115.

3,406 CYAN. Before sailing [a poem]. NIGERIAN FIELD 24 (1959), p. 79.

3,407 DAMAS, L. Balance sheet [a poem]. BO 2 (1958), p. 25.

3,408 DAMAS, L. Black dolls [a poem]. BO 2 (1958), p. 24.

3,409 DAMAS, L. Black Label. PRESENCE AFR. 4 (1948), pp. 617-624.

3,410 DAMAS, L. Six African poems. BO 6 (1959), pp. 13-15.

3,411 DANE, P. Feet [a poem]. TRANSITION 1 (1961), p. 7.

3,412 DATHORNE, O. R. The acquaintanceship of Constable. BLACK ORPHEUS 17 (1965), pp. 18-26.

3,413 DATHORNE, O. R. Biography. PRESENCE AFR. N.S. 48 (1963), p. 169.

3,414 DATHORNE, O. R. Poem of exile. TRANSITION 15 (1964), p. 54.

3,415 DATHORNE, O. R. Poem of exile (for Abu from London). BLACK ORPHEUS 17 (1965), pp. 57-58.

3,416 DAVIDSON, N. Air journey across Africa. PRESENCE AFR. N. S. 3 (1955), p. 45.

3,417 DEMPSTER, R. T. Africa, it's time—your time. PRESENCE AFR. N.S. 32-33 (1960), pp. 145-146.

3,418 DIPOKO, M. S. Our destiny [a poem]. TRANSITION 12 (1964), pp. 20-21.

3,419 ENRIGHT, D. J. An honest government [a poem]. TRANSITION 21 (1965), p. 9.

3,420 EPELLE, S. Greetings to all Afric's lands: East, North, South, West. PRESENCE AFR. N.S. 32-33 (1960), pp. 147-148.

3,421 GORDIMER, N. Some Monday for sure. TRANSITION 18 (1965), pp. 9-15.

3,422 HARRIS, W. Kanaiwa. BLACK ORPHEUS 13 (1963), pp. 17-21.

3,423 HEAD, B. The green tree [fiction]. TRANSITION 16 (1964), p. 33.

3,424 HEATON, J. Among schoolchildren [a poem]. TRANSITION 16 (1964), p. 37.

3,425 HICKMAN, A. S. The drought has broken [a poem]. NADA 6 (1928), p. 44.

3,426 HIGO, A. Four poems [Ritual murder, Bank of Waste Africa, Myself my slogan, Listen and hear]. TRANSITION 8 (1963), pp. 48-49.

3,427 HINDMARSH, R. Poems. TRANSITION 1 (1961), pp. 6-7.

3,428 HOH, I. K. A lament for mother Africa. PRESENCE AFR. N.S. 41 (1962), pp. 103-105.

3,429 HONWANA, L. B. The hands of the blacks. BLACK ORPHEUS 17 (1965), pp. 11-12.

3,430 HUGHES, L. Africa [a poem]. AFR. SOUTH 1, no. 3 (1957), p. 128.

3,431 HUGHES, L. Africa [a poem]. BO 5 (1959), p. 28.

3,432 HUGHES, L. African question mark [a poem]. BO 5 (1959), p. 29.

3,433 HUGHES, L. Terre du Sud. PRESENCE AFR. N.S. 5 (1955-1956), p. 94.

3,434 IMOKHUEDE, F. A. Negritude [a poem]. BO 10 (1961), p. 6.

3,435 JAMESON, H. Two poems [Yesterday and tomorrow, Africa liberanda est]. PRESENCE AFR. N.S. 31 (1960), pp. 61-65.

3,436 JONES, LE ROI. Poems. BLACK ORPHEUS 17 (1965), pp. 49-50.

3,437 KAIKINI, P. R. Flame of Afro-Asia. AFRICA QUART. 2, no. ii (1962), p. 106.

3,438 KAYPER-MENSAH, A. W. Shapes. PRESENCE AFR. N.S. 20 (1958), p. 61.

3,439 KHALI, B. Negroes' music. PRESENCE AFR. N.S. 3 (1955), pp. 46-47.

3,440 MAMMERI, M. Zebra. BLACK ORPHEUS 13 (1963), pp. 44-49.

3,441 MATTHEWS, J. The party [fiction]. TRANSITION 10 (1963), pp. 9-12.

3,442 MEDHIN, T. G. Home-coming son [a poem]. TRANSITION 13 (1964), p. 51.

3,443 MILLER, A. November in Tangier [a poem]. TRANSITION 20 (1965), p. 36.

3,444 MPHAHLELE, E. The immigrant [a poem]. BO 6 (1959), pp. 23-27.

3,445 MUTIGA, J. G. Enjoy the African night [a poem]. TRANSITION 5 (1962), p. 14.

3,446 NEOGY, R. Poems. TRANSITION 1 (1961), p. 37.

3,447 NEOGY, R. 7T One = 7E Ton. TRANSITION 1 (1961), p. 8.

3,448 NKOSI, L. Potgieter's castle [fiction]. TRANSITION 15 (1964), pp. 13-16.

3,449 NKOSI, L. Two poems. BLACK ORPHEUS 17 (1965), p. 21.

3,450 NORTJE, K. A. Five poems. BO 12 (1962), pp. 24-26.

3,451 NWANKWO, N. Three poems. BLACK ORPHEUS 17 (1965), pp. 22-23.

3,452 OBI, D. S. Winds of Africa [a poem]. BO 10 (1961), p. 10.

3,453 OGOT, G. Ward nine [fiction]. TRANSITION 13 (1964), pp. 41-45.

3,454 OKARA, G. The fisherman's invocation. BLACK ORPHEUS 13 (1963), pp. 34-43.

3,455 OKARA, G. Two poems [Piano and drums, You laughed and laughed and laughed]. BO 6 (1959), pp. 33-34.

3,456 OKIGBO, C. Distances [a poem]. TRANSITION 16 (1964), pp. 9-13.

3,457 OKIGBO, C. Lament of the drums. BLACK ORPHEUS 17 (1965), pp. 13-17.

3,458 OKIGBO, C. Lament of the drums [a poem]. TRANSITION 18 (1965), pp. 16-17.

3,459 OKIGBO, C. The limits [a poem]. TRANSITION 5 (1962), pp. 18-19; 6-7 (1962), pp. 39-40.

3,460 OKIGBO, C. Silences (lament of the silent sisters). TRANSITION 8 (1963), pp. 13-16.

3,461 OLISA, M. Five poems. BO 14 (1964), pp. 46-47.

3,462 PICARDIE, M. Anglo-Saxon dreams [a poem]. AFR. SOUTH 2, no. 1 (1957), p. 106.

3,463 REYNOLDS, R. Emigrant ship. AFR. SOUTH 3, no. 4 (1959), p. 4.

3,464 RIVE, R. Moon over district six. TRANSITION 8 (1963), p. 11.

3,465 ROUMAIN, J. Guinea [a poem]. BO 2 (1958), p. 27.

3,466 ROUMAIN, J. When the Tam-Tam beats [a poem]. BO 2 (1958), p. 28.

3,467 ROY, C. Africa [a poem]. TRANSITION 4 (1962), p. 17.

3,468 SAPRASSASSON, B. Creation. BLACK ORPHEUS 13 (1963), pp. 54-56.

3,469 SCOTT, A. Two poems [African love, Three African memories]. TRANSITION 4 (1962), p. 10.

3,470 SEHEME, L. My pass [a poem]. TRANSITION 8 (1963), p. 49.

3,471 SOYINKA, W. Three poems [The immigrant, ...and the other immigrant, My next door neighbour]. BO 5 (1959), pp. 9-13.

3,472 TAPSON, R. R. A restless spirit. NADA 8 (1930), pp. 75-76.

3,473 TAYLOR, B. John Hanning Speke 1862-1962 [a poem]. TRANSITION 5 (1962), p. 21.

3,474 TAYLOR, B. To Musa [a poem]. TRANSITION 3 (1962), pp. 24-25.

3,475 THEROUX, P. Four poems. BLACK ORPHEUS 17 (1965), pp. 8-10.

3,476 TIROLIEN, G. Prayer of a black boy [a poem]. BO 2 (1958), pp. 26-27.

3,477 TODHUNTER, J. H. An African idyll. NADA 6 (1928), p. 55.

3,478 TONG, R. Bronze Goddess. AFR. AFFAIRS 52 (1953), p. 58.

3,479 U TAM'SI. Madness [from "Brush fire"]. BLACK ORPHEUS 13 (1963), pp. 13-16.

3,480 WELBOURN, H. Three stories for adults. TRANSITION 8 (1963), pp. 44-46.

3,481 WILLIAMS, D. Other leopards [fiction]. TRANSITION 11 (1963), pp. 10-19.

3,482 WILLIAMS, G. A. Seven poems. BLACK ORPHEUS 13 (1963), pp. 50-53.

Literature in French

3,483 ALBERT, A. Poème. PRESENCE AFR. N.S. 49 (1964), pp. 195-198.

3,484 ALBERT, A. La poème de la Basse Mer. PRESENCE AFR. N.S. 45 (1963), pp. 160-163.

3,485 ALEXIS, J. S. La rouille des ans. PRESENCE AFR. N.S. 16 (1957), pp. 89-93.

3,486 ALIMA, E. Négritude. ABBIA 5 (1964), p. 176.

3,487 ASSOUAN, R. Retour. PRESENCE AFR. N.S. 37 (1961), p. 88.

3,488 AZEVEDO, W. D'. Sargasso. PRESENCE AFR. N.S. 47 (1963), pp. 179-180.

3,489 B., A. Afrique Noire, littérature rose [La France et les Noirs by Jean Guéhenno, Le Regard du Roi by Camara Laye]. PRESENCE AFR. N.S. 1 (1955), pp. 133-145.

3,490 BALANDIER, G. La littérature noire de langue française. PRESENCE AFR. 8 (1950), pp. 393-402.

3,491 BASTIDE, R. Dans la forêt sacrée [Pourquoi by Lydia Cabrera]. PRESENCE AFR. N.S. 3 (1955), pp. 83-85.

3,492 BAYE, A. M. Trois poèmes [Témoignage, Sablier, Silhouette]. PRESENCE AFR. N.S. 32-33 (1960), pp. 143-144.

3,493 BOTO, E. Tanga. PRESENCE AFR. N.S. 1 (1955), pp. 126-132.

3,494 BOTO, E. Ville cruelle. PRESENCE AFR. 16 (1954), pp. 7-158.

3,495 BOUCQUEY, E. Présence du "Cahier d'un retour au pays natal" d'Aimé Césaire. La littérature de la négritude. ZAIRE 15 (1961), pp. 95-106.

3,496 CANIE, A. Pour que la vie soit claire. PRESENCE AFR. N.S. 18-19 (1958), pp. 195-196.

3,497 CARTEY, W. G. O. Voix obscures. PRESENCE AFR. N.S. 56 (1965), pp. 82-97.

3,498 CESAIRE, A. Addis-Abéba 1963. PRESENCE AFR. N.S. 47 (1963), pp. 173-175.

3,499 CESAIRE, A. Des crocs. PRESENCE AFR. N.S. 1 (1955), p. 117.

3,500 CESAIRE, A. Eight poems translated by Sangodare Akanji. BO 11 (1962), pp. 36-40.

3,501 CESAIRE, A. Faveur des sèves. PRESENCE AFR. N.S. 1 (1955), p. 119.

3,502 CESAIRE, A. Four poems [Since Akkad, since Elam, since Sumer; Word; Africa; from: Notes on a return to the native country]. BO 2 (1958), pp. 37-41.

3,503 CESAIRE, A. Mémorial de Louis Delgrès. PRESENCE AFR. N.S. 23 (1958-1959), pp. 69-72.

3,504 CESAIRE, A. Message sur l'Etat de l'Union. PRESENCE AFR. N.S. 6 (1956), pp. 119-120.

3,505 CESAIRE, A. Pour saluer le Tiers Monde. PRESENCE AFR. N.S. 26 (1959), pp. 90-91.

3,506 CESAIRE, A. Pour un gréviste assassiné. PRESENCE AFR. N.S. 1 (1955), pp. 120-121.

3,507 CESAIRE, A. Réponse à Depestre poète haïtien. Eléments d'un art poétique. PRESENCE AFR. N.S. 1 (1955), pp. 113-115.

3,508 CESAIRE, A. Statue de Lafcadio Hearn. PRESENCE AFR. N.S. 1 (1955), p. 118.

3,509 CESAIRE, A. Sur la poésie nationale. PRESENCE AFR. N.S. 4 (1955), pp. 39-41.

3,510 CESAIRE, A. Va-t-en chien des nuits. PRESENCE AFR. N.S. 1 (1955), p. 116.

3,511 CISSE, D. La mort du Damel. PRESENCE AFR. 1 (1947), pp. 62-77.

3,512 CORNELL, A. Nevrose. PRESENCE AFR. N.S. 37 (1961), pp. 119-124.

3,513 DADIE, B. B. L'ablation. PRESENCE AFR. 4 (1948), pp. 603-606.

3,514 DADIE, B. B. Chanter l'Afrique. PRESENCE AFR. 6 (1949), pp. 126-127.

3,515 DADIE, B. B. Les Enchères. PRESENCE AFR. N.S. 32-33 (1960), pp. 149-155.

3,516 DADIE, B. B. Le fond importe plus. PRESENCE AFR. N.S. 6 (1956), pp. 116-118.

3,517 DADIE, B. B. La legende "au pays de Kaydara." PRESENCE AFR. N.S. 20 (1958), pp. 53-56.

3,518 DADIE, B. B. Puissance! PRESENCE AFR. 1 (1947), pp. 60-61.

3,519 DADIE, B. B. Reconnaissance et ingratitude. La Vie. PRESENCE AFR. N.S. 20 (1958), pp. 52-53.

3,520 DADIE, B. B. "La route." PRESENCE AFR. 14 (1953), pp. 207-212.

3,521 DELISLE, G. Les Pays que Dieu oublia. PRESENCE AFR. N.S. 18-19 (1958), pp. 199-200.

3,522 DEPESTRE, R. Au soleil des innocents. PRESENCE AFR. N.S. 14-15 (1957), pp. 343-357.

3,523 DEPESTRE, R. Mon cinéma d'enfant noir. PRESENCE AFR. N.S. 5 (1955-1956), pp. 90-93.

3,524 DEPESTRE, R. Poèmes. PRESENCE AFR. N.S. 5 (1955-1956), pp. 90-93.

3,525 DEPESTRE, R. Port de mer. PRESENCE AFR. N.S. 11 (1957), p. 108.

3,526 DEPESTRE, R. Une rose des vents noirs [Coups de pilon by D. Diop, La Ronde des Jours by B. B. Dadié and Lamba et Antsa by J. Rabemananjara]. PRESENCE AFR. N.S. 11 (1957), pp. 110-115.

3,527 DERMENGHEM, E. L'histoire du singe fidèle. PRESENCE AFR. 2 (1948), pp. 267-271.

3,528 DESPORTES, G. Mon Île. PRESENCE AFR. N.S. 6 (1956), pp. 121-122.

3,529 DIAKHATE, L. Pour la jeune fille de soie noire. PRESENCE AFR. N.S. 3 (1955), p. 48.

3,530 DIOP, B. Le prétexte. PRESENCE AFR. 6 (1949), pp. 94-99.

3,531 DIOP, B. Le taureau de Bouki. PRESENCE AFR. N.S. 18-19 (1958), pp. 201-207.

3,532 DIOP, D. Africa [a poem]. BO 5 (1959), p. 49.

3,533 DIOP, D. Afrique. PRESENCE AFR. 6 (1949), p. 125.

3,534 DIOP, D. A un enfant noir. PRESENCE AFR. N.S. 4 (1955), p. 63.

3,535 DIOP, D. Auprès de toi. PRESENCE AFR. 14 (1953), p. 190.

3,536 DIOP, D. Certitude. PRESENCE AFR. 14 (1953), p. 187.

3,537 DIOP, D. La cuiller sale. PRESENCE AFR. 6 (1949), pp. 100-107.

3,538 DIOP, D. En mémoire du poète trop tôt disparu. [A ma mère]. PRESENCE AFR. N.S. 32-33 (1960), p. 139.

3,539 DIOP, D. Les heures. PRESENCE AFR. 14 (1953), p. 188.

3,540 DIOP, D. Poètes africains [A. R. Bolamba, F. N'dsitouna, K. P. Joachim, M. Sinda]. PRESENCE AFR. N.S. 3 (1955), pp. 79-80.

3,541 DIOP, D. Le rénégat. PRESENCE AFR. 7 (1949), p. 305.

3,542 DIOP, D. The renegade [a poem]. BO 5 (1949), p. 48.

3,543 DIOP, D. Trois poèmes [Le temps du martyr, Celui qui a tout perdu..., Souffre pauvre nègre...]. PRESENCE AFR. 2 (1948), pp. 235-236.

3,544 DIOP, D. Vagues. PRESENCE AFR. 14 (1953), p. 189.

3,545 DIOP, D. The vultures [a poem]. BO 5 (1959), p. 50.

3,546 DIOP, D. Your presence [a poem]. BO 5 (1959), p. 51.

3,547 FELIX-TCHICAYA, G. Le vertige. PRESENCE AFR. N.S. 13 (1957), pp. 77-80.

3,548 GHARTEY, D. E. B. Lion du pays. PRESENCE AFR. N.S. 32-33 (1960), pp. 163-165.

3,549 GLISSANT, E. Afrique. PRESENCE AFR. N.S. 17 (1957-1958), pp. 93-98.

3,550 GRATIANT, G. L'Arc-en-ciel noir. PRESENCE AFR. N.S. 7 (1956), pp. 98-101.

3,551 GRATIANT, G. Ça n'est plus de jeu! PRESENCE AFR. N.S. 20 (1958), pp. 57-60.

3,552 GUILLEN, N. Elégie à Jacques Roumain. PRESENCE AFR. N.S. 4 (1955), pp. 64-69.

3,553 GUILLEN, N. The name [a poem]. BO 7 (1960), pp. 8-10.

3,554 HUGHES, L. Terre du Sud. PRESENCE AFR. N.S. 5 (1955-1956), p. 94.

3,555 JOACHIM, P. L'heure negrè. PRESENCE AFR. N.S. 16 (1957), pp. 80-82.

3,556 JOACHIM, P. Un poème inédit: Pour saluer l'Afrique à l'envol rendu libre. PRESENCE AFR. N.S. 32-33 (1960), pp. 140-142.

3,557 JOACHIM, P. Le sang de Bandoeng. PRESENCE AFR. N.S. 4 (1955), pp. 73-74.

3,558 JUIN, H. Le songe de Toussaint Louverture. PRESENCE AFR. N.S. 16 (1957), pp. 83-88.

3,559 KALUNGANO. Où suis-je? PRESENCE AFR. N.S. 20 (1958), pp. 62-63.

3,560 KANIE, A. Les égocentriques. PRESENCE AFR. 14 (1953), p. 191.

3,561 LAPLAYNE, J.-R. Le noir n'est pas qu'une couleur. PRESENCE AFR. 6 (1949), p. 134.

3,562 LAPLAYNE, J.-R. Poèmes noirs. PRESENCE AFR. 6 (1949), p. 83.

3,563 LARGIE, S. A. Je parlerai. PRESENCE AFR. 7 (1949), p. 304.

3,564 LARGIE, S. A. La route du soleil. PRESENCE AFR. 6 (1949), p. 78.

3,565 LAYE, C. The black lion [fiction]. BO 14 (1964), pp. 21-24.

3,566 LAYE, C. Et demain? PRESENCE AFR. N.S. 14-15 (1957), pp. 290-295.

3,567 LAYE, C. Les yeux de la statue. PRESENCE AFR. N.S. 13 (1957), pp. 102-110.

3,568 MARAN, R. Les saisons et les jours. PRESENCE AFR. N.S. 17 (1957-1958), pp. 99-110.

3,569 MARSHALLDAVIS, F. Pour toi. PRESENCE AFR. 7 (1949), p. 303.

3,570 M'BITI, J. S. Wavata et l'limu. PRESENCE AFR. N.S. 32-33 (1960), pp. 160-162.

3,571 MEDEDJI, C. A Anoma. PRESENCE AFR. N.S. 1 (1955), p. 122.

3,572 MEDEDJI, C. Nou do gbe si. PRESENCE AFR. 14 (1953), pp. 192.

3,573 MINNE, J. Terre bantoue. AFRICA (Rome) 14 (1959), pp. 29-30.

3,574 NIGER, P. Au rendez-vous des Palmeraies. PRESENCE AFR. 6 (1949), pp. 113-116.

3,575 NIGER, P. Je n'aime pas l'Afrique. PRESENCE AFR. 3 (1948), pp. 432-440.

3,576 NIGER, P. Poème de Paul Niger. PRESENCE AFR. N.S. 29 (1959-1960), pp. 62-63.

3,577 NYUNAI, R. Chansons cubaines et autres poèmes de Nicolas Guillen. PRESENCE AFR. N.S. 3 (1955), pp. 81-82.

3,578 OUEGIN, M. Négresses. PRESENCE AFR. N.S. 13 (1957), pp. 74-75.

3,579 OUSMANE, S. La mère. PRESENCE AFR. N.S. 17 (1957-1958), pp. 111-112.

3,580 PALACIOS, A. La forêt et la pluie. PRESENCE AFR. N.S. 5 (1955-1956), pp. 95-100.

3,581 PATRI, A. Deux poètes noirs en langue française. PRESENCE AFR. 3 (1948), pp. 378-387.

3,582 PATRI, A. Le message philosophique et poétique de Malcolm de Chazal. PRESENCE AFR. 1 (1947), pp. 137-142.

3,583 PHILOMBE, R. Hymne d'Addis-Abéba. ABBIA 5 (1964), pp. 172-173.

3,584 RABEMANANJARA, J. Pâques 48. PRESENCE AFR. 6 (1949), pp. 108-110.

3,585 RABEMANANJARA, J. Pour Marcelle. PRESENCE AFR. N.S. 4 (1955), pp. 70-72.

3,586 RANAIVO, F. Songes d'emprunt. PRESENCE AFR. N.S. 13 (1957), p. 76.

3,587 ROUMAIN, J. Bois d'ébène. PRESENCE AFR. 2 (1948), pp. 230-234.

3,588 ROY, F. J. La disgrace de stones. PRESENCE AFR. N.S. 31 (1960), pp. 66-81.

3,589 SENGHOR, L. S. Chant de l'initié. PRESENCE AFR. 1 (1947), pp. 56-59.

3,590 SENGHOR, L. S. Elégie des circoncis. PRESENCE AFR. N.S. 22 (1958), pp. 74-75.

3,591 SENGHOR, L. S. Latinité et Négritude. (Discours à l'Université de Bahia.) PRESENCE AFR. N.S. 52 (1964), pp. 5-13.

3,592 SENGHOR, L. S. Night of sine [a poem]. BO 5 (1959), p. 18.

3,593 SENGHOR, L. S. Prayer to masks [a poem]. BO 1 (1957), p. 22.

3,594 SY, L. Frère Blanc. PRESENCE AFR. N.S. 12 (1957), p. 88.

3,595 TIDIANY, C. S. Belafong et frénésie. PRESENCE AFR. 14 (1953), pp. 196-197.

3,596 TIDIANY, C. S. Espoir. PRESENCE AFR. 14 (1953), pp. 193-194.

3,597 TIDIANY, C. S. Martyrs. PRESENCE AFR. 14 (1953), p. 195.

3,598 TIROLIEN, G. Deux poèmes [Gouaches, Fama Moussa]. PRESENCE AFR. N.S. 31 (1960), pp. 58-60.

3,599 TRAORE-LEROUX, C. Deux poèmes [including Noire Solitude]. PRESENCE AFR. 7 (1949), p. 299.

3,600 U TAM'SI, T. L'affiche. PRESENCE AFR. N.S. 30 (1960), pp. 72-73.

3,601 U TAM'SI, T. Le pardon de l'adieu. PRESENCE AFR. N.S. 30 (1960), pp. 74-76.

3,602 WADE, A. M. J'aime... PRESENCE AFR. 14 (1953), p. 198.

3,603 WADE, A. M. Les "civilisateurs." PRESENCE AFR. 14 (1953), p. 202.

3,604 WADE, A. M. Rappelle-toi. PRESENCE AFR. 14 (1953), p. 199.

3,605 WRIGHT, R. Claire étoile du matin [translated by Boris Vian]. PRESENCE AFR. 1 (1947), pp. 120-135; 2 (1948), pp. 299-316.

3,606 IIe Congrès des Ecrivains et Artistes noirs [special number]. PRESENCE AFR. N.S. 24-25 (1959).

3,607 Sokamé. Adaptation d'un conte indigène. PRESENCE. AFR. 4 (1948), pp. 627-641.

Literature in other languages

3,608 BRANDT, W. De donkere lier. KONGO-OVERZEE 24 (1958), pp. 162-169.

3,609 BURSSENS, A. Nederlandsche koloniale literatuur. Joos van Ghistele. KONGO-OVERZEE 3 (1936-1937), pp. 226-229.

3,610 CAMOES, L. DE. Tomada de Ceuta. PORT. EM AFR. 4 (1947), p. 219.

3,611 CASIMIRO, A. Oração da noite africana [a poem]. PORT. EM AFR. 16 (1959), pp. 53-54.

3,612 CASTRO, A. O. DE. Luso Africanas [a poem]. PORT. EM AFR. 10 (1953), p. 186.

3,613 COUCEIRO, H. DE P. O sonho do soldado. PORT. EM AFR. 1 (1944), pp. 87-89.

3,614 DUYOS, R. Poesías de tema africano. ARCH. INST. EST. AFR. 8, no. 33 (1955), pp. 41-65.

3,615 MONTEYNE, L. Nederlandsche koloniale literatuur. M. H. Székely-Lulofs. - L. Székely. - Fr. Demers. KONGO-OVERZEE 3 (1936-1937), pp. 99-102.

3,616 MULLER, S. A febre de Africa. PORT. EM AFR. 2 (1945), p. 278.

3,617 NOBRE, A. Lisboa Imperial. PORT. EM AFR. 3 (1946), p. 99.

3,618 SAN-BENTO, O. Poemas... PORT. EM AFR. 11 (1954), p. 288.

3,619 SILVA, P. A. DA. Literatura africana. PORT. EM AFR. 3 (1946), pp. 217-221.

3,620 VEIGA, J. Poesia Negra em Jorge de Lima. PORT. EM AFR. 11 (1954), pp. 173-180.

L A W

3,621 THE AFRICAN STUDIES BRANCH. Methods of recording native customary law. J. AFR. ADM. 1 (1949), pp. 130-136.

3,622 ALLOTT, A. N. African legal education. [Foreword to special number.] J. AFR. LAW 6 (1962), pp. 75-80.

3,623 ALLOTT, A. N. African legal studies in the United Kingdom. BULL. AFR. STUD. ASSOC. 2 (1964), pp. 12-15.

3,624 ALLOTT, A. N. Arbitral proceedings in customary law. J. AFR. ADM. 9 (1957), pp. 96-100.

3,625 ALLOTT, A. N. The authority of English decisions in colonial courts. J. AFR. LAW 1 (1957), pp. 23-39.

3,626 ALLOTT, A. N. The changing law in a changing Africa. SOCIOLOGUS 11 (1961), pp. 115-131.

3,627 ALLOTT, A. N. Codification and unification of laws in Africa. AFRICA QUART. 3, no. iii (1963), pp. 187-200.

3,628 ALLOTT, A. N. The extent of the operation of native customary law. J. AFR. ADM. 2 (1950), pp. 4-11.

3,629 ALLOTT, A. N. The future of African law. AFR. LAW: ADAPTATION AND DEVELOPMENT, 1965, pp. 216-240.

3,630 ALLOTT, A. N. Legal development and economic growth in Africa. CHANGING LAW IN DEVELOPING COUNTRIES, 1963, pp. 194-209.

3,631 ALLOTT, A. N. The London Conference on the future of law in Africa. AFR. STUD. BULL. 3, no. ii (1960), pp. 13-15.

3,632 ALLOTT, A. N. Methods of legal research into customary law. J. AFR. ADM. 5 (1953), pp. 172-177.

3,633 ALLOTT, A. N. Native land courts. J. AFR. ADM. 1 (1949), pp. 82-86.

3,634 ALLOTT, A. N. The place of African customary law in modern African legal systems. PROC. INT. CONG. AFR. 1 (1962), pp. 190-196.

3,635 ALLOTT, A. N. The problem of practical training for law students in Africa. J. AFR. LAW 5 (1961), pp. 123-124.

3,636 ALLOTT, A. N. The recording of customary law in British Africa and the restatement of African law project. LA REDACTION DES COUTUMES DANS LE PASSE ET DANS LE PRESENT, 1962, pp. 197-232.

3,637 ALLOTT, A. N. Towards a definition of "absolute ownership." J. AFR. LAW 5 (1961), pp. 99-102, 145-150.

3,638 ALLOTT, A. N. L'unité de droit africain. PRESENCE AFR. 27-28 (1959), pp. 343-358.

3,639 ALLOTT, A. N. United Kingdom [: African legal education]. J. AFR. LAW 6 (1962), pp. 156-157.

3,640 ALLOTT, A. N. The unity of African law. J. AFR. ADM. 11 (1959), pp. 72-83.

3,641 AMADEO, G. La notion de résidence habituelle dans le Code du travail des territoires d'Outre-Mer. RJPUF 11 (1957), pp. 761-785.

3,642 ANDERSON, J. N. D. The adaptation of Muslim law in sub-Saharan Africa. AFR. LAW: ADAPTATION AND DEVELOPMENT, 1965, pp. 149-164.

3,643 ANDERSON, J. N. D. Customary law and Islamic law in British African territories. THE FUTURE OF CUSTOMARY LAW IN AFRICA, 1956, pp. 70-87.

3,644 ANDERSON, J. N. D. Islamic law in African colonies. CORONA 3 (1951), pp. 262-266.

3,645 ANDERSON, J. N. D. Islamic law in Africa: problems of today and tomorrow. CHANGING LAW IN DEVELOPING COUNTRIES, 1963, pp. 164-183.

3,646 ANDERSON, J. N. D. Law and custom in Muslim areas in Africa. Recent developments in Nigeria. CIVILISATIONS 7 (1957), pp. 17-31.

3,647 ANDERSON, J. N. D. Muslim procedure and evidence. J. AFR. ADM. 1 (1949), pp. 123-129, 176-183.

3,648 ANDERSON, J. N. D. Relationship between Islamic and customary law in Africa. J. AFR. ADM. 12 (1960), pp. 228-234.

3,649 ANOZIE, I. O. and READ, J. S. Colloquium on African law, London, June, 1963. Codification and unification of laws in Africa. J. AFR. LAW 7 (1963), pp. 72-83.

3,650 ARBOUSSIER, G. D'. L'évolution de la législation dans les pays africains d'expression française et à Madagascar. AFR. LAW: ADAPTATION AND DEVELOPMENT, 1965, pp. 165-183.

3,651 ARBOUSSIER, G. D'. Les problèmes nouveaux du droit africain. PRESENCE AFR. N.S. 50 (1964), pp. 5-19.

3,652 ARBOUSSIER, G. D'. The significance of the Lagos Conference. J. INT. COMM. JURISTS 3, no. i (1961), pp. 22-24.

3,653 ATANGANA, N. Analyse juridique des décrets de la "loi-cadre." PRESENCE AFR. N.S. 18-19 (1958), pp. 75-81.

3,654 BENOIT, F. P. Des conditions du développement d'un droit administratif autonome dans les états nouvellement indépendants. ANNALES AFR., 1962, pp. 129-138.

3,655 BETHUNE, E. DE and STAMPA, L. Quelques problèmes constitutionnels des pays neufs. ZAIRE 14 (1960), pp. 439-466.

3,656 BHELY-QUENUM, O. Africa and human rights. TRANSITION 18 (1965), pp. 18-19.

3,657 BLONDEL, A. Problèmes posés par le développement de l'aviation en Afrique. ANNALES AFR., 1962, pp. 139-150.

3,658 BOISDON, D. Note sur les conflits entre le statut civil français et les statuts civils coutumiers dans les pays d'Outre-Mer dépendant de la République française. THE FUTURE OF CUSTOMARY LAW IN AFRICA, 1956, pp. 130-141.

3,659 BOURJOL, M. Essai sur les transformations et l'évolution dialectique de la famille africaine de la gens au ménage. RJPUF 11 (1957), pp. 81-100.

3,660 BRAUSCH, G. E. J.-B. African ethnocracies: some sociological implications of constitutional change in emergent territories of Africa. CIVILISATIONS 13 (1963), pp. 82-94; French summary, pp. 95-97.

3,661 BROOKE, N. J. The changing character of customary courts. J. AFR. ADM. 6 (1954), pp. 67-73.

3,662 BROSSEL, C. Le nouveau droit social international des colonies. ZAIRE 1 (1947), pp. 1085-1110.

3,663 BROWNE, G. ST. J. O. Witchcraft and British colonial law. AFRICA 8 (1935), pp. 481-487.

3,664 BULCK, G. VAN. L'empêchement de parenté en droit coutumier africain. ZAIRE 13 (1959), pp. 339-385.

3,665 CATRICE, P. Un an de législation sociale à l'Assemblée de l'Union Française. ZAIRE 3 (1949), pp. 909-913.

3,666 CHABAS, J. La sanction pénale des actes réglementaires pris par les représentants du Gouvernement dans les départements et les territoires d'outre-mer. RJPUF 2 (1948), pp. 29-58.

3,667 CHABAS, J. Le statut personnel des autochtones de l'Afrique noire Française. CIVILISATIONS 3 (1953), pp. 199-210; English summary, pp. 210-213.

3,668 CHITEPO, H. W. The responsibility of the judiciary and of the bar for protection of the rights of the individual in society. AFR. CONF. ON THE RULE OF LAW, 1961, pp. 69-81.

3,669 COTRAN, E. African Conference on local courts and customary law. J. LOCAL ADM. OV. 4 (1965), pp. 128-133.

3,670 DAVID, R. La réfonte du Code civil dans les Etats africain. ANNALES AFR., 1962, pp. 160-170.

3,671 DECOTTIGNIES, R. L'application du Code de la nationalité dans les Territoires d'outre-mer. ANNALES AFR., 1954, pp. 49-90.

3,672 DECOTTIGNIES, R. Nationalité et citoyenneté 1959 en Afrique Noire. ANNALES AFR., 1959, pp. 41-71.

3,673 DECOTTIGNIES, R. La personnalité morale en Afrique Noire. ANNALES AFR., 1958, pp. 11-36.

3,674 DECOTTIGNIES, R. Requiem pour la famille africaine. ANNALES AFR., 1965, pp. 251-286.

3,675 DERRETT, J. D. M. Justice, equity and good conscience. CHANGING LAW IN DEVELOPING COUNTRIES, 1963, pp. 114-153.

3,676 DOUGLASS, M. L'homme primitif et la loi. ZAIRE 10 (1956), pp. 367-374.

3,677 DRIBERG, J. H. The African conception of law. J. AFR. SOC. 34 (1935), supplement.

3,678 ELIAS, T. O. Customary law: the limits of its validity in colonial law. AFR. STUD. 13 (1954), pp. 97-107.

3,679 ELIAS, T. O. The evolution of law and government in modern Africa. AFR. LAW: ADAPTATION AND DEVELOPMENT, 1965, pp. 184-195.

3,680 ELIAS, T. O. Insult as an offence in African customary law. AFR. AFFAIRS 53 (1954), pp. 66-69.

3,681 ELIAS, T. O. Reflections on the Law of Lagos. J. INT. COMM. JURISTS 3, no. i (1961), pp. 25-28.

3,682 ENTREVAN, C. Réflexions sur la valeur des Constitutions. ANNALES AFR., 1963, pp. 107-133.

3,683 FERREIRA, F. Necessidade de se aperfeiçoar a legislação e a jurisprudência nas nossas Províncias Ultramarinas. BSEM 100 (1956), pp. 45-52.

3,684 GASSE, V. L'immatriculation foncière et la jurisprudence. RJPUF 7 (1953), pp. 157-175.

3,685 GEORGES, P. La communauté conventionnelle: évolution et structure. ANNALES AFR., 1961, pp. 85-104.

3,686 GERARD, J. Essai sur la coutume des traditions précaires mobilières. ZAIRE 11 (1957), pp. 613-621.

3,687 GLEDHILL, A. Fundamental rights. CHANGING LAW IN DEVELOPING COUNTRIES, 1963, pp. 81-96.

3,688 GLUCKMAN, M. Reasonableness and responsibility in the law of segmentary societies. AFR. LAW: ADAPTATION AND DEVELOPMENT, 1965, pp. 120-146.

3,689 GONIDEC, P. F. Les assemblées locales des territoires d'outre-mer. RJPUF 6 (1952), pp. 317-355; 7 (1953), pp. 443-491.

3,690 GONIDEC, P. F. La Convention collective dans les Territoires d'outre-mer. ANNALES AFR., 1955, pp. 7-39.

3,691 GONIDEC, P. F. L'évolution des Territoires d'outre-mer depuis 1946. RJPUF 11 (1957), pp. 429-477, 701-728.

3,692 GONIDEC, P. F. Métamorphoses du Commonwealth. RJPUF 4 (1950), pp. 229-253.

3,693 GONIDEC, P. F. Un mystique de l'égalité: le Code du travail des territoires d'outre-mer. RJPUF 7 (1953), pp. 176-196.

3,694 GOODHART, A. L. The importance of a definition of law. J. AFR. ADM. 3 (1951), pp. 106-109.

3,695 GORCE, J. Les accidents du travail dans les territoires français d'Afrique. RJPUF 5 (1951), pp. 169-193.

3,696 GOURON, A. Le concours d'un droit écrit et d'un droit coutumier et l'expérience médiévale française. ANNALES AFR., 1962, pp. 197-205.

3,697 GRAY, J. *Islamic Law in Africa* by J. N. D. Anderson. J. AFR. ADM. 7 (1955), pp. 33-36.

3,698 HODGSON, P. C. Error jurisdiction in native courts. J. AFR. ADM. 7 (1955), pp. 131-135.

3,699 HOMONT, A. L'application du régime de la tutelle aux territoires sous mandat. RJPUF 6 (1952), pp. 149-179.

3,700 J., H. M. G. On interpretation and mendacity. NADA 4 (1926), p. 121.

3,701 JARVIS, K. Transfer of lawyers within the Commonwealth. COMM. AND EMP. LAW CONF. 2 (1960), pp. 346-390.

3,702 JAUFFRET, A. La réforme de la législation maritime dans les pays en voie de développement et notamment dans les nouveaux Etats d'Afrique. ANNALES AFR., 1962, pp. 213-218.

3,703 JEAREY, J. H. Trial by jury and trial with the aid of assessors in the superior courts of British African territories. J. AFR. LAW 4 (1960), pp. 133-146; 5 (1961), pp. 36-47, 82-98.

3,704 JUNOD, H. P. African penal conceptions and the emancipation of African states. GENEVE-AFR. 1 (1962), pp. 156-175; French summary, pp. 176-178.

3,705 KERR, A. J. Some recent studies of native law. AFR. STUD. 15 (1956), pp. 139-144.

3,706 KNOX-MAWER, R. The jury system in British colonial Africa. J. AFR. LAW 2 (1958), pp. 160-163.

3,707 KOLLEWIJN, R. D. Le statut personnel des autochtones. CIVILISATIONS 3 (1953), pp. 227-231; English summary, pp. 231-232.

3,708 LAFORCADE, R. DE. Problèmes juridiques et politiques posés par la multiplication des juridictions internationales. ANNALES AFR., 1960, pp. 155-174.

3,709 LAMPUE, P. L'étendue d'application du statut personnel des autochtones dans les territoires français d'outre-mer. CIVILISATIONS 7 (1957), pp. 1-13; English summary, pp. 13-15.

3,710 LAMPUE, P. La promulgation des lois et des décrets dans les Territoires d'outre-mer. ANNALES AFR., 1956, pp. 7-26.

3,711 LARGUIER, J. Chronique de jurisprudence criminelle. ANNALES AFR., 1955, pp. 109-132; 1956, pp. 121-139; 1957, pp. 79-95; 1958, pp. 159-177; 1959, pp. 129-149; 1960, pp. 123-153; 1961, pp. 105-115.

3,712 LAVROFF, D. G. Documentation législative et administrative africaine. ANNALES AFR., 1960, pp. 273-467.

3,713 LEGOUX, P. La réglementation minière des territoires français d'Afrique noire et de Madagascar. RJPUF 4 (1950), pp. 24-49, 198-228.

3,714 LERUGAR, L. Europa y Africa: juicios federalistas. CUAD. EST. AFR. 23 (1953), pp. 9-24.

3,715 LETOCHA, T. Seminar on problems of state and law in contemporary Africa. AFR. BULL. 2 (1965), pp. 99-101.

3,716 LEVY, D. Documentation législative et administrative africaine. ANNALES AFR., 1959, pp. 295-462.

3,717 LEWIN, J. Native courts and British justice in Africa. AFRICA 14 (1944), pp. 448-452.

3,718 LEWIN, J. The recognition of native law and custom in British Africa. J. AFR. SOC. 37 (1938), supplement.

3,719 LITTLEWOOD, Sir S. The legal profession in African territories. CHANGING LAW IN DEVELOPING COUNTRIES, 1963, pp. 154-163.

3,720 LIVERSAGE, V. Les tenures tribales et leur décomposition. PRESENCE AFR. 13 (1952), pp. 152-169.

3,721 LOUSSOUARN, Y. La nationalité des sociétés dans les législations du développement. ANNALES AFR., 1962, pp. 219-228.

3,722 LOVERIDGE, A. J. The future of native courts. J. AFR. ADM. 1 (1949), pp. 7-18.

3,723 LUCHAIRE, F. Le champ d'application des statuts personnels en Algérie et dans les territoires d'Outre-mer. RJPUF 9 (1955), pp. 1-52.

3,724 MACAULAY, B. Students for law schools and faculties in Africa. J. AFR. LAW 6 (1962), pp. 81-90.

3,725 MCPETRIE, J. C. Survey of constitutions drafted at the Colonial Office since 1944. CHANGING LAW IN DEVELOPING COUNTRIES, 1963, pp. 29-42.

3,726 MANGIN, G. Problèmes judiciaires dans les états africains de la communauté. J. INT. COMM. JURISTS 2, no. ii (1959-1960), pp. 76-95.

3,727 MEEK, C. K. The Amsterdam land tenure symposium. J. AFR. ADM. 4 (1952), pp. 113-114.

3,728 MEINHOF, C. Changes in the African conception of law, due to the influence of missions. INT. REV. MISSIONS 18 (1929), pp. 430-435.

3,729 MEINHOF, K. The codification of native law in the German colonies. J. AFR. SOC. 7 (1908), pp. 159-164.

3,730 MOREIRA, A. Customary law in the Portuguese overseas. THE FUTURE OF CUSTOMARY LAW IN AFRICA, 1956, pp. 229-231.

3,731 MURCIER, J. P. Le Code du travail pour les territoires français d'Outre-Mer. ZAIRE 7 (1953), pp. 737-754.

3,732 NADEL, S. F. Reason and unreason in African law. AFRICA 26 (1956), pp. 160-172.

3,733 NYUNAÏ. Le grand divorce. PRESENCE AFR. N.S. 4 (1955), pp. 75-76.

3,734 OLESA MUNIDO, F. F. El concepto legal de indígena en el ordenamiento jurídico penal de los territorios del Africa británica. CUAD. EST. AFR. 9 (1950), pp. 77-94.

3,735 PAULUS, J. M. Aperçu de la situation de fait de l'organisation judiciaire par rapport a l'application du droit coutumier. THE FUTURE OF CUSTOMARY LAW IN AFRICA, 1956, pp. 16-41.

3,736 PAUTRAT, R. Les vicissitudes du statut personnel. ANNALES AFR., 1957, pp. 331-361.

3,737 PHILLIPS, A. The future of customary law in Africa. THE FUTURE OF CUSTOMARY LAW IN AFRICA, 1956, pp. 88-101. Also in J. AFR. ADM. 7 (1955), pp. 151-159.

3,738 PHILLIPS, A. The legal factor in a changing Africa. AFR. AFFAIRS 54 (1955), pp. 280-287.

3,739 PHILLIPS, A. Some aspects of legal dualism in British Colonial Territories. CIVILISATIONS 3 (1953), pp. 189-195; French summary, pp. 195-197.

3,740 POIRIER, J. L'avenir du droit coutumier négro-africain. THE FUTURE OF CUSTOMARY LAW IN AFRICA, 1956, pp. 155-169.

3,741 POIRIER, J. Les catégories de la pensée juridique et l'interprétation des droits coutumiers africains. CONGR. INT. SC. ANTHR. ETHN. 6, no. ii (1960), pp. 349-354.

3,742 POIRIER, J. La rédaction des coutumes juridiques en Afrique d'expression française. LA REDACTION DES COUTUMES DANS LE PASSE ET DANS LE PRESENT, 1962, pp. 275-292.

3,743 POIRIER, J. Projet de questionnaire d'ethnologie juridique appliqué à l'enquête de droit coutumier africain. LA REDACTION DES COUTUMES DANS LE PASSE ET DANS LE PRESENT, 1962, pp. 293-331.

3,744 POIRIER, J. Situation actuelle des études de droit africain en France. J. AFR. LAW 6 (1962), pp. 100-102.

3,745 POSSELT, F. Native marriage. NADA 6 (1928), pp. 67-73.

3,746 POSSOZ, E. La Droit nègre. AEQUATORIA 2 (1939), p. 53.

3,747 POSSOZ, E. Etudes de droit foncier. AFR. STUD. 3 (1944), pp. 172-177.

3,748 POSSOZ, E. La nature juridique de la "dot" et son avenir. KONGO-OVERZEE 17 (1951), pp. 221-235.

3,749 POSSOZ, E. Principe de droit clanique. KONGO-OVERZEE 12-13 (1946-1947), pp. 221-224.

3,750 POTEKHIN, I. I. Land relations in African countries. JMAS 1 (1963), pp. 39-59.

3,751 R., A. La création d'un Centre d'Etudes de Droit Comparé Africain à l'Université Lovanium. ET. CONG. 3, no. 7 (1962), pp. 81-84.

3,752 RAU, E. Une coutume meutrière : le "charo." ANNALES AFR., 1955, pp. 175-183.

3,753 RAU, E. Le juge et le sorcier. ANNALES AFR., 1957, pp. 305-319; 1958, pp. 179-206.

3,754 RAU, E. Variations sur deux nullités. ANNALES AFR., 1954, pp. 153-168.

3,755 READ, J. S. Criminal law in the Africa of today and tomorrow. J. AFR. LAW 7 (1963), pp. 5-17.

3,756 READ, J. S. Women's status and law reform. CHANGING LAW IN DEVELOPING COUNTRIES, 1963, pp. 210-239.

3,757 ROBERT, A. A comparative study of legislation and customary law courts in the French, Belgian and Portuguese territories in Africa. J. AFR. ADM. 11 (1959), pp. 124-131.

3,758 ROBERT, A. P. Attitude du Legislateur français en face du droit coutumier d'Afrique Noire. THE FUTURE OF CUSTOMARY LAW IN AFRICA, 1956, pp. 170-189.

3,759 ROBERTS-WRAY, Sir K. The adaptation of imported law in Africa. J. AFR. LAW 4 (1960), pp. 66-78.

3,760 ROBERTS-WRAY, Sir K. The authority of the United Kingdom in dependent territories. CHANGING LAW IN DEVELOPING COUNTRIES, 1963, pp. 11-28.

3,761 ROBERTS-WRAY, Sir K. The independence of the judiciary in Commonwealth countries. CHANGING LAW IN DEVELOPING COUNTRIES, 1963, pp. 63-80.

3,762 ROBERTS-WRAY, Sir K. The legal machinery for the transition from dependence to independence. CHANGING LAW IN DEVELOPING COUNTRIES, 1963, pp. 43-62.

3,763 ROBERTS-WRAY, Sir K. The need for study of native law. J. AFR. LAW 1 (1957), pp. 82-86.

3,764 ROBINSON, R. E. The administration of African customary law. J. AFR. ADM. 1 (1949), pp. 158-176.

3,765 SACRE-COEUR, M. A. DU. L'activité politique de la femme en Afrique Noire. RJPUF 8 (1954), pp. 476-491.

3,766 SAUMAGNE, C. Sur la formation du colonat. CT 10 (1962), pp. 115-205.

3,767 SCHAEFFER, E. Considérations générales sur le droit du travail dans les pays en voie de développement d'Afrique Noire. ANNALES AFR., 1962, pp. 234-245.

3,768 SCHAEFFER, E. Procédure pénale et développement. Libre propos sur la procédure pénale dans les Etats d'Afrique Noire d'expression française. ANNALES AFR., 1962, pp. 246-249.

3,769 SCHILLER, A. A. African law in the United States. J. AFR. LAW 3 (1959), pp. 81-83.

3,770 SCHILLER, A. A. Essays in African Law [by A. N. Allott]. J. AFR. LAW 4 (1960), pp. 175-182.

3,771 SEIDMAN, R. B. The inarticulate premise. JMAS 3 (1965), pp. 567-587.

3,772 SIMPSON, S. R. Towards a definition of "absolute ownership" [a commentary on A. N. Allott's original article; with reply by Dr. Allott]. J. AFR. LAW 5 (1961), pp. 145-150.

3,773 SMITH, D. N. Confessions received through interpreters: an African hearsay problem. NLJ 1 (1964), pp. 26-37.

3,774 SMITH, M. G. The sociological framework of law. AFR. LAW: ADAPTATION AND DEVELOPMENT, 1965, pp. 24-48.

3,775 SOLUS, H. Le problème actuel de la dot en Afrique noire. RJPUF 4 (1950), pp. 453-471.

3,776 SPADARO, S. Le pouvoir judiciare et spécialement l'action des tribunaux administratifs dans les pays africains anciens et nouveaux. CIVILISATIONS 14 (1964), pp. 342-352; English summary, pp. 353-357.

3,777 SPURLING, A. C. The sentence of the court is... CORONA 1, no. 3 (1949), pp. 23-24.

3,778 STOUFFLET, J. De l'élaboration d'une législation de droit privé dans un pays en voie de développement. ANNALES AFR., 1962, pp. 250-255.

3,779 TWINING, W. The restatement of African customary law: a comment. J. MOD. AFR. STUD 1 (1963), pp. 221-228.

3,780 VANDERLINDEN, J. The recording of customary law in France during the fifteenth and sixteenth centuries and the recording of African customary laws. J. AFR. LAW 3 (1959), pp. 165-175.

3,781 VERDIER, R. Ethnologie et droits africains. J. SOC. AFR. 33 (1963), pp. 105-128.

3,782 WADE, A. L'Afrique doit-elle élaborer un droit positif? PRESENCE AFR. N.S. 8-10 (1956), pp. 301-317.

3,783 WADE, A. Human rights and government security: the legislature, executive and judiciary. AFR. CONF. ON THE RULE OF LAW, 1961, pp. 56-68.

3,784 WHITE, C. M. N. African customary law: the problem of concept and definition. J. AFR. LAW 9 (1965), pp. 86-89.

3,785 African Conference on the rule of law. J. AFR. LAW 4 (1960), pp. 127-128.

3,786 African Conference on the Rule of Law, Lagos, Nigeria, 1961. J. INT. COMM. JURISTS 3, no. i (1961), pp. 10-18.

3,787 African legal education [special number: Vol. 6, no. 2]. J. AFR. LAW 6 (1962), pp. 75-160.

3,788 African legal studies in the University of London. J. AFR. LAW 1 (1957), pp. 147-149.

3,789 American Program for Cooperation in African Legal Education and Research. J. AFR. LAW 5 (1961), pp. 121-123.

3,790 Bibliography of African law, 1956 [-1965]. J. AFR. LAW 1 (1957), pp. 74-76, 144, 205-206; 2 (1958), pp. 72, 136-137, 204; 3 (1959), pp. 79, 143-144, 215-216; 4 (1960), pp. 61-64, 125, 183-184; 5 (1961), pp. 71-72, 119-120, 194-197; 6 (1962), pp. 71-73, 233-236; 7 (1963), pp. 67-68, 210-213; 8 (1964), pp. 50-53, 151-152; 9 (1965), pp. 76-79.

3,791 Brussels Colloquium on the recording of customary law [May, 1960]. J. AFR. LAW 4 (1960), p. 65.

3,792 Civil procedure in native courts. J. AFR. ADM. 5 (1953), supplement, pp. 25-30.

3,793 Collection du Centre de Recherches d'Etudes et de Documentation sur les institutions et la législation africaines (C.R.E.D.I.L.A.). J. AFR. LAW 8 (1964), pp. 4-5.

3,794 Colloque des facultés de droit, 23-26 mai 1962. ANNALES AFR., 1962, pp. 1-608.

3,795 Colloquium on African Law, London, June, 1961: The legal status of women in Africa; and practice, procedure and evidence in the native, African, local or customary courts. J. AFR. LAW 5 (1961), pp. 125-138.

3,796 Colonial research in progress. J. AFR. LAW 1 (1957), pp. 77-78.

3,797 Conference on the future of law in Africa [held in London from the 28th December 1959 to the 8th January]. J. AFR. ADM. 12 (1960), pp. 107-108.

3,798 Conferences on African law. J. AFR. LAW 7 (1963), pp. 133-135.

3,799 Constitution and personnel of the native courts. J. AFR. ADM. 5 (1953), supplement, pp. 15-18.

3,800 Control over native courts: appeals, revision and administration. J. AFR. ADM. 5 (1953), supplement, pp. 5-9.

3,801 Council of Legal Education, London. J. AFR. LAW 6 (1962), p. 157.

3,802 Création d'un Département de Droit et Economie des Pays d'Afrique. J. AFR. LAW 8 (1964), pp. 1-4.

3,803 Creation of a "Centre d'histoire et d'ethnologie juridiques." J. AFR. LAW 4 (1960), pp. 5-6.

3,804 Criminal procedure and evidence in native courts. J. AFR. ADM. 5 (1953), supplement, pp. 30-31.

3,805 Draft outline for the national reports for the African Conference on the Rule of Law. J. INT. COMM. JURISTS 3, no. i (1961), pp. 19-21.

3,806 First meeting of the Inter-African Conference on Social Sciences, Bukavu [1955]. J. AFR. LAW 1 (1957), pp. 7-8.

3,807 Informal meeting of British and African law teachers at Oxford. J. AFR. LAW 7 (1963), pp. 69-70.

3,808 Integration of customary and modern legal systems in Africa [a conference at Ibadan, August, 1964]. J. AFR. LAW 8 (1964), pp. 55-56.

3,809 The International African Law Association. J. AFR. LAW 3 (1959), pp. 146-148.

3,810 International African Law Association. BULL. AFR. STUD. ASSOC. 5 (1965), pp. 16-17.

3,811 International African Law Association... Formation of Belgian section. J. AFR. LAW 4 (1960), pp. 7-8.

3,812 International African Law Association... Formation of British section. J. AFR. LAW 5 (1961), p. 3.

3,813 Judicial Advisers' Conference [1956]. J. AFR. LAW 1 (1957), pp. 4-6.

3,814 Judicial systems of the British territories in Africa. THE FUTURE OF CUSTOMARY LAW IN AFRICA, 1956, pp. 117-129.

3,815 Jurisdiction of native courts. J. AFR. ADM. 5 (1953), supplement, pp. 18-21.

3,816 Justice and the rule of law in British dependent territories. J. AFR. LAW 2 (1958), pp. 75-77.

3,817 The Lagos Conference on the rule of law [January, 1961]. J. AFR. LAW 5 (1961), p. 1.

3,818 [The] Law of Lagos. J. INT. COMM. JURISTS 3, no. 1 (1961), p. 9.

3,819 Law reporting. J. AFR. LAW 1 (1957), p. 79.

3,820 Law reporting in Africa. J. AFR. LAW 1 (1957), pp. 10-11.

3,821 Legal education in Africa. J. AFR. LAW 6 (1962), pp. 1-4.

3,822 [The] London Conference on the future of law in Africa. J. AFR. LAW 3 (1959), pp. 148-149; 4 (1960), pp. 1-3.

3,823 Meeting of the working committee of the Conference on Legal Education in Africa. J. AFR. LAW 7 (1963), pp. 3-4.

3,824 The move towards codification. J. AFR. LAW 2 (1958), pp. 73-75.

3,825 Native courts and native customary law in Africa. Record of the Judicial Advisers' Conference, 1956. J. AFR. ADM. 8 (1956), supplement; 9 (1957), supplement.

3,826 Position and functions of Judicial Advisers. J. AFR. ADM. 5 (1953), supplement, pp. 10-15.

3,827 Problems of courts in Moslem areas. J. AFR. ADM. 5 (1953), supplement, pp. 33-36.

3,828 Progress in African legal studies. J. AFR. LAW 3 (1959), pp. 145-146.

3,829 Record of the Judicial Advisers' Conference, 1953. J. AFR. ADM. 5 (1953), supplement.

3,830 Report of the Committee on Legal Education for Students from Africa [some recommendations of the Conference on the Future of Law in Africa, held in London, 28th December 1959 to the 8th January, 1960]. J. AFR. ADM. 13 (1961), pp. 118-122.

3,831 A report on African legal studies in the United Kingdom. J. AFR. LAW 5 (1961), pp. 151-156.

3,832 The restatement of African law project. J. AFR. LAW 3 (1959), pp. 149-151.

3,833 School of Oriental and African Studies, University of London. J. AFR. LAW 6 (1962), p. 157.

3,834 The study of African law at the University of Paris. J. AFR. LAW 1 (1957), pp. 8-10.

3,835 The study of Islamic law in Belgium. J. AFR. LAW 1 (1957), p. 80.

3,836 Symposium on the future of customary law Africa; Amsterdam, 1955. J. AFR. ADM. 7 (1955), pp. 197-198.

3,837 The teaching of African law in British and African universities. J. AFR. LAW 1 (1957), pp. 6-7.

3,838 The teaching of law in African universities. J. AFR. LAW 1 (1957), pp. 78-79.

3,839 The territorial police force and native courts. J. AFR. ADM. 5 (1953), supplement, pp. 32-33.

3,840 United States. Programme for cooperation in African legal education and research. J. AFR. LAW 6 (1962), p. 160.

See also 414, 1479, 1574, 2007, 4738, 10720.

RELIGION

General. Christianity. Missions

3,841 AFRIKANUS. Instituto de Educação e de Serviço Social. PORT. EM AFR. 19 (1962), pp. 362-377.

3,842 ALVES, H. Libermann em Portugal. PORT. EM AFR. 9 (1952), pp. 45-52.

3,843 AMORIM, S. Os católicos leigos e as Missões. PORT. EM AFR. 14 (1957), pp. 193-211.

3,844 AMU, E. The position of Christianity in modern Africa. INT. REV. MISSIONS 29 (1940), pp. 477-485.

3,845 ANGUS, J. A. The relevance of Christ in Africa to-day. INT. REV. MISSIONS 32 (1943), pp. 288-292.

3,846 ASHANIN, C. B. Christianity and African nationalism. UNIVERSITAS 4 (1960), pp. 85-87.

3,847 BABO, F. DE. Alminhas Padrões de Portugal Cristão. PORT. EM AFR. 15 (1958), pp. 344-349.

3,848 BANTON, M. African prophets. RACE 5, no. 2 (1963-1964), pp. 42-55.

3,849 BAPTISTA, M. Responsabilidades. PORT. EM AFR. 19 (1962), pp. 287-294.

3,850 BASCOM, W. African culture and the Missionary. CIVILISATIONS 3 (1953), pp. 491-502; French summary, pp. 502-504.

3,851 BASCOM, W. Le religion africaine au nouveau monde. RELIGIONS AFR. TRAD., 1965, pp. 119-137.

3,852 BATES, M. S. The training of Christian ministers in non-British Africa. INT. REV. MISSIONS 43 (1954), pp. 294-300.

3,853 BELTRAMI, S. I problemi della nuova Africa alla luce della Mater et Magistra. AFRICA (Rome) 17 (1962), pp. 107-112.

3,854 BETHAM, T. A. The Church in Africa faces 1957. INT. REV. MISSIONS 46 (1957), pp. 17-29.

3,855 BONCHAUD, J. Maria Salvação da Africa. PORT. EM AFR. 12 (1955), pp. 111-114.

3,856 BOOTH, N. S. Mission priorities in Africa [review article on Knowing the African by E. W. Smith. INT. REV. MISSIONS 37 (1948), pp. 93-98.

3,857 BOUAERT, J. C. Statistiques des Missions. ZAIRE 9 (1955), pp. 953-967.

3,858 BRANCO, A. M. XV Congresso da U.M.O.F.C. PORT. EM AFR. 17 (1960), pp. 68-81.

3,859 BRASIO, A. Ainda a promoção sacerdotal do africano. PORT. EM AFR. 20 (1963), pp. 135-155.

3,860 BRASIO, A. A Causa de Canonização do Padre Libermann. PORT. EM AFR. 12 (1955), pp. 5-14.

3,861 BRASIO, A. Crítica das Ideias e dos Factos. PORT. EM AFR. 11 (1954), pp. 12-20, 163-172, 240-248.

3,862 BRASIO, A. O Culto de Nossa Senhora na Africa Portuguesa. PORT. EM AFR. 11 (1954), pp. 138-144.

3,863 BRASIO, A. Congresso missionário internacional. PORT. EM AFR. 19 (1962), pp. 206-209.

3,864 BRASIO, A. A Promoção Sacerdotal do Africano. PORT. EM AFR. 19 (1962), pp. 12-22.

3,865 BRASIO, A. Centenário de martírio. PORT. EM AFR. 1 (1944), pp. 40-55.

3,866 BRASIO, A. Um centenário espiritano (1848-1948). PORT. EM AFR. 5 (1948), pp. 292-306.

3,867 BRASIO, A. Conselheiro Júlio de Vilhena. PORT. EM AFR. 2 (1945), pp. 214-222.

3,868 BRASIO, A. O Esforco Missionário dos Irmãos de S. João de Deus. PORT. EM AFR. 7 (1950), pp. 270-279, 348-359.

3,869 BRASIO, A. O inimigo dos antigos Colonos e Missionários de Africa. PORT. EM AFR. 1 (1944), pp. 215-229.

3,870 BRASIO, A. Irmãs do Espirito Santo Missionárias e Enfermeiras. PORT. EM AFR. 5 (1948), pp. 140-148.

3,871 BRASIO, A. Missiologia ou Missionologia? PORT. EM AFR. 5 (1948), pp. 347-352.

3,872 BRASIO, A. Por Missiologia. PORT. EM AFR. 6 (1949), pp. 283-304.

3,873 BRASIO, A. Por um estatuto indigena cristão. PORT. EM AFR. 2 (1945), pp. 65-76.

3,874 BRASIO, A. Senhora de Africa. PORT. EM AFR. 4 (1947), pp. 193-200.

3,875 BRENNECKE, G. Mission, Kirche und Oekumene in Afrika. BASILEIA: FESTSCHRIFT FUR WALTER FREYTAG, 1959, pp. 81-90.

3,876 BROCHADO, C. A Espiritualidade dos Descobrimentos e Conquistas dos Portugueses. PORT. EM AFR. 2 (1945), pp. 7-21.

3,877 BUERKLE, H. The message of the false prophets of the independent churches of Africa. MAKERERE J. 11 (1965), pp. 51-55.

3,878 BULCK, G. VAN. Journées d'études missionnaires en 1953. Paris, Louvain, Rome. ZAIRE 8 (1954), pp. 201-210.

3,879 BUSIA, K. A. The African world view. PRESENCE AFR. N.S. 4 (1955), pp. 16-23.

3,880 BUSIA, K. A. Has the Christian faith been adequately presented? INT. REV. MISSIONS 50 (1961), pp. 86-89.

3,881 C., J. Le protestantisme en Afrique. ZAIRE 8 (1954), pp. 945-946.

3,882 C., R. V. De missiologische studiedagen in het Institut Catholique te Parijs. ZAIRE 5 (1951), pp. 839-851.

3,883 CAENEGHEM, R. V. De Missiologische studiedagen in het Institut Catholique et Parijs van 1 tot 5 Juli 1952. AEQUATORIA 16 (1953), pp. 11-22.

3,884 CAPERAN, C. D. L. A Missão da Igreja e as Missões. PORT. EM AFR. 6 (1949), pp. 273-282, 335-346.

3,885 CARPENTER, G. W. Church and State in Africa today. CIVILISATIONS 3 (1953), pp. 519-538; French summary, 539-543.

3,886 CASTRO, M. L. P. DE. O Açoriano em Africa. PORT. EM AFR. 21 (1964), pp. 208-214.

3,887 CAUSARD, M. Síntese sobre a origem do Padroado Português. PORT. EM AFR. 7 (1950), pp. 20-29.

3,888 CHADWICK, H. The African Training Institute, Colwyn Bay. J. AFR. SOC. 3 (1903), pp. 104-106.

3,889 CHARLES, P. A verdadeira natureza do Dever Missionário. PORT. EM AFR. 1 (1944), pp. 129-143.

3,890 CHIRGWIN, A. M. Christian literature in Africa. AFRICA 5 (1932), pp. 323-337.

3,891 CIDADE, H. O Itinerário de Fr. Gaspar de S. Bernardino. PORT. EM AFR. 5 (1948), pp. 129-139.

3,892 CLERC, A. An experiment in the religious education of African boys. INT. REV. MISSIONS 32 (1943), pp. 404-411.

3,893 CODJO, R. Colonisation et conscience chrétienne. PRESENCE AFR. N.S. 6 (1956), pp. 9-19.

3,894 COMHAIRE, J. Les missions protestantes américaines en Afrique. ZAIRE 6 (1952), pp. 273-280, 391-398.

3,895 COMHAIRE, J. L. Religious trends in African and Afro-American urban societies. ANTHR. QUART. 26 (1953), pp. 95-108.

3,896 CORREIA, P. J. A. O dever Missionário. Conclusões teológicas ou conclusões do senso comum cristão. PORT. EM AFR. 1 (1944), pp. 65-72.

3,897 CORREIA, P. J. A. O Legado do Sumo Pontífice em visita às Missões Portuguesas. PORT. EM AFR. 1 (1944), pp. 257-258.

3,898 CORREIA, P. J. A. O Santo Padre, o seu Legado e as Missões. PORT. EM AFR. 1 (1944), pp. 335-339.

3,899 CORREIA, P. J. A. A teologia e o dever missionário. PORT. EM AFR. 1 (1944), pp. 11-17.

3,900 CRANE, W. H. Indigenization in the African Church. INT. REV. MISSIONS 53 (1964), pp. 408-422.

3,901 CUTHBERT, D. Education into Christianity. THE CHURCH IN CHANGING AFRICA, 1958, pp. 23-33.

3,902 DAMMERS, A. H. Training for the ministry in Africa and Asia. INT. REV. MISSIONS 47 (1958), pp. 312-315.

3,903 DANIELOU, J. O Espírito Missionário na Igreja. PORT. EM AFR. 8 (1951), pp. 223-228.

3,904 DAVID DE SOUSA, M. Os Religiosos na Epopeia Missionária Portuguesa. PORT. EM AFR. 15 (1958), pp. 83-102.

3,905 DAVIDSON, J. Dieu est-il Blanc? AEQUATORIA 19 (1956), pp. 88-90.

3,906 DAVIS, J. M. The cinema and missions in Africa. INT. REV. MISSIONS 25 (1936), pp. 378-383.

3,907 DIAS, G. S. Padre Ernesto Lecomte. PORT. EM AFR. 2 (1945), pp. 230-236.

3,908 DIAS NOGUEIRA, E. O Estado e as Missões Católicas no Ultramar Português. PORT. EM AFR. 15 (1958), pp. 195-220.

3,909 DIOP, A. L'Occident chrétien et nous. PRESENCE AFR. N.S. 6 (1956), pp. 143-147.

3,910 DOIG, A. B. The Christian Church and demobilization in Africa. INT. REV. MISSIONS 35 (1946), pp. 174-182.

3,911 DOUGALL, J. W. C. African separatist churches. INT. REV. MISSIONS 45 (1956), pp. 257-266.

3,912 DOUGALL, J. W. C. The relationship of Church and school in Africa. INT. REV. MISSIONS 26 (1937), pp. 204-214.

3,913 DOUGALL, J. W. C. Thomas Jesse Jones: crusader for Africa. INT. REV. MISSIONS 39 (1950), pp. 311-317.

3,914 ESTERMANN, C. Biobibliografia do Missionário-etnólogo. PORT. EM AFR. 19 (1962), pp. 67-78.

3,915 ESTERMANN, P. C. Manifestacão tardia do Monoteísmo na evolucão da humanidade? PORT. EM AFR. 3 (1946), pp. 135-148.

3,916 FARIA, D. Quando o Cardeal-Legado passou pelas Missões da Africa portuguesa. PORT. EM AFR. 1 (1944), pp. 352-355.

3,917 FERNANDES DE SA, A. Dois Evangelizadores do Mundo Pagão. S. Paulo E Libermann. PORT. EM AFR. 12 (1955), pp. 93-100, 169-178.

3,918 FERNANDEZ, J. W. African religious movements—types and dynamics. J. MOD. AFR. STUD. 2 (1964), pp. 531-549.

3,919 FILESI, T. Esordi del colonialismo e azione della Chiesa. AFRICA (Rome) 20 (1965), pp. 143-162, 269-293, 370-403.

3,920 FRANCOLINI, B. I rapporti culturali tra mondo cattolico e Africa musulmana. AFRICA (Rome) 10 (1955), pp. 23-24.

3,921 FRASER, A. A missionary's wife among African women. INT. REV. MISSIONS 3 (1914), pp. 456-469.

3,922 FRASER, D. The Church and games in Africa. INT. REV. MISSIONS 10 (1921), pp. 110-117.

3,923 FRASER, D. The evangelistic approach to the African. INT. REV. MISSIONS 15 (1926), pp. 438-449.

3,924 FRIBERG, D. Church and mission in the Afro-Asian revolution. INT. REV. MISSIONS 51 (1962), pp. 485-489.

3,925 FRIMODT-MOLLER, C. The work of medical missions: the tuberculosis problem. INT. REV. MISSIONS 17 (1928), pp. 186-197.

3,926 FUCHS, P. L. Uma guestão de Vida ou de Morte. PORT. EM AFR. 7 (1950), pp. 335-342.

3,927 FUETER, P. D. African genesis and Western theology. INT. REV. MISSIONS 52 (1963), pp. 60-68.

3,928 FUETER, P. D. The all-Africa Lutheran Conference, Marangu 1955. INT. REV. MISSIONS 45 (1956), pp. 289-296.

3,929 FUETER, P. D. Négritude et education chrétienne. ABBIA 7 (1964), pp. 109-124.

3,930 FUETER, P. D. Theological education in Africa. INT. REV. MISSIONS 45 (1956), pp. 377-395.

3,931 FULANI BIN FULANI. Christianity and labour conditions in Africa. INT. REV. MISSIONS 9 (1920), pp. 544-551.

3,932 G., J. La recherche missionnaire aux Etats-Unis. ZAIRE 8 (1954), p. 310.

3,933 GARRONE, D. G. M. Diocese e Missões. PORT. EM AFR. 19 (1962), pp. 259-274.

3,934 GASPAR, J. M. O problema missionário e a educação. PORT. EM AFR. 21 (1964), pp. 154-167.

3,935 GENSICHEN, H. W. Theological education in Africa. The special Africa programme of the Theological Education Fund. INT. REV. MISSIONS 52 (1963), pp. 155-162.

3,936 GERDENER, G. B. A. Some basic principles of the literature auxiliary in the Christian mission. CHRISTIAN LIT. FOR THE BANTU OF S. AFR., 1957, pp. 17-26.

3,937 GOMES DOS SANTOS, P. A. O Criador do Apostolado Africano. PORT. EM AFR. 8 (1951), pp. 87-96, 156-165.

3,938 GOUVEIA, D. T. DE. A grande abandonada. PORT. EM AFR. 3 (1946), pp. 197-205.

3,939 GOUVEIA, T. DE. O Problema Missionário Português. PORT. EM AFR. 9 (1952), pp. 151-160.

3,940 GREAVES, L. B. The All Africa Church Conference: Ibadan, Nigeria: 10th to 20th January, 1958. INT. REV. MISSIONS 47 (1958), pp. 257-264.

3,941 GRESCHAT, H. J. Die originalsprachliche Literatur des christlichen Synkretismus in Afrika. AFR. UND UB. 48 (1964-1965), pp. 275-283.

3,942 H., G. Semaine interafricaine de formation religieuse. AEQUATORIA 20 (1957), pp. 96-103.

3,943 HARES, B. Men and women in Africa today: a consultation (Ibadan, Nigeria, January 1958). INT. REV. MISSIONS 47 (1958), pp. 306-311.

3,944 HARRIES, L. Linguistic research in the Church in Africa. INT. REV. MISSIONS 36 (1947), pp. 258-262.

3,945 HARRIES, L. Mission research and the African marriage survey. INT. REV. MISSIONS 39 (1950), pp. 94-99.

3,946 HARRIS, R. G. Cool, sober and methodical. TRANSITION 15 (1964), pp. 43-45.

3,947 HAYWARD, V. E. W. African independent Church movements. INT. REV. MISSIONS 52 (1963), pp. 163-172.

3,948 HERBIGNY, M. M. D'. O dever Missionário dos membros da Igreja. PORT. EM AFR. 4 (1947), pp. 221-234.

3,949 HOLAS, B. Nom, invocation, prière: transposition du problème général sur le terrain des recherches négro-africaines. BULL. IFAN, Série B: Sciences humaines 17 (1955), pp. 109-128.

3,950 HOLDING, E. M. Women's institutions and the African Church. INT. REV. MISSIONS 31 (1942), pp. 290-300.

3,951 HOOPER, H. D. The expression of Christian life in primitive African society. INT. REV. MISSIONS 13 (1924), pp. 67-73.

3,952 HORSTED, J. L. C. Co-operation with Africans. INT. REV. MISSIONS 24 (1935), pp. 203-212.

3,953 HORTON, R. Ritual man in Africa. AFRICA 34 (1964), pp. 85-103.

3,954 HUBBLE, G. The Ghana Assembly: a report on group discussion. INT. REV. MISSIONS 47 (1958), pp. 143-149, 150-152.

3,955 JAMES, M. Christianity in the emergent Africa. PRESENCE AFR. N.S. 8-10 (1956), pp. 238-244.

3,956 JAMES, M. Religion en Afrique. PRESENCE AFR. N.S. 24-25 (1959), pp. 185-191.

3,957 JANEIRO, M. Laicado Missionário. PORT. EM AFR. 16 (1959), pp. 216-231.

3,958 JOHNSON, R. P. Renewal of the Christian mission to Islam. Reflections on the Asmara Conference. INT. REV. MISSIONS 48 (1959), pp. 438-444.

3,959 KARIUKI, O. The Church, youth and the family. Christian home life. THE CHURCH IN CHANGING AFRICA, 1958, pp. 18-22.

3,960 KEABLE, R. The worth of an African. INT. REV. MISSIONS 7 (1918), pp. 319-332.

3,961 LAZZARINI, P. D. O Dever individual da Cooperacão Missionária. PORT. EM AFR. 2 (1945), pp. 326-335.

3,962 LEFEBVRE, M. M. A Missão em Africa. PORT. EM AFR. 22 (1965), pp. 133-139.

3,963 LERRIGO, P. H. J. An African medical staff. INT. REV. MISSIONS 17 (1928), pp. 197-204.

3,964 LERRIGO, P. H. J. The ministry of health and welfare work. INT. REV. MISSIONS 15 (1926), pp. 515-532.

3,965 LOPES, E. C. Os Missionários e o respeito pelas culturas indígenas. PORT. EM AFR. 1 (1944), pp. 113-116.

3,966 LORAM, C. T. The separatist Church movement. INT. REV. MISSIONS 15 (1926), pp. 476-482.

3,967 LUIS LUPI. Assistência às Missões Católicas. PORT. EM AFR. 12 (1955), pp. 223-228.

3,968 M., A. La personalità africana in seno alla vita cattolica. AFRICA (Rome) 17 (1962), pp. 113-114.

3,969 MABONA, P. M. La spiritualité africaine. PRESENCE AFR. N. S. 52 (1964), pp. 157-161.

3,970 MACGREGOR, J. K. Christian missions and marriage usage in Africa. INT. REV. MISSIONS 24 (1935), pp. 379-391.

3,971 MAIO, P. A. T. Um ano de Apostolado dos Padres do Espírito Santo. PORT. EM AFR. 4 (1947), pp. 357-364; 6 (1949), pp. 5-12.

3,972 MARQUES, F. Consciência do Dever Missionário. PORT. EM AFR. 12 (1955), pp. 253-258.

3,973 MARQUES, M. A. DA C. Perspectivas missionárias dos tempos livres e jogos: Como ajudar a eclodir a vocação missionária. PORT. EM AFR. 20 (1963), pp. 39-49.

3,974 MATTHEWS, Z. K. Christian education in a changing Africa. INT. REV. MISSIONS 52 (1963), pp. 38-46.

3,975 MELADY, T. P. The impact of Africa on recent developments in the Roman Catholic Church. RACE 7, no. 1 (1965), pp. 147-156.

3,976 MESTRAL, C. DE. Christian literature for Africa. INT. REV. MISSIONS 43 (1954), pp. 436-442.

3,977 MESTRAL, C. DE. Christian literature in Africa. CHRISTIAN LIT. FOR THE BANTU OF S. AFR., 1957, pp. 33-59.

3,978 MICHEL, J. C. The story of events [of the Pan-African Catholic Education Conference]. CATHOLIC ED. IN THE SERVICE OF AFR., 1965, pp. 23-42.

3,979 MIRANDA SANTOS, A. Convergência sintomática. PORT. EM AFR. 16 (1959), pp. 271-285.

3,980 MIRANDA SANTOS, A. Para além dos nacionalismos. PORT. EM AFR. 16 (1959), pp. 91-106.

3,981 MIRANDA SANTOS, A. O P.^{e} Poullart des Places... PORT. EM AFR. 16 (1959), pp. 257-270.

3,982 MIRANDA SANTOS, A. Sentido de renovação. PORT. EM AFR. 19 (1962), pp. 143-154.

3,983 MONTAGNE, R. Le Christianisme en Afrique. AFR. ET ASIE 1, no. 2 (1948), pp. 6-25.

3,984 MORALES OLIVER, L. Carlos V. ARCH. INST. EST. AFR. 13, no. 50 (1959), pp. 7-21.

3,985 MOREIRA CANDELARIA, M. O Problema central da Africa. PORT. EM AFR. 16 (1959), pp. 307-310.

3,986 M'TIMKULU, D. G. S. All Africa Church Conference. INT. REV. MISSIONS 51 (1962), pp. 63-66.

3,987 MUKASA, D. K. Give an account of thy stewardship. THE CHURCH IN CHANGING AFRICA, 1958, pp. 75-76.

3,988 MULAGO, V. La théologie et seo responsabilités. PRESENCE AFR. 27-28 (1959), pp. 188-205.

3,989 NEILL, S. African theological survey. INT. REV. MISSIONS 39 (1950), pp. 207-211.

3,990 NEIVA, A. T. O Cinema ao Serviço das Missões. PORT. EM AFR. 11 (1954), pp. 29-36.

3,991 NFOULOU, J. L'Athéisme tentation du monde, réveil des chrétiens. PRESENCE AFR. N.S. 51 (1964), pp. 121-130.

3,992 NIELSON, J. For an African christianity. ABBIA 7 (1964), pp. 101-108.

3,993 NILES, D. T. The All Africa Conference of Churches. INT. REV. MISSIONS 52 (1963), pp. 409-413.

3,994 NKETIA, J. H. The contribution of African culture to Christian worship. THE CHURCH IN CHANGING AFRICA, 1958, pp. 59-65. Also in INT. REV. MISSIONS 47 (1958), pp. 265-278.

3,995 O., R. K. The I[nternational] M[issionary] C[ouncil] Assembly in Ghana. INT. REV. MISSIONS 46 (1957), pp. 197-200.

3,996 OLDHAM, J. H. The Christian mission in Africa as seen at the International Conference at Le Zoute. INT. REV. MISSIONS 16 (1927), pp. 24-35.

3,997 OLDHAM, J. H. Dr. Siegfried Knak on the Christian task in Africa. INT. REV. MISSIONS 20 (1931), pp. 547-555.

3,998 OLDHAM, J. H. Some reflections on the report of the Phelps-Stokes Commission. INT. REV. MISSIONS 14 (1925), pp. 173-187.

3,999 OLIVEIRA, A. G. D'. Uma igreja africana? PORT. EM AFR. 21 (1964), pp. 12-20.

4,000 OLIVEIRA, H. L. D'. Imprensa e Missões. PORT. EM AFR. 22 (1965), pp. 178-184.

4,001 ORNELAS, M. C. DE J. C. DE O. As Missionárias de S. José de Cluny. PORT. EM AFR. 1 (1944), pp. 273-284.

4,002 PAIXAO, B. Novos aspectos do problema missionário português. PORT. EM AFR. 6 (1949), pp. 129-140.

4,003 PARRINDER, G. Religion in village and town. WAISER 2 (1953), pp. 115-127.

4,004 PARSONS, R. T. Missionary-African relations. CIVILISATIONS 3 (1953), pp. 505-516; French summary, pp. 517-518.

4,005 PATON, A. S. The attitude of the Church and the Christian towards the state. THE CHURCH IN CHANGING AFRICA, 1958, pp. 48-56.

4,006 P'BITEK, O. Fr. Tempels' Bantu philosophy. TRANSITION 13 (1964), pp. 15-17.

4,007 P'BITEK, O. The self in African imagery, on The Primal Vision by John Taylor. TRANSITION 15 (1964), pp. 32-35.

4,008 PEIRONE, F. O Problema missionário à luz da Geografia Humana. PORT. EM AFR. 14 (1957), pp. 144-166.

4,009 PELICHY, A. G. DE. Orações pagãs da Africa negra. PORT. EM AFR. 16 (1959), pp. 331-342; 17 (1960), pp. 17-29.

4,010 PINHO, D. M. A. DE. Apontamentos para uma conferência. PORT. EM AFR. 5 (1948), pp. 65-76.

4,011 PIUS XII, Pope. Carta Encíclica, Fidei Donum. PORT. EM AFR. 14 (1957), pp. 129-143.

4,012 POSTIOMA, A. DE. Para uma Africa autênticamente cristã. Para uma Igreja autênticamente africana! PORT. EM AFR. 20 (1963), pp. 283-289.

4,013 PRICE, T. The task of mission schools in Africa. INT. REV. MISSIONS 27 (1938), pp. 233-238.

4,014 QUEIROZ, M. I. P. DE. Autour du messianisme. PRESENCE AFR. N.S. 20 (1958), pp. 72-76.

4,015 RALIBERA, P. R. Théologien-prêtre africain et développement de la culture négro-africaine. PRESENCE AFR. 27-28 (1959), pp. 154-187.

4,016 RAUM, J. Christianity and African puberty rites. INT. REV. MISSIONS 16 (1927), pp. 581-591.

4,017 REDACCAO, A. Paiva Couceiro. PORT. EM AFR. 1 (1944), pp. 73-86.

4,018 RESENDE, D. S. DE. O problema escolar nas Missões. PORT. EM AFR. 6 (1949), pp. 162-168.

4,019 RETIF, A. Le Clergé indigène. AFR. ET ASIE 21 (1953), pp. 6-12.

4,020 REY, P. A. Os Protomártires Franciscanos e a Casa Real Portuguesa. PORT. EM AFR. 7 (1950), pp. 30-35.

4,021 RICHTER, J. Missionary work and race education in Africa. INT. REV. MISSIONS 18 (1929), pp. 74-82.

4,022 ROCHA, F. N. DA. Das trevas à luz (conversão do venerável Libermann) 1824-1826. PORT. EM AFR. 9 (1952), pp. 8-21.

4,023 RODRIGUES DE CAMPOS, O. Presenca de Mousinho. PORT. EM AFR. 12 (1955), pp. 489-501.

4,024 ROELANDT, R. L'enseignement religieux en pays de missions. La XXVe Semaine de Missiologie de Louvain (23-26 août 1955). ZAIRE 10 (1956), pp. 187-201.

4,025 ROEYKENS, P. A. Le problème des missions chrétiennes et de l'éducation des indigènes à la Conférence géographique de Bruxelles. AEQUATORIA 20 (1957), pp. 41-56.

4,026 ROUSE, R. Dispersions: Oriental and African. INT. REV. MISSIONS 18 (1929), pp. 216-230.

4,027 RUSSEL, B. Revolução na Africa. PORT. EM AFR. 18 (1961), pp. 355-357.

4,028 SA COUTO, H. Libermann e o Apostolado moderno Africano. PORT. EM AFR. 13 (1956), pp. 1-10.

4,029 SANCHES, G. O problema Religioso do Séc XX. PORT. EM AFR. 13 (1956), pp. 211-220.

4,030 SANTOS, A. G. DOS. Libermann e o Clero Indígena. PORT. EM AFR. 9 (1952), pp. 53-65.

4,031 SARMENTO RODRIGUES, M. Arte Sacra Missionária. PORT. EM AFR. 8 (1951), pp. 329-333.

4,032 SASTRE, R. Spiritualité africaine et christianisme. PRESENCE AFR. N.S. 13 (1957), pp. 23-30.

4,033 SAWYERR, H. The basis of a theology for Africa. INT. REV. MISSIONS 52 (1963), pp. 266-278.

4,034 SCOTT, M. N. O. C. Church and mission relationship. THE CHURCH IN CHANGING AFRICA, 1958, pp. 76-78.

4,035 SENIOR, M. M. Women in the African village Church. INT. REV. MISSIONS 37 (1948), pp. 403-409.

4,036 SEUMOIS, A. A Missiologia na Hollanda. PORT. EM AFR. 8 (1951), pp. 105-114, 177-185.

4,037 SEUMOIS, P. A. Accão Missionária tentativa de definicão. PORT. EM AFR. 5 (1948), pp. 100-112, 159-166, 226-234, 275-281, 335-346.

4,038 SICARD, H. VON. Language and theological training in Africa. INT. REV. MISSIONS 44 (1955), pp. 147-152.

4,039 SILVA, C. DA. As Missões Católicas e o Ensino dos Indígenas. PORT. EM AFR. 4 (1947), pp. 5-8.

4,040 SILVA, F. DA. O grande advento. PORT. EM AFR. 18 (1961), pp. 227-237.

4,041 SIMEAO VITORIA. Missionários. PORT. EM AFR. 12 (1955), pp. 24-28.

4,042 SPANTON, E. F. Building the African Church. INT. REV. MISSIONS 15 (1926), pp. 467-475.

4,043 SPITZ, M. The growth of Roman Catholic missions in Africa. INT. REV. MISSIONS 13 (1924), pp. 360-372.

4,044 STETSON, G. R. Christianity and Islam in Africa. LIBERIA BULL. 6 (1895), pp. 50-52.

4,045 TATE, H. R. The position and prospects of the church in Africa. J. AFR. SOC. 35 (1936), pp. 26-33.

4,046 THOMAS, L. V. Pour un programme d'études théoriques des religions et d'un humanisme africains. PRESENCE AFR. N.S. 37 (1961), pp. 48-86.

4,047 THURNWALD, R. The missionary's concern in sociology and psychology. AFRICA 4 (1931), pp. 418-433.

4,048 VANNESTE, M. Het opperwezen en de Regen. KONGO-OVERZEE 10-11 (1944-1945), pp. 127-131.

4,049 VAZ, J. M. Problemas Africanos. PORT. EM AFR. 15 (1958), pp. 273-301, 322-333; 16 (1959), pp. 38-52, 71-90.

4,050 VAZ, M. M. Missionário que Libermann sonhava. PORT. EM AFR. 10 (1953), pp. 7-17, 112-119.

4,051 VAZ, M. M. O Missionário de Libermann. PORT. EM AFR. 14 (1957), pp. 48-62.

4,052 VEIGA, J. Arte Negra e Missionacão. PORT. EM AFR. 12 (1955), pp. 244-252.

4,053 VILAKAZI, A. Changing concepts of the self and the supernatural in Africa. ANTHROPOLOGY AND AFRICA TODAY, 1962, pp. 670-675.

4,054 WARREN, M. A. C. '...your attention to Africa.' INT. REV. MISSIONS 46 (1957), pp. 129-135.

4,055 WASHINGTON, B. T. David Livingstone and the Negro. INT. REV. MISSIONS 2 (1913), pp. 224-235.

4,056 WELBOURN, F. Who am I? An essay on nationalism and identity. TRANSITION 12 (1964), pp. 33-36.

4,057 WELCH, J. W. Can Christian marriage in Africa be African? INT. REV. MISSIONS 22 (1933), pp. 17-32.

4,058 WELMERS, W. E. African languages and Christian missions. CIVILISATIONS 3 (1953), pp. 545-561; French summary, pp. 561-564.

4,059 WEST, I. G. Asmara study conference, April 1-9, 1959. INT. REV. MISSIONS 48 (1959), pp. 433-437.

4,060 WILLOUGHBY, W. C. Building the African Church. INT. REV. MISSIONS 15 (1926), pp. 450-466.

4,061 WILSON, C. E. The provision of a Christian literature for Africa. INT. REV. MISSIONS 15 (1926), pp. 506-514.

4,062 WILSON, H. S. E. W. Blyden on religion in Africa. SIERRA L. BULL. REL. 2 (1960), pp. 58-66.

4,063 WRONG, M. The Church's task in Africa south of the Sahara. INT. REV. MISSIONS 36 (1947), pp. 206-231.

4,064 YOUNG, T. C. How far can African ceremonial be incorporated in the Christian system? AFRICA 8 (1935), pp. 210-217.

4,065 The African continent: a survey of ten years [based on material received from missionaries and officers of mission boards]. INT. REV. MISSIONS 13 (1924), pp. 481-499.

4,066 Associação de Nossa Senhora de Africa. PORT. EM AFR. 9 (1952), pp. 94-95.

4,067 Autocritique des spiritains sur la politique culturelle des Missions. ABBIA 7 (1964), pp. 125-127.

4,068 De la contribution de la personnalité africaine à la vitalité du catholicisme. ABBIA 1 (1963), pp. 96-107.

4,069 Um Benemérito da Accão Missionária. PORT. EM AFR. 4 (1947), pp. 30-31.

4,070 Cardeal Gouveia. PORT. EM AFR. 3 (1946), pp. 82-87.

4,071 Catéchèse bantoue. ZAIRE 3 (1949), pp. 771-788.

4,072 Catolicismo no Ultramar Português. PORT. EM AFR. 13 (1956), pp. 51-62.

4,073 Conclusões e votos do XV Congresso da U.M.O.F.C. PORT. EM AFR. 17 (1960), pp. 82-86.

4,074 Escola de Enfermagem e Accão Social Ultramarima. PORT. EM AFR. 9 (1952), pp. 85-93.

4,075 "Humanisme chrétien" africain. ZAIRE 3 (1949), pp. 673-685.

4,076 Inauguração do Instituto Superior Missionário dos Padres do Espírito Santo. PORT. EM AFR. 14 (1957), pp. 280-288.

4,077 O Instituto das Franciscanas Missionárias de Maria. PORT. EM AFR. 4 (1947), pp. 65-77.

4,078 João XXIII. PORT. EM AFR. 15 (1958), p. 321.

4,079 Journées d'études sur la cartographie des religions en Afrique noire (29 juin-3 juillet 1953) [by X...]. BULL. IFAN 16 (1954), pp. 418-422.

4,080 Latrocínio infame. PORT. EM AFR. 19 (1962), pp. 23-25.

4,081 Morreu Pio XII. PORT. EM AFR. 15 (1958), pp. 257-259.

4,082 Novo Ministro do Ultramar [Raul Ventura]. PORT. EM AFR. 12 (1955), pp. 209-210.

4,083 Padre José Alves Têrcas. PORT. EM AFR. 1 (1944), pp. 117-118.

4,084 Perspectives catholiques en Afrique. ZAIRE 6 (1952), pp. 290-291.

4,085 Pontificado Missionário de Pio XI. PORT. EM AFR. 6 (1949), pp. 43-48, 361-368.

4,086 Quand "les Dieux" parlent à France-Soir. PRESENCE AFR. N. S. 54 (1965), pp. 262-264.

4,087 Training of the ministry in Africa: a claim for women. AFR. WOMEN 1 (1955), pp. 47-48.

4,088 1505: A Carta de Poderes do Capitão-Mor. PORT. EM AFR. 12 (1955), pp. 485-488.

Islam

4,089 A., P. Petite critériologie pour une sociologie de l'Islam négro-africain. AFR. ET ASIE 44 (1958), pp. 42-50.

4,090 BLYDEN, E. W. The Koran in Africa. J. AFR. SOC. 4 (1905), pp. 157-171.

4,091 DELAFOSSE, M. Islam in Africa. INT. REV. MISSIONS 15 (1926), pp. 533-546.

4,092 GAIRDNER, W. H. T. Islam in Africa: the sequel to a challenge. INT. REV. MISSIONS 13 (1924), pp. 3-25.

4,093 GRAY, A. Moslem Conference. AFR. AFFAIRS 58 (1959), pp. 106-107.

4,094 MILLER, W. R. Islam in Africa. INT. REV. MISSIONS 15 (1926), pp. 556-568.

4,095 MONTEIL, V. L'Islam noir. REV. TUN. SC. SOC. 4 (1965), pp. 31-66.

4,096 N'GOMA, A. L'Islam noir. PRESENCE AFR. 8 (1950), pp. 333-343.

4,097 ZWEMMER, S. M. Islam in Africa. INT. REV. MISSIONS 15 (1926), pp. 547-555.

4,098 Conferenza islamico-cristiana ad Alessandria. AFRICA (Rome) 10 (1955), p. 73.

See also 494, 517, 543, 700, 3066, 3920, 3958, 4044, 4419, 4437, 4495, 4569, 4570, 4680, 4686.

SCIENCE

General

4,099 BAFFOUR, R. P. Science and technology in relation to Africa's development. PROC. INT. CONG. AFR. 1 (1962), pp. 301-308.

4,100 BEHANZIN, L. S. Responsabilités des Noirs d'Afrique en fait de culture scientifique. PRESENCE AFR. N.S. 16 (1957), pp. 70-79.

4,101 DIOP, C. A. Alerte sous les Tropiques. PRESENCE AFR. 5 (1955-1956), pp. 8-33.

4,102 KEAY, R. W. K. The natural sciences in Africa. AFR. AFFAIRS, Special Issue (1965), pp. 50-54.

4,103 MABONA, P. A. Vocation et présence de l'Afrique dans la vie scientifique moderne. PRESENCE AFR. N.S. 48 (1963), pp. 206-209.

4,104 MALVEZZI DE MEDICI, Marquis DE and LOUWERS, O. Foreign scientific missions in Africa, 1927-1933. J. AFR. SOC. 32 (1933), pp. 405-408.

4,105 MENDES, M. J. F. Relatório adicional ao Capítulo II da agenda. BSEM 119 (1959), pp. 49-56.

4,106 MONOD, TH. Autour de la recherche scientifique africaine. GENEVE-AFR. 1 (1962), pp. 9-15; abridged English version, pp. 16-19.

4,107 MONOD, TH. Two African international scientific conferences. GEOG. REV. 40 (1950), pp. 309-312.

4,108 OGILVIE, A. G. 'Science in Africa' by E. B. Worthington: a review. AFRICA 12 (1939), pp. 233-238.

4,109 SANTOS, M. P. DOS. Capítulo II da Ordem do Dia: construção e conservação das estradas: Relatório Geral. BSEM 119 (1959), pp. 31-46.

4,110 TROUP, R. S. Science in Africa [by E. B. Worthington]. J. AFR. SOC. 38 (1939), pp. 227-239.

4,111 U.N.E.S.C.O. Lagos plan for scientific research and training in Africa. AFRICA QUART. 4, no. iii (1964), pp. 205-216.

4,112 WORTHINGTON, E. B. Science in African international relations. INTERNAT. AFFAIRS 29 (1953), pp. 52-58.

4,113 Colonial research [need for central control of research]. AFR. AFFAIRS 45 (1946), pp. 3-4; 46 (1947), pp. 182-183.

4,114 Conférence Internationale sur le rôle de la science dans le développement des nouveaux Etats. Institut de Science Weizmann Réhovoth, Israël 15-28 août 1960. RECH. ET. CAM. 2 (1960), pp. 93-96.

4,115 Conseil scientifique pour l'Afrique au Sud du Sahara. BULL. IFAN 14 (1952), pp. 363-365.

4,116 The state of research in British Africa. AFR. AFFAIRS 52 (1953), pp. 58-63.

4,117 U.N.S.C.A.T. (United Nations Conference on the Application of Science and Technology for the Benefit of the Less Developed Areas). GENEVE-AFR. 2 (1963), pp. 97-117.

Human and veterinary medicine.
Hygiene. Public health

4,118 AFRICANUS. The African sleeping-sickness. CONTEMP. REV. 137 (1930), pp. 615-622.

4,119 AMOUSSOUGA, P. Recherches entomologiques et grandes endémies. Conférence donnée à l'I.R.A.D. le 9 Février 1965. ET. DAHOM. N.S. 4 (1965), pp. 87-79.

4,120 ANNETT, H. E. The work of the Liverpool School of Tropical Medicine. J. AFR. SOC. 1 (1902), pp. 208-213.

4,121 ARAUJO, J. S. Métodos profiláticos na Peripneumonia contagiosa em Africa. BOL. INST. ANGOLA 6 (1955), pp. 25-42.

4,122 BAKER, P. Skin marking of Africans. WEST. AFR. MILITARY MED. BULL. 2 (1942), p. 46.

4,123 BEIT, Sir A. Health services for Africans. RACE RELATIONS 16 (1949), pp. 32-37.

4,124 BENOIST, J. Données comparatives sur la croissance somatique des enfants de couleur et des enfants de race blanche nés et élevés à la Martinique. J. SOC. AFR. 29 (1959), pp. 7-9.

4,125 BERTE, M. Histopathology of the cutaneous lesions of Kwashiorkor. MALNUTRITION IN AFRICAN WOMEN..., 1952, pp. 111-114.

4,126 BIGWOOD, E. J. Sulphur deficiency and Kwashiorkor. MALNUTRITION IN AFRICAN WOMEN..., 1952, pp. 249-253.

4,127 BOYLE, A. K. A useful vein-seeker. WEST AFR. MILITARY MED. BULL. 2 (1942), pp. 46-47.

4,128 BRODEN, . The sleeping-sickness. J. AFR. SOC. 5 (1906), pp. 409-417.

4,129 BRUCE, D. Sleeping-sickness in Africa. J. AFR. SOC. 7 (1908), pp. 249-259.

4,130 CAMAIN, R. and PIERCHON, M. Lesions of the pancreas in Kwashiorkor. MALNUTRITION IN AFRICAN WOMEN..., 1952, pp. 146-151.

4,131 CAMARA, T. Recherches sur les relations antigènes et immunigènes des virus de la maladie de Carré et de la peste bovine. RECH. AFR. 1-4 (1964), pp. 99-150.

4,132 CAWSTON, F. G. The problem of controlling bilharzia infection. TANG. NOTES 16 (1943), pp. 96-98.

4,133 CHAMBERLAIN, J. The London School of Tropical Medicine. LIBERIA BULL. 18 (1901), pp. 25-31.

4,134 CHRISTY, C. Sleeping sickness. J. AFR. SOC. 3 (1903), pp. 1-11.

4,135 CORREIA, P. J. A. Acção médica nas colónias e a dos Missionários Cristãos. PORT. EM AFR. 2 (1945), pp. 279-283.

4,136 COSTA, F. M. C. DA. Conferência sobre a lepra em Brazzaville. BCBP 14 (1959), pp. 633-667.

4,137 COSTA, F. C. DA. Estudo do valor comparative do exame de suco ganglionar a fresco e de sangue em gota espessa corada, no diagnóstico da tripanosomíase humana à T. gambiense. BCBP 18 (1963), pp. 195-201.

4,138 COUTELLER, I. H. LE. Febre hemo-globinúrica. PORT. EM AFR. 5 (1948), pp. 44-48.

4,139 CRUZ, C. S. Fomento e sanidade pecuárias: principios e disposições básicas duma organização imperial dos Serviços Veterinários Coloniais. BSEM 69 (1951), pp. 65-88.

4,140 CUNHA, C. A. DO C. L. O teste de Thorn nas eosinofílias parasitárias do africano. BCGP 17 (1962), pp. 437-447.

4,141 DARKER, G. F. The practice of tropical hygiene. J. AFR. SOC. 13 (1913), pp. 51-53.

4,142 DAVEY, D. G. Antrycide and the problems of tsetse fly disease. AFR. AFFAIRS 48 (1949), pp. 205-212, 297-300.

4,143 DAVIES, J. N. P. Introductory statement on the pathology of Kwashiorkor. MALNUTRITION IN AFRICAN WOMEN..., 1952, pp. 109-110.

4,144 DIAKITE, L. Contribution a l'étude de éosinophilie tropicale. RECH. AFR. 2 (1962), pp. 7-22.

4,145 DIONISIO BARRETO, A. and SIMOES ALBERTO, M. Contribuição para o estudo dos grupos sanguineos como caracteristica etnológica de raças humanas. BSEM 80 (1953), pp. 27-39.

4,146 EKODO-NKOULOU-ESSAMA, F. La médecine par les plantes en Afrique Noire. PRESENCE AFR. 27-28 (1959), pp. 252-262.

4,147 FALADE, S. Rapport sur le fonctionnement de l'Institut d'ethno-psychopathologie africaine. CAH. ET. AFR. 4 (1964), pp. 603-620.

4,148 FERREIRA, F. S. C. et al. Síndroma de Guillain-Barré numa africana, by F. S. C. Ferreira, C. C. L. Cunha, F. A. Conceição. BCGP 18 (1963), pp. 185-194.

4,149 FERREIRA, M. C. A importância da sistemática na resolução do problema da Bilharziose. BSEM 96 (1956), pp. 53-57.

4,150 GANZIN, M. J. A contribution to the study of plasma proteins in the African. MALNUTRITION IN AFRICAN WOMEN..., 1952, pp. 200-202.

4,151 GEFFEN, D. H. Disease control in the tropics. CORONA 4 (1952), pp. 309-311.

4,152 GIBBS, P. The London School of Tropical Medicine. J. AFR. SOC. 2 (1903), pp. 316-324.

4,153 GILKS, J. L. The relation of economic development to public health in rural Africa. J. AFR. SOC. 34 (1935), pp. 31-40.

4,154 GIROLAMI, M. I problemi medici ed igienici e la campagna contro la fame. AFRICA (Rome) 18 (1963), pp. 132-134.

4,155 HAWKING, F. Filariasis. TANG. NOTES 7 (1939), pp. 28-34.

4,156 HOFFMANN, W. H. Leprosy and the cultural development of Africa. AFRICA 5 (1932), pp. 455-463.

4,157 HORN, A. E. The control of disease in Tropical Africa. J. AFR. SOC. 32 (1933), pp. 21-30, 123-134, 252-260.

4,158 IRVINE, F. R. Health and agriculture in Africa. AFR. AFFAIRS 53 (1954), pp. 132-142.

4,159 JEFFREYS, M. D. W. Bilharzia Schistosomum. NADA 31 (1954), pp. 95-96.

4,160 JOHNSTON, Sir H. H. A note on a possible specific for blackwater fever. J. AFR. SOC. 7 (1908), pp. 147-149.

4,161 JONES, Dame K. War hospitals in Africa. AFR. AFFAIRS 43 (1944), pp. 81-84.

4,162 KIRK, R. Notes on yellow fever. SUDAN NOTES 34 (1953), pp. 47-61.

4,163 LADKIN, R. S. The medical officer and Local Government. J. AFR. ADM. 5 (1953), pp. 21-30.

4,164 LAMBRECHT, F. L. Aspects of evolution and ecology of tsetse flies and trypanosomiasis in prehistoric African environment. J. AFR. HIST. 5 (1964), pp. 1-24.

4,165 LEMAIRE, R. et al. Les effets toxiques des extraits de Physalia pelagica by R. Lemaire, P. Camain, R. Postel, Y. Leduc, S. Ehrhard. BULL. IFAN 15 (1953), pp. 1128-1137.

4,166 LINDAN, O. Experiments on dietary liver injury. MALNUTRITION IN AFRICAN WOMEN..., 1952, pp. 129-141.

4,167 LORAM, C. T. The training of Africans in medicine and public health. INT. REV. MISSIONS 18 (1929), pp. 410-415.

4,168 LOTTE, A. J. Casque colonial et insolation. ET. GUIN. 2 (1947), pp. 69-75.

4,169 MACDONALD, G. Malaria control for rural populations. AFR. AFFAIRS 44 (1945), pp. 171-176.

4,170 MAEGRAITH, B. G. The diagnosis and treatment of snake bite. WEST AFR. MILITARY MED. BULL. 2 (1942), pp. 24-30.

4,171 MAEGRAITH, B. G. The liver in malaria. MALNUTRITION IN AFRICAN WOMEN..., 1952, pp. 144-145.

4,172 MANSON, Sir P. The malaria parasite. J. AFR. SOC. 6 (1907), pp. 225-233.

4,173 MANSON, Sir P. A school of tropical medicine. ROYAL COL. INST. PR. 31 (1899-1900), pp. 178-206.

4,174 MANSON, Sir P. Schools of tropical medicine. LIBERIA BULL. 18 (1901), pp. 56-62.

4,175 MATILLA, V. Los problemas de la Salud en el Trópico Africano. ARCH. INST. EST. AFR. 14, no. 52 (1960), pp. 43-60.

4,176 MATILLA, V. Síntesis de la labor sanitaria de España en Africa. ARCH. INST. EST. AFR. 19, no. 74 (1965), pp. 7-28.

4,177 MEILLON, B. DE. Yellow fever. RHODES-LIV. J. 6 (1948), pp. 60-63.

4,178 METTAM, R. W. M. A short history of Rinderpest with special reference to Africa. UGANDA J. 5 (1937), pp. 22-26.

4,179 MINCHIN, E. A. The prevention of malaria. J. AFR. SOC. 10 (1911), pp. 157-172.

4,180 MINGONI, G. Contro la malaria in Africa. AFRICA (Rome) 11 (1956), pp. 216-218.

4,181 MINGONI, G. Il programma dell'U.N.I.C.E.F. in Africa. AFRICA (Rome) 13 (1958), pp. 199-201.

4,182 MORAIS, T. DE. Alguno métodos práticos de investigação na Bilharziose, compatíveis com os meios ao dispor das clínicas rurais. BSEM 97 (1956), pp. 61-86.

4,183 MORENO MARTIN, F. et al. Nuestra aportación a la lucha contra la lepra; by F. Moreno Martin, J. Ramos Boned, A. Santos Merino. ARCH. INST. EST. AFR. 3, no. 7 (1949), pp. 93-99.

4,184 MUIR, E. The leprosy situation in Africa. J. AFR. SOC. 39 (1940), pp. 134-142.

4,185 NICOLAS, J. P. Esquisse écologique des complexes pathologènes intertropicaux. BULL. IFAN 21 (1959), pp. 155-166.

4,186 NWEDO, A. A Cultura Africana e a Religião Crista. PORT. EM AFR. SUPPL. (1960-1961), pp. 379-384.

4,187 OLDHAM, J. H. Population and health in Africa. INT. REV. MISSIONS 15 (1926), pp. 402-417.

4,188 POWER, A. D. A British empire leprosarium. J. AFR. SOC. 38 (1939), pp. 465-468.

4,189 POWER, A. D. The leprosy problem in Africa. AFR. AFFAIRS 44 (1945), pp. 81-85.

4,190 RIEL, J. VAN. De tropische omgeving. KONGO-OVERZEE 22 (1956), pp. 207-229.

4,191 RODHAIN, A. La prophylaxie antimalarienne dans les régions tropicales, envisagée à la lumière des récents progrès thérapeutiques. BULL. SEANCES IRCB 4 (1933), pp. 649-667.

4,192 RODRIGUES MARTINS, J. L. R. Primeira reunião dos especialistas do C.S.A. sobre a utilizacão dos radioisótopos (Prétória 1957). BSEM 122 (1960), pp. 79-124.

4,193 ROSS, Sir R. Malaria in India and the Colonies. ROYAL COL. INST. 35 (1903-1904), pp. 7-26.

4,194 ROSS, Sir R. The progress of tropical medicine. J. AFR. SOC. 4 (1905), pp. 271-289.

4,195 RUAS, A. A Difeniltioureia (D.P.T. ou CIBA 1906) no tratamento da lepra. BCGP 17 (1962), pp. 375-383.

4,196 RUSSELL, H. B. L. Epidemiology and the provision of health services in Africa. MAN AND AFRICA, 1965, pp. 146-169.

4,197 RUSSELL, H. B. L. The work of the World Health Organization in Africa. COOPERAZIONE INT. AFR., 1960, pp. 133-137.

4,198 SAAKWA-MANTE, K. A survey of the levels and age distribution of African infant mortality based on reports of special studies in fifteen areas. GHANA MED. J. 4 (1965), pp. 2-8, 42-46.

4,199 SANTOS DIAS, J. A. T. Algumas considerações sobre o controle da Glossina austeni Newst., baseado no conhecimento da sua ecologia. BSEM 91 (1955), pp. 125-134.

4,200 SCHWETZ, J. Le Quatrième Congrès international de médicine tropicale et de paludisme à Washington du 10 au 18 mai 1948. ZAIRE 3 (1949), pp. 35-45.

4,201 SELLERS, W. Teaching hygiene. AFR. WOMEN 1 (1956), pp. 87-89.

4,202 SILVA, A. DE N. W. DA. Tuberculose-Readaptação. BCGP 15 (1960), pp. 805-818.

4,203 SILVERA, W. D. Fatty liver in new-born African infants. MALNUTRITION IN AFRICAN WOMEN..., 1952, p. 143.

4,204 SIMOES ALBERTO, M. Elementos para o reajustamento da Carta Hematológica dos povos Negros da Africa a Sul do Equador. BSEM 128 (1961), pp. 67-75.

4,205 SINGER, R. The sickle cell trait in Africa. AMER. ANTHR. 55 (1953), pp. 634-648.

4,206 SMITH, H. Medicine in Africa as I have seen it. AFR. AFFAIRS 54 (1955), pp. 28-36.

4,207 STAMMERS, F. A. R. Surgical operations in the tropics. WEST AFR. MILITARY MED. BULL. 1 (1942), pp. 11-12.

4,208 STETSON, G. R. Hygiene in Equatorial Africa. LIBERIA BULL. 11 (1897), pp. 1-9.

4,209 STEUDEL, Prof. Dr. Epidemiologische Betrachtungen über die Wege der Schlafkrankheit und ihre Ausbreitung durch den Weltkrieg. AFRICA 2 (1929), pp. 105-128; English summary, pp. 128-129.

4,210 TROWELL, H. C. Prevention of Kwashiorkor in children. MALNUTRITION IN AFRICAN WOMEN..., 1952, pp. 315-321.

4,211 TROWELL, H. C. Public health in British Tropical Africa. INT. REV. MISSIONS 28 (1939), pp. 407-414.

4,212 VERHAGEN, P. Une conférence sur les problèmes de la santé mentale en Afrique noire (Bukavu, 10-18 mars 1958). ZAIRE 12 (1958), pp. 409-412.

4,213 WATERLOW, J. C. Nomenclature of Kwashiorkor. MALNUTRITION IN AFRICAN WOMEN..., 1952, p. 357.

4,214 WATSON, Sir M. Malaria and nutrition in Africa. J. AFR. SOC. 36 (1937), pp. 405-420.

4,215 WILSON, J. F. Blindness in colonial Africa. AFR. AFFAIRS 52 (1953), pp. 141-149.

4,216 WOODALL, J. P. O'nyong-nyong. TRANSITION 6-7 (1962), pp. 33-34.

4,217 Blackwater fever and its treatment. J. AFR. SOC. 4 (1905), pp. 437-440.

4,218 The fight against malaria: an industrial necessity for our African colonies. Translated by Sir William MacGregor from the Cologne Gazette. J. AFR. SOC. 2 (1903), pp. 149-160.

4,219 The Liverpool School of Tropical Medicine. AFR. AFFAIRS 47 (1948), pp. 222-227.

4,220 Yellow fever control [a recommendation by the Colonial Office]. J. AFR. SOC. 41 (1942), p. 107.

Nutrition

4,221 BASCOULERGUE, P. IVe Conférence Interafricaine sur l'alimentation et la nutrition (Douala 4-13 septembre 1961). RECH. ET CAM. 5 (1961-1962), pp. 132-134.

4,222 BENIPARRELL, C. DE. Los problemas alimenticios del continente africano. CUAD. EST. AFR. 28 (1954), pp. 19-28.

4,223 BIGWOOD, E. J. and ADRIAENS, E. L. Amino-acid content of cassava meal. MALNUTRITION IN AFRICAN WOMEN..., 1952, pp. 243-248.

4,224 CULWICK, G. M. Nutrition work in British African colonies since 1939. AFRICA 14 (1943), pp. 24-26.

4,225 DEAN, R. F. A. Preparation of soya bean and banana diet. MALNUTRITION IN AFRICAN WOMEN..., 1952, p. 279.

4,226 FERRAO, J. E. M. Estudos sobre alimentação tropical. BOL. INST. ANGOLA 14 (1960), pp. 61-73.

4,227 FROSSART, M. Colloque sur la banane de table [12-19 october 1960]. RECH. AFR. 3 (1961), pp. 70-71.

4,228 JONES, E. B. Preparation of fermented soya bean curd (tempe). MALNUTRITION IN AFRICAN WOMEN..., 1952, pp. 278-279.

4,229 LABOURET, H. L'alimentation des autochtones dans les possessions tropicales. AFRICA 11 (1938), pp. 160-173.

4,230 PLATT, B. S. Nitrogen metabolism in malnourished infants and children. MALNUTRITION IN AFRICAN WOMEN..., 1952, pp. 153-159.

4,231 PLATT, B. S. Some nutritional implications of the mother-infant interrelationship. MALNUTRITION IN AFRICAN WOMEN..., 1952, pp. 285-289.

4,232 RICHARD-MOLARD, J. A propos de la faim de l'Afrique. Alimentation et nutrition en Afrique noire, d'après la conférence de Dschang. BULL. IFAN 13 (1951), pp. 906-915.

4,233 SAUNDERS, L. H. My citrus recipes. NIGERIAN FIELD 1, no. 3 (1932), pp. 45-47.

4,234 THOMAS, L. V. Essai sur la conduite négro-africaine du repas (l'alimentation comme fait humain total). BULL. IFAN 27 (1965), pp. 573-635.

4,235 TROWELL, H. C. A note on definitions and terminology of a malnutritional disorder in childhood. MALNUTRITION IN AFRICAN WOMEN..., 1952, pp. 351-354.

4,236 XABREGAS, J. Nutrição, agronomia e educação alimentar. BOL. INST. ANGOLA 12 (1959), pp. 67-74.

4,237 L'alimentazione in Africa: I Convegni di Ancona, Bari e Roma tra il luglio e l'ottobre 1963. AFRICA (Rome) 19 (1964), pp. 17-43.

Biology. Botany. Zoology.
Conservation of nature

4,238 ALFARO CARDOSO, J. G. Considerações sobre a protecção da natureza. BSEM 126 (1961), H 3.

4,239 ANDRADA, E. DE C. Como encarar e defender as florestas coloniais. BSEM 51, no. i (1946), pp. 255-268.

4,240 BAILLAUD, E. The mangrove: its botanical characteristics and economic uses. J. AFR. SOC. 4 (1905), pp. 172-182.

4,241 BERTRAND, L. Contribution à l'étude anatomique des Marantacées africaines. BULL. I.E.C. N.S. 15-16 (1958), pp. 99-144.

4,242 BOURKE, D. O'D. On keeping owls in captivity. NIGERIAN FIELD 21 (1956), pp. 28-35.

4,243 BOWEN, W. W. Some recorded cases of albinism, melanism and abnormal coloration in African animals. SUDAN NOTES 9 (1926), part 2, pp. 69-73.

4,244 BRANCO, A. C. A entomologia—sua evolução. BCGP 10 (1955), pp. 635-640.

4,245 BUXTON, E. N. The preservation of species in Africa. J. AFR. SOC. 20 (1921), pp. 279-283.

4,246 CARPENTER, G. D. H. Two remarkable African butterflies and the study of geographical distribution of animals. J. AFR. SOC. 26 (1926), pp. 27-39.

4,247 CHAPIN, J. P. and MARCHANT, S. The lyre-tailed honey guide. NIGERIAN FIELD 15 (1950), pp. 19-21.

4,248 CHARADRIUS. The Senegal golden oriole, Oriolus Auratus Auratus. NIGERIAN FIELD 3 (1934), pp. 121-122.

4,249 CHRISTY, C. The African buffalo. J. AFR. SOC. 22 (1923), pp. 203-217.

4,250 CHRISTY, C. The African elephant. J. AFR. SOC. 21 (1922), pp. 92-104, 187-198, 291-301; 22 (1922), pp. 30-42.

4,251 COLA ALBERICH, J. Problemas de la fauna y la ganadería en Africa. CUAD. EST. AFR. 15 (1951), pp. 45-53.

4,252 COLA ALBERICH, J. Repercusiones sociológicas de la ruptura del equilibrio natural en la vegetación africana. CUAD. EST. AFR. 13 (1951), pp. 27-34.

4,253 COLLINS, W. B. The tropical forest: an animal and plant association. NIGERIAN FIELD 21 (1956), pp. 4-27.

4,254 DAVID, P. Quatre nouvelles Sagra africaines (Col. Chrysomelidae). BULL. IFAN 15 (1953), pp. 1506-1511.

4,255 DEKEYSER, P. L. A propos de la tête osseuse d'un Cynocéphale du Tibesti. BULL. IFAN 14 (1952), pp. 537-544.

4,256 DEKEYSER, P. L. Essai sur les Singes fossiles et les Hommes-Singes d'Afrique. BULL. IFAN 15 (1953), pp. 185-219.

4,257 DEKEYSER, P. L. Influences saisonnières sur le cycle sexuel des Oiseaux. BULL. IFAN 13 (1951), pp. 535-542.

4,258 DEKEYSER, P. L. and VILLIERS, A. La zoologie africaine et la systematique. BULL. IFAN 13 (1951), pp. 253-257.

4,259 DENDROPHILUS. The African tulip tree (Spathodea campanulata Beauv.). NIGERIAN FIELD 3 (1934), pp. 67-69.

4,260 DIAS, J. A. T. S. A propósito de uma pequena colecção de carraças do Museu de Hamburgo. BSEM 101 (1956), pp. 47-60.

4,261 DOLLMAN, G. African antelopes. J. AFR. SOC. 35 (1936), supplement.

4,262 F., W. A. African scops owl: Otus Senegalensis. NIGERIAN FIELD 3 (1934), pp. 73-76.

4,263 FAIRBAIRN, W. A. The African hobby. NIGERIAN FIELD 8 (1939), p. 107.

4,264 FERREIRA, M. C. Catálogo dos Escarabídeos da Região Etiópica: tribo Onitini. BSEM 123 (1960), pp. 97-148.

4,265 FERREIRA, M. C. Morfologia dos Coleópteros Africanos. BSEM 81 (1953), pp. 139-171; 83 (1954), pp. 53-81; 90 (1955), pp. 97-133.

4,266 FIGUEIREDO GOMES E SOUSA, A. DE. O género "Khaya" na Africa portuguesa (apontamentos para o seu estudo). BSEM 3 (1932), pp. 41-55.

4,267 FISHER, H. M. The African elephant and its hunters. TANG. NOTES 18 (1944), p. 98.

4,268 GOWERS, Sir W. Elephants in Africa [by Frank Melland]. J. AFR. SOC. 38 (1939), pp. 145-149.

4,269 HALDANE, J. B. S. Biological research in developing countries. MAN AND AFRICA, 1965, pp. 222-238.

4,270 HOBLEY, C. W. National sanctuaries. The key of the wild life position. J. AFR. SOC. 32 (1933), pp. 171-177.

4,271 HOBLEY, C. W. The preservation of wild life in the empire. J. AFR. SOC. 34 (1935), pp. 403-407.

4,272 HOWARD, Sir A. The circulation of organic matter in nature. J. AFR. SOC. 40 (1941), pp. 19-26.

4,273 JACQUES-FELIX, H. Sur quelques Melastomaceae d'Afrique. BULL. IFAN 15 (1953), pp. 972-1001.

4,274 JEFFREYS, M. D. W. African Pterodactyls. AFR. AFFAIRS 43 (1944), pp. 72-74.

4,275 JEFFREYS, M. D. W. The Basenji or kur-dogge. NIGERIAN FIELD 19 (1954), pp. 70-76.

4,276 JEFFREYS, M. D. W. Honey-guides. NIGERIAN FIELD 17 (1952), pp. 66-69.

4,277 JEFFREYS, M. D. W. Indicatoridae: two early references. NIGERIAN FIELD 27 (1962), pp. 45-46.

4,278 JEFFREYS, M. D. W. The muscovy duck. NIGERIAN FIELD 21 (1956), pp. 108-111.

4,279 JEFFREYS, M. D. W. Notes on the Situtunga. NIGERIAN FIELD 9 (1940), pp. 65-68.

4,280 JEFFREYS, M. D. W. Some re-discoveries. NADA 33 (1956), pp. 92-94.

4,281 JOERGENS, W. Crocodile gall. TANG. NOTES 18 (1944), pp. 99-100.

4,282 JOHNSTON, A. The common date palm (Phoenix dactylifera). J. AFR. SOC. 3 (1904), pp. 177-182.

4,283 JOHNSTON, Sir H. H. The Mammalian fauna of Africa. J. AFR. SOC. 19 (1920), pp. 253-277.

4,284 LEROY, J. F. La conception synthétique de l'espèce: étude morphologique et biogeographique sur un groupe de Celtis de la section Solenostigma (Ulmacées-Celtidoïdées). BULL. IFAN 10 (1948), pp. 212-234.

4,285 LISTER, U. G. African grey parrots breeding in captivity. NIGERIAN FIELD 27 (1962), pp. 127-134.

4,286 MARTINHO, J. As reacções das raças bovinas selectas da Europa nos climas tropicais e subtropicais. BSEM 52, no. i (1947), pp. 49-76.

4,287 MASSON, H. Condensations atmosphériques non enregistrables au pluviomètre. [L'eau de condensation et la végétation.] BULL. IFAN. 10 (1948), pp. 1-181.

4,288 MONOD, TH. A propos des Campos Cerrados. BULL. IFAN 12 (1950), pp. 844-849.

4,289 MONOD, TH. Sur l'appareil branchiospinal de quelques Téléosteens tropicaux. BULL. IFAN 11 (1949), pp. 36-76.

4,290 MOREWOOD-DOWSETT, J. Elephant past and present. J. AFR. SOC. 38 (1939), supplement.

4,291 ONSLOW, Earl of. Preservation of African fauna. J. AFR. SOC. 37 (1938), pp. 380-386.

4,292 PAIX, H. Note sur une anomalie dentaire chez un gorille. BULL. I.E.C. 1, no. 1 (1945), pp. 109-110.

4,293 PIC, M. Nouveaux Coléoptères africains. BULL. IFAN 15 (1953), pp. 495-506.

4,294 PIRES, F. A. Uma nova espécie de glossina do grupo morsitans (Diptera, Muscidae, Glossina borgesi sp. nov.). BSEM 125 (1960), D 4.

4,295 PIRES, F. A. and SILVA, J. M. DA. Subsídios para o estudo das Glossinas do Ultramar português. Sobre a morfologia da armadura genital da G. pallidipes Austen, 1903 (Diptera). BSEM 125 (1960), D 3.

4,296 PITOT, A. Les Racines échasses de Rhizophora racemosa. BULL. IFAN 13 (1951), pp. 978-1010.

4,297 PITOT, A. Recherches anatomiques sur la plantule du Cupressus Mac-Nabiana. BULL. IFAN 11 (1949), pp. 255-280.

4,298 PITOT, A. Sur l'ovaire de deux Borraginales. BULL. IFAN 12 (1950), pp. 75-101.

4,299 PORTERES, R. Eleusine coracana Gaertner, céréale des humanités pauvres des pays tropicaux. BULL. IFAN 13 (1951), pp. 1-78.

4,300 PRIESTLEY, N. New light on the tiger fish? NIGERIAN FIELD 22 (1957), p. 183.

4,301 QUENUM, S. Les glandes extra-florales chez quelques plantes tropicales. ET. DAHOM. N.S. 2 (1964), pp. 21-32.

4,302 REYNOLDS, V. Some behavioral comparisons between the Chimpanzee and the Mountain Gorilla in the wild. AMER. ANTHR. 67 (1965), pp. 691-706.

4,303 REYNOLDS, V. Troop life among chimpanzees. EAISR, July (1962), pp. 1-8.

4,304 ROMER, J. D. et al. Racial variation in the common African toad. NIGERIAN FIELD 17 (1952), pp. 82-83.

4,305 ROSA PINTO, A. A. DA. Descrição de uma nova sub-espécie de mirafra africanoides. BSEM 75 (1952), pp. 5-7.

4,306 RUSHBY, G. G. The African elephant and its hunters. TANG. NOTES 17 (1944), pp. 59-63.

4,307 SANTOS DIAS, J. A. T. Chave para os Ixodideos Adultos género Haemaphysalis Koch conhecidos até 1954 na Africa Etiopica. BSEM 92 (1955), pp. 53-68.

4,308 SANTOS DIAS, J. A. T. Chave para os subgéneros do género Rhipicephalus Koch, 1844 (Acarina, Ixodoidea). BSEM 114 (1959), pp. 73-90.

4,309 SANTOS DIAS, J. A. T. Estudo sobre alguns rhipicephalus do grupo simus sub-grupo planus nov. BSEM 74 (1952), pp. 53-63.

4,310 SAUNDERS, L. H. Some euphorbias for the verandah. NIGERIAN FIELD 3 (1934), pp. 83-84.

4,311 SERLE, W. The blue-throated Roller (Eurystomus gularis) Vieillot. NIGERIAN FIELD 20 (1955), pp. 172-173.

4,312 SHARPE, A. Big game shooting in Africa. J. AFR. SOC. 22 (1922), pp. 1-4.

4,313 SIKES, S. K. Pluto the hornbill (Bucorvus Abyssinicus [Boddaert]). NIGERIAN FIELD 21 (1956), pp. 79-84.

4,314 SILLANS, R. Economie des plantes à parfums d'Afrique centrale. BULL. I.E.C. N.S. 9 (1955), pp. 107-140.

4,315 SILVA TEIXEIRA, A. J. DA and R. DE C. S. DA. Glossário do algodão. BSEM 79 (1953), pp. 1-148.

4,316 SIMMONS, F. J. Notes on the bush-pig (potamochoerus). UGANDA J. 17 (1953), pp. 80-81.

4,317 SPENCER, H. A. The driver ant of Africa. CONTEMP. REV. 153 (1938), pp. 609-612.

4,318 STIGAND, C. H. Scent and sight amongst game and other animals. SUDAN NOTES 1 (1918), pp. 16-20.

4,319 TENDEIRO, J. Etudes sur les mallophages. Deux espèces parasites d'Apus affinis (Aves, Apodidae): Eureum cimicoides Burmeister et Dennyus hirundinis (L.) (Amblycera, Menoponidae). BCGP 13 (1958), pp. 477-487.

4,320 TENDEIRO, J. Etudes sur les mallophages. Nouvelles observations sur le genre Columbicola Ewing avec description de deux nouvelles espèces. BCGP 15 (1960), pp. 529-624.

4,321 TENDEIRO, J. Etudes sur les mallophages. Observations aditionelles sur le genre Mulcticola (Ischnocera, Philopteridae), avec la description de quelques nouvelles espèces. BCGP 17 (1962), pp. 345-373.

4,322 TENDEIRO, J. Etudes sur les mallophages. Observations sur des Ischnocera africains, avec description de 12 espèces et 2 sous-espèces nouvelles. BCGP 17 (1962), pp. 669-704.

4,323 TENDEIRO, J. Etudes sur les mallophages. Observations sur des Ischnocera africains, avec description de 12 espèces et 2 sous-espèces nouvelles (suite et fin). BCGP 18 (1963), pp. 13-106.

4,324 TENDEIRO, J. Etudes sur les mallophages. Sur quelques espèces et sous-espèces du genre Nosopon Hopkins (Amblycera, Menoponidae), parasites de Falconiformes. BCGP 14 (1959), pp. 193-211.

4,325 TENDEIRO, J. Etudes sur les mallophages. Sur deux espèces et deux sous-espèces nouvelles du Penenirmus Th. Clay et Meinertzhagen (Ischnocera, Philopteridae) obtenues sur des Capitonidés. BCGP 15 (1960), pp. 785-803.

4,326 TENDEIRO, J. Etudes sur les mallophages. Sur deux espèces et trois sous-espèces du genre Degeeriella Neumann 1906 (Ischnocera, Philopteridae), parasites de Falconiformes. BCGP 13 (1958), pp. 25-62.

4,327 TENDEIRO, J. Etudes sur les mallphages. Sur deux espèces et trois sous-espèces nouvelles du genre Columbicola Ewing, parasites de Columbidés africains. BCGP 14 (1959), pp. 669-699.

4,328 TENDEIRO, J. Etudes sur les mallophages. Quelques espèces recontrées sur le Tantale Ibis, Ibis ibis (L.). BCGP 13 (1958), pp. 157-173.

4,329 TENDEIRO, J. Nota sobre a distribuição geográfica dos aponomas africanos. BCGP 13 (1958), pp. 269-303.

4,330 TENDEIRO, J. Sobre alguns ixodídeos dos géneros Hyalomma C. L. Koch 1844 e Aponomma Neumann 1899. BCGP 10 (1955), pp. 319-461.

4,331 TENDEIRO, J. and VALDEZ, V. Nota sobre os helmintes de alguns peixes da costa portuguesa e do Atlântico Sul. BCGP 12 (1957), pp. 333-345.

4,332 TROCHAIN, J. L. La cartographie botanique. Application à la feuille de Thies (A.O.F.: Senegal). BULL. I.E.C. N.S. 7-8 (1954), pp. 187-200.

4,333 TROCHAIN, J. Nomenclature et classification des types de végétation en Afrique Noire Française. BULL. I.E.C. N.S. 2 (1951), pp. 9-18.

4,334 VILLIERS, A. L'Assemblée générale de l'Union Internationale pour la Protection de la Nature (Caracas, 1952). BULL. IFAN 15 (1953), pp. 461-464.

4,335 VILLIERS, A. La collection de Serpents de l'IFAN. (Acquisitions 1952.) BULL. IFAN 15 (1953), pp. 1103-1127.

4,336 VILLIERS, A. Les Endomychidae africains III. Notes sur diverses espèces du genre Trycherus. BULL. IFAN 15 (1953), pp. 1463-1505.

4,337 WELMAN, J. Crocodiliana. CORONA 2 (1950), pp. 400-402.

4,338 WILDEMAN, E. DE. Les bambous en Afrique. CONGO 1 (1921), pp. 10-44.

4,339 WILLIAMS, C. B. The migrations of Libytheine butterflies in Africa. NIGERIAN FIELD 16 (1951), pp. 152-159.

4,340 WORTHINGTON, E. B. Dynamic conservation in Africa. NYASA J. 14, no. 2 (1961), pp. 7-12.

4,341 ZICCARDI, F. Antilopi e gazzelle d'Africa. Le antilopi piccole e medie. AFRICA (Rome) 15 (1960), pp. 193-196, 241-243.

4,342 ZICCARDI, F. Incalzata dall' avenzare dell' uomo scompare la fauna africana. AFRICA (Rome) 13 (1958), pp. 72-74.

4,343 ZICCARDI, F. I rischi della caccia grossa. AFRICA (Rome) 17 (19620, pp. 83-86, 311-314.

4,344 Association pour l'Etude Taxonomique de la Flore d'Afrique Tropicale (A.E.T.F.A.T.). BULL. AFR. STUD. ASSOC. 3 (1964), pp. 9-11.

4,345 La conférence scientifique des Nations Unies pour la conservation et l'utilisation des ressources naturelles. BULL. IFAN 12 (1950), pp. 242-243.

4,346 La conférence technique internationale pour la protection de la nature. BULL. IFAN 12 (1950), pp. 243-247.

4,347 International Office for the Protection of Nature: its origin, programme and organization. NIGERIAN FIELD 2, no. 8 (1933), pp. 4-12.

Geology. Soil science. Mineralogy. Hydrology.
Mathematics. Physics

4,348 BERNARD, E. A. Interprétation astronomique des pluviaux et interpluviaux du Quaternaire africain. PROC. PAN-AFR. CONGR. PRE-HIST. 4 (1962), pp. 67-95.

4,349 BEYER, G. Algumas possibilidades do emprêgo da Geofísica no sul do Continente Africano. BSEM 31 (1936), pp. 155-166.

4,350 BOUFFIL, P. Etude du mouvement des éléments minéraux dits assimilables et de l'azote total dans un sol à différentes profondeurs. BULL. IFAN 1 (1939), pp. 769-836.

4,351 CHOUBERT, G. Note sur le mécanisme probable des granitisations: application à certains granites africains. PROC. SYMP. GRANITES W. AFR., 1965, pp. 53-93.

4,352 COLA ALBERICH, J. Los minerales de interes estratégico en Africa. CUAD. EST. AFR. 19 (1952), pp. 9-17.

4,353 DANDY, A. J. Physico-chemical investigations of East African clays. PROC. E. AFR. ACAD. 2 (1964), pp. 3-10.

4,354 DOWSETT, J. M. Soil erosion. AFR. AFFAIRS 43 (1944), pp. 29-39.

4,355 FUSTER, J. M. Las técnicas fotogeológicas y los problemas geológicos africanos. ARCH. INST. EST. AFR. 11, no. 47 (1958), pp. 41-54.

4,356 GUISCAFRE, J. 1ère Conférence Interafricaine sur l'Hydrologie (Nairobi, 16-25 janvier 1961). RECH. ET. CAM. 4 (1961), pp. 102-106.

4,357 HAARER, A. E. Africa's chief problem [: water]. CONTEMP. REV. 185 (1954), pp. 104-107.

4,358 JOHNSTONE, S. J. Metals of the British Empire. BULL. IMP. INST. 39 (1941), pp. 152-160.

4,359 MEEO, J. F. DE. As pérolas finas selvagens e de cultura e os bancos perolíferos do Ultramar Português. BSEM 91 (1955), pp. 143-173.

4,360 MONOD, TH. A propos du livre de R. Furon, Géologie de l'Afrique. BULL. IFAN 12 (1950), pp. 1150-1154.

4,361 MONOD, TH. Résumés des exposés faits par Th. Monod à la séance du C.L.O.E.C. du 21 novembre 1949. I. Les remontées d'eaux littorales. II. Note sur le phénomène d'eaux rouge et les mortalités massives de poissons. BULL. IFAN 12 (1950), pp. 838-841.

4,362 MOUMOUNI, A. L'énergie solaire dans les pays africains. PRESENCE AFR. N.S. 50 (1964), pp. 96-126.

4,363 MULHACEN, Marqués DEL. La obra científica del general marques de Mulhacen y la union geodésica y astronómica de España con Africa. ARCH. INST. EST. AFR. 9, no. 37 (1956), pp. 57-75.

4,364 MUSSETT, A. E. et al. Palaeomagnetism in East Africa: a progress report on the tertiary volcanics. PROC. E. AFR. ACAD. 2 (1964), pp. 27-35.

4,365 SURET-CANALE, J. La troisième conférence interafricaine des sols (Dalaba: 2-11 novembre 1959). RECH. AFR. 2 (1960), pp. 54-59.

4,366 THOMPSON, A. B. The development of subsoil water in Africa. J. AFR. SOC. 32 (1933), pp. 334-341.

4,367 WHITE, K. K. Geometry, the African and civilisation. NADA 32 (1955), pp. 68-71.

4,368 La conférence interafricaine des sols de Dalaba. RECH. AFR. 1 (1960), pp. 3-11.

4,369 The constitution and work of the Imperial Institute, with special reference to mineral resources. BULL. IMP. INST. 15 (1917), pp. 335-353.

4,370 Rapport du Colloque C.S.A. sur l'Oceanographie et les Pêches maritimes sur la côte occidentale d'Afrique, tenu à Luanda du 21 au 27 novembre 1957 (Afrique Equatoriale Française). BULL. I.E.C. N.S. 17-18 (1959), pp. 155-156.

4,371 XVe Congrès de géologie international. BULL. ACAD. MALG. 10 (1927), pp. 43-44.

See also 464, 621, 628, 662, 730, 1698, 2767, 3925, 3963, 4214, 4455, 4492, 4512.

SOCIOLOGY:
demography. games. community development. social welfare. philosophy (social)

4,372 ABDEL-MALEK, A. La vision du problème colonial par le monde Afro-Asiatique. CAH. INT. SOCIOL. 35 (1963), pp. 145-156.

4,373 ABOU-SIRIL. Civilisations africaines au pluriel. PRESENCE AFR. 8 (1950), pp. 71-77.

4,374 ABRAHAMS, P. The conflict of culture in Africa. INTERNAT. AFFAIRS 30 (1954), pp. 304-312.

4,375 ABRAHAMS, P. Le conflit de cultures en Afrique. PRESENCE AFR. N.S. 14-15 (1957), pp. 107-118.

4,376 ACHILLE, L. T. Les Negro-spirituals et l'expansion de la culture noire. PRESENCE AFR. N.S. 8-10 (1956), pp. 227-237.

4,377 AFRIKANUS. Triangulação em devir. PORT. EM AFR. 19 (1962), pp. 36-40.

4,378 AGBLEMAGNON, F. N. La condition socio-culturelle negro-africaine et le cinéma. PRESENCE AFR. N.S. 55 (1965), pp. 32-41.

4,379 AGBLEMAGNON, N'S. F. Pessoa, tradiçao e cultura na Africa Negra. PORT. EM AFR. SUPPL. (1960-1961), pp. 319-326.

4,380 AGBLEMAGNON, N'S. Les responsabilités du sociologue africain. PRESENCE AFR. 27-28 (1959), pp. 206-214.

4,381 AGBLEMAGNON, F.N. Totalité et systèmes dans les sociétés d'Afrique Noire. PRESENCE AFR. N.S. 41 (1962), pp. 13-22.

4,382 AKALA, E. Colonisation, décolonisation et préjugés raciaux en Afrique Noire. PRESENCE AFR. N.S. 54 (1965), pp. 54-74.

4,383 ALBERT, A. A propos de Study in Brown. PRESENCE AFR. N.S. 44 (1962), pp. 81-99.

4,384 ALEXANDRE, P. DES émancipations africaines à la réforme de l'enseignement ethnologique français. AFR. ET ASIE 49 (1960), pp. 26-37.

4,385 ALEXIS, J.S. Du réalisme merveilleux des Haïtiens. PRESENCE AFR. N.S. 8-10 (1956), pp. 245-271.

4,386 ALLEGRET, E. Black and white in Africa: a French point of view. INT. REV. MISSIONS 15 (1926), pp. 327-343.

4,387 ALLEN, S.W. Muntu. PRESENCE AFR. N.S. 44 (1962), pp. 210=214.

4,388 ALLIATA DI MONTEREALE. Discours du prince Alliata di Montereale, à l'occasion du IIe Congrès de la Société africaine de culture. PRESENCE AFR. N.S. 24-25 (1959), pp. 31-33.

4,389 ALVAREZ, M. DE T. La problación del Continente Africano, su evolucion, distribución regional y perspectivas para el futuro. ARCH. INST. EST. AFR. 17, no. 68 (1963), pp. 25-35.

4,390 ARMSTRONG, R.G. Le développement de l'unité culturelle en Afrique, au sud du Sahara. PRESENCE AFR. N.S. 24-25 (1959), pp. 316-320.

4,391 ARNETT, E. J. Demography in Africa. J. AFR. SOC. 39 (1940), pp. 176-180.

4,392 ATANGANA, N. Cultures africaines et développement. ABBIA 2 (1963), pp. 18-24; English translation, pp. 25-30.

4,393 ATANGANA, N. La femme africaine dans la société. PRESENCE AFR. N.S. 13 (1957), pp. 133-142.

4,394 ATKINSON, G. A. African housing. AFR. AFFAIRS 49 (1950), pp. 228-237.

4,395 B., A. Problèmes de l'étudiant noir. PRESENCE AFR. 14 (1953), pp. 2-32.

4,396 BACHELARD, G. et al. Témoignages sur la Philosophie Bantoue du Père Tempels, by Gaston Bachelard, Albert Camus and others. PRESENCE AFR. 7 (1949), pp. 252-278.

4,397 BALANDIER, G. Africanism confronted with problems of political anthropology and political sociology. PROC. INT. CONG. AFR. 1 (1962), pp. 267-271.

4,398 BALANDIER, G. L'Africanisme face aux problèmes de l'anthropologie et de la sociologie politique. PRESENCE AFR. N.S. 46 (1963), pp. 197-201.

4,399 BALANDIER, G. Déséquilibres socio-culturels et modernisation des "pays sous-développés." CAH. INT. SOCIOL. 20 (1956), pp. 30-44.

4,400 BALANDIER, G. Erreurs noires. PRESENCE AFR. 3 (1948), pp. 392-404.

4,401 BALANDIER, G. Messianismes et nationalismes en Afrique noire. CAH. INT. SOCIOL. 14 (1953), pp. 40-65.

4,402 BALANDIER, G. Les mythes politiques de colonisation et de décolonisation en Afrique. CAH. INT. SOCIOL. 33 (1962), pp. 85-96.

4,403 BALANDIER, G. Le noir est un homme. PRESENCE AFR. 1 (1947), pp. 31-36.

4,404 BALANDIER, G. Problematique des classes sociales en Afrique noire. CAH. INT. SOCIOL. 38 (1965), pp. 131-142.

4,405 BALANDIER, G. Sociologie dynamique et histoire à partir de faits Africains. CAH. INT. SOCIOL. 34 (1963), pp. 3-11.

4,406 BANTON, M. Africa south of the Sahara excluding Southern Rhodesia and the Union of South Africa. INT. SOC. SC. J. 13 (1961), pp. 197-214.

4,407 BANTON, M. White Englishmen and brown. AFR. SOUTH 1, no. 4 (1957), pp. 82-88.

4,408 BARTOCCI, E. L'Africa del lavoro attraverso il cinema. AFRICA (Rome) 10 (1955), pp. 156-157.

4,409 BASCOM, W. African material culture, technology, and ecological adaptation. ANTHROPOLOGY AND AFRICA TODAY, 1962, pp. 581-589.

4,410 BASCOM, W. The urban African and his world. CAH. ET. AFR. 4, no. 14 (1963), pp. 163-185.

4,411 BASTIDE, R. Amérique du Sud. PRESENCE AFR. 8 (1950), pp. 385-391.

4,412 BATTEN, T. R. The community and development. CORONA 3 (1951), pp. 330-334.

4,413 BATTEN, T. R. The community and the external agent. CORONA 4 (1952), pp. 328-332.

4,414 BATTEN, T. R. Community development in the colonies. AFR. AFFAIRS 50 (1951), pp. 321-326.

4,415 BEIT, A. Health services for Africans. RACE RELATIONS 16 (1949), pp. 32-37.

4,416 BENNABI, M. [Problems of African culture]. PRESENCE AFR. N.S. 24-25 (1959), pp. 286-291.

4,417 BERGER, J. The penance of Europe [review article on Muntu: An Outline of Neo-African Culture by Janheinz Jahn]. AFR. SOUTH 5, no. 4 (1961), pp. 124-128.

4,418 BERNOLLES, J. Les Noirs et le Sahara. ET. DAHOM. N.S. 4 (1965), pp. 69-86.

4,419 BIOBAKU, S. O. Aspects historiques de l'acculturation: L'historique d'un cas. PRESENCE AFR. N.S. 47 (1963), pp. 194-198.

4,420 BISSAINTHE, R. P. G. Le Christianisme face aux aspirations culturelles des peuples noirs. PRESENCE AFR. N.S. 8-10 (1956), pp. 326-329.

4,421 BLANC, P. A propos des migrations dans l'ancienne Afrique Française. AFR. ET ASIE 54 (1961), pp. 16-36.

4,422 BLOOM, L. Some psychological concepts of urban Africans. ETHNOLOGY 3 (1964), pp. 66-95.

4,423 BLYDEN, E. W. The African and the European. LIBERIA BULL. 30 (1907), pp. 20-22.

4,424 BOELAERT, E. De "Bantoe-Filosofie" volgens E. P. Tempels. ZAIRE 1 (1947), pp. 387-398.

4,425 BOELAERT, E. La philosophie Bantoue selon le R. P. Placide Tempels. AEQUATORIA 9 (1946), pp. 81-90.

4,426 BOURGEOIS-PICHAT, J. Problems of population size, growth and distribution in Africa. MAN AND AFRICA, 1965, pp. 65-97.

4,427 BOYER, J. Le jeu africain des godets. PRESENCE AFR. 7 (1949), pp. 310-314.

4,428 BRAUSCH, G. Promotion du bien-être rural Africain. KONGO-OVERZEE 23 (1957), pp. 146-199.

4,429 BRELSFORD, V. The philosophy of the savage. NADA 15 (1938), pp. 62-65.

4,430 BROWN, W. O. The outlook for the white man in Africa, particularly as settler. AFR. STUD. BULL. 3, no. iii (1960), pp. 1-11.

4,431 BROWNE, G. B. O. The African prisoner. CONTEMP. REV. 151 (1937), pp. 577-582.

4,432 BRUYNE E. DE. Kantteekeningen bij de Bantu-Philosophie. KONGO-OVERZEE 10-11 (1944-1945), pp. 255-260.

4,433 BUNBURY, I. Women's position as workers in Africa south of the Sahara. CIVILISATIONS 11 (1961), pp. 159-168; French summary, pp. 168-170.

4,434 C., J. La population scolaire en Afrique portugaise. ZAIRE 9 (1955), p. 170.

4,435 CAILLENS, J. Culture et civilisation noire à travers l'édition française. PRESENCE AFR. 4 (1948), pp. 706-709.

4,436 CALLAWAY, A. Unemployment among African school leavers. J. MOD. AFR. STUD. 1 (1963), pp. 351-371.

4,437 CANALE, J. S. Contexte et conséquences sociales de la traite africaine. PRESENCE AFR. N.S. 50 (1964), pp. 127-150.

4,438 CARDAIRE, M. L'Islam et la cellule sociale africaine. AFR. ET ASIE 29 (1955), pp. 20-28.

4,439 CARRINGTON, C. E. Frontiers in Africa. INTERNAT. AFFAIRS 36 (1960), pp. 424-439.

4,440 CARTER, G. E. Traditional African social thought. PAN-AFRICANISM RECONSIDERED, 1962, pp. 255-266.

4,441 CARTER, G. M. Multi-racialism in Africa. INTERNAT. AFFAIRS 36 (1960), pp. 457-463.

4,442 CECCHELLA, A. Il lavoro obbligatorio e l'ascesa economica e sociale dell'Africa. AFRICA (Rome) 17 (1962), pp. 283-290.

4,443 CEPOLLARO, A. Il Peul Bororo nelle sue migrazioni. AFRICA (Rome) 18 (1963), pp. 291-292.

4,444 CERBELLA, G. Il tukul primitiva abitazione dei nostri padri. AFRICA (Rome) 18 (1963), pp. 33-37.

4,445 CESAIRE, A. Culture et colonisation. PRESENCE AFR. N.S. 8-10 (1956), pp. 190-205.

4,446 CESAIRE, A. L'homme de culture et ses responsabilités. PRESENCE AFR. N.S. 24-25 (1959), pp. 116-122.

4,447 CHARLES, P. Le traumatisme noir. Essai de psychologie culturelle. ZAIRE 7 (1953), pp. 449-468.

4,448 CHISIZA, D. K. Plural societies, multiracial governments, racial partnership. AFRICA QUART. 2, no. i (1962), pp. 5-9.

4,449 CHOMBART DE LAUWE, P. H. Esquisse d'un plan de recherches sur la vie sociale en milieu urbain. CT 8, nos. 29-30 (1960), pp. 5-16.

4,450 CHRISTY, C. White settlement in Tropical Africa. J. AFR. SOC. 27 (1928), pp. 338-341.

4,451 CLARK, J. D. Human ecology during pleistocene and later times in Africa south of the Sahara. CURRENT ANTHR. 1 (1960), pp. 307-324.

4,452 CLAYTON, H. R. A psychological approach to race relations. PRESENCE AFR. 3 (1948), pp. 418-431; 4 (1948), pp. 549-563.

4,453 COLA ALBERICH, J. Aspectos de la acción cultural europea en Africa. CUAD. EST. AFR. 21 (1953), pp. 9-22.

4,454 COLA ALBERICH, J. Le déclin des Sociétés Négro-Africaines. AEQUATORIA 18 (1955), pp. 98-104.

4,455 COLA ALBERICH, J. El declive de las sociedades negro-africanas. CUAD. EST. AFR. 25 (1954), pp. 23-33.

4,456 COLA ALBERICH, J. L'hydrographie comme facteur bio-dynamique et sociologique en Afrique. PRESENCE AFR. 13 (1952), pp. 34-42.

4,457 COLA ALBERICH, J. Problemas de contacto de culturas en Africa. CUAD. AFR. OR. 30 (1955), pp. 9-23.

4,458 COLSON, E. Family change in contemporary Africa. ANTHROPOLOGY AND AFRICA TODAY, 1962, pp. 641-652.

4,459 COMHAIRE, J. La délinquance dans les grandes villes d'Afrique britannique. ZAIRE 3 (1949), pp. 1101-1108.

4,460 COMHAIRE, J. L. The community concept in the study and government of African and Afro-american societies. PRIMITIVE MAN 25 (1952), pp. 41-48.

4,461 CONCEICAO TAVARES DA SILVA, M. Feminilidade e cultura. PORT. EM AFR. SUPPL. (1960-1961), pp. 347-363.

4,462 COOK, M. Les relations raciales aux Etats-Unis vues par les voyageurs français depuis la deuxième guerre mondiale. PRESENCE AFR. N.S. 14-15 (1957), pp. 119-128.

4,463 CORY, H. The necessity. Co-ordination of economic and political development. TANG. NOTES 30 (1951), pp. 78-82.

4,464 CRAHAY, F. De la décolonisation culturelle. ZAIRE 14 (1960), pp. 539-548.

4,465 CROOKENDEN, H. The Capricorn contract. AFR. AFFAIRS 55 (1956), pp. 297-302.

4,466 CROWLEY, D. J. L'héritage africain dans les Bahamas. PRESENCE AFR. N.S. 23 (1958-1959), pp. 41-58.

4,467 CULWICK, A. T. The labourer and his hire. TANG. NOTES 17 (1944), pp. 26-33.

4,468 CUNNINGHAM, M. M. Problems of the African family. LIBERIA BULL. 34 (1909), pp. 19-21.

4,469 DADIE, B. B. Un negro a Roma. AFRICA (Rome) 15 (1960), pp. 287-291.

4,470 DAVIES, O. Food-supply and human rights in barbaric and developed societies. UNIVERSITAS 1, no. 5 (1955), pp. 9-11.

4,471 DAVIS, J. The participation of the Negro in the democratic process in the United States. PRESENCE AFR. N.S. 14-15 (1957), pp. 129-147.

4,472 DELAUNEY, C. Préjuges. PRESENCE AFR. 7 (1949), pp. 309-310.

4,473 DESMOULIEZ, G. Les accords culturels de la France avec les Etats d'expression française. ANNALES AFR., 1962, pp. 521-528.

4,474 DESSARRE, E. Aperçus du drame africaine. PRESENCE AFR. N. S. 22 (1958), pp. 101-106.

4,475 DEVERNOIS, G. The social evolution in the Algerian Departments and in the Overseas territories of the French Republic. CIVILISATIONS 7 (1957), pp. 597-606.

4,476 DIA, M. Economie et culture devant les élites africaines. PRESENCE AFR. N.S. 14-15 (1957), pp. 58-72.

4,477 DIAGNE, P. L'Afro-franglais. PRESENCE AFR. N.S. 52 (1964), pp. 150-156.

4,478 DIAKHATE, L. Politique et culture. CIVILISATIONS 14 (1964), pp. 94-100.

4,479 DIOP, A. Colonialisme et nationalisme culturels. PRESENCE AFR. N.S. 4 (1955), pp. 5-15.

4,480 DIOP, A. De l'expansion du travail. PRESENCE AFR. 13 (1952), pp. 5-17.

4,481 DIOP, A. Niam n'goura ou les raisons d'être de Présence Africaine. PRESENCE AFR. 1 (1947), pp. 7-14; English translation, pp. 185-192.

4,482 DIOP, A. Solidarité du culturel et du politique. PRESENCE AFR. N.S. 41 (1962), pp. 117-122.

4,483 DIOP, C. A. Apports et perspectives culturels de l'Afrique. PRESENCE AFR. N.S. 8-10 (1956), pp. 339-346.

4,484 DIOP, C. A. Résponses à quelques critiques. BULL IFAN 24 (1962), pp. 542-474.

4,485 DIOP, C. A. Sociologie africaine et méthodes de recherche. PRESENCE AFR. N.S. 48 (1963), pp. 180-186.

4,486 DIOP, C. A. L'unité culturelle africaine. PRESENCE AFR. N.S. 24-25 (1959), pp. 60-65.

4,487 DIOP, D. Etudiant africain devant le fait colonial. PRESENCE AFR. 14 (1953), pp. 114-117.

4,488 DONOHUGH, A. C. L. Essentials of African culture. AFRICA 8 (1935), pp. 329-338.

4,489 DOVER, C. Culture and creativity. PRESENCE AFR. N.S. 8-10 (1956), pp. 281-300.

4,490 DU BOIS, W. E. B. Africa and the American Negro intelligentsia. PRESENCE AFR. N.S. 5 (1955-1956), pp. 34-51.

4,491 DU SAUTOY, P. A guide for the administrator to the principles of community development. J. LOCAL ADM. OV. 2 (1963), pp. 204-211.

4,492 DU SAUTOY, P. Some administrative aspects of community development. J. LOCAL ADM. OV. 1 (1962), pp. 39-46.

4,493 EDOZIEN, J. C. Malaria, population growth and economic development in Africa. PROC. INT. CONG. AFR. 1 (1962), pp. 329-333.

4,494 EHRENFELS, U. R. The African synthesis. AFR. QUART. 1, no. 1 (1961), pp. 10-19.

4,495 EISENSTADT, S. N. Social change and modernization in African societies south of the Sahara. CAH. ET. AFR. 5 (1965), pp. 453-471.

4,496 EKOLLO, T. De l'importance de la culture pour l'assimilation du message chrétien en Afrique Noire. PRESENCE AFR. N.S. 8-10 (1956), pp. 179-189.

4,497 EKONDY-AKALA. Les élites africaines et les relations raciales. PRESENCE AFR. N.S. 56 (1965), pp. 45-67.

4,498 EREKOSIMA, T. V. The political role of the medicine man in Africa: his relation to the function of cultural values in public affairs. PROC. 3RD. GRAD. ACAD. UCLA, 1965, pp. 163-179.

4,499 ETIEMBLE, M. Esquisse d'une pédagogie antiraciste. PRESENCE AFR. N.S. 26 (1959), pp. 114-118.

4,500 EVANS, M. S. International conference on the negro. J. AFR. SOC. 11 (1912), pp. 416-429.

4,501 FALL, K. Problème de l'élite en Afrique noire. PRESENCE AFR. 14 (1953), pp. 33-39.

4,502 FALLERS, L. A. Are African cultivators to be called "peasants"? CURRENT ANTHR. 2 (1961), pp. 108-110.

4,503 FANON, F. Fondement réciproque de la culture nationale et des luttes de libération. PRESENCE AFR. N.S. 24-25 (1959), pp. 82-89.

4,504 FANON, F. Racisme et culture. PRESENCE AFR. N.S. 8-10 (1956), pp. 122-131.

4,505 FARIA, R. Aspectos humanos do problema africano. PORT. EM AFR. 19 (1962), pp. 196-205.

4,506 FARRER-BROWN, L. Dispensing bounty in Africa. AFR. AFFAIRS 59 (1960), pp. 201-212.

4,507 FELE, B. Qu'est-ce que le "luso tropicalismo"? PRESENCE AFR. N.S. 4 (1955), pp. 24-35.

4,508 FERENCZI, V. Quelques implications psycho-sociales du film et l'action éducative. PRESENCE AFR. N.S. 34-35 (1960-1961), pp. 104-123.

4,509 FERREIRA, H. H. The use of social case drama in training African social workers. RHODES-LIV. J. 13 (1953), pp. 35-40.

4,510 FERREIRA, J. Juventude, educação e liberdade. BCGP 19 (1964), pp. 129-142.

4,511 FERRINHO, H. Considerações sobre métodos de desénvolvimento das comunidades rurais. BSEM 139 (1964), pp. 9-159.

4,512 FILESI, T. L'istituto della famiglia nelle Costituzioni africane. AFRICA (Rome) 19 (1964), pp. 63-79.

4,513 FIRTH, R. The sociological study of native diet. AFRICA 7 (1934), pp. 401-414.

4,514 FONTAINE, W. T. Philosophical aspects of contemporary African social thought. PAN-AFRICANISM RECONSIDERED, 1962, pp. 244-254.

4,515 FRANKLIN, A. Le paternalisme contre l'étudiant africain. PRESENCE AFR. 14 (1953), pp. 71-82.

4,516 FRANTZ, C. Changes and continuities in Africa. RHODES-LIV. J. 27 (1960), pp. 50-58.

4,517 FRAZIER, E. F. Human, all too human. PRESENCE AFR. 6 (1949), pp. 47-60.

4,518 FREYRIA, C. La protection sociale de la main-d'oeuvre dans les pays en cours de développement. ANNALES AFR., 1962, pp. 181-196.

4,519 GELDERS, V. Christianisation et famille indigène en Afrique. KONGO-OVERZEE 14 (1948), pp. 82-86.

4,520 GELDERS, V. Programmes et plans de relèvement rural en pays tropicaux et sub-tropicaux. ZAIRE 8 (1954), pp. 75-89.

4,521 GIBBONS, R. M. African good manners. TANG. NOTES 1 (1936), pp. 81-83.

4,522 GIRAO, A. DE A. Papel das Elites na colonizacao Africana. PORT. EM AFR. 2 (1945), pp. 321-325.

4,523 GLUCKMAN, M. An advance in African sociology. AFR. STUD. 6 (1947), pp. 57-76.

4,524 GLUCKMAN, M. The difficulties, achievements, and limitations of social anthropology. RHODES-LIV. J. 1 (1944), pp. 22-43.

4,525 GLUCKMAN, M. Malinowski's 'functional' analysis of social change. AFRICA 17 (1947), pp. 103-121.

4,526 GOLDTHORPE, J. E. The present position of elite studies. EAISR, July (1962), pp. 1-4.

4,527 GOODY, J. Tribal, racial, religious and language problems in Africa. MAN AND AFRICA, 1965, pp. 98-120.

4,528 GOODY, J. and WATT, I. The consequences of literacy. COMP. STUD. SOC. HIST. 5 (1962-1963), pp. 304-345.

4,529 GORE-BROWNE, S. The relations of black and white in Tropical Africa. J. AFR. SOC. 34 (1935), pp. 378-386.

4,530 GRAVIERE, E. LA. The problem of alcoholism in the countries and territories south of the Sahara. INT. REV. MISSIONS 46 (1957), pp. 290-298.

4,531 GRAVIERE, E. LA. Le régime de l'alcool et la répression de l'alcoolisme dans la France d'Outre-Mer. BULL. IFAN 13 (1951), pp. 1309-1317.

4,532 GRIAULE, M. L'Action sociologique en Afrique noire. PRESENCE AFR. 3 (1948), pp. 388-391.

4,533 GRILO, V. H. V. Problemas da Societização da Cultura. BSEM 131 (1962), pp. 61-70.

4,534 GRUNDY, K. The 'class struggle' in Africa: an examination of conflicting theories. J. MOD. AFR. STUD. 2 (1964), pp. 379-393.

4,535 GUERIN, D. Controverse autour de l'héritage africain aux U.S.A. PRESENCE AFR. N.S. 18-19 (1958), pp. 166-172.

4,536 GUGLER, J. Life in a dual system. EAISR, Jan. (1965), pp. 1-14.

4,537 GUILLEME, M. Simples notes sur l'émigration des indigènes de l'Afrique centrale vers les centres industriels. AFRICA 5 (1932), pp. 40-49.

4,538 GUTKIND, P. C. W. African urban family life. CAH. ET. AFR. 3 (1962), pp. 149-217.

4,539 GUTKIND, P. C. W. The African urban milieu: a force in rapid change. CIVILISATIONS 12 (1962), pp. 167-191; French summary, pp. 192-195.

4,540 GUTKIND, P. C. W. African urbanism, mobility and the social network. INT. J. COMP. SOC. 6(1965), pp. 48-60.

4,541 GUTMANN, B. The African standpoint. AFRICA 8 (1935), pp. 1-19.

4,542 GUTTERIDGE, W. The place of the armed forces in society in African states. RACE 4, no. 1 (1962-1963), pp. 22-33.

4,543 HARLOW, V. Tribalism in Africa. J. AFR. ADM. 7 (1955), pp. 17-20.

4,544 HAW, R. C. The impact of civilization on the African. NADA 26 (1949), pp. 31-33; 27 (1950), pp. 82-84.

4,545 HAZOUME, P. L'humanisme occidental et l'humanisme africain. PRESENCE AFR. N.S. 14-15 (1957), pp. 29-45.

4,546 HEBGA, M. Une seule pensée, une seule civilisation. PRESENCE AFR. N.S. 14-15 (1957), pp. 301-306.

4,547 HEISLER, H. Strategy of social administration in Africa. CIVILISATIONS 13 (1963), pp. 474-488.

4,548 HERMANN, F. Les relations anthropologiques et culturelles de l'Afrique noire (Anthropologische und kulturelle Zusammenhange im schwarzen Afrika). PRESENCE AFR. N.S. 24-25 (1959), pp. 309-315.

4,549 HERSKOVITS, M. J. Le noir dans le nouveau monde. PRESENCE AFR. 8 (1950), pp. 347-356.

4,550 HERSKOVITS, M. J. Some contemporary developments in sub-Saharan Africa. AFR. STUD. 13 (1954), pp. 49-64.

4,551 HERSKOVITS, M. J. Traditions et bouleversements de la culture en Afrique. PRESENCE AFR. N.S. 34-35 (1960-1961), pp. 124-131.

4,552 HEUSCH, L. DE. Les vacances de la science? ZAIRE 10 (1956), pp. 717-728.

4,553 HOBLEY, C. W. Game and its relation to mankind. J. AFR. SOC. 29 (1929), pp. 139-148.

4,554 HODSON, H. V. Race relations in the Commonwealth. INTERNAT. AFFAIRS 26 (1950), pp. 305-315.

4,555 HOWLETT, J. Absence et présence. PRESENCE AFR. 1 (1947), pp. 50-55.

4,556 HOWLETT, J. Notes sur Chester B. Himes et l'aliénation noir. PRESENCE AFR. 4 (1948), pp. 697-704.

4,557 HUBBARD, J. W. The cause and the cure of African immorality. INT. REV. MISSIONS 20 (1931), pp. 241-253.

4,558 HUDSON, W. Psychological research on the African worker. CIVILISATIONS 8 (1958), pp. 193-201; French summary, pp. 201-203.

4,559 HULSTAERT, G. L'attraction des centres urbains. AEQUATORIA 16 (1953), pp. 76-79.

4,560 HULSTAERT, G. Le problème des Mulâtres. AFRICA 15 (1945), pp. 129-143; English summary, pp. 143-144; 16 (1946), pp. 39-44.

4,561 INDIAN COUNCIL FOR AFRICA. Seminar on Africa (Organized by Indian Council for Africa, February, 1961). AFRICA QUART. 1, no. ii (1961), pp. 47-53.

4,562 IVY, J. W. The National Association for the Advancement of Colored People. PRESENCE AFR. N.S. 8-10 (1956), pp. 330-335.

4,563 JEAL, E. F. Anthropological gulf [phobia on white Africans]. CONTEMP. REV. 198 (1960), pp. 490-493.

4,564 JEFFRIES, C. Recent social welfare developments in British Tropical Africa. AFRICA 14 (1943), pp. 4-10.

4,565 JOACHIM, P. Les clients noirs. PRESENCE AFR. N.S. 34-35 (1960-1961), pp. 161-167.

4,566 JOHNSTON, Sir H. H. Race problems in the new Africa. FOREIGN AFFAIRS 2 (1923-1924), pp. 598-612.

4,567 JOKL, E. African man-power. RACE RELATIONS 11 (1944), pp. 21-29.

4,568 JONES-QUARTEY, K. A. B. Black and white [review of some books on the subject]. UNIVERSITAS 4 (1961), pp. 141-147.

4,569 JUDD, H. The African woman designs her future. AFR. WOMEN 4 (1960), pp. 6-8.

4,570 JUNOD, H. P. Bantu marriage and Christian society. BANTU STUD. 15 (1941), pp. 25-36.

4,571 JUNOD, H. P. Christian home and family life in Africa. INT. REV. MISSIONS 53 (1964), pp. 89-93.

4,572 JUNOD, H. P. La Croix-Rouge et l'Afrique sub-saharienne, souvenirs et remarques au moment du centenaire. GENEVE-AFR. 2 (1963), pp. 163-182.

4,573 JUNOD, H. P. Influence du passé et du présent en Afrique. GENEVE-AFR. 1 (1962), pp. 80-98; English summary, pp. 99-100.

4,574 KALA-LOBE, I. La vocation africaine du sport. PRESENCE AFR. N.S. 41 (1962), pp. 34-57.

4,575 KELFA-CAULKER, O. African women in the new society. WOMEN TODAY 6 (1965), pp. 103-104.

4,576 KIDD, B. The future of the lower races. LIBERIA BULL. 5 (1894), pp. 49-63.

4,577 KINGSLEY, M. H. The relationship between European and African culture. LIBERIA BULL. 17 (1900), pp. 31-34.

4,578 KI-ZERBO, J. African personality and the new African society. PAN-AFRICANISM RECONSIDERED, 1962, pp. 267-282.

4,579 KI-ZERBO, J. La personnalité negro-africaine. PRESENCE AFR. N.S. 41 (1962), pp. 137-143.

4,580 KLINEBERG, O. Race differences: the present position of the problem. RHODES-LIV. J. 12 (1951), pp. 12-19.

4,581 KNAPPERT, J. Languages and societies. EAISR, June (1963), pp. 1-6.

4,582 KOHLER, O. Soziale vorgänge in Afrika und ihr Einflub auf religiöse Stammesvorstellungen. SOCIOLOGUS 3 (1953), pp. 29-49.

4,583 KUCZYNSKI, R. R. Population movements: the contribution of demography to the study of social problems. RHODES-LIV. J. 2 (1944), pp. 16-34.

4,584 LABOURET, H. Sur la main-d'oeuvre autochtone. PRESENCE AFR. 13 (1952), pp. 124-136.

4,585 LADIKPO, R. Table ronde sur l'artisanat et l'industrialisation. GENEVE-AFR. 3 (1964), pp. 105-106.

4,586 LAHBABI, M. A. Propos sur la civilisation et les cultures. PRESENCE AFR. N.S. 16 (1957), pp. 94-111; N.S. 17 (1957-1958), pp. 9-30.

4,587 LAMBO, T. A. Socioeconomic changes in Africa and their implications for mental health. MAN AND AFRICA, 1965, pp. 121-145.

4,588 LANDES, R. Negro slavery and female status. AFR. AFFAIRS 52 (1953), pp. 54-57.

4,589 LANGO, T. A. Important areas of ignorance and doubt in the psychology of the African. PROC. INT. CONG. AFR. 1 (1962), pp. 337-344.

4,590 LEMAIRE, Lieut. Woman in Africa. LIBERIA BULL. 11 (1897), pp. 43-50.

4,591 LOMBARD, J. Le collectivisme africain. Valeur socio-culturelle traditionnelle instrument de progrès économique. PRESENCE AFR. N.S. 26 (1959), pp. 22-51.

4,592 LOMBARD, J. Un "diptyque" de sociologie familiale. ZAIRE 9 (1955), pp. 1075-1087.

4,593 LORETO, R. Le civiltà nere. AFRICA (Rome) 19 (1964), pp. 7-11.

4,594 LOVERIDGE, A. J. Chiefs and politics. J. AFR. ADM. 11 (1959), pp. 201-207.

4,595 LYSTAD, R. A. Basic African values. NEW FORCES IN AFRICA, 1962, pp. 10-24.

4,596 M., M. De ontwikkeling van het Verstand bij het Negerkind. AEQUATORIA 5 (1942), pp. 30-32.

4,597 MABILLE, G. Lebollo contre stylographe. Le conflit de la coutume et des influences extérieures. PRESENCE AFR. 8 (1950), pp. 425-435.

4,598 MABONA, A. Eléments de culture africaine. PRESENCE AFR. N.S. 41 (1962), pp. 144-150.

4,599 MABONA, P. A. Philosophie africaine. PRESENCE AFR. N.S. 30 (1960), pp. 40-59.

4,600 MACINNES, C. Britain's mixed half-million. AFR. SOUTH 5, no. 2 (1961), pp. 107-115.

4,601 MACMILLAN, W. M. African growing pains. AFR. AFFAIRS 52 (1953), pp. 192-201.

4,602 MACRAE, D. G. Sociology in transitional societies. UNIVERSITAS 2 (1956), pp. 107-109.

4,603 MAGA, H. La promotion sociale africaine. CIVILISATIONS 8 (1958), pp. 182-190; English summary, pp. 191-192.

4,604 MAIR, L. P. Social change in Africa. INTERNAT. AFFAIRS 36 (1960), pp. 447-456.

4,605 MAIR, L. P. The study of culture contact as a practical problem. AFRICA 7 (1934), pp. 415-422.

4,606 MALCOLM, L. W. G. and PARKES, A. S. Sex-ratio in African peoples. AMER. ANTHR. 26 (1924), pp. 454-473.

4,607 MAQUET, J. J. De la dépandence à l'infériorité. ZAIRE 7 (1953), pp. 1066-1075.

4,608 MAQUET, J. J. La nouvelle civilisation de l'Afrique sera-t-elle celle de l'acier? PRESENCE AFR. N.S. 47 (1963), pp. 206-210.

4,609 MAQUET, J. J. Le relativisme culturel. PRESENCE AFR. N.S. 22 (1958), pp. 65-73; N.S. 23 (1958-1959), pp. 59-68.

4,610 MARS, J. A population stop policy for developing countries. NJESR 5 (1963), pp. 145-185.

4,611 MARWICK, M. G. New light on social relations: an appreciation of George C. Homans's The Human Group. RHODES-LIV. J. 14 (1954), pp. 41-48.

4,612 MARWICK, M. G. The study of social attitudes. RHODES-LIV. J. 5 (1947), pp. 44-47.

4,613 MASEFIELD, G. B. A comparison between settlement in villages and isolated homesteads. J. AFR. ADM. 7 (1955), pp. 64-68.

4,614 MASEFIELD, G. B. Farming systems and land tenure. J. AFR. ADM. 4 (1952), supplement, pp. 8-14.

4,615 MASON, P. The colour problem in Britain as it affects Africa and the Commonwealth. AFR. AFFAIRS 58 (1959), pp. 110-122.

4,616 MAUNY, R. Ancienneté de la variolisation en Afrique. PRESENCE AFR. 36 (1961), pp. 127-130.

4,617 MAYER, P. Migrancy and the study of Africans in towns. AMER. ANTHR. 64 (1962), pp. 576-592.

4,618 MELLAND, F. Ethical and political aspects of African witchcraft. AFRICA 8 (1935), pp. 495-503.

4,619 MEMEL-FOTE, H. De la Paix perpétuelle dans la philosophie pratique des Africains. PRESENCE AFR. N.S. 55 (1965), pp. 15-31.

4,620 MEMMI, A. Sociologie des rapports entre colonisateurs et colonisés. CAH. INT. SOCIOL. 23 (1957), pp. 85-96.

4,621 MERCIER, P. Les classes sociales et les changements politiques récents en Afrique noire. CAH. INT. SOCIOL. 38 (1965), pp. 143-154.

4,622 MERCIER, P. Remarques sur la signification du "tribalisme" actuel en Afrique noire. CAH. INT. SOCIOL. 31 (1961), pp. 61-80.

4,623 MERCIER, P. La sociologie et ses applications. BULL. IFAN 13 (1951), pp. 550-558.

4,624 MEZZA, E. L'Africa nella cinematografia italiana. AFRICA (Rome) 10 (1955), p. 125.

4,625 MILLER, K. The primary needs of the Negro race. LIBERIA BULL. 17 (1900), pp. 34-51.

4,626 MILLIN, S. G. Fear in Africa. FOREIGN AFFAIRS 28 (1949-1950), pp. 102-113.

4,627 MINGONI, G. Il bambino africano e l'opera dell'Unicef. AFRICA (Rome) 11 (1956), pp. 172-174.

4,628 MIRACLE, M. P. Seasonal hunger: a vague concept and an unexplored problem. BULL. IFAN 23 (1961), pp. 273-283.

4,629 MIRANDA SANTOS, A. A acção das estereotipias. PORT. EM AFR. 22 (1965), pp. 296-310.

4,630 MIRANDA SANTOS, A. Desenraizamentos. PORT. EM AFR. 22 (1965), pp. 364-379.

4,631 MIRANDA SANTOS, A. Obsolescência da negritude? PORT. EM AFR. 22 (1965), pp. 328-348.

4,632 MITCHELL, J. C. The anthropological study of urban communities. AFR. STUD. 19 (1960), pp. 169-172.

4,633 MITCHELL, J. C. The meaning in misfortune for urban Africans. AFRICAN SYSTEMS OF THOUGHT, 1965, pp. 192-203.

4,634 MNTAMBO, P. C. The African and how to promote his welfare. TANG. NOTES 18 (1944), pp. 1-10.

4,635 MONTEIL, C. La civilisation négro-africaine. BULL. IFAN 27 (1965), pp. 701-705.

4,636 MORAIS, E. O Negro no Pensamento Europeu. BOL. INST. ANGOLA 4 (1954), pp. 53-60.

4,637 MOREIRA, A. Problemas sociais do Ultramar. PORT. EM AFR. SUPPL. (1960-1961), pp. 335-346.

4,638 MORIN, J. V. Aide sociale. CANADA ET LES PAYS AFR. FRANCOPHONES, 1965, pp. 113-119.

4,639 MOUNIER, E. Lettre à un ami africain. PRESENCE AFR. 1 (1947), pp. 37-43.

4,640 MPHAHLELE, M. E. La culture noire dans une société multiraciale en Afrique. PRESENCE AFR. N.S. 24-25 (1959), pp. 208-214.

4,641 MPHAHLELE, M. E. The fabric of African cultures. FOREIGN AFFAIRS 42 (1963-1964), pp. 614-627.

4,642 MUMFORD, W. B. Education and the social adjustment of the primitive peoples of Africa to European culture. AFRICA 2 (1929), pp. 138-159.

4,643 NAIDOO, H. A. Keep Britain white. AFR. SOUTH 3, no. 2 (1959), pp. 65-68.

4,644 NAVILLE, P. Avertissement. PRESENCE AFR. 13 (1952), pp. 19-24.

4,645 NAVILLE, P. "Présence africaine." PRESENCE AFR. 1 (1947), pp. 44-46.

4,646 NEESEN, V. Le problème des statistiques démographiques en Africa. ZAIRE 6 (1952), pp. 339-349.

4,647 NENE-KHALY, B. Débats sur la jeunesse africaine. PRESENCE AFR. N.S. 20 (1958), pp. 86-103.

4,648 NERFIN, M. Towards a housing policy. JMAS 3 (1965), pp. 543-565.

4,649 NGANGO, G. Colonialisme culturel en Afrique. PRESENCE AFR. N.S. 47 (1963), pp. 199-205.

4,650 NGANGO, G. L'Occident chrétien face à l'éveil des non-occidentaux. PRESENCE AFR. N.S. 45 (1963), pp. 205-211.

4,651 NICOL, D. Our critics and lovers: three re-assessments [Albert Schweitzer, Graham Greene, Joyce Cary]. TRANSITION 22 (1965), pp. 32-37.

4,652 OGUNSHEYE, A. Société traditionnelle et démocratie moderne. PRESENCE AFR. N.S. 23 (1958-1959), pp. 6-15.

4,653 OKEDIJI, F. O. The social adjustment of the African students in two United States communities. NJESS 6 (1964), pp. 363-392.

4,654 OKEDIJI, F. O. Some correlates of ethnic cohesiveness: a further analysis of African students' adjustment in two United States communities. NJESS 7 (1965), pp. 347-362.

4,655 PARR, M. Marriage ordinances for Africans. AFRICA 17 (1947), pp. 1-7.

4,656 PATRI, A. Ya-t-il une philosophie bantoue? PRESENCE AFR. 2 (1948), pp. 203-208.

4,657 PATTERSON, C. J. What is Africa to me? TRANSITION 15 (1964), pp. 20-22.

4,658 PAUL, E. C. L'ethnologie et les cultures noires. PRESENCE AFR. N.S. 8-10 (1956), pp. 143-153.

4,659 PAULME, D. La femme africaine au travail. PRESENCE AFR. 13 (1952), pp. 116-123.

4,660 PAULME, D. La notion de parenté dans les sociétés Africaines. CAH. INT. SOCIOL. 15 (1953), pp. 150-173.

4,661 PEDRO ROMANO, G. M. Vantagens dos aldeamentos indígenas do ponto de vista das obras públicas. BSEM 120 (1960), pp. 47-52.

4,662 PHILLIPS, A. The African marriage survey. J. AFR. ADM. 1 (1949), pp. 39-40.

4,663 PHILIPPS, T. British influence as a vehicle of European civilisation in the Asian and African tropics. CIVILISATIONS 6 (1956), pp. 27-42; French summary, p. 43.

4,664 POLLINS, H. Coloured people in post-war English literature. RACE 1, no. 2 (1959-1960), pp. 3-13.

4,665 POSSOZ, E. La morale nègre. AEQUATORIA 2 (1939), p. 54.

4,666 POTEKHIN, I. De quelques problèmes méthodologiques pour l'étude de la formation des nations en Afrique au sud du Sahara. PRESENCE AFR. N.S. 17 (1957-1958), pp. 60-75.

4,667 PRESSAT, R. Les données démographiques du sous-développement. PRESENCE AFR. N.S. 21 (1958), pp. 14-22.

4,668 PRICE-MARS, J. Survivances africaines et dynamisme de la culture noire outre-Atlantique. PRESENCE AFR. N.S. 8-10 (1956), pp. 272-280.

4,669 PROST, A. Jeux et Jouets. PRESENCE AFR. 8 (1950), pp. 241-248.

4,670 PROTHERO, R. M. Continuity and change in African population mobility. GEOGRAPHERS AND THE TROPICS, 1964, pp. 189-213.

4,671 R., B. China's impact on Africa—a summing up. RACE 5, no. 4 (1963-1964), pp. 75-82.

4,672 RABEMANANJARA, J. Les fondements de notre unité tirés de l'époque coloniale. PRESENCE AFR. N.S. 24-25 (1959), pp. 66-81.

4,673 RAINERO, R. Observations sur l'opinion publique dans les pays Afro-Asiatiques. AFR. ET ASIE 60 (1962), pp. 5-16.

4,674 RICHARD-MOLARD, J. Collectivités et collectivismes en Afrique noire. AFR. ET ASIE 43 (1958), pp. 3-15.

4,675 RICHARD-MOLARD, J. Plaidoyer pour une nouvelle paysannerie en Afrique noire. PRESENCE AFR. 13 (1952), pp. 170-179.

4,676 RICHARD-MOLARD, J. Recherches sur le peuplement de l'Afrique. BULL. IFAN 12 (1950), pp. 232-240.

4,677 RICHARDS, A. I. Social mechanisms for the transfer of political rights in some African tribes. JRAI 90 (1960), pp. 175-190.

4,678 ROBINSON, A. E. Arabic family and individual names. TANG. NOTES 5 (1938), pp. 70-71.

4,679 RONAIVOARIVONY, G. DE P. Sociologie de la formation professionnelle et sous-developpement. GENEVE-AFR. 4 (1965), pp. 78-83.

4,680 ROSEVEARE, R. Anglican bishops and racial conflicts. AFR. SOUTH 3, no. 2 (1959), pp. 80-84.

4,681 ROSNER, M. S. Community development and the delinquent. RHODES-LIV. J. 38 (1965), pp. 1-10.

4,682 RUBBENS, A. De sociale bevordering van de mulatten. ZAIRE 8 (1954), pp. 507-512.

4,683 SACRE-COEUR, M. A. DU. La situation de la Femme en Afrique Noire francaise. CIVILISATIONS 1, no. 4 (1951), pp. 46-53; English summary, pp. 53-54.

4,684 SARTRE, J. P. Orphée noir. PRESENCE AFR. 6 (1949), pp. 9-14.

4,685 SARTRE, J. P. Presence noire. PRESENCE AFR. 1 (1947), pp. 28-29.

4,686 SASTRE, R. Théologie et culture africaine. PRESENCE AFR. N.S. 24-25 (1959), pp. 132-141.

4,687 SCHOLS, J. P. A contemporary approach to the question of dialogue. GHANA J. SOC. 1 (1965), pp. 1-9.

4,688 SEGY, L. African phallic symbolism. ZAIRE 9 (1955), pp. 1039-1067.

4,689 SENGHOR, L. S. Eléments constructifs d'une civilisation d'inspiration négro-africaine. PRESENCE AFR. N.S. 24-25 (1959), pp. 249-279.

4,690 SENGHOR, L. S. L'esprit de la civilisation ou les lois de la culture négro-africaine. PRESENCE AFR. N.S. 8-10 (1956), pp. 51-65.

4,691 SENGHOR, L. S. Négritude et civilisation de l'Universel. PRESENCE AFR. N.S. 46 (1963), pp. 8-13.

4,692 SHELTON, A. J. Las modificaciones metodológicas en las investigaciones de costumbres y Sociedades Africanas. ARCH. INST. EST. AFR. 19, no. 75 (1965), pp. 75-81.

4,693 SHELTON, A. J. Le principe cyclique de la personnalité africaine. PRESENCE AFR. N.S. 45 (1963), pp. 98-104; N.S. 46 (1963), pp. 64-67.

4,694 SILBERMAN, L. Logic and problems of sampling in social research. RHODES-LIV. J. 5 (1947), pp. 1-17.

4,695 SILBERMAN, L. The urban social survey in the colonies. ZAIRE 8 (1954), pp. 279-299.

4,696 SIMON, E. La Négritude et les problèmes culturels de l'Afrique contemporaine. PRESENCE AFR. N.S. 47 (1963), pp. 145-172.

4,697 SIMPSON, S. R. Land reform and procedure. J. LOCAL ADM. OV. 1 (1962), pp. 84-87.

4,698 SISSOKO, F. D. L'humour africain. PRESENCE AFR. 8 (1950), pp. 227-239.

4,699 SKALNIKOVA, O. Ethnographical research into the present changes in the mode of life of urban population in Africa. PROC. INT. CONG. AFR. 1 (1962), pp. 286-297.

4,700 SMITH, E. W. A survey of African marriage and family life. J. AFR. ADM. 5 (1953), pp. 102-112.

4,701 SMITH, R. B. Englishmen in Africa. CONTEMP. REV. 59 (1891), pp. 69-76.

4,702 SOUSBERGHE, L. DE. A propos de "la Philosophie Bantoue." ZAIRE 5 (1951), pp. 821-828.

4,703 SOUTHALL, A. W. On chastity in Africa. UGANDA J. 24 (1960), pp. 207-216.

4,704 SPENGLER, J. J. The Commonwealth: demographic dimensions; implications. COMMONWEALTH PERSPECTIVES, 1958, pp. 86-124.

4,705 SPENGLER, J. J. Population movements and problems in sub-Saharan Africa. ECON. DEV. FOR AFRICA, 1965, pp. 281-311.

4,706 STEEL, R. W. An inventory of land and people. J. AFR. ADM. 12 (1960), pp. 211-223.

4,707 STENNING, D. J. Relationship of social research to planning, organization and evaluation of national social welfare and community development programmes. EAISR, Jan. (1963), pp. 1-11.

4,708 STETSON, G. R. The eyes and ears of whites and blacks. LIBERIA BULL. 10 (1897), pp. 25-40.

4,709 TANBURN, E. The practical aspect of social and economic surveys in under-developed territories. WAISER 2 (1953), pp. 98-128.

4,710 TATE, H. R. Colour conflict: race relations in Africa, by G. W. Broomfield. AFR. AFFAIRS 43 (1944), pp. 40-44.

4,711 TAYLOR, A. Some aspects of personnel selection. UNIVERSITAS 2 (1955), pp. 13-15.

4,712 TCHIDIMBO, R. L'étudiant africain face à la culture latine. PRESENCE AFR. 14 (1953), pp. 55-64.

4,713 TEMA, S. S. The disintegration of African family life. INT. REV. MISSIONS 30 (1941), pp. 191-197.

4,714 TEMPELS, P. L'être est force, extraits de la Philosophie Bantoue... PRESENCE AFR. 7 (1949), pp. 249-251.

4,715 TEMPELS, P. P. Moeten we op zoek naar een Bantu-Filosofie? AEQUATORIA 7 (1944), pp. 143-151.

4,716 THEUWS, T. Philosophie Bantoue et Philosophie Occidentale. CIVILISATIONS 1, no. 3 (1951), pp. 54-61; English summary, pp. 62-63.

4,717 THIAM, D. De l'avenir des institutions coutumières en Afrique noire. PRESENCE AFR. 6 (1949), pp. 36-46.

4,718 THOMAS, I. B. Empire Britannique: Les développements aux points de vue social et médical en 1951-1952. CIVILISATIONS 3 (1953), pp. 361-368.

4,719 THOMAS, L. V. Les constantes de la culture nègre ou réflexions à propos du livre de Janheinz Jahn: Muntu. L'homme africain et la culture néo-africaine. BULL. IFAN 26 (1964), pp. 258-271.

4,720 THOMAS, L. V. De l'usage de quelques tests projectifs pour la compréhension de la personnalité noire. Aperçus méthodologiques. BULL. IFAN 21 (1959), pp. 1-19.

4,721 THOMAS, L. V. Problèmes de sociologie africaine. PRESENCE AFR. N.S. 51 (1964), pp. 24-41.

4,722 THOMAS, M. Some methodological comments on the use of personality tests in Africa. NISER 6 (1958), p. 234.

4,723 THURNWALD, R. The social problems of Africa. AFRICA 2 (1929), pp. 130-136.

4,724 THURNWALD, R. Social systems of Africa. AFRICA 2 (1929), pp. 221-242, 352-378

4,725 TIDIANY, C. S. Noir Africain et culture latine. PRESENCE AFR. 14 (1953), pp. 40-54.

4,726 TIDIANY, C. S. Le Noir africain et les cultures indo-européennes. PRESENCE AFR. N.S. 14-15 (1957), pp. 7-28.

4,727 TIDJANI, A. S. L'Africain face au problème du travail. PRESENCE AFR. 13 (1952), pp. 108-115.

4,728 TINKER, H. Community development: a new philosopher's stone? INTERNAT. AFFAIRS 37 (1961), pp. 309-322.

4,729 TORRES, M. F. La faceta africana en el destino español. ARCH. INST. EST. AFR. 4, no. 13 (1950), pp. 69-84.

4,730 TOURE, S. Le leader politique considéré comme le représentant d'une culture. PRESENCE AFR. N.S. 24-25 (1959), pp. 104-115.

4,731 TOWA, M. Liberté 1, de Léopold Sedar Senghor. GENEVE-AFR. 4 (1965), pp. 225-233.

4,732 TRAORE, B. Les damnés de la terre. PRESENCE AFR. N.S. 45 (1963), pp. 197-204.

4,733 TRAORE, B. Le théâtre negro-africain et ses fonctions sociologiques. PRESENCE AFR. N.S. 14-15 (1957), pp. 180-201.

4,734 TREVELYAN, M. African student at home. AFR. AFFAIRS 54 (1955), pp. 37-41.

4,735 TRUJEDA INCERA, L. Sobre las relaciones interraciales en el Africa negra. CUAD. EST. AFR. 16 (1951), pp. 43-53.

4,736 [U.N.E.S.C.O.] Il ne peut y avoir de justification biologique aux discriminations raciales. PRESENCE AFR. 10 (1951), pp. 248-254.

4,737 VAN DEN BERGHE, P. L. Racialism and assimilation in Africa and the Americas. SOUTHWESTERN J. ANTHR. 19 (1963), pp. 424-432.

4,738 VERDIER, R. Civilisations agraires et droits fonciers négro-africains. PRESENCE AFR. N.S. 31 (1960), pp. 24-33.

4,739 VERGER, P. Culture africaine, element de stabilité intérieure chez les descendants d'Africains déplacés au Nouveau Monde. PRESENCE AFR. N.S. 24-25 (1959), pp. 292-298.

4,740 VIALLE, J. Femmes africaines. CIVILISATIONS 1, no. 4 (1951), pp. 55-57; English summary, p. 58.

4,741 VILAKAZI, A. L. Social research and problems of African economic and social development. PROC. INT. CONG. AFR. 1 (1962), pp. 184-189.

4,742 VINCENT, F. L'éducation, moteur du développement. GENEVE-AFR. 3 (1964), pp. 60-80.

4,743 VINCENT, J. Les problèmes de l'enfance inadaptée dans les pays en voie de développement. ANNALES AFR., 1962, pp. 267-286.

4,744 WADLOW, R. Pierre Ceresole and Le Travail Cadeau. GENEVE-AFR. 2 (1963), pp. 144-148.

4,745 WALTON, G. The scout movement in Africa. J. AFR. SOC. 36 (1937), pp. 477-481.

4,746 WATTEAU, M. Situations raciales et condition de l'homme dans l'oeuvre de J.-P. Sartre. PRESENCE AFR. 2 (1948), pp. 209-229, 405-417.

4,747 WILLIAMS, E. Le leader politique considéré comme un homme de culture. PRESENCE AFR. N.S. 24-25 (1959), pp. 90-103.

4,748 WINNINGTON-INGRAM, C. Land tenure and farming systems in Scotland and Africa. J. AFR. ADM. 4 (1952), pp. 63-68.

4,749 WINTERBOTTOM, J. M. Can we measure the African's intelligence? RHODES-LIV. J. 6 (1948), pp. 53-59.

4,750 WISTE, M. Assimilation des indigènes ou ségrégation. ZAIRE 5 (1951), pp. 829-838.

4,751 WOLDE-GIORGHIS, H. An african encounters the United States. TRANSITION 15 (1964), pp. 22-25.

4,752 WOLFE, A. W. Man's relation to man in Africa. AMER. ANTHR. 61 (1959), pp. 606-614.

4,753 WRIGHT, R. Tradition and industrialization. PRESENCE AFR. N.S. 8-10 (1956), pp. 347-360.

4,754 WYNDHAM, H. A. The colour problem in Africa. INTERNAT. AFFAIRS 4 (1925), pp. 174-190.

4,755 X. The South African problem from three different angles. INT. REV. MISSIONS 15 (1926), pp. 344-362.

4,756 ZERBO, J. K. Témoignage d'un étudiant catholique. PRESENCE AFR. 14 (1953), pp. 65-70.

4,757 ZIEGLER, J. Sociologie de la Nouvelle Afrique. PRESENCE AFR. N.S. 54 (1965), pp. 245-251.

4,758 L'Afrique et les Jeux Olympiques. PRESENCE AFR. N.S. 53 (1965), pp. 237-240.

4,759 All Africa church conference and status of women. AFR. WOMEN 2 (1956-1958), pp. 82-83.

4,760 Community centres. AFR. AFFAIRS 44 (1945), pp. 95-96.

4,761 Le culte de la doctrine. PRESENCE AFR. N.S. 51 (1964), pp. 172-173.

4,762 Des nègres au ciel...ou le sens d'une canonisation. PRESENCE AFR. N.S. 53 (1965), pp. 240-245.

4,763 Deux nouvelles perspectives de recherche en Afrique indépendante. PRESENCE AFR. N.S. 50 (1964), pp. 255-257.

4,764 L'exode rural blanc en Afrique du Sud. ZAIRE 7 (1953), p. 1087.

4,765 Final Report of the British African Land Utilisation Conference, Jos, Nigeria, November 1949. J. AFR. ADM. 3 (1951), pp. 46-47.

4,766 First United States conference on the role of women in Africa. AFR. WOMEN 3 (1960), pp. 88-89.

4,767 Formation professionnelle rapide en Afrique française. ZAIRE 6 (1952), pp. 974-975.

4,768 Le fosse. PRESENCE AFR. N.S. 41 (1962), pp. 169-171.

4,769 Girl Guides of Africa. AFR. WOMEN 4 (1962), pp. 81-82.

4,770 Les indigènistes et la culture. PRESENCE AFR. N.S. 54 (1965), pp. 251-255.

4,771 Individualidade socio-cultural. PORT. EM AFR. SUPPL. (1960-1961), pp. 309-318.

4,772 Le mouvement coopératif en Afrique Anglaise. ZAIRE 7 (1953), pp. 1090-1092.

4,773 Le Nègre, ce méconnu. PRESENCE AFR. 15 (1953), pp. 61-66.

4,774 Nous les Noirs. PRESENCE AFR. N.S. 40 (1962), pp. 167-168.

4,775 Population de l'Afrique 1958-1960 [tableau]. GENEVE-AFR. 1 (1962), pp. 239-240.

4,776 La population de l'Afrique. Note démographique. PRESENCE AFR. 13 (1952), pp. 25-33.

4,777 The problem of the customary chiefdom in French Overseas Territories. J. AFR. ADM. 9 (1957), pp. 136-139.

4,778 Propositions pour l'Afrique. PRESENCE AFR. 15 (1953), pp. 365-382.

4,779 A racialist's progress. RACE 6, no. 1 (1964-1965), pp. 267-268.

4,780 Role of women in urban development in Africa. WOMEN TODAY 6 (1964), pp. 32-33.

4,781 La sécurité. Perspectives d'une Afrique nouvelle. PRESENCE AFR. 15 (1953), pp. 335-346.

4,782 Social development through family and home. Report of a conference held at Oxford in September 1959. J. AFR. ADM. 12 (1960), pp. 249-250.

4,783 Villes d'Afrique Noire. PRESENCE AFR. 15 (1953), pp. 295-306.

See also 455, 686, 1161, 1283, 1504, 1505, 1506, 1714, 2866, 3660, 3668, 3673, 3674, 3745, 3752, 3756, 3879, 3945, 4057, 4234, 4252.

North Africa

GENERAL

4,784 HALPERN, M. New perspectives in the study of North Africa. JMAS 3 (1965), pp. 103-114.

Agriculture

4,785 BENIPARRELL, C. DE. La destrucción de los suelos norteafricanos. CUAD. EST. AFR. 22 (1953), pp. 51-66.

4,786 CHEREL, J. De qui s'agit-il? ou la mise en valeur agricole, problème d'ensembles humains. CT 8, nos. 29-30 (1960), pp. 17-49.

4,787 COLA ALBERICH, J. El problema de la destrucción de los suelos norteafricanos. CUAD. AFR. OR. 34 (1956), pp. 69-85.

4,788 DESPOIS, J. Les greniers fortifiés de l'Afrique du Nord. CT 1 (1953), pp. 38-58.

4,789 GAILLARD, C. Quelques aspects du problème de l'eau dans les Oasis. CT 5 (1957), pp. 7-21.

4,790 MARTHELOT, P. Contribution à l'étude de l'irrigation. CT 5 (1957), pp. 113-117.

4,791 UVAROV, B. P. Desert locust: the 1951 campaign. CORONA 4 (1952), pp. 67-68.

4,792 VALDEYRON, G. Pour une utilisation rationnelle de l'eau en agriculture méditerranéenne. CT 5 (1957), pp. 79-95.

See also 5083.

Anthropology

4,793 ARKELL, A. J. Some Tuareg ornaments and their connection with India. JRAI 65 (1935), pp. 297-308.

4,794 ASHLEY MONTAGU, M. F. Infibulation and defibulation in the Old and New Worlds. AMER. ANTHR. 47 (1945), pp. 464-467.

4,795 BLANC, A. C. L'industrie sur obsidienne des Iles Dahlac (Mer Rouge). PROC. PAN-AFR. CONGR. PRE-HIST. 2 (1952), pp. 355-357.

4,796 BRIGGS, L. C. Living tribes of the Sahara and the problem of prehistoric origins. PROC. PAN-AFR. CONGR. PRE-HIST. 3 (1955), pp. 195-199.

4,797 CABANNES, R. J. The distribution of abnormal haemoglobin in Algeria, the Hoggar, and High Volta: anthropological incidences. JRAI 90 (1960), pp. 306-319.

4,798 CANTERO, V. B. Miscelánea costumbrista de Beni Aarós. ARCH. INST. EST. AFR. 6, no. 22 (1952), pp. 15-28.

4,799 CAUNEILLE, A. and DUBIEF, J. Les Requibat Legouacem: chronologie et nomadisme. BULL. IFAN, Série B: Sciences humaines 17 (1955), pp. 528-550.

4,800 COLA ALBERICH, J. Antecedentes de paletnología ibero africana. ARCH. INST. EST. AFR. 5, no. 19 (1951), pp. 79-90.

4,801 DRAKE, S. C. Détruire le mythe chamitique, devoir des hommes cultivés. PRESENCE AFR. N.S. 24-25 (1959), pp. 215-230.

4,802 GAY, Le Capitaine. Sur la "Sébiba." J. SOC. AFR. 5 (1935), pp. 61-66.

4,803 HOWELL, F. C. European and Northwest African middle pleistocene hominids. CURRENT ANTHR. 1 (1960), pp. 195-232.

4,804 HUGOT, H. J. Faits nouveaux dans la préhistoire saharienne. BULL. IFAN, Série B: Sciences humaines 20 (1958), pp. 1-6.

4,805 IBANEZ, E. Orígenes y evolución del pueblo ereber. ARCH. INST. EST. AFR. 8, no. 33 (1955), pp. 7-23.

4,806 IBANEZ, P. E. El problema etnológico Bereber. ARCH. INST. EST. AFR. 6, no. 25 (1953), pp. 19-41.

4,807 JOLEAUD, L. Le rôle des singes dans les traditions populaires nord-africaines. J. SOC. AFR. 1 (1931), pp. 117-150.

4,808 LE COEUR, C. Le Tibesti et les Téda: une circoncision. J. SOC. AFR. 5 (1935), pp. 41-60.

4,809 LINDBLOM, G. An ethnographical exhibition. ETHNOS 9 (1944), pp. 46-48.

4,810 MARCAIS, P. Réflexions sur la structure de la vie familiale chez les indigènes de l'Afrique du Nord. MEMORIAL ANDRE BASSET, 1957, pp. 69-82.

4,811 MELDON, J. A. Some remarks on the Nilotic negro and a review of Mr. Westermann's Shilluk people. J. AFR. SOC. 12 (1913), pp. 165-176.

4,812 MICHELL, G. B. The Berbers. J. AFR. SOC. 2 (1903), pp. 161-194.

4,813 NORRIS, H. T. Tuareg nomadism in the modern world. AFR. AFFAIRS 51 (1952), pp. 152-155.

4,814 PALMER, H. R. The Tuareg of the Sahara. J. AFR. SOC. 31 (1932), pp. 153-166, 293-308; 33 (1934), pp. 276-291.

4,815 PAQUES, V. Mythe et structures dans les sociétés africaines traditionnelles. BULL. IFAN 26 (1964), pp. 71-77.

4,816 PAQUES, V. Mythes et structures dans les sociétés sahariennes sédentarisées. CONGR. INT. SC. ANTHR. ET ETHN. 6, no. ii (1960), pp. 441-445.

4,817 RAHMANI, H. S. Dissolution de la famille. Le divorce en Kabylie. CONGR. INT. SC. ANTHR. ET ETHN. 6, no. ii (1960), pp. 355-362.

4,818 VASSAL, P. A. Persistance du type de Mechta-el-Arbi en Afrique du Nord. CONG. INT. SC. ANTHR. ET ETHN. 4, no. i (1952), pp. 241-256.

4,819 ZELTNER, Fr. DE. Les Touareg du Sud. JRAI 44 (1914), pp. 351-375.

See also 4847, 15820.

Art. Archaeology. Prehistory. Visual arts. Music

4,820 ALCOBE, S. Antropología del Paleolítico en el norte de Africa y en el levante español. ARCH. INST. EST. AFR. 7, no. 30 (1954), pp. 73-86.

4,821 ALIMEN, H. Considérations sur les nucléus du Paléolithique ancien au Sahara nord-occidental. PROC. PAN-AFR. CONGR. PRE-HIST. 5 (1965), pp. 103-114.

4,822 ALIMEN, H. Sines abstraits accompagnant les gravures rupestres de Marhouma (Sahara occidental). PROC. PAN-AFR. CONGR. PRE-HIST. 2 (1952), pp. 687-691.

4,823 ALIMEN, M. H. Chronologie préhistorique du Sahara. PROC. PAN-AFR. CONGR. PRE-HIST. 3 (1955), pp. 80-85.

4,824 ALIMEN, M. H. and CHAVAILLON, J. Position stratigraphique et évolution de la Pebble Culture au Sahara nord-occidental. PROC. PAN-AFR. CONGR. PRE-HIST. 4, no. iii (1962), pp. 3-22.

4,825 ALVERNY, F. D'. Vestiges d'art rupestre au Tibesti oriental. J. SOC. AFR. 20 (1950), pp. 239-272.

4,826 ARAMBOURG, C. Etat actuel des recherches sur le Quaternaire en Afrique du Nord. PROC. PAN-AFR. CONGR. PRE-HIST. 4 (1962), pp. 255-277.

4,827 ARAMBOURG, C. Récentes découvertes de paléotologie humaine réalisées en Afrique du Nord française (L'Atlanthropus de Ternifine—L'Hominien de Casablanca). PROC. PAN-AFR. CONGR. PRE-HIST. 3 (1955), pp. 186-194.

4,828 ARAMBOURG, C. and BALOUT, L. L'ancien lac de Tihodaïne et ses gisements préhistoriques. PROC. PAN-AFR. CONGR. PRE-HIST. 2 (1952), pp. 281-292.

4,829 ARKELL, A. J. The relations of the Nile valley with the southern Sahara in Neolithic times. PROC. PAN-AFR. CONGR. PRE-HIST. 2 (1952), pp. 345-346.

4,830 ARKELL, A. J. and UCKO, P. J. Review of predynastic development in the Nile valley. CURRENT ANTHR. 6 (1965), pp. 145-166.

4,831 BALOUT, L. Données nouvelles sur le problème du Moustérien en Afrique du Nord. PROC. PAN-AFR. CONGR. PRE-HIST. 5 (1965), pp. 137-143.

4,832 BEGUINOT, F. Gli studi sull'epigrafia libica e sulle iscrizioni Tuâreg fatti in Italia nell'ultimo quarantennio. LIBIA 1, no. 1 (1953), pp. 83-90.

4,833 BESSAC, H. Contribution à l'inventaire préhistorique du Sahara occidental. BULL. IFAN 15 (1953), pp. 1582-1604.

4,834 BOBO, J. Un faciès Mésolithique saharien: le faciès d'El-Oued sa place dans l'ensemble des industries du Souf. PROC. PAN-AFR. CONGR. PRE-HIST. 2 (1952), pp. 493-502.

4,835 BREUIL, H. Les roches peintes du Tassil-n-Ajjer. PROC. PAN-AFR. CONGR. PRE-HIST. 2 (1952), pp. 65-219.

4,836 BUTZER, K. W. The Pleistocene sequence in Egypt and its implication for pluvial-glacial correlation in the Sahara. PROC. PAN-AFR. CONGR. PRE-HIST. 4 (1962), pp. 133-139.

4,837 CAPOT-REY, [R.] A propos des figurations rupestres de chars a boeufs. BULL. IFAN 14 (1952), pp. 362-363.

4,838 CHASSELOUP LAUBAT, F. DE. Le sens du Haut-Mertoutek. J. SOC. AFR. 12 (1942), pp. 139-147.

4,839 DART, R. A. The Garamantes of central Sahara. AFR. STUD. 11 (1952), pp. 29-34.

4,840 DURAND, J. H. Les différents types de croûtes, leurs caractères principaux, leur signification climatique. PROC. PAN-AFR. CONGR. PRE-HIST. 2 (1952), pp. 277-278.

4,841 ESPERANDIEV, G. Domestication et élevage dans le Nord de l'Afrique au Néolithique et dans la Protohistoire d'après les figurations rupestres. PROC. PAN-AFR. CONGR. PRE-HIST. 2 (1952), pp. 551-573.

4,842 EVANS, Sir A. The early Nilotic, Libyan and Egyptian relations with Minoan Crete. JRAI 55 (1925), pp. 199-288.

4,843 FEVRIER, P. A. Remarques sur la céramique d'Afrique du Nord. CT 12, nos. 45-46 (1964), pp. 129-137.

4,844 HOLIDAY, G. The Tuareg of the Ahaggar. AFR. MUSIC, 1956, pp. 48-52.

4,845 HUARD, P. Contribution a l'étude du cheval, du fer et du chameau au Sahara oriental. BULL. IFAN 22 (1960), pp. 134-178.

4,846 HUARD, P. Les figurations d'animaux à disques frontaux et attributs rituels au Sahara oriental. BULL. IFAN 23 (1961), pp. 476-517.

4,847 JOLEAUD, L. Gravures rupestres et rites de l'eau en Afrique du Nord. J. SOC. AFR. 3 (1933), pp. 197-282; 4 (1934), pp. 285-302.

4,848 LHOTE, H. L'abbé Breuil et le Sahara. J. SOC. AFR. 32 (1962), pp. 63-74.

4,849 LHOTE, H. L'abri a peintures de l'Oued Tadjerdjert (Tassili-n-Ajjer). PROC. PAN-AFR. CONGR. PRE-HIST. 2 (1952), pp. 733-735.

4,850 LHOTE, H. Le cheval et le chameau dans les peintures et gravures rupestres du Sahara. BULL. IFAN 15 (1953), pp. 1138-1228.

4,851 LHOTE, H. Gravure rupestre de Tihoubar-n-Attaram (Tassili-n-Ajjer). PROC. PAN-AFR. CONGR. PRE-HIST. 2 (1952), pp. 737-738.

4,852 LHOTE, H. Gravures, peintures et inscriptions rupestres du Kaouar, de l'Aïr et de l'Adras des Iforas. BULL. IFAN 14 (1952), pp. 1268-1340.

4,853 LHOTE, H. Nouvelles statuettes en pierre polie découvertes au Sahara Central et contribution aux cultes anciens des populations sahariens. PROC. PAN-AFR. CONGR. PRE-HIST. 2 (1952), pp. 725-732.

4,854 LHOTE, H. Varia sur la Sandale et la marche chez les Touareg. BULL. IFAN 14 (1952), pp. 596-622.

4,855 MASSEY, R. E. A note on the early history of cotton. SUDAN NOTES 6 (1923), pp. 231-233.

4,856 MAUNY, R. Un âge du cuivre au Sahara occidental? BULL. IFAN 13 (1951), pp. 168-180.

4,857 MAUNY, R. Autour de la répartition des chars rupestres du Nord-Ouest Africain. PROC. PAN-AFR. CONGR. PRE-HIST. 2 (1952), pp. 741-746.

4,858 MONOD, TH. Sur les inscriptions arabes peintes de Ti-m-Missao Sahara central. J. SOC. AFR. 8 (1938), pp. 83-95.

4,859 MONOD, TH. and CAUNEILLE, Cap. Nouvelles figurations rupestres de chars du Sahara occidental. BULL. IFAN 13 (1951), pp. 181-197.

4,860 MORDINI, A. Les inscriptions rupestres tifinagh du Sahara et leur signification ethnologique. ETHNOS 2 (1937), pp. 333-337.

4,861 MORI, F. Sahara presente e passato. AFRICA (Rome) 12 (1957), pp. 137-140.

4,862 NOUGIER, L. R. Influence Egyptienne dans le néo-énéolithique Saharien. PROC. PAN-AFR. CONGR. PRE-HIST. 2 (1952), pp. 641-645.

4,863 PALACIN, A. DE L. Antigua musica Española en el Norte de Africa. ARCH. INST. EST. AFR. 14, no. 52 (1960), pp. 33-42.

4,864 PALMER, H. R. Notes on some Asben records. J. AFR. SOC. 9 (1910), pp. 388-400.

4,865 PARIS-TEYNAC, E. J. Essai sur le koufique ancien dit koufique carré. Ses applications dans la décoration artisanale. BULL. IFAN 21 (1959), pp. 501-543.

4,866 PERRET, R. Une carte des gravures rupestres et des peintures a l'ocre de l'Afrique du Nord. J. SOC. AFR. 7 (1937), pp. 107-123.

4,867 ROBINSON, A. E. The camel in antiquity. SUDAN NOTES 19 (1936), pp. 47-69.

4,868 RODD, F. Some rock drawings from Aïr in the southern Sahara. JRAI 68 (1938), pp. 99-111.

4,869 SAEZ-MARTIN, B. Sobre una supuesta del Bronce en Africa Menor y Sahara. PROC. PAN-AFR. CONGR. PRE-HIST. 2 (1952), pp. 659-662.

4,870 SALOMONSON, J. W. Un plat de terre cuite trouvé à El-Djem, pièce d'importation ou produit local? CT 12, nos. 45-46 (1964), pp. 107-127.

4,871 TSCHUDI, J. Die Felsmalereien im Edjeri, Tamrit, Assakao, Meddak (Tassili-n-Ajjer). PROC. PAN-AFR. CONGR. PRE-HIST. 2 (1952), pp. 761-767.

4,872 VITA-FINZI, C. and KENNEDY, R. A. Seven Saharan sites. JRAI 95 (1965), pp. 195-213.

See also 4796, 4996, 7592, 16620.

Biography

4,873 ANDREW, G. Dr. John Ball: an appreciation, with bibliography. SUDAN NOTES 24 (1941), pp. 213-217.

4,874 GLEICHEN, Lord E. Lord Cromer: by the Marquess of Zetland. J. AFR. SOC. 32 (1933), pp. 37-47.

4,875 JOLEAUD, L. Nécrologie: Stéphane Gsell. J. SOC. AFR. 2 (1932), pp. 243-244.

4,876 LESOURD, M. Charles de Foucauld, éminent linguiste. AFR. ET ASIE 61 (1963), pp. 41-46.

4,877 NEWBOLD, D. Dr. John Ball: a personal memoir. SUDAN NOTES 24 (1941), pp. 209-212.

Economics

4,878 ADAM, A. Etude économique et sociologique d'un Souq du Haut-Atlas occidental: Imi-n-Tanout. CONG. INT. SC. ANTH. ET ETHN. 4, no. iii (1952), pp. 9-16.

4,879 ATKINS, H. J. B. The French North African background. Economics. AFR. AFFAIRS 46 (1947), p. 155-163.

4,880 BIANCACCI, F. Valorizzare il Sahara. AFRICA (Rome) 15 (1960), pp. 74-79.

4,881 BLANCO DEL VALLE, J. Los cetacéos en el norte de Africa. ARCH. INST. EST. AFR. 7, no. 30 (1954), pp. 47-71.

4,882 BOVY, L. Histoire du mouvement syndical nord-ouest africain. AFRICA (Rome) 18 (1963), pp. 123-131.

4,883 C., J. Les ailes françaises au Sahara. ZAIRE 9 (1955), pp. 171-172.

4,884 CLAUZEL, J. La situation en pays touareg. AFR. ET ASIE 58 (1962), pp. 23-40.

4,885 COHEN, V. Eldorado in the Sahara? CONTEMP. REV. 192 (1957), pp. 212-215.

4,886 CONSIGLIO, G. Francia ed Italia in Africa. AFRICA (Rome) 10 (1955), pp. 253-254.

4,887 DESPOIS, J. Problèmes techniques, économiques et sociaux des oasis sahariennes. REV. TUN. SC. SOC. 2 (1965), pp. 51-57.

4,888 GARCIA-FUENTE, S. La investigacion petrolifera en el Sahara. ARCH. INST. EST. AFR. 16, no. 59 (1961), pp. 99-115.

4,889 GAUTIER, E. F. The trans-Saharan railway. GEOG. REV. 15 (1925), pp. 51-69.

4,890 GIBBONS, A. ST. H. The Nile and Zambezi systems as waterways. ROYAL COL. INST. PR. 32 (1900-1901), pp. 79-98.

4,891 GOTTMANN, J. Economic problems of French North Africa. GEOG. REV. 33 (1943), pp. 175-196.

4,892 HALPERN, J. Economic planning in Africa. AFR. BULL. 1 (1964), pp. 41-71.

4,893 HAWKES, C. P. The old Timbuctu trail: traffic and transport in the Sahara. CONTEMP. REV. 124 (1923), pp. 479-488.

4,894 KNIGHT, M. M. Economic space for Europeans in French North Africa. ECONOMIC DEVELOPMENT AND CULTURAL CHANGE 1 (1952-1953), pp. 360-375.

4,895 KNIGHT, M. M. Water and the course of empire in North Africa. QUART. J. ECON. 43 (1928-1929), pp. 44-93.

4,896 KRAFT, L. French Sahara and its mineral wealth. INTERNAT. AFFAIRS 36 (1960), pp. 197-205.

4,897 LADREIT DE LACHARRIERE, J. La renaissance de l'olivier et la propriété foncière dans l'Afrique du Nord. AFRICA 1 (1928), pp. 463-477.

4,898 MOYAL, M. The need for cooperation in the Sahara. AFR. AFFAIRS 58 (1959), pp. 329-333.

4,899 PEDRAZZI, O. Considerazioni sul discorso inaugurale del Sottosegretario di Stato Sen. Giardina. AFRICA (Rome) 12 (1957), pp. 85-86.

4,900 PENFIELD, F. C. Railway enterprise in Egypt. LIBERIA BULL. 7 (1895), pp. 67-69.

4,901 POLK, W. R. The nature of modernization. The Middle East and North Africa. FOREIGN AFFAIRS 44 (1965), pp. 100-110.

4,902 SAINTE-MARIE, J. F. L'immigration des travailleurs nord-africains en France. AFR. ET ASIE 1, no. 3 (1948), pp. 17-28.

4,903 SICARD, H. Problèmes fonciers au Maghreb. AFR. ET ASIE 72 (1965), pp. 22-36.

4,904 SKEET, T. H. H. Developing the French Sahara. CONTEMP. REV. 191 (1957), pp. 278-283.

4,905 SOUSTELLE, J. The wealth of the Sahara. FOREIGN AFFAIRS 37 (1958-1959), pp. 626-636.

4,906 THOMAS, B. E. Modern trans-Saharan routes. GEOG. REV. 42 (1952), pp. 267-282.

4,907 VALLE FERNANDEZ, R. DEL. Investigaciones petrolíferas en el Magreb. CUAD. EST. AFR. 24 (1953), pp. 51-59.

4,908 Employment of women in North Africa. AFR. WOMEN 4 (1961), pp. 32-34.

4,909 Studies in war-time organisation: the United Kingdom Commercial Corporation. AFR. AFFAIRS 43 (1944), pp. 116-123.

Geography

4,910 AFER. Sarà possibile popolare il Sahara? AFRICA (Rome) 10 (1955), p. 10.

4,911 BOVILL, E. W. The encroachment of the Sahara on the Sudan. J. AFR. SOC. 20 (1921), pp. 174-185, 259-269.

4,912 BROSSET, D. Essai sur les ergs du Sahara occidental [with a note by Th. Monod]. BULL. IFAN 1 (1939), pp. 657-690.

4,913 CAPOT-REY, R. Dry and humid morphology in the Western Erg. GEOG. REV. 35 (1945), pp. 391-407.

4,914 CARLP, R. L'économie des transports dans le Nord-Est du Sahara. ACTA GEOGRAPHICA 16 (1951), pp. 55-64.

4,915 CLARK, E. The Mzabite cities of the Sahara. CONTEMP. REV. 189 (1956), pp. 360-363.

4,916 CORO, F. Il Sahara nel passato, nel presente e nel suo avvenire. LIBIA 2, no. 2 (1954), pp. 57-66; 2, no. 3 (1954), pp. 39-45.

4,917 DEASY, G. F. Spanish territorial boundary changes in North Africa. GEOG. REV. 32 (1942), pp. 303-306.

4,918 DESPOIS, J. L'utilisation du sol dans les montagnes du Maghreb. ACTA GEOGRAPHICA 46-47 (1963), pp. 27-34.

4,919 FORBES, R. H. The Transsaharan conquest. GEOG. REV. 33 (1943), pp. 197-213.

4,920 GAUTIER, E. F. The Ahaggar: heart of the Sahara. GEOG. REV. 16 (1926), pp. 378-394.

4,921 GAUTIER, E. F. The monument of Tin Hinan in the Ahaggar. GEOG. REV. 24 (1934), pp. 439-443.

4,922 GAUTIER, E. F. Native life in French North Africa. GEOG. REV. 13 (1923), pp. 27-39.

4,923 GAUTIER, E. F. Nomad and sedentary folks of Northern Africa. GEOG. REV. 11 (1921), pp. 3-15.

4,924 GOTTMANN, J. New facts and some reflections on the Sahara. GEOG. REV. 32 (1942), pp. 659-662.

4,925 HILL, R. Nile and Congo: comparisons in river transport. J. AFR. SOC. 35 (1936), pp. 204-211.

4,926 JIMENEZ BENAMU, L. Plazas Africanas de soberania. ARCH. INST. EST. AFR. 16, no. 58 (1961), pp. 7-27.

4,927 LANGLANDS, B. W. Concepts of the Nile. UGANDA J. 26 (1962), pp. 1-22.

4,928 LEMEE, G. Contribution à l'étude ecologique de la végétation des confins Saharo-Marocains. DESERT RESEARCH, 1953, pp. 302-306.

4,929 LOMBARDI, G. Un comodo itinerario turistico dal Mediterraneo al Lago Victoria. AFRICA (Rome) 16 (1961), pp. 181-187.

4,930 MONOD, TH. Autour de l'Alaska saharien. BULL. IFAN 14 (1952), pp. 679-684.

4,931 MONOD, TH. Nouvelles remarques sur Teghaza (Sahara occidental). BULL. IFAN 2 (1940), pp. 248-250.

4,932 MONOD, TH. and CAILLEUX, A. Sur les conditions désertiques anciennes au Sahara. BULL. IFAN 12 (1950), pp. 530-531.

4,933 PERRET, R. Images sahariennes. ACTA GEOGRAPHICA 39 (1961), pp. 3-7.

4,934 PERRET, R. Voyages au Sahara central. ACTA GEOGRAPHICA 1 (1947), pp. 11-21.

4,935 SABBADINI, E. Il Mare Sahariano; progetto concreto o fantasia? AFRICA 10 (1955), pp. 7-8.

4,936 SANDFORD, K. S. Problems of the Nile valley. GEOG. REV. 26 (1936), pp. 67-76.

4,937 STADELMANN, E. Sur la plasmolyse des plantes sahariennes par des electrolytes (note préliminaire). DESERT RESEARCH, 1953, pp. 332-334.

4,938 STORME, M. Angelo Vinco op zoek naar de Nijlbronnen. ZAIRE 5 (1951), pp. 929-940.

4,939 TUNINETTI, D. M. Cinquant'anni di esplorazioni desertiche. AFRICA (Rome) 13 (1958), pp. 339-340.

4,940 VARGUES, H. Etude microbiologique de quelques sols sahariens en relation avec la présence d'Anabasis aretioides Coss. et Moq. DESERT RESEARCH, 1953, pp. 318-324.

Government. Administration. Politics

4,941 ABDERRAHIM BOUABID. Prospects for a united Maghrib. NEW FORCES IN AFRICA, 1962, pp. 101-113.

4,942 COLL, F. M. Mendès-France y la política del norte de Africa. CUAD. AFR. OR. 29 (1955), pp. 61-66.

4,943 CONSIGLIO, G. Dopo Mendès-France. AFRICA (Rome) 10 (1955), pp. 1-2.

4,944 EPTON, N. Nationalism in French North Africa. CONTEMP. REV. 173 (1948), pp. 361-365.

4,945 GRAY, A. North Africa and France. AFR. AFFAIRS 54 (1955), p. 86.

4,946 HAHN, L. Last chance in North Africa. FOREIGN AFFAIRS 36 (1957-1958), pp. 302-314.

4,947 JAMES, L. The future of French North Africa. CONTEMP. REV. 171 (1947), pp. 93-97.

4,948 LENOIR, G. Institutions en Afrique du Nord. AFR. ET ASIE 31 (1955), pp. 49-58.

4,949 MARTIN DE LA ESCALERA, C. La evolución política actual del Africa septentrional francesa. CUAD. EST. AFR. 5 (1949), pp. 9-36.

4,950 MARTIN DE LA ESCALERA, C. Rumbos de la Unión Francesa y el Magreb. CUAD. EST. AFR. 24 (1953), pp. 23-41.

4,951 MONTAGNE, R. French policy in North Africa and in Syria. INTERNAT. AFFAIRS 16 (1937), pp. 263-279.

4,952 MONTAGNE, R. The teaching of democracy in Islamic countries. J. AFR. ADM. 4 (1952), pp. 58-62.

4,953 NALDONI, N. Quo vadis Gallia? AFRICA (Rome) 10 (1955), p. 6.

4,954 ROCHER, L. L'Afrique du Nord et l'Union Française. AFR. ET ASIE 16 (1951), pp. 39-53.

4,955 ROCHER, L. Perspectives d'évolution politique en Afrique du Nord. AFR. ET ASIE 12 (1950), pp. 5-36.

4,956 SALVY, G. Où en est le Sahara? AFR. ET ASIE 34 (1956), pp. 60-71.

4,957 WHITTLESEY, D. Lands athwart the Nile. WORLD POLITICS 5 (1952-1953), pp. 214-241.

4,958 Voeu émis par le bureau directeur de l'Institut de Recherches sahariennes de l'Université d'Alger. BULL. IFAN 14 (1952), pp. 1118-1120.

See also 7777.

History

4,959 ABDULWAHAB, H. H. La Vaga du Bellum Africum. CT 8, no. 31 (1960), pp. 19-23.

4,960 ALLEN, G. A glimpse of North Africa. CONTEMP. REV. 53 (1888), pp. 526-536.

4,961 ALVES, H. O Infante D. Henrique e a acção missionária de Portugal. BOL. INST. ANGOLA 13 (1960), pp. 33-37.

4,962 ANDERSON, M. S. Great Britain and the Barbary States in the eighteenth century. BULL. INST. HIST. RES. 29 (1956), pp. 87-107.

4,963 AURIGEMMA, S. Il Bornu e Tripoli. AFRICA (Rome) 13 (1958), pp. 132-134.

4,964 BENNETT, N. R. Christian and negro slavery in eighteenth-century North Africa. J. AFR. HIST. 1 (1960), pp. 65-82.

4,965 BONO, S. Gli stati barbareschi nella Histoire Philosophique dell'abate Thomas François Raynal. AFRICA (Rome) 14 (1959), pp. 189-192.

4,966 BOVILL, E. W. Italy in Africa. J. AFR. SOC. 32 (1933), pp. 178-186, 351-361.

4,967 BOVILL, E. W. North Africa in the middle ages. J. AFR. SOC. 30 (1931), pp. 128-141.

4,968 BOVILL, E. W. Saharan explorers of the fifteenth century. J. AFR. SOC. 28 (1928), pp. 19-27.

4,969 CARO BAROJA, J. La Historia entre los nómadas saharianos. ARCH. INST. EST. AFR. 8, no. 35 (1955), pp. 57-67.

4,970 CHAOUACHE, H. Les structures économiques de la Byzacène à travers l'Antiquité et le Moyen-Age. CT 12, nos. 47-48 (1964), pp. 41-57.

4,971 CHARLES-ROUX, F. Les travaux d'Herculais ou une extraordinaire mission en Barbarie. RHCF 20 (1927), pp. 1-32, 201-258, 321-368, 543-580.

4,972 COOLIDGE, A. C. The European reconquest of North Africa. AM. HIST. REV. 17 (1911-1912), pp. 723-734.

4,973 CORBYN, E. Inland from the Eighth Army: the Fighting French in the Libyan hinterland. AFR. AFFAIRS 43 (1944), pp. 20-22.

4,974 CRUZ, F. A náuta Henriquina. BOL. INST. ANGOLA 13 (1960), pp. 81-100.

4,975 DESANGES, J. La dernière retraite de Gélimer. CT 7 (1959), pp. 429-435.

4,976 DESANGES, J. Deux inscriptions de Thuburbo Majus. CT 7 (1959), pp. 275-279.

4,977 DESANGES, J. Etendue et importance du Byzacium avant la création, sous Declétien, de la province de Byzacène. CT 11, no. 44 (1963), pp. 7-22.

4,978 DESFEUILLES, P. Scandinaves et Barbaresques à la fin de l'Ancien Régime. CT 4 (1956), pp. 327-349.

4,979 DIAZ DE VILLEGAS, J. La guerra en la Paz. El momento estrategico en Africa del norte. ARCH. INST. EST. AFR. 17, no. 68 (1963), pp. 7-23.

4,980 EMERIT, M. Un collaborateur d'Alexandre Dumas, Ducouret Abd El Hamid. CT 4 (1956), pp. 243-249.

4,981 FERRON, J. L. La Byzacène à l'époque punique. Etat actuel des connaissances. CT 11, no. 44 (1963), pp. 31-46.

4,982 FERRON, J. L. Le Byzacium protoromain. CT 11, no. 44 (1963), pp. 47-62.

4,983 FOUCHER, L. César en Afrique: autour d'Aggar. CT 8, no. 31 (1960), pp. 11-17.

4,984 FOUCHER, L. Projet d'enquête sur les ports de Byzacène au début du IIIe siècle. CT 12, nos. 45-46 (1964), pp. 39-44.

4,985 FREND, W. H. C. North Africa and Europe in the early middle ages. TRHS, 5th series, 5 (1955), pp. 61-80.

4,986 FREZOULS, E. Pour une enquête sur les villes de la Byzacène. CT 11, no. 44 (1963), pp. 75-84.

4,987 GHIRELLI, A. Monografía de la kabila de Bokoia. ARCH. INST. EST. AFR. 8, no. 32 (1955), pp. 27-83.

4,988 GOULVEN, J. L'établissement des premiers Européens à Mazagan au cours du XIXe siècle. RHCF 6 (1918), pp. 385-416.

4,989 GRAY, A. French rule challenged. AFR. AFFAIRS 54 (1956), pp. 11-12.

4,990 GUGLIELMI, G. La colonizzazione dell'Africa del nord. AFRICA (Rome) 13 (1958), p. 6.

4,991 HARDY, G. La pénétration saharienne et la psychologie du nomade saharien. RHCF 22 (1929), pp. 113-146.

4,992 HESS, R. L. The itinerary of Benjamin of Tudela: a twelfth-century Jewish description of north-east Africa. J. AFR. HIST. 6 (1965), pp. 15-24.

4,993 LANCEL, S. Originalité de la province ecclésiastique de Byzacène aux IVe et Ve siècles. CT 12, nos. 45-46 (1964), pp. 139-153.

4,994 LEWICKI, T. L'Etat nord-africain de Tāhert et ses relations avec le Soudan occidental à la fin du VIIIe et au IXe siècle. CAH. ET. AFR. 2 (1962), pp. 513-535.

4,995 MARCAIS, G. Sîdî Uqba, Abû l-Muhâjir et Kusaila. CT 1 (1953), pp. 11-17.

4,996 MAUNY, R. Une route préhistorique à travers le Sahara occidental. BULL. IFAN 9 (1947), pp. 341-357.

4,997 MIDDLETON, W. L. France and North Africa. CONTEMP. REV. 188 (1955), pp. 222-226.

4,998 MOFFITT, F. W. Some despatches from Khedive Ismail to major-general Charles Gordon. J. AFR. SOC. 34 (1935), pp. 107-116.

4,999 MONSABERT, DE. North Africa in Atlantic strategy. FOREIGN AFFAIRS 31 (1952-1953), pp. 418-426.

5,000 MONTAGNE, R. L'accélération de l'histoire dans les pays musulmans. AFR. ET ASIE 17 (1952), pp. 5-23.

5,001 MONTEIL, V. Chroniques de Tichit (Sahara occidental). BULL. IFAN 1 (1939), pp. 282-312.

5,002 MORALES OLIVER, L. La guerra de Africa en Pedro Antonio de Alarcón. ARCH. INST. EST. AFR. 14, no. 54 (1960), pp. 7-18.

5,003 MOREWOOD-DOWSETT, J. Ancient Roman policy in Africa. J. AFR. SOC. 36 (1937), pp. 201-212.

5,004 MORO, N. B. Tradiciones hispano-argelinas. ARCH. INST. EST. AFR. 5, no. 16 (1951), pp. 53-74.

5,005 MOTA, M. O Infante dos mares. BOL. INST. ANGOLA 13 (1960), pp. 39-43.

5,006 NEVEU, C. A. LE. France and Italy in North Africa. FOREIGN AFFAIRS 7 (1927), pp. 132-138.

5,007 NEWMAN, E. W. P. Egypt, Libya and the Mediterranean. CONTEMP. REV. 161 (1942), pp. 8-12.

5,008 PALMER, H. R. The central Sahara and Sudan in the twentieth century A.D. J. AFR. SOC. 28 (1929), pp. 368-378.

5,009 PALMER, H. R. The white races of North Africa. SUDAN NOTES 9 (1926), pp. 69-74.

5,010 PHILBY, H. ST. J. B. African contacts with Arabia. J. AFR. SOC. 38 (1939), pp. 33-46.

5,011 PICARD, G. C. Néron et le blé d'Afrique. CT 4 (1956), pp. 163-173.

5,012 PONCET, J. Notes sur la vie rurale dans l'est du Maghreb contemporain. CT 11, nos. 41-42 (1963), pp. 79-93.

5,013 PROROK, B. K. DE. Ancient trade routes from Carthage into the Sahara. GEOG. REV. 15 (1925), pp. 190-205.

5,014 QUIROS, C. Dinastías bereberes. Los almoravides. ARCH. INST. EST. AFR. 8, no. 32 (1955), pp. 7-26.

5,015 QUIROS, C. El pueblo bereber; noticias y comentarios. ARCH. INST. EST. AFR. 5, no. 16 (1951), pp. 75-88.

5,016 QUONIAM, P. Le statut municipal de Thuburbo Majus. CT 8, no. 31 (1960), pp. 25-27.

5,017 RODD, F. A Fezzani military expedition to Kanem and Bagirmi in 1821. J. AFR. SOC. 35 (1936), pp. 153-165.

5,018 RODRIGUEZ, C. Q. B. Batuta un viajero tangerino del siglo XIV. ARCH. INST. EST. AFR. 6, no. 20 (1952), pp. 11-27.

5,019 RODRIGUEZ, C. Q. B. Jaldun, político e historiador. ARCH. INST. EST. AFR. 6, no. 24 (1953), pp. 7-19.

5,020 SALAMA, P. La Via Hadrumetina en Byzacène. CT 12, nos. 45-46 (1964), pp. 73-85.

5,021 SANCHO DE SOPRANIS, H. Algunas noticias sobre las fortificaciones de la Mámora. ARCH. INST. EST. AFR. 7, no. 31 (1954), pp. 31-50.

5,022 SAUMAGNE, C. Esquisse des circonscriptions domaniales dans l'Afrique romaine. CT 10 (1962), pp. 245-255.

5,023 SAUMAGNE, C. Points de vue sur la reconquête byzantine de l'Afrique au VIe siècle. CT 7 (1959), pp. 281-297.

5,024 SAUMAGNE, C. Sur le colonat Byzantin en Afrique. CT 10 (1962), pp. 295-298.

5,025 SCOTT, A. M. The French in North Africa. CONTEMP. REV. 120 (1921), pp. 217-222.

5,026 SOPRANIS, H. S. DE. Un foco de cooperación a la obra portuguesa en Africa. ARCH. INST. EST. AFR. 6, no. 24 (1953), pp. 21-75.

5,027 SOSA, L. DE. Prim: una actuación de España en Africa. ARCH. INST. EST. AFR. 6, no. 20 (1952), pp. 59-75.

5,028 STANDING, P. C. France and North Africa: 1830-1930. CONTEMP. REV. 137 (1930), pp. 629-637.

5,029 TOLEMEE, P. Hier et avant-hier. Fantaisie en sept tableaux. PRESENCE AFR. 8 (1950), pp. 79-93.

5,030 VENTURA, R. O espírito do Infante. BOL. INST. ANGOLA 13 (1960), pp. 69-79.

5,031 VITA-EVRARD, G. DI. Nouvelles précisions sur la famille de Septime-Sévère. CT 12, nos. 45-46 (1964), pp. 69-72.

5,032 VYCICHL, W. Three problems of North African chronology. The Canary Islands, the Haggar in the Central Sahara, old Egypt. CONG. INT. SC. ANTH. ET ETHN., 4, no. iii (1952), pp. 5-8.

See also 7787, 7857, 13006.

Language. Literature

Language: Berber

5,033 BASSET, A. La langue berbère (conférence inédite, Oct. 1950). AFR. ET ASIE 34 (1956), pp. 39-45.

5,034 BASSET, A. Présentation des premières cartes d'un Atlas Linguistique—en cours de réalisation—des parlers du Sahara et du Soudan. INT. CONG. LING. 4 (1936), pp. 177-182.

5,035 CORO, F. La lingua latina nella Provincia d'Africa. AFRICA (Rome) 17 (1962), pp. 141-142.

5,036 GRIMME, H. Nachtrag zu A. Klingenhebens Studie über die berberischen Zählmethoden. AFR. UND UB. 17 (1926-1927), pp. 230-234.

5,037 HOMBURGER, L. La structure morphologique en Berbère. INT. CONG. LING. 5 (1939), pp. 70-71.

5,038 KLINGENHEBEN, A. Zu den Zählmethoden in den Berbersprachen. AFR. UND UB. 17 (1926-1927), pp. 40-51.

5,039 LAROCHETTE, J. La racine du type CV dans les langues soudanaises. ZAIRE 4 (1950), pp. 583-612.

5,040 LUKAS, J. Umrisse einer ostsaharanischen Sprachgruppe. AFR. UND UB. 36 (1951-1952), pp. 3-7.

5,041 MEINHOF, H. Sudansprachen und Hamitensprachen. AFR. UND UB. 1 (1910), pp. 161-166.

5,042 MICHELL, G. B. Notes on a comparative table of Berber dialects of North Africa. J. AFR. SOC. 1 (1902), pp. 395-398.

5,043 MOUCHET, J. Vocabulaires comparatifs de quinze parlers du Nord-Cameroun. ET. CAMER. 29-30 (1950), pp. 5-74.

5,044 PRASSE, K. G. The origin of Berber noun-prefixes. PROC. INT. CONG. AFR. 1 (1962), pp. 97-104.

5,045 RODD, P. R. Translations of Tuareg poems. BULL. SOAS 5 (1928-1930), pp. 109-113.

5,046 TOVAR, A. Los estudios bereberes en relación con españa. CUAD. EST. AFR. 1 (1946), pp. 113-121.

5,047 ZYHLARZ, E. Altere und jüngere Pluralbildung im Berberischen. AFR. UND UB. 22 (1931-1932), pp. 1-15.

5,048 ZYHLARZ, E. Eine Auslese aus Max Müller's Kondjara-Werk. AFR. UND UB. 32 (1942), pp. 164-182.

5,049 ZYHLARZ, E. Der Zenāga-Dialekt des Berberischen. AFR. UND UB. 33 (1942-1943), pp. 81-111.

See also 16106.

Literature

5,050 CATRICE, P. Femmes écrivains d'Afrique du Nord et du Proche-Orient. AFR. ET ASIE 59 (1962), pp. 23-44.

5,051 KREA, H. Préface au panorama de la nouvelle littérature maghrébine (la génération de 1954). PRESENCE AFR. N.S. 34-35 (1960-1961), pp. 168-182.

5,052 LAFUENTE, T. C. D. La literatura oral del pueblo berberí. ARCH. INST. EST. AFR. 4, no. 13 (1950), pp. 7-15.

5,053 RETIF, A. La leçon des romans nord-africains. AFR. ET ASIE 33 (1956), pp. 20-22.

See also 5029.

Law

5,054 BERQUE, J. Droit des terres et intégration sociale au Maghreb. CAH. INT. SOCIOL. 25 (1958), pp. 38-74.

5,055 BOUSQUET, G. H. Le droit coutumier des Berbères. THE FUTURE OF CUSTOMARY LAW IN AFRICA, 1956, pp. 142-154.

5,056 COLLIARD, C. A. Les anciennes colonies italiennes. RJPUF 6 (1952), pp. 246-286.

5,057 FLORY, M. La notion de protectorat et son évolution en Afrique du Nord. RJPUF 8 (1954), pp. 449-475; 9 (1955), pp. 53-82.

5,058 LACHARRIERE, R. DE. Le problème de l'organisation gouvernementale en vue de l'Union française. RJPUF 3 (1949), pp. 401-431.

5,059 QUERMONNE, J. L. L'organisation commune des régions sahariennes selon la loi du 10 janvier 1957. RJPUF 11 (1957), pp. 273-293.

5,060 ROUSSIER, J. L'immutabilité du droit musulman et le développement économique. ANNALES AFR., 1962, pp. 229-233.

See also 5093.

Religion

5,061 ATKINS, H. J. B. The French North African background. Islam. AFR. AFFAIRS 46 (1947), pp. 21-29.

5,062 BOUHDIBA, A. Intervention de Monsieur Bouhdiba [L'Islam maghrébin: essai d'une typologie]. REV. TUN. SC. SOC. 4 (1965), pp. 3-30.

5,063 BROWN, L. C. The Islamic reformist movement in North Africa. J. MOD. AFR. STUD. 2 (1964), pp. 55-63.

5,064 ELLIS, I. P. Professor Groves and the North African church. SIERRA L. BULL. REL. 5 (1963), pp. 66-71.

5,065 GALADANCI, S. A. S. The origin and doctrines of Mu'tazilah. KANO STUD. 1 (1965), pp. 9-12.

5,066 HAIR, P. E. H. Christianity in medieval Nubia and the Sudan: a bibliographical note. BULL. SOC. AFR. CHURCH HIST. 1 (1964), pp. 67-73.

5,067 LE GRIP, A. L'avenir de l'Islam en Afrique Noire. AFR. ET ASIE 10 (1950), pp. 5-19.

5,068 LE GRIP, A. Le Mahdisme en Afrique Noire. AFR. ET ASIE 18 (1952), pp. 3-16.

5,069 PADWICK, C. E. North African reverie. INT. REV. MISSIONS 27 (1938), pp. 341-354.

5,070 PROBST-BIRABEN, J. H. Le Serpent, persistance de son culte dans l'Afrique du Nord. J. SOC. AFR. 3 (1933), pp. 289-295.

Science

5,071 AMSEL, H. G. Neue Kleinschmetterlinge aus Nordwest-Africa. BULL. IFAN 15 (1953), pp. 1441-1460.

5,072 DURAND, J. Etude de la pedologie des environs de Beni-Ounif. DESERT RESEARCH, 1953, pp. 438-452.

5,073 F., W. A. Some bird notes: trans-Sahara from Dahomey to Algeria. NIGERIAN FIELD 2, no. 8 (1933), pp. 13-16.

5,074 GAUDIO, A. Farmacopea berbera sahariana (studio comparativo). LIBIA 4, nos. 1-2 (1956), pp. 41-45.

5,075 GERS, J. A plea for the camel. CORONA 1, no. 6 (1949), pp. 30-33.

5,076 HUARD, P. Archéologie et zoologie: contribution à l'étude des singes au Sahara oriental et central. BULL. IFAN 24 (1962), pp. 86-104.

5,077 LA VINA VILLA, J. La investigación de fosfatos en el Sahara. ARCH. INST. EST. AFR. 16, no. 59 (1961), pp. 65-83.

5,078 MAUNY, R. A. Répartition de la grande faune éthiopienne du Nord-Ouest Africain du Paléolithique à nos jours. PROC. PAN-AFR. CONGR. PRE-HIST. 3 (1955), pp. 102-105.

5,079 MONOD, TH. and CAILLEUX, A. Etude de quelques sables et grès du Sahara occidental. BULL. IFAN 7 (1945), pp. 174-190.

5,080 SABBADINI, E. Il Cape Canaveral del Sahara. AFRICA (Rome) 14 (1959), pp. 144-145.

5,081 SALVY, G. Les fichiers sahariens à Paris. AFR. ET ASIE 62 (1963), pp. 58-60.

5,082 VILLIERS, A. A propos de Leptotyphlops macrorhynchus Jan. BULL. IFAN. 14 (1952), pp. 243-246.

5,083 VONDERHEYDEN, M. Le henné chez les musulmans de l'Afrique du Nord. J. SOC. AFR. 4 (1934), pp. 35-61, 179-202.

Sociology

5,084 ANTONIO DE VEGA, L. Españoles en el Norte de Africa. ARCH. INST. EST. AFR. 16, no. 62 (1962), pp. 25-57.

5,085 ATKINS, H. J. B. The North African background. Private life. AFR. AFFAIRS 47 (1948), pp. 106-113.

5,086 ATKINS, H. J. B. The North African background. Public life. AFR. AFFAIRS 47 (1948), pp. 153-160.

5,087 BELKHODJA, B. Les représentations de la grossesse. REV. TUN. SC. SOC. 3 (1965), pp. 57-61.

5,088 BERQUE, J. L'Afrique du Nord entre les deux guerres mondiales. CAH. INT. SOCIOL. 30 (1961), pp. 3-22.

5,089 BERQUE, J. Le Maghreb d'hier à demain. CAH. INT. SOCIOL. 37 (1964), pp. 51-78.

5,090 BERQUE, J. The North of Africa. INT. SOC. SC. J. 13 (1961), pp. 177-198.

5,091 BERQUE, J. Les sociétés nord-Africaines vues du Haut-Atlas. CAH. INT. SOCIOL. 19 (1955), pp. 59-65.

5,092 HIRSCHBERG, H. Z. [J. W.] The problem of the Judaized Berbers. J. AFR. HIST. 4 (1963), pp. 313-339.

5,093 KRONENBERG, A. Zur kulturhistorischen Stellung des Mutterrechtes der Tuareg. CONG. INT. SC. ANTH. ET ETHN. 4, no. iii (1952), pp. 24-27.

5,094 LESOURD, M. Evolution des populations sahariennes. AFR. ET ASIE 57 (1962), pp. 11-26.

5,095 LESOURD, M. Les noirs du Sahara deviendront-ils propriétaires terriens? AFR. ET ASIE 60 (1962), pp. 36-44.

5,096 LETOURNEAU, R. Social change in the Muslim cities of North Africa. AM. J. SOC. 60 (1954-1955), pp. 527-535.

5,097 MARTIN DE LA ESCALERA, C. La juventud norte africana de hoy y el posible mañana. CUAD. EST. AFR. 10 (1950), pp. 55-65.

5,098 MARTIN DE LA ESCALERA, C. Problema real y soluciones artificiales. CUAD. EST. AFR. 14 (1951), pp. 63-74.

5,099 MARTIN DE LA ESCALERA, C. En torno de la demografía del Norte de Africa francés. CUAD. EST. AFR. 8 (1949), pp. 55-76.

5,100 NATAF, A. On laisse mourir la culture du Maghreb. PRESENCE AFR. N.S. 23 (1958-1959), pp. 123-129.

5,101 PAQUES, V. Caractères sociaux et mythiques du boucher dans le Nord-Ouest africain. J. SOC. AFR. 29 (1959), pp. 217-228.

5,102 PIGANIOL, A. La religion et les mouvements sociaux dans le Maghreb antique. J. WORLD HIST. 3 (1956-1957), pp. 813-832.

5,103 ROBINSON, A. E. The "Utfa" or camel-litter of the Arabs. J. AFR. SOC. 30 (1931), pp. 69-78.

5,104 SERVIER, J. H. La civilisation berbère. CONG. INT. SC. ANTH. ET ETHN. 4, no. iii (1952), pp. 17-18.

5,105 SHINAR, P. Note on the socio-economic and cultural role of Sufi brotherhoods and Marabutism in the Modern Maghrib. PROC. INT. CONG. AFR. 1 (1962), pp. 272-285.

5,106 STERNBERG-SAREL, B. Les Oasis du Djérid. CAH. INT. SOCIOL. 30 (1961), pp. 131-145.

5,107 VENDEIX, J. En écoutant les chefs et les anciens: essai d'étude sur l'adultère et la prostitution chez les Noirs d'Afrique. J. SOC. AFR. 5 (1935), pp. 163-174.

5,108 WAUGHRAY, V. The French racial scene. North African immigrants in France. RACE 2, no. 1 (1960-1961), pp. 60-70.

5,109 ZIADEH, N. A. Cultural trends in North Africa. J. WORLD HIST. 7 (1962-1963), pp. 109-133.

See also 7423.

UNITED ARAB REPUBLIC (Egypt)

General: institutions. libraries

5,110 MONOD, TH. Inauguration de l'Institut Fouad 1er du Désert. BULL. IFAN 13 (1951), pp. 1306-1307.

5,111 SABET, A. A. The library movement in Egypt. UNESCO BULL. LIBS. 10 (1956), pp. 182-183.

5,112 The cultural department of the League of Arab States: its organization and programme. INT. SOC. SC. BULL. 5 (1953), pp. 723-728.

5,113 The National Centre of Social and Criminological Research, Cairo. INT. SOC. SC. J. 13 (1961), pp. 660-662.

See also 18634.

Agriculture

5,114 CHEVALIER, A. A cultivation of the cotton plant and the agricultural future of Senegambia and of the Soudan. J. AFR. SOC. 1 (1902), pp. 431-441.

5,115 DUDGEON, G. C. The cotton worm in Egypt. BULL. IMP. INST. 10 (1912), pp. 584-620.

5,116 DUDGEON, G. C. The decline in the yield of Egyptian cotton and its causes. BULL. IMP. INST. 19 (1921), pp. 160-174.

5,117 DUDGEON, G. C. The extension of cotton cultivation in Egypt. BULL. IMP. INST. 17 (1919), pp. 195-204.

5,118 DUDGEON, G. C. The maintenance of the quality of Egyptian cotton. BULL. IMP. INST. 16 (1918), pp. 160-170.

5,119 DUDGEON, G. C. The pink boll worm and the cotton crop of Egypt. BULL. IMP. INST. 16 (1918), pp. 362-370.

5,120 DUDGEON, G. C. The progress of Egyptian agriculture, with special reference to cotton. BULL. IMP. INST. 11 (1913), pp. 90-101.

5,121 DUDGEON, G. C. The water supply of Egypt in its relation to agriculture. BULL. IMP. INST. 17 (1919), pp. 358-366.

5,122 HILZHEIMER, M. Der Ur in Agypten. FESTSCHRIFT EDUARD HAHN, 1917, pp. 9-16.

5,123 MUSTAFA' AL-ALIEL. La riforma agraria in Egitto. AFRICA (Rome) 11 (1956), p. 40.

5,124 PERRETT, M. Egypt and the Nile flood. CONTEMP. REV. 173 (1948), pp. 244-247.

5,125 TIGNOR, R. L. British agricultural and hydraulic policy in Egypt. AGRIC. HIST. 37 (1963), pp. 63-74.

Anthropology

5,126 ADAMS, J. B. Culture and conflict in an Egyptian village. AMER. ANTHR. 59 (1957), pp. 225-235.

5,127 AMMAR, A. Physical measurements and serology of the people of Sharqiya (Egypt). JRAI 70 (1940), pp. 147-170.

5,128 AMMAR, A. Racial elements in the north-eastern province of Egypt. A study of ethnic stocks in Sharqiya. J. AFR. SOC. 40 (1941), pp. 159-169, 347-361; 41 (1942), pp. 119-128.

5,129 BATRAWI, A. The racial history of Egypt and Nubia. Part 1. The cranialogy of lower Nubia from predynastic times to the sixth century a.d. JRAI 75 (1945), pp. 81-101.

5,130 BATRAWI, A. The racial history of Egypt and Nubia. Part 2. The racial relationship of the ancient and modern populations of Egypt and Nubia. JRAI 76 (1946), pp. 131-156.

5,131 FIELD, H. The University of California African expedition: 1, Egypt. AMER. ANTHR. 50 (1948), pp. 479-493.

5,132 FUMAGALLI, S. I Crani neolitici di Gebelên (Alto Egitto). CONG. INT. SC. ANTH. ET ETHN. 4, no. i (1952), pp. 221-227.

5,133 GUIRGUIS, M. El-Bega tribes; a little known people of Egypt and the Sudan. CIVILISATIONS 6 (1956), pp. 237-242.

5,134 HORNELL, J. Traps and snares from upper Egypt. ETHNOS 2 (1937), pp. 65-73.

5,135 KOCK, G. Some reflections on the problem of the animal-headed gods in Egypt. ETHNOS 8 (1943), pp. 153-160.

5,136 MACIVER, D. Recent anthropometrical work in Egypt. JRAI 30 (1900), pp. 95-103.

5,137 MURRAY, G. W. The Northern Beja. JRAI 57 (1927), pp. 39-53.

5,138 MYERS, C. S. Contributions to Egyptian anthropology: tatuing. JRAI 33 (1903), pp. 82-89.

5,139 MYERS, C. S. Contributions to Egyptian anthropology. JRAI 36 (1906), pp. 237-271; 38 (1908), pp. 99-147.

5,140 MYERS, C. S. Contributions to Egyptian anthropometry. The comparative anthropometry of the most ancient and modern inhabitants. JRAI 35 (1905), pp. 80-91.

5,141 OWEN, Professor. Contributions to the ethnology of Egypt. JRAI 4 (1874), pp. 223-254.

5,142 PRICE, F. G. H. Notes upon some ancient Egyptian implements. JRAI 14 (1885), pp. 56-83.

5,143 RIAD, M. Aids to the study of semi-assimilated nomads in Upper Egypt. CONG. INT. SC. ANTH. ET ETHN. 6, no. i (1960), pp. 235-236.

5,144 RIVERS, W. H. R. The colour vision of the natives of Upper Egypt. JRAI 31 (1901), pp. 229-247.

5,145 RIZKANA, I. Two new Egyptian cultures. PROC. PAN-AFR. CONGR. PRE-HIST. 3 (1955), pp. 391-393.

5,146 SHRUBSALL, F. C. Notes on crania from the Nile-Welle watershed. JRAI 31 (1901), pp. 256-260.

5,147 UCKO, P. J. Anthropomorphic ivory figurines from Egypt. JRAI 95 (1965), pp. 214-239.

5,148 WILSON, Sir C. W. On the tribes of the Nile Valley, north of Khartûm. JRAI 17 (1888), pp. 3-25.

Art. Archaeology. Pre-history. Egyptology. Pre-Roman history

5,149 AMER, M. The excavations of the Egyptian University in the prehistoric site at Maadi, near Cairo. The first two seasons' work (1930-1 and 1932). JRAI 66 (1936), pp. 65-69.

5,150 AMER BEY, M. Recent discoveries at Maadi, near Cairo. PROC. PAN-AFR. CONGR. PRE-HIST. 1 (1947), pp. 238-239.

5,151 AMER BEY, M. and HUZZAYIN, S. A. Some physiographic problems related to the predynastic site of Ma'adi. PROC. PAN-AFR. CONGR. PRE-HIST. 1 (1947), pp. 222-224.

5,152 BADIAN, E. Egypt under the Ptolemies. HISTORY TODAY 10 (1960), pp. 451-459.

5,153 BALODIS, F. Die "Ka"- and "Ba"-darstellungen in der ägyptischen Kunst. ETHNOS 9 (1944), pp. 67-83.

5,154 BARBOUR, N. The Arabic theatre in Egypt. BULL. SOAS 8 (1935-1937), pp. 173-187, 991-1012.

5,155 BARTOCCI, E. Successi italiani al 1° Rallye Automobilistico Cairo-Tripoli-Cairo. AFRICA (Rome) 11 (1956), pp. 175-176.

5,156 BJERKE, S. Remarks on the Egyptian ritual of opening the mouth and its interpretation. NUMEN 12 (1965), pp. 201-216.

5,157 BLEEKER, C. J. Die Idee des Schicksals in der altägyptischen Religion. NUMEN 2 (1955), pp. 28-46.

5,158 BLEEKER, C. J. The pattern of ancient Egyptian culture. J. WORLD HIST. 9 (1965), pp. 107-113; NUMEN 11 (1964), pp. 75-82.

5,159 BLEEKER, C. J. The position of the queen in ancient Egypt. CONG. INT. HIST. REL. 8 (1955), pp. 227-228.

5,160 BROWNE, A. J. J. Flint implements from Egypt. JRAI 7 (1877), pp. 396-412.

5,161 BURTON, R. F. Flint flakes from Egypt. JRAI 7 (1877), pp. 323-324.

5,162 CAZENEUVE, J. La connaissance technique dans l'Egypte ancienne. CAH. INT. SOCIOL. 28 (1960), pp. 23-32.

5,163 CERBELLA, G. Le iscrizioni sui portali delle case di Massaua. AFRICA (Rome) 17 (1962), pp. 137-140.

5,164 CERNY, J. Prices and wages in Egypt in the Ramesside period. J. WORLD HIST. 1 (1953-1954), pp. 903-921.

5,165 CLERE, J. J. Histoire des XIe et XIIe dynasties égyptiennes. J. WORLD HIST. 1 (1953-1954), pp. 643-668.

5,166 DABROWSKA-SMEKTALA, E. Polish excavations in Egypt and Sudan (1963/1964). AFR. BULL. 2 (1965), pp. 102-112.

5,167 FAIRMAN, H. W. Ancient Egypt and Africa. AFR. AFFAIRS, Special Issue (1965), pp. 69-75.

5,168 GREG, R. P. Neolithic flint implements of the Nile Valley and Egypt. JRAI 10 (1881), pp. 424-429.

5,169 GRIFFITH, F. L. The system of writing in ancient Egypt. JRAI 30 (1900), pp. 153-160.

5,170 HORGAN, E. S. Medicine and surgery in the most ancient East-Babylonia and Egypt. SUDAN NOTES 30 (1949); supplement, pp. 29-46.

5,171 HUZAYYIN, S. A. New light on the Upper Palaeolithic of Egypt. PROC. PAN-AFR. CONGR. PRE-HIST. 1 (1947), pp. 202-204.

5,172 JACOBSOHN, H. Die symbolische Bedeutung des göttlichen Pharaonentums für den ägyptischen Menschen. CONG. INT. HIST. REL. 8 (1955), pp. 230-233.

5,173 JOLEAUD, L. L'évolution des idées récentes en Egyptologie sous l'influence d'Alexandre Moret (1868-1938). J. SOC. AFR. 8 (1938), pp. 57-63.

5,174 KIRBY, P. R. The trumpets of Tut-Ankh-Amen and their successors. JRAI 77 (1947), pp. 33-45.

5,175 LANCZKOWSKI, G. Eschatology in ancient Egyptian religion. CONG. INT. HIST. REL. 9 (1958), pp. 129-134.

5,176 LECLANT, J. The suckling of the Pharaoh as a part of the coronation rites in ancient Egypt. [French text.] CONG. INT. HIST. REL. 9 (1958), pp. 135-145.

5,177 LEVA, A. E. Miti greci e scenari africani. AFRICA (Rome) 18 (1963), pp. 8-23.

5,178 LIGHTHEIM, M. Ancient Egypt: a survey of current historiography. AM. HIST. REV. 69 (1963-1964), pp. 30-46.

5,179 LIVCHITZ, I. G. Nouveaux documents sur l'histoire de l'Egyptologie. J. WORLD HIST. 6 (1960-1961), pp. 605-627.

5,180 LUBBOCK, J. Notes on the discovery of stone implements in Egypt. JRAI 4 (1874), pp. 215-222.

5,181 MACALISTER, A. Notes on Egyptian mummies. JRAI 23 (1894), pp. 101-121.

5,182 MIDDLETON, R. Brother-sister and father-daughter marriage in ancient Egypt. AMER. SOC. REV. 27 (1962), pp. 603-611.

5,183 MORMINO, G. Giuseppe Ferlini e le sue scoperte in Egitto. AFRICA (Rome) 14 (1959), pp. 35-37.

5,184 NAVILLE, E. The origin of Egyptian civilisation. JRAI 37 (1907), pp. 201-214.

5,185 NAVILLE, E. L'origine de la civilisation égyptienne. CONG. INT. HIST. REL. 1923, pp. 35-50.

5,186 PETRIE, W. F. On our present knowledge of the early Egyptians. JRAI 28 (1899), pp. 202-203.

5,187 PETRIE, W. M. F. On the mechanical methods of the ancient Egyptians. JRAI 13 (1884), pp. 88-109.

5,188 PETRIE, W. M. F. The races of early Egypt. JRAI 31 (1901), pp. 248-255.

5,189 PITT RIVERS, Lieut.-General. On the Egyptian boomerang and its affinities. JRAI 12 (1883), pp. 454-463.

5,190 PITT RIVERS, Major-General. On the discovery of chert implements in stratified gravel in the Nile Valley near Thebes. JRAI 11 (1882), pp. 382-400.

5,191 POOLE, R. S. Ancient Egypt. CONTEMP. REV. 34 (1879), pp. 304-321, 570-581, 741-762; 35 (1879), pp. 107-120.

5,192 POOLE, R. S. Ancient Egypt in its comparative relations. CONTEMP. REV. 39 (1881), pp. 804-821; 40 (1881), pp. 45-62, 282-299, 361-377.

5,193 PROCTOR, R. A. The problem of the Great Pyramid. CONTEMP. REV. 36 (1879), pp. 93-119.

5,194 RANDALL-MacIVER, D. The manufacture of pottery in Upper Egypt. JRAI 35 (1905), pp. 20-29.

5,195 REDER, D. G. Ancient Egypt, a centre of agriculture. J. WORLD HIST. 4 (1957-1958), pp. 801-817.

5,196 SABBADINI, E. Con gli antichi Egiziani alla scoperta della terra di Punt. AFRICA (Rome) 19 (1964), pp. 113-119.

5,197 SABBADINI, E. I graffiti di Abu Simbel. AFRICA (Rome) 18 (1963), pp. 135-137.

5,198 SELIGMAN, C. G. The older palaeolithic age in Egypt. JRAI 51 (1921), pp. 115-153.

5,199 SHINNIE, P. L. and M. SHINNIE. New light on medieval Nubia. J. AFR. HIST. 6 (1965), pp. 263-273.

5,200 STUART, V. Note on some Egyptian antiquities. JRAI 12 (1883), pp. 324-326.

5,201 SZCZUDLOWSKA, A. and POMORSKA, I. Les fouilles archéologiques polonaises en Egypte et au Soudan. AFR. BULL. 1 (1964), pp. 168-176.

5,202 THOMAS, E. S. A comparison of drawings from ancient Egypt, Libya, and the South Spanish caves. JRAI 56 (1926), pp. 385-394.

5,203 WILLIAMS, R. J. Literature as a medium of political propaganda in ancient Egypt. THE SEED OF WISDOM: ESSAYS IN HONOUR OF T. J. MEEK, 1964, pp. 14-30.

5,204 WILSON, J. A. Egyptian culture and religion. THE BIBLE AND THE ANCIENT NEAR EAST: ESSAYS IN HONOUR OF W. F. ALBRIGHT, 1961, pp. 298-315.

5,205 ZANDEE, J. Le roi-dieu et le dieu-roi dans l'Egypt ancienne. CONG. INT. HIST. REL. 8 (1955), pp. 233-234.

See also 13632.

Biography

5,206 ESCOTT, T. H. S. Lord Cromer behind the scenes. CONTEMP. REV. 111 (1917), pp. 336-344.

5,207 Obituary: Georges Douin. SUDAN NOTES 26 (1945), pp. 183-184.

5,208 Obituary: W. F. Hume. SUDAN NOTES 30 (1949), p. 281.

See also 5976.

Economics

5,209 BAER, W. The promoting and the financing of the Suez Canal. BUSINESS HIST. REV. 30 (1956), pp. 361-381.

5,210 BARBOUR, K. M. A new approach to the Nile waters problem. INTERNAT. AFFAIRS 33 (1957), pp. 319-330.

5,211 BEZY, F. Les formes du développement économique dans l'Egypt nassérienne. GENEVE-AFR. 4 (1965), pp. 206-224.

5,212 BRESCIANI-TURRONI, C. Egypt's balance of trade. J. POLIT. ECON. 42 (1934), pp. 371-384.

5,213 CONDIE, R. H. B. Egypt's trade with the Sudan. SUDAN NOTES AND RECORDS 36 (1955), pp. 57-63.

5,214 D., H. The Assuan dam, by H. D. J. AFR. SOC. 12 (1913), pp. 200-201.

5,215 DORI, L. Tipografi e giornalisti italiani in Egitto. AFRICA (Rome) 14 (1959), pp. 146-148.

5,216 EDWARDS, F. M. The Egyptian rural problem. CONTEMP. REV. 140 (1931), pp. 191-199.

5,217 GLASGOW, G. Egypt and the Canal. CONTEMP. REV. 190 (1956), pp. 133-136.

5,218 GRAY, A. The Nile waters. AFR. AFFAIRS 55 (1956), pp. 91-93.

5,219 GRAY, A. Nile Waters Agreement. AFR. AFFAIRS 59 (1960), pp. 5-6.

5,220 HANSEN, B. and EL TOMY, M. The seasonal employment profile in Egyptian agriculture. J. DEVELOPMENT STUDS. 1 (1965), pp. 399-409.

5,221 HASSAN, A. M. Egypt 1952-1957. CIVILISATIONS 7 (1957), pp. 419-443.

5,222 INTRONA, S. Situazione politica ed economica dell'Egitto. AFRICA (Rome) 10 (1955), pp. 20-22.

5,223 KAY, H. C. Land tenure and taxation in Egypt. CONTEMP. REV. 43 (1883), pp. 411-427.

5,224 LEGRAND, F. The economic condition of Egypt. J. AFR. SOC. 11 (1911), pp. 1-20.

5,225 McFARLANE, J. The production of cotton in Egypt. J. AFR. SOC. 8 (1909), pp. 372-382.

5,226 MULHALL, M. G. Egyptian finance. CONTEMP. REV. 42 (1882), pp. 525-535.

5,227 NEWMAN, E. W. P. Egypt: crisis and capitulations. CONTEMP. REV. 141 (1932), pp. 42-48.

5,228 O'BRIEN, P. K. An economic appraisal of the Egyptian revolution. J. DEVELOPMENT STUDS. 1 (1964), pp. 93-113.

5,229 RASHAD, I. The co-operative movement in Egypt. J. AFR. SOC. 38 (1939), pp. 469-476.

5,230 SANCHIZ, J. C. Money and banking in the United Arab Republic. IMF STAFF PAPERS 12 (1965), pp. 314-328.

5,231 SIEGFRIED, A. The Suez: international roadway. FOREIGN AFFAIRS 31 (1952-1953), pp. 605-618.

5,232 SIRRY BEY, H. The Qattara power scheme. GEOG. REV. 19 (1929), pp. 290-292.

5,233 WARRINER, D. Land reform in Egypt and its repercussions. INTERNAT. AFFAIRS 29 (1953), pp. 1-10.

5,234 WELD, H. The Blue Nile, and irrigation. J. AFR. SOC. 27 (1928), pp. 97-103.

5,235 WILSON, A. The Suez Canal. CONTEMP. REV. 155 (1939), pp. 280-287.

5,236 WILSON, Sir A. The Suez Canal. INTERNAT. AFFAIRS 18 (1939), pp. 380-395.

5,237 War and finance in Egypt. ECON. J. 25 (1915), pp. 79-96.

See also 5432, 11429.

Education

5,238 DIN, S. EL. La nouvelle fonction des Universités d'Egypte. CIVILISATIONS 5 (1955), pp. 345-351; English summary, pp. 351-352.

5,239 MARVIN, F. S. Education in Egypt. CONTEMP. REV. 139 (1931), pp. 456-463.

5,240 NAWAR, A. Adult education in Egypt. CIVILISATIONS 8 (1958), pp. 119-131.

5,241 NAWAR, A. A brief survey of education in post-revolutionary Egypt. CIVILISATIONS 7 (1957), pp. 93-111.

5,242 SAILER, T. H. P. Problems of education in Egypt. INT. REV. MISSIONS 1 (1912), pp. 498-510.

5,243 SMITH, R. Education in Egypt. CONTEMP. REV. 143 (1933), pp. 204-210.

Geography

5,244 BOAK, A. E. R. Irrigation and population in the Faiyûm, the Garden of Egypt. GEOG. REV. 16 (1926), pp. 353-364.

5,245 CRARY, D. D. Irrigation and land use in Zeiniya Bahari, Upper Egypt. GEOG. REV. 39 (1949), pp. 568-583.

5,246 FORBES, R. H. Egyptian-Libyan borderlands. GEOG. REV. 32 (1942), pp. 294-302.

5,247 GIL BENUMEYA, R. El Africa del Nilo. CUAD. EST. AFR. 5 (1949), pp. 57-69.

5,248 GUSSMAN, B. Contrasts in Cairo. CONTEMP. REV. 169 (1946), pp. 47-50.

5,249 HOBBS, W. H. A pilgrimage in northeastern Africa, with studies of desert conditions. GEOG. REV. 3 (1917), pp. 337-355.

5,250 HOSKINS, H. L. Suez Canal problems. GEOG. REV. 30 (1940), pp. 665-671.

5,251 LOMHOLT, A. Captain F. L. Norden's journey to Egypt and Nubia 1737-38: some facts about a remarkable work. LIBRI 11 (1961), pp. 364-376.

5,252 PIKE, A. H. Notes on the exploration of the sources of the Nile. TANGANYIKA NOTES AND RECORDS 49 (1957), pp. 223-225.

5,253 RIAD, M. An introduction to Nubia. AFRICA QUART. 3, no. i (1963), pp. 14-29.

5,254 TOTHILL, B. H. Some extracts from the life and travels of Theodore Kotschy. SUDAN NOTES 25 (1942), pp. 109-121.

5,255 WILSON, E. M. Zagazig: a cotton market. GEOG. REV. 24 (1934), pp. 566-575.

Government. Administration. Politics

5,256 BEAMAN, A. H. The political situation in Egypt. CONTEMP. REV. 132 (1928), pp. 15-23.

5,257 BILAINKIN, G. Realities in Egypt. CONTEMP. REV. 181 (1952), pp. 202-207.

5,258 COLOMBE, L. L'Egypte et la crise actuelle de l'arabisme. AFR. ET ASIE 11 (1950), pp. 31-41.

5,259 COLOMBE, M. L'Egypte et les origines du nationalisme arabe. AFR. ET ASIE 14 (1951), pp. 19-33.

5,260 COLOMBE, M. Où en est le Wafd égyptien? AFR. ET ASIE 10 (1950), pp. 36-44.

5,261 ELGOOD, P. G. The situation in Egypt [an address given on June 28th, 1927]. INTERNAT. AFFAIRS 6 (1927), pp. 299-313.

5,262 FEKI, A. H. EL-. Afro-Asian solidarity and the United Arab Republic. AFRO-ASIAN AND W. AFF. 1 (1964), pp. 55-61.

5,263 GIBB, H. A. R. Anglo-Egyptian relations. INTERNAT. AFFAIRS 27 (1951), pp. 440-450.

5,264 GIBB, H. A. R. The situation in Egypt. INTERNAT. AFFAIRS 15 (1936), pp. 351-373.

5,265 GIL BENUMEYA, R. Nueve meses de Egipto nacional con Mohammed Naguib. CUAD. EST. AFR. 22 (1953), pp. 9-18.

5,266 GIL BENUMEYA, R. Política y partidos políticos en Egipto. CUAD. EST. AFR. 10 (1950), pp. 39-51.

5,267 GIL BENUMEYA, R. Visita a los hombres de la revolución egipcia. CUAD. EST. AFR. 27 (1954), pp. 9-20.

5,268 GRAY, A. Egypto-Sudanese dispute. AFR. AFFAIRS 57 (1958), p. 96.

5,269 GUIRGUIS, M. Egypt. CIVILISATIONS 6 (1956), pp. 655-662.

5,270 GUSSMAN, B. Egypt's dilemma. CONTEMP. REV. 172 (1947), pp. 145-148.

5,271 HYSLOP, J. R. Egypt and the Sudan. CONTEMP. REV. 180 (1951), pp. 205-210.

5,272 KOROSTOVTSEV, M. A. A propos des objets égyptiens découverts en U.R.S.S. J. WORLD HIST. 3 (1956-1957), pp. 967-984.

5,273 McILWRAITH, M. A decade of Egyptian politics. CONTEMP. REV. 142 (1932), pp. 172-180.

5,274 MACKAY, M. Cairo and the three dreams. AFR. AFFAIRS 62 (1963), pp. 270-274.

5,275 MAZRUI, A. A. Africa and the Egyptian's four circles. AFR. AFFAIRS 63 (1964), pp. 129-141.

5,276 MERTON, A. Constitutionalism in Egypt. CONTEMP. REV. 139 (1931), pp. 32-40.

5,277 MERTON, A. Great Britain and Egypt. CONTEMP. REV. 149 (1936), pp. 314-322.

5,278 MERTON, A. Independent Egypt. CONTEMP. REV. 152 (1937), pp. 165-173.

5,279 NEWMAN, E. W. P. Progress in Egypt. CONTEMP. REV. 136 (1929), pp. 174-181.

5,280 PARKER, J. S. F. The United Arab Republic. INTERNAT. AFFAIRS 38 (1962), pp. 15-28.

5,281 PHILBY, H. ST. J. B. Labour, Lord Lloyd and Egypt. CONTEMP. REV. 136 (1929), pp. 332-337.

5,282 PONSONBY, A. Egypt to-day. CONTEMP. REV. 134 (1929), pp. 282-287.

5,283 ROWLATT, M. Impressions of Egypt. CONTEMP. REV. 185 (1954), pp. 196-200.

5,284 ROWLATT, M. Thoughts on the Anglo-Egyptian Agreement. CONTEMP. REV. 186 (1954), pp. 331-333.

5,285 SAVORY, Sir D. Sequel to the Suez crisis. CONTEMP. REV. 199 (1961), pp. 80-83, 255-257.

5,286 STRANGE, S. Suez and after. THE YEAR BOOK OF WORLD AFFAIRS 11 (1957), pp. 76-103.

5,287 WARRINER, D. Observations on land reform administration in Egypt. J. LOCAL ADM. OV. 2 (1963), pp. 100-111.

History

5,288 AGUIRRE DE CARCER, N. Los Tribunales Mixtos y la evolucion politico-internacional en Egipto. CUAD. EST. AFR. 2 (1946), pp. 93-113.

5,289 ALLEN, B. M. The Royal Engineers in Egypt and the Sudan [by E. W. C. Sandes]. J. AFR. SOC. 37 (1938), pp. 471-476.

5,290 AMOS, S. Egypt and England. CONTEMP. REV. 42 (1882), pp. 318-334.

5,291 AMOS, S. The new Egyptian constitution. CONTEMP. REV. 43 (1883), pp. 909-922.

5,292 AMOS, S. "Spoiling the Egyptians": revised version. CONTEMP. REV. 42 (1882), pp. 509-524.

5,293 BELL, K. British policy towards the construction of the Suez Canal, 1859-65. TRHS, 5th series, 15 (1965), pp. 121-143.

5,294 BESANT, W. H. The early days of the Egyptian army, 1883-1892. J. AFR. SOC. 33 (1934), pp. 160-168.

5,295 BESSON, M. Un corps Anglo-Indien en Egypte, en 1802. RHCF 26 (1933), pp. 71-78.

5,296 BILAINKIN, G. Genesis of President Nasser. CONTEMP. REV. 202 (1962), pp. 304-309.

5,297 BIRDWOOD, Lord. Britain and the Middle East. AFR. AFFAIRS 58 (1959), pp. 123-133.

5,298 BROCHADO, C. A Espiritualidade dos Descobrimentos e a Cruzada contra o Sultão do Egipto. PORT. EM AFR. 3 (1946), pp. 16-19.

5,299 BORCHADO, C. Ainda a Cruzada de El-Rei D. Manuel 1. PORT EM AFR. 3 (1946), pp. 292-297.

5,300 BROWN, C. H. Egypt from Cromer to Neguib. HISTORY TODAY 3 (1953), pp. 469-475.

5,301 BRUNYATE, W. E. Sidelights on Egypt. CONTEMP. REV. 119 (1921), pp. 451-461.

5,302 CAIRENE. The English failure in Egypt. CONTEMP. REV. 67 (1895), pp. 390-395.

5,303 CAMBIER, R. Stanley et Emin Pacha. ZAIRE 3 (1949), pp. 533-548.

5,304 CANA, F. R. Egyptian and Sudan frontiers. CONTEMP. REV. 105 (1914), pp. 688-697.

5,305 CHALONER, W. H. De Lesseps and the Suez Canal. HISTORY TODAY 6 (1956), pp. 680-684.

5,306 CHANDLER, D. G. The Egyptian campaign of 1801. HISTORY TODAY 12 (1962), pp. 116-123, 177-186.

5,307 CHARLES-ROUX, F. L'expédition de Bonaparte en Egypte et la politique anglaise dans la Mer Rouge. RHCF 15 (1923), pp. 173-204.

5,308 CHIROL, V. The Egyptian question. INTERNAT. AFFAIRS 1 (1922), pp. 55-71.

5,309 COCATRE-ZILGIEN, A. Amr-ibn-al-Ass et la conquête de l'Egypte par les Arabes. ANNALES AFR., 1959, pp. 201-244.

5,310 COLOMBE, M. L'Egypte et l'abdication du roi Farouk. AFR. ET ASIE 20 (1952), pp. 27-38.

5,311 COLOMBE, M. Onze mois d'évolution de l'Egypte (29 juillet 1952-18 juin 1953). AFR. ET ASIE 23 (1953), pp. 4-14.

5,312 COLOMBE, M. Où va l'Egypte? AFR. ET ASIE 1, no. 4 (1948), pp. 29-42.

5,313 COOPER, A. F. The future of Egypt. INTERNAT. AFFAIRS 4 (1925), pp. 161-173.

5,314 CRABITES, P. Egypt, the Sudan and the Nile. FOREIGN AFFAIRS 3 (1924-1925), pp. 320-330.

5,315 CRABITES, P. The Nile Waters Agreement. FOREIGN AFFAIRS 8 (1929-1930), pp. 145-149.

5,316 DORI, L. Come apparvero il Cairo e Porto Said agli occhi di Ruggero Leoncavallo. AFRICA (Rome) 13 (1958), pp. 179-181.

5,317 DUNCKLEY, H. Egypt, Europe, and Mr. Gladstone. CONTEMP. REV. 46 (1884), pp. 1-22.

5,318 EBERS, G. Cairo: the old in the new. CONTEMP. REV. 43 (1883), pp. 674-684, 842-857.

5,319 ELGOOD, P. G. Egyptian affairs. J. AFR. SOC. 32 (1933), pp. 190-194.

5,320 ELGOOD, P. G. Treaty of alliance between the United Kingdom and Egypt. White Paper: Egypt no. 1 (1936). J. AFR. SOC. 36 (1937), pp. 33-35.

5,321 FARRAG, R. Civiltà egizia millenaria. AFRICA (Rome) 10 (1955), p. 22.

5,322 FORBES, A. The failure of the Nile campaign. CONTEMP. REV. 61 (1892), pp. 39-48.

5,323 GAZZINI, M. Italiani in Egitto ante 1940: nel paese. AFRICA (Rome) 10 (1955), p. 216.

5,324 GAZZINI, M. Italiani in Egito ante 1940. Suez. AFRICA (Rome) 10 (1955), p. 176.

5,325 GLEICHEN, E. Egypt since Cromer. By Lord Lloyd of Dolobran. J. AFR. SOC. 32 (1933), pp. 113-122.

5,326 GLEICHEN, E. The Egyptian situation. CONTEMP. REV. 127 (1925), pp. 24-31.

5,327 GOODMAN, C. The problem of Egypt. CONTEMP. REV. 117 (1920), pp. 356-363.

5,328 GRAY, A. Col. Nasser's escape. AFR. AFFAIRS 54 (1955), pp. 6-8.

5,329 GRAY, A. The Suez Canal. AFR. AFFAIRS 56 (1957), pp. 2-4.

5,330 GRAY, A. Suez Canal question. AFR. AFFAIRS 55 (1956), pp. 255-257.

5,331 GROOT, E. DE. Europe and Egypt in the 19th century. HISTORY TODAY 2 (1952), pp. 34-44.

5,332 HENNE, H. Petites recherches sur le directeur des cultes dans l'Egypte romaine. MELANGES OFFERTS A M. NICOLAS IORGA, 1933, pp. 435-464.

5,333 HODGKIN, T. Theon and Son, Egyptian bankers of the second century. CONTEMP. REV. 75 (1899), pp. 84-89.

5,334 HOLT, P. M. The Beylicate in Ottoman Egypt during the seventeenth century. BULL. SOAS 24 (1961), pp. 214-248.

5,335 HOMBERT, M. and PREAUX, C. Les mariages consanguins dans l'Egypte romaine. HOMMAGES A JOSEPH BIDEZ ET A FRANZ CUMONT, 1949, pp. 135-142.

5,336 HOSKINS, H. L. Some recent works on Mohamed Ali and modern Egypt. J. MOD. HIST. 4 (1932), pp. 93-103.

5,337 HOSKINS, H. L. The Suez Canal in time of war. FOREIGN AFFAIRS 14 (1935-1936), pp. 93-101.

5,338 JESMAN, C. American officers of Khedive Ismail. AFR. AFFAIRS 57 (1958), pp. 302-307.

5,339 JESMAN, C. Egyptian invasion of Ethiopia. AFR. AFFAIRS 58 (1959), pp. 75-81.

5,340 JOHNSTON, Sir H. H. Lord Cromer's "Modern Egypt." J. AFR. SOC. 7 (1908), pp. 239-248.

5,341 KEAY, J. S. "Spoiling the Egyptians": a rejoinder. CONTEMP. REV. 42 (1882), pp. 764-785.

5,342 KHALIL, O. Egypte. CIVILISATIONS 7 (1957), pp. 259-263; 8 (1958), pp. 320-324.

5,343 LANDAU, J. M. The young Egypt party. BULL. SOAS 15 (1953), pp. 161-164.

5,344 LANGER, W. L. The struggle for the Nile. FOREIGN AFFAIRS 14 (1935-1936), pp. 259-273.

5,345 "MALORTIE". The outlook in Egypt. CONTEMP. REV. 45 (1884), pp. 266-279.

5,346 MICHALOWSKI, K. La Nubie chrétienne. AFR. BULL. 3 (1965), pp. 9-26.

5,347 MILLER, T. B. The Egyptian question and British foreign policy, 1892-1894. J. MOD. HIST. 32 (1960), pp. 1-15.

5,348 MIROT, L. Deux représentations de la bataille d'Aboukir. RHCF 4 (1916), pp. 301-318.

5,349 MULCHACEN, M. DE. La aventura de Suez. ARCH. INST. EST. AFR. 13, no. 49 (1959), pp. 53-79.

5,350 NASSER, G. A. The Egyptian revolution. FOREIGN AFFAIRS 33 (1954-1955), pp. 199-211.

5,351 NEWMAN, E. W. P. Egypt. CONTEMP. REV. 138 (1930), pp. 570-577.

5,352 NEWMAN, E. W. P. Egypt: a new era. CONTEMP. REV. 154 (1938), pp. 425-432.

5,353 NEWMAN, E. W. P. Egypt and the treaty. CONTEMP. REV. 150 (1936), pp. 407-415.

5,354 NEWMAN, E. W. P. Egypt and the war. CONTEMP. REV. 158 (1940), pp. 488-494; 159 (1941), pp. 624-630.

5,355 NORMAN, H. The evacuation of Egypt. CONTEMP. REV. 61 (1892), pp. 487-497.

5,356 O'ROURKE, V. A. The British position in Egypt. FOREIGN AFFAIRS 14 (1935-1936), pp. 698-701.

5,357 OSBORN, R. D. The value of Egypt to Great Britain. CONTEMP. REV. 41 (1882), pp. 27-36.

5,358 PAGEARD, R. Civilisation mossie et Egypte ancienne. GENEVE AFR. 2 (1963), pp. 183-206.

5,359 PAUL, A. Aidhab: a medieval Red Sea port. SUDAN NOTES AND RECORDS 36 (1955), pp. 64-70.

5,360 PETRIE, W. M. F. Egypt and Israel. CONTEMP. REV. 69 (1896), pp. 617-627.

5,361 PLUMB, J. H. The search for the Nile. HISTORY TODAY 2 (1952), pp. 738-745.

5,362 PRICE, M. P. The Suez crisis in perspective. CONTEMP. REV. 190 (1956), pp. 194-197.

5,363 QUINTANO RIPOLLES, A. Etapas de la evolución de Egipto. CUAD. EST. AFR. 12 (1950), pp. 29-43.

5,364 RAYMOND, J. Cromer: the miracle of Egypt. HISTORY TODAY 10 (1960), pp. 240-246.

5,365 REID, R. T. The Suez Canal question. CONTEMP. REV. 44 (1883), pp. 157-168.

5,366 ROBERTSON, J. M. The problem of Egypt. CONTEMP. REV. 115 (1919), pp. 490-496.

5,367 ROBINSON, P. The Army, the Volunteers, and the Press: lessons of the Egyptian campaign. CONTEMP. REV. 42 (1882), pp. 973-978.

5,368 RODD, R. The present situation in Egypt. CONTEMP. REV. 121 (1922), pp. 409-417.

5,369 ROWLATT, M. The Egyptian situation. CONTEMP. REV. 184 (1953), pp. 19-23.

5,370 RUSSELL, W. H. Why did we depose Ismail? CONTEMP. REV. 48 (1885), pp. 305-325.

5,371 SANDERSON, G. N. "Emir Suleyman Ibn Inger Abdullah": an episode in the Anglo-French conflict on the Upper Nile, 1896-1898. SUDAN NOTES AND RECORDS 35, part 1 (1954), pp. 22-74.

5,372 SAYCE, A. H. Upper Egypt under British rule. CONTEMP. REV. 45 (1884), pp. 504-512.

5,373 SHOCK, M. Gladstone's invasion of Egypt, 1882. HISTORY TODAY 7 (1957), pp. 351-357.

5,374 STACEY, C. P. Canada and the Nile expedition of 1884-85. CANADIAN HIST. REV. 33 (1952), pp. 319-340.

5,375 STERN, A. Colonel Cradock's missions to Egypt. ENG. HIST. REV. 15 (1900), pp. 277-287.

5,376 STEWART, D. Mohammed Ali: Pasha of Egypt. HISTORY TODAY 8 (1958), pp. 321-327.

5,377 SWANZY, H. The situation in Egypt. AFR. AFFAIRS 46 (1947), pp. 123-124.

5,378 TAYLOR, A. J. P. Prelude to Fashoda: the question of the Upper Nile, 1894-5. ENG. HIST. REV. 65 (1950), pp. 52-80.

5,379 TEMPLE, R. Principles of British policy in Egypt. CONTEMP. REV. 42 (1882), pp. 495-508.

5,380 TIGNOR, R. L. The Indianization of the Egyptian administration under British rule. AM. HIST. REV. 68 (1962-1963), pp. 636-661.

5,381 VYCICHL, W. Qui était Fa'awngiyus? ANNALES D'ETHIOPIE 2 (1957), pp. 181-185.

5,382 WACHS, O. The strategic value of Egypt. CONTEMP. REV. 62 (1892), pp. 442-455.

5,383 WEDGWOOD, J. C. The occupation of Egypt. CONTEMP. REV. 131 (1927), pp. 152-157.

5,384 WESTLAKE, J. England's duty in Egypt. CONTEMP. REV. 42 (1882), pp. 823-839.

5,385 WHITEHOUSE, C. The expansion of Egypt. CONTEMP. REV. 52 (1887), pp. 415-427.

5,386 WICKENS, G. M. Mamluk Egypt at the eleventh hour: some eyewitness observations. THE SEED OF WISDOM: ESSAYS IN HONOUR OF T. J. MEEK, 1964, pp. 141-158.

5,387 WIET, G. Les secrétaires de la Chancellerie en Egypte sous les Mamlouks circassiens (784-922/1382-1517). MELANGES RENE BASSET, 1923, pp. 271-314.

5,388 WILLIS, C. Egypt. AFR. AFFAIRS 53 (1954), pp. 311-318.

5,389 YAHYA, G. E-D. Egitto ed Etiopia. AFRICA (Rome) 11 (1956), pp. 8-10.

5,390 ZAVATTI, S. Lettere inedite di Romolo Gessi relative alla spedizione del Kaffa. AFRICA (Rome) 17 (1962), pp. 300-301.

5,391 Can we desert Egypt? CONTEMP. REV. 56 (1889), pp. 314-334.

5,392 An English Resident in Egypt. Egypt and constitutional rule. CONTEMP. REV. 41 (1882), pp. 541-559.

5,393 A German Field Officer. The English military power and the Egyptian campaign of 1882. CONTEMP. REV. 43 (1883), pp. 457-475.

5,394 Italiani in Egito ante 1940. Assuan. AFRICA (Rome) 10 (1955), pp. 157-158.

5,395 The position of General Gordon, a conversation. CONTEMP. REV. 45 (1884), pp. 866-878.

See also 2788, 6244, 16793.

Language. Literature

Language

5,396 GREENBERG, J. H. The interpretation of the Coptic vowel system. J. AFR. LANGS. 1 (1962), pp. 22-29.

5,397 HEYWORTH-DUNNE, J. A selection of Cairo's street cries (referring to vegetables, fruit, flowers and food). BULL. SOAS 9 (1937-1939), pp. 351-362.

5,398 LAMBDIN, T. O. Egypt: its language and literature. THE BIBLE AND THE ANCIENT NEAR EAST: ESSAYS IN HONOUR OF W. F. ALBRIGHT, 1961, pp. 279-297.

5,399 LESLAU, W. A prefix h in Egyptian, modern south Arabian, and Hausa. AFRICA 32 (1962), pp. 65-68.

5,400 SABBADINI, E. L'unità linguistica della valle del Nilo nell'antichità. AFRICA (Rome) 18 (1963), pp. 233-239.

5,401 ZYHLARZ, E. Die Sprachreste der unteräthiopischen Nachbarn Altägyptens. AFR. UND UB. 25 (1934-1935), pp. 161-188, 241-261.

5,402 ZYHLARZ, E. Ursprung und Sprachcharakter des Altägyptischen. AFR. UND UB. 23 (1932-1933), pp. 25-45, 81-110, 161-194, 241-254.

Literature

5,403 ARCHER, R. Caesar in Egypt. AFR. AFFAIRS 55 (1956), p. 157.

5,404 CATRICE, P. Women writers of North Africa. AFR. WOMEN 5 (1963), pp. 34-35.

5,405 COSSERY, A. The girl and the hashish smoker [fiction]. BO 16 (1964), pp. 11-16.

5,406 DUSOGI, M. M. EL-. Dr. Taha Hussain and his literary method. KANO STUD. 1 (1965), p. 8.

5,407 EBAN, A. S. The modern literary movement in Egypt. INTERNAT. AFFAIRS 20 (1944), pp. 166-178.

5,408 FARES, B. The bark [fiction]. BO 14 (1964), pp. 56-58.

5,409 Egyptian poetry. BO 18 (1965), pp. 4-8.

Law

5,410 BAER, G. Tanzimat in Egypt: the penal code. BULL. SOAS 26 (1963), pp. 29-49.

5,411 GARLE, H. E. Judicial reform and the Egyptian settlement. INTERNAT. AFFAIRS 11 (1932), pp. 229-250.

5,412 GINSBURG, N. S. The Egyptian land reform law. ECON. DEVELOPMENT AND CULTURAL CHANGE 1 (1952-1953), pp. 295-319.

5,413 MANSUR. La supresión de los tribunales mixtos en Egipto. CUAD. EST. AFR. 9 (1950), pp. 127-128.

Religion

5,414 CAIRENE. Egypt and religious liberty. INT. REV. MISSIONS 22 (1933), pp. 530-548.

5,415 ELDER, E. E. The evangelical church in Egypt: a study in the development of a younger church. INT. REV. MISSIONS 26 (1937), pp. 514-525.

5,416 HASSAN, S. Remains of religious customs of ancient and modern Egypt. CONG. INT. HIST. REL. 5 (1929), pp. 162-167.

5,417 JEFFERY, A. Three Cairo modernists ['Ali 'Abd ar-Raziq, Taha Hussain, Muhammad Abu Zaid]. INT. REV. MISSIONS 21 (1932), pp. 498-515.

5,418 MAENARDUS, O. F. A. Ecclesiastica Aethiopica in Aegypto. J. ETHIOP. STUD. 3, no. 1 (1965), pp. 23-35.

5,419 MORENZ, S. Die Erwählung Zwischen Gott und König in Agypten. CONG. INT. HIST. REL. 8 (1955), pp. 228-230.

Science

5,420 ALLEN, R. W. Cairo drainage scheme. J. AFR. SOC. 28 (1929), pp. 340-346.

5,421 MEYERHOF, M. Ein Beitrag zum Volksheilglauben der heutigen Agypter. FESTSCHRIFT EDUARD HAHN, 1917, pp. 320-331.

5,422 NAWAR, G. On the fecundity of the Nile catfish Synodontis schall (Bloch-Schneider 1801). SUDAN NOTES AND RECORDS 40 (1959), pp. 139-141.

5,423 NAWAR, G. On the fecundity of the Nile cyprinid Labeo coubie (Rüppell 1832). SUDAN NOTES AND RECORDS 40 (1959), pp. 136-138.

5,424 RUFFER, A. Study of abnormalities and pathology of ancient Egyptian teeth. AMER. J. PHYS. ANTHR. 3 (1920), pp. 335-382.

5,425 TAYLOR, M. and BURNS, C. The decline of cotton yield in Egypt. SUDAN NOTES 5 (1922), pp. 234-235.

5,426 TODD, T. W. Egyptian medicine: a critical study of recent claims. AMER. ANTHR. 23 (1921), pp. 460-470.

Sociology

5,427 ABDEL-AZIZ, A. Problèmes sociaux, économiques et culturels en R.A.U. PRESENCE AFR. N.S. 56 (1965), pp. 9-25.

5,428 ASAAD, R. W. The picture of the foreigner: a study of prejudice in an Alexandrian secondary school. CIVILISATIONS 8 (1958), pp. 67-76; French summary, pp. 77-78.

5,429 ASAAD, R. W. Social survey of Egypt. CIVILISATIONS 7 (1957), pp. 47-56.

5,430 AWAD, M. The assimilation of nomads in Egypt. GEOG. REV. 44 (1954), pp. 240-252.

5,431 BAUER, I. La Sociedad bereber. CUAD. EST. AFR. 6 (1949), pp. 61-68.

5,432 BEER, C. W. Social development in the Gezira scheme. AFR. AFFAIRS 54 (1955), pp. 42-51.

5,433 BREESE, G. Some notes on a case study of European urban "transplants" in Cairo. COMP. STUD. SOC. HIST. 7 (1964-1965), pp. 458-460.

5,434 MANSUR. La población egipcia según el ultimo censo general. CUAD. EST. AFR. 11 (1950), pp. 49-52.

5,435 RODRIGUEZ MELLADO, I. Notas sobre la evolución social de la mujer egipcia. CUAD. EST. AFR. 17 (1952), pp. 49-62.

5,436 SEDKI, L. K. Egyptian women. AFR. WOMEN 3 (1958-1960), pp. 53-55.

5,437 Progress in Egypt. AFR. WOMEN 5 (1963), pp. 30-31.

SUDAN

General

5,438 ARKELL, A. J. Some suggested lines of research in the Sudan. SUDAN NOTES 30 (1949), supplement, pp. 1-3.

5,439 HILL, R. L. Recent Italian literature concerning the Sudan. SUDAN NOTES 22 (1939), pp. 167-169.

5,440 IBRAHIM, A. and EL NASRI, A. R. Sudan bibliography 1959-1963. SUDAN NOTES 46 (1965), pp. 130-166.

5,441 SANDERSON, G. N. Sudan Notes and Records as a vehicle of research on the Sudan. SUDAN NOTES 45 (1964), pp. 164-172.

5,442 SEWELL, P. H. The development of library service in Sudan. UNESCO BULL. LIBS. 15 (1961), pp. 87-90.

5,443 SHEBEIKA, M. E. A Sudan historical manuscript. SUDAN NOTES 30 (1949), supplement, pp. 4-5.

5,444 STRUCK, B. A bibliography of the languages of the Southern Sudan. SUDAN NOTES 11 (1928), pp. 217-226.

5,445 The Institute of Sudanese Studies. INT. SOC. SC. BULL. 5 (1953), pp. 729-730.

5,446 Philosophical Society of the Sudan. Annual Conference, 1955. SUDAN NOTES 37 (1956), pp. 102-121.

5,447 Philosophical Society of the Sudan. Report upon the 1946/7 and 1947/8 sessions. SUDAN NOTES 29 (1948), pp. 228-232.

5,448 Philosophical Society of the Sudan. Third Annual Conference, December, 1954: Physical sciences in the Sudan. SUDAN NOTES 39 (1958), pp. 101-108.

5,449 Proceedings of the Philosophical Society of the Sudan, 1946-1947. SUDAN NOTES 30 (1949), supplement, pp. 1-20.

5,450 Recent books and articles of interest to Sudan readers. SUDAN NOTES 29 (1948), pp. 233-236; 30 (1949), pp. 122-129; 31 (1950), pp. 164-172; 32 (1951), pp. 166-172; 33 (1952), pp. 172-180; 34 (1953), pp. 136-145; 39 (1958), pp. 115-130.

5,451 Sudan bibliography. SUDAN NOTES AND RECORDS 35, part 1 (1954), pp. 157-167; 36 (1955), pp. 89-100.

See also 18634.

Agriculture

5,452 ALLEN, R. W. Irrigation in the Sudan. J. AFR. SOC. 23 (1924), pp. 257-264.

5,453 BASINSKI, J. J. Some problems of agricultural development in the southern provinces of the Sudan. SUDAN NOTES 38 (1957), pp. 21-46.

5,454 BAUMER, M. Etude et amélioration des pâturages en République du Soudan. BULL. I.E.C. N.S 17-18 (1959), pp. 145-153.

5,455 BEER, C. W. The social and administrative effects of large-scale planned agricultural development. J. AFR. ADM. 5 (1953), pp. 112-118.

5,456 BELL, G. W. Nuba agricultural methods and beliefs. SUDAN NOTES 21 (1938), pp. 237-249.

5,457 BOND, W. R. G. Rotation of crops in gum gardens of the White Nile. SUDAN NOTES 1 (1918), pp. 80-87.

5,458 BOND, W. R. G. Some curious methods of cultivation in Dongola Province. SUDAN NOTES 8 (1925), pp. 97-103.

5,459 DARLING, H. S. The storage of food grains in the Sudan. FOOD AND SOCIETY IN THE SUDAN, 1955, pp. 91-104.

5,460 JACKSON, J. K. and SHAWKI, M. K. Shifting cultivation in the Sudan, with particular reference to forestry. SUDAN NOTES 31 (1950), pp. 210-222.

5,461 JEFFERSON, J. H. K. A short description of Harig and Mahal methods of cultivation. SUDAN NOTES 30 (1949), pp. 276-280.

5,462 JEFFERSON, J. H. K. The Sudan's grain supply. SUDAN NOTES 30 (1949), pp. 77-100.

5,463 LEACH, T. A. Date-trees in Halfa Province. SUDAN NOTES 2 (1919), pp. 98-104.

5,464 MARTIN, F. J. and MASSEY, R. E. Experiments of wheat growing. SUDAN NOTES 4 (1921), pp. 113-115.

5,465 MASSEY, R. E. A note on the maintenance of quality of cotton grown in the Sudan. SUDAN NOTES 4 (1921), pp. 44-45.

5,466 MILLER, R. New land for Africa: irrigation in the Gezira. CORONA 3 (1951), pp. 148-150.

5,467 MOIR, T. R. G. Some aspects of agricultural development in the Sudan. FOOD AND SOCIETY IN THE SUDAN, 1955, pp. 213-242.

5,468 NICHOLLS, W. The Sakia in Dongola Province. SUDAN NOTES 1 (1918), pp. 21-24.

5,469 REED, W. The pearl shell farm at Dongonab Bay. SUDAN NOTES 45 (1964), pp. 158-163.

5,470 SCHLIPPE, P. DE. Hedge strip farming: a plan for Zandeland. SUDAN NOTES AND RECORDS 36 (1955), pp. 6-35.

5,471 SCHLIPPE, P. DE and BATWELL, B. L. Preliminary study of the Nyangwara system of agriculture. AFRICA 25 (1955), pp. 321-350.

5,472 SNOW, O. W. Some problems in agricultural research in the Sudan. SUDAN NOTES 30 (1949), supplement, p. 13.

5,473 WHITEHEAD, G. O. Crops and cattle among the Bari-speaking tribes. SUDAN NOTES 43 (1962), pp. 131-142.

5,474 The Zande scheme. CORONA 3 (1951), pp. 260-261.

Anthropology

5,475 A., A. J. Only a fern. SUDAN NOTES 7 (1924), part 2, pp. 128-129.

5,476 A., A. J. Two notes on iron implements with magic properties. SUDAN NOTES 7 (1924), part 1, pp. 137-139.

5,477 AGLEN, E. F. Kordofan superstitions. SUDAN NOTES 19 (1936), pp. 343-345.

5,478 ALBAN, A. H. A. The Langu. SUDAN NOTES 5 (1922), pp. 49-51.

5,479 ARKELL, A. J. The Baza festival in Jebel Meidob. SUDAN NOTES 28 (1947), pp. 127-134.

5,480 ARKELL, A. J. Fung origins. SUDAN NOTES 15 (1932), pp. 201-250.

5,481 ARKELL, A. J. Magic and medicine in Dar Masalit. SUDAN NOTES 9 (1926), pp. 89-94.

5,482 ARKELL, A. J. Māni magic in Northern Darfur. SUDAN NOTES 19 (1936), pp. 317-319.

5,483 ARKELL, A. J. More about Fung origins. SUDAN NOTES 27 (1946), pp. 87-97.

5,484 ARKELL, A. J. The removal of the uvula in infants in Darfur. SUDAN NOTES 19 (1936), pp. 322-323.

5,485 ARKELL, A. J. Throwing-sticks and throwing-knives in Darfur. SUDAN NOTES 22 (1939), pp. 251-266.

5,486 ARKELL, A. J. The *Tigda* or reaping knife in Darfur. SUDAN NOTES 20 (1937), pp. 306-307.

5,487 ASAD, T. Seasonal movements of the Kababish Arabs of Northern Kordofan. SUDAN NOTES 45 (1964), pp. 48-58.

5,488 B., E. F. N. Divination. SUDAN NOTES 1 (1918), p. 135.

5,489 BACON, C. R. K. The Anuak. SUDAN NOTES 5 (1922), pp. 113-129.

5,490 BACON, C. R. K. The investiture of an Anuak Nyeya or Sultan. SUDAN NOTES 7 (1924), part 2, pp. 114-117.

5,491 BACON, C. R. K. Kingship amongst the Anuak. SUDAN NOTES 4 (1921), pp. 162-164.

5,492 BEATON, A. C. The Bari: clan and age-class systems. SUDAN NOTES 19 (1936), pp. 109-145.

5,493 BEATON, A. C. A Bari game—Soro. SUDAN NOTES 22 (1939), pp. 133-143.

5,494 BEATON, A. C. The Fur. SUDAN NOTES 29 (1948), pp. 1-39.

5,495 BEATON, A. C. Fur dance songs. SUDAN NOTES 23 (1940), pp. 305-329.

5,496 BEATON, A. C. Record of the Toposa tribe. SUDAN NOTES 31 (1950), pp. 129-132.

5,497 BEATON, A. C. Tigri folk tales (Digam). SUDAN NOTES 28 (1947), pp. 146-150.

5,498 BEATON, A. C. Youth organisation among the Fur. SUDAN NOTES 24 (1941), pp. 181-187.

5,499 BEDRI, I. Notes on Dinka religious beliefs in their hereditary chiefs and rain makers. SUDAN NOTES 22 (1939), pp. 125-131.

5,500 BEDRI, I. More notes on the Padang Dinka. SUDAN NOTES 29 (1948), pp. 40-57.

5,501 BEER, C. W. Note on manufacture of Nuba stone knob sticks. SUDAN NOTES 18 (1935), pp. 294-296.

5,502 BELL, G. Nuba fertility stones. SUDAN NOTES 19 (1936), pp. 313-316.

5,503 BELL, G. W. Ordeal by fire. SUDAN NOTES 20 (1937), pp. 316-318.

5,504 BELTRAME, G. Some notes on the distribution of the Nilotic peoples in the mid-nineteenth century. SUDAN NOTES 42 (1961), pp. 118-121.

5,505 BLOSS, J. F. E. Notes on a Dinka game trap. SUDAN NOTES 22 (1939), p. 163.

5,506 BOLTON, A. R. C. The Dubab and Nuba of Jebel Daier. SUDAN NOTES 19 (1936), pp. 93-108.

5,507 BONHAM-CARTER, E. Note on Frazer's folk lore in the Old Testament. SUDAN NOTES 7 (1924), part 2, pp. 5-17.

5,508 BOWER, J. E. Circumcision school in the western Bahr al Ghazal. SUDAN NOTES 6 (1923), pp. 249-250.

5,509 BRELSFORD, W. V. Bird lore of the Babemba in Northern Rhodesia. NADA 22 (1945), pp. 28-35.

5,510 BROCK, R. G. C. Some notes on the Zande tribe as found in the Meridi District (Bahr El Ghazal Province). SUDAN NOTES 1 (1918), pp. 249-262.

5,511 BUXTON, J. "Clientship" among the Mandari of the Southern Sudan. SUDAN NOTES 38 (1957), pp. 100-110.

5,512 BUXTON, J. The Mandari of the Southern Sudan. TRIBES WITHOUT RULERS, 1958, pp. 67-96.

5,513 C., E. G. A stray buffalo. SUDAN NOTES 2 (1919), pp. 76-77.

5,514 CANN, G. P. A day in the life of an idle Shilluk. SUDAN NOTES 12 (1929), pp. 251-253.

5,515 CHATAWAY, J. D. P. Fung origins. SUDAN NOTES 17 (1934), pp. 111-117.

5,516 CHATAWAY, J. D. P. Notes on the history of the Fung. SUDAN NOTES 13 (1930), pp. 247-258.

5,517 CLARK, W. T. Manners, customs and beliefs of the Northern Bega. SUDAN NOTES 21 (1938), pp. 1-29.

5,518 COOK, R. C. A Bari stone. SUDAN NOTES 23 (1940), p. 191.

5,519 COOKE, R. C. and BEATON, A. C. Bari rain cults and Fur rain cults and ceremonies. SUDAN NOTES 22 (1939), pp. 181-203.

5,520 CORFIELD, F. D. The Koma. SUDAN NOTES 21 (1938), pp. 123-163.

5,521 CORKILL, N. L. A game trap in the Upper Nile Province. SUDAN NOTES 27 (1946), pp. 233-234.

5,522 CORKILL, N. L. A Kadugli cobra trap. SUDAN NOTES 18 (1935), pp. 131-134.

5,523 CORKILL, N. L. The Kambala and other seasonal festivals of the Kadugli and Miri Nuba. SUDAN NOTES 22 (1939), pp. 205-219.

5,524 CORKILL, N. L. Snake stories from Kordofan. SUDAN NOTES 18 (1935), pp. 243-258.

5,525 CORKILL, N. L. Traps from the Anglo-Egyptian Sudan. JRAI 73 (1943), pp. 107-118.

5,526 COTTAM, R. and COTTAM, L. Some native superstitions about the white-spotted gecko lizard with notes on its habits. SUDAN NOTES 6 (1923), pp. 40-50.

5,527 CRAZZOLARA, P. Die Bedeutung des Rindes bei den Nuer. AFRICA 7 (1934), pp. 300-320.

5,528 CRAZZOLARA, P. Die Gar-Zeremonie bei den Nuer. AFRICA 5 (1932), pp. 28-39; English summary, p. 39.

5,529 CRAZZOLARA, P. Pygmies on the Bahr el Ghazal. SUDAN NOTES 16 (1933), pp. 85-88.

5,530 CROWFOOT, G. M. The handspinning of cotton in the Sudan. SUDAN NOTES 7 (1924), part 2, pp. 83-89.

5,531 CROWFOOT, G. M. Spinning and weaving in the Sudan. SUDAN NOTES 4 (1921), pp. 20-38.

5,532 CROWFOOT, G. M. The Sudanese camel girth in double weave. SUDAN NOTES 32 (1951), pp. 71-76.

5,533 CROWFOOT, J. W. Angels of the Nile. SUDAN NOTES 2 (1919), pp. 183-197.

5,534 CROWFOOT, J. W. Customs of the Rubātāb. SUDAN NOTES 1 (1918), pp. 119-134.

5,535 CROWFOOT, J. W. Further notes on pottery. SUDAN NOTES 8 (1925), pp. 125-136.

5,536 CROWFOOT, J. W. Old sites in the Butana. SUDAN NOTES 3 (1920), pp. 85-93.

5,537 CUMMINS, S. L. Sub-tribes of the Bahr-el-Ghazal Dinkas. JRAI 34 (1904), pp. 149-166.

5,538 CUNNISON, I. Giraffe hunting among the Humr tribe. SUDAN NOTES 39 (1958), pp. 49-60.

5,539 CUNNISON, I. The Humr and their land. SUDAN NOTES AND RECORDS 35, part 2 (1954), pp. 50-68.

5,540 D., R. Firesticks. SUDAN NOTES 8 (1925), pp. 214-217.

5,541 DANIELL, J. P. S. A new use for empty cartridge cases. SUDAN NOTES 22 (1939), pp. 273-276.

5,542 DAVIES, H. R. J. Some tribes of the Ethiopian borderland between the Blue Nile and Sobat Rivers. SUDAN NOTES 41 (1960), pp. 21-34.

5,543 DAVIES, R. Elephant and giraffe hunting in the Homr tribe (south-west Kordofan). SUDAN NOTES 2 (1919), pp. 17-19.

5,544 DAVIES, R. Omens at Jebel Mun. SUDAN NOTES 5 (1922), pp. 167-168.

5,545 DAVIES, R. Some Arab games and puzzles. SUDAN NOTES 8 (1925), pp. 137-152.

5,546 DAVIES, R. A system of sand divination. SUDAN NOTES 3 (1920), pp. 157-162.

5,547 DAVIES, R. Totemism in the Homr tribe. SUDAN NOTES 2 (1919), pp. 231-234.

5,548 DEANE, L. A. Superstitions. SUDAN NOTES 2 (1919), pp. 138-139.

5,549 DISNEY, A. W. M. The coronation of the Fung King of Fazoghli. SUDAN NOTES 26 (1945), pp. 37-42.

5,550 DRIBERG, J. H. Clan functionaries. J. AFR. SOC. 38 (1939), pp. 65-74.

5,551 DRIBERG, J. H. Lafon Hill. SUDAN NOTES 8 (1925), pp. 47-57.

5,552 DRIBERG, J. H. A preliminary account of the Didinga. SUDAN NOTES 5 (1922), pp. 208-222.

5,553 DUNN, S. C. Native gold washings in the Nuba Mountains Province. SUDAN NOTES 4 (1921), pp. 138-145.

5,554 DUNN, S. C. Some instances of Nuba magic. SUDAN NOTES 1 (1918), pp. 202-204.

5,555 EVANS-PRITCHARD, E. E. Bibliographical note on the ethnology of the Southern Sudan. AFRICA 13 (1940), pp. 62-67.

5,556 EVANS-PRITCHARD, E. E. The Bongo. SUDAN NOTES 12 (1929), pp. 1-61.

5,557 EVANS-PRITCHARD, E. E. Bridewealth among the Nuer. AFR. STUD. 6 (1947), pp. 181-187.

5,558 EVANS-PRITCHARD, E. E. Burial and mortuary rites of the Nuer. AFR. AFFAIRS 48 (1949), pp. 56-63.

5,559 EVANS-PRITCHARD, E. E. Cannibalism: A Zande text. AFRICA 26 (1956), pp. 73-74.

5,560 EVANS-PRITCHARD, E. E. A contribution to the study of Zande culture. AFRICA 30 (1960), pp. 309-323.

5,561 EVANS-PRITCHARD, E. E. Daily life of the Nuer in dry season camps. CUSTOM IS KING: ESSAYS...TO R. R. MARETT, 1936, pp. 291-299.

5,562 EVANS-PRITCHARD, E. E. The dance. AFRICA 1 (1928), pp. 446-462.

5,563 EVANS-PRITCHARD, E. E. Economic life of the Nuer: cattle. SUDAN NOTES 20 (1937), pp. 209-245; 21 (1938), pp. 31-77.

5,564 EVANS-PRITCHARD, E. E. The ethnic composition of the Azande of Central Africa. ANTHR. QUART. 31 (1958), pp. 95-118.

5,565 EVANS-PRITCHARD, E. E. Ethnological observations in Dar Fung. SUDAN NOTES 15 (1932), pp. 1-61.

5,566 EVANS-PRITCHARD, E. E. A final contribution to the study of Zande culture. AFRICA 35 (1965), pp. 1-7.

5,567 EVANS-PRITCHARD, E. E. A further contribution to the study of Zande culture. AFRICA 33 (1963), pp. 183-197.

5,568 EVANS-PRITCHARD, E. E. Further observations on the political system of the Anuak. SUDAN NOTES 28 (1947), pp. 62-97.

5,569 EVANS-PRITCHARD, E. E. A history of the kingdom of Gbudwe (Azande of the Sudan). ZAIRE 10 (1956), pp. 451-491, 673-710, 815-860.

5,570 EVANS-PRITCHARD, E. E. Kinship and the local community among the Nuer. AFRICAN SYSTEMS OF KINSHIP AND MARRIAGE, 1950, pp. 360-391.

5,571 EVANS-PRITCHARD, E. E. Mani, a Zande secret society. SUDAN NOTES 14 (1931), pp. 105-148.

5,572 EVANS-PRITCHARD, E. E. The Mberidi (Shilluk group) and Mbegumba (Basiri group) of the Bahr-el-Ghazal. SUDAN NOTES 14 (1931), pp. 15-48; 15 (1932), pp. 273-274.

5,573 EVANS-PRITCHARD, E. E. The meaning of sacrifice among the Nuer. JRAI 84 (1954), pp. 21-33.

5,574 EVANS-PRITCHARD, E. E. The morphology and function of magic: a comparative study of Trobriand and Zande ritual and spells. AMER. ANTHR. 31 (1929), pp. 619-641.

5,575 EVANS-PRITCHARD, E. E. Nilotic studies. JRAI 80 (1950), pp. 1-6.

5,576 EVANS-PRITCHARD, E. E. The non-Dinka peoples of the Amadi and Rumbek districts. SUDAN NOTES 20 (1937), pp. 156-158.

5,577 EVANS-PRITCHARD, E. E. A note on courtship among the Nuer. SUDAN NOTES 28 (1947), pp. 115-126.

5,578 EVANS-PRITCHARD, E. E. A note on Ingessana marriage customs. SUDAN NOTES 21 (1938), pp. 307-313.

5,579 EVANS-PRITCHARD, E. E. The Nuer: age-sets. SUDAN NOTES 19 (1936), pp. 233-269.

5,580 EVANS-PRITCHARD, E. E. Nuer bridewealth. AFRICA 16 (1946), pp. 247-257.

5,581 EVANS-PRITCHARD, E. E. The Nuer conception of spirit in its relation to the social order. AMER. ANTHR. 55 (1953), pp. 201-214.

5,582 EVANS-PRITCHARD, E. E. Nuer curses and ghostly vengeance. AFRICA 19 (1949), pp. 288-292.

5,583 EVANS-PRITCHARD, E. E. The Nuer family. SUDAN NOTES 31 (1950), pp. 21-42.

5,584 EVANS-PRITCHARD, E. E. Nuer marriage ceremonies. AFRICA 18 (1948), pp. 29-40.

5,585 EVANS-PRITCHARD, E. E. Nuer modes of address. UGANDA J. 12 (1948), pp. 166-171.

5,586 EVANS-PRITCHARD, E. E. The Nuer of the Southern Sudan. AFRICAN POLITICAL SYSTEMS, 1940, pp. 272-296.

5,587 EVANS-PRITCHARD, E. E. Nuer spear symbolism. ANTHR. QUART. 26 (1953), pp. 1-19.

5,588 EVANS-PRITCHARD, E. E. Nuer time-reckoning. AFRICA 12 (1939), pp. 189-216.

5,589 EVANS-PRITCHARD, E. E. The Nuer: tribe and clan. SUDAN NOTES 16 (1933), pp. 1-53; 17 (1934), pp. 1-57; 18 (1935), pp. 37-87.

5,590 EVANS-PRITCHARD, E. E. Oracle-magic of the Azande. SUDAN NOTES 11 (1928), pp. 1-53.

5,591 EVANS-PRITCHARD, E. E. The organization of a Zande kingdom. CAH. ET. AFR. 1 (1960), pp. 5-37.

5,592 EVANS-PRITCHARD, E. E. The origin of the ruling clan of the Azande. SOUTHWESTERN J. ANTHR. 13 (1957), pp. 322-343.

5,593 EVANS-PRITCHARD, E. E. A preliminary account of the Ingassana tribe in Fung Province. SUDAN NOTES 10 (1927), pp. 69-83.

5,594 EVANS-PRITCHARD, E. E. The relationship between the Anuak and the Föri (Sudan). SUDAN NOTES 23 (1940), pp. 337-340.

5,595 EVANS-PRITCHARD, E. E. The sacrificial role of cattle among the Nuer. AFRICA 23 (1953), pp. 181-197.

5,596 EVANS-PRITCHARD, E. E. Some features and forms of Nuer sacrifices. AFRICA 21 (1951), pp. 112-121.

5,597 EVANS-PRITCHARD, E. E. Some features of Nuer religion. JRAI 81 (1951), pp. 1-13.

5,598 EVANS-PRITCHARD, E. E. Some Zande folk-tales. SUDAN NOTES 44 (1963), pp. 43-68; 45 (1964), pp. 59-78; 46 (1965), pp. 50-66.

5,599 EVANS-PRITCHARD, E. E. Witchcraft. AFRICA 8 (1935), pp. 417-422.

5,600 EVANS-PRITCHARD, E. E. Witchcraft (mangu) amongst the Azande. SUDAN NOTES 12 (1929), pp. 163-249.

5,601 EVANS-PRITCHARD, E. E. Zande blood-brotherhood. AFRICA 6 (1933), pp. 369-401.

5,602 EVANS-PRITCHARD, E. E. Zande border raids. AFRICA 27 (1957), pp. 217-230.

5,603 EVANS-PRITCHARD, E. E. Zande cannibalism. JRAI 90 (1960), pp. 238-258.

5,604 EVANS-PRITCHARD, E. E. The Zande corporation of witch doctors. JRAI 62 (1932), pp. 291-336; 63 (1933), pp. 63-100.

5,605 EVANS-PRITCHARD, E. E. Zande historical texts. SUDAN NOTES 37 (1956), pp. 20-47; 38 (1957), pp. 74-99.

5,606 EVANS-PRITCHARD, E. E. Zande kings and princes. ANTHR. QUART. 30 (1957), pp. 61-90.

5,607 EVANS-PRITCHARD, E. E. The Zande royal court. ZAIRE 11 (1957), pp. 361-389, 493-511, 687-713.

5,608 EVANS-PRITCHARD, E. E. Zande theology. SUDAN NOTES 19 (1936), pp. 5-46.

5,609 EVANS-PRITCHARD, E. E. Zande therapeutics. ESSAYS PRESENTED TO C. G. SELIGMAN, 1934, pp. 49-61.

5,610 EVANS-PRITCHARD, E. E. and BEATON, A. C. Folk stories of the Sudan. SUDAN NOTES 23 (1940), pp. 55-74, 271-278.

5,611 EVANS-PRITCHARD, E. E. and MYNORS, T. H. B. Folk stories of the Sudan. SUDAN NOTES 24 (1941), pp. 69-84.

5,612 FERGUSSON, V. Mattiang Goh witchcraft. SUDAN NOTES 6 (1923), pp. 112-114.

5,613 FERGUSSON, V. Nuer beast tales. SUDAN NOTES 7 (1924), pp. 105-112.

5,614 FERGUSSON, V. The Holy Lake of the Dinka. SUDAN NOTES 5 (1922), pp. 163-166.

5,615 FERGUSSON, V. The Nuong Nuer. SUDAN NOTES 4 (1921), pp. 146-155.

5,616 FERNEA, R. A. The ethnological survey of Egyptian Nubia: a progress report. CURRENT ANTHR. 4 (1963), pp. 122-129.

5,617 FIELD, H. The University of California African expedition: 2, Sudan and Kenya. AMER. ANTHR. 51 (1949), pp. 72-84.

5,618 FINCH, F. J. Bari child names. SUDAN NOTES 20 (1937), pp. 166-168.

5,619 FINCH, F. J. Travelling in the "old days" in the Kuku country. SUDAN NOTES 21 (1938), pp. 213-215.

5,620 FLEMING, G. J. Benī 'Amer marriage custom. SUDAN NOTES 2 (1919), pp. 74-76.

5,621 FUCHS, P. Entwicklungen und Veränderungen der Institution des Priester-Häuptlings in Süd-Wadai, Sudan. SOCIOLOGUS 11 (1961), pp. 174-186.

5,622 GLUCKMAN, M. The logic of African science and witchcraft: an appreciation of Evans-Pritchard's Witchcraft oracles and magic among the Azande of the Sudan. RHODES-LIV. J. 1 (1944), pp. 61-71.

5,623 GOLDSMITH, J. H. Marriage customs among the Beni 'Amer tribe. SUDAN NOTES 3 (1920), pp. 293-295.

5,624 GRABHAM, C. W. Fossil bones. SUDAN NOTES 3 (1920), pp. 131-133.

5,625 GRIFFITHS, J. G. The use of plates and saucers to decorate houses in Lower Nubia. SUDAN NOTES 21 (1938), pp. 217-220.

5,626 GROVE, E. T. N. Customs of the Acholi. SUDAN NOTES 2 (1919), pp. 157-182.

5,627 GUSINDE, M. Die giftproben der Kakwa-Niloten. ETHNOS 7 (1942), pp. 44-48.

5,628 H. Dreams. SUDAN NOTES 5 (1922), pp. 108-110.

5,629 H., J. A. DE C. Notes on the Fellata Melle of Kassala. SUDAN NOTES 9 (1926), pp. 85-86.

5,630 H., N. B. A Nuba wake. SUDAN NOTES 8 (1925), pp. 184-186.

5,631 H., S. The trial of a Jur "Witch-Doctor." SUDAN NOTES 12 (1929), pp. 99-101.

5,632 HADOW, A. L. Oracle magic of the Azande. SUDAN NOTES 12 (1929), p. 258.

5,633 HALL, E. Women's custom in Omdurman. SUDAN NOTES 1 (1918), pp. 199-201.

5,634 HARWOOD, F. L. The story of Tajoj. SUDAN NOTES 24 (1941), pp. 197-199.

5,635 HAWKESWORTH, D. A description of a ceremony by which a Nuba chief became a Kujur. SUDAN NOTES 23 (1940), pp. 345-347.

5,636 HAWKESWORTH, D. The Nuba proper of Southern Kordofan. SUDAN NOTES 15 (1932), pp. 159-199.

5,637 HAWLEY, D. F. Zanneia. SUDAN NOTES 27 (1946), pp. 236-238.

5,638 HAY-DRUMMOND-HAY, E. W. Were-hyenas. SUDAN NOTES 2 (1919), pp. 144-145.

5,639 HEBBERT, G. K. C. The Bandala of the Bahr el Ghazal. SUDAN NOTES 8 (1925), pp. 187-194.

5,640 HENDERSON, K. D. D. A note on the migration of the Messira tribe into southwest Kordofan. SUDAN NOTES 22 (1939), pp. 49-77.

5,641 HENDERSON, K. D. D. Origin of the Dagu. SUDAN NOTES 15 (1932), pp. 151-152.

5,642 HERZOG, R. Die Nubier im Bereich des Künftigen Stausees. CONG. INT. SC. ANTH. ET ETHN. 6, no. i (1960), pp. 127-129.

5,643 HILLELSON, S. Notes on the Dago with special reference to the Dago settlement in Western Kordofan. SUDAN NOTES 8 (1925), pp. 59-73.

5,644 HILLELSON, S. The people of Abū Jarīd. SUDAN NOTES 1 (1918), pp. 175-193.

5,645 HILLS-YOUNG, E. Charms and customs associated with childbirth. SUDAN NOTES 23 (1940), pp. 331-335.

5,646 HORNELL, J. The frameless boats of the Middle Nile. SUDAN NOTES 25 (1942), pp. 1-36.

5,647 HORNELL, J. String figures from the Anglo-Egyptian Sudan. SUDAN NOTES 23 (1940), pp. 99-122.

5,648 HOWELL, P. P. The age-set system and the institution of Nak among the Nuer [with a note by E. E. Evans-Pritchard]. SUDAN NOTES 29 (1948), pp. 173-182.

5,649 HOWELL, P. P. The death and burial of reth Dak wad Fadiet of the Shilluk. SUDAN NOTES 33 (1952), pp. 156-164.

5,650 HOWELL, P. P. The election and installation of Reth Kur Wad Fafiti of the Shilluk. SUDAN NOTES 34 (1953), pp. 189-204.

5,651 HOWELL, P. P. A note on elephants and elephant hunting among the Nuer. SUDAN NOTES 26 (1945), pp. 95-103.

5,652 HOWELL, P. P. Notes on the Ngork Dinka of Western Kordofan. SUDAN NOTES 32 (1951), pp. 239-293.

5,653 HOWELL, P. P. Observations on the Shilluk of the Upper Nile. Customary law: marriage and the violation of rights in women. AFRICA 23 (1953), pp. 94-109.

5,654 HOWELL, P. P. Observations on the Shilluk of the Upper Nile. The laws of homicide and the legal functions of the Reth. AFRICA 22 (1952), pp. 97-119.

5,655 HOWELL, P. P. The Shilluk settlement. SUDAN NOTES 24 (1941), pp. 47-67.

5,656 HOWELL, P. P. Some observations on divorce among the Nuer. JRAI 83 (1953), pp. 136-146.

5,657 HOWELL, P. P. The Zeraf hills [with a note by A. J. Arkell]. SUDAN NOTES 26 (1945), pp. 319-328.

5,658 HOWELL, P. P. and LEWIS, B. A. Nuer Ghouls: a form of witchcraft. SUDAN NOTES 28 (1947), pp. 157-168.

5,659 HOWELL, P. P. and THOMSON, W. P. G. The death of a Reth of the Shilluk and the installation of his successor. SUDAN NOTES 27 (1946), pp. 5-85.

5,660 HUDDLESTON, C. Catching white ants in Jebel Marra. SUDAN NOTES 27 (1946), p. 235.

5,661 HUSSEY, E. R. J. Crocodile charmers. SUDAN NOTES 1 (1918), pp. 206-207.

5,662 HUSSEY, E. R. J. A Fiki's clinic. SUDAN NOTES 6 (1923), pp. 35-39.

5,663 IBRAHIM FAHEIL. The Nahas of the Kababish as told by Sheikh Ibrahim Faheil. SUDAN NOTES 11 (1928), pp. 213-215.

5,664 IRELAND, A. W. Climate and building design in the Northern Sudan. SUDAN NOTES 30 (1949), Supplement, pp. 46-49.

5,665 JAAFAR ALI and HAMILTON, J. A. DE C. Note on the Halenga tribe, by Sheikh Jaafar Ali, Nazir of the Halenga. SUDAN NOTES 8 (1925), pp. 180-184.

5,666 JACKSON, H. C. The Khawālda tribe. SUDAN NOTES 1 (1918), pp. 167-174.

5,667 JACKSON, H. C. The Mahas of 'Eilafūn. SUDAN NOTES 2 (1919), pp. 285-292.

5,668 JACKSON, H. C. The Nuer of the Upper Nile Province. SUDAN NOTES 6 (1923), pp. 59-107, 123-189.

5,669 JACKSON, H. C. Two Gezira families. SUDAN NOTES 3 (1920), pp. 94-109.

5,670 JANSSEN, E. Inleiding tot de Soedanese Legenden van Emiel van der Straeten. KONGO-OVERZEE 22 (1956), pp. 75-85.

5,671 JENNINGS-BRAMLY, W. E. Bisharin fables. SUDAN NOTES 8 (1925), pp. 177-178.

5,672 JOHNSTON, R. T. The religious and spiritual beliefs of the Bor Dinka. SUDAN NOTES 17 (1934), pp. 124-128.

5,673 KAUCZOR, D. Der achtköpfige Unhold. BIBLIOTHECA AFR. 3 (1929), pp. 23-35.

5,674 KAUCZOR, D. The Afitti Nuba of Gebel Dair and their relation to the Nuba proper. SUDAN NOTES 6 (1923), pp. 1-34.

5,675 KAUCZOR, D. Bergnubische Texte. BIBLIOTHECA AFR. 2 (1926), pp. 239-244, 315-321.

5,676 KEANE, A. H. Ethnology of Egyptian Sudán. JRAI 14 (1885), pp. 91-113.

5,677 KERICK, J. W. A Nuba age-grade initiation ceremony. The Sibrs of the tail and of the shield. SUDAN NOTES 26 (1945), pp. 311-318.

5,678 KOHLER, O. Gottesnamen und Gottesvorstellungen bei den Niloten. SOCIOLOGUS 6 (1956), pp. 34-44.

5,679 KRONENBERG, A. Nyimang circumcision. SUDAN NOTES 39 (1958), pp. 79-82.

5,680 KRONENBERG, A. Verdienstfeste und Grabmonumente in der Bahr-el-Ghazal Provinz. CONGR. INT. SC. ANTH. ET ETHN. 6, no. ii (1960), pp. 229-232.

5,681 LAGAE, C. R. Les Azande sont-ils animistes? SUDAN NOTES 3 (1920), pp. 143-156.

5,682 LAGAE, C. R. Notes sur les êtres suprasensibles chez les Azande. CONGO 1 (1921), pp. 396-413.

5,683 LAMPEN, E. A short account of Meidob. SUDAN NOTES 11 (1928), pp. 55-67.

5,684 LAMPEN, G. D. The Baggara tribes of Darfur. SUDAN NOTES 16 (1933), pp. 97-118.

5,685 LARKEN, P. M. An account of the Zande. SUDAN NOTES 9 (1926), pp. 1-55.

5,686 LARKEN, P. M. Impressions of the Azande. SUDAN NOTES 10 (1927), pp. 85-134; 13 (1930), pp. 99-115.

5,687 LARKEN, P. M. Zande notes. SUDAN NOTES 6 (1923), pp. 235-247.

5,688 LEGESSE, A. Class systems based on time. J. ETHIOPIAN STUD. 1, part 2 (1963), pp. 1-29.

5,689 LEWIS, B. A. Murle folk tales. SUDAN NOTES 28 (1947), pp. 135-145.

5,690 LEWIS, B. A. Nuer spokesmen. A note on the institution of the Ruic. SUDAN NOTES 32 (1951), pp. 77-84.

5,691 LIENHARDT, G. Anuak village headman. AFRICA 28 (1958), pp. 23-36, 341-354.

5,692 LIENHARDT, G. Nilotic kings and their mothers' kin. AFRICA 25 (1955), pp. 29-41.

5,693 LIENHARDT, G. On the concept of objectivity in social anthropology. JRAI 94 (1964), pp. 1-10.

5,694 LIENHARDT, G. Some notions of witchcraft among the Dinka. AFRICA 21 (1951), pp. 303-318.

5,695 LIENHARDT, G. The western Dinka. TRIBES WITHOUT RULERS, 1958, pp. 97-135.

5,696 LISOWSKI, F. P. A report on the skulls from excavations at Sesebi (Anglo-Egyptian Sudan). CONG. INT. SC. ANTH. ET ETHN. 4, no. i (1952), pp. 228-240.

5,697 LOGAN, M. H. The Biers. SUDAN NOTES 1 (1918), pp. 238-248.

5,698 LORIMER, F. C. S. The Rubatab. SUDAN NOTES 19 (1936), pp. 162-167.

5,699 LUCAS, L. On natives of Suakin, and Bishareen vocabulary. JRAI 6 (1876), pp. 191-194.

5,700 LUXMOORE, H. B. Swimming cattle across the Nile. SUDAN NOTES 34 (1953), pp. 117-118.

5,701 MacDIARMID, D. N. Notes on Nuba customs and language. SUDAN NOTES 10 (1927), pp. 224-233.

5,702 MacDIARMID, D. N. Nuba boys at play. SUDAN NOTES 5 (1922), pp. 231-233.

5,703 MacDIARMID, D. N. Some Nuba ideas. SUDAN NOTES 7 (1924), pp. 125-126.

5,704 MacINTOSH, E. H. A note on the Dago tribe. SUDAN NOTES 14 (1931), pp. 171-177.

5,705 MacLAREN, J. F. P. The nomad tent of Northern Kordofan. SUDAN NOTES 10 (1927), pp. 235-240.

5,706 MacMICHAEL, H. A. Arab dumb show. SUDAN NOTES 17 (1934), p. 129.

5,707 MacMICHAEL, H. A. Hamad Wad Um Tunko. SUDAN NOTES 3 (1920), p. 136.

5,708 MacMICHAEL, H. A. Notes on Gebel Haraza. SUDAN NOTES 10 (1927), pp. 61-67.

5,709 MacMICHAEL, H. A. Notes on the Zaghāwa and the people of Crebel Mīdōb, Anglo-Egyptian Sudan. JRAI 42 (1912), pp. 288-344.

5,710 MacMICHAEL, H. A. Pottery making on the Blue Nile. SUDAN NOTES 5 (1922), pp. 33-38.

5,711 MacMICHAEL, H. A. A seasonal festival at Gebel Mīdōb. SUDAN NOTES 2 (1919), pp. 91-97.

5,712 MacMICHAEL, H. A. The Tungur-Fur of Dar Furnung. SUDAN NOTES 3 (1920), pp. 24-32.

5,713 MacPHAIL, J. G. S. The Bandala method of hunting elephant on foot. SUDAN NOTES 13 (1930), pp. 279-283.

5,714 MADDEN, J. F. The exhumation of a Latuka rain chief. SUDAN NOTES 23 (1940), pp. 351-354.

5,715 MARTINI, G. An impression of the Nuba and their country in 1875. SUDAN NOTES 42 (1961), pp. 122-126.

5,716 MARWICK, M. G. The social context of Cewa witch beliefs. AFRICA 22 (1952), pp. 120-135, 215-233.

5,717 MERRILL, W. The wooden locks of the Halfa region. SUDAN NOTES 45 (1964), pp. 29-34.

5,718 MILLS, W. L. A Dinka witch-doctor. SUDAN NOTES 2 (1919), pp. 31-34.

5,719 MILLWARD, G. R. The birth of a dhow. SUDAN NOTES 32 (1951), pp. 197-206.

5,720 MONTEITH, W. N. Sibr al Maut at Fungor. SUDAN NOTES 31 (1950), pp. 307-308.

5,721 MOSTYN, J. P. Some notes on Burun customs and beliefs. SUDAN NOTES 4 (1921), pp. 209-211.

5,722 MUNRO, P. Installation of the Ret of the Chol (King of the Shilluks). SUDAN NOTES 1 (1918), pp. 145-152.

5,723 MURATORI, C. A case of magical poisoning in a Lotuko village. SUDAN NOTES 31 (1950), pp. 133-140.

5,724 MYNORS, T. H. B. Moru arrowheads. SUDAN NOTES 34 (1953), p. 311.

5,725 MYNORS, T. H. B. Moru proverbs and games. SUDAN NOTES 24 (1941), pp. 205-207.

5,726 NADEL, S. F. Dual descent in the Nuba Hills. AFRICAN SYSTEMS OF KINSHIP AND MARRIAGE, 1950, pp. 333-359.

5,727 NADEL, S. F. The hill tribes of Kadero. SUDAN NOTES 25 (1942), pp. 37-79.

5,728 NADEL, S. F. Notes on Beni Amer society. SUDAN NOTES 26 (1945), pp. 51-94.

5,729 NALDER, L. F. Fung origins. SUDAN NOTES 14 (1931), pp. 61-66.

5,730 NALDER, L. F. Tales from the Fung Province. SUDAN NOTES 14 (1931), pp. 67-86.

5,731 NALDER, L. F. Throwing knives in the Sudan. SUDAN NOTES 18 (1935), pp. 297-302.

5,732 NICHOLLS, W. A Sennar marriage custom. SUDAN NOTES 1 (1918), pp. 205-206.

5,733 NOBBS, K. J. The burial of a Nuba Mek at Dunger. SUDAN NOTES 21 (1938), pp. 325-326.

5,734 NUNN, N. A Dinka sacrifice. SUDAN NOTES 31 (1950), pp. 141-142.

5,735 OGOT, B. A. The concept of Jok. AFR. STUD. 20 (1961), pp. 123-130.

5,736 OWEN, T. R. H. The Hadendowa. SUDAN NOTES 20 (1937), pp. 183-208.

5,737 OWEN, T. R. H. A Bega game—"andot." SUDAN NOTES 21 (1938), pp. 201-205.

5,738 OWEN, T. R. H. Notes on an Arab stellar calendar. SUDAN NOTES 16 (1933), pp. 67-71.

5,739 OYLER, D. S. Examples of Shilluk folk-lore. SUDAN NOTES 2 (1919), pp. 216-223.

5,740 OYLER, D. S. Nikawng's place in the Shilluk religion. SUDAN NOTES 1 (1918), pp. 283-292.

5,741 OYLER, D. S. The Shilluk peace ceremony. SUDAN NOTES 3 (1920), pp. 296-299.

5,742 OYLER, D. S. The Shilluk's belief in the evil eye. The evil medicine man. SUDAN NOTES 2 (1919), pp. 122-137.

5,743 OYLER, D. S. The Shilluk's belief in the good medicine men. SUDAN NOTES 3 (1920), pp. 110-116.

5,744 OYLER, D. S. Shilluk notes. SUDAN NOTES 9 (1926), pp. 57-68.

5,745 PALMER, H. R. The Fung Kakar. SUDAN NOTES 12 (1929), pp. 255-257.

5,746 PARR, M. W. Still more notes on Tebeldis [with replies by D. Newbold and G. M. Crowfoot]. SUDAN NOTES 7 (1924), part 2, pp. 117-123.

5,747 PAUL, A. Horse-breeding among the Shankhab. SUDAN NOTES 18 (1935), pp. 138-142.

5,748 PAUL, A. The Mar of the Shilluk. SUDAN NOTES 33 (1952), pp. 165-166.

5,749 PAUL, A. Notes on the Beni Amer. SUDAN NOTES 31 (1950), pp. 223-245.

5,750 PAUL, A. Sagio custom in Shendi district. SUDAN NOTES 19 (1936), pp. 346-350.

5,751 PENN, A. E. D. Traditional stories of the 'Abdullab tribe. SUDAN NOTES 17 (1934), pp. 59-82.

5,752 PETTINEN, A. Lieder und Rätsel der Aandonga. AFR. UND UB. 17 (1926-1927), pp. 202-230.

5,753 PETTINEN, A. Märchen der Aandonga. AFR. UND UB. 16 (1925-1926), pp. 133-148, 197-240, 256-275.

5,754 PETTINEN, A. Sagen und Mythen der Aandonga. AFR. UND UB. 17 (1926-1927), pp. 51-78, 108-129.

5,755 PETTINEN, A. Sprichwörter der Aandonga. AFR. UND UB. 17 (1926-1927), pp. 249-266.

5,756 PETTINEN, A. and NITSCHE, G. Gebete und Zaubersprüche der Aandonga. AFR. UND UB. 15 (1924-1925), pp. 161-179.

5,757 PHILIPPS, J. E. T. The Azande. J. AFR. SOC. 26 (1926), pp. 21-26.

5,758 PHILIPPS, J. E. T. Observations on some aspects of religion among the Azande (Niam-niam) of Equatorial Africa. JRAI 56 (1926), pp. 171-187.

5,759 POWELL, J. Ornaments and arms among the Acholi and their neighbours. SUDAN NOTES 4 (1921), pp. 213-216.

5,760 PUMPHREY, M. E. C. Shilluk "royal" language conventions. SUDAN NOTES 20 (1937), pp. 319-321.

5,761 PUMPHREY, M. E. C. The Shilluk tribe. SUDAN NOTES 24 (1941), pp. 1-45.

5,762 RAGLAN. The Langu (a correction). SUDAN NOTES 6 (1923), pp. 117-118.

5,763 REID, J. A. Some notes on the tribes of the White Nile Province. SUDAN NOTES 13 (1930), pp. 149-209.

5,764 RICHARDS, A. I. A problem of anthropological approach. BANTU STUD. 15 (1941), pp. 45-52.

5,765 RICHARDS, M. G. Bongo magic. SUDAN NOTES 18 (1935), pp. 143-147.

5,766 RICHARDS, M. G. Medical treatment by Bor witch doctors. SUDAN NOTES 10 (1927), pp. 241-242.

5,767 RICHARDS, M. G. The truth diviner (amongst the Agar Dinkas). SUDAN NOTES 7 (1924), pp. 139-141.

5,768 RICHARDSON, J. N. Bari notes. SUDAN NOTES 16 (1933), pp. 181-186.

5,769 ROBERTS, D. F. and BAINBRIDGE, D. R. Nilotic physique. AM. J. PHY. ANT. 21 (1963), pp. 341-364.

5,770 ROBERTSON, J. W. Fung origins. SUDAN NOTES 17 (1934), pp. 260-265.

5,771 ROBERTSON, J. W. Further notes on the Ingessana tribe. SUDAN NOTES 17 (1934), pp. 118-123.

5,772 ROBINSON, A. E. Notes on the Gamuia tribe, Sudan. J. AFR. SOC. 26 (1927), pp. 138-144; 28 (1928), pp. 55-67.

5,773 ROBINSON, A. E. Some notes on the regalia of the Fung Sultans of Sennar. J. AFR. SOC. 30 (1931), pp. 361-376.

5,774 ROWLEY, J. V. Notes on the Madi of Equatoria Province. SUDAN NOTES 23 (1940), pp. 279-294.

5,775 S.-H., E. G. The Dumbari or locust banisher of Darfur. SUDAN NOTES 3 (1920), pp. 291-292.

5,776 SANDARS, G. E. R. The Bisharin. SUDAN NOTES 16 (1933), pp. 119-149.

5,777 SANTANDREA, S. The Belanda, Ndogo, Bai and Sere in the Bahr-el-Ghazal. SUDAN NOTES 16 (1933), pp. 161-179.

5,778 SANTANDREA, S. Evil and witchcraft among the Ndogo group of tribes. AFRICA 11 (1938), pp. 459-481.

5,779 SANTANDREA, S. A further note on the Ngala (or Ngara) tribe. SUDAN NOTES AND RECORDS 35, part 1 (1954), p. 148.

5,780 SANTANDREA, S. Gleanings in the western Bahr el Ghazal. SUDAN NOTES 31 (1950), pp. 54-64.

5,781 SANTANDREA, S. Little known tribes of the Bahr el Ghazal. SUDAN NOTES 29 (1948), pp. 78-106.

5,782 SANTANDREA, S. Minor Shilluk sections in the Bahr el Ghazal. SUDAN NOTES 21 (1938), pp. 267-289.

5,783 SANTANDREA, S. A new tribe? The Ngala or Ngara. SUDAN NOTES 33 (1952), pp. 317-321.

5,784 SANTANDREA, S. Notes on the Bongo. SUDAN NOTES 39 (1958), pp. 61-78.

5,785 SANTANDREA, S. A preliminary account of the Indri, Togoyo, Feroge, Mangaya and Woro. SUDAN NOTES 34 (1953), pp. 230-264.

5,786 SANTANDREA, S. Tribes of the Bongo group in the Sudan. SUDAN NOTES 43 (1962), pp. 147-152.

5,787 SANTANDREA, S. What is the real name of the Nzakara (or N'sakara)? SUDAN NOTES 33 (1952), pp. 315-316.

5,788 SANTANDREA, S. and GIORGI, L. DE. Morte violenta per i re divini Scilluk e Dinka—Sudan. AFRICA (Rome) 20 (1965), pp. 15-32, 163-187.

5,789 SAVILLE, R. V. A Zaghawa custom. SUDAN NOTES 5 (1922), p. 169.

5,790 SCHUSTER, C. Modern parallels for ancient Egyptian tatooing [with an appendix by O. H. Myers]. SUDAN NOTES 29 (1948), pp. 71-77.

5,791 SELIGMAN, B. Z. Sacred litters among the Semites with reference to the Utfa of the Kababish. SUDAN NOTES 1 (1918), pp. 268-282.

5,792 SELIGMAN, C. G. Note on dreams. SUDAN NOTES 4 (1921), pp. 156-161.

5,793 SELIGMAN, C. G. Note on Jebel Tabi. SUDAN NOTES 7 (1924), part 2, pp. 111-114.

5,794 SELIGMAN, C. G. The physical characters of the Nuba of Kordofan. JRAI 40 (1910), pp. 505-524.

5,795 SELIGMAN, C. G. The religion of the Pagan tribes of the White Nile. AFRICA 4 (1931), pp. 1-20.

5,796 SELIGMAN, C. G. Some aspects of the Hamitic problem in the Anglo-Egyptian Sudan. JRAI 43 (1913), pp. 593-705.

5,797 SELIGMAN, C. G. and SELIGMAN, B. Z. Note on the history and present condition of the Beni Amer (southern Beja). SUDAN NOTES 13 (1930), pp. 83-97.

5,798 SELIGMAN, C. G. and SELIGMAN, B. Z. The social organization of the Lotuko. SUDAN NOTES 8 (1925), pp. 1-45.

5,799 SHAW, A. Dinka animal stories (Bor dialect). SUDAN NOTES 2 (1919), pp. 255-275.

5,800 SOMERSET, F. R. R. The Lotuko. SUDAN NOTES 1 (1918), pp. 153-159.

5,801 SPANOLO, L. M. Some notes on the initiation of young men and girls in the Bari tribe. AFRICA 5 (1932), pp. 393-403.

5,802 SPENCE, B. Stone worship among the Zaghawa. SUDAN NOTES 1 (1918), pp. 197-199.

5,803 SPIRE, F. Rain-making in equatorial Africa. J. AFR. SOC. 5 (1905), pp. 15-21.

5,804 STANTON, E. A. E. The peoples of the Anglo-Egyptian Sudan. J. AFR. SOC. 2 (1903), pp. 121-131.

5,805 STEBBING, J. B. The encouragement to forestry research that could be given by the Society [Philosophical Society of Sudan]. SUDAN NOTES 30 (1949), supplement, p. 18.

5,806 STEVENSON, R. C. The Nyamang of the Nuba Mountains of Kordofan. SUDAN NOTES 23 (1940), pp. 75-98.

5,807 STIGAND, C. H. Notes on the Burun. SUDAN NOTES 5 (1922), pp. 223-224.

5,808 STIGAND, C. H. The story of Kir and the White Spear. SUDAN NOTES 2 (1919), pp. 224-226.

5,809 STIGAND, C. H. Warrior classes of the Nuers. SUDAN NOTES 1 (1918), pp. 116-118.

5,810 STRUCK, B. An unlocated tribe on the White Nile. J. AFR. SOC. 8 (1908), pp. 75-78.

5,811 STUBBS, J. M. The ordeal by boiling water. SUDAN NOTES 25 (1942), pp. 135-136.

5,812 STUBBS, J. M. and MORISON, C. G. T. The Western Dinkas, their land and their agriculture. SUDAN NOTES 21 (1938), pp. 251-265.

5,813 STUBBS, J. N. Notes on beliefs and customs of the Malwal Dinka of the Bahr el Ghazal Province. SUDAN NOTES 17 (1934), pp. 243-254.

5,814 T., A. J. and T., F. S. Boundary settlement. SUDAN NOTES 9 (1926), p. 131.

5,815 T., G. W. Burial alive among Dinka of the Bahr-el-Ghazal Province. SUDAN NOTES 8 (1925), pp. 196-197.

5,816 T., G. W. Magicians, etc., among the Raik Dinka. SUDAN NOTES 8 (1925), pp. 194-195.

5,817 T., G. W. Nuba houses. SUDAN NOTES 14 (1931), p. 196.

5,818 TAYIB, A. AL-. The changing customs of the riverain Sudan. SUDAN NOTES 45 (1964), pp. 12-28.

5,819 TAYIB, A. EL-. Changing customs of the Riverain Sudan. SUDAN NOTES 37 (1956), pp. 56-69.

5,820 THOMSON, W. P. G. Further notes on the death of a Reth of the Shilluk. SUDAN NOTES 29 (1948), pp. 151-160.

5,821 TITHERINGTON, G. W. The Kubinat. Old forts in the Fourth Cataract. SUDAN NOTES 22 (1939), pp. 269-272.

5,822 TITHERINGTON, G. W. The Raik Dinka of Bahr el Ghazal Province. SUDAN NOTES 10 (1927), pp. 159-209.

5,823 TONIOLO, E. V. An early manuscript on the Dinka written by a member of this tribe. SUDAN NOTES 41 (1960), pp. 107-113.

5,824 TRACEY, C. B. Two ghost stories. SUDAN NOTES 23 (1940), pp. 185-187.

5,825 TUCKER, A. N. Children's games and songs in the southern Sudan. JRAI 63 (1933), pp. 165-187.

5,826 TUCKER, A. N. The tribal confusion around Wau. SUDAN NOTES 14 (1931), pp. 49-60.

5,827 TUCKER, A. N. Witchcraft applied to animals. SUDAN NOTES 14 (1931), pp. 191-195.

5,828 TUCKER, A. W. and MYERS, C. S. A contribution to the anthropology of the Sudan. JRAI 40 (1910), pp. 141-163.

5,829 UCIN, F. The Bviri tribe. SUDAN NOTES 28 (1947), pp. 98-114.

5,830 VAN DEN PLAS, V. H. Quel est le nom de famille des chefs Azande? CONGO 1 (1921), pp. 1-9.

5,831 W., M. J. The Balanda. SUDAN NOTES 6 (1923), pp. 251-253.

5,832 WAGNER, G. Witchcraft among the Azande [by E. E. Evans-Pritchard]. J. AFR. SOC. 36 (1937), pp. 469-476.

5,833 WALSH, R. H. The Beri or, more correctly Pari. SUDAN NOTES 5 (1922), pp. 47-48.

5,834 WEDDERBURN-MAXWELL, H. G. The Maban of Southern Sudan. SUDAN NOTES 19 (1936), pp. 179-183.

5,835 WHALLEY, R. C. R. Note on the Adonga Anuak. SUDAN NOTES 19 (1936), pp. 351-353.

5,836 WHITEHEAD, G. O. Property and inheritance among the Bari. SUDAN NOTES 31 (1950), pp. 143-147.

5,837 WHITEHEAD, G. O. Social change among the Bari. SUDAN NOTES 12 (1929), pp. 91-97.

5,838 WHITEHEAD, G. O. Suppressed classes among the Bari and Bari-speaking tribes. SUDAN NOTES 34 (1953), pp. 265-280.

5,839 WILLIS, C. A. The cult of Deng. SUDAN NOTES 11 (1928), pp. 195-212.

5,840 WYLD, J. W. G. The recollections of two Zande chiefs. SUDAN NOTES 42 (1961), pp. 127-131.

5,841 YUNIS, N. Notes on the Kuku and other minor tribes inhabiting the Kajo Kaji District, Mongalla Province. SUDAN NOTES 7 (1924), pp. 1-41.

5,842 YUZBASHI [pseud.]. Tribes on the Upper Nile. The Bari. J. AFR. SOC. 4 (1905), pp. 226-231.

5,843 YUZBASHI NEGIB EFF. YUNIS. Notes on the Baggara and Nuba of Western Kordofan. SUDAN NOTES 5 (1922), pp. 200-207.

5,844 ZENKOVSKY, S. Marriage customs in Omdurman. SUDAN NOTES 26 (1945), pp. 241-255; 30 (1949), pp. 39-46.

5,845 ZENKOVSKY, S. Zar and Tambura as practised by the women of Omdurman. SUDAN NOTES 31 (1950), pp. 65-81.

5,846 ZUGNONI, J. and HIBBERT, G. K. C. Yilede, a secret society among the Gbaya (Kreish), Aja, and Banda tribes of the Western District of Equatoria. SUDAN NOTES 26 (1945), pp. 105-111.

5,847 Installation of a new Shilluk King. SUDAN NOTES 37 (1956), pp. 99-101.

5,848 The manufacture of iron by the Juers. SUDAN NOTES 4 (1921), p. 50.

5,849 Notes on the Azande. SUDAN NOTES 2 (1919), pp. 24-30.

5,850 Nuba pots in the Gordon College. SUDAN NOTES 7 (1924), part 2, pp. 18-28.

5,851 A Nuba superstition. SUDAN NOTES 5 (1922), p. 233.

5,852 Peace-making ceremony of Raik Dinka, Bahr el Ghazal Province. SUDAN NOTES 7 (1924), part 2, pp. 127-128.

5,853 The reason for the Beir's hatred of the Dinka. SUDAN NOTES 4 (1921), p. 51.

5,854 Secret societies of the Southern Sudan. SUDAN NOTES 4 (1921), pp. 204-208.

5,855 The Ujang tribe. SUDAN NOTES 5 (1922), pp. 169-170.

5,856 Women and blood revenge. SUDAN NOTES 4 (1921), pp. 107-108.

See also 519, 5128, 5129, 5133, 5456, 6212, 6275, 6277, 9628, 13871, 13964, 15793, 15816, 16508, 17228.

Art. Archaeology. Pre-history

5,857 ADDISON, F. Antiquities at Sennar. SUDAN NOTES 18 (1935), pp. 288-293.

5,858 ADDISON, F. Antiquities found near Gordon's Tree, Khartoum Province. SUDAN NOTES 14 (1931), p. 197.

5,859 ADDISON, F. Archaeological notes. SUDAN NOTES 8 (1925), pp. 197-200.

5,860 ADDISON, F. Archaeology in the Fung Province. SUDAN NOTES 15 (1932), pp. 152-154.

5,861 ADDISON, F. A Christian site near Khartoum. SUDAN NOTES 13 (1930), pp. 285-288.

5,862 ADDISON, F. The Temple of Taharga at Kawa. SUDAN NOTES 12 (1929), pp. 85-90.

5,863 ADDISON, F. and DUNHAM, D. Alem. A Meroitic site. SUDAN NOTES 5 (1922), pp. 39-46.

5,864 ANDERSON, L. S. Cisterns at Ibn Abbas Island. SUDAN NOTES 22 (1939), pp. 277-280.

5,865 ANDREW, G. A note on Zeolite artefacts. SUDAN NOTES 32 (1951), pp. 308-310.

5,866 ANDREW, G. and DELANY, F. Note on a Neolithic site in the Sabaloka gorge. SUDAN NOTES 33 (1952), p. 167.

5,867 ARKELL, A. J. Beads made in Darfur and Wadai. SUDAN NOTES 26 (1945), pp. 305-310.

5,868 ARKELL, A. J. Darfur antiquities. SUDAN NOTES 19 (1936), pp. 301-311; 20 (1937), pp. 91-105; 27 (1946), pp. 185-202.

5,869 ARKELL, A. J. Darfur pottery. SUDAN NOTES 22 (1939), pp. 79-88.

5,870 ARKELL, A. J. The discovery of a new Christian site at Umm 'Ali in Shendi District. SUDAN NOTES 30 (1949), supplement, pp. 3-4.

5,871 ARKELL, A. J. The double spiral amulet. SUDAN NOTES 20 (1937), pp. 151-155.

5,872 ARKELL, A. J. The excavation of an ancient site at Khartoum. SUDAN NOTES 26 (1945), pp. 329-331.

5,873 ARKELL, A. J. The excavation of a Neolithic site at Esh Shaheinab. SUDAN NOTES 30 (1949), pp. 212-221.

5,874 ARKELL, A. J. An extinct Darfur hoe. SUDAN NOTES 20 (1937), pp. 146-150.

5,875 ARKELL, A. J. Hebron beads in Darfur. SUDAN NOTES 20 (1937), pp. 300-305.

5,876 ARKELL, A. J. Kohl pins. SUDAN NOTES 19 (1936), pp. 150-151.

5,877 ARKELL, A. J. The results of the excavation of an early site at Khartoum in 1944-1945. SUDAN NOTES 30 (1949), supplement, pp. 19-20.

5,878 ARKELL, A. J. Rock pictures in Northern Darfur. SUDAN NOTES 20 (1937), pp. 281-288.

5,879 ARKELL, A. J. The steel and tinder in Darfur. SUDAN NOTES 19 (1936), pp. 320-321.

5,880 ARKELL, A. J. Three burials in Sennar district. SUDAN NOTES 17 (1934), pp. 103-110.

5,881 ARNAUD, M. [tr.]. Kangombiyo. PRESENCE AFR. 3 (1948), pp. 470-477.

5,882 BASIL, Dr. the Rev. B. Towards a solution of African music problems. An assessment of the work of Father Giorgietti. AFR. MUSIC, 1959, pp. 90-92.

5,883 BLOSS, J. F. E. Relics of ancient gold miners. SUDAN NOTES 20 (1937), pp. 313-315.

5,884 BONNET, A. Les gravures rupestres de Niola Doha en Ennedi et les peintures corporelles actuelles de certaines tribus du Soudan nilotique. CONG. INT. SC. ANTH. ET ETHN. 6, no. i (1960), pp. 351-357.

5,885 CHATAWAY, J. D. P. Archaeology in the Southern Sudan. SUDAN NOTES 13 (1930), pp. 259-267.

5,886 CHMIELEWSKI, W. Excavation researches conducted by the paleolithic section of the Institute of the History of Material Culture, Polish Academy of Sciences, in north Sudan. AFR. BULL. 3 (1965), pp. 112-116.

5,887 C[ROWFOOT], J. W. [Two inscriptions from rock at Bayuda]. SUDAN NOTES 3 (1920), p. 293.

5,888 DELANY, F. Graves in the Langeb-Baraka area. SUDAN NOTES 33 (1952), pp. 58-59.

5,889 DUNBAR, J. H. Some Nubian rock pictures. SUDAN NOTES 17 (1934), pp. 139-167; 18 (1935), pp. 303-307.

5,890 DUNHAM, D. The history of the Kingdom of Kush (Sudan) from 800 B.C. to 350 A.D. as disclosed by Dr. Reisner's excavations. SUDAN NOTES 30 (1949), supplement, pp. 14-15.

5,891 EDMONDS, J. M. A quartz arrowhead from Zankor. SUDAN NOTES 23 (1940), p. 193.

5,892 EDMONDS, J. M. A ruin in the Wadi el Qasr. SUDAN NOTES 23 (1940), pp. 161-167.

5,893 EDMONDS, J. M. Some stone-walled enclosures in Dar Hawawir. SUDAN NOTES 23 (1940), pp. 295-303.

5,894 GRABHAM, G. W. An ancient Sudani. SUDAN NOTES 23 (1940), p. 349.

5,895 GRAY, T. The First Cataract. SUDAN NOTES 30 (1949), pp. 120-121.

5,896 GRIFFITH, F. L. Excavations at Kawa, 1930-1931. SUDAN NOTES 14 (1931), pp. 87-89.

5,897 HASSAN, T. The discovery of a Meroitic child's grave in Khartoum. SUDAN NOTES 30 (1949), pp. 112-113.

5,898 HENDERSON, K. D. D. "Nubian origins." SUDAN NOTES 14 (1931), pp. 90-93.

5,899 HODGKIN, R. A. Caves in the sandstone hills north of Omdurman. SUDAN NOTES 30 (1949), pp. 265-266.

5,900 JEFFERSON, J. H. K. A note based on field experience on planning Hafir excavation programmes. SUDAN NOTES 33 (1952), pp. 224-243.

5,901 JUNGRAITHMAYR, H. Bericht über eine Forschungsreise nach Darfur und Wadai. AFR. UND UB. 44 (1960), pp. 81-93.

5,902 JUNGRAITHMAYR, H. Felsbilder von Süd-Darfur. AFR. UND UB. 44 (1960), pp. 193-207.

5,903 JUNGRAITHMAYR, H. Rock paintings in the Sudan. CURRENT ANTHR. 2 (1961), pp. 388-389.

5,904 MacMICHAEL, H. A. Note on the burial-place of the Fur Sultans at Tura, in Jebel Marra. SUDAN NOTES 9 (1926), part 2, pp. 75-77.

5,905 MADIGAN, C. T. A description of some old towers in the Red Sea Province, north of Port Sudan. SUDAN NOTES 5 (1922), pp. 78-87.

5,906 MYERS, O. H. The consolidation and protection of ancient monuments of the Sudan. SUDAN NOTES 29 (1948), pp. 206-217.

5,907 MYERS, O. H. Excavations in the Second Cataract area. SUDAN NOTES 29 (1948), p. 129.

5,908 NEWBOLD, D. The history and archaeology of the Sudan. SUDAN NOTES 26 (1945), pp. 229-239.

5,909 NEWBOLD, D. The Zebaydia in the Apocrypha. SUDAN NOTES 7 (1924), pp. 131-132.

5,910 PAUL, A. Ancient tombs in Kassala Province. SUDAN NOTES 33 (1952), pp. 54-57.

5,911 PAUL, H. G. B. Decorated pipes of the Fung Kingdom. SUDAN NOTES 32 (1951), p. 325.

5,912 PAUL, H. G. B. Early cultures on the Northern Blue Nile. SUDAN NOTES 33 (1952), pp. 202-215.

5,913 PENN, A. E. D. The ruins of Zankor. SUDAN NOTES 14 (1931), pp. 179-184.

5,914 REISNER, G. A. Discovery of the tombs of the Egyptian XXVth dynasty at El-Kurruw in Dongola Province. SUDAN NOTES 2 (1919), pp. 237-254.

5,915 REISNER, G. A. Excavations at Semna and Uronarti by the Harvard-Boston expedition. SUDAN NOTES 12 (1929), pp. 143-161.

5,916 REISNER, G. A. Outline of the ancient history of the Sudan. SUDAN NOTES 1 (1918), pp. 3-15, 57-79, 217-237; 2 (1919), pp. 35-67.

5,917 REISNER, G. A. The pyramids of Meroe and the Candaces of Ethiopia. SUDAN NOTES 5 (1922), pp. 173-196.

5,918 REISNER, G. A. Uronarti. SUDAN NOTES 14 (1931), pp. 1-14.

5,919 SABBADINI, E. Atene dell' Africa l'antico Regno di Meroe. AFRICA (Rome) 19 (1964), pp. 12-16.

5,920 SANDARS, G. E. R. and OWEN, T. R. H. Note on ancient villages in Khor Nubt and Khor Omek [with a note by P. L. Shinnie]. SUDAN NOTES 32 (1951), pp. 326-331.

5,921 SELIGMAN, C. G. A neolithic site in the Anglo-Egyptian Sudan. JRAI 40 (1910), pp. 209-214.

5,922 S.-H., E. G. The sacred drum of Dar Turrti J. Meidob. SUDAN NOTES 3 (1920), pp. 225-227.

5,923 S.-H., E. G. The sacred stone of Furnung in northern Darfur. SUDAN NOTES 3 (1920), pp. 223-224.

5,924 SETON-KARR, H. W. Discovery of the lost flint mines of Egypt. JRAI 27 (1898), pp. 90-92.

5,925 SHAW, W. B. K. The ruins of Abu Sufyan. SUDAN NOTES 19 (1936), pp. 324-326.

5,926 SHINNIE, P. L. Archaeological discoveries during winter 1947-48. SUDAN NOTES 29 (1948), p. 128.

5,927 SHINNIE, P. L. Excavating in Nubia. UNIVERSITAS 5 (1962), pp. 3-4.

5,928 SHINNIE, P. L. Mogroka Church. SUDAN NOTES 32 (1951), p. 150.

5,929 SHINNIE, P. L. A note on some fragments of stamped pottery from Christian Nubia. SUDAN NOTES 31 (1950), pp. 279-299.

5,930 SMITH, H. F. C. and ABDELRAHMAN, A. Four ancient sites in the island of Meroe. SUDAN NOTES 31 (1950), pp. 303-306.

5,931 T., G. W. City mounds in the Bahr el Ghazal province. SUDAN NOTES 6 (1923), pp. 111-112.

5,932 TITHERINGTON, G. W. A Roman fort in the Sudan. SUDAN NOTES 21 (1938), pp. 331-332.

5,933 VERCOUTTER, J. Archaeological survey in the Sudan, 1955-57. SUDAN NOTES 38 (1957), pp. 111-117.

5,934 WAINWRIGHT, G. A. Iron in the Napatan and Meroitic ages. SUDAN NOTES 26 (1945), pp. 5-36.

5,935 WAINWRIGHT, G. A. Some ancient records of Kordofan. SUDAN NOTES 28 (1947), pp. 11-24.

5,936 WHEELER, N. F. Excavations of the Harvard-Boston expedition in Halfa Province, 1930-31. SUDAN NOTES 15 (1932), pp. 251-259.

5,937 WHITEHEAD, G. O. Nagaa and Masawwarat. SUDAN NOTES 9 (1926), part 2, pp. 59-67.

5,938 WHITEHEAD, G. O. and ADDISON, F. Meroitic remains. SUDAN NOTES 9 (1926), part 2, pp. 51-58.

5,939 ZYHLARZ, E. I reami della Nubia prima dell' Islam: uno sguardo storico sul Sudan antico e medioevale. RASS. STUDI ETIOP. 3 (1943), pp. 237-271.

5,940 The excavation of an ancient site at Khartoum. SUDAN NOTES 26 (1945), p. 182.

Art. Music

5,941 BEATON, A. C. Bari songs. SUDAN NOTES 19 (1936), pp. 327-334.

5,942 BEATON, A. C. Bari studies. SUDAN NOTES 15 (1932), pp. 63-95.

5,943 BEATON, A. C. The poetry of the Bari dance. SUDAN NOTES 21 (1938), pp. 105-122.

5,944 BEATON, A. C. Some Bari songs. SUDAN NOTES 18 (1935), pp. 277-287.

5,945 BEIER, U. Ibrahim Salahi. BO 10 (1961), pp. 48-50.

5,946 GIORGETTI, F. African music, with special reference to the Zande tribe. SUDAN NOTES 33 (1952), pp. 216-223.

5,947 HILLELSON, S. Songs of the Baggara. SUDAN NOTES 12 (1929), pp. 73-83.

5,948 KAMITIN, F. R. The Rongo. SUDAN NOTES 28 (1947), pp. 179-180.

5,949 PAUL, H. G. B. Islam at Uri. SUDAN NOTES AND RECORDS 35, part 1 (1954), pp. 139-140.

5,950 PAUL, H. G. B. Two curiosities from Dar Masalit. SUDAN NOTES AND RECORDS 35, part 1 (1954), pp. 141-143.

5,951 POUX-CRANSAC, G. Tage Rabebe, chanson de Rabah, recueillie et commentée. J. SOC. AFR. 7 (1937), pp. 173-187.

5,952 R., A. E. The Fung drum or Nehas. SUDAN NOTES 4 (1921), pp. 211-212.

5,953 STANTON, E. A. The Sudan Camel Stamp. SUDAN NOTES 18 (1935), pp. 135-137.

5,954 THORBURN, D. H. Sudanese soldiers' songs. J. AFR. SOC. 24 (1925), pp. 314-321.

5,955 WILLIAMS, D. A Sudanese calligraphy: a contemporary interpretation of Mohammedan art. TRANSITION 9 (1963), pp. 19-20.

See also 5166, 5201.

Biography

5,956 HILL, R. Death of a governor-general. SUDAN NOTES 39 (1958), pp. 83-87.

5,957 HILLELSON, S. Tabaqât Wad Dayf Allah. Studies in the lives of the scholars and saints. SUDAN NOTES 6 (1923), pp. 191-230.

5,958 The diary of 'Abbas Bey.' SUDAN NOTES 32 (1951), pp. 179-196.

5,959 BREDIN, G. R. F. The life-story of Yuzbashi 'Abdullah Adlan. SUDAN NOTES 42 (1961), pp. 37-52.

5,960 MYNORS, T. H. B. The adventures of a Darfur slave [Bakir Ahmed]. SUDAN NOTES 30 (1949), pp. 273-275.

5,961 Obituary: William Beam. SUDAN NOTES 3 (1920), p. 83.

5,962 Obituary: A. J. Chalmers. SUDAN NOTES 3 (1920), p. 139.

5,963 Obituary: Pierre Crabitès. SUDAN NOTES 26 (1945), pp. 343-344.

5,964 H., P. P. Obituary: Jack Herbert Driberg. SUDAN NOTES 28 (1947), pp. 197-198.

5,965 In memoriam: Saad ed Din Fawzi. CIVILISATIONS 9 (1959), p. 123.

5,966 Major Stanley Smyth Flower (1871-1946). SUDAN NOTES 27 (1946), pp. 245-246.

5,967 SHINNIE, P. L. Sir Francis Galton and the Sudan. SUDAN NOTES 33 (1952), pp. 168-169.

5,968 Obituary: Sir Hubert Huddleston. AFR. AFFAIRS 50 (1951), pp. 73-74.

5,969 MARCO, E. Frank Miller Lupton. SUDAN NOTES 28 (1947), pp. 50-61.

5,970 A., G. Obituary: Cecil Thomas Madigan. SUDAN NOTES 28 (1947), pp. 198-199.

5,971 WINGATE, R. Major General Bertram Reveley Mitford. SUDAN NOTES 19 (1936), pp. 1-3.

5,972 Newbold. AFR. AFFAIRS 52 (1953), pp. 188-190.

5,973 Douglas Newbold. SUDAN NOTES 26 (1945), pp. 205-211.

5,974 HOPE, A. C. The adventurous life of Faraj Sadik. SUDAN NOTES 32 (1951), pp. 154-158.

5,975 A gallant soldier [Sir Nevill Smyth]. J. AFR. SOC. 41 (1942), p. 9.

5,976 Obituary: Prince Omar Toussoun. SUDAN NOTES 27 (1946), p. 241.

5,977 KIRK, R. Sir Henry Wellcome and the Sudan. SUDAN NOTES 37 (1956), pp. 79-89.

5,978 G. O. Whitehead. SUDAN NOTES 27 (1946), pp. 242-244.

5,979 WINGATE, Sir R. An eightieth birthday [Sir R. Wingate]. J. AFR. SOC. 40 (1941), p. 203.

See also 5207 [Douin], 5208 [Hume].

Economics

5,980 AGLEN, E. F. The economic limitations to future development. FOOD AND SOCIETY IN THE SUDAN, 1955, pp. 269-292.

5,981 ALI AHMED SULIMAN. Stabilization policies for cotton in the Sudan. AFR. PRIMARY PRODUCTS AND INT. TRADE, 1965, pp. 159-180.

5,982 ALLEN, R. W. The Gezira irrigation scheme, Sudan. J. AFR. SOC. 25 (1926), pp. 229-236.

5,983 BESHIR, M. O. The Gezira Scheme: an experiment in socio-economic development. CIVILISATIONS 11 (1961), pp. 63-67.

5,984 BRAUSCH, G. E. J.-B. Problèmes du travail au Gezira (Soudan). CIVILISATIONS 13 (1963), pp. 250-262; English summary, pp. 263-266.

5,985 CATFORD, J. R. The introduction of cotton as a cash-crop in the Maridi area of Equatoria. SUDAN NOTES 34 (1953), pp. 153-171.

5,986 CONDIE, R. H. B. Cotton exports and economic development in the Sudan. SUDAN NOTES 37 (1956), pp. 70-78.

5,987 CONROY, F. D. Aid program in the Sudan. AFR. STUD. BULL. 7, no. i (1964), pp. 6-10.

5,988 CULWICK, G. M. Social change in the Gezira scheme. CIVILISATIONS 5 (1955), pp. 173-181; French summary, pp. 181-182.

5,989 D., W. A. and C., J. W. Soap making in the Sudan. SUDAN NOTES 5 (1922), pp. 224-226.

5,990 FAWZI, S. E. D. Problems of economic development in the Sudan. PRESENCE AFR. N.S. 6 (1956), pp. 28-45.

5,991 FAWZI, S. E. D. The wage structure and wage policy in the Sudan. SUDAN NOTES AND RECORDS 36 (1955), pp. 159-175.

5,992 GAITSKELL, A. The Sudan Gezira scheme. AFR. AFFAIRS 51 (1952), pp. 306-313.

5,993 GEORGE, L. The Andat Oil bug or Gutran El Andat. SUDAN NOTES 37 (1956), pp. 96-98.

5,994 GRAY, A. The Sudan economy. AFR. AFFAIRS 61 (1962), pp. 279-281.

5,995 HANCE, W. A. The Gezira: an example in development. GEOG. REV. 44 (1954), pp. 253-270.

5,996 HAUSER, A. Colons africains au Soudan. WAISER 5 (1956), pp. 45-53.

5,997 HENIN, R. A. Recent developments in Sudan's foreign trade (1949-61). SUDAN NOTES 45 (1964), pp. 113-132.

5,998 HOFSTEDE, A. E. The conservation and development of inland fisheries. SUDAN NOTES 37 (1956), pp. 113-119.

5,999 KHALIL, I. M. Developing the animal wealth of the Sudan. SUDAN NOTES 41 (1960), pp. 6-20.

6,000 KUHN, M. Selected aspects of market planning in Omdurman, Sudan. PROC. 3RD. GRAD. ACAD. UCLA, 1965, pp. 223-233.

6,001 LEWIS, B. A. Deim el Arab and the Beja stevedores of Port Sudan. SUDAN NOTES 43 (1962), pp. 16-49.

6,002 LISHMAN, J. F. Some economic considerations concerning the development of communications in the Southern Sudan. SUDAN NOTES 30 (1949), supplement, pp. 23-28.

6,003 McCALL, A. G. Some notes on Zandeland. FOOD AND SOCIETY IN THE SUDAN, 1955, pp. 243-256.

6,004 McLOUGHLIN, P. F. M. Economic development and the heritage of slavery in the Sudan republic. AFRICA 32 (1962), pp. 355-391.

6,005 McLOUGHLIN, P. F. M. Labour force participation rates in the Sudan's nine economic regions. NJESR 5 (1963), pp. 354-363.

6,006 McLOUGHLIN, P. F. M. The Sudan's Gezira scheme: an economic profile. SOCIAL AND ECON. STUD. 12 (1963), pp. 179-199.

6,007 MAHHOUK, A. and DREES, F. Domestic policies and payments problems of the Sudan, 1947-62. INT. MONETARY FUND STAFF PAPERS 11 (1964), pp. 150-176.

6,008 MORRICE, H. A. W. The development of Sudan communications. SUDAN NOTES 30 (1949), pp. 1-38, 141-178.

6,009 MORRICE, H. A. W. The use of investigation teams for planning the development of remote and sparsely populated areas. FOOD AND SOCIETY IN THE SUDAN, 1955, pp. 257-268.

6,010 OGDEN, G. W. Relationship of frequency and speed of transport. SUDAN NOTES 30 (1949), supplement, pp. 7-9.

6,011 OSMAN, O. M. Some economic aspects of private pump schemes. SUDAN NOTES 39 (1958), pp. 40-48.

6,012 REED, W. A study of marine fisheries in the Sudan. SUDAN NOTES 43 (1962), pp. 1-15.

6,013 REHFISCH, F. A study of some southern migrants in Omdurman. SUDAN NOTES 43 (1962), pp. 50-104.

6,014 REINING, C. C. The role of money in the Zande economy. AMER. ANTHR. 61 (1959), pp. 39-43.

6,015 SALIH, M. M. The Sudanese press. SUDAN NOTES 46 (1965), pp. 1-7.

6,016 SANDON, H. [ed.]. The problems of fisheries in the area affected by the Equatorial Nile Project. SUDAN NOTES 32 (1951), pp. 5-36.

6,017 SATTI, S. A. Some aspects of the Sudan economy. AFR. AFFAIRS 56 (1957), pp. 32-39.

6,018 STANIFORTH, G. R. A trial economic survey of twenty families among the Morokodu tribe of Amadi district, Equatoria Province. SUDAN NOTES 29 (1948), pp. 221-224.

6,019 STANTON, E. A. Progress in the Sudan. J. AFR. SOC. 13 (1914), pp. 365-368.

6,020 TURNER, L. E. Soap making at Karkoj. SUDAN NOTES 23 (1940), pp. 189-190.

6,021 VERSLUYS, J. D. N. The Gezira scheme in the Sudan and the Russian Kolkhoz: a comparison of two experiments. ECON. DEVELOPMENT AND CULTURAL CHANGE 2 (1953-1954), pp.120-135, 216-235.

6,022 VICARI, E. Il Sudan e il lavoro italiano. AFRICA (Rome) 10 (1955), pp. 15-19.

6,023 WHITE, C. M. N. Factors determining the content of African land tenure systems in Northern Rhodesia. AFR. AGRARIAN SYSTEMS, 1963, pp. 364-373.

6,024 ZILIOTTO, G. Un paese in marcia. AFRICA (Rome) 14 (1959), pp. 132-134.

6,025 The Institute of Public Administration of the Republic of the Sudan. INT. SOC. SC. J. 12 (1960), pp. 607-608.

6,026 La terra del rinoceronte bianco [intervista di B. Russi con Ibrahim Mohammed Khalil]. AFRICA (Rome) 13 (1958), pp.21-22.

See also 5213, 11429.

Education

6,027 ALI, N. EL HAG. Educational problems in the Sudan. SUDAN NOTES 41 (1960), pp. 66-77.

6,028 BESHIR, M. O. Workers and adult education in the Sudan. CIVILISATIONS 9 (1959), pp. 29-36.

6,029 CURRIE, Sir J. The educational experiment in the Anglo-Egyptian Sudan, 1900-33. J. AFR. SOC. 33 (1934), pp. 361-371; 34 (1935), pp. 41-59.

6,030 GRANT, M. The first year of Khartoum University. SUDAN NOTES 37 (1956), pp. 90-91.

6,031 HODGKIN, R. Literacy experiment in the Sudan. CORONA 1, no. 2 (1949), pp. 13-15.

6,032 KASHIF, H. The Sudanese women's movement. AFR. WOMEN 3 (1958-1960), pp. 55-56.

6,033 MATHEWS, A. T. Objective examinations. SUDAN NOTES 30 (1949), supplement, pp. 16-17.

6,034 MYNORS, T. H. B. A School of Administration in the Anglo Egyptian Sudan. J. AFR. ADM. 2 (1950), pp. 24-26.

6,035 PATERFAMILIAS. The Sirdar's College at Khartoum. CONTEMP. REV. 75 (1899), pp. 194-202.

6,036 RICHARDS, G. E. Adult education amongst country women: an experiment at Umm Gerr. SUDAN NOTES 29 (1948), pp. 225-227.

6,037 SANDERSON, L. Careers for women in the Sudan today. AFR. WOMEN 5 (1963), pp. 25-29.

6,038 SANDERSON, L. Educational development and administrative control in the Nuba mountains region of the Sudan. J. AFR. HIST. 4 (1963), pp. 233-247.

6,039 SANDERSON, L. Educational development in the Southern Sudan: 1900-1948. SUDAN NOTES 43 (1962), pp. 105-117.

6,040 SANDERSON, L. Some aspects of the development of girls' education in the Northern Sudan. SUDAN NOTES 42 (1961), pp. 91-101.

6,041 SANDERSON, L. A survey of material available for the study of educational development in the modern Sudan, 1900-1963. SUDAN NOTES 44 (1963), pp. 69-81.

6,042 SCOTT, G. C. Intelligence testing in the Sudan. SUDAN NOTES 29 (1948), pp. 107-119.

6,043 STANTON, E. A. The Sir-et-Tugar. J. AFR. SOC. 35 (1936), pp. 34-36.

6,044 STYLER, W. E. Adult education in the Sudan. AFR. AFFAIRS 56 (1957), pp. 289-294.

6,045 TAYIB, G. EL-. Women's education in the Sudan. KANO STUD. 1 (1965), pp. 43-46.

6,046 WILCHER, L. C. Some problems of university education. SUDAN NOTES 34 (1953), pp. 62-72.

6,047 "Do-it-yourself" girls' school. AFR. WOMEN 4 (1960), p. 13.

Geography. Topography. Travel

6,048 BACON, C. R. Days and nights on the Akobo river. SUDAN NOTES 6 (1923), pp. 51-55.

6,049 BACON, C. R. Poisoned fish. SUDAN NOTES 1 (1918), pp. 207-209.

6,050 BARBOUR, K. M. Maps of Africa before surveys: the location of Omodias map of Sudan. GEOG. REV. 51 (1961), pp. 71-86.

6,051 BARBOUR, K. M. The Wadi Azum from Zalingei to Murnei. SUDAN NOTES 31 (1950), pp. 105-128.

6,052 BAUMER, M. The ranges of Dar Meganin. SUDAN NOTES 44 (1963), pp. 120-135; 45 (1964), pp. 133-147.

6,053 BERRY, L. The Red Sea coast of the Sudan. SUDAN NOTES 45 (1964), pp. 148-157.

6,054 BOOTH, G. A. The forests of Upper Nile Province, 1862-1950. SUDAN NOTES 33 (1952), pp. 113-128.

6,055 BOYCE, A. A. R. Daylight hunting lions. SUDAN NOTES 9 (1926), part 2, pp. 83-84.

6,056 BOYCE, A. A. R. A survey note. SUDAN NOTES 7 (1924), part 2, p. 131.

6,057 COLCHESTER, G. V. Malha Crater, Darfur. SUDAN NOTES 10 (1927), pp. 233-235.

6,058 COOKE, B. K. The Red Sea coast in 1540. SUDAN NOTES 16 (1933), pp. 151-159.

6,059 COX, F. J. Munzinger's observations on the Sudan, 1871: The Little America of Africa. SUDAN NOTES 33 (1952), pp. 189-201.

6,060 D'ALMASY, L. E. Bir Bidi. SUDAN NOTES 18 (1935), pp. 259-276.

6,061 D'ALMASY, L. E. By motor car from Wadi Halfa to Cairo. SUDAN NOTES 13 (1930), pp. 269-278.

6,062 DURAND, J. Le vent et sa conséquence, l'érosion éolienne, facteur de formation des sols au Sahara. DESERT RESEARCH, 1953, pp. 434-437.

6,063 FERGUSON, H. The food crops of the Sudan and their relation to environment. FOOD AND SOCIETY IN THE SUDAN, 1955, pp. 7-60.

6,064 FIDDES, E. S. Eighteenth-century geography of the Sudan. SUDAN NOTES 19 (1936), pp. 176-178.

6,065 FLEMING, G. J. Kassala. SUDAN NOTES 5 (1922), pp. 65-77.

6,066 FLEMING, G. J. Tokar. SUDAN NOTES 3 (1920), pp. 12-23.

6,067 GILLAN, J. A. Jabel Marra and the Deriba Lakes. SUDAN NOTES 1 (1918), pp. 263-267.

6,068 GLENNIE, J. F. The Equatorial Nile Project. SUDAN NOTES 38 (1957), pp. 67-73.

6,069 GRABHAM, C. W. The Bayuda volcanic field. SUDAN NOTES 3 (1920), pp. 133-136.

6,070 GRABHAM, C. W. Desiccation. SUDAN NOTES 3 (1920), pp. 130-131.

6,071 GREENWOOD. Escape in the grass. SUDAN NOTES 24 (1941), pp. 189-196.

6,072 HAMDAN, G. The growth and functional structure of Khartoum. GEOG. REV. 50 (1960), pp. 21-40.

6,073 HASSOUN, ISAM AHMAD. "Western" migration and settlement in the Gezira. SUDAN NOTES 33 (1952), pp. 60-112.

6,074 HEBBERT, H. E. El Rih—a Red Sea island. SUDAN NOTES 18 (1935), pp. 308-313.

6,075 HILL, R. The Suakin-Berber Railway, 1885. SUDAN NOTES 20 (1937), pp. 107-124.

6,076 HILL, R. L. An unpublished itinerary to Kordofan 1824-1825. SUDAN NOTES 29 (1948), pp. 58-70.

6,077 HILLELSON, S. David Reubeni, an early visitor to Sennar. SUDAN NOTES 16 (1933), pp. 55-66.

6,078 HODGKIN, R. A. The ascent of Jebel Kassala. SUDAN NOTES 25 (1942), pp. 123-129.

6,079 HODSON, A. An incident with lion. SUDAN NOTES 8 (1925), pp. 75-78.

6,080 INNES, N. M. The Monasir country, 1930. SUDAN NOTES 14 (1931), pp. 185-190.

6,081 JACKSON, H. C. Seed-time and harvest. SUDAN NOTES 2 (1919), pp. 1-16.

6,082 JACKSON, H. C. A trek in Abu Hamed district. SUDAN NOTES 9 (1926), part 2, pp. 1-35.

6,083 JACKSON, Sir H. W. Description of the Bordein and the Telahawieh, 1884-1885. SUDAN NOTES 15 (1932), pp. 269-271.

6,084 JACKSON, J. K. Changes in the climate and vegetation of the Sudan. SUDAN NOTES 38 (1957), pp. 47-66.

6,085 JACKSON, J. K. Mount Lotuke, Didinga Hills. SUDAN NOTES 32 (1951), pp. 339-341.

6,086 LEACH, T. A. The Selima Oasis [with notes by G. W. Grabham and F. Addison]. SUDAN NOTES 9 (1926), part 2, pp. 37-49.

6,087 LEBON, J. H. G. Recent contributions to the geography of the Sudan. GEOG. REV. 46 (1956), pp. 246-252.

6,088 LEBON, J. H. G. Some concepts of modern geography applied to Sudan. SUDAN NOTES 42 (1961), pp. 3-28.

6,089 LYNES, H. Notes on the natural history of Jebel Marra. SUDAN NOTES 4 (1921), pp. 119-137.

6,090 MacMICHAEL, H. A. The Kheiran. SUDAN NOTES 3 (1920), pp. 231-244.

6,091 MARLING, Sir P. The Sudan revisited, after fifty years. J. AFR. SOC. 32 (1933), pp. 261-269.

6,092 NEWBOLD, D. A desert odyssey of a thousand miles. SUDAN NOTES 7 (1924), pp. 43-92.

6,093 NEWBOLD, D. A note on "The Gizzu" or jizu. SUDAN NOTES 7 (1924), part 2, pp. 129-130.

6,094 NEWBOLD, D. and SHAW, W. B. K. An exploration in the South Libyan Desert. SUDAN NOTES 11 (1928), pp. 103-194.

6,095 OLIVER, J. The climate of Khartoum Province. SUDAN NOTES 46 (1965), pp. 90-129.

6,096 ORNELLA, G. B. DE P. D'. An historic Tamarind tree and notes on some of the explorers of the Upper Nile region. SUDAN NOTES 28 (1947), pp. 174-178.

6,097 PAGE, C. H. Inland water navigation of the Sudan. SUDAN NOTES 2 (1919), pp. 293-306.

6,098 PAGE, C. H. The Rahad. A note on navigation and the possibilities of the river. SUDAN NOTES 1 (1918), pp. 99-106.

6,099 RANDELL, J. R. El Gedid—a Blue Nile Gezira village. SUDAN NOTES 39 (1958), pp. 25-39.

6,100 RANDELL, J. R. A rainfall map of the Sudan Gezira. SUDAN NOTES 42 (1961), pp. 29-36.

6,101 RATH, U. C. W. The climate of the Sudan: a factor in the social and economic development of the country. FOOD AND SOCIETY IN THE SUDAN, 1955, pp. 105-112.

6,102 ROBINSON, A. E. Desiccation or destruction. Notes on the increase of desert areas in the Nile Valley. SUDAN NOTES 18 (1935), pp. 119-130.

6,103 SHAW, W. B. K. Darb el Arba'in. The forty days' road. SUDAN NOTES 12 (1929), pp. 63-71.

6,104 STANTON, E. A. The Anglo-Egyptian Sudan. J. AFR. SOC. 11 (1912), pp. 261-274.

6,105 STANTON, E. A. England in the Sudan. J. AFR. SOC. 10 (1911), pp. 274-284.

6,106 STANTON, E. A. The great marshes of the White Nile. J. AFR. SOC. 2 (1903), pp. 375-379.

6,107 STIGAND, C. H. The Dabba of the sudd area. SUDAN NOTES 1 (1918), pp. 209-210.

6,108 SUDAN. INTELLIGENCE DEPARTMENT. Glossary of Arabic geographical terms used in maps and route reports in the A.E. Sudan. J. AFR. SOC. 11 (1912), pp. 201-205.

6,109 TOTHILL, B. H. Additional note on the death of Mlle. Tinne [extracted and translated from G. Nachtigal's account in Sahara und Sudan]. SUDAN NOTES 28 (1947), pp. 45-49.

6,110 TOTHILL, B. H. An expedition in Central Africa by three Dutch ladies [extracted and translated from Plantae Tinneanae]. SUDAN NOTES 28 (1947), pp. 25-44.

6,111 WELLS, J. Road construction across the cotton soils of the Southern Sudan. SUDAN NOTES 4 (1921), pp. 108-111.

6,112 WEST, L. C. Dongola province of the Anglo-Egyptian Sudan. GEOG. REV. 5 (1918), pp. 22-37.

6,113 WHITEHEAD, G. O. Italian travellers in the Berta country. SUDAN NOTES 17 (1934), pp. 217-227.

6,114 WILLIMOTT, S. G. Cultivable land and land use in Equatoria Province. MALAYAN J. TR. GEOG. 8 (1956), pp. 40-50.

6,115 WILLIMOTT, S. G. Soils and vegetation of the Boma Plateau and Eastern District Equatoria. SUDAN NOTES 38 (1957), pp. 10-20.

6,116 WORRALL, G. A. A simple introduction to the geology of the Sudan. SUDAN NOTES 38 (1957), pp. 2-9.

6,117 WORRALL, G. A. Soils and land use in the vicinity of the three towns. SUDAN NOTES 39 (1958), pp. 2-10.

6,118 WRIGHT, J. W. Air survey in the Sudan. SUDAN NOTES 30 (1949), pp. 58-76.

6,119 WRIGHT, J. W. The White Nile and the Sobat. SUDAN NOTES 32 (1951), pp. 113-130.

6,120 Drifting sand. SUDAN NOTES 24 (1941), pp. 201-204.

6,121 Jebel Nishki Well. SUDAN NOTES 33 (1952), p. 322.

6,122 A short account of the Equatorial Nile Project and its effects in the Sudan by members of the Jonglei Investigation Team. SUDAN NOTES 33 (1952), pp. 3-41.

6,123 Three impressions of Khartoum during the Turkiya from the letters and diaries of Italian missionaries [Luigi Montuori, G. Beltrame and B. Rolleri]. SUDAN NOTES 41 (1960), pp. 101-106.

See also 5254, 19088.

Government. Politics. Administration

6,124 ABEL, D. Free Sudan: the first year. CONTEMP. REV. 191 (1957), pp. 164-168.

6,125 ARIES. The Sudan and democracy. AFR. AFFAIRS 61 (1962), pp. 247-254.

6,126 BENUMEYA, R. G. Perspectives generales del Sudán en 1955. CUAD. AFR. OR. 29 (1955), pp. 17-25.

6,127 BENUMEYA, R. G. Presente y futuro del Sudán independiente. CUAD. AFR. OR. 33 (1956), pp. 53-61.

6,128 BRANNEY, L. Local government in the Sudan. J. AFR. ADM. 1 (1949), pp. 143-156.

6,129 BROADBENT, P. B. Sudanese self-government. INTERNAT. AFFAIRS 30 (1954), pp. 320-330.

6,130 BUCHANAN, L. M. Local Government in the Sudan since 1947. J. AFR. ADM. 5 (1953), pp. 152-158.

6,131 C., E. N. Report on the administration of the Sudan in 1935; by E. N. C. J. AFR. SOC. 36 (1937), pp. 87-91.

6,132 C., J. Accord sur le Soudan. ZAIRE 7 (1953), pp. 411-412.

6,133 COLLINS, R. and HERZOG, R. Early British administration in the Southern Sudan. J. AFR. HIST. 2 (1961), pp. 119-135.

6,134 CORBYN, E. N. The administration of the Sudan in 1937. J. AFR. SOC. 38 (1939), pp. 281-288.

6,135 FERIK IBRAHIM ABBOUD and MIRALAI EL MAGBOUL EL AMIN EL HAG. Decentralization in the Sudan—1. J. LOCAL ADM. OV. 1 (1962), pp. 71-74.

6,136 GADDI, S. Un nuovo Stato africano indipendente la Republica del Sudan. AFRICA (Rome) 11 (1956), p. 19.

6,137 GIL BENUMEYA, R. Resumen de la cuestión actual del Sudán. CUAD. EST. AFR. 19 (1952), pp. 31-41.

6,138 GRAY, A. The new Sudan. AFR. AFFAIRS 55 (1956), pp. 90-91.

6,139 GRAY, A. Sudan coup. AFR. AFFAIRS 58 (1959), pp. 4-6.

6,140 GRAY, A. Sudan: independence? AFR. AFFAIRS 54 (1955), pp. 253-255.

6,141 GRAY, A. Sudan on the eve [of self-government]. AFR. AFFAIRS 55 (1956), pp. 2-3.

6,142 HENDERSON, K. D. D. The Sudan today. AFR. AFFAIRS 64 (1965), pp. 170-181.

6,143 HYSLOP, J. Problems and prospects in the Sudan. CONTEMP. REV. 185 (1954), pp. 333-338.

6,144 HYSLOP, J. The Sudan. CONTEMP. REV. 182 (1952), pp. 68-74.

6,145 KILNER, P. The seven generals: a study of the Sudan. AFR. SOUTH 5, no. 3 (1961), pp. 93-99.

6,146 MADDICK, H. Decentralization in the Sudan—11; a critical appraisal. J. LOCAL ADM. OV. 1 (1962), pp. 75-83.

6,147 MAZRUI, A. Religion and democracy in the First Republic of the Sudan. MAKERERE J. 11 (1965), pp. 39-50.

6,148 MEYEROWITZ, E. L. R. The Southern Sudan today. AFR. AFFAIRS 62 (1963), pp. 274-279, 310-311.

6,149 MISKIN, A. B. Land registration. J. AFR. ADM. 5 (1953), pp. 72-80.

6,150 MUSTAFA, B. M. Le Soudan et l'unité africaine. PRESENCE AFR. N.S. 46 (1963), pp. 93-107.

6,151 NEWBOLD, Sir D. The share of the Sudanese in the Sudan government. BULL. UGANDA SOC. 3 (1944), pp. 7-11.

6,152 WALLIS, C. A. G. Local administration in the Sudan. J. AFR. ADM. 13 (1961), pp. 158-164.

6,153 The Sudan elections. CONTEMP. REV. 185 (1954), pp. 71-76.

See also 5268, 5271, 10444, 11638.

History

6,154 A., A. J. The southern route to Kufra. From El Fasher to the Senussi and back with Ali Dinar's Caravan, 1915-16. Told by Bidi Awdi, the guide. SUDAN NOTES 5 (1922), pp. 130-136.

6,155 'ABDIN, 'ABD AL-MAGID. Some general aspects of the Arabisation of the Sudan. SUDAN NOTES AND RECORDS 40 (1959), pp. 48-74.

6,156 ADAWI, I. A. AL. Description of the Sudan by Muslim geographers and travellers. SUDAN NOTES AND RECORDS 35, part 2 (1954), pp. 5-16.

6,157 AGLEN, E. F. Sheikan battlefield. SUDAN NOTES 20 (1937), pp. 138-145.

6,158 ALI GULLA and NALDER, L. F. The defeat of Hicks Pasha. SUDAN NOTES 8 (1925), pp. 119-123.

6,159 ALLEN, B. M. How Khartoum fell. J. AFR. SOC. 40 (1941), pp. 327-334.

6,160 ARIE, R. L'opinion publique en France et l'affaire de Fachoda. REV. HIST. COL. 41 (1954), pp. 329-367.

6,161 ARKELL, A. J. The coinage of 'Alī Dīnār, Sultan of Darfur, 1898-1916. SUDAN NOTES 23 (1940), pp. 151-160.

6,162 ARKELL, A. J. The history of Darfur. SUDAN NOTES 32 (1951), pp. 37-70, 207-238; 33 (1952), pp. 129-155, 244-275.

6,163 ARKELL, A. J. Forged Mahdi pounds. SUDAN NOTES 26 (1945), pp. 43-49.

6,164 ARKELL, A. J. The medieval history of Darfur in its relation to other cultures and to the Nilotic Sudan. SUDAN NOTES AND RECORDS 40 (1959), pp. 44-47.

6,165 ARKELL, A. J. A Roman coin of the Emperor Diocletian at El Obeid. SUDAN NOTES 16 (1933), p. 187.

6,166 ARKELL, A. J. Roman coins at Sennar. SUDAN NOTES 15 (1932), pp. 271-272.

6,167 ATIYA, S. B. Senin and Ali Dinar. SUDAN NOTES 7 (1924), part 2, pp. 63-69.

6,168 BAKER, S. W. The Soudan and its future. CONTEMP. REV. 45 (1884), pp. 64-80.

6,169 BASHIR, M. O. Nasihat Al Awam. SUDAN NOTES 41 (1960), pp. 59-65.

6,170 BEATON, A. C. A chapter in Bari history. The history of Sindiru, Bilinian and Möngiri. SUDAN NOTES 17 (1934), pp. 169-200.

6,171 BELL, G. W. Shaibun gold. SUDAN NOTES 20 (1937), pp. 125-137.

6,172 BELL, G. W. Suleiman Hariga. SUDAN NOTES 20 (1937), pp. 296-299.

6,173 BERGE, J. L. Crise au Sud-Soudan. AFR. ET ASIE 64 (1963), pp. 19-35.

6,174 BESHIR, M. O. Abdel Rahman Ibn Hussein El Jabri and his book "History of the Mahdi." SUDAN NOTES 44 (1963), pp. 136-139.

6,175 BLOSS, J. F. E. The story of Suakin. SUDAN NOTES 19 (1936), pp. 271-300; 20 (1937), pp. 247-280.

6,176 BOLTON, A. R. C. El Menna Ismail; Fiki and Emir in Kordofan. SUDAN NOTES 17 (1934), pp. 229-241.

6,177 BOUSTEAD, J. E. H. The youth and last days of Sultan Ali Dinar. "A Fur view." SUDAN NOTES 22 (1939), pp. 149-153.

6,178 BROADBENT, P. B. Reminiscences of a Berber merchant. SUDAN NOTES 23 (1940), pp. 123-130.

6,179 C., J. W. A history of the Arabs in the Sudan by H. A. MacMichael. SUDAN NOTES 5 (1922), pp. 61-64.

6,180 CAMERON, V. L. Our duty in the Soudan. CONTEMP. REV. 47 (1885), pp. 573-578.

6,181 COLLINS, R. O. Patrols against the Beirs. SUDAN NOTES 41 (1960), pp. 35-58.

6,182 COLLINS, R. O. The transfer of the Lado Enclave to the Anglo-Egyptian Sudan, 1910. ZAIRE 14 (1960), pp. 193-210.

6,183 COMBE, E. T. Four Arabic inscriptions from the Red Sea. SUDAN NOTES 13 (1930), pp. 288-291.

6,184 CORBYN, E. N. The Sudan annual report [1933]. J. AFR. SOC. 34 (1935), pp. 179-183.

6,185 CORIAT, P. Gwek, the witch-doctor and the Pyramid of Denkgur. SUDAN NOTES 22 (1939), pp. 221-237.

6,186 CRAWFORD, O. G. S. The Ashraf of the Sudan. SUDAN NOTES AND RECORDS 36 (1955), pp. 180-182.

6,187 CRAWFORD, O. G. S. Lul. SUDAN NOTES 26 (1945), pp. 335-336.

6,188 CUMMING, D. C. The history of Kassala and the Province of Taka. SUDAN NOTES 20 (1937), pp. 1-45; 23 (1940), pp. 1-54, 225-269.

6,189 DAFALLA, H. Notes on the history of Wadi Halfa town. SUDAN NOTES 46 (1965), pp. 8-26.

6,190 DAVIES, R. The Masalit Sultanate. SUDAN NOTES 7 (1924), part 2, pp. 49-62.

6,191 DUNHAM, D. Outline of the ancient history of the Sudan. SUDAN NOTES 28 (1947), pp. 1-10.

6,192 EDWARDS, F. A. The foundation of Khartoum. SUDAN NOTES 5 (1922), pp. 157-162.

6,193 ELLES, R. J. The Kingdom of Tegali. SUDAN NOTES 18 (1935), pp. 1-35.

6,194 EMILY, C. et al. Les Missions du Haut-Nil en 1897-1898, by C. Emily, C. Michel, A. Martineau. RHCF 24 (1931), pp. 233-284.

6,195 EVANS-PRITCHARD, E. E. Zande historical texts. SUDAN NOTES AND RECORDS 36 (1955), pp. 123-145.

6,196 FITZGERALD, W. W. A. The commercial possibilities of the Sudan. ROYAL COL. INST. PR. 35 (1903-1904), pp. 349-376.

6,197 G., H. W. General Gordon and the slave trade. CONTEMP. REV. 46 (1884), pp. 682-686.

6,198 GAGE, M. F. Sudd cutting. Experiences of the expedition from Uganda 1899-1900. SUDAN NOTES 31 (1950), pp. 7-20.

6,199 GATACRE, W. After the Atbara and Omdurman. CONTEMP. REV. 75 (1899), pp. 299-304.

6,200 GAZZINI, M. Italiani nel Sudan ante 1940. AFRICA (Rome) 10 (1955), p. 44.

6,201 GIFFORD, G. The Sudan at war: the composite infantry battalion of the Eastern Arab Corps, Sudan Defence Force, in the Abyssinian campaign. J. AFR. SOC. 42 (1943), pp. 155-164.

6,202 GILLAN, Sir A. The Sudan: past, present and future. AFR. AFFAIRS 43 (1944), pp. 123-128.

6,203 GILLAN, J. A. Darfur, 1916. SUDAN NOTES 22 (1939), pp. 1-25.

6,204 GRAY, A. Sudan change. AFR. AFFAIRS 55 (1956), pp. 252-253.

6,205 GRAY, Sir J. Ismail Pasha and Sir Samuel Baker. UGANDA J. 25 (1961), pp. 199-213.

6,206 GUEMARD. Correspondance inédite relative a Alexandre Vaudey et aux Frères Poncet explorateurs du Haut Nil Blanc et du Bahr-El-Ghazal. RHCF 29 (1936), pp. 165-174.

6,207 H., A. J. C. The Rubātāb. SUDAN NOTES 1 (1918), p. 293.

6,208 HAMILTON-GRIERSON, P. F. A local calendar. SUDAN NOTES 6 (1923), pp. 118-121.

6,209 HASAN, Y. F. The Umayyad genealogy of the Funj. SUDAN NOTES 46 (1965), pp. 27-32.

6,210 HASHIM, I. E. The defence of Nyala. SUDAN NOTES 25 (1942), pp. 81-108.

6,211 HENDERSON, K. D. D. The Sudan and the Abyssinian campaign. J. AFR. SOC. 42 (1943), pp. 12-20.

6,212 HERZOG, R. Ethnographical notes on the Sudan in an early traveller's account. SUDAN NOTES 38 (1957), pp. 119-129.

6,213 HILL, R. The period of Egyptian occupation 1820-1881. SUDAN NOTES AND RECORDS 40 (1959), pp. 101-106.

6,214 HILL, R. L. Rulers of Sudan, 1820-1885. SUDAN NOTES 32 (1951), pp. 85-95.

6,215 HILL, R. L. An unpublished chronicle of the Sudan. SUDAN NOTES 37 (1956), pp. 2-19; 38 (1957), pp. 130-146.

6,216 HILL, R. L. An unpublished fragment of a manuscript concerning events in the Sudan, 1843-1848. SUDAN NOTES AND RECORDS 36 (1955), pp. 112-122.

6,217 HILLELSON, S. Nubian origins. SUDAN NOTES 13 (1930), pp. 137-148.

6,218 HOLT, P. M. The archives of the Mahdia. SUDAN NOTES AND RECORDS 36 (1955), pp. 71-80.

6,219 HOLT, P. M. Funj origins: a critique and new evidence. J. AFR. HIST. 4 (1963), pp. 39-55.

6,220 HOLT, P. M. The place in history of the Sudanese Mahdia. SUDAN NOTES AND RECORDS 40 (1959), pp. 107-112.

6,221 HOLT, P. M. A Sudanese historical legend: the Funj conquest of Sūba. BULL. SOAS 23 (1960), pp. 1-12.

6,222 HUGODOT, M. L'opinion publique anglaise et l'affaire de Fachoda. REV. ET. COL. 44 (1957), pp. 113-137.

6,223 HYSLOP, J. The Sudan treaty. CONTEMP. REV. 183 (1953), pp. 203-206.

6,224 I., D. Conspiracy against the Mek of the Shilluks in 1917. SUDAN NOTES 5 (1922), p. 111.

6,225 JACKSON, H. W. Fashoda, 1898. SUDAN NOTES 3 (1920), pp. 1-11.

6,226 JENNINGS-BRAMLEY, W. E. Tales of the Wadai slave trade in the 'nineties. SUDAN NOTES 23 (1940), pp. 169-183.

6,227 JOB, H. S. The coinage of the Mahdi and the Khalifa. SUDAN NOTES 3 (1920), pp. 163-196; supplementary note, 7 (1924), part 2, pp. 124-127.

6,228 JUNGFLEISCH, M. Hasan Suliman, Kashif of Nubia. SUDAN NOTES 27 (1946), pp. 239-240.

6,229 KEAYS, G. A. V., BEY. Note on the history of the Camel Corps. SUDAN NOTES 22 (1939), pp. 103-123.

6,230 KENRICK, J. W. The Kingdom of Tegali, 1921-1946. SUDAN NOTES 29 (1948), pp. 143-150.

6,231 KINGDON, F. D. The Western Nuer patrol 1927-28. SUDAN NOTES 26 (1945), pp. 171-178.

6,232 KIRK, R. The Sudanese in Mexico. SUDAN NOTES 24 (1941), pp. 113-130.

6,233 KIRWAN, L. P. A contemporary account of the conversion of the Sudan to Christianity. SUDAN NOTES 20 (1937), pp. 289-295.

6,234 KIRWAN, L. P. The international position of Sudan in Roman and medieval times. SUDAN NOTES AND RECORDS 40 (1959), pp. 23-37.

6,235 KIRWAN, L. P. A survey of Nubian origins. SUDAN NOTES 20 (1937), pp. 47-62.

6,236 LAMPEN, G. D. History of Darfur. SUDAN NOTES 31 (1950), pp. 177-209.

6,237 LORIMER, F. C. S. The Megadhib of El Damer. SUDAN NOTES 19 (1936), pp. 335-342.

6,238 LUBBOCK, J. England and the Soudan. CONTEMP. REV. 47 (1885), pp. 562-572.

6,239 MacKENZIE, P. Z. The Battle of Aguat, 1952. SUDAN NOTES 34 (1953), pp. 309-310.

6,240 MacKENZIE, P. Z. The part played by the animals of the Sudan with the Allied Armies, 1940-1946. SUDAN NOTES 43 (1962), pp. 153-157.

6,241 MacMICHAEL, H. A. Old Khartoum. SUDAN NOTES 6 (1923), pp. 110-111.

6,242 MARLING, Sir P. The Nile campaign: 1884-1885. J. AFR. SOC. 35 (1936), pp. 143-152.

6,243 MITFORD, B. R. Extracts from the diary of a subaltern on the Nile in the 'eighties and 'nineties. SUDAN NOTES 18 (1935), pp. 167-193; 19 (1936), pp. 199-231; 20 (1937), pp. 63-89.

6,244 MONTAGUE-STUART-WORTLEY, E. J. My reminiscences of Egypt and the Sudan (1882 to 1899). SUDAN NOTES 34 (1953), pp. 17-46, 172-188.

6,245 MURATORI, C. Ikang, queen of Tirrangore. SUDAN NOTES AND RECORDS 35, part 1 (1954), pp. 144-147.

6,246 MURATORI, C. Lomoro Xujang (1853-1912), a Lotuxo chief, Tirrangore. SUDAN NOTES 30 (1949), pp. 107-109.

6,247 MUSAD, M. M. The downfall of the Christian Nubian kingdoms. SUDAN NOTES AND RECORDS 40 (1959), pp. 124-128.

6,248 NEWBOLD, D. The crusaders in the Red Sea and the Sudan. SUDAN NOTES 26 (1945), pp. 213-227.

6,249 NICHOLSON, H. B. A fragment from Christian Nubia. SUDAN NOTES 16 (1933), pp. 83-85.

6,250 OYLER, D. S. Nikawng and the Shilluk migration. SUDAN NOTES 1 (1918), pp. 107-115.

6,251 PALMER, H. R. The Bornu mahram and the pre-Tunjur rulers of Wadai. SUDAN NOTES 5 (1922), pp. 197-199.

6,252 PALMER, H. R. The kingdom of Gaòga of Leo Africanus. J. AFR. SOC. 29 (1930), pp. 280-284, 350-369.

6,253 PALMER, H. R. Two Sudanese manuscripts of the seventeenth century. BULL. SOAS 5 (1928-1930), pp. 541-560.

6,254 PAUL, A. The Hadāreb—a study in Arab-Beja relationships. SUDAN NOTES AND RECORDS 40 (1959), pp. 75-78.

6,255 PAUL, A. Some aspects of the Fung sultanate. SUDAN NOTES AND RECORDS 35, part 2 (1954), pp. 17-31.

6,256 PAUL, A. Tewfik Bey. SUDAN NOTES AND RECORDS 35, part 1 (1954), pp. 132-138.

6,257 PETERMANN, A. Travels in the Sudan in the 'sixties. SUDAN NOTES 24 (1941), pp. 145-179.

6,258 REHFISCH, F. A. A sketch of the early history of Omdurman. SUDAN NOTES 45 (1964), pp. 35-47.

6,259 REHFISCH, F. A. A note on comtemporary source-materials of the Sudanese Mahdia. SUDAN NOTES 44 (1963), pp. 143.

6,260 REID, J. A. The Mahdi's Emirs. SUDAN NOTES 20 (1937), pp. 308-312.

6,261 REID, J. A. Reminiscences of the Sudan Mahdi, Sheikh Mohammed Ahmed. By his personal servant Mohammed El Mekki Ghuleib, who is still living in the Sudan. J. AFR. SOC. 35 (1936), pp. 71-75.

6,262 REID, J. A. Some notes on the Khalifa Abdullahi from contemporary Sudanese sources. SUDAN NOTES 21 (1938), pp. 207-211.

6,263 REID, J. A. Story of a Mahdist Amir. SUDAN NOTES 9 (1926), part 2, pp. 79-82.

6,264 REISNER, A. Historical inscriptions from Gebel Barkal. SUDAN NOTES 4 (1921), pp. 59-75.

6,265 ROBERTSON, Sir J. The Sudan in transition. AFR. AFFAIRS 52 (1953), pp. 317-327.

6,266 ROBINSON, A. E. "Abu El Kalkik," the kingmaker of the Fung of Sennar. AMER. ANTHR. 31 (1929), pp. 232-264.

6,267 ROBINSON, A. E. Ahmed Pasha Abu Udan. SUDAN NOTES 5 (1922), pp. 226-230.

6,268 ROBINSON, A. E. The Arab dynasty of Dar For (Darfur). A.D. 1448-1874 or A.H. 852-1201. J. AFR. SOC. 27 (1928), pp. 353-363; 28 (1928), pp. 274-280, 379-384; 29 (1929), pp. 53-70.

6,269 ROBINSON, A. E. British Consuls at Suakin. SUDAN NOTES 4 (1921), p. 108.

6,270 ROBINSON, A. E. The conquest of the Sudan by the Wali of Egypt, Muhammad Ali Pasha, 1820-1824. J. AFR. SOC. 25 (1925), pp. 47-58, 164-182.

6,271 ROBINSON, A. E. The Mamelukes in the Sudan. SUDAN NOTES 5 (1922), pp. 88-94.

6,272 ROBINSON, A. E. Nimr, the last king of Shendi. SUDAN NOTES 8 (1925), pp. 105-118.

6,273 ROBINSON, A. E. The rulers of the Sudan since the Turkish occupation until the evacuation by order of the Khedive. J. AFR. SOC. 24 (1924), pp. 39-49.

6,274 ROBINSON, A. E. The Tekruri Sheikhs of Gallabat (S.E. Sudan). J. AFR. SOC. 26 (1926), pp. 47-53.

6,275 SAGAR, J. W. Notes on the history, religion, and customs of the Nuba. SUDAN NOTES 5 (1922), pp. 137-156.

6,276 SALMON, R. The story of Sheikh Abdullahi Ahmed Abu Gelaha, a Sudanese vicar of Bray. SUDAN NOTES 21 (1938), pp. 79-103.

6,277 SANDARS, G. E. R. The Amarar. SUDAN NOTES 18 (1935), pp. 195-219.

6,278 SANDERSON, G. N. The European powers and the Sudan in the later nineteenth century. SUDAN NOTES AND RECORDS 40 (1959), pp. 79-100.

6,279 SANDERSON, G. N. The modern Sudan, 1820-1956: the present position of historical studies. J. AFR. HIST. 4 (1963), pp. 435-461.

6,280 SANTANDREA, S. The Bandiya at Deim Zubeir. SUDAN NOTES AND RECORDS 40 (1959), pp. 129-135.

6,281 SANTANDREA, S. The Belgians in Western Bahr el Ghazal. SUDAN NOTES AND RECORDS 36 (1955), pp. 188-191.

6,282 SANTANDREA, S. Sanusi, ruler of Dar Banda and Dar Kuti, in the history of the Bahr-el-Ghazal. SUDAN NOTES 38 (1957), pp. 151-155.

6,283 TAME, G. B. Legends of the Halawin of Blue Nile Province. SUDAN NOTES 17 (1934), pp. 201-216.

6,284 TEMPLE, R. The Mahdi and British India. CONTEMP. REV. 47 (1885), pp. 305-314.

6,285 THABIT, T. H. International relations of the Sudan in Napatan times. SUDAN NOTES AND RECORDS 40 (1959), pp. 19-22.

6,286 THEOBALD, A. B. Dārfūr and its neighbours under Sultān 'Alī Dinār, 1898-1916. SUDAN NOTES AND RECORDS 40 (1959), pp. 113-120.

6,287 THEOBALD, A. B. The Khalifa 'Abdallahi. SUDAN NOTES 31 (1950), pp. 254-273.

6,288 THOMAS, H. B. Note on the Sudanese corps in Mexico (1863-67) and on Fort Magungu. UGANDA J. 8 (1940), pp. 28-32.

6,289 TONIOLO, E. The first centenary of the Roman Catholic Mission to Central Africa, 1846-1946. SUDAN NOTES 27 (1946), pp. 99-126.

6,290 TRACEY, C. B. The curious case of Bayin Abdulla. SUDAN NOTES 21 (1938), pp. 327-329.

6,291 VERCOUTTER, J. Ancient Egyptian influence in the Sudan. SUDAN NOTES AND RECORDS 40 (1959), pp. 8-18.

6,292 WALKER, J. The coinage of Ali Dinar. SUDAN NOTES 19 (1936), pp. 147-149.

6,293 WALKLEY, C. E. J. The story of Khartoum. SUDAN NOTES 18 (1935), pp. 221-241; 19 (1936), pp. 71-92.

6,294 WATSON, Sir C. M. The campaign of Gordon's steamers. SUDAN NOTES 12 (1929), pp. 119-141.

6,295 WHITEHEAD, G. O. André Melly's visit to Khartoum 1850. SUDAN NOTES 21 (1938), pp. 291-305.

6,296 WHITEHEAD, G. O. Mansfield Parkyns and his projected history of the Sudan. SUDAN NOTES 23 (1940), pp. 131-138.

6,297 WHITEHEAD, G. O. A note on Bari history. SUDAN NOTES 19 (1936), pp. 152-157.

6,298 WINGATE, F. R. The seige and fall of Khartoum. SUDAN NOTES 13 (1930), pp. 1-82.

6,299 YAGI, M. A. Les origines de Khartoum. PRESENCE AFR. N.S. 22 (1958), pp. 81-85.

6,300 Extract from the Bahr el Ghazal Province Diary for May 1919. SUDAN NOTES 2 (1919), p. 309.

6,301 A fragment from Ali Dinar. SUDAN NOTES 34 (1953), pp. 114-116.

6,302 The history of Gallabat. SUDAN NOTES 7 (1924), pp. 93-101.

6,303 The name Mongalla. SUDAN NOTES 11 (1928), pp. 228-229.

6,304 "A conversation." The position of General Gordon. CONTEMP. REV. 45 (1884), pp. 866-878.

6,305 A sidelight on history [death of Ismail Sadiq Pasha]. SUDAN NOTES 4 (1921), pp. 106-107.

6,306 The Sudan's service in a global war: the story of a section of the trans-African air ferry route. AFR. AFFAIRS 43 (1944), pp. 16-20.

6,307 Unpublished letters of Charles George Gordon. SUDAN NOTES 10 (1927), pp. 1-59.

6,308 War in the Jebels. SUDAN NOTES 22 (1939), pp. 89-101.

See also 4973, 5303, 5304, 5314, 5315, 5908, 13587, 16087, 19184, 19308.

Language. Literature

Language

6,309 ABEL, H. Nubisch-Agyptisches Sprachgut. AFR. UND UB. 24 (1933-1934), pp. 303-306.

6,310 BEATON, A. C. Bari names. SUDAN NOTES 17 (1934), pp. 255-259.

6,311 BELL, G. W. Some examples of Arabic slang used in the Sudan. SUDAN NOTES 34 (1953), pp. 299-308.

6,312 BORK, F. Zu den neuen Sprachen von Süd-Kordofan. AFR. UND UB. 3 (1912-1913), pp. 140-156.

6,313 BRYAN, M. A. A linguistic no-man's land. AFRICA 15 (1945), pp. 188-205.

6,314 CHRISTALLER, J. G. Bemerkungen zu R. Lepsius' Einleitung über die Völker und Sprachen Afrikas, Nubische Grammatik, 1880. ZAS 1 (1887-1888), pp. 241-251.

6,315 COSTERMANS, B. Logo-Avokaya als taalgroep. KONGO-OVERZEE 21 (1955), pp. 1-27.

6,316 COWAN, W. A note on the phonemes of Moro. J. AFR. LANG. 4 (1965), pp. 114-117.

6,317 D., R. Sudan Arabic. SUDAN NOTES 9 (1926), pp. 131-136; 10 (1927), pp. 211-219; 12 (1929), pp. 109-110.

6,318 DREXEL, A. and KAUCZOR, D. Die Daiersprache in Kordofan. BIBLIOTHECA AFR. 4, no. 2 (1930-1931), pp. 42-53.

6,319 EVANS-PRITCHARD, E. E. Ideophones in Zande. SUDAN NOTES 43 (1962), pp. 143-146.

6,320 EVANS-PRITCHARD, E. E. Sanza, a characteristic feature of Zande language and thought. BULL. SOAS 18 (1956), pp. 161-180.

6,321 GASIM, AWN AL-SHARIF. Some aspects of Sudanese colloquial Arabic. SUDAN NOTES 46 (1965), pp. 40-49.

6,322 GLUCKMAN, M. Prefix concordance in Lozi, lingua franca of Barotseland. AFR. STUD. 1 (1942), pp. 105-114.

6,323 HESS, J. J. Geographische Benennungen u. Pflanzennamen in der nördlichen Bischâri-Sprache. AFR. UND UB. 9 (1918-1919), pp. 209-225.

6,324 KAUCZOR, D. Bergnubisches Wörterverzeichnis. BIBLIOTHECA AFR. 3 (1929-1930), pp. 342-383.

6,325 LEHR, J. Die sprachliche Stellung des Schilluk. BIBLIOTHECA AFR. 1 (1924), pp. 18-26; 2 (1926), pp. 235-238.

6,326 LUKAS, J. Beitrage zur Kenntnis der Sprachen von Wadâi (Mararēt, Mába). J. SOC. AFR. 3 (1933), pp. 25-55.

6,327 LUKAS, J. Tonbezeichnete Mabatexte (Wadai). AFR. UND UB. 37 (1952-1953), pp. 51-60.

6,328 LUKAS, J. Verbalwurzel und Verbalaffixe im Maba (Waddai). AFR. UND UB. 36 (1951-1952), pp. 93-98.

6,329 LUKAS, J. and VOLCKERS, O. G. Nachtigal's Aufzeichnungen über die Sprache der Mimi in Wadai. AFR. UND UB. 29 (1939), pp. 145-154.

6,330 MacDIARMID, P. A. and MacDIARMID, D. N. The languages of the Nuba Mountains. SUDAN NOTES 14 (1931), pp. 149-162.

6,331 MacMICHAEL, H. A. Darfur linguistics. SUDAN NOTES 3 (1920), pp. 197-216.

6,332 MEINHOF, C. Das Heiban in Kordofan. AFR. UND UB. 34 (1943-1944), pp. 94-130.

6,333 MEINHOF, C. Die Sprache von Meroe. AFR. UND UB. 12 (1921-1922), pp. 1-16.

6,334 MEINHOF, C. Sprachstudien im egyptischen Sudan. AFR. UND UB. 6 (1915-1916), pp. 161-205, 264-284; 7 (1916-1917), pp. 36-80, 105-133, 212-250, 326-335; 8 (1917-1918), pp. 46-74, 110-139, 170-196, 257-267; 9 (1918-1919), pp. 43-64, 88-117, 167-204, 227-255.

6,335 MEINHOF, C. and TUTSCHEK, K. Sprachproben von der Sprache in Darfur. AFR. UND UB. 20 (1929-1930), pp. 81-91.

6,336 MURATORI, C. A linguistic curiosity in Equatoria Province: an interlabial b. SUDAN NOTES 30 (1949), p. 119.

6,337 MURRAY, G. W. The Nilotic languages—a comparative essay. JRAI 50 (1920), pp. 327-368.

6,338 MURRAY, G. W. The Nubian and Bari languages compared. SUDAN NOTES 3 (1920), pp. 260-270.

6,339 MURRAY, W. A. English in the Sudan: trends and policies: relations with Arabic. LANGUAGE IN AFRICA, 1963, pp. 86-95.

6,340 NEWBOLD, D. Some links with the Anag at Gebel Haraza. SUDAN NOTES 7 (1924), pp. 126-131.

6,341 NICHOLSON, H. A. Saqia terminology in Dongola. SUDAN NOTES 18 (1935), pp. 314-322.

6,342 SANTANDREA, S. A note on Kare grammar. SUDAN NOTES 45 (1964), pp. 103-112.

6,343 SANTANDREA, S. Short notes on the Bodo, Huma and Kare languages. SUDAN NOTES 44 (1963), pp. 82-99.

6,344 SELIGMANN, B. Z. Note on the language of the Nubas of southern Kordofan. AFR. UND UB. 1 (1910), pp. 167-188.

6,345 SELIGMANN, B. Z. Note on two languages spoken in the Sennar province of the Anglo-Egyptian Sudan. AFR. UND UB. 2 (1911-1912), pp. 297-308.

6,346 STEVENSON, R. C. Linguistic research in the Nuba Mountains. SUDAN NOTES 43 (1962), pp. 118-130; 45 (1964), pp. 79-102.

6,347 STEVENSON, R. C. A survey of the phonetics and grammatical structure of the Nuba Mountain languages, with particular reference to Otoro, Katcha and Nyiman. AFR. UND UB. 40 (1956), pp. 73-84, 93-115; 41 (1957), pp. 27-65, 117-152, 171-196.

6,348 TUCKER, A. N. The function of voice quality in the Nilotic languages. INT. CONG. PHONETIC SCIENCES 2 (1935), pp. 125-131.

6,349 TUCKER, A. N. The linguistic situation in the Southern Sudan. AFRICA 7 (1934), pp. 28-39.

6,350 TUCKER, A. N. Notes on Murle (Beir). AFR. UND UB. 36 (1951-1952), pp. 99-114.

6,351 TUCKER, A. N. Survey of the language groups in the Southern Sudan. BULL. SOAS 7 (1933-1935), pp. 861-896.

6,352 TUTSCHEK, K. Sprachproben von der Sprache in Darfur. AFR. UND UB. 12 (1921-1922), pp. 81-97; 16 (1925-1926), pp. 161-196.

6,353 WEISS, P. H. Grammaire et lexique diola du Fogny (Casamance). BULL. IFAN 1 (1939), pp. 412-578.

6,354 WRIGHT, J. W. and JANSON-SMITH, G. The spelling of place names in the Sudan. SUDAN NOTES 32 (1951), pp. 311-324.

6,355 ZYHLARZ, E. Die Lautverschiebungen des Nubischen. AFR. UND UB. 35 (1949-1950), pp. 1-20, 129-146, 280-313.

6,356 ZYHLARZ, E. Die Sprache der Blemmyer. AFR. UND UB. 31 (1941), pp. 1-21.

6,357 ZYHLARZ, E. Sprachproben von der Sprache in Darfur. AFR. UND UB. 32 (1942), pp. 81-89.

See also 6108.

Literature

6,358 CALAME-GRIAULE, G. La structure symbolique des fables soudanaises. CONG. INT. SC. ANTH. ET ETHN. 6, no. ii (1960), pp. 163-167.

6,359 CLUTTON, S. G. Vernacular literature in the Southern Sudan since 1940. SUDAN NOTES 30 (1949), pp. 260-264.

6,360 D., R. and H., S. Two texts from Kordofan. SUDAN NOTES 13 (1930), pp. 117-122.

6,361 DOKE, C. M. An unusual Bantu tale of the Little-hare series. AFR. STUD. 3 (1944), pp. 31-36.

6,362 EVANS-PRITCHARD, E. E. Four Zande tales. ANTHR. QUART. 37 (1964), pp. 157-174. Also in JRAI 93 (1965), pp. 44-74.

6,363 HILLELSON, S. Arabic nursery rhymes. SUDAN NOTES 1 (1918), pp. 25-29.

6,364 HILLELSON, S. Arabic proverbs, sayings, riddles and popular beliefs. SUDAN NOTES 4 (1921), pp. 76-86.

6,365 HILLELSON, S. Classical reminiscences in popular literature. SUDAN NOTES 30 (1949), pp. 271-272.

6,366 HILLELSON, S. Historical poems and traditions of the Shukriya. SUDAN NOTES 3 (1920), pp. 33-75.

6,367 JACKSON, H. C. Sudan proverbs. SUDAN NOTES 2 (1919), pp. 105-111.

6,368 JENNINGS-BRAMLY, W. E. Stories of the Gerarish. SUDAN NOTES 8 (1925), pp. 178-180.

6,369 ROPER, E. M. Poetry of the Hadendiwa. SUDAN NOTES 10 (1927), pp. 147-158.

6,370 SHOUSH, M. I. EL. Some background notes on modern Sudanese poetry. SUDAN NOTES 44 (1963), pp. 21-42.

6,371 WHITEHEAD, G. O. Some authors of the Southern Sudan. SUDAN NOTES 11 (1928), pp. 83-101.

Law

6,372 ABU RANNAT, S. M. The relationship between Islamic and customary law in the Sudan. J. AFR. LAW 4 (1960), pp. 9-16.

6,373 ANDERSON, J. N. D. Recent developments in Shari'a law in the Sudan. SUDAN NOTES 31 (1950), pp. 82-104.

6,374 ATIYAH, P. S. Some problems of family law in the Sudan Republic. SUDAN NOTES 39 (1958), pp. 88-100.

6,375 DISNEY, A. W. M. English law in the Sudan, 1899-1958. SUDAN NOTES AND RECORDS 40 (1959), pp. 121-123.

6,376 DRIBERG, J. H. Didinga customary law. SUDAN NOTES 8 (1925), pp. 153-175.

6,377 FARRAN, C. D'O. The Nile Waters question in international law. SUDAN NOTES 41 (1960), pp. 88-100.

6,378 FAWZI, S. ED D. The status of foreigners in the newly independent Sudan. CIVILISATIONS 7 (1957), pp. 343-356.

6,379 GNAWI, J. B. Notes on the law and custom of the Jur tribe in the central district of Bahr el Ghazal Province. SUDAN NOTES 7 (1924), part 2, pp. 71-81.

6,380 GOW, J. J. Law and the Sudan. SUDAN NOTES 33 (1952), pp. 299-310.

6,381 GUTTMANN, E. Land tenure among the Azande people of Equatoria Province in the Sudan. SUDAN NOTES 37 (1956), pp. 48-55.

6,382 JEFFREYS, M. D. W. Law among the Nuer. AFR. STUD. 16 (1957), pp. 115-118.

6,383 KHALIL, M. I. A plea for a shorter LL.B. course in Khartoum. J. AFR. LAW 7 (1963), pp. 125-132.

6,384 MACKRELL, J. E. C. The Dinka oath on ashes. SUDAN NOTES 25 (1942), pp. 131-134.

6,385 MISKIN, A. B. Land registration. SUDAN NOTES 31 (1950), pp. 274-286.

6,386 NUR, M. I. EL. The role of the native courts in the administration of justice in the Sudan. SUDAN NOTES 41 (1960), pp. 78-87.

6,387 OWEN, T. R. H. Lynch law in the Eastern Jebels. SUDAN NOTES 23 (1940), pp. 195-198.

6,388 REID, J. A. and MacLAREN, J. F. P. Arab court procedure and customary law. SUDAN NOTES 19 (1936), pp. 158-161.

6,389 SIMPSON, S. R. Land law and registration in the Sudan. J. AFR. ADM. 7 (1955), pp. 11-17.

6,390 SIMPSON, S. R. Land tenure aspects of the Gezira scheme in the Sudan. J. AFR. ADM. 9 (1957), pp. 92-95.

6,391 TWINING, W. L. Law reporting in the Sudan. J. AFR. LAW 3 (1959), pp. 176-178.

6,392 TWINING, W. L. Legal studies at the University of Khartoum. J. AFR. LAW 6 (1962), pp. 145-150.

6,393 "Documenting Sudan law" project. J. AFR. LAW 5 (1961), pp. 1-2.

6,394 Two murder trials in Kordofan. SUDAN NOTES 3 (1920), pp. 245-259.

See also 5653, 5654, 5836, 6604.

Religion

6,395 ABESSOLO, S. Emprise de la religion sur le Noir. PRESENCE AFR. N.S. 1 (1955), pp. 11-23.

6,396 C[ROWFOOT], J. W. The sign of the cross. SUDAN NOTES 1 (1918), pp. 55-56.

6,397 GADALLAH, F. F. The Egyptian contribution to Nubian Christianity. SUDAN NOTES AND RECORDS 40 (1959), pp. 38-43.

6,398 HASSAN, Y. F. The penetration of Islam in the Eastern Sudan. SUDAN NOTES 44 (1963), pp. 1-8.

6,399 JENSEN, A. E. Bezichungen zwischen dem Alten Testamentes und der Nilotischen Kultur in Afrika. CULTURE IN HISTORY: ESSAYS IN HONOR OF PAUL RADIN, 1960, pp. 449-466.

6,400 MICHELMORE, A. P. G. A possible relic of Christianity in Darfur. SUDAN NOTES 15 (1932), pp. 272-273.

6,401 MISCHLICH, A. Religiöse und weltliche Gesänge der Mohammedaner aus dem Sudan. AFRIKA (Berlin) 2 (1943), pp. 129-198.

6,402 NADEL, S. F. A Shaman cult in the Nuba Mountains. SUDAN NOTES 24 (1941), pp. 85-112.

6,403 NADEL, S. F. Two Nuba religions: an essay in comparison. AMER. ANTHR. 57 (1955), pp. 661-679.

6,404 NALDER, L. F. The influence of animism in Islam. SUDAN NOTES 9 (1926), pp. 75-87.

6,405 PALMER, H. R. A Muslim Divine of the Sudan in the fifteenth century. AFRICA 3 (1930), pp. 203-216.

6,406 PAUL, H. G. B. A prehistoric cult still practised in Muslim Darfur. JRAI 86, part 1 (1956), pp. 77-86.

6,407 S[TERRY], W. and H[ILLELSON], S. The charm of Sālih ibn Husaina embroidered with names of the djinns, a miraculous weaving. SUDAN NOTES 1 (1918), pp. 53-55.

6,408 STEVENSON, R. C. Some aspects of the spread of Islam in the Nuba Mountains. SUDAN NOTES 44 (1963), pp. 9-20.

6,409 WILLIS, C. A. Religious confraternities of the Sudan. SUDAN NOTES 4 (1921), pp. 175-194.

6,410 Religious practices in Rejaf District. SUDAN NOTES 11 (1928), pp. 227-228.

See also 11118, 14230.

Science

6,411 ABD EL-FARAG ALI. An elephant with four tusks. SUDAN NOTES 2 (1919), pp. 230-231.

6,412 ABDEL HALIM, AHMED. Native medicine and ways of treatment in the Northern Sudan. SUDAN NOTES 22 (1939), pp. 27-48.

6,413 ABDEL NABI, A. Protection of game in the Sudan. SUDAN NOTES 37 (1956), pp. 119-121.

6,414 ACLAND, P. B. E. Notes on the camel in the Eastern Sudan. SUDAN NOTES 15 (1932), pp. 119-149.

6,415 ANDERSON, A. B. Marabout nesting colonies of the Southern Sudan. SUDAN NOTES 30 (1949), pp. 114-118.

6,416 ANDERSON, A. B. Small mammals of the Southern Sudan. SUDAN NOTES 30 (1949), pp. 252-259.

6,417 ANDREW, G. The development of the Sudan plain in the Quaternary. PROC. PAN-AFR. CONGR. PRE-HIST. 1 (1947), pp. 73-75.

6,418 ARKELL, A. J. Some land and freshwater snails of the Western Sudan. SUDAN NOTES 26 (1945), pp. 339-341.

6,419 B. Natural history notes. SUDAN NOTES 1 (1918), pp. 161-166.

6,420 BACON, C. R. Latet anguis in herba. SUDAN NOTES 6 (1923), pp. 56-58.

6,421 BELL, G. W. Elixir. SUDAN NOTES 30 (1949), pp. 110-111.

6,422 BLOSS, J. F. E. Notes on the health of the Sudan prior to the present Government. SUDAN NOTES 24 (1941), pp. 131-143.

6,423 BLOSS, J. F. E. Nutrition and society among the Nilotics. FOOD AND SOCIETY IN THE SUDAN, 1955, pp. 151-166.

6,424 BLOSS, J. F. E. The rural dispensary, its development in the Sudan. CORONA 2 (1950), pp. 68-70.

6,425 BLOSS, J. F. E. The tsetse fly in the Sudan. SUDAN NOTES 26 (1945), pp. 139-166.

6,426 BLUNT, H. S. Tabeldis. SUDAN NOTES 6 (1923), pp. 114-117.

6,427 BOND, W. R. G. The Chinese banana and its future in the Sudan. SUDAN NOTES 8 (1925), pp. 200-205.

6,428 BOND, W. R. G. Coloration of Gazelles. SUDAN NOTES 8 (1925), pp. 205-209.

6,429 BOND, W. R. G. Distribution of Sudan acacias [with a note by R. E. Massey]. SUDAN NOTES 2 (1919), pp. 81-90.

6,430 BOND, W. R. G. Hawks and verandahs. SUDAN NOTES 4 (1921), pp. 51-52.

6,431 BOWEN, W. W. The game-birds and water-fowl of the Sudan. SUDAN NOTES 8 (1925), pp. 85-95; 9 (1926), pp. 107-124; 11 (1928), pp. 69-82.

6,432 BOWEN, W. W. Nesting habits of the Bustard. SUDAN NOTES 9 (1926), pp. 88-89.

6,433 BOWEN, W. W. An ornithological puzzle. SUDAN NOTES 12 (1929), pp. 106-108.

6,434 BOWEN, W. W. The swallow-tailed Kite. SUDAN NOTES 9 (1926), pp. 86-88.

6,435 BOWERS, J. B. The wader birds in the Sudan. SUDAN NOTES 22 (1939), pp. 239-250.

6,436 CAVE, F. O. A further list of new records of birds for the Southern Sudan. SUDAN NOTES 22 (1939), pp. 159-162.

6,437 CAVE, F. O. A note on birds not previously recorded from the Southern Sudan. SUDAN NOTES 21 (1938), pp. 167-188.

6,438 CAVE, F. O. Some interesting birds from the Southern Sudan. SUDAN NOTES 27 (1946), pp. 225-228.

6,439 CAVE, F. O. and CRUICKSHANK, A. A note on game migration in the south eastern Sudan. SUDAN NOTES 23 (1940), pp. 341-344.

6,440 CLOUDSLEY-THOMPSON, J. L. Desert invertebrates of Khartoum Province. SUDAN NOTES 45 (1964), pp. 1-11.

6,441 COLLEY, W. M. Snakes in Geneina. SUDAN NOTES 27 (1946), pp. 213-220.

6,442 CORBYN, E. N. The Kitchener School of Medicine at Khartoum, Sudan. AFR. AFFAIRS 43 (1944), pp. 66-68.

6,443 CORKILL, N. L. Blood group patterns in Sudanese. SUDAN NOTES 30 (1949), pp. 267-270.

6,444 CORKILL, N. L. Dietary change in a Sudan village following locust visitation. AFRICA 9 (1949), pp. 1-11.

6,445 CORKILL, N. L. The Egyptian cobra and a fatal case of snake bite. SUDAN NOTES 26 (1945), p. 338.

6,446 CORKILL, N. L. Sudan Thanatophidia. SUDAN NOTES 30 (1949), pp. 101-106.

6,447 CORYTON, E. G. Some stages of evolution as evidenced by the fishes. SUDAN NOTES 2 (1919), pp. 211-215.

6,448 CORYTON, E. G. Tebeldis. SUDAN NOTES 16 (1933), p. 188.

6,449 COTTAM, R. A note on the Peregrine falcon in Khartoum. SUDAN NOTES 5 (1922), p. 52.

6,450 COTTAM, R. Observations on an entomophilus plant, Kanahia laniflora R. Br., in Khartoum. SUDAN NOTES 5 (1922), pp. 29-32.

6,451 CROSSLAND, C. Botanical note [on the fern Ophioglussum and another note by Mrs. Crowfoot]. SUDAN NOTES 1 (1918), pp. 135-137.

6,452 CROSSLAND, C. Comfort and health in the Tropics. SUDAN NOTES 2 (1919), pp. 198-210; 3 (1920), p. 79.

6,453 CROSSLAND, C. Dangers of pearl diving. SUDAN NOTES 2 (1919), pp. 234-236.

6,454 CROSSLAND, C. The pearl shell farm at Dongonab on the Red Sea. SUDAN NOTES 14 (1931), pp. 163-170.

6,455 CROSSLAND, C. Some common Red Sea fishes. SUDAN NOTES 3 (1920), pp. 117-129.

6,456 CRUICKSHANK, A. The birth of a leper settlement—Li-Rangu, Equatoria. SUDAN NOTES 29 (1948), pp. 183-188.

6,457 CULWICK, G. M. Social factors affecting diet. FOOD AND SOCIETY IN THE SUDAN, 1955, pp. 173-192.

6,458 DARLING, H. S. Insects and grain storage in the Sudan. SUDAN NOTES 32 (1951), pp. 131-149.

6,459 DARLING, R. C. M. The desert locust. SUDAN NOTES 19 (1936), pp. 168-175.

6,460 DARLING, R. C. X. Notes on the food of camels on the Red Sea coast and in north eastern Kordofan. SUDAN NOTES 21 (1938), pp. 189-205.

6,461 DAVIES, R. Methods of exterminating white ants. SUDAN NOTES 3 (1920), p. 137.

6,462 FANE, R. Mesquite: bush of many uses—a Sudan experiment. AFR. AFFAIRS 46 (1947), p. 234.

6,463 FLOWER, W. H. Exhibition of a deformed skull of a chimpanzee. JRAI 13 (1884), p. 276.

6,464 FORBES, A. and TAYLOR, R. E. Food supplies from wild animals and fish. FOOD AND SOCIETY IN THE SUDAN, 1955, pp. 113-116.

6,465 FOWLER, H. W. The fishes of the Red Sea. SUDAN NOTES 26 (1945), pp. 113-137.

6,466 FRANKLIN, C. B. Method of exterminating white ants. SUDAN NOTES 2 (1919), pp. 309-310.

6,467 GEORGE, L. The sesame seed moth (Corcyra Cephalonica, Stains). SUDAN NOTES AND RECORDS 36 (1955), pp. 81-82.

6,468 GEORGE, L. The woolly bear (Anthrenus Fasciatus, Herbst). SUDAN NOTES AND RECORDS 36 (1955), p. 83.

6,469 GIRGIS, S. A list of common fish of the Upper Nile with their Shilluk, Dinka and Nuer names. SUDAN NOTES 29 (1948), pp. 120-125.

6,470 HASEEB, M. A. Haemoglobin standards in the Sudan. SUDAN NOTES 31 (1950), pp. 300-302.

6,471 HASEEB, M. A. A scorpion in captivity. SUDAN NOTES 32 (1951), p. 338.

6,472 HEBBERT, H. E. The Port Sudan water supply. SUDAN NOTES 18 (1935), pp. 89-101.

6,473 HENRY, A. J. Sudan food values. FOOD AND SOCIETY IN THE SUDAN, 1955, pp. 167-172.

6,474 HOOGSTRAAL, H. Medical investigations of the United States Navy in the Anglo-Egyptian Sudan 1948-1950. SUDAN NOTES 32 (1951), pp. 333-337.

6,475 HUTCHINSON, J. B. Speculations on the rate of evolution. SUDAN NOTES 30 (1949), supplement, pp. 17-18.

6,476 IRELAND, A. W. Health and comfort in hot climates. SUDAN NOTES AND RECORDS 36 (1955), pp. 105-111.

6,477 JACK, J. D. M. Food resources of animal origin in the Sudan. FOOD AND SOCIETY IN THE SUDAN, 1955, pp. 61-90.

6,478 JOHNSTON, H. B. A note on locusts. SUDAN NOTES 7 (1924), part 2, pp. 91-101.

6,479 JOSEPH, A. F. Gas poisoning in a Kordofan well. SUDAN NOTES 4 (1921), pp. 112-113.

6,480 JOSEPH, A. F. Soil investigations in the Sudan. SUDAN NOTES 4 (1921), pp. 217-218.

6,481 KENCHINGTON, F. E. Further observations on the Nile perch. SUDAN NOTES 18 (1935), pp. 323-326.

6,482 KENCHINGTON, F. E. Studies on the Nile perch or aigle (Lates Nilotica) at Sennar. SUDAN NOTES 16 (1933), pp. 73-81.

6,483 KENDALL, E. M. A short history of the training of midwives in the Sudan. SUDAN NOTES 33 (1952), pp. 42-53.

6,484 KING, H. H. Natural history notes. SUDAN NOTES 4 (1921), pp. 39-43.

6,485 KING, H. H. Note on the origin of the migratory locust. SUDAN NOTES 5 (1922), pp. 54-56.

6,486 KING, H. H. Notes on Sudan scorpions. SUDAN NOTES 8 (1925), pp. 79-84.

6,487 KING, H. H. The Spanish sparrow in Dongola. SUDAN NOTES 4 (1921), pp. 45-46.

6,488 KIRK, R. Some vegetable poisons of the Sudan. SUDAN NOTES 27 (1946), pp. 127-152.

6,489 KIRK, R. Two epidemics of cerebrospinal meningitis. SUDAN NOTES 31 (1950), pp. 43-53.

6,490 LEWIS, D. J. The destruction of mosquito larvae by terrapins. SUDAN NOTES 25 (1942), p. 141.

6,491 LEWIS, D. J. Medical entomology in the Sudan Republic. SUDAN NOTES 39 (1958), pp. 11-24.

6,492 LEWIS, D. J. Early references to malaria near Dongola. SUDAN NOTES 29 (1948), pp. 218-220.

6,493 LEWIS, D. J. Early travellers' accounts of Surret flies (Tabanidae) in the Anglo-Egyptian Sudan. SUDAN NOTES 33 (1952), pp. 276-298.

6,494 LEWIS, D. J. Nimitti and some other small annoying flies in the Sudan. SUDAN NOTES AND RECORDS 35, part 2 (1954), pp. 76-89.

6,495 LEWIS, D. J. Notes on tsetse flies in the Anglo-Egyptian Sudan. SUDAN NOTES 32 (1951), pp. 96-105.

6,496 LEWIS, D. J. The tsetse fly problem in the Anglo-Egyptian Sudan. SUDAN NOTES 30 (1949), pp. 179-211.

6,497 LOVERIDGE, A. On snakes collected in the Anglo-Egyptian Sudan by J. S. Owen, Esq. SUDAN NOTES AND RECORDS 36 (1955), pp. 37-56.

6,498 LYTH, R. E. The migration of game in the Boma area. SUDAN NOTES 28 (1947), pp. 191-192.

6,499 MacDONALD, J. D. Problematical Sudan birds. SUDAN NOTES 26 (1945), pp. 301-304.

6,500 MacINTOSH, E. H. A note on the birds of Khartoum Province. SUDAN NOTES 9 (1926), pp. 95-105.

6,501 MacKENZIE, P. Z. A record of the species of birds observed and collected at Um Badr Lake in north-west Kordofan in January, 1955. SUDAN NOTES AND RECORDS 36 (1955), pp. 176-179.

6,502 MacLAREN, J. F. P. Some notes on the Barbary sheep in Northern Kordofan. SUDAN NOTES 8 (1925), pp. 209-212.

6,503 MacLEAY, K. N. G. Corrections and emendations to the Flora of the Sudan. SUDAN NOTES 44 (1963), pp. 140-142.

6,504 MacLEAY, K. N. G. The ferns and the fern-allies of the Sudan. SUDAN NOTES 34 (1953), pp. 286-289.

6,505 MacLEAY, K. N. G. Ophioglossum polyphyllum A. Br. in the Sudan. SUDAN NOTES 37 (1956), pp. 94-95.

6,506 MacLEAY, K. N. G. Pteridophyta recently recorded from the Sudan. SUDAN NOTES 32 (1951), pp. 160-164.

6,507 MADDEN, J. F. Additional notes on the shore birds of the Red Sea Province. SUDAN NOTES 12 (1929), pp. 104-106.

6,508 MADDEN, J. F. Bird migration at el Fasher 1944. SUDAN NOTES 27 (1946), pp. 221-223.

6,509 MADDEN, J. F. Bird migration in the Red Sea Province. SUDAN NOTES 13 (1930), pp. 123-135.

6,510 MADDEN, J. F. Notes on the birds of Southern Darfur. SUDAN NOTES 17 (1934), pp. 83-101; 18 (1935), pp. 103-118.

6,511 MADDEN, J. F. Notes on some shore birds of the Red Sea Province. SUDAN NOTES 10 (1927), pp. 135-146.

6,512 MADDEN, J. F. Some common birds of Torit District, Equatoria Province. SUDAN NOTES 26 (1945), pp. 283-300.

6,513 MARTIN, F. J. and GRAY, H. R. Methods of accelerating the germination of seeds. SUDAN NOTES 4 (1921), pp. 165-168.

6,514 MASSEY, R. E. Bacterial disease of cotton. SUDAN NOTES 7 (1924), pp. 123-124.

6,515 MASSEY, R. E. Helminthosporium sp. on wheat and barley in the Sudan. SUDAN NOTES 5 (1922), pp. 105-106.

6,516 MASSEY, R. E. Notes on some plant diseases caused by fungi in the Sudan. SUDAN NOTES 4 (1921), pp. 219-224.

6,517 MAURICE, G. K. The entry of relapsing fever into the Sudan. SUDAN NOTES 15 (1932), pp. 97-118.

6,518 MAURICE, G. K. The history of sleeping sickness in the Sudan. SUDAN NOTES 13 (1930), pp. 211-245.

6,519 MAXWELL-DARLING, R. C. Locusts in the Sudan. SUDAN NOTES 34 (1953), pp. 5-16.

6,520 MELLOR, J. E. M. Natural history notes. Notes on a Bengalia-like fly. SUDAN NOTES 5 (1922), pp. 95-100.

6,521 MELLOR, J. E. M. A note on the ruff. SUDAN NOTES 4 (1921), pp. 195-198.

6,522 MELLOR, J. E. M. A note on the food of certain birds shot in the Sudan during 1920 and 1921. SUDAN NOTES 12 (1929), pp. 102-103.

6,523 MELLOR, J. E. M. Notes on four Sudan Solitary Wasps. SUDAN NOTES 4 (1921), pp. 87-105.

6,524 MILLWARD, G. R. Oysters, pearls, and pearling in Sudan waters. SUDAN NOTES 27 (1946), pp. 203-212.

6,525 MOHAMMED ABDULLAH GOBAL. The Wa'ab. SUDAN NOTES 10 (1927), pp. 221-223.

6,526 MUTWAKIL, H. Types of dura used by Shilluk and Dinka. SUDAN NOTES 28 (1947), pp. 184-186.

6,527 NEWBOLD, D. The Ethiopian ant-lion [with a note by H. H. King]. SUDAN NOTES 7 (1924), pp. 133-135.

6,528 NEWBOLD, D. A historical note on the guinea-fowl. SUDAN NOTES 9 (1926), pp. 125-129.

6,529 NEWBOLD, D. More notes on Tebeldis. SUDAN NOTES 7 (1924), pp. 135-137.

6,530 NUNN, N. A Dinka public health measure. SUDAN NOTES 25 (1942), pp. 139-140.

6,531 OGDEN, G. W. Some notes on the messurement of time. SUDAN NOTES 31 (1950), pp. 246-253.

6,532 OWEN, J. S. A field key to the genera of Sudan rodents. SUDAN NOTES 34 (1953), pp. 104-113.

6,533 OWEN, J. S. Further notes on poisonous snakes. SUDAN NOTES 33 (1952), pp. 311-314.

6,534 OWEN, J. S. Torit snakes. SUDAN NOTES 37 (1956), pp. 92-93.

6,535 OWEN, T. R. H. Bird talk. SUDAN NOTES 28 (1947), pp. 193-196.

6,536 OWEN, T. R. H. A few cures for snake-bite. SUDAN NOTES 25 (1942), pp. 137-138.

6,537 OWEN, T. R. H. The Red Sea ibex. SUDAN NOTES 20 (1937), pp. 159-165.

6,538 PEAKE, F. G. G. Notes on die-back in Sunt (Acacia arabica) and forest pests in Equatoria. SUDAN NOTES AND RECORDS 35, part 2 (1954), pp. 90-98.

6,539 PEKKOLA, W. Notes on the habits, breeding, and food of some White Nile fish. SUDAN NOTES 2 (1919), pp. 113-121.

6,540 PEKKOLA, W. Seasonal occurrence and edibility of fish at Khartoum. SUDAN NOTES 1 (1918), pp. 88-98.

6,541 ROBBIE, J. The cultivated Adeniums (poison trees) in Khartoum. SUDAN NOTES 26 (1945), pp. 179-181.

6,542 ROBBIE, J. The tolerance of garden plants, fruit trees and some indigenous species to immersion in flood water in Blue Nile Province. SUDAN NOTES 28 (1947), pp. 187-190.

6,543 S., C. H. Mimics of the Genus Limnas. SUDAN NOTES 2 (1919), pp. 227-228.

6,544 SANDON, H. and TAYIB, AMIN AL. The food of some common Nile fish. SUDAN NOTES 34 (1953), pp. 205-229.

6,545 SANTOS DIAS, J. A. T. A propósito de uma colecção de carraças do Sudão Anglo-Egípcio. Algumas considerações sobre o Rhipicephalus longus Neumann, 1907. BSEM 92 (1955), pp. 103-118.

6,546 SCOTT, J. R. Kinana cattle. SUDAN NOTES 28 (1947), pp. 181-183.

6,547 SELIGMAN, C. G. A simple form of Distillatio per descensum in the Sudan. SUDAN NOTES 1 (1918), p. 202.

6,548 SMITH, D. A. Clinical observations on nutritional status in the central and northern Sudan. FOOD AND SOCIETY IN THE SUDAN, 1955, pp. 135-150.

6,549 SMITH, J. Distribution of tree species in the Sudan in relation to moisture and soil-texture. SUDAN NOTES 30 (1949), supplement, pp. 9-12.

6,550 SPENCE, B. Investigations at Halfa Quarantine. SUDAN NOTES 4 (1921), pp. 47-49.

6,551 STIGAND, C. H. A caterpillar with a portable house. SUDAN NOTES 2 (1919), pp. 142-143.

6,552 STUBBS, J. M. Fresh water fisheries in the northern Bahr el Ghazal waters. SUDAN NOTES 30 (1949), pp. 245-251.

6,553 THESIGER, W. P. Galloping lion. SUDAN NOTES 22 (1939), pp. 155-157.

6,554 THORNTON, I. W. B. Notes on the ecology of the Acacia Bagworm in the environs of Khartoum. SUDAN NOTES 38 (1957), pp. 147-150.

6,555 TITHERINGTON, G. W. Sudan bees. SUDAN NOTES 22 (1939), pp. 145-148.

6,556 TOTHILL, J. D. A collector's notes on the large land snails of the Anglo-Egyptian Sudan. SUDAN NOTES 29 (1948), pp. 189-205.

6,557 TOTHILL, J. D. The fossil-bearing clay at Erkowit. SUDAN NOTES 27 (1946), pp. 229-232.

6,558 TOTHILL, J. D. The origin of the Gezira soil. SUDAN NOTES 30 (1949), supplement, pp. 6-7.

6,559 TOTHILL, J. D. The origin of the Sudan Gezira clay plain. SUDAN NOTES 27 (1946), pp. 153-184.

6,560 VAN DEN PLAS, V. H. Note sur des Chenilles de Psychidae. SUDAN NOTES 3 (1920), pp. 79-81.

6,561 WHALLEY, R. C. R. Southern Sudan game and its habitat. SUDAN NOTES 15 (1932), pp. 261-267.

6,562 WILSON, C. E. Birds causing crop damage in the Sudan. SUDAN NOTES 29 (1948), pp. 161-172.

6,563 WILSON, C. E. Butterflies of the Northern and Central Sudan. SUDAN NOTES 30 (1949), pp. 222-244.

6,564 WILSON, C. E. Butterflies of the Southern Sudan. SUDAN NOTES 34 (1953), pp. 73-103.

6,565 WILSON, C. E. The Sudan Dioch in grain-growing areas. SUDAN NOTES 28 (1947), pp. 151-156.

6,566 WOODMAN, H. M. More rare birds of the southern Bahr el Ghazal. SUDAN NOTES 21 (1938), pp. 315-324.

6,567 WOODMAN, H. M. Rare birds of the Zande district. SUDAN NOTES 19 (1936), pp. 184-188.

6,568 The Khartoum Nursing College. AFR. WOMEN 3 (1960), pp. 87-88.

6,569 Mole rats in the Southern Sudan. SUDAN NOTES 26 (1945), p. 337.

6,570 A note on the range and nesting habits of the Spanish sparrow. SUDAN NOTES 5 (1922), pp. 101-103.

See also 4162.

Sociology

6,571 ARBER, H. B. The Baramka. SUDAN NOTES 23 (1940), pp. 139-150.

6,572 ARTHUR, A. J. V. Slum clearance in Khartoum. J. AFR. ADM. 6 (1954), pp. 73-80.

6,573 AUDAS, R. S. Oryx hunting in Northern Darfur. SUDAN NOTES 2 (1919), pp. 20-23.

6,574 B. Census superstitions. SUDAN NOTES 3 (1920), pp. 137-138.

6,575 BLOSS, J. F. E. The Sudanese angler. SUDAN NOTES 26 (1945), pp. 257-281.

6,576 BOND, W. R. G. "Karāma." SUDAN NOTES 2 (1919), pp. 276-284.

6,577 BRAUSCH, G. Change and continuity in the Gezira region of the Sudan. INT. SOC. SC. BULL. 16 (1964), pp. 341-356.

6,578 CATFORD, J. R. Katiri cultivation in the Moru district of Equatoria. SUDAN NOTES 32 (1951), pp. 106-112.

6,579 CORKILL, N. L. Cretan parallels in the Nuba Mountains. SUDAN NOTES 26 (1945), pp. 167-170.

6,580 CORKILL, N. L. Weight equivalent of Sudan foods sold by measures of capacity. SUDAN NOTES 29 (1948), pp. 126-127.

6,581 CRAWFORD, O. G. S. Tagia Umm Gerein. SUDAN NOTES 26 (1945), pp. 333-334.

6,582 CROWFOOT, J. W. Beliefs about the Mansions of the Moon. SUDAN NOTES 3 (1920), pp. 271-279.

6,583 CROWFOOT, J. W. A local Nile gauge. SUDAN NOTES 1 (1918), pp. 295-296.

6,584 CROWFOOT, J. W. Wedding customs in the Northern Sudan. SUDAN NOTES 5 (1922), pp. 1-28.

6,585 CULWICK, G. M. Some problems of social survey in the Sudan. SUDAN NOTES 35, part 1 (1954), pp. 110-131.

6,586 D., R. Id el Faig. SUDAN NOTES 2 (1919), p. 73.

6,587 FARRELL, H. B. McD. Dearth of children among the Azande: preliminary report. SUDAN NOTES AND RECORDS 35, part 1 (1954), pp. 7-21.

6,588 FAWZI, S. EL D. Joint consultation in Sudan industry: a critical analysis of the attempt to form Works committees in the Sudan. SUDAN NOTES AND RECORDS 35, part 2 (1954, pp. 32-49.

6,589 FAWZI, S. EL D. Social aspects of urban housing in the Northern Sudan. SUDAN NOTES AND RECORDS 35, part 1 (1954), pp. 91-109.

6,590 HALE, S. The nature of the social, political, and religious changes among urban women: Northern Sudan. PROC. 3RD. GRAD. ACAD. UCLA, 1965, pp. 127-140.

6,591 HARVIE, C. H. The proposed sampling census in the Sudan. SUDAN NOTES 32 (1951), pp. 294-307.

6,592 HAYCOCK, B. G. The kingship of Cush in the Sudan. COMP. STUD. SOC. HIST. 7 (1964-1965), pp. 461-480.

6,593 HENIN, R. A. Economic development and internal migration in the Sudan. SUDAN NOTES 44 (1963), pp. 100-119.

6,594 HENIN, R. A. The future population size of Khartoum, Khartoum North, Omdurman and Port Sudan. SUDAN NOTES 42 (1961), pp. 85-90.

6,595 HILLARD, R. J. Welfare and development. SUDAN NOTES 30 (1949), supplement, pp. 15-16.

6,596 KENRICK, J. W. The need for slum clearance in Omdurman. SUDAN NOTES 34 (1953), pp. 281-285.

6,597 KROTKI, K. J. A correction to infant mortality. SUDAN NOTES 42 (1961), pp. 53-84.

6,598 LYALL, C. E. Rights, dues and customs prevailing among Arab tribes in the White Nile Province. SUDAN NOTES 4 (1921), pp. 199-203.

6,599 MacGAFFEY, W. The history of Negro migrations in the Northern Sudan. SOUTHWESTERN J. ANTHR. 17 (1961), pp. 178-197.

6,600 McLOUGHLIN, F. M. The Gash-Tokar economic region: some aspects of its labour force and income. SUDAN NOTES 46 (1965), pp. 67-83.

6,601 McLOUGHLIN, F. M. The Sudan's three towns: a demographic and economic profile of an African urban complex. ECON. DEVELOPMENT AND CULTURAL CHANGE 12 (1963-1964), pp. 70-83, 158-172, 286-304.

6,602 MacMICHAEL, H. A. Nubian elements in Darfur. SUDAN NOTES 1 (1918), pp. 30-48.

6,603 MacMICHAEL, H. A. Sudan Arabs in Nigeria. SUDAN NOTES 6 (1923), pp. 109-110.

6,604 MATTHEW, J. G. Land customs and tenure in Singa District. SUDAN NOTES 4 (1921), pp. 1-19.

6,605 NEWBOLD, D. The white Nuba of Jebel Haraza, and white races of North Africa [with a note by R. G. Archibald]. SUDAN NOTES 7 (1924), part 2, pp. 29-47.

6,606 REHFISCH, F. An unrecorded population count of Omdurman. SUDAN NOTES 46 (1965), pp. 33-39.

6,607 SANDISON, P. J. Problems of low-cost housing in the Sudan. SUDAN NOTES AND RECORDS 35, part 1 (1954), pp. 75-90.

6,608 SHERBINI, A. A. EL. The demand for soft drinks in the Sudan: a case study. SUDAN NOTES 42 (1961), pp. 102-117.

6,609 TRACEY, C. B. Merissa. SUDAN NOTES 8 (1925), pp. 212-214.

6,610 VIELROSE, E. Birth rates in Sudan. AFR. BULL. 1 (1964), pp. 95-104.

6,611 W., C. A. Kordofan [an incident]. SUDAN NOTES 5 (1922), p. 53.

6,612 W., C. A. Nubian elements in Darfur. SUDAN NOTES 1 (1918), pp. 293-295.

6,613 W., R. S. The use of mirrors. SUDAN NOTES 3 (1920), p. 81.

6,614 WYLD, J. W. The Zande scheme. SUDAN NOTES 30 (1949), pp. 47-57.

6,615 New Sudanese women's organisation. AFR. WOMEN 5 (1963), p. 29.

LIBYA

General

6,616 CONTINI, F. Storia delle istituzioni Scolastiche della Libia. LIBIA 1, no. 3 (1953), pp. 7-102.

6,617 EVANS-PRITCHARD, E. E. A select bibliography of writings on Cyrenaica. AFR. STUD. 4 (1945), pp. 146-150; 5 (1946), pp. 189-194; 8 (1949), pp. 62-65.

See also 6637.

Agriculture

6,618 ZINEVRAKIS, E. Gebelia. AFRICA (Rome) 10 (1955), pp. 368-369.

Art. Archaeology

6,619 ARKELL, A. J. The petroglyphs of Wadi Zirmei in North-Eastern Tibesti. PROC. PAN-AFR. CONGR. PRE-HIST. 4, no. iii (1962), pp. 391-393.

6,620 BONO, F. Architettura popolare della Libia. LIBIA 3, no. 1 (1955), pp. 63-71.

6,621 BONO, F. La casa araba della Libia. AFRICA (Rome) 15 (1960), pp. 231-233.

6,622 BREUIL, H. and PAQUES, V. Gravures rupestres préhistoriques du Fezzan. J. SOC. AFR. 28 (1958), pp. 25-32.

6,623 CERBELLA, G. Canti di marinai tripolini. LIBIA 2, no. 3 (1954), pp. 21-24.

6,624 CORO, F. Gadames Archeologica. Storia degli studi delle esplorazioni e dei risultati su alcuni fra i più tipici antichi monumenti dell' Oasi famosa. LIBIA 4, nos. 3-4 (1956), pp. 3-26.

6,625 CORO, F. La prima missione libica di ricerca della preistoria del Sud tripolitano. AFRICA (Rome) 18 (1963), pp. 293-298.

6,626 CORO, F. La storia dell' artigianato libico attraverso i tempi e le dominazioni. LIBIA 1, no. 1 (1953), pp. 113-118.

6,627 CORSO, R. I tuaregh della conca di Gat e le loro caratteristiche costumanze. LIBIA 1, no. 1 (1953), pp. 91-102.

6,628 GAUDIO, A. Missione etno-linguistica all' Oasi di Siwa. LIBIA 1, no. 3 (1953), pp. 107-120.

6,629 MORAINI, O. Impressioni libiche. LIBIA 3, no. 1 (1955), pp. 95-99.

6,630 PAQUES, V. Le bélier cosmique: son rôle dans les structures humaines et territoriales du Fezzan. J. SOC. AFR. 26 (1956), pp. 211-253.

6,631 PARADISI, U. I recenti ritrovamenti d'arte preistorica nel margine orientale della Hamada el-Hamra (Sud Tripòlino). LIBIA 3, no. 1 (1955), pp. 55-62.

6,632 RHOTERT, H. Neue Felsbilderfunde im Wadi Tarhoscht (Südwest-Libyen). FESTSCHRIFT FUR A. E. JENSEN, 1964, pp. 501-512.

6,633 VERGARA-CAFFARELLI, E. Le antichità della Tripolitania negli ultimi due anni. LIBIA 2, no. 1 (1954), pp. 77-81.

6,634 VERGARA-CAFFARELLI, E. Prigioni sotterranee scoperte nel Castello di Tripoli. LIBIA 3, no. 2 (1955), pp. 53-55.

6,635 VERGARA-CAFFARELLI, E. Due nuove colonne miliarie scoperte presso Leptis. LIBIA 4, nos. 3-4 (1956), pp. 41-44.

See also 5177, 5202.

Biography

6,636 FILESI, T. Francesco Bono. AFRICA (Rome) 17 (1962), pp. 24-26.

6,637 La morte di Plinio Maggi pioniere dell'arte Tipografica in Libia. LIBIA 3, no. 4 (1955), pp. 67-68.

6,638 ZINEVRAKIS, E. Giuseppe de' Micheli e la valorizzazione agricola della Libia. AFRICA (Rome) 10 (1955), p. 82.

6,639 ZINEVRAKIS, E. Carlo Petrocchi. AFRICA (Rome) 11 (1956), p. 25.

6,640 CIASCA, R. Ettore Rossi. AFRICA (Rome) 10 (1955), p. 300.

Economics

6,641 AMIRANTE, S. Economica della Libia e sua politica finanziaria. AFRICA (ROME) 11 (1956), pp. 156-157.

6,642 BLOWERS, G. A. and McLEOD, A. N. Currency unification in Libya. I.M.F. STAFF PAPERS 2 (1951-1952), pp. 439-467.

6,643 DEIS, E. Gli scambi italo-libici. AFRICA (Rome) 10 (1955), pp. 24-25.

6,644 GIULIANELLI, A. Il commercio estero libico e gli scambi con l'Italia. AFRICA (Rome) 11 (1956), pp. 157-159.

6,645 MUELLER-MINERVO, O. La publicità in Libia. Aspetti del Paese per l'uomo d'Affari. AFRICA (Rome) 15 (1960), pp. 33-35.

6,646 SCAGLIONE, F. A. L'istituzione di una Cassa di Risparmio in Libia. AFRICA (Rome) 12 (1957), pp. 82-84.

6,647 VALLE, C. DELLA. L'industria in Libia tra il 1911 e il 1940. LIBIA 3, no. 3 (1955), pp. 61-66?; 3, no. 4 (1955), pp. 45-66?

6,648 L'oeuvre de la France au Fezzan. ZAIRE 5 (1951), pp. 751-753.

See also 12944.

Education

6,649 UNESCO. Women's education centre in the Fezzan. AFR. WOMEN 3 (1958-1960), p. 38.

Geography. Topography. Travel

6,650 BAGNOLD, R. A. The Libyan desert. J. AFR. SOC. 35 (1936), pp. 294-305.

6,651 CERBELLA, G. Mare e marinai in Libia. LIBIA 3, no. 1 (1955), pp. 3-54; 3, no. 2 (1955), pp. 3-34.

6,652 CLARKE, J. I. Geographical studies of Libya. CT 7 (1959), pp. 475-480.

6,653 DAINELLI, G. The Italian colonies. GEOG. REV. 19 (1929), pp. 404-419.

6,654 DESPOIS, J. Types of native life in Tripolitania. GEOG. REV. 35 (1945), pp. 352-367.

6,655 FANTOLI, A. Un'isola fra due Continenti ed un Santuario fra due popoli. LIBIA 3, no. 4 (1955), pp. 25-43.

6,656 KOROSTOVETZ, V. DE. Snapshots in Tripolitania. CONTEMP. REV. 172 (1947), pp. 213-217.

6,657 LEONE, G. Origin and reclamation of the dunes in Tripolitania. DESERT RESEARCH, 1953, pp. 401-403.

6,658 LEWICKI, T. A propos du nom de l'Oasis de Koufra chez les géographes arabes du XIe et du XIIe siecle. J. AFR. HIST. 6 (1965), pp. 295-306.

6,659 STANLEY, C. V. B. The oasis of Siwa. J. AFR. SOC. 11 (1912), pp. 290-324.

6,660 STECHMAN, S. Map of population distribution in Libya. AFR. BULL. 3 (1965), pp. 49-56.

6,661 ZIEGERT, H. Climatic changes and palaeolithic industries in East Fezzan, Libya. CURRENT ANTHR. 6 (1965), pp. 104-105.

See also 5246.

Government. Politics. Administration

6,662 BONFIGLIO, E. Libia. AFRICA (Rome) 10 (1955), pp. 203-204.

6,663 CUMMING, D. C. British stewardship of the Italian colonies: an account rendered. INTERNAT. AFFAIRS 29 (1953), pp. 11-21.

6,664 ERMONT, L. Où en est la Libye? AFR. ET ASIE 2, no. 1 (1949), pp. 42-45.

6,665 KIRKBRIDE, A. "Libya—which way facing?" AFR. AFFAIRS 56 (1957), pp. 49-55.

6,666 M., Q. Gli accordi italo libici. AFRICA (Rome) 11 (1956), pp. 11-12.

6,667 OWEN, R. Libyan note-book. AFR. SOUTH 5, no. 3 (1961), pp. 100-106.

6,668 QUINTANO RIPOLES, A. Libia, nuevo Estado africano. CUAD. EST. AFR. 14 (1951), pp. 27-37.

6,669 R., P. Nouvelles étapes vers l'indépendance libyenne. AFR. ET ASIE 14 (1951), pp. 12-18.

6,670 R., P. Perspectives de l'indépendance libyenne. AFR. ET ASIE 11 (1950), pp. 51-59.

6,671 RUBIO GARCIA, L. Libia y los intereses franceses el Fezzán. CUAD. EST. AFR. 17 (1952), pp. 19-36.

6,672 SILLERY, A. Libyan aspirations. AFR. AFFAIRS 46 (1947), pp. 13-21.

6,673 Proclamation de l'indépendance de la Libye. ZAIRE 6 (1952), pp. 186-187.

See also 6789, 6790.

History

6,674 BERGNA, P. C. I Caramànli. LIBIA 1, no. 2 (1953), pp. 5-59.

6,675 BONO, S. Bolognesi schiavi a Tropoli nei sec. XVII e XVIII. LIBIA 2, no. 3 (1954), pp. 25-37.

6,676 BONO, S. Difficoltà e speranze per lo Stato Libico nel giudizio del primo rappresentante americano a Tripoli. AFRICA (Rome) 13 (1958), pp. 19-20.

6,677 BONO, S. Fonti inedite di storia della Tripolitania. LIBIA 1, no. 2 (1953), pp. 117-121.

6,678 CAPUTO, G. Un' epigrafe cufica del 326 Eg. (937-8 d.C.) rinvenuta in Tripolitania. LIBIA 1, no. 4 (1953), pp. 45-51.

6,679 CERBELLA, G. I colori della bandiera libica nella storia e nella letteratura arabo-musulmana. LIBIA 2, no. 1 (1954), pp. 45-76.

6,680 CERBELLA, G. Interpretazione storico-etnologica d'un rito islamo-cristiano. LIBIA 1, no. 2 (1953), pp. 61-108.

6,681 DUBOIS, J. La colonizzazione italiana in Libia. AFRICA (Rome) 10 (1955), pp. 287-289.

6,682 EVANS-PRITCHARD, E. E. Italy and the Bedouin in Cyrenaica. AFR. AFFAIRS 45 (1946), pp. 12-21.

6,683 EVANS-PRITCHARD, E. E. Italy and the Sanusiya order in Cyrenaica. BULL. SOAS 11 (1943-1946), pp. 843-853.

6,684 PATRIARCA, G. Fac-simili di iscrizioni di Creta e Cirene. LIBIA 1, no. 3 (1953), pp. 103-106.

6,685 PHILIPPS, T. Fourth shore—Italy's mass colonisation of Libya by Martin Moore. J. AFR. SOC. 39 (1940), pp. 129-133.

6,686 ROSSI, E. Le epigrafi musulmane del Museo di Tripoli. LIBIA 1, no. 1 (1953), pp. 103-107.

6,687 ROSSI, E. Storia della Libia dalla conquista araba al 1911. LIBIA 2, no. 1 (1954), pp. 3-43.

6,688 TACCONI, S. Italia en Africa. CUAD. EST. AFR. 25 (1954), pp. 53-74.

6,689 VADALA, R. Essais sur l'histoire des Karamanlis pachas de Tripolitaine de 1714 a 1835. RHCF 7, no. 1 (1919), pp. 177-288.

6,690 VERDAT, M. La réoccupation de la Tripolitaine par les Italiens. RHCF 25 (1932), pp. 113-152.

6,691 WINGATE, Sir R. Libya in the last war. The Talbot mission and the agreements of 1917 [an extract from a memoir of M. G. Talbot]. J. AFR. SOC. 40 (1941), pp. 128-131.

See also 16074.

Language. Literature

6,692 CERBELLA, G. Gûma, poeta e patriota libico, nella storia e nella leggenda. LIBIA 3, no. 4 (1955), pp. 3-23.

6,693 HAMP, E. P. Zuara Berber personals. BULL. SOAS 22 (1959), pp. 140-141.

6,694 MITCHELL, T. F. Particle-noun complexes in a Berber dialect (Zuara). BULL. SOAS 15 (1953), pp. 375-390.

6,695 MURABET, M. Sull' etimologia storica di Libia. LIBIA 1, no. 1 (1953), pp. 109-112.

See also 6617.

Law

6,696 CHILLEMI, A. La condition juridique des étrangers en Libye. CIVILISATIONS 7 (1957), pp. 327-341; English summary, pp. 341-342.

6,697 GIANTURCO, V. La Corte Suprema Federale del Regno Unito di Libia. LIBIA 2, no. 2 (1954), pp. 15-50.

Religion

6,698 BASSET, H. Quelques notes sur l'Ammon libyque. MELANGES RENE BASSET, 1923, pp. 1-30.

6,699 BERGNA, P. C. L'origine della Missione Francescana in Libia. LIBIA 4, nos. 1-2 (1956), pp. 33-39.

6,700 EVANS-PRITCHARD, E. E. The distribution of Sanusi lodges. AFRICA 15 (1945), pp. 183-187.

6,701 EVANS-PRITCHARD, E. E. The Sanusi of Cyrenaica. AFRICA 15 (1945), pp. 61-79.

6,702 ROVERE, P. F. Il Cristianesimo in Cirenaica. LIBIA 3, no. 2 (1955), pp. 43-52.

Science

6,703 PANETTA, E. Medicina empirica e farmacologia della Libia. LIBIA 2, no. 3 (1954), pp. 47-55; 3, no. 1 (1955), pp. 77-94.

Sociology

6,704 AGOSTINI, E. DE. Sulle popolazioni della Libia. LIBIA 2, no. 2 (1954), pp. 3-15.

6,705 CERBELLA, G. Caratteristiche della società musulmana Libica. LIBIA 1, no. 1 (1953), pp. 7-81.

6,706 CERBELLA, G. Il tè nella vita, nella poesia e nelle tradizioni del popolo libico. LIBIA 1, no. 4 (1953), pp. 53-62; 2, no. 1 (1954), pp. 83-94; 2, no. 2 (1954), pp. 67-72; 2, no. 3 (1954), pp. 57-76.

6,707 LOLLINI, C. Del matrimonio precoce in Libia. LIBIA 3, no. 1 (1955), pp. 73-75.

See also 6957.

TUNISIA

General

6,708 PIGNON, J. L'oeuvre de Pierre Grandchamp. CT 13 (1965), pp. 13-25.

6,709 Bibliographie des oeuvres de Pierre Grandchamp. CT 13 (1965), pp. 27-35.

6,710 Tunis [a deuxième conférence des peuples africains du 25 au 30 janvier 1960]. PRESENCE AFR. N.S. 30 (1960), p. 105.

Agriculture

6,711 ATTIA, H. Modernisation agricole et structures sociales. Exemple des oasis du Djerid. REV. TUN. SC. SOC. 2 (1965), pp. 59-93.

6,712 ATTYA, H. L'organisation de l'Oasis. CT 5 (1957), pp. 39-43.

6,713 AVENTUR, J. La politique agricole tunisienne depuis l'independance. ANNALES AFR., 1962, pp. 305-314.

6,714 BARDIN, P. Le cadastre de la haute vallée de la Madjerda. CT 1 (1953), pp. 261-285.

6,715 BARDIN, P. Les groupements coopératifs agricoles dans la haute vallée de la Medjerda (Tunisie). AFR. ET ASIE 18 (1952), pp. 31-44.

6,716 BERNIS, G. D. DE. Problèmes économiques concernant l'utilisation de l'eau en périmètre irrigué. CT 5 (1957), pp. 97-111.

6,717 BUGEAT, L. Les irrigations dans le Centre de la Tunisie. CT 5 (1957), pp. 63-74.

6,718 BUTHAUD, E. Introduction à l'étude des problèmes humains de l'immatriculation foncière en Tunisie. CT 1 (1953), pp. 229-260.

6,719 CHAUVIN, P. L'irrigation à El-Alem par les eaux de l'Oued Nebana. CT 5 (1957), pp. 75-78.

6,720 FAIVRE-DUPAIGRE, J. P. L'irrigation traditionnelle dans l'Oasis de Gabès. CT 5 (1957), pp. 23-37.

6,721 GODARD, C. Le Djebbad du Fezzan. CT 5 (1957), pp. 45-55.

6,722 PAUPHILET, D. La disposition des terres collectives chez les Ouled Chehida. CT 1 (1953), pp. 207-228.

6,723 PONCET, J. Comment la mise en valeur de la Basse-Medjerda et l'industrialisation agricole pourraient-elles être rentables? CT 7 (1959), pp. 175-180.

6,724 PROST, G. Utilisation de la terre et production dans le Sud tunisien: Matmata et Ouderna. CT 2 (1954), pp. 28-66.

6,725 SURIN, R. Une nouvelle orientation de la politique de mise en valeur: la basse-vallée de la Madjerda. CT 1 (1953), pp. 286-319.

6,726 VALDEYRON, G. A propos de l'économie agricole de la Tunisie. CT 2 (1954), pp. 203-212.

6,727 ZGHAL, A. Modernisation de l'agriculture et population semi-nomade. REV. TUN. SC. SOC. 2 (1965), pp. 31-49.

Anthropology

6,728 ADJMIA, M. B. Structure des villages et origine de leur population dans le Sahel septentrional. CT 12, nos. 47-48 (1964), pp. 101-108.

6,729 BALFET, H. Poterie artisanale en Tunisie. CT 6 (1958), pp. 317-347.

6,730 CORNET, H. Les Juifs de Gafsa. CT 3 (1955), pp. 276-315.

6,731 CUISENIER, J. and ZGHAL, A. Changements culturels en milieu rural tunisien. CT 8, nos. 29-30 (1960), pp. 51-74.

6,732 GINESTOUS, L. and GINESTOUS, P. Le vêtement féminin usuel à Bizerte. CT 7 (1959), pp. 519-535.

6,733 GOBERT, E. G. Les pierres talismaniques (Folklore tunisien). J. SOC. AFR. 16 (1946), pp. 39-47.

6,734 MASSABIE, G. La vannerie de roseau à Chenini de Gabès. CT 6 (1958), pp. 365-371.

6,735 MUHL, J. Moeurs et coutumes d'un village du sud tunisien: El Golaa. CT 2 (1954), pp. 67-91.

6,736 PROST, G. L'emigration chez les Matmata et les Ouderna (Sud Tunisien). CT 3 (1955), pp. 316-325.

6,737 PROST, G. Habitat et habitation chez les Ouderna et les Matmata. CT 2 (1954), pp. 239-253.

6,738 RONDOT, P. Les conseils de fraction (mîâd) dans quelques tribus de la Tunisie du Nord (Nefza, Amdûn, Ustâta). CT 3 (1955), pp. 267-275.

6,739 SETHOM, H. Les artisans-potiers de Moknine. REV. TUN. SC. SOC. 1 (1964), pp. 53-70.

Art. Archaeology

6,740 BALIL, A. Notas iconograficos sobre algunos mosaicos de Sussa. CT 12, nos. 45-46 (1964), pp. 7-10.

6,741 CINTAS, P. A propos de trois vases du Musée de Sousse. CT 8, no. 31 (1960), pp. 7-9.

6,742 COUSTILLAC, L. Note sur la teinture végétale dans le Sud Tunisien. CT 6 (1958), pp. 353-363.

6,743 GIAMPIETRO, M. Il problema idrico dell' antica Tunisia. AFRICA (Rome) 16 (1961), pp. 289-292.

6,744 GOBERT, E. G. Bibliographie critique de la préhistoire Tunisienne. CT 11, nos. 41-42 (1963), pp. 37-77.

6,745 GOBERT, E. G. Notions générales acquises sur la préhistoire de la Tunisie. PROC. PAN-AFR. CONGR. PRE-HIST. 2 (1952), pp. 221-239.

6,746 GOBERT, E. G. and HOWE, B. L'Ibéro-maurusien de l'Oued El Akarit (Tunisie). PROC. PAN-AFR. CONGR. PRE-HIST. 2 (1952), pp. 575-596.

6,747 GRAIRI, A. Carrières et taille de pierres à Téboulba. CT 6 (1958), pp. 349-352.

6,748 KREA, H. Abdallah Benanteur, peintre maghrébin, artiste de l'universel. PRESENCE AFR. N.S. 56 (1965), pp. 150-151.

6,749 LEZINE, A. Résistance à l'hellenisme de l'architecture religieuse de Carthage. CT 7 (1959), pp. 247-261.

6,750 RENARD, M. L'Asarôtos oikos d'El-Djem. CT 12, nos. 45-46 (1964), pp. 35-38.

6,751 REVAULT, J. Broderies tunisiennes. CT 8, nos. 29-30 (1960), pp. 137-157.

6,752 REVAULT, J. Notes sur les instruments traditionnels de musique populaire dans le Sud tunisien. CONG. INT. SC. ANTH. ET ETHN. 6, no. ii (1960), pp. 113-120.

6,753 REVAULT, J. Tapis tunisiens à haute laine et à poil ras. CT 6 (1958), pp. 119-138.

6,754 SALOMONSON, J. W. La mosaïque du banquet costumé d'El Djem. CT 8, no. 31 (1960), pp. 57-61.

6,755 STERN, H. L'image du mois d'octobre sur une mosaique d'El-Djem. CT 12, nos. 45-46 (1964), pp. 21-32.

Biography

6,756 Nicolas Béranger et sa correspondance. CT 13 (1965), pp. 85-117.

6,757 V., F. León Bercher, 1889-1955. CT 3 (1955), pp. 7-13.

6,758 BILAINKIN, G. President Bourguiba. CONTEMP. REV. 202 (1962), pp. 86-90.

6,759 FREZOULS, E. Christian Courtois et son oeuvre. CT 6 (1958), pp. 373-386.

6,760 MARTEL, A. Note autobiographique. Les origines d'un viceconsul de France à Sfax, A. d'Espina (1819-1867). CT 7 (1959), pp. 511-515.

6,761 DESPOIS, J. Pierre Grandchamp 1875-1964. CT 13 (1965), pp. 9-11.

6,762 PIGNON, J. Osta Moratto turcho genovese, Dey de Tunis (1637-1640). CT 3 (1955), pp. 331-362.

Economics

6,763 AOUANI, M. EL. Structure agraire dans un village côtier du nord-est de la Tunisie: Galaat El Andleuss. REV. TUN. SC. SOC. 3 (1965), pp. 71-108.

6,764 BARRE, R. La conjoncture economique. REV. TUN. DROIT 1 (1953), pp. 27-32, 141-147, 257-266; 2 (1954), pp. 40-46, 150-156.

6,765 BERNIS, G. D. DE. Economie tunisienne et expérience chinoise. CT 7 (1959), pp. 187-214.

6,766 BERNIS, G. D. DE. La Tunisie et la zone franc. CT 7 (1959), pp. 5-122.

6,767 BRUGNES-ROMIEU, M. P. Les investissements en Tunisie de 1955 à 1961. REV. TUN. SC. SOC. 3 (1965), pp. 159-166.

6,768 CUISENIER, J. Le sous-développement économique dans un groupement rural: le Djebel Lansarine. CT 6 (1958), pp. 219-265.

6,769 DEBERNARDI. L. Le premier chemin de fer tunisien le T.G.M. (1870-1898). REV. FRANC. HIST. OUTRE-MER 50 (1963), pp. 197-226.

6,770 DUCHAC, R. La presse tunisienne et la bombe. CT 8, no. 32 (1960), pp. 99-127.

6,771 HERBERT, M. Le soutien financier de la France à la Tunisie. AFR. ET ASIE 27 (1954), pp. 49-55.

6,772 INTRONA, S. L'Italia della produzione a Tunisi. AFRICA (Rome) 10 (1955), pp. 364-365.

6,773 MUELLER-MINERVO, O. Luci ed ombre dell' economia tunisina. AFRICA (Rome) 17 (1962), pp. 143-145.

6,774 SEBAG, P. L'industrialisation de la Tunisie. Une experience-pilote dans l'industrie de la chaussure. CT 7 (1959), pp. 147-173.

6,775 YOUNES, Y. Note sur le calcul économique. REV. TUN. SC. SOC. 1 (1964), pp. 27-52.

6,776 Colloque international sur les niveaux de vie en Tunisie. CIVILISATIONS 5 (1955), pp. 595-598.

Education

6,777 CAMILLERI, C. Les représentations éducatives dans des groupes de jeunes parents de Tunis. REV. TUN. SC. SOC. 3 (1965), pp. 7-44.

6,778 MONTETY, H. DE. Révolution moderniste à l'Université ez Zitouna. AFR. ET ASIE 13 (1951), pp. 24-35.

Geography

6,779 ABDUL WAHAB, H. H. Les steppes Tunisiennes (région de Gammouda) pendant le Moyen-Age. CT 2 (1954), pp. 5-16.

6,780 DOUIB, A. La région de Zarzis: l'occupation du sol avant 1880. CT 6 (1958), pp. 311-316.

6,781 MARTEL, A. Préoccupations sahariennes à Tunis (1911). CT 7 (1959), pp. 517-518.

6,782 MARTHELOT, P. Problèmes de la steppe tunisienne. CT 2 (1954), pp. 17-27.

6,783 MARTHELOT, P. Les Tunisiens. Réflexions sur quelques disparités géographiques et sociologiques. CT 7 (1959), pp.123-140.

6,784 PISSALOUX, R. Les cartes d'occupation du sol en Tunisie. CT 2 (1954), pp. 265-306.

6,785 RONDEAU, A. Climat et érosion. CT 11, nos. 41-42 (1963), pp. 95-102.

6,786 TAIEB, J. Une banlieue de Tunis l'Ariana. CT 8, no. 32 (1960), pp. 33-76.

Government

6,787 BELING, W. A. W.F.T.U. and decolonisation: a Tunisian case study. J. MOD. AFR. STUD. 2 (1964), pp. 551-564.

6,788 BEN BARKA, EL MEHDI. The unity of the Maghreb. AFR. SOUTH 5, no. 2 (1961), pp. 96-101.

6,789 BRAILSFORD, H. N. Impressions of Tunis and Libya. INTERNAT. AFFAIRS 18 (1939), pp. 361-379.

6,790 CORO, F. Tunisia e Tripolitania attraverso i secoli nelle loro relazioni politiche ed economiche. AFRICA (Rome) 18 (1963), pp. 89-91.

6,791 GIL BENUMEYA, R. Túnez después de la declaración de independencia. CUAD. AFR. OR. 34 (1956), pp. 21-30.

6,792 GILMER, J. H. The French Union in 1954-55. 2. North Africa and Indo-China. CIVILISATIONS 6 (1956), pp. 111-121.

6,793 GILMER, J. H. French Union, less French West Africa. CIVILISATIONS 5 (1955), pp. 114-126.

6,794 GRAY, A. Bold French move [Tunisia to be granted autonomy]. AFR. AFFAIRS 54 (1955), p. 165.

6,795 LENOIR, G. Signification du précédent tunisien. AFR. ET ASIE 33 (1956), pp. 23-25.

6,796 MARTIN DE LA ESCALERA, C. Estados Unidos, su anticolonialismo y Túnez. CUAD. EST. AFR. 19 (1952), pp. 43-55.

6,797 MARTIN DE LA ESCALERA, C. Reforms en Túnez. CUAD. EST. AFR. 12 (1950), pp. 57-65.

6,798 WIAN, G. Realta' economica tunisina e collaborazione dell' Italia. AFRICA (Rome) 10 (1955), pp. 270-272.

6,799 Gli accordi franco-tunisini. AFRICA (Rome) 10 (1955), p. 150.

6,800 Tunisia. CIVILISATIONS 3 (1953), pp. 125-128.

See also 7271.

History

6,801 BONO, S. L'incursione dei corsari tunisini a Carloforte e il riscatto degli schiavi carolini. AFRICA (Rome) 15 (1960), pp. 234-238.

6,802 BRIEY, P. DE. La bataille de Bizerte dans le cadre nord africain. CIVILISATIONS 11 (1961), pp. 429-439; English summary, pp. 440-443.

6,803 CORO, F. Lettere inedite di Garibaldi sull' occupazione di Tunisi. AFRICA (Rome) 16 (1961), pp. 178-180.

6,804 COUSINS, W. M. Tunis in transition. CONTEMP. REV. 163 (1943), pp. 336-342.

6,805 DAVIES, G. Greek slaves at Tunis in 1823. ENG. HIST. REV. 34 (1919), pp. 84-89.

6,806 DEMONTES, V. Un essai de Protectorat tunisien à Oran (9 février-22 août 1831). RHCF 15 (1923), pp. 251-288.

6,807 DENIZET, J. L'histoire navale de la Tunisie de 1815 à 1888 aux Archives de la Marine [Nationale]. CT 4 (1956), pp. 409-412.

6,808 DESPOIS, J. Le Djebel Ousselat, les Ousseltiya et les Kooub. CT 7 (1959), pp. 407-427.

6,809 DUVAL, N. Observations sur l'urbanisme tardif de Sufetula (Tunisie). CT 12, nos. 45-46 (1964), pp. 87-103.

6,810 EMERIT, M. L'essai d'une marine marchande barbaresque au XVIIIe siècle. CT 3 (1955), pp. 363-370.

6,811 EMERIT, M. Au temps de saint Vincent de Paul. La Mission de Savary de Brèves en Afrique du Nord (1606). REV. FRANC. HIST. OUTRE-MER 52 (1965), pp. 297-314.

6,812 EMERIT, M. Trois notes d'histoire tunisienne. CT 3 (1955), pp. 466-473.

6,813 FENDRI, M. Inventaire préliminaire du trésor et présentation des différentes types de monnaies. CT 12, nos. 45-46 (1964), pp. 59-67.

6,814 FENDRI, M. Les thermes des mois à Thina. CT 12, nos. 45-46 (1964), pp. 47-57.

6,815 FOUCHER, L. Les galères de Themetra. CT 4 (1956), pp. 271-277.

6,816 G., P. Documents concernant la course dans la Régence de Tunis de 1764 à 1769 et de 1783 à 1843. CT 5 (1957), pp. 269-340.

6,817 GANIAGE, J. Les Européens en Tunisie au milieu du XIXe siècle (1840-1870). CT 3 (1955), pp. 388-421.

6,818 GHALLOUSSI, B. Archives du Sahel au XIXe siècle. CT 8, no. 31 (1960), pp. 97-108.

6,819 HUGON, H. Un document numismatique du voyage d'Ahmed Bey a Paris (1846). RHCF 10, no. 2 (1922), pp. 107-114.

6,820 JOHNSTON, A. French rule in Tunis. J. AFR. SOC. 4 (1905), pp. 357-365.

6,821 LATHAM, J. D. Towards a study of Andalusian immigration and its place in Tunisian history. CT 5 (1957), pp. 203-249.

6,822 LEGENDRE, M. Note sur la cadastration romaine en Tunisie. CT 5 (1957), pp. 135-166.

6,823 LEGLAY, M. Stèles à Saturne d'Aïn Gassa (Tunisie). CT 11, no. 44 (1963), pp. 63-68.

6,824 LE TOURNEAU, R. La révolte d'Abû-Yazîd au Xme siècle. CT 1 (1953), pp. 103-125.

6,825 LEZINE, A. Deux ribât du Sahel Tunisien. CT 4 (1956), pp. 279-288.

6,826 LEZINE, A. Notes sur l'amphithéâtre de Thysdrus. CT 8, no. 31 (1960), pp. 29-50.

6,827 McKAY, D. V. The French in Tunisia. GEOG. REV. 35 (1945), pp. 368-390.

6,828 MAHJOUBI, A. Découvertes archéologiques dans la région de Béja. CT 7 (1959), pp. 481-487.

6,829 MAHJOUBI, A. Nouveau témoignage épigraphique sur la communauté chrétienne de Kairouan au XIe siècle. CT 12, nos. 45-46 (1964), pp. 159-162.

6,830 MANTRAN, R. Documents turcs relatifs à l'armée tunisienne. CT 4 (1956), pp. 359-372.

6,831 MANTRAN, R. L'évolution des relations entre la Tunisie et l'Empire Ottoman du XVIe au XIXe siècle. CT 7 (1959), pp. 319-333.

6,832 MANTRAN, R. Une relation inédite d'un voyage en Tunisie au milieu du 19me siècle. CT 3 (1955), pp. 474-480.

6,833 MANTRAN, R. La titulature des beys de Tunis au XIXe siècle d'après les documents d'archives turcs du Dar-el-Bey (Tunis). CT 5 (1957), pp. 341-348.

6,834 MARSDEN, A. Britain and the Tunis base, 1894-1899. ENG. HIST. REV. 79 (1964), pp. 67-96.

6,835 MARTEL, A. L'armée d'Ahmed Bey d'après un instructeur français. CT 4 (1956), pp. 373-407.

6,836 MARTEL, A. Le commerce maritime du Sud-Tunisien 1885-1910. CT 12, nos. 47-48 (1964), pp. 109-145.

6,837 MARTEL, A. Le Makhzen du Sud Tunisien (1881-1910). CT 8, no. 32 (1960), pp. 7-31; 11, no. 43 (1963), pp. 63-70.

6,838 MARTEL, A. Sources inédites de l'histoire tunisienne. Les papiers Nyssen aux Archives Nationales. CT 5 (1957), pp. 349-380.

6,839 MARTIN DE LA ESCALERA, C. Las Convenciones franco-tunecinas. CUAD. AFR. OR. 31 (1955), pp. 59-66.

6,840 MIDDLETON, W. L. French policy in Tunisia. CONTEMP. REV. 186 (1954), pp. 133-135.

6,841 MONCHICOURT, C. Un autre du Mémoire sur Tunis publié par Chateaubriand. RHCF 16 (1923), pp. 67-104.

6,842 MONCHICOURT, C. Fragmens historiques et statistiques sur la Régence de Tunis, suivis d'un itinéraire dans quelques régions du Sahra par le comte Filippi, Agent et Consul général de S.M. à Tunis. RHCF 17 (1924), pp. 193-236, 381-428, 551-592; 19 (1926), pp. 235-260, 387-422, 537-592.

6,843 MONCHICOURT, C. Notice sur Tunez et biographie du Bach Mamelouk Hassine par Louis Calligaris. RHCF 21 (1928), pp. 525-588.

6,844 PALLOTTINO, M. Les relations entre les Etrusques et Carthage du VIIe au IIIe siècle avant J.-C. Nouvelles données et essai de périodisation. CT 11, no. 44 (1963), pp. 23-29.

6,845 PICARD, G. C. Rubellius Plantus patron de Mactar. CT 11, no. 44 (1963), pp. 69-74.

6,846 PIGNON, J. Aperçu sur les relations entre Malte et la Côte Orientale de la Tunisie au début du XVIIme siècle. CT 12, nos. 47-48 (1964), pp. 59-87.

6,847 PIGNON, J. Dix ans de relations franco-tunisiennes (1606-1616). CT 4 (1956), pp. 199-212.

6,848 PIGNON, J. Un document inédit sur la Tunisie au début du XVIIe siècle. CT 9, nos. 33-35 (1961), pp. 109-219.

6,849 PIGNON, J. La milice des janissaires de Tunis au temps des Deys (1590-1650). CT 4 (1956), pp. 301-326.

6,850 PONCET, J. Un problème d'histoire rurale: le habous Aziza Othmana, au Sahel. CT 8, no. 31 (1960), pp. 137-156.

6,851 PONCET, J. Aux sources de l'histoire nord-africaine: prospérité et décadence ifrikiyennes. CT 9, nos. 33-35 (1961), pp. 221-243.

6,852 PRADEL DE LAMASE, M. DE. La station navale française de Tunis. CT 4 (1956), pp. 351-357.

6,853 RAYMOND, A. Les libéraux anglais et la question tunisienne (1880-1881). CT 3 (1955), pp. 422-465.

6,854 RAYMOND, A. Tunisiens et Maghrébins au Caire au dix-huitième siècle. CT 7 (1959), pp. 335-371.

6,855 RAYMOND, R. Une liste des deys de Tunis de 1590 à 1832. CT 8, no. 32 (1960), pp. 129-136.

6,856 ROMANELLI, P. A proposito della Schola juvenum di Mactaris. CT 12, nos. 45-46 (1964), pp. 11-17.

6,857 RONDOT, P. L'émigration ancienne des Mekna (1880-1890). CT 1 (1953), pp. 18-35.

6,858 SAUMAGNE, C. Du principe iter populo debetur. CT 10 (1962), pp. 429-461.

6,859 SAUMAGNE, C. La Fossa Regia. CT 10 (1962), pp. 407-416.

6,860 SAUMAGNE, C. La manoeuvre du Muthul. CT 10 (1962), pp. 391-405.

6,861 SAUMAGNE, C. La manoeuvre de Zama. CT 10 (1962), pp. 373-390.

6,862 SAUMAGNE, C. Note sur la cadastration de la Colonia Trajana Thamugadi. CT 10 (1962), pp. 509-515.

6,863 SAUMAGNE, C. La paix vandale. CT 10 (1962), pp. 417-425.

6,864 SAUMAGNE, C. Le plan de la colonie Gracchane de Carthage. CT 10 (1962), pp. 473-487.

6,865 SAUMAGNE, C. Le plan de la colonie Julienne de Carthage. CT 10 (1962), pp. 463-471.

6,866 SAUMAGNE, C. Le plan de la colonie Trajane de Timgad. CT 10 (1962), pp. 489-508.

6,867 SAUMAGNE, C. La population rurale de la Region de Musti. CT 10 (1962), pp. 263-293.

6,868 SAUMAGNE, C. Los pretextes juridiques de la IIIe Guerre punique. CT 10 (1962), pp. 301-371.

6,869 SAUMAGNE, C. Les vestiges de la cité latine de Gafsa. CT 10 (1962), pp. 519-531.

6,870 SAYOUS, A. Le commerce européen en Tunisie au moyen-âge et au début de l'ère moderne. RHCF 22 (1929), pp. 225-250.

6,871 SEBAG, P. Une description de Tunis au XIXe siècle. CT 6 (1958), pp. 161-181.

6,872 SEBAG, P. Les Juifs de Tunisie au XIXe siècle d'après J.-J. Benjamin II. CT 7 (1959), pp. 489-510.

6,873 SEBAG, P. Une ville européenne à Tunis au XVIe siècle. CT 9, nos. 33-35 (1961), pp. 97-107.

6,874 SLAMA, B. L'insurrection de 1280-1864 dans le Sahel. CT 8, no. 31 (1960), pp. 109-136.

6,875 SLIM, H. Les facteurs de l'épanouissement économique de Thysarus. CT 8, no. 31 (1960), pp. 51-56.

6,876 SLIM, H. Quelques aspects de la vie économique à Thysdrus avant le second siècle de l'ère chrétienne. CT 12, nos. 45-46 (1964), pp. 155-158.

6,877 SLIM, T. Current events in Tunisia. AFR. AFFAIRS 57 (1958), pp. 120-124.

6,878 TALBI, M. Intérêt des oeuvres juridiques traitant de la guerre pour l'historien des armées médievales ifrikiennes. CT 4 (1956), pp. 289-293.

6,879 VAJDA, G. Problèmes et tâches de l'investigation du passé juif en Tunisie. CT 2 (1954), pp. 309-313.

6,880 VALENSI, L. Le Djebel Ousselat au XVIIIme siècle. CT 12, nos. 47-48 (1964), pp. 89-100.

6,881 VALENSI, L. Les relations commerciales entre la Régence de Tunis et Malte au XVIIIème siècle. CT 11, no. 43 (1963), pp. 71-83.

6,882 VIVIAN, H. The French in Tunisia. CONTEMP. REV. 74 (1898), pp. 563-575.

6,883 ZECCA, G. L'emigrazione italiana in Tunisia. AFRICA (Rome) 18 (1963), pp. 55-62.

6,884 Arbre généalogique de la famille Hassinite, 1705-1944. CT 13 (1965), pp. 132-133.

6,885 Les différends de 1832-1833 entre la Régence de Tunis et les royaumes de Sardaigne et des Deux-Siciles. CT 13 (1965), pp. 119-132.

6,886 Un mameluk tunisien d'origine française. CT 13 (1965), pp. 133-139.

6,887 La prétendue captivité de Saint Vincent de Paul à Tunis (1605-1607). CT 13 (1965), pp. 51-83.

6,888 La Révolution de 1864 en Tunisie. CT 13 (1965), pp. 141-169.

Language

6,889 BUSELLI, G. Berber texts from Jebel Nefûsi. J. AFR. SOC. 23 (1924), pp. 285-293.

6,890 GARMANDI, S. La langue des enseignes de quelques rues importantes de Tunis. REV. TUN. SC. SCO. 3 (1965), pp. 133-146.

6,891 SEIDEL, A. Beiträge zur Kenntniss der tunesischen Volkslitteratur. ZAOS 3 (1897), pp. 186-188, 268-271.

6,892 STUMME, H. Neue tunisische Sammlungen (Kinderlieder, Strassenlieder, Auszählreime, Räthsel, Arôbis, Geschichtchen u.s.w.). ZAOS 2 (1896), pp. 97-144.

Law

6,893 AUSSEL, J. M. La réforme des prisons et la Tunisie. REV. TUN. DROIT 5-6 (1957-1958), pp. 3-21.

6,894 BATTIFOL, H. De l'actualité du droit international privé. REV. TUN. DROIT 1 (1953), pp. 11-19.

6,895 BUSQUET, R. La compétence ratione loci en matière d'actions dirigées par les allocataires contre les caisses d'allocations et le problème de la nature juridique des allocations. REV. TUN. DROIT 1 (1953), pp. 233-254.

6,896 CANAZZI, A. Les assesseurs tunisiens et la procédure d'application de l'assessorat. REV. TUN. DROIT 4 (1956), pp. 263-277.

6,897 CANAZZI, A. La Convention Judiciaire franco-tunisienne. REV. TUN. DROIT 3 (1955), pp. 124-142.

6,898 CANAZZI, A. Le mariage des Italiens en Tunisie et le décret beylical du 19 février 1953. REV. TUN. DROIT 1 (1953), pp. 129-140.

6,899 CASCIO, A. De la valeur de l'expertise en matière pénale. REV. TUN. DROIT 4 (1956), pp. 126-129.

6,900 CORET, A. L'évolution du régime foncier tunisien. RJPUF 11 (1957), pp. 294-332.

6,901 DRAGO, R. L'exception d'illégalité devant les Tribunaux judiciaires en Tunisie. REV. TUN. DROIT 2 (1954), pp. 1-15.

6,902 DRAGO, R. La réparation des dommages causés par les attroupements et les attentats en Tunisie. REV. TUN. DROIT 1 (1953), pp. 109-128, 255-256.

6,903 GOUAUX, A. et al. Le problème de l'enfance malheureuse en Tunisie by A. Gouaux, Déchezelles and M. B. Boccara. REV. TUN. DROIT 5-6 (1957-1958), pp. 28-50.

6,904 JAMBU-MERLIN, A. Le décret du 26 janvier 1956 sur la nationalité tunisienne. REV. TUN. DROIT 4 (1956), pp. 3-10.

6,905 JAMBU-MERLIN, R. Le droit privé en Tunisie depuis l'entrée en vigueur des Conventions franco-tunisiennes. REV. TUN. DROIT 4 (1956), pp. 117-125.

6,906 JAMBU-MERLIN, R. Introduction [à l'étude des Convention franco-tunisiennes]. REV. TUN. DROIT 3 (1955), pp. 121-123.

6,907 JAMBU-MERLIN, R. La loi du 1er Mars 1954 sur les juridictions algériennes et son influence éventuelle en Tunisie. REV. TUN. DROIT 2 (1954), pp. 215-222.

6,908 JAMBU-MERLIN, R. La nationalité en Tunisie, d'après la Convention franco-tunisienne sur la situation des personnes. REV. TUN. DROIT 3 (1955), pp. 143-162.

6,909 JAMBU-MERLIN, R. Quelques problèmes actuels du transport maritime de marchandises. REV. TUN. DROIT 2 (1954), pp. 260-274.

6,910 JAMBU-MERLIN, R. Les sociétés commerciales en Tunisie sous le régime des Conventions franco-tunisiennes. REV. TUN. DROIT 3 (1955), pp. 164-170.

6,911 KARILA-COHEN, C. Le lévirat dans le droit hébraïque ancien et la pratique de cette institution en droit tunisien moderne. REV. TUN. DROIT 4 (1956), pp. 211-253.

6,912 LAKHDAR, T. De l'économie juridique de la Mogharça. REV. TUN. DROIT 2 (1954), pp. 16-21.

6,913 MOISSENET, P. Les accidents d'automobile à l'étranger devant les juridictions françaises. REV. TUN. DROIT 2 (1954), pp. 113-122.

6,914 ROUSSE, J. P. L'Assemblée Nationale Constituante. REV. TUN. DROIT 4 (1956), pp. 24-35.

6,915 ROUSSE, J. P. Le décret du 21 septembre 1955, portant organisation provisoire des pouvoirs publics. REV. TUN. DROIT 3 (1955), pp. 291-297.

6,916 ROUSSIER, J. Le Code tunisien du statut personnel. RJPUF 11 (1957), pp. 213-230.

6,917 SAMARAN, C. La responsabilité civile à raison des dommages causés par les animaux. REV. TUN. DROIT 5-6 (1957-1958), pp. 22-27.

6,918 SAMARAN, C. De la responsabilité civile à raison des dommages causés par les bâtiments. REV. TUN. DROIT 4 (1956), pp. 254-262.

6,919 SAMARAN, C. De la responsabilité du fait d'autrui en droit tunisien. REV. TUN. DROIT 4 (1956), pp. 11-23.

6,920 SAUMAGNE, C. Essai sur une legislation agraire. CT 10 (1962), pp. 10-114.

6,921 SILVERA, V. De l'administration directe et du contrôle dans le régime du protectorat français en Tunisie. RJPUF 6 (1952), pp. 57-71.

6,922 SILVERA, V. De l'autonomie interne à l'indépendance de la Tunisie. RJPUF 10 (1956), pp. 687-704.

6,923 SILVERA, V. Les conditions de l'évolution de la nationalité tunisienne. RJPUF 6 (1952), pp. 356-363.

6,924 SILVERA, V. La Convention sur la coopération administrative et technique. REV. TUN. DROIT 3 (1955), pp. 246-291.

6,925 SILVERA, V. Le domaine de l'état français en Tunisie. REV. TUN. DROIT 1 (1953), pp. 214-232.

6,926 SILVERA, V. De l'incompétence, absolue ou relative de la Juridiction française en Tunisie. REV. TUN. DROIT 1 (1953), pp. 20-26.

6,927 SILVERA, V. La Justice française et l'indépendance de la Tunisie. RJPUF 12 (1958), pp. 1-17.

6,928 SILVERA, V. Le Ministère des Affaires marocaines et tunisiennes. REV. TUN. DROIT 3 (1955), pp. 17-27.

6,929 SILVERA, V. Le protectorat français en Tunisie et au Maroc (essai de droit comparé). RJPUF 7 (1953), pp. 350-396.

6,930 SILVERA, V. La récente réforme gouvernementale tunisienne. RJPUF 2 (1948), pp. 175-212.

6,931 SILVERA, V. La réforme des Assemblées locales en Tunisie (conseils municipaux et conseils de caïdats). RJPUF 7 (1953), pp. 23-105.

6,932 SILVERA, V. Des réformes du 4 mars 1954 aux futures conventions franco-tunisiennes. REV. TUN. DROIT 2 (1954), pp. 223-227.

6,933 SILVERA, V. Les réformes institutionelles tunisiennes. RJPUF 8 (1954), pp. 25-103.

6,934 SILVERA, V. Les réformes institutionelles tunisiennes (mars 1954). REV. TUN. DROIT 2 (1954), pp. 22-39.

6,935 SILVERA, V. Les réformes tunisiennes de février 1951. RJPUF 5 (1951), pp. 1-54.

6,936 SILVERA, V. Le statut des contrôleurs civils en Tunisie. REV. TUN. DROIT 3 (1955), pp. 13-16.

6,937 TALLON, D. La condition des personnes d'après les Conventions franco-tunisiennes. REV. TUN. DROIT 3 (1955), pp. 231-245.

Religion

6,938 ATTAL, R. Note sur une enquête de sociologie religieuse en milieu israélite à Tunis. CT 3 (1955), pp. 247-261.

6,939 BISHOP, E. F. F. With Methodism from Tunis to Algiers. INT. REV. MISSIONS 42 (1953), pp. 162-171.

6,940 BOUHDIBA, A. Islam in Tunisia. PROC. INT. CONG. AFR. 1 (1962), pp. 134-145.

6,941 GRAFF, R. Le protestantisme en Tunisie. CT 3 (1955), pp. 235-246.

6,942 RONDOT, P. Jeûne du Ramadan et lutte contre le sous-développement en Tunisie. AFR. ET ASIE 50 (1960), pp. 45-49.

Science

6,943 BURNET, E. Pour une étude scientifique de l'alimentation en Tunisie. CT 3 (1955), pp. 493-500.

6,944 DEGLIN, C. and POITRINEAU, A. Un terroir de la zone côtière du Nord: El Aousdja. CT 2 (1954), pp. 254-264.

6,945 GEORGE, P. Le problème de l'énergie. CT 7 (1959), pp. 141-146.

6,946 GOBERT, E. G. Les références historiques des nourritures tunisiennes. CT 3 (1955), pp. 501-542.

6,947 GRUET, M. Amoncellement pyramidal de sphères calcaires dans une source fossile moustérienne a El-Guettar (Sud Tunisien). PROC. PAN-AFR. CONGR. PRE-HIST. 2 (1952), pp. 449-456.

6,948 PAUPHILET, D. Observations sur le niveau alimentaire des populations tunisiennes. CT 3 (1955), pp. 615-626.

6,949 PISSALOUX, R. Production agricole et alimentation humaine. CT 3 (1955), pp. 543-614.

6,950 SOLIGNAC, M. J. Remarques de méthode sur l'étude des installations hydrauliques Ifriqiyennes au Haut Moyen-Age. CT 12, nos. 47-48 (1964), pp. 25-36.

6,951 UZAN, M. and PAUPHILET, D. Aperçu d'ensemble sur le problème alimentaire en Tunisie. CT 3 (1955), pp. 627-632.

Sociology

6,952 AGUESSE, P. Etude critique d'un recensement: la pratique dominicale dans les paroisses catholiques de Tunis en 1952. CT 3 (1955), pp. 229-234.

6,953 BERQUE, J. Médinas villeneuves et bidonvilles. CT 6 (1958), pp. 5-42.

6,954 CALLENS, M. L'hébergement traditionnel à Tunis. CT 3 (1955), pp. 165-179.

6,955 CAMILLERI, C. Etude sur l'intégration familiale du jeune Tunisien cultivé. CT 9, nos. 33-35 (1961), pp. 7-95.

6,956 CHAULET, C. L'utilisation des données numériques en sociologie rurale tunisienne: la région d'Enfidaville. CT 6 (1958), pp. 43-88.

6,957 CLARKE, J. I. Some observations on Libyans in Tunisia. CT 6 (1958), pp. 89-99.

6,958 DANON, V. Les niveaux de vie dans la Hara de Tunis. CT 3 (1955), pp. 180-210.

6,959 DARDEL, J. B. and KLIBI, S. C. Un faubourg clandestin de Tunis: le Djebel Lahmar. CT 3 (1955), pp. 211-224.

6,960 DUVIGNAUD, J. Classes et conscience de classe dans un pays du Maghreb: la Tunisie. CAH. INT. SOCIOL. 38 (1965), pp. 185-200.

6,961 FENNICHE, N. Attitudes des jeunes parents tunisois de 20 à 30 ans devant le mariage mixte. REV. TUN. SC. SOC. 3 (1965), pp. 45 56.

6,962 GANIAGE, J. Etude démographique sur les Européens de Tunis. Natalité, fécondité, mortalité infantile au milieu du XIXe siècle. CT 5 (1957), pp. 167-201.

6,963 LUNET, P. Aspects sociaux du Sahel de Tunisie. AFR. ET ASIE 28 (1954), pp. 55-63.

6,964 MOREAU, P. Le problème du nomadisme dans le Sud tunisien. AFR. ET ASIE 11 (1950), pp. 42-50.

6,965 POMPEI, S. Problèmes d'urbanisme dans le Sahel. CT 12, nos. 47-48 (1964), pp. 147-163.

6,966 PONCET, J. L'evolution des genres de vie en Tunisie. CT 2 (1954), pp. 315-328.

6,967 RIZA, S. Les représentations de jeunes parents tunisois sur la profession future de leurs enfants. REV. TUN. SC. SOC. 3 (1965), pp. 62-70.

6,968 RONDOT, P. Le fonctionnement de l'opinion et l'ijma moderne en Tunisie. AFR. ET ASIE 60 (1962), pp. 17-24.

6,969 SEBAG, P. Le bidonville de Borgel. CT 6 (1958), pp. 267-309.

6,970 SEBAG, P. Le faubourg de Sîdî Fathallâh. CT 8, nos. 29-30 (1960), pp. 75-136.

6,971 SEKLANI, M. Petite Kabylie: aspects démographiques et problèmes d'emploi. REV. TUN. SC. SOC. 3 (1965), pp. 147-158.

6,972 ZGHAL, A. Les effets de la modernisation de l'agriculture sur la stratification sociale dans les campagnes tunisiennes. CAH. INT. SOCIOL. 38 (1965), pp. 201-206.

6,973 General Union of Tunisian Women. AFR. WOMEN 4 (1961), pp. 65-66.

6,974 Women of Tunisia. AFR. WOMEN 5 (1963), pp. 31-34.

ALGERIA

Agriculture

6,975 BODLEY, E. F. The locust plague in Algeria. CONTEMP. REV. 59 (1891), pp. 912-916.

6,976 COUNIL, J. Défense et restauration des sols en Algérie. AFR. ET ASIE 15 (1951), pp. 43-52.

6,977 JANSSENS, G. B. DE. Les Musulmans d'Algérie et le crédit agricole mutuel. AFR. ET ASIE 35 (1956), pp. 42-52.

6,978 LE TOURNEAU, R. Coup d'oeil sur le paysanat algérien. AFR. ET ASIE 10 (1950), pp. 54-60.

6,979 MIETTE, R. Le problème de la traction, clef du développement agricole chez les Musulmans d'Algérie. AFR. ET ASIE 40 (1957), pp. 43-48.

6,980 RIVIERE, T. and FAUBLEE, J. L'apiculture chez les Ouled Abderrahman montagnards du versant sud de l'Aurès. J. SOC. AFR. 13 (1943), pp. 95-107.

Anthropology

6,981 ALPORT, E. A. The Mzab. JRAI 84 (1954), pp. 34-44.

6,982 BRIGGS, L. C. On three skulls from Mechta-el-'Arbi. A reexamination of Cole's adult series. AM. J. PHY. ANTH. 8 (1950), pp. 305-314.

6,983 CHAMPAULT, D. Un collier d'enfant du Sahara algéro-marocain. J. SOC. AFR. 26 (1956), pp. 197-209.

6,984 CHAMPAULT, D. La naissance à Tabelbala (Sahara Algéro-Marocain). J. SOC. AFR. 23 (1953), pp. 87-101.

6,985 FAUBLEE-URBAIN, M. Magasins collectifs de l'Oued el Abiod (Aures). J. SOC. AFR. 21 (1951), pp. 139-150.

6,986 FAUBLEE-URBAIN, M. Sceaux de magasins collectifs (Aurès). J. SOC. AFR. 25 (1955), pp. 19-23.

6,987 FAUBLEE-URBAIN, M. and FAUBLEE, J. La vie des Aït Frah d'après le volume d'Andre Basset: textes berbères de l'Aurès. J. SOC. AFR. 34 (1964), pp. 85-116.

6,988 GAST, M. Mesures de capacités et de poids en Ahaggar. J. SOC. AFR. 33 (1963), pp. 209-229.

6,989 HILTON-SIMPSON, M. W. Some Arab and Shawia remedies and notes on the trepanning of the skull in Algeria. JRAI 43 (1913), pp. 706-721.

6,990 JANBON, M. H. Les rites de passage et l'acculturation dans une oasis saharienne: Ouargla. CONGR. INT. SC. ANTH. ET ETHN. 6, no. ii (1960), pp. 217-220.

6,991 KOLLER, R. P. A. La Jemâ berbère. CIVILISATIONS 4 (1954), pp. 43-50; English summary, p. 50.

6,992 NICOLAS, F. Folklore Twāreg: poésies et chansons de l'Azāwarh. BULL. IFAN 6 (1944), pp. 1-463.

6,993 PROBST-BIRABEN, J. H. Les rites d'obtention de la pluie dans la province de Constantine. J. SOC. AFR. 2 (1932), pp. 95-102.

6,994 RAHMANI, S. Le mariage des autochtones en Algérie. CONG. INT. SC. ANTH. ET ETHN. 4, no. iii (1952), pp. 21-23.

6,995 RIVIERE, T. L'Habitation chez les Ouled Abderrahman Chaouïa de l'Aurès. AFRICA 11 (1938), pp. 294-311.

6,996 RIVIERE, T. and FAUBLEE, J. Les tatouages des Chaouia de l'Aurès. J. SOC. AFR. 12 (1942), pp. 67-80.

6,997 SERVIER, J. Les rites du labour en Algérie. (Région du Dahra et du Moyen-Chélif.) J. SOC. AFR. 21 (1951), pp. 175-196.

6,998 TILLION, G. Les sociétés berbères dans l'Aurès Méridional. AFRICA 11 (1938), pp. 42-54.

Art. Archaeology. Pre-history

6,999 ARAMBOURG, C. Aperçu sur les résultas des fouilles du gisement de Ternifine. PROC. PAN-AFR. CONGR. PRE-HIST. 5 (1965), pp. 129-135.

7,000 AYME, A. Le Quaternaire littoral des environs d'Alger. PROC. PAN-AFR. CONGR. PRE-HIST. 2 (1952), pp. 243-246.

7,001 BALOUT, L. Note préliminaire sur le paléolithique inférieur de Champlain (Department d'Alger). PROC. PAN-AFR. CONGR. PRE-HIST. 2 (1952), pp. 263-267.

7,002 BREUIL, H. Restes d'une sépultune en grotte au Sahara. J. SOC. AFR. 24 (1954), pp. 113-117.

7,003 CADENAT, P. Les gravures rupestres des environs de la région de Tiaret (Départment d'Oran). PROC. PAN-AFR. CONGR. PRE-HIST. 2 (1952), pp. 701-713.

7,004 CAMPS, G. La céramique des monuments Mégalithiques. Collections du Musée du Bardo (Alger). PROC. PAN-AFR. CONGR. PRE-HIST. 2 (1952), pp. 513-550.

7,005 DALLONI, M. L'extension du Paléolithique ancien dans la zone littorale de l'Algérie. PROC. PAN-AFR. CONGR. PRE-HIST. 2 (1952), pp. 251-258.

7,006 DALLONI, M. La station moustérienne de Retaimia près d'Inkermann (Algérie). PROC. PAN-AFR. CONGR. PRE-HIST. 2 (1952), pp. 419-427.

7,007 HUGOT, H. J. Du Capsien au Tidikelt? PROC. PAN-AFR. CONGR. PRE-HIST. 2 (1952), pp. 601-603.

7,008 JOLEAUD, L. and CASTELLANI. Escargotière prehistorique de Champlain, près de Medea (Alger). J. SOC. AFR. 5 (1935), pp. 159-162.

7,009 JOLEAUD, L. and LAFFITTE, R. Grotte préhistorique de Khanquet Si Mohammed Tahar (Aures septentrional). J. SOC. AFR. 4 (1934), pp. 111-114.

7,010 LACOSTE, C. Sabres Kabyles. J. SOC. AFR. 28 (1958), pp. 111-191.

7,011 LE DU, R. Le gisement préhistorique de l'Ain Guedara. PROC. PAN-AFR. CONGR. PRE-HIST. 2 (1952), pp. 605-611.

7,012 LEPAGNOT, L. Les théatres en Algérie de 1830 à 1860. REV. HIST. COL. 39 (1952), pp. 76-102.

7,013 LHOTE, H. Gravures rupestres d'Aguennar (Ahaggar). J. SOC. AFR. 34 (1964), pp. 37-83.

7,014 LHOTE, H. Nouvelle contribution à l'étude des gravures et peintures rupestres du Sahara Central. La station de Tit (Ahaggar). J. SOC. AFR. 29 (1959), pp. 147-192.

7,015 LHOTE, H. Peintures rupestres de l'Oued Takéchérouet (Ahaggar). BULL. IFAN 15 (1953), pp. 283-291.

7,016 MOREL, J. La station préhistorique du Demnet El-Hassan dans la Commune Mixte de La Calle (Départment de Constantine) et le problème de l'Ibèro-maurusien. PROC. PAN-AFR. CONGR. PRE-HIST. 2 (1952), pp. 631-639.

7,017 MYRES, J. L. Notes on the history of the Kabyle pottery. JRAI 32 (1902), pp. 248-262.

7,018 PERRET, R. Recherches archéologiques et ethnographiques au Tassili des Ajjers (Sahara central). Les gravures rupestres de l'Oued Djaret, la population et les ruines d'Iherir. J. SOC. AFR. 6 (1936), pp. 41-64.

7,019 PUIGAUDEAU, O. DU. and SENONES, M. Le cimetière de Bir 'Umm Garn. J. SOC. AFR. 17 (1947), pp. 51-56.

7,020 RANDALL-MacIVER, D. On a rare fabric of Kabyle pottery. JRAI 32 (1902), pp. 245-247.

7,021 REYGASSE, M. Sur une industrie campignienne découverte dans la région de l'Oued Mahrouguet (Sud de Tebessa). J. SOC. AFR. 4 (1934), pp. 115-116.

7,022 ROUANEL, J. Arab music, tr. by M. L. Smith. J. AFR. SOC. 5 (1906), pp. 148-150.

7,023 ROUBET, F. E. Les foyers préhistoriques de la crique des pêcheurs, a Bou-Aïchem près de Kristel (Oran). PROC. PAN-AFR. CONGR. PRE-HIST. 2 (1952), pp. 655-657.

7,024 ROUBET, F. E. Observations sur la stratigraphie des gisements préhistoriques du littoral de l'Oranie orientale. PROC. PAN-AFR. CONGR. PRE-HIST. 2 (1952), pp. 279-280.

7,025 TIXIER, J. Un gisement préhistorique in situ au sud de Bou-Saada (Algérie). PROC. PAN-AFR. CONGR. PRE-HIST. 2 (1952), pp. 681-684.

7,026 VUILLEMONT, G. La station prehistorique de Bégeyville. PROC. PAN-AFR. CONGR. PRE-HIST. 2 (1952), pp. 485-488.

See also 6748.

Biography

7,027 CESAIRE, A. et al. Hommages à Jean Amrouche. PRESENCE AFR. N.S. 46 (1963), pp. 187-196.

7,028 BERQUE, J. et al. Hommages à Frantz Fanon. PRESENCE AFR. N.S. 40 (1962), pp. 118-141.

7,029 Le mort de Mouloud Feraoun. PRESENCE AFR. N.S. 40 (1962), p. 173.

Economics

7,030 AGRICOLA. Vers une nouvelle réforme foncière en Algérie. AFR. ET ASIE 46 (1959), pp. 44-48.

7,031 ANCEL, R. La Kabylie vivra-t-elle? AFR. ET ASIE 17 (1952), pp. 43-51.

7,032 BOIREAU, A. Pour une révolution technique: nécessité d'une augmentation des rendements. AFR. ET ASIE 39 (1957), pp. 48-55.

7,033 CEPOLLARO, A. Ammodernamento e attrezzatura dell'Algeria. AFRICA (Rome) 10 (1955), pp. 257-259.

7,034 FERVEL, J. Les allocations familiales aux travailleurs agricoles en Algérie. AFR. ET ASIE 29 (1955), pp. 37-45.

7,035 KAMEN-KAYE, M. Petroleum development in Algeria. GEOG. REV. 48 (1958), pp. 463-473.

7,036 LIGER, P. Problèmes ruraux, problèmes fonciers. AFR. ET ASIE 39 (1957), pp. 55-58.

7,037 MAITRE-DEVALLON, C. Sur la réforme agraire algérienne. AFR. ET ASIE 41 (1958), pp. 45-49.

7,038 MARTIN DE LA ESCALERA, C. Economía, demografía y emigración argelina. CUAD. AFR. OR. 29 (1955), pp. 39-51.

7,039 MASSEI, E. A tu per tu con l'Algeria. AFRICA (Rome) 10 (1955), pp. 151-155.

7,040 MESSUD, G. Perspectives de l'économie algérienne. AFR. ET ASIE 24 (1953), pp. 36-61.

7,041 MIETTE, R. Une formule pour la réforme agraire en Algérie: la Coopérative ouvrière agricole. AFR. ET ASIE 60 (1962), pp. 45-48.

7,042 MIETTE, R. Pour une révolution sociale: réforme agraire et revenus familiaux. AFR. ET ASIE 39 (1957), pp. 42-48.

7,043 MIETTE, R. Quelques réflexions sur l'avenir économique de l'Algérie. AFR. ET ASIE 25 (1954), pp. 62-66.

7,044 MONTAGNE, R. L'Emigration des musulmans d'Algérie en France. AFR. ET ASIE 22 (1953), pp. 5-20.

7,045 WERTHEIMER, M. A terres nouvelles, personnel technique supplémentaire. AFR. ET ASIE 39 (1957), pp. 59-62.

7,046 ZERKOVITZ, P. La formation professionnelle accélérée en Algérie. AFR. ET ASIE 12 (1950), pp. 37-44.

See also 22111.

Education

7,047 BLACKMORE, J. T. C. The educational work of the French government in Algeria. INT. REV. MISSIONS 19 (1930), pp. 266-276.

Geography

7,048 ABA, N. Voyelles pour Gazelle. PRESENCE AFR. N.S. 50 (1964), p. 214.

7,049 CIVERA SIMON, G. Argelia y sus fronteras. CUAD. AFR. OR. 35 (1956), pp. 41-62.

7,050 GRAY, A. Earthquake in Algeria. AFR. AFFAIRS 54 (1955), pp. 15-16.

7,051 HOGARTH, R. Compte rendu de Mission en Algérie. J. SOC. AFR. 12 (1942), pp. 241-247.

7,052 KILLIAN, M. and HODENT. Le recensement des paturages sur les Hauts-Plateaux algériens, les steppes présahariennes et le role de l'aviation. J. SOC. AFR. 17 (1947), pp. 1-5.

7,053 TAYLOR, G. Sea to Sahara: settlement zones in eastern Algeria. GEOG. REV. 29 (1939), pp. 177-195.

See also 8418.

Government. Politics. Administration

7,054 BARBOUR, N. Algeria and De Gaulle. AFR. SOUTH 3, no. 1 (1958), pp. 97-102.

7,055 BARRAT, R. The declaration of the 121. AFR. SOUTH 5, no. 2 (1961), pp. 92-95.

7,056 BEHR, E. The Algerian dilemma. INTERNAT. AFFAIRS 34 (1958), pp. 280-290.

7,057 BOURDET, C. Algeria and France. AFR. SOUTH 2, no. 3 (1958), pp. 75-82.

7,058 BOURDET, C. Algeria and the future of France. AFR. SOUTH 5, no. 2 (1961), pp. 85-91.

7,059 CHANDERLI, A. K. Algerian objectives. AFR. SOUTH 6 (1961), pp. 98-101.

7,060 CIVERA, G. España ante el futuro de Argelia. CUAD. AFR. OR. 33 (1956), pp. 33-51.

7,061 COLL, F. Modalidades de la acción de Francia en Argelia. CUAD. AFR. OR. 32 (1955), pp. 57-65.

7,062 CROZIER, B. and MANSELL, G. France and Algeria. INTERNAT. AFFAIRS 36 (1960), pp. 310-321.

7,063 DANIEL, J. The Algerian problem begins. FOREIGN AFFAIRS 40 (1961-1962), pp. 605-611.

7,064 F., R. Quelques réflexions sur l'accès des Francais musulmans à la fonction publique en Algérie. AFR. ET ASIE 35 (1956), pp. 57-61.

7,065 G., J. L. Double collège ou collège unique en Algérie? AFR. ET ASIE 36 (1956), pp. 47-50.

7,066 GALLAGHER, C. F. Toward a settlement in Algeria. FOREIGN AFFAIRS 38 (1959-1960), pp. 273-284.

7,067 GLORIES, J. Quelques observations sur la révolution algérienne et la communisme. AFR. ET ASIE 41 (1958), pp. 16-44; 42 (1958), pp. 3-23.

7,068 JEAN-MARIE. Une experience de réforme municipale en Grande Kabylie. AFR. ET ASIE 47 (1959), pp. 48-52.

7,069 JEAN-MARIE. La réforme municipale atout majeur de la pacification en Algérie. AFR. ET ASIE 46 (1959), pp. 31-38.

7,070 KRAFT, J. Settler politics in Algeria. FOREIGN AFFAIRS 39 (1960-1961), pp. 591-600.

7,071 LACHERAF, M. L'Algérie devant sa liberté. PRESENCE AFR. N.S. 6 (1956), pp. 147-157.

7,072 LACOUTURE, J. At and after Evian. AFR. SOUTH 5, no. 4 (1961), pp. 95-100.

7,073 MANDOUZE, A. La "nuit coloniale" de Ferhat Abbas. PRESENCE AFR. N.S. 44 (1962), pp. 190-203.

7,074 MARCAIS, P. Robert Montagne et l'Algérie. AFR. ET ASIE 32 (1955), pp. 9-15.

7,075 MASSIA MARTIN, A. Puntos de vista sobre la crisis argelina. CUAD. AFR. OR. 40 (1957), pp. 29-42.

7,076 MESSUD, G. Algérie et patrie française. AFR. ET ASIE 33 (1956), pp. 29-50.

7,077 MIDDLETON, W. L. France and Algeria. CONTEMP. REV. 193 (1958), pp. 284-288.

7,078 MIDDLETON, W. L. The Franco-Algerian negotiations. CONTEMP. REV. 199 (1961), pp. 189-191.

7,079 MIDDLETON, W. L. General De Gaulle and Algeria. CONTEMP. REV. 197 (1960), pp. 131-134.

7,080 MILLIOT, L. Algeria 1956-1957. CIVILISATIONS 7 (1957), pp. 477-482.

7,081 MORIZOT, J. Le benbellisme et l'opinion algérienne. AFR. ET ASIE 65 (1964), pp. 31-41.

7,082 PARANT, R. Assimilation—intégration. AFR. ET ASIE 40 (1957), pp. 49-51.

7,083 PHILIP, D. The real drama of Algeria. CONTEMP. REV. 189 (1956), pp. 266-270.

7,084 VALIN, R. Alger: huit mois d'indépendance. AFR. ET ASIE 62 (1963), pp. 16-37.

7,085 VALIN, R. Socialisme musulman en Algérie. AFR. ET ASIE 66 (1964), pp. 21-42; 69 (1965), pp. 14-32.

7,086 YAKER, L. The Algerians' struggle for freedom. AFRICA QUART. 2, no. i (1962), pp. 35-41.

7,087 L'Affreux et le Transhumant. PRESENCE AFR. N.S. 53 (1965), pp. 245-246.

7,088 Où en est l'Algérie? (Nov., 1947). AFR. ET ASIE 1, no. 1 (1948), pp. 36-39.

7,089 Où va l'Algérie? AFR. ET ASIE 30 (1955), pp. 31-38.

See also 2048, 6788, 6792, 6793.

History

7,090 AYANDELE, E. A. Abdel Kader and French occupation of Algeria, 1830-1847. TARIKH 1, no. 1 (1965), pp. 53-63.

7,091 BARBOUR, N. The significance of the conflict in Algeria. AFR. AFFAIRS 56 (1957), pp. 20-31.

7,092 BAUDENS and DEMONTES, V. La relation de l'expédition de Médéa. RHCF 8, no. 2 (1920), pp. 187-308.

7,093 BENN, A. W. The Algerian war. AFR. SOUTH 4, no. 4 (1960), pp. 98-103.

7,094 BONO, S. Algeri alla metà del XVIII secolo nella testimonianza del Console Carlo Antonio Stendardi. AFRICA (Rome) 20 (1965), pp. 250-268.

7,095 BUGEAUD, M. Lettre inédite: la colonisation de l'Algérie et les Maronites. RHCF 25 (1932), pp. 183-186.

7,096 CARRET, J. Le problème de l'indépendance du culte musulman en Algérie. AFR. ET ASIE 37 (1957), pp. 43-58.

7,097 DARMON, J. P. Note sur le Tarif de Zaraï. CT 12, nos. 47-48 (1964), pp. 7-23.

7,098 DEHERAIN, H. La mission du commissaire général Dubois Thainville auprès du dey d'Alger (An VIII et an X: 1800 et 1801). RHCF 19 (1926), pp. 75-100.

7,099 DEMONTES, V. Lettre de Bugeaud a Soult (26 Novembre 1841): réponse aux Instructions ministérielles du 13 août. RHCF 7, no. 2 (1919), pp. 195-236.

7,100 DENY, J. Chansons des janissaires turcs d'Alger (fin du XVIIIe siècle). MELANGES RENE BASSET, 1925, pp. 33-175.

7,101 GAUTHEROT, G. Le maréchal de Bourmont et l'admiral Duperré. Quelques documents sur le commandement en chef de l'expédition de 1830. RHCF 10, no. 2 (1922), pp. 189-232.

7,102 GRAY, A. Algeria at UNO. AFR. AFFAIRS 56 (1957), pp. 99-100.

7,103 GRAY, A. Algerian unrest. AFR. AFFAIRS 55 (1956), pp. 162-163.

7,104 GRAY, A. Call to greatness. AFR. AFFAIRS 57 (1958), pp. 173-174.

7,105 GRAY, A. Settlement in Algeria. AFR. AFFAIRS 61 (1962), pp. 178-182.

7,106 GRAY, A. Trouble for France. AFR. AFFAIRS 55 (1956), pp. 93-95.

7,107 GRAY, A. The war in Algeria. AFR. AFFAIRS 57 (1958), pp. 88-89.

7,108 HARDY, G. Une région historique de l'Algérie: le pays Chaouia. REV. HIST. COL. 37 (1950), pp. 81-100.

7,109 JAMMES, R. Cheikh Ben Badis et la France en avril 1936. AFR. ET ASIE 57 (1962), pp. 40-42.

7,110 JOHNSON, D. Algeria: some problems of modern history. J. AFR. HIST. 5 (1964), pp. 221-242.

7,111 MANTRAN, R. Heurs et malheurs de l'Algérie. CT 9, nos. 33-35 (1961), pp. 245-255.

7,112 MONTAGNE, R. Evolution in Algeria. INTERNAT. AFFAIRS 23 (1947), pp. 42-51.

7,113 NOUSCHI, A. Archives de l'ex-Gouvernement Général de l'Algérie. CT 9, no. 36 (1961), pp. 1-3.

7,114 NOUSCHI, A. Constantine à la veille de la conquête française. CT 3 (1955), pp. 371-387.

7,115 OVEJERO, A. Cisneros en Africa. ARCH. INST. EST. AFR. 5, no. 16 (1951), pp. 31-51.

7,116 RAYNAL, P. La conquête d'Alger. RHCF 23 (1930), pp. 1-44.

7,117 SCHEFER, C. La conquête totale de l'Algérie (1839-1843): Valée, Bugeaud et Soult. RHCF 4 (1916), pp. 19-76.

7,118 SINGH, D. Algeria's fight for freedom. AFR. QUART. 1, no. 1 (1961), pp. 36-39.

7,119 WEILL, G. Les républicains français et l'Algérie. RHCF 24 (1931), pp. 285-292.

7,120 La fin des guillements. PRESENCE AFR. N.S. 40 (1962), pp. 163-165.

Language. Literature

7,121 KREA, H. Revenge [fiction]. BO 14 (1964), pp. 26-31.

7,122 MOHAMMED DIB. A beautiful wedding [fiction]. BO 18 (1965), pp. 20-25.

See also 5404.

Law

7,123 CARRET, J. Le particularisme ibadite au M'zab. AFR. ET ASIE 49 (1960), pp. 38-46.

7,124 CUNCTATOR, F. Réflexions sur la réforme communale en Algérie: risques et limites. AFR. ET ASIE 38 (1957), pp. 44-52.

7,125 DOUBLIER, R. Les récentes réformes du régime foncier algérien. RJPUF 11 (1957), pp. 612-623.

7,126 FAIVRE, C. Le Khammessat en Algérie, sa réforme et son avenir. AFR. ET ASIE 34 (1956), pp. 46-54.

7,127 FRISON, R. La réforme territoriale de l'Algérie. AFR. ET ASIE 36 (1956), pp. 29-37.

7,128 IDENBURG, P. J. Agrarisch Recht in Algerije. ZAIRE 6 (1952), pp. 25-46.

7,129 JANSSENS, G. B. DE. L'indépendance du culte musulman en Algérie. RJPUF 5 (1951), pp. 305-339.

7,130 JAUSSERAND, M. Réflexions sur la réforme communale en Algérie: raisons d'être et chances de la réforme. AFR. ET ASIE 38 (1957), pp. 53-62.

7,131 KOLLEWIJN, R. D. Le droit intergentiel en Algérie. RJPUF 8 (1954), pp. 321-346.

7,132 LAMPUE, P. Les lois applicables en Algérie. RJPUF 4 (1950), pp. 1-23.

7,133 MARCHAT, H. La frontière algéro-marocaine. RJPUF 11 (1957), pp. 257-272.

7,134 PASSERON, R. La structure administrative de l'Algérie. RJPUF 5 (1951), pp. 449-465.

7,135 PRALUS, M. Le visa des actes de prêts d'argent en Algérie. RJPUF 11 (1957), pp. 115-121.

7,136 RUSSINGER, A. En marge de la pacification: Justice francaise et justice tribale en Kabylie. AFR. ET ASIE 40 (1957), pp. 55-66.

See also 3723.

Religion

7,137 CARRET, J. L'Association des Oulama Réformistes d'Algérie. AFR. ET ASIE 43 (1958), pp. 23-44.

7,138 FAUQUE, L. P. Ou en est l'Islam traditionnel en Algérie? AFR. ET ASIE 55 (1961), pp. 17-22.

7,139 LEONE, E. DE. La Santa Sede e la spedizione di Algeri. AFRICA (Rome) 16 (1961), pp. 19-25.

7,140 PADWICK, C. E. Lilias Trotter of Algiers. INT. REV. MISSIONS 21 (1932), pp. 119-128.

See also 6939.

Science

7,141 FAUREL, L. et al. Les lichens du Sahara Algérien, by L. Faurel, P. Ozenda, G. Schotter. DESERT RESEARCH, 1953, pp. 310-317.

7,142 FERVEL, J. Les chances de l'Hôpital Moderne en Algérie. AFR. ET ASIE 58 (1962), pp. 48-53.

7,143 MEDINA, M. A. El congreso geológico de Argel y una excursión al Haggar. ARCH. INST. EST. AFR. 6, no. 23 (1952), pp. 7-19.

Sociology

7,144 ABA, N. Débat imaginaire sur la culture algérienne. PRESENCE AFR. N.S. 49 (1964), pp. 212-221.

7,145 BELLIN, P. L'enfant saharien a travers ses jeux. J. SOC. AFR. 33 (1963), pp. 47-103.

7,146 BOIREAU, A. La démographie et l'économie algérienne. AFR. ET ASIE 19 (1952), pp. 14-22.

7,147 DESCLOITRES, R., DESCLOITRES, C. and REVERDY, J. C. Organisation urbaine et structures sociales en Algérie. CIVILISATIONS 12 (1962), pp. 211-230; English summary, pp. 231-236.

7,148 DESCLOITRES, R. and REVERDY, J. C. Recherche sur les attitudes du sous-prolétariat algérien à l'égard de la société urbaine. CIVILISATIONS 13 (1963), pp. 30-76; English summary, pp. 77-81.

7,149 F., J. Algérie, natalité et politique. AFR. ET ASIE 42 (1958), pp. 54-63.

7,150 FERVEL, J. Allocations familiales ou limitation des naissances Outre-Mer? AFR. ET ASIE 30 (1955), pp. 46-52.

7,151 GIRARD, A. La migration algérienne vers la France. CT 3 (1955), pp. 664-671.

7,152 JOVY, R. L'urbanisme algérien. AFR. ET ASIE 47 (1959), pp. 37-47.

7,153 LUXEMBOURG, R. L'expropriation des terres et la pénétration capitaliste en Afrique. PRESENCE AFR. 13 (1952), pp. 137-151.

7,154 MICHEL, A. Les classes sociales en Algérie. CAH. INT. SOCIOL. 38 (1965), pp. 207-220.

7,155 PAYRE, G. Algérie, communauté multi-raciale. AFR. ET ASIE 36 (1956), pp. 38-41.

7,156 RUSSINGER, A. Un problème d'évolution des coutumes Kabyles: le cas des arbres abandou. AFR. ET ASIE 42 (1958), pp. 47-51.

7,157 The Social and Economic Research Institute of Algiers. INT. SOC. SC. BULL. 7 (1955), p. 658.

See also 4474.

M O R O C C O (Tangier)

Agriculture

7,158 BIANCACCI, F. I molti problemi dell'agricoltura marocchina. AFRICA (Rome) 13 (1958), pp. 355-356.

7,159 CHALLOT, J. P. Quelques aspects marocains des problèmes de défense et de restauration des sols. AFR. ET ASIE 30 (1955), pp. 39-45.

7,160 MEUNIE, J. Les greniers collectifs au Maroc. Compte rendu de mission (1941-1942). J. SOC. AFR. 14 (1944), pp. 1-16.

7,161 MOHAMMAD IBN AZZUZ HAQUIM. Refranero agrícola de Gumara. CUAD. EST. AFR. 28 (1954), pp. 65-68.

7,162 SETHOM, H. Les rapports entre les modes d'exploitation agricole et l'érosion des sols en Tunisie. CT 11, no. 43 (1963), pp. 85-95.

Anthropology

7,163 ALPORT, E. A. The Ammeln. JRAI 94 (1964), pp. 160-171.

7,164 BARDON, P. C. M. Antiguas poblaciones del Rif. ARCH. INST. EST. AFR. 3, no. 10 (1949), pp. 35-56.

7,165 BARDON, P. C. M. Etnografia y folklore de Marruecos. ARCH. INST. EST. AFR. 4, no. 15 (1950), pp. 7-31.

7,166 BERTHELEMY, A. Industries des croûtes calcaires du Maroc préatlasique. PROC. PAN-AFR. CONGR. PRE-HIST. 2 (1952), pp. 269-273.

7,167 BRUNOT, L. Noms des vêtements masculins à Rabat. MELANGES RENE BASSET, 1923, pp. 87-144.

7,168 CABANAS, R. Aportación al estudio del habitat en la region occidental del Protectorado español en Marruecos. ARCH. INST. EST. AFR. 6, no. 22 (1952), pp. 37-52.

7,169 COLA ALBERICH, J. Supersticiones y legendas marroquíes. ARCH. INST. EST. AFR. 3, no. 8 (1949), pp. 51-63.

7,170 FAUBLEE-URBAIN, M. La vie des Ait Sadden d'après le volume d'André Basset: "Textes berbères du Maroc (parler des Ait Sadden)." J. SOC. AFR. 34 (1964), pp. 117-121.

7,171 FOGG, W. The organization of a Moroccan tribal market. AMER. ANTHR. 44 (1942), pp. 47-61.

7,172 FOGG, W. A tribal market in the Spanish zone of Morocco. AFRICA 11 (1938), pp. 428-458.

7,173 HARRIS, W. B. The Berbers of Morocco. JRAI 27 (1898), pp. 61-73.

7,174 JACQUES-MEUNIE, D. La coutume écrite des Berbères montagnards du Sud marocain. CONGR. INT. SC. ANTHR. ET ETHN. 6, no. ii (1960), pp. 329-335.

7,175 JOUIN, J. Chansons de fillettes a Rabat. J. SOC. AFR. 12 (1942), pp. 49-53.

7,176 LESOURD, M. Les femmes d'in Calah mangeuses de chats a l'occasion de la fête Es Sabaa. J. SOC. AFR. 7 (1937), pp. 33-35.

7,177 MEAKIN, J. E. B. The Morocco Berbers. JRAI 24 (1895), pp. 1-14.

7,178 MOHAMMAD IBN AZZUZ HAQUIM. Del Tetúan de otros días (Tipos pintorescos y costumbres viejas, de intenso sabor marroquí, desaparecidos ya o en trance de serlo). ARCH. INST. EST. AFR. 6, no. 21 (1952), pp. 7-26.

7,179 RUHLMANN, A. Prehistoric Morocco. PROC. PAN-AFR. CONGR. PRE-HIST. 1 (1947), pp. 140-147.

7,180 WESTERMARCK, E. The blood-feud among some Berbers of Morocco. ESSAYS PRESENTED TO C. G. SELIGMAN, 1934, pp. 361-368.

See also 6991.

Art. Archaeology. Pre-history

7,181 BERTHELEMY, A. Une nouvelle industrie du Paléolithique supérieur dans la région de Marrakech. PROC. PAN-AFR. CONGR. PRE-HIST. 2 (1952), pp. 401-402.

7,182 BIBERSON, P. Observations sur le Pléistocéne et la prehistoire de la province de Tarfaïa (Maroc meridional). PROC. PAN-AFR. CONGR. PRE-HIST. 5 (1965), pp. 157-167.

7,183 CORNET, H. Tissage de la laine à Djerba et artisanat. CT 6 (1958), pp. 139-160.

7,184 CRUZ HERRERA, J. Treinta y tres años de pintura en Marruecos. ARCH. INST. EST. AFR. 16, no. 62 (1962), pp. 59-66.

7,185 FROIDEVAUX, H. L'Exposition d'art morocain au Pavillon de Marsan; ses enseignements historiques. RHCF 5 (1917), pp. 331-348.

7,186 GLORY, A. Une nouvelle industrie préhistorique les triêdres Toulkiniens. PROC. PAN-AFR. CONGR. PRE-HIST. 2 (1952), pp. 429-434.

7,187 GLORY, A. and ALLAIN, C. Les quartzites taillés de la haute bordure du Draa supérieur (Maroc). PROC. PAN-AFR. CONGR. PRE-HIST. 2 (1952), pp. 435-448.

7,188 GLORY, A. et al. Les gravures Libyco-Berbères du Haut-Drâa (Maroc). PROC. PAN-AFR. CONGR. PRE-HIST. 2 (1952), pp. 715-722.

7,189 MALHOMME, J. Les gravures rupestres Grand Atlas (Maroc). PROC. PAN-AFR. CONGR. PRE-HIST. 2 (1952), pp. 739-740.

7,190 MARTINEZ, N. Notes sur la poterie et les potiers d'Azemmour. J. SOC. AFR. 35 (1965), pp. 251-281.

7,191 MOHAMMAD IBN AZZUZ HAQUIM. El I Congresso de Arqueología marroquí. CUAD. EST. AFR. 24 (1953), pp. 61-63.

7,192 PALACIN, A. DE L. Proyecciones Hispanicas en la cultura musical Marroqui. ARCH. INST. EST. AFR. 14, no. 56 (1960), pp. 21-29.

7,193 PRUSSO, P. Inscriptions rupestres modernes dans le sous. J. SOC. AFR. 4 (1934), pp. 269-272.

7,194 PUIGAUDEAU, O. DU and SENONES, M. Gravures rupestres de l'Oued Tamanart (Sud marocain). BULL. IFAN 15 (1953), pp. 1242-1261.

7,195 PUIGAUDEAU, O. DU and SENONES, M. Nouvelles gravures rupestres de l'oued Tamanart (Sud-Marocain). BULL. IFAN 27 (1965), pp. 282-286.

7,196 ROCHE, J. Note préliminaire sur la grotte de Taforalt (Maroc Oriental). PROC. PAN-AFR. CONGR. PRE-HIST. 2 (1952), pp. 647-652.

7,197 RUHLMANN, A. The Moroccan Aterian and its sub-divisions. PROC. PAN-AFR. CONGR. PRE-HIST. 1 (1947), pp. 210-222.

7,198 SENONES, M. and PUIGAUDEAU, O. DU. Gravures rupestres de la montagne d'Icht (sud-marocain). J. SOC. AFR. 11 (1941), pp. 147-155.

7,199 SENONES, M. and PUIGAUDEAU, O. DU. Gravures rupestres de la vallée moyenne du Draa (sud-marocain). J. SOC. AFR. 11 (1941), pp. 157-167.

7,200 TARRADELL, M. La Arqueología romana en el Protectorado de España en Marruecos. ARCH. INST. EST. AFR. 4, no. 12 (1950), pp. 31-44.

7,201 TARRADELL, M. Yacimentos liticos de superficie ineditos en el N.O. de Marruecos. PROC. PAN-AFR. CONGR. PRE-HIST. 2 (1952), pp. 377-380.

See also 6748.

Biography

7,202 AMAWI, J. AL. Homenaje y recuerdo a Mariano Bertuchi como símbolo hispano-marroqui. CUAD. AFR. OR. 31 (1955), pp. 67-69.

7,203 GARCIA FIGUERAS, T. Bertuchi en Marruecos (1898-1955). ARCH. INST. EST. AFR. 16, no. 61 (1962), pp. 31-45.

7,204 In memoriam: Fernand Daguin. BULL. IFAN 11 (1949), p. 210.

7,205 BARBUDO DUARTE, E. El Capitán de Navío Fernández Duro explorador de la costa Noroeste de Africa. ARCH. INST. EST. AFR. 1, no. 1 (1947), pp. 67-81.

7,206 GARCIA FIGUERAS, T. El Padre Lerchundi, arabista, investigador y propulsor de los estudios cientificos de Marruecos. ARCH. INST. EST. AFR. 19, no. 74 (1965), pp. 29-41.

7,207 GARCIA FIGUERAS, T. José María de Murga y Mugartegui. El Hach Mohammed el Bagdadi. El moro vizcaíno (1827-1876). ARCH. INST. EST. AFR. 1, no. 1 (1947), pp. 83-106.

7,208 LAFORGUE, P. In memoriam: Armand Ruhlmann. BULL. IFAN 12 (1950), pp. 230-231.

7,209 LESTER, P. Nécrologie: Auguste Terrier. J. SOC. AFR. 2 (1932), p. 244.

Economics

7,210 AZAM, P. Réflexions sur un cas concret d'assistance technique (Maroc 1956-1959). AFR. ET ASIE 56 (1961), pp. 46-51.

7,211 BERENGUIER, H. Le syndicalisme marocain. AFR. ET ASIE 53 (1961), pp. 25-36.

7,212 DOMENECH LAFUENTE, A. Zona Norte de nuestro Protectorado: las industrias del país. CUAD. EST. AFR. 23 (1953), pp. 25-36.

7,213 FOGG, W. The economic revolution in the countryside of French Morocco. J. AFR. SOC. 35 (1936), pp. 123-129.

7,214 FOGG, W. The importance of tribal markets in the commercial life of the countryside of north-west Morocco. AFRICA 12 (1939), pp. 445-449.

7,215 FOGG, W. Tribal markets in Spanish Morocco. J. AFR. SOC. 38 (1939), pp. 322-326.

7,216 GUDIN FERNANDEZ, T. Las obras hidraulicas en Marruecos. ARCH. INST. EST. AFR. 16, no. 64 (1962), pp. 101-112.

7,217 INTRONA, S. Piani per il Marocco. AFRICA (Rome) 10 (1955), pp. 265-266.

7,218 MATTEIS, V. DE. L'economia del Marocco e l'Italia. AFRICA (Rome) 10 (1955), pp. 9-10.

7,219 MIKESELL, M. W. The role of tribal markets in Morocco. GEOG. REV. 48 (1958), pp. 494-511.

7,220 MILLERON, J. La mise en valeur du nouveau Maroc. AFR. ET ASIE 33 (1956), pp. 5-13.

7,221 MOHAMMAD IBN AZZUZ HAQUIM. El Zoco, centro de actividad commercial en Marruecos. CUAD. EST. AFR. 17 (1952), pp. 63-71.

7,222 MONTAGNE, R. Naissance du prolétariat marocain. AFR. ET ASIE 13 (1951), pp. 6-23.

7,223 NOUACER, K. The changing status of women and the employment of women in Morocco. AFR. WOMEN 5 (1962), pp. 17-20.

7,224 PEREZ, V. T. Política económica marroquí, consideraciones sobre el factor "precio del trigo" en la vida del campesino marroquí. CUAD. EST. AFR. 2 (1946), pp. 133-146.

7,225 STALEY, E. Mannesmann mining interests and the Franco-German conflict over Morocco. J. POLIT. ECON. 40 (1932), pp. 52-72.

7,226 TIANO, M. Le lutte d'un pays africain contre le sous-emploi: le Maroc. ANNALES AFR., 1962, pp. 406-450.

7,227 The economic crisis in Morocco. J. AFR. SOC. 34 (1935), pp. 201-204.

Education

7,228 FAUQUENOT, E. La jeunesse et l'Enseignement au Maroc. AFR. ET ASIE 33 (1956), pp. 14-19.

7,229 PEREZ LOZANO, L. La Impronta Hispánica en la Educación y Cultura de Marruecos durante medio siglo de Protectorado. ARCH. INST. EST. AFR. 16, no. 64 (1962), pp. 57-73.

Geography. Topography. Travel

7,230 BLACHE, J. Modes of life in the Moroccan countryside: interpretations of aerial photographs. GEOG. REV. 11 (1921), pp. 477-502.

7,231 CORO, F. La miracolosa Acacia Albida della minuscola oasi di Auenat. AFRICA (Rome) 17 (1962), pp. 315-317.

7,232 DEFERT, S. Les chaines hotelières et le tourisme au Maroc. ACTA GEOGRAPHICA 18 (1952), pp. 98-107.

7,233 DIAZ DE VILLEGAS, J. Africa septentrional: Marruecos el nexo del estrecho. ARCH. INST. EST. AFR. 14, no. 52 (1960), pp. 7-17.

7,234 EZQUERRA ABADIA, R. Domingo Badía: sus audaces viajes y proyectos. ARCH. INST. EST. AFR. 1, no. 1 (1947), pp. 107-123.

7,235 FOGG, W. Morocco: the basin of the "amnis magnificus." A study in physiography. J. AFR. SOC. 33 (1934), pp. 130-136.

7,236 HARRIS, P. Snapshots in Morocco. CONTEMP. REV. 181 (1952), pp. 213-217.

7,237 HERNANDEZ PACHECO, E. La exploración del N.O. africano al Sur del Atlas. ARCH. INST. EST. AFR. 1, no. 1 (1947), pp. 7-28.

7,238 HIRST, D. Moroccan snapshots. CONTEMP. REV. 199 (1961), pp. 31-34.

7,239 LOMBARDERO VICENTE, M. La exploración científica de la Geografía de Marruecos. ARCH. INST. EST. AFR. 1, no. 2 (1947), pp. 23-67.

7,240 WRENCH, W. Behind the scenes in French Morocco. J. AFR. SOC. 37 (1938), pp. 180-183.

Government. Politics. Administration

7,241 ADAM, A. Robert Montagne et le Maroc. AFR. ET ASIE 32 (1955), pp. 16-35.

7,242 ARQUES, E. Zona de influencia en vez de protectorado. CUAD. EST. AFR. 28 (1954), pp. 9-17.

7,243 B., D. Lettre à un jeune Marocain sur les dangers de l'heure presente. AFR. ET ASIE 36 (1956), pp. 52-66.

7,244 BALAFREJ, A. Morocco plans for independence. FOREIGN AFFAIRS 34 (1955-1956), pp. 483-489.

7,245 BARBOUR, N. Two problems in modern Morocco. CIVILISATIONS 11 (1961), pp. 265-275; French summary, pp. 276-281.

7,246 BARON, R. La réorganisation des collectivités urbaines au Maroc. AFR. ET ASIE 35 (1956), pp. 36-41.

7,247 BASTIDE, H. DE LA. Les civilisations dans la Promotion nationale au Maroc. AFR. ET ASIE 63 (1963), pp. 2-7.

7,248 BENITEZ CANTERO, V. El nuevo Gobierno marroquí de la zona jalifiana y sus funciones. CUAD. AFR. OR. 29 (1955), pp. 9-15.

7,249 BIANCACCI, F. Indipendenza del Marocco. AFRICA (Rome) 11 (1956), pp. 161-162.

7,250 BILAINKIN, G. The magic of Morocco. CONTEMP. REV. 185 (1954), pp. 200-206.

7,251 BOWLES, P. Tangier diary: a post-colonial interlude. AFR. SOUTH 2, no. 3 (1958), pp. 83-88.

7,252 BULL, M. The new situation in Morocco. CONTEMP. REV. 190 (1956), pp. 136-139.

7,253 BUTTIN, P. La Relève au Maroc des Cadres francais par les Cadres marocains. CIVILISATIONS 11 (1961), pp. 52-60; English summary, pp. 61-62.

7,254 CARR, R. C. Spain and Morocco: a new phase. CONTEMP. REV. 205 (1964), pp. 409-412.

7,255 CHENBAUX, A. Maroc 1965. AFR. ET ASIE 70 (1965), pp. 36-50.

7,256 CLAVERIA, M. M. Notes on the political and legal organization of the Spanish Territories in Africa. CIVILISATIONS 1, no. iv (1951), pp. 120-125.

7,257 CORDERO TORRES, J. M. Honni soit qui mal y pense...(Como informa un periódico británico a sus lectores sobre el Marruecos jalifiano). CUAD. EST. AFR. 8 (1949), pp. 83-91.

7,258 CORDERO TORRES, J. M. La influencia española en Marruecos: Lo que permiten y no que prohiben las estipulaciones internacionales de 1912. CUAD. AFR. OR. 29 (1955), pp. 53-59.

7,259 CORDERO TORRES, J. M. Marruecos. La Unión Francesa y España. CUAD. EST. AFR. 13 (1951), pp. 35-42.

7,260 CORDERO TORRES, J. M. Nueva fase en el interminable problema marroquí. CUAD. AFR. OR. 32 (1955), pp. 9-19.

7,261 CORDERO TORRES, J. M. El pensamiento español sobre Marruecos: problemas nuevos, criterios perennes. CUAD. AFR. OR. 35 (1956), pp. 9-40.

7,262 GRAY, A. Morocco's Sultan. AFR. AFFAIRS 55 (1956), pp. 12-14.

7,263 GRAY, A. Troubled Morocco. AFR. AFFAIRS 54 (1955), p. 255.

7,264 HALSTEAD, J. P. The changing character of Moroccan reformism, 1921-1934. J. AFR. HIST. 5 (1964), pp. 435-447.

7,265 HARRIS, W. B. Tangier and internationalisation. INTERNAT. AFFAIRS 2 (1923), pp. 233-250.

7,266 HOBHOUSE, C. E. The international status of Tangier. CONTEMP. REV. 148 (1935), pp. 156-163.

7,267 JULIEN, C. A. Morocco: the end of an era. FOREIGN AFFAIRS 34 (1955-1956), pp. 199-211.

7,268 LACOUTURE, J. Morocco: monarchy and revolution. AFR. SOUTH 6 (1961), pp. 90-96.

7,269 LANDAU, R. The Moroccan problem. THE YEAR BOOK OF WORLD AFFAIRS 6 (1952), pp. 170-188.

7,270 MARTIN DE LA ESCALERA, C. Una constante en el porvenir de Marruecos. CUAD. EST. AFR. 21 (1953), pp. 45-62.

7,271 MARTIN DE LA ESCALERA, C. Marruecos, Tunicia y la interdependencia magrebí. CUAD. AFR. OR. 36 (1956), pp. 15-29.

7,272 MARTIN DE LA ESCALERA, C. En torno a las negociaciones franco-marroquíes. CUAD. AFR. OR. 33 (1956), pp. 21-32.

7,273 MOHAMMAD IBN AZZUZ HAQUIM. La capacitación técnico-administrativa de los marroquíes en la zona jalifiana de Marruecos. CUAD. AFR. OR. 31 (1955), pp. 27-36.

7,274 MOHAMMAD IBN AZZUZ HAQUIM. Hacia una posible autonomía de la zona jalifiana. CUAD. AFR. OR. 30 (1955), pp. 35-40.

7,275 MOHAMMAD IBN AZZUZ HAQUIM. Las Yemaas o colectividades indigenas de la Zona. CUAD. EST. AFR. 13 (1951), pp. 55-63.

7,276 MONTAGNE, R. La politique Berbère de la France. J. AFR. SOC. 33 (1934), pp. 338-352.

7,277 MONTAGNE, R. The power of the chieftains in Morocco. J. AFR. ADM. 1 (1949), pp. 114-119.

7,278 N. La situation politique au Maroc. AFR. ET ASIE 36 (1956), p. 51.

7,279 PHILIP, D. The changing face of Morocco. CONTEMP. REV. 189 (1956), pp. 209-215.

7,280 R., J. Un aspect de la crise marocaine. AFR. ET ASIE 45 (1959), pp. 37-39.

7,281 R., J. Un aspect du Maroc actuel: le Bled sans caïd. AFR. ET ASIE 40 (1957), pp. 52-54.

7,282 RECOULES, J. Les chances du communisme au Maroc. AFR. ET ASIE 42 (1958), pp. 24-34.

7,283 RECOULES, J. Siba au Maroc. AFR. ET ASIE 51 (1960), pp. 13-19.

7,284 REYNER, A. S. Morocco's international boundaries: a factual background. J. MOD. AFR. STUD. 1 (1963), pp. 313-326.

7,285 SIMON, H. La pacification du Maroc. J. AFR. SOC. 33 (1934), pp. 329-337.

7,286 SINGH, K. R. Morocco since independence—a study of the political cross-currents. AFRO-ASIAN AND W. AFF. 1 (1964), pp. 120-130.

7,287 SZYMANSKI, E. Formation de l'état marocain. AFR. BULL. 3 (1965), pp. 27-48.

7,288 T., J. M. C. Transfretania: emancipación, unificación y transformación en Marruecos. CUAD. AFR. OR. 40 (1957), pp. 17-28.

7,289 TARN, P. Une année difficile pour le Maroc. AFR. ET ASIE 45 (1959), pp. 27-36.

7,290 TORRES, J. M. C. The Spanish dependencies 1938-1951. CIVILISATIONS 2 (1952), pp. 413-417, 623-624.

7,291 TORRES, J. M. C. The Spanish Territories in Africa 1940-50. CIVILISATIONS 2 (1952), pp. 268-275.

7,292 TORRES, J. M. C. Spanish dependencies. CIVILISATIONS 3 (1953), pp. 133-138, 389-390.

7,293 TORRES, J. M. C. The Spanish dependencies in 1953. CIVILISATIONS 4 (1954), pp. 123-124, 311-315, 486-489, 618-619.

7,294 TORRES, J. M. C. Spanish dependencies. CIVILISATIONS 5 (1955), pp. 127-129, 271-274, 437, 439; 7 (1958), p. 319.

7,295 TORRES, J. M. C. Tangier: the last Co-Imperium in a country of differing civilisations. CIVILISATIONS 3 (1953), pp. 129-132.

7,296 TORRES, J. M. C. Spanish Africa in 1952. CIVILISATIONS 3 (1953), pp. 291-292.

7,297 TORRES, J. M. C. Spanish Territories—1952. CIVILISATIONS 3 (1953), pp. 597-598.

7,298 WENDEL, H. C. M. The protégé system in Morocco. J. MOD. HIST. 2 (1930), pp. 48-60.

7,299 WOOLBERT, R. G. Spain as an African power. FOREIGN AFFAIRS 24 (1945-1946), pp. 723-735.

7,300 French Morocco. CIVILISATIONS 3 (1953), pp. 121-123.

7,301 Où en est le Maroc? AFR. ET ASIE 35 (1956), pp. 24-35.

See also 6788, 6792, 6793, 8427, 15720.

History

7,302 AGUIRRE DE CARCER, M. El obstaculo internacional en la Guerra de 1859-60. ARCH. INST. EST. AFR. 14, no. 54 (1960), pp. 87-144.

7,303 ARRIBAS PALAU, M. Una mediación de Marruecos entre España y Argel. ARCH. INST. EST. AFR. 6, no. 23 (1952), pp. 49-57.

7,304 ARRIBAS PALAU, M. Nuevos datos sobre moros en la Alhambra en el Siglo XVIII. ARCH. INST. EST. AFR. 7, no. 29 (1954), pp. 7-24.

7,305 AUZOUX, A. L'affaire de Larache (1765). RHCF 21 (1928), pp. 505-524.

7,306 BAUER, I. La embajada de un marino en Marruecos (Jorge Juan y el Tratado de 1767). ARCH. INST. EST. AFR. 5, no. 18 (1951), pp. 31-52.

7,307 BENSUSAN, S. L. Great Britain, France, and the Moorish empire. CONTEMP. REV. 84 (1903), pp. 675-686.

7,308 BOWMAN, I. A note on Tangier and the Spanish zones in Africa. FOREIGN AFFAIRS 2 (1923-1924), pp. 500-503.

7,309 BROWN, C. H. Morocco: Lyantey and after. HISTORY TODAY 4 (1954), pp. 30-37.

7,310 CAILLE, J. Le consul Jean-Baptiste Estelle et le commerce de la France au Maroc a la fin du XVIIe siècle. REV. FRANC. HIST. OUTRE-MER 46 (1959), pp. 7-48.

7,311 CASTRO-RIAL CANOSA, J. M. Las capitulaciones marroquíes. CUAD. EST. AFR. 3 (1947), pp. 3-41.

7,312 CORDERO TORRES, J. M. Marruecos: su unidad y sus límites. CUAD. EST. AFR. 1 (1946), pp. 1-43; 2 (1946), pp. 3-43; 3 (1947), pp. 57-123.

7,313 CORDERO TORRES, J. M. Las ultimas derivaciones internacionales del problema marroquí. CUAD. EST. AFR. 25 (1954), pp. 9-22.

7,314 COSSE-BRISSAC, P. DE. Robert Blake and the Barbary Company. AFR. AFFAIRS 48 (1949), pp. 25-37.

7,315 DELAFOSSE, M. Les Rochelais au Maroc au XVIIe siècle: commerce et rachat de captifs. REV. HIST. COL. 35 (1948), pp. 70-83.

7,316 DESIRE-VUILLEMIN, G. M. Cheikh Ma El Aïnin et le Maroc ou l'échec d'un moderne Almoravide. REV. HIST. COL. 45 (1958), pp. 29-52.

7,317 DRAGUE, G. Maroc d'hier et de demain. AFR. ET ASIE 53 (1961), pp. 37-45.

7,318 EDWARDS, E. W. The Franco-German agreement on Morocco, 1909. ENG. HIST. REV. 78 (1963), pp. 483-513.

7,319 FERRANDIS TORRES, M. Consecuencias politicas y sociales de la Guerra de 1860. ARCH. INST. EST. AFR. 14, no. 54 (1960), pp. 39-52.

7,320 G., E. Some notes from a Tangier diary, 1893. J. AFR. SOC. 31 (1932), pp. 366-370.

7,321 GALLISSOT, R. La question ouvrière au Maroc (1931-1935). Le prolétariat Marocain à sa naissance, et l'attitude du patronat européen. CT 11, no. 43 (1963), pp. 5-36.

7,322 GARCIA BELLIDO, A. Las primeras invasiones moras (época romana) en España. ARCH. INST. EST. AFR. 8, no. 33 (1955), pp. 31-39.

7,323 GARCIA FIGUERAS, T. La prensa (periodicos y periodistas) en la Guerra de Africa (1859-60). ARCH. INST. EST. AFR. 11, no. 46 (1958), pp. 7-27.

7,324 GAVIRA, J. El explorador africano, D. Alberto Suarez de Lorenzana. ARCH. INST. EST. AFR. 4, no. 12 (1950), pp. 45-88.

7,325 GAVIRA, J. El Kaid Ismail, Comandante de Artillería del Sultan (el explorador africano D. Joaquín Gatell, 1826-1879). ARCH. EST. INST. AFR. 1, no. 2 (1947), pp. 71-90.

7,326 GLEICHEN, Lord E. France in Morocco [foreword to articles by Marquis de Segonzac, H. Simon, R. Montagne]. J. AFR. SOC. 33 (1934), pp. 319-320.

7,327 H. The campaign in Morocco. FOREIGN AFFAIRS 4 (1925-1926), pp. 248-253.

7,328 HARBRON, J. D. Spain, Spanish Morocco and Arab policy. AFR. AFFAIRS 55 (1956), pp. 135-143.

7,329 HARDY, G. Les relations de la France et du Maroc sous Louis XIV. RHCF 20 (1927), pp. 489-508.

7,330 HARRIS, W. B. Morocco in war time. CONTEMP. REV. 112 (1917), pp. 270-279.

7,331 HOBHOUSE, C. The situation in Morocco. CONTEMP. REV. 128 (1925), pp. 437-445; 130 (1926), pp. 14-21.

7,332 IBANEZ, E. El padre Lerchundi, explorador marroquí y embajador espiritual de la cultura de España en Africa. ARCH. INST. EST. AFR. 1, no. 1 (1947), pp. 45-65.

7,333 JOHNSTONE, M. Une ambassade au Maroc. RHCF 23 (1930), pp. 45-56.

7,334 LACHERAF, M. Maroc: d'une "révolution" sur commande à une révolution populaire. PRESENCE AFR. N.S. 5 (1955-1956), pp. 105-108.

7,335 LOUTSKAIA, N. S. A propos de la structure inférieure de la République du Rif. RECH. AFR. 4 (1960), pp. 14-21.

7,336 MacLEOD, J. M. The work of France in Morocco. J. AFR. SOC. 17 (1918), pp. 97-112.

7,337 MARSAN, E. Relations commerciales de la France avec le Maroc au XVe siècle. RHCF 25 (1932), pp. 451-464.

7,338 MARTIN DE LA ESCALERA, C. Marruecos en la política peninsular de Isabel de Inglaterra. CUAD. EST. AFR. 2 (1946), pp. 147-153.

7,339 MARTY, P. Une tentative de pénétration pacifique dans le Sud marocain en 1839. RHCF 9, no. 2 (1921), pp. 101-116.

7,340 MEDRANO EZQUERRA, C. Aspecto militar de la Guerra de Africa 1859-1860. ARCH. INST. EST. AFR. 14, no. 54 (1960), pp. 53-85.

7,341 MOHAMMAD IBN AZZUZ HAQUIM. Una Embajada marroquí en el Vaticano. CUAD. EST. AFR. 5 (1949), pp. 73-84.

7,342 MONTAGNE, R. Morocco between East and West. FOREIGN AFFAIRS 26 (1947-1948), pp. 360-372.

7,343 PARSONS, F. V. The Morocco question in 1884: an early crisis. ENG. HIST. REV. 77 (1962), pp. 659-683.

7,344 PARSONS, F. V. The proposed Madrid Conference on Morocco, 1887-88. HIST. J. 8 (1965), pp. 72-94.

7,345 R., J. Notes sur la frontière méridionale du Maroc. AFR. ET ASIE 64 (1963), pp. 53-56.

7,346 RECOULES, J. Les frontières de l'état Marocain. AFR. ET ASIE 52 (1960), pp. 44-52.

7,347 RECOULES, J. Nuages dans le ciel marocain. AFR. ET ASIE 33 (1956), pp. 26-28.

7,348 ROSS, E. D. An embassy from King John to the Emperor of Morocco. BULL. SOAS 3 (1923-1925), pp. 555-559.

7,349 ROUTH, E. The English occupation of Tangier (1661-1683). TRHS N.S. 19 (1905), pp. 61-78.

7,350 SEGONZAC, Marquis DE. Lyautey. L'Evolution Marocaine. J. AFR. SOC. 33 (1934), pp. 321-328.

7,351 SEVILLA ANDRES, D. Antecedentes politicos de la Guerra de 1859-60. ARCH. INST. EST. AFR. 14, no. 54 (1960), pp. 19-38.

7,352 SEVILLA ANDRES, D. Los Partidos políticos y el Protectorado. ARCH. INST. EST. AFR. 17, no. 65 (1963), pp. 61-86.

7,353 SOLANO Y AZA, M. Tanger: La Desaparición de un régimen internacional. ARCH. INST. EST. AFR. 10, no. 41 (1957), pp. 29-49.

7,354 SPILLMANN, G. Lyautey et la Jeunesse marocaine. AFR. ET ASIE 57 (1962), pp. 34-39.

7,355 STUART, G. H. The future of Tangier. FOREIGN AFFAIRS 23 (1944-1945), pp. 675-679.

7,356 TARDE, A. DE. The work of France in Morocco. GEOG. REV. 7 (1919), pp. 1-30.

7,357 TAYLOR, A. J. P. British policy in Morocco, 1886-1902. ENG. HIST. REV. 66 (1951), pp. 342-374.

7,358 TORRES, J. M. C. L'Indépendance du Maroc espagnol. CIVILISATIONS 6 (1956), pp. 243-247.

7,359 WILLSON, B. The truth about Morocco. CONTEMP. REV. 128 (1925), pp. 146-154.

7,360 Marta Franceschini sultana del Marocco. AFRICA (Rome) 10 (1955), p. 158.

7,361 Morocco. J. AFR. SOC. 32 (1933), pp. 428-433.

7,362 Moroccan affairs [June, 1935]. J. AFR. SOC. 34 (1935), pp. 339-342.

7,363 Moroccan affairs [September, 1935]. J. AFR. SOC. 34 (1935), pp. 452-454.

7,364 Moroccan notes. J. AFR. SOC. 35 (1936), pp. 86-90.

7,365 Moroccan notes [June, 1936]. J. AFR. SOC. 35 (1936), pp. 320-322.

7,366 Moroccan notes. J. AFR. SOC. 36 (1937), pp. 95-98.

See also 7262.

Language. Literature

7,367 DEHERAIN, H. Un enquête de Silvestre de Sacy sur la langue du Maroc en l'an VII. RHCF 2 (1914), pp. 231-238.

7,368 MOHAMMAD IBN AZZUZ HAQUIM. Leyendas y tradiciones de Gumata. ARCH. INST. EST. AFR. 14, no. 53 (1960), pp. 41-84.

7,369 WILLMS, A. Sekundäre Kontrastierung in Ergänzung der Konsonantenlänge im Berberischen Südmarokkos. AFR. UND UB. 48 (1964-1965), pp. 289-293.

7,370 Tadla (Maroc). PRESENCE AFR. N.S. 18-19 (1958), pp. 197-198.

See also 7167.

Law

7,371 AGUIRRE DE CARCER, M. Uso y abuso del derecho de protección en Marruecos. El incidente de Mazagan. ARCH. INST. EST. AFR. 16, no. 60 (1961), pp. 97-129.

7,372 ANDERSON, J. N. D. Reforms in family law in Morocco. J. AFR. LAW 2 (1958), pp. 146-159.

7,373 BEAUREPAIRE, C. DE. Le rôle économique du régime de l'immatriculation foncière au Maroc. RJPUF 11 (1957), pp. 231-256.

7,374 BONAN, J. Les idées maîtresses du dahir formant code de commerce maritime au Maroc. RJPUF 5 (1951), pp. 220-227.

7,375 BREMARD, F. La procédure législative au Maroc depuis 1912. RJPUF 5 (1951), pp. 228-250.

7,376 CAGIGAS, I. DE LAS. Introducción al estudio jurídico-administrativo de la institución del habús en Marruecos. CUAD. EST. AFR. 10 (1950), pp. 9-22.

7,377 CAILLE, J. Le glas de la procédure marocaine. RJPUF 4 (1950), pp. 337-350.

7,378 CAILLE, J. Le recours contre les décisions des conservateurs de la propriété foncière au Maroc. RJPUF 10 (1956), pp. 299-306.

7,379 CEPOLARRO, A. La giustizia nel Marocco francese. AFRICA (Rome) 10 (1955), pp. 45-48.

7,380 CHENEBAUX, A. La colonisation francaise et le dahir du 9 mai 1959 sur les terres collectives au Maroc. AFR. ET ASIE 55 (1961), pp. 40-48.

7,381 DECROUX, P. L'état civil et les Marocains. RJPUF 6 (1952), pp. 1-19.

7,382 DECROUX, P. Les inscriptions sur le livre fonciers marocains. RJPUF 11 (1957), pp. 624-663.

7,383 DURAND, E. L'évolution du droit public marocain. RJPUF 10 (1956), pp. 75-86.

7,384 DURAND, E. Souveraineté et pouvoirs public dans le Maroc nouveau. RJPUF 11 (1957), pp. 478-500.

7,385 GARCIA BARRIUSO, P. La libertad jurídica e histórica de Cultos en Marruecos. ARCH. INST. EST. AFR. 17, no. 66 (1963), pp. 41-85.

7,386 GARCIA BARRIUSO, P. Proyección interconfesional e internacional del nuevo estatuto personal marroquí. ARCH. INST. EST. AFR. 16, no. 60 (1961), pp. 7-96.

7,387 LAUBADERE, A. DE. La réforme de l'organisation judiciaire marocaine. RJPUF 2 (1948), pp. 443-465.

7,388 LAUBADERE, A. DE. Les réformes des pouvoirs publics au Maroc. RJPUF 2 (1948), pp. 1-28, 136-174.

7,389 LAUBADERE, A. DE. Le statut international du Maroc et l'arrêt de la Cour internationale de Justice du 27 août 1952. RJPUF 6 (1952), pp. 429-473.

7,390 MARCHAT, H. Le régime économique de l'Acte d'Algésiras. RJPUF 12 (1958), pp. 18-30.

7,391 MORERE, M. Le Statut juridique chrétien au Maroc. CONGR. INT. SC. ANTHR. ET ETHN. 6, no. ii (1960), pp. 341-347.

7,392 PAGE, A. Le statut des relations economiques internationales du Maroc. RJPUF 9 (1955), pp. 445-494.

7,393 PANIAGUA Y SANTOS, J. M. Notas sobre el derecho consuetudinario de la propiedad en el Rif. ARCH. INST. EST. AFR. 2, no. 4 (1948), pp. 7-44.

7,394 PLANTEY, A. La justice coutumière marocaine. RJPUF 6 (1952), pp. 20-56, 189-211.

7,395 QUIROS, C. La adquisición originaria de la tierra, en el derecho musulmán maleki. ARCH. INST. EST. AFR. 3, no. 10 (1949), pp. 57-68.

7,396 RACINE, J. Application de la loi et des décrets français au Maroc. RJPUF 5 (1951), pp. 399-407.

7,397 RACINE, J. Mesures législatives et réglementaires prises par les autorités en exercice au Maroc. RJPUF 6 (1962), pp. 212-245, 364-382.

7,398 RODRIGUEZ AGUILERA, C. Ante una posible reforma de la Justicia marroquí en la Zona española de Protectorado en Marruecos. CUAD. EST. AFR. 24 (1953), pp. 43-49.

7,399 VIGUERA FRANCO, E. DE. Sistemas orgánico-judiciales en Marruecos. CUAD. EST. AFR. 8 (1949), pp. 9-54.

7,400 ZARAGOZA, J. DE M. El poder Judicial en Marruecos. ARCH. INST. EST. AFR. 19, no. 76 (1965), pp. 43-76.

See also 7133.

Religion

7,401 CORO, F. Alla celebre Zavia islamica di Ubari nel Fezzan. AFRICA (Rome) 16 (1961), pp. 26-28.

7,402 ESTEBAN IBANEZ, P. Los franciscanos españoles en las Misiones de Marruecos. ARCH. INST. EST. AFR. 13, no. 48 (1959), pp. 65-79.

7,403 GALLENT, G. G. Nuevos datos para el Episcopologio Marroquí. ARCH. INST. EST. AFR. 6, no. 25 (1953), pp. 75-88.

7,404 HAGOPIAN, E. C. The status and role of the Marabout in pre-protectorate Morocco. ETHNOLOGY 3 (1964), pp. 42-52.

See also

Science

7,405 DIAZ MARIN, J. Aportaciones a la Epidemiología del Paludismo en Marruecos. ARCH. INST. EST. AFR. 10, no. 43 (1957), pp. 7-89.

7,406 HERRERO MUNOZ, L. Acción Sanitaria Española en Marruecos. ARCH. INST. EST. AFR. 13, no. 51 (1959), pp. 57-95.

7,407 HERRERO MUNOZ, L. La sanidad española en Marruecos. ARCH. INST. EST. AFR. 16, no. 64 (1962), pp. 37-55.

7,408 MARIA TORROJA, J. Un eclipse que no pudo observarse. ARCH. INST. EST. AFR. 14, no. 56 (1960), pp. 7-19.

7,409 MEDINA, M. A. Interpretación de algunas estructuras petrograficas del Sahara meridional español. ARCH. INST. EST. AFR. 6, no. 20 (1952), pp. 7-10.

7,410 MOHAMMAD IBN AZZUZ HAQUIM. La sanidad española en Marruecos. CUAD. EST. AFR. 22 (1953), pp. 33-50.

7,411 ROLDAN, J. DE L. Y. Notas sobre aguas subterraneas. ARCH. INST. EST. AFR. 5, no. 17 (1951), pp. 49-67.

7,412 SOLSAN CONILLERA, J. Del maestro-sangrador al medico el trabajo y la generosidad de españa en la evolucion sanitaria de Marruecos. ARCH. INST. EST. AFR. 16, no. 64 (1962), pp. 7-35.

7,413 VILLAR, E. H. DEL. Estado de la edafología en la Zona española de Marruecos y Tánger. ARCH. INST. EST. AFR. 3, no. 9 (1949), pp. 61-105.

Sociology

7,414 BENEITEZ CANTERO, V. Algo sobre la infancia de la mujer marroqui. CUAD. EST. AFR. 26 (1954), pp. 41-50.

7,415 BENSABAT, S. J. Los judíos en Marruecos. CUAD. EST. AFR. 17 (1952), pp. 37-48.

7,416 ESTEBAN IBANEZ, P. Acción española de los franciscanos en Marruecos (Labor político-diplomática, benéfico-social y cultural-pedagógica). ARCH. INST. EST. AFR. 2, no. 6 (1948), pp. 7-27.

7,417 FIGUERAS, T. G. The participation of the native in the evolution of his country. CIVILISATIONS 6 (1956), pp. 193-203; French summary, pp. 204-206.

7,418 FORGET, N. Attitudes towards work by women in Morocco. INT. SOC. SC. J. 14 (1962), pp. 92-124.

7,419 FORNES ANDRES, A. En torno a la juventud marroquí: a proposito de un articulo de Bernard Simiot. CUAD. AFR. OR. 30 (1955), pp. 51-57.

7,420 JOUIN, J. Le costume de la femme israélite au Maroc. J. SOC. AFR. 6 (1936), pp. 167-185.

7,421 LAHBABI, M. A. Cultural problems in the new Morocco. CIVILISATIONS 7 (1957), pp. 82-92.

7,422 LAHLOU, A. La bourgeoisie, symbole et reflet direct de l'occidentalisation de la société marocaine. CIVILISATIONS 14 (1964), pp. 62-80; English summary, pp. 81-84.

7,423 LERICHE, A. De l'origine du thé au Maroc et au Sahara. BULL. IFAN 15 (1953), pp. 731-736.

7,424 MOHAMMAD IBN AZZUZ HAQUIM. Beneficencia y acción social en Marruecos. CUAD. EST. AFR. 27 (1954), pp. 21-40.

7,425 MOHAMMAD IBN AZZUZ HAQUIM. La evolución social en la zona jalifiana: las Juntas Rurales de Fracción. CUAD. EST. AFR. 21 (1953), pp. 23-29.

7,426 MOHAMMAD IBN AZZUZ HAQUIM. La formación cultural de la juventud marroquí de la zona jalifiana. CUAD. EST. AFR. 14 (1951), pp. 55-61.

7,427 MOHAMMAD IBN AZZUZ HAQUIM. Juntas Rurales (Transformación del agro marroquí). CUAD. EST. AFR. 12 (1950), pp. 9-27.

7,428 MONTAGNE, R. Où en est l'évolution sociale du Maroc. AFR. ET ASIE 3, no. 1 (1950), pp. 52-65.

7,429 NOUACER, K. The changing status of women and the employment of women in Morocco. INT. SOC. SC. J. 14 (1962), pp. 124-130.

See also 7223.

SPANISH SAHARA (Ifni)

Anthropology

7,430 CARO BAROJA, J. Una vision etnologica del Sahara Español. ARCH. INST. EST. AFR. 7, no. 28 (1954), pp. 67-80.

7,431 DOMENECH LAFUENTE, A. Sáhara español: del vivir nómada de las tribus. CUAD. EST. AFR. 21 (1953), pp. 31-43.

7,432 GAUDIO, A. Notes sur le Sahara espagnol. J. SOC. AFR. 22 (1952), pp. 17-25.

Art

7,433 BOETA, J. R. Un magnetofón entre los Baamaranis de Ifni. ARCH. INST. EST. AFR. 4, no. 13 (1950), pp. 55-67.

7,434 GARCIA, L. P. Industria iberomauritánica en el Sudeste de España. PROC. PAN-AFR. CONGR. PRE-HIST. 3 (1955), pp. 378-379.

7,435 GARCIA, L. P. Los trabajos de los ultimos quince años sobre la prehistoria del Africa española. PROC. PAN-AFR. CONGR. PRE-HIST. 3 (1955), pp. 274-276.

7,436 JORDA CERDA, F. Notas sobre el levalloiso-musteriense del Yebel Zini (Sahara Español). ARCH. INST. EST. AFR. 8, no. 35 (1955), pp. 81-97.

7,437 JORDA CERDA, F. Los problemas de la investigación prehistórica en el Sahara español. ARCH. INST. EST. AFR. 8, no. 33 (1955), pp. 81-97.

7,438 LARREA, A. DE. El bordado en Sidi Ifni. ARCH. INST. EST. AFR. 7, no. 31 (1954), pp. 15-29.

See also 7432.

Biography

7,439 Memoria anual del servicio Provincial de Sanidad del Gobierno General de la Provincia de Sahara. ARCH. INST. EST. AFR. 18, no. 70 (1964), pp. 109-136.

See also 7205.

Economics

7,440 ANDRES, C. A. Caracteristicas economicas y legales de las concesiones petroliferas en las Provincias Africanas. ARCH. INST. EST. AFR. 16, no. 59 (1961), pp. 85-98.

7,441 TABERNERO CHACOBO, H. Ifni: La obra de España. ARCH. INST. EST. AFR. 11, no. 45 (1958), pp. 33-48.

Geography

7,442 ALIA MEDINA, M. Geografica del Sahara español. ARCH. INST. EST. AFR. 11, no. 45 (1958), pp. 7-15.

7,443 HERNANDEZ-PACHECO, F. Caracteristicas fisiograficas del litoral y costa del Sahara español. ARCH. INST. EST. AFR. 16, no. 59 (1961), pp. 25-64.

7,444 HERNANDEZ-PACHECO, F. Características generales geográfico-geológicas del Territorio de Ifni. ARCH. INST. EST. AFR. 11, no. 45 (1958), pp. 49-63.

7,445 LHOTE, H. Michel Vieuchange et Sahara. ACTA GEOGRAPHICA 16 (1951), pp. 46-54.

7,446 MARIA FUSTER, J. Vulcanología del Atlántico meridional. ARCH. INST. EST. AFR. 8, no. 33 (1955), pp. 67-79.

7,447 SOLER, B. Cien dias en el Sahara español. ARCH. INST. EST. AFR. 6, no. 25 (1953), pp. 43-58.

See also 15711.

Government

7,448 FUEYO ALVAREZ, J. Ideología comunista y sociología política del éspacio africano. ARCH. INST. EST. AFR. 18, no. 69 (1964), pp. 71-85.

See also 7256, 7290.

History

7,449 A., Y. B. Y. Ifni. CUAD. AFR. OR. 40 (1957), pp. 9-16.

7,450 BIANCACCI, F. La questione di Ifni dalle origini ad oggi. AFRICA (Rome) 13 (1958), pp. 143-144.

7,451 GHIRELLI, A. Apuntes Sobre la cabila de Beni Iteft. ARCH. INST. EST. AFR. 9, no. 37 (1956), pp. 7-56.

7,452 HERNANDEZ-PACHECO, F. La Geografía y la Historia de las Hespérides y el Atlas de Africa española. ARCH. INST. EST. AFR. 9, no. 36 (1956), pp. 25-65.

Law

See 15740.

Religion

7,453 DOMENECH LAFUENTE, A. Del territorio de Ifni: Cofradías religiosas en Ait Ba Aamrán. CUAD. EST. AFR. 18 (1952), pp. 51-66.

7,454 DOMENECH LAFUENTE, A. Del territorio de Ifni: Religión y creencias de Ait Ba Aamrán. CUAD. EST. AFR. 7 (1949), pp. 9-21.

7,455 DOMENECH LAFUENTE, A. Del territorio de Ifni: Yenún y cuevas en Ait Ba Aamran. CUAD. EST. AFR. 14 (1951), pp. 39-53.

7,456 MUNIZ, A. Misioneros españoles en Ifni y Sahara español. ARCH. INST. EST. AFR. 13, no. 48 (1959), pp. 23-38.

See also 15724.

Science

7,457 ALIA MEDINA, M. La arquitecturo geologica del Sahara meridional español. ARCH. INST. EST. AFR. 6, no. 21 (1952), pp. 27-39.

7,458 ALIA MEDINA, M. Sobre la existencia de formaciones de hamada neogena en el Sahara meridional español. ARCH. INST. EST. AFR. 7, no. 29 (1954), pp. 49-54.

7,459 COMBA EZQUERRA, J. A. La investigacion minera en la provincia del Sahara. ARCH. INST. EST. AFR. 16, no. 59 (1961), pp. 7-24.

7,460 COMBA EZQUERRA, J. A. XXV años de investigación geológica y minera de las provincias africanas. ARCH. INST. EST. AFR. 19, no. 77 (1965), pp. 7-20.

7,461 MATEOS, J. P. Estudio mineralogico de algunas muestras de arena del Sahara Meridional español. ARCH. INST. EST. AFR. 4, no. 14 (1950), pp. 77-93.

7,462 ORTIZ DE RIVERO, M. Gobierno general de la Provincia de Ifni. Memorial anual de Hospital Central correspondiente al año 1959. ARCH. INST. EST. AFR. 14, no. 56 (1960), pp. 53-64.

7,463 VALVERDE, J. A. Aves del Sahara español. ARCH. INST. EST. AFR. 9, no. 36 (1956), pp. 67-82.

7,464 VALVERDE, J. A. Expedición zoológica en la provincia del Sahara. ARCH. INST. EST. AFR. 19, no. 74 (1965), pp. 71-78.

CEUTA, MELILLA, CANARY ISLANDS

General

7,465 JACKSON, W. D. A survey of the literature available at UCLA on the Spanish territories in Africa. PROC. 3RD. GRAD. ACAD. UCLA, 1965, pp. 301-311.

Anthropology

7,466 HOOTON, E. A. Preliminary remarks on the archeology and physical anthropology of Tenerife. AMER. ANTHR. 18 (1916), pp. 358-365.

See also 8338.

Art

7,467 MARCY, G. La vraie destination des Pintaderas des iles Canaries. J. SOC. AFR. 10 (1940), pp. 163-180.

7,468 ROBERT, D. Poteries récentes des iles Canaries. J. SOC. AFR. 30 (1960), pp. 15-55.

Economics

7,469 FRANCES ALONSO, J. Diversos aspectos de los sellos de Ifni, Guinea y Sahara. ARCH. INST. EST. AFR. 9, no. 39 (1956), pp. 77-90.

7,470 GARCIA CABRERA, C. El banco pesquero. Canario-Sahariano. ARCH. INST. EST. AFR. 18, no. 70 (1964), pp. 23-65.

Geography

7,471 BRAVO, T. Modificaciones litorales por efusiones volcánicas Cuaternarias. PROC. PAN-AFR. CONGR. PRE-HIST. 5 (1965), pp. 207-224.

7,472 CARVAJAL FERRER, F. J. Proyecto de una nueva ciudad en la bahía de Benzú (Ceuta). ARCH. INST. EST. AFR. 9, no. 38 (1956), pp. 41-49.

7,473 D'ANVERS, C. The mysterious islands. J. AFR. SOC. 19 (1919), pp. 44-54.

7,474 FERNANDEZ DEL CASTILLO, J. DE V. Y. Canarie paradiso trovato. AFRICA (Rome) 11 (1956), pp. 14-15.

7,475 JOHNSTON, A. Future rôle of Tenerife. J. AFR. SOC. 19 (1920), pp. 189-195.

7,476 JOHNSTON, A. Sylviculture and acclimatisation in the Canaries. J. AFR. SOC. 24 (1925), pp. 322-327.

Government

7,477 LERIA, M. Ceuta y su mito. CUAD. AFR. OR. 36 (1956), pp. 31-39.

7,478 OSUNA, M. G. Algunas facetas de la integración de Ceuta en la Monarquía Española. ARCH. INST. EST. AFR. 17, no. 66 (1963), pp. 7-24.

History

7,479 BRASIO, A. Santa Maria de Africa. PORT. EM AFR. 1 (1944), pp. 151-161.

7,480 SKEEL, C. A. J. The Canary Company. ENG. HIST. REV. 31 (1916), pp. 529-544.

Religion

7,481 BRASIO, A. A primitive Catedral de Ceuta. PORT. EM AFR. 7 (1950), pp. 231-244.

7,482 MALDONADO VAZQUEZ, E. Constantes Norteafricanas. ARCH. INST. EST. AFR. 16, no. 61 (1962), pp. 47-62.

West Africa

GENERAL

7,483 HAUSER, A. La cinquième conference annuelle du Waiser. BULL. IFAN 19 (1957), pp. 312-313.

7,484 HAUSER, A. Quelques notes sur l'Afrique Occidentale britannique et le Libéria. BULL. IFAN 19 (1957), pp. 673-678.

7,485 HOFFMANN, M. Research on opinions and attitudes in West Africa. INT. SOC. SC. J. 15 (1963), pp. 59-69.

7,486 HOLAS, B. Ve C.I.A. O [Ve Conférence des Africanistes de l'Ouest]. BULL. IFAN 16 (1954), pp. 424-428.

7,487 HUNWICK, J. O. Centre of Arabic documentation for West Africa. AFRICAN NOTES 1, no. 1 (1963), pp. 27-28; 2, no. 3 (1965), pp. 7-8.

7,488 STOPFORD, R. W. The Institute of West African Arts, Industries and Social Science. J. AFR. SOC. 42 (1943), pp. 183-190.

7,489 TEIXEIRA DA MOTA, A. A 2.a Conferência Internacional dos Africanistas Ocidentais. BOL. CULT. GUINE PORT. 3 (1948), pp. 13-74.

7,490 The journal of West African languages and the West African language monograph series. BULL. AFR. STUD. ASSOC. 1 (1964), pp. 24-25.

7,491 Select bibliography of periodical literature relating to Ghana and West Africa. GHANA NOTES 1 (1961), pp. 14-17; 2 (1961), p. 14.

7,492 Sixième session de la Conférence Internationale des Africanistes de l'Ouest, Recommendations et Conclusions (Extrait). BULL. IFAN 19 (1957), pp. 313-314.

7,493 Some bibliographical notices of Arabic manuscript material bearing on the history of the Western Sudan. J. HIST. SOC. NIG. 1 (1958), pp. 247-248.

See also 8143.

Agriculture

7,494 BAILLAUD, E. The problem of agricultural development in West Africa. J. AFR. SOC. 5 (1906), pp. 117-129.

7,495 BAKER, H. G. Comments on the thesis that there was a major centre of plant domestication near the headwaters of the river Niger. J. AFR. HIST. 3 (1964), pp. 229-233.

7,496 BRIDGES, A. F. B. Garden planning. NIGERIAN FIELD 18 (1953), pp. 37-41.

7,497 KNAPP, A. W. Cacao fermentation in West Africa. BULL. IMP. INST. 32 (1934), pp. 411-429.

7,498 KNAPP, A. W. Scientific aspects of cacao fermentation. BULL. IMP. INST. 33 (1935), pp. 31-49, 147-161, 306-319, 453-466; 34 (1936), pp. 154-180, 307-331.

7,499 LONERGON, M. B. The novice angler in West Africa. NIGERIAN FIELD 30 (1965), pp. 112-120.

7,500 MacLAREN, P. I. R. Fishing for bonga. NIGERIAN FIELD 17 (1952), pp. 79-81.

7,501 MORGAN, W. B. The forest and agriculture in West Africa. J. AFR. HIST. 3 (1962), pp. 235-239.

7,502 NICOL, J. M. Ephestia elutella and E. cautella infesting cacao. BULL. IMP. INST. 33 (1935), pp. 171-174.

7,503 NOSTI, J. Nuevos cultivos coloniales. CUAD. EST. AFR. 4 (1948), pp. 29-48.

7,504 PASSMORE, F. R. A survey of damage by insects and moulds to West African cacao before storage in Europe, season 1930-31. BULL. IMP. INST. 30 (1932), pp. 296-305.

7,505 SARBAH, J. M. The oil-palm and its uses. J. AFR. SOC. 8 (1909), pp. 232-250.

7,506 SAUNDERS, L. H. Hedges and borders, gardening notes... NIGERIAN FIELD 1, no. 3 (1932), pp. 41-44.

7,507 WILLETT, F. The introduction of maize into West Africa: an assessment of recent evidence. AFRICA 32 (1962), pp. 1-13.

See also 7670.

Anthropology

7,508 ADANDE, A. La tradition gnomique. PRESENCE AFR. 8 (1950), pp. 323-332.

7,509 APPIA, B. Notes sur le génie des eaux en Guinée. J. SOC. AFR. 14 (1944), pp. 33-41.

7,510 ARKELL, A. J. Forms of the talhākim and tanāghilit as adopted from the Tuareg by various West African tribes. JRAI 65 (1935), pp. 307-309.

7,511 BA, A. H. Sur l'animisme. A travers les mythes de l'Afrique Noire. PRESENCE AFR. N.S. 24-25 (1959), pp. 142-152.

7,512 BALFOUR, H. Modern brass-casting in West Africa. JRAI 40 (1910), pp. 525-528.

7,513 BALFOUR, H. The origin of West African crossbows. J. AFR. SOC. 8 (1909), pp. 337-356.

7,514 BARNICOT, N. A. and LAWLER, S. D. A study of the Lewis, Kell, Lutheran and P blood group systems and the ABH secretion in West African negroes. AM. J. PHY. ANTHR. 11 (1953), pp. 83-90.

7,515 BASCOM, W. R. West Africa and the complexity of primitive cultures. AMER. ANTHR. 50 (1948), pp. 18-23.

7,516 BEUCHELT, E. Traditionelle und moderne Jugendzietung im West-Sudan. SOCIOLOGUS 11 (1961), pp. 147-160.

7,517 BISHOP OF LAGOS, THE. Polygamy in West Africa. INT. REV. MISSIONS 12 (1923), pp. 403-411.

7,518 BIYI, E. The Kru and related peoples, West Africa. J. AFR. SOC. 29 (1929), pp. 71-77.

7,519 BLOXAM, G. W. Exhibition of West African symbolic messages. JRAI 16 (1887), pp. 295-299.

7,520 BOYLE, C. V. Historical notes on the Yola Fulanis. J. AFR. SOC. 10 (1910), pp. 73-92.

7,521 BROWN, P. Patterns of authority in West Africa. AFRICA 21 (1951), pp. 261-278.

7,522 BUNNING, P. S. C. Some observations on the West African calcaneus and the associated talo-calcaneal interosseous ligamentous apparatus. AM. J. PHY. ANTHR. 22 (1964), pp. 467-472.

7,523 CARREIRA, A. As primeiras referências escritas à excisão clitoridiana no ocidente africano. BCGP 18 (1963), pp. 309-315; 20 (1965), pp. 147-150.

7,524 COOKSON, C. E. The Gold Coast hinterland and the negroid race. J. AFR. SOC. 14 (1914-1915), pp. 298-307.

7,525 DAVIES, O. Neolithic hoe-cultures in West Africa. CONG. INT. SC. ANTHR. ET ETHN. 6, no. i (1960), pp. 383-385.

7,526 DIETERLEN, G. L'Initiation chez les pasteurs peul (Afrique Occidentale). AFRICAN SYSTEMS OF THOUGHT, 1965, pp. 314-327.

7,527 DIETERLEN, G. Mythe et organisation sociale en Afrique occidentale. J. SOC. AFR. 29 (1959), pp. 119-138.

7,528 FASHOLE-LUKE, E. W. The theme of myths: their status and right appraisal in West African religion. SIERRA L. BULL. REL. 7 (1965), pp. 33-41.

7,529 FORTES, M. Human ecology in West Africa. AFR. AFFAIRS 44 (1945), pp. 27-31.

7,530 FROELICH, J. C. Les problèmes posés par les refoulés montagnards de culture paléonigritique. CAH. ET. AFR. 4 (1964), pp. 383-399.

7,531 GAUDIO, A. Apuntes para un estudio sobre los aspectos etnológicos del Sáhara Occidental—su constitución básica. CUAD. EST. AFR. 19 (1952), pp. 57-65.

7,532 GIBSON, A. E. M. Slavery in Western Africa. By a West African. J. AFR. SOC. 3 (1903), pp. 17-52.

7,533 GOODY, J. The mother's brother and the sister's son in West Africa. JRAI 89 (1959), pp. 61-88.

7,534 HASELBERGER, H. Die Wandzierkunst der Neger in Savanne und Waldland Westafrikas. CONG. INT. SC. ANTHR. ET ETHN. 6, no. i (1960), pp. 123-126.

7,535 HERSKOVITS, M. J. Freudian mechanisms in primitive Negro psychology. ESSAYS PRESENTED TO C. G. SELIGMAN, 1934, pp. 75-84.

7,536 HILL, P. Contact with French anthropologists. UNIV. GHANA RES. REV. 1, no. 2 (1965), pp. 28-31.

7,537 HIMMELHEBER, H. Le système de la religion des Dan. RELIGIONS AFR. TRAD., 1965, pp. 75-96.

7,538 HISKETT, M. Material relating to the state of learning among the Fulani before their Jihād. BULL. SOAS 19 (1957), pp. 550-578.

7,539 HOLAS, B. Remarques sur la valeur sociologique du nom dans les sociétés traditionelles de l'Ouest Africain. J. SOC. AFR. 23 (1953), pp. 77-86.

7,540 HUTTON, J. H. West Africa and Indonesia: a problem in distribution. JRAI 76 (1946), pp. 5-12.

7,541 KENNEDY, R. A. West Africa in prehistory. HISTORY TODAY 8 (1958), pp. 646-653.

7,542 LABOURET, H. L'ethnologie dans l'Ouest-Africain (Bibliographie sommaire 1920-1927). AFRICA 1 (1928), pp. 240-248.

7,543 LABOURET, H. La parenté à plaisanteries en Afrique Occidentale. AFRICA 2 (1929), pp. 244-253; English summary, pp. 253-254.

7,544 LABOURET, H. A propos des labrets en verre de quelques populations voltaïques. BULL. IFAN 14 (1952), pp. 1385-1401.

7,545 LABOURET, H. Sacrifices humains en Afrique occidentale. J. SOC. AFR. 11 (1941), pp. 193-196.

7,546 LABOURET, H. Situation matérielle morale et coutumière de la femme dans l'Ouest-Africain. AFRICA 13 (1940), pp. 97-124.

7,547 LIVINGSTONE, F. B. Anthropological implications of sickle cell gene distribution in West Africa. AMER. ANTHR. 60 (1958), pp. 533-562.

7,548 MARINUCCI, C. I Fulbe popolo pastore. AFRICA (Rome) 14 (1959), pp. 69-72.

7,549 MARRIOTT, H. P. The secret societies of West Africa. JRAI 29 (1899), pp. 21-27.

7,550 MARTI, M. P. Conduites abusives permises en Afrique. BULL. IFAN 22 (1960), pp. 299-327.

7,551 MIGEOD, F. W. H. Personal names among some West African tribes. J. AFR. SOC. 17 (1917), pp. 38-45.

7,552 MONTEIL, C. Anthroponymie du Soudan occidental. Les Rouges et les Noirs. BULL. IFAN 11 (1949), pp. 379-381.

7,553 MONTEIL, C. Réflexions sur le problème des Peuls. J. SOC. AFR. 20 (1950), pp. 153-192.

7,554 MOREIRA, J. M. Os Fulas da Guiné Portuguesa na panorâmica geral do mundo Fula. BCGP 19 (1964), pp. 289-327, 417-432.

7,555 PALMER, H. R. M. Delafosse's account of the Fulani. J. AFR. SOC. 13 (1914), pp. 195-203.

7,556 PARRINDER, E. G. Divine kingship in West Africa. NUMEN 3 (1956), pp. 111-121.

7,557 PORTERES, R. Les appellations pour manioc dans l'Ouest africain. CONG. INT. SC. ANTHR. ET ETHN. 6, no. ii (1960), pp. 45-46.

7,558 QUINTINO, F. R. Sobrevivências da cultura Etiópica no Ocidente Africano. BCGP 17 (1962), pp. 5-40, 281-343; 19 (1964), pp. 5-35.

7,559 RATTRAY, R. S. Totemism and blood groups in West Africa. CUSTOM IS KING: ESSAYS...TO R. R. MARETT, 1936, pp. 19-32.

7,560 REED, L. N. Notes on some Fulani tribes and customs. AFRICA 5 (1932), pp. 422-454.

7,561 SAWYERR, H. Ancestor worship. SIERRA L. BULL. REL. 6, no. 2 (1964), pp. 25-33.

7,562 SCHNELL, R. Sur quelques croyances et pratiques Ouest-africaines concernant les serpents et les moyens de se protéger de leurs morsures. J. SOC. AFR. 19 (1949), pp. 89-98.

7,563 TALBOT, P. A. Notes on the anthropometry of some central Sudan tribes. JRAI 46 (1916), pp. 173-183.

7,564 THOMAS, L. V. Acculturations et déplacements de populations en Afrique de l'Ouest. CONGR. INT. SC. ANTHR. ET ETHN. 6, no. ii (1960), pp. 609-610.

7,565 THOMAS, L. V. Brève esquisse sur la pensée cosmologique du Diola. AFRICAN SYSTEMS OF THOUGHT, 1965, pp. 366-382.

7,566 THOMAS, N. W. The week in West Africa. JRAI 54 (1924), pp. 183-209.

7,567 TRAORE, M. Jeux et jouets des enfants foula. BULL. IFAN 2 (1940), pp. 237-247.

7,568 VANDENHOUTE, P. J. Poro en masker. KONGO-OVERZEE 18 (1952), pp. 153-198.

7,569 VIEILLARD, G. Note sur deux institutions propres aux populations Peules d'entre Niger et Tchad: le soro et le gerewol. J. SOC. AFR. 2 (1932), pp. 85-93.

7,570 WEINER, J. S. and THAMBIPILLAI, V. Skeletal maturation of West African negroes. AM. J. PHY. ANTHR. 10 (1952), pp. 407-418.

7,571 WERDER, P. VON. Herrschaft und Gemeinschaft im Westsudan. AFRICA 10 (1937), pp. 293-306; English summary, pp. 306-307.

7,572 WESTERMANN, D. Gottesvorstellungen in Oberguinea. AFRICA 1 (1928), pp. 189-209.

7,573 L'homme ouest-africain. PRESENCE AFR. 15 (1953), pp. 45-60.

See also 4797, 4815, 7970.

Art. Antiquities. Archaeology.
Architecture. Music. Sculpture

7,574 CARDEW, M. West African pottery. AFR. SOUTH 3, no. 1 (1958), pp. 109-113.

7,575 CLARKE, D. Negro art: sculpture from West Africa. J. AFR. SOC. 34 (1935), pp. 129-137.

7,576 DARK, P. The art of Africa: West African bronzes. AFR. SOUTH 3, no. 2 (1959), pp. 109-116.

7,577 DAVIES, O. The biological sciences and archaeology. UNIVERSITAS 5 (1962), pp. 37-39.

7,578 DAVIES, O. The old stone-age between the Volta and the Niger. BULL. IFAN 19 (1957), pp. 592-616.

7,579 DAVIES, O. West African sculpture is perishing. UNIVERSITAS 2 (1957), pp. 183-184.

7,580 DELANGE, J. L'art peul. CAH. ET. AFR. 4 (1963), pp. 5-13.

7,581 DIETERLEN, G. Contribution à la préhistoire et à l'histoire de la région du lac Débo (République Soudanaise). CONG. INT. SC. ANTHR. ET ETHN. 6, no. i (1960), pp. 387-388.

7,582 ENGESTROM, T. Origin of pre-Islamic architecture in West Africa. ETHNOS 24 (1959), pp. 64-69.

7,583 FAGG, B. E. B. The Nok terra-cottas in West African art history. PROC. PAN-AFR. CONGR. PRE-HIST. 4, no. iii (1962), pp. 445-449.

7,584 FOYLE, A. M. Architecture in West Africa. AFR. SOUTH 3, no. 3 (1959), pp. 97-105.

7,585 JEFFREYS, M. D. W. Some notes on the Neolithic of West Africa. PROC. PAN-AFR. CONGR. PRE-HIST. 3 (1955), pp. 262-273.

7,586 JOHNSON, M. A note on cowries. UNIV. GHANA RES. REV. 2 (1965), pp. 37-40.

7,587 LAFORGUE, P. La préhistoire de l'Ouest Africain. AFRICA 4 (1931), pp. 456-465.

7,588 LHOTE, H. L'anneau de bras des Touareg, ses techniques et ses rapports avec la préhistoire. BULL. IFAN 12 (1950), pp. 456-487.

7,589 MAUNY, R. Akori beads. J. HIST. SOC. NIG. 1 (1958), pp. 210-214.

7,590 MAUNY, R. Bibliographie préhistorique et protohistorique de l'A.O.F. (à partir de 1940). BULL. IFAN 15 (1953), pp. 863-867.

7,591 MAUNY, R. La monnaie marginelloïde de l'Ouest africain. BULL. IFAN 19 (1957), pp. 659-669.

7,592 MAUNY, R. Perles ouest-africaines en Amazonite. BULL. IFAN 18 (1956), pp. 140-147.

7,593 MAUNY, R. Les recherches archéologiques et historiques en A.O.F. de 1953 à 1957. BULL. IFAN, Série B: Sciences humaines 20 (1958), pp. 291-302.

7,594 MONOD, T. New rock engravings of the western Sahara. PROC. PAN-AFR. CONGR. PRE-HIST. 1 (1947), pp. 232-234.

7,595 MONOD, T. The rock paintings of French Zemmour, western Sudan. PROC. PAN-AFR. CONGR. PRE-HIST. 1 (1947), pp. 227-229.

7,596 MONOD, T. Un type aberrant de Stromatolithe ouest-africain. BULL. IFAN 15 (1953), pp. 895-900.

7,597 MONOD, T. and MAUNY, R. Découverte de nouveaux instruments en os dans l'Ouest Africain. PROC. PAN-AFR. CONGR. PRE-HIST. 3 (1955), pp. 242-247.

7,598 MURRAY, H. D. Experiments on degumming Anaphe silk. BULL. IMP. INST. 30 (1932), pp. 307-311.

7,599 MURRAY, K. C. West African wood carving. AFR. SOUTH 2, no. 4 (1958), pp. 102-105.

7,600 PARRINDER, E. G. Music in West African churches. AFR. MUSIC, 1956, pp. 37-38.

7,601 PRIETZE, R. Landwirtschaftliche Hausa-Lieder. FESTSCHRIFT EDUARD HAHN, 1917, pp. 167-189.

7,602 RATTON, C. L'or fétiche. PRESENCE AFR. 10 (1951), pp. 136-155.

7,603 RYDER, A. F. C. A note on the Afro-Portuguese ivories. J. AFR. HIST. 5 (1964), pp. 363-365.

7,604 SMITH, E. A. Popular music in West Africa. AFR. MUSIC, 1962, pp. 11-17.

7,605 SMITH, E. M. Musical training in tribal West Africa. AFR. MUSIC, 1962, pp. 6-10.

7,606 VAN DAM, T. The influence of the West African songs of derision in the New World. AFR. MUSIC, 1954, pp. 53-56.

7,607 West African Archaeological Newsletter. RES. BULL. CENTRE ARABIC DOC. IBADAN 1 (1964), pp. 14-15.

7,608 The West African Archaeological newsletter. BULL. AFR. STUD. ASSOC. 5 (1965), p. 12.

See also 4837, 4856, 4857, 4859, 8849.

Biography

7,609 L., R. P. Captain G. H. F. Abadie [obituary]. J. AFR. SOC. 4 (1905), pp. 146-149.

7,610 RODA Y JIMENEZ, R. DE. Marcelino Andrés. Su personalidad y su obra. ARCH. INST. EST. AFR. 1, no. 2 (1947), pp. 7-22.

7,611 Batty, J. H. AFR. AFFAIRS 46 (1947), p. 50.

7,612 SHOOTER-FAULKNER, M. The first West African to build a pipe organ [Augustus Beresford]. SIERRA LEONE STUD. 8 (1957), pp. 221-225.

7,613 LYNCH, H. R. Edward W. Blyden: pioneer West African nationalist. J. AFR. HIST. 6 (1965), pp. 373-388.

7,614 BONELLI RUBIO, J. M. Emilio Bonelli Hernando: un Español que vivio para Africa. ARCH. INST. EST. AFR. 1, no. 1 (1947), pp. 29-44.

7,615 SHELFORD, F. Sir George Dashwood Taubman Goldie. J. AFR. SOC. 25 (1926), pp. 132-137.

7,616 C., M. S. Mary Kingsley. J. AFR. SOC. 41 (1942), pp. 12-13.

7,617 GREEN, A. S. Mary Kingsley. J. AFR. SOC. 1 (1901), pp. 1-16.

7,618 HOWARD, C. Mary Kingsley. HISTORY TODAY 4 (1954), pp. 129-137.

7,619 FLINT, J. E. Mary Kingsley—a reassessment. J. AFR. HIST. 4 (1963), pp. 95-104.

7,620 The late Miss Mary H. Kingsley. LIBERIA BULL. 18 (1901), pp. 63-69.

7,621 MONOD, TH. Un naturaliste ouest-africain oublié: Adolphe Kummer. BULL. IFAN 13 (1951), pp. 897-901.

7,622 LUGARD, Sir F. D. Speech at presentation of Gold Medal of [African] Society. J. AFR. SOC. 24 (1925), pp. 354-359.

7,623 BOVILL, E. W. Mohammed el Maghili. J. AFR. SOC. 34 (1935), pp. 27-30.

7,624 Obituary: F. W. H. Migeod. AFR. AFFAIRS 51 (1952), pp. 340-341.

7,625 HARRIS, P. G. A note on Mungo Park and the Upper Niger. J. AFR. SOC. 35 (1936), pp. 435-439.

7,626 Obituary: Viscount Trenchard. AFR. AFFAIRS 55 (1956), pp. 121-122.

See also 19677.

Economics

7,627 ADERIBIGBE, A. B. West African integration; an historical perspective. NJESR 5 (1963), pp. 9-14.

7,628 ALUKO, S. A. Problems of financial and monetary integration in West Africa. NJESS 5 (1963), pp. 55-63.

7,629 BADOUIN, R. Les modifications des structures économiques internes dans les états de l'Afrique Occidentale. ANNALES AFR., 1960, pp. 61-82.

7,630 BAILLAUD, E. Cultivation of cotton in Western Africa. J. AFR. SOC. 2 (1903), pp. 132-148.

7,631 BALDWIN, K. D. S. The role of the economist in government service in underdeveloped territories. NISER 6 (1958), pp. 74-79.

7,632 BARLTROP, E. W. Labour in West Africa. CORONA 1, no. 6 (1949), pp. 11-13.

7,633 BAUER, P. T. Concentration in tropical trade: some aspects and implications of oligopoly. ECONOMICA 20 (1953), pp. 302-321.

7,634 BAUER, P. T. Origins of the statutory export monopolies of British West Africa. BUSINESS HIST. REV. 28 (1954), pp. 197-213.

7,635 BRENNER, Y. Problems of under-employment in West Africa. AFR. QUART. 5, no. 2 (1965), pp. 106-113.

7,636 BRIGHT, G. Trade and progress. WASU 3-4 (1927), pp. 19-20.

7,637 BUSIA, K. A. The impact of industrialization in West Africa. GHURYE FELICITATION VOLUME, 1954, pp. 111-115.

7,638 CAINE, Sir S. Trade and state action in an underdeveloped economy. ECONOMICA 23 (1956), pp. 71-75.

7,639 COX-GEORGE, N. A. Economic structures of West African countries. NJESS 5 (1963), pp. 15-26.

7,640 DAVISON, R. B. The study of industrial relations in West Africa. WAISER EC. 2 (1953), pp. 5-24.

7,641 EDOKPAYI, S. I. Industrialisation in West Africa. AFR. AFFAIRS 56 (1957), pp. 317-324.

7,642 FABUNMI, L. A. Foreign aid and self-help in West Africa. AFR. SOUTH 3, no. 2 (1959), pp. 100-108.

7,643 HELM, E. The cultivation of cotton in West Africa. J. AFR. SOC. 2 (1902), pp. 1-10.

7,644 HUTTON, J. A. Financial statistics of British West African crown colonies. J. AFR. SOC. 4 (1965), pp. 366-370.

7,645 HUTTON, J. A. West African finances. J. AFR. SOC. 1 (1902), pp. 151-159.

7,646 JACKSON, J. R. The vegetable resources of West Africa. J. AFR. SOC. 1 (1902), pp. 288-301.

7,647 JOHNSTON, A. A negro exodus. J. AFR. SOC. 3 (1904), pp. 398-404.

7,648 KNAPP, A. W. et al. Kind of cacao desired by manufacturers, by A. W. Knapp, E. Wiehr, Léon Olivier. BULL. IMP. INST. 31 (1933), pp. 359-369.

7,649 LA ROSA, C. Missione economica italiana nell' Africa occidentale (30 novembre-17 dicembre 1958). AFRICA (Rome) 14 (1959), pp. 21-28.

7,650 LEDUC, G. Le Congrès Economique d'Achimota. CIVILISATIONS 3 (1953), pp. 247-248.

7,651 MacDONALD, G. Gold in West Africa. J. AFR. SOC. 1 (1902), pp. 416-430.

7,652 MAGUIRE, P. West African dyeing. J. AFR. SOC. 5 (1906), pp. 151-153.

7,653 MARCELLA. Supply, demand, and the wholesaler. UNIVERSITAS 2 (1956), pp. 45-48.

7,654 MARCELLA. The wholesaler in the distribution system in West Africa. UNIVERSITAS 2 (1955), pp. 8-10.

7,655 MARCUS, E. Development planning and the "inherent" instability of the West African economies. NJESR 5 (1963), pp. 187-195.

7,656 MERCATOR. Fruitful co-existence. UNIVERSITAS 5 (1962), pp. 43-44.

7,657 MILBOURNE, A. H. Palm kernels from West Africa. Movement to establish the industry in Great Britain. J. AFR. SOC. 15 (1916), pp. 133-144.

7,658 NEVILLE, G. W. West African currency. J. AFR. SOC. 17 (1918), pp. 223-226.

7,659 ONITIRI, H. M. A. Towards a West African economic community. NJESR 5 (1963), pp. 27-54.

7,660 POLANYI, K. Sortings and 'ounce trade' in the West African slave trade. J. AFR. HIST. 5 (1964), pp. 381-393.

7,661 PEDLER, F. J. Foreign investment in West Africa. INTERNAT. AFFAIRS 31 (1955), pp. 459-468.

7,662 ROBINSON, S. West African resources. J. AFR. SOC. 18 (1919), pp. 190-197.

7,663 ROOT, J. W. British trade with West Africa. J. AFR. SOC. 1 (1901), pp. 40-63.

7,664 RUETE, T. Fibre plants in West Africa: a possible industry. J. AFR. SOC. 9 (1910), pp. 168-175.

7,665 SECK, A. Problèmes de modernisation de l'Ouest Africain. PRESENCE AFR. 14 (1953), pp. 83-113.

7,666 SHELFORD, F. The development of West Africa by railways. ROYAL COL. INST. PR. 35 (1903-1904), pp. 248-280.

7,667 STERN, R. M. The determinants of cocoa supply in West Africa. AFRICAN PRIMARY PRODUCTS AND INT. TRADE, 1965, pp. 65-82.

7,668 STOPFORD, R. W. Some problems involved in the development of secondary industries in West Africa. AFRICA 14 (1943), pp. 165-169.

7,669 TIXIER, G. La politique budgétaire des Etats de l'Afrique de l'Ouest. ANNALES AFR., 1962, pp. 256-266.

7,670 WELLS, J. C. Appraising an agricultural project in Northern Nigeria: a problem in investment evaluation. NJESR 5 (1963), pp. 127-140.

7,671 WILLIAMS, D. M. West African marketing boards. AFR. AFFAIRS 52 (1953), pp. 45-54.

7,672 WILLIAMS, J. W. Problems of economic development of Ghana, Nigeria, Sierra Leone, Liberia, Spanish territories. ECON. DEV. FOR AFRICA, 1965, pp. 184-197.

7,673 WRIGHT, W. D. C. A determinant of demand for food imports into West Africa. AFRICAN PRIMARY PRODUCTS AND INT. TRADE, 1965, pp. 117-124.

7,674 WYNDHAM, H. A. The problem of the West African liquor traffic. INTERNAT. AFFAIRS 9 (1930), pp. 801-818.

7,675 Cocoa control in West Africa. AFR. AFFAIRS 44 (1945), pp. 1-2.

7,676 Germany and the palm kernel trade. J. AFR. SOC. 14 (1914-1915), pp. 193-198.

7,677 An imperial industry. J. AFR. SOC. 15 (1916), pp. 320-334.

7,678 Réflexions sur le syndicalisme africain. GENEVE-AFR. 4 (1965), pp. 278-280.

7,679 Trade problems in West Africa. ECON. BULL. AFR. 2, no. 1 (1962), pp. B1-B22.

7,680 Traitements comparés, français et anglais. ZAIRE 7 (1953), pp. 286-287.

See also 4884, 4892, 5114, 7821, 7991.

Education

7,681 ASHBY, Sir E. The functions of West African universities in the field of higher education. INTER-UNIV. CO-OP. IN W. AFR., 1961, paper SL/i.

7,682 BALMER, W. T. Text-books: a study with an African background. INT. REV. MISSIONS 14 (1925), pp. 37-44.

7,683 BEVAN, C. W. L. Plans for the organisation of West African inter-university co-operation and the contribution it can make to the improvement of the various fields of higher education. INTER-UNIV. CO-OP. IN W. AFR., 1961, paper SL/x.

7,684 BIOBAKU, S. O. Definition of the fields in which inter-university co-operation is necessary and desirable, forms which it should take, and methods of co-operation. INTER-UNIV. CO-OP. IN W. AFR., 1961, paper SL/v.

7,685 BUSIA, K. A. The fuctions of West African universities in the field of higher education. INTER-UNIV. CO-OP. IN W. AFR., 1961, paper SL/ii.

7,686 CAPELLE, M. G. Methods of co-operation among West African universities with regard to problems arising from the use of English and French. INTER-UNIV. CO-OP. IN W. AFR., 1961, paper SL/viii.

7,687 COLESON, E. The impact of European education in West Africa. HIST. EDUC. J. 6 (1954-1955), pp. 169-178.

7,688 DOWUONA, M. Planning for common standards and exchange of personnel, including students and teachers. INTER-UNIV. CO-OP. IN W. AFR., 1961, paper SL/ix.

7,689 GUBERINA, P. and RIVENC, P. Projet de programme pour le développement de l'enseignement des langues en Afrique Occidentale. PRESENCE AFR. N.S. 39 (1961), pp. 118-124.

7,690 HATCH, J. Extra-mural education in a developing country. INTER-UNIV. CO-OP. IN W. AFR., 1961, paper SL/xv.

7,691 HILLIARD, F. H. Some educational problems in the Islamic areas of British West Africa. UNIVERSITAS 1, no. 1 (1953), pp. 8-10.

7,692 HUMPHREYS, K. School examinations—a joint responsibility. UNIVERSITAS 1, no. 3 (1954), pp. 5-6.

7,693 HUSSEY, E. R. J. Higher education in West Africa. AFR. AFFAIRS 44 (1945), pp. 165-170.

7,694 KING, V. E. Extension of general education by the development of extra-mural activities, special courses, etc., the position of universities and their acceptance by public opinion in the country. INTER-UNIV. CO-OP. IN W. AFR., 1961, paper SL/xiii.

7,695 KUFOUR, F. A. Planning the division of labour among institutions of higher education in West Africa, particularly in specialized teaching and research, scientific and technical education. INTER-UNIV. CO-OP. IN W. AFR., 1961, paper SL/xvi.

7,696 LEVY, D. Problems of co-operation between the English and French speaking universities of West Africa. INTER-UNIV. CO-OP. IN W. AFR., 1961, paper SL/xii.

7,697 MAXWELL, I. C. M. Co-operation on methods of recruitment and conditions of expatriate personnel. INTER-UNIV. CO-OP. IN W. AFR., 1961, paper SL/xi.

7,698 NEAL, E. E. Possibilities of liaison between West African governments in the presentation of West African higher educational needs to foreign organisations and foundations. INTER-UNIV. CO-OP. IN W. AFR., 1961, paper SL/xiv.

7,699 NICOL, D. The need for a West African intellectual community and the role of inter-African university co-operation in its formation. INTER-UNIV. CO-OP. IN W. AFR., 1961, paper SL/iii.

7,700 PORTER, A. The creation of a clearing house and bibliographical services on West African subjects. INTER-UNIV. CO-OP. IN W. AFR., 1961, paper SL/vi.

7,701 SCHULZE, W. Geography at the West African universities. SIERRA LEONE GEOG. ASSOC. BULL. 9 (1965), pp. 45-53.

7,702 SHILS, E. A further step toward a West African intellectual community: inter-university co-operation in West Africa. INTER-UNIV. CO-OP. IN W. AFR., 1961, paper SL/iv.

7,703 STAVELEY, R. O. The study of science [by West Africans]. WASU 3-4 (1927), pp. 29-30.

7,704 STEWART, M. L. The primary school and girls. AFR. WOMEN 1 (1956), pp. 84-86.

7,705 Dans les universités anglaises d'Afrique occidentale. ZAIRE 5 (1951), p. 627.

Geography

7,706 ALLISON, P. A. Historical inferences to be drawn from the effect of human settlement on the vegetation of Africa. J. AFR. HIST. 3 (1962), pp. 241-249.

7,707 BOUVEIGNES, O. DE. Le filleul noir de Louis XIV. ZAIRE 4 (1950), pp. 51-58.

7,708 C., J. Dans le delta central du Niger. ZAIRE 9 (1955), p. 174.

7,709 CROCKER, H. E. A fishing adventure in West Africa. AFR. AFFAIRS 43 (1944), pp. 27-29.

7,710 DIAZ DE VILLEGAS, J. Africa Atlántica: las riberas fronteras de Canarias. Islas y territorios del Gulfo de Biafra. ARCH. INST. EST. AFR. 14, no. 52 (1960), pp. 19-32.

7,711 DUNCAN-JOHNSTONE, A. Diary of overland journey from Lorha, Northern Territories, Gold Coast, to Dakar, Senegal, 2nd August to 26th September, 1919. GOLD COAST REV. 3 (1927), pp. 269-293; 4 (1928), pp. 31-56.

7,712 DURU, R. C. National atlas of Nigeria and international atlas of West Africa. AFRICAN NOTES 2, no. 1 (1964), pp. 8-14.

7,713 FORBES, R. H. The desiccation problem in West Africa. GEOG. REV. 22 (1932), pp. 97-106.

7,714 GALWAY, Sir H. L. West Africa fifty years ago. J. AFR. SOC. 41 (1942), pp. 90-100.

7,715 GAMBLE, D. P. Urbanisation in West Africa. SIERRA LEONE GEOG. ASSOC. BULL. 7 (1964), pp. 7-8.

7,716 GODDARD, S. In the footsteps of Mungo Park. NIGERIAN FIELD 30 (1965), pp. 18-27.

7,717 HANDOVER, D. H. A new empire link. West African colonies linked with empire's air system. J. AFR. SOC. 35 (1936), pp. 413-417.

7,718 HEYMANS, P. Excursion to Timbuctoo. UNIVERSITAS 4 (1960), pp. 44-46.

7,719 JARRETT, H. R. The present setting of the oil-palm industry with special reference to West Africa. J. TROP. GEOG. 11 (1958), pp. 59-69.

7,720 JEFFREYS, M. D. W. Arab knowledge of the Niger's course. AFRICA 25 (1955), pp. 84-89.

7,721 LAMOTTE, M. and ROUGERIE, G. Les niveaux d'érosion intérieurs dans l'Ouest Africain. RECH. AFR. 4 (1961), pp. 51-69.

7,722 LE COEUR, C. Compte rendu d'une mission au Niger. BULL. IFAN 14 (1952), pp. 1108-1111.

7,723 MASSON, H. Contribution à l'étude du réchauffement de l'eau sous l'effet de la radiation solaire. BULL. IFAN 14 (1952), pp. 389-404.

7,724 MENENDEZ GARCIA, N. Campaña oceanográfica internacional en el Golfo de Guinea. ARCH. INST. EST. AFR. 18, no. 71 (1964), pp. 49-63.

7,725 NICOL, D. Mungo Park and the River Niger. AFR. AFFAIRS 55 (1956), pp. 47-50.

7,726 NORRIS, A. W. Three tours on the west coast of Africa. GOLD COAST REV. 4 (1928), pp. 124-153, 204-231.

7,727 PARKINSON, J. The geological structure of West Africa. J. AFR. SOC. 13 (1913), pp. 14-22.

7,728 RENNER, G. T. A famine zone in Africa: the Sudan. GEOG. REV. 16 (1926), pp. 583-596.

7,729 ROBERTY, G. Les cartes de la végétation ouest-africaine a l'échelle du 1/1.000.000^e. BULL. IFAN 14 (1952), pp. 686-694.

7,730 ROWE, R. H. Some considerations governing survey work in West Africa. GOLD COAST REV. 2 (1926), pp. 122-132.

7,731 SCHNELL, R. Remarques préliminaires sur les groupements végétaux de la forêt dense ouest-africaine. BULL. IFAN 12 (1950), pp. 297-314.

7,732 SHELFORD, F. On West African railways. J. AFR. SOC. 1 (1902), pp. 339-354.

7,733 SHELFORD, F. Ten years' progress in West Africa. J. AFR. SOC. 6 (1907), pp. 341-349.

7,734 STAMP, L. D. The southern margin of the Sahara: comments on some recent studies on the question of desiccation in West Africa. GEOG. REV. 30 (1940), pp. 297-300.

7,735 SWANZY, F. A French voyage to West Africa in 1666-1667. J. AFR. SOC. 7 (1908), pp. 190-204.

7,736 TALBOT, P. A. From the Gulf of Guinea to the central Sudan. J. AFR. SOC. 11 (1912), pp. 373-393.

7,737 TEIXEIRA DA MOTA, A. O Noroeste Africano na cartografia portuguesa antiga. BOL. CULT. GUINE PORT. 3 (1948), pp. 173-199.

7,738 WELMAN, J. Harmattan. CORONA 1, no. 8 (1949), pp. 39-41.

7,739 WHITE, H. P. Terre de Barre the basis of a West African agricultural region. BULL. IFAN 27 (1965), pp. 169-182.

7,740 ZAHAN, D. Problèmes sociaux posés par la transplantation des Mossi sur les terres irriguées de l'Office du Niger. AFR. AGRARIAN SYSTEMS, 1963, pp. 392-403.

See also 4911, 12949.

Government. Politics. Administration

7,741 AKIWUMI, A. West Africa and the world. WASU 2 (1926), pp. 14-16.

7,742 ARNETT, E. J. Native administration in West Africa. A comparison of French and British policy. J. AFR. SOC. 32 (1933), pp. 240-251.

7,743 ASAFU-ADJAYE, E. O. Shall West Africa co-operate? WASU 1 (1926), pp. 8-10.

7,744 AWOLOWO, O. The place of the second chamber in West Africa. WHAT ARE THE PROBLEMS OF PARL. GOVT. IN W. AFR.?, 1958, pp. 114-123.

7,745 BIRMINGHAM, W. The economic basis of parliamentary government in British West Africa. WHAT ARE THE PROBLEMS OF PARL. GOVT. IN W. AFR.?, 1958, pp. 27-37.

7,746 BOND, H. M. Reflections, comparative, on West African nationalist movements. PRESENCE AFR. N.S. 8-10 (1956), pp. 133-142.

7,747 BOYCE, R. The colonization of Africa. J. AFR. SOC. 10 (1911), pp. 392-397.

7,748 CANHAM, P. H. Parliament and the civil service in West Africa. WHAT ARE THE PROBLEMS OF PARL. GOVT. IN W. AFR.?, 1958, pp. 85-95.

7,749 CROWDER, M. Colonial rule in West Africa: factor for division or unity. CIVILISATIONS 14 (1964), pp. 167-178; French summary, pp. 179-182.

7,750 CUNHA, S. A evolução politica do Ultramar Francês e a Africa Occidental (1945-1958). BCGP 15 (1960), pp. 115-138.

7,751 EVANS, H. Studies in war-time organisation: the resident ministry in West Africa. AFR. AFFAIRS 43 (1944), pp. 152-158.

7,752 FRY, E. M. Town planning in West Africa. AFR. AFFAIRS 45 (1946), pp. 197-204.

7,753 GARDINER, R. K. Relationship between political parties and the government in West Africa. WHAT ARE THE PROBLEMS OF PARL. GOVT. IN W. AFR.?, 1958, pp. 79-84.

7,754 GARIGUE, P. Changing political leadership in West Africa. AFRICA 24 (1954), pp. 220-232.

7,755 GRAY, A. Royal visitors. AFR. AFFAIRS 61 (1962), p. 6.

7,756 HALL, N. West African development. AFR. AFFAIRS 44 (1945), pp. 158-163.

7,757 HAYFORD, C. Nationalism as a West African ideal. WASU 2 (1926), pp. 23-28.

7,758 HODGKIN, T. A note on West African political parties. WHAT ARE THE PROBLEMS OF PARL. GOVT. IN W. AFR.?, 1958, pp. 51-64.

7,759 JUERGENSMEYER, J. C. African presidentialism: a comparison of the "executive" under the constitutions of the Federation of Nigeria, the Federal Republics of the Congo and Cameroon, and the Republics of Ghana, Chad, Congo and the Entente. J. AFR. LAW 8 (1964), pp. 157-177.

7,760 KOLARZ, W. The impact of communism on West Africa. INTERNAT. AFFAIRS 38 (1962), pp. 156-169.

7,761 KORSAH, K. A. Indirect rule—a means to an end. AFR. AFFAIRS 43 (1944), pp. 177-182.

7,762 LITTLE, K. Parliamentary government and social change in West Africa. WHAT ARE THE PROBLEMS OF PARL. GOVT. IN W. AFR.?, 1958, pp. 38-51.

7,763 O'CONNELL, J. The changing role of the State in West Africa. NJESS 3 (1961), pp. 1-12.

7,764 O'CONNELL, J. Senghor, Nkrumah and Azikiwe: unity and diversity in West African states. NJESS 5 (1963), pp. 77-93.

7,765 OGUNSHEYE, A. The place of federation in West Africa. WHAT ARE THE PROBLEMS OF PARL. GOVT. IN W. AFR.?, 1958, pp. 124-135.

7,766 PALMER, Sir R. Some observations on Capt. R. S. Rattray's paper, "Present tendencies of African colonial government." J. AFR. SOC. 33 (1934), pp. 37-48.

7,767 PILKINGTON, F. Nationalism in West Africa. CONTEMP. REV. 180 (1951), pp. 161-165.

7,768 PREISWERK, R. Problèmes de la recherche en Suisse: à propos de Demokratische Staatsformen in Westafrika d'Eugen Fehr. GENEVE-AFR. 4 (1965), pp. 84-86.

7,769 RATTRAY, R. S. Present tendencies of African colonial government. J. AFR. SOC. 33 (1934), pp. 22-36.

7,770 SCOTT, D. J. R. Problems of West African elections. WHAT ARE THE PROBLEMS OF PARL. GOVT. IN W. AFR.?, 1958, pp. 65-78.

7,771 SENGHOR, L. S. West Africa in evolution. FOREIGN AFFAIRS 39 (1960-1961), pp. 240-246.

7,772 WEINBERG, L. Party politics in West Africa. GENEVE-AFR. 3 (1964), pp. 180-242.

7,773 WILLIAMS, D. How deep the split in West Africa? FOREIGN AFFAIRS 40 (1961-1962), pp. 118-127.

7,774 WISEMAN, H. V. The development of the cabinet in West Africa. WHAT ARE THE PROBLEMS OF PARL. GOVT. IN W. AFR.?, 1958, pp. 103-113.

7,775 WRAITH, R. E. Leaders or agitators? CORONA 4 (1952), pp. 408-411.

7,776 WRAITH, R. E. Training for Local Government in West Africa. J. AFR. ADM. 3 (1951), pp. 158-162.

7,777 ZARTMAN, I. W. The politics of boundaries in North and West Africa. J. MOD. AFR. STUD. 3 (1965), pp. 155-173.

See also 15998.

History

7,778 ABDALLAH, L. Le règne du Cheik Ousman Dan Fodio. PRESENCE AFR. N.S. 39 (1961), pp. 159-165.

7,779 ABUN-NASR, J. Some aspects of the Umari branch of the Tijaniyya. J. AFR. HIST. 3 (1962), pp. 329-331.

7,780 ADESINA, S. Reflections on the Fulani Jihad of 1804. B. How religious? AFR. HISTORIAN 1, no. ii (1964), pp. 36-39.

7,781 ANENE, J. C. Liaison and competition between sea and land routes in international trade from the 15th century: the Central Sudan and North Africa. LES GRANDES VOIES MARITIMES DANS LE MONDE XVe-XIXe, 1965, pp. 191-207.

7,782 ARNETT, E. J. West Africa in review. J. AFR. SOC. 34 (1935), pp. 60-70.

7,783 BELCHIOR, M. D. Sobre a origem do termo Guiné. BCGP 17 (1962), pp. 41-56.

7,784 BENTZMANN, P. DE. La pacification du Sahara occidental. RHCF 28 (1935), pp. 249-284.

7,785 BERTHO, J. La parenté des Yoruba aux peuplades de Dahomey et Togo. AFRICA 19 (1949), pp. 121-132; English summary, p. 132.

7,786 BLYDEN, E. W. West Africa before Europe. J. AFR. SOC. 2 (1903), pp. 359-374.

7,787 BOAHEN, A. A. The caravan trade in the nineteenth century. J. AFR. HIST. 3 (1962), pp. 349-359.

7,788 BOAHEN, A. A. The Ghana kola trade. GHANA NOTES 1 (1961), pp. 8-10.

7,789 BOUCHAUD, J. Les Portugais dans la Baie de Biafra au XVIème siècle. AFRICA 16 (1946), pp. 217-227.

7,790 BOUGE, L. G. Théophile Conneau alias Théodore Canot négrier en Afrique, fonctionnaire en Nouvelle-Calédonie, 1804-1860. REV. HIST. COL. 40 (1953), pp. 249-263.

7,791 BOVILL, E. W. The Moorish invasion of the Sudan. J. AFR. SOC. 26 (1927), pp. 245-262, 380-387; 27 (1927), pp. 47-56.

7,792 BOVILL, E. W. The Niger and the Songhai empire. J. AFR. SOC. 25 (1926), pp. 138-146.

7,793 BOVILL, E. W. The silent trade of Wangara. J. AFR. SOC. 29 (1929), pp. 27-38.

7,794 BROWN, G. N. Clio as a working girl in Ghana. TR. HIST. SOC. GHANA 4 (1960), pp. 3-13.

7,795 BRUNSCHWIG, H. Les origines du partage de l'Afrique Occidentale. J. AFR. HIST. 5 (1964), pp. 121-125.

7,796 BRUNSCHWIG, H. La troque et la traite. CAH. ET. AFR. 2 (1962), pp. 339-346.

7,797 BUSIA, K. A. West Africa in the twentieth century. J. WORLD HIST. 4 (1957-1958), pp. 203-217, 471-472, 473-474.

7,798 CHILVER, E. M. et al. Sources of the nineteenth-century slave trade: two comments. J. AFR. HIST. 6 (1965), pp. 117-120.

7,799 COWAN, A. A. Early trading conditions in the Bight of Biafra. J. AFR. SOC. 34 (1935), pp. 391-402; 35 (1936), pp. 53-64.

7,800 CURTIN, P. D. and VANSINA, J. Sources of the nineteenth century Atlantic slave trade. J. AFR. HIST. 5 (1964), pp. 185-208.

7,801 DEAN, D. Joseph Wall of Goree Island. AFR. AFFAIRS 57 (1958), pp. 295-301.

7,802 DIAZ DE VILLEGAS, J. Misioneros y exploradores españoles en Guinea. ARCH. INST. EST. AFR. 13, no. 48 (1959), pp. 7-21.

7,803 EDWARDS, E. and BARKER, T. H. The trade in spirits with West Africa. LIBERIA BULL. 8 (1896), pp. 35-59.

7,804 EGWUONWU, A. N. Islamic influences on the ancient Sudanese empires. AFR. HISTORIAN 1, no. iii (1965), pp. 25-29.

7,805 ELIAS, T. O. British West Africa, past and present. AFR. SOUTH 3, no. 2 (1959), pp. 85-92.

7,806 FAGE, J. D. Some remarks on beads and trade in Lower Guinea. J. AFR. HIST. 3 (1962), pp. 343-347.

7,807 FAGE, J. D. Some thoughts on state-formation in the Western Sudan before the seventeenth century. BOSTON UNIV. PAPERS IN AFR. HIST. 1 (1964), pp. 17-34.

7,808 FARO, J. Manuel Severim de Faria e a Evangelização da Guiné. BCGP 14 (1959), pp. 459-497.

7,809 FLUTRE, L. F. De quelques termes de la langue commerciale usités sur les côtes de l'Afrique occidentale aux XVIIe et XVIIIe siècles d'après les récits des voyageurs du temps. ANN. UNIV. MADAG. 3 (1964), pp. 65-95; 4 (1965), pp. 113-141.

7,810 FURLEY, J. T. Provisional list of some Portuguese governors of the Captaincy Da Mina. TR. HIST. SOC. GHANA 2 (1956), pp. 53-62.

7,811 G., H. L. A memorial in memory of Major Alexander Gordon Laing, 2nd. W. I. Regt. J. AFR. SOC. 29 (1930), p. 507.

7,812 GANIER, G. Papiers d'Afrique. BULL. IFAN 25 (1963), pp. 145-171.

7,813 GAUTIER, E. F. The ancestors of the Tuaregs. GEOG. REV. 25 (1935), pp. 12-20.

7,814 GOLDSMITH, H. S. The river Niger: Macgregor Laird and those who inspired him. J. AFR. SOC. 31 (1932), pp. 383-393.

7,815 GREENBERG, J. H. Linguistic evidence for the influence of the Kanuri on the Hausa. J. AFR. HIST. 1 (1960), pp. 205-212.

7,816 H., J. O. A note on two Arabic manuscripts: al-Lam' fī 'l-ishāra li hukm tibgh; Fath al-shakūr fī ma'rifat a'yān 'ulamā' al-Takrur. RES. BULL. CENTRE ARABIC DOC. IBADAN 1 (1964), pp. 18-19.

7,817 HARDY, G. La politique de la France en Afrique Occidentale de 1763 à 1870. RHCF 21 (1928), pp. 325-332.

7,818 HARGREAVES, J. D. Winwood Reade and the discovery of Africa. AFR. AFFAIRS 56 (1957), pp. 306-316.

7,819 HISKETT, M. An Islamic tradition of reform in the western Sudan from the sixteenth to the eighteenth century. BULL. SOAS 25 (1962), pp. 577-596.

7,820 HODGKIN, T. The fact of African history: Islam in West Africa. AFR. SOUTH 2, no. 3 (1958), pp. 89-99.

7,821 HOWES, F. N. The early introduction of cocoa to West Africa. AFR. AFFAIRS 45 (1946), pp. 152-153.

7,822 HUTCHISON, W. F. The introduction of civilization into West Africa. WASU 2 (1926), pp. 7-13.

7,823 IRIA, J. A. O Algarve no descobrimento e christianização da Guiné no século XV. PORT. EM AFR. 3 (1946), pp. 261-273.

7,824 JANVIER, J. Autour des missions Voulet-Chanoine en Afrique Occidentale (1896-1899). PRESENCE AFR. N.S. 22 (1958), pp. 86-100.

7,825 JEFFREYS, M. D. W. How ancient is West African maize? AFRICA 33 (1963), pp. 115-131.

7,826 JEFFREYS, M. D. W. The Jewish origin of the Fulani? BULL. IFAN 15 (1953), pp. 1715-1717.

7,827 JEFFREYS, M. D. W. Niger: origins of the word. CAH. ET. AFR. 4 (1964), pp. 443-451.

7,828 JEFFREYS, M. D. W. L'origine du nom Fulani. BSEC 5 (1944), pp. 5-22.

7,829 JOHNSTON, Sir H. H. British West Africa and the trade of the interior. ROYAL COL. INST. PR. 20 (1888-1889), pp. 90-128.

7,830 JOHNSTON, Sir H. H. Note on Ptolemy's West Africa. J. AFR. SOC. 14 (1914-1915), pp. 423-426.

7,831 JOHNSTON, Sir H. H. The Portuguese in West Africa. J. AFR. SOC. 12 (1913), pp. 113-119.

7,832 JONES-QUARTEY, K. A. B. A note on press-archives research as an approach to West African history. UNIV. GHANA RES. REV. 2 (1965), pp. 48-57.

7,833 KLEIST, A. M. The English African trade under the Tudors. TR. HIST. SOC. GHANA 3 (1957), pp. 137-150.

7,834 LAWRENCE, A. W. Some source books for West African history. J. AFR. HIST. 2 (1961), pp. 227-234.

7,835 LEVTZION, N. The thirteenth- and fourteenth-century kings of Mali. J. AFR. HIST. 4 (1963), pp. 341-353.

7,836 LORETO, R. L'Africa Occidentale nel Modioevo. AFRICA (Rome) 18 (1963), pp. 75-77.

7,837 LUGARD, Lady. West African Negroland. ROYAL COL. INST. PR. 35 (1903-1904), pp. 300-326.

7,838 LY, A. Sur la politique guinéenne de Louis XIV, conditions et débuts. BULL. IFAN 16 (1954), pp. 22-54.

7,839 LYNCH, H. R. The attitude of Edward W. Blyden to European imperialism in Africa. J. HIST. SOC. NIG. 3 (1965), pp. 249-259.

7,840 McCALL, D. F. The traditions of the founding of Sijilmassa and Ghana. TR. HIST. SOC. GHANA 5 (1961), pp. 3-32.

7,841 MacDONNELL, R. G. Our relations with the Ashanties. ROYAL COL. INST. PR. 5 (1873-1874), pp. 71-102.

7,842 MACHADO, R. DE S. Henrique—o Navegador e a Génese dos Descobrimentos. BCGP 15 (1960), pp. 683-733.

7,843 MARTIN, B. G. A Mahdist document from Futa Jallon. BULL. IFAN 25 (1963), pp. 47-65.

7,844 MAUNY, R. Essai sur l'histoire des métaux en Afrique occidentale. BULL. IFAN 14 (1952), pp. 545-595.

7,845 MAUNY, R. Etat actuel de la question de Ghana. BULL. IFAN 13 (1951), pp. 463-475.

7,846 MAUNY, R. Noms de pays d'Afrique occidentale. PRESENCE AFR. N.S. 34-35 (1960-1961), pp. 61-72.

7,847 MAUNY, R. Les prétendues navigations dieppoises à la Côte occidentale d'Afrique au XIVe siècle. BULL. IFAN 12 (1950), pp. 122-134.

7,848 MAUNY, R. Relation du Sr. Destival, 1672. BULL. IFAN 13 (1951), pp. 1298-1301.

7,849 MEEK, C. K. The Niger and the classics: the history of a name. J. AFR. HIST. 1 (1960), pp. 1-17.

7,850 MIGEOD, F. W. H. Notes on West Africa according to Ptolemy. J. AFR. SOC. 14 (1914-1915), pp. 414-422.

7,851 MIRACLE, M. P. Interpretation of evidence on the introduction of maize into West Africa. AFRICA 33 (1963), pp. 132-135.

7,852 MISCHLICH, A. Contributions to the history of the Hausa states. J. AFR. SOC. 4 (1905), pp. 455-479.

7,853 MONOD, TH. Etapes. PRESENCE AFR. 1 (1947), pp. 15-20.

7,854 MONOD, TH. Un vieux problème: les navigations dieppoises sur la côte occidentale d'Afrique au XIVe siècle. BULL. IFAN 25 (1963), pp. 427-434.

7,855 MORTON-WILLIAMS, P. The Oyo Yoruba and the Atlantic trade, 1670-1830. J. HIST. SOC. NIG. 3 (1964), pp. 25-45.

7,856 MOUNTMORRES, Viscount. The commercial possibilities of West Africa. ROYAL COL. INST. PR. 38 (1906-1907), pp. 219-237.

7,857 MUHAMMAD BELLO, Emir of Sokoto. Western Sudan history. The Raudthât' ul Afkâri, tr. and ed. by H. R. Palmer. J. AFR. SOC. 15 (1916), pp. 261-273.

7,858 NEWBURY, C. W. The development of French policy on the Lower and Upper Niger, 1880-98. J. MOD. HIST. 31 (1959), pp. 16-26.

7,859 NEWBURY, C. W. Victorians, republicans, and the partition of West Africa. J. AFR. HIST. 3 (1962), pp. 493-501.

7,860 NICOL, A. West Indians in West Africa. SIERRA LEONE STUD. 13 (1960), pp. 14-23.

7,861 NWOSU, B. E. The economic effects of the Jihad in West Africa. AFR. HISTORIAN 1, no. i (1963), pp. 17-18.

7,862 OKIGBO, P. Factors in West African economic history. J. WORLD HIST. 4 (1957-1958), pp. 218-230, 475-477.

7,863 OZOR, C. N. Reflections on the Fulani Jihad of 1804. A. Political and economic aspects. AFR. HISTORIAN 1, no. ii (1964), pp. 32-35.

7,864 PAGEARD, R. Contribution critique à la chronologie historique de l'Ouest africain, suivie d'une traduction des Tables chronologiques de Barth. J. SOC. AFR. 32 (1962), pp. 91-132.

7,865 PALMER, H. R. The Lixitae of Hanno. J. AFR. SOC. 27 (1927), pp. 7-15.

7,866 PARSONS, F. V. The North-West African Company and the British government, 1875-95. HISTORICAL J. 1 (1958), pp. 136-153.

7,867 PERSON, Y. Les ancêtres de Samori. CAH. ET. AFR. 4 (1963), pp. 125-156.

7,868 PERSON, Y. L'aventure de Porèkèrè et le drame de Waïma. CAH. ET. AFR. 5 (1965), pp. 248-316.

7,869 PLUMB, J. H. The Niger quest. HISTORY TODAY 2 (1952), pp. 243-251.

7,870 QUINTINO, F. R. R. O problema da origem dos termos Guiné e Guinéus. BCGP 20 (1965), pp. 117-145.

7,871 ROBINSON, C. H. Mohammedanism in the central Soudan. LIBERIA BULL. 9 (1896), pp. 57-63.

7,872 ROBINSON, C. H. The slave trade in the West African hinterland. CONTEMP. REV. 73 (1898), pp. 698-705.

7,873 RODNEY, W. Portuguese attempts at monopoly on the Upper Guinea coast, 1580-1650. J. AFR. HIST. 6 (1965), pp. 307-322.

7,874 SAINT-MARTIN, Y. Note sur deux éditions des Voyages du sieur Lemaire aux Iles Canaries, Cap-Verd, Senegal et Gambie. BULL. IFAN 26 (1964), pp. 709-713.

7,875 SALMON, C. S. British policy in West Africa. CONTEMP. REV. 42 (1882), pp. 878-893.

7,876 SALMON, C. S. Our West African settlements. CONTEMP. REV. 48 (1885), pp. 370-377.

7,877 SALVADORI, R. La storia e il volto di una colonia. AFRICA (Rome) 10 (1955), pp. 225-226.

7,878 SCARISBRICK, J. J. and CARTER, P. L. An expedition to Wangara. GHANA NOTES 1 (1961), pp. 4-5.

7,879 SEMONIN, P. The Almoravid movement in the Western Sudan. TRANS. HIST. SOC. GHANA 7 (1964), pp. 42-59.

7,880 SILVA, A. A. DA. Apontamentos sobre as populações oeste-africanas segundo os autores portugueses dos séculos XVI e XVII. BCGP 14 (1959), pp. 373-406.

7,881 SMITH, H. F. C. Nineteenth-century Arabic archives of West Africa. J. AFR. HIST. 3 (1962), pp. 333-336.

7,882 SMITH, H. F. C. Source material for the history of the Western Sudan. J. HIST. SOC. NIG. 1 (1958), pp. 238-246.

7,883 SMITH, J. S. Sir John Kirk in West Africa. NIGERIAN FIELD 23 (1958), p. 191.

7,884 SOLANKE, L. Unity and co-operation among West African ancients as disclosed by history and tradition. WASU 5 (1927), pp. 18-21.

7,885 THOMAS, L. V. Temps, mythe et histoire en Afrique de l'Ouest. PRESENCE AFR. N.S. 39 (1961), pp. 12-58.

7,886 TROWELL, M. The Rosette cylinder from Ntusi. BULL. UGANDA SOC. 4 (1945), pp. 18-19.

7,887 URVOY, Y. Chronologie du Bornou. J. SOC. AFR. 11 (1941), pp. 21-32.

7,888 VERGER, P. Rôle joué par le tabac de Bahia dans la traite des esclaves au Golfe du Bénin. CAH. ET. AFR. 4 (1964), pp. 349-369.

7,889 WALDMAN, M. R. The Fulani Jihād: a reassessment. J. AFR. HIST. 6 (1965), pp. 333-355.

7,890 WALLS, A. F. A history of Islam in West Africa, by J. Spencer Trimingham [review article]. SIERRA LEONE STUD. 17 (1963), pp. 278-281.

7,891 WASON, J. C. The importance of West Africa. J. AFR. SOC. 5 (1906), pp. 422-431.

7,892 WASON, J. C. Native policy in West Africa. J. AFR. SOC. 12 (1913), pp. 285-289.

7,893 WESTLAKE, J. England and France in West Africa. CONTEMP. REV. 73 (1898), pp. 582-592.

7,894 WILKS, I. A medieval trade-route from the Niger to the Gulf of Guinea. J. AFR. HIST. 3 (1962), pp. 337-341.

7,895 WILLIAMSON, B. A vanished age—West Africa in the 1920's. NIGERIAN FIELD 25 (1960), pp. 112-124.

7,896 The Park-Lander memorial. J. AFR. SOC. 29 (1930), p. 508.

7,897 Some recent publications concerning the history of West Africa. TR. HIST. SOC. GHANA 2 (1956), p. 49, pp. 121-122; 3 (1957), pp. 152-153; 3 (1957), pp. 220-222.

7,898 Tables chronologiques sur l'histoire du Sonrhay et des royaumes voisins. J. SOC. AFR. 32 (1962), pp. 133-177.

7,899 West African Frontier Force in India. AFR. AFFAIRS 43 (1944), pp. 52-53.

See also 4961, 4968, 4974, 5005, 5030, 7507, 7590, 7735.

Language. Literature

Language

7,900 ARNOTT, D. W. Fula dialects in the Polyglotta Africana. SIERRA LEONE LANG. REV. 4 (1965), pp. 109-121.

7,901 ARNOTT, D. W. Proverbial lore and word-play of the Fulani. AFRICA 27 (1957), pp. 379-395.

7,902 ARNOTT, D. W. Some features of the nominal class system of Fula in Nigeria, Dahomey and Niger. AFR. UND UB. 43 (1959-1960), pp. 241-278.

7,903 BENDOR-SAMUEL, P. M. Phonemic interpretation problems in some West African languages. SIERRA LEONE LANG. REV. 4 (1965), pp. 85-90.

7,904 BRITO, E. Onomástica Fula e graus de parentesco. BCGP 10 (1955), pp. 599-615.

7,905 CARNOCHAN, J. Glottalization in Hausa. TRANS. PHILOLOGICAL SOC., 1952, pp. 78-109.

7,906 CHRISTALLER, J. G. Die Volta-Sprachen-Gruppe, drei altbekannte und zwei neubekannte Negersprachen... ZAS 1 (1887-1888), pp. 161-188.

7,907 DALBY, D. The Mel languages: a reclassification of southern West Atlantic. AFR. LANG. STUD. 6 (1965), pp. 1-17.

7,908 DALBY, D. The noun Ganī in Hausa: a semantic study. J. AFR. LANGS., 1964, pp. 273-305.

7,909 DIAGNE, P. La Ve conférence de linguistique Ouest Africaine. PRESENCE AFR. N.S. 55 (1965), pp. 154-158.

7,910 DREXEL, A. Haussa-Probleme. BIBLIOTHECA AFR. 1 (1925), pp. 149-172; 2 (1926), pp. 245-257.

7,911 DREXEL, A. Psychologische Erwägungen zum ful'schen Anlautewechsel. BIBLIOTHECA AFR. 3 (1929-1930), pp. 299-316.

7,912 DUCOS, G. E. Parallèle Badiaranké—peul, limité à deux points de structure. J. AFR. LANGS. 3 (1964), pp. 75-79.

7,913 ESSEN, O. VON. Implosive Verschlusslaute in Hausa. AFR. UND UB. 45 (1961-1962), pp. 285-291.

7,914 GOUFFÉ, C. Observations sur le dergé causatif dans un parler Haoussa du Niger. J. AFR. LANGS. 1 (1962), pp. 182-200.

7,915 GREENBERG, J. West African Languages congress [Freetown, 1963]. AFR. STUD. BULL. 6, no. iii (1963), pp. 30-31.

7,916 HAIR, P. E. H. The contribution of Freetown and Fourah Bay College to the study of West African languages. SIERRA LEONE LANG. REV. 1 (1962), pp. 7-18.

7,917 HISKETT, M. The historical background to the naturalization of Arabic loan-words in Hausa. AFR. LANG. STUD. 6 (1965), pp. 18-26.

7,918 HOMBURGER, L. Eléments dravidiens en peul. J. SOC. AFR. 18 (1948), pp. 135-143.

7,919 HOUIS, M. Du rapport entre les classes et le conditionnement de l'initiale radicale en peul. BULL. IFAN 21 (1959), pp. 167-178.

7,920 HOUIS, M. Quelques données de toponymie ouest-africaine. BULL. IFAN, Série B: Sciences humaines, 20 (1958), pp. 562-575.

7,921 HOUIS, M. Rapport presente a la commission du linguistic survey. WAISER 5 (1956), pp. 149-155.

7,922 HOUIS, M. Schèmes et fonctions tonologiques. BULL. IFAN 18 (1956), pp. 335-368.

7,923 HUNWICK, J. O. The influence of Arabic in West Africa. TRANS. HIST. SOC. GHANA 7 (1964), pp. 24-41.

7,924 JEFFREYS, M. D. W. Speculative origins of the Fulani language. AFRICA 17 (1947), pp. 47-53.

7,925 JOHNSTON, Sir H. H. The Fulas and their language. J. AFR. SOC. 20 (1921), pp. 212-216.

7,926 JUNGRAITHMAYR, H. Bericht vom 3. Kongress für das Stadium westafrikanischer Sprachen (Third West African Languages Congress) 25 März bis 1 April 1963 in Freetown, Sierra Leone. AFR. UND UB. 46 (1962-1963), pp. 314-316.

7,927 KING, P. V. Some Hausa idioms. J. AFR. SOC. 8 (1909), pp. 193-201.

7,928 KIRK-GREENE, A. The Hausa Language Board. AFR. UND UB. 47 (1964), pp. 187-203.

7,929 KLINGENHEBEN, A. Die Inversion im Ful. AFR. UND UB. 45 (1961-1962), pp. 161-169.

7,930 KLINGENHEBEN, A. Die Präfixklassen des Ful. AFR. UND UB. 14 (1923-1924), pp. 189-222, 290-315.

7,931 KLINGENHEBEN, A. Die Silbenauslautgesetze des Hausa. AFR. UND UB. 18 (1927-1928), pp. 272-297.

7,932 KLINGENHEBEN, A. Die Tempora Westafrikas und die semitischen Tempora. AFR. UND UB. 19 (1928-1929), pp. 241-268.

7,933 KRAFT, C. The morpheme Nā in relation to a broader classification of Hausa verbals. J. AFR. LANGS. 3 (1964), pp. 231-240.

7,934 KRAFT, C. A new study of Hausa syntax. J. AFR. LANGS. 3 (1964), pp. 66-74.

7,935 LANG, K. Zur Wortbedeutung in Fulfulde. BIBLIOTHECA AFR. 2 (1926), pp. 229-232.

7,936 LA VERGNE DE TRESSAN, DE. De langage descriptif en Peul. BULL. IFAN 14 (1952), pp. 636-659.

7,937 LA VERGNE DE TRESSAN, DE. Pour une transcription phonétique Peule unifiée. BULL. IFAN 13 (1951), pp. 916-923.

7,938 LUKAS, J. Neue Aussichten zur sprachlichen Gliederung des Sudan. INT. CONG. LING. 4 (1936), pp. 186-191.

7,939 MANESSY, G. Adjectifs épithètes et adjectifs conjoints dans les langues voltaïques. BULL. IFAN 26 (1964), pp. 505-517.

7,940 MANESSY, G. L'alterance consonantique initiale en Manya, Kpelle, Loma, Bandi et Mende. J. AFR. LANGS. 3 (1964), pp. 162-178.

7,941 MANESSY, G. Nom et verbe dans les langues Mandé. J. AFR. LANGS. 1 (1962), pp. 57-68.

7,942 MANESSY, G. Les particules affirmatives postverbales dans le groupe voltaïque. BULL. IFAN 25 (1963), pp. 107-124.

7,943 MANESSY, G. Remarques sur la formation du pluriel en bandi, loma, mende et kpelle. BULL. IFAN 26 (1964), pp. 119-126.

7,944 MANESSY, G. Structure de la proposition relative dans quelques langues Voltaïgnes. J. AFR. LANGS. 2 (1963), pp. 260-267.

7,945 MANESSY, G. Les substantifs à préfixe et suffixe dans les langues voltaïques. J. AFR. LANGS. 4 (1965), pp. 170-181.

7,946 MEEUSSEN, A. E. A note on permutation in Kpele-Mende. AFR. LANG. STUD. 6 (1965), pp. 112-116.

7,947 MERRICK, G. Notes on Hausa and pidgin English. J. AFR. SOC. 8 (1909), pp. 303-307.

7,948 OSADEBAY, D. C. et al. West African voices by D. C. Osadebay, E. L. Lasebikan, J. H. Nketia. AFR. AFFAIRS 48 (1949), pp. 151-158, 242-249.

7,949 PALMER, H. The "Fulas" and their language. J. AFR. SOC. 22 (1923), pp. 121-130.

7,950 PARSONS, F. W. Further observations on the 'causative' grade of the verb in Hausa. J. AFR. LANGS. 1 (1962), pp. 253-272.

7,951 PARSONS, F. W. An introduction to gender in Hausa. AFR. LANG. STUD. 1 (1960), pp. 117-136.

7,952 PARSONS, F. W. The operation of gender in Hausa: the personal pronouns and genitive copula. AFR. LANG. STUD. 2 (1961), pp. 100-124.

7,953 PARSONS, F. W. The operation of gender in Hausa: stabilizer, dependent nominals and qualifiers. AFR. LANG. STUD. 4 (1963), pp. 166-207.

7,954 PRIETZE, R. Dichtung der Haussa. AFRICA 4 (1931), pp. 86-95.

7,955 PRIETZE, R. Zwei Haussa-Texte. ZAOS 3 (1897), pp. 140-156.

7,956 ROSS, A. S. C. Note on a Hausa problem. J. AFR. LANGS. 3 (1964), p. 201.

7,957 SCHLUNK, M. Die Sprachenfrage in den Missionsschulen Afrikas. FESTSCHRIFT MEINHOF, 1927, pp. 502-506.

7,958 TAYLOR, F. W. The orthography of African languages. With special reference to Hausa and Fulani. J. AFR. SOC. 28 (1929), pp. 241-252.

7,959 TAYLOR, F. W. Some English words in Fulani and Hausa. J. AFR. SOC. 20 (1920), pp. 25-32.

7,960 TRESSAN, Marquis DE. Au sujet des Peuls. BULL. IFAN 14 (1952), pp. 1512-1559.

7,961 ULDALL, H. J. Report of the Linguistic Survey Committee. WAISER 5 (1956), pp. 145-148.

7,962 VISCHER, H. Rules for Hausa spelling. J. AFR. SOC. 11 (1912), pp. 339-347.

7,963 YOHSEN, E. Proben der Fulah-Sprache. ZAS 1 (1887-1888), pp. 217-237.

7,964 WANGLER, H. H. Neuere Ergebnisse zur Tonologie des Hausa. INT. CONG. PHONETIC SC. 4 (1961), pp. 787-794.

7,965 WARD, I. C. Tone in West African languages. INT. CONG. PHONETIC SC. 3 (1938), pp. 383-388.

7,966 WARD, I. C. Tones and grammar in West African languages. TRANS. PHILOLOGICAL SOC., 1936, pp. 43-53.

7,967 WARD, I. C. Verbal tone patterns in West African languages. BULL. SOAS 12 (1947-1948), pp. 831-837.

7,968 WELMERS, W. E. Associative a and ka in Niger-Congo. LANGUAGE 39 (1963), pp. 432-447.

7,969 WERNER, A. Language and folklore in West Africa. J. AFR. SOC. 6 (1906), pp. 65-83.

7,970 WESCOTT, R. W. Problems in linguistic anthropology. WAISER 5 (1956), pp. 138-144.

7,971 WESTERMANN, D. Form und Funktion der Reduplikation in einigen westafrikanischen sprachen. AFRIKA (Berlin) 3 (1944), pp. 83-104.

7,972 WESTERMANN, D. The linguistic situation and vernacular literature in British West Africa. AFRICA 2 (1929), pp. 337-351.

7,973 WESTERMANN, D. Laut, Ton und Sinn in Westafrikanischen Sudansprachen. FESTSCHRIFT MEINHOF, 1927, pp. 315-328.

7,974 WESTERMANN, D. Morphologische Struktur der nigritischen Sudansprachen. INT. CONG. LING. 5 (1939), pp. 71-72.

7,975 WILSON, W. A. A. The fifth West African Languages Congress. UNIV. GHANA RES. REV. 1, no. 2 (1965), pp. 46-48.

7,976 WINSTON, F. D. D. Third West African Languages Congress, Freetown 1963. SIERRA LEONE LANG. REV. 2 (1963), pp. 55-58.

See also 310, 311, 313, 5039, 7551, 7557, 7815.

Literature

7,977 ANIMAGEDDI. West African just so stories: Why the iguana is deaf; How the dove repaid the tortoise. [Fiction.] NIGERIAN FIELD 6 (1937), pp. 42-44; 8 (1939), pp. 38-39.

7,978 BEIER, U. The conflict of cultures in West African poetry. BO 1 (1957), pp. 17-21.

7,979 EDWARDS, P. Hasana's lover: a West African tale in verse. TRANSITION 23 (1965), pp. 30-31.

7,980 MOORE, G. Mister Johnson [by Joyce Cary] reconsidered. BO 4 (1958), pp. 16-23.

7,981 NADE, A. M. Chants populaires d'Afrique Noire: Marie-toi au pays, Chant de guerre, Gnama. PRESENCE AFR. N.S. 12 (1957), pp. 86-87.

7,982 NICOL, D. The soft pink palms. PRESENCE AFR. N.S. 8-10 (1956), pp. 108-121.

7,983 NICOL, D. West African poetry. AFR. SOUTH 5, no. 3 (1961), pp. 115-122.

7,984 PFEFFER, G. Prose and poetry of the Ful'be. AFRICA 12 (1939), pp. 285-306.

7,985 RATTRAY, R. S. Hausa poetry. ESSAYS PRESENTED TO C. G. SELIGMAN, 1934, pp. 255-265.

7,986 SHELTON, A. J. Behaviour and cultural value in West African stories: literary sources for the study of culture contact. AFRICA 34 (1964), pp. 353-359.

7,987 VAJDA, G. Contribution a la connaissance de la littérature arabe en Afrique Occidentale. J. SOC. AFR. 20 (1950), pp. 229-237.

7,988 Un prix littéraire destiné à l'A.O.F.: le prix Margaret Wrong. BULL. IFAN 13 (1951), pp. 1308-1309.

Law

7,989 B., P. La réorganisation foncière en A.O.F., en AEF, au Togo et au Cameroun. RJPUF 11 (1957), pp. 101-114.

7,990 DANIELS, W. C. E. Some principles of the law of trusts in West Africa. J. AFR. LAW 6 (1962), pp. 164-178.

7,991 GEARY, W. N. M. Land tenure and legislation in British West Africa. J. AFR. SOC. 12 (1913), pp. 236-248.

7,992 OLLENNU, N. M. The influence of English law on West Africa. J. AFR. LAW 5 (1961), pp. 21-35.

7,993 STOPFORD, J. G. B. English governor and African chiefs. J. AFR. SOC. 2 (1903), pp. 308-311.

7,994 STOPFORD, J. G. B. Glimpses of native law in West Africa. J. AFR. SOC. 1 (1901), pp. 80-97.

7,995 Res Judicata. J. AFR. LAW 1 (1957), pp. 130-132.

See also 7759, 10748.

Religion

7,996 ALLEN, R. Islam and christianity in the Sudan. INT. REV. MISSIONS 9 (1920), pp. 531-543.

7,997 BLYDEN, E. W. Islam in Western Soudan. J. AFR. SOC. 2 (1902), pp. 11-37.

7,998 BRITO, E. Festas religiosas do Islamisco Fula. BCGP 11 (1956), pp. 91-105.

7,999 BRITO, E. Notas a Vida Religiosa dos Fulas e Mandingas. BCGP 12 (1957), pp. 149-189.

8,000 CORREIA, P. O Forte de S. João Baptista de Ajudá. PORT. EM AFR. 10 (1953), pp. 167-171.

8,001 DENNETT, R. E. A common basis of religion. Or, the Order in Genesis one with the Order in the Categories in West Africa. J. AFR. SOC. 12 (1913), pp. 256-275; 13 (1913), pp. 33-44.

8,002 FILESI, T. Di una breve relazione sulle missioni in terra di Guinea all' inizio del 1600. AFRICA (Rome) 20 (1965), pp. 40-53.

8,003 FISHER, H. J. Some novelties introduced into West African Islam by Ahmadiya. NISER 6 (1958), pp. 220-231.

8,004 FYFE, C. The West African Methodists in the nineteenth century. SIERRA L. BULL. REL. 3 (1961), pp. 22-28.

8,005 HAIR, P. E. H. C.M.S. native clergy in West Africa to 1900. SIERRA L. BULL. REL. 4 (1962), pp. 71-72.

8,006 HODGKIN, T. Islam and national movements in West Africa. J. AFR. HIST. 3 (1962), pp. 323-327.

8,007 HUDSON, A. The missionary in West Africa. J. AFR. SOC. 2 (1903), pp. 454-455; 3 (1903), pp. 100-103.

8,008 JONES, F. M. The work of the Church Missionary Society in West Africa. INT. REV. MISSIONS 1 (1912), pp. 240-257.

8,009 MAUNY, R. Le Judaïsme, les Juifs et l'Afrique occidentale. BULL. IFAN 11 (1949), pp. 354-378.

8,010 NICKELS, A. Snapshots from West Africa. CONTEMP. REV. 164 (1943), pp. 364-368.

8,011 PALMER, H. R. An early Fulani conception of Islam. J. AFR. SOC. 13 (1914), pp. 407-414.

8,012 PARRINDER, E. G. Islam and West African indigenous religion. NUMEN 6 (1959), pp. 130-141.

8,013 PARRINDER, E. G. The religious situation in West Africa. AFR. AFFAIRS 59 (1960), pp. 38-42.

8,014 PARRINDER, E. G. Les Sociétés religieuses en Afrique Occidentale. PRESENCE AFR. N.S. 18-19 (1958), pp. 17-22.

8,015 SAWYERR, H. Christian evangelistic strategy in West Africa. Reflections on the centenary of the consecration of Bishop Samuel Adjayi Crowther on St. Peter's Day, 1864. INT. REV. MISSIONS 54 (1965), pp. 343-352.

8,016 SKINNER, E. P. The diffusion of Islam in an African society. ANTHROPOLOGY AND AFRICA TODAY, 1962, pp. 659-669.

8,017 SMITH, E. L. The evangelization of West Africa to-day. INT. REV. MISSIONS 54 (1965), pp. 484-496.

8,018 THOMAS, L. V. Animisme et christianisme. Réflexions sur quelques problèmes d'évangélisation en Afrique Occidentale. PRESENCE AFR. N.S. 26 (1959), pp. 5-21.

8,019 TONKIN, T. J. Muhammadanism in the Western Sudan. J. AFR. SOC. 3 (1904), pp. 123-141.

8,020 TURNER, H. W. The catechism of an independent West African church. SIERRA L. BULL. REL. 2 (1960), pp. 45-57.

8,021 TURNER, H. W. The litany of an independent West African church. SIERRA L. BULL. REL. 1 (1959), pp. 48-55.

8,022 TURNER, H. W. Searching and syncretism: a West African documentation. INT. REV. MISSIONS 49 (1960), pp. 189-194.

8,023 WESTERMANN, D. Islam in the Eastern Sudan. INT. REV. MISSIONS 2 (1913), pp. 454-485.

8,024 WESTERMANN, D. Islam in the West and Central Sudan. INT. REV. MISSIONS 1 (1912), pp. 618-653.

See also 13011.

Science

8,025 ADAM, W. Les Céphalopodes de l'Institut Français d'Afrique Noire. BULL. IFAN 13 (1951), pp. 771-787.

8,026 ADAMS, C. D. Diospyros mespiliforms. UNIVERSITAS 3 (1959), pp. 180-181.

8,027 ADAMS, C. D. Vernonia colorata. UNIVERSITAS 3 (1958), pp. 49-50.

8,028 AIDIN, R. Abnormal red cells in faeces and urine. WEST AFR. MILITARY MED. BULL. 3 (1945), pp. 40-41.

8,029 ALMEIDA, F. F. M. DE. Precambrian geology of north-eastern Brazil and Western Africa and the theory of continental drift. PROC. SYMP. GRANITES W. AFR., 1965, pp. 151-162.

8,030 ARCHER, G. T. L. A note on phage types of Bact. typhosum in West Africa. WEST AFR. MILITARY MED. BULL. 3 (1945), pp. 14-18.

8,031 ARENES, J. A propos des Centaurea (section Calcitrapa) de l'Afrique tropicale occidentale. BULL. IFAN 14 (1952), pp. 28-33.

8,032 BASILEWSKY, P. Contribution à l'étude des Coléoptères Carabidae de l'Afrique occidentale. 1. Coléoptères Carabiques recueillis au Liberia by M. M. Dekeyer and Holas. 2. Coléoptères recueillis by M. A. Villiers and Richard-Toll (Sénégal). BULL. IFAN 11 (1949), pp. 327-330.

8,033 BASILEWSKY, P. Contribution à l'étude des Coléoptères Carabiques de l'Afrique occidentale. V. Listes diverses. BULL. IFAN 15 (1953), pp. 1031-1036.

8,034 BEGG, A. H. A note on heterophile agglutination in trypanosomiasis. WEST AFR. MILITARY MED. BULL. 3 (1945), pp. 37-40.

8,035 BENOIT, P. L. G. Contribution à la connaissance des Ichneumonides de l'Afrique occidentale. BULL. IFAN 15 (1953), pp. 543-548.

8,036 BERRIE, A. and BERRIE, G. K. The West African cycad. NIGERIAN FIELD 21 (1956), pp. 36-41.

8,037 BIGOURDAN, J. Le Phacochère et les Suidés dans l'Ouest africain. BULL. IFAN 10 (1948), pp. 285-360.

8,038 BOORMAN, J. Mantispids. NIGERIAN FIELD 25 (1960), pp. 104-112.

8,039 BOORMAN, J. Mosquitoes. NIGERIAN FIELD 28 (1963), pp. 120-128.

8,040 BOWMAN, A. I. Duikers Joe and Josephine. NIGERIAN FIELD 23 (1958), pp. 66-70.

8,041 BROWN, A. P. Palaearctic migrants in West Africa. NIGERIAN FIELD 29 (1964), pp. 174-177.

8,042 BROWN, J. Preservation of tent pegs against infestation white ants. WEST. AFR. MILITARY MED. BULL. 1 (1942), p. 13.

8,043 CADENAT, J. Notes d'Ichtyologie ouest africaine. VI. Poissons des campagnes du Gérard Tréca. BULL. IFAN 15 (1953), pp. 1051-1102.

8,044 CAMERON, M. New species of African Staphylinidae (col). BULL. IFAN 11 (1949), pp. 313-326.

8,045 CAMERON, M. Three new Staphylinidae from West Africa. BULL. IFAN 13 (1951), pp. 126-128.

8,046 CHEVALIER, A. On some alleged rubber-producing plants of West Africa. J. AFR. SOC. 5 (1906), pp. 252-256.

8,047 CHEW, C. W. Le rocouyer (Bixa Orellana Linné) avec une planche en couleurs. ET. CAMER. 27-28 (1949), pp. 177-178.

8,048 COLLINS, W. B. Sounds in the forest. NIGERIAN FIELD 20 (1955), pp. 84-88.

8,049 DAGET, J. Description d'un Cichlidé pétricole du Niger. Labrochromis polli. BULL. IFAN 14 (1952), pp. 226-228.

8,050 DAGET, J. Poissons d'eau douce nouvellement entrés dans les collections de l'Ifan. BULL. IFAN 13 (1951), pp. 1141-1151.

8,051 DALZIEL, J. M. Some West African trees, shrubs and vines now growing in America. NIGERIAN FIELD 7 (1938), pp. 81-84, 126-130.

8,052 DEKEYSER, P. L. Considérations sur les Chats (Felis libyca Forster) de l'Afrique occidentale. BULL. IFAN 12 (1950), pp. 700-709.

8,053 DEKEYSER, P. L. Notes d'Ornithologie Ouest-Africaine. BULL. IFAN 9 (1947), pp. 358-382.

8.054 DELAIS, M. Notes d'ichtyologie ouest-africaine. III. Notes sur les Lutjanidae. BULL. IFAN 14 (1952), pp. 1214-1227.

8.055 DIXON, P. A. Volvariella volvacea: Abe-mirre. UNIVERSITAS 4 (1960), pp. 51-52.

8,056 DOUCET, J. and LEPESME, P. Sur un cas d'envenimation par Atractaspis Vipéridé ouest-africain. BULL. IFAN 15 (1953), pp. 855-859.

8,057 DONALD, R. G. and ELGOOD, J. H. The painted snipe in West Africa. NIGERIAN FIELD 27 (1962), pp. 173-177.

8,058 DUONG-HUU-THOI. Contribution a l'étude de l'Hibiscus Rosa Sinensis L. Fécondation-germination du Pollen Cytologie. BULL. IFAN 9 (1947), pp. 138-169.

8,059 ENGLAND, P. J. M. The treatment of gonorrhoea by intramuscular injections of suspension of M. and B.693. WEST. AFR. MILITARY MED. BULL. 2 (1942), pp. 32-34.

8,060 EVANS-ANFOM, E. Intestinal perforation (some observations on aetiology and management). GHANA MED. J. 2 (1963), pp. 99-103.

8,061 FAIRBAIRN, W. A. The fine-spotted woodpecker. NIGERIAN FIELD 4 (1935), p. 70.

8,062 FAIRBAIRN, W. A. The northern black-bellied bustard. NIGERIAN FIELD 6 (1937), p. 116.

8,063 FAIRBAIRN, W. A. Two interesting birds. NIGERIAN FIELD 6 (1937), p. 18.

8,064 FINDLAY, G. M. The diagnosis and treatment of the dysenteries and diarrhoeas. WEST AFR. MILITARY MED. BULL. 2 (1942), pp. 34-46.

8,065 FINDLAY, G. M. The diagnosis and treatment of yellow fever. WEST AFR. MILITARY MED. BULL. 2 (1942), pp. 3-11.

8,066 FINDLAY, G. M. Notes on the treatment of blackwater fever. WEST AFR. MILITARY MED. BULL. 1 (1942), pp. 18-25.

8,067 FINDLAY, G. M. The treatment of malaria with large doses of quinine. WEST AFR. MILITARY MED. BULL. 1 (1942), pp. 26-28.

8,068 FINDLAY, G. M. Yaws. WEST AFR. MILITARY MED. BULL. 3 (1945), pp. 5-13.

8,069 FORBES, J. G. Medical report of the Anglo-French Boundary Commission on the western frontier of the Gold Coast Colony—January, 1902-May, 1903. J. AFR. SOC. 3 (1904), pp. 381-397.

8,070 FORBES, J. G. Native methods of treatment in West Africa. With notes on the tropical diseases most prevalent among the inhabitants of the Gold Coast Colony. J. AFR. SOC. 3 (1904), pp. 361-380.

8,071 FOREST, J. Caractères et affinités de Pseudopagurus, genre nouveau établi pour un Paguridae de la Côte occidentale d'Afrique, Pagurus granulimanus Miers. BULL. IFAN 14 (1952), pp. 799-812.

8,072 GRAY, J. D. Pulsometers. WEST AFR. MILITARY MED. BULL. 3 (1945), p. 32.

8,073 HAMER, A. B. Emulsion of palm oil and flavine in the treatment of wounds. WEST AFR. MILITARY MED. BULL. 2 (1942), pp. 30-31.

8,074 HENDERSON-BEGG, A. Modification of Field's stain. WEST AFR. MILITARY MED. BULL. 3 (1945), pp. 30-31.

8,075 HENDRICKSE, R. G. Anaemia in children in West Africa. GHANA MED. J. 2 (1963), pp. 124-130.

8,076 HEPPER, F. N. The story of Thunbergia erecta. NIGERIAN FIELD 29 (1964), pp. 147-150.

8,077 HOLLAND, J. H. Scirpus lacustris (Linn.). J. AFR. SOC. 4 (1905), p. 310.

8,078 HOWIE, J. W. Fields modified stain for malaria parasites. WEST AFR. MILITARY MED. BULL. 1 (1942), pp. 14-16.

8,079 IRVINE, F. R. Green turtle. NIGERIAN FIELD 4 (1935), pp. 29-32.

8,080 IRVINE, F. R. Leathery turtle. NIGERIAN FIELD 4 (1935), pp. 32-33.

8,081 IRVINE, F. R. Mosses and liverworts: a field for research in West Africa. NIGERIAN FIELD 19 (1954), pp. 15-23.

8,082 JELLICOE, M. R. The plainbacked pipit in Sierra Leone. NIGERIAN FIELD 19 (1954), pp. 31-35.

8,083 KEAY, R. W. J. Getting to know plants in West Africa. NIGERIAN FIELD 21 (1956), pp. 75-77.

8,084 LALLEMAND, A. Nouveaux Homoptères de l'Ouest africain. BULL. IFAN 12 (1950), pp. 630-633.

8,085 LALLEMAND, V. Un nouveau Flatide de l'Ouest africain. BULL. IFAN 11 (1949), p. 331.

8,086 LAWSON, G. W. The Caulerpas of West Africa. NIGERIAN FIELD 25 (1960), pp. 23-31.

8,087 McARDLE, T. D. The bare-headed rockfowl Picathartes gymnocephalus. NIGERIAN FIELD 23 (1958), pp. 19-20.

8,088 MADGE, D. S. Soil zoology: a critical appraisal. NIGERIAN FIELD 29 (1964), pp. 180-188.

8,089 MARCHANT, S. The birds of tropical West Africa by D. A. Bannerman. NIGERIAN FIELD 15 (1950), pp. 109-112.

8,090 MARMO, V. On the granites of Northern Ivory Coast, Jos Plateau of Nigeria, and Northern Cameroon. PROC. SYMP. GRANITES W. AFR., 1965, pp. 95-103.

8,091 MARSHALL, Sir H. The carmelite sunbird: Chalcomitra fuliginosa. NIGERIAN FIELD 26 (1961), pp. 128-129.

8,092 MARSHALL, Sir H. The Orioles of West Africa. NIGERIAN FIELD 24 (1959), pp. 6-13.

8,093 MARSHALL, Sir H. The rufous-crowned Eremomela (Eremomela badiceps badiceps). NIGERIAN FIELD 28 (1963), pp. 115-116.

8,094 MAUNY, R. Notes historiques autour des principales plantes cultivées d'Afrique occidentale. BULL. IFAN 15 (1953), pp. 684-730.

8,095 MILLOUS, P. Le coefficient de robustesse ou indice Pignet chez les Noirs de la côte occidentale d'Afrique. J. SOC. AFR. 3 (1933), pp. 57-72.

8,096 MILLS, W. G. The African knee. WEST AFR. MILITARY MED. BULL. 3 (1945), pp. 33-37.

8,097 MILLS, W. G. The minor surgery of West Africa. WEST AFR. MILITARY MED. BULL. 3 (1945), pp. 21-24.

8,098 MINCHIN, E. A. The prevention of malaria. J. AFR. SOC. 8 (1909), pp. 251-258.

8,099 MONCEAUX, R. H. Le beurre d'arachides. BULL. IFAN 13 (1951), pp. 901-906.

8,100 MONOD, TH. Au sujet des Talinum ouest-africains. BULL. IFAN 13 (1951), pp. 546-550.

8,101 MONOD, TH. Notes d'ichtyologie ouest-africaine. BULL. IFAN 12 (1950), pp. 1-71.

8,102 MONOD, TH. Sur deux Garra d'Afrique occidentale. BULL. IFAN 12 (1950), pp. 976-983.

8,103 MONOD, TH. Sur quelques. Stomatopodes ouest-africains. BULL. IFAN 13 (1951), pp. 139-144.

8,104 OGAN, O. The West African weaver bird. NIGERIAN FIELD 8 (1939), pp. 52-56.

8,105 PAPP, C. S. Petite contribution à l'étude des Chrysomélides de la faune africaine. BULL. IFAN 14 (1952), pp. 120-125.

8,106 PEPPER, J. L. W. Walking plasters. WEST AFR. MILITARY MED. BULL. 3 (1945), pp. 27-28.

8,107 PERES, J. M. Contribution à l'étude des Ascidies de la côte occidentale d'Afrique. BULL. IFAN 11 (1949), pp. 159-207.

8,108 PIC, M. Coléoptères rares ou nouveaux d'Afrique. BULL. IFAN 13 (1951), pp. 1099-1102.

8,109 PIC, M. Nouveaux Coléoptères d'Afrique. BULL. IFAN 12 (1950), pp. 72-74.

8,110 PIC, M. Nouveaux Coléoptères de l'Ouest africain. BULL. IFAN 11 (1949), pp. 307-312.

8,111 PIC, M. Sur quelques Hétéromères africains (Coleoptera). BULL. IFAN 12 (1950), pp. 927-929.

8,112 PRIETZE, R. Arzneipflanzen der Haussa. AFR. UND UB. 4 (1913-1914), pp. 81-90.

8,113 RAGUIN, E. Les granites de l'Ouest Africain en Côte-d'Ivoire, au Nigéria et au Cameroun. PROC. SYMP. GRANITES W. AFR., 1965, pp. 105-117.

8,114 RENNER, W. Native poison, West Africa. J. AFR. SOC. 4 (1904), pp. 109-111.

8,115 RILEY, N. D. A polymorphic Charaxes. NIGERIAN FIELD 16 (1951), pp. 67-69.

8,116 ROBERTY, G. Les Eragrostis ouest-africains. BULL. IFAN 15 (1953), pp. 83-92.

8,117 SAIDU, C. De la pathologie vésiculaire en Afrique Noire. RECH. AFR. 4 (1960), pp. 22-27.

8,118 SCHNELL, R. Contribution à l'étude des Uragoga (Rubiacées) de l'Ouest africain. BULL. IFAN 15 (1953), pp. 98-132.

8,119 SCHNELL, R. Plantes employées en Afrique occidentale pour se protéger des serpents. BULL. IFAN, Série B: Sciences humaines 20 (1958), pp. 205-214.

8,120 SCHNELL, R. Sarcophrynium (Marantacées) ouest-africains. BULL. IFAN 15 (1953), pp. 1390-1395.

8,121 SCHUBART, O. Ueber einige Diplopoden von Bergmassiv Aïr in der Sud Sahara, gesammelt von L. Chopard und A. Villiers im 1947. BULL. IFAN 13 (1951), pp. 116-125.

8,122 SCOTT, J. G. Snake venom in the eye. WEST AFR. MILITARY MED. BULL. 3 (1945), p. 29.

8,123 SEMPLE, T. Simple psychotherapeutic suggestion in African troops. WEST AFR. MILITARY MED. BULL. 3 (1945), pp. 19-20.

8,124 SERLE, W. The Lower Guinea bare-headed crow (Picathartes oreas Reichenow). NIGERIAN FIELD 17 (1952), pp. 131-132.

8,125 SERLE, W. The splendid sunbird (Cinnyris Coccinigaster (Latham)). NIGERIAN FIELD 21 (1956), p. 78.

8,126 SHARLAND, R. E. Bird-singing in West Africa, 1959. NIGERIAN FIELD 25 (1960), pp. 125-127.

8,127 SHARLAND, R. E. Bird singing in West Africa, 1961. NIGERIAN FIELD 27 (1962), pp. 134-137.

8,128 SHARLAND, R. E. Birds seen at sea. NIGERIAN FIELD 20 (1955), pp. 168-171.

8,129 STAMMERS, F. A. R. Tropical Bubo or lymphogranuloma inguinale. WEST AFR. MILITARY MED. BULL. 1 (1942), pp. 5-11.

8,130 TENDEIRO, J. and VALDEZ, V. Helmintologia ictiológica: Helmintes de alguns peixes da Costa Oeste-Africana. BCGP 10 (1955), pp. 129-163.

8,131 TENDEIRO, J. and VALDEZ, V. Helmintologia ictiológica. Sobre os helmintes de alguns peixes da costa portuguesa. BCGP 10 (1955), pp. 81-127.

8,132 VILLIERS, A. La collection de Serpents de l'I.F.A.N. (Acquisitions 1950). BULL. IFAN 13 (1951), pp. 813-836.

8,133 VILLIERS, A. La collection de Serpents de l'I.F.A.N. (Acquisitions 1951). BULL. IFAN 14 (1952), pp. 881-898.

8,134 WILSON, A. F. Geological report on granites in W. Africa. PROC. SYMP. GRANITES W. AFR., 1965, pp. 123-147.

8,135 Halcyon senegelensis senegalensis: the Senegal kingfisher. NIGERIAN FIELD 1, no. 3 (1932), p. 15.

8,136 Health of troops: prevention of mosquito-borne diseases. WEST AFR. MILITARY MED. BULL. 2 (1942), pp. 48-56.

8,137 Index of botanical collectors in West Africa. BULL. AFR. STUD. ASSOC. 4 (1965), p. 15.

8,138 M. Chevalier's scientific work in West Africa. J. AFR. SOC. 8 (1908), pp. 62-74.

See also 5073, 7570, 12977.

Sociology

8,139 BAKARI, K. L'Afrique occidentale pré-coloniale et le fait urbain. PRESENCE AFR. N.S. 22 (1958), pp. 76-80.

8,140 BRITO, E. Notas sobre a vida familiar e jurídica da tribo fula. Instituicões civis. BCGP 12 (1957), pp. 301-314; 13 (1958), pp. 7-23.

8,141 BUSIA, K. A. The impact of industrialization on West Africa. WAISER SOC. 2 (1953), pp. 31-37.

8,142 CARREIRA, A. Aspectos da influência da cultura portuguesa na área compreendida entre o rio Senegal e o norte da Serra Leoa. BCGP 19 (1964), pp. 373-416.

8,143 DELMOND, P. De l'imposition de noms de personnes aux Africains. BULL. IFAN 15 (1953), pp. 453-460.

8,144 DRAKE, S. C. Representative government and the traditional cultures and institutions of West African societies. AFR., THE DYNAMICS OF CHANGE, 1963, pp. 9-33.

8,145 FALLERS, L. A. Comments on "the Lebanese in West Africa." COMP. STUD. SOC. HIST. 4 (1961-1962), pp. 334-336.

8,146 FIRTH, R. Social problems and research in British West Africa. AFRICA 17 (1947), pp. 77-91, 170-180.

8,147 FORDE, D. The conditions of social development in West Africa. Retrospect and prospect. CIVILISATIONS 3 (1953), pp. 471-485; French summary, pp. 485-489.

8,148 GARIGUE, P. The West African Students' Union: a study in culture contact. AFRICA 23 (1953), pp. 55-69.

8,149 GOODWIN, A. J. H. Mother, child and civilization. UNIVERSITAS 2 (1955), pp. 15-19; rejoinder, 2 (1956), pp. 113-116.

8,150 KHURI, F. I. Kinship, emigration, and trade partnership among the Lebanese of West Africa. AFRICA 35 (1965), pp. 385-395.

8,151 KUCZYNSKI, R. R. La population de la British West Africa en 1940. BULL. IFAN 12 (1950), p. 240.

8,152 LETNEV, A. Problems in the development of family relations in West Africa. INT. SOC. SC. J. 16 (1964), pp. 400-410.

8,153 LITTLE, K. The organisation of voluntary associations in West Africa. CIVILISATIONS 9 (1959), pp. 283-297; French summary, pp. 297-300.

8,154 LITTLE, K. The role of voluntary associations in West African urbanization. AMER. ANTHR. 59 (1957), pp. 579-596.

8,155 LITTLE, K. The study of 'social change' in British West Africa. AFRICA 23 (1953), pp. 274-283.

8,156 LITTLE, K. Some traditionally based forms of mutual aid in West African urbanization. ETHNOLOGY 1 (1962), pp. 197-211.

8,157 LITTLE, K. The urban role of tribal associations in West Africa. AFR. STUD. 21 (1962), pp. 1-9.

8,158 LITTLE, K. West African urbanization as a social process. CAH. ET. AFR. 1 (1960), pp. 90-102.

8,159 MEYEROWITZ, H. V. Progress for Africans. INT. REV. MISSIONS 32 (1943), pp. 165-171.

8,160 MONTEIL, C. Le village africain de l'Ouest. BULL. IFAN 27 (1965), pp. 706-714.

8,161 MONTEIL, V. Contribution à la sociologie des Peuls (Le Fonds Viellard de l'IFAN). BULL. IFAN 25 (1963), pp. 351-414.

8,162 PROTHERO, R. M. Migrant labour in West Africa. J. LOCAL ADM. OV. 1 (1962), pp. 149-155.

8,163 ROLLINGS, P. J. A comment on class attitudes. UNIVERSITAS 2 (1956), pp. 113-116; rejoinder: 2 (1955), pp. 15-19.

8,164 SHILS, E. The formation of the West African intellectual community: tasks and possibilities. AFR., THE DYNAMICS OF CHANGE, 1963, pp. 179-208.

8,165 SKINNER, E. P. Strangers in West African societies. AFRICA 33 (1963), pp. 307-320.

8,166 SMITH, M. G. Historical and cultural conditions of political corruption among the Hausa. COMPT. STUD. SOC. HIST. 6 (1963-1964), pp. 164-194.

8,167 WALLERSTEIN, E. La recherche d'une identité nationale en Afrique occidentale. PRESENCE AFR. N.S. 34-35 (1960-1961), pp. 79-91.

8,168 WALLERSTEIN, I. Ethnicity and national integration in West Africa. CAH. ET. AFR. 1 (1960), pp. 129-139.

8,169 WATKINS, M. H. The West African "bush" school. AM. J. SOC. 48 (1942-1943), pp. 666-675.

8,170 WESTERMANN, D. Kulturelle Wandlungen und Anpassungen in Westafrika. SOCIOLOGUS 1 (1951), pp. 32-43, 96-116.

8,171 WINDER, R. B. The Lebanese in West Africa. COMP. STUD. SOC. HIST. 4 (1961-1962), pp. 296-333.

8,172 ZAREMBA, P. The urban development of West and Equatorial Africa. AFR. BULL. 1 (1964), pp. 105-134.

8,173 Un anniversaire Haoussa. ZAIRE 7 (1953), p. 199.

8,174 Bibliography of West African sociological material: aim and scope. AFR. NOTES 3, no. 1 (1965), p. 9.

8,175 Status of women in West Africa. AFR. WOMEN 1 (1955), pp. 63-66.

8,176 L'urbanisation de l'A.O.F. ZAIRE 4 (1950), pp. 1139-1140.

See also 17004.

FRENCH WEST AFRICA

General

8,177 MONOD, TH. Notes bibliographiques sur le Sahara occidental. J. SOC. AFR. 3 (1933), pp. 129-196, 335-340; 5 (1935), pp. 117-124.

8,178 Au Conseil scientifique africain. ZAIRE 6 (1952), pp. 414-415.

8,179 Bibliographie de A. Leriche. BULL. IFAN 19 (1957), pp. 335-336.

Agriculture

8,180 BAILLAUD, E. An agricultural experiment in French West Africa. J. AFR. SOC. 1 (1902), pp. 325-338.

8,181 C., J. Foires agricoles en A.O.F. ZAIRE 8 (1954), pp. 523-524.

8,182 LEBEUF, J. P. Quelques types de poulaillers africains. J. SOC. AFR. 12 (1942), pp. 33-47.

Anthropology

8,183 BA, A. H. Culture Peule. PRESENCE AFR. N.S. 8-10 (1956), pp. 85-97.

8,184 CANTRELLE, P. and DUPIRE, M. L'endogamie des Peuls du Fouta-Djallon. RECH. AFR. 1-4 (1964), pp. 69-98.

8,185 CHERON, G. Le Dyidé. J. SOC. AFR. 1 (1931), pp. 285-289.

8,186 CHERON, G. Les Tyèblenké. J. SOC. AFR. 1 (1931), pp. 281-283.

8,187 DIETERLEN, G. The Mande creation myth. AFRICA 27 (1957), pp. 124-137.

8,188 FODEBA, P. K. La moisson. PRESENCE AFR. 6 (1949), pp. 79-82.

8,189 LABOURET, H. La sorcellerie au Soudan occidental. AFRICA 8 (1935), pp. 462-472.

8,190 MERCIER, P. Etude du mariage et enquête urbaine. CAH. ET. AFR. 1, no. 1 (1960), pp. 28-43.

8,191 MEYER, L. M. Points cardinaux. PRESENCE AFR. 8 (1950), pp. 289-295.

8,192 MONTEIL, V. Charles Monteil et les questions de toponymie et d'anthroponymie en Afrique. BULL. IFAN 11 (1949), pp. 545-546.

8,193 PEIFFER, E. Données obtenues au test de Rorschach chez des noirs d'Afrique occidentale française. BULL. IFAN 21 (1959), pp. 20-60.

8,194 PROUTEAUX, M. Quelques exemples de l'utilité pratique des études ethnologiques. J. SOC. AFR. 1 (1931), pp. 195-206.

8,195 ROUCH, J. La danse. PRESENCE AFR. 8 (1950), pp. 219-226.

8,196 Les groupes ethniques en A.O.F. PRESENCE AFR. 15 (1953), pp. 107-137.

8,197 La maison paysanne en A.O.F. PRESENCE AFR. 15 (1953), pp. 252-258.

Art

8,198 APPIA, B. La représentation humaine dans les dessins d'enfants noirs. BULL. IFAN 1 (1939), pp. 405-411.

8,199 LHOTE, H. Les gravures rupestres d'Aouineght (Sahara occidental). Nouvelle contribution à l'étude des chars rupestres du Sahara. BULL. IFAN 19 (1957), pp. 617-658.

8,200 MAUNY, R. Un âge de cuivre au Sahara occidental? (Addendum). BULL. IFAN 13 (1951), pp. 1301-1302.

8,201 MAUNY, R. Catalogue des restes osseux humains préhistoriques trouvés dans l'Ouest africain. BULL. IFAN 23 (1961), pp. 388-410.

8,202 MAUNY, R. Les recherches archéologiques en A.O.F. particulièrement de 1938 à 1952. BULL. IFAN 15 (1953), pp. 859-863.

8,203 MONOD, TH. Peintures rupestres du Zemmour français (Sahara occidental). BULL. IFAN 13 (1951), pp. 198-213.

8,204 REMONDON, R. A propos de quelques objets d'art de l'A.O.F. PRESENCE AFR. 1 (1947), pp. 143-145.

8,205 ZELTNER, F. DE. La bijouterie indigène en Afrique occidentale. J. SOC. AFR. 1 (1931), pp. 43-48.

See also 4844, 4858, 8297.

Biography

8,206 MARTINEAU, A. et al. En l'honneur de Général Archinard. RHCF 23 (1930), pp. 113-136.

8,207 RICHARD-MOLARD, J. In memoriam: Denis Berlan. BULL. IFAN 11 (1949), pp. 541-543.

8,208 DEBIEN, G. [ed.]. Journal du docteur Corre en pays sérère (décembre 1876-janvier 1877). BULL. IFAN 26 (1964), pp. 532-600.

8,209 MARTONNE, E. DE. In memoriam: Le colonel Fouquet. BULL. IFAN 13 (1951), pp. 251-252.

8,210 MONOD, TH. In memoriam: Claude Francis-Boeuf. BULL. IFAN 14 (1952), pp. 677-678.

8,211 Georges Gayet. CIVILISATIONS 12 (1962), p. 165.

8,212 DUNCAN-JOHNSTONE, A. Gordon Laing memorial plaque. Account of unveiling at Timbuctoo. J. AFR. SOC. 31 (1932), pp. 282-292.

8,213 D., G. Albert Leriche (1901-1957). BULL. IFAN 19 (1957), pp. 333-335.

8,214 Nécrologie: [Bernard Maupoil]. J. SOC. AFR. 15 (1945), p. 38.

8,215 In memoriam: Charles Monteil. BULL. IFAN 11 (1949), pp. 543-544.

8,216 DEBIEN, G. Papiers d'Afrique. III. Papiers Ernest Noirot. BULL. IFAN 26 (1964), pp. 676-693.

8,217 S., G. Jacques Richard-Molard. BULL. IEC N.S. 2 (1951), pp. 5-8.

8,218 OLIVIER, Gouverneur Général. Nécrologie: le gouverneur général Roume. J. SOC. AFR. 12 (1942), pp. 253-255.

8,219 LESTER, P. Nécrologie: Louis Tauxier. J. SOC. AFR. 12 (1942), pp. 255-258.

See also 7209.

Economics

8,220 ARNETT, E. J. Economic conditions in French West Africa. J. AFR. SOC. 34 (1935), pp. 434-445.

8,221 BERG, E. Equal pay for equal work in French West Africa. AFR. SOUTH 1, no. 2 (1957), pp. 86-95.

8,222 C., J. L'assistance au paysan d'Afrique francaise. ZAIRE 8 (1954), pp. 522-523.

8,223 C., J. Balance commerciale de l'A.O.F. ZAIRE 8 (1954), pp. 953-954.

8,224 C., J. Banques et épargne en A.O.F. ZAIRE 9 (1955), pp. 166-167.

8,225 C., J. Le commerce extérieur de l'A.O.F. en 1952. ZAIRE 7 (1953), pp. 412-413.

8,226 CAPET, M. and FABRE, J. L'économie de l'A.O.F. depuis la guerre. ANNALES AFR., 1957, pp. 135-193.

8,227 DELAFOSSE, M. Memorandum ou land tenure in French West Africa. Translated by F. H. Ruxton. J. AFR. SOC. 10 (1911), pp. 258-273.

8,228 EHRHARD, M. J. The economic and financial structure of French West Africa. WAISER EC. 2 (1953), pp. 141-147.

8,229 GAYET, G. Autonomies financières territoriales en Afrique Occidentale Francaise. CIVILISATIONS 3 (1953), pp. 343-347; English summary, pp. 347-348.

8,230 GRAY, A. Economic co-operation. AFR. AFFAIRS 60 (1961), pp. 377-378.

8,231 GUILLARD, J. Où en est l'économie de l'A.O.F.? AFR. ET ASIE 2, no. 2 (1949), pp. 27-50.

8,232 LABOURET, H. Le coton et l'indigène (Afrique Occidentale Française). AFRICA 1 (1928), pp. 320-337.

8,233 LEDUC, G. L'Utilisation des ressources locales dans le financement du développement economique de l'Outre-mer, (avec applications aux Territoires d'Outre-mer de l'Union Française). WAISER EC. 2 (1953), pp. 39-55.

8,234 MALARA, A. Regime doganale e traffici nell'Africa Occidentale francese. AFRICA (Rome) 10 (1955), pp. 149-150.

8,235 MALARA, A. Scambi e valute nell' A.E.F. AFRICA (Rome) 11 (1956), p. 41.

8,236 MASSA, C. A. Notes sur les conditions de vie du travailleur africain en A.O.F. AFR. ET ASIE 19 (1952), pp. 37-45.

8,237 MATIP, B. Le syndicalisme en Afrique Noire. Aperçu des mouvements ouvriers dans les pays d'origine coloniale francaise. AFRICA (Rome) 14 (1959), pp. 65-67.

8,238 ROCHE, J. Aspects financiers de la loi-cadre. ANNALES AFR., 1958, pp. 53-86.

8,239 ROCHE, J. Le budget général de l'Afrique Occidentale Française. ANNALES AFR., 1956, pp. 213-255.

8,240 SECK, A. Communications in French West Africa. MALAYAN J. TR. GEOG. 8 (1956), pp. 51-54.

8,241 SINGH, P. Development planning in French Tropical Africa. AFRICA QUART. 2, no. i (1962), pp. 10-20.

8,242 WIPPER, A. A comparative study of nascent unionism in French West Africa and the Philippines. ECON. DEVELOPMENT AND CULTURAL CHANGE 13 (1964-1965), pp. 20-55.

8,243 Le chemin de fer Dakar-Niger. ZAIRE 8 (1954), pp. 193-194.

8,244 La circulation automobile en A.O.F. ZAIRE 7 (1953), pp. 1086-1087.

8,245 Commerce extérieur de l'A.O.F. ZAIRE 6 (1952), p. 1091.

8,246 Conference de l'élevage à Bamako. ZAIRE 5 (1951), pp. 531-532.

8,247 Le Génie rural en A.O.F. ZAIRE 5 (1951), pp. 1075-1076.

8,248 Personnel et main-d'oeuvre en A.O.F. ZAIRE 7 (1953), p. 286.

8,249 La politique fiscale de l'A.O.F. ZAIRE 7 (1953), pp. 284-285.

8,250 Problèmes financiers en A.O.F. ZAIRE 6 (1952), pp. 287-288.

8,251 Programme d'équipement de l'A.O.F. ZAIRE 7 (1953), pp. 1085-1086.

8,252 Les transports aériens en A.O.F. ZAIRE 8 (1954), pp. 194-195.

Education

8,253 CHABAS, J. French West Africa in 1953. CIVILISATIONS 4 (1954), pp. 615-617.

8,254 COMHAIRE, J. La situation de l'enseignement en A.O.F. ZAIRE 5 (1951), pp. 275-278.

8,255 DADIE, B. Misère de l'enseignement en A.O.F. PRESENCE AFR. N.S. 11 (1957), pp. 57-70.

8,256 LABOURET, H. L'éducation des masses en Afrique Occidentale Française. AFRICA 8 (1935), pp. 98-102.

8,257 ZAJACZKOWSKI, A. Jeune élite africaine; une étude sur l'Afrique francophone. AFR. BULL. 2 (1965), pp. 57-70.

8,258 Boursiers africains en France. ZAIRE 5 (1951), pp. 629-630.

8,259 L'enseignement public en A.O.F. ZAIRE 7 (1953), p. 413.

8,260 Observations sur les méthodes d'enseignement en A.O.F. PRESENCE AFR. 15 (1953), pp. 347-356.

Geography

8,261 C., J. Aux portes du Sahara. ZAIRE 7 (1953), pp. 866-867.

8,262 GARNIER, P. Le déficit de saturation absolu en A.O.F. BULL. IFAN 13 (1951), pp. 733-749.

8,263 JONES, G. I. and CHADWICK, E. R. Trans-Sahara, Eastern Route. Account of a trip made by the authors. NIGERIAN FIELD 4 (1935), pp. 148-157.

8,264 MAZEN, L. A visit to French West Africa and Nigeria. J. AFR. SOC. 36 (1937), pp. 170-175.

8,265 PITOT, A. Feux sauvages, végétation et sols en A.O.F. BULL. IFAN 15 (1953), pp. 1369-1383.

8,266 SPRAY, E. G. and MICHIE, C. W. Trans-Sahara, Western Route. Account of a trip made by the authors. NIGERIAN FIELD 4 (1935), pp. 157-164.

8,267 Une chaîne de froid de Dakar au Niger. ZAIRE 5 (1951), pp. 976-977.

8,268 Enquête sur le dessèchement en A.O.F. Première tranche: Mauritanie, Sénégal, Soudan, Niger. BULL. IFAN 12 (1950), pp. 1171-1175.

8,269 La navigation sur le Niger. ZAIRE 7 (1953), p. 288.

Government. Politics. Administration

8,270 ARNETT, E. J. A French view of colonial administration. J. AFR. SOC. 36 (1937), pp. 447-451.

8,271 ARNETT, E. J. A note on French administration in West Africa. J. AFR. SOC. 36 (1937), pp. 217-220.

8,272 BALLARD, J. A. Politics and government in former French West and Equatorial Africa: a critical bibliography. JMAS 3 (1965), pp. 589-605.

8,273 BASILE, K. L'Afrique Noire et son destin face à la France. Essai de critique du réformisme dans les colonies. PRESENCE AFR. 12 (1957), pp. 109-126.

8,274 CORBY, C. Une assemblée locale dans l'Union francaise: le grand Conseil de l'A.O.F. AFR. ET ASIE 22 (1953), pp. 45-52.

8,275 DAVIDSON, B. French West Africa: the background. AFR. SOUTH 3, no. 3 (1959), pp. 77-85.

8,276 DAVIDSON, B. French West Africa: the view to-day. AFR. SOUTH 4, no. 1 (1959), pp. 87-96.

8,277 DELMOND, P. Quelques observations sur l'etat-civil indigène au Soudan occidental. BULL. IFAN 7 (1945), pp. 54-79.

8,278 KIBA, S. Dakar and Bamako. AFR. SOUTH 5, no. 4 (1961), pp. 92-94.

8,279 MOREL, E. D. The French in Western and Central Africa. J. AFR. SOC. 1 (1902), pp. 192-207.

8,280 NEWBURY, C. The Government General and political change in French West Africa. ST. ANTONY'S PAPERS 10 (1961), pp. 41-59.

8,281 NEWBURY, C. The formation of the Government General of French West Africa. J. AFR. HIST. 1 (1960), pp. 111-128.

8,282 ROBINSON, K. E. French West Africa. AFR. AFFAIRS 50 (1951), pp. 123-132.

8,283 ROBINSON, K. E. Local Government reform in French Tropical Africa. J. AFR. ADM. 8 (1956), pp. 179-185.

8,284 ROGER, A. et al. Naissance du Movement africain de liberation nationale (M.L.N.). PRESENCE AFR. N.S. 20 (1958), pp. 139-140.

8,285 WATSON, J. H. A. French-speaking Africa since independence. AFR. AFFAIRS 62 (1963), pp. 211-222.

8,286 WALLERSTEIN, I. L'unité et la balkanisation de l'A.O.F. ET. CONG. 2, no. 1 (1962), pp. 36-40.

8,287 Courants politiques en Afrique française. ZAIRE 5 (1951), pp. 1074-1075.

8,288 La nouvelle constitution de l'Union française. ZAIRE 1 (1947), pp. 90-93.

8,289 La politique routière en A.O.F. ZAIRE 6 (1952), p. 974.

History

8,290 ARNETT, E. J. Recent developments in French West Africa. J. AFR. SOC. 35 (1936), pp. 290-293.

8,291 BOUCHE, D. Les villages de Liberté en A.O.F. BULL. IFAN 11 (1949), pp. 491-540; 12 (1950), pp. 135-215.

8,292 CISSOKO, S. M. Le siècle de Kankou Moussa: le XIVe siècle. PRESENCE AFR. N.S. 52 (1964), pp. 94-103.

8,293 DAVIDSON, B. Jacobins in Africa. HISTORY TODAY 9 (1959), pp. 83-93.

8,294 KAKE, B. I. A propos de l'exil de Dinah Salifou roi des Nalous. PRESENCE AFR. N.S. 51 (1964), pp. 146-158.

8,295 KOUROUBARI, A. Histoire de l'Iman Samori. BULL. IFAN 21 (1959), pp. 544-571.

8,296 LE QUESNE, C. M. French West Africa. AFR. AFFAIRS 64 (1965), pp. 78-90.

8,297 MAUNY, R. Les recherches archéologiques et historiques en Afrique occidentale d'expression française de 1957 a 1961. BULL. IFAN 24 (1962), pp. 279-298.

8,298 PORTERES, R. La monnaie de fer dans l'Ouest-Africain au XXe siècle. RECH. AFR. 4 (1960), pp. 3-13.

8,299 SAINT-MARTIN, Y. Les relations diplomatiques entre la France et l'Empire toucouleur de 1860 à 1887. BULL. IFAN 27 (1965), pp. 183-222.

8,300 SURET-CANALE, J. A propos des Guinze en Guinée. RECH. AFR. 2-3 (1963), pp. 32-33.

8,301 Une inventaire des archives historiques du Gouvernement général de l'Afrique Occidentale française. RHCF 10, no. 2 (1922), pp. 167-172.

Language. Literature

Language

8,302 HOUIS, M. Remarques sur la transcription toponymique en Afrique occidentale française. BULL. IFAN 14 (1952), pp. 351-356.

8,303 LABOURET, H. La situation linguistique en Afrique Occidentale Française. AFRICA 4 (1931), pp. 56-62.

8,304 LABOURET, H. and WARD, I. C. Quelques observations sur la langue mandingue. AFRICA 6 (1933), pp. 38-50.

See also 335, 8901, 9647.

Literature

8,305 CHATAIGNIER, A. L'imperissable beaute. AFR. STUD. 5 (1946), pp. 195-206.

8,306 DADIE, B. B. L'aveu. PRESENCE AFR. 1 (1947), pp. 78-80.

8,307 DIOP, B. L'os. PRESENCE AFR. 1 (1947), pp. 81-88.

8,308 JAHN, J. Discussion on Camara Laye. Camara Laye: an interpretation. BO 6 (1959), pp. 35-38.

8,309 MOORE, G. Towards realism in French African writing. JMAS 1 (1963), pp. 61-73.

8,310 NIANE, D. T. Mythes, légendes et sources orales dans l'oeuvre de Mahmoud Kati. RECH. AFR. 1-4 (1964), pp. 36-42.

8,311 RAMSARAN, J. A. Camara Laye's symbolism. An interpretation of The radiance of the king. BO 3 (1958), pp. 55-57.

8,312 SADJI, A. Nini (roman). PRESENCE AFR. 1 (1947), pp. 89-110; 2 (1948), pp. 276-298; 3 (1948), pp. 485-504; 4 (1948), pp. 647-666.

8,313 Ballade khassonkaise de Dioudi. PRESENCE AFR. 2 (1948), pp. 237-241.

Law

8,314 BRUYAS, J. Chronique de législation, A.O.F.-A.E.F. ANNALES AFR., 1955, pp. 133-174; 1956, pp. 257-341; 1957, pp. 195-304; 1958, pp. 327-429.

8,315 CARLIER, J. La détermination du prix des loyers d'habitation en A.O.F. ANNALES AFR., 1957, pp. 321-330.

8,316 CHABAS, J. La conciliation devant les tribunaux de droit local de L'Afrique Occidentale Française. RJPUF 7 (1953), pp. 333-349.

8,317 CHABAS, J. De la transformation des droits fonciers coutumiers en droit de propriété. ANNALES AFR., 1959, pp. 73-107.

8,318 CHABAS, J. La justice française en Afrique Occidentale Française. ANNALES AFR., 1955, pp. 79-108.

8,319 CHABAS, J. La justice indigène en Afrique Occidentale Française. ANNALES AFR., 1954, pp. 91-151.

8,320 CHABAS, J. La réforme foncière et le régime des concessions en Afrique Occidentale Française. ANNALES AFR., 1958, pp. 37-51.

8,321 CHABAS, J. Le régime foncier coutumier en A.O.F. ANNALES AFR., 1957, pp. 53-78.

8,322 CHABAS, J. Transformation du droit local et évolution économique. ANNALES AFR., 1962, pp. 151-159.

8,323 CHAULEUR, P. L'application du régime des allocations familiales du secteur privé dans les territoires d'outre-mer. RJPUF 11 (1957), pp. 47-68.

8,324 DECOTTIGNIES, R. La condition des étrangers en Afrique Occidentale Française. ANNALES AFR., 1956, pp. 27-73.

8,325 DECOTTIGNIES, R. L'état civil en Afrique Occidentale Française. ANNALES AFR., 1955, pp. 41-78.

8,326 DECOTTIGNIES, R. French West and Equatorial Africa. CIVILISATIONS 5 (1955), pp. 323-330.

8,327 DEMAISON, D. Le régime de l'immatriculation foncière en Afrique Occidentale Française. RJPUF 10 (1956), pp. 421-478.

8,328 DEMAISON, D. Le régime des concessions foncières en Afrique occidentale française. RJPUF 9 (1955), pp. 761-784.

8,329 DEMAISON, D. Le régime foncier coutumier des autochtones en Afrique Occidentale Française. RJPUF 10 (1956), pp. 257-298.

8,330 DEPREZ, J. Evolution et particularisme du droit du travail en Afrique Occidentale. ANNALES AFR., 1960, pp. 7-32.

8,331 DROUET, P. L'expropriation forcée des immeubles immatriculés. ANNALES AFR., 1960, pp. 175-198.

8,332 DROUET, P. L'immatriculation foncière en A.O.F. depuis le décret du 20 mai 1955. ANNALES AFR., 1958, pp. 207-217.

8,333 KIRSCH, B. Les tribunaux du travail en Afrique Occidentale Francaise. RJPUF 9 (1955), pp. 317-334.

8,334 PHILLIPS, A. Recent French legislation concerning African marriage. AFRICA 22 (1952), pp. 66-70.

8,335 POIRIER, J. L'Organisation judiciaire de l'Afrique Occidentale Française. THE FUTURE OF CUSTOMARY LAW IN AFRICA, 1956, pp. 190-197.

8,336 ROBERT, A. P. Attitude de législateur français en face du droit coutumier d'Afrique Noire. RJPUF 9 (1955), pp. 743-760.

8,337 ROBERT, A. P. La justice de droit local en Afrique Occidentale Française. RJPUF 10 (1956), pp. 748-780.

8,338 WICKERS, S. Les nullités de l'instruction contradictoire en Afrique Occidentale Française. RJPUF 10 (1956), pp. 479-520.

8,339 Suggestions pour une réforme des institutions de l'A.O.F. RJPUF 9 (1955), pp. 139-146.

Religion

8,340 GRIAULE, M. Philosophie et religion des noirs. PRESENCE AFR. 8 (1950), pp. 307-321.

8,341 LEENHARDT, M. Sociologie religieuse. Questionnaire en vue de l'établissement d'une carte religieuse de l'A.O.F. BULL. IFAN 15 (1953), pp. 767-797.

8,342 LE GRIP, A. Aspects actuels de l'Islam en A.O.F.: 1. mouvements et influences anti-traditionnalistes. 2. L'Islam traditionnel et ses moyens de défense. AFR. ET ASIE 24 (1953), pp. 6-20; 25 (1954), pp. 43-61.

Science

8,343 C., J. Effectifs médicaux en A.O.F. ZAIRE 7 (1953), p. 646.

8,344 CAMERON, M. New species of Staphylinidae (col.) from French West Africa. BULL. IFAN 15 (1953), pp. 519-521.

8,345 CAZANOVE, J. L. F. La question du lait dans les colonies africaines. AFRICA 9 (1936), pp. 227-236.

8,346 CHAMPION, P. Contribution à l'étude de la tache pigmentaire congénitale en Afrique occidentale française et au Togo. J. SOC. AFR. 8 (1938), pp. 145-162.

8,347 DAGET, J. Observations sur une pêche d'Alestes leuciscus Gunther. BULL. IFAN 13 (1951), pp. 260-262.

8,348 DECLOITRE, L. Matériaux pour une faune rhizopodique d'A.O.F. BULL. IFAN 10 (1948), pp. 235-284; 11 (1949), pp. 281-301.

8,349 DEKEYSER, P. L. La tête osseuse chez les Chacals d'A.O.F. Etude comparative. BULL. IFAN 13 (1951), pp. 376-383.

8,350 DELEVE, J. Dryopidae de l'Ouest africain. BULL. IFAN 15 (1953), pp. 1461-1462.

8,351 HUSTACHE, A. Cucurlionidés de l'Afrique Occidentale Française. BULL. IFAN 4 (1942), pp. 182-189.

8,352 MONOD, TH. and RICHARD-MOLARD, J. Une synthèse du Précambrien ouest-africain. BULL. IFAN 12 (1950), pp. 523-530.

8,353 RAOULT, A. Clinical aspects of kwashiorkor in French West Africa. MALNUTRITUION IN AFRICAN MOTHERS..., 1952, pp. 37-44.

8,354 RISBEC, J. Chalcidoïdes d'A.O.F. BULL. IFAN 13 (1951), pp. 1110-1130.

8,355 RISBEC, J. Chalcidoïdes et Proctotrupoïdes de l'Afrique occidentale française. BULL. IFAN 15 (1953), pp. 549-609.

8,356 RISBEC, J. Les Microgasteridae d'A.O.F. (Rectifications). BULL. IFAN 14 (1952), p. 701.

8,357 RISBEC, J. Notes relatives a la communication 49 de la première Conférence Internationale des Africanistes de l'Ouest. BULL. IFAN 12 (1950), pp. 542-545.

8,358 ROBERTY, G. Notes sur la flore de l'Ouest africain. BULL. IFAN 15 (1953), pp. 1396-1431.

8,359 RODE, P. Sur la répartition des groupes sanguins chez les indigènes de l'Afrique occidentale française. J. SOC. AFR. 7 (1937), pp. 37-40.

8,360 ROEWER, C. F. Opiliones aus französisch-Westafrika, gessammelt durch Herrn Dr. A. Villiers. BULL. IFAN 15 (1953), pp. 610-630.

8,361 VILLIERS, A. Notes d'Entomologie ouest-africaine. II. Observations sur la répartition de quelques Hémiptères Hétéroptères et description de nouvelles espèces. BULL. IFAN 13 (1951), pp. 326-342.

8,362 Deux thèses intéressant l'A.O.F. BULL. IFAN 11 (1949), p. 552.

8,363 Note d'Entomologie Ouest-africaine. BULL. IFAN 12 (1950), pp. 634-659.

8,364 Stations de quinquina en A.O.F. ZAIRE 5 (1951), p. 747.

See also 5071.

Sociology

8,365 BEART, C. D'une sociologie des peuples africains à partir de leurs jeux. BULL. IFAN 21 (1959), pp. 271-328.

8,366 BERTHO, J. Le problème du mariage chrétien en Afrique occidentale française. AFRICA 17 (1947), pp. 252-259.

8,367 BISMUTH, H. and MENAGE, C. Les boissons alcooliques en A.O.F. BULL. IFAN 23 (1961), pp. 60-118.

8,368 C., J. Evolution de l'alimentation indigène en A.O.F. ZAIRE 7 (1953), pp. 413-414.

8,369 C., J. La recherche sociologique en Afrique francaise. ZAIRE 7 (1953), pp. 865-866.

8,370 LOMBARD, J. Acculturation et affaiblissement des pouvoirs traditionnels en Afrique Occidentale Francaise. BCGP 12 (1957), pp. 7-19.

8,371 MERCIER, P. Aspects des problèmes de stratification sociale dans l'ouest Africain. CAH. INT. SOCIOL. 17 (1954), pp. 47-65.

8,372 MOAL, G. LE. Les habitations semi-souterraines en Afrique de l'Ouest. J. SOC. AFR. 30 (1960), pp. 193-203.

8,373 PARRINDER, E. G. S. Christian marriage in French West Africa. AFRICA 17 (1947), pp. 260-268.

8,374 RICHARD-MOLARD, J. Le progrès de l'alcoolisme en Afrique Noire Française. BULL. IFAN 12 (1950), pp. 841-844.

8,375 ROBINSON, K. The Sociétés de Prévoyance in French West Africa. J. AFR. ADM. 2 (1950), pp. 29-34.

8,376 SEURIN, J. L. Elites sociales et partis politiques d'A.O.F. ANNALES AFR., 1958, pp. 123-157.

8,377 TOP, W. La valeur du travail des salariés africains. PRESENCE AFR. 13 (1952), pp. 251-264.

8,378 WALLERSTEIN, I. Elites in French-speaking West Africa: the social basis of ideas. JMAS 3 (1965), pp. 1-33.

8,379 WEISS, H. F. L'évolution des élites. Comparaison entre la situation en Afrique occidentale francophone et au Congo avant l'indépendance. ET. CONG. 8, no. 5 (1965), pp. 1-14.

8,380 Démographie de l'A.O.F. PRESENCE AFR. 15 (1953), pp. 67-82.

8,381 La population non africaine en A.O.F. ZAIRE 6 (1952), p. 416.

8,382 Statistiques de superficie et de démographie en A.O.F. BULL. IFAN 11 (1949), pp. 548-552.

See also 5101.

MAURITANIA

General

8,383 TOUPET, C. Orientation bibliographique sur la Mauritanie. BULL. IFAN 21 (1959), pp. 201-239; 24 (1962), pp. 594-613.

Anthropology

8,384 LERICHE, A. Coutumes maures relatives à l'élevage. BULL. IFAN 15 (1953), pp. 1316-1320.

8,385 LERICHE, A. Notes sur les classes sociales et sur quelques tribus de Mauritanie. BULL. IFAN, Série B: Sciences humaines 17 (1955), pp. 173-203.

8,386 LOTTE, Lieutenant. Coutumes des Imraguen (Côtes de Mauritanie, A.O.F.). J. SOC. AFR. 7 (1937), pp. 41-51.

8,387 LUCAS, A. J. Considérations sur l'ethnique maure et en particulier sur une race ancienne: les Bafours. J. SOC. AFR. 1 (1931), pp. 151-194.

8,388 MARTIN, H. Les tribus du Sahel mauritanien et du Rio de Oro. 1. Les Oulad Bou Sba. BULL. IFAN 1 (1939), pp. 587-629.

8,389 MONTEIL, V. La Cryptographie chez les Maures. Note sur quelques alphabets secrets du Hodh. BULL. IFAN 13 (1951), pp. 1157-1264.

8,390 PARIS, E. Recherches sur l'origine des marques de tribus (Feux). BULL. IFAN 15 (1953), pp. 1619-1632.

See also 4833.

Art

8,391 BESSAC, H. Contribution à la prehistoire et à la protohistoire des régions d'Akjoujt et d'Atar (Mauritanie). BULL. IFAN, Série B: Sciences humaines 20 (1958), pp. 317-367.

8,392 BIBERSON, P. Recherches sur le Paléolithique inférieur de l'Adrar de Mauritanie. PROC. PAN-AFR. CONGR. PRE-HIST. 5 (1965), pp. 173-189.

8,393 DUCHEMIN, G. J. A propos des décorations murales des habitations de Oualata (Mauritanie). BULL. IFAN 12 (1950), pp. 1095-1110.

8,394 JACQUES-MEUNIE, D. Cités caravanières de Mauritanie Tichite et Oualata. J. SOC. AFR. 27 (1957), pp. 19-35.

8,395 JACQUES-MEUNIE, D. Quelques gravures et peintures rupestres de la Mauritanie sahélienne. Une pierre taillée de Tinigar. J. SOC. AFR. 29 (1959), pp. 19-31.

8,396 LAFORGUE, P. Notes sur Aoudaghost, ancienne capitale des Berbères Lemtouna (Mauritanie saharienne). BULL. IFAN 2 (1940), pp. 217-236.

8,397 LAFORGUE, P. and MAUNY, R. Contribution à la préhistoire de la région de Tichitt (Mauritanie). BULL. IFAN 1 (1939), pp. 691-696.

8,398 LAMBERT, N. Nomenclature et première étude de quelques sites préhistoriques de la région d'Akjoujt. BULL. IFAN 27 (1965), pp. 800-812.

8,399 LAMBERT, N. Note sur quelques céramiques de Mauritanie occidentale. BULL. IFAN 27 (1965), pp. 413-444.

8,400 LAMBERT, N. Le site néolithique de Médinet sbat dans l'Ifozouiten (Mauritanie). BULL. IFAN 23 (1961), pp. 423-455.

8,401 MAUNY, R. Contribution à l'étude du Paléolithique de Mauritanie. PROC. PAN-AFR. CONGR. PRE-HIST. 2 (1952), pp. 461-480.

8,402 MAUNY, R. Les industries paléolithiques de la région El-Beyyed-Tazazmout (Adrar de Mauritanie). PROC. PAN-AFR. CONGR. PRE-HIST. 4, no. iii (1962), pp. 179-193.

8,403 MAUNY, R. Notes d'histoire et d'archéologie sur Azougui, Chinguetti et Ouadane. BULL. IFAN, Série B: Sciences humaines 17 (1955), pp. 142-162.

8,404 MAUNY, R. and HALLEMANS, J. Préhistoire et protohistoire de la région d'Akjoujt (Mauritanie). PROC. PAN-AFR. CONGR. PRE-HIST. 3 (1955), pp. 248-261.

8,405 MAUNY, R. and VILLIERS, A. Contribution à la préhistoire de la Mauritanie occidentale (Missions A. Villiers 1948-1949). BULL. IFAN 12 (1950), pp. 1007-1014.

8,406 PUIGAUDEAU, O. DU. Architecture maure. BULL. IFAN 22 (1960), pp. 92-133.

8,407 PUIGAUDEAU, O. DU. Contribution à l'étude du symbolisme dans le décor mural et l'artisanat de Walâta. BULL. IFAN 19 (1957), pp. 137-183.

8,408 RICHARD-MOLARD, J. and MAUNY, R. Contribution à la préhistoire de l'Adrar mauritanien septentrional et du Makteir. BULL. IFAN 15 (1953), pp. 1229-1241.

8,409 SENONES, M. and PUIGAUDEAU, O. DU. Peintures rupestres du Tagant (Mauritanie). J. SOC. AFR. 9 (1939), pp. 43-70.

8,410 WESTERMARCK, E. The magic origin of Moorish designs. JRAI 34 (1904), pp. 211-222.

Biography

8,411 VUILLEMIN, G. Un pionnier de Mauritanie: le commandant Frèrejean. REV. HIST. COL. 36 (1949), pp. 1-23.

Economics

8,412 C., J. Perspectives minières en Mauritanie. ZAIRE 9 (1955), p. 172.

8,413 TOUPET, C. Agrarian and social transformations in the Tamourt Basin, Mauritania. MALAYAN J. TR. GEOG. 8 (1956), pp. 82-86.

8,414 TOUPET, C. Le problème des transports en Mauritanie. BULL. IFAN 25 (1963), pp. 80-106.

Education

8,415 LERICHE, A. De l'enseignement arabe féminin en Mauritanie. BULL. IFAN 14 (1952), pp. 975-983.

Geography

8,416 BAYARD, Lieutenant. Aspects principaux et consistance des dunes (Mauritanie). BULL. IFAN 9 (1947), pp. 1-17.

8,417 BORRICAND, P. Notes sur l'Ouaran et l'Erg Chech. BULL. IFAN 14 (1952), pp. 660-668.

8,418 DUCHEMIN, G. J. L'inondation de l'Aftout es Sahel et du poste de Nouakchott (Mauritanie: Trarza occidental). BULL. IFAN 13 (1951), pp. 1303-1305.

8,419 McCALLIEN, W. J. A visit to iron and copper fields of Mauritania. UNIVERSITAS 1, no. 6 (1955), pp. 9-12.

8,420 MAUNY, R. Plages soulevées de la région de Nouakchott-Sebkha de Ndghamcha (Mauritanie occidentale). PROC. PAN-AFR. CONGR. PRE-HIST. 4 (1962), pp. 279-287.

8,421 MONOD, TH. and POURQUIE, A. La cratère d'Aouelloul (Adrar, Sahara occidental). BULL. IFAN 13 (1951), pp. 293-311.

8,422 SEVENET, Lieutenant. Etude sur le "Djouf" (Sahara occidental). BULL. IFAN 5 (1943), pp. 1-26.

8,423 TOUPET, C. La vallée de la Tamourt: transformations agraires et sociales. BULL. IFAN 18 (1956), pp. 509-513.

8,424 TOUPET, C. La vallée de la Tamourt en Naaj Tagant. Problèmes d'aménagement. BULL. IFAN, Série B: Sciences humaines 20 (1958), pp. 68-110.

Government

8,425 MERIC, E. La Mauritanie nouvelle n'est pas mal partie. AFR. ET ASIE 64 (1963), pp. 36-40.

8,426 MOORE, C. H. One-partyism in Mauritania. JMAS 3 (1965), pp. 409-420.

8,427 SERJAC, J. Mauritanie et Maroc. AFR. ET ASIE 45 (1959), pp. 11-21.

History

8,428 DESIRE-VUILLEMIN, G. M. Note sur les origines des pelotons méharistes de Mauritanie. REV. HIST. COL. 45 (1958), pp. 53-60.

8,429 FAURE, C. Les essais de pêche au banc d'Arguin en 1825, 1826 et 1827. RHCF 16 (1923), pp. 41-66.

8,430 FREREJEAN, L. Coppolani en Mauritanie. REV. HIST. COL. 42 (1955), pp. 291-342.

8,431 LEPORTIER, J. Atar, Mauritanie. ANNALES AFR., 1958, pp. 221-233.

8,432 LERICHE, A. Deux lettres du temps de la pacification (Mauritanie). BULL. IFAN 14 (1952), pp. 627-635.

8,433 LERICHE, A. Notes pour servir à l'histoire maure (notes sur les forgerons, les Kunta et les Maures du Hōd). BULL. IFAN 15 (1953), pp. 737-750.

8,434 LERICHE, A. De l'origine du thé en Mauritanie. BULL. IFAN 13 (1951), pp. 868-871.

8,435 LERICHE, A. Petite note pour servir à l'histoire d'Atar (Mauritanie). BULL. IFAN 14 (1952), pp. 623-626.

8,436 LERICHE, A. Toponymie et histoire maure. BULL. IFAN 14 (1952), pp. 337-343.

8,437 LERICHE, A. and HAMIDOUN, M. O. Coutumes d'autrefois en Mauritanie. BULL. IFAN 14 (1952), pp. 344-350.

8,438 LOYEWSKI, D'O. Coppolani et la Mauritanie. REV. HIST. COL. 31, no. 2 (1938), pp. 1-70.

8,439 MARTY, P. Tentatives commerciales anglaises à Portendick et en Mauritanie (1800-1826). RHCF 10, no. 1 (1922), pp. 1-38, 265-302.

8,440 MAUNY, R. L'expédition marocaine d'Ouadane (Mauritanie) vers 1543-1544. BULL. IFAN 11 (1949), pp. 129-140.

8,441 NICOLAS, R. P. F. J. A propos de la date d'introduction du thé en Mauritanie. BULL. IFAN 14 (1952), pp. 684-685.

8,442 NORRIS, H. T. The history of Shingīt, according to the Idaw 'Ali tradition. BULL. IFAN 24 (1962), pp. 393-413.

8,443 PUIGAUDEAU, O. DU. La Ziâra de Cheik Mohammed Fadel. BULL. IFAN 13 (1951), pp. 1218-1226.

8,444 REYNIER, E. L'Esclavage en Mauritanie. ET. DAHOM. N.S. 3 (1964), pp. 31-50.

8,445 Mauritanie indépendante. PRESENCE AFR. N.S. 34-35 (1960-1961), pp. 217-220.

See also

Language. Literature

8,446 DIOP, M. N. Le canari d'or. PRESENCE AFR. N.S. 45 (1963), pp. 164-174.

8,447 DUBIE, P. L'Îlot berbérophone de Mauritanie. BULL. IFAN 2 (1940), pp. 316-325.

8,448 FERAL, G. Notes sur la morphologie du verbe dans le dialecte Hassane (Mauritanie). BULL. IFAN 13 (1951), pp. 214-250.

8,449 LE BORGNE, Captain. Vocabulaire technique du chameau en Mauritanie (dialecte Hassanya). BULL. IFAN 15 (1953), pp. 292-380.

8,450 LERICHE, A. Note sur la langue berbère de Mauritanie; au sujet de la filiation et des noms de tribus. BULL. IFAN, Série B: Sciences humaines 20 (1958), pp. 241-248.

8,451 LERICHE, A. Vocabulaire du chameau en Mauritanie. BULL. IFAN 14 (1952), pp. 984-995.

8,452 TRANCART, A. Note sur le vocabulaire camélin en Haute Mauritanie. BULL. IFAN 3 (1941), pp. 45-52.

8,453 VYCICHL, W. Les Gétules de la Mauritanie. BULL. IFAN, Série B: Sciences humaines 17 (1955), pp. 163-167.

Law

8,454 LERICHE, A. Des châtiments prévus par la loi musulmane et de leur application en Mauritanie. BULL. IFAN 19 (1957), pp. 446-463.

Religion

8,455 LERICHE, A. L'Islam en Mauritanie. BULL. IFAN 11 (1949), pp. 458-470.

Science

8,456 ARENES, J. Contribution à l'étude des Composées-Carduacées d'Afrique. BULL. IFAN 15 (1953), pp. 59-71.

8,457 BALFOUR-BROWNE, J. Contribution à l'étude du peuplement de la Mauritanie. Coléoptères Hydrophilides. BULL. IFAN 14 (1952), pp. 513-517.

8,458 BASILEWSKY, P. Contribution à l'étude du peuplement de la Mauritanie. Coléoptères Carabidae. BULL. IFAN 14 (1952), pp. 1170-1190.

8,459 BEAUMONT, J. DE. Contribution à l'étude du peuplement de la Mauritanie. Hyménoptères Sphecidae. BULL. IFAN 15 (1953), pp. 171-177.

8,460 BENOIST, R. Contribution à l'étude du peuplement de la Mauritanie. Apides recueillis en 1948-49 par MM. L. Berland et A. Villiers. BULL. IFAN 12 (1950), pp. 940-943.

8,461 CAMERON, M. Contribution à l'étude du peuplement de la Mauritanie. Coleoptera Staphylinidae. BULL. IFAN 14 (1952), pp. 822-826.

8,462 CHOPARD, L. Contribution à l'étude du peuplement de la Mauritanie. Orthoptéroïdes. BULL. IFAN 14 (1952), pp. 457-478.

8,463 DEKEYSER, P. L. and VILLIERS, A. Contribution à l'étude du peuplement de la Mauritanie. BULL. IFAN 12 (1950), pp. 660-699.

8,464 FRASER, F. C. Contribution à l'étude du peuplement de la Mauritanie. Odonata, Neuroptera, Nemoptera and Ephemeroptera. BULL. IFAN 14 (1952), pp. 479-484.

8,465 GRIDELLI, E. Contribution à l'étude du peuplement de la Mauritanie. Coléoptères Ténébrionides. BULL. IFAN 14 (1952), pp. 60-96.

8,466 GUIGNOT, F. Contribution à l'étude du peuplement de la Mauritanie. Dytiscides et Gyrinides. BULL. IFAN 14 (1952), pp. 529-536.

8,467 LA VARDE, R. P. DE. Découverte du genre Gymnostomiella en Mauritanie. BULL. IFAN 15 (1953), pp. 1387-1389.

8,468 LERICHE, A. Mesures maures. Note préliminaire. BULL. IFAN 13 (1951), pp. 1227-1256.

8,469 MONOD, TH. Contribution à l'étude du peuplement de la Mauritanie. Notes botaniques sur l'Adrar (Sahara occidental). BULL. IFAN 14 (1952), pp. 405-449.

8,470 MONOD, TH. Contribution à l'étude du peoplement de la Mauritanie. Poissons d'eau douce. BULL. IFAN 13 (1951), pp. 802-812.

8,471 MONOD, TH. Notes sur le Quaternaire de la région Tazazmout-El Beyyed (Adrar de Mauritanie). PROC. PAN-AFR. CONGR. PREHIST. 4 (1962), pp. 177-188.

8,472 PERES, J. M. Nouvelle contribution à l'étude des Ascidies de la Côte occidentale d'Afrique. BULL. IFAN 13 (1951), pp. 1051-1071.

8,473 PIC, M. Contribution à l'étude du peuplement de la Mauritanie. Coléoptères divers. BULL. IFAN 13 (1951), pp. 798-801; 14 (1952), pp. 489-494.

8,474 SEGUY, E. Contribution à l'étude du peuplement de la Mauritanie. BULL. IFAN. 13 (1951), pp. 317-318.

8,475 SMITH, W. C. and HEY, M. H. The silica-grass from the crater of Aouelloul (Adrar, western Sahara). BULL. IFAN 14 (1952), pp. 762-776.

8,476 VACHON, M. Contribution à l'étude du peuplement de la Mauritanie. BULL. IFAN 15 (1953), pp. 1012-1028.

8,477 VILLIERS, A. Contribution à l'étude du peuplement de la Mauritanie. BULL. IFAN 12 (1950), pp. 984-998; 13 (1951), pp. 129-138.

8,478 VILLIERS, A. Contribution à l'étude du peuplement de la Mauritanie. Note sur la faune aquatique et ripicole de l'Adrar mauritanien. BULL. IFAN 15 (1953), pp. 631-646.

8,479 WALTER, C. Hydracariens de Mauritanie. BULL. IFAN 2 (1940), pp. 416-422.

8,480 Un prix scientifique en A.O.F. BULL. IFAN 13 (1951), p. 1308.

Sociology

8,481 DUCHEMIN, G. J. La récolte du sel et les conditions de travail dans les salines du Trarza occidental (Mauritanie). BULL. IFAN 13 (1951), pp. 853-867.

8,482 MARTIN, H. L'Association agricole ou "širka fe-l harāta" en Mauritanie. BULL. IFAN 1 (1939), pp. 762-768.

8,483 NORRIS, H. T. Yemenis in the western Sahara. J. AFR. HIST. 3 (1962), pp. 317-322.

SENEGAL

General

8,484 ABI-SAAB, R. Le Sénégal, des origines a l'Indépendance [a bibliography]. GENEVE-AFR. 3 (1964), pp. 288-297.

8,485 BOULEGUE, M. La presse au Sénégal avant 1939. Bibliographie. BULL. IFAN 27 (1965), pp. 715-754.

8,486 LE ROY, J. Matan, Sénégal. ANNALES AFR., 1958, pp. 235-243.

8,487 PASQUIER, R. Les débuts de la presse au Sénégal. CAH. ET. AFR. 2 (1962), pp. 477-490.

8,488 L'Institut français d'Afrique noire de Dakar et la Société d'Etudes Camerounaises. BSEC 5 (1944), pp. 95-96.

8,489 L'Institut Français d'Afrique Noire et nous. BSEC 6 (1944), pp. 93-95.

8,490 L'Institut Universitaire de Dakar. ZAIRE 4 (1950), pp. 898.

Agriculture

8,491 CHABAS, J. Le domaine national du Sénégal; réforme foncière et agraire. ANNALES AFR., 1965, pp. 33-70.

8,492 DAVID, P. Fraternité d'hivernage (le Contrat de navétanat), théorie et pratique. PRESENCE AFR. N.S. 31 (1960), pp. 45-57.

8,493 GUEYE, Y. Essai sur les causes et les conséquences de la micropropriété au Fouta Toro. BULL. IFAN. 19 (1957), pp. 28-42.

8,494 PAPY, L. La vallée du Sénégal: agriculture traditionnelle et riziculture mécanisée. ET. SENEG. 2 (1952), pp. 1-48.

8,495 PELISSIER, P. L'arachide au Sénégal: rationalisation et modernisation de sa culture. ET. SENEG. 2 (1952), pp. 49-80.

8,496 Calendrier agricole pour le Sénégal. BULL. IFAN 8 (1946), pp. 138-163.

See also 17688.

Anthropology

8,497 AMES, D. W. The economic base of Wolof polygyny. SOUTHWESTERN J. ANTHR. 11 (1955), pp. 391-403.

8,498 AMES, D. W. The selection of mates, courtship and marriage among the Wolof. BULL. IFAN 18 (1956), pp. 156-168

8,499 APPIA, B. Superstitions guinéennes et Sénégalaises. BULL. IFAN 2 (1940), pp. 358-395.

8,500 COLLOMB, H. and AYATS, H. Les migrations au Senegal: étude psychopathologique. CAH. ET. AFR. 2 (1962), pp. 570-597.

8,501 DIAGNE, P. Royaumes Seréres: les institutions traditionnelles du Sine Saloum. PRESENCE AFR. N.S. 54 (1965), pp. 142-172.

8,502 DUPIN, H. and MASSE, L. Aspects méthodologiques des études de poids de naissance: portée en Santé publique et en Anthropologie physique. BULL. IFAN. 24 (1962), pp. 383-392.

8,503 ENGESTROM, T. Some aspects of the Mande myth problem. ETHNOS 26 (1961), pp. 219-226.

8,504 GESSAIN, M. Note sur les Badyaranké (Guinée, Guinée Portugaise et Sénégal). J. SOC. AFR. 28 (1958), pp. 43-89.

8,505 TAYIB, A. EL. The changing customs of the Riverain Sudan. SUDAN NOTES AND RECORDS 36 (1955), pp. 146-158.

8,506 THOMAS, L. V. L'animisme, religion caduque. Etude qualitative et quantitative sur les opinions et pratique religieuse en Basse Casamance (pays diola). BULL. IFAN 27 (1965), pp. 1-42.

8,507 THOMAS, L. V. Esquisse sur les mouvements de populations et les contacts socio-culturels en pays Diola (Basse-Casamance). BULL. IFAN 22 (1960), pp. 486-508.

8,508 THOMAS, L. V. Essai d'analyse structurale appliquée à la cuisine diola. BULL. IFAN 22 (1960), pp. 328-345.

8,509 THOMAS, L. V. Essai sur quelques notions de morale théorique en pays diola (Basse-Casamance). BULL. IFAN 19 (1957), pp. 1-27.

8,510 THOMAS, L. V. Etude sur la vie pulsionnelle du Diola (Basse-Casamance). BULL. IFAN 24 (1962), pp. 105-154.

8,511 THOMAS, L. V. La frustration chez les Diola. BULL. IFAN 23 (1961), pp. 518-572.

8,512 THOMAS, L. V. Note sur l'enfant et l'adolescent Diola. BULL. IFAN 25 (1963), pp. 66-79.

8,513 THOMAS, L. V. Pour une systématique de l'habitat diola. BULL. IFAN 26 (1964), pp. 78-118.

8,514 THOMAS, L. V. Réflexions sur quelques activités techniques en basse Casamance (Sénégal). BULL. IFAN 19 (1957), pp. 507-557.

8,515 THOMAS, L. V. Réflexions sur quelques aspects de la moralité diola. BULL. IFAN, Série B: Sciences humaines 20 (1958), pp. 249-290.

8,516 THOMAS, L. V. Un système philosophique sénégalais: la cosmologie des Diola. PRESENCE AFR. N.S. 32-33 (1960), pp. 64-75.

8,517 THOMAS, L. V. Le test de Rorschach comme mode d'approche de la psychologie noire. Aperçus sur la personnalité Diola. BULL. IFAN 25 (1963), pp. 288-350.

Art

8,518 APPIA-DABIT, B. Notes sur quelques bijoux sénégalais. BULL. IFAN 5 (1943), pp. 27-32.

8,519 APPIA-DABIT, B. Quelques artisans noirs. BULL. IFAN 3 (1941), pp. 1-44.

8,520 APPIA-DABIT, B. Quelques faîtes de cases en Casamance. BULL. IFAN 5 (1943), pp. 34-37.

8,521 BIRAME, S. Sur le théatre africain. PRESENCE AFR. 14 (1953), pp. 304-306.

8,522 CORBEIL, R. Les récentes découvertes au Cap-Vert concernant le Paléolithique. BULL. IFAN 13 (1951), pp. 384-437.

8,523 CORBEIL, R. et al. Préhistoire et protohistoire de la presqu'île du Cap-Vert et de l'extrême ouest sénégalais by R. Corbeil, R. Mauny, J. Charbonnier. BULL. IFAN 10 (1948), pp. 378-460.

8,524 DAGAN, T. Le site préhistorique de Tiemassas (Senegal). BULL. IFAN 18 (1956), pp. 432-461.

8,525 JOIRE, J. Découvertes archéologiques dans la région de Rao (Bas-Sénégal). BULL. IFAN, Série B: Sciences humaines 17 (1955), pp. 249-333.

8,526 LERICHE, A. Instruments de musique maure et Griots. BULL. IFAN 12 (1950), pp. 744-750.

8,527 LERICHE, A. Poésie et Musique maure. BULL. IFAN 12 (1950), pp. 710-743.

8,528 MAUNY, R. Poteries néolithiques du Cap Vert (Senegal). BULL. IFAN 13 (1951), pp. 155-167.

8,529 MAUNY, R. Les ruines du fort de M'Bidjem (Senegal). BULL. IFAN 8 (1946), pp. 133-137.

8,530 MAUNY. R. Sur la préhistoire de la Presqu'île du Cap Vert. ET. SENEG. 1 (1949), pp. 239-251.

8,531 RICHARD, R. Contribution à l'étude de quelques gisements néolithiques de tradition capsienne de la presqu'île du Cap-Vert. BULL. IFAN 13 (1951), pp. 1181-1202.

8,532 RICHARD, R. Contribution à l'étude du gisement néolithique guinéen du Cap Manuel a Dakar. BULL. IFAN 14 (1952), pp. 247-258.

8,533 SZUMOWSKI, G. Gisement paléolithique de Bargny-Ouest. BULL. IFAN 14 (1952), pp. 1228-1267.

8,534 La danse et la musique au Senegal. PRESENCE AFR. N.S. 54 (1965), pp. 240-244.

See also 9023.

Biography

8,535 MASSON, P. Une double énigme: André Brue. RHCF 25 (1932), pp. 9-34.

8,536 In memoriam [: David Diop]. RECH. AFR. 4 (1960), pp. 28-32.

8,537 Leopold Sedar Senghor. PRESENCE AFR. N.S. 39 (1961), pp. 213-214.

Economics

8,538 AMES, D. W. The use of a transitional cloth-money token among the Wolof. AMER. ANTHR. 57 (1955), pp. 1016-1024.

8,539 BALANDIER, G. and MERCIER, P. Particularisme et évolution: les pêcheurs Lebou. ET. SENEG. 3 (1952), pp. 1-213.

8,540 BRIGAUD, F. Le Sénégal économique. ET. SENEG. 9, no. vi (1967), pp. 3-146.

8,541 CROWDER, M. French Senegal. CONTEMP. REV. 190 (1956), pp. 287-291.

8,542 DENIS, P. A. Les "anciennes contributions directes" au Sénégal. ANNALES AFR., 1961, pp. 129-249.

8,543 FOUQUET, J. La traite des Arachides dans le pays de Kaolack, et ses conséquences économiques, sociales et juridiques. ET. SENEG. 8 (1958), pp. 1-261.

8,544 HAUSER, A. Absenteeism and labour turnover in the manufacturing industries of the Dakar area. HUMAN FACTORS OF PRODUCTIVITY IN AFR., 1962, pp. 113-129.

8,545 HAUSER, A. Les industries de transformation de la région de Dakar. ET. SENEG. 5 (1954), pp. 69-83.

8,546 MERSADIER, Y. Budgets familiaux africains: étude chex 136 familles de salariés dans trois centres urbains du Sénégal. ET. SENEG. 7 (1957), pp. 5-102.

8,547 MERSADIER, Y. Structure de budgets familiaux à Thiès. BULL. IFAN, Série B: Sciences humaines 17 (1955), pp. 388-432.

8,548 ROBIN, J. Le Marbat: Marché au Betail de Louga. AFRICA 15 (1945), pp. 47-60.

8,549 THOMAS, L. V. Essai sur quelques problemes relatifs au regime foncier des Diola de Basse-Casamance (Senegal). AFRICAN AGRARIAN SYSTEMS, 1963, pp. 314-330.

8,550 Arachides et vivres au Sénégal. ZAIRE 6 (1952), pp. 1089-1090.

8,551 Baisse des prix à Dakar. ZAIRE 9 (1955), p. 308.

8,552 La culture du riz au Sénégal. ZAIRE 6 (1952), pp. 1090-1091.

8,553 The Institut d'Etudes Administratives Africaines, University of Dakar. INT. SOC. SC. J. 12 (1960), pp. 448-449.

8,554 The Institut des Science Economiques et Commerciales Appliquées a l'Afrique Noire, University of Dakar. INT. SOC. SC. J. 12 (1960), pp. 445-448.

8,555 A new African institute of economic development and planning [Dakar]. BULL. AFR. STUD. ASSOC. 1 (1964), p. 23; 5 (1965), p. 28.

8,556 La plaque tournante du Sénégal. ZAIRE 5 (1951), pp. 750-751.

See also 9234.

Education

8,557 COCATRE-ZILGIEN, A. De la contribution apportée par l'Université de Dakar a la formation des cadres moyens et supérieurs. ANNALES AFR., 1962, pp. 501-520.

8,558 GRELIER, S. Essai de classification des fautes d'Anglais d'élèves Wolof, avec exercises d'accompagnement. CENTRE DE LINGUISTIQUE APPLIQUEE DE DAKAR, no. 19, pp. 1-35.

8,559 GUEYE, M. The education of women in rural areas of Senegal. AFR. WOMEN 4 (1962), pp. 84-87.

8,560 A l'Université de Saint-Louis. ZAIRE 4 (1950), pp. 1019-1020.

8,561 Expérience d'education de base au Sénégal. ZAIRE 7 (1953), pp. 1084-1085.

8,562 Inauguration de l'Université de Dakar. ANNALES AFR., 1959, pp. 7-13.

Geography

8,563 ADAM, J. G. Connaissance du Sénégal: végétation. ET. SENEG. 9, fasc. 3 (1965), pp. 155-214.

8,564 BERRIT, G. R. Esquisse des conditions hydrologiques du plateau continental du Cap Vert à la Gambie. Températures et salinités. BULL. IFAN 14 (1952), pp. 735-761.

8,565 BRASSEUR, G. Le problème de l'eau au Sénégal. ET. SENEG. 4 (1952), pp. 5-99.

8,566 BRIGAUD, F. Connaissance du Sénégal: climat. ET. SENEG. 9, fasc. 3 (1965), pp. 1-109.

8,567 BRIGAUD, F. Connaissance du Sénégal: hydrographie. ET. SENEG. 9, fasc. 2 (1961), pp. 3-102.

8,568 COOMBS, G. M. Dakar. CONTEMP. REV. 162 (1942), pp. 350-352.

8,569 DEVOIS, J. C. Peuplements forestiers de la Basse Casamance. BULL. IFAN 10 (1948), pp. 182-211.

8,570 FROELICH, J. C. Le journal de route du missionnaire A. Mischlich. ET. DAHOM. 3 (1950), pp. 75-87.

8,571 GORODISKI, A. La presqu'ile du Cap-Vert: Structure. ET. SENEG. 1 (1949), pp. 23-56.

8,572 JAEGER, P. La presqu'ile du Cap-Vert: Le climat. ET. SENEG. 1 (1949), pp. 63-91.

8,573 LERICHE, A. and MOKHATAR OULD HAMIDOUN. Notes sur le Trârza. Essai de géographie historique. BULL. IFAN 10 (1948), pp. 461-538.

8,574 LOMBARD, J. Connaissance du Sénégal: géographie humaine. ET. SENEG. 9, fasc. 5 (1963), pp. 3-183.

8,575 NICOLAS, J. P. Deux ports d'estuaire: Saint-Louis du Sénégal et Doula. BULL. IFAN 19 (1957), pp. 259-274.

8,576 PITOT, A. and MASSON, H. Quelques données sur la température au cours des feux de brousse aux environs de Dakar. BULL. IFAN 13 (1951), pp. 711-732.

8,577 RICHARD-MOLARD, J. La presqu'ile du Cap-Vert: Introduction. ET. SENEG. 1 (1949), pp. 9-21.

8,578 ROBERTY, G. La végétation du Ferlo. BULL. IFAN 14 (1952), pp. 777-798.

8,579 SAVONNET, G. La ville de Thiès: étude de géographie urbaine. ET. SENEG. 6 (1955), pp. 5-178.

8,580 TOUPET, C. Dakar, premier port de l'Union française. BULL. IFAN 19 (1957), pp. 670-673.

8,581 WHITTLESEY, D. Dakar and the other Cape Verde settlements. GEOG. REV. 31 (1941), pp. 609-638.

8,582 WHITTLESEY, D. Dakar revisited. GEOG. REV. 38 (1948), pp. 626-632.

8,583 Déboisement de la région de Dakar. ZAIRE 5 (1951), pp. 977-978.

Government. Politics. Administration

8,584 BOURLON, A. L'évolution politique du Sénégal. AFR. ET ASIE 68 (1964), pp. 23-41.

8,585 GRIAULE, M. Mission Dakar-Djibouti, (loi du 31 mars 1931) rapport général (mai 1931-mai 1932). J. SOC. AFR. 2 (1932), pp. 113-122, 229-236.

8,586 MILLE, P. The "black-vote" in Senegal, tr. by E. D. M[orel]. J. AFR. SOC. 1 (1901), pp. 64-79.

8,587 ROBSON, P. The problem of Senegambia. JMAS 3 (1965), pp. 393-407.

8,588 SKURNIK, W. A. E. Léopold Sédas Senghor and African socialism. JMAS 3 (1965), pp. 349-369.

8,589 WOLF, J. Le Sénégal dans le contexte africain et mondial. CIVILISATIONS 13 (1963), pp. 463-473.

8,590 ZUCCARELLI, F. Le régime des engagés à temps au Sénégal (1817-1848). CAH. ET. AFR. 2 (1962), pp. 420-461.

8,591 Le Comité de défense des libertés démocratiques. PRESENCE AFR. N.S. 20 (1958), p. 137.

History

8,592 ASSANE, S. Une Republique africaine au XIXe siècle (1795-1857). PRESENCE AFR. N.S. 1 (1955), pp. 47-65.

8,593 ASSANE, S. Vérités sur Dakar. PRESENCE AFR. N.S. 23 (1958-1959), pp. 81-87.

8,594 ATKINS, P. M. Dakar and the strategy of West Africa. FOREIGN AFFAIRS 20 (1941-1942), pp. 358-366.

8,595 BA, M. A. Notice sur Maghama et le canton du Littama. BULL. IFAN 1 (1939), pp. 743-761.

8,596 BA TAMSIR OUSMANE. Essai historique sur le Rip (Sénégal). BULL. IFAN 19 (1957), pp. 564-591.

8,597 BRIGAUD, F. Connaissance du Sénégal: histoire traditionnelle du Sénégal. ET. SENEG. 9, fasc. 9 (1962), pp. 1-335.

8,598 DEROURE, F. La vie quotidienne à Saint-Louis par ses Archives (1779-1809). BULL. IFAN 26 (1964), pp. 397-439.

8,599 DESSERTINE, A. Naissance d'un port: Kaolack, des origines a 1900. ANNALES AFR., 1960, pp. 225-259.

8,600 DIOP, A. Enquête sur la migration Toucouleur à Dakar. BULL. IFAN 22 (1960), pp. 393-418.

8,601 DODWELL, H. Le Sénégal sous la domination anglais. RHCF 4 (1916), pp. 267-300.

8,602 F., H. Le gouverneur Roger, la Société de Géographie et Duranton. RHCF 9, no. 2 (1921), pp. 264-268.

8,603 FARIA, F. L. DE. Relação do Porto de Rio Senegal, feita por João Baptista Lavanha. BCGP 14 (1959), pp. 359-371.

8,604 FAURE, C. La garnison européenne du Sénégal et le recrutement des premières troupes noires (1779-1858). RHCF 8, no. 2 (1920), pp. 5-108.

8,605 FAURE, C. Notice sur les Archives du Sénégal. RHCF 2 (1914), pp. 353-374.

8,606 FAURE, C. Le premier séjour de Duranton au Sénégal (1819-1826). RHCF 9, no. 2 (1921), pp. 189-263.

8,607 FROIDEVAUX, H. Une lettre inédite d'Adanson pendant son voyage au Sénégal. RHCF 5 (1917), pp. 79-90.

8,608 FROIDEVAUX, H. Un plan de colonisation du Sénégal en 1802. Notes critiques. RHCF 7, no. 2 (1919), pp. 177-194.

8,609 GANIER, G. Lat Dyor et le chemin de fer de l'arachide, 1876-1886. BULL. IFAN 27 (1965), pp. 223-281.

8,610 GIRARD, J. Note sur l'histoire locale du Fouladou (cercle de Velingara, Haute-Casamance). J. SOC. AFR. 34 (1964), pp. 302-306.

8,611 GUEYE, M. L'affaire Chautemps (avril 1904) et la suppression de l'esclavage de case au Sénégal. BULL. IFAN 27 (1965), pp. 543-559.

8,612 HARGREAVES, J. D. Assimilation in eighteenth-century Senegal. J. AFR. HIST. 6 (1965), pp. 177-184.

8,613 JORE, L. Les établissements français sur la côte occidentale d'Afrique de 1758 a 1809. REV. FRANC. HIST. OUTRE-MER 51 (1964), pp. 5-446.

8,614 JORE, L. and DEBIEN, G. Autour de la chaumière africaine. BULL. IFAN 27 (1965), pp. 287-318.

8,615 LE MIRE, P. Petite chronique du Djilor. BULL. IFAN 8 (1946), pp. 55-63.

8,616 LY, A. A propos d'un événement: La France et les Etablissements Français au Sénégal entre 1713 et 1763, de M. Delcourt. BULL. IFAN 14 (1952), pp. 1560-1580.

8,617 LY, A. Conséquences des cas Labat et Loyer. BULL. IFAN 15 (1953), pp. 751-766.

8,618 MARTY, P. Un centenaire colonial: La découverte des sources de la Gambie et du Sénégal: Mollien (1818-1819). RHCF 9, no. 1 (1921), pp. 53-98.

8,619 MARTY, P. Episodes de l'histoire du Sénégal. La mission de Sauvigny dans le Sin-Saloun en 1822. RHCF 15 (1923), pp. 223-246.

8,620 MARTY, P. L'établissement des Français dans le Haut-Sénégal (1817-1822). RHCF 18 (1925), pp. 51-118, 210-268.

8,621 MARTY, P. L'expédition de Repentigny dans le Saloun et la première cession du pays à la France en 1785. RHCF 17 (1924), pp. 43-66.

8,622 MARTY, P. Le suicide d'un gouverneur du Sénégal. RHCF 8, no. 1 (1920), pp. 129-144.

8,623 MARTY, P. Tentatives de christianisation et de constitution de l'état-civil des captifs sénégalis en 1823-1824. RHCF 18 (1925), pp. 395-410.

8,624 MONOD, TH. Un empéreur: Moussa I. PRESENCE AFR. 8 (1950), pp. 109-114.

8,625 MONTEILHET, J. Le ministre Decrès historiographe de Napoléon à l'usage du Sénégal. RHCF 9, no. 1 (1921), pp. 269-286.

8,626 PASQUIER, R. Villes du Sénégal aux XIXe siècle. REV. FRANC. HIST. OUTRE-MER 47 (1960), pp. 387-426.

8,627 RAU, E. Quand se dénouent les chaînes... ANNALES AFR., 1959, pp. 245-257.

8,628 ROBIN, J. D'un royaume amphibie et fort disparate. AFR. STUD. 5 (1946), pp. 250-256.

8,629 ROUSSEAU, R. Le Sénégal d'autrefois. Seconde étude sur le Cayor (compléments tirés des manuscrits de Yoro Dyâo). BULL. IFAN 3 (1941), pp. 79-144.

8,630 SAINT-MARTIN, Y. L'artillerie d'El Hadj Omar et d'Ahmadou. BULL. IFAN 27 (1965), pp. 560-572.

8,631 SAINT-MARTIN, Y. Une source de l'histoire coloniale du Sénégal: les rapports de situation politique (1874-1891). REV. FRANC. HIST. OUTRE-MER 52 (1965), pp. 153-224.

8,632 SAULNIER, E. Les français en Casamance et dans l'archipel des Bissagos (Mission Dangles, 1828). RHCF 2 (1914), pp. 41-76.

8,633 SAULNIER, M. Une réception royale a l'Ile de Gorée en 1831. RHCF 6 (1918), pp. 339-348.

8,634 THOMAS, L. V. L'organisation foncière des Diola (Basse-Casamance). ANNALES AFR., 1960, pp. 199-223.

8,635 VERDAT, M., CARIOU, M., and MONOD, TH. La presqu'ile du Cap Vert: L'histoire. ET. SENEG. 1 (1949), pp. 253-288.

8,636 WADE, A. Chronique du Wâlo sénégalais (1186?-1855). BULL. IFAN 26 (1964), pp. 440-498.

8,637 ZUCCARELLI, F. L'entrepôt fictif de Gorée entre 1822 et 1852. ANNALES AFR., 1959, pp. 261-282.

8,638 ZUCCARELLI, F. Le recrutement de travailleurs sénégalais par l'état indépendant du Congo (1888-1896). REV. FRANC. HIST. OUTRE-MER 47 (1960), pp. 475-481.

Language. Literature

Language

8,639 ANTA, D. C. Extrait du dictionnaire étymologique [de la langue Valaf]. PRESENCE AFR. 4 (1948), pp. 680-684.

8,640 ANTA, D. C. Origines de la langue et de la race Valaf. PRESENCE AFR. 4 (1948), pp. 672-679.

8,641 CALVET, M. Interférences du phonétisme wolof dans le français parlé au Sénégal dans la région du Cap Vert. BULL. IFAN 26 (1964), pp. 518-531.

8,642 CANU, G. Les systèmes phonologiques des principales langues du Sénégal: étude comparative. CENTRE DE LINGUISTIQUE APPLIQUEE DE DAKAR, no. 13, pp. 1-44.

8,643 CHATAIGNER, A. Le Créole Portugais du Senegal: observations et textes. J. AFR. LANGS. 2 (1963), pp. 44-71.

8,644 DELAFOSSE, M. Classes nominales en Wolof. FESTSCHRIFT MEINHOF, 1927, pp. 29-44.

8,645 HOMBURGER, L. Le sérère-peul. J. SOC. AFR. 9 (1939), pp. 85-102.

8,646 KENNEDY, A. M. Dialect in Diola. J. AFR. LANGS. 3 (1964), pp. 96-101.

8,647 KLINGENHEBEN, A. Die Mande-Völker und ihre Sprachen. AFR. UND UB. 34 (1943-1944), pp. 1-23.

8,648 LESTRANGE, M. DE and TRESSAN, Marquis DE. Proverbes peuls du Badyar et du Fouta Djallon. BULL. IFAN, Série B: Sciences humaines 17 (1955), pp. 433-476.

8,649 MUKAROVSKY, H. Vers une linguistique comparative ouest-africaine: le Diola; langue bantoue-guinéenne. BULL. IFAN 26 (1964), pp. 127-165.

8,650 PICHL, W. Verschiedene Wolof-Texte. AFR. UND UB. 46 (1962-1963), pp. 204-218.

8,651 PICHL, W. Wolof-Erzählungen. AFR. UND UB. 44 (1960), pp. 253-282; 45 (1961-1962), pp. 67-95, 189-205.

8,652 PICHL, W. Wolof-Sprichwörter und -Rätsel. AFR. UND UB. 46 (1962-1963), pp. 93-109.

8,653 RUDIGOZ, C. Fondements théoriques d'une méthode d'anglais pour le Sénégal. CENTRE DE LINGUISTIQUE APPLIQUEE DE DAKAR, no. 16, pp. 1-116.

8,654 SENGHOR, L. S. L'article conjonctif en wolof. J. SOC. AFR. 17 (1947), pp. 19-22.

8,655 SENGHOR, L. S. Les classes nominales en Wolof et les substantifs a initiale nasale. J. SOC. AFR. 13 (1943), pp. 109-122.

8,656 SENGHOR, L. S. L'harmonie vocalique en Sérère (Dialecte du Dyéguème). J. SOC. AFR. 14 (1944), pp. 17-23.

8,657 SHAFER, R. Phonétique comparée du Nigéro-Sénégalien (Mande). BULL. IFAN 21 (1959), pp. 179-200.

8,658 TASTEVIN, R. P. C. Vocabulaires inédits de sept dialectes sénégalais, dont six de la Casamance. J. SOC. AFR. 6 (1936), pp. 1-33.

8,659 WIOLAND, F. Enquête sur les langues parlées au Sénégal par les élèves de l'enseignement primaire. Etude statistique 1965. CENTRE DE LINGUISTIQUE APPLIQUEE DE DAKAR, no. 11, pp. 1-252.

8,660 WIOLAND, F. Le genre en français parlé et en Wolof: étude comparative. CENTRE DE LINGUISTIQUE APPLIQUEE DE DAKAR

8,661 Balade toucoulore de Samba-Foul [translated by Peul]. PRESENCE AFR. 3 (1948), pp. 478-484.

See also 8768, 9690.

Literature

8,662 ANTA KA, A. L'Envers du masque. PRESENCE AFR. N.S. 3 (1955), pp. 49-66.

8,663 BEKRIN, A. O. A. "El 'Omda" poème sur la médicine Maure [with an introduction by Paul Dubié]. BULL. IFAN 5 (1943), pp. 38-66.

8,664 BRAMBILLA, C. Il poema di Chaka-Senghor. AFRICA (Rome) 17 (1962), pp. 217-219.

8,665 DADIE, B. Mémoires d'une rue. PRESENCE AFR. 4 (1948), pp. 599-602.

8,666 DIAKHATE, L. M'Bàye Rab Gueye. Poète et penseur Sénégalais d'expression ouolove. PRESENCE AFR. N.S. 4 (1955), pp. 76-80.

8,667 DIAKHATE, L. Le mythe dans la poésie populaire au Sénégal et sa présence dans l'oeuvre de Léopold Sedar Senghor et de Birago Diop. PRESENCE AFR. N.S. 39 (1961), pp. 59-78.

8,668 DIALLO, B. M'bala. PRESENCE AFR. 6 (1949), pp. 128-133.

8,669 DIOP, B. Mamelles [fiction]. BO 10 (1961), pp. 61-65.

8,670 DIOP, B. Retour au Blason. PRESENCE AFR. N.S. 51 (1964), pp. 97-98.

8,671 KHANE, S. A. Ambigious adventure: an extract from a novel. BO 15 (1964), pp. 9-12.

8,672 LAGNEAU, L. La Negritude de Léopold Sédar Senghor. PRESENCE AFR. N.S. 39 (1961), pp. 166-181.

8,673 NIANG, L. Les pierres du Guadalquivir. PRESENCE AFR. N.S. 39 (1961), pp. 154-156.

8,674 OUMAR, BA. Dix-huit poèmes peul modernes, presentes par Pierre F. Lacroix. CAH. ET. AFR. 2 (1962), pp. 536-550.

8,675 PICHL, W. Ein Wolof-Gedicht und -Lieder. AFR. UND UB. 45 (1961-1962), pp. 271-285.

8,676 SADJI, A. Nini, mulâtresse du Sénégal. PRESENCE AFR. 16 (1954), pp. 287-415.

8,677 SAINT-JOSEPH, L. M. DE. Fables et contes maures. Les histoires du chacal. BULL. IFAN 10 (1948), pp. 560-594.

8,678 SENGHOR, L. S. Elégie à Aynina Fall. PRESENCE AFR. N.S. 11 (1957), pp. 103-107.

8,679 SENGHOR, L. S. Les nouveaux contes d'Amadou Koumba. PRESENCE AFR. N.S. 18-19 (1958), pp. 208-216.

8,680 SENGHOR, L. S. Ten poems from Chants pour naett tr. by Sangodare Akanji. BO 9 (1960), pp. 25-30.

8,681 SOUCE, O. The descendants [a story]. BO 18 (1965), pp. 44-47.

8,682 WADE, A. M. A ma soeur Fatou. PRESENCE AFR. 14 (1953), pp. 200-201.

8,683 WADE, A. M. Poème pour David. PRESENCE AFR. N.S. 34-35 (1960-1961), pp. 154-155.

See also 3272.

Law

8,684 ARRIGHI, G. and CARLIER, J. Chronique de jurisprudence de la Cour Suprême du Sénégal. ANNALES AFR., 1961, pp. 117-127; 1964, pp. 187-210.

8,685 AURILLAC, M. Les aspects juridiques du socialisme sénégalais. Théorie et pratique du socialisme africain au Sénégal. ANNALES AFR., 1962, pp. 93-112.

8,686 CHABAS, J. Le droit de la responsabilité devant la cour suprême du Sénégal. ANNALES AFR., 1963, pp. 91-105.

8,687 CHABAS, J. Le droit des successions chez les Ouolofs. ANNALES AFR., 1956, pp. 75-119.

8,688 CHABAS, J. Le mariage et le divorce dans les coutumes des Ouolofs habitant les grands centres du Sénégal. RJPUF 6 (1952), pp. 474-532.

8,689 CHABAS, J. Les pouvoirs du Conservateur en matière d'immatriculation et d'inscription. ANNALES AFR., 1960, pp. 41-60.

8,690 DECOTTIGNIES, R. L'apport européen dans l'élaboration du droit privé sénégalais. ANNALES AFR., 1964, pp. 79-113.

8,691 DECOTTIGNIES, R. Réflexions sur le projet du Code sénégalais des obligations. ANNALES AFR., 1962, pp. 171-180.

8,692 DECOTTIGNIES, R. Université de Dakar, Faculté de Droit et des Sciences Economiques. J. AFR. LAW 6 (1962), pp. 129-130.

8,693 FARNSWORTH, E. A. Law reform in a developing country: a new code of obligations for Senegal. J. AFR. LAW 8 (1964), pp. 6-19.

8,694 FARNSWORTH, E. A. Le nouveau code des obligations du Sénégal. ANNALES AFR., 1963, pp. 73-90.

8,695 GEORGES, P. La procédure législative au Sénégal. ANNALES AFR., 1965, pp. 173-188.

8,696 NOBLE, B. P. Memoire sur quelques aspects du régime foncier au Sénégal, en Angleterre et en Gambie. ANNALES AFR., 1965, pp. 229-249.

8,697 PASQUIER, R. En marge de la guerre de Sécession: les essais de culture du coton au Sénégal. ANNALES AFR., 1955, pp. 185-202.

8,698 PEISER, G. L'ordonnance sénégalaise du 15 mai 1963 portant loi organique relative aux lois de finances. ANNALES AFR., 1964, pp. 115-136.

8,699 RAU, E. La question des terrains de Tound. ANNALES AFR., 1956, pp. 141-163.

Religion

8,700 BOURLON, A. Actualité des Mourides et du Mourisdisme. AFR. ET ASIE 46 (1959), pp. 10-30.

8,701 HERBINIERE, E. Apóstolo, inteiramente... PORT. EM AFR. 19 (1962), pp. 93-97.

8,702 JANIN, J. Le clergé dans les vielles colonies françaises. RHCF 29 (1936), pp. 175-188.

8,703 REEVE, H. Forest temples. J. AFR. SOC. 6 (1907), pp. 286-290.

8,704 Pèlerinages musulmans au Sénégal. ZAIRE 5 (1951), pp. 530-531.

Science

8,705 BALACHOWSKY, A. S. Sur un Dysmicoccus nouveau (Hom. Coccoïdea-Pseudococcini) nuisible au Casuarina en A.O.F. BULL. IFAN 15 (1953), pp. 1046-1050.

8,706 BASILEWSKY, P. Contribution à l'etude des Coléoptères Carabidae de l'Afrique occidentale. III. Carabiques. BULL. IFAN 13 (1951), pp. 1107-1109.

8,707 BENOIST, R. Apides de l'A.O.F. communiqués par A. Villiers. BULL. IFAN 12 (1950), p. 629.

8,708 BRIGAUD, F. Connaissance du Sénégal: géologie. ET. SENEG. 9, fasc. 1 (1960), pp. 13-93.

8,709 CADENAT, J. Liste des espèces de Poissons recueillies par le chalutier Gérard Tréca. BULL. IFAN 12 (1950), pp. 216-222.

8,710 CADENAT, J. Notes d'Ichthyologie ouest africaine. IV. Les Rémoras des côtes du Sénégal. BULL. IFAN 15 (1953), pp. 672-683.

8,711 CADENAT, J. Notes sur les Cétacés observés sur les côtes du Sénégal de 1941 à 1948. BULL. IFAN 11 (1949), pp. 1-15.

8,712 CADENAT, J. Notes sur les Tortues marines des côtes du Sénégal. BULL. IFAN 11 (1949), pp. 16-35.

8,713 CADENAT, J. Notes sur Paragaleus gruveli Budker. BULL. IFAN 12 (1950), pp. 412-417.

8,714 CADENAT, J. La pêche sur les côtes de la Presqu'ile du Cap Vert. ET. SENEG. 1 (1949), pp. 191-207.

8,715 CADENAT, J. Rapport sur les Sélaciens des côtes du Sénégal et plus spécialement sur les Requins. BULL. IFAN 12 (1950), pp. 944-975.

8,716 CADENAT, J. Remarques biologiques sur Leptocharias Smithii Mül. et Henle. BULL. IFAN 12 (1950), pp. 408-411.

8,717 CAPART, A. Quelques Copépodes parasites de Poissons marins de la région de Dakar. BULL. IFAN 15 (1953), pp. 647-671.

8,718 CEDANT, J. Notes sur une petite collection de poissons des îles du Cap Vert. BULL. IFAN 11 (1949), pp. 332-339.

8,719 CHARREAU, C. and FAUCK, R. Connaissance du Sénégal: sols. ET. SENEG. 9, fasc. 3 (1965), pp. 111-154.

8,720 DAGET, J. La passe à poissons de Markala. BULL. IFAN 12 (1950), pp. 1166-1171.

8,721 DECLOITRE, L. Matériaux pour une faune rhizopodique d'A.O.F. Faune du lac Tamna (Sénégal). BULL. IFAN 13 (1951), pp. 87-108.

8,722 DEKEYSER, P. L. and VILLIERS, A. Mission J. Cadenat aux Iles du Cap Vert. Reptiles. BULL. IFAN 13 (1951), pp. 1152-1158.

8,723 DEKEYSER, P. L. and VILLIERS, A. Nidification d'aigrettes blanches au Sénégal. BULL. IFAN 13 (1951), pp. 151-154.

8,724 DELAIS, M. Notes d'ichthyologie ouest-africaine. I. Note sur les Antennariides en collection au Laboratoire de Biologie marine de l'I.F.A.N. à Goree. BULL. IFAN 13 (1951), pp. 145-150.

8,725 DELAIS, M. Notes d'ichthyologie ouest africaine. II. Les Gobiidae d'Afrique Occidentale Française en collection au laboratoire de biologie marine de l'IFAN à Goree. BULL. IFAN 13 (1951), pp. 343-370.

8,726 DELCOURT, A. Quelques inédits d'Adanson. BULL. IFAN 2 (1940), pp. 326-333.

8,727 DOLLFUS, R. P. Métacercaire de Trématode (Gasterostomata) enkystée chez les Sparisoma, Rupiscartes et Blennius de Gorée (Sénégal). BULL. IFAN 13 (1951), pp. 762-770.

8,728 FAUVEL, P. Additions à la faune des Polychètes du Sénégal. BULL. IFAN 13 (1951), pp. 312-316.

8,729 FAUVEL, P. Contribution à la Faune des Annélides Polychètes du Sénégal. BULL. IFAN 12 (1950), pp. 335-394.

8,730 FRASER, F. C. Report on a collection of Odonata and Neuroptera from Senegal. BULL. IFAN 13 (1951), pp. 1093-1098.

8,731 GARINE, I. DE. Usages alimentaires dans la région de Khombole (Senegal). CAH. ET. AFR. 3 (1962), pp. 218-265.

8,732 JAEGER, P. La presqu'ile du Cap-Vert: La végétation. ET. SENEG. 1 (1949), pp. 93-157.

8,733 JOIRE, J. Amas de coquillages du littoral sénégalais dans la banlieue de Saint-Louis. BULL. IFAN 9 (1947), pp. 170-340.

8,734 LEVI, C. Spongiaires de la côte du Sénégal. BULL. IFAN 14 (1952), pp. 34-59.

8,735 LINHARD, J. et al. Calcium and magnesium in the sera of Dakar Africans by J. Lihard, F. Busson and P. Giraud. MALNUTRITION IN AFRICAN WOMEN..., 1952, pp. 301-307.

8,736 MONARD, A. Un nouvel Harpactacide du Senegal. Amphiascus monodi. BULL. IFAN 14 (1952), pp. 817-818.

8,737 MONOD, TH. Un catalogue des plantes de Richard-Toll (Sénégal) en 1824. BULL. IFAN 13 (1951), pp. 1281-1298.

8,738 MONOD, TH. Note complémentaire sur un travail algologique (Abbé P. Fremy, 1945). BULL. IFAN 13 (1951), p. 534.

8,739 MONOD, TH. Note sur les couches à Lépidocyclines. ET. SENEG. 1 (1949), pp. 57-61.

8,740 MONOD, TH. Sur un Colopisthus sénégalais. BULL. IFAN 14 (1952), pp. 813-816.

8,741 MONOD, TH. and VILLIERS, A. Notes sur la faune de la Presqu'ile du Cap Vert. ET. SENEG. 1 (1949), pp. 159-189.

8,742 PELISSIER, P. La géologie de l'Ouest sénégalais d'après F. Tessier. BULL. IFAN 13 (1951), pp. 894-897.

8,743 PELTIER, Médecin-Général-Inspecteur. La pathologie de la Presqu'ile du Cap Vert. ET. SENEG. 1 (1949), pp. 209-238.

8,744 PERES, J. M. Note sur deux Ascidies nouvelles récoltées dans la zone intercotidale du Sénégal. BULL. IFAN 15 (1953), pp. 1002-1011.

8,745 PICARD, J. Hydraires littoraux du Sénégal récoltés par H. Sourie aux environs de Dakar. BULL. IFAN 13 (1951), pp. 109-115.

8,746 ROUSSEAU, R. Le chameau au Sénégal. BULL. IFAN 5 (1943), pp. 67-79.

8,747 ROUSSEAU, R. Le porc au Sénégal, etude statistique. BULL. IFAN 8 (1946), pp. 71-87.

8,748 VILLIERS, A. Notes éthologiques sur quelques Coleoptères du Sénégal. BULL. IFAN 15 (1953), pp. 1329-1333.

See also 8472.

Sociology

8,749 BEART, C. Intimité: les lettres de la fiancée. PRESENCE AFR. 8 (1950), pp. 271-288.

8,750 COLLOMB, H. et al. Intoxication par le chanvre indien au Sénégal, by Henri Collomb, Moussa Diop, Henri Ayats. CAH. ET. AFR. 3 (1962), pp. 139-144.

8,751 DIENE, EL HADJ AMADOU LAMINE et al. Vers une évolution du mariage Sénégalais. BULL. IFAN 13 (1951), pp. 542-546.

8,752 DUCHEMIN, G. J. and MONOD, TH. La presqu'ile du Cap Vert: Le milieu humain. ET. SENEG. 1 (1949), pp. 289-316.

8,753 GIRARD, J. De la Communauté traditionnelle à la collectivité moderne en Casamance. ANNALES AFR., 1963, pp. 135-165.

8,754 GIRARD, J. Diffusion en milieu diola de l'association du Koumpo baïnouk. BULL. IFAN 27 (1965), pp. 42-98.

8,755 HAUSER, A. Quelques relations des travailleurs de l'industrie à leur travail en A.O.F. (Sénégal, Soudan, Guinée). BULL. IFAN, Série B: Sciences humaines 17 (1955), pp. 129-141.

8,756 HAUSER, J. Notes sur quelques attitudes de la collégienne dakaroise. BULL. IFAN, Série B: Sciences humaines 17 (1955), pp. 203-209.

8,757 LEQUES, R. La mode actuelle chez les Dakaroises (Etude de psychologie sociale). BULL. IFAN 19 (1957), pp. 431-445.

8,758 MASSE, L. La connaissance de l'âge en milieu urbain. Méthode d'approche concernant Dakar. BULL. IFAN 25 (1963), pp. 125-133.

8,759 MASSE, L. Contribution à l'étude de la nuptialité et de la fertilité dans l'agglomération dakaroise. ET. SENEG. 5 (1954), pp. 41-67.

8,760 MASSE, L. Contribution à l'étude de la ville de Thiès. Note concernant un sondage socio-démographique. Premier dépouillement numérique sur la situation matrimoniale. BULL. IFAN 18 (1956), pp. 255-280.

8,761 MASSE, L. Contribution à l'étude de la ville de Thiès. Suite du dépouillement numérique sur la situation matrimoniale. BULL. IFAN 19 (1957), pp. 275-283.

8,762 MERCIER, P. Aspects de la société africaine dans l'agglomération dakaroise: groupes familiaux et unités de voisinage. ET. SENEG. 5 (1954), pp. 11-40.

8,763 MERCIER, P. Le groupement Européen de Dakar: orientation d'une enquête. CAH. INT. SOCIOL. 19 (1955), pp. 130-146.

8,764 MERCIER, P. La vie politique dans les centres urbains du Sénégal. CAH. INT. SOCIOL. 27 (1959), pp. 55-84.

8,765 ROBIN, J. L'evolution du mariage coutumier chez les musulmans du Senegal. AFRICA 17 (1947), pp. 192-201; English summary, p. 201.

8,766 SANKALE, M. Souveraineté nationale et problèmes sanitaires internationaux. PRESENCE AFR. 36 (1961), pp. 34-50.

8,767 SAVONNET, G. Les villages de la banlieue thiessoise. BULL. IFAN, Série B: Sciences humaines 17 (1955), pp. 371-387.

8,768 THIRIET, A. Le Sénégal: population, langues, programmes scolaires. CENTRE DE LINGUISTIQUE APPLIQUEE DE DAKAR, no. 1, pp. 1-19.

8,769 THORE, L. Dagoudane-Pikine. Etude démographique et sociologique. BULL. IFAN 24 (1962), pp. 155-198.

8,770 THORE, L. Mariage et divorce dans la banlieue Dakar. CAH. ET. AFR. 4 (1964), pp. 479-551.

8,771 VALANTIN, S. and COLLOMB, H. Etude psycho-sociologique de la situation pédagogique au Senegal. CAH. ET. AFR. 2 (1962), pp. 624-630.

8,772 L'élevage indigène au Sénégal. ZAIRE 6 (1952), pp. 288-289.

M A L I

General

8,773 GOUNDIAM, O. San, Soudan français. ANNALES AFR., 1958, pp. 287-291.

8,774 PAGEARD, R. Ségou, Soudan français. ANNALES AFR., 1958, pp. 293-304.

8,775 PETOT, F. Sikasso, Soudan français. ANNALES AFR., 1958, pp. 305-326.

8,776 POUSSIBET, F. Notes sur l'Azaouad. BULL. IFAN 23 (1961), pp. 573-595.

Agriculture

8,777 AUBERT, G. Quelques problèmes pédologiques de mise en valeur de sols du Delta Central Nigerien (Soudan Français). DESERT RESEARCH, 1953, pp. 392-400.

8,778 GRIAULE, M. Le verger des Ogol (Soudan Français). J. SOC. AFR. 17 (1947), pp. 65-79.

Anthropology

8,779 BA, A. H. and DAGET, J. Note sur les chasses rituelles Bozo. J. SOC. AFR. 25 (1955), pp. 89-97.

8,780 CALAME-GRIAULE, G. Notes sur l'habitation du plateau central nigérien. BULL. IFAN, Série B: Sciences humaines 17 (1955), pp. 477-499.

8,781 CAPRON, J. Quelques notes sur la société du do chez les populations Bwa du cercle de San. J. SOC. AFR. 27 (1957), pp. 81-129.

8,782 CHELHOD, J. Le monde mythique arabe, examiné à la lumière d'un mythe africain. J. SOC. AFR. 24 (1954), pp. 49-61.

8,783 CISSE, Y. Notes sur les sociétés de chasseurs Malinké. J. SOC. AFR. 34 (1964), pp. 175-226.

8,784 CISSOKHO, B. Notes sur le Diankhouran. BULL. IFAN 4 (1942), pp. 155-159.

8,785 DAGET, J. and LIGERS, Z. Une ancienne industrie malienne: les pipes en terre. BULL. IFAN 24 (1962), pp. 12-53.

8,786 DIETERLEN, G. L'arme et l'outil chez les anciens Bambara. AFRICA 18 (1948), pp. 105-111.

8,787 DIETERLEN, G. Mécanisme de l'impureté chez les Dogon. J. SOC. AFR. 17 (1947), pp. 81-90.

8,788 DIETERLEN, G. Mythe et organisation sociale au Soudan français. J. SOC. AFR. 25 (1955), pp. 39-76.

8,789 DIETERLEN, G. Note sur le génie des eaux chez les Bozo. J. SOC. AFR. 12 (1942), pp. 149-155.

8,790 DIETERLEN, G. Parenté et mariage chez les Dogon (Soudan français). AFRICA 26 (1956), pp. 107-147; English summary, pp. 147-148.

8,791 DIETERLEN, G. Les rites symboliques du mariage chez les Bambara (Soudan Francais). ZAIRE 8 (1954), pp. 815-841.

8,792 DIETERLEN, G. and LIGERS, Z. Un objet rituel bozo: le maniyalo. J. SOC. AFR. 28 (1958), pp. 33-42.

8,793 DUPUIS, J. Un problème de minorité; les nomades dans l'état soudanais. AFR. ET ASIE 50 (1960), pp. 19-44.

8,794 ENGESTROM, T. Contribution aux connaissances des styles de construction au Soudan Français. ETHNOS 20 (1955), pp. 122-126.

8,795 GANAY, S. DE. Graphies bambara des nombres. J. SOC. AFR. 20 (1950), pp. 295-305.

8,796 GANAY, S. DE. Un jardin d'essai et son autel chez les Bambara. J. SOC. AFR. 17 (1947), pp. 57-63.

8,797 GANAY, S. DE. Notes sur le culte du Lebe chez les Dogon du Soudan français. J. SOC. AFR. 7 (1937), pp. 203-211.

8,798 GANAY, S. DE. Symbolisme des biens de la fiancée chez les Bambara (République soudanaise). CONGR. INT. SC. ANTH. ET ETHN. 6, no. ii (1960), pp. 187-190.

8,799 GRIAULE, G. Le vêtement Dogon, confection et usage. J. SOC. AFR. 21 (1951), pp. 151-162.

8,800 GRIAULE, M. L'alliance cathartique. AFRICA 18 (1948), pp. 242-258; English summary, p. 258.

8,801 GRIAULE, M. Blasons totémiques des Dogon. J. SOC. AFR. 7 (1937), pp. 69-78.

8,802 GRIAULE, M. Le Domfé des Kouroumba. J. SOC. AFR. 11 (1941), pp. 7-20.

8,803 GRIAULE, M. L'image du monde au Soudan. J. SOC. AFR. 19 (1949), pp. 81-87.

8,804 GRIAULE, M. Notes complémentaires sur les masques Dogons. J. SOC. AFR. 10 (1940), pp. 79-85.

8,805 GRIAULE, M. Note sur le couteau de circoncision Bozo. J. SOC. AFR. 26 (1956), pp. 7-8.

8,806 GRIAULE, M. Nouvelles remarques sur la harpeluth des Dogon. J. SOC. AFR. 24 (1954), pp. 119-122.

8,807 GRIAULE, M. Réflexions sur des symboles Soudanais. CAH. INT. SOCIOL. 13 (1952), pp. 8-30.

8,808 GRIAULE, M. Remarques sur le mécanisme du sacrifice dogon (Soudan français). J. SOC. AFR. 10 (1940), pp. 127-129.

8,809 GRIAULE, M. Le savoir des Dogon. J. SOC. AFR. 22 (1952), pp. 27-42.

8,810 GRIAULE, M. and DIETERLEN, G. L'agriculture rituelle des Bozo. J. SOC. AFR. 19 (1949), pp. 209-222.

8,811 GRIAULE, M. and DIETERLEN, G. Un système soudanais de Sirius. J. SOC. AFR. 20 (1950), pp. 273-294.

8,812 GRIAULE, M. and LIGERS, Z. Le bulu, jeu bozo. J. SOC. AFR. 25 (1955), pp. 35-37.

8,813 HAMA, B. L'esprit de la culture sonraïe. PRESENCE AFR. N.S. 14-15 (1957), pp. 149-154.

8,814 HEUZEY, J. A. Note sur le tissage au Soudan. BULL. IFAN 3 (1941), pp. 145-150.

8,815 LEBEUF, J. P. Notes sur la circoncision chez les Kouroumba du Soudan français. J. SOC. AFR. 11 (1941), pp. 61-93.

8,816 LEIRIS, M. and SCHAEFFNER, A. Les rites de circoncision chez les Dogon de Sanga. J. SOC. AFR. 6 (1936), pp. 141-161.

8,817 LIFSZYC, D. and PAULME, D. Les fêtes des semailles en 1935 chez les Dogon de Sanga. J. SOC. AFR. 6 (1936), pp. 95-110.

8,818 LIGERS, Z. La chasse à l'éléphant chez les Bozo. J. SOC. AFR. 30 (1960), pp. 95-99.

8,819 LIGERS, Z. La chasse à l'hippopotame chez les Bozo. J. SOC. AFR. 27 (1957), pp. 37-66.

8,820 LIGERS, Z. Comment les Peuls de Koa castrent leurs taureaux. BULL. IFAN, Série B: Sciences humaines 20 (1958), pp. 191-204.

8,821 MALGRAS, R. P. D. La condition sociale du paysan minyanka dans le cercle de San. BULL. IFAN 22 (1960), pp. 276-298.

8,822 MENGRELIS, T. Contes de la forêt. PRESENCE AFR. 8 (1950), pp. 185-192.

8,823 ORTOLI, H. Le décès d'une femme enceinte chez les Dogon de Bandiagara. BULL. IFAN 3 (1941), pp. 64-73.

8,824 ORTOLI, H. Les rites de la maternité chez les Dogon de Bandiagara. BULL. IFAN 3 (1941), pp. 53-63.

8,825 PAGEARD, R. Note sur les Diawambé ou Diokoramé. J. SOC. AFR. 29 (1959), pp. 239-260.

8,826 PAGEARD, R. Note sur les Kagoro et la chefferie de Soro. J. SOC. AFR. 29 (1959), pp. 261-272.

8,827 PAGEARD, R. Notes sur les rapports de "Senankouya" au Soudan français particulièrement dans les cercles de Segou et de Macina. BULL. IFAN, Série B: Sciences humaines 20 (1958), pp. 123-141.

8,828 PAQUES, V. Bouffons sacrés du cercle de Bougouni (Soudan français). J. SOC. AFR. 24 (1954), pp. 63-110.

8,829 PAQUES, V. L'estrade royale des Niare. BULL. IFAN 15 (1953), pp. 1642-1654.

8,830 PAQUES, V. Les Samake. BULL. IFAN 18 (1956), pp. 369-390.

8,831 PAULME, D. La divination par les chacals chez les Dogon de Sanga. J. SOC. AFR. 7 (1937), pp. 1-13.

8,832 PAULME, D. Parenté à plaisanteries et alliance par le sang en Afrique Occidentale. AFRICA 12 (1939), pp. 433-444.

8,833 PAULME, D. Sur quelques rites de purification des Dogon (Soudan français). J. SOC. AFR. 10 (1940), pp. 65-78.

8,834 POLLET, G. Bibliographie des Sarakolé)Soninké, Marka). J. SOC. AFR. 34 (1964), pp. 283-292.

8,835 PROST, R. P. Notes sur les Songay. BULL. IFAN 16 (1954), pp. 167-213.

8,836 ROUCH, J. Rites de pluie chez les Songhay. BULL. IFAN 15 (1953), pp. 1655-1689.

8,837 SIDIBE, M. Contes de la Savane. PRESENCE AFR. 8 (1950), pp. 193-204.

8,838 STAPLETON, J. H. D. In their end is their beginning—a Fulani crisis. NIGERIAN FIELD 13 (1948), pp. 53-59.

8,839 STAUDE, W. La légende royale des Kouroumba. J. SOC. AFR. 31 (1961), pp. 209-259.

8,840 TAIT, D. An analytical commentary on the social structure of the Dogon. AFRICA 20 (1950), pp. 175-198.

8,841 TAIT, D. Language and social symbiosis among the Dogon of Sanga. BULL. IFAN, Série B: Sciences humaines 17 (1955), pp. 525-528.

8,842 TAUXIER, L. Des Dorhosié et Dorhosié-Finng du cercle de Bobo-Dioulasso (Soudan français). J. SOC. AFR. 1 (1931), pp. 61-110.

8,843 YARO, J. and DIKO, S. A propos des crocodiles sacrés de Bandiagara. BULL. IFAN 2 (1940), pp. 211-216.

8,844 ZAHAN, D. Aperçu sur la pensée théogonique des Dogon. CAH. INT. SOCIOL. 6 (1949), pp. 113-133.

8,845 ZAHAN, D. Ataraxie et silence chez les Bambara. ZAIRE 14 (1960), pp. 491-504.

8,846 ZAHAN, D. Parole et silence chez les Bambara (République soudanaise). CONGR. INT. SC. ANTHR. ET ETHN. 6, no. ii (1960), pp. 507-508.

See also 8390, 13501.

Art. Antiquities. Anthropology

8,847 CAPOT-REY, R. A propos de l'age de l'homme d'Asselar. BULL. IFAN 12 (1950), pp. 1128-1131.

8,848 DESPLAGNES, L. Fouilles du tumulus d'El Oualedji (Soudan). BULL. IFAN 13 (1951), pp. 1159-1173.

8,849 DIETERLEN, G. and LIGERS, Z. Notes sur les tambours-de-calebasse en Afrique occidentale. J. SOC. AFR. 33 (1963), pp. 255-274.

8,850 ENGESTROM, T. Wall decorations of the Oualata type at Bamako. ETHNOS 21 (1956), pp. 216-219.

8,851 GALLAY, A. Peintures rupestres récentes du Bassin du Niger (propos de recherches). J. SOC. AFR. 34 (1964), pp. 123-139.

8,852 GANAY, S. DE. Rôle protecteur de certaines peintures rupestres du Soudan français. J. SOC. AFR. 10 (1940), pp. 87-98.

8,853 GRIAULE, M. Un masque du Mont Tabi. J. SOC. AFR. 14 (1944), pp. 25-32.

8,854 HUARD, P. Gravures rupestres des Confins nigéro-tchadiens. BULL. IFAN 15 (1953), pp. 1569-1581.

8,855 HOPKINS, N. S. Le théâtre moderne au Mali. PRESENCE AFR. N.S. 53 (1965), pp. 162-193.

8,856 LABOURET, H. and TRAVELE, M. Le théâtre mandingue (Soudan Francais). AFRICA 1 (1928), pp. 73-97.

8,857 LEM, F. H. Au sujet d'une statuette Senoufo. BULL. IFAN 4 (1942), pp. 175-181.

8,858 LESCHI, J. Etude de crânes de Tellem recueillis en pays Dogon (Soudan. Republique du Mali). BULL. IFAN 23 (1961), pp. 411-422.

8,859 LHOTE, H. Les boîtes moulées en peau du Soudan, dites Bata. BULL. IFAN 14 (1952), pp. 919-955.

8,860 LHOTE, H. Le gisement néolithique de l'Oued Chet Iler (Tanezrouft N-Ahenet). J. SOC. AFR. 11 (1941), pp. 125-140.

8,861 LHOTE, H. Quelques objets a faciès paléolithique trouvés dans le Sahara central. J. SOC. AFR. 11 (1941), pp. 141-146.

8,862 LHOTE, H. and KELLEY, H. Les collections africaines du département de prehistoire exotique du Musée d'ethnographie du Trocadéro. XI: Gisement acheuléen de l'Erg d'Admer (Tassili des Ajjers). J. SOC. AFR. 6 (1936), pp. 217-221.

8,863 MAUNY, R. Les gisements néolithiques de Karkarichinkat (Tilemsi, Soudan français). PROC. PAN-AFR. CONGR. PRE-HIST. 2 (1952), pp. 617-629.

8,864 MAUNY, R. Notes d'archéologie au sujet de Gao. BULL. IFAN 13 (1951), pp. 837-852.

8,865 MAUNY, R. Notes d'archéologie sur Tombouctou. BULL. IFAN 14 (1952), pp. 899-918.

8,866 MEILLASSOUX, C. La farce villageoise à la ville: le Koteba de Bamako. PRESENCE AFR. N.S. 52 (1964), pp. 27-59.

8,867 SZUMOWSKI, G. Fouilles au Nord du Macina et dans la région de Ségou. BULL. IFAN 19 (1957), pp. 224-258.

8,868 SZUMOWSKI, G. Industrie préhistorique en forme de coup de poing aux environs de Bamako. PROC. PAN-AFR. CONGR. PRE-HIST. 2 (1952), pp. 481-484.

8,869 SZUMOWSKI, G. Notes sur la grotte préhistorique de Bamako. PROC. PAN-AFR. CONGR. PRE-HIST. 2 (1952), pp. 673-680.

8,870 SZUMOWSKI, G. La question de l'industrie microlithique aux environs de Bamako. PROC. PAN-AFR. CONGR. PRE-HIST. 2 (1952), pp. 663-672.

8,871 SZUMOWSKI, G. Les tombeaux de Diguidiguiba. J. SOC. AFR. 31 (1961), pp. 97-107.

8,872 THOMASSEY, P. and MAUNY, R. Campagne de fouilles à Koumbi Saleh. BULL. IFAN 13 (1951), pp. 438-462.

8,873 THOMASSEY, P. and MAUNY, R. Campagne de fouilles de 1950 à Koumbi Saleh (Ghana?). BULL. IFAN 18 (1956), pp. 117-140.

8,874 URVOY, Y. Gravures rupestres dans l'Aribinda (Boucle du Niger). J. SOC. AFR. 11 (1941), pp. 1-5.

8,875 URVOY, Y. Peintures rupestres de Takoutala (Soudan francais), avec une note de T. Monod. J. SOC. AFR. 8 (1938), pp. 97-101.

8,876 VIEILLARD, G. Sur quelques objets en terre cuite de Dienné. BULL. IFAN 2 (1940), pp. 347-349.

8,877 ZAHAN, D. Un gnomon soudanais. AFRICA 20 (1950), pp. 126-130; English summary, p. 131.

8,878 ZAHAN, D. Notes sur un luth dogon. J. SOC. AFR. 20 (1950), pp. 193-227.

8,879 ZAHAN, D. Principes de médicine bambara. ZAIRE 11 (1957), pp. 967-977.

8,880 ZAHAN, D. and GANAY, S. DE. Etude sur la cosmologie des Dogon et des Bambara du Soudan français. AFRICA 21 (1951), pp. 13-23 including English summaries.

8,881 ZELTNER, F. DE. Les boites en cuir moulé du Soudan. J. SOC. AFR. 2 (1932), pp. 23-34.

See also 4833.

Biography

8,882 MONOD, TH. Un homme de Dieu: Tierno Bokar. PRESENCE AFR. 8 (1950), pp. 149-158.

Economics

8,883 CHARLES, V. La Conférence du Travail de Bamako. ZAIRE 7 (1953), p. 389.

8,884 DAGET, J. La pêche dans le delta central du Niger. J. SOC. AFR. 19 (1949), pp. 1-79.

8,885 GENEVIERE, J. Les Kountas et leurs activités commerciales. BULL. IFAN 12 (1950), pp. 1111-1127.

Education

8,886 FOFANA, A. The university of Mali. PAN-AFRICANISM RECONSIDERED, 1962, pp. 214-220.

8,887 GRIAULE, M. Etendue de l'instruction traditionnelle au Soudan. ZAIRE 6 (1952), pp. 563-568.

Geography

8,888 AMBLARD-RAMBERT, A. et al. Les pointes de la Basse Vallée du Tilemsi by A. Amblard-Rambert, J. Gaussen, M. Gaussen. J. SOC. AFR. 30 (1960), pp. 123-143.

8,889 BRASSEUR, G. Etude de géographie régionale: le village de Tenentou (Mali). BULL. IFAN 23 (1961), pp. 607-675.

8,890 CHAILLEY, M. La mission du Haut-Soudan (1898) le drame de Zinder. ACTA GEOGRAPHICA 17 (1951), pp. 25-44.

8,891 GOSSELIN, M. Bamako, ville soudanaise moderne. AFR. ET ASIE 21 (1953), pp. 31-37.

8,892 THOMASSEY, P. Notes sur la géographie et l'habitat de la région de Koumbi Saleh. BULL. IFAN 13 (1951), pp. 476-486.

See also 8422.

Government. Politics. Administration

8,893 DELVAL, J. Le R.D.A. au Soudan Francais. AFR. ET ASIE 16 (1951), pp. 54-67.

8,894 GRAY, A. Visitors from Mali. AFR. AFFAIRS 60 (1961), pp. 481-482.

8,895 KANOUTE, P. African socialism. TRANSITION 13 (1964), pp. 49-51.

8,896 KEITA, M. The foreign policy of Mali. INTERNAT. AFFAIRS 37 (1961), pp. 432-439.

8,897 Discours du Général de Gaulle devant l'Assemblée Nationale du Mali. PRESENCE AFR. N.S. 29 (1959-1960), pp. 123-126.

8,898 Mali [le Mali s'apprête à l'indépendance]. PRESENCE AFR. N.S. 30 (1960), pp. 102-103.

See also 13540.

History

8,899 BECKINGHAM, C. F. Le pèlerinage et la mort de Sakoura, roi de Mali. BULL. IFAN 16 (1954), pp. 390-391.

8,900 CHAILLEY, Commandant. La mission du Haut-Soudan et le drame de Zinder. BULL. IFAN 16 (1954), pp. 243-254.

8,901 CISSOKO, S. M. L'humanisme sur les bords du Niger au XVIe siècle. PRESENCE AFR. N.S. 49 (1964), pp. 81-88.

8,902 CLARKE, J. H. Le Nigeria ancien et le Soudan occidental. PRESENCE AFR. N.S. 32-33 (1960), pp. 187-193.

8,903 DECRAENE, P. Le Mali médiéval. CIVILISATIONS 12 (1962), pp. 250-255; English summary, pp. 256-258.

8,904 DOUCOURE, A. Niongo Mari chevalier Peulh. PRESENCE AFR. 14 (1953), pp. 203-206.

8,905 DOUCOURE, M. B. Notice sur l'origine des habitants de Goumbou, subdivision de Nara, Cercle de Néma. BULL. IFAN 2 (1940), pp. 350-357.

8,906 JEFFREYS, M. D. W. The Marginelle currency of Timbuctu. BULL. IFAN 15 (1953), pp. 143-151.

8,907 LHOTE, H. Contribution à l'étude des Touaregs soudanais. BULL. IFAN, Série B: Sciences humaines 17 (1955), pp. 334-370.

8,908 LHOTE, H. Contribution a l'histoire des Touaregs soudanais. Les limites de l'Empire du Mâli; la route de Gao a l'Aïr et au Caire; les Tademekket dans la région de Tombouctou; les Songaï dans l'Adrar des Iforas. BULL. IFAN 18 (1956), pp. 391-407.

8,909 MONTEIL, C. Notes sur le Tarikh es-Soudan. BULL. IFAN 27 (1965), pp. 479-530.

8,910 NIANE, D. T. Recherches sur l'Empire du Mali au Moyen Age. RECH. AFR. 1-4 (1959), pp. 35-46; 1 (1960), pp. 17-36; 2 (1961), pp. 31-51.

8,911 PAGEARD, R. Le marche orientale du Mali (Ségou-Djenné) en 1644, d'après le Tarikh es-Soudan. J. SOC. AFR. 31 (1961), pp. 73-81.

8,912 PAGEARD, R. Note sur le peuplement de l'est du pays de Ségou. J. SOC. AFR. 31 (1961), pp. 83-90.

8,913 PERSON, Y. Correspondances de la résidence du Kissi relatives à l'affaire de Waïma (1893). CAH. ET. AFR. 5 (1965), pp. 472-489.

8,914 SAUVAGET, J. Les épitaphes royales de Gao. BULL. IFAN 12 (1950), pp. 418-440.

8,915 SURET-CANALE, J. El Hadj Omar. PRESENCE AFR. N.S. 20 (1958), pp. 69-72.

8,916 VIRE, M. M. Notes sur trois épitaphes royales de Gao. BULL. IFAN, Série B: Sciences humaines 20 (1958), pp. 368-376.

8,917 VIRE, M. M. Stèles funéraires musulmanes soudano-sahariennes. BULL. IFAN 21 (1959), pp. 459-500.

8,918 Notes et souvenirs du capitaine Granderye. REV. HIST. COL. 34 (1947), pp. 87-131.

Language. Literature

Language

8,919 BERTHO, J. La place des dialectes Dogon (dogõ) de la falaise de Bandiagara parmi les autres groupes linguistiques de la zone soudanaise. BULL. IFAN 15 (1953), pp. 405-441.

8,920 CALAME-GRIAULE, G. Les dialectes Dogon. AFRICA 26 (1956), pp. 62-72; English summary, p. 72.

8,921 CALAME-GRIAULE, G. Syntaxe des particules 'subordinatives' en Dogon. J. AFR. LANGS. 2 (1963), pp. 268-271.

8,922 CLAUZEL, J. Des noms Songay dans l'Ahaggar. J. AFR. LANGS. 1 (1962), pp. 43-44.

8,923 DIANOUX, H. J. DE. Le mots d'emprunt d'origine arabe dans la langue songhay. BULL. IFAN 23 (1961), pp. 596-606.

8,924 HOUIS, M. Notes sur le songay. BULL. IFAN, Série B: Sciences humaines 20 (1958), pp. 225-240.

8,925 LEIRIS, M. L'expression de l'idée de travail dans une langue d'initiés soudanais. PRESENCE AFR. 13 (1952), pp. 69-83.

8,926 LIFCHITZ, D. La littérature orale chez les Dogon du Soudan Français. AFRICA 13 (1940), pp. 235-249.

8,927 LIFSZYC, D. Les formules propitiatoires chez les Dogon des falaises de Bandiagara (Soudan français). J. SOC. AFR. 8 (1938), pp. 33-55.

8,928 POUSSIBET, F. Notes sur le vocabulaire botanique des Brâbich et Kounta Regagda. BULL. IFAN 24 (1962), pp. 265-278.

8,929 POUSSIBET, F. Répertoire des termes géographiques maures de la région de Tombouctou. BULL. IFAN 24 (1962), pp. 199-262.

8,930 POUSSIBET, F. Vocabulaire maure relatif a la météorologie. BULL. IFAN 24 (1962), pp. 263-264.

8,931 PROST, A. Légendes songay. BULL. IFAN 18 (1956), pp. 188-201.

See also 5399.

Literature

8,932 BA, A. H. Bambara knights: a Bambara tale. BO 6 (1959), pp. 5-12.

8,933 BA, A. H. Le Peul et le Bozo ou le coccyx calamiteux. PRESENCE AFR. 6 (1949), pp. 117-124.

8,934 BA, A. H. Poesie peule du Macina. PRESENCE AFR. 8 (1950), pp. 169-184.

8,935 CALAME-GRIAULE, G. Esotérisme et fabulation au Soudan. BULL. IFAN 16 (1954), pp. 307-321.

8,936 MONOD, TH. Un poème mystique soudanais. PRESENCE AFR. 3 (1948), pp. 441-450.

8,937 NYUNAI, [R.] L'essor. PRESENCE AFR. N.S. 1 (1955), pp. 124-125.

8,938 NYUNAI, [R.] Les liens du passé. PRESENCE AFR. N.S. 1 (1955), p. 123.

8,939 VIELLARD, G. Le chant de l'Eau et du Palmier doum. Poème bucolique du marais nigérien. BULL. IFAN 2 (1940), pp. 219-315.

8,940 YAMBO, [O.] 1901. PRESENCE AFR. N.S. 51 (1964), pp. 99-100.

8,941 YAMBO, O. Paysage humain. PRESENCE AFR. N.S. 48 (1963), pp. 167-168.

Law

8,942 FOURNIER, M. F. Aspects politique du problème des chefferies au Soudan présahélien. RJPUF 9 (1955), pp. 147-182.

8,943 PAGEARD, R. Enlèvement coutumier et Code pénal au Soudan français (pays Bambara). RJPUF 11 (1957), pp. 122-127.

Religion

See 8703.

Science

8,944 BASILEWSKY, P. Contribution à l'étude de la zone d'inondation du Niger (mission G. Remaudière, 1950). VI. Coléoptères Carabidae. BULL. IFAN 15 (1953), pp. 1552-1560.

8,945 DAGET, J. Mémoires sur la biologie des poissons du Niger Moyen. I. Biologie et croissance des espèces du genre Alestes. BULL. IFAN 14 (1952), pp. 191-225.

8,946 DESCARPENTRIES, A. Contribution à l'étude de la zone d'inondation du Niger (mission G. Remaudière, 1950). VIII. BULL. IFAN 15 (1953), pp. 1566-1568.

8,947 DIETERLIN, G. Classification des végétaux chez les Dogon. J. SOC. AFR. 22 (1952), pp. 115-158.

8,948 DIETERLEN, G. and CALAME-GRIAULE, G. L'alimentation dogon. CAH. ET. AFR. 1 (1960), pp. 46-89.

8,949 DOUTRESSOULLE, G. Le Cheval au Soudan Français et ses origines. BULL. IFAN 2 (1940), pp. 342-346.

8,950 FRASER, F. C. Contribution à l'étude de la zone d'inondation du Niger (mission G. Remaudière 1950). I. Odonata, Neuroptera and Mecoptera. BULL. IFAN 15 (1953), pp. 1523-1528.

8,951 GRIAULE, M. Classification des insectes chez les Dogon. J. SOC. AFR. 31 (1961), pp. 7-71.

8,952 JAEGER, P. and JAROVOY, M. Les grès de Kita (Soudan occidental); leur influence sur la répartition du peuplement végétal. BULL. IFAN 14 (1952), pp. 1-18.

8,953 JANSSENS, A. Contribution à l'étude de la zone d'inondation du Niger (mission G. Remaudière, 1950). V. Coléoptères Scarabaeinae. BULL. IFAN 15 (1953), pp. 1548-1551.

8,954 JOLIVET, P. Contribution à l'étude de la zone d'inondation du Niger (mission G. Remaudière, 1950). IV. Coléoptères Chrysomeloidea. BULL. IFAN 15 (1953), pp. 1539-1547.

8,955 LEGROS, C. Contribution à l'étude de la zone d'inondation du Niger (mission G. Remaudière, 1950). VII. Coléoptères Haliplidae, Dytiscidae, Hydrophilidae, Spercheidae. BULL. IFAN 15 (1953), pp. 1561-1565.

8,956 PIC, M. Contribution à l'étude de la zone d'inondation du Niger (mission G. Remaudière, 1950). II. Coléoptères Malacodermoidea. BULL. IFAN 15 (1953), pp. 1529-1534.

8,957 ROBERTY, G. Notes de botanique ouest-africaine. VI. Plantes banales dans le sahel de Nioro. BULL. IFAN 15 (1953), pp. 442-452.

8,958 ROUSSELOT, R. Notes sur la faune ornithologique du Cercle de Mopti (Soudan Français). BULL. IFAN 1 (1939), pp. 1-88.

8,959 TRANCART, A. Le pâturage en haut Adrar. BULL. IFAN 2 (1940), pp. 285-288.

8,960 VRYDAGH, J. M. Contribution à l'étude de la zone d'inondation du Niger (mission G. Remaudière, 1950). III. Coléoptères Bostrychidae. BULL. IFAN 15 (1953), pp. 1535-1538.

8,961 La recherche piscicole au Soudan français. ZAIRE 6 (1952), pp. 289-290.

See also 15749.

Sociology

8,962 BA, A. H. Note sur la migration des villages sambourou. BULL. IFAN 13 (1951), p. 487.

8,963 DAGET, J. La pêche à Diafarabé, étude monographique. BULL. IFAN 18 (1956), pp. 1-97.

8,964 GRIAULE, M. Remarques sur l'oncle utérin au Soudan. CAH. INT. SOCIOL. 16 (1954), pp. 35-49.

8,965 LEM, F. H. Le culte des arbres et des génies protecteurs du sol au Soudan français. BULL. IFAN 10 (1948), pp. 539-559.

8,966 LETNEV, A. The extended family in Mali and Guinea. WOMEN TODAY 6 (1965), pp. 87-89.

8,967 MAKANGUILE, A. Nara. Aperçu sur la vie agricole au Soudan. ANNALES AFR., 1959, pp. 283-288.

8,968 MALZY, P. Les Bozos du Niger et leurs modes de pêche (région de Diafarabé). BULL. IFAN 8 (1946), pp. 100-132.

8,969 ORTOLI, H. Le gage des personnes au Soudan Français. BULL. IFAN 1 (1939), pp. 313-324.

8,970 L'habitat urbain à Bamako. ZAIRE 5 (1951), pp. 861-862.

8,971 Renseignements statistiques sur la population du Soudan. BULL. IFAN 13 (1951), pp. 257-260.

See also 8755, 8766.

GUINEA

General

8,972 AUTRA, M. T. R. L'Institut National de Recherches et de Documentation (1944-1964). [Guinée]. RECH. AFR. 1-4 (1964), pp. 5-35.

8,973 BALANDIER, G. Les études guinéennes. ET. GUIN. 1 (1947), pp. 5-6.

Agriculture

8,974 ALPHA, D. Perspectives sur l'élevage en République de Guinée. RECH. AFR. 1-4 (1959), pp. 47-62.

8,975 BAILLAUD, E. Observations and reflections on European agriculture in Guinea. J. AFR. SOC. 6 (1907), pp. 267-280.

8,976 BALANDIER, G. Ethnologie et psychologie. ET. GUIN. 1 (1947), pp. 47-54.

8,977 BALDE, S. L'élevage au Fouta-Djallon (régions de Timbo et Labé). BULL. IFAN 1 (1939), pp. 630-644.

8,978 NOUMOUKE, D. Le service de l'élevage et des industries animales en Guinée. RECH. AFR. 1 (1962), pp. 5-10.

8,979 PORTERES, M. R. Le problème de la restauration du Fouta-Djalon. RECH. AFR. 3 (1960), pp. 49-57.

8,980 SORY, B. Le problème de la conservation des sols en Guinée. RECH. AFR. 1-4 (1959), pp. 70-75.

8,981 Rapport sur la protection des sols au Fouta-Djalon. RECH. AFR. 3 (1960), pp. 38-47.

Anthropology

8,982 AUTRA, M. T. R. and SAMPIL, M. Notes ethnographiques recueillies en pays kissien. RECH. AFR. 3 (1960), pp. 58-67; 1 (1961), pp. 50-58.

8,983 BALDE, S. Les associations d'âge chez les Foulbé du Fouta-Djallon. BULL. IFAN 1 (1939), pp. 89-109.

8,984 BARRY, S. Le chasse en Guinée. RECH. AFR. 1 (1960), pp. 51-57.

8,985 BOUBAKAR, D. T. Le divorce chez les Peuls au Fouta-Djallon. RJPUF 11 (1957), pp. 333-355.

8,986 CHERON, G. La circoncision et l'excision chez les Malinké. J. SOC. AFR. 3 (1933), pp. 297-303.

8,987 COUTOULY, F. DE. Les populations de l'ancien Cercle de Kadé-Touba (1908). ET. GUIN. 8 (1952), pp. 40-48.

8,988 DELACOUR, A. Sociétés secrètes chez les Tenda. ET. GUIN. 2 (1947), pp. 37-52.

8,989 GAVINET, M. Quelques superstitions chez les Soussou de Basse-Guinée. ET. GUIN. 2 (1947), p. 67.

8,990 GERMAIN, J. L'Au-Delà chez les Geerzé. ET. GUIN. 2 (1947), pp. 27-35.

8,991 GESSAIN, M. A propos de l'évolution actuelle des femmes coniagui et bassari. J. SOC. AFR. 34 (1964), pp. 255-276.

8,992 HOLAS, B. Décès d'une femme Guerzé (cercle de Nzérékoré, Guinée française). AFRICA 23 (1953), pp. 145-155; English summary, pp. 154-155.

8,993 HOLAS, B. Echantillons du folklore Kono (Haute-Guinée française). ET. GUIN. 9 (1952), pp. 3-90.

8,994 HOLAS, B. Pratiques divinatoires Kissi (Guinée Française). BULL. IFAN 14 (1952), pp. 272-308.

8,995 HOLAS, B. Quelques remarques complémentaires autour de la circoncision kissi. ET. GUIN. 13 (1955), pp. 60-67.

8,996 IFAN. Autour d'un casse-tête africain. BULL. IFAN 14 (1952), pp. 358-362.

8,997 KEITA, M. M. La famille et le mariage chez les Tyapi. ET. GUIN. 2 (1947), pp. 63-66.

8,998 KEITA, M. M. Le Noir et le secret. ET. GUIN. 1 (1947), pp. 69-78.

8,999 LAMBIN, R. Notes sur les cérémonies et les épreuves rituelles d'émancipation et d'initiation chez les Kissiens. BULL. IFAN 8 (1946), pp. 64-70.

9,000 LESTRANGE, M. DE. Génies de l'eau et de la brousse en Guinée Français. ET. GUIN. 4 (1950), pp. 3-24.

9,001 LESTRANGE, M. DE. Pour une méthode socio-démographique. (Etude du mariage chez les Coniagui et les Bassari). J. SOC. AFR. 21 (1951), pp. 97-109.

9,002 LESTRANGE, M. DE. Les Sarankole de Badyar (technique de teinturiers). ET. GUIN. 6 (1950), pp. 17-27.

9,003 LHOTE, H. L'extraordinaire aventure des Peuls. PRESENCE AFR. N.S. 22 (1958), pp. 48-57.

9,004 MADEIRA-KEITA, M. Aperçu sommaire sur les raisons de la polygamie chez les Malinké. ET. GUIN. 4 (1950), pp. 49-55.

9,005 MENGRELIS, T. Esquisse sur l'habitat Guerzé. AFRICA 33 (1963), pp. 45-53.

9,006 MENGRELIS, T. Le sens des masques dans l'initiation chez les Guerzé de la Guinée Française. AFRICA 22 (1952), pp. 257-262.

9,007 MENGRELIS, T. La sortie des jeunes filles excisées en pays Mano[n]. ET. GUIN. 8 (1952), pp. 55-58.

9,008 MOITY, M. Notes sur les Mani (Guinée française). BULL. IFAN 19 (1957), pp. 302-307.

9,009 PAULME, D. Les Kissi—"gens du riz." PRESENCE AFR. 6 (1949), pp. 26-35; 7 (1949), pp. 226-248.

9,010 PAULME, D. La notion de sorcier chez les Baga. BULL. IFAN, Série B: Sciences humaines 20 (1958), pp. 406-416.

9,011 PAULME, D. La société Kissi: son organisation politique. CAH. ET. AFR. 1 (1960), pp. 73-85.

9.012 PAULME, D. Structures sociales en pays baga. (Guinée française). BULL. IFAN 18 (1956), pp. 98-116.

9,013 POREKO, D. O. Evolution sociale chez les Peuls du Fouta-Djallon. RECH. AFR. 4 (1961), pp. 73-94.

9,014 SAMPIL, M. Une société secrète en pays nalou: Le Simo. RECH. AFR. 1 (1961), pp. 46-49.

9,015 SCHAEFFNER, A. Les rites de circoncision en pays Kissi (Haute Guinée française). ET. GUIN. 12 (1953), pp. 3-56.

9,016 STAINER, M. Notice sur les Coniagui. ET. GUIN. 2 (1947), pp. 57-61.

9,017 TELLI, D. Le divorce chez les Peuls. PRESENCE AFR. N.S. 22 (1958), pp. 29-47.

9,018 VIEILLARD, G. Notes sur les Peuls du Fouta-Djallon (Guinée Française). BULL. IFAN 2 (1940), pp. 85-210.

9,019 WANE, Y. Etat actuel de la documentation au sujet des Toucouleurs. BULL. IFAN 25 (1963), pp. 457-477.

9,020 Essai sur la vie paysanne au Fouta-Djalon. PRESENCE AFR. 15 (1953), pp. 155-251.

9,021 Les traits d'ensemble du Fouta-Djalon. PRESENCE AFR. 15 (1953), pp. 141-154.

See also 7509, 8499, 8504, 12527.

Art

9,022 APPIA, B. Les forgerons du Fouta-Djallon. J. SOC. AFR. 35 (1965), pp. 317-352.

9,023 APPIA, B. Masques de Guinée française et de Casamance. J. SOC. AFR. 13 (1943), pp. 155-182.

9,024 BALDE, C. et al. Les sites archéologiques de Guémé Sangan et de Pété Bonodji (Région administrative de Télimélé) by C. Balde, Camara Nene-Khaly, J. Suret-Canale. RECH. AFR. 3 (1962), pp. 51-67.

9,025 DAVIES, O. The distribution of old stone-age material in Guinea. BULL. IFAN 21 (1959), pp. 102-108.

9,026 FODEBA, K. Chansons du Dioliba. PRESENCE AFR. 4 (1948), pp. 595-598.

9,027 HALLE, C. Notes sur Koly Tenguella, Olivier de Sanderval et les ruines de Gueme-Sangan. RECH. AFR. 1 (1960), pp. 37-71.

9,028 HOLAS, B. Danses masquées de la Basse-Côte. ET. GUIN. 1 (1947), pp. 61-67.

9,029 HOLAS, B. Note complémentaire sur l'abri sous roche Blandè (fouilles de 1951). BULL. IFAN 14 (1952), pp. 1341-1352.

9,030 HOLAS, B. Notes préliminaires sur les fouilles de la grotte de Blandè. BULL. IFAN 12 (1950), pp. 999-1006.

9,031 HOLAS, B. and MAUNY, R. Nouvelles fouilles à l'abri sous roche de Blandè (Guinée). BULL. IFAN 15 (1953), pp. 1605-1618.

9,032 PERSON, Y. Les Kissi et leurs statuettes de pierre dans le cadre de l'histoire ouest-africaine. BULL. IFAN 23 (1961), pp. 1-59.

9,033 ROUGET, G. Les ballets africains de Keita Fodeba. PRESENCE AFR. N.S. 7 (1956), pp. 138-140.

9,034 SANO, M. De la mélodie populaire Alpha Yaya, à l'hymne national Liberté. RECH. AFR. 2-3 (1963), pp. 28-32.

9,035 SCHAEFFNER, A. Musiques rituelles Baga. CONG. INT. SC. ANTH. ET ETHN. 6, no. ii (1960), pp. 123-125.

9,036 SCHNELL, R. Vestiges archéologiques et agricultures anciennes dans le nord du Fouta-Djallon. BULL. IFAN 19 (1957), pp. 295-301.

9,037 SILVA, A. A. DA. Arte Nalú. BCGP 11, no. 44 (1956), pp. 27-47.

9,038 SZUMOWSKI, G. Fouilles de l'Abri sous roche de Kourounkorokalé (Soudan français). BULL. IFAN 18 (1956), pp. 462-508.

See also 8519, 8849.

Biography

9,039 In memoriam: Monseigneur Lerouge, premier Evêque de Guinée, n'est plus. ET. GUIN. 4 (1950), p. 81.

9,040 Diallo Ousmane Poréko (1922-1961). RECH. AFR. 4 (1961), pp. 71-72.

9,041 MONOD, TH. Introduction [sur Richard-Molard]. RECH. AFR. 4 (1961), pp. 6-7.

9,042 PERSON, Y. La jeunesse de Samori. REV. FRANC. HIST. OUTRE-MER 49 (1962), pp. 151-180.

9,043 NIANE, D. T. A propos de Koli Tenguella. RECH. AFR. 4 (1960), pp. 33-36.

Economics

9,044 AUTRA, M. T. R. La République de Guinée...en bref. RECH. AFR. 1-4 (1959), pp. 7-17.

9,045 BALANDIER, G. L'or de la Guinée française. PRESENCE AFR. 4 (1948), pp. 539-548.

9,046 BINET, J. Marchés en pays Soussou. CAH. ET. AFR. 3 (1962), pp. 104-114.

9,047 BOUTILLIER, J. L. Les rapports du système foncier Toucouler et de l'organisation sociale et économique traditionnelle: leur évolution actuelle. AFR. AGRARIAN SYSTEMS, 1963, pp. 116-136.

9,048 C., J. Combinat industriel en Guinée française. ZAIRE 8 (1954), p. 642.

9,049 GERMAIN, J. Extrait d'une monographie des habitants du cercle de N'Zérékoré (Guerzé, Kono, Manon). Les artisans les techniques et les arts. ET. GUIN. 13 (1955), pp. 3-54.

9,050 HAUSER, A. Les industries extractives de la région de Conakry. ET. GUIN. 13 (1955), pp. 55-59.

9,051 KOUROUMA, K. Le revenu annuel d'une famille guerzé. ET. GUIN. 1 (1947), pp. 55-59.

9,052 SALVADORI, R. Esplorazione pratica della Guinea francese. AFRICA (Rome) 10 (1955), pp. 115-119.

9,053 SALVADORI, R. Promuoviamo in Africa la collaborazione del lavoro. AFRICA (Rome) 10 (1955), pp. 147-148.

9,054 SURET-CANALE, J. Fria 1963. Etablissement industriel Guinéen. RECH. AFR. 2-3 (1963), pp. 3-27.

9,055 SURET-CANALE, J. Notes sur l'économie guinéenne. RECH. AFR. 1-4 (1964), pp. 43-68.

9,056 T., J. Conditions des études statistiques en Guinée. ET. GUIN. 12 (1953), pp. 60-63.

9,057 Entreprise minière en Guinée française. ZAIRE 7 (1953), pp. 75-76.

9,058 Quelques données statistiques sur la Guinée. RECH. AFR. 2 (1961), pp. 74-80.

See also 9234.

Education

9,059 DIOP, D. M. Autour de la réforme de l'enseignement en Guinée. PRESENCE AFR. N.S. 29 (1959-1960), pp. 105-108.

9,060 RIVIERE, C. Les investissements éducatifs en Republique de Guinée. CAH. ET. AFR. 5 (1965), pp. 618-634.

9,061 SAINVILLE, L. La presse française et la Guinée. PRESENCE AFR. N.S. 29 (1959-1960), pp. 109-115.

Geography

9,062 CORFEC, J. LE. Notes sur le Canton Tanda-Kade (Cerde de Gaoual). ET. GUIN. 8 (1952), pp. 13-39.

9,063 DIOP, A. Impressions de voyage. PRESENCE AFR. N.S. 29 (1959-1960), pp. 3-7.

9,064 DOLLFUS, O. Conakry en 1951-1952. Etude humaine et économique. ET. GUIN. 10-11 (1952), pp. 3-110.

9,065 GAUTIER, E. F. Climatic and physiographic notes on French Guinea. GEOG. REV. 23 (1933), pp. 248-258.

9,066 LAMINE, T. M. Les ports de Guinée. RECH. AFR. 1-4 (1959), pp. 63-69.

9,067 LAVAU, G. DE. Boké, Guinée française. ANNALES AFR., 1958, pp. 245-258.

9,068 MAIGNIEN, R. Le Fouta-Djalon dans l'Ouest Africain. RECH. AFR. 3 (1960), pp. 25-38.

9,069 PELISSIER, P. and ROUGERIE, G. Problèmes morphologiques dans le bassin de Siguiri (Haut-Niger). BULL. IFAN 15 (1953), pp. 1-47.

9,070 PICOT, J. N'Zérékoré, Guinée française. ANNALES AFR., 1958, pp. 273-286.

9,071 RICHARD-MOLARD, J. Découverte de la Guinée. Extraits d'un carnet de route. RECH. AFR. 4 (1961), pp. 8-23.

9,072 ROUGERIE, G. Modelés et dynamiques de savane en Guinée orientale. RECH. AFR. 4 (1961), pp. 24-50.

9,073 SCHNELL, R. Etudes préliminaires sur la végétation et la flore des hauts plateaux de Mali (Fouta-Djallon). BULL. IFAN 12 (1950), pp. 905-926.

9,074 VIGNERON, B. Kindia, Guinée française. ANNALES AFR., 1958, pp. 259-272.

See also 9256.

Government

9,075 CESAIRE, A. La pensée politique de Sékou Touré. PRESENCE AFR. N.S. 29 (1959-1960), pp. 65-73.

9,076 FISCHER, G. Quelques aspects de la doctrine politique guinéenne. CIVILISATIONS 9 (1959), pp. 457-474; English summary, pp. 475-478.

9,077 RABEMANANJARA, J. Variations sur le thème guinéen. PRESENCE AFR. N.S. 29 (1959-1960), pp. 75-88.

9,078 TOURE, S. The Republic of Guinea. INTERNAT. AFFAIRS 36 (1960), pp. 168-173.

9,079 WALLERSTEIN, I. L'idéologie politique du P.D.G. PRESENCE AFR. N.S. 40 (1962), pp. 44-56.

9,080 WEINSTEIN, B. Guinea's School of Public Administration. J. LOCAL ADM. OV. 4 (1965), pp. 239-243.

9,081 Action conjointe dans le Fouta-Djalon (Mamou, République de Guinée, 2-7 mai 1960). RECH. AFR. 3 (1960), pp. 15-57.

9,082 Au Conseil général de la Guinée française. ZAIRE 5 (1951), p. 189.

9,083 Quelques aspects du problème des cadres en République de Guinée. RECH. AFR. 4 (1960), pp. 40-47.

9,084 Les statuts du Parti Democratique de Guinée. RECH. AFR. 4 (1963), pp. 34-47.

See also 10398.

History

9,085 ALLAINMENT, Y. Note sur l'identification des tombes de Campbell et Peddie à Boké (Guinée). BULL. IFAN 3 (1941), pp. 74-78.

9,086 ARLABOSSE, General. Une phase de la lutte contre Samory 1890-1892. RHCF 25 (1932), pp. 385-432, 465-514.

9,087 BRIERE, D. Souvenirs guinéens. Les débuts du Cercle de Télimélê. ET. GUIN. 8 (1952), pp. 3-12.

9,088 DAVIDSON, B. Guinea: past and present. HISTORY TODAY 9 (1959), pp. 392-398.

9,089 FISCHER, G. La signification de l'indépendance guinéenne. PRESENCE AFR. N.S. 29 (1959-1960), pp. 53-61.

9,090 MAIGRET, J. A la recherche du temps perdu. ET. GUIN. 1 (1947), pp. 7-8.

9,091 MAUPOIL, B. Notes concernant l'histoire des Coniagui-Bassari et en particulier l'occupation de leur pays par les Français. BULL. IFAN 16 (1954), pp. 378-389.

9,092 MEILLASSOUX, C. Histoire et institutions du kafo de Bamako d'après la tradition des Niaré. CAH. ET. AFR. 4, no. 14 (1963), pp. 186-227.

9,093 NIANE, D. T. Mise en place des populations de la Huate-Guinée. RECH. AFR. 2 (1960), pp. 40-53.

9,094 OUSMANE, D. Connaissance historique de la Guinée. PRESENCE AFR. N.S. 29 (1959-1960), pp. 45-52.

9,095 PERSON, Y. Soixante ans d'evolution en pays Kissi. CAH. ET. AFR. 1 (1960), pp. 86-112.

9,096 POUJADE, J. La Guinée est-elle le dernier jalon d'un ancien Empire? Nos méthodes de travail. ET. GUIN. 2 (1947), pp. 3-7.

9,097 QUINQUAD, J. La pacification du Fouta-Djallon. REV. HIST. COL. 31, no. 4 (1938), pp. 49-134.

9,098 SURET-CANALE, J. L'Almamy Samory Toure. RECH. AFR. 1-4 (1959), pp. 18-22.

9,099 SURET-CANALE, J. La Guinée dans le système colonial. PRESENCE AFR. N.S. 29 (1959-1960), pp. 9-44.

9,100 VERDAT, M. Le Ouali de Goumba (essai historique). ET. GUIN. 3 (1949), pp. 3-65.

9,101 VIEILLARD, G. Notes sur l'exode toucouleur. CAH. ET. AFR. 1 (1960), pp. 193-197.

9,102 Les rivières du Sud en 1885. RECH. AFR. 1 (1961), pp. 32-45; 2 (1961), pp. 59-73; 3 (1961), pp. 60-69; 1 (1962), pp. 40-63.

9,103 Traités conclus entre le Gouvernement français et les chefs des Rivières du Sud de 1854 à 1885. RECH. AFR. 2 (1962), pp. 23-37.

9,104 Le vrai visage de Sanderval. RECH. AFR. 3 (1960), pp. 3-14.

Language. Literature

Language

9,105 BALANDIER, G. Toponymie des Iles de Kabak et Kakossa. ET. GUIN. 8 (1952), pp. 49-54.

9,106 HOUIS, M. Caractères et possibilités de la langue Soso. RECH. AFR. 1 (1962), pp. 3-4.

9,107 HOUIS, M. Les minorités ethniques de la Guinée côtière. Situation linguistique. ET. GUIN. 4 (1950), pp. 25-48.

9,108 HOUIS, M. Notes lexicologiques sur les rapports du soso avec les langues mãde-sud du groupe mana-busa. BULL. IFAN 16 (1954), pp. 391-401.

9,109 HOUIS, M. Le rapport d'annexion en baga. BULL. IFAN 15 (1953), pp. 848-854.

9,110 HOUIS, M. Le système pronominal et les classes dans les dialectes baga. BULL. IFAN 15 (1953), pp. 381-404.

9,111 JOFFRE, J. Sur un nouvel alphabet ouest-africain: le Toma (frontière franco-libérienne). BULL. IFAN 7 (1945), pp. 160-173.

9,112 LASSORT. La langue Kpèlè. ET. GUIN. 2 (1947), pp. 21-25.

9,113 MENGRELIS, T. Curiosités linguistiques. AFRICA 21 (1951), p. 138.

9,114 POREKO, D. O. A propos des phonèmes spéciaux de la langue Peule. RECH. AFR. 4 (1960), pp. 37-39.

9,115 PORTERES, R. Notes de toponymie rurale au Fouta-Djallon. RECH. AFR. 1-4 (1964), pp. 151-159.

9,116 SISSOKO, F. D. Glossaire des mots français passés en Malinké. BULL. IFAN 1 (1939), pp. 325-366.

9,117 SOW, A. I. Notes sur les procédés poétiques dans la littérature des Peuls du Foûta-Djalon. PRESENCE AFR. N.S. 54 (1965), pp. 181-197; CAH. ET. AFR. 5 (1965), pp. 370-385.

See also 8648, 12623, 12769.

Literature

9,118 APPIA, B. Quelques proverbes guinéens. BULL. IFAN 2 (1940), pp. 396-415.

9,119 B., A. L'enfant noir. PRESENCE AFR. 16 (1954), pp. 419-420.

9,120 CESAIR, A. Salut à la Guinée. PRESENCE AFR. N.S. 26 (1959), p. 89.

9,121 FODEBA, K. Etrange destin—Minuit. PRESENCE AFR. 3 (1948), pp. 466-469.

9,122 GESSAIN, M. La littérature orale des Coniagui (République de Guinée). RECH. AFR. 3 (1961), pp. 24-37; 3 (1962), pp. 25-50.

9,123 HOUIS, M. Contes Baga. ET. GUIN. 6 (1950), pp. 3-15.

9,124 KEITA, O. Les secret d'une mère. Conte... RECH. AFR. 1 (1960), pp. 58-60.

9,125 LAYE, C. The eyes of the statue. BO 5 (1959), pp. 19-27.

9,126 LESTRANGE, M. DE. Contes et légendes des Fulakunda du Badyar avec une introduction et des notes sur leurs croyances et coutumes. ET. GUIN. 7 (1951), pp. 3-66.

9,127 MAMADOU, S. Contes et légendes d'Afrique. RECH. AFR. 2 (1962), pp. 38-44.

9,128 MENGRELIS, T. Contes de la forêt. ET. GUIN. 5 (1950), pp. 3-86.

9,129 MENGRELIS, T. Deux contes toma. ET. GUIN. 1 (1947), pp. 27-45.

9,130 NENE-KHALY. La voie conquerante. PRESENCE AFR. N.S. 20 (1958), pp. 64-65.

9,131 SORY, A. et al. Trois contes soussou, by A. Sory, Y. Lay, F. Momo. ET. GUIN. 1 (1947), pp. 23-25.

9,132 TAYIRE. Du temps ou les animaux parlaient: Le lièvre, l'hyène et la chèvre..., La chèvre, l'hyène et le bijoutier. GENEVE-AFR. 2 (1963), pp. 218-222.

9,133 TAYIRE, A.A.D. DE. N'naliguiyan. GENEVE-AFR. 2 (1963), pp. 215-217.

9,134 Chants révolutionnaires guinéens. PRESENCE AFR. N.S. 29 (1959-1960), pp. 89-103.

9,135 Three Soussou tales [Sweetness, The moon, The well]. BO 15 (1964), p. 8.

9,136 Un mariage chez les Mandegnis. PRESENCE AFR. 4 (1948), pp. 642-646.

Law

9,137 CLAVIER, J. L. Coutumier Coniagui (Resumé du droit privé des Coniagui). BULL. IFAN 14 (1952), pp. 321-336.

9,138 DELACOUR, A. La propriété et ses modes de transmission chez les Coniagui et les Bassari. ET. GUIN. 2 (1947), pp. 53-56.

9,139 DIALLO, A. A. Introduction a l'étude de la constitution Guinée du 10 novembre 1958. RECH. AFR. 2 (1961), pp. 52-58.

9,140 FODE, F. La révolution pacifique en marche: la nouvelle législation sociale de la République de Guinée. RECH. AFR. 3 (1961), pp. 38-59.

9,141 GIBBS, J. L. Poro values and courtroom procedures in a Kpelle chiefdom. SOCIOLOGUS 18 (1962), pp. 341-350.

9,142 JEREMINE, E. Etude des statuettes Kissiennes au point de vue mineralogique et pétrographique. J. SOC. AFR. 15 (1945), pp. 3-14.

Religion

9,143 Islam ou colonisation au Fouta-Djalon. PRESENCE AFR. 15 (1953), pp. 357-364.

Science

9,144 ABBAYES, H. DES. Lichens récoltés en Guinée française et en Côte d'Ivoire. III. Physciacées. BULL. IFAN 13 (1951), pp. 749-761.

9,145 ABBAYES, H. DES. Lichens récoltés en Guinée française et en Côte d'Ivoire. IV. Parméliacées. BULL. IFAN 13 (1951), pp. 965-977.

9,146 ABBAYES, H. DES. Lichens récoltés en Guinée française et en Côte d'Ivoire. V. Genres: Roccella, Coenogonium, Sticta, Cladonia, Ramalina. BULL. IFAN 14 (1952), pp. 19-27.

9,147 ABBAYES, H. DES. Lichens récoltés en Guinée française et en Côte d'Ivoire. VI. Collémancées, Heppiacées, Pannariacées. BULL. IFAN 14 (1952), pp. 450-456.

9,148 ABBAYES, H. DES. Lichens récoltés en Guinée française et en Côte d'Ivoire. VII. Pyrenulacées, Trypéthéliacées, Astrothéliacées, Cyphéliacées. BULL. IFAN 15 (1953), pp. 48-58.

9,149 ABBAYES, H. DES and MOTYKA, J. Lichens récoltés en Guinée française et en Côte d'Ivoire. BULL. IFAN 12 (1950), pp. 601-610.

9,150 ABBAYES, H. DES et al. Contribution à la flore des Ptéridophytes d'A.O.F. (Guinée et Côte d'Ivoire) by H. des Abbayes, A. H. G. Alston, M. L. Tardieu-Blot. BULL. IFAN 13 (1951), pp. 79-86; 15 (1953), pp. 1384-1386.

9,151 BALACHOWSKY, A. S. Deux Pseudaonidia Ckll. (Hom. Coccoidea-Diaspidinae) nouveaux du massif du Béna (Moyenne Guinée) A.O.F. BULL. IFAN 15 (1953), pp. 1512-1522.

9,152 CUILLE, J. Contribution à l'étude de l'ethologie de Cosmopolites sordidus Germ. ET. GUIN. 1 (1947), pp. 9-22.

9,153 DEKEYSER, P. L. Présence de Thos adustus en Guinée Française. BULL. IFAN 13 (1951), pp. 371-375.

9,154 GOLEMANSKY, V. Etudes sur la faune des rhizopodes de Guinée forestière. RECH. AFR. 3 (1962), pp. 3-24.

9,155 GOLEMANSKY, V. Faune muscicole de Guinée forestière (Rhizopodes testacés). RECH. AFR. 4 (1962), pp. 33-60.

9,156 KILLIAN, C. Contribution à l'etude de la biologie de quelques Utricularia tropicaux. BULL. IFAN 15 (1953), pp. 72-82.

9,157 KILLIAN, C. Germination et développement post-embryonnaire de Genlisea africana. BULL. IFAN 13 (1951), pp. 1029-1036.

9,158 KILLIAN, C. Mesures écologiques sur des végétaux types du Fouta-Djallon (Guinée Française) et sur leur milieu, en saison sèche. BULL. IFAN 13 (1951), pp. 601-681.

9,159 KILLIAN, C. Observations biologiques sur un Ascomycète, parasite du Cyathea Dregeri. BULL. IFAN 13 (1951), pp. 1037-1050.

9,160 KILLIAN, C. Observations sur l'écologie et les besoins édaphiques du Quinquina. BULL. IFAN 15 (1953), pp. 901-971.

9,161 LAMOTTE, M. and ROY, R. Les traits principaux du peuplement animal de la prairie montagnarde du Mont Nimba (Guinée). RECH. AFR. 1 (1962), pp. 11-30.

9,162 LAMOTTE, M. and ZUBER-VOGELI, M. Contribution à l'étude des Batraciens de l'Ouest africain. Le développement larvaire de Rana oxyrhynchus gribinguiensis Angel. BULL. IFAN 15 (1953), pp. 178-184.

9,163 MARSHALL, G. A. K. New Curculionidae (Col.) from French West Africa. BULL. IFAN 13 (1951), pp. 319-325.

9,164 MONOD, TH. Sur une Podestémonacée nouvelle pour l'A.O.F. BULL. IFAN 7 (1945), pp. 156-159.

9,165 PITOT, A. Sur l'anatomie de Psilotum triquetrum Sw. BULL. IFAN 12 (1950), pp. 315-334.

9,166 POUJADE, J. Technologie. ET. GUIN. 2 (1947), pp. 85-89.

9,167 RISTORCELLI, M. La traitement indigène de la trypanosomiase chez les Peuls du Fouta-Djallon (Guinée française). J. SOC. AFR. 9 (1939), pp. 1-2.

9,168 ROUANET, R. Le problème de la conservation des sols en Guinée. ET. GUIN. 8 (1952), pp. 59-65.

9,169 SCHNELL, R. Contribution préliminaire a l'étude botanique de la Basse-Guinée française. ET. GUIN. 6 (1950), pp. 31-73.

9,170 SCHNELL, R. Noms vernaculaires et usages indigènes de plantes d'Afrique Occidentale. ET. GUIN. 4 (1950), pp. 57-80.

9,171 SCHNELL, R. Plantes nouvelles ou peu connues d'Afrique occidentale française (Guinée et Côte d'Ivoire). BULL. IFAN 15 (1953), pp. 93-97.

9,172 SILVERSTOV, Y. Eléments de géomorphologie de la Guinée et ses principaux problèmes. RECH. AFR. 4 (1963), pp. 51-67.

9,173 TOURE, L. Les resources hydro-électriques de la République de Guinée. RECH. AFR. 1 (1960), pp. 42-50.

9,174 TUZET, O. et al. Trichophytes et Ciliés parasites intestinaux de Pachybolus sp., Scaphiostreptus obesus Attems et Termatodiscus nimbanus Attems (Myriapodes Diplopodes)... by O. Tuzet, J. F. Manier, M. Vogeli-Zuber. BULL. IFAN 15 (1953), pp. 133-142.

9,175 La réserve naturelle intégrale et la station scientifique nationale des Monts Mimba. RECH. AFR. 2 (1960), pp. 69-71.

See also 8709.

Sociology

9,176 C., J. L'alcoolisme en Guinée francaise. ZAIRE 8 (1954), p. 857.

9,177 HOUIS, M. Toponymie et sociologie. BULL. IFAN 22 (1960), pp. 443-445.

9,178 LERICHE, A. Anthroponymie toucouleur. BULL. IFAN 18 (1956), pp. 169-188.

9,179 LESTRANGE, M. DE. La population de la région de Youkounkoun en Guinée française. ET. GUIN. 7 (1951), pp. 67-69.

9,180 Les densités de population au Fouta-Djalon. PRESENCE AFR. 15 (1953), pp. 95-106.

9,181 En Guinée française: le grenier de Conakry. ZAIRE 6 (1952), pp. 975-976.

9,182 Notes démographiques sur la région de Labe. PRESENCE AFR. 15 (1953), pp. 83-94.

See also 8755, 8966.

IVORY COAST

General

9,183 DELRIEU, S. The Ivory Coast Central Library: a Unesco pilot project. UNESCO BULL. LIBS. 18 (1964), pp. 201-206.

9,184 GRIVOT, R. Le Cercle de Lahou (Côte d'Ivoire). BULL. IFAN 4 (1942), pp. 1-154.

9,185 Centre des Sciences Humaines, Abidjan. BULL. AFR. STUD. ASSOC. 1 (1964), pp. 27-28.

Agriculture

9,186 DUPIRE, M. Planteurs autochtones et étrangers en Basse-Côte d'Ivoire orientale. ET. EBURN. 8 (1960), pp. 7-237.

9,187 TRICART, J. Deux types de production agricole aux environs d'Odienne (Haute Côte-d'Ivoire). BULL. IFAN 19 (1957), pp. 284-294.

Anthropology

9,188 ABDOULAYE, N. Etude sur le cercle du Bas-Sassandra. AFR. BULL. 3 (1965), pp. 57-66.

9,189 ABEL, H. Déchiffrement des poids a peser l'or en Côte d'Ivoire. J. SOC. AFR. 29 (1959), pp. 273-286.

9,190 ABEL, H. Poids à peser l'or en Côte d'Ivoire. BULL. IFAN 16 (1954), pp. 55-82.

9,191 ALLAND, A., Jr. Abron witchcraft and social structure. CAH. ET. AFR. 5 (1965), pp. 495-502.

9,192 BERNUS, E. Ahouati, notes sur un village Dida. ET. EBURN. 6 (1957), pp. 213-229.

9,193 BERNUS, E. Kong et sa région. ET. EBURN. 8 (1960), pp. 239-324.

9,194 BOCHET, G. Le poro des Diéli. BULL. IFAN 21 (1959), pp. 61-101.

9,195 BOUSCAYROL, R. Notes sur le peuple ébrié. BULL. IFAN 11 (1949), pp. 382-408.

9,196 BRISLEY, T. Some notes on the Baoulé tribe. J. AFR. SOC. 8 (1909), pp. 296-302.

9,197 DELUZ-CHIVA, A. Mariage et économie monétaire chez les Gouro de Côte-d'Ivoire. AFR. ET ASIE 70 (1965), pp. 3-16.

9,198 DELUZ-CHIVA, A. Villages et lignages chez les Guro de Côte d'Ivoire. CAH. ET. AFR. 5 (1965), pp. 388-452.

9,199 HEBERT, R. P. Du mariage Toussian. BULL. IFAN 23 (1961), pp. 696-731.

9,200 HOLAS, B. Le Bois, matière, première des accessoires cérémoniels en Côte d'Ivoire. AFRICAN SYSTEMS OF THOUGHT, 1965, pp. 351-365.

9,201 HOLAS, B. Bref aperçu sur les principaux cultes syncrétiques de la basse Côte d'Ivoire. AFRICA 24 (1954), pp. 55-60; English summary, p. 60.

9,202 HOLAS, B. Eléments du système spirituel bété. PRESENCE AFR. N.S. 53 (1965), pp. 136-148.

9,203 HOLAS, B. L'évolution du schéma initiatique chez les femmes Oubi (région de Taï, Côte d'Ivoire). AFRICA 27 (1957), pp. 241-250; English summary, p. 250.

9,204 HOLAS, B. Fondements spirituels de la vie sociale sénoufo (région de Korhogo, Côte d'Ivoire). J. SOC. AFR. 26 (1956), pp. 9-32.

9,205 HOLAS, B. Note sur le vêtement et la parure baoulé (Côte d'Ivoire). BULL. IFAN 11 (1949), pp. 438-457.

9,206 HOLAS, B. Sur quelques divinités baoulé de rang inférieur; leurs figurations, leur role liturgique. BULL. IFAN 18 (1956), pp. 408-432.

9,207 KNOPS, P. L'enfant chez les Sénoufos de la Côte d'Ivoire. AFRICA 11 (1938), pp. 482-492.

9,208 KOBBEN, A. J. F. The development of an under-developed territory. SOCIOLOGUS 8 (1958), pp. 29-40.

9,209 KOBBEN, A. J. F. L'héritage chez les Agni: l'influence de l'économie de profit. AFRICA 24 (1954), pp. 359-363; English summary, p. 363.

9,210 KOBBEN, A. J. F. Le planteur noir. Essai d'une ethnographie d'aspect. ET. EBURN. 5 (1956), pp. 7-189.

9,211 MARTIN, R. P. and BOUTILLIER, J. L. L'amélioration de l'habitat dans la Subdivision de Bongouahou. ET. EBURN. 5 (1956), pp. 191-215.

9,212 NIANGORAN-BOUAH, G. Les Abouré. Une société lagunaire de Cote d'Ivoire. ANN. UNIV. ABIDJAN 1 (1965), pp. 37-171.

9,213 NIANGORAN-BOUAH, G. Poids à pesser l'or. PRESENCE AFR. N.S. 46 (1963), pp. 202-220.

9,214 NIANGORAN-BOUAH, G. Le village abouré. CAH. ET. AFR. 1 (1960), pp. 113-127.

9,215 OLBRECHTS, F. M. De Glee-dienst bij de Bevolking van de Boven-Cavally, Ivoorkust. KONGO-OVERZEE 5 (1939), pp. 127-137.

9,216 OLBRECHTS, F. M. Ivoorkust-expeditie der Rijksuniversiteit te Gent en van het Vleeschuis-Museum te Antwerpen. KONGO-OVERZEE 5 (1939), pp. 177-187.

9,217 PAULME, D. Une religion syncrétique en Côte d'Ivoire: le culte deima. CAH. ET. AFR. 3 (1962), pp. 5-90.

9,218 PAULME, D. Sur un mythe africain récent d'origine de la mort. CONGR. INT. SC. ANTHR. ET ETHN. 6, no. ii (1960), pp. 449-452.

9,219 PROUTEAUX, M. Les épreuves par le poison chez les indigènes du Bas-Cavally. J. SOC. AFR. 2 (1932), pp. 59-74.

9,220 ROUCH, J. Introduction a l'étude de la communauté de Bregbo. J. SOC. AFR. 33 (1963), pp. 129-202.

9,221 SIDIBE, M. Famille, vie sociale et vie religieuse chez les Birifor et les Oulé (région de Diébougou, Côte d'Ivoire). BULL. IFAN 1 (1939), pp. 697-742.

9,222 TARAORE, D. Yaro Hā ou mariages entre femmes chez les Bobo Niéniégué. J. SOC. AFR. 11 (1941), pp. 197-200.

9,223 TAUXIER, L. La religion des Touras. J. SOC. AFR. 1 (1931), pp. 259-280.

Art

9,224 CAZALAS, A. Prehistoric stations in the Ivory Coast French West Africa. AMER. ANTHR. 29 (1927), pp. 142-145.

9,225 FERGUSON, I. Dancers of the Ivory Coast. AFR. MUSIC, 1962, pp. 18-19.

9,226 HIMMELHEBER, H. Sculptors and sculptures of the Dan. PROC. INT. CONGR. AFR. 1 (1962), pp. 243-255.

9,227 HOLAS, B. Deux haches polies de grande taille de la Basse Cotê d'Ivoire. BULL. IFAN 13 (1951), pp. 1174-1180.

9,228 HOLAS, B. Senufo sculpture. BO 5 (1959), pp. 30-32.

9,229 SCHNELL, R. Sur un marteau de pierre emmanché recueilli en Côte d'Ivoire. J. SOC. AFR. 18 (1948), pp. 127-128.

9,230 ZEMP, H. Musiciens autochtones et griots malinké chez les Dan de Côte d'Ivoire. CAH. ET. AFR. 4 (1964), pp. 370-382.

See also 8504, 9425.

Biography

9,231 ROUX, A. Un prophète: Harris. PRESENCE AFR. 8 (1950), pp. 133-140.

Economics

9,232 ABEL, H. Déchiffrement des poids a peser l'or en Côte d'Ivoire. J. SOC. AFR. 22 (1952), pp. 95-114; 24 (1954), pp. 7-23.

9,233 C., J. Développement de la Côte d'Ivoire. ZAIRE 8 (1954), pp. 638-639.

9,234 FODERATO, S. Missione economica in Africa occidentale (Costa d'Avorio, Guinea, Sierra Leone e Senegal). AFRICA (Rome) 15 (1960), pp. 3-22.

9,235 HAUSER, A. Les industries de transformation de la Côte-d'Ivoire. Mission en Côte-d'Ivoire (Octobre 1954). ET. EBURN. 4 (1955), pp. 108-113.

9,236 MEILLASSOUX, C. L'économie des échanges pré-coloniaux en pays Gouro. CAH. ET. AFR. 3 (1963), pp. 551-576.

9,237 ROUGERIE, G. 1949: Jalon dans la vie économique de la Côte d'Ivoire. BULL. IFAN 12 (1950), pp. 1132-1138.

9,238 SOURNIES, J. A propos des huileries de palme. ET. EBURN. 5 (1956), pp. 216-219.

9,239 A propos de l'ouverture du port d'Abidjan. ZAIRE 5 (1951), pp. 408-410.

9,240 Difficultés de ravitaillement en Côte d'Ivoire. ZAIRE 5 (1951), pp. 298-299.

9,241 Essor industriel de la ville d'Abidjan. ZAIRE 7 (1953), pp. 1083-1084.

Education

9,242 NICOLAS, A. Teacher training in the Ivory Coast. AFR. ED. 2, no. 2 (1964), pp. 15-17.

9,243 L'Institut de Recherche d'Apiopodoume. ZAIRE 5 (1951), pp. 628-629.

Geography

9,244 ADJANONHOUN, E. Végétation des savanes et des rochers découverts en Côte d'Ivoire. ET. DAHOM. N.S. 3 (1964), pp. 119-122.

9,245 BERNUS, E. Abidjan. Note sur l'agglomération d'Abidjan et sa population. BULL. IFAN 24 (1962), pp. 54-85.

9,246 BONNEFOY, C. Tiagba: notes sur un village aizi. ET. EBURN. 3 (1954), pp. 7-129.

9,247 FUSTER CASAS, J. Impresiones de un viaje a la costa de Marfil. ARCH. INST. EST. AFR. 7, no. 31 (1954), pp. 7-14.

9,248 GRIVOT, R. Agboville, esquisse d'une cité d'Afrique noire. ET. EBURN. 4 (1955), pp. 84-107.

9,249 HALLOUIN, C. Géographie humaine de la subdivision de Daloa. BULL. IFAN 9 (1947), pp. 18-55.

9,250 LAPLANTE, A. and ROUGERIE, G. Etude pédologique du bassin français de la Bia. BULL. IFAN 12 (1950), pp. 883-904.

9,251 RIOU, G. Notes sur les sols complexes des savanes préforestières en Cote d'Ivoire. ANN. UNIV. ABIDJAN 1 (1965), pp. 17-35.

9,252 ROUGERIE, G. Le niveau des 200 m et les niveaux récents en Côte d'Ivoire. ET. EBURN. 7 (1958), pp. 223-233.

9,253 ROUGERIE, G. Les pays Agni du Sud-Est de la Côte d'Ivoire forestière. ET. EBURN. 6 (1957), pp. 7-211.

9,254 ROUGERIE, G. Le port d'Abidjan. Le problème des débouchés maritimes de la Côte d'Ivoire. Sa solution lagunaire. BULL. IFAN 12 (1950), pp. 751-837.

9,255 ROUGERIE, G. Séisme en basse Côte d'Ivoire. BULL. IFAN 12 (1950), p. 1171.

9,256 SCHNELL, R. Structure et évolution de la végétation des monts Nimba (Afrique Occidentale Française) en fonction du modelé et du sol. BULL. IFAN 7 (1945), pp. 80-100.

9,257 SKOTNICKI, M. La subdivision de Soubré. Notes d'un séjour en Côte d'Ivoire. AFR. BULL. 2 (1965), pp. 35-56.

9,258 TATE, G. H. H. The lower Cavally river, West Africa. GEOG. REV. 32 (1942), pp. 574-584.

9,259 TRICART, J. Quelques éléments de l'évolution géomorphologique de l'Ouest de la Côte d'Ivoire. RECH. AFR. 1 (1962), pp. 31-39.

9,260 VARLET, F. Mission de préprospection du domaine de San Pedro (février 1955). Rapport océanographique. ET. EBURN. 7 (1958), pp. 235-247.

9,261 VARLET, F. Le régime de l'Atlantique près d'Abidjan (Côte d'Ivoire). Essai d'oceanographie littorale. ET. EBURN. 7 (1958), pp. 97-222.

Government. Politics. Administration

9,262 ALEXANDER, A. S., Jr. The Ivory Coast constitution: an accelerator, not a brake. J. MOD. AFR. STUD. 1 (1963), pp. 293-311.

9,263 GRAY, A. Visitor from Ivory Coast. AFR. AFFAIRS 61 (1962), pp. 281-283.

9,264 ZOLBERG, A. R. Effets de la structure d'un parti politique sur l'integration nationale. CAH. ET. AFR. 1 (1960), pp. 140-149.

See also 10388.

History

9,265 ATGER, P. Les comptoirs fortifiés de la Cote d'Ivoire, 1843-1871. REV. FRANC. HIST. OUTRE-MER 47 (1960), pp. 427-474.

9,266 BERNUS, E. Notes sur l'histoire de Korhogo. BULL. IFAN 23 (1961), pp. 284-290.

9,267 WONDJI, C. La Côte d'Ivoire occidentale. Période de pénétration pacifique (1890-1908). REV. FRANC. HIST. OUTRE-MER 50 (1963), pp. 346-381.

Language. Literature

Language

9,268 BERTHO, J. La place des dialectes Géré et Wobê par rapport aux autres dialectes de la Côte d'Ivoire. BULL. IFAN 13 (1951), pp. 1272-1280.

9,269 BERTHO, J. La place du dialecte adiukru par rapport aux autres dialectes de la Côte d'Ivoire. BULL. IFAN 12 (1950), pp. 1075-1094.

9,270 CLAMENS, G. Essai de grammaire senufo tagwana. BULL. IFAN 14 (1952), pp. 1402-1465.

9,271 MIEGE, J. Notes de toponymie Baoulé. ET. EBURN. 3 (1954), pp. 131-140.

9,272 MONOD, TH. Un nouvel alphabet ouest-africain: le bété (Côte d'Ivoire). BULL. IFAN, Série B: Sciences humaines 20 (1958), pp. 432-553.

9,273 PAULIAN, R. Elements d'un vocabulaire zoologique des dialectes forestiers de Basse Côte d'Ivoire. J. SOC. AFR. 16 (1946), pp. 23-28.

9,274 STEWART, J. M. Notes on Baule phonology. BULL. SOAS 18 (1956), pp. 353-365.

9,275 THOIRE, G. Le dialecte Plaoui (Côte d'Ivoire). J. SOC. AFR. 3 (1933), pp. 319-333.

Literature

9,276 BOGNINI, J. M. Three poems [When you want to sleep at night, Song of the sun, My days overgrown by coffee blossoms]. BO 18 (1965), pp. 17-19.

9,277 BOGNINI, J. M. Transparence, Rien qu'un murmure. PRESENCE AFR. N.S. 53 (1965), pp. 233-234.

9,278 BOGNINI, J. M. Trois poèmes. PRESENCE AFR. N.S. 34-35 (1960-1961), pp. 151-153.

9,279 DADIE, B. La risaia. AFRICA (Rome) 13 (1958), pp. 342-343.

9,280 DADIE, B. B. Christmas! PRESENCE AFR. N.S. 47 (1963), pp. 176-177.

9,281 DADIE, B. B. Hommes de tous les continents; Tisons dans la nuit. PRESENCE AFR. N.S. 54 (1965), pp. 234-235.

9,282 DADIE, B. B. Le roi d'un jour. PRESENCE AFR. N.S. 47 (1963), pp. 177-178.

9,283 SILLARET, M. Un bienfait n'est jamais perdu. PRESENCE AFR. 7 (1949), pp. 279-287.

Law

9,284 CLOZEL, F. J. Land tenure among the natives of the Ivory Coast. J. AFR. SOC. 1 (1912), pp. 399-415.

9,285 KOBBEN, A. J. F. Land as an object of gain in a non-literate society. Land tenure among the Bete and Dida (Ivory Coast, West Africa). AFR. AGRARIAN SYSTEMS, 1963, pp. 245-266.

9,286 TIXIER, G. Centre d'Enseignement Supérieur d'Abidjan, Ecole de Droit. J. AFR. LAW 6 (1962), p. 95.

Science

9,287 ARNOULD, M. Les granites de haute Côte-d'Ivoire. PROC. SYMP. GRANITES W. AFR., 1965, pp. 22-28.

9,288 BOURDIEC, P. LE. Contribution à l'étude géomorphologique du bassin sédimentaire et des régions littorales de Côte d'Ivoire. ET. EBURN. 7 (1958), pp. 7-96.

9,289 DELAMARE-DEBOUTTEVILLE, C. Nouveaux Paronelliens de la Côte d'Ivoire. BULL. IFAN 13 (1951), pp. 1072-1075.

9,290 MANGENOT, G. Etude sur les forêts des plaines et plateaux de la Côte-d'Ivoire. ET. EBURN. 4 (1955), pp. 5-83.

9,291 MONOD, TH. Un nouveau Stenasellus ouest-africain. BULL. IFAN 7 (1945), pp. 101-114.

9,292 PORTERES, R. Les variations des Ceintures hydrophytiques et gramino-hélephytiques des eaux vives du système lagunaire de la Côte d'Ivoire. BULL. IFAN 13 (1951), pp. 1011-1028.

9,293 ROUGERIE, G. Etude morphologique du Bassin français de la Bia et des régions littorales de la Lagune Aby (Basse Côte d'Ivoire orientale). ET. EBURN. 2 (1951), pp. 5-110.

9,294 SCHNELL, R. Sur quelques plantes a usage religieux de la région forestière d'Afrique occidentale. J. SOC. AFR. 16 (1946), pp. 29-38.

9,295 TUZET, O. et al. Sur quelques parasites intestinaux de Mardonius piceus Attems 1952, Myriapode-Diplopode de Daloa (Côte d'Ivoire), by O. Tuzet, J. F. Manier and M. Vogeli-Zuber. BULL. IFAN 14 (1952), pp. 1143-1151.

9,296 TUZET, O. and ZUBER-VOGELI, M. La spermatogenèse de Zonocerus variegatus L. BULL. IFAN 15 (1953), pp. 487-494.

9,297 VILLIERS, A. Un nouvel Endomychidé de l'Ouest africain. BULL. IFAN 11 (1949), pp. 208-209.

See also 9162, 9163, 9171, 9175.

Sociology

9,298 ATTOUNGBRE, G. Beoumi. Aperçu sur les structures rurales en Côte d'Ivoire. ANNALES AFR., 1959, pp. 289-293.

9,299 BADIE, B. B. Le sort du travailleur noir de Cote-d'Ivoire. PRESENCE AFR. 13 (1952), pp. 242-250.

9,300 CLIGNET, R. Introduction to the inquiry on the attitudes of society towards women in the Ivory Coast. INT. SOC. SC. J. 14 (1962), pp. 137-148.

9,301 CLIGNET, R. Urbanization and family structure in the Ivory Coast. COMP. STUD. SOC. HIST. 8 (1965-1966), pp. 385-401.

9,302 GERVAIS, J. Position and problems of the woman in...Ivory Coast. WOMEN TODAY 6 (1964), pp. 49-51.

9,303 HIERNAUX, C. R. Notes sur l'evolution des Gagou. Habitat, régime de propriété, vie agraire et sociale. BULL. IFAN 12 (1950), pp. 488-512.

9,304 HOLAS, B. La Goumbé. Une association de jeunesse musulmane en basse Côte d'Ivoire. KONGO-OVERZEE 19 (1953), pp. 116-131.

9,305 ROUCH, J. Problèmes relatifs à l'étude des migrations traditionnelles et des migrations actuelles en Afrique occidentale. BULL. IFAN 22 (1960), pp. 367-378.

9,306 ROUCH, J. and BERNUS, E. Note sur les prostitutes Toutou de Treichville et d'Adjamé. ET. EBURN. 6 (1957), pp. 231-242.

See also 12655, 13446,

TOGOLAND

Anthropology

9,307 CORNEVIN, R. Avec le Lieutenant Plehn à la recherche d'un cercle du Moyen Togo. ET. DAHOM. 4 (1950), pp. 43-60.

9,308 CORNEVIN, G. Le canton de l'Akébou. ET. DAHOM. 7 (1952), pp. 81-132.

9,309 CORNEVIN, R. Capitales et centres de dispersion des peuples Adja, Evhé et Fon (Républiques du Togo et du Dahomey). CONGR. INT. SC. ANTH. ET. ETHN. 6, no. ii (1960), pp. 175-177.

9,310 CORNEVIN, R. Contribution a l'étude des populations parlant des langues Gouang au Togo et au Dahomey. J. AFR. LANGS. 3 (1964), pp. 226-230.

9,311 CORNEVIN, R. L'enterrement d'un chef Koukomba. AFRICA 24 (1954), pp. 247-249; English summary, p. 249.

9,312 CORNEVIN, R. Evolution dans le Nord du Togo. SOCIOLOGUS 4 (1954), pp. 59-67.

9,313 CORNEVIN, R. Le Litimé. ET. DAHOM. 14 (1955), pp. 21-65.

9,314 CORNEVIN, R. Names among the Bassari. SOUTHWESTERN J. ANTHR. 10 (1954), pp. 160-163.

9,315 CORNEVIN, R. Totémisme, liens communautaires et coutumes chez quelques groupes ethniques Togolais. ET. DAHOM. 17 (1956), pp. 9-11.

9,316 FROELICH, J. C. Généralités sur les Kabrè du Nord-Togo. BULL. IFAN 11 (1949), pp. 77-105.

9,317 FROELICH, J. C. Les Konkomba du Nord-Togo. BULL. IFAN 11 (1949), pp. 409-437.

9,318 FROELICH, J. C. Notes sur les Naoudeba du Nord-Togo. BULL. IFAN 12 (1950), pp. 102-121.

9,319 FROELICH, J. C. Les sociétés d'initiation chez les Moba et les Gourma du Nord-Togo. J. SOC. AFR. 19 (1949), pp. 99-141.

9,320 FUNKE, E. Einiges über Geschichte, religiöse Gebräuche und Anschauungen des Avatimevolkes in Togo. AFR. UND UB. 1 (1910), pp. 81-105.

9,321 FUNKE, E. Die Familie im Spiegel der afrikanischen Volksmärchen. AFR. UND UB. 2 (1911-1912), pp. 37-63.

9,322 HUBER, H. Cérémonie pour les filles pubères d'origine Andangme à Anécho (Togo). BULL. IFAN, Série B: Sciences humaines 20 (1958), pp. 417-431.

9,323 MERCIER, P. Notice sur le peuplement Yoruba au Dahomey-Togo. ET. DAHOM. 4 (1950), pp. 29-40.

9,324 NETTL, B. Family relationships in Lamba tales. ANTHR. QUART. 29 (1956), pp. 24-30.

9,325 TAIT, D. The family, household, and minor lineage of the Konkomba. AFRICA 26 (1956), pp. 219-248, 332-341.

9,326 TAIT, D. The political system of Konkomba. AFRICA 23 (1953), pp. 213-222.

9,327 WOLF, F. Totémisme, liens communautaires et coutumes chez quelques tribus du Togo (Afrique occidentale). ET. DAHOM. 17 (1956), pp. 12-34.

See also 9499, 10025, 10118.

Art

9,328 LESOURD, M. Dessins géométriques composés par les élèves des écoles coraniques d'In Calah. J. SOC. AFR. 6 (1936), pp. 213-216.

9,329 MAUNY, R. Etat actuel de nos connaissances sur la préhistoire du Dahomey et du Togo. ET. DAHOM. 4 (1950), pp. 5-11.

Economics

9,330 FESTA, G. Il regime del franco nei territori africani francesi e la situazione del Togo e del Camerun. AFRICA (Rome) 10 (1955), pp. 41-43.

9,331 SCHOBER, R. Native co-operation in Togoland. AFRICA 9 (1936), pp. 485-494.

9,332 U TUN WAI et al. The economy of Togo. IMF STAFF PAPERS 12 (1965), pp. 409-469.

Education

9,333 DICKSON, A. G. Mass education in Togoland. AFR. AFFAIRS 49 (1950), pp. 136-150.

9,334 Boursiers togolais en France. ZAIRE 6 (1952), pp. 1092-1093.

9,335 La question des Ewes au Conseil de Tutelle de l'O.N.U. ZAIRE 4 (1950), pp. 1023-1025.

9,336 VIIe congres de l'Association des étudiants togolais en France [July, 1958]. PRESENCE AFR. N.S. 20 (1958), pp. 135-136.

Geography

9,337 GRIVOT, R. Etude sur la crue du Mono en 1944. BULL. IFAN 11 (1949), pp. 245-254.

9,338 VILLIERS, A. Mission A. Villiers au Togo et au Dahomey (1950). ET. DAHOM. 5 (1951), pp. 5-90.

9,339 WHITE, H. P. Avatime: a highland environment in Togoland. MALAYAN J. TR. GEOG. 8 (1956), pp. 32-39.

9,340 ZECH, VON. Pays et populations de la frontière nord-ouest du Togo. ET. DAHOM. 2 (1949), pp. 9-36.

Government

9,341 AFRICANUS, P. La fin d'une idylle. AFR. ET ASIE 43 (1958), pp. 16-22.

9,342 AFRICANUS, P. Vers une fédération franco-africaine: naissance de la République togolaise. AFR. ET ASIE 36 (1956), pp. 5-28.

9,343 BONO, S. Il Togo da colonia tedesca a stato indipendente. AFRICA (Rome) 15 (1960), pp. 181-189.

9,344 DEVERNOIS, G. Republic of Togoland 1958-1959; political and institutional evolution. CIVILISATIONS 9 (1959), pp. 235-238.

9,345 L'assassinat du President Sylvano Olympio. GENEVE-AFR. 2 (1963), pp. 81-82.

9,346 Enquête sur le régime électoral au Togo. ZAIRE 6 (1952), pp. 531-532.

9,347 Native affairs in French Togoland. GOLD COAST REV. 1 (1925), pp. 146-175.

9,348 Le Togo français en 1950. ZAIRE 5 (1951), pp. 1072-1074.

See also 10378, 10393, 18219.

History

9,349 ALEXANDRE, P. Le facteur islamique dans l'histoire d'un Etat du Moyen-Togo. AFR. ET ASIE 65 (1964), pp. 31-41.

9,350 ALEXANDRE, P. Organisation politique des Kotokoli du Nord-Togo. CAH. ET. AFR. 4, no. 14 (1963), pp. 228-274.

9,351 CARDINALL, A. W. The story of the German occupation of Togoland. GOLD COAST REV. 2 (1926), pp. 192-207; 3 (1927), pp. 56-72.

9,352 CORNEVIN, R. Contribution à l'histoire de la chefferie cotokoli. CAH. ET. AFR. 4 (1964), pp. 456-460.

9,353 CRABTREE, W. A. The conquest of Togoland. J. AFR. SOC. 14 (1914-1915), pp. 386-391.

9,354 CRABTREE, W. A. Togoland. J. AFR. SOC. 14 (1914-1915), pp. 168-184.

9,355 FROELICH, J. C. and ALEXANDRE, P. Histoire traditionnelle des Kotokoli et des Bi-Tchambi du Nord-Togo. BULL. IFAN 22 (1960), pp. 211-275.

Language. Literature

Language

9,356 BERTHO, J. Les dialectes du Moyen-Togo. BULL. IFAN 14 (1952), pp. 1046-1107.

9,357 CHRISTALLER, J. G. Die Adelesprache im Togogebiet. ZAOS 1 (1895), pp. 16-33.

9,358 CHRISTALLER, J. G. Die Sprachen des Togogebiets in kurzer allgemeiner Uebersicht. ZAOS 1 (1895), pp. 5-8.

9,359 CORNEVIN, R. Note sur la toponymie des villages Konkomba de la circonscription de Bassari. BULL. IFAN 26 (1964), pp. 694-708.

9,360 DEBRUNNER, H. W. Vergessene Sprachen und Tricksprachen bei den Togorestvölkern. AFR. UND UB. 46 (1962-1963), pp. 109-118.

9,361 DREXEL, A. Der Ewe-Typus in seiner systematischen Eigenart und in seiner sprachgeschichtlichen Stellung. BIBLIOTHECA AFR. 4, no. 2 (1930-1931), pp. 31-41.

9,362 FUNKE, E. Original-Texte aus den Klassensprachen in Mittel Togo. AFR. UND UB. 10 (1919-1920), pp. 261-313.

9,363 PRIETZE, R. Beiträge zur Erforschung von Sprache und Volksgeist in der Togo-Kolonie. ZAOS 3 (1897), pp. 17-64.

9,364 PROST, A. Les classes nominales en Bassari-Tobote. J. AFR. LANGS. 2 (1963), pp. 210-217.

9,365 PROST, R. P. A. Vocabulaires comparés du quatre langues voltaïques du Togo. BULL. IFAN 26 (1964), pp. 212-257.

9,366 RAPP, E. L. Die Adangme-Gã-Mundart von Agotime in Togo. AFRIKA (Berlin) 2 (1943), pp. 4-58.

9,367 SEIDEL, A. Beiträge zur Kenntniss der Sprachen in Togo. ZAOS 4 (1898), pp. 201-286.

9,368 SEIDEL, H. Der Yew'e-Dienst im Togolande. ZAOS 3 (1897), pp. 157-185.

9,369 TAIT, D. Konkomba nominal classes. With a phonetic commentary by P. D. Strevens. AFRICA 24 (1954), pp. 130-147.

9,370 WESTERMANN, D. Ein Beitrag zur Kenntnis des Zarma-Songai am Niger. AFR. UND UB. 11 (1920-1921), pp. 188-220.

9,371 WESTERMANN, D. Die Grussisprachen im westlichen Sudan. AFR. UND UB. 4 (1913-1914), pp. 161-180, 312-332; 5 (1914-1915), pp. 45-76.

9,372 WIEGRABE, P. A reader in the vernacular for West Africa. AFRICA 4 (1931), pp. 435-444.

Literature

9,373 LE BRETON, A. Fragments de la phrase ensemble. PRESENCE AFR. 4 (1948), pp. 607-616.

9,374 SENGHOR, L. S. La phrase ensemble [de Le Breton]. PRESENCE AFR. 4 (1948), pp. 685-687.

Law

9,375 DECOTTIGNIES, R. La condition des personnes au Togo et au Cameroun. ANNALES AFR., 1957, pp. 7-52.

9,376 LUCHAIRE, F. Le Togo francais. De la tutelle à l'autonomie. RJPUF 11 (1957), pp. 1-46, 501-587.

Science

9,377 BALFOUR-BROWNE, J. Mission A. Villiers au Dahomey (1950). VII. Coléoptères Hydrophilides. BULL. IFAN 14 (1952), pp. 126-139.

9,378 BASILEWSKY, P. Mission A. Villiers au Togo et au Dahomey (1950). XXII. Coléoptères Carabidae. BULL. IFAN 15 (1953), pp. 522-542.

9,379 BERNARDI, G. Mission A. Villiers au Togo et au Dahomey (1950). XVIII. Lépidoptères Pieridae. BULL. IFAN 14 (1952), pp. 837-841.

9,380 CAMERON, M. Mission A. Villiers au Togo et au Dahomey (1950). XVII. Coléoptères Staphylinidae. BULL. IFAN 14 (1952), pp. 827-836.

9,381 CONDAMIN, M. Mission A. Villiers au Togo et au Dahomey (1950). X. Lépidoptères Rhopalocères. BULL. IFAN 14 (1952), pp. 170-183.

9,382 DESCARPENTRIES, A. Mission A. Villiers au Togo et au Dahomey (1950). XIX. Coléoptères Buprestides. BULL. IFAN 14 (1952), pp. 1152-1169.

9,383 FRASER, F. C. Mission A. Villiers au Togo et au Dahomey (1950). V. Odonata and Neuroptera. BULL. IFAN 13 (1951), pp. 1076-1093.

9,384 GUIGNOT, F. Mission A. Villiers au Togo et au Dahomey (1950). XV. Coléoptères Hydrocanthares. BULL. IFAN 14 (1952), pp. 518-528.

9,385 LALLEMAND, V. Mission A. Villiers au Togo et au Dahomey (1950). IX. Hémiptères Homoptères. BULL. IFAN 14 (1952), pp. 164-169.

9,386 LOVERIDGE, A. Mission A. Villiers au Togo et au Dahomey (1950). XII. Tortoises and Lizards. BULL. IFAN 14 (1952), pp. 229-242.

9,387 PIC, M. Mission A. Villiers au Togo et au Dahomey (1950). VI. Coléoptères divers. BULL. IFAN 14 (1952), pp. 97-119.

9,388 PIC, M. Mission A. Villiers au Togo et au Dahomey (1950). XIV. Coléoptères Chrysomélides. BULL. IFAN 14 (1952), pp. 495-512.

9,389 POISSON, R. Mission A. Villiers au Togo et au Dahomey (1950). IV. Hémiptères Cryptocérates. BULL. IFAN 13 (1951), pp. 1131-1140.

9,390 SCHEDL, K. E. Fauna Aethiopica. VII. Bark- and Ambrosia-Beetles from Dahomey and Togo collected by Mr. A. Villiers. BULL. IFAN 13 (1951), pp. 1103-1106.

9,391 STEMPFFER, H. Mission A. Villiers au Togo et au Dahomey (1950). XI. Lépidoptères Lycaenidae. BULL. IFAN 14 (1952), pp. 184-190.

9,392 VILLIERS, A. Mission A. Villiers au Togo et au Dahomey (1950). VIII. Hémiptères Réduviides. BULL. IFAN 14 (1952), pp. 140-163.

9,393 VILLIERS, A. Mission A. Villiers au Togo et au Dahomey (1950). XIII. Coléoptères Lyctides et Bostrychides. BULL. IFAN 14 (1952), pp. 485-488.

9,394 VILLIERS, A. Mission A. Villiers au Togo et au Dahomey (1950). XVI. Coléoptères Erotylidae subfam. Languriinae. BULL. IFAN 14 (1952), pp. 819-821.

9,395 VILLIERS, A. Mission A. Villiers au Togo et au Dahomey (1950). XXI. Hémiptères. BULL. IFAN 14 (1952), pp. 1196-1213.

See also 8346.

Sociology

9,396 AGEBLEMAGNON, F.N. Du "temps" dans la culture "Ewe." PRESENCE AFR. N.S. 14-15 (1957), pp. 222-232.

9,397 AGEBLEMAGNON, F.N. Mythe et réalité de la classe sociale en Afrique noire: le cas du Togo. CAH. INT. SOCIOL. 38 (1965), pp. 155-168.

9,398 ABEBLEMAGNON, F.N. Research on attitudes toward the Togolese woman. INT. SOC. SC. J. 14 (1962), pp. 148-156.

9,399 CORNEVIN, R. Etude sur le centre urbain de Bassari (Togo). BULL. IFAN 19 (1957), pp. 72-110.

9,400 PAUVERT, J. C. Migrations et éducation. BULL. IFAN 22 (1960), pp. 467-475.

9,401 WARD, B. Some notes on migration from Togoland. AFR. AFFAIRS 49 (1950), pp. 129-135.

See also 4390, 9305.

UPPER VOLTA

Anthropology

9,402 AKINDELE, A. and AGUESSY, C. Données traditionnelles relatives aux Fon Dovinou de Savalou. BULL. IFAN, Série B: Sciences humaines 17 (1955), pp. 551-560.

9,403 BALANDIER, G. and SAUTTER, G. Mission M. Cartry-G. Remy en Haute-Volta (1962). CAH. ET. AFR. 3 (1963), pp. 435-442.

9,404 CAPRON, J. Bibliographie générale des Bwa. ET. VOLT. 5 (1964), pp. 201-205.

9,405 CAPRON, J. Univers religieux et cohésion interne dans les communautés villageoses Bwa traditionnelles. AFRICA 32 (1962), pp. 132-171; ETUDES VOLTAIQUES N.S. 4 (1963), pp. 73-124; AFRICAN SYSTEMS OF THOUGHT, 1965, pp. 291-313.

9,406 CARTRY, M. Note sur les signes graphiques du géomancien gourmantchè. J. SOC. AFR. 33 (1963), pp. 275-306.

9,407 DIETERLEN, G. Note sur les Kouroumba du Yatenga septentrional. J. SOC. AFR. 10 (1940), pp. 181-189.

9,408 GIRAULT, R. P. L. Essai sur la religion des Dagara. BULL. IFAN 21 (1959), pp. 329-356.

9,409 GOSSELIN, G. Bibliographie générale des Bisa. ET. VOLT. 5 (1964), pp. 199-200.

9,410 GRIAULE, M. and DIETERLEN, G. La mort chez les Kouroumba. J. SOC. AFR. 12 (1942), pp. 9-24.

9,411 IZARD, M. Bibliographie générale des Mossi. ETUDES VOLTAIQUES N.S. 3 (1962), pp. 103-111.

9,412 JAQUINOD, R. P. F. Les Bolon (Cercle d'Orodara, Haute-Volta). BULL. IFAN 25 (1963), pp. 134-144.

9,413 KABORE, G. V. Caractère "féodal" du système politique mossi. CAH. ET. AFR. 2 (1962), pp. 609-623.

9,414 MENJAUD, H. Documents ethnographiques sur le Gourma. J. SOC. AFR. 2 (1932), pp. 35-47.

9,415 MOAL, G. LE. Note sur les populations "Bobo." ETUDES VOLTAIQUES N.S. 1 (1960), pp. 5-17.

9,416 NICOLAS, F. J. Mythes et êtres mythiques des L'éla de la Haute-Volta. BULL. IFAN 14 (1952), pp. 1353-1384.

9,417 NICOLAS, F. J. La question de l'ethnique 'Gourounsi' en Haute-Volta (A.O.F.). AFRICA 22 (1952), pp. 170-172.

9,418 OUEDRAOGO, J. Les funérailles en pays mossi. BULL. IFAN 12 (1950), pp. 441-455.

9,419 PAGEARD, R. Note sur les Setba. ETUDES VOLTAIQUES N.S. 2 (1961), pp. 57-60.

9,420 PAGEARD, R. Recherches sur les Nioniossé. ETUDES VOLTAIQUES N.S. 4 (1963), pp. 5-71.

9,421 PEGARD, O. [Soeur Jean Bernard]. Structures et relations sociales en pays Bisa (Haute-Volta). CAH. ET. AFR. 5 (1965), pp. 161-247.

9,422 RASILLY, R. P. B. DE. Bwa laada: coutumes et croyances bwa. BULL. IFAN 27 (1965), pp. 99-154.

9,423 ROUAMBA, T. Mission d'enquête en Haute-Volta. CAH. ET. AFR. 3 (1962), pp. 299-301.

9,424 SANOGO, M. and PAGEARD, R. Notes sur les coutumes des Marka de Lanfiéra (cercle de Tougan, Haute-Volta). J. SOC. AFR. 34 (1964), pp. 306-310.

9,425 SAVONNET, G. La colonisation du pays Koulango (Haute Côte d'Ivoire) par les Lobi de Haute-Volta. ETUDES VOLTAIQUES N.S. 3 (1962), pp. 79-102.

9,426 SAVONNET, G. Quelques notes sur les Gan et sur le rituel d'intronisation de leur chef. ETUDES VOLTAIQUES N.S. 4 (1963), pp. 125-132.

9,427 SAVONNET, G. Un système de culture perfectionnée, pratique par les Bwaba-Bobo-Oulé de la région de Houndé (Haute-Volta). ETUDES VOLTAIQUES N.S. 1 (1960), pp. 19-52.

9,428 SCHWEEGER-HEFEL, A. Les insignes royaux des Kouroumba (Haute-Volta). J. SOC. AFR. 32 (1962), pp. 275-323.

9,429 SKINNER, E. P. The effect of co-residence of Sisters' sons on African corporate patrilineal descent groups. CAH. ET. AFR. 4 (1964), pp. 467-478.

9,430 TAUXIER, L. Deux petites populations peu connues de l'Afrique Occidentale française: Les Oura ou Guala, et les Natioro. J. SOC. AFR. 9 (1939), pp. 159-195.

9,431 TAUXIER, L. Les Gouin et les Tourouka, résidence de Banfora, cercle de Bobo-Dioulasso. Etude ethnographique, suivie d'un double vocabulaire. J. SOC. AFR. 3 (1933), pp. 77-128.

9,432 ZAHAN, D. L'habitation mossi. BULL. IFAN 12 (1950), pp. 223-229.

9,433 ZAHAN, D. Notes sur les marchés Mossi du Yatenga. AFRICA 24 (1954), pp. 370-376.

9,434 ZWERNEMANN, J. Les notions du dieu-ciel chez quelques tribus voltaïques. BULL. IFAN 23 (1961), pp. 243-272; ETUDES VOLTAIQUES N.S. 2 (1961), pp. 71-100.

9,435 ZWERNEMANN, J. Shall we use the word 'Gurunsi'? AFRICA 28 (1958), pp. 123-125.

Art

9,436 BARRAL, B. Le cinéma en milieu rural africain. ETUDES VOLTAIQUES N.S. 5 (1964), pp. 185-197.

9,437 ROUCH, J. Restes anciens et gravures rupestres d'Aribinda (Haute-Volta). ETUDES VOLTAIQUES N.S. 2 (1961), pp. 61-70.

Economics

9,438 BOUTILLIER, J. L. Les structures foncières en Haute-Volta. ETUDES VOLTAIQUES N.S. 5 (1964), pp. 5-181.

9,439 BRESSON, Y. De la répartition optimale des surfaces cultivées en Haute-Volta. ANNALES AFR., 1965, pp. 189-227.

9,440 C., J. Inauguration du chemin de fer du Mossi. ZAIRE 9 (1955), pp. 172-173.

9,441 Le chemin de fer du pays Mossi. ZAIRE 6 (1952), pp. 1091-1092.

Geography

9,442 BARLET, P. La Haute-Volta. Essai de présentation géographique. ETUDES VOLTAIQUES N.S. 3 (1962), pp. 5-77.

9,443 HILTON, T. E. Mossi country. UNIVERSITAS 4 (1959), pp. 7-8.

9,444 NYE, P. Road to Timbuktu. UNIVERSITAS 1, no. 2 (1954), pp. 19-20.

See also 10357.

History

9,445 HEBERT, P. Samory en Haute-Volta. ETUDES VOLTAIQUES N.S. 2 (1961), pp. 5-55.

9,446 HEBERT, R. P. J. Esquisse de l'histoire du pays toussian. BULL. IFAN 23 (1961), pp. 309-327.

9,447 HEBERT, R. P. J. Une page d'histoire voltaïque: Amoro, chef des Tiéfo. BULL. IFAN, Série B: Sciences humaines 20 (1958), pp. 377-405.

9,448 PAGEARD, R. Un enquête historique en pays mossi. J. SOC. AFR. 35 (1965), pp. 11-66.

9,449 PROST, A. Notes sur l'origine des Mossi. BULL. IFAN 15 (1953), pp. 1333-1338.

9,450 PROST, R. P. A. Notes sur les Boussansé. BULL. IFAN 7 (1945), pp. 47-53.

9,451 TIENDREBEOGO, Y. Histoire traditionnelle des Mossi de Ouagadougou. J. SOC. AFR. 33 (1963), pp. 7-46.

See also 5358.

Language

9,452 CUENOT, R. P. J. Essai de grammaire bobo-oulé (Dialecte de Massala). BULL. IFAN 14 (1952), pp. 996-1045.

9,453 CUENOT, R. P. J. Note sur les noms donnés aux "Bobo-Oulé," d'aprés la note de M. G. Le Moal. BULL. IFAN, Série B: Sciences humaines 20 (1958), pp. 635-640.

9,454 GIRAULT, R. P. L. Note sur la particule postverbale na en dagara. BULL. IFAN 26 (1964), pp. 499-504.

9,455 JAQUINOD, R. P. F. and PROST, A. La langue des Bô ou Bôkâ. BULL. IFAN, Série B: Sciences humaines 20 (1958), pp. 623-635.

9,456 MANESSY, G. Le bwamu et ses dialectes. BULL. IFAN 23 (1961), pp. 119-178.

9,457 NICOLAS, F. J. Onomastique personnelle des L'éla de la Haute-Volta. BULL. IFAN 15 (1953), pp. 818-847.

9,458 NICOLAS, F. J. Un texte des L'ela de la Haute-Volta (A.O.F.). AFR. UND UB. 36 (1951-1952), pp. 163-172.

9,459 PROST, R. P. A. Quelques notes sur le Don (Samogho). BULL. IFAN, Série B: Sciences humaines 20 (1958), pp. 612-623.

9,460 ZWERNEMANN, J. Notizen über das Verbum des Nuna. AFR. UND UB. 45 (1961-1962), pp. 258-271.

9,461 ZWERNEMANN, J. Personennamen der Kassena. AFR. UND UB. 47 (1964), pp. 133-142.

9,462 ZWERNEMANN, J. Remarques sur la structure classificatoire et sur une ancienne classe nominale du lyélé. BULL. IFAN, Série B: Sciences humaines 20 (1958), pp. 215-224.

9,463 ZWERNEMANN, J. Untersuchungen zur Sprache der Kasena. AFR. UND UB. 41 (1957), pp. 3-26, 97-116.

9,464 ZWERNEMANN, J. Zum Bedeutungsinhalt soziologischer und religiöser Termini in einigen Gur-Sprachen. AFR. UND UB. 48 (1964-1965), pp. 284-288.

See also 9431.

Religion

9,465 SKINNER, E. P. Christianity and Islam among the Mossi. AMER. ANTHR. 60 (1958), pp. 1102-1119.

See also 10767.

Sociology

9,466 MOAL, G. LE. Note sur les populations Bobo. BULL. IFAN 19 (1957), pp. 418-430.

9,467 SAVONNET, G. Un système de culture perfectionnée, pratiqué par les Bwaba-Bobo-Oulé de la région de Houndé (Haute-Volta). BULL. IFAN 21 (1959), pp. 425-458.

9,468 SKINNER, E. P. Labour migration and its relationship to socio-cultural change in Mossi society. AFRICA 30 (1960), pp. 375-399.

See also 10856.

DAHOMEY

Agriculture

9,469 ADANDE, A. Regard retrospectif sur l'économie africaine et perspective de développement agricole au Dahomey. ET. DAHOM. N.S. 1 (1963-1964), pp. 7-16.

9,470 BERNARD, M. Le cocotier dans le golfe du Bénin. ET. DAHOM. 1 (1948), pp. 20-46.

9,471 CROZON, H. Le tabac au Dahomey: Historique et culture actuelle. ET. DAHOM. 4 (1950), pp. 23-27.

9,472 DAGBA, E. Une étude sur le maïs dans la region d'Allada. ET. DAHOM. N.S. 1 (1963-1964), pp. 91-100.

9,473 IBRAHIM, S. Technique simple d'etablissement des programmes agricoles pluriannuels au Dahomey. ET. DAHOM. N.S. 4 (1965), pp. 119-138.

9,474 JESEL. Le maïs au Dahomey. ET. DAHOM. 8 (1952), pp. 5-18.

9,475 LAFIA KOTTO, S. L'expérience chinoise de la culture de riz et sa possible application au Dahomey. ET. DAHOM. N.S. 2 (1964), pp. 5-19.

9,476 MENSAH, M. Problèmes du développement de l'agriculture dahoméenne. ET. DAHOM. N.S. 1 (1963-1964), pp. 59-78.

9,477 PISSARD, R. Ahikun-Yovo (Le haricot du blanc). ET. DAHOM. 1 (1948), pp. 56-86.

Anthropology

9,478 BEART, C. Adolescence. PRESENCE AFR. 8 (1950), pp. 261-269.

9,479 BENNETT, A. L. Ethnographical notes on the Fang. FRAI 29 (1899), pp. 66-98.

9,480 BERNOLLES, J. Un mythe nago de Dassa-Zoumé (Etude morphologique et critique). ET. DAHOM. N.S. 2 (1964), pp. 33-49.

9,481 BERNOLLES, J. Note sur le cycle végétatif et humain des danses en pays Dompago. ET. DAHOM. N.S. 3 (1964), pp. 91-105.

9,482 BERNOLLES, J. Note sur les enfants anormaux dans le Nord du Dahomey. ET. DAHOM. N.S. 5 (1965), pp. 51-67.

9,483 BERNOLLES, J. Première étude sur les rites et danses funéraires des Pila-Pila de Béléfoungou, arrondissement de Djougou (Dahomey). ET. DAHOM. N.S. 1 (1963-1964), pp. 125-134.

9,484 BERTHO, J. La science du destin au Dahomey. AFRICA 9 (1936), pp. 359-378.

9,485 BOHANNAN, L. Dahomean marriage: a revaluation. AFRICA 19 (1949), pp. 273-287.

9,486 BURTON, R. F. Les Coutumes Royales d'Abomey. ET. DAHOM. 4 (1950), pp. 61-69.

9,487 GANI, O. Notes sur les coutumes funéraires des Pila. ET. DAHOM. 4 (1950), pp. 13-21.

9,488 GANI, O. Varun ou la Grotte vénérée des Monts Tanika-Koko Dör. ET. DAHOM. N.S. 1 (1963-1964), pp. 135-136.

9,489 HAZOUME, P. L'âme du Dahoméen animiste révélée par sa religion. PRESENCE AFR. N.S. 14-15 (1957), pp. 233-251.

9,490 HERSKOVITS, M. J. A note on 'woman marriage' in Dahomey. AFRICA 10 (1937), pp. 335-341.

9,491 HERSKOVITS, M. J. Some aspects of Dahomean ethnology. AFRICA 5 (1932), pp. 266-296.

9,492 M., P. Note sur les Kwayaribè (Nord-Dahomey). ET. DAHOM. 1 (1948), pp. 87-91.

9,493 MARIN, J. Etude des moyens de Pêche dans la basse et moyenne vallée de l'Ouémé. ET. DAHOM. 16 (1956), pp. 7-20.

9,494 MAUPOIL, B. Contribution a l'étude de l'origine musulmane de la géomancie dans le Bas-Dahomey. J. SOC. AFR. 13 (1943), pp. 1-94.

9,495 MERCIER, P. Le consentment au mariage et son évolution chez les Betammadibe. AFRICA 20 (1950), pp. 219-227; English summary, p. 227.

9,496 MERCIER, P. L'habitat et l'occupation de la terre chez les Somba. BULL. IFAN 15 (1953), pp. 798-817.

9,497 MERCIER, P. L'habitation à étage dans l'Atakora. ET. DAHOM. 11 (1954), pp. 29-79.

9,498 MERCIER, P. The social role of circumcision among the Besorube. AMER. ANTHR. 53 (1951), pp. 326-337.

9,499 MERLO, C. Aspects de l'activité fétichiste. BULL. IFAN 12 (1950), pp. 1155-1166.

9,500 MERLO, C. Hiérarchie fétichiste de Ouidah. BULL. IFAN 2 (1940), pp. 1-84.

9,501 MOULERO, R. P. Histoire et légende de Chabé (Savè). ET. DAHOM. N.S. 2 (1964), pp. 51-92.

9,502 PALAU-MARTI, M. Notes sur les rois de Daṣa. J. SOC. AFR. 27 (1957), pp. 197-209.

9,503 PARRINDER, G. Yoruba-speaking peoples in Dahomey. AFRICA 17 (1947), pp. 122-129.

9,504 PERSON, Y. Brève note sur les Logba et leurs classes d'âge (Dompago, Cercle de Djougou). ET. DAHOM. 17 (1956), pp. 35-49.

9,505 PERSON, Y. Esquisse sociale et historique des Gbazâtfe de Sämle (Semere) (Cercle de Djougou). BULL. IFAN 18 (1956), pp. 202-227.

9,506 PERSON, Y. Note sur les Nyantruku. ET. DAHOM. 16 (1956), pp. 21-45.

9,507 PERSON, Y. Notes sur les Baseda (Bassila, Cercle de Djougou). ET. DAHOM. 15 (1956), pp. 35-68.

9,508 PERSON, Y. Première esquisse du peuple Biyôbè (Soruba, cercles de Djougou et Lama-kara). BULL. IFAN, Série B: Sciences humaines 17 (1955), pp. 499-524.

9,509 POGNON, A. Le problème Popo. ET. DAHOM. 13 (1955), pp. 13-14.

9,510 RENAUD, le Ct. and AKINDELE, A. La collectivité actuelle chez les Goun du royaume de Porto-Novo. BULL. IFAN 15 (1953), pp. 1690-1709.

9,511 ROUGET, G. Une chante-fable d'un signe divinatoire (Dahomey). J. AFR. LANGS. 1 (1962), pp. 273-292.

9,512 SILVA, G. DA. La mythe du Fa et ses dérivés patronymiques. ET. DAHOM. N.S. 1 (1963-1964), pp. 115-124.

9,513 TEREAU and HUTTEL. Monographie du Hollidgé. ET. DAHOM. 2 (1949), pp. 59-72; 3 (1950), pp. 7-37.

9,514 TIDJANI, A. S. Notes sur le mariage au Dahomey. ET. DAHOM. 6 (1951), pp. 27-107; 7 (1952), pp. 5-79.

9,515 TIDJANI, A. S. Un procédé de divination au Dahomey: la gourde-pendule. BULL. IFAN 5 (1943), pp. 122-135.

9,516 TIDJANI, A. S. Rituels. PRESENCE AFR. 8 (1950), pp. 297-305.

9,517 VERGER, P. Le culte des Vodoun d'Abomey aurait-il été apporté à Saint-Louis de Maranhon par la mère du roi Ghézo? ET. DAHOM. 8 (1952), pp. 19-24.

9,518 VERGER, P. Rôle joué par l'état d'hébétude au cours de l'initiation des novices aux Cultes des Orisha et Vodun. BULL. IFAN 16 (1954), pp. 322-340.

9,519 VERGER, P. Une sortie de Iyawo dans un village Nago au Dahomey. ET. DAHOM. 6 (1951), pp. 11-26.

9,520 WESTERMANN, D. The chamelion and the sun-god Lisa on the West African Slave Coast. CUSTOM IS KING: ESSAYS...TO R. R. MAPETT, 1936, pp. 143-153.

9,521 Note sur les Pila-Pila et les Taneka. ET. DAHOM. 3 (1950), pp. 39-71.

9,522 A study of the fetish convents in Dahomey. GOLD COAST REV. 5 (1929), pp. 118-124.

See also 9309, 9310, 9323, 10025.

Art

9,523 ADANDE, A. Protection et développement de l'artisanat d'art au Dahomey. ET. DAHOM. N.S. 2 (1964), pp. 93-100.

9,524 BEIER, U. The Bochio: a little known type of African carving. BO 3 (1958), pp. 28-31.

9,525 CRUZ, C. DA. Les bois de construction dans le cercle de Porto-Novo. ET. DAHOM. 8 (1952), pp. 25-56.

9,526 CRUZ, C. DA. Les instruments de musique dans le Bas-Dahomey (Populations Fon, Adja, Kotafon, Péda, Aïzo). ET. DAHOM. 12 (1954), pp. 3-79.

9,527 DAVIES, O. Notes sur la préhistoire du Dahomey. ET. DAHOM. 17 (1956), pp. 3-8.

9,528 KARL, E. Les Récades: témoins d'une civilisation. ET. DAHOM. N.S. 1 (1963-1964), pp. 107-113.

9,529 LOMBARD, J. Aperçu sur la technologie et l'artisanat Bariba. ET. DAHOM. 18 (1957), pp. 5-60.

9,530 MERCIER, P. Images de l'art animalier au Dahomey. ET. DAHOM. 5 (1951), pp. 93-103.

9,531 ROUGET, G. Musique vodũ (Dahomey). CONG. INT. SC. ANTH. ET ETHN. 6, no. ii (1960), pp. 121-122.

9,532 Le Musée historique d'Abomey. ET. DAHOM. 22 (1959), pp. 5-40.

Biography

9,533 Notice biographique sur Edouard Dunglas. ET. DAHOM. 19 (1957), pp. 5-6.

9,534 SURET-CANALE, J. Un pionnier méconnu du mouvement démocratique et national en Afrique: Louis Hunkanrin. ET. DAHOM. N.S. 3 (1964), pp. 5-30.

Economics

9,535 C., J. Situation économique du Dahomey. ZAIRE 8 (1954), pp. 641-642.

9,536 IBRAHIM, S. Note sur les méthodes de projections utilisées dans la planification économique et sociale au Dahomey. ET. DAHOM. N.S. 3 (1964), pp. 107-119.

9,537 LOMBARD, J. Les bases traditionnelles de l'économie rurale bariba et ses fondements nouveaux. Conclusions à une enquête effectuée dans la région de Bembereke (Haut-Dahomey). BULL. IFAN 23 (1961), pp. 179-242.

9,538 PONOUKOUN, K. B. G. La vie d'un militant syndicaliste. PRESENCE AFR. 13 (1952), pp. 355-358.

9,539 TARDITS, C. Développement du régime d'appropriation privée des terres de la palmeraie du Sud-Dahomey. AFR. AGRARIAN SYSTEMS, 1963, pp. 297-313.

9,540 VERGER, P. and BASTIDE, R. Les réseaux des marchés Nago (Dahomey). NISER 6 (1958), pp. 208-219.

9,541 Le téléphone automatique au Dahomey. ZAIRE 7 (1953), p. 76.

Education

9,542 TARDITS, C. Réflexions sur le problème de la scolarisation des filles au Dahomey. CAH. ET. AFR. 3 (1962), pp. 266-281.

Geography

9,543 GUILCHER, A. La région côtière du Bas-Dahomey occidental. Etude de géographie physique et humaine appliquée. BULL. IFAN 21 (1959), pp. 357-424.

9,544 LOMBARD, J. Cotonou, ville africaine. ET. DAHOM. 10 (1953), pp. 3-210.

9,545 REPIN. Voyage au Dahomey. ET. DAHOM. 3 (1950), pp. 89-95.

9,546 TUAL. Deux notes de la Mission Géographique. ET. DAHOM. 11 (1954), pp. 21-27.

Government

9,547 C., J. La famille royale du Dahomey. ZAIRE 7 (1953), pp. 528-529.

9,548 DIOP, D. M. Le congrès de Cotonou. Interview de M. Bertin Borna. PRESENCE AFR. N.S. 20 (1958), pp. 117-119.

9,549 LOMBARD, J. Un système politique traditionnel de type féodal: les Bariba du Nord-Dahomey. Aperçu sur l'organisation sociale et le pouvoir central. BULL. IFAN 19 (1957), pp. 464-506.

9,550 LOMBARD, J. La vie politique dans une ancienne société de type féodal: les Bariba du Dahomey. CAH. ET. AFR. 1 (1960), pp. 5-45.

9,551 Congrès du P.R.A. [Cotonou, July, 1958]. PRESENCE AFR. N.S. 20 (1958), pp. 134-135.

9,552 Le Dahomey et Monseigneur Steinmetz. ZAIRE 6 (1952), pp. 636-637.

History

9,553 AGUESSY, C. Esclavage, colonisation et tradition au Dahomey (sud). PRESENCE AFR. N.S. 6 (1956), pp. 58-86.

9,554 BALLARD, J. A. Les incidents de 1923 à Porto-Novo: la politique a l'époque coloniale. ET. DAHOM. N.S. 5 (1965), pp. 69-87.

9,555 BALLARD, J. A. The Porto Novo incidents of 1923: politics in the colonial era. ODU 2, no. 1 (1965), pp. 52-75.

9,556 COISSY, A. L'arrivée des Alladahonou à Houawé. ET. DAHOM. 13 (1955), pp. 33-34.

9,557 COISSY, A. Un règne de femme dans l'ancien royaume d'Abomey. ET. DAHOM. 2 (1949), pp. 5-8.

9,558 COLLERY, M. Origine historique des Cantons de la Subdivision d'Athiènné. ET. DAHOM. 8 (1952), pp. 89-108.

9,559 COQUERY, C. La blocus de Whydah (1876-1877) et la rivalité franco-anglaise au Dahomey. CAH. ET. AFR. 2 (1962), pp. 373-419.

9,560 CORNEVIN, R. A propos de l'histoire du Dahomey. ET. DAHOM. N.S. 3 (1964), pp. 123-125.

9,561 CORNEVIN, R. Au sujet des Bazantché ou Gbazantché de Sémeré (Cercle de Djougou-Dahomey). BULL. IFAN 24 (1962), pp. 627-630.

9,562 CORNEVIN, R. Les divers épisodes de la lutte contre le royaume d'Abomey (1887-1894). REV. FRANC. HIST. OUTRE-MER 47 (1960), pp. 161-212.

9,563 CORREIA, P. As Aspiraçoes dos Portugueses do Daomé. PORT. EM AFR. 11 (1954), pp. 87-92.

9,564 DUNGLAS, E. Contribution a l'histoire du Moyen-Dahomey (Royaumes d'Abomey, de Ketou et de Ouidah). ET. DAHOM. 19 (1957), pp. 11-185; 20 (1957), pp. 3-152; 21 (1958), pp. 7-116.

9,565 ELLINGWORTH, P. Christianity and politics in Dahomey, 1843-1867. J. AFR. HIST. 5 (1964), pp. 209-220.

9,566 GANIER, G. Les rivalités franco-anglaise et franco-allemande de 1894-1898, dernière phase de la course au Niger: la mission Ganier dans le Haut Dahomey 1897-1898. REV. FRANC. HIST. OUTRE-MER 49 (1962), pp. 181-261.

9,567 LEFAIVRE, H. Dictateurs noirs. Les derniers rois du Dahomey. RHCF 30 (1937), pp. 25-76.

9,568 LOPES, E. C. O Passado Português no Daomé. PORT. EM AFR. 2 (1945), pp. 105-110.

9,569 MAUPOIL, B. De Haïti au Dahomey. BULL. IFAN 2 (1940), pp. 423-430.

9,570 MONDJANNAGNI, A. Quelques aspects historiques, economiques et politiques de la frontière Dahomey, Nigeria. ET. DAHOM. N.S. 1 (1963-1964), pp. 17-57.

9,571 MOULERO, R. P. Histoire des Wémènous ou Dékanmènous. ET. DAHOM. N.S. 3 (1964), pp. 51-76.

9,572 MOULERO, T. Conquête de Kétou par Glèlè et Conquête d'Abomey par la France. ET. DAHOM. N.S. 4 (1965), pp. 61-68.

9,573 MOULERO, T. Guézo ou Guédizo Massigbé. ET. DAHOM. N.S. 4 (1965), pp. 51-59.

9,574 NEWBURY, C. C. An early enquiry into slavery and captivity in Dahomey. ZAIRE 14 (1960), pp. 53-67.

9,575 NEWBURY, C. W. A note on the Abomey protectorate. AFRICA 29 (1959), pp. 146-154.

9,576 NORRIS, R. Voyage à la Cour de Bossa-Ahadée, roi de Dahomé. ET. DAHOM. 14 (1955), pp. 67-84.

9,577 PALAU-MARTI, M. Note à propos d'un ancien récit de voyage au Dahomey (1797). REV. FRANC. HIST. OUTRE-MER 50 (1963), pp. 53-63.

9,578 PERSON, Y. Réponse de Y. Person [à R. Cornevin]. BULL. IFAN 24 (1962), pp. 631-632.

9,579 SOSSOUHOUNTO, F. Les anciens rois de la dynastie d'Abomey. Essai généalogique et historique. ET. DAHOM. 13 (1955), pp. 25-30.

9,580 SOUZA, N. F. DE. Contribution à l'histoire de la famille de Souza. ET. DAHOM. 13 (1955), pp. 17-21.

9,581 [TIDJANI, A. S.] Un exemple d'émigration. La tribu des Ouin-Vi, Aïnon-Vi ou Adikoun-Vi de Cove. BULL. IFAN 22 (1960), pp. 514-530.

9,582 VERGER, P. Le Fort Portugais de Ouidah. ET. DAHOM. N.S. 4 (1965), pp. 5-50; N.S. 5 (1965), pp. 5-50.

9,583 WALDMAN, L. K. An unnoticed aspect of Archibald Dalzel's the history of Dahomey. J. AFR. HIST. 6 (1965), pp. 185-192.

9,584 ZOHONCON, C. A propos de l'histoire de Cotonou. ET. DAHOM. 13 (1955), pp. 7-9.

9,585 L'histoire dahoméenne de la fin du XIXe siècle a travers les textes. ET. DAHOM. 9 (1953), pp. 5-156.

See also 9238, 11758, 11802.

Language. Literature

Language

9,586 BEAUDET, M. et al. Origine des noms des villages, by M. Beaudet, G. Mouleres, B. Gbaguidi, M. Bartel. ET. DAHOM. 8 (1952), pp. 58-88.

9,587 BERTHO, J. Quatre dialectes mandé du Nord-Dahomey et de la Nigeria anglaise. BULL. IFAN 13 (1951), pp. 1265-1271.

9,588 BERTHO, J. Trois îlots linguistiques du Moyen-Dahomey. Le Tshummbuli, le Bazantché et le Basila. BULL. IFAN 13 (1951), pp. 872-892.

9,589 COMHAIRE-SYLVAIN, S. and J. COMHAIRE-SYLVAIN. Survivances africaines dans le vocabulaire religieux d'Haïti. ET. DAHOM. 14 (1955), pp. 3-20.

9,590 CRUZ, C. DA. Essai de petit vocabulaire Français-Fongbé. ET. DAHOM. 11 (1954), pp. 15-19.

9,591 CRUZ, C. DA. Petit recueil des pseudonymes (population Fon, région d'Abomey). ET. DAHOM. 15 (1956), pp. 3-34.

9,592 FUNKE, E. Die Sprachverhältnisse in Sugu. Dahome (Franz. Westafrika). AFR. UND UB. 5 (1914-1915), pp. 257-269.

9,593 MERCIER, P. Vocabulaire de quelques langues du Nord-Dahomey. ET. DAHOM. 2 (1949), pp. 73-83.

9,594 ROUGET, G. Le problème du 'ton moyen' en Gü. J. AFR. LANGS. 2 (1963), pp. 218-221.

9,595 A propos de l'etymologie d'Agoué. ET. DAHOM. 16 (1956), pp. 3-6.

Literature

9,596 ACOGNY, T. Souvenir du pays. PRESENCE AFR. 6 (1949), pp. 111-112.

9,597 BHELY-QUENUM, O. Le chant du lac. PRESENCE AFR. N.S. 49 (1964), pp. 201-211.

9,598 COYSSI, A. La honte plus meurtrière que le couteau. PRESENCE AFR. 3 (1948), pp. 451-459.

9,599 JOACHIM, P. A David Diop [poème]. PRESENCE AFR. N.S. 52 (1964), pp. 167-168.

9,600 OLOGOUDOU, E. La Flambée. PRESENCE AFR. N.S. 52 (1964), pp. 169.

Religion

9,601 BASTIDE, R. Réflexions sans titre autour d'une des formes de la spiritualité africaine. PRESENCE AFR. N.S. 18-19 (1958), pp. 9-16.

9,602 CORREIA, P. S. João Baptista de Ajudá. PORT. EM AFR. 11 (1954), pp. 273-280.

9,603 HAZOUME, P. La révolte des Prêtres. PRESENCE AFR. N.S. 8-10 (1956), pp. 29-42.

Science

9,604 AMOUSSOUGA, P. Etat de l'entomologie médicale et vétérinaire au Dahomey. ET. DAHOM. N.S. 4 (1965), pp. 99-117.

9,605 OLORY-TOGBE, G. La contribution de la thèse de M. Slansky à la connaissance des substances utiles du Bassin sedimentaire Côtier du Dahomey. ET. DAHOM. N.S. 1 (1963-1964), pp. 79-90.

See also 9377.

Sociology

9,606 ADANDE, A. Le maïs et ses usages dans le Bas-Dahomey. BULL. IFAN 15 (1953), pp. 220-282.

9,607 BRASSEUR, G. Un type d'habitat au Bas-Dahomey. BULL. IFAN 14 (1952), pp. 669-676.

9,608 CRUZ, C. DA. Notes sur l'habitat dans le Cercle de Porto-Novo (Dahomey). ET. DAHOM. 11 (1954), pp. 4-14.

9,609 GRIVOT, R. La pêche chez les Pedah du lac Ahémé. BULL. IFAN 11 (1949), pp. 106-128.

9,610 LOMBARD, J. Cotonou, ville africaine. Tendances évolutives et réaction des coutumes traditionnelles. BULL. IFAN 16 (1954), pp. 341-377.

9,611 LOMBARD, J. Les moyens de controle social dans l'ancien Dahomey: survivances actuelles et formes nouvelles. WAISER 5 (1956), pp. 120-133.

9,612 LOMBARD, J. Le problème des migrations locales, leur rôle dans les changements d'une société en transition (Dahomey). BULL. IFAN 22 (1960), pp. 455-466.

9,613 MERCIER, P. L'affaiblissement des processus d'intégration dans des sociétés en changement. BULL. IFAN 16 (1954), pp. 143-166.

9,614 MERCIER, P. Mouvements de population dans les traditions des Bêtâmmaribè. ET. DAHOM. 1 (1948), pp. 47-55.

9,615 MERCIER, P. Travail et service public dans l'ancien Dahomey. PRESENCE AFR. 13 (1952), pp. 84-91.

9,616 VIGNON, R. Etude sociologique d'une région agricole de Sakété. ET. DAHOM. N.S. 3 (1964), pp. 77-89.

NIGER

Anthropology

9,617 CASTINEL, J. Le mariage et la mort dans la région du Yanga (cercle de Fada N'Gourma, colonie du Niger). BULL. IFAN 7 (1945), pp. 148-155.

9,618 DUPIRE, M. Contribution à l'étude des marques de propriété du bétail chez les pasteurs peuls. J. SOC. AFR. 24 (1954), pp. 123-143.

9,619 GRALL, Lieutenant. Le secteur nord du Cercle de Gouré. BULL. IFAN 7 (1945), pp. 1-46.

9,620 GRIAULE, M. L'arche du monde chez les populations nigériennes. J. SOC. AFR. 18 (1948), pp. 117-126.

9,621 JOUBERT, Lieutenant. Les coutumes et le droit chez les Kel Tadélé. BULL. IFAN 1 (1939), pp. 245-281.

9,622 ROUCH, J. Banghawi, chasse à l'Hippopotame au harpon par les pêcheurs sorko du Moyen-Niger. BULL. IFAN 10 (1948), pp. 361-377.

9,623 ROUCH, J. Culte des génies chez les Sonray. J. SOC. AFR. 15 (1945), pp. 15-32.

Art

9,624 BOUESNARD, L. and MAUNY, R. Gravures rupestres et sites néolithiques des abords est de l'Aïr. BULL. IFAN 24 (1962), pp. 1-11.

9,625 CHEVALIER, A. Sur deux outils en pierre polie a manche avec étranglement trouvés près de Djado (Sahara Central). J. SOC. AFR. 3 (1933), pp. 73-75.

9,626 ECHARD, N. Note sur les forgerons de l'Ader (Pays Hausa, République du Niger). J. SOC. AFR. 35 (1965), pp. 353-372.

9,627 HUARD, P. Nouvelles gravures rupestres du Djado, de l'Afafi et du Tibesti. BULL. IFAN 19 (1957), pp. 184-223.

9,628 HUARD, P. Répertoire des stations rupestres du Sahara oriental français (Confins Nigéro-Tchadiens-Tibesti-Borkou-Ennedi). J. SOC. AFR. 23 (1953), pp. 43-76.

9,629 KELLEY, H. Collections africaines du départment de Préhistoire exotique du Musée d'ethnographie du Trocadéro. 1—Harpons, objets en os travaillé et silex taillés de Taferjit et Tamaya Mellet (Sahara nigérien). J. SOC. AFR. 4 (1934), pp. 135-143.

9,630 LHOTE, H. and HUARD, P. Gravures rupestres de l'Aïr. BULL. IFAN 27 (1965), pp. 445-478.

9,631 MAUNY, R. Etat actuel de nos connaissances sur la préhistoire de la colonie du Niger. BULL. IFAN 11 (1949), pp. 141-158.

9,632 ROUCH, J. Gravures rupestres de Kourki (Niger). BULL. IFAN 11 (1949), pp. 340-353.

9,633 VEDY, J. Contribution à l'inventaire de la station rupestre de Dao Timni-Woro-Yat (Niger). BULL. IFAN 24 (1962), pp. 325-382.

9,634 VEDY, J. La station rupestre de Ziri-Betidai (Niger). BULL. IFAN 23 (1961), pp. 456-475.

See also 11225.

Economics

9,635 GERY, R. Une industrie autochtone nigérienne: les sauniers du Manga. BULL. IFAN 14 (1952), pp. 309-320.

9,636 GRANDIN, Captain. Notes sur l'industrie et le commerce du sel au Kawar et en Agram. BULL. IFAN 13 (1951), pp. 488-533.

9,637 Financement de la production agricole au Niger francais. ZAIRE 9 (1955), p. 305.

Geography

9,638 DRESCH, J. Les transformations du Sahel Nigérien. ACTA GEOGRAPHICA 30 (1959), pp. 3-12.

9,639 GAUTIER, E. F. The people of the Veil: a review. GEOG. REV. 18 (1928), pp. 478-484.

9,640 HILL, P. By air to Niamey. UNIVERSITAS 5 (1962), pp. 41-42.

9,641 ROBIN, J. Description de la province de Dosso. BULL. IFAN 9 (1947), pp. 56-98.

See also 13535.

History

9,642 CHAILLEY, Commandant. La mission du Haut-Soudan et le drame de Zinder (II). BULL. IFAN, Série B: Sciences humaines 17 (1955), pp. 1-58.

9,643 LE SOURD, M. Tarikh el Kawar. BULL. IFAN 8 (1946), pp. 1-54.

9,644 PERIE, J. Notes historiques sur la région de Maradi (Niger). BULL. IFAN 1 (1939), pp. 377-400.

9,645 PERIE, J. and SELLIER, M. Histoire des populations du cercle de Dosso (Niger). BULL. IFAN 12 (1950), pp. 1015-1074.

9,646 ROBIN, M. Note sur les premières populations de la région de Dosso (Niger). BULL. IFAN 1 (1939), pp. 401-404.

9,647 URVOY, Y. Chroniques d'Agadès. J. SOC. AFR. 4 (1934), pp. 145-177.

Language. Literature

Language

9,648 DUPIRE, M. and TRESSAN, M. DE. Devinettes peules et bororo. AFRICA 25 (1955), pp. 375-391; English summary, pp. 391-392.

9,649 GAUDICHE, Le capitaine. La langue boudouma. J. SOC. AFR. 8 (1938), pp. 11-32.

Literature

9,650 TIROLIEN, G. Vive Bélisaire! PRESENCE AFR. N.S. 51 (1964), pp. 104-120.

Law

9,651 DAVEAU, S. and TOUPET, C. Anciens terroirs Gangara. BULL. IFAN 25 (1963), pp. 193-214.

9,652 MAUGHAM, R. C. F. Native land tenure in the Timbuktu districts. J. AFR. SOC. 23 (1924), pp. 125-130.

See also 9621.

Religion

9,653 LEROUX, H. Animisme et Islam dans la subdivision de Maradi (Niger). BULL. IFAN 10 (1948), pp. 595-697.

9,654 RAULIN, H. Un aspect historique des rapports de l'anisme et de l'Islam au Niger. J. SOC. AFR. 32 (1962), pp. 249-274.

Science

9,655 COLLIER, F. S. A shooting trip to Termitt. NIGERIAN FIELD 7 (1938), pp. 113-119.

9,656 DUPIRE, M. Pharmacopée Peule du Niger et du Cameroun. BULL. IFAN 19 (1957), pp. 382-417.

9,657 GRIAULE, M. Tanières de crocodiles dans les falaises nigériennes. J. SOC. AFR. 11 (1941), pp. 187-192.

9,658 LE COEUR, C. and M. LE COEUR. Initiation a l'hygiène et a la morale de l'alimentation chez les Djerma et les Peuls de Niamey. BULL. IFAN 8 (1946), pp. 164-180.

9,659 ROUSSELOT, R. Notes sur la faune ornithologique des cercles de Maradi et de Tanout (Niger français). BULL. IFAN 9 (1947), pp. 99-137.

Sociology

9,660 MEILLASSOUX, C. The social structure of modern Bamako. AFRICA 35 (1965), pp. 125-142.

9,661 NICOLAS, F. Notes sur la société et l'état chez les Twareg du Dinnik (Iullemeden de l'Est). BULL. IFAN 1 (1939), pp. 579-586.

GAMBIA

Agriculture

9,662 JARRETT, H. R. The strange farmers of the Gambia. GEOG. REV. 39 (1949), pp. 649-657.

Anthropology

9,663 AMES, D. Belief in 'witches' among the rural Wolof of the Gambia. AFRICA 29 (1959), pp. 263-273.

See also 8497.

Archaeology

9,664 OZANNE, P. The Anglo-Gambian stone circles expedition. UNIV. GHANA RES. REV. 1 (1965), no. 2, pp. 32-36.

9,665 PARKER, H. Stone circles in Gambia. JRAI 53 (1923), pp. 173-228.

Biography

See 11349.

Economics

See 8538.

Education

9,666 Community development in the Gambia. CORONA 1, no. 9 (1949), p. 32.

Geography

9,667 DIKSHIT, R. D. The river-state of Gambia. AFR. QUART. 4, no. iv (1965), pp. 229-239.

9,668 JARRETT, H. R. Population and settlement in the Gambia. GEOG. REV. 38 (1948), pp. 633-636.

See also 8564.

Government. Politics. Administration

9,669 FOON, M. Operation Ping-pong to beat votes fiddlers. J. AFR. ADM. 13 (1961), pp. 35-37.

9,670 GRAY, A. Constitutional advances. AFR. AFFAIRS 59 (1960), pp. 7-9.

9,671 KEITH-LUCAS, B. Sierra Leone and the Gambia. WHAT ARE THE PROBLEMS OF PARL. GOVT. IN W. AFR.?, 1958, pp. 19-26.

9,672 ORDE, M. H. Development of local government in rural areas in the Gambia. J. LOCAL ADM. OV. 4 (1965), pp. 51-59.

9,673 PRICE, J. H. The influence of women in Gambian politics. AFR. WOMEN 4 (1960), pp. 11-12.

9,674 PRICE, J. H. Some notes on the influence of women in Gambian politics. NISER 6 (1958), pp. 151-158.

9,675 YOUNG, F. Report on the Gambia question. ROY. COL. INST. PROC. 7 (1875-1876), pp. 68-85.

9,676 Elections en Gambie. ZAIRE 6 (1952), pp. 190-191.

History

9,677 CATALA, R. La question de l'échange de la Gambie britannique contre les comptoirs français du Golfe de Guinée de 1866 a 1876. REV. HIST. COL. 35 (1948), pp. 114-137.

9,678 GRAY, Sir J. Eighteenth-century Gambia journey. AFR. AFFAIRS 58 (1959), pp. 65-74.

9,679 GREENWOOD, O. Hannak Kilham's plan. SIERRA L. BULL. REL. 4 (1962), pp. 9-22, 61-71.

9,680 H., E. Annual report on the Gambia, 1935; by E. H. J. AFR. SOC. 36 (1937), pp. 79-81.

9,681 LANGLEY, M. The Gambia: trading post to independent nation. HISTORY TODAY 15 (1965), pp. 420-425.

9,682 LY, A. Retour sur la fondation au XVIIe siècle du Comptoir français d'Albreda. BULL. IFAN 15 (1953), pp. 1262-1277.

9,683 MAHONEY, F. Notes on Mulattoes of the Gambia before the mid-nineteenth century. TR. HIST. SOC. GHANA 8 (1965), pp. 120-129.

9,684 MARTY, P. Le comptoir français d'Albréda en Gambie (1817-1826). RHCF 17 (1924), pp. 237-272.

9,685 PALMER, Sir H. R. A history of the Gambia: by J. M. Gray. J. AFR. SOC. 39 (1940), pp. 272-279.

9,686 SCUTHORN, Sir T. The Gambia: background for progress. AFR. AFFAIRS 43 (1944), pp. 10-15.

Language. Literature

9,687 PETERS, L. Six poems. BO 14 (1964), pp. 17-20.

9,688 PETERS, L. Six poems. BO 16 (1964), pp. 25-30.

9,689 PETERS, L. Wider excursions, etc. [poems]. BO 11 (1962), pp. 61-64.

9,690 WARD, I. C. A short phonetic study of Wolof (Jolof) as spoken in the Gambia and in Senegal. AFRICA 12 (1939), pp. 320-334.

See also 8650.

Law

9,691 The Gambia [alteration of judicial system]. J. AFR. LAW 8 (1964), pp. 106-109.

See also 8696.

Religion

See 9679.

Science

9,692 BALFOUR, M. Growth, nitrogen balance and histological picture of organs of rats fed on Gambian diets. MALNUTRITION IN AFRICAN WOMEN..., 1952, pp. 120-128.

9,693 BIDWELL, B. Health centre in the Gambia. AFR. WOMEN 4 (1961), pp. 30-32.

9,694 GRANT, M. W. Gambian methods of preparing flour from grain. MALNUTRITION IN AFRICAN WOMEN..., 1952, pp. 275-276.

9,695 HOPKINSON, E. Birds of the Gambia. J. AFR. SOC. 16 (1917), pp. 297-305.

9,696 HOPKINSON, E. The ducks of the Gambia. J. AFR. SOC. 35 (1936), pp. 48-52.

9,697 McGREGOR, I. A. Observations of the effect of malaria on Gambian infants and young children. MALNUTRITION IN AFRICAN MOTHERS..., 1952, pp. 92-94.

9,698 PLATT, B. S. and GRANT, M. W. Food consumption in the Gambia. MALNUTRITION IN AFRICAN WOMEN..., 1952, pp. 225-229.

9,699 PLATT, B. S. and GRANT, M. W. Results of feeding animal protein factor concentrate to Gambian school children. MALNUTRITION IN AFRICAN WOMEN..., 1952, pp. 254-261.

9,700 WALTERS, J. H. and WATERLOW, J. C. Fibrosis of the liver in Gambian children. MALNUTRITION IN AFRICAN WOMEN..., 1952, p. 142.

9,701 Demonstration of Gambian foods. MALNUTRITION OF AFRICAN WOMEN..., 1952, pp. 264-265.

Sociology

9,702 JAWARA, A. The Gambia Women's Federation. WOMEN TODAY 6 (1965), pp. 79-81.

9,703 LITTLE, K. L. The organization of communal farms in the Gambia. J. AFR. ADM. 1 (1949), pp. 76-82.

9,704 REES, J. G. Housing in a Gambia village. AFR. AFFAIRS 51 (1952), pp. 230-237.

SIERRA LEONE

General

9,705 HAIR, P. E. H. A bibliographical guide to Sierra Leone, 1460-1650. SIERRA LEONE STUD. 9 (1957), pp. 62-72.

9,706 HAIR, P. E. H. A bibliographical guide to Sierra Leone, 1650-1800. SIERRA LEONE STUD. 13 (1960), pp. 41-49.

9,707 Recent developments in African studies [in Sierra Leone]. SIERRA L. BULL. REL. 4 (1962), p. 36.

Agriculture

9,708 C., J. Politique agricole de Sierra-Leone. ZAIRE 8 (1954), p. 948.

9,709 HOPKINS, W. Agriculture in Sierra Leone. J. AFR. SOC. 14 (1914-1915), pp. 143-147.

9,710 LITTLE, L. L. The Mende rice farm and its cost. ZAIRE 5 (1951), pp. 227-273, 371-389.

9,711 TINDALL, H. D. Early introduction and cultivation of economic and ornamental plants in Sierra Leone. SIERRA LEONE STUD. 9 (1957), pp. 49-58.

9,712 Soil Conservation and Land Use in Sierra Leone [a report]. J. AFR. ADM. 4 (1952), p. 118.

See also 17671.

Anthropology

9,713 AMARA, I. B. Possession: its nature and some modes. SIERRA L. BULL. REL. 6, no. 2 (1964), pp. 1-12.

9,714 ANWYL, T. C. The Timne and other tribes of Sierra Leone. J. AFR. SOC. 16 (1916), pp. 36-51.

9,715 BANTON, M. The ethnography of the Protectorate: review article on Peoples of the Sierra Leone Protectorate by M. McCulloch]. SIERRA LEONE STUD. 4 (1955), pp. 240-249.

9,716 BASSIR, O. Marriage rites among the Aku (Yoruba) of Freetown. AFRICA 24 (1954), pp. 251-255.

9,717 BIYI, E. The Temne people and how they make their kings. J. AFR. SOC. 12 (1913), pp. 190-199.

9,718 BROWN, S. The Nomoli of Mende country. AFRICA 18 (1948), pp. 18-20.

9,719 BURROWS, D. The human leopard society of Sierra Leone. J. AFR. SOC. 13 (1914), pp. 143-151.

9,720 BUXTON, T. F. V. The Creole in West Africa. J. AFR. SOC. 12 (1913), pp. 385-394.

9,721 CROSBY, K. H. Polygamy in Mende country. AFRICA 10 (1937), pp. 249-264.

9,722 DORJAHN, V. R. The changing political system of the Temne. AFRICA 30 (1960), pp. 110-139.

9,723 DORJAHN, V. R. The organization and functions of the Ragbenle society of the Temne. AFRICA 29 (1959), pp. 156-169.

9,724 DORJAHN, V. R. Some aspects of Temne divination. SIERRA L. BULL. REL. 4 (1962), pp. 1-9.

9,725 DORJAHN, V. R. and FYFE, C. Landlord and stranger: change in tenancy relations in Sierra Leone. J. AFR. HIST. 3 (1962), pp. 391-397.

9,726 EBERL-ELBER, R. Die masken der männerbünde in Sierra Leone. ETHNOS 2 (1937), pp. 38-46.

9,727 EBERL-ELBER, R. Eine Tierfabel in der Mende-Sprache. ETHNOS 3 (1938), pp. 47-52.

9,728 FINNEGAN, R. Swears among the Limba. SIERRA L. BULL. REL. 6 (1964), pp. 8-26.

9,729 FINNEGAN, R. The traditional concept of chiefship among the Limba. SIERRA LEONE STUD. 17 (1963), pp. 241-253.

9,730 GAMBLE, D. P. The Temne family in a modern town (Lunsar) in Sierra Leone. AFRICA 33 (1963), pp. 209-226.

9,731 GRIFFITH, T. R. On the races inhabiting Sierra Leone. JRAI 16 (1887), pp. 300-310.

9,732 HARRIS, W. T. Ceremonies and stories connected with trees, rivers and hills in the Protectorate of Sierra-Leone. SIERRA LEONE STUD. 2 (1954), pp. 91-97.

9,733 HARRIS, W. T. How the Mende people first started to pray to Ngewo. SIERRA L. BULL. REL. 5 (1963), pp. 61-63.

9,734 HOFSTRA, S. Personality and differentiation in the political life of the Mendi. AFRICA 10 (1937), pp. 436-457.

9,735 HORNELL, J. String figures from Sierra Leone, Liberia and Zanzibar. JRAI 60 (1930), pp. 81-114.

9,736 INNES, G. The function of the song in Mende folktales. SIERRA LEONE LANG. REV. 4 (1965), pp. 54-63.

9,737 KILSON, M. D. DE B. Supernatural beings in Mende domeisia. SIERRA L. BULL. REL. 3 (1961), pp. 1-11.

9,738 KOROMA, M. S. and PROUDFOOT, L. Freetown morning. AFR. AFFAIRS 59 (1960), pp. 43-51.

9,739 LANGLEY, E. R. The Kono people of Sierra Leone: their clans and names. AFRICA 5 (1932), pp. 61-67.

9,740 LITTLE, K. L. The changing position of women in the Sierra Leone Protectorate. AFRICA 18 (1948), pp. 1-16.

9,741 LITTLE, K. L. Land and labour among the Mende. AFR. AFFAIRS 47 (1948), pp. 23-31.

9,742 LITTLE, K. L. Mende political institutions in transition. AFRICA 17 (1947), pp. 8-23.

9,743 LITTLE, K. L. The political function of the Poro. AFRICA 35 (1965), pp. 349-365.

9,744 LITTLE, K. L. The Poro society as an arbiter of culture. AFR. STUD. 7 (1948), pp. 1-15.

9,745 LITTLEJOHN, J. The Temne Ansasa. SIERRA LEONE STUD. 13 (1960), pp. 32-35.

9,746 LITTLEJOHN, J. Temne space. ANTHR. QUART. 36 (1963), pp. 1-17.

9,747 LOVERIDGE, A. J. The present position of the Temne chiefs of Sierra Leone. J. AFR. ADM. 9 (1957), pp. 115-120.

9,748 NDANEMA, I. The rationale of Mende swears. SIERRA L. BULL. REL. 6, no. 2 (1964), pp. 21-25.

9,749 PARSONS, R. T. Death and burial in Kono religion. SIERRA L. BULL. REL. 3 (1961), pp. 55-64; 4 (1962), pp. 34-36.

9,750 PARSONS, R. T. Kono religion and adult crises. SIERRA L. BULL. REL. 4 (1962), pp. 51-53.

9,751 PARSONS, R. T. Kono religion and preparation for adult life. SIERRA L. BULL. REL. 3 (1961), pp. 11-16.

9,752 PARSONS, R. T. Kono religion, marriage and procreation. SIERRA L. BULL. REL. 2 (1960), pp. 11-17.

9,753 PARSONS, R. T. Religion in Kono village life. SIERRA L. BULL. REL. 1 (1959), pp. 36-47.

9,754 SAWYERR, H. The dogma of super-size. SIERRA L. BULL. REL. 4 (1962), pp. 41-51; 5 (1963), pp. 1-18.

9,755 SAWYERR, H. Graveside libations in and near Freetown. SIERRA L. BULL. REL. 7 (1965), pp. 48-55.

9,756 SAWYERR, H. The Supreme God and spirits. SIERRA L. BULL. REL. 3 (1961), pp. 41-55.

9,757 SAWYERR, H. Traditional sacrificial rituals and Christian worship. SIERRA L. BULL. REL. 2 (1960), pp. 18-27.

9,758 SAWYERR, H. and SAWYERR, A. W. Disong. SIERRA L. BULL. REL. 5 (1963), pp. 47-54.

9,759 TAPPEN, N. C. Primate studies in Sierra Leone. CURRENT ANTHR. 5 (1964), pp. 339-340.

9,760 THOMAS, N. W. Who were the Manes? J. AFR. SOC. 19 (1920), pp. 176-188; 20 (1920), pp. 33-42.

9,761 TIMOTHY, E. B. The deeds of Bokari. AFR. AFFAIRS 51 (1952), pp. 61-72.

9,762 WALLIS, C. B. In the court of the native chiefs in Mendiland. J. AFR. SOC. 4 (1905), pp. 397-409.

9,763 WALLIS, C. B. The Poro of the Mendi. J. AFR. SOC. 4 (1905), pp. 183-189.

9,764 WILLANS, R. H. K. The Kounoh people. J. AFR. SOC. 8 (1909), pp. 130-144, 288-295.

9,765 WILSON, H. S. and PROUDFOOT, S. L. Changing social functions of a Creole feast. AFR. AFFAIRS 58 (1959), pp. 153-160.

Art

9,766 AKAR, J. The arts in Sierra Leone. AFR. FORUM 1 (1965), pp. 87-91.

9,767 DUNWELL, H. Stone church built at Segbwema. SIERRA LEONE STUD. 6 (1956), pp. 169-172.

9,768 LITTLEJOHN, J. The Temne house. SIERRA LEONE STUD. 14 (1960), pp. 63-79.

9,769 MARGAI, M. A. S. Music in the Protectorate of Sierra Leone. WASU 2 (1926), pp. 38-40.

Biography

9,770 LINDROTH, S. Adam Afzelius: a Swedish botanist in Sierra-Leone, 1792-96. SIERRA LEONE STUD. 4 (1955), pp. 194-207.

9,771 HAIR, P. E. H. E. W. Blyden and the C.M.S.: Freetown 1871-2. SIERRA L. BULL. REL. 4 (1962), pp. 22-28.

9,772 SCOTLAND, D. W. Notes on Bai Bureh, of 1898 fame. SIERRA LEONE STUD. 4 (1955), pp. 11-19.

9,773 MARKWEI, M. The Rev. Daniel Coker of Sierra Leone. SIERRA L. BULL. REL. 7 (1965), pp. 41-48.

9,774 EASMON, M. C. F. Paul Cuffee. SIERRA LEONE STUD. 12 (1959), pp. 196-200.

9,775 BEETHAM, T. A. A Sierra Leone missionary to Kenya [Rev. W. H. During]. SIERRA L. BULL. REL. 1 (1959), pp. 56-57.

9,776 FYFE, C. H. The life and times of John Ezzidio. SIERRA LEONE STUD. 4 (1955), pp. 213-223.

9,777 EASMON, M. C. F. Paramount Chief Bai Kur. A biographical sketch of one of Sierra Leone's oldest chiefs. SIERRA LEONE STUD. 8 (1967), pp. 194-199.

9,778 HARGREAVES, J. D. Sir Samuel Lewis and the Legislative Council. SIERRA LEONE STUD. 1 (1953), pp. 40-52.

9,779 ORR, G. B. A biographical note on the Rt. Hon. Sir Matthew Nathan (1862-1939). SIERRA LEONE STUD. 8 (1957), pp. 252-254.

9,780 RYDINGS, H. H. Prince Niambanna in England. SIERRA LEONE STUD. 8 (1957), pp. 200-208.

9,781 FENTON, J. S. Obituary: E. F. Sayers, 1889-1954. SIERRA LEONE STUD. 4 (1955), pp. 237-239.

9,782 FYFE, C. H. A. B. C. Sibthorpe: a neglected historian. SIERRA LEONE STUD. 9 (1957), pp. 99-109.

9,783 WRIGHT, E. J. The late Ernest Jenner Wright. SIERRA LEONE STUD. 6 (1956), pp. 111-112.

9,784 EASMON, M. C. F. Madam Yoko: ruler of the Mendi confederacy. SIERRA LEONE STUD. 11 (1958), pp. 165-168.

Economics

9,785 ALLDRIDGE, T. J. Sierra Leone and its undeveloped products. ROYAL COL. INST. PR. 37 (1905-1906), pp. 36-52.

9,786 BANTON, M. P. Economic development and social change in Sierra Leone. ECON. DEVELOPMENT AND CULTURAL CHANGE 2 (1953-1954), pp. 136-138.

9,787 BERESFORD-STOOKE, Sir G. Sierra Leone to-day. AFR. AFFAIRS 53 (1954), pp. 56-65.

9,788 BONO, S. Nelle risorse economiche della Sierra Leone il fundamento del suo sviluppo economico e sociale. AFRICA (Rome) 16 (1961), pp. 70-74.

9,789 BYRNE, J. Sierra Leone: trade and communications. J. AFR. SOC. 29 (1929), pp. 1-6.

9,790 CAMINO, S. W. Uno sguardo alla Sierra Leone. AFRICA (Rome) 14 (1959), pp. 75-78.

9,791 DECKER, T. This is Freetown calling. SIERRA LEONE STUD. 7 (1956), pp. 166-168.

9,792 JACK, D. T. Economic Survey. J. AFR. ADM. 11 (1959), pp. 108-109.

9,793 JARRET, H. R. Rents, roads and railways: a study of their interrelationship in Freetown. SIERRA LEONE STUD. 4 (1955), pp. 36-43.

9,794 JARRET, H. R. Rice production in Sierra Leone. MALAYAN J. TR. GEOG. 8 (1956), pp. 73-81.

9,795 PETCH, G. A. Economic planning in Sierra Leone 1945-1953. WAISER EC. 2 (1953), pp. 25-38.

9.796 REICHMAN, S. Domestic transport in Sierra Leone. SIERRA LEONE GEOG. ASSOC. BULL. 9 (1965), pp. 27-33.

9,797 VENNER, W. The Sierra Leone railway. CORONA 3 (1951), pp. 335-336.

See also 9234.

Education

9,798 GYASI-TWUM, K. Sierra Leone students leaving Fourah Bay College between 1944 and 1956. SIERRA LEONE STUD. 9 (1957), pp. 85-98.

9,799 HAIR, P. E. H. An analysis of the register of Fourah Bay College, 1827-1950. SIERRA LEONE STUD. 6 (1956), pp. 155-160.

Geography

9,800 DAVEAU, S. The Loma Mountains. SIERRA LEONE GEOG. ASSOC. BULL. 9 (1965), pp. 2-11.

9,801 EASMON, M. C. F. Freetown in 1856. SIERRA LEONE STUD. 9 (1957), p. 59.

9,802 FITZJOHN, W. H. A village in Sierra Leone. SIERRA LEONE STUD. 6 (1956), pp. 145-154.

9,803 FYFE, C. H. A view of Freetown, Sierra Leone. SIERRA LEONE STUD. 1 (1953), pp. 26-27.

9,804 GAMBLE, D. P. Kenema: a growing town in Mende country. SIERRA LEONE GEOG. ASSOC. BULL. 7 (1964), pp. 9-12.

9,805 GAMBLE, D. P. Lunsar: a mining town in Temne country. SIERRA LEONE GEOG. ASSOC. BULL. 7 (1964), pp. 13-17.

9,806 GWYNNE-JONES, D. R. G. Rubber production in Sierra Leone. SIERRA LEONE GEOG. ASSOC. BULL. 9 (1965), pp. 23-26.

9,807 JARRET, H. R. Freetown: a study in space relationships. SIERRA LEONE STUD. 2 (1954), pp. 98-108.

9,808 JARRET, H. R. Some aspects of the urban geography of Freetown, Sierra Leone. GEOG. REV. 46 (1956), pp. 334-354.

9,809 MIGEOD, F. W. H. A view of the colony of Sierra Leone. J. AFR. SOC. 25 (1925), pp. 1-9.

9,810 MITCHELL, P. K. Matotoka: a Sierra Leone chiefdom town. SIERRA LEONE STUD. 17 (1963), pp. 269-277.

9,811 MITCHELL, P. K. and SWINDELL, K. Recent changes in Sierra Leone's mineral industry. SIERRA LEONE GEOG. ASSOC. BULL. 9 (1965), pp. 12-22.

9,812 RANSON, H. The growth of Mayomba. SIERRA LEONE GEOG. ASSOC. BULL. 9 (1965), pp. 54-62.

9,813 SCOTLAND, D. W. A view of Freetown on the river Sierra-Leone. SIERRA LEONE STUD. 4 (1955), pp. 211-212.

Government. Politics. Administration

9,814 THE AFRICAN STUDIES BRANCH. A note on two recent Local Government ordinances in Sierra Leone. J. AFR. ADM. 3 (1951), pp. 94-96.

9,815 BANTON, M. P. The origins of tribal administration in Freetown. SIERRA LEONE STUD. 2 (1954), pp. 109-119.

9,816 BANTON, M. P. Tribal headmen in Freetown. J. AFR. ADM. 6 (1954), pp. 140-144.

9,817 C., J. Le premier ministère de Sierra Leone. ZAIRE 7 (1953), p. 526.

9,818 COX-GEORGE, N. A. The economic significance of grants-in-aid of Sierra Leone in the nineteenth century. SIERRA LEONE STUD. 8 (1957), pp. 237-244.

9,819 DAVIDSON, H. W. Report on the functions and finances of District Councils in Sierra Leone. J. AFR. ADM. 6 (1954), pp. 42-44.

9,820 FYFE, C. H. The administration in 1885. SIERRA LEONE STUD. 4 (1955), pp. 226-228.

9,821 FYFE, C. H. The old secretariat. SIERRA LEONE STUD. 2 (1954), p. 120.

9,822 GRAY, A. Sierra Leone advances. AFR. AFFAIRS 56 (1957), pp. 13-14.

9,823 GRAY, A. The Sierra Leone Constitutional Conference. AFR. AFFAIRS 59 (1960), p. 288.

9,824 GRAY, A. Sierra Leone independence. AFR. AFFAIRS 60 (1961), pp. 141-144.

9,825 HARGREAVES, J. D. Colonial office opinions on the constitution of 1863. SIERRA LEONE STUD. 4 (1955), pp. 2-10.

9,826 HARGREAVES, J. D. Western democracy and African society. Some reflections from Sierra Leone. INTERNAT. AFFAIRS 31 (1955), pp. 327-334.

9,827 HARGREAVES, J. D. The work of an early District Commissioner. SIERRA LEONE STUD. 4 (1955), p. 231.

9,828 HEDGES, D. M. Progress of Kambia District Council, Sierra Leone. J. AFR. ADM. 5 (1953), pp. 30-34.

9,829 KIRBY, D. Ballots in the bush. J. AFR. ADM. 9 (1957), pp. 174-182.

9,830 McDOUGALL, R. S. Sierra Leone: Report regarding the transfer of functions from the Sierra Leone Central Government to the Freetown Municipality. J. AFR. ADM. 3 (1951), pp. 49-50.

9,831 PORTER, A. T. The social background of political decision makers in Sierra Leone. SIERRA LEONE STUD. 13 (1960), pp. 2-13.

9,832 Report of the Commission of Inquiry into Disturbances in the Provinces (November 1955 to March, 1956). [Commission appointed by Governor of Sierra Leone under chairmanship of Sir Herbert Cox]. J. AFR. ADM. 9 (1957), pp. 49-54.

9,833 Statement of the Sierra Leone Government on the Report of the Commission of Inquiry into Disturbances in the Protectorate (November 1955 to March 1956). J. AFR. ADM. 9 (1957), pp. 54-55.

See also 9671, 9778.

History

9,834 ALLDRIDGE, T. J. Sierra Leone up to date. ROYAL COL. INST. PR. 40 (1908-1909), pp. 37-55.

9,835 AZEVEDO, W. L. D'. Some historical problems in the delineation of a central west Atlantic region. ANTHROPOLOGY AND AFRICA TODAY, 1962, pp. 512-538.

9,836 BLYDEN, E. W. At last Sierra Leone. AFR. SOUTH 4, no. 4 (1960), pp. 92-97.

9,837 BROOKS, G. E. Samuel Swan's letter book: an American view of Sierra Leone and the coast of Africa. SIERRA LEONE STUD. 12 (1959), pp. 245-259.

9,838 BROOKS, G. S. A view of Sierra Leone ca. 1815. SIERRA LEONE STUD. 13 (1960), pp. 24-31.

9,839 CLARKE, W. R. E. The foundation of the Luawa chiefdoms (the story of Kailondo and Ndawa). SIERRA LEONE STUD. 8 (1957), pp. 245-251.

9,840 COTAY, A. B. Sierra Leone in the post-war world. AFR. AFFAIRS 58 (1959), pp. 210-220.

9,841 COX-GEORGE, N. A. Direct taxation in the early history of Sierra-Leone. SIERRA LEONE STUD. 4 (1955), pp. 20-35.

9,842 DORJAHN, V. R. A brief history of the Temne of Yoni. SIERRA LEONE STUD. 14 (1960), pp. 80-89.

9,843 DORJAHN, V. R. and THOLLEY, A. S. A provisional history of the Limba, with special reference to Tonko Limba chiefdom. SIERRA LEONE STUD. 12 (1959), pp. 273-283.

9,844 EASMON, M. C. F. The departure of Governor Kennedy from Freetown in 1854. SIERRA LEONE STUD. 6 (1956), p. 110.

9,845 EASMON, M. C. F. Sierra Leone's connection with royalty. SIERRA LEONE STUD. 16 (1962), pp. 184-188.

9,846 FILESI, T. Sierra Leone: origini storiche ed evoluzione politica. AFRICA (Rome) 15 (1960), pp. 159-169.

9,847 FYFE, C. Four Sierra Leone recaptives. J. AFR. HIST. 2 (1961), pp. 77-85.

9,848 FYFE, C. H. European and Creole influence in the hinterland of Sierra Leone before 1896. SIERRA LEONE STUD. 6 (1956), pp. 113-123.

9,849 FYFE, C. H. A royal visit in 1860. SIERRA LEONE STUD. 12 (1959), pp. 260-272.

9,850 FYFE, C. H. The Sierra Leone press in the nineteenth century. SIERRA LEONE STUD. 8 (1967), pp. 226-236.

9,851 FYFE, C. H. Thomas Peters: history and legend. SIERRA LEONE STUD. 1 (1953), pp. 4-13.

9,852 FYFE, C. H. View of the new burial ground. SIERRA LEONE STUD. 2 (1954), pp. 85-90.

9,853 GRIFFITH, T. R. Sierra Leone—past, present, and future. ROY. COL. INST. PROC. 13 (1881-1882), pp. 56-98.

9,854 HAIR, P. E. H. A history of Sierra Leone, 1962; by Christopher Fyfe. SIERRA LEONE STUD. 17 (1963), pp. 281-296.

9,855 HALIBURTON, G. The Nova Scotia settlers of 1792. SIERRA LEONE STUD. 9 (1957), pp. 16-25.

9,856 HALL, Sir R. Nineteenth century chiefs' medals. SIERRA LEONE STUD. 12 (1959), pp. 201-210.

9,857 HALL, Sir R. A note on some early XIXth century cannon at Government House, Freetown. SIERRA LEONE STUD. 6 (1956), pp. 173-176.

9,858 HARGREAVES, J. D. The establishment of the Sierra Leone Protectorate and the insurrection of 1898. CAMB. HIST. J. 12 (1956), pp. 56-80.

9,859 HARGREAVES, J. D. The French occupation of the Mellacourie, 1865-67. SIERRA LEONE STUD. 9 (1957), pp. 3-15.

9,860 HIRST, E. An attempt at reconstructing the history of the Loko people from about 1790 to the present day. SIERRA LEONE STUD. 9 (1957), pp. 26-39.

9,861 JONES-QUARTEY, K. A. B. Sierra-Leone and Ghana: nineteenth-century pioneers in West African journalism. SIERRA LEONE STUD. 12 (1959), pp. 230-244.

9,862 JONES-QUARTEY, K. A. B. Sierra Leone's role in the development of Ghana, 1820-1930. SIERRA LEONE STUD. 9 (1957), pp. 73-84.

9,863 KIRK-GREENE, A. David George: the Nova Scotian experience. SIERRA LEONE STUD. 14 (1960), pp. 93-120.

9,864 KUP, A. P. Early Portuguese trade in the Sierra Leone and Great Scarcies Rivers. BCGP 18 (1963), pp. 107-124; includes Portuguese translation.

9,865 KUP, A. P. Edward Fenton's visit to Sierra Leone, 1852. SIERRA LEONE STUD. 6 (1956), pp. 161-166.

9,866 KUP, A. P. Freetown in 1794. SIERRA LEONE STUD. 11 (1958), pp. 161-164.

9,867 KUP, A. P. Instructions to the Royal African Company's factory at Bunce, 1702. SIERRA LEONE STUD. 4 (1955), pp. 44-53; 6 (1956), pp. 71-80.

9,868 LYNCH, H. R. The native pastorate controversy and cultural ethno-centrism in Sierra Leone, 1871-1874. J. AFR. HIST. 5 (1964), pp. 395-413.

9,869 MANNAH-KPAKA, J. K. Memoirs of the 1898 rising. SIERRA LEONE STUD. 1 (1953), pp. 28-39.

9,870 MARKE, M. C. A primitive people. WASU 1 (1926), pp. 19-22.

9,871 MITCHELL, P. K. Trade routes of the early Sierra Leone Protectorate. SIERRA LEONE STUD. 16 (1962), pp. 204-217.

9,872 ORFOND, P. S. D'. New light on the origin of the Waiima affair, 1893. SIERRA LEONE STUD. 11 (1958), pp. 128-135.

9,873 PEARSALL, A. W. H. Sierra-Leone and the suppression of the slave trade. SIERRA LEONE STUD. 12 (1959), pp. 211-229.

9,874 PROBYN, L. Sierra Leone and the natives of West Africa. J. AFR. SOC. 6 (1907), pp. 250-258.

9,875 PROUDFOOT, L. The Fourah Bay dispute: an Aku faction fight in East Freetown. SIERRA L. BULL. REL. 4 (1962), pp. 75-88.

9,876 QUILLIAM, A. A chapter in the history of Sierra Leone. J. AFR. SOC. 3 (1903), pp. 83-99.

9,877 SCOTLAND, D. W. Notes on the Banana Islands A.D. 1462-1846. SIERRA LEONE STUD. 11 (1958), pp. 149-160.

9,878 SHELFORD, F. Sierra Leone in the making. J. AFR. SOC. 28 (1929), pp. 235-240.

9,879 WILSON, H. S. The changing image of the Sierra Leone colony in the works of E. W. Blyden. SIERRA LEONE STUD. 11 (1958), pp. 136-148.

9,880 WRIGHT, E. J. Granville Town. SIERRA LEONE STUD. 12 (1959), pp. 188-195.

9,881 WURIE, A. The Bundukas of Sierra Leone. SIERRA LEONE STUD. 1 (1953), pp. 14-25.

See also 12586.

Language. Literature

Language

9,882 BERRY, J. Nominal classes in Hu-Limba. SIERRA LEONE STUD. 11 (1958), pp. 169-173.

9,883 BERRY, J. A note on voice and aspect in Hu-Limba. SIERRA LEONE STUD. 13 (1960), pp. 36-40.

9,884 BERRY, J. The origins of Krio vocabulary. SIERRA LEONE STUD. 12 (1959), pp. 298-307.

9,885 BERRY, J. A short phonetic study of Sherbro (Bolom) as spoken in Sierra Leone. SIERRA LEONE STUD. 12 (1959), pp. 284-294.

9,886 BERRY, J. The structure of the noun in Kisi. SIERRA LEONE STUD. 12 (1959), pp. 308-315.

9,887 BOCKARI, J. The derivation of Mende names for the months of the year. SIERRA LEONE STUD. 4 (1955), pp. 208-210.

9,888 BRADSHAW, A. T. VON S. Vestiges of Portuguese in the languages of Sierra Leone. SIERRA LEONE LANG. REV. 4 (1965), pp. 5-37.

9,889 DALBY, T. D. P. Banta and Mabanta. SIERRA LEONE LANG. REV. 2 (1963), pp. 23-25.

9,890 DALBY, T. D. P. The extinct language of Dama. SIERRA LEONE LANG. REV. 2 (1963), pp. 50-54.

9,891 DALBY, T. D. P. Language distribution in Sierra Leone: 1961-1962. SIERRA LEONE LANG. REV. 1 (1962), pp. 62-67.

9,892 DALBY, T. D. P. Mel languages in the Polyglotta Africana. Part 1. Baga, Landuma and Temne. SIERRA LEONE LANG. REV. 4 (1965), pp. 129-135.

9,893 DAWSON, J. L. Temne witchcraft vocabulary. SIERRA LEONE LANG. REV. 2 (1963), pp. 16-22.

9,894 DECKER, T. Julius Caesar in Krio. SIERRA LEONE LANG. REV. 4 (1965), pp. 64-78.

9,895 FINNEGAN, R. Limba religious vocabulary. SIERRA LEONE LANG. REV. 2 (1963), pp. 11-15.

9,896 HAIR, P. E. H. Bibliography of the Mende language. SIERRA LEONE LANG. REV. 1 (1962), pp. 39-61.

9,897 HAIR, P. E. H. Christian literature in the Yalunka language: a note on earlier knowledge of the Yalunka and Kuranko tongues. SIERRA L. BULL. REL. 3 (1961), pp. 70-72.

9,898 HAIR, P. E. H. Freetown and the study of West African languages 1800-1875. BULL. IFAN 21 (1959), pp. 579-586.

9,899 HAIR, P. E. H. Notes on the discovery of the Vai script, with a bibliography. SIERRA LEONE LANG. REV. 2 (1963), pp. 36-49.

9,900 HAIR, P. E. H. Notes on the early study of some West African languages (Susu, Byllom/Sherbro, Temne, Mende, Vai and Yoruba). BULL. IFAN 23 (1961), pp. 683-695.

9,901 HAIR, P. E. H. Sierra Leone items in the Gullah dialect of American English. SIERRA LEONE LANG. REV. 4 (1965), pp. 79-84.

9,902 HAIR, P. E. H. The Sierra Leone settlement: the earliest attempts to study African languages. SIERRA LEONE LANG. REV. 2 (1963), pp. 5-10.

9,903 HAIR, P. E. H. Susu studies and literature: 1799-1900. SIERRA LEONE LANG. REV. 4 (1965), pp. 38-53.

9,904 HAIR, P. E. H. Temne and African language classification before 1864. J. AFR. LANGS. 4 (1965), pp. 46-56.

9,905 HARRIGAN, W. N. Christian literature in the Yalunka language: a handlist of modern translations. SIERRA L. BULL. REL. 3 (1961), pp. 68-69.

9,906 HARRIGAN, W. N. Form, function and distribution of the definite nominal suffix in Yalunka. SIERRA LEONE LANG. REV. 2 (1963), pp. 30-35.

9,907 HARRIS, W. T. Ngewo and Leve (Mende names for God: a study of origins). SIERRA L. BULL. REL. 5 (1963), pp. 34-36, 64-65.

9,908 HOBLEY, J. A preliminary tonal analysis of the Bassa language. J. W. AFR. LANG. 1 (1964), pp. 51-55.

9,909 INNES, G. A note on consonant mutation in Bandi. SIERRA LEONE STUD. 14 (1960), pp. 90-92.

9,910 INNES, G. An outline grammar of Loko with texts. AFR. LANG. STUD. 5 (1964), pp. 115-173.

9,911 JONES, E. D. Mid-nineteenth century evidences of a Sierra Leone Patois. SIERRA LEONE LANG. REV. 1 (1962), pp. 19-26.

9,912 JONES, E. D. The potentialities of Krio as a literary language. SIERRA LEONE STUD. 9 (1957), pp. 40-48.

9,913 JONES, E. D. Some aspects of the Sierra Leone Patois or Krio. SIERRA LEONE STUD. 6 (1956), pp. 97-109.

9,914 JONES, E. D. Some English fossils in Krio. SIERRA LEONE STUD. 12 (1959), pp. 295-297.

9,915 LANG-WIEN, K. Die Substantivbildung in der Soso-sprache BIBLIOTHECA AFR. 2 (1927), pp. 285-296.

9,916 LAW, J. R. S. The translation of the Bible into Mende. SIERRA L. BULL. REL. 2 (1960), pp. 40-44.

9,917 MacLURE, H. L. The New Testament in Temne. SIERRA LEONE STUD. 6 (1956), pp. 177-182.

9,918 MOURADIAN, J. Note sur quelques emprunts de la langue wolof à l'arabe. BULL. IFAN 2 (1940), pp. 269-284.

9,919 SAWYERR, H. A. E. Postpositions and prepositions in the Mende language. SIERRA LEONE STUD. 8 (1957), pp. 209-220.

9,920 SENIOR, M. M. Some Mende proverbs. AFRICA 17 (1947), pp. 202-205.

9,921 SHOUP, H. Christian literature in the Kuranko language. SIERRA L. BULL. LIT. 4 (1962), pp. 73-74.

9,922 WILSON, W. A. A. Temne and the West Atlantic group. SIERRA LEONE LANG. REV. 2 (1963), pp. 26-29.

9,923 WILSON, W. A. A. Temne, Landuma and the Baga languages. SIERRA LEONE LANG. REV. 1 (1962), pp. 27-38.

Literature

9,924 EBERL-ELBER, R. Two Mende tales. BULL. SOAS 10 (1940-1942), pp. 223-234.

9,925 GHAZALI, ABDUL KARIM. A Muslim propaganda play, with a commentary by Leslie Proudfoot. SIERRA L. BULL. REL. 3 (1961), pp. 72-79.

9,926 NICOL, A. Comme la nuit le jour. PRESENCE AFR. N.S. 54 (1965), pp. 221-232.

Law

9,927 BIYI, E. Têmnê land tenure. J. AFR. SOC. 12 (1913), pp. 407-420.

9,928 BROOKE, N. J. Native courts in Sierra Leone. J. AFR. ADM. 6 (1954), pp. 185-191.

9,929 COLE, C. O. E. Sierra Leone. Noteworthy legislation of the year 1956. J. AFR. LAW 1 (1957), pp. 113-115.

9,930 HARRIS, W. T. Mende marriage and the law of inheritance. SIERRA L. BULL. REL. 1 (1959), pp. 33-36.

9,931 SAWYERR, H. Sierra Leone's marriage laws: Amendment Acts 1965. SIERRA L. BULL. REL. 7 (1965), pp. 22-27.

9,932 Land tenure in Sierra Leone Protectorate. J. AFR. ADM. 1 (1949), pp. 119-123.

9,933 The University College of Sierra Leone (Fourah Bay), Department of Law. J. AFR. LAW 6 (1962), pp. 130-131.

Religion

9,934 FISHER, H. Ahmadiyya in Sierra Leone. SIERRA L. BULL. REL. 2 (1960), pp. 1-10.

9,935 FYFE, C. The Baptist churches in Sierra Leone. SIERRA L. BULL. REL. 5 (1963), pp. 55-60.

9,936 FYFE, C. The Countess of Huntingdon's Connexion in nineteenth century Sierra Leone. SIERRA L. BULL. REL. 4 (1962), pp. 53-61.

9,937 GHAZALI, A. K. Sierra Leone Muslims and sacrificial rituals. SIERRA L. BULL. REL. 2 (1960), pp. 27-32.

9,938 HAIR, P. E. H. Archdeacon Crowther and the Delta Pastorage 1892-9. SIERRA L. BULL. REL. 5 (1963), pp. 18-27.

9,939 HAIR, P. E. H. Freetown Christianity and Africa. SIERRA L. BULL. REL. 6, no. 2 (1964), pp. 13-21.

9,940 HAIR, P. E. H. Sierra Leone and Bulama 1792-4: further notes. SIERRA L. BULL. REL. 6 (1964), pp. 26-31.

9,941 HEMELBERG, E. The Jesuits in Sierra Leone 1605-17; a whirlwind of grace. SIERRA L. BULL. REL. 6 (1964), pp. 1-8.

9,942 KUP, A. P. Jesuit and Capuchin missions of the seventeenth century. SIERRA L. BULL. REL. 5 (1963), pp. 27-34.

9,943 MacLURE, H. L. Religion and disease in Sierra Leone. SIERRA L. BULL. REL. 4 (1962), pp. 29-34.

9,944 NDANEMA, I. M. The Martha Davies Confidential Benevolent Association. SIERRA L. BULL. REL. 3 (1961), pp. 64-67.

9,945 PORTER, A. T. Religious affiliation in Freetown, Sierra Leone. AFRICA 23 (1953), pp. 3-14.

9,946 PROUDFOOT, L. Ahmed Alhadi and the Ahmaddiya in Sierra Leone. SIERRA L. BULL. REL. 2 (1960), pp. 66-68.

9,947 PROUDFOOT, L. Mosque-building and tribal separatism in Freetown east. AFRICA 29 (1959), pp. 405-415.

9,948 PROUDFOOT, L. Towards Muslim solidarity in Freetown. AFRICA 31 (1961), pp. 147-156.

9,949 ROWE, S. Judas die don tidday (A radio feature programme... depicting the observance of Good Friday in Freetown). SIERRA L. BULL. REL. 7 (1965), pp. 1-12.

9,950 TRIMINGHAM, J. S. and FYFE, C. The early expansion of Islam in Sierra Leone. SIERRA L. BULL. REL. 2 (1960), pp. 33-40.

9,951 W., A. F. A second narrative of Samuel Ajayi Crowther's early life. BULL. SOC. AFR. CHURCH HIST. 2 (1965), pp. 5-14.

9,952 WALLS, A. F. Documentary materials for the study of Sierra Leone church history. SIERRA L. BULL. REL. 1 (1959), pp. 57-61.

9,953 WALLS, A. F. Some attitudes to sacrifice. SIERRA L. BULL. REL. 2 (1960), pp. 69-70.

9,954 WALLS, A. F. The usefulness of schoolmasters: notes on the early Sierra Leone documents of the Methodist Missionary Society. SIERRA L. BULL. REL. 3 (1961), pp. 28-40.

9,955 WOOD, A. S. Sierra Leone and Bulama: a fragment of missionary history. SIERRA L. BULL. REL. 3 (1961), pp. 16-22.

9,956 WOOD, C. T. A Crowther manuscript in Cape Town. BULL. SOC. AFR. CHURCH HIST. 1 (1964), pp. 99-100.

See also 12223.

Science

9,957 BURKE, L. J. A short account of the discovery of the major diamond deposit. SIERRA LEONE STUD. 12 (1959), pp. 316-328.

9,958 EASMON, M. C. F. Sierra Leone doctors. SIERRA LEONE STUD. 6 (1956), pp. 81-96.

9,959 GLANVILLE, R. R. Birds of Bintiman: peak, Sierra Leone. NIGERIAN FIELD 26 (1961), pp. 53-64.

9,960 JELLICOE, M. R. An introduction to the study of Sierra-Leone birds. SIERRA LEONE STUD. 2 (1954), pp. 66-84.

9,961 JELLICOE, M. R. Some less common birds of Sierra Leone. NIGERIAN FIELD 19 (1954), pp. 169-176.

9,962 JONES, T. Notes on bat-eating snakes. NIGERIAN FIELD 26 (1961), pp. 69-70.

9,963 NEWHS, F. Bird watching around Freetown. NIGERIAN FIELD 28 (1963), pp. 172-183.

9,964 NICHOL, E. P. Notes on some African vegetables in Sierra Leone. SIERRA LEONE STUD. 6 (1956), pp. 66-70.

9,965 POLLETT, J. D. The diamond deposits of Sierra Leone. BULL. IMP. INST. 35 (1937), pp. 333-348.

9,966 ROSE, J. R. The commoner birds of the Kailahun district. SIERRA LEONE STUD. 4 (1955), pp. 231-236.

9,967 ROSE, J. R. Kwashiorkor in the South-east Province of Sierra-Leone. SIERRA LEONE STUD. 6 (1956), pp. 130-144.

9,968 ROSE, J. R. A review of the causes of blindness in the South-eastern Province of Sierra Leone. SIERRA LEONE STUD. 4 (1955), pp. 224-225.

9,969 SCOTLAND, D. W. The introduction of plants and seeds into the colony of Sierra Leone in the early years of its foundation. SIERRA LEONE STUD. 6 (1956), pp. 183-187.

See also 8114.

Sociology

9,970 BANTON, M. Adaptation and integration in the social system of Temne immigrants in Freetown. AFRICA 26 (1956), pp. 354-367.

9,971 BENJAMIN, E. The Sierra Leone census, 1963. SIERRA LEONE GEOG. ASSOC. BULL. 9 (1965), pp. 63-71.

9,972 BETTS, V. O. The home development programme: Sierra Leone. WOMEN TODAY 6 (1964), pp. 64-66.

9,973 C., J. Enquête sociale à Freetown. ZAIRE 7 (1953), p. 529.

9,974 CARNEY, D. The economics of health in conditions of low population growth: the example of Sierra Leone. INT. SOC. SC. J. 17 (1965), pp. 277-283.

9,975 CARNEY, D. The integration of social development plans with over-all development planning: the example of Sierra Leone. INT. SOC. SC. J. 16 (1964), pp. 357-377.

9,976 CARTER, M. Professional women of Sierra Leone. AFR. WOMEN 3 (1958-1960), pp. 41-42.

9,977 CLARKE, J. I. Sex-ratios in Sierra Leone. SIERRA LEONE GEOG. ASSOC. BULL. 9 (1965), pp. 72-77.

9,978 DAWSON, J. Race and inter-group relations in Sierra Leone. RACE 6, no. 1 (1964-1965), pp. 83-99, 217-231.

9,979 G., J. Premiers résultats de l'enquête de Freetown. ZAIRE 8 (1954), pp. 309-310.

9,980 GAMBLE, D. P. Sociological research in an urban community (Lunsaŋ) in Sierra Leone. SIERRA LEONE STUD. 17 (1963), pp. 254-268.

9,981 JELLICOE, M. R. Women's groups in Sierra Leone. AFR. WOMEN 1 (1955), pp. 35-43.

9,982 LITTLE, K. L. The significance of the West African Creole for Africanist and Afro-American Studies. AFR. AFFAIRS 49 (1950), pp. 308-319.

9,983 LITTLE, K. L. Social change and social class in the Sierra Leone Protectorate. AMER. J. SOC. 54 (1948-1949), pp. 10-21.

9,984 LITTLE, K. L. Structural change in Sierra Leone Protectorate. AFRICA 25 (1955), pp. 217-233.

9,985 MARGAI, M. A. S. Welfare work in a secret society. AFR. AFFAIRS 47 (1948), pp. 227-230.

9,986 Women's Institutes in Sierra Leone. AFR. WOMEN 1 (1954), pp. 17-18.

GHANA

General

9,987 AMEDEKEY, E. Y. Current problems of University libraries in Ghana. GHANA LIBRARY J. 1 (1964), pp. 36-41.

9,988 BALME, D. M. The Balme Library [address at opening ceremony]. UNIVERSITAS 4 (1960), pp. 39-41.

9,989 BENGE, R. C. The role of the librarian in Ghana. GHANA LIBRARY J. 1 (1964), pp. 64-69.

9,990 CORNELIUS, D. On trek with the mobile library in Ghana. UNESCO BULL. LIBS. 12 (1958), pp. 206-207.

9,991 DRAKE, ST. C. Two terms in the Institute. UNIV. GHANA RES. REV. 1 (1965), no. 2, p. 40.

9,992 EVANS, E. J. A. The training of Gold Coast girls as librarians. AFR. WOMEN 1 (1955), pp. 66-67.

9,993 HODGKIN, T. Work in progress [at the Institute of African Studies, Ghana]. UNIV. GHANA RES. REV. 1 (1965), no. 2, pp. 26-28.

9,994 HOWE, G. N. A select bibliography of recent literature on the Gold Coast. UNIVERSITAS 2 (1955), pp. 21-24; 2 (1956), pp. 55-58, 87-89, 122-125; 2 (1957), pp. 157-163; 3 (1957), pp. 17-21; 3 (1958), pp. 50-55, 97-103, 192-195.

9,995 KORANTENG, E. K. The tasks ahead [of the Ghana Library Association]. GHANA LIBRARY J. 1 (1964), pp. 57-59.

9,996 LAWRENCE, A. W. The National Museum of the Gold Coast. UNIVERSITAS 1, no. 2 (1954), pp. 10-12.

9,997 LEESE, F. E. A select bibliography of recent literature on Ghana. UNIVERSITAS 3 (1958), pp. 132-135; 3 (1959), pp. 161-163.

9,998 MENSAH-KANE, J. J. Secondary school and training college libraries in Ghana. GHANA LIBRARY J. 1 (1964), pp. 27-31.

9,999 OFORI, G. T. Library co-operation in Ghana: the public libraries point of view. GHANA LIBRARY J. 1 (1964), pp. 60-64.

10,000 SELLIER, R. The Gold Coast. CONTEMP. REV. 171 (1947), pp. 285-290.

10,001 WAKKAD, M. EL-. Arabic manuscripts in Ghana. GHANA NOTES 2 (1961), p. 11.

10,002 WILKS, I. Arabic mss. collection [at the Institute of African Studies, Ghana]. UNIV. GHANA RES. REV. 2 (1965), pp. 17-31.

10,003 The Arabic collection [at the Institute of African Studies, Ghana]. UNIV. GHANA RES. REV. 1 (1965), p. 15.

10,004 Bulletin of the Institute of African Studies, University of Ghana (BIAS). RES. BULL. CENTRE ARABIC DOC. IBADAN 1 (1964), pp. 13-14.

10,005 Gift from the Kingdom of Morocco. UNIV. GHANA RES. REV. 1 (1965), no. 2, pp. 41-42.

10,006 David Tait, 1912-56: a bibliography. TR. HIST. SOC. GHANA 3 (1957), p. 151.

10,007 Institut d'Etudes Africaines à l'Université de Ghana. GENEVE-AFR. 1 (1962), p. 215.

See also 7491, 10605.

Agriculture

10,008 CLARKSON, M. L. An experiment in evaluation of the cocoa extension campaign in the Gold Coast. WAISER 5 (1956), pp. 18-30.

10,009 FIELD, M. J. The agricultural system of the Manya-Krobo of the Gold Coast. AFRICA 14 (1943), pp. 54-65.

10,010 HAMILTON, H. Agriculture in the Ankaful (Gold Coast) leper settlement. NIGERIAN FIELD 18 (1953), pp. 180-182.

10,011 HILL, P. Three types of southern Ghanaian cocoa farmer. AFR. AGRARIAN SYSTEMS, 1963, pp. 203-223.

10,012 JONES, G. H. Educational needs in West Africa: an agricultural view. J. AFR. SOC. 26 (1927), pp. 341-367.

10,013 PHILLIPS, J. Problems and prospects of the agricultural industry. UNIVERSITAS 1, no. 1 (1953), pp. 10-13; 1, no. 4 (1954), pp. 5-8.

10,014 WHITE, H. P. Provisional agricultural regions of Ghana. J. TROP. GEOG. 11 (1958), pp. 90-99.

Anthropology

10,015 ADJEI, A. Mortuary usages of the Ga people of the Gold Coast. AMER. ANTHR. 45 (1943), pp. 84-98.

10,016 AGBLEMAGNON, F. N. Le concept de crise appliqué à une société africaine: les Ewés. CAH. INT. SOCIOL. 23 (1957), pp. 157-166.

10,017 AGYEMANG-DUAH, J. The ceremony of enstoolment of the Asantehene. GHANA NOTES 7 (1965), pp. 8-11.

10,018 AKESSON, S. K. The Akan concept of the soul. AFR. AFFAIRS 64 (1965), pp. 280-291.

10,019 AKESSON, S. K. The secret of Akom. AFR. AFFAIRS 49 (1950), pp. 237-246, 325-333.

10,020 AMOO, J. W. A. The effect of western influence on Akan marriage. AFRICA 16 (1946), pp. 228-237.

10,021 ANDOH, A. S. Y. A note on ntam. ASHANTI RES. PROJ. 1ST. CONF., 1964, pp. 41-43.

10,022 ARHIN, K. The new Mim oath. UNIV. GHANA RES. REV. 1 (1965), p. 35.

10,023 ARMATTOE, R. E. G. Akwasidae. AFR. AFFAIRS 50 (1951), pp. 61-63.

10,024 ARMATTOE, R. E. G. Epe-Ekpe. AFR. AFFAIRS 50 (1951), pp. 326-329.

10,025 ARMATTOE, R. E. G. Some aspects of the ethnography of the Ewes of West Africa. CONG. INT. SC. ANTH. ET ETHN. 4, no. iii (1952), pp. 28-29.

10,026 BERRY, J. A Gã folk tale. BULL. SOAS 12 (1947-1948), pp. 409-416.

10,027 BLAY, R. S. The truth about the Gold Coast marriage custom. WASU 2 (1926), pp. 20-23.

10,028 BOHANNAN, L. A [Tiv] genealogical charter. AFRICA 22 (1952), pp. 301-315.

10,029 BROKENSHA, D. Akwapim studies. UNIVERSITAS 5 (1962), pp. 4-7.

10,030 BROKENSHA, D. A study of Larteh, Ghana. CURRENT ANTHR. 4 (1963), pp. 533-534.

10,031 BROWN, A. A. A. Signs and omens. GOLD COAST REV. 2 (1926), pp. 285-289.

10,032 BROWN, E. J. P. Mfantsi-Akan totems. GOLD COAST REV. 2 (1926), pp. 181-191.

10,033 BRUCE-MYERS, J. M. The origin of the Gãs. J. AFR. SOC. 27 (1927), pp. 69-76, 167-173.

10,034 CARDINALL, A. W. Folk lore of the Gold Coast. GOLD COAST REV. 2 (1926), pp. 14-27.

10,035 CARDINALL, A. W. Some random notes on the customs of the Konkomba. J. AFR. SOC. 18 (1918), pp. 45-62.

10,036 CARDINALL, A. W. The state of our present ethnographical knowledge of the Gold Coast peoples. AFRICA 2 (1929), pp. 405-412.

10,037 CHRISTENSEN, J. B. Marketing and exchange in a West African tribe. SOUTHWESTERN J. ANTHR. 17 (1961), pp. 124-139.

10,038 CHRISTENSEN, J. B. The role of proverbs in Fante culture. AFRICA 28 (1958), pp. 232-242.

10,039 CLARKE, E. The sociological significance of ancestor-worship in Ashanti. AFRICA 3 (1930), pp. 431-470.

10,040 CLARKE, J. H. La célébration d'une veillée funèbre dans la tribu ga du Ghana. PRESENCE AFR. N.S. 23 (1958-1959), pp. 107-112.

10,041 COTTON, S. A. The deer festival at Winneba. NIGERIAN FIELD 30 (1965), pp. 82-84.

10,042 DANQUAH, J. B. The culture of Akan. AFRICA 22 (1952), pp. 360-366.

10,043 DUNN, J. S. Fante star lore. NIGERIAN FIELD 25 (1960), pp. 52-64.

10,044 FFOULKES, A. Borgya and Abirwa; or, the latest fetich on the Gold Coast. J. AFR. SOC. 8 (1909), pp. 387-397.

10,045 FFOULKES, A. The company system in Cape Coast Castle. J. AFR. SOC. 7 (1908), pp. 261-277.

10,046 FFOULKES, A. The Fanti family system. J. AFR. SOC. 7 (1908), pp. 394-409.

10,047 FFOULKES, A. Fanti marriage customs. J. AFR. SOC. 8 (1908), pp. 31-48.

10,048 FFOULKES, A. Funeral customs of the Gold Coast Colony. J. AFR. SOC. 8 (1909), pp. 154-164.

10,049 FIELD, M. J. A further note on Burukung. GHANA NOTES 4 (1962), pp. 29-30.

10,050 FIELD, M. J. Some new shrines of the Gold Coast and their significance. AFRICA 13 (1940), pp. 138-149.

10,051 FLEISCHER, C. and WILKIE, M. B. Specimens of folk-lore of the Gā-people on the Gold Coast. AFRICA 3 (1930), pp. 360-368.

10,052 FORTES, M. Communal fishing and fishing magic in the Northern Territories of the Gold Coast. JRAI 67 (1937), pp. 131-142.

10,053 FORTES, M. Culture contact as a dynamic process: an investigation in the Northern Territories of the Gold Coast. AFRICA 9 (1936), pp. 24-55.

10,054 FORTES, M. Kinship and marriage among the Ashanti. AFRICAN SYSTEMS OF KINSHIP AND MARRIAGE, 1950, pp. 252-284.

10,055 FORTES, M. Kinship, incest and exogamy of the Northern Territories of the Gold Coast. CUSTOM IS KING: ESSAYS...TO R. R. MARETT, 1936, pp. 239-256.

10,056 FORTES, M. Pietas in ancestor worship. JRAI 91 (1961), pp. 166-191.

10,057 FORTES, M. The political system of the Talensi of the Northern Territories of the Gold Coast. AFRICAN POLITICAL SYSTEMS, 1940, pp. 239-271.

10,058 FORTES, M. Ritual festivals and social cohesion in the hinterland of the Gold Coast. AMER. ANTHR. 38 (1936), pp. 590-604.

10,059 FORTES, M. The significance of descent in Tale social structure. AFRICA 14 (1944), pp. 362-384.

10,060 FORTES, M. Social and psychological aspects of education in Taleland. AFRICA 11 (1938), supplement.

10,061 FORTES, M. The tribes of the Ashanti hinterland; by R. S. Rattray. J. AFR. SOC. 32 (1933), pp. 87-93.

10,062 FORTES, M. and FORTES, S. L. Food in the domestic economy of the Tallensi. AFRICA 9 (1936), pp. 237-276.

10,063 FRANCE, H. Customs of the Awuna tribes. J. AFR. SOC. 5 (1905), pp. 38-40.

10,064 FRANCE, H. Worship of the thunder-god among the Awuna. J. AFR. SOC. 8 (1908), pp. 79-81.

10,065 FRASER, A. G. The cult of the Kwahu hunter on the question of Sasa animals, especially the elephant. GOLD COAST REV. 4 (1928), pp. 155-171.

10,066 GOODY, E. Research into the fostering of children by kin in Northern and Southern Ghana. UNIV. GHANA RES. REV. 2 (1965), pp. 40-42.

10,067 GOODY, J. Anomie in Ashanti. AFRICA 27 (1957), pp. 356-362.

10,068 GOODY, J. Ethnohistory and the Akan of Ghana. AFRICA 29 (1959), pp. 67-80.

10,069 GOODY, J. Fields of social control among the LoDagaba. JRAI 87 (1957), pp. 75-104.

10,070 GRIFFITH, W. B. Native stools on the Gold Coast. J. AFR. SOC. 4 (1905), pp. 290-294.

10,071 GROTTANELLI, L. NOme e anima fra gli Nzema. CONGR. INT. ANTHR. ET ETHN. 6, no. ii (1960), pp. 389-392.

10,072 GROTTANELLI, V. L. Nzema provergs. AFR. UND UB. 42 (1958), pp. 17-26.

10,073 HAMMOND, P. B. Mossi joking. ETHNOLOGY 3 (1964), pp. 259-267.

10,074 HARPER, C. H. et al. Notes on the totemism of the Gold Coast. JRAI 36 (1906), pp. 178-188.

10,075 HERSKOVITS, M. J. The Ashanti ntoro: a re-examination. JRAI 67 (1937), pp. 287-296.

10,076 HIRSCHBERG, W. Der Abfallhügel von Dawu (akuapim, Ghana) und der Reisebericht Pieter de Marees (1605). FESTSCHRIFT FUR A. E. Jensen, 1964, pp. 193-198.

10,077 HORTON, R. Destiny and the unconscious in West Africa. AFRICA 31 (1961), pp. 110-116.

10,078 HUBER, H. Der Kult der Jenseits-Frau bei den Adangme-und Ewe-Stämmen des Unteren Volta. CONGR. INT. SC. ANTHR. ET ETHN. 6, no. ii (1960), pp. 405-408.

10,079 HUBER, H. Ritual oaths as instruments of coercion and self-defence among the Adarjme of Ghana. AFRICA 29 (1959), pp. 41-49.

10,080 HUBER, H. Das Totenritual einer Ewe-Gruppe des südöstlichen Ghana. ETHNOS 30 (1965), pp. 79-104.

10,081 HUTCHINSON, J. T. A Gold Coast detective. J. AFR. SOC. 17 (1918), pp. 227-230.

10,082 JAHODA, G. Boys' images of marriage partners and girls' self-images in Ghana. SOCIOLOGUS 8 (1958), pp. 155-169.

10,083 JOHNSON, J. C. DE G. The Fanti Asafu. AFRICA 5 (1932), pp. 307-322.

10,084 JOHNSON, J. C. DE G. The significance of some Akan titles. GOLD COAST REV. 2 (1926), pp. 208-223.

10,085 LAMTIS, M. Fanti omens. AFRICA 13 (1940), pp. 150-159.

10,086 LAWSON, G. Village life in West Africa. AFR. WOMEN 1 (1956), pp. 91-95.

10,087 MANGIN, T. R. O. The Supon fetish. GOLD COAST REV. 2 (1926), pp. 118-121.

10,088 MARSHALL, Sir J. On the natives of the Gold Coast. JRAI 16 (1887), pp. 180-182.

10,089 MATSON, J. N. Testate succession in Ashanti. AFRICA 23 (1953), pp. 224-232.

10,090 MEAD, M. A Twi relationship system. JRAI 67 (1937), pp. 297-304.

10,091 MEYEROWITZ, E. L. R. Akan oral historical traditions. UNIVERSITAS 5 (1962), pp. 44-49.

10,092 MEYEROWITZ, E. L. R. Concepts of the soul among the Akan of the Gold Coast. AFRICA 21 (1951), pp. 24-31.

10,093 MEYEROWITZ, E. L. R. A further note on Burukung. GHANA NOTES 2 (1961), p.

10,094 MIGEOD, F. W. H. Tribal mixture on the Gold Coast. J. AFR. SOC. 19 (1920), pp. 109-125.

10,095 MYERS, J. M. B. The connubial institutions of the Gas. J. AFR. SOC. 30 (1931), pp. 399-409.

10,096 OPOKU-AMPOMAH, J. K. 'Amoafo': a folk etymology. GHANA NOTES 1 (1961), pp. 7-8.

10,097 OPOKU-AMPOMAH, J. K. Introducing an Ashanti girl into womanhood. GHANA NOTES 2 (1961), pp. 7-9.

10,098 OWIREDU, P. A. The Akan system of inheritance today and tomorrow. AFR. AFFAIRS 58 (1959), pp. 161-165.

10,099 PARENKO, P. and HEBERT, R. P. J. Une famille ethnique: les Gan, les Padoro, les Dorobé, les Komono. BULL. IFAN 24 (1962), pp. 414-448.

10,100 PARKINSON, J. An obsolete official. J. AFR. SOC. 32 (1933), pp. 362-365.

10,101 PITT, W. J. The Mfantra [people]. GOLD COAST REV. 2 (1926), pp. 71-77.

10,102 PUPLAMPU, D. A. The national epic of the Adangme. AFR. AFFAIRS 50 (1951), pp. 236-241.

10,103 QUARTEY-PAPAFIO, A. B. Apprenticeship amongst the Gās. J. AFR. SOC. 13 (1914), pp. 415-422.

10,104 QUARTEY-PAPAFIO, A. B. The Gā homowo festival. J. AFR. SOC. 19 (1920), pp. 126-134, 227-232.

10,105 QUARTEY-PAPAFIO, A. B. The use of names among the Gās or Accra people of the Gold Coast. J. AFR. SOC. 13 (1914), pp. 167-182.

10,106 RATTRAY, R. S. The drum language of West Africa. J. AFR. SOC. 22 (1923), pp. 226-236, 302-316.

10,107 RATTRAY, R. S. Some aspects of West African folk-lore. J. AFR. SOC. 28 (1928), pp. 1-11.

10,108 RATTRAY, R. S. The tribes of the Ashanti hinterland. (Some results of a two-year anthropological survey of the Northern Territories of the Gold Coast). J. AFR. SOC. 30 (1931), pp. 40-57.

10,109 RATTRAY, R. S. and BUXTON, L. H. D. Cross-cousin marriages. J. AFR. SOC. 24 (1925), pp. 83-91.

10,110 RICHARDS, A. and MORTON-WILLIAMS, P. Anthropology in Asante Abakosem. ASHANTI RES. PROJ. 1ST. CONF., 1964, pp. 19-20.

10,111 SCHEIBLER, P. Basa-Märchen und Rätsel. AFR. UND UB. 7 (1916-1917), pp. 161-166.

10,112 SCHEIBLER, P. and ZIEGLER, J. Basa-Sprichwörter. AFR. UND UB. 8 (1917-1918), pp. 1-35, 209-256.

10,113 SHRUBSALL, F. Notes on Ashanti skulls and crania. JRAI 28 (1899), pp. 95-103.

10,114 SMITH, E. W. Religious beliefs of the Akan. AFRICA 15 (1945), pp. 23-28.

10,115 STEEMERS, J. C. S. Notes on the kenekra, boasekye and boasekuri and okra traditions among the Guans of the Volta basin. GHANA BULL. THEOL. 2, no. 8 (1965), pp. 1-10.

10,116 STEEMERS, J. C. S. The okra traditions among the Guans of the Volta basin. GHANA BULL. THEOL. 2, nos. 9-10 (1965-1966), pp. 1-11.

10,117 SWITHENBANK, M. Asante Abakosem: the traditional architecture of Ashanti. ASHANTI RES. PROJ. 1ST. CONF., 1964, pp. 34-40.

10,118 TAIT, D. Konkomba friendship relations. AFR. STUD. 13 (1954), pp. 77-84.

10,119 TAIT, D. Konkomba sorcery. JRAI 84 (1954), pp. 66-74.

10,120 TAIT, D. The place of libation in Konkomba ritual. BULL. IFAN, Série B: Sciences humaines 17 (1955), pp. 168-172.

10,121 TAIT, D. A sorcery hunt in Dagomba. AFRICA 33 (1963), pp. 136-147.

10,122 TAIT, D. Spirit of the bush: a note on personal religion among the Konkomba. UNIVERSITAS 1, no. 1 (1953), pp. 17-18.

10,123 WARD, B. E. Some observations on religious cults in Ashanti. AFRICA 26 (1956), pp. 47-60.

10,124 WARD, W. E. Rites of the Oyeni fetish. GOLD COAST REV. 4 (1928), pp. 232-235.

10,125 WELMAN, C. W. James Fort, Accra, and the Oyeni fetish. GOLD COAST REV. 3 (1927), pp. 73-88.

10,126 WESTERMANN, D. Soul, spirit, fate. According to the notions of the Tshi and Ehwe tribes (Gold Coast and Togo, W. Africa), tr. by A. Jehle. J. AFR. SOC. 6 (1907), pp. 405-415.

10,127 WILD, R. P. Funerary equipment from Agona-Smedru, Winnebah district. JRAI 67 (1937), pp. 67-75.

10,128 WILKS, I. Akwamu and Otublohum: an eighteenth-century Akan marriage arrangement. AFRICA 29 (1959), pp. 391-403.

10,129 WILKS, I. Burukung. GHANA NOTES 1 (1961), pp. 11-12.

10,130 WOHLGEMUTH, N. Ein Fante-tiermärchen. ETHNOS 1 (1936), pp. 128-132.

10,131 WORSLEY, P. M. The kinship system of the Tallensi: a revaluation. JRAI 86, no. 1 (1956), pp. 37-75.

10,132 WRIGHT, V. Some Ga customs. GOLD COAST REV. 3 (1927), pp. 224-228.

10,133 ZAJACZKOWSKI, A. La famille, le lignage et la communaute villageoise chez les Ashanti de la période de transition. CAH. ET. AFR. 1 (1960), pp. 99-114.

10,134 A Melusine story from the Gold Coast. J. AFR. SOC. 5 (1905), pp. 104-107.

10,135 Volta resettlement symposium, 21st.-27th. March, 1965. BULL. AFR. STUD. ASSOC. 4 (1965), p. 17.

See also 9311, 9325, 9326.

Art

10,136 ANQUANDAH, H. Ghana's terra-cotta cigars. GHANA NOTES 7 (1965), p. 26.

10,137 ANQUANDAH, J. R. An archaeological survey of the Techiman-Wenchi area. UNIV. GHANA RES. REV. 1 (1965), Supplement, pp. 111-134.

10,138 BALFOUR, H. Notes on a collection of ancient stone implements from Ejura, Ashanti. J. AFR. SOC. 12 (1912), pp. 1-16.

10,139 BEIER, U. Vincent Akweti Kofi: a sculptor from Ghana. BO 9 (1961), pp. 35-36.

10,140 BUMPUS, B. S. G. Biconically pierced stones of the Gold Coast. NIGERIAN FIELD 18 (1953), pp. 78-86.

10,141 BURTON, R. F. On stone implements from the Gold Coast, West Africa. JRAI 12 (1883), pp. 449-454.

10,142 CARDINALL, A. W. Aggrey beads of the Gold Coast. J. AFR. SOC. 24 (1925), pp. 287-298.

10,143 CARPENTER, P. East and West: a brief view of theatre in Ghana and Uganda since 1960. MAKERERE J. 8 (1963), pp. 35-39.

10,144 CARPENTER, P. Theatre in Ghana. UNIVERSITAS 5 (1962), pp. 35-37.

10,145 CARTER, P. L. and CARTER, P. J. Rock painting from Northern Ghana. TRANS. HIST. SOC. GHANA 7 (1964), pp. 1-3.

10,146 DAAKU, K. Y. Pre-European currencies of West Africa and Western Sudan. GHANA NOTES 2 (1961), pp. 12-14.

10,147 DAVIES, O. The archaeological evidence for the iron age in Ashanti. ASHANTI RES. PROJ. 1ST. CONF., 1964, pp. 44-49.

10,148 DAVIES, O. An archaeological link with ancient Ghana. UNIVERSITAS 3 (1959), pp. 175-176.

10,149 DAVIES, O. The climatic and cultural sequence in the late Pleistocene of the Gold Coast. PROC. PAN-AFR. CONGR. PRE-HIST. 3 (1955), pp. 1-5.

10,150 DAVIES, O. Earliest man and how he reached Ghana. UNIVERSITAS 3 (1958), pp. 35-37.

10,151 DAVIES, O. Gonja painted pottery. TRANS. HIST. SOC. GHANA 7 (1964), pp. 4-11.

10,152 DAVIES, O. Neolithic cultures of Ghana. PROC. PAN-AFR. CONGR. PRE-HIST. 4, no. iii (1962), pp. 291-301.

10,153 DAVIES, O. Recent archaeological research in the Volta basin. UNIV. GHANA RES. REV. 1 (1965), no. 2, pp. 16-19.

10,154 DAVIES, O. Soil and water. UNIVERSITAS 4 (1960), pp. 80-81.

10,155 DERBI, M. D. Pottery in Ghana. AFR. WOMEN 2 (1956-1958), pp. 84-85.

10,156 DJAN, O. S. Drums and victory. Africa's call to the empire; ed. M. S. Cockin. J. AFR. SOC. 41 (1942), pp. 29-41.

10,157 EHSANULLAH, L. Ashanti goldweights. NIGERIAN FIELD 29 (1964), pp. 82-88.

10,158 ELSBEMD, A. J. Archaeological finds at Somanya, Gold Coast. NIGERIAN FIELD 21 (1956), pp. 69-74.

10,159 FIELD, M. J. The investigation of the ancient settlements of the Accra Plain. GHANA NOTES 4 (1962), pp. 4-5.

10,160 GBEHO, P. The indigenous Gold Coast music. AFR. MUSIC, 1952, pp. 30-34.

10,161 GBEHO, P. Music of the Gold Coast. AFR. MUSIC, 1954, pp. 62-64.

10,162 GROTTANELLI, V. L. Asonu worship among the Nzema: a study in Akan art and religion. AFRICA 31 (1961), pp. 46-59.

10,163 HAMILTON, R. Bilingas on the Gold Coast. NIGERIAN FIELD 19 (1954), p. 180.

10,164 HAMILTON, R. Small clay pillars in the Gold Coast. NIGERIAN FIELD 17 (1952), pp. 90-91; 19 (1954), pp. 133-135.

10,165 JEFFREYS, M. D. W. Notes on Ashanti gold weights. NIGERIAN FIELD 29 (1964), pp. 191-192.

10,166 LAWRENCE, A. W. Premier rapport annuel du Musée National de la Gold Coast (1951). BULL. IFAN 14 (1952), pp. 1581-1582.

10,167 LAWRENSON, T. E. The idea of a national theatre. UNIVERSITAS 1, no. 3 (1954), pp. 6-10.

10,168 LYSTAD, M. H. Paintings of Ghanaian children. AFRICA 30 (1960), pp. 238-241.

10,169 McHARDY, C. The performing arts in Ghana. AFR. FORUM 1 (1965), pp. 113-117.

10,170 MATHEWSON, R. W. Report on the departmental [Archaeology, University of Ghana] work carried out while on trek from 3rd August-5th September 1965. UNIV. GHANA RES. REV. 2 (1965), pp. 46-48.

10,171 MAUNY, R. Un exemple a méditer en A.O.F.: le Musée historique national de la Gold Coast. BULL. IFAN 14 (1952), pp. 1580-1581.

10,172 MENSAH, A. A. Musicality and musicianship in north-western Ghana. UNIV. GHANA RES. REV. 2 (1965), pp. 42-45.

10,173 MEYEROWITZ, E. L. R. The art of Africa: gold and the Akan of Ghana. AFR. SOUTH 3, no. 1 (1958), pp. 103-108.

10,174 NEWLANDS, H. S. An archaeological puzzle from West Africa. J. AFR. SOC. 19 (1919), pp. 40-43.

10,175 NKETIA, J. H. The ideal in African folk music: a note on Klama. UNIVERSITAS 3 (1958), pp. 40-42.

10,176 NKETIA, J. H. Modern trends in Ghana music. AFR. MUSIC, 1957, pp. 13-17.

10,177 NKETIA, J. H. The organisation of music in Adangme society. UNIVERSITAS 3 (1957), pp. 9-11.

10,178 NKETIA, J. H. Organisation of music in Adangme society. AFR. MUSIC, 1958, pp. 28-30.

10,179 NKETIA, J. H. The role of the drummer in Akan society. AFR. MUSIC, 1954, pp. 34-43.

10,180 NKETIA, J. H. Traditional music of the Ga people. AFR. MUSIC, 1958, pp. 21-27. Also in UNIVERSITAS 3 (1958), pp. 76-81.

10,181 OSAFO, F. O. An African orchestra in Ghana. AFR. MUSIC, 1957, pp. 11-12.

10,182 OZANNE, P. Adwuki: fortified hill-top village in Shai. GHANA NOTES 7 (1965), pp. 4-5.

10,183 OZANNE, P. The archaeological contribution to the Ashanti Research Scheme. ASHANTI RES. PROJ. 1ST. CONF., 1964, pp. 50-59.

10,184 OZANNE, P. An earthenware oil-lamp from near Nsawan. TR. HIST. SOC. GHANA 5 (1962), pp. 75-77.

10,185 OZANNE, P. Excavation at Dawu. TR. HIST. SOC. GHANA 6 (1962), pp. 119-123.

10,186 OZANNE, P. Ladoku: an early town near Prampram. GHANA NOTES 7 (1965), pp. 6-7.

10,187 OZANNE, P. Notes on the early historic archaeology of Accra. TR. HIST. SOC. GHANA 6 (1962), pp. 51-70.

10,188 OZANNE, P. Notes on the later prehistory of Accra. J. HIST. SOC. NIG. 3 (1964), pp. 3-23.

10,189 OZANNE, P. Report on field-work at Banda and Wenchi, 8-16 August, 1964. UNIV. GHANA RES. REV. 1 (1965), pp. 19-23.

10,190 OZANNE, P. et al. A Shai tradition in ritual pottery by P. Ozanne, A. K Quarcoo, M. Johnson. UNIV. GHANA RES. REV. 2 (1965), pp. 64-67.

10,191 PAULME, D. A propos des Kuduo Ashanti. PRESENCE AFR. 10 (1951), pp. 156-162.

10,192 PLASS, M. W. Poids à or des Ashanti. PRESENCE AFR. 10 (1951), pp. 163-166.

10,193 QUARCOO, A. K. and AMEYAW, K. Museum reports: [mortuary and cult figures]. UNIV. GHANA RES. REV. 2 (1965), pp. 62-63.

10,194 RATTRAY, R. S. Arts and crafts of Ashanti. J. AFR. SOC. 23 (1924), pp. 265-270.

10,195 RIVERSON, I. D. The growth of music in the Gold Coast. TR. HIST. SOC. GHANA 1 (1952-1955), pp. 121-132.

10,196 SHAW, C. T. Archaeology in the Gold Coast. AFR. STUD. 2 (1943), pp. 139-147.

10,197 SHAW, C. T. Bead-making with a bow-drill in the Gold Coast. JRAI 75 (1945), pp. 45-50.

10,198 SHINNIE, P. L. Yendi Dabari. GHANA NOTES 1 (1961), pp. 10-11; 3 (1961), pp. 4-5.

10,199 SHINNIE, P. L. and OZANNE, P. C. Excavations at Yendi Dabari. TR. HIST. SOC. GHANA 6 (1962), pp. 87-118.

10,200 STEVENS, G. A. The future of African art, with special reference to problems arising in Gold Coast Colony. AFRICA 3 (1930), pp. 150-160.

10,201 STEWART, J. L. Northern Gold Coast songs. AFR. MUSIC, 1952, pp. 39-42.

10,202 THOMAS, N. W. Ashanti and Baule gold weights. JRAI 50 (1920), pp. 52-68.

10,203 WARD, W. E. Music in the Gold Coast. GOLD COAST REV. 3 (1927), pp. 199-223.

10,204 WIEGRABE, P. Ewelieder. AFR. UND UB. 37 (1952-1953), pp. 99-108; 38 (1953-1954), pp. 17-26, 113-120, 155-164.

10,205 WILD, R. P. The archaeology of the Nsuta manganese mine. GOLD COAST REV. 5 (1929), pp. 150-155.

10,206 WILD, R. P. Cuttle fish bone mould casting as practised on the Gold Coast. GOLD COAST REV. 5 (1929), pp. 144-149.

10,207 WILD, R. P. A disc-shaped stone artefact from Tarkwa. GOLD COAST REV. 5 (1929), pp. 180-183.

10,208 WILD, R. P. Nyame Akuma or God axes. GOLD COAST REV. 5 (1929), pp. 156-165.

10,209 WILD, R. P. An old native pot dug up near Obuasi in Ashanti. GOLD COAST REV. 2 (1926), p. 13.

10,210 WILD, R. P. Stone age pottery from the Gold Coast and Ashanti. JRAI 64 (1934), pp. 203-215.

10,211 WILD, R. P. Stone artefacts of the Gold Coast and Ashanti. GOLD COAST REV. 3 (1927), pp. 157-194.

10,212 WILD, R. P. A stone implement of palaeolithic type from the Gold Coast Colony. GOLD COAST REV. 5 (1929), pp. 174-179.

10,213 WILD, R. P. An unusual type of primitive iron smelting furnace at Abomposu, Ashanti. GOLD COAST REV. 5 (1929), pp. 184-192.

10,214 WILD, R. P. Vestiges of a pre-Ashanti race at Obuasi (Ashanti). GOLD COAST REV. 5 (1929), pp. 1-17.

10,215 YORK, R. N. Excavations at Bui: a preliminary report. UNIV. GHANA RES. REV. 1 (1965), no. 2, pp. 36-39.

10,216 School of Music and Drama. UNIV. GHANA RES. REV. 1 (1965), no. 2, pp. 6-10.

See also 10499.

Biography

10,217 SMITH, E. W. Un éducateur: Dr. J. Aggrey. PRESENCE AFR. 8 (1950), pp. 123-131.

10,218 LOCHNER, N. Anton Wilhelm Amo: a Ghana scholar in eighteenth century Germany. TR. HIST. SOC. GHANA 3 (1958), pp. 169-179.

10,219 BERESFORD-STOOKE, G. Obituary: Sir Charles Arden-Clarke. AFRICA 33 (1963), p. 93.

10,220 Sir Charles Arden-Clarke. AFR. AFFAIRS 62 (1963), p. 5.

10,221 CHAPLIN, J. H. Notes on a Ghanaian been-to [R. E. G. Armattoe]. MAKERERE J. 11 (1965), pp. 17-22.

10,222 KWAKU, W. A. Raphael Ernst Glikpo Armattoe (1913-1953). AFR. UND UB. 38 (1953-1954), pp. 111-112.

10,223 KORSAH, Sir A. D. M. Balme. UNIVERSITAS 3 (1957), pp. 3-4.

10,224 AKITA, J. M. Biographical sketch of George Blankson of Anomabu. TR. HIST. SOC. GHANA 1 (1952-1955), pp. 217-222.

10,225 GAULD, D. T. Angus Booth—an appreciation. UNIVERSITAS 3 (1958), pp. 84-85.

10,226 PRIESTLEY, M. A. Richard Brew; an eighteenth-century trader at Anomabu. TR. HIST. SOC. GHANA 4 (1959), pp. 29-46.

10,227 Un homme de sciences africain. [K. A. Busia]. ZAIRE 4 (1950), pp. 1021-1022.

10,228 BARTELS, F. L. Jacobus Eliza Johannes Capitein 1717-47. TR. HIST. SOC. GHANA 4 (1959), pp. 3-13.

10,229 SEIDEL, A. J. G. Christaller und die afrikanische Sprachwissenschaft. ZAOS 2 (1896), pp. 267-270.

10,230 Gold Coast's first Assembly woman [Miss Mabel Dove]. AFR. WOMEN 1 (1954), pp. 15-16.

10,231 SAMPSON, M. J. George Ekem Ferguson of Anomabu. TR. HIST. SOC. GHANA 2 (1956), pp. 30-45.

10,232 Casely Hayford: an appreciation. WASU 3-4 (1927), pp. 15-16.

10,233 NEWLANDS, H. S. A rolling stone [Joseph Sebastian Mensa]. J. AFR. SOC. 23 (1924), pp. 299-304.

10,234 PADMORE, G. Ghana—l'autobiographie de Kwame Nkruma. PRESENCE AFR. N.S. 12 (1957), pp. 27-31.

10,235 BARTELS, F. L. Philip Quaque, 1741-1816. TR. HIST. SOC. GHANA 1 (1952-1955), pp. 153-177.

10,236 JONES-QUARTEY, K. A. B. A note on J. M. Sarbah and J. E. Casely Hayford: Ghanaian leaders, politicians, and journalists—1864-1930. SIERRA LEONE STUD. 14 (1960), pp. 57-62.

10,237 BAETA, C. G. In memoriam: Sydney George Williamson: 1906-1959. UNIVERSITAS 4 (1959), pp. 11-13.

Economics

10,238 ALEXANDER, J. T. The retailer. UNIVERSITAS 3 (1959), pp. 172-175.

10,239 ALLEN, K. Gold mining in Ghana. AFR. AFFAIRS 57 (1958), pp. 221-240.

10,240 BARBARA. Oil palm plantations. UNIVERSITAS 4 (1959), pp. 13-15.

10,241 BEVIN, H. J. The Gold Coast economy about 1880. TR. HIST. SOC. GHANA 2 (1956), pp. 73-86.

10,242 BIRMINGHAM, W. B. and TAIT, D. Standards of living in the Gold Coast—a comment. UNIVERSITAS 1, no. 3 (1954), pp. 20-22; 1, no. 4 (1954), pp. 8-11.

10,243 CANTOR, D. J. Effects of import-replacing industrialisation on the foreign trade of Ghana. NJESS 6 (1964), pp. 231-238.

10,244 CONCILIATOR. Towards improved industrial relations. UNIVERSITAS 4 (1960), pp. 41-43.

10,245 DALTON, J. H. Colony and metropolis: some aspects of British rule in Gold Coast and their implications for an understanding of Ghana today. J. ECON. HIST. 21 (1961), pp. 552-565.

10,246 DE FREITAS, Sir G. Britain and Ghana's economy. AFR. AFFAIRS 62 (1963), pp. 290-299.

10,247 DICKSON, K. B. The development of road transport in Southern Ghana and Ashanti since about 1850. TR. HIST. SOC. GHANA 5 (1961), pp. 33-42.

10,248 ECONOMIST. Government revenue and expenditure in Ghana. UNIVERSITAS 3 (1958), pp. 109-112.

10,249 FAHM, L. A. Capital formation, balance of payments, and absorptive capacity in Ghana and Nigeria. PAN-AFRICANISM RECONSIDERED, 1962, pp. 169-187.

10,250 FORD, S. H. Manganese ore in the Gold Coast. J. AFR. SOC. 19 (1920), pp. 278-284.

10,251 GARLICK, P. C. The matrilineal family system and business enterprise. NISER 6 (1958), pp. 121-131.

10,252 GAULD, D. T. Fisheries research. UNIVERSITAS 1, no. 2 (1954), pp. 12-14.

10,253 GAULD, D. T. Herring. UNIVERSITAS 4 (1960), pp. 76-78.

10,254 GRAY, A. Ghana in difficulties. AFR. AFFAIRS 56 (1957), pp. 181-183.

10,255 GRAY, A. Volta Project Report. AFR. AFFAIRS 55 (1956), pp. 254-255.

10,256 GRAY, A. Volta scheme greenlight. AFR. AFFAIRS 61 (1962), pp. 112-113.

10,257 HAMMOND, N. J. D. Ghana on the move. AFR. AFFAIRS 62 (1963), pp. 249-258.

10,258 HILL, P. The history of the migration of Ghana cocoa farmers. TR. HIST. SOC. GHANA 4 (1959), pp. 14-28.

10,259 HILL, P. The migrant cocoa farmers of southern Ghana. AFRICA 31 (1961), pp. 209-230.

10,260 HILL, P. The migration of Ghana cocoa farmers or the system of migration by company. NISER 6 (1958), pp. 1-9.

10,261 HILL, P. The migration of southern Ghanaian cocoa farmers. BULL. IFAN 22 (1960), pp. 419-425.

10,262 HILL, P. Systems of labour employment on Gold Coast cocoa farms. WAISER 5 (1956), pp. 54-67.

10,263 HILL, P. Two economists in the field [Cocoa development in Ahafo, West Ashanti by F. R. Bray and African traders in Kumasi by P. C. Garlick]. UNIVERSITAS 4 (1960), pp. 53-55.

10,264 HILL, P. and McGLADE, C. "Companies" and cocoa growing in Akim Abuakwa. UNIVERSITAS 2 (1956), pp. 109-111.

10,265 JUGE, P. E. The 1961 Sekondi-Takoradi strike: crisis in Ghanaian mobilization. PROC. 3RD. GRAD. ACAD. UCLA, 1965, pp. 83-95.

10,266 KATZ, S. I. Development and stability in Central and West Africa: a study in colonial monetary institutions. SOCIAL AND ECON. STUD. 5 (1956), pp. 281-294.

10,267 KULICK, G. D. The impact of the Volta River project on the economy of Ghana. PROC. 3RD. GRAD. ACAD. UCLA, 1965, pp. 113-125.

10,268 LAWSON, R. Some economic problems of development in the Gold Coast fishing industry. WAISER EC. 2 (1953), pp. 129-133.

10,269 LAWSON, R. M. The structure, migration and resettlement of Ewe fishing units. AFR. STUD. 17 (1958), pp. 21-27.

10,270 LIRONI, H. E. An experimental power surf boat. CORONA 1, no. 5 (1949), pp. 22-23.

10,271 MARCELLA. The benefits of big business. UNIVERSITAS 2 (1957), pp. 154-156.

10,272 MARCELLA. The Ghanaian in business. UNIVERSITAS 3 (1958), pp. 37-40.

10,273 MARCELLA. The Gold Coast, industrialisation and overseas enterprise. UNIVERSITAS 2 (1956), pp. 73-76.

10,274 MARCELLA. Private investment in the Gold Coast. UNIVERSITAS 2 (1956), pp. 111-113.

10,275 MARCELLA. The role of the overseas businessman in Ghana's economic development. UNIVERSITAS 2 (1957), pp. 185-187.

10,276 MATEKOLE, Nene A. The Gold Coast: development in the native states. CORONA 2 (1950), pp. 446-449.

10,277 MERCATOR. The economic development of agriculture assets. UNIVERSITAS 4 (1960), pp. 106-109.

10,278 MERCATOR. The wholesaler's changing role. UNIVERSITAS 5 (1962), pp. 11-12.

10,279 MUNGER, E. S. Land use in Accra. ZAIRE 8 (1954), pp. 911-919.

10,280 NICULESCU, B. M. Food and roads in the Gold Coast. WAISER 5 (1956), pp. 68-73.

10,281 OMABOE, F. N. Market research in Ghana. NISER 6 (1958), pp. 132-139.

10,282 RADO, E. R. The African contractor and the Gold Coast building industry. WAISER 5 (1956), pp. 95-96.

10,283 RATTRAY, R. S. A solo flight from England to the Gold Coast in Cirrus-Moth G. Ebzz... GOLD COAST REV. 5 (1929), pp. 18-72.

10,284 ROWLATT, M. Radio and Mrs. Mensah. CORONA 1, no. 8 (1949), pp. 28-31.

10,285 SIRCAR, P. K. Ghana and the Volta project. AFR. QUART. 1, no. ii (1961), pp. 30-37.

10,286 STEEL, R. W. Economic change in Ghana. THE YEAR BOOK OF WORLD AFFAIRS 19 (1965), pp. 89-112.

10,287 SZERESZEWSKI, R. The process of growth in Ghana, 1891-1911. J. DEVELOPMENT STUD. 1 (1965), pp. 123-141.

10,288 TAIT, D. Food in the Northern Territories. UNIVERSITAS 2 (1955), pp. 76-77.

10,289 TAIT, D. On the growth of some Konkomba markets. WAISER SOC. 2 (1953), pp. 38-50.

10,290 THOMAS, I. B. Ghana. CIVILISATIONS 7 (1957), pp. 387-388, 616.

10,291 TUDHOPE, W. T. D. The development of the cocoa industry in the Gold Coast and Ashanti. J. AFR. SOC. 9 (1909), pp. 34-45.

10,292 WHITE, H. P. Environment and land use in the south eastern savannas of the Gold Coast. WAISER 5 (1956), pp. 74-84.

10,293 WILLIAMS, J. W. The cocoa price policy in the Gold Coast. WAISER EC. 2 (1953), pp. 82-96.

10,294 WILLIAMS, J. W. The question of a Gold Coast currency. UNIVERSITAS 1, no. 2 (1954), pp. 15-17.

10,295 Ghana development plan. AFR. QUART. 3, no. 4 (1964), pp. 257-271.

10,296 Projet d'industrialisation en Gold Coast. ZAIRE 7 (1953), pp. 198-199.

10,297 The Volta Basin survey. UNIV. GHANA RES. REV. 1 (1965), p. 14.

10,298 The Volta River Project. AFR. AFFAIRS 55 (1956), pp. 287-293.

10,299 The Volta scheme. CORONA 3 (1951), pp. 181-182.

See also 1237, 11415.

Education

10,300 ALEXANDER, J. T. Careers and a university education. UNIVERSITAS 4 (1961), pp. 131-134.

10,301 ASAMDA, E. A. The problem of language in education in the Gold Coast. AFRICA 25 (1955), pp. 60-78.

10,302 AUDAX. The academic mind considered: occasional thoughts by an occasional thinker. UNIVERSITAS 4 (1960), pp. 87-88.

10,303 BALME, D. M. Preliminaries to a university. UNIVERSITAS 1, no. 2 (1954), pp. 6-9.

10,304 BALME, D. M. Reflecting on work done. UNIVERSITAS 3 (1957), pp. 4-6.

10,305 BALME, D. M. University aims in the Gold Coast. UNIVERSITAS 1, no. 3 (1954), pp. 13-15.

10,306 BARTELS, F. L. Education in the Gold Coast. AFR. AFFAIRS 48 (1949), pp. 300-311.

10,307 BURTON, E. M. Housecraft in Ghana. AFR. WOMEN 2 (1956-1958), pp. 58-61.

10,308 C., J. L'éducation des masses en Gold Coast. ZAIRE 6 (1952), pp. 865-866.

10,309 DOUGLAS, A. B. The anansesem in Gold Coast schools. GOLD COAST REV. 5 (1929), pp. 125-143.

10,310 DU SAUTOY, P. The academic and the bureaucrat. UNIVERSITAS 1, no. 5 (1955), pp. 4-5.

10,311 ENGMANN, E. A. W. The work of a teacher in Africa. INT. REV. MISSIONS 36 (1947), pp. 324-328.

10,312 FRASER, A. G. Denationalisation. GOLD COAST REV. 1 (1925), pp. 71-75.

10,313 FRASER, A. G. What Achimota has done. GOLD COAST REV. 3 (1927), pp. 229-268.

10,314 GBEDEMAH, K. A. The University College [a toast]. UNIVERSITAS 4 (1961), p. 167.

10,315 GIBBONS, P. C. A university in Ghana. UNIVERSITAS 4 (1960), pp. 103-104.

10,316 HILLIARD, F. H. Some educational principles of Greece and Rome and their relevance today. UNIVERSITAS 1, no. 6 (1955), pp. 14-17.

10,317 HIPPODAMUS. Legon Hill. UNIVERSITAS 1, no. 1 (1953), pp. 13-15.

10,318 KIMBLE, H. A reading survey in Accra. UNIVERSITAS 2 (1956), pp. 77-81.

10,319 MARTIN, E. C. Early educational experiments on the Gold Coast. J. AFR. SOC. 23 (1924), pp. 294-298.

10,320 MASON, I. Teaching and reading material in Fante, Gold Coast. TOWARDS A LITERATE AFRICA, 1948, pp. 40-44.

10,321 NKETIA, J. H. Progress in Gold Coast education. TR. HIST. SOC. GHANA 1 (1952-1955), pp. 63-71.

10,322 OWEN, G. African women in broadcasting. AFR. WOMEN 2 (1956-1958), pp. 49-51.

10,323 OWUSU, C. A. P. Nursery schools in tropical countries—Ghana. AFR. WOMEN 3 (1958-1960), pp. 26-29.

10,324 PICKARD-CAMBRIDGE, A. W. The place of Achimota in West African education. J. AFR. SOC. 39 (1940), pp. 143-153.

10,325 SEWELL, W. G. From China to Ghana. UNIVERSITAS 3 (1957), pp. 7-8.

10,326 TAY, J. The National Women's Training Centre, Pamfokrom, Ghana. AFR. WOMEN 5 (1962), pp. 1-3.

10,327 VARLEY, W. J. Operation inauguration [University College of the Gold Coast]. UNIVERSITAS 1, no. 1 (1953), pp. 18-19.

10,328 WARD, A. H. "Throw physic(s) to the dogs." UNIVERSITAS 5 (1962), pp. 39-41.

10,329 WHITE, K. Building up of voluntary effort amongst women in Ashanti. TOWARDS A LITERATE AFRICA, 1948, pp. 49-54.

10,330 WILSON, J. Gold Coast information. AFR. AFFAIRS 43 (1944), pp. 111-115.

10,331 WOOD, N. P. Cape Coast day nurseries. AFR. WOMEN 1 (1955), pp. 43-44.

10,332 YOUNG, R. R. Central, local, and voluntary initiative. TOWARDS A LITERATE AFRICA, 1948, pp. 45-49.

10,333 Ghana women and higher education [extract from the report of the Commission on University education in Ghana, 1961]. AFR. WOMEN 4 (1961), p. 62.

10,334 Grants for universities. CORONA 1, no. 2 (1949), p. 20.

10,335 Progrès de l'enseignement en Gold Coast. ZAIRE 6 (1952), pp. 746-747.

10,336 Status of women in Togoland and the Cameroons. AFR. WOMEN 1 (1956), pp. 95-98.

10,337 L'Université de Gold Coast. ZAIRE 4 (1950), p. 896.

10,338 The University College [of the Gold Coast] bye-laws. UNIVERSITAS 1, no. 2 (1954), pp. 5-6.

See also 9333.

Geography

10,339 ANDERSON, M. M. and BRUCKNER, W. D. Note on raised shorelines of the Gold Coast. PROC. PAN-AFR. CONGR. PRE-HIST. 3 (1955), pp. 86-92.

10,340 AUCHINLECK, G. G. Seasonal and geographical distribution of rainfall in the Gold Coast. GOLD COAST REV. 2 (1926), pp. 28-33.

10,341 AUSTIN, W. G. C. To Senya Beraku. UNIVERSITAS 5 (1962), pp. 8-11.

10,342 BOATENG, E. A. Geographical research in West Africa. UNIVERSITAS 3 (1958), pp. 45-46.

10,343 BOATENG, E. A. Some notes on the classification of Gold Coast settlements. UNIVERSITAS 2 (1955), pp. 19-21.

10,344 BOATENG, E. A. The study of human settlements. UNIVERSITAS 1, no. 3 (1954), pp. 16-18.

10,345 CLENDINNING, J. Note on the magnetic variation in the Gold Coast. GOLD COAST REV. 2 (1926), pp. 271-274.

10,346 CLENDINNING, J. Sunrise and sunset in the Gold Coast. GOLD COAST REV. 2 (1926), pp. 275-276.

10,347 COFIE, J. "The Desert of Gofan": was it ever densely inhabited? GHANA NOTES 5 (1963), pp. 10-15.

10,348 DAVIES, O. The raised beaches of the Gold Coast in relation to those of Natal and of the Mediterranean. PROC. PAN-AFR. CONGR. PRE-HIST. 2 (1952), pp. 259-261.

10,349 DICKSON, K. B. Development of the copra industry in Ghana. J. TROP. GEOG. 19 (1964), pp. 27-34.

10,350 HAMILTON, R. Bovals on the Gold Coast. NIGERIAN FIELD 20 (1955), pp. 141-142.

10,351 HILTON, T. E. Bawku. UNIVERSITAS 3 (1958), pp. 108-109.

10,352 HILTON, T. E. The economic development of the southeastern coastal plains of Ghana. J. TROP. GEOG. 16 (1962), pp. 18-31.

10,353 HILTON, T. E. Frafra resettlement and the population problem in Zuarungu. UNIVERSITAS 3 (1959), pp. 144-146.

10,354 HILTON, T. E. Le peuplement de Frafra, district du Nord-Ghana. BULL. IFAN 27 (1965), pp. 678-700.

10,355 JOHNSTON, A. D. A coasting voyage from Sekondi to Marseilles. GOLD COAST REV. 4 (1928), pp. 94-119, 172-203.

10,356 MIGEOD, F. W. H. The Gold Coast: — its physical features, flora, fauna, and ethnology. J. AFR. SOC. 13 (1914), pp. 369-384.

10,357 RILEY, W. T. C. Account of an expedition to the town of Tombouctou by motor cycle and sidecar made by Captain W. T. C. Riley, F. R. G. S., K. M. Vaugham and Captain Sayers Gowing. GOLD COAST REV. 2 (1926), pp. 53-70.

10,358 RODGER, J. P. The Gold Coast of today. J. AFR. SOC. 9 (1909), pp. 1-18.

10,359 SLATER, Sir R. Changing problems of the Gold Coast. J. AFR. SOC. 29 (1930), pp. 461-466.

10,360 WILLMER, J. E. Three geographers in search of a school text. UNIVERSITAS 3 (1959), pp. 182-184.

10,361 Quelques données sur le Ghana. PRESENCE AFR. 12 (1957), pp. 6-10.

10,362 Three thousand miles in the Gold Coast. GOLD COAST REV. 4 (1928), pp. 66-93.

Government. Politics. Administration

10,363 ACQUAH, I. The development and functioning of municipal government in Accra. WAISER 5 (1956), pp. 97-98.

10,364 AFRICAN STUDIES BRANCH. Local Authority Police Forces. J. AFR. ADM. 6 (1954), pp. 64-66.

10,365 AFRICAN STUDIES BRANCH. A note on four recent Local and Regional Government reports from the Gold Coast. J. AFR. ADM. 3 (1951), pp. 192-201.

10,366 AFRICANUS, P. Emancipations africaines: naissance du Ghana. AFR. ET ASIE 38 (1957), pp. 3-14.

10,367 ALTON, E. B. S. The Local Government Training School in the Gold Coast. J. AFR. ADM. 4 (1952), pp. 108-113.

10,368 AMAMOO, J. G. Fresh national problems. AFR. AFFAIRS 55 (1956), pp. 303-304.

10,369 AMAMOO, J. G. Ghana and western democracies. AFR. AFFAIRS 58 (1959), pp. 54-60.

10,370 APTER, D. E. Some economic factors in the political development of the Gold Coast. J. ECON. HIST. 14 (1954), pp. 409-427.

10,371 ARDEN-CLARKE, Sir C. Eight years of transition in Ghana. AFR. AFFAIRS 57 (1958), pp. 29-37.

10,372 ARDEN-CLARKE, Sir C. Gold Coast into Ghana. Some problems of transition. INTERNAT. AFFAIRS 34 (1958), pp. 49-56.

10,373 ASAFU-ADJAYE, E. O. Ghana since independence. AFR. AFFAIRS 57 (1958), pp. 182-188.

10,374 ASANTE, K. B. Towards the future in Ghana. AFR. AFFAIRS 57 (1958), pp. 52-57.

10,375 AUSTIN, D. G. Elections in an African rural area. AFRICA 31 (1961), pp. 1-17.

10,376 AUSTIN, D. G. The Ghana government. AFR. SOUTH 3, no. 3 (1959), pp. 90-96.

10,377 AUSTIN, D. G. Institutional history of the Gold Coast/ Ghana. WHAT ARE THE PROBLEMS OF PARL. GOVT. IN W. AFR.?, 1958, pp. 6-18.

10,378 AUSTIN, D. G. The uncertain frontier: Ghana-Togo. J. MOD. AFR. STUD. 1 (1963), pp. 139-145.

10,379 AUSTIN, D. G. The Working Committee of the United Gold Coast Convention. J. AFR. HIST. 2 (1961), pp. 273-297.

10,380 BEHANZIN, L. S. Signification historique d'une indépendance. PRESENCE AFR. N.S. 12 (1957), pp. 58-63.

10,381 C., J. A propos du gouvernement local en Gold Coast. ZAIRE 8 (1954), pp. 947-948.

10,382 C., J. Nouveaux progrès en Gold Coast. ZAIRE 8 (1954), pp. 637-638.

10,383 CANHAM, P. H. Local government in Ashanti. CORONA 1, no. 4 (1949), pp. 16-18.

10,384 CANHAM, P. H. and PATTESON, J. E. The Gold Coast General Election, 1951. 2. The election itself in two areas of Ashanti—the Municipality of Kumasi and the Rural Electoral District of Kumasi South. J. AFR. ADM. 3 (1951), pp. 73-77.

10,385 CARDINALL, A. W. Our mandate in north Togoland. J. AFR. SOC. 21 (1922), pp. 302-308; 22 (1922), pp. 43-49.

10,386 CATLIN, G. Gold Coast democracy. CONTEMP. REV. 189 (1956), pp. 338-341.

10,387 CAYTON, H. What problems face the new nation, Ghana? PRESENCE AFR. N.S. 12 (1957), pp. 78-85.

10,388 CLIGNET, R. P. and FOSTER, P. Potential elites in Ghana and the Ivory Coast, a preliminary comparison. AMER. J. SOC. 70 (1964-1965), pp. 349-362.

10,389 COLVIN, I. Ghana: the morning after. AFR. SOUTH 2, no. 3 (1958), pp. 69-74.

10,390 CONFALONIERI, V. B. Costa d'Oro. AFRICA (Rome) 10 (1955), pp. 219-220.

10,391 DANQUAH, J. B. Autopsy on old Ashanti [review of <u>The position of the Chief in the modern political system of Ashanti</u>, by K. A. Busia]. AFR. AFFAIRS 51 (1952), pp. 134-143.

10,392 DENNIS, P. C. W. A note on land revenue and Local Government in Ghana. J. AFR. ADM. 9 (1957), pp. 84-88.

10,393 ENSOR, M. The Togolands: an Anglo-French experiment. CORONA 1, no. 7 (1949), pp. 29-32.

10,394 ERZUAH, J. B. Comparative study of constitutional and administrative structures in Ghana. CIVILISATIONS 14 (1964), pp. 85-91; French summary, pp. 92-93.

10,395 FRANKLIN, A. The Gold Coast revolution. PRESENCE AFR. 14 (1953), pp. 307-311.

10,396 G., J. Voyage de deux ministres de la Gold Coast. ZAIRE 5 (1951), p. 754.

10,397 GODFREY, J. L. The emergence of Ghana. COMMONWEALTH PERSPECTIVES, 1958, pp. 125-144.

10,398 GRAY, A. Ghana and Guinea. AFR. AFFAIRS 58 (1959), pp. 3-4.

10,399 GRAY, A. Ghana developments. AFR. AFFAIRS 61 (1962), pp. 6-10.

10,400 GRAY, A. Ghana republic. AFR. AFFAIRS 59 (1960), pp. 289-291.

10,401 GRAY, A. Ghana scene [government's attitude to South Africa]. AFR. AFFAIRS 60 (1961), pp. 380-381.

10,402 GRAY, A. Ghana still disturbed. AFR. AFFAIRS 57 (1958), pp. 4-5.

10,403 GRAY, A. Ghana unrest. AFR. AFFAIRS 56 (1957), pp. 250-251.

10,404 GRAY, A. Gold Coast differences. AFR. AFFAIRS 54 (1955), pp. 248-250; 56 (1957), pp. 5-6.

10,405 GRAY, A. Gold Coast elections. AFR. AFFAIRS 55 (1956), pp. 166-169, 253-254.

10,406 GRAY, A. Gold Coast report. AFR. AFFAIRS 55 (1956), pp. 98-100.

10,407 GRAY, A. Gold Coast unrest. AFR. AFFAIRS 54 (1955), pp. 85-86.

10,408 GRAY, A. Royal visit to Ghana. AFR. AFFAIRS 59 (1960), pp. 2-3.

10,409 GRAY, A. Togoland plebiscite. AFR. AFFAIRS 55 (1956), pp. 169-171.

10,410 GRAY, A. Togoland tomorrow. AFR. AFFAIRS 55 (1956), pp. 14-15.

10,411 GREENWOOD, A. F. Ten years local government in Ghana. J. LOCAL ADM. OV. 1 (1962), pp. 23-28.

10,412 GROGAN, V. The evolution of the constitution of Ghana. AFR. QUART. 3, no. i (1963), pp. 4-13.

10,413 GUERIN, D. Au Ghana. "Syndicalisme et Socialisme." Réponse à S. G. Ikoku. PRESENCE AFR. N.S. 51 (1964), pp. 14-23.

10,414 GUGGISBERG, F. G. The goal of the Gold Coast. J. AFR. SOC. 21 (1922), pp. 81-91.

10,415 HANNIGAN, A. St. J. J. Efficiency against self expression in local government. UNIVERSITAS 3 (1958), pp. 68-72.

10,416 HANNIGAN, A. St. J. J. Local Government in the Gold Coast. J. AFR. ADM. 7 (1955), pp. 116-123.

10,417 HANNIGAN, A. St. J. J. The present system of succession amongst the Akan people of the Gold Coast. J. AFR. ADM. 6 (1954), pp. 166-171.

10,418 HATCH, J. Policies and politics in the Gold Coast. AFR. SOUTH 1, no. 1 (1956), pp. 107-115.

10,419 HAYFORD, C. Decentralisation: its advantages and disadvantages. GOLD COAST REV. 2 (1926), pp. 34-36.

10,420 HEER, N. A. DE. Ghana. CIVILISATIONS 8 (1958), pp. 132-136, 325-330, 421-428, 611-615; 9 (1959), pp. 238-245.

10,421 LEGASSICK, M. The ideology of the Convention People's Party: a historical perspective. PROC. 3RD. GRAD. ACAD. UCLA, 1965, pp. 69-81.

10,422 LEGUM, C. Ghana: the morning after: the Accra Conference. AFR. SOUTH 2, no. 4 (1958), pp. 82-93.

10,423 McLAREN, C. A. Local Government training in the Gold Coast. J. AFR. ADM. 9 (1957), pp. 63-71.

10,424 MAIR, L. P. Representative local government as a problem in social change. RHODES-LIV. J. 21 (1957), pp. 1-17.

10,425 MERCER, T. M. K. The Gold Coast development programme. AFR. AFFAIRS 55 (1956), pp. 27-32.

10,426 MURRAY, A. H. and DRYSDALE, J. G. S. Town boards in Agona State. J. AFR. ADM. 3 (1951), pp. 110-112.

10,427 NKRUMAH, K. La naissance de mon parti et son programme d'action positive. PRESENCE AFR. N.S. 12 (1957), pp. 11-26.

10,428 O'DONOVAN, P. The new Africa. CORONA 3 (1951), pp. 179-180.

10,429 OFOSU-APPIAH, L. H. International cooperation in Africa: aims, problems and achievements with special reference to Ghana. COOPERAZIONE INT. AFR., 1960, pp. 425-429.

10,430 PACKHAM, E. S. Notes on the development of the Native Authorities in Northern Territories of the Gold Coast. J. AFR. ADM. 2 (1950), pp. 26-30.

10,431 PAUVERT, J. C. L'évolution politique des Ewé. CAH. ET. AFR. 1 (1960), pp. 161-191.

10,432 PETERS, W. Tradition and change in the Saltpond subdistrict of the Gold Coast Colony. J. AFR. ADM. 6 (1954), pp. 5-11.

10,433 PRASAD, A. Nationalism and politics in Ghana. AFRICA 1, no. iv (1962), pp. 46-58.

10,434 PRICE, J. H. The future of democracy in Ghana. UNIVERSITAS 4 (1961), pp. 136-138.

10,435 PRICE, J. H. The Ghana White Paper. UNIVERSITAS 2 (1957), pp. 194-195.

10,436 PRICE, J. H. How democracy works in Ghana. UNIVERSITAS 4 (1960), pp. 105-106.

10,437 ROHDIE, S. The Gold Coast Aborigines abroad. J. AFR. HIST. 6 (1965), pp. 389-411.

10,438 RUSSELL, A. C. The Gold Coast General Election, 1951. 1. The delimitation of electoral areas, the registration of electors, and the conduct of the elections. J. AFR. ADM. 3 (1951), pp. 65-73.

10,439 SALOWAY, Sir R. The new Gold Coast. INTERNAT. AFFAIRS 31 (1955), pp. 469-476.

10,440 SAMPSON, A. Ghana: the morning after. AFR. SOUTH 2, no. 2 (1958), pp. 91-96.

10,441 SENGAT-KUO, F. Ghana: un exemple et un test. PRESENCE AFR. N.S. 12 (1957), pp. 69-70.

10,442 TIGER, L. Nkrumah's Ghana and the theory of charisma. BULL. AFR. STUD. CANADA 2, no. 1 (1964), pp. 2-10.

10,443 WALLERSTEIN, I. Le Ghana face au présent. PRESENCE AFR. N.S. 18-19 (1958), pp. 184-194.

10,444 WALLIS, C. A. G. The British form of Local Government finds new adherents. J. AFR. ADM. 4 (1952), pp. 68-70.

10,445 WALLIS, C. A. G. Reorganization of Local Government in Ghana. J. AFR. ADM. 11 (1959), pp. 22-26.

10,446 WRAITH, R. E. West Africa d'Outre Mer. CORONA 3 (1951), pp. 426-427.

10,447 WRONG, M. The evolution of local government in British African colonies. INTERNAT. AFFAIRS 22 (1946), pp. 418-421.

10,448 La constitution de l'état de Ghana. PRESENCE AFR. N.S. 12 (1957), pp. 48-58.

10,449 Constitutional reform in the Gold Coast: the recommendations of the Coussey Committee. J. AFR. ADM. 2 (1950), pp. 2-11.

10,450 Evènements au Ghana. PRESENCE AFR. N.S. 44 (1962), pp. 215-216.

10,451 Fin de la crise politique à Abéokouta. ZAIRE 5 (1951), pp. 295-296.

10,452 The governor's powers, their basis and their delegation to District Commissioners. GOLD COAST REV. 5 (1929), pp. 96-104.

10,453 Local Government reform in the Gold Coast. A survey of the proposals of the Coussey Committee. J. AFR. ADM. 2 (1950), pp. 35-44.

10,454 Nouvelle constitution de la Gold-Coast. ZAIRE 5 (1951), p. 406.

10,455 Nouvelles de Gold Coast. ZAIRE 6 (1952), p. 189.

10,456 Opening of British colonial administrative services to Africans. J. AFR. SOC. 41 (1942), pp. 219-220.

10,457 Partis politiques indigènes en Gold Coast. ZAIRE 5 (1951), p. 70.

10,458 Personnel politique de la Gold Coast. ZAIRE 7 (1953), pp. 1089-1090.

10,459 Le premier ministère de la Gold Coast. ZAIRE 5 (1951), pp. 626-627.

10,460 Réforme du gouvernement local en Gold Coast. ZAIRE 6 (1952), p. 633.

10,461 Régionalisme et politique en Gold Coast. ZAIRE 9 (1955), pp. 307-308.

10,462 Report of the Regional Constitutional Commission; 1958. J. AFR. ADM. 11 (1959), pp. 107-108.

10,463 Report (with the Legislative Council Decisions thereon) of the Select Committee of the Legislative Council appointed to examine the questions of Elections and Constituencies. J. AFR. ADM. 3 (1951), pp. 44-45.

10,464 Two new constitutions [for the Gold Coast and Northern Rhodesia]. AFR. AFFAIRS 44 (1945), pp. 2-3.

10,465 West African democracy. AFR. AFFAIRS 44 (1945), pp. 49-50.

See also 8587, 9335.

History

10,466 ABRAHAM, W. The life and times of Anton Wilhelm Amo. TR. HIST. SOC. GHANA 7 (1964), pp. 60-81.

10,467 ACKAH, C. A. The historical significance of some Ghanaian festivals. GHANA NOTES 5 (1963), pp. 16-27.

10,468 ADAMS, C. D. Activities of Danish botanists in Guinea 1783-1850. TR. HIST. SOC. GHANA 3 (1957), pp. 30-46.

10,469 AGBODEKA, F. The Fanti Confederacy, 1865-69. TR. HIST. SOC. GHANA 7 (1964), pp. 82-123.

10,470 AGYEMANG-DUAH, J. History of the Mpintin drums. GHANA NOTES 2 (1961), p. 12.

10,471 AGYEMANG-DUAH, J. Mampong, Ashanti: a traditional history to the reign of Nana Safo Kantanka. TR. HIST. SOC. GHANA 4 (1960), pp. 21-25.

10,472 AKITA, J. M. Documentary material available for historical research in the Gold Coast. TR. HIST. SOC. GHANA 1 (1952-1955), pp. 21-23.

10,473 AKITA, J. M. The National Archives of Ghana. GHANA LIBRARY J. 1 (1963), pp. 8-12.

10,474 ALBERICH, J. C. Notes sobre Ghana. CUAD. AFR. OR. 39 (1957), pp. 41-53.

10,475 ARHIN, K. A note on Ahafo oral traditions. UNIV. GHANA RES. REV. 1 (1965), pp. 27-29.

10,476 ATTAFUA, A. B. Traditional history. TR. HIST. SOC. GHANA 1 (1952-1955), pp. 18-20.

10,477 AUSTIN, D. The new Ghana. AFR. AFFAIRS 59 (1960), pp. 20-25.

10,478 AZU, A. A. Adangbe (Adangme) history. GOLD COAST REV. 2 (1926), pp. 239-270; 3 (1927), pp. 89-116; 4 (1928), pp. 3-29.

10,479 BAGYIRE VI, O. Abiriwhene. The Guans: a preliminary note. GHANA NOTES 7 (1965), pp. 21-24.

10,480 BEHANZIN, L. S. Signification d'une indépendance. PRESENCE AFR. N.S. 12 (1957), pp. 58-63.

10,481 BOAHEN, A. A. Asante-Dahomey contacts in the 19th century. GHANA NOTES 7 (1965), pp. 1-3.

10,482 BOAHEN, A. A. Ashanti Research Scheme: Court proceedings. ASHANTI RES. PROJ. 1ST. CONF., 1964, pp. 60-61.

10,483 BOAHEN, A. A. Juaben and Kumasi relations in the 19th century. ASHANTI RES. PROJ. 1ST. CONF., 1964, pp. 25-33.

10,484 BOAHEN, A. The roots of Ghanaian nationalism. J. AFR. HIST. 5 (1964), pp. 127-132.

10,485 BROKENSHA, D. Chief Akrofi of Larteh. TR. HIST. SOC. GHANA 7 (1964), pp. 12-23.

10,486 BROOKS, G. E. The letter book of Captain Edward Harrington. TR. HIST. SOC. GHANA 6 (1962), pp. 71-77.

10,487 BROWN, A. A. A. Historical account of Mohammedanism in the Gold Coast. GOLD COAST REV. 3 (1927), pp. 195-197.

10,488 CARTLAND, G. B. The Gold Coast—an historical approach. AFR. AFFAIRS 46 (1947), pp. 89-97.

10,489 CARDINALL, A. W. A survival [the village of Butie]. GOLD COAST REV. 5 (1929), pp. 193-197.

10,490 CAYTON, H. What problems face the new nation, Ghana? PRESENCE AFR. N.S. 12 (1957), pp. 78-85.

10,491 CLIFFORD, H. Recent developments on the Gold Coast. J. AFR. SOC. 18 (1919), pp. 241-253.

10,492 COLLINS, E. The panic element in nineteenth-century British relations with Ashanti. TR. HIST. SOC. GHANA 5 (1962), pp. 79-144.

10,493 COOMBS, D. The place of the 'Certificate of Apologie' in Ghanaian history. TR. HIST. SOC. GHANA 3 (1958), pp. 180-193.

10,494 CROWTHER, F. G. Affairs in Wassaw. GOLD COAST REV. 2 (1926), pp. 168-180.

10,495 CROWTHER, F. G. The Epwe speaking people. GOLD COAST REV. 3 (1927), pp. 11-55.

10,496 DAAKU, K. Y. The European traders and the coastal traders 1630-1720. TR. HIST. SOC. GHANA 8 (1965), pp. 11-23.

10,497 DANQUAH, J. B. The historical significance of the Bond of 1844. TR. HIST. SOC. GHANA 3 (1957), pp. 3-29.

10,498 DANQUAH, J. B. Notes on 'Oburoni' and 'Buronya'. TR. HIST. SOC. GHANA 2 (1956), pp. 71-72.

10,499 DAVIES, O. The invaders of Northern Ghana. What archaeologists are teaching the historians. UNIVERSITAS 4 (1961), pp. 134-136.

10,500 DEBRUNNER, H. Notable Danish chaplains on the Gold Coast. TR. HIST. SOC. GHANA 2 (1956), pp. 13-29.

10,501 DICKSON, K. B. Origin of Ghana's cocoa industry. GHANA NOTES 5 (1963), pp. 4-9.

10,502 FAGE, J. D. The administration of George Maclean on the Gold Coast, 1830-44. TR. HIST. SOC. GHANA 1 (1952-1955), pp. 104-120.

10,503 FAGE, J. D. Ancient Ghana: a review of the evidence. TR. HIST. SOC. GHANA 3 (1957), pp. 77-98.

10,504 FAGE, J. D. A new check list of the forts and castles of Ghana. TR. HIST. SOC. GHANA 4 (1959), pp. 57-67.

10,505 FAGE, J. D. Some general considerations relevant to historical research in the Gold Coast. TR. HIST. SOC. GHANA 1 (1952-1955), pp. 24-29.

10,506 FAGE, J. D. Some notes on a scheme for the investigation of oral tradition in the Northern Territories of the Gold Coast. J. HIST. SOC. NIG. 1 (1956), pp. 15-19.

10,507 FAGE, J. D. Some problems of Gold Coast history. UNIVERSITAS 1, no. 6 (1955), pp. 5-9.

10,508 FARO, J. Estêvão da Gama capitão de S. Jorge da Mina e a sua organização administrativa em 1529. BCGP 12 (1957), pp. 385-442.

10,509 FARO, J. A organização Comercial de S. Jorge da Mina em 1529 e as suas relações com a Ilha de S. Tomé. BCGP 13 (1958), pp. 305-363.

10,510 FELE, B. Ghana et les zones de silence en Afrique Noire. PRESENCE AFR. N.S. 12 (1957), pp. 71-72.

10,511 FILESI, T. Ghana nuovo membro del Commonwealth. AFRICA (Rome) 12 (1957), pp. 112-118.

10,512 FRIMPONG, K. The final obsequies of the late Nana Sir Ofori Atta, K.B.E. Abuakwahene. AFRICA 15 (1945), pp. 80-85.

10,513 FURLEY, J. T. Notes on some Portuguese Governors of the Captaincy Da Mina. TR. HIST. SOC. GHANA 3 (1958), pp. 194-214.

10,514 FYNN, J. K. The reign and times of Kusi Obodum, 1750-64. TR. HIST. SOC. GHANA 8 (1965), pp. 24-32.

10,515 GOODY, J. A note on the penetration of Islam into the west of the Northern Territories of the Gold Coast. TR. HIST. SOC. GHANA 1 (1952-1955), pp. 45-46.

10,516 GOODY, J. and ARHIN, K., eds. Ashanti and the Northwest [a research project with introduction by Jack Goody]. UNIV. GHANA RES. REV. 1 (1965), Supplement, pp. 1-185.

10,517 GOODY, J. and BOATENG, C. Y. The history and traditions of Nkoranza. UNIV. GHANA RES. REV. 1 (1965), Supplement, pp. 170-184.

10,518 GORDON, J. Some oral traditions of Denkyira. TR. HIST. SOC. GHANA 1 (1952-1955), pp. 89-95.

10,519 GRAY, A. Ghana arises. AFR. AFFAIRS 56 (1957), pp. 95-97.

10,520 HILTON, T. E. Notes on the history of Kusasi. TR. HIST. SOC. GHANA 6 (1962), pp. 79-86.

10,521 HOBBS, H. J. History of Nkoranza. GOLD COAST REV. 3 (1927), pp. 117-121.

10,522 HODSON, Sir A. R. The account of the part played by the Gold Coast Brigade in the East African campaign, August, 1940 to May, 1941. J. AFR. SOC. 40 (1941), pp. 300-311; 41 (1942), pp. 14-28.

10,523 HODSON, Sir A. W. The war effort of the Gold Coast. J. AFR. SOC. 39 (1940), pp. 303-305.

10,524 HOLDEN, J. J. The Zabarima conquest of North-west Ghana. TR. HIST. SOC. GHANA 8 (1965), pp. 60-86.

10,525 HOLMES, W. F. Notes on the early history of Tarkwa as a gold mining district. GOLD COAST REV. 2 (1926), pp. 78-117.

10,526 HOLTSBAUM, F. P. Sefwi and its peoples. GOLD COAST REV. 1 (1925), pp. 76-94.

10,527 IRWIN, G. Current trends in African historiography. GHANA NOTES 6 (1964), pp. 4-7.

10,528 IRWIN, G. The origins of the Akan and of Akan culture. UNIVERSITAS 4 (1961), pp. 138-141.

10,529 JOHNSON, M. Ashanti east of the Volta. TR. HIST. SOC. GHANA 8 (1965), pp. 33-59.

10,530 JOHNSON, M. Salaga 1875-1900. UNIV. GHANA RES. REV. 2 (1965), pp. 72-73.

10,531 JONES, D. H. Jakpa and the foundation of Gonja. TR. HIST. SOC. GHANA 6 (1962), pp. 1-29.

10,532 JONES-QUARTEY, K. A. B. Anglo-African journals and journalists in the nineteenth and early twentieth centuries. TR. HIST. SOC. GHANA 4 (1959), pp. 47-56.

10,533 JONES-QUARTEY, K. A. B. Thought and expression in the Gold Coast press: 1874-1930. UNIVERSITAS 3 (1958), pp. 72-75, 113-116.

10,534 KI ZERBO, J. L'histoire recommence. PRESENCE AFR. N.S. 12 (1957), pp. 64-66.

10,535 KOLE, A. M. The historical background of Krobo customs. TR. HIST. SOC. GHANA 1 (1952-1955), pp. 133-140.

10,536 LANDER, J. R. Patterns in historical studies. UNIVERSITAS 1, no. 3 (1954), pp. 19-20.

10,537 LEVTZION, N. Early nineteenth century Arabic manuscripts from Kumasi. TR. HIST. SOC. GHANA 8 (1965), pp. 99-119.

10,538 LIEVRE, P. D. The Kpando Division. GOLD COAST REV. 1 (1925), pp. 29-52.

10,539 LILLEY, C. C. A short history of the Nkonya Division in the Ho District. GOLD COAST REV. 1 (1925), pp. 108-126.

10,540 LOPES, E. C. O problema português na Mina. PORT. EM AFR. 4 (1947), pp. 157-160.

10,541 LOPES, E. C. S. João Baptista de Ajudá. PORT. EM AFR. 1 (1944), pp. 246-250.

10,542 McINTYRE, W. D. British policy in West Africa: the Ashanti expedition of 1873-4. HIST. J. 5 (1962), pp. 19-46.

10,543 MANSFIELD, E. T. History of the bell of Ho. GOLD COAST REV. 2 (1926), pp. 290-292.

10,544 MARTIN, B. G. Arabic materials for Ghanaian history. UNIV. GHANA RES. REV. 2 (1965), pp. 74-83.

10,545 MARTIN, E. C. The English establishments on the Gold Coast in the second half of the eighteenth century. TRHS, 4th series, 5 (1922), pp. 167-208.

10,546 MATSON, J. N. The French at Amoku. TR. HIST. SOC. GHANA 1 (1952-1955), pp. 47-60.

10,547 MATSON, J. N. History in Akan words. TR. HIST. SOC. GHANA 2 (1956), pp. 63-70.

10,548 MAUNY, R. A. The question of Ghana. AFRICA 24 (1954), pp. 200-212.

10,549 MAXWELL, J. Ashanti, Kumasi—the garden city of West Africa. J. AFR. SOC. 27 (1928), pp. 219-233.

10,550 METCALFE, G. E. After Maclean: some aspects of British Gold Coast policy in the mid-nineteenth century. TR. HIST. SOC. GHANA 1 (1952-1955), pp. 178-192.

10,551 MEYEROWITZ, E. L. R. A note on the early history of the Jamasi people. TR. HIST. SOC. GHANA 1 (1952-1955), pp. 141-143.

10,552 MEYEROWITZ, E. L. R. A note on the origins of Ghana. AFR. AFFAIRS 51 (1952), pp. 319-323.

10,553 MEYEROWITZ, E. L. R. The tradition of Tafo from about 1600 to 1740 from material given to me by the Tafohene Nana Yao Dabanka and his elders in 1946. TR. HIST. SOC. GHANA 4 (1960), pp. 30-32.

10,554 MEYEROWITZ, E. L. R. Villages founded in Nkwanta state (1650-1750). GHANA NOTES 7 (1965), pp. 12-20.

10,555 MIGEOD, F. W. H. A history of the Gold Coast—and Ashanti. J. AFR. SOC. 15 (1916), pp. 234-243.

10,556 MILES, A. C. Recollections of the Gold Coast forty years ago. NIGERIAN FIELD 20 (1955), pp. 105-111.

10,557 NATHAN, Sir M. The Gold Coast at the end of the seventeenth century under the Danes and Dutch. J. AFR. SOC. 4 (1904), pp. 1-32.

10,558 NATHAN, Sir M. Historical chart of the Gold Coast and Ashanti, compiled from various sources. J. AFR. SOC. 4 (1904), pp. 33-43.

10,559 NKRUMAH, K. De l'histoire culturelle du Ghana. PRESENCE AFR. N.S. 41 (1962), pp. 5-12.

10,560 NORRIS, A. W. Notes on Ashanti heraldry. GOLD COAST REV. 2 (1926), pp. 235-238.

10,561 NORRIS, A. W. A theory with interludes of phantasy lightly bound with fragments of history and legend. GOLD COAST REV. 2 (1926), pp. 224-234.

10,562 O'BRIEN, C. C. The teaching of history. GHANA NOTES 6 (1964), pp. 2-3.

10,563 PACHAI, B. An outline of the history of municipal government at Cape Coast. TR. HIST. SOC. GHANA 8 (1965), pp. 130-161.

10,564 PADMORE, G. Ghana—l'autobiographie de Kwame Nkrumah. PRESENCE AFR. N.S. 12 (1957), pp. 27-31.

10,565 PAGE, R. E. The Osu and kindred peoples. GOLD COAST REV. 1 (1925), pp. 66-70.

10,566 PERREGAUX, W. A few notes on Kwahu ("Quahoe," a territory in the Gold Coast Colony, West Africa). J. AFR. SOC. 2 (1903), pp. 444-450.

10,567 PITT, W. J. The Bedu people, their history, customs and language. GOLD COAST REV. 2 (1926), pp. 277-284.

10,568 PRIESTLEY, M. A. The Ashanti question and the British: eighteenth-century origins. J. AFR. HIST. 2 (1961), pp. 35-59.

10,569 PRIESTLEY, M. A. An early strike in Ghana. GHANA NOTES 7 (1965), p. 25.

10,570 PRIESTLEY, M. A. English gifts for the King of Ashanti in the 18th century. GHANA NOTES 2 (1962), pp. 4-7.

10,571 PRIESTLEY, M. A. A note on Fort William, Anomabu. TR. HIST. SOC. GHANA 2 (1956), pp. 46-48.

10,572 PRIESTLEY, M. A. and WILKS, I. The Ashanti kings in the eighteenth century: a revised chronology. J. AFR. HIST. 1 (1960), pp. 83-96.

10,573 RICHARDS, T. H. H. The Gold Coast colony. ROYAL COL. INST. PR. 29 (1897-1898), pp. 31-35.

10,574 ROACH, H. Christiansborg. AFR. AFFAIRS 44 (1945), pp. 131-133.

10,575 RYDER, A. F. C. The re-establishment of Portuguese factories on the Costa da Mina to the mid eighteenth century. J. HIST. SOC. NIG. 1 (1958), pp. 157-181.

10,576 SANDERSON, R. W. The history of Nzima up to 1874. GOLD COAST REV. 1 (1925), pp. 95-107.

10,577 SARBAH, J. M. The Gold Coast when Edward IV was king. J. AFR. SOC. 3 (1904), pp. 194-197.

10,578 SASTRE, R. God bless Ghana. PRESENCE AFR. N.S. 12 (1957), pp. 67-68.

10,579 SAXTON, S. W. Historical survey of the Shai people. GOLD COAST REV. 1 (1925), pp. 127-145.

10,580 SENGAT-KUO, F. Ghana: un exemple et un test. PRESENCE AFR. N.S. 12 (1957), pp. 69-70.

10,581 SHAW, J. V. Akim-Abuakwa: a brief note on its constitution and customs. GOLD COAST REV. 1 (1925), pp. 53-65.

10,582 SHELFORD, F. The Gold Coast in the making. J. AFR. SOC. 28 (1928), pp. 28-35.

10,583 SLATER, Sir R. The Gold Coast: some facts and figures. J. AFR. SOC. 29 (1930), pp. 343-349.

10,584 SLATER, Sir R. The Gold Coast to-day. J. AFR. SOC. 27 (1928), pp. 321-328.

10,585 SWANZY, H. Incident at Mouri. AFR. AFFAIRS 58 (1959), pp. 147-152.

10,586 SWANZY, H. A trading family in the nineteenth century Gold Coast. TR. HIST. SOC. GHANA 2 (1956), pp. 87-120.

10,587 TATE, H. R. Some early reminiscences of a transport officer. Ashanti Field Force and Ogaden Punitive Force. J. AFR. SOC. 41 (1942), pp. 101-107.

10,588 THOMAS, T. S. The Gold Coast. Recent developments and some comparisons. J. AFR. SOC. 29 (1929), pp. 7-11.

10,589 TORDOFF, W. The Ashanti confederacy. J. AFR. HIST. 3 (1962), pp. 399-417.

10,590 TORDOFF, W. Brandford Griffith's offer of British protection to Ashanti (1891). TR. HIST. SOC. GHANA 6 (1962), pp. 31-49.

10,591 TORDOFF, W. The exile and repatriation of Nana Prempeh I of Ashanti (1896-1924). TR. HIST. SOC. GHANA 4 (1960), pp. 33-58.

10,592 TORDOFF, W. A note on the relations between Samory and King Prempeh I of Ashanti. GHANA NOTES 3 (1961), pp. 5-7.

10,593 TRANAKIDES, G. Observations on the history of some Gold Coast peoples. TR. HIST. SOC. GHANA 1 (1952-1955), pp. 33-44.

10,594 VAN DANTZIG, A. Le traité d'échange de territoires sur la Côte de l'Or entre la Grande-Bretagne et les Pays-Bas en 1867. CAH. ET. AFR. 4 (1963), pp. 69-96.

10,595 VARLEY, W. J. The castles and forts of the Gold Coast. TR. HIST. SOC. GHANA 1 (1952-1955), pp. 1-17.

10,596 WADDY, B. B. Some reminiscences of the western northern territories of the Gold Coast. NIGERIAN FIELD 22 (1957), pp. 70-86.

10,597 WAKKAD, M. EL- and WILKS, I. Quissatu Salga Tarikhu Gonja: the story of Salaga and the history of Gonja. GHANA NOTES 3 (1961), pp. 8-31; 4 (1962), pp. 6-25.

10,598 WALKER, A. J. The Kwahus. GOLD COAST REV. 1 (1925), pp. 15-28.

10,599 WALLIS, J. R. The Kwahus: their connection with the Afram Plain. TR. HIST. SOC. GHANA 1 (1952-1955), pp. 72-88.

10,600 WARD, W. E. Problems in Gold Coast history. GOLD COAST REV. 2 (1926), pp. 37-52.

10,601 WASSERMAN, B. The Ashanti war of 1900: a study in cultural conflict. AFRICA 31 (1961), pp. 167-178.

10,602 WATHERSTON, A. E. G. The Northern Territories of the Gold Coast. J. AFR. SOC. 7 (1908), pp. 344-373.

10,603 WENCHI, Omanhene of. The three old men of Nkoranza by the Omanhene of Wenchi. GOLD COAST REV. 4 (1928), pp. 120-123.

10,604 WILKS, I. The Ashanti of Rattray and the Ashanti of reality. ASHANTI RES. PROJ. 1ST. CONF., 1964, pp. 21-24.

10,605 WILKS, I. The Institute of African Studies collection of Arabic manuscripts from Ghana: a note on material relevant to Ashanti history. ASHANTI RES. PROJ. 1ST. CONF., 1964, pp. 17-18.

10,606 WILKS, I. The northern factor in Ashanti history: Begho and the Mande. J. AFR. HIST. 2 (1961), pp. 25-34.

10,607 WILKS, I. A note on the early spread of Islam in Dagomba. TR. HIST. SOC. GHANA 8 (1965), pp. 87-98.

10,608 WILKS, I. A note on the traditional history of Mampong. TR. HIST. SOC. GHANA 4 (1960), pp. 26-29.

10,609 WILKS, I. A note on Twifo and Akwamu. TR. HIST. SOC. GHANA 3 (1958), pp. 215-217.

10,610 WILKS, I. The rise of the Akwamu Empire, 1650-1710. TR. HIST. SOC. GHANA 3 (1957), pp. 99-136.

10,611 WILKS, I. Tribal history and myth. UNIVERSITAS 2 (1956), pp. 84-86, 116-118.

10,612 WOODS, W. W. and NATHAN, Sir M. Dutch and English on the Gold Coast in the eighteenth century. J. AFR. SOC. 3 (1904), pp. 325-351.

10,613 ZAJACZKOWSKI, A. La structure du pouvoir chez les Ashanti de la période de transition. CAH. ET. AFR. 3 (1963), pp. 458-473.

10,614 ZERBO, J. K. L'histoire recommence. PRESENCE AFR. N.S. 12 (1957), pp. 64-66.

10,615 Collections of oral traditions from the Volta Basin. UNIV. GHANA RES. REV. 1 (1965), no. 2, pp. 20-22.

10,616 The crucial research room [of the Nigerian National Archives]. AFRICAN NOTES 2, no. 2 (1965), pp. 12-16.

10,617 The English purchase of the Danish possessions in the East Indies and Africa, 1845-1850. RHCF 26 (1933), pp. I-LXVII.

10,618 The history of Africa: select reading list (mainly for teachers). GHANA NOTES 6 (1964), pp. 17-18.

10,619 Inaugural meeting of the Gold Coast and Togoland Historical Society. TR. HIST. SOC. GHANA 1 (1952-1955), pp. 30-31.

10,620 The late King Sakitey and the Ashanti war. GOLD COAST REV. 5 (1929), pp. 105-117.

10,621 Methods of teaching history. GHANA NOTES 6 (1964), pp. 14-17.

10,622 National Archives of Ghana. ARCHIVES 7 (1965), p. 52.

10,623 Notes on Ashanti heraldry. UNIV. GHANA RES. REV. 1 (1965), no. 2, pp. 48-52.

10,624 Proceedings of the Conference on the teaching of history in Ghanaian schools and colleges. GHANA NOTES 6 (1964), pp. 1-20.

10,625 Proposed [history] syllabus for Secondary Schools. GHANA NOTES 6 (1964), pp. 9-12.

10,626 Proposed [history] syllabus for Training Colleges. GHANA NOTES 6 (1964), pp. 12-14.

10,627 Quelques données sur le Ghana. PRESENCE AFR. N.S. 12 (1957), pp. 6-10.

10,628 Talking drums [account of the death of a Gold Coast paper]. AFR. AFFAIRS 52 (1953), pp. 191-192.

See also 9370, 9861, 9862, 10236, 11812, 12922.

Language. Literature

10,629 AMONOO, R. F. Problems of Ghanaian lingue franche. LANGUAGE IN AFRICA, 1963, pp. 78-85.

10,630 ANSRE, G. Reduplication in Ewe. J. AFR. LANGS. 2 (1963), pp. 128-132.

10,631 BENDOR-SAMUEL, J. T. The Grusi sub-group of the Gur languages. J. W. AFR. LANG. 2 (1965), pp. 47-55.

10,632 BERRY, J. Some notes on the phonology of the Nzema and Ahanta dialects. BULL. SOAS 17 (1955), pp. 160-165.

10,633 BERRY, J. Some preliminary notes on Ada personal nomenclature. AFR. LANG. STUD. 1 (1960), pp. 177-184.

10,634 BERRY, J. Vowel harmony in Twi. BULL. SOAS 19 (1957), pp. 124-130.

10,635 BOADI, L. A. Palatality as a factor in Twi vowel harmony. J. AFR. LANGS. 2 (1963), pp. 133-138.

10,636 BOADI, L. A. Some Twi phrase structure rules. J. W. AFR. LANG. 2 (1965), pp. 37-46.

10,637 BROSNAHAN, L. F. A fifteenth century West African word list. J. W. AFR. LANG. 2 (1965), p. 5.

10,638 CALLOW, J. C. Kasem nominals—a study in analyses. J. W. AFR. LANG. 2 (1965), pp. 29-36.

10,639 CHINEBUAH, I. K. The category of number in Nzema. J. AFR. LANGS. 2 (1963), pp. 244-259.

10,640 CHRISTALLER, J. G. Negersagen von der Goldküste, mitgeteilt und mit Sagen andrer afrikanischer Völker verglichen. ZAS 1 (1887-1888), pp. 49-63.

10,641 CHRISTALLER, J. G. Sprichwörter der Tshwi-Neger. ZAOS 1 (1895), pp. 184-187; 2 (1896), pp. 51-53, 241-243.

10,642 DICKENS, K. J. Orthography in the Gold Coast. AFRICA 6 (1933), pp. 317-322.

10,643 GOODY, J. R. Ethnological notes on the distribution of the Guang languages. J. AFR. LANGS. 2 (1963), pp. 173-189.

10,644 KROPP, M. E. Ga and Adangme [a linguistic research]. UNIV. GHANA RES. REV. 2 (1965), pp. 32-33.

10,645 KROPP, M. E. The morphology of the Adangme verb complex. J. AFR. LANGS. 3 (1964), pp. 80-95.

10,646 MATTHEWS, J. H. English-Mole vocabulary. GOLD COAST REV. 5 (1929), pp. 73-95.

10,647 OFOSU-APPIAH, L. H. On translating the Homeric epithet and simile into Twi. AFRICA 30 (1960), pp. 41-45.

10,648 ORMSBY, G. Some notes on the Angass language. J. AFR. SOC. 12 (1913), pp. 421-424; 13 (1913), pp. 54-61, 204-210, 313-315.

10,649 OWIREDU, P. A. Proposals for a national language for Ghana. AFR. AFFAIRS 63 (1964), pp. 142-145.

10,650 OWIREDU, P. A. Towards a common language for Ghana. AFR. AFFAIRS 56 (1957), pp. 295-299.

10,651 PILSZCZIKOWA, N. Some preliminary notes on Lete grammar. AFR. BULL. 3 (1965), pp. 67-107.

10,652 RAPP, E. L. Adangme-Texte. AFRIKA (Berlin) 1 (1942), pp. 55-100(?).

10,653 STEWART, J. M. Some restrictions on objects in Twi. J. AFR. LANGS. 2 (1963), pp. 145-149.

10,654 STREVENS, P. D. Konkomba or Dagomba? A linguistic corollary to "History and Social Organisation." TR. HIST. SOC. GHANA 1 (1952-1955), pp. 211-216.

10,655 TAYLOR, C. J. Some Akan names. NIGERIAN FIELD 18 (1953), pp. 34-37.

10,656 TOSO, V. Ewe-texte. AFR. UND UB. 7 (1916-1917), pp. 1-24.

10,657 WESTERMANN, D. Texte in der Gẽ-Mundart des Ewe. AFR. UND UB. 39 (1954-1955), pp. 1-5, 119-127.

10,658 WESTERMANN, D. Die velarbaialen lenaLaute in der Ewe-Tschigruppe der Sudansprachen. AFR. UND UB. 10 (1919-1920), pp. 243-261.

10,659 WESTERMANN, D. A visit to the Gold Coast. AFRICA 1 (1928), pp. 107-111.

10,660 WILKS, I. The Mande loan element in Twi [with a note by John Stewart]. GHANA NOTES 4 (1962), pp. 26-28.

10,661 WILSON, A. Research in Ghanaian languages. UNIV. GHANA RES. REV. 1 (1965), no. 2, pp. 22-25.

10,662 WILSON, W. A. A. Relative constructions in Dagbani. J. AFR. LANGS. 2 (1963), pp. 139-144.

10,663 African languages. UNIV. GHANA RES. REV. 1 (1965), pp. 16-18.

See also 9371, 10105, 10229.

Literature

10,664 ADALI-MORTTI, G. Ewe poetry. BO 4 (1958), pp. 36-45.

10,665 AIDOO, C. A. A. No sweetness here [a story]. BO 12 (1962), pp. 27-36.

10,666 AIDOO, C. A. A. Sebonwoma. PRESENCE AFR. N.S. 49 (1964), pp. 199-200.

10,667 ANNAN, K. Ding dong bell [a story]. AFR. SOUTH 3, no. 2 (1959), pp. 117-124.

10,668 APPRONTI, J. A Ghanaian [a poem]. TRANSITION 14 (1964), p. 47.

10,669 ASANTE, D. Illusion. AFR. AFFAIRS 52 (1953), pp. 334-336.

10,670 AWOONOR-WILLIAMS, G. The years behind. PRESENCE AFR. N.S. 47 (1963), p. 181.

10,671 BROWN, G. N. Insomnia [a poem]. UNIVERSITAS 4 (1960), p. 109.

10,672 DANQUAH, J. B. Achimota [a poem]. WASU 3-4 (1927), p. 29.

10,673 DU BOIS, W. E. B. Ghana calls. PRESENCE AFR. N.S. 34-35 (1960-1961), pp. 156-159.

10,674 JONES-QUARTEY, K. A. B. Twin memories [a poem]. UNIVERSITAS 2 (1957), p. 163.

10,675 KHAN, R. The poetry of Dr. R. E. G. Armattoe. PRESENCE AFR. N.S. 12 (1957), pp. 32-47.

10,676 KOMEY, E. A. Poems [The change, Midzakuman]. BO 9 (1961), p. 37.

10,677 MOORE, G. Three poems [Visit; Jolof rice; Jamestown, Accra]. BO 14 (1964), p. 25.

10,678 MOSLEY, J. S. Three poems [Evolution, Zygote, Cemetry]. BO 9 (1961), pp. 55-56.

10,679 NKETIA, K. Akan poetry. BO 3 (1958), pp. 5-27.

10,680 RAS KHAN. The poetry of Dr. R. E. G. Armattoe. PRESENCE AFR. N.S. 12 (1957), pp. 32-47.

10,681 SEY, K. A. Le père sauvé. PRESENCE AFR. N.S. 40 (1962), pp. 146-151.

10,682 STEWART, K. M. Ode to stools and stool worship. AFR. AFFAIRS 52 (1953), pp. 185-187.

10,683 STEWART, M. Three sonnets. PRESENCE AFR. N.S. 39 (1961), pp. 157-158.

10,684 STORCH, R. F. Stone houses at Elmina [a poem]. UNIVERSITAS 4 (1960), pp. 82-84.

10,685 STORCH, R. F. Writing in Ghana. UNIVERSITAS 2 (1957), pp. 148-151.

10,686 SUTHERLAND, E. T. "Anansegoro." PRESENCE AFR. N.S. 50 (1964), pp. 221-236.

10,687 WIEGRABE, P. Neuere Literatur in Ewe. AFR. UND UB. 44 (1960), pp. 132-135.

10,688 WILLIAMS, G. A. I heard a bird cry [a poem]. BO 15 (1964), pp. 23-31.

10,689 WRIGHT, J. To Malcolm X. PRESENCE AFR. N.S. 54 (1965), p. 239.

10,690 Two Gold Coast poems [An idea of happiness, by K. Mac-Neill Stewart and The redeemed, by E. T. Morgue]. AFR. AFFAIRS 51 (1952), pp. 155-157.

See also 10858.

Law

10,691 ADJETEY, P. A. Some legal consequences of polygamous marriages in Ghana. UNIVERSITAS 4 (1961), pp. 168-171.

10,692 AFREH, D. K. Statutory Corporations Act, 1964 (Act 232). UGLJ 1 (1964), pp. 144-147.

10,693 ALLOTT, A. N. Customary law of the Akan peoples. AFR. STUD. 12 (1953), pp. 26-30.

10,694 ALLOTT, A. N. Marriage and internal conflict of laws in Ghana. J. AFR. LAW 2 (1958), pp. 164-184.

10,695 ALLOTT, A. N. Native tribunals in the Gold Coast, 1844-1927. Prolegomena to a study of native courts in Ghana. J. AFR. LAW 1 (1957), pp. 163-171.

10,696 ALLOTT, A. N. A note on the Gā law of succession. BULL. SOAS 15 (1953), pp. 164-169.

10,697 ALLOTT, A. N. Proof of customary law. J. AFR. LAW 1 (1957), pp. 202-204.

10,698 AMISSAH, A. N. E. The contents of an indictment and C.O.P. v. Akowuah: the recent judicial attitude to criminal justice in Ghana. UGLJ 2 (1965), pp. 84-129.

10,699 AMISSAH, A. N. E. The machinery of criminal justice in Ghana. UGLJ 1 (1964), pp. 80-109.

10,700 ARHIN, K. On the Hwesoni, caretaker, category of land holding in Ahafo land tenure. UNIV. GHANA RES. REV. 2 (1965), pp. 68-72.

10,701 ASANTE, S. K. B. Stare decisis in the Ghana Supreme Court. UGLJ 1 (1964), pp. 52-67.

10,702 ASMIS, W. Law and policy. Relating to the natives of the Gold Coast and Nigeria. J. AFR. SOC. 12 (1912), pp. 17-51, 137-164.

10,703 DANIELS, W. C. E. The Administration of Estates Act, 1961. J. AFR. LAW 6 (1962), pp. 30-34.

10,704 DANIELS, W. C. E. Constitution (Amendment) Act, 1964 (Act 224). UGLJ 1 (1964), pp. 136-144.

10,705 DANIELS, W. C. E. Criminal Procedure (Amendment) Act, 1964 (Act 238). UGLJ 1 (1964), pp. 147-150.

10,706 DANIELS, W. C. E. Habeas Corpus Act, 1964 (Act 244). UGLJ 1 (1964), pp. 150-151.

10,707 DANIELS, W. C. E. Towards the integration of the laws relating to husband and wife in Ghana. UGLJ 2 (1965), pp. 20-60.

10,708 DAVIES, S. G. The growth of law in the Gold Coast. UNIVERSITAS 2 (1955), pp. 4-6. Also in J. AFR. ADM. 9 (1957), pp. 88-92.

10,709 GONIDEC, P. F. Vers la création de Dominions noirs: la Gold Coast. RJPUF 5 (1951), pp. 503-542; 6 (1952), pp. 72-104.

10,710 GRIFFITH, W. B. Some account of the various editions of the Gold Coast ordinances. J. AFR. SOC. 16 (1917), pp. 326-335.

10,711 HANNIGAN, A. St. J. J. The impact of English law upon the existing Gold Coast custom and the possible development of the resulting system. J. AFR. ADM. 8 (1956), pp. 126-132. Also in WAISER 5 (1956), pp. 135-137.

10,712 HANNIGAN, A. St. J. J. Introduction of registration of title to land. UNIVERSITAS 2 (1956), pp. 41-43.

10,713 HANNIGAN, A. St. J. J. Native custom, its similarity to English conventional custom and its mode of proof. J. AFR. LAW 2 (1958), pp. 101-115.

10,714 HARVEY, W. B. A value analysis of Ghanaian legal development since independence. UGLJ 1 (1964), pp. 4-22.

10,715 JOHNSON, J. W. DE G. Akan land tenure. TR. HIST. SOC. GHANA 1 (1952-1955), pp. 99-103.

10,716 LOVERIDGE, A. J. A note on the development of land tenures in the Gold Coast. J. AFR. SOC. 42 (1943), pp. 31-33.

10,717 LOVERIDGE, A. J. Wills and the customary law in the Gold Coast. J. AFR. ADM. 2 (1950), pp. 24-28.

10,718 MACAULAY, B. Assessors in criminal trials in Ghana—a study from without. J. AFR. LAW 7 (1963), pp. 18-46.

10,719 MAIR, L. P. Land tenure in the Gold Coast. CIVILISATIONS 2 (1952), pp. 183-187; French summary, pp. 187-188.

10,720 NKRUMAH, K. Law in Africa. J. AFR. LAW 6 (1962), pp. 103-109.

10,721 OFOSU-AMAAH, G. K. A. Observations on exception clauses in treaties. UGLJ 1 (1964), pp. 110-124.

10,722 OLLENNU, N. A. Law of succession in Ghana. UGLJ 2 (1965), pp. 4-19.

10,723 POGUCKI, P. J. H. Customary law of a society in transition. UNIVERSITAS 2 (1956), pp. 119-121.

10,724 POGUCKI, R. J. H. A note on the codification of customary land law on the Gold Coast. J. AFR. ADM. 8 (1956), pp. 192-196.

10,725 PRICE, J. H. The Ghana Independence Bill. UNIVERSITAS 2 (1957), pp. 144-147.

10,726 QUAMIE-KYIAMAH, A. The customary oath in the Gold Coast. AFR. AFFAIRS 50 (1951), pp. 139-147.

10,727 QUARTEY-PAPAFIO, A. B. Law of succession among the Akras or the Ga tribes proper of the Gold Coast. J. AFR. SOC. 10 (1910), pp. 64-72.

10,728 QUARTEY-PAPAFIO, A. B. The native tribunals of the Akras of the Gold Coast. J. AFR. SOC. 10 (1911), pp. 320-330, 434-446; 11 (1911), pp. 75-94.

10,729 READ, J. S. Changes in the law of contract [Ghana: The Contracts Act, 1960]. J. AFR. LAW 5 (1961), pp. 48-50.

10,730 R[EAD], J. S. Ghana: Criminal Code, 1960; Criminal Procedure Code, 1960. J. AFR. LAW 5 (1961), pp. 157-158.

10,731 SARBAH, J. M. Maclean and Gold Coast judicial assessors. J. AFR. SOC. 9 (1910), pp. 349-359.

10,732 SEIDMAN, R. B. Insanity as a defence under the Criminal Code, 1960 (Ghana). UGLJ 1 (1964), pp. 42-51.

10,733 SEKYI, K. A. Courts (Amendment) Act, 1965 (Act 262). UGLJ 2 (1965), pp. 140-141.

10,734 SEKYI, K. A. Criminal Procedure (Amendment) (No. 2) Act, 1964 (Act 254). UGLJ 2 (1965), pp. 138-140.

10,735 SHELFORD, F. Land tenure on the Gold Coast. J. AFR. SOC. 10 (1911), pp. 473-476.

10,736 SOWAH, E. N. P. The contents of an indictment and C.O.P. v. Akowuah: a miscarriage of justice. UGLJ 2 (1965), pp. 130-137.

10,737 TAIT, D. The territorial pattern and lineage system of Konkomba. TRIBES WITHOUT RULERS, 1958, pp. 167-202.

10,738 THOYER, J. R. The use of Ghana statutory materials including a bibliography of Ghanaian law. UGLJ 1 (1964), pp. 125-135.

10,739 WOODMAN, G. R. The acquisition of family land in Ghana. J. AFR. LAW 7 (1963), pp. 136-151.

10,740 WOODMAN, G. R. The alienation of family land in Ghana. UGLJ 1 (1964), pp. 23-41.

10,741 Ashanti court records [with introduction by Adu Boahen]. UNIV. GHANA RES. REV. 1 (1965), no. 2, pp. 12-16; 2 (1965), pp. 11-16.

10,742 La constitution de l'Etat de Ghana. PRESENCE AFR. N.S. 12 (1957), pp. 48-57.

10,743 Ghana: The Chieftaincy Act, 1961. J. AFR. LAW 6 (1962), pp. 29-30.

10,744 Ghana [Courts Act, 1960]. J. AFR. LAW 4 (1960), pp. 147-149.

10,745 Ghana Marriage, Divorce and Inheritance Bill. AFR. WOMEN 5 (1963), pp. 37-38.

10,746 The Ghana School of Law, Accra. J. AFR. LAW 6 (1962), pp. 110-112.

10,747 Ghana's Preventive Detention Act. J. INT. COMM. JURISTS 3, no. ii (1961), pp. 65-99.

10,748 Internal conflict of laws: the application of customary law. J. AFR. LAW 1 (1957), pp. 126-128.

10,749 Legal developments in Ghana. J. AFR. LAW 1 (1957), p. 10.

10,750 Legal education in Ghana. J. AFR. LAW 2 (1958), p. 145; 4 (1960), pp. 4-5.

10,751 The legislation providing for the grant of independence to Ghana. J. AFR. LAW 1 (1957), pp. 99-112.

10,752 New marriage bill for Ghana [1962]. AFR. WOMEN 5 (1962), pp. 13-14.

10,753 Recording of customary law in Ghana? J. AFR. LAW 4 (1960), pp. 128-129.

10,754 Reform of company law in Ghana. J. AFR. LAW 2 (1958), pp. 140-142.

10,755 The reform of the law of succession in Ghana. J. AFR. LAW 3 (1959), pp. 90-92.

10,756 Statement by the Government on the Report of the Commission on Native Courts. [Appointed by Government of the Gold Coast under chairmanship of Sir K. Arku Korsah]. J. AFR. ADM. 8 (1956), pp. 161-162.

10,757 University of Ghana, department of law. J. AFR. LAW 6 (1962), pp. 109-110.

See also 7995.

Religion

10,758 ASHANIN, C. B. The social significance of religious studies in West Africa. UNIVERSITAS 4 (1959), pp. 9-11.

10,759 BELSHAW, H. Church and State in Ashanti. INT. REV. MISSIONS 35 (1946), pp. 408-415.

10,760 BELSHAW, H. Religious education in the Gold Coast. INT. REV. MISSIONS 34 (1945), pp. 267-272.

10,761 BREWER, J. H. The ordination of Philip Quaque, 1765: some problems. BULL. SOC. AFR. CHURCH HIST. 1 (1964), pp. 89-91.

10,762 DEBRUNNER, H. W. Sieckentrooster, Predikants and Chaplains: a documentation of the history of Dutch and English Chaplains to Guinea before 1750. BULL. SOC. AFR. CHURCH HIST. 1 (1964), pp. 73-89.

10,763 GRAU, E. The German protestant heritage of the church in Ghana. GHANA BULL. THEOL. 2, nos. 9-10 (1965-1966), pp. 12-18.

10,764 HALIBURTON, G. M. The Anglican Church in Ghana and the Harris movement in 1914. BULL. SOC. AFR. CHURCH HIST. 1 (1964), pp. 101-106.

10,765 HALIBURTON, G. M. The calling of a prophet: Sampson Oppong. BULL. SOC. AFR. CHURCH HIST. 2 (1965), pp. 84-96.

10,766 KING, N. Q. Synthesis and symbiosis: theology in an African university. INT. REV. MISSIONS 49 (1960), pp. 385-392.

10,767 LADURIE, M. LE R. Etude sur les vocations religieuses au pays Mossi. CAH. ET. AFR. 4, no. 14 (1963), pp. 275-316.

10,768 MENSAH, A. A. The Akan Church lyric. INT. REV. MISSIONS 49 (1960), pp. 183-188.

10,769 ODONKOR, S. S. A missionary tour of Adangme land. INT. REV. MISSIONS 34 (1945), pp. 144-149.

10,770 WILLIAMSON, S. G. The lyric in the Fante Methodist Church. AFRICA 28 (1958), pp. 126-133.

10,771 WILLIAMSON, S. G. Missions and education in the Gold Coast. INT. REV. MISSIONS 41 (1952), pp. 364-373.

See also 479, 9465, 12223, 12225.

Science

10,772 ABRAHAMS, C. A. and LAING, E. Antibiotic resistance in staphylococcus pyogenes isolated in Accra (1. 1956-1959). GHANA MED. J. 3 (1964), pp. 67-71.

10,773 ADAMS, C. D. Ceropegia gemmifera. UNIVERSITAS 3 (1958), pp. 81-82.

10,774 ADAMS, C. D. Curculigo pilosa. UNIVERSITAS 3 (1957), pp. 15-16.

10,775 ADAMS, C. D. Eulophia cristata. UNIVERSITAS 2 (1957), pp. 190-191.

10,776 ADAMS, C. D. Mussaenda erythrophylla. UNIVERSITAS 3 (1959), pp. 151-152.

10,777 ADAMS, C. D. Ophioglossum costatum. UNIVERSITAS 3 (1958), pp. 116-117.

10,778 BARNOR, M. A. A history of medical societies in Ghana. GHANA MED. J. 1 (1962), pp. 4-7.

10,779 BRACHOTT. A ten-year health programme for Ghana (1961-1970). GHANA MED. J. 1 (1962), pp. 8-14.

10,780 BURTON, G. J. et al. A survey for the vector of yellow fever in the Damongo area, Northern Region, Ghana, by G. J. Burton, G. K. Noamesi and T. M. Macrae. GHANA MED. J. 3 (1964), pp. 9-15.

10,781 CANHAM, P. An Ashanti case-history. AFRICA 17 (1947), pp. 35-40.

10,782 CANSDALE, G. S. Field notes on some Gold Coast snakes. NIGERIAN FIELD 13 (1948), pp. 43-50.

10,783 CANSDALE, G. S. Further notes on Gold Coast snakes. NIGERIAN FIELD 14 (1949), pp. 52-54, 106-113.

10,784 CANSDALE, G. S. Gold Coast snakes—a complete list. NIGERIAN FIELD 19 (1954), pp. 118-132.

10,785 CANSDALE, G. S. Some Gold Coast animals. NIGERIAN FIELD 9 (1940), pp. 56-65.

10,786 CANSDALE, G. S. Some Gold Coast lizards. NIGERIAN FIELD 16 (1951), pp. 21-34.

10,787 COOPER, W. G. G. Gold Coast bauxite. BULL. IMP. INST. 34 (1936), pp. 331-347.

10,788 COURSEY, D. G. Research on yams. UNIV. GHANA RES. REV. 1 (1965), no. 2, p. 54.

10,789 CROW, A. T. Geology and earthquakes in the Gold Coast. NIGERIAN FIELD 21 (1956), pp. 52-68.

10,790 DAVID, J. B. Acute respiratory obstruction in the child (some early experiences in Ghana). GHANA MED. J. 2 (1963), pp. 138-143.

10,791 DIXON, P. A. Toadstools and termites. UNIVERSITAS 3 (1959), pp. 146-148.

10,792 EASMON, C. O. and LAHIRI, H. S. Volvulus of the sigmoid colon (a review of 29 cases). GHANA MED. J. 2 (1963), pp. 62-67.

10,793 EDINGTON, G. M. Anaemias of pregnancy in Gold Coast Africans. MALNUTRITION IN AFRICAN WOMEN..., 1952, pp. 299-300.

10,794 EDINGTON, G. M. Haemosiderosis in the Gold Coast African. MALNUTRITION IN AFRICAN WOMEN..., 1952, pp. 115-119.

10,795 FORSTER, E. B. A historical survey of psychiatric practice in Ghana. GHANA MED. J. 1 (1962), pp. 25-29.

10,796 GASS, M. D. I. The bee-eaters of Ghana. NIGERIAN FIELD 28 (1963), pp. 30-34.

10,797 GASS, M. D. I. Gold Coast bird notes. NIGERIAN FIELD 19 (1954), pp. 23-30, 76-83.

10,798 GASS, M. D. I. Some migrant birds of Ghana. NIGERIAN FIELD 22 (1957), pp. 166-168.

10,799 GREGORY, M. E. The work of health visitors in schools of the Gold Coast. AFR. WOMEN 2 (1956), pp. 10-11.

10,800 GRIMES, L. G. Some observations on Picathartes gymnocephalus. NIGERIAN FIELD 28 (1963), pp. 63-65.

10,801 GRIMES, L. G. and Gardiner, N. Looking for Picathartes gymnocephalus in Ghana. NIGERIAN FIELD 28 (1963), pp. 55-63.

10,802 HAMER, A. B. Onchoceriasis. W. AFR. MILITARY MED. BULL. 1 (1942), pp. 16-17.

10,803 HARRIS, B. J. and BAKER, H. G. Pollination of flowers by bats in Ghana. NIGERIAN FIELD 24 (1959), pp. 151-159.

10,804 HATHORN, M. Haemoglobin levels in pregnant women in Accra. GHANA MED. J. 2 (1963), pp. 55-61.

10,805 HAWE, A. J. Carbon monoxide poisoning in Ghana. GHANA MED. J. 2 (1963), pp. 52-54.

10,806 HAWE, A. J. Looking back [history of medicine in Ghana]. GHANA MED. J. L (1962), pp. 16-18.

10,807 HIRST, T. The geology of the Konongo gold belt and surrounding country. BULL. IMP. INST. 40 (1942), pp. 36-61.

10,808 JOHNSON, S. B. G. DE G. Down's syndrome (Mongolism) in Accra. GHANA MED. J. 3 (1964), pp. 157-162.

10,809 JOLLY, H. Neonatal problems in West Africa. GHANA MED. J. 1 (1962), pp. 46-49.

10,810 KAY, R. W. W. et al. Fatal poisoning from ingestion of Benzene hexchloride, by R. W. W. Kay, G. G. Kuder and R. A. Lewis. GHANA MED. J. 3 (1964), pp. 72-74.

10,811 KAYE, B. Mental health in rural Ghana. UNIVERSITAS 4 (1961), pp. 171-172.

10,812 KISSEIH, D. A. N. A brief survey of nursing in Ghana. GHANA MED. J. 1 (1962), pp. 22-24.

10,813 LAHIRI, H. S. Non-penetrating abdominal injury. GHANA MED. J. 3 (1964), pp. 166-170.

10,814 LAWSON, J. B. Maternal mortality in West Africa. GHANA MED. J. 1 (1962), pp. 31-36.

10,815 LESAGE, M. C. Snake not quite charmed. NIGERIAN FIELD 21 (1956), pp. 111-121.

10,816 LESAGE, M. C. Snake-bite fatalities in the Gold Coast. NIGERIAN FIELD 20 (1955), pp. 69-75.

10,817 LEWIS, R. A. et al. Clinical experiences with phenothiazines in the treatment of sickle cell crisis. GHANA MED. J. 4 (1965), pp. 47-52.

10,818 MORRISON, C. M. Field notes on Gold Coast birds. NIGERIAN FIELD 17 (1952), pp. 25-37.

10,819 MORRISON, C. M. Field notes on some Gold Coast birds. NIGERIAN FIELD 12 (1947), pp. 59-64.

10,820 NOAMESI, G. K. The tube bioassay technique in tests to evaluate entomologically the effects of simulium control operations in northwest Ghana. GHANA MED. J. 3 (1964), pp. 163-165.

10,821 ONORI, E. The results of a mass campaign against yaws in the Volta Region of Ghana. GHANA MED. J. 1 (1962), pp. 36-45.

10,822 RATNESAR, V. C. An epidemic of polyradiculoneuritis in Ghana (Gullain-Barre-Landry Syndrome). GHANA MED. J. 3 (1964), pp. 148-156.

10,823 RODGER, F. C. Onchocerciasis in the northern Gold Coast. NIGERIAN FIELD 20 (1955), pp. 161-165.

10,824 RUSSELL, A. C. Birds of Cape Coast reservoir. NIGERIAN FIELD 14 (1949), pp. 146-150.

10,825 RUSSELL, A. C. Collecting for a zoo. NIGERIAN FIELD 14 (1949), pp. 10-19.

10,826 SAI, F. T. The history of the Ghana Medical School project. GHANA MED. J. 2 (1963), pp. 34-37.

10,827 SAUNDERS, G. F. T. The native attitude to modern medicine. GOLD COAST REV. 4 (1928), pp. 57-65.

10,828 SCOTT, D. The history and work of the medical field units in Ghana. GHANA MED. J. 1 (1962), pp. 19-22.

10,829 TRENT, R. D. A study of communication and comprehensibility of public health information. GHANA MED. J. 4 (1965), pp. 9-13.

10,830 WINTERBOTTOM, J. M. Bird population studies: travelling bird censuses in the Gold Coast. GOLD COAST REV. 5 (1929), pp. 166-173.

10,831 WOLFE, M. S. et al. Studies with TWSb (Astiban) and recommendations for its use in the treatment of urinary schistosomiasis in Ghana, by M. S. Wolfe, E. Moser and R. Biek. GHANA MED. J. 4 (1965), pp. 14-19.

10,832 YOUNN, S. S. Congenital malformations observed in Accra (post mortem studies at the Korle Bu Hospital). GHANA MED. J. 2 (1963), pp. 134-137.

10,833 YOUNN, S. S. Intra-abdominal malignant lymphomas in autopsies at Korle Bu Hospital, Accra. GHANA MED. J. 3 (1964), pp. 21-25.

10,834 Community health nursing in Ghana. AFR. WOMEN 4 (1961), p. 61.

See also 12399.

Sociology

10,835 ADDO, N. O. Madina study. UNIV. GHANA RES. REV. 2 (1965), pp. 34-36.

10,836 AMARTEIFIO, E. Customary marriage in Ghana. AFR. WOMEN 3 (1958-1960), pp. 4-5.

10,837 ANDERSON, C. The king of Abiriu (W.A.L. Congress, Ghana), April, 1965. KANO STUD. 1 (1965), pp. 3-8.

10,838 ANKRAH, E. M. The American community in Ghana. GHANA J. SOC. 1 (1965), pp. 10-18.

10,839 ARHIN, K. Market settlements in Northwestern Ashanti: Kintampo. UNIV. GHANA RES. REV. 1 (1965), Supplement, pp. 135-155.

10,840 BOOKER, H. S. Debt in Africa. AFR. AFFAIRS 48 (1949), pp. 141-149.

10,841 CHRISTIAN, A. The place of women in Ghana society. AFR. WOMEN 3 (1958-1960), pp. 57-59.

10,842 CLIFFORD, H. Some facts concerning the Gold Coast. J. AFR. SOC. 14 (1914-1915), pp. 15-23.

10,843 DATTA, A. K. Aspects of urbanisation in Ghana in relation to social integration. AFRO-ASIAN AND W. AFF. 2 (1965), pp. 28-34.

10,844 EKWENSI, C. Life from Legon. UNIVERSITAS 2 (1957), pp. 152-153.

10,845 FORTES, M. The Ashanti Social Survey: a preliminary report. RHODES-LIV. J. 6 (1948), pp. 1-36.

10,846 HARMAN, H. A. The Gold Coast, 1931. AFRICA 7 (1934), pp. 60-69.

10,847 HILTON, T. E. Frafra resettlement and the population problem in Zuarungu. BULL. IFAN 22 (1960), pp. 426-442.

10,848 HUNTER, J. M. Regional patterns of population growth in Ghana 1948-60. ESSAYS IN GEOGRAPHY FOR AUSTIN MILLER, 1965, pp. 272-290.

10,849 JAHODA, G. Love, marriage, and social change: letters to the advice column of a West African newspaper. AFRICA 29 (1959), pp. 177-189.

10,850 JAHODA, G. Urban adolescents' views on social changes in the Gold Coast. WAISER SOC. 2 (1953), pp. 51-72.

10,851 JOHNSON, K. E. DE G. Social control in a changing society. GHANA J. SOC. 1 (1965), pp. 47-55.

10,852 JONES, A. D. Literacy and personality. RHODES-LIV. J. 30 (1961), pp. 59-60.

10,853 JUDD, H. Something concrete in the ground. UNIVERSITAS 3 (1958), pp. 107-108.

10,854 KAYE, B. Growing up in Ghana [review of Child Training in Ghana: an Impressionistic Survey]. UNIVERSITAS 4 (1960), pp. 116-117.

10,855 LYSTAD, M. H. Traditional values of Ghanaian children. AMER. ANTHR. 62 (1960), pp. 454-464.

10,856 MOAL, G. LE. Un aspect de l'émigration: la fixation de Voltaïques au Ghana. BULL. IFAN 22 (1960), pp. 446-454.

10,857 MUSTAPHA, T. M. and GOODY, J. Wenchi and its inhabitants. UNIV. GHANA RES. REV. 1 (1965), Supplement, pp. 156-169.

10,858 REA, C. J. The culture line: a note on Dilemma of a Ghost [by Christina Aidoo]. AFR. FORUM 1 (1965), pp. 111-113.

10,859 ROBERTSON, W. S. The joy of bearded men. UNIVERSITAS 4 (1960), pp. 110-111.

10,860 ROUCH, J. Migrations au Ghana (Gold Coast). Enquête 1953-1955. J. SOC. AFR. 26 (1956), pp. 33-196.

10,861 STAPLETON, G. B. Nigerians in Ghana with special reference to the Yoruba. NISER 6 (1958), pp. 159-163.

10,862 SUTHERLAND, A. C. Housing and town planning as instrument of social control in Africa. WAISER 5 (1956), pp. 85-94.

10,863 TAIT, D. History and social organisation. TR. HIST. SOC. GHANA 1 (1952-1955), pp. 193-210.

10,864 WARD, B. Some notes on migration from Togoland. AFR. AFFAIRS 49 (1950), pp. 129-135.

10,865 The Ashanti research project. UNIV. GHANA RES. REV. 1 (1965), pp. 11-14; 1 (1965), no. 2, pp. 11-12; 2 (1965), pp. 9-10.

10,866 National Council of Ghana Women. AFR. WOMEN 3 (1960), pp. 86-87.

See also 9305, 9468, 12498.

N I G E R I A

General

10,867 AMANKWE, N. Revision of classification schemes for Nigerian needs. NIGERIAN LIBS. 1 (1965), pp. 165-173.

10,868 AREJE, R. A. Western Regional Library. NIGERIAN LIBS. 1 (1965), pp. 177-178.

10,869 BENGE, R. C. Foundations for a library school. NIGERIAN LIBS. 1 (1964), pp. 81-85.

10,870 CANNON, D. A. The development of medical library facilities in Nigeria. LIBRI 3 (1954), pp. 184-187.

10,871 CLARK, H. M. The development of medical library facilities in Nigeria. LIBRI 3 (1954), p. 183.

10,872 EDWARDES, P. M. J. The Library of the Institute for Agricultural Research, Ahmadu Bello University, Samaru, Zaria. NIGERIAN LIBS. 1 (1964), pp. 24-29.

10,873 HARRIS, J. Ibadan University Library. NIGERIAN LIBS. 1 (1965), pp. 181-184.

10,874 HARRIS, J. Medical facilities in the library of University College, Ibadan. LIBRI 3 (1954), pp. 188-190.

10,875 HARRIS, J. Why a professional association? NIGERIAN LIBS. 1 (1964), pp. 4-7.

10,876 HORROCKS, S. H. Unesco public library pilot project in the Eastern Region of Nigeria. UNESCO BULL. LIBS. 13 (1959), pp. 5-7.

10,877 MAJASAN, J. A. The history of the Nigerian College of Arts, Science and Technology. AFR. HISTORIAN 1, no. i (1963), pp. 10-11.

10,878 MOID, S. A. Northern Regional Library. NIGERIAN LIBS. 1 (1965), pp. 175-177.

10,879 MOMAH, C. C. New trends in Nigerian libraries. The problems of the new university libraries. NIGERIAN LIBS. 1 (1964), pp. 30-33.

10,880 MOYS, E. M. University of Lagos Library. NIGERIAN LIBS. 1 (1965), pp. 178-181.

10,881 NWOYE, S. C. Library co-operation: some proposals for organisation in Nigeria. NIGERIAN LIBS. 1 (1964), pp. 119-124.

10,882 OBI, D. S. The library scene in Eastern Nigeria. NIGERIAN LIBS. 1 (1964), pp. 16-23.

10,883 OKORIE, K. Eastern Nigeria library service. UNESCO BULL. LIBS. 14 (1960), pp. 260-263.

10,884 OKORIE, K. Library resources in Nigeria: present position and future trends. NIGERIAN LIBS. 1 (1965), pp. 101-112.

10,885 OKU, E. E. New developments in Nigerian libraries: progress report. Public libraries. NIGERIAN LIBS. 1 (1965), pp. 174-175.

10,886 SHARR, F. A. The development of a new library service. NIGERIAN LIBS. 1 (1964), pp. 8-15.

10,887 SHARR, F. A. The library needs of Northern Nigeria. UNESCO BULL. LIBS. 18 (1964), pp. 259-262.

10,888 WHITE, C. M. Education and training of library personnel in Nigeria. NIGERIAN LIBS. 1 (1964), pp. 75-80.

10,889 Accessions to the microfilm collection [Arabic manuscripts at the Centre of Arabic Documentation, Ibadan]. RES. BULL. CENTRE ARABIC DOC. IBADAN 1 (1965), pp. 48-76.

10,890 Ahmadu Bello University, Zaria, Northern Nigeria. BULL. AFR. STUD. ASSOC. 5 (1965), pp. 19-27.

10,891 The Arabic and Islamic collection of the University of Ibadan Library. RES. BULL. CENTRE ARABIC DOC. IBADAN 1 (1964), p. 15.

10,892 A centre of Arabic documentation for West Africa [University of Ibadan]. BULL. AFR. STUD. ASSOC. 1 (1964), pp. 20-21.

10,893 Nigerian Field Society: a talk broadcast from the Lagos Studio on 16th August, 1938. NIGERIAN FIELD 8 (1939), pp. 33-37.

10,894 Odu, the University of Ife journal of African studies. RES. BULL. CENTRE ARABIC DOC. IBADAN 1 (1964), p. 13.

10,895 Report on the National Library of Nigeria. NIGERIAN LIBS. 1 (1964), pp. 124-125.

Agriculture. Animal husbandry. Fisheries. Forestry. Horticulture

10,896 ALUKO, S. A. Agriculture and economic development in Nigeria. NJESS 1 (1959), pp. 27-40.

10,897 ARIKPO, O. Nigeria agricola. AFRICA (Rome) 11 (1956), pp. 65-66.

10,898 BALDWIN, K. D. S. Land-tenure problems in relation to agricultural development in the Northern Region of Nigeria. AFR. AGRARIAN SYSTEMS, 1963, pp. 65-82.

10,899 BALL, J. H. Rearing the two-spotted palm civet (Nandinia binotata). NIGERIAN FIELD 20 (1955), pp. 64-68.

10,900 BROWNE, G. Soil conservation in Nigeria. CORONA 2 (1950), pp. 110-111.

10,901 C., J. Recherche et propagande agricoles en Nigeria. ZAIRE 7 (1953), pp. 414-415.

10,902 CARTER, G. L. Poultry keeping in Nigeria. NIGERIAN FIELD 1, no. 3 (1932), pp. 35-40.

10,903 CHAPMAN, P. R. Cow Fulani: an impression. NIGERIAN FIELD 24 (1959), pp. 120-121.

10,904 COX, P. G. Observations of the agriculture of the Jos plateau. NIGERIAN FIELD 30 (1965), pp. 84-94.

10,905 COZENS, A. B. A query on fish weights. NIGERIAN FIELD 22 (1957), p. 182.

10,906 DANIEL, F. DE F. An improved bit suitable for native use. NIGERIAN FIELD 9 (1940), pp. 93-95.

10,907 DENNETT, R. E. Agricultural progress in Nigeria. J. AFR. SOC. 18 (1919), pp. 266-289.

10,908 FOGG, C. D. Economic and social factors affecting the development of smallholder agriculture in Eastern Nigeria. ECON. DEVELOPMENT AND CULTURAL CHANGE 13 (1964-1965), pp. 278-292.

10,909 HOLDEN, M. J. Fishing methods in Sokoto province, N. Nigeria. NIGERIAN FIELD 26 (1961), pp. 147-158.

10,910 HYDE, R. H. Bini snares. NIGERIAN FIELD 18 (1953), pp. 130-134.

10,911 JEFFREYS, M. D. W. Cross River prawn and shrimp fishing. NIGERIAN FIELD 17 (1952), pp. 135-140.

10,912 KING, W. S. Stumpy crocodile farm. NIGERIAN FIELD 18 (1953), pp. 171-174.

10,913 KIRK-GREENE, A. H. M. The Bornu stud farm. NIGERIAN FIELD 26 (1961), pp. 4-9.

10,914 LAMB, P. H. Agriculture in Hansaland, Northern Nigeria. BULL. IMP. INST. 11 (1913), pp. 626-634.

10,915 LAMB, P. H. Agricultural development in Nigeria. J. AFR. SOC. 30 (1931), pp. 119-127.

10,916 LAMB, P. H. The present position and prospects of cotton growing in the Northern Provinces of Nigeria. BULL. IMP. INST. 19 (1921), pp. 469-474.

10,917 LITTLEJOHN, K. G. Notes on the Nile perch: fishing at Olokemeji in 1937-38. NIGERIAN FIELD 8 (1939), pp. 11-13.

10,918 MACKAY, J. H. Vegetation and land planning. NIGERIAN FIELD 9 (1940), pp. 84-91.

10,919 MACLAREN, P. I. R. Game fishing in Nigeria. NIGERIAN FIELD 18 (1953), pp. 110-129.

10,920 MACLAREN, P. I. R. Nigerian fishing gear. NIGERIAN FIELD 20 (1955), pp. 148-160.

10,921 OLUWASANMI, H. A. Agriculture and economic development in tropical Africa. NJESS 1 (1959), pp. 41-50.

10,922 OREKYEH, R. O. Gardening for Africans. NIGERIAN FIELD 6 (1937), pp. 37-39.

10,923 OREKYEH, R. O. Vegetable growing in Nigeria. NIGERIAN FIELD 8 (1939), pp. 25-26.

10,924 OREKYEH, R. O. Vegetable growing in Nigeria. II. NIGERIAN FIELD 8 (1939), pp. 115-118.

10,925 PETTIT, E. R. Niger perch in the Ogun river. NIGERIAN FIELD 6 (1937), pp. 40-41.

10,926 REES, P. M. The agricultural census of Nigeria, 1950. WAISER EC. 2 (1953), pp. 148-165.

10,927 SAUNDERS, L. H. Blue in the Nigerian flower garden. NIGERIAN FIELD 4 (1935), pp. 133-136.

10,928 SAUNDERS, L. H. Citrus culture for Nigerian gardens: notes for beginners. NIGERIAN FIELD 3 (1934), pp. 79-82.

10,929 SAUNDERS, L. H. Judging standards for Nigerian horticultural shows, Part II. NIGERIAN FIELD 4 (1935), pp. 75-81.

10,930 SAUNDERS, L. H. The Nigerian flower garden. NIGERIAN FIELD 2, no. 8 (1933), pp. 24-37.

10,931 SAUNDERS, L. H. The Nigerian horticultural shows of 1933. NIGERIAN FIELD 3 (1934), pp. 56-62.

10,932 SAUNDERS, L. H. Quickly grown salads. NIGERIAN FIELD 6 (1937), p. 35.

10,933 SAUNDERS, L. H. Vegetable culture in Nigeria. NIGERIAN FIELD 4 (1935), pp. 71-74.

10,934 SAUNDERS, L. H. Vegetable growing in Nigeria: asparagus. NIGERIAN FIELD 4 (1935), pp. 138-139.

10,935 STANTON, W. R. The analysis of the present distribution of varietal variation in maize, sorghum, and cowpea in Nigeria as an aid to the study of tribal movement. J. AFR. HIST. 3 (1962), pp. 251-262.

10,936 UDO, R. K. The migrant tenant farmer of Eastern Nigeria. AFRICA 34 (1964), pp. 326-338.

10,937 UNWIN, A. H. The forests and forest department of Nigeria. J. AFR. SOC. 18 (1918), pp. 9-31.

10,938 WELMAN, J. Fly-fishing in Nigeria. CORONA 4 (1952), pp. 227-231.

10,939 Agricultural education in Northern Nigeria. WOMEN TODAY 6 (1965), pp. 86-87.

10,940 Nigerian Field Society's flower show, 1938, 1939. NIGERIAN FIELD 8 (1939), pp. 7-8; 9 (1940), pp. 4-5.

See also 12940.

Anthropology

10,941 ADEDEJI, G. O. The Arç ceremony in Ilǫfa. NIGERIAN FIELD 4 (1935), pp. 35-39.

10,942 AJOSE, O. A. Preventive medicine and superstition in Nigeria. AFRICA 27 (1957), pp. 268-273.

10,943 ALAGOA, E. J. Idu: a creator festival at Okpoma (Brass) in the Niger Delta. AFRICA 34 (1964), pp. 1-7.

10,944 ALUKO, S. A. How many Nigerians? An analysis of Nigeria's census problems, 1901-63. JMAS 3 (1965), pp. 371-392.

10,945 ANDERSON, M. G. Belief and crime. J. AFR. SOC. 37 (1938), pp. 374-379.

10,946 ANIMAGEDDI. West African Just So stories. NIGERIAN FIELD 4 (1935), pp. 43-44, 92-94, 140-142, 190-191; 6 (1937), pp. 88-89, 136, 183-184; 7 (1938), pp. 91-94, 143-144, 183-185; 8 (1939), pp. 87-91, 127-128.

10,947 ARDENER, E. W. The kinship terminology of a group of southern Ibo. AFRICA 24 (1954), pp. 85-98.

10,948 ARDENER, E. W. Lineage and locality among the Mba-ise Ibo. AFRICA 29 (1959), pp. 113-132.

10,949 ARMSTRONG, R. G. A West African inquest. AMER. ANTHR. 56 (1954), pp. 1051-1075.

10,950 ASABIA, S. O. Foundation of Yoruba government. ODU 7 (1959), pp. 23-27.

10,951 ASKARI, E. K. The social organization of the Owe. AFRICAN NOTES 2, no. 3 (1965), pp. 9-12.

10,952 BAKER, T. M. Political control among the Birom. WAISER 5 (1956), pp. 111-119.

10,953 BASCOM, W. R. The esusu: a credit institution of the Yoruba. JRAI 82 (1952), pp. 63-69.

10,954 BASCOM, W. R. The sanctions of Ifa divination. JRAI 71 (1941), pp. 43-54.

10,955 BASCOM, W. R. Yoruba cooking. AFRICA 21 (1951), pp. 125-137.

10,956 BASCOM, W. R. Yoruba food. AFRICA 21 (1951), pp. 41-53.

10,957 BATTY, R. B. Notes on the Yoruba country. JRAI 19 (1890), pp. 160-164.

10,958 BEATON, W. G. Tanning and dyeing of goat skins: Native method, Kano, Northern Nigeria. BULL. IMP. INST. 31 (1933), pp. 56-59.

10,959 BEDDOES, H. R. Hausa notes. J. AFR. SOC. 2 (1903), pp. 451-453.

10,960 BEIER, H. U. The egungun cult among the Yorubas. PRESENCE AFR. N.S. 18-19 (1958), pp. 33-36.

10,961 BEIER, H. U. Obatala: five myths of the Yoruba Creator God. BO 7 (1960), pp. 34-35.

10,962 BEIER, H. U. The position of Yoruba women. PRESENCE AFR. N.S. 1 (1955), pp. 39-46.

10,963 BEIER, H. U. Le sens historique et psychologique des mythes Yoruba. PRESENCE AFR. N.S. 7 (1956), pp. 125-132.

10,964 BEIER, H. U. Shango shrine of the Timi of Ede. BO 4 (1958), pp. 30-35.

10,965 BEIER, H. U. Spirit children among the Yoruba. AFR. AFFAIRS 53 (1954), pp. 328-331.

10,966 BEIER, H. U. The Yoruba attitude to dogs. ODU 7 (1959), pp. 31-37.

10,967 BLUMBERG, B. S. et al. The blood groups of the pastoral Fulani of Northern Nigeria and the Yoruba of Western Nigeria. AMER. J. PHY. ANTHR. 19 (1961), pp. 195-201.

10,968 BOHANNAN, L. Political aspects of Tiv social organization. TRIBES WITHOUT RULERS, 1958, pp. 33-66.

10,969 BOHANNAN, P. Concepts of time among the Tiv of Nigeria. SOUTHWESTERN J. ANTHR. 9 (1953), pp. 251-262.

10,970 BOHANNAN, P. The emigration and expansion of the Tiv. AFRICA 24 (1954), pp. 2-16.

10,971 BOHANNAN, P. Some principles of exchange and investment among the Tiv. AMER. ANTHR. 57 (1955), pp. 60-70.

10,972 BOSTON, J. S. The hunter in Igala legends of origin. AFRICA 34 (1964), pp. 116-125.

10,973 BOYLE, C. V. and BOYLE, A. M. The marking of girls at Ga-Anda. J. AFR. SOC. 15 (1916), pp. 361-366.

10,974 BOYLE, C. V. and BOYLE, A. M. Ordeal of manhood [at Ga-Anda]. J. AFR. SOC. 15 (1916), pp. 244-255.

10,975 BOYLE, C. V. and BOYLE, A. V. The Lala people and their customs. J. AFR. SOC. 15 (1951), pp. 54-69.

10,976 BRACKENBURY, E. A. Notes on the "Bororo Fulbe" or nomad "Cattle Fulani." J. AFR. SOC. 23 (1924), pp. 208-217, 271-277.

10,977 BRADBURY, R. E. Father and senior son in Edo mortuary ritual. AFRICAN SYSTEMS OF THOUGHT, 1965, pp. 96-121.

10,978 BRISTOW, W. M. Some notes on the Jarawa people near Jos, Plateau Province, Nigeria. AFR. UND UB. 37 (1952-1953), pp. 61-64.

10,979 BUTCHER, H. L. M. Some aspects of the Otu system of the Isa sub-tribes of the Edo people of Southern Nigeria. AFRICA 8 (1935), pp. 149-161.

10,980 BYNG-HALL, F. F. W. Notes on the Bassa Komo tribe. J. AFR. SOC. 8 (1908), pp. 13-20.

10,981 CARDI, C. N. DE. Ju-ju laws and customs in the Niger Delta. JRAI 29 (1899), pp. 51-64.

10,982 CHADWICK, E. R. Bebege. NIGERIAN FIELD 6 (1937), pp. 165-168.

10,983 CHADWICK, E. R. Ijo Lilliput villages. NIGERIAN FIELD 7 (1938), pp. 133-134.

10,984 CHILVER, E. M. and KABERRY, P. M. Traditional government in Bafut, West Cameroon. NIGERIAN FIELD 28 (1963), pp. 4-30.

10,985 CIROMA, M. A. L. The dying God of Zagun. NIGERIAN FIELD 19 (1954), p. 185.

10,986 CLARKE, J. D. Three Yoruba fertility ceremonies. JRAI 74 (1944), pp. 91-96.

10,987 CLIFFORD, M. A Nigerian chiefdom. Some notes on the Igala tribe in Nigeria and their "divine-king." JRAI 66 (1936), pp. 393-435.

10,988 COBHAM, H. Animal-stories from Calabar. J. AFR. SOC. 4 (1905), pp. 307-309.

10,989 COBHAM, H. The idem secret society. J. AFR. SOC. 5 (1905), pp. 41-42.

10,990 COHEN, R. Marriage instability among the Kanuri of Northern Nigeria. AMER. ANTHR. 63 (1961), pp. 1231-1249.

10,991 CONANT, F. P. The manipulation of ritual among plateau Nigerians. AFRICA 33 (1963), pp. 227-236.

10,992 COTTON, J. C. The Calabar marriage law and custom. J. AFR. SOC. 4 (1905), pp. 427-430.

10,993 COTTON, J. C. Calabar stories. J. AFR. SOC. 5 (1906), pp. 191-196.

10,994 COTTON, J. C. The people of Old Calabar. J. AFR. SOC. 4 (1905), pp. 302-306.

10,995 COZENS, A. B. Bamenda wedding. NIGERIAN FIELD 14 (1949), pp. 163-167.

10,996 COZENS, A. B. Lorry names in southern Nigeria. NIGERIAN FIELD 26 (1961), pp. 158-162.

10,997 DANIEL, F. DE F. The regalia of Katsina, northern provinces, Nigeria. J. AFR. SOC. 31 (1932), pp. 80-83.

10,998 DARKER, G. F. Niger delta natives. With special reference to maintaining and increasing the population of southern Nigeria. J. AFR. SOC. 4 (1905), pp. 206-220.

10,999 DENNETT, R. E. How the Yoruba count. And the Universal Order in Creation, etc. J. AFR. SOC. 16 (1917), pp. 242-250.

11,000 DENNETT, R. E. The Ogboni and other secret societies in Nigeria. J. AFR. SOC. 16 (1916), pp. 16-29.

11,001 DENNETT, R. E. Yoruba salutations. J. AFR. SOC. 8 (1909), pp. 187-189.

11,002 DOOB, L. W. Eidetic images among the Ibo. ETHNOLOGY 3 (1964), pp. 357-368.

11,003 EKANDEM, M. J. Ibibo farmers and some of their customs. NIGERIAN FIELD 22 (1957), pp. 169-175.

11,004 EKANDEM, M. J. The use of plants as symbols in Ibibio and Ibo country. NIGERIAN FIELD 20 (1955), pp. 53-64.

11,005 ELGEE, C. H. Ensigns of royalty in West Africa. J. AFR. SOC. 4 (1905), pp. 392-396.

11,006 ELLISON, R. E. Marriage and child-birth among the Kanuri. AFRICA 9 (1936), pp. 524-535.

11,007 ESENWA, F. E. Marriage customs in Asaba division. NIGERIAN FIELD 13 (1948), pp. 71-81.

11,008 FABIYI, T. F. and SAWYERR, H. The sense of concreteness in Yoruba worship. SIERRA L. BULL. REL. 7 (1965), pp. 13-21.

11,009 FEGAN, E. S. Some notes on the Bachama tribe, Adamawa province, northern provinces, Nigeria. J. AFR. SOC. 29 (1930), pp. 269-279, 376-400.

11,010 FITZPATRICK, J. F. J. Customs of pagan tribes in the Kwongoma district in N. Nigeria. J. AFR. SOC. 11 (1912), pp. 332-338.

11,011 FITZPATRICK, J. F. J. Some notes on the Kwolla district and its tribes. J. AFR. SOC. 10 (1910), pp. 16-52, 213-221.

11,012 FOKKEN, H. A. Erzählungen und Märchen der Larusa. AFR. UND UB. 7 (1916-1917), pp. 81-104, 192-211.

11,013 FORDE, D. Une analyse sociologique des formalités matrimoniales chez les Yakö. CAH. ET. AFR. 3 (1963), pp. 447-457.

11,014 FORDE, D. Double descent among the Yakö. AFRICAN SYSTEMS OF KINSHIP AND MARRIAGE, 1950, pp. 285-332.

11,015 FORDE, D. Fission and accretion in the patrilineal clans of a semi-Bantu community in Southern Nigeria. JRAI 68 (1938), pp. 311-338.

11,016 FORDE, D. The governmental roles of associations among the Yakö. AFRICA 31 (1961), pp. 309-322.

11,017 FORDE, D. Integrative aspects of the Yakö first fruits rituals. JRAI 79 (1949), pp. 1-10.

11,018 FORDE, D. Rôle des sociétés dans le cérémonial funéraire des Yakö. CAH. ET. AFR. 3 (1963), pp. 307-317.

11,019 FORDE, D. Ward organization among the Yakö. AFRICA 20 (1950), pp. 267-289.

11,020 GAJERE. Kongoni and the zebra. A tale from East Africa. NIGERIAN FIELD 6 (1937), pp. 160-164.

11,021 GAJERE. Ngabi the bushbuck. NIGERIAN FIELD 6 (1937), pp. 129-133.

11,022 GAJERE. The red fortress. NIGERIAN FIELD 6 (1937), pp. 58-64.

11,023 GARLANDA, U. Areopago di idoli in Nigeria. AFRICA (Rome) 13 (1958), pp. 27-31.

11,024 GIDLEY, C. G. B. Mantanfas—a study in oral tradition. AFR. LANG. STUD. 6 (1965), pp. 32-51.

11,025 GODDARD, S. Town-farm relationships in Yoruba-land: a case study from Oyo. AFRICA 35 (1965), pp. 21-29.

11,026 GOLLMER, C. A. On African symbolic messages. JRAI 14 (1885), pp. 169-182.

11,027 GRAHAM, C. Some bird traps of Katsina province. NIGERIAN FIELD 4 (1935), pp. 173-174.

11,028 GRANVILLE, R. K. Notes on the Jekris, Sobos and Ijos of the Warri district of the Niger coast Protectorate. JRAI 28 (1899), pp. 104-126.

11,029 GRIFFITH, W. J. Jillawol and dare. NIGERIAN FIELD 21 (1956), pp. 122-124.

11,030 GROOM, A. H. The main characteristics of the "inland" Igbirras in Kabba province, Northern Nigeria. J. AFR. SOC. 9 (1910), pp. 176-183.

11,031 HALL, F. F. W. B. Notes on the Okpoto and Igara tribes. J. AFR. SOC. 7 (1908), pp. 165-174.

11,032 HARRIS, J. S. Papers on the economic aspect of life among the Ozuitem Ibo. AFRICA 14 (1943), pp. 12-23.

11,033 HARRIS, J. S. Some aspects of the economics of sixteenth century Ibo individuals. AFRICA 14 (1944), pp. 302-335.

11,034 HARRIS, P. G. The Kebbi fishermen (Sokoto Province, Nigeria). JRAI 72 (1942), pp. 23-31.

11,035 HARRIS, P. G. Notes on the Dakarkari peoples of Sokoto Province, Nigeria. JRAI 68 (1938), pp. 113-152.

11,036 HARRIS, P. G. Notes on Yauri (Sokoto Province), Nigeria. JRAI 60 (1930), pp. 283-334.

11,037 HARRIS, R. The influence of ecological factors and external relations on the Mbembe tribes of south-east Nigeria. AFRICA 32 (1962), pp. 38-52.

11,038 HARTLAND, E. S. Ibo-speaking peoples of Southern Nigeria. J. AFR. SOC. 14 (1914-1915), pp. 271-277.

11,039 HAY-DRUMMOND-HAY, E. W. West African experiences. SUDAN NOTES 2 (1919), pp. 139-141.

11,040 HIDE, R. H. The Bini as a botanist. NIGERIAN FIELD 11 (1943), pp. 169-179.

11,041 HOLAS, B. Alatangana: the Kono creation myth. BO 2 (1958), pp. 7-8.

11,042 HOLLIS, R. Sketching Fulani. NIGERIAN FIELD 30 (1965), pp. 41-45.

11,043 HOPEN, C. E. A note on Alkali Fulfulde: a reformation movement among the nomadic Fulbe (Fulani) of Sokoto province. AFRICA 34 (1964), pp. 21-26.

11,044 HORTON, R. Kalabari diviners and oracles. ODU 1, no. 1 (1964), pp. 3-16.

11,045 HORTON, R. The Kalabari Ekine society: a borderland of religion and art. AFRICA 33 (1963), pp. 94-114.

11,046 HORTON, R. The Kalabari world-view: an outline and interpretation. AFRICA 32 (1962), pp. 197-220.

11,047 HORTON, W. R. G. God, man, and the land in a northern Ibo village-group. AFRICA 26 (1956), pp. 17-26.

11,048 HORTON, W. R. G. The Ohu system of slavery in a northern Ibo village-group. AFRICA 24 (1954), pp. 311-335.

11,049 HUBER, H. Initiation to womanhood among the SE (Ghana). NIGERIAN FIELD 23 (1958), pp. 99-119.

11,050 IMEGWU, C. The Aros and the oracle. AFR. HISTORIAN 1, no. iii (1965), pp. 43-46.

11,051 ITTMANN, J. Aus dem Rätselschatz der Kosi. AFR. UND UB. 21 (1930-1931), pp. 25-54.

11,052 ITTMANN, J. Das Leben eines Kosi-Kindes in den ersten zwei Wochen. AFR. UND UB. 20 (1929-1930), pp. 256-282.

11,053 JEFFREYS, M. D. W. Additional steps in the Umundri coronation ceremony. AFRICA 9 (1936), pp. 403-406.

11,054 JEFFREYS, M. D. W. Age-groups among the Ika and kindred people. AFR. STUD. 9 (1950), pp. 157-166.

11,055 JEFFREYS, M. D. W. The bull-roarer among the Ibo. AFR. STUD. 8 (1949), pp. 23-34.

11,056 JEFFREYS, M. D. W. The burial bird for an okuku. AFR. STUD. 14 (1955), pp. 134-137.

11,057 JEFFREYS, M. D. W. The divine Umundri king. AFRICA 8 (1935), pp. 346-354.

11,058 JEFFREYS, M. D. W. Ikenga: the Ibo ram-headed god. AFR. STUD. 13 (1954), pp. 25-40.

11,059 JEFFREYS, M. D. W. The Nyama society of the Ibibio women. AFR. STUD. 15 (1956), pp. 15-28.

11,060 JEFFREYS, M. D. W. The origin of the Ikelebeji festival. NIGERIAN FIELD 26 (1961), pp. 188-191.

11,061 JEFFREYS, M. D. W. Palm wine among the Ibibio. NIGERIAN FIELD 22 (1957), pp. 40-45.

11,062 JEFFREYS, M. D. W. Some notes on the Bum. NIGERIAN FIELD 27 (1962), pp. 177-184.

11,063 JEFFREYS, M. D. W. Some notes on the Ekoi. JRAI 69 (1939), pp. 95-108.

11,064 JEFFREYS, M. D. W. Some notes on the Fon of Bikom. AFR. AFFAIRS 50 (1951), pp. 241-249.

11,065 JEFFREYS, M. D. W. Some notes on the Rom people. NIGERIAN FIELD 28 (1963), pp. 78-86.

11,066 JEFFREYS, M. D. W. The winged solar disk or Ibo Itshi facial sacrification. AFRICA 21 (1951), pp. 93-110.

11,067 JEFFREYS, M. D. W. The Wiya tribe. AFR. STUD. 21 (1962), pp. 83-104, 174-222.

11,068 JONES, G. I. The attitude of the natives is friendly. [Berde District reports 1907-13.] NIGERIAN FIELD 12 (1947), pp. 64-70.

11,069 JONES, G. I. Dual organization in Ibo social structure. AFRICA 19 (1949), pp. 150-156.

11,070 JONES, G. I. Ecology and social structure among the north-eastern Ibo. AFRICA 31 (1961), pp. 117-134.

11,071 JONES, G. I. Ibo age organization, with special reference to the Cross River and North-Eastern Ibo. JRAI 92 (1962), pp. 191-211.

11,072 JONES, G. I. Ifogu Nkporo. NIGERIAN FIELD 8 (1939), pp. 119-121.

11,073 JONES, G. I. Mbari houses. NIGERIAN FIELD 6 (1937), pp. 77-79.

11,074 JONES, G. I. Ogbukere Ihuaba. NIGERIAN FIELD 8 (1939), pp. 81-82.

11,075 JONES, G. I. Ohaffia Obu houses. NIGERIAN FIELD 6 (1937), pp. 169-171.

11,076 JONES, G. I. Time and oral tradition with special reference to Eastern Nigeria. J. AFR. HIST. 6 (1965), pp. 153-160.

11,077 JONES, G. I. Who are the Aro? NIGERIAN FIELD 8 (1939), pp. 100-103.

11,078 JONES, G. I. and MULHALL, H. An examination of the physical type of certain peoples of South-Eastern Nigeria. JRAI 79 (1949), pp. 11-19.

11,079 JUDD, A. S. Notes on the Munshi tribe and language. J. AFR. SOC. 16 (1916), pp. 52-61, 143-148.

11,080 JUNGRATHMAYR, H. Materialien zur Kenntnis des Chip, Montol, Gerka und Burrum (Südplateau, Nordnigerien). AFR. UND UB. 48 (1964-1965), pp. 161-182.

11,081 KALU, E. An Ibo autobiography. NIGERIAN FIELD 7 (1938), pp. 158-170.

11,082 KENNETT, B. L. A. The Afoshi dancers of Kabba Division, Northern Nigeria. JRAI 61 (1931), pp. 435-442.

11,083 KETLEY, H. C. Boat building in Nigeria. NIGERIAN FIELD 7 (1938), pp. 186-188.

11,084 KIRK-GREENE, A. H. M. The Mba ceremony of the Marghi. NIGERIAN FIELD 24 (1959), pp. 80-87.

11,085 LA CHARD, L. W. The correlation of finger impressions and racial characteristics. J. AFR. SOC. 19 (1919), pp. 55-63.

11,086 LEGER, A. Notes sur le mariage chez des païens du Nord-Cameroun. AFRICA 8 (1935), pp. 340-345.

11,087 LEITH-ROSS, S. Notes on the Osu system among the Ibo of Owerri Province, Nigeria. AFRICA 10 (1937), pp. 206-220.

11,088 LLOYD, P. C. Sacred kinship and government among the Yoruba. AFRICA 30 (1960), pp. 221-237.

11,089 LLOYD, P. C. The traditional political system of the Yoruba. SOUTHWESTERN J. ANTHR. 10 (1954), pp. 366-384.

11,090 LLOYD, P. C. The Yoruba lineage. AFRICA 25 (1955), pp. 235-251.

11,091 LUCAS, J. O. The cult of "Adamu-Orisha." NIGERIAN FIELD 11 (1943), pp. 184-196.

11,092 LUKAS, J. Aus dem Leben der Kanuri, ihre grossen Tage, ihre Wohnung. AFR. UND UB. 29 (1939), pp. 161-188.

11,093 LUKAS, J. Fabeln der Kanuri. AFR. UND UB. 30 (1940), pp. 161-181, 273-295.

11,094 LUKAS, J. Sprichwörter, Aussprüche, und Rätsel der Kanuri. AFR. UND UB. 28 (1937-1938), pp. 161-174.

11,095 MacGREGOR, B. D. Some notes on nsibidi. JRAI 39 (1909), pp. 209-219.

11,096 MALCOLM, L. W. G. Notes on the ethno-botany of the cattle Fulbe, Adamawa, W. Africa. BIBLIOTHECA AFR. 1 (1925), pp. 126-148.

11,097 MARTI, P. Ọba só, Ọba kò só (Le roi s'est pendu, le roi ne s'est pas pendu). CONGR. INT. SC. ANTHR. ET ETHN. 6, no. ii (1960), pp. 253-257.

11,098 MATHEWS, H. F. Duodecimal numeration in Northern Nigeria. NIGERIAN FIELD 24 (1964), pp. 188-191.

11,099 MEEK, C. K. The Katab and their neighbours. J. AFR. SOC. 27 (1928), pp. 104-126, 269-286, 364-379; 28 (1928), pp. 43-54, 265-273, 385-393.

11,100 MEEK, C. K. The Kulū in Northern Nigeria. AFRICA 7 (1934), pp. 257-269.

11,101 MEEK, C. K. Marriage by exchange in Nigeria: a disappearing institution. AFRICA 9 (1936), pp. 64-74.

11,102 MEEK, C. K. The religions of Nigeria. AFRICA 14 (1943), pp. 106-117.

11,103 MEEK, C. K. A religious festival in Northern Nigeria. AFRICA 3 (1930), pp. 323-345.

11,104 MERRICK, G. The Bolewa tribe. J. AFR. SOC. 4 (1905), pp. 417-426.

11,105 MIGEOD, F. W. H. The ancient So people of Bornu. J. AFR. SOC. 23 (1923), pp. 19-29.

11,106 MILBURN, S. A Yoruba household altar. NIGERIAN FIELD 17 (1952), pp. 43-44.

11,107 MONCKTON, J. C. Burial ceremonies of the Attah of Idah. J. AFR. SOC. 27 (1927), pp. 16-23, 155-166.

11,108 MORTON-WILLIAMS, P. An outline of the cosmology and cult organization of the Ọyọ Yoruba. AFRICA 34 (1964), pp. 243-260.

11,109 MORTON-WILLIAMS, P. The Yoruba Ogboni cult in Ọyọ. AFRICA 30 (1960), pp. 362-374.

11,110 MORTON-WILLIAMS, P. Yoruba responses to the fear of death. AFRICA 30 (1960), pp. 34-40.

11,111 MURRAY, K. C. Ayolugbe. NIGERIAN FIELD 12 (1947), pp. 73-75.

11,112 MURRAY, K. C. Idah masks. NIGERIAN FIELD 14 (1949), pp. 85-92.

11,113 MYERS, O. A note on some cosmetics used in Yorubaland. ODU 1, no. 2 (1965), pp. 92-103.

11,114 NADEL, S. F. The *Gani* ritual of Nupe: a study in social symbiosis. AFRICA 19 (1949), pp. 177-186.

11,115 NADEL, S. F. Gunnu, a fertility cult of the Nupe in Northern Nigeria. JRAI 67 (1937), pp. 91-130.

11,116 NADEL, S. F. The Kede: a riverain state in Northern Nigeria. AFRICAN POLITICAL SYSTEMS, 1940, pp. 165-195.

11,117 NADEL, S. F. Nupe state and community. AFRICA 8 (1935), pp. 257-303.

11,118 NADEL, S. F. Witchcraft and anti-witchcraft in Nupe society. AFRICA 8 (1935), pp. 423-445.

11,119 NADEL, S. F. Witchcraft in four African societies: an essay in comparison. AMER. ANTHR. 54 (1952), pp. 18-29.

11,120 NEHER, G. Chibuk face marks. NIGERIAN FIELD 28 (1963), pp. 72-78.

11,121 NEWBERRY, R. J. Games and pastimes of Southern Nigeria. NIGERIAN FIELD 8 (1939), pp. 75-80; 9 (1940), pp. 40-43.

11,122 NEWBERRY, R. J. Some games and pastimes of Southern Nigeria. NIGERIAN FIELD 7 (1938), pp. 85-90, 131-132.

11,123 NICHOLSON, W. E. Notes on some of the customs of the Busa and Kyenga tribes at Illo. J. AFR. SOC. 26 (1927), pp. 93-100.

11,124 NOON, J. A. A preliminary examination of the death concepts of the Ibo. AMER. ANTHR. 47 (1942), pp. 638-654.

11,125 ODUKOYA, M. A. Okosi festival at Epe town. ODU 7 (1959), pp. 28-30.

11,126 OJO-ILORI, I. O. The ancestral shrines of Ife. AFR. HISTORIAN 1, no. ii (1964), pp. 50-52.

11,127 OKARO, G. Ogboinba: the Ijaw creation myth. BO 2 (1958), pp. 9-17.

11,128 ORR, C. W. The Hausa race. J. AFR. SOC. 7 (1908), pp. 278-283; 8 (1909), pp. 274-278.

11,129 OTTENBERG, S. Improvement associations among the Afikpo Ibo. AFRICA 25 (1955), pp. 1-27.

11,130 OTTENBERG, S. Supplementary bibliography on the Ibo-speaking people of south-eastern Nigeria. AFR. STUD. 14 (1955), pp. 63-85.

11,131 OWOADE, A. and OGUNREMI, 'D. Oke 'Badan. AFR. HISTORIAN 1 (1963), pp. 22-25.

11,132 PALMER, H. R. Notes on the Korôrofawa and Jukoñ. J. AFR. SOC. 11 (1912), pp. 401-415.

11,133 PARKINSON, J. Note on the Asaka people (Ibos) of the Niger. JRAI 36 (1906), pp. 312-324.

11,134 PARKINSON, J. A note on the Efik and Ekoi tribes of the eastern province of Southern Nigeria. JRAI 37 (1907), pp. 261-267.

11,135 PARKINSON, J. Yoruba folklore. J. AFR. SOC. 8 (1909), pp. 165-186.

11,136 PARKINSON, J. Yoruba string figures. JRAI 36 (1906), pp. 132-141.

11,137 PARRINDER, E. G. Ibadan annual festival. AFRICA 21 (1951), pp. 54-58.

11,138 PARTRIDGE, C. A note on the Igara tribe. J. AFR. SOC. 8 (1908), pp. 1-2.

11,139 PILKINGTON, F. Pagan and anti-pagan. AFR. AFFAIRS 58 (1959), pp. 61-64.

11,140 PRICE-WILLIAMS, D. R. A case study of ideas concerning disease among the Tiv. AFRICA 32 (1962), pp. 123-131.

11,141 PROTHERO, R. M. African ethnographic maps, with a new example from Northern Nigeria. AFRICA 32 (1962), pp. 61-64.

11,142 ROUCH, J. Les Sorkawa pêcheurs itinérants du Moyen Niger. AFRICA 20 (1950), pp. 5-25; English summary, p. 25.

11,143 RUEL, M. Witchcraft, morality and doubt. ODU 2, no. 1 (1965), pp. 3-27.

11,144 RUMANN, W. B. Funeral ceremonies for the late ex-Oba of Benin. J. AFR. SOC. 14 (1914-1915), pp. 35-39.

11,145 RUXTON, F. H. An anthropological no-man's-land. AFRICA 3 (1930), pp. 1-11.

11,146 RUXTON, F. H. Notes on the tribes of the Muri province. J. AFR. SOC. 7 (1908), pp. 374-386.

11,147 SAI, B. A. The 'descent' of the Tiv from Ibenda Hill. AFRICA 24 (1954), pp. 295-310.

11,148 SASSOON, M. Lorry names collected in Northern Nigeria. NIGERIAN FIELD 28 (1963), pp. 95-96.

11,149 SAUTTER, G. Pression démographique et système foncier Tiv. CAH. ET. AFR. 2 (1961), pp. 326-332.

11,150 SCHNEIDER, G. Kom burial. NIGERIAN FIELD 21 (1956), pp. 84-88.

11,151 SCHNEIDER, G. Mambila album. NIGERIAN FIELD 20 (1955), pp. 112-132.

11,152 SCHWAB, W. B. Continuity and change in the Yoruba lineage system. ANTHROPOLOGY AND AFRICA TODAY, 1962, pp. 590-605.

11,153 SCHWAB, W. B. The growth and conflicts of religion in a modern Yoruba community. ZAIRE 6 (1952), pp. 829-835.

11,154 SCHWAB, W. B. Kinship and lineage among the Yoruba. AFRICA 25 (1955), pp. 352-373.

11,155 SCHWAB, W. B. The terminology of kinship and marriage among the Yoruba. AFRICA 28 (1958), pp. 301-312.

11,156 SETON, R. S. Notes on the Igala tribe, Northern Nigeria. J. AFR. SOC. 29 (1929), pp. 42-52, 149-163.

11,157 SHELTON, A. J. Anthropological "values" and culture change: a note. AMER. ANTHR. 67 (1965), pp. 103-107.

11,158 SHELTON, A. J. The meaning and method of afa divination among the Northern Nsukka Ibo. AMER. ANTHR. 67 (1965), pp. 1441-1455.

11,159 SIEBER, D. and SIEBER, J. Das Leben des Kindes im Nsungli-Stamm. AFRICA 11 (1938), pp. 208-220.

11,160 SIMMONS, D. C. Efik knots. NIGERIAN FIELD 21 (1956), pp. 127-134.

11,161 SIMMONS, D. C. Notes on the Aro. NIGERIAN FIELD 23 (1958), pp. 27-33.

11,162 SIMMONS, D. C. Oron proverbs. AFR. STUD. 19 (1960), pp. 126-137.

11,163 SIMMONS, D. C. Sexual life, marriage, and childhood among the Efik. AFRICA 30 (1960), pp. 153-165.

11,164 SIMPSON, G. E. Selected Yoruba rituals: 1964. NJESS 7 (1965), pp. 311-324.

11,165 SIMPSON, G. E. The Shango Cult in Nigeria and in Trinidad. AMER. ANTHR. 64 (1962), pp. 1204-1219.

11,166 SMITH, M. G. The Hausa system of social status. AFRICA 29 (1959), pp. 239-251.

11,167 SMITH, M. G. Secondary marriage in Northern Nigeria. AFRICA 23 (1953), pp. 298-323.

11,168 SMITH, M. G. The social functions and meaning of Hausa praise-singing. AFRICA 27 (1957), pp. 26-43.

11,169 SOLANKE, L. The customary constitution of the Yoruba or Aku Commonwealth. WASU 3-4 (1927), pp. 30-36.

11,170 SOLANKE, L. The Ogboni institution in Yoruba. WASU 2 (1926), pp. 28-34.

11,171 SPEED, F. Ford Foundation film-making scheme. AFRICAN NOTES 1, no. 2 (1964), pp. 14-15.

11,172 STENNING, D. J. Transhumance, migratory drift, migration; patterns of pastoral Fulani nomadism. JRAI 87 (1957), pp. 57-73.

11,173 TALBOT, P. A. Some beliefs of to-day and yesterday (Niger-delta tribes). J. AFR. SOC. 15 (1916), pp. 305-319.

11,174 TALBOT, P. A. Some foreign influences on Nigeria. J. AFR. SOC. 24 (1925), pp. 178-201.

11,175 TALBOT, P. A. Some Ibibio customs and beliefs. J. AFR. SOC. 13 (1914), pp. 241-258.

11,176 TEPOWA, A. The titles of Ozor and Ndiche at Ouitsha. J. AFR. SOC. 9 (1910), pp. 189-192.

11,177 THOMAS, M. A. Birth customs of the Edo-speaking peoples. JRAI 52 (1922), pp. 250-258.

11,178 THOMAS, N. W. The Edo-speaking peoples of Nigeria. J. AFR. SOC. 10 (1910), pp. 1-15.

11,179 THOMAS, N. W. Notes on Edo burial customs. JRAI 50 (1920), pp. 377-411.

11,180 THOMAS, N. W. Some Ibo burial customs. JRAI 47 (1917), pp. 160-213.

11,181 TREMEARNE, Major A. J. N. Notes on the Kagoro and other Nigerian head-hunters. JRAI 42 (1912), pp. 136-199.

11,182 TREMEARNE, B. A. Notes on some Nigerian tribal marks. JRAI 41 (1911), pp. 162-178.

11,183 TULEY, P. How to tap an oil palm. NIGERIAN FIELD 30 (1965), pp. 28-37.

11,184 TULEY, P. How to tap a Raphia palm. NIGERIAN FIELD 30 (1965), pp. 120-132.

11,185 UCHENDU, V. C. Concubinage among Ngwa Igbo of southern Nigeria. AFRICA 35 (1965), pp. 187-197.

11,186 UCHENDU, V. C. The status implications of Igbo religious beliefs. NIGERIAN FIELD 29 (1964), pp. 27-37.

11,187 UDO, B. U. A profile of the Ibibios. AFR. HISTORIAN 1, no. iii (1965), pp. 20-24.

11,188 UPWARD, A. The province of Kabba, Northern Nigeria. J. AFR. SOC. 2 (1903), pp. 235-260.

11,189 VAUGHAN, J. H. The religion and world view of the Marghi. ETHNOLOGY 3 (1964), pp. 389-397.

11,190 VERGER, P. Grandeur et décadence du culte de Iyámi Osòròngà (Ma mère la sorcière) chez les yoruba. J. SOC. AFR. 35 (1965), pp. 141-243.

11,191 WALLACE, J. G. The Tiv system of election. J. AFR. ADM. 10 (1958), pp. 63-70.

11,192 WALSH, M. J. The Edi festival at Ile Ife. AFR. AFFAIRS 47 (1948), pp. 231-238.

11,193 WELCH, J. W. An African tribe in transition [: the Isoko tribe]. INT. REV. MISSIONS 20 (1931), pp. 556-574.

11,194 WELCH, J. W. The Isoko tribe. AFRICA 7 (1934), pp. 160-173.

11,195 WESCOTT, J. and MORTON-WILLIAMS, P. The symbolism and ritual context of the Yoruba Laba Shango. JRAI 92 (1962), pp. 23-37.

11,196 WHITEHOUSE, A. A. An African fetish. J. AFR. SOC. 4 (1905), pp. 410-416.

11,197 WHITEHOUSE, A. A. An Ibo festival. J. AFR. SOC. 4 (1904), pp. 134-135.

11,198 WILLIAMSON, K. Changes in the marriage system of the Okrika Ijo. AFRICA 32 (1962), pp. 53-60.

11,199 WILSON-HAFFENDEN, J. R. Ethnological notes on the Kwottos of Toto (Panda) district, Keffi division, Benue province, Northern Nigeria. J. AFR. SOC. 26 (1927), pp. 368-379; 27 (1927), pp. 24-46, 142-154, 281-286, 380-393.

11,200 WILSON-HAFFENDEN, J. R. Ethnological notes on the Shuwalbe group of the Borroro Fulani in the Kurafi district of Keffi Emirate, Northern Nigeria. JRAI 57 (1927), pp. 275-293.

11,201 WILSON-HAFFENDEN, J. R. Initiation ceremonies in Northern Nigeria. J. AFR. SOC. 29 (1930), pp. 370-375.

11,202 WOODHOUSE, C. A. Some account of the inhabitants of the Waja district of Banchi province, Nigeria. J. AFR. SOC. 23 (1924), pp. 110-121, 194-207.

11,203 Crime religieux à Lagos. ZAIRE 8 (1954), pp. 418-419.

11,204 Kalabari culture and history. AFR. NOTES 2, no. 3 (1965), pp. 16-17.

11,205 Native crowns. J. AFR. SOC. 2 (1903), pp. 312-315.

11,206 Propaganda against leopard-men [extracted from the Nigerian Eastern Mail]. AFR. AFFAIRS 46 (1947), pp. 218-219.

11,207 Some Yoruba Customs. I, II. NIGERIAN FIELD 13 (1948), pp. 24-27, 59-61; 14 (1949), pp. 33-35, 74-79, 113-119.

See also 481, 9518, 13062, 13114, 14019.

Art

11,208 ABIMBOLA, W. The ruins of Oyo division. AFR. NOTES 2, no. 1 (1964), pp. 16-19.

11,209 ALLEN, J. G. C. The Nigerian Eisteddfod. CORONA 2 (1950), p. 256.

11,210 ARAGBABALU, O. The art of Susanne Wenger. AFR. SOUTH 4, no. 3 (1960), pp. 99-102.

11,211 ARNOT, A. S. Uri body painting and Aro embroidery. NIGERIAN FIELD 15 (1950), pp. 133-137.

11,212 B., F. More amateur boat-building. NIGERIAN FIELD 2, no. 8 (1933), pp. 38-44.

11,213 BALFOUR, H. The tandu industry in Northern Nigeria and its affinities elsewhere. ESSAYS PRESENTED TO C. G. SELIGMAN, 1934, pp. 5-18.

11,214 BANHAM, M. Theater on wheels. AFR. FORUM 1 (1965), pp. 108-109.

11,215 BASCOM, W. Odu Ifa: the order of the figures of Ifa. BULL. IFAN 23 (1961), pp. 676-682.

11,216 BEIER, H. U. Yoruba vocal music. AFR. MUSIC, 1956, pp. 23-28.

11,217 B[EIER], U. The dancers of Agbor. ODU 7 (1959), p. 41.

11,218 BEIER, U. Demas Nwoko: a young Nigerian artist. BO 8 (1960), pp. 10-11.

11,219 BEIER, U. Gelede masks. ODU 6 (1958), pp. 5-23.

11,220 BEIER, U. Ibo and Yoruba art. BO 8 (1960), pp. 46-50.

11,221 BEIER, U. The Talking Drums of the Yoruba. AFR. MUSIC, 1954, pp. 29-31.

11,222 BEIER, U. Yoruba folk operas. AFR. MUSIC, 1954, pp. 32-34.

11,223 BEIER, U. The Yoruba painters. BO 6 (1959), pp. 29-32.

11,224 BEIER, U. Yoruba wall paintings. ODU 8 (1960), pp. 36-39.

11,225 BIVAR, A. D. H. and SHINNIE, P. L. Old Kanuri capitals. J. AFR. HIST. 3 (1962), pp. 1-10.

11,226 BOSTON, J. S. Some Northern Ibo masquerades. JRAI 90 (1960), pp. 54-65.

11,227 C., E. The Nsude pyramids. NIGERIAN FIELD 4 (1935), pp. 82-85.

11,228 CARROL, K. Yoruba religious music. AFR. MUSIC, 1956, pp. 45-47.

11,229 CARROLL, K. Ekiti Yoruba woodcarving. ODU 4 (1957), pp. 3-10.

11,230 CARROLL, K. Yoruba masks. ODU 3 (1956), pp. 3-15.

11,231 CHADWICK, E. R. A divisional museum [Udi Divisional Museum, Nigeria]. NIGERIAN FIELD 17 (1952), pp. 84-89.

11,232 CHADWICK, E. R. The "George Shotton" Hulk. NIGERIAN FIELD 7 (1938), pp. 181-182.

11,233 CHADWICK, E. R. A hippo play in Brass division. NIGERIAN FIELD 18 (1953), pp. 30-33.

11,234 CHADWICK, E. R. An Ibo village art gallery. NIGERIAN FIELD 4 (1935), pp. 175-182.

11,235 CHADWICK, E. R. Wall decorations of Ibo houses. NIGERIAN FIELD 6 (1937), pp. 134-135.

11,236 CLARKE, J. D. A visit to Old Ọyọ. NIGERIAN FIELD 7 (1938), pp. 139-142.

11,237 COCKIN, M. S. Nigeria's need of a museum. J. AFR. SOC. 37 (1938), pp. 502-503.

11,238 CONANT, E. P. Contemporary communities and abandoned settlement sites. ANTHROPOLOGY AND AFRICA TODAY, 1962, pp. 539-574.

11,239 CROCKER, H. E. The bronzes of Ife. J. AFR. SOC. 42 (1943), pp. 38-39.

11,240 DANFORD, J. A. Art in Nigeria. AFR. AFFAIRS 48 (1949), pp. 37-47. Also in ZAIRE 3 (1949), pp. 447-452.

11,241 DANIEL, F. The stone figures of Esie, Ilorin Province, Nigeria. JRAI 67 (1937), pp. 43-49.

11,242 DARK, P. J. C. A preliminary catalogue of Benin art and technology: some problems of material culture analysis. JRAI 87 (1957), pp. 175-189.

11,243 EDET, E. M. Music in Nigeria. AFR. MUSIC, 1964, pp. 111-113.

11,244 ELGEE, C. H. The Ife stone carvings. J. AFR. SOC. 7 (1908), pp. 338-343.

11,245 ELLISON, R. E. A Bornu puppet show. NIGERIAN FIELD 4 (1935), pp. 89-91.

11,246 FAGG, B. E. B. The cave paintings and rock gongs of Birnin Kudu. PROC. PAN-AFR. CONGR. PRE-HIST. 3 (1955), pp. 306-312.

11,247 FAGG, B. E. B. The discovery of multiple rock gongs in Nigeria. AFR. MUSIC, 1956, pp. 6-9.

11,248 FAGG, B. E. B. The Nok culture in prehistory. J. HIST. SOC. NIG. 1 (1959), pp. 288-293.

11,249 FAGG, B. E. B. A preliminary note on a new series of pottery figures from Northern Nigeria. AFRICA 15 (1945), pp. 21-22.

11,250 FAGG, B. E. B. The rock gong complex today and in prehistoric times. J. HIST. SOC. NIG. 1 (1956), pp. 27-42.

11,251 FAGG, W. De l'art des Yoruba. PRESENCE AFR. 10 (1951), pp. 103-135.

11,252 FAGG, W. L'art nigérien avant Jesus-Christ. PRESENCE AFR. 10 (1951), pp. 91-95.

11,253 FAGG, W. Art without age. CORONA 2 (1950), pp. 24-26.

11,254 FAGG, W. and WILLETT, F. Ancient Ife: an ethnographical summary. PROC. PAN-AFR. CONGR. PRE-HIST. 4, no. iii (1962), pp. 357-372.

11,255 FITZGERALD, R. T. D. Dakakari grave pottery. JRAI 74 (1944), pp. 43-57; NIGERIAN FIELD 23 (1958), pp. 76-84.

11,256 GOODWIN, A. J. H. Archaeology and Benin architecture. J. HIST. SOC. NIG. 1 (1957), pp. 65-85.

11,257 GOODWIN, A. J. H. Walls, paving, water-paths and landmarks. ODU 6 (1958), pp. 45-53.

11,258 HARPER, P. Traditional dance and new theatre. AFR. NOTES 2, no. 1 (1964), pp. 15-16.

11,259 HARRIS, P. G. Notes on drums and musical instruments seen in Sokoto Province, Nigeria. JRAI 62 (1932), pp. 105-125.

11,260 HAU, K. A royal title on a palace tusk from Benin (southern Nigeria). BULL. IFAN 26 (1964), pp. 21-39.

11,261 HAY-BARCLAY, H. Hides and skins of Nigeria. BULL. IMP. INST. 36 (1938), pp. 472-482.

11,262 HOGARTH, R. F. African schoolboy acting. NIGERIAN FIELD 9 (1940), pp. 43-46.

11,263 HOLLIS, R. Dakakari grave pottery. NIGERIAN FIELD 23 (1958), pp. 23-26.

11,264 HORTON, R. A note on recent finds of brasswork in the Niger delta. ODU 2, no. 1 (1965), pp. 76-91.

11,265 JEFFREYS, M. D. W. Carved bottle corks. NIGERIAN FIELD 18 (1953), pp. 41-43.

11,266 JEFFREYS, M. D. W. Cordage among the Ibo. NIGERIAN FIELD 25 (1960), pp. 42-44.

11,267 JEFFREYS, M. D. W. The degeneration of the Ofo Anam. NIGERIAN FIELD 21 (1956), pp. 173-177.

11,268 JEFFREYS, M. D. W. Notes on the neolithic stone age culture of Bamenda. NIGERIAN FIELD 29 (1964), pp. 38-41.

11,269 JEFFREYS, M. D. W. Oku blacksmiths. NIGERIAN FIELD 26 (1961), pp. 137-144.

11,270 JEFFREYS, M. D. W. The origins of the Benin bronzes. AFR. STUD. 10 (1951), pp. 87-92.

11,271 JEFFREYS, M. D. W. Primitive hoes. NIGERIAN FIELD 20 (1955), pp. 39-41.

11,272 JEFFREYS, M. D. W. Some beads from Awka. NIGERIAN FIELD 19 (1954), pp. 37-44.

11,273 JONES, G. I. The distribution of Negro sculpture in Southern Nigeria. NIGERIAN FIELD 7 (1938), pp. 102-108.

11,274 JONES, G. I. Ibo bronzes from the Awka Division. NIGERIAN FIELD 8 (1939), pp. 164-167.

11,275 JOWETT, P. and POOLE, E. J. Cloth manufacture from Nigerian wool. BULL. IMP. INST. 29 (1931), pp. 288-299.

11,276 KENNEDY, R. A. A necked and a lugged axe from Nigeria, and some preliminary observations on the outils à gorge family in Africa. BULL. IFAN 22 (1960), pp. 202-210.

11,277 KING, A. Employments of the "standard pattern" in Yoruba music. AFR. MUSIC, 1960, pp. 51-54.

11,278 KING, A. A report on the use of stone clappers for the accompaniment of sacred songs. AFR. MUSIC, 1961, pp. 64-71.

11,279 KING, A. V. Nigerian traditional dances and music. AFR. NOTES 1, no. 2 (1964), pp. 15-19.

11,280 KINGSLAKE, B. The art of the Yoruba. AFR. MUSIC, 1951, pp. 13-18.

11,281 KINGSLAKE, B. Musical memories of Nigeria. AFR. MUSIC, 1957, pp. 17-20.

11,282 LALOUM, C. La musique de deux chants liturgiques yoruba. J. SOC. AFR. 35 (1965), pp. 109-139.

11,283 LANE, M. The Aku-Ahwa and Aku-Maga post-burial rites of the Jukun peoples of Northern Nigeria. AFR. MUSIC, 1959, pp. 29-32. Also in NIGERIAN FIELD 25 (1960), pp. 100-104.

11,284 LANE, M. The origin of present day musical taste in Nigeria. NIGERIAN FIELD 21 (1956), pp. 99-105. Also in AFR. MUSIC, 1956, pp. 18-22.

11,285 LANE, M. G. M. The music of Tiv. AFR. MUSIC, 1954, pp. 12-15. Also in NIGERIAN FIELD 20 (1955), pp. 177-182.

11,286 LAOYE, I, Timi of Ede. Yoruba drums. ODU 7 (1959), pp. 5-14.

11,287 LINNE, S. Masterpiece of primitive art. ETHNOS 23 (1958), pp. 172-174.

11,288 LLOYD, P. Sungbo's Eredo. ODU 7 (1959), pp. 15-22.

11,289 MACKAY, M. The Shantu music of the Harims of Nigeria. AFR. MUSIC, 1955, pp. 56-57.

11,290 MACKAY, M. The traditional musical instruments of Nigeria. NIGERIAN FIELD 15 (1950), pp. 112-133.

11,291 MACKAY, M. and ENE, A. The Atilogwu dance. AFR. MUSIC, 1957, pp. 20-22.

11,292 MADUMERE, A. Ibo village music. AFR. AFFAIRS 52 (1953), pp. 63-67.

11,293 MALIK, H. Art in Nigeria. AFR. QUART. 1, no. 1 (1961), pp. 30-35.

11,294 MALMSTEN, K. A Benin bench. Part I. Description. ETHNOS 2 (1937), pp. 199-207.

11,295 MESSENGER, J. C. Anang art, drama, and social control. AFR. STUD. BULL. 5, no. ii (1962), pp. 29-35.

11,296 MEYEROWITZ, E. L. R. Wood-carving in the Yoruba country to-day. AFRICA 14 (1943), pp. 66-69.

11,297 MURRAY, K. C. Art in Nigeria: the need for a museum. J. AFR. SOC. 41 (1942), pp. 241-249.

11,298 MURRAY, K. C. Arts and crafts of Nigeria: their past and future. AFRICA 14 (1943), pp. 155-163.

11,299 MURRAY, K. C. An exhibition of masks and head-dresses of Nigeria. NIGERIAN FIELD 15 (1950), pp. 26-39.

11,300 MURRAY, K. C. Exhibition of wood-carvings, terracottas, and water-colours. NIGERIAN FIELD 7 (1938), pp. 12-15.

11,301 MURRAY, K. C. Music and dancing in Nigeria. AFR. MUSIC, 1952, pp. 44-45.

11,302 MURRAY, K. C. Ogbom. NIGERIAN FIELD 10 (1941), pp. 127-131.

11,303 MURRAY, K. C. The provision of a Nigerian Museum. NIGERIAN FIELD 8 (1939), pp. 169-175.

11,304 MYERS, O. H. The importance of archaeology to the history of Nigeria. AFR. HISTORIAN 1, no. ii (1964), pp. 13-18.

11,305 NEHER, G. Brass casting in north-east Nigeria. NIGERIAN FIELD 29 (1964), pp. 16-27.

11,306 NKETIA, K. Yoruba musicians in Accra. ODU 6 (1958), pp. 35-44.

11,307 NWOKWU, M. E. Awka wood carving. NIGERIAN FIELD 4 (1935), pp. 86-89.

11,308 OGBOMO. Benin moats. AFR. HISTORIAN 1, no. 1 (1963), p. 16.

11,309 ONYIDO, U. The Nigerian Institute of Music. RHODES-LIV. J. 19 (1955), pp. 46-47.

11,310 ORMISTON, W. Past and present postage stamps of Nigeria. NIGERIAN FIELD 6 (1937), pp. 81-82.

11,311 PALMER, H. R. Hansa legend and earth pyramids in the western and central Sudan. BULL. SOAS 2 (1921-1923), pp. 225-233.

11,312 PEPPER, H. Sur un xylophone Ibo. AFR. MUSIC, 1952, pp. 35-38.

11,313 ROUGET, G. Notes et documents pour servir a l'étude de la musique yoruba. J. SOC. AFR. 35 (1965), pp. 67-107.

11,314 SCHNEIDER, G. The village Smithy of Kwadja. NIGERIAN FIELD 16 (1951), pp. 179-183.

11,315 SHAW, T. Two Nigerian caves. AFR. NOTES 1, no. 2 (1964), pp. 13-14.

11,316 SMITH, R. Erin and Iwawun, forgotten towns of the Okè Ogùn. ODU 1, no. 1 (1964), pp. 17-32.

11,317 SOPER, R. C. The Stone Age in Northern Nigeria. J. HIST. SOC. NIG. 3 (1965), pp. 175-194.

11,318 SOWANDE, F. Three Yoruba songs. ODU 3 (1956), pp. 36-40.

11,319 STOCKER, J. A Nigerian Eisteddfod. CORONA 2 (1950), p. 186.

11,320 SYDOW, E. VON. Ancient and modern art in Benin City. AFRICA 11 (1938), pp. 55-62.

11,321 TOBIAS, P. V. A re-examination of the Kanam Mandible. PROC. PAN-AFR. CONGR. PRE-HIST. 4 (1962), pp. 341-360.

11,322 VERGER, P. Note on the Bas reliefs in the royal palaces of Abomey. ODU 5 (1958), pp. 3-8.

11,323 VERNON-JACKSON, H. Craft work in Bida. AFRICA 30 (1960), pp. 51-60.

11,324 WESCOTT, J. The sculpture and myths of Eshu-Elegba, the Yoruba trickster. Definition and interpretation in Yoruba iconography. AFRICA 32 (1962), pp. 336-354.

11,325 WHYTE, H. Types of Ibo music. NIGERIAN FIELD 18 (1953), pp. 182-186.

11,326 WILLETT, F. The discovery of new brass figures at Ife. ODU 6 (1958), pp. 29-34.

11,327 WILLETT, F. Ife and its archaeology. J. AFR. HIST. 1 (1960), pp. 231-248.

11,328 WILLETT, F. The microlithic industry from old Oyo, Western Nigeria. PROC. PAN-AFR. CONGR. PRE-HIST. 4, no. iii (1962), pp. 261-271.

11,329 WILLETT, F. Recent archaeological discoveries at Ilesha. ODU 8 (1960), pp. 5-20.

11,330 WILLIAMS, D. The iconology of the Yoruba Edan Ogboni. AFRICA 34 (1964), pp. 139-165.

11,331 WILLIAMS, D. The Nigerian image. Problems in Nigerian art history. ODU 1, no. 2 (1965), pp. 83-91.

11,332 WOLFF, H. Rárà: a Yoruba chant. J. AFR. LANGS. 1 (1962), pp. 45-56.

11,333 YOUNG, J. Lively sculpture from Nigeria. CORONA 4 (1952), p. 224.

11,334 Daybreak in Udi. NIGERIAN FIELD 15 (1950), pp. 40-41.

11,335 La musique au Nigeria. PRESENCE AFR. N.S. 55 (1965), pp. 200-203.

See also

Biography

11,336 ARMSTRONG, R. G. Roy Clive Abraham, 1890-1963. J. W. AFR. LANG. 1 (1964), pp. 49-53.

11,337 AYORINDE, O. J. A. Oba Sir Isaac Babalola Akinyele Kt. Olubadan-Ibadan. ODU 1, no. 2 (1965), pp. 78-82.

11,338 Obituary: E. J. Alex-Taylor. AFR. AFFAIRS 47 (1948), p. 55.

11,339 Obituary /Dr. P. Amaury-Talbot/. AFR. AFFAIRS 45 (1946), p. 97.

11,340 JONES-QUARTEY, K. A. B. The moulding of Azikiwe. TRANSITION 15 (1964), pp. 50-53.

11,341 IGE, O. Joseph Babalola: a twentieth century prophet. AFR. HISTORIAN 1, no. iii (1965), pp. 38-42.

11,342 DIKE, K. O. John Beecroft, 1790-1854: Her Brittanic Majesty's Consul to the Bights of Benin and Biafra 1849-1854. J. HIST. SOC. NIG. 1 (1956), pp. 5-14.

11,343 Obituary: Sir Bernard Bourdillon. AFR. AFFAIRS 47 (1948), pp. 118-119.

11,344 BRIDGES, A. F. B. Jottings on a Nigerian career. NIGERIAN FIELD 17 (1952), pp. 7-14.

11,345 Obituary: Sir Donald Cameron. AFR. AFFAIRS 47 (1948), pp. 117-118.

11,346 Obituary: Frank Simon Collier. NIGERIAN FIELD 29 (1964), pp. 95-96.

11,347 KIRK-GREENE, A. Kitty Cooke looks back: a personal mining memoir. NIGERIAN FIELD 26 (1961), pp. 110-128.

11,348 CUDJOE, R. Some reminiscences of a senior interpreter. NIGERIAN FIELD 18 (1953), pp. 148-164.

11,349 DENTON, G. C. Twenty-three years in Lagos and the Gambia. J. AFR. SOC. 11 (1912), pp. 129-140.

11,350 RYDER, A. F. C. The story of Dom Domingos. ODU 4 (1957), pp. 33-39.

11,351 Dom Domingos, prince of Warri. ODU 4 (1957), pp. 27-28.

11,352 DANIEL, F. Shehu dan Fodio. J. AFR. SOC. 25 (1926), pp. 278-283.

11,353 PARK, E. Taffy Jones: first town engineer of Ibadan. NIGERIAN FIELD 28 (1963), pp. 103-114.

11,354 Statuette of Lord Lugard. J. AFR. SOC. 38 (1939), pp. 179-181.

11,355 Nouvel Emir de Kano [Muhammada Sanusi]. ZAIRE 8 (1954), pp. 417-418.

11,356 NEVILLE, G. W. Nanna Oloma of Benin. J. AFR. SOC. 14 (1914-1915), pp. 162-167.

11,357 JEFFREYS, M. D. W. A note on Onoyom Iya Nya Ita. NIGERIAN FIELD 21 (1956), pp. 41-47.

11,358 IGWI, M. A. O. The outline history of Nnochiri Oriaku. NIGERIAN FIELD 16 (1951), pp. 168-179.

11,359 JEFFREYS, M. D. W. Isaac Fielding Pefok, a brief autobiography. NIGERIAN FIELD 27 (1962), pp. 81-90.

11,360 Obituary: Duncan George Stewart. NIGERIAN FIELD 15 (1950), p. 48.

11,361 WEBSTER, J. B. Dictionary of Nigerian biography. BULL. AFR. STUD. ASSOC. 6 (1965), pp. 30-31.

11,362 Towards a dictionary of national biography [for Nigeria]. AFR. NOTES 1, no. 3 (1964), pp. 4-5.

Economics

11,363 A., E. J. A Nigerian trade report [1935]; by E. J. A. J. AFR. SOC. 36 (1937), pp. 82-85.

11,364 ABOYADE, O. Problems in plan revision. NJESS 7 (1965), pp. 121-130.

11,365 ABOYADE, O. Some implications of Nigerian imports structure. NJESS 4 (1962), pp. 51-61.

11,366 ADEDEJI, A. The future of personal income taxation in Nigeria. NJESS 7 (1965), pp. 159-174.

11,367 ADEWALE, T. J. A vernacular news bulletin in Nigeria. TOWARDS A LITERATE AFRICA, 1948, pp. 62-65.

11,368 ADU, S. A. Statistics in a developing economy, with special reference to Nigeria. NJESS 1 (1959), pp. 51-59.

11,369 AKINOLA, R. A. Factors affecting the location of a textile industry: the example of the Ikeja textile mill. NJESS 7 (1965), pp. 245-256.

11,370 ALUKO, S. A. Economics in an immature society. NJESS 2 (1960), pp. 19-25.

11,371 ALUKO, S. A. Financing economic development in Nigeria. NJESS 3 (1961), pp. 39-67.

11,372 ALUKO, S. A. and IJERE, M. O. The economics of mineral oil. NJESS 7 (1965), pp. 209-220.

11,373 AMOGU, O. O. Some notes on savings in an African economy. SOCIAL AND ECON. STUD. 5 (1956), pp. 202-209.

11,374 ARNETT, E. J. Annual report (No. 1625) on the social and economic progress of the people of Nigeria, 1932. J. AFR. SOC. 33 (1934), pp. 82-85.

11,375 AYIDA, A. A. Contractor finance and supplier credit in economic growth. NJESS 7 (1965), pp. 175-188.

11,376 BALDWIN, K. D. S. Some problems of government in land settlement. WAISER 5 (1956), pp. 36-44.

11,377 BARATZ, M. S. Public investment in private enterprise: a Western Nigeria case study. NJESS 6 (1964), pp. 60-71.

11,378 BARBACK, R. H. Marx and economic development. NJESS 6 (1964), pp. 177-183.

11,379 BARTON, P. A canoe on the Imo river. NIGERIAN FIELD 20 (1955), pp. 77-84.

11,380 BHAMBRI, R. S. Marxist economic doctrines and their relevance to problems of economic development of Nigeria. NJESS 6 (1964), pp. 185-198.

11,381 BISPHAM, W. M. L. The concept and measurement of labour commitment and its relevance to Nigerian development. NJESS 6 (1964), pp. 51-59.

11,382 BOHANNAN, P. The impact of money on an African subsistence economy. J. ECON. HIST. 19 (1959), pp. 491-503.

11,383 BOVILL, E. W. Jega market. J. AFR. SOC. 22 (1922), pp. 50-60.

11,384 BROWN, C. V. The recent Nigerian banking amendments—a tentative appraisal. NJESS 4 (1962), pp. 156-164.

11,385 C., J. La radio-distribution en Nigéria. ZAIRE 8 (1954), pp. 951-952.

11,386 CALLAWAY, A. From traditional crafts to modern industries. ODU 2, no. 1 (1965), pp. 28-51.

11,387 CHARLE, E. G. An appraisal of British imperial policy with respect to the extraction of mineral resources in Nigeria. NJESS 6 (1964), pp. 37-42.

11,388 COHEN, A. The social organization of credit in a West African cattle market. AFRICA 35 (1965), pp. 8-19.

11,389 COHEN, R. Some aspects of institutionalized exchange: a Kanuri example. CAH. ET. AFR. 5 (1965), pp. 353-369.

11,390 COMHAIRE, J. La rapport de la Banque International sur la Nigéria. ZAIRE 9 (1955), pp. 49-58.

11,391 COMHAIRE, J. Trois budgets municipaux [Lagos, 1950-1951; Cape Town, 1950; New York, 1950-1951]. ZAIRE 4 (1950), pp. 1107-1110.

11,392 COMHAIRE-SYLVAN, S. Le travail des femmes a Lagos, Nigeria. ZAIRE 5 (1951), pp. 169-187, 475-502.

11,393 DEIS, E. Scambi Italia-Nigeria. AFRICA (Rome) 11 (1956), pp. 64-65.

11,394 DUGGAN, E. DE C. The cotton growing industry of Nigeria. J. AFR. SOC. 21 (1922), pp. 199-207.

11,395 DUGGAN, E. DE C. The cotton prospects of Northern Nigeria. J. AFR. SOC. 26 (1926), pp. 10-20.

11,396 EDOKPAYI, S. I. The Niger and the Benue in Nigeria's economy: past, present and future. NJESS 3 (1961), pp. 68-77.

11,397 EDOKPAYI, S. I. The problems facing our coal industry. NJESS 2 (1960), pp. 12-17.

11,398 EKUNDARE, R. O. The price equalisation fund in Nigeria. NJESS 2 (1960), pp. 6-11.

11,399 FELL, Sir G. The tin mining industry in Nigeria. J. AFR. SOC. 38 (1939), pp. 246-258.

11,400 GARRONI, Z. Attualità della Nigeria. AFRICA (Rome) 11 (1956), pp. 106-107.

11,401 GERVERS, J. H. Vertical integration with Europe. NJESS 5 (1963), pp. 65-75.

11,402 GRAY, A. Development in Nigeria. AFR. AFFAIRS 61 (1962), pp. 290-293.

11,403 GRAY, A. Nigeria buoyant. AFR. AFFAIRS 55 (1956), pp. 171-172.

11,404 GRAY, A. Nigerian oil. AFR. AFFAIRS 57 (1958), pp. 96-97.

11,405 GRAY, A. World Bank's Nigeria plan. AFR. AFFAIRS 54 (1955), pp. 14-15.

11,406 GRAY, C. S. Credit creation for Nigeria's economic development: a Polak model of money, income and the balance of payments in Nigeria. NJESR 5 (1963), pp. 247-353.

11,407 HAIG, E. F. G. Co-operatives in Nigeria. AFR. AFFAIRS 49 (1950), pp. 41-50.

11,408 HAWKINS, E. K. The growth of a money economy in Nigeria and Ghana. OXFORD ECONOMIC PAPERS N.S. 10 (1958), pp. 339-354.

11,409 HAWKINS, E. K. Nigéria. Chronique économique et politique. CIVILISATIONS 5 (1955), pp. 275-280.

11,410 HEADS, J. Urbanization and economic progress. NJESS 6 (1958), pp. 65-73.

11,411 HELLEINER, G. K. Nigeria and the African common market. NJESS 4 (1962), pp. 283-298.

11,412 HELLEINER, G. K. Peasant agriculture development, and export instability: the Nigerian case. AFR. PRIMARY PRODUCTS AND INT. TRADE, 1965, pp. 44-64.

11,413 HELLEINER, G. K. A wide-ranging development institution: the Northern Nigeria development corporation, 1949-62. NJESS 6 (1964), pp. 239-257.

11,414 HICKS, U. K. The new tax system of Eastern Nigeria. J. AFR. ADM. 8 (1956), pp. 202-205.

11,415 HOBLEY, C. W. Mining. J. AFR. SOC. 34 (1935), pp. 70-71.

11,416 HOGG, V. W. Towards assessing the highway needs of Nigeria. NISER 6 (1958), pp. 91-103.

11,417 IJERE, M. O. Credit development in Nigerian agriculture. NJESR 5 (1963), pp. 211-219.

11,418 IJEWERE, G. O. Rail-road problems in Nigeria. NJESS 1 (1959), pp. 17-26.

11,419 ISONG, C. N. Modernisation of the Ensusu Credit Society. NJESS 6 (1958), pp. 111-120.

11,420 JEFFREYS, M. D. W. A forgotten canal. NIGERIAN FIELD 20 (1955), pp. 137-138.

11,421 JOHNSRUD, R. O. A decade of Nigerian cotton, 1949-1958. NIG. GEOGR. J. 3, no. 2 (1960), pp. 1-14.

11,422 JONES, G. I. The beef-cattle trade in Nigeria. AFRICA 16 (1946), pp. 29-38.

11,423 JONES, G. I. Native and trade currencies in Southern Nigeria during the eighteenth and nineteenth centuries. AFRICA 28 (1958), pp. 43-53.

11,424 KIRK-GREENE, A. H. M. Tax and travel among the hill-tribes of northern Adamawa. AFRICA 26 (1956), pp. 369-378.

11,425 LLOYD, P. Craft organization in Yoruba towns. AFRICA 23 (1953), pp. 30-44.

11,426 LONGDEN, J. Urban consumers' surveys in Nigeria. WAISER EC. 2 (1953), pp. 166-176.

11,427 LUGARD, Sir F. Taxation in Northern Nigeria. J. AFR. SOC. 5 (1906), pp. 311-324.

11,428 MacFIE, J. W. S. The pottery industry of Ilorin, Northern Nigeria. BULL. IMP. INST. 11 (1913), pp. 110-121.

11,429 MASON, P. F. Kano to Karachi by imperial airways. NIGERIAN FIELD 8 (1939), pp. 23-24.

11,430 MILLER, N. S. The history of the Lagos steam tramways. NIGERIAN FIELD 23 (1958), pp. 124-141.

11,431 MILLIKEN, M. Some notes on land as a factor of production in Nigeria. WAISER EC. 2 (1953), pp. 72-81.

11,432 MORGAN, W. B. The movement of passenger traffic and railway hinterlands on the Lagos-Kano-Nguru line: a method analysis. NIG. GEOGR. J. 2, no. 2 (1958), pp. 105-112.

11,433 MORTON, M. A. Report on the Home Economics-Nutrition Conference: held in Nigeria, May 17 to 21, 1965. WOMEN TODAY 6 (1965), pp. 108-109.

11,434 NETTING, R. M. Household organization and intensive agriculture: the Kofyar case. AFRICA 35 (1965), pp. 422-429.

11,435 NIVEN, C. R. Struttura e sviluppo dell' economia nigeriana. AFRICA (Rome) 11 (1956), pp. 61-64.

11,436 NWOGU, E. D. Oil in Nigeria. NIG. GEOGR. J. 3, no. 2 (1960), pp. 15-25.

11,437 OBAYAN, E. O. The machinery of planning in the Federation of Nigeria. NJESS 4 (1962), pp. 277-282.

11,438 OGUNSHEYE, A. Marketing boards and the stabilisation of producer prices and incomes in Nigeria. NJESS 7 (1965), pp. 131-139.

11,439 OKEDIJI, O. O. Some socio-cultural problems in the Western Nigeria land settlement scheme: a case study. NJESS 7 (1965), pp. 301-310.

11,440 OKONJO, C. On the teaching of economics in Nigeria. NJESS 5 (1963), pp. 197-210.

11,441 OKONJO, C. On the teaching of economics in Nigeria: a reply. NJESS 6 (1964), pp. 128-130.

11,442 OKOYE, M. Le Nigéria d'aujourd'hui. PRESENCE AFR. N.S. 44 (1962), pp. 100-108.

11,443 OLAKANPO, O. Concept, measurement and determinants of personal saving, with reference to the Nigerian economy. NJESS 4 (1962), pp. 26-39.

11,444 OLAKANPO, O. Distributive trade—a critique of government policy. NJESS 5 (1963), pp. 237-246.

11,445 OLDFIELD, G. A. The native railway worker in Nigeria. AFRICA 9 (1936), pp. 379-401.

11,446 OLUWASANMI, H. A. Agriculture and industrial development in Nigeria. NISER 6 (1958), pp. 50-64.

11,447 OLUWASANMI, H. A. and ALAO, J. A. The role of credit in the transformation of traditional agriculture: the Western Nigerian experience. NJESS 7 (1965), pp. 31-50.

11,448 ONI of Ife. Iwofa [system of money lending]. ODU 3 (1956), pp. 16-18.

11,449 ONITIRI, H. M. A. The Central Bank of Nigeria and the problem of domestic monetary stability. NISER 6 (1958), pp. 80-90.

11,450 ONITIRI, H. M. A. Import duties and the Nigerian balance of external payments. NJESS 2 (1960), pp. 26-40.

11,451 ONITIRI, H. M. A. Nigeria's international economic relations: a survey. NJESS 3 (1961), pp. 13-38.

11,452 ONITIRI, H. M. A. Recent trends in Nigeria's balance of payments. NJESS 7 (1965), pp. 145-157.

11,453 OREWA, G. Property rating in Western Nigeria. NISER 6 (1958), pp. 104-110.

11,454 ORME-SMITH, R. Maiduguri market—Northern Nigeria. J. AFR. SOC. 37 (1938), pp. 318-325.

11,455 OWOADE, A. Isundunrin Iron Foundry. AFR. HISTORIAN 1, no. ii (1964), pp. 27-32.

11,456 OYELESE, J. O. Land use survey project. AFR. NOTES 2, no. 3 (1965), pp. 3-6.

11,457 PEDLER, F. J. A study of income and expenditure in northern Zaria. AFRICA 18 (1948), pp. 259-271.

11,458 RIVKIN, A. Economic development planning in the Federation of Nigeria. J. LOCAL ADM. OV. 3 (1964), pp. 27-34.

11,459 ROBINSON, M. S. Nigerian oil: prospects and perspectives. NJESS 6 (1964), pp. 219-229.

11,460 SAP, S. The West African mahogany industry. NIGERIAN FIELD 4 (1935), pp. 127-132.

11,461 SCHATZ, S. P. Aiding Nigerian business: the Yaba industrial estate. NJESS 6 (1964), pp. 199-217.

11,462 SCHATZ, S. P. Nigeria's first national development plan (1962-68); an appraisal. NJESS 5 (1963), pp. 221-235.

11,463 SCHATZ, S. P. Obstacles to Nigerian private investment. NJESS 4 (1962), pp. 66-72.

11,464 SCHATZ, S. P. and EDOKPAYI, S. I. Economic attitudes of Nigerian businessmen. NJESS 4 (1962), pp. 257-268.

11,465 SMITH, M. G. A study of Hausa domestic economy in northern Zaria. AFRICA 22 (1952), pp. 333-347.

11,466 SOKUNBI, D. O. B. The impact of the oil industry on the economy of Nigeria. NJESS 4 (1962), pp. 77-82.

11,467 SONUBI, O. A note on Nigeria's youth employment problems. NJESS 4 (1962), pp. 228-232.

11,468 STOLPER, W. F. Economic development in Nigeria. J. ECON. HIST. 23 (1963), pp. 391-413.

11,469 STOLPER, W. F. How bad is the plan? NJESS 6 (1964), pp. 261-276.

11,470 UGOH, S. U. The Nigerian cement company. NJESS 6 (1964), pp. 72-91.

11,471 UGOH, S. U. Prospects for some Nigerian agricultural products in the world market. NJESS 7 (1965), pp. 237-243.

11,472 UNITED AFRICA COMPANY. The future of the Nigerian oil industry. AFR. AFFAIRS 46 (1948), pp. 41-51.

11,473 UPTON, M. Linear programming rations for pigs. NJESS 7 (1965), pp. 221-226.

11,474 UZOAGA, W. O. Bank money in Nigeria. NJESS 6 (1964), pp. 92-97.

11,475 WELLS, F. A. Report presented by the governments of the United Kingdom and of the Federation of Nigeria [on Nigerian industrial conditions]. HUMAN FACTORS OF PRODUCTIVITY IN AFR., 1962, pp. 169-192.

11,476 WELLS, J. C. Investment criteria and the Nigerian development plan. NJESS 6 (1964), pp. 277-304.

11,477 WELLS, J. C. Price stabilization of Nigeria's export crops. NJESS 4 (1962), pp. 40-49.

11,478 WHYTE, W. H. Some reflections on the economy of Nigeria. WAISER EC. 2 (1953), pp. 134-140.

11,479 WRIGLEY, C. C. On the teaching of economics in Nigeria: a comment. NJESS 6 (1964), pp. 124-127.

11,480 YESUFU, T. M. Nigerian manpower problems (a preliminary assessment). NJESS 4 (1962), pp. 207-219.

11,481 ZIELINSKI, J. G. Problems of long- and short-term planning based on Polish experience. NJESS 7 (1965), pp. 103-119.

11,482 Budgets multiples en Nigéria. ZAIRE 6 (1952), pp. 747-748.

11,483 Eastern Nigeria Development Plan, 1962-68. J. LOCAL ADM. OV. 1 (1962), pp. 266-268.

11,484 Symposium on the new Nigerian development plan. NJESS 4 (1962), pp. 85-146.

11,485 Ten year development plan for Nigeria. AFR. AFFAIRS 45 (1946), pp. 132-133.

11,486 Two Nigerian lists. AFR. AFFAIRS 44 (1945), pp. 164-165.

See also 1558, 10249, 10896, 10908, 14503.

Education

11,487 ADIGUN, B. A. Religione e istruzione nella Federazione della Nigeria. AFRICA (Rome) 16 (1961), pp. 163-167.

11,488 AKPOFURE, R. E. O. Textbooks and the teaching of African history in Nigeria. J. HIST. SOC. NIG. 1 (1957), pp. 138-144.

11,489 ARMSTRONG, R. Running a summer school in Kano. KANO STUD. 1 (1965), pp. 40-42.

11,490 ARMSTRONG, R. G. Some technical gaps in Nigerian school curricula. WAISER SOC. 2 (1953), pp. 170-205.

11,491 BURNESS, H. M. The war against ignorance. AFR. WOMEN 3 (1958-1960), pp. 49-53.

11,492 CALLAWAY, A. Nigeria's indigenous education: the apprentice system. ODU 1, no. 1 (1964), pp. 62-79.

11,493 CHADWICK, E. R. Community development in South eastern Nigeria. NIGERIAN FIELD 16 (1951), pp. 113-123.

11,494 CHADWICK, E. R. Community development in the Eastern Provinces. CORONA 3 (1951), pp. 421-425.

11,495 CHADWICK, E. R. Mass education in Udi division. AFR. AFFAIRS 46 (1948), pp. 31-41.

11,496 CLARKE, A. F. An experimental school in Nigeria. J. AFR. SOC. 39 (1940), pp. 36-53.

11,497 COCKIN, G. The land and education in the Ibo country of south-east Nigeria. INT. REV. MISSIONS 33 (1944), pp. 274-279.

11,498 COMHAIRE, J. Enseignement féminin et mariage à Lagos, Nigéria. ZAIRE 9 (1955), pp. 261-277.

11,499 DICKSON, A. G. Man O'War Bay. NIGERIAN FIELD 18 (1953), pp. 4-19.

11,500 ENGLISH, M. C. What history does the Nigerian pupil need? J. HIST. SOC. NIG. 1 (1957), pp. 111-118.

11,501 GARDINER, R. K. Extra-mural studies in Nigeria. CORONA 4 (1952), pp. 253-255.

11,502 HOWARD, F. H. Education in Nigeria. J. AFR. SOC. 15 (1916), pp. 216-224.

11,503 HUNTER, F. P. G. Two centres of higher learning:—I: University College, Ibadan, by F. P. G. Hunter. AFR. AFFAIRS 48 (1949), pp. 223-226.

11,504 JUDD, A. S. Native education in the northern provinces of Nigeria. J. AFR. SOC. 17 (1917), pp. 1-10.

11,505 LOCKWOOD, Sir J. et al. Significant university developments in the Commonwealth, 1958-63: Nigeria, by Sir John Lockwood, Davidson Nicol, E. Njoku. CONGR. OF THE UNIVS. OF THE COMMONWEALTH 9 (1963), pp. 50-69.

11,506 MAGDALEN, M. C. Education of girls in Southern Nigeria. INT. REV. MISSIONS 17 (1928), pp. 505-514.

11,507 MILLER, W. J. Developments in primary education in Northern Nigeria. J. LOCAL ADM. OV. 3 (1964), pp. 221-225.

11,508 MONTEIL, V. Problèmes d'éducation au Nigéria. PRESENCE AFR. N.S. 40 (1962), pp. 152-159.

11,509 MPHAHLELE, E. Travels of an extra-mural donkey. TRANSITION 11 (1963), pp. 46-50.

11,510 NEISSER, C. S. Community development and mass education in British Nigeria. ECON. DEVELOPMENT AND CULTURAL CHANGE 3 (1954-1955), pp. 352-365.

11,511 ONYENACHO, B. N. Education amongst the Mbaise-Ibo. AFR. HISTORIAN 1, no. iii (1965), pp. 34-37.

11,512 READ, M. Education and social control. WAISER 5 (1956), pp. 1-17.

11,513 RITSERT, K. E. Adult education experiment in Northern Nigeria. AFR. WOMEN 3 (1960), pp. 82-85.

11,514 RITSERT, K. E. "It's the attitude that matters." AFR. WOMEN 2 (1956-1958), pp. 25-28.

11,515 SMITH, H. F. C. School certificate history syllabuses in Nigeria. J. HIST. SOC. NIG. 1 (1957), pp. 119-129.

11,516 WILSON, T. The advanced teachers' colleges, Nigeria. AFR. ED. 2, no. 2 (1964), pp. 12-14.

11,517 YELD, E. R. Educational problems among women and girls in Sokoto Province of Northern Nigeria. SOCIOLOGUS 11 (1961), pp. 160-173.

11,518 Adult education in Western Nigeria [1955-1958]. AFR. WOMEN 3 (1960), p. 86.

11,519 Assemblée scolaire en Nigeria. ZAIRE 7 (1953), pp. 727-728.

11,520 Community development in Udi. CORONA 1, no. 2 (1949), pp. 10-13; 1, no. 3 (1949), pp. 11-14.

11,521 Growing up in Nigeria. AFR. WOMEN 2 (1956-1958), pp. 73-78.

11,522 Institut Nigérien de Recherches Economiques et Sociales. GENEVE-AFR. 1 (1962), pp. 215-216.

11,523 Nigeria: education. AFR. WOMEN 2 (1956-1958), pp. 38-39.

11,524 Nigerian educational policy. AFR. AFFAIRS 46 (1948), pp. 52-54.

11,525 Problems of girls' education in Nigeria, Northern Region. AFR. WOMEN 1 (1955), pp. 68-70.

11,526 Reading for self-improvement in Eastern Nigeria. UNESCO BULL. LIBS. 16 (1962), pp. 244-246.

See also 10334.

Geography

11,527 AGBOOLA, S. A. The middle belt of Nigeria: the basis of unity. NIG. GEOGR. J. 4, no. 1 (1961), pp. 41-46.

11,528 AMAMKPA, E. W. An outline of geography taught in the Lutheran Teacher Training College, Ibakachi! NIG. GEOGR. J. 4, no. 1 (1961), pp. 47-48.

11,529 ARMSTRONG, R. G. Vegetation of the Olokemeji forest reserve [a research project]. AFR. NOTES 1, no. 2 (1964), pp. 3-4.

11,530 BROUNGER, S. G. Nigeria past and present. J. AFR. SOC. 12 (1913), pp. 249-255.

11,531 BUCHANAN, K. An outline of the geography of the Western Region of Nigeria. MALAYAN J. TR. GEOGR. 1 (1953), pp. 9-24.

11,532 BUCHANAN, K. Recent developments in Nigerian peasant farming. MALAYAN J. TR. GEOGR. 2 (1954), pp. 17-34.

11,533 C., H. L. Nigeria. Annual report of Land and Survey Department, 1935; by H. L. C. J. AFR. SOC. 36 (1937), pp. 81-82.

11,534 CARTER, J. Erosion and sedimentation from aerial photographs, a micro-study from Nigeria. J. TROP. GEOGR. 11 (1958), pp. 100-106.

11,535 CLAYTON, W. D. The swamps and sand dunes of Hadejia. NIG. GEOGR. J. 1, no. 2 (1957), pp. 31-37.

11,536 EGBUNU, A. The importance of the rivers Niger and Benue in the internal and external trade of the Koton, Karifi district. NIG. GEOGR. J. 1, no. 1 (1957), pp. 17-18.

11,537 GARNIER, B. J. Geography and national development. NIG. GEOGR. J. 1, no. 1 (1957), pp. 3-6.

11,538 GARNIER, J. B. La géographie en Nigeria: les progrès et son avenir. BULL. IFAN 19 (1957), pp. 308-312.

11,539 GRANT, J. A. P. Okitipupa: a brief survey. NIG. GEOGR. J. 1, no. 1 (1957), pp. 7-13.

11,540 GWYNNE-JONES, D. R. G. A picture of new Idanre. NIG. GEOGR. J. 1, no. 2 (1957), p. 45.

11,541 HALLAM, W. K. R. A remote stretch of the middle Niger. NIGERIAN FIELD 28 (1963), pp. 184-190.

11,542 HEIGHAM, J. B. A trip to Orosun. NIGERIAN FIELD 30 (1965), pp. 132-142.

11,543 HIDE, R. H. Local leave at Jos Hill Station. NIGERIAN FIELD 10 (1941), pp. 134-139.

11,544 HIGGINS, G. M. Experimental farm coverage in Northern Nigeria. NIG. GEOGR. J. 4, no. 2 (1961), pp. 11-25.

11,545 ILOEJE, N. P. The structure and relief of the Nsukka: Okigwi Cuesta. NIG. GEOGR. J. 4, no. 1 (1961), pp. 21-39.

11,546 JARRETT, H. R. Possibilities of field work in Nigeria. NIG. GEOGR. J. 2, no. 1 (1958), pp. 40-44.

11,547 JENNINGS, J. H. Enugu: a geographical outline. NIG. GEOGR. J. 3, no. 1 (1959), pp. 28-38.

11,548 LEDGER, D. C. Aspects of Nigerian hydrology. NIG. GEOGR. J. 3, no. 1 (1959), pp. 18-27.

11,549 LUKAS, J. Reise durch Bornu (Nigerien) und Nordkamerun. AFR. UND UB. 37 (1952-1953), pp. 5-6.

11,550 MABOGUNJE, A. L. The evolution of rural settlement in Egba division, Nigeria. J. TROP. GEOGR. 13 (1959), pp. 65-77.

11,551 MABOGUNJE, A. L. The growth of residential districts in Ibadan. GEOG. REV. 52 (1962), pp. 56-77.

11,552 MABOGUNJE, A. L. Rice cultivation in Southern Nigeria. NIG. GEOGR. J. 2, no. 2 (1958), pp. 59-69.

11,553 MABOGUNJE, A. L. and OYAWOYE, M. O. The problems of the Northern Yoruba towns: the example of Shaki. NIG. GEOGR. J. 4, no. 2 (1961), pp. 2-10.

11,554 MacBRIDE, D. F. H. Land survey in the Kano Emirate, northern provinces, Nigeria. J. AFR. SOC. 37 (1938), pp. 75-91.

11,555 MacGREGOR, W. Lagos, Abeokuta and the Alake. J. AFR. SOC. 3 (1904), pp. 465-481.

11,556 MacLAREN, P. I. R. Aba to Opobo by canoe. NIGERIAN FIELD 15 (1950), pp. 21-26.

11,557 MARSHALL, C. P. A canoe trip in Benin province, Southern Nigeria. NIGERIAN FIELD 7 (1938), pp. 31-34.

11,558 MORGAN, W. B. The distribution of food-crop storage methods in Nigeria. J. TROP. GEOGR. 13 (1959), pp. 58-64.

11,559 MORGAN, W. B. A field trip from Ibadan. NIG. GEOGR. J. 2, no. 1 (1958), pp. 45-52.

11,560 MORGAN, W. B. A picture of part of Lagos Island. NIG. GEOGR. J. 2, no. 1 (1958), p. 55.

11,561 MORGAN, W. B. Settlement patterns of the Eastern Region of Nigeria. NIG. GEOGR. J. 1, no. 2 (1957), pp. 23-30.

11,562 MORGAN, W. B. and MOSS, R. P. Savanna and forest in western Nigeria. AFRICA 35 (1965), pp. 286-294.

11,563 NANA, S. J. A summary of the Escravos Bar project. NIG. GEOGR. J. 4, no. 1 (1961), pp. 53-55.

11,564 NESS, P. Lake Chad picnic. J. AFR. SOC. 40 (1941), pp. 316-326.

11,565 NIVEN, C. R. Nigerian pilgrimage to Mecca. CORONA 2 (1950), pp. 408-410.

11,566 OBOLI, H. O. N. The teaching of local geography in secondary schools. NIG. GEOGR. J. 1, no. 1 (1957), pp. 14-16.

11,567 OGUNDANA, B. Lagos: Nigeria's premier port. NIG. GEOGR. J. 4, no. 2 (1961), pp. 26-40.

11,568 OLUMIDE, A. O. Geography in the secondary school curriculum. NIG. GEOGR. J. 2, no. 1 (1958), pp. 37-39.

11,569 ONAEKO, E. A. Shagamu and its district: a short geographical account. NIG. GEOGR. J. 2, no. 1 (1958), pp. 14-25.

11,570 OYAWOYE, M. O. A note on some inselbergs around Bauchi, Northern Nigeria. NIG. GEOGR. J. 3, no. 2 (1960), pp. 33-37.

11,571 PALMER, Sir R. Arriving in Northern Nigeria. J. AFR. SOC. 41 (1942), pp. 108-110.

11,572 PEAL, J. Local leave on Mambila plateau. NIGERIAN FIELD 26 (1961), pp. 129-137.

11,573 PRESCOTT, J. R. V. The evolution of Nigeria's boundaries. NIG. GEOGR. J. 2, no. 2 (1958), pp. 80-104.

11,574 PRESCOTT, J. R. V. The geographical basis of Nigerian federation. NIG. GEOGR. J. 2, no. 1 (1958), pp. 1-13.

11,575 PRESCOTT, J. R. V. Nigeria's regional boundary problems. GEOG. REV. 49 (1959), pp. 485-505.

11,576 PROTHERO, R. M. Problems of population mapping in an under-developed territory (Northern Nigeria). NIG. GEOGR. J. 3, no. 1 (1959), pp. 1-7.

11,577 PUGH, J. C. River captures in Nigeria. NIG. GEOGR. J. 4, no. 2 (1961), pp. 41-48.

11,578 PUGH, J. C. The volcanoes of Nigeria. NIG. GEOGR. J. 2, no. 1 (1958), pp. 26-36.

11,579 S., W. J. S. The city of Sokoto. CORONA 2 (1950), pp. 107-109, 135-137, 187-189.

11,580 SPOTTISWOODE, H. E. The general trend and distribution of rainfall in Nigeria. NIGERIAN FIELD 9 (1940), pp. 50-56.

11,581 SPOTTISWOODE, H. E. The route from Nigeria to Khartoum. NIGERIAN FIELD 6 (1937), pp. 5-11.

11,582 STAMP, D. Land utilization and soil erosion in Nigeria. GEOG. REV. 28 (1938), pp. 32-45.

11,583 THOMPSON, H. N. The forests of southern Nigeria. J. AFR. SOC. 10 (1911), pp. 122-145.

11,584 UDO, R. K. Disintegration of nucleated settlement in Eastern Nigeria. GEOG. REV. 55 (1965), pp. 53-67.

11,585 UDO, R. K. Land and population in Otoro district. NIG. GEOGR. J. 4, no. 1 (1961), pp. 3-19.

11,586 VOUTE, C. Geological and morphological evolution of the Niger and Benue valleys. PROC. PAN-AFR. CONGR. PRE-HIST. 4 (1962), pp. 189-207.

11,587 WATSON, D. N. Result of an inquiry into geography in Nigerian schools. NIG. GEOGR. J. 2, no. 2 (1958), pp. 75-79.

11,588 WATSON, G. D. An account of field work in the teaching of geography. NIG. GEOGR. J. 1, no. 2 (1957), pp. 38-43.

11,589 WHITE, H. P. and PRESCOTT, J. R. V. The lower middle Niger. NIG. GEOGR. J. 3, no. 1 (1959), pp. 39-47.

11,590 WHITTLESEY, D. Kano: a Sudanese metropolis. GEOG. REV. 27 (1937), pp. 177-199.

11,591 Nigerian maps suitable for teaching purposes. NIG. GEOGR. J. 2, no. 2 (1958), pp. 70-74.

11,592 Practical notes on the Yoruba country and its development, by "White Ant." J. AFR. SOC. 1 (1902), pp. 316-324.

11,593 Statistics of mean monthly rainfall in Nigeria. NIG. GEOGR. J. 4, no. 1 (1961), pp. 49-52.

See also 8264.

Government. Politics. Administration

11,594 ADEDEJI, A. The public service and the administration of development programmes in Nigeria. NJESS 6 (1964), pp. 321-331.

11,595 THE AFRICAN STUDIES BRANCH. Administration of urban areas in the Northern Region of Nigeria. J. AFR. ADM. 6 (1954), pp. 94-95.

11,596 THE AFRICAN STUDIES BRANCH. Lagos Town Council. J. AFR. ADM. 5 (1953), pp. 133-134.

11,597 THE AFRICAN STUDIES BRANCH. Local Government reorganisation in the Eastern Provinces of Nigeria and Kenya. J. AFR. ADM. 1 (1949), pp. 18-29.

11,598 THE AFRICAN STUDIES BRANCH. Local rating and primary education [digest of an inquiry]. J. AFR. ADM. 4 (1952), pp. 32-34.

11,599 THE AFRICAN STUDIES BRANCH. Provincial authorities in the Northern Region of Nigeria. J. AFR. ADM. 9 (1957), pp. 139-144.

11,600 AKPAN, E. E. The development of Local Government in Eastern Nigeria. J. LOCAL ADM. OV. 4 (1965), pp. 118-127.

11,601 AKPAN, N. U. Chieftaincy in Eastern Nigeria. J. AFR. ADM. 9 (1957), pp. 120-124.

11,602 ALDERTON, E. C. Developments in Local Government in the Eastern Region of Nigeria. J. AFR. ADM. 8 (1956), pp. 169-175.

11,603 ANGLIN, D. G. Nigeria: political non-alignment and economic alignment. J. MOD. AFR. STUD. 2 (1964), pp. 247-263.

11,604 ARIKPO, O. The development of representative government in Nigeria. WHAT ARE THE PROBLEMS OF PARL. GOVT. IN W. AFR.?, 1958, pp. 1-5.

11,605 AWA, E. High level administration in the public services of Nigeria. NJESS 6 (1964), pp. 43-50.

11,606 AWA, E. O. Local government problems in Nigeria. AFR., THE DYNAMICS OF CHANGE, 1963, pp. 211-231.

11,607 AZIKIWE, N. Essentials for Nigerian survival. FOREIGN AFFAIRS 43 (1964-1965), pp. 447-461.

11,608 AZIKIWE, N. La part du Nigéria dans la politique mondiale. PRESENCE AFR. N.S. 34-35 (1960-1961), pp. 5-16.

11,609 BALEWA, Sir A. T. Nigeria looks ahead. FOREIGN AFFAIRS 41 (1962-1963), pp. 131-140.

11,610 BALMER, P. H. Report on the Holding of the 1956 Parliamentary Election to the Western House of Assembly. J. AFR. ADM. 10 (1958), pp. 107-111.

11,611 BARATZ, M. S. Power and stability in Nigeria [review of Power and stability in Nigeria: the politics of decolonization by H. L. Bretton]. NJESS 6 (1964), pp. 309-319.

11,612 BELL, H. H. Recent progress in Northern Nigeria. J. AFR. SOC. 10 (1911), pp. 377-391.

11,613 BENNION, M. J. The Institute of Administration, Zaria—1. Northernization—1954-1961. J. LOCAL ADM. OV. 2 (1963), pp. 40-42.

11,614 BLUNT, M. E. The place of ideology in the origins and development of public enterprise in Nigeria. NJESS 6 (1964), pp. 333-349.

11,615 BOOTH, J. D. L. Oiling the wheels of Local Government in Eastern Nigeria. J. AFR. ADM. 7 (1955), pp. 55-64.

11,616 BOURDILLON, Sir B. The future of native authorities. AFRICA 15 (1945), pp. 123-128.

11,617 BOURDILLON, Sir B. The Nigerian constitution. AFR. AFFAIRS 45 (1946), pp. 87-96.

11,618 BOURDILLON, Sir B. and PALMER, Sir R. Nigerian constitutional proposals. AFR. AFFAIRS 44 (1945), pp. 120-124.

11,619 BRANNEY, L. Registration of title to land in Lagos. J. AFR. ADM. 10 (1958), pp. 136-143.

11,620 BROWN, R. E. Local Government in the West Region of Nigeria, 1950-1955. J. AFR. ADM. 7 (1955), pp. 180-188.

11,621 BROWN, R. E. Local Government in the Western Provinces of Nigeria. J. AFR. ADM. 2 (1950), pp. 15-21.

11,622 BUTCHER, H. L. Report on the Commission of Inquiry into the allegations of misconduct against Chief Salami Agbaje, the Otun Balogun of Ibadan, and allegations of inefficiency and maladministration on the part of the Ibadan and District Native Authority. J. AFR. ADM. 3 (1951), pp. 209-210.

11,623 C., J. Elections en Nigéria. ZAIRE 9 (1955), pp.170-171.

11,624 C., J. Femmes politiques en Nigéria. ZAIRE 8 (1954), p. 637.

11,625 C., J. Politique financière en Nigéria. ZAIRE 7 (1953), pp. 644-645.

11,626 CLIFFORD, H. United Nigeria. J. AFR. SOC. 21 (1921), pp. 1-14.

11,627 COLE, C. W. Village and District Councils in the Northern Provinces of Nigeria. J. AFR. ADM. 3 (1951), pp. 91-94.

11,628 DALDRY, L. C. Nigeria's federal parliament. AFR. AFFAIRS 59 (1960), pp. 292-293.

11,629 DARWIN, L. Sir George Goldie on government in Africa. J. AFR. SOC. 34 (1935), pp. 138-143.

11,630 DENT, M. J. Elections in Northern Nigeria. J. LOCAL ADM. OV. 1 (1962), pp. 213-224.

11,631 DRY, P. Northern Nigeria. CONTEMP. REV. 185 (1954), pp. 302-304.

11,632 DUDLEY, B. J. The concept of federalism. NJESS 5 (1963), pp. 95-103.

11,633 DUDLEY, B. J. Marxism and political change in Nigeria. NJESS 6 (1964), pp. 155-165.

11,634 DUDLEY, B. J. The nomination of parliamentary candidates in Northern Nigeria. J. COMM. POL. STUD. 2 (1963-1964), pp. 45-58.

11,635 DUDLEY, B. J. Violence in Nigerian politics. TRANSITION 21 (1965), pp. 21-23.

11,636 DYSON, P. Local Government training in the Western Region of Nigeria. J. AFR. ADM. 11 (1959), pp. 193-200.

11,637 EBONG, I. J. The birth of the federation of Nigeria. AFR. AFFAIRS 60 (1961), pp. 52-55.

11,638 FABUNMI, L. A. A look at the current power politics in Nigeria through the Soudan. PRESENCE AFR. N.S. 14-15 (1957), pp. 73-83.

11,639 FAIRHOLM, G. W. Local Government and community development in the Northern Emirates of Northern Nigeria. J. LOCAL ADM. OV. 3 (1964), pp. 156-163.

11,640 FAIRHOLM, G. W. A profile of the portfolio councillor in Northern Nigeria. J. LOCAL ADM. OV. 4 (1965), pp. 270-279.

11,641 FARRINGTON, J. L. Northern Nigeria—an awakening giant. AFR. AFFAIRS 62 (1963), pp. 125-136.

11,642 FILESI, T. L'indipendenza della Nigeria. AFRICA (Rome) 15 (1960), pp. 211-219.

11,643 FOOT, H. M. Democracy in the colonies. ZAIRE 4 (1950), pp. 837-842.

11,644 FORDE, D. Government in Umor: a study of social change and problems of indirect rule in a Nigerian village community. AFRICA 12 (1939), pp. 129-161.

11,645 GILMOUR, T. L. The two Nigerias. J. AFR. SOC. 11 (1912), pp. 275-284.

11,646 GRAY, A. Cameroons' future. AFR. AFFAIRS 59 (1960), pp. 10-11.

11,647 GRAY, A. E. Nigeria dispute. AFR. AFFAIRS 55 (1956), pp. 247-249.

11,648 GRAY, A. Nigeria commissions. AFR. AFFAIRS 57 (1958), pp. 6-7.

11,649 GRAY, A. Nigeria gets a premier. AFR. AFFAIRS 56 (1957), pp. 255-256.

11,650 GRAY, A. Nigeria on the march [a new constitution]. AFR. AFFAIRS 54 (1955), pp. 10-11.

11,651 GRAY, A. Nigerian conference. AFR. AFFAIRS 56 (1957), pp. 179-181.

11,652 GRAY, A. Nigerian independence. AFR. AFFAIRS 60 (1961), p. 5.

11,653 GRAY, A. Nigeria's constitution. AFR. AFFAIRS 55 (1956), pp. 96-98; 56 (1957), p. 103.

11,654 GRAY, A. Northern Nigeria self government. AFR. AFFAIRS 58 (1959), pp. 208-209.

11,655 HAASTRUP, A. A. Nigeria's role in world affairs. AFR. QUART. 4, no. iv (1965), pp. 240-248.

11,656 HOLLAND, S. W. C. Recent developments in Local Government in Eastern Nigeria. J. LOCAL ADM. OV. 2 (1963), pp. 3-15.

11,657 HUNT, Sir W. E. "Delta Do." An address at the presentation of an ambulance from Nigeria. AFR. AFFAIRS 43 (1944), pp. 68-71.

11,658 IMAM, A. Nigerian constitutional proposals. AFR. AFFAIRS 45 (1946), pp. 22-27.

11,659 JAKANDE, L. K. Nigeria: the background to federation. AFR. SOUTH 3, no. 3 (1959), pp. 86-89.

11,660 JONES, G. I. Report on the Position, Status and Influence of Chiefs and Natural Rulers in the Eastern REgion of Nigeria (The Jones Report). J. AFR. ADM. 10 (1958), pp. 171-174.

11,661 KIRK-GREENE, A. H. M. The Institute of Administration, Zaria—II. How Northern Nigeria has trained administrative officers. J. LOCAL ADM. OV. 2 (1963), pp. 43-48.

11,662 KIRK-GREENE, A. H. M. A redefinition of provincial administration. The Northern Nigerian approach. J. LOCAL ADM. OV. 4 (1965), pp. 5-26.

11,663 KIRK-GREENE, A. H. M. A training course for Northern Nigerian administrative officers. J. AFR. ADM. 11 (1959), pp. 63-71.

11,664 LABOURET, H. La politique britannique en Nigéria. AFRICA 11 (1938), pp. 88-89.

11,665 LLOYD, P. C. The integration of the new economic classes into local government in Western Nigeria. AFR. AFFAIRS 52 (1953), pp. 327-334.

11,666 LLOYD, P. C. Some comments on the elections in Nigeria. J. AFR. ADM. 4 (1952), pp. 82-92.

11,667 LLOYD, P. C. Some modern changes in the government of Yoruba towns. WAISER SOC. 2 (1953), pp. 7-20.

11,668 LLOYD, P. C. and POST, K. W. J. Where should one vote? J. AFR. ADM. 12 (1960), pp. 95-106.

11,669 LUGARD, Sir F. Administration and progress in Nigeria. J. AFR. SOC. 13 (1914), pp. 307-312.

11,670 LUGARD, Sir F. British policy in Nigeria. AFRICA 10 (1937), pp. 377-400.

11,671 MABOGUNJE, A. Nigeria and tomorrow's African. AFR. SOUTH 5, no. 1 (1960), pp. 99-106.

11,672 MACKINTOSH, J. P. Electoral trends and the tendency to a one party system in Nigeria. J. COMM. POL. STUD. 1 (1961-1963), pp. 194-210.

11,673 MACKINTOSH, J. P. The struggle for power in Nigeria. TRANSITION 22 (1965), pp. 21-25.

11,674 MARSHALL, J. R. N. Land acquisition for the Bornu railway extension in Northern Nigeria. J. LOCAL ADM. OV. 2 (1963), pp. 222-232.

11,675 METCALFE, F. Development of parliamentary procedure in the Nigerian Federal House of Representatives. WHAT ARE THE PROBLEMS OF PARL. GOVT. IN W. AFR.?, 1958, pp. 96-102.

11,676 MOCKLER-FERRYMAN, A. F. British Nigeria. J. AFR. SOC. 1 (1902), pp. 160-173.

11,677 MONTAGNE, R. Où en est le Nigéria? AFR. ET ASIE 1, no. 3 (1948), pp. 37-45.

11,678 MOORE, F. J. Development planning in Eastern Nigeria. J. LOCAL ADM. OV. 3 (1964), pp. 136-145.

11,679 MORTIMER, M. Voting in Nigeria. CONTEMP. REV. 206 (1965), pp. 18-20.

11,680 MORTON-WILLIAMS, P. Some Yoruba kingdoms under modern conditions. J. AFR. ADM. 7 (1955), pp. 174-179.

11,681 NAYAK, S. Foundations of foreign policy of Nigeria. AFR. QUART. 2, no. ii (1962), pp. 118-124.

11,682 NICHOLAS, W. B. Progress of a District Council in Northern Nigeria, 1950-1953. J. AFR. ADM. 5 (1953), pp. 166-171.

11,683 NICHOLSON, M. Return to the new Nigeria. AFR. AFFAIRS 54 (1955), pp. 293-299.

11,684 NIGERIA. NORTHERN REGION. MINISTRY FOR LOCAL GOVERNMENT. A review of the state of development of the Native Authority system in the Northern Region of Nigeria on the 1st. of January, 1955. J. AFR. ADM. 7 (1955), pp. 77-86.

11,685 NIGERIA. NORTHERN REGION. PUBLIC RELATIONS OFFICE. Training for Local Government in Northern Nigeria. J. AFR. ADM. 6 (1954), pp. 92-93.

11,686 NIVEN, C. R. Elections in Northern Nigeria. CORONA 4 (1952), pp. 179-181.

11,687 NZIMIRO, F. I. The political system of the Ibo [a research programme]. AFR. NOTES 1, no. 2 (1964), p. 3.

11,688 O'CONNELL, J. Northern Regional elections, 1961: an analysis. NJESS 4 (1962), pp. 181-187.

11,689 OKOYE, N. Nigeria in crisis. AFR. SOUTH 6 (1961), pp. 83-89.

11,690 OLUSANYA, G. O. India and Nigeria nationalism. AFR. QUART. 5 (1965), pp. 188-191.

11,691 ONWUTEAKA, V. C. The Aba riot of 1929 and its relation to the system of indirect rule. NJESS 7 (1965), pp. 273-282.

11,692 OREWA, G. Property rating in Western Nigeria. J. AFR. ADM. 13 (1961), pp. 29-34.

11,693 OTTENBERG, S. Comments on Local Government in Afikpo Division, south eastern Nigeria. J. AFR. ADM. 8 (1956), pp. 3-10.

11,694 PAYNE, E. G. S. Local Government in the County of Eket, Eastern Region, Nigeria. J. AFR. ADM. 5 (1953), pp. 177-182.

11,695 PILKINGTON, F. An independent Nigeria: CONTEMP. REV. 197 (1960), pp. 185-187.

11,696 PILKINGTON, F. The problem of unity in Nigeria. AFR. AFFAIRS 55 (1956), pp. 219-222.

11,697 POST, K. W. J. Forming a government in Nigeria. NJESS 2 (1960), pp. 1-5.

11,698 POST, K. W. J. Nationalism and politics in Nigeria: a Marxist approach. NJESS 6 (1964), pp. 167-176.

11,699 POST, K. W. J. Nigeria: the first decade. AFR. SOUTH 6 (1961), pp. 75-82.

11,700 PRESCOTT, J. R. V. Nigeria's boundaries: a colonial heritage. NISER 6 (1958), pp. 140-150.

11,701 RICHARDSON, S. S. The Institute of Administration, Zaria—III. Semi-autonomy within Ahmadu Bello University, 1962. J. LOCAL ADM. OV. 3 (1964), pp. 42-44.

11,702 RICHARDSON, S. S. Training for penal reform in Northern Nigeria. J. AFR. ADM. 13 (1961), pp. 38-45.

11,703 ROBERTSON, Sir J. Nigeria in 1965. AFR. AFFAIRS 64 (1965), pp. 250-260.

11,704 ROBERTSON, Sir J. Sovereign Nigeria. AFR. AFFAIRS 60 (1961), pp. 145-154.

11,705 SELBORNE, Lord [R. C. Palmer]. The native problem on the West coast. J. AFR. SOC. 21 (1922), pp. 261-267.

11,706 SERTORIO, G. L'evoluzione constituzionale della Nigeria. AFRICA (Rome) 19 (1964), pp. 120-132.

11,707 SKLAR, R. L. Contradictions in the Nigerian political system. J. MOD. AFR. STUD. 3 (1965), pp. 201-213.

11,708 SKLAR, R. L. Le nationalisme au Nigéria et les droits de l'homme. ET. CONG. 6, no. 1 (1964), pp. 31-47.

11,709 SMITH, E. W. Indirect rule in Nigeria. J. AFR. SOC. 36 (1937), pp. 371-378.

11,710 SONG, M. Nigerian Local Government in transition. J. AFR. ADM. 12 (1960), pp. 74-76.

11,711 SOWERBY, T. W. Northern Nigeria assignment. J. LOCAL ADM. OV. 3 (1964), pp. 88-91.

11,712 STEVENS, R. A. Progress in local government in the Eastern Region of Nigeria. J. AFR. ADM. 5 (1953), pp. 15-21.

11,713 SWANZY, H. The Nigerian constitution. AFR. AFFAIRS 46 (1947), pp. 2-3, 63-64.

11,714 SWANZY, H. Nigerian nationalism. AFR. AFFAIRS 45 (1946), pp. 168-169.

11,715 TUGBIYELE, E. A. Local Government in Nigeria. Some suggestions for solving the problems of structure and finance. J. LOCAL ADM. OV. 1 (1962), pp. 225-230.

11,716 TUGBIYELE, E. A. The Nigerian Federal Union. NJESR 5 (1963), pp. 364-373.

11,717 WALLIS, L. G. C. Nigerianization of the public services in Western Nigeria. J. AFR. ADM. 12 (1960), pp. 144-146.

11,718 WALLIS, L. G. C. The Public Service Commission in Nigeria. CIVILISATIONS 10 (1960), pp. 233-237; French summary, pp. 237-238.

11,719 WALLIS, L. G. C. The public service commission. Its role and development in Western Nigeria. AFR. AFFAIRS 60 (1961), pp. 532-538.

11,720 WHITAKER, P. The preparation of the register of electors in the Western region of Nigeria. J. AFR. ADM. 9 (1957), pp. 23-29.

11,721 WILLIAMS, B. A random note on African nationalism. AFR. HISTORIAN 1, no. ii (1964), pp. 22-26.

11,722 WILLIAMS, D. Nigeria today. AFR. AFFAIRS 55 (1956), pp. 109-119.

11,723 WRAITH, R. E. Institutional training in Africa. 1. The institutes. 2. The training. J. LOCAL ADM. OV. 4 (1965), pp. 27-37, 79-87.

11,724 Annual reports on native administration Nigeria Northern Provinces, 1932. J. AFR. SOC. 33 (1934), pp. 80-82.

11,725 Certaines conséquences de la grève générale nigérienne. PRESENCE AFR. N.S. 51 (1964), pp. 170-171.

11,726 Conférences de M. Hugh M. Foot. ZAIRE 4 (1950), pp. 1022-1023.

11,727 Courants politiques en Nigéria. ZAIRE 5 (1951), pp. 296-297.

11,728 Crise des institutions indigènes en Nigeria. ZAIRE 5 (1951), p. 71.

11,729 Crise politique en Nigéria. ZAIRE 7 (1953), pp. 1087-1088.

11,730 Duties and functions of administrative officers in the Western Region, Nigeria. J. AFR. ADM. 8 (1956), pp. 45-48.

11,731 Elections en Nigeria. ZAIRE 6 (1952), p. 190.

11,732 Le gouvernement local en Nigéria occidentale. ZAIRE 6 (1952), pp. 1087-1088.

11,733 Local Government reform in the Eastern Provinces of Nigeria. J. AFR. ADM. 2 (1950), pp. 44-53.

11,734 Native system of government and land tenure in the Yoruba country, by "A native Yoruba." J. AFR. SOC. 1 (1902), pp. 312-315.

11,735 The Nigerian constitutional review, a progress report. J. AFR. ADM. 2 (1950), pp. 11-14; 2 (1950), pp. 31-37.

11,736 Nouvelle constitution en Nigeria. ZAIRE 5 (1951), pp. 1069-1070.

11,737 Policy for Local Government. Sessional Paper No. 2 of 1956. J. AFR. ADM. 8 (1956), pp. 212-213.

11,738 Politique indigène à Ibadan. ZAIRE 6 (1952), p. 413.

11,739 The practice and possibilities of Local Government—an experiment in publicity. J. AFR. ADM. 3 (1951), pp. 165-170.

11,740 Le premier parlement nigérien. ZAIRE 6 (1952), pp. 529-531.

11,741 Rapport sur le Nigéria. ZAIRE 3 (1949), pp. 454-455.

11,742 Le recensement au Nigeria. PRESENCE AFR. N.S. 50 (1964), pp. 242-246.

11,743 Reformes et mouvements locaux en Nigéria. ZAIRE 7 (1953), pp. 1088-1089.

11,744 Report of a Commission Appointed to Enquire into the Affairs of the Akim Abuakwa State by Commissioner J. Jackson. J. AFR. ADM. 11 (1959), p. 55.

11,745 Report of the Commission of Enquiry into the Okrika-Kalabari Dispute. J. AFR. ADM. 3 (1951), pp. 149-150.

11,746 Report of the Commission on Revenue Allocation. J. AFR. ADM. 3 (1951), pp. 204-206.

11,747 Report of the Nigerian Minorities Commission [under chairmanship of Sir Henry Willink]. J. AFR. ADM. 11 (1959), pp. 50-54.

11,748 Report of the Urban African Affairs Commission 1958. J. AFR. ADM. 11 (1959), pp. 54-55.

11,749 Report on the General Election to the Eastern House of Assembly 1957. J. AFR. ADM. 10 (1958), pp. 174-176.

11,750 Report on the Nigeria Federal Elections, 1960. J. AFR. ADM. 12 (1960), p. 249.

11,751 Revenu national et politique en Nigéria. ZAIRE 8 (1954), pp. 415-416.

11,752 Royal tour of Nigeria. AFR. AFFAIRS 55 (1956), pp. 78-80.

11,753 Vers le morcellement du Nigeria? PRESENCE AFR. N.S. 41 (1962), pp. 164-166.

11,754 Women's franchise in Northern Nigeria. AFR. WOMEN 3 (1958-1960), pp. 5-6.

See also 10364, 10368, 10428, 10447, 14699, 18150, 18219.

History

11,755 ABI-SAAB, R. Le Nigéria, des origines à l'Indépendance. GENEVE-AFR. 4 (1965), pp. 102-107.

11,756 ADERIBIGBE, A. B. Trade and British expansion in the Lagos area in the second half of the nineteenth century. NJESS 4 (1962), pp. 188-193.

11,757 ADESINA, S. The Adubi rising of 1918. AFR. HISTORIAN 1, no. iii (1965), pp. 47-51.

11,758 ADESINA, S. The Egbas and the Dahomian menace. AFR. HISTORIAN 1, no. i (1963), pp. 25-27.

11,759 AFIGBO, A. E. Herbert Richmond Palmer and indirect rule in Eastern Nigeria: 1915-1928. J. HIST. SOC. NIG. 3 (1965), pp. 295-312.

11,760 AJAYI, J. F. A. Henry Venn and the policy of development. J. HIST. SOC. NIG. 1 (1959), pp. 331-342.

11,761 AJAYI, J. F. A. L'occupazione britannica di Lagos. AFRICA (Rome) 16 (1961), pp. 293-297.

11,762 AJAYI, J. F. A. Professional warriors in nineteenth century Yoruba politics. TARIKH 1, no. 1 (1965), pp. 72-81.

11,763 AKINJOGBIN, I. A. Enactment ceremonies as a source of unwritten history. NISER 6 (1958), pp. 168-179.

11,764 AKINJOGBIN, I. A. The prelude to the Yoruba civil wars of the nineteenth century. ODU 1, no. 2 (1965), pp. 24-46.

11,765 AKPALA, A. The background of the Enugu colliery shooting incident in 1949. J. HIST. SOC. NIG. 3 (1965), pp. 335-363.

11,766 ALLISON, P. The last days of old Oyo. ODU 4 (1957), pp. 16-27.

11,767 ALLISON, P. A. The first travelling commissioners of the Ekiti country. NIGERIAN FIELD 17 (1952), pp. 100-115.

11,768 ANENE, J. The Protectorate government of Southern Nigeria and the Aros 1900-1902. J. HIST. SOC. NIG. 1 (1956), pp. 20-26.

11,769 ANENE, J. C. The eclipse of the Borgawa. J. HIST. SOC. NIG. 3 (1965), pp. 211-220.

11,770 ANENE, J. C. The foundations of British rule in "Southern Nigeria" (1885-1891). J. HIST. SOC. NIG. 1 (1959), pp. 253-262.

11,771 ARNETT, E. J., tr. A Hausa chronicle [Daura Makas Sariki]. J. AFR. SOC. 9 (1910), pp. 161-167.

11,772 AWE, B. The Ajele system (a study of Ibadan imperialism in the nineteenth century). J. HIST. SOC. NIG. 3 (1964), pp. 47-60.

11,773 AWE, B. The end of an experiment: the collapse of the Ibadan empire, 1877-1893. J. HIST. SOC. NIG. 3 (1965), pp. 221-230.

11,774 AYANDELE, E. A. An assessment of James Johnson and his place in Nigerian history, 1874-1917; part II, 1890-1917. J. HIST. SOC. NIG. 3 (1964), pp. 73-101.

11,775 BAMGBOYE, A. and AKINGBADE, P. I. The Kiriji War. AFR. HISTORIAN 1, no. ii (1964), pp. 18-22.

11,776 BASCOM, W. La chute de l'ancien Oyo ou de Katunga. PRESENCE AFR. N.S. 24-25 (1959), pp. 299-304.

11,777 BASCOM, W. Lander's routes through Yoruba country. NIGERIAN FIELD 25 (1960), pp. 12-22.

11,778 BEIER, H. U. Before Oduduwa. ODU 3 (1956), pp. 25-32.

11,779 BEIER, H. U. The use and interpretation of myths: the historical and psychological significance of Yoruba myths. ODU 1 (1955), pp. 17-25.

11,780 BIOBAKU, S. O. An historical sketch of Egba traditional authorities. AFRICA 22 (1952), pp. 35-49.

11,781 BIOBAKU, S. O. An historical sketch of the peoples of Western Nigeria. ODU 6 (1958), pp. 24-28.

11,782 BIOBAKU, S. O. The pattern of Yoruba history. AFR. SOUTH 2, no. 2 (1958), pp. 63-67.

11,783 BIOBAKU, S. O. The problem of traditional history with special reference to Yoruba traditions. J. HIST. SOC. NIG. 1 (1956), pp. 43-47.

11,784 BIOBAKU, S. O. The use and interpretation of myths: myths and oral history. ODU 1 (1955), pp. 12-17.

11,785 BIOBAKU, S. O. The Yoruba Historical Research Scheme. J. HIST. SOC. NIG. 1 (1956), pp. 59-60.

11,786 BIRTWISTLE, C. A. Cotton growing and Nigeria. ROYAL COL. INST. PR. 39 (1907-1908), pp. 80-104.

11,787 BIVAR, A. D. H. Arabic documents of Northern Nigeria. BULL. SOAS 22 (1959), pp. 324-349.

11,788 BIVAR, A. D. H. The Wathīgat ahl al-Sūdān: a manifesto of the Fulani jihād. J. AFR. HIST. 2 (1961), pp. 235-243.

11,789 BOURDILLON, Sir B. Nigeria's war effort. J. AFR. SOC. 39 (1940), pp. 115-122.

11,790 BRADBURY, R. E. Chronological problems in the study of Benin history. J. HIST. SOC. NIG. 1 (1959), pp. 263-287.

11,791 BROOKS, G. E. A note on French influence in the Oil Rivers in the 1840's and 1860's. J. HIST. SOC. NIG. 3 (1965), pp. 421-430.

11,792 BUCKLE, D. Nigeria's road to independence. AFR. SOUTH 1, no. 1 (1956), pp. 96-107.

11,793 BURDON, J. A. Sokoto history. Tables of dates and genealogy. J. AFR. SOC. 6 (1907), pp. 367-374.

11,794 BUSTIN, E. Les étapes de l'indépendance nigérienne. CIVILISATIONS 10 (1960), pp. 415-442; English summary, pp. 443-445.

11,795 C., J. Dans les Emirats de Nigeria du Nord. ZAIRE 8 (1954), p. 636.

11,796 CARTER, Sir G. The colony of Lagos. ROYAL COL. INST. PR. 28 (1896-1897), pp. 275-304.

11,797 CHILVER, E. M. Meta village chiefdoms of the Bome valley in the Bamenda prefecture of West Cameroon. NIGERIAN FIELD 30 (1965), pp. 4-18, 52-59.

11,798 CRABTREE, W. A. Great Britain in West Africa. J. AFR. SOC. 19 (1920), pp. 196-205.

11,799 DAVIDSON, A. M. The origin and early history of Lagos. NIGERIAN FIELD 19 (1954), pp. 52-69.

11,800 DIKE, K. O. Problems of archive administration in Nigeria. WAISER SOC. 2 (1953), pp. 106-114.

11,801 DUGGAN, E. DE C. Notes on the Munshi ("Tivi") tribe of Northern Nigeria. Some historical outlines. J. AFR. SOC. 31 (1932), pp. 173-182.

11,802 DUNGLAS, E. Deuxième attaque des Dahoméens contre Abéokuta (15 mars 1864). ET. DAHOM. 2 (1949), pp. 37-58.

11,803 DUNGLAS, E. La première attaque des Dahoméens contre Abéokuta (3 mars 1851). ET. DAHOM. 1 (1948), pp. 7-19.

11,804 EKWENSI, C. Lagos diary. AFR. SOUTH 2, no. 2 (1958), pp. 97-100.

11,805 ELLIOT, W. The parliamentary visit to Nigeria. J. AFR. SOC. 27 (1928), pp. 205-218.

11,806 ELLISON, R. E. Three forgotten explorers of the latter half of the 19th century with special reference to their journeys to Bornu. J. HIST. SOC. NIG. 1 (1959), pp. 322-330.

11,807 ESIKE, S. O. The Aba riots of 1929. AFR. HISTORIAN 1, no. iii (1965), pp. 7-13.

11,808 EZERA, K. Nigeria's constitutional road to independence. AFR. SOUTH 3, no. 2 (1959), pp. 93-99.

11,809 FABELURIN, N. O. Ogedengbe of Ilesha. AFR. HISTORIAN 1, no. i (1963), pp. 14-15.

11,810 FAGG, W. and WILLETT, F. Ancient Ife. ODU 8 (1960), pp. 21-35.

11,811 FOLORUNSO, F. O. and ALAKA. The need for local history. AFR. HISTORIAN 1, no. i (1963), pp. 9-10.

11,812 FORTES, M. The impact of the war on British West Africa. INTERNAT. AFFAIRS 21 (1945), pp. 206-219.

11,813 FREEMANTLE, J. M. A history of the region comprising the Katagum division of Kano province. J. AFR. SOC. 10 (1911), pp. 298-319, 398-421; 11 (1911), pp. 62-74, 187-200.

11,814 GADDI, S. Nigeria: vitalita' di un Paese e debolezza di uno Stato nascente. AFRICA (Rome) 11 (1956), pp. 60-61.

11,815 GALWAY, Sir H. The rising of the Brassmen. J. AFR. SOC. 34 (1935), pp. 144-162.

11,816 GALWAY, H. L. Nigeria in the "nineties." J. AFR. SOC. 29 (1930), pp. 221-247.

11,817 GERTZEL, C. Relations between African and European traders in the Niger Delta, 1880-1896. J. AFR. HIST. 3 (1962), pp. 361-366.

11,818 GIROUARD, P. The development of Northern Nigeria. J. AFR. SOC. 7 (1908), pp. 331-337.

11,819 GLENNY, H. Q. Notes on the history of Miga. AFR. AFFAIRS 48 (1949), pp. 323-328.

11,820 GRAHAM, J. D. The slave trade, depopulation and human sacrifice in Benin history. CAH. ET. AFR. 5 (1965), pp. 317-334.

11,821 GRAY, A. Nigerian independence. AFR. AFFAIRS 58 (1959), pp. 10-14.

11,822 GREAT BRITAIN. COLONIAL OFFICE. INFORMATION DEPT. Research into the history of Benin. AFR. STUD. 15 (1956), p. 144.

11,823 HAIR, P. E. H. Elephant hunters visit the Delta, 1892. NIGERIAN FIELD 28 (1963), pp. 132-134.

11,824 HERMAN, J. M. The voice of nationalism in the Nigerian Legislative Council in the 1920's. PROC. 3RD. GRAD. ACAD. UCLA, 1965, pp. 21-41.

11,825 HISKETT, M. The teaching of Islamic history in Northern Nigeria: problems and approaches. J. HIST. SOC. NIG. 1 (1957), pp. 130-137.

11,826 HOLT, C. A note on the John Holt Archives. J. HIST. SOC. NIG. 1 (1957), pp. 154-155.

11,827 HOPKINS, A. G. The Lagos Chamber of Commerce 1888-1903. J. HIST. SOC. NIG. 3 (1965), pp. 241-248.

11,828 IKIME, O. Chief Dogho: the Lugardian system in Warri 1917-1932. J. HIST. SOC. NIG. 3 (1965), pp. 313-333.

11,829 IKIME, O. Traditional system of government and justice among the Urhobo and Isoko of Delta Province, Nigeria. NJESS 7 (1965), pp. 283-300.

11,830 IONGH, P. DE. Nigeria: two imperialists and their creation [George Goldie and Lord Lugard]. HISTORY TODAY 14 (1964), pp. 835-843.

11,831 JEFFREYS, M. D. W. Banyo: a local historical note. NIGERIAN FIELD 18 (1953), pp. 87-91.

11,832 JEFFREYS, M. D. W. Fort Stuart: a lost site. NIGERIAN FIELD 20 (1955), pp. 89-90.

11,833 JEFFREYS, M. D. W. A note on Abagana town. NIGERIAN FIELD 22 (1957), pp. 184-185.

11,834 JEFFREYS, M. D. W. Two Arabic documents: Diyyâ s-Sultan and Tazyîn l-Waragat. AFR. STUD. 9 (1950), pp. 77-85.

11,835 JEFFREYS, M. D. W. The Umundri tradition of origin. AFR. STUD. 15 (1956), pp. 119-131.

11,836 JEFFREYS, M. D. W. When was Ile Ife founded. NIGERIAN FIELD 23 (1958), pp. 21-23.

11,837 JONES, G. I. European and African tradition on the Rio Real. J. AFR. HIST. 4 (1963), pp. 391-402.

11,838 JONES, G. I. Oral tradition and history. AFR. NOTES 2, no. 2 (1965), pp. 7-11.

11,839 KIRK-GREENE, A. H. M. The British consulate at Lake Chad. AFR. AFFAIRS 58 (1959), pp. 334-339.

11,840 KIRK-GREENE, A. H. M. Expansion on the Benue 1830-1900. J. HIST. SOC. NIG. 1 (1958), pp. 215-237.

11,841 KIRK-GREENE, A. H. M. The kingdom of Sukur: a Northern Nigerian Ichabod. NIGERIAN FIELD 25 (1960), pp. 67-96.

11,842 KIRK-GREENE, A. H. M. A preliminary note on new sources for Nigerian military history. J. HIST. SOC. NIG. 3 (1964), pp. 129-147.

11,843 KIRK-GREENE, A. H. M. Von Uechtritz's expedition to Adamawa, 1893. J. HIST. SOC. NIG. 1 (1957), pp. 86-98.

11,844 KLINGENHEBEN, A. Zwei geschichtliche Hausatexte. AFR. UND UB. 31 (1941), pp. 114-129.

11,845 LAST, D. M. Arabic source material and historiography in Sokoto to 1864: an outline. RES. BULL. CENTRE ARABIC DOC. IBADAN 1 (1965), pp. 3-19.

11,846 LAST, D. M. and AL-HAJJ, M. A. Attempts at defining a Muslim in 19th century Hausaland and Bornu. J. HIST. SOC. NIG. 3 (1965), pp. 231-240.

11,847 LATHAM, N. The use of source material in the teaching of history. J. HIST. SOC. NIG. 1 (1957), pp. 145-153.

11,848 LEITH-ROSS, S. A glimpse of Nigeria fifty years ago. NIGERIAN FIELD 22 (1957), pp. 160-164.

11,849 LLOYD, P. C. Captaine Landolphe and the Compagnie d'Owhere et de Benin. ODU 5 (1958), pp. 14-21.

11,850 LLOYD, P. C. The Itsekiri in the nineteenth century; an outline social history. J. AFR. HIST. 4 (1963), pp. 207-231.

11,851 LLOYD, P. C. Osifakorede of Ijebu. ODU 8 (1960), pp. 59-64.

11,852 LLOYD, P. C. The Portuguese in Warri. ODU 4 (1957), pp. 28-33.

11,853 LUGARD, Sir F. Northern Nigeria. J. AFR. SOC. 5 (1906), pp. 387-403.

11,854 McINTYRE, W. D. Commander Glover and the colony of Lagos, 1861-73. J. AFR. HIST. 4 (1963), pp. 57-79.

11,855 MACKINTOSH, J. P. Nigeria's external relations. J. COMM. POL. STUD. 2 (1963-1964), pp. 207-218.

11,856 MARTIN, B. G. A new Arabic history of Ilorin. RES. BULL. CENTRE ARABIC DOC. IBADAN 1 (1965), pp. 20-27.

11,857 MATHEWS, A. B. The Kisra legend. AFR. STUD. 9 (1950), pp. 144-147.

11,858 MAUNY, R. Rayonnement d'Ifé. Capitale artistique et religieuse ancienne du Golfe de Guinée. PRESENCE AFR. N.S. 4 (1955), pp. 80-82.

11,859 MEEK, C. K. The soul of Nigeria. By I. O. Delano. J. AFR. SOC. 37 (1938), pp. 119-122.

11,860 METCALFE, G. E. The making of a nation [review of some books on Nigerian history and politics]. UNIVERSITAS 4 (1960), pp. 113-116.

11,861 MILLER, N. S. et al. Aspects of the development of Lagos. NIGERIAN FIELD 28 (1963), pp. 144-172.

11,862 MILVERTON, Lord. Nigeria. AFR. AFFAIRS 47 (1948), pp. 80-89.

11,863 MURRAY, K. C. Frobenius and Ile Ife. NIGERIAN FIELD 11 (1943), pp. 200-203.

11,864 MURRAY, K. C. Opobo to-day. AFR. AFFAIRS 43 (1944), pp. 134-137.

11,865 NAGER, O. A. EL-. A note on source material for the study of Rabeh's career. BULL. AFR. STUD. ASSOC. 6 (1965), pp. 20-23.

11,866 NIVEN, C. R. Nigeria past and present. AFR. AFFAIRS 56 (1957), pp. 265-275.

11,867 NIVEN, C. R. Recent developments in Nigeria. AFR. AFFAIRS 54 (1955), pp. 121-128.

11,868 NWABARA, S. N. British foundation of Nigeria: a sage of hardship, 1788-1914. CIVILISATIONS 13 (1963), pp. 308-317; French summary, pp. 318-320.

11,869 NWABARA, S. N. The Fulani conquest and rule of the Hausa kingdom of Northern Nigeria (1804-1900). J. SOC. AFR. 33 (1963), pp. 231-241.

11,870 NWOSU, B. E. External influences on the history of Nigeria. AFR. HISTORIAN 1, no. ii (1964), pp. 7-13.

11,871 OBA ALAIYELUWA ADEGORIOLA I, Ogoga of Ikere. A note on the administration of Ikere before the advent of the British. ODU 3 (1956), pp. 19-24.

11,872 OGUNKOYA, T. O. The early history of Ijebu. J. HIST. SOC. NIG. 1 (1956), pp. 48-58.

11,873 OJO-COLE, J. A glimpse of Yoruba civilisation. WASU 3-4 (1927), pp. 16-19.

11,874 OKOLI, J. The Christian missionary penetration of Nigeria before 1900 A.D. AFR. HISTORIAN 1, no. iii (1965), pp. 14-19.

11,875 OKOLI, J. People of the Anambra. AFR. HISTORIAN 1, no. 1 (1963), pp. 19-22; 1, no. 2 (1964), pp. 41-46.

11,876 OLAJUBU, O. Obokun. AFR. HISTORIAN 1, no. ii (1964), pp. 46-50.

11,877 OLAMIJULO, J. Yoruba sayings with historical bearing. AFR. HISTORIAN 1, no. i (1963), pp. 18-19.

11,878 ORR, Sir C. The northern provinces of Nigeria. J. AFR. SOC. 36 (1937), pp. 8-16.

11,879 PALMER, H. R. The Bornu Girgam. J. AFR. SOC. 12 (1912), pp. 71-83.

11,880 PALMER, H. R. History of Katsina. J. AFR. SOC. 26 (1927), pp. 216-236.

11,881 PALMER, H. R. The origin of the name Bornu. J. AFR. SOC. 28 (1928), pp. 36-42.

11,882 PALMER, Sir R. British enterprise in Nigeria, by A. N. Cook. AFR. AFFAIRS 43 (1944), pp. 86-92.

11,883 PAYNE, P. Calabar coronation: being the programme of the coronation of His Highness Archibong the Fifth, Obong of Calabar [Jan., 1950). NIGERIAN FIELD 19 (1954), pp. 85-96.

11,884 PERRY, R. New sources for research in Nigerian history. AFRICA 25 (1955), pp. 430-432.

11,885 RIAD, M. The Jukun: an example of African migrations in the sixteenth century. BULL. IFAN 22 (1960), pp. 476-485.

11,886 ROSS, D. A. The career of Domingo Martinez in the Bight of Benin 1833-64. J. AFR. HIST. 6 (1965), pp. 79-90.

11,887 RYDER, A. F. C. Dutch trade on the Nigerian coast during the seventeenth century. J. HIST. SOC. NIG. 3 (1964), pp. 195-210.

11,888 RYDER, A. F. C. An early Portuguese trading voyage to the Forcados River. J. HIST. SOC. NIG. 1 (1959), pp. 294-321.

11,889 RYDER, A. F. C. A reconsideration of the Ife-Benin relationship. J. AFR. HIST. 6 (1965), pp. 25-37.

11,890 SALUBI, A. The establishment of British administration in the Urhobo Country (1891-1913). J. HIST. SOC. NIG. 1 (1958), pp. 184-209.

11,891 SHARWOOD-SMITH, J. Kano. CORONA 4 (1952), pp. 461-465.

11,892 SHEFFIELD, A. F. W. Nigeria revisited. NIGERIAN FIELD 29 (1964), pp. 117-126.

11,893 SIMMONS, D. Fort Stuart, Calabar—a further note. NIGERIAN FIELD 20 (1955), pp. 139-140.

11,894 SMITH, H. F. C. The Benin study. J. HIST. SOC. NIG. 1 (1956), pp. 60-61.

11,895 SMITH, M. G. Field histories among the Hausa. J. AFR. HIST. 2 (1961), pp. 87-101.

11,896 SMITH, R. The Alafin in exile: a study of the Igboho period in Oyo history. J. AFR. HIST. 6 (1965), pp. 57-77.

11,897 SMITH, R. The Bara, or Royal Mausoleum, New Oyo. J. HIST. SOC. NIG. 3 (1965), pp. 415-420.

11,898 SMITH, R. The Battle of Oshogbo. AFR. HISTORIAN 1, no. 1 (1963), pp. 12-14.

11,899 SMITH, R. A list of Alafin of Oyo. AFR. HISTORIAN 1, no. iii (1965), pp. 52-55.

11,900 TAMUNO, T. N. Some aspects of Nigerian reaction to the imposition of British rule. J. HIST. SOC. NIG. 3 (1965), pp. 271-294.

11,901 TAYLOR, F. W. The word "Nigeria." J. AFR. SOC. 38 (1939), pp. 154-159.

11,902 TAYLOR, O. W. History teaching in Nigeria: an American view. J. HIST. SOC. NIG. 1 (1957), pp. 99-111.

11,903 TEPOWA, A. A short history of Brass and its people. J. AFR. SOC. 7 (1907), pp. 32-88.

11,904 THOMSON, G. Some problems of administration and development in Nigeria. J. AFR. SOC. 26 (1927), pp. 305-314.

11,905 THORBURN, J. W. A. Nigerian memories in lighter vein: 1925-1947. NIGERIAN FIELD 28 (1963), pp. 45-48.

11,906 THORBURN, J. W. A. Some memories of Western Nigeria in the twenties and thirties. NIGERIAN FIELD 23 (1958), pp. 85-89.

11,907 TONG, R. The ancient city of Benin. CORONA 3 (1951), pp. 30-32.

11,908 TONG, R. Gwato, the old port of Benin. CORONA 3 (1951), pp. 59-61.

11,909 VERGER, P. Notes on some documents in which Lagos is referred to by the name 'Onim' and which mention relations between Onim and Brazil. J. HIST. SOC. NIG. 1 (1959), pp. 343-350.

11,910 VERGER, P. Oral tradition in the cult of the Orishas and its connection with the history of the Yoruba. J. HIST. SOC. NIG. 1 (1956), pp. 61-63.

11,911 VERGER, P. Yoruba influences in Brazil. ODU 1 (1955), pp. 3-11.

11,912 VIGNOLS, L. Une expédition négrière en 1821 d'après son registre de bord. RHCF 21 (1928), pp. 265-324.

11,913 VITORIA, J. L. A tin-mining anniversary of Jos: report of proceedings at a commemoration of the 50th anniversary of the arrival of Colonel H. W. Laws on the Plateau. Held at Bukuru on 22nd January 1954. NIGERIAN FIELD 19 (1954), pp. 99-117.

11,914 WESCOTT, R. W. Did the Yoruba come from Egypt. ODU 4 (1957), pp. 10-15.

11,915 WHITTING, C. E. J. Extracts from an Arabic history of Sokoto. AFR. AFFAIRS 47 (1948), pp. 160-169.

11,916 WILCOX, D. Kwakwambelo—an instance of religious syncretism. AFR. HISTORIAN 1, no. ii (1964), pp. 39-41.

11,917 The balance of British rule [Have we failed in Nigeria? by W.R. Miller]. AFR. AFFAIRS 46 (1947), pp. 145-148.

11,918 Eastern history research scheme: Nri-Awka pilot project. AFR. NOTES 1, no. 1 (1963), pp. 9-12.

See also 8902, 9570, 9581, 21146.

Language. Literature

Language

11,919 ADAMS, R. F. G. and WARD, I. C. The Arochuku dialect of Ibo: phonetic analysis and suggested orthography. AFRICA 2 (1929), pp. 57-70.

11,920 ADAMS, R. F. G. Efik vocabulary of living things. NIGERIAN FIELD 11 (1943), pp. 156-169; 12 (1947), pp. 23-34; 13 (1948), pp. 61-67.

11,921 ADAMS, R. F. G. Ibo texts. AFRICA 7 (1934), pp. 452-463.

11,922 ADAMS, R. F. G. Oberi Okaime: a new African language and script. AFRICA 17 (1947), pp. 24-34.

11,923 AJAYI, J. F. A. How Yoruba was reduced to writing. ODU 8 (1960), pp. 49-58.

11,924 ANWYL, T. C. Chapters on Yoruba. TRANS. PHILOLOGICAL SOC. 1917-1920, pp. 107-125.

11,925 ARMSTRONG, R. G. Comparative word lists of two dialects of Yoruba with Igala. J. W. AFR. LANG. 2 (1965), pp. 51-78.

11,926 ARMSTRONG, R. G. Notes on Etulo. J. W. AFR. LANG. 1 (1964), pp. 57-60.

11,927 ARMSTRONG, R. G. The subjunctive in Idoma. J. AFR. LANGS. 2 (1963), pp. 155-159.

11,928 ARNOTT, D. W. The classification of verbs in Tiv. BULL. SOAS 21 (1958), pp. 111-133.

11,929 ARNOTT, D. W. Downstep in the Tiv verbal system. AFR. LANG. STUD. 5 (1964), pp. 34-51.

11,930 ARNOTT, D. W. Morphological features in the verbal system of Fula. J. W. AFR. LANG. 2 (1965), pp. 5-14.

11,931 ARNOTT, D. W. Sentence intonation in the Gombe dialect of Fula—a tentative analysis. AFR. LANG. STUD. 6 (1965), pp. 73-100.

11,932 ARNOTT, D. W. The subjunctive in Fula: a study of the relation between meaning and syntax. AFR. LANG. STUD. 2 (1961), pp. 125-138.

11,933 BAMGBOSE, A. Assimilation and contraction in Yoruba. J. W. AFR. LANG. 2 (1965), pp. 21-27.

11,934 BAMGBOSE, A. Verb-nominal collocations in Yoruba: a problem of syntactic analysis. J. W. AFR. LANG. 1 (1964), pp. 27-32.

11,935 BERTHO, J. Aperçu d'ensemble sur les dialectes de l'Ouest de la Nigéria. BULL. IFAN 14 (1952), pp. 259-271.

11,936 BOUQUIAUX, L. A word list of Aten (Ganawuri). J. W. AFR. LANG. 1 (1964), pp. 5-25.

11,937 BRACKENBURY, E. A. Notes on Fulfulde. J. AFR. SOC. 15 (1915), pp. 70-82.

11,938 BRISTOW, W. M. Birom texts (Plateau Province near Jos, Nigeria). AFR. UND UB. 37 (1952-1953), pp. 145-150.

11,939 BROSNAHAN, L. F. Outlines of the phonology of the Gokana dialect of Ogoni. J. W. AFR. LANG. 1 (1964), pp. 43-48.

11,940 BUCHNER, H. Vokabulare der Sprachen in und um Gava (Nordnigerien). AFR. UND UB. 48 (1964-1965), pp. 36-45.

11,941 BURSSENS, A. Het Ibo als toontaal. KONGO-OVERZEE 3 (1936-1937), pp. 103-106.

11,942 BUTCHER, H. L. M. Four Edo fables. Vernacular version by E. O. Gbinigie. AFRICA 10 (1937), pp. 342-352.

11,943 CARNOCHAN, J. The category of number in Igbo grammar. AFR. LANG. STUD. 3 (1962), pp. 110-115.

11,944 CARNOCHAN, J. Pitch, tone and intonation in Igbo. INT. CON. PHONETIC SCIENCES 4 (1961), pp. 547-554.

11,945 CARNOCHAN, J. A study in the phonology of an Igbo speaker. BULL. SOAS 12 (1947-1948), pp. 417-426.

11,946 CARNOCHAN, J. A study of quantity in Hausa. BULL. SOAS 13 (1949-1951), pp. 1032-1044.

11,947 CARNOCHAN, J. Towards a syntax for Igbo. J. AFR. LANGS. 2 (1963), pp. 222-226.

11,948 CARNOCHAN, J. Vowel harmony in Igbo. AFR. LANG. STUD. 1 (1960), pp. 155-163.

11,949 CORREIA, J. A. Vocables religieux et philosophiques des peuples Ibos. BIBLIOTHECA AFR. 1 (1925), pp. 104-113.

11,950 CRABB, D. W. The dia-phonemic principle in field work. SIERRA LEONE LANG. REV. 4 (1965), pp. 91-94.

11,951 DANGEL-WIEN, R. Grammatische Skizze der Yergum-Sprache. BIBLIOTHECA AFR. 3 (1929), pp. 135-145.

11,952 DENNETT, R. E. How the Yoruba count. J. AFR. SOC. 17 (1917), pp. 60-71.

11,953 DENNETT, R. E. Notes on the language of the Efa (people) or the Bini commonly called Uze Ado. J. AFR. SOC. 3 (1904), pp. 142-153.

11,954 DENNETT, R. E. West African categories and the Yoruba language. J. AFR. SOC. 14 (1914-1915), pp. 75-80.

11,955 EAST, R. M. A first essay in imaginative African literature. AFRICA 9 (1936), pp. 350-357.

11,956 EAST, R. M. Modern tendencies in the languages of Northern Nigeria. The problem of European words. AFRICA 10 (1937), pp. 97-105.

11,957 FUNKE, E. Einige Tanz- und Liebeslieder der Hausa. AFR. UND UB. 11 (1920-1921), pp. 259-278.

11,958 GASKIN, E. A. L. Twelve proverbs and one folk-story from the Efik country. AFRICA 5 (1932), pp. 68-70.

11,959 GOUFFE, C. La lexicographie du Haoussa et le préalable phonologique. J. AFR. LANG. 4 (1965), pp. 191-210.

11,960 GREEN, M. M. The classification of West African tone languages: Igbo and Efik. AFRICA 19 (1949), pp. 213-219.

11,961 GREEN, M. M. The present linguistic situation in Ibo country. AFRICA 9 (1936), pp. 508-523.

11,962 GREEN, M. M. Suffixes in Igbo. AFR. LANG. STUD. 5 (1964), pp. 92-114.

11,963 GREEN, M. M. Sayings of the Okonko Society of the Igbo-speaking people. BULL. SOAS 21 (1958), pp. 157-173.

11,964 GREENBERG, J. H. Arabic loan-words in Hausa. WORD 3 (1947), pp. 85-97.

11,965 HARRIS, P. G. Notes on the Reshe language. AFR. STUD. 5 (1946), pp. 221-242.

11,966 HAU, K. Evidence of the use of pre-Portuguese written characters by the Bini? BULL. IFAN 21 (1959), pp. 109-154.

11,967 HAU, K. Oberi Ikaime script, texts, and counting system. BULL. IFAN 23 (1961), pp. 291-308.

11,968 HOFFMANN, C. The noun class system of central Kambari. J. AFR. LANGS. 2 (1963), pp. 160-169.

11,969 HOFFMANN, C. A word list of central Kambari. J. W. AFR. LANG. 2 (1965), pp. 7-31.

11,970 HOFMANN, I. Das Verhältnis der Langvokale zu den Kurzvokalen im Hausa. AFR. UND UB. 48 (1964-1965), pp. 202-211.

11,971 JAMES, A. L. The tones of Yoruba. BULL. SOAS 3 (1923-1925), pp. 119-128.

11,972 JAMES, A. L. and BARGERY, G. P. A note on the pronunciation of Hausa. BULL. SOAS 3 (1923-1925), pp. 721-728.

11,973 JEFFREYS, M. D. W. A note on the Ekoi language. AFR. UND UB. 35 (1949-1950), pp. 260-263.

11,974 JOHNSTON, Sir H. H. The semi-Bantu languages of Eastern Nigeria. J. AFR. SOC. 20 (1921), pp. 186-194.

11,975 JUDD, A. S. Language of the Arago or Alago tribe. J. AFR. SOC. 23 (1923), pp. 30-38.

11,976 JUNGRAITHMAYR, H. Internal *a* in Ron plurals. J. AFR. LANG. 4 (1965), pp. 102-107.

11,977 JUNGRAITHMAYR, H. On the ambiguous position of Angas. J. AFR. LANGS. 2 (1963), pp. 272-278.

11,978 JUNGRAITHMAYR, H. Die Sprache der Sura (Maghavul) in Nordnigerien. AFR. UND UB. 47 (1964), pp. 8-89, 204-220.

11,979 JUNGRAITHMAYR, H. Texte und Sprichwörter im Angas von Kabwir (Nordnigerien) mit einer grammatischen Skizze. AFR. UND UB. 48 (1964-1965), pp. 17-35, 114-127.

11,980 KIRK-GREENE, A. H. M. Neologisms in Hausa: a sociological approach. AFRICA 33 (1963), pp. 25-44.

11,981 KOHLER, O. Das 'Pferd' in den Gur-Sprachen. Eine sprachkulturgeographische Studie. AFR. UND UB. 38 (1953-1954), pp. 93-109.

11,982 LADEFOGED, P. Igbirra notes and word-list. J. W. AFR. LANG. 1 (1964), pp. 27-37.

11,983 LASEBIKAN, E. L. The tonal structure of Yoruba poetry. PRESENCE AFR. N.S. 8-10 (1956), pp. 43-50.

11,984 LAVER, J. D. M. Some observations on alveolar and dental consonant-articulations in Higi. J. W. AFR. LANG. 2 (1965), pp. 59-61.

11,985 LUKAS, J. Das Hitkalanci, eine Sprache um Gwoza (Nordostnigerien). AFR. UND UB. 48 (1964-1965), pp. 81-114.

11,986 LUKAS, J. Der II. Stamm des Verbums im Hausa. AFR. UND UB. 47 (1964), pp. 162-186.

11,987 LUKAS, J. Lautlehre des Bádawi-Kanurí in Borno. AFR. UND UB. 25 (1934-1935), pp. 3-29.

11,988 LUKAS, J. and WILLMS, A. Outline of the language of the Jarawa in Northern Nigeria (Plateau Province). AFR. UND UB. 45 (1961-1962), pp. 1-66.

11,989 MACKAY, H. D. A word-list of Eloyi. J. W. AFR. LANG. 1 (1964), pp. 5-12.

11,990 MEEK, C. K. The semi-Bantu languages of the Benue valley. J. AFR. SOC. 21 (1922), pp. 222-223.

11,991 MERRICK, G. Languages in Northern Nigeria. J. AFR. SOC. 5 (1905), pp. 43-47.

11,992 NEWMAN, P. A brief note on the Maha language. J. W. AFR. LANG. 2 (1965), pp. 57-58.

11,993 NEWMAN, P. A word list of Tera. J. W. AFR. LANG. 1 (1964), pp. 33-50.

11,994 OLMSTED, D. L. Comparative notes on Yoruba and Lucumí. LANGUAGE 29 (1953), pp. 157-164.

11,995 PARSONS, F. W. The verbal system in Hausa. AFR. UND UB. 44 (1960), pp. 1-36.

11,996 PHILPOT, W. T. A. Notes on the Igala language. BULL. SOAS 7 (1933-1935), pp. 897-913.

11,997 PRIETZE, R. Die sprachlichen Sammlungen Barth's, Nachtigal's und Rohlfs'. ZAOS 2 (1896), pp. 195-196.

11,998 ROWLANDS, E. C. Notes on some class languages of Northern Nigeria. AFR. LANG. STUD. 3 (1962), pp. 71-83.

11,999 ROWLANDS, E. C. Tone and intonation systems in Brass-Nembe Ijaw. AFR. LANG. STUD. 1 (1960), pp. 137-154.

12,000 ROWLANDS, E. C. Yoruba and English: a problem of co-existence. AFR. LANG. STUD. 4 (1963), pp. 208-214.

12,001 ROWLANDS, E. C. Yoruba dialects in the Polyglotta Africana. SIERRA LEONE LANG. REV. 4 (1965), pp. 103-108.

12,002 SHELTON, A. J. Some problems of inter-communication. J. MOD. AFR. STUD. 2 (1964), pp. 395-403.

12,003 SIERTSEMA, B. Some notes on Yoruba phonetics and spelling. BULL. IFAN, Série B: Sciences humaines 20 (1958), pp. 576-592.

12,004 SIERTSEMA, B. Three Yoruba dictionaries [by Lydia Cabrera, I. O. Delano, R. C. Abraham]. BULL. IFAN 21 (1959), pp. 572-579.

12,005 SIMMONS, D. C. Ibibio verb morphology. AFR. STUD. 16 (1957), pp. 1-19.

12,006 SIMMONS, D. C. Oron noun morphology. J. W. AFR. LANG. 2 (1965), pp. 33-37.

12,007 SIMMONS, D. C. Oron verb morphology. AFRICA 26 (1956), pp. 250-263.

12,008 STEVICK, E. W. Pitch and duration in two Yoruba idiolects. J. AFR. LANG. 4 (1965), pp. 85-101.

12,009 STRUCK, B. Linguistic bibliography of Northern Nigeria; including Hausa and Fula, with notes on the Yoruba dialects. J. AFR. SOC. 11 (1911), pp. 47-61, 213-230.

12,010 TANGHE, P. B. Bij de Ngbadi (Mbaati) en de Yoruba. CONGO 1 (1921), pp. 431-432.

12,011 TAYLOR, F. W. Hausa and the late Canon C. H. Robinson. J. AFR. SOC. 26 (1927), pp. 145-159.

12,012 TEPOWA, A. Notes on the (Nembe) Brass language. J. AFR. SOC. 4 (1904), pp. 117-133.

12,013 THOMAS, N. W. The Bantu languages of Nigeria. FESTSCHRIFT MEINHOF, 1927, pp. 65-72.

12,014 WARD, I. C. A linguistic tour in Southern Nigeria: certain problems re-stated. AFRICA 8 (1935), pp. 90-96.

12,015 WARD, I. C. Some notes on the pronunciation of the Kanuri language of West Africa. BULL. SOAS 4 (1926-1928), pp. 139-146.

12,016 WESCOTT, R. W. Speech-tempo and the phonemics of Bini. J. AFR. LANG. 4 (1965), pp. 182-190.

12,017 WESTERMANN, D. A standard Hausa dictionary. AFRICA 7 (1934), pp. 371-374.

12,018 WILLIAMSON, K. The syntax of verbs of motion in Ijo. J. AFR. LANG. 2 (1963), pp. 150-154.

12,019 WINSTON, F. D. D. The 'mid tone' in Efik. AFR. LANG. STUD. 1 (1960), pp. 185-192.

12,020 WINSTON, F. D. D. Nigerian Cross River languages in the Polyglotta Africana: Part II. SIERRA LEONE LANG. REV. 4 (1965), pp. 122-128.

12,021 WINSTON, F. D. D. The nominal class system of Loke. AFR. LANG. STUD. 3 (1962), pp. 49-70.

12,022 WOLFF, H. Synopsis of the Ogoni languages. J. AFR. LANG. 3 (1964), pp. 38-51.

12,023 Grammar of the Tula language (Northern Provinces, Nigeria). AFR. UND UB. 39 (1954-1955), pp. 101-118, 149-168.

See also 6329, 9587.

Literature

12,024 ABIMBOLA, W. The Odu of Ifa. AFR. NOTES 1, no. 3 (1964), pp. 6-12.

12,025 ABIMBOLA, W. Yoruba oral literature. AFR. NOTES 2, no. 2 (1965), pp. 3-4; 2, no. 3 (1965), pp. 12-16.

12,026 ACHEBE, C. La Mort d'Ikemefuna. PRESENCE AFR. N.S. 56 (1965), pp. 99-104.

12,027 ADEKAMBI, C. Ikini (Yoruba salutation). ODU 5 (1958), pp. 42-45.

12,028 ADEMOLA, F. J. P. Clark and his audiences. AFR. FORUM 1 (1965), pp. 84-86.

12,029 ADESANYA, A. Mo juba k'iba se [a poem]. ODU 4 (1957), p. 40.

12,030 AJAO, D. O. Orin Idagbere; a Yoruba dirge. ODU 3 (1956), pp. 33-34.

12,031 ANIEBO, I. N. C. Four dimensions [a story]. BO 18 (1965), pp. 9-16.

12,032 ASTRACHAN, A. Like goats to the slaughter: three plays, by John Pepper Clark. BO 16 (1964), pp. 21-24.

12,033 BABALOLA, A. The characteristic features of outer form of Yoruba Ijala chants. ODU 1, no. 1 (1964), pp. 33-44; 2, no. 1 (1965), pp. 47-77.

12,034 BABALOLA, A. Ijala: the traditional poetry of Yoruba hunters. BO 1 (1957), pp. 5-16.

12,035 BABALOLA, A. New Yoruba poems [The elephant, vanity, dignity, kindness]. AFR. AFFAIRS 53 (1954), pp. 332-337.

12,036 BABALOLA, A. La poésie Yoruba. PRESENCE AFR. N.S. 47 (1963), pp. 211-217.

12,037 BABALOLA, A. Village characters [poems]. AFR. AFFAIRS 52 (1953), pp. 156-162.

12,038 BABALOLA, A. When I first heard of forest farms. AFR. AFFAIRS 49 (1950), pp. 338-343.

12,039 BEIER, U. Fagunwa: a Yoruba novelist. BLACK ORPHEUS 17 (1965), pp. 51-56.

12,040 BEIER, U. Public opinion on lovers: popular Nigerian literature sold in Onitsha market. BO 14 (1964), pp. 4-16.

12,041 BEIER, U. Quelques poètes nigériens. PRESENCE AFR. N.S. 32-33 (1960), pp. 183-186.

12,042 BIRD, B. History under the microscope [a story]. NIGERIAN FIELD 21 (1956), pp. 88-90, 135.

12,043 BIVAR, A. D. H. and HISKETT, M. The Arabic literature of Nigeria to 1804: a provisional account. BULL. SOAS 25 (1962), pp. 104-148.

12,044 BLAKELEY, J. A ghost at school. NIGERIAN FIELD 28 (1963), pp. 139-141.

12,045 BRADBURY, R. E. Ehi: three stories from Benin. ODU 8 (1960), pp. 40-48.

12,046 CLARK, J. P. [Poems:] Abiku, Fulani cattle, The imprisonment of Obatala. BO 10 (1961), pp. 4-5.

12,047 CLARK, J. P. Girl bathing. PRESENCE AFR. N.S. 52 (1964), p. 171.

12,048 CLARK, J. P. I woke to the sight. PRESENCE AFR. N.S. 52 (1964), p. 170.

12,048-A CLARK, J. P. A step in the night [a story]. BO 16 (1964), pp. 35-37.

12,049 COLLIER, F. S. Yoruba hunters' salutes. NIGERIAN FIELD 18 (1953), pp. 52-67.

12,050 COOK, D. Of the strong breed [review article on Soyinka's Three Plays]. TRANSITION 13 (1964), pp. 38-40.

12,051 COZENS, A. B. It all hinged on a bee [a story]. NIGERIAN FIELD 26 (1961), pp. 45-47.

12,052 CROSS, L. The pleasure of Mamfe [a poem]. NIGERIAN FIELD 19 (1954), p. 84.

12,053 DATHORNE, O. R. Seven poems. BO 10 (1961), pp. 45-47.

12,054 EAST, R. M. Recent activities of the Literature Bureau, Zaria, Northern Nigeria. AFRICA 14 (1943), pp. 71-76.

12,055 ECHERUO, M. J. C. Debut or love and the hermitage [poems]. BO 12 (1962), pp. 4-9.

12,056 EKWENSI, C. Drums and voices: a chapter from an unpublished novel. BO 7 (1960), pp. 40-45.

12,057 EKWENSI, C. Gens de la Cité. PRESENCE AFR. N.S. 13 (1957), pp. 111-125.

12,058 EKWEREKWU, O. and YESUFU-GIWA, M. Two Nigerian poems [Evening on the Niger, Africa has a god]; [Not alone, Comedy of Error]. AFR. AFFAIRS 45 (1946), pp. 134-135, 205-207.

12,059 EPELLE, K. Two poems [Hymn of the matchet, Death-song of the rivers]. AFR. AFFAIRS 51 (1952), pp. 335-340.

12,060 FAGUNWA, D. O. Igbako: an extract from The brave hunter in the jungle of the four hundred gods. BO 15 (1964), pp. 5-7.

12,061 FALETI, A. Independence [a poem]. BO 8 (1960), pp. 4-5.

12,062 FONLON, B. The fear of future years [a poem]. ABBIA 2 (1963), pp. 140-141.

12,063 GBADAMOSI, B. and BEIER, U., tr. The poetry of masqueraders. ODU 7 (1959), pp. 38-40.

12,064 GREEN, M. M. The unwritten literature of the Igbo-speaking people of south-eastern Nigeria. BULL. SOAS 12 (1947-1948), pp. 838-846.

12,065 HOPE, J. Poems. BO 16 (1964), pp. 55-58.

12,066 JOLAOSO, M. I. Conflict [a poem]. ODU 3 (1956), p. 35.

12,067 JONES, H. E. B. The Mockers: opening chapter of an unpublished novel. BO 10 (1961), pp. 11-21.

12,068 JONES-QUARTEY, K. A. B. A new- and major?- African writer [Vincent Ikeotuonye]. UNIVERSITAS 5 (1962), pp. 50-54.

12,069 LADIPO, D. Oba koso: the closing scene of a drama. BO 15 (1964), pp. 41-45.

12,070 LUKAS, J. Aus der Literatur der Bádawi-Kanuri in Borno. AFR. UND UB. 26 (1935-1936), pp. 35-57, 133-150.

12,071 MacJAJAH, N. O. M. Trial of the wizard. AFR. AFFAIRS 50 (1951), pp. 147-153.

12,072 MacLEAN, U. Soyinka's international drama. BO 15 (1964), pp. 46-51.

12,073 MADAKI, P. R. and KIRK-GREENE, A. H. M. Nkashe ta: the story of the leg. NIGERIAN FIELD 27 (1962), pp. 161-169.

12,074 MAIMO, S. Because—she has turned her back on me [a poem]. ABBIA 1 (1963), p. 90.

12,075 MAIMO, S. Harken boys, to the Bugle call [a poem]. ABBIA 1 (1963), p. 89.

12,076 MAIMO, S. I am vindicated [a story]. ABBIA 3 (1963), pp. 93-101; French translation, pp. 102-112.

12,077 MAUNICK, E. As far as Yoruba land. PRESENCE AFR. N.S. 55 (1965), pp. 170-187.

12,078 MOORE, G. Amos Tutuola: a Nigerian visionary. BO 1 (1957), pp. 27-35.

12,079 NCHAMI, V. C. The way to Senior Service. AFR. AFFAIRS 49 (1950), pp. 67-74.

12,080 NDU, P. N. Nativity poems. BO 18 (1965), pp. 26-29.

12,081 NDU, P. N. Royal drums. ABBIA 7 (1964), pp. 142-143.

12,082 NDU, P. N. Turning point. ABBIA 7 (1964), p. 141.

12,083 NICOL, A. D. Easter evening. AFR. AFFAIRS 53 (1954), p. 328.

12,084 NKWAIN, F. I. W. Ku the hunter: a Kom folk tale. NIGERIAN FIELD 18 (1953), pp. 186-187.

12,085 NKWAIN, F. I. W. and BRIGGS, W. H. The adventures of Funkoti. NIGERIAN FIELD 25 (1960), pp. 44-45, 137-138.

12,086 NKWAIN, F. I. W. and BRIGGS, W. H. The Kom legend. NIGERIAN FIELD 23 (1958), pp. 7-18.

12,087 NWANKWO, N. The gambler [a story]. BO 9 (1961), pp. 49-54.

12,088 NWANODI, G. O. Three poems [A memorial, Salute to Songhai, The worshipper]. BO 16 (1964), pp. 31-33.

12,089 NWOGA, D. I. Onitsha market literature. TRANSITION 19 (1965), pp. 26-33.

12,090 OJO-COLE, J. Three gems. WASU 2 (1926), pp. 16-19.

12,091 OJO-COLE, J. To Moriamo [a poem]. WASU 5 (1927), p. 22.

12,092 OKAFOR, M. Jigida; or the string of beads [a story]. BO 9 (1961), pp. 22-24.

12,093 OKARA, G. The crooks [a story]. BO 8 (1960), pp. 6-9.

12,094 OKARA, G. Okolo or the voice: opening chapter of an unpublished novel. BO 10 (1961), pp. 38-44.

12,095 OKARA, G. Three poems [Spirit of the wind, the call of the river nun, were I to choose]. BO 1 (1957), pp. 36-38.

12,096 OKIGBO, C. Four canzones (1957-1961). BO 11 (1962), pp. 5-9.

12,097 OLAAIYE, N. The world is restless. PRESENCE AFR. N.S. 40 (1962), pp. 144-145.

12,098 OLISA, M. Songs of Nmeka. BO 8 (1960), pp. 21-24.

12,099 PADEN, J. N. A survey of Kano Hausa poetry. KANO STUD. 1 (1965), pp. 33-39.

12,100 PARRY, J. Nigerian novelists. CONTEMP. REV. 200 (1961), pp. 377-381.

12,101 PROBYN, E. H. On the Queen's visit to Nigeria [a poem]. NIGERIAN FIELD 21 (1956), p. 172.

12,102 SHELTON, A. J. The offended Chi in Achebe's novels. TRANSITION 13 (1964), pp. 36-37.

12,103 SHORTHOSE, W. T. A camp by the Afu hills [a poem]. NIGERIAN FIELD 19 (1954), pp. 44-46.

12,104 SHORTHOSE, W. T. Jos, after twenty-two years of absence [a poem]. NIGERIAN FIELD 19 (1954), pp. 135-137.

12,105 SHORTHOSE, W. T. Lake Chael in january [a poem]. NIGERIAN FIELD 22 (1957), pp. 17-19.

12,106 SIMMONS, D. C. A Efik Judas play: the metamorphosis of an ancient Efik ceremony into a New Year's eve celebration and a Judas play. NIGERIAN FIELD 26 (1961), pp. 100-110.

12,107 SIMMONS, D. C. Efik riddles. NIGERIAN FIELD 21 (1956), pp. 168-171.

12,108 SIMMONS, D. C. Ibibio tone riddles. NIGERIAN FIELD 25 (1960), pp. 132-134.

12,109 SOYINKA, W. [Poems:] Abiku, Death in the dawn, Season, Night. BO 10 (1961), pp. 7-9.

12,110 SWAYNE, A. C. C. Hunters' tales. NIGERIAN FIELD 3 (1934), pp. 77-78.

12,111 TAHIR, I. Kasim: the opening chapter of an unpublished novel. BO 9 (1961), pp. 4-12.

12,112 TAHIR, I. A. The captive [a poem]. BO 14 (1964), p. 32.

12,113 THEROUX, P. Christopher Okigbo. TRANSITION 22 (1965), pp. 18-20.

12,114 TONG, R. Fabled city. AFR. AFFAIRS 53 (1954), pp. 130-132.

12,115 TUTUOLA, A. Faut pas rendre le mal pour le mal. PRESENCE AFR. N.S. 30 (1960), pp. 77-81.

12,116 UKENI, L. O. Triumph over death. AFR. AFFAIRS 53 (1954), pp. 142-147.

12,117 YEMITAN, E. O. Ijala [a poem]. ODU 8 (1960), pp. 64-66.

12,118 Alajere [messages from a Yoruba god]. BO 16 (1964), pp. 38-41.

12,119 Yoruba poems. ODU 8 (1960), pp. 67-69.

Law

12,120 AJAYI, F. A. The future of customary law in Nigeria. THE FUTURE OF CUSTOMARY LAW IN AFRICA, 1956, pp. 42-69.

12,121 AJAYI, F. A. The interaction of English law with customary law in Western Nigeria. J. AFR. LAW 4 (1960), pp. 40-50, 98-114.

12,122 A[LLOTT], A. N. Western region of Nigeria [law reform]. J. AFR. LAW 3 (1959), pp. 116-118.

12,123 ANDERSON, J. N. D. Conflict of laws in Northern Nigeria. J. AFR. LAW 1 (1957), pp. 87-98.

12,124 ARMSTRONG, R. G. Intestate succession among the Idoma. STUD. IN THE LAWS OF SUCCESSION IN NIGERIA, 1965, pp. 212-229.

12,125 ARNOTT, D. W. Councils and courts among the Tiv—traditional concepts and alien institutions in a non-Moslem tribe of Northern Nigeria. J. AFR. LAW 2 (1958), pp. 19-25.

12,126 BOOTH, J. D. L. Application of the direct taxation ordinance in Eastern Nigeria. J. AFR. ADM. 8 (1956), pp. 74-82.

12,127 BOSTON, J. S. Igala inheritance and succession. STUD. IN THE LAWS OF SUCCESSION IN NIGERIA, 1965, pp. 174-211.

12,128 BROOKE, N. T. Some legal aspects of land tenure in Nigeria. AFR. STUD. 5 (1946), pp. 211-220.

12,129 DENNETT, R. E. Notes on the land laws in the western province of southern Nigeria. J. AFR. SOC. 9 (1910), pp. 129-145.

12,130 DERRETT, J. D. M. Succession in Nigeria. The patchwork of the present scene and the common problems of the future. STUD. IN THE LAWS OF SUCCESSION IN NIGERIA, 1965, pp. 1-32.

12,131 EKINEH, A. Human rights and civil liberties and the role of the lawyer in protecting them. COMM. AND EMP. LAW CONF. 2 (1960), pp. 114-121.

12,132 ELIAS, T. O. Legal education in Nigeria. J. AFR. LAW 6 (1962), pp. 117-125.

12,133 ELIAS, T. O. La nouvelle constitution du Nigéria et la protection des droits de l'homme et des libertés fondamentales. J. INT. COMM. JURISTS 2, no. ii (1959-1960), pp. 30-47.

12,134 EZEANI, A. O. N. The legal effect of religious marriages: recent cases in Nigeria. NLJ 1 (1965), pp. 227-231.

12,135 FORDE, D. Justice and judgment among the southern Ibo under colonial rule. AFR. LAW: ADAPTATION AND DEVELOPMENT, 1965, pp. 79-96.

12,136 FOWLER, W. Some observations on the Western Region Local Government Law, 1952 (No. 1 of 1953). J. AFR. ADM. 5 (1953), pp. 119-123.

12,137 GOWER, L. C. B. Nigerian statutes and customary law. NLJ 1 (1964), pp. 73-92.

12,138 GROVE, D. L. The "sentinels" of liberty? The Nigerian judiciary and fundamental rights. J. AFR. LAW 7 (1963), pp. 152-171.

12,139 HARRINGTON, E. M. Ogwu v. Leventis Motors Limited: a case study of conditions and warranties. NLJ 1 (1965), pp. 289-292.

12,140 HARRIS, R. Intestate succession among the Mbembe of South-Eastern Nigeria. STUD. IN THE LAWS OF SUCCESSION IN NIGERIA, 1965, pp. 91-138.

12,141 HEDGES, R. Y. Liability under the Nigeria criminal code: a historical and comparative study. CHANGING LAW IN DEVELOPING COUNTRIES, 1963, pp. 184-193.

12,142 HUBBARD, P. C. Conflict of laws in Northern Nigeria [with some observations by J. N. D. Anderson]. J. AFR. LAW 3 (1959), pp. 85-90.

12,143 IJALAYE, D. A. Precedent in the Nigerian courts. NLJ 1 (1965), pp. 284-288.

12,144 JAMES, R. W. The changing role of land in Southern Nigeria. ODU 1, no. 2 (1965), pp. 3-23.

12,145 JONES, G. I. Ibo land tenure. AFRICA 19 (1949), pp. 309-323.

12,146 KASUNMU, A. B. Intestate succession in Nigeria. NLJ 1 (1964), pp. 50-58.

12,147 KEITH, A. B. Land tenure in Nigeria. J. AFR. SOC. 11 (1912), pp. 325-351.

12,148 KIRK-GREENE, A. H. M. On swearing: an account of some judicial oaths in Northern Nigeria. AFRICA 25 (1955), pp. 43-53.

12,149 LLOYD, P. C. Family property among the Yoruba. J. AFR. LAW 3 (1959), pp. 105-115.

12,150 LLOYD, P. C. Some modern developments in Yoruba customary land law. J. AFR. ADM. 12 (1960), pp. 11-20.

12,151 LLOYD, P. C. Some notes on the Yoruba rules of succession and on "family property." J. AFR. LAW 3 (1959), pp. 7-32.

12,152 LLOYD, P. C. Some problems of tenancy in Yoruba land tenure. AFR. STUD. 12 (1953), pp. 93-103.

12,153 LLOYD, P. C. Yoruba inheritance and succession. STUD. IN THE LAWS OF SUCCESSION IN NIGERIA, 1965, pp. 139-173.

12,154 LUNING, H. A. The impact of socio-economic factors on the land tenure pattern in Northern Nigeria. J. LOCAL ADM. OV. 4 (1965), pp. 173-182.

12,155 MABOGUNJE, A. L. Some comments on land tenure in Egba division, Western Nigeria. AFRICA 31 (1961), pp. 258-269.

12,156 MARSHALL, O. R. A critique of the property legislation of Western Nigeria. NLJ 1 (1965), pp. 151-172.

12,157 McDOWELL, C. M. An introduction to the problems of ownership of land in Northern Nigeria. NLJ 1 (1965), pp. 202-226.

12,158 MEEK, C. K. Ibo law. ESSAYS PRESENTED TO C. G. SELIGMAN, 1934, pp. 209-226.

12,159 MEEK, C. K. Law and authority in a Nigerian tribe. A study in indirect rule. J. AFR. SOC. 37 (1938), pp. 115-118.

12,160 MESSENGER, J. C. The role of proverbs in a Nigerian judicial system. SOUTHWESTERN J. ANTHR. 15 (1959), pp. 64-73.

12,161 MILNER, A. Ahmadu Bello University, Zaria, Northern Nigeria. Faculty of Law. J. AFR. LAW 7 (1963), pp. 116-118.

12,162 MILNER, A. The sanctions of customary criminal law: a study in social control. NLJ 1 (1965), pp. 173-193.

12,163 NAISH, M. E. A redefinition of provocation under the criminal code. NLJ 1 (1964), pp. 10-25.

12,164 NWOGUGU, E. I. Legitimacy in Nigerian law. J. AFR. LAW 8 (1964), pp. 91-105.

12,165 OBI, S. N. C. Women's property and succession thereto in modern Ibo law (Eastern Nigeria). J. AFR. LAW 6 (1962), pp. 6-18.

12,166 OGWURIKE, C. The aims of Nigerian federalism. NLJ 1 (1965), pp. 194-201.

12,167 OHONBALU, O. Current trends in the Nigerian customary law of mortgage. NLJ 1 (1964), pp. 1-9.

12,168 OKONKWO, C. O. Accidental manslaughter. NLJ 1 (1965), pp. 253-259.

12,169 OKONKWO, C. O. A note on reform of the Nigerian Criminal Code. NLJ 1 (1965), pp. 293-299.

12,170 OTTENBERG, S. Inheritance and succession in Afikpo. STUD. IN THE LAWS OF SUCCESSION IN NIGERIA, 1965, pp. 33-90.

12,171 PARK, A. E. W. The cession of territory and private land rights: a reconsideration of the Tijani case. NLJ 1 (1964), pp. 38-49.

12,172 PARK, A. E. W. A dual system of land tenure: the experience of southern Nigeria. J. AFR. LAW 9 (1965), pp. 1-19.

12,173 PARTRIDGE, C. Native law and custom in Egbaland. J. AFR. SOC. 10 (1911), pp. 422-433.

12,174 REWANE, O. N. Contempt of court in Nigerian criminal law. J. AFR. LAW 1 (1957), pp. 172-185.

12,175 RICHARDSON, S. S. "Opting out": an experiment with jurisdiction in Northern Nigeria. J. AFR. LAW 8 (1964), pp. 20-28.

12,176 ROWLING, C. W. An analysis of factors effecting changes in land tenure in Africa. J. AFR. ADM. 4 (1952), Supplement, pp. 21-28.

12,177 SALACUSE, J. W. Birth, death, and the Marriage Act: some problems in conflict of laws. NLJ 1 (1964), pp. 59-72.

12,178 SEIDMAN, R. B. Constitutional standards of judicial review of administrative action in Nigeria. NLJ 1 (1965), pp. 232-252.

12,179 SMITH, M. G. Hausa inheritance and succession. STUD. IN THE LAWS OF SUCCESSION IN NIGERIA, 1965, pp. 230-281.

12,180 SOFOLUWE, G. O. A study of divorce cases in Igbo-Ora. NJESS 7 (1965), pp. 51-62.

12,181 UCHENDU, V. C. Livestock tenancy among Igbo of southern Nigeria. AFR. STUD. 23 (1964), pp. 89-94.

12,182 UPWARD, A. In the provincial court: notes of cases tried in the provincial court of Kabba, Northern Nigeria. J. AFR. SOC. 3 (1904), pp. 405-409.

12,183 UTTON, A. E. Nigeria and the United States: some constitutional comparisons. J. AFR. LAW 9 (1965), pp. 40-59.

12,184 WILLOUGHBY, P. G. Land registration in Nigeria: past, present and future. NLJ 1 (1965), pp. 260-283.

12,185 The centre and the regions in Nigeria. CORONA 4 (1952), pp. 100-104.

12,186 The constitutional changes of 1st. October, 1963. NLJ 1 (1964), pp. 93-99.

12,187 The creation of the Mid-West Region. NLJ 1 (1964), pp. 100-102.

12,188 Eastern region of Nigeria: Report of the Committee on Bride Price. J. AFR. LAW 1 (1957), pp. 11-12.

12,189 Ecoles de Droit à Lovanium et à Lagos (Nigeria). GENEVE-AFR. 1 (1962), p. 216.

12,190 Federal Law School, Lagos. J. AFR. LAW 6 (1962), p. 125.

12,191 Federation of Nigeria: A Report on the Registration of Title to Land in the Federal Territory of Lagos, by S. Rowton Simpson. J. AFR. LAW 2 (1958), pp. 79-81.

12,192 Federation of Nigeria [The Nigeria (Constitution) Order in Council, 1960]. J. AFR. LAW 4 (1960), p. 149.

12,193 The Institute of Administration, Zaria, Northern Nigeria. J. AFR. LAW 6 (1962), pp. 121-123.

12,194 Judicial and legal development in the Northern Region of Nigeria. J. AFR. LAW 7 (1963), pp. 70-71.

12,195 Land tenure in Western Nigeria. J. AFR. LAW 1 (1957), pp. 80-81.

12,196 Legal education in Nigeria. J. AFR. LAW 3 (1959), pp. 84-85.

12,197 Legal education in Nigeria. Federation of Nigeria: Report of the Committee on the Future of the Nigeria Legal Profession. J. AFR. LAW 4 (1960), pp. 3-4.

12,198 Native Courts in Nigeria. J. AFR. ADM. 5 (1953), pp. 80-94, 140-143.

12,199 Proof of customary law. J. AFR. LAW 1 (1957), pp. 128-130.

12,200 Reorganisation of the Legal and Judicial Systems of the Northern Region; 1958 [a statement laid on the Table of Northern Nigeria's Legislative Houses]. J. AFR. ADM. 11 (1959), pp. 159-165.

12,201 School of Arabic Studies, Kano. J. AFR. LAW 6 (1962), pp. 123-124.

12,202 University of Ife. J. AFR. LAW 6 (1962), p. 125.

12,203 University of Lagos. J. AFR. LAW 6 (1962), p. 125.

12,204 University of Nigeria, Nsukka, Faculty of Law. J. AFR. LAW 6 (1962), p. 124.

See also 3646, 10702, 10898, 10992, 11734.

Religion

12,205 HAJJ, M. AL-. The Fulani concept of Jihād: Shehu Uthmān dān Fodio. ODU 1, no. 1 (1964), pp. 45-58.

12,206 AJAYI, W. O. The beginnings of the African bishopric on the Niger. BULL. SOC. AFR. CHURCH HIST. 1 (1964), pp. 92-99.

12,207 AJAYI, W. O. The Niger Delta Pastorage Church, 1892-1902. BULL. SOC. AFR. CHURCH HIST. 2 (1965), pp. 37-54.

12,208 AYANDELE, E. A. Missionary enterprise versus indirect rule among the Angass of the Bauchi Plateau, 1906-14. BULL. SOC. AFR. CHURCH HIST. 2 (1965), pp. 73-83.

12,209 COMHAIRE, J. La vie religieuse à Lagos. ZAIRE 3 (1949), pp. 549-556.

12,210 FISHER, H. J. The Ahmadiyya movement in Nigeria. ST. ANTONY'S PAPERS 10 (1961), pp. 60-88.

12,211 ILOGU, E. The contribution of the Church to national unity in Nigeria. INT. REV. MISSIONS 53 (1964), pp. 272-280.

12,212 ILOGU, E. Nationalism and the Church in Nigeria. INT. REV. MISSIONS 51 (1962), pp. 439-450.

12,213 MACDONALD, R. K. Church union: Nigeria. THE CHURCH IN CHANGING AFRICA, 1958, pp. 78-83.

12,214 MESSENGER, J. C., Jr. Reinterpretations of Christian and indigenous belief in a Nigerian nativist church. AMER. ANTHR. 62 (1960), pp. 268-278.

12,215 MURRAY, A. V. A missionary educational policy for Southern Nigeria. INT. REV. MISSIONS 21 (1932), pp. 516-531.

12,216 O'CONNELL, J. Government and politics in the Yoruba African churches: the claims of tradition and modernity. ODU 2, no.1 (1965), pp. 92-108.

12,217 ODUTOLA, S. O. Islam as it affects life in Nigeria. THE CHURCH IN CHANGING AFRICA, 1958, pp. 65-67.

12,218 PALMER, H. R. An early Fulani conception of Islam. J. AFR. SOC. 14 (1914-1915), pp. 53-59, 185-192.

12,219 PARNIS, R. O. A visit to Aiyetoro. NIGERIAN FIELD 30 (1965), pp. 37-40.

12,220 PILKINGTON, F. The church in Nigeria. AFR. AFFAIRS 56 (1957), pp. 158-160.

12,221 PILKINGTON, F. Islam in Nigeria. CONTEMP. REV. 192 (1957), pp. 41-46.

12,222 PRIOR, K. H. An African diocese adapts a rural programme. INT. REV. MISSIONS 36 (1947), pp. 370-378.

12,223 TURNER, H. W. The church of the Lord: the expansion of a Nigerian independent church in Sierra Leone and Ghana. J. AFR. HIST. 3 (1962), pp. 91-110.

12,224 TURNER, H. W. Prophets and politics: a Nigerian testcase. BULL. SOC. AFR. CHURCH HIST. 2 (1965), pp. 97-118.

12,225 WESCOTT, R. W. Ancient Egypt and modern Africa. [The Religion of the Yoruba by J. O. Lucas; The Divine Kingship in Ghana by E. L. R. Meyerowitz]. J. AFR. HIST. 2 (1961), pp. 311-321.

12,226 WILKIE, A. W. and MacGREGOR, J. K. In the Calabar mission of the United Free Church of Scotland. INT. REV. MISSIONS 3 (1914), pp. 742-747.

See also 9601.

Science

12,227 ADAMS, R. F. G. et al. Hartlaub's Duck in southern Nigeria. NIGERIAN FIELD 4 (1935), pp. 22-29.

12,228 ALLISON, P. A. Elephant in the Kabba province. NIGERIAN FIELD 14 (1949), pp. 5-10.

12,229 ALLISON, P. A. Elephant in the Ondo province. NIGERIAN FIELD 11 (1943), pp. 180-184.

12,230 ALLISON, P. A. Regional governments and wild life. NIGERIAN FIELD 24 (1959), pp. 43-45.

12,231 AMOS, R. L. Elephant adventure at Owo. NIGERIAN FIELD 23 (1958), pp. 186-190.

12,232 BALDRY, D. A. The vesicating rove beetle (Paederus sabaeus). NIGERIAN FIELD 27 (1962), pp. 184-189.

12,233 BALL, J. C. H. Rearing a harnessed antelope. NIGERIAN FIELD 16 (1951), pp. 159-163.

12,234 BALL, J. C. H. Rearing leopard cubs. NIGERIAN FIELD 17 (1952), pp. 18-22.

12,235 BASSIR, O. Une diététique africaine. PRESENCE AFR. N.S. 34-35 (1960-1961), pp. 207-210.

12,236 BEAL, W. P. B. The manatee as a food animal. NIGERIAN FIELD 8 (1939), pp. 124-126.

12,237 BIRKET-SMITH, J. S. R. and HAMBLER, D. J. A biological garden in Ibadan. NIGERIAN FIELD 26 (1961), pp. 10-13.

12,238 BOORMAN, J. The hawkmoths of Nigeria. NIGERIAN FIELD 25 (1960), pp. 148-172; 26 (1961), pp. 17-42.

12,239 BOSTOCK, D. H. Nigerian pets. IV. NIGERIAN FIELD 6 (1937), pp. 83-84.

12,240 BOURDILLON, Sir B. Terns on Lagos Beach, Nigeria. NIGERIAN FIELD 12 (1947), pp. 20-22.

12,241 BOURKE, D. O'D. The life of the black-faced Dioch (Quelea quelea). NIGERIAN FIELD 25 (1960), pp. 3-12.

12,242 BRICE-SMITH, H. M. Birdmen and meteors in N. Nigeria. NIGERIAN FIELD 25 (1960), pp. 128-131.

12,243 BRIDGES, A. F. B. Garden planning. NIGERIAN FIELD 16 (1951), pp. 83-87.

12,244 BROWN, A. The nesting of a grey hornbill. NIGERIAN FIELD 9 (1940), pp. 80-84.

12,245 BROWN, H. The bagworm moth (Psychidae). NIGERIAN FIELD 22 (1957), pp. 86-90.

12,246 BROWN, H. The life history of Phromnia superba Mel. (Flatidae). NIGERIAN FIELD 20 (1955), pp. 99-105.

12,247 BUNSURU. Wild life in the Benue valley fifty years ago. NIGERIAN FIELD 24 (1959), pp. 35-43.

12,248 C., A. J. More bush path flowers. NIGERIAN FIELD 3 (1934), pp. 112-115.

12,249 C., F. Bushbuck (Tragelaphus scriptus scriptus). NIGERIAN FIELD 1, no. 3 (1932), pp. 17-18.

12,250 C., F. Field notes on Nigerian mammals. NIGERIAN FIELD 9 (1940), pp. 10-16.

12,251 C., F. Field notes on roan. NIGERIAN FIELD 8 (1939), p. 10.

12,252 C., F. Field notes on white oryx. NIGERIAN FIELD 8 (1939), pp. 10-11.

12,253 C., F. Notes on gorilla. NIGERIAN FIELD 3 (1934), pp. 92-102.

12,254 CAILLEUX, A. and MONOD, TH. Note sur la lithologie des grès de la série fluvio-volcanique du plateau de Jos (Nigeria). BULL. IFAN 12 (1950), pp. 1146-1150.

12,255 CARPENTER, A. J. Wild flowers of Nigeria, III. NIGERIAN FIELD 7 (1938), pp. 35-40.

12,256 CHARADRIUS. The Nigerian white-throated frankolin (Francolinus Albogularis Gambagae). NIGERIAN FIELD 2, no. 8 (1933), pp. 16-17.

12,257 CHUBB, L. T. A visit to the Obudu grass plateau. NIGERIAN FIELD 14 (1949), pp. 133-141.

12,258 CLARKE, J. D. Migration and other problems: some notes and queries. NIGERIAN FIELD 1, no. 3 (1932), pp. 19-21.

12,259 COLLIER, F. S. Field notes on the hartebeests and gazelles. NIGERIAN FIELD 7 (1938), pp. 149-152.

12,260 COLLIER, F. S. Field notes on waterbuck, kob and reedbuck. NIGERIAN FIELD 7 (1938), pp. 156-157.

12,261 COLLIER, F. S. Notes on the preservation of the fauna of Nigeria. NIGERIAN FIELD 4 (1935), pp. 3-13, 51-62, 101-113.

12,262 COLLIER, F. S. A shooting trip to Termitt. NIGERIAN FIELD 8 (1939), pp. 14-20.

12,263 COOPER, L. G. Some Nigerian high forest trees. NIGERIAN FIELD 22 (1957), pp. 21-36.

12,264 COOPER, L. G. A Sunbird's nest. NIGERIAN FIELD 20 (1955), p. 143.

12,265 COTTERELL, G. C. B. Leopard. NIGERIAN FIELD 1, no. 3 (1932), pp. 11-15.

12,266 COZENS, A. B. A mouse new to Nigeria. NIGERIAN FIELD 17 (1952), pp. 159-160.

12,267 COZENS, A. B. The otter shrew. NIGERIAN FIELD 15 (1950), pp. 76-83.

12,268 COZENS, A. B. The ranges of the dwarf and royal antelopes. NIGERIAN FIELD 16 (1951), pp. 14-19.

12,269 COZENS, A. B. and MARCHANT, S. A contribution to the fauna of Owerri province. NIGERIAN FIELD 17 (1952), pp. 70-79, 116-130.

12,270 DAWS, H. H. Ozala Udi's last elephant. NIGERIAN FIELD 1, no. 3 (1932), p. 16.

12,271 DELF, B. H. and HARRIS, K. M. Notes on Nigerian hawkmoths. NIGERIAN FIELD 29 (1964), pp. 150-160.

12,272 DEMA, I. S. The application of recent advances in the knowledge of nutrition to community development in Nigeria. PROC. INT. CONG. AFR. 1 (1962), pp. 318-328.

12,273 DENDROPHILUS. The camwood (Pterocarpus soyauxii). NIGERIAN FIELD 1, no. 3 (1932), pp. 28-33.

12,274 DOBBS, K. A. Birds of Sokoto, 1948. NIGERIAN FIELD 14 (1949), pp. 102-105.

12,275 DOBBS, K. A. Some birds of Sokoto, Northern Nigeria, with brief notes on their status. NIGERIAN FIELD 24 (1959), pp. 102-119, 185-191.

12,276 DUNGER, G. T. Wase rock—its history, geology, fauna and climbs. NIGERIAN FIELD 30 (1965), pp. 148-184.

12,277 ELGOOD, J. H. The birds of the Obudu plateau, eastern region of Nigeria. NIGERIAN FIELD 30 (1965), pp. 60-69.

12,278 FAIRBAIRN, W. A. The Ahanta francolin. NIGERIAN FIELD 6 (1937), p. 117.

12,279 FAIRBAIRN, W. A. The black bee-eater. NIGERIAN FIELD 4 (1935), pp. 62-63.

12,280 FAIRBAIRN, W. A. The flight of birds. NIGERIAN FIELD 8 (1939), pp. 56-58.

12,281 FAIRBAIRN, W. A. Lavaillant's cuckoo. NIGERIAN FIELD 6 (1937), pp. 65-67.

12,282 FAIRBAIRN, W. A. The speed of birds. NIGERIAN FIELD 7 (1938), pp. 120-121.

12,283 GAMBLES, R. M. A dragonfly migration at Vom. NIGERIAN FIELD 16 (1951), pp. 135-138.

12,284 GILL, H. C. A local leave in Northern game country. NIGERIAN FIELD 7 (1938), pp. 21-27.

12,285 GOLDING, F. D. Nigerian pets. II—Aloysius, the hornbill. NIGERIAN FIELD 4 (1935), pp. 123-126.

12,286 GOLDING, F. D. Nigerian pets. V—"Whiskers" the palm squirrel. NIGERIAN FIELD 7 (1938), pp. 121-123.

12,287 GOLDING, F. D. A nomad's notes on Nigerian game birds. NIGERIAN FIELD 3 (1934), pp. 70-72.

12,288 GOLDING, F. D. Some random observations on driver ants. NIGERIAN FIELD 9 (1940), pp. 91-93.

12,289 GOLDING, F. D. The voyage of the "Mallard." [Tour made by an entomologist.] NIGERIAN FIELD 12 (1947), pp. 75-79.

12,290 GREGORY, H. Eocene fossil shells of Southern Nigeria. NIGERIAN FIELD 14 (1949), pp. 70-73.

12,291 GREY, R. F. A. Manillas. NIGERIAN FIELD 16 (1951), pp. 52-66.

12,292 HAIG, E. F. G. The butterflies of Nigeria. III. NIGERIAN FIELD 6 (1937), pp. 71-76.

12,293 HAIG, E. F. G. The butterflies of Nigeria: IV. Nymphalidae. NIGERIAN FIELD 7 (1938), pp. 41-42.

12,294 HAIG, E. F. G. The butterflies of Nigeria: V. Nymphalidae: Charaxidinae. NIGERIAN FIELD 7 (1938), pp. 61-80.

12,295 HAIG, E. F. G. A little-known Nigerian nymphalid. NIGERIAN FIELD 13 (1948), pp. 68-69.

12,296 HAIG, E. F. G. Some large Nigerian moths. NIGERIAN FIELD 2, no. 8 (1933), pp. 18-23.

12,297 HARDIE, A. D. K. Okoubaka, a rare juju tree. NIGERIAN FIELD 28 (1963), pp. 70-72.

12,298 HARDY, J. The ABO blood groups of Southern Nigerians and their relation to the history of the area. JRAI 92 (1962), pp. 223-231.

12,299 HARPER, F. J. Concerning Terebra Micans. NIGERIAN FIELD 14 (1949), pp. 167-168.

12,300 HARPER, F. J. The genus eulophia. NIGERIAN FIELD 16 (1951), pp. 103-106, 149-152; 17 (1952), pp. 181-182.

12,301 HARPER, F. J. The genus eulophidium and a footnote to the genus eulophia. NIGERIAN FIELD 18 (1953), pp. 174-176.

12,302 HARPER, F. J. Notes on certain species of the botanical genera Gladiolus and Eulophia. NIGERIAN FIELD 14 (1949), pp. 68-69.

12,303 HARPER, F. J. Notes on some common Nigerian orchids. III. NIGERIAN FIELD 17 (1952), pp. 23-24.

12,304 HATCH, W. R. Bird notes, Obudu. NIGERIAN FIELD 4 (1935), pp. 14-15.

12,305 HEPPER, F. N. A botanist in Adamawa. NIGERIAN FIELD 27 (1962), pp. 54-78, 100-122.

12,306 HOLLIS, R. Reflections on baobabs. NIGERIAN FIELD 28 (1963), pp. 134-138.

12,307 HOPKINS, B. The screw pine in Nigeria. NIGERIAN FIELD 27 (1962), pp. 36-44.

12,308 HUGHES, J. C. S. My first bushcow. NIGERIAN FIELD 20 (1955), pp. 182-184.

12,309 JEFFREYS, M. D. W. Crabs. NIGERIAN FIELD 8 (1939), pp. 62-64.

12,310 JEFFREYS, M. D. W. Discoveries and re-discoveries. [Birds.] NIGERIAN FIELD 6 (1937), pp. 157-159.

12,311 JEFFREYS, M. D. W. The jigger or sand-flea. NIGERIAN FIELD 14 (1949), pp. 31-32.

12,312 JEFFREYS, M. D. W. Locusts. NIGERIAN FIELD 10 (1941), pp. 112-121.

12,313 JEFFREYS, M. D. W. Notes on some Nigerian crabs. NIGERIAN FIELD 16 (1951), pp. 183-185.

12,314 JEFFREYS, M. D. W. Notes on some Nigerian river fish. NIGERIAN FIELD 16 (1951), pp. 130-135.

12,315 JEFFREYS, M. D. W. Some sources of salt in Nigeria. NIGERIAN FIELD 9 (1940), pp. 37-40.

12,316 JEFFREYS, M. D. W. Some West African meteorites. NIGERIAN FIELD 26 (1961), pp. 13-14.

12,317 JEFFREYS, M. D. W. and HAIG, E. F. G. The cream swallowtail butterfly. NIGERIAN FIELD 13 (1948), pp. 20-23.

12,318 JELLIFE, D. B. Infant feeding among the Yoruba of Ibadan. MALNUTRITION IN AFRICAN WOMEN..., 1952, pp. 230-241.

12,319 JONES, G. I. Camera notes: on the making of records. NIGERIAN FIELD 9 (1940), pp. 33-37.

12,320 KEAY, R. W. Nigerian orchids: introductory. NIGERIAN FIELD 16 (1951), pp. 101-102.

12,321 KETLEY, H. C. Bird life of Okene reservoir. NIGERIAN FIELD 7 (1938), pp. 124-125.

12,322 LA CHARD, L. W. The arrow-poisons of Northern Nigeria. J. AFR. SOC. 5 (1905), pp. 22-27.

12,323 LAMBERT, W. A leper colony in Nigeria. J. AFR. SOC. 36 (1937), pp. 213-216.

12,324 LEESON, F. The external characters of Colubride snakes. NIGERIAN FIELD 12 (1947), pp. 6-19.

12,325 LEGER, R. G. T. The larger butterflies of the Obudu plateau. NIGERIAN FIELD 30 (1965), pp. 69-81.

12,326 LEWIS, F. A. Notes on the larger fauna of the Benue valley. NIGERIAN FIELD 20 (1955), pp. 18-24.

12,327 LISHMAN, M. Nigerian pets, III—"Fussy" the leopard. NIGERIAN FIELD 6 (1937), pp. 29-32.

12,328 MACKAY, J. H. and WARDROP, T. N. The forest trees of Southern Nigeria. NIGERIAN FIELD 7 (1938), pp. 171-180.

12,329 MacKENZIE, R. F. The Sokoto government gardens. NIGERIAN FIELD 22 (1957), pp. 135-139.

12,330 MacLAREN, P. I. R. Bird notes from Nigeria. NIGERIAN FIELD 18 (1953), pp. 165-171.

12,331 MacLAREN, P. I. R. The fish and fisheries of the Lower Ogun River. NIGERIAN FIELD 15 (1950), pp. 177-181.

12,332 MacLAREN, P. I. R. Nigerian fishes and their palatability. NIGERIAN FIELD 19 (1954), pp. 4-15.

12,333 MacLAREN, P. I. R. The sea and creek birds of Nigeria. NIGERIAN FIELD 17 (1952), pp. 160-174; 18 (1953), pp. 20-28.

12,334 MacLAREN, P. I. R. Wader migrants at Lagos. NIGERIAN FIELD 15 (1950), pp. 85-87.

12,335 MANN, M. A. Birds of Ofemiri, Owerri Province. NIGERIAN FIELD 17 (1952), pp. 175-180.

12,336 MANN, M. A. Four Owerri kingfishers. NIGERIAN FIELD 18 (1953), pp. 28-30.

12,337 MARCHANT, S. Aspects of the fauna of the Owerri province. NIGERIAN FIELD 14 (1949), pp. 47-51.

12,338 MARCHANT, S. Bird notes from a Kaduna garden. NIGERIAN FIELD 28 (1963), pp. 63-65; 65-68.

12,339 MARCHANT, S. Calls of some forest birds. NIGERIAN FIELD 16 (1951), pp. 70-79; 107-112.

12,340 MARCHANT, S. Charaxid butterflies of Owerri. NIGERIAN FIELD 14 (1949), pp. 160-162.

12,341 MARCHANT, S. Notes on a migration of the butterfly: Libythea labdaca. NIGERIAN FIELD 15 (1950), pp. 88-90.

12,342 MARCHANT, S. On keeping bird notes. NIGERIAN FIELD 15 (1950), pp. 173-176.

12,343 MARCHANT, S. The scaly francolin: francolinus squamatus squamatus cassin. NIGERIAN FIELD 16 (1951), pp. 164-166.

12,344 MARCHANT, S. Six West African migratory birds. NIGERIAN FIELD 14 (1949), pp. 19-27.

12,345 MARCHANT, S. Some bird notes from the Upper Imo River, Owerri Province. NIGERIAN FIELD 10 (1941), pp. 121-125.

12,346 MARCHANT, S. The West African wood-owl. NIGERIAN FIELD 13 (1948), pp. 16-20.

12,347 MARSHALL, H. F. River birds of the Benin division. NIGERIAN FIELD 9 (1940), pp. 22-32.

12,348 MASON, P. F. A brief faunal survey of North-western Benin. NIGERIAN FIELD 9 (1940), pp. 17-22, 68-80.

12,349 MASON, P. F. Nature teasers No. 2: three black long-tailed birds. NIGERIAN FIELD 15 (1950), pp. 90-92.

12,350 MERRETT, W. E. S. Bird notes, Gadau. NIGERIAN FIELD 4 (1935), pp. 13-14.

12,351 NEWTON, R. Notes on bishop-birds and whydahs in the Cameroons. NIGERIAN FIELD 6 (1937), pp. 151-156.

12,352 NEWTON, T. C. A further criticism of Mr. Collier's "Notes on the preservation of the fauna of Nigeria." NIGERIAN FIELD 6 (1937), pp. 19-22.

12,353 NICOL, D. Foods of Western Nigeria. MALNUTRITION IN AFRICAN WOMEN..., 1952, pp. 262-264.

12,354 NICOL, D. Review of nutritional research and surveys in Nigeria. MALNUTRITION IN AFRICAN MOTHERS..., 1952, pp. 70-77.

12,355 NIELSON, M. S. Common seaweeds at Lagos. NIGERIAN FIELD 23 (1958), pp. 34-44.

12,356 ODEKU, E. L. Peculiar subgalfal inclusion cysts. GHANA MED. J. 4 (1965), pp. 37-41.

12,357 OLIVER, B. Nigeria's useful plants. NIGERIAN FIELD 23 (1958), pp. 147-171; 24 (1959), pp. 13-34, 54-71, 121-143, 160-182; 25 (1960), pp. 46-48, 174-192; 26 (1961), pp. 70-90, 170-180; 27 (1962), p. 48.

12,358 PASQUAL, J. H. The chameleons of Nigeria. NIGERIAN FIELD 6 (1937), pp. 32-34.

12,359 PASQUAL, J. R. H. The biting mechanism of Atractaspis. NIGERIAN FIELD 27 (1962), pp. 137-142.

12,360 PEARSON, V. Bird notes, Lagos. NIGERIAN FIELD 8 (1939), pp. 21-22.

12,361 POLLARD, W. G. An over-fed Ark. NIGERIAN FIELD 22 (1957), pp. 120-128.

12,362 POMEROY, A. W. J. The irritating hairs of the wild silk moths of Nigeria. BULL. IMP. INST. 19 (1921), pp. 311-318.

12,363 POWER, A. D. Health and education in Nigeria. J. AFR. SOC. 34 (1935), pp. 408-422.

12,364 PRIESTLEY, N. DE B. Elephant in North Nigeria. NIGERIAN FIELD 27 (1962), pp. 170-172.

12,365 PRING, R. W. and ROCHE, P. The butterflies of Nigeria. NIGERIAN FIELD 17 (1952), pp. 53-66.

12,366 RAINS, A. B. A field key to the commoner genera of Nigerian grasses. NIGERIAN FIELD 22 (1957), pp. 99-119, 148-159.

12,367 ROCHE, P. Life history of a Nigerian lymantriid moth. NIGERIAN FIELD 20 (1955), pp. 35-38.

12,368 ROCHE, P. Notes on Nigerian butterflies of the genus Charaxes. NIGERIAN FIELD 21 (1956), pp. 163-167.

12,369 ROCHE, P. A processionary butterfly caterpillar in Nigeria. NIGERIAN FIELD 23 (1958), pp. 120-123.

12,370 ROMER, J. D. et al. Introducing some common Nigerian reptiles. NIGERIAN FIELD 18 (1953), pp. 70-75.

12,371 ROSEVEAR, D. R. The ant-eaters of Nigeria. NIGERIAN FIELD 6 (1937), pp. 11-14.

12,372 ROSEVEAR, D. R. The antelopes of Nigeria. NIGERIAN FIELD 6 (1937), pp. 106-113, 147-150; 7 (1938), pp. 16-17, 52-54, 109-112, 153-155; 8 (1939), pp. 9-10.

12,373 ROSEVEAR, D. R. The civets of Nigeria. NIGERIAN FIELD 4 (1935), pp. 114-122.

12,374 ROSEVEAR, D. R. The flesh-eating mammals of Nigeria. NIGERIAN FIELD 4 (1935), pp. 64-69.

12,375 ROSEVEAR, D. R. The hoofed mammals of Nigeria. NIGERIAN FIELD 8 (1939), pp. 48-51, 104-107, 136-138; 9 (1940), pp. 7-10.

12,376 ROSEVEAR, D. R. The insect eaters of Nigeria. NIGERIAN FIELD 10 (1941), pp. 98-103.

12,377 ROSEVEAR, D. R. The lemurs of Nigeria. NIGERIAN FIELD 4 (1935), pp. 16-21.

12,378 ROSEVEAR, D. R. The mongooses of Nigeria. NIGERIAN FIELD 4 (1935), pp. 165-170.

12,379 ROSEVEAR, D. R. Nigerian animals that don't exist. NIGERIAN FIELD 13 (1948), pp. 6-14.

12,380 ROSEVEAR, D. R. Note on a new otter. NIGERIAN FIELD 8 (1939), p. 47.

12,381 ROSEVEAR, D. R. On bringing up a hare. NIGERIAN FIELD 14 (1949), pp. 41-47.

12,382 ROSEVEAR, D. R. The rodents of Nigeria. NIGERIAN FIELD 14 (1949), pp. 93-101; 15 (1950), pp. 4-18, 101-108, 148-172.

12,383 RUSSELL, C. E. B. The leprosy problem in Nigeria. J. AFR. SOC. 37 (1938), pp. 66-71.

12,384 RUSSELL, T. A. The Lagos botanic station: a forgotten garden. NIGERIAN FIELD 22 (1957), pp. 130-135.

12,385 S., F. The identification of stars in Nigeria. NIGERIAN FIELD 3 (1934), pp. 63-66.

12,386 SANDER, F. A list of birds of Lagos and its environs, with brief notes on their status. NIGERIAN FIELD 21 (1956), pp. 147-162; 22 (1957), pp. 5-17, 55-69.

12,387 SANDER, F. Some effects of swamp drainage on the distribution of birds in the Lagos area. NIGERIAN FIELD 20 (1955), pp. 4-15.

12,388 SAUNDERS, L. H. Miscellaneous fruit for the Nigerian garden: some notes for the amateur. NIGERIAN FIELD 3 (1934), pp. 125-127.

12,389 SERLE, W. The Cameroon mountain francolin. NIGERIAN FIELD 27 (1962), pp. 34-36.

12,390 SERLE, W. The chattering grass-warbler. NIGERIAN FIELD 14 (1949), pp. 28-29.

12,391 SERLE, W. The double-collared sunbird. NIGERIAN FIELD 16 (1951), pp. 20-21.

12,392 SERLE, W. Gilbert's babbler. NIGERIAN FIELD 15 (1950), p. 84.

12,393 SERLE, W. Some breeding records of birds at Calabar, Eastern Nigeria. NIGERIAN FIELD 24 (1959), pp. 45-48.

12,394 SERLE, W. Some breeding records of birds at Ndian, British Southern Cameroons. NIGERIAN FIELD 24 (1959), pp. 76-79.

12,395 SERLE, W. Some breeding records of birds at Sapele, Western Nigeria. NIGERIAN FIELD 23 (1958), pp. 70-75.

12,396 SERLE, W. The white-spotted pigmy rail. NIGERIAN FIELD 20 (1955), pp. 76-77.

12,397 SERLE, W. and YOUNG, C. G. The stripe-breasted swallow. NIGERIAN FIELD 13 (1948), pp. 15-16.

12,398 SERVICE, M. W. The problem of stink bugs in Northern Nigeria. NIGERIAN FIELD 26 (1961), pp. 183-188.

12,399 SHARLAND, R. E. Bird singing in Nigeria and Ghana, 1962, 1963, 1964. NIGERIAN FIELD 28 (1963), pp. 129-131; 29 (1964), pp. 177-180; 30 (1965), pp. 187-189.

12,400 SHARLAND, R. E. Birds of the Benue river. NIGERIAN FIELD 18 (1953), pp. 67-70.

12,401 SHARLAND, R. E. and HARRIS, B. J. Bird ringing in Nigeria and Ghana during 1960. NIGERIAN FIELD 26 (1961), pp. 65-68.

12,402 SHARLAND, R. E. and HARRIS, B. J. West African bird-ringing report for 1958. NIGERIAN FIELD 24 (1959), pp. 72-75.

12,403 SHORTHOSE, W. T. The fauna of Nigeria. NIGERIAN FIELD 1, no. 3 (1932), pp. 3-9.

12,404 SHORTHOSE, W. T. Ningi bush revisited. NIGERIAN FIELD 23 (1958), pp. 172-184.

12,405 SHORTHOSE, W. T. Operation Chad. NIGERIAN FIELD 19 (1954), pp. 148-168.

12,406 SIKES, S. K. The calving of the hinds: sylvicapra grimmia var. coronata—The gray duiker. NIGERIAN FIELD 23 (1958), pp. 55-66.

12,407 SIKES, S. K. A game survey of the Yankan reserve of Northern Nigeria. NIGERIAN FIELD 29 (1964), pp. 54-82, 127-141.

12,408 SIKES, S. K. Nigerian forest and savannah elephants. NIGERIAN FIELD 29 (1964), pp. 9-16.

12,409 SKILLETER, M. Some notes on Kaduna birds. NIGERIAN FIELD 28 (1963), pp. 34-42.

12,410 SMITH, K. G. A dragonfly migration at Lagos. NIGERIAN FIELD 16 (1951), pp. 138-139.

12,411 SMITH, V. W. Further notes on birds breeding near Vom, Northern Nigeria. NIGERIAN FIELD 29 (1964), pp. 100-117, 161-174.

12,412 SMITH, V. W. Some birds which breed near Vom, northern Nigeria. NIGERIAN FIELD 27 (1962), pp. 4-34.

12,413 SMITHIES, F. Ten years' weather in Ibadan. NIGERIAN FIELD 10 (1941), pp. 103-112.

12,414 SPOTTISWOODE, H. Game preservation—ambition or achievement? NIGERIAN FIELD 6 (1937), pp. 114-115.

12,415 SPOTTISWOODE, H. Gunpowder plot. NIGERIAN FIELD 22 (1957), pp. 177-180.

12,416 STAHL, F. Report of the President of the Sapele Sanitary Board for the year 1905. J. AFR. SOC. 6 (1907), pp. 59-64.

12,417 STONES, P. B. Nigerian snakes—a brief conspectus. NIGERIAN FIELD 14 (1949), pp. 151-157.

12,418 STORY, T. H. S. Extermination of game in Northern Nigeria. NIGERIAN FIELD 23 (1958), pp. 142-143.

12,419 T., E. The square stickleback. NIGERIAN FIELD 1, no. 3 (1932), p. 34.

12,420 TAWA, A. A. Dreadful incident: elephant's attack on party at Igbonla area, 19-2-46. NIGERIAN FIELD 17 (1952), pp. 157-158.

12,421 TUGARINOV, A. Age absolu et particularités génétiques des granites du Nigeria et du Cameroun septentrional. PROC. SYMP. GRANITES W. AFR., 1965, pp. 119-123.

12,422 TURNER, D. C. Review of the younger granites of Northern Nigeria. PROC. SYMP. GRANITES W. AFR., 1965, pp. 19-21.

12,423 WELMAN, J. Tiger-fish. CORONA 1, no. 1 (1949), pp. 31-33.

12,424 WILLAN, R. G. M. Game preservation in Nigeria. NIGERIAN FIELD 7 (1938), pp. 28-31.

12,425 WILLIAMS, C. B. Notes on a small collection of Sphingidae from Nigeria. NIGERIAN FIELD 19 (1954), pp. 176-179.

12,426 WILLOUGHBY, R. W. H. Birds of Ibadan reservoir. NIGERIAN FIELD 14 (1949), pp. 142-145.

12,427 WOOD, M. G. A little grebe's nest in Kano. NIGERIAN FIELD 14 (1949), pp. 54-65.

12,428 WOODS, F. J. Manatee. NIGERIAN FIELD 6 (1937), pp. 23-28.

12,429 WOODWARD, S. F. A bat-eating snake. NIGERIAN FIELD 25 (1960), pp. 172-174.

12,430 Bird notes, Enugu, January 1934. NIGERIAN FIELD 3 (1934), pp. 75-76, 123-124.

12,431 Extracts from president's report to the Sapele Sanitary Board (Benin), 1903. J. AFR. SOC. 4 (1904), pp. 136-138.

12,432 Key to the identification of the principal Nigerian high forest trees. NIGERIAN FIELD 8 (1939), pp. 139-164.

12,433 The long-crested helmet shrike. NIGERIAN FIELD 8 (1939), pp. 110-115.

12,434 Nigerian forest trees. II. NIGERIAN FIELD 8 (1939), pp. 65-74.

12,435 Nutrition in the service of the community [a research feature]. AFR. NOTES 2, no. 2 (1965), pp. 5-6.

12,436 Some mammals and reptiles which may be seen within 30 miles from Zaria. NIGERIAN FIELD 21 (1956), pp. 136-138.

Sociology

12,437 AJAYI, J. F. A. History for determining age. AFR. NOTES 1, no. 2 (1964), pp. 11-13.

12,438 ALIGWEKWE, E. Lagging emulation in Southern Nigeria. AMER. ANTHR. 67 (1965), pp. 1518-1521.

12,439 APTHORPE, R. Opium of the state: some remarks on law and society in Nigeria. NJESS 6 (1964), pp. 139-153.

12,440 ARDENER, S. G. The social and economic significance of the contribution club among a section of the southern Ibo. WAISER SOC. 2 (1953), pp. 128-142.

12,441 ARNETT, E. J. The census of Nigeria, 1931. J. AFR. SOC. 32 (1933), pp. 398-404.

12,442 BARTON, P. Christmas canoeing, 1959. NIGERIAN FIELD 26 (1961), pp. 162-170.

12,443 BASCOM, W. Les premiers fondements historiques de l'urbanisme yorouba. PRESENCE AFR. N.S. 23 (1958-1959), pp. 22-40.

12,444 BASCOM, W. Some aspects of Yoruba urbanism. AMER. ANTHR. 64 (1962), pp. 699-706.

12,445 BASCOM, W. Urbanization among the Yoruba. AMER. J. SOC. 60 (1954-1955), pp. 446-454.

12,446 BASCOM, W. R. Social status, wealth and individual differences among the Yoruba. AMER. ANTHR. 53 (1951), pp. 490-505.

12,447 BATLEY, S. K. The privately owned maternity home in Nigeria. AFR. WOMEN 3 (1958-1960), pp. 39-41.

12,448 BELLO, M. Community development in Northern Nigeria. CORONA 4 (1952), pp. 373-374.

12,449 BREWSTER, P. G. Some Nigerian games, with their parallels and analogues. J. SOC. AFR. 24 (1954), pp. 25-48.

12,450 BROWN, A. The development of the scout movement in Nigeria. AFR. AFFAIRS 46 (1947), pp. 38-42.

12,451 C., J. A propos du recensement en Nigéria du Nord. ZAIRE 8 (1954), pp. 519-520.

12,452 C., J. Réforme municipale à Lagos. ZAIRE 7 (1953), p. 525.

12,453 CHILDS, S. H. Christian marriage in Nigeria. AFRICA 16 (1946), pp. 238-246.

12,454 CLINTON, J. V. Untouchability in Nigeria. CONTEMP. REV. 191 (1957), pp. 217-220.

12,455 COOPER, B. K. New Eruwa. CORONA 4 (1952), pp. 225-227.

12,456 CRABB, D. Ogoja research project. AFR. NOTES 2, no. 3 (1965), pp. 6-7.

12,457 DARK, P. Brief report on the Fourth Annual Conference of the West African Institute of Social and Economic Research. BULL. IFAN 18 (1956), pp. 289-290.

12,458 DAY, P. An opinion survey of the students in the University of Ife: 1962-1963. NJESS 7 (1965), pp. 333-346.

12,459 DELANO, I. O. The Yoruba family as the basis of Yoruba culture. ODU 5 (1958), pp. 21-28.

12,460 ENEMO, E. O. The social problems of Nigeria. AFRICA 18 (1948), pp. 190-198.

12,461 FERGUSON, J. Race relations in Nigeria. AFR. QUART. 2 (1962-1963), pp. 230-239.

12,462 GLEAVE, M. B. Hill settlements and their abandonment in western Yorubaland. AFRICA 33 (1963), pp. 343-352.

12,463 HAIR, P. E. H. Enugu: an industrial and urban community in East Nigeria 1914-1953. WAISER SOC. 2 (1953), pp. 143-169.

12,464 HASTA. 1936 racing in Northern Nigeria. NIGERIAN FIELD 6 (1937), pp. 85-87.

12,465 HENDRICKSE, B. The Mbari story. AFR. FORUM 1 (1965), pp. 109-111.

12,466 HORTON, R. Kalabari culture and history. AFR. NOTES 2, no. 1 (1964), pp. 5-7.

12,467 IGUN, A. A. Draft proposals for the collection of vital statistics data in the Western Region. NJESS 5 (1963), pp. 105-125.

12,468 ILOGU, E. The problem of indigenization in Nigeria. INT. REV. MISSIONS 49 (1960), pp. 167-182.

12,469 IMOHIOSEN, A. Functionalism in the social sciences. NJESS 7 (1965), pp. 227-234.

12,470 IZZETT, A. The fears and anxieties of delinquent Yoruba children. ODU 1 (1955), pp. 26-34.

12,471 JEFFREYS, M. D. W. Psychical phenomena among negroes. J. AFR. SOC. 39 (1940), pp. 354-360.

12,472 KRIEGER, K. Die Bedentung statistischer Erhebungen für die Völkerkunde am Beispiel der Stadt Anka in Nord-Nigeria. SOCIOLOGUS 4 (1954), pp. 67-81.

12,473 LEITH-ROSS, S. The rise of a new élite amongst the women of Nigeria. AFR. WOMEN 2 (1956-1958), pp. 51-56.

12,474 LEITH-ROSS, S. Women of affairs. J. AFR. SOC. 37 (1938), pp. 477-482.

12,475 LIELL, J. et al. A research design for a comparative study of urbanism and fertility: a progress report. NJESS 7 (1965), pp. 63-69.

12,476 LLOYD, P. C. Tribalism in Warri. WAISER 5 (1956), pp. 99-110.

12,477 MABOGUNJE, A. L. The economic implications of the pattern of urbanisation in Nigeria. NJESS 7 (1965), pp. 9-20.

12,478 MABOGUNJE, A. L. Urbanization in Nigeria: a constraint on economic development. ECON. DEVELOPMENT AND CULTURAL CHANGE 13 (1964-1965), pp. 413-438.

12,479 MABOGUNJE, A. The Yoruba home. ODU 5 (1958), pp. 28-41.

12,480 MAIR, L. P. Some social implications of economic change in Nigeria. NJESS 1 (1959), pp. 8-16.

12,481 MARRIS, P. The approach of sociologists and anthropologists to the study of family relationships. NISER 6 (1958), pp. 164-167.

12,482 McEWEN, W. Marriage problems in the Federation of Nigeria. WOMEN TODAY 6 (1964), pp. 35-37.

12,483 MORGAN, R. W. Occupational prestige ratings by Nigerian students. NJESS 7 (1965), pp. 325-332.

12,484 MORTON-WILLIAMS, P. The Atinga Cult among the southwestern Yoruba: a sociological analysis of a witch-finding movement. BULL. IFAN 18 (1956), pp. 315-334.

12,485 MORTON-WILLIAMS, P. Varieties of sanctions among the Yoruba. WAISER 5 (1956), p. 134.

12,486 MPHAHLELE, E. A South African in Nigeria. AFR. SOUTH 3, no. 3 (1959), pp. 99-104.

12,487 NZIMIRO, I. A study of mobility among the Ibos of Southern Nigeria. INT. J. COMP. SOC. 6 (1965), pp. 117-130.

12,488 OGUNSHEYE, F. A. Les femmes du Nigéria. PRESENCE AFR. N.S. 32-33 (1960), pp. 121-138.

12,489 OKONJO, C. Patterns of population growth. NJESS 6 (1964), pp. 6-22.

12,490 OLOKO, O. The impact of advanced technology on the social structure of traditional societies. NJESS 6 (1964), pp. 23-36.

12,491 OMER-COOPER, J. D. Nigeria, Marxism and social progress: an historical perspective. NJESS 6 (1964), pp. 133-138.

12,492 ORME, U. M. Women's athletics in Nigeria. AFR. WOMEN 1 (1955), pp. 70-72.

12,493 PERHAM, M. The census of Nigeria, 1931. AFRICA 6 (1933), pp. 415-430.

12,494 PHILOPHER. Sunday at home: reflections of an occasional recluse. NIGERIAN FIELD 8 (1939), pp. 27-32.

12,495 PILKINGTON, F. In the Nigerian background. AFR. AFFAIRS 57 (1958), pp. 138-140.

12,496 PILKINGTON, F. Progress in Nigeria. CONTEMP. REV. 187 (1955), pp. 189-195.

12,497 PLOTNICOU, L. "Nativism" in contemporary Nigeria. ANTHR. QUART. 37 (1964), pp. 121-137.

12,498 POWELL, E. C. Athletics: Nigeria v. Gold Coast. NIGERIAN FIELD 16 (1951), pp. 186-190.

12,499 PRICE, J. H. Groundnut city Salah. UNIVERSITAS 1, no. 4 (1954), pp. 11-13.

12,500 PRINCE, R. H. Cultural mechanisms for the mastery of grief among the Yoruba. NISER 6 (1958), pp. 232-233.

12,501 PROTHERO, R. M. Informants and statistics: population changes in Gwadabawa district, Sokoto Province, Northern Nigeria 1953/54. NIG. GEOGR. J. 3, no. 2 (1960), pp. 26-32.

12,502 PROTHERO, R. M. Land use, land holdings and land tenure at Soba, Zaria Province, Northern Nigeria. BULL. IFAN 19 (1957), pp. 558-563.

12,503 PROTHERO, R. M. Migratory labour from north-western Nigeria. AFRICA 27 (1957), pp. 251-261.

12,504 ROGERS, C. A. A study of race attitudes in Nigeria. RHODES-LIV. J. 26 (1959), pp. 51-64.

12,505 SMITH, M. G. The Hausa system of social status. NISER 6 (1958), pp. 180-194.

12,506 STANFIELD, D. P. Six climbs on Jiju rock, Enugi. NIGERIAN FIELD 13 (1948), pp. 69-71.

12,507 TIDJANI, A. S. Note sur la migration humaine à la côte du Bénin. BULL. IFAN 22 (1960), pp. 509-513.

12,508 "TITUS". Coarse fishing in West Africa. NIGERIAN FIELD 13 (1948), pp. 50-53.

12,509 USORO, E. J. The place of women in Nigerian society. AFR. WOMEN 4 (1961), pp. 27-30.

12,510 VAN KLAVEREN, J. J. Comment [corruption in Nigeria]. COMP. STUD. SOC. HIST. 6 (1963-1964), pp. 195-198.

12,511 WELMAN, J. Mai Umoru Uda: a profile. CORONA 1, no. 3 (1949), pp. 31-33.

12,512 WILLIAMS, P. M. The social consequences of industrialism among the S.W. Yoruba; with comparisons from Hausa society. WAISER SOC. 2 (1953), pp. 21-30.

12,513 WRATH, R. E. Community development in Nigeria. J. LOCAL ADM. OV. 3 (1964), pp. 92-102.

12,514 Les communautés rurales en Nigéria occidentale. ZAIRE 6 (1952), pp. 633-634.

12,515 Cricket. Nigeria v. Gold Coast. Played at Lagos on Saturday, Monday and Tuesday, April 7th, 9th and 10th. NIGERIAN FIELD 3 (1934), pp. 116-120.

12,516 Cricket. Northern Nigeria v. Southern Nigeria. Played at Enugu on December 23rd, 24th and 25th 1933. NIGERIAN FIELD 3 (1934), pp. 50-55.

12,517 Recensement de Lagos. ZAIRE 5 (1951), p. 408.

12,518 Some women's organisations in Nigeria. WOMEN TODAY 6 (1964), pp. 38-39.

12,519 Udi today. CORONA 3 (1951), pp. 454-457.

12,520 Women's co-operative societies in E. Nigeria. AFR. WOMEN 1 (1955), p. 72.

See also 6603, 10861.

LIBERIA

Agriculture

12,521 GIBSON, D. and CLARKE, J. D. The vice-consul's garden: H.B.M. Embassy, Monrovia. NIGERIAN FIELD 19 (1954), pp. 181-184.

12,522 JOHNSON, H. R. W. Liberia coffee. LIBERIA BULL. 7 (1895), pp. 49-56.

12,523 KING, A. B. Liberian coffee. LIBERIA BULL. 6 (1895), pp. 40-43.

Anthropology

12,524 BUTTIKOFER, J. A few observations on the native tribes of Liberia. LIBERIA BULL. 10 (1897), pp. 57-66.

12,525 CHRISTY, C. Pawning of human beings in Liberia. J. AFR. SOC. 30 (1931), pp. 169-174.

12,526 HARLEY, G. W. Masks as agents of social control in northeast Liberia. ET. GUIN. 7 (1951), pp. 71-74.

12,527 LASSORT and LELONG. Chez les Kpèlè du Libéria et les Guerzé de la Guinée Française. ET. GUIN. 2 (1947), pp. 9-20.

12,528 MEKEEL, H. S. Social administration of the Kru. A preliminary survey, part II. AFRICA 10 (1937), pp. 75-96; 12 (1939), pp. 460-468.

12,529 WELMERS, W. E. Secret medicines, magic, and rites of the Kpelle tribe in Liberia. SOUTHWESTERN J. ANTHR. 5 (1949), pp. 208-243.

12,530 ZWERNEMANN, J. Zum Gottesbegriff der Vai. AFR. UND UB. 43 (1959-1960), pp. 127-132.

See also 9764.

Art. Antiquities

12,531 ARUNDELL, R. D. H. Rock paintings in Bukoba district. JRAI 66 (1936), pp. 113-115.

See also 9735.

Biography

12,532 In memoriam: Thomas G. Addison. LIBERIA BULL. 9 (1896), pp. 77-78.

12,533 President Cheeseman of Liberia. LIBERIA BULL. 3 (1893), pp. 1-2.

12,534 Hon. Garretson W. Gibson. LIBERIA BULL. 17 (1900), pp. 1-2.

12,535 WILSON, J. O. The Hon. Thomas W. Haynes, Attorney General of Liberia. LIBERIA BULL. 20 (1902), pp. 7-9.

12,536 Hon. Alfred Benedict King. LIBERIA BULL. 21 (1902), pp. 1-4.

12,537 Chief Justice Z. B. Roberts, of Liberia. LIBERIA BULL. 13 (1898), p. 1.

12,538 WILSON, J. O. Hon. J. J. Ross. LIBERIA BULL. 16 (1900), pp. 15-16.

12,539 Liberia's first woman M.P. [Mrs. Ellen Mills Scarborough]. AFR. WOMEN 4 (1961), pp. 38-39.

12,540 General Reginald A. Sherman. LIBERIA BULL. 6 (1895), pp. 1-2.

12,541 Una grave perdita per i rapporti tra Italia e Liberia [Carlo Sommaruga]. AFRICA (Rome) 10 (1955), p. 40.

12,542 WILLIAMS, D. Profile of a president: Tubman of Liberia. AFR. SOUTH 4, no. 1 (1959), pp. 97-103.

Economics

12,543 BALANDIER, G. La main-d'oeuvre chez Firestone-Libéria. PRESENCE AFR. 13 (1952), pp. 347-354.

12,544 BROWN, G. Firestone-Libéria. PRESENCE AFR. 13 (1952), pp. 342-347.

12,545 DALTON, G. History, politics, and economic development in Liberia. J. ECON. HIST. 25 (1965), pp. 569-591.

12,546 HAGER, L. M. Taxation of foreign investment in Liberia. LLJ 1 (1965), pp. 151-178.

12,547 HANSON, E. P. An economic survey of the western province of Liberia. GEOG. REV. 37 (1947), pp. 53-69.

12,548 MARINELLI, L. A. Liberia's open-door policy. J. MOD. AFR. STUD. 2 (1964), pp. 91-98.

12,549 MERCATOR. Il commercio estero della Liberia e lo sviluppo degli scambi italo-liberiani. AFRICA (Rome) 11 (1956), pp. 204-205.

12,550 POOLEY, R. P. Recent trade of Sierra Leone. LIBERIA BULL. 8 (1896), pp. 73-75.

12,551 QURESHI, M. A. et al. The Liberian economy. INT. MONETARY FUND STAFF PAPERS 11 (1964), pp. 285-326.

12,552 STANLEY, W. R. Air transportation in Liberia: the role of the scheduled airline in the development of the Liberian transportation. SIERRA LEONE GEOG. ASSOC. BULL. 9 (1965), pp. 34-44.

12,553 TRICART, J. Développement économique récent du Libéria. RECH. AFR. 2 (1960), pp. 60-68.

12,554 A propos des mines du Libéria. ZAIRE 7 (1953), pp. 79-80.

12,555 A propos du Libéria. ZAIRE 5 (1951), pp. 862-863.

12,556 Attualità economica della Liberia. AFRICA (Rome) 10 (1955), pp. 155-156.

12,557 Progrès récents du Libéria. ZAIRE 5 (1951), pp. 633-635.

See also 11408.

Education

12,558 CAMPHOR, A. P. Fifteen thousand dollars needed for a worthy cause. LIBERIA BULL. 19 (1901), pp. 44-50.

12,559 SADLER, W. The Loma literacy programme. INT. REV. MISSIONS 48 (1959), pp. 318-324.

Geography

12,560 ABBE, C. Climate and health in Liberia. LIBERIA BULL. 1 (1892), pp. 34-39.

12,561 COOK, O. F. Monrovia and St. Paul River. LIBERIA BULL. 8 (1896), pp. 30-35.

12,562 HARLEY, G. W. Roads and trials in Liberia. GEOG. REV. 29 (1939), pp. 447-460.

12,563 JOHNSTON, Sir H. Liberia. LIBERIA BULL. 28 (1906), pp. 3-25.

12,564 LYON, E. A journey to Kpondia Hill. LIBERIA BULL. 26 (1905), pp. 59-70.

12,565 ROSS, E. The climate of Liberia and its effect on man. GEOG. REV. 7 (1919), pp. 387-402.

See also 9258.

Government. Politics. Administration

12,566 ELLIS, G. W. Liberia in the political psychology of West Africa. J. AFR. SOC. 12 (1912), pp. 52-70.

12,567 HARRIS, J. H. Liberian slavery: the essentials. CONTEMP. REV. 139 (1931), pp. 303-309.

12,568 MACKAY, M. Liberia and her eastward neighbours. AFR. AFFAIRS 64 (1965), pp. 116-119.

12,569 MEKEEL, H. S. Social administration of the Kru. A preliminary survey. AFRICA 10 (1937), pp. 75-96.

12,570 ROBINSON, K. Constitutional autochthony in Ghana. J. COMM. POL. STUD. 1 (1961-1963), pp. 41-55.

12,571 VERPLAETSE, J. El punto cuatro del Presidente Truman. CUAD. EST. AFR. 9 (1950), pp. 97-118.

12,572 WILSON, J. O. The United States mission in Liberia. LIBERIA BULL. 13 (1898), pp. 17-18.

12,573 Los poderes antiguos y el punto cuarto de Truman. CUAD. EST. AFR. 10 (1950), pp. 23-37.

History

12,574 BLYDEN, E. W. The future of Liberia. LIBERIA BULL. 26 (1905), pp. 45-52.

12,575 BLYDEN, E. W. The problems before Liberia. LIBERIA BULL. 34 (1909), pp. 36-59.

12,576 CHEESEMAN, J. J. The growth of Liberia. LIBERIA BULL. 5 (1894), pp. 42-47.

12,577 COOK, O. F. The American Negro in Liberia. LIBERIA BULL. 13 (1898), pp. 21-29.

12,578 COOK, O. F. What should emigrants carry to Liberia? LIBERIA BULL. 12 (1898), pp. 32-37.

12,579 COOK, O. F. Who should go to Liberia? LIBERIA BULL. 9 (1896), pp. 1-7.

12,580 DENNIS, G. L. Liberia to-day. J. AFR. SOC. 35 (1936), pp. 432-434.

12,581 DU BOIS, W. E. B. Liberia, the League and the United States. FOREIGN AFFAIRS 11 (1932-1933), pp. 682-695.

12,582 DYKE, F. M. The problem of Liberia. J. AFR. SOC. 34 (1935), pp. 169-178.

12,583 FILESI, T. Liberia di ieri e di oggi. AFRICA (Rome) 11 (1956), pp. 197-202.

12,584 FILESI, T. Origini storiche della Repubblica di Liberia. AFRICA (Rome) 13 (1958), pp. 331-338.

12,585 HAIR, P. E. H. An account of the Liberian hinterland c. 1780. SIERRA LEONE STUD. 16 (1962), pp. 218-226.

12,586 HARGREAVES, J. D. African colonization in the nineteenth century: Liberia and Sierra Leone. BOSTON UNIV. PAPERS IN AFR. HIST. 1 (1964), pp. 55-76. Also in SIERRA LEONE STUD. 16 (1962), pp. 189-205.

12,587 HARTZELL, J. C. The outlook in Liberia. LIBERIA BULL. 13 (1898), pp. 2-7; 17 (1900), pp. 28-31.

12,588 JOHNSTON, Sir H. Commerce of Liberia. LIBERIA BULL. 30 (1907), pp. 36-49.

12,589 KING, A. B. The twenty-sixth of July in my boyhood days. LIBERIA BULL. 17 (1900), pp. 51-56.

12,590 LYNDEN, B. H. DE. The Liberian centenary [with a note by L. A. Smart]. AFR. AFFAIRS 46 (1947), pp. 207-218.

12,591 MacKENZIE, M. D. Liberia and the League of Nations. J. AFR. SOC. 33 (1934), pp. 372-381.

12,592 MOELLER, A. La question du Libéria. BULL. SEANCES IRCB 6 (1935), pp. 573-609.

12,593 NARDIN, J. C. Le Libéria et l'opinion publique en France 1821-1847. CAH. ET. AFR. 5 (1965), pp. 96-144.

12,594 NOYES, I. P. Liberia. LIBERIA BULL. 25 (1904), pp. 55-58.

12,595 PARKINSON, J. The end of a war. J. AFR. SOC. 34 (1935), pp. 72-74.

12,596 RICHARDSON, R. B. Liberia's position and present opportunities. LIBERIA BULL. 18 (1901), pp. 15-25.

12,597 SEATON, S. W. Maryland County, Liberia. LIBERIA BULL. 12 (1898), pp. 38-39.

12,598 STEVENS, J. C. The American Negro and Liberia. LIBERIA BULL. 16 (1900), pp. 56-57.

12,599 SUNDERLAND, B. Liberian colonization. LIBERIA BULL. 16 (1900), pp. 16-32.

12,600 WILSON, J. O. Liberia as a factor in the progress of the Negro race. LIBERIA BULL. 3 (1893), pp. 2-11.

12,601 The defence of Liberia. J. AFR. SOC. 42 (1943), pp. 54-55.

12,602 The 1930 enquiry commission to Liberia. J. AFR. SOC. 30 (1931), pp. 277-290.

12,603 Sir Harry Johnston's "Liberia." J. AFR. SOC. 6 (1907), pp. 177-185.

See also 9835.

Language

12,604 AZEVEDO, W. L. D'. Uses of the past in Gola discourse. J. AFR. HIST. 3 (1962), pp. 11-34.

12,605 BLOK, H. P. Annotations to Mr. Turner's Africanisms in the Gullah dialect (1949). LINGUA 8 (1959), pp. 306-321.

12,606 DALBY, D. and HAIR, P. E. H. 'Le langaige de Guynee': a sixteenth century vocabulary from the Pepper Coast. AFR. LANG. STUD. 5 (1964), pp. 174-191.

12,607 DAMMANN, E. Vai-Erzählungen. AFR. UND UB. 23 (1932-1933), pp. 254-278.

12,608 DAMMANN, E. Vai-Sprichwörter. AFR. UND UB. 24 (1933-1934), pp. 76-79.

12,609 ESSEN, O. VON. Stimmhafte Implosive im Vai. AFR. UND UB. 26 (1935-1936), pp. 150-158.

12,610 HAIR, P. E. H. An early seventeenth-century vocabulary of Vai. AFR. STUD. 23 (1964), pp. 129-139.

12,611 HERZOG, G. Drum-signaling in a West African tribe. WORD 1 (1945), pp. 217-238.

12,612 HEYDORN, R. Das Manya. AFR. UND UB. 34 (1943-1944), pp. 25-53; 35 (1949-1950), pp. 47-66.

12,613 HEYDORN, R. Die Sprache der Bandi in Nordwestlichen Liberia. AFR. UND UB. 31 (1941), pp. 81-114, 188-217.

12,614 HOBLEY, J. Bassa verbal formations. J. W. AFR. LANG. 2 (1965), pp. 39-50.

12,615 INNES, G. Morphological units in Grebo. AFR. LANG. STUD. 3 (1962), pp. 84-109.

12,616 INNES, G. An outline of the Grebo verbal system. AFR. LANG. STUD. 1 (1960), pp. 164-176.

12,617 KLINGENHEBEN, A. The Vai script. AFRICA 6 (1933), pp. 158-170.

12,618 KLINGENHEBEN, A. Vai-Texte. AFR. UND UB. 16 (1925-1926), pp. 58-133.

12,619 MASSAQUOI, M. The Vai people and their syllabic writing. J. AFR. SOC. 10 (1911), pp. 459-466.

12,620 MIGEOD, F. W. H. The syllabic writing of the Vai people. J. AFR. SOC. 9 (1909), pp. 46-58.

12,621 SAPIR, E. Notes on the Gweabo language of Liberia. LANGUAGE 7 (1931), pp. 30-41.

12,622 SAPIR, E. and BLOOAH, C. G. The Voice of Africa: some Gweabo proverbs. AFRICA 2 (1929), pp. 183-185.

12,623 WELMERS, W. E. The phonology of Kpelle. J. AFR. LANGS. 1 (1962), pp. 69-93.

12,624 WELMERS, W. E. The syntax of emphasis in Kpelle. J. W. AFR. LANG. 1 (1964), pp. 13-26.

See also 9111.

Law

12,625 FRAENTEL, M. Marriage in Monrovia. WOMEN TODAY 6 (1965), pp. 92-93.

12,626 GIBBS, J. L. The Kpelle moot: a therapeutic model for the informal settlement of disputes. AFRICA 33 (1963), pp. 1-11.

12,627 KONVITZ, M. R. The Liberian code of laws. J. AFR. LAW 2 (1958), pp. 116-118.

12,628 KONVITZ, M. R. and ROSENZWEIG, M. Background and summary of the new Civil Procedure Law. LLJ 1 (1965), pp. 3-15.

12,629 LYON, E. Liberia law of apprenticeship. LIBERIA BULL. 26 (1905), pp. 76-77.

12,630 MATZ, D. E. The judicial contempt power. LLJ 1 (1965), pp. 179-200.

12,631 MORGAN, L. Benefits of the pretrial conference. LLJ 1 (1965), pp. 39-42.

12,632 PIERRE, J. A. A. Introduction to the new pleading. LLJ 1 (1965), pp. 16-38.

12,633 ZARR, G. H. Juvenile delinquency and Liberian law. LLJ 1 (1965), pp. 201-233.

12,634 Constitution of Liberia. LIBERIA BULL. 2 (1893), pp. 41-48.

12,635 The effect of the new Debt Act upon Liberian Civil Procedure: a problem in statutory interpretation. LLJ 1 (1965), pp. 111-140.

12,636 The expanded discovery provisions in the new Civil Procedure Law. LLJ 1 (1965), pp. 65-110.

12,637 How the new Liberian Civil Procedure Law benefits plaintiffs in tort litigation. LLJ 1 (1965), pp. 141-150.

12,638 The Louis Arthur Grimes School of Law of the University of Liberia, Monrovia, Liberia. J. AFR. LAW 7 (1963), pp. 113-116.

12,639 [The] Pretrial conference. LLJ 1 (1965), pp. 43-52.

12,640 Transcript of a pretrial conference. LLJ 1 (1965), pp. 53-64.

12,641 University of Monrovia, Liberia. J. AFR. LAW 6 (1962), p. 116.

Religion

12,642 DONOHUGH, T. S. The Christian mission in Liberia. INT. REV. MISSIONS 34 (1945), pp. 136-143.

12,643 EARTHY, E. D. The impact of Mohammedanism on paganism in the Liberian hinterland. NUMEN 2 (1955), pp. 206-216.

12,644 JONES, G. S. Laywomen in church and society (Liberia). THE CHURCH IN CHANGING AFRICA, 1958, pp. 87-89.

12,645 Nouvelle Mission Catholique au Libéria. ZAIRE 5 (1951), p. 301.

Science

12,646 CONDAMIN, M. Mission P. L. Dekeyser et B. Holas au Libéria. Lépidoptères Rhopalocères. BULL. IFAN 13 (1951), pp. 788-797.

12,647 FRASER, F. C. Report on a collection of Odonata from Liberia. BULL. IFAN 12 (1950), pp. 611-624.

12,648 LEPESME, P. Longicornes récoltés au Liberia par P. L. Dekeyser et B. Holas. BULL. IFAN 12 (1950), pp. 395-400.

12,649 OBERHOLSER, H. C. The birds of Liberia. LIBERIA BULL. 12 (1898), pp. 16-25.

12,650 PICARD, J. Hesperiidae du Libéria collectés par P. L. Dekeyser et B. Holas. BULL. IFAN 12 (1950), pp. 625-628.

12,651 STEMPFFER, H. Contribution à l'étude des Lycaenidae du Libéria. BULL. IFAN 12 (1950), pp. 402-407.

12,652 VILLIERS, A. Hémiptères récoltés au Liberia par P. L. Dekeyser et B. Holas. BULL. IFAN 12 (1950), pp. 930-939.

12,653 WILDER, H. H. Racial differences in palm and sole configurations: II—palm and sole prints of Liberian natives. AMER. ANTHR. 15 (1913), pp. 189-207.

See also 9175.

Sociology

12,654 GANT, I. A. Liberian womanhood. LIBERIAN BULL. 32 (1908), pp. 25-28.

12,655 HIMMELHEBER, H. and TAME-TABMEN, W. Wunkirle, die gastlichste Frau. FESTSCHRIFT ALFRED BUHLER, 1965, pp. 171-181.

12,656 SCARBROUGH, E. M. Women of Liberia. AFR. WOMEN 3 (1958-1960), pp. 35-37.

PORTUGUESE GUINEA

General

12,657 TEIXEIRA DA MOTA, A. O Centro de Estudes da Guiné Portuguesa—historia e perspectivas. BCGP 10 (1955), pp. 641-660.

Agriculture

12,658 CABRAL, A. L. A propos du cycle cultural arachide-mils en Guiné Portugaise. BCGP 13 (1958), pp. 149-156.

12,659 CABRAL, A. L. Acerca da contribuição dos povos guineenses para a produção agrícola da Guiné. BCGP 9 (1954), pp. 771-777.

12,660 CABRAL, A. L. Queimadas e Pousios na Circunscrição de Fulacunda em 1953. BCGP 9 (1954), pp. 627-643.

12,661 CABRAL, A. L. Recenseamento Agrícola da Guiné. Estimativa em 1953. BCGP 11, no. 43 (1956), pp. 7-243.

12,662 FRADE, F. Investigaçãoes para o melhoramento da pesca indígena nas águas interiores da Guiné Portuguesa. BCGP 9 (1954), pp. 671-706.

12,663 LOPES, L. DOS. Arrolamento Geral do Gado e Animais de Capoeira. BCGP 19 (1964), pp. 151-196.

12,664 MARTINS BATISTA, M. Problemas agrícolas coloniais. A Guiné desconhecida. BCGP 3 (1948), pp. 881-924.

12,665 NEVES, J. B. Hidráulica e Hidráulica agrícola. Problemas do rio Geba. BCGP 14 (1959), pp. 213-230.

12,666 SANTARENO, J. A. L. M. A agricultura na Guiné Portuguesa. BCGP 12 (1957), pp. 355-383.

12,667 TEIXEIRA DA MOTA, A. A agricultura de Brames e Balantas vista através da fotografia aérea. BCGP 5 (1950), pp. 131-172.

Anthropology

12,668 ALMEIDA, A. DE. As Aves em algumas superticões indigenas da Guiné e de Cabo-Verde. PORT. EM AFR. 1 (1944), pp. 31-39, 90-98.

12,669 ALMEIDA, A. DE. Sobre a matemática dos indígenas da Guiné Portuguesa. BCGP 2 (1947), pp. 375-434.

12,670 BARROS, A. DE. A invasão fula na circunscrição de Bafatá. Queda dos Beafadas e Mardingas. Tribos "Gabu'ngabé." BCGP 2 (1947), pp. 737-743.

12,671 CARREIRA, A. O Céu, Deus e a Terra (lenda de manjacas). BCGP 2 (1947), pp. 461-463.

12,672 CARREIRA, A. Contos e historietas dos Mardingas, tal qual foram recolhidas deles. BCGP 1 (1946), pp. 327-329, 767-772.

12,673 CARREIRA, A. Do arrancamento da pele aos cadáveres e da necrofagia na Guiné Portuguesa. BCGP 20 (1965), pp. 151-153.

12,674 CARREIRA, A. A etnonímia dos povos de entre o Gâmbia e o estuário do Geba. BCGP 19 (1964), pp. 233-275.

12,675 CARREIRA, A. Multilações étnicas dos Manjacos. BCGP 16 (1961), pp. 83-101.

12,676 CARREIRA, A. Símbolos, ritualistas e ritualismos ânimofeiticistas na Guiné Portuguesa. BCGP 16 (1961), pp. 505-539.

12,677 COSTA, E. C. E. A medicina entre os Mandingas. PORT. EM AFR. 2 (1945), pp. 274-277.

12,678 COSTA, F. C. Subsídos para o estudo da higiene e patologia da tribo Bijagó. BCGP 12 (1957), pp. 483-537.

12,679 CUNHA, A. A memória de Edmundo Correia Lopes. BCGP 3 (1948), pp. 1037-1062.

12,680 CUNHA TABORDA, A. Apontamentos etnográficos sobre os felupes de Susana. BCGP 5 (1950), pp. 187-223.

12,681 CUNHA TABORDA, A. Contos felupes. BCGP 2 (1947), pp. 1009-1020.

12,682 DIAS DINIS, P. A. J. As tribos da Guiné portuguesa na História. PORT. EM AFR. 3 (1946), pp. 206-215.

12,683 DIAS DINIS, P. A. J. Primeiras informações etnográficas sôbre a Guiné portuguesa. PORT. EM. AFR. 1 (1944), pp. 26-30.

12,684 FERREIRA, D. J. O mistério da família. BCGP 20 (1965), pp. 67-76.

12,685 GOMES BARBOSA, O. C. Breve notícia dos caracteres étnicos dos indígenas da tribo Biafada. BCGP 1 (1946), pp. 205-271.

12,686 GOMES PEREIRA, A. Contos fulas. BCGP 3 (1948), pp. 445-452.

12,687 MARTINS MEIRELES, A. Baiú (gentes de Kaiú). BCGP 3 (1948), pp. 607-638; 4 (1949), pp. 7-25.

12,688 MENDES, F. A. Vida material dos Brâmes. BCGP 3 (1948), pp. 81-113.

12,689 NOGUEIRA, A. Báná Sirabanda (lenda dos banhurs). BCGP 2 (1947), pp. 455-460.

12,690 NOGUEIRA, A. A família Cassanga. BCGP 3 (1948), pp. 359-394.

12,691 NOGUEIRA, A. O "Irã" na Circunscrição de S. Domingos. BCGP 2 (1947), pp. 711-716.

12,692 NOGUEIRA, A. O lobo, a ganga (grou coroado), o hipopótamo e a lebre (conto cassanga). BCGP 2 (1947), pp. 193-196.

12,693 NOGUEIRA, A. Monografia sobre a tribo Banhum. BCGP 2 (1947), pp. 973-1008.

12,694 NOGUEIRA, A. A povoação de Jobel (Baiotes). BCGP 2 (1947), pp. 745-747.

12,695 ROGADO QUINTINO, F. Como se trajam e se adornam os povos da Guiné Portuguesa. BCGP 19 (1964), pp. 37-47.

12,696 ROGADO QUINTINO, F. Justiça de "Iran." BCGP 2 (1947), pp. 197-205.

12,697 ROGADO QUINTINO, F. No segredo das crenças—Das instituições religiosas na Guiné Portuguesa. BCGP 4 (1949), pp. 419-488, 687-721.

12,698 ROGADO QUINTINO, F. Serão os balantas negros sudaneses? BCGP 2 (1947), pp. 299-313.

12,699 ROGADO QUINTINO, F. O Totemismo na Guiné Portuguesa. BCGP 19 (1964), pp. 117-128.

12,700 SANTOS LIMA, A. J. Os Bijagós e o regime do matriarcado. BCGP 2 (1947), pp. 593-615.

12,701 SANTOS LIMA, A. J. O "Iran." BCGP 2 (1947), pp. 173-177.

12,702 VIEIRA, R. A. Estudo dos grupos sanguíneos dos indígenas Bijagos da Guiné Portuguesa. Contribuição para o estudo da sua soro-antropologia. BCGP 10 (1955), pp. 585-597.

Art

12,703 CORREIA, B. A cerâmica na vida dos Balantas e Manjacos. BCGP 13 (1958), pp. 133-148.

12,704 GRANDAO, F. Uma peça histórica. BCGP 2 (1947), pp. 449-454.

12,705 MATEUS, A. Acerca da Pre-História da Guiné. BCGP 9 (1954), pp. 457-472.

12,706 MOTA, A. T. DA. Descoberta de bronzes antigos na Guiné Portuguesa. BCGP 15 (1960), pp. 625-632.

12,707 PIRES DE FIGUEIREDO, J. Os selos postais da Guiné Portuguesa. BCGP 3 (1948), pp. 581-605; 4 (1949), pp. 489-512, 649-686.

12,708 ROGADO QUINTINO, F. Música e dança na Guiné Portuguesa. BCGP 18 (1963), pp. 551-569.

12,709 ROGADO QUINTINO, F. A pintura e a escultura na Guiné Portuguesa. BCGP 19 (1964), pp. 277-288.

Biography

12,710 MOTA, A. T. DA. O centenário da morte de Honório Barreto. BCGP 13 (1958), pp. 195-201.

12,711 MARIA ROSA. Folhas do meu diário. BCGP 3 (1948), pp. 759-773.

Economics

12,712 AREAL, J. A. Possibilidades industriais da Guiné. BCGP 9 (1954), pp. 707-770.

12,713 CARREIRA, A. Guiné Portuguesa. Região dos Manjacos e dos Brâmes (Alguns aspectos da sua economia). BCGP 15 (1960), pp. 735-784.

12,714 GUERRA, F. M. The plan for the development of Portuguese oversea territories. CIVILISATIONS 6 (1956), pp. 565-574.

12,715 HORTA, C. A. P. Análise estrutural e conjuntural da economia da Guiné. (Diagnóstico da situação económica.) BCGP 20 (1965), pp. 333-495.

12,716 MARQUES, B. Aplicabilidade local da teorética do crescimento económico. BCGP 18 (1963), pp. 203-222.

12,717 MENDONCA, P. C. DE. A estrutura do comércio externo da Guiné. BCGP 12 (1957), pp. 277-292.

12,718 REGO, C. A. DE F. S. O estado actual da indústria de pesca na Província Ultramarina da Guiné e o seu provável incremento. BCGP 13 (1958), pp. 63-74.

12,719 ROGARDO QUINTINO, F. Das possibilidades do aumento da produção na Guiné. BCGP 6 (1951), pp. 365-370.

12,720 SA, C. DE. Comércio externo da Guiné em 1947. BCGP 3 (1948), pp. 411-443.

12,721 SANTARENO, J. A. L. M. Possibilidades da elaeicultura da Guiné Portuguesa. BCGP 20 (1965), pp. 155-171.

12,722 SARDINHA, R. M. DE A. Primeiro relatório dos resultados da prospecção efectuada à Ilha de Bubaque. BCGP 20 (1965), pp. 259-292.

Education

12,723 DIAS DINIS, P. A. J. O problema do ensino ao indígena da Guiné. PORT. EM AFR. 5 (1948), pp. 84-90, 149-158.

12,724 DURIEUX, A. De la politique du Portugal, en matière d'enseignement, en égard à la convention de Saint-Germain-en-Laye. ZAIRE 1 (1947), pp. 801-805.

12,725 SOARES, A. C. Acerca da Educacão de Base na Guiné Portuguesa. BCGP 15 (1960), pp. 461-475.

Geography

12,726 CABRAL, A. L. Para o conhecimento do problema da erosão do Solo da Guiné. 1. Sobre o conceito de erosão. BCGP 9 (1954), pp. 163-202.

12,727 CASTRO, A. Notas sobre degradação dos solos na Guiné Portuguesa. BCGP 6 (1951), pp. 371-397.

12,728 COUTINHO, G. Nuno Tristão e o mar de Sargaço. BCGP 4 (1949), pp. 1-5.

12,729 CRESPO, M. P. O rio Cacheu. BCGP 10 (1955), pp. 279-292.

12,730 CRESPO, M. P. Roteiro da costa da Guiné (Breve nota sobre a maneira de demandar o Porto de Bissau). BCGP 8 (1953), pp. 311-315.

12,731 CRESPO, M. P. Roteiro da Costa da Guiné. Breve nota sobre a maneira de demandar o porto de Bolama. BCGP 10 (1955), pp. 35-47.

12,732 CRESPO, M. P. Roteiro da Costa da Guiné. Breve nota sobre a maneira de demandar o porto de Bubaque. BCGP 12 (1957), pp. 191-198.

12,733 CRESPO, M. P. Trabalhos da Missão geo-hidrográfica da Guiné—Carta hidrográfica no. 216. BCGP 4 (1949), pp. 512-547.

12,734 GUIMARAES, C. As Chuvas na Guiné Portuguesa. BCGP 12 (1957), pp. 315-332.

12,735 GUIMARAES, C. O clima da Guiné Portuguesa. BCGP 14 (1959), pp. 295-334.

12,736 GUIMARAES, C. As linhas de convergência e as marés (na Guiné). BCGP 13 (1958), pp. 471-475.

12,737 MARQUES MANO, M. Uma visita a Guiné. BCGP 2 (1947), pp. 467-512.

12,738 OLIVEIRA BOLEO, J. DE. Viagens de descobrimento e exploração nas costas da Guiné. BCGP 1 (1946), pp. 713-728.

12,739 TEIXEIRA DA MOTA, A. A descoberta da Guiné. [Cont.] BCGP 1 (1946), pp. 273-326.

Government

12,740 BRAZAO, A. A vida administrativa da colónia da Guiné. BCGP 2 (1947), pp. 751-782.

12,741 CUNHA, J. DA S. Portuguese Africa. CIVILISATIONS 6 (1956), pp. 651-654.

12,742 DUARTE, F. Guiné Portuguesa. A influência política, social e económica dos Regimentos na formação da Colónia. BCGP 5 (1950), pp. 225-256.

12,743 FIRMINO CARDOSO. Visita Presidencial. PORT. EM AFR. 12 (1955), pp. 137-144.

12,744 FORTUNA, V. N. P. The Portuguese Overseas Territories. CIVILISATIONS 6 (1956), pp. 436-454; 7 (1957), pp. 409-418; 8 (1958), pp. 411-420; 9 (1959), pp. 505-510.

12,745 MOREIRA, A. Portuguese overseas territories in 1955. CIVILISATIONS 6 (1956), pp. 287-292; 7 (1957), pp. 251-258; 8 (1958), pp. 311-318; 9 (1959), pp. 223-228.

12,746 MOREIRA, A. Portuguese policy in the light of recent developments in Africa. CIVILISATIONS 10 (1960), pp. 259-263.

12,747 REGO, A. DA S. Overseas Portugal 1956, 1957. CIVILISATIONS 7 (1957), pp. 75-81; 8 (1958), pp. 112-118; 9 (1959), pp. 79-84; 10 (1960), pp. 105-109.

12,748 RICHARD-MOLARD, J. Le départ du Gouverneur M. M. Sarmento Rodriguez. BULL. IFAN 12 (1950), pp. 240-241.

12,749 RODRIGUES, J. F. Native policy in the Portuguese oversea territories. CIVILISATIONS 5 (1955), pp. 71-77.

12,750 On se bat en Guinée. PRESENCE AFR. N.S. 40 (1962), pp. 165-167.

See also 23517.

History

12,751 CARVALHO VIEGAS, L. A. DE. A memória do Comandante Carlos de Almeida Pereira, Governador da Guiné de 1910 a 1913. BCGP 4 (1949), pp. 131-132.

12,752 DIAS DINIS, P. A. J. As tribos da Guiné Portuguesa na história. PORT. EM AFR. 4 (1947), pp. 88-95, 129-138, 205.

12,753 DUARTE, F. Alexandre Herculano e a Guiné Portuguesa. BCGP 4 (1949), pp. 723-735.

12,754 FARO, J. A aclamação de D. João IV na Guiné. BCGP 13 (1958), pp. 489-515.

12,755 FARO, J. Duas expedições enviadas à Guiné anteriormente a 1474 e custeadas pela Fazeda de D. Afonso V. BCGP 12 (1957), pp. 47-104.

12,756 FARO, J. Expedições realizadas por espanhóis à Guiné de 1475 a 1479. BCGP 14 (1959), pp. 721-734.

12,757 FARO, J. O movimento comercial do porto de Bissau de 1788 a 1794. BCGP 14 (159), pp. 231-258.

12,758 FARO, J. A Organização administrativa da Guiné de 1615 a 1676. BCGP 14 (1959), pp. 97-122.

12,759 FARO, J. Os problemas de Bissau, Cacheu e suas dependências vistos em 1831 por Manuel Antônio Martins. BCGP 13 (1958), pp. 203-216.

12,760 FARO, J. Uma carta de quitação do infante D. Henrique mencionando produtos, obtidos nos tractos da Guiné pelo seu tesoureiro-mor. BCGP 12 (1957), pp. 255-258.

12,761 HAIR, P. E. H. Beaver on Bulama. BCGP 15 (1960), pp. 361-383; Portuguese summary, p. 360.

12,762 MORAIS TRIGO, A. B. A morte de Nuno Tristão. BCGP 2 (1947), pp. 189-192.

12,763 NOGUEIRA, A. Figuras da ocupação: Abdu lujai. BCGP 4 (1949), pp. 49-60.

12,764 TEAGUE, M. Bulama in the 18th century. BCGP 13 (1958), pp. 177-193; Portuguese summary, p. 176.

12,765 TEIXEIRA DA MOTA, A. Cronologia e âmbito das viagens portuguesas de descoberta na Africa Ocidental, de 1445 a 1462. BCGP 2 (1947), pp. 315-341.

12,766 TEIXEIRA DA MOTA, A. Um relatório de Sousa Lage. BCGP 3 (1948), pp. 329-352.

See also 10508.

Language. Literature

Language

12,767 BASSO MARQUES, J. Aspectos do problema da semelhança da língua dos papéis, manjacos e brames. BCGP 2 (1947), pp. 77-109.

12,768 BASSO MARQUES, J. Familiaridade idiomática entre Cobianas e Cassangas. BCGP 2 (1947), pp. 875-913.

12,769 CARREIRA, A. Alguns aspectos da influência da língua Mandinga na Pajadinca. BCGP 18 (1963), pp. 345-383.

12,770 ESPIRITO SANTO, J. DO. Nomes vernáculos de algumas plantas da Guiné Portuguesa. BCGP 3 (1948), pp. 983-1036; 18 (1963), pp. 405-510.

12,771 KLINGENHEBEN, A. Die Permutation des Biafada und des Ful. AFR. UND UB. 15 (1924-1925), pp. 180-213, 266-272.

12,772 KRAUSE, G. A. Die Fada-Sprache am Geba-Flusse im portugiesischen Westafrika. ZAOS 1 (1895), pp. 363-372.

12,773 ROGADO QUINTINO, F. Conhecimento da língua Balanta, através da sua estrutura vocabular. BCGP 16 (1961), pp. 737-768.

12,774 SOUSA BELLA, L. DE. Apontamentos sobre a língua dos Balantas de Jabadá. BCGP 1 (1946), pp. 729-765.

12,775 WILSON, W. A. A. Numeration in the languages of Guiné. AFRICA 31 (1961), pp. 372-377.

12,776 WILSON, W. A. A. Outline of the Balanta language. AFR. LANG. STUD. 2 (1961), pp. 139-168.

12,777 WILSON, W. A. A. A reconstruction of the Pajade mutation system. J. W. AFR. LANG. 2 (1965), pp. 15-20.

12,778 WILSON, W. A. A. Uma volta linguística na Guiné. BCGP 14 (1959), pp. 569-601.

12,779 Nomes vernáculos de algumas plantas da Guiné Portuguesa. BCGP 11, no. 42 (1956), pp. 73-81.

See also 8646, 12679.

Literature

12,780 ALVARO, E. O calor, o abandono e um olhar meigo. BCGP 19 (1964), pp. 63-71.

12,781 ALVARO, E. No escuro da noite. BCGP 19 (1964), pp. 143-149.

12,782 BARBOSA, A. Louvam-se Irãs. BCGP 5 (1950), pp. 257-262.

12,783 BARBOSA, A. A. M. Planície conquistada. BCGP 3 (1948), pp. 453-459.

12,784 BARRAGAO, F. R. Magda Bagi—um Balanta. BCGP 4 (1949), pp. 739-742.

12,785 BARRAGAO, F. R. Matagal sobre o Asfalto. BCGP 16 (1961), pp. 193-262.

12,786 BARRAGAO, F. R. Tribulações de um balanta. BCGP 6 (1951), pp. 399-404.

12,787 CONDUTO, J. E. Contos Bijagós. BCGP 10 (1955), pp. 489-504.

12,788 LEDO PONTES, L. Foi assim a sua vitória. BCGP 3 (1948), pp. 1063-1071.

12,789 VALOURA, F. Uma noite em Camarancunda. BCGP 8 (1953), pp. 357-363.

Law

12,790 BARBOSA, H. J. Os indígenas da Guiné perante a lei Portuguesa. BCGP 2 (1947), pp. 343-362.

12,791 BARBOSA, H. J. Informações jurídicas para o conhecimento da orgânica administrativa da Guiné Portuguesa. BCGP 1 (1946), pp. 663-705.

12,792 BRITO, E. O direito costumeiro e o conceito especial de personalidade. BCGP 20 (1965), pp. 213-234.

12,793 BRITO, E. Regime jurídico da propriedade dos Vizinhos das regedorias da Guiné. BCGP 20 (1965), pp. 5-65.

12,794 CARREIRA, A. Alguns aspectos do regime jurídico da propriedade imobiliária dos Manjacos. BCGP 1 (1946), pp. 707-712.

12,795 CARREIRA, A. A protecção de propriedade do nativo da Guine nossas leis. BCGP 5 (1950), pp. 173-185.

12,796 DUARTE, F. Duas Causas. BCGP 6 (1951), pp. 405-454.

12,797 GERAIS, C. Direitos de familia e propriedade entre os Fulas da Guiné Portuguesa. BCGP 10 (1955), pp. 1-22.

12,798 SILVA, A. A. DA. O Direito penal entre os Fulas da Guiné. BCGP 9 (1954), pp. 481-495.

12,799 SILVA, A. A. DA. Direitos reais e das sucessões entre os Fulas de Guiné Portuguesa. BCGP 11, no. 42 (1956), pp. 7-24.

12,800 SILVA, A. A. DA. Usos e costumes jurídicos dos Felupes da Guiné. BCGP 15 (1960), pp. 7-52.

12,801 TAVARES, A. Do indigenato à cidadania. O Diploma legislativo no. 1,364, de 7 de Outubro de 1946. BCGP 2 (1947), pp. 853-865.

Religion

12,802 GONCALVES, J. J. O islamismo na Guiné Portuguesa. BCGP 13 (1958), pp. 397-470.

12,803 SARMENTO RODRIGUES, M. M. Os Maometanos no futuro da Guiné Portuguesa. BCGP 3 (1948), pp. 219-236.

See also 12697.

Science

12,804 ABREU, M. M. M. DE A. Contribuição para o estudo da oncocercose na Guiné Portuguesa. BCGP 19 (1964), pp. 433-447.

12,805 ABREU, M. M. M. DE A. Contribuição para o estudo das glossinas da Guiné. Reconhecimento no Concelho de Bissau. BCGP 19 (1964), pp. 49-61.

12,806 ABREU, M. M. M. DE A. Glossinas do Gabú. Ensaio de profilaxia agronómica nos Regulados de Propana e Sama Dembel. BCGP 18 (1963), pp. 595-645.

12,807 ALMEIDA, C. L. DE. Aureomicinoterápia do Molluscum Contogiosum. BCGP 11 (1956), pp. 107-114.

12,808 ALMEIDA, C. L. DE. Inquérito etnográfico sobre a alimentacão dos Felupes. BCGP 10 (1955), pp. 617-663.

12,809 ALMEIDA, F. DA N. and ALMEIDA, J. M. DA N. Plano para a luta contra a tuberculose no província da Guiné. BCGP 17 (1962), pp. 575-657.

12,810 ARAUJO FERREIRA, J. Fauna da reserva de Cufada. BCGP 3 (1948), pp. 739-758.

12,811 BRITO, E. Taxas de natalidade e mortalidade dos fulas do Gabú. BCGP 11, no. 44 (1956), pp. 7-26.

12,812 CARVALHO GUERRA, A. Elementos de climatologia aeronáutica. BCGP 2 (1947), pp. 915-964.

12,813 CARVALHO GUERRA, A. DE. Subsídios para o estudo do clima da Guiné Portuguesa. BCGP 2 (1947), pp. 3-75.

12,814 CASTEL-BRANCO, A. J. F. Entomofauna da Guiné Portuguesa e S. Tomé e Príncipe (contribuição para o seu conhecimento) Hemípteros e Himenópteros. BCGP 11, no. 44 (1956), pp. 67-85.

12,815 CASTEL-BRANCO, A. J. F. and ALVES, M. L. G. Contribuição para o melhor conhecimento do género dysdercus na Guiné Portuguesa e em S. Tomé e Principe. BCGP 12 (1957), pp. 21-37.

12,816 COSTA, F. C. DA. Contribuição para o estudo do regime alimentar dos bijagós. BCGP 18 (1963), pp. 385-403.

12,817 COSTA, F. C. DA. A oxiurose em Bissau e o seu tratamento com o pamoato de pervinio (Vanquin). BCGP 18 (1963), pp. 5-12.

12,818 COSTA, F. C. DA and MEIRA, L. V. DE. Paludismo e Campanha Anti-Palúdica em Bissau. BCGP 17 (1962), pp. 119-165.

12,819 COSTA, F. M. C. DA. Alguns dados relativos à evolução da tripanosomíase humana na Guiné Portuguesa. BCGP 17 (1962), pp. 449-457.

12,820 COSTA, F. M. C. DA. La bilharziose en Guinée Portugaise. BCGP 15 (1960), pp. 521-527.

12,821 COSTA, F. M. C. DA. Contribuição para o conhecimento da Endemia Palustre na área da Circunscrição de Cacheu. BCGP 16 (1961), pp. 297-311.

12,822 CRESPO, M. P. Trabalhos da Missão Geo-Hidrográfica da Guiné—Campanha de 1950-1951. BCGP 6 (1951), pp. 321-337.

12,823 CRESPO, M. P. Missão geo-hidrográfica da Guiné. BCGP 3 (1948), pp. 973-982.

12,824 CRUZ FERREIRA, F. S. DA. Acerca da doença do sono na Guiné Portuguesa. BCGP 2 (1947), pp. 363-374.

12,825 CRUZ FERREIRA, F. S. DA. A propósito da pseudo-profilaxia quinínica da malaria. BCGP 2 (1947), pp. 1023-1034.

12,826 CRUZ FERREIRA, F. S. DA et al. A campanha contra a ancilostomiase na Ilha de Bissau. BCGP 2 (1947), pp. 965-972.

12,827 CRUZ FERREIRA, F. S. DA et al. Contribuição para o estudo da Ancilostomiase na Guiné Portuguesa. BCGP 3 (1948), pp. 925-968.

12,828 CRUZ FERREIRA, F. S. DA et al. Os Índices de infestação palustre entre os indígenas das ilhas de Bolama e de Bissau. BCGP 3 (1948), pp. 205-215.

12,829 DIAS, M. G. and D'ALMEIDA, C. L. A propósito de um caso de apoplexia úteroplacentária acompanhada de descolamento prematuro da placenta normalmente inserida. BCGP 12 (1957), pp. 559-564.

12,830 ESPIRITO SANTO, J. DO. Algumas plantas venenosas e medicinais usadas pelos indígenas da Guiné Portuguesa. BCGP 3 (1948), pp. 395-410.

12,831 ESPIRITO SANTO, J. DO. Contribução para o conhacimento fitogeográfico da Guiné Portuguesa. BCGP 4 (1949), pp. 95-129.

12,832 ESPIRITO SANTO, J. DO. Subsídio para o conhecimento da flora económica da Guiné Portuguesa. BCGP 2 (1947), pp. 179-187.

12,833 FERREIRA, F. S. DA C. História da Doenca do Sono na Guiné Portuguesa. BCGP 15 (1960), pp. 67-113, 325-357; 16 (1961), pp. 139-157, 313-347, 569-606, 783-804.

12,834 FERREIRA, F. S. DA C. and COSTA, F. M. C. DA. Résultats du traitement des malades du sommeil en Guinée Portugaise. BCGP 17 (1962), pp. 659-667.

12,835 FONSECA, J. P. C. DA. Breve notícia sobre algumas térmites da Guiné Portuguesa. BCGP 14 (1959), pp. 701-704.

12,836 FONSECA, J. P. C. DA. Contribuição para o conhecimento do estado fitosanitário dos povoamentos espontâneos de cibes (Borassus aethiopum Mart.) da Guiné Portuguesa. BCGP 11, no. 42 (1956), pp. 83-98.

12,837 FONSECA, J. P. C. DA. As térmites na paisagen da Guiné. Documentário fotográfico. BCGP 14 (1959), pp. 705-719.

12,838 FORTUNA, J. T. et al. Relatório sobre as hérnias abdominais externas na Guiné Portuguesa. BCGP 12 (1957), pp. 565-581.

12,839 FRASER, F. C. Two new species of Libelluliness from Portuguese Guinea (Order Odonata). BULL. IFAN 11 (1949), pp. 302-306.

12,840 LECUONA, M. DE O. A Oncocercose e o seu interesse médico-social na Guiné Portuguesa. Subsídios para o estudo epidemiológico do foco de Sonaco. BCGP 15 (1960), pp. 193-240.

12,841 MARTINS BAPTISTA, M. Aspectos do problema florestal da Guiné Portuguesa. BCGP 2 (1947), pp. 717-736.

12,842 NEVES, C. M. B. Nota sobre a Biocenose do Algodão na Guiné. BCGP 9 (1954), pp. 473-480.

12,843 NEVES, C. M. B. et al. Os prejuízos causados pelos insectos no amendoim importado da Guiné, by C. M. B. Neves, J. P. C. da Fonseca, J. P. P. Amaro. BCGP 8 (1953), pp. 181-310.

12,844 NUNES, H. F. J. S. DE F. P. Leguminosas Florestais da Guiné Portuguesa. BCGP 10 (1955), pp. 187-278.

12,845 PINTO, A. R. and COSTA, F. C. DA. La lutte contre la lèpre en Guinée Portugaise. BCGP 14 (1959), pp. 603-631.

12,846 REIS, C. S. and ALMEIDA, C. L. DE. O peso dos recém-nascidos africanos de Bissau (Guiné Portuguesa). BCGP 15 (1960), pp. 477-520.

12,847 REIS, C. S. and COSTA, F. C. DA. A Alimentação dos Manjacos. BCGP 16 (1961), pp. 377-504.

12,848 RUAS, A. Esboço dum programa de recuperação dos leprosos inválidos da Guiné Portuguesa. BCGP 17 (1962), pp. 167-182.

12,849 SANTARENO, J. A. L. M. Primeiros elementos para o estudo do comportamento, em viveiro, das principais espécies florestais da Guiné Portuguesa. BCGP 16 (1961), pp. 541-567.

12,850 SANTARENO, J. A. L. M. Subsídio para o conhecimento da composição das manchas florestais da circunscrição de Farim. BCGP 11, no. 42 (1956), pp. 25-72.

12,851 SCARPA, A. Novos conhecimentos provenientes de casos recentes de lactatio agravidica ou serotina na Guiné Portuguesa. BCGP 14 (1959), pp. 167-191.

12,852 TENDEIRO, J. Acerca dos hematazoários de algumas aves da Guiné Portuguesa. BCGP 3 (1948), pp. 115-171.

12,853 TENDEIRO, J. Anotações parasitológicas. BCGP 9 (1954), pp. 779-789, 791-793, 795-848.

12,854 TENDEIRO, J. Entomofauna da Guiné Portuguesa e S. Tomé e Príncipe (contribuição para o seu conhecimento). Malófagos. BCGP 11, no. 44 (1956), pp. 121-138.

12,855 TENDEIRO, J. Estudo preliminar dos tabanídeos da Guiné Portuguesa. BCGP 2 (1947), pp. 435-447.

12,856 TENDEIRO, J. Estudos de Ixodologia. Notas sobre o Rhipicephalus Simus Simus C. L. Koch 1844 e o Rhipicephalus Simus Senegalensis C. L. Koch 1844 na Guiné Portuguesa. BCGP 11, no. 42 (1956), pp. 99-109.

12,857 TENDEIRO, J. Estudos sobre uma collecção de Malófagos de Aves. BCGP 9 (1954), pp. 497-625.

12,858 TENDEIRO, J. A Guiné no Plano General da Zoogeografia Parasitológica. BCGP 12 (1957), pp. 199-253.

12,859 TENDEIRO, J. Ixodídeos da Guiné Portuguesa. Notas teratológicas. BCGP 2 (1947), pp. 617-709; 6 (1951), pp. 339-363.

12,860 TENDEIRO, J. Malófagos da Guiné Portuguesa. BCGP 8 (1953), pp. 335-355.

12,861 TENDEIRO, J. Malófagos da Guiné Portuguesa. BCGP 9 (1954), pp. 3-162.

12,862 TENDEIRO, J. Monstro hidrocéfalo, cidocéfalo e anosmático (Contribução ao estudo da teratologia nos trópicos). BCGP 4 (1949), pp. 27-47.

12,863 TENDEIRO, J. Nota sobre o Leucocytozoon martyi Commes 1918. BCGP 3 (1948), pp. 969-972.

12,864 TENDEIRO, J. Notas de helmintologia guineense. BCGP 8 (1953), pp. 317-334.

12,865 TENDEIRO, J. Subsídios para o conhecimento da fauna parasitológica da Guiné. BCGP 3 (1948), pp. 639-738.

12,866 TENDEIRO, J. Trypanosoma agueda-ferreirae N. SP., parasita da perdiz africana (Francolinus bicalcaratus L.). BCGP 2 (1947), pp. 867-874.

12,867 TENDEIRO, J. Tripanosomíases animais da Guiné Portuguesa. BCGP 2 (1947), pp. 111-172.

12,868 TENDEIRO, J. and VALDEZ, V. Helmintologia ictiológica: alguns helmintes do sável, alosa alosa (L.), das águas portuguesas. Descrição de uma nova especie, Mazocräes vilelai n. sp. (Trematoda, Monogenea). BCGP 10 (1955), pp. 49-80.

12,869 TORDO, G. C. Entomofauna da Guiné Portuguesa e S. Tomé e Príncipe (Contribuição para o seu conhecimento). Coleópteros e Hemípteros. BCGP 11, no. 44 (1956), pp. 107-120.

12,870 TRINCAO, C. et al. Hemoglobinas anormais nas principais tribos da Província da Guiné, by C. Trincão, L. T. A. Franco, and A. R. Nogueira. BCGP 15 (1960), pp. 61-66.

12,871 VENTIM NEVES, M. J. G. Actavadade da brigada de construção de moradias até fins do ano de 1948. BCGP 4 (1949), pp. 559-579.

12,872 VIEIRA, R. A. Alguns aspectos da alimentação dos indígenas bijagós de Guiné Portuguesa. BCGP 10 (1955), pp. 463-487.

12,873 VIEIRA, R. A. Pesquisa de Vitamina C na urina dos indígenas Bijagós da Guiné Portuguesa. BCGP 12 (1957), pp. 539-557.

12,874 VILLIERS, A. Note sur quelques Ophidiens de la Guiné Portugaise. BCGP 3 (1948), pp. 201-204.

12,875 VILLIERS, A. Note sur quelques Réduviides et Henicocephalides de la Guinée Portugaise. Description de deux espèces nouvelles. BCGP 3 (1948), pp. 75-79.

12,876 VILLIERS, S. Note sur quelques mollusques de Guinée Portugaise. BCGP 3 (1948), pp. 353-357.

12,877 WALTER, J. Breve estudo da flora medicinal da Guiné. BCGP 1 (1946), pp. 635-662.

12,878 Primeira reunião médica (em Bissau de 27 a 29 de dezembro de 1948). (Trabalhos da Missão de Estudo e Combate da Doença do Sono na Guiné Portuguesa.) BCGP 4 (1949), pp. 61-93.

See also 12916, 24256.

Sociology

12,879 BRITO, E. Inquérito à fecundidade da mulher Fula do Gabú. BCGP 18 (1963), pp. 571-593.

12,880 CAMPOS, F. S. DE. O estudo do habitat como base do planeamento. BCGP 17 (1962), pp. 513-573.

12,881 CARREIRA, A. O Censo General da População de 1960. BCGP 16 (1961), pp. 125-135.

12,882 CARREIRA, A. Movimento natural da população não civilizada da Circunscrição Administrativa de Cacheu (Nupcialidade, fecundidade, natalidade, mortalidade). BCGP 11 (1956), pp. 7-90.

12,883 CARREIRA, A. Organização social e económica dos povos da Guiné Portuguesa. BCGP 16 (1961), pp. 641-736.

12,884 CARREIRA, A. População autóctone segundo os recenseamentos para fins fiscais. BCGP 15 (1960), pp. 53-60, 241-323; 16 (1961), pp. 103-124, 263-296; 17 (1962), pp. 57-118, 221-280, 405-436.

12,885 CARREIRA, A. A população civilizada da Guiné Portuguesa em 1950. BCGP 14 (1959), pp. 547-568.

12,886 CARREIRA, A. Recenseamentos de população Indices da Poligamia. BCGP 16 (1961), pp. 769-782.

12,887 CARREIRA, A. and MEIRELES, A. M. DE. Notas sobre os movimentos migratórios da população da Guiné Portuguesa. BCGP 14 (1959), pp. 7-19.

12,888 CARREIRA, A. and MEIRELES, A. M. DE. Quelques notes sur les mouvements migratoires des populations de la province portugaise de Guinée. BULL. IFAN 22 (1960), pp. 379-392.

12,889 MARQUES, J. E. A. DA S. A gerontocracia na organização social dos bijagós. BCGP 10 (1955), pp. 293-297.

12,890 MENDONCA, P. C. DE. Elevacão do nível de vida do trabalhador na Guiné Portuguesa. BCGP 11, no. 42 (1956), pp. 111-127.

12,891 MOREIRA, J. M. Estrutura das comunidades rurais da Guiné Portuguesa. Sua promoção e integreção no complexo social portugues. BCGP 17 (1962), pp. 459-472.

12,892 VIEIRA, R. A. Alguns aspectos demográficos dos Bijagós da Guiné Portuguesa (Inquérito realizado na Ilha de Bubaque). BCGP 10 (1955), pp. 23-33.

CAPE VERDE ISLANDS

12,893 ALVES, P. H. A actividade dos Padres do Espírito Santo em Cabo-Verde. PORT. EM AFR. 2 (1945), pp. 146-154.

12,894 BELCHIOR, M. Presença da Guiné. PORT. EM AFR. 20 (1963), pp. 240-250.

12,895 BRASIO, P. A. O Padre António Vieira e as Missões de Cabo Verde. PORT. EM AFR. 3 (1946), pp. 298-305.

12,896 DIAS DINIS, P. A. J. Crencas e costumes dos indígenas da ilha de Bissau no século XVIII. PORT. EM AFR. 2 (1945), pp. 159-165, 223-229.

12,897 FERREIRA, J. Um grande Missionário [D. Faustino Moreira dos Santos]. PORT. EM AFR. 12 (1955), pp. 381-393.

12,898 FONSECA, A. X. DA. A lepra em Cabo Verde. PORT. EM AFR. 6 (1949), pp. 204-207.

12,899 NOGUEIRA, A. A religião em Cabo Verde. PORT. EM AFR. 13 (1956), pp. 147-160.

12,900 PEREIRA DE OLIVEIRA, J. Primeiro Centenário da elavação da vila de Santa Maria da Praia à categoria de cidade da Praia de Santiago, capital da Provincia de Cabo Verde. PORT. EM AFR. 15 (1958), pp. 302-307.

12,901 PEREIRA DE OLIVEIRA, J. Renascimento Religioso [de Cabo Verde]. PORT. EM AFR. 13 (1956), pp. 161-194.

12,902 REGO, F. A. DO. A Actividade dos Padres do Espírito Santo em Cabo Verde. PORT. EM AFR. 8 (1951), pp. 373-380; 9 (1952), pp. 306-316.

12,903 REGO, F. A. DO. A Actividade dos Padres do Espírito Santo em Cabo Verde—1954. PORT. EM AFR. 12 (1955), pp. 75-87.

12,904 REGO, F. A. DO. Cabo Verde. PORT. EM AFR. 12 (1955), pp. 235-243, 437-442.

12,905 REGO, F. A. DO. Carta de Cabo Verde. PORT. EM AFR. 15 (1958), pp. 238-240.

12,906 REGO, F. A. DO. Os padres do Espírito Santo em Cabo Verde. PORT. EM AFR. 10 (1953), pp. 334-342.

12,907 REGO, F. A. DO. A última crise em Cabo Verde. PORT. EM AFR. 13 (1956), pp. 117-119.

12,908 RIBAS, T. Notas para uma introdução ao estudo das danças na Africa portuguesa. PORT. EM AFR. 21 (1964), pp. 305-310.

12,909 SOUSA, A. N. DE. Cabo Verde não apenas o arquipélago. PORT. EM AFR. 18 (1961), pp. 285-289.

12,910 SOUSA, A. N. DE. O Novo Seminário de Cabo Verde. PORT. EM AFR. 14 (1957), pp. 289-294.

12,911 SOUSA, P. A. N. Costumes de Santiago de Cabo-Verde. PORT. EM AFR. 3 (1946), pp. 77-80.

12,912 Arquipelago de Cabo Verde. PORT. EM AFR. 13 (1956), pp. 129-130.

12,913 Descobrimento de Cabo Verde. PORT. EM AFR. 13 (1956), pp. 131-140.

12,914 Plano de fomento para 1959-1964. PORT. EM AFR. 17 (1960), pp. 54-64, 113-123.

12,915 Povo caboverdiano. PORT. EM AFR. 13 (1956), pp. 141-146.

See also 8581, 23630.

SAO TOME. PRINCIPE

12,916 ALVES, M. L. G. Entomofauna da Guiné Portuguesa e S. Tomé e Príncipe (Contribuição para o seu conhecimento). Coleópteros (Lucanidae, scarabaeidae, cicindelidae, buprestidae). BCGP 11, no. 44 (1956), pp. 87-105.

12,917 BRASIO, A. D. Frei Bernardo da Cruz, Bishop de S. Tomé. PORT. EM AFR. 6 (1949), pp. 321-333.

12,918 BRASIO, A. D. João Baptista, O.P., Bispo de S. Tomé? PORT. EM AFR. 8 (1951), pp. 275-287; 9 (1952), pp. 127-130.

12,919 BRASIO, A. D. Pedro de Sousa Bispo de S. Tomé? PORT. EM AFR. 4 (1947), pp. 235-238.

12,920 BRASIO, A. Estado religioso de S. Tomé e Príncipe em meados do século XVIII. PORT. EM AFR. 3 (1946), pp. 100-109.

12,921 BRASIO, A. As fontes arquivistas da história de S. Tomé. PORT. EM AFR. 21 (1964), pp. 148-153.

12,922 FARO, J. A organizacão fiscal de S. Jorge da Mina em 1529. BCGP 13 (1958), pp. 75-108.

12,923 FELE, B. Massacres à Sao Tomé. PRESENCE AFR. N.S. 1 (1955), pp. 146-152.

12,924 LEITE DE FARIA, F. Os Barbadinhos Italianos em S. Tomé e Príncipe de 1714 a 1794. PORT. EM AFR. 11 (1954), pp. 69-85, 390-404; 12 (1955), pp. 46-55.

12,925 TENDEIRO, J. Ixodídeos encontrados em S. Tomé e Principe. BCGP 12 (1957), pp. 39-46.

See also 10508, 12814, 12815, 12854, 12908.

Central Africa

GENERAL

Agriculture

12,926 MIRACLE, M. P. Economics and agriculture in Central Africa: some problems. ZAIRE 14 (1960), pp. 35-51.

12,927 SILLANS, R. Sur quelques plantes alimentaires spontanées de l'Afrique Centrale. BULL. IEC N.S. 5 (1953), pp. 77-99.

Anthropology

12,928 ALEXANDRE, P. Proto-histoire du groupe beti-bulu-fang: essai de synthèse provisoire. CAH. ET. AFR. 5 (1965), pp. 503-560.

12,929 BRAUSCH, G. De integratie van de gewoonterechtelijke instellingen in het maatschappelijk dienstbetoon in Centraal-Afrika. KONGO-OVERZEE 23 (1957), pp. 24-34.

12,930 CRABTREE, W. A. Lake Bangweulu and its inhabitants. J. AFR. SOC. 16 (1917), pp. 216-226.

12,931 CUNNINGTON, W. A. String figures and tricks from Central Africa. JRAI 36 (1906), pp. 121-131.

12,932 DOUGLAS, M. Matriliny and pawnship in Central Africa. AFRICA 34 (1964), pp. 301-313.

12,933 FERNANDEZ, J. W. and BEKALE, P. Christian acculturation and Fang witchcraft. CAH. ET. AFR. 2 (1961), pp. 244-270.

12,934 GARLANDA, U. Il coccodrillo, genio dei fiumi, nume degli idolatri centro-africani. AFRICA (Rome) 11 (1956), pp. 20-22.

12,935 GREBERT, F. La famille Pahouine en 1931. AFRICA 5 (1932), pp. 192-201.

12,936 GREBERT, F. and KELLER, J. La famille galoase et son évolution désirée par la jeunesse. AFRICA 10 (1937), pp. 329-334.

12,937 THOMAS, J. M. C. and SEVY, G. V. Contes, fables et histoires ngbaka. PRESENCE AFR. N.S. 50 (1964), pp. 183-206.

12,938 ZAAL, C. Bij de Nzakara. Bendo, een fetisj voor de vrouwen. KONGO-OVERZEE 24 (1958), pp. 80-89.

See also 15809, 15821.

Art

12,939 ARKELL, A. J. The distribution in Central Africa of one early Neolithic ware (dotted wavy line pottery) and its possible connection with the beginning of pottery. PROC. PAN-AFR. CONGR. PRE-HIST. 4, no. iii (1962), pp. 283-285.

12,940 A musical pilgrim's progress. AFR. MUSIC, 1963, pp. 43-47.

See also 15836.

Biography

12,941 DELHAYE, F. Le Chanoine Achille Salée 1883-1932 [obituary]. BULL. SEANCES IRCB 4 (1933), pp. 28-37.

12,942 The late Mrs. M. French Sheldon. J. AFR. SOC. 35 (1936), pp. 202-203.

Economics

12,943 CECCHELLA, A. Le migrazioni della manodopera nei paesi dell' Africa centrale: Aspetti economici e sociali. AFRICA (Rome) 17 (1962), pp. 173-177.

12,944 CORO, F. Il commercio carovaniero fra la Libia e i paesi dell' Africa centrale. AFRICA (Rome) 16 (1961), pp. 87-90.

12,945 HALCROW, Sir W. Hydro-electric power in Central Africa. CORONA 4 (1952), pp. 292-293.

12,946 ORR, C. W. Light railways for Tropical Africa. J. AFR. SOC. 10 (1911), pp. 179-190.

Education

See 15930.

Geography

12,947 CAMERON, Lt. Colonisation of Central Africa. ROYAL COL. INST. PR. 7 (1875-1876), pp. 274-296.

12,948 DEBENHAM, F. The Bangweulu swamps of Central Africa. GEOG. REV. 37 (1947), pp. 351-368.

12,949 LAVAUDEN, L. The equatorial forest of Africa: its past, present and future. J. AFR. SOC. 36 (1937), supplement.

12,950 MIGEOD, F. W. H. Across Africa along the equator. J. AFR. SOC. 20 (1921), pp. 270-278; 21 (1921), pp. 15-22.

12,951 ROOME, J. W. A white man in a pygmy forest. J. AFR. SOC. 35 (1936), pp. 262-267.

12,952 WARTHIN, M. Transportation developments in Central Africa. GEOG. REV. 18 (1928), pp. 307-309.

See also 4925, 15963.

Government. Politics. Administration

12,953 CHIDZERO, B. T. G. Central Africa: the race question and the franchise. RACE 1, no. 1 (1959-1960), pp. 53-60.

12,954 SPILSBURY, A. G. The development of Central Africa from the east. J. AFR. SOC. 1 (1902), pp. 358-367.

12,955 TORDAY, E. The influence of the kingdom of Kongo on Central Africa. AFRICA 1 (1928), pp. 157-169.

12,956 Il futuro dell' Africa Centrale nelle raccomandazioni Monckton. AFRICA (Rome) 15 (1960), p. 297.

See also 7759, 8585.

History

12,957 ANSTEY, R. T. British trade and policy in West Central Africa between 1816 and the early 1880's. TR. HIST. SOC. GHANA 3 (1957), pp. 47-71.

12,958 BURTT, J. Slave labour on cocoa plantations. CONTEMP. REV. 96 (1909), pp. 468-473.

12,959 EVANS-PRITCHARD, E. E. An historical introduction to a study of Zande society. AFR. STUD. 17 (1958), pp. 1-15.

12,960 TAYLOR, A. R. and DUORIN, E. P. Political development in British Central Africa 1890-1956. A select survey of the literature and background materials. RACE 1, no. 1 (1959-1960), pp. 61-78.

12,961 Search for early records of Central and Southern Africa. ARCHIVES 1, no. 2 (1949), pp. 49-50.

Language

12,962 BULCK, G. VAN. Le problème linguistique dans les Missions d'Afrique centrale. ZAIRE 6 (1952), pp. 49-65.

12,963 GUTHRIE, M. Teke radical structure and common Bantu. AFR. LANG. STUD. 1 (1960), pp. 1-15.

12,964 LAMAN, K. E. Languages used in the Congo Basin: a linguistic survey. AFRICA 1 (1928), pp. 372-380.

12,965 LUKAS, J. Linguistic research between Nile and Lake Chad. AFRICA 12 (1939), pp. 335-349.

12,966 LUKAS, J. The linguistic situation in the Lake Chad area in Central Africa. AFRICA 9 (1936), pp. 332-348.

12,967 MEINHOF, C. Die Sprache der Bira. AFR. UND UB. 29 (1939), pp. 241-287.

12,968 MELZIAN, H. J. Zehn Sprichwörter und ein Märchen aus dem Duala. AFRICA 2 (1929), pp. 71-73.

12,969 RENDINGER, DE. Contribution a l'étude des langues nègres du Centre-africain. J. SOC. AFR. 19 (1949), pp. 143-194.

12,970 STUHLMANN, F. Wortlisten zentralafrikanischer Stämme. AFR. UND UB. 7 (1916-1917), pp. 257-308.

12,971 WESTERMANN, D. Neue Sprachforschungen in Zentralafrika. AFRIKA (Berlin) 2 (1943), pp. 123-128?.

Law

See 7759, 7989, 8314, 8326.

Religion

12,972 MILFORD, T. R. In Central and Southern Africa for the theological education fund. INT. REV. MISSIONS 50 (1961), pp. 286-292.

12,973 MOORE, R. J. B. The development of the conception of God in Central Africa. INT. REV. MISSIONS 31 (1942), pp. 412-420.

Science

12,974 DOLLMAN, G. The Basenji dog. J. AFR. SOC. 36 (1937), pp. 148-149.

12,975 RIEL, J. V. De bestrijding van de tuberculose in Centraal Afrika. ZAIRE 9 (1955), pp. 589-618.

12,976 SALVO, C. S. Primera reunión del Comité Regional del Africa Central para la conservacion y utilizacion de los suelos. ARCH. INST. EST. AFR. 7, no. 29 (1954), pp. 55-63.

12,977 SICE, A. L'assistance médicale en Afrique noire française. AFRICA 14 (1943), pp. 27-36.

See also 8113.

Sociology

12,978 BOELAERT, E. Dernières données sur la démographie mongo. ZAIRE 9 (1955), pp. 741-743.

12,979 COULTER, C. W. Problems arising from industrialization of native life in Central Africa. AMER. J. SOC. 40 (1934-1935), pp. 582-592.

See also 4536, 8172.

FRENCH EQUATORIAL AFRICA

Anthropology

12,980 DENNETT, R. E. The religion of the Fjort or Fiote "Mavungu." J. AFR. SOC. 1 (1902), pp. 452-454.

12,981 MURAZ, G. Les cache-sexe du Centre-africain. J. SOC. AFR. 2 (1932), pp. 103-111.

12,982 PANYELLA, A. and SABATER, J. Los cuatro grados de la familia en los Fang de la Guinea española, Camarones y Gabón. ARCH. INST. EST. AFR. 10, no. 40 (1957), pp. 7-17.

12,983 SICE, A. Notes sur les groupements ethniques en Afrique équatoriale française. AFRICA 14 (1944), pp. 454-458; English summary, p. 458.

12,984 SORET, M. Carte ethno-démographique de l'Afrique Equatoriale Française. Note préliminaire. BULL. IEC N.S. 11 (1956), pp. 26-52.

Art. Antiquities

12,985 FOURNEAU, J. and KRAVETZ, L. La pagne sur la Côte de Guinée et au Congo du XVe siècle à nos jours. BULL. IEC N.S. 7-8 (1954), pp. 5-22.

12,986 ITALIAANDER, R. Experiments in modern African art: etchings in French Equatorial Africa. AFRICA 30 (1960), pp. 46-50.

12,987 PEPPER, H. L'enregistrement du son et l'art musical ethnique. BULL. IEC N.S. 4 (1952), pp. 143-149.

Economics

12,988 C[OMHAIRE], J. Progrès et problèmes de l'Afrique Equatoriale française. ZAIRE 5 (1951), pp. 715-721.

12,989 DEL VALLE, R. La estructura económica agraria en el Africa Ecuatorial Francesa. CUAD. EST. AFR. 20 (1952), pp. 43-51.

12,990 FREY, R. Les armes de Brazzaville viennent d'Italie. AFRICA (Rome) 16 (1961), p. 304.

12,991 GUILBOT, J. Absenteeism and labour turnover in Equatorial Africa. HUMAN FACTORS OF PRODUCTIVITY IN AFR., 1962, pp. 131-155.

12,992 HAARER, A. E. The development of Equatorial Africa. CONTEMP. REV. 180 (1951), pp. 356-359.

12,993 S., E. Aviazione civile in A.E.F. AFRICA (Rome) 10 (1955), p. 159.

12,994 SILLANS, R. Economie des plantes à parfums d'Afrique Centrale. BULL. IEC N.S. 6 (1953), pp. 181-208.

See also 8230.

Education

12,995 PERLSTEIN, M. L'enseignement en Afrique équatoriale française. AFRICA 14 (1943), pp. 130-135.

12,996 L'enseignement féminin en A.E.F. ZAIRE 6 (1952), p. 1093.

Geography

12,997 NIVEN, C. R. Visit to Brazzaville. CORONA 2 (1950), pp. 17-19.

12,998 TATE, G. H. H. From the Cameroons to the Ivory Coast by air. GEOG. REV. 32 (1942), pp. 150-153.

12,999 VASSAL, G. French Equatorial Africa. J. AFR. SOC. 31 (1932), pp. 167-172.

Government

13,000 COMHAIRE, J. L'Afrique équatoriale francaise dix ans après Eboué. ZAIRE 8 (1954), pp. 171-179.

13,001 HAARER, A. E. Problems of Equatorial Africa. CONTEMP. REV. 187 (1955), pp. 409-414.

13,002 SILBERMAN, L. Changes in the French colonies. RACE RELATIONS 12 (1945), pp. 37-44.

13,003 The Eboue Memoranda of 1941. SUDAN NOTES 25 (1943), part 2, pp. 1-80.

See also 8273, 8279.

History

13,004 BRUEL, G. L'Olumo aviso de flottille un épisode de la mission de l'Ouest africain (1883-1886). RHCF 29 (1936), pp. 317-358.

13,005 BRUNSCHWIG, H. Les factures de Brazza, 1875-1878. CAH. ET. AFR. 4 (1963), pp. 14-21.

13,006 JOOS, C. D. Le Ouadai, le Dar el Kouti et la Senoussia en 1904. Matériaux pour une étude de l'histoire des Etats d'Afrique Centrale. Documents traduits et présentés. ET. CAMER. 53-54 (1956), pp. 3-17.

13,007 PIERRET, F. Les sociétés historiques en A.E.F. RHCF 30 (1937), pp. 291-298.

13,008 SURET-CANALE, J. Brazza ou la dernière idole. RECH. AFR. 1 (1960), pp. 12-16.

Language. Literature

See 8397.

Law

13,009 LEGIER, H. J. Afrique equatoriale d'expression française. [Legal education.] J. AFR. LAW 6 (1962), p. 91.

13,010 MANGIN, G. L'organisation judiciaire de l'Afrique Equatoriale francaise et du Cameroun. THE FUTURE OF CUSTOMARY LAW IN AFRICA, 1956, pp. 198-207.

See also 8314.

Religion

13,011 KONKA, R. Les débuts de la Mission catholique de Landana (1873-1876). CAH. ET. AFR. 2 (1962), pp. 362-372.

Science

13,012 BLANCOU, L. Notes biogéographiques sur les Mammifères de l'A.E.F. BULL. IEC N.S. 15-16 (1958), pp. 7-42.

13,013 CECCALDI, J. et al. Contribution à l'étude des groupes sanguins chez les populations de l'Afrique Equatoriale Française. BULL. IEC 1, no. 1 (1945), pp. 111-117.

13,014 CHEVALIER, A. Identification du Champignon employé en Afrique équatoriale pour la confection de ceintures de parure. J. SOC. AFR. 5 (1935), pp. 247-249.

13,015 CHEVALIER, A. Les plantes magiques cultivées par les Noirs d'Afrique et leur origine. J. SOC. AFR. 7 (1937), pp. 93-105.

13,016 COLLIGNON, J. La pêche au chalut sur les côtes d'A.E.F. BULL. IEC N.S. 17-18 (1959), pp. 21-33.

13,017 MAILLOT, L. Les Glossines, vecteurs de la maladie du sommeil, en A.E.F. BULL IEC N.S. 2 (1951), pp. 63-72.

13,018 MURAZ, G. Remarque sur un champignon, ceinture de parure. J. SOC. AFR. 5 (1935), pp. 93-95.

13,019 OVAZZA and TAUFFLIEB. Tabanides d'A.E.F. BULL. IEC N.S. 4 (1952), pp. 131-141.

13,020 PALES, L. Premières recherches sur la tache pigmentaire congénitale (tache mongolique) en Afrique equatoriale française. J. SOC. AFR. 2 (1932), pp. 55-58.

13,021 PRIESNER, H. On some central African *Thysanoptera*. BULL. IFAN 14 (1952), pp. 842-880.

13,022 ROUX, C. Considérations pratiques sur la Pêche le long du littorale de l'A.E.F. BULL. IEC N.S. 1 (1950), pp. 65-78.

13,023 ROUX, C. and COLLIGNON, J. La station océanographique de Pointe-Noire durant l'année 1951. BULL. IEC N.S. 4 (1952), pp. 119-129.

13,024 SOYER, L. Note sur les activités de l'Institut pour la Recherche Scientifique en Afrique Centrale. COOPERAZIONE INT. AFR., 1960, pp. 207-209.

13,025 TROCHAIN, J. L. La géobotanique et son intérêt économique. BULL. IEC N.S. 15-16 (1958), pp. 91-97.

13,026 TROCHAIN, J. L. Sur l'intérêt d'introduire ou développer certaines productions végétales en A.E.F. BULL. IEC N.S. 11 (1956), pp. 61-80.

Sociology

13,027 LEBEUF, J. Centres urbains d'Afrique Equatoriale Française. AFRICA 23 (1953), pp. 285-296; English summary, pp. 296-297.

13,028 PAUVERT, J. C. La notion de travail en Afrique noire. PRESENCE AFR. 13 (1952), pp. 92-107.

13,029 PAUVERT, J. C. Le problème des classes sociales en Afrique équatoriale. CAH. INT. SOCIOL. 19 (1955), pp. 76-91.

See also 8272.

CAMEROUN

General

13,030 COMHAIRE, J. Vues générales sur le Cameroun. ZAIRE 7 (1953), pp. 55-64.

13,031 MOHAMADOU, E. Pour sauver nos cultures: Le Centre Federal Linguistique et Culturel Camerounais. ABBIA 5 (1964), pp. 181-183.

13,032 The American Society of African Culture. AMSAC. ABBIA 3 (1963), pp. 169-171; French translation, pp. 171-73.

13,033 Arrêté du 9 Mai 1944: Arrêté portant création d'un centre local au Cameroun de l'Institut français d'Afrique noire. BSEC 6 (1944), pp. 5-6.

13,034 The birth of two cultural associations: the Cameroon Cultural Association and the Cameroon Cultural Society. ABBIA 1 (1963), pp. 112-113; French translation, pp. 113-114.

13,035 Le Cameroun a son Centre Fédéral Linguistique et Culturel. ABBIA 1 (1963), pp. 115-116.

13,036 The cercle d'études du grand séminaire d'Otélé. ABBIA 3 (1963), pp. 154-156.

13,037 Clé, Centre de littérature évangélique pour l'Afrique d'expression francaise Yaoundé. ABBIA 3 (1963), pp. 167-168.

13,038 La Commission Nationale Camerounaise pour l'U.N.E.S.C.O. est née. ABBIA 1 (1963), pp. 107-109.

13,039 Les travaux de l'Institut de Recherches Scientifiques du Cameroun (I.R.CAM.). ABBIA 3 (1963), pp. 157-161.

See also 8488, 8489.

Agriculture

13,040 DUGAST, R. L'agriculture chez les Ndiki de population Banen. BSEC 8 (1944), pp. 7-103.

13,041 EVANS, F. Agricultural development in the Cameroons. BULL. IMP. INST. 20 (1922), pp. 165-173.

13,042 HALLAIRE, A. Koubadje. Etude d'un terroir agricole de l'Adamaoua. RECH. ET. CAM. 5 (1961-1962), pp. 47-72.

13,043 KOCH, H. Le petit bétail chez les Badjoué et Bilélé de Messaména. BSEC 13-14 (1946), pp. 27-108.

13,044 SEGALEN, P. Dix années de travaux pédologiques au Cameroun. RECH. ET CAM. 1 (1960), pp. 115-122.

13,045 VAILLANT, A. Une enquête agricole chez les Mofu de Wazam. BSEC 17-18 (1947), pp. 41-98.

13,046 WHITE, S. L'Economie agricole des montagnes Kirdis de l'Emirat de Dikoa au Cameroun sous Mandat Britannique. BSEC 3 (1943), pp. 77-84.

13,047 YONKE, J. P. Les problèmes posés par le développement harmonieux de l'Agriculture du Cameroun Oriental. ABBIA 4 (1963), pp. 95-113.

13,048 Questionnaire sur l'agriculture indigène. BSEC 5 (1944), pp. 91-94.

See also 8182, 17671.

Anthropology

13,049 ABBO, H. et al. Coutumes du Mandara by H. Abbo, J. P. Lebeuf, M. Rodinson. BULL. IFAN 11 (1949), pp. 471-490.

13,050 ALEXANDRE, P. Contradiction. CAH. ET. AFR. 4 (1964), pp. 435-442.

13,051 ALTHABE, G. Changements sociaux chez le Pygmées Baka de l'Est-Cameroun. CAH. ET. AFR. 5 (1965), pp. 561-592.

13,052 AMATO, F. Croyances Bafias. AFRICA (Rome) 18 (1963), pp. 25-32.

13,053 ANYA-NOA, L. and ANTANGANA, S. La sagesse Béti dans le chant des oiseaux. ABBIA 8 (1965), pp. 97-139.

13,054 ANYA-NOA, L. et al. Enigmes Beti, by L. Anya-Noa, G. Mfomo, G. Many. RECH. ET. CAM. 5 (1961-1962), pp. 111-127.

13,055 ARANZADI, I. DE. Tradiciones orales del bosque fang. ARCH. INST. EST. AFR. 10, no. 41 (1957), pp. 61-77.

13,056 AWONA, S. La guerre d'Akoma Mba contre Abo Mama. ABBIA 9-10 (1965), pp. 180-214.

13,057 BAHOKEN, J. C. La notion de Bedimo chez les Bantu du Cameroun. J. SOC. AFR. 31 (1961), pp. 91-96.

13,058 BEKOMBO, M. Conflits d'autorité au sein de la société familiale chez les Dwala du Sud-Cameroun. CAH. ET. AFR. 4, no. 14 (1963), pp. 317-329.

13,059 BERTAUT, M. Contribution a l'étude des Negrilles de la Région du Haut-Nyong. BSEC 4 (1943), pp. 73-91.

13,060 BINET, J. L'habitation dans la Subdivision de Foumbot. ET. CAMER. 31-32 (1950), pp. 189-199.

13,061 BINET, J. L'habitation dans la Subdivision de N'Kongsamba. BSEC 21-22 (1948), pp. 35-48.

13,062 BLANCHFLOWER, T. G. Some random fishing notes. NIGERIAN FIELD 4 (1935), pp. 136-137.

13,063 BOT BA NJOK, H. M. Prééminences sociales et système politico-religieux dans la société traditionnelle Bulu et Fang. J. SOC. AFR. 30 (1960), pp. 151-171.

13,064 BRUTSCH, J. R. Les relations de parenté chez les Duala. ET. CAMER. 31-32 (1950), pp. 211-230.

13,065 BRYGOO, E. R. R. La tache pigmentaire congénitale chez les nouveau-nés de la Subdivision d'Akonolinga. ET. CAMER. 25-26 (1949), pp. 69-80.

13,066 BUISSON, E. M. Caractères descriptifs de quelques Foulbé nobles de Maroua (Haut-Cameroun). J. SOC. AFR. 3 (1933), pp. 283-288.

13,067 BUREAU, R. Ethno-sociologie religieuse des Duala et apparentés. RECH. ET. CAM. 7-8 (1962), pp. 5-372.

13,068 BWINDI, J. Fishing among the Bimbians. NIGERIAN FIELD 4 (1935), pp. 188-189.

13,069 CHILVER, E. M. A Bamileke community in a Bali-Nyonga: a note on the Bawok. AFR. STUD. 23 (1964), pp. 121-127.

13,070 COURNARIE, P. Notes sommaires sur les pratiques divinatoires des populations de la circonscription de Yaoundé. J. SOC. AFR. 6 (1936), pp. 35-39.

13,071 COUSTEIX, P. J. L'art et la pharmacopée des guérisseurs ewondo (Région de Yaoundé). RECH. ET. CAM. 6 (1961-1963), pp. 3-87.

13,072 COZENS, A. B. A village Smithy in the Cameroons. NIGERIAN FIELD 20 (1955), pp. 25-34.

13,073 DELAROZIERE, R. Les institutions politiques et sociales des populations dites Bamileke. ET. CAMER. 25-26 (1949), pp. 5-68; 27-28 (1949), pp. 127-175.

13,074 DELCROIX, G. Enquête sur le Lahoré de N'Gaoundéré. BSEC 1 (1935), pp. 43-52.

13,075 DUGAST, R. A la recherche d'une épouse. BSEC 11 (1945), pp. 57-75.

13,076 DUGAST, R. Autobiographie d'une femme Banen. BSEC 6 (1944), pp. 73-84.

13,077 DUGAST, R. Une corbeille divinatoire. BSEC 15-16 (1946), pp. 87-104.

13,078 DUGAST, R. L'habitation chez les Ndiki du Cameroun. J. SOC. AFR. 10 (1940), pp. 99-125.

13,079 EBDING, F. Duala-Märchen. AFR. UND UB. 18 (1927-1928), pp. 140-152.

13,080 EKALLE, S. Croyances et pratiques obstétricales des Duala. BSEC 19-20 (1947), pp. 61-92.

13,081 ERYGOO, J. and ERYGOO, E. Notes d'anthropologie: gémelleite, polydactylie, albinisme dans la région d'Ayos. ET. CAMER. 33-34 (1951), pp. 41-52.

13,082 FOURNEAU, J. Une tribu païenne du Nord-Cameroun: les Guissiga (Moutouroua), contribution ethnologique. J. SOC. AFR. 8 (1938), pp. 163-195.

13,083 FROELICH, J. C. Le commandement et l'organisation sociale chez les Fali du Nord Cameroun. ET. CAMER. 53-54 (1956), pp. 20-60.

13,084 FROELICH, J. C. Le commandement et l'organisation sociale chez les Foulbé de l'Adamaoua (Cameroun). ET. CAMER. 45-46 (1954), pp. 3-91.

13,085 FROELICH, J. C. Notes sur les Mboum du Nord-Cameroun. J. SOC. AFR. 29 (1959), pp. 91-117.

13,086 GARDI, R. Uber den Totenkult bei den Doayo in Nordkamerun. FESTSCHRIFT ALFRED BUHLER, 1965, pp. 117-126.

13,087 GARINE, I. DE. Le prestige et les vaches. CONGR. INT. SC. ANTHR. ET ETHN. 6, no. ii (1960), pp. 191-196.

13,088 GAUTHIER, J. G. Notes sur la religion des Fali. ABBIA 3 (1963), pp. 48-54.

13,089 GEHR, C. Zwei Dualamärchen. AFR. UND UB. 7 (1916-1917), pp. 25-35.

13,090 GUILBOT, J. Le Bilaba. J. SOC. AFR. 21 (1951), pp. 163-174.

13,091 GUILBOT, J. Les conditions de vie des indigènes de Douala. ET. CAMER. 27-28 (1949), pp. 179-239.

13,092 GUILLEMIN. Le rite Esye. ET. CAMER. 23-24 (1948), pp. 71-85.

13,093 GUILLOU. L'industrie du fer dans la Subdivision de Babimbi. ET. CAMER. 31-32 (1950), pp. 207-209.

13,094 HARTER, P. Les courses de pirogues coutumières chez les Duala ou pembisan a myoloo Duala. RECH. ET. CAM. 1 (1960), pp. 71-91.

13,095 HECKLINGER, P. Dualasprichwörter. AFR. UND UB. 11 (1920-1921), pp. 35-70, 125-160, 220-239, 306-315.

13,096 HINDERLING, P. Ueber die Herstellung von Schnur- und Ledertaschen in Nordkamerun. FESTSCHRIFT ALFRED BUHLER, 1965, pp. 183-186.

13,097 HINDERLING, P. Versuch einer Analyse der sozialen Struktur der Matakam. AFRICA 25 (1955), pp. 405-425; English summary, pp. 425-426.

13,098 HIRSCHBERG, W. The problem of relationship between Pygmies and Bushmen. AFRICA 7 (1934), pp. 444-451.

13,099 HORNER, G. R. The allocation of power and responsibility in Bulo society. CAH. ET. AFR. 4 (1964), pp. 400-434.

13,100 HORNER, N. A. Polygyny among the Bantu of French Cameroun. INT. REV. MISSIONS 43 (1954), pp. 173-178.

13,101 HURAULT, J. Quelques aspects de la structure sociale des montagnards Kirdi du nord Cameroun. BULL. IFAN, Série B: Sciences humaines 20 (1958), pp. 111-122.

13,102 ITTMANN, J. Ein Bakoko-Märchen aus Kamerun. AFR. UND UB. 38 (1953-1954), pp. 141-154.

13,103 ITTMANN, J. Bemerkungen zu den Altersklassen der Duala und ihrer Nachbarn. AFR. UND UB. 39 (1954-1955), pp. 83-88.

13,104 ITTMANN, J. Rezepte aus dem Waldland von Kamerun. AFR. UND UB. 40 (1956), pp. 141-162.

13,105 ITTMANN, J. Spiele der Kosi in Kamerun. AFR. UND UB. 45 (1961-1962), pp. 123-158.

13,106 ITTMANN, J. Von der Gottesvorstellung der Bakwiri. AFRICA 8 (1935), pp. 355-372.

13,107 ITTMANN, J. Von Totengebräuchen und Ahnenkult der Kosi in Kamerun. AFRICA 26 (1956), pp. 380-396; English summary, pp. 396-397.

13,108 JEFFREYS, M. D. W. The Bali of Bamenda. AFR. STUD. 16 (1957), pp. 108-113.

13,109 JEFFREYS, M. D. W. The Bamum coronation ceremony as described by King Njoya. AFRICA 20 (1950), pp. 38-45.

13,110 JEFFREYS, M. D. W. Notes on Bakweri funeral customs. AFR. STUD. 20 (1961), pp. 61-65.

13,111 JEFFREYS, M. D. W. Notes on twins: Bamenda. AFR. STUD. 6 (1947), pp. 189-195.

13,112 JEFFREYS, M. D. W. Le serpent a deux têtes Bamum. BSEC 9 (1945), pp. 7-12.

13,113 JEFFREYS, M. D. W. Some African tribal names. J. AFR. SOC. 41 (1942), pp. 47-49.

13,114 JEFFREYS, M. D. W. Some notes on births among the Fulani. AFR. STUD. 14 (1955), p. 42.

13,115 JEFFREYS, M. D. W. Some notes on the customs of the Grassfield Bali of Northwestern Cameroons. AFR. UND UB. 46 (1962-1963), pp. 161-168.

13,116 JEFFREYS, M. D. W. Who are the Tikar? AFR. STUD. 23 (1964), pp. 141-153.

13,117 JENKS, A. E. Bulu knowledge of the gorilla and chimpanzee. AMER. ANTHR. 13 (1911), pp. 56-64.

13,118 KABERRY, P. M. Retainers and royal households in the Cameroons grassfields. CAH. ET. AFR. 3 (1962), pp. 282-298.

13,119 KAHLER-MEYER, E. Spiele bei den Bali in Kamerun. AFR. UND UB. 39 (1954-1955), pp. 179-190.

13,120 KELLER, I. Knowledge and theories of astronomy on the part of the Isubu natives of the Western slopes of the Cameroon mountains, in German West Africa (Kamerun). J. AFR. SOC. 3 (1903), pp. 59-61.

13,121 LAMY, P. Notes sur l'anthropologie Mesmé. BULL. IEC 1, no. 2 (1947), pp. 115-117.

13,122 LAVERGNE, G. Le pays et la population matakam. BSEC 7 (1944), pp. 7-73.

13,123 LEBEUF, A. Le système classificatoire des Fali (Nord-Cameroun). AFRICAN SYSTEMS OF THOUGHT, 1965, pp. 328-340.

13,124 LEBEUF, J. P. Bibliographie Sao et Kotoko. BSEC 21-22 (1948), pp. 121-137.

13,125 LEBEUF, J. P. La circoncision chez les Kotoko dans l'ancien pays Sao. J. SOC. AFR. 8 (1938), pp. 1-9.

13,126 LEBEUF, J. P. Labrets et greniers des Fali (Nord Cameroun). BULL. IFAN 15 (1953), pp. 1321-1328.

13,127 LEBEUF, J. P. Le nom chez les Fali. J. SOC. AFR. 9 (1939), pp. 103-117.

13,128 LEBEUF, J. P. Les rites funéraires chez les Fali. J. SOC. AFR. 8 (1938), pp. 103-122.

13,129 LEDERBOGEN, W. Duala fables. J. AFR. SOC. 4 (1904), pp. 56-77.

13,130 LEIRIS, M. Rites de circoncision namchi. J. SOC. AFR. 4 (1934), pp. 63-80.

13,131 LEMBEZAT, B. Les rites du serment chez les animistes de Mora. BSEC 21-22 (1948), pp. 91-104.

13,132 MALCOLM, L. W. G. Notes on birth, marriage and death ceremonies of the EYAP tribe, Central Cameroon. JRAI 53 (1923), pp. 388-401.

13,133 MALCOLM, L. W. G. Notes on the ancestral cult ceremonies of the Eyāp, Central Cameroons. JRAI 55 (1925), pp. 373-404.

13,134 MALZY, P. Les Fali du Tingelin (Nord Cameroun). ET. CAMER. 51 (1956), pp. 3-37.

13,135 MALZY, P. Quelques villages Fali du Tingelin (Nord Cameroun, Region de la Benoue). ET. CAMER. 51 (1956), pp. 38-41.

13,136 MARCHESSEAU, G. Quelques éléments d'ethnographie sur les Mofu du massif de Durum. BSEC 10 (1945), pp. 7-53.

13,137 MARTIN, H. Le pays des Bamum et le Sultan Njoya. ET. CAMER. 33-34 (1951), pp. 5-40.

13,138 MEYER, E. Bemerkungen zum Fök im Hochland von Mittel-Kamerun. AFR. UND UB. 35 (1949-1950), pp. 264-280.

13,139 MOHAMADOU, E. Contes Foulbé de la Bénoué. ABBIA 9-10 (1965), pp. 11-46.

13,140 MOUCHET, J. J. Duvangar. Rites agraires et classes d'âge. BSEC 6 (1944), pp. 51-61.

13,141 MOUCHET, J. J. Pratiques de divination Massa et Tupuri. BSEC 4 (1943), pp. 63-72.

13,142 MOUCHET, J. J. Prospection ethnologique sommaire dans les montagnes du Mandara. BSEC 19-20 (1947), pp. 93-104; 21-22 (1948), pp. 105-119.

13,143 MOUCHET, J. J. Prospection ethnologique sommaire des Massifs du Mandara. ET. CAMER. 55 (1957), pp. 3-15.

13,144 MOUCHET, J. J. Prospection ethnologique sommaire du Massif Zelgwa. ET. CAMER. 25 (1949), pp. 39-54.

13,145 MOUCHET, J. J. Prospections ethnologiques sommaires de quelques massifs du Mandara. BSEC 17-18 (1947), pp. 99-139.

13,146 MUKOKO-MOKEBA, M. P. Philosophical basis of Bakweri mysticism. ABBIA 3 (1963), pp. 39-44; French summary, pp. 44-47.

13,147 NICOLAS, J. P. Nécessité actuelle et anthropologie au Cameroun. ET. CAMER. 23-24 (1948), pp. 5-21.

13,148 NKOUDOU, J. R. O. Le problème du mariage dotal au Cameroun français. ET. CAMER. 39-40 (1953), pp. 41-83.

13,149 OLIVIER, G. Anthropologie physique des Negrilles du Cameroun (d'après les documents des Docteurs Aujoulat et Chabeuf). ET. CAMER. 29-30 (1950), pp. 113-118.

13,150 OLIVIER, G. Documents anthropométriques pour servir a l'étude des principales populations du Sud-Cameroun. BSEC 15-16 (1946), pp. 17-86.

13,151 OLIVIER, G. Etude anthropologique comparée des principales tribus de la région de Yaoundé. BSEC 10 (1945), pp. 55-76.

13,152 PANYELLA, A. El individuo y la sociedad fang. ARCH. INST. EST. AFR. 11, no. 46 (1958), pp. 51-64.

13,153 PANYELLA, A. El proceso de la transformación de la cultura Fang y sus problemas. ARCH. INST. EST. AFR. 17, no. 66 (1963), pp. 25-40.

13,154 PARE, I. L'araignée divinatrice. ET. CAMER. 53-54 (1956), pp. 61-83.

13,155 PEDRALS, H. DE. Contribution a l'établissement d'un inventaire ethnique du Cameroun. BSEC 15-16 (1946), pp. 7-15.

13,156 PEIFFER, E. et al. Quelques résultats obtenus au test de Rorschach, chez les Bamilékés du Cameroun by E. Peiffer, S. Pélage, Mme Pélage. BULL. IFAN 25 (1963), pp. 454-457.

13,157 PERONO, J. Les Basa. BSEC 4 (1943), pp. 94-106.

13,158 PODLEWSKI, A. M. Enquête sur l'émigration des Mafa hors du pays Matakam. RECH. ET. CAM. 5 (1961-1962), pp. 73-95.

13,159 REHFISCH, F. Competitive gift exchange among the Mambila. CAH. ET. AFR. 3 (1962), pp. 91-103.

13,160 REHFISCH, F. The dynamics of multilineality on the Mambila Plateau. AFRICA 30 (1960), pp. 246-260.

13,161 RELLY, H. Quelques notes sur les noms et titres du Grassfield. BSEC 10 (1945), pp. 77-83.

13,162 RITZENTHALER, R. E. Anlu: a women's uprising in the British Cameroons. AFR. STUD. 19 (1960), pp. 151-156.

13,163 ROYER, P. and BUISSON, E. M. Etude comparée de cranes Kirdi et Moundan du Haut-Cameroun. J. SOC. AFR. 4 (1934), pp. 129-133.

13,164 RUEL, M. J. Genealogical concepts or 'category words'? A study of Banyang kinship terminology. JRAI 92 (1962), pp. 157-176.

13,165 RUEL, M. J. The modern adaptation of associations among the Banyang of the West Cameroon. SOUTHWESTERN J. ANTHR. 20 (1964), pp. 1-14.

13,166 SAKAH, B. T. Nso magico-religious practices. ABBIA 2 (1963), pp. 67-70; French translation, pp. 71-74.

13,167 SCHMIDT, A. The water of life [a fertility ceremony]. AFR. STUD. 14 (1955), pp. 23-28.

13,168 SCHURLE, G. and KLAMROTH, M. Afrikanische Liebeslieder [Duala-Lieder by G. Schürle, Ein Dzalamo-Lied by M. Klamroth]. AFR. UND UB. 3 (1912-1913), pp. 244-247.

13,169 SIEBER, J. Märchen und Fabeln der Wute. AFR. UND UB. 12 (1921-1922), pp. 53-72, 162-239.

13,170 TOWO-ATANGANA, G. Le Mvet genre majeur de la littérature orale des populations Pahouines (Bula, Béti, Fang-Ntumu). ABBIA 9-10 (1965), pp. 163-179.

13,171 TSALA, T. Moeurs et coutumes des Ewondo. ET. CAMER. 56 (1958), pp. 8-112.

13,172 VOORHOEVE, J. Note sur les noms-d'éloge bamiléké. CAH. ET. AFR. 4 (1964), pp. 452-455.

13,173 WARMINGTON, W. A. Saving and indebtedness among Cameroon plantation workers. AFRICA 28 (1958), pp. 329-342.

13,174 WOLFE, A. W. The institution of Demba among the Ngonje Ngombe. ZAIRE 8 (1954), pp. 843-856.

13,175 Esquisse ethnologique pour servir à l'étude des principales tribus des Territoires du Cameroun sous Mandat Français. BSEC 3 (1943), pp. 11-59.

13,176 Les funérailles des Bamoun. ET. CAMER. 56 (1958), pp. 122-132.

13,177 Inventaire ethnique et linguistique du Cameroun sous mandat français. J. SOC. AFR. 4 (1934), pp. 203-208.

13,178 Une ordalie en pays Namchi. BSEC 3 (1943), pp. 61-75.

See also 9618.

Art

13,179 DELAROZIERE, S. and LUC, G. Une forme peu connue de l'expression artistique africaine: l'Abbia. Jeu de dés des populations forestières du Sud-Cameroun. ET. CAMER. 49-50 (1955), pp. 3-52.

13,180 FOURNEAU, J. Le néolithique au Cameroun. J. SOC. AFR. 5 (1935), pp. 67-83.

13,181 GOPFERT, H. A cave in the Cameroons. NIGERIAN FIELD 25 (1960), pp. 34-42.

13,182 GUILLEMIN, L. Le tambour d'appel des Ewondo. BSEC 20-21 (1948), pp. 69-84.

13,183 GWELLEM, J. F. Bemenda Museum. ABBIA 3 (1963), pp. 162-163.

13,184 HARTWEG, R. Ossements humains recueillis au Tchad par la Mission Sahara-Cameroun (Villages de Midigué et de Damazé). ET. CAMER. 29-30 (1950), pp. 95-111.

13,185 ITTMANN, J. Lieder aus dem Kameruner Waldland. AFR. UND UB. 42 (1958), pp. 1-15, 69-79.

13,186 JAUZE, J. B. L'art inconnu d'une culture primitive africaine dans la région de Yaounde. ET. CAMER. 23-24 (1948), pp. 47-49.

13,187 JAUZE, J. B. Contribution à l'étude de l'Archéologie du Cameroun. BSEC 8 (1944), pp. 105-123.

13,188 JEFFREYS, M. D. W. Neolithic stone implements (Bemenda, British Cameroons). BULL. IFAN 13 (1951), pp. 1203-1217.

13,189 LAGRAVE, R. Quelques remarques sur les dessins spontanés d'écoliers du Nord-Cameroun. ET. CAMER. 55 (1957), pp. 16-33.

13,190 LAUWE, P. H. DE. Pierres et poteries sacrées du Mandara (Cameroun Nord). (Mission Sahara-Cameroun.) J. SOC. AFR. 7 (1937), pp. 53-67.

13,191 LEBEUF, A. and LEBEUF, J. P. Monuments symboliques du palais royal de Logone-Birni (Nord-Cameroun). J. SOC. AFR. 25 (1955), pp. 25-34.

13,192 LETOUZEY, Y. Propos et suggestions tirés d'expériences relatives a l'enseignement du dessin au Cameroun. BULL. IFAN 15 (1953), pp. 1710-1715.

13,193 MVENG, E. L'Art Camerounais. ABBIA 3 (1963), pp. 3-24.

13,194 PARE, I. Un artiste camerounais peu connu: Ibrahim Njoya. ABBIA 6 (1964), pp. 173-185.

13,195 PARE, I. La place et le rôle des musées dans le Plan du Developpement Economique et Social de l'Afrique. ABBIA 7 (1964), pp. 49-65.

13,196 SCHAEFFNER, A. Sur deux instruments de musique des Bata (Nord Cameroun). J. SOC. AFR. 13 (1943), pp. 123-151.

13,197 TSALA, T. Minlan mi mved (Chants lyriques). RECH. ET. CAM. 2 (1960), pp. 35-63; 4 (1961), pp. 71-89.

13,198 La danse traditionnelle Camerounaise triomphe au Théâtre des Nations. ABBIA 3 (1963), pp. 141-147.

13,199 Musée d'Art et de Folklore Bamiléké, Bafoussam. ET. CAMER. 52 (1956), p. 26.

13,200 Musée Camerounais, Doula. ET. CAMER. 52 (1956), pp. 8-18.

13,201 Musée des Arts et Traditions Bamum (Foumban). ET. CAMER. 52 (1956), pp. 19-22.

13,202 Musée du Diamare, Maroua. ET. CAMER. 52 (1956), pp. 23-25.

13,203 Le Musée du Palais de Foumban. ET. CAMER. 52 (1956), p. 27.

See also 13520.

Biography

13,204 CARRET, J. M. Le Père Julien Perono. BSEC 4 (1943), p. 93.

Economics

13,205 ARDENER, S. Banana co-operatives in the Southern Cameroons. NISER 6 (1958), pp. 10-25.

13,206 BARKAN, J. D. The economic integration of the Federal Republic of Cameroon. PROC. 3RD. GRAD. ACAD. UCLA, 1965, pp. 43-56.

13,207 BINET, J. Le marché de Foumbot. ET. CAMER. 37-38 (1952), pp. 63-70.

13,208 BOUCHART, P. Le F.I.D.E.S. au Cameroun. CIVILISATIONS 6 (1956), pp. 393-407; English summary, pp. 407-409.

13,209 CHILVER, E. M. and KABERRY, P. M. From tribute to tax in a Tikar chiefdom. AFRICA 30 (1960), pp. 1-18.

13,210 FROELICH, J. C. Ngaoundéré. La vie économique d'une cité peul. ET. CAMER. 43-44 (1954), pp. 3-66.

13,211 GUILLAUME, M. Observations sur l'exploitation des funtumias. BSEC 5 (1944), pp. 71-85.

13,212 KISOB, J. A. The Cameroon worker. ABBIA 2 (1963), pp. 111-121.

13,213 KISOB, J. A. Towards a better housing policy. ABBIA 6 (1964), pp. 186-195.

13,214 MAIMO, S. Early education and commerce in the Bamenda Grasslands. ABBIA 2 (1963), pp. 92-99.

13,215 MUKOKO-MOKEBA, M. P. The Cameroon worker isn't lazy. ABBIA 6 (1964), pp. 5-14.

13,216 MULLENDORFF, P. The development of German West Africa (Kamerun). J. AFR. SOC. 2 (1902), pp. 70-92.

13,217 O'KELLY, E. Corn mill societies in the Southern Cameroons. AFR. WOMEN 1 (1955), pp. 33-35.

13,218 ROSSIGNOL, M. Le Cameroun maritime: ressources et possibilités économiques. RECH. ET. CAM. 2 (1960), pp. 64-85.

13,219 SCHMIDT, A. Some notes on the influence of religion on economics in a Tikar subtribe, West Africa. AFR. STUD. 10 (1951), pp. 13-26.

13,220 Le Centre de production de Manuels et d'Auxiliaires de l'Enseignement installé à Yaoundé. ABBIA 1 (1963), pp. 91-95.

See also 1562, 9330.

Education

13,221 KUO, S. A propos de l'education de base au Cameroun. PRESENCE AFR. N.S. 6 (1956), pp. 87-105; 7 (1956), pp. 74-84.

13,222 LAGNEAU-KESTELOOT, L. Une expérience au lycée de Garoua. ABBIA 6 (1964), p. 196.

13,223 NDONGMO, A. L'Education au Pays Bamiléké. ET. CAMER. 47-48 (1955), pp. 43-51.

13,224 TOWA, M. La fonction normale de l'ecole dans la nation. ABBIA 2 (1963), pp. 75-83; English translation, pp. 84-91.

13,225 VOUILLOUX. Etude de la psycho-motricité d'enfants africains au Cameroun. Test de Gesell et réflexes archaïques. J. SOC. AFR. 29 (1959), pp. 11-18.

13,226 Girls' education in the Cameroons. AFR. WOMEN 4 (1961), pp. 62-63.

13,227 IXe Congres de l'Union nationale des Etudiants Kamerunais. PRESENCE AFR. N.S. 22 (1958), pp. 138-141.

See also 10336.

Geography

13,228 BACHELIER, G. et al. Les sols de savane du Sud-Cameroun [by G. Bachelier, M. Curis, D. Martin]. BULL. IEC N.S. 13-14 (1957), pp. 7-27.

13,229 BAUDRY, R. Etude climatologique de la région de Doula. BSEC 4 (1943), pp. 7-47.

13,230 D., R. and L., M. Présentation du Diamaré. RECH. ET. CAM. 9 (1962-1963), pp. 3-11.

13,231 DEBOUDAUD, J. Carte schématique des populations du Cameroun. J. SOC. AFR. 9 (1939), pp. 197-203.

13,232 DUBREUIL, P. Hydrologie de surface dans le Diamaré. RECH. ET. CAM. 9 (1962-1963), pp. 31-41.

13,233 FOURY, P. Indications données par l'état actuel de la végétation sur la répartition ancienne des groupements humains. BSEC 2 (1937), pp. 7-13.

13,234 HAIG, E. F. G. The Cameroon Mountain; a general conspectus. NIGERIAN FIELD 6 (1937), pp. 118-128, 172-181.

13,235 LEBEUF, J. P. Rapport sur les travaux de la 4e mission Griaule, Sahara-Cameroun (10 juillet 1936-16 octobre 1937). J. SOC. AFR. 7 (1937), pp. 213-219.

13,236 MIGEOD, F. W. H. British Cameroons, its tribes and natural features. J. AFR. SOC. 23 (1924), pp. 176-187.

13,237 NICOLAS, J. P. Questions de toponymie. ET. CAMER. 25 (1949), pp. 7-18.

13,238 SALASC. Le Bebenda formation du Lamidat de Bibemi. ET. CAMER. 31-32 (1950), pp. 201-206.

13,239 SRAM, J. Remarques sur la glaciation au Cameroun. ET. CAMER. 49-50 (1955), pp. 53-55.

See also 8575, 11549.

Government. Politics. Administration

13,240 A., E. J. The Cameroons under British mandate, 1935; by E. J. A. J. AFR. SOC. 36 (1937), pp. 76-78.

13,241 ARNETT, E. J. Cameroons under British mandate. Report by H. M. government to the Council of the League of Nations for the year 1932. J. AFR. SOC. 33 (1934), pp. 85-87.

13,242 ARNETT, E. J. The French mandate in Cameroons. J. AFR. SOC. 37 (1938), pp. 191-198.

13,243 BINET, J. Les Cadres au Cameroun. CIVILISATIONS 11 (1961), pp. 21-37; English summary, pp. 37-38.

13,244 DELAVIGNETTE, R. A letter from French Cameroun. AFR. AFFAIRS 46 (1947), pp. 151-155.

13,245 DEVERNOIS, G. Cameroons 1958-1959: from trusteeship to independence. CIVILISATIONS 9 (1959), pp. 229-235; 10 (1960), pp. 256-258.

13,246 FILESI, T. L'indipendenza del Camerun fattore di equilibrio o di turbamento per l'Africa? AFRICA (Rome) 15 (1960), pp. 121-125.

13,247 GONIDEC, P. F. Les institutions politiques de la République fédérale du Cameroun. CIVILISATIONS 11 (1961), pp. 370-395; English summary, pp. 396-400; 12 (1962), pp. 13-22; English summary, pp. 23-26.

13,248 GRAY, A. Republic of Cameroun. AFR. AFFAIRS 61 (1962), p. 10.

13,249 KABERRY, P. M. Traditional politics in Nsaw. AFRICA 29 (1959), pp. 366-382.

13,250 KABERRY, P. M. and CHILVER, E. M. An outline of the traditional political system of Bali-Nyonga, southern Cameroons. AFRICA 31 (1961), pp. 355-370.

13,251 MASSON-DETOURBET, A. Croyances relatives à l'organisation politique du royaume Lagoune (Kotoko du Nord-Cameroun). J. SOC. AFR. 23 (1953), pp. 7-34.

13,252 MUKOKO-MOKEBA, M. P. A government concern. ABBIA 5 (1964), pp. 101-111.

13,253 O'KELLY, E. Administrative problems in community development in the Southern Cameroons. J. AFR. ADM. 12 (1960), pp. 29-33.

13,254 RETIF, A. Communisme et religion au Cameroun. AFR. ET ASIE 33 (1956), pp. 51-55.

13,255 RITZENTHALER, R. Anlu: women's uprising in the British Cameroons. ZAIRE 14 (1960), pp. 481-490.

See also 11646.

History

13,256 B., P. J. R. Autour du procès de Rudolf Duala Manga. ET. CAMER. 51 (1956), pp. 44-51.

13,257 BAKARI, LE M. Histoire des sultans de Maroua. ABBIA 3 (1963), pp. 77-92.

13,258 BASSORO, M. H. Un manuscript peul sur l'histoire de Garoua. ABBIA 8 (1965), pp. 45-75.

13,259 BOND, E. The conquest of the Cameroon. CONTEMP. REV. 109 (1916), pp. 620-627.

13,260 BOUCHAUD, J. Notes d'histoire du Cameroun. BSEC 10 (1945), pp. 85-105; 11 (1945), pp. 77-109; 13-14 (1946), pp. 109-137; 15-16 (1946), pp. 109-151; 17-18 (1947), pp. 141-163; 19-20 (1947), pp. 105-140; 21-22 (1948), pp. 139-150; 25 (1949), pp. 19-37; ET. CAMER. 23-24 (1948), pp. 93-130.

13,261 BRUTSCH, J. R. Les Traités Camerounais. Recueillis, traduits et commentés. ET. CAMER. 47-48 (1955), pp. 9-42.

13,262 CHILVER, E. M. Nineteenth century trade in the Bamenda Grassfields, Southern Cameroons. AFR. UND UB. 45 (1961-1962), pp. 233-258.

13,263 DUGAST, R. Essai sur le peuplement du Cameroun. BSEC 21-22 (1948), pp. 19-33.

13,264 DUNSTAN, E. A Bangwa account of early encounters with the German colonial administration. J. HIST. SOC. NIG. 3 (1965), pp. 403-413.

13,265 FABIA, C. Documents d'histoire: l'installation des Allemands au Cameroun. BSEC 6 (1944), pp. 85-91.

13,266 JEFFREYS, M. D. W. The capture of Fumbam. AFR. STUD. 6 (1947), pp. 35-40.

13,267 JEFFREYS, M. D. W. Nsaangu's head. AFR. STUD. 5 (1946), pp. 57-62.

13,268 JEFFREYS, M. D. W. Nsaw history and social categories. AFRICA 22 (1952), pp. 71-75.

13,269 JEFFREYS, M. D. W. Traditional sources prior to 1890 for the Grassfield Bali of Northwestern Cameroons. AFR. UND UB. 46 (1962-1963), pp. 168-199, 296-313.

13,270 JOOS, L. Traité Germano-Peul de Tibati (11-9-1899). ET. CAMER. 51 (1956), pp. 42-43.

13,271 JOOS, L. C. D. Note sur le traité entre l'Allemagne et le Lamidat de Tibati. ET. CAMER. 53-54 (1956), pp. 18-19.

13,272 KABERRY, P. M. and CHILVER, E. M. Historical research in Bamenda Division. ABBIA 4 (1963), pp. 117-133; French summary, pp. 134-135.

13,273 LACROIX, P. F. Matériaux pour servir à l'histoire des Peul de l'Adamawa. ET. CAMER. 37-38 (1952), pp. 3-61; 39-40 (1953), pp. 5-40.

13,274 LEBEUF, J. P. Généalogies royales des villes Kotoko (Goulfeil, Kousseri, Makari). ET. CAMER. 23-24 (1948), pp. 31-46.

13,275 LEBEUF, J. P. Les souverains de Logone-Birni (Nord-Cameroun). ET. CAMER. 47-48 (1955), pp. 3-8.

13,276 LEEMING, A. J. A historical sketch of Victoria, British Cameroons. NIGERIAN FIELD 15 (1950), pp. 184-189; 16 (1951), pp. 37-45.

13,277 MAFIAMBA, P. C. Notes on the Esimbi of Wum Division. ABBIA 8 (1965), pp. 5-12.

13,278 MALCOLM, L. W. G. Notes on certain substitutes used by the Germans in the Cameroon campaign. J. AFR. SOC. 19 (1920), pp. 206-209.

13,279 MOHAMADOU, E. L'histoire des lamidats Foulbé de Tchamba et Tibati. ABBIA 6 (1964), pp. 15-158.

13,280 MOHAMADOU, E. Pour servir à l'histoire du Cameroun: la chronique de Bouba Njidda Rey. ABBIA 4 (1963), pp. 17-55.

13,281 NJOYA, I. M. Le bultanat du pays Amoun et son origine. BSEC 1 (1935), pp. 63-64.

13,282 NKWENGA, J. Histoire de la chefferie de Bangangté. ABBIA 9-10 (1965), pp. 91-110.

13,283 RODINSON, M. Généalogie royale de Logone Birni (Cameroun). ET. CAMER. 29-30 (1950), pp. 75-82.

13,284 SAVANI, M. Notes sur les populations Namchi. BSEC 2 (1937), pp. 15-42.

13,285 VAUGHAN, J. H. Culture history, and grass-roots politics in a Northern Cameroons kingdom. AMER. ANTHR. 66 (1964), pp. 1078-1095.

13,286 VERNON-JACKSON, H. O. H. A chronology of the history of academic education in Cameroon 1844-1940. ABBIA 3 (1963), pp. 148-153.

13,287 VOSSART, J. Histoire du sultanat du Mandara, province de l'empire du Bornou. ET. CAMER. 35-36 (1952), pp. 19-52.

13,288 ZELTNER, J. C. Notes relatives à l'histoire du Nord-Cameroun. ET. CAMER. 35-36 (1952), pp. 5-18.

13,289 Evolution récente du Cameroun. ZAIRE 5 (1951), pp. 974-976.

See also 15725.

Language. Literature

Language

13,290 ALEXANDRE, P. Aperçu sommaire sur le Pidgin A70 du Cameroun. CAH. ET. AFR. 3 (1963), pp. 577-582.

13,291 ALEXANDRE, P. Rapport de mission ethno-linguistique au Sud-Cameroun. CAH. ET. AFR. 2 (1962), pp. 630-634.

13,292 ALEXANDRE, P. Sur la voyelle suffixielle du Bulu. J. AFR. LANGS. 1 (1962), pp. 243-252.

13,293 BAUDELAIRE, H. La numération de 1 à 10 dans les dialectes Habé de Garoua, Guider, Poli et Rey Bouba. BSEC 5 (1944), pp. 23-30.

13,294 BRUENS, A. Het Londo (Brits-Kameroen). KONGO-OVERZEE 14 (1948), pp. 87-106.

13,295 BRUTSCH, J. R. Bibliographie de la langue Duala. BSEC 23-24 (1948), pp. 87-92.

13,296 BUFE, E. Die Dualasprache in ihrem Verhältnis zu den Dialekten des Nordgebiets der Station Bombe. AFR. UND UB. 1 (1910), pp. 25-36.

13,297 CLEMENT, N. Lore and learning in Mankon tongue Bamenda, West Cameroon. ABBIA 9-10 (1965), pp. 147-162.

13,298 COLINET, G. De la traduction. ABBIA 5 (1964), pp. 113-124.

13,299 DAUZATS, A. Quelques notes de toponymie du Nord-Cameroun. BSEC 4 (1943), pp. 49-61.

13,300 DORSCH, H. Grammatik der Nkosi-Sprache mit einer das Nkosi mit Duala vergleichenden Einleitung. AFR. UND UB. 1 (1910), pp. 241-283.

13,301 DORSCH, H. Vocabularium der Nkosi-Sprache (Kamerun). AFR. UND UB. 2 (1911-1912), pp. 161-193, 324-330; 3 (1912-1913), pp. 34-62.

13,302 DUGAST, I. La langue secrète du Sultan Njoya. ET. CAMER. 31-32 (1950), pp. 231-260.

13,303 DUGAST, I. Petit vocabulaire Bandem. ET. CAMER. 33-34 (1951), pp. 60-66.

13,304 DUGAST, R. Etude grammaticale d'une fable du Cameroun francais. AFR. STUD. 5 (1946), pp. 44-53.

13,305 DUNSTAN, E. Conjugation in Ngwe. J. AFR. LANGS. 2 (1963), pp. 235-243.

13,306 DUNSTAN, E. Towards a phonology of Ngwe. J. W. AFR. LANG. 1 (1964), pp. 39-42.

13,307 FONLON, B. A case for early bilingualism. ABBIA 4 (1963), pp. 56-94.

13,308 FONLON, B. Pour un bilinguisme de bonne heure. ABBIA 7 (1964), pp. 7-47.

13,309 GENGENBACH, K. Märchen in der Nyang-Sprache. AFR. UND UB. 29 (1939), pp. 1-37, 119-145, 216-233.

13,310 GLENN, E. Interpretation and translation. ABBIA 5 (1964), pp. 125-127; French translation, pp. 128-130.

13,311 GOHRING, M. Aus der Volkslitteratur der Duala in Kamerun. ZAOS 5 (1900), pp. 342-353.

13,312 GRIAULE, M. Vocabulaires Papé, Woko, Koutinn, Namtchi et Séwé du Cameroun septentrional. J. SOC. AFR. 11 (1941), pp. 169-183.

13,313 GUERPILLON, M. Les languages dits Kotoko. ET. CAMER. 23-24 (1948), pp. 23-30.

13,314 HEEPE, M. Die Trommelsprache der Jaunde in Kamerun. AFR. UND UB. 10 (1919-1920), pp. 43-60.

13,315 HEEPE, M. Weitere Jaundexte. AFR. UND UB. 10 (1919-1920), pp. 122-147.

13,316 HOFMEISTER, J. Kurzgefasste Wute-Grammatik. AFR. UND UB. 9 (1918-1919), pp. 1-19.

13,317 ITTMANN, J. Das Haus der Kosi in Kamerun. AFR. UND UB. 44 (1960), pp. 161-193.

13,318 ITTMANN, J. Skizze der Sprache des Nixenkultbundes am Kamerunberg. AFR. UND UB. 43 (1959-1960), pp. 161-190.

13,319 ITTMANN, J. Uber Kameruner Personennamen. AFR. UND UB. 39 (1954-1955), pp. 19-30.

13,320 ITTMANN, J. Verschlingemärchen aus dem vorderen Kamerun. AFR. UND UB. 36 (1951-1952), pp. 17-30, 115-135, 173-189.

13,321 JACQUOT, A. Les langues Bantu du nord-ouest. Etat des connaissances perspectives de la recherche. RECH. ET. CAM. 2 (1960), pp. 5-34.

13,322 JEFFREYS, M. D. W. The death of a dialect. AFR. STUD. 4 (1945), pp. 37-40.

13,323 KAHLER-MEYER, E. Beobachtungen am Konsonantenbestand der Graslandsprachen von Kamerun. AFR. UND UB. 39 (1954-1955), pp. 7-18.

13,324 KISOB, J. A. A live language: Pidgin English. ABBIA 1 (1963), pp. 25-31; French translation, pp. 32-37.

13,325 KOCH, H. Proverbes Badjue et Bikele. BSEC 5 (1944), pp. 31-51.

13,326 LACROIX, P. F. Note sur le langue Galke (^{n}dai). J. AFR. LANGS. 1 (1962), pp. 94-121.

13,327 LEBEUF, J. P. Vocabulaires comparés des parlers de 16 villages Fali du Cameroun septentrional. J. SOC. AFR. 11 (1941), pp. 33-60.

13,328 LEGER, A. Contribution a l'étude de la langue bamiléké. J. SOC. AFR. 2 (1932), pp. 209-227.

13,329 MAKEMBE, P. Duala-texte. AFR. UND UB. 11 (1920-1921), pp. 161-181.

13,330 MALCOLM, L. W. G. Short notes on the syllabic writing of the Eyap—central Cameroons. J. AFR. SOC. 20 (1921), pp. 127-129; 24 (1924), pp. 34-38.

13,331 MEINHOF, C. Die Sprachverhältnisse in Kamerun. ZAOS 1 (1895), pp. 138-163.

13,332 MEYER, E. Mambila—Studie. AFR. UND UB. 30 (1940), pp. 1-52, 117-148, 210-232.

13,333 MEYER, E. Märchen in der Balisprache aus Grasland von Kamerun. AFR. UND UB. 32 (1942), pp. 135-160, 224-236.

13,334 MEYER, E. Stand und Aufgaben der Sprachforschung in Kamerun. AFR. UND UB. 32 (1942), pp. 241-285.

13,335 MOHAMADOU, E. Introduction à la littérature Peule du Nord-Cameroun. ABBIA 3 (1963), pp. 66-72.

13,336 MOUCHET, J. Vocabulaires comparatifs de 15 parlers du Nord-Cameroun. J. SOC. AFR. 8 (1938), pp. 123-143.

13,337 MOUCHET, J. Vocabulaires comparatifs de sept parlers du Nord-Cameroun. ET. CAMER. 41-42 (1953), pp. 137-206.

13,338 MOUCHET, J. and ERICKSON, E. Esquisse grammaticale du Masana. ET. CAMER. 33-34 (1951), pp. 67-76.

13,339 NEKES, P. H. Zur Entwicklung der Jaunde-Sprache unter dem Einfluss der europäischen Kultur. FESTSCHRIFT MEINHOF, 1927, pp. 301-314.

13,340 NICOLAS, J. P. Couverture linguistique du pays dit Bamileke. BULL. IFAN 15 (1953), pp. 1633-1641.

13,341 NJOCK, H. M. B. B. Les tous en Gasa. J. AFR. LANGS. 3 (1964), pp. 252-259.

13,342 PANCONCELLI-CALZIA, G. Experimentalphonetische Untersuchungen. AFR. UND UB. 11 (1920-1921), pp. 182-188.

13,343 PARE, I. Nsa'Ngu Ngungure fugitif et errant. ABBIA 9-10 (1965), pp. 131-146.

13,344 PIERRE, N. Nécessité d'une langue nationale. ABBIA 7 (1964), pp. 83-99.

13,345 RICHARDSON, C. H. Zur Grammatik der Sprache der Bakundu (Kamerun). ZAS 1 (1887-1888), pp. 43-48.

13,346 ROGOZINSKI, S. Characteristic features of the Bantu dialect "Bakwiri" used in the Cameroon mountains: compared with some other related dialects. J. AFR. SOC. 2 (1903), pp. 400-415.

13,347 ROUSSEAU, J. A. Les migrations Foulbe et la linguistique botanique. BSEC 1 (1935), pp. 55-61.

13,348 SCHULER, E. Aus der Volkslitteratur der Yabakalaki-Bakoko in Kamerun. ZAOS 3 (1897), pp. 275-276.

13,349 STORBECK, F. Fulsprichwörter aus Adamaua, Nord-Kamerun. AFR. UND UB. 10 (1919-1920), pp. 106-122.

13,350 STORBECK, F. Fultexte aus Adamaua, Nordkamerun. AFR. UND UB. 11 (1920-1921), pp. 24-34.

13,351 STRUMPELL, F. Wörterverzeichnis der Heidensprachen des Mandara-Gebirges (Adamaua). AFR. UND UB. 13 (1922-1923), pp. 47-74, 109-149.

13,352 TISCHHAUSER, G. and KAHLER-MEYER, E. Kurze Wortliste der Sprache von Bebedjato in der Landschaft Mbembe, Kamerun. AFR. UND UB. 38 (1953-1954), pp. 69-71.

13,353 TISCHHAUSER, G. et al. Sprachproben aus der Landschaft Mbembe im Bezirk Bamenda, Kamerun [by G. Tischhauser, A. Vielhauer and E. Kahler-Meyer]. AFR. UND UB. 37 (1952-1953), pp. 109-118, 151-182.

13,354 VOORHOEVE, J. La classification nominale dans le Bangangté. J. AFR. LANGS. 2 (1963), pp. 206-209.

13,355 VOORHOEVE, J. The structure of the morpheme in Bamileke (Bangangté dialect). LINGUA 13 (1964), pp. 319-334.

13,356 ZINTGRAFF, E. Einiges aus der Balisprache (Hinterland von Kamerun). ZAOS 1 (1895), pp. 318-323.

13,357 A propos des langues vernaculaires. BSEC 11 (1945), pp. 9-15.

13,358 Principes pour l'établissement d'une notation phonétique. BSEC 4 (1943), pp. 111-114.

13,359 Tsho Ngo Pangante. ABBIA 9-10 (1965), pp. 111-130.

See also 13177.

Literature

13,360 ALEXANDRE, P. Un conte bulu de Sangmélima: la jeune albinos et le Pygmée. J. SOC. AFR. 33 (1963), pp. 243-254.

13,361 ALIMA, E. Four poems. ABBIA 11 (1965), pp. 101-106.

13,362 ALIMA, E. Je t'ai élu député... ABBIA 7 (1964), pp. 144-146.

13,363 AYISSI, L. M. Minkana. ABBIA 7 (1964), pp. 147-159.

13,364 BEBEY, F. Musica africa [a poem]. ABBIA 4 (1963), pp. 114-115.

13,365 BEIER, U. The novel in the French Cameroons. BO 2 (1958), pp. 42-52.

13,366 BETI, M. Seduction: from Le pauvre Christ de Bomba. BO 15 (1964), pp. 52-56.

13,367 DIKUM, L. Four poems. ABBIA 11 (1965), pp. 107-110.

13,368 DIPOKO, M. S. Childhood; Perfume of time. PRESENCE AFR. N.S. 51 (1964), p. 103.

13,369 DIPOKO, M. S. Poèmes. PRESENCE AFR. N.S. 48 (1963), p. 170.

13,370 DIPOKO, M. S. Pris au piège. PRESENCE AFR. N.S. 41 (1962), pp. 106-116.

13,371 DONGMO, J. L. La bouteille noire. ABBIA 6 (1964), pp. 202-203.

13,372 DONGMO-MVA, J. L. A la danseuse. ABBIA 6 (1964), pp. 200-201.

13,373 FLOTTUM, S. Le lapin et la famine, conte en langue Mbum. ET. CAMER. 29-30 (1950), pp. 83-93.

13,374 FONLON, B. Nightmare [a poem]. ABBIA 3 (1963), pp. 123-124.

13,375 GAUTHIER, J. La littérature orale des Fali. ABBIA 7 (1964), pp. 129-134.

13,376 GUEYE, Y. A. La légende de Oumarel. PRESENCE AFR. N.S. 6 (1956), pp. 126-142; 7 (1956), pp. 102-119.

13,377 KAYO, P. La guerre. PRESENCE AFR. N.S. 45 (1963), pp. 158-159.

13,378 KAYO, P. L'heure s'évade [a poem]. ABBIA 3 (1963), p. 127.

13,379 MATIP, B. Le jugement suprême: drame en trois actes et vingt tableaux. ABBIA 2 (1963), pp. 64-66.

13,380 MAYSSAL, H. Poèmes Foulbé de la Bénoué. ABBIA 9-10 (1965), pp. 47-90.

13,381 MBIDA, D. E. Aux morts [a poem]. ABBIA 3 (1963), pp. 125-126.

13,382 MOORE, G. Ferdinand Oyono et la tragi-comédie coloniale. PRESENCE AFR. N.S. 46 (1963), pp. 221-233.

13,383 MOUASSO-PRISO, F. Le cultivateur et la belle-mère. PRESENCE AFR. 2 (1948), pp. 272-275.

13,384 NGANDE, C. Echos africains, Sous-developpement, Pagne des fiancailles, Mes ancetres [poems]. ABBIA 2 (1963), pp. 138-139.

13,385 NGANDE, C. Nous partizons. ABBIA 5 (1964), p. 178.

13,386 NGANDE, C. La poésie camerounaise. ABBIA 2 (1963), pp. 135-136; English translation, pp. 136-137.

13,387 NGANDE, C. Quand la Paix reviendra. ABBIA 5 (1964), p. 177.

13,388 NKWENGA, J. Qu'est-ce que l'Agent spécial? [a play by J. M. Nzouankeu]. ABBIA 5 (1964), pp. 145-167.

13,389 NZOUANKEU, J. M. La dame d'eau [nouvelle]. ABBIA 2 (1963), pp. 101-110; 3 (1963), pp. 113-122.

13,390 PHILOMBE, R. A l'aubade du tam-tam. ABBIA 5 (1964), p. 174.

13,391 PHILOMBE, R. Réponse à Charles Ngandé: L'avenir de la Poésie Camerounaise. ABBIA 5 (1964), pp. 167-171.

13,392 PHILOMBE, R. Sur la tombe de mon père. ABBIA 5 (1964), p. 175.

13,393 WUTA, S. K. Légende de Badoblum. ABBIA 7 (1964), p. 140.

13,394 YUNIA, E. Mouandjo Berthe. ABBIA 1 (1963), p. 88.

13,395 Chansons populaires camerounaises. PRESENCE AFR. N.S. 6 (1956), pp. 123-125.

13,396 Questionnaire pour une enquête sur la littérature orale. BSEC 4 (1943), pp. 107-109.

Law

13,397 ANTOINE, M. P. La nature juridique des sociétés africaines de prévoyance au Cameroun. RJPUF 8 (1954), pp. 360-379.

13,398 EGBE, E. T. From a lawyer's note book: Some principles and characteristics of justice. ABBIA 5 (1964), pp. 91-95; French translation, pp. 96-100.

13,399 ENGO, P. B. An aspect of personal freedom. Leading star: Habeas corpus. ABBIA 5 (1964), pp. 57-72; French translation, pp. 73-89.

13,400 ENGO, P. B. Quelques aspects de la reforme du système juridique du Cameroun. ABBIA 7 (1964), pp. 67-81.

13,401 ENGO, P. B. Some aspects of legal reform in Cameroon. ABBIA 6 (1964), pp. 159-171.

13,402 ENONCHONG, H. N. A. The position of the Cameroon state in litigation. ABBIA 11 (1965), pp. 59-67; French translation, pp. 68-78.

13,403 KABERRY, P. M. Land tenure among the Nsaw of the British Cameroons. AFRICA 20 (1950), pp. 307-322.

13,404 KABERRY, P. M. Some problems of land tenure in Nsaw, Southern Cameroons. J. AFR. ADM. 12 (1960), pp. 21-28.

13,405 TCHERNONOG. La nature juridique des chefferies du Cameroun. RJPUF 7 (1953), pp. 197-203.

13,406 Eléments de droit coutumier Bassa. ABBIA 4 (1963), pp. 136-156.

13,407 Integration of laws in Cameroon. J. AFR. LAW 8 (1964), pp. 153-154.

See also 9375.

Religion

13,408 AFRIKANUS. Ainda o Alambamento. PORT. EM AFR. 18 (1961), pp. 336-340.

13,409 BRUTSCH, J. R. Les débuts du christianisme au Cameroun. ET. CAMER. 33-34 (1951), pp. 53-59.

13,410 BRUTSCH, J. R. A glance at missions in Cameroon. INT. REV. MISSIONS 39 (1950), pp. 302-310.

13,411 DUBIE, P. Christianisme, Islam et Animisme chez les Bamoum (Cameroun). BULL. IFAN 19 (1957), pp. 337-381.

13,412 EBDING, F. and ITTMANN, J. Religiöse Gesänge aus dem nördlichen Waldland von Kamerun. AFR. UND UB. 39 (1954-1955), pp. 169-177; 40 (1956), pp. 39-44, 125-132.

13,413 MALCOLM, L. W. G. Islam in the Cameroons, West AFrica. J. AFR. SOC. 21 (1921), pp. 35-46.

13,414 MORANT, A. Die Ex-Seminaristen: Erfahrungen in Kamerun. DAS LAIENAPOSTOLAT IN DEN MISSIONEN, 1961, pp. 281-297.

13,415 MOUCHET, J. Note sur la conversion a l'islamisme, en 1715 de la Tribu Wandala. BSEC 15-16 (1946), pp. 105-107.

13,416 RAAFLAUB, F. Ordnung der Presbyterianischen Kirche in Kamerun. BASILEIA: FESTSCHRIFT FUR WALTER FREYTAG, 1959, pp. 285-292.

13,417 SEPPO, P. Christian citizenship in the French Cameroun. THE CHURCH IN CHANGING AFRICA, 1958, pp. 47-48.

See also 13742.

Science

13,418 BREUNING, ST. Un nouvel Oxylamia du Cameroun. BULL. IFAN 12 (1950), p. 401.

13,419 BRYGOO. Le nouveau-né et la femme enceinte aux environs d'Ayos. BSEC 21-22 (1948), pp. 49-68.

13,420 CAPPONI, A. Le lignite de Dschang. BSEC 7 (1944), pp. 75-86.

13,421 CHEW, C. W. Notes sur la flore du Cameroun. BSEC 6 (1944), pp. 63-72.

13,422 CHEW, C. W. Les Orchidées Angroecoides du Mont Cameroun et de région du Wouri. BSEC 21-22 (1948), pp. 7-12.

13,423 CONDAMIN, M. Lépidoptères Rhopalocères récoltés au Cameroun par C. de Raemy. BULL. IFAN 15 (1953), pp. 1037-1045.

13,424 DENAEYER, M. A. and BLONDEL, F. Bibliographie géologique du Cameroun. BSEC 6 (1944), pp. 33-50.

13,425 DUGAST, R. L'Anatomie du corps humain et les causes des maladies expliquées par trois guérisseurs de la tribu des Ndiki. ET. CAMER. 23-24 (1948), pp. 51-69.

13,426 DUMORT, J. C. Monographie géologique du Diamaré. RECH. ET CAM. 9 (1962-1963), pp. 13-30.

13,427 EYIDI, B. et al. Une enquête sur l'alimentation à Doula (quartier New-Bell) by R. B. Eyidi, M. L. Pierme, R. Masseyeff. RECH. ET. CAM. 5 (1961-1962), pp. 5-45.

13,428 GAZEL, J. La Calcaire au Cameroun français. BSEC 17-18 (1947), pp. 21-39.

13,429 GOOD, A. I. Les Rongeurs du Cameroun. BSEC 17-18 (1947), pp. 5-20.

13,430 HAUGOU, P. Le Cameroun à travers les périodes géologiques. BSEC 6 (1944), pp. 7-32.

13,431 JACQUES-FELIX, H. Ignames sauvages et cultivées du Cameroun. BSEC 21-22 (1948), pp. 13-18.

13,432 JAMOT, E. La maladie du sommeil au Cameroun. AFRICA 3 (1930), pp. 161-177.

13,433 LISLE, M. DE. Les cétoines du Cameroun. BSEC 12 (1945), pp. 73-102.

13,434 LISLE, M. DE. Note sur la faune coléoptérologique du Cameroun. BSEC 5 (1944), pp. 53-69.

13,435 LISLE, M. DE. Notes complémentaires sur la faune coléoptérologique du Cameroun. BSEC 7 (1944), pp. 91-92.

13,436 LISLE, M. DE. Notes complémentaires sur les cétoines du Cameroun. BSEC 19-20 (1947), pp. 7-54.

13,437 LISLE, M. DE. Sur un Phosphorus trouvé à Batouri. BSEC 7 (1944), pp. 87-90.

13,438 LOMBARD, J. Les granites du nord du Cameroun. PROC. SYMP. GRANITES W. AFR., 1965, pp. 29-35.

13,439 MASSEYEFF, R. et al. Une enquête sur l'alimentation dans la region de Batouri (Est-Cameroun) by R. Masseyeff, M. L. Piermé, B. Bergeret. RECH. ET. CAM. 1 (1960), pp. 6-70.

13,440 MILLOUS. Le lutte contre les maladies sociales au Cameroun en 1934. AFRICA 8 (1935), pp. 171-182.

13,441 MOUCHET, J. and GARIOU, J. Anophélisme et paludisme dans le départment Bamiléké (Ouest Cameroun). RECH. ET. CAM. 1 (1960), pp. 92-114.

13,442 MOUCHET, J. and RAGEAU, J. Les arthropodes d'intérêt médical du Diamarê. RECH. ET. CAM. 9 (1962-1963), pp. 73-108.

13,443 NEWTON, R. By mountain tarns in the Cameroons. NIGERIAN FIELD 6 (1937), pp. 14-17.

13,444 NICKLES, M. Mollusques marins de la région de Kribi. ET. CAMER. 25-26 (1949), pp. 113-118.

13,445 OLIVIER, G. and AUJOULAT, L. L'obstétrique en pays Yaoundé. Etude ethnologique medicale et d'anthropologie somatique. BSEC 12 (1945), pp. 7-72.

13,446 PAULIAN, R. L'origine des peuplements entomologiques d'A.O.F. BULL. IFAN 12 (1950), pp. 540-542.

13,447 PERRET, J. L. La biologie d'Acanthixalus spinosus (Amphibia salientia). RECH. ET. CAM. 4 (1961), pp. 90-101.

13,448 REIS, J. A. Les oiseaux du Cameroun français. BSEC 11 (1945), pp. 17-55.

13,449 ROUGEOT, P. C. Notules d'ornithologie en pays Fang. BULL. IEC N.S. 3 (1952), pp. 101-102.

13,450 SEGALEN, P. et al. Les sols du Diamaré, by P. Segalen, D. Martin, G. Sieffermann. RECH. ET. CAM. 9 (1962-1963), pp. 43-71.

13,451 SERLE, W. A crowned hawk-eagle, Stephanoaëtus coronatus (Linnaeus), in British Southern Cameroons. NIGERIAN FIELD 22 (1957), p. 165.

13,452 SIEFFERMANN, G. and SUSINI, J. Appareil d'analyse thermique differentielle réalisé a la section de pedologie de l'I.R.CAM. RECH. ET. CAM. 1 (1960), pp. 123-139.

13,453 SOHLER, J. Dans la flore du Cameroun. BSEC 5 (1944), pp. 87-89.

13,454 SOHLER, J. Un peu de zoologie...à propos d'un proverbe. BSEC 7 (1944), pp. 93-95.

13,455 SRAM, J. Remarques sur la glaciation au Cameroun. ET. CAMER. 49-50 (1955), pp. 53-55.

13,456 SUSINI, J. Dosage spectrographique du Cuivre dans les sols, les végétaux et les tissus animaux. RECH. ET. CAM. 5 (1961-1962), pp. 97-109.

13,457 TARDIEU-BLOT et al. Contribution à la flore et à l'écologie des fougères du Cameroun by Tardieu-Blot, M. Nicklès, Jacques-Felix. ET. CAMER. 25-26 (1949), pp. 81-112.

13,458 VAILLANT, A. La flore méridionale du Lac Tchad. BSEC 9 (1945), pp. 13-98.

13,459 VOELCKEL, J. La répartition des muridés citadins à Douala et ses rapports possibles avec la compétition mondiale des deux espèces Rattus. ET. CAMER. 56 (1958), pp. 113-121.

13,460 WHEELER, W. R. The battle against sleeping sickness in French Cameroons. INT. REV. MISSIONS 18 (1929), pp. 121-130.

13,461 Plantes récoltés dans le Nord-Cameroun par Henri Lhote. BULL. IFAN 14 (1952), pp. 694-700.

See also 8110, 9656.

Sociology

13,462 ARDENER, E. Marriage stability in the Southern Cameroons. NISER 6 (1958), pp. 195-207.

13,463 ARDENER, E. W. The origins of modern sociological problems connected with the plantation system in the Victoria division of the Cameroons. WAISER SOC. 2 (1953), pp. 89-105.

13,464 AWOUMA, J. Esquisse d'une étude socio-culturelle d'un conte Bulu (Sud Cameroun). PRESENCE AFR. N.S. 55 (1965), pp. 83-91.

13,465 BINET, J. Groupes socio-professionnels au Cameroun. CAH. INT. SOCIOL. 24 (1958), pp. 88-103.

13,466 BINET, J. Condition des femmes dans la région Cacaoyere du Cameroun. CAH. INT. SOCIOL. 20 (1956), pp. 109-123.

13,467 BURNLEY, G. E. Women's work in West Cameroon. WOMEN TODAY 6 (1964), pp. 34-35.

13,468 DIZIAN, R. Etude sur la population du quarter New-Bell à Douala. RECH. ET. CAM. 3 (1960), pp. 1-210.

13,469 DUGAST, R. Objets, sens, buts et méthodes proposés pour les investigations sociologiques au Cameroun. BSEC 1 (1935), pp. 15-54.

13,470 FONLON, B. Idea of culture. ABBIA 11 (1965), pp. 5-29; French translation, pp. 31-58.

13,471 FONLON, B. Will we make or mar? [a Cameroon cultural review]. ABBIA 5 (1964), pp. 9-34; French translation, pp. 35-56.

13,472 KALA-LOBE, I. Grandeur et décadence de "Mun' a moto" cultivateur camerounais. PRESENCE AFR. N.S. 37 (1961), pp. 90-118.

13,473 KISOB, J. A. An appreciation of Bemenda traditional costume. ABBIA 3 (1963), pp. 55-65.

13,474 MANGA, F. B. Cameroon: a marriage of three cultures. ABBIA 5 (1964), pp. 131-144.

13,475 PAUPHILET, D. Sociologie de l'Afrique Noire. CT 5 (1957), pp. 130-132.

13,476 PLATZER, H. The care of motherless children in the Southern Cameroons. AFR. WOMEN 2 (1956-1958), pp. 56-58.

13,477 PODLEWSKI, M. Etude demographique de trois ethnies païennes du Nord-Cameroun: Matakam, Kapsiki, Goude. RECH. ET. CAM. 4 (1961), pp. 3-70.

13,478 Etude de la stabilité de la population Bamiléké de la Subdivision de Bafoussam pendant les années 1946 et 1947. ET. CAMER. 31-32 (1950), pp. 137-187.

13,479 Rapport sur les questions de l'enfance au Cameroun. ABBIA 2 (1963), pp. 142-145.

See also 4390.

CHAD

Agriculture

13,480 GILG, J. P. Mobilité pastorale au Tchad occidental et central. CAH. ET. AFR. 3 (1963), pp. 491-510.

13,481 GRIAULE, M. Notes sur l'agriculture des Goula et des Koulfa. BULL. IFAN 8 (1946), pp. 88-99.

Anthropology

13,482 B., J. L. Cohabitation de nomades et de sédentaires en Afrique noire. Les problèmes actuels du Tchad. AFR. ET ASIE 63 (1963), pp. 33-38.

13,483 BRIGGS, L. C. Aperçu sur l'anthropologie des Tedâ. BULL. IFAN 18 (1956), pp. 280-283.

13,484 FORTIER, J. Rites et coutumes d'une tribu sara, les Mbaye de Moissala. BULL. IFAN, Série B: Sciences humaines 20 (1958), pp. 142-169.

13,485 FUCHS, P. Der Ursprung der Tubu. CONGR. INT. SC. ANTHR. ET ETHN. 6, no. ii (1960), pp. 183-186.

13,486 GARCIA. Moeurs et coutumes des Tedâ du Tou. BULL. IEC N.S. 9 (1955), pp. 167-209.

13,487 HERSE, P. L. Etude sur les margayes de Melfi (Tchad). BULL. IEC 1, no. 1 (1945), pp. 33-46.

13,488 HERSE, P. Observations sur les Margayes de Melfi. BULL. IEC 1, no. 2 (1947), pp. 1-97.

13,489 HUARD, P. Les groupes sanguins des Teda du Tibesti. BULL. IFAN 23 (1961), pp. 328-329.

13,490 HUARD, P. and CHARPIN, M. Aspect sociologique d'une enquête anthropologique sur les Teda du Tibesti. BULL. IFAN 24 (1962), pp. 575-583.

13,491 HUARD, P. and CHARPIN, M. Contribution à l'étude anthropologique des Teda du Tibesti. BULL. IFAN 22 (1960), pp. 179-201.

13,492 ITTMANN, J. Sprichwörter der Subu. AFR. UND UB. 36 (1951-1952), pp. 189-190.

13,493 JAULIN, R. Eléments et aspects divers de l'organisation civile et pénale des groupes du Moyen Chari, groupe Sara Madjingaye et groupe Mbaye (district de Koumra, Tchad, A.E.F.). BULL. IFAN, Série B: Sciences humaines 20 (1958), pp. 170-190.

13,494 JAULIN, R. Note sur Marabé, le village Mara. CAH. ET. AFR. 1 (1960), pp. 85-98.

13,495 LEBEUF, J. P. Saó et Kotoko du Tchad. ZAIRE 1 (1947), pp. 297-311.

13,496 LE COEUR, C. Autour de l'enfant. PRESENCE AFR. 8 (1950), pp. 249-259.

13,497 MARTIN, R. Note sur les Mundang de la région de Léré (Tchad). BULL. IEC 1, no. 2 (1947), pp. 99-105.

13,498 MOULINARD. Essai sur l'habitat indigène dans la colonie du Tchad. J. SOC. AFR. 17 (1947), pp. 7-18.

13,499 PAIRAULT, C. A. Boum Kabir en présence de la mort. J. SOC. AFR. 34 (1964), pp. 141-167.

13,500 PAIRAULT, C. A. Structure de la parente chez les Goula Iro. AFRICA 34 (1964), pp. 360-369; English summary, p. 369.

13,501 TUBIANA, M. J. Un sacrifice de bête pleine chez les Zaghawa Kobé du Ouaddai. CONGR. INT. SC. ANTHR. ET ETHN. 6, no. ii (1960), pp. 487-490.

See also 4808, 13125, 13163, 13536.

Art

13,502 ARKELL, A. J. The Aterian of Great Wanyanga (Ounianga Kebir). PROC. PAN-AFR. CONGR. PRE-HIST. 4, no. iii (1962), pp. 233-236.

13,503 BABET, V. Description d'un ustensile en pierre trouvé au Tchad. BULL. IEC 1, no. 1 (1945), pp. 105-108.

13,504 CARRIQUE, le Capitaine. Notice sur la "Ville inconnue" découverte a N'Galaka (Borkou). J. SOC. AFR. 5 (1935), pp. 85-92.

13,505 COPPENS, Y. Deux gisements de Vertébrés Villafranchiens au Tchad. PROC. PAN-AFR. CONGR. PRE-HIST. 4 (1962), pp. 299-313.

13,506 COPPENS, Y. L'Hominien du Tchad. PROC. PAN-AFR. CONGR. PRE-HIST. 5 (1965), pp. 329-330.

13,507 COPPENS, Y. Les proboscidiens du Tchad. Leur contribution à la chronologie du Quaternaire Africain. PROC. PAN-AFR. CONGR. PRE-HIST. 5 (1965), pp. 331-387.

13,508 DERENDINGER, le général. Les curieuses mines de fer de Télé-Nugar (Tchad). J. SOC. AFR. 6 (1936), pp. 197-204.

13,509 GRIAULE, M. and LEBEUF, J. P. Fouilles dans la région du Tchad. J. SOC. AFR. 18 (1948), pp. 1-116; 20 (1950), pp. 1-151; 21 (1951), pp. 1-96.

13,510 HARTWEG, R. Les squelettes humains anciens du village de Sao. J. SOC. AFR. 12 (1942), pp. 1-7.

13,511 HUARD, P. A propos de deux objects modernes du Tchad ed cuivre coulé à la cire perdue. ODU 1, no. 1 (1964), pp. 59-61.

13,512 HUARD, P. Gravures et peintures rupestres du Borkou. BULL. IEC N.S. 6 (1953), pp. 150-160.

13,513 HUARD, P. Nouvelle contribution a l'étude du fer au Sahara et au Tchad. BULL. IFAN 26 (1964), pp. 297-396.

13,514 HUARD, P. Nouvelles données séro-anthropologiques sur les Teda du Tibesti. BULL. IFAN 25 (1963), pp. 451-453.

13,515 HUARD, P. Préhistoire et archéologie au Tchad. BULL. IEC N.S. 17-18 (1959), pp. 5-20.

13,516 HUARD, P. and BACQUIE, le cap. Matériaux pour l'étude de l'age du fer au Djourab. II. Maledinga. BULL. IFAN 25 (1963), pp. 442-451.

13,517 HUARD, P. et al. Matériaux pour l'étude de l'age du fer au Djourab (Tchad). I. Toungour by P. Huard, les cap. Bacquié, Scheibling. BULL. IFAN 25 (1963), pp. 435-442.

13,518 KELLEY, H. Outils à gorge africains. J. SOC. AFR. 21 (1951), pp. 197-206.

13,519 LEBEUF, J. P. L'Archéologie de la région du Tchad. PROC. PAN-AFR. CONGR. PRE-HIST. 4, no. iii (1962), pp. 427-435.

13,520 LEBEUF, J. P. L'art du delta du Chari. PRESENCE AFR. 10 (1951), pp. 96-102.

13,521 LEBEUF, J. P. Bracelets anthropomorphes de Gawi (Tchad). J. SOC. AFR. 35 (1965), pp. 7-10.

13,522 LEBEUF, J. P. Les collections Sao du Musée Lebaudy (Cabrerets, Lot). J. SOC. AFR. 13 (1943), pp. 183-186.

13,523 LEBEUF, J. P. Fouilles archéologiques dans la région du Tchad. ZAIRE 1 (1947), pp. 543-553.

13,524 LEBEUF, J. P. and RODINSON, M. Les mosquées de Fort-Lamy (A.E.F.). BULL. IFAN 14 (1952), pp. 970-974.

13,525 LEBEUF, M. D. Enceintes de briques de la région tchadienne. PROC. PAN-AFR. CONGR. PRE-HIST. 4, no. iii (1962), pp. 437-442.

13,526 MAUNY, R. Poteries engobées et peintes de tradition nilotique de la région de Koro Toro (Tchad). BULL. IFAN 25 (1963), pp. 39-46.

13,527 NENEKHALY-CAMARA, C. Mission archéologique au Tchad. RECH. AFR. 3 (1961), pp. 75-78.

13,528 PALES, L. Découverte d'un important gisement prehistorique a Fort-Lamy (Tchad). J. SOC. AFR. 7 (1937), pp. 125-172.

13,529 PASSEMARD, E. and SAINT-FLORIS, H. DE. Les peintures rupestres de l'Ennedi. J. SOC. AFR. 5 (1935), pp. 97-112.

13,530 SELIQUER, Capitaine. Eléments d'une étude archéologique des Pays bas du Tchad. BULL. IFAN 7 (1945), pp. 191-209.

See also 9627, 9628, 11225.

Economics

13,531 CABOT, J. Kim, village du Moyen-Logone (région du Mayo-Kebbi). BULL. IEC N.S. 5 (1953), pp. 41-67.

13,532 TUBIANA, M. J. Le marché de Hili-ba: moutons, mil, sel et conrebande. CAH. ET. AFR. 2 (1961), pp. 198-243.

Geography

13,533 ADLER, A. Rapport sur une mission en pays Mbay (sud du Tchad) juillet 1963-février 1964. CAH. ET. AFR. 5 (1965), pp. 341-347.

13,534 ALEXANDER, B. Lake Chad. J. AFR. SOC. 7 (1908), pp. 225-238.

13,535 ARBAUMONT, J. D'. Le Tibesti et le domaine Teda-Daza. BULL. IFAN 16 (1954), pp. 255-306.

13,536 GANAY, S. DE and GRIAULE, M. Notes sur les pirogues et la pêche dans la région du bahr Salamat. J. SOC. AFR. 13 (1943), pp. 187-204.

13,537 HAUGOU, P. Etude de l'assèchement possible du Lac Tchad. BSEC 13-14 (1946), pp. 7-26.

13,538 TUBIANA, J. La mission du Centre National de la Recherche Scientifique aux confins du Tchad. CAH. ET. AFR. 1 (1960), pp. 115-120.

Government

13,539 ARBAUMONT, J. D'. Organisation politique au Tibesti. Une convention entre Arna et Tomagra. BULL. IFAN 18 (1956), pp. 148-155.

13,540 HUGOT, P. Tchad et Soudan. AFR. ET ASIE 37 (1957), pp. 3-10.

History

13,541 BOULNOIS, J. La migration des Sao au Tchad [see also mise au point by L. Pales]. BULL. IFAN 5 (1943), pp. 80-121.

13,542 DAGNAC, le Capitaine. Les traditions historiques des clans habitant actuellement le Tibesti. BULL. IEC 1, no. 1 (1945), pp. 7-31.

13,543 HUARD, P. and BACQUIE, le cap. Un établissement islamique dans le désert tchadien: Ouogayi. BULL. IFAN 26 (1964), pp. 1-20.

13,544 KELINGUEN, Y. Renaissance d'un sultanat dans l'Afrique Centrale Francaise: le Ouaddaï. AFR. ET ASIE 13 (1951), pp. 36-40.

13,545 LAMI, P. Le Chefferie Pève de Lame (Tchad). BULL. IEC 1, no. 1 (1945), pp. 47-51.

13,546 LEBEUF, J. P. Prehistory, protohistory and history of Chad. PROC. INT. CONG. AFR. 1 (1962), pp. 72-81.

13,547 MENIER, M. A. La marche au Tchad de 1887 à 1891. BULL. IEC N.S. 5 (1953), pp. 5-18.

13,548 PALES, L. Mise au point [reference to the article la migration des Sao au Tchad by J. Boulnois]. BULL. IFAN 11 (1949), pp. 546-547.

13,549 RODINSON, M. and LEBEUF, J. P. L'origine et les souverains du Mandara. BULL. IFAN 18 (1956), pp. 227-255.

13,550 TUBIANA, M. J. Un document inédit sur les sultans du Waddāy. CAH. ET. AFR. 1 (1960), pp. 49-112.

See also 6251.

Language. Literature

Language

13,551 DERENDINGER, Colonel. Traduction d'un texte baghirmien. J. SOC. AFR. 2 (1932), pp. 147-151.

13,552 JUNGRAITHMAYR, H. Beobachtungen zur tschadohamitischen Sprache der Jegu (und Jonkor) von Abu Telfan (Republique du Tchad). AFR. UND UB. 45 (1961-1962), pp. 95-123.

13,553 LEBEUF, J. P. Vocabulaires Kotoko: Makari, Goulfeil, Kousseri, Afadé. BULL. IFAN 4 (1942), pp. 160-174.

13,554 LUKAS, J. Der Hamitische Gehalt der tschadohamitischen Sprachen. AFR. UND UB. 28 (1937-1938), pp. 286-299.

13,555 LUKAS, J. Mitteilungen über die Stämme und Sprache der östlichen Kanembu (Tschadseegebiet). AFR. UND UB. 43 (1959-1960), pp. 106-115.

13,556 LUKAS, J. Tubu-Texte und Ubungsstücke. AFR. UND UB. 38 (1953-1954), pp. 1-16, 53-68, 121-134.

13,557 MOUCHET, J. Contribution à l'étude du Gula (Tchad). BULL. IFAN, Série B: Sciences humaines 20 (1958), pp. 593-611.

13,558 MOUCHET, J. Esquisse grammaticale du parler Juman. BULL. IEC N.S. 7-8 (1954), pp. 171-185.

13,559 STEVENSON, R. A. Bagirmi specimen texts. AFR. UND UB. 40 (1956), pp. 45-47.

Literature

13,560 JOSEPH, S. B. Le Bonnet, la Bourse et la Canne magiques. PRESENCE AFR. N.S. 32-33 (1960), pp. 156-159.

13,561 JOSEPH, S. B. L'eclipse de la lune. Conte du Tchad. PRESENCE AFR. N.S. 26 (1959), pp. 92-93.

Science

13,562 BODIN, V. Examen de fragments de terre cuite provenant de la région du Tchad. ET. CAMER. 25-26 (1949), pp. 119-125.

13,563 GAUTHIER, H. Contribution à l'étude de la faune dulçaquicole de la région du Tchad et particulièrement des Branchiopodes et des Ostracodes. BULL. IFAN 1 (1939), pp. 110-244.

13,564 HYDE, H. P. T. Boubou. AFR. AFFAIRS 47 (1948), pp. 114-116.

13,565 KOECHLIN, J. Rapport de mission botanique dans le Territoire du Tchad, Novembre-Décembre 1955. BULL. IEC N.S. 12 (1956), pp. 129-199.

13,566 TAUFFLIEB, R. Rapport sur la campagne antisimulidienne de 1956 au Mayo-Kebbi. BULL. IEC N.S. 11 (1956), pp. 53-59.

Sociology

13,567 POUILLON, J. Rapport d'enquête au Tchad. CAH. ET. AFR. 1, no. 3 (1960), pp. 153-155.

CENTRAL AFRICAN REPUBLIC

Agriculture

13,568 TISSERANT, C. L'agriculture dans les savanes de l'Oubangui. BULL. IEC N.S. 6 (1953), pp. 209-273.

Anthropology

13,569 CHABRELIE, L. Notes sur quelques croyances des Sara. J. SOC. AFR. 3 (1933), pp. 314-318.

13,570 DAMPIERRE, E. DE. Coton noir, café blanc. Deux cultures du Haut-Oubangui à la veille de la loi-cadre. CAH. ET. AFR. 1 (1960), pp. 128-147.

13,571 GRANGEON, G. Les Babinga des rives de l'Oubangui. AFR. ET ASIE 71 (1965), pp. 34-42.

13,572 JAULIN, R. Essai d'analyse formelle d'un procédé géomantique. BULL. IFAN 19 (1957), pp. 43-71.

13,573 LAURENTIN-RETEL, A. Un jugement coutumier Nzakara. Réflexions sur un enregistrement d'audience. CAH. ET. AFR. 3 (1963), pp. 391-412.

13,574 LEYNAUD, E. Ligwa, un village zande de la R.C.A. CAH. ET. AFR. 3 (1963), pp. 318-390.

13,575 SAMARIN, W. J. Ngaragé, a Gbeya society. AFR. STUD. 18 (1959), pp. 190-196.

13,576 SEVY, G. V. Le wama des Ngbaka de la Lobaye. CAH. ET. AFR. 1 (1960), pp. 103-128.

13,577 TANGHE, B. O. Overzicht van de Volken en Stammen in Ubangi. KONGO-OVERZEE 12-13 (1946-1947), pp. 193-203.

13,578 TISSERANT, C. Le mariage dans l'Oubangui-Chari. BULL. IEC N.S. 2 (1951), pp. 73-102.

13,579 TISSERANT, C. Quelques remarques au sujet de la dot. BULL. IEC N.S. 4 (1952), pp. 187-200.

13,580 L'habitat indigène à Bangui. ZAIRE 8 (1954), p. 195.

See also 13973.

Art

13,581 GANAY, S. DE. Le xylophone chez les Sara du Moyen Chari. J. SOC. AFR. 12 (1942), pp. 203-239.

13,582 KUBIK, G. Harp music of the Azande and related peoples in the Central African Republic. AFR. MUSIC, 1964, pp. 37-76.

13,583 LALOUEL. Les forgerons Mondjombo. BULL. IEC 1, no. 2 (1947), pp. 106-114.

13,584 MARQUER, P. Note sur deux empreintes de pieds humains trouvées dans la République Centre-Africaine. J. SOC. AFR. 30 (1960), pp. 7-14.

13,585 PEPPER, H. and BARAT-PEPPER, E. Trois danses chantées avec accompagnement de Linga (dialecte Banda-Linda, Oubangui-Chari). BSEC 21-22 (1948), pp. 85-89.

Geography

13,586 AIME, J. Le seuil de Zinga. BULL. IEC N.S. 5 (1953), pp. 69-75.

History

13,587 FORAN, W. R. Edwardian ivory poachers over the Nile. AFR. AFFAIRS 57 (1958), pp. 125-134.

13,588 TANGHE, M. B. Histoire générale des migrations des peuples de l'Ubangi. CONGO 2 (1938), pp. 361-391.

Language. Literature

Language

13,589 BOUQUIAUX, L. A propos de la phonologie du Sara. J. AFR. LANGS. 3 (1964).

13,590 BRUEL, G. Noms donnés par des populations de l'Oubangui et du Chari à des planètes, à des étoiles et à des constellations. J. SOC. AFR. 2 (1932), pp. 49-53.

13,591 BURSSENS, A. Kleine bijdrage over het zoogenaamde Bwaka (Ubangi). CONGO 2, no. 4 (1933), pp. 558-567.

13,592 CHABRELIE, L. Notes sur la langue des Sara. J. SOC. AFR. 5 (1935), pp. 125-151.

13,593 HAUSER, A. La frontière linguistique Bantoue-Oubanguienne entre le Bas Oubangui et ses affluents de droite. ZAIRE 8 (1954), pp. 21-26.

13,594 JACQUOT, A. Esquisse phonologique du Sango urbain (Bangui). J. SOC. AFR. 30 (1960), pp. 173-191.

13,595 JACQUOT, A. Notes sur la situation du Sango à Bangui: résultats d'un sondage. AFRICA 31 (1961), pp. 158-165; English summary, pp. 165-166.

13,596 SAMARIN, W. J. The attitudinal and autobiographic in Gbeya dog names. J. AFR. LANGS. 4 (1965), pp. 57-72.

13,597 SAMARIN, W. J. Prospecting Gbaya dialects. AFR. STUD. 18 (1959), pp. 68-73.

13,598 SAMARIN, W. J. Sango, an African lingua franca. WORD 11 (1955), pp. 254-267.

13,599 SAMARIN, W. J. The vocabulary of Sango. WORD 17 (1961), pp. 16-22.

Literature

13,600 BAMBOTE, M. Enfance. PRESENCE AFR. N.S. 47 (1963), pp. 182-193.

13,601 BAMBOTE, M. Youlou (l'amour maternel). PRESENCE AFR. N.S. 53 (1965), pp. 221-231.

Science

13,602 DUPONT, R. Le cancer chez les Saras. J. SOC. AFR. 12 (1942), pp. 25-31.

13,603 GRJEBINE, A. Les moustiques des régions de Bouar et de Bozoum (Oubangui-Chari). BULL. IEC N.S. 4 (1952), pp. 151-180.

13,604 THOMAS, J. M. C. Quelques plantes connues des Ngbaka de la Lobaye. J. SOC. AFR. 30 (1960), pp. 75-93.

13,605 THOMAS, J. M. C. Sur quelques plantes cultivées chez les Ngbaka de la Lobaye (République Centrafricaine). BULL. IEC 19-20 (1960), pp. 5-43.

C O N G O (Brazzaville)

General

13,606 SORET, M. Premières Tables décennales du Bulletin de l'Institut d'Etudes Centrafricaines (Nouvelle Série). BULL. IEC 19-20 (1960), pp. 189-218.

13,607 TROCHAIN, J. L. Compte rendu d'activité (Septembre 1950-Août 1951) et programmes de recherches (Août 1951-Août 1952) de l'Institut d'Etudes Centrafricaines. BULL. IEC N.S. 3 (1952), pp. 5-74.

13,608 TROCHAIN, J. L. Compte rendu d'activité (Septembre 1957-Septembre 1958) et Programmes de recherches (Septembre 1958-Septembre 1959) de l'Institut d'Etudes Centrafricaines. BULL. IEC N.S. 17-18 (1959), pp. 87-144.

13,609 TROCHAIN, J. L. Les études poursuivies par l'Institut d'Etudes Centrafricaines, depuis sa création, sur le Territoire de la République du Congo. BULL. IEC 19-20(1960), pp. 127-129.

13,610 TROCHAIN, J. L. Procès-Verbal de la Dixième Réunion (1956) du Conseil Consultatif de Recherches de l'Institut d'Etudes Centrafricaines. BULL. IEC N.S. 13-14 (1957), pp. 103-146.

13,611 TROCHAIN, J. L. Procès-Verbal de la Huitième Réunion (1954) du Conseil Consultatif de Recherches de l'Institut d'Etudes Centrafricaines. BULL. IEC N.S. 7-8 (1954), pp. 211-232.

13,612 TROCHAIN, J. L. Procès-Verbal de la Neuvième Réunion (1955) du Conseil Consultatif de Recherches de l'Institut d'Etudes Centrafricaines. BULL. IEC N.S. 10 (1955), pp. 237-285.

13,613 TROCHAIN, J. L. Procès-Verbal de la Onzième Réunion (1957) du Conseil Consultatif de Recherches de l'Institut d'Etudes Centrafricaines. BULL. IEC N.S. 15-16 (1958), pp. 145-177.

13,614 TROCHAIN, J. L. Procès-Verbal de la Sixième Réunion (1952) du Conseil Consultatif de Recherches de l'Institut d'Etudes Centrafricaines. BULL. IEC N.S. 5 (1953), pp. 101-131.

13,615 Organisation Generale du Centre d'Enseignement Superieur de Brazzaville. BULL. AFR. STUD. ASSOC. 1 (1964), pp. 28-29.

Agriculture

13,616 MAZERE, J. Observations sommaires sur la pêche chez les Likoualas du Bas-Kouyou (Terre Lokakoua, District de Fort-Rousset, Moyen-Congo). BULL. IEC N.S. 7-8 (1954), pp. 165-169.

13,617 SAUTTER, G. Notes l'agriculture des Bakamba de la Vallée du Niari. BULL. IEC N.S. 9 (1955), pp. 67-105.

Anthropology

13,618 BONNEFOND, R. P. and LOMBARD, J. Notes de folklore lari. J. SOC. AFR. 4 (1934), pp. 81-109.

13,619 BONNEFOND, R. P. and LOMBARD, J. Notes sur les coutumes Lari. BULL. IEC N.S. Supplement (1950), pp. 141-177.

13,620 BROWN, H. D. The Nkumu of the Tumba: ritual chieftainship on the Middle Congo. AFRICA 14 (1944), pp. 431-446.

13,621 DOUGLAS, M. Social and religious symbolism of the Lele of the Kasai. ZAIRE 9 (1955), pp. 385-402.

13,622 EVEN, A. Le caractère sacré des chefs chez les Babamba et les Mindassa d'Okondja (Moyen Congo). J. SOC. AFR. 6 (1936), pp. 187-195.

13,623 FAURE, H. M. Rites mortuaires chez les M'Bérés. J. SOC. AFR. 1 (1931), pp. 111-115.

13,624 HOTTOT, R. Teke fetishes. JRAI 86, part 1 (1956), pp. 25-36.

13,625 LEYNAUD, E. Parenté et alliance chez les Bandas du District de Bria, Région de la Kotto, Dar el Kouti. BULL. IEC N.S. 7-8 (1954), pp. 109-164.

13,626 LINDBLOM, G. An old African basket from the West Indies in the Stockholm Museum. ETHNOS 2 (1937), pp. 367-368.

13,627 SWARTENBROECKX, P. Quand l'Ubangi vint au Kwango...Bayansi ou Babangi? ZAIRE 2 (1948), pp. 723-755.

13,628 TREZENEM, E. Contribution à l'étude des nègres africains: les Bateke Balali. J. SOC. AFR. 10 (1940), pp. 1-63.

13,629 WEEKS, J. H. Savage man in Central Africa. J. AFR. SOC. 15 (1916), pp. 150-156.

Art. Antiquities

13,630 BREUIL, H. Un gisement de l'âge de la pierre taillée à Fort Rousset (Oubangui-Chari). J. SOC. AFR. 25 (1955), pp. 7-11.

13,631 DROUX, G. and KELLEY, H. Recherches préhistoriques dans la région de Boko-Songho et à Pointe-Noire (Moyen-Congo). J. SOC. AFR. 9 (1939), pp. 71-84.

13,632 FOURNEAU, J. Recherches sur l'origine des perles de Zanaga. BULL. IFAN 16 (1954), pp. 1-21.

13,633 FOURNEAU, J. Sur des perles anciennes de pâte de verre provenant de Zanaga (Moyen Congo). BULL. IFAN 14 (1952), pp. 956-969.

13,634 FREY, R. Une évolution de l'art nègre; les pierres taillées de Mbigou. BULL. IEC 1, no. 1 (1945), pp. 97-104.

13,635 JUNG, R. Notes sur la case des Bembé. J. SOC. AFR. 16 (1946), pp. 9-21.

13,636 JUNG, R. Piege a porc-épic. J. SOC. AFR. 18 (1948), pp. 129-133.

13,637 LEBEUF, J. L'école des peintres de Poto-Poto. AFRICA 26 (1956), pp. 277-280; English summary, p. 280.

13,638 LOMBARD, J. Matériaux préhistoriques du Congo français. J. SOC. AFR. 1 (1931), pp. 49-59.

13,639 MASSON-DETOURBET, A. Le tissage du raphia chez les Batéké (Moyen-Congo). J. SOC. AFR. 27 (1957), pp. 67-79.

13,640 PEPPER, H. Musique et pensée africaines. PRESENCE AFR. 1 (1947), pp. 149-157.

13,641 SODERBERG, B. Musical instruments used by the Babembe. AFR. MUSIC, 1953, pp. 46-56.

Biography

13,642 Centenaire de la naissance de Brazza. ZAIRE 6 (1952), pp. 631-632.

13,643 Médecin—Colonel J. Ceccaldi. BULL. IEC N.S. 13-14 (1957), pp. 5-6.

Economics

13,644 BALANDIER, G. Le travail non-salarié dans les "Brazzavilles Noires." ZAIRE 6 (1952), pp. 675-690.

13,645 HAUSER, A. Les exploitations mécanisées du Moyen Congo français. AFRICA 24 (1954), pp. 114-128; English summary, p. 128.

13,646 Les marchés indigènes de la Circonscription du Djoué en 1916. BULL. IEC N.S. 11 (1956), pp. 91-109.

Education

13,647 VAUTHERIN, R. Une Université ouvrière en Afrique. CIVILISATIONS 9 (1959), pp. 17-26; English summary, pp. 27-28.

Geography

13,648 COLLIGNON, J. Indications concernant les caractères physico-chimiques de quelques eaux douces du Moyen-Congo. BULL. IEC N.S. 9 (1955), pp. 5-14.

13,649 SAUTTER, G. Note sur l'érosion en cirque des sables au nord de Brazzaville. BULL. IEC N.S. 2 (1951), pp. 49-61.

13,650 SAUTTER, G. Le plateau congolais de Mbé. CAH. ET. AFR. 1 (1960), pp. 5-48.

13,651 SAUTTER, G. Le régime des terres et ses modifications récentes aux environs de Brazzaville et au Woleau N'Tem. BULL. IEC N.S. 7-8 (1954), pp. 201-209.

13,652 TROCHAIN, J. L. and KOECHLIN, J. Les pâturages naturels du Sud de l'A.E.F. BULL. IEC N.S. 15-16 (1958), pp. 59-83.

Government

13,653 Le differend Congo-Gabon. PRESENCE AFR. N.S. 44 (1962), pp. 224-225.

13,654 The position of British merchants in the French Congo. J. AFR. SOC. 2 (1902), pp. 38-43.

History

13,655 BRUNSCHWIG, H. La négociation du traité Makoko. CAH. ET. AFR. 5 (1965), pp. 5-56.

13,656 COQUERY-VIDROVITCH, C. Les idées économiques de Brazza et les premières tentatives de compagnies de colonisation au Congo Français, 1885-1898. CAH. ET. AFR. 5 (1965), pp. 57-82.

13,657 MENIER, M. A. Conceptions politiques et administratives de Brazza, 1885-1898. CAH. ET. AFR. 5 (1965), pp. 83-95.

13,658 SORET, M. Les sciences humaines en République du Congo de 1948 à 1960. BULL. IEC 19-20 (1960), pp. 169-182.

13,659 VINCENT, J. F. Traditions historiques chez les Djem de Souanke (République du Congo-Brazzaville). REV. FRANC. HIST. OUTRE-MER 50 (1963), pp. 64-73.

Language

13,660 BURSSENS, A. Een paar Bedenkingen bij het Essai de Grammaire tsogo van A. Walker. KONGO-OVERZEE 14 (1948), pp. 42-44.

13,661 DENNETT, R. E. The Bavili alphabet restored. J. AFR. SOC. 5 (1905), pp. 48-58.

13,662 GUTHRIE, M. The lingua franca of the Middle Congo. AFRICA 14 (1943), pp. 118-123.

13,663 HULSTAERT, G. On the classification of Congo languages. AFR. STUD. 19 (1960), pp. 173-176.

13,664 JACQUOT, A. La langue des pygmées de la Sangha. Essai d'identification. BULL. IEC N.S. 17-18 (1959), pp. 35-42.

13,665 JACQUOT, A. Notes sur la phonologie du Deembe (Congo). J. AFR. LANGS. 1 (1962), pp. 232-242.

13,666 JACQUOT, A. Précisions sur l'inventaire des langues teke du Congo. CAH. ET. AFR. 5 (1965), pp. 335-340.

13,667 LAMAN, K. E. The musical tone of the Teke language. FESTSCHRIFT MEINHOF, 1927, pp. 118-124.

13,668 SAMARIN, J. W. The Gbaya languages. AFRICA 28 (1958), pp. 148-155.

Law

See 15239.

Science

13,669 AIME, J. Les recherches hydrologiques sur le Territoire de la Republique du Congo de 1948 à 1960. BULL. IEC 19-20 (1960), pp. 130-140.

13,670 BERRIT, G. Les recherches océanographiques sur les côtes de la République du Congo de 1950 à 1960. BULL. IEC 19-20 (1960), pp. 141-149.

13,671 BRUGIERE, J. M. Les recherches pédologiques sur le Territoire de la République du Congo de 1949 à 1960. BULL. IEC 19-20 (1960), pp. 150-161.

13,672 COLLIGNON, J. Contribution à la connaissance des Otolithus des côtes d'Afrique Equatoriale. BULL. IEC 19-20 (1960), pp. 55-84.

13,673 COLLIGNON, J. Observations hydrologiques dans la baie de Pointe-Noire. BULL. IEC N.S. 9 (1955), pp. 153-166.

13,674 COLLIGNON, J. Préliminaires à une étude ecologique de la baie de Pointe-Noire. Répartition de quelques Echinodermes caractéristiques. BULL. IEC N.S. 13-14 (1957), pp. 29-37.

13,675 GRJEBINE, A. Moustiques du Moyen-Congo. BULL. IEC N.S. 1 (1950), pp. 25-48.

13,676 KOECHLIN, J. and CAVALAN, P. Les essais d'introduction et de culture de plantes fourragères dans la Vallée du Niari. BULL. IEC N.S. 17-18 (1959), pp. 43-70.

13,677 KOECHLIN, J. Morphoscopie des sables et végétation dans la région de Brazzaville. BULL. IEC N.S. 13-14 (1957), pp. 39-48.

13,678 KOECHLIN, J. Les recherches de biologie végétale sur le Territoire de la République du Congo de 1947 à 1960. BULL. IEC 19-20 (1960), pp. 162-168.

13,679 KOECHLIN, J. Sur quelques usages de plantes spontanées de la région de Brazzaville. BULL. IEC N.S. 2 (1951), pp. 103-109.

13,680 MAILLOT, L. Elevage de Glossina fuscipes quanzensis Pires à Brazzaville. BULL. IEC N.S. 15-16 (1958), pp. 85-90.

13,681 MAILLOT, L. Infection naturelle de Glossina fuscipes quanzensis Pires par Trypanosoma cazalboui-vivax. BULL. IEC N.S. 17-18 (1959), pp. 71-86.

13,682 MAILLOT, L. and CECCALDI, J. Enquête sur les Glossines dans la vallée du M'Filou au niveau de Gamaba à proximité de Brazzaville (Janvier-Avril 1956). BULL. IEC N.S. 12 (1956), pp. 201-208

13,683 RAVISSE, P. Notes sur les serpents de Brazzaville. BULL. IEC 19-20 (1960), pp. 45-53.

13,684 TAUFFLIEB, R. Notes sur les puces d'Afrique Equatoriale, principalement de la région de Brazzaville. BULL. IEC 19-20 (1960), pp. 85-90.

13,685 TAUFFLIEB, R. Recherches d'entomologie médicale et vétérinaire sur le Territoire de la République du Congo de 1947 à 1960. BULL. IEC 19-20 (1960), pp. 183-188.

13,686 TAUFFLIEB, R. and FINELLE, P. Etude écologique et biologique des Tabanides d'Afrique Equatoriale Française. BULL. IEC N.S. 12 (1956), pp. 209-251.

Sociology

13,687 BALANDIER, G. Approche sociologique des Brazzavilles noires: étude préliminaire. AFRICA 22 (1952), pp. 23-34.

13,688 BALANDIER, G. Le travailleur africain dans les "Brazzavilles noires." PRESENCE AFR. 13 (1952), pp. 315-330.

13,689 SAUTTER, G. L'utilisation des documents administratifs pour l'étude numérique de la population au Moyen-Congo et au Gabon. BULL. IEC N.S. 7-8 (1954), pp. 23-32.

13,690 VENNETIER, P. Un quartier suburbain de Brazzaville: Moukondji-Ngouaka. BULL. IEC 19-20 (1960), pp. 91-124.

13,691 VINCENT, J. F. Women in Brazzaville, Congo. WOMEN TODAY 6 (1965), p. 116.

13,692 L'Organisation Mondiale de la Santé à Brazzaville. ZAIRE 7 (1953), pp. 728-729.

13,693 Sport et tribalisme. PRESENCE AFR. N.S. 44 (1962), pp. 216-217.

GABON

Agriculture

13,694 BUDKER, P. and COLLIGNON, J. Trois campagnes baleinières au Gabon (1949-1950-1951). BULL. IEC N.S. 3 (1952), pp. 75-100.

13,695 SAUTTER, G. Le Cacao dans l'économie rurale du Woleu-N'Tem. BULL. IEC N.S. 1 (1950), pp. 7-24.

Anthropology

13,696 BALANDIER, G. Aspects de l'évolution sociale chez les Fang du Gabon. CAH. INT. SOCIOL. 9 (1950), pp. 76-106.

13,697 CHEVALIER, A. Les rapports des Noirs avec la nature. Sur l'utilisation par les indigènes du Gabon d'une fougère pour piégeage et d'un champignon pour des ceintures de parure. J. SOC. AFR. 4 (1934), pp. 123-127.

13,698 DENIS, J. La nouvelle carte ethnique de l'Afrique Equatoriale Française. ZAIRE 9 (1955), pp. 1069-1073.

13,699 ECKENDORFF, J. Note sur les tribus des Subdivisions de Makokou et de Mékambo (Gabon). BULL. IEC 1, no. 1 (1945), pp. 87-95.

13,700 FERNANDEZ, J. W. The idea and symbol of the Saviour in a Gabon syncretistic cult. INT. REV. MISSIONS 53 (1964), pp. 281-289.

13,701 FERNANDEZ, J. W. Symbolic consensus in a Fang reformative cult. AMER. ANTHR. 67 (1965), pp. 902-929.

13,702 HAUSER, A. Notes sur les Omyéné du bas Gabon. BULL. IFAN 16 (1954), pp. 402-415.

13,703 HEE, R. P. Le Ngo: société secrete du Haut-Ogowé (Gabon). AFRICA 10 (1937), pp. 472-480.

13,704 MACLATCHY, A. L'organisation sociale des populations de la région de Mimongo (Gabon). BULL. IEC 1, no. 1 (1945), pp. 53-86.

13,705 MILETTO. Notes sur les ethnies de la région du Haut-Ogooué. BULL. IEC N.S. 2 (1951), pp. 19-48.

13,706 TREZENEM, E. Notes ethnographiques sur les tribus Fan du Moyen Ogooué (Gabon). J. SOC. AFR. 6 (1936), pp. 65-93.

13,707 WALKER, A. Conte tsogo. J. SOC. AFR. 9 (1939), pp. 153-157.

13,708 WEINSTEIN, B. Social communication methodology in the study of nation-building. CAH. ET. AFR. 4 (1964), pp. 569-589.

See also 12933.

Art. Antiquities

13,709 BLANKOFF, B. Quelques découvertes préhistoriques récentes au Gabon. PROC. PAN-AFR. CONGR. PRE-HIST. 5 (1965), pp. 191-206.

13,710 GREBERT, F. Arts en voie de disparition au Gabon. AFRICA 7 (1934), pp. 82-88.

13,711 PEISSI, P. Les masques blancs des tribus de l'Ogoué. PRESENCE AFR. 10 (1951), pp. 182-184.

13,712 SEGY, L. Bakota funerary figures. ZAIRE 6 (1952), pp. 451-461.

Biography

13,713 BALLARD, C. M. Albert Schweitzer. CONTEMP. REV. 207 (1965), pp. 225-228.

13,714 SCHWEITZER, A. Albert Schweitzer [acknowledges award of Wellcome bronze medal]. AFR. AFFAIRS 53 (1954), pp. 1-3.

13,715 GELL, C. W. M. Albert Schweitzer at eighty. CONTEMP. REV. 187 (1955), pp. 18-22.

13,716 ROSS, E. Albert Schweitzer, the man and his mind. INT. REV. MISSIONS 37 (1948), pp. 330-333.

13,717 SILKIN, J. The Forests (on the occasion of Dr. Schweitzer's visit to England). AFR. AFFAIRS 55 (1956), p. 46.

13,718 WALTHER, D. A visit to Albert Schweitzer. CONTEMP. REV. 170 (1946), pp. 160-166.

Economics

13,719 BALANDIER, G. Problèmes économiques et problèmes politiques au niveau du village Fang. BULL. IEC N.S. 1 (1950), pp. 49-64.

13,720 C., J. La politique de l'okoumé au Gabon. ZAIRE 9 (1955), p. 173.

Geography

13,721 BERRIT, G. R. Les eaux de la Baie du Cap Lopez en février 1956. BULL. IEC N.S. 11 (1956), pp. 5-19.

Government

See 13653.

History

13,722 BRUNSCHWIG, H. Expéditions punitives au Gabon (1875-1877). CAH. ET. AFR. 2 (1962), pp. 347-361.

13,723 COQUERY-VIDROVITCH, C. De Brazza à Gentil: la politique française en Haute-Sangha à la fin du XIXe siècle. REV. FRANC. HIST. OUTRE-MER 52 (1965), pp. 22-40.

13,724 DESCHAMPS, H. Quinze ans de Gabon (Les débuts de l'établissement français, 1839-1853). REV. FRANC. HIST. OUTRE-MER 50 (1963), pp. 283-345; 52 (1965), pp. 92-126.

13,725 REYNARD, R. Note sur l'activité économique des côtes du Gabon au début du XVIIe siècle. BULL. IEC N.S. 13-14 (1957), pp. 49-54.

13,726 REYNARD, R. Nouvelles recherches sur l'influence portugaise au Gabon. BULL. IEC N.S. 11 (1956), pp. 21-25.

13,727 REYNARD, R. Recherches sur la présence des Portugais au Gabon XVe-XIXe siècles. BULL. IEC N.S. 9 (1955), pp. 15-66.

13,728 WALKER, A. and REYNARD, R. Anglais, Espagnols et Nord-Américains au Gabon au XIXe siècle. BULL. IEC N.S. 12 (1956), pp. 253-279.

See also 14871.

Language. Literature

13,729 ADAM, M. J. Dialectes du Gabon. La famille des langues Téké. BULL. IEC N.S. 7-8 (1954), pp. 33-107.

13,730 BONNEAU, R. P. J. Grammaire Pounou. J. SOC. AFR. 10 (1940), pp. 131-161; 17 (1947), pp. 23-50; 22 (1952), pp. 43-93.

13,731 ITTMANN, J. Einiges aus der Bankon-Literatur. AFR. UND UB. 17 (1926-1927), pp. 81-108.

13,732 ITTMANN, J. Lieder der Subu. AFR. UND UB. 36 (1951-1952), pp. 135-136.

13,733 MARTROU, L. Le langue Fan et ses dialectes. J. SOC. AFR. 6 (1936), pp. 205-211.

13,734 MILLER, C. B. Duration as a semantic element in the Bankon language. INT. CONG. LING. 4 (1936), p. 177.

13,735 TREZENEM, E. Vocabulaire Inzabi. J. SOC. AFR. 2 (1932), pp. 75-84.

13,736 WALKER, A. L'alphabet des idiomes gabonais. J. SOC. AFR. 2 (1932), pp. 139-146.

13,737 WALKER, A. Concordance de proverbes gabonais et Européens. BULL. IEC N.S. 15-16 (1958), pp. 43-58.

13,738 WALKER, A. Essai de grammaire Tsogo. BULL. IEC N.S. Supplement (1950), pp. 5-69.

13,739 WALKER, A. Les néologismes dans les idiomes gabonais. J. SOC. AFR. 3 (1933), pp. 305-314.

13,740 WALKER, A. R. Les idiomes Gabonais. Similitudes et divergences. BULL. IEC N.S. 10 (1955), pp. 211-236.

13,741 WALKER, A. R. Remarques sur les noms propres gabonais. BULL. IEC. N.S. 11 (1956), pp. 81-91.

Religion

13,742 MacKENZIE, J. K. Some African women. INT. REV. MISSIONS 12 (1923), pp. 98-111.

Science

13,743 GODIVIER, R. and DONCHE, L. LE. Six mois d'enregistrements du champ magnétique terrestre à la Station géophysique de l'I.E.C. à Bangui (Février-Septembre 1952). BULL. IEC N.S. 13-14 (1957), pp. 95-101.

13,744 LINDBLOM, G. An ethnographical proof of the honey buzzard's migrations to Cameroun. ETHNOS 3 (1938), pp. 4-7.

13,745 ROUGEOT, P. C. Note sur les papillons gabonais du genre Drepanoptera Roths. BULL. IEC 1, no. 2 (1947), pp. 129-134.

13,746 ROUGEOT, P. C. Notes sur les Laridès du Gabon. BULL. IEC 1, no. 2 (1947), pp. 125-128.

13,747 WALKER, A. Usages pharmaceutiques des plantes spontanées du Gabon. BULL. IEC N.S. 4 (1952), pp. 181-186; N.S. 5 (1953), pp. 19-40; N.S. 6 (1953), pp. 275-329.

Sociology

13,748 ADIBE, M. L. and TESSA, A. Position and problems of the woman in...Gabon. WOMEN TODAY 6 (1964), pp. 51-53.

13,749 LOTTE, A. J. Situation démographique du district de Franceville (Gabon). BULL. IEC N.S. 6 (1953), pp. 161-180.

See also 13689, 13693.

ZAIRE

General

13,750 BILSEN, J. VAN. Chronique congolaise. ZAIRE 4 (1950), pp. 73-77.

13,751 BULCK, G. VAN. Rapport sur une mission d'etudes effectuée au Congo Belge (janvier 1932-août 1933). BULL. SEANCES IRCB 6 (1935), pp. 116-139.

13,752 COPPENS, P. Le Congrès Colonial National. ZAIRE 1 (1947), pp. 555-566.

13,753 DEPASSE, C. Les bibliothèques publiques au Congo. Un court historique... ZAIRE 2 (1948), pp. 277-302.

13,754 HEYSE, T. Le travail bibliographique colonial belge de 1876 jusqu'en 1933.* ZAIRE 2 (1948), pp. 639-656.

13,755 MARZORATI, A. Perspectieven voor het jaar 2000. Belgisch Kongo. ZAIRE 4 (1950), pp. 843-846.

13,756 RYELANDT. D. Bibliographie générale des articles et ouvrages politiques sur la République du Congo-Léopoldville (1959-1962). ET. CONG. 4, Special Number (1963), pp. 1-130.

13,757 Elizabethville Anthropological Museum. TANG. NOTES 17 (1944), p. 66.

Agriculture. Forestry.

13,758 ADRIAENS, L. Les huiles siccatives d'Aleurites. CONGO 1 (1938), pp. 499-519.

13,759 BAZA, P. and MAVUNGU, A. Mambu ma mabu ku tsi Mayombe (De palmbomen in Mayombe: translated by L. Leclercq). ZAIRE 2 (1948), pp. 159-173.

13,760 BERTRAND, A. De la nécessité d'une documentation scientifique ou statistique préalable à toute mesure interessant les indigènes. BULL. SEANCES IRCB 2 (1931), pp. 489-500.

13,761 BRANDEN, F. V. DEN. ...le traitement des trypanosomiases bovines expérimentales à type congolense-dimorphon, par l'association du moranyl 309 fourneau et de l'émétique de potasse. BULL. SEANCES IRCB 1 (1930), pp. 267-268.

13,762 BRUYNS, L. Kollektieve hoeven, een landbouwexperiment bij de Bakongo. ZAIRE 4 (1950), pp. 3-15.

13,763 DELEVOY, G. Pourquoi la richesse forestière n'est pas toujours fonction de la richesse des sols. BULL. SEANCES IRCB 2 (1931), pp. 545-547.

13,764 KHONDE, G. and KINI, N. Mambu ma maba ku tsi Mayombe (De palmboomen in Mayombe: translated by L. Declercq). ZAIRE 1 (1947), pp. 755-772.

13,765 LACOPS, B. Het hoekje over inlandse landbouw en Veeteelt (N.S.). AEQUATORIA 10 (1947), pp. 141-143.

13,766 LACOPS, M. Lager landbouwonderwijs in Belgisch Congo. CONGO 1 (1938), pp. 55-67; 1 (1939), pp. 514-529.

13,767 LACOPS, M. Landbouwonderwijs op de Normaalschool voor inlandsche onderwijzers in Belgisch Congo. CONGO 2 (1939), pp. 56-69.

13,768 LEPLAE, E. Agriculture in the Belgian Congo. BULL. IMP. INST. 12 (1914), pp. 60-75.

13,769 LEPLAE, E. L'avenir de l'agriculture congolaise conformément au Discours du Duc de Brabant. CONGO 1 (1937), pp. 233-286.

13,770 LEPLAE, E. Cotton growing in the Belgian Congo. BULL. IMP. INST. 18 (1920), pp. 352-402.

13,771 LEPLAE, E. Native agricultural policy and European agriculture in the Belgian Congo. J. AFR. SOC. 38 (1939), pp. 357-369.

13,772 LEPLAE, E. Note sur l'irrigation au Congo et spécialement sur l'application de l'irrigation mécanique. BULL. SEANCES IRCB 6 (1935), pp. 476-485.

13,773 LEPLAE, E. La question forestière au Congo belge. BULL. SEANCES IRCB 2 (1931), pp. 142-149.

13,774 LEPLAE, E. Recent improvement of African oil palms and palm oil production in the Belgian Congo. BULL. IMP. INST. 35 (1937), pp. 174-180.

13,775 LUBAMBA, G. and PHANZU, F. Mambu ma moba ku tsi Mayombe (De palmbomen in Mayombe: translated by L. Leclercq). ZAIRE 2 (1948), pp. 869-896.

13,776 MALONDA, M. Oliepalm en palmgaarde. KONGO-OVERZEE 10-11 (1944-1945), pp. 145-178.

13,777 MOSTAZA, B. El Congo, fruta cortada en agraz. ARCH. INST. EST. AFR. 16, no. 63 (1962), pp. 53-65.

13,778 PEETERS, G. L'agriculture congolaise et ses problèmes. ZAIRE 12 (1958), pp. 451-477.

13,779 PEETERS, G. Problèmes d'économie agraire congolaise paysan submarginal au fermier? ZAIRE 11 (1957), pp. 391-397.

13,780 PINXTEN, K. and BRUYNS, L. Inlandse boerenbedrijven. ZAIRE 5 (1951), pp. 451-473.

13,781 TORDEUR, J. Les plantations indigènes de palmiers au Mayumbe. ZAIRE 1 (1947), pp. 607-627.

13,782 TROESCH, J. La peche au Ma-yombe (enclave de Cabinda). ZAIRE 9 (1955), pp. 943-952.

13,783 VANDERLINDEN, J. Problèmes posés par l'introduction de nouveaux modes d'usage des terres chez les Zande vungara du Congo. AFRICAN AGRARIAN SYSTEMS, 1963, pp. 331-347.

13,784 VANDERYST, H. Importance pratique des formations et associations agrostologiques dans la Province Congo-Kasaï, et l'Angola. BULL. SEANCES IRCB 2 (1931), pp. 548-550.

13,785 VANDERYST, H. Le système de culture des Bantous et la destruction des formations forestières dans le Moyen-Congo. CONGO 1 (1921), pp. 525-541.

13,786 VERMOESEN, F. M. C. Sur la vitalité des formations forestières dans le Bas- et Moyen-Congo. CONGO 2 (1921), pp. 65-77.

13,787 WILDE, L. O. J. DE. De inlandse landbouwstelsels in Belgisch-Kongo. ZAIRE 3 (1949), pp. 995-1002.

13,788 WILDE, L. O. J. DE. Het Lundbouwonderzoek in Belgisch-Kongo. KONGO-OVERZEE 20 (1954), pp. 237-246.

13,789 WILDEMAN, E. DE. Protection de la Nature, protection de l'Agriculture. Les problèmes qu'elles soulèvent. BULL. SEANCES IRCB 4 (1933), pp. 386-428.

13,790 WILDEMAN, E. DE. Restriction des cultures. Extension des cultures. BULL. SEANCES IRCB 5 (1934), pp. 171-195.

Anthropology

13,791 ADALBERT. Devinettes Nkundo. AEQUATORIA 15 (1952), pp. 41-51.

13,792 ALDEN, K. The prophet movement in the Congo. INT. REV. MISSIONS 25 (1936), pp. 347-353.

13,793 AVERMAET, G. VAN. Nota over de Bofomela. AEQUATORIA 2 (1939), pp. 133-136.

13,794 B., E. Les Batwa. AEQUATORIA 9 (1946), pp. 153-154.

13,795 BAYAKA, J. et al. Politesse Mongo: by J. Bayaka, A. Emenge, F. Longonda and B. Bolanjei. AEQUATORIA 8 (1945), pp. 103-108.

13,796 BENGALA, A. Le noble des Booli. AEQUATORIA 25 (1962), pp. 105-111.

13,797 BERGER, P. Uberlieferungen der Kindiga. Mit einem Anhang: Ein Jagdbericht. AFRIKA (Berlin) 2 (1943), pp. 97-122?.

13,798 BIEBUYCK, D. Les divisions du jour et de la nuit chez les Nyanga. AEQUATORIA 21 (1958), pp. 134-138.

13,799 BIEBUYCK, D. Fondements de l'organisation politique des Lunda du Mwaanlayaav en territoire de Kapanga (Province du Katanga, Congo belge). ZAIRE 11 (1957), pp. 787-817.

13,800 BIEBUYCK, D. De Mbu'i wa abeca bij de Babembe. ZAIRE 6 (1952), pp. 691-697.

13,801 BIEBUYCK, D. De Mumbo-instelling bij de Banyanga (Kivu). KONGO-OVERZEE 21 (1955), pp. 441-448.

13,802 BIEBUYCK, D. Organisation politique des Nyanga: La chefferie Ihana. KONGO-OVERZEE 22 (1956), pp. 301-341; 23 (1957), pp. 58-98.

13,803 BIEBUYCK, D. Repartitions et droits du pangolin chez les Balega. ZAIRE 7 (1953), pp. 899-924.

13,804 BIEBUYCK, D. La société kumu face au Kitawala. ZAIRE 11 (1957), pp. 7-40.

13,805 BITTREMIEUX, L. De Baphende's van Luanda (Opper-Kasaï). CONGO 1 (1939), pp. 27-39, 153-181.

13,806 BITTREMIEUX, L. Enkele aanteekeningen over de te weinig bekende Bateke's. CONGO 2 (1936), pp. 663-667.

13,807 BITTREMIEUX, L. De geschiedenis van Luziolo, de Mayombsche Schoone. KONGO-OVERZEE 2 (1935-1936), pp. 25-40.

13,808 BITTREMIEUX, L. Nganda Tsundi: Volk en Vermomden. KONGO-OVERZEE 6 (1940), pp. 49-65, 113-134.

13,809 BITTREMIEUX, L. Een verhaal van de Baphende. CONGO 1 (1940), pp. 150-153.

13,810 BITTREMIEUX, L. Wederwraak op z'n heidensch. CONGO 2 (1937), pp. 291-299.

13,811 BITTREMIEUX, L. De Wondervogel. Vaders Vogel. CONGO 2 (1939), pp. 274-319.

13,812 BOELAERT, E. Batetela—Zuid-Mongo. KONGO-OVERZEE 5 (1939), pp. 77-81.

13,813 BOELAERT, E. Les Batswa. Quelques notes démographiques. AEQUATORIA 10 (1947), pp. 134-136.

13,814 BOELAERT, E. Bene-en Maledictie bij de Nkundo. CONGO 2 (1939), pp. 376-379.

13,815 BOELAERT, E. Les Bongili. AEQUATORIA 10 (1947), pp. 17-34.

13,816 BOELAERT, E. Le clan équivoque. AEQUATORIA 11 (1948), pp. 13-19.

13,817 BOELAERT, E. Coups de Sonde. AEQUATORIA 5 (1942), pp. 26-31.

13,818 BOELAERT, E. De Elima der Nkundo. CONGO 1 (1936), pp. 42-52.

13,819 BOELAERT, E. Eloko, de boeman der Nkundo. ZAIRE 3 (1949), pp. 129-137.

13,820 BOELAERT, E. Les épouvantails-amulettes. CONGO 1 (1936), pp. 677-679.

13,821 BOELAERT, E. Hekserij bij de Nkundo. KONGO-OVERZEE 2 (1935-1936), pp. 139-155.

13,822 BOELAERT, E. L'histoire de l'immatriculation. AEQUATORIA 14 (1951), pp. 6-12.

13,823 BOELAERT, E. Klan-exogamie der Batswa. KONGO-OVERZEE 15 (1944), pp. 24-33.

13,824 BOELAERT, E. De Mongo. Kantteekeningen bij Les Peuplades du Congo Belge. KONGO-OVERZEE 4 (1938), pp. 19-22.

13,825 BOELAERT, E. De Nkundo-Maatschappij. KONGO-OVERZEE 6 (1940), pp. 148-161.

13,826 BOELAERT, E. La procession de Lianja. AEQUATORIA 25 (1962), pp. 1-9.

13,827 BOELAERT, E. Systematiek der Bloedverwantschapsbenamingen bij de Nkundo. AEQUATORIA 20 (1957), pp. 125-128.

13,828 BOELAERT, E. Terminologue classificatoire des Nkundo. AFRICA 21 (1951), pp. 218-223; English summary, p. 223.

13,829 BOELAERT, E. Validiteit der Pseudo-huwelijken. AEQUATORIA 2 (1939), pp. 30-33.

13,830 BOELAERT, E. Waar komen onze Pygmoiden vandaan? KONGO-OVERZEE 3 (1936-1937), pp. 22-25.

13,831 BOELAERT, E. Yebola. KONGO-OVERZEE 1 (1934), pp. 16-19.

13,832 BOGAERTS, H. Un aspect de la structure sociale chez les Bakwa Luntu. ZAIRE 5 (1951), pp. 563-609.

13,833 BOGAERTS, H. Bij de Basala Mpasu, de Koppensnellers van Kasai. ZAIRE 4 (1950), pp. 379-419.

13,834 BOGAERTS, H. Gewoontelijke strafbepalingen tegen het overspel bij de Babindi. CONGO 2 (1939), pp. 533-536.

13,835 BOGAERTS, H. Iets over Stamboomen. CONGO 2 (1939), pp. 410-425.

13,836 BOGAERTS, H. Is het bruidschat-systeem een definitieve instelling in Kongo? ZAIRE 6 (1952), pp. 1017-1040.

13,837 BOONE, O. Carte ethnique du Congo Belge et du Ruanda-Urundi. ZAIRE 8 (1954), pp. 451-465.

13,838 BOUCCIN. Les Babadi. CONGO 2 (1935), pp. 685-712; 1 (1936), pp. 26-41.

13,839 BOUILLON, A. La corporation des chasseurs Baluba. ZAIRE 8 (1954), pp. 563-594.

13,840 BOUILLON, A. Les Mammifères dans le folklore Luba. ZAIRE 7 (1953), pp. 563-601.

13,841 BRANDT, L. DE. Het heelal van den Muluba. CONGO 1 (1921), pp. 249-268.

13,842 BRAUSCH, G. Plan voor de studie van de maatschappelijke ethnologie in Belgisch-Kongo. KONGO-OVERZEE 12-13 (1946-1947), pp. 103-106.

13,843 BRETT, P. M. An acquired cranial deformity. SUDAN NOTES 3 (1920), pp. 81-82.

13,844 BRUYNS, L. De vaststelling van den bruidschat in de streek van Kisantu. ZAIRE 3 (1949), pp. 617-628.

13,845 BULCK, G. VAN. Les Ba. Dzing dans nos sources de littérature ethnographique. CONGO 2 (1934), pp. 297-331.

13,846 BULCK, G. VAN. Ethnologie et Ethnographie dans les Pays-Bas. CONGO 1 (1938), pp. 241-260.

13,847 BULCK, G. VAN. Journées d'étude d'ethnologie et de missiologie (Paris-Louvain, juillet-août 1954). ZAIRE 8 (1954), pp. 955-979.

13,848 BULCK, G. VAN. Notes d'ethnologie: style oral et symbolisme au Mayombe. CONGO 1 (1938), pp. 481-498.

13,849 BULCK, G. VAN. Tendances nouvelles en ethnologie. ZAIRE 13 (1959), pp. 287-293.

13,850 BULCK, V. VAN. Het Probleem der Pygmeeënreligie volgens P. Schebesta. KONGO-OVERZEE 15 (1949), pp. 108-118.

13,851 BULCK, V. VAN. Het Probleem van het Pygmeeënras volgens Gusinde. KONGO-OVERZEE 15 (1949), pp. 45-58.

13,852 BULCK, V. VAN. La religion des Bakongo orientaux. ZAIRE 2 (1948), pp. 663-673.

13,853 BULCK, V. VAN. Où en est le problème des pygmées de l'Ituri. ZAIRE 2 (1948), pp. 423-436.

13,854 BURK, E. I. The Lega school of circumcision. ZAIRE 10 (1956), pp. 375-377.

13,855 BURROWS, G. On the natives of the Upper Welle district of the Belgian Congo. JRAI 28 (1899), pp. 35-47.

13,856 BURSSENS, A. Eerste Kiluba-vertelsel. KONGO-OVERZEE 18 (1952), pp. 122-129.

13,857 BURSSENS, H. The so-called Bangala and a few problems of art-historical and ethnographical Order. KONGO-OVERZEE 20 (1954), pp. 221-236.

13,858 BURTON, W. F. P. A Luba folk-tale. BANTU STUD. 9 (1935), pp. 69-80.

13,859 BURTON, W. F. P. The secret societies of Lubaland, Congo Belge. BANTU STUD. 4 (1930), pp. 217-250.

13,860 C., E. La limitation du taux des dots. ZAIRE 2 (1948), pp. 955-968.

13,861 CAENEGHEM, R. VAN. De Gastvrijheid in de spreekwoorden der Luba-menschen. CONGO 1 (1939), pp. 295-310, 412-432.

13,862 CAENEGHEM, R. VAN. Gebeden der Baluba II. AEQUATORIA 10 (1947), pp. 4-16.

13,863 CAENEGHEM, R. VAN. Geven aan anderman in der de spreekwoorden der Baluba-Menschen. CONGO 2 (1937), pp. 377-411.

13,864 CAENEGHEM, R. VAN. Het Godsbegrip bij de Baluba van Kasai. ZAIRE 3 (1949), pp. 743-764.

13,865 CAENEGHEM, R. VAN. Het vrijgezellen-leven in de spreekwoorden van Luba en Moyo-volk. CONGO 1 (1940), pp. 47-73.

13,866 CAENEGHEM, R. VAN. De psychologie der Baluba in hun spreekwoorden over de ziekten. CONGO 1 (1940), pp. 284-306.

13,867 CAENEGHEM, R. VAN. Der Psychologie der Baluba in hun spreekwoorden over de ziekten. ZAIRE 1 (1947), pp. 55-72.

13,868 CAENEGHEM, R. VAN. Vertellingen van de Baluba's. CONGO 1 (1935), pp. 503-519.

13,869 CAENEGHEM, R. VAN and BURSSENS, A. Luba-Teksten. Lusumuinu lua Kabundi. KONGO-OVERZEE 1 (1934), pp. 45-54.

13,870 CAPELLE, E. Les indigènes ont-ils un nom de famille? ZAIRE 1 (1947), pp. 923-927.

13,871 CARMIGNANI, R. Il Cannibalismo degli Asandè. AFRICA 27 (1957), pp. 397-399; English summary, p. 400.

13,872 CARRINGTON, J. F. The initiation language: Lokele tribe. AFR. STUD. 6 (1947), pp. 196-207.

13,873 CELIS, M. J. Enkele nota's over den godsdienst der Vanande. KONGO-OVERZEE 2 (1935-1936), pp. 100-105.

13,874 CELIS, M. J. Nota's over de plechtigheid der Manddraging bij de Zuid-Vanande. KONGO-OVERZEE 9 (1943), pp. 176-182.

13,875 CLARKE, R. T. The drum language of the Tumba people. AMER. J. SOC. 40 (1934-1935), pp. 34-48.

13,876 CLEENE, N. DE. Les chefs indigènes au Mayombe. Hier. Aujourd'hui. Demain. AFRICA 8 (1935), pp. 63-75.

13,877 CLEENE, N. DE. L'élément religieux dans l'organisation sociale des Bayombe. CONGO 1 (1936), pp. 706-711.

13,878 CLEENE, N. DE. La famille dans l'organisation sociale du Mayombe. Hier.-Aujourd'hui.-Demain. AFRICA 10 (1937), pp. 1-15.

13,879 CLEENE, N. DE. La société Yombe. CONGO 1 (1938), pp. 409-415.

13,880 CLERCQ, A. DE. Hoe het Tshiluba zich in Kasai verspreidde. KONGO-OVERZEE 3 (1936-1937), pp. 241-244.

13,881 CLERCQ, A. DE. Mupongo, Buloji. CONGO 1 (1936), pp. 1-10.

13,882 COCKER, M. DE. Defensieve magie in de Ngbakanamen. ZAIRE 4 (1950), pp. 203-209.

13,883 COCKER, M. DE. Speeksel, als magische kracht, bij enkele volksstammen in Congo-Ubangi. ZAIRE 3 (1949), pp. 29-34.

13,884 COCKER, M. DE. Vlees-en vistaboe bij de Ngbaka (Gemena-Gewest). ZAIRE 3 (1949), pp. 1119-1122.

13,885 COCKER, P. DE. Enkele gegevens over een zekere vorm van totemisme bij de Ngbaka (Gemena-gewest). ZAIRE 4 (1950), pp. 303-306.

13,886 COCKER, P. DE. Oorzakelijkheid en Moraalbeschouwingen in de Ngbakaverhalen. ZAIRE 4 (1950), pp. 39-50.

13,887 COCQUYT, A. Proverbes des Ntomba e Njale. AEQUATORIA 16 (1953), pp. 147-152; 17 (1954), pp. 7-27.

13,888 COEMAN, P. F. Historische Ngbaka-Legenden. AEQUATORIA 8 (1945), pp. 135-150.

13,889 COLARD, R. J. H. Note sur les Batsamba. CONGO 1 (1936), pp. 523-525.

13,890 COLLINS, R. O. Ivory poaching in the Lado enclave. UGANDA J. 24 (1960), pp. 217-228.

13,891 COMHAIRE, J. Une decade d'evolution en territoire d'Oshe. ZAIRE 7 (1953), pp. 255-263.

13,892 COMHAIRE, J. Sociétés secrètes et mouvements prophétiques au Congo Belge. AFRICA 25 (1955), pp. 54-58; English summary, pp. 58-59.

13,893 COMHAIRE-SYLVAIN, J. Les danses Nkundu du territoire d'Oshwe du Congo Belge. AFR. STUD. 6 (1947), pp. 124-130.

13,894 COMHAIRE-SYLVAIN, S. Quelques devinettes des enfants noirs de Léopoldville. AFRICA 19 (1949), pp. 40-52.

13,895 COMHAIRE-SYLVAIN, S. and COMHAIRE-SYLVAIN, J. Kinship change in the Belgian Congo. AFR. STUD. 16 (1957), pp. 20-24.

13,896 COSTERMANS, B. J. De Besnijdenis bij de Mamwu-Mangutu en omstreken. AEQUATORIA 13 (1950), pp. 14-20.

13,897 COSTERMANS, B. J. Dai ou Angai? ZAIRE 4 (1950), pp. 515-523.

13,898 COSTERMANS, B. J. Dorp en gebouwen van de Logo-Avokaya. ZAIRE 5 (1951), pp. 675-689.

13,899 COSTERMANS, B. J. De eed bij de Logo-Avokaya. ZAIRE 8 (1954), pp. 709-718.

13,900 COSTERMANS, B. J. De Efe van Watsa-Gombari. CONGO 2 (1937), pp. 526-532.

13,901 COSTERMANS, B. J. De gebouwen bij de Mamvu-Mangutu-Walese. ZAIRE 1 (1947), pp. 281-295.

13,902 COSTERMANS, B. J. Het behekste kind. ZAIRE 3 (1949), pp. 379-393.

13,903 COSTERMANS, B. J. Het slecht voorteken of de Ruba van de Logo-Avokaya. ZAIRE 6 (1952), pp. 809-827.

13,904 COSTERMANS, B. J. De Kazibah. KONGO-OVERZEE 4 (1938), pp. 177-184.

13,905 COSTERMANS, B. J. Ndogo. AEQUATORIA 16 (1953), pp. 137-138.

13,906 COSTERMANS, B. J. Rouwbedrijf en lijkplechtigheid bij de Logo-Avokaya. ZAIRE 5 (1951), pp. 3-30, 137-167.

13,907 COSTERMANS, B. J. Sipema. Puberteits-ceremonie bij de Logo-Avokaya. ZAIRE 4 (1950), pp. 167-179.

13,908 COSTERMANS, B. J. Spelen bij de Mamvu en Logo in de gewesten Watsa-Faradje. ZAIRE 2 (1948), pp. 249-275, 525-550, 757-785.

13,909 COSTERMANS, B. J. Termieten-larvenoogst bij de Logo. KONGO-OVERZEE 16 (1950), pp. 185-197.

13,910 COSTERMANS, B. J. Torè, God en Geesten bij de Mamvu en hun dwergen. CONGO 1 (1938), pp. 532-547.

13,911 COSTERMANS, B. J. De verering van de tweelingen bij de Logo-Avokaya. AEQUATORIA 14 (1951), pp. 57-73.

13,912 COSTERMANS, B. J. Yitri. De Visvangst door Bedwelming bij de Vele-volken. KONGO-OVERZEE 15 (1949), pp. 129-154.

13,913 CROCKER, H. E. Among the cannibals of the Congo. AFR. AFFAIRS 43 (1944), pp. 75-79.

13,914 CUYPERS, J. B. Les relations sociales et les attitudes entre Shi (bantu) et Rhwa (pygmées) à l'Ouest du lac Kivu. EAISR Jan. (1964), pp. 1-15.

13,915 DAVIDSON, J. La circoncision chez les Ngombe. AEQUATORIA 14 (1951), pp. 93-94.

13,916 DAVIDSON, J. Les proverbes dans la langue des Ngombe. AEQUATORIA 14 (1951), pp. 48-56.

13,917 DECAPMAKER, I. Sanctions coutumières contre l'adultère chez les Bas-Congo de la région de Kasi. CONGO 2 (1939), pp. 134-147.

13,918 DECAPMAKER, J. La famille dans le matriarcat. AEQUATORIA 12 (1949), pp. 95-102.

13,919 DECAPMAKER, J. Les funérailles chez les Bakongo. AEQUATORIA 14 (1951), pp. 81-84.

13,920 DECAPMAKER, J. Le matriarcat en face de l'évolution. AEQUATORIA 22, no. iii (1959), pp. 98-100.

13,921 DECAPMAKER, J. Zedelijkheid bij de Bakongo. AEQUATORIA 16 (1953), pp. 93-98.

13,922 DEDAVE, A. Les pêcheurs de Stanleyville: quelques aspects de la vie sociale et coutumière des Wagenia. AFRICA 27 (1957), pp. 262-267; English summary, p. 267.

13,923 DELANGHE, A. and COMHAIRE, J. De Batwa van het Gewest Oshwe. ZAIRE 1 (1947), pp. 1145-1147.

13,924 DELOBBE. L'oncle maternel dans la famille Kundu. CONGO 1 (1937), pp. 100-102.

13,925 DENIS, L. Devinettes des Bakongo. CONGO 1 (1936), pp. 187-205.

13,926 DENIS, L. Jeux des enfants Bakongo. CONGO 2 (1937), pp. 412-426.

13,927 DENIS, L. Proverbes des Bakongo. CONGO 2 (1936), pp. 351-368.

13,928 DENIS, L. Proverbes des Bakongo expliqués par eux-mêmes. CONGO 2 (1935), pp. 313-329.

13,929 DENIS, L. La supputation du temps et le calendrier chez les Bakongo. CONGO 2 (1938), pp. 481-489.

13,930 DENIS, P. La tortue et le leopard dans les legendes mangbetu. ZAIRE 6 (1952), pp. 155-172.

13,931 DENIS, P. J. L'organisation d'un peuple primitif. CONGO 1 (1935), pp. 481-502.

13,932 DENNETT, R. E. Laws and customs of the Fjort or Bavili family, kingdom of Loango. J. AFR. SOC. 1 (1902), pp. 259-287.

13,933 DENOLF, F. De slaven bij de Basho, Bakuba en Baluba. CONGO 2 (1938), pp. 67-79, 197-212, 296-308.

13,934 DENOLF, P. Aan den rand der Dibese. ZAIRE 4 (1950), pp. 613-641, 721-752, 965-988.

13,935 DENOLF, P. Een Kongolese stam die de Bruidschat niet kende. De Balualua (Kasayi). KONGO-OVERZEE 18 (1952), pp. 249-262.

13,936 DEVAUX, V. Le clan matrilinéal dans la société indigène. ZAIRE 1 (1947), pp. 318-322.

13,937 DILLEN, K. Het hof van Tshibanda a Tshibanda, Kanyoka-hoofd. KONGO-OVERZEE 18 (1952), pp. 369-381.

13,938 DILLEN, K. Tweelingen bij de Bena Ngungi (Basonge). KONGO-OVERZEE 17 (1951), pp. 97-110.

13,939 DONCKERWOLCKE, A. De Instellingen der Wankutshu. KONGO-OVERZEE 1 (1934), pp. 235-250.

13,940 DONOHUGH, A. C. L. and BERRY, P. A Luba tribe in Katanga: customs and folklore. AFRICA 5 (1932), pp. 176-183.

13,941 DOUGLAS, M. Age-status among the Lele. ZAIRE 13 (1959), pp. 386-413.

13,942 DOUGLAS, M. Alternate generations among the Lele of the Kasai, south-west Congo. AFRICA 22 (1952), pp. 59-65.

13,943 DOUGLAS, M. Animals in Lele religious symbolism. AFRICA 27 (1957), pp. 46-57.

13,944 DOUGLAS, M. Blood-debts and clientship among the Lele. JRAI 90 (1960), pp. 1-28.

13,945 DOUGLAS, M. The environment of the Lele. ZAIRE 9 (1955), pp. 801-823.

13,946 DOUGLAS, M. The pattern of residence among the Lele. ZAIRE 11 (1957), pp. 819-843.

13,947 DOUGLAS, M. The spirit of contradiction. ZAIRE 13 (1959), pp. 295-300.

13,948 DOUTRELOUX, A. Magie Yombe. Notes sur la fonction sociologique de formes "para-religieuses." ZAIRE 15 (1961), pp. 45-57.

13,949 DOUTRELOUX, A. Prophétisme et culture. AFRICAN SYSTEMS OF THOUGHT, 1965, pp. 224-239.

13,950 DWORKIN, M. S. Masters of the Congo jungle. CONTEMP. REV. 198 (1960), pp. 494-497.

13,951 EKONYO, P. Bote wa likili. AEQUATORIA 2 (1939), pp. 66-67.

13,952 EKONYO, P. De Likili. AEQUATORIA 2 (1939), pp. 68-70.

13,953 EMILE, P. Paternité et critique. AEQUATORIA 25 (1962), pp. 10-12.

13,954 ESSER, J. Un fléau africain: la polygamie. ZAIRE 3 (1949), pp. 239-255.

13,955 FISHER, W. S. Black magic feuds. AFR. STUD. 8 (1949), pp. 20-22.

13,956 FLAMENT, E. B. Contribution à l'étude des Babunda. CONGO 1 (1934), pp. 679-692.

13,957 FLOWER, W. H. Description of two skeletons of Akkas, a pygmy race from Central Africa. JRAI 18 (1889), pp. 3-19.

13,958 FOURCHE, J. A. T. and MORLIGHEM, H. Conceptions des indigènes du Kasai sur l'Homme et la mort. J. SOC. AFR. 7 (1937), pp. 189-202.

13,959 FRAZAO, S. O Antigo Sóio. PORT. EM AFR. 4 (1947), pp. 96-98.

13,960 GELDERS, V. Une théorie ethnologique du droit indigène. ZAIRE 2 (1948), pp. 175-187.

13,961 GERARD, J. La grande initiation chez les Bakumu du nord-est et les populations avoisinantes. ZAIRE 10 (1956), pp. 87-94.

13,962 GEURTS, L. Etude démographique des populations Batétéla, Baluba, Bakwa Mputu du territoire de Lusambo. ZAIRE 3 (1949), pp. 963-993, 1067-1089; 4 (1950), pp. 17-38.

13,963 GILLET, J. Een oud zandee-verhaal: De zoons van Bagbaya: Tule en Atali. CONGO 2 (1939), pp. 537-539.

13,964 GIORGETTI, F. Il cannibalismo dei Niam Niam. AFRICA 27 (1957), pp. 178-185; English summary, pp. 185-186.

13,965 GOETHEM, E. VAN. Devinettes Nkundo. AEQUATORIA 15 (1952), pp. 41-48.

13,966 GOETHEM, E. VAN. Le Dieu des Nkundo. AEQUATORIA 13 (1950), pp. 1-6.

13,967 GONZALEZ DE PABLO, A. El Mbueti y sus doctrinas. CUAD. EST. AFR. 2 (1946), pp. 69-92.

13,968 GREGORIUS, P. Ethnologische resultaten van P. Schebesta's expeditie's onder de Bambuti-Pygmeeën aan de Ituri-rivier. ZAIRE 6 (1952), pp. 379-390.

13,969 GROOTEART, J. E. A. Les Indigènes ont-ils un nom de famille? AEQUATORIA 10 (1947), pp. 35-36.

13,970 GUILMIN, M. La polygamie sous l'Equateur. ZAIRE 1 (1947), pp. 1001-1023.

13,971 GUILMIN, M. Quelques proverbes des Bwaka expliqués par eux-mêmes. CONGO 2, no. 4 (1933), pp. 535-557.

13,972 GUSINDE, M. Pygmies and pygmoids: twides of tropical Africa. ANTHR. QUART. 28 (1955), pp. 3-61.

13,973 HAUSER, A. Les Babinga. ZAIRE 7 (1953), pp. 147-179.

13,974 HEIJBOER, B. M. A propos d'un cri d'alarme. ZAIRE 1 (1947), pp. 1148-1149.

13,975 HEIJBOER, B. M. Demographische gegevens over de Ngōmbē van het district der Tshuapa. ZAIRE 1 (1947), pp. 969-1000.

13,976 HEIJBOER, B. M. De Ngombe-stammen van het Lulonga-stroomgebied. AEQUATORIA 9 (1946), pp. 128-134.

13,977 HERTSENS, L. Bijdrage tot de analyse van sommige culturen uit de Noordoostelijke hoek van Belgisch-Kongo. KONGO-OVERZEE 14 (1948), pp. 1-9.

13,978 HEUSCH, L. DE. Autorité et prestige dans la societé tetela. ZAIRE 8 (1954), pp. 1011-1027.

13,979 HEUSCH, L. DE. Eléments de potlatch chez les Hamba. AFRICA 24 (1954), pp. 337-347; English summary, p. 347.

13,980 HEUSCH, L. DE. Un système de parenté insolite: les Onga (Kasaï, Congo belge). ZAIRE 9 (1955), pp. 1011-1027.

13,981 HOLDREDGE, C. P. and YOUNG, K. Circumcision rites among the BaJok. AMER. ANTHR. 29 (1927), pp. 661-669.

13,982 HULSTAERT, G. L'adoption par le mariage. AEQUATORIA 23 (1960), pp. 41-43.

13,983 HULSTAERT, G. Les cercueils anthropomorphes. AEQUATORIA 23 (1960), pp. 121-129.

13,984 HULSTAERT, G. Les cercueils des Eleku. AEQUATORIA 22 (1959), pp. 11-15.

13,985 HULSTAERT, G. La clôture de chasse. AEQUATORIA 25 (1962), pp. 13-18.

13,986 HULSTAERT, G. Un conte Mongo. AEQUATORIA 25 (1962), pp. 101-104.

13,987 HULSTAERT, G. La coutume Nkundo (Mongo) et le décret sur la protection de la fille indigène non-pubère. CONGO 2 (1937), pp. 269-276.

13,988 HULSTAERT, G. Le divorce chez les Nkundo. CONGO 2 (1934), pp. 657-673; 1 (1935), pp. 38-56.

13,989 HULSTAERT, G. L'extraction de l'huile chez les Mongo. AEQUATORIA 25 (1962), pp. 41-42.

13,990 HULSTAERT, G. La grande famille. AEQUATORIA 23 (1960), pp. 25-26.

13,991 HULSTAERT, G. Het Betalen van den Bruidschat bij de Nkundo. KONGO-OVERZEE 1 (1934), pp. 129-136.

13,992 HULSTAERT, G. Hondennamen bij de Nkundo. KONGO-OVERZEE 2 (1935-1936), pp. 226-239.

13,993 HULSTAERT, G. Les idées religieuses des Nkundo. CONGO 2 (1936), pp. 668-676.

13,994 HULSTAERT, G. Lingala-invloed op Lomongo. ZAIRE 7 (1953), pp. 225-244.

13,995 HULSTAERT, G. Noms de personnes chez les Nkundo. AEQUATORIA 19 (1956), pp. 91-102, 135-136.

13,996 HULSTAERT, G. Note sur les redevances de chasse. ZAIRE 10 (1956), pp. 283-289.

13,997 HULSTAERT, G. Prières païennes. AEQUATORIA 25 (1962), p. 140.

13,998 HULSTAERT, G. La sorcellerie chez les Mongo. AFRICAN SYSTEMS OF THOUGHT, 1965, pp. 165-170.

13,999 HULSTAERT, G. Sur les droits du chef de famille. AEQUATORIA 17 (1954), pp. 154-156.

14,000 ITTMANN, J. Nyang-Märchen. AFR. UND UB. 22 (1931-1932), pp. 47-67.

14,001 ITTMANN, J. Spiele der Stämme rings um die Ambasbucht. AFR. UND UB. 43 (1959-1960), pp. 37-68.

14,002 ITTMANN, J. Sprichwörter der Nyang. AFR. UND UB. 22 (1931-1932), pp. 120-155, 215-230, 281-312.

14,003 JACOBS, J. Enigmes Tetela, espèces et fonction. AEQUATORIA 25 (1962), pp. 81-91.

14,004 JACOBS, J. Notre univers. Essai de cosmologie Tetela (Kasai). AEQUATORIA 23 (1960), pp. 81-99.

14,005 JACOBS, J. Le récit épique de Lofokefoke, le héros des Mbde (Bambuli). AEQUATORIA 24 (1961), pp. 81-92.

14,006 JACOBS, J. La vannerie, la poterie et le tissage dans les proverbes Tetela. KONGO-OVERZEE 21 (1955), pp. 272-288.

14,007 JAK, J. Eenige Ethnographica over de Walengola-Babira. CONGO 1 (1938), pp. 13-22; 2 (1939), pp. 47-55.

14,008 JAK, J. Enkele Bemerkingen over de Anioto. CONGO 1 (1938), pp. 520-531.

14,009 JEFFREYS, M. D. W. The Batwa: who are they? AFRICA 23 (1953), pp. 45-54.

14,010 JONGHE, E. DE. Formations récentes de sociétés secrètes au Congo Belge. AFRICA 9 (1936), pp. 56-63.

14,011 JONGHE, E. DE. Over stam- en kwanwezen in Belgisch Congo. CONGO 2 (1938), pp. 434-446.

14,012 JONGHE, E. DE. Plan d'exploration ethnographique et ethnologique du Congo belge. ZAIRE 1 (1947), pp. 1151-1158.

14,013 JONGHE, E. DE. Questionnaire ethnographique [includes a bibliography]. CONGO 2 (1939), pp. 473-511.

14,014 JONK, J. and BOURITIUS, G. Waarzeggerij en beheksing bij Bandaka en Arabises. ZAIRE 8 (1954), pp. 595-613.

14,015 JOSET, P. E. Buda Efeba. (Contes et légendes pygmées.) ZAIRE 2 (1948), pp. 25-56, 137-157.

14,016 KALALA, K. Kaayowa. Kongo-Overzee 21 (1955), pp. 28-41.

14,017 KALANDA, A. Deux contes luba. KONGO-OVERZEE 19 (1953), pp. 458-463.

14,018 KAMAINDA, T. Djigi et le Balambo. PRESENCE AFR. N.S. 34-35 (1960-1961), pp. 73-78.

14,019 KEITH, A. On certain physical characters of the negroes of the Congo Free State and Nigeria. JRAI 41 (1910), pp. 40-71.

14,020 KERKEN, G. VAN DER. Enkele Beschouwingen in verband met de studie der inlandsche volken van Belgisch Afrika. KONGO-OVERZEE 1 (1934), pp. 93-102, 151-167, 299-307; 2 (1935-1936), pp. 156-167, 271-281; 3 (1936-1937), pp. 215-225, 292-302; 4 (1938), pp. 139-149, 260-274; 5 (1939), pp. 85-100.

14,021 KERKEN, G. VAN DER. Kantteekeningen bij een studie over de Badia. KONGO-OVERZEE 2 (1935-1936), pp. 179-182.

14,022 KERKEN, G. VAN DER. kritiek op een inventaris der Kongoleesche volksstammen. KONGO-OVERZEE 2 (1935-1936), pp. 94-99.

14,023 LABRECQUE, E. Le mariage chez les Babemba. AFRICA 4 (1931), pp. 209-221.

14,024 LEBEUF, J. P. Le mythe de la création chez les Likouba et les Likouala (Congo). CONGR. INT. SC. ANTHR. ET ETHN. 6, no. ii (1960), pp. 421-427.

14,025 LERRIGO, P. H. J. The Prophet Movement in Congo. INT. REV. MISSIONS 11 (1922), pp. 270-277.

14,026 LIESENBORGHS, O. Aanvullende nota's over enkele volksstammen uit Noordoost-Kongo. KONGO-OVERZEE 3 (1936-1937), pp. 84-90.

14,027 LIESENBORGHS, O. Bijdrage tot de Kennis der lichamelijke ontwikkeling van de Kong-leesche Schooljeugd. KONGO-OVERZEE 5 (1939), pp. 193-204.

14,028 LIESENBORGHS, O. Enkele Nota's over de Bale en Banioro van Belgisch Kongo. KONGO-OVERZEE 1 (1934), pp. 205-218.

14,029 LIESENBORGHS, O. Nog over de Banioro. KONGO-OVERZEE 5 (1939), pp. 82-84.

14,030 LINDEN, T. V. D. De jacht onder de Mongonegers. CONGO 1 (1921), pp. 61-69.

14,031 LODEWIJCKX, C. Sur la dénatalité Nkundo. AEQUATORIA 12 (1949), pp. 77-81.

14,032 M., V. Valeurs culturelles. AEQUATORIA 15 (1952), pp. 146-147.

14,033 MacBEATH, A. The revival of Bolobo, Belgian Congo. INT. REV. MISSIONS 27 (1938), pp. 415-423.

14,034 MAES. La sanza du Congo Belge. CONGO 1 (1921), pp. 542-572.

14,035 MAES, J. L'ethnologie de l'Afrique centrale et le Musée du Congo Belge. AFRICA 7 (1934), pp. 174-190.

14,036 MAES, J. Kantleekeningen bij de Kritiek op een inventaris der Kongoleesche volksstammen. KONGO-OVERZEE 3 (1936-1937), pp. 91-98.

14,037 MAES, J. Mythes et legendes sur l'allume-feu des populations du Congo Belge. AFRICA 9 (1936), pp. 495-507.

14,038 MAES, J. Note sur les populations Lalia et Yasayama du Territoire des Dsalia-Boyela. CONGO 1 (1934), pp. 172-179.

14,039 MAES, V. De Ngbaka. AEQUATORIA 8 (1945), pp. 96-103.

14,040 MAES, V. De Spin. AEQUATORIA 13 (1950), pp. 7-11.

14,041 MAEYENS, L. De Babvesa (Uit den rijken verhalenschat der Babira: hoe een nieuwe familie ontstond). CONGO 1 (1937), pp. 543-547.

14,042 MAEYENS, L. Een geval van Beheksing bij de Babira. KONGO-OVERZEE 4 (1938), pp. 82-89.

14,043 MAQUET, M. Sur les flancs du Pic Sorensen. CONGO 2 (1939), pp. 271-273.

14,044 MARCHAL, P. G. Liturgia do casamento entre os gentios do Zaire. PORT. EM AFR. 3 (1946), pp. 282-291.

14,045 MARCHAL, P. G. Origem da raca Solongo (Zaire) segundo a lenda. PORT. EM AFR. 4 (1947), pp. 78-86.

14,046 MARCHAL, P. G. Sur l'origine des Basolongo. AEQUATORIA 11 (1948), pp. 121-125.

14,047 MARCHOVELLETTE, E. D'. DE. La divination chez les Baluba au moyen du "lubuko" ou "Katotola." ZAIRE 8 (1954), pp. 487-505.

14,048 MARTINS VAZ, J. Aforismos populares do Enclave de Cabinda. PORT. EM AFR. 13 (1956), pp. 109-116.

14,049 MASUKA, A. A. Proverbes Bagumbu. AEQUATORIA 15 (1952), pp. 135-140.

14,050 MATHIJSEN, H. Tooverij en hekserij bij Topoke en Bambole. AEQUATORIA 2 (1939), pp. 44-48.

14,051 MBIYE, B. L'arbre qui porte des houes. KONGO-OVERZEE 21 (1955), pp. 54-70.

14,052 MEEUSSEN, A. E. Aktiespreuken bij de Lega. KONGO-OVERZEE 25 (1959), pp. 73-76.

14,053 MERRIAM, A. P. The concept of culture clusters applied to the Belgian Congo. SOUTHWESTERN J. ANTHR. 15 (1959), pp. 373-395.

14,054 MERTENS, J. L'esclavage chez les Ba Dzing de la Kamtsha. CONGO 1 (1936), pp. 641-676.

14,055 MERTENS, J. Syonya. CONGO 1 (1939), pp. 21-26.

14,056 MERTENS, V. Dénomination des relations de famille chez les Bakongo et spécialement chez les Bambata. ZAIRE 3 (1949), pp. 55-58.

14,057 MERTENS, V. Le mariage chez les Bambata (Bakongo) et ses leçons sociales. ZAIRE 2 (1948), pp. 1099-1126.

14,058 MILLMAN, W. The tribal initiation ceremony of the Lokele. INT. REV. MISSIONS 16 (1927), pp. 364-380.

14,059 MOL, P. D. VAN. Hondennamen bij de Abarambo. ZAIRE 3 (1949), pp. 515-532.

14,060 MOLET, L. La cohésion familiale chez les Yakoma. AFRICAN SYSTEMS OF THOUGHT, 1965, pp. 145-157.

14,061 MOLET, L. Kanda et Sangere, génies Yakoma. AFRICAN SYSTEMS OF THOUGHT, 1965, pp. 158-164.

14,062 MOLLER, M. Einige Korbtypen bei den Buende. ETHNOS 2 (1937), pp. 218-229.

14,063 MORTIER, R. Anthropologische metingen in Ubangi. AEQUATORIA 16 (1953), pp. 49-60.

14,064 MORTIER, R. De Bambenga-Pygmoïden in Ubangi. KONGO-OVERZEE 3 (1936-1937), pp. 245-251.

14,065 MORTIER, R. Volken en Volksverhuizingen in Ubangi (Belgisch Kongo). KONGO-OVERZEE 3 (1936-1937), pp. 209-214.

14,066 MULLER, E. W. L'application de la terminologie de Murdock à la structure sociale des Ekonda. AEQUATORIA 22 (1959), pp. 1-10.

14,067 MUNDAY, J. T. Spirit names among the central Bantu. AFR. STUD. 7 (1948), pp. 39-44.

14,068 NAESSENS, H. Spreuken der Bayaka. KONGO-OVERZEE 15 (1949), pp. 282-285.

14,069 NAUWELAERT, P. La société Yombe. CONGO 1 (1938), pp. 405-409.

14,070 NGOI, P. La limitation du taux de la dot. ZAIRE 4 (1950), pp. 643-650.

14,071 NOLLEVAUX, P. J. La cosmogonie des Bazela. AEQUATORIA 12 (1949), pp. 121-128.

14,072 NOORDMAN, H. De Ngombe van Lulonga, Ikelemba en Lopori. AEQUATORIA 7 (1944), pp. 113-116.

14,073 OLBRECHTS, M. Vraag om inlichtingen: Over het voorkomen van de Confessio Parturientis in Congo. KONGO-OVERZEE 1 (1934), pp. 296-298; also in CONGO 1 (1935), pp. 689-691.

14,074 OMARI, A. Le mariage coutumier chez les Bakusu. KONGO-OVERZEE 14 (1948), pp. 10-20.

14,075 PAGES, P. Notes sur le régime des biens dans la province du Bugoyi. CONGO 2 (1938), pp. 392-433.

14,076 PARADIS, J. La situation démographique du district de l'Uele. ZAIRE 1 (1947), pp. 849-883.

14,077 PAUWELS, M. Description détaillée d'un mariage de montagnard Muhutu de la région de Byumba (Rwanda). KONGO-OVERZEE 20 (1954), pp. 31-64.

14,078 PAUWELS, M. L'habitation au Rwanda. KONGO-OVERZEE 19 (1953), pp. 20-62.

14,079 PAUWELS, M. Imana. KONGO-OVERZEE 18 (1952), pp. 318-337.

14,080 PAUWELS, M. Le mariage chez les montagnards Bahutu. KONGO-OVERZEE 19 (1953), pp. 317-342.

14,081 PAUWELS, M. La mode au Rwanda. KONGO-OVERZEE 19 (1953), pp. 234-258.

14,082 PEERAER, S. Dood en onderwereld bij de Baluba Shankadi. KONGO-OVERZEE 2 (1935-1936), pp. 193-225.

14,083 PEERAER, S. Enkele Benamingen voor het opperwezen bij de Baluba-Shankaji. KONGO-OVERZEE 1 (1934), pp. 20-30.

14,084 PEERAER, S. Gouwzang der Bene-Lupulu. CONGO 1 (1938), pp. 261-287, 416-440.

14,085 PEERAER, S. Luba-samba Teksten. KONGO-OVERZEE 1 (1934), pp. 42-44.

14,086 PEERAER, S. Spreuken der Baluba Shankaji over het Opperwezen. KONGO-OVERZEE 1 (1934), pp. 274-295.

14,087 PEERAER, S. Toespraken tot Jonggehuwden bij de Baluba (Katanga). KONGO-OVERZEE 5 (1939), pp. 241-276; 9 (1943), pp. 1-59.

14,088 PHILIPPE, R. Les fiancailles précoces chez les Boloki Congo belge. KONGO-OVERZEE 24 (1958), pp. 214-224.

14,089 PHILIPPE, R. Le mariage chez les Ntomb'e Njale du Lac Léopold II. AEQUATORIA 17 (1954), pp. 86-106, 129-153.

14,090 PHILIPPE, R. Les Ntomb'e Njale du Lac Léopold II. AEQUATORIA 16 (1953), pp. 41-48.

14,091 PHILIPPE, R. La secte Ekitelakitela des Budja (Congo ex-belge). CONGR. INT. SC. ANTHR. ET ETHN. 6, no. ii (1960), pp. 459-464.

14,092 PHILLIPS, R. C. The lower Congo; a sociological study. JRAI 17 (1888), pp. 214-237.

14,093 PIERRARD, G. A. Contribution à l'étude des coutumes de chasse chez les Babira. KONGO-OVERZEE 21 (1955), pp. 389-419.

14,094 PINTASSILGO, A. R. Seitas secretas no Congo. PORT. EM AFR. 10 (1953), pp. 361-371.

14,095 POSSOZ, E. Les Ababua. AEQUATORIA 3 (1940), pp. 85-87.

14,096 POSSOZ, E. Batoa, Batwa, Batswa. AFRICA 24 (1954), pp. 257-259; English summary, p. 260.

14,097 POSSOZ, E. Ethnologie et méthode. KONGO-OVERZEE 16 (1950), pp. 253-275.

14,098 POSSOZ, E. Huwelijksrecht bij de Mongo. AEQUATORIA 2 (1939), pp. 3-11.

14,099 POSSOZ, E. Mariage par consentement. KONGO-OVERZEE 12-13 (1946-1947), pp. 117-121.

14,100 QUIRINI, P. DE. Les fiançailles de droit chez les Bayansi. ZAIRE 6 (1952), pp. 499-504.

14,101 RADCLIFFE-BROWN, A. R. A commentary on alternate generations among the Lele. AFRICA 23 (1953), pp. 351-354.

14,102 RENIER, M. Pour un essai de paysannat indigene chez les Bapende et les Basuku sur la base de plantations de bambous. ZAIRE 6 (1952), pp. 363-378.

14,103 REYNOLDS, H. Notes on the Azandé tribe of the Congo. J. AFR. SOC. 3 (1904), pp. 238-246.

14,104 RICHARDS, A. I. Some types of family structure amongst the central Bantu. AFRICAN SYSTEMS OF KINSHIP AND MARRIAGE, 1950, pp. 207-251.

14,105 RIEHL, P. A. A família indígena no Congo. PORT. EM AFR. 3 (1946), pp. 88-98.

14,106 ROMBAUTS, H. Les Ekonda. AEQUATORIA 8 (1945), pp. 121-127.

14,107 ROMBAUTS, H. Ekonda e Mputela. AEQUATORIA 9 (1946), pp. 138-152.

14,108 ROOD, N. Contes Ngombe. AEQUATORIA 25 (1962), pp. 43-44.

14,109 ROOD, N. Lidoko et Mowea. AEQUATORIA 25 (1962), pp. 125-139.

14,110 ROP, A. DE. Kanttekeningen bij les Pygmées du Congo Belge. AEQUATORIA 16 (1953), pp. 129-133.

14,111 ROP, A. DE. Nota's over de smidse der Nkundo. AEQUATORIA 17 (1954), pp. 1-6.

14,112 ROY, H. VAN. De godservaring bij de Bakongo. AEQUATORIA 22, no. iv (1959), pp. 132-143.

14,113 ROY, H. VAN. L'origine des Balunda du Kwango. AEQUATORIA 24 (1961), pp. 136-141.

14,114 RUBBENS, A. Le mariage entre indigène et non-indigène au Congo belge. ZAIRE 10 (1956), pp. 147-149.

14,115 RYCKMANS, A. Choix de devinettes des Bankanu et Bayaka du Territoire de Popokabaya. ZAIRE 11 (1957), pp. 563-592.

14,116 S., N. H. D. Native graves in the Congo Belge. NADA 8 (1930), pp. 77-78.

14,117 SAENEN, J. Volkslitteratuur bij de Ngbaka. CONGO 2 (1939), pp. 148-157.

14,118 SAMAIN, A. Zeden en gebruiken der Baluba's. CONGO 2 (1921), pp. 21-35.

14,119 SCHAETZEN, A. DE. L'enterrement des morts chez les Ntomba-njale du Lac Léopold II. ZAIRE 3 (1949), pp. 1017-1021.

14,120 SCHEBESTA, P. A propos de "l'ethnic Mongo." ZAIRE 2 (1948), pp. 77-89.

14,121 SCHEBESTA, P. Bambuti-Initiation. KONGO-OVERZEE 24 (1958), pp. 136-161.

14,122 SCHEBESTA, P. Die Belueli vom Apare (Ituri). KONGO-OVERZEE 19 (1953), pp. 357-375.

14,123 SCHEBESTA, P. La civilisation aramba en Afrique. ZAIRE 3 (1949), pp. 483-502.

14,124 SCHEBESTA, P. Données essentielles sur la religion des Pygmées. CONGO 1 (1936), pp. 321-331.

14,125 SCHEBESTA, P. Initiationen bei den Bambuti-Pygmäen vom Ituri. KONGO-OVERZEE 25 (1959), pp. 113-123.

14,126 SCHEBESTA, P. Tore, le dieu forestier des Bambuti. ZAIRE 1 (1947), pp. 181-195.

14,127 SCHEBESTA, P. Wanderungen und schichtung der völker im "Herzen Afrikas." KONGO-OVERZEE 19 (1953), pp. 63-88.

14,128 SCHINGEN, S. J. VAN. La circoncision chez les Bayaka et les Basuku (Kwango). CONGO 2 (1921), pp. 51-64.

14,129 SCHUMACHER, P. Les Batwa. Sont-ils des Pygmées authentiques? AEQUATORIA 10 (1947), pp. 130-133.

14,130 SCHUMACHER, P. Encore les Twides. ZAIRE 3 (1949), pp. 1023-1026.

14,131 SCHUMACHER, P. Psyché au centre africain. ZAIRE 1 (1947), pp. 679-686.

14,132 SCHUMACHER, P. Les Twides. ZAIRE 1 (1947), pp. 1049-1053.

14,133 SIX, E. P. De geheime Mani-sekte te Boma. CONGO 2 (1921), pp. 226-241.

14,134 SOHIER, A. Le rôle de la femme dans la famille indigène congolaise. ZAIRE 1 (1947), pp. 440-445.

14,135 SOORS, M. Notes sur les Pygmées. ZAIRE 4 (1950), pp. 299-301.

14,136 SORET, M. La chasse en pays Ba-Kongo. ZAIRE 13 (1959), pp. 801-811.

14,137 SORET, M. La propriété foncière chez les Kongo du Nord-Ouest. Caractéristiques générales et évolution. AFR. AGRARIAN SYSTEMS, 1963, pp. 281-296.

14,138 SOUSBERGHE, L. DE. Etuis péniens ou gaines de chasteté chez les Ba-pende. AFRICA 24 (1954), pp. 214-218; English summary, p. 219.

14,139 SOUSBERGHE, L. DE. Les frères de belles-mères dans les sociétés du Kwango et l'interprétation des structures de parenté. ZAIRE 9 (1955), pp. 927-942.

14,140 SOUSBERGHE, L. DE. Pactes d'union dans la mort ou pactes de sang chez les Bapende et leurs voisins. ZAIRE 8 (1954), pp. 391-400.

14,141 STANISLAS, P. De Atetela-Asambala. AEQUATORIA 9 (1946), pp. 91-99.

14,142 STANISLAS, P. Kleine nota over de Ankutshu. AEQUATORIA 2 (1939), pp. 124-130.

14,143 STAPPERS, L. Bandala-Mumba, vrouwen van gezagdragers bij de Baamilembwe. KONGO-OVERZEE 16 (1950), pp. 249-252.

14,144 STAPPERS, L. Bij een boek over de Godsgedachte bij de Baluba van Kasai. KONGO-OVERZEE 18 (1952), pp. 438-441.

14,145 STAPPERS, L. De geheime sekte van de Bukisi bij de Beena Milembwe. KONGO-OVERZEE 16 (1950), pp. 73-96.

14,146 STAPPERS, L. Het introden van het kind bij de Baa Milembwe. KONGO-OVERZEE 18 (1952), pp. 1-5.

14,147 STAPPERS, L. De Kasongo-Fetisj bij de Baa Milembwe. KONGO-OVERZEE 17 (1951), pp. 373-378.

14,148 STAPPERS, L. Kimoshi, de rouwzang van de Baamilembwe. ZAIRE 4 (1950), pp. 1083-1091.

14,149 STAPPERS, L. De Kisheeta-Fetisj bij de Baa Milembwe. KONGO-OVERZEE 17 (1951), pp. 379-393.

14,150 STAPPERS, L. Iets over de Ntambwe fetisj in Kasai. AEQUATORIA 14 (1951), pp. 90-92.

14,151 STAPPERS, L. De mpunga fetisj. ZAIRE 5 (1951), pp. 351-369.

14,152 STAPPERS, L. Nsompo, het Aqua lustralis bij de Baa-milembwe. KONGO-OVERZEE 16 (1950), pp. 299-300.

14,153 STAPPERS, L. Prayer of a Milembwe woman after a child's birth. KONGO-OVERZEE 18 (1952), pp. 6-7.

14,154 STAPPERS, L. Tshiluba-tekst. De hongersnood te Kenda-Kamba. KONGO-OVERZEE 18 (1952), pp. 426-431.

14,155 STAPPERS, L. Uit het verleden der Baa Milembwe. KONGO-OVERZEE 17 (1951), pp. 1-8.

14,156 STAS, J. B. Les Nkumu chez les Ntomba de Bikoro. AEQUATORIA 2 (1939), pp. 109-123.

14,157 STAYT, H. A. Notes on the Balemba. JRAI 61 (1931), pp. 231-238.

14,158 STORMS, A. Famille chrétienne et société matriarcale au Katanga. ZAIRE 2 (1948), pp. 239-248.

14,159 STRUYF, V. Kahemba. Envahisseurs et conquérants Balunda. ZAIRE 2 (1948), pp. 308-390.

14,160 STRUYFS, Y. L'Etre Suprême chez les Tutshokwe (Batshioko). CONGO 1 (1939), pp. 361-411.

14,161 SWARTENBROECKX, P. Quand l'Ubangi vint au Kwango. ZAIRE 2 (1948), pp. 721-755.

14,162 TANGHE, B. Le Droit d'aînesse chez les indigènes du Haut-Ubbangi (Congo Belge). AFRICA 3 (1930), pp. 78-82.

14,163 TANGHE, B. De laatste volksverhuizingen, die zich in Opper-en Neder-Ubangi hebben neergezet. KONGO-OVERZEE 2 (1935-1936), pp. 168-171.

14,164 TANGHE, B. Les Mbangi (Babangi) et leurs apparentés dans l'ancien district de l'Ubangi. CONGO 1 (1934), pp. 654-656.

14,165 TANGHE, B. Zijn de Nyi oorspronkelijic Bantoenegers? KONGO-OVERZEE 5 (1939), pp. 40-41.

14,166 TANGHE, B. O. Ngombe en Nyi in Ubangi. AEQUATORIA 2 (1939), pp. 13-17.

14,167 TANGHE, B. O. Yakoma. AEQUATORIA 2 (1939), pp. 142-143.

14,168 TANGHE, J. Eighth Mabale story. KONGO-OVERZEE 19 (1953), pp. 146-148.

14,169 TANGHE, J. Sixth Mabale story. KONGO-OVERZEE 17 (1951), pp. 369-372.

14,170 TANGHE, J. Tenth Mabale story. KONGO-OVERZEE 21 (1955), pp. 298-299.

14,171 TEMPELS, P. Hoe de Baluba-Shankadi zich de wereld voorstellen. KONGO-OVERZEE 2 (1935-1936), pp. 129-138.

14,172 TEMPELS, P. Raadsels in Midden-Katanga. KONGO-OVERZEE 4 (1938), pp. 203-214.

14,173 TEW, M. A form of polyandry among the Lele of the Kasai. AFRICA 21 (1951), pp. 1-12.

14,174 THEUWS, T. Croyance et culte chez les Baluba. PRESENCE AFR. N.S. 18-19 (1958), pp. 23-32.

14,175 THEUWS, T. Naître et mourir dans le rituel luba. ZAIRE 14 (1960), pp. 115-173.

14,176 THEUWS, T. Le reel dans la conception Luba. ZAIRE 15 (1961), pp. 3-44.

14,177 THIEL, H. VAN. Derde Lingombe-vertelsel. KONGO-OVERZEE 17 (1951), pp. 236-239.

14,178 THIEL, H. VAN. Het Offer van Itota. KONGO-OVERZEE 17 (1951), pp. 60-77, 165-185, 258-281, 394-434.

14,179 THIEL, H. VAN. Tweede Lingombe vertelsel. KONGO-OVERZEE 17 (1951), pp. 157-161.

14,180 THIEL, H. VAN. Vierde Lingombe-vertelsel. KONGO-OVERZEE 17 (1951), pp. 358-359.

14,181 TORDAY, E. Culture and environment: cultural differences among the various branches of the Batetela. JRAI 51 (1921), pp. 370-384.

14,182 TORDAY, E. and JOYCE, T. A. Notes on the ethnography of the Ba-Huana. JRAI 36 (1906), pp. 272-301.

14,183 TORDAY, E. and JOYCE, T. A. Notes on the ethnography of the Ba-Mbala. JRAI 35 (1905), pp. 398-426.

14,184 TORDAY, E. and JOYCE, T. A. Notes on the ethnography of the Ba-Yaka. JRAI 36 (1906), pp. 39-58.

14,185 TORDAY, E. and JOYCE, T. A. On the ethnology of the Southwestern Congo. JRAI 37 (1907), pp. 133-156.

14,186 TROESCH, J. Le Nkutu du comte de Soyo. AEQUATORIA 24 (1961), pp. 41-49.

14,187 TROESCH, J. Pesca no Maiombe: Enclave de Cabinda. PORT. EM AFR. 13 (1956), pp. 76-86.

14,188 TURNBULL, C. M. The elima: a pre-marital festival among the Bamputi pygmies. ZAIRE 14 (1960), pp. 175-192.

14,189 TURNBULL, C. M. Initiation among the Ba Mbuti pygmies of the central Ituri. JRAI 87 (1957), pp. 191-216.

14,190 TURNBULL, C. M. Legends of the Bambuti. JRAI 89 (1959), pp. 45-60.

14,191 VANCOILLIE, G. Grepen uit de Mbagani-traditie. AEQUATORIA 10 (1947), pp. 89-101, 122-129.

14,192 VANCOILLIE, G. Recueil de signaux clariques ou kúmbu des tribus Mbagani et du Kasai (Congo Belge). AFR. STUD. 8 (1949), pp. 35-45, 80-100.

14,193 VANSINA, J. Les croyances religieuses des Kuba. ZAIRE 12 (1958), pp. 725-758.

14,194 VANSINA, J. La famille nucléaire chez les Bushoong. AFRICA 28 (1958), pp. 95-108.

14,195 VANSINA, J. Initiation rituals of the Bushong. AFRICA 25 (1955), pp. 138-152.

14,196 VANSINA, J. Miko mi Yool, une association religieuse Kuba. AEQUATORIA 22, no. ii (1959), pp. 7-20, 81-92.

14,197 VANSINA, J. Note sur les Twa du territoire de Mweka (Kasai). ZAIRE 8 (1954), pp. 729-732.

14,198 VANSINA, J. Les valeurs culturelles des Bushong. ZAIRE 8 (1954), pp. 899-910.

14,199 VAZ, M. M. Filosofia Popular do Fiote. Casamento indigena no Enclave de Cabinda. PORT. EM AFR. 12 (1955), pp. 29-36.

14,200 VECIANA, A. DE. La Organización familiar de los Kombe. ARCH. INST. EST. AFR. 9, no. 36 (1956), pp. 83-91.

14,201 VERBEECK. Anticonceptionele middelen. AEQUATORIA 14 (1951), pp. 26-28.

14,202 VERBEECK, A. Le problème de la dénatalité chez les Nkundo. AEQUATORIA 18 (1955), pp. 6-13, 41-49.

14,203 VERBEKEN, A. La signification mystique des couleurs chez les Bantou. ZAIRE 1 (1947), pp. 1139-1144.

14,204 VERHAEGEN, P. Utilite actuelle des tests pour l'étude psychologique des autochtones congolais. ZAIRE 10 (1956), pp. 787-801.

14,205 VERWILGHEN, P. Bingana bi Bayaka. Bayaka-spreuken. KONGO-OVERZEE 16 (1950), pp. 128-138.

14,206 VIAENE, L. La religion des Bahunde. KONGO-OVERZEE 18 (1952), pp. 388-425.

14,207 VIAENE, L. La vie domestique des Bahunde. KONGO-OVERZEE 17 (1951), pp. 111-156.

14,208 VIAENE, R. P. L. Coup d'oeil sur la vie intellectuelle des Bahunde (Kivu). KONGO-OVERZEE 22 (1956), pp. 360-383.

14,209 VICCARS, J. D. Witchcraft in Bolobo, Belgian Congo. AFRICA 19 (1949), pp. 220-229.

14,210 VORBICHLER, A. Fetischismus und Hexerei. KONGO-OVERZEE 23 (1957), pp. 35-57.

14,211 VORBICHLER, A. Symbolisches Denken der Balonso-Bayaka, Belg. Kongo. KONGO-OVERZEE 22 (1956), pp. 187-206.

14,212 VRIESE, G. DE. Demographische studie in de Mayumbe. ZAIRE 8 (1954), pp. 3-20, 123-156.

14,213 WALDECKER, B. Serments et ordalies des Abahuma en comparaison avec ceux d'autres tribus au Congo belge. ZAIRE 1 (1947), pp. 1025-1035.

14,214 WARD, H. Ethnographical notes relating to the Congo tribes. JRAI 24 (1895), pp. 285-299.

14,215 WAUTERS, G. De Bilima van de Batswa der Evenaarsprovincie. KONGO-OVERZEE 6 (1940), pp. 95-103.

14,216 WEEKS, J. H. Anthropological notes on the Bangala of the Upper Congo River. JRAI 39 (1909), pp. 97-136, 416-459; 40 (1910), pp. 360-427.

14,217 WEEKX, G. Le peuplade des Ambundu (District du Kwango). CONGO 1 (1937), pp. 353-373; 2 (1937), pp. 13-35, 150-166.

14,218 WEGHSTEEN, J. Croyances religieuses des Watabwa. KONGO-OVERZEE 20 (1954), pp. 205-220.

14,219 WEGHSTEEN, J. De toren van Babel in de overleveringen van de Watabwa (Katanga). KONGO-OVERZEE 21 (1955), pp. 157-159.

14,220 WERNER, A. The Bushongo. J. AFR. SOC. 11 (1912), pp. 206-212.

14,221 WINDELS, A. Jeux et divertissements chez les Mpama-Bakutu. AEQUATORIA 2 (1939), pp. 18-23.

14,222 WINDELS, A. La puberté chez les Mpama-Bakutu. AEQUATORIA 2 (1939), pp. 37-43.

14,223 WINDELS, A. La secte secrète des Mani à Lukolela. AEQUATORIA 3 (1940), pp. 79-84.

14,224 WING, J. V. Folklore Kiyansi (Congo Belge). BIBLIOTHECA AFR. 4 (1930-1931), pp. 46-78.

14,225 WING, J. VAN. Le Kibangisme vu par un témoin. ZAIRE 12 (1958), pp. 563-618.

14,226 WING, J. VAN. Les mouvements messianiques populaires dans le Bas-Congo. Notes marginales. ZAIRE 14 (1960), pp. 225-237.

14,227 WING, J. VAN. La polygamie au Congo Belge. AFRICA 17 (1947), pp. 93-101.

14,228 WING, J. V. VAN. Nzo Longo ou les rites de la puberté chez les Bakongo. CONGO 1 (1921), pp. 48-59, 365-389.

14,229 WITTE, P. DE. Religie en magie onder de Basakata. AEQUATORIA 16 (1953), pp. 26-29.

14,230 ZAAL, C. Zegui, God bij de Nzakara. KONGO-OVERZEE 23 (1957), pp. 226-231.

14,231 Zedelijke Toestand der Inlanders. KONGO-OVERZEE 5 (1939), pp. 138-172.

See also 15565, 15588, 15822, 18747, 18749, 18752, 18802.

Art. Antiquities

14,232 ANCIAUX DE FAVEAUX, D. A. Gisements et industries préhistoriques des Hauts plateaux des Biano (Katentania). PROC. PAN-AFR. CONGR. PRE-HIST. 2 (1952), pp. 391-400.

14,233 ANCIAUX DE FAVEAUX, D. A. Gisements et industries préhistoriques des Hauts plateaux des Kundelungu. PROC. PAN-AFR. CONGR. PRE-HIST. 2 (1952), pp. 383-390.

14,234 ANCIAUX DE FAVEAUX, D. A. Les gisements préhistoriques de Kansenia. PROC. PAN-AFR. CONGR. PRE-HIST. 2 (1952), pp. 333-343.

14,235 BEQUAERT, M. Fouilles à Dinga (Congo Belge). PROC. PAN-AFR. CONGR. PRE-HIST. 2 (1952), pp. 347-353.

14,236 BEQUAERT, M. Fouilles à Thysville du Musée royal du Congo belge, en 1938. PROC. PAN-AFR. CONGR. PRE-HIST. 4, no. iii (1962), pp. 323-340.

14,237 BEQUAERT, M. Préhistoire au Congo-Belge. Fouilles de 1950-1952. CONG. INT. SC. ANTH. ET ETHN. 4, no. iii (1952), pp. 30-35.

14,238 BIEBUYCK, D. Some remarks on Segy's "Warega Ivories." ZAIRE 7 (1953), pp. 1076-1082.

14,239 BIEBUYCK, D. De verwording der kunst bij de Balega. ZAIRE 8 (1954), pp. 273-278.

14,240 BISSOT, L. A propos du théâtre indigène. ZAIRE 6 (1952), pp. 623-630.

14,241 BITTREMIEUX, L. Symbolisme in de Negerkunst of beeldspreuken der Bawoyo's. CONGO 2 (1934), pp. 168-204.

14,242 BLACKING, J. Eight flute tunes from Butembo, east Belgian Congo. AFR. MUSIC, 1955, pp. 24-52.

14,243 BOUVEIGNES, O. DE. La musique indigène au Congo Belge. AFR. MUSIC, 1950, pp. 19-27.

14,244 BURSSENS, H. Beschouwingen bij boetseerwerk van kinderen in Kivu (Belgisch-Kongo). KONGO-OVERZEE 22 (1956), pp. 97-105.

14,245 BURSSENS, H. Sculptuur in Ngbandi-Stijl. Een bijdrage tot de studie van de plastiek van Noord-Kongo. KONGO-OVERZEE 24 (1958), pp. 1-52.

14,246 C., J. Expositions d'art congolais à New York. ZAIRE 5 (1951), pp. 635-636.

14,247 CABU, F. Some aspects of the Stone Age in the Belgian Congo. PROC. PAN-AFR. CONGR. PRE-HIST. 1 (1947), pp. 195-201.

14,248 CAENEGHEM, R. VAN. De Lupangu vrouw. ZAIRE 6 (1952), pp. 463-486, 569-595.

14,249 CARRINGTON, J. F. The drum language of the Lokole tribe. AFR. STUD. 3 (1944), pp. 75-88.

14,250 CARRINGTON, J. F. Four-toned announcements on Mbole talking drums. AFR. MUSIC, 1957, pp. 23-26.

14,251 CARRINGTON, J. F. Individual names given to talking-gongs in the Yalemba area of Belgian Congo. AFR. MUSIC, 1956, pp. 10-17.

14,252 CARRINGTON, J. F. Notes on an idiophone used in Kabile initiation rites by the Mbae. AFR. MUSIC, 1954, pp. 27-28.

14,253 CLEENE, N. DE. Symbolisme in de negerkunst. CONGO 1 (1934), pp. 348-356.

14,254 COMHAIRE-SYLVAIN, J. L'habitation chez les Nkundu du territoire d'Oshwe, Congo Belge. AFR. STUD. 8 (1949), pp. 66-69.

14,255 COSTERMANS, B. Muziekinstrumenten van Watsa-Gombari en omstreken. ZAIRE 1 (1947), pp. 515-542, 629-663.

14,256 COSTERMANS, B. Relevé de stations préhistoriques dans les territoires de Watsa-Gombari et de Dungu. ZAIRE 3 (1949), pp. 153-174.

14,257 COSTERMANS, P. De gebouwen bij de Mamvu-Mangutu-Walese. ZAIRE 1 (1947), pp. 281-295.

14,258 DENIS, L. Chansons des Bakongo. CONGO 2 (1939), pp. 380-409.

14,259 DOIZE, R. L. Rapports entre les industries préhistoriques du Kasai et celles de l'Afrique du Sud. CONGO 1 (1937), pp. 374-383.

14,260 FAVEAUX, A. A. DE. Une industrie sur galets spéciale aux plateaux des Biano (Katanga, Congo Belge). PROC. PAN-AFR. CONGR. PRE-HIST. 3 (1955), pp. 210-213.

14,261 FAVEAUX, A. A. DE. Travaux d'approche pour une synthèse climatique, stratigraphique et archéologique des Plateaux des Biano. PROC. PAN-AFR. CONGR. PRE-HIST. 4, no. iii (1962), pp. 165-176.

14,262 GILBERT, D. R. The Lukumbi, a six-toned slit drum of the Batetela. AFR. MUSIC, 1955, pp. 21-23.

14,263 GUEBELS, L. African music and the Christian outlook. Three points of view from the Congo [Native Music and the Catholic Religion, by R. P. Peters; Indigenous and Sacred Music, by l'Abbé Idohou; Reflections of a missionary]. AFR. MUSIC, 1949, pp. 9-15.

14,264 H., G. Exposition d'art religieux missionnaire. AEQUATORIA 12 (1949), p. 106.

14,265 HAENE, J. DE. Découvertes préhistoriques en Haut-Ituri. ZAIRE 3 (1949), pp. 1003-1010.

14,266 HIERNAUX, J. Un haut-fourneau préhistorique au Buhunde (Kivu, Congo belge). ZAIRE 8 (1954), pp. 615-619.

14,267 HIERNAUX, J. Note sur "l'Homme de la Ruzizi." ZAIRE 11 (1957), pp. 845-846.

14,268 HIERNAUX, J. and BUYST, J. DE. Note sur une campagne de fouilles à Katoto (région de Bukama, Katanga). ZAIRE 14 (1960), pp. 251-253.

14,269 HULSTAERT, G. Chants de portage. AEQUATORIA 19 (1956), pp. 53-64.

14,270 HULSTAERT, G. Morceaux rythmiques Mongo. AEQUATORIA 10 (1947), pp. 54-58.

14,271 HULSTAERT, G. Musique indigène et musique sacrée. AEQUATORIA 12 (1949), pp. 86-88.

14,272 HULSTAERT, G. Note sur les instruments de musique a l'Equateur. CONGO 2 (1935), pp. 185-200, 354-375.

14,273 HULSTAERT, G. Théâtre Nkundo. AEQUATORIA 16 (1953), pp. 142-146.

14,274 JACOBS, J. Signaaltrommeltaal bij de Tetela. KONGO-OVERZEE 20 (1954), pp. 409-422.

14,275 JADOT, J. M. Les arts populaires au Congo Belge, au Ruanda et dans l'Urundi. ZAIRE 4 (1950), pp. 181-188.

14,276 JADOT, J. M. Lettres et arts en Belgique coloniale et au Congo belge en 1954. ZAIRE 9 (1955), pp. 67-77.

14,277 JADOT, J. M. Les lettres et les arts en Belgique coloniale et au Congo belge en 1955, 1956. ZAIRE 10 (1956), pp. 151-163, 1051-1065.

14,278 JANS, P. Essai de musique religieuse pour Indigènes dans le Vicariat Apostolique de Coquilhatville. AEQUATORIA 19 (1956), pp. 1-43.

14,279 KELLEY, H. and DOIZE, R. L. Collections africaines du département de préhistoire exotique du Musée d'ethnographie du Trocadero. II. Nouvelles recherches préhistoriques au Congo. J. SOC. AFR. 4 (1934), pp. 303-312.

14,280 KOCHNITZKY, L. Mushenge et la cour du Niymi. AFR. MUSIC, 1952, pp. 11-13.

14,281 KOSHLAND, M. Six chants from the Congo. BO 2 (1958), pp. 18-21.

14,282 LODS, P. Les peintres de Poto-Poto. PRESENCE AFR. N.S. 24-25 (1959), pp. 326-330.

14,283 MAES, J. Wederwoord. KONGO-OVERZEE 6 (1940), pp. 167-169.

14,284 MAES, T. Les figurines sculptées du Bas-Congo. AFRICA 3 (1930), pp. 347-359.

14,285 MAQUET, J. N. Initiation a la musique congolaise. AFR. MUSIC, 1954, pp. 64-68.

14,286 MARTINS, J. O simbolismo entre os pretos do distrito de Cabinda. BOL. INST. ANGOLA 15 (1961), pp. 45-67.

14,287 MASSON, P. Armes, outils et instruments de musique employés par les Shi. KONGO-OVERZEE 24 (1958), pp. 239-255.

14,288 MAURICE, A. Union Africaine des Arts et des Lettres. AFR. AFFAIRS 50 (1951), pp. 233-236.

14,289 MBIYE, B. Kasala des Mulumba (Ntiite). KONGO-OVERZEE 21 (1955), pp. 160-165.

14,290 MERRIAM, A. P. African music re-examined in the light of new materials from the Belgian Congo and Ruanda Urundi. AFR. MUSIC, 1953, pp. 57-64, 245-253.

14,291 MERRIAM, A. P. Recording in the Belgian Congo. AFR. MUSIC, 1952, pp. 15-17.

14,292 MERRIAM, A. P. Song texts of the Bashi. AFR. MUSIC, 1954, pp. 44-52; also in ZAIRE 8 (1954), pp. 27-43.

14,293 MEYLEMANS, M. Kongoleesche kunst en hare aanpassing aan de missie. ZAIRE 1 (1947), pp. 141-157.

14,294 MONTEYNE, L. Frans Demers' koloniaal tooneel. KONGO-OVERZEE 1 (1934), pp. 55-64.

14,295 MOORSEL, H. VAN. Nota's bij voorhistorische opzoekingen in het plein van Leopoldstad. AEQUATORIA 8 (1945), pp. 128-134.

14,296 MORTELMANS, G. Archéologie des Grottes Dimba et Ngove (Region de Thysville, Bas-Congo). PROC. PAN-AFR. CONGR. PRE-HIST. 4, no. iii (1962), pp. 407-422.

14,297 MORTELMANS, G. Le Cénozoïque du Congo Belge. PROC. PAN-AFR. CONGR. PRE-HIST. 3 (1955), pp. 23-50.

14,298 MORTELMANS, G. The early pebble cultures of Katanga. PROC. PAN-AFR. CONGR. PRE-HIST. 3 (1955), pp. 214-216.

14,299 MORTELMANS, G. Les industries à galets taillés (pebble culture) du Katanga. PROC. PAN-AFR. CONGR. PRE-HIST. 2 (1952), pp. 295-300.

14,300 MORTELMANS, G. Vue d'ensemble sur la préhistoire du Congo occidental. PROC. PAN-AFR. CONGR. PRE-HIST. 4, no. iii (1962), pp. 129-164.

14,301 MORTELMANS, G. and MONTEYNE, R. Le Quaternaire du Congo occidental et sa chronologie. PROC. PAN-AFR. CONGR. PRE-HIST. 4 (1962), pp. 97-126.

14,302 NENQUIN, J. Notes on some early pottery cultures in northern Katanga. J. AFR. HIST. 4 (1963), pp. 19-32.

14,303 NENQUIN, J. Quelques poteries protohistoriques a face humaine trouvées au Katanga (Congo). J. SOC. AFR. 30 (1960), pp. 145-150.

14,304 OLBRECHTS, F. M. De Kabila-beelden van Dr. J. Maes. KONGO-OVERZEE 6 (1940), pp. 38-48.

14,305 PERIER, G. D. A la Commission pour la protection des arts et métiers indigènes. Rapport du Secrétaire sur sa visite à Elisabethville. ZAIRE 4 (1950), pp. 1093-1105.

14,306 RAKOWSKI, R. F. On a collection of neolithic axes and celts from the Welle basin, Belgian Congo. JRAI 51 (1921), pp. 154-164.

14,307 ROP, A. DE. Lilwa-beeldjes bij de Boyela. ZAIRE 9 (1955), pp. 115-120.

14,308 RYCKMANS, A. Etude sur les signaux de "Mondo" (tambour-telephone) chez les Bayaka et Bankanu du Territoire de Popokabaka. ZAIRE 10 (1956), pp. 493-515.

14,309 RYCROFT, D. The guitar improvisations of Mwenda Jean Bosco. AFR. MUSIC, 1961, pp. 81-98; 1962, pp. 86-101.

14,310 SEGY, L. Circle-dot symbolic sign on African ivory carvings. ZAIRE 7 (1953), pp. 35-54.

14,311 SHAFFER, J. Experiments in indigenous church music among the Batetela. AFR. MUSIC, 1956, pp. 39-42.

14,312 SHAFFER, J. Bamboo pipes of the Batetela children. AFR. MUSIC, 1954, pp. 74-75.

14,313 SOORS, M. A propos des découvertes préhistoriques en Haut-Ituri. ZAIRE 4 (1950), p. 58.

14,314 SOUSBERGHE, L. DE. De la signification de quelques masques Pende shave des Shona et mbuya des Pende. ZAIRE 14 (1960), pp. 505-531.

14,315 SOUSBERGHE, L. DE. Forgerons et fondeurs de fer chez les Ba-Pende et leurs voisins. ZAIRE 9 (1955), pp. 25-31.

14,316 SPAANDONCK, M. VAN, tr. Tumbako ya mu mpua. Een toneelschets in het Potopot-Kingwana van Katanga [by Christophe Makonga]. KONGO-OVERZEE 25 (1959), pp. 1-16.

14,317 STAPPERS, L. Vijftig motieven uit de dansliederen van de Baamilembwe. KONGO-OVERZEE 20 (1954), pp. 1-30.

14,318 SULZMANN, E. Les danseurs ekonda a "Changwe Yetu." ZAIRE 13 (1959), pp. 57-71.

14,319 TANGHE, J. Kanttekeningen bij Mr. Kunst's beschouwingen over "de inheemse kunst en de zending." ZAIRE 2 (1948), pp. 909-914.

14,320 VANDEN BOSSCHE, J. L'art plastique chez les Bapende. PRESENCE AFR. 10 (1951), pp. 167-174.

14,321 VANDENHOUDT, N. Aangepaste christelijke kunst in Kongo. ZAIRE 3 (1949), pp. 279-284.

14,322 VANDERYST, H. Nouvelles observations préhistoriques dans le Congo occidental. BULL. SEANCES IRCB 5 (1934), pp. 445-468.

14,323 VANDERYST, H. La station préhistorique du Lazaret Saint-Jean Berchmans, à Kisantu. BULL. SEANCES IRCB 2 (1931), pp. 327-345.

14,324 VERBEECK, A. Fatalisme in de denataliteit van de Mongo? AEQUATORIA 20 (1957), pp. 19-24.

14,325 VERBEKEN, A. Le language tambouriné des Congolais. AFR. MUSIC, 1953, pp. 28-41.

14,326 VERLY, R. La statuaire de pierre du Bas-Congo (Bamboma-Mussurongo). ZAIRE 9 (1955), pp. 451-528.

14,327 VERWILGHEN, A. Wat elk Europeaan weten moet over Kongolese muziek. ZAIRE 4 (1950), pp. 489-499.

14,328 WALSCHAP, A. Gedachten over Negermuziek. AEQUATORIA 2 (1939), pp. 25-29.

14,329 WANNIJN, R. Objets anciens en métal du Bas-Congo. ZAIRE 5 (1951), pp. 391-393.

14,330 WELLE, J. Rumbas congolaises et jazz americain. AFR. MUSIC, 1952, pp. 42-43.

14,331 WING, J. VAN. Bakongo music. JRAI 71 (1941), pp. 85-97.

14,332 WING, J. VAN. Les danses Bakongo. CONGO 2 (1937), pp. 121-131.

14,333 Bibliographie ethnographique du Congo belge et des Régions avoisinantes. CONGO 2 (1934), pp. 457-593; 2 (1935), pp. 473-584; 2 (1936), pp. 473-592.

14,334 Contribution to the study of the chronology of African plastic art [by F.M.O.]. AFRICA 14 (1943), pp. 183-193.

14,335 Exposition d'arts indigènes. Extraits du catalogue des oeuvres de l'atelier P. Romain-Desfossés, Elizabethville, Belgian Congo. AFR. MUSIC, 1949, pp. 31-33.

14,336 Warega ivories. ZAIRE 5 (1951), pp. 1041-1045.

See also

Biography

14,337 FRAZAO, S. D. Maria Amália, Princesa do Congo? PORT. EM AFR. 3 (1946), pp. 363-367.

14,338 Le centenaire de Monseigneur Augouard. ZAIRE 7 (1953), pp. 76-77.

14,339 In memoriam: P. Ern. van Avermaet. AEQUATORIA 16 (1953), p. 79.

14,340 BOELAERT, E. Le Capitaine Boshart. AEQUATORIA 18 (1955), pp. 121-124.

14,341 CUVELIER, Mgr. Notes sur Cavazzi. ZAIRE 3 (1949), pp. 175-184.

14,342 In Memoriam. Mgr. A. de Clercq. KONGO-OVERZEE 5 (1939), pp. 319-320.

14,343 RONDELEZ, V. Le centenaire d'un missionnaire-explorateur: le R. P. C. De Deken missionnaire de Scheut (1852-1896). ZAIRE 7 (1953), pp. 115-146.

14,344 Paul Fontainas. CIVILISATIONS 13 (1963), p. 537.

14,345 HILDEBRAND, P. Nieuwe Bijdrage over Jons van Geel. KONGO-OVERZEE 1 (1934), pp. 103-118.

14,346 ESSER, J. Un indigèniste éminent, Monseigneur Van Goethem. AEQUATORIA 12 (1949), pp. 103-105.

14,347 CLEENE, N. DE. and MALENGREAU, G. In memoriam: Edouard De Jonghe. ZAIRE 4 (1950), pp. 119-121.

14,348 STENGERS, J. Un collaborateur de Léopold II: Otto Lindner. ZAIRE 13 (1959), pp. 415-424.

14,349 CLEMENT, P. Patrice Lumumba (Stanleyville 1952-1953). PRESENCE AFR. N.S. 40 (1962), pp. 57-78.

14,350 VAN LIERDE, J. Témoignage Patrice Lumumba, leader et ami. PRESENCE AFR. 36 (1961), pp. 112-119.

14,351 Léopold Mottoulle. CIVILISATIONS 13 (1963), pp. 536-537.

14,352 Mort de Jules Renkin. CONGO 2 (1934), pp. 227-242.

14,353 JANSSENS, A. In memoriam. L. Scharpé, stichter en Hoofdredacteur van Onze Kongo (1910-1914). KONGO-OVERZEE 1 (1934), pp. 314-318.

14,354 Antoine Sohier. CIVILISATIONS 13 (1963), p. 535.

14,355 WILDEMAN, E. DE. R. P. Hyacinthe Vanderyst (1860-1934). BULL. SEANCES IRCB 6 (1935), pp. 28-38.

14,356 Le gouvernement provincial du Kongo Central. Notices biographiques. ET. CONG. 5, no. 6 (1963), pp. 38-43.

Economics

14,357 ALLARD, E. L'aviation coloniale. BULL. SEANCES IRCB 2 (1931), pp. 197-205.

14,358 ALLARD, E. La liaison aérienne Belgique-Congo. BULL. SEANCES IRCB 6 (1935), pp. 264-276.

14,359 AMEYE, L. The economic problems of the Belgian Congo. AFR. AFFAIRS 58 (1959), pp. 293-299.

14,360 BACKER, E. DE. La rivière Kasai entre Kwamouth et Port-Francqui. L'amélioration de ses conditions de navigabilité par balisage, signalisation et travaux d'aménagement. BULL. SEANCES IRCB 3 (1932), pp. 252-278.

14,361 BERTIEAUX, R. The economic situation of the Belgian Congo in 1953. CIVILISATIONS 4 (1954), pp. 321-328.

14,362 BETTE, R. Captation de l'énergie de la Lufira à Chutes Cornet (Madingusha). BULL. SEANCES IRCB 2 (1931), pp. 626-644.

14,363 BETTE, R. La centrale hydro-électrique de la M'Pozo (Bas Congo). BULL. SEANCES IRCB 5 (1934), pp. 492-514.

14,364 BEZY, F. Aspects de l'économie congolaise à la fin de 1952. ZAIRE 7 (1953), pp. 65-72.

14,365 BEZY, F. Aspects de l'économie congolaise au premier semestre de 1954. ZAIRE 8 (1954), pp. 733-752.

14,366 BEZY, F. Conjoncture congolaise. ZAIRE 5 (1951), pp. 853-858.

14,367 BEZY, F. Conjoncture congolaise. ZAIRE 6 (1952), pp. 173-183.

14,368 BEZY, F. La conjoncture congolaise pendant le premier semestre de 1952. ZAIRE 6 (1952), pp. 849-862.

14,369 BEZY, F. La conjoncture économique du Congo Belge. ZAIRE 7 (1953), pp. 955-983.

14,370 BEZY, F. La conjoncture économique du Congo Belge en 1950. ZAIRE 5 (1951), pp. 395-403.

14,371 BEZY, F. L'économie congolaise à la fin de 1954. ZAIRE 8 (1954), pp. 1081-1090.

14,372 BEZY, F. L'économie congolaise en 1951. ZAIRE 6 (1952), pp. 505-523.

14,373 BEZY, F. Les fondements d'une politique des rémunérations au Congo belge. ZAIRE 12 (1958), pp. 115-150.

14,374 BEZY, F. Native economy in the Belgian Congo 1950-1953. CIVILISATIONS 4 (1954), pp. 316-320.

14,375 BEZY, F. Principes pour l'orientation du developpement economique au Congo. ZAIRE 13 (1959), pp. 3-56.

14,376 BEZY, F. Problems of economic development of Congo. ECON. DEV. FOR AFRICA, 1965, pp. 71-88.

14,377 BIEBUYCK, D. La monnaie musanga des Balega. ZAIRE 7 (1953), pp. 675-686.

14,378 BIEBUYCK, D. Systèmes de tenure foncière et problèmes fonciers au Congo. AFR. AGRARIAN SYSTEMS, 1963, pp. 83-100.

14,379 BILSEN, J. VAN. Caoutchouc et... ZAIRE 4 (1950), pp. 771-772.

14,380 BILSEN, J. VAN. C.S.K.-Jubileum. ZAIRE 4 (1950), pp. 874-878.

14,381 BILSEN, J. VAN. Deux missions industrielles au Congo Belge. ZAIRE 3 (1949), pp. 1033-1036.

14,382 BILSEN, J. VAN. Divers autres évènements... ZAIRE 4 (1950), pp. 773-774.

14,383 BILSEN, J. VAN. La "guerre des couvertures." ZAIRE 4 (1950), pp. 535-537.

14,384 BILSEN, J. VAN. Het privilege der B[anque] C[ongo] B[elge]. ZAIRE 4 (1950), pp. 1116-1118.

14,385 BILSEN, J. VAN. Plan décennal. ZAIRE 4 (1950), pp. 534-535.

14,386 BILSEN, J. VAN. Quinine [production]. ZAIRE 4 (1950), pp. 772-773.

14,387 BOELAERT, E. Ntange. AEQUATORIA 15 (1952), pp. 58-62, 96-100.

14,388 BOELAERT, E. La question cruciale des terres indigènes. Pourquoi les indigènes sont-ils mécontents? ZAIRE 9 (1955), pp. 969-972.

14,389 BRAUCOURT, J. DE H. DE. Comptages typologiques par catégories; extension aux industries eurafricaines. PROC. PAN-AFR. CONGR. PRE-HIST. 4, no. iii (1962), pp. 113-127.

14,390 BUCK, A. DE. Naissance à Bukavu de la première caisse de compensation pour allocations familiales payées aux travailleurs indigènes. ZAIRE 8 (1954), pp. 929-938.

14,391 BUELENS, K. Analyse économique du problème de propriété foncière au Congo. ZAIRE 12 (1958), pp. 227-249.

14,392 BUTTGENBACH, H. Les minéraux à columbium et tantale du Congo belge. BULL. SEANCES IRCB 4 (1933), pp. 209-219.

14,393 BUTTGENBACH, H. Les recherches géologiques et minières au Congo belge. BULL. SEANCES IRCB 3 (1932), pp. 545-570.

14,394 CAPELLE, M. The industrial employment of women in the Belgian Congo. AFR. WOMEN 3 (1958-1960), pp. 59-61.

14,395 CAUWENBERGH, A. VAN. Le développement du commerce et de l'artisanat indigènes à Leopoldville. ZAIRE 10 (1956), pp. 637-664.

14,396 CHARLES, V. L'action syndicale congolaise. ZAIRE 6 (1952), pp. 1085-1086.

14,397 CHARLES, V. Les allocations familiales. ZAIRE 6 (1952), pp. 70-73.

14,398 CHARLES, V. Au parlement. ZAIRE 5 (1951), pp. 279-281.

14,399 CHARLES, V. Au parlement [les budgets coloniaux pour l'année 1952]. ZAIRE 7 (1953), pp. 381-383.

14,400 CHARLES, V. La Caisse d'Epargne. ZAIRE 6 (1952), pp. 736-738.

14,401 CHARLES, V. La création de la Caisse d'Epargne. ZAIRE 4 (1950), pp. 1135-1136.

14,402 CHARLES, V. Les débuts de la Caisse d'Epargne. ZAIRE 5 (1951), pp. 960-963.

14,403 CHARLES, V. L'évolution du mouvement syndical congolais. ZAIRE 5 (1951), pp. 963-966.

14,404 CHARLES, V. L'exécution du plan décennal. ZAIRE 6 (1952), pp. 399-412.

14,405 CHARLES, V. L'inspection du travail. ZAIRE 7 (1953), p. 391.

14,406 CHARLES, V. Le problème de la main-d'oeuvre. ZAIRE 6 (1952), pp. 733-735.

14,407 CHARLES, V. La vie syndicale. ZAIRE 6 (1952), pp. 76-77.

14,408 CLAIR, M. H. Notre colonie dans les publications anglaises. KONGO-OVERZEE 21 (1955), pp. 304-305.

14,409 CLEENE, N. DE. La notion de propriété chez quelques peuplades matrilinéales du Congo Belge. AFRICA 16 (1946), pp. 23-28; English summary, p. 28.

14,410 CORNELIS, H. De ekonomische evolutie der inlandsche gemeenschap in Midden-Afrika. KONGO-OVERZEE 5 (1939), pp. 12-27.

14,411 CRABBE, J. Per una futura politica economica nel Congo. AFRICA (Rome) 15 (1960), pp. 71-73.

14,412 DAVIDSON, B. Le Congo Belge au carrefour de son destin. PRESENCE AFR. N.S. 1 (1955), pp. 94-108.

14,413 DELEVOY, G. Sur quelques essais de résineux au Katanga. BULL. SEANCES IRCB 5 (1934), pp. 122-130.

14,414 DEUREN, P. VAN. Activité du Syndicat d'Etudes du Bas-Congo. BULL. SEANCES IRCB 4 (1933), pp. 305-314.

14,415 DHANIS, E. Recrutements de main d'oeuvre chez les Bayaka. ZAIRE 7 (1953), pp. 489-496.

14,416 DOUGLAS, M. Raffia cloth distribution in the Lele economy. AFRICA 28 (1958), pp. 109-122.

14,417 DOUTRELOUX, A. Note sur le domaine foncier au Mayumbe. ZAIRE 13 (1959), pp. 499-508.

14,418 DUJARDIN. L'industrie de la brasserie dans la Colonie. BULL. SEANCES IRCB 2 (1931), pp. 393-396.

14,419 ENGELS, A. La problème financier et le problème économique au Congo belge en 1932 [with notes by F. Dellicour, O. Louwers]. BULL. SEANCES IRCB 3 (1932), pp. 576-598.

14,420 EVERWYN, G. Which way in Katanga? AFR. AFFAIRS 61 (1962), pp. 149-157.

14,421 FRANCK, L. La Banque du Congo Belge de 1909 à 1934. CONGO 1 (1934), pp. 641-653.

14,422 GELDERS, V. Un essai de réforme agraire et rurale au Congo. KONGO-OVERZEE 12-13 (1946-1947), pp. 88-102.

14,423 GELDERS, V. Les Noirs et la terre. KONGO-OVERZEE 14 (1948), pp. 213-222.

14,424 GERARD-LIBOIS, J. L'assistance technique belge et la République du Congo. ET. CONG. 2, no. 3 (1962), pp. 1-11.

14,425 GODDING, R. Aspecten van de economische en sociale politiek in Belgisch-Kongo. KONGO-OVERZEE 12-13 (1946-1947), pp. 65-87.

14,426 H., F. L'aide financière au Congo et l'accord Congo-ONU du 10 juin 1961. ET. CONG. 1, no. 3 (1961), pp. 11-18.

14,427 HENRY, E. Régime de l'alcohol au Congo. CONGO 1 (1921), pp. 617-622.

14,428 HERBOTS, J. H. Le Congo et le Marché commun européen. ET. CONG. 7, no. 9 (1964), pp. 27-42.

14,429 HERMAN, F. La création d'un marché libre des changes à Léopoldville. ET. CONG. 2, no. 1 (1962), pp. 25-35.

14,430 HERMAN, F. La situation économique du Congo au cours du premier semestre 1963. ET. CONG. 5, no. 7 (1963), pp. 1-21.

14,431 H[ERMAN], F. La situation économique et financière de la République du Congo depuis l'indépendance. ET. CONG. 1, no. 1 (1961), pp. 13-19; 1, no. 2 (1961), pp. 15-25; 1, no. 4 (1961), pp. 13-24; 2, no. 2 (1962), pp. 1-34; 2, no. 3 (1962), pp. 12-15; 3, no. 8 (1962), pp. 17-26; 4, no. 3 (1963), pp. 1-27; 6, no. 4 (1964), pp. 1-36; 7, no. 8 (1964), pp. 1-19; 8, no. 4 (1965), pp. 1-35.

14,432 HEYSE, T. Cessions et concessions foncières. CONGO 1 (1934), pp. 13-40; 2 (1935), pp. 330-353; 2 (1939), pp. 252-270.

14,433 HEYSE, T. De l'application de l'emphytéose au Congo. BULL. SEANCES IRCB 2 (1931), pp. 476-486.

14,434 HUYBRECHTS, A. La conjoncture congolaise au premier semestre de 1956. ZAIRE 10 (1956), pp. 861-876.

14,435 HUYBRECHTS, A. La conjoncture congolaise en 1955. ZAIRE 10 (1956), pp. 291-314.

14,436 HUYBRECHTS, A. La conjoncture congolaise en 1956. ZAIRE 11 (1957), pp. 273-295.

14,437 HUYBRECHTS, A. La conjoncture congolaise pendant les trois premiers trimestres de 1957. ZAIRE 11 (1957), pp. 847-864.

14,438 HUYBRECHTS, A. L'économie congolaise au milieu de 1958. ZAIRE 12 (1958), pp. 513-528.

14,439 HUYBRECHTS, A. L'économie congolaise en 1959. Crise politique, redressement conjoncturel, difficultés financières. ZAIRE 13 (1959), pp. 843-861.

14,440 HUYBRECHTS, A. La situation économique du Congo belge en 1958. ZAIRE 13 (1959), pp. 169-183.

14,441 JAER, E. DE. Les fibres textiles au Congo. CONGO 2, no. 4 (1933), pp. 603-605.

14,442 JUSSIANT, A. L'organisation de Coopératives en Milieux Indigènes. AEQUATORIA 7 (1944), pp. 137-142.

14,443 KALONJI, B. Bilan du syndicalisme congolais. ET. CONG. 7, no. 8 (1964), pp. 48-57.

14,444 LADDERSOUS, A. M. DE. Economic conditions in the Congo and some of the factors underlying them. AFR. AFFAIRS 64 (1965), pp. 6-16.

14,445 LECLERCQ, H. Principes pour l'orientation d'une politique fiscale au Congo. ZAIRE 13 (1959), pp. 451-497.

14,446 LEFEBVRE, J. Plan Décennal du Congo Belge. CIVILISATIONS 6 (1956), pp. 357-367; English summary, pp. 368-370.

14,447 LEONARD, H. Les concessions de mines au Congo Belge. CONGO 1 (1921), pp. 589-616.

14,448 LEPLAE, E. Rendements des Elaeis africains comparés à ceux de Malaisie. CONGO 1 (1921), pp. 467-473.

14,449 LEPLAE, E. Résultats obtenus au Congo Belge par les cultures obligatoires alimentaires et industriels. ZAIRE 1 (1947), pp. 115-139.

14,450 L'HEUREUX, L. Le Congo peut-il nous fournir les apprêts indispensables à notre industrie textile? CONGO 1 (1940), pp. 1-8.

14,451 LOUWERS, O. Le financement des colonies tropicales modernes. BULL. SEANCES IRCB 5 (1934), pp. 586-638.

14,452 LUX, A. Le niveau de vie des chomeurs de Luluabourg. ZAIRE 14 (1960), pp. 3-34.

14,453 M., G. Les syndicats et la politique congolaise. ET. CONG. 6, no. 2 (1964), pp. 19-26.

14,454 MALENGREAU, G. L'accession des indigènes à la propriété foncière individuelle. ZAIRE 7 (1953), pp. 607-612.

14,455 MALENGREAU, G. Le régime foncier dans la société indigène. CONGO 2 (1939), pp. 1-46.

14,456 MAURY, J. Quelques remarques au sujet des méthodes d'étude des traces de chemins de fer aux colonies. BULL. SEANCES IRCB 3 (1932), pp. 464-474.

14,457 MEERHAEGHE, M. VAN. De Kongolese Economie in 1947. KONGO-OVERZEE 14 (1948), pp. 168-188.

14,458 MEERHAEGHE, M. VAN. De Kongolese Economie in 1948. KONGO-OVERZEE 15 (1949), pp. 200-225.

14,459 MEERHAEGHE, M. VAN. Overzicht von de economische toestand van Belgisch-Kongo. KONGO-OVERZEE 12-13 (1946-1947), pp. 287-313.

14,460 MENDIAUX, E. Le Comité National du Kivu. ZAIRE 10 (1956), pp. 803-813, 927-964, 1045-1050.

14,461 MOULAERT, G. Les exploitations aurifères au Congo belge. BULL. SEANCES IRCB 3 (1932), pp. 491-509.

14,462 MOULAERT, J. Les exploitations minières de Kilo-Moto et de la Province Orientale. CONGO 1 (1935), pp. 1-31.

14,463 NICAISE, J. L'affaire de Ngweshe ou les contrats d'entreprise, de société et de métayage. ZAIRE 8 (1954), pp. 622-627.

14,464 NICAISE, J. Le conflit du Kivu. ZAIRE 8 (1954), pp. 187-189.

14,465 NICAISE, J. Les coopératives indigènes. ZAIRE 8 (1954), pp. 185-186.

14,466 NICAISE, J. Les journées d'études des mutualités. ZAIRE 9 (1955), pp. 158-161.

14,467 NICAISE, J. Politique familiale et législation fiscale. ZAIRE 8 (1954), p. 181.

14,468 NICAISE, J. Questions diverses. ZAIRE 9 (1955), pp. 161-162.

14,469 NICAISE, J. Rémunération des travailleurs congolais. ZAIRE 8 (1954), pp. 186-187.

14,470 NICAISE, J. Les salaires au Kivu. ZAIRE 8 (1954), pp. 621-622.

14,471 NORBET LAUDE, T. C. El plan decenal del Congo belga. CUAD. EST. AFR. 16 (1951), pp. 9-13.

14,472 OMBREDANE, A. La stimulation économique en milieu coutûmier et capitaliste. PRESENCE AFR. 13 (1952), pp. 338-341.

14,473 ORSINI, D'A. Per attuare il programma di Inga è stato creato l'Istituto per lo Sviluppo del Basso Congo. AFRICA (Rome) 13 (1958), p. 64.

14,474 PEETERS, G. Comment déterminer la valeur du "capital terre" du cultivateur congolais? ZAIRE 11 (1957), pp. 204-208.

14,475 PHILIPPE, R. L'accession des Congolais à la propriété foncière individuelle. AEQUATORIA 21 (1958), pp. 5-28.

14,476 PHILIPPE, R. Notes sur le régime foncier au Lac Léopold II. AEQUATORIA 17 (1954), pp. 51-57.

14,477 PHILIPPSON, M. Les radio-communications au et avec le Congo belge. BULL. SEANCES IRCB 4 (1933), pp. 295-300.

14,478 PILLAY, V. The Belgian treasury. AFR. SOUTH 4, no. 2 (1960), pp. 79-86.

14,479 PUTTE, M. VAN DE. Recherches sur le Copal du Congo. BULL. SEANCES IRCB 4 (1933), pp. 265-291.

14,480 RENIER, M. La région de la Black-River et ses perspectives d'avenir. KONGO-OVERZEE 17 (1951), pp. 329-344.

14,481 S., J. Plan et développement au Congo. ET. CONG. 4, no. 5 (1963), pp. 1-24.

14,482 SABBADINI, E. Interessi coloniali Belgi. AFRICA (Rome) 11 (1956), p. 118.

14,483 SLUYSMANS. Les constructions démontables et transportables système Sluysmans. CONGO 1 (1921), pp. 462-467.

14,484 SMAL. Le problème de la navigation fluviale au Congo Belge. Moyens de transport; bateaux de 1000 et de 500 tonnes; sternwheel, barges; trains de navigation. CONGO 1 (1921), pp. 457-462; 2 (1921), pp. 110-120.

14,485 STENMANS, A. Quelques données statistiques sur l'évolution de l'occupation foncière dans la province du Kasai depuis sa création. ZAIRE 5 (1951), pp. 691-707.

14,486 TATAY PUCHOL, R. Las comunicaciones aéreas con Guinea y el problema del aeropuerto. ARCH. INST. EST. AFR. 2, no. 6 (1948), pp. 155-165.

14,487 URBAIN, Y. The Belgian Congo. CIVILISATIONS 2 (1952), pp. 142-147.

14,488 VANSINA, J. Le régime foncier dans la Kuba. ZAIRE 10 (1956), pp. 899-926.

14,489 VAREBEKE, F. J. DE. Le régime de la main-d'oeuvre au Katanga. CONGO 2 (1921), pp. 176-193.

14,490 VERHAEGEN, B. Les syndicats et le nouveau contrat de louage de services. ET. CONG. 1, no. 3 (1961), pp. 19-31.

14,491 VOUSSURE, G. Note sur la construction des routes au Congo belge. CONGO 1 (1937), pp. 1-33.

14,492 W., J. C. La presse dans les provinces du Congo. ET. CONG. 7, no. 6 (1964), pp. 98-110.

14,493 WILLAERT, M. Création d'une caisse d'épargne et de crédit au Congo. ZAIRE 2 (1946), pp. 127-136.

14,494 ZANNA, E. L. Mercati da seguire: Nel Congo Belga e Ruanda Urundi in progresso la produzione italiana. AFRICA (Rome) 13 (1958), pp. 147-148.

14,495 La bataille du cobalt. ZAIRE 7 (1953), p. 77.

14,496 The Belgian Agreements. J. AFR. SOC. 40 (1941), pp. 99-100.

14,497 Chronique économique: étude statistique sur le volume des exportations du premier semestre 1963. ET. CONG. 7, no. 7 (1964), pp. 72-75.

14,498 Conférence économique et financière du Kongo Central. ET. CONG. 7, no. 9 (1964), pp. 43-62.

14,499 Draft outline of the first five-year plan of the Republic of the Congo. ECON. BULL. AFR. 5 (1965), pp. 80-83.

14,500 Economic developments in the Republic of the Congo (Leopoldville), 1957-60. ECON. BULL. AFR. 1, no. 1 (1961), pp. 90-102.

14,501 Economic organisation of the Congo. AFR. AFFAIRS 48 (1949), pp. 72-73.

14,502 Una grande manifestazione fieristica a Stanleyville. AFRICA (Rome) 10 (1955), p. 79.

14,503 Leopoldville and Lagos. Comparative study of urban conditions in 1960. ECON. BULL. AFR. 1, no. 2 (1961), pp. 50-65.

14,504 The problem of native labour in the Belgian Congo. INT. REV. MISSIONS 14 (1925), pp. 536-544.

14,505 Salaires et consommation. ZAIRE 5 (1951), pp. 611-613.

14,506 Statistiques de la colonie pour 1946. ZAIRE 2 (1948), pp. 91-94.

14,507 Structure of the Congo economy, by provinces (with special reference to Katanga). ECON. BULL. AFR. 1, no. 2 (1961), pp. 66-82.

14,508 Traitements, grèves et politique d'austérité... ET. CONG. 2, no. 5 (1962), pp. 1-32.

14,509 La voix du capital et du travail... ZAIRE 5 (1951), pp. 616-619.

Education

14,510 BALLEGEER, L. L'enseignement supérieur au Congo. KONGO-OVERZEE 14 (1948), pp. 310-313.

14,511 BERNARDIN, . Belang en moeilijkheden van het normaalonderwijs in Kongo. KONGO-OVERZEE 6 (1940), pp. 30-37.

14,512 BULCK, V. VAN. Het taalprobleem in het Kongolees universitair onderwijs. KONGO-OVERZEE 19 (1953), pp. 343-356.

14,513 CHARLES, V. L'enseignement professionnel. ZAIRE 7 (1953), p. 385.

14,514 COLIN, M. A technical school for Congolese girls. AFR. WOMEN 2 (1956-1958), pp. 39-40.

14,515 DAVIS, O. J. Educational development in the Belgian Congo. INT. REV. MISSIONS 43 (1954), pp. 421-428.

14,516 DEHASSE, J. and MAITER, B. Données complémentaires sur l'enseignement supérieur dans la République du Congo. ET. CONG. 5, no. 10 (1963), pp. 1-36.

14,517 DEHEYN, J. J. The education of women in the Belgian Congo. AFR. WOMEN 3 (1958-1960), pp. 33-35.

14,518 DELANAYE, P. De l'emploi des langues dans l'enseignement des Africains au Congo Belge. ZAIRE 9 (1955), pp. 227-259.

14,519 DERINE, R. A propos d'un livre sur les institutions congolaises. ZAIRE 14 (1960), pp. 533-538.

14,520 EKWA, M. Les principes constitutionnels en matière d'enseignement. ET. CONG. 8, no. 2 (1965), pp. 119-125.

14,521 HULSTAERT, G. Formation générale et école primaire. AEQUATORIA 8 (1945), pp. 87-91.

14,522 JADOT, J. M. The Belgian Congo (July 1953-July 1954). CIVILISATIONS 4 (1954), pp. 620-624.

14,523 JONES, T. J. L'éducation des nègres. CONGO 2 (1921), pp. 162-175.

14,524 JONGHE, E. DE. La question des subsides scolaires au Congo Belge. ZAIRE 1 (1947), pp. 35-54.

14,525 KELLY, L. Congo Polytechnic Institute: Home Economics Department. WOMEN TODAY 6 (1964), pp. 44-45.

14,526 LACOPS, B. Hoevescholen. AEQUATORIA 9 (1946), pp. 121-127; 10 (1947), pp. 1-3.

14,527 LIESENBORGHS, O. Beschouwingen over het Onderwijs in Belgisch Kongo. Bij het jongste Ontwerp van Hervorming. KONGO-OVERZEE 5 (1939), pp. 58-76.

14,528 LIESENBORGHS, O. L'instruction publique des indigènes du Congo belge. CONGO 1 (1940), pp. 233-272.

14,529 LIESENBORGHS, O. Naar een Afrikaansche Opvoedkunde. KONGO-OVERZEE 4 (1938), pp. 1-16.

14,530 LIESENBORGHS, O. De Vorming van den Kongoleeschen Onderwijzer. KONGO-OVERZEE 4 (1938), pp. 127-138.

14,531 M., Z. Uit een schoolverslag. AEQUATORIA 2 (1939), pp. 55-59.

14,532 MAES, F. Het Kongolees in het Onderwijs. AEQUATORIA 20 (1957), pp. 81-84.

14,533 MAES, F. Het rekenen bij de Inlandse Leerlingen. AEQUATORIA 15 (1952), pp. 141-145.

14,534 MAES, F. Het rekenprogramma in Kongo. AEQUATORIA 19 (1956), pp. 49-52.

14,535 MAES, F. De Lagere School bij de Nkundo. AEQUATORIA 16 (1953), pp. 108-111.

14,536 MAUS, A. La nouveau programme de l'enseignement libre. CONGO 2 (1938), pp. 490-525; 1 (1939), pp. 1-20.

14,537 MOULAERT, G. Instruction et éducation. ZAIRE 10 (1956), pp. 525-528.

14,538 P., L. V. Bij het Ontwerp van een nieuw Schoolprogramma. KONGO-OVERZEE 5 (1939), pp. 188-192.

14,539 PHILIPPE, R. Le problème de l'enseignement au Congo Belge. AEQUATORIA 22 (1959), pp. 16-20.

14,540 RHODIUS, G. The evolution of the native woman in the Belgian Congo and Ruanda-Urundi. AFR. WOMEN 1 (1955), pp. 73-74.

14,541 SCALAIS, F. La réorganisation scolaire au Congo Belge. ZAIRE 4 (1950), pp. 421-428; also in AEQUATORIA 17 (1954), pp. 107-111.

14,542 SCHNEIDER, W. L'enseignement du calcul à l'école primaire et la méthode Schneider. AEQUATORIA 18 (1955), pp. 131-133.

14,543 TAKIZALA, H. D. Situation de l'enseignement durant la première législature. ET. CONG. 7, no. 8 (1964), pp. 61-79.

14,544 VERHAEGEN, B. La situation et les perspectives de l'enseignement supérieur à Léopoldville. ET. CONG. 3, no. 6 (1962), pp. 1-27.

14,545 A propos de l'égalité des missions nationales et étrangères au Congo. ZAIRE 1 (1947), pp. 323-324.

14,546 La fondation de l'Ecole Nationale de Droit et d'Administration. ET. CONG. 1, no. 1 (1961), pp. 3-5.

14,547 Het probleem van de inlandse onderwijstaal in Leopoldstad. KONGO-OVERZEE 19 (1953), pp. 7-9.

14,548 Le premier congrès des Etudiants congolais à Léopoldville. ET. CONG. 1, no. 2 (1961), pp. 52-65.

14,549 Le programme de recherches du Centre d'études politiques de l'Institut de recherches économiques et sociales de l'Université Lovanium. CIVILISATIONS 14 (1964), pp. 209-212.

14,550 L'Université officielle du Congo à Elisabethville. ET. CONG. 5, no. 8 (1963), pp. 1-33.

Geography

14,551 BARNS, T. A. A trans-African expedition. J. AFR. SOC. 24 (1925), pp. 272-286.

14,552 BOELAERT, E. Les premières explorations du Ruki et de ses affluents. AEQUATORIA 21 (1958), pp. 121-133.

14,553 BOELAERT, E. La Sanford exploring expedition. AEQUATORIA 22, no. iv (1959), pp. 121-131.

14,554 BOURDONNEC, D. P. Sens de quelques termes géographiques du Katanga. ZAIRE 13 (1959), pp. 73-80.

14,555 BOUVEIGNES, O. DE. Jérome de Montesarchio et la découverte du Stanley-Pool. ZAIRE 2 (1948), pp. 989-1013.

14,556 BOUVEIGNES, O. DE. Tuckey et Stanley. ZAIRE 5 (1951), pp. 31-44.

14,557 BOUVEIGNES, O. DE. Le voyage de Pierre Farde au Congo. ZAIRE 5 (1951), pp. 709-714.

14,558 BRIEY, R. DE. Stanleyville capitale du Congo Belge. CONGO 1 (1921), pp. 390-395.

14,559 CORNELIS. Orthographie des noms géographiques du Congo. KONGO-OVERZEE 20 (1954), pp. 71-73.

14,560 CORNELIS. De schrijfwijze van de Kongolese geografische namen. KONGO-OVERZEE 20 (1954), pp. 68-70.

14,561 CROCKER, H. E. A canoe voyage on the Congo. J. AFR. SOC. 42 (1943), pp. 69-71.

14,562 DEHALU, M. L'année polaire et la création d'une station magnétique temporaire au Congo belge. BULL. SEANCES IRCB 3 (1932), pp. 479-488.

14,563 DEHALU, M. Sur la mesure du 30e méridien à travers l'Afrique. BULL. SEANCES IRCB 1 (1930), pp. 427-437.

14,564 DENIS, J. Coquilhatville. Elements pour une étude de géographie sociale. AEQUATORIA 19 (1956), pp. 137-148; 20 (1957), pp. 1-4.

14,565 DENIS, J. Léopoldville. Etude de géographie urbaine et sociale. ZAIRE 10 (1956), pp. 563-611.

14,566 DENOLF, P. Arme Bakuba. KONGO-OVERZEE 18 (1952), pp. 338-354.

14,567 DRESCH, M. J. Villes congolaises. ACTA GEOGRAPHICA 3 (1947), pp. 1-4.

14,568 DU BOIS, C. G. B. Recent volcanic activity in the Kivu District, Belgian Congo. UGANDA J. 23 (1959), pp. 118-123.

14,569 FONTAINAS, P. La formation des alluvions diamantifères du Kasai. BULL. SEANCES IRCB 5 (1934), pp. 573-585.

14,570 FONTAINAS, P. Le rôle des grands lacs du plateau central africain dans le régime du Nil. BULL. SEANCES IRCB 4 (1933), pp. 608-639.

14,571 FRAZAO, S. O Rio Zaire. PORT. EM AFR. 2 (1945), pp. 284-291.

14,572 GARLANDA, U. Il miracolo del Congo rivelato al mondo dal viaggio di Baldovino Re dei Re congolesi. AFRICA (Rome) 10 (1955), pp. 267-269.

14,573 GOHR, A. Du régime juridique des rivières non navigables ni flottables au Congo. BULL. SEANCES IRCB 6 (1935), pp. 536-556.

14,574 JONGHE, E. DE. A la recherche du lac Central Africain. CONGO 2 (1934), pp. 39-50.

14,575 LEPLAE, E. La Grande Forêt Equatoriale Congolaise; son influence sur le régime des pluies défrichements nécessaires à la prospérité des indigènes. CONGO 1 (1937), pp. 473-542.

14,576 LEPLAE, E. Observations et publications météorologiques au Congo belge. BULL. SEANCE IRCB 3 (1932), pp. 179-215.

14,577 MAURY, J. Emploi du nivellement barométrique pour les besoins de la cartographie dans les régions tropicales. BULL. SEANCES IRCB 2 (1931), pp. 369-390.

14,578 MAURY, J. Etude établie par le lieutenant du génie Delvaux sur les travaux de la Mission cartographique de Dilolo. BULL. SEANCES IRCB 1 (1930), pp. 541-565.

14,579 MAURY, J. Le réseau fondamental de la Région de Kilo-Moto. BULL. SEANCES IRCB 6 (1935), pp. 726-743.

14,580 MAURY, J. Triangulation du Katanga. Notes complémentaires par M. Vanderstraeten. BULL. SEANCES IRCB 1 (1930), pp. 566-610.

14,581 MAURY, J. La triangulation et la coordination des travaux cartographiques du Congo oriental. BULL. SEANCES IRCB 4 (1933), pp. 668-691.

14,582 NASI, G. Il Congo è il Congo. AFRICA (Rome) 11 (1956), pp. 115-117.

14,583 OLSEN, F. Les avatars et les desiderata de la navigation sur le Haut Fleuve. BULL. SEANCES IRCB 3 (1932), pp. 228-248.

14,584 PENDLETON, R. L. The Belgian Congo: impressions of a changing region. GEOG. REV. 39 (1949), pp. 371-400.

14,585 PLANCQUAERT, M. Le grand Lac Central et le Kwango. En réponse au Dr. Maes. CONGO 2 (1935), pp. 161-171.

14,586 POUSSIN, J. DE LA V. Notes stratigraphiques à propos des conches relevées dans le massif du Ruwenzori (Graben central africain). BULL. SEANCES IRCB 4 (1933), pp. 768-775.

14,587 POWELL-COTTON, P. H. G. Notes on a journey through the great Ituri forest. J. AFR. SOC. 7 (1907), pp. 1-12.

14,588 ROBERT, M. Bibliographie de Jules Cornet relative au Bassin du Congo. BULL. SEANCES IRCB 2 (1931), pp. 31-36.

14,589 ROBERT, M. Considérations au sujet des fascicules 1 et 2 de l'<u>Atlas du Katanga</u>, publié par le Comité Special du Katanga. BULL. SEANCES IRCB 2 (1931), pp. 358-363.

14,590 SCHEBESTA, P. Meine Forschungsreise in Belgisch-Kongo, 1929-1930. AFRICA 4 (1931), pp. 401-416.

14,591 SCHWETZ. Un voyage d'études au Lomami. CONGO 2 (1921), pp. 194-225.

14,592 STETSON, G. R. The Congo State: its people and products. LIBERIA BULL. 8 (1896), pp. 14-23.

14,593 STORME, M. Le problème de la rivière Kasayi. Etude de géographie historique. ZAIRE 11 (1957), pp. 227-262.

14,594 STRUYF, I. De verhuizingen bij de Kamtsha. CONGO 2 (1936), pp. 343-350.

14,595 VANDEPLAS, A. Les chutes Zrinski. ZAIRE 9 (1955), pp. 411-414.

14,596 VANDERYST, H. Le mystérieux lac Akakalunda. BULL. SEANCES IRCB 2 (1931), pp. 615-623.

14,597 VANDERYST, H. Nouvelle contribution à l'étude de la région littorale du Congo belge. BULL. SEANCES IRCB 4 (1933), pp. 815-851.

14,598 VANSINA, I. Taalgeografische toestand in het Kuba-gebied. AEQUATORIA 21 (1958), pp. 1-4.

14,599 VITTA, G. Kinshasa. CONGO 2 (1921), p. 161.

14,600 WHITAKER, P. and SILVEY, J. A visit to Congo, Rwanda and Burundi. MAKERERE J. 9 (1964), pp. 71-82.

14,601 Mission scientifique au Congo [Départ pour 12 à 14 mois, janvier 1952]. ZAIRE 6 (1952), p. 194.

See also 18065.

Government

14,602 ACHTEN, L. De la colonisation européenne au Congo. CONGO 1 (1935), pp. 358-365.

14,603 ANET, H. The Congo native and Belgian administration. INT. REV. MISSIONS 10 (1921), pp. 196-206.

14,604 BAILLEUL, H. Les Bayaka. Apercu de l'évolution politique et économique de leur pays jusqu'en 1958. ZAIRE 13 (1959), pp. 823-841.

14,605 BALLEGEER, L. Les principes de la politique coloniale belge. KONGO-OVERZEE 15 (1949), pp. 195-199.

14,606 BEAUNE, R. J. DE. La Constitution provinciale du Kwilu du 26 avril 1963. ET. CONG. 7, no. 6 (1964), pp. 1-26.

14,607 BECKERS, H. Le Fonds du Bien-Etre indigène. ZAIRE 5 (1951), pp. 787-812.

14,608 BELGIUM. MINISTRY OF COLONIES. The organisation of native administration in the Belgian Congo. J. AFR. ADM. 8 (1956), pp. 88-95.

14,609 BEMBE, L. Elections au Congo Belge. PRESENCE AFR. N.S. 17 (1957-1958), pp. 115-117.

14,610 BERTIEAUX, R. Belgian Congo. CIVILISATIONS 5 (1955), pp. 281-284; 6 (1956), pp. 473-482; 7 (1957), pp. 400-408; 8 (1958), pp. 446-454; 9 (1959), pp. 385-390.

14,611 BERTRAND, A. De la nécessité d'une documentation scientifique ou statistique, préalable à toute mesure intéressant les indigènes [with note by A. Engels]. BULL. SEANCES IRCB 4 (1933), pp. 44-59, 89-95.

14,612 BEZY, F. Belgian Congo 1951-52. CIVILISATIONS 3 (1953), pp. 293-297.

14,613 BILSEN, A. A. J. VAN. Some aspects of the Congo problem. INTERNAT. AFFAIRS 38 (1962), pp. 41-51.

14,614 BILSEN, J. VAN. Chronique congolaise—Congolees tijdspiegel. ZAIRE 3 (1949), pp. 925-931.

14,615 BILSEN, J. VAN. Congolees Tijdspiegel. ZAIRE 3 (1949), pp. 1123-1126.

14,616 BILSEN, J. VAN. [Het officiële tegenbezoek van de gouverneur generaal van Angola aan Kongo in September 1949]. ZAIRE 4 (1950), p. 1111.

14,617 BILSEN, J. VAN. Incidenten en clandestiene goudexploitatie. ZAIRE 4 (1950), p. 873.

14,618 BILSEN, J. VAN. Koloniale politiek. ZAIRE 4 (1950), pp. 878-881.

14,619 BRAUSCH, G. Political changes in the Upper Lukenyi area of the Congo. AFR. STUD. 3 (1944), pp. 65-74.

14,620 BOELAERT, E. Volk en Staat in Kongo. KONGO-OVERZEE 5 (1939), pp. 120-126.

14,621 CARPENTER, G. W. Whose Congo? INT. REV. MISSIONS 50 (1961), pp. 271-285.

14,622 CHARLES, V. Afrique Belge. CIVILISATIONS 3 (1953), pp. 399-403.

14,623 CHARLES, V. Autour de la crise de main-d'oeuvre. ZAIRE 5 (1951), pp. 959-960.

14,624 CHARLES, V. Autour du Conseil de Gouvernement. ZAIRE 6 (1952), pp. 1077-1079.

14,625 CHARLES, V. Le Conseil de Gouvernement. ZAIRE 4 (1950), pp. 1133-1134.

14,626 CHARLES, V. Deuxième trimestre 1950. ZAIRE 4 (1950), p. 883.

14,627 CHARLES, V. Note de politique sociale. Le salariat indigène et le dernier Conseil de Gouvernement. ZAIRE 2 (1948), pp. 1135-1139.

14,628 CHARLES, V. La politique sociale congolaise pendant le premier trimestre 1949. ZAIRE 3 (1949), pp. 663-672, 901-908, 1127-1137; 4 (1950), pp. 307-317, 539-551.

14,629 CHARLES V. La politique sociale congolaise pendant le second semestre 1948. ZAIRE 3 (1949), pp. 285-292.

14,630 CHARLES, V. Le rapport aux Chambres de 1949. ZAIRE 5 (1951), pp. 619-620.

14,631 CHARLES, V. Troisième trimestre 1950. ZAIRE 4 (1950), p. 1127.

14,632 CLEENE, N. DE. Volkenkunde en Koloniale Staatkunde. CONGO 1 (1934), pp. 672-678.

14,633 COMITE PERMANENT DU CONGRES COLONIAL NATIONAL. L'interpénétration des carrières coloniales et métropolitaines. CONGO 1 (1939), pp. 241-275.

14,634 COPPENS, P. Le Congrès Colonial National. ZAIRE 1 (1947), pp. 555-566.

14,635 COUSSEE, P. Au service des troupes congolaises. ZAIRE 1 (1947), pp. 911-916.

14,636 CRABBE, J. Indépendance et salaires au Congo. AFRICA (Rome) 15 (1960), pp. 146-148.

14,637 CRABBE, J. L'opinion belge et le Congo. ET. CONG. 6, no. 5 (1964), pp. 91-97.

14,638 D., N. Carte du mérite civique. AEQUATORIA 11 (1948), pp. 103-105.

14,639 DABIN, P. L'idée fédérale dans le processus constitutionnel congolais. ET. CONG. 6, no. 4 (1964), pp. 37-60.

14,640 DABIN, P. Vers un présidentialisme d'inspiration africaine. ET. CONG. 6, no. 3 (1964), pp. 45-53.

14,641 DUMONT, A. Le gouvernement du Congo Belge et les institutions indigènes. AFRICA 14 (1943), pp. 78-90; English summary, pp. 88-89.

14,642 DUPRIEZ, L. Quelques considérations sur le rôle et l'activité du Conseil colonial. BULL. SEANCES IRCB 3 (1932), pp. 525-544.

14,643 DURIEUX, A. Le Conseil d'Etat et le Congo Belge. ZAIRE 1 (1947), pp. 665-677.

14,644 DURIEUX, A. La réorganisation du Ministère des Colonies. ZAIRE 1 (1947), pp. 271-279.

14,645 FAWCETT, D. Western evolution and Africa. KONGO-OVERZEE 20 (1954), pp. 159-164.

14,646 FELE, B. Le manifeste de "Conscience africaine." PRESENCE AFR. N.S. 11 (1957), pp. 146-147.

14,647 GELDERS, V. Le respect des institutions indigènes et la famille noire en Afrique. KONGO-OVERZEE 12-13 (1946-1947), pp. 11-23.

14,648 GERARD-LIBOIS, J. L'avant-projet de Constitution pour la République du Congo. ET. CONG. 3, no. 10 (1962), pp. 1-27.

14,649 GERARD-LIBOIS, J. Les structures du Congo et le Plan Thant. ET. CONG. 3, no. 8 (1962), pp. 1-16.

14,650 GHENEA, R. El Congo en el mundo actual. ARCH. INST. EST. AFR. 17, no. 67 (1963), pp. 15-29.

14,651 GLICKMAN, H. The roots of crisis in the Congo. NEW FORCES IN AFRICA, 1962, pp. 67-87.

14,652 CLINNE, E. Le pourquoi de l'affaire katangaise. PRECENCE AFR. N.S. 32-33 (1960), pp. 49-63.

14,653 GOETHEM, F. VAN. Kongo zoals het is en zoals het uit de U.N.O. wordt gezien. KONGO-OVERZEE 20 (1954), pp. 165-180.

14,654 GRAY, A. Congo development. AFR. AFFAIRS 62 (1963), pp. 8-15.

14,655 GRAY, A. Congo jubilee. AFR. AFFAIRS 57 (1958), pp. 263-264.

14,656 GRAY, A. Congo troubles. AFR. AFFAIRS 59 (1960), p. 281.

14,657 GRAY, A. Congo unrest. AFR. AFFAIRS 58 (1959), pp. 99-102.

14,658 GRAY, A. Katanga and the Congo. AFR. AFFAIRS 61 (1962), pp. 14-15.

14,659 GROOTAERT, J. Le canevas de l'organisation coutumière, administrative et judiciaire. KONGO-OVERZEE 19 (1953), pp. 392-412.

14,660 HASTINGS, S. The United Nations in Katanga. AFR. AFFAIRS 61 (1962), pp. 191-200.

14,661 HOFFMANS, J. La structure institutionnelle de la colonisation. ZAIRE 1 (1947), pp. 159-179.

14,662 HULSTAERT, G. Discours du Gouverneur Général. AEQUATORIA 14 (1951), pp. 95-102; 15 (1952), pp. 101-104.

14,663 HULSTAERT, G. Discours du Gouverneur Général 1955. AEQUATORIA 18 (1955), pp. 134-138.

14,664 ILUNGA, A. R. et al. Le projet de Constitution de Luluabourg. ET. CONG. 6, no. 5 (1964), pp. 1-26.

14,665 JADOT, J. M. Belgian Congo. CIVILISATIONS 2 (1952), pp. 611-616.

14,666 JADOT, J. M. Belgian Congo (January 1952-July 1953). CIVILISATIONS 3 (1953), pp. 599-604.

14,667 JADOT, J. M. The Belgian Congo (October 1954-December 1955). CIVILISATIONS 5 (1955), pp. 617-622.

14,668 JADOT, J. M. Belgian Congo 1956. CIVILISATIONS 7 (1957), pp. 123-128; 8 (1958), pp. 137-143; 9 (1959), pp. 90-98.

14,669 JESMAN, C. Background to events in the Congo. AFR. AFFAIRS 60 (1961), pp. 382-391.

14,670 KALANDA, A. Quelques réflexions à propos de la declaration gouvernementale sur le Congo. PRESENCE AFR. N.S. 26 (1959), pp. 102-113.

14,671 KERKEN, G. VAN DER. Belgian Congo and Ruanda-Urundi. CIVILISATIONS 3 (1953), pp. 139-145.

14,672 KERKEN, G. VAN DER. La structure des sociétés indigènes et quelques problèmes de politique indigène [with notes by Jonghe, E. de; A. Bertrand]. BULL. SEANCES IRCB 3 (1932), pp. 291-333.

14,673 KILOLO, B. Les partis politiques dans l'ancienne province du Katanga. ET. CONG. 8, no. 2 (1965), pp. 125-135.

14,674 L., J. G. L'affaire Katangaise: de Kitona à Léopoldville. ET. CONG. 2, no. 4 (1962), pp. 23-29.

14,675 L., J. G. Le Plan Thant pour la réintégration du Katanga. ET. CONG. 4, no. 1 (1963), pp. 12-17.

14,676 LEGUM, C. The Belgian Congo: towards independence. AFR. SOUTH 4, no. 4 (1960), pp. 78-91.

14,677 LEGUM, C. The Congo: after independence. AFR. SOUTH 5, no. 1 (1960), pp. 77-87.

14,678 LEMARCHAND, R. The bases of nationalism among the Bakongo. AFRICA 31 (1961), pp. 344-354.

14,679 LOUWERS, M. L'annuaire de documentation coloniale comparée. BULL. SEANCES IRCB 1 (1930), pp. 59-71.

14,680 LOVENS, M. Les élections communales du 31 janvier 1965 à Léopoldville. ET. CONG. 8, no. 2 (1965), pp. 1-118.

14,681 LUMUMBA, P. et al. Lettre du Congo belge, au Ministre des Colonies. PRESENCE AFR. N.S. 20 (1958), pp. 138-139.

14,682 LUTHERA, V. P. The Congo and sub-Saharan colonial Africa. AFR. QUART. 2, no. ii (1962), pp. 107-117.

14,683 M., L. and L., J. G. La province du Kwilu. ET. CONG. 4, no. 1 (1963), pp. 37-42.

14,684 MALENGREAU, G. De l'accession des indigènes à la propriété foncière individuelle du Code civil. ZAIRE 1 (1947), pp. 235-270, 399-433.

14,685 MALENGREAU, G. Le discours du Gouverneur général Pétillon. ZAIRE 6 (1952), pp. 970-971.

14,686 MALENGREAU, G. Le malaise de la Territoriale. ZAIRE 7 (1953), pp. 616-621.

14,687 MALENGREAU, G. Political evolution in the Belgian Congo. J. AFR. ADM. 6 (1954), pp. 160-166.

14,688 MARZORATI, A. F. G. The political organization and the evolution of African society in the Belgian Congo. AFR. AFFAIRS 53 (1954), pp. 104-112.

14,689 MARZORATI, A. and GELDERS, V. La colonisation nationale du Congo belge. CONGO 2 (1936), pp. 198-209.

14,690 MOELLER, A. La politique indigène de la Belgique au Congo. J. AFR. SOC. 35 (1936), pp. 233-240.

14,691 MOREL, E. D. The "commercial" aspect of the Congo question. J. AFR. SOC. 3 (1904), pp. 430-448.

14,692 MOULAERT, G. Colonisation européenne au Congo. CONGO 2 (1939), pp. 361-375.

14,693 NICAISE, J. The Belgian Congo and Ruanda Urundi. CIVILISATIONS 3 (1953), pp. 391-397.

14,694 NICAISE, J. Belgian Congo and Ruanda-Urundi 1955-56. CIVILISATIONS 6 (1956), pp. 663-669; 7 (1957), pp. 607-615.

14,695 NICAISE, J. Ephémérides. ZAIRE 8 (1954), pp. 191-192.

14,696 O'DONOVAN, P. The precedent of the Congo. INTERNAT. AFFAIRS 37 (1961), pp. 181-188.

14,697 P., C. La commission constitutionnelle à Luluabourg. ET. CONG. 6, no. 1 (1964), pp. 22-30.

14,698 PERIN, F. La crise congolaise et les institutions politiques africaines. CIVILISATIONS 11 (1961), pp. 281-292; English summary, pp. 293-295.

14,699 POST, K. W. J. Nigerian pamphleteers and the Congo. JMAS 2 (1964), pp. 405-418.

14,700 PETILLON [Governor General of Belgian Congo]. New institutions of Local Government in the Belgian Congo. J. AFR. ADM. 9 (1957), pp. 79-84.

14,701 PRADHAN, R. C. Freedom movement in the Congo (Leopoldville) (1956-1960). AFR. QUART. 4, no. ii (1964), pp. 68-83.

14,702 PRADHAN, R. C. OAU and the Congo crisis. AFR. QUART. 5, no. 1 (1965), pp. 30-42.

14,703 ROULEAU, E. The Congo compromise. AFR. SOUTH 6 (1961), pp. 57-63.

14,704 RUBBENS, A. Belgian Congo. CIVILISATIONS 6 (1956), pp. 282-286; 7 (1957), pp. 264-268; 8 (1958), pp. 335-340; 9 (1959), pp. 245-250.

14,705 RUBBENS, A. Belgian Congo 1953-54. CIVILISATIONS 5 (1955), pp. 130-136.

14,706 RUBBENS, A. De Kolonisatie in Kongo in het licht van de Wetteksten. CONGO 2 (1936), pp. 56-64.

14,707 RUBBENS, A. Political awakening in the Belgian Congo. CIVILISATIONS 10 (1960), pp. 63-76.

14,708 SALMON, J. Les attributions normatives du Président de la République. ET. CONG. 8, no. 4 (1965), pp. 36-52.

14,709 SARTRE, J. P. La pensée politique de Patrice Lumumba. PRESENCE AFR. N.S. 47 (1963), pp. 18-58.

14,710 SOUTHALL, A. W. Belgian and British administration in Alurland. ZAIRE 8 (1954), pp. 467-486.

14,711 SPEYER, H. La revision de la Charte coloniale. BULL. SEANCES IRCB 2 (1931), pp. 73-90.

14,712 SWANZY, H. The Belgian Congo. AFR. AFFAIRS 46 (1947), pp. 3-4.

14,713 TAKIZALA, M. Le Cercle Culturel National face à la situation politique actuelle du pays. ET. CONG. 7, no. 7 (1964), pp. 79-83.

14,714 UGEUX, W. A propos de deux Tables Rondes. CIVILISATIONS 10 (1960), pp. 327-337.

14,715 V., B. La Cuvette Centrale. ET. CONG. 4, no. 1 (1963), pp. 33-37.

14,716 V., B. and M., L. La Province du Kongo Central. ET. CONG. 4, no. 1 (1963), pp. 18-32.

14,717 VANDERVELDE, E. Belgian and British interests in Africa. J. AFR. SOC. 14 (1914-1915), pp. 266-270.

14,718 VERHAEGEN, B. Autour d'une décolonisation. PRESENCE AFR. N.S. 23 (1958-1959), pp. 97-106.

14,719 VERHAEGEN, B. Le dossier concernant M. Gizenga. ET. CONG. 2, no. 2 (1962), pp. 35-43.

14,720 VERHAEGEN, B. Le Parlement à Lovanium. ET. CONG. 2, no. 1 (1962), pp. 1-24.

14,721 VERMEULEN, V. Au tournant de la politique coloniale. ZAIRE 5 (1951), pp. 503-511.

14,722 VIAENE, R. P. L. L'organisation politique des Bahunde. KONGO-OVERZEE 18 (1952), pp. 8-34, 111-121.

14,723 W., J. C. L'évolution des partis politiques au Congo. ET. CONG. 5, no. 10 (1963), pp. 37-43.

14,724 WALLIS, C. A. G. The administration of towns in the Belgian Congo. J. AFR. ADM. 10 (1958), pp. 95-100.

14,725 WHITAKER, P. The problem of public accountability in colonial administration and Belgian approach. MAKERERE J. 4 (1960), pp. 46-58.

14,726 WHITAKER, P. Some aspects of the administration of the Belgian Congo. EAISR Jan. (1959), pp. 1-23.

14,727 WIGNY, P. Belgium and the Congo. INTERNAT. AFFAIRS 37 (1961), pp. 273-284.

14,728 WIGNY, P. Hoe doet zich het Probleem Kongo in 1948 voor? KONGO-OVERZEE 14 (1948), pp. 120-123.

14,729 WIGNY, P. Methods of government in the Belgian Congo. AFR. AFFAIRS 50 (1951), pp. 310-317.

14,730 WIGNY, P. The political future of the Belgian Congo. CORONA 3 (1951), pp. 458-460.

14,731 WISTE, M. La politique indigène au Congo Belge et l'exemple du Portugal. ZAIRE 4 (1950), pp. 651-658.

14,732 Burundi: détermination des relations entre le Royaume du Burundi et la République du Congo-Léo. ET. CONG. 7, no. 7 (1964), pp. 75-77.

14,733 Le Congo au Conseil de Sécurité. PRESENCE AFR. N.S. 39 (1961), pp. 207-213.

14,734 Congo belge [la table ronde belgo-congolaise a décidé, le 27 janvier dernier, que le 30 juin 1960 le Congo passerait sans transition du statut colonial au statut de pleine souveraineté]. PRESENCE AFR. N.S. 30 (1960), pp. 97-100.

14,735 Le Congo et l'O.N.U. PRESENCE AFR. N.S. 34-35 (1960-1961), pp. 211-214.

14,736 The Congo state and the Domaine Privé. J. AFR. SOC. 1 (1902), pp. 355-357.

14,737 Conseil de Gouvernement 1947. Un important discours du Vice-gouverneur général Pétillon. ZAIRE 2 (1948), pp. 65-76.

14,738 Constitution de la République du Congo du 1er août 1964. ET. CONG. 7, no. 10 (1964), pp. 1-55.

14,739 Le discours du Gouverneur Général. AEQUATORIA 20 (1957), pp. 90-95; 22 (1959), p. 105.

14,740 Le dossier de la sécession Katangaise. ET. CONG. 6, no. 1 (1964), pp. 1-21.

14,741 Les institutions politiques et administratives du Congo Belge. ZAIRE 3 (1949), pp. 565-568.

14,742 Katanga 1960. La proclamation de l'indépendance du Katanga. ET. CONG. 1, no. 1 (1961), pp. 32-57.

14,743 Lumumba, deux fois assassiné. PRESENCE AFR. N.S. 51 (1964), pp. 173-174.

14,744 Les nouvelles provinces. ET. CONG. 3, no. 8 (1962), pp. 26-36.

14,745 Les regroupements politiques au Congo au 30 juin 1964. ET. CONG. 7, no. 7 (1964), pp. 1-71.

See also 15610.

History

14,746 AZEVEDO, F. A. DE. Os Portugueses têem direitos históricos no Zaire. PORT. EM AFR. 2 (1945), pp. 77-81.

14,747 BAL, W. Le royaume du Congo aux XVe et XVIe siècles. PRESENCE AFR. N.S. 45 (1963), pp. 82-97.

14,748 BALLEGEER, L. Pour une histoire du Congo. KONGO-OVERZEE 15 (1949), pp. 119-121.

14,749 BARBER, F. Return to the Congo. AFR. SOUTH 5, no. 1 (1960), pp. 89-95.

14,750 BIRMINGHAM, D. The date and significance of the Imbaangala invasion of Angola. J. AFR. HIST. 6 (1965), pp. 143-152.

14,751 BIRMINGHAM, D. Speculations on the kingdom of Kongo. TR. HIST. SOC. GHANA 8 (1965), pp. 1-10.

14,752 BITTREMIEUX, L. Brief van Musiri (Geschiedenis van een Negerkoning uit Katanga) door Zijn zoon en opvolger Mukandabantu. (Met het relaas der groote daden van den Schrijver.) Uit het Kisanga vertaald. KONGO-OVERZEE 3 (1936-1937), pp. 69-83, 252-291.

14,753 BITTREMIEUX, L. De Goden van Kakongo en Ngoyo. KONGO-OVERZEE 12-13 (1946-1947), pp. 1-10.

14,754 BITTREMIEUX, L. De inwijking der Baphende's. CONGO 1 (1938), pp. 154-167.

14,755 BITTREMIEUX, L. Inwijking der Mbamba's volgens Hoofd Cajetanus Mbamba Kalunga. KONGO-OVERZEE 1 (1934), pp. 145-150.

14,756 BITTREMIEUX, L. Nog over den Brief van Musiri, door Mukanda-Bantu. Een terechtwijzing. KONGO-OVERZEE 4 (1938), pp. 17-18.

14,757 BOELAERT, E. Les Arabes à l'Equateur? AEQUATORIA 20 (1957), pp. 10-18.

14,758 BOOVEN, H. VAN. Over het ontstaan van "Tropenwee." ZAIRE 6 (1952), pp. 1069-1076.

14,759 BRASIO, A. O Brazão de Armas do Rei do Congo. PORT. EM AFR. 4 (1947), pp. 100-106.

14,760 BRASIO, A. O Congo e o Concílio Tridentino. PORT. EM AFR. 3 (1946), pp. 39-52.

14,761 BRASIO, A. Uma embaixada colonizadora ao Congo no Século XVI. PORT. EM AFR. 7 (1950), pp. 37-46.

14,762 BRASIO, A. Embaixada do Congo ao Vaticano em 1513? PORT. EM AFR. 10 (1953), pp. 386-389.

14,763 BRASIO, A. A Primeira Embaixada do Congo ao Vaticano. PORT. EM AFR. 4 (1947), pp. 170-176.

14,764 BRASIO, A. Quarto centenário da Se do Congo. PORT. EM AFR. 5 (1948), pp. 91-99.

14,765 BRASIO, A. Um Regimento Missionário do Século XVI. PORT. EM AFR. 7 (1950), pp. 171-183.

14,766 BRASIO, A. Tricentenário da "Missão" do Congo. PORT. EM AFR. 2 (1945), pp. 166-175.

14,767 BROSSEL, C. Les British documents on the origins of the war et le Congo belge. CONGO 1 (1940), pp. 9-46.

14,768 BULCK, G. VAN. L'ancien Congo d'après les archives romaines. ZAIRE 9 (1955), pp. 529-537.

14,769 BURSSENS, A. De beschryvinghe vant groot ende vermaert Coninckrijck van Congo (1596). KONGO-OVERZEE 7-8 (1941-1942), pp. 1-86, 113-203.

14,770 BURSSENS, A. De oudste Nederlandsche Teksten over het Oude Koninkrijk Kongo. KONGO-OVERZEE 1 (1934), pp. 3-15, 137-144, 193-204.

14,771 CAMPOS, E. DE. Monografia de Cabinda. PORT. EM AFR. 17 (1960), pp. 30-37, 91-96.

14,772 CEULEMANS, P. Les idées du Général Lahure sur l'oeuvre civilisatrice de la Belgique en Afrique (1880) et l'opinion anglaise. ZAIRE 13 (1959), pp. 813-822.

14,773 CEULEMANS, P. Les tentatives de Léopold II pour engager le Colonel Charles Gordon au service de l'Association internationale africaine (1880). ZAIRE 12 (1958), pp. 251-274.

14,774 COLLINS, O. R. Anglo-Congolese negociations 1900-1906. ZAIRE 12 (1958), pp. 479-512, 619-652.

14,775 COMHAIRE, J. Evolution politique et sociale du Congo belge en 1949-1951. ZAIRE 5 (1951), pp. 941-949.

14,776 COMHAIRE, J. Evolution politique et sociale du Congo belge en 1950-1952. ZAIRE 6 (1952), pp. 1041-1050.

14,777 COMHAIRE, J. Evolution politique et sociale du Congo Belge en 1951-1953. ZAIRE 8 (1954), pp. 45-53.

14,778 COMHAIRE, J. Evolution politique et sociale du Congo Belge en 1952-1954. ZAIRE 8 (1954), pp. 921-927.

14,779 COOKEY, S. J. S. West African immigrants in the Congo. J. HIST. SOC. NIG. 3 (1965), pp. 261-270.

14,780 CORNEVIN, R. Chronique de l'histoire coloniale: le Congo ex-belge. REV. FRANC. HIST. OUTRE-MER 49 (1962), pp. 262-279.

14,781 CUVELIER, J. Overzicht van de geschiedenis van het Oud-Koninkrijk Kongo. KONGO-OVERZEE 16 (1950), pp. 1-16.

14,782 DENNETT, R. E. The court of the slave Mamboma. J. AFR. SOC. 3 (1904), pp. 159-162.

14,783 DENNETT, R. E. A few notes on the history of Luango (northern portion of Congo coast). J. AFR. SOC. 3 (1904), pp. 277-280.

14,784 DENNETT, R. E. King Maluango's court. J. AFR. SOC. 3 (1904), pp. 154-158.

14,785 DESCAMPE, E. Note sur les Bayanzi. CONGO 1 (1935), pp. 685-688.

14,786 DIJKMAN, B. Korte geschiednis van de bevolking der bestuursgebieden van Bondo en Ango. KONGO-OVERZEE 19 (1953), pp. 182-233, 434-452.

14,787 ERMENS, P. L'effort de guerre de la force publique du Congo Belge. Situation militaire de la colonie en mai 1940. ZAIRE 1 (1947), pp. 7-34.

14,788 FOX, R. C. et al. La deuxième indépendance. Etude d'un cas: La rébellion au Kwilu, by R. C. Fox, W. de Craemer, J.-M. Ribeaucourt. ET. CONG. 8, no. 1 (1965), pp. 1-35.

14,789 FOX, R. C. et al. "The second independence": a case study of the Kwilu rebellion in the Congo, by Renée C. Fox, Willy de Craemer and Jean-Marie Ribeaucourt. COMP. STUD. SOC. HIST. 8 (1965-1966), pp. 78-109.

14,790 FREDERIC, B. Essai historique sur les Lusankani. AEQUATORIA 23 (1960), pp. 100-111.

14,791 GANN, L. The end of the slave trade in British Central Africa: 1889-1912. RHODES-LIV. J. 17 (1954), pp. 27-51.

14,792 GERARD-LIBOS, J. Comment le Congo a accédé à l'indépendance. CIVILISATIONS 10 (1960), pp. 338-342.

14,793 HARRIS, J. H. The zone of peace in Africa. CONTEMP. REV. 108 (1915), pp. 190-194.

14,794 HEIJBOER, B. M. Esquisse d'histoire des migrations Ngombe depuis le début du XVIIIme siècle. AEQUATORIA 10 (1947), pp. 63-68.

14,795 HEYSE, T. Les visées allemandes sur les colonies portugaises et le Congo belge, d'après les documents diplomatiques français. BULL. SEANCES IRCB 6 (1935), pp. 613-634.

14,796 HILDEBRAND, P. Les droits historiques du Portugal sur le Congo. CONGO 1 (1938), pp. 23-54.

14,797 HILDEBRAND, P. Oude Plaatsnamen in Kongo in verband met Jon's van Geel. KONGO-OVERZEE 4 (1938), pp. 105-126.

14,798 HILDEBRAND, P. De zoogezegde Kongoreis van den Gentenaar Farde' in 1688. KONGO-OVERZEE 6 (1940), pp. 135-147.

14,799 HOSKYNS, C. Sources for a study of the Congo since independence. JMAS 1 (1963), pp. 373-382.

14,800 HOSKYNS, C. Violence in the Congo. TRANSITION 21 (1965), pp. 47-50.

14,801 IHLE, A. Das alte Königreich Kongo. AFRIKA (Berlin) 3 (1944), pp. 49-72.

14,802 ISEKOLONGO, M. Note historique sur les Nsamba. AEQUATORIA 23 (1960), p. 57.

14,803 JACOBS, J. Les épopées de Soundjata et de Chaka. Une étude comparée. AEQUATORIA 25 (1962), pp. 121-124.

14,804 JADIN, L. Essais d'évangélisation du Loango et du Kakongo 1766-1775. ZAIRE 7 (1953), pp. 1053-1065.

14,805 JANSSEN, F. Le commerce extérieur du Congo belge pedant l'année 1919. CONGO 2 (1921), pp. 36-50.

14,806 JAUGEON, R. Les sociétés d'exploitation au Congo et l'opinion française de 1890 a 1906. REV. FRANC. HIST. OUTRE-MER 48 (1961), pp. 353-437.

14,807 LAVELEYE, E. DE. The Congo neutralized. CONTEMP. REV. 43 (1883), pp. 767-782.

14,808 LEGUM, C. The Belgian Congo: revolt of the elite. AFR. SOUTH 4, no. 1 (1959), pp. 104-113.

14,809 LEONARD, H. Qui a le premier révélé l'existence de l'or à Kilo? CONGO 1 (1939), pp. 125-152.

14,810 LIPPINS, Count. The Belgian Congo. J. AFR. SOC. 38 (1939), pp. 419-426.

14,811 LOTAR, L. Souvenirs de l'Uélé. CONGO 1 (1934), pp. 1-2; 1 (1935), pp. 641-667; 2 (1935), pp. 665-684; 1 (1938), pp. 361-404; 2 (1938), pp. 7-58, 121-178; 2 (1939), pp. 241-251.

14,812 LOTAR, P. Communication relative à l'expédition entreprise par Miani dans l'Uele en 1872. BULL. SEANCES IRCB 2 (1931), pp. 249-253.

14,813 LOUIS, W. R. The Anglo-Congolese agreement of 1894 and the Cairo corridor. ST. ANTONY'S PAPERS 15 (1963), pp. 81-100.

14,814 LOUIS, W. R. Great Britain and the Stokes case. UGANDA J. 28 (1964), pp. 135-149.

14,815 LOUIS, W. R. Roger Casement and the Congo. J. AFR. HIST. 5 (1964), pp. 99-120.

14,816 MAES, J. Le camp de Mashita Mbansa et les migrations des Bapende. CONGO 2 (1935), pp. 713-724.

14,817 MAEYENS, L. Den Babira geschiedenis. Hun zwerftocht. CONGO 1 (1938), pp. 145-153.

14,818 MARTINS, I. Monarquia do Ngoio. PORT. EM AFR. 13 (1956), pp. 197-210.

14,819 MAURICE, A. Leopold II, Stanley et les Etats-Unis. AFRICA (Rome) 12 (1957), pp. 135-136.

14,820 MAZERY, A. DES. Emeutes a Leopoldville. PRESENCE AFR. N.S. 23 (1958-1959), pp. 113-122.

14,821 MAZRUI, A. A. Edmund Burke and reflections on the revolution in the Congo. COMP. STUD. SOC. HIST. 5 (1962-1963), pp. 121-133.

14,822 MAZULA, A. J. História dos nianjas. PORT. EM AFR. 19 (1962), pp. 155-166, 235-247.

14,823 MENDIAUX, E. Pour une revision de la Charte coloniale. ZAIRE 11 (1957), pp. 1031-1051.

14,824 MESTRAL, C. DE. The Belgian Congo. AFR. SOUTH 1, no. 3 (1957), pp. 74-79.

14,825 MOREL, E. D. Belgium and the Congo. CONTEMP. REV. 93 (1908), pp. 48-54.

14,826 MOREL, E. D. The Belgian parliament and the Congo. CONTEMP. REV. 94 (1908), pp. 344-355.

14,827 MORTIER, R. Historische legenden. AEQUATORIA 7 (1944), pp. 101-111, 129-136.

14,828 MOULAERT, G. A propos de la découverte des mines d'or de Kilo-Moto. CONGO 2 (1939), pp. 121-133.

14,829 MOULAERT, G. A propos des mutineries au Congo Belge. ZAIRE 2 (1948), pp. 1139-1140.

14,830 MOULAERT, G. Note au sujet des mutineries au Congo belge. ZAIRE 2 (1948), pp. 657-662.

14,831 NAEMEN, L. VAN. Migration des Bayansi (Bayeye). CONGO 1 (1934), pp. 189-196.

14,832 O'BRIEN, C. C. The UN, Congo and Tshombe. TRANSITION 15 (1964), pp. 29-31.

14,833 OLIVEIRA, P. H. L. DE. Cabinda e o seu Baronato. PORT. EM AFR. 7 (1950), pp. 331-334.

14,834 OWOADE, A. The Congo situation—its historical background. AFR. HISTORIAN 1, no. iii (1965), pp. 30-33.

14,835 PAIAS, J. D. As Pedras de Ielala. BOL. INST. ANGOLA 12 (1959), pp. 47-52.

14,836 PERRAUDIN, J. Le Cardinal Lavigerie et Leopold II. ZAIRE 11 (1957), pp. 901-932; 12 (1958), pp. 37-64, 165-177, 275-291, 393-408.

14,837 PHILIPPE, R. Deux pages tragiques de l'histoire des Uele. AEQUATORIA 22, no. iii (1959), pp. 101-104.

14,838 RIVKIN, A. The Congo crisis in world affairs. CIVILISATIONS 10 (1960), pp. 473-479.

14,839 ROEYKENS, A. Le Baron Léon de Béthune et la politique religieuse de Leopold II en Afrique. ZAIRE 10 (1956), pp. 3-68, 227-281.

14,840 ROEYKENS, A. Les réunions préparatoires de la délégation belge à la Conférence Géographique de Bruxelles en 1876 [contribution a l'histoire des origines du Congo Belge]. ZAIRE 7 (1953), pp. 787-827.

14,841 ROEYKENS, P. A. Un précieux témoignage sur les débuts véridiques de l'oeuvre Africaine de Léopold II. AEQUATORIA 19 (1956), pp. 125-134.

14,842 ROOD, N. Une histoire racontée par les anciens. AEQUATORIA 25 (1962), pp. 20-21.

14,843 ROTBERG, R. I. Plymouth Brethren and the occupation of Katanga, 1886-1907. J. AFR. HIST. 5 (1964), pp. 285-297.

14,844 SAMUEL, H. The Congo State and the commission of inquiry. CONTEMP. REV. 88 (1905), pp. 872-883.

14,845 SHEPPERSON, G. Scotland and early Katanga. MAKERERE J. 10 (1964), pp. 23-27.

14,846 SIEGEL, M. Shamba Bolongongo: African king of peace. AFR. SOUTH 2, no. 3 (1958), pp. 100-106.

14,847 SLADE, R. King Leopold II and the attitude of English and American Catholics towards the anti-Congolese campaign. ZAIRE 11 (1957), pp. 593-612.

14,848 SLUYS, M. La première exploration scientifique au Congo. L'expédition du capitaine J. K. Tuckey, en 1816. CONGO 2 (1936), pp. 649-662.

14,849 SOORS, M. Les poussées Soudanaises ont-elles traversé les régions Kundu? ZAIRE 3 (1949), pp. 59-60.

14,850 SPENDER, H. The great Congo iniquity. CONTEMP. REV. 90 (1906), pp. 43-55.

14,851 STENGERS, J. Quelques observations sur la correspondance de Stanley. ZAIRE 9 (1955), pp. 899-926.

14,852 STORME, M. B. L'Abbé Forget (1852-1933) et le Séminaire Africain de Louvain. ZAIRE 6 (1952), pp. 785-808.

14,853 STORME, M. B. Léopold II, les Missions du Congo et la fondation du Seminaire Africain de Louvain. ZAIRE 6 (1952), pp. 3-24.

14,854 TANGHE, B. Région de la Haute Ebola. Notes d'histoire (1890-1900). AEQUATORIA 2 (1939), pp. 61-64.

14,855 THOMAS, M. E. Anglo-Belgian military relations and the Congo question, 1911-1913. J. MOD. HIST. 25 (1953), pp. 157-165.

14,856 THOMAS, N. W. Sir Harry Johnston on "George Grenfell and the Congo." J. AFR. SOC. 8 (1908), pp. 21-30.

14,857 TROESCHE, J. História Política do Maiombe. PORT. EM AFR. 10 (1953), pp. 18-25, 187-197.

14,858 TROESCHE, J. Le Royaume de Soyo. AEQUATORIA 25 (1962), pp. 95-100.

14,859 TSCHOFFEN, P. Albert 1er le Colonial. CONGO 1 (1934), pp. 161-164.

14,860 V., I. Ndo of Okebo. KONGO-OVERZEE 23 (1957), pp. 213-223.

14,861 VANDEPLAS, A. A propos des nouvelles recherches d'A. Roeykens sur la genèse et la nature du dessein africain de Léopold II. Notes marginales. ZAIRE 11 (1957), pp. 715-738.

14,862 VANDEPLAS, A. A propos d'un voyage de Léopold II en Allemagne. ZAIRE 10 (1956), pp. 379-385.

14,863 VANDEPLAS, A. L'envoi de canons Krupp au Congo en 1883. ZAIRE 9 (1955), pp. 43-47.

14,864 VANDERVELDE, E. Belgium and the reforms on the Congo. CONTEMP. REV. 96 (1909), pp. 652-659.

14,865 VANDEWALLE, F. A. Deuxième note au sujet des mutineries au Congo Belge. ZAIRE 2 (1948), pp. 903-907.

14,866 VANDEWALLE, F. A. Mutineries au Congo Belge. ZAIRE 1 (1947), pp. 487-514.

14,867 VANNINI, V. Encore des Souvenirs de l'Ubangi 1902-1904. CONGO 1 (1934), pp. 550-556.

14,868 VANSINA, J. La fondation du royaume de Kasanje. AEQUATORIA 25 (1962), pp. 45-62.

14,869 VANSINA, J. The foundation of the Kingdom of Kasanje. J. AFR. HIST. 4 (1963), pp. 355-374.

14,870 VANSINA, J. De handelingen der voorouders. Een handschrift waarin de genesis der Bieng verhaald wordt. KONGO-OVERZEE 22 (1956), pp. 257-300.

14,871 VANSINA, J. Long-distance trade-routes in Central Africa. J. AFR. HIST. 3 (1962), pp. 375-390.

14,872 VANSINA, J. Notes sur l'origine du royaume de Kongo. J. AFR. HIST. 4 (1963), pp. 33-38.

14,873 VANSINA, J. Recording the oral history of the Bakuba. J. AFR. HIST. 1 (1960), pp. 45-53, 257-270.

14,874 VERHAEGEN, B. Histoire des Tables Rondes du Congo indépendant. ET. CONG. 1, no. 2 (1961), pp. 1-14; 1, no. 4 (1961), pp. 1-12; 1, no. 5 (1961), pp. 33-39.

14,875 ZANDIJCKE, A. VAN. Note historique sur les origines de Luluabourg (Malandi). ZAIRE 6 (1952), pp. 227-249.

14,876 ZANDIJCKE, R. P. VAN. La révolte de Luluabourg (4 juillet 1895). ZAIRE 4 (1950), pp. 931-963, 1063-1082.

14,877 ZOUSMANOVITCH, A. Z. L'insurrection des Batetelas au Congo Belge au XIXe siècle. PRESENCE AFR. N.S. 51 (1964), pp. 159-169.

14,878 Belgium and the war [2nd. World War]. J. AFR. SOC. 41 (1942), pp. 215-217.

14,879 Communication au sujet de la publication des archives congolaises. BULL. SEANCES IRCB 1 (1930), pp. 56-58.

14,880 Congo ou le jeu de massacre. PRESENCE AFR. N.S. 44 (1962), pp. 222-224.

14,881 La crise des Nations Unies et la Congo. ET. CONG. 5, no. 6 (1963), pp. 1-28.

14,882 Les événements congolais. Chronologie des événements politiques depuis le 1er janvier 1961. ET. CONG. 1, no. 1 (1961), pp. 20-31; 1, no. 2 (1961), pp. 26-32; 1, no. 3 (1961), pp. 32-40; 1, no. 4 (1961), pp. 25-35; 1, no. 5 (1961), pp. 40-64; 2, no. 1 (1962), pp. 41-67; 2, no. 2 (1962), pp. 50-64; 2, no. 3 (1962), pp. 24-37; 2, no. 4 (1962), pp. 37-51; 2, no. 6 (1962), pp. 40-53; 3, no. 7 (1962), pp. 85-105; 3, no. 8 (1962), pp. 37-67; 3, no. 9 (1962), pp. 11-37; 4, no. 1 (1963), pp. 54-74; 4, no. 2 (1963), pp. 31-64; 4, no. 3 (1963), pp. 41-70; 4, no. 4 (1963), pp. 32-64; 4, no. 5 (1963), pp. 43-72; 5, no. 6 (1963), pp. 44-68; 4, no. 6 (1963), pp. 45-81; 5, no. 8 (1963), pp. 46-75; 5, no. 9 (1963), pp. 20-54; 5, no. 10 (1963), pp. 61-95; 6, no. 1 (1964), pp. 48-101; 6, no. 2 (1964), pp. 51-82; 6, no. 3 (1964), pp. 54-73; 6, no. 5 (1964), pp. 98-109; 7, no. 6 (1964), pp. 69-97; 7, no. 8 (1964), pp. 80-111; 7, no. 9 (1964), pp.63-92; 7, no. 10 (1964), pp. 56-94; 8, no. 1 (1965), pp. 62-101; 8, no. 3 (1965), pp. 65-98; 8, no. 4 (1965), pp. 92-115; 8, no. 5 (1965), pp. 71-107; 8, no. 6 (1965), pp. 108-133.

14,883 L'imbroglio Katangais. PRESENCE AFR. N.S. 39 (1961), pp. 218-225.

14,884 Le Katanga, le Congo et l'O.N.U. PRESENCE AFR. N.S. 45 (1963), pp. 230-232.

14,885 La protection des missions religieuses et les actes internationaux. CONGO 1 (1936), pp. 161-186.

See also 23549.

Language. Literature

Language

14,886 ADALBERT. De bijwoordelijke functie in het Tshiluba. AEQUATORIA 12 (1949), pp. 145-147; 13 (1950), pp. 25-27.

14,887 ADALBERT. Het polysynthetisch aspect van het Tshiluba. AEQUATORIA 15 (1952), pp. 93-95, 132-134; 16 (1953), pp. 73-75, 105-107, 139-141.

14,888 ADALBERT, B. Stamverdubbeling met bijwoordelijke functie in Tshiluba. AEQUATORIA 12 (1949), pp. 82-85.

14,889 AMBROSIUS, P. Inleiding tot de Chichoksche spraakleer. CONGO 1 (1935), pp. 366-374.

14,890 AVERMAET, E. VAN. Langage rythmé des Baluba. AEQUATORIA 18 (1955), pp. 1-5.

14,891 AVERMAET, G. VAN. Spraakkundige termen in het Lomongo. AEQUATORIA 5 (1942), pp. 21-25.

14,892 BEERST, G. DE. Essai de Grammaire Tabwa. ZAOS 2 (1896), pp. 271-287, 291-383.

14,893 BERVOETS, S. Enige spreekwoorden van bij de Zande. ZAIRE 6 (1952), pp. 719-732; 7 (1953), pp. 181-195; 8 (1954), pp. 1043-1065.

14,894 BIEBUYCK, D. and MEEUSSEN, A. E. Bembe-tekst. KONGO-OVERZEE 20 (1954), pp. 74-77.

14,895 BILSEN, J. VAN. Taalkunde en spelling. ZAIRE 4 (1950), pp. 1111-1112.

14,896 BITTREMIEUX, L. Het Kikongo. CONGO 2 (1937), pp. 427-432.

14,897 BITTREMIEUX, L. De Kongoleesche spraakkunde op nieuwe banen. CONGO 2 (1937), pp. 36-64.

14,898 BITTREMIEUX, L. Oude voornamen in Mayombe. AEQUATORIA 8 (1945), pp. 81-87.

14,899 BITTREMIEUX, L. De Weglating van het Prefix in het Kikongo. KONGO-OVERZEE 9 (1943), pp. 60-80.

14,900 BLOK, H. P. Iets over de zogenaamde "geïntsi-veerde" fonemen in het Ganda en Nyoro. KONGO-OVERZEE 17 (1951), pp. 193-220.

14,901 BOECK, L. B. DE. Un B vibrant dans le Bantou septentrional. AFR. STUD. 9 (1950), pp. 40-42.

14,902 BOECK, L. B. DE. Taaltoestand te Leopoldstad. KONGO-OVERZEE 19 (1953), pp. 1-7.

14,903 BOECK, E. DE. Twee taaleigenaardigheden bij de Mondunga. KONGO-OVERZEE 2 (1935-1936), pp. 282-284.

14,904 BOECK, J. DE. Spraakkunst van het Lokonda. AEQUATORIA 2 (1939), pp. 97-106.

14,905 BOECK, L. DE. Dialectgroepen in het ngiri-gebied. AEQUATORIA 12 (1949), pp. 89-94.

14,906 BOECK, L. B. DE. Eigenaardige toonstructuur van enkele Bantoetalen in het Noord-Westen van Belgisch-Kongo. KONGO-OVERZEE 16 (1950), pp. 37-53, 112-124, 212-223, 281-291.

14,907 BOECK, L. B. DE. Kantteekeningen bij de Grammatica van het Idzing. KONGO-OVERZEE 6 (1940), pp. 66-79.

14,908 BOECK, L. B. DE. Het lingala op de weegschaal! ZAIRE 6 (1952), pp. 115-153.

14,909 BOECK, L. B. DE. Ngombe-tekst uit Boso-kufe. AEQUATORIA 10 (1947), pp. 59-62.

14,910 BOECK, L. B. DE. Les préprefixes dans les langues bantoues du nord-ouest du Congo Belge. AFRICA 20 (1950), pp. 143-147; English summary, p. 147.

14,911 BOELAERT, E. Bij vergelijkende taalstudie III. AEQUATORIA 3 (1940), pp. 88-89.

14,912 BOELAERT, E. Naar een nationale inlandsche taal in Kongo? KONGO-OVERZEE 2 (1935-1936), pp. 240-248.

14,913 BOELAERT, E. Nsong'a Lianja. CONGO 1 (1934), pp. 49-70, 197-215.

14,914 BOELAERT, E. Persistance des tons en Lomongo. AEQUATORIA 24 (1961), pp. 11-15.

14,915 BOGAERTS, H. Onomasticon van 't l'Luntuvolk. CONGO 2 (1937), pp. 167-192.

14,916 BOURDONNEC, P. M. La langue sanga. AEQUATORIA 11 (1948), pp. 41-49.

14,917 BUFE, E. Material zur Erforschung der Bakundu-Sprache. AFR. UND UB. 5 (1914-1915), pp. 161-189.

14,918 BULCK, G. VAN. Cinq nouvelles classifications des langues bantoues. ZAIRE 2 (1948), pp. 969-987.

14,919 BULCK, G. VAN. De invloed van de Westersche cultuur op de gesproken woordkunst. KONGO-OVERZEE 2 (1935-1936), pp. 285-293; 3 (1936-1937), pp. 26-41.

14,920 BULCK, G. VAN. Verslag van de Ethnologische Afdeeling der Vlaamsche Wetenschappelijke Congressen. KONGO-OVERZEE 2 (1935-1936), pp. 294-302.

14,921 BULCK, G. VAN. Het oudste Kakongo-woordenboek (1768-1775) E. H. Jean-Joseph Descourvières (1743-1804). KONGO-OVERZEE 20 (1954), pp. 97-125.

14,922 BULCK, G. VAN. Het Probleem der Pygmeeëntaal volgens Schebesta. KONGO-OVERZEE 14 (1948), pp. 305-309.

14,923 BURSSENS, A. Etude tonologique des démonstratifs en Amashi. KONGO-OVERZEE 19 (1953), pp. 155-169.

14,924 BURSSENS, A. Kern en Affixen in het tshiLuba. KONGO-OVERZEE 5 (1939), pp. 113-119.

14,925 BURSSENS, A. Het Partikel-a in het tshiLuba (Toontaal). KONGO-OVERZEE 4 (1938), pp. 169-176.

14,926 BURSSENS, A. Het Probleem der Kongoleesche niet-Bantoetalen. KONGO-OVERZEE 1 (1934), pp. 31-41.

14,927 BURSSENS, A. Het Tshiluba en de phonologische Afrika-Spelling. KONGO-OVERZEE 3 (1936-1937), pp. 1-21.

14,928 BURSSENS, A. De klinkerphonemen in het 'Ngbandi. KONGO-OVERZEE 2 (1935-1936), pp. 257-270.

14,929 BURSSENS, A. Linguistisch Onderzoek in Centraal-Katanga. Het kíluvà als Toontaal. KONGO-OVERZEE 5 (1939), pp. 277-315.

14,930 BURSSENS, A. Les numéraux en Amashi (Kivu). KONGO-OVERZEE 18 (1952), pp. 66-76.

14,931 BURSSENS, A. Tonologisch Onderzoek van de copula di in het tshiLuba. KONGO-OVERZEE 4 (1938), pp. 275-285.

14,932 BURSSENS, A. Tonologisch onderzoek van de Possessief met nominale stam in het Amashi (Kivu). KONGO-OVERZEE 18 (1952), pp. 355-363.

14,933 BURSSENS, A. Tonologisch Onderzoek van de verbale -a 'ku-en-a' ka- vormen in het Tshiluba. KONGO-OVERZEE 6 (1940), pp. 162-166.

14,934 BURSSENS, A. Tonologisch Onderzoek van het Aanwijzend Woord in het tshiLuba. KONGO-OVERZEE 5 (1939), pp. 28-35.

14,935 BURSSENS, A. Tonologisch Onderzoek van het Luba. Het Hoofdtelwoord. KONGO-OVERZEE 4 (1938), pp. 25-38.

14,936 BURSSENS, A. Tonologisch Onderzoek van het Luba. Telwoorden en Telliederen bij de Baluba. KONGO-OVERZEE 4 (1938), pp. 41-48.

14,937 BURSSENS, A. Tonologisch Onderzoek van het Substitutieve Pronomen in het tshiLuba. KONGO-OVERZEE 5 (1939), pp. 49-57.

14,938 BURSSENS, A. Tonologische Tshiluba-Tekst. KONGO-OVERZEE 7-8 (1941-1942), pp. 100-107.

14,939 BURSSENS, A. Le Tshílúbà, langue à intonation. AFRICA 12 (1939), pp. 267-284.

14,940 BURSSENS, A. Vorm en tonen van de infinitief in het Amashi. KONGO-OVERZEE 16 (1950), pp. 228-233.

14,941 BURSSENS, A. and BULCK, G. VAN. Accent in de kongoleesche talen. KONGO-OVERZEE 3 (1936-1937), pp. 113-164, 177-208.

14,942 BURSSENS, A. and BULCK, G. VAN. De Africa-spelling en de Kongoleesche talen. KONGO-OVERZEE 2 (1935-1936), pp. 65-93.

14,943 BURTON, W. F. P. Kanya oral literature in Lubaland. AFR. STUD. 2 (1943), pp. 93-96.

14,944 CAENEGHEM, R. VAN. De bruidschat en de verloving in de spreekwoorden der Lulua- en Baluba-Menschen. CONGO 1 (1937), pp. 287-326, 384-424.

14,945 CAENEGHEM, R. VAN. De gierigheid in de spreekwoorden der Baluba en Baluba-Moyo. CONGO 2 (1935), pp. 376-388, 585-597, 725-736.

14,946 CAENEGHEM, R. VAN. De Kasala-zang der Bakwa-Tshimini. CONGO 1 (1937), pp. 103-133.

14,947 CAENEGHEM, R. VAN. De Kasalazang der Baluba. CONGO 1 (1936), pp. 680-705.

14,948 CAENEGHEM, R. VAN. De Kasala-zang van den Bakwanga-stam. CONGO 2 (1936), pp. 677-715.

14,949 CAENEGHEM, R. VAN. Regels van de toonabsorptie in het Tshiluba. KONGO-OVERZEE 19 (1953), pp. 97-115.

14,950 CARRINGTON, J. F. Esquisse de la langue Mba (Kimanga). KONGO-OVERZEE 15 (1949), pp. 90-107.

14,951 CARRINGTON, J. F. Notes on Dr. Sims's Yalulema vocabulary. AFR. STUD. 18 (1959), pp. 74-78.

14,952 CARRINGTON, J. F. Notes sur la langue Olombo (Turumbu). AEQUATORIA 10 (1947), pp. 102-113.

14,953 CARRINGTON, J. F. The tonal structure of Kele (Lokele). AFR. STUD. 2 (1943), pp. 193-209.

14,954 CARROCERA, P. B. DE. O primeiro dicionário conguês. PORT. EM AFR. 3 (1946), pp. 337-351.

14,955 CHADORO. Ein Brief des Mpokomo Chadoro au seine Freunde. ZAOS 2 (1896), pp. 85-87.

14,956 CHATELAIN, H. Die Begriffe und Wörter für Leben, Geist, Sede und Tod im Ki-mbundu. ZAOS 2 (1896), pp. 42-45.

14,957 CHATELAIN, H. Ueber Adverbialbildungen im Ki-mbundu. ZAOS 1 (1895), pp. 314-317.

14,958 CLEIRE, R. and BURSSENS, A. Noms de famille chez les Abashi (Kivu). KONGO-OVERZEE 16 (1950), pp. 125-127.

14,959 CLEIRE, R. Talen en taalunificatie in het Vicariaat Kivu. KONGO-OVERZEE 17 (1951), pp. 32-37.

14,960 CLERCQ, A. DE. Les langues communes au Congo Belge. CONGO 2 (1934), pp. 161-167.

14,961 CLERCQ, A. DE. Lubataal-Studie. KONGO-OVERZEE 1 (1934), pp. 75-92, 168-176, 219-227; 2 (1935-1936), pp. 14-24.

14,962 CLERCQ, A. and BURSSENS, A. Langage Luba. KONGO-OVERZEE 12-13 (1946-1947), pp. 204-215.

14,963 CLERCQ, L. DE. Le verbe Kikongo. CONGO 2 (1935), pp. 1-52.

14,964 COILLIE, G. VAN. Korte Mbagani-Spraakkunst, de Taal van de Babindji in Kasayi. KONGO-OVERZEE 14 (1948), pp. 257-279; 15 (1949), pp. 172-194.

14,965 COMHAIRE-SYLVAIN, S. Le Lingala des enfants noirs à Leopoldville. KONGO-OVERZEE 15 (1949), pp. 239-250.

14,966 COSTERMANS, J. B. Het termieten-stoken bij de Logo-Avokaya. AEQUATORIA 18 (1955), pp. 14-25, 50-55.

14,967 COUPEZ, A. Les phonèmes bantou G. et J. non precedes de nasale. ZAIRE 8 (1954), pp. 157-161.

14,968 COUPEZ, A. A propos du problème linguistique au Congo belge. ZAIRE 7 (1953), pp. 603-605.

14,969 DAELEMAN, I. Dag-en jaarverdeling bij de Bakoongo. AEQUATORIA 21 (1958), pp. 98-101.

14,970 DAELEMAN, J. Mfinu-teksten. KONGO-OVERZEE 24 (1958), pp. 225-238.

14,971 DAELEMAN, J. Verkorting en viermoren-wet in het Kikóongo. AEQUATORIA 22, no. iii (1959), pp. 93-96.

14,972 DAVIDSON, J. Les verbes defectifs dans la langue des Ngombe. AEQUATORIA 16 (1953), pp. 8-10.

14,973 DECAPMAKER, J. L'emploi du passif dans le langage des Bakongo. AEQUATORIA 17 (1954), pp. 28-30.

14,974 DECLERCQ, A. Esquisse de la langue Bakete. ZAOS 4 (1898), pp. 316-336.

14,975 DECLERCQ, A. Quelques notes sur la langue des Bena Lulua. ZAOS 5 (1900), pp. 16-19.

14,976 DECLERCQ, P. A. Vingt-deux contes Luba. AFR. UND UB. 4 (1913-1914), pp. 181-231.

14,977 DELANAYE, P. Position des Missions Catholiques en matière d'emploi des langues indigènes. AEQUATORIA 18 (1955), pp. 91-95.

14,978 DELILLE, A. and BURSSENS, A. Tshokwe-teksten. KONGO-OVERZEE 2 (1935-1936), pp. 41-60.

14,979 DENOLF, P. Ann den rand der Dibeso. CONGO 1 (1936), pp. 206-226, 358-379, 526-552.

14,980 DENOLF, P. Linguistische schets van het gebied tussen de Kasai en de Lomani. ZAIRE 5 (1951), pp. 55-58.

14,981 DIJKMAN, B. Nota over de taalverhoudingen binnen de grenzen van de Bestuursgebieden Bondo en Ango. KONGO-OVERZEE 17 (1951), pp. 250-257.

14,982 DILLEN, K. De groet bij de Bena Kanyoka. KONGO-OVERZEE 18 (1952), pp. 243-248.

14,983 DILLEN, K. Spreuken der Bena Kanioka. KONGO-OVERZEE 19 (1953), pp. 453-457.

14,984 GROOTAERT, J. De Spelling van Belgisch-Kongo. KONGO-OVERZEE 12-13 (1946-1947), pp. 30-31.

14,985 GRUBE, W. Ein Beitrag zur Kenntniss der Kai-Dialekte. ZAOS 1 (1895), pp. 83-96, 118-131.

14,986 GUILBERT, D. J. C. Civilisation occidentale et langage au Congo belge. ZAIRE 6 (1952), pp. 899-928.

14,987 GUTHRIE, M. Some features of the Mfinu verbal system. BULL. SOAS 18 (1956), pp. 84-102.

14,988 GUTHRIE, M. Tone ranges in a two-tone language (Lingala). BULL. SOAS 10 (1940-1942), pp. 469-478.

14,989 HARRIES, J. Nyali, Bantoid language (Belgian Congo). KONGO-OVERZEE 25 (1959), pp. 174-205.

14,990 HARRIES, L. Congo Swahili. TANGANYIKA NOTES AND RECORDS 44 (1956), pp. 50-53.

14,991 HARRIES, L. Grammar of Gesogo. KONGO-OVERZEE 21 (1955), pp. 420-440.

14,992 HARRIES, L. Kumu. A sub-Bantu language. KONGO-OVERZEE 24 (1958), pp. 265-296.

14,993 HARRIES, L. Notes on the Balese Language of the Ituri forest. KONGO-OVERZEE 22 (1956), pp. 152-170.

14,994 HARRIES, L. Le Swahili au Congo belge. KONGO-OVERZEE 22 (1956), pp. 395-400.

14,995 HARRIES, L. Swahili in the Belgian Congo. TANGANYIKA NOTES AND RECORDS 39 (1955), pp. 12-15.

14,996 HEIJBOER, B. M. Kp en gb in Noord-Bantoe. AEQUATORIA 11 (1948), pp. 126-127.

14,997 HEIJBOER, B. M. Londo en Lingombe. AEQUATORIA 11 (1948), pp. 60-66, 108-110.

14,998 HERROELEN, P. Commentaire sur Quelques noms vernaculaires d'animaux très communs au Congo Belge en dialectes du groupe Lingala et en Kisuku. AEQUATORIA 20 (1957), pp. 85-89.

14,999 HERROELEN, P. Quelques notes sur les noms d'oiseaux dans le Nsong'a Lianja. AEQUATORIA 20 (1957), p. 25.

15,000 HERTSENS, L. Quelques notes sur la phonétique Lendu. AFRICA 15 (1940), pp. 268-288.

15,001 HULSTAERT, G. A propos d'Onomastique. AEQUATORIA 15 (1952), pp. 52-57.

15,002 HULSTAERT, G. Bestaat er wel in de Congoleesche talen een tegenwoordige tijd? AEQUATORIA 3 (1940), pp. 90-95.

15,003 HULSTAERT, G. Bibliographie van het Lonkundo-Lomongo. CONGO 2 (1937), pp. 533-555.

15,004 HULSTAERT, G. De bronnen van het Lingala. ZAIRE 13 (1959), pp. 509-515.

15,005 HULSTAERT, G. Connectieve bijzinnen in Lomongo. AEQUATORIA 9 (1946), pp. 135-137.

15,006 HULSTAERT, G. Le dialecte des pygmoïdes Batswá de l'Equateur. AFRICA 18 (1948), pp. 21-28.

15,007 HULSTAERT, G. La langue Ntomba. AEQUATORIA 20 (1957), pp. 57-62.

15,008 HULSTAERT, G. La langue véhiculaire de l'enseignement. AEQUATORIA 2 (1939), pp. 85-89.

15,009 HULSTAERT, G. Les langues de la cuvette centrale congolaise. AEQUATORIA 14 (1951), pp. 18-24.

15,010 HULSTAERT, G. Les langues indigènes et les Européens au Congo Belge. AFR. STUD. 5 (1946), pp. 126-135.

15,011 HULSTAERT, G. Lingala. AEQUATORIA 3 (1940), pp. 65-73.

15,012 HULSTAERT, G. Lomongo en Ngbandi. AEQUATORIA 8 (1945), pp. 153-155; 9 (1946), p. 103.

15,013 HULSTAERT, G. Over het dialekt der Boyela. AEQUATORIA 5 (1942), pp. 41-43.

15,014 HULSTAERT, G. Over de tonen in het Lonkundo. KONGO-OVERZEE 11 (1934), pp. 257-273.

15,015 HULSTAERT, G. La persistance des tons en Lomongo. AEQUATORIA 24 (1961), pp. 102-105.

15,016 HULSTAERT, G. Que signifie le nom Batswa? AEQUATORIA 16 (1953), pp. 101-104.

15,017 HULSTAERT, G. Rechtstreeksche rede in chronologische orde in de Kongo-talen. AEQUATORIA 9 (1946), pp. 100-103.

15,018 HULSTAERT, G. Schets van het Lontomba (Belgisch Kongo). KONGO-OVERZEE 5 (1939), pp. 205-221; 6 (1940), pp. 1-29.

15,019 HULSTAERT, G. Sur le parler Doko. AEQUATORIA 24 (1961), pp. 121-135.

15,020 HULSTAERT, G. Sur quelques langues bantoues du Congo. AEQUATORIA 24 (1961), pp. 53-58.

15,021 HULSTAERT, G. Het talenvraagstuk in Belgisch Kongo. KONGO-OVERZEE 3 (1936-1937), pp. 49-68.

15,022 HULSTAERT, G. Taaleenmaking in het Mongo-gebied. KONGO-OVERZEE 16 (1950), pp. 292-298.

15,023 HULSTAERT, G. Tonologie van het Lomongo. KONGO-OVERZEE 16 (1950), pp. 139-147.

15,024 HULSTAERT, G. Vergelijkende Taalstudie III. AEQUATORIA 2 (1939), pp. 73-83.

15,025 HULSTAERT, G. Vlaams Filologencongres. AEQUATORIA 20 (1957), pp. 63-65.

15,026 ITTAMEIER, E. Abriss einer Lautlehre und Grammatik des Kinilāmba. AFR. UND UB. 13 (1922-1923), pp. 1-47.

15,027 ITTMANN, J. Kenyan, die Sprache der Nyang. AFR. UND UB. 26 (1935-1936), pp. 2-35, 97-133, 174-202, 272-300.

15,028 JACOBS, J. Long consonants and their tonal function in Tetela. KONGO-OVERZEE 23 (1957), pp. 200-212.

15,029 JACOBS, J. Nkumi-zang, Tetela (Mbvunge-dialect, gewest Lodja). Weergave van geregistreerde tekst. KONGO-OVERZEE 21 (1955), pp. 42-53.

15,030 JACOBS, J. Principes généraux de la nouvelle orthographe Otetela-Kikusu (Kasai-Kivu, Congo). KONGO-OVERZEE 25 (1959), pp. 145-169.

15,031 JACOBS, J. Tetela-Tekst. KONGO-OVERZEE 22 (1956), pp. 171-186.

15,032 JACOBS, J. Texte tetela. KONGO-OVERZEE 23 (1957), pp. 14-23.

15,033 JONGHE, E. DE. Les langues communes au Congo belge. CONGO 2, no. 4 (1933), pp. 509-523.

15,034 JONGHE, E. DE. Vers une langue nationale congolaise. BULL. SEANCES IRCB 6 (1935), pp. 340-351.

15,035 KITUMBOY, L. W. H. Kiswahili usages, Congo Belge and Rwanda Urundi. SWAHILI 31 (1960), pp. 227-230.

15,036 KITUMBOY, L. W. H. Swahili in Ruanda Urundi and Congo Republic. SWAHILI 32 (1961), pp. 65-66.

15,037 KNAPPERT, J. De bronnen van het Lingala. KONGO-OVERZEE 24 (1958), pp. 193-202.

15,038 LAMAN, K. E. and MEINHOF, C. An essay in Kongo phonology. AFR. UND UB. 19 (1928-1929), pp. 12-40.

15,039 LAROCHETTE, J. La détermination du nom dans les langues soudanaises du Congo belge. KONGO-OVERZEE 22 (1956), pp. 106-128.

15,040 LAROCHETTE, J. Les langues du groupe Moru-Mangbetu. KONGO-OVERZEE 24 (1958), pp. 118-135.

15,041 LECOSTE, B. A grammatical study of two recordings of Belgian-Congo Swahili. SWAHILI 31 (1960), pp. 219-226.

15,042 LECOSTE, B. Le Ngwana, variété congolaise du Swahili. KONGO-OVERZEE 20 (1954), pp. 391-408.

15,043 LECOSTE, B. Vocabulaire Ngwana. KONGO-OVERZEE 21 (1955), pp. 289-297.

15,044 LEKENS, B. Nota over het Ngbandi als voertaal in Ubangi. KONGO-OVERZEE 17 (1951), pp. 162-164.

15,045 LIESENBORGHS, O. Beschouwingen over Wezen, Nut en Toekomst der Zoogenaamde Linguae francae van Belgisch Kongo. KONGO-OVERZEE 7-8 (1941-1942), pp. 87-99.

15,046 LIESENBORGHS, O. Over taal en oorsprong der Mabendi. CONGO 2 (1934), pp. 35-38.

15,047 LIESENBORGHS, O. What is Kingwana? KONGO-OVERZEE 4 (1938), pp. 233-249.

15,048 LOOTENS, P. Noms vernaculaires d'animaux. AEQUATORIA 21 (1958), pp. 60-61.

15,049 MAES. Test-proef over de aandacht der inlandse leerlingen. AEQUATORIA 14 (1951), pp. 13-17.

15,050 MAES, J. Vocabularie des populations de la région du Kasai-Lulua-Sankuru. J. SOC. AFR. 4 (1934), pp. 209-267.

15,051 MAES, V. Het Ngbaka, een Soedantaal in Ubangi. KONGO-OVERZEE 17 (1951), pp. 292-304.

15,052 MAEYENS, L. De bilabiale, stemhebbende implosief in het kiBira. KONGO-OVERZEE 4 (1938), pp. 23-24.

15,053 MAEYENS, L. Het inlandsch Lied en het muzikaal accent met semantische functie bij de Babira. KONGO-OVERZEE 4 (1938), pp. 250-259.

15,054 MAEYER, F. DE. Een eigenaardig geval van tweetaligheid op de taalgrens der Soedan-en Bantoetalen in Belgisch Kongo. KONGO-OVERZEE 9 (1943), pp. 166-175.

15,055 MAHIEU, W. DE. Un cas isolé de click en langue Kongo. AEQUATORIA 25 (1962), pp. 19-20.

15,056 MEEUSSEN, A. E. Hoe een inlandse taal te beschrijven. KONGO-OVERZEE 12-13 (1946-1947), pp. 216-220, 282-286; 14 (1948), pp. 37-41, 223-235.

15,057 MEEUSSEN, A. E. Iets over de tonologie van den tweeden nominalen werkwoordvorm in het Tshiluba. KONGO-OVERZEE 9 (1943), pp. 183-186.

15,058 MEEUSSEN, A. E. Over een werkwoordvorm in het Tshiluba. KONGO-OVERZEE 12-13 (1946-1947), pp. 45-52.

15,059 MEEUSSEN, A. E. Syntaxis van het Tshiluba (Kasayi). KONGO-OVERZEE 9 (1943), pp. 81-105, 113-159; 10-11 (1944-1945), pp. 89-114, 218-249; 12-13 (1946-1947), pp. 173-184; 23 (1957), pp. 303-315; 24 (1958), pp. 256-264.

15,060 MEEUSSEN, A. E. Taalgeografie in Kongo. ZAIRE 8 (1954), pp. 163-170.

15,061 MEEUSSEN, A. E. De talen van Maniema. KONGO-OVERZEE 19 (1953), pp. 385-391.

15,062 MEEUSSEN, A. E. De tonen van de imperatief in het Ciluba (Kasayi). KONGO-OVERZEE 16 (1950), pp. 110-111.

15,063 MEEUSSEN, A. E. Tooncontractie in het Ciluba. KONGO-OVERZEE 17 (1951), pp. 289-291.

15,064 MEEUSSEN, A. E. Werkwoordafleiding in Mongo en Oerbantoe. AEQUATORIA 17 (1954), pp. 81-86.

15,065 MEEUSSEN, A. E. and NDEMBE, D. Principles de tonologie Yombe (Kongo occidental). J. AFR. LANGS. 3 (1964), pp. 135-161.

15,066 MIGEOD, F. W. H. Ngala, and its dead language. JRAI 52 (1922), pp. 230-241.

15,067 MORTIER, R. Methode voor het aanleren der tonen in een toontaal. Toepassing op het Ngbandi. AEQUATORIA 11 (1948), pp. 137-142; 12 (1949), pp. 138-144.

15,068 MORTIER, R. Ubangi onder linguistisch opzicht. AEQUATORIA 9 (1946), pp. 104-112.

15,069 NIDA, E. A. Tribal and trade languages. AFR. STUD. 14 (1955), pp. 155-158.

15,070 NNUNDUMA, B. E. Written Swahili in the Belgian Congo. SWAHILI 29 (1959), pp. 24-33.

15,071 PAUWELS, J. L. De Spelling van Belgisch-Kongo. KONGO-OVERZEE 12-13 (1946-1947), pp. 32-35.

15,072 PEERAER, S. and BURSSENS, A. Nominale Klassen en Prefixen in het kiLuba (Katanga). KONGO-OVERZEE 4 (1938), pp. 150-165.

15,073 PHILIPPE, R. Au sujet de deux cartes linguistiques du Congo Belge. AEQUATORIA 18 (1955), pp. 67-68.

15,074 PICAVET, R. Het dialekt der Batswa. AEQUATORIA 10 (1947), pp. 137-141.

15,075 POSSOZ, E. De la langue dans les juridictions indigènes. AEQUATORIA 3 (1940), p. 95.

15,076 POSSOZ, E. Questiones disputandae: le préfixe YA. AEQUATORIA 2 (1939), p. 131.

15,077 PRICE, E. W. The tonal structure of the Ngombe verb. AFR. STUD. 3 (1944), pp. 28-30.

15,078 ROMBAUTS, H. Batwá, Batúa, Batóa. AEQUATORIA 13 (1950), pp. 21-23.

15,079 ROMBAUTS, H. Elimo chez les Ekonda. AEQUATORIA 15 (1952), pp. 121-126.

15,080 ROMBAUTS, H. Tonétique du Lokonda (Congo Belge). KONGO-OVERZEE 15 (1949), pp. 10-23.

15,081 ROMBAUTS, H. Tonétique du Lokonda (Congo belge). Deuxiéme étude. KONGO-OVERZEE 20 (1954), pp. 376-390.

15,082 ROMMES, M. La situation linguistique dans les vicariats de Stanleyville et de Wamba. KONGO-OVERZEE 17 (1951), pp. 240-249.

15,083 ROOD, N. La phonétique du Lingombe. AEQUATORIA 24 (1961), pp. 50-52.

15,084 ROP, A. DE. De Bakongo en het Lingala. KONGO-OVERZEE 19 (1953), pp. 170-174.

15,085 ROP, A. DE. Bantoe g en j vergeleken met het Lomongo. KONGO-OVERZEE 20 (1954), pp. 432-435.

15,086 ROP, A. DE. Het Lomongo als Cultuurtaal. KONGO-OVERZEE 21 (1955), pp. 265-271.

15,087 ROP, A. DE. Het toonsysteem van het Lomongo en het Oerbantoe. KONGO-OVERZEE 19 (1953), pp. 413-419.

15,088 ROP, A. DE. Les langues du Congo. AEQUATORIA 23 (1960), pp. 1-24.

15,089 ROP, A. DE. L'orthographe du Ciluba. AEQUATORIA 22, no. ii (1959), pp. 1-6.

15,090 ROP, A. DE. Over Riviernamen in het Mongo-Gebied. AEQUATORIA 20 (1957), pp. 5-9.

15,091 ROP, A. DE. De zogezegde stamnaam Balolo. AEQUATORIA 20 (1957), pp. 136-137.

15,092 SCHEBESTA, P. La langue des Pygmees. ZAIRE 3 (1949), pp. 119-128.

15,093 SCHMID, S. Gedanken über das Problem vom Ursprung der Sprache und über die Methoden und Ziele der linguistischen Forschung. ZAOS 5 (1900), pp. 304-341.

15,094 SMITH, E. W. The language of pygmies of the Ituri. J. AFR. SOC. 37 (1938), pp. 464-470.

15,095 SPAANDONCK, M. Palatalization: a phonological process in the agentive noun of Bushóóng. J. AFR. LANGS. 3 (1964), pp. 191-201.

15,096 STAPLETON, W. H. Note on the Kele verb. J. AFR. SOC. 5 (1906), pp. 290-299.

15,097 STAPPERS, L. L'emploi des personnels isolés en Ciluba. KONGO-OVERZEE 24 (1958), pp. 72-79.

15,098 STAPPERS, L. Enige eigenaardigheden van het West-Kanyok (Kasayi). KONGO-OVERZEE 18 (1952), pp. 382-387.

15,099 STAPPERS, L. Het toonsysteem van het Buina Milembwe (Zuid-Kisongye). KONGO-OVERZEE 18 (1952), pp. 199-242.

15,100 STAPPERS, L. Het Tshiluba als omgangstaal of unificatie van de Luba-dialekten? KONGO-OVERZEE 18 (1952), pp. 50-65.

15,101 STAPPERS, L. In hoeverre verschilt het Kisongye van het Tshiluba? AEQUATORIA 16 (1953), pp. 1-7.

15,102 STAPPERS, L. Miadi. Rouwplechtigheden. KONGO-OVERZEE 19 (1953), pp. 10-19.

15,103 STAPPERS, L. De Middlehooge toon in het Tshiluba. KONGO-OVERZEE 10-11 (1944-1945), pp. 261-264.

15,104 STAPPERS, L. Een Ruund dialekt: de taal der Beena Tubeya. KONGO-OVERZEE 20 (1954), pp. 369-375.

15,105 STAPPERS, L. Schets van het Budya. KONGO-OVERZEE 21 (1955), pp. 97-143.

15,106 STAPPERS, L. De toongroepen en hun wijzigingen in de taal van de Aphende. KONGO-OVERZEE 19 (1953), pp. 376-379.

15,107 STAPPERS, L. Toonparallelisme als mnemotechnisch middel in spreekwoorden. AEQUATORIA 16 (1953), pp. 99-100.

15,108 STAPPERS, L. Tussen Luba en Songye. ZAIRE 4 (1950), pp. 271-276.

15,109 TANGHE, B. O. Les Ababua (Uele). Quelle langue parlaient ils autrefois? AEQUATORIA 2 (1939), p. 107.

15,110 TEMPELS, P. Het tellen van 1 tot 10 bij de Baluba-Shankadi. KONGO-OVERZEE 2 (1935-1936), pp. 61-63.

15,111 TEMPELS, P. De Telgebaren der Bashila. KONGO-OVERZEE 4 (1938), pp. 49-53.

15,112 TERCAFS, J. and MEYER, E. Material zur Yogo-Sprache. AFR. UND UB. 33 (1942-1943), pp. 1-24.

15,113 TEW, M. Elicited responses in Lele language. KONGO-OVERZEE 16 (1950), pp. 224-227.

15,114 THIEL, H. VAN. Kongolese Woordkunst: Lingombe-Vertelsel. KONGO-OVERZEE 16 (1950), pp. 276-280.

15,115 THIEL, H. VAN. Tonetiek van het Lingombe. AEQUATORIA 10 (1947), pp. 70-77.

15,116 THIEL, H. VAN. Vijfde Lingombe-vertelsel. KONGO-OVERZEE 18 (1952), pp. 308-311.

15,117 TOULMOND, L. Essai de grammaire d'Ebudja. CONGO 2 (1937), pp. 361-376, 481-525.

15,118 TROESCH, J. Barafunda dos nomes indígenas (em busca de uma solução). PORT. EM AFR. 15 (1958), pp. 241-245.

15,119 TROESCH, J. Le négation dans le dialecte fiote. AEQUATORIA 16 (1953), pp. 134-136.

15,120 VANHOUTEGHEM, A. Overzicht der Bantu dialekten van het Distrikt-Lisala. AEQUATORIA 10 (1947), pp. 41-50.

15,121 VANNESTE, M. De benamingen der familiebetrekkingen bij de Alur. CONGO 2 (1936), pp. 369-377.

15,122 VANNESTE, M. De Getallen in de Alur-Taal. CONGO 2 (1934), pp. 692-700.

15,123 VANNESTE, M. Persoonsnamen bij de Alur in Belgisch-Kongo. KONGO-OVERZEE 14 (1948), pp. 129-143, 193-212.

15,124 VANNESTE, M. Vergelijking van een paar Alur-woorden met de taal der Farao's. KONGO-OVERZEE 9 (1943), pp. 160-165.

15,125 VANSINA, J. Systématique des termes de parenté Bushoong. KONGO-OVERZEE 23 (1957), pp. 286-302.

15,126 VERWILGHEN, P. Bingana bi Bayaka, Bayaka-spreuken (II). KONGO-OVERZEE 17 (1951), pp. 360-368.

15,127 VORBICHLER, A. Die sprachlichen Beziehungen zwischen den Waldnegern und Pygmäen in der Republik Kongo-Leo. CONG. INT. SC. ANTH. ET ETHN. 6, no. ii (1960), pp. 85-91.

15,128 WARMELO, N. J. V. Zur Gwamba-Lautlehre. AFR. UND UB. 20 (1929-1930), pp. 221-231.

15,129 WING, J. VAN. Het Kikongo en het Lingala te Leopoldstad. KONGO-OVERZEE 19 (1953), pp. 175-178.

15,130 WING, J. VAN. Nota over de "Commissie voor unificatie van het Kikongo" (1935-1936). KONGO-OVERZEE 17 (1951), pp. 38-40.

15,131 WITTE, P. DE. Une nouvelle grammaire Kilongo en préparation. AEQUATORIA 16 (1953), pp. 69-72.

15,132 WITTE, P. DE. Nog over de tonologie van het Kikongo. KONGO-OVERZEE 19 (1953), pp. 306-316.

15,133 WITTE, P. DE. Over de tonologie van het Kikongo. KONGO-OVERZEE 17 (1951), pp. 345-357.

15,134 WOUTERS, J. Bingana bi Bayaka. Spreuken der Bayaka. KONGO-OVERZEE 19 (1953), pp. 149-154.

15,135 Mambu ma maba ku tsi Mayombe. (De palmboomen in Mayombe.) Zes teksten van zwarten. (Vertaald door L. Declercq.) ZAIRE 1 (1947), pp. 755-772; 2 (1948), pp. 159-173, 868-896.

15,136 Manifeste d'un groupe de Bakongo. KONGO-OVERZEE 19 (1953), pp. 178-181.

See also 6315, 13663, 13872, 13875, 19348.

Literature

15,137 BEMBA, S. The darkroom [a story]. BO 15 (1964), pp. 15-22.

15,138 BITTREMIEUX, L. Koloniale Literatuur. KONGO-OVERZEE 5 (1939), pp. 222-226.

15,139 BITTREMIEUX, L. Ritueele Dichtkunst in Mayombe. KONGO-OVERZEE 5 (1939), pp. 1-11.

15,140 BOELAERT, E. Nog over het epos van de Mongo: het hoe heldenzanger werd. KONGO-OVERZEE 20 (1954), pp. 289-292.

15,141 BOELAERT, E. Nsong'a Lianja. L'Epopée nationale des Nkundo. AEQUATORIA 12 (1949), pp. 1-76.

15,142 BOELAERT, E. De structuur van de Nicundo-Poëzie. KONGO-OVERZEE 21 (1955), pp. 262-264.

15,143 BOLAMBA, A. R. Two poems [Portrait, A fistful of news]. BO 11 (1962), pp. 51-52.

15,144 BOUVEIGNES, O. DE. La Muse et le Congo. ZAIRE 1 (1947), pp. 773-789.

15,145 BOUVEIGNES, O. DE. Sur la source d'un roman africain de 1769. (Zingha, reine d'Angola...par L. Castilhon.) ZAIRE 2 (1948), pp. 797-800.

15,146 BRAASEM, W. A. Primitieve woordkunst en haar waardering. Bij twee Vlaamse publikaties. KONGO-OVERZEE 23 (1957), pp. 1-13.

15,147 BRIERE, J. F. Patrice Lumumba. PRESENCE AFR. N.S. 37 (1961), p. 87.

15,148 BURK, E. I. et al. Proverbes Lega by E. I. Burk, D. Byakilema, P. Ardoise, P. Kisubi, A. Mbambalwa. ZAIRE 10 (1956), pp. 711-715.

15,149 BURSSENS, A. Een nieuwe Nederlandsche Roman over Belgisch Kongo. KONGO-OVERZEE 1 (1934), pp. 119-124.

15,150 BURSSENS, A. Koloniale Literatuur. KONGO-OVERZEE 4 (1938), pp. 286-288.

15,151 CAENEGHEM, R. VAN. Uit de taalschat van de Baluba en de Bena-Moyo. CONGO 2 (1935), pp. 53-68.

15,152 CELEN, V. Nederlands letterkundig werk in verband met onze kolonie. ZAIRE 2 (1948), pp. 391-406.

15,153 COMELIAU, J. Littérature pour Indigènes. AEQUATORIA 13 (1950), pp. 23-24.

15,154 COMHAIRE-SYLVAIN, S. Proverbes récueillis à Léopoldville. ZAIRE 3 (1949), pp. 629-647.

15,155 DEPOORTER, K. Nkenda mi Bayaka. Bayaka-sprookjes. KONGO-OVERZEE 19 (1953), pp. 136-145.

15,156 DIPUMBA, B. Poème luba. KONGO-OVERZEE 19 (1953), pp. 464-468.

15,157 E., I. Littérature indigène. AEQUATORIA 5 (1942), pp. 39-40.

15,158 HINDMARSH, R. The Congo of the mind [review of Graham Greene's A Burnt-Out Case]. TRANSITION 1 (1961), p. 41.

15,159 HULSTAERT, G. Style oral. AEQUATORIA 8 (1945), pp. 151-152.

15,160 JACOBS, J. La littérature orale tetela (Kasai, Congo). CONGR. INT. SC. ANTH. ET ETHN. 6, no. ii (1960), pp. 215-216.

15,161 JACOBS, J. Le message tambouriné, genre de littérature orale bantoue (Tetela, Sankuru, Congo Belge). KONGO-OVERZEE 25 (1959), pp. 90-112.

15,162 JACOBS, J. and VANSINA, J. Het Koninklijk Epos der Bushong. KONGO-OVERZEE 22 (1956), pp. 1-39.

15,163 JADOT, J. M. Le Congo dans les lettres belges de langue francaise (1952-1953). ZAIRE 8 (1954), pp. 63-73.

15,164 JADOT, J. M. Les lettres coloniales belges d'expression française durant l'occupation allemande. ZAIRE 1 (1947), pp. 567-573, 917-922.

15,165 JADOT, J. M. Les lettres et les arts en Belgique coloniale et au Congo belge en 1957, 1958. ZAIRE 12 (1958), pp. 179-190; 13 (1959), pp. 185-196.

15,166 KALANDA, A. Bartholomée Dipumba ou les perspectives nouvelles de la poésie congolaise. KONGO-OVERZEE 25 (1959), pp. 77-85.

15,167 MALONGA, J. Coeur d'Aryenne. PRESENCE AFR. 16 (1954), pp. 159-285.

15,168 MATEENE, K. Sur un poème Kihunde. PRESENCE AFR. N.S. 55 (1965), pp. 73-82.

15,169 MEEUSSEN, A. E. Rundi-teksten van André Bariumwete. KONGO-OVERZEE 19 (1953), pp. 420-427.

15,170 MONTEYNE, L. Koloniale Literatuur. KONGO-OVERZEE 4 (1938), pp. 215-219.

15,171 MONTEYNE, L. Koloniale Literatuur. A. B. van der Weerelt-E. Tilemans-Frans de Prez-Manny Demers-Mans. KONGO-OVERZEE 1 (1934), pp. 308-313.

15,172 MONTEYNE, L. Koloniale Litteratuur. Sylva de Jonghe en Jef de Pillecijn. KONGO-OVERZEE 11 (1934), pp. 177-185.

15,173 MONTEYNE, L. Nederlandsche koloniale litteratuur. KONGO-OVERZEE 2 (1935-1936), pp. 303-309.

15,174 O'FERRALL, R. An old war song of the Babemba. BULL. SOAS 4 (1926-1928), pp. 839-844.

15,175 OLIVEIRA, C. P. DE. Literatura Cabindana. PORT. EM AFR. 13 (1956), pp. 221-230, 299-309.

15,176 PEERAER, P. S. Vijf Kabunji-sprookjes. CONGO 2 (1935), pp. 201-217.

15,177 RODE, P. DE. Le drame de la Tuilo. AEQUATORIA 14 (1951), pp. 85-89.

15,178 ROOD, N. Gedichten in Lingombe. AEQUATORIA 11 (1948), pp. 6-12.

15,179 ROP, A. DE. L'Epopée des Nkundo, l'original et la copie. KONGO-OVERZEE 24 (1958), pp. 170-178.

15,180 SAENEN, J. Een legende van de Ngbaka. CONGO 1 (1935), pp. 215-220.

15,181 SENGHOR, L. S. Congo. PRESENCE AFR. 4 (1948), pp. 625-626.

15,182 STAPPERS, L. Drie vertellingen in het Luba-Kasayi en Luba-Katanga. KONGO-OVERZEE 20 (1954), pp. 193-204.

15,183 STAPPERS, L. Eerste geluiden uit de Luba-poëzie. KONGO-OVERZEE 18 (1952), pp. 97-110.

15,184 TANGHE, J. Mabale stories with a few notes on Mabale grammar. BULL. SOAS 5 (1928-1930), pp. 359-378, 571-586.

15,185 TANGHE, J. Ninth Mabale story. KONGO-OVERZEE 20 (1954), pp. 265-266.

15,186 TANGHE, J. Seventh Mabale story. KONGO-OVERZEE 18 (1952), pp. 305-307.

15,187 THISSEN, L. Alguns elementos da literatura oral dos Basuku. PORT. EM AFR. 17 (1960), pp. 176-185.

15,188 U'TAMSI, F. T. Agony [a poem]. BO 15 (1964), pp. 13-14.

15,189 U-TAM'SI, T. Deux poèmes [dédiés à la mémoire de Patrice Lumumba]. PRESENCE AFR. N.S. 40 (1962), pp. 142-143.

15,190 VANSINA, J. Làãm: Gezongen kwaadsprekerij bij de Bushong. AEQUATORIA 18 (1955), pp. 125-130.

15,191 VERTENTEN, P. Nkundo-Vertelsels. KONGO-OVERZEE 1 (1934), pp. 65-74.

15,192 VIAENE, R. P. L. Coup d'oeil sur la littérature orale des Bahunde (Kivu). KONGO-OVERZEE 21 (1955), pp. 212-240.

15,193 L'auteur de Ngandu nous parle. PRESENCE AFR. 7 (1949), pp. 314-316.

Law

15,194 ANDRIES, A. A propos du statut des villes. ZAIRE 7 (1953), pp. 621-624.

15,195 BASTID, S. La succession du Congo belge aux obligations de l'Etat indépendant du Congo devant la Cour de Paris. RJPUF 11 (1957), pp. 356-375.

15,196 BIEBUYCK, D. Grondrecht en grondbezit in Belgisch Congo. ZAIRE 12 (1958), pp. 151-164.

15,197 BIEBUYCK, D. and DUFOUR, J. Le régime foncier du Congo belge. Etude ethnologique et juridique. ZAIRE 12 (1958), pp. 365-382.

15,198 BILSEN, J. VAN. Polygamie. ZAIRE 4 (1950), pp. 769-771.

15,199 BOELAERT, E. Législation foncière de l'Etat indépendant et droit naturel. AEQUATORIA 17 (1954), pp. 41-50.

15,200 BOELAERT, E. De rechtsproeven bij de Nkundo. CONGO 2 (1938), pp. 526-546.

15,201 BOELAERT, E. Un statut pour monogames. AEQUATORIA 2 (1939), pp. 91-93.

15,202 BOELAERT, E. Les trois fictions du droit foncier congolais. ZAIRE 11 (1957), pp. 399-427.

15,203 BRAUSCH, G. La justice coutumière chez les Bakwa Luntu. AFR. STUD. 1 (1942), pp. 235-242.

15,204 C., M. S. En lisant Autour de la dot. AEQUATORIA 3 (1940), pp. 74-78.

15,205 CAPELLE, E. La limitation du taux des dots. ZAIRE 2 (1948), pp. 955-968.

15,206 CHARLES, P. Réactions mutuelles de l'évangélisation et de la colonisation dans le domaine juridique. BULL. SEANCES IRCB 2 (1931), pp. 459-475.

15,207 CHARLES, V. Les allocations familiales. ZAIRE 7 (1953), pp. 391-392.

15,208 CHARLES, V. L'application de la législation sociale [allocations familiales, réparation des dommages, d'accidents de travail ou de maladies professionnelles]. ZAIRE 6 (1952), pp. 1082-1085.

15,209 CHARLES, V. L'élaboration de la législation sociale. ZAIRE 5 (1951), pp. 281-285; 7 (1953), pp. 389-390.

15,210 CHARLES, V. La législation sociale en voie d'application. ZAIRE 4 (1950), pp. 886-887.

15,211 CHARLES, V. Le permis de main-d'oeuvre. ZAIRE 7 (1953), pp. 390-391.

15,212 CHARLES, V. Les sanctions pénales. ZAIRE 6 (1952), pp. 73-76.

15,213 CHARLES, V. Sanctions pénales et contrat de travail en Afrique belge. ZAIRE 8 (1954), pp. 939-943.

15,214 CLEENE, N. DE. A propos de l'étude du droit coutumier congolais. ZAIRE 2 (1948), pp. 551-556.

15,215 CYFER-DIDERICH, G. The legal situation of the native woman in the Belgian Congo. CIVILISATIONS 1, no. iv (1951), pp. 59-67; French summary, pp. 67-68.

15,216 D., F. La nouvelle législation sur le contrat de louage de services. ET. CONG. 1, no. 1 (1961), pp. 6-12.

15,217 D., N. A propos de Vol. AEQUATORIA 5 (1942), pp. 33-38.

15,218 DECAPMAKER, P. Le droit foncier et le matriarcat. AEQUATORIA 21 (1958), p. 139.

15,219 DELACAUW, A. Droit coutumier des Barundi. CONGO 1 (1936), pp. 332-357, 481-522.

15,220 DELLICOUR, F. La réforme du Code pénal congolais [with a note by A. Sohier]. BULL. SEANCES IRCB 4 (1933), pp. 726-739, 740-742.

15,221 DEVAUX, V. Le commentaire du code pénal congolais de M. G. Mineur. ZAIRE 1 (1947), pp. 1054-1059.

15,222 DUFOUR, J. P. Quelques aspects juridiques du problème foncier au Congo. AFR. AGRARIAN SYSTEMS, 1963, pp. 173-184.

15,223 DUFRENOY, P. Terres vacantes et circonscriptions urbaines. CONGO 1 (1935), pp. 169-214.

15,224 DUPRIEZ, G. La législation du travail. ET. CONG. 8, no. 6 (1965), pp. 1-15.

15,225 DURIEUX, A. L' "Aperçu de droit civil du Congo belge" de M. M. Verstraete. ZAIRE 2 (1948), pp. 557-561.

15,226 DURIEUX, A. La Belgique et le Congo belge. Note de droit public. ZAIRE 7 (1953), pp. 337-379.

15,227 GELDERS, V. Une théorie ethnologique du droit indigène. ZAIRE 2 (1948), pp. 175-187.

15,228 GOHR, A. Rapports de droit privé entre indigènes et non-indigènes. BULL. SEANCES IRCB 4 (1933), pp. 323-333, 344-345.

15,229 HERBOTS, J. H. Les droits fonciers et l'administration à Léopoldville. ET. CONG. 6, no. 3 (1964), pp. 22-40.

15,230 HEYSE, T. L'aire d'application du décret du 6 février 1920 sur la constatation et le transfert de la propriété civile. BULL. SEANCES IRCB 4 (1933), pp. 334-343.

15,231 HEYSE, T. Cessions et concessions foncières. CONGO 2 (1936), pp. 313-342; 1 (1938), pp. 1-12, 121-144; 2 (1938), pp. 241-256; 1 (1939), pp. 480-498.

15,232 HEYSE, T. Le Décret du 31 mai 1934 sur la constatation de la vacance des terres et la vacance des terres et la renonciation des droits indigènes. BULL. SEANCES IRCB 6 (1935), pp. 282-296.

15,233 HEYSE, T. Quelques vues générales et critiques sur le régime de la propriété immobilière au Congo belge. BULL. SEANCES IRCB 5 (1934), pp. 317-355.

15,234 HEYSE, T. Terres vacantes et terres sans maître. CONGO 2 (1937), pp. 132-149.

15,235 HULSTAERT, G. Droit coutumier. AEQUATORIA 20 (1957), pp. 121-124.

15,236 HULSTAERT, G. Evolution du droit coutumier. AEQUATORIA 7 (1944), p. 112.

15,237 HULSTAERT, G. Sur le droit foncier Nkundo. AEQUATORIA 17 (1954), pp. 58-65.

15,238 HULSTAERT, G. and SOHIER, A. La réaction indigène contre les divorces. CONGO 1 (1936), pp. 11-25.

15,239 JAEGER, A. DE. Le contrat de mariage chez les Yakoma. CONGO 1 (1921), pp. 584-588.

15,240 JENTGEN, P. De la délégation des pouvoirs en droit public congolais. ZAIRE 1 (1947), pp. 77-83.

15,241 KOPYTOFF, I. Family and lineage among the Suku of the Congo. THE FAMILY ESTATE IN AFRICA, 1964, pp. 83-116.

15,242 LOUWERS, O. La répression de l'adultère et de la bigamie et la protection du mariage monogamique au Congo Belge. ZAIRE 2 (1948), pp. 1067-1091.

15,243 M., G. Le problème du statut du district de Léopoldville. ET. CONG. 4, no. 5 (1963), pp. 25-31.

15,244 MALENGREAU, G. De l'accession des indigènes à la propriété foncière individuelle du code civil. ZAIRE 1 (1947), pp. 235-270, 399-433.

15,245 MALENGREAU, G. L'immatriculation des indigènes. ZAIRE 6 (1952), pp. 957-965.

15,246 MALENGREAU, G. Propositions pour une solution du problème foncier. ZAIRE 10 (1956), pp. 387-403.

15,247 MALENGREAU, G. Le statut des villes. ZAIRE 7 (1953), pp. 612-616.

15,248 MARZORATI, A. Le problème judiciaire au Congo belge [with notes by O. Louwers, A. Gohr, F. Dellicour, A. Engels, P. Charles, A. Sohier, P. Ryckmans]. BULL. SEANCES IRCB 3 (1932), pp. 43-130, 281-290.

15,249 MERTENS, J. La juridiction indigène chez les Bakongo Orientaux. KONGO-OVERZEE 10-11 (1944-1945), pp. 49-88, 179-217; 12-13 (1946-1947), pp. 133-150, 241-250; 14 (1948), pp. 21-36, 107-119, 144-167, 236-245; 15 (1949), pp. 34-44, 155-171, 273-281; 16 (1950), pp. 17-36, 97-109, 198-211; 17 (1951), pp. 41-59, 305-328; 18 (1952), pp. 130-152, 282-304.

15,250 MOELLER, A. Aperçus du droit coutumier des pasteurs du Kivu. BULL. SEANCES IRCB 5 (1934), pp. 664-680.

15,251 NICAISE, J. Autour de la législation sociale: contrat de travail. ZAIRE 8 (1954), p. 186.

15,252 NICAISE, J. Le Décret du 6 juin 1956 sur la pension des travailleurs autochtones. ZAIRE 10 (1956), pp. 1011-1033.

15,253 NICAISE, J. Le nouveau décret sur le contrat de travail. ZAIRE 9 (1955), pp. 153-158.

15,254 NICAISE, J. Le projet de modification du décret du 25 juin 1949 sur le contrat d'emploi. ZAIRE 8 (1954), pp. 627-633.

15,255 NZAU, T. Les conventions collectives du travail au Congo. ET. CONG. 5, no. 10 (1963), pp. 53-60.

15,256 PAUWELS, J. M. La Constitution du Congo et le Droit coutumier. ET. CONG. 7, no. 9 (1964), pp. 1-26.

15,257 PHILIPPE, R. Les modes de propriété chez les Mongo. Essai d'étude comparée. KONGO-OVERZEE 25 (1959), pp. 17-72.

15,258 POSSOZ, E. Etude sur l'article premier du décret sur les juridictions indigènes. ZAIRE 2 (1948), pp. 407-422.

15,259 POSSOZ, E. Hoofdbestanddelen van het Inlands Recht. KONGO-OVERZEE 15 (1949), pp. 1-9.

15,260 POSSOZ, E. Impressionisme et ethnologie juridique. KONGO-OVERZEE 19 (1953), pp. 428-433.

15,261 POSSOZ, E. Mariage et droits féodaux. AEQUATORIA 2 (1939), pp. 137-142.

15,262 POSSOZ, E. Polygamie. AEQUATORIA 2 (1939), pp. 48-53.

15,263 POSSOZ, E. Quaestiones disputandae: divorce. AEQUATORIA 2 (1939), pp. 89-91.

15,264 POSSOZ, E. and PHILIPPE, R. Les occidentaux et le droit clanique. AEQUATORIA 23 (1960), pp. 44-56.

15,265 RUBBENS, A. La formation du droit indigène. ZAIRE 1 (1947), pp. 435-439.

15,266 RYCKBOST, J. La liberté syndicale et la grève en droit congolais. ZAIRE 13 (1959), pp. 227-242.

15,267 RYCKBOST, J. Le régime des libertés publiques en droit congolais. ET. CONG. 2, no. 4 (1962), pp. 1-22.

15,268 SOHIER, A. Une branche inexplorée du droit. Le droit coutumier congolais. CONGO 1 (1935), pp. 321-357.

15,269 SOHIER, A. Le droit coutumier au Congo Belge. THE FUTURE OF CUSTOMARY LAW IN AFRICA, 1956, pp. 1-15.

15,270 SOHIER, A. Le droit pénal coutumier. AEQUATORIA 11 (1948), pp. 32-33, 67-69.

15,271 SOHIER, A. L'évolution du droit coutumier congolais par voie de décision des autorités indigènes. ZAIRE 1 (1947), pp. 313-317.

15,272 SOHIER, A. Les juridictions indigènes congolaises [with a note by A. Moeller]. BULL. SEANCES IRCB 6 (1935), pp. 55-107.

15,273 SOHIER, A. Mariage coutumier et mariage religieux. ZAIRE 1 (1947), pp. 73-76.

15,274 SOHIER, A. Notes sur l'organisation et la procédure judiciaires coutumières des indigènes du Congo Belge. AFRICA 13 (1940), pp. 25-42.

15,275 SOHIER, A. La problème des indigènes évolués et la Commission du statut des Congolais civilisés. ZAIRE 3 (1949), pp. 843-880.

15,276 SOHIER, A. Rapport de la Commission des Tribunaux Indigènes. ZAIRE 3 (1949), pp. 303-311.

15,277 SOHIER, A. Le statut civil coutumier des Congolais. CIVILISATIONS 7 (1957), pp. 33-46.

15,278 SOHIER, A. Le statut des Congolais civilises. ZAIRE 4 (1950), pp. 815-822.

15,279 SOUPART, H. De la contrainte par corps pour dettes chez les Budja. CONGO 1 (1940), pp. 113-135.

15,280 SOUSBERGHE, L. DE. L'étude du droit coutumier indigène: méthode et obstacles. ZAIRE 9 (1955), pp. 339-358.

15,281 TEMPELS, P. Le mariage indigène et la loi. KONGO-OVERZEE 10-11 (1944-1945), pp. 265-282.

15,282 VANDERLINDEN, J. Vers la rédaction des droits coutumiers congolais. LA REDACTION DES COUTUMES DANS LE PASSE ET DANS LE PRESENT, 1962, pp. 233-274.

15,283 VANSINA, I. A traditional legal system: the Kuba. AFR. LAW: ADAPTATION AND DEVELOPMENT, 1965, pp. 97-119.

15,284 VERSTRAETE, M. Une date dans le droit coutumier du Congo belge. KONGO-OVERZEE 16 (1950), pp. 155-161.

15,285 VERSTRAETE, M. Over openbare en staatsburgerlijke rechten in Kongo. KONGO-OVERZEE 15 (1949), pp. 65-89.

15,286 VERWILGHEN, J. P. Les dissolutions successives du Comité Spécial du Katanga. ET. CONG. 8, no. 3 (1965), pp. 1-55.

15,287 VINDEVOGHEL, J. Etude juridique du problème de l'habitation indigène. ZAIRE 3 (1949), pp. 421-432.

15,288 WILDE, L. DE. Synthese van de rechtsregels inzake huwelijk bij de Tshokwe-bevolking van Kahemba. KONGO-OVERZEE 23 (1957), pp. 129-145.

15,289 WILDE, L. O. J. De mobilisatie van het grond capitaal der inheemsen. KONGO-OVERZEE 23 (1957), pp. 265-285.

15,290 A propos de la codification de la coutume. ZAIRE 3 (1949), pp. 313-328.

15,291 L'enseignement du droit dans la République du Congo (Léopoldville). J. AFR. LAW 6 (1962), pp. 92-95.

15,292 Vers l'assimilation légale des élites congolaises? ZAIRE 4 (1950), pp. 1003-1006.

See also 14378, 15075.

Religion

15,293 ANET, H. Protestant missions in Belgian Congo. INT. REV. MISSIONS 28 (1939), pp. 415-425.

15,294 AZED, M. Les missions protestantes au Congo. CONGO 1 (1938), pp. 288-296.

15,295 BILSEN, J. VAN. Andere actualiteiten. ZAIRE 4 (1950), pp. 321-322.

15,296 BOELAERT, E. Le Syndicat des Tabacs et la fondation de la Mission d'Ikoko. AEQUATORIA 24 (1961), pp. 59-64.

15,297 BOELAERT, P. Pleidooi voor de Batswa. ZAIRE 3 (1949), pp. 1091-1100.

15,298 BROWN, H. D. The Church and its missionary task in Congo. INT. REV. MISSIONS 41 (1952), pp. 301-309.

15,299 BROWNE, S. G. The indigenous medical evangelist in Congo. INT. REV. MISSIONS 35 (1946), pp. 59-67.

15,300 BUHLMANN, W. Science missionnaire et apostolat missionnaire. AEQUATORIA 18 (1955), pp. 139-142.

15,301 CAENEGHEM, R. VAN. Beschouwingen bij le rôle de la femme dans les Missions. AEQUATORIA 15 (1952), pp. 127-131.

15,302 CARPENTER, G. W. Co-operation in Christian literature production in Belgian Congo. INT. REV. MISSIONS 43 (1954), pp. 414-420.

15,303 CARROCERA, P. B. DE. Os Capuchinhos no Congo e o clero indígena. PORT. EM. AFR. 6 (1949), pp. 232-241.

15,304 CLEENE, N. DE. Africa and Christianity. CONGO 2 (1937), pp. 277-290.

15,305 CLEENE, N. DE. Un stade de l'évolution de la vie religieuse au Mayombe. CONGO 1 (1935), pp. 668-684.

15,306 COCKER, M. DE. Essai de parallelisme biblico-congolais. ZAIRE 4 (1950), pp. 277-298.

15,307 COMHAIRE, J. Note sur les musulmans de Léopoldville. ZAIRE 2 (1948), pp. 303-304.

15,308 COXILL, H. W. Protestants in the Belgian Congo. INT. REV. MISSIONS 34 (1945), pp. 273-279.

15,309 CUVELIER, J. La pratique baptismale des missionnaires capucins dans l'ancien Congo. ZAIRE 4 (1950), pp. 429-435.

15,310 DUMONT, G. Statistiques de la Mission de Lemfu en 1934. CONGO 2 (1935), pp. 172-184.

15,311 FORD, W. H. Conversion and its recognition in Congo converts. INT. REV. MISSIONS 22 (1933), pp. 377-387.

15,312 GEVAERTS, T. F. De UNESCO en de zedelijke opvoeding der inlanders in Belgisch Kongo. ZAIRE 7 (1953), pp. 829-838.

15,313 GREGORIUS. Een nieuwe missieactie in wording. CONGO 2 (1934), pp. 361-366.

15,314 HILDEBRAND, P. Wordt Joris Van Geel ooit zaligverklaard? ZAIRE 1 (1947), pp. 687-697.

15,315 JONGHE, E. DE. Pie XI, le pape des missions 1922-1939. CONGO 1 (1939), pp. 121-124.

15,316 KILGER, P. L. As dificuldades da Antiga Missão do Congo. PORT. EM AFR. 5 (1948), pp. 17-25.

15,317 LAGAE, R. Vijf en twintig jaar Dominikaansch Apostolaat in Uéle. CONGO 2 (1937), pp. 259-268.

15,318 LEITE DE FARIA, F. Fr. João de Santiago e a sua Relação sobre os Capuchinhos no Congo. PORT. EM AFR. 10 (1953), pp. 316-333.

15,319 LEITE DE FARIA, F. Glorioso Tricentenário. O Capuchinho Jorge de Geel, morto pela fé em Terras do Congo. PORT. EM AFR. 10 (1953), pp. 69-85.

15,320 LERRIGO, P. H. J. Protestant missions in relation to the future of Congo. INT. REV. MISSIONS 25 (1936), pp. 227-234.

15,321 MARCHAL, P. G. Santo António do Zaire. PORT. EM AFR. 4 (1947), pp. 274-280.

15,322 MARTINS, P. J. A Missão do Lucula. PORT. EM AFR. 4 (1947), pp. 139-143.

15,323 MORTELMANS, G. and MONTEYNE, R. La Grotto peinte de Mbafu, témoignage iconographique de la première évangélisation du Bas-Congo. PROC. PAN-AFR. CONGR. PRE-HIST. 4, no. iii (1962), pp. 457-486.

15,324 POSTIOMA, A. DE. A heresia do antonianismo. PORT. EM AFR. 19 (1962), pp. 378-381.

15,325 POSTIOMA, A. DE. Metodologia missionária dos capuchinhos no Congo-Matamba-Angola 1645-1834. PORT. EM AFR. 21 (1964), pp. 293-304, 343-360.

15,326 RAYMAKERS, P. L'Eglise de Jésus-Christ sur la terre par le prophète Simon Kimbangu. Contribution à l'étude des mouvements messianiques dans le Bas-Kongo. ZAIRE 13 (1959), pp. 675-756.

15,327 RIEL, P. A. Evangelização do Maiombe. PORT. EM AFR. 5 (1948), pp. 10-15.

15,328 ROEYKENS, P. A. Les Capucins et les Missions Congolaises au XIX siècle. AEQUATORIA 11 (1948), pp. 128-136.

15,329 ROEYKENS, P. A. Les Pères du Saint-Esprit et l'acceptation de la mission du Congo au XIXe siècle. AEQUATORIA 13 (1950), pp. 93-100; 14 (1951), pp. 1-47.

15,330 ROP, A. DE. Kanttekening bij de "Bantu-Mis." ZAIRE 7 (1953), pp. 497-501.

15,331 SCHEBESTA, P. Tore, le dieu forestier des Bambuti. ZAIRE 1 (1947), pp. 181-195.

15,332 STONELAKE, A. The missionary situation in Congo. INT. REV. MISSIONS 8 (1919), pp. 314-330.

15,333 TEIXEIRA MAIO, A. Experiência eloquente: o drama do Kasai. PORT. EM AFR. Supplement (1960-1961), pp. 260-268.

15,334 TROESCH, J. B. História religiosa do Congo... PORT. EM AFR. 16 (1959), pp. 232-245, 358-362; 17 (1960), pp. 41-51.

15,335 TURNBULL, C. M. The molimo: a men's religious association among the Ituri Bambuti. ZAIRE 14 (1960), pp. 307-340.

15,336 VIERSTRAETE, G. De rol van de leken in de missielanden. ZAIRE 6 (1952), pp. 944-955.

15,337 VLEESCHAUWER, M. A. DE. The Christian church in Belgian Congo. J. AFR. SOC. 37 (1938), pp. 510-511.

15,338 A propos de l'égalité des missions nationales et étrangères au Congo. ZAIRE 1 (1947), pp. 323-324.

15,339 Le Congo Belge, foyer de persécution! ZAIRE 4 (1950), pp. 1025-1026.

15,340 Discours de M. J. Masa au Congrès des Syndicats Chrétiens à Bruxelles. ZAIRE 4 (1950), pp. 61-71.

15,341 Os Proto-Missionários do Congo. PORT. EM AFR. 1 (1944), pp. 99-112.

15,342 De Protestantsche Zendingen in Kongo. CONGO 1 (1921), pp. 573-583.

15,343 Recordando: Rev. Dr. Clemente Pereira da Silva. PORT. EM AFR. 14 (1957), pp. 261-266.

Science

15,344 ADRIAENS, L. Le Croton Tiglium L. CONGO 2 (1934), pp. 674-691.

15,345 ADRIAENS, L. Le Pentadesma Butyracea du Congo Belge. CONGO 1 (1934), pp. 180-188.

15,346 ADRIAENS, L. Les plantes à huile chaulmoogrique. CONGO 2, no. 4 (1933), pp. 524-534.

15,347 ADRIAENS, L. La valeur économique de l'Aleurites montana. CONGO 1 (1939), pp. 499-513.

15,348 AUTRET, M. and BURGESS, R. C. Supplementary feeding programmes in Africa: the example of the Belgian Congo. MALNUTRITION IN AFRICAN WOMEN..., 1952, pp. 324-331.

15,349 B., F. The Parc National Albert: Belgian Congo. NIGERIAN FIELD 3 (1934), pp. 103-111.

15,350 BASTIN, R. Etude de la fécule de Pachira aquatica Aubl. CONGO 2 (1937), pp. 1-12.

15,351 BILSEN, J. VAN. Het sociaal aspect van het doktersgeschil. ZAIRE 4 (1950), pp. 1118-1120.

15,352 BOGAERTS, H. De luipaard bij de negervolkeren uit Kasai. CONGO 2 (1936), pp. 210-227.

15,353 BRANDE, P. V. Contribution à l'étude de quelques espèces végétales du Katanga méridional. BULL. SEANCES IRCB 6 (1935), pp. 652-665.

15,354 BRANDEN, F. VAN DEN. Action des sels de métaux rares (Gallium, Vanadium) sur les infections à Trypanosoma congolense chez le cobaye et le rat. BULL. SEANCES IRCB 2 (1931), pp. 595-605.

15,355 BRANDEN, F. VAN DEN. Action des sels de métaux rares (gallium, vanadium) sur les infections à Trypanosoma Rhodesiense chez le rat. BULL. SEANCES IRCB 3 (1932), pp. 399-402.

15,356 BRANDEN, F. VAN DEN. Sur les essais de traitement des infections à Trypanosoma congolense par le Bayer 205, le Naganol et la Fouadine. BULL. SEANCES IRCB 1 (1930), pp. 517-522.

15,357 BURGEON, L. Note sur la faune entomologique du Ruwenzeri. BULL. SEANCES IRCB 4 (1933), pp. 455-469.

15,358 BUTTGENBACH, H. Sur un sulfate d'urane du Katanga. BULL. SEANCES IRCB 6 (1935), pp. 449-455.

15,359 CALUWAERT, R. Milonge's. CONGO 1 (1921), pp. 45-47.

15,360 CASTAGNE, E. Contribution à l'étude chimique de la Liane Efiri. CONGO 1 (1934), pp. 41-48, 341-347; 2 (1934), pp. 357-360; 1 (1935), pp. 32-37.

15,361 CHARLES, V. L'orientation et la protection médicale des travailleurs. ZAIRE 6 (1952), pp. 739-741.

15,362 CHARLES, V. Le service médical des entreprises. ZAIRE 7 (1953), p. 393.

15,363 COUTREZ, G. L'éclipse annulaire totale de soleil du 24 février 1933 au Congo belge. BULL. SEANCES IRCB 3 (1932), pp. 511-518.

15,364 CRUZ, F. Uma espécie extinta da fauna do Congo no século XVI. BOL. INST. ANGOLA 12 (1959), pp. 99-101.

15,365 DELEVOY, G. La gestion des forêts congolaises. BULL. SEANCES IRCB 2 (1931), pp. 120-141.

15,366 DELEVOY, G. Sur les essais d'introduction des quinquinas au Katanga. BULL. SEANCES IRCB 1 (1930), pp. 472-476.

15,367 DELHAYE, F. and SLUYS, M. Les Calcaires du Bas-Congo. CONGO 1 (1921), pp. 211-237, 414-430.

15,368 DEROOVER, M. L'eau potable au Congo belge. BULL. SEANCES IRCB 2 (1931), pp. 670-688.

15,369 DROOGMANS, H. Sur l'importance des plantations de quinquinas. BULL. SEANCES IRCB 1 (1930), pp. 456-457.

15,370 DUBOIS, A. Contribution à la connaissance des souches de bacilles tuberculeux au Congo. BULL. SEANCES IRCB 4 (1933), pp. 445-454.

15,371 DUBOIS, A. La lèpre dans la région de Pawa-Wamba. BULL. SEANCES IRCB 2 (1931), pp. 173-179.

15,372 DUBOIS, A. La pauvreté en calcium des terrains et des eaux du Congo. BULL. SEANCES IRCB 6 (1935), pp. 711-712.

15,373 DUBOIS, A. La prophylaxie de la lèpre au Congo. BULL. SEANCES IRCB 6 (1935), pp. 458-472.

15,374 DUBOIS, A. La thérapeutique de l'infection à trypanosome congolense (Broden), par le Bayer 205 et l'émétique de potassium associés. BULL. SEANCES IRCB 1 (1930), pp. 326-335.

15,375 ESSER, J. Le centre africain crie famine. AEQUATORIA 13 (1950), pp. 12-13.

15,376 FONTAINAS, P. Contribution à la description géologique de l'Afrique Centrale. BULL. SEANCES IRCB 5 (1934), pp. 408-434.

15,377 FONTAINAS, P. La question de l'étain et le Congo Belge. BULL. SEANCES IRCB 2 (1931), pp. 227-229.

15,378 FOURMARIER, P. Note préliminaire sur la tectonique du Ruwenzori. BULL. SEANCES IRCB 4 (1933), pp. 237-243.

15,379 FOURMARIER, P. Présentation de la minute de la première feuille de la carte géologique du Congo belge à l'échelle du 500000e. BULL. SEANCES IRCB 2 (1931), pp. 313-316.

15,380 FOURMARIER, P. Rapport sur les travaux de la Commission de Géologie du Ministère des Colonies pendant les années 1931 et 1932. BULL. SEANCES IRCB 4 (1933), pp. 187-194.

15,381 GELISSEN, G. Note sur le copal. CONGO 1 (1940), pp. 273-283.

15,382 GYSIN, M. Note préliminaire sur la géologie et la pétrographie du Katanga méridional. BULL. SEANCES IRCB 5 (1934), pp. 701-703.

15,383 HEINZELIN, J. DE. Les formations du Western Rift et de la cuvette congolaise. PROC. PAN-AFR. CONGR. PRE-HIST. 4 (1962), pp. 219-243.

15,384 HEMERIJCKX, F. Les causes médicales et sociales de la dénatalité. ZAIRE 2 (1948), pp. 471-523.

15,385 L'HEUREUX, L. Les Agrumes. CONGO 2 (1938), pp. 59-66, 179-196, 256-295.

15,386 HIERNAUX, J. Etat de nutrition des Kuba (Kasai). ZAIRE 8 (1954), pp. 719-727.

15,387 HULSTAERT, G. L'alimentation de l'indigène. AEQUATORIA 7 (1944), pp. 155-157.

15,388 JONCKHEERE, F. Recherches préliminaires chimiques et médicales sur l'Efiri. BULL. SEANCES IRCB 2 (1931), pp. 575-581.

15,389 LEDOUX, P. A propos de Butyrospermum Parkii (G. Don) Kotschy [Karité] signalé dans la région de Mahagi (Congo Belge). BULL. SEANCES IRCB 1 (1930), pp. 338-344.

15,390 LEPLAE, E. Dispositions qui seront suivies pour l'introduction du quinquina dans les villages du Congo belge. BULL. SEANCES IRCB 2 (1931), pp. 98-112.

15,391 LEPLAE, E. Enquête sur divers essais de culture de quinquinas exécutés dans le Bas-Congo. BULL. SEANCES IRCB 4 (1933), pp. 498-509.

15,392 LEPLAE, E. Résultats de l'analyse chimique de vingt-cinq échantillons d'écorces de quinquinas provenant de la région de Kilo. BULL. SEANCES IRCB 2 (1931), pp. 307-312.

15,393 M., V. Problèmes alimentaires. AEQUATORIA 20 (1957), pp. 129-135.

15,394 MARCHAL, M. L'étude de Mm. Staner et Verplancke relative à un état pathologique du Sisal au Congo Belge. BULL. SEANCES IRCB 1 (1930), pp. 279-300.

15,395 MATHOT, R. E. L'utilisation des huiles végétales pour la force motrice au Congo Belge. CONGO 2 (1921), pp. 125-135.

15,396 MEYER, E. DE and CLOSE, J. Nitrogen and fat balance in the 'normal' adults in the Belgian Congo. MALNUTRITION IN AFRICAN WOMEN..., 1952, pp. 191-195.

15,397 MOTTOULE. Historique, organisation et résultats obtenus d'une oeuvre de protection de l'enfance noire dans la population indigène industrielle de Union Minière du Haut-Katanga. BULL. SEANCES IRCB 2 (1931), pp. 531-544.

15,398 NGOI, P. La grossesse et l'enfantement chez les Nkundo. AEQUATORIA 7 (1944), pp. 117-124.

15,399 PASSAU, G. La région volcanique du Sud-Ouest du lac Kivu. BULL. SEANCES IRCB 3 (1932), pp. 414-424.

15,400 PHILIPPS, T. Les sciences naturelles sous les tropiques africains. ZAIRE 4 (1950), pp. 359-377.

15,401 PIERAERTS, J. and ROBYNS. Le Pappea Radlkoferi Schweinf. BULL. SEANCES IRCB 1 (1930), pp. 313-321.

15,402 PIERAERTS, M. J. and TANRET, M. G. Contribution à l'étude du Tetrapleura Thonningii Benth. BULL. SEANCES IRCB 1 (1930), pp. 121-142.

15,403 PIERAERTS, J. et al. Contribution à l'étude chimique des Légumineuses oléagineuses du Congo belge, by J. Pieraerts, E. Castagne, L. Adriaens. BULL. SEANCES IRCB 1 (1930), pp. 143-186.

15,404 POLINARD, E. Description de pierres taillées provenant de la région du Kasai. BULL. SEANCES IRCB 6 (1935), pp. 669-679.

15,405 PYNAERT, L. Dispersion de la culture du quinquina chez les indigènes de la colonie. BULL. SEANCES IRCB 1 (1930), pp. 470-471.

15,406 PYNAERT, L. Les sauterelles au Congo belge. La lutte. BULL. SEANCES IRCB 3 (1932), pp. 425-458.

15,407 ROBERT, M. Le système du Kundelungu au Katanga. BULL. SEANCES IRCB 4 (1933), pp. 436-440.

15,408 ROBYNS, W. Sur les espèces de Podocarpus du Congo belge et du Ruanda-Urundi. BULL. SEANCES IRCB 6 (1935), pp. 226-242.

15,409 RODHAIN, A. Sur l'extension à donner à la culture du Cinchona Succirubra, pour lutter contre la malaria chez les indigènes. BULL. SEANCES IRCB 1 (1930), pp. 458-469.

15,410 RODHAIN, A. J. and NYSSEN, R. Essais thérapeutiques avec l'Efiri dans la malaria humaine. BULL. SEANCES IRCB 5 (1934), pp. 435-444.

15,411 RYCKMANS, P. Etudes démographiques du Fonds Reine Elisabeth pour l'assistance médicale aux indigènes (Foréami) dans le Bas-Congo. BULL. SEANCES IRCB 5 (1934), pp. 366-384.

15,412 SANTESSON, C. G. Pfeilgiftstudien. Cortex Erythrophlaei aus Zentralafrika. ETHNOS 2 (1937), pp. 230-234.

15,413 SANTOS DIAS, J. A. T. Uma nova espécie de Haematopota (Diptera, Tabanidae) do Congo Belga. BSEM 120 (1960), pp. 55-60 including English summary.

15,414 SCHOUTEDEN, H. A propos de la faune ornithologique du Parc National Albert. BULL. SEANCES IRCB 4 (1933), pp. 149-156.

15,415 SCHOUTEDEN, H. A propos des sauterelles migratrices [with a note by H. Droogmans]. BULL. SEANCES IRCB 3 (1932), pp. 137-156.

15,416 SCHOUTEDEN, H. Les mollusques aquatiques vivants et subfossiles de la région du lac Kivu. BULL. SEANCES IRCB 4 (1933), pp. 519-527.

15,417 SCHUMACHER, P. La fillette exposée dans la cime de l'arbre. AEQUATORIA 11 (1948), pp. 143-146.

15,418 SCHWETZ, J. Les problèmes médicaux actuels au Congo belge; ce qui a été fait et ce qui reste à faire. ZAIRE 2 (1948), pp. 3-13.

15,419 SCHWETZ, J. Un voyage médical et paramédical dans la forêt de l'Ituri. CONGO 2 (1934), pp. 16-34.

15,420 TROLLI, G. L'alimentation chez les travailleurs imdigènes dans les exploitations commerciales, agricoles, industrielles et minières au Congo. AFRICA 9 (1936), pp. 197-217.

15,421 TROLLI, G. Résultats d'une enquête sur la présence et la vitalité des insectes et rats et notamment des moustiques à bord des avions de la ligne Léo-Stanleyville. BULL. SEANCES IRCB 3 (1932), pp. 601-630.

15,422 VANDERYST, H. La capture, à Thielen Saint-Jacques, de deux râles des prés, bagués, l'un à Jägebord (Suède), l'autre à Helgoland et les futures explorations ornithologiques à organiser au Congo belge. BULL. SEANCES IRCB 2 (1931), pp. 283-295.

15,423 VERBEECK, A. Inlandse geneesmiddelen. AEQUATORIA 11 (1947), pp. 23-31, 70-75, 98-102, 148-152.

15,424 WILDE, L. DE. Het wetenschappelijk onderzoek in Belgisch-Kongo. KONGO-OVERZEE 14 (1948), pp. 65-81.

15,425 WILDEMAN, E. DE. A propos de plantes fébrifuges congolaises: Kongololo et Efiri. BULL. SEANCES IRCB 2 (1931), pp. 560-574.

15,426 WILDEMAN, E. DE. Considérations sur des espèces du genre Afzelia Smith. BULL. SEANCES IRCB 6 (1935), pp. 182-210.

15,427 WILDEMAN, E. DE. La culture des quinquinas à Katana et à Tshibinda. BULL. SEANCES IRCB 2 (1931), pp. 296-304.

15,428 WILDEMAN, E. DE. Encore la forêt tropicale congolaise. BULL. SEANCES IRCB 2 (1931), pp. 556-559.

15,429 WILDEMAN, E. DE. Une étude de M. Ledoux relative à la présence du Karité ou arbre à beurre dans la région de Mahagi. BULL. SEANCES IRCB 1 (1930), pp. 336-337.

15,430 WILDEMAN, E. DE. Plantes pour la soif. BULL. SEANCES IRCB 5 (1934), pp. 131-157.

15,431 WILDEMAN, E. DE. Quelques considérations sur les résines dénommées copals. BULL. SEANCES IRCB 4 (1933), pp. 478-497.

15,432 WILDEMAN, E. DE. Sur des plantes à huiles chaulmoogriques du Congo belge. BULL. SEANCES IRCB 1 (1930), pp. 94-115.

15,433 WILDEMAN, E. DE. Sur la question forestière en Afrique. BULL. SEANCES IRCB 1 (1930), pp. 504-516.

15,434 WILDEMAN, E. DE. Sur les poivres indigènes du Congo. Notes préliminaires. BULL. SEANCES IRCB 2 (1931), pp. 346-354.

15,435 WILDEMAN, E. DE. and PIERAERTS, J. Les Hydnocarpus à huile chaulmoogrique, cultivés au Congo. BULL. SEANCES IRCB 1 (1930), pp. 303-312.

15,436 La conservation des gorilles du Parc National Albert est menacée. BULL. IEC 19-20 (1960), pp. 125-126.

Sociology

15,437 BACKER, E. DE. Considérations générales sur l'urbanisme au Congo belge. BULL. SEANCES IRCB 4 (1933), pp. 531-572.

15,438 BAECK, L. Léopoldville, phenomène urbain africain. ZAIRE 10 (1956), pp. 613-636.

15,439 BAECK, L. Une société rurale en transition: étude socio-économique de Thysville. ZAIRE 11 (1957), pp. 115-186.

15,440 BILSEN, J. VAN. "Colour—Conflict." ZAIRE 4 (1950), pp. 881-882.

15,441 BILSEN, J. VAN. De gentse koloniale academische dag. ZAIRE 4 (1950), pp. 1120-1125.

15,442 BILSEN, J. VAN. Polemiek rond het syndicalisme. ZAIRE 4 (1950), pp. 319-320.

15,443 BILSEN, J. VAN. Urbanisme... ZAIRE 4 (1950), pp. 320-321.

15,444 BOELAERT, E. Assimilation. AEQUATORIA 14 (1951), pp. 1-5.

15,445 BOELAERT, E. Faut-il créer des réserves pour les indigènes? ZAIRE 9 (1955), pp. 133-142.

15,446 BOELAERT, E. Ontvolking door kolonizatie? AEQUATORIA 8 (1945), pp. 92-94.

15,447 BOUVAERT, A. C. Le colour-bar au Congo Belge. ZAIRE 3 (1949), pp. 895-900.

15,448 BRAUSCH, G. Culturele genootschappen in de moderne Afrikaanse samenleving. KONGO-OVERZEE 15 (1949), pp. 233-238.

15,449 BRAUSCH, G. Groepethnologie. De maatschappelijke groep als scheppende synthese. KONGO-OVERZEE 10-11 (1944-1945), pp. 20-48.

15,450 BRUEL, J. VAN DEN. Het maatschappelijk dienstbetoon in onze koloniale nijverheidsondernemingen. ZAIRE 1 (1947), pp. 903-909.

15,451 BRUYNS, L. Les mutualités au Congo: problèmes et évolution. CIVILISATIONS 10 (1960), pp. 225-231.

15,452 BRUYNS, L. Les mutualités ont-elles un sens au Congo? ZAIRE 10 (1956), pp. 1035-1044.

15,453 BRUYNS, L. and PINXTEN, K. De geleide immigratie van de Banya Ruanda in Kivu. ZAIRE 6 (1952), pp. 251-272.

15,454 BULCK, G. VAN. La promotion de la femme au Congo belge et au Ruanda-Urundi. A propos de la XIIe Session du Congrès Colonial National (23-24 novembre 1956). ZAIRE 10 (1956), pp. 1067-1074.

15,455 CAENEGHEM, E. VAN. Der psychologie der Baluba in heen spreekwoorden over de ziekten. ZAIRE 1 (1947), pp. 55-72.

15,456 CATOIRE, P. Le contrat social indigène. A propos d'une causerie de M. E. Capelle. ZAIRE 1 (1947), pp. 806-808.

15,457 CHARLES, V. A la Commission pour la Protection des Indigènes. ZAIRE 7 (1953), pp. 383-384.

15,458 CHARLES, V. L'assistance sociale. ZAIRE 4 (1950), pp. 889-891.

15,459 CHARLES, V. Autour du problème de l'habitat ouvrier. ZAIRE 5 (1951), pp. 288-291.

15,460 CHARLES, V. Belgian Africa. CIVILISATIONS 2 (1952), pp. 401-406.

15,461 CHARLES, V. Considérations sur le recensement de la population ouvrière. ZAIRE 6 (1952), pp. 67-70.

15,462 CHARLES, V. L'enquête sur le standing de l'indigène. ZAIRE 4 (1950), p. 1136.

15,463 CHARLES, V. L'équilibre des sexes parmi les adultes dans les milieux extra-coutumiers. ZAIRE 3 (1949), pp. 47-51.

15,464 CHARLES, V. L'exode rural. ZAIRE 4 (1950), pp. 884-886.

15,465 CHARLES, V. Familles ouvrières et évolution sociale à Thysville. ZAIRE 9 (1955), pp. 731-739.

15,466 CHARLES, V. Les Journées du Service Social à Bruxelles. ZAIRE 7 (1953), pp. 387-388.

15,467 CHARLES, V. Le "mal démographique" de Léopoldville. ZAIRE 2 (1948), pp. 897-901.

15,468 CHARLES, V. Le marché du travail à Léopoldville. ZAIRE 7 (1953), pp. 858-859.

15,469 CHARLES, V. L'office des cités africaines. ZAIRE 6 (1952), pp. 742-744.

15,470 CHARLES, V. L'organisation professionnelle. ZAIRE 4 (1950), pp. 888-889.

15,471 CHARLES, V. Le problème de l'habitat. ZAIRE 6 (1952), pp. 1079-1082.

15,472 CHARLES, V. Le problème de l'habitation. ZAIRE 7 (1953), pp. 854-855.

15,473 CHARLES, V. La protection de l'enfance delinquante a Leopoldville. ZAIRE 9 (1955), pp. 1029-1037.

15,474 CHARLES, V. Revendications syndicales. ZAIRE 5 (1951), pp. 285-288.

15,475 CHARLES, V. Les travaux du Conseil de Gouvernement. ZAIRE 7 (1953), pp. 851-853.

15,476 CLERCQ, A. DE. L'attitude des Baluba vis-à-vis de la pénétration des idées européennes. BULL. SEANCES IRCB 2 (1931), pp. 46-51.

15,477 COMHAIRE, J. Note sur les Musulmans de Léopoldville. ZAIRE 2 (1948), pp. 303-304.

15,478 COMHAIRE, J. Some aspects of urbanization in the Belgian Congo. AMER. J. SOC. 62 (1956-1957), pp. 8-13.

15,479 COMHAIRE-SYLVAIN, S. Jeux congolais. ZAIRE 6 (1952), pp. 351-362.

15,480 COMHAIRE-SYLVAIN, S. Les jeux des enfants noirs de Leopoldville. ZAIRE 3 (1949), pp. 139-152.

15,481 COMITE PERMANENT DU CONGRES COLONIAL NATIONAL. Paysannat indigène. CONGO 1 (1934), pp. 390-396.

15,482 COPPENS, P. Le problème des mulâtres. ZAIRE 1 (1947), pp. 733-753.

15,483 COSTERMANS, B. De spelen bij de Mamvu en Logo in de gewesten Watsa-Faradje. ZAIRE 2 (1948), pp. 249-275, 757-785.

15,484 CRINE, F. Aspects politico-sociaux du système du tenure des terres des Luunda Septentrionaux. AFR. AGRARIAN SYSTEMS, 1963, pp. 157-172.

15,485 DAVIDSON, J. Protestant missions and marriage in the Belgian Congo. AFRICA 18 (1948), pp. 120-128.

15,486 DENOLF, P. Ontvolking en veelwijverij in Kongo. CONGO 1 (1934), pp. 528-549.

15,487 DEVAUX, V. Rapport sur un projet de décret sur l'immatriculation des indigènes. ZAIRE 3 (1949), pp. 197-206.

15,488 ENGELS, A. Quelques observations sur les migrations indigènes dans la région de l'Equateur. BULL. SEANCES IRCB 5 (1934), pp. 218-226.

15,489 ESSER, J. Vision de deux mondes qui s'affrontent. AEQUATORIA 12 (1949), pp. 133-137.

15,490 GILLE, A. and GREVISSE, F. The social and scientific role of C.E.P.S.I. AFR. AFFAIRS 49 (1950), pp. 151-157.

15,491 GREVISSE, F. Les aspects multiples et changeants du problème du logement des populations Katangaises. CIVILISATIONS 12 (1962), pp. 88-107; English summary, pp. 108-110.

15,492 GUGLIELMI, G. L'evoluzione degli africani: identità formali e differenze sostanziali. AFRICA (Rome) 13 (1958), pp. 121-123.

15,493 H., G. Contre la prolétarisation des Congolais. AEQUATORIA 11 (1948), pp. 106-107.

15,494 HEIJBOER, B. M. Demographische gegevens over de Ngōmbē van het District der Tshuapa. ZAIRE 1 (1947), pp. 969-1000.

15,495 HEUSCH, L. DE. A propos d'une mise en question par le R. P. de Sousberghe des thèses sociologiques de M. Lévi-Strauss. ZAIRE 9 (1955), pp. 849-861.

15,496 HOVE, J. VAN. Social service in the Belgian Congo: present situation and future plans. CIVILISATIONS 1, no. 1 (1951), pp. 22-26; French summary, p. 27.

15,497 HULSTAERT, G. Civilisation occidentale et langage au Congo Belge. AEQUATORIA 16 (1953), pp. 23-25.

15,498 HULSTAERT, G. Dénatalité dans l'Uele. AEQUATORIA 18 (1955), pp. 105-106.

15,499 HULSTAERT, G. La Dénatalité dans les milieux indigènes. AEQUATORIA 7 (1944), pp. 158-161.

15,500 HULSTAERT, G. Dénatalité Mongo. AEQUATORIA 19 (1956), pp. 45-48.

15,501 HULSTAERT, G. Note démographique. AEQUATORIA 11 (1948), pp. 20-22, 50-52.

15,502 JONGHE, E. DE. A propos de l'esclavage au Congo. BULL. SEANCES IRCB 4 (1933), pp. 65-88.

15,503 LAMAL, F. Considerations critiques sur des récents travaux de démographie congolaise. ZAIRE 9 (1955), pp. 563-588.

15,504 LAMAL, F. La densité de la population rurale au Congo belge. ZAIRE 9 (1955), pp. 723-729.

15,505 LAMAL, F. L'exode massif des hommes adultes vers Léopoldville. ZAIRE 8 (1954), pp. 365-377.

15,506 LAROCHETTE, J. Problèmes culturels et problèmes linguistiques. ZAIRE 4 (1950), pp. 123-165.

15,507 LEBLANC, M. La problématique d'adaptation du T.A.T. au Congo. ZAIRE 12 (1958), pp. 339-348.

15,508 LE GRAND, L. La dépopulation du Congo Belge et les recensements de 1917. CONGO 1 (1921), pp. 202-210.

15,509 LEPLAE, E. Les avantages et les modalités d'introduction du paysannat intégral au Congo belge. CONGO 1 (1934), pp. 504-527.

15,510 LEPLAE, E. Un exemple à méditer par le Congo belge: heureux effets d'une culture obligatoire dans une Colonie française. BULL. SEANCES IRCB 6 (1935), pp. 637-651.

15,511 LODEWIJCKW, C. Est-il possible de relever la natalité Nkundo? AEQUATORIA 11 (1948), pp. 1-5.

15,512 LOTAR, P. L'enquête coloniale instituée dans l'Afrique Occidentale et Equatoriale Française sur l'organisation familiale indigène. BULL. SEANCES IRCB 2 (1931), pp. 275-278.

15,513 LUCENTINI, M. Congo dei grattacieli. AFRICA (Rome) 10 (1955), pp. 183-184.

15,514 LUX, A. Migrations, accroissement et urbanisation de la population congolaise de Luluabourg. ZAIRE 12 (1958), pp. 675-724, 819-877.

15,515 M., V. Délinquance juvénile. AEQUATORIA 8 (1945), p. 95.

15,516 MAN, M. DE. Het sociaal statuut van de vrouw in Belgisch-Kongo. ZAIRE 4 (1950), pp. 851-869.

15,517 MAQUET, J. J. The modern evolution of African populations in the Belgian Congo. AFRICA 19 (1949), pp. 265-271.

15,518 MAQUET, M. Les populations des environs de Léopoldville. CONGO 2 (1937), pp. 241-258.

15,519 MARZORATI, A. F. L'évolution des relations entre les communautés européennes et la société du Congo belge. ZAIRE 6 (1952), pp. 929-939.

15,520 MERNIER, P. L'évolution de la société noire au Congo belge. ZAIRE 2 (1948), pp. 835-868.

15,521 MOELLER, A. L'adaptation des Sociétés indigènes de la Province Orientale à la situation créée par la colonisation. BULL. SEANCES IRCB 2 (1931), pp. 52-66.

15,522 MOELLER, A. Blancs et Noirs au Congo Belge. CONGO 2 (1934), pp. 1-15.

15,523 MOELLER, A. Les grandes lignes des migrations des Bantous de la Province Orientale. BULL. SEANCES IRCB 5 (1934), pp. 63-111.

15,524 MULLER, E. W. L'organisation sociale des Ekonda et la terminologie sociologique. AEQUATORIA 21 (1958), pp. 41-59.

15,525 MUNGUL-DIAKA, B. Projet de regroupement des villages en centres ruraux. ET. CONG. 4, no. 5 (1963), pp. 32-42.

15,526 NICAISE, J. Belgian Congo and Ruanda Urundi. CIVILISATIONS 4 (1954), pp. 490-494; 5 (1955), pp. 447-452.

15,527 NICAISE, J. Mise au point. ZAIRE 8 (1954), pp. 633-634.

15,528 NICAISE, J. La question de l'habitation indigène. ZAIRE 8 (1954), pp. 181-184.

15,529 OMBREDANE, A. Les techniques de fortune dans le travail coutumier des Noirs. PRESENCE AFR. 13 (1952), pp. 58-68.

15,530 PHILLIPS, A. African marriage in the Belgian Congo. J. AFR. ADM. 2 (1950), pp. 15-19.

15,531 REYES MORALES, R. El pseudo estado tribal y racista del Congo. ARCH. INST. EST. AFR. 16, no. 63 (1962), pp. 7-31.

15,532 ROMANIUK, A. Evolution et perspectives démographiques de la population au Congo. ZAIRE 13 (1959), pp. 563-626.

15,533 RUBBENS, A. L'action syndicale près des Congolais. ZAIRE 1 (1947), pp. 1111-1119.

15,534 RUBBENS, A. Le colour-bar au Congo Belge. ZAIRE 3 (1949), pp. 503-513.

15,535 RUTTEN, A. Démographie congolaise. CONGO 2 (1921), pp. 1-13.

15,536 RYCKMANS, A. Etude sur les statistiques démographiques au Congo belge. ZAIRE 7 (1953), pp. 3-33.

15,537 RYCKMANS, A. Démographie congolaise. AFRICA 6 (1933), pp. 241-258.

15,538 RYCKMANS, A. Note sur la démographie congolaise. BULL. SEANCES IRCB 2 (1931), pp. 254-269.

15,539 SAUTTER, G. Aperçu sur les villes africaines du Moyen Congo. AFR. ET ASIE 14 (1951), pp. 34-53.

15,540 SCHEBESTA, P. Blancs et Noirs au Congo belge. CONGO 1 (1934), pp. 321-340.

15,541 SCHOENTJES, R. Considérations générales sur l'urbanisme au Congo belge. BULL. SEANCES IRCB 5 (1934), pp. 534-560.

15,542 SCHWERS, G. A. Les facteurs de la dénatalité au Congo Belge. AEQUATORIA 7 (1944), pp. 89-100.

15,543 SOHIER, A. Mariage coutumier et mariage religieux. ZAIRE 1 (1947), pp. 73-76.

15,544 SOHIER, A. La politique d'intégration. ZAIRE 5 (1951), pp. 899-928.

15,545 SOHIER, A. Le statut personnel des autochtones au Congo Belge. CIVILISATIONS 3 (1953), pp. 179-186; English summary, pp. 186-187.

15,546 SOHIER, J. Quelques considérations sur les travaux démographiques. ZAIRE 3 (1949), pp. 293-301.

15,547 SOORS, M. La dénatalité chez les Mongo. ZAIRE 4 (1950), pp. 525-532.

15,548 STORMS, A. Famille chrétienne et société matriarcale au Katanga. ZAIRE 2 (1948), pp. 239-248.

15,549 TROLLI, G. Contribution à l'étude de la démographie des Bakongo. BULL. SEANCES IRCB 5 (1934), pp. 239-316.

15,550 VANSINA, J. Migrations dans la province du Kasai. Une hypothèse. ZAIRE 10 (1956), pp. 69-85.

15,551 VERHAEGEN, B. Présentation morphologique des nouvelles provinces. ET. CONG. 4, no. 4 (1963), pp. 1-24.

15,552 WILLEMS, M. Belgian Congo, an up-to-date survey from the economic, social and political points of view. KONGO-OVERZEE 12-13 (1946-1947), pp. 156-172.

15,553 ZIEGLER, J. Le mercenariat Katangais. GENEVE-AFR. 2 (1963), pp. 68-77.

15,554 Considérations sur la justice sociale. ZAIRE 3 (1949), pp. 803-804.

15,555 Fédération des associations de colons. ZAIRE 4 (1950), pp. 1006-1007.

15,556 Note démographique. ZAIRE 3 (1949), pp. 433-440.

15,557 Resumé du rapport de la Sous-Commission chargée de l'étude des habitations indigènes dans les cités indigènes et centres extra-coutumiers. ZAIRE 3 (1949), pp. 413-420.

15,558 Le sort des jeunes délinquants. ZAIRE 5 (1951), pp. 613-616.

15,559 Social policy of Union Minière du Haut Katanga. AFR. AFFAIRS 46 (1947), pp. 87-89.

15,560 Statistiques de la polygamie au Congo. ZAIRE 9 (1955), p. 1089.

See also 4559, 8379, 13475, 21227.

Agriculture

15,561 LEURQUIN, P. Economie de subsistance et alimentation au Ruanda-Urundi. Quelques cas concrets. ZAIRE 12 (1958), pp. 3-35.

15,562 LEURQUIN, P. La vie économique du paysan ruanda. L'exemple de Karama, Nyaruguru. ZAIRE 11 (1957), pp. 41-67.

Anthropology

15,563 ALBERT, E. M. Une étude de valeurs en Urundi. CAH. ET. AFR. 1 (1960), pp. 148-160.

15,564 ARIANOFF, A. D'. Origines des clans Hamites du Ruanda. ZAIRE 5 (1951), pp. 45-54.

15,565 BUCK, A. DE. Les mutualités au Kivu et au Ruanda-Urundi. ZAIRE 9 (1955), pp. 33-42.

15,566 BULCK, G. VAN. La conception coutumière d'enfant légitime, d'enfant nKuli et d'enfant umusambanano au Rwanda. ZAIRE 10 (1956), pp. 729-737.

15,567 GRAVEL, P. B. Life on the manor in Gisaka (Rwanda). J. AFR. HIST. 6 (1965), pp. 323-331.

15,568 HERTEFELT, M. D'. Huwelijk, familie en aanverwants chap bij de Reera (noordwestelijk Rwaanda). ZAIRE 13 (1959), pp. 115-147, 243-285.

15,569 HIERNAUX, J. Note sur une ancienne population du Ruanda-Urundi: les Renge. ZAIRE 10 (1956), pp. 351-360.

15,570 KAGAME, A. Le code ésotérique de la dynastie du Rwanda. ZAIRE 1 (1947), pp. 363-386.

15,571 KAGAME, A. Importantes manifestations religieuses au Ruanda. ZAIRE 1 (1947), pp. 84-89.

15,572 KAGAME, A. La poésie pastorale au Rwanda. ZAIRE 1 (1947), pp. 791-800.

15,573 MAQUET, J. J. Les groupes de parenté du Rwanda ancien. AFRICA 23 (1953), pp. 25-28; English summary, p. 29.

15,574 MAQUET, J. J. Le problème de la domination Tutsi. ZAIRE 6 (1952), pp. 1011-1016.

15,575 PAGES, A. A Ruanda, à la cour du Mwami. ZAIRE 4 (1950), pp. 471-487.

15,576 PAGES, A. Rwanda Belge. Cérémonies qui entourent la naissance d'un enfant et réclusion de la mère. CONGO 2 (1934), pp. 205-226.

15,577 PAGES, R. P. Proverbes et sentences du Ruanda. AEQUATORIA 10 (1947), pp. 81-88, 144-150; 11 (1948), pp. 53-59, 81-86.

15,578 PAUWELS, M. La chasse au Rwanda. KONGO-OVERZEE 22 (1956), pp. 40-74, 230-243.

15,579 PAUWELS, M. Etude complémentaire sur le mariage au Rwanda. KONGO-OVERZEE 20 (1954), pp. 126-158.

15,580 PAUWELS, M. Le symbolisme du tabouret Munyarwanda. KONGO-OVERZEE 21 (1955), pp. 144-156.

15,581 PAUWELS, P. H. Fiancée et jeune mariée au Rwanda. ZAIRE 5 (1951), pp. 115-135.

15,582 PAUWELS, P. M. L'héritage au Rukiga des environs de Byumba, Ruanda. ZAIRE 4 (1950), pp. 847-850.

15,583 PAUWELS, R. P. M. La divination au Rwanda. KONGO-OVERZEE 20 (1954), pp. 293-368.

15,584 SANTOS, E. DOS. Gli Europei ei popoli della Lunda. AFRICA (Rome) 19 (1964), pp. 91-97.

15,585 SCHUMACHER, P. Au Ruanda. Considérations sur la nature de l'homme. ZAIRE 3 (1949), pp. 257-278.

15,586 SCHUMACHER, P. Caracterologie au Ruanda. ZAIRE 2 (1948), pp. 591-624.

15,587 SCHUMACHER, P. Les Twides. ZAIRE 1 (1947), pp. 1049-1053.

15,588 SOUSBERGHE, L. DE. Cousins croisés et descendants: les systèmes du Rwanda et du Burundi comparés à ceux du Bas-Congo. AFRICA 35 (1965), pp. 396-421.

15,589 TROUWBORST, A. Kinship and geographical mobility in Burundi (East Central Africa). INT. J. COMP. SOC. 6 (1965), pp. 166-182.

15,590 WILDE, L. DE. Het huwelijk in de Tshohwe-Maatschappij van het gewest Kahemba. KONGO-OVERZEE 22 (1956), pp. 384-391.

See also 18738.

Art. Antiquities

15,591 BERGEAUD, G. Note sur les outils à encoches (grattoirs) trouvés dans la vallée du Niari. BULL. IEC 1, no. 2 (1947), pp. 119-124.

15,592 BOUVEIGNES, O. DE. Les danses negres [with English summary by H. P. Junod]. AFR. MUSIC, 1952, pp. 21-30.

15,593 HIERNAUX, J. Recent research at protohistoric sites in Ruanda, the Belgian Congo (Katanga province) and in Uganda (Kibiro). DISCOVERING AFRICA'S PAST, 1959, pp. 26-30.

15,594 MAQUET, E. Une représentation théâtrale au Rwanda. ZAIRE 4 (1950), pp. 1001-1002.

15,595 MERRIAM, A. P. Yovu songs from Ruanda. ZAIRE 11 (1957), pp. 933-966.

See also 14264, 14275, 14290.

Economics

15,596 COMHAIRE, J. Evolution générale du Ruanda-Urundi en 1953. ZAIRE 8 (1954), pp. 1067-1074.

15,597 COMHAIRE, J. Situation générale du Ruanda-Urundi. ZAIRE 5 (1951), pp. 1047-1054.

15,598 HARROY, J. P. La lutte contre la dissipation des ressources naturelles au Ruanda-Urundi. CIVILISATIONS 4 (1954), pp. 363-373; English summary, pp. 373-374.

15,599 HARROY, J. P. Ruanda-Urundi. UGANDA J. 21 (1957), pp. 226-228.

15,600 NICAISE, J. Au Ruanda-Urundi. ZAIRE 8 (1954), p. 190.

15,601 PINXTEN, K. Tienjarenplan en toekomst van Ruanda-Urundi. ZAIRE 7 (1953), pp. 925-953.

15,602 RUBBENS, A. Enkele opzoekingen nopens de gewoontelijke modaliteiten der belasting in het sultanaat Ruanda. CONGO 1 (1940), pp. 136-149.

15,603 TICHELEN, H. E. VAN. Problèmes du développement économique du Ruanda-Urundi. ZAIRE 11 (1957), pp. 451-474.

15,604 VANSINI, I. Les régimes fonciers Ruanda et Kuba: une comparison. AFR. AGRARIAN SYSTEMS, 1963, pp. 348-363.

15,605 WALLE, E. VAN DE. Chomage dans une petite ville d'Afrique: Usumbura. ZAIRE 14 (1960), pp. 341-359.

15,606 WALLE, E. VAN DE. Un essai de resorption du chomage: Usumbura 1959. ZAIRE 14 (1960), pp. 467-480.

See also 14382, 14494.

Geography

15,607 BURIJE, J. Note sur l'orthographe des principaux noms géographiques du Burundi. KONGO-OVERZEE 23 (1957), pp. 224-225.

15,608 COUPEZ, A. and KAMANZI, T. Quelques noms géographiques rwanda. ZAIRE 13 (1959), pp. 149-168.

15,609 SHANTZ, H. L. Urundi, territory and people. GEOG. REV. 12 (1922), pp. 329-357.

See also 14600, 15959.

Government. Politics. Administration

15,610 BILSEN, J. VAN. De mwami en andere reizen. ZAIRE 4 (1950), pp. 872-873.

15,611 BILSEN, J. VAN. Roeanda-Oeroendi en Kongo. ZAIRE 4 (1950), pp. 1112-1115.

15,612 BILSEN, J. VAN. Le Ruanda-Urundi à Genève. ZAIRE 4 (1950), pp. 533-534.

15,613 COMHAIRE, J. Au Ruanda-Urundi: faits, programme, opinions. ZAIRE 6 (1952), pp. 1051-1068.

15,614 COMHAIRE, J. Le Ruanda-Urundi en 1952. ZAIRE 8 (1954), pp. 55-61.

15,615 GELDERS, V. Native political organization in the Ruanda-Urundi. CIVILISATIONS 4 (1954), pp. 125-132.

15,616 GRAY, A. Rwanda and Burundi. AFR. AFFAIRS 61 (1962), pp. 296-297.

15,617 HERTEFELT, M. D'. Les élections communales et le consensus politique au Rwanda. ZAIRE 14 (1960), pp. 403-438.

15,618 MALENGREAU, G. L'organisation politique indigène des territoires du Ruanda-Urundi. ZAIRE 6 (1952), pp. 965-970.

15,619 PAGES, A. Au Rwanda. Droits et pouvoirs des chefs sous la suzeraineté du roi hamite. Quelques abus du système. ZAIRE 3 (1949), pp. 359-377.

15,620 SEBIVA, G. Burundi: détente entre le Gouvernement et le Parlement. ET. CONG. 5, no. 8 (1963), pp. 42-45.

15,621 TANNER, R. E. S. The Belgian and British administrations in Ruanda-Urundi and Tanganyika. J. LOCAL ADM. OV. 4 (1965), pp. 202-211.

15,622 Accord de tutelle pour le territoire du Ruanda-Urundi. ZAIRE 2 (1948), pp. 563-568.

15,623 Le Burundi à recherche d'une stabilite. PRESENCE AFR. N.S. 47 (1963), pp. 235-241.

15,624 Les élections au Rwanda et au Burundi. PRESENCE AFR. N.S. 39 (1961), pp. 202-205.

15,625 Mission de visite dans le Territoire sous tutelle du Ruanda-Urundi. ZAIRE 3 (1949), pp. 687-691.

15,626 Territoires coloniaux et Territoires sous tutelle. ZAIRE 3 (1949), pp. 805-817.

See also 14607, 14622, 14638, 14671, 14672, 14694, 14732.

History

15,627 DELLICOUR, F. La conquête du Ruanda-Urundi (d'après des ouvrages récents) [with a note by O. Louwers and others]. BULL. SEANCES IRCB 6 (1935), pp. 142-178, 359-378.

15,628 KAGAME, A. A. Un nouveau livre sur le Rwanda. AEQUATORIA 16 (1953), pp. 89-92.

15,629 MARAL, P. La Révolution Bantoue au Rwanda. AFR. ET ASIE 69 (1965), pp. 3-13.

15,630 VANSINA, J. Notes sur l'histoire du Burundi. AEQUATORIA 24 (1961), pp. 1-10.

See also 14540.

Language. Literature

Language

15,631 BARAKANA, G. L'unification des langues au Ruanda-Urundi. CIVILISATIONS 2 (1952), pp. 67-77; French summary, p. 78.

15,632 BULCK, G. VAN. La dialectique des baRundi. ZAIRE 11 (1957), pp. 1021-1029.

15,633 COUPEZ, A. Application de la lexicostatistique au mongo et au rwanda. AEQUATORIA 19 (1956), pp. 85-87.

15,634 COUPEZ, A. Deux textes Rwanda. KONGO-OVERZEE 22 (1956), pp. 129-151.

15,635 COUPEZ, A. Réflexions sur un dictionnaire. ZAIRE 13 (1959), pp. 517-526.

15,636 COUPEZ, A. Texte ruúndi. Les rois du pays ruúndi et les hommes qui y sont venus les premiers. ZAIRE 11 (1957), pp. 623-636.

15,637 COUPEZ, A. Texte ruúndi no. 2. AEQUATORIA 21 (1958), pp. 81-97.

15,638 GUILLEBAUD, R. Conte Rundi. KONGO-OVERZEE 24 (1958), pp. 53-65.

15,639 MEEUSSEN, A. E. Systematiek van de verwantschapstermen in het Rwonda. KONGO-OVERZEE 21 (1955), pp. 300-303.

15,640 ROEHL, K. Das Dahlsche Gesetz und verwandte Erscheinungen im Ruanda-Rundi-Ha. AFR. UND UB. 8 (1917-1918), pp. 197-207.

15,641 ROEHL, K. Eine fast verloren gegangene Klasse des Ur-Bantu. FESTSCHRIFT MEINHOF, 1927, pp. 233-240.

See also 15035, 15036.

Literature

15,642 COUPEZ, A. Poème pastoral rwanda. AEQUATORIA 24 (1961), pp. 93-101.

15,643 KAGAME, A. Importantes manifestations religieuses au Ruanda. ZAIRE 1 (1947), pp. 84-89.

15,644 KAGAME, A. La voix de l'Afrique: un poème du Rwanda avec traduction par l'abbé Alexis Kagame. AFRICA 7 (1947), pp. 41-46.

15,645 KAGAME, A. A. Avec un Troubadour du Rwanda. ZAIRE 3 (1949), pp. 765-769.

15,646 KAGAME, A. A. Bref aperçu sur la poésie dynastique du Rwanda. ZAIRE 4 (1950), pp. 243-270.

15,647 KAGAME, A. A. La poésie guerrière. PRESENCE AFR. N.S. 11 (1957), pp. 119-122.

15,648 PAGES, A. La vie intellectuelle des Noirs du Ruanda. CONGO 1 (1934), pp. 357-389, 481-503, 657-671.

15,649 ZUURE, B. Poésies chez les Barundi. AFRICA 5 (1932), pp. 344-354.

See also 15572.

Law

15,650 KAGAME, A. Le code ésotérique de la dynastie du Rwanda. ZAIRE 1 (1947), pp. 363-386.

15,651 MAQUET, J. J. and NAIGIZIKI, S. Les droits fonciers dans le Ruanda ancien. ZAIRE 11 (1957), pp. 339-359.

15,652 VANHOVE, J. Les juridictions indigènes au Ruanda. CONGO 2 (1939), pp. 158-172.

Religion

15,653 BILSEN, J. VAN. Jubileum in Roeanda. ZAIRE 4 (1950), p. 874.

15,654 MIRANDA SANTOS, A. Um facto e sua significação. PORT. EM AFR. 15 (1958), pp. 7-17.

15,655 SCHUMACHER, P. Urundi. AEQUATORIA 12 (1949), pp. 129-132.

15,656 Diocèse de Malange. PORT. EM AFR. 15 (1958), pp. 103-123.

Science

15,657 ARIAN, A. D'. Une enquete pilote sur l'alimentation des indigènes du Ruanda-Urundi. ZAIRE 8 (1954), pp. 339-351.

See also 15408.

Sociology

15,658 ALBERT, E. M. Socio-political organization and receptivity to change: some differences between Ruanda and Urundi. SOUTHWESTERN J. ANTHR. 16 (1960), pp. 46-74.

15,659 BAECK, L. Quelques aspects sociaux de l'urbanisation au Ruanda-Urundi. ZAIRE 10 (1956), pp. 115-145.

15,660 EGGINS, E. C. The disappearance of a feudal aristocracy. CORONA 4 (1952), pp. 301-303.

15,661 MAQUET, J. J. La participation de la classe paysanne au mouvement d'indépendance du Rwanda. CAH. ET. AFR. 4 (1964), pp. 552-568.

15,662 NEESEN, V. Le premier recensement par échantillonnage au Ruanda-Urundi. ZAIRE 7 (1953), pp. 469-488.

15,663 NEESEN, V. Quelques donnees démographiques sur la population du Ruanda-Urundi. ZAIRE 7 (1953), pp. 1011-1025.

15,664 TROUWBORST, A. A. La mobilité de l'individu en fonction de l'organisation politique des Burundi. ZAIRE 13 (1959), pp. 787-800.

15,665 Statistiques et recensement en Afrique du sud. ZAIRE 6 (1952), p. 414.

15,666 De uitwijking bij de Baroendi. ZAIRE 3 (1949), pp. 207-211.

15,667 The women of Ruanda-Urundi. AFR. WOMEN 4 (1962), pp. 87-91.

See also 15454, 15462, 15526, 15555.

SPANISH GUINEA (Fernando Poo)

General

See 7465.

Agriculture

15,668 FICKENDEY, E. Consideraciones sobre la lucha contra los animales dañinos y las enfermedades en las plantas cultivadas. ARCH. INST. EST. AFR. 6, no. 20 (1952), pp. 29-37.

15,669 NOSTI NAVA, J. Recientes progresos técnicos-agrícolas en la agricultura tropical y en su aplicación a Guinea. ARCH. INST. EST. AFR. 9, no. 39 (1956), pp. 7-23.

15,670 ORTIZ DE ZARATE LOPEZ, A. La fauna malacológica terrestre de la Isla de Fernando Poo. ARCH. INST. EST. AFR. 13, no. 50 (1959), pp. 23-36.

15,671 ZARCO SEGALERVA, E. Los insectos en la economía forestal de Guinea. ARCH. INST. EST. AFR. 13, no. 51 (1959), pp. 19-32.

Anthropology

15,672 ALCOBE, S. Los pamues en el complejo racial del Africa negra. ARCH. INST. EST. AFR. 4, no. 13 (1950), pp. 17-35.

15,673 CASTILLO BARRIL, M. Síntesis valorativa de las culturas autóctonas de la Guinea Ecuatorial. ARCH. INST. EST. AFR. 19, no. 76 (1965), pp. 77-92.

15,674 CORELLA, D. L. B. Algunas costumbres pamues. ARCH. INST. EST. AFR. 4, no. 11 (1950), pp. 81-100.

15,675 IBARROLA, R. Aportación al estudio del nivel mental de los indigenas de Guinea. ARCH. INST. EST. AFR. 5, no. 18 (1951), pp. 7-29.

15,676 MORENO, J. A. M. Formas de antropofagia en los territorios españoles del Golfo de Guinea. ARCH. INST. EST. AFR. 5, no. 17 (1951), pp. 69-85.

15,677 PALACIN, A. DE L. Algunas costumbres y mitos de los bujebas de nuestra Guinea Continental. ARCH. INST. EST. AFR. 7, no. 28 (1954), pp. 35-66.

15,678 PANYELLA, A. Notas de tipología cultural. La casa y el poblado Fang (Guinea espanola). ARCH. INST. EST. AFR. 5, no. 16 (1951), pp. 7-30.

15,679 PANYELLA, A. and SABATER, J. Esquema de la antroponimia Fang de la Guinea española desde el punto de vista etnológico. ARCH. INST. EST. AFR. 8, no. 34 (1955), pp. 73-84.

15,680 PANYELLA, S. A. Y A. Estudio cuantitativo de la exogamia de los pamues (Frang) de la Guinea Continental Española. ARCH. INST. EST. AFR. 5, no. 18 (1951), pp. 53-77.

15,681 PAYA, J. E. Algunos aspectos de la caza en la Guinea continental española. ARCH. INST. EST. AFR. 4, no. 15 (1950), pp. 33-46.

15,682 PONS, J. Huellas dactilares en negros de la Guinea Española. ARCH. INST. EST. AFR. 5, no. 18 (1951), pp. 79-88.

15,683 SAENZ MARTINEZ, J. La vivienda en el territorio español de Ifni. ARCH. INST. EST. AFR. 3, no. 7 (1949), pp. 7-69.

15,684 TATAY, R. Caza menor y mayor en Guinea. ARCH. INST. EST. AFR. 6, no. 24 (1953), pp. 77-92.

15,685 VECIANA, A. DE. Le estructura sociológica del mosaico étnico de la Costa de Guinea (Guinea española). ARCH. INST. EST. AFR. 10, no. 40 (1957), pp. 43-48.

Art

15,686 FRANCES, J. La Guinea española y Carlos Tauler, su pintor. ARCH. INST. EST. AFR. 3, no. 10 (1949), pp. 7-24.

15,687 IBARROLA MONASTERIO, R. El arte de los pueblos pamues. ARCH. INST. EST. AFR. 10, no. 41 (1957), pp. 51-60.

15,688 PALACIN, A. DE L. Canciones del Africa Occidental Española. ARCH. INST. EST. AFR. 11, no. 44 (1958), pp. 21-47.

15,689 PANYELLA, A. La Prehistoria de Fernando Poo. ARCH. INST. EST. AFR. 13, no. 49 (1959), pp. 17-33.

15,690 PANYELLA, A. Primeros resultados de la campaña de excavaciones del I.D.E.A. en Fernando Poo. ARCH. INST. EST. AFR. 16, no. 62 (1962), pp. 7-23.

Economics

15,691 ALVAREZ CORUGEDO, J. El impacto sectorial del Plan de Desarrollo económico de Fernando Poo y Río Muni. ARCH. INST. EST. AFR. 18, no. 71 (1964), pp. 57-78.

15,692 BONELLI, J. M. Diferencia del concepto económico en la colonización de Fernando Poo y Guinea Continental. ARCH. INST. EST. AFR. 3, no. 7 (1949), pp. 71-79.

15,693 COSSIO Y DE COSIO, R. DE. Los problemas macroeconómicos del Plan de Desarrollo económico y social de Fernando Poo y Río Muni. ARCH. INST. EST. AFR. 18, no. 71 (1964), pp. 37-55.

15,694 DIAZ DE VILLEGAS, J. La Guinea de Iradier y la de hoy. ARCH. INST. EST. AFR. 9, no. 36 (1956), pp. 7-23.

15,695 FICKENDEY, E. Perspectivas de la explotación del aciete de palma en la Guinea Española. ARCH. INST. EST. AFR. 7, no. 28 (1954), pp. 23-33.

15,696 FICKENDEY, E. Posibilidades del cultivo de la palmera de aceite en la Guinea Española. ARCH. INST. EST. AFR. 7, no. 29 (1954), pp. 25-30.

15,697 MARIA FRANCES, J. El Correo y los sellos en la provincia de Guinea. ARCH. INST. EST. AFR. 14, no. 53 (1960), pp. 7-22.

15,698 MOLINA ARRABAL, J. Principales circunstancia económico-jurídicas peculiares de la Guinea española. ARCH. INST. EST. AFR. 10, no. 41 (1957), pp. 7-21.

15,699 MOLINA ARRABAL, J. Sobre las provincias de Fernando Poo y Rio Muni. ARCH. INST. EST. AFR. 16, no. 58 (1961), pp. 45-59.

15,700 NOSTI, J. Cooperativas indígenas de Guinea. ARCH. INST. EST. AFR. 2, no. 4 (1948), pp. 45-60.

15,701 PERPINA. Mano de obra africana, factor de coste colonial: investigación sobre el peso de los branceros contratados en Fernando Póo. CUAD. EST. AFR. 3 (1947), pp. 127-144.

15,702 VELARDE FUERTES, J. El Plan de Desarrollo económico y social de Fernando Poo y Río Muni. ARCH. INST. EST. AFR. 18, no. 71 (1964), pp. 7-36.

Education

15,703 ALVAREZ, H. R. La cultura, problema fundamental en colonización. ARCH. INST. EST. AFR. 3, no. 8 (1949), pp. 25-49.

15,704 ALVAREZ, H. R. Enseñanza en la Guinea española. ARCH. INST. EST. AFR. 6, no. 22 (1952), pp. 29-36.

15,705 ALVAREZ, H. R. El problema de la orientación, iniciación y enseñanza profesional en Guinea. CUAD. AFR. OR. 29 (1955), pp. 27-37.

15,706 TRUJEDA INCERA, L. Sobre la política educativa indígena. CUAD. EST. AFR. 10 (1950), pp. 66-73.

Geography

15,707 ALCOBE NOGUER, S. Informe de la labor realizada por la expedicion cientifica a los territorios españoles del Golfo de Guinea, organizada por la Direccion General de Marruecos y Colonias. ARCH. INST. EST. AFR. 8, no. 32 (1955), pp. 85-96.

15,708 ALVAREZ SANCHEZ, J. Impresiones de un viaje a la Isla de Annobón. ARCH. INST. EST. AFR. 15, no. 57 (1961), pp. 53-70.

15,709 CASTILLO-FIEL, Conde. Geografía humana de la Guinea portuguesa. ARCH. INST. EST. AFR. 2, no. 4 (1948), pp. 75-95.

15,710 CHURCH, R. J. H. Fernando Po. CORONA 4 (1952), pp. 175-178.

15,711 DIAZ DE VILLEGAS, J. Momento actual de las Plazas y Provincias Africanas. ARCH. INST. EST. AFR. 18, no. 69 (1964), pp. 7-23.

15,712 FERNANDEZ BLANCO, F. L. Impresiones de un viaje a Fernando Poo y Río Muni. ARCH. INST. EST. AFR. 16, no. 62 (1962), pp. 67-89.

15,713 FRY, C. H. Annobon: a south sea island in the Gulf of Guinea. NIGERIAN FIELD 27 (1962), pp. 147-161.

15,714 FUSTER, J. M. Un accidente volcánico exceptional: La Caldera de San Carlos (Fernando Póo). ARCH. INST. EST. AFR. 10, no. 40 (1957), pp. 65-74.

15,715 LOMBARDERO VICENTE, M. El servicio geografico del ejercito en la Guinea española. ARCH. INST. EST. AFR. 2, no. 6 (1948), pp. 65-97.

15,716 OCANA GARCIA, M. Factores que influencian la distribucion de la vegetation en Fernando Poo. ARCH. INST. EST. AFR. 14, no. 55 (1960), pp. 67-85.

15,717 PERIS, S. V. La Isla de Annobón. ARCH. INST. EST. AFR. 15, no. 57 (1961), pp. 27-51.

15,718 UNZUETA Y YUSTE, A. DE. La geografía y la Historia de la capital fernandina. ARCH. INST. EST. AFR. 2, no. 6 (1948), pp. 29-64.

Government

15,719 ALTOZANO, H. El Patronato de Indígenas de Guinea. Institución Ejemplar. ARCH. INST. EST. AFR. 10, no. 40 (1957), pp. 49-63.

15,720 CORDERO TORRES, J. M. Lección en Marruecos: advertencia para Guinea. CUAD. AFR. OR. 34 (1956), pp. 9-19.

15,721 ORTIZ DE RIVERO, M. Gobierno General de Africa Occidental Española. ARCH. INST. EST. AFR. 11, no. 47 (1958), pp. 55-76; 13, no. 51 (1959), pp. 33-55.

15,722 PHILIPPE, R. Où en est la Guinée espagnole? AEQUATORIA 20 (1957), pp. 66-67.

15,723 TABERNERO CHACOBO, H. Africa Occidental española en la actualidad. ARCH. INST. EST. AFR. 16, no. 58 (1961), pp. 29-43.

See also 7256, 7290, 7291, 7292, 7293, 7294, 7295, 7296, 7297, 7299.

History

15,724 ARRIBAS PALAU, M. El salvoconducto enviado por Mawlay Muslama a 'Abd Allah al-Quitarani. ARCH. INST. EST. AFR. 11, no. 47 (1958), pp. 23-24.

15,725 BRUTSCH, J. R. Fernando Poo et le Cameroun. ET. CAMER. 43-44 (1954), pp. 67-78.

15,726 CENCILLO DE PINEDA, M. El brigadier Conde de Argelejo y su expedición militar a Fernando Póo en 1778. ARCH. INST. EST. AFR. 2, no. 6 (1948), pp. 121-136.

15,727 COQUERY-VIDROVITCH, C. L'intervention d'une société privée à propos du contesté franco-espagnol dan le Rio Muni: la Société d'Explorations Coloniales (1899-1924). CAH. ET. AFR. 4 (1963), pp. 22-68.

15,728 GONZALEZ RAMOS, M. Relación del viaje a Guinea del navío Santiago en 1779. ARCH. INST. EST. AFR. 3, no. 7 (1949), pp. 81-91.

15,729 MARTINEZ VAL, J. M. Esquema histórico del Africanismo Español. ARCH. INST. EST. AFR. 18, no. 69 (1964), pp. 25-56.

15,730 MORENO, J. A. M. Origen y vicisitudes del antiguo reino de Moka. ARCH. INST. EST. AFR. 6, no. 27 (1953), pp. 7-30.

15,731 MORENO, J. A. M. Viejos cementerios fernandinos. ARCH. INST. EST. AFR. 6, no. 26 (1953), pp. 79-87.

15,732 PELISSER, R. Spanish Guinea: an introduction. RACE 6, no. 1 (1964-1965), pp. 117-128.

Language. Literature

15,733 BAUMANN, O. Beiträge zur Kenntnis der Bube-Sprache auf Fernando Póo. ZAOS 1 (1887-1888), pp. 138-141.

15,734 ECHEGARAY, C. G. Bibliografía lingüística de los Territorios Españoles de Guinea. ARCH. INST. EST. AFR. 6, no. 27 (1953), pp. 57-82.

15,735 ECHEGARAY, C. G. Hacia la unificación ortográfica de la lengua pamue. ARCH. INST. EST. AFR. 5, no. 19 (1951), pp. 21-33.

15,736 ECHEGARAY, C. G. La clasificación nominal en el baseque. ARCH. INST. EST. AFR. 6, no. 23 (1952), pp. 73-88.

15,737 ECHEGARAY, C. G. El Africa Ecuatorial española a través de la novela y la poesía actuales. ARCH. INST. EST. AFR. 18, no. 70 (1964), pp. 67-107.

15,738 ECHEGARAY, C. G. Les sistemas de numeración y los numerales en los pueblos de la Guinea española. ARCH. INST. EST. AFR. 4, no. 12 (1950), pp. 19-29.

15,739 MARTINEZ Y SANZ, J. Vokabular des Banapá (Sta. Isabel). Dialektes der Bube-Sprache von Fernando Póo. ZAOS 1 (1887-1888), pp. 142-155.

Law

15,740 GARCIA-GALLO DE DIEGO, A. Les títulos jurídicos de la integración de los territorios africanos en la Monarquía Española. ARCH. INST. EST. AFR. 18, no. 69 (1964), pp. 57-70.

Religion

15,741 OLANGUA, A. Cien años de Historia de las Misiones de la Guinea Española. ARCH. INST. EST. AFR. 13, no. 48 (1959), pp. 39-64.

Science

15,742 ALCOBE, S. Une expedición científica a los Territorios Españoles del Golfo de Guinea. ARCH. INST. EST. AFR. 3, no. 10 (1949), pp. 25-33.

15,743 BASILEWSKY, P. Contribution à l'étude des Coléoptères Carabiques de l'Afrique occidentale. IV. Description d'un Lébien nouveau de Fernando-Poo. BULL. IFAN 15 (1953), pp. 1029-1030.

15,744 BERNARDI, G. Lépidoptères Pieridae recueillis à Fernando Poo par MM. P. L. Dekeyser, P. Lepesme. BULL. IFAN 15 (1953), pp. 1437-1440.

15,745 CASAS, J. M. F. Aportaciones a la petrografía de la isla de Fernando Póo, Guinea española. ARCH. INST. EST. AFR. 4, no. 11 (1950), pp. 28-39.

15,746 CASAS, J. M. F. Las rocas ultrabasicas de Annobon y su relacion con los magmas basalticos de ofras islas del Golfo de Guinea. ARCH. INST. EST. AFR. 4, no. 13 (1950), pp. 37-54.

15,747 CASTRO, A. H. DE. Impresiones edafológicas de los Territorios españoles del Golfo de Guinea. ARCH. INST. EST. AFR. 6, no. 23 (1952), pp. 59-72.

15,748 GARRORENA, R. C. Eclipse de sol en Guinea. ARCH. INST. EST. AFR., no. 21 (1952), pp. 63-66.

15,749 GUIGNOT, F. Dytiscides et Gyrinides de Fernando-Poo et du Soudan français. BULL. IFAN 14 (1952), pp. 1191-1195.

15,750 KUBIENA, W. L. Los suelos de los Territorios Españoles del Golfo de Guinea. ARCH. INST. EST. AFR. 11, no. 46 (1958), pp. 65-75.

15,751 LEPESME, P. and BREUNING, S. Coléoptères Cérambycides récoltés par P. L. Dekeyser, P. Lepesme et A. Villiers dans l'Ile de Fernando-Poo. BULL. IFAN 15 (1953), pp. 507-518.

15,752 LOPEZ-MONIS, C. Aspectos de la lucha sanitaria en Guinea. ARCH. INST. EST. AFR. 3, no. 9 (1949), pp. 7-16.

15,753 MATEU, J. Algo sobre la fauna de la Guinea Española. ARCH. INST. EST. AFR. 3, no. 8 (1949), pp. 93-107.

15,754 MATILLA, V. Pasado, presente y porvenir de la Sanidad en Guinea. ARCH. INST. EST. AFR. 4, no. 11 (1950), pp. 41-67.

15,755 MATILLA, V. Progresos sanitarios en la Guinea Española. ARCH. INST. EST. AFR. 14, no. 55 (1960), pp. 45-65.

15,756 MEDINA, M. A. Impresiones geológicas de un viaje a la Guinea Continental Española. ARCH. INST. EST. AFR. 4, no. 11 (1950), pp. 69-79.

15,757 MENOR, J. G. Algunas características de la fauna entomológica de la Guinea Española. ARCH. INST. EST. AFR. 3, no. 8 (1949), pp. 7-23.

15,758 MENOR, J. G. Características de la fauna hemipterológica de la Guinea Española. ARCH. INST. EST. AFR. 5, no. 19 (1951), pp. 7-19.

15,759 MOLINER, R. R. Aspectos sociales de la alimentación en Fernando Póo. ARCH. INST. EST. AFR. 5, no. 17 (1951), pp. 21-31.

15,760 NOSTI NAVA, J. El origen de las plantas cultivadas en los territorios españoles del Golfo de Guinea. ARCH. INST. EST. AFR. 5, no. 19 (1951), pp. 53-78.

15,761 ORTIZ DE RIVERO, M. Gobierno General del Africa Occidental española Hospital General. ARCH. INST. EST. AFR. 11, no. 44 (1958), pp. 49-71.

15,762 ORTIZ DE RIVERO, M. Resumen estadístico-sanitario del Africa Occidental Española, en Sidi Ifni Años 1949-1954. ARCH. INST. EST. AFR. 8, no. 35 (1955), pp. 7-55.

15,763 PIC, M. Coléoptères nouveaux de Fernando-Poo. BULL. IFAN 15 (1953), pp. 152-170.

15,764 SABATER PI, J. Notas para un estudio de los indicadores de miel (familia indicatoridae) de la Guinea Española. ARCH. INST. EST. AFR. 7, no. 30 (1954), pp. 7-12.

15,765 SANTOS DIAS, J. A. T. Notas sobre a ixodofauna da ilha de S. Tomé. BSEM 110 (1958), pp. 159-165.

15,766 VARDE, R. P. DE LA. Petite contribution à la flore bryologique de Fernando-Poo. BULL. IFAN 15 (1953), pp. 483-486.

See also 7460.

Sociology

15,767 ALVAREZ, H. R. Enseñanza y política social en Guinea. CUAD. EST. AFR. 11 (1950), pp. 35-48.

15,768 MOLINER, R. R. Apuntes sobre la estructura social de Fernando Po. CUAD. EST. AFR. 7 (1949), pp. 23-52.

15,769 MOLINER, R. R. Notas sobre la situación social de la mujer indígena en Fernando Póo. CUAD. EST. AFR. 18 (1952), pp. 21-38.

15,770 PALACIN, A. DE L. and ECHEGARAY, C. G. Aspecto económico-social de la pesca entre los indígenas de la Guinea española. ARCH. INST. EST. AFR. 11, no. 44 (1958), pp. 7-19.

15,771 PANYELLA, A. El problemiento de la Isla de Fernando Poo y el problema de las migraciones Africanas. ARCH. INST. EST. AFR. 14, no. 55 (1960), pp. 31-44.

15,772 TRUJEDA, L. El problema demográfico y la política indígena en los Territorios españoles del Golfo de Guinea. CUAD. EST. AFR. 1 (1946), pp. 57-66.

East Africa

GENERAL

15,773 BAREGU, M. and WISE, M. Bibliography—East Africana published between January 1963 and April 1964. TANG. NOTES 63 (1964), pp. 249-253.

15,774 HEYER, S. S. Select bibliography of recent publications relating to economic problems in East Africa (documents published since January 1963). E. AFR. EC. REV. N.S. 1, no. 3 (1965), pp. 84-87.

15,775 HOCKEY, S. W. Library resources in English-speaking countries of East Africa. UNESCO BULL. LIBS. 15 (1961), pp. 232-236.

15,776 HOCKEY, S. W. Report of the Working Party appointed by the Conference on Library Training in East Africa. NIGERIAN LIBS. 1 (1964), pp. 86-89.

15,777 MAQUET, J. J. La Conférence de Noël de l'"East African Institute of Social Research." ZAIRE 5 (1951), pp. 194-196.

15,778 Azania, a new journal. BULL. AFR. STUD. ASSOC. 5 (1965), p. 11.

15,779 East Africa Institute of Social Research. SUDAN NOTES 32 (1951), pp. 151-153; TANG. NOTES 32 (1952), p. 85.

Agriculture

15,780 KENNEDY, T. J. A study of economic motivation involved in peasant cultivation of cotton. EAISR Jan. (1964), pp. 1-8.

15,781 KYESIMIRA, Y. Agricultural export developments in East Africa. EAISR Jan. (1965), pp. 1-14.

15,782 LOSSE, G. F. A purse seine fishery in East African coastal waters. PROC. E. AFR. ACAD. 2 (1964), pp. 88-91.

15,783 MELVILLE, A. R. Planning for agricultural development. PROBLEMS OF EC. DEVELOPMENT IN E. AFR., 1965, pp. 49-59.

15,784 SWYNNERTON, R. J. M. Agricultural advances in Eastern Africa. AFR. AFFAIRS 61 (1962), pp. 201-215.

15,785 WORSLEY, R. R. LE G. Some East African essential oils. BULL. IMP. INST. 32 (1934), pp. 253-270.

Anthropology

15,786 ALLISON, A. C. et al. Blood groups in some East African tribes. JRAI 82 (1952), pp. 55-61.

15,787 ALLISON, A. C. et al. Further observations on blood groups in East African tribes. JRAI 84 (1954), pp. 158-162.

15,788 BAKER, E. C. Tribal calendars. TANG. NOTES 33 (1952), pp. 30-33.

15,789 BARKER, R. DE LA B. Bush paths in East Africa. TANG. NOTES 10 (1940), pp. 94-95.

15,790 BEATTIE, J. H. M. Ethnographic and sociological research in East Africa: a review. AFRICA 26 (1956), pp. 265-275.

15,791 BEECH, M. W. H. Slavery on the east coast of Africa. J. AFR. SOC. 15 (1916), pp. 145-149.

15,792 BEIDELMAN, T. O. Intertribal insult and opprobrium in an East African chiefdom (Ukaguru). ANTHR. QUART. 37 (1964), pp. 33-52.

15,793 BERNARDI, B. The age-system of the Nilo-Hamitic peoples. A critical evaluation. AFRICA 22 (1952), pp. 316-332.

15,794 DAHYA, B. W. The evil eye in an Asian community in East Africa. EAISR Jan. (1963), pp. 1-17.

15,795 DRIBERG, J. H. The status of women among the Nilotics and Nilo-Hamitics. AFRICA 5 (1932), pp. 404-421.

15,796 DUNDAS, Honorable CHARLES. The organization and laws of some Bantu tribes in East Africa. JRAI 45 (1915), pp. 234-306.

15,797 FRENCH-SHELDON. Customs among the natives of East Africa, from Teita to Kilemegalia, with special reference to their women and children. JRAI 21 (1892), pp. 358-390.

15,798 GORDON, H. L. The mental capacity of the African. J. AFR. SOC. 33 (1934), pp. 226-242.

15,799 GROTTANELLI, V. L. Ricerche 1951-52 fra i Bantu costieri dell' Oltregiuba (Bagiuni). CONG. INT. SC. ANTH. ET ETHN. 4, no. iii (1952), pp. 49-50.

15,800 HARRIES, L. The Arabs and Swahili culture. AFRICA 34 (1964), pp. 224-229.

15,801 HERSKOVITS, M. J. The cattle complex in East Africa. AMER. ANTHR. 28 (1926), pp. 230-272, 361-388, 494-528, 633-664.

15,802 HORNELL, J. Indonesian influence of East African culture. JRAI 64 (1934), pp. 305-332.

15,803 HUNTINGFORD, G. W. B. The distribution of certain culture elements in East Africa. JRAI 91 (1961), pp. 251-295.

15,804 JOHANSSEN, E. The idea of God in the myths and proverbs of some East African Bantu tribes. INT. REV. MISSIONS 20 (1931), pp. 344-355, 534-546.

15,805 JOHNSTON, Sir H. H. The people of Eastern Equatorial Africa. JRAI 15 (1886), pp. 3-15.

15,806 LAGERCRANTZ, S. An East African accessory fishing implement. ETHNOS 5 (1940), pp. 29-34.

15,807 LEYS, N. M. and JOYCE, T. A. Note on a series of physical measurements from East Africa. JRAI 43 (1913), pp. 195-267.

15,808 MacDONALD, J. R. L. Notes on the ethnology of tribes met with during progress of the Juba expedition of 1897-99. JRAI 29 (1899), pp. 226-247.

15,809 MARWICK, M. G. Another modern anti-witchcraft movement in East Central Africa. AFRICA 20 (1950), pp. 100-112.

15,810 MILNE, G. African Village layout. TANGANYIKA NOTES AND RECORDS 13 (1942), pp. 3-5.

15,811 MORRIS, H. S. The divine kingship of the Aga Khan: a study of theocracy in East Africa. SOUTHWESTERN J. ANTHR. 14 (1958), pp. 454-472.

15,812 OGOT, G. A. The year of sacrifice: an East African fairy tale. BO 11 (1962), pp. 41-50.

15,813 PEARSALL, M. Distributional variations of bride-wealth in the East African cattle area. SOUTHWESTERN J. ANTHR. 3 (1947), pp. 15-31.

15,814 POCOCK, D. F. "Difference" in East Africa: a study of caste and religion in modern Indian society. SOUTHWESTERN J. ANTHR. 13 (1957), pp. 289-300.

15,815 RAYMOND, W. D. Native materia medica. TANG. NOTES 1 (1936), pp. 77-80; 2 (1936), pp. 50-54; 5 (1938), pp. 72-75.

15,816 ROBERTS, D. F. Serology and the history of the northern Nilotes. J. AFR. HIST. 3 (1962), pp. 301-305.

15,817 SKENE, R. Arab and Swahili dances and ceremonies. JRAI 47 (1917), pp. 413-434.

15,818 STEERE, E. On East African tribes and languages. JRAI 1 (1871), pp. cxliii-cliv.

15,819 THURNWALD, R. Social transformations in East Africa. AMER. J. SOC. 38 (1932-1933), pp. 175-184.

15,820 TUBIANA, J. Moyens et méthodes d'une ethnologie historique de l'Afrique orientale. CAH. ET. AFR. 2 (1961), pp. 5-11.

15,821 TURNER, V. W. Witchcraft and sorcery: taxonomy versus dynamics. AFRICA 34 (1964), pp. 314-324.

15,822 VETO, M. Le role de l'homme dans les mythes de mort chez les Bantou de l'Afrique orientale et du Congo. ZAIRE 15 (1961), pp. 75-93.

15,823 VETO, M. Unité et dualité de la conception du mal chez les Bantou orientaux. CAH. ET. AFR. 2 (1962), pp. 551-569.

15,824 WERNER, A. The Bantu coast tribes of the East Africa Protectorate. JRAI 45 (1915), pp. 326-354.

15,825 WERNER, A. The Galla of the East Africa protectorate. J. AFR. SOC. 13 (1914), pp. 121-142, 262-287.

15,826 WIJEYEWARDENE, G. E. T. Swahili conceptions of health and disease. EAISR Dec. (1959), pp. 83-87.

See also 4801, 4811, 5688, 5693.

Art

15,827 BANFIELD, J. Film in East Africa. TRANSITION 13 (1964), pp. 18-21.

15,828 BATE, D. M. A. The Pleistocene mammal faunas of Palestine and East Africa. PROC. PAN-AFR. CONGR. PRE-HIST. 1 (1947), pp. 38-39.

15,829 CARSON, J. Entertainment in East Africa. CORONA 3 (1951), pp. 183-184.

15,830 EMSHEIMER, E. Drei tanzgesänge der Akamba. ETHNOS 2 (1937), pp. 137-143.

15,831 FREEMAN-GRENVILLE, G. S. P. East African coin finds and their historical significance. J. AFR. HIST. 1 (1960), pp. 31-43.

15,832 FREEMAN-GRENVILLE, G. S. P. The times of ignorance: a review of pre-Islamic and early Islamic settlement on the East African coast. DISCOVERING AFRICA'S PAST, 1959, pp. 4-17.

15,833 HIERNAUX, J. Le début de l'Age des Méfaux dans la région des Grands Lacs Africains. PROC. PAN-AFR. CONGR. PRE-HIST 4, no. iii (1962), pp. 381-388.

15,834 KORITSCHONER, H. Some East African native songs. TANG. NOTES 4 (1937), pp. 51-64.

15,835 KLEINDIENST, M. R. Components of the East African Acheulian assemblage: an analytic approach. PROC. PAN-AFR. CONGR. PRE-HIST. 4, no. iii (1962), pp. 81-105.

15,836 KUBIK, G. The phenomenon of inherent rhythms in East and Central African instrumental music. AFR. MUSIC, 1962, pp. 33-42.

15,837 LAMBERT, H. E. The Beni dance songs. SWAHILI 33, no. 1 (1962-1963), pp. 18-21.

15,838 LEAKEY, L. S. B. The sequence of stone-age cultures in East Africa. ESSAYS PRESENTED TO C. G. SELIGMAN, 1934, pp. 143-147.

15,839 LEAKEY, L. S. B. Stone-age man in East Africa. BULL. UGANDA SOC. 2 (1944), pp. 11-12.

15,840 LEAKEY, L. S. B. The Tumbian culture in East Africa. PROC. PAN-AFR. CONGR. PRE-HIST. 1 (1947), pp. 201-202.

15,841 LINDBLOM, G. Die strosstrommel, insbesondere in Afrika. ETHNOS 10 (1945), pp. 17-38.

15,842 LURY, E. E. Music in African churches [with a note by Hugh Tracey]. AFR. MUSIC, 1956, pp. 34-36.

15,843 NTIRO, S. East African art. TANG. NOTES 61 (1963), pp. 121-134.

15,844 POSNANSKY, M. The neolithic cultures of East Africa. PROC. PAN-AFR. CONGR. PRE-HIST. 4, no. iii (1962), pp. 272-279.

15,845 POSNANSKY, M. Pottery types from archaeological sites in East Africa. J. AFR. HIST. 2 (1961), pp. 177-198.

15,846 ROBINSON, A. E. Some notes on ancient means of water transport in relation to the vessels of East Africa. TANG. NOTES 4 (1937), pp. 65-71.

15,847 TRACEY, H. Recording in East Africa and northern Congo. AFR. MUSIC, 1953, pp. 6-15.

15,848 TRACEY, H. Recording tour, May to November 1950, East Africa. AFR. MUSIC, 1951, pp. 38-51.

15,849 Exhibition at the Imperial Institute, London of paintings, carvings and terracottas from Makerere College, Uganda—extracts from the press. AFR. MUSIC, 1949, pp. 34-35.

See also 7598, 19629.

Biography

15,850 SNOW-WHITE, A. et al. In memoriam: K. Amri Abedi 1924-1964. SWAHILI 35, no. 1 (1965), pp. 4-13.

15,851 MNYAMPALA, M. E. Maisha ya mheshimiwa Sheikh K. Amri Abedi Kwa Kifupi. SWAHILI 35, no. 1 (1965), pp. 14-18.

15,852 RISLEY, R. C. H. Burton: an appreciation. TANGANYIKA NOTES AND RECORDS 49 (1957), pp. 257-300.

15,853 SIMMONS, J. A suppressed passage in Livingstone's Last Journals relating to the death of Baron von der Decken. J. AFR. SOC. 40 (1941), pp. 335-346.

15,854 GRAY, Sir J. M. Correspondence relating to the death of Bishop Hannington. Uganda J. 13 (1949), pp. 1-22.

15,855 FUCHS, V. E. Foreword to Admiral von Höhnel's manuscript. J. AFR. SOC. 37 (1938), pp. 16-20.

15,856 Obituary: W. S. Marchant. AFR. AFFAIRS 52 (1953), p. 337.

15,857 THOMAS, H. B. James Martin. His medals. UGANDA J. 22 (1958), pp. 183-185.

15,858 GRAY, Sir J. M. Obituary: Michael Moses, O.B.E. UGANDA J. 22 (1958), pp. 97-103.

15,859 FILESI, T. Un libro di Vittorio Merlo Pich; Il più grande amico degli Africani. AFRICA (Rome) 16 (1961), p. 82.

15,860 SNOXALL, R. A. Obituary—The Rev. B. J. Ratcliffe. SWAHILI 23 (1953), pp. 3-4.

15,861 In memoriam [: Sheikh Shaaban Robert]. SWAHILI 33, no. 1 (1962-1963), p. x.

15,862 INGHAM, K. John Hanning Speke: a Victorian and his inspiration. TANGANYIKA NOTES AND RECORDS 49 (1957), pp. 301-311.

15,863 THOMAS, H. B. Dictionary of East African biography. MAKERERE J. 8 (1963), pp. 65-69.

15,864 Dictionary of East African biography project. BULL. AFR. STUD. ASSOC. 3 (1964), pp. 37-38.

Economics

15,865 THE AFRICAN STUDIES BRANCH. The East Africa Royal Commission and African land tenure. J. AFR. ADM. 8 (1956), pp. 69-74.

15,866 ARKADIE, B. V. Import substitution and export promotion as aids to industrialization in East Africa. E. AFR. EC. REV. N.S. 1, no. 1 (1964), pp. 40-56.

15,867 ARKADIE, B. V. The structure of the economies [of East Africa]. EAISR Jan. (1965), pp. 1-34.

15,868 ARKADIE, B. V. and NDEGWA, P. Future trade, balance of payments and aid requirements in East Africa. E. AFR. EC. REV. N.S. 1, no. 2 (1965), pp. 32-64.

15,869 BOVILL, E. W. The essential oil market. J. AFR. SOC. 33 (1934), pp. 217-225.

15,870 BULCK, G. VAN. Le troupeau de vaches, est-il un placement de capital en Afrique Orientale? ZAIRE 10 (1956), pp. 517-523.

15,871 BUXTON, T. F. V. Missions and industries in East Africa. J. AFR. SOC. 8 (1909), pp. 279-287.

15,872 CHRISTY, C. Rubber cultivation and native industries. J. AFR. SOC. 17 (1918), pp. 113-117.

15,873 CLARK, P. G. Co-ordination of development plans in East Africa. EAISR Jan. (1964), pp. 1-33.

15,874 CLARK, P. G. The rationale and uses of a projection model for the East African economies. E. AFR. EC. REV. N.S. 1, no. 2 (1965), pp. 1-20.

15,875 CLARK, P. G. The role of a central bank in accelerating economic development. PROBLEMS OF EC. DEVELOPMENT IN E. AFR., 1965, pp. 83-99.

15,876 CLARK, W. After independence in East Africa. AFR. AFFAIRS 61 (1962), pp. 126-137.

15,877 COURT, B. Television in East Africa. TRANSITION 5 (1962), p. 33.

15,878 DESAI, R. H. The family and business enterprise among the Asians in East Africa. EAISR Jan. (1965), pp. 1-6.

15,879 DUE, J. F. The reform of East African taxation. E. AFR. EC. REV. N.S. 1, no. 1 (1964), pp. 57-68.

15,880 ELKAN, W. The East African trade in woodcarvings. AFRICA 28 (1958), pp. 314-323.

15,881 ENGBERG, H. L. Commercial banking in East Africa, 1950-1963. JMAS 3 (1965), pp. 175-200.

15,882 EVANS, C. Fish! CORONA 3 (1951), pp. 416-417.

15,883 FRANK, C. R. Analysis and projection of the demand for sugar in East Africa. EAISR Jan. (1965), pp. 1-22.

15,884 FRANK, C. R. The production and distribution of sugar in East Africa. EAISR Jan. (1964), pp. 1-15.

15,885 GASKIN, M. Monetary flexibility in dependent economies. E. AFR. EC. REV. N.S. 1, no. 2 (1965), pp. 94-106; also in EAISR Jan. (1965), pp. 1-12.

15,886 GHAI, D. P. Tax structure for rapid economic growth. PROBLEMS OF EC. DEVELOPMENT IN E. AFR., 1965, pp. 73-78.

15,887 GRAY, A. East African development. AFR. AFFAIRS 55 (1956), pp. 250-251.

15,888 HEINZ, G. L'association entre le Marché Commun Européen et les Etats Africains et Malgache Associés (E.A.M.A.). ET. CONG. 4, no. 1 (1963), pp. 1-11.

15,889 HITCHCOCK, Sir E. The sisal industry of East Africa. TANGANYIKA NOTES AND RECORDS 52 (1959), pp. 4-17.

15,890 HOYT, E. Economic sense and the East African impressions of a visiting American economist. AFRICA 22 (1952), pp. 165-169.

15,891 HOYT, E. E. Certain social and cultural aspects of technological development in British East Africa. ZAIRE 6 (1952), pp. 487-490.

15,892 KARMILOFF, C. Regional development and industrial location in East Africa. PROBLEMS OF EC. DEVELOPMENT IN E. AFR., 1965, pp. 60-73.

15,893 KENNEDY, T. A. The East African customs union: some features of its history and operation. MAKERERE J. 3 (1959), pp. 19-41.

15,894 LOMORO, G. M. Monetary expansion in East African economic development. EAISR Jan. (1965), pp. 1-12.

15,895 MacDONA, B. East Africa and Rhodesia. AFR. AFFAIRS 57 (1958), pp. 41-52.

15,896 MUMFORD, W. B. East Africa: some problems in native economic development and a possible solution in co-operative societies. AFRICA 6 (1933), pp. 27-37.

15,897 MURUMBI, J. Some thoughts on problems of economic development in East Africa. PROBLEMS OF EC. DEVELOPMENT IN E. AFR., 1965, pp. 5-12.

15,898 NDEGWA, P. Development effects of the East African common market. EAISR Jan. (1965), pp. 1-17.

15,899 NDEGWA, P. Some aspects of inter-territorial trade in Africa in recent years. EAISR Jan. (1964), pp. 1-36.

15,900 NESS, P. New East African roads. J. AFR. SOC. 33 (1934), pp. 152-159.

15,901 NEWMAN, P. Foreign investment and economic growth: the case of East Africa, 1963-1970. E. AFR. EC. REV. N.S. 1, no. 1 (1964), pp. 22-39.

15,902 NEWMAN, P. K. Trends in the economy of East Africa. PROBLEMS OF EC. DEVELOPMENT IN E. AFR., 1965, pp. 13-30.

15,903 NUTMAN, F. J. The field for sisal research in East Africa. BULL. IMP. INST. 29 (1931), pp. 299-307.

15,904 NYANZI, S. The East African market: for better or for worse. TRANSITION 2 (1961), pp. 18-20.

15,905 NYANZI, S. A review of the East African common market. TRANSITION 6-7 (1962), pp. 13-14.

15,906 NYE, J. S., Jr. East African economic integration. JMAS 1 (1963), pp. 475-502.

15,907 ORMSBY-GORE, W. G. A. The work of the East Africa Commission. J. AFR. SOC. 24 (1925), pp. 165-177.

15,908 OSBORNE, J. F. The role of scientific research in the sisal industry of East Africa. PROC. E. AFR. ACAD. 2 (1964), pp. 149-156.

15,909 PATEL, S. J. An outline of economic prospects in East Africa. PROBLEMS OF EC. DEVELOPMENT IN E. AFR., 1965, pp. 31-40.

15,910 ROBINS, Sir R. E. Development of the transport system and its part and position in the history and development of East Africa. UGANDA J. 14 (1950), pp. 129-138.

15,911 ROWE, J. W. F. The coffee industries of East Africa in the world market setting. AFR. PRIMARY PRODUCTS AND INT. TRADE, 1965, pp. 83-94.

15,912 SCOTT, R. D. The determination of statutory minimum wages in East Africa: a case study in the politics of resource allocation. EAISR Jan. (1965), pp. 1-12.

15,913 WALKER, D. Economics in East Africa. MAKERERE J. 2 (1959), pp. 14-25.

15,914 WEDGWOOD, J. C. Land settlement in East Africa. CONTEMP. REV. 110 (1916), pp. 315-324.

15,915 WEIGT, E. Tropical East Africa. Possibilities of development. THE MALAYAN J. OF TR. GEOG. 8 (1956), pp. 87-89.

15,916 YOSHIDA, M. and BELSHAW, D. G. R. The introduction of the trade licensing system for primary products in East Africa, 1900-1939. EAISR Jan. (1965), pp. 1-29.

15,917 YOUNG, T. L. East African tax-method revision. J. AFR. SOC. 35 (1936), pp. 381-385.

15,918 Z., E. Attività turistica Italia-East Africa. AFRICA (Rome) 10 (1955), pp. 303-304.

15,919 Relations commerciales Israël-Afrique. ZAIRE 5 (1951), p. 864.

15,920 Sviluppo aereo in Africa Centrale. AFRICA (Rome) 10 (1955), pp. 87-88.

See also 1237, 4909.

Education

15,921 ALLEN, J. W. T. World literacy. TANG. NOTES 17 (1944), pp. 1-5.

15,922 ANDERSON, C. A. and FOSTER, P. J. Potentials for federation of East African educational programmes. J. DEVELOPMENT STUDS. 2 (1965), pp. 59-81.

15,923 BENSON, T. G. The Jeanes School and the education of the East African native. J. AFR. SOC. 35 (1936), pp. 418-431.

15,924 CARLIN, M. M. Arts in East Africa: a symposium. MAKERERE J. 4 (1960), pp. 1-19.

15,925 CARLIN, M. M. The Midas touch. Some observations on the Como Report. MAKERERE J. 9 (1964), pp. 45-52.

15,926 CARTER, J. Arts in East Africa: a symposium. MAKERERE J. 4 (1960), pp. 30-36.

15,927 COOK, D. Reflections after visiting some East African secondary schools. MAKERERE J. 8 (1963), pp. 57-64.

15,928 DE BUNSEN, B. Higher education and political change in East Africa. AFR. AFFAIRS 60 (1961), pp. 494-500.

15,929 DICKSON, A. G. Studies in war-time organisation: the Mobile Propaganda Unit, East Africa Command. AFR. AFFAIRS 44 (1945), pp. 9-18.

15,930 DOUGALL, J. W. C. Religious education. INT. REV. MISSIONS 15 (1926), pp. 493-505.

15,931 FRY, E. Freedom and responsibility. TRANSITION 3 (1962), p. 40.

15,932 GOLD, R. L. On screening candidates for T.E.A. EAISR Jan. (1964), pp. 1-16.

15,933 GOLD, R. L. and NELSON, F. B. Determining validity of field work data. EAISR Jan. (1965), pp. 1-9.

15,934 GRAY, A. Education in East Africa. AFR. AFFAIRS 57 (1958), pp. 180-181.

15,935 GREAVES, L. B. The educational adviserhip in East Africa. INT. REV. MISSIONS 36 (1947), pp. 329-337.

15,936 HARRIS, R. G. Standards in transition: analysis of a dilemma. MAKERERE J. 8 (1963), pp. 17-27.

15,937 HUSSEY, E. R. J. Higher education in East Africa. Report of the commission appointed by the secretary of state for the colonies. J. AFR. SOC. 36 (1937), supplement.

15,938 JAHADHMY, A. A. A note on Arab schooling and the Arab role in East Africa. AFR. AFFAIRS 51 (1952), pp. 150-152.

15,939 LANGLANDS, B. Arts in East Africa: a symposium. MAKERERE J. 4 (1960), pp. 20-29.

15,940 LATHAM, G. C. Indirect rule and education in East Africa. AFRICA 7 (1934), pp. 423-430.

15,941 MORGAN, G. D. Value orientations of B group teachers. EAISR Jan. (1964), pp. 1-7.

15,942 MUMFORD, W. B. Native schools in Central Africa. J. AFR. SOC. 26 (1927), pp. 237-244.

15,943 MUSGROVE, F. What sort of facts? AFR. AFFAIRS 51 (1952), pp. 313-318.

15,944 NELSON, F. B. American values and the role of school master in East Africa. EAISR Jan. (1964), pp. 1-7.

15,945 OLIENSIS, D. Some aspects of inter-racial attitudes of senior secondary schools. EAISR Jan. (1965), pp. 1-9.

15,946 PRATT, R. C. African universities and Western tradition—some East African reflections. JMAS 3 (1965), pp. 421-428.

15,947 RADO, E. R. The scope for short term manpower and educational policies. EAISR Jan. (1965), pp. 1-18.

15,948 RANGER, T. African attempts to control education in East and Central Africa 1900-1939. PAST AND PRESENT 32 (1965), pp. 57-85.

15,949 RICKETTS, E. The East African woman looks ahead. AFR. WOMEN 3 (1960), pp. 73-75.

15,950 SCOTT, H. S. The effect of education on the African. J. AFR. SOC. 37 (1938), pp. 504-509.

15,951 SILVEY, J. Preliminary thoughts on aptitude testing and educational selection in East Africa. EAISR Jan. (1963), pp. 1-12.

15,952 STUART, D. Liberal studies and language. MAKERERE J. 8 (1963), pp. 45-55.

15,953 TURNER, G. C. Education in Africa. AFR. AFFAIRS 48 (1949), pp. 213-222.

15,954 Education in British Africa. AFR. AFFAIRS 53 (1954), pp. 147-156.

15,955 Educational psychology. SWAHILI 17 (1943), pp. 11-14.

15,956 Université de l'Afrique Orientale. GENEVE-AFR. 1 (1962), p. 215.

15,957 Women's education in East Africa [Report of the East Africa Royal Commission 1953-1955]. AFR. WOMEN 1 (1955), pp. 55-57.

15,958 World literacy. TANG. NOTES 18 (1944), pp. 95-97.

Geography

15,959 BAKER, S. J. K. The distribution of native population over East Africa. AFRICA 10 (1937), pp. 37-54.

15,960 BRENARD, R. The romance of the air mail to East and South Africa. J. AFR. SOC. 38 (1939), pp. 47-64.

15,961 CORY, H. and MASALU, M. M. Place names in the Lake Province. TANG. NOTES 30 (1951), pp. 53-72.

15,962 CRAWFORD, O. G. S. The strange adventures of Zaga Christ. SUDAN NOTES 31 (1950), pp. 287-296.

15,963 CROSTHWAIT, H. L. Aerial survey of East and Central African territories. J. AFR. SOC. 29 (1930), pp. 333-342.

15,964 DONQUE, G. Le contexte océanique des anciennes migrations: vents et courants dans l'Océan Indien. ANN. UNIV. MADAG., Hors série (1965), pp. 43-59.

15,965 FREEMAN-GRENVILLE, G. S. P. Ibn Batuta's visit to East Africa A.D. 1332: a translation. UGANDA J. 19 (1955), pp. 1-6.

15,966 GILLMAN, C. An annotated list of ancient and modern indigenous stone structures in Eastern Africa. TANG. NOTES 17 (1944), pp. 44-55.

15,967 GILLMAN, C. White colonization in East Africa with special reference to Tanganyika Territory. GEOG. REV. 32 (1942), pp. 585-597.

15,968 GRAY, J. M. A precursor of Krapf and Rebmann. UGANDA J. 1 (1934), p. 71.

15,969 HETHERWICK, A. Opening up of Central Africa from the east coast. J. AFR. SOC. 2 (1903), pp. 326-330.

15,970 HOHNEL, L. VON. The Lake Rudolf region. Its discovery and subsequent exploration, 1888-1909. J. AFR. SOC. 37 (1938), pp. 21-45, 206-226.

15,971 HUXLEY, E. Some impressions of East Africa to-day. AFR. AFFAIRS 46 (1947), pp. 197-207; 47 (1948), pp. 15-23.

15,972 HUXLEY, H. Visite à l'Est africain en 1946. PRESENCE AFR. 13 (1952), pp. 180-185.

15,973 HUXLEY, J. Travel and politics in East Africa. J. AFR. SOC. 30 (1931), pp. 245-261.

15,974 JOHNSTON, Sir H. H. Dr. Weule's expedition to German East Africa. J. AFR. SOC. 8 (1909), pp. 383-386.

15,975 JOHNSTON, Sir H. H. The land of Zinj. J. AFR. SOC. 12 (1913), pp. 354-358.

15,976 KENWORTHY, J. M. Rainfall and the water resources of East Africa. GEOGRAPHERS AND THE TROPICS, 1964, pp. 111-137.

15,977 KOBISHCHANOW, Y. M. On the problem of sea voyages of ancient Africans in the Indian Ocean. J. AFR. HIST. 6 (1965), pp. 137-141.

15,978 MASSEI, E. In Africa per imparare. AFRICA (Rome) 11 (1956), pp. 151-155.

15,979 O'CONNOR, A. M. New railway construction and the pattern of economic development in East Africa. EAISR Jan. (1965), pp. 1-10.

15,980 POWELL-COTTON, P. H. G. Notes on a journey through East Africa and northern Uganda. J. AFR. SOC. 3 (1904), pp. 315-324.

15,981 ROSSINI, C. C. L'Africa Orientale in carte arabe dei secoli XII e XIII. RASS. STUDI ETIOP. 3 (1943), pp. 167-171.

15,982 RUSMINI, E. Attraverso l'East Africa. 1. Da Aden ad Arusha. 2. Da Arusha alle Murchison. AFRICA (Rome) 10 (1955), pp. 83-86, 121-124.

15,983 STOPFORD, J. G. B. What Africa can do for white men. J. AFR. SOC. 2 (1902), pp. 50-63.

15,984 TEMPLE, P. H. Lake Victoria levels. PROC. E. AFR. ACAD. 2 (1964), pp. 50-58.

15,985 THOMAS, H. B. A sketch-map of Gordon's Equatorial Provinces. UGANDA J. 23 (1959), pp. 178-179.

15,986 WALTER, A. A note on the seasonal rains in East Africa and their causation. TANG. NOTES 8 (1939), pp. 21-26.

15,987 WORTHINGTON, E. B. The Central African lakes. BULL. UGANDA SOC. 3 (1944), pp. 3-6.

15,988 ZANCANELLA, A. Da Mogadiscio alle cascate Vittoria. AFRICA (Rome) 13 (1958), pp. 202-205.

15,989 Origins of place names in East Africa. SWAHILI 18 (1944), pp. 11-13.

See also 4929, 12950, 19700, 19703, 19705, 22274.

Government

15,990 AFRICANUS, pseud. A central African confederation. J. AFR. SOC. 17 (1918), pp. 276-306.

15,991 BEAUDOIN, A. Les institutions politiques en Afrique Orientale Britannique. AFR. ET ASIE 27 (1954), pp. 3-24.

15,992 BEECHER, A. L. J. The East African political scene. The East African prospect. AFR. AFFAIRS 45 (1946), pp. 141-152.

15,993 BOVILL, E. W. East Africa to-day. AFR. AFFAIRS 50 (1951), pp. 225-232.

15,994 BRAINE, B. Storm clouds over the Horn of Africa. INTERNAT. AFFAIRS 34 (1958), pp. 435-443.

15,995 CHIDZERO, B. T. G. African nationalism in East and Central Africa. INTERNAT. AFFAIRS 36 (1960), pp. 464-475.

15,996 COLA ALBERICH, J. Africa oriental británica. CUAD. AFR. OR. 37 (1957), pp. 49-59.

15,997 CORYNDON, R. T. Problems of Eastern Africa. J. AFR. SOC. 21 (1922), pp. 177-186.

15,998 CRABTREE, W. A. The Germans in East and West Africa. J. AFR. SOC. 15 (1915), pp. 1-10.

15,999 GRAY, A. East Africa report. AFR. AFFAIRS 54 (1955), pp. 256-258.

16,000 GRAY, A. East African advance. AFR. AFFAIRS 56 (1957), pp. 104-105.

16,001 GRAY, A. East African co-operation. AFR. AFFAIRS 60 (1961), pp. 485-487.

16,002 GRAY, A. Princess [Margaret] in East Africa. AFR. AFFAIRS 55 (1956), pp. 246-247.

16,003 GREAT BRITAIN. HOUSE OF LORDS. Eastern and Central Africa. House of Lords debate on the report of commission on closer union. J. AFR. SOC. 28 (1929), pp. 253-264.

16,004 HUNTER, G. East Africa—its difficulties and possibilities. AFR. AFFAIRS 43 (1944), pp. 128-133.

16,005 IBINGIRA, G. Political movements and their role in promoting unity in East Africa. TRANSITION 20 (1965), pp. 37-42.

16,006 JOHNS, D. H. Defence and police organization in East Africa. EAISR Jan. (1964), pp. 1-16.

16,007 KHAMISI, F. J. The East African political scene. The African viewpoint. AFR. AFFAIRS 45 (1946), pp. 139-141.

16,008 KIANO, J. G. From PAFMECA to PAFMECSA—and beyond. AFR. FORUM 1 (1965), pp. 36-49.

16,009 LABOURET, H. Problèmes d'Afrique Orientale. AFR. ET ASIE 2, no. 1 (1949), pp. 26-41.

16,010 LUGARD, Lord. Native policy in East Africa. FOREIGN AFFAIRS 9 (1930-1931), pp. 65-78.

16,011 MEZZA, E. La polizia dell' Africa Orientale Italiana: scuola di civismo. AFRICA (Rome) 10 (1955), pp. 359-360.

16,012 NEWMAN, E. W. P. Changes in North-East Africa. CONTEMP. REV. 151 (1937), pp. 162-170.

16,013 NYE, J. S. Attitudes of Makerere students towards the East African Federation. EAISR Jan. (1963), pp. 1-12.

16,014 NYERERE, J. K. Two views on Capricorn: the entrenchment of privilege. AFR. SOUTH 2, no. 2 (1958), pp. 85-90.

16,015 O'CONNOR, J. Catholicism and African socialism. TRANSITION 16 (1954), pp. 19-21.

16,016 OLDHAM, J. H. Report of the Commission on Closer Union of the Eastern and Central African Dependencies. INTERNAT. AFFAIRS 8 (1929), pp. 227-259.

16,017 OLIVIER. Settled policy in East Africa. CONTEMP. REV. 140 (1931), pp. 694-701.

16,018 OWEN, W. E. Some thoughts on native development in East Africa. J. AFR. SOC. 30 (1931), pp. 225-237.

16,019 PONSONBY, C. E. The future of British East Africa. J. AFR. SOC. 41 (1942), pp. 234-237.

16,020 RICHARDS, A. I. East African Conference on Colonial Administration. J. AFR. ADM. 5 (1953), pp. 62-65.

16,021 ROTBERG, R. I. An account of the attempt to achieve closer union in British East Africa. EAISR Jan. (1963), pp. 1-9.

16,022 ROTHCHILD, D. East African federation. A report on the Nairobi conference, the second in a series of three conferences organised by the University of East Africa. TRANSITION 12 (1964), pp. 39-42.

16,023 SEGAL, A. A federal capital for East Africa. EAISR Jan. (1964), pp. 1-7.

16,024 SILBERMAN, L. Change and conflict in the Horn of Africa. FOREIGN AFFAIRS 37 (1958-1959), pp. 649-659.

16,025 SMITH, A. East Africa emergent. THE YEAR BOOK OF WORLD AFFAIRS 16 (1962), pp. 122-188.

16,026 STANNER, W. E. H. Observations on colonial planning. INTERNAT. AFFAIRS 25 (1949), pp. 318-328.

16,027 STIRLING, D. The Capricorn contract. AFR. AFFAIRS 56 (1957), pp. 191-199.

16,028 TATE, H. R. Closer union in East Africa. J. AFR. SOC. 31 (1932), pp. 38-53.

16,029 TOLEN, A. Une révolution, trois interventions, une Afrique à construire. PRESENCE AFR. N.S. 53 (1965), pp. 36-46.

16,030 VINCENT, Sir A. East African development. AFR. AFFAIRS 48 (1949), pp. 47-55.

16,031 WARD, R. E. K. The East African political scene. The European point of view. AFR. AFFAIRS 45 (1946), pp. 136-139.

16,032 WOOD, M. Two views on Capricorn: towards a common citizenship. AFR. SOUTH 2, no. 2 (1958), pp. 82-85.

16,033 L'avenir politique de l'Est-Africain. ZAIRE 5 (1951), p. 528.

See also 12954, 19712.

History

16,034 BEACHEY, R. W. The arms trade in East Africa in the late nineteenth century. EAISR Jan. (1959), pp. 1-27; also in J. AFR. HIST. 3 (1962), pp. 451-467.

16,035 BENNETT, N. R. Some notes on French policy in Buganda and East Africa, 1879-1890. MAKERERE J. 6 (1962), pp. 1-17.

16,036 BRIDGES, R. C. Krapf and the strategy of the mission to East Africa, 1844-55. MAKERERE J. 5 (1961), pp. 37-50.

16,037 BUELL, R. L. The destiny of East Africa. FOREIGN AFFAIRS 6 (1927-1928), pp. 408-426.

16,038 CHITTICK, N. The 'Shirazi' colonization of East Africa. J. AFR. HIST. 6 (1965), pp. 275-294.

16,039 COLQUHOUN, A. R. Our East African empire. ROYAL COL. INST. PR. 39 (1907-1908), pp. 198-228.

16,040 EBERLIE, R. F. The German achievement in East Africa. TANGANYIKA NOTES AND RECORDS 55 (1960), pp. 181-214.

16,041 ELIOT, Sir C. The progress and problems of the East Africa Protectorate. ROYAL COL. INST. PR. 37 (1905-1906), pp. 81-111.

16,042 ELLIOTT, J. A. G. A visit to the Bajun islands. J. AFR. SOC. 25 (1925), pp. 10-22, 147-163, 245-263, 338-358.

16,043 FREEMAN-GRENVILLE, G. S. P. Cosmas Indicopleustes: a problem in East African history. TANGANYIKA NOTES AND RECORDS 52 (1959), pp. 57-60.

16,044 FREEMAN-GRENVILLE, G. S. P. East African studies. UNIV. GHANA RES. REV. 1 (1965), no. 2, p. 53.

16,045 FREEMAN-GRENVILLE, G. S. P. Historiography of the East African coast. TANGANYIKA NOTES AND RECORDS 55 (1960), pp. 279-289.

16,046 FREEMAN-GRENVILLE, G. S. P. Some problems of East African coinage: from early times to 1890. TANGANYIKA NOTES AND RECORDS 53 (1959), pp. 250-260.

16,047 FREEMAN-GRENVILLE, G. S. P. Swahili literature and the history and archaeology of the East African coast. SWAHILI 28, no. 2 (1958), pp. 7-25.

16,048 GHAI, D. P. Asians in East Africa: the Asians of East Africa by L. W. Hollingsworth [a review article]. TRANSITION 3 (1962), pp. 35-36.

16,049 GILLARD, D. R. Salisbury's African policy and the Heligoland offer of 1890. ENG. HIST. REV. 75 (1960), pp. 631-653.

16,050 GRAY, J. Trading expeditions from the coast to Lakes Tanganyika and Victoria before 1857. TANGANYIKA NOTES AND RECORDS 49 (1957), pp. 226-246.

16,051 HARRIES, L. The founding of Rabai: a Swahili chronicle of Midani bin Nwidad. SWAHILI 31 (1960), pp. 140-149.

16,052 HOLLIS, A. C. Notes on the history of Vumba, East Africa. JRAI 30 (1900), pp. 275-297.

16,053 HOWE, S. Premiers essais de pénétration des Anglais en Afrique Occidentale, d'après des renseignements inédits du Foreign Office. REV. HIST. COL. 33 (1940-1946), pp. 50-69.

16,054 HUXLEY, E. The invaders of East Africa [by R. Coupland]. J. AFR. SOC. 38 (1939), pp. 347-356.

16,055 INGHAM, K. East African history from local sources. MAKERERE J. 3 (1959), pp. 72-85.

16,056 JEFFREYS, M. D. W. Muhindi or grain of Arabia. UGANDA J. 20 (1956), pp. 198-201.

16,057 LAMDEN, S. C. Some aspects of porterage in East Africa. TANG. NOTES 61 (1963), pp. 155-164.

16,058 LEGGETT, Sir H. The British East African territories and their strategical implications. J. AFR. SOC. 39 (1940), pp. 206-210.

16,059 LIBRA. I Cinesi e l'Africa orientale. AFRICA (Rome) 18 (1963), pp. 38-40.

16,060 MATHEW, G. The east coast cultures. AFR. SOUTH 2, no. 2 (1958), pp. 59-62.

16,061 NORTHEY, E. The East African campaign. J. AFR. SOC. 18 (1919), pp. 81-87.

16,062 OLIVER, R. Some aspects in the British occupation of East Africa. UGANDA J. 15 (1951), pp. 49-64.

16,063 PLATT, Sir W. Studies in war-time organisation: East African Command. AFR. AFFAIRS 45 (1946), pp. 27-35.

16,064 RAMM, A. Great Britain and the planting of Italian power in the Red Sea, 1868-1885. ENG. HIST. REV. 59 (1944), pp. 211-236.

16,065 RANGELEY, W. H. J. The Arabs. NYASA J. 16, no. 2 (1963), pp. 11-25.

16,066 ROBINSON, A. E. Migrations of African peoples from the sea to the interior. J. AFR. SOC. 28 (1929), pp. 394-395.

16,067 ROBINSON, A. E. The Shirazi colonization of East Africa: Vumba. TANG. NOTES 7 (1939), pp. 92-112.

16,068 ROBINSON, A. E. The Shirazi colonizations of East Africa. TANG. NOTES 3 (1937), pp. 40-81.

16,069 ROBINSON, A. E. Some historical notes on East Africa. TANG. NOTES 2 (1936), pp. 21-43.

16,070 ROUSSIER, P. Les origines du Dépot des Papiers Publics des Colonies. Le Dépot de Rochefort (1763-1790). RHCF 18 (1925), pp. 21-50.

16,071 SHEPPERSON, G. The military history of British Central Africa. RHODES-LIV. J. 26 (1959), pp. 23-33.

16,072 SMITH, E. W. The exploitation of East Africa [by R. Coupland]. J. AFR. SOC. 38 (1939), pp. 483-489.

16,073 STANTON, E. A. Secret letters from the Khedive Ismail in connection with an occupation of the east coast of Africa. J. AFR. SOC. 34 (1935), pp. 269-282.

16,074 TATE, H. R. The Italian colonial empire. J. AFR. SOC. 40 (1941), pp. 146-158.

16,075 THOMAS, H. B. Church Missionary Society boats in East Africa. UGANDA J. 25 (1961), pp. 43-53.

16,076 THOMAS, H. B. The death of Dr. Livingstone: Carus Farrar's narrative. UGANDA J. 14 (1950), pp. 115-128.

16,077 THOMAS, H. B. Emile Jonveaux: an armchair African explorer. BULL. UGANDA SOC. 4 (1945), pp. 29-30.

16,078 THOMAS, H. B. A federal capital for Eastern Africa—some early proposals. UGANDA J. 2 (1935), pp. 247-249.

16,079 THOMAS, H. B. The Imperial British East Africa Company Medal. UGANDA J. 16 (1952), pp. 28-29; 19 (1955), pp. 209-210.

16,080 THOMAS, H. B. The Maria Theresa dollar. UGANDA J. 16 (1952), pp. 96-98.

16,081 THOMSON, J. East Africa as it was and is. CONTEMP. REV. 55 (1889), pp. 41-51.

16,082 TWYNAM, C. D. Early East African mails. NYASA J. 4, no. 2 (1951), pp. 67-70.

16,083 WASON, C. The East Africa and Uganda Protectorates. ROYAL COL. INST. PR. 35 (1903-1904), pp. 186-196.

16,084 WATERFIELD, G. The Horn of Africa. AFR. AFFAIRS 57 (1958), pp. 11-19.

16,085 WRIGHT, A. C. A. Maize names as indicators of economic contacts. UGANDA J. 13 (1949), pp. 61-81.

16,086 ZUCCARI, P. L. Anna d'Aosta fra gli operai italia nel cuore dell' Africa. AFRICA (Rome) 10 (1955), pp. 119-121.

16,087 The Sudan Defence Force and the Italian East African Campaign. J. AFR. SOC. 41 (1942), pp. 162-171.

See also 4966, 4992, 5010, 19738.

Language. Literature

Language: General

16,088 BOUET, K. English abstract [of German contributions to the study of East African languages]. SWAHILI 35, no. 2 (1965), pp. 58-59.

16,089 BUTTNER, C. G. Deutsch-Kikamba Wörterbuch. Nach den Vorarbeiten von L. Krapf. ZAS 1 (1887-1888), pp. 81-123.

16,090 CRABTREE, W. A. Missing links. J. AFR. SOC. 21 (1922), pp. 208-216.

16,091 DAMMANN, E. Deutsche beitrage zur kenntnis Ostafrikanischer sprachen. SWAHILI 35, no. 2 (1965), pp. 54-57.

16,092 DOKE, C. M. The linguistic work of H. W. Woodward. AFR. STUD. 20 (1961), pp. 197-202.

16,093 GLAUNING, VON. Forms of salutation amongst natives of East Africa. J. AFR. SOC. 3 (1904), pp. 288-299.

16,094 GREENBERG, J. H. Nilotic, 'Nilo-Hamitic', and Hamito-Semitic: a reply. AFRICA 27 (1957), pp. 364-377.

16,095 HADDON, E. B. Note on the verbal -E stem in East African Bantu. AFRICA 25 (1955), pp. 79-83.

16,096 HADDON, E. B. The perfect tense in the Eastern Bantu languages. UGANDA J. 4 (1936), pp. 120-125.

16,097 HOHENBERGER, J. Some notes on Nolitic, 'Nilo-Hamitic', and Hamito-Semitic, by John Greenberg. AFRICA 28 (1958), pp. 37-41.

16,098 HONEYMAN, A. M. The letter-order of the Semitic alphabets in Africa and the Near East. AFRICA 22 (1952), pp. 136-147.

16,099 LESLAU, W. Observations of a Semitist on recent etymologies proposed by Africanists. AFRICA 28 (1958), pp. 324-328.

16,100 MEEUSSEN, A. E. Hamietisch en Nilotisch. ZAIRE 11 (1957), pp. 263-272.

16,101 MEINHOF, C. Dissimilation der Nasalverbindungen im Bantu. AFR. UND UB. 3 (1912-1913), pp. 272-278.

16,102 MELDON, J. A. The Latuka and Bari languages. J. AFR. SOC. 9 (1910), pp. 193-195.

16,103 ROEHL, K. The linguistic situation in East Africa. AFRICA 3 (1930), pp. 191-202.

16,104 SNOXALL, R. A. Some thoughts on the orthography of the Bantu languages of East Africa. SWAHILI 19 (1945), pp. 3-7.

16,105 STRUCK, B. Collections towards a bibliography of the Bantu languages of British East Africa. J. AFR. SOC. 6 (1907), pp. 390-404.

16,106 TUCKER, A. N. Problèmes de typologie dans la classification des langues non Bantu de l'Afrique du Nord-est. J. SOC. AFR. 30 (1960), pp. 57-74.

16,107 TUCKER, A. N. Taaleenmaking in Oost-Afrika. KONGO-OVERZEE 18 (1952), pp. 312-317.

16,108 TUCKER, A. N. De unificatie der Zuidnilotische talen. KONGO-OVERZEE 12-13 (1946-1947), pp. 257-264.

16,109 TUCKER, A. N. and BRYAN, M. A. Noun classification in Kalenjin: Päkot. AFR. LANG. STUD. 3 (1962), pp. 137-181.

16,110 WAINWRIGHT, G. A. The diffusion of -uma as a name for iron. UGANDA J. 18 (1954), pp. 113-136.

16,111 WERNER, A. Notes on the Shambala and some allied languages of East Africa. J. AFR. SOC. 5 (1906), pp. 154-166.

16,112 WERNER, A. Specimens of East African dialects. BANTU STUD. 3 (1927), pp. 1-3.

16,113 WHITELEY, W. H. Kinship terminology and the initial vowel. AFRICA 29 (1959), pp. 253-262.

16,114 WHITELEY, W. H. A linguistic bibliography of East Africa. SWAHILI 27 (1957), pp. 103-105.

16,115 WHITELEY, W. H. Linguistic research in East Africa. SWAHILI 24 (1954), pp. 9-20.

16,116 WHITELEY, W. H. Shape and meaning in Yao nominal classes. AFR. LANG. STUD. 2 (1961), pp. 1-24.

16,117 WHITELEY, W. H. Some problems of syntax of sentences in a Bantu language of East Africa. LINGUA 9 (1960), pp. 148-174.

16,118 WHITELEY, W. H. Suggestions for recording a Bantu language in the field. TANG. NOTES 62 (1964), pp. 1-19.

16,119 WILLIAMSON, J. Grammatical nomenclature in text-books of East African Bantu languages. SWAHILI 26 (1956), pp. 18-19.

See also 12962, 12965.

Language: Swahili

16,120 ALI AHMED JAHADHMY. The basis of English-Swahili translation work. SWAHILI 23 (1953), pp. 34-35.

16,121 ALI AHMED JAHADHMY. The teaching of Swahili as a foreign language. SWAHILI 22 (1952), pp. 4-5.

16,122 ALI AHMED JAHADHMY and TRAVERS, R. Some Swahili nautical terms. SWAHILI 23 (1953), pp. 71-72.

16,123 ALLEN, J. W. T. The elision of the subjective prefix and the use of negative questions in Swahili. SWAHILI 32 (1961), pp. 67-68.

16,124 ALLEN, J. W. T. The rapid spread of Swahili. SWAHILI 30 (1959), pp. 70-73.

16,125 ALLEN, J. W. T. et al. Bantu linguistic terminology by C. M. Doke. SWAHILI 10 (1936), pp. 7-24.

16,126 ASHTON, E. O. The e and o of LuGanda and the o of Swahili. BULL. SOAS 8 (1935-1937), pp. 1121-1123.

16,127 ASHTON, E. O. The idea approach to Swahili. BULL. SOAS 7 (1933-1935), pp. 837-859.

16,128 BRAIN, J. L. Swahili at Syracuse. SWAHILI 35, no. 1 (1965), pp. 68-72.

16,129 BROOMFIELD, G. W. The change of the prefix KI to CH before vowels. SWAHILI 6 (1933), pp. 10-12.

16,130 BROOMFIELD, G. W. The development of the Swahili language. AFRICA 3 (1930), pp. 516-522.

16,131 BROOMFIELD, G. W. Notes on the -ka- and -ki- tenses. SWAHILI 6 (1933), pp. 7-9.

16,132 BROOMFIELD, G. W. The re-Bantuization of the Swahili language. AFRICA 4 (1931), pp. 77-85.

16,133 BROOMFIELD, G. W. Some points of translation [the -ka- prefix]. SWAHILI 6 (1933), pp. 15-16.

16,134 BROOMFIELD, G. W. Suggestions with regard to certain non-Bantu words of which the origins have not previously been traced. SWAHILI 9 (1935), pp. 3-5.

16,135 BRYAN, M. A. The archaic perfect tense in old and modern Swahili. BULL. SOAS 9 (1937-1939), pp. 195-199.

16,136 BRYAN, M. A. The T/K languages: a new substratum. AFRICA 29 (1959), pp. 1-20.

16,137 BUHLMANN, W. Principles of phonetic adaptation in Swahili applied to Christian names. AFRICA 23 (1953), pp. 127-134.

16,138 BULL, A. F. Looking back thirty years—and forward: the story of the East African Swahili Committee. SWAHILI 32 (1961), pp. 20-23.

16,139 BULL, A. F. Mbona?—The rhetorical question. SWAHILI 16 (1942), pp. 8-9.

16,140 CEPOLLARO, A. I Swahili e la loro lingua. AFRICA (Rome) 17 (1962), pp. 67-82.

16,141 CHUM, H. and LAMBERT, H. E. A vocabulary of the Kikae (Kimakunduchi, Kihadimu) dialect with examples illustrating the morphology. SWAHILI 33, no. 1 (1962-1963), pp. 51-68.

16,142 COPLAND, B. D. Some Swahili nautical terms. BULL. SOAS 7 (1933-1935), pp. 377-380.

16,143 DAMMANN, E. German contributions to Swahili studies in recent decades. SWAHILI 26 (1956), pp. 9-17.

16,144 DAMMANN, E. Eine Sprachprobe aus der siu-Mundart des Suaheli. AFR. UND UB. 30 (1940), pp. 72-77.

16,145 DAMMANN, E. Verwendung und Bedeutung von B. yi. AFR. UND UB. 39 (1954-1955), pp. 31-40.

16,146 DOKE, C. M. Word-division and grammatical classification in Swahili. SWAHILI 11 (1936), pp. 3-8.

16,147 EAST AFRICAN MARINE FISHERIES RESEARCH ORGANIZATION. Swahili names for marine fishes. SWAHILI 28, no. 1 (1958), pp. 43-47.

16,148 FREEMAN-GRENVILLE, G. S. P. Medieval evidences for Swahili. SWAHILI 29 (1959), pp. 10-23.

16,149 GOWER, R. H. Swahili borrowings from English. AFRICA 22 (1952), pp. 154-157; TANGANYIKA NOTES AND RECORDS 50 (1958), pp. 118-120.

16,150 GOWER, R. H. Swahili slang. SWAHILI 28, no. 2 (1958), pp. 41-48.

16,151 GRIGORIEVA, T. N. The study of Swahili in the Soviet Union. SWAHILI 35, no. 2 (1965), pp. 59-66.

16,152 HADDON, E. B. Notes on the noun classes. SWAHILI 23 (1953), pp. 66-69.

16,153 HADDON, E. B. Some notes on the initial vowel preprefix. SWAHILI 26 (1956), pp. 32-48.

16,154 HARRIES, L. Locative agreements in Swahili. SWAHILI 35, no. 2 (1965), pp. 70-73.

16,155 HARRIES, L. Some grammatical features of recent Swahili prose. AFR. LANG. STUD. 2 (1961), pp. 37-41.

16,156 HARRIS, L. Supplementary vocabulary: Swahili-English. SWAHILI 28, no. 2 (1958), pp. 49-84; 29, no. 2 (1959), pp. 55-80.

16,157 HEEPE, M. Alte Verbalformen mit vollständiger Vokalassimilation im Suaheli. AFR. UND UB. 9 (1918-1919), pp. 118-125.

16,158 HELLIER, A. B. The alphabet. SWAHILI 7 (1934), pp. 22-23.

16,159 HELLIER, A. B. Bantu weights and measures. SWAHILI 9 (1935), pp. 12-13.

16,160 HELLIER, A. B. The case of two A's in Swahili. SWAHILI 6 (1933), pp. 5-6.

16,161 HELLIER, A. B. Numeration in the Swahili language. SWAHILI 6 (1933), pp. 13-15.

16,162 HELLIER, A. B. Stray notes: 1. Nikitopenda 2. -KA- following upon -ME- 3. The mood of the -KA- and -KI- tenses 4. The -KI- tense in clauses of time 5. Will and would. SWAHILI 7 (1934), pp. 24-29.

16,163 HICHENS, W. Swahili prosody. SWAHILI 33, no. 1 (1962-1963), pp. 107-137.

16,164 HILL, P. Some notes on structural differences between English and Swahili. SWAHILI 35, no. 1 (1965), pp. 24-27.

16,165 JENSEN, H. Ausgewählte Kapitel aus der Syntax des Suaheli. AFR. UND UB. 13 (1922-1923), pp. 241-259.

16,166 JENSEN, H. Negationspartikeln im Suaheli und in einigen anderen Bantusprachen. FESTSCHRIFTEN MEINHOF, 1927, pp. 111-117.

16,167 JOHNSON, F. Miscellaneous notes: 1. the verb kutoa and the negative of the infinitive. 2. Cha and chwa. 3. Verbs ending in -ua and -ca. SWAHILI 6 (1933), pp. 17-24.

16,168 JOHNSON, F. Notes on the derivation of certain Swahili words. SWAHILI 9 (1935), pp. 9-11.

16,169 JOHNSON, F. The uses of licha and sembuse. SWAHILI 8 (1935), pp. 4-5.

16,170 JOHNSON, F. Verbs ending in -UA and -OA. SWAHILI 8 (1935), pp. 5-6.

16,171 KAHLER-MEYER, E. Das Phonem /j/ im Swahili. AFR. UND UB. 48 (1964-1965), pp. 192-202.

16,172 KLINGENHEBEN-V. TILING, M. Lautliche Eigentümlichkeiten im gesprochenen Suaheli. AFR. UND UB. 20 (1929-1930), pp. 1-10.

16,173 KNAPPERT, J. The adaptation of Swahili to modern times. AFR. UND UB. 48 (1964-1965), pp. 182-191.

16,174 KNAPPERT, J. Derivation of nouns of action in -o in Swahili. SWAHILI 33, no. 1 (1962-1963), pp. 74-106.

16,175 KNAPPERT, J. The divine names. SWAHILI 31 (1960), pp. 180-199.

16,176 KNAPPERT, J. Leidende beginselen voor een spelling van het Swahili. KONGO-OVERZEE 22 (1956), pp. 342-359.

16,177 KNAPPERT, J. Le swahili, langue de culture. PRESENCE AFR. N.S. 50 (1964), pp. 178-182.

16,178 KNAPPERT, J. Woordscheiding en woordverdeling in literair Swahili. KONGO-OVERZEE 25 (1959), pp. 86-89.

16,179 KOPOKA, O. B. The -E form of the verb in standard Swahili. SWAHILI 25 (1955), pp. 44-60.

16,180 KOPOKA, O. B. The possessive in standard Swahili. SWAHILI 24 (1954), pp. 21-32.

16,181 LAMBERT, H. E. The archaic perfect tense in Swahili. SWAHILI 35, no. 1 (1965), pp. 73-74.

16,182 LAMBERT, H. E. Comments on "supplementary vocabulary: Swahili-English." SWAHILI 32 (1961), pp. 60-64.

16,183 LAMBERT, H. E. The -E verb ending in archaic Swahili. SWAHILI 25 (1955), pp. 61-90.

16,184 LAMBERT, H. E. The possessive in dialect. SWAHILI 24 (1954), pp. 33-57.

16,185 LAMBERT, H. E. Scraps from a Swahili scrap-book. SWAHILI 33, no. 1 (1962-1963), pp. 48-49.

16,186 LAMBERT, H. E. The translation threat to Swahili idiom. SWAHILI 22 (1952), pp. 8-12.

16,187 LAMBERT, H. E. The Vumba verb. SWAHILI 23 (1953), pp. 14-33.

16,188 LESLIE, J. A. K. Swahili slang. SWAHILI 29 (1959), pp. 81-84.

16,189 LOOGMAN, A. Notes on the locative classes. SWAHILI 9 (1935), pp. 6-7.

16,190 MANYAMPALA, M. E. and KNAPPERT, J. Orodha ya manemo ya utenzi wa Enjili: word list to the epic of the Gospel. SWAHILI 34, no. 1 (1964), pp. 69-85.

16,191 MAW, J. Some problems involved in comparing linguistic systems. SWAHILI 35, no. 2 (1965), pp. 73-76.

16,192 OHLY, R. Patterns of new-coined abstract terms (nominal forms) in modern Swahili language. AFR. BULL. 2 (1965), pp. 71-86.

16,193 OVIR, E. Die abgeleiteten Verba im Kiswahili. ZAOS 2 (1896), pp. 249-266.

16,194 PAKENHAM, R. H. W. Kiswahili names of birds and beasts in the Zanzibar protectorate. SWAHILI 29 (1959), pp. 34-54.

16,195 PANCOLLI-CALZIA, G. Uber die aspirierten und nichtaspirierten Verschlußlaute sowie den Frageton im Suaheli. AFR. UND UB. 1 (1910), pp. 305-315.

16,196 PATEL, R. B. The borrowing of Swahili words in spoken Gujarati. SWAHILI 35, no. 2 (1965), pp. 14-16.

16,197 PAULINUS, B. Suggested list of terms for stars and constellations. SWAHILI 35, no. 1 (1965), pp. 75-76.

16,198 PICKS, M. Standardization of Christian names and grammatical terms. SWAHILI 11 (1936), pp. 9-10.

16,199 PRINS, A. H. J. An analysis of Swahili kinship terminology. SWAHILI 26 (1956), pp. 20-27; 28 (1958), pp. 9-16.

16,200 RATCLIFFE, B. J. History, purpose and activities of the Inter-territorial Language Committee. SWAHILI 16 (1942), pp. 3-8.

16,201 RATCLIFFE, B. J. Swahili words suggested as being derived from Portuguese. SWAHILI 16 (1942), pp. 11-13.

16,202 RATCLIFFE, B. J. The use of the onomatopoetic in Swahili. SWAHILI 12 (1938), pp. 8-9.

16,203 RAUM, J. Kleine Beiträge zur Swahiligrammatik. ZAOS 4 (1898), pp. 133-135.

16,204 ROBERT, S. Swahili as unifying force in East Africa. SWAHILI 33, no. 1 (1962-1963), pp. 11-12.

16,205 SCOTT, R. R. Medical and hospital terms. SWAHILI 19 (1945), pp. 23-27; 20 (1947), pp. 7-9.

16,206 SCOTTON, C. M. M. Some Swahili political words. JMAS 3 (1965), pp. 527-541.

16,207 SEIDEL, A. Das arabische Element in Suaheli. ZAOS 1 (1895), pp. 9-15, 97-104.

16,208 SEIDEL, A. Uza und uliza im Suaheli. ZAOS 5 (1900), pp. 158-160.

16,209 SEIDEL, A. Zur Lehre von den Präpositionem im Suahili. ZAOS 5 (1900), pp. 44-47.

16,210 SNOXALL, R. A. Comments on the verb 'kutoa' and the negative of the infinitive. SWAHILI 8 (1935), pp. 3-4.

16,211 SNOXALL, R. A. How Swahili is changing. BULL. EAST. AFR. INTER-TERRITORIAL LANG. COMM. 21 (1951), pp. 8-11.

16,212 SNOXALL, R. A. The ideophone in Swahili. SWAHILI 12 (1938), pp. 5-7.

16,213 SNOXALL, R. A. Tone in Swahili. Does it exist? SWAHILI 17 (1943), pp. 4-6.

16,214 SNOXALL, R. A. et al. [List of words with suggested Swahili equivalents]. SWAHILI 12 (1938), pp. 3-7; 13 (1939), pp. 3-19; 14 (1940), pp. 3-25; 15 (1941), pp. 3-26; 16 (1942), pp. 9-10.

16,215 TANZANIA EPISCOPAL CONFERENCE. Provisional religious vocabulary: Swahili-English, English-Swahili based on the Katekisimu ya Kikristu (Ndanda). SWAHILI 35, no. 1 (1965), pp. 77-91.

16,216 TUCKER, A. N. Foreign sounds in Swahili. BULL. SOAS 11 (1943-1946), pp. 854-871.

16,217 TUCKER, A. N. [Memorandum]. BULL. EAST AFR. INTER-TERRITORIAL LANG. COMM. 21 (1951), pp. 5-7.

16,218 TUCKER, A. N. and ASHTON, E. O. Swahili phonetics. AFR. STUD. 1 (1942), pp. 77-103, 161-182.

16,219 VIRMANI, K. K. The teaching of Swahili in Delhi. SWAHILI 35, no. 2 (1965), pp. 66-69.

16,220 VORST, G. VAN DER. Le Kiswahili, langue classique. KONGO-OVERZEE 24 (1958), pp. 203-213.

16,221 WALFORD, A. S. Queries and suggestions about certain agricultural terms. SWAHILI 11 (1936), pp. 11-12.

16,222 WESTON, A. B. Law in Swahili: problems in developing the national language. SWAHILI 35, no. 2 (1965), pp. 2-13.

16,223 WHITELEY, W. H. The changing position of Swahili in East Africa. AFRICA 26 (1956), pp. 343-353.

16,224 WHITELEY, W. H. Further problems in the study of Swahili sentences. LINGUA 10 (1961), pp. 148-173.

16,225 WHITELEY, W. H. Kimvita: an enquiry into dialectal status and characteristics. SWAHILI 25 (1955), pp. 10-38.

16,226 WHITELEY, W. H. Notes on the Ci-Miini dialect of Swahili. AFR. LANG. STUD. 6 (1965), pp. 67-72.

16,227 WHITELEY, W. H. Political concepts and connotations: observations on the use of some political terms in Swahili. ST. ANTONY'S PAPERS 10 (1961), pp. 7-21.

16,228 WHITELEY, W. H. Problems of a lingua franca: Swahili and the trade unions. J. AFR. LANGS. 3 (1964), pp. 215-225.

16,229 WHITELEY, W. H. Swahili and the classical tradition. TANGANYIKA NOTES AND RECORDS 53 (1959), pp. 214-223.

16,230 WHITELEY, W. H. The work of the East African Swahili Committee,1930-1957. KONGO-OVERZEE 23 (1957), pp. 242-255.

16,231 WILLIAMSON, J. Congo Swahili. BULL. EAST AFR. INTER-TERRITORIAL LANG. COMM. 21 (1951), pp. 15-17.

16,232 WILLIAMSON, J. The ka prefix. SWAHILI 22 (1952), p. 8.

16,233 WILLIAMSON, J. Place [mahali in Swahili]. SWAHILI 22 (1952), pp. 6-8.

16,234 WILLIAMSON, J. The "U" prefix. SWAHILI 22 (1952), p. 13.

16,235 WRIGHT, M. Swahili language policy, 1890-1940. SWAHILI 35, no. 1 (1965), pp. 40-48.

16,236 WURTZ, F. Beiträge zur Kenntnis des Lamu-Dialektes der Suaheli-Sprache. ZAOS 1 (1895), pp. 169-183.

16,237 ZANI, Z. M. S. A comparative note on the possessive in Chi-Digo. SWAHILI 24 (1954), pp. 58-63.

16,238 Check list of Swahili bird names. SWAHILI 27 (1957), pp. 83-88.

16,239 The development of Swahili [a memorandum and an answer by G. W. Broomfield]. SWAHILI 7 (1934), pp. 3-21.

16,240 Establishment of research group in Swahili studies at Makerere College, Uganda. SWAHILI 32 (1961), pp. 4-5.

16,241 Proposed supplement to the standard Swahili-English dictionary. SWAHILI 26 (1956), pp. 53-81.

16,242 Provisional list of mathematical terms [English-Swahili]. SWAHILI 35, no. 1 (1965), pp. 92-95; 35, no. 2 (1965), pp. 77-78.

16,243 Revised list of swahili equivalents for words and terms. SWAHILI 8 (1935), pp. 7-15; 10 (1936), p. 3.

16,244 Swahili terms in psychology. SWAHILI 17 (1943), pp. 7-11.

16,245 Swahili words and equivalents for English terms and phrases. SWAHILI 18 (1944), pp. 5-10.

See also 3022, 16047, 16051.

Literature: Swahili

16,246 ABDALLAH BIN HEMED BIN ALI LIAJJEMI. Habari za Wakilindi. SWAHILI 27 (1957), pp. 13-61; 28 (1958), pp. 57-58.

16,247 ABEDI, K. A. Kilio cha Shaaban Robert. SWAHILI 33, no. 1 (1962-1963), pp. 1-2.

16,248 ALI, M. Jumua ya taaluma ya Kiswahili: 2nd. lecture: Kiswahili toka ng'ambo hata ng'ambo. SWAHILI 28, no. 1 (1958), pp. 22-24.

16,249 ALI, M. Matatizo na matatuzi ya Kutfsiri sheria. SWAHILI 35, no. 1 (1965), pp. 19-23.

16,250 ALLEN, J. W. T. The Bible in Swahili. SWAHILI 33, no. 2 (1963), pp. 125-127.

16,251 ALLEN, J. W. T. The collection of Swahili literature and its relation to oral tradition and history. EAISR July (1959), pp. 1-10.

16,252 ALLEN, J. W. T. The complete works of the late Shaaban Robert. SWAHILI 33, no. 2 (1963), pp. 128-142.

16,253 ALLEN, J. W. T. A note on Dr. Nyerere's translation of Julius Caesar [into Swahili]. MAKERERE J. 9 (1964), pp. 53-61.

16,254 ALLEN, R. Inkishafi—a translation from the Swahili. AFR. STUD. 5 (1946), pp. 243-249.

16,255 AUGUSTINY, J. Geschichte der Häuptlinge von Madschame. AFR. UND UB. 17 (1926-1927), pp. 161-201.

16,256 BHALO, A. N. J. Ukumbusho wa Sheikh Shaaban Robert. SWAHILI 33, no. 1 (1962-1963), pp. 8-10.

16,257 BIGILIMANA, R. B. K. Historia ya familia kutokana na utumwa. SWAHILI 33, no. 2 (1963), pp. 12-19.

16,258 BUTTNER, C. G. Chuo cha Herkal. Das Buch von Herkal. AFR. UND UB. 2 (1911-1912), pp. 1-36, 108-136, 194-232, 261-296.

16,259 CHIRAGHDIN, S. Maisha ya sheikh Mbaruk bin Rashid Al-Mazrui. SWAHILI 31 (1960), pp. 150-179.

16,260 CHUM, H. Some Hadimu proverbs. SWAHILI 33, no. 2 (1963), pp. 123-125.

16,261 CHUM, H. and LAMBERT, H. E. Utenzi wa Tariku Salati. SWAHILI 33, no. 1 (1962-1963), pp. 28-34.

16,262 CHUM, H. and LAMBERT, H. E. Wano: a specimen of Kae (Hadimu) prose. SWAHILI 33, no. 1 (1962-1963), pp. 25-28.

16,263 DAMMANN, E. Bemerkungen zur textlichen Gestaltung der Suahelidichtung Kozi na Ndiwa. AFR. UND UB. 44 (1960), pp. 207-218.

16,264 DAMMANN, E. Ein Fluchgedicht auf die Somali in der Siu-Mundart des Suaheli. AFR. UND UB. 32 (1942), pp. 286-300.

16,265 DAMMANN, E. Kurzlieder der Suaheli auf Lamu. AFR. UND UB. 33 (1942-1943), pp. 24-37.

16,266 DAMMANN, E. Philologische Spielereien der Suaheli in dichterischer Form. AFR. UND UB. 38 (1953-1954), pp. 135-136.

16,267 DAMMANN, E. Prosatexte in der Lamu-Mundart des Suaheli. AFR. UND UB. 39 (1954-1955), pp. 65-82.

16,268 DAMMANN, E. Suaheli-Dichtungen des Scheichs Muhammed bin Abubekr bin Omar Kidjumwa Masihii aus Lamu. AFRIKA (Berlin) 1 (1942), pp. 125-196.

16,269 DAMMANN, E. Eine Suaheli-Dichtung über Moses, den Habicht und die Taube. AFR. UND UB. 28 (1937-1938), pp. 1-14.

16,270 DAMMANN, E. Suaheli-Lieder aus Lamu. AFR. UND UB. 31 (1941), pp. 161-188, 278-287.

16,271 DAMMANN, E. Ein Suahelivers mit Gallawörtern. AFR. UND UB. 30 (1940), pp. 233-234.

16,272 DAMMANN, E. Utenzi wa mwana Ayesha binti Abi Bakari na mtume Muhamadi salia Allahu Alehi wa Sallama. SWAHILI 34, no. 1 (1964), pp. 130-140.

16,273 DOWSETT, F. D. Jumua ya taaluma ya Kiswahili: 3rd. lecture: Historia ya nchi hizi za Afrika ya mashariki. SWAHILI 28, no. 1 (1958), pp. 25-32.

16,274 ELKINDY, A. M. Metanguliya Shebani Rabbi atamrahamu. SWAHILI 33, no. 1 (1962-1963), p. 7.

16,275 HARRIES, L. Cultural verse-forms in Swahili. AFR. STUD. 15 (1956), pp. 176-187.

16,276 HARRIES, L. Dialogue verse in Swahili. AFRICA 24 (1954), pp. 157-159.

16,277 HARRIES, L. The legend of the monk Barsis—a Swahili version. AFR. LANG. STUD. 5 (1964), pp. 17-33.

16,278 HARRIES, L. Maulid Barzanji, the Swahili abridgement of Seyyid Mansab. AFR. UND UB. 42 (1958), pp. 27-39.

16,279 HARRIES, L. A poem from Siu from the Swahili-Arabic text. BULL. SOAS 13 (1949-1951), pp. 759-770.

16,280 HARRIES, L. Popular verse of the Swahili tradition. AFRICA 22 (1952), pp. 158-164.

16,281 HARRIES, L. Strung pearls. A poem from the Swahili-Arabic text. BULL. SOAS 15 (1953), pp. 146-156.

16,282 HARRIES, L. Swahili epic literature. AFRICA 20 (1950), pp. 55-59; also in TANG. NOTES 30 (1951), pp. 73-77.

16,283 HARRIES, L. The Swahili Quatrain. AFR. UND UB. 41 (1957), pp. 67-71.

16,284 HARRIES, L. A Swahili takhmis. AFR. STUD. 11 (1952), pp. 59-67.

16,285 HELLIER, A. B. Swahili prose literature. BANTU STUD. 14 (1940), pp. 247-257.

16,286 JERRARD, R. C. Three Swahili fables. TANG. NOTES 6 (1938), pp. 93-98.

16,287 JUMA, S. K. Maisha ya kabila la Waruri (Mbakwaya). SWAHILI 33, no. 2 (1963), pp. 61-83.

16,288 JUMA, S. K. Mauti yangechaguwa Robert Asingekwenda [a poem]. SWAHILI 33, no. 1 (1962-1963), pp. 2-3.

16,289 KIBWANA, S. Jumua ya taaluma ya Kiswahili: 4th lecture: Kiswahili cha karne hii. SWAHILI 28, no. 1 (1958), pp. 33-36.

16,290 KIIMBILA, J. K. Kanuni za Kufundisha Kiswahili. SWAHILI 35, no. 1 (1965), pp. 28-39.

16,291 KNAPPERT, J., ed. Adhabu za jahannamu: the punishments of hell by Moza Binti Ali. SWAHILI 34, no. 1 (1964), pp. 35-38.

16,292 KNAPPERT, J. ed. An admonition to be faithful. SWAHILI 33, no. 2 (1963), pp. 53-55.

16,293 KNAPPERT, J. The chronicle of Mombasa. SWAHILI 34, no. 2 (1964), pp. 21-27.

16,294 KNAPPERT, J., ed. Chuo cha Dua. SWAHILI 33, no. 2 (1963), pp. 28-32.

16,295 KNAPPERT, J., ed. An exhortation and a prayer. SWAHILI 34, no. 2 (1964), pp. 41-44.

16,296 KNAPPERT, J. The first Christian Utenzi, a new development in Swahili literature. AFR. UND UB. 47 (1964), pp. 221-232.

16,297 KNAPPERT, J., ed. Five Kasida's by Hashimiya. SWAHILI 33, no. 1 (1962-1963), pp. 69-74.

16,298 KNAPPERT, J. Het gebedenboek van mijnheer Muwinga. Een Swahili-gedicht over de hellestraffen welke hen wachten die niet vasten. KONGO-OVERZEE 25 (1959), pp. 124-139.

16,299 KNAPPERT, J. Mawaidha ya dini. Religious remonstrance. SWAHILI 34, no. 2 (1964), pp. 38-40.

16,300 KNAPPERT, J., ed. The poem of the birth of the Prophet Muhammad. SWAHILI 33, no. 2 (1963), pp. 51-52.

16,301 KNAPPERT, J., ed. The poem of the robe. SWAHILI 33, no. 2 (1963), pp. 55-60.

16,302 KNAPPERT, J. Swahili Loflied op de Profeet Mohammed. KONGO-OVERZEE 25 (1959), pp. 170-173.

16,303 KNAPPERT, J. Utendi wa Mkonumbi. SWAHILI 34, no. 2 (1964), pp. 1-10.

16,304 KNAPPERT, J. Utenzi wa Barasisi. SWAHILI 34, no. 2 (1964), pp. 28-37.

16,305 KNAPPERT, J., ed. Utenzi wa Isa. SWAHILI 33, no. 2 (1963), pp. 33-36.

16,306 KNAPPERT, J. Utenzi wa Kutawafu Mtume Salla Allahu Alehi Wasalama. SWAHILI 34, no. 2 (1964), pp. 11-18.

16,307 KNAPPERT, J., ed. Utenzi wa Mikidadi bin Alasuadi na Mayasa Mkwewe. SWAHILI 34, no. 1 (1964), pp. 120-129.

16,308 KNAPPERT, J., ed. Utenzi wa mwana Hasina na Barasisi. SWAHILI 34, no. 2 (1964), pp. 87-97.

16,309 KOTI, A. The mzigo song. SWAHILI 35, no. 2 (1965), pp. 47-54.

16,310 LAMBERT, H. E. Chigano cha chitungua na membe: a story in Funzi chichifundi. SWAHILI 33, no. 1 (1962-1963), pp. 21-22.

16,311 LAMBERT, H. E. Chigano cha mrambo wa panya: a story in Wasin chichifundi. SWAHILI 33, no. 1 (1962-1963), pp. 23-24.

16,312 LAMBERT, H. E. Full-length portrait of a lady. SWAHILI 33, no. 1 (1962-1963), pp. 34-46.

16,313 LAMBERT, H. E. Habari za Mrima. SWAHILI 32 (1961), pp. 34-59.

16,314 LAMBERT, H. E. Hadithi ya pate na siu. SWAHILI 33, no. 2 (1963), pp. 43-47.

16,315 LAMBERT, H. E. Kigano kya Lumbwi: a story in Kivumba. SWAHILI 33, no. 1 (1962-1963), pp. 24-25.

16,316 LAMBERT, H. E. Kumwe na kumwe: a story in Kivumba. SWAHILI 33, no. 2 (1963), pp. 21-23.

16,317 LAMBERT, H. E. Mzee na zijana zitalu: a story in Kiamu. SWAHILI 33, no. 1 (1962-1963), pp. 13-14.

16,318 LAMBERT, H. E. A nonsense rhyme from P'emba. SWAHILI 33, no. 1 (1962-1963), pp. 49-50.

16,319 LAMBERT, H. E. Ode to Mwana Mnga: a poem. SWAHILI 23 (1953), pp. 56-65.

16,320 LAMBERT, H. E. Some Gunya verses. SWAHILI 33, no. 1 (1962-1963), pp. 46-48.

16,321 LAMBERT, H. E. Some initiation songs of the southern Kenya coast. SWAHILI 35, no. 1 (1965), pp. 49-67.

16,322 LAMBERT, H. E. Some riddles from the southern Kenya coast. SWAHILI 33, no. 1 (1962-1963), pp. 14-18.

16,323 LAMBERT, H. E. Some songs from the northern Kenya coast. SWAHILI 26 (1956), pp. 49-52.

16,324 LAMBERT, H. E. A specimen of Lamu prose. SWAHILI 22 (1952), pp. 14-15.

16,325 LAMBERT, H. E. Swahili popular verse. AFRICA 22 (1952), pp. 372-373.

16,326 LAMBERT, H. E. The taking of Tumbe town. SWAHILI 23 (1953), pp. 36-45.

16,327 MANGWELA, B. M. Watunzi tuna huzuni! SWAHILI 33, no. 1 (1962-1963), pp. 4-5.

16,328 MEINHOF, C. Das Lied des Liongo. AFR. UND UB. 15 (1924-1925), pp. 241-265.

16,329 MKWAWA, S. N. Mungu amuweke pema. SWAHILI 33, no. 1 (1962-1963), pp. 5-6.

16,330 MNYAMPALA, M. E. Dance songs. SWAHILI 33, no. 2 (1963), pp. 36-42.

16,331 MNYAMPALA, M. E. Four poems. SWAHILI 33, no. 2 (1963), pp. 47-50.

16,332 MNYAMPALA, M. E. Kifo cha bwana Robert. SWAHILI 33, no. 1 (1962-1963), pp. 3-4.

16,333 MNYAMPALA, M. E. Kito cha hekima: gem of wisdom. SWAHILI 34, no. 1 (1964), pp. 39-68.

16,334 MNYAMPALA, M. E. Two versifications of the Gospel. SWAHILI 33, no. 2 (1963), pp. 24-27.

16,335 MOHAMMEDI, A. A. Utenzi wa maisha ya Nabii Adamu na Hawaa. SWAHILI 34, no. 1 (1964), pp. 86-119.

16,336 MTANDIKA, A. J. Mti wa ajabu. SWAHILI 35, no. 2 (1965), pp. 17-23.

16,337 MTILA, M. M. Bismillah Arrahamani Arrahim: mawaidha ya Ramadhani. SWAHILI 34, no. 1 (1964), pp. 13-17.

16,338 MUSTAFA BIN KISI BIN HAMADI IMUTAFI. The bombardment of Zanzibar. SWAHILI 27 (1957), pp. 66-77.

16,339 MWENDA, E. A. Historia na maendeleo ya Ubena. SWAHILI 33, no. 2 (1963), pp. 99-123.

16,340 MWINDADI, J. Jumuia ya taaluma ya Kiswahili: 1st lecture: Ubora wa lugha ya Kiswahili Katika lugha za dunia. SWAHILI 28, no. 1 (1958), pp. 17-21.

16,341 NGARE, N. Uhuru [a film script]. SWAHILI 34, no. 2 (1964), pp. 45-86.

16,342 NYASURU, M. B. K. Afadhali niwe kijana tena. SWAHILI 35, no. 2 (1965), pp. 33-47.

16,343 OTHMAN, G. Praise of Zanzibar. SWAHILI 33, no. 2 (1963), p. 127.

16,344 PARET, R. Die arabische Quelle der Suaheli-Dichtung Chuo cha Herkal (Das Buch von Herkal). AFR. UND UB. 17 (1926-1927), pp. 241-249.

16,345 PRINS, A. H. J. On Swahili historiography. SWAHILI 28, no. 2 (1958), pp. 26-40.

16,346 ROBERT, S. Halmashauri ya Kiswahili ya Afrika Mashariki. SWAHILI 26 (1956), pp. 28-31.

16,347 ROBERT, S. Jamua ya taaluma ya Kiswahili: 5th lecture: Hotuba juu ya ushairi. SWAHILI 28, no. 1 (1958), pp. 37-42.

16,348 ROBERT, S. Maisha katika mlingano. SWAHILI 27 (1957), pp. 9-12.

16,349 ROBERT, S. Swahili poetry. BO 11 (1962), pp. 22-23.

16,350 ROBERT, S. Two wonders, Our fame [poems translated from Swahili by Shaaban Robert and Gerald Moore]. BO 11 (1962), p. 24.

16,351 ROBERT, S. Ushairi Utakiwao. SWAHILI 32 (1961), pp. 32-33.

16,352 SNOW-WHITE, A. Kisa cha mwanamema na hadithi nyingine. SWAHILI 35, no. 2 (1965), pp. 24-33.

16,353 SNOW-WHITE, A. "Siku ya Kukumbukwa." SWAHILI 34, no. 1 (1964), pp. 11-12.

16,354 SUDI, A. A. "Tuongoze Mathiasi." SWAHILI 34, no. 1 (1964), pp. 12-13.

16,355 SUDI, A. A. "Ya-Allahu ya Robati." SWAHILI 33, no. 1 (1962-1963), pp. 6-7.

16,356 TAYLOR, W. E. A Swahili tale in the dialect of Mombasa. AFR. UND UB. 23 (1932-1933), pp. 1-24.

16,357 TILING, M. VON. Frauen- und Kinderlieder der Suaheli. FESTSCHRIFT MEINHOF, 1927, pp. 288-300.

16,358 TILING, M. VON. Suaheli-Lieder. AFR. UND UB. 17 (1926-1927), pp. 295-304.

16,359 VERSTEIJNEN, F. Kufika kwa wamisionari wakatoliki katika nchi hizi ya Afrika ya mashariki. SWAHILI 33, no. 2 (1963), pp. 83-87.

16,360 WERNER, A. An alphabetical acrostic in a northern dialect of Swahili. BULL. SOAS 5 (1928-1930), pp. 561-569.

16,361 WERNER, A. A Duruma tale of "the old woman and her pig." BANTU STUD. 2 (1923), pp. 1-22.

16,362 WERNER, A. A "hare" story in African folklore. J. AFR. SOC. 4 (1904), pp. 139-141.

16,363 WERNER, A. Native poetry in East Africa. AFRICA 1 (1928), pp. 348-357.

16,364 WERNER, A. Some missing stanzas from the northern version of the Inkishafi poem. AFR. UND UB. 17 (1926-1927), pp. 291-294.

16,365 WERNER, A. Swahili poetry. BULL. SOAS 1, no. 2 (1918), pp. 113-127; J. AFR. SOC. 26 (1927), pp. 101-111.

16,366 WERNER, A. The Swahili saga of Liongo Fumo. BULL. SOAS 4 (1926-1928), pp. 247-255.

16,367 WERNER, A. A traditional poem attributed to Liongo Fumo, with some notes on his legend. FESTSCHRIFT MEINHOF, 1927, pp. 45-54.

16,368 WERNER, A. Utendi wa Ayubu [in English]. BULL. SOAS 2 (1921-1923), pp. 85-115, 297-320, 347-416.

16,369 ZACHE, R. Beiträge zur Suahili-Litteratur. ZAOS 3 (1897), pp. 131-139, 250-267.

16,370 ZAKWANY, A. S. Kiyama. SWAHILI 34, no. 2 (1964), pp. 19-20.

16,371 Aridhlihali ya Jumuia ya taaluma ya Kiswahili Tanganyika kwa Ujumbe wa mataifa ya umoja uliotembelea Tanganyika mwezi, Septemba, 1954. SWAHILI 25 (1955), pp. 40-43.

16,372 List of current periodicals published wholly or partly in Swahili. SWAHILI 31 (1960), pp. 231-232; 32 (1961), pp. 70-74.

16,373 Shairi la bwana Shabaan Robert. SWAHILI 33, no. 1 (1962-1963), pp. 10-11.

Law

16,374 ALLOTT, A. N. Legal education in East Africa. J. AFR. LAW 4 (1960), pp. 130-132.

16,375 ANDERSON, J. N. D. Muslim marriages and the courts in East Africa. J. AFR. LAW 1 (1957), pp. 14-22.

16,376 ANDERSON, J. N. D. Waqfs in East Africa. J. AFR. LAW 3 (1959), pp. 152-164.

16,377 BUSHE, H. G. Criminal justice in East Africa. J. AFR. SOC. 34 (1935), pp. 117-128.

16,378 COTRAN, E. The unification of laws in East Africa. JMAS 1 (1963), pp. 209-220.

16,379 DRIBERG, J. H. Primitive law in Eastern Africa. AFRICA 1 (1928), pp. 63-72.

16,380 DUNDAS, C. Native laws of some Bantu tribes of East Africa. JRAI 51 (1921), pp. 217-278.

16,381 GRAY, Sir J. Opinions of assessors in criminal trials in East Africa as to native custom. J. AFR. LAW 2 (1958), pp. 5-18.

16,382 HAMILTON, Sir R. and an ex-district officer. Criminal justice in East Africa. J. AFR. SOC. 34 (1935), pp. 7-26.

16,383 McAUSLAN, J. P. W. B. Prolegomena to the rule of law in East Africa. EAISR Jan. (1964), pp. 1-9.

16,384 MAIR, L. P. Native land tenure in East Africa. AFRICA 4 (1931), pp. 314-329.

16,385 NYERERE, J. Freedom and unity. TRANSITION 14 (1964), pp. 40-45.

16,386 PHILLIPS, A. Marriage and divorce laws in East Africa. J. AFR. LAW 3 (1959), pp. 93-98.

16,387 Ethnographic and sociological research in East Africa. J. AFR. LAW 1 (1957), pp. 9-10.

See also 15796.

Religion

16,388 BUXTON, C. R. Missionaries in East Africa. CONTEMP. REV. 143 (1933), pp. 438-446.

16,389 FULLANI BIN FULLANI. Religion and common life: a problem in East African missions. INT. REV. MISSIONS 8 (1919), pp. 155-172.

16,390 GOLLOCK, G. A. Uganda, Masasi and the Upper Nile. INT. REV. MISSIONS 16 (1927), pp. 235-249.

16,391 HARRIES, L. Bishop Lucas and the Masasi experiment. INT. REV. MISSIONS 34 (1945), pp. 389-398.

16,392 HARRIES, L. The missionary on the East African coast. INT. REV. MISSIONS 35 (1946), pp. 183-186.

16,393 HINDMARSH, R. The future of the Catholic missionary in East Africa. TRANSITION 1 (1961), pp. 13-16.

16,394 SUNDKLER, B. G. M. Marriage problems in the Church in Tanganyika. INT. REV. MISSIONS 34 (1945), pp. 253-266.

See also 15871.

Science

16,395 BANAGE, W. B. Some aspects of the ecology of soil nematodes. PROC. E. AFR. ACAD. 2 (1964), pp. 67-74.

16,396 BEADLE, L. C. The evolution of species in the lakes of East Africa. UGANDA J. 26 (1962), pp. 44-54.

16,397 BEAUCHAMP, R. S. A. Fishery research in East Africa. UGANDA J. 19 (1955), pp. 169-176.

16,398 C., J. La recherche médicale dans l'Est-Africain. ZAIRE 7 (1953), pp. 645-646.

16,399 COLCHESTER, T. C. Bacchus Pasha. CORONA 2 (1950), pp. 39-40.

16,400 COOKE, H. B. S. The problem of Quaternary glacio-pluvial correlation in East and Southern Africa. PROC. PAN-AFR. CONGR. PRE-HIST. 3 (1955), pp. 51-55.

16,401 CULWICK, G. M. Nutrition in East Africa. AFRICA 14 (1944), pp. 401-410.

16,402 DECLOITRE, A. L. Rhizopodes de l'Afrique orientale anglaise. BULL. IFAN 15 (1953), pp. 1432-1436.

16,403 FISH, G. R. The food of Tilapia in East Africa. UGANDA J. 19 (1955), pp. 85-89.

16,404 FURLONG, J. R. East African hides and the post war market: elimination of gouging damage. BULL. IMP. INST. 41 (1943), pp. 228-231.

16,405 G., P. J. Calumba root. TANGANYIKA NOTES AND RECORDS 46 (1957), p. 74.

16,406 G., P. J. Mangroves. TANGANYIKA NOTES AND RECORDS 46 (1957), pp. 72-73.

16,407 GAPPERT, G. An American on science in East Africa. TRANSITION 5 (1962), pp. 28-30.

16,408 GARTLAN, J. S. Dominance in East African monkeys. PROC. E. AFR. ACAD. 2 (1964), pp. 75-79.

16,409 GOULDING, E. The development of bast and leaf fibre cultivation in the British Empire. BULL. IMP. INST. 25 (1927), pp. 14-31.

16,410 HESSE, P. R. Some facts and fallacies about termite mounds. TANGANYIKA NOTES AND RECORDS 39 (1955), pp. 16-24.

16,411 HOPKINS, G. H. E. Annotated and illustrated keys to the known fleas of East Africa. UGANDA J. 11 (1947), pp. 133-190.

16,412 HOPKINS, G. H. E. Lice. BULL. UGANDA SOC. 5 (1945), pp. 2-9.

16,413 JOLLY, A. Sex ratio and dominance in social lemurs. PROC. E. AFR. ACAD. 2 (1964), pp. 81-87.

16,414 LEAKEY, L. S. B. The climatic sequence of the Pleistocene in East Africa. PROC. PAN-AFR. CONGR. PRE-HIST. 2 (1952), pp. 293-294.

16,415 NILSSON, E. Pleistocene climatic changes in East Africa. PROC. PAN-AFR. CONGR. PRE-HIST. 1 (1947), pp. 45-55.

16,416 OTIENO, N. C. Contributions to a knowledge of poroid agarics in East Africa. The genus Favolaschia (Pat.) Henn. PROC. E. AFR. ACAD. 2 (1964), pp. 92-108.

16,417 OTIENO, N. C. Contributions to a knowledge of termite fungi in East Africa. The genus Termitomyces Heim. PROC. E. AFR. ACAD. 2 (1964), pp. 108-121.

16,418 PAGE, L. R. Earth sciences in African development. PROC. E. AFR. ACAD. 2 (1964), pp. 46-49.

16,419 SAVORY, B. A note on the Dugong. TANGANYIKA NOTES AND RECORDS 51 (1958), pp. 255-258.

16,420 SMITH, D. A. East African Nutrition School. CORONA 1, no. 8 (1949), pp. 17-18.

16,421 SOUTHON, H. A. W. The epidemiology of sleeping sickness on the north-east shores of Lake Victoria, 1961-63. PROC. E. AFR. ACAD. 2 (1964), pp. 131-140.

16,422 WINTERBOTTOM, J. M. The fresh waters of Eastern Africa: an appreciation of fishing researches in Eastern and Central Africa. RHODES-LIV. J. 2 (1944), pp. 56-64.

16,423 WOODALL, J. P. The viruses isolated from arthropods at the East African Virus Research Institute in the 26 years ending December 1963. PROC. E. AFR. ACAD. 2 (1964), pp. 141-146.

16,424 WORTHINGTON, E. B. Faunistic evidence of the former distribution of lakes and river systems in East Africa. PROC. PAN-AFR. CONGR. PRE-HIST. 1 (1947), pp. 82-85.

16,425 WORTHINGTON, E. B. On the food and nutrition of African natives. AFRICA 9 (1936), pp. 150-165.

16,426 The drying of East African hides with reference to the prevention of blister. Report by the Imperial Institute Advisory Committee on hides and skins. BULL. IMP. INST. 32 (1934), pp. 43-56.

Sociology

16,427 ANDREWS, C. F. Indians in Zanzibar and East Africa. CONTEMP. REV. 147 (1935), pp. 684-691.

16,428 ATKINSON, G. A. Jobbing builders or self help for African housing. J. AFR. ADM. 13 (1961), pp. 46-49.

16,429 BHARATI, A. Patterns of identification among the East African Asians. SOCIOLOGUS 15 (1965), pp. 128-142.

16,430 BUXTON, T. F. V. A social effort in East Africa. J. AFR. SOC. 10 (1911), pp. 342-344.

16,431 COOK, D. Ten weeks. TRANSITION 2 (1961), pp. 31-34.

16,432 DESAI, R. H. Leadership in an Asian community [in East Africa]. EAISR June (1963), pp. 1-12.

16,433 EDGERTON, R. B. "Cultural" vs. "Ecological" factors in the expression of values, attitudes, and personality characteristics. AMER. ANTHR. 67 (1965), pp. 442-447.

16,434 ELKAN, W. Some social policy implications of industrial development in East Africa. INT. SOC. SC. J. 16 (1964), pp. 390-399.

16,435 FANE, R. The return of the soldier: East Africa. AFR. AFFAIRS 43 (1944), pp. 56-60.

16,436 FORTT, J. M. East African Institute of Social Research. UGANDA J. 15 (1951), pp. 205-206.

16,437 GHAI, D. P. and GHAI, Y. P. Asians in East Africa: problems and prospects. JMAS 3 (1965), pp. 35-51.

16,438 GOLDTHORPE, J. E. Race relations in East Africa. TRANSITION 1 (1961), pp. 31-36; 3 (1962), p. 31, pp. 38-39.

16,439 GRAY, R. East Africa without the whites. RACE 6, no. 1 (1964-1965), pp. 159-162.

16,440 GUTMANN, B. Aufgaben der Gemeinschaftsbildung in Afrika. AFRICA 1 (1928), pp. 429-445.

16,441 INGUTIA, A. K. Caste: in India and Africa. TRANSITION 23 (1965), pp. 15-18.

16,442 KAYAMBA, H. M. T. The modern life of the East African native. AFRICA 5 (1932), pp. 50-59.

16,443 MELLAND, F. East African census reports, 1931. AFRICA 7 (1934), pp. 213-219.

16,444 MPOLOGOMA, F. Power to move? A review of Paul Foster's ideas in White to move? TRANSITION 1 (1961), pp. 43-48.

16,445 NELSON, F. B. Religion and American secondary teachers in East Africa. EAISR Jan. (1963), pp. 1-13.

16,446 PRASAD, A. Indians in East Africa. AFR. QUART. 1, no. 1 (1961), pp. 20-29.

16,447 REBELO, D. J. S. Nota sobre as comunidades Portuguesas do Este Africano a Norte do Rio Rovuma. BSEM 143 (1965), pp. 71-141.

16,448 SALVADORI, M. Quelques aspects de l'immigration européenne en Afrique et en particulier sur les hauts plateaux de l'Afrique Orientale. BULL. SEANCES IRCB 6 (1935), pp. 305-235.

16,449 SINGH, D. Indians in East Africa. AFR. QUART. 1, no. 4 (1962), pp. 43-45.

16,450 SYMES, Sir S. An African review. AFR. AFFAIRS 53 (1954), pp. 303-309.

16,451 TANNER, R. Crime and punishment in East Africa. TRANSITION 21 (1965), pp. 35-38.

16,452 WARD, B. E. East Africa. INT. SOC. SC. BULL. 10 (1958), pp. 372-386.

16,453 Administration and finance [urban problems in East and Central Africa; report of the Ndola Conference, February, 1958]. J. AFR. ADM. 10 (1958), pp. 208-218.

16,454 Administration of justice and the maintenance of law and order [urban problems in East and Central Africa; report of the Ndola Conference, February, 1958]. J. AFR. ADM. 10 (1958), pp. 219-227.

16,455 The control of peri-urban areas and the development of small towns [report of the Ndola Conference, February, 1958]. J. AFR. ADM. 10 (1958), pp. 201-202.

16,456 The East African Institute of Social Research Report 1950-1955. J. AFR. ADM. 9 (1957), pp. 107-108.

16,457 Housing [urban problem in East and Central Africa; report of the Ndola Conference, February, 1958]. J. AFR. ADM. 10 (1958), pp. 194-200.

16,458 Liaison between urban and rural authorities [report of the Ndola Conference, February, 1958]. J. AFR. ADM. 10 (1958), pp. 228-229.

16,459 Problems arising from settlement of Africans in towns with their families. J. AFR. ADM. 10 (1958), pp. 203-205.

16,460 Social security [urban problem in East and Central Africa; report of the Ndola Conference, February, 1958]. J. AFR. ADM. 10 (1958), pp. 206-207.

16,461 Stabilization town planning and land tenure [urban problems in East and Central Africa; report of the Ndola Conference, February, 1958]. J. AFR. ADM. 10 (1958), pp. 187-193.

16,462 Urban problems in East and Central Africa. Report of a conference held at Ndola, Northern Rhodesia, in February, 1958. J. AFR. ADM. 10 (1958), pp. 182-251.

See also 15790, 15791,

ETHIOPIA

General

16,463 CASTRO, F. Scritti di M. M. Moreno. RASS. STUDI ETIOP. 20 (1964), pp. 12-21.

16,464 CERULLI, E. I manoscritti etiopici della Biblioteca Nazionale di Atene. RASS. STUDI ETIOP. 2 (1942), pp. 181-190.

16,465 CONTI ROSSINI, C. Miniature armene nel ms. et n. 50 della Biblioteca Vaticana. RASS. STUDI ETIOP. 2 (1942), pp. 191-197.

16,466 CONTI ROSSINI, C. Pubblicazioni etiopistiche dal 1936 al 1945. RASS. STUDI ETIOP. 4 (1944), pp. 1-132.

16,467 FUSELLA, L. Recenti pubblicazioni amariche in Abissinia. RASS. STUDI ETIOP. 5 (1945), pp. 93-102.

16,468 HAMMERSCHMIDT, E. Die äthiopistischen Studien in Deutschland (von ihren Anfängen bis zur Gegenwart). ANN. ETHIOPIE 6 (1965), pp. 255-277.

16,469 HAMMERSCHMIDT, E. A brief history of German contributions to the study of Ethiopia. J. ETHIOP. STUD. 1, no. 2 (1963), pp. 30-48.

16,470 KAMIL, M. Les manuscrits éthiopiens du Siraï. ANN. ETHIOPIE 2 (1957), pp. 83-90.

16,471 LESLAU, W. Ten years of ethiopic linguistics (1946-1956). ANN. ETHIOPIE 2 (1957), pp. 277-318.

16,472 MIKAEL, K. and LECLANT, J. La section d'archéologie (1952-1955). ANN. ETHIOPIE 1 (1955), pp. 1-6.

16,473 ROBERTS, A. D. Documentation on Ethiopia and Eritrea. THE JOURNAL OF DOCUMENTATION 1 (1945-1946), pp. 185-193.

16,474 STRELCYN, S. Note sur le manuscrit éthiopien d'Abbadie 7 de la B. N. RASS. STUDI ETIOP. 10 (1951), pp. 52-55.

16,475 TUBIANA, J. Ouvrages manuscrits concernant l'Ethiopie à la Bibliothèque Nationale de Paris. RASS. STUDI ETIOP. 15 (1959), pp. 96-105.

16,476 TURAIEV, B. Testi etiopici in manoscritti di Leningrado. RASS. STUDI ETIOP. 7 (1948), pp. 1-12.

16,477 WRIGHT, S. Book and manuscript collections in Ethiopia. J. AFR. STUD. 2, no. 1 (1964), pp. 11-24.

16,478 Institute of Ethiopian studies, Haile Sellassie I University. BULL. AFR. STUD. ASSOC. 1 (1964), pp. 26-27.

Agriculture

16,479 GULILAT, T. The role of FAO in Ethiopia's agriculture. COOPERAZIONE INT. AFR., 1960, pp. 417-424.

16,480 JONES, D. W. R. H. Some aspects of Eritrean fruit production. SUDAN NOTES 46 (1965), pp. 84-89.

16,481 SYLVAIN, P. G. Note sur le café d'Ethiope. ZAIRE 9 (1955), pp. 301-303.

16,482 Enquête agronomique en Ethiopie. ZAIRE 8 (1954), p. 197.

Anthropology

16,483 AESCOLY, A. Z. Notices sur les Falacha ou Juifs d'Abyssinie, d'après le "Journal de Voyage" d'Antoine d'Abbadie. CAH. ET. AFR. 2 (1961), pp. 84-147.

16,484 AHMED, Y. A foča. J. ETHIOP. STUD. 3, no. ii (1965), pp. 125-132.

16,485 ALLBROOK, D. B. The East African vertebral column: a study in racial variability. AMER. J. PHY. ANTHR. 13 (1955), pp. 489-513.

16,486 BAXTER, P. T. W. Repetition in certain Boran ceremonies. AFRICAN SYSTEMS OF THOUGHT, 1965, pp. 64-78.

16,487 BORELLO, M. Proverbi Galla. RASS. STUDI ETIOP. 5 (1945), pp. 103-121; 7 (1948), pp. 68-88.

16,488 CACCIAPUOTI, R. Medicina e farmacologia indigena in Etiopia. RASS. STUDI ETIOP. 1 (1941), pp. 322-329.

16,489 CHIOMIO, G. I Magi (Masi) nell' Etiopia del sud-ovest. RASS. STUDI ETIOP. 1 (1941), pp. 271-304.

16,490 CIPRIANI, L. Sui Berta, Coma e Mao dell' ovest etiopico. RASS. STUDI ETIOP. 2 (1942), pp. 273-276.

16,491 CONTI ROSSINI, C. I camminatori sul fuoco in Etiopia. RASS. STUDI ETIOP. 3 (1943), pp. 106-110.

16,492 CONTI ROSSINI, C. Monarchidismo e regalità presso i Giangerò. RASS. STUDI ETIOP. 2 (1942), pp. 101-103.

16,493 CONTI ROSSINI, C. Sul calendario astrologico degli Habab. RASS. STUDI ETIOP. 5 (1945), pp. 83-92.

16,494 ELLERO, G. Note sull' Endertà. RASS. STUDI ETIOP. 1 (1941), pp. 146-172.

16,495 ELLERO, G. I Tacruri in Eritrea. RASS. STUDI ETIOP. 6 (1947), pp. 189-199.

16,496 FUSELLA, L. Proverbi amarici. RASS. STUDI ETIOP. 2 (1942), pp. 282-311.

16,497 GRIAULE, M. Attaches et noeuds Abyssins. J. SOC. AFR. 1 (1931), pp. 27-42.

16,498 GRIAULE, M. Le mariage en pays Tigre (Abyssinie). J. SOC. AFR. 1 (1931), pp. 21-25.

16,499 GRIAULE, M. Moules et tour a travailler le corne (Abyssinie). J. SOC. AFR. 11 (1941), pp. 201-207.

16,500 GRIAULE, M. Noms propres d'animaux domestiques (Abyssinie). J. SOC. AFR. 12 (1942), pp. 55-65.

16,501 GRIAULE, M. Notes sur l'arîthmomancie éthiopieene. J. SOC. AFR. 4 (1934), pp. 25-31.

16,502 GRIAULE, M. Notes sur la naissance et la mort au Wollo (Abyssinie). J. SOC. AFR. 12 (1942), pp. 87-94.

16,503 GRIAULE, M. Le travail sur l'aire au Wollo (Abyssinie). J. SOC. AFR. 12 (1942), pp. 81-86.

16,504 HABERLAND, E. Bemerkungen zur Kultur und Sprache der Galila im Wonči-See (Mittel-Athiopien). RASS. STUDI ETIOP. 16 (1960), pp. 5-22.

16,505 HABERLAND, E. Uber einen unbekannten Gunza-stamm in Wallegga. RASS. STUDI ETIOP. 12 (1953), pp. 139-148.

16,506 HOFFMANN, H. Formal versus informal estimates of cultural stability. AMER. ANTHR. 67 (1965), pp. 110-115.

16,507 JENSEN, A. E. Elementi della cultura spirituale dei Conso nell' Etiopa Meridionale. RASS. STUDI ETIOP. 2 (1942), pp. 217-259.

16,508 KOHLER, O. Zur Frage der Galla-Wanderungen im Nilotischen Sudan. AFR. UND UB. 36 (1951-1952), pp. 9-15.

16,509 LECLANT, J. Deux têtes de pierres dressées du Sidamo (J.E., Nos. 1 et 2). ANN. ETHIOPIE 1 (1955), pp. 53-58.

16,510 LESLAU, W. Chaha riddles. RASS. STUDI ETIOP. 21 (1965), pp. 27-93.

16,511 LESLAU, W. Tigre games. RASS. STUDI ETIOP. 17 (1961), pp. 61-68.

16,512 MONNERET DE VILLARD, U. Il culto del sole a Meroe. RASS. STUDI ETIOP. 2 (1942), pp. 107-142.

16,513 PECCI, D. Note sul sistema delle Gada e delle classi di età presso le popolazioni Borana. RASS. STUDI ETIOP. 1 (1941), pp. 305-321.

16,514 PLOWMAN, C. H. F. Notes on the Gedamoch ceremonies among the Boran. J. AFR. SOC. 18 (1919), pp. 114-121.

16,515 REY, C. F. The Arussi and other Galla of Abyssinia. J. AFR. SOC. 23 (1924), pp. 85-95.

16,516 RICCI, M. Notizie etnografiche sugli Amar. RASS. STUDI ETIOP. 11 (1952), pp. 49-95.

16,517 RICCI, M. Notizie etnografiche sugli Arbore. RASS. STUDI ETIOP. 9 (1950), pp. 5-40.

16,518 RICCI, M. Usanze funerarie degli Arbore, degli Amar e dei Gheleba nel sud etiopico. RASS. STUDI ETIOP. 3 (1943), pp. 214-222.

16,519 SACCHETTI, A. Sull' antropologia degli Arbore. RASS. STUDI ETIOP. 3 (1943), pp. 295-301.

16,520 SANTESSON, C. G. Pfeilgiftstudien: pfeilgift aus Süd-Abessinien. ETHNOS 1 (1936), pp. 86-94.

16,521 SAVARD, G. C. War chants in praise of ancient Afar heroes. J. ETHIOP. STUD. 3, no. i (1965), pp. 105-108.

16,522 SAVOIA-GENEVO, E. DI and SIMONINI, G. Proverbi tigrini. RASS. STUDI ETIOP. 3 (1943), pp. 3-35.

16,523 SCHULZ-WEIDNER, W. Die Zala ein Kuschitisches Volkstum in Südwest-Abessinien. CONG. INT. SC. ANTH. ET ETHN. 4, no. iii (1952), pp. 36-41.

16,524 SCHWARTZ, J. A propos du carré sator chez les éthiopiens. ANN. ETHIOPIE 2 (1957), pp. 219-223.

16,525 SHACK, W. A. Religious ideas and social action in Gurage bond-friendship. AFRICA 33 (1963), pp. 198-208.

16,526 SHACK, W. A. Some aspects of ecology and social structure in the ensete complex in South-west Ethiopia. JRAI 93 (1963), pp. 72-79.

16,527 SIMOONS, F. J. The agricultural implements and cutting tools of Begember and Semyen, Ethiopia. SOUTHWESTERN J. ANTHR. 14 (1958), pp. 386-406.

16,528 STEINMANN, A. Einige merkwürdige Töpfereierzeugnisse der Galla im westlichen Aethiopien. FESTSCHRIFT ALFRED BUHLER, 1965, pp. 385-388.

16,529 STINSON, L. Source materials: folk tales of the Hadiya. J. ETHIOP. STUD. 3, no. ii (1965), pp. 87-124.

16,530 TUBIANA, J. Un culte des génies agrestes en Ethiopie. RASS. STUDI ETIOP. 13 (1954), pp. 76-90.

16,531 A survey of some genetical characters in Ethiopian tribes. AMER. J. PHY. ANTHR. 20 (1962), pp. 167-208.

See also 5855.

Art. Antiquities

16,532 ABBABA, B. La peinture éthiopienne: point de vue d'un Ethiopien. CAH. ET. AFR. 2 (1961), pp. 160-165.

16,533 ADMASSOU SHIFERAOU. Rapport sur la découverte d'antiquités trouvées dans les locaux du gouvernement général de Magallé. ANN. ETHIOPIE 1 (1955), pp. 13-15.

16,534 ANFRAY, F. Une campagne de fouilles à Yěhā (Février-Mars 1960). ANN. ETHIOPIE 5 (1963), pp. 171-232.

16,535 ANFRAY, F. Chronique archéologique (1960-1964) avec des notes de G. Annequin, G. Bailloud et R. Schneider. ANN. ETHIOPIE 6 (1965), pp. 3-48.

16,536 ANFRAY, F. Le musée archéologique d'Asmara. RASS. STUDI ETIOP. 21 (1965), pp. 5-15.

16,537 ANFRAY, F. Note sur quelques poteries axoumites. ANN. ETHIOPIE 6 (1965), pp. 217-220.

16,538 ANFRAY, F. La première campagne de fouilles à Matarā, près de Sénafé (Novembre 1959-Janvier 1960). ANN. ETHIOPIE 5 (1963), pp. 87-166.

16,539 ANFRAY, F. and ANNEQUIN, G. Matarā. Deuxième, troisième et quatrième campagnes de fouilles. ANN. ETHIOPIE 6 (1965), pp. 49-86.

16,540 BARRIVIERA, L. B. Le chiese in roccia di Lalibelà di altri luoghi del Lasta. RASS. STUDI ETIOP. 18 (1962), pp. 5-76; 19 (1963), pp. 5-118.

16,541 BREUIL, H. and KELLEY, H. Les collections africaines du départment de préhistoire exotique du Musée d'ethnographie du Trocadéro. V: Documents préhistoriques recueillis par la mission du Bourg de Bozas, en Abyssinie (1901-1902). J. SOC. AFR. 6 (1936), pp. 111-140.

16,542 CAQUOT, A. Les Actes d'Ezrā de Gunda-Gundē. ANN. ETHIOPIE 4 (1961), pp. 69-121.

16,543 CAQUOT, A. L'inscription éthiopieene de Mārib. ANN. ETHIOPIE 6 (1965), pp. 223-227.

16,544 CAQUOT, A. and DREWES, A. J. Les monuments recueillis à Magallé (Tigné). ANN. ETHIOPIE 1 (1955), pp. 16-41.

16,545 CERBELLA, G. La diffusione in Eritrea della casa musulmana tipica. AFRICA (Rome) 17 (1962), pp. 291-299.

16,546 CERBELLA, G. I Waldebit dei notabili eritrei e qualche cenno ancora sulle iscrizioni delle abitazioni musulmane in Eritrea. AFRICA (Rome) 18 (1963), pp. 78-88.

16,547 CERULLI, E. Il Gesù percosso nell' arte etiopica e le sue origini nell' Europa del XV secolo. RASS. STUDI ETIOP. 6 (1947), pp. 109-129.

16,548 CHOJNACKI, S. Short introduction to Ethiopian traditional painting. J. ETHIOP. STUD. 2, no. ii (1964), pp. 1-11.

16,549 CONTENSON, H. DE. Aperçus sur les fouilles à Axoum et dans la région d'Axoum en 1958 et 1959. ANN. ETHIOPIE 3 (1959), pp. 101-106.

16,550 CONTENSON, H. DE. Les fouilles à Axoum en 1957. Rapport préliminaire. ANN. ETHIOPIE 3 (1959), pp. 25-42.

16,551 CONTENSON, H. DE. Les fouilles à Axoum en 1958—rapport préliminaire. ANN. ETHIOPIE 5 (1963), pp. 1-40.

16,552 CONTENSON, H. DE. Les fouilles à Haoulti-Melazo en 1958. ANN. ETHIOPIE 4 (1961), pp. 39-60.

16,553 CONTENSON, H. DE. Les fouilles à Haoulti en 1959—rapport préliminaire. ANN. ETHIOPIE 5 (1963), pp. 41-86.

16,554 CONTENSON, H. DE. Les fouilles à Ouchatei Golo près d'Axoum, en 1958. ANN. ETHIOPIE 4 (1961), pp. 3-15.

16,555 CONTENSON, H. DE. Les principales étapes de l'Ethiopie antique. CAH. ET. AFR. 2 (1961), pp. 12-23.

16,556 CONTENSON, H. DE. Trouvailles fortuites aux environs d'Axoum (1957-1959). ANN. ETHIOPIE 4 (1961), pp. 15-38.

16,557 CONTI ROSSINI, C. Iehà, Tsehùf Emnì e Derà. RASS. STUDI ETIOP. 6 (1947), pp. 12-22.

16,558 CONTI ROSSINI, C. Incisioni rupestri all' Hagghèr. RASS. STUDI ETIOP. 3 (1943), pp. 102-106.

16,559 CONTI ROSSINI, C. Statuette di terracotta in scavo presso Bonga (Caffa). RASS. STUDI ETIOP. 6 (1947), pp. 97-101.

16,560 DAVICO, A. Ritrovamenti sud-arabici nella zona del Cascasé. RASS. STUDI ETIOP. 5 (1945), pp. 1-6.

16,561 EURINGER, S. Osservazioni sui "Sigilli abissini" di E. Littmann. RASS. STUDI ETIOP. 2 (1942), pp. 333-335.

16,562 FRANCHINI, V. Altre pitture rupestri nell' Akkelè Guzay. IL BOLL. 2 (1957), pp. 1-12.

16,563 FRANCHINI, V. Pitture rupestri a Ba 'atti Scellùm nel Deghien. RASS. STUDI ETIOP. 11 (1952), pp. 47-48.

16,564 FRANCHINI, V. Pitture rupestri a Sullum Baatti. RASS. STUDI ETIOP. 10 (1951), pp. 122-123.

16,565 FRANCHINI, V. Pitture rupestri e antichi resti architettonici dell' Acchelè Guzài. RASS. STUDI ETIOP. 17 (1961), pp. 5-10.

16,566 FRANCHINI, V. Ritrovamenti archeologici in Eritrea. RASS. STUDI ETIOP. 12 (1953), pp. 5-28.

16,567 FRANCHINI, V. Stazioni litiche di superficie in Eritrea. IL BOLL. 1 (1953), pp. 25-30.

16,568 FRANCHINI, V. La zona archeologica di Macheda'. IL BOLL. 1 (1953), pp. 21-24.

16,569 GABRIEL, G. Il Museo Archeologico di Asmara. IL BOLL. 1 (1953), pp. 13-16.

16,570 GAUDIO, A. Comunicazione sulla collezione archeologica Sud-Arabica del Museo archeologico dell' Asmara nel suo ordine di classificazione. IL BOLL. 1 (1953), pp. 31-43.

16,571 GAUDIO, A. Quattro ritrovamenti archeologici e paleografici in Eritrea. IL. BOLL. 1 (1953), pp. 44-49.

16,572 GAZZINI, M. Il grande orologio. AFRICA (Rome) 10 (1955), p. 327.

16,573 GEZAU HAILEMARIAM, A. Objects found in the neighborhood of Axum. ANN. ETHIOPIE 1 (1955), pp. 50-51.

16,574 GRAZIOSI, P. Le pitture rupestri dell' Amba Focadà (Eritrea). RASS. STUDI ETIOP. 1 (1941), pp. 61-70.

16,575 HEINITZ, W. Analyse eines abessinischen Harfenliedes. FESTSCHRIFT MEINHOF, 1927, pp. 263-274.

16,576 JAGER, O. A. and DEININGER-ENGLHART, L. Some notes on illuminations of manuscripts in Ethiopia. RASS. STUDI ETIOP. 17 (1961), pp. 45-60.

16,577 KEBBEDE, M. and LECLANT, J. La Section d'archéologie (1952-1955). ANN. ETHIOPIE 1 (1955), pp. 1-6.

16,578 LECLANT, J. Deux têtes de pierres dressées du Sidamo (J. E. nos. 1 et 2). ANN. ETHIOPIE 1 (1955), pp. 53-55.

16,579 LECLANT, J. Les fouilles à Axoum en 1955-1956. Rapport préliminaire. ANN. ETHIOPIE 3 (1959), pp. 3-24.

16,580 LECLANT, J. Haoulti-Melazo (1955-1956). ANN. ETHIOPE 3 (1959), pp. 43-82.

16,581 LECLANT, J. Note sur l'amulette en cornaline J.E., 2832 (Pl. LXVII, 1). ANN. ETHIOPIE 6 (1965), pp. 86-87.

16,582 LECLANT, J. and MIQUEL, A. Reconnaissances dans l'Agamé: Goulo-Makeda et Sabéa. ANN. ETHIOPE 3 (1959), pp. 107-130.

16,583 LEROY, I. Une Madonne italienne conservée dans un manuscrit éthiopien du British Museum. RASS. STUDI ETIOP. 18 (1962), pp. 77-82.

16,584 LEROY, J. Les "Ethiopiens" de Persépolis. ANN. ETHIOPIE 5 (1963), pp. 293-298.

16,585 LEROY, J. L'évangéliaire éthiopien illustré du British Museum (Or. 510) et ses sources iconographiques. ANN. ETHIOPIE 4 (1961), pp. 155-180.

16,586 LEROY, J. Notes d'achéologie et d'iconographie éthiopiennes. ANN. ETHIOPIE 6 (1965), pp. 229-254.

16,587 LEROY, J. Objectifs des recherches sur la peinture religieuse éthiopienne. ANN. ETHIOPIE 1 (1955), pp. 127-136.

16,588 LITTMANN, E. Nuove osservazioni sui sigilli abissini. RASS. STUDI ETIOP. 2 (1942), pp. 331-332.

16,589 LITTMANN, E. Sigilli abissini. RASS. STUDI ETIOP. 1 (1941), pp. 217-225.

16,590 MIQUEL, A. Reconnaissance dans le Lasta (décembre 1955). ANN. ETHIOPIE 3 (1959), pp. 131-134.

16,591 MONNERET DE VILLARD, U. La chiesa monolitica di Yakkā Mikā'ēl. RASS. STUDI ETIOP. 1 (1941), pp. 226-233.

16,592 MONNERET DE VILLARD, U. La majestas Domini in Abissinia. RASS. STUDI ETIOP. 3 (1943), pp. 36-45.

16,593 MORDINI, A. Un' antica pittura etiopica. RASS. STUDI ETIOP. 11 (1952), pp. 29-32.

16,594 MORDINI, A. Appunti di numismatica aksumita. ANN. ETHIOPIE 3 (1959), pp. 179-184.

16,595 MORDINI, A. L'architecture religieuse chrétienne dans l'Ethiopie du Moyen Age: un programme de recherches. CAH. ET. AFR. 2 (1961), pp. 166-171.

16,596 MORDINI, A. La chiesa di Aramò (con considerazioni sulla datazione di monumenti dell' arte religiosa etiopica). RASS. STUDI ETIOP. 15 (1959), pp. 39-54.

16,597 MORDINI, A. La chiesa di Barakhaha nello Scimezana. ANN. ETHIOPIE 4 (1961), pp. 131-138.

16,598 MORDINI, A. Il convento di Gunde gundiè. RASS. STUDI ETIOP. 12 (1953), pp. 29-70.

16,599 MORDINI, A. Il soffitto del secondo vestibolo dell' Endā abuna Aragāwi in Dabra Damnoó. RASS. STUDI ETIOP. 6 (1947), pp. 29-35.

16,600 MORDINI, A. Informazioni preliminari sui risultati delle mie ricerche in Etiopia dal 1939 al 1944. RASS. STUDI ETIOP. 4 (1944), pp. 145-154.

16,601 MORDINI, A. Un riparo sotto roccia con pitture rupestri nell' Ambà Focadà. RASS. STUDI ETIOP. 1 (1941), pp. 54-60.

16,602 MORDINI, A. Su di un nuovo titolo regale aksumita. RASS. STUD. ETIOP. 8 (1949), pp. 7-11.

16,603 MORDINI, A. Un tissu musulman du moyen âge provenant du couvent de Dabra Dāmmō (Tigrai, Ethiopie). ANN. ETHIOPIE 2 (1957), pp. 75-79.

16,604 MORDINI, A. Un vasetto con figurazioni votive proveniente da Daroca' (Tigrai). IL BOLL. 1 (1953), pp. 17-20.

16,605 ORNELLA ACANFORA, M. Avanzi di civiltà antica a Debra Tsiēn (Asmara). RASS. STUDI ETIOP. 6 (1947), pp. 23-28.

16,606 OSTINI, F. Nuove redazioni di vecchi statuti: lo statuto di Adghenā-Ghelebā nell' Acchelè Guzai. IL BOLL. 1 (1953), pp. 79-84.

16,607 PETRACEK, K. Quelques faux sud-arabes de San'ā'. ANN. ETHIOPIE 4 (1961), pp. 125-129.

16,608 PIRENNE, J. Chronique d'archéologie sud-arabe 1955-1956. ANN. ETHIOPIE 2 (1957), pp. 37-68.

16,609 PLAYNE, B. Suggestions on the origin of the false doors of the Axumite Stelae. ANN. ETHIOPIE 6 (1965), pp. 279-280.

16,610 PUIGAUDEAU, O. DU and SENONES, M. Vestiges préislamiques de la région d'Assa. J. SOC. AFR. 22 (1952), pp. 7-15.

16,611 RICCI, L. Antichità nello 'Agāmē. RASS. STUDI ETIOP. 17 (1961), pp. 116-118.

16,612 RICCI, L. Der'ā. RASS. STUDI ETIOP. 16 (1960), p. 122.

16,613 RICCI, L. I ritrovamenti archeologici nel Tigrai. AFRICA (Rome) 11 (1956), pp. 159-160.

16,614 RICCI, L. Iscrizioni rupestri dell' Eritrea. RASS. STUDI ETIOP. 15 (1959), pp. 55-95; 16 (1960), pp. 77-119.

16,615 RICCI, L. Notevoli risultati degli scavi compiuti negli anni 1957-1959 a cura della Section d'Archéologie di Addis Abeba. RASS. STUDI ETIOP. 15 (1959, pp. 114-117.

16,616 RICCI, L. Nuovi materiali da altri luoghi dell' Eritrea. RASS. STUDI ETIOP. 16 (1960), pp. 122-123.

16,617 RICCI, L. Piccole note archeologiche dall' Eritrea. RASS. STUDI ETIOP. 13 (1954), pp. 121-122.

16,618 RICCI, L. Ritrovamenti a Meterā a Yehā. RASS. STUDI ETIOP. 16 (1960), pp. 120-122.

16,619 RICCI, L. La statuetta di bovino in bronzo da Zēbān Kutùr. RASS. STUDI ETIOP. 15 (1959), pp. 112-113.

16,620 ROBINSON, A. E. Notes on saucer and bowl decorations on houses, mosques and tombs. TANG. NOTES 10 (1940), pp. 79-87.

16,621 ROSSI, E. L'iscrizione sepolcrale di Zain ul-Mulk figlia d'un sultano di Dahlach (sec. XII) nel Museo di Treviso. RASS. STUDI ETIOP. 3 (1943), pp. 46-49.

16,622 ROSSI, E. Iscrizioni funerarie arabe musulmane del paese degli Arussi nel Museo Coloniale di Roma. RASS. STUDI ETIOP. 2 (1942), pp. 277-281.

16,623 RYCKMANS, G. Une "éthiopienne" en Arabie. ANN. ETHIOPIE 2 (1957), pp. 3-6.

16,624 SAUTER, R. L'église monolithe de Yekka-Mikaël. ANN. ETHIOPIE 2 (1957), pp. 15-36.

16,625 SAUTER, R. Où en est notre connaissance des églises rupestres d'Ethiope. ANN. ETHIOPIE 5 (1963), pp. 235-292.

16,626 SCHNEIDER, R. Inscriptions d'Enda Cerqos. ANN. ETHIOPIE 4 (1961), pp. 61-66.

16,627 SCHNEIDER, R. Notes épigraphiques sur les découvertes de Matarā. ANN. ETHIOPIE 6 (1965), pp. 89-142.

16,628 SCHNEIDER, R. Remarques sur les inscriptions d'Enda Cerqos. ANN. ETHIOPIE 6 (1965), pp. 221-222.

16,629 SHIFERAOU, A. Rapport sur la découverte d'antiquités trouvées dans les locaux du gouvernement général de Magallé. ANN. ETHIOPIE 1 (1955), pp. 13-15.

16,630 SIMOONS, F. J. Some questions of the economic prehistory of Ethiopia. J. AFR. HIST. 6 (1965), pp. 1-13.

16,631 STAUDE, W. Etude sur la décoration picturale des églises Abbā Antonios de Gondar et Dabra Sinā de Gorgora. ANN. ETHIOPIE 3 (1959), pp. 185-220.

16,632 STAUDE, W. Iconographie de la légende éthiopienne de la reine d'Aziel ou de Sala. J. SOC. AFR. 27 (1957), pp. 139-181.

16,633 TRINGALI, G. Cenni sulle 'ona di Asmara e dintorni. ANN. ETHIOPIE 6 (1965), pp. 143-161.

16,634 VACCARO, F. Monete Aksumite. IL. BOLL. 1 (1953), pp. 74-78.

16,635 WRIGHT, S. Notes on some cave churches in the province of Wallo. ANN. ETHIOPIE 2 (1957), pp. 8-13.

16,636 L'importanza della nuova zona archeologica di Hautî Melāzō. RASS. STUDI ETIOP. 15 (1959), pp. 111-112.

16,637 Notes complémentaires ou rectificatives sur les monuments de Lalibela. ANN. ETHIOPIE 3 (1959), pp. 135-171.

16,638 Qualche osservazione sull' iconografia della Maiestas Domini. RASS. STUDI ETIOP. 15 (1959), pp. 106-111.

16,639 Un peintre ethiopien. PRESENCE AFR. N.S. 44 (1962), pp. 226-228.

See also 5917.

Biography

16,640 CERULLI, E. Francesco Gallina. RASS. STUDI ETIOP. 2 (1942), pp. 347-348.

16,641 RICCI, L. Martino Mario Moreno. RASS. STUDI ETIOP. 20 (1964), pp. 5-21.

16,642 GROTTANELLI, V. L. Carlo Conti Rossini. RASS. STUDI ETIOP. 8 (1949), pp. 5-6.

16,643 Alfonso Tacoli. AFRICA (Rome) 10 (1955), p. 202.

16,644 FONTANA, M. Una signora africana. AFRICA (Rome) 10 (1955), p. 358.

Economics

16,645 BETHELL, A. D. The future possibilities of Ethiopian commerce and industry. AFR. AFFAIRS 44 (1945), pp. 31-36.

16,646 C., J. Progrès recents de l'Ethiopie. ZAIRE 9 (1955), p. 171.

16,647 DEIS, E. Le esportazioni italiane in Etiopia. AFRICA (Rome) 10 (1955), p. 175.

16,648 DEIS, E. Situazione e prospettive dei traffici italo-etiopici. AFRICA (Rome) 10 (1955), pp. 323-324.

16,649 G., A. I cinquant' anni delle Saline Eritree. AFRICA (Rome) 11 (1956), pp. 10-11.

16,650 G., A. Il turismo nella Federazione Etiopica. AFRICA (Rome) 10 (1955), p. 330.

16,651 GULILAT, T. Coffee in the Ethiopian economy. J. ETHIOP. STUD. 1, no. 1 (1963), pp. 47-56.

16,652 HAILU, A. G. Y. Etiopia marinara. AFRICA (Rome) 11 (1956), p. 215.

16,653 INTRONA, S. Fiera del Giubileo. AFRICA (Rome) 10 (1955), pp. 319-320.

16,654 M., Q. Ali tricolori a Johannesburg e a Nairobi. AFRICA (Rome) 11 (1956), p. 75.

16,655 MARRO, E. Gli interessi italiani in Etiopia. AFRICA (Rome) 12 (1957), pp. 182-183.

16,656 MERCATOR. La fiera etiopica del Giubileo d'Argento. AFRICA (Rome) 10 (1955), pp. 213-214.

16,657 MESSING, S. D. Non-maximizing marketing patterns in a provincial Abyssinian town and the traditional division of labor. CONG. INT. SC. ANTHR. ET. ETHN. 6, no. 1 (1960), pp. 585-590.

16,658 PANKHURST, R. Ethiopian monetary and banking innovations in the nineteenth and early twentieth centuries. J. ETHIOP. STUD. 1, no. 2 (1963), pp. 64-120.

16,659 RADO, E. R. and JOLLY, A. R. The demand for manpower: an East African case study. J. DEVELOPMENT STUD. 1 (1965), pp. 226-250.

16,660 RASCHI, R. La Coniel in Etiopia. Problemi di ieri e di oggi. AFRICA (Rome) 12 (1957), pp. 177-181.

16,661 ROWSE, E. A. A. Comprehensive environmental development as applied to Africa. MAN AND AFRICA, 1965, pp. 345-363.

16,662 TREVES, P. Le relazioni economiche italo-etiopiche. AFRICA (Rome) 10 (1955), pp. 353-357.

16,663 VEECHI, B. V. Etiopia 1955. AFRICA (Rome) 10 (1955), p. 74.

16,664 WASSERMAN, M. J. The new Ethiopian monetary system. J. POLIT. ECON. 54 (1946), pp. 358-362.

16,665 L'aviazione civile in Etiope. AFRICA (Rome) 10 (1955), p. 335.

16,666 I rapporti italo-etiopici. AFRICA (Rome) 10 (1955), p. 174.

Education

16,667 AMARE, G. Memorization in Ethiopian schools. J. ETHIOP. STUD. 1, no. 1 (1963), pp. 27-31.

16,668 COMHAIRE-SYLVAIN, S. Higher education and professional training of women in Ethiopia. WOMEN TODAY 6 (1964), pp. 58-59.

16,669 ERIKSSON, O. Education in Abyssinia. AFRICA 5 (1932), pp. 338-343.

16,670 GREENFIELD, R. Afro-Ethiopia. A note on current state of higher education and university research in Ethiopia. MAKERERE J. 8 (1963), pp. 1-15.

16,671 HABTE, A. et al. Higher education in Ethiopia, by Aklilu Habte, Menguesha Gebre Hewit, and Monica Kehoe. J. ETHIOP. STUD. 1, no. 1 (1963), pp. 3-7.

16,672 Women's education in Ethiopia. AFR. WOMEN 3 (1958-1960), p. 55.

Geography

16,673 AUSTIN, H. H. A glimpse of western Abyssinia. J. AFR. SOC. 37 (1938), pp. 348-365.

16,674 BECKINGHAM, C. F. The Itinerario of Jerónimo Lobo. RASS. STUDI ETIOP. 21 (1965), pp. 167-168.

16,675 BECKINGHAM, C. F. Notes on an unpublished manuscript of Francisco Alvares: Verdadera infomacam das terras do Preste Joam das Indias. ANN. ETHIOPIE 4 (1961), pp. 139-154.

16,676 BROOKE, C. The rural village in the Ethiopian highlands. GEOG. REV. 49 (1959), pp. 58-75.

16,677 CHOJNACKI, S. Dr. Zagiell's "Journey" to Abyssinia. A piece of Polish Pseudo-Ethiopica. J. ETHIOP. STUD. 2, no. i (1964), pp. 25-32.

16,678 CHOJNACKI, S. Forests and the forestry problem as seen by some travellers in Ethiopia. J. ETHIOP. STUD. 1, no. 1 (1963), pp. 32-39.

16,679 CONTI ROSSINI, C. Carte Abissine. RASS. STUDI ETIOP. 3 (1943), pp. 171-175.

16,680 CONTI ROSSINI, C. Gli itinerari di Alessandro Zorzi. RASS. STUDI ETIOP. 3 (1943), pp. 175-199.

16,681 DUPUIS, C. E. Lake Tana and the Nile. J. AFR. SOC. 35 (1936), pp. 18-25.

16,682 GARCIA FIGUERAS, V. Don Juan Abargues de Sostén explorador de Abisinia. ARCH. INST. EST. AFR. 1, no. 2 (1947), pp. 91-107.

16,683 ROSS, Sir E. D. Early travellers in Abyssinia. J. AFR. SOC. 21 (1922), pp. 268-278; 22 (1922), pp. 5-6.

16,684 SIMOONS, F. J. Snow in Ethiopia: a review of the evidence. GEOG. REV. 50 (1960), pp. 402-411.

16,685 THOMAS, T. H. Modern Abyssinia: a selected geographical bibliography. GEOG. REV. 27 (1937), pp. 120-128.

16,686 TRASSELLI, C. Un Italiano in Etiopia nel XV secolo: Pietro Rombulo da Messina. RASS. STUDI ETIOP. 1 (1941), pp. 173-202.

16,687 TUBIANA, J. Le voyage d'Emile Jonveaux en Ethiopie: effets récents d'une ancienne mystification. J. AFR. HIST. 4 (1963), pp. 287-288.

16,688 La capitale de l'Ethiopie. ZAIRE 8 (1954), pp. 196-197.

See also 6653.

Government. Politics. Administration

16,689 BENIPARRELL, C. DE. Notas sobre Etiopía. CUAD. AFR. OR. 38 (1957), pp. 23-33.

16,690 CERULLI, E. La constituzione dell' Etiopia. AFRICA (Rome) 11 (1956), pp. 7-8.

16,691 CLARK, R. T. Abyssinia and the Powers. CONTEMP. REV. 130 (1926), pp. 196-204.

16,692 CONSIGLIO, G. Etiopia d'Oggi. AFRICA (Rome) 10 (1955), pp. 349-351.

16,693 CONSIGLIO, G. Nozze d'argento. AFRICA (Rome) 10 (1955), p. 317.

16,694 CORA, G. L'Imperatore d'Etiopia. AFRICA (Rome) 10 (1955), pp. 351-352.

16,695 DAVON, R. Où en est l'Afrique Orientale? AFR. ET ASIE 1, no. 4 (1948), pp. 43-49.

16,696 HAYLU, G. Y. Giubileo dell' Imperatore giubilo del popolo. AFRICA (Rome) 10 (1955), pp. 318-319.

16,697 HUSSEY, E. R. J. Eritrea self-governing. AFR. AFFAIRS 53 (1954), pp. 320-328.

16,698 LONGRIGG, S. H. The future of Eritrea. AFR. AFFAIRS 45 (1946), pp. 120-127.

16,699 MARIAM, M. W. The background of the Ethio-Somalian boundary dispute. JMAS 2 (1964), pp. 189-219.

16,700 RICCARDI, T. Contributi dell' Italia all' evoluzione civile dell' Eritrea. AFRICA (Rome) 10 (1955), pp. 325-327.

16,701 STANDING, P. C. Abyssinia and the Royal visit. CONTEMP. REV. 138 (1930), pp. 639-644.

16,702 VECCHI, B. V. L' Italia ad Addis Abeba. AFRICA (Rome) 10 (1955), pp. 357-358.

16,703 ZILIOTTO, G. Fine della Federazione Etiopia-Eritrea. AFRICA (Rome) 17 (1962), pp. 277-281.

16,704 The government of Ethiopia. AFR. AFFAIRS 47 (1948), pp. 169-173.

16,705 Incorporation de l'Erythrée à l'Ethiopie. ZAIRE 6 (1952), pp. 1093-1094.

See also 6663.

History

16,706 ABIR, M. Brokerage and brokers in Ethiopia in the first half of the 19th century. J. ETHIOP. STUD. 3, no. 1 (1965), pp. 1-5.

16,707 ABIR, M. The emergence and consolidation of the monarchies of Enarea and Jimma in the first half of the fifteenth century. J. AFR. HIST. 6 (1965), pp. 205-219.

16,708 ALAQA WALDA MARYAM. History of King Theodore, ed. by H. W. Blundell. J. AFR. SOC. 6 (1906), pp. 12-42.

16,709 ALLEN, B. Gordon and Abyssinia. J. AFR. SOC. 35 (1936), pp. 130-142.

16,710 BENTWICH, N. Ethiopia and Italy's former colonies. CONTEMP. REV. 172 (1947), pp. 79-82.

16,711 BENTWICH, N. Ethiopia today. INTERNAT. AFFAIRS 20 (1944), pp. 509-518.

16,712 BOMBACI, A. Notizie sull' Abissinia in fonti turche. RASS. STUDI ETIOP. 3 (1943), pp. 79-86.

16,713 BOSI, R. Appunti per una protostoria d'Etiopia. AFRICA (Rome) 13 (1958), pp. 344-346.

16,714 CAQUOT, A. Aperçu préliminaire sur le Mashafa Tēfut de Gechen Amba. ANN. ETHIOPIE 1 (1955), pp. 89-108.

16,715 CAQUOT, A. Les "chroniques abrégées" d'Ethiopie. ANN. ETHIOPIE 2 (1957), pp. 187-192.

16,716 CAQUOT, A. Histoire amharique de Grāñ et des Gallas. ANN. ETHIOPIE 2 (1957), pp. 123-143.

16,717 CAQUOT, A. Note sur Berber Māryām. ANN. ETHIOPIE 1 (1955), pp. 109-116.

16,718 CAQUOT, A. La reine de Saba et le bois de la croix selon une tradition éthiopienne. ANN. ETHIOPIE 1 (1955), pp. 137-147.

16,719 CAQUOT, A. La royauté sacrale en Ethiopie. ANN. ETHIOPIE 2 (1957), pp. 205-218.

16,720 CAQUOT, A. and LECLANT, J. Arabie du Sud et Afrique: examen d'une hypothèse récente. ANN. ETHIOPIE 1 (1955), pp. 119-120.

16,721 CAQUOT, A. and LECLANT, J. Ethiopie et Cyrénaïque? A propos d'un texte de Synésius. ANN. ETHIOPIE 3 (1959), pp. 173-177.

16,722 CENCILLO DE PINEDA, M. Etiopia el Imperio del Preste Juan y del Trono de David. ARCH. INST. EST. AFR. 14, no. 53 (1960), pp. 29-40.

16,723 CERULLI, E. L'Etiopia medievale in alcuni brani di scrittori arabi. RASS. STUDI ETIOP. 3 (1943), pp. 272-294.

16,724 CERULLI, E. Gli Emiri di Harar dal secolo XVI alla conquista egiziana (1875). RASS. STUDI ETIOP. 2 (1942), pp. 3-20.

16,725 CERULLI, E. Il Sultanato dello Scioa nel secolo XIII secondo un nuovo documento storico. RASS. STUDI ETIOP. 1 (1941), pp. 5-42.

16,726 CHOJNACKI, S. Some notes on the history of the Ethiopian national flag. J. ETHIOP. STUD. 1, no. 2 (1963), pp. 49-63.

16,727 CONSIGLIO, G. Vincitore è solo Dio, fra gli uomini non vi sono vincitori. AFRICA (Rome) 10 (1955), pp. 71-72.

16,728 CONTI ROSSINI, C. Leggendarie regine di Aksum. RASS. STUDI ETIOP. 2 (1942), p. 97.

16,729 CONTI ROSSINI, C. Portoghesi sul Guiba. RASS. STUDI ETIOP. 2 (1942), pp. 99-101.

16,730 CONTI ROSSINI, C. Sulla comunità abissina di Cipro. RASS. STUDI ETIOP. 2 (1942), pp. 98-99.

16,731 CRAWFORD, O. G. S. The Habab tribe. SUDAN NOTES AND RECORDS 36 (1955), pp. 183-187.

16,732 CUMMING, Sir D. The U.N. disposal of Eritrea. AFR. AFFAIRS 52 (1953), pp. 127-136.

16,733 DAVIS, A. J. The 16th century Jihad in Ethiopia and the impact on its culture. J. HIST. SOC. NIG. 3 (1964), pp. 113-128.

16,734 DAVON, R. Où en est l'Ethiopie? AFR. ET ASIE 2, no. 3 (1949), pp. 34-48.

16,735 DREWES, A. J. Les inscriptions de Melazo. ANN. ETHIOPIE 3 (1959), pp. 83-99.

16,736 DREWES, A. J. Problèmes de paléographie éthiopienne. ANN. ETHIOPIE 1 (1955), pp. 121-126.

16,737 DU BOIS, W. E. B. Inter-racial implications of the Ethiopian crisis. A negro view. FOREIGN AFFAIRS 14 (1935-1936), pp. 62-92.

16,738 ELLERO, G. Il Uolcaìt. RASS. STUDI ETIOP. 7 (1948), pp. 89-112.

16,739 FERRY, R. Quelques hypothèses sur les origines des conquêtes musulmanes en Abyssinie au XVIe siècle. CAH. ET. AFR. 2 (1961), pp. 24-36.

16,740 FOTI, C. La cronaca abbreviata dei Re d'Abissinia in un manoscritto di Dabra Berhān di Gondar. RASS. STUDI ETIOP. 1 (1941), pp. 87-123.

16,741 FRIES, F. T. The Hewett mission to Abyssinia, 1884. J. AFR. SOC. 35 (1936), pp. 268-289, 397-412.

16,742 FUSELLA, L. Abissinia e Metemma in uno scritto dei belattā Heruy. RASS. STUDI ETIOP. 3 (1943), pp. 200-213.

16,743 FUSELLA, L. L'ambasciata francese a Něgusē. RASS. STUDI ETIOP. 7 (1948), pp. 176-191.

16,744 FUSELLA, L. Il Dāgmāwi Menilek di Afawårg Gabra Iyasus. RASS. STUDI ETIOP. 19 (1963), pp. 119-149.

16,745 GARRATT, G. T. Abyssinia. J. AFR. SOC. 36 (1937), pp. 36-49.

16,746 GIANNINI, C. La conquista Scioana dell' Aussa (ricordi di missione). RASS. STUDI ETIOP. 3 (1943), pp. 223-236.

16,747 GIGLIO, C. Article 17 of the Treaty of Uccialli. [Transl. by Richard Caulk.] J. AFR. HIST. 6 (1965), pp. 221-231.

16,748 GRIAULE, M. Un camp militaire abyssin. J. SOC. AFR. 4 (1934), pp. 117-122.

16,749 GWYNN, Sir C. The frontiers of Abyssinia. A retrospect. J. AFR. SOC. 36 (1937), pp. 150-161.

16,750 HARRIS, J. Italy and Abyssinia. CONTEMP. REV. 148 (1935), pp. 148-155.

16,751 HOOKER, J. R. The Foreign Office and the "Abyssinian Captives." J. AFR. HIST. 2 (1961), pp. 245-258.

16,752 HUNTINGFORD, G. W. B. The constitutional history of Ethiopia. J. AFR. HIST. 3 (1962), pp. 311-315.

16,753 JAENEN, C. J. Blondeel: the Belgian attempt to colonize Ethiopia. AFR. AFFAIRS 55 (1956), pp. 214-218.

16,754 JESMAN, C. Leopold II and Ethiopia. AFR. AFFAIRS 58 (1959), pp. 145-146.

16,755 JOSEPH, A. T. M. De Presbytero Johanne. IL BOLL. 1 (1953), pp. 50-52; 2 (1957), pp. 27-32.

16,756 LEFEVRE, R. Documenti pontifici sui rapporti con l'Etiopia nei secoli XV e XVI. RASS. STUDI ETIOP. 5 (1945), pp. 17-41.

16,757 LEFEVRE, R. L'Etiopia nella stampa del primo Cinquecento. AFRICA (Rome) 20 (1965), pp. 345-369.

16,758 LEFEVRE, R. Note su alcuni pellegrini etiopi in Roma al tempo di Leone X. RASS. STUDI ETIOP. 21 (1965), pp. 16-26.

16,759 LEFEVRE, R. Roma e la communità etiopica di Cipro nei secoli XV e XVI. RASS. STUDI ETIOP. 1 (1941), pp. 71-86.

16,760 LEWIS, H. S. Historical problems in Ethiopia and the Horn of Africa. ANTHROPOLOGY AND AFRICA TODAY, 1962, pp. 504-511.

16,761 LO GUIDICE, B. I preliminari di pace di Faras-Mai del 1896. RASS. STUDI ETIOP. 2 (1942), pp. 90-96.

16,762 LOZZA, L. La Confessione di Claudio re d'Etiopia. RASS. STUDI ETIOP. 5 (1945), pp. 67-78.

16,763 MARCUS, H. G. A background to direct British diplomatic involvement in Ethiopia, 1894-1896. J. ETHIOP. STUD. 1, no. 2 (1963), pp. 121-132.

16,764 MARCUS, H. G. Ethio-British negotiations concerning the western border with Sudan, 1896-1902. J. AFR. HIST. 4 (1963), pp. 81-94.

16,765 MARCUS, H. G. Preliminary history of the Tripartite Treaty of December 13, 1906. J. ETHIOP. STUD. 2, no. ii (1964), pp. 21-40.

16,766 MARCUS, H. G. The Rodd mission of 1897. J. ETHIOP. STUD. 3, no. ii (1965), pp. 25-35.

16,767 MEINARDUS, O. F. A. Notizen über das eustathische Kloster Debra Bizen. ANN. ETHIOPIE 6 (1965), pp. 285-291.

16,768 MEINARDUS, O. F. A. Ein portugiesischer Altar in Bahar Dar Georgis. ANN. ETHIOPIE 6 (1965), pp. 281-284.

16,769 MELLY, J. M. Ethiopia and the war from the Ethiopian point of view. INTERNAT. AFFAIRS 15 (1936), pp. 103-121.

16,770 MOLIGNONI, G. La storia di re Bacaffa nel racconto di James Bruce. RASS. STUDI ETIOP. 6 (1947), pp. 36-41.

16,771 MORENO, M. M. La cronaca di re Teodoro attribuita al dabtarā "Zaneb." RASS. STUDI ETIOP. 2 (1942), pp. 143-180.

16,772 MUSTOE, N. E. Modern Ethiopia. AFR. AFFAIRS 61 (1962), pp. 216-222.

16,773 NEWMAN, E. W. P. Abyssinia and the war. CONTEMP. REV. 159 (1941), pp. 38-45.

16,774 NOEL-BUXTON, Lord. Abyssinia rediviva. CONTEMP. REV. 159 (1941), pp. 610-615.

16,775 NOEL-BUXTON, Lord. Slavery in Abyssinia. INTERNAT. AFFAIRS 11 (1932), pp. 512-526.

16,776 OUDENRIJN, M. C. VAN DEN. L'évêque dominicain fr. Barthélemy, fondateur supposé d'un couvent dans le Tigré au 14e siècle. RASS. STUDI ETIOP. 5 (1945), pp. 7-16.

16,777 PAKENHAM, T. Ethiopia. AFR. SOUTH 2, no. 3 (1958), pp. 107-111.

16,778 PANKHURST, R. Emperor Menelik II of Ethiopia. TARIKH 1, no. 1 (1965), pp. 1-15.

16,779 PANKHURST, R. Guns in Ethiopia. TRANSITION 20 (1965), pp. 26-33.

16,780 PANKHURST, R. L'indépendance de l'Ethiopie et son importation d'armes au XIXe siècle. PRESENCE AFR. N.S. 32-33 (1960), pp. 77-102.

16,781 PANKHURST, R. Italian settlement policy in Eritrea and its repercussions 1889-1896. BOSTON UNIV. PAPERS IN AFR. HIST. 1 (1964), pp. 119-156.

16,782 PANKHURST, R. The Maria Theresa dollar in pre-war Ethiopia. J. ETHIOP. STUD. 1, no. i (1963), pp. 8-26.

16,783 PANKHURST, R. Menelik and the foundation of Addis Ababa. J. AFR. HIST. 2 (1961), pp. 103-117.

16,784 PANKHURST, R. Menelik II, Empereur d'Ethiopie. PRESENCE AFR. N.S. 41 (1962), pp. 151-163.

16,785 PANKHURST, R. 'Primitive money' in Ethiopia. J. SOC. AFR. 32 (1962), pp. 213-247.

16,786 PANKHURST, R. Theodore II, Empereur d'Ethiopie. PRESENCE AFR. N.S. 47 (1963), pp. 123-144.

16,787 PANKHURST, R. The trade of Northern Ethiopia in the 19th and early 20th centuries. J. ETHIOP. STUD. 2, no. i (1964), pp. 49-159; 2, no. ii (1964), pp. 41-91.

16,788 PANKHURST, R. The trade of southern and western Ethiopia and the Indian Ocean Ports in the 19th and early 20th centuries. J. ETHIOP. STUD. 3, no. ii (1965), pp. 37-74.

16,789 PANKHURST, R. The trade of the Gulf of Aden Ports of Africa in the 19th and early 20th centuries. J. ETHIOP. STUD. 3, no. i (1965), pp. 36-81.

16,790 PANKHURST, R. Transport and communications in Ethiopia, 1835-1935. J. TRANSP. HIST. 5 (1961-1962), pp. 69-88, 166-181, 233-254.

16,791 REY, C. F. Abyssinia of to-day. J. AFR. SOC. 21 (1922), pp. 279-290; 22 (1922), pp. 17-29; 22 (1923), pp. 109-120.

16,792 RICHARD, J. L'Extrême-Orient légendaire au Moyen Age: roi David et Prêtre Jean. ANN. ETHIOPIE 2 (1957), pp. 225-242.

16,793 ROBINSON, A. E. The Egyptian-Abyssinian war of 1874-1876. J. AFR. SOC. 26 (1927), pp. 263-280.

16,794 ROSS, Sir E. D. Almeida's History of Ethiopia: recovery of the preliminary matter. BULL. SOAS 2 (1921-1923), pp. 783-804.

16,795 ROSS, Sir E. D. The manuscripts collected by William Marsden with special reference to two copies of Almeida's History of Ethiopia. BULL. SOAS 2 (1921-1923), pp. 513-538.

16,796 RUBENSON, S. The Lion of the Tribe of Judah, Christian symbol and/or Imperial title. J. ETHIOP. STUD. 3, no. ii (1965), pp. 75-85.

16,797 RUBENSON, S. The protectorate paragraph of the Wichalē treaty. J. AFR. HIST. 5 (1964), pp. 243-283.

16,798 SANDERSON, G. N. The foreign policy of the Negus Menelik, 1896-1898. J. AFR. HIST. 5 (1964), pp. 87-97.

16,799 SANDFORD, D. A. Ethiopia; reforms from within versus foreign control. INTERNAT. AFFAIRS 15 (1936), pp. 183-201.

16,800 SCAETTA, H. Geography, Ethiopia's ally. FOREIGN AFFAIRS 14 (1935-1936), pp. 62-70.

16,801 SEQUEIRA, J. H. The Ethiopian refugees in Kenya. J. AFR. SOC. 38 (1939), pp. 329-333.

16,802 SILBERMAN, L. Why the Haud was ceded. CAH. ET. AFR. 2 (1961), pp. 37-83.

16,803 SNOWDEN, F. M. Quelques observations grecques et romaines sur les Ethiopiens. BULL. IFAN 24 (1962), pp. 584-594.

16,804 TUBIANA, J. Quatre généalogies royales éthiopiennes. CAH. ET. AFR. 2 (1962), pp. 491-508.

16,805 TUBIANA, J. Théodore II d'Ethiopie, yä-mäysa-lag. RASS. STUDI ETIOP. 19 (1963), pp. 155-163.

16,806 TUBIANA, J. Turning points in Ethiopian history. RASS. STUDI ETIOP. 21 (1965), pp. 162-166.

16,807 ULLENDORFF, E. Index of C. Conti Rossini's Storia d'Etiopia. RASS. STUDI ETIOP. 18 (1962), pp. 97-141.

16,808 VILLARI, L. and ABRAHAM, E. Abyssinia and Italy: (i) the Italian case; (ii) the case for Ethiopia. J. AFR. SOC. 34 (1935), pp. 366-377.

16,809 VYCICHL, W. Le pays de Kouch dans une inscription éthiopienne. ANN. ETHIOPIE 2 (1957), pp. 177-179.

16,810 VYCICHL, W. Qui était Fa'awngiyus? ANN. ETHIOPIE 2 (1957), pp. 181-185.

16,811 VYCICHL, W. Le titre de roi des rois. Etude historique et comparative sur la monarchie en Ethiopie. ANN. ETHIOPIE 2 (1957), pp. 193-203.

16,812 WEISSLEDER, W. The socio-political character of an historical Ethiopian capital. EAISR Jan. (1964), pp. 1-12.

16,813 WHITE, F. Peace terms for Abyssinia. CONTEMP. REV. 149 (1936), pp. 540-547.

16,814 WOOLBERT, R. G. Feudal Ethiopia and her army. FOREIGN AFFAIRS 14 (1935-1936), pp. 71-81.

16,815 WOOLBERT, R. G. The future of Ethiopia. FOREIGN AFFAIRS 20 (1941-1942), pp. 535-551.

16,816 WOOLBERT, R. G. Italy in Abyssinia. FOREIGN AFFAIRS 13 (1934-1935), pp. 499-508.

16,817 WOOLBERT, R. G. The rise and fall of Abyssinian imperialism. FOREIGN AFFAIRS 14 (1935-1936), pp. 692-697.

16,818 ZIMMERN, A. The League's handling of the Italo-Abyssinian dispute. INTERNAT. AFFAIRS 14 (1935), pp. 753-768.

16,819 Abyssinia and the Powers. FOREIGN AFFAIRS 5 (1926-1927), pp. 324-326.

16,820 Abyssinia and the war. J. AFR. SOC. 40 (1941), pp. 102-103.

16,821 En Erythrée, après onze ans d'occupation. ZAIRE 7 (1953), p. 198.

16,822 Ethiopian Women's Work Association. J. AFR. SOC. 40 (1941), pp. 296-297.

16,823 The liberation of Abyssinia. J. AFR. SOC. 41 (1942), pp. 86-87.

16,824 La relazione di Pietro Felter sullo sgombro di Macalè. RASS. STUDI ETIOP. 3 (1943), pp. 327-334.

16,825 Three books on Abyssinia. European Realities, E. W. Polson Newman. Black Shirt Black Skin, Boake Carter. A History of Abyssinia, A. H. M. Jones and Elizabeth Monroe. J. AFR. SOC. 37 (1938), pp. 366-373.

16,826 The treaty with Abyssinia. J. AFR. SOC. 41 (1942), pp. 111-113.

See also 5339, 5389, 6201, 6688.

Language. Literature

Language

16,827 ANDRZEJEWSKI, B. W. The categories of number in noun forms in the Borana dialect of Galla. AFRICA 30 (1960), pp. 62-75.

16,828 ANDRZEJEWSKI, B. W. Ideas about warfare in Borana: Galla stories and fables. AFR. LANG. STUD. 3 (1962), pp. 116-136.

16,829 ASSIRELLI, O. Contributo agli studi etiopici nell' opera di Alfredo Trombetti. RASS. STUDI ETIOP. 3 (1943), pp. 61-78.

16,830 BASLINI, F. Pinocchio in amarico. RASS. STUDI ETIOP. 13 (1954), pp. 56-75.

16,831 BRAUNER, H. P. Schizzo morfologico dello šinaša. RASS. STUDI ETIOP. 9 (1950), pp. 65-83.

16,832 CAQUOT, J. Un texte éthiopien sur les enseignes du camp d'Israel. ANN. ETHIOPIE 2 (1957), pp. 246-247.

16,833 CERULLI, E. Il linguaggio degli Amar Cocchè e quello degli Arbore nella zona del Lago Stefania. RASS. STUDI ETIOP. 2 (1942), pp. 260-272.

16,834 CERULLI, E. Il linguaggio dei Masongo nell' Etiopia Occidentale. RASS. STUDI ETIOP. 7 (1948), pp. 131-166.

16,835 CERULLI, E. Three Berta dialects in Western Ethiopia. AFRICA 17 (1947), pp. 157-169.

16,836 COHEN, M. and SCHNEIDER, R. Le troisième chapitre de la Grammaire par Abbā Takla Māryām W. S. RASS. STUDI ETIOP. 13 (1954), pp. 31-55; 14 (1955-1958), pp. 27-57.

16,837 COHEN, M. et al. Esquisse d'une étude chiffrée du verbe guèze (éthiopien classique), by M. Cohen, R. Schneider, S. Strelcyn, G. Troupeau, B. Velat. RASS. STUDI ETIOP. 9 (1950), pp. 41-64.

16,838 CONTI ROSSINI, C. Un' iscrizione su obelisco di Anzà. RASS. STUDI ETIOP. 2 (1942), pp. 21-28.

16,839 CONTI ROSSINI, C. Sui linguaggi parlati a nord dei laghi Rodolfo e Stefania. FESTSCHRIFT MEINHOF, 1927, pp. 247-255.

16,840 CONTI ROSSINI, C. Sulle misure di capacità tigrine. RASS. STUDI ETIOP. 3 (1943), pp. 94-102.

16,841 COTTERELL, F. P. Amharic word classes. J. ETHIOP. STUD. 2, no. i (1964), pp. 33-48.

16,842 COTTERELL, F. P. Expansion processes in Amharic syntax. AFR. LANG. STUD. 5 (1964), pp. 1-16.

16,843 DEMOZ, A. European loanwords in an Amharic daily newspaper. LANGUAGE IN AFRICA, 1963, pp. 116-122.

16,844 DREWES, A. J. Problèmes de paléographie éthiopienne. ANN. ETHIOPIE 1 (1955), pp. 121-126.

16,845 FLEMING, H. C. Baiso and Rendille: Somali outliers. RASS. STUDI ETIOP. 20 (1964), pp. 35-96.

16,846 FULLAS, H. The particle yä—in Amharic. RASS. STUDI ETIOP. 20 (1964), pp. 103-119.

16,847 FURLANI, G. Et hasīn = ferro e acc ḥassīnu = ascia. RASS. STUDI ETIOP. 6 (1947), pp. 1-11.

16,848 GASPARINI, A. Di due vocaboli etiopici oscuri. RASS. STUDI ETIOP. 5 (1945), pp. 79-82.

16,849 GOLDENBERG, G. Studies in Amharic syntax. J. ETHIOP. STUD. 3, no. i (1965), pp. 6-22.

16,850 GOVER, M. B. An Abyssinian vocabulary of the seventeenth century. BULL. SOAS 2 (1921-1923), pp. 763-782.

16,851 GREBAUT, S. Quelques nomenclatures pour l'intelligence de l'Hymnologie de l'Eglise éthiopienne. J. SOC. AFR. 12 (1942), pp. 123-132.

16,852 GROTTANELLI, V. L. Gli Scinascia del Nilo Azzurro ed alcuni lessici poco noti della loro lingua. RASS. STUDI ETIOP. 1 (1941), pp. 234-270.

16,853 GROTTANELLI, V. L. Materiali di lingua Coma. RASS. STUDI ETIOP. 5 (1945), pp. 122-155.

16,854 HERTRON, R. La voyelle du sixième ordre en Amharique. J. AFR. LANGS. 3 (1964), pp. 179-190.

16,855 HOFNER, M. Uberlieferungen bei Tigrē-Stämmen (1) 'Ad šek. ANN. ETHIOPIE 4 (1961), pp. 181-203.

16,856 HUNTINGFORD, G. W. B. Ethiopian place-names. AFR. LANG. STUD. 3 (1962), pp. 182-194.

16,857 KLINGENHEBEN, A. Amharisch des täglichen Lebens. AFR. UND UB. 11 (1920-1921), pp. 296-305.

16,858 KLINGENHEBEN, A. Eine amharische Form der Wiedererkennungsgeschichte der Placidas-Legende. AFR. UND UB. 10 (1919-1920), pp. 181-208.

16,859 KLINGENHEBEN, A. Die w- und y-haltigen Konsananten abessinischer Semitensprachen mit besonderer Berücksichtigung des Amharischen. RASS. STUDI ETIOP. 14 (1955-1958), pp. 28-47.

16,860 KLINGENHEBEN, A. Zur Nominalbildung im Galla. AFR. UND UB. 35 (1949-1950), pp. 21-47, 107-127, 235-260; 36 (1951-1952), pp. 45-66.

16,861 KLINGENHEBEN-V. TILING, M. Galla-Texte. AFR. UND UB. 19 (1928-1929), pp. 1-12.

16,862 LESLAU, W. An analysis of the Harari vocabulary. ANN. ETHIOPIE 3 (1959), pp. 275-298.

16,863 LESLAU, W. Chansons Harari. RASS. STUDI ETIOP. 6 (1947), pp. 130-161.

16,864 LESLAU, W. Echo-words in Ethiopic. ANN. ETHIOPIE 4 (1961), pp. 205-238.

16,865 LESLAU, W. An Ethiopian argot of a Gurage secret society. J. AFR. LANGS. 3 (1964), pp. 52-65.

16,866 LESLAU, W. An Ethiopian argot of people possessed by a spirit. AFRICA 19 (1949), pp. 204-212.

16,867 LESLAU, W. Ethiopic proverbs of Chaha. WORD 5 (1949), pp. 214-223.

16,868 LESLAU, W. Examen du supposé Argobba de Seetzen et de Lefebvre. WORD 5 (1949), pp. 46-54.

16,869 LESLAU, W. The farmer in Chaha song. AFRICA 34 (1964), pp. 230-242.

16,870 LESLAU, W. Gleanings from the Harari vocabulary. RASS. STUDI ETIOP. 16 (1960), pp. 23-37.

16,871 LESLAU, W. Harari idioms. RASS. STUDI ETIOP. 19 (1963), pp. 150-154.

16,872 LESLAU, W. The influence of Cushitic on the Semitic languages of Ethiopia: a problem of substratum. WORD 1 (1945), pp. 59-82.

16,873 LESLAU, W. Linguistic observations on a Tigre codex. RASS. STUDI ETIOP. 11 (1952), pp. 33-46.

16,874 LESLAU, W. Moča, a tone language of the Kafa group in south-western Ethiopia. AFRICA 28 (1958), pp. 135-147.

16,875 LESLAU, W. Notes de grammaire et d'étymologie éthiopienne. WORD 5 (1949), pp. 273-279.

16,876 LESLAU, W. Notes on Kambatta of southern Ethiopia. AFRICA 22 (1952), pp. 348-359.

16,877 LESLAU, W. Observations on a comparative phonology of semitic ethiopie. ANN. ETHIOPIE 2 (1957), pp. 147-166.

16,878 LESLAU, W. Observations on a study on the Ethiopian quadriradicals. RASS. STUDI ETIOP. 20 (1964), pp. 120-128.

16,879 LESLAU, W. Observations on Gurage documents. WORD 6 (1950), pp. 234-238.

16,880 LESLAU, W. Observations on 'Gurage notes' (by E. Ullendorff in Africa 20 (1950), pp. 335-344). AFRICA 21 (1951), pp. 139-145.

16,881 LESLAU, W. A preliminary description of Argobba. ANN. ETHIOPIE 3 (1959), pp. 251-273.

16,882 LESLAU, W. La réforme de l'alphabet éthiopien. RASS. STUDI ETIOP. 12 (1953), pp. 96-106.

16,883 LESLAU, W. Report on a second trip to Ethiopia. WORD 8 (1952), pp. 72-79.

16,884 LESLAU, W. Ten years of Ethiopic linguistics (1946-1956). ANN. ETHIOPIE 2 (1957), pp. 277-318.

16,885 LESLAU, W. Toward a history of the Amharic vocabulary. J. ETHIOP. STUD. 2, no. ii (1964), pp. 12-20.

16,886 LESLAU, W. Le type läbsä en gouragué. RASS. STUDI ETIOP. 10 (1951), pp. 85-98.

16,887 LESLAU, W. A year of research in Ethiopia. WORD 4 (1948), pp. 212-225.

16,888 LESLAU, W. Yes and no in the Ethiopian languages. LANGUAGE 38 (1962), pp. 147-148.

16,889 LITTMANN, E. L'iscrizione di Anza. RASS. STUDI ETIOP. 11 (1952), pp. 5-8.

16,890 LITTMANN, E. La leggenda del dragone di Aksum in lingua tigrai. RASS. ETUDI ETIOP. 6 (1947), pp. 42-45.

16,891 MARRO, E. Lingua e scuda italiana nella Federazione Etiopica. AFRICA (Rome) 10 (1955), pp. 72-73.

16,892 MITTWOCH, E. Popular Amharic texts. J. AFR. SOC. 41 (1942), pp. 261-267.

16,893 MORENO, M. M. L'azione del cuscitico sul sistema morfologico delle lingue semitiche dell' Etiopia. RASS. STUDI ETIOP. 7 (1948), pp. 121-130.

16,894 MORENO, M. M. Brevi notazioni di ğiddu. RASS. STUDI ETIOP. 10 (1951), pp. 99-107.

16,895 MORENO, M. M. Nuove notizie sull' Alaba e sugli Alaba. RASS. STUDI ETIOP. 1 (1941), pp. 43-53.

16,896 MORENO, M. M. Strutta e terminologia del Sawāsew. RASS. STUDI ETIOP. 8 (1949), pp. 12-62.

16,897 MORENO, M. M. La terminologia dei nuovi codici etiopici. RASS. STUDI ETIOP. 20 (1964), pp. 22-34.

16,898 PALMER, F. R. Bilin 'to be' and 'to have.' AFR. LANG. STUD. 6 (1965), pp. 101-111.

16,899 PALMER, F. R. Comparative statement and Ethiopian Semitic. TRANS. PHILOLOGICAL SOC. 1958, pp. 119-143.

16,900 PALMER, F. R. The 'derived forms' of the Tigrinya verb. AFR. LANG. STUD. 1 (1960), pp. 109-116.

16,901 PETRACEK, K. Zur Entwicklung des phonologischen Systems des Altäthiopischen (Ge'ez). RASS. STUDI ETIOP. 20 (1964), pp. 129-132.

16,902 PIOVANI, P. G. Nomi galla di vegetali. RASS. STUDI ETIOP. 2 (1942), pp. 312-330.

16,903 PLAZIKOWSKY-BRAUNER, H. Grammatik der Alābā-Sprache. RASS. STUDI ETIOP. 18 (1962), pp. 83-96.

16,904 PLAZIKOWSKY-BRAUNER, H. Die Hadiya-Sprache. RASS. STUDI ETIOP. 16 (1960), pp. 38-76.

16,905 PLAZIKOWSKY-BRAUNER, H. Texte der Hadiya-Sprache. RASS. STUDI ETIOP. 17 (1961), pp. 83-115.

16,906 PLAZIKOWSKY-BRAUNER, H. Die verbalen Bildungen in den sog. Kuschitischen Sprachen. RASS. STUDI ETIOP. 21 (1965), pp. 94-110.

16,907 PLAZIKOWSKY-BRAUNER, H. Wörterbuch der Hadiya-sprache. RASS. STUDI ETIOP. 20 (1964), pp. 133-182.

16,908 RICCI, L. Nomi personali fra genti a lingua tigrina. RASS. STUDI ETIOP. 21 (1965), pp. 111-161.

16,909 SCHWARTZ, J. A propos du carré Sator chez les Ethiopiens. ANN. ETHIOPIE 2 (1957), pp. 219-223.

16,910 STRELCYN, S. Ethiopian medical treatises as a source for the study of early Amharic. PROC. INT. CONG. AFR. 1 (1962), pp. 105-112.

16,911 TRENTO, P. G. DA. Vocaboli in Lingue dell'Etiopia Meridionale. RASS. STUD. ETIOP. 1 (1941), pp. 203-207.

16,912 ULLENDORFF, E. Gurage notes. AFRICA 20 (1950), pp. 335-344; 21 (1951), pp. 248-249.

16,913 ULLENDORFF, E. The labio-velars in the Ethiopian languages. RASS. STUDI ETIOP. 10 (1951), pp. 71-84.

16,914 ULLENDORFF, E. The Semitic languages of Ethiopia and their contribution to general Semitic studies. AFRICA 25 (1955), pp. 154-160.

16,915 ULLENDORFF, E. Studies in the Ethiopic syllabary. AFRICA 21 (1951), pp. 207-217.

16,916 VYCICHL, W. Amharique denk "nain," égyptien d-n-g. ANN. ETHIOPIE 2 (1957), pp. 248-249.

16,917 VYCICHL, W. Un amharisme dans un texte copte. ANN. ETHIOPIE 2 (1957), pp. 247-248.

16,918 VYCICHL, W. Egzi'abehēr "Dieu." ANN. ETHIOPIE 2 (1957), pp. 249-250.

16,919 VYCICHL, W. Note sur la transcription de l'Amharique. ANN. ETHIOPIE 2 (1957), p. 245.

16,920 VYCICHL, W. Le pays de Kouch dans une inscription éthiopienne. ANN. ETHIOPIE 2 (1957), pp. 177-179.

16,921 VYCICHL, W. Trois notes de linguistique amharique. ANN. ETHIOPIE 2 (1957), pp. 167-176.

16,922 WEBSTER, E. J. The particle in Boran. AFR. STUD. 19 (1960), pp. 33-43.

16,923 WELMERS, W. E. Notes on the structure of Saho. WORD 8 (1952), pp. 145-162.

16,924 WRIGHT, S. The transliteration of Amharic. J. ETHIOP. STUD. 2, no. i (1964), pp. 1-10.

16,925 ZYHLARZ, E. Meroïtisches Sprachgut im heutigen Abessinien. AFR. UND UB. 24 (1933-1934), pp. 230-232.

See also 6313.

Literature

16,926 BROTTO, E. 1. Menestrelli e canzoni del Caffa. 2. Magianghir. RASS. STUDI ETIOP. 6 (1947), pp. 62-96.

16,927 CAQUOT, A. Aperçu préliminaire sur le Mashafa Tēfut de Gechen Amba. ANN. ETHIOPIE 1 (1955), pp. 89-108.

16,928 CAQUOT, A. Histoire amharique de Grañ et des Gallas. ANN. ETHIOPIE 2 (1957), pp. 123-143.

16,929 CAQUOT, A. L'homélie en l'honneur de l'archange Ouriel (Dersāna Urā'ēl). ANN. ETHIOPIE 1 (1955), pp. 61-88.

16,930 CAQUOT, A. L'homélie en l'honneur de l'archange Raquel (Dersāna Rāqu'ēl). ANN. ETHIOPIE 2 (1957), pp. 91-122.

16,931 CAQUOT, A. Note sur Berber Māryām. ANN. ETHIOPIE 1 (1955), pp. 109-116.

16,932 CERULLI, E. Un frammento degli Atti di Batērgēlā Māryām. RASS. STUDI ETIOP. 3 (1943), pp. 131-138.

16,933 CONTI ROSSINI, C. Lo 'Awda Nagast scritto divinatorio etiopico. RASS. STUDI ETIOP. 1 (1941), pp. 127-145.

16,934 CONTI ROSSINI, C. Due capitoli del Libro del Mistero di Giyorgis da Saglā. RASS. STUDI ETIOP. 7 (1948), pp. 13-53.

16,935 CONTI ROSSINI, C. Il Fisiologo etiopico. RASS. STUDI ETIOP. 10 (1951), pp. 5-51.

16,936 FUSELLA, L. Il Dāgmawi Mĕnilĕk di Afawarq Gabra Iyasus. RASS. STUDI ETIOP. 17 (1961), pp. 11-44.

16,937 FUSELLA, L. Il Lĕbb wăllad tārik. RASS. STUDI ETIOP. 10 (1951), pp. 56-70.

16,938 FUSELLA, L. Le lettere del dabtarā Assaggākhañ. RASS. STUDI ETIOP. 12 (1953), pp. 80-95; 13 (1954), pp. 20-30.

16,939 GABRE-MEDHIN, T. Fear shall fail. PRESENCE AFR. N.S. 54 (1965), pp. 237-238.

16,940 GABRE-MEDHIN, T. L... L... [poème]. PRESENCE AFR. N.S. 53 (1965), p. 232.

16,941 KAMIL, M. Les manuscrits éthiopiens du Sinaï. ANN. ETHIOPIE 2 (1957), pp. 83-90.

16,942 KLINGENHEBEN, A. Zur amharischen Poesie. RASS. STUDI ETIOP. 15 (1959), pp. 5-20.

16,943 LEMMA, M. The technical aspects of Amharic versification. J. ETHIOP. STUD. 1, no. 2 (1963), pp. 133-151.

16,944 RICCI, L. La leggenda della Vergine al Libano el del santo Gigār. RASS. STUDI ETIOP. 8 (1949), pp. 83-118.

16,945 RICCI, L. Studi di letteratura etiopica ed amarica. RASS. STUDI ETIOP. 4 (1944), pp. 162-188.

16,946 SADWA, P. Un manoscritto etiopico degli evangeli. RASS. STUDI ETIOP. 11 (1952), pp. 9-28.

16,947 SCHNEIDER, R. Une page du Gadla Sādgān. ANN. ETHIOPIE 5 (1963), pp. 167-169.

16,948 VELAT, B. Fuoco sacro ed acque prodigiose a Gerusalemme e nel Gelo Makādā. RASS. STUDI ETIOP. 7 (1948), pp. 167-175.

16,949 ULLENDORFF, E. The Ethiopic manuscripts in the Royal Library, Windsor Castle. RASS. STUDI ETIOP. 12 (1953), pp. 71-79.

Law

16,950 BAUDISSIN, G. G. VON. An introduction to labour developments in Ethiopia. J. ETHIOP. LAW 2 (1965), pp. 101-110.

16,951 BUHAGIAR, W. Marriage under the civil code of Ethiopia. J. ETHIOP. LAW 1 (1964), pp. 73-99.

16,952 DAVID, R. L'enseignement du droit en Ethiopie. J. AFR. LAW 6 (1962), pp. 96-100.

16,953 DUNCANSON, D. J. Sir 'At 'Adkeme Milga'—a native law code of Eritrea. AFRICA 19 (1949), pp. 141-149.

16,954 EMILIA, A. D'. Intorno ai Nomoi ton Homeriton. RASS. STUDI ETIOP. 7 (1948), pp. 54-67.

16,955 FUSELLA, G. La statuto del Barequà. RASS STUDI ETIOP. 6 (1947), pp. 46-61.

16,956 GRAVEN, J. The penal code of the Empire of Ethiopia. J. ETHIOP. LAW 1 (1964), pp. 267-298.

16,957 GRAVEN, P. Joinder of criminal and civil proceedings. J. ETHIOP. LAW 1 (1964), pp. 135-150.

16,958 GRAVEN, P. Prosecuting criminal offences punishable only upon private complaint. J. ETHIOP. LAW 2 (1965), pp. 121-127.

16,959 KRZECZUNOWICZ, G. Code and custom in Ethiopia. J. ETHIOP. LAW 2 (1965), pp. 425-439.

16,960 KRZECZUNOWICZ, G. The Ethiopian civil code: its usefulness, relation to customs and applicability. J. AFR. LAW 7 (1963), pp. 172-177.

16,961 KRZECZUNOWICZ, G. Ethiopian legal education: retrospection and prospects. J. ETHIOP. STUD. 1, no. i (1963), pp. 68-74.

16,962 KRZECZUNOWICZ, G. Hierarchy of laws in Ethiopia. J. ETHIOP. LAW 1 (1964), pp. 111-117.

16,963 KRZECZUNOWICZ, G. A new legislative approach to customary law: the "repeals" provision of the Ethiopian civil code of 1960. J. ETHIOP. STUD. 1, no. i (1963), pp. 57-67.

16,964 KRZECZUNOWICZ, G. Statutory interpretation in Ethiopia. J. ETHIOP. LAW 1 (1964), pp. 315-323.

16,965 LOWENSTEIN, S. The penal system of Ethiopia. J. ETHIOP. LAW 2 (1965), pp. 383-399.

16,966 NADEL, S. F. Land tenure on the Eritrean plateau. AFRICA 16 (1946), pp. 1-21, 99-108.

16,967 OSTINI, F. La condition juridique des étrangers en Erythrée. CIVILISATIONS 9 (1959), pp. 343-353.

16,968 OSTINI, F. La questione terriera sull' altipiano Eritreo e le sue possibili soluzioni legislative e giudiziarie. IL BOLL. 2 (1957), pp. 39-46.

16,969 PAUL, J. C. N. First annual report from the Dean [of the Faculty of Law of Haile Sellaissie I University]; [second report]. J. ETHIOP. LAW 1 (1964), pp. 335-340; 2 (1965), pp. 515-532.

16,970 RUSSELL, F. F. Eritrean customary law. J. AFR. LAW 3 (1959), pp. 99-104.

16,971 SEDLER, R. A. The chilot jurisdiction of the Emperor of Ethiopia: a legal analysis in historical and comparative perspective. J. AFR. LAW 8 (1964), pp. 59-76.

16,972 SEDLER, R. A. Criminal jurisdiction in Ethiopia: a commentary. J. ETHIOP. LAW 2 (1965), pp. 467-486.

16,973 SEDLER, R. A. Nationality, domicile and the personal law in Ethiopia. J. ETHIOP. LAW 2 (1965), pp. 161-179.

16,974 Marriage in Ethiopia. AFR. WOMEN 4 (1960), pp. 5-7.

See also 5056.

Religion

16,975 AMBROSIO, V. Sull' ordinamento ecclesiastico nel Limmu-Enaria (in memoriam). RASS. STUDI ETIOP. 2 (1942), pp. 336-347.

16,976 CAQUOT, A. La reine de Saba et le bois de la croix: selon une tradition éthiopienne. ANN. ETHIOPIE 1 (1955), pp. 137-147.

16,977 CAQUOT, A. Un texte éthiopien sur les enseignes du camp d'Israël. ANN. ETHIOPIE 2 (1957), pp. 246-247.

16,978 CAQUOT, A. Une version ge'ez du Traité d'Hippolyte de Rome sur l'Antichrist. ANN. ETHIOPIE 6 (1965), pp. 165-214.

16,979 CERULLI, E. Gli Atti de Batra Māryām. RASS. STUDI ETIOP. 4 (1944), pp. 133-144; 5 (1945), pp. 42-66.

16,980 CONTI ROSSINI, C. Il libro di re Zar'a-Yā'gob sulla custodia del Mistero. RASS. STUDI ETIOP. 3 (1943), pp. 148-166.

16,981 CORREIA, P. J. A. A revelação da Etiópia na Verdadeira Informação. PORT. EM AFR. 1 (1944), pp. 178-180.

16,982 CRUMMEY, D. E. Foreign missions in Ethiopia 1829-68. BULL. SOC. AFR. CHURCH HIST. 2 (1965), pp. 15-36.

16,983 EURINGER, S. Un frammento di Midrasch di Melchisedech nella liturgia dell' Osanna etiopica. RASS. STUDI ETIOP. 3 (1943), pp. 50-60.

16,984 GRIAULE, M. Disposition de l'assistance a l'office abyssin. J. SOC. AFR. 4 (1934), pp. 273-278.

16,985 HAMMERSCHMIDT, E. Jewish elements in the cult of the Ethiopian Church. J. ETHIOP. STUD. 3, no. ii (1965), pp. 1-12.

16,986 LEONESSA, P. M. DA. La versione etiopica dei canoni apocrifi del concilio di Nicea secondo i codici vaticani ed il fiorentino. RASS. STUDI ETIOP. 2 (1942), pp. 29-89.

16,987 PAPI, M. R. Una santa abissina anticattolica: Walatta-Pētros. RASS. STUDI ETIOP. 3 (1943), pp. 87-93.

16,988 RICCI, L. Le Vite di Enbāqom e di Yohannēs, abbati di Dabra Libānos di Scioa. RASS. STUDI ETIOP. 13 (1954), pp. 91-120; 14 (1955?1958), pp. 69-107.

16,989 STRELCYN, S. Sur une prière 'falacha' publiée par C. Conti Rossini dans les Appunti di storia e letteratura falascia. RASS. STUDI ETIOP. 8 (1949), pp. 63-82.

16,990 SUMMER, C. The Ethiopic liturgy: an analysis. J. ETHIOP. STUD. 1, no. i (1963), pp. 40-46.

16,991 TEDESCHI, S. Profilo storico di Dayr as-Sultan. J. ETHIOP. STUD. 2, no. ii (1964), pp. 92-160.

16,992 I 25 anni del Pontificio Collegio Etiopico. AFRICA (Rome) 10 (1955), p. 72.

Science

16,993 GRABHAM, G. W. Abyssinian cereals. SUDAN NOTES 5 (1922), pp. 104-105.

16,994 GRIAULE, M. D'un mode aberrant de conservation de l'hydromel au Godjam. J. SOC. AFR. 4 (1934), pp. 279-284.

16,995 GRIAULE, M. Note sur la variolisation au Godjam et au Choa (Abyssinie). J. SOC. AFR. 12 (1942), pp. 117-121.

16,996 HILL, B. G. Cat (Catha edulis Forsk). J. ETHIOP. STUD. 3, no. ii (1965), pp. 13-23.

16,997 HUZAYYIN, S. A. Recent physiographic stages in the lower Nile valley and their relation to hydrographic and climatic changes in Abyssinia and East Africa. PROC. PAN-AFR. CONGR. PREHIST. 1 (1947), pp. 75-78.

16,998 LEONESSA, M. DA. Un trattato sul calendario redatto al tempo di re 'Amda-Syon I. RASS. STUDI ETIOP. 3 (1943), pp. 302-326.

16,999 PUGLISI, G. Le cisterne di Dahlac Chebir e di Adal nell' Arcipelago delle Dahlac. IL BOLL. 1 (1953), pp. 53-70.

17,000 STRELCYN, S. Les écrits médicaux éthiopiens. J. ETHIOP. STUD. 3, no. 1 (1965), pp. 82-103.

17,001 STRELCYN, S. Un traité éthiopien d'hygiène et de diététique. AFR. BULL. 1 (1964), pp. 73-94.

17,002 STRELCYN, S. Les traités médicaux éthiopiens. CAH. ET. AFR. 2 (1961), pp. 148-159.

Sociology

17,003 FELLOWS, P. A. Urbanism: engineering trends in Ethiopia. INTERNAT. J. COMP. SOCIOL. 4 (1963), pp. 162-177.

17,004 GRISMAN, C. S. West Africans in Eritrea. NIGERIAN FIELD 20 (1955), pp. 41-45.

17,005 NEWMAN, E. W. P. Slavery in Abyssinia. CONTEMP. REV. 148 (1935), pp. 650-657.

17,006 NOEL-BUXTON, Lord. Slavery in Abyssinia. CONTEMP. REV. 141 (1932), pp. 698-707.

17,007 RICCI, L. Organisation de l'état et structures sociales en Ethiopie. CIVILISATIONS 14 (1964), pp. 19-22; English summary, pp. 23-24.

17,008 WOOLBERT, R. G. The peoples of Ethiopia. FOREIGN AFFAIRS 14 (1935-1936), pp. 340-344.

17,009 Addis-Abeba. PRESENCE AFR. N.S. 47 (1963), pp. 230-233.

SOMALIA

General

17,010 Al IV Convegno economico italo-africano si è parlato sopratutto di Somalia. AFRICA (Rome) 10 (1955), p. 144.

17,011 Il Centro Studi della Somalia a fine d'anno 1954-55. AFRICA (Rome) 10 (1955), p. 214.

Agriculture

17,012 DAINELLI, G. The agricultural possibilities of Italian Somalia. GEOG. REV. 21 (1931), pp. 56-69.

17,013 GIORIO, C. Alcune considerazioni sulla cooperazione internazionale in Africa e riflessi sociali dell' agricoltura in Somalia. COOPERAZIONE INT. AFR., 1962, pp. 435-441.

17,014 HASSAN, A. M. L'agriculture. Considerations générales. PRESENCE AFR. N.S. 38 (1961), pp. 147-156.

Anthropology

17,015 AFRICANUS [pseud.]. Somal marriage. J. AFR. SOC. 21 (1921), pp. 23-34.

17,016 AHMED MOHAMED. Sha: a Somali game. SOMALILAND J. 1 (1955), pp. 110-113.

17,017 AMIN, A. The rado branch of gu'oso. SOMALILAND J. 1 (1955), pp. 114-115.

17,018 GROTTANELLI, V. L. Asiatic influences on Somali culture. ETHNOS 12 (1947), pp. 153-181.

17,019 KIRK, J. W. C. The Yibirs and Midgāns of Somaliland, their traditions and dialects. J. AFR. SOC. 4 (1904), pp. 91-108.

17,020 LEWIS, I. M. Clanship and contract in northern Somaliland. AFRICA 29 (1959), pp. 274-293.

17,021 LEWIS, I. M. Dualism in Somali nations of power. JRAI 93 (1963), pp. 109-116.

17,022 LEWIS, I. M. The Galla in Northern Somaliland. RASS. STUDI ETIOP. 15 (1959), pp. 21-38.

17,023 LEWIS, I. M. Notes on the social organisation of the 'Ise Somali. RASS. STUDI ETIOP. 17 (1961), pp. 69-82.

17,024 LUCAS, M. Renseignements ethnographiques et linguistiques sur les Danakils de Tadjourah. J. SOC. AFR. 5 (1935), pp. 181-202.

17,025 MARIN, G. Somali games. JRAI 61 (1931), pp. 499-511.

17,026 PARENTI, R. I Bagiuni, contributo alla conoscenza delle popolazioni della Somalia Meridionale. RASS. STUDI ETIOP. 5 (1945), pp. 156-190.

17,027 PARKINSON, J. Customs in Western British Somaliland. J. AFR. SOC. 35 (1936), pp. 241-245.

17,028 PRINS, A. H. J. The didemic diarchic Boni. JRAI 93 (1963), pp. 174-185.

17,029 VILLENEUVE, A. DE. Etude sur une coutume somalie: les femmes cousues. J. SOC. AFR. 7 (1937), pp. 15-32.

17,030 Notes on the somali. NADA 25 (1948), pp. 85-92.

17,031 Some aspects of Somali rural society today. SOMALILAND J. 1 (1955), pp. 94-98.

Art

17,032 CLARK, J. D. Recent prehistoric research in the Somalilands. PROC. PAN-AFR. CONGR. PRE-HIST. 1 (1947), pp. 146-161.

17,033 GRAZIOSI, P. Une nouvelle industrie paléolithique de Somalie: l'Eibien. PROC. PAN-AFR. CONGR. PRE-HIST. 2 (1952), pp. 367-372.

17,034 MONNERET DE VILLARD, U. I minareti di Mogadiscio. RASS. STUDI ETIOP. 3 (1943), pp. 127-130.

Economics

17,035 BIGI, F. Attualità e prospettive della bananicoltura somala nel quadro dei rapporti tra Italia e Somalia. AFRICA (Rome) 18 (1963), pp. 240-249.

17,036 BIGI, F. Situazione e prospettive economiche della Somalia alla vigilia dell' indipendenza. AFRICA (Rome) 15 (1960), pp. 123-138.

17,037 CONSIGLIO, G. Insistiamo: attenzione alla Somalia! AFRICA (Rome) 10 (1955), pp. 65-68.

17,038 FRANCESCHI, F. La pêche et les activites annexes. PRESENCE AFR. N.S. 38 (1961), pp. 173-175.

17,039 G., C. Bilancio S.A.I.S. 1954. AFRICA (Rome) 10 (1955), p. 68.

17,040 GORI, F. Profumo di Migiurtina. AFRICA (Rome) 11 (1956), p. 171.

17,041 LAWRIE, J. J. Frankincense. SOMALILAND J. 1 (1954), pp. 26-30.

17,042 M., Q. Al convegno italo-africano di Milano i rapporti Italia-Somalia. AFRICA (Rome) 11 (1956), pp. 97-98.

17,043 MOHAMED FARAH SIAD. Somalia e Occidente. AFRICA (Rome) 11 (1956), p. 69.

17,044 MOHAMUD YUSUF ADEN MURO. La cooperazione internazionale e lo sviluppo dell' istruzione con riguardo particolare alla Somalia. COOPERAZIONE INT. AFR., 1960, pp. 429-435.

17,045 ODONE, A. Somalia's economy: prospects and problems. CIVILISATIONS 11 (1961), pp. 444-448; French summary, pp. 449-450.

17,046 YUSUF, A. A. Le mouvement syndical. PRESENCE AFR. N.S. 38 (1961), pp. 216-219.

17,047 ZICCARDI, F. Lo sforzo italiano in Somalia. AFRICA (Rome) 15 (1960), pp. 65-70.

17,048 ZICCARDI, F. Vittorio Emanuele III a caccia di elefanti. AFRICA (Rome) 10 (1955), pp. 29-33.

17,049 Attività dell' Agip in Somalia. AFRICA (Rome) 10 (1955), p. 68.

17,050 Radio Somali. AFR. AFFAIRS 53 (1954), pp. 318-320.

See also 1319.

Education

17,051 BELL, C. R. V. Schools and Somalis. CORONA 2 (1950), pp. 395-397.

17,052 COSTANZO, G. A. L'educazione chiave dello sviluppo della Somalia. AFRICA (Rome) 15 (1960), pp. 139-145.

17,053 DORATO, M. L'istruzione professionale in Somalia. AFRICA (Rome) 13 (1958), pp. 15-18.

17,054 HALANE, M. O. L'organisation scolaire. PRESENCE AFR. N.S. 38 (1961), pp. 164-167.

17,055 MAGNINO, L. Ancora l'Università di Mogadiscio. AFRICA (Rome) 11 (1956), p. 210.

17,056 MAGNINO, L. Università a Mogadiscio. AFRICA (Rome) 10 (1955), pp. 33-34.

17,057 Burao Girls' School, Somaliland Protectorate. AFR. WOMEN 2 (1956-1958), p. 36.

17,058 Girls' education in the Somaliland Protectorate. AFR. WOMEN 1 (1955), pp. 51-52.

17,059 Women in Italian Somaliland. AFR. WOMEN 2 (1956-1958), pp. 83-84.

Geography

17,060 BALDACCI, G. The promontory of Cape Guardafui. J. AFR. SOC. 9 (1909), pp. 59-72.

17,061 BONANNI, C. Boscaglia somala. AFRICA (Rome) 10 (1955), p. 89.

17,062 FAILLACE, C. Cooperazione internazionale nell' attuazione di un programma organico di ricerche idriche in Somalia. COOPERAZIONE INT. AFR., 1960, pp. 447-451.

17,063 GIRACE, A. Schedine da Mogadiscio. AFRICA (Rome) 10 (1955), pp. 69-70.

See also 6653.

Government. Politics. Administration

17,064 AHMED DAHIR HASSAN. La pasizione della Somalia nelle organizzazioni internazionali. COOPERAZIONE INT. AFR., 1960, pp. 451-454.

17,065 ALI, M. W. Le développement de l'organisation municipale en Somalie. PRESENCE AFR. N.S. 38 (1961), pp. 196-202.

17,066 ALI, M. W. Notes sur le développement politique et constitutionnel de la Somalie. PRESENCE AFR. N.S. 38 (1961), pp. 157-163.

17,067 ALI, M. W. Au sujet de la durée de l'Assemblée législative. PRESENCE AFR. N.S. 38 (1961), pp. 176-179.

17,068 BERTOLA, A. Religion et droits de l'homme dans la Constitution de la Somalie. CIVILISATION 11 (1961), pp. 296-309; English summary, pp. 310-311.

17,069 BRAINE, B. The Somali question. AFR. AFFAIRS 57 (1958), pp. 189-199.

17,070 CONFALONIERI, V. B. L'indipendenza della Somalia. Il punto di vista del Ministero degli Esteri italiano. AFRICA (Rome) 10 (1955), pp. 137-138.

17,071 CONSIGLIO, G. Creazione di uno Stato. AFRICA (Rome) 10 (1955), pp. 169-172.

17,072 COSTANZO, G. A. L'évolution politique de la Somalie durant les six premières années de l'Administration italienne. CIVILISATIONS 6 (1956), pp. 301-309; 7 (1957), pp. 483-487; 8 (1958), pp. 331-334.

17,073 FRANCESCHI, F. Dix ans de A.F.I.S. (Administration Fiduciaire Italienne de Somalie). PRESENCE AFR. N.S. 38 (1961), pp. 137-139.

17,074 FRANCESCHI, F. Il Governo Somalo e il suo ordinamento. AFRICA (Rome) 11 (1956), p. 150.

17,075 FRANCESCHI, F. Nationalisme. PRESENCE AFR. N.S. 38 (1961), pp. 107-109.

17,076 GIAMA, M. O. Les partis politiques. PRESENCE AFR. N.S. 38 (1961), pp. 121-129.

17,077 GIASTI, M. H. La Pansomalisme. PRESENCE AFR. N.S. 38 (1961), pp. 135-136.

17,078 GRAY, A. Somalia [preliminary step to Somaliland joining up with Somalia]. AFR. AFFAIRS 59 (1960), pp. 287-288.

17,079 GRAY, A. Somaliland claim. AFR. AFFAIRS 55 (1956), pp. 15-16.

17,080 GRAY, A. Somaliland policy. AFR. AFFAIRS 58 (1959), pp. 105-106.

17,081 HALL, Sir D. Somaliland's last year as a protectorate. AFR. AFFAIRS 60 (1961), pp. 26-37.

17,082 JAENEN, C. J. The Somali problem. AFR. AFFAIRS 56 (1957), pp. 147-157.

17,083 LEGUM, C. Somali liberation songs. JMAS 1 (1963), pp. 503-519.

17,084 LEWIS, I. M. Modern political movements in Somaliland. AFRICA 28 (1958), pp. 244-260, 344-362.

17,085 LEWIS, I. M. Pan-Africanism and Pan-Somalism. JMAS 1 (1963), pp. 147-161.

17,086 LEWIS, I. M. Problems in the development of modern leadership and loyalties in the British Somaliland Protectorate and U.N. Trusteeship territory of Somalia. CIVILISATIONS 10 (1960), pp. 49-60; French summary, pp. 61-62.

17,087 LUCE, R. British Somaliland awakens. CONTEMP. REV. 195 (1959), pp. 294-296.

17,088 MOHAMED FARAH SIAD. Le elezioni politiche in Somalia. AFRICA (Rome) 11 (1956), pp. 16-17.

17,089 MOHAMED HASSAN EL ZAYYAT. Statement of the chairman of the United Nations Advisory Council (UNAC) for Somalia under Italian trusteeship. COOPERAZIONE INT. AFR., 1960, pp. 85-96.

17,090 MOHAMUD, S. M. L'indépendance politique est-elle suffisante? PRESENCE AFR. N.S. 38 (1961), pp. 189-195.

17,091 MORGANTINI, A. M. Somalie sous tutelle italienne Schéma de l'économie et chronique économique 1950-1955. CIVILISATIONS 6 (1956), pp. 455-472; 8 (1958), pp. 429-445; 10 (1960), pp. 117-130.

17,092 PIRONE, M. Evolution sociale des Somalis. CIVILISATIONS 7 (1957), pp. 617-626; 8 (1958), pp. 145-150, 616-622; 9 (1959), pp. 85-89; 10 (1960), pp. 264-268; 11 (1961), pp. 209-212; 12 (1962), pp. 141-144.

17,093 PIRONE, M. Somalie sous tutelle italienne. Développement de l'éducation, de l'instruction et de la culture de la population somalie. CIVILISATIONS 7 (1957), pp. 112-122.

17,094 SALOME, F. Governo somalo in Somalia. AFRICA (Rome) 11 (1956), pp. 96-97.

17,095 SAMANTAR, M. S. Réflexions sur la Somalie à la veille de l'indépendance. PRESENCE AFR. N.S. 38 (1961), pp. 207-209.

17,096 SAMANTAR, Y. O. Comment on nous a enseigné la démocratie. PRESENCE AFR. N.S. 38 (1961), pp. 110-117.

17,097 SAMANTAR, Y. O. La Somalie et le mouvement Afro-Asiatique. PRESENCE AFR. N.S. 38 (1961), pp. 140-143.

17,098 WATERFIELD, G. Trouble in the Horn of Africa? The British Somali case. INTERNAT. AFFAIRS 32 (1956), pp. 52-60.

17,099 Un an d'administration italienne en Somalie. ZAIRE 5 (1951), pp. 1076-1078.

17,100 L'irredentisme Somali au Kenya. PRESENCE AFR. N.S. 39 (1961), pp. 205-207.

See also 6663, 16695, 16699, 17402.

History

17,101 ALI SHEIKH MOHAMED. The origin of the Isaaq peoples. SOMALILAND J. 1 (1954), pp. 22-25.

17,102 FEARSON, D. Notes on the history of Berbera. SOMALILAND J. 1 (1954), pp. 11-20, 70-80.

17,103 FREEMAN-GRENVILLE, G. S. P. Coins from Mogadishu, c. 1300 to c. 1700. UNIV. GHANA RES. REV. 1 (1965), p. 36.

17,104 GRAY, A. Somaliland freedom. AFR. AFFAIRS 59 (1960), pp. 181-183.

17,105 HESS, R. L. The 'Mad Mullah' and northern Somalia. J. AFR. HIST. 5 (1964), pp. 415-433.

17,106 JARDINE, D. Somaliland: the Cinderella of the empire. J. AFR. SOC. 24 (1925), pp. 100-109.

17,107 KITTERMASTER, H. B. British Somaliland. J. AFR. SOC. 27 (1928), pp. 329-337.

17,108 KITTERMASTER, H. B. The development of the Somalis. J. AFR. SOC. 31 (1932), pp. 234-244.

17,109 LEVA, A. E. La Somalia negli scritti di Enrico Cerulli. AFRICA (Rome) 13 (1958), pp. 139-140.

17,110 LEWIS, I. M. The Somali conquest of the Horn of Africa. J. AFR. HIST. 1 (1960), pp. 213-229.

17,111 LEYDEN, J. L. Somaliland Protectorate. CORONA 2 (1950), pp. 370-371.

17,112 OKONGA, S. La Somalie, hier et aujourd'hui. PRESENCE AFR. N.S. 38 (1961), pp. 220-235.

17,113 PIRONE, M. What the Ogaden Somali say about their past. SOMALILAND J. 1 (1955), pp. 83-91.

17,114 RECE, Sir G. The Horn of Africa. INTERNAT. AFFAIRS 30 (1954), pp. 440-449.

17,115 SCEK, M. A. L'Italie et nous. PRESENCE AFR. N.S. 38 (1961), pp. 180-184.

17,116 SYAD, W. La Somalie à l'heure de la vérité. PRESENCE AFR. N.S. 38 (1961), pp. 74-97.

17,117 WATSON, J. M. The historical background to the ruined towns in the west of the Protectorate. SOMALILAND J. 1 (1955), pp. 120-125.

17,118 WRIGHT, A. C. A. A footnote to East African history. AFR. AFFAIRS 46 (1947), pp. 97-101.

17,119 YUSUF, K. A. Les limites de la Somalie. PRESENCE AFR. N.S. 38 (1961), pp. 130-134.

17,120 Il premio Duca d'Aosta alla tesi su la Somalia e l'opera di Luigi Amedeo di Savoia. AFRICA (Rome) 10 (1955), p. 70.

17,121 La Somalie de conquête coloniale à l'indépendance, chronologie sommaire. PRESENCE AFR. N.S. 38 (1961), pp. 236-237.

17,122 The temporary withdrawal from British Somaliland. J. AFR. SOC. 39 (1940), pp. 294-295.

See also 1319, 6688, 16802.

Language. Literature

Language

17,123 ANDRZEJEWSKI, B. W. Accentual patterns in verbal forms in the Isaaq dialect of Somali. BULL. SOAS 18 (1956), pp. 103-129.

17,124 ANDRZEJEWSKI, B. W. Notes on the substantive pronouns in Somali. AFR. LANG. STUD. 2 (1961), pp. 80-99.

17,125 ANDRZEJEWSKI, B. W. Pronominal and prepositional particles in northern Somali. AFR. LANG. STUD. 1 (1960), pp. 96-108.

17,126 ANDRZEJEWSKI, B. W. Some problems of Somali orthography. SOMALILAND J. 1 (1954), pp. 34-47.

17,127 ANDRZEJEWSKI, B. W. and GALAAL, M. H. I. A Somali poetic combat—1, 2, 3. J. AFR. LANGS. 2 (1963), pp. 15-28, 93-100, 190-205.

17,128 BERGHOLD, K. Somâli—Studien. ZAOS 3 (1897), pp. 1-16.

17,129 CERULLI, E. Il gergo delle genti di bassa casta della Somalia. FESTSCHRIFT MEINHOF, 1927, pp. 99-110.

17,130 CERULLI, E. Somali songs and little texts. J. AFR. SOC. 19 (1920), pp. 135-140, 221-226; 20 (1920), pp. 46-49; 21 (1921), pp. 47-54.

17,131 HETZRON, R. The particle bàa in Northern Somali. J. AFR. LANG. 5 (1965), pp. 118-130.

17,132 ISAAK, B. F. A. Le problème de la langue. PRESENCE AFR. N.S. 38 (1961), pp. 168-172.

17,133 KLINGENHEBEN-V. TILING, M. Adjektiv-Endungen im Somali. AFR. UND UB. 10 (1919-1920), pp. 208-240.

17,134 KLINGENHEBEN-V. TILING, M. Jabarti-texte. AFR. UND UB. 15 (1924-1925), pp. 50-64, 139-158.

17,135 KLINGENHEBEN-V. TILING, M. Ein Somali-Text von Muhãmmed Nur. AFR. UND UB. 18 (1927-1928), pp. 230-233.

17,136 KLINGENHEBEN-V. TILING, M. Die Sprache der Jabartï. AFR. UND UB. 12 (1921-1922), pp. 17-52, 97-162.

17,137 KLINGENHEBEN-V. TILING, M. Die Vokale des bestimmten Artikels im Somali. AFR. UND UB. 9 (1918-1919), pp. 132-166.

17,138 LANG, K. Repetition, Reduplikation und Lautmalerei in der Somali-Sprache. BIBLIOTHECA AFR. 1 (1925), pp. 98-104.

17,139 LEWIS, I. M. The Gadabuursi Somali script. BULL. SOAS 21 (1958), pp. 134-156.

17,140 LEWIS, I. M. The names of God in northern Somali. BULL. SOAS 22 (1959), pp. 134-140.

17,141 MAINO, M. L'alfebeto osmania in Somalia. RASS. STUDI ETIOP. 10 (1951), pp. 108-121.

17,142 MORENO, M. M. Il dialetto degli Ašrāf di Mogadiscio. RASS. STUDI ETIOP. 12 (1953), pp. 107-138; 13 (1954), pp. 5-19.

17,143 RICCI, L. Corrispondenza epistolare in osmania. RASS. STUDI ETIOP. 14 (1955-1958), pp. 108-150.

17,144 Con quali caratteri sarà scritto il Somalo. LIBIA 4, nos. 3-4(1956), pp. 65-69.

Literature

17,145 BONANNI, C. Poesia Somala. AFRICA (Rome) 15 (1960), pp. 229-230.

17,146 HASSAN, S. M. A. Poem from Somali. PRESENCE AFR. N.S. 38 (1961), p. 239.

17,147 IBRAHIM MOHAMED. A dove golay [fiction]. SOMALILAND J. 1 (1955), pp. 116-117.

17,148 MBITI, J. Tre poemetti inediti. AFRICA (Rome) 18 (1963), pp. 269-270.

17,149 PIKE, V. F. Hargeisa [a poem]. SOMALILAND J. 1 (1954), p. 21.

17,150 SYAD, W. The birth of a nation. PRESENCE AFR. N.S. 38 (1961), p. 72.

17,151 SYAD, W. Hier. PRESENCE AFR. N.S. 38 (1961), p. 238.

17,152 TURNBULL, R. W. Erigavo environs [a poem]. SOMALILAND J. 1 (1954), p. 31.

Law

17,153 CONTINI, P. Integration of laws in the Somali Republic: report on the work of the Consultative Commission for Integration from its inception until 31st March, 1964. J. AFR. LAW 8 (1964), pp. 56-58.

17,154 NOOR MUHAMMAD, H. N. A. The rule of law in the Somali Republic. J. INT. COMM. JURISTS 5 (1964), pp. 275-302.

17,155 RAYNE, H. Somali tribal law. J. AFR. SOC. 20 (1921), pp. 101-106.

17,156 Integration Commission in Somali Republic. J. AFR. LAW 5 (1961), pp. 2-3.

17,157 Somali Republic [courses in law]. J. AFR. LAW 6 (1962), p. 131.

Religion

17,158 EIDARUS, S. M. L'Islam et les confraternités religieuses. PRESENCE AFR. N.S. 38 (1961), pp. 203-206.

17,159 LEWIS, I. M. Sufism in Somaliland: a study in tribal Islam. BULL. SOAS 17 (1955), pp. 581-602; 18 (1956), pp. 145-160.

17,160 SANCEAU, E. As actividades missionárias de Frei António do Loureiro, 1506-1519(?). PORT. EM AFR. 14 (1957), pp. 181-190.

Science

17,161 AHMED ALI. The yeib. SOMALILAND J. 1 (1955), pp. 118-119.

17,162 CURTIS, G. E. A note on the Dibatag (Ammodorcas clarkei). SOMALILAND J. 1 (1954), pp. 48-51.

17,163 LAPICCIRELLA, V. La medicina in Somalia nella luce della cooperazione internazionale in Africa. COOPERAZIONE INT. AFR., 1960, pp. 441-446.

17,164 NUR, M. A. Le développement de l'organisation sanitaire en Somalie. PRESENCE AFR. N.S. 38 (1961), pp. 185-188.

17,165 SANTOS DIAS, J. A. T. Nota sobre duas carraças do género Aponomma Neumann, 1899, da Somália Italiana. BSEM 110 (1958), pp. 111-118.

17,166 The distribution of the beira, Dorcatragus megalotis Menges [remarks and notes by R. E. Drake-Brockman and G. E. Curtis]. SOMALILAND J. 1 (1955), pp. 126-127.

Sociology

17,167 ALI, M. W. L'institution du "Scir," son fondement et ses fonctions. PRESENCE AFR. N.S. 38 (1961), pp. 118-120.

17,168 C., J. L'urbanisation en Somalie Italienne. ZAIRE 8 (1954), p. 859.

17,169 JONES, R. L. Structural continuity in the Somali Republic. PROC. 3RD. GRAD. ACAD. UCLA, 1965, pp. 99-111.

17,170 LESOURD, M. Notes sur les Nawakhid, navigateurs de la mer Rouge. BULL. IFAN 22 (1960), pp. 346-355.

17,171 LEWIS, I. M. Historical aspects of genealogies in northern Somali social structure. J. AFR. HIST. 3 (1962), pp. 35-48.

17,172 LEWIS, I. M. Shaikhs and warriors in Somaliland. AFRICAN SYSTEMS OF THOUGHT, 1965, pp. 204-223.

17,173 LEWIS, I. M. Sociology in Somaliland. SOMALILAND J. 1 (1954), pp. 3-10, 100-103.

17,174 MOHAMOUD ABDI HIRAD. Somali marriage custom in outline. SOMALILAND J. 1 (1955), pp. 92-93.

17,175 MOHAMUD, M. Y. La femme dans la société. PRESENCE AFR. N.S. 38 (1961), pp. 144-146.

17,176 ZANCANELLA, A. Impressioni di Somalia dal diario del regista. AFRICA (Rome) 10 (1955), pp. 221-224.

FRENCH SOMALILAND (Territory of the Afars and Issas)

17,177 BERNARD, M. Description de la cérémonie dite Möhâ (Cote française des Somalis). J. SOC. AFR. 4 (1934), pp. 33-34.

17,178 BOHME, R. Die französische Somaliküste. KOLONIALE STUDIEN: HANS MEYER FESTSCHRIFT, 1928, pp. 147-160.

17,179 CHAILLEY, Commandant. L'habitation à la Côte française des Somalis. BULL. IFAN 14 (1952), pp. 1490-1511.

17,180 EMERIT, M. Le premier projet d'établissement français sur la Côte des Somalis. REV. FRANC. HIST. OUTRE-MER 50 (1963), pp. 189-196.

17,181 G., M. Italiani a Gibuti ante 1940. AFRICA (Rome) 10 (1955), p 90.

17,182 MALARA, A. Il regime del franco nei territori francesi dell' Oceano Indiano. AFRICA (Rome) 10 (1955), pp. 111-112.

17,183 UZEL, B. La fondation de Djibouti. REV. HIST. COL. 39 (1952), pp. 63-75.

See also 16695.

KENYA

Agriculture

17,184 BALL, R. S. Pyrethrum cultivation in Kenya. BULL. IMP. INST. 42 (1944), pp. 13-24.

17,185 BECKLEY, V. A. Pyrethrum in Kenya. BULL. IMP. INST. 36 (1938), pp. 31-44.

17,186 CHAMBERS, P. C. Group farming in Kenya. CORONA 2 (1950), pp. 253-255.

17,187 CHAMPION, A. M. The reconditioning of native reserves in Africa. J. AFR. SOC. 38 (1939), pp. 442-464.

17,188 FANE, R. Forest development in Kenya. AFR. AFFAIRS 47 (1948), pp. 242-243.

17,189 HEYER, J. A linear programming model for peasant agriculture in Kenya. EAISR Jan. (1965), pp. 1-13.

17,190 McENTEE, P. D. Improved farming in Central Nyanza District—Kenya Colony. J. AFR. ADM. 12 (1960), pp. 68-73.

17,191 MAHER, C. Tung oil in Kenya. BULL. IMP. INST. 34 (1936), pp. 181-188.

17,192 MISKIN, T. Gli aspetti agricoli del Kenya e il successo degli agricoltori italiani. AFRICA (Rome) 11 (1956), pp. 67-68.

17,193 MONSON, C. J. The prospects for tobacco cultivation in Kenya. BULL. IMP. INST. 22 (1924), pp. 33-38.

17,194 STRANGE, B. F. Kenya women in agriculture. WOMEN TODAY 6 (1963), pp. 7-9.

17,195 SWYNNERTON, J. R. M. Kenya's agricultural planning. AFR. AFFAIRS 56 (1957), pp. 209-215.

17,196 WARD, E. H. Kenya's greatest problem. J. AFR. SOC. 38 (1939), pp. 370-380.

17,197 WILSON, F. A district team at work [in Kenya]. CORONA 3 (1951), pp. 295-300, 337-339.

17,198 Kenya woman farmer. AFR. WOMEN 4 (1961), p. 38.

Anthropology

17,199 AUGUSTINY, J. Kambamärchen. AFR. UND UB. 15 (1924-1925), pp. 81-116, 213-223.

17,200 B., R. DE LA B. Nyanza lion hunters. TANG. NOTES 34 (1953), pp. 75-76.

17,201 BAGGE, S. The circumcision ceremony among the Naivasha Masai. JRAI 34 (1904), pp. 167-169.

17,202 BANOW, H. Status reversal and political reaction: a case study of the Masai of Kenya and Tanzania. EAISR Jan. (1965), pp. 1-8.

17,203 BARRETT, W. E. H. Notes on the customs and beliefs of the Wa-Giriama, etc., British East Africa. JRAI 41 (1911), pp. 20-39.

17,204 BARTON, J. Notes on the Kipsikis or Lumbwa tribe of Kenya colony. JRAI 53 (1923), pp. 42-78.

17,205 BARTON, J. Notes on the Suk tribe of Kenia colony. JRAI 51 (1921), pp. 82-99.

17,206 BARTON, J. Notes on the Turkana tribe of British East Africa. J. AFR. SOC. 20 (1921), pp. 107-115, 204-211.

17,207 BATES, J. D. Democracy among the Pare. CORONA 2 (1950), pp. 53-56.

17,208 BEECH, M. W. H. Sketch of Elgeyo law and custom. J. AFR. SOC. 20 (1921), pp. 195-203.

17,209 BEWES, T. F. C. Kikuyu religion, old and new. AFR. AFFAIRS 52 (1953), pp. 202-210.

17,210 CAGNOLO, C. Kikuyu tales. AFR. STUD. 11 (1952), pp. 1-15, 123-135; 12 (1953), pp. 10-21, 62-71, 122-131.

17,211 CONANT, F. P. Korok: a variable unit of physical and social space among the Pokot of East Africa. AMER. ANTHR. 67 (1965), pp. 429-434.

17,212 COPLAND, B. D. Note on the officials of the Kilindi Kingdom and the first rulers. SWAHILI 27 (1957), pp. 64-65.

17,213 DAMMANN, E. Digo—Märchen. AFR. UND UB. 26 (1935-1936), pp. 81-97, 202-231; 32 (1942), pp. 31-58.

17,214 DAMMANN, E. Erzählungen eines Digo zur Geschichte seines Stammes. AFR. UND UB. 29 (1939), pp. 293-311.

17,215 DANBY, P. M. A study of the physique of some native East Africans. JRAI 83 (1953), pp. 194-214.

17,216 DUNDAS, K. R. The Wawanga and other tribes of the Elgon district, British East Africa. JRAI 43 (1913), pp. 19-75.

17,217 EDGERTON, R. B. Pokot intersexuality: an East African example of the resolution of sexual incongruity. AMER. ANTHR. 66 (1964), pp. 1288-1299.

17,218 EDGERTON, R. B. and CONANT, F. P. Kilapat: the "shaming party" among the Pokot of East Africa. SOUTHWESTERN J. ANTHR. 20 (1964), pp. 404-418.

17,219 EMLEY, E. D. The Turkana of Kolosia District. JRAI 57 (1927), pp. 157-201.

17,220 EVANS-PRITCHARD, E. E. Luo tribes and clans. RHODES-LIV. J. 7 (1949), pp. 24-40.

17,221 EVANS-PRITCHARD, E. E. Marriage customs of the Luo of Kenya. AFRICA 20 (1950), pp. 132-142.

17,222 EVANS-PRITCHARD, E. E. The political structure of the Nandi-speaking peoples of Kenya. AFRICA 13 (1940), pp. 250-267.

17,223 FORAN, W. R. Imprints on the sands of time. AFR. AFFAIRS 56 (1957), pp. 68-80.

17,224 FOX, D. S. Further notes on the Masai of Kenya Colony. JRAI 60 (1930), pp. 447-465.

17,225 GERLACH, L. P. Some basic Digo conceptions of health and disease. EAISR Dec. (1959), pp. 9-34.

17,226 GRIFFITHS, J. B. Glimpses of a Nyika tribe (Waduruma). JRAI 65 (1935), pp. 267-296.

17,227 GULLIVER, P. H. Counting with the fingers by two East African tribes. TANGANYIKA NOTES AND RECORDS 51 (1958), pp. 259-262.

17,228 GULLIVER, P. H. The Karamajong cluster. AFRICA 22 (1952), pp. 1-22.

17,229 GULLIVER, P. H. Nomad anthropologist. CORONA 4 (1952), pp. 129-132.

17,230 GUTH, W. Der Asu-Gruss. AFR. UND UB. 30 (1940), pp. 148-160.

17,231 GUTH, W. Der Bodengott der Asu. AFRICA 12 (1939), pp. 450-459.

17,232 HARRIES, L. Swahili traditions of Mombasa. AFR. UND UB. 43 (1959-1960), pp. 81-105.

17,233 HARRIS, G. Possession "hysteria" in a Kenya tribe. AMER. ANTHR. 59 (1957), pp. 1046-1066.

17,234 HINAWIY, M. A. Notes on customs in Mombasa. SWAHILI 34, no. 1 (1964), pp. 17-35.

17,235 HOBLEY, C. W. Anthropological studies in Kavirondo and Nandi. JRAI 33 (1903), pp. 325-359.

17,236 HOBLEY, C. W. Further researches into Kikuyu and Kamba religious beliefs and customs. JRAI 41 (1911), pp. 406-457.

17,237 HOBLEY, C. W. Kikuyu customs and beliefs. Thahu and its connection with circumcision rites. JRAI 40 (1910), pp. 428-452.

17,238 HOBLEY, C. W. Some native problems in Eastern Africa. J. AFR. SOC. 22 (1923), pp. 189-202, 278-301.

17,239 HOLLIS, A. C. A note on the Masai system of relationship and other matters connected therewith. JRAI 40 (1910), pp. 473-482.

17,240 HOLLIS, A. C. Taveta enigmas. J. AFR. SOC. 10 (1911), pp. 200-212.

17,241 HOLLIS, Sir C. The Masai. J. AFR. SOC. 42 (1943), pp. 119-126.

17,242 HOMAN, F. D. Land consolidation and redistribution of population in the Imenti sub-tribe of the Meru (Kenya). AFR. AGRARIAN SYSTEMS, 1963, pp. 224-244.

17,243 HUNTINGFORD, G. W. B. Miscellaneous records relating to the Nandi and Kony tribes. JRAI 57 (1927), pp. 417-461.

17,244 HUNTINGFORD, G. W. B. The social organization of the Dorobo. AFR. STUD. 1 (1942), pp. 183-200.

17,245 JAMES, L. The Kenya Masai: a nomadic people under modern administration. AFRICA 12 (1939), pp. 49-72.

17,246 JOHANSSEN, E. and DORING, P. Das Leben der Schambala beleuchtet durch ihre Sprichworter. AFR. UND UB. 5 (1914-1915), pp. 137-150, 190-226, 306-318.

17,247 JOHNSTONE, H. B. Notes on the customs of the tribes occupying Mombasa sub-district, British East Africa. JRAI 32 (1902), pp. 263-272.

17,248 KENYATTA, J. Kikuyu religion, ancestor-worship, and sacrificial practices. AFRICA 10 (1937), pp. 308-328.

17,249 LA FONTAINE, S. H. Taveta customs and beliefs in connection with religion, burial, and disease. J. AFR. SOC. 13 (1914), pp. 385-394.

17,250 LEAKEY, L. S. B. The Kikuyu problem of the initiation of girls. JRAI 61 (1931), pp. 277-285.

17,251 LEAKEY, L. S. B. Some notes on the Masai of Kenya colony. JRAI 60 (1930), pp. 185-209.

17,252 LEAKEY, L. S. B. Some problems arising from the part played by goats and sheep in the social life of the Kikuyu. J. AFR. SOC. 33 (1934), pp. 70-79.

17,253 LEVINE, R. A. Witchcraft and co-wife proximity in Southwestern Kenya. ETHNOLOGY 1 (1962), pp. 39-45.

17,254 LEVINE, R. A. and SANGREE, W. H. The diffusion of age-group organization in East Africa. AFRICA 32 (1962), pp. 97-110.

17,255 McGLASHAN, N. Indigenous Kikuyu education. AFR. AFFAIRS 63 (1964), pp. 47-57.

17,256 MAYER, I. From kinship to common descent: four-generation genealogies among the Gusii. AFRICA 35 (1965), pp. 366-384.

17,257 MAYER, P. The joking of "pals" in Gusii age-sets. AFR. STUD. 10 (1951), pp. 27-41.

17,258 MAYER, P. Privileged obstruction of marriage rites among the Gusii. AFRICA 20 (1950), pp. 113-125.

17,259 MAYER, P. Two studies in applied anthropology in Kenya; a digest by the African Studies Branch. J. AFR. ADM. 3 (1951), pp. 135-137.

17,260 NEEDHAM, R. The left hand of the Mugwe: an analytical note on the structure of Meru symbolism. AFRICA 30 (1960), pp. 20-33.

17,261 NOTTINGHAM, J. C. Sorcery among the Akamba in Kenya. J. AFR. ADM. 11 (1959), pp. 2-14.

17,262 OLIVER, S. C. Individuality, freedom of choice, and cultural flexibility of the Kamba. AMER. ANTHR. 67 (1965), pp. 421-428.

17,263 ORCHARDSON, I. Q. Some traits of the Kipsigis in relation to their contact with Europeans. AFRICA 4 (1931), pp. 466-474.

17,264 ORDE-BROWNE, G. S. J. Mount Kenya and its people. Some notes on the Chuka tribe. J. AFR. SOC. 15 (1916), pp. 225-233.

17,265 PERISTIANY, J. G. The age-set system of the pastoral Pokot. AFRICA 21 (1951), pp. 188-206, 279-302.

17,266 PERISTIANY, J. G. Pokot sanctions and structure. AFRICA 24 (1954), pp. 17-25.

17,267 PRINS, A. H. J. An outline of the descent system of the Teita, a north-eastern Bantu tribe. AFRICA 20 (1950), pp. 26-37.

17,268 RAYNE, H. Turkana. J. AFR. SOC. 18 (1919), pp. 183-189, 254-265.

17,269 ROSCOE, J. Notes on the Bageshu. JRAI 39 (1909), pp. 181-196.

17,270 RUEL, M. J. Kuria generation classes. AFRICA 32 (1962), pp. 14-37.

17,271 RUEL, M. J. Kuria generation sets. EAISR Jan. (1958), pp. 1-16.

17,272 RUEL, M. J. Piercing. EAISR June (1958), pp. 1-15.

17,273 RUEL, M. J. Religion and society among the Kuria of East Africa. AFRICA 35 (1965), pp. 295-306.

17,274 SABERWAL, S. C. Some Embu social institutions: a preliminary report. EAISR June (1963), pp. 1-5.

17,275 SCHNEIDER, H. K. The subsistence role of cattle among the Pokot and in East Africa. AMER. ANTHR. 59 (1957), pp. 278-300.

17,276 SELIGMANN, C. G. Note on the preparation and use of the Kenya dart-poison ipoh. JRAI 32 (1902), pp. 239-244.

17,277 SHELFORD, F. Notes on the Masai. J. AFR. SOC. 9 (1910), pp. 267-269.

17,278 SPENCER, P. Samburu notions of health and disease and their relationship to inner cleanliness. EAISR Dec. (1959), pp. 95-97.

17,279 STEVENSON, M. S. Specimens of Kikuyu proverbs. FESTSCHRIFT MEINHOF, 1927, pp. 241-246.

17,280 TANNER, R. E. S. Cousin marriage in the Afro-Arab community of Mombasa, Kenya. AFRICA 34 (1964), pp. 127-138.

17,281 TATE, H. R. Further notes on the Kikuyu tribe of British East Africa. JRAI 34 (1904), pp. 255-265.

17,282 TATE, H. R. Further notes on the southern Gikuyu of British East Africa. J. AFR. SOC. 10 (1911), pp. 285-297.

17,283 TATE, H. R. Notes on the Kikuyu and Kamba tribes of British East Africa. JRAI 34 (1904), pp. 130-148.

17,284 THOMAS, D. K. Illegal hunting in Tanganyika. TANG. NOTES 61 (1963), pp. 190-194.

17,285 WAGNER, G. The changing family among the Bantu Kavirondo. AFRICA 12 (1939), no. 1 supplement.

17,286 WAGNER, G. The political organisation of the Bantu of Kavirondo. AFRICAN POLITICAL SYSTEMS, 1940, pp. 197-236.

17,287 WAGNER, G. The study of culture contact and the determination of policy. AFRICA 9 (1936), pp. 317-330.

17,288 WAGNER, G. Wesenszüge der politischen Struktur der Kavirondo-Bantu. AFRIKA (Berlin) 1 (1942), pp. 7-54.

17,289 WERNER, A. The Akikuyu. J. AFR. SOC. 10 (1911), pp. 447-458.

17,290 WERNER, A. The native tribes of British East Africa. J. AFR. SOC. 19 (1920), pp. 285-294.

17,291 WERNER, A. Some notes on the Wapokomo of the Tana valley. J. AFR. SOC. 12 (1913), pp. 359-384.

17,292 WHITE, R. F. Notes on the Turkana tribe. SUDAN NOTES 3 (1920), pp. 217-222.

See also 5617, 15825, 18812.

Art. Antiquities

17,293 HORNELL, J. The sea-going mtepe and dáu of the Lamu Archipelago. TANGANYIKA NOTES AND RECORDS 14 (1942), pp. 27-37.

17,294 HYSLOP, G. H. African musical instruments in Kenya. AFR. MUSIC, 1958, pp. 31-36.

17,295 HYSLOP, G. H. Brief report of a music course conducted at Siriba for the Nyanza Musical Society. AFR. MUSIC, 1955, pp. 58-59.

17,296 HYSLOP, G. H. Choice of music for festivals in Africa. AFR. MUSIC, 1955, pp. 53-55.

17,297 HYSLOP, G. H. Kenya's colony music and drama officer. AFR. MUSIC, 1958, pp. 37-39.

17,298 HYSLOP, G. H. More Kenya musical instruments. AFR. MUSIC, 1959, pp. 24-28.

17,299 KINGDON, J. and NEOGY, R. Gregory Maloba talks about his childhood and his growth as a sculptor... TRANSITION 11 (1963), pp. 20-22.

17,300 KIRKMAN, J. Kilwa: the cutting behind the defensive wall. TANGANYIKA NOTES AND RECORDS 50 (1958), pp. 94-101.

17,301 KIRKMAN, J. S. Archaeological research on the coast of Kenya. DISCOVERING AFRICA'S PAST, 1959, pp. 18-25.

17,302 LEAKEY, L. S. B. The environment of the Kenya Lower Miocene apes. PROC. PAN-AFR. CONGR. PRE-HIST. 2 (1952), pp. 323-324.

17,303 LEAKEY, L. S. B. The Olorgesailie prehistoric site. PROC. PAN-AFR. CONGR. PRE-HIST. 1 (1947), p. 209.

17,304 LEAKEY, L. S. B. The religious element in Mau Mau. AFR. MUSIC, 1954, p. 77.

17,305 OWEN, A. W. E. An amateur field collector in Kavirondo. J. AFR. SOC. 38 (1939), pp. 124-132; 39 (1940), pp. 220-226.

17,306 OWUOR, H. Luo songs. BO 10 (1961), pp. 51-56.

17,307 ROBERTS, J. Kenya's pop music. TRANSITION 19 (1965), pp. 40-43.

17,308 SWANZY, H. Prehistory. AFR. AFFAIRS 46 (1947), pp. 64-65.

17,309 TRACEY, A. Kamba carvers. AFR. MUSIC, 1960, pp. 55-58.

17,310 Report from the Jeanes School, Lower Kabete, Kenya. Report on teachers' vacation course in music 22nd August to 5th September, 1953. AFR. MUSIC, 1954, pp. 78-79.

17,311 The Stoneham museum. AFR. AFFAIRS 43 (1944), pp. 5-6.

See also 7592, 17028.

Biography

17,312 I morti italiani in East Africa riposano a Nyeri. AFRICA (Rome) 10 (1955), p. 81.

See also 9775.

Economics

17,313 ARKADIE, B. V. The structure of the Kenya economy. EAISR Jan. (1964), pp. 1-9.

17,314 B., L. Commentary on the Report of the Working Party on African Land Tenure in Kenya, 1957-58. J. AFR. ADM. 11 (1959), pp. 215-224.

17,315 BARWELL, C. W. A note on some changes in the economy of the Kipsigis tribe. J. AFR. ADM. 8 (1956), pp. 95-101.

17,316 BERNADI, B. La riforma terriera nel Kenya. AFRICA (Rome) 15 (1960), pp. 175-178.

17,317 BRANNEY, L. Towards the systematic individualization of African land tenure. The background to the Report of the Working Party on African Land Tenure in Kenya. J. AFR. ADM. 11 (1959), pp. 208-214.

17,318 BRETT, E. A. Economic policy in Kenya Colony: a study in the politics of resource allocation. EAISR Jan. (1965), pp. 1-8.

17,319 C., J. Le travail indigène au Kenya. ZAIRE 7 (1953), p. 865.

17,320 CLAYTON, E. S. Safeguarding agrarian development in Kenya. J. AFR. ADM. 11 (1959), pp. 144-150.

17,321 CLOUGH, R. H. Some notes on a recent economic survey of land settlement in Kenya. E. AFR. EC. REV. N.S. 1, no. 3 (1965), pp. 78-83.

17,322 ELKAN, W. The Kamba trade in wood carvings. EAISR Jan. (1958), pp. 1-21.

17,323 ETHERINGTON, D. M. Projected changes in urban and rural population in Kenya and the implications for development policy. EAISR Jan. (1965), pp. 1-9.

17,324 FOULKES, J. Suggestions for profitable enterprise in British East Africa. J. AFR. SOC. 4 (1905), pp. 434-436.

17,325 GERLACH, L. P. Traders on bicycle: a study of entrepreneurship and culture change among the Digo and Duruma of Kenya. SOCIOLOGUS 13 (1963), pp. 32-49.

17,326 GRAY, A. Kenya development. AFR. AFFAIRS 56 (1957), pp. 183-185.

17,327 GRAY, A. Kenya's economy. AFR. AFFAIRS 55 (1956), pp. 163-165.

17,328 GRIGG, E. Land policy and economic development in Kenya. J. AFR. SOC. 31 (1932), pp. 1-14.

17,329 HENNINGS, R. O. Foot safari. CORONA 1, no. 1 (1949), pp. 14-16.

17,330 HILL, M. F. The white settler's role in Kenya. FOREIGN AFFAIRS 38 (1959-1960), pp. 638-645.

17,331 HOMAN, F. D. Inheritance in the Kenya native land units. J. AFR. ADM. 10 (1958), pp. 131-135.

17,332 HOMAN, F. D. Succession to registered land in the African areas of Kenya. J. LOCAL ADM. OV. 2 (1963), pp. 49-54.

17,333 HOWE, C. W. and KARANI, H. A projection model for the Kenya economy: a study in development planning and comparative economic structures. E. AFR. EC. REV. N.S. 1, no. 2 (1965), pp. 21-31.

17,334 KAMAU, J. Problems of African business enterprise. EAISR Jan. (1965), pp. 1-6.

17,335 KARANI, H. and HOWE, C. A statistical projection model for the Kenya economy. EAISR Jan. (1965), pp. 1-8.

17,336 KENNEDY, T. A. Economic development in British East Africa. CIVILISATIONS 6 (1956), pp. 371-389; French summary, pp. 390-392.

17,337 KIBAKI, M. Manpower and economic development. PROBLEMS OF ECON. DEVELOPMENT IN E. AFR., 1965, pp. 79-82.

17,338 KRISHNA, K. G. V. The industrial sector in Kenya's plan: some comments. EAISR Jan. (1965), pp. 1-7.

17,339 McWILLIAM, M. D. Economic viability and the race factor in Kenya. ECON. DEVELOPMENT AND CULTURAL CHANGE 12 (1963-1964), pp. 55-69.

17,340 McWILLIAM, M. D. The World Bank and the transfer of power in Kenya. J. COMM. POL. STUD. 2 (1963-1964), pp. 165-169.

17,341 MASSEI, E. Il Kenya: che cos'è-che cosa può essere. AFRICA (Rome) 12 (1957), pp. 172-174.

17,342 MBOYA, T. Trade unionism in Kenya. AFR. SOUTH 1, no. 2 (1957), pp. 77-86.

17,343 MOODY, R. W. Labour migration in Samia. EAISR Jan. (1962), pp. 1-7.

17,344 PEDRAZA, G. J. W. Land consolidation in the Kikuyu areas of Kenya. J. AFR. ADM. 8 (1956), pp. 82-87.

17,345 REBELO, J. S. O chá na economia do Quénia (um estudo economico). BSEM 142 (1965), pp. 137-163; includes English summary.

17,346 RUBIO GARCIA, L. R. Una experiencia y una lección del Africa negra Kenya. CUAD. EST. AFR. 28 (1954), pp. 29-51.

17,347 SILLITOE, K. K. Land and the community in Nyeri. EAISR Jan. (1963), pp. 1-14.

17,348 SILLITOE, K. K. Preliminary notes on the sociological and economic aspects of land tenure and usage in Meru district, Kenya. EAISR Jan. (1962), pp. 1-10.

17,349 SMITH, E. W. Land in Kenya. J. AFR. SOC. 35 (1936), pp. 246-250.

17,350 SORRENSEN, M. P. K. Counter revolution in Mau Mau: land consolidation in Kikuyuland, 1952-1960. EAISR June (1963), pp. 1-13.

17,351 SPELLER, C. Land policy and economic development in Kenya. J. AFR. SOC. 30 (1931), pp. 377-385.

17,352 STORRAR, A. A guide to the principles and practices of land settlement in Kenya. J. LOCAL ADM. OV. 3 (1964), pp. 14-19.

17,353 SYTEK, W. L. Social factors in Luo land consolidation. EAISR Jan. (1965), p. 1.

17,354 TANNER, R. E. S. Cousin marriage in the Kenya Afro-Arab community. EAISR July (1962), pp. 1-11.

17,355 VASEY, E. A. Economic and political trends in Kenya. AFR. AFFAIRS 55 (1956), pp. 101-108.

17,356 WATKINS, O. F. The report of the Kenya Land Commission, September, 1933. J. AFR. SOC. 33 (1934), pp. 207-216.

17,357 WATT, K. S. African coffee. J. AFR. SOC. 36 (1937), pp. 194-200.

17,358 WEST, R. L. Estimates of national accounts for Kenya 1923-1939. E. AFR. EC. REV. N.S. 1, no. 3 (1965), pp. 23-45.

17,359 WHEELER, S. H. Sisal planting in B.E.A. J. AFR. SOC. 17 (1918), pp. 314-318.

17,360 WHITEHOUSE, G. C. The building of Kenya and Uganda railway. UGANDA J. 12 (1948), pp. 1-15.

17,361 WIGGLESWORTH, A. Kenya's tribulation. J. AFR. SOC. 21 (1922), pp. 217-221.

17,362 WILSON, R. G. Land consolidation in the Fort Hall District of Kenya. J. AFR. ADM. 8 (1956), pp. 144-151.

17,363 African labour efficiency [summary of survey by C. H. Northcott]. AFR. AFFAIRS 48 (1949), pp. 234-239.

17,364 Centre for economic research, Nairobi. AFR. STUD. BULL. 7, no. iii (1964), pp. 18-19.

17,365 Land tenure and control outside native lands. J. AFR. ADM. 12 (1960), pp. 53-56; 13 (1961), p. 60.

17,366 Land titles in Native Land Units (a report by a sub-committee of the Kenya African Affairs Committee). J. AFR. ADM. 2 (1950), pp. 19-24.

17,367 Trade of East Africa. ECON. BULL. AFR. 2, no. 1 (1962), pp. B23-B56.

See also 16654, 18989.

Education

17,368 ASKWITH, T. G. Training for Local Government at Jeanes' School. J. AFR. ADM. 3 (1951), pp. 162-165.

17,369 BELCHER, A. The future of pottery for African women. AFR. WOMEN 2 (1956-1958), pp. 28-29.

17,370 DOUGALL, J. W. C. School education and native life. AFRICA 3 (1930), pp. 49-57.

17,371 HOLDING, M. Central, local and voluntary initiative in Meru, Kenya. TOWARDS A LITERATE AFRICA, 1948, pp. 54-61.

17,372 LIENHARDT, P. The mosque college of Lamu and its social background. TANGANYIKA NOTES AND RECORDS 53 (1959), pp. 228-242.

17,373 OLIVER, R. A. C. Mental tests in the study of the African. AFRICA 7 (1934), pp. 40-46.

17,374 SHRUBSOLE, A. C. Some problems of teacher education in a rapidly changing African society. WOMEN TODAY 6 (1965), pp. 97-99.

17,375 WAMUYU, C. D. Audio-visual aids in formal education. AFR. WOMEN 5 (1962), pp. 7-9.

17,376 WEEKS, S. G. A preliminary report on a sociological case study of an urban day secondary school. EAISR Jan. (1963), pp. 1-11.

17,377 Progress [of African women] in Kenya. AFR. WOMEN 1 (1954), pp. 14-15.

17,378 Training of ex-servicemen at Kabete. CORONA 1, no. 2 (1949), pp. 15-17.

17,379 A visit to Nairobi. AFR. WOMEN 1 (1955), pp. 59-61.

17,380 Women in Kenya cotton campaign. AFR. WOMEN 3 (1958-1960), pp. 10-11.

See also 17561.

Geography

17,381 BRISTOW, C. M. A visit to Oldonyo Lengai on Sunday, June 26th, 1960. TANGANYIKA NOTES AND RECORDS 58/59 (1962), pp. 119-123.

17,382 FLETCHER, J. and HANGARTNER, R. Oldonyo Lengai. TANGANYIKA NOTES AND RECORDS 58/59 (1962), pp. 116-118.

17,383 FOSBROOKE, H. A. Richard Thornton in East Africa. TANGANYIKA NOTES AND RECORDS 58/59 (1962), pp. 43-63.

17,384 MUNGER, E. S. Water problems of Kitui district, Kenya. GEOG. REV. 40 (1950), pp. 575-582.

17,385 PARKINSON, J. Problems of geology in British East Africa ("Kenya Colony"). J. AFR. SOC. 21 (1922), pp. 105-114.

17,386 PORTER, P. W. Environmental potentials and economic opportunities—a background for cultural adaptation. AMER. ANTHR. 67 (1965), pp. 409-420.

17,387 SADLER, E. H. Notes on the geography of British East Africa. J. AFR. SOC. 11 (1912), pp. 173-186.

17,388 SARGENT, D. Sketches from Mariakani. AFR. AFFAIRS 50 (1951), pp. 63-70.

17,389 THOMAS, H. B. George Wilson and Dagoretti Fort. UGANDA J. 23 (1959), pp. 173-177.

See also 18106.

Government. Politics. Administration. Mau Mau

17,390 AINSLIE, R. An African diary. AFR. SOUTH 3, no. 1 (1958), pp. 61-68.

17,391 ALPORT, C. J. M. Kenya's answer to the Mau Mau challenge AFR. AFFAIRS 53 (1954), pp. 241-248.

17,392 ALTORFER, A. Financial officers in the Ministry of Local Government, Kenya. J. AFR. ADM. 13 (1961), pp. 11-23.

17,393 ASKWITH, T. Course for chiefs in Kenya. CORONA 3 (1951), pp. 106-107.

17,394 BLOUNT, B. G. Tribalism in Kenya politics. PROC. 3RD. GRAD. UCLA, 1965, pp. 183-192.

17,395 BLUNDELL, M. Making a nation in Kenya. AFR. AFFAIRS 58 (1959), pp. 221-228.

17,396 BROCKWAY, F. Les revendications agraires africaines au Kenya. PRESENCE AFR. 13 (1952), pp. 186-192.

17,397 BROWN, P. H. Stock reduction in Nandi. J. AFR. ADM. 10 (1958), pp. 25-33.

17,398 BROWN, R. T. Local Government in the African areas of Kenya. J. AFR. ADM. 12 (1960), pp. 147-149.

17,399 C., J. Déclarations du ministère du Kénya. ZAIRE 8 (1954), p. 950.

17,400 C., J. Nouvelle phase de la crise au Kenya. ZAIRE 7 (1953), pp. 643-644.

17,401 C., J. Réunion du parlement du Kenya. ZAIRE 8 (1954), p. 635.

17,402 CASTAGNO, A. A. The Somali-Kenyan controversy: implications for the future. JMAS 2 (1964), pp. 165-188.

17,403 CHAMBERS, R. J. H. The use of case studies in public administration training in Kenya. J. LOCAL ADM. OV. 3 (1964), pp. 169-174.

17,404 COLCHESTER, T. C. The Kenya Local Native Council budgets for 1949. J. AFR. ADM. 1 (1949), pp. 106-114.

17,405 CORFIELD, F. D. Historical Survey of the Origins and Growth of Mau Mau [a survey commissioned by the Kenya Government]. J. AFR. ADM. 12 (1960), pp. 250-257.

17,406 COWLEY, K. The Native Authority system in Kenya. EAISR June (1952), pp. 1-6.

17,407 DAVIDSON, B. The Kenya crisis [The Mau Mau rebellion]. AFR. SOUTH 1, no. 3 (1957), pp. 68-73.

17,408 DESSY, G. B. Considerazioni sul fenomeno Mau Mau. AFRICA (Rome) 10 (1955), pp. 86-87.

17,409 ENGLAND, J. O. Graduated personal tax in Kenya. J. LOCAL ADM. OV. 3 (1964), pp. 204-213.

17,410 EVANS, C. Police dogs in Kenya. CORONA 3 (1951), pp. 187-189.

17,411 EVANS, M. N. Local Government in the African areas of Kenya. J. AFR. ADM. 7 (1955), pp. 123-127.

17,412 FALLERS, L. A. Village chiefs in Busoga. EAISR June (1952), pp. 19-27.

17,413 FANE, R. Nationalism in Kenya. AFR. AFFAIRS 55 (1956), pp. 294-296.

17,414 FILESI, T. Ed ora parliamo male del Kenya. AFRICA (Rome) 10 (1955), pp. 25-26.

17,415 FILETEO. Kenya in chiave marxista. AFRICA (Rome) 10 (1955), pp. 143-144.

17,416 FULLER, C. and CHAMBERS, R. Training for the administration of development in Kenya. J. LOCAL ADM. OV. 4 (1965), pp. 109-117.

17,417 GERTZEL, C. Regional administration in Kenya 1963-1964. EAISR Jan. (1965), pp. 1-5.

17,418 GHAI, Y. Kenya's socialism. TRANSITION 20 (1965), pp. 20-23.

17,419 GILL, R. W. The problem of the minor chiefs. EAISR June (1952), pp. 15-18.

17,420 GRAY, A. Hola tragedy. AFR. AFFAIRS 58 (1959), pp. 273-276.

17,421 GRAY, A. Kenya advances. AFR. AFFAIRS 59 (1960), pp. 188-191.

17,422 GRAY, A. Kenya constitution. AFR. AFFAIRS 57 (1958), pp. 89-91.

17,423 GRAY, A. Kenya developments. AFR. AFFAIRS 60 (1961), pp. 476-478.

17,424 GRAY, A. Kenya differences. AFR. AFFAIRS 60 (1961), pp. 379-380.

17,425 GRAY, A. Kenya elections. AFR. AFFAIRS 57 (1958), pp. 178-180; 60 (1961), pp. 135-136.

17,426 GRAY, A. Kenya improvements. AFR. AFFAIRS 56 (1957), pp. 8-11.

17,427 GRAY, A. Kenya politics. AFR. AFFAIRS 58 (1959), pp. 8-10.

17,428 GRAY, A. Kenya problems. AFR. AFFAIRS 61 (1962), pp. 11-12.

17,429 GRAY, A. Kenya relaxes. AFR. AFFAIRS 56 (1957), pp. 97-99.

17,430 GRAY, A. The Kenya scene. AFR. AFFAIRS 58 (1959), pp. 205-207.

17,431 GRAY, A. Kenya state council. AFR. AFFAIRS 57 (1958), pp. 257-261.

17,432 GRAY, A. Kenya talks [and a new constitution]. AFR. AFFAIRS 59 (1960), pp. 93-95.

17,433 GRAY, A. Kenya vote plan. AFR. AFFAIRS 55 (1956), pp. 175-177.

17,434 GRAY, A. Last phase in Kenya [of the fight against Mau-Mau]. AFR. AFFAIRS 54 (1955), pp. 166-167.

17,435 GRAY, A. Mau Mau in retreat. AFR. AFFAIRS 54 (1955), pp. 250-251.

17,436 GRAY, A. Mau Mau origins. AFR. AFFAIRS 59 (1960), pp. 276-279.

17,437 GRAY, A. Mau Mau reviewed. AFR. AFFAIRS 55 (1956), pp. 5-6.

17,438 GRAY, A. Mercy for Mau Mau. AFR. AFFAIRS 54 (1955), pp. 83-84.

17,439 GRAY, A. New Kenya settlement. AFR. AFFAIRS 57 (1958), pp. 2-3.

17,440 GRAY, A. Progress in Kenya. AFR. AFFAIRS 59 (1960), pp. 3-5.

17,441 GRAY, A. Queen Mother's tour. AFR. AFFAIRS 58 (1959), pp. 95-97.

17,442 GRAY, A. Report on Kenya. AFR. AFFAIRS 56 (1957), p. 253.

17,443 GRAY, A. Two years of Mau Mau. AFR. AFFAIRS 54 (1955), pp. 2-4.

17,444 GRIGG, E. British policy in Kenya. J. AFR. SOC. 26 (1927), pp. 193-208.

17,445 GUPTA, V. P. Kenya's struggle for freedom. AFR. QUART. 3, no. iv (1964), pp. 210-224.

17,446 H., R. S. The Kenya Coastal Strip: Report of the Commissioner [Sir James Robertson]. J. LOCAL ADM. OV. 1 (1962), pp. 128-131.

17,447 HANNIGAN, A. S. J. The role of rural Local Government in an independent Kenya. J. LOCAL ADM. OV. 4 (1965), pp. 165-172.

17,448 HARRIS, G. The position of lower chiefs in Taita. EAISR June (1952), pp. 6-14.

17,449 HARRIS, J. H. The challenge of Kenya. CONTEMP. REV. 138 (1930), pp. 598-604.

17,450 HENNINGS, R. O. Grazing management in the pastoral areas of Kenya. J. AFR. ADM. 13 (1961), pp. 191-203.

17,451 HOWES, R. J. C. A Kenya experiment in training for Local Government. J. AFR. ADM. 3 (1951), pp. 87-90.

17,452 KENYA. Framework of the Kenya constitution. AFR. QUART. 2, no. i (1962), pp. 59-64.

17,453 KENYA. MINISTRY OF AGRICULTURE. African Land Development in Kenya, 1946-1955. J. AFR. ADM. 9 (1957), p. 156.

17,454 KIANO, G. Political trends in Kenya. AFR. SOUTH 3, no. 1 (1958), pp. 69-76.

17,455 KNOWLES, E. J. F. Foundations of government in Kenya. J. AFR. ADM. 6 (1954), pp. 137-139.

17,456 M., V. La leçon du Kenya [le mouvement Mau Mau]. AEQUATORIA 19 (1956), pp. 103-105.

17,457 MBOYA, T. African socialism. TRANSITION 8 (1963), pp. 17-19.

17,458 MBOYA, T. The future of Kenya. AFR. AFFAIRS 63 (1964), pp. 6-12.

17,459 MBOYA, T. Kenya at the cross-roads. AFR. SOUTH 3, no. 4 (1959), pp. 94-98.

17,460 MUSTOE, K. W. L. The audit of African District Council accounts in Kenya. J. AFR. ADM. 13 (1961), pp. 139-147.

17,461 NAZARETH, J. M. Minority rights in Kenya. AFR. SOUTH 4, no. 2 (1960), pp. 87-91.

17,462 NYAMWEYA, J. The constitution of Kenya. CIVILISATIONS 14 (1964), pp. 331-338; French summary, pp. 339-341.

17,463 O'HAGAN, D. African's part in Nairobi Local Government. J. AFR. ADM. 1 (1949), pp. 156-158.

17,464 PARKER, M. Municipal government and the growth of African municipal institutions in the urban areas of Kenya. ZAIRE 3 (1949), pp. 649-662.

17,465 PELHAM-BURN, H. Kenya and Kenyatta. CONTEMP. REV. 204 (1963), pp. 205-208.

17,466 PENWILL, D. J. Paper—the other side. J. AFR. ADM. 6 (1954), pp. 115-123.

17,467 PENWILL, D. J. Sub-chiefs in Kikuyu and Ukambani. EAISR June (1952), pp. 60-68.

17,468 PHADNIS, U. N. Contemporary Kenya and Jomo Kenyatta. AFR. QUART. 3, no. iii (1963), pp. 156-163.

17,469 PICH, V. M. La fine dei Mau Mau. AFRICA (Rome) 15 (1960), pp. 79-80.

17,470 POWER, M. G. English Local Government in Taita District, Kenya. J. AFR. ADM. 6 (1954), pp. 28-38.

17,471 PROSSER, R. C. Training for Local Government. J. AFR. ADM. 13 (1961), pp. 98-104.

17,472 SALVADORI, M. W. Back from Kenya: by a Kenya farmer. CONTEMP. REV. 151 (1937), pp. 728-736.

17,473 SANGER, C. and NOTTINGHAM, J. The Kenya general election of 1963. JMAS 2 (1964), pp. 1-40.

17,474 SEELY, H. C. Local Government development finance (Kenya). J. LOCAL ADM. OV. 3 (1964), pp. 191-203.

17,475 SILLITOE, K. K. Local organisation in Nyeri. EAISR July (1962), pp. 1-8.

17,476 SIMMANCE, A. J. F. The Kenya Institute of Administration. J. LOCAL ADM. OV. 3 (1964), pp. 164-168.

17,477 WERLIN, H. The Nairobi City Council: a study in comparative local government. PROC. 3RD. GRAD. ACAD. UCLA, 1965, pp. 239-261.

17,478 WERLIN, H. The politics of Nairobi. EAISR Jan. (1964), pp. 1-11.

17,479 WHITELEY, W. H. Language and politics in East Africa. TANGANYIKA NOTES AND RECORDS 47-48 (1957), pp. 159-173.

17,480 WHITTLESEY, D. Kenya, the land and Mau Mau. FOREIGN AFFAIRS 32 (1953-1954), pp. 80-90.

17,481 WYATT, E. G. Mau Mau and the African mind. CONTEMP. REV. 184 (1953), pp. 206-211.

17,482 L'administration indigène à Nairobi. ZAIRE 5 (1951), pp. 1067-1069.

17,483 Annual Report of the Social Services and Housing Department of Nairobi City Council, 1958. J. AFR. ADM. 12 (1960), p. 53.

17,484 Les districts du Nord-Est du Kénya. GENEVE-AFR. 2 (1963), pp. 84-85.

17,485 Extension de la crise au Kenya. ZAIRE 6 (1952), p. 973.

17,486 A graduated personal tax for rural Local Government in Kenya. J. LOCAL ADM. OV. 3 (1964), pp. 45-52.

17,487 Le Kenya accède a l'indépendance. PRESENCE AFR. N.S. 49 (1964), pp. 225-228.

17,488 Kenya colony and protectorate. Native affairs department annual report, 1934. J. AFR. SOC. 35 (1936), pp. 440-443.

17,489 Kenya Constitution—1. Regions and Local Government. 2. The present and future pattern of public authorities. J. LOCAL ADM. OV. 2 (1963), pp. 160-166.

17,490 La Kenya lendemain de la conference constitutionnelle. PRESENCE AFR. N.S. 41 (1962), pp. 171-173.

17,491 The Kenya question mark. AFR. SOUTH 5, no. 4 (1961), pp. 86-91.

17,492 Kenya [une conférence constitutionnelle]. PRESENCE AFR. N.S. 30 (1960), pp. 100-102.

17,493 Local Government finance in Kenya. J. LOCAL ADM. OV. 2 (1963), pp. 233-237.

17,494 Native affairs in Kenya. Annual report of the Native Affairs department of Kenya colony and protectorate, 1932. J. AFR. SOC. 33 (1934), pp. 404-410.

17,495 North Nyanza local native council budget. AFR. AFFAIRS 48 (1949), pp. 311-317.

17,496 Politique et ethnographie au Kenya. ZAIRE 5 (1951), p. 859.

17,497 La politique raciale au Kénya. ZAIRE 5 (1951), pp. 627-628.

17,498 The reconstitution of local authorities [in Kenya]. J. LOCAL ADM. OV. 1 (1962), pp. 62-67.

17,499 Report of Committee on Agricultural Credit for Africans. J. AFR. ADM. 3 (1951), pp. 100-101.

17,500 Report of the Commission of Inquiry into alleged corruption or other malpractices in relation to the Affairs of the Nairobi City Council. J. AFR. ADM. 8 (1956), pp. 210-212.

17,501 Report of the Land Development Board (non-scheduled areas) 1957-58. J. AFR. ADM. 12 (1960), pp. 51-52.

17,502 Road Authority Annual Report 1958/59. J. AFR. ADM. 13 (1961), pp. 123-126.

See also 10415, 17100.

History

17,503 BEACHEY, R. W. Freeland: a socialist experiment in East Africa—1894. MAKERERE J. 2 (1959), pp. 56-68.

17,504 BENNETT, G. Kenyatta and the Kikuyu [review article on Jomo Kenyatta: Towards truth about The Light of Kenya by George Delf and East African Rebels: A Study of Some Independent Churches by F. B. Welbourn]. INTERNAT. AFFAIRS 37 (1961), pp. 477-482.

17,505 BENNETT, G. Pre-independence Kenya. CIVILISATIONS 13 (1963), pp. 122-132; French summary, pp. 133-135.

17,506 BENNETT, N. R. The Church Missionary Society at Mombasa 1873-1894. BOSTON UNIV. PAPERS IN AFR. HIST. 1 (1964), pp. 157-194.

17,507 BLUNDELL, M. The present situation in Kenya. AFR. AFFAIRS 54 (1955), pp. 99-108.

17,508 BOXER, C. R. Portuguese in the land of Zanj. HISTORY TODAY 9 (1959), pp. 752-759.

17,509 CASHMORE, T. H. R. A note on the chronology of the Wanyika of the Kenya coast. TANGANYIKA NOTES AND RECORDS 57 (1961), pp. 152-172.

17,510 CHHABRA, H. S. Kenya: a new nation is born. AFRO-ASIAN AND W. AFF. 1 (1964), pp. 77-85.

17,511 CHITTICK, N. British Institute of History and Archaeology (Nairobi). BULL. AFR. STUD. ASSOC. 5 (1965), pp. 9-11.

17,512 F., T. Contradittorio Kenya. AFRICA (Rome) 12 (1957), pp. 175-176.

17,513 FEARN, H. The gold-mining era in Kenya Colony. J. TROP. GEOG. 11 (1958), pp. 43-58.

17,514 FREEMAN-GRENVILLE, G. S. P. The Augustinian missions in East Africa, 1596-1730. UNIV. GHANA RES. REV. 1 (1965), pp. 36-37.

17,515 FREEMAN-GRENVILLE, G. S. P. The chronology of the Sultans of Kilwa. TANGANYIKA NOTES AND RECORDS 50 (1958), pp. 85-93.

17,516 FREEMAN-GRENVILLE, G. S. P. The history of Pate, Kenya. UNIV. GHANA RES. REV. 1 (1965), pp. 38-39.

17,517 GRAY, Sir J. M. Portuguese records relating to the Wasegeju. TANG. NOTES 29 (1950), pp. 85-97.

17,518 HALL, B. E. F. How peace came to Kikuyu. Extracts of letters from Francis George Hall. J. AFR. SOC. 37 (1938), pp. 432-448.

17,519 HARRIS, J. H. Making the lazy nigger work. CONTEMP. REV. 105 (1914), pp. 819-825.

17,520 HATCHELL, G. W. The boundary between Tanganyika and Kenya. TANGANYIKA NOTES AND RECORDS 43 (1956), p. 41.

17,521 HICHENS, W. Khabar al-Lamu, a chronicle of Lamu by Shaibu Faraji bin Hamed al-Bakariy al-Lamuy. BANTU STUD. 12 (1938), pp. 1-33.

17,522 HOLLIS, C. Notes on the history and customs of the people of Taveta, East Africa. J. AFR. SOC. 1 (1901), pp. 98-125.

17,523 JACKSON, Sir F. J. The ghost of Leven House, Mombasa. UGANDA J. 15 (1951), pp. 159-164.

17,524 JOHNSTON, A. The colonization of British East Africa. J. AFR. SOC. 5 (1905), pp. 28-37.

17,525 LONSDALE, J. M. Archdeacon Owen and the Kavirondo Taxpayers Welfare Association. EAISR Jan. (1963), pp. 1-16.

17,526 MAZRUI, A. On heroes and uhuru-worship. TRANSITION 11 (1963), pp. 23-28.

17,527 OGOT, A. How Kenya became a blackman's country [review article on Kenya, a political history: the colonial period]. TRANSITION 14 (1964), p. 48.

17,528 OGOT, B. A. British administration in the central Nyasaland district of Kenya, 1900-60. J. AFR. HIST. 4 (1963), pp. 249-273.

17,529 OMARI BIN STAMBOUL. An early history of Mombasa and Tanga. TANG. NOTES 31 (1951), pp. 32-36.

17,530 PROTHERO, M. The Kenya controversy. CONTEMP. REV. 123 (1923), pp. 198-204.

17,531 RENISON, Sir P. Kenya in transition. AFR. AFFAIRS 62 (1963), pp. 341-355.

17,532 SCOTT, H. S. European settlement and native development in Kenya. J. AFR. SOC. 35 (1936), pp. 178-190.

17,533 SORRENSON, M. The official mind and Kikuyu land tenure, 1895-1939. EAISR Jan. (1963), pp. 1-12.

17,534 T., H. R. The opening up of British East Africa. J. AFR. SOC. 4 (1904), pp. 44-55.

17,535 THOMAS, H. B. The Kenya History Society. UGANDA J. 22 (1958), pp. 181-183.

17,536 WALLBANK, T. W. American reflections on Kenya. J. AFR. SOC. 37 (1938), supplement.

17,537 WERNER, A. A Swahili history of Pate. J. AFR. SOC. 14 (1914-1915), pp. 148-161, 278-297, 392-413.

17,538 British Institute of History and Archaeology in East Africa. BULL. AFR. STUD. ASSOC. 1 (1964), pp. 15-18.

See also 16801, 18230, 19181.

Language. Literature

Language

17,539 AUGUSTINY, J. Erlebnisse eines Kambajungen. AFR. UND UB. 10 (1919-1920), pp. 161-180.

17,540 BARLOW, A. R. The spelling of "Kenya." J. AFR. SOC. 42 (1943), pp. 72-75.

17,541 BARLOW, A. R. The use of the copula with the Kikuyu verb. FESTSCHRIFT MEINHOF, 1927, pp. 223-227.

17,542 BEECHER, L. J. The stories of the Kikuyu. AFRICA 11 (1938), pp. 80-87.

17,543 BOCKING. Sagen der Wa-Pokomo. ZAOS 2 (1896), pp. 33-39.

17,544 BULL, A. F. Asu (Pare) proverbs and songs. AFRICA 6 (1933), pp. 323-328.

17,545 BUSSE, J. Inamwanga-Texte. AFR. UND UB. 27 (1936-1937), pp. 241-261.

17,546 BUSSE, J. Lautlehre des Inamwanga. AFR. UND UB. 31 (1941), pp. 21-50.

17,547 COPLAND, B. D. A note on the origin of the Mbugu with a text. AFR. UND UB. 24 (1933-1934), pp. 241-245.

17,548 DAMMANN, E. Einige Notizen über die Sprache der Sanye (Kenya). AFR. UND UB. 35 (1949-1950), pp. 227-234.

17,549 DAMMANN, E. Ein Nachtrag zur Geschichte der Digo. AFR. UND UB. 44 (1960), pp. 37-40.

17,550 DAMMANN, E. Schwangerschaft, Geburt und Aufzucht der Kleinkinder bei den Digo. AFR. UND UB. 44 (1960), pp. 93-109.

17,551 GREENBERG, J. H. The Mogogodo, a forgotten Cushitic people. J. AFR. LANGS. 2 (1963), pp. 29-43.

17,552 GREENBERG, J. H. The origin of the Masai passive. AFRICA 29 (1959), pp. 171-175.

17,553 HARRIES, L. Some tonal principles of the Kikuyu language. WORD 8 (1952), pp. 140-144; also in AFR. STUD. 13 (1954), pp. 41-44.

17,554 HOHENBERGER, J. Comparative Masai word list: Nilotic-Nilo-Hamitic-Masai-Hamitic-Semitic. AFRICA 26 (1956), pp. 281-287.

17,555 HOHENBERGER, J. Zur Lautlehre und Grammatik des Asu. AFR. UND UB. 20 (1929-1930), pp. 175-208.

17,556 HOLLIS, A. C. Taveta sayings and proverbs. J. AFR. SOC. 9 (1910), pp. 255-266.

17,557 HUNTINGFORD, G. W. B. Nandi place-names. AFR. LANG. STUD. 2 (1961), pp. 64-79.

17,558 HUNTINGFORD, G. W. B. Studies in Nandi etymology. BIBLIOTHECA AFR. 3 (1929), pp. 35-50, 146-160; 3 (1929-1930), pp. 317-326.

17,559 ITOTIA, J. The voice of Africa: Kikuyu proverbs translated and explained by James W. C. Dougall. AFRICA 1 (1928), pp. 486-490.

17,560 KOPOKA, O. B. English as a lingua franca in Kenya. SWAHILI 24 (1954), pp. 76-81.

17,561 LAUGHTON, W. H. The teaching of African languages in schools: a note on the position in Kenya. AFRICA 11 (1937), pp. 221-225.

17,562 LYNE, R. N. The spelling of Kenya. J. AFR. SOC. 41 (1942), p. 46, 259-260; 42 (1943), pp. 42-44.

17,563 MBITI, J. S. "L'éveil de la littérature indigène de la tribu akamba." PRESENCE AFR. N.S. 24-25 (1959), pp. 231-248.

17,564 NDUMBU, J. M. G. and WHITELEY, W. H. Some problems of stability and emphasis in Kamba one-word tenses. J. AFR. LANGS. 1 (1962), pp. 167-180.

17,565 RAUM, J. Einige Masai-Märchen in Kimadshame. ZAOS 4 (1898), pp. 124-132.

17,566 SHARP, A. E. Vowel-length and syllabicity in Kikuyu. AFR. LANG. STUD. 1 (1960), pp. 42-59.

17,567 TUCKER, A. N. and BRYAN, M. A. Noun classification in Kalenjin: Nandi-Kipsigis. AFR. LANG. STUD. 5 (1964), pp. 192-247; 6 (1965), pp. 117-187.

17,568 WERNER, A. Giryama Texte: In Britisch-Ostafrika gesammelt. AFR. UND UB. 5 (1914-1915), pp. 1-25.

17,569 WHITELEY, W. H. Loan-words in Kamba: a preliminary survey. AFR. LANG. STUD. 4 (1963), pp. 146-165.

17,570 WILLIAMSON, J. Dabida numerals. AFR. STUD. 2 (1943), pp. 215-216.

17,571 WURTZ, F. Grammatik des Pokomo. ZAOS 2 (1896), pp. 62-79, 168-194.

17,572 WURTZ, F. Lieder der Pokomo. ZAOS 1 (1895), pp. 324-328.

17,573 WURTZ, F. Wörterbuch des Ki-Tikuu und des Ki-Pokomo. ZAOS 1 (1895), pp. 193-230, 289-313.

See also 16845.

Literature

17,574 BOTO, E. "Sans haine et sans amour." PRESENCE AFR. 14 (1953), pp. 213-220.

17,575 GUILLEN, N. Mau-Mau. PRESENCE AFR. N.S. 1 (1955), pp. 109-112.

17,576 MBITI, J. S. The brink of youth [a poem]. AFRICA (Rome) 13 (1958), pp. 183-184.

17,577 MBITI, J. S. The heat of Port Sudan [a poem]. AFRICA (Rome) 13 (1958), p. 183.

17,578 NGUGI, J. T. The return [fiction]. TRANSITION 3 (1962), pp. 5-7.

17,579 NJAU, R. Muma. PRESENCE AFR. N.S. 50 (1964), pp. 215-220.

17,580 NJAU, R. The scar: a tragedy. TRANSITION 8 (1963), pp. 23-29.

17,581 RICHARDS, C. G. The East African Literature Bureau. UNESCO BULL. LIBS. 15 (1961), pp. 237-238.

17,582 RUORO, P. Two women [fiction]. TRANSITION 20 (1965), pp. 43-45.

17,583 SOYINKA, W. Luo plains (Kenya) [a poem]. TRANSITION 13 (1964), p. 17.

Law

17,584 THE AFRICAN STUDIES BRANCH. Developments in the administration of customary law in Kenya. J. AFR. ADM. 1 (1949), pp. 86-88.

17,585 BEECH, M. H. Kikuyu system of land tenure. J. AFR. SOC. 17 (1917), pp. 46-59, 136-144.

17,586 CARSON, J. B. Further notes on the African courts system in Kenya. J. AFR. ADM. 10 (1958), pp. 34-38.

17,587 COTRAN, E. African Courts (Amendment) Ordinance No. 50 of 1962. J. AFR. LAW 7 (1963), pp. 187-191.

17,588 COTRAN, E. Report of customary criminal offences in Kenya. J. LOCAL ADM. OV. 2 (1963), p. 175.

17,589 FLIEDNER, H. Some legal aspects of land reform in Kenya. EAISR June (1963), pp. 1-10.

17,590 HANNIGAN, A. S. J. The Royal College, Nairobi. J. AFR. LAW 6 (1962), p. 115.

17,591 HANNIGAN, A. S. J. The state and the rights of the individual. EAISR Jan. (1964), pp. 1-8.

17,592 HARRIS, A. and HARRIS, G. Property and the cycle of domestic groups in Taita. THE FAMILY ESTATE IN AFRICA, 1964, pp. 117-153.

17,593 HENNINGS, R. O. Some trends and problems of African land tenure in Kenya. J. AFR. ADM. 4 (1952), pp. 122-134.

17,594 HOMAN, F. D. Consolidation, enclosure and registration of title in Kenya. J. LOCAL ADM. OV. 1 (1962), pp. 4-14.

17,595 KNOWLES, O. S. Some modern adaptations of customary law in the settlement of matrimonial disputes in the Luo, Kisii and Kuria tribes of South Nyanza. J. AFR. ADM. 8 (1956), pp. 11-15.

17,596 LAMBERT, H. E. Land tenure among the Akamba. AFR. STUD. 6 (1947), pp. 131-147, 157-175.

17,597 LEVINE, R. A. The Gusii family. THE FAMILY ESTATE IN AFRICA, 1964, pp. 63-82.

17,598 MAYER, P. and MAYER, I. Land law in the making. AFR. LAW: ADAPTATION AND DEVELOPMENT, 1965, pp. 51-78.

17,599 OULTON, A. D. M. Loans in Kenya on the security of chattels. J. AFR. LAW 4 (1960), pp. 17-39, 79-97.

17,600 PHILLIPS, A. The African court system in Kenya. J. AFR. ADM. 4 (1952), pp. 135-138.

17,601 RAKE, A. The lessons of libel. AFR. SOUTH 3, no. 1 (1958), pp. 77-82.

17,602 READ, J. S. Changes in the law of contract [Kenya: The Law of Contract Ordinance, 1960]. J. AFR. LAW 5 (1961), p. 48.

17,603 ROBERTS, C. C. Witchcraft and colonial legislation. AFRICA 8 (1935), pp. 488-493.

17,604 ROWLANDS, J. S. S. Notes on native law and custom in Kenya. J. AFR. LAW 6 (1962), pp. 192-209.

17,605 SIMMANCE, A. J. F. The adoption of children among the Kikuyu of Kiambu district. J. AFR. LAW 3 (1959), pp. 33-38.

17,606 SIMMANCE, A. J. F. Land redemption among the Fort Hall Kikuyu. J. AFR. LAW 5 (1961), pp. 75-81.

17,607 SLATER, M. Le procès de Jomo Kenyatta. PRESENCE AFR. N.S. 6 (1956), pp. 46-55; 11 (1957), pp. 32-46.

17,608 TATE, E. R. The native law of the southern Gikuyu of British East Africa. J. AFR. SOC. 9 (1910), pp. 233-254.

17,609 TENNENT, J. R. M. The administration of criminal law in some Kenya African courts. J. AFR. LAW 5 (1961), pp. 139-144.

17,610 WADE, Sir A. Trial by ordeal. CORONA 3 (1951), pp. 189-190.

17,611 African Courts Training Centre, Maseno. J. AFR. LAW 6 (1962), pp. 115-116.

17,612 Customary criminal law in Kenya. J. AFR. LAW 7 (1963), pp. 1-3.

17,613 Qualifications for admission to practice. J. AFR. LAW 6 (1962), pp. 113-114.

17,614 Report of Working Party on African land tenure in Kenya. J. AFR. LAW 3 (1959), pp. 2-6.

See also 17208.

Religion

17,615 BEWES, T. F. C. The work of the Christian Church among the Kikuyu. INTERNAT. AFFAIRS 29 (1953), pp. 316-325.

17,616 BRITTON, J. The missionary task in Kenya. INT. REV. MISSIONS 12 (1923), pp. 412-420.

17,617 BUXTON, E. R. Kikuyu christians. CONTEMP. REV. 183 (1953), pp. 339-343.

17,618 DAIN, F. R. Land hunger and social disturbance in Kenya viewed as a challenge to the Christian churches. THE CHURCH IN CHANGING AFRICA, 1958, pp. 37-46.

17,619 FUETER, P. S. A Christian Council in action: the Christian Council of Kenya. INT. REV. MISSIONS 49 (1960), pp. 291-300.

17,620 HAKE, A. An urban mission course in Nairobi. INT. REV. MISSIONS 52 (1963), pp. 173-181.

17,621 LANGFORD-SMITH, N. Revival in East Africa. INT. REV. MISSIONS 43 (1954), pp. 77-81.

17,622 MacPHERSON, R. Unity and union in Kenya. THE CHURCH IN CHANGING AFRICA, 1958, pp. 83-86.

17,623 MBITI, J. S. Christianisme et religions indigènes au Kenya. PRESENCE AFR. 27-28 (1959), pp. 129-153.

17,624 WILLIS, J. J. [Bishop of Uganda]. A statement by Christian converts in Kavirondo addressed to their heathen friends. INT. REV. MISSIONS 4 (1915), pp. 382-395.

See also 16486.

Science

17,625 BOURKE, D. O'D. Some observations in East Africa and Madagascar. NIGERIAN FIELD 30 (1965), pp. 99-112.

17,626 CARSON, J. B. Game preservation in Kenya. CORONA 4 (1952), pp. 374-375.

17,627 SOMEREN, V. G. L. VAN. Systematic notes on the associated blue-banded black papilios of the bromius-brontes-sosia complex of Kenya and Uganda, with descriptions of two new species. BSEM 123 (1960), pp. 63-93.

17,628 TROWELL, H. C. Aspects médicaux de l'inefficience. PRESENCE AFR. 13 (1952), pp. 331-337.

17,629 VARLEY, E. R. Vermiculite deposits in Kenya. BULL. IMP. INST. 46 (1948), pp. 348-352.

17,630 WADE, Sir A. Bwana pumps. CORONA 4 (1952), pp. 277-278.

17,631 WILLIAMS, L. A. J. Rock fragments of unknown origin found at Mida creek, near Malindi, Kenya. PROC. E. AFR. ACAD. 2 (1964), pp. 59-63.

17,632 Red Cross worker in Kenya. AFR. WOMEN 1 (1956), pp. 86-87.

See also 4153.

Sociology

17,633 ASKWITH, T. African housing in Nairobi. J. AFR. ADM. 2 (1950), pp. 37-39.

17,634 ASKWITH, T. A community centre in Kenya. CORONA 4 (1952), pp. 332-334.

17,635 ASKWITH, T. Tribalism in Nairobi. CORONA 2 (1950), pp. 292-295.

17,636 ASKWITH, T. G. Self-help housing. J. AFR. ADM. 13 (1961), pp. 204-210.

17,637 BARNETT, A. Christian home and family life in Kenya today. INT. REV. MISSIONS 49 (1960), pp. 420-426.

17,638 C., J. A la cité indigène de Nairobi. ZAIRE 7 (1953), pp. 861-863.

17,639 C., J. Niveau de vie et commerce indigène à Nairobi. ZAIRE 7 (1953), pp. 863-864.

17,640 CAROE, O. Land tenure and the franchise. A basis for partnership in African plural societies. J. AFR. ADM. 6 (1954), pp. 152-160.

17,641 CHOWDHRY, S. P. Kenya and the immigrants. AFR. QUART. 4, no. iii (1964), pp. 157-166.

17,642 COOKE, S. V. Human relations in Kenya. CORONA 3 (1951), pp. 461-463.

17,643 ETHERINGTON, D. M. Projected changes in urban and rural population in Kenya and the implications for development policy. E. AFR. EC. REV. N.S. 1, no. 2 (1965), pp. 65-83.

17,644 FORDHAM, P. and WILTSHIRE, H. C. Some texts of prejudice in an East African adult college. RACE 5, no. 2 (1963-1964), pp. 70-77.

17,645 FRANCIS, E. C. Kenya's problems as seen by a schoolmaster in Kikuyu country. AFR. AFFAIRS 54 (1955), pp. 186-196.

17,646 GOLDS, J. M. African urbanization in Kenya. J. AFR. ADM. 13 (1961), pp. 24-28.

17,647 HEYER, S. S. The Asian in Kenya. AFR. SOUTH 5, no. 2 (1961), pp. 77-84.

17,648 HUGHES, O. E. B. Villages in the Kikuyu country. J. AFR. ADM. 7 (1955), pp. 170-174.

17,649 LAMBERT, H. E. A note on children's pastimes. SWAHILI 30 (1959), pp. 74-78.

17,650 LEVINE, R. A. and LEVINE, B. B. Studying child rearing and personality development in an East African community. ANTHROPOLOGY AND AFRICA TODAY, 1962, pp. 620-628.

17,651 LEWIS, I. M. The problem of the Northern Frontier District of Kenya. RACE 5, no. 1 (1963-1964), pp. 48-60.

17,652 NGATHO, Z. Family housing. AFR. WOMEN 1 (1955), p. 48.

17,653 OMINDE, S. H. Population movements to the main urban areas of Kenya. CAH. ET. AFR. 5 (1965), pp. 593-617.

17,654 OMINDE, S. H. Rural population patterns and problems of the Kikuyu, Embu and Meru districts of Kenya. PROC. E. AFR. ACAD. 2 (1964), pp. 36-45.

17,655 PARKER, M. Race relations and political development in Kenya. AFR. AFFAIRS 50 (1951), pp. 41-52, 133.

17,656 PENWILL, D. J. A pilot scheme for two Kikuyu improved villages near Nairobi. J. AFR. ADM. 12 (1960), pp. 61-67.

17,657 QUALI. The native question in British East Africa. CONTEMP. REV. 113 (1918), pp. 453-460.

17,658 REISDORF, G. Kenya 1951. ZAIRE 9 (1955), pp. 359-384, 619-648.

17,659 SHANNON, M. Rebuilding the social life of the Kikuyu. AFR. AFFAIRS 56 (1957), pp. 276-284.

17,660 SHANNON, M. Rehabilitating the Kikuyu. AFR. AFFAIRS 54 (1955), pp. 129-138.

17,661 SILBERMAN, L. The social survey of the old town of Mombasa. J. AFR. ADM. 2 (1950), pp. 14-21.

17,662 SMITH, E. W. Kenya: a community development project. CORONA 4 (1952), pp. 267-268.

17,663 WIJEYEWARDENE, G. A preliminary report on tribal differentiation and social groupings on the southern Kenya coast. EAISR June (1958), pp. 1-20.

17,664 African social welfare in Nairobi. AFR. AFFAIRS 49 (1950), pp. 50-56.

17,665 Kenya African Women's Seminar [April, 1963]. WOMEN TODAY 6 (1963), pp. 5-6.

See also 17332, 18598, 21240.

T A N Z A N I A

General

17,666 MNTAMBO, P. C. The founding of King George V Memorial Museum, Dar es Salaam, East Africa. TANGANYIKA NOTES AND RECORDS 12 (1941), pp. 20-22.

17,667 SASSOON, H. Bibliography. TANG. NOTES 64 (1965), pp. 154-162.

17,668 Bibliography of publications relating to Tanganyika published during the year 1951. TANG. NOTES 32 (1952), pp. 88-92.

17,669 Tanganyika Society. TANG. NOTES 32 (1952), pp. ix-xvi.

Agriculture

17,670 BREWIN, D. R. Kilimanjaro agriculture. TANG. NOTES 64 (1965), pp. 115-117.

17,671 BUSSE, W. The organisation of experimental work in agriculture in the German colonies. BULL. IMP. INST. 11 (1913), pp. 462-478.

17,672 CALTON, W. E. Hydroponics as a gardening adjunct. TANGANYIKA NOTES AND RECORDS 58-59 (1962), pp. 218-223.

17,673 HARTNOLL, A. V. and COUCHMAN, N. R. F. The "Mashokora" cultivations of the coast. TANG. NOTES 3 (1937), pp. 34-39.

17,674 KESBY, J. D. Warangi reaction to agricultural change. EAISR Jan. (1965), pp. 1-12.

17,675 McCLELLAN, F. C. Agricultural resources of the Zanzibar Protectorate. BULL. IMP. INST. 12 (1914), pp. 407-429.

17,676 MARSLAND, H. Mlau cultivation in the Rufiji Valley. TANG. NOTES 5 (1938), pp. 56-59.

17,677 PATERSON, R. L. Ukara Island. TANGANYIKA NOTES AND RECORDS 44 (1956), pp. 54-62.

17,678 PIKE, A. H. Soil conservation amongst the Matengo tribe. TANG. NOTES 6 (1938), pp. 79-81; 7 (1939), pp. 117-118.

17,679 PITT, J. Provisional macroscopic key to the identification of certain timbers of Tanganyika Territory, with an index by L. Wigg. TANG. NOTES 8 (1939), pp. 27-46.

17,680 PITT-SCHENKEL, C. J. W. Pole and fuel plantations and windbreaks, Kwimba district. TANG. NOTES 2 (1936), pp. 55-59.

17,681 STURDY, D. Agricultural notes. TANG. NOTES 1 (1936), pp. 52-56.

17,682 TANNER, R. E. S. Land rights on the Tanganyika coast. AFR. STUD. 19 (1960), pp. 14-25.

17,683 TAWNEY, J. J. Trees for the people. CORONA 2 (1950), pp. 450-452.

17,684 THORNTON, D. and ROUNCE, N. V. Ukara Island and the agricultural practices of the Wankara. TANG. NOTES 1 (1936), pp. 25-32.

17,685 WAKEFIELD, A. J. Tanganyika territory and native uplift. J. AFR. SOC. 39 (1940), pp. 231-243.

17,686 WOOD, P. J. The forest glades of West Kilimanjaro. TANG. NOTES 64 (1965), pp. 108-111.

17,687 WOOD, P. J. A note on forestry on Kilimanjaro. TANG. NOTES 64 (1965), pp. 111-114.

17,688 A propos d'arachides: la leçon de deux expériences. ZAIRE 5 (1951), pp. 625-626.

Anthropology

17,689 ABDURAHMAN, M. Anthropological notes from the Zanzibar Protectorate. TANG. NOTES 8 (1939), pp. 59-84.

17,690 ABDY, D. M. Witchcraft amongst the Wahadimu. J. AFR. SOC. 16 (1917), pp. 234-241.

17,691 ABRAHAMS, R. G. Neighbourhood organization: a major subsystem among the northern Nyamwezi. AFRICA 35 (1965), pp. 168-186.

17,692 ABRAHAMS, R. G. Some aspects of Nyamwezi witch belief. EAISR Jan. (1959), pp. 1-10.

17,693 ADAM, V. Rain making rites in Ihanzu. EAISR Jan. (1963), pp. 1-23.

17,694 ADAM, V. Social composition of Isanzu villages. EAISR Jan. (1962), pp. 1-12.

17,695 BACHMANN, T. Nyiha-Märchen. AFR. UND UB. 6 (1915-1916), pp. 81-101.

17,696 BAGENAL, C. J. Nwariye: a sacred mountain of Tanganyika. J. AFR. SOC. 24 (1925), pp. 299-305; TANG. NOTES 36 (1954), pp. 58-63.

17,697 BAGSHAWE, F. J. The peoples of the happy valley (East Africa). J. AFR. SOC. 24 (1924), pp. 25-33, 117-130, 219-227, 328-347; 25 (1925), pp. 59-74.

17,698 BAKER, E. C. Notes on the Shirazi of East Africa. TANG. NOTES 11 (1941), pp. 1-10.

17,699 BAKER, G. An experiment in applied anthropology. AFRICA 8 (1935), pp. 304-314.

17,700 BARKER, R. D. Insects as food. TANG. NOTES 11 (1941), p. 68.

17,701 BAXTER, H. C. Introduction to witchcraft in Africa. TANG. NOTES 18 (1944), pp. 69-76.

17,702 BAXTER, H. C. Religious practices of the pagan Wazigua: the story of a dying creed. TANG. NOTES 15 (1943), pp. 49-57.

17,703 BEIDELMAN, T. O. The Baraguyu. TANGANYIKA NOTES AND RECORDS 55 (1960), pp. 244-278; 57 (1961), p. 238.

17,704 BEIDELMAN, T. O. Beer drinking and cattle theft in Ukaguru: intertribal relations in a Tanganyika chiefdom. AMER. ANTHR. 63 (1961), pp. 534-547.

17,705 BEIDELMAN, T. O. The blood covenant and the concept of blood in Ukaguru. AFRICA 33 (1963), pp. 321-342.

17,706 BEIDELMAN, T. O. Further adventures of hyena and rabbit: the folktale as a sociological model. AFRICA 33 (1963), pp. 54-69.

17,707 BEIDELMAN, T. O. Hyena and rabbit: a Kaguru representation of matrilineal relations. AFRICA 31 (1961), pp. 61-73.

17,708 BEIDELMAN, T. O. Ironworking in Ukaguru. TANGANYIKA NOTES AND RECORDS 58-59 (1962), pp. 288-289.

17,709 BEIDELMAN, T. O. A note on Baraguyu house-types and Baraguyu economy. TANGANYIKA NOTES AND RECORDS 56 (1961), pp. 55-66.

17,710 BEIDELMAN, T. O. Pig (Guluwe): an essay on Ngulu sexual symbolism and ceremony. SOUTHWESTERN J. ANTHR. 20 (1964), pp. 359-392.

17,711 BEIDELMAN, T. O. Right and left hand among the Kaguru: a note on symbolic classification. AFRICA 31 (1961), pp. 250-257.

17,712 BEIDELMAN, T. O. Some notes on the Kamba in Kilosa District. TANGANYIKA NOTES AND RECORDS 57 (1961), pp. 181-194.

17,713 BEIDELMAN, T. O. Three tales of the living and the dead: the ideology of Kaguru ancestral propitiation. JRAI 94 (1964), pp. 109-137.

17,714 BLEEK, D. F. The Hadzapi or Watindega of Tanganyika Territory. AFRICA 4 (1931), pp. 273-285.

17,715 BOWIE, D. F. The lip plug, or "ndonya" among the tribes of the Southern Province. TANG. NOTES 27 (1949), pp. 75-77.

17,716 BRAIN, J. L. Cannibalism amongst the Doe. TANGANYIKA NOTES AND RECORDS 57 (1961), p. 238.

17,717 BRAIN, J. L. The Kwere of the Eastern Province. TANGANYIKA NOTES AND RECORDS 58-59 (1962), pp. 231-241.

17,718 BROWN, G. G. Bride-wealth among the Hehe. AFRICA 5 (1932), pp. 145-157.

17,719 BROWN, G. G. Hehe cross-cousin marriage. ESSAYS PRESENTED TO C. G. SELIGMAN, 1934, pp. 27-39.

17,720 BROWNE, G. S. J. O. The tsetse fly and native morals. J. AFR. SOC. 23 (1923), pp. 39-43.

17,721 BUNTING, S. A. East African prospects. CONTEMP. REV. 114 (1918), pp. 521-526.

17,722 CARNELL, W. J. Four Gogo folktales. TANGANYIKA NOTES AND RECORDS 40 (1955), pp. 30-42.

17,723 CARNELL, W. J. Sympathetic magic among the Gogo of Mpwapwa District. TANGANYIKA NOTES AND RECORDS 39 (1955), pp. 25-38.

17,724 CHISHOLM, J. A. Notes on the manners and customs of the Winamwanga and Wiwa. J. AFR. SOC. 9 (1910), pp. 360-387.

17,725 CLARKE, J. C. A note on the Ntore system in Bugufi, Biharamulo District. TANG. NOTES 5 (1938), pp. 76-78.

17,726 COLE, H. Notes on the Wagogo of German East Africa. JRAI 32 (1902), pp. 305-338.

17,727 CONAN-DAVIES, E. Queen Mab in Masasi. TANG. NOTES 17 (1944), pp. 64-65.

17,728 CONNOR, R. M. B. Nyakyusa pagan religion. INT. REV. MISSIONS 43 (1954), pp. 170-172.

17,729 COOPER, B. The Kindiga. TANG. NOTES 27 (1949), pp. 8-15.

17,730 CORY, H. The Buswezi. AMER. ANTHR. 57 (1955), pp. 923-952.

17,731 CORY, H. The Buyeye: a secret society of snake-charmers in Sukumaland, Tanganyika Territory. AFRICA 16 (1946), pp. 160-176.

17,732 CORY, H. Figurines used in the initiation ceremonies of the Nguu of Tanganyika Territory. AFRICA 14 (1944), pp. 459-464.

17,733 CORY, H. The ingredients of magic medicines. AFRICA 19 (1949), pp. 13-32.

17,734 CORY, H. Jando, Part I. JRAI 77 (1947), pp. 159-168.

17,735 CORY, H. The people of the Lake Victoria region. TANG. NOTES 33 (1952), pp. 22-29.

17,736 CORY, H. Religious beliefs and practices of the Sukuma/Nyamwezi tribal group. TANGANYIKA NOTES AND RECORDS 54 (1960), pp. 14-26.

17,737 CORY, H. The Sambaa initiation rites for boys. TANGANYIKA NOTES AND RECORDS 58-59 (1962), pp. 2-7.

17,738 CORY, H. Sukuma twin ceremonies—Mabasa. TANG. NOTES 17 (1944), pp. 34-43.

17,739 CORY, H. Sumbwa birth figurines. JRAI 91 (1961), pp. 67-76.

17,740 CORY, H. Tambiko (Fika). TANGANYIKA NOTES AND RECORDS 58-59 (1962), pp. 274-282.

17,741 CROSSE-UPCOTT, A. R. W. Male circumcision among the Ngindo. JRAI 89 (1959), pp. 169-189.

17,742 CROSSE-UPCOTT, A. R. W. Social aspects of Ngindo bee-keeping. JRAI 86, no. 2 (1956), pp. 81-108.

17,743 CULWICK, A. T. Ngindo honey-hunters. TANG. NOTES 5 (1938), pp. 66-67.

17,744 CULWICK, A. T. and CULWICK, G. M. Fostermothers in Ulanga. TANG. NOTES 1 (1936), pp. 19-24.

17,745 CULWICK, A. T. and CULWICK, G. M. The functions of bride-wealth in Ubena of the rivers. AFRICA 7 (1934), pp. 140-159.

17,746 CULWICK, G. M. Letter-writing in Ulanga. TANG. NOTES 5 (1938), p. 79.

17,747 DAHL, E. Hundert Rätsel der Wanamwezi. AFR. UND UB. 3 (1912-1913), pp. 257-271.

17,748 DAMMANN, E. Bonde-Erzählungen. AFR. UND UB. 28 (1937-1938), pp. 299-318.

17,749 DAMMANN, E. Sprichwörter der Zigula. AFR. UND UB. 29 (1939), pp. 71-76.

17,750 DAMMANN, E. Zigula-Märchen. AFR. UND UB. 28 (1937-1938), pp. 139-157.

17,751 DANIELSON, E. R. Proverbs of the Waniramba people of East Africa. TANGANYIKA NOTES AND RECORDS 47-48 (1957), pp. 187-197.

17,752 DOBSON, E. B. Comparative land tenure of ten Tanganyika tribes. TANGANYIKA NOTES AND RECORDS 38 (1955), pp. 31-38.

17,753 DUNDAS, Hon. K. R. Notes on the tribes inhabiting the Baringo district, East Africa Protectorate. JRAI 40 (1910), pp. 49-72.

17,754 FINCH, F. G. Hambageu: some additional notes on the god of the Wasonjo. TANGANYIKA NOTES AND RECORDS 47-48 (1957), pp. 203-208.

17,755 FOSBROOKE, H. A. Blessing the year: a Wasi/Rangi ceremony. TANGANYIKA NOTES AND RECORDS 50 (1958), pp. 21-29.

17,756 FOSBROOKE, H. A. The defensive measures of certain tribes in north-eastern Tanganyika. TANGANYIKA NOTES AND RECORDS 39 (1955), pp. 1-11.

17,757 FOSBROOKE, H. A. ed. Hambageu, the God of the Wasonjo. TANG. NOTES 35 (1953), pp. 38-42.

17,758 FOSBROOKE, H. A. Laying the ghosts. TANG. NOTES 31 (1951), pp. 72-73.

17,759 FOSBROOKE, H. A. The Masai age-group system as a guide to tribal chronology. AFR. STUD. 15 (1956), pp. 188-206.

17,760 FOSBROOKE, H. A. A note on the Ngasa. AFR. STUD. 13 (1954), pp. 153-154.

17,761 FOSBROOKE, H. A. A Rangi circumcision ceremony: blessing a new grove. TANGANYIKA NOTES AND RECORDS 50 (1958), pp. 30-38.

17,762 GARNETT, C. B. "Dudu." TANG. NOTES 2 (1936), pp. 108-109.

17,763 GRANT, C. H. B. Some African royal burials and coronations in western Tanganyika. AFR. STUD. 10 (1951), pp. 185-193.

17,764 GRAY, Sir J. M. Nairuzi or Siku ya mwaka. TANGANYIKA NOTES AND RECORDS 38 (1955), pp. 1-22.

17,765 GRAY, Sir J. M. Nairuzi—some additional notes. TANGANYIKA NOTES AND RECORDS 41 (1955), pp. 69-72.

17,766 GRAY, Sir J. M. The Wadebuli and the Wadiba. TANG. NOTES 36 (1954), pp. 22-42.

17,767 GRAY, R. F. Hajaro: a new Sonjo colony. EAISR Jan. (1965), p. 1.

17,768 GRAY, R. F. Positional succession among the Wambugwe. AFRICA 23 (1953), pp. 233-243.

17,769 GRAY, R. F. Some parallels in Sonjo and Christian mythology. AFRICAN SYSTEMS OF THOUGHT, 1965, pp. 49-63.

17,770 GRAY, R. F. Sonjo bride-price and the question of African "wife purchase." AMER. ANTHR. 62 (1960), pp. 34-57.

17,771 GREEN, E. C. The Wambugu of Usambara (with notes on Kimbugu). TANG. NOTES 61 (1963), pp. 175-189.

17,772 GRIFFITHS, J. E. S. The Aba-Ha of the Tanganyika Territory: some aspects of their tribal organizations and sleeping sickness concentrations. TANG. NOTES 2 (1936), pp. 72-76.

17,773 GRIFFITHS, J. E. S. Masai cattle auction. TANG. NOTES 6 (1938), pp. 99-101.

17,774 GULLIVER, P. Dancing clubs of the Nyasa. TANGANYIKA NOTES AND RECORDS 41 (1955), pp. 58-59.

17,775 GULLIVER, P. H. Structural dichotomy and jural processes among the Arusha of northern Tanganyika. AFRICA 31 (1961), pp. 19-34.

17,776 GULLIVER, P. H. A tribal map of Tanganyika. TANGANYIKA NOTES AND RECORDS 52 (1959), pp. 61-74.

17,777 GUTMANN, B. Bruchstücke aus den Kerbstocklehren für Mädchen, nach dem Mreho fo Ljangō. AFR. UND UB. 15 (1924-1925), pp. 1-19.

17,778 GUTMANN, B. Chagga folk-lore [extracts from Dichten und Denken der Dschagganeger and Volksbuch der Wadschagga]. TANG. NOTES 64 (1965), pp. 50-55.

17,779 GUTMANN, B. Die Kerbstocklehren der Dschagga in Ostafrika. AFR. UND UB. 13 (1922-1923), pp. 81-109, 205-235, 260-302.

17,780 GUTMANN, B. Das Rechtsleben der Wadschagga im Spiegel ihrer Sprichwörter. AFR. UND UB. 14 (1923-1924), pp. 44-68.

17,781 HALL, R. DE Z. A bibliography of ethnographical literature for Tanganyika Territory. TANG. NOTES 7 (1939), pp. 75-83.

17,782 HALL, R. DE Z. The dance societies of the Wasukuma, as seen in the Maswa district. TANG. NOTES 1 (1936), pp. 94-96.

17,783 HALL, R. DE Z. The study of native court records as a method of ethnological inquiry. AFRICA 11 (1938), pp. 412-426.

17,784 HALL, R. DE Z. A tribal museum at Bweranyange, Bukoba District. TANG. NOTES 5 (1938), pp. 1-4.

17,785 HARRIES, L. Makua song-riddles from the initiation rites. AFR. STUD. 1 (1942), pp. 27-46.

17,786 HARRIES, L. Notes on the mythology of the Bantu in the Ruvuma District. TANGANYIKA NOTES AND RECORDS 12 (1941), pp. 38-44.

17,787 HARRIES, L. Some riddles of the Makua people. AFR. STUD. 1 (1942), pp. 275-291.

17,788 HARRIES, L. Some riddles of the Mwera people. AFR. STUD. 6 (1947), pp. 21-34.

17,789 HARRIS, W. V. Some notes on insects as food. TANG. NOTES 9 (1940), pp. 45-48.

17,790 HARTNOLL, A. V. Praying for rain in Ugogo. TANGANYIKA NOTES AND RECORDS 13 (1942), pp. 59-60.

17,791 HARWOOD, A. Beer-drinking and famine in a Safwa village: a case of adaptation in a time of crisis. EAISR Jan. (1964), pp. 1-6.

17,792 HATCHELL, G. W. Some account of the people living under the protection of Mount Mkungwe. TANG. NOTES 11 (1941), pp. 41-46.

17,793 HODGSON, A. G. O. Some notes on the hunting customs of the Wandamba of the Ulanga valley, Tanganyika Territory, and other East African tribes. JRAI 56 (1926), pp. 59-70.

17,794 HODGSON, A. G. O. Some notes on the Wahehe of Mahenge district, Tanganyika territory. JRAI 56 (1926), pp. 37-58.

17,795 HOKORORO, A. M. The influence of the church on tribal customs at Lukuledi. TANGANYIKA NOTES AND RECORDS 54 (1960), pp. 1-13.

17,796 HORE, E. C. On the twelve tribes of Tanganyika. JRAI 12 (1883), pp. 2-21.

17,797 HUCKS, G. W. Y. Haya surnames. TANG. NOTES 7 (1939), pp. 72-74.

17,798 HUGGINS, P. M. Sukuma fables. TANG. NOTES 1 (1936), pp. 90-93.

17,799 HUNTER, G. A Sandawe climbing rope. TANG. NOTES 33 (1952), p. 93.

17,800 JACKSON, C. H. N. The Mangati. TANGANYIKA NOTES AND RECORDS 13 (1942), pp. 6-13.

17,801 JELLICOE, M. R. Women of the Turu. WOMEN TODAY 6 (1963), pp. 9-12.

17,802 JERRARD, R. C. The Muheza Bee Fundi. The story of Seluchungi son of Machungi. TANG. NOTES 7 (1939), pp. 116-117.

17,803 JOHNSON, F. Kiniramba folk tales. BANTU STUD. 5 (1931), pp. 327-356.

17,804 JOHNSON, V. E. African harvest dance. TANG. NOTES 37 (1954), pp. 138-142.

17,805 JOHNSTON, Sir H. H. The Tanganyika Plateau [Awemba]. J. AFR. SOC. 11 (1912), pp. 141-150.

17,806 JOHNSTON, P. H. Some aspects of dhow building. TANG. NOTES 27 (1949), pp. 47-51.

17,807 JONES, W. W. African dugouts. TANG. NOTES 11 (1941), pp. 11-12.

17,808 JUMA, W. The Sukuma societies for young men and women. TANGANYIKA NOTES AND RECORDS 54 (1960), pp. 27-29.

17,809 KANNENBERG, H. Beiträge zur afrikanischen Sagenkunde. ZAOS 5 (1900), pp. 161-162.

17,810 KIRSCHSTEIN, E. F. Meteorites as celestial ram-bones in the belief of Tanganyika natives. TANGANYIKA NOTES AND RECORDS 13 (1942), p. 61.

17,811 KIRSCHSTEIN, E. F. A note on native power of discernment. TANG. NOTES 6 (1938), pp. 102-103.

17,812 KIRSCHSTEIN, E. F. Some tales of Tanganyika natives. TANG. NOTES 4 (1937), pp. 82-83.

17,813 KLAMROTH, M. Beiträge zum Verständnis der religiösen Vorstellungen der Saramo im Bezirk Daressalam (Deutsch-Ostafrika). AFR. UND UB. 1 (1910), pp. 37-70, 118-153, 189-223.

17,814 KLIMA, G. Jural relations between sexes among the Barabaig. AFRICA 34 (1964), pp. 9-19.

17,815 KORIT-SCHONER, H. and HARTNOLL, M. M. Tribal structure in Ohaya. TANGANYIKA NOTES AND RECORDS 14 (1942), pp. 1-18.

17,816 KRUMM, B. Zwei Matumbi-Märchen. AFR. UND UB. 23 (1932-1933), pp. 154-158.

17,817 LAMBURN, A. R. G. P. Some notes on the Yao. TANG. NOTES 29 (1950), pp. 73-84.

17,818 LANCASTER, D. G. Tentative chronology of the Ngoni, genealogy of their chiefs, and notes. JRAI 67 (1937), pp. 77-90.

17,819 LEES, E. C. L. A note on the Wambulu. TANG. NOTES 2 (1936), pp. 106-107.

17,820 LEHMAN, F. Notes on the daily life of the Nyakusa (Tanganyika Territory). SOCIOLOGUS 1 (1951), pp. 138-148.

17,821 LEHMANN, F. R. Some field-notes on the Chaga of Kilimanjaro. BANTU STUD. 15 (1941), pp. 385-396.

17,822 LUSSY, K. Some aspects of work and recreation among the Wapogoro of Southern Tanganyika. ANTHR. QUART. 26 (1953), pp. 109-128.

17,823 LYONS, C. P. A witch-doctor at work. TANG. NOTES 1 (1936), pp. 97-98.

17,824 MacQUARIE, C. Water gipsies of the Malagarasi. TANG. NOTES 9 (1940), pp. 61-67.

17,825 MAGUIRE, R. A. J. Il-Torōbo. J. AFR. SOC. 27 (1928), pp. 127-141, 249-268.

17,826 MAREALLE, Chief P. I. Chagga customs, beliefs and traditions... TANG. NOTES 64 (1965), pp. 56-61.

17,827 MAREALLE, Chief P. I. Notes on Chagga customs. TANGANYIKA NOTES AND RECORDS 60 (1963), pp. 67-90.

17,828 MAREALLE, T. L. M. The Wachagga of Kilimanjaro. TANG. NOTES 32 (1952), pp. 57-64.

17,829 MAURICE, M. La maladie et la mort chez les Bapimbwe. BIBLIOTHECA AFR. 4, no. 2 (1930-1931), pp. 22-31.

17,830 MAURICE, M. Les médecines Abasinganga chez les Bapimbwe. BIBLIOTHECA AFR. 3 (1929), pp. 190-198.

17,831 MAURICE, M. La naissance au pays de Bapimbwe. BIBLIOTHECA AFR. 4 (1930-1931), pp. 79-86.

17,832 MAURICE, M. La religion des Bapimbwe. BIBLIOTHECA AFR. 3 (1929-1930), pp. 286-298.

17,833 MAURICE, M. Les sorciers abalodi chez les Bapimbwe. BIBLIOTHECA AFR. 3 (1929), pp. 11-22.

17,834 MBEE, G. Letter from Mbugwe, Tanganyika. AFRICA 35 (1965), pp. 198-208.

17,835 MDEE, A. M. Some experiences of witchcraft. TANGANYIKA NOTES AND RECORDS 57 (1961), pp. 149-151.

17,836 MELLAND, F. H. Notes on the ethnography of the Awemba (and part of the Wa-Wisa). J. AFR. SOC. 4 (1905), pp. 337-345.

17,837 MOLLER, M. S. G. Bahaya customs and beliefs in connection with pregnancy and childbirth. TANGANYIKA NOTES AND RECORDS 50 (1958), pp. 112-117.

17,838 MOREAU, R. E. The joking relationship (Utani) in Tanganyika. TANGANYIKA NOTES AND RECORDS 12 (1941), pp. 1-10.

17,839 MOREAU, R. E. Joking relationships in Tanganyika. AFRICA 14 (1944), pp. 386-400.

17,840 MOREAU, R. E. Suicide by "breaking the cooking pot." TANGANYIKA NOTES AND RECORDS 12 (1941), pp. 49-50.

17,841 MORISON, Sir T. The Wachaga of Kilimanjaro. Reminiscences of a war-time district officer. J. AFR. SOC. 32 (1933), pp. 140-147.

17,842 MTAWA, A. B. M. How the Wadoe got their name. TANG. NOTES 31 (1951), pp. 79-80.

17,843 MTEKTEKA, J. Some Pangwa customs. TANGANYIKA NOTES AND RECORDS 50 (1958), pp. 102-103.

17,844 MUMFORD, W. B. The Hehe-Bena-Sangu peoples of East Africa. AMER. ANTHR. 36 (1934), pp. 203-222.

17,845 NORTHCOTE, R. C. The evolution of tribal control. AFRICA 6 (1933), pp. 312-316.

17,846 NTUNDU, Y. The position of Rainmaker among the Wanyiramba translated by J. W. T. Allen. TANG. NOTES 7 (1939), pp. 84-87.

17,847 OAKES, F. A note on earth eating in the Southern Province. TANG. NOTES 7 (1939), p. 113.

17,848 OPPER, C. J. Father of the man. BANTU STUD. 15 (1941), pp. 185-190.

17,849 PAKENHAM, R. H. W. Two Zanzibar ngomas. TANGANYIKA NOTES AND RECORDS 52 (1959), pp. 111-116.

17,850 PARK, G. K. Kinga bridewealth: approaches to a social problem. EAISR Jan. (1963), pp. 1-19.

17,851 PARK, G. K. The problem of late marriage of Kinga women. EAISR July (1962), pp. 1-14.

17,852 POPPLEWELL, G. D. Notes on the Fipa. TANG. NOTES 3 (1937), pp. 99-105.

17,853 PROCTER, J. Did you see me from afar? TANGANYIKA NOTES AND RECORDS 54 (1960), pp. 48-50.

17,854 RAUM, O. F. The Church and African society [a critical study of Dr. Gutmann's work on Kilimanjaro]. INT. REV. MISSIONS 26 (1937), pp. 500-507.

17,855 RAUM, O. F. Female initiation among the Chaga. AMER. ANTHR. 41 (1939), pp. 554-565.

17,856 RAUM, O. F. Some aspects of indigenous education among the Chaga. JRAI 68 (1938), pp. 209-221.

17,857 REDMAYNE, A. Preliminary report on a Hehe community. EAISR July (1962), pp. 1-8.

17,858 REUSCH, R. The Menelik legend. TANG. NOTES 2 (1936), pp. 77-79.

17,859 REVINGTON, T. M. Concerning the Banangoma and Basumba Batale Societies of the Bukwimba Wasukuma. TANG. NOTES 5 (1938), pp. 60-62.

17,860 REVINGTON, T. M. The pain of individualism. TANG. NOTES 3 (1937), pp. 120-121.

17,861 RIGBY, P. J. A. Aspects of residence and co-operation in a Gogo village. EAISR Jan. (1962), pp. 1-13.

17,862 RIGBY, P. J. A. The Mbuya relationship and marriage in Gogo. EAISR Jan. (1963), pp. 1-14.

17,863 RIGBY, P. J. A. Witchcraft, kinship and authority in Gogo. EAISR July (1962), pp. 1-14.

17,864 ROLLESTON, I. H. O. The Watumbatu of Zanzibar. TANG. NOTES 8 (1939), pp. 85-97.

17,865 RUSHBY, G. G. Five fables. TANG. NOTES 27 (1949), pp. 78-82.

17,866 RWIZA, K. J. Natal customs in Bukoba. TANGANYIKA NOTES AND RECORDS 50 (1958), pp. 104-105.

17,867 SCHNEIDER, H. K. The lion men of Singida: a reappraisal. TANGANYIKA NOTES AND RECORDS 58-59 (1962), pp. 124-128.

17,868 SCRIVENOR, T. V. Some notes on Utani, or the vituperative alliances existing between the clans in the Masai district. TANG. NOTES 4 (1937), pp. 72-74.

17,869 SENIOR, H. S. The Sukuma homestead. TANG. NOTES 9 (1940), pp. 42-44.

17,870 SILLERY, A. Musira and its burial caves. TANGANYIKA NOTES AND RECORDS 13 (1942), pp. 57-58.

17,871 SIMENAUER, E. The miraculous birth of Hambageu, hero-god of the Sonjo: a Tanganyika theogony. TANGANYIKA NOTES AND RECORDS 38 (1955), pp. 23-30.

17,872 SMITH, A. The missionary contribution to education (Tanganyika) to 1914. TANGANYIKA NOTES AND RECORDS 60 (1963), pp. 91-109.

17,873 SPIES, E. Observations on Utani customs among the Ngoni of Songea District. TANG. NOTES 16 (1943), pp. 49-53.

17,874 STAMBERG, F. Märchen der Dschagga (Mwika-Dialekt). AFR. UND UB. 23 (1932-1933), pp. 202-231, 278-306; 29 (1939), pp. 38-71.

17,875 STAMBERG, F. Rätsel der Djaga (Mwika-Dialekt). AFR. UND UB. 33 (1942-1943), pp. 66-77, 146-156; 34 (1943-1944), pp. 69-76; 35 (1949-1950), pp. 146-157; 36 (1951-1952), pp. 137-143.

17,876 STEINER, F. B. Chagga truth: a note on Gutmann's account of the Chagga concept of truth in Das Recht der Dschagga. AFRICA 24 (1954), pp. 364-369.

17,877 STIERLING, D. The Hehe royal graves. TANGANYIKA NOTES AND RECORDS 46 (1957), pp. 25-28.

17,878 TANNER, R. E. S. Ancestor propitiation ceremonies in Sukumaland, Tanganyika. AFRICA 28 (1958), pp. 225-231.

17,879 TANNER, R. E. S. Archery amongst the Sukuma. TANG. NOTES 35 (1953), pp. 63-65.

17,880 TANNER, R. E. S. Hysteria in Sukuma medical practice. AFRICA 25 (1955), pp. 274-279.

17,881 TANNER, R. E. S. The installation of Sukuma chiefs in Mwanga District, Tanganyika. AFR. STUD. 16 (1957), pp. 197-209.

17,882 TANNER, R. E. S. An introduction to the Northern Basukund's idea of the Supreme Being. ANTHR. QUART. 29 (1956), pp. 45-56.

17,883 TANNER, R. E. S. An introduction to the spirit beings of the Northern Basukuma. ANTHR. QUART. 29 (1956), pp. 69-81.

17,884 TANNER, R. E. S. The magician in Northern Sukumaland, Tanganyika. SOUTHWESTERN J. ANTHR. 13 (1957), pp. 344-351.

17,885 TANNER, R. E. S. Maturity and marriage among the northern Basukuma of Tanganyika. AFR. STUD. 14 (1955), pp. 123-133, 159-170.

17,886 TANNER, R. E. S. The spirits of the dead: an introduction to the ancestor worship of the Sukuma of Tanganyika. ANTHR. QUART. 32 (1959), pp. 108-124.

17,887 TANNER, R. E. S. Sukuma ancestor worship and its relationship to social structure. TANGANYIKA NOTES AND RECORDS 50 (1958), pp. 52-62.

17,888 TAWNEY, J. J. Insignia and ceremonies of the Heru chiefdom of Buha, in the Kasulu District. TANG. NOTES 18 (1944), pp. 81-88.

17,889 TAWNEY, J. J. Ugabire: a feudal custom among the Waha. TANG. NOTES 17 (1944), pp. 6-9.

17,890 TEALE, Sir E. An unusual place and form of burial. TANG. NOTES 31 (1951), p. 71.

17,891 TREVOR, J. C. The physical characters of the Sandawe. JRAI 77 (1947), pp. 61-78.

17,892 TRIPE, W. B. A curious form of chiefly succession in Mambwe-Nyanda, Ufipa district. TANG. NOTES 7 (1939), pp. 88-91.

17,893 TRIPE, W. B. The tribal insignia of Heru. TANG. NOTES 16 (1943), pp. 2-6.

17,894 WAGNER, G. An anthropologist's criticism [of Dr. Gutmann's work on Kilimanjaro]. INT. REV. MISSIONS 26 (1937), pp. 508-513.

17,895 WALDOW, A. VON. Mädchenerziehung bei den Zaramo. AFR. UND UB. 45 (1961-1962), pp. 292-306.

17,896 WENBAN-SMITH, W. Nairunzi. TANGANYIKA NOTES AND RECORDS 41 (1955), p. 74.

17,897 WERNER, A. Mambwe proverbs. BULL. SOAS 10 (1940-1942), pp. 455-467.

17,898 WERNER, A. The native races of German East Africa. J. AFR. SOC. 10 (1910), pp. 53-63.

17,899 WERNER, A. The Wahadimu of Zanzibar. J. AFR. SOC. 15 (1916), pp. 356-360.

17,900 WILLIS, R. G. Community and descent in Ufipa: a problem of pattern. EAISR June (1963), pp. 1-8.

17,901 WILSON, G. An African morality. AFRICA 9 (1936), pp. 75-98.

17,902 WILSON, G. An introduction to Nyakyusa society. BANTU STUD. 10 (1936), pp. 253-291.

17,903 WILSON, G. Nyakyusa conventions of burial. BANTU STUD. 13 (1939), pp. 1-31.

17,904 WILSON, G. M. The Tatoga of Tanganyika. TANG. NOTES 33 (1952), pp. 34-47; 34 (1953), pp. 35-56.

17,905 WILSON, M. Nyakyusa age-villages. JRAI 79 (1949), pp. 21-25.

17,906 WILSON, M. Nyakyusa ritual and symbolism. AMER. ANTHR. 56 (1954), pp. 228-241.

17,907 WINANS, E. V. and EDGERTON, R. B. Hehe magical justice. AMER. ANTHR. 66 (1964), pp. 745-764.

17,908 WISE, R. Marriage guidance by exorcism. TANGANYIKA NOTES AND RECORDS 58-59 (1962), pp. 40-42.

17,9   WISE, R. Some rituals of iron-making in Ufipa. TANGANYIKA NOTES AND RECORDS 51 (1958), pp. 232-238.

17,910 WOODBURN, J. The future of the Tindiga. TANGANYIKA NOTES AND RECORDS 58-59 (1962), pp. 268-273.

17,911 WOODBURN, J. C. The Hadza: first impressions. EAISR Jan. (1958), pp. 1-10.

17,912 WOODBURN, J. C. Hadza conceptions of health and disease. EAISR Dec. (1959), pp. 89-94.

17,913 WRIGHT, A. C. A. The magical importance of pangolins among the Basukuma. TANG. NOTES 36 (1954), pp. 71-72.

17,914 WYATT, A. W. The lion men of Singida. TANG. NOTES 28 (1950), pp. 3-9.

17,915 WYATT, A. W. Some stories from the Haya. TANG. NOTES 2 (1936), pp. 104-105.

17,916 The grave of Ngaonalupembe, chief of the Wahehe area 1800-1820. TANG. NOTES 30 (1951), p. 83.

17,917 Iraqw housing as affected by inter-tribal raiding. TANG. NOTES 36 (1954), pp. 52-57.

17,918 O Povo Maconde. PORT. EM AFR. 18 (1961), pp. 358-361.

See also 17202, 17227, 17244, 17254, 17270, 17271, 17273.

Art

17,919 ALLEN, J. W. T. Rhapta. TANG. NOTES 27 (1949), pp. 52-59.

17,920 BAXTER, H. C. Pangani: the trade centre of ancient history. TANG. NOTES 17 (1944), pp. 15-25.

17,921 BLEACKLEY, R. "Then to this Earthen Bowl..." TANG. NOTES 16 (1943), pp. 99-101.

17,922 CHITTICK, H. N. Notes on Kilwa. TANGANYIKA NOTES AND RECORDS 53 (1959), pp. 179-203.

17,923 CHITTICK, H. N. Recent discoveries in Tanganyika. PROC. PAN-AFR. CONGR. PRE-HIST. 4, no. iii (1962), pp. 215-223.

17,924 CHITTICK, H. N. [Stone-built remains]. TANG. NOTES 61 (1963), p. 217.

17,925 CLAUSEN, G. Ruins of North Iraqw. TANG. NOTES 61 (1963), pp. 216-217.

17,926 CROSSE-UPCOTT, A. R. W. Darikiwa pottery. TANGANYIKA NOTES AND RECORDS 40 (1955), pp. 24-29.

17,927 CULWICK, A. T. Some rock-paintings in Central Tanganyika. JRAI 61 (1931), pp. 443-453.

17,928 CULWICK, A. T. and CULWICK, G. M. Indonesian echoes in Central Tanganyika. TANG. NOTES 2 (1936), pp. 60-66.

17,929 DORMAN, M. H. The Kilwa civilization and the Kilwa ruins. TANG. NOTES 6 (1938), pp. 61-71.

17,930 FORSTER, N. A note on some ruins near Bagamoyo. TANG. NOTES 3 (1937), pp. 106-109.

17,931 FOSBROOKE, H. A. The age and meaning of the paintings. TANG. NOTES 29 (1950), pp. 11-14.

17,932 FOSBROOKE, H. A. A brief review of archaeological remains in Tanganyika. TANG. NOTES 33 (1952), pp. 60-66.

17,933 FOSBROOKE, H. A. Early iron age in Tanganyika relative to traditional history. PROC. PAN-AFR. CONGR. PRE-HIST. 3 (1955), pp. 318-325.

17,934 FOSBROOKE, H. A. Kondoa Boma. TANG. NOTES 32 (1952), pp. 50-51.

17,935 FOSBROOKE, H. A. The Kondoa sites: where they are and how to get there. TANG. NOTES 29 (1950), pp. 30-38.

17,936 FOSBROOKE, H. A. Methods of preservation and reproduction. TANG. NOTES 29 (1950), pp. 20-26.

17,937 FOSBROOKE, H. A. Paintings in districts other than Kondoa. TANG. NOTES 29 (1950), pp. 46-54.

17,938 FOSBROOKE, H. A. Prehistoric wells, rainponds and associated burials in Northern Tanganyika. PROC. PAN-AFR. CONGR. PRE-HIST. 3 (1955), pp. 326-335.

17,939 FOSBROOKE, H. A. Rift valley ruins. TANG. NOTES 6 (1938), pp. 58-60.

17,940 FOSBROOKE, H. A. Rock engravings or petroglyphs. TANG. NOTES 29 (1950), pp. 27-29.

17,941 FOSBROOKE, H. A. Some historic Moshi buildings. TANGANYIKA NOTES AND RECORDS 51 (1958), pp. 198-205.

17,942 FOSBROOKE, H. A. and SASSOON, H. Archaeological remains on Kilimanjaro. TANG. NOTES 64 (1965), pp. 62-64.

17,943 FOSBROOKE, J. Some Kondoa paintings more fully described. TANG. NOTES 29 (1950), pp. 39-45.

17,944 FOZZARD, P. M. H. Some rock paintings in South and Southwest Kondoa-Irangi District, Central Province. TANGANYIKA NOTES AND RECORDS 52 (1959), pp. 74-110.

17,945 FREEMAN-GRENVILLE, G. S. P. Chinese porcelain in Tanganyika. TANGANYIKA NOTES AND RECORDS 41 (1955), pp. 63-66.

17,946 FREEMAN-GRENVILLE, G. S. P. Husuni. TANGANYIKA NOTES AND RECORDS 58-59 (1962), pp. 227-230.

17,947 FREEMAN-GRENVILLE, G. S. P. Some preliminary observations on medieval mosques near Dar es Salaam. TANG. NOTES 36 (1954), pp. 64-70.

17,948 FREYVOGEL, T. A collection of plaited mats from the Ulanga District of Tanganyika. TANGANYIKA NOTES AND RECORDS 57 (1961), pp. 139-148.

17,949 GARLAKE, P. and GARLAKE, M. Early ship engravings of the East African coast. TANG. NOTES 63 (1964), pp. 197-206.

17,950 GINNER, P. An artistic appreciation of the Kondoa rock paintings. TANG. NOTES 29 (1950), pp. 3-10.

17,951 GRAY, R. F. Notes on Irangi houses. TANG. NOTES 35 (1953), pp. 45-52.

17,952 GREIG, R. C. H. Iron smelting in Fipa. TANG. NOTES 4 (1937), pp. 77-81.

17,953 HATCHELL, G. W. The ngalawa and the mtepe. TANGANYIKA NOTES AND RECORDS 57 (1961), pp. 210-215.

17,954 HOWELL, F. C. et al. Isimila: an Acheulian occupation site in the Iringa Highlands, Southern Highlands Province, Tanganyika. PROC. PAN-AFR. CONGR. PRE-HIST. 4, no. iii (1962), pp. 43-80.

17,955 HUNTER, G. Hidden drums in Singida District. TANG. NOTES 34 (1953), pp. 28-32.

17,956 HUNTER, G. A note on some tombs at Kaole. TANG. NOTES 37 (1954), pp. 134-137.

17,957 INSKEEP, R. The age of the Kondoa rock paintings in the light of recent excavations at Kisese II rock shelter. PROC. PAN-AFR. CONGR. PRE-HIST. 4, no. iii (1962), pp. 249-254.

17,958 KARIARA, J. Kibo Art Gallery. TANG. NOTES 64 (1965), pp. 147-149.

17,959 KIMWANI, E. G. A pictorial description of the manufacture of barkcloth in the Bukoba district. TANG. NOTES 30 (1951), pp. 85-98.

17,960 KIRKMAN, J. Excavations at Ras Mkumbuu on the Island of Pemba. TANGANYIKA NOTES AND RECORDS 53 (1959), pp. 161-178.

17,961 LEAKEY, L. S. B. The archaeological aspect of the Tanganyika paintings. TANG. NOTES 29 (1950), pp. 15-19.

17,962 LEAKEY, L. S. B. Preliminary report on examination of the Engaruka ruins. TANG. NOTES 1 (1936), pp. 57-60.

17,963 LOWE, C. VAN R. The Kafuan culture. PROC. PAN-AFR. CONGR. PRE-HIST. 3 (1955), pp. 207-209.

17,964 MATHEW, G. Songo Mnara. TANGANYIKA NOTES AND RECORDS 53 (1959), pp. 155-160.

17,965 MIGEOD, F. W. H. The Dinosaurs of Tendaguru. J. AFR. SOC. 26 (1927), pp. 323-340.

17,966 MORGAN, J. C. The Machinga Cave (with a note on those on Songo-Songo Island, and the Tawa-Pondo Cave). TANG. NOTES 7 (1939), pp. 59-71.

17,967 MORGAN, J. C. The Ngalawa of the Kilwa coast. TANG. NOTES 9 (1940), pp. 27-36.

17,968 NJAU, E. Kibo Art Gallery. TANG. NOTES 64 (1965), p. 147.

17,969 REEVE, W. H. Prehistory in Tanganyika. TANG. NOTES 6 (1938), pp. 49-57.

17,970 ROBINSON, A. E. Indonesian influences in Africa. TANG. NOTES 3 (1937), pp. 122-123.

17,971 ROSEMOND, C. C. DE. Iron smelting in the Kahama District. TANG. NOTES 16 (1943), pp. 79-84.

17,972 SADLIER, T. R. A note on the Handeni Museum. TANG. NOTES 33 (1952), pp. 91-92.

17,973 SMOLLA, G. Steingeraete vom Tendaguru. PROC. PAN-AFR. CONGR. PRE-HIST. 4, no. iii (1962), pp. 243-247.

17,974 STOWELL, R. F. Notes on some ruins at Tongoni, near Tanga. TANG. NOTES 4 (1937), pp. 75-76.

17,975 TANNER, R. E. S. A prehistoric culture in Mwanza District, Tanganyika. TANGANYIKA NOTES AND RECORDS 47-48 (1957), pp. 175-186.

17,976 TANNER, R. E. S. A series of rock paintings near Mwanza. TANG. NOTES 34 (1953), pp. 62-67.

17,977 TANNER, R. E. S. Some Chinese pottery found at Kilwa Kisiwani. TANG. NOTES 32 (1952), pp. 83-84.

17,978 TENRAA, W. F. E. R. Sandawe musical and other sound producing instruments. TANGANYIKA NOTES AND RECORDS 60 (1963), pp. 23-48; 62 (1964), pp. 91-95.

17,979 TRACEY, H. Recording tour in Tanganyika by a team of the African Music Society. TANG. NOTES 32 (1952), pp. 43-49.

17,980 VICKERS-HAVILAND, L. A. W. The making of an African historical film. TANG. NOTES 6 (1938), pp. 82-86.

17,981 WHEELER, M. Archaeology in East Africa. TANGANYIKA NOTES AND RECORDS 40 (1955), pp. 43-47.

17,982 WHITELEY, W. H. Southern Province rock-paintings. TANG. NOTES 31 (1951), pp. 58-60.

17,983 WISE, R. Iron smelting in Ufipa. TANGANYIKA NOTES AND RECORDS 50 (1958), pp. 106-111.

17,984 WORSLEY, P. M. and RUMBERGER, J. P. Remains of an earlier people in Uhehe. TANG. NOTES 27 (1949), pp. 42-46.

17,985 Bibliography [of rock paintings]. TANG. NOTES 29 (1950), pp. 60-61.

17,986 Rules: the Protected Monuments (Kondoa District Rock-Paintings) Rules, 1949. TANG. NOTES 29 (1950), p. 59.

17,987 Tanganyika rock paintings: a guide and record. TANG. NOTES 29 (1950), pp. 1-61.

See also 9735.

Biography

17,988 ATIMAN, A. The Wellcome Medal for 1955 [Edward Atiman]. AFR. AFFAIRS 54 (1955), p. 143.

17,989 BAX, S. N. The grave of Fred Barker, one of Stanley's followers. TANG. NOTES 7 (1939), pp. 56-58.

17,990 BENNETT. Philippe Broyon: pioneer trader in East Africa. AFR. AFFAIRS 62 (1963), pp. 156-164.

17,991 In memoriam: B. D. Burtt. TANG. NOTES 6 (1938), p. 4.

17,992 GRAY, Sir J. M. A note on Joseph Francois Charpentier de Cossigny (1736-1809). TANGANYIKA NOTES AND RECORDS 51 (1958), pp. 246-249.

17,993 T[RACEY], H. Obituary: Hans Cory, O.B.E. 1889-1962. AFR. MUSIC, 1962, p. 111.

17,994 In memoriam [: Hans Cory]. SWAHILI 33, no. 1 (1962-1963), p. ix.

17,995 HOLLIS, C. Von der Decken. TANGANYIKA NOTES AND RECORDS 50 (1958), pp. 63-67.

17,996 WADE, F. B. James Frederic Elton. TANG. NOTES 8 (1939), pp. 98-101.

17,997 FOSBROOKE, H. A. The life of Justin: an African autobiography. TANGANYIKA NOTES AND RECORDS 41 (1955), pp. 31-57; 42 (1956), pp. 19-30.

17,998 SILLERY, A. Maizan. TANG. NOTES 10 (1940), pp. 89-91.

17,999 SNOXALL, R. A. James Martin (Antonio Martini) 1857-1924. UGANDA J. 1 (1934), pp. 145-149.

18,000 HARVEY, R. J. Mirambo. TANG. NOTES 28 (1950), pp. 10-28.

18,001 Obituary: William Bryant Mumford. AFR. AFFAIRS 50 (1951), p. 251.

18,002 Julius Nyerere: the Transition profile. TRANSITION 2 (1961), pp. 21-24.

18,003 SCHMIEDEL, H. Bwana Sakkarani: Captain Tom von Prince and his times. TANGANYIKA NOTES AND RECORDS 52 (1959), pp. 35-52.

18,004 Obituary: Miss Jessie Robertson. TANG. NOTES 16 (1943), p. 1.

18,005 GRAY, Sir J. M. Albrecht Roscher. TANGANYIKA NOTES AND RECORDS 50 (1958), pp. 71-84.

18,006 GRAY, Sir J. M. Memoirs of an Arabian princess [Emily Ruete, née Princess of Oman and Zanzibar]. TANG. NOTES 37 (1954), pp. 49-70.

18,007 FRANK, C. N. Bishop Steere and Kiswahili. TANG. NOTES 32 (1952), pp. 38-42.

18,008 C. F. Massy Swynnerton. J. AFR. SOC. 37 (1938), p. 343.

18,009 In memoriam: C. F. M. Swynnerton. TANG. NOTES 6 (1938), pp. 3-4.

18,010 T., H. B. Obituary: Sir Mark Wilson. UGANDA J. 21 (1957), p. 121.

Economics

18,011 ADAM, V. Migrant labour from Ihanzu. EAISR Jan. (1963), pp. 1-19.

18,012 ALEXANDER, C. S. Fish poisoning along northeastern coast of Tanganyika. TANG. NOTES 62 (1964), pp. 57-60.

18,013 BIENEN, H. The role of Tanu and the five year [development] plan in Tanganyika. EAISR Jan. (1965), pp. 1-21.

18,014 BROWNE, G. S. J. O. Native labour in Tanganyika. J. AFR. SOC. 26 (1927), pp. 112-116.

18,015 CLARK, P. G. The Tanganyika plan: a statistical projection model. EAISR Jan. (1965), pp. 1-13.

18,016 COLE, G. F. Notes on sea-angling off the Tanganyika coast. TANG. NOTES 3 (1937), pp. 15-33.

18,017 EHRLICH, C. Some aspects of economic policy in Tanganyika, 1945-60. JMAS 2 (1964), pp. 265-277.

18,018 EISEN, A. Institutional transfer in Tanzania. PROC. 3RD. GRAD. ACAD. UCLA, 1965, pp. 287-299.

18,019 FRAMWELL, C. Fishing on Kilimanjaro. TANG. NOTES 64 (1965), pp. 90-91.

18,020 FRIEDLAND, W. H. The institutionalization of labor protest in Tanganyika and some resultant problems. SOCIOLOGUS 11 (1961), pp. 132-147.

18,021 GULLIVER, P. H. Nyakyusa labour migration. RHODES-LIV. J. 21 (1957), pp. 32-63.

18,022 HATCHELL, G. W. Further notes on fishing near Tanga. TANG. NOTES 9 (1940), pp. 49-52.

18,023 HATCHELL, G. W. Sea-fishing on the Tanganyika coast. TANG. NOTES 37 (1954), pp. 1-39.

18,024 HATCHELL, G. W. Some notes on sea-fishing near Tanga. TANG. NOTES 5 (1938), pp. 63-65.

18,025 HITCHEN, C. S. Tanganyika coalfields. CORONA 4 (1952), pp. 294-297.

18,026 HUCKS, G. W. Y. A fortune in a Tanganyika swamp. CORONA 1, no. 3 (1949), pp. 19-22.

18,027 JONES, N. S. C. Land settlement schemes in Kenya. AFR. QUART. 4, no. i (1964), pp. 9-19.

18,028 KARMILOFF, G. Regional plan implementation: Tanzania's experiment. E. AFR. EC. REV. N.S. 1, no. 2 (1965), pp. 85-93.

18,029 MAURY, M. J. Sur The report on the preliminary surveys for a railway line to open up the south-west of Tanganyika Territory. BULL. SEANCES IRCB 1 (1930), pp. 357-364.

18,030 NYE, J. Tanganyika's self-help. TRANSITION 11 (1963), pp. 35-39.

18,031 PIGGOTT, D. W. I. Spoonfishing in the Mafia group. TANG. NOTES 37 (1954), pp. 39-48.

18,032 PURVIS, J. T. The Sukumaland development scheme. CORONA 3 (1951), pp. 67-71.

18,033 REBELO, D. J. S. O chá na economia do Tanganhica (um estudo económico). BSEM 144-145 (1965), pp. 89-108; includes English summary.

18,034 SAMUEL, F. The East African groundnuts scheme. AFR. AFFAIRS 46 (1947), pp. 135-145.

18,035 SEABROOK, A. T. P. The groundnut scheme in retrospect. TANGANYIKA NOTES AND RECORDS 47-48 (1957), pp. 87-91.

18,036 SENIOR, H. S. Sukuma salt caravans to Lake Eyasi. TANG. NOTES 6 (1938), pp. 87-90.

18,037 SPALDING, J. Mining and minerals in Tanganyika. TANGANYIKA NOTES AND RECORDS 42 (1956), pp. 31-37.

18,038 WENBAN-SMITH, H. B. The coastal fisheries near Dar es Salaam. TANG. NOTES 61 (1963), pp. 165-174.

18,039 WILLIAMS, R. O. The Zanzibar Clove Growers' Association. CORONA 1, no. 7 (1949), pp. 24-25.

18,040 WINANS, E. V. The political context of economic adaptation in the Southern Highlands of Tanganyika. AMER. ANTHR. 67 (1965), pp. 435-441.

18,041 ZANNA, E. L. Mercati da conoscere: il Tanganyika. AFRICA (Rome) 13 (1958), pp. 33-34.

18,042 Nouveaux plans de développement au Tanganyika [le plan décennal (1947-1956)]. ZAIRE 5 (1951), pp. 528-529.

18,043 Salt production among the Wasambaa. TANG. NOTES 8 (1939), pp. 102-103.

See also 17336, 17357, 17367, 18971, 22205.

Education

18,044 GRIFFITH, A. W. M. Primitive native education in the Bukoba district. TANG. NOTES 1 (1936), pp. 87-89.

18,045 HENDRY, W. Some aspects of education in Zanzibar. J. AFR. SOC. 27 (1928), pp. 342-352.

18,046 HORNSBY, G. A brief history of Tanga school up to 1914. TANGANYIKA NOTES AND RECORDS 58-59 (1962), pp. 148-150.

18,047 HORNSBY, G. German educational achievement in East Africa. TANG. NOTES 62 (1964), pp. 83-90.

18,048 MICAPA, B. Tanganyika's integrated education: its objective and significance. TRANSITION 2 (1961), pp. 13-14.

18,049 MUMFORD, W. B. Education in Tanganyika [1933]. J. AFR. SOC. 34 (1935), pp. 198-200.

18,050 MUMFORD, W. B. Malangali School: a first year's work in the development of a school from native custom and looking towards adjustment to European culture. AFRICA 3 (1930), pp. 265-290.

18,051 RAUM, J. Educational problems in Tanganyika Territory. INT. REV. MISSIONS 19 (1930), pp. 563-575.

18,052 SHANN, G. N. The early development of education among the Chagga. TANGANYIKA NOTES AND RECORDS 45 (1956), pp. 21-32.

18,053 STANLEY, M. Student-staff relations in an African university. Some comments on the social context of higher education. EAISR Dec. (1960), pp. 1-21.

18,054 African schoolgirls in Tanganyika. AFR. WOMEN 2 (1956-1958), pp. 31-34.

18,055 Girls' education in Tanganyika. AFR. WOMEN 1 (1954), pp. 10-13.

18,056 Women in Zanzibar. AFR. WOMEN 1 (1955), pp. 49-51.

Geography

18,057 AITKEN, W. G. Geomorphology of parts of Kondoa District. TANG. NOTES 29 (1950), pp. 55-58.

18,058 ANSTEY, D. Mkomazi Game Reserve. TANGANYIKA NOTES AND RECORDS 50 (1958), pp. 68-70.

18,059 BALLETTO, G. M. Mountains of central Tanganyika. TANGANYIKA NOTES AND RECORDS 58-59 (1962), pp. 64-66.

18,060 BARKER, R. D. The light phenomenon on Mpara Hill near Kilwa. TANG. NOTES 11 (1941), pp. 66-67.

18,061 BARKER, R. DE LA B. The delta of the Rufiji River. TANG. NOTES 2 (1936), pp. 1-6; 4 (1937), pp. 10-16.

18,062 BARKER, R. DE LA B. Stiegler's Gorge, Rufiji. TANGANYIKA NOTES AND RECORDS 55 (1960), pp. 290-292.

18,063 BARNS, T. A. Ngorongoro, the giant crater; and the gorilla, the giant ape. J. AFR. SOC. 22 (1923), pp. 179-188.

18,064 BATTYE, R. K. M. Kilombero. TANG. NOTES 30 (1951), pp. 1-5.

18,065 BOLLENGIER, I. K. Een niew boek, van Ir E. J. Devroey, over het Tanganikameer en de Lukuga, in verband met de bevaarbaarheid van de Congostroom (Middenpand van de Lualaba, Kindu-Ponthierville). ZAIRE 5 (1951), pp. 513-524.

18,066 BURTON, R. Description of a visit to Kilwa in 1859. TANGANYIKA NOTES AND RECORDS 12 (1941), pp. 45-48.

18,067 CHESHAM, Lord. Settlement in Tanganyika. J. AFR. SOC. 37 (1938), pp. 184-190.

18,068 COLLINGWOOD, F. W. N. Kilimanjaro, ordinary: 4th to 8th December, 1950. TANGANYIKA NOTES AND RECORDS 51 (1958), pp. 159-166.

18,069 COOKE, H. J. Kilimanjaro, extraordinary. TANGANYIKA NOTES AND RECORDS 51 (1958), pp. 167-173.

18,070 CORY, H. Buhaya and the African explorer. TANGANYIKA NOTES AND RECORDS 43 (1956), pp. 20-27.

18,071 COUTTS, P. G. Whitsun on Elgon. CORONA 3 (1951), pp. 215-219.

18,072 ELLIOTT, H. F. I. An island in Lake Victoria. TANG. NOTES 10 (1940), pp. 28-40.

18,073 FOSBROOKE, H. A. The early exploration of Kilimanjaro, a bibliographical note. TANG. NOTES 64 (1965), pp. 1-4.

18,074 FOSBROOKE, H. A. Ol Donyo L'Engai. TANGANYIKA NOTES AND RECORDS 41 (1955), pp. 74-75.

18,075 FOURMARIER, P. Note au sujet du bassin charbonnier du Tanganyika. BULL. SEANCES IRCB 6 (1935), pp. 486-493.

18,076 GEILINGER, W. The retreat of the Kilimanjaro glaciers. TANG. NOTES 2 (1936), pp. 7-20.

18,077 GIFFARD, G. G. Ships that have passed. TANG. NOTES 11 (1941), pp. 32-34.

18,078 GILLMAN, C. Clouds and cloudscapes. TANG. NOTES 9 (1940), pp. 1-14.

18,079 GILLMAN, C. A population map of Tanganyika Territory. GEOG. REV. 26 (1936), pp. 353-375.

18,080 GILLMAN, C. A synopsis of the geography of Tanganyika Territory. TANG. NOTES 1 (1936), pp. 5-13.

18,081 GILLMAN, C. A vegetation-types map of Tanganyika Territory. GEOG. REV. 39 (1949), pp. 7-37.

18,082 GRANT, C. H. B. Notes on Uvinza, Tongwe and Ubende, western Tanganyika. TANG. NOTES 27 (1949), pp. 69-73.

18,083 GRANT, D. K. S. Mangrove woods of Tanganyika Territory, their silviculture and dependent industries. TANG. NOTES 5 (1938), pp. 5-16.

18,084 GRANTHAM, D. R. Some Pleistocene lakes in Tanganyika. PROC. PAN-AFR. CONGR. PRE-HIST. 1 (1947), pp. 78-82.

18,085 GREENWAY, P. J. The vegetation and flora of Mt. Kilimanjaro. TANG. NOTES 64 (1965), pp. 97-107.

18,086 GRIFFITHS, J. E. S. A visit to the Island of Godziba in Lake Victoria. TANG. NOTES 28 (1950), pp. 58-63.

18,087 GUEST, N. J. Climbing Oldonyo l'Engai. TANG. NOTES 31 (1951), pp. 55-57.

18,088 GUNN, B. Malagarasi journey. TANGANYIKA NOTES AND RECORDS 58-59 (1962), pp. 153-161.

18,089 HALDEMANN, E. G. Translation of "Description of Lake Victoria and the Wembere Steppe irrigation scheme, 1913." TANGANYIKA NOTES AND RECORDS 47-48 (1957), pp. 103-107.

18,090 HARKIN, D. A. The Sarabwe lava flow, Kiejo, Rungwe District. TANGANYIKA NOTES AND RECORDS 40 (1955), pp. 20-23.

18,091 HARPUM, J. R. The origin of limestone caves with special reference to those of Cheddar and Amboni. TANG. NOTES 27 (1949), pp. 1-7.

18,092 HARRIS, J. H. Lake Manyara. TANG. NOTES 30 (1951), pp. 6-14.

18,093 HASSFORTHER, E. E. An account of a journey through N.W. German East Africa in 1913-14. TANG. NOTES 61 (1963), pp. 209-215.

18,094 HASSING, P. and BENNETT, N. R. A journey across Tanganyika in 1886. TANGANYIKA NOTES AND RECORDS 58-59 (1962), pp. 129-147.

18,095 HATCHELL, G. W. Resettlement in areas reclaimed from tsetse fly. TANGANYIKA NOTES AND RECORDS 53 (1959), pp. 243-247.

18,096 HORNBY, H. E. and HORNBY, R. M. A contribution to the study of the vegetation of Mpwapwa. TANG. NOTES 15 (1943), pp. 25-48.

18,097 JOHNSTON, Sir H. H. The Kilimanjaro expedition. Introductory note by R. F. Eberlie. TANG. NOTES 64 (1965), pp. 15-24.

18,098 KERSTEN, O. Climbing Kilimanjaro one hundred years ago. Introduction and notes by H. A. Fosbrooke. TANG. NOTES 64 (1965), pp. 5-14.

18,099 LANE, L. P. Naval visit, Dar es Salaam—November 1914. TANG. NOTES 16 (1943), pp. 76-78.

18,100 LE ROY, A. Au Kilima-ndjaro, translated from the French by J. A. Hutchinson. TANG. NOTES 64 (1965), pp. 29-34.

18,101 LYNE, R. N. The argument of the appetite. A true story of Africa. J. AFR. SOC. 40 (1941), pp. 140-145.

18,102 McMASTER, D. N. Change of regional balance in the Bukoba district of Tanganyika. GEOG. REV. 50 (1960), pp. 73-88; TANGANYIKA NOTES AND RECORDS 56 (1961), pp. 79-92.

18,103 MEYER, H. Mount Kilimanjaro (the Shining Mountain). Preface written in 1890 by Dr. Hans Meyer to his book: Across East African Glaciers. TANG. NOTES 64 (1965), pp. 25-28.

18,104 MOFFETT, J. P. One hundred years ago in Tanganyika. TANG. NOTES 33 (1952), pp. 83-90.

18,105 MOFFETT, J. P. A raft on the Malagarasi. TANG. NOTES 16 (1943), pp. 54-75.

18,106 MOREAU, R. E. Kilimanjaro and Mount Kenya: some comparisons, with special reference to the mammals and birds; and with a note on Mount Meru with a bibliography of Kilimanjaro, by C. Gillman. TANG. NOTES 18 (1944), pp. 28-68.

18,107 MOREAU, R. E. Local sinkage of the reef off Pangani. TANG. NOTES 7 (1939), p. 116.

18,108 MOREAU, R. E. and GREENWAY, P. J. A note on Longido and Ketumbeine Mountains. TANG. NOTES 3 (1937), pp. 8-14.

18,109 MORGAN, P. R. A Rufiji experiment. TANGANYIKA NOTES AND RECORDS 52 (1959), pp. 33-34.

18,110 O'HAGAN, C. C. Mkungwe Mountain. TANG. NOTES 9 (1940), pp. 53-60.

18,111 PEET, G. A. New caves near Tanga and their relation to the Amboni group. TANGANYIKA NOTES AND RECORDS 47-48 (1957), pp. 149-158.

18,112 PIGGOTT, D. W. I. Magari. TANG. NOTES 11 (1941), pp. 61-63.

18,113 PIKE, A. G. Kilimanjaro and the furrow system. TANG. NOTES 64 (1965), pp. 95-96.

18,114 PROCTER, J. The second ascent of Kungwe mountain. TANGANYIKA NOTES AND RECORDS 51 (1958), pp. 239-245.

18,115 PUGH, K. T. How high is Kilimanjaro. TANG. NOTES 64 (1965), pp. 144-146.

18,116 QUIRING, D. P. The Cleveland Clinic-Museum expedition to Northern Tanganyika. TANG. NOTES 2 (1936), pp. 101-103.

18,117 RAMSAY, J. C. Kilimanjaro—sources of water supplies. TANG. NOTES 64 (1965), pp. 92-94.

18,118 REUSCH, R. Mount Kilimanjaro and its ascent. TANG. NOTES 64 (1965), pp. 131-134.

18,119 REVINGTON, T. M. Some notes on the Mafia Island group (Mafia, Chole, Juani and Jibondo). TANG. NOTES 1 (1936), pp. 33-37.

18,120 REVINGTON, T. M. Stick-in-the-mud. TANG. NOTES 6 (1938), pp. 103-104.

18,121 ROSE, Sister. Voyage de Marseille au lac Tanganyika en 1902 via Mozambique et lac Nyasa. TANG. NOTES 3 (1937), pp. 110-113.

18,122 SAMPSON, D. N. The geology, volcanology and glaciology of Kilimanjaro. TANG. NOTES 64 (1965), pp. 118-124.

18,123 SALT, G. The Shira Plateau of Kilimanjaro. TANGANYIKA NOTES AND RECORDS 39 (1955), pp. 39-53.

18,124 SAWE, J. A. The Outward Bound Mountain School of East Africa. TANG. NOTES 64 (1965), pp. 141-143.

18,125 SCOTT, R. R. The reefs of San Raphael. TANGANYIKA NOTES AND RECORDS 14 (1942), pp. 19-26.

18,126 SEGAL, D. "Expedition Ramonage." Ten days spent in the crater of Kibo in 1963. TANG. NOTES 64 (1965), pp. 125-130.

18,127 SMITH, A. The Amboni caves—a third theory. TANG. NOTES 61 (1963), pp. 195-204.

18,128 SMITH, E. W. The earliest ox-wagons in Tanganyika—an experiment which failed. TANGANYIKA NOTES AND RECORDS 40 (1955), pp. 1-14; 41 (1955), pp. 1-15.

18,129 SOMERVILLE, A. A. et al. The parliamentary visit to Tanganyika, 1928. J. AFR. SOC. 28 (1929), pp. 122-148.

18,130 STEVENS, T. E. Oxford University Tanganyika expeditions 1958-9. TANGANYIKA NOTES AND RECORDS 58-59 (1962), pp. 110-115.

18,131 STOCKLEY, G. M. Geological notes on the coastal region of Tanganyika. TANG. NOTES 3 (1937), pp. 82-86.

18,132 STOCKLEY, G. M. The geology of the Rufiji District, including a small portion of northern Kilwa District (Matumbi Hills). TANG. NOTES 16 (1943), pp. 7-28.

18,133 TEALE, E. O. Geographical and geological problems in East Africa, with special reference to Tanganyika territory. J. AFR. SOC. 23 (1923), pp. 6-17.

18,134 TEALE, E. O. and HARVEY, E. A physiographical map of Tanganyika Territory. GEOG. REV. 23 (1933), pp. 402-413.

18,135 THOMAS, Father. Un voyage de Marseille au lac Tanganyika en 1906. TANG. NOTES 5 (1938), pp. 25-30.

18,136 THRELFALL, H. R. Some physical features of the Dar es Salaam district. TANG. NOTES 29 (1950), pp. 68-72.

18,137 WATERMEYER, A. M. and ELLIOTT, H. F. I. Lake Manyara. TANG. NOTES 15 (1943), pp. 58-71.

18,138 WELCH, J. R. A note on the subsequent history of the resettlement area. TANGANYIKA NOTES AND RECORDS 53 (1959), pp. 247-249.

18,139 WRIGHT, C. A. Climbing Kilimanjaro—"the easy way"—1963. TANG. NOTES 64 (1965), pp. 135-139.

18,140 WYATT, A. W. Earthquake at Songea. TANG. NOTES 16 (1943), pp. 91-95.

18,141 The 'Eiger' of Africa. TANG. NOTES 64 (1965), p. 140.

18,142 Struck by lightning. TANG. NOTES 27 (1949), pp. 77-78.

18,143 Three French parachutists land on Kilimanjaro. TANG. NOTES 64 (1965), p. 143.

See also 15986, 17383.

Government

18,144 AUSTEN, R. A. Notes on the pre-history of TANU. MAKERERE J. 9 (1964), pp. 1-6.

18,145 AUSTEN, R. A. The study of indirect rule in a Tanganyika province. EAISR Jan. (1963), pp. 1-14.

18,146 BENNETT, G. An outline history of TANU. MAKERERE J. 7 (1963), pp. 15-32.

18,147 BIENEN, H. National security in Tanganyika after the mutiny. TRANSITION 21 (1965), pp. 39-46.

18,148 BIENEN, H. The party and the no party state: Tanganyika and the Soviet Union. TRANSITION 13 (1964), pp. 25-32.

18,149 BURKE, F. ...While other countries aim to reach the moon...we must aim to reach the villages. EAISR Jan. (1963), part A, pp. 1-13.

18,150 CAMERON, Sir D. Native administration in Tanganyika and Nigeria. J. AFR. SOC. 36 (1937), supplement.

18,151 CLIFF, L. Nationalism and the reaction to enforced agricultural improvement in Tanganyika during the colonial period. EAISR Jan. (1965), pp. 1-10.

18,152 COLE, J. S. R. Progress to independence: Tanganyika. TANGANYIKA NOTES AND RECORDS 58-59 (1962), pp. 179-186.

18,153 CORY, H. Reform of tribal political institutions in Tanganyika. J. AFR. ADM. 12 (1960), pp. 77-84.

18,154 CULWICK, A. T. New beginning [in Tanganyika]. RHODES-LIV. J. 1 (1944), pp. 44-49.

18,155 CULWICK, A. T. and CULWICK, G. M. What the Wabena think of indirect rule. J. AFR. SOC. 36 (1937), pp. 176-193.

18,156 DUDBRIDGE, B. J. and GRIFFITHS, J. E. S. The development of local government in Sukumaland. J. AFR. ADM. 3 (1951), pp. 141-146.

18,157 DUFF, P. C. Land and politics among the Luguru of Tanganyika. TANGANYIKA NOTES AND RECORDS 56 (1961), pp. 111-114.

18,158 FLETCHER-COOKE, J. Tanganyika and the Trusteeship Council. TANGANYIKA NOTES AND RECORDS 56 (1961), pp. 40-48.

18,159 GLYNN, F. J. Africanization and job analysis in Tanganyika. J. LOCAL ADM. OV. 2 (1963), pp. 149-153.

18,160 GOWER, R. H. An experiment in district training. J. AFR. ADM. 4 (1952), pp. 6-9.

18,161 GRAY, A. Republic move in Tanganyika. AFR. AFFAIRS 61 (1962), pp. 297-299.

18,162 GRAY, A. Tanganyika. AFR. AFFAIRS 55 (1956), pp. 173-175.

18,163 GRAY, A. Tanganyika advances. AFR. AFFAIRS 60 (1961), pp. 374-377.

18,164 GRAY, A. Tanganyika [constitutional] changes. AFR. AFFAIRS 59 (1960), pp. 100-101, 274-275.

18,165 GRAY, A. Tanganyika independence. AFR. AFFAIRS 61 (1962), pp. 104-107.

18,166 GRAY, A. Tanganyika's progress. AFR. AFFAIRS 57 (1958), pp. 175-178.

18,167 GRAY, A. Zanzibar government. AFR. AFFAIRS 56 (1957), pp. 18-19.

18,168 HARRIS, C. C. Development of local councils and reorganisation of local government, Bukoba district. EAISR June (1952), pp. 37-42.

18,169 HARRIS, C. C. Tanganyika today; the background. INTERNAT. AFFAIRS 36 (1960), pp. 35-43.

18,170 HUCKS, G. W. Y. Legislative Council elections—1958. TANGANYIKA NOTES AND RECORDS 54 (1960), pp. 38-47.

18,171 INGHAM, K. Tanganyika in the 'twenties: the era of Byatt and Cameron. TANGANYIKA NOTES AND RECORDS 52 (1959), pp. 18-30.

18,172 JOHNSTON, P. H. Chagga constitutional development. J. AFR. ADM. 5 (1953), pp. 134-140.

18,173 KAWAWA, R. M. Africanisation. AFR. SOUTH 5, no. 1 (1960), pp. 96-98.

18,174 KINGDOM, Z. E. The initiation of a system of local government by African Rural Councils in the Rungwe district of Tanganyika. J. AFR. ADM. 3 (1951), pp. 186-191.

18,175 KIRBY, Sir A. Tanganyika triumph. AFR. AFFAIRS 61 (1962), pp. 114-125.

18,176 LAWRANCE, J. C. D. A pilot scheme for grant of land titles in Uganda. J. AFR. ADM. 12 (1960), pp. 135-143.

18,177 LIEBENOW, J. G. The chief in Sukuma local government. J. AFR. ADM. 11 (1959), pp. 84-92.

18,178 LIEBENOW, J. G. The establishment of legitimacy in a dependency situation: a case study of the Nyaturu of Tanganyika. AFR. STUD. 20 (1961), pp. 33-52.

18,179 LIEBENOW, J. G. Some problems in introducing local government reform in Tanganyika. J. AFR. ADM. 8 (1956), pp. 132-139.

18,180 LIEBENOW, J. G. Tribalism, traditionalism, and modernism in Chagga local government. J. AFR. ADM. 10 (1958), pp. 71-82.

18,181 LOFCHIE, M. F. Party conflict in Zanzibar. JMAS 1 (1963), pp. 185-207.

18,182 LOFCHIE, M. F. Party conflict in Zanzibar: the origins and background of Zanzibar nationalism. EAISR Jan. (1963), pp. 1-14.

18,183 MacKENZIE, W. J. M. Changes in local government in Tanganyika. J. AFR. ADM. 6 (1954), pp. 123-129.

18,184 MATHER, K. G. A note on African councils in the Rungwe district in Tanganyika. J. AFR. ADM. 9 (1957), pp. 182-188.

18,185 MAWHOOD, P. N. Choosing the town councillor. The development of representative local government in the towns of Tanganyika. J. AFR. ADM. 13 (1961), pp. 131-138.

18,186 MAZRUI, A. A. Tanzania versus East Africa. A case of unwitting Federal sabotage. J. COMM. POL. STUD. 3 (1965), pp. 209-225.

18,187 MEEK, C. I. A practical experiment in local government. J. AFR. ADM. 2 (1950), pp. 21-28.

18,188 MEEK, C. I. Stock reduction in the Mbulu Highlands, Tanganyika. J. AFR. ADM. 5 (1953), pp. 158-166.

18,189 MILLER, N. N. Village leadership in Tanzania: a preliminary evaluation. EAISR Jan. (1965), pp. 1-16.

18,190 MOHAMED, A. R. Election postscript. AFR. SOUTH 5, no. 3 (1961), pp. 90-92.

18,191 MOLOHAN, M. J. B. Report on Detribalization. J. AFR. ADM. 10 (1958), pp. 111-115.

18,192 MONTAGUE, F. A. Native authorities: the new democracy. CORONA 1, no. 5 (1949), pp. 18-20.

18,193 MONTAGUE, F. A. Some difficulties in the democratisation of Native Authorities in Tanganyika. J. AFR. ADM. 3 (1951), pp. 21-27.

18,194 NORTON, I. H. An inter-racial local council in Tanganyika. J. AFR. ADM. 8 (1956), pp. 26-32.

18,195 NYERERE, J. K. The relationship between the civil service, political parties and members of Legislative Council. J. AFR. ADM. 13 (1961), pp. 108-111.

18,196 NYERERE, J. K. Tanganyika today; the nationalist view. INTERNAT. AFFAIRS 36 (1960), pp. 43-47.

18,197 OLDAKER, A. A. Tribal customary land tenure in Tanganyika. TANGANYIKA NOTES AND RECORDS 47-48 (1957), pp. 117-144.

18,198 PENNEY, J. C. Notes on the election in the Protectorate of Zanzibar, 1957. J. AFR. ADM. 10 (1958), pp. 144-152.

18,199 PERHAM, M. F. The system of native administration in Tanganyika. AFRICA 4 (1931), pp. 302-312.

18,200 REINING, P. Village organisation in Buhaya. EAISR June (1952), pp. 43-47.

18,201 SHADBOLT, K. E. Local government elections in a Tanganyika district. J. AFR. ADM. 13 (1961), pp. 78-84.

18,202 SHAW, J. V. The development of African local government in Sukumaland. J. AFR. ADM. 6 (1954), pp. 171-178.

18,203 SMITH, R. W. The Native Authority system in Biharamulo, Tanganyika. EAISR June (1952), pp. 1-4 of addendum.

18,204 SPRY, J. F. Some notes on land tenure, adjudication of rights and registration of titles with specific reference to Tanganyika. J. AFR. ADM. 8 (1956), pp. 175-179.

18,205 SWARTZ, M. J. Preliminary reflections on Bena political power. EAISR June (1963), pp. 1-9.

18,206 TANGANYIKA. MINISTRY OF LOCAL GOVERNMENT AND ADMINISTRATION. Report on the Development of Local Government in Tanganyika, 1956. J. AFR. ADM. 10 (1958), pp. 117-118.

18,207 TANNER, R. E. S. Local government elections in Ngara, Tanganyika. A study in the process of social change. J. LOCAL ADM. OV. 1 (1962), pp. 173-182.

18,208 TANZANIA. Tanganyika-Zanzibar union. AFR. QUART. 4, no. i (1964), pp. 48-50.

18,209 TAWNEY, J. Election in Tanganyika. CORONA 4 (1952), pp. 181-183.

18,210 TORDOFF, W. Parliament in Tanzania. J. COMM. POL. STUD. 3 (1965), pp. 85-103.

18,211 TORDOFF, W. Regional administration in Tanganyika. EAISR Jan. (1965), pp. 37-57; JMAS 3 (1965), pp. 63-89.

18,212 TWINING, Sir E. The situation in Tanganyika. AFR. AFFAIRS 50 (1951), pp. 297-310.

18,213 TYLER, J. W. Minor chiefs in Rusubi chiefdom, Buzinza. EAISR June (1952), pp. 52-59.

18,214 VARMA, S. N. Independent Zanzibar. AFR. QUART. 3, no. iii (1963), pp. 148-155.

18,215 WARRELL-BOWRING, W. J. The reorganization of the administration in Tanganyika. J. LOCAL ADM. OV. 2 (1963), pp. 188-194.

18,216 WHITELEY, W. Modern local government among the Makua. AFRICA 24 (1954), pp. 349-358.

18,217 WINNINGTON-INGRAM, C. Reforming local government in a Tanganyika district. J. AFR. ADM. 2 (1950), pp. 10-15.

18,218 Administrative and departmental staffs—co-ordination of work. [Tanganyika Government Circular No. 7 of 1954.] J. AFR. ADM. 7 (1955), pp. 75-76.

18,219 Dans les territoires sous tutelle britannique. ZAIRE 5 (1951), pp. 406-407.

18,220 The Lake Province Council, Tanganyika. J. AFR. ADM. 2 (1950), pp. 21-24.

18,221 The Makonde Water Corporation: Report of Committee of Inquiry. J. AFR. ADM. 12 (1960), pp. 187-188.

18,222 Recommendations for the development of local government in Tanganyika. A digest...of the report of the Committee for Constitutional Development in Tanganyika. J. AFR. ADM. 4 (1952), pp. 29-31.

18,223 Report on Local Government in Zanzibar, 1960. J. AFR. ADM. 13 (1961), pp. 126-127.

18,224 Report on the administration of Tanganyika Territory, 1935. J. AFR. SOC. 36 (1937), pp. 91-94.

18,225 République du Tanganyika. GENEVE-AFR. 1 (1962), pp. 216-217.

18,226 Some notes on native administration in Tanganyika. AFR. AFFAIRS 48 (1949), pp. 240-242.

18,227 The Sukumaland Federation Land Settlement Rules, December 20th, 1950. J. AFR. ADM. 3 (1951), pp. 207-208.

18,228 Tanganyika territory: Annual reports of the provincial commissioners on native administration for the year 1932. J. AFR. SOC. 32 (1933), pp. 372-376.

See also 15621, 17479.

History

18,229 ABDALLAH BIN HEMEDI BIN ALI LIAJJEMI. The story of Mbega, translated by Roland Allen. TANG. NOTES 1 (1936), pp. 38-51; 2 (1936), pp. 80-91; 3 (1937), pp. 87-98.

18,230 BAKER, E. C. Notes on the history of the Wasegeju. TANG. NOTES 27 (1949), pp. 16-41.

18,231 BARNWELL, P. J. Origins of Dar es Salaam. TANGANYIKA NOTES AND RECORDS 58-59 (1962), pp. 297-298.

18,232 BAUMANN, O. Mafia Island. TANGANYIKA NOTES AND RECORDS 46 (1957), pp. 1-24.

18,233 BAX, S. N. Notes on the presence of tsetse fly, between 1857 and 1915, in the Dar es Salaam area. TANG. NOTES 16 (1943), pp. 33-48.

18,234 BECKER, A. The capture and death of the rebel leader Bushiri. TANGANYIKA NOTES AND RECORDS 60 (1963), pp. 2-9.

18,235 BECKER, A. A new Sultan succeeds to the throne in Zanzibar... TANG. NOTES 61 (1963), pp. 147-154.

18,236 BECKER, A. The subjugation of Chief Meli of Moshi, 1893. TANGANYIKA NOTES AND RECORDS 57 (1961), pp. 199-209.

18,237 BEIDELMAN, T. O. A history of Ukaguru: 1857-1916. TANGANYIKA NOTES AND RECORDS 58-59 (1962), pp. 11-39.

18,238 BELL, R. M. The Maji-Maji Rebellion in the Liwale District. TANG. NOTES 28 (1950), pp. 38-57.

18,239 BENNETT, N. R. Americans in Zanzibar: 1825-1845. TANGANYIKA NOTES AND RECORDS 56 (1961), pp. 93-108; 57 (1961), pp. 121-138.

18,240 BENNETT, N. R. Americans in Zanzibar: 1865-1915. TANGANYIKA NOTES AND RECORDS 60 (1963), pp. 49-66.

18,241 BENNETT, N. R. The British on Kilimanjaro: 1884-1892. TANG. NOTES 63 (1964), pp. 229-244.

18,242 BENNETT, N. R. Captain Storms in Tanganyika: 1882-1885. TANGANYIKA NOTES AND RECORDS 54 (1960), pp. 51-63.

18,243 BERGER, R. Oral traditions in Karagwe. EAISR June (1963), pp. 1-7.

18,244 BOJARSKI, E. A. The last of the cannibals in Tanganyika. TANGANYIKA NOTES AND RECORDS 51 (1958), pp. 227-231.

18,245 BRIGGS, J. H. German East Africa during the War. J. AFR. SOC. 16 (1917), pp. 193-199.

18,246 BRUWER, J. Note on Maravi origin and migration. AFR. STUD. 9 (1950), pp. 32-34.

18,247 BYATT, H. Tanganyika. J. AFR. SOC. 24 (1924), pp. 1-9.

18,248 C., J. Le héros des Wahehe. ZAIRE 8 (1954), p. 951.

18,249 C., J. Occidentalisation de Zanzibar. ZAIRE 8 (1954), pp. 640-641.

18,250 CAMERON, D. Position and prospects in Tanganyika. J. AFR. SOC. 26 (1927), pp. 315-322.

18,251 CANA, F. R. German East Africa and its future. J. AFR. SOC. 17 (1918), pp. 125-135.

18,252 CEULEMANS, P. Le séjour de Stanley à Zanzibar (18 mars-fin mai 1879). ZAIRE 11 (1957), pp. 675-685.

18,253 CHARLEWOOD, C. J. Naval actions on the Tanganyika coast, 1914-1917. TANGANYIKA NOTES AND RECORDS 54 (1960), pp. 120-138; 55 (1960), pp. 153-180.

18,254 CHHABRA, H. S. Tanganyika attains independence. AFR. QUART. 1, no. iii (1961), pp. 30-38.

18,255 CHITTICK, N. Kilwa and the Arab settlement of the East African coast. J. AFR. HIST. 4 (1963), pp. 179-190.

18,256 CRIPWELL, H. A. Operations around Mpepo, German East Africa, 1917. RHODESIANA 10 (1964), pp. 54-79.

18,257 DU TOIT, P. J. Notes on the coinage of German East Africa (Tanganyika). TANG. NOTES 31 (1951), pp. 37-41.

18,258 EDWARDS, C. A. The Germans on Lake Nyasa. TANG. NOTES 61 (1963), pp. 217-218.

18,259 ELLIS, P. J. C. Ubungu in Chunya District. TANGANYIKA NOTES AND RECORDS 47-48 (1957), pp. 201-202.

18,260 FILESI, T. I rapporti tra l'Italia e il Sultanato di Zanzibar (1885-1893). AFRICA (Rome) 14 (1959), pp. 135-143.

18,261 FOSBROOKE, H. A. Chagga forts and bolt holes. TANG. NOTES 37 (1954), pp. 115-129.

18,262 FOSBROOKE, H. A. The defensive measures of certain tribes in North-Eastern Tanganyika. TANG. NOTES 35 (1953), pp. 1-6; 36 (1954), pp. 50-51.

18,263 FOSBROOKE, H. A. The "Masai walls" of Moa: walled towns of the Segeju. TANGANYIKA NOTES AND RECORDS 54 (1960), pp. 29-37.

18,264 FOSBROOKE, H. A. Tanganyika's population problem: an historical explanation. RHODES-LIV. J. 23 (1958), pp. 54-58.

18,265 FREEMAN-GRENVILLE, G. S. P. In search of the history of the "Tabora sovereign." TANGANYIKA NOTES AND RECORDS 50 (1958), pp. 49-51.

18,266 GAVIN, R. J. The Bartle Frere mission to Zanzibar, 1873. HISTORICAL J. 2 (1962), pp. 122-148.

18,267 GAVIN, R.J. Sayyid Sa'id. TARIKH 1, no. 1 (1965), pp. 16-29.

18,268 GILLMAN, C. "San Rafael" once more. TANG. NOTES 17 (1944), p. 66.

18,269 GILLMAN, C. A short history of the Tanganyika Railways. TANGANYIKA NOTES AND RECORDS 13 (1942), pp. 14-56.

18,270 GOWER, R. H. Ukutu in the nineteenth century. TANGANYIKA NOTES AND RECORDS 51 (1958), pp. 206-215.

18,271 GRAY, Sir J. M. Another letter of Emin Pasha. UGANDA J. 14 (1950), pp. 219-220.

18,272 GRAY, Sir J. M. The British Vice-consulate at Kilwa Kivinji, 1884-1885. TANGANYIKA NOTES AND RECORDS 51 (1958), pp. 174-194.

18,273 GRAY, Sir J. M. Commercial intercourse between Angola and Kilwa in the sixteenth century. TANGANYIKA NOTES AND RECORDS 57 (1961), pp. 173-174.

18,274 GRAY, Sir J. M. Dar es Salaam under the Sultans of Zanzibar. TANG. NOTES 33 (1952), pp. 1-21.

18,275 GRAY, Sir J. M. Early Portuguese visitors to Kilwa. TANGANYIKA NOTES AND RECORDS 52 (1959), pp. 117-128; 57 (1961), pp. 175-176.

18,276 GRAY, Sir J. M. A European graveyard at Kigoma. TANG. NOTES 37 (1954), pp. 130-133.

18,277 GRAY, Sir J. M. Fort Santiago at Kilwa. TANGANYIKA NOTES AND RECORDS 58-59 (1962), pp. 175-178.

18,278 GRAY, Sir J. M. A French account of Kilwa at the end of the eighteenth century. TANG. NOTES 63 (1964), pp. 224-228.

18,279 GRAY, Sir J. M. The French at Kilwa, 1776-1784. TANGANYIKA NOTES AND RECORDS 44 (1956), pp. 28-49.

18,280 GRAY, Sir J. M. The French at Kilwa in 1797. TANGANYIKA NOTES AND RECORDS 58-59 (1962), pp. 172-173.

18,281 GRAY, Sir J. M. A history of Kilwa. TANG. NOTES 31 (1951), pp. 1-24; 32 (1952), pp. 11-37.

18,282 GRAY, Sir J. M. Mikindani Bay before 1887. TANG. NOTES 28 (1950), pp. 29-37.

18,283 GRAY, Sir J. M. Official use of the Persian solar calendar by the sultans of Zanzibar. TANGANYIKA NOTES AND RECORDS 58-59 (1962), p. 211.

18,284 GRAY, Sir J. M. The opening of Dar es Salaam as a sea port. TANGANYIKA NOTES AND RECORDS 58-59 (1962), p. 224.

18,285 GRAY, Sir J. M. The recovery of Kilwa by the Arabs in 1785. TANG. NOTES 62 (1964), pp. 20-26.

18,286 GRAY, Sir J. M. Sir John Henderson and the Princess of Zanzibar. TANGANYIKA NOTES AND RECORDS 40 (1955), pp. 15-19.

18,287 GRAY, Sir J. M. Sir John Kirk and Mutesa. UGANDA J. 15 (1951), pp. 1-16.

18,288 GRAY, Sir J. M. Stanley versus Tippoo Tib. BULL. UGANDA SOC. 2 (1944), pp. 18-20; TANG. NOTES 18 (1944), pp. 11-27.

18,289 GRAY, Sir J. M. Visit of a French ship to Kilwa in 1527. TANG. NOTES 63 (1964), pp. 222-223.

18,290 GRAY, Sir J. M. Zanzibar local histories. SWAHILI 30 (1959), pp. 24-40; 31 (1960), pp. 111-139.

18,291 GRAY, R. F. The Mbugwe tribe: origin and development. TANGANYIKA NOTES AND RECORDS 38 (1955), pp. 39-50.

18,292 GROOT, E. DE. Great Britain and Germany, in Zanzibar: Consul Holmwood's papers, 1886-1887. J. MOD. HIST. 25 (1953), pp. 120-138.

18,293 GULLIVER, P. H. A history of the Songea Ngoni. TANGANYIKA NOTES AND RECORDS 41 (1955), pp. 16-30.

18,294 HAARER, A. E. Tanganyika yesterday and to-day. CONTEMP. REV. 179 (1951), pp. 165-167.

18,295 HALL, R. DE Z. Angoni raids in the Rufiji District. TANG. NOTES 27 (1949), pp. 74-75.

18,296 HAMOUD BIN MAHOMED BIN SAID. The abolition of slavery in Zanzibar. LIBERIA BULL. 11 (1897), pp. 22-24.

18,297 HAMSHERE, C. E. The campaign in German East Africa. HISTORY TODAY 15 (1965), pp. 249-258.

18,298 HARTNOLL, M. A story of the origin of the name of Bandar-es-Salaam, which in the old days was called Mzi-zima. TANG. NOTES 3 (1937), pp. 117-119.

18,299 HATCHELL, G. W. The British occupation of the South-Western Area of Tanganyika Territory. TANGANYIKA NOTES AND RECORDS 51 (1958), pp. 131-155.

18,300 HATCHELL, G. W. History of the ruling family of Ukerewe. TANGANYIKA NOTES AND RECORDS 47-48 (1957), pp. 198-200.

18,301 HATCHELL, G. W. Maritime relics of the 1914-18 War. TANG. NOTES 36 (1954), pp. 1-21.

18,302 HATCHELL, G. W. San Raphael once again. TANG. NOTES 31 (1951), pp. 51-52.

18,303 HELLBERG, C. J. The German Evangelical Mission and the north-western boundaries of Tanganyika. TANGANYIKA NOTES AND RECORDS 58-59 (1962), pp. 207-210.

18,304 HOFMEYR, I. H. Germany's colonial claims: a South African view. FOREIGN AFFAIRS 17 (1938-1939), pp. 788-798.

18,305 HOLLIS, C. Zanzibar: present conditions and interests. J. AFR. SOC. 28 (1929), pp. 217-223.

18,306 HONE, E. D. Raid! TANG. NOTES 2 (1936), pp. 98-100.

18,307 HOWES, A. M. D. Some details of the first twenty-five years of flying in Tanganyika, 1914-1939. TANGANYIKA NOTES AND RECORDS 50 (1958), pp. 39-47.

18,308 HUGHES, T. A profile of Zanzibar. AFR. SOUTH 5, no. 3 (1961), pp. 85-89.

18,309 HUGHES, T. Tanganyika on the eve [of independence]. AFR. SOUTH 6 (1961), pp. 64-74.

18,310 INGHAM, K. Tanganyika in the twenties. MAKERERE J. 1 (1958), pp. 8-24.

18,311 JERVIS, T. S. A history of robusta coffee in Bukoba. TANG. NOTES 8 (1939), pp. 47-58.

18,312 JIDDAWI, A. M. Extracts from an Arab account book, 1840-1854. TANG. NOTES 31 (1951), pp. 25-31.

18,313 JOELSON, F. S. War comes to Tanganyika. TANGANYIKA NOTES AND RECORDS 58-59 (1962), pp. 295-297.

18,314 KIDAMALA, D. and DANIELSON, E. R. A brief history of the Waniramba people up to the time of the German occupation. TANGANYIKA NOTES AND RECORDS 56 (1961), pp. 67-78.

18,315 KIRO, S. Tribal history and legend: the history of the Zigua tribe, translated from the Swahili of Selemani Kiro by Petro Sh. Mntambo. TANG. NOTES 34 (1953), pp. 70-74.

18,316 KOENIG, O. The ancient wells of Ngassumat in South Masailand. TANG. NOTES 31 (1951), pp. 53-54.

18,317 LAMBOURN, A. R. Zanzibar to Masasi in 1876, the founding of Masasi Mission. TANG. NOTES 31 (1951), pp. 42-46.

18,318 LANE, L. P. The T.R.S. Mwanza. TANG. NOTES 6 (1938), pp. 72-78.

18,319 LEVERETT, C. W. An outline of the history of railways in Tanganyika 1890-1956. TANGANYIKA NOTES AND RECORDS 47-48 (1957), pp. 108-116.

18,320 LONGLAND, F. A note on the Tembe at Kwihara, Tabora. TANG. NOTES 1 (1936), pp. 84-86.

18,321 MacKENZIE, G. S. British East Africa. ROYAL COL. INST. PR. 22 (1890-1891), pp. 3-30.

18,322 MARTIN, B. G. Review article: The mediaeval history of the Tanganyika coast (G. S. P. Freeman-Grenville). TRANS. HIST. SOC. GHANA 7 (1964), pp. 124-131.

18,323 MARVIN, D. K. The Boma at Masoko-Rungwe District. TANGANYIKA NOTES AND RECORDS 57 (1961), pp. 216-225.

18,324 MASEFIELD, G. Livingstone and the Baganda. BULL. UGANDA SOC. 4 (1945), pp. 14-17.

18,325 MATSON, A. T. A note on non-native vessels on Lake Victoria. TANGANYIKA NOTES AND RECORDS 58-59 (1962), pp. 225-226.

18,326 MIDDLETON, J. Society and politics in Zanzibar. CIVILISATIONS 12 (1962), pp. 375-383; French summary, pp. 384-387.

18,327 MWENE KAROLO ILONGA II BIN SASAWATA. The story of the Wawungu. TANGANYIKA NOTES AND RECORDS 52 (1959), pp. 75-93.

18,328 NTEMO, F. D. Some notes on Ngulu. TANGANYIKA NOTES AND RECORDS 45 (1956), pp. 15-19.

18,329 OSBORNE, J. M. The Berlin Mission. TANGANYIKA NOTES AND RECORDS 54 (1960), pp. 64-68.

18,330 O'SULLEVAN, J. J. Campaign on German East Africa—Rhodesian border. J. AFR. SOC. 15 (1916), pp. 209-215.

18,331 PENNINGTON, A. L. Refugees in Tanganyika during the Second World War. TANG. NOTES 32 (1952), pp. 52-56.

18,332 PHATAK, D. M. A note on a privately issued token. TANGANYIKA NOTES AND RECORDS 57 (1961), p. 180.

18,333 PHATAK, D. M. Note on Tabora emergency coinage. TANGANYIKA NOTES AND RECORDS 50 (1958), p. 48.

18,334 PHATAK, D. M. Weights of five Heller coins minted at Tabora in 1916. TANGANYIKA NOTES AND RECORDS 52 (1959), pp. 31-32.

18,335 PIGGOTT, D. W. I. History of Mafia. TANG. NOTES 11 (1941), pp. 35-40.

18,336 PRINS, A. H. J. Uncertainties in coastal cultural history: the "ngalawa" and the "mtepe." TANGANYIKA NOTES AND RECORDS 53 (1959), pp. 204-213.

18,337 REUSCH, R. How the Swahili people and language came into existence. TANG. NOTES 34 (1953), pp. 20-27.

18,338 REUSCH, R. The struggle of Mombasa for its freedom. TANG. NOTES 35 (1953), pp. 53-62.

18,339 RICHARDSON, R. B. Livingstone's Tembe at Kwihara, Tabora. TANG. NOTES 9 (1940), p. 68.

18,340 RUSSELL, A. The landing at Tanga, 1914. TANGANYIKA NOTES AND RECORDS 58-59 (1962), pp. 103-109.

18,341 RUSSELL, A. War comes to Tanganyika—1914. TANGANYIKA NOTES AND RECORDS 57 (1961), pp. 195-198.

18,342 SAADI, K. A. O. Mafia—history and traditions. TANGANYIKA NOTES AND RECORDS 12 (1941), pp. 23-27.

18,343 SALEH, I. The Comoro Islands: notes of a lecture delivered at the Zanzibar Museum. TANGANYIKA NOTES AND RECORDS 12 (1941), pp. 51-60.

18,344 SHANN, G. N. Tanganyika place names of European origin. TANGANYIKA NOTES AND RECORDS 54 (1960), pp. 79-88.

18,345 STAHL, K. M. Outline of Chagga history. TANG. NOTES 64 (1965), pp. 35-49.

18,346 TAUTE, M. A German account of the medical side of the war in East Africa, 1914-18. TANG. NOTES 8 (1939), pp. 1-20.

18,347 TERLINDEN, C. Les campagnes belges dans l'Est africain allemand (1914-1917). RHCF 25 (1932), pp. 77-98.

18,348 THOMAS, H. B. The Kionga Triangle. TANG. NOTES 31 (1951), pp. 47-50.

18,349 THOMSON, C. A special sort of day. TRANSITION 6-7 (1962), pp. 58-59.

18,350 TWINING, Lord. The last nine years in Tanganyika. AFR. AFFAIRS 58 (1959), pp. 15-24.

18,351 WALKER, J. and FREEMAN-GRENVILLE, G. S. P. The history and coinage of the sultans of Kilwa. TANGANYIKA NOTES AND RECORDS 45 (1956), pp. 33-65.

18,352 WEBSTER, J. B. Mirambo and Nyamwezi unification. TARIKH 1, no. 1 (1965), pp. 64-71.

18,353 WENBAN-SMITH, W. Diary of the 1857-1858 expedition to the Great Lakes. TANGANYIKA NOTES AND RECORDS 49 (1957), pp. 247-255.

18,354 WILLIS, R. G. Traditional history and social structure in Ufipa. EAISR Jan. (1964), pp. 1-15; also in AFRICA 34 (1964), pp. 340-351.

18,355 YEO, P. H. Caput Nili—the travels of Richard Kandt in German East Africa. TANG. NOTES 63 (1964), pp. 207-212.

18,356 YONGE, D. D. The history of Tabora 15-rupee piece. TANG. NOTES 62 (1964), pp. 49-56.

18,357 YONGE, D. D. Tabora emergency coinage. TANGANYIKA NOTES AND RECORDS 44 (1956), p. 63.

18,358 Some notes on Kilwa. TANG. NOTES 2 (1936), pp. 92-95.

18,359 Le Tanganyika indépendant. PRESENCE AFR. N.S. 39 (1961), pp. 215-218.

18,360 Tanganyika territory. Annual report, 1936. J. AFR. SOC. 37 (1938), pp. 100-101.

18,361 Tanganyika territory. Annual reports of provincial commissioners on native administration, 1935. J. AFR. SOC. 35 (1936), pp. 444-446.

18,362 Tanganyika territory [1933]. J. AFR. SOC. 34 (1935), pp. 195-198.

See also 16076, 17508, 17520, 17529, 21146.

Language. Literature

Language

18,363 AUGUSTINY, J. Sukuma-Texte. AFR. UND UB. 14 (1923-1924), pp. 1-43, 153-189.

18,364 BEIDELMAN, T. O. A Kaguru version of the Sons of Noah. A study in the inculcation of the idea of racial superiority. CAH. ET. AFR. 3 (1963), pp. 474-490.

18,365 BEIDELMAN, T. O. Some Baraguyu cattle songs. J. AFR. LANGS. 4 (1965), pp. 1-18.

18,366 BEIDELMAN, T. O. Some Ngulu texts. TANG. NOTES 63 (1964), pp. 165-196.

18,367 BEIDELMAN, T. O. Ten Kaguru texts: tales of an East African Bantu people. J. AFR. LANGS. 3 (1964), pp. 1-37.

18,368 BERGER, P. Konde-Texte. AFR. UND UB. 23 (1932-1933), pp. 110-154.

18,369 BERGER, P. Ndali-Texte. AFR. UND UB. 25 (1934-1935), pp. 229-239, 284-307.

18,370 BOESCH, F. Etwas zur Genesis des Kilwana. BIBLIOTHECA AFR. 4 (1930-1931), pp. 31-45.

18,371 BRAIN, J. L. Swahili slang. TANGANYIKA NOTES AND RECORDS 56 (1961), pp. 114-115.

18,372 BUSSE, J. Aus dem Leben von Asyukile Malango (Nyakyusa-Texte). AFR. UND UB. 35 (1949-1950), pp. 191-227.

18,373 BUSSE, J. Kaguru-Texte. AFR. UND UB. 27 (1936-1937), pp. 61-75.

18,374 BUSSE, J. Kimbu-Sprachproben. AFR. UND UB. 37 (1952-1953), pp. 183-186.

18,375 BUSSE, J. Konde-Texte. AFR. UND UB. 32 (1942), pp. 201-224.

18,376 BUSSE, J. Lambya-Texte. AFR. UND UB. 30 (1940), pp. 250-272.

18,377 CAPUS, A. Contes, chants et proverbes des Basumbwa dans l'Afrique Orientale. ZAOS 3 (1897), pp. 358-381.

18,378 CAPUS, A. Grammaire de Shisumbwa. ZAOS 4 (1898), pp. 1-96, 97-123.

18,379 CLARKE, P. H. C. A note on school slang. TANGANYIKA NOTES AND RECORDS 58-59 (1962), pp. 205-206.

18,380 CLEVE, G. L. Beiträge zur Logik der Sprache bei den Wa-Suaheli und Wa-Zaramo in Deutsch-Ostafrika. ZAOS 3 (1897), pp. 272-274.

18,381 DAMMANN, E. Sprachproben aus dem Segedju. AFR. UND UB. 27 (1936-1937), pp. 223-233.

18,382 DAMMANN, E. Zur Kenntnis des Zaramo. AFR. UND UB. 25 (1934-1935), pp. 135-147.

18,383 DEMPWOLFF, O. Beiträge zur Kenntnis der Sprachen in Deutsch-Ostafrika. AFR. UND UB. 2 (1911-1912), pp. 81-107, 257-260; 3 (1912-1913), pp. 161-181; 5 (1914-1915), pp. 26-44, 113-136, 227-253, 270-298; 6 (1915-1916), pp. 1-27, 102-123; 7 (1916-1917), pp. 134-160, 167-192, 309-315.

18,384 DREXEL, A. Das grammatische Geschlecht im Nama und Sandawe. BIBLIOTHECA AFR. 3 (1929), pp. 51-58.

18,385 GOWER, R. H. Swahili slang. TANGANYIKA NOTES AND RECORDS 51 (1958), pp. 250-254.

18,386 GRAY, Sir J. M. Burton on Kiswahili. TANGANYIKA NOTES AND RECORDS 51 (1958), pp. 156-158.

18,387 GUTMAN, B. Grusslieder der Wadschagga. FESTSCHRIFT MEINHOF, 1927, pp. 228-232.

18,388 HEESE, D. Die Sango-Sprache. AFR. UND UB. 10 (1919-1920), pp. 87-105.

18,389 HOLLIS, A. C. Nyika enigmas. J. AFR. SOC. 16 (1917), pp. 135-142.

18,390 HOLLIS, A. C. Nyika proverbs. J. AFR. SOC. 16 (1916), pp. 62-70.

18,391 HUTCHINSON, J. A. The meaning of Kilimanjaro. TANC. NOTES 64 (1965), pp. 65-67.

18,392 INGRAMS, W. H. The dialects of the Zanzibar Sultanato. BULL. SOAS 3 (1923-1925), pp. 533-550.

18,393 JOHNSON, F. Notes on Kimakonde. BULL. SOAS 2 (1921-1923), pp. 417-466; 3 (1923-1925), pp. 1-32.

18,394 JOHNSON, F. Notes on Kiniramba. BANTU STUD. 2 (1928), pp. 167-192, 233-263.

18,395 JOHNSTON, Sir H. H. The Ki-shashi (Ki-sasi) language (S. E. Victoria Nyanza). J. AFR. SOC. 19 (1920), pp. 210-213.

18,396 KAHLER-MEYER, E. Töne und Akzente in der Formenlehre des Chasu (Tanganyika). AFR. UND UB. 47 (1964), pp. 89-133.

18,397 KOOTZ-KRETSCHMER, E. Safwa-Texte in Briefen. AFR. UND UB. 33 (1942-1943), pp. 112-145.

18,398 KOOTZ-KRETSCHMER, E. Safwa-Texte in Kleinen Erzählungen und Briefen. AFR. UND UB. 24 (1933-1934), pp. 161-201, 245-281.

18,399 KOOTZ-KRETSCHMER, E. Safwa- und Nyixa-Texte. AFR. UND UB. 22 (1931-1932), pp. 241-274.

18,400 MAASS, M. and SEIDEL, A. Beiträge zur Kenntniss des Ki-Zaramo in Deutsch-Ostafrika. ZAOS 3 (1897), pp. 311-317.

18,401 MBAGA, K. and WHITELEY, W. H. Formality and informality in Yao speech. AFRICA 31 (1961), pp. 135-146.

18,402 MEINHOF, C. Dzalamo-texte. AFR. UND UB. 11 (1920-1921), pp. 278-295.

18,403 MOREAU, R. E. Bird nomenclature in an East African area. BULL. SOAS 10 (1940-1942), pp. 998-1006.

18,404 OLSON, H. S. Rimi proverbs. TANG. NOTES 62 (1964), pp. 73-82.

18,405 OVIR, E. Märchen und Räthsel der Wamadschame. ZAOS 3 (1897), pp. 65-96.

18,406 RAUM, O. F. Educational psychology in the speech of the Chaga. BANTU STUD. 13 (1939), pp. 237-241.

18,407 RAUM, O. F. Language perversions in East Africa. AFRICA 10 (1937), pp. 221-226.

18,408 REHSE, H. Eigentümlichkeiten in der Sprache der Bazinza in Deutsch-Ostafrika. AFR. UND UB. 4 (1913-1914), pp. 257-285.

18,409 REHSE, H. Die Priestersprache und die Frauensprache der Bazinza. AFR. UND UB. 6 (1915-1916), pp. 244-250.

18,410 REHSE, H. Die Sprache der Baziba in Deutsch-Ostafrika. AFR. UND UB. 3 (1912-1913), pp. 1-33, 81-123, 201-229.

18,411 REYNOLDS, F. A. Lavu huzungusha dunia. TANGANYIKA NOTES AND RECORDS 58-59 (1962), pp. 203-204.

18,412 SANTANDREA, S. Brief notes on Bina. AFR. UND UB. 40 (1956), pp. 25-37.

18,413 SCHUMANN, C. Der musikalische Ton in der Benasprache. AFR. UND UB. 8 (1917-1918), pp. 145-169.

18,414 SEIDEL, A. Beiträge zur Kenntniss der Shambala-Sprache in Usambara (Deutsch-Ostafrika). ZAOS 1 (1895), pp. 34-82.

18,415 SEIDEL, A. Beiträge zur Kenntniss des Ki-Kami in Deutsch-Ostafrika. ZAOS 2 (1896), pp. 3-32.

18,416 SEIDEL, A. Eine Erzählung der Wa-Shambala. ZAOS 2 (1896), pp. 145-149.

18,417 SEIDEL, A. Grundzüge der Grammatik der Sprache von Kavagwe und Nkole in Deutsch-Ostafrika. ZAOS 5 (1900), pp. 1-15.

18,418 SEIDEL, A. Grundzüge der Sprache von Usindja. Mit Texten und einem Wörterverzeichniss. ZAOS 4 (1898), pp. 151-178.

18,419 SEIDEL, A. Die Sprache von Ufiomi in Deutsch-Ostafrika. ZAOS 5 (1900), pp. 165-175.

18,420 SEIDEL, A. Sprichwörter der Wa-Bondeï in Deutsch-Ostafrika. ZAOS 4 (1898), pp. 287-288; 5 (1900), pp. 76-78.

18,421 SHANN, G. N. Tanganyika place names of European origin. TANGANYIKA NOTES AND RECORDS 58-59 (1962), pp. 283-284.

18,422 SHARP, A. E. A tonal analysis of the disyllabic noun in the Machame dialect of Chaga. BULL. SOAS 16 (1954), pp. 157-169.

18,423 SILLERY, A. Note on learning tribal languages. TANG. NOTES 1 (1936), pp. 14-18.

18,424 SILLERY, A. Notes for a grammar of the Kuria language. BANTU STUD. 10 (1936), pp. 9-29.

18,425 SILLERY, A. A sketch of the Kikwaya language. BANTU STUD. 6 (1932), pp. 273-307.

18,426 SOWA, R. V. Skizzen der Grammatik des Ki-Bena (Ki-Hehe) in Deutsch-Ostafrika. ZAOS 5 (1900), pp. 63-75.

18,427 SOWA, R. V. Skizzen der Grammatik des Ki-Mwera in Deutsch-Ostafrika. ZAOS 2 (1896), pp. 197-204.

18,428 STOLZ, A. Die Namen einiger afrikanischer Nutzpflanzen in der Konde-Sprache. AFR. UND UB. 24 (1933-1934), pp. 81-99.

18,429 WALTHER, K. Beiträge zur Kenntniss des Moshi-Dialekts des Ki-Chagga (Kilimandjaro, Deutsch-Ostafrika). ZAOS 5 (1900), pp. 28-43.

18,430 WHITELEY, W. H. Chagga languages, a note. TANG. NOTES 64 (1965), p. 68.

18,431 WHITELEY, W. H. An introduction to the rural dialects of Zanzibar. SWAHILI 30 (1959), pp. 41-69; 31 (1960), pp. 200-218.

18,432 WHITELEY, W. H. Linguistic hybrids. AFR. STUD. 19 (1960), pp. 95-97.

18,433 WHITELEY, W. H. The verbal radical in Iraqw. AFR. LANG. STUD. 1 (1960), pp. 79-95.

18,434 WOODWARD, H. W. Kitaita or Kisighau as spoken on the Shambala hills above Bwiti. AFR. UND UB. 4 (1913-1914), pp. 91-117.

18,435 WOODWARD, H. W. Makua tales. BANTU STUD. 6 (1932), pp. 71-87; 9 (1935), pp. 115-158.

18,436 WOODWARD, H. W. An outline of Makua grammar. BANTU STUD. 2 (1928), pp. 269-325.

18,437 WORMS, A. Grundzüge der Grammatik des Ki-Zaramo in Deutsch-Ostafrika. ZAOS 3 (1897), pp. 289-310.

18,438 WORMS, A. Wörterverzeichniss der Sprache von Uzaramo. ZAOS 4 (1898), pp. 339-365.

18,439 Vocabulary control in primary school readers. SWAHILI 33, no. 2 (1963), pp. 87-98.

18,440 Wörterverzeichnisse aus dem Ki-Dschagga und Pare. ZAS 1 (1887-1888), pp. 72-76.

See also 17786.

Literature

18,441 ALLEN, J. W. T. The collection of Swahili literature and its relation to oral tradition and history. TANGANYIKA NOTES AND RECORDS 53 (1959), pp. 224-227.

18,442 ALLEN, J. W. T. Tenzi. TANG. NOTES 28 (1950), pp. 81-83.

18,443 BEIDELMAN, T. O. Four Kaguru tales. TANG. NOTES 61 (1963), pp. 135-146.

18,444 BEIDELMAN, T. O. Three Kaguru tales. Some examples of the literature of an East African tribe. AFR. UND UB. 46 (1962-1963), pp. 218-229.

18,445 GUTMANN, B. Lieder der Dschagga. AFR. UND UB. 18 (1927-1928), pp. 161-195.

18,446 HALDANE, L. A. [Four short bird stories.] TANG. NOTES 30 (1951), pp. 44-47.

18,447 IONIDES, C. J. P. Stories of the Wangindo. TANG. NOTES 31 (1951), pp. 81-82.

18,448 LEECHMAN, B. A pioneer Tanganyika journalist. TANGANYIKA NOTES AND RECORDS 43 (1956), pp. 28-30.

18,449 SHORE, H. L. The sea that burst out roaring [fiction]. BO 18 (1965), pp. 30-34.

Law

18,450 THE AFRICAN STUDIES BRANCH. A digest of the Tanganyika Local Courts Ordinance 1951. J. AFR. ADM. 4 (1952), pp. 22-25.

18,451 BEIDELMAN, T. O. Kaguru justice and the concept of legal fictions. J. AFR. LAW 5 (1961), pp. 5-20.

18,452 COTRAM, E. Some recent developments in the Tanganyika judicial system. J. AFR. LAW 6 (1962), pp. 19-28.

18,453 DOBSON, E. B. Comparative land tenure of ten Tanganyika tribes. J. AFR. ADM. 6 (1954), pp. 80-91.

18,454 DOBSON, E. B. Land tenure of the Wasambaa. TANG. NOTES 10 (1940), pp. 1-27.

18,455 FUNDIKIRA, A. S. The reorganization of courts in Tanganyika. J. LOCAL ADM. OV. 1 (1962), pp. 257-258.

18,456 GRAY, Sir J. M. Zanzibar Protectorate: Report on the Inquiry into Claims to certain Land at or near Ngezi, Vitongoji, in the Mudiria of Chake Chake, in the District of Pemba. J. AFR. LAW 1 (1957), pp. 12-13.

18,457 GRAY, R. F. Sonjo lineage structure and property. THE FAMILY ESTATE IN AFRICA, 1964, pp. 231-262.

18,458 GRIFFITHS, J. E. S. Notes on land tenure and land rights among the Sonjo of Tanganyika Territory. TANG. NOTES 9 (1940), pp. 15-19.

18,459 GULLIVER, P. H. The Arusha family. THE FAMILY ESTATE IN AFRICA, 1964, pp. 197-229.

18,460 HALL, R. DE Z. Nyakyusa law from court records. AFR. STUD. 2 (1943), pp. 153-161.

18,461 HAMILTON, R. W. Land tenure among the Bantu Wanyika of East Africa. J. AFR. SOC. 20 (1920), pp. 13-18.

18,462 HAMP, E. P. A point of Sandawe law. J. AFR. LANGS. 1 (1962), p. 181.

18,463 HARTLEY, B. J. Land tenure in Usukuma. TANG. NOTES 5 (1938), pp. 17-24.

18,464 LEWIS-BARNED, J. F. DE S. Integration of judicial systems: the recent reform of the local courts appeal system of Tanganyika. J. AFR. LAW 7 (1963), pp. 84-93.

18,465 LIENHART, P. Family Waqf in Zanzibar. EAISR June (1958), pp. 1-18.

18,466 MAGUIRE, R. A. J. The Masai penal code. Some notes on the recognized punishments for crimes, with examples of Masai oaths or ordeals. J. AFR. SOC. 28 (1928), pp. 12-18.

18,467 MOFFETT, J. P. Native Courts in Tanganyika. A history of the development... J. AFR. ADM. 4 (1952), pp. 17-21.

18,468 NYERERE, J. K. Extracts from speech...at the opening ceremony of the University College, Dar-es-Salaam, 25th October, 1961. J. AFR. LAW 6 (1962), pp. 150-151.

18,469 READ, J. S. Minimum sentences in Tanzania. J. AFR. LAW 9 (1965), pp. 20-39.

18,470 SLATER, M. K. Informal arbitration of disputes among the Wanyika. EAISR June (1963), pp. 1-7.

18,471 TANNER, R. E. S. Law enforcement by communal action in Sukumaland, Tanganyika Territory. J. AFR. ADM. 7 (1955), pp. 159-165.

18,472 WESTON, A. B. Faculty of Law, University of East Africa, at the University College, Dar-es-Salaam. J. AFR. LAW 6 (1962), pp. 151-155.

18,473 WILSON, G. Introduction to Nyakyusa law. AFRICA 10 (1937), pp. 16-36.

18,474 WINANS, E. V. The Shambala family. THE FAMILY ESTATE IN AFRICA, 1964, pp. 35-61.

18,475 Faculty of Law in Dar es Salaam. J. AFR. LAW 5 (1961), pp. 73-74.

18,476 Muslim Academy, Zanzibar. J. AFR. LAW 6 (1962), p. 160.

Religion

18,477 BAX, S. N. The early Church Missionary Society missions at Buzilima and Usambiro in the Mwanza district. TANG. NOTES 7 (1939), pp. 39-55.

18,478 DAVEY, A. C. Church Missionary Society, Ngambo. TANG. NOTES 5 (1938), pp. 68-69.

18,479 FRANK, C. N. Young pioneers in Tanganyika. TANG. NOTES 34 (1953), pp. 16-19.

18,480 HUNTER, M. An African Christian morality. AFRICA 10 (1937), pp. 265-291.

18,481 SCHOLTEN, H. The growth and expansion of the East African Church. INT. REV. MISSIONS 39 (1950), pp. 270-276.

18,482 SMITH, H. M. Frank Weston, Bishop of Zanzibar: an appreciation. INT. REV. MISSIONS 14 (1925), pp. 188-197.

18,483 Mission catholique américaine au Tanganyika. ZAIRE 4 (1950), p. 1019.

Science

18,484 ABRAHAMS, R. G. African concepts of health and disease. EAISR Dec. (1959), pp. 1-7.

18,485 B., R. DE LA B. Bitterns, Coqui francolins and Temminck's coursers. TANG. NOTES 33 (1952), p. 94.

18,486 B., R. DE LA B. Crocodiles. TANG. NOTES 34 (1953), pp. 76-78.

18,487 B., R. DE LA B. Geckos. TANG. NOTES 31 (1951), p. 85.

18,488 B., R. DE LA B. The hammer-headed stork. TANG. NOTES 32 (1952), p. 87.

18,489 B., R. DE LA B. Instinct. TANG. NOTES 31 (1951), p. 85.

18,490 B., R. DE LA B. A nesting Abdim's stork. TANG. NOTES 32 (1952), p. 87.

18,491 B., R. DE LA B. Note on colours and light effects. TANG. NOTES 33 (1952), p. 94.

18,492 BAIRD, D. A. A check list of the birds of Zanzibar and Pemba. TANGANYIKA NOTES AND RECORDS 58-59 (1962), pp. 187-196.

18,493 BASSET, H. European little bittern makes forced landing at Dedoma. TANG. NOTES 34 (1953), p. 81.

18,494 BURTT, E. Observations relating to some Tanganyika millepedes (Swahili: Jongoo). TANG. NOTES 6 (1938), pp. 91-92.

18,495 CALTON, W. E. A year's experience of small-scale nutrient culture (hydroponics) at Oyster Bay. TANGANYIKA NOTES AND RECORDS 51 (1958), pp. 216-226.

18,496 CHILD, G. S. Some notes on the mammals of Kilimanjaro. TANG. NOTES 64 (1965), pp. 77-89.

18,497 COLE, G. F. San Rafael. TANG. NOTES 15 (1943), p. 82.

18,498 COOPER, W. H. A bush-buck running with a troop of baboons. TANG. NOTES 18 (1944), p. 101.

18,499 CROSSE-UPCOTT, A. R. W. Ngindo famine subsistence. TANGANYIKA NOTES AND RECORDS 50 (1958), pp. 1-20.

18,500 CULWICK, G. M. A further note on German storks at Kiberege. TANG. NOTES 4 (1937), p. 84.

18,501 CULWICK, G. M. German storks at Kiberege. TANG. NOTES 3 (1937), p. 122.

18,502 DOUGHTY, L. R. The origin of the East African sisal. TANG. NOTES 18 (1944), p. 98.

18,503 DUDBRIDGE, B. J. Some notes on the duck and geese of Usukuma. TANG. NOTES 31 (1951), pp. 74-78.

18,504 EGGELING, W. J. Ringed birds recovered in Uganda. UGANDA J. 15 (1951), pp. 17-25.

18,505 FRASER, H. The introduction of trout into Tanganyika. TANG. NOTES 4 (1937), pp. 1-9.

18,506 FREYVOGEL, T. A. A collection of snakes from Ifakara, Eastern Province. TANGANYIKA NOTES AND RECORDS 54 (1960), pp. 89-90.

18,507 FUGGLES-COUCHMAN, N. R. The habitat-distribution of the birds of Northern, Eastern and Central Tanganyika, with field keys. TANG. NOTES 33 (1952), pp. 48-59; 35 (1953), pp. 14-37; 37 (1954), pp. 71-114; 46 (1957), pp. 32-68; 58-59 (1962), pp. 67-97.

18,508 FUGGLES-COUCHMAN, N. R. Notes on the nesting habits of some Tanganyika birds. TANG. NOTES 1 (1936), pp. 61-76.

18,509 G., C. Indian elephants in Tanganyika. TANGANYIKA NOTES AND RECORDS 12 (1941), pp. 61-63.

18,510 GILLMAN, C. San Rafael. TANG. NOTES 15 (1943), pp. 82-83.

18,511 GREENWAY, P. J. Arrow-root. TANG. NOTES 35 (1953), pp. 43-44.

18,512 GUEST, N. J. and LEEDAL, G. P. Notes on the fauna of Kilimanjaro. TANG. NOTES 36 (1954), pp. 43-49.

18,513 GUNN, B. Locusts ascending: how a red locust outbreak was crushed. TANGANYIKA NOTES AND RECORDS 58-59 (1962), pp. 162-171.

18,514 GUNN, D. L. A history of Lake Rukwa and the red locust. TANGANYIKA NOTES AND RECORDS 42 (1956), pp. 1-18.

18,515 H., G. Avian housing shortage. TANG. NOTES 34 (1953), p. 78.

18,516 HALDANE, L. A. Birds of the Njombe District. TANGANYIKA NOTES AND RECORDS 44 (1956), pp. 1-27.

18,517 HALDANE, L. A. Butterflies of the Njombe highlands. TANGANYIKA NOTES AND RECORDS 43 (1956), pp. 31-40.

18,518 HALDANE, L. A. Notes on the birds of the Ngara District. TANG. NOTES 30 (1951), pp. 15-44.

18,519 HALDANE, R. H. and HALDANE, L. A. Snout safari—migration of Libythea labdaca. TANGANYIKA NOTES AND RECORDS 47-48 (1957), p. 174.

18,520 HALDEMANN, E. G. Mud-volcanoes in the Sekenke area. TANGANYIKA NOTES AND RECORDS 58-59 (1962), pp. 242-257.

18,521 HALDEMANN, E. G. Recent landslide phenomena in the Rungwe volcanic area, Tanganyika. TANGANYIKA NOTES AND RECORDS 45 (1956), pp. 1-14.

18,522 HARRIS, W. V. Biological brevities. TANG. NOTES 15 (1943), pp. 76-79; 16 (1943), pp. 85-90; 17 (1944), pp. 56-58.

18,523 HATCHELL, C. W. An early "Sleeping-Sickness Settlement" in South-Western Tanganyika. TANG. NOTES 27 (1949), pp. 60-64.

18,524 HATCHELL, G. W. Giant fish in Lake Tanganyika. TANG. NOTES 36 (1954), pp. 73-74.

18,525 HILL, J. E. Record ivory in the collection of the British Museum (Natural History). TANGANYIKA NOTES AND RECORDS 46 (1957), pp. 29-31.

18,526 HOLLINS, F. R. Lepidoptera of the Eastern Province: Part I.—Papilionoidea (Butterflies) Section (i). Danaidae (Monarchs). TANGANYIKA NOTES AND RECORDS 58-59 (1962), pp. 212-217.

18,527 IONIDES, C. J. P. Pages from a Tanganyika game ranger's notebook. TANG. NOTES 29 (1950), pp. 62-67; 30 (1951), pp. 48-52.

18,528 IONIDES, C. J. P. Snakes of the Southern Province. TANG. NOTES 29 (1950), pp. 98-108.

18,529 JERRARD, R. C. Anti-locust measures memoirs. TANG. NOTES 3 (1937), pp. 114-116.

18,530 KERFOOT, O. A first check-list of the vascular plants of Mbeya Range, Southern Highlands Region, Tanganyika. TANG. NOTES 62 (1964), pp. 27-43.

18,531 KORITSCHONER, H. Details of a native medical treatment. TANG. NOTES 2 (1936), pp. 67-71.

18,532 LAMERTON, J. F. Bichir in Tanganyika. TANGANYIKA NOTES AND RECORDS 58-59 (1962), p. 151.

18,533 LAMPREY, H. F. Birds of the forest and Alpine zones of Kilimanjaro. TANG. NOTES 64 (1965), pp. 69-76.

18,534 LAMPREY, H. F. Elephant control in Tanganyika—a discussion. TANGANYIKA NOTES AND RECORDS 47-48 (1957), pp. 145-148.

18,535 LAMPREY, H. F. The Tarangire Game Reserve. TANGANYIKA NOTES AND RECORDS 60 (1963), pp. 10-22.

18,536 LANE, L. P. Fishing on Lake Tanganyika. TANG. NOTES 7 (1939), pp. 3-27.

18,537 LANE, L. P. Fungu Kizimkazi, or Latham Island. TANG. NOTES 18 (1944), pp. 89-94.

18,538 LINDEMAN, H. A. Notes on some flowering and ornamental shrubs and trees including shade and fruit trees, with special reference to those suitable to Tabora. TANG. NOTES 5 (1938), pp. 37-55.

18,539 LOVERIDGE, A. Comments on the reptiles and amphibians of Lindi. TANGANYIKA NOTES AND RECORDS 14 (1942), pp. 38-51.

18,540 LOVERIDGE, A. The crocodiles of Tanganyika Territory. TANG. NOTES 10 (1940), pp. 41-46.

18,541 LOVERIDGE, A. On a third collection of reptiles taken in Tanganyika by C. J. P. Ionides, Esq. TANGANYIKA NOTES AND RECORDS 43 (1956), pp. 1-19.

18,542 LOVERIDGE, A. Some Geckos of Tanganyika Territory. TANGANYIKA NOTES AND RECORDS 12 (1941), pp. 32-37.

18,543 M., A. F. Frigate bird at Dar es Salaam. TANG. NOTES 32 (1952), p. 86.

18,544 M., J. P. The black-bellied florican or long-legged bustard (Lissotis melanogaster melanogaster). TANG. NOTES 31 (1951), p. 83.

18,545 McCALLUM, D. Rain-making in Tanganyika. TANGANYIKA NOTES AND RECORDS 52 (1959), pp. 53-56.

18,546 MHINA, J. E. F. Provision of health services in rural communities in Tanganyika. PROC. 3RD. GRAD. ACAD. UCLA, 1965, pp. 279-286.

18,547 MITCHELL, A. J. Locating and proving an underground source of water supply. TANG. NOTES 10 (1940), pp. 73-78.

18,548 MOFFETT, J. P. A review of scientific progress in Tanganyika during 1952. TANG. NOTES 34 (1953), pp. 1-15.

18,549 MOFFETT, J. P. A strategic retreat from tsetse fly. Uyowa and Bugomba concentrations 1937. TANG. NOTES 7 (1939), pp. 35-38.

18,550 MOREAU, R. E. Bird-names used in coastal north-eastern Tanganyika Territory. TANG. NOTES 10 (1940), pp. 47-72; 11 (1941), pp. 47-60.

18,551 MOREAU, R. E. The distribution of the Chimpanzee in Tanganyika Territory. TANGANYIKA NOTES AND RECORDS 14 (1942), pp. 52-55.

18,552 MOREAU, R. E. Migrant birds in Tanganyika Territory. TANG. NOTES 4 (1937), pp. 17-50.

18,553 MOREAU, R. E. A note on the fauna of Mafia. TANG. NOTES 7 (1939), p. 115.

18,554 MOREAU, R. E. Ornithology in Tanganyika. TANG. NOTES 28 (1950), pp. 64-79.

18,555 MOREAU, R. E. Sacrosanct birds on islets near Mafia. TANG. NOTES 7 (1939), pp. 114-115.

18,556 MOREAU, R. E. A vanilla as a plantation protector. TANG. NOTES 15 (1943), pp. 80-81.

18,557 MORGAN-DAVIES, A. M. Notes on some breeding birds of Lake Manyara National Park. TANG. NOTES 62 (1964), pp. 96-104.

18,558 MORRISON, A. F. A review of recent scientific progress in Tanganyika. TANG. NOTES 32 (1952), pp. 1-10.

18,559 OATES, F. The Meteoric iron at Mbosi. TANG. NOTES 2 (1936), pp. 44-49.

18,560 OATES, F. A record of the meteorites of Tanganyika Territory. TANGANYIKA NOTES AND RECORDS 12 (1941), pp. 28-31.

18,561 PROBYN, M. Birds in an Arusha garden. TANGANYIKA NOTES AND RECORDS 54 (1960), pp. 113-119.

18,562 REES, A. F. A check list of the mammals and amphibia of Ulanga District. TANG. NOTES 63 (1964), pp. 245-248.

18,563 REES, A. F. Some notes on elephants and their feeding habits. TANG. NOTES 61 (1963), pp. 205-208.

18,564 ROBSON, J. R. K. Malnutrition in Tanganyika. TANGANYIKA NOTES AND RECORDS 58-59 (1962), pp. 258-267.

18,565 ROCH, R. Report on West Usambara from the point of view of health. TANG. NOTES 35 (1953), pp. 7-13.

18,566 RUSHBY, G. G. Game in relation to tsetse. TANG. NOTES 18 (1944), pp. 77-80.

18,567 RUSHBY, G. G. Pan Satyrus (Chimpanzee). TANG. NOTES 16 (1943), pp. 101-103.

18,568 S., G. H. Serengeti Safari. TANG. NOTES 31 (1951), pp. 84-85.

18,569 SAMPSON, D. N. Notes on the flora of Kilimanjaro. TANG. NOTES 34 (1953), pp. 68-69.

18,570 SILLERY, A. Indian elephants in Tanganyika. TANG. NOTES 11 (1941), pp. 64-65.

18,571 SPRY, J. F. The sea shells of Dar es Salaam. TANG. NOTES 63 (1964), pp. 123-164.

18,572 SPRY, J. F. The sea shells of Dar es Salaam: Gastropods. TANGANYIKA NOTES AND RECORDS 56 (1961), pp. 1-33.

18,573 SWYNNERTON, B. A key to the recognition in the field of two hundred and sixty of the commoner birds of Tanganyika. TANG. NOTES 6 (1938), pp. 5-48.

18,574 SWYNNERTON, C. F. M. Tsetse-flies of East Africa. J. AFR. SOC. 37 (1938), pp. 92-94.

18,575 TANNER, R. E. S. Patterson's Eland. TANG. NOTES 28 (1950), p. 80.

18,576 TANNER, R. E. S. Some Southern Province trees with their African names and uses. TANG. NOTES 31 (1951), pp. 61-70.

18,577 TEALE, Sir E. O. Progress of mining in Tanganyika Territory. BULL. IMP. INST. 37 (1939), pp. 611-621.

18,578 TEALE, Sir E. O. Recent developments in gold mining in Tanganyika Territory. BULL. IMP. INST. 34 (1936), pp. 44-54.

18,579 THOMAS, D. K. Birds—further notes on breeding in Tanganyika. TANGANYIKA NOTES AND RECORDS 58-59 (1962), pp. 197-202.

18,580 THOMAS, D. K. Birds—notes on breeding in Tanganyika 1958-1959. TANGANYIKA NOTES AND RECORDS 55 (1960), pp. 225-243.

18,581 THOMAS, D. K. The Gombe Stream Game Reserve. TANGANYIKA NOTES AND RECORDS 56 (1961), pp. 34-39.

18,582 THOMAS, D. K. The Ugalla River Controlled Area. TANGANYIKA NOTES AND RECORDS 57 (1961), pp. 226-230.

18,583 V-H., N. H. A strange bush tableau. TANG. NOTES 33 (1952), pp. 94-95.

18,584 VERDCOURT, B. The Gulellae (Moll., Streptaxidae) of the Usambara Mountains, N. E. Tanganyika. TANGANYIKA NOTES AND RECORDS 47-48 (1957), pp. 92-102.

18,585 VERDCOURT, B. Observations on the ecology of the land and freshwater Mollusca of North-east Tanganyika. TANG. NOTES 33 (1952), pp. 67-82.

18,586 VESEY-FITZGERALD, D. F. Mammals of the Rukwa Valley. TANG. NOTES 62 (1964), pp. 61-72.

18,587 VESEY-FITZGERALD, D. F. and BEESLEY, J. S. S. An annotated list of the birds of the Rukwa valley. TANGANYIKA NOTES AND RECORDS 54 (1960), pp. 91-110.

18,588 WHYBROW, C. An English flower garden in the Tropics. TANG. NOTES 2 (1936), pp. 96-97.

18,589 WHYBROW, C. Preliminary list of some butterflies taken near Malangali—with notes. TANG. NOTES 9 (1940), pp. 37-41.

18,590 WILLETT, K. C. Trypanosomiasis research at Tinde. TANG. NOTES 34 (1953), pp. 33-34.

18,591 WORSLEY, R. R. LE G. Cinchona in Amani. BULL. IMP. INST. 33 (1935), pp. 14-31.

18,592 Andersson's bat hawk. TANG. NOTES 34 (1953), pp. 78-81.

18,593 European storks in East Africa. TANG. NOTES 11 (1941), p. 66.

18,594 Out of the strong came forth sweetness [the death of an elephant]. TANG. NOTES 31 (1951), pp. 83-84.

See also 17625.

Sociology

18,595 ALLNUT, R. B. Gulio. TANG. NOTES 10 (1940), pp. 92-93.

18,596 ASKWITH, T. Community development in Kenya. CORONA 3 (1951), pp. 220-223.

18,597 BEIDELMAN, T. O. A demographic map of the Baraguyu. TANGANYIKA NOTES AND RECORDS 58-59 (1962), pp. 8-10.

18,598 CAVE, B. S. The end of slavery in Zanzibar and British East Africa. J. AFR. SOC. 9 (1909), pp. 20-33.

18,599 CULWICK, A. T. New beginning. TANG. NOTES 15 (1943), pp. 1-6.

18,600 CULWICK, A. T. The population trend. TANG. NOTES 11 (1941), pp. 13-17.

18,601 FOSBROOKE, H. A. Government sociologists in Tanganyika. 2. A sociological view. J. AFR. ADM. 4 (1952), pp. 103-108.

18,602 GLASS, J. M. Tanganyika: the citizen, the common good, and political development. PROC. 3RD. GRAD. ACAD. UCLA, 1965, pp. 193-208.

18,603 GULLIVER, P. H. The population of the Arusha chiefdom: a high density area in East Africa. RHODES-LIV. J. 28 (1961), pp. 1-21.

18,604 HALL, R. DE Z. Bao. TANG. NOTES 34 (1953), pp. 57-61.

18,605 HALL, R. DE Z. Local migration in Tanganyika. AFR. STUD. 4 (1945), pp. 53-69.

18,606 HARTNOLL, M. M. Some African pastimes. TANG. NOTES 5 (1938), pp. 31-36.

18,607 JERRARD, R. C. Tanganyika's greatest asset. TANG. NOTES 16 (1943), pp. 29-32.

18,608 LANE, L. P. Reconstruction in relation to revision. TANG. NOTES 17 (1944), pp. 10-14.

18,609 LESLIE, J. A. K. Dick Whittington comes to Dar es Salaam. TANGANYIKA NOTES AND RECORDS 54 (1960), pp. 69-78; 55 (1960), pp. 215-224; 56 (1961), pp. 49-55.

18,610 LEVA, A. E. Dell' isola di Socotra e dei costumi dei suoi abitanti nel secolo XVII. Un case di involuzione sociologica. AFRICA (Rome) 16 (1961), pp. 15-18.

18,611 MAAS, A. The Nyegezi Social Training Centre, Tanganyika. WOMEN TODAY 6 (1964), pp. 13-14.

18,612 MASON, H. Progress in Pare [an experiment in community development]. CORONA 4 (1952), pp. 212-219.

18,613 MOFFETT, J. P. Government sociologists in Tanganyika. 1. A government view. J. AFR. ADM. 4 (1952), pp. 100-103.

18,614 PIGGOTT, D. W. I. Spoonfishing in the Mafia Group. TANGANYIKA NOTES AND RECORDS 12 (1941), pp. 11-19.

18,615 PRATT, C. Multi-racialism and local government in Tanganyika. RACE 2, no. 1 (1960-1961), pp. 33-49.

18,616 RAYMOND, W. D. Nutrition and Tanganyika. TANG. NOTES 11 (1941), pp. 18-24.

18,617 SAADA SALIM BIN OMAR. The Swahili life. TANG. NOTES 9 (1940), pp. 20-26.

18,618 SCHNEIDER, H. K. A model of African indigenous economy and society. COMP. STUD. SOC. HIST. 7 (1964-1965), pp. 37-55.

18,619 SHIMAN, D. A. The Asians in Tanzania: a problem of role definition. PROC. 3RD. GRAD. ACAD. UCLA, 1965, pp. 141-148.

18,620 SILBERMAN, L. Civic survey of Mombasa Old Town. ZAIRE 6 (1952), pp. 699-717.

18,621 SMITH, J. R. A note on the water-carriers of Tabora. TANGANYIKA NOTES AND RECORDS 58-59 (1962), p. 102.

18,622 TANNER, R. E. S. Conflict with small European communities in Tanganyika. EAISR July (1962), pp. 1-16.

18,623 TANNER, R. E. S. The relationships between the sexes in a coastal Islamic society: Pangani District, Tanganyika. AFR. STUD. 21 (1962), pp. 70-82.

18,624 TANNER, R. E. S. Who goes home? An analysis of up-country European communities in Tanganyika. TRANSITION 8 (1963), pp. 31-33; 9 (1963), pp. 32-36.

18,625 WILLIS, R. G. Community and descent in Ufipa: a problem of pattern. EAISR June (1963), pp. 1-8.

18,626 YELD, R. Implications of experience with refugee settlement. EAISR Jan. (1965), pp. 1-13.

18,627 La femme bantoue au Tanganyika. ZAIRE 7 (1953), p. 78.

18,628 Marriage customs in Tanganyika. AFR. WOMEN 3 (1958-1960), pp. 61-62.

See also 1550.

UGANDA

General

18,629 CARLIN, M. M. Kampala diary. AFR. SOUTH 2, no. 1 (1957), pp. 84-89.

18,630 DUNBAR, A. R. Mutala survey of Bujenje (Kisonga), Bunyoro. UGANDA J. 29 (1965), pp. 61-74.

18,631 GRAY, Sir J. M. The first twenty-five volumes [of The Uganda Journal]. UGANDA J. 25 (1961), pp. 125-135.

18,632 LANGLANDS, B. W. Uganda bibliography 1961-1962, 1962-1963, 1963-1964, 1964, 1964-1965. UGANDA J. 27 (1963), pp. 245-260; 28 (1964), pp. 115-124, 233-242; 29 (1965), pp. 115-132, 239-255.

18,633 LARSEN, K. The East African School of Librarianship. UNESCO BULL. LIBS. 18 (1964), pp. 105-109.

18,634 SIMPSON, D. H. A bibliography of Emin Pasha. UGANDA J. 24 (1960), pp. 138-165.

18,635 African studies at Makerere University College, Uganda, 1965-6. BULL. AFR. STUD. ASSOC. 5 (1965), pp. 27-28.

18,636 The East African Institute of Social Research. INT. SOC. SC. BULL. 3 (1951), pp. 611-612.

18,637 List of books in the [Uganda] Society's Library, 31st December 1947. UGANDA J. 12 (1948), pp. 237-278; 13 (1949), pp. 245-247.

Agriculture

18,638 FRENCH, M. H. Cattle breeding problems in Uganda. UGANDA J. 19 (1955), pp. 73-84.

18,639 GULLIVER, P. H. Jie agriculture. UGANDA J. 18 (1954), pp. 65-70.

18,640 HARMSWORTH, J. Peasant agricultural labour organisation in four selected areas of Eastern Uganda. EAISR July (1962), pp. 1-11.

18,641 LAMB, P. H. Recent agricultural developments in Uganda. BULL. IMP. INST. 10 (1912), pp. 422-433.

18,642 LUDWIG, H. D. Mixed farming on Ukara island. EAISR Jan. (1965), pp. 1-2.

18,643 McMASTER, D. N. The distribution of traditional types of food storage containers in Uganda. UGANDA J. 26 (1962), pp. 154-160.

18,644 MORS, P. O. Cattle in Buhaya. ANTHR. QUART. 27 (1954), pp. 23-29.

18,645 OTHIENO, T. M. and BELSHAW, D. G. R. Technical innovation in two systems of African peasant agriculture in Bukedi district. EAISR Jan. (1965), pp. 1-24.

18,646 SMALL, W. Coffee cultivation in Uganda. BULL. IMP. INST. 12 (1914), pp. 242-250.

18,647 T.-W.-FIENNES, R. N. Soil erosion and agricultural planning. UGANDA J. 6 (1939), pp. 137-147.

18,648 WATSON, J. M. The Agoro systems of irrigation. UGANDA J. 16 (1952), pp. 159-163.

18,649 WILLIAMS, F. L. Sowing and harvesting in Ankole. UGANDA J. 3 (1936), pp. 203-210.

18,650 WILSON, P. N. An agricultural survey of Moruita Erony, Teso. UGANDA J. 22 (1958), pp. 22-38.

18,651 WILSON, P. N. and WATSON, J. M. Two surveys of Kasilang Erony, Teso, 1937 and 1953. UGANDA J. 20 (1956), pp. 182-197.

18,652 Goat survey in Uganda. CORONA 4 (1952), pp. 223-224.

Anthropology

18,653 AKENA, N. Lango religion. UGANDA J. 23 (1959), pp. 188-190.

18,654 B., J. P. Some notes on the Metu people of West Madi. UGANDA J. 5 (1937), pp. 134-136.

18,655 BABIIHA, J. K. The Bayaga clan of Western Uganda. UGANDA J. 22 (1958), pp. 123-130.

18,656 BAMUNOBA, Y, K. Blood brotherhood in Ankole. UGANDA J. 28 (1964), pp. 217-218.

18,657 BAMUNOBA, Y. K. and WELBOURN, F. B. Emandwa initiation in Ankole. UGANDA J. 29 (1965), pp. 13-25.

18,658 BARBER, J. P. Female circumcision among the Sebei. UGANDA J. 25 (1961), pp. 94-98.

18,659 BEATTIE, J. H. M. The blood pact in Bunyoro. AFR. STUD. 17 (1958), pp. 198-203.

18,660 BEATTIE, J. H. M. Bunyoro: an African feudality? J. AFR. HIST. 5 (1964), pp. 25-35.

18,661 BEATTIE, J. H. M. Bunyoro through the looking glass. J. AFR. ADM. 12 (1960), pp. 85-94.

18,662 BEATTIE, J. H. M. Divination in Bunyoro, Uganda. SOCIOLOGUS 14 (1964), pp. 44-62.

18,663 BEATTIE, J. H. M. The ghost cult in Bunyoro. ETHNOLOGY 3 (1964), pp. 127-151.

18,664 BEATTIE, J. H. M. Group aspects of the Nyoro Spirit Mediumship Cult. RHODES-LIV. J. 30 (1961), pp. 11-38.

18,665 BEATTIE, J. H. M. Initiation into the Cwezi spirit possession cult in Bunyoro. AFR. STUD. 16 (1957), pp. 150-161.

18,666 BEATTIE, J. H. M. Matiyo and his two wives: a further case study from Bunyoro. AFRICA 35 (1965), pp. 252-262.

18,667 BEATTIE, J. H. M. Nyoro kinship. AFRICA 27 (1957), pp. 317-339.

18,668 BEATTIE, J. H. M. Nyoro marriage and affinity. AFRICA 28 (1958), pp. 1-22.

18,669 BEATTIE, J. H. M. Nyoro mortuary rites. UGANDA J. 25 (1961), pp. 171-183.

18,670 BEATTIE, J. H. M. Nyoro personal names. UGANDA J. 21 (1957), pp. 99-106.

18,671 BEATTIE, J. H. M. On the Nyoro concept of _mahano_. AFR. STUD. 19 (1960), pp. 145-150.

18,672 BEATTIE, J. H. M. Rituals of Nyoro kinship. AFRICA 29 (1959), pp. 134-144.

18,673 BEATTIE, J. H. M. The story of Mariya and Yozefu: a case study from Bunyoro, Uganda. AFRICA 34 (1964), pp. 105-115.

18,674 BEATTIE, J. H. M. Twin ceremonies in Bunyoro. JRAI 92 (1962), pp. 1-12.

18,675 BENNETT, F. J. A Muganda housewife's day and its health implications. MAKERERE J. 9 (1964), pp. 63-70.

18,676 BERE, R. M. Acholi hunts. UGANDA J. 1 (1934), pp. 153-154.

18,677 BERE, R. M. Kungu—the sacred rock. UGANDA J. 7 (1940), pp. 188-189.

18,678 BERE, R. M. Land and chieftainship among the Acholi. UGANDA J. 19 (1955), pp. 49-56.

18,679 BESSELL, M. J. Nyabingi. UGANDA J. 6 (1938), pp. 73-86.

18,680 BIRCH, J. P. Madi blacksmiths. UGANDA J. 5 (1937), pp. 48-49.

18,681 BIRCH, J. P. Migration movements of the Madi, with some tentative conclusions. UGANDA J. 6 (1938), pp. 119-122.

18,682 BOCCASSINO, R. The nature and characteristics of the Supreme Being worshipped among the Acholi of Uganda. UGANDA J. 6 (1939), pp. 195-201.

18,683 BOCCASSINO, R. Il peccato chiamato _kir_ e la sua espiazione secondo gli Acioli dell' Uganda. CONG. INT. SC. ANTH. ET ETHN. 4, no. iii (1952), pp. 42-48.

18,684 BRIGHT, R. G. T. An exploration in central Equatorial Africa. J. AFR. SOC. 9 (1910), pp. 225-232.

18,685 BRUTON, C. L. Some notes on the Basoga. UGANDA J. 2 (1935), pp. 291-296.

18,686 CARMICHAEL, J. A crocodile trap. UGANDA J. 2 (1935), pp. 250-251.

18,687 CLARK, D. Death and burial ceremonies among the Karamojong. UGANDA J. 17 (1953), pp. 75-76.

18,688 CLARK, D. Karamojong age-groups and clans. UGANDA J. 14 (1950), pp. 215-218.

18,689 CLARK, D. A Karamojong wedding. UGANDA J. 16 (1952), pp. 176-177.

18,690 CLARK, D. Memorial service for an ox in Karamoja. UGANDA J. 16 (1952), pp. 69-71.

18,691 COX, T. R. F. Lango proverbs. BULL. UGANDA SOC. 5 (1945), pp. 21-29; also in UGANDA J. 10 (1946), pp. 113-123.

18,692 COX, T. R. F. Progress in Africa. UGANDA J. 9 (1942), p. 85.

18,693 CRAZZOLARA, J. P. The Lwoo people. UGANDA J. 5 (1937), pp. 1-21.

18,694 CULWICK, A. T. and CULWICK, G. M. Culture contact on the fringe of civilization. AFRICA 8 (1935), pp. 163-170.

18,695 DAVIS, M. B. Lunyoro proverbs. UGANDA J. 9 (1941), pp. 115-132.

18,696 DOCHERTY, A. J. The Karamojong and the Suk. UGANDA J. 21 (1957), pp. 30-40.

18,697 DRIBERG, J. H. Rain-making among the Lango. JRAI 49 (1919), pp. 52-73.

18,698 DYSON-HUDSON, N. The Karamojong and the Suk. UGANDA J. 22 (1958), pp. 173-180.

18,699 EDEL, M. M. Property among the Ciga in Uganda. AFRICA 11 (1938), pp. 325-341.

18,700 EHRLICH, C. Some social and economic implications of paternalism in Uganda. J. AFR. HIST. 4 (1963), pp. 275-285.

18,701 EMLEY, E. D. The Turkana of Kolosia district. JRAI 57 (1927), pp. 157-201.

18,702 EVANS-PRITCHARD, E. E. Customs and beliefs relating to twins among the Nilotic Nuer. UGANDA J. 3 (1936), pp. 230-238.

18,703 FALLERS, L. A. Some determinants of marriage stability in Busoga: a reformulation of Gluckman's hypothesis. AFRICA 27 (1957), pp. 106-121.

18,704 FEW, H. S. S. On avoiding detection. UGANDA J. 23 (1959), pp. 85-87.

18,705 FORD, J. Tsetse fly in Ankole: a Hima song. UGANDA J. 17 (1953), pp. 186-188.

18,706 FURLEY, O. W. Kasagama of Toro. UGANDA J. 25 (1961), pp. 184-198.

18,707 GALE, H. P. Mutesa I—was he a god? The enigma of Kiganda paganism. UGANDA J. 20 (1956), pp. 72-87.

18,708 GRAY, Sir J. M. The Basoga. UGANDA J. 3 (1936), pp. 308-312.

18,709 GULLIVER, P. H. Bell-oxen and ox-names among the Jie. UGANDA J. 16 (1952), pp. 72-75.

18,710 GULLIVER, P. H. Jie marriage. AFR. AFFAIRS 52 (1953), pp. 149-155.

18,711 GULLIVER, P. H. The name 'Lango' as a title for the Nilo-Hamites. UGANDA J. 15 (1951), pp. 111-114.

18,712 GULLIVER, P. H. The Teso and the Karamojong cluster. UGANDA J. 20 (1956), pp. 213-215.

18,713 GUMBA, E. and KAFUHO, E. Two Lusoga fables. UGANDA J. 10 (1946), pp. 17-24.

18,714 HADDON, E. B. System of chieftainship amongst the Bari of Uganda. J. AFR. SOC. 10 (1911), pp. 467-472.

18,715 HADDOW, A. J. Whistled signals among the Bakonjo. UGANDA J. 16 (1952), pp. 164-167.

18,716 HARRIS, C. M. Sesse canoes. UGANDA J. 10 (1946), pp. 29-31.

18,717 HAYLEY, T. T. S. Changes in Lango marriage customs. UGANDA J. 7 (1940), pp. 145-163.

18,718 HAYLEY, T. T. S. The power concept in Lango religion. UGANDA J. 7 (1940), pp. 98-122.

18,719 HORNELL, J. The sewn canoes of Victoria-Nyansa: construction and origin. TANG. NOTES 15 (1943), pp. 7-24.

18,720 IKOMBE, N. The legend of Nkanda. TANG. NOTES 15 (1943), pp. 72-75.

18,721 JACOBS, B. L. A Madi spring. UGANDA J. 17 (1953), pp. 76-77.

18,722 JACOBS, B. L. and FLEAY, M. A hot sulphur spring in Toro. UGANDA J. 16 (1952), pp. 67-68.

18,723 JAMES, E. T. Bahima cattle transactions. UGANDA J. 17 (1953), pp. 74-75.

18,724 JAMES, E. T. The time of day in Ankole. UGANDA J. 17 (1953), pp. 73-74.

18,725 JENKINS, A. O. A note on the Saza of Bugerere, Buganda Kingdom. UGANDA J. 6 (1939), pp. 204-206.

18,726 KAGGWA, L. B. and WELBOURN, F. B. Lubaale initiation in Buganda. UGANDA J. 28 (1964), pp. 218-220.

18,727 KAGOLO, B. M. Tribal names and customs in Teso District. UGANDA J. 19 (1955), pp. 41-48.

18,728 KANYAMUNYU, P. K. The tradition of the coming of the Abalisa clan to Buhwezu, Ankole. UGANDA J. 15 (1951), pp. 191-192.

18,729 KORITSCHONER, H. Ngoma ya sheitani: an East African native treatment for psychical disorder. JRAI 66 (1936), pp. 209-219.

18,730 KULUBYA, S. W. Some aspects of Baganda customs. UGANDA J. 9 (1942), pp. 49-56.

18,731 LANNING, E. C. Bark-cloth hammers. UGANDA J. 23 (1959), pp. 79-83.

18,732 LANNING, E. C. The death of Chieftain Kateboha. UGANDA J. 23 (1959), pp. 186-188.

18,733 LANNING, E. C. Masaka Hill—an ancient centre of worship. UGANDA J. 18 (1954), pp. 24-30.

18,734 LAWRENCE, J. C. D. The Karamojong cluster: a note. AFRICA 23 (1953), pp. 244-249.

18,735 LOWTH, N. L. C. The story of the entry of the Alur into the West Nile. UGANDA J. 2 (1935), pp. 245-246.

18,736 LUDGER, K. Rainmakers in Teso. UGANDA J. 18 (1954), pp. 185-186.

18,737 McCONNELL, R. E. Notes on the Lugwari tribe of Central Africa. JRAI 55 (1925), pp. 439-467.

18,738 MAIR, L. What anthropologists are after. UGANDA J. 7 (1939), pp. 85-92.

18,739 MAIR, L. Clientship in East Africa. CAH. ET. AFR. 2 (1961), pp. 315-325.

18,740 MALANDRA, A. The ancestral shrine of the Acholi. UGANDA J. 7 (1939), pp. 27-43.

18,741 MALING, R. W. The Were leopard. UGANDA J. 7 (1939), pp. 93-95.

18,742 MATSON, A. T. The Samson and Delilah story. UGANDA J. 25 (1961), pp. 217-220.

18,743 MELDON, J. A. The Latuka. J. AFR. SOC. 9 (1910), pp. 270-274.

18,744 MELDON, J. A. Notes on the Bahima of Ankole. J. AFR. SOC. 6 (1907), pp. 136-153, 234-249.

18,745 MELDON, J. A. Notes on the Sudanese in Uganda. J. AFR. SOC. 7 (1908), pp. 123-146.

18,746 MENZIES, I. R. and PATIKO, J. A pagan harvest thanksgiving in Acholi district. UGANDA J. 18 (1954), pp. 182-185.

18,747 MIDDLETON, J. The concept of 'bewitching' in Lugbara. AFRICA 25 (1955), pp. 252-260.

18,748 MIDDLETON, J. Myth, history and mourning taboos in Lugbara. UGANDA J. 19 (1955), pp. 194-203.

18,749 MIDDLETON, J. The political system of the Lugbara of the Nile-Congo divide. TRIBES WITHOUT RULERS, 1958, pp. 203-229.

18,750 MIDDLETON, J. Social change among the Lugbara of Uganda. CIVILISATIONS 10 (1960), pp. 446-454; French summary, pp. 455-456.

18,751 MIDDLETON, J. The social significance of Lugbara personal names. UGANDA J. 25 (1961), pp. 34-42.

18,752 MIDDLETON, J. Some social aspects of Lugbara myth. AFRICA 24 (1954), pp. 189-198.

18,753 MILLER, R. G. Crocodile fishing. UGANDA J. 3 (1936), p. 317.

18,754 MORRIS, H. F. The Balisa Bakama of Buzimba. UGANDA J. 17 (1953), pp. 71-73.

18,755 MORRIS, H. F. The Kingdom of Mpororo. UGANDA J. 19 (1955), pp. 204-207.

18,756 MORRIS, T. D. H. Bakonjo shrines. UGANDA J. 17 (1953), p. 78.

18,757 MORS, P. O. Grasshoppers as food in Buhaya. ANTHR. QUART. 31 (1958), pp. 56-58.

18,758 MORS, P. O. Notes on hunting and fishing in Buhaya. ANTHR. QUART. 26 (1953), pp. 89-93.

18,759 MUKASA, S. K. B. A legendary hero of Buganda [Wakiwugulu]. UGANDA J. 7 (1939), p. 49.

18,760 NASON, C. S. Proverbs of the Baganda. UGANDA J. 3 (1936), pp. 247-258.

18,761 NILE, L. U. Out with an Acholi hunt. AFR. AFFAIRS 45 (1946), pp. 178-184.

18,762 NORTHCOTE, G. A. S. The Nilotic Kavirondo. JRAI 37 (1907), pp. 58-66.

18,763 NSIMBI, M. B. Baganda traditional personal names. UGANDA J. 14 (1950), pp. 204-214.

18,764 NSIMBI, M. B. The clan system in Buganda. UGANDA J. 28 (1964), pp. 25-30.

18,765 NSIMBI, M. B. Village life and customs in Buganda. UGANDA J. 20 (1956), pp. 27-36.

18,766 NYE, G. W. A legend of some hills in Bulemezi. UGANDA J. 7 (1940), pp. 140-141.

18,767 NYE, G. W. A note on Kikasa in Bulemezi. UGANDA J. 7 (1940), p. 190.

18,768 NYENDWOHA, S. On paying a visit in Bunyoro. UGANDA J. 22 (1958), pp. 81-83.

18,769 O., A. V. The Hima method of counting. UGANDA J. 4 (1936), p. 91.

18,770 OBERG, K. Analysis of the Bahima marriage ceremony. AFRICA 19 (1949), pp. 107-120.

18,771 OBERG, K. The kingdom of Ankole in Uganda. AFRICAN POLITICAL SYSTEMS, 1940, pp. 121-162.

18,772 OBERG, K. Kinship organization of the Banyankole. AFRICA 11 (1938), pp. 129-158.

18,773 OKELLO, Y. K. Lango marriage. UGANDA J. 15 (1951), pp. 65-73.

18,774 OLIVER, R. Ancient sites of Ankole. UGANDA J. 23 (1959), pp. 51-63.

18,775 olyech, e. the anointing of clan heads among the Lango. UGANDA J. 4 (1937), pp. 317-318.

18,776 ORYEM, P. and WRIGHT, M. J. Lucoro and Min-kwet. An Akoli folk-tale. UGANDA J. 24 (1960), pp. 120-122.

18,777 OSMASTON, H. A. The termite and its uses for food. UGANDA J. 15 (1951), pp. 80-83.

18,778 P'BITEK, O. Acholi concept of fate, Wilobo and Ru-piny. UGANDA J. 29 (1965), pp. 85-93.

18,779 P'BITEK, O. Acholi folk tales. EAISR July (1962), pp. 1-8.

18,780 P'BITEK, O. The concept of Jok among the Acholi and Lango. UGANDA J. 27 (1963), pp. 15-29.

18,781 PEARSON, P. The Black Forest Pigmies. UGANDA J. 4 (1936), pp. 115-119.

18,782 PENREATH, R. Superstitions in North Kavirondo. UGANDA J. 3 (1936), pp. 318-321.

18,783 PERLMAN, M. L. Some aspects of marriage stability in Toro. EAISR Dec. (1960), pp. 1-21; Jan. (1962), pp. 1-17.

18,784 PERRYMAN, P. W. Native witchcraft. UGANDA J. 4 (1936), pp. 7-26.

18,785 PERSSE, E. M. The Bagwe. Ethnological notes and some folk-tales. UGANDA J. 3 (1936), pp. 282-302.

18,786 PERSSE, E. M. Ethnological notes on the Karimojong. UGANDA J. 1 (1934), pp. 110-115.

18,787 RAPER, A. B. and LADKIN, R. G. The Banakalanga of Kyagwe. UGANDA J. 15 (1951), pp. 144-158.

18,788 ROSCOE, J. The Bahima: a cow tribe of Enkole in the Uganda Protectorate. JRAI 37 (1907), pp. 93-118.

18,789 ROSCOE, J. Notes on the manners and customs of the Baganda. JRAI 31 (1901), pp. 117-130.

18,790 SANDERSON, M. Relationships among the Wayao. JRAI 50 (1920), pp. 369-376.

18,791 SHACKELL, R. S. A Buganda fable. UGANDA J. 2 (1935), pp. 304-305.

18,792 SHILLITO, J. F. "Etuku"...a problem propounded. UGANDA J. 5 (1938), p. 300.

18,793 SNOXALL, R. A. The coronation ritual and customs of Buganda. UGANDA J. 4 (1937), pp. 277-288.

18,794 SOUTHALL, A. W. Alur tradition and its historical significance. UGANDA J. 18 (1954), pp. 137-165.

18,795 SOUTHALL, A. W. Oedipus in Alur folklore. UGANDA J. 22 (1958), pp. 167-169.

18,796 SPIRE, F. Notes on the Madi negroes (Equatorial Nile). J. AFR. SOC. 4 (1905), p. 301.

18,797 STAFFORD, D. N. Bunyoro grain pits. UGANDA J. 19 (1955), p. 208.

18,798 STAFFORD, D. N. The casting of metals by Africans. UGANDA J. 19 (1955), pp. 208-209.

18,799 STANNUS, H. S. and DAVEY, J. B. The initiation ceremony for boys among the Yao of Nyasaland. JRAI 43 (1913), pp. 119-123.

18,800 STEIGER-HAYLEY, T. T. Wage labour and the desire for wives among the Lango. UGANDA J. 8 (1940), pp. 15-18.

18,801 STENNING, D. J. Salvation in Ankole. AFRICAN SYSTEMS OF THOUGHT, 1965, pp. 258-275.

18,802 STRUCK, B. On the ethnographic nomenclature of the Uganda-Congo border. J. AFR. SOC. 9 (1910), pp. 275-288.

18,803 SWITZER, C. W. The story of Lwabinumi. UGANDA J. 4 (1937), pp. 262-265.

18,804 TARANTINO, A. Lango clans. UGANDA J. 13 (1949), pp. 109-111.

18,805 TARANTINO, A. Notes on the Lango. UGANDA J. 13 (1949), pp. 145-153.

18,806 TARANTINO, A. The origin of the Lango. UGANDA J. 10 (1946), pp. 12-16.

18,807 THIEL, E. P. The Jinja stone. UGANDA J. 26 (1962), pp. 101-102.

18,808 THOMAS, A. S. Some photographs of Bwamba initiates. UGANDA J. 4 (1936), p. 90.

18,809 THOMAS, I. The flat-roofed houses of the Sebei at Benet [finds of the Brathay Expedition, 1962]. UGANDA J. 27 (1963), pp. 115-122.

18,810 TROWELL, M. The development of an ethnological museum with a technological bias. RHODES-LIV. J. 4 (1945), pp. 55-65.

18,811 USHER-WILSON, L. C. An Acholi hunt. UGANDA J. 11 (1947), pp. 30-37.

18,812 USHER-WILSON, L. C. Dini ya Misambwa. UGANDA J. 16 (1952), pp. 125-129.

18,813 VELSEN, J. V. Some economic aspects of Kumam marriage and family. EAISR June (1958), pp. 1-19.

18,814 W., K. The procedure in accession to the throne of a nominated king in the Kingdom of Bunyoro-Kitara. UGANDA J. 4 (1937), pp. 289-299.

18,815 WALLACE, J. M. Fire-making by friction. UGANDA J. 12 (1948), pp. 102-104.

18,816 WALSHE, C. I. Notes on the Kumam. UGANDA J. 11 (1947), pp. 101-105.

18,817 WATSON, J. M. Lake Mutukula. UGANDA J. 8 (1940), pp. 33-34.

18,818 WEATHERBY, J. M. Discussion on Nandi speaking groups. EAISR June (1963), pp. 1-10.

18,819 WEATHERBY, J. M. Sebei conceptions of health and disease. EAISR Dec. (1959), pp. 71-81.

18,820 WEATHERBY, J. M. et al. The Sirikwa by J. W. Weatherby, B. E. Kipkorir and J. E. G. Sutton. UGANDA J. 28 (1964), pp. 61-74.

18,821 WELBOURN, F. B. Kibuuka comes home. TRANSITION 5 (1962), pp. 15-17, 20.

18,822 WELBOURN, F. B. Some aspects of Kiganda religion. UGANDA J. 26 (1962), pp. 171-182.

18,823 WERNER, A. The custom of "Hlonipa" in its influence on language. J. AFR. SOC. 4 (1905), pp. 346-356.

18,824 WHISSON, M. G. The will of God and the wiles of men (...beliefs concerning the supernatural held by the Luo...). EAISR Jan. (1962), pp. 1-34.

18,825 WILLIAMS, F. L. Ankole folk tales. AFRICA 21 (1951), pp. 32-40.

18,826 WILLIAMS, F. L. Blood-brotherhood in Ankole (Omukago). UGANDA J. 2 (1934), pp. 33-41.

18,827 WILLIAMS, F. L. The coronation of the Abakama of Koki. UGANDA J. 4 (1937), pp. 313-316.

18,828 WILLIAMS, F. L. The drum Wango. UGANDA J. 6 (1938), pp. 54-55.

18,829 WILLIAMS, F. L. Hima cattle. UGANDA J. 6 (1938), pp. 17-42, 87-117.

18,830 WILLIAMS, F. L. The inauguration of the Omugabe of Ankole to office. UGANDA J. 4 (1937), pp. 300-312.

18,831 WILLIAMS, F. L. Metamorphosis. UGANDA J. 4 (1936), pp. 91-93.

18,832 WILLIAMS, F. L. Myth, legend and lore in Uganda. BULL. UGANDA SOC. 3 (1944), pp. 12-23; also in UGANDA J. 10 (1946), pp. 64-75.

18,833 WILLIAMS, F. L. Nuwa Mbaguta, Nganzi of Ankole. BULL. UGANDA SOC. 4 (1945), pp. 3-13.

18,834 WILLIAMS, F. R. J. The pagan religion of the Madi. UGANDA J. 13 (1949), pp. 202-210.

18,835 WINTER, E. The aboriginal political structure of Bwamba. TRIBES WITHOUT RULERS, 1958, pp. 136-166.

18,836 WRIGHT, A. C. A. Notes on the Iteso social organization. UGANDA J. 9 (1942), pp. 57-80.

18,837 WRIGHT, A. C. A. A rainmaking ceremony in Teso. UGANDA J. 10 (1946), pp. 25-28.

18,838 WRIGHT, A. C. A. Some notes on Acholi religious ceremonies. UGANDA J. 3 (1936), pp. 175-202.

18,839 WRIGHT, A. C. A. The Supreme Being among the Acholi of Uganda—another viewpoint. UGANDA J. 7 (1940), pp. 130-137.

18,840 WRIGHT, M. J. Ishekindi will give birth to Ishekindi. An Ankole folk-tale. UGANDA J. 25 (1961), pp. 112-114.

18,841 WRIGHT, M. J. Lango folk-tales—an analysis. UGANDA J. 24 (1960), pp. 99-113.

18,842 WRIGHT, M. J. The leopard and the hare. A Kiga folk-tale. UGANDA J. 23 (1959), pp. 191-194.

18,843 WRIGLEY, C. C. Kimera. UGANDA J. 23 (1959), pp. 38-43.

18,844 ZIBONDO, E. and LAIGHT. Basoga death and burial rites. UGANDA J. 2 (1934), pp. 120-144.

18,845 Sesse canoes. UGANDA J. 11 (1947), p. 61.

See also 5626, 5803, 17227.

Art. Antiquities

18,846 BERE, R. M. Acholi dances (Myel). UGANDA J. 1 (1934), pp. 64-65.

18,847 BERE, R. M. Note on the origin of the Payera Acholi. UGANDA J. 1 (1934), pp. 65-67.

18,848 BISHOP, W. W. Pleistocene correlation in the Uganda section of the Albert-Edward Rift Valley. PROC. PAN-AFR. CONGR. PRE-HIST. 4 (1962), pp. 245-253.

18,849 BISHOP, W. W. Recent palaeontological, palaeolithic and stratigraphical research in Uganda. DISCOVERING AFRICA'S PAST, 1959, pp. 2-3.

18,850 BISHOP, W. W. A summary of the present position regarding Quaternary stratigraphical research in Uganda. PROC. PAN-AFR. CONGR. PRE-HIST. 4 (1962), pp. 209-217.

18,851 BISHOP, W. W. and POSNANSKY, M. Pleistocene environments and early man in Uganda. UGANDA J. 24 (1960), pp. 44-61.

18,852 BISSET, C. B. Hill-top hollows in Masaka District. UGANDA J. 5 (1937), pp. 130-133.

18,853 BRACHI, R. M. Excavation of a rock shelter at Hippo Bay, Entebbe. UGANDA J. 24 (1960), pp. 62-70.

18,854 CLARK, J. D. A re-examination of the industry from the type site of Magosi, Uganda. PROC. PAN-AFR. CONGR. PRE-HIST. 3 (1955), pp. 228-241.

18,855 COLE, G. H. Recent archaeological work in southern Uganda. UGANDA J. 29 (1965), pp. 149-161.

18,856 COUTTS, P. G. Some musical instruments of Usuku. UGANDA J. 14 (1950), pp. 160-162.

18,857 DUNCAN, J. M. Music in Uganda: old and new. UGANDA J. 3 (1936), pp. 314-317.

18,858 GGOMOTOKA, J. T. K. History and legends of the rocks of Kakumiro and of some other places in the Sazas of Mubende. UGANDA. J. 14 (1950), pp. 85-96.

18,859 GRAY, Sir J. M. The cairns of Koki. UGANDA J. 22 (1958), pp. 180-181.

18,860 GRAY, Sir J. M. Early history of Buganda. UGANDA J. 2 (1935), pp. 259-271.

18,861 GRAY, Sir J. M. Nsimbi and his pipe. UGANDA J. 19 (1955), pp. 91-93.

18,862 GRAY, Sir J. M. The riddle of Biggo. UGANDA J. 2 (1935), pp. 226-233.

18,863 JACOBS, B. L. A note from Luuka County, Busoga. UGANDA J. 13 (1949), pp. 111-112.

18,864 KUBIK, G. The Endara xylophone of Bukonjo. AFR. MUSIC, 1962, pp. 43-48.

18,865 KUBIK, G. The structure of Kiganda xylophone music. AFR. MUSIC, 1960, pp. 6-30.

18,866 KUBIK, G. Xylophone playing in Southern Uganda. JRAI 94 (1964), pp. 138-159.

18,867 LANNING, E. C. Ancient earthworks in western Uganda. UGANDA J. 17 (1953), pp. 51-62.

18,868 LANNING, E. C. A burial site at Mweya, Toro. UGANDA J. 22 (1958), pp. 170-172.

18,869 LANNING, E. C. The cairns of Koki, Buganda. UGANDA J. 21 (1957), pp. 176-183.

18,870 LANNING, E. C. Caves and rock shelters of western Uganda. UGANDA J. 26 (1962), pp. 183-193.

18,871 LANNING, E. C. The Munsa earthworks. UGANDA J. 19 (1955), pp. 177-182.

18,872 LANNING, E. C. Notes on certain shafts in Buganda and Toro. UGANDA J. 18 (1954), pp. 187-190.

18,873 LANNING, E. C. Protohistoric pottery in Uganda. PROC. PAN-AFR. CONGR. PRE-HIST. 3 (1955), pp. 313-317.

18,874 LAWRANCE, J. C. D. Rock paintings in Teso. UGANDA J. 17 (1953), pp. 8-13; 19(1955), p. 90.

18,875 LAWRANCE, J. C. D. Rock paintings in Teso and Bukedi. UGANDA J. 22 (1958), pp. 39-42.

18,876 LEAKEY, L. S. B. Prelimary notes on a survey of prehistoric art in Tanganyika. PROC. PAN-AFR. CONGR. PRE-HIST. 2 (1952), pp. 723-724.

18,877 LEAKEY, L. S. B. Preliminary report on a Chellean I living site at B.K. II, Olduvai gorge, Tanganyika Territory. PROC. PAN-AFR. CONGR. PRE-HIST. 3 (1955), pp. 217-218.

18,878 LUSH, A. J. Kiganda drums. UGANDA J. 3 (1935), pp. 7-25.

18,879 MARRIOTT, J. W. F. The Kampala Museum. UGANDA J. 2 (1934), pp. 79-82.

18,880 MARSHALL, K. The prehistory of the Entebbe peninsula. UGANDA J. 18 (1954), pp. 44-57.

18,881 MORRIS, H. F. Historic sites in Ankole. UGANDA J. 20 (1956), pp. 177-181.

18,882 O'BRIEN, T. P. Prehistory and Uganda. UGANDA J. 2 (1935), pp. 183-195.

18,883 OLIVER, R. The royal tombs of Buganda. UGANDA J. 23 (1959), pp. 124-133.

18,884 OLLIER, C. D. Some implements in Lugbara. UGANDA J. 23 (1959), pp. 182-183.

18,885 OLLIER, C. D. and HARROP, J. F. The caves of Mount Elgon. UGANDA J. 22 (1958), pp. 158-163.

18,886 OSMASTON, H. A. Ensa za Kateboha. UGANDA J. 29 (1965), pp. 223-223.

18,887 PARRY, R. E. Further notes on two antique chairs in Namirembe Cathedral. UGANDA J. 7 (1940), pp. 191-192.

18,888 PATZ, M. J. Hill-top hollows—further investigations. UGANDA J. 29 (1965), pp. 225-228.

18,889 PAUWELS, M. The Masaka cylinder: an interpretation of its use. UGANDA J. 13 (1949), pp. 23-30.

18,890 PEARCE, S. and POSNANSKY, M. The re-excavation of Nzongezi rock-shelter, Ankole. UGANDA J. 27 (1963), pp. 85-94.

18,891 POSNANSKY, M. Progress and prospects in historical archaeology in Uganda. DISCOVERING AFRICA'S PAST, 1959, pp. 31-39.

18,892 POSNANSKY, M. Recent palaeolithic discoveries in Uganda. PROC. PAN-AFR. CONGR. PRE-HIST. 4, no. iii (1962), pp. 207-212.

18,893 POSNANSKY, M. Rock paintings on Lolui Island, Lake Victoria. UGANDA J. 25 (1961), pp. 105-111.

18,894 POSNANSKY, M. Some archaeological aspects of the ethnohistory in Uganda. PROC. PAN-AFR. CONGR. PRE-HIST. 4, no. iii (1962), pp. 375-379.

18,895 POSNANSKY, M. and SEKIBENGO, J. W. Ground stone axes and bored stones in Uganda. UGANDA J. 23 (1959), pp. 179-181.

18,896 POWELL-COTTON, C. The Powell-Cotton Museum. DISCOVERING AFRICA'S PAST, 1959, p. 40.

18,897 SCHOFIELD, A. T. Photography in Uganda. UGANDA J. 2 (1935), pp. 285-290.

18,898 SCOTT, R. R. Kenya exhibition of musical instruments from Uganda and demonstration of Uganda music. AFR. MUSIC, 1949, pp. 22-27.

18,899 SEMPEBWA, E. K. K. Baganda folk-songs: a rough classification. UGANDA J. 12 (1948), pp. 16-24.

18,900 SHINNIE, P. L. Excavations at Bigo, 1957. UGANDA J. 24 (1960), pp. 16-28.

18,901 SOYINKA, W. Towards a true theatre. TRANSITION 8 (1963), pp. 21-22.

18,902 THOMAS, H. B. Two antique chairs for Namirembe Cathedral. UGANDA J. 7 (1940), pp. 138-139.

18,903 TODD, C. Modern sculpture and sculptors in East Africa. AFR. MUSIC, 1961, pp. 72-76.

18,904 TROWELL, M. The rosette cylinder from Ntusi. UGANDA J. 10 (1946), pp. 151-152.

18,905 TROWELL, M. Some royal craftsmen of Buganda. UGANDA J. 8 (1941), pp. 47-64.

18,906 WACHSMANN, K. P. Ancient earthworks in Western Uganda: notes on finds. UGANDA J. 18 (1954), pp. 190-192.

18,907 WACHSMANN, K. P. Musicology in Uganda. JRAI 83 (1953), pp. 50-57.

18,908 WAYLAND, E. J. Neoanthropic man of the early Stone Age. UGANDA J. 1 (1934), pp. 69-70.

18,909 WAYLAND, E. J. Note on a prehistoric 'Inscription' in Ankole and Uganda. UGANDA J. 5 (1938), pp. 252-253.

18,910 WAYLAND, E. J. Notes on the Biggo bya Mugenyi: some ancient earthworks in Northern Buddu. UGANDA J. 2 (1934), pp. 21-32.

18,911 WAYLAND, E. J. Pleistocene pluvial periods in Uganda. JRAI 60 (1930), pp. 467-475.

18,912 WAYLAND, E. J. Rifts, rivers, rains and early man in Uganda. JRAI 64 (1934), pp. 333-352.

18,913 WAYLAND, E. J. and BURKITT, M. C. The Magosian culture of Uganda. JRAI 62 (1932), pp. 369-390.

18,914 WEATHERBY, J. M. and WILSON, J. G. A note on the Sebei caves. Their formation and evidence of recent habitation. UGANDA J. 26 (1962), pp. 213-217.

18,915 Z., X. Y. Native music. UGANDA J. 1 (1934), p. 63.

18,916 An art exhibition in Uganda. J. AFR. SOC. 37 (1938), p. 463.

18,917 Beyond the fringe: the Transition profile. TRANSITION 1 (1961), pp. 21-22.

See also 889, 10143, 12940, 15593.

Biography

18,918 HUDDLE, J. G. The life of Yakobo Adoko of Lango District. UGANDA J. 21 (1957), pp. 184-190.

18,919 ANYWAR, R. S. The life of Rwot Iburaim Awich. UGANDA J. 12 (1948), pp. 72-81.

18,920 BERE, R. M. Awich—a biographical note and a chapter of Acholi history. UGANDA J. 10 (1946), pp. 76-78.

18,921 KINLOCH, B. G. Obituary: Karamoja Bell, Captain W. D. M. Bell. UGANDA J. 19 (1955), pp. 106-109.

18,922 COOK, A. R. Obituary: Dr. "Jack" Cook. UGANDA J. 11 (1947), pp. 127-128.

18,923 Obituary: Sir Albert Ruskin Cook. AFR. AFFAIRS 50 (1951), pp. 250-251; UGANDA J. 15 (1951), p. 211.

18,924 BUDD, M. S. Obituary: Mr. K. Hay Dale, O.B.E. UGANDA J. 20 (1956), pp. 218-219.

18,925 W., F. L. Obituary: J. H. Driberg. UGANDA J. 10 (1946), pp. 40-41.

18,926 Obituary [J. H. Driberg]. AFR. AFFAIRS 45 (1946), pp. 97-98.

18,927 LANNING, E. C. Sultan Fademulla Murjan of Aringa. UGANDA J. 18 (1954), pp. 178-180.

18,928 THOMAS, H. B. The Rev. A. B. Fisher in Uganda: a memoir. UGANDA J. 21 (1957), pp. 107-110.

18,929 Obituary: Norman Godinho, M. B. E. UGANDA J. 16 (1952), p. 182.

18,930 PITMAN, C. R. S. Obituary: Sir William Gowers: a tribute. UGANDA J. 19 (1955), pp. 105-106.

18,931 THOMAS, H. B. The death of Bishop Hannington. Supplementary evidence. UGANDA J. 23 (1959), pp. 29-37.

18,932 THOMAS, H. B. The last days of Bishop Hannington. UGANDA J. 8 (1940), pp. 19-27.

18,933 STAFFORD, D. N. The burial of Kabarega. UGANDA J. 19 (1955), p. 208.

18,934 THOMAS, H. B. Capax imperii—the story of Semei Kakunguru. UGANDA J. 6 (1939), pp. 125-136.

18,935 GRAY, Sir J. M. Mother Mary Kevin, C.B.E. UGANDA J. 22 (1958), pp. 103-104.

18,936 GRAY, Sir J. M. Ernest Linant de Bellefonds. UGANDA J. 28 (1964), pp. 31-54.

18,937 LOW, D. A. Alexander Mackay. MAKERERE J. 2 (1959), pp. 50-55.

18,938 WILLIAMS, F. L. Nuwa Mbaguta, Nganzi of Ankole. UGANDA J. 10 (1946), pp. 124-135.

18,939 SEBULIBA, C. The late Ham Mukasa. UGANDA J. 23 (1959), pp. 184-186.

18,940 EGGELING, W. J. Death of Mumia. UGANDA J. 14 (1950), p. 105.

18,941 GRAY, Sir J. M. Rwot Ochama of Payera. UGANDA J. 12 (1948), pp. 121-128.

18,942 WRIGHT, M. J. The early life of Rwot Isaya Ogwangguji, M.B.E. UGANDA J. 22 (1958), pp. 131-138.

18,943 SHINNIE, P. L. Roddie Owen's grave. UGANDA J. 21 (1957), p. 220.

18,944 THOMAS, H. B. Roddy Owen. UGANDA J. 18 (1954), pp. 186-187.

18,945 Obituary: J. R. P. Postlethwaite. AFR. AFFAIRS 55 (1956), pp. 122-123.

18,946 PITMAN, C. R. S. Samaki—Captain R. J. D. Salmon, M.V.O., M.C. UGANDA J. 17 (1953), pp. 68-70.

18,947 ROWE, J. A. Mika Sematimba. UGANDA J. 28 (1964), pp. 179-199.

18,948 THOMAS, H. B. The death of Speke in 1864. UGANDA J. 13 (1949), pp. 105-107.

18,949 THIEL, E. P. Frederick Spire, C.M.G. UGANDA J. 26 (1962), pp. 99-101.

18,950 GRAY, Sir J. M. In memoriam: Archbishop Henri Streicher, C.B.E. UGANDA J. 17 (1953), pp. 63-67.

18,951 THOMAS, H. B. Jacob Wainwright in Uganda. UGANDA J. 15 (1951), pp. 204-205.

18,952 THOMAS, H. B. Obituary: J. J. Uganda, Bishop Willis. UGANDA J. 19 (1955), pp. 103-104.

18,953 THOMAS, H. B. The Wilsons of early Uganda. UGANDA J. 20 (1956), pp. 210-213.

See also 11343, 18010.

Economics

18,954 BELSHAW, D. G. R. An outline of resettlement policy in Uganda: 1945-63. EAISR June (1963), pp. 1-16.

18,955 DAVIES, K. A. World mineral production and Uganda's contribution. UGANDA J. 5 (1938), pp. 289-295.

18,956 EHRLICH, C. Cotton and the Uganda economy, 1903-1909. UGANDA J. 21 (1957), pp. 162-175.

18,957 EHRLICH, C. The economy of Buganda, 1893-1903. UGANDA J. 20 (1956), pp. 17-26.

18,958 EHRLICH, C. Some social and economic implications of paternalism in Uganda. EAISR Jan. (1959), pp. 1-17.

18,959 ELKAN, W. The employment of women in Uganda. AFR. WOMEN 2 (1956), pp. 6-9.

18,960 ELLIOTT, G. F. S. The best route to Uganda. CONTEMP. REV. 68 (1895), pp. 15-20.

18,961 FURLEY, O. W. The origins of economic paternalism in a British territory: Western Uganda. SOC. AND ECON. STUD. 11 (1962), pp. 57-72.

18,962 GHAI, D. Economic growth and tax revenue in Uganda: 1962-70. EAISR Jan. (1965), pp. 1-33.

18,963 HALL, Sir J. M. Some aspects of economic development in Uganda. AFR. AFFAIRS 51 (1952), pp. 124-134.

18,964 HARMSWORTH, J. Cows for Christmas. EAISR Jan. (1963), pp. 1-15.

18,965 HARMSWORTH, J. Dynamics of Kisoga land tenure. EAISR Jan. (1962), pp. 1-9.

18,966 HAWES, C. G. Some effects of the Owen Falls Scheme. UGANDA J. 16 (1952), pp. 107-112.

18,967 HICKS, P. H. The railway extension to western Uganda. UGANDA J. 18 (1954), pp. 71-75.

18,968 HOYLE, B. S. The economic expansion of Jinja, Uganda. GEOG. REV. 53 (1963), pp. 377-388.

18,969 ILLINGWORTH, S. Kenyans in Busoga. EAISR June (1963), pp. 1-6.

18,970 KAJUBI, W. S. Coffee and prosperity in Buganda: some aspects of economic and social change. UGANDA J. 29 (1965), pp. 135-147.

18,971 LIVINGSTONE, I. The marketing of crops in Uganda and Tanganyika. AFR. PRIMARY PRODUCTS AND INT. TRADE, 1965, pp. 125-147.

18,972 MAIR, L. P. The growth of economic individualism in African society. J. AFR. SOC. 33 (1934), pp. 261-273.

18,973 MOODY, R. Samaia fishermen. EAISR Jan. (1963), pp. 1-9.

18,974 MORGAN, A. R. Uganda's cotton industry—fifty years back. UGANDA J. 22 (1958), pp. 107-112.

18,975 OCHENG, D. An economist looks at Uganda's future. TRANSITION 1 (1961), pp. 17-20.

18,976 OLIVIER, H. Some aspects of the Owen Falls Scheme. UGANDA J. 17 (1953), pp. 28-37.

18,977 PEAL, W. J. The Kampala to Bombo railway. UGANDA J. 27 (1963), pp. 61-70.

18,978 RADO, E. R. Wages and employment in Uganda. PROBLEMS OF ECON. DEVELOPMENT IN E. AFR., 1965, pp. 100-107.

18,979 RAMCHANDANI, R. R. Uganda's economy—its problems and prospects. AFR. QUART. 2, no. iii (1962), pp. 183-200.

18,980 REBELO, D. J. S. O chá na economia da Uganda (um estudo económico). BSEM 143 (1965), pp. 33-55; includes English summary.

18,981 RICHARDS, A. I. Some effects of the introduction of individual freehold into Buganda. AFR. AGRARIAN SYSTEMS, 1963, pp. 267-280.

18,982 ROGERS, F. H. The stamps of Uganda. UGANDA J. 5 (1938), pp. 141-159.

18,983 SCAFF, A. H. The re-development of Kisenyi: progress report of the United Nations urban planning mission to Uganda. EAISR Jan. (1964), pp. 1-9.

18,984 SWANZY, H. Uganda development. AFR. AFFAIRS 46 (1947), pp. 184-185.

18,985 T., A. D. F. Bark-cloth making in Buganda. UGANDA J. 1 (1934), pp. 17-21.

18,986 TEMPLE, P. H. Nakasero market, Kampala. UGANDA J. 28 (1964), pp. 165-178.

18,987 THOMAS, H. B. An experiment in African native land settlement. J. AFR. SOC. 27 (1928), pp. 234-248.

18,988 WALKER, D. Some preliminary reactions to Uganda's development plans. EAISR Jan. (1959), pp. 1-19.

18,989 WHITE, H. P. The way to the West. UNIVERSITAS 2 (1956), pp. 51-52.

18,990 The search for oil in Uganda. J. AFR. SOC. 39 (1940), pp. 299-300.

18,991 The s.s. "Winifred" and s.s. "Clement Hill." UGANDA J. 4 (1937), pp. 268-269.

See also 17336, 17343, 17360, 17367.

Education

18,992 BANAGE, W. B. Some thoughts on science education in Uganda schools. MAKERERE J. 10 (1964), pp. 53-60.

18,993 BELL, J. Further education for the women of Uganda. AFR. WOMEN 4 (1962), pp. 73-77.

18,994 BELL, P. W. Some musings on the Midas touch: a brief note. MAKERERE J. 10 (1964), pp. 49-50.

18,995 BUNSEN, B. DE. The reply of Makerere. AFR. SOUTH 4, no. 1 (1959), pp. 53-56.

18,996 BURNET, A. M. Women at Makerere. AFR. WOMEN 2 (1956-1958), pp. 78-80.

18,997 BUTLER, J. Willingly to school: the day-student in Uganda. TRANSITION 9 (1963), pp. 27-29.

18,998 CARLIN, M. M. Some further musings [on the Midas touch]: a briefer note. MAKERERE J. 10 (1964), pp. 50-51.

18,999 CARR, D. E. B. Adult literacy in Buganda. CORONA 4 (1952), pp. 144-148.

19,000 CARR, D. E. B. Community development campaigns in Buganda. CORONA 4 (1952), pp. 459-460.

19,001 CARR, D. E. B. Demonstration teams [in Uganda]. CORONA 3 (1951), pp. 140-142.

19,002 CARTER, F. The education of African Muslims in Uganda. UGANDA J. 29 (1965), pp. 193-199.

19,003 GOLDTHORPE, J. E. Makerere revisited. A symposium discussing J. E. Goldthorpe, An African Elite, Makerere College Students 1922-1960. MAKERERE J. 11 (1965), pp. 1-16.

19,004 GOLDTHORPE, J. E. and MacPHERSON, M. Makerere College and its old students. ZAIRE 12 (1958), pp. 349-363.

19,005 GOODE, P. M. The Gayaza farm-diet scheme in Uganda. AFR. WOMEN 3 (1958-1960), pp. 7-10.

19,006 HERON, D. B. Some reflections on academic freedom [at Makerere University College]. MAKERERE J. 9 (1964), pp. 33-43.

19,007 JOLLY, R. Stocks and flows in Uganda education and manpower. EAISR Jan. (1964), pp. 1-16.

19,008 JOLLY, R. and RADO, E. Education in Uganda: reflections on the report of the Uganda Education Commission. E. AFR. EC. REV. N.S. 1, no. 1 (1964), pp. 69-79; also in EAISR Jan. (1964), pp. 1-9.

19,009 KAMOGA, F. K. School leaving as affected by separation of parents in Buganda. EAISR Jan. (1963), pp. 1-9.

19,010 KAMOGA, F. K. Wastage among teachers in Buganda. EAISR Jan. (1964), pp. 1-17.

19,011 McADAM, K. J. The need for selection and guidance services in Uganda. MAKERERE J. 7 (1963), pp. 33-60.

19,012 McFIE, J. African performance on an intelligence test. UGANDA J. 18 (1954), pp. 34-43.

19,013 MALECHE, A. J. A study of wastage in primary schools in Uganda. EAISR Dec. (1960), pp. 1-20.

19,014 MALECHE, A. J. Wastage among school leavers in West Nile: 1959 and 1960. EAISR Jan. (1962), pp. 1-12.

19,015 MULIRA, E. M. K. Graduates in Uganda. CIVILISATIONS 2 (1952), pp. 339-345; French summary, pp. 345-347.

19,016 MUSGROVE, F. Education and the culture concept. AFRICA 23 (1953), pp. 110-125.

19,017 MUSGROVE, F. Some reflections on the sociology of African education. AFR. STUD. 11 (1952), pp. 165-178.

19,018 MUSGROVE, F. A Uganda secondary school as a field of culture change. AFRICA 22 (1952), pp. 234-249.

19,019 PHIPPS, B. A. The teaching profession in Uganda: some preliminary thoughts. EAISR Jan. (1963), pp. 1-10.

19,020 PHIPPS, P. E. Preliminary survey into reading habits. EAISR Jan. (1963), pp. 1-10.

19,021 SAUNDERS, M. M. Development plan for girls' education in Uganda. AFR. WOMEN 1 (1954), pp. 4-9.

19,022 SAUNDERS, M. M. Technical education for girls in Uganda. AFR. WOMEN 2 (1956-1958), pp. 30-31.

19,023 SCOTT, R. D. Agitators or educators? A critical review of the African Labour College. MAKERERE J. 10 (1964), pp. 15-21.

19,024 SOMERSET, H. C. A. Home structure, parental separation, and examination success in Buganda. EAISR Jan. (1965), pp. 1-19.

19,025 SOMERSET, H. C. A. The junior secondary schools leavers project: a progress report. EAISR Jan. (1964), pp. 1-11.

19,026 THOMPSON, F. New years thoughts in Uganda. TRANSITION 3 (1962), pp. 41-42.

19,027 VOWLES, P. F. Makerere College in transformation. MAKERERE J. 3 (1959), pp. 1-7.

19,028 WALKER, R. H. A history of education in Uganda. J. AFR. SOC. 16 (1917), pp. 283-286.

19,029 WEATHERHEAD, H. W. The educational value of industrial work as illustrated in King's School, Uganda. INT. REV. MISSIONS 3 (1914), pp. 343-348.

19,030 WEEKS, S. G. A preliminary examination of the role of minority students at a day secondary school in Kampala, Uganda. EAISR Jan. (1963), pp. 1-14.

19,031 WINGARD, P. Problems of the media of instruction in some Uganda school classes: a preliminary survey. LANGUAGE IN AFRICA, 1963, pp. 96-115.

19,032 Community development in Uganda. J. AFR. ADM. 5 (1953), pp. 50-61.

19,033 The education of women and girls in Uganda. WOMEN TODAY 6 (1964), pp. 42-44.

19,034 Extracts from "Mengo Notes." UGANDA J. 10 (1946), pp. 32-38, 144-147; 11 (1947), pp. 47-59, 110-122; 12 (1948), pp. 82-98, 172-196; 13 (1949), pp. 82-104, 211-229.

19,035 Literacy programme for the women of Uganda. WOMEN TODAY 6 (1964), pp. 57-58.

19,036 Women's technical education in Uganda. AFR. WOMEN 1 (1955), pp. 46-47.

Geography

19,037 ACKROYD, R. The British Museum (Natural History) expedition to the Birunga Volcanoes, 1933-34. UGANDA J. 1 (1934), pp. 107-109.

19,038 AP GRIFFITH, G. Soils and men. UGANDA J. 14 (1950), pp. 97-102.

19,039 B., R. M. An ascent of Mount Mikeno. UGANDA J. 2 (1935), pp. 300-301.

19,040 BAKER, S. J. K. Bunyoro: a regional appreciation. UGANDA J. 18 (1954), pp. 101-112.

19,041 BAKER, S. J. K. The geographical background of Western Uganda. UGANDA J. 22 (1958), pp. 1-10.

19,042 BAKER, S. J. K. The population map of Uganda: a geographical interpretation. UGANDA J. 1 (1934), pp. 134-144.

19,043 BEADLE, L. C. and LIND, E. M. Research on the swamps of Uganda. UGANDA J. 24 (1960), pp. 84-98.

19,044 BERE, R. M. Exploration of the Ruwenzori. UGANDA J. 19 (1955), pp. 119-136.

19,045 BERE, R. M. Ruwenzori: routes on Mount Stanley. UGANDA J. 15 (1951), pp. 74-79.

19,046 BERE, R. M. and HICKS, P. H. Ruwenzori. BULL. UGANDA SOC. 5 (1945), pp. 10-20; also in UGANDA J. 10 (1946), pp. 84-96.

19,047 BISHOP, W. W. Gully erosion in the Queen Elizabeth National Park. UGANDA J. 26 (1962), pp. 161-165.

19,048 BISSET, C. B. Note on earth tremors on and about 18th March, 1945. BULL. UGANDA SOC. 4 (1945), pp. 25-26; also in UGANDA J. 10 (1946), pp. 154-157.

19,049 BRASNETT, N. V. Modern trends in forestry with particular application to Uganda. UGANDA J. 7 (1940), pp. 164-175.

19,050 CHORLEY, C. W. The effect of cloud on the behaviour of tsetse fly. UGANDA J. 5 (1938), pp. 245-251.

19,051 CHORLEY, C. W. Waterspouts. UGANDA J. 5 (1937), pp. 46-48.

19,052 CHORLEY, C. W. Winds and storms of Lake Victoria. UGANDA J. 8 (1941), pp. 76-80.

19,053 DAVIES, K. A. Geology and its service to Uganda. UGANDA J. 10 (1946), pp. 3-11.

19,054 DAWE, M. T. An ascent of Ruwenzori. J. AFR. SOC. 5 (1906), pp. 182-186.

19,055 DAWE, M. T. The forests of Uganda. J. AFR. SOC. 9 (1910), pp. 120-128.

19,056 DAWKINS, H. C. The Northern Province mountains: speculations on climate and vegetation. UGANDA J. 18 (1954), pp. 58-64.

19,057 DESHLER, W. Livestock trypanosomiasis and human settlement in north-eastern Uganda. GEOG. REV. 50 (1960), pp. 541-554.

19,058 GREENLAND, D. J. and CHANCELLOR, R. J. West Nile District. Some soil and vegetation types. UGANDA J. 22 (1958), pp. 64-73.

19,059 GROVES, A. W. The physiography of Uganda. The evolution of the Great Lakes and the Victoria Nile drainage system. J. AFR. SOC. 33 (1934), pp. 59-69.

19,060 HENDERSON, J. P. Some aspects of climate in Uganda, with special reference to rainfall. UGANDA J. 13 (1949), pp. 154-176.

19,061 HIPPEL, E. V. Kaweri. UGANDA J. 10 (1946), pp. 158-160.

19,062 HUMPHREY-SMITH, G. An Arab historian's reference to the sources of the Nile in 950 A.D. UGANDA J. 7 (1939), pp. 47-48.

19,063 JACOBS, B. L. By car from Uganda. CORONA 3 (1951), pp. 103-105.

19,064 JARDINE, J. Hippo hunting by night. UGANDA J. 5 (1938), pp. 302-303.

19,065 KIRKPATRICK, R. T. Lake Choga and surrounding country. UGANDA J. 10 (1946), pp. 160-162.

19,066 LANGLANDS, B. W. Maize in Uganda. UGANDA J. 29 (1965), pp. 215-221.

19,067 LANNING, E. C. The earthworks at Kibengo, Mubende District. UGANDA J. 24 (1960), pp. 183-196.

19,068 LIND, E. M. Studies in Uganda swamps. UGANDA J. 20 (1956), pp. 166-176.

19,069 LINDSELL, R. F. J. Uganda place names. UGANDA J. 19 (1955), p. 102.

19,070 McMASTER, D. N. Speculations on the coming of the banana to Uganda. J. TROP. GEOG. 16 (1962), pp. 57-69.

19,071 MENZIES, I. R. The glaciers of Ruwenzori. UGANDA J. 15 (1951), pp. 177-181.

19,072 MOTTRAM, B. H. The Rwizi drainage basin of south-west Uganda in relation to the Oruchinga and Kagera rivers. UGANDA J. 27 (1963), pp. 177-186.

19,073 MUSGROVE, F. Teaching geography to the peoples of western Uganda. AFR. STUD. 11 (1952), pp. 68-74.

19,074 OSMASTON, H. A. Notes on the Ruwenzori glaciers. UGANDA J. 25 (1961), pp. 99-104.

19,075 OSMASTON, H. A. Two inselbergs near Acholi—Karamoja border. UGANDA J. 23 (1959), pp. 183-184.

19,076 PALLISTER, J. W. The physiography of Mengo District, Buganda. UGANDA J. 21 (1957), pp. 16-29.

19,077 PARRY, R. E. Fusiform cumulo-nimbus clouds in Uganda. UGANDA J. 4 (1937), pp. 257-262.

19,078 PITMAN, C. R. S. The Mabira Forest. UGANDA J. 1 (1934), pp. 7-16.

19,079 POSNETT, R. N. Some notes on West Nile hills and history. UGANDA J. 15 (1951), pp. 165-176.

19,080 RAVENSTEIN, E. G. Messrs. Jackson and Gedge's journey to Uganda via Masailand. UGANDA J. 12 (1948), pp. 129-133.

19,081 SCOTT, R. The Mubuku River and the angler. UGANDA J. 4 (1937), pp. 247-256.

19,082 STONES, R. Y. Kibo. UGANDA J. 3 (1935), pp. 84-86.

19,083 SYNGE, P. M. Some notes on the mountains of Uganda. UGANDA J. 2 (1934), pp. 145-157.

19,084 TEMPLE, P. H. Evidence of lake-level changes from the northern shoreline of Lake Victoria, Uganda. GEOGRAPHERS AND THE TROPICS, 1964, pp. 31-56.

19,085 TEMPLE, P. H. Kampala: influences upon its growth and development. EAISR June (1963), pp. 1-11.

19,086 THOMAS, H. B. An early visit to Ruwenzori. UGANDA J. 11 (1947), pp. 61-63.

19,087 THOMAS, H. B. Emile Jonveaux—an armchair African explorer. UGANDA J. 10 (1946), pp. 152-154.

19,088 THOMAS, H. B. Giovanni Miani and the White Nile. UGANDA J. 6 (1939), pp. 176-194.

19,089 THOMAS, H. B. Ruwenzori and Elgon—footnotes. UGANDA J. 2 (1935), pp. 249-250.

19,090 THOMAS, H. B. and LINDSELL, R. F. J. Early ascents of Mount Elgon. UGANDA J. 20 (1956), pp. 113-128.

19,091 THOMAS, I. General account [of the Brathay Exploration Group's expedition to Uganda, 1962]. UGANDA J. 27 (1963), pp. 107-108.

19,092 TRICKER, B. J. K. et al. Fossils from Karamoja by B. J. K. Tricker, W. H. Taylor and W. W. Bishop [finds of the Brathay Expedition, 1962]. UGANDA J. 27 (1963), pp. 109-114.

19,093 WATNEY, N. B. The dry crossing of the Nile near Nimule. UGANDA J. 4 (1937), pp. 350-351.

19,094 WAYLAND, E. J. A dry crossing of the Nile. UGANDA J. 1 (1934), pp. 68-69.

19,095 WAYLAND, E. J. The dry crossing of the Nile near Nimule. UGANDA J. 5 (1938), pp. 301-302.

19,096 WAYLAND, E. J. Katwe. UGANDA J. 1 (1934), pp. 96-106.

19,097 WAYLAND, E. J. Notes on the thermal and mineral springs in Uganda. UGANDA J. 4 (1937), pp. 197-207.

19,098 WAYLAND, E. J. Past climates and some future possibilities in Uganda [with a note on the Noachian Deluge and its possible equivalent in Eastern Africa]. UGANDA J. 3 (1935), pp. 93-118; 3 (1936), pp. 313-314.

19,099 WHITTOW, J. B. and SHEPHERD, A. The Speke glacier, Ruwenzori. UGANDA J. 23 (1959), pp. 153-161.

19,100 WILSON, M. An aerial phenomenon. UGANDA J. 2 (1935), pp. 302-304.

19,101 La métropole de l'Uganda. ZAIRE 6 (1952), pp. 187-189.

See also 4927, 6068, 18071.

Government. Politics. Administration

19,102 ADIMOLA, A. B. Uganda: the newest "independent." AFR. AFFAIRS 62 (1963), pp. 326-332.

19,103 APTER, D. E. Some problems of local government in Uganda. J. AFR. ADM. 11 (1959), pp. 27-37.

19,104 BADENOCH, A. C. Graduated taxation in the Teso district of Uganda. J. LOCAL ADM. OV. 1 (1962), pp. 15-22.

19,105 BEATTIE, J. Democratization in Bunyoro. The impact of democratic institutions and values on a traditional African kingdom. CIVILISATIONS 11 (1961), pp. 8-18; French summary, pp. 19-20.

19,106 BROCKWAY, F. Rapport sur la situation en Uganda. PRESENCE AFR. 13 (1952), pp. 401-406.

19,107 BUCHANAN, L. M. Report on urban local government in Uganda. J. AFR. ADM. 8 (1956), pp. 162-163.

19,108 BURKE, F. The application of the English committee system to local government in Uganda. J. AFR. ADM. 10 (1958), pp. 39-46.

19,109 BURKE, F. The new role of the chief in Uganda. J. AFR. ADM. 10 (1958), pp. 153-160.

19,110 BUSTIN, E. L'africanisation des cadres administratifs de l'Ouganda. CIVILISATIONS 9 (1959), pp. 133-147; English summary, pp. 147-150.

19,111 COHEN, Sir A. Uganda's progress and problems. AFR. AFFAIRS 56 (1957), pp. 111-112.

19,112 COURT, B. Independence. TRANSITION 1 (1961), pp. 23-25.

19,113 COX, T. R. F. A reason for paying poll tax. UGANDA J. 10 (1946), p. 39.

19,114 ENGHOLM, G. Political parties and Uganda's independence. TRANSITION 3 (1962), pp. 15-17.

19,115 ENGHOLM, G. F. Administrative aspect of the 1958 Uganda elections. EAISR Jan. (1959), pp. 1-21.

19,116 FALLERS, L. The predicament of the modern African chief: an instance from Uganda. AMER. ANTHR. 57 (1955), pp. 290-305.

19,117 GEE, T. W. Uganda's Legislative Council between the Wars. UGANDA J. 25 (1961), pp. 54-64.

19,118 GRAY, A. The Buganda question. AFR. AFFAIRS 60 (1961), pp. 139-141.

19,119 GRAY, A. Kabaka decision reversed. AFR. AFFAIRS 54 (1955), pp. 5-6.

19,120 GRAY, A. Kabaka home. AFR. AFFAIRS 55 (1956), pp. 3-4.

19,121 GRAY, A. Kabaka returning. AFR. AFFAIRS 54 (1955), pp. 247-248.

19,122 GRAY, A. Lukiko rebuffed. AFR. AFFAIRS 56 (1957), pp. 185-186.

19,123 GRAY, A. New Uganda government. AFR. AFFAIRS 61 (1962), pp. 186-187.

19,124 GRAY, A. Uganda changes. AFR. AFFAIRS 59 (1960), pp. 183-185.

19,125 GRAY, A. Uganda [constitutional] problems. AFR. AFFAIRS 59 (1960), pp. 288-289.

19,126 GRAY, A. Uganda [constitutional] proposals. AFR. AFFAIRS 59 (1960), pp. 103-104.

19,127 GRAY, A. Uganda election plans. AFR. AFFAIRS 56 (1957), pp. 261-263.

19,128 GRAY, A. Uganda elections. AFR. AFFAIRS 60 (1961), pp. 8-10.

19,129 GRAY, A. Uganda independence. AFR. AFFAIRS 61 (1962), pp. 14-15, 287-290; 62 (1963), pp. 15-18.

19,130 GRAY, A. Uganda legislature. AFR. AFFAIRS 57 (1958), pp. 97-98.

19,131 GRAY, A. Uganda relations. AFR. AFFAIRS 60 (1961), pp. 482-484.

19,132 GRAY, A. Uganda self-government. AFR. AFFAIRS 61 (1962), pp. 110-111.

19,133 GRAY, A. Uganda unrest. AFR. AFFAIRS 58 (1959), pp. 202-204.

19,134 GREENSTONE, J. D. Corruption and self-interest in Kampala and Nairobi: a comment on local politics in East Africa. COMP. STUD. SOC. HIST. 8 (1965-1966), pp. 199-210.

19,135 HOPKINS, T. K. La politique en Uganda: La question du Buganda. ET. CONG. 8, no. 5 (1965), pp. 15-43.

19,136 INGHAM, K. British administration in Lango District, 1907-1935. UGANDA J. 19 (1955), pp. 156-168.

19,137 INGHAM, K. Early proposals for a federal Uganda. UGANDA J. 21 (1957), pp. 223-226.

19,138 INGHAM, K. Uganda's masque of independence. AFR. AFFAIRS 62 (1963), pp. 29-39.

19,139 JACOBS, B. 13 points on the problems of administration in new African states. TRANSITION 16 (1964), pp. 31-32.

19,140 JACOBS, B. L. The state of the Uganda civil service two years after independence. EAISR Jan. (1965), pp. 1-13.

19,141 KIRONDE, E. Towards a definition of foreign policy. TRANSITION 5 (1962), p. 13.

19,142 LAWRENCE, J. C. D. The position of chiefs in local government in Uganda. J. AFR. ADM. 8 (1956), pp. 186-192.

19,143 LAWRENCE, J. C. D. A provincial course for chiefs in Uganda. J. AFR. ADM. 5 (1953), pp. 69-72.

19,144 LEE, J. M. Buganda's position in Federal Uganda. J. COMM. POL. STUD. 3 (1965), pp. 165-181.

19,145 LEYS, C. and VALENTINE, M. The party after independence: the case of the UPC. EAISR Jan. (1965), pp. 1-2.

19,146 LOW, A. The British and the Baganda. INTERNAT. AFFAIRS 32 (1956), pp. 308-317.

19,147 LOW, A. The composition of the Buganda Lukiko in 1902. UGANDA J. 23 (1959), pp. 64-68.

19,148 LOW, D. A. The anatomy of administrative origins: Uganda 1890-1902. EAISR Jan. (1958), pp. 1-24.

19,149 MIDDLETON, J. Notes on the political organization of the Madi of Uganda. AFR. STUD. 14 (1955), pp. 29-36.

19,150 MIDDLETON, J. The role of chiefs and headmen among the Lugbara of West Nile District, Uganda. J. AFR. ADM. 8 (1956), pp. 32-38.

19,151 MITCHELL, P. E. Indirect rule. UGANDA J. 4 (1936), pp. 101-107.

19,152 MUKASA, H. The rule of the kings of Buganda. UGANDA J. 10 (1946), pp. 136-143.

19,153 OBOTE, M. A plan for nationhood. TRANSITION 6-7 (1962), pp. 15-18.

19,154 OCHENG, D. Economic forces and Uganda's foreign policy. TRANSITION 6-7 (1962), pp. 27-29.

19,155 ROSCOE, J. Uganda and some of its problems. J. AFR. SOC. 22 (1923), pp. 96-108, 218-225.

19,156 SADLER, J. H. Present-day administration in Uganda. ROYAL COL. INST. PR. 36 (1904-1905), pp. 68-86.

19,157 SAVAGE, D. C. A profile of Buganda. AFR. SOUTH 5, no. 4 (1961), pp. 81-85.

19,158 SAULDIE, M. M. Independence: a challenge to Uganda. AFR. QUART. 2, no. iii (1962), pp. 173-182.

19,159 SOUTHALL, A. W. Micropolitics in Uganda: traditional and modern politics. EAISR Jan. (1963), pp. 1-23.

19,160 UGANDA. Framework of Uganda constitution. AFR. QUART. 2, no. ii (1962), pp. 127-137.

19,161 WELBOURN, F. B. A Christian in politics: the Hour after midnight by Colin Morris. TRANSITION 2 (1961), pp. 44-45.

19,162 WINTER, E. H. Local African administration in Bwamba. EAISR June (1952), pp. 31-36.

19,163 Report of the Uganda Relationships Commission, 1961. J. AFR. ADM. 13 (1961), pp. 243-254.

19,164 Senior chiefs in Uganda look to the future. J. AFR. ADM. 9 (1957), pp. 124-129.

19,165 L'Uganda a l'heure de M. Obote. PRESENCE AFR. N.S. 41 (1962), pp. 173-175.

See also 17479.

History

19,166 ADIMOLA, A. B. The Lamogi Rebellion 1911-12. UGANDA J. 18 (1954), pp. 166-177.

19,167 ALPERS, E. A. Charles Chaillé-Long's mission to Mutesa of Buganda. UGANDA J. 29 (1965), pp. 1-11.

19,168 BAKER, J. N. L. Sir Richard Burton and the Nile sources. UGANDA J. 12 (1948), pp. 61-71.

19,169 BAKER, J. R. Baker and Ruyonga. UGANDA J. 25 (1961), pp. 214-216.

19,170 BAMUNOBA, Y. K. Diviners for the Abagabe. UGANDA J. 29 (1965), pp. 95-97.

19,171 BARBER, J. P. The Karamoja district of Uganda: a pastoral people under colonial rule. J. AFR. HIST. 3 (1962), pp. 111-124.

19,172 BARBER, J. P. Karamoja in 1910. UGANDA J. 28 (1964), pp. 15-23.

19,173 BARBER, J. P. The Macdonald expedition to the Nile 1897-1899. UGANDA J. 28 (1964), pp. 1-14.

19,174 BARBER, J. P. The moving frontier of British imperialism in northern Uganda. UGANDA J. 29 (1965), pp. 27-43.

19,175 BAXENDALE, A. S. and JOHNSON, D. Uganda and Breat Britain. UNIV. BIRM. HIST. J. 8 (1962), pp. 162-188.

19,176 BENNETT, G. The eastern boundary of Uganda in 1902. UGANDA J. 23 (1959), pp. 69-72.

19,177 BERE, R. M. Awich: a biographical note and a chapter of Acholi history. BULL. UGANDA SOC. 1 (1943), pp. 14-16.

19,178 BERE, R. M. Buganda. CORONA 3 (1951), pp. 383-389.

19,179 BERE, R. M. An outline of Acholi history. UGANDA J. 11 (1947), pp. 1-8.

19,180 BIRD, C. H. Uganda twenty-five years ago. UGANDA J. 20 (1956), pp. 47-51.

19,181 BRASNETT, J. The Karasuk problem. UGANDA J. 22 (1958), pp. 113-122.

19,182 BRIDGES, R. C. Sir John Speke and the Royal Geographical Society. UGANDA J. 26 (1962), pp. 23-43.

19,183 COLLINS, R. O. Mahdist and Belgian leaders in the Upper Nile during the late nineteenth century. UGANDA J. 27 (1963), pp. 227-229.

19,184 COLLINS, R. O. Sudan-Uganda boundary rectification and the Sudanese occupation of Madial, 1914. UGANDA J. 26 (1962), pp. 140-153.

19,185 COLLINS, R. O. The Turkana patrol, 1918. UGANDA J. 25 (1961), pp. 16-33.

19,186 COOK, Sir A. R. An early newspaper in Uganda and comments on the news contained therein. UGANDA J. 4 (1936), pp. 27-40.

19,187 COOK, Sir A. R. Further memories of Uganda. UGANDA J. 2 (1934), pp. 97-115.

19,188 COOK, Sir A. R. The journey to Uganda in 1896 and Kampala during the closing years of last century. UGANDA J. 1 (1934), pp. 83-95.

19,189 COOK, Sir A. R. Uganda memories (1897-1940). BULL. UGANDA SOC. 4 (1945), pp. 33-35.

19,190 COOTE, J. M. The Kivu mission, 1909-10. UGANDA J. 20 (1956), pp. 105-112.

19,191 COX, A. H. The growth and expansion of Buganda. UGANDA J. 14 (1950), pp. 153-159.

19,192 CRAZZOLARA, J. P. Lwoo migrations. UGANDA J. 25 (1961), pp. 136-148.

19,193 DAVIES, K. A. A glimpse of Uganda's past. UGANDA J. 2 (1934), pp. 71-73.

19,194 DELME-RADCLIFFE, C. Extracts from Lt.-Col. C. Delmé-Radcliffe's typescript diary report on the delimitation of the Anglo-German boundary, Uganda, 1902-1904. UGANDA J. 11 (1947), pp. 9-29.

19,195 DICKSON, A. A photograph of Mumia. UGANDA J. 11 (1947), pp. 60-61.

19,196 DUNBAR, A. R. The British and Bunyoro-Kitara, 1891 to 1899. UGANDA J. 24 (1960), pp. 229-241.

19,197 DUNBAR, A. R. Emin Pasha and Bunyoro-Kitara, 1877 to 1889. UGANDA J. 24 (1960), pp. 71-83.

19,198 DUNBAR, A. R. European travellers in Bunyoro-Kitara, 1862-1877. UGANDA J. 23 (1959), pp. 101-117.

19,199 EGGELING, W. J. Another photograph of Mumia. UGANDA J. 12 (1948), pp. 197-199.

19,200 FLETCHER, T. B. Mwanga—the man and his times. UGANDA J. 4 (1936), pp. 162-167.

19,201 FURLEY, O. W. The Sudanese troops in Uganda. AFR. AFFAIRS 58 (1959), pp. 311-327.

19,202 FURLEY, O. W. The Sudanese troops in Uganda. From Lugard's enlistment to the mutiny, 1891-97. EAISR Jan. (1959), pp. 1-26.

19,203 GEE, T. W. A century of Muhammadan influence in Buganda, 1852-1951. UGANDA J. 22 (1958), pp. 139-150.

19,204 GERARD, R. E. Le sens du nom "mvuta nzighe" donné au Lac Albert. ZAIRE 3 (1949), p. 557.

19,205 GOWERS, W. Some thoughts on Uganda. J. AFR. SOC. 29 (1930), pp. 467-470.

19,206 GOWERS, W. Uganda and its future. J. AFR. SOC. 26 (1927), pp. 85-92.

19,207 GRAY, Sir J. M. Acholi history, 1860-1901. UGANDA J. 15 (1951), pp. 121-143; 16 (1952), pp. 32-50, 132-144.

19,208 GRAY, Sir J. M. Acholiland in 1897. UGANDA J. 18 (1954), pp. 21-23.

19,209 GRAY, Sir J. M. Ahmed bin Ibrahim—the first Arab to reach Buganda. UGANDA J. 11 (1947), pp. 80-97.

19,210 GRAY, Sir J. M. An Anglo-German agreement relating to traffic on Lake Victoria, 1890. UGANDA J. 11 (1947), pp. 124-125.

19,211 GRAY, Sir J. M. Anglo-German relations in Uganda, 1890-1892. J. AFR. HIST. 1 (1960), pp. 281-297.

19,212 GRAY, Sir J. M. Arabs on Lake Victoria. Some revisions. UGANDA J. 22 (1958), pp. 76-81.

19,213 GRAY, Sir J. M. A corrigendum to Speke's Journal of the Discovery of the Sources of the Nile. UGANDA J. 1 (1934), p. 70.

19,214 GRAY, Sir J. M. The diaries of Emin Pasha—extracts. UGANDA J. 25 (1961), pp. 1-15, 149-170; 26 (1962), pp. 72-96, 121-139; 27 (1963), pp. 1-13, 143-161; 28 (1964), pp. 75-97, 201-216; 29 (1965), pp. 75-83, 201-214.

19,215 GRAY, Sir J. M. Early treaties in Uganda. UGANDA J. 17 (1953), p. 189.

19,216 GRAY, Sir J. M. Early treaties in Uganda, 1888-1891. UGANDA J. 12 (1948), pp. 25-42.

19,217 GRAY, Sir J. M. Gordon's fort at Mruli. UGANDA J. 19 (1955), pp. 62-67.

19,218 GRAY, Sir J. M. A history of Ibanda, Saza of Mitoma, Ankole [as related by Nuwa Mbaguta to F. A. Knowles]. UGANDA J. 24 (1960), pp. 166-182.

19,219 GRAY, Sir J. M. Kabarega's embassy to the Mahdists in 1897. UGANDA J. 19 (1955), pp. 93-95.

19,220 GRAY, Sir J. M. Kakunguru in Bukedi. UGANDA J. 27 (1963), pp. 31-59.

19,221 GRAY, Sir J. M. Kibuka. UGANDA J. 20 (1956), pp. 52-71.

19,222 GRAY, Sir J. M. The Kivu Mission, 1909-10. UGANDA J. 21 (1957), pp. 119-120.

19,223 GRAY, Sir J. M. The Lango wars with Egyptian troops, 1877-8. UGANDA J. 21 (1957), pp. 111-114.

19,224 GRAY, Sir J. M. Livingstone's Muganda servant. UGANDA J. 13 (1949), pp. 119-129.

19,225 GRAY, Sir J. M. Mackay's canoe voyage along the western shore of Lake Victoria in 1883. UGANDA J. 18 (1954), pp. 13-20.

19,226 GRAY, Sir J. M. Magimbi Kamanyiro. UGANDA J. 24 (1960), pp. 242-252.

19,227 GRAY, Sir J. M. Mutesa of Buganda. UGANDA J. 1 (1934), pp. 22-50; 5 (1937), p. 68.

19,228 GRAY, Sir J. M. The sieges of Bukumi, Mubende District, in 1898. UGANDA J. 25 (1961), pp. 65-85.

19,229 GRAY, Sir J. M. The solar eclipse in Ankole in 1492. UGANDA J. 27 (1963), pp. 217-221; 28 (1964), p. 125.

19,230 GRAY, Sir J. M. Speke and Grant. UGANDA J. 17 (1953), pp. 146-160.

19,231 GRAY, Sir J. M. Tippu Tib and Unganda. UGANDA J. 19 (1955), pp. 95-96.

19,232 GRAY, Sir J. M. Toro in 1897. UGANDA J. 17 (1953), pp. 14-27.

19,233 GRAY, Sir J. M. The year of the three kings of Buganda, Mwanga-Kiwewa-Kalema, 1888-1889. UGANDA J. 14 (1950), pp. 15-52.

19,234 GUTKIND, P. C. W. Notes on the Kibuga of Buganda. UGANDA J. 24 (1960), pp. 29-43.

19,235 HADDON, E. B. Kibuka. UGANDA J. 21 (1957), pp. 114-119.

19,236 HEAD, M. E. Inter-tribal history through tribal stories. BULL. UGANDA SOC. 2 (1944), pp. 13-17; also in UGANDA J. 10 (1946), pp. 106-112.

19,237 HEWETSON, C. An early cash book from Nandi Station. UGANDA J. 16 (1952), pp. 30-31.

19,238 HIPPEL, E. V. Kaweri. BULL. UGANDA SOC. 4 (1945), pp. 20-22.

19,239 HONE, H. R. The history of the Uganda Volunteer Reserve. UGANDA J. 8 (1941), pp. 65-75.

19,240 HOYLE, W. E. Early days in Kampala. UGANDA J. 21 (1957), pp. 91-98.

19,241 INGHAM, K. The amagasani of the Abakama of Bunyoro. UGANDA J. 17 (1953), pp. 138-145.

19,242 INGHAM, K. Some aspects of the history of Buganda. UGANDA J. 20 (1956), pp. 1-16.

19,243 INGHAM, K. Some aspects of the history of Western Uganda. UGANDA J. 21 (1957), pp. 131-149.

19,244 INGHAM, K. Uganda's old Eastern Province: the transfer to East Africa Protectorate in 1902. UGANDA J. 21 (1957), pp. 41-46.

19,245 KABUGA, C. E. S. The genealogy of Kabaka Kintu and the early Bakabaka of Buganda. UGANDA J. 27 (1963), pp. 205-216.

19,246 KATUMBA, A. and WELBOURN, F. B. Muslim martyrs of Buganda. UGANDA J. 28 (1964), pp. 151-163.

19,247 KEANE, G. J. The progress of Uganda. J. AFR. SOC. 35 (1936), pp. 311-319.

19,248 KEANE, G. K. The African native medical corps. J. AFR. SOC. 19 (1920), pp. 295-304.

19,249 KEANE, G. T. Uganda protectorate [1933]. J. AFR. SOC. 34 (1935), pp. 190-194.

19,250 KIRONDE, E. Before. TRANSITION 6-7 (1962), pp. 9-10.

19,251 KUSAMBIZA, N. F. M. Mother Kevin. UGANDA J. 11 (1947), p. 123.

19,252 LANGLANDS, B. W. Early travellers in Uganda: 1860-1914. UGANDA J. 26 (1962), pp. 55-71.

19,253 LANNING, E. C. Notes on the history of Koki. UGANDA J. 23 (1959), pp. 162-172.

19,254 LAWRENCE, J. C. D. A history of Teso to 1937. UGANDA J. 19 (1955), pp. 7-40.

19,255 LEGUM, C. The dangers of independence. TRANSITION 6-7 (1962), pp. 11-12.

19,256 LOUIS, W. R. The Anglo-German hinterland settlement of 1890 and Uganda. UGANDA J. 27 (1963), pp. 71-83.

19,257 LOUIS, W. R. The diary of the Kivu Mission. UGANDA J. 27 (1963), pp. 187-193.

19,258 LOW, A. British public opinion and the Uganda question: October-December 1892. UGANDA J. 18 (1954), pp. 81-100.

19,259 McMASTER, D. N. Speculations on the coming of the banana to Uganda. UGANDA J. 27 (1963), pp. 163-175.

19,260 MASEFIELD, G. Livingstone and the Baganda. UGANDA J. 10 (1946), pp. 79-83.

19,261 MATSON, A. T. Harry Johnston and Clement Hill. UGANDA J. 23 (1959), pp. 190-191.

19,262 MATSON, A. T. Macdonald's expedition to the Nile 1892-1899. UGANDA J. 29 (1965), pp. 98-103.

19,263 MATSON, A. T. Uganda's old Eastern Province and East Africa's federal capital. UGANDA J. 22 (1958), pp. 43-53.

19,264 MATSON, A. T. and SUTTON, J. E. G. The role of forts in safeguarding the Uganda road. UGANDA J. 29 (1965), pp. 163-184.

19,265 MAYANJA, A. M. K. [tr.] Chronology of Buganda, 1800-1907, from Kagwa's Ebika. UGANDA J. 16 (1952), pp. 148-158.

19,266 MOORE, G. The quiet day of freedom. TRANSITION 3 (1962), pp. 22-23.

19,267 MORRIS, H. F. The making of Ankole. UGANDA J. 21 (1957), pp. 1-15.

19,268 MORRIS, H. F. The murder of H. St. G. Galt. UGANDA J. 24 (1960), pp. 1-15.

19,269 MOSES, M. A history of Wadelai. UGANDA J. 17 (1953), pp. 78-80.

19,270 MUKASA, E. W. S. The origin of the title Mugema in the royal family of Buganda. BULL. UGANDA SOC. 1 (1943), p. 17.

19,271 MUKASA, E. W. S. The reason for the creation of the post of Mugema in Buganda. UGANDA J. 10 (1946), p. 150.

19,272 MUKASA, H. Ebifa ku Mulembe gwa Kabaka Mutesa: some notes on the reign of Mutesa. UGANDA J. 1 (1934), pp. 116-133; 2 (1934), pp. 60-71.

19,273 MUKASA, H. The rule of the kings of Buganda. BULL. UGANDA SOC. 2 (1944), pp. 21-23; 3 (1944), pp. 24-27.

19,274 MUKASA, H. Speke at the court of Muteesa I. UGANDA J. 26 (1962), pp. 97-99.

19,275 MUNGONYA, Z. C. K. The Bacwezi in Ankole. UGANDA J. 22 (1958), pp. 18-21.

19,276 NTARE SCHOOL HISTORY SOCIETY. H. M. Stanley's journey through Ankole in 1889. UGANDA J. 29 (1965), pp. 185-192.

19,277 OLIVER, R. The Baganda and the Bakonjo. UGANDA J. 18 (1954), pp. 31-33.

19,278 OLIVER, R. A question about the Bachwezi. UGANDA J. 17 (1953), pp. 135-137.

19,279 OLIVER, R. The traditional histories of Buganda, Bunyoro and Nkole. JRAI 85 (1955), pp. 111-117.

19,280 PITMAN, C. R. S. The Maria Theresa Dollar. UGANDA J. 17 (1953), p. 78.

19,281 QUIX, J. P. Au pays de Mahagi. CONGO 1 (1939), pp. 276-294.

19,282 ROBERTS, A. D. The evolution of the Uganda Protectorate. UGANDA J. 27 (1963), pp. 95-106.

19,283 ROBERTS, A. D. The "lost counties" of Bunyoro. UGANDA J. 26 (1962), pp. 194-199.

19,284 ROWE, J. A. Baganda chiefs who survived Kabaka Nwanga's purge of 1886. EAISR June (1963), pp. 1-14.

19,285 ROWE, J. A. Land and politics in Buganda, 1875-1955. MAKERERE J. 10 (1964), pp. 1-13.

19,286 ROWE, J. A. The purge of Christians at Mwanga's court: a reassessment of this episode in Buganda history. J. AFR. HIST. 5 (1964), pp. 55-71.

19,287 SKEENS, S. R. Reminiscences of Busoga and its chiefs. UGANDA J. 4 (1937), pp. 185-196.

19,288 SNOXALL, R. A. and GRAY, Sir J. M. The Uganda Staff List for 1895. UGANDA J. 1 (1934), pp. 61-63.

19,289 SOUTHALL, A. The Alur legend of Sir Samuel Baker and the Mukama Kabarega. UGANDA J. 15 (1951), pp. 187-190.

19,290 SPEKE, J. H. Journal of the Discovery of the Source of the Nile [an extract]. UGANDA J. 26 (1962), p. [i].

19,291 TARANTINO, A. Lango wars. UGANDA J. 13 (1949), pp. 230-235.

19,292 THOMAS, H. B. Arabic correspondence captured in south-west Bunyoro in 1895: with a note on Arab traders in Bunyoro. UGANDA J. 13 (1949), pp. 31-38.

19,293 THOMAS, H. B. An autograph letter of Emin Pasha. UGANDA J. 13 (1949), pp. 235-236.

19,294 THOMAS, H. B. The Baganda martyrs, 1885-1887 with special reference to the Protestant victims. UGANDA J. 15 (1951), pp. 84-91.

19,295 THOMAS, H. B. Captain Eric Smith's expedition to Lake Victoria in 1891. UGANDA J. 23 (1959), pp. 134-152.

19,296 THOMAS, H. B. Early treaties made by F. J. Jackson. UGANDA J. 24 (1960), pp. 260-262.

19,297 THOMAS, H. B. Emin Pasha—a last portrait. UGANDA J. 16 (1952), pp. 175-176.

19,298 THOMAS, H. B. Ernest Linant de Bellefonds and Stanley's letter to the "Daily Telegraph." UGANDA J. 2 (1934), pp. 7-13.

19,299 THOMAS, H. B. Gordon's farthest South in Uganda in 1876. UGANDA J. 5 (1938), pp. 284-288.

19,300 THOMAS, H. B. Imperatrix v. Juma and Urzee. UGANDA J. 7 (1939), pp. 70-84.

19,301 THOMAS, H. B. Jackson and von Tiedemann. UGANDA J. 2 (1934), pp. 158-159.

19,302 THOMAS, H. B. The Kagera triangle and the Kagera salient. UGANDA J. 23 (1959), pp. 73-78.

19,303 THOMAS, H. B. Livingstone's Muganda servant—a postscript. UGANDA J. 28 (1964), pp. 99-100.

19,304 THOMAS, H. B. The mission to Uganda in 1893—in memory. UGANDA J. 17 (1953), pp. 1-7.

19,305 THOMAS, H. B. Mohammed Biri. UGANDA J. 24 (1960), pp. 123-126.

19,306 THOMAS, H. B. The Mutiny Memorial at Bukaleba. UGANDA J. 22 (1958), pp. 74-75.

19,307 THOMAS, H. B. Our predecessors. UGANDA J. 22 (1958), pp. 185-187.

19,308 THOMAS, H. B. A relic of SS. Khedive. UGANDA J. 14 (1950), pp. 103-104.

19,309 THOMAS, H. B. Richard Buchta and early photography in Uganda. UGANDA J. 24 (1960), pp. 114-119.

19,310 THOMAS, H. B. Two finds in northern Uganda [A sun-dial of 1713 and a Charles II halfpenny]. UGANDA J. 16 (1952), pp. 173-175.

19,311 THOMAS, I. F. Baker's fort at Patiko. UGANDA J. 27 (1963), pp. 195-204.

19,312 THOMSON, J. The Uganda problem. CONTEMP. REV. 62 (1892), pp. 786-796.

19,313 TOWELL, M. Clues to African tribal history. BULL. UGANDA SOC. 1 (1943), pp. 4-11.

19,314 TURPIN, C. A. The occupation of the Turkwel River area by the Karamojong tribe. UGANDA J. 12 (1948), pp. 161-165.

19,315 TWINING, E. F. Uganda medals and decorations. UGANDA J. 2 (1935), pp. 209-225.

19,316 VANNESTE, M. Nyabongo, de eerste Bito-Koning: werkelijkheid en legende. KONGO-OVERZEE 16 (1950), pp. 148-154.

19,317 W., K. Abakama ba Bunyoro-Kitara [the kings of Bunyoro-Kitara]. UGANDA J. 3 (1935), pp. 149-160; 4 (1936), pp. 65-83; 5 (1937), pp. 53-67, 69-84.

19,318 WAINWRIGHT, G. A. The coming of the banana to Uganda. UGANDA J. 16 (1952), pp. 145-147.

19,319 WEATHERBY, J. M. Inter-tribal warfare on Mount Elgon in the 19th and 20th centuries (with particular reference to the part played by the Sebei-speaking groups). UGANDA J. 26 (1962), pp. 200-212.

19,320 WELBOURN, F. B. Abamalaki in Buganda, 1914-1919. UGANDA J. 21 (1957), pp. 150-161.

19,321 WELBOURN, F. B. Ezera Kabali's diary of the 1916 War. UGANDA J. 27 (1963), pp. 223-226.

19,322 WELBOURN, F. B. Speke and Stanley at the court of Mutesa. UGANDA J. 25 (1961), pp. 220-223.

19,323 WHISSON, M. G. The journeys of the JoRamogi. EAISR July (1962), pp. 1-12.

19,324 WHITEHEAD, E. F. A short history of Uganda military units formed during World War II. UGANDA J. 14 (1950), pp. 1-14.

19,325 WILLIAMS, F. L. The drum Wango. UGANDA J. 6 (1938), pp. 54-55.

19,326 WILLIAMS, F. L. Early explorers in Ankole. With a few notes on the routes traversed. UGANDA J. 2 (1935), pp. 196-208.

19,327 WILLIAMS, F. L. The Kabaka of Buganda. Death of His Highness Sir Daudi Chwa II, K.C.M.G., K.B.E. and accession of Edward Mutesa II. UGANDA J. 7 (1940), pp. 176-187.

19,328 WILLIAMS, W. H. Uganda. ROYAL COL. INST. PR. 25 (1893-1894), pp. 105-136.

19,329 WILSON, G. The progress of Uganda. J. AFR. SOC. 6 (1907), pp. 113-135.

19,330 WORKER, J. C. With the 4th (Uganda) K.A.R. in Abyssinia and Burma. UGANDA J. 12 (1948), pp. 52-56.

19,331 WRIGHT, A. C. A. Lwoo migrations—a review. UGANDA J. 16 (1952), pp. 82-88.

19,332 WRIGLEY, C. C. Some thoughts on the Bacwezi. UGANDA J. 22 (1958), pp. 11-17.

19,333 Indépendance de l'Ouganda. GENEVE-AFR. 1 (1962), p. 217.

19,334 More about H.M.S. Uganda. UGANDA J. 11 (1947), pp. 123-124.

19,335 Our predecessors [two photographs taken: 1. on the occasion of H.H. The Kabaka of Buganda's birthday, 1901. 2. at the opening of the Entebbe European Hospital, 1904]. UGANDA J. 3 (1936), pp. 239-242.

19,336 Uganda's jubilee. J. AFR. SOC. 42 (1943), pp. 104-106.

19,337 The war record of H.M.S. Uganda. UGANDA J. 11 (1947), pp. 63-64.

See also 19034.

Language. Literature

Language

19,338 B., A. An approach to linguistics. UGANDA J. 1 (1934), p. 155.

19,339 BARTON, J. Turkana grammatical notes and vocabulary. BULL. SOAS 2 (1921-1923), pp. 43-73.

19,340 BLOK, H. P. Kanttekeningen bij de jongste Luganda-Spraakkunst. KONGO-OVERZEE 21 (1955), pp. 306-317.

19,341 COLE, D. T. Some features of Ganda linguistic structure. AFR. STUD. 24 (1965), pp. 3-54, 71-116, 199-240.

19,342 CRABTREE, W. A. The language of the Uganda protectorate. J. AFR. SOC. 13 (1914), pp. 152-166.

19,343 CRABTREE, W. A. The "L" sound in Lu-ganda. J. AFR. SOC. 12 (1913), pp. 276-284, 395-406.

19,344 CRABTREE, W. A. The N sound in Lu-Ganda. J. AFR. SOC. 30 (1931), pp. 148-163.

19,345 DAMMANN, E. Zur Geschichte der Digo. AFR. UND UB. 34 (1943-1944), pp. 53-69.

19,346 HUNTINGFORD, G. W. B. The Orusyan language of Uganda. J. AFR. LANGS. 4 (1965), pp. 145-169.

19,347 JEFFREYS, M. D. W. Maize names. UGANDA J. 18 (1954), pp. 192-194.

19,348 KNAPPERT, J. The verb in Dhô-Alûr. J. AFR. LANGS. 2 (1963), pp. 101-127.

19,349 KOLLMANN. Eine Erzählung der Waganda. ZAOS 3 (1897), pp. 382-384.

19,350 MAIR, L. Linguistics without sociology: some notes of the standard Luganda dictionary. BULL. SOAS 7 (1933-1935), pp. 913-921.

19,351 MEEUSSEN, A. E. Les phonèmes du Ganda et du Bantou commun. AFRICA 25 (1955), pp. 170-180; English summary, p. 180.

19,352 MEEUSSEN, A. E. A preliminary tonal analysis of Ganda verb forms. J. AFR. LANGS. 4 (1965), pp. 108-113.

19,353 MILL HILL FATHERS. Derivations of some Teso place-names. UGANDA J. 16 (1952), pp. 168-172.

19,354 MORRIS, H. F. A note on Lunyole. UGANDA J. 27 (1963), pp. 127-134.

19,355 MORRIS, H. F. Some aspects of Runyankore. UGANDA J. 22 (1958), pp. 54-63.

19,356 MURATORI, C. Maize names and history: a further discussion. UGANDA J. 16 (1952), pp. 76-81.

19,357 RAGLAN, Lord. The Lotuko language. BULL. SOAS 2 (1921-1923), pp. 267-296.

19,358 ROBERTS, A. D. The sub-imperialism of the Baganda. J. AFR. HIST. 3 (1962), pp. 435-450.

19,359 SABBADINI, E. Considerazioni sulle lingue Maasai e Luganda. AFRICA (Rome) 13 (1958), pp. 93-94.

19,360 SEIDEL, A. Grundzüge der Grammatik der Sprache von Karagwe und Nkole in Deutsch-Ostafrika. ZAOS 4 (1898), pp. 366-382.

19,361 SNOXALL, R. A. Some Buganda place-names. BULL. UGANDA SOC. 2 (1944), pp. 1-10; also in UGANDA J. 10 (1946), pp. 43-53.

19,362 SNOXALL, R. A. Some problems and principles of lexicography in Luganda. AFR. LANG. STUD. 6 (1965), pp. 27-31.

19,363 SNOXALL, R. A. Word importation into Bantu language with particular reference to Banda. UGANDA J. 5 (1938), pp. 267-283.

19,364 STEPHENS, J. E. M. Derivations of some Teso place-names. UGANDA J. 17 (1953), pp. 191-192.

19,365 THOMAS, H. B. and DALE, I. R. Uganda place names: some European eponyms. UGANDA J. 17 (1953), pp. 101-123.

19,366 TUCKER, A. N. Notes on Konzo. AFR. LANG. STUD. 1 (1960), pp. 16-41.

19,367 TUCKER, A. N. The syllable in Luganda: a prosodic approach. J. AFR. LANGS. 1 (1962), pp. 122-166.

19,368 WALTHER, K. Eine Fabel vom Löwen im Mamba-Dialekt am Kilimandjaro. ZAOS 4 (1898), pp. 337-338.

See also 16126.

Literature

19,369 BAGCHI, G. The deviant [drama]. TRANSITION 2 (1961), inset.

19,370 CLARK, J. P. Song of a goat [drama]. TRANSITION 4 (1962), pp. 19-22.

19,371 LUBAMBULA, Y. B. The voice of Africa: a Ganda poem, by Y. B. Lubambula. AFRICA 18 (1948), pp. 45-48.

19,372 MORRIS, H. F. The praise poems of Bahima women. AFR. LANG. STUD. 6 (1965), pp. 52-66.

19,373 MUSHANGA, M. Folk tales from Ankole. TRANSITION 13 (1964), pp. 22-24; 22 (1965), pp. 26-30.

19,374 MUTIGA, J. G. To the ceremonial Mugumo (Fig tree) [a poem]. TRANSITION 3 (1962), p. 8.

19,375 NAGENDA, J. And he said hello [fiction]. TRANSITION 6-7 (1962), pp. 19-20.

19,376 NAGENDA, J. And this, at last [fiction]. TRANSITION 2 (1961), pp. 5-6.

19,377 ODIN, K. Stella queen's [fiction]. TRANSITION 4 (1962), pp. 7-9.

19,378 P'BITEK, O. Acholi folk tales. TRANSITION 6-7 (1962), pp. 21-24.

19,379 SNOXALL, R. A. Ganda literature. AFR. STUD. 1 (1942), pp. 55-63.

19,380 SYKES, J. The Sanders Saga. UGANDA J. 7 (1939), pp. 1-26.

Law

19,381 BEATTIE, J. H. M. Informal judicial activity in Bunyoro. J. AFR. ADM. 9 (1957), pp. 188-195.

19,382 BEATTIE, J. H. M. The Kibanja system of land tenure in Bunyoro, Uganda. J. AFR. ADM. 6 (1954), pp. 18-28.

19,383 BEATTIE, J. H. M. A further note on the Kibanja system of land tenure in Bunyoro, Uganda. J. AFR. ADM. 6 (1954), pp. 178-185.

19,384 BROWN, W. Status of Uganda women in relation to marriage laws. AFR. WOMEN 4 (1960), pp. 1-4.

19,385 COTRAN, E. Recent changes in the Uganda legal system. J. AFR. LAW 6 (1962), pp. 210-215.

19,386 FALLERS, L. A. Changing customary law in Busoga District of Uganda. J. AFR. ADM. 8 (1956), pp. 139-144.

19,387 FORDHAM, P. Uganda and its new constitution. TRANSITION 3 (1962), pp. 9-12.

19,388 GRAY, A. Land in Uganda. AFR. AFFAIRS 55 (1956), pp. 95-96.

19,389 HAYDON, E. S. Legal publications in an African vernacular. J. AFR. LAW 6 (1962), pp. 179-191.

19,390 HONE, H. R. The native of Uganda and the criminal law. UGANDA J. 6 (1938), pp. 1-16.

19,391 HOPKINS, E. The assessment of criminal guilt in the district court of Ankole. EAISR July (1962), pp. 1-14.

19,392 KALANDA, P. Adaptation of Church law to the Ganda marriage prohibitions. EAISR Jan. (1964), pp. 1-15.

19,393 MAIR, L. P. Baganda land tenure. AFRICA 6 (1933), pp. 187-205.

19,394 MOODY, R. W. Land tenure in Samia. EAISR July (1962), pp. 1-12.

19,395 MORRIS, H. F. Jurisdiction of the Buganda courts and the scope of customary law in Uganda. J. AFR. LAW 9 (1965), pp. 154-161.

19,396 MORRIS, H. F. Marriage and divorce in Uganda. UGANDA J. 24 (1960), pp. 197-206.

19,397 MORRIS, H. F. Uganda. Changes in the structure and jurisdiction of the courts and in the criminal law they administer. J. AFR. LAW 9 (1965), pp. 65-73.

19,398 OCHENG, D. O. Land tenure in Acholi. UGANDA J. 19 (1955), pp. 57-61.

19,399 PERLMAN, M. L. Land tenure in Toro. EAISR Jan. (1962), pp. 1-16.

19,400 SOUTHWOLD, M. The inheritance of land in Buganda. UGANDA J. 20 (1956), pp. 88-96.

19,401 STENNING, D. J. Coral Tree Hill (preliminary field report of land tenure enquiry in West Ankole District). EAISR June (1958), pp. 1-14.

19,402 WEST, H. W. Reflections upon the problems of land registration in Buganda. EAISR Jan. (1964), pp. 1-9.

19,403 Land tenure in Uganda. J. AFR. LAW 2 (1958), pp. 1-4.

19,404 Local law school, Entebbe. J. AFR. LAW 6 (1962), p. 156.

Religion

19,405 MIDDLETON, J. The Yakan or Allah Water Cult among the Lugbara. JRAI 93 (1963), pp. 80-108.

19,406 MOCKLER-FERRYMAN, A. F. Christianity in Uganda. J. AFR. SOC. 2 (1903), pp. 276-291.

19,407 POULTON, J. Like father, like son: some reflections on the Church of Uganda. INT. REV. MISSIONS 50 (1961), pp. 297-307.

19,408 ROWLING, F. The building of the Uganda cathedral. INT. REV. MISSIONS 8 (1919), pp. 227-237.

19,409 TAYLOR, J. V. The Uganda Church to-day. INT. REV. MISSIONS 46 (1957), pp. 136-144.

19,410 WELBOURN, F. B. Towards a definition of religion. MAKERERE J. 4 (1960), pp. 37-45.

19,411 WILLIS, J. J. The organization of the Anglican Church in Uganda: a study in contrasts. INT. REV. MISSIONS 7 (1918), pp. 481-491.

Science

19,412 ALLBROOK, D. Some problems associated with pelvic form and size in the Ganda of East Africa. JRAI 92 (1962), pp. 102-114.

19,413 ALLEN, P. M. and FRIPP, P. J. The birds of Makerere Hill: notes and check-list. UGANDA J. 28 (1964), pp. 55-60.

19,414 BARNLEY, G. R. The Mbwa Fly and problems of its control. UGANDA J. 16 (1952), pp. 113-120.

19,415 BATEMAN, H. R. Research and reminiscences: Uganda 1908-1910. UGANDA J. 15 (1951), pp. 26-40.

19,416 BENNETT, F. J. et al. An inventory of Kiganda foods by F. J. Bennett, A. A. Mugalula-Mukiibi, J. S. W. Lutwama and G. Nansubaga. UGANDA J. 29 (1965), pp. 45-53.

19,417 BIRCH, J. P. A lone giraffe. UGANDA J. 4 (1937), pp. 265-266.

19,418 BISSET, C. B. Water boring in Uganda 1920-1940. SUDAN NOTES 25 (1942), pp. 159-160.

19,419 BRASNETT, N. V. Mahogany. UGANDA J. 2 (1934), pp. 42-48.

19,420 CARPENTER, G. D. H. Do birds eat butterflies? UGANDA J. 5 (1938), pp. 253-254.

19,421 CHORLEY, T. W. Bee-keeping in Uganda. UGANDA J. 3 (1936), pp. 303-307.

19,422 CHORLEY, T. W. Bees nesting in key-holes. UGANDA J. 2 (1935), pp. 299-300.

19,423 CHORLEY, C. W. Kingfishers. UGANDA J. 7 (1939), pp. 44-46.

19,424 CHORLEY, C. W. Observations on bird migration on Nsadzi Isle, Lake Victoria. UGANDA J. 2 (1934), pp. 164-166.

19,425 CHORLEY, C. W. Some birds of prey of Lake Victoria. UGANDA J. 7 (1940), pp. 123-129.

19,426 COTT, H. B. The status of the Nile crocodile in Uganda. UGANDA J. 18 (1954), pp. 1-12.

19,427 CRABBE, J. R. The total eclipse of the sun, Uganda, May 1947. UGANDA J. 12 (1948), pp. 99-100.

19,428 DAVIES, J. N. P. Analysis of morbidity and mortality in children at Mulago hospital 1950-1. MALNUTRITION IN AFR. MOTHERS..., 1952, pp. 84-91.

19,429 DEAN, R. F. A. Diagnosis of acute Kwashiorkor in children at Mulago. MALNUTRITION IN AFR. WOMEN..., 1952, pp. 78-83.

19,430 DEAN, R. F. A. Treatment of kwashiorkor at Mulago. MALNUTRITION IN AFR. WOMEN..., 1952, pp. 308-314.

19,431 DIAS, J. A. T. S. Um novo nome para a Haematopota nigra T. Dias, 1956 nomen bis lectum. BSEM 103 (1957), pp. 133-135.

19,432 DOGGETT, W. G. Notes on some antelopes of the western part of the Uganda Protectorate. J. AFR. SOC. 3 (1904), pp. 163-165.

19,433 DONISTHORPE, J. A pilot study of the Mountain Gorilla (Gorilla gorilla beringei) in south-west Uganda. UGANDA J. 23 (1959), pp. 1-28.

19,434 DUKE, H. L. Hypsignathus monstrosus. UGANDA J. 1 (1934), pp. 72-74.

19,435 DUKE, H. L. An interesting hybrid [offspring of a situtunga and a bushbuck]. UGANDA J. 2 (1934), pp. 159-162.

19,436 DYSON-HUDSON, V. R. An Akarimojong-English check list of the trees of southern Karamoja. UGANDA J. 26 (1962), pp. 166-170.

19,437 DYSON-HUDSON, V. R. East coast fever in Karamoja. UGANDA J. 24 (1960), pp. 253-259.

19,438 EGGELING, W. J. Ambatch and African blackwood and some other light and heavy Uganda woods. UGANDA J. 2 (1935), pp. 278-284.

19,439 EGGELING, W. J. Bird notes from the Northern Province. UGANDA J. 3 (1936), pp. 242-243.

19,440 EGGELING, W. J. Ducks eating groundnuts. UGANDA J. 5 (1938), p. 299.

19,441 EGGELING, W. J. Epiphytes in the Budongo forest. UGANDA J. 12 (1948), pp. 106-114.

19,442 EGGELING, W. J. Notes on the flora and fauna of a Uganda swamp. UGANDA J. 1 (1934), pp. 51-60.

19,443 EGGELING, W. J. A plant—collection from Karamoja. UGANDA J. 6 (1938), pp. 43-53.

19,444 EGGELING, W. J. A review of some vegetational studies in Uganda. UGANDA J. 12 (1948), pp. 139-152.

19,445 EGGELING, W. J. The water-clearing roots of Courbonia. UGANDA J. 12 (1948), pp. 100-101.

19,446 EGGELING, W. J. Two plant problems. UGANDA J. 6 (1939), p. 164.

19,447 FORAN, W. R. Futki the friendly failure. AFR. AFFAIRS 55 (1956), pp. 38-42.

19,448 GIBBINS, E. G. "Mbwa" flies. UGANDA J. 2 (1935), pp. 272-277.

19,449 GLEESON, W. Abo phenotype distribution in Tororo secondary schools. UGANDA J. 25 (1961), pp. 114-115.

19,450 GOWERS, Sir W. Measuring African elephants. UGANDA J. 18 (1954), pp. 181-182.

19,451 GREENWOOD, P. H. The fishes of Uganda. UGANDA J. 19 (1955), pp. 137-155; 20 (1956), pp. 129-165: 21 (1957), pp. 47-80, 191-219.

19,452 GUDGER, E. W. The giant freshwater perch of Africa. UGANDA J. 11 (1947), pp. 106-109.

19,453 HANCOCK, G. L. R. The major pests of the cotton plant in Uganda. UGANDA J. 3 (1935), pp. 26-46.

19,454 HARRIS, W. V. Insects which alter the landscape. UGANDA J. 12 (1948), pp. 57-60.

19,455 HENDERSON, G. J. A strange story of an attack by a lion on a hippopotamus on the shores of Lake Naivasha. UGANDA J. 4 (1936), pp. 93-94.

19,456 HILL, J. E. Two mammals from Bwamba County, Uganda. UGANDA J. 17 (1953), p. 166.

19,457 HIPPEL, E. V. Stomach contents of crocodiles. UGANDA J. 10 (1946), pp. 148-149.

19,458 HOLMES, E. G. Considerations of protein deficiency in Uganda. MALNUTRITION IN AFR. WOMEN..., 1952, pp. 160-176.

19,459 HOPKINS, G. H. E. Lice. UGANDA J. 10 (1946), pp. 97-105.

19,460 HOPKINS, G. H. E. Mankind at war with the insects. UGANDA J. 2 (1935), pp. 234-244.

19,461 HOPKINS, G. H. E. "Moles" in Uganda. UGANDA J. 11 (1947), pp. 98-100.

19,462 HOPKINS, G. H. E. A note on the African buffalo. UGANDA J. 2 (1935), pp. 297-298.

19,463 HOPKINS, G. H. E. Notes on Uganda mosquitos and on methods of control. UGANDA J. 2 (1934), pp. 49-59.

19,464 JACKSON, Sir F. J. Two nature notes: i Leaf-cutter bee. ii The tippling grasshopper. UGANDA J. 16 (1952), pp. 94-96.

19,465 JACKSON, T. H. E. A trout from the Siti river. UGANDA J. 13 (1949), pp. 107-109.

19,466 LADKIN, R. G. Health education in Uganda. AFR. WOMEN 2 (1956), pp. 9-10.

19,467 LEHMANN, H. and RAPER, A. B. Distribution of the sickle-cell trait in Uganda, and its ethnological significance. UGANDA J. 15 (1951), pp. 41-43.

19,468 LOEWENTHAL, L. J. A. The African's skin. UGANDA J. 3 (1935), pp. 161-164.

19,469 MACDONALD, W. W. Lake-flies. UGANDA J. 17 (1953), pp. 124-134.

19,470 MALING, R. W. Old Azigara of the West Nile. UGANDA J. 6 (1938), pp. 123-124.

19,471 MARGACH, T. P. Nile perch in Lake Albert. UGANDA J. 12 (1948), pp. 105-106.

19,472 METTAM, R. W. M. Plant poisoning in Africa. UGANDA J. 4 (1937), pp. 208-219.

19,473 ODHIAMBO, T. R. An association between mites and carpenter-bees. UGANDA J. 22 (1958), pp. 164-166.

19,474 PERCY, R. C. and RIDLEY, M. W. On a few fish from Bwamba. UGANDA J. 19 (1955), pp. 96-101.

19,475 PERKINS, E. A. T. The crocodiles of Nabugabo. UGANDA J. 11 (1947), pp. 69-79.

19,476 PERKINS, E. A. T. The first finding of a live pigmy crocodile in Uganda. UGANDA J. 15 (1951), pp. 182-186.

19,477 PERKINS, E. A. T. Island elephants again. UGANDA J. 11 (1947), pp. 38-41.

19,478 PERKINS, E. A. T. A strange story about elephants. UGANDA J. 3 (1935), pp. 79-82.

19,479 PERLMAN, E. H. Preliminary inquiry into conceptions of health, disease, pregnancy and child care in Toro. EAISR Dec. (1959), pp. 47-70.

19,480 PERRY, J. S. The growth and reproduction of elephants in Uganda. UGANDA J. 16 (1952), pp. 51-66.

19,481 PITMAN, C. R. S. About crocodiles. UGANDA J. 9 (1941), pp. 89-114.

19,482 PITMAN, C. R. S. The amazing muscular reflexes of a dead crocodile. UGANDA J. 9 (1942), pp. 81-84.

19,483 PITMAN, C. R. S. Bird migration. UGANDA J. 1 (1934), p. 154.

19,484 PITMAN, C. R. S. The chimpanzees of the Kayonsa region, Western Kigezi. UGANDA J. 4 (1937), pp. 266-268.

19,485 PITMAN, C. R. S. A guide to the snakes of Uganda. UGANDA J. 3 (1935), pp. 47-78, 130-148; 3 (1936), pp. 211-229, 259-281; 4 (1936), pp. 41-64, 126-150; 4 (1937), pp. 220-246, 319-349; 5 (1937), pp. 27-45, 93-129; 5 (1938), pp. 160-244.

19,486 PITMAN, C. R. S. High altitude leopards. UGANDA J. 15 (1951), pp. 114-115.

19,487 PITMAN, C. R. S. Lions catching monkeys. UGANDA J. 3 (1935), pp. 164-165.

19,488 PITMAN, C. R. S. Pigmy crocodiles in Uganda. UGANDA J. 16 (1952), pp. 121-124.

19,489 PITMAN, C. R. S. Recovery of ringed white storks. UGANDA J. 3 (1935), pp. 83-84.

19,490 PRENTICE, A. N. Clover in Kampala. UGANDA J. 15 (1951), pp. 203-204.

19,491 RIDLEY, M. W. The birds of Bwamba—further additions. UGANDA J. 17 (1953), pp. 161-165.

19,492 ROBERTS, R. O. Amblygonite and associated minerals from the Mbale mine, Uganda. BULL. IMP. INST. 46 (1948), pp. 342-347.

19,493 ROBERTS, R. O. Meteorites in Uganda. UGANDA J. 11 (1947), pp. 42-46.

19,494 ROLLINSON, D. H. L. Cattle earth licks with some observations in Lango. UGANDA J. 17 (1953), pp. 167-172.

19,495 ROWELL, T. E. The habitat of baboons in Uganda. PROC. E. AFR. ACAD. 2 (1964), pp. 121-127.

19,496 SIMMONS, W. C. Mimicry. UGANDA J. 2 (1934), pp. 162-163.

19,497 SIMMONS, W. C. A note on chamaeleons. UGANDA J. 3 (1935), pp. 165-167.

19,498 SNOXALL, R. A. "Old Azigara" of the West Nile. UGANDA J. 9 (1941), p. 133.

19,499 SOMMERFELT, K. The Bakonjo's ideas of health and disease. EAISR Dec. (1959), pp. 35-42.

19,500 SOUTHWOLD, M. Ganda conceptions of health and disease. EAISR Dec. (1959), pp. 43-46.

19,501 STANIER, M. W. The blood of the Karamojong. UGANDA J. 17 (1953), pp. 173-177.

19,502 SYKES, J. The eclipse at Biharwe. UGANDA J. 23 (1959), pp. 44-50.

19,503 T., A. D. F. The uses of the banana. UGANDA J. 2 (1934), pp. 116-119.

19,504 THOMAS, H. B. "Futki" and some other elephants. UGANDA J. 4 (1936), pp. 151-155.

19,505 THOMPSON, M. D. Pancreatic function in a type of Kwashiorkor (Kampala area). MALNUTRITION IN AFR. WOMEN..., 1952, pp. 208-212.

19,506 TROWELL, H. C. Food, protein and Kwashiorkor. UGANDA J. 21 (1957), pp. 81-90.

19,507 TROWELL, H. C. Undernutrition and Kwashiorkor in Uganda. MALNUTRITION IN AFR. MOTHERS..., 1952, pp. 45-51.

19,508 WATSON, J. M. Notes on the birds of the riverain forests of Karamoja and north-east Uganda. UGANDA J. 12 (1948), pp. 43-51.

19,509 WATSON, J. M. The wild mammals of Teso and Karamoja. UGANDA J. 12 (1948), pp. 200-229; 13 (1949), pp. 30-60, 182-201; 14 (1950), pp. 53-84, 163-203; 15 (1951), pp. 92-106, 193-202; 16 (1952), pp. 89-93.

19,510 WAYLAND, E. J. Note on Bismutotantalite (and some remarks on Bismuth). UGANDA J. 1 (1934), pp. 150-152.

19,511 WEEKES, J. T. The birds of Ruwenzori. UGANDA J. 13 (1949), pp. 130-144.

19,512 WILLIAMS, A. W. Storks. UGANDA J. 2 (1934), pp. 74-78.

19,513 WILLIAMS, J. G. The birds of Bwamba: some additions. UGANDA J. 15 (1951), pp. 107-111.

19,514 WILSON, P. N. and WATSON, J. M. The flora of Kasilang Erony, Teso. UGANDA J. 19 (1955), pp. 183-193.

19,515 WRIGHT, A. C. A. Blood grouping and the tribal historian. UGANDA J. 15 (1951), pp. 44-48.

19,516 The Ruwenzori colobus. UGANDA J. 12 (1948), p. 230.

See also 15357, 15378, 17627.

Sociology

19,517 BOOTH, A. J. The possibilities of sailplaning and gliding in Uganda. UGANDA J. 5 (1937), pp. 85-92.

19,518 BUTLER, B. A letter home [Beryl Butler's letters to her mother in England]. TRANSITION 1 (1961), pp. 51-52; 3 (1962), pp. 45-46.

19,519 COX, T. R. F. Village competitions in the Eastern Provinces of Uganda. J. AFR. ADM. 4 (1952), pp. 27-29.

19,520 DAHYA, B. W. The Nkasero XI: a street football team. A discussion of some aspects of a spontaneous youth group in Kampala. EAISR Jan. (1962), pp. 1-17.

19,521 DAHYA, B. W. Some characteristics of tribal associations in Kampala. EAISR Jan. (1963), pp. 1-10.

19,522 FALLERS, L. A. Ideology and culture in Uganda rationalism. AMER. ANTHR. 63 (1961), pp. 677-686.

19,523 GULLIVER, P. H. The population of Karamoja. UGANDA J. 17 (1953), pp. 178-185.

19,524 GUTKIND, P. C. W. African urban marriage and family life: a note on some social and demographic characteristics from Kampala, Uganda. BULL. IFAN 25 (1963), pp. 266-287.

19,525 GUTKIND, P. C. W. Some problems of African urban family life: an example from Kampala, Uganda, British East Africa. ZAIRE 15 (1961), pp. 59-74.

19,526 GUTKIND, P. C. W. Town life in Buganda. UGANDA J. 20 (1956), pp. 37-46.

19,527 HASTIE, C. Training courses for women's club leaders in Uganda. AFR. WOMEN 4 (1962), pp. 77-81.

19,528 ILLINGWORTH, S. Preliminary report on research: the South Busoga resettlement scheme. EAISR Jan. (1963), pp. 1-6.

19,529 KAUMI, B. K. Days in the life of a cotton grower. UGANDA J. 13 (1949), pp. 177-181.

19,530 KENNEDY, F. R. Some notes on the making and maintenance of golf greens in Uganda. UGANDA J. 8 (1941), pp. 81-83.

19,531 LANNING, E. C. Rock-cut *mweso* boards. UGANDA J. 20 (1956), pp. 97-98.

19,532 LOW, D. A. Populism in Buganda. COMP. STUD. SOC. HIST. 6 (1963-1964), pp. 424-444.

19,533 LUDGER, K. Control of crime in primitive society—an example from Teso. UGANDA J. 16 (1952), pp. 130-131.

19,534 MATSON, A. T. The game of Mweso. UGANDA J. 21 (1957), p. 221.

19,535 MIDDLETON, J. Social change in Northern Uganda. CONTEMP. REV. 194 (1958), pp. 92-96.

19,536 PARKIN, D. J. Some aspects of status and role on a Kampala housing estate. EAISR Jan. (1963), pp. 1-16.

19,537 P'BITEK, O. Acholi love. TRANSITION 17 (1964), pp. 29-33.

19,538 PERRYMAN, P. W. Double swindle. UGANDA J. 12 (1948), pp. 134-138.

19,539 PRASAD, A. People of Indian origin in Uganda. AFR. QUART. 2 (1962-1963), pp. 240-250.

19,540 PURSEGLOVE, J. W. Kigezi resettlement. UGANDA J. 14 (1950), pp. 139-152.

19,541 PURSEGLOVE, J. W. Re-settlement in Kigezi, Uganda. J. AFR. ADM. 3 (1951), pp. 13-21.

19,542 ROTH, N. R. Social values, social services and social change. EAISR Jan. (1965), pp. 1-7.

19,543 RUSSELL, Sir A. Sailing on the Victoria Nyanza in 1908. UGANDA J. 6 (1939), pp. 202-203.

19,544 SENKATUKA, M. E. Women's clubs in Uganda. AFR. WOMEN 1 (1955), pp. 45-46.

19,545 SHACKELL, R. S. Mweso—the board game. UGANDA J. 2 (1934), pp. 14-20.

19,546 SHACKELL, R. S. More about Mweso. UGANDA J. 3 (1935), pp. 119-129.

19,547 SOFER, C. and SOFER, R. Recent population growth in Jinja. UGANDA J. 17 (1953), pp. 38-50.

19,548 THOMAS, A. S. Garden making in Uganda. UGANDA J. 8 (1940), pp. 1-14.

19,549 TURYAGYENDA, J. D. Overpopulation and its effects in the Gombolola of Buhara, Kigezi. UGANDA J. 28 (1964), pp. 127-133.

19,550 WAYLAND, E. J. Notes on the board game known as "Mweso" in Uganda. UGANDA J. 4 (1936), pp. 84-89.

19,551 WOOD, H. H. The Uganda War Memorial recreation ground, Kampala. UGANDA J. 5 (1938), pp. 296-298.

See also 21240.

Southern Africa

GENERAL

19,552 AGAR-HAMILTON, J. A. I. An African centenary. RACE RELATIONS 8 (1941), pp. 6-12.

19,553 JUNOD, H. P. Henri-Alexandre Junod (1863-1934), bibliographie de ses ouvrages. GENEVE AFR. 4 (1965), pp. 271-277.

19,554 Après la Conférence de Victoria Falls. ZAIRE 6 (1952), pp. 81-82.

Agriculture

19,555 BROWNLEE, F. Kalahari irrigation. J. AFR. SOC. 38 (1939), pp. 109-113.

19,556 HALL, T. D. Soil fertility in Southern Africa. J. AFR. SOC. 39 (1940), pp. 160-169.

Anthropology. Bushmen. Hottentots

19,557 ALBERTO, M. S. Necessidade duma revisão da sequência do povoamento humano na Africa Meridional. BSEM 111 (1958), pp. 161-170.

19,558 BLEEK, D. F. Bushman folklore. AFRICA 2 (1929), pp. 302-313.

19,559 BLEEK, D. F. [ed.] Customs and beliefs of the !Xam Bushmen [from material collected by W. H. I. Bleek and L. C. Lloyd]. BANTU STUD. 5 (1931), pp. 167-179; 6 (1932), pp. 47-63, 233-249, 323-342; 7 (1933), pp. 297-312, 375-392; 9 (1935), pp. 1-47; 10 (1936), pp. 131-162.

19,560 BLEEK, D. F. Special speech of animals and moon used by the !Xam Bushmen [from material collected by W. H. I. Bleek and L. C. Lloyd bet. 1870 and 1880]. BANTU STUD. 10 (1936), pp. 163-203.

19,561 BODESTEIN, W. and RAUM, O. F. A present day Zulu philosopher. AFRICA 30 (1960), pp. 166-180.

19,562 BREUTZ, P. L. Ancient people in the Kalahari Desert. AFR. UND UB. 42 (1958), pp. 49-67.

19,563 BRODERICK, G. E. P. The drums of death. NADA 34 (1957), pp. 64-65.

19,564 BROWNLEE, F. The Kehle and the war. J. AFR. SOC. 42 (1943), pp. 29-30.

19,565 BROWNLEE, F. Nkunzi, the maker of Assegais. AFR. AFFAIRS 45 (1946), pp. 43-46.

19,566 BROWNLEE, F. The social organization of the Kung (!Un): Bushmen of the north-western Kalahari. AFRICA 14 (1943), pp. 124-129.

19,567 BROWNLEE, F. Uncanny. J. AFR. SOC. 36 (1937), pp. 452-460.

19,568 BROWNLEE, W. T. Witchcraft among the natives of South Africa. Suggested historical origin of superstitions. J. AFR. SOC. 24 (1925), pp. 306-313.

19,569 BRUWER, J. P. Remnants of a rain-cult among the Acewa. AFR. STUD. 11 (1952), pp. 179-182.

19,570 CARDOSO, J. J. A. Monografia etnográfica sobre os Tsuas. BSEM 108 (1958), pp. 153-207.

19,571 CHINYANDURA. The origin of the Mashona. The dowry custom. Damages. NADA 22 (1945), pp. 52-55.

19,572 COLSON, E. and GLUCKMAN, M. Seven tribes in Central Africa. AFRICA 22 (1952), pp. 271-274.

19,573 DART, R. A. The hut distribution genealogy and homogeneity of the /?Auni-≠Khomani Bushmen. BANTU STUD. 11 (1937), pp. 159-174.

19,574 DART, R. A. A note on Jan, the Bushman. BANTU STUD. 2 (1923), pp. 107-109.

19,575 DART, R. A. The physical characters of the /?Auni-≠Khomani Bushmen. BANTU STUD. 11 (1937), pp. 175-246.

19,576 DOKE, C. M. Games, plays and dances of the ≠Khomani Bushmen. BANTU STUD. 10 (1936), pp. 461-471.

19,577 DORNAN, S. S. Moon lore amongst the Bantu. NADA 5 (1927), pp. 29-35.

19,578 DORNAN, S. S. Rainmaking in South Africa. BANTU STUD. 3 (1927), pp. 185-195.

19,579 DRENMAN, M. R. Finger mutilation in the Bushman. BANTU STUD. 11 (1937), pp. 247-249.

19,580 EARTHY, E. D. A Chopi love-song and a story in Ki-Lenge. AFRICA 4 (1931), pp. 475-482.

19,581 ELSDON-DEW, R. Serological differences between various groups of the Bantu of Southern Africa. BANTU STUD. 8 (1934), pp. 361-366.

19,582 FLEISCHER, A. C. Bambata and his bones. AFR. AFFAIRS 47 (1948), pp. 244-245.

19,583 GRILO, V. H. V. Antigos registos portugueses na história da etnologia científica e variação cultural na Africa Jo Sul. BSEM 111 (1958), pp. 133-146.

19,584 GRILO, V. H. V. A dispersão dos "Wa-Remba" ou ("Vha-Lemba") e tribos afins, a sul do Zambeze. BSEM 108 (1958), pp. 113-127.

19,585 HECHTER-SCHULZ, K. Cosmetic practices of some Bantu tribes of Southern Africa. BSEM 142 (1965), pp. 117-133.

19,586 HELLMAN, E. Methods of urban field work. BANTU STUD. 9 (1935), pp. 185-202.

19,587 HILLIER, A. P. The native races of South Africa. ROYAL COL. INST. PR. 30 (1898-1899), pp. 30-67.

19,588 HOERNLE, R. F. A. The concept of the "primitive." BANTU STUD. 2 (1923), pp. 327-332.

19,589 HOWELL, F. C. The age of the australopithecines of Southern Africa. AMER. J. PHY. ANTHR. 13 (1955), pp. 635-662.

19,590 JAQUES, A. A. Terms of kinship and corresponding patterns of behaviour among the Thonga. BANTU STUD. 3 (1927), pp. 327-348.

19,591 JASPAN, M. A. La culture noire en Afrique du Sud avant la conquête européenne. PRESENCE AFR. N.S. 18-19 (1958), pp. 143-165.

19,592 JEFFREYS, M. D. W. The origin of the name Hottentot. AFR. AFFAIRS 46 (1947), pp. 163-165.

19,593 JUNOD, H. A. Moral sense among the Bantu. INT. REV. MISSIONS 16 (1927), pp. 85-90.

19,594 KAMTEDZA, J. DE D. G. O significado filosófico dos costumes bantos. PORT. EM AFR. 22 (1965), pp. 51-64, 118-127.

19,595 KOHLER, O. Sprachkritische Aspekte zur Hamitentheorie über die Herkunft der Hottentotten. SOCIOLOGUS 10 (1960), pp. 69-77.

19,596 LARSON, T. J. Epic tales of the Mbukushu. AFR. STUD. 22 (1963), pp. 176-189.

19,597 MACCRONE, I. D. A note on the tsamma and its uses among the Bushmen. BANTU STUD. 11 (1937), pp. 251-252.

19,598 MACDONALD, J. East Central African customs. JRAI 22 (1893), pp. 99-122.

19,599 MACDONALD, J. Manners, customs, superstitions, and religions of South African tribes. JRAI 19 (1890), pp. 264-296; 20 (1891), pp. 113-140.

19,600 MAFOHLA. Erythraea: countries and times of the ritual regicide (by Leo Frobenius). NADA 9 (1931), pp. 108-109.

19,601 MARSHALL, L. The kin terminology system of the !Kung Bushmen. AFRICA 27 (1957), pp. 1-24.

19,602 MARSHALL, L. Marriage among !Kung Bushmen. AFRICA 29 (1959), pp. 335-364.

19,603 MARSHALL, L. Sharing, talking, and giving: relief of social tensions among !Kung Bushmen. AFRICA 31 (1961), pp. 231-248.

19,604 MENDELSSOHN, S. Judaic or Semiti legends and customs amongst South African natives. J. AFR. SOC. 13 (1914), pp. 395-406.

19,605 MEYLER, H. M. The Zulu: the gentleman of the African Veld. J. AFR. SOC. 24 (1925), pp. 202-212.

19,606 SAMUELSON, L. M. Some Zulu customs. J. AFR. SOC. 10 (1911), pp. 191-199.

19,607 SCHAPERA, I. Customs relating to twins in South Africa. J. AFR. SOC. 26 (1927), pp. 117-137.

19,608 SCHAPERA, I. The present state and future development of ethnographical research in South Africa. Report of a sub-committee appointed by the Inter-University Committee for African Studies in January, 1932. BANTU STUD. 8 (1934), pp. 219-342.

19,609 SCHMIDT, W. Zur Erforschung der alten Buschmann-Religion. AFRICA 2 (1929), pp. 291-301; English summary, p. 301.

19,610 SHAW, [E. M.] Fertility dolls in Southern Africa. NADA 25 (1948), pp. 63-68.

19,611 SICARD, H. VON. The ancient East African bantu drum. ETHNOS 7 (1942), pp. 49-54.

19,612 SICARD, H. VON. Honorific cremation in Southeastern Africa. AFR. STUD. 12 (1953), pp. 135-136.

19,613 SICARD, H. VON. Die initiation im Monomutapa-Reich. ETHNOS 6 (1941), pp. 42-47.

19,614 SKUTIL, J. Une contribution archéologique tchèque à la connaissance de l'Afrique du Sud. PROC. PAN-AFR. CONGR. PRE-HIST. 2 (1952), pp. 759-760.

19,615 SUNDKLER, B. Chief and prophet in Zululand and Swaziland. AFRICAN SYSTEMS OF THOUGHT, 1965, pp. 276-290.

19,616 TOBIAS, P. U. On the survival of the Bushmen. AFRICA 26 (1956), pp. 174-186.

19,617 WALTON, J. The forked sledge in Southern Africa. ETHNOS 19 (1954), pp. 24-33.

19,618 WATT, J. M. and BREYER-BRANDWIJK, M. G. Native medicines. NADA 27 (1950), pp. 72-74.

19,619 WERNER, A. Lobgesänge (Izbongo) der Könige der Zulu. ZAOS 3 (1897), pp. 277-284.

19,620 WERNER, A. "Now is the time." NADA 4 (1926), pp. 118-120.

See also 12930.

Art

19,621 BALFOUR, H. The goura, a stringed-wind musical instrument of the Bushmen and Hottentots. JRAI 32 (1902), pp. 156-176.

19,622 BARRADAS, L. On the need of a terminology for Quaternary transgressions and regressions in Southern Africa. PROC. PAN-AFR. CONGR. PRE-HIST. 4 (1962), pp. 295-297.

19,623 BASIL, DR. THE REV. BR. The dilemma of Bantu church music. AFR. MUSIC, 1957, pp. 36-39.

19,624 BLAXALL, F. M. African music in institutions. AFR. MUSIC, 1949, p. 16.

19,625 BOND. G. Quaternary sands at the Victoria Falls. PROC. PAN-AFR. CONGR. PRE-HIST. 3 (1955), pp. 115-122.

19,626 BOSAZZA, V. L. The Kalahari system in Southern Africa and its importance in relationship to the evolution of man. PROC. PAN-AFR. CONGR. PRE-HIST. 3 (1955), pp. 127-132.

19,627 CLARK, J. D. The Kalambo Falls prehistoric site: an interim report. PROC. PAN-AFR. CONGR. PRE-HIST. 4, no. iii (1962), pp. 195-199.

19,628 COOKE, H. B. S. Quaternary events in South Africa. PROC. PAN-AFR. CONGR. PRE-HIST. 1 (1947), pp. 26-36.

19,629 EISELEY, L. C. Early man in South and East Africa. AMER. ANTHR. 50 (1948), pp. 11-17.

19,630 FAGAN, B. Pre-European ironworking in Central Africa with special reference to Northern Rhodesia. J. AFR. HIST. 2 (1961), pp. 199-210.

19,631 GOODWIN, A. J. H. The Stone Ages in South Africa. AFRICA 2 (1929), pp. 174-182.

19,632 HECHTER-SCHULZ, K. Note on Tuyeres found at prehistoric iron smelting sites in Southern Africa. BSEM 143 (1965), pp. 57-69.

19,633 HIRSCHLAND, H. A Bantu suite for piano, xylophone, whistles and voices. AFR. MUSIC, 1957, pp. 40-44.

19,634 KIRBY, P. R. The Gora and its Bantu successors: a study in South African native music. BANTU STUD. 5 (1931), pp. 89-109.

19,635 KIRBY, P. R. A further note on the Gora and its Bantu successors. BANTU STUD. 9 (1935), pp. 53-61.

19,636 KIRBY, P. R. The musical practices of the /?Auni and ǂKhomani Bushmen. BANTU STUD. 10 (1936), pp. 373-431.

19,637 KIRBY, P. R. Physical phenomena which appear to have determined the bases and development of an harmonic sense among Bushmen, Hottentots and Bantu. AFR. MUSIC, 1961, pp. 6-9.

19,638 KIRBY, P. R. A study of Bushman music. BANTU STUD. 10 (1936), pp. 205-252.

19,639 KUBIK, G. Generic names for the Mbira. AFR. MUSIC, 1964, pp. 25-36.

19,640 MABBUTT, J. A. Physiographic evidence for the age of the Kalahari sands of the Southwestern Kalahari. PROC. PAN-AFR. CONGR. PRE-HIST. 3 (1955), pp. 123-126.

19,641 NORTON, W. A. African melodies. J. AFR. SOC. 18 (1919), pp. 122-137.

19,642 PALES, L. and SAINT-PEREUSE, T. DE. Inventaire provisoire des sites préhistoriques d'Afrique australe visités, relevés ou signalés par l'abbé Breuil. J. SOC. AFR. 32 (1962), pp. 53-61.

19,643 PAVER, F. R. Monumentos portugueses na Africa meridional. BSEM 57-58 (1948), pp. 27-29.

19,644 PETERS, C. Ophir and Punt in South Africa. J. AFR. SOC. 1 (1902), pp. 174-183.

19,645 ROUMEGUERE, P. and ROUMEGUERE-EBERHARDT, J. Poupées de fertilité et figurines d'argile. Leurs lois initiatiques. J. SOC. AFR. 30 (1960), pp. 205-223.

19,646 TRACEY, H. T. A case for the name Mbira. AFR. MUSIC, 1961, pp. 17-25.

19,647 TRACEY, H. T. Musical wood. AFR. MUSIC, 1949, pp. 17-21.

19,648 TRACEY, H. T. Organised research in African music. RHODES-LIV. J. 6 (1948), pp. 48-52.

19,649 TRACEY, H. T. Recording tour 1949. AFR. MUSIC, 1950, pp. 33-37.

19,650 TRACEY, H. T. Short survey of southern African folk music for the international catalogue of folk music records. AFR. MUSIC, 1953, pp. 41-46.

19,651 WALTON, J. Some forms of Bushman art. AFR. MUSIC, 1957, pp. 27-32.

19,652 WELLS, L. H. Late stone age human types in Central Africa. PROC. PAN-AFR. CONGR. PRE-HIST. 3 (1955), pp. 183-185.

19,653 WERNER, A. Bushman paintings. J. AFR. SOC. 7 (1908), pp. 387-393.

19,654 WESTPHAL, E. Linguistics and the African Music Research. AFR. MUSIC, 1948, pp. 12-18.

19,655 Records of African music. AFR. MUSIC, 1948, pp. 24-26.

See also 15836.

Biography

19,656 Obituary: Canon G. E. P. Broderick. NADA 36 (1959), pp. 134-135.

19,657 JOHNSTON, Sir H. H. In memory of James Chapman. J. AFR. SOC. 17 (1918), pp. 118-124.

19,658 THACKERAY, R. H. Henry Hartley. African hunter and explorer. J. AFR. SOC. 37 (1938), pp. 283-297.

19,659 The death of Professor Hoernlé. AFR. AFFAIRS 43 (1944), p. 5.

19,660 WILLOUGHBY, W. C. Khama: a Bantu reformer. INT. REV. MISSIONS 13 (1924), pp. 74-83.

19,661 Obituary: Gérard Paul Lestrade: 1897-1962. AFR. STUD. 22 (1963), pp. 91-95.

19,662 MURRAY, A. V. Livingstone the missionary. RACE RELATIONS 8 (1941), pp. 2-6.

19,663 AMERY, L. S. The late Sir Dougal Malcolm. AFR. AFFAIRS 54 (1955), pp. 288-289.

19,664 Obituary: Julian Mockford. AFR. AFFAIRS 49 (1950), p. 253.

19,665 GARRETT, F. E. The character of Cecil Rhodes. CONTEMP. REV. 81 (1902), pp. 761-779.

19,666 LANGTON, A. V. Cecil John Rhodes, 1853-1902. AFR. AFFAIRS 43 (1944), pp. 8-9.

19,667 RANGER, T. The last word on Rhodes? PAST AND PRESENT 28 (1964), pp. 116-127.

19,668 WYNDHAM, H. A. "Rhodes" by Sarah Gertrude Millin. J. AFR. SOC. 32 (1933), pp. 236-239.

19,669 Praise names of Cecil John Rhodes. NADA 36 (1959), pp. 99-102.

19,670 Lord Robins of Rhodesia. AFR. AFFAIRS 61 (1962), pp. 274-275.

19,671 SCLATER, W. L. Captain Selous: a memoir. J. AFR. SOC. 18 (1919), pp. 198-201.

19,672 SHAW, J. R. Obituary: Edwin Smith. RHODES-LIV. J. 22 (1957), pp. viii-ix.

19,673 Obituary: Rev. Dr. Edwin Smith. AFR. AFFAIRS 57 (1958), p. 62.

19,674 BILSEN, J. VAN. Sur la mort de Smuts. ZAIRE 4 (1950), pp. 1009-1010.

19,675 REYNARDSON, H. B. Mrs. Millin's life of General Smuts. J. AFR. SOC. 36 (1937), pp. 255-259.

19,676 Mort du Maréchal Smuts. ZAIRE 4 (1950), pp. 1137-1138.

19,677 Obituary: J. Grenfell Williams. AFR. AFFAIRS 54 (1955), p. 145.

19,678 WINGATE, Sir R. Sir Robert Williams, Bt., D.L., J.P. A personal appreciation. J. AFR. SOC. 37 (1938), pp. 339-343.

19,679 GLUCKMAN, M. Obituary: Godfrey Baldwin Wilson. RHODES-LIV. J. 1 (1944), pp. 1-3.

19,680 W., A. R. Rodney C. Wood. NYASA J. 15, no. 2 (1962), pp. 38-39.

Economics

19,681 ALLAN, W. African land usage. RHODES-LIV. J. 3 (1945), pp. 13-20.

19,682 BALLINGER, M. The Union and the Protectorates: some economic aspects. RACE RELATIONS 2, no. iii (1934-1935), p. 162.

19,683 FODERARO, S. Missione economica italiana nell' Africa sud' orientale. AFRICA (Rome) 17 (1962), pp. 161-172.

19,684 JONES, J. D. R. The development of Central and Southern Africa. Suggestions for research and action on some of the problems common to these territories. RHODES-LIV. J. 7 (1949), pp. 1-23.

19,685 NICHOLLS, G. H. The part of the Union in the development of Africa. INTERNAT. AFFAIRS 21 (1945), pp. 343-354.

19,686 TAGART, E. S. B. "The African Labourer" by Major G. St. J. Orde Browne. J. AFR. SOC. 32 (1933), pp. 299-305.

19,687 TWYNAM, C. D. The telegraph in British Central Africa. NYASA J. 6, no. 2 (1953), pp. 52-55.

19,688 WYNDHAM, H. A. The report of the native economic commission of the Union of South Africa. J. AFR. SOC. 31 (1932), pp. 375-382.

See also 4890, 15907.

Education

19,689 AFRICANUS [pseud.] Native education in Central Africa. J. AFR. SOC. 20 (1921), pp. 95-100.

19,690 BEIT, Sir A. Education services for Africans. RACE RELATIONS 16 (1949), pp. 26-31.

19,691 DAVIDSON, B. African education in British central and southern Africa. PRESENCE AFR. N.S. 6 (1956), pp. 106-112.

19,692 JUNOD, H. A. The native language and native education. J. AFR. SOC. 5 (1905), pp. 1-14.

19,693 MORRIS, S. E. At the vacation course of Bantu studies, University of Cape Town. NADA 8 (1930), pp. 30-45.

19,694 TREVOR, T. G. Native education from an employer's point of view. NADA 5 (1927), pp. 97-99.

Geography

19,695 BALSAN, F. La première traversée de la poche du Kalahari. ACTA GEOGRAPHICA 8 (1949), pp. 9-14.

19,696 CAMPBELL, E. A young lady's journey to Umtali, 1895. RHODESIANA 8 (1963), pp. 9-15.

19,697 DIXON, J. R. Building the lower Zambesi bridge. J. AFR. SOC. 34 (1935), pp. 163-168.

19,698 EDWARDS, W. Wiri: reminiscences. NADA 37 (1960), pp. 81-101; 38 (1961), pp. 5-21; 39 (1962), pp. 19-44.

19,699 FRIPP [C. E.] Bishop Knight Bruce's journey to the Zambesi in 1888. NADA 16 (1939), pp. 76-91.

19,700 KRENKEL, E. Das Faltengebirge Ost- und Südafrikas: Afriziden und Kapiden. KOLONIALE STUDIEN: HANS MEYER FESTSCHRIFT, 1928, pp. 132-146.

19,701 LACY, G. A century of exploration in South Africa. J. AFR. SOC. 1 (1902), pp. 215-229.

19,702 LUNA, I. R. DE. Metalogenia y aventuras en el Continente negro. ARCH. INST. EST. AFR. 6, no. 25 (1953), pp. 7-18.

19,703 PARKINSON, J. A note on the volcanic history of South and East Africa. J. AFR. SOC. 23 (1924), pp. 96-105.

19,704 POLDERVAART, A. Kalahari sands. PROC. PAN-AFR. CONGR. PRE-HIST. 3 (1955), pp. 106-114.

19,705 PONSONBY, C. E. From Cape to Kampala. AFR. AFFAIRS 54 (1955), pp. 179-185.

19,706 ROMANO, M. P. Da necessidade de estreita colaboração internacional em Hidrologia. BSEM 96 (1956), pp. 41-44.

See also 15960, 15963, 15964, 15969.

Government. Politics. Administration

19,707 AFRICANUS [pseud.] Further thoughts on a Central African confederation. J. AFR. SOC. 19 (1920), pp. 101-108.

19,708 AFRICANUS [pseud.] Reconstruction in Central Africa. J. AFR. SOC. 19 (1920), pp. 92-100.

19,709 BUTLER, R. A. Report of the Central Africa conference 1963. AFR. QUART. 3, no. ii (1963), pp. 122-135.

19,710 CHATTERJEE, S. Mahatma Gandhi and South Africa. AFR. QUART. 2, no. ii (1962), pp. 94-98.

19,711 ELIAS, T. O. Gandhi as seen by an African. AFR. QUART. 3, no. ii (1963), pp. 80-81.

19,712 FABRE-LUCE, A. The bird-catcher and the cage. AFR. AFFAIRS 60 (1961), pp. 424-434.

19,713 GANDHI, M. Mahatma Gandhi on freedom in Africa. AFR. QUART. 1, no. ii (1961), pp. 5-7.

19,714 HARRIS, J. Britain's greatest African problem. CONTEMP. REV. 150 (1936), pp. 699-706.

19,715 HARRIS, J. The South African danger. CONTEMP. REV. 154 (1938), pp. 410-416.

19,716 KUPER, H. The colonial situation in Southern Africa. JMAS 2 (1964), pp. 149-164.

19,717 PYARELAL [pseud. - NAIR, P.] Gandhiji and the African question. AFR. QUART. 2, no. ii (1962), pp. 77-85.

19,718 RAWSON, H. E. Native affairs in South Africa. J. AFR. SOC. 10 (1911), pp. 146-156.

19,719 SELBORNE, Lord [PALMER, R.] The South African protectorates. J. AFR. SOC. 13 (1914), pp. 353-364.

19,720 SMUTS, J. C. Native policy in Africa. J. AFR. SOC. 29 (1930), pp. 248-268.

19,721 TREDGOLD, Sir C. The constitutional position of the Protectorates. RACE RELATIONS 2, no. iii (1934-1935), pp. 145-148.

19,722 TREDGOLD, Sir C. The constitutional position of the South African protectorates. J. AFR. SOC. 33 (1934), pp. 382-397.

19,723 WALSTON, Lord. Thoughts on Southern Africa. AFR. AFFAIRS 63 (1964), pp. 23-31.

19,724 WHEELWRIGHT, C. A. Native administration in Zululand. J. AFR. SOC. 24 (1925), pp. 92-99.

19,725 The British protectorates in South Africa [based on an address by Lord Harlech]. AFR. STUD. 4 (1945), pp. 128-134.

See also 2537, 15990, 16003, 16008, 16027.

History

19,726 AFRIKANDER. Cecil Rhodes: colonist and imperialist. CONTEMP. REV. 69 (1896), pp. 374-390.

19,727 AGAR-HAMILTON, J. A. I. The South African protectorates. J. AFR. SOC. 29 (1929), pp. 12-26.

19,728 BENZIES, W. R. Funeral of Cecil John Rhodes. NADA 9, no. 1 (1964), pp. 37-38.

19,729 BUTT, J. David Livingstone and the idea of African evolution. HISTORY TODAY 13 (1963), pp. 376-382.

19,730 FULLER, C. E. The early Portuguese in Southern Africa. AFR. STUD. 12 (1953), pp. 31-37.

19,731 HARLECH, Lord [GORE, D.] The British South African territories: the present internal position. AFR. AFFAIRS 44 (1945), pp. 68-73.

19,732 JOHNSTON, Sir H. H. England's work in Central Africa. ROYAL COL. INST. PR. 28 (1896-1897), pp. 50-75.

19,733 JUNOD, H. P. Some notes on Tjopi origins. BANTU STUD. 3 (1927), pp. 57-71.

19,734 KAKE, B. I. Evocations historiques [Le Monomotapa, Royaume de Loango, Zimbabwe]. PRESENCE AFR. N.S. 53 (1965), pp. 208-214.

19,735 LORD, W. B. and BAINES, T. Shifts and expedients of camp life. RHODESIANA 9 (1963), pp. 44-51.

19,736 MARODZI. The Barozwi. NADA 2 (1924), pp. 88-91.

19,737 MICHELL, Sir L. Greater South Africa. ROYAL COL. INST. PR. 40 (1908-1909), pp. 261-286.

19,738 ROTBERG, R. I. The federation movement in British East and Central Africa 1889-1953. J. COMM. POL. STUD. 2 (1963-1964), pp. 141-160.

19,739 SCHAPERA, I. Livingstone and the Boers. AFR. AFFAIRS 59 (1960), pp. 144-156.

19,740 SMITH, E. W. Sebetwane and the Makololo. AFR. STUD. 15 (1956), pp. 49-74.

19,741 SMUTS, J. C. African settlement. J. AFR. SOC. 29 (1929), pp. 109-131.

19,742 WALKER, E. A. The British South African territories: external relations. AFR. AFFAIRS 44 (1945), pp. 62-68.

19,743 WALKER, E. A. The franchise in Southern Africa. CAMB. HIST. J. 11 (1953), pp. 93-113.

19,744 WHITE, R. Letters from South Africa in 1895. J. AFR. SOC. 37 (1938), pp. 167-173.

19,745 WINSPEAR, C. F. A short history of the Universities Mission to Central Africa. NYASA J. 9, no. 1 (1956), pp. 11-50.

19,746 WYNDHAM, H. A. A history of South Africa by E. A. Walker. J. AFR. SOC. 40 (1941), pp. 11-18.

See also 16071.

Language. Literature

Language: Bushman, Korana, Ronga, Zulu

19,747 BEUCHAT, P. D. A restatement of the Zulu verb conjugation. AFR. STUD. 22 (1963), pp. 137-169; 23 (1964), pp. 67-68.

19,748 BISHOP, H. L. On the use of the "proclitic a" in Si Ronga. BANTU STUD. 2 (1923), pp. 111-114.

19,749 BLEEK, D. F. /Auni vocabulary. BANTU STUD. 11 (1937), pp. 259-278.

19,750 BLEEK, D. F. Bushman terms of relationship. BANTU STUD. 2 (1923), pp. 57-70.

19,751 BLEEK, D. F. The distribution of Bushman languages in South Africa. FESTSCHRIFT MEINHOF, 1927, pp. 55-64.

19,752 BLEEK, D. F. Grammatical notes and texts in the /Auni language. BANTU STUD. 11 (1937), pp. 253-258.

19,753 BLEEK, D. F. Note on Bushman orthography. BANTU STUD. 2 (1923), pp. 71-74.

19,754 BLEEK, W. H. I. A fragment [continuation of Comparative Grammar of South African Languages]. BANTU STUD. 10 (1936), pp. 1-7.

19,755 BOURQUIN, W. Click-words which Xhosa, Zulu and Sotho have in common. AFR. STUD. 10 (1951), pp. 59-81.

19,756 BOURQIN, W. The prefix of the locative in Kafir. BANTU STUD. 1, no. ii (1922), pp. 2-3.

19,757 COERTZE, P. J. Die betekenis en funksie van die Voorvoegsel van die sewende klas van selfstandige naamwoorde Sotho-Tswana-groep van bantoetale. BANTU STUD. 10 (1936), pp. 75-88.

19,758 COLE, D. T. Fanagalo and the Bantu languages in South Africa. AFR. STUD. 12 (1953), pp. 1-9.

19,759 DOKE, C. M. Conjunctive writing for Bantu languages. RHODES-LIV. J. 1 (1944), pp. 10-15.

19,760 DOKE, C. M. A dissertation on the phonetics of the Zulu language. BULL. SOAS 2 (1921-1923), pp. 685-729.

19,761 DOKE, C. M. The linguistic situation in South Africa. AFRICA 1 (1928), pp. 478-485.

19,762 DOKE, C. M. The native languages of South Africa. A report on their present position with special reference to research and the development of literature. AFR. STUD. 1 (1942), pp. 135-141.

19,763 DOKE, C. M. An outline of ǂKhomani Bushman phonetics. BANTU STUD. 10 (1936), pp. 433-460.

19,764 DOKE, C. M. An outline of the phonetics of the language of the chü: Bushmen of north-west Kalahari. BANTU STUD. 2 (1923), pp. 129-165.

19,765 DOKE, C. M. A preliminary investigation into the state of the native languages of South Africa with suggestions as to research and the development of literature. BANTU STUD. 7 (1933), pp. 1-98.

19,766 EEDEN, B. I. C. VAN. The terminating vowel of the Bantu verbal stem. BANTU STUD. 8 (1934), pp. 367-375.

19,767 JAQUES, A. A. Shangana-Tsonga ideophones and their tones. BANTU STUD. 15 (1941), pp. 205-244.

19,768 JONES, D. The phonetic structure of the Sechuana language. TRANS. PHILOLOGICAL SOC. 1917-1920, pp. 99-106.

19,769 KOHLER, O. Observations on the central Khoisan language group. J. AFR. LANGS. 2 (1963), pp. 227-234.

19,770 LANHAM, L. W. The copulative construction in Bantu with special reference to Zulu. AFR. STUD. 12 (1953), pp. 141-162.

19,771 LANHAM, L. W. and HALLOWES, D. P. Linguistic relationships and contacts expressed in the vocabulary of eastern Bushmen. AFR. STUD. 15 (1956), pp. 45-48.

19,772 LAROCHETTE, J. Racines et Radicaux dans les Langues Bantoues. KONGO-OVERZEE 17 (1951), pp. 9-31.

19,773 LESTRADE, G. P. Some notes on the political organization of the Venda-speaking tribes. AFRICA 3 (1930), pp. 306-321.

19,774 MACDONALD, D. Yao and Nyanja tales. BANTU STUD. 12 (1938), pp. 251-285.

19,775 MAINGARD, L. F. A comparative study of Naron, Hietshware and Korana. AFR. STUD. 22 (1963), pp. 97-108.

19,776 MEEUSSEN, A. E. Lexicostatistiek van het Bantoe: Bobangi en Zulu. KONGO-OVERZEE 22 (1956), pp. 86-89.

19,777 MEINHOF, C. Die Bedeutung des Sotho für die Erforschung der Bantu-Sprachen. ZAOS 2 (1896), pp. 150-167.

19,778 MEINHOF, C. Die Paarung der Begriffe. AFR. UND UB. 30 (1940), pp. 241-249.

19,779 NIENABER, G. S. Kom die Zoeloe i(li)hhashi uit Engels? AFR. STUD. 12 (1953), pp. 22-25.

19,780 PLANERT, W. Die Schnalzsprachen. BIBLIOTHECA AFR. 2 (1927), pp. 296-315.

19,781 ROCHLIN, S. A. Some South African language pioneers of the nineteenth century. AFR. STUD. 14 (1955), pp. 171-173.

19,782 RYCROFT, D. K. Melodic features in Zulu eulogistic recitation. AFR. LANG. STUD. 1 (1960), pp. 60-78.

19,783 RYCROFT, D. K. Tone in Zulu nouns. AFR. LANG. STUD. 4 (1963), pp. 43-68.

19,784 SEIDEL, A. Etymologische Forschungen auf dem Gebiete der Bantusprachen. ZAOS 5 (1900), pp. 20-27.

19,785 TAYLOR, J. D. Inkondlo Kazulu [by B. W. Vilakazi]. BANTU STUD. 9 (1935), pp. 163-168.

19,786 VEDDER, H. Korana-Katechismus von C. F. Wuras. FESTSCHRIFT MEINHOF, 1927, pp. 3-28.

19,787 WERNER, A. Hottentot roots in Bantu click-words. J. AFR. SOC. 4 (1904), pp. 142-143.

19,788 WESTPHAL, E. The indicative mood and its classification in southern Bantu. AFR. STUD. 4 (1945), pp. 189-192.

19,789 WESTPHAL, E. The unification of Bantu languages. AFR. STUD. 5 (1946), pp. 54-56.

19,790 WESTPHAL, E. O. J. The linguistic prehistory of Southern Africa: Bush, Kwadi, Hottentot, and Bantu linguistic relationships. AFRICA 33 (1963), pp. 237-265.

19,791 WESTPHAL, E. O. J. On classifying Bushman and Hottentot languages. AFR. LANG. STUD. 3 (1962), pp. 30-48.

19,792 WESTPHAL, E. O. J. On linguistic relationship. ZAIRE 11 (1957), pp. 513-524.

19,793 WESTPHAL, E. O. J. A re-classification of Southern African non-Bantu languages. J. AFR. LANGS. 1 (1962), pp. 1-8.

19,794 WHITE, C. M. N. A comparative survey of the verb forms in four languages of the west central Bantu group. AFR. STUD. 6 (1947), pp. 1-20.

19,795 WHITE, C. M. N. Notes on the qualificative concords in four languages of the west central zone. AFR. STUD. 4 (1945), pp. 88-96.

19,796 WHITE, C. M. N. The noun prefixes of the west-central zone of Bantu languages. AFR. STUD. 3 (1944), pp. 153-160.

See also 3151, 19654.

Literature

19,797 GODFREY, R. Rev. John Bennie, the father of Kafir literature. BANTU STUD. 8 (1934), pp. 123-134.

19,798 JAQUES, A. A. A survey of Shangana-Tsonga, Ronga and Tswa literature. BANTU STUD. 14 (1940), pp. 259-270.

19,799 MERWE, D. F. V. D. Hurutshe poems. BANTU STUD. 15 (1941), pp. 307-337.

19,800 MOREIRA, E. Gênio Banto [a poem]. PORT. EM AFR. 19 (1962), p. 167.

19,801 REYNOLDS, R. Meddlers from abroad [a poem]. AFR. SOUTH 3, no. 1 (1958), pp. 95-96.

19,802 VILAKAZI, B. W. The conception and development of poetry in Zulu. BANTU STUD. 12 (1938), pp. 105-134.

19,803 WERNER, A. Some native writers in South Africa. J. AFR. SOC. 30 (1931), pp. 27-39.

Law

19,804 COCKCROFT, I. G. Is the right of disinheritance recognised in native law? NADA 12 (1934), p. 36.

19,805 GLUCKMAN, M. African land tenure. RHODES-LIV. J. 3 (1945), pp. 1-12.

19,806 JACKSON, H. M. G. Some reflections on the relation of law to social anthropology. NADA 5 (1927), pp. 26-29.

19,807 KERR, A. J. The reception and codification of systems of law in Southern Africa. J. AFR. LAW 2 (1958), pp. 82-100.

19,808 KERR, A. J. South Africa. Introductory note [on legal education]. J. AFR. LAW 6 (1962), pp. 132-133.

19,809 KUPER, B. Bibliography of native law in South Africa, 1941-1961. AFR. STUD. 23 (1964), pp. 155-165.

19,810 LEWIN, J. The recording of native law and custom. J. AFR. SOC. 37 (1938), pp. 483-493.

19,811 LEWIN, J. A short survey of native law in South Africa. BANTU STUD. 15 (1941), pp. 65-90.

Religion

19,812 ANSTEY, R. T. Christianity and Bantu philosophy. Observations on the thought and work of Placide Tempels. INT. REV. MISSIONS 52 (1963), pp. 316-322.

19,813 BARNES, J. A. African separatist churches. RHODES-LIV. J. 9 (1950), pp. 26-30.

19,814 JUNOD, H. A. Bantu heathen prayers. INT. REV. MISSIONS 11 (1922), pp. 561-571.

19,815 JUNOD, H. A. God's ways in the Bantu soul. INT. REV. MISSIONS 3 (1914), pp. 96-106.

19,816 LEONARD, D. A. Sweet heaven. AFR. SOUTH 5, no. 2 (1961), pp. 116-122.

19,817 OLIVEIRA, O. R. DE. Cabo de Tsvimbo ancestral de chefe tribal. BSEM 135 (1963), pp. 29-37.

19,818 PAUW, B. A. Patterns of christianization among the Tswana and the Xhosa-speaking peoples. AFRICAN SYSTEMS OF THOUGHT, 1965, pp. 240-257.

19,819 SHEPPERSON, G. Church and sect in Central Africa: a review article [on The Christian Ministry in Africa and other books]. RHODES-LIV. J. 33 (1963), pp. 82-94.

19,820 SHEPPERSON, G. The politics of African church separatist movements in British Central Africa, 1892-1916. AFRICA 24 (1954), pp. 233-245.

19,821 WERNER, A. A Mosuto novelist. INT. REV. MISSIONS 14 (1925), pp. 428-436.

19,822 YOUNG, T. C. The communal bond in Bantu Africa. INT. REV. MISSIONS 22 (1933), pp. 105-114.

See also 12972.

Science

19,823 BREYER-BRANDWIJK, M. G. A note on the Bushman arrow poison, diamphidia simplex péringuey. BANTU STUD. 11 (1937), pp. 279-284.

19,824 CORINTA FERREIRA, M. Contribuição para o estudo dos Cerambicíneos da Africa do Sul; descrição de espécies novas e notas sinonímicas. BSEM 92 (1955), pp. 135-142.

19,825 CORINTA FERREIRA, M. Contribuição para o estudo dos Cerambicíneos da Africa do Sul: uma espécie nova do genero derolus Gahan. BSEM 91 (1955), pp. 215-217.

19,826 CORINTA FERREIRA, M. Contribuição para o estudo dos Cerambicíneos da Africa do Sul; tribo dos Oemini. BSEM 82 (1953), pp. 181-191.

19,827 CORINTA FERREIRA, M. Duas espécies novas de Scarabaeus da Africa do sul. BSEM 75 (1952), pp. 19-24.

19,828 CORINTA FERREIRA, M. Monografia dos escarabaeídeos da Africa do sul. BSEM 87 (1954), pp. 83-99; 94-95, no. i (1955), pp. 311-349.

19,829 CORINTA FERREIRA, M. Monografia dos escarabaeídeos da Africa do sul. Tribo Scarabaeni. BSEM 78 (1953), pp. 3-83.

19,830 CORINTA FERREIRA, M. Os escarabideos do Transvaal Museum. BSEM 108 (1958), pp. 131-150.

19,831 CRUZ, C. S. O melhoramento pecuário. BSEM 11 (1933), pp. 3-13; 12 (1933), pp. 3-10.

19,832 JOHNSTON, Sir H. H. The flora of South Africa. J. AFR. SOC. 13 (1914), pp. 259-261.

19,833 KOCH, C. The Tenebrionidae of Southern Africa. BSEM 80 (1953), pp. 107-113; 81 (1953), pp. 173-182; 96 (1956), pp. 3-17; 101 (1956), pp. 5-17.

19,834 KOKOT, D. F. Possibilidades de energia hidro-eléctrica na Africa do Sul. BSEM 57-58 (1948), pp. 43-58.

19,835 LEAL, E. F. Chuva artificial. Condições mais favoráveis à sua produção na região da Barra do Cuanza. BOL. INST. ANGOLA 4 (1954), pp. 41-51.

19,836 MAINGARD, J. F. Some notes on health and disease among the Bushmen of the southern Kalahari. BANTU STUD. 11 (1937), pp. 285-295.

19,837 SCHAPERA, I. Bushman arrow poisons. BANTU STUD. 2 (1923), pp. 199-214.

19,838 SEGAL, B. A possible base for "Bushman" paint. BANTU STUD. 9 (1935), pp. 49-51.

19,839 SELOUS, F. C. Big game in South Africa and its relation to the tse-tse fly. J. AFR. SOC. 8 (1909), pp. 113-129.

19,840 WATT, J. M. A note on raphionacme purpurea—3006. BANTU STUD. 2 (1923), pp. 333-334.

See also 4272, 16400.

Sociology

19,841 ALTMAN, P. The cloudy isle. AFR. SOUTH 6 (1961), pp. 31-38.

19,842 BROWN, A. R. Some problems of Bantu sociology. BANTU STUD. 1, no. iii (1922), pp. 5-9.

19,843 FARQUHAR, J. H. Integration of native life in a Reserve. NADA 21 (1944), pp. 40-45.

19,844 JONES, J. D. R. The effects of urbanisation in South and Central Africa. AFR. AFFAIRS 52 (1953), pp. 37-44.

19,845 MILLER, D. The good people. AFR. SOUTH 5, no. 1 (1960), pp. 119-123.

19,846 "MSITELI". The growth of race consciousness. NADA 2 (1924), pp. 29-30.

19,847 OPPENHEIMER, H. F. Industrial relations in a multi-racial society. AFR. AFFAIRS 55 (1956), pp. 313-319.

19,848 SCHAPERA, I. Economic changes in South African native life. AFRICA 1 (1928), pp. 170-188.

19,849 Bibliography [relevant to social and psychological problems in British Central Africa]. RHODES-LIV. J. 3 (1945), pp. 91-102.

See also 4625, 16450.

RHODESIA
(Formerly Southern Rhodesia)
Works relating to all three territories of the former Federation of Rhodesia and Nyasaland are classified here

General

19,850 BRELSFORD, W. V. Northern Rhodesiana. RHODESIANA 1 (1956), pp. 7-19.

19,851 McCULLOCH, M. The sixth Conference of Research Officers of the Rhodes-Livingstone Institute (Lusaka, January 1953). ZAIRE 7 (1953), pp. 647-649.

19,852 FOSBROOKE, H. A. History of research scheme R370. RHODES-LIV. J. 23 (1958), pp. 1-11.

19,853 GLUCKMAN, M. The Rhodes-Livingstone Institute and Museum. RHODES-LIV. J. 1 (1944), pp. 4-9.

19,854 GLUCKMAN, M. Seven-year research plan of the Rhodes-Livingstone Institute of social studies in British Central Africa. RHODES-LIV. J. 4 (1945), pp. 1-32.

19,855 TABLER, E. C. Rare or little-known Rhodesiana relating to the prepioneer period. RHODESIANA 5 (1960), pp. 60-64.

19,856 WHITE, J. The rationale of the missionary conference of Southern Rhodesia. NADA 2 (1924), pp. 67-69.

19,857 Director's report to the trustees on the work [of the Rhodes-Livingstone Institute] of the years 1944-5-6; 1947-8-9; 1950, 1951, 1952. RHODES-LIV. J. 6 (1948), pp. 64-79; 10 (1950), pp. 74-93; 17 (1954), pp. 23-50.

19,858 The Outpost [a magazine]. NADA 39 (1962), p. 93.

19,859 Public libraries in the Federation of Rhodesia and Nyasaland. UNESCO BULL. LIBS. 15 (1961), pp. 239-241.

Agriculture

19,860 ALVORD, E. D. Agricultural life of Rhodesian natives. NADA 7 (1929), pp. 9-16.

19,861 HAMILTON, P. The changing pattern of African land use in Rhodesia. ESSAYS IN GEOGRAPHY FOR AUSTIN MILLER, 1965, pp. 247-271.

19,862 HARRIS, P. G. Two aspects of Rhodesian economy. Rhodesian farming and the Van Riet experience. AFR. AFFAIRS 47 (1948), pp. 95-98.

19,863 HUTCHINS, D. E. Forestry in Rhodesia: extracts from a report to the Rhodes trustees. J. AFR. SOC. 3 (1904), pp. 410-429.

19,864 JACKSON, A. P. Ample food without ploughing. NADA 31 (1954), pp. 62-66.

19,865 MORTEN, I. H. A fair return to farmers. AFR. AFFAIRS 49 (1950), pp. 334-337.

19,866 ROBINSON, D. A. Soil conservation and implications of the Land Husbandry Act. NADA 37 (1960), pp. 27-35.

19,867 VENZO, E. La valorizzazione del bacino del Sabi e Lundi in Rhodesia. AFRICA (Rome) 14 (1959), pp. 31-34, 52.

19,868 WALLACE, R. Rhodesia and its agricultural possibilities. ROYAL COL. INST. PR. 40 (1908-1909), pp. 80-108.

19,869 Msengezi Experimental School. NADA 38 (1961), pp. 93-94.

Anthropology

19,870 A., H. and STAYT, E. The Bavenda. NADA 9 (1931), pp. 107-108.

19,871 ADAM, J. S. and HOWMAN, E. G. The sacrifice of Rudwidzo. NADA 4 (1926), pp. 70-72.

19,872 AQUINA, M. A note on missionary influence on Shona marriage. RHODES-LIV. J. 33 (1963), pp. 68-79.

19,873 AQUINA, M. A study of the Vatavara kinship system. NADA 37 (1960), pp. 8-26.

19,874 AQUINA, M. The tribes in Chilimanzi reserve and their relation to the Rozvi. NADA 9, no. 2 (1965), pp. 40-51.

19,875 AQUINA, M. The tribes in the Victoria reserve. NADA 9, no. 2 (1965), pp. 6-15.

19,876 B., H. J. Some scraps of native life. NADA 17 (1940), pp. 100-101.

19,877 BAKER, R. H. The mutupo among the Wamanyika. NADA 3 (1925), pp. 48-54.

19,878 BAKER, R. H. Suggestions for anthropological investigation among the Makaranga. NADA 1 (1923), pp. 55-60; 12 (1934), pp. 88-94.

19,879 BAZELEY, W. S. The Mainini custom. NADA 2 (1924), pp. 65-67.

19,880 BAZELEY, W. S. A Manyika marriage custom. NADA 4 (1926), pp. 48-52.

19,881 BENT, J. T. On the finds at the Great Zimbabwe ruins (with a view to elucidating the origin of the race that built them). JRAI 22 (1893), pp. 124-136.

19,882 BENZIES, W. R. and J., H. M. G. Proverbs from the Matabele. NADA 2 (1924), p. 31.

19,883 BERLYN, P. Traditional religion of the MaShona. NADA 2 (1965), pp. 94-96.

19,884 BISSETT, C. J. Some Chikararga proverbs, with explanations. NADA 11 (1933), pp. 98-100.

19,885 BLAKE-THOMPSON, J. Some notes on African ritual sacrifice. NADA 34 (1957), pp. 123-129.

19,886 BLAKE-THOMPSON, J. and SUMMERS, R. Mlimo and Mwari: notes on a native religion in Southern Rhodesia. NADA 33 (1956), pp. 53-58.

19,887 BRELSFORD, W. V. The succession of Bemba chiefs, a guide for district officers. NADA 27 (1950), p. 85.

19,888 BRENDON, N. J. Do not look inside the drum. NADA 37 (1960), pp. 5-7.

19,889 BRODERICK, G. E. P. Betrothal ceremony among the Wazeruru of the Salisbury district. NADA 22 (1945), pp. 49-50.

19,890 BRODERICK, G. E. P. Description of a pagan funeral. NADA 33 (1956), pp. 60-62.

19,891 BRUBAKER, H. H. The native ceremony Ukubuyisa. NADA 7 (1929), pp. 113-114.

19,892 BULLOCK, C. Notes on the Ba-Venda. NADA 4 (1926), pp. 62-66.

19,893 BULLOCK, C. On the origin and nature of totemism. NADA 9 (1931), pp. 10-15.

19,894 BULLOCK, C. The origin and nature of totemism among the Mashona. NADA 28 (1951), pp. 45-51.

19,895 BUNDU. Waduma ceremonies. NADA 15 (1938), pp. 11-14.

19,896 BURBRIDGE, A. How to become a witch doctor. NADA 1 (1923), pp. 94-100; 8 (1930), pp. 85-91.

19,897 BURBRIDGE, A. In spirit-bound Rhodesia. NADA 15 (1938), pp. 15-27.

19,898 BURBRIDGE, A. The witch doctor's power. NADA 3 (1925), pp. 22-31.

19,899 BURBRIDGE, A. The witch doctor's power: a study of its source and scope. NADA 17 (1940), pp. 8-17.

19,900 CAMPBELL, A. C. Chimombe. NADA 34 (1957), pp. 31-37.

19,901 CAMPBELL, D. D. and HOWMAN, E. G. Some native beliefs regarding birds and their calls. NADA 10 (1932), pp. 59-61.

19,902 CAPELL, A. E. Tales of the Makorrie-Korrie. NADA 22 (1945), pp. 25-27.

19,903 CHAPARADZA, W. Makoromokwa. NADA 35 (1958), p. 44.

19,904 "CHIGUMI". "Kugarira" or "Ugariri." NADA 1 (1923), pp. 79-81.

19,905 CHILD, H. F. Amandebele custom. NADA 10 (1932), pp. 36-39.

19,906 CHILD, H. F. Etiquette and relationship terms. NADA 25 (1948), pp. 18-21.

19,907 CHILD, H. F. Family and tribal structure—status of women. NADA 35 (1958), pp. 65-70.

19,908 CHINYANDURA. The children's corner [a collection of games]. NADA 12 (1934), pp. 12-16.

19,909 CHINYANDURA. A Mukaranga doctor of thunder and lightning. NADA 11 (1933), pp. 119-120.

19,910 CHINYANDURA. Spirit cattle (Ngombe yo Mudzimu). NADA 16 (1939), pp. 92-93.

19,911 CHINYANDURA. The tribes of Mambo. NADA 24 (1947), pp. 73-75.

19,912 CHINYANDURA. Zwitukwane: ghosts. NADA 14 (1936-1937), pp. 88-91.

19,913 CHITEWHE, S. S. M. Rain-making in Mashonaland. NADA 31 (1954), pp. 24-26.

19,914 CLOSE, A. G. L. Tales from the Eastern border. NADA 35 (1958), pp. 104-109.

19,915 COWGILL, J. I. W. Notes on the Mugariri custom. NADA 8 (1930), pp. 78-79.

19,916 CRAWFORD, J. R. Marriage to the Ngozi and the Mainini custom. NADA 40 (1963), pp. 27-28.

19,917 CRIPPS, H. Mbewa. NADA 16 (1939), pp. 13-16.

19,918 CRIPPS, H. Should Lobolo be restricted by legislation. NADA 24 (1947), pp. 41-47.

19,919 D., A. A superstition. NADA 1 (1923), pp. 83-84.

19,920 DAVIES, W. N. G. and QUINCHE, C. Amandebele taboos and etiquette. BANTU STUD. 7 (1933), pp. 277-284.

19,921 DAVIS, C. S. The Amandabele habitat. NADA 12 (1934), pp. 74-79.

19,922 DAVIS, C. S. The concluding rites of marriage. NADA 11 (1933), pp. 61-64.

19,923 DAVIS, C. S. and CHANIKIRA: Chikwambo and Chitsina. NADA 9 (1931), pp. 41-43.

19,924 DOMINUS. Madala. NADA 40 (1963), pp. 84-85.

19,925 DUNCAN, J. R. Mazariri, Tsikiro: Chibi district. NADA 9 (1931), pp. 71-73.

19,926 DUNCAN, J. R. Native food and culinary methods. NADA 11 (1933), pp. 101-106.

19,927 "DYKE NEUK". Dumbghe. NADA 1 (1923), pp. 51-54.

19,928 EDWARDS, W. From birth to death: notes on the natives of the Mrewa district, Southern Rhodesia. NADA 7 (1929), pp. 16-42.

19,929 EDWARDS, W. Kuwaka Imba (to build a hut). NADA 6 (1928), pp. 73-74.

19,930 EDWARDS, W. Sacred places. NADA 6 (1928), pp. 23-27.

19,931 FARQUHAR, J. H. The African hand. NADA 24 (1947), pp. 29-33; 25 (1948), pp. 25-28.

19,932 FERREIRA, V. Two legends. NADA 19 (1942), pp. 39-40.

19,933 FOGGIN, B. J. M. Totemism. NADA 14 (1936-1937), pp. 62-69.

19,934 FORTUNE, G. Some Zezuru and Kalanga riddles. NADA 28 (1951), pp. 30-44.

19,935 FRANKLIN, H. Chikaranga cocktails. NADA 11 (1933), pp. 116-117.

19,936 FRANKLIN, H. Chisi or Zwisi. NADA 11 (1933), p. 32.

19,937 FRANKLIN, H. The conspiracy of the five sons; or how Neshoro lost the chieftainship of the Nebghwimi tribe. NADA 5 (1927), pp. 45-47.

19,938 FRANKLIN, H. Manyusa (Amanxusa). NADA 10 (1932), pp. 77-83.

19,939 FRANKLIN, H. A selection from notes on Manyika customs. NADA 5 (1927), pp. 56-60.

19,940 FRANKLIN, H. Traps in common use among the Vakaranga. NADA 9 (1931), pp. 74-80.

19,941 FRANKLIN, H. Vakaranga superstitions. NADA 11 (1933), pp. 122-124.

19,942 GELFAND, M. The charm and the bead in African practice. NADA 29 (1952), pp. 18-25.

19,943 GELFAND, M. Chikwambo (Runhare). NADA 31 (1954), pp. 59-61.

19,944 GELFAND, M. Chitsina. NADA 34 (1957), pp. 6-7.

19,945 GELFAND, M. Mahungbwe. NADA 37 (1960), pp. 36-37.

19,946 GELFAND, M. The Mararano (medicine at the cross roads). NADA 24 (1947), pp. 76-80.

19,947 GELFAND, M. The Mhondoro-Chaminuku. NADA 36 (1959), pp. 6-10.

19,948 GELFAND, M. The Mhondoro cult of the Shona-speaking people of Southern Rhodesia. AFRICAN SYSTEMS OF THOUGHT, 1965, pp. 341-350.

19,949 GELFAND, M. The normal man: a new concept of Shona philosophy. NADA 9, no. 2 (1965), pp. 78-93.

19,950 GELFAND, M. The religion of the Mashona. NADA 33 (1956), pp. 27-31.

19,951 GELFAND, M. The totem of the tutelary spirit (Mhondoro) and that of the clan of the Sokoto District. AFR. STUD. 20 (1961), pp. 214-216.

19,952 GELFAND, M. and SWART, Y. The Nyora. NADA 30 (1953), pp. 5-11.

19,953 GLUCKMAN, M. Social anthropology in Central Africa. RHODES-LIV. J. 20 (1956), pp. 1-27.

19,954 GUMPRICH, D. Ziki, chief of the Waduma. Succession ceremony held in Bikita Reserve on 26th October, 1957. NADA 36 (1959), pp. 85-86.

19,955 HANNAN, M. Unhu ne Tsumo. NADA 25 (1948), pp. 58-60.

19,956 HAYES, M. E. Marriage amongst the Makorekore. NADA 21 (1944), pp. 47-48.

19,957 HEMANS, T. J. Nyamkungangedati and his weapons. NADA 26 (1949), pp. 66-67.

19,958 HETHERWICK, A. Some animistic beliefs among the Yaos of British Central Africa. JRAI 32 (1902), pp. 89-95.

19,959 HLAZO, T. J. The naming of the hill Intaba Yezinduna, Matabeleland. NADA 12 (1934), pp. 72-73.

19,960 HOWMAN, E. G. Notes and anecdotes. NADA 14 (1936-1937), pp. 16-24.

19,961 HOWMAN, E. G. Replies to some questions in the native customs examinations of 1923. NADA 9 (1931), pp. 69-71.

19,962 HOWMAN, E. G. Rufimbi. NADA 27 (1950), pp. 31-33.

19,963 HOWMAN, E. G. Some notes on the consequences of childless marriages among natives. NADA 7 (1929), p. 8.

19,964 HOWMAN, R. Mteu: the supreme court of the Mashona. NADA 13 (1935), pp. 23-25.

19,965 HUGHES, A. J. B. Uzimu: some preliminary notes on vengeance magic among the Rhodesian Ndebele. RHODES-LIV. J. 19 (1955), pp. 27-45.

19,966 HUGO, H. C. The Mashona spirits. NADA 13 (1935), pp. 52-58.

19,967 HUGO, H. C. The spirit world of the Mashona (Vakaranga). NADA 3 (1925), pp. 14-17.

19,968 HUNT, N. A. More notes on the witchdoctor's bones. NADA 39 (1962), pp. 14-16.

19,969 HUNT, N. A. Some Karanga riddles. NADA 29 (1952), pp. 90-98; 34 (1957), pp. 66-74.

19,970 HUNT, N. A. Some notes on the witchdoctor's bones. NADA 27 (1950), pp. 40-46; 31 (1954), pp. 16-23.

19,971 JACKSON, A. C. Proverbs of the Vakaranga. NADA 13 (1935), pp. 26-34.

19,972 JACKSON, A. P. Kinship terms of the Karanga tribes. NADA 27 (1950), pp. 66-72.

19,973 JACKSON, A. P. Native hunting customs. NADA 27 (1950), pp. 39-40.

19,974 JACKSON, H. M. G. Notes on the marriage laws of the Amandebele, with endogamous and exogamous bars to marriage. NADA 3 (1925), pp. 35-36.

19,975 JACKSON, H. M. G. Odds and ends concerning Matabele and their customs. NADA 4 (1926), pp. 81-82.

19,976 JACKSON, H. M. G. Odds and ends of Matabele customs and customary law. NADA 6 (1928), pp. 7-11.

19,977 JACKSON, S. N. G. The fall of a witch doctor. NADA 11 (1933), pp. 57-59.

19,978 JACKSON, S. N. G. The mystery of the sacred tongs. NADA 3 (1925), pp. 45-46.

19,979 JEFFREYS, M. D. W. Cowry: ndoro. NADA 30 (1953), pp. 35-52.

19,980 JEFFREYS, M. D. W. Mumbo Jumbo or Mambo, the heart eater. NADA 40 (1963), pp. 74-83.

19,981 JEFFREYS, M. D. W. The Sarwa are foreigners. NADA 32 (1955), pp. 4-6.

19,982 JENKINSON, J. N. Installation ceremony of chief Maranke. NADA 36 (1959), pp. 46-48.

19,983 JONES, N. More Sindebele proverbs. NADA 23 (1946), pp. 7-9.

19,984 JONES, N. Sindebele proverbs. NADA 3 (1925), pp. 65-73.

19,985 JONES, N. and SUMMERS, R. F. H. The Magosian culture of Khami, near Bulawayo, Southern Rhodesia. JRAI 76 (1946), pp. 59-68.

19,986 JOWETT, L. V. Mashona background. NADA 35 (1958), pp. 110-117.

19,987 JUNOD, H. P. A contribution to the study of Ndau demography, totemism, and history. BANTU STUD. 8 (1934), pp. 17-37.

19,988 KANDAMAKUMBO. Courtship and marriage amongst the Vakaranga. NADA 17 (1940), p. 61.

19,989 KANDAMAKUMBO. Courtship and marriage amongst the Vakaranga. Kutiza Makumbo. NADA 15 (1938), p. 87.

19,990 KANDAMAKUMBO. Mamwe Matsika: Vakaranga custom. NADA 17 (1940), pp. 53-54.

19,991 KANDAMAKUMBO. Ordeals. NADA 15 (1938), pp. 70-71.

19,992 KENDAL, J. Anthropology, superstition and all that. NADA 15 (1938), pp. 5-10.

19,993 LEAVER, K. D. Native religion: its constitution. NADA 18 (1941), pp. 46-48.

19,994 LEAVER, K. D. Proverbs of the Amandebele. NADA 24 (1947), pp. 95-99.

19,995 LEWIS, D. G. Matabele customs. NADA 12 (1934), p. 85.

19,996 McADAMS, L. J. and HOWMAN, R. Notes on the handspinning and weaving of cotton. NADA 17 (1940), pp. 96-100.

19,997 MacALPINE, A. G. Tonga religious beliefs and customs. J. AFR. SOC. 5 (1906), pp. 187-190, 257-268, 377-380.

19,998 MACHARANGWADA. Mudzimu, Shabe, Ngozi and other spirits. NADA 10 (1932), pp. 7-10.

19,999 MAFOHLA. The curse of Chigodoro: an incident in the history of the Vambire tribe. NADA 5 (1928), pp. 20-23.

20,000 MAFOHLA. Ku Tiza Botso: a Vazezuru custom. NADA 7 (1929), pp. 138-139.

20,001 MAFOHLA. The Ngozi of Chinyowa. NADA 4 (1926), pp. 104-106.

20,002 MAFOHLA. A raid and what led to it: an incident of native history in Mashonaland. NADA 4 (1926), pp. 102-103.

20,003 MARAPARA, M. Wazezuru names and their meanings. NADA 31 (1954), pp. 7-9.

20,004 MARCONNES, F. The Karangas. NADA 10 (1932), pp. 11-18.

20,005 MARR, F. Some notes on Chief Sileya (Chireya: Shona) Gokwe district, S. Rhodesia. NADA 39 (1962), pp. 81-84.

20,006 MATTHEWS, J. B. The Mhondoro of Mutota and his village. NADA 37 (1960), pp. 66-74.

20,007 MATTHEWS, J. B. Notes on some African stone games. NADA 9, no. 1 (1964), pp. 64-68.

20,008 MAUCH, K. The Makalaka; translated from the German by F. O. Bernhard with notes by M. Gelfand. RHODESIANA 12 (1965), pp. 63-75.

20,009 "MBIZO". The lightning doctor. NADA 2 (1924), pp. 60-62.

20,010 "MBIZO". Mashona proverbs. NADA 4 (1926), pp. 29-30.

20,011 MEREDITH, L. C. The rain spirit of Mabota Murangadzwa, Melsetter District. NADA 3 (1925), pp. 77-81.

20,012 MERWE, W. J. The Shona idea of God. NADA 34 (1957), pp. 39-63.

20,013 MITCHELL, J. C. Chidzere's tree: a note on a Shona land-shrine and its significance. NADA 38 (1961), pp. 28-35.

20,014 MORKEL, E. R. Koromu—a portrait. NADA 27 (1950), pp. 46-49.

20,015 MORKEL, E. R. The Mondoro or ancestral spirit of the Wabuja, Mtoko. NADA 8 (1930), pp. 11-14.

20,016 MORKEL, E. R. Spiritualism amongst the Wabudya. NADA 11 (1933), pp. 106-116.

20,017 MPUZARIMA. The proof of chastity. NADA 8 (1930), p. 77.

20,018 MURRAY, G. S. Totemism. NADA 13 (1935), pp. 78-84.

20,019 MUSHOMA. The native approach to religion. NADA 10 (1932), pp. 27-32.

20,020 "NDAU". The Mula custom. NADA 4 (1926), p. 69.

20,021 NEUK, D. Dumbghe. NADA 13 (1935), pp. 101-104.

20,022 NICOLLE, W. H. H. Dzikaramba, the witch doctor. NADA 12 (1934), pp. 96-99.

20,023 NICOLLE, W. H. H. A few notes on Baka Chimombe: the idol worshippers of the Zambesi valley. NADA 14 (1936-1937), pp. 26-33.

20,024 ODENDALL, P. J. The bow and arrow in Southern Rhodesia. NADA 8 (1930), pp. 59-61; 18 (1941), pp. 23-24.

20,025 PARKHURST, D. C. H. Beliefs about the elephant. NADA 25 (1948), p. 49.

20,026 PEELE, C. R. DE. Porcupine trap. NADA 14 (1938), pp. 28-29.

20,027 PENDERED, A. Kubika wawa: beer making. NADA 9 (1931), p. 30.

20,028 PENDERED, A. Kuwhombera. NADA 13 (1935), pp. 74-76.

20,029 PENDERED, A. Kuzodza kwe Nzou. NADA 8 (1930), pp. 46-47.

20,030 POSSELT, F. W. T. The Banyemba legend and ceremony. NADA 2 (1924), pp. 11-13.

20,031 POSSELT, F. W. T. Chaminuka the wizard. NADA 4 (1926), pp. 35-37.

20,032 POSSELT, F. W. T. Life on the by-ways of Rhodesia. NADA 9 (1931), pp. 25-29.

20,033 POSSELT, F. W. T. Mashona folk-lore. NADA 5 (1927), pp. 35-39.

20,034 POSSELT, F. W. T. The story of the Princess Mepo. NADA 7 (1929), pp. 115-117.

20,035 POSSELT, F. W. T. The Watawara and the Batonga. NADA 7 (1929), pp. 80-95.

20,036 POWELL, R. J. The Kuteurira midzimu ceremony at a Vashankwe kraal. NADA 29 (1952), pp. 87-89.

20,037 POWELL, R. J. Marriage customs in the Bushu reserve. NADA 31 (1954), pp. 10-15.

20,038 POWELL, R. J. Notes on burial customs in the Bushu Reserve. NADA 33 (1956), pp. 6-10.

20,039 POWELL, R. J. Notes on life at one of the Batonka kraals in the Sebungwe district. NADA 28 (1951), pp. 26-29.

20,040 POWELL, R. J. Notes on the Kutaya, Kukomba, and Kugare Nhaka ceremonies of the Vashankwe. NADA 30 (1953), pp. 14-21.

20,041 POWELL, R. J. Some of the marriage customs of the Batonka of Chief Sinempande's country: Sebungwe district. NADA 30 (1953), pp. 59-63.

20,042 POWYS-JONES, L. Tsa Mutombo. NADA 6 (1928), p. 31.

20,043 RICHARDS, J. B. The Mlimo: belief and practice of the Kalanga. NADA 19 (1942), pp. 51-55.

20,044 ROBERTS, J. G. A Southern Rhodesian totem. NADA 24 (1947), pp. 65-70.

20,045 ROBERTS, J. G. Threshing episode with variations. NADA 32 (1955), pp. 93-111.

20,046 ROBERTS, J. G. Totemism and sexuality. NADA 15 (1938), pp. 44-61.

20,047 ROBERTS, J. G. Totemism, Zimbabwe and the Barozwi. NADA 24 (1947), pp. 48-52.

20,048 ROBINSON, L. K. The hyena's spell. NADA 6 (1928), pp. 53-54.

20,049 SADZA, D. Digma. NADA 31 (1954), pp. 38-40.

20,050 SCHEBESTA, P. Religiöse Anschauungen der Asena: Mul-ungu und seine Verehrung. BIBLIOTHECA AFR. 3 (1929), pp. 1-10.

20,051 SCHEBESTA, P. Zur Ethnographie der Asena am Unteren Sambesi. BIBLIOTHECA AFR. 2 (1926), pp. 201-208, 322-334.

20,052 SEAGER, C. E. The original marriage customs of the Makalana. NADA 19 (1942), pp. 55-57.

20,053 SEBINA, A. M. Makalaka. AFR. STUD. 6 (1947), pp. 82-94.

20,054 SEED, J. H. The kingship system of a Bantu tribe. NADA 10 (1932), pp. 65-73; 11 (1933), pp. 35-56.

20,055 SEYMOUR, L. F. The tradition of the VaMare of Chibi. NADA 17 (1940), pp. 73-76.

20,056 SHROPSHIRE, D. The exorcism of a Bswoka spirit by a Wabarwe doctor. NADA 10 (1932), pp. 33-34.

20,057 SHROPSHIRE, D. The initiation of a doctor of the WaBarwe tribe. NADA 8 (1930), pp. 8-10.

20,058 SHROPSHIRE, D. The medical outfit of a Wamanyika doctor. NADA 6 (1928), pp. 27-30.

20,059 SHROPSHIRE, D. Midzimu worship in a village of the WaBarwe tribe. NADA 6 (1928), pp. 74-77; 11 (1933), pp. 95-97.

20,060 SHROPSHIRE, D. The story of an anthropological research trek. NADA 7 (1929), pp. 52-63.

20,061 SICARD, H. VON. African tree dwellers. NADA 32 (1955), pp. 65-67.

20,062 SICARD, H. VON. The bird in the Zimbawe culture. ETHNOS 8 (1943), pp. 104-114.

20,063 SICARD, H. VON. The brother-sister marriage in the South Erythrean culture. ETHNOS 13 (1948), pp. 27-35.

20,064 SICARD, H. VON. The Jawunda. NADA 36 (1959), pp. 103-128.

20,065 SICARD, H. VON. Lemba clans. NADA 39 (1962), pp. 68-80.

20,066 SICARD, H. VON. The Rhodesian tally. NADA 31 (1954), pp. 52-54.

20,067 SICARD, H. VON. The tree cult in the Zimbawe culture. AFR. STUD. 5 (1946), pp. 257-267.

20,068 SIMEY, P. A. T. Rhodesian mythical monsters. J. AFR. SOC. 39 (1940), pp. 61-63.

20,069 SIMMONDS, R. G. S. Charewa, voice of the rain god. NADA 9, no. 1 (1964), pp. 60-63.

20,070 SLOAN, A. The black woman. NADA 1 (1923), pp. 60-69.

20,071 SNOWDEN, A. E. A double-storey hut. NADA 15 (1938), pp. 65-68.

20,072 SPEARS, J. The burial and succession rites of a Mushona chief. NADA 6 (1928), pp. 89-91.

20,073 STEAD, W. H. The clan organization and kinship system of some Shona tribes. AFR. STUD. 5 (1946), pp. 1-20.

20,074 STEAD, W. H. Good manners, use of the chidawu. NADA 13 (1935), p. 26.

20,075 STEAD, W. H. Os primitivos povos da Rodésia. BSEM 57-58 (1948), pp. 17-26.

20,076 STEAD, W. H. Some notes on the Manyika. NADA 25 (1948), p. 24.

20,077 STEAD, W. H. Succeeding to the name Mandeya. NADA 23 (1946), pp. 11-12.

20,078 SWIFT, P. Kupisa guwa. NADA 10 (1932), pp. 61-62.

20,079 T., J. E. S. Spirit trees. NADA 14 (1936-1937), pp. 33-35.

20,080 TABERER, W. S. Mashonaland natives. J. AFR. SOC. 4 (1905), pp. 311-336.

20,081 TAYLOR, G. A. The genealogical method of anthropological enquiry. NADA 2 (1924), pp. 33-48.

20,082 TAYLOR, G. A. The Matabele head ring (Isidhlodhlo) and some fragments of history. NADA 3 (1925), pp. 37-42.

20,083 TAYLOR, G. A. A Mushona hut. NADA 5 (1927), pp. 22-26.

20,084 TAYLOR, G. A. Some Mashona songs and dances. NADA 4 (1926), pp. 38-42.

20,085 TAYLOR, M. Angoni stories. NADA 4 (1926), pp. 75-76.

20,086 THOMAS, T. M. Ceremonies of Ndebele marriage. NADA 4 (1926), pp. 44-47.

20,087 THOMAS, W. E. A game reserve. NADA 33 (1956), p. 59.

20,088 THOMPSON, J. B. Physical appearances of some Mashona totemic groups. NADA 25 (1948), pp. 29-33.

20,089 THOMPSON, L. C. The Ba-Lemba of Southern Rhodesia. NADA 19 (1942), pp. 76-86.

20,090 TRACEY, H. T. The bones. NADA 12 (1934), pp. 23-26.

20,091 TRACEY, H. T. The Hakata of Southern Rhodesia. NADA 40 (1963), pp. 105-107.

20,092 TRACEY, H. T. The rules of the native game Tsoro. NADA 9 (1931), pp. 33-34.

20,093 TRACEY, H. T. String figures (Madandi) found in Southern Rhodesia. NADA 14 (1936-1937), pp. 78-88.

20,094 TRACEY, H. T. What are Mashawi spirits? NADA 12 (1934), pp. 39-52.

20,095 TRACEY, L. T. Blindness: a sanction. NADA 24 (1947), p. 94.

20,096 TUCKER, C. B. A cure for lightning. NADA 35 (1958), pp. 16-17.

20,097 WANE, F. J. The ceremony of Kuroba Guba or Kudibura Guba. NADA 9 (1931), pp. 100-102.

20,098 WATERS, M. W. The tragedy of the home (a sketch from a reserve). NADA 6 (1928), pp. 77-79.

20,099 WEIDENREICH, F. The relation of Sinanthropus Pekinensis to Pithecanthropus, Javanthropus and Rhodesian Man. JRAI 67 (1937), pp. 51-65.

20,100 WELLS, A. Murder Inc. NADA 27 (1950), pp. 23-25.

20,101 WERBNER, R. P. Atonement ritual and guardian-spirit possession among Kalanga. AFRICA 34 (1964), pp. 206-222.

20,102 WIESCHHOFF, H. Names and naming customs among the Mashona in Southern Rhodesia. AMER. ANTHR. 39 (1937), pp. 497-503.

20,103 WILSON, A. A decree from the all-highest. NADA 11 (1933), pp. 65-66.

20,104 WILSON, A. The ghost hill. NADA 10 (1932), pp. 24-25.

20,105 WILSON, A. The human sacrifice. NADA 9 (1931), pp. 6-10.

20,106 WILSON, N. H. Note on Darwin ritual murder. NADA 4 (1926), pp. 61-62.

20,107 WOLLACOTT, R. C. Dzewaquru: god of rain. NADA 40 (1963), pp. 116-121.

20,108 WOODS, G. G. B. Extracts from customs and history; Amandebele. NADA 9 (1931), pp. 16-23.

20,109 ZENGENI, S. The game Matomba. NADA 17 (1940), p. 7.

20,110 The ancient Barwe accession to chieftaincy. NADA 31 (1954), pp. 54-56.

20,111 Exogamy: rules amongst the Wa-Rozwi: Msarurgwa's people: Charter district. NADA 13 (1935), pp. 92-93.

20,112 Handbook to the Bantu chieftaincies of Southern Rhodesia. NADA 38 (1961), p. 109.

20,113 Manyika headwomen. NADA 17 (1940), pp. 3-5.

20,114 Muchape. NADA 13 (1935), pp. 17-18.

20,115 Native bee hives. NADA 10 (1932), pp. 49-50.

20,116 A native trap. NADA 10 (1932), p. 51.

20,117 Notes on Butwa, an African secret society. NADA 25 (1948), pp. 44-48.

See also 23750.

Art

20,118 ALBERTO, M. S. Antigas ruínas portuguesas na Rodésia do Sul. BSEM 85 (1954), pp. 129-136.

20,119 ARMSTRONG, A. L. Rhodesian archaeological expedition, 1929. NADA 9 (1931), pp. 103-104.

20,120 ARMSTRONG, A. L. Rhodesian archaeological expedition (1929): excavations in Bambata cave and researches on prehistoric sites in Southern Rhodesia. JRAI 61 (1931), pp. 239-276.

20,121 BALFOUR, H. Note upon an implement of palaeolithic type from the Victoria Falls, Zambesi. JRAI 36 (1906), pp. 170-171.

20,122 BATE, T. W. A Manyika stronghold. NADA 8 (1930), pp. 21-22.

20,123 BEATTY, M. C. A ruin and a legend. NADA 12 (1934), pp. 86-88.

20,124 BEEK, J. L. R. W. The Bushman and Zimbabwe. NADA 6 (1928), pp. 104-109.

20,125 BERNHARD, F. O. Notes on the pre-ruin Ziwa culture of Inyanga. RHODESIANA 11 (1964), pp. 22-30.

20,126 BERNHARD, F. O. The Ziwa ware of Inyanga. NADA 38 (1961), pp. 84-92.

20,127 BLEEK, D. F. The Ndanga rock paintings. NADA 5 (1927), pp. 79-80.

20,128 BOGOMAS, E. V. M. New light on the mystery of Zimbabwe. NADA 39 (1962), pp. 85-93.

20,129 BOND, G. Pleistocene research in Southern Rhodesia. PROC. PAN-AFR. CONGR. PRE-HIST. 4 (1962), pp. 141-150.

20,130 BULLOCK, C. Bushman paintings, Zimbabwe and romanticists. NADA 26 (1949), pp. 50-53.

20,131 BULLOCK, C. Thoughts on a show. NADA 7 (1929), pp. 49-52.

20,132 CAMPBELL, A. C. A cave found on the Malunda river. NADA 36 (1959), pp. 97-98.

20,133 CATON-THOMPSON, G. Recent excavations at Zimbabwe and other ruins in Rhodesia. J. AFR. SOC. 29 (1929), pp. 132-138.

20,134 CHINYANDURA. The Sinoia caves: a historiette. NADA 9 (1931), pp. 67-68.

20,135 COCKCROFT, I. G. Hunting. NADA 12 (1934), pp. 94-95.

20,136 COOKE, C. K. Evidence of human migrations from the rock art of Southern Rhodesia. AFRICA 35 (1965), pp. 263-285.

20,137 COOKE, C. K. The prehistoric artist of Southern Matabeleland: his materials and technique as a basis for dating. PROC. PAN-AFR. CONGR. PRE-HIST. 3 (1955), pp. 282-294.

20,138 COOPER, G. Filming the Matabele. NADA 12 (1934), pp. 60-63.

20,139 CRIPPS, L. Rock paintings of southern Rhodesia. NADA 18 (1941), pp. 25-35.

20,140 DART, R. A. Foreign influences of the Zimbabwe and pre-Zimbabwe eras. NADA 32 (1955), pp. 19-30.

20,141 FRANKLIN, H. The native ironworkers of Enkeldoorn district and their art. NADA 22 (1945), pp. 5-10.

20,142 FRIPP, C. E. and MARTIN, C. The preservation of old beads in Southern Rhodesia. NADA 16 (1939), pp. 48-49.

20,143 GARDNER, Father. Digging. NADA 10 (1932), pp. 44-49.

20,144 GARDNER, Father. Excavations in a Wilton industry at Gokommere, Fort Victoria, Southern Rhodesia. JRAI 58 (1928), pp. 497-510.

20,145 GARDNER, T. Stone age implements. NADA 9 (1931), pp. 51-59.

20,146 GOODALL, E. A distinctive mythical figure appearing in the rock paintings of Southern Rhodesia. PROC. PAN-AFR. CONGR. PRE-HIST. 4, no. iii (1962), pp. 399-405.

20,147 GOODALL, E. The geometric motif in rock art. PROC. PAN-AFR. CONGR. PRE-HIST. 3 (1955), pp. 300-303.

20,148 GOODALL, E. Notes sur une gravure rupestre récemment découverte dans la Rhodésie du Sud. PROC. PAN-AFR. CONGR. PRE-HIST. 4, no. iii (1962), pp. 395-397.

20,149 GOODALL, E. Pictorial documents of prehistoric people. NADA 24 (1947), pp. 23-28.

20,150 GOODALL, E. Report on an ancient burial ground, Salisbury, Southern Rhodesia. PROC. PAN-AFR. CONGR. PRE-HIST. 4, no. iii (1962), pp. 315-322.

20,151 GOODALL, E. Rhodesian pots with moulded decorations. NADA 23 (1946), pp. 36-49.

20,152 GOODALL, E. Styles in rock paintings. PROC. PAN-AFR. CONGR. PRE-HIST. 3 (1955), pp. 295-299.

20,153 HALL, R. N. The great Zimbabwe. J. AFR. SOC. 4 (1905), pp. 295-300.

20,154 HALL, R. N. Stone fort and pits on the Inyanga estate, Rhodesia. JRAI 35 (1905), pp. 92-102.

20,155 HANNAN, M. Ngano Dzokupunza: Shona fireside songs. NADA 31 (1954), pp. 30-37.

20,156 HOLZ, P. The riddle of the Zimbabwe ruins. CONTEMP. REV. 190 (1956), pp. 362-364.

20,157 JONES, N. On the occurrence of rostro-carinate implements at Hope Fountain, Rhodesia. JRAI 60 (1930), pp. 73-80.

20,158 JONES, N. On the palaeolithic deposits of sawmills, Rhodesia. JRAI 54 (1924), pp. 276-286.

20,159 JONES, N. Some aspects of the Stone Age in Southern Rhodesia. PROC. PAN-AFR. CONGR. PRE-HIST. 1 (1947), pp. 136-140.

20,160 KAUFFMAN, R. Hymns of the Wabvuwi. AFR. MUSIC, 1960, pp. 31-35.

20,161 LAMPLUGH, G. W. Notes on the occurrence of stone implements in the valley of the Zambesi around Victoria Falls. JRAI 36 (1906), pp. 159-169.

20,162 LENHERR, J. On a traditional Karanga song. AFR. MUSIC, 1964, pp. 15-19.

20,163 LOWE, C. VAN R. Pinturas rupestres e a cultura do Zimbáuè. BSEM 57-58 (1948), pp. 3-16.

20,164 M., H. B. The early inhabitants of Southern Rhodesia. NADA 2 (1924), pp. 5-11.

20,165 M., H. B. Zimbabwe culture, ruins and reactions [The Zimbabwe Culture by G. Caton-Thompson]. NADA 9 (1931), pp. 110-111.

20,166 McHARG, J. African music in Rhodesian native education. AFR. MUSIC, 1958, pp. 46-50.

20,167 MARTIN, C. Manyika beads of the XIXth century. NADA 17 (1940), pp. 18-26.

20,168 NGUBANE, S. S. Music north of the Limpopo. AFR. MUSIC, 1948, pp. 18-22.

20,169 NORTON, E. A. Inyanga, S. Rhodesia. J. AFR. SOC. 25 (1926), pp. 237-244.

20,170 OIDTMAN, C. VON. Proposta para o estudo do problema de Zimbáuè. BSEM 121 (1960), pp. 115-125.

20,171 OIDTMAN, C. VON. Vorschläge zur Lösung des Zimbabwe—Problems. AFR. UND UB. 44 (1960), pp. 225-253.

20,172 PATERSON, E. Cyrene art. NADA 26 (1949), pp. 45-50.

20,173 RHODES, W. Changing times. AFR. MUSIC, 1959, pp. 6-9.

20,174 ROBINSON, K. R. Excavations at Khami ruins, Matabeleland. PROC. PAN-AFR. CONGR. PRE-HIST. 3 (1955), pp. 357-365.

20,175 S., N. H. D. Mutivi. NADA 27 (1950), pp. 56-59.

20,176 S., N. H. D. Nkosi Sikelel' iAfrika. NADA 26 (1949), pp. 56-57.

20,177 SANDES, S. D. Zwenyika remembers [Zimbabwe]. NADA 32 (1955), pp. 31-40.

20,178 SCHOFIELD, J. F. The "Acropolis" at Zimbabwe. J. AFR. SOC. 23 (1924), pp. 122-124.

20,179 SICARD, H. VON. Occam's razor. NADA 30 (1953), pp. 53-56.

20,180 SICARD, H. VON. Ruins and their traditions on the Lower Mzingwane and in the Beitbridge area. NADA 38 (1961), pp. 50-73.

20,181 SICARD, H. VON. The Vuxwa Hills and their inhabitants. NADA 35 (1958), pp. 71-83.

20,182 SNOWDEN, A. E. Some common musical instruments found among the native tribes of Southern Rhodesia. NADA 15 (1938), pp. 99-103; 16 (1939), pp. 72-76.

20,183 SNOWDEN, A. E. Some technical notes on weapons and implements used in Mashonaland. NADA 17 (1940), pp. 62-70.

20,184 STEAD, W. H. Notes on the types of clay pots found in the Inyanga district, 1945... NADA 24 (1947), pp. 100-102.

20,185 STEVENS, C. G. The Zimbabwe temple. JRAI 61 (1931), pp. 181-186.

20,186 SUMMERS, R. Archaeology in Southern Rhodesia, 1900-1955. PROC. PAN-AFR. CONGR. PRE-HIST. 3 (1955), pp. 396-411.

20,187 SUMMERS, R. Carl Maunch on Zimbabwe ruins. NADA 29 (1952), pp. 9-17.

20,188 SUMMERS, R. Imbahuru hill, Belingwe. NADA 29 (1952), pp. 78-82.

20,189 SUMMERS, R. The Southern Rhodesian Iron Age. J. AFR. HIST. 2 (1961), pp. 1-13.

20,190 SUMMERS, R. Zimbabwe: capital of an ancient Rhodesian kingdom. AFR. SOUTH 2, no. 2 (1958), pp. 50-58.

20,191 TRACEY, A. Mbira music of Jege A. Tapera. AFR. MUSIC, 1961, pp. 44-63.

20,192 TRACEY, A. Three tunes for "Mbira dza vadzimu." AFR. MUSIC, 1963, pp. 23-26.

20,193 TRACEY, H. Native dancing: a wasted asset. NADA 17 (1940), pp. 28-34.

20,194 TRACEY, H. Ngoma. NADA 26 (1949), p. 65.

20,195 TRACEY, H. Poetic justice. NADA 22 (1945), pp. 45-49.

20,196 TRACEY, H. Recording in the Lost Valley. AFR. MUSIC, 1957, pp. 45-47.

20,197 TRACEY, H. A study of native music in Rhodesia. NADA 26 (1949), pp. 27-29.

20,198 TRACEY, H. Tina's lullaby. AFR. MUSIC, 1961, pp. 99-101.

20,199 TRACEY, H. The tuning of musical instruments. NADA 13 (1935), pp. 35-44.

20,200 TRACEY, H. T. Some observations on native music of Southern Rhodesia. NADA 7 (1929), pp. 96-103.

20,201 TREVOR, T. G. Some observations on the relics of pre-European culture in Rhodesia and South Africa. JRAI 60 (1930), pp. 389-399.

20,202 TREVOR-JONES, R. Skeletal remains from Salisbury, Southern Rhodesia. PROC. PAN-AFR. CONGR. PRE-HIST. 4 (1962), pp. 365-373.

20,203 VENNING, J. H. Notes on Southern Rhodesian ruins in Victoria district. J. AFR. SOC. 7 (1908), pp. 150-158.

20,204 WALTON, J. Some features of the Monomotapa culture. PROC. PAN-AFR. CONGR. PRE-HIST. 3 (1955), pp. 336-356.

20,205 WHITE, F. Notes on the great Zimbabwe elliptical ruin. JRAI 35 (1905), pp. 39-47.

20,206 WHITE, F. On the ruins of Dhlo-Dhlo, in Rhodesia. JRAI 31 (1901), pp. 21-28.

20,207 WHITTY, A. The origins of the stone architecture of Zimbabwe. PROC. PAN-AFR. CONGR. PRE-HIST. 3 (1955), pp. 366-377.

20,208 WILLIAMSON, L. Kwanongomo College, Bulawayo. AFR. MUSIC, 1963, pp. 48-49.

20,209 African and European musical culture in the Federation of Rhodesia and Nyasaland. AFR. MUSIC, 1959, p. 58.

20,210 The approach to music in the Federation. AFR. MUSIC, 1959, pp. 59-60.

20,211 Cyrene exhibition in London. Extracts from the press. AFR. MUSIC, 1949, pp. 28-30.

20,212 Draft programme for the development of music in the Federation. AFR. MUSIC, 1959, pp. 60-61.

20,213 The head office of native administration: an historic building. NADA 10 (1932), p. 26.

20,214 New tests date occupation of Zimbabwe. NADA 32 (1955), pp. 112-113.

20,215 When Rome came to Bindura. NADA 8 (1930), pp. 45-46.

Biography

20,216 Donald P. Abraham. NADA 38 (1961), p. 4.

20,217 Obituary: Emery Delmont Alvord. NADA 37 (1960), pp. 115-116.

20,218 A remarkable career [E. D. Alvord]. NADA 37 (1960), pp. 38-39.

20,219 HICKMAN, A. The death of Charles Annesty. RHODESIANA 12 (1965), pp. 93-102.

20,220 REGULUS. Frank William Baxter, V.C. RHODESIANA 2 (1957), pp. 16-28.

20,221 Memoirs of the late W. R. Benzies. NADA 40 (1963), pp. 50-68.

20,222 William Robertson Benzies. NADA 38 (1961), pp. 106-108.

20,223 Obituary: J. Blake-Thompson. NADA 9, no. 1 (1964), p. 70.

20,224 Charles Bullock. NADA 36 (1959), p. 5.

20,225 CHANAKIRA, B. The story of my father. NADA 3 (1925), pp. 82-85.

20,226 Obituary: Sir John Chancellor. AFR. AFFAIRS 51 (1952), p. 340.

20,227 Chief Chinamora. NADA 27 (1950), p. 55.

20,228 Musoni Shumba Ye Chinanga. NADA 38 (1961), p. 49.

20,229 FINN, D. E. Kambandakoto: a study of A. S. Cripps, 1869-1952. RHODESIANA 7 (1962), pp. 34-43.

20,230 WILSON, B. J. Kwezane Frank, African pioneer. NADA 39 (1962), p. 45.

20,231 Sergeant Gargwe. NADA 26 (1949), pp. 54-55.

20,232 Ginyilitshe. NADA 26 (1949), p. 69.

20,233 HICKMAN, A. S. Louis Samuel Glover, C.B.E.; a biographical introduction. RHODESIANA 11 (1964), pp. 31-36.

20,234 TURNER, R. W. S. Henry Hartley 1815-1876. RHODESIANA 12 (1965), pp. 27-36.

20,235 BURKE, E. E. William Hartley's grave. RHODESIANA 8 (1963), pp. 1-8.

20,236 KENDAL. Father Hartmann's notes. NADA 22 (1945), pp. 10-18.

20,237 Obituary: Edward George Howman. NADA 37 (1960), pp. 112-114.

20,238 MASON, P. Two sets of values [a review of Huggins of Rhodesia: The man and his country by L. H. Gann]. RACE 6, no. 1 (1964-1965), pp. 152-158.

20,239 Obituary: Arthur John Huxtable. NADA 36 (1959), p. 135.

20,240 W., E. M. B. Rev. Percy Ibbotson, O.B.E., M.P. NADA 33 (1956), p. 96.

20,241 Obituary: Herbert Stanley Keigwin. NADA 40 (1963), p.122.

20,242 T., J. E. S. John Vass Kerr, M.C. NADA 33 (1956), p. 95.

20,243 Chief Ndaniso Kumalo, Gwanda district. NADA 26 (1949), p. 34.

20,244 Sidojiwe Kumalo. NADA 38 (1961), p. 105.

20,245 The death of Lewanika. J. AFR. SOC. 16 (1917), pp. 149-154.

20,246 Obituary: Rev. Andrew Louw. NADA 34 (1957), p. 130.

20,247 Jessie Lovemore. NADA 38 (1961), p. 108.

20,248 Obituary: Leonard John Barrington McAdams. NADA 37 (1960), pp. 114-115.

20,249 McDONALD, L. J. Bishop Mackenzie's grave. NYASA J. 14, no. 1 (1961), pp. 60-67; 15, no. 2 (1962), pp. 12-13; 16, no. 1 (1963), p. 80.

20,250 CLIMENHAGA, A. M. Maladze Dube. NADA 35 (1958), pp. 57-60.

20,251 Manditshona alias Mary Jane. NADA 32 (1955), pp. 16-18.

20,252 Chief Mangwende, Mrewa district. NADA 26 (1949), pp. 20-21.

20,253 F., J. H. Mrs. Mangwende. NADA 33 (1956), p. 97.

20,254 Chief Mzimuni Masuku. NADA 25 (1948), pp. 50-51.

20,255 REED, J. Portrait of an agitator: Patrick Matimba. AFR. SOUTH 4, no. 2 (1960), pp. 73-78.

20,256 KANDAMAKWMBO. Mazariri, son of Makonese, the Tswikiro of Chikanga, Chibi district, Southern Rhodesia. NADA 13 (1935), p. 21.

20,257 Sgt. Findo Mpofu. NADA 9, no. 2 (1965), p. 77.

20,258 Sergeant Tom Munyambi retires. NADA 40 (1963), p. 90.

20,259 Mutanda alias Mutari. NADA 30 (1953), pp. 12-13.

20,260 Kadzima Mutasa. NADA 27 (1950), p. 60.

20,261 Muzimba alias Muteto. NADA 31 (1954), pp. 50-51.

20,262 Obituary: Major Randolph Cosby Nesbitt. NADA 34 (1957), p. 131.

20,263 Chief Ntelele: head of the Malaba Section. NADA 25 (1948), pp. 22-23.

20,264 Obituary: Mr. J. Lindsay Oliver. NADA 34 (1957), p. 131.

20,265 John Granville Roberts. NADA 37 (1960), p. 4.

20,266 Obituary: Rev. Thomson D. Samkange. NADA 34 (1957), pp. 130-131.

20,267 Father Joseph Henry Seed. NADA 38 (1961), pp. 105-106.

20,268 MYBURGH, C. A. L. J. R. H. Shaul: an appreciation. RHODES-LIV. J. 35 (1964), pp. 73-77.

20,269 A Shona chief. NADA 25 (1948), pp. 34-35.

20,270 Siatsha. NADA 29 (1952), p. 7.

20,271 SIKOBOLE NDHLOVU. Sikobole Ndhlovu. NADA 35 (1958), pp. 39-43.

20,272 Johnnie Tapedza, prince of interpreters. NADA 32 (1955), pp. 48-51.

20,273 G. A. Taylor. NADA 34 (1957), pp. 4-5.

20,274 Obituary: Francis John Wane. NADA 36 (1959), p. 136.

20,275 McADAM, J. An early enthusiast for Rhodesian aviation: Mr. C. F. Webb in 1912. RHODESIANA 12 (1965), pp. 103-110.

20,276 BARTON, F. Portrait of a failure: Sir Roy Welensky. AFR. SOUTH 3, no. 4 (1959), pp. 64-69.

20,277 N. H. Wilson. NADA 33 (1956), p. 4.

20,278 Neil Housman Wilson. NADA 38 (1961), p. 104.

20,279 BERLYN, P. ...of women who left their mark. RHODESIANA 13 (1965), pp. 54-56.

20,280 BRETTELL, N. H. Three Rhodesian poets [Kingsley Fairbridge, Lewis Hastings, Arthur Shearly Cripps]. RHODESIANA 3 (1958), pp. 29-39.

20,281 SPICER, C. A tribute to the wives of officials of the former department of native affairs. NADA 9, no. 2 (1965), pp. 28-30.

See also 18009.

Economics

20,282 BARBER, W. J. Economic rationality and behavior patterns in an underdeveloped area: a case study of African economic behavior in the Rhodesias. ECON. DEVELOPMENT AND CULTURAL CHANGE 8 (1959-1960), pp. 237-251.

20,283 BETTISON, D. G. The poverty datum line in Central Africa. RHODES-LIV. J. 27 (1960), pp. 1-40.

20,284 BETTISON, D. G. A reply to the note of B. Thomson and G. Kay. RHODES-LIV. J. 30 (1961), pp. 49-53.

20,285 C., J. Problèmes de main-d'oeuvre en Rhodésie du Sud. ZAIRE 7 (1953), pp. 415-416.

20,286 CARBUTT, C. L. Communal land tenure. NADA 5 (1927), pp. 42-45.

20,287 CARBUTT, C. L. [Economic value of the Native.] Address delivered by Col. C. L. Carbutt, Chief Native Commissioner, to the Rotary Club, Salisbury, in March, 1932. NADA 10 (1932), pp. 57-59.

20,288 CHANTRY, C. Last chance in Rhodesia. TRANSITION 9 (1963), pp. 37-38.

20,289 COLE, R. L and PEARSON, D. S. The tobacco industry of Central Africa 1953-1963. E. AFR. EC. REV. N.S. 1, no. 3 (1965), pp. 46-77.

20,290 COLSON, E. Land rights and land use among the Valley Tonga of the Rhodesian Federation: the background to the Kariba resettlement programme. AFR. AGRARIAN SYSTEMS, 1963, pp. 137-156.

20,291 COOMBS, G. M. Southern Rhodesia. CONTEMP. REV. 175 (1949), pp. 211-214.

20,292 CROCKER, H. E. Southern Rhodesia. CONTEMP. REV. 188 (1955), pp. 311-315.

20,293 DEANE, P. The industrial revolution in British Central Africa. CIVILISATIONS 12 (1962), pp. 331-347; French summary, pp. 348-355.

20,294 DEANE, P. National income: problems of social accounting in Central Africa. RHODES-LIV. J. 5 (1947), pp. 24-43.

20,295 DEANE, P. Problems of surveying village economies. RHODES-LIV. J. 8 (1949), pp. 42-49.

20,296 FLOYD, B. N. Changing patterns of African land use in Southern Rhodesia. RHODES-LIV. J. 25 (1959), pp. 20-39.

20,297 FRANCERIES, G. Les déplacements de main d'oeuvre dans les territoires d'Afrique Centrale britannique. AFR. ET ASIE 15 (1951), pp. 31-42.

20,298 GRAY, A. Copper in Rhodesia. AFR. AFFAIRS 55 (1956), pp. 259-261.

20,299 GRAY, A. Financing Kariba. AFR. AFFAIRS 55 (1956), pp. 87-89.

20,300 GRAY, A. Kariba contracts. AFR. AFFAIRS 55 (1956), pp. 257-259.

20,301 GRAY, A. £137,700,000 federal plan. AFR. AFFAIRS 56 (1957), p. 254.

20,302 GRAY, A. Rhodesian steel de-nationalised. AFR. AFFAIRS 56 (1957), pp. 15-17.

20,303 HAW, R. G. Some thoughts on native development. NADA 27 (1950), pp. 20-22.

20,304 HUNT, N. A. Age and land in a native reserve. NADA 40 (1963), pp. 108-112.

20,305 JOHNSON, R. W. M. An economic survey of Chiweshe Reserve. RHODES-LIV. J. 36 (1965), pp. 82-108.

20,306 JORDAN, J. D. Zimutu Reserve: a land-use appreciation. RHODES-LIV. J. 36 (1965), pp. 59-81.

20,307 MASON, P. Development plans for the Federation of Rhodesia and Nyasaland. CIVILISATIONS 6 (1956), pp. 341-356.

20,308 MASSER, F. I. Changing patterns of African employment in Southern Rhodesia. GEOGRAPHERS AND THE TROPICS, 1964, pp. 215-234.

20,309 MORTEN, I. H. A fair return to farmers. AFR. AFFAIRS 49 (1950), pp. 334-337.

20,310 NATIVE AFFAIRS DEPARTMENT (ECONOMIC DEVELOPMENT). African economic development in Southern Rhodesia. NADA 35 (1958), pp. 45-56.

20,311 NESHAM, W. T. Kariba resettlement (Southern Rhodesia). NADA 38 (1961), pp. 22-27.

20,312 NIDDRIE, D. The road to work: a survey of the influence of transport on migrant labour in Central Africa. RHODES-LIV. J. 15 (1954), pp. 31-42.

20,313 PRAIN, Sir R. Economic priorities in Central Africa. AFR. AFFAIRS 62 (1963), pp. 40-52.

20,314 SCOTT, P. Migrant labor in Southern Rhodesia. GEOG. REV. 44 (1954), pp. 29-48.

20,315 SOUTO, A. M. DO. Nas Rodésias. PORT. EM AFR. 22 (1965), pp. 90-102.

20,316 STEAD, W. H. Change and exchange. NADA 12 (1934), pp. 27-28.

20,317 THOMAS, Sir M. Two aspects of Rhodesian economy. Africa's industrial revolution. AFR. AFFAIRS 47 (1948), pp. 89-95.

20,318 VALLE FERNANDEZ, R. DEL. Estructura económica de una nueva federación. CUAD. AFR. OR. 34 (1956), pp. 31-44.

20,319 VENZO, E. Le ferrovie della Rhodesia. AFRICA (Rome) 16 (1961), pp. 83-86.

20,320 WELLINGTON, J. H. Zambezi-Okovango development projects. GEOG. REV. 39 (1949), pp. 552-567.

20,321 Gold mining in Rhodesia. Reprinted from The South African Mining and Engineering Journal. J. AFR. SOC. 42 (1943), pp. 76-77.

20,322 Unilateral declaration of independence and Rhodesia's economy. AFRO-ASIAN AND W. AFF. 2 (1965), pp. 373-380.

See also 10266, 15895.

Education

20,323 BEVAN, L. E. W. The education of natives in the pastoral pursuits. NADA 2 (1924), pp. 13-16; 17 (1940), pp. 34-37.

20,324 C., E. A. The younger generation, urban Africa. NADA 16 (1939), pp. 112-114.

20,325 C., J. L'enseignement indigène en Rhodésie. ZAIRE 6 (1952), pp. 866-867.

20,326 CHINYANDURA. A plea for a collegiate for Rhodesian natives. NADA 17 (1940), pp. 5-7.

20,327 DOSS, M. Nutrition education in Southern Rhodesia. AFR. WOMEN 2 (1956-1958), pp. 34-35.

20,328 FARQUHAR, J. H. A mass literacy campaign for Southern Rhodesia. NADA 9, no. 2 (1965), pp. 100-109; 23 (1946), pp. 13-24.

20,329 FARQUHAR, M. A. The African hand. NADA 27 (1950), pp. 25-30.

20,330 FLETCHER, B. A. A university in Central Africa. CONTEMP. REV. 190 (1956), pp. 163-165.

20,331 GARDENER, G. Community development...lecturing and learning. NADA 30 (1953), pp. 22-25.

20,332 HAMMOND, J. African education. NADA 35 (1958), pp. 12-15.

20,333 HARMON, R. J. An experiment in testing aural perception in English with a group of Shona-speaking African pupils. RHODES-LIV. J. 34 (1964), pp. 36-43.

20,334 IRVINE, S. H. Education for citizenship. NADA 38 (1961), pp. 74-83.

20,335 IRVINE, S. H. Some practical and theoretical problems of general ability testing at the African standard six level in Southern Rhodesia. EAISR Jan. (1963), pp. 1-11.

20,336 KEIGWIN, H. S. Native development. NADA 1 (1923), pp. 10-17.

20,337 LISULO, B. J. W. The Barotse National School. NADA 5 (1927), pp. 54-56.

20,338 LLOYD, B. W. Early history of Domboshawa School; period 1920-1939. NADA 39 (1962), pp. 4-13.

20,339 NGONYAMA, S. The education of the African girl. NADA 31 (1954), pp. 57-58.

20,340 P., E. T. Native labour. NADA 4 (1926), pp. 122-123.

20,341 PARKER, F. African community development and education in Southern Rhodesia, 1920-1935. INT. REV. MISSIONS 51 (1962), pp. 335-347.

20,342 PHILLIPS, G. The great experiment begins. AFR. AFFAIRS 56 (1957), pp. 228-231.

20,343 POSSELT, F. W. T. Native education. NADA 16 (1939), pp. 99-106.

20,344 REGULUS. Native customs examination, 1952. NADA 30 (1953), pp. 26-34.

20,345 ROBERTS, H. M. Adult literacy workshops. WOMEN TODAY 6 (1965), pp. 73-76.

20,346 STUHARDT, J. G. Essay on native agricultural schools. NADA 6 (1928), pp. 109-113.

20,347 WILLIAMS, A. G. M. Msonneddi homecraft village. AFR. AFFAIRS 46 (1947), pp. 37-38.

20,348 African nurses in the Central African Federation. AFR. WOMEN 3 (1958-1960), pp. 11-12.

20,349 Educational needs of women in Rhodesia. WOMEN TODAY 6 (1965), pp. 104-105.

20,350 A Fairbridge Memorial College in Southern Rhodesia. J. AFR. SOC. 39 (1940), pp. 111-112.

20,351 Homecraft work in Southern Rhodesia. AFR. WOMEN 4 (1960), p. 13.

20,352 Mapolisa. NADA 9, no. 1 (1964), p. 69.

20,353 The rural women of Rhodesia. AFR. WOMEN 5 (1962), p. 16.

20,354 The task of education. NADA 31 (1954), pp. 97-98.

20,355 The third-class school. NADA 5 (1927), pp. 50-54.

Geography

20,356 ANDERSON, C. A. Development of water supplies in Native Reserves. NADA 3 (1925), pp. 74-77.

20,357 BASIKORO. Bike and hike touring in the Rhodesias. NADA 9, no. 2 (1965), pp. 73-77.

20,358 BERGHEGGE, F. Account of a journey in Central Africa. RHODESIANA 3 (1958), pp. 1-13.

20,359 CAPELL, A. E. Tales of the Makorrie-Korrie. NADA 21 (1944), pp. 38-40; 23 (1946), pp. 67-71.

20,360 CARBUTT, C. L. Reminiscences of a native commissioner. NADA 2 (1924), pp. 76-82; 17 (1940), pp. 54-60.

20,361 CARBUTT, C. L. Some more reminiscences of a native commissioner. NADA 4 (1926), pp. 77-80.

20,362 COLQUHOUN, A. R. Matabeleland. Description of the Mashonaland and Matabeleland plateau. ROYAL COL. INST. PR. 25 (1893-1894), pp. 45-103.

20,363 CRIPPS, H. Shangwa (drought). NADA 9 (1931), pp. 43-51.

20,364 CROXTON, A. H. Rhodesia's light railways. RHODESIANA 13 (1965), pp. 57-68.

20,365 DOMINUS. A hard day. NADA 9, no. 1 (1964), pp. 48-51.

20,366 FLOYD, B. N. Land apportionment in Southern Rhodesia. GEOG. REV. 52 (1962), pp. 566-582.

20,367 HOWLAND, R. C. The Mazoe patrol. RHODESIANA 8 (1963), pp. 16-31.

20,368 INKOMOYAHLABA. An historical tour. NADA 9, no. 2 (1965), pp. 61-69.

20,369 J., L. V. and C., C. C. In the country of the Mtukwa wa Chigodoro. NADA 9 (1931), pp. 31-32.

20,370 JENNINGS, A. C. Water supply development in native reserves. NADA 1 (1923), pp. 7-9.

20,371 JENNINGS, A. C. Water supplies in native reserves. NADA 2 (1924), pp. 32-33.

20,372 LIVINGSTONE, D. With David Livingstone to the Falls. AFR. AFFAIRS 54 (1955), pp. 306-311.

20,373 McADAM, J. Early birds in Central Africa. An account of flying activities in the Rhodesias during the years 1920 to 1922. RHODESIANA 13 (1965), pp. 38-53.

20,374 MARR, M. Kalahari memories. NADA 39 (1962), pp. 52-54.

20,375 "MATANDIDWALA". On trek. NADA 4 (1926), pp. 116-117.

20,376 McELLANDJ, F. H. Extracts from letters...an official in the N.E. Rhodesian Service of the British South African Company. J. AFR. SOC. 2 (1903), pp. 380-399.

20,377 MUROMBO. Old Bikita. NADA 40 (1963), pp. 113-115.

20,378 OLIVER, Sir H. F. The Zambesi in 1889. Reprinted from "The Navy." NYASA J. 14, no. 2 (1961), pp. 36-38.

20,379 POSSELT, F. W. T. The land of magic: the Nata river and Lake Makarikari. NADA 16 (1939), pp. 3-12.

20,380 POSSELT, F. W. T. The early days of Mashonaland and a visit to the Zimbabwe ruins. NADA 2 (1924), pp. 70-76.

20,381 PRESCOTT, J. R. V. Population distribution in Southern Rhodesia. GEOG. REV. 52 (1962), pp. 559-565.

20,382 RAWSON, H. D. Diary of a journey from Southampton to Salisbury, 1895. RHODESIANA 12 (1965), pp. 76-92.

20,383 SHROPSHIRE, D. W. T. A journey in Mashonaland. AFR. AFFAIRS 51 (1952), pp. 52-61.

20,384 SOUSA NEVES, A. DE. Geosyndines of the Zambezi river basin area. BSEM 144-145 (1965), pp. 237-252.

20,385 STUART, P. A. My Matabeleland experiences (1897-1903). NADA 19 (1942), pp. 60-72.

20,386 TAMAYI. A visit to the Vadoma Massif. NADA 36 (1959), pp. 52-57.

20,387 TAWSE-JOLLIE, E. Southern Rhodesia: a white man's country in the tropics. GEOG. REV. 17 (1927), pp. 89-106.

20,388 WOOD, R. A recent visit to Central Africa. AFR. AFFAIRS 57 (1958), pp. 20-28.

20,389 The Chindamora Reserve. NADA 5 (1927), p. 49.

20,390 Native nomenclature: series no. 1. NADA 12 (1934), pp. 55-59; 25 (1948), pp. 76-77; 26 (1949), pp. 72-74; 27 (1950), pp. 76-77.

20,391 Wedza-Rusapi bridge. NADA 23 (1946), pp. 50-59.

Government. Politics. Administration

20,392 ALPORT, Lord. Britain in Central Africa in the sixties. AFR. AFFAIRS 62 (1963), pp. 300-308.

20,393 BARTON, F. Rhodesian liberals in dilemma. The roads to union. AFR. SOUTH 3, no. 2 (1959), pp. 61-64.

20,394 BAXTER, G. H. and HODGENS, P. W. The constitutional status of the Federation of Rhodesia and Nyasaland. INTERNAT. AFFAIRS 33 (1957), pp. 442-452.

20,395 BAZELEY, W. S. First principles of native policy. NADA 13 (1935), pp. 47-51.

20,396 BEIT, Sir A. The future of the Rhodesias. AFR. AFFAIRS 44 (1945), pp. 37-42.

20,397 BRADFORD, J. E. S. Survey and registration of African land units in Southern Rhodesia. J. AFR. ADM. 7 (1955), pp. 165-170.

20,398 BRANNEY, L. Second Report of the Select Committee of the Southern Rhodesia Legislative Assembly on the Resettlement of Natives, 1960. J. AFR. ADM. 13 (1961), pp. 184-187.

20,399 BRODERICK, G. E. P. Some suggestions towards the development of a native policy in Southern Rhodesia. NADA 17 (1940), pp. 77-81.

20,400 C., A. J. La Fédération des Rhodésies et du Nyassaland à l'heure de la vérité. ET. CONG. 2, no. 5 (1962), pp. 33-41.

20,401 C., J. La Fédération centre-africaine devant la Chambre des Lords. ZAIRE 6 (1952), pp. 863-864.

20,402 CALLAGHAN, J. Central Africa: federation and the British Labour Party. AFR. SOUTH 2, no. 4 (1958), pp. 62-67.

20,403 CAMPBELL, E. R. Rhodesia—its past and its present. AFR. AFFAIRS 64 (1965), pp. 182-190.

20,404 CANHAM, P. H. Inside Rhodesia. CONTEMP. REV. 207 (1965), pp. 179-185.

20,405 CASTLE, B. Labour and Central Africa. AFR. SOUTH 3, no. 3 (1959), pp. 84-93.

20,406 CHILD, H. F. Policy. NADA 8 (1930), pp. 70-74.

20,407 CREECH JONES, A. Central Africa. II. The challenge of federation. AFR. SOUTH 2, no. 1 (1957), pp. 73-83.

20,408 CRIPPS, A. S. African land tenure (a plea for tolerance). NADA 4 (1926), pp. 96-101.

20,409 CRIPPS, A. S. A difficult and delicate operation. NADA 2 (1924), pp. 98-106.

20,410 CRIPPS, A. S. The native problem in South Africa: the Reserves Commission in S. Rhodesia. CONTEMP. REV. 117 (1920), pp. 553-556.

20,411 CRIPPS, A. S. Native Rhodesia's now or never. NADA 1 (1923), pp. 44-51.

20,412 DUMBUTSHENA, E. Southern Rhodesia explodes. AFR. SOUTH 5, no. 1 (1960), pp. 63-67.

20,413 FULLER, C. C. Notes on (a) education and (b) land. NADA 1 (1923), pp. 28-29.

20,414 GOODENOUGH, K. M. Rhodesia looks ahead. AFR. AFFAIRS 46 (1947), pp. 29-37.

20,415 GOODENOUGH, K. M. Southern Rhodesia revisited. AFR. AFFAIRS 48 (1949), pp. 318-323.

20,416 GORE-BROWNE, S. The federated states of Rhodesia. J. AFR. SOC. 36 (1937), pp. 2-7.

20,417 GORE-BROWNE, S. Southern Rhodesia's native affairs report, 1936. J. AFR. SOC. 36 (1937), pp. 490-492.

20,418 GRAY, A. Federal affairs. AFR. AFFAIRS 57 (1958), pp. 255-257.

20,419 GRAY, A. Federal status. AFR. AFFAIRS 56 (1957), pp. 188-190.

20,420 GRAY, A. Federation and its foes. AFR. AFFAIRS 58 (1959), pp. 199-201.

20,421 GRAY, A. Federation in flux. AFR. AFFAIRS 60 (1961), pp. 10-17.

20,422 GRAY, A. Future of Federation. AFR. AFFAIRS 61 (1962), pp. 293-296.

20,423 GRAY, A. Lord Malvern retires. AFR. AFFAIRS 56 (1957), p. 19.

20,424 GRAY, A. Mr. Todd steps down. AFR. AFFAIRS 57 (1958), p. 95.

20,425 GRAY, A. Monckton Commission. AFR. AFFAIRS 59 (1960), pp. 6-7.

20,426 GRAY, A. Queen Mother in Rhodesia. AFR. AFFAIRS 56 (1957), pp. 249-250.

20,427 GRAY, A. Rhodesian affairs. AFR. AFFAIRS 59 (1960), pp. 99-100.

20,428 GRAY, A. Rhodesian changes. AFR. AFFAIRS 57 (1958), pp. 93-94.

20,429 GRAY, A. Rhodesian commission. AFR. AFFAIRS 58 (1959), pp. 279-284.

20,430 GRAY, A. Rhodesian [constitutional] developments. AFR. AFFAIRS 60 (1961), pp. 136-139.

20,431 GRAY, A. Rhodesian election. AFR. AFFAIRS 58 (1959), pp. 6-7.

20,432 GRAY, A. Rhodesian events. AFR. AFFAIRS 60 (1961), pp. 480-491.

20,433 GRAY, A. Rhodesian franchise. AFR. AFFAIRS 56 (1957), pp. 256-257.

20,434 GRAY, A. The Rhodesian scene. AFR. AFFAIRS 57 (1958), pp. 170-172.

20,435 GRAY, A. Rhodesia's future. AFR. AFFAIRS 61 (1962), pp. 185-186.

20,436 GRAY, A. Royal visit (Queen Elizabeth the Queen Mother in Central Africa). AFR. AFFAIRS 59 (1960), pp. 180-181.

20,437 GRAY, A. Southern Rhodesia debate at U.N. AFR. AFFAIRS 61 (1962), pp. 284-287.

20,438 GRAY, A. Status of Rhodesia. AFR. AFFAIRS 55 (1956), pp. 262-265.

20,439 GRUNDY, D. The doctor's discards. AFR. SOUTH 5, no. 1 (1960), pp. 73-76.

20,440 GRUNDY, D. An interview with Todd. AFR. SOUTH 3, no. 4 (1959), pp. 70-76.

20,441 GRUNDY, D. Salisbury and London. AFR. SOUTH 4, no. 3 (1960), pp. 91-94.

20,442 GRUNDY, D. Salisbury diary. AFR. SOUTH 4, no. 1 (1959), pp. 76-80.

20,443 HERBERT, R. L. D. The Native Affairs Department: a few facts. NADA 22 (1945), pp. 65-68.

20,444 HLAZO, T. J. Native councils. NADA 4 (1926), pp. 94-95.

20,445 HOLLAND, F. C. The prospects of Rhodesia. CONTEMP. REV. 72 (1897), pp. 470-481.

20,446 HOMBARUME. Sidelights on native administration. NADA 19 (1942), pp. 32-34.

20,447 HOWMAN, R. African leadership in transition—an outline. J. AFR. ADM. 8 (1956), pp. 117-126.

20,448 HOWMAN, R. African local government in Southern Rhodesia. J. AFR. ADM. 11 (1959), pp. 132-138.

20,449 HOWMAN, R. The Native Affairs Department and the African. NADA 31 (1954), pp. 42-49.

20,450 HUGGINS, Sir G. Southern Rhodesia. AFR. AFFAIRS 51 (1952), pp. 143-149.

20,451 HULLEY, F. A plea for dissemination of policy. NADA 4 (1926), pp. 124-125.

20,452 JACKSON, H. M. G. Indirect rule in Southern Rhodesia. NADA 3 (1925), pp. 57-58.

20,453 KEATLEY, P. The guilty partner. AFR. SOUTH 6 (1961), pp. 45-55.

20,454 KEATLEY, P. Monckton and Cleopatra. AFR. SOUTH 5, no. 2 (1961), pp. 63-71.

20,455 LEMKIN, J. A Tory looks at federation. AFR. SOUTH 4, no. 4 (1960), pp. 69-74.

20,456 LEWANIKA, G. The problems of a multi-racial society in Central Africa. AFR. AFFAIRS 57 (1958), pp. 279-289.

20,457 LEYS, C. Natives no longer kill twins. AFR. SOUTH 3, no. 3 (1959), pp. 77-83.

20,458 LLEWELLIN, Lord. Some facts about the Federation of Rhodesia and Nyasaland. AFR. AFFAIRS 55 (1956), pp. 266-272.

20,459 LUTHERA, V. P. Is Southern Rhodesia self-governing? AFR. QUART. 1, no. iv (1962), pp. 14-27.

20,460 McWILLIAM, M. D. The Central African liberals. AFR. SOUTH 3, no. 1 (1958), pp. 83-86.

20,461 MAGUIRE, R. Rhodesia. J. AFR. SOC. 22 (1923), pp. 81-95.

20,462 MAKONE, M. An iota of difference. AFR. SOUTH 3, no. 4 (1959), pp. 62-63.

20,463 MASON, P. Partnership in Central Africa. INTERNAT. AFFAIRS 33 (1957), pp. 154-164, 310-318.

20,464 MASON, P. Prospects and progress in the Federation of Rhodesia and Nyasaland. AFR. AFFAIRS 61 (1962), pp. 17-28.

20,465 MORKEL, E. R. R. Native administration and some customs and beliefs. NADA 26 (1949), pp. 39-44.

20,466 MPONGO, D. S. Issues before Southern Rhodesia. AFRO-ASIAN AND W. AFF. 2 (1965), pp. 61-65.

20,467 MTEPUKA, E. M. Central African Federation. (1) The attack. AFR. SOUTH 1, no. 4 (1957), pp. 73-81.

20,468 NKOMO, J. The case for majority rule in Southern Rhodesia. AFR. QUART. 4, no. ii (1964), pp. 90-101.

20,469 NKOMO, J. The crucible of privilege: Southern Rhodesia. AFR. SOUTH 3, no. 4 (1959), pp. 57-61.

20,470 PAGET, E. F. Native policy in Southern Rhodesia. RACE RELATIONS 12 (1945), pp. 44-46.

20,471 PATTERSON, T. T. The role of the Ministry of Local Government in Southern Rhodesia. J. LOCAL ADM. OV. 2 (1963), pp. 31-39.

20,472 POWYS-JONES, L. The native purchase areas of Southern Rhodesia. J. AFR. ADM. 7 (1955), pp. 20-26.

20,473 RANGER, T. Devlin in Southern Rhodesia. AFR. SOUTH 4, no. 2 (1960), pp. 67-72.

20,474 REED, J. The Salisbury talks. AFR. SOUTH 5, no. 3 (1961), pp. 56-61.

20,475 RENNIE, Sir G. The first year of federation. AFR. AFFAIRS 54 (1955), pp. 18-27.

20,476 RICHARDSON, C. B. Southern Rhodesia elects. AFR. SOUTH 3, no. 1 (1958), pp. 87-94.

20,477 ROBINSON, A. E. P. 1961, the year of decision in Rhodesia and Nyasaland. AFR. AFFAIRS 60 (1961), pp. 400-409.

20,478 ROGERS, C. A. The organization of political attitudes in Southern Rhodesia. RHODES-LIV. J. 25 (1959), pp. 1-19.

20,479 SANGER, C. A long time dying: Central African Federation. AFR. SOUTH 6 (1961), pp. 39-44.

20,480 SHAMUYARIRA, N. M. The coming showdown in Central Africa. FOREIGN AFFAIRS 39 (1960-1961), pp. 291-298.

20,481 SHAW, S. The Rhodesias and Nyasaland. CONTEMP. REV. 182 (1952), pp. 151-155.

20,482 SMITH, I. D. Southern Rhodesia and its future. AFR. AFFAIRS 63 (1964), pp. 13-22.

20,483 SOMERVILLE, J. J. B. The Central African Federation. INTERNAT. AFFAIRS 39 (1963), pp. 386-402.

20,484 STONEHOUSE, J. A Central African report. AFR. SOUTH 4, no. 1 (1959), pp. 81-86.

20,485 SWANZY, H. Southern Rhodesian native policy. AFR. AFFAIRS 46 (1947), pp. 183-184.

20,486 THOMSON, J. The developing federation and partnership. How is it progressing? AFR. AFFAIRS 57 (1958), pp. 266-278.

20,487 TODD, R. S. G. The only turning. AFR. SOUTH 5, no. 1 (1960), pp. 68-72.

20,488 USBORNE, M. The Africanisation of the public services in Northern Rhodesia and Nyasaland. CIVILISATIONS 11 (1961), pp. 39-48; French summary, pp. 49-51.

20,489 VAMBE, L. C. An African looks at federation. AFR. AFFAIRS 58 (1959), pp. 285-292.

20,490 WATSON, G. C. Southern Rhodesia. CONTEMP. REV. 184 (1953), pp. 23-27.

20,491 WELENSKY, R. Toward federation in Central Africa. FOREIGN AFFAIRS 31 (1952-1953), pp. 142-149.

20,492 WHITEHEAD, Sir E. Southern Rhodesia. INTERNAT. AFFAIRS 36 (1960), pp. 188-196.

20,493 WILSON, N. H. The development of native resources: one phase of native policy for Southern Rhodesia. NADA 1 (1923), pp. 86-94.

20,494 WILSON, N. H. Native political movements in Southern Rhodesia. NADA 1 (1923), pp. 17-19.

20,495 Central African council. AFR. AFFAIRS 44 (1945), p. 3; 45 (1946), p. 3.

20,496 Un Dominion des Rhodésies? ZAIRE 3 (1949), pp. 453-454.

20,497 Extracts from the report of the secretary for internal affairs and chief native commissioner for the year 1962, 1963. NADA 9, no. 1 (1964), pp. 7-13; 9, no. 2 (1965), pp. 21-27.

20,498 The Information Services Branch, Division of Native Affairs, Southern Rhodesia. NADA 37 (1960), pp. 56-65.

20,499 Hypocrisie en Afrique centrale. PRESENCE AFR. N.S. 40 (1962), pp. 168-172.

20,500 Native Affairs annual report, 1961. NADA 40 (1963), pp. 91-104.

20,501 Pour qui sonne le glas en Afrique centrale? PRESENCE AFR. N.S. 45 (1963), pp. 217-218.

20,502 Le premier parlement d'Afrique centrale. ZAIRE 8 (1954), p. 417.

20,503 En Rhodésie du Sud, après le referendum. ZAIRE 7 (1953), p. 727.

See also 15995, 16014, 16016, 16032.

History

20,504 ABRAHAM, D. D. The Monomotapa dynasty. NADA 36 (1959), pp. 59-84.

20,505 ABRAHAM, D. P. Maramuca: an exercise in the combined use of Portuguese records and oral tradition. J. AFR. HIST. 2 (1961), pp. 211-225.

20,506 ABRAHAM, D. P. The principality of Maungwe: its history and traditions. NADA 28 (1951), pp. 56-83.

20,507 ALVORD, E. D. The great hunger. NADA 6 (1928), pp. 35-43.

20,508 B., E. H. Notes on the Matebele occupation of Southern Rhodesia. NADA 13 (1935), pp. 14-17.

20,509 BAKER, R. H. The Mutasa and Makoni dynasties. NADA 2 (1924), pp. 85-87.

20,510 BAXTER, T. W. The National Archives. NYASA J. 14, no. 1 (1961), pp. 50-59.

20,511 BAXTER, T. W. The preservation of archives with particular reference to Central Africa. RHODES-LIV. J. 8 (1949), pp. 57-66.

20,512 BRENDON, N. J. Chiuzingu. NADA 36 (1959), pp. 19-25.

20,513 BRODERICK, G. E. P. Some notes [on the chiefs of Hunyani]. NADA 16 (1939), pp. 106-112.

20,514 CARBUTT, C. L. A brief account of the rise and fall of the Matabele. NADA 25 (1948), pp. 38-44.

20,515 CARNEGIE, W. A. Brief notes on Lobengula and his people. NADA 11 (1933), pp. 13-22.

20,516 CHANCELLOR, J. Progress and development of Southern Rhodesia. J. AFR. SOC. 28 (1929), pp. 149-154.

20,517 CHIDZIWA, J. History of the Vashawasha. NADA 9, no. 1 (1964), pp. 16-33.

20,518 COLEY, D. M. The fate of the last Bashankwe chief. NADA 5 (1927), pp. 65-66.

20,519 CRIPPS, A. S. Native interests in Southern Rhodesia and the renewal of the Rhodesian charter. CONTEMP. REV. 106 (1914), pp. 537-544.

20,520 CRIPPS, H. Some reminiscences of life on an outstation in S. Rhodesia. NADA 9, no. 2 (1965), pp. 36-39.

20,521 CRIPPS, L. The Umtasa Treaty: a study in empire building and other things. NADA 11 (1933), pp. 91-95.

20,522 CRIPPS, M. Umtali during the rebellion: 1896. RHODESIANA 9 (1963), pp. 52-55.

20,523 DART, R. A. The earlier stages of Indian transoceanic traffic. NADA 34 (1957), pp. 95-115.

20,524 DAVIES, C. Odds and ends: things observed and things heard round the fire. NADA 17 (1940), pp. 26-28.

20,525 DEYO, M. History of the Mutambara tribe. NADA 32 (1955), pp. 55-64.

20,526 DICKINSON, R. W. Sofala. RHODESIANA 10 (1964), pp. 45-53.

20,527 DIZA. The death of Mandevana (H. H. Ruping). NADA 9, no. 1 (1964), pp. 34-36.

20,528 DUNCAN, J. R. Graves, unmarked, uncared for and unknown. NADA 36 (1959), p. 129.

20,529 DUNCAN, J. R. The story of Mugodi Diamond, a Swazi. NADA 36 (1959), pp. 49-51.

20,530 DUNCAN, J. R. The story of Simba Jim. NADA 35 (1958), pp. 99-103.

20,531 E., B. M. and O'MAHONEY, K. E. The Southern Column's flight at Singuesi, 2nd. November, 1893. RHODESIANA 9 (1963), pp. 28-36.

20,532 EDWARDS, J. A. Colquhoun in Mashonaland: a portrait of failure. RHODESIANA 9 (1963), pp. 1-17.

20,533 EDWARDS, J. A. The Lomagundi district; an historical sketch. RHODESIANA 7 (1962), pp. 1-21.

20,534 EDWARDS, W. Memories of the '96 rebellion. NADA 1 (1923), pp. 20-27.

20,535 EDWARDS, W. The Wanoe: a short historical sketch. NADA 4 (1926), pp. 13-28.

20,536 FOX, H. W. Rhodesia and the war. J. AFR. SOC. 14 (1914-1915), pp. 345-354.

20,537 FRANKLIN, H. Nyaningwe: notes on the Chibi family. NADA 6 (1928), pp. 80-87.

20,538 FRANKLIN, H. The war of the Tell-Tale between chiefs Makoni and Mtasa. NADA 15 (1938), pp. 39-40.

20,539 G., N. Magango Hutari. NADA 11 (1933), pp. 29-31.

20,540 GAMBO, F. Some true history about the royal house of the Gambos. NADA 39 (1962), pp. 46-51.

20,541 GARLAKE, P. S. Pioneer forts in Rhodesia. RHODESIANA 12 (1965), pp. 37-62.

20,542 GLOVER, L. S. Memories of the Mashonaland mounted police, 1896-97. RHODESIANA 11 (1964), pp. 37-48.

20,543 GWATI, C. Native history of Salisbury. NADA 16 (1939), pp. 17-19.

20,544 HAWKIN, R. C. Rhodesia. CONTEMP. REV. 104 (1913), pp. 183-191.

20,545 HICK, E. Black ivory: a tale of the slave-trade. NADA 5 (1927), pp. 14-21.

20,546 HICKMAN, A. S. The Mashonaland Irish. RHODESIANA 5 (1960), pp. 1-6.

20,547 HICKMAN, A. S. Norton district in the Mashona rebellion. RHODESIANA 3 (1958), pp. 14-28.

20,548 HICKMAN, A. S. The siege of the Abercorn store. RHODESIANA 9 (1963), pp. 18-27.

20,549 HICKMAN, A. S. Some notes on police pioneer doctors and others. RHODESIANA 2 (1957), pp. 3-15.

20,550 HOLE, H. M. Pioneer days in Southern Rhodesia. J. AFR. SOC. 35 (1936), pp. 37-47.

20,551 HONYERA. The story of the Masunda headmanship. NADA 9, no. 1 (1964), pp. 55-59.

20,552 HOSTE, H. F. Rhodesia in 1890. RHODESIANA 12 (1965), pp. 1-26.

20,553 HOWLAND, R. C. The Market Hall: Salisbury's oldest building. RHODESIANA 9 (1963), pp. 37-43.

20,554 HOWLAND, R. C. Salisbury: old and new contrasted in photographs. RHODESIANA 11 (1964), pp. 50-55.

20,555 HOWMAN, E. G. and STANLEY, J. H. The hand of glory. NADA 6 (1928), pp. 32-34.

20,556 HOWMAN, R. The effects of history on an African. RHODESIANA 2 (1957), pp. 1-2.

20,557 JACKSON, H. M. G. A Boer invasion of Rhodesia. NADA 2 (1924), pp. 58-60.

20,558 JACKSON, H. M. G. Notes on Chiefs Gambo and Sikombo. NADA 3 (1925), pp. 18-19.

20,559 JACKSON, H. M. G. A sketch of Lobengula. NADA 10 (1932), pp. 39-44.

20,560 JACKSON, S. N. G. The first visit of the Mandebele to Rhodesia. NADA 5 (1927), p. 21.

20,561 JACKSON, S. N. G. Reminiscences of the 1896 rebellion. NADA 5 (1927), pp. 61-64.

20,562 JOHNSON, F. Rhodesia: its present and future. ROYAL COL. INST. PR. 33 (1901-1902), pp. 4-33.

20,563 KAPLAN, M. Their Rhodesia: a Transition special report. TRANSITION 23 (1965), pp. 33-43.

20,564 KENDAL, J. Getting across [Jesuit missionaries in Matabeleland]. NADA 15 (1938), pp. 40-43.

20,565 KENDAL, J. King and people. NADA 10 (1932), pp. 94-98.

20,566 LEWIS, D. G. The battle at Zwangendaba. NADA 33 (1956), pp. 51-52.

20,567 LEWIS, D. G. Lobengula's regiments: recruiting and Lobolo. NADA 33 (1956), p. 5.

20,568 LEWIS, D. G. Nkulumana, Umta Ka Umziligazi. NADA 33 (1956), pp. 11-12.

20,569 LEWIS, D. G. The Shangani fight. NADA 12 (1934), pp. 82-83.

20,570 LEWIS, M. B. Mrs. Mary Blackwood Lewis's letters about Mashonaland, 1897-1901. RHODESIANA 5 (1960), pp. 14-53.

20,571 LISULO, B. J. W. The history of the Barotse nation. NADA 5 (1927), pp. 81-84.

20,572 LLOYD, E. M. Mbava. NADA 3 (1925), pp. 62-64.

20,573 MARCONNES, F. The Rozvis or Destroyers. NADA 11 (1933), pp. 72-90.

20,574 MARCONNES, F. The two East African Sofalas and King Solomon's Ophir. NADA 13 (1935), pp. 59-74.

20,575 MAUND, E. A. Mashonaland and its development. ROYAL COL. INST. PR. 23 (1891-1892), pp. 248-270.

20,576 MBABAZANE. Luveve. NADA 14 (1938), pp. 37-38.

20,577 "MBIZO". Mtikana ka Mafu, Induna of the Godhlwayo Section during Lobengula's reign. NADA 4 (1926), pp. 53-57.

20,578 MBOFANA, P. W. G. The capture of my grandmother by the Matabeles. NADA 22 (1945), pp. 60-63.

20,579 MERWE, D. J. VAN DER. Some history of the Vakaranga in Gutu reserve. NADA 14 (1936-1937), pp. 71-74.

20,580 MHLAHLO and WHITNEY, E. C. P. Major Wilson's last stand on the Shangani river, 1896. NADA 13 (1935), pp. 45-47.

20,581 MHLANGA, W. The story of Ngwaqazi. (2) The history of the Amatshangana. NADA 25 (1948), pp. 70-73.

20,582 MILLER, E. H. Rhodesia and its resources. ROYAL COL. INST. PR. 38 (1906-1907), pp. 124-138.

20,583 MILLS, M. G. With the R.A.R. in Arakan. NADA 26 (1949), pp. 22-26.

20,584 MUHLANGA, S. and LLOYD, E. M. In the early days. NADA 4 (1926), pp. 107-110.

20,585 MUHLANGA, S. and LLOYD, E. M. Mbava and others. NADA 4 (1926), pp. 91-93.

20,586 NCUBE, R. M. M. The true story re Chaminuka and Lobengula. NADA 39 (1962), pp. 59-67.

20,587 NEUK, D. Dumbghe. NADA 17 (1940), pp. 85-88.

20,588 NICOLLE, W. H. H. Tribes in the Zambesi valley. NADA 36 (1959), pp. 11-15.

20,589 O'KEEFFE, S. M. L. Southern Rhodesia's war effort. J. AFR. SOC. 39 (1940), pp. 211-215.

20,590 PAQUET, J. A propos de deux ouvrages récents sur l'histoire de l'occupation européenne de la Rhodésie. ZAIRE 14 (1960), pp. 239-249.

20,591 PARKER, S. C. What's in a name. NADA 11 (1933), pp. 121-122.

20,592 PITOUT, J. A. The arrival of the Mandebele in S. Rhodesia as told by Siatsha. NADA 30 (1953), pp. 57-58.

20,593 PITOUT, J. A. Lobengula's flight and the Shangani battle. NADA 40 (1963), pp. 69-73.

20,594 POLLETT, H. The Mazoe patrol. RHODESIANA 2 (1957), pp. 29-38.

20,595 POSSELT, F. W. T. Marondera. NADA 5 (1927), pp. 47-48.

20,596 POSSELT, F. W. T. Nkulumana. The disputed succession. A chapter of Amandebele history. NADA 1 (1923), pp. 29-42.

20,597 POSSELT, H. The rebellion of 1896 and the relief charter. NADA 8 (1930), pp. 79-84.

20,598 POSSELT, W. The early days of Mashonaland and a visit to the Zimbabwe ruins. NADA 24 (1947), pp. 34-40.

20,599 RANGER, T. The recent history of Central Africa. J. COMM. POL. STUD. 3 (1965), pp. 148-152.

20,600 REA, W. F. [Gonçalo da Silveira.] RHODESIANA 6 (1961), pp. 1-40.

20,601 REA, W. F. Rhodesian pioneer. RHODESIANA 5 (1960), pp. 54-59.

20,602 REID, R. E. The capture of Chief Makoni. NADA 32 (1955), pp. 52-53.

20,603 REYNOLDS, R. [ed.] The British South Africa Company's central settlement farm, Marandellas, 1907-1910; from the papers of H. K. Scorror. RHODESIANA 10 (1964), pp. 1-16.

20,604 ROBINSON, K. R. A history of the Bikita district. NADA 34 (1957), pp. 75-87.

20,605 SAWANHU, J. The Waharawa history. NADA 3 (1925), pp. 59-62.

20,606 SCHOFIELD, J. F. The ancient workings of South-East Africa. NADA 3 (1925), pp. 5-12.

20,607 SEED, J. H. A glimpse of native history; the Vashawasha. NADA 14 (1936-1937), pp. 5-16.

20,608 SELOUS, F. C. The history of the Matabele and the cause and effect of the Matabele war. ROYAL COL. INST. PR. 25 (1893-1894), pp. 251-290.

20,609 SHROPSHIRE, D. Native development in Southern Rhodesia. J. AFR. SOC. 32 (1933), pp. 409-423.

20,610 SICARD, H. VON. The ancient Sabi-Zimbabwe trade route. NADA 40 (1963), pp. 6-16.

20,611 SICARD, H. VON. The derivation of the name Mashona. AFR. STUD. 9 (1950), pp.138-143.

20,612 SICARD, H. VON. The origin of some of the tribes in the Belingwe Reserve. NADA 25 (1948), pp. 93-104; 27 (1950), pp. 7-19; 28 (1951), pp. 5-25; 29 (1952), pp. 43-64; 30 (1953), pp. 64-71; 32 (1955), pp. 77-92.

20,613 SICARD, H. VON. Places of ancient occupation in chief Negove's country. NADA 33 (1956), pp. 32-50; 34 (1957), pp. 8-30.

20,614 SICARD, H. VON. Rhodesian sidelights on Bechuanaland history. NADA 31 (1954), pp. 67-94.

20,615 SICARD, H. VON. Tentative chronological tables. NADA 23 (1946), pp. 30-35.

20,616 SIGOLA, S. How Lobengula came to rule the Matabele. NADA 36 (1959), pp. 87-91.

20,617 SMART, H. W. Early days in Bulawayo (1896-1900). RHODESIANA 7 (1962), pp. 22-33.

20,618 SMITH, H. S. Monomotapas—a king-list. NADA 35 (1958), pp. 84-86.

20,619 SPEARES, J. How Chivero came to take the Chidao of Gwenzi. NADA 6 (1928), p. 114.

20,620 SUMMERS, R. The military doctrine of the Matabele. NADA 32 (1955), pp. 7-15.

20,621 SURRIDGE, F. H. Matabeleland and Mashonaland. ROYAL COL. INST. PR. 22 (1890-1891), pp. 305-331.

20,622 TABLER, E. C. Impressions of Hendrik's Pass. RHODESIANA 5 (1960), pp. 7-13.

20,623 TABLER, E. C. Sir Theophilus Shepstone and the Matabele succession, 1868-1870. RHODESIANA 9 (1963), pp. 56-57.

20,624 TAGWIREYI, J. H. Origin of the Vamari clan. NADA 27 (1950), pp. 63-66.

20,625 TAPSON, R. R. Some notes on the Mrozwi occupation of the Sebungwe District. NADA 21 (1944), pp. 29-32.

20,626 TAYLOR, C. T. C. Lomagundi. RHODESIANA 10 (1964), pp. 17-44.

20,627 TAYLOR, G. A. The Matabele head ring (Isidhlodhlo) and some fragments of history. NADA 16 (1939), pp. 49-55.

20,628 TENDENGUWO. The Shona rebellion in the Mrewa district. NADA 9, no. 1 (1964), pp. 4-6.

20,629 THOKOZANE, J. A short history of Chief Chipunza. NADA 9, no. 2 (1965), pp. 59-60.

20,630 TIZIRAI, P. The story of the Chilimanzi people. NADA 26 (1949), pp. 36-38.

20,631 TREDGOLD, Sir R. Address on the occasion of the unveiling of the memorial at the Mangwe Pass on the 18th July, 1954. RHODESIANA 1 (1956), pp. 1-6.

20,632 W., A. The expulsion of Nkulumana. NADA 13 (1935), pp. 93-95.

20,633 WALLIS, J. P. R. The story of Central African Archives. AFR. AFFAIRS 47 (1948), pp. 238-242.

20,634 WARHURST, P. R. Extracts from the South African letters and diaries of Victor Morier, 1890-1891. RHODESIANA 13 (1965), pp. 1-37.

20,635 WOODS, G. G. B. Matabele history and customs. NADA 7 (1929), pp. 43-49.

20,636 Another link with the past is broken. NADA 9, no. 2 (1965), p. 97.

20,637 Before the Charter Laager, 1896. NADA 13 (1935), pp. 95-100.

20,638 Diaries of the Jesuit Missionaries at Bulawayo 1879-1881; translated from the French by M. Lloyd. RHODESIANA 4 (1959), pp. 7-84.

20,639 L'exposition de Bulawayo. ZAIRE 7 (1953), p. 729.

20,640 Historical Association of Rhodesia and Nyasaland. NADA 9, no. 1 (1964), p. 69.

20,641 The jubilee of Southern Rhodesia. J. AFR. SOC. 40 (1941), pp. 5-7.

20,642 The Kutama lineage. NADA 39 (1962), pp. 55-58.

20,643 Laager and Garrison, 1896. NADA 17 (1940), pp. 38-49.

20,644 Some happenings of 1896. NADA 15 (1938), pp. 29-37.

Language. Literature

Language

20,645 BAKER, R. H. Portuguese words in Chimanyika. NADA 24 (1947), pp. 62-64.

20,646 BARNES, B. H. A campaign against Babel: the unification of the dialects of Mashonaland. NADA 6 (1928), pp. 45-50.

20,647 BARNES, B. H. The progress of the new Shona orthography. NADA 12 (1934), pp. 30-35.

20,648 BULLOCK, C. The birth of a language. NADA 9 (1931), pp. 104-107.

20,649 CARTER, H. Stabilization in the Manyika dialect of the Shona group. AFRICA 26 (1956), pp. 398-404.

20,650 CRIPWELL, H. A. SiNtu sounds and symbols. NADA 6 (1928), pp. 51-53.

20,651 DOKE, C. M. The earliest vocabulary from Mashonaland. NADA 11 (1933), pp. 67-71.

20,652 FORTUNE, G. A Rozi text with translation and notes. NADA 33 (1956), pp. 67-91.

20,653 FORTUNE, G. "To be" and "to have" in Shona. AFR. STUD. 9 (1950), pp. 86-91.

20,654 HANNAN, Father. Shona dictionary. NADA 35 (1958), pp. 18-38.

20,655 HANNAN, M. Learning Shona in the computer age. NADA 9, no. 2 (1965), pp. 3-5.

20,656 HUNT, N. A. Chizezuru as she is spoke. NADA 34 (1957), pp. 93-94.

20,657 HUNT, N. A. Some Karanga idiomatic phrases. NADA 28 (1951), pp. 52-55.

20,658 HUNT, N. A. Some notes on the naming of dogs in Chikaranga. NADA 29 (1952), pp. 67-73.

20,659 JACKSON, S. K. The names of the vashona. NADA 34 (1957), pp. 116-122.

20,660 KNAPPERT, J. Derivation and tone deflection in Cindau and some other Bantu languages. AFR. UND UB. 45 (1961-1962), pp. 169-189.

20,661 LEAVER, K. D. A plea for the unification of Sindebele. NADA 23 (1946), pp. 9-10.

20,662 LEAVER, K. D. Proverbs collected from the Amandebele. AFR. STUD. 5 (1946), pp. 136-139.

20,663 MALALA, S. N. Some recent trends in the development of the Ndebele language. NADA 35 (1958), pp. 6-11.

20,664 MORRIS, S. E. The origin of some Mashona names of chiefs and places. NADA 10 (1932), pp. 18-20.

20,665 ROBERTS, J. G. Chishona names. NADA 9 (1931), pp. 89-92.

20,666 ROBERTS, J. G. A note on names of mines and claims, principally in the Hartley district. NADA 37 (1960), pp. 102-104.

20,667 S., N. H. D. A theory regarding native mental reaction to the sound of native proper names. NADA 12 (1934), pp. 79-81.

20,668 SICARD, H. VON. The Hakata names. NADA 36 (1959), pp. 26-29.

20,669 STEVICK, E. W. Inflection of the Manyika verb. NADA 36 (1959), pp. 30-45.

20,670 TAYLOR, G. A. Primitive colour vision. NADA 1 (1923), pp. 69-72.

20,671 THOMPSON, W. L. A uniform phonetic alphabet for the native languages of Rhodesia. NADA 5 (1927), pp. 67-76.

20,672 TSHAKALISA and MBIZWO. Sindebele names and expressions used in farming. NADA 33 (1956), pp. 63-66.

20,673 WESTPHAL, E. The stative conjugation in Zulu, Sotho and Venda. AFR. STUD. 9 (1950), pp. 125-137.

20,674 WINTERBOTTOM, J. M. Some problems of the use of African vernaculars. RHODES-LIV. J. 7 (1949), pp. 67-74.

20,675 The problem of the Mashona dialects. NADA 5 (1927), pp. 77-78.

20,676 Schedules from the Central African broadcasting station. AFR. AFFAIRS 48 (1949), pp. 231-233.

20,677 The work of the Shona orthography committee. NADA 32 (1955), pp. 114-119.

Literature

20,678 ADAMS, G. Night duty: African hospital [a poem]. NADA 38 (1961), p. 21.

20,679 ALVORD, E. D. The trail of the baboon [a poem]. NADA 6 (1928), pp. 114-115.

20,680 BUNDII. How the seasons came to the valley [fiction]. NADA 18 (1941), pp. 49-51.

20,681 BUNDU. The history of Muroyindapikwa [fiction]. NADA 12 (1934), pp. 68-72.

20,682 CAMPBELL, A. C. Ithwaza: the young diviner [a poem]. NADA 9, no. 1 (1964), pp. 14-15.

20,683 CHIEZA, G. P. The history of Chieza and his red dangers [fiction]. NADA 18 (1941), pp. 52-68.

20,684 CHIMANGA, E. Rungano Rgwe Kondo ne njiwa [fiction]. NADA 15 (1938), pp. 69-70, 104-107; 16 (1939), pp. 33-36.

20,685 CHITEWHE, S. S. M. A tale related to me by my grandfather, Zinyongo Chitewhe [fiction]. NADA 25 (1948), pp. 52-57.

20,686 CHOTO, E. Rungano Rgwa Sekuru no Muzukuru [fiction]. NADA 16 (1939), pp. 55-57.

20,687 CRIPPS, A. S. Homage to J. W. Posselt, N.C. of Charter district (A.D. 1902-1933) [poetry]. NADA 11 (1933), pp. 90-91.

20,688 CRIPPS, H. Mapakatsine [fiction]. NADA 6 (1928), pp. 95-100.

20,689 DOMINUS. Khamba, the slayer [fiction]. NADA 38 (1961), pp. 36-37.

20,690 EDWARDS, W. Wanoe stories [fiction]. NADA 6 (1928), pp. 87-88.

20,691 FARQUHAR, J. H. Dipping day at Mutsago [fiction]. NADA 24 (1947), pp. 71-72.

20,692 HARTLEY, G. H. and RUSIKE, I. Rungano Rgwe Nerera Yakapiwa Gonzo Ne Tsindi [fiction]. NADA 17 (1940), pp. 50-52.

20,693 HARTLEY, G. H. and RUSIKE, I. Rungano Rgwe Tsuro No Murume Ne Makudo [fiction]. NADA 17 (1940), pp. 102-105.

20,694 HAWKEY, J. E. Mutero [fiction]. NADA 11 (1933), pp. 117-118.

20,695 HICK, E. The frozen puddle [fiction]. NADA 8 (1930), pp. 24-29; 18 (1941), pp. 69-73.

20,696 HICK, E. M'boi; a story retold [fiction]. NADA 9 (1931), pp. 84-88.

20,697 HICK, E. Pagan pipes [fiction]. NADA 11 (1933), pp. 7-12.

20,698 HICK, E. White magic: a tale of African life [fiction]. NADA 6 (1928), pp. 11-20.

20,699 HINDE, C. A. I remember...youthful pastimes [fiction]. NADA 10 (1932), pp. 99-107.

20,700 HOLDERNESS, R. Shumba ne Dendera (the lion and the bird) [fiction]. NADA 2 (1965), pp. 16-20.

20,701 JACKSON, H. M. G. Strictly official [fiction]. NADA 12 (1934), p. 54.

20,702 KABVUTA. The beer drink [fiction]. NADA 14 (1936-1937), pp. 45-46.

20,703 LALA. The fable of the cat [fiction]. NADA 25 (1948), p. 33.

20,704 LEWIS, D. G. Mlimo [fiction]. NADA 12 (1934), p. 84.

20,705 LEWIS, V. A. Tears [a poem]. NADA 10 (1932), pp. 35-36.

20,706 LITTNER, M. L. Shakespeare has come to Africa. CONTEMP. REV. 205 (1964), pp. 201-203.

20,707 MACKENZIE, W. F. Kakomwe Ka Chitemamtanda: a Wanoe analogy of Aladdin's lamp [fiction]. NADA 7 (1929), pp. 75-80.

20,708 MALIWA, S. and PARKER, S. C. Ingwenya le Nkuku [fiction]. NADA 12 (1934), pp. 20-22.

20,709 MUKWEREZA, E. Nhena, Mudiwa Wangu (Nhena my beloved) [a poem]. NADA 26 (1949), pp. 82-83.

20,710 MUNGATI, J. Rungano Rgwe Tezwara no Mukwasha Wake [fiction]. NADA 14 (1936-1937), pp. 75-76.

20,711 NICHOLLS, L. One proud son [fiction]. NADA 28 (1951), pp. 108-114.

20,712 POSSELT, F. W. T. and SPICER, N. H. D. Nofiswa—the king's favorite [fiction]. NADA 27 (1950), pp. 78-82.

20,713 R., C. F. Baboon and hare [fiction]. NADA 17 (1940), pp. 72-73.

20,714 R., C. F. The man, the hare and the lion: Munho, Shuro ne Shumba [fiction]. NADA 17 (1940), p. 71.

20,715 R., C. F. Two fables [1. Elephant, hippopotamus and hare. 2. The eagle and the rooster.] [fiction]. NADA 14 (1936-1937), pp. 47-48.

20,716 REYNOLDS, R. Take it easy, Sir Roy [a poem]. AFR. SOUTH 2, no. 3 (1958), pp. 67-68.

20,717 RGWATINYANYA, A. Rungano Rgwe Vanakomana Vaviri [fiction]. NADA 15 (1938), pp. 109-112.

20,718 TAYLOR, M. E. Mashona stories [fiction]. NADA 6 (1928), pp. 91-95.

20,719 TAYLOR, M. E. More Angoni stories [fiction]. NADA 5 (1927), pp. 39-41.

20,720 TSHAPARADZA, W. The double wise: African story [fiction]. NADA 24 (1947), pp. 81-93.

20,721 WILSON, A. The border murderer [fiction]. NADA 10 (1932), pp. 83-94.

20,722 WILSON, A. George's courts [fiction]. NADA 14 (1936-1937), pp. 91-94.

20,723 WILSON, A. His native hearth [fiction]. NADA 16 (1939), pp. 114-120.

20,724 Imbali Yenyoni Lensedhlu [fiction]. NADA 11 (1933), pp. 32-34.

20,725 Umpumpu Ka Ngumbati [fiction]. NADA 12 (1934), pp. 81-82.

20,726 Uplift in Bantuland [fiction]. NADA 8 (1930), pp. 48-59.

20,727 Uplift in Bantuland or Mambuya at home [fiction]. NADA 18 (1941), pp. 36-46.

Law

20,728 ADAM, M. A. Trial by jury in Southern Rhodesia. RNLJ 2 (1962), pp. 38-52.

20,729 ALLEN, C. J. Juries and lay magistrates. RNLJ 1 (1961), pp. 118-129.

20,730 BARON, L. S. Southern Rhodesia and the rule of law. J. INT. COMM. JURISTS 6 (1965), pp. 219-244.

20,731 BAZELEY, W. S. Manyika law and custom regarding inheritance of wives and property and the guardianship of children. NADA 7 (1929), pp. 110-112.

20,732 BULLOCK, C. Can a native make a will? Concepts of testate succession in native law. NADA 7 (1929), pp. 104-109.

20,733 CHILD, H. F. The history and extent of recognition of native law in Southern Rhodesia. NADA 40 (1963), pp. 29-45.

20,734 CHINYANDURA. The native oath. NADA 12 (1934), p. 53.

20,735 DEVINE, W. A. The habitual criminal. NADA 10 (1932), pp. 21-23.

20,736 DEVINE, W. A. Native marriage tangles. NADA 4 (1926), pp. 43-44.

20,737 EEKELAAR, J. M. The tort of intimidation. RLJ 4 (1964), pp. 119-132.

20,738 FYNN, J. W. L. Evidence of customs, etc. NADA 11 (1933), pp. 125-130; 15 (1938), pp. 88-97.

20,739 GARBETT, G. K. The Land Husbandry Act of Southern Rhodesia. AFR. AGRARIAN SYSTEMS, 1963, pp. 185-202.

20,740 GASSON, J. G. H. Cruelty as a ground of divorce in Southern Rhodesia. RNLJ 1 (1961), pp. 35-45; 2 (1962), pp. 28-37.

20,741 GOLDIN, B. Recent trends in income tax. RNLJ 1 (1961), pp. 84-90.

20,742 GRAY, A. U.K. supports Federal Bill. AFR. AFFAIRS 57 (1958), pp. 7-10.

20,743 HACKWILL, G. R. J. Southern Rhodesian native law: conflict of laws in relation to the guardianship of children after divorce. RNLJ 1 (1961), pp. 71-79.

20,744 HAWKIN, R. C. The laws and administration of Rhodesia. J. AFR. SOC. 13 (1913), pp. 45-50.

20,745 HEARN, J. M. N. The order to fire and the defence of superior orders. RNLJ 2 (1962), pp. 53-75.

20,746 HICK, E. Twin sacrifice. NADA 10 (1932), pp. 62-64.

20,747 HOFFMAN, H. J. Water rights in Southern Rhodesia. RNLJ 2 (1962), pp. 106-112; 3 (1963), pp. 27-73, 107-190.

20,748 HOLLEMAN, J. F. An anthropological approach to Bantu law; with special reference to Shona law. RHODES-LIV. J. 10 (1950), pp. 51-64.

20,749 HOLLEMAN, J. F. Hera court procedure. NADA 29 (1952), pp. 26-42.

20,750 HOLLEMAN, J. F. Indigenous administration of justice. NADA 32 (1955), pp. 41-47.

20,751 HOPE, W. A. Hearsay evidence in outline. RNLJ 1 (1961), pp. 130-139.

20,752 HOPE, W. A. Liability to third parties under comprehensive motor policies. RNLJ 2 (1962), pp. 153-173.

20,753 HORN, J. W. Commentary on part III of the Law and Order (Maintenance) Act [Chapter 39]. RLJ 4 (1964), pp. 14-68.

20,754 HORN, J. W. Discrediting one's own witness. RNLJ 1 (1961), pp. 80-83.

20,755 HOWMAN, E. G. Replies to some questions in the Native Customs Examinations of 1923. NADA 1 (1923), pp. 84-86.

20,756 HOWMAN, R. The Matri-estate. NADA 38 (1961), pp. 38-48.

20,757 HOWMAN, R. The significance of law for native administration in Africa. RHODES-LIV. J. 8 (1949), pp. 14-25.

20,758 HOWMAN, R. Trial by jury in Southern Rhodesia; an historical and sociological analysis of an institution. RHODES-LIV. J. 7 (1949), pp. 41-66.

20,759 HOWMAN, R. Witchcraft and the law. NADA 25 (1948), pp. 7-18.

20,760 JACKSON, H. M. G. Matela v. Mntogufa. NADA 1 (1923), pp. 5-6.

20,761 JACKSON, H. M. G. Notes on Matebele customary law. NADA 5 (1927), pp. 7-14.

20,762 JACKSON, H. M. G. Notes on Matebele customary law: inheritance—guardianship—wills. NADA 4 (1926), pp. 30-34.

20,763 JENNINGS, A. C. Land apportionment in Southern Rhodesia. J. AFR. SOC. 34 (1935), pp. 296-312.

20,764 JENNINGS, A. C. The native area. NADA 10 (1932), pp. 74-77.

20,765 LEWIS, V. A. Evidence of native witnesses in court—its fickleness. NADA 8 (1930), pp. 6-8.

20,766 MAFOHLA. Anticipated. NADA 8 (1930), p. 29.

20,767 MASON, P. Modifications in the civil law of Southern Rhodesia. RACE 1, no. 2 (1959-1960), pp. 51-58.

20,768 MUNYAI. Our mother land, our birthright. NADA 27 (1950), pp. 33-34.

20,769 PALLEY, C. Comparative study of mistake. RNLJ 1 (1961), pp. 140-206.

20,770 PALLEY, C. Stare decisis and the Federal Supreme Court. RNLJ 2 (1962), pp. 126-152.

20,771 PENDERED, A. and MEMERTY, W. VON. Native land husbandry Act of Southern Rhodesia. J. AFR. ADM. 7 (1955), pp. 99-109.

20,772 POPE-SIMMONDS, E. W. Asking for what you want. RNLJ 1 (1961), pp. 46-70.

20,773 POSSELT, F. W. T. Some observations on punishment. NADA 9 (1931), pp. 81-83.

20,774 PRICE, O. J. Quamtum of damages in bodily injury cases. RNLJ 1 (1961), pp. 91-102.

20,775 ROWLAND, J. H. The usefulness of duty of care. RLJ 5 (1965), pp. 20-30.

20,776 S., C. T. The truth, the whole truth, and nothing but the truth. NADA 4 (1926), pp. 73-74.

20,777 SEYMOUR, L. F. Legislation affecting Africans in urban areas in Southern Rhodesia. RNLJ 1 (1961), pp. 103-117.

20,778 SQUIRES, H. G. Suggested reforms of the Insolvency Act. RNLJ 2 (1962), pp. 113-125.

20,779 TAPSON, R. Grounds for divorce? NADA 6 (1928), pp. 100-103.

20,780 THOMPSON, A. Commentary on the Deserted Wives and Children Protection Act [Chapter 173]. RLJ 4 (1964), pp. 69-97.

20,781 THOMPSON, A. Commentary on the Maintenance Orders (Facilities for Enforcement) Act [Chapter 175]. RLJ 4 (1964), pp. 133-161.

20,782 UNYEREKUPI. Kutawura versus Mfanyana. NADA 25 (1948), pp. 78-80.

20,783 WEINBERG, S. Judicial review and legislative process. RNLJ 1 (1961), pp. 16-34.

20,784 Duplication of statutory offences. RLJ 5 (1965), pp. 31-34.

20,785 A federal [Rhodesia and Nyasaland] legal bibliography. RNLJ 2 (1962), pp. 77-80.

20,786 High court judgment on what constitutes a native marriage. NADA 31 (1954), pp. 27-29.

20,787 Report of the commission appointed to inquire into and report on administrative and judicial functions in the Native Affairs and District Court departments. J. AFR. LAW 6 (1962), pp. 143-144.

20,788 University College of Rhodesia and Nyasaland, Salisbury. J. AFR. LAW 6 (1962), p. 143.

20,789 When custom and law clash: death sentences for killing native twins. NADA 5 (1927), pp. 95-96.

See also 19976.

Religion

20,790 BARR, Father. Mureri, the rain goddess. NADA 23 (1946), pp. 60-62.

20,791 BURBRIDGE, A. In spirit-bound Rhodesia. NADA 2 (1924), pp. 17-29.

20,792 HOOKER, J. R. Witnesses and watchtower in the Rhodesias and Nyasaland. J. AFR. HIST. 6 (1955), pp. 91-106.

20,793 MAKULU, H. Industrialization and the Church with particular reference to the conditions in British Central Africa. THE CHURCH IN CHANGING AFRICA, 1958, pp. 34-37.

20,794 MEADE, H. M. T. An arboreal place of worship. NADA 4 (1926), pp. 106-107.

20,795 MENYHARTH, L. Missão do Baixo Zambeze: Miruru. BSEM 131 (1962), pp. 185-188.

20,796 REA, F. B. The future of mission education in Southern Rhodesia. INT. REV. MISSIONS 49 (1960), pp. 195-200.

20,797 REA, F. B. The need for a unified Church in Southern Rhodesia. INT. REV. MISSIONS 47 (1958), pp. 84-89.

20,798 WILKINSON, F. O. G. Christianity in Central Africa. AFR. AFFAIRS 62 (1963), pp. 114-124.

20,799 WORSLEY, P. M. Religion and politics in Central Africa. PAST AND PRESENT 15 (1959), pp. 73-81.

Science

20,800 BUNDU. Patrol [small-pox outbreak]. NADA 19 (1942), pp. 86-94.

20,801 CORINTA FERREIRA, M. Contribuição para o estudo dos Cerambicíneos da Africa do Sul. BSEM 83 (1954), pp. 83-86; 84 (1954), pp. 141-146.

20,802 FERREIRA, G. DA V. Contribuição para o estudo dos Cerambicíneos da Africa do Sul. BSEM 83 (1954), pp. 87-89.

20,803 GELFAND, M. Medical problems in the native of Southern Rhodesia. NADA 21 (1944), pp. 33-38.

20,804 HANNAN, M. Shiri. NADA 27 (1950), pp. 61-63.

20,805 HOWMAN, R. The native labourer and his food. NADA 19 (1942), pp. 3-24.

20,806 JONES, E. B. The food of the Rhodesian native from the diatetic point of view. NADA 19 (1942), pp. 34-39.

20,807 JONES, E. B. Foods from Southern Rhodesia. MALNUTRITION IN AFR. WOMEN..., 1952, pp. 269-271.

20,808 MacGREGOR, A. M. Gorceixite in Southern Rhodesia. BULL. IMP. INST. 39 (1941), pp. 399-401.

20,809 MAKUMETE. An African clinic. NADA 25 (1948), pp. 68-69.

20,810 MJELE. Haplosterna Delagorguei. NADA 12 (1934), pp. 37-38.

20,811 MORRIS, R. M. Onyalai in Southern Rhodesia. NADA 12 (1934), pp. 17-19.

20,812 MUNDAY, M. C. A problem in sanitation. NADA 22 (1945), pp. 50-52.

20,813 PARKHURST, D. C. H. Mangoromera. NADA 11 (1933), pp. 59-61.

20,814 THOMPSON, J. B. B. Native herbal medicines. NADA 9 (1931), pp. 93-99.

20,815 THOMPSON, L. C. Ingots of native manufacture. NADA 26 (1949), pp. 7-19.

20,816 THOMPSON, L. C. A native-made tin ingot. NADA 31 (1954), p. 41.

20,817 YORKE, W. The relation of big game to sleeping sickness. J. AFR. SOC. 13 (1913), pp. 23-32.

20,818 A naturalist's list of Ndebele names for the indigenous creatures and plants of Matebeleland. NADA 24 (1947), pp. 53-61.

See also 16422.

Sociology

20,819 AQUINA, M. The social background of agriculture in Chilimanzi Reserve. RHODES-LIV. J. 36 (1965), pp. 7-39.

20,820 BARFORD, M. F. Dismantling the colour bar in Southern Rhodesia. CONTEMP. REV. 199 (1961), pp. 238-241.

20,821 BARR. Family statistics. NADA 25 (1948), pp. 81-84.

20,822 BAZELEY, W. Townships in the native area. NADA 17 (1940), pp. 81-84.

20,823 BETTISON, D. G. Factors in the determination of wage rates in central Africa. RHODES-LIV. J. 28 (1961), pp. 22-46.

20,824 C., J. L'urbanisation en Afrique centrale britannique. ZAIRE 8 (1954), pp. 639-640.

20,825 CARBUTT, C. L. The racial problem in Southern Rhodesia. NADA 12 (1934), pp. 6-11.

20,826 CHANCELLOR, J. and COGHLAN, C. Southern Rhodesia and its problems. J. AFR. SOC. 26 (1926), pp. 1-9.

20,827 COCKCROFT, I. G. Maintenance: Sondhlo, Mombe yo Kurera. NADA 12 (1934), pp. 67-68.

20,828 DOMINUS. What's in a dream? NADA 39 (1962), pp. 17-18.

20,829 DOTSON, F. and DOTSON, L. Indians and coloured in Rhodesia and Nyasaland. RACE 5, no. 1 (1963-1964), pp. 61-75.

20,830 FABER, M. The distribution of income between racial groups in Southern Rhodesia. RACE 2, no. 2 (1960-1961), pp. 41-52.

20,831 FILESI, T. Difficile il salto della barriera del colore. AFRICA (Rome) 10 (1955), pp. 209-210.

20,832 FRANTZ, C. Native policy in the U.S.A. and Southern Rhodesia. NADA 37 (1960), pp. 40-55.

20,833 FRANTZ, C. Race attitudes and social structure in Southern Rhodesia. CONG. INT. SC. ANTH. ET ETHN. 6, no. i (1960), pp. 91-95.

20,834 FRANTZ, C. Southern Rhodesia. INT.SOC. SC. J. 13 (1961), pp. 215-224.

20,835 FRANTZ, C. and ROGERS, C. A. Length of residence and race attitudes of Europeans in Southern Rhodesia. RACE 3, no. 2 (1961-1962), pp. 46-54.

20,836 FYNN, J. W. L. Parcere subjectis et debellare superbos. NADA 7 (1929), pp. 6-7.

20,837 GILCHRIST, R. D. Rhodesia's place in the native problem. J. AFR. SOC. 32 (1933), pp. 135-139.

20,838 GRAY, R. Race relations in Central Africa. AFR. AFFAIRS 62 (1963), pp. 333-340.

20,839 GUSSMAN, B. Industrial efficiency and the urban African: a study of conditions in Southern Rhodesia. AFRICA 23 (1953), pp. 135-144.

20,840 GUSSMAN, B. Problems of adjustment in British Central Africa. CIVILISATIONS 9 (1959), pp. 445-454; French summary, pp. 455-456.

20,841 HAMILTON, P. Population pressure and land use in Chiweshe Reserve. RHODES-LIV. J. 36 (1965), pp. 40-58.

20,842 HARTLEY, G. H. The development of an African urban community. NADA 35 (1958), pp. 87-98.

20,843 HAW, R. C. Race relations. NADA 29 (1952), pp. 74-77.

20,844 HAWKEY, J. E. Sipambaniso. NADA 13 (1935), pp. 22-23.

20,845 HOOKER, J. R. The African worker in Southern Rhodesia: black aspirations in a white economy 1927-36. RACE 6, no. 1 (1964-1965), pp. 142-151.

20,846 HOWMAN, R. Industry and human erosion. NADA 21 (1944), pp. 19-28.

20,847 HOWMAN, R. Mwari and his people. NADA 28 (1951), pp. 84-93.

20,848 IBBOTSON, P. The coloured people of Southern Rhodesia. RACE RELATIONS 9 (1942), pp. 47-51.

20,849 IBBOTSON, P. Native welfare societies of Southern Rhodesia. RACE RELATIONS 9 (1942), pp. 71-74.

20,850 IBBOTSON, P. The urban native problem. NADA 22 (1945), pp. 35-44.

20,851 IBBOTSON, P. Urbanization in Southern Rhodesia. AFRICA 16 (1946), pp. 73-82.

20,852 JONES, N. Training native women in community service in Southern Rhodesia. INT. REV. MISSIONS 21 (1932), pp. 566-574.

20,853 KEIGWIN, H. S. Segregation. NADA 2 (1924), pp. 52-57.

20,854 McEWAN, P. J. M. European intelligence in Southern Rhodesia: patterns and causes. RACE 4, no. 1 (1962-1963), pp. 98-120.

20,855 McEWAN, P. J. M. The European population of Southern Rhodesia. CIVILISATIONS 13 (1963), pp. 429-441; French summary, pp. 442-444.

20,856 McEWAN, P. J. M. The urban African population of Southern Rhodesia. CIVILISATIONS 13 (1963), pp. 267-290; French summary, pp. 291-293.

20,857 MacMILLAN, W. M. Southern Rhodesia and the development of Africa. J. AFR. SOC. 32 (1933), pp. 294-298.

20,858 MANYUCHI. Good manners. NADA 26 (1949), pp. 30-31.

20,859 MARR, M. My Bushman. NADA 29 (1952), pp. 65-66.

20,860 MOKWILE, J. S. Native ideals. NADA 2 (1924), pp. 95-97.

20,861 MOYO, P. H. Native life in the Reserves. NADA 3 (1925), p. 47.

20,862 NOBLE, G. W. African housing in the urban areas of Southern Rhodesia. J. AFR. ADM. 3 (1951), pp. 124-128.

20,863 PANDOMBIRI. Priority no. 1. NADA 25 (1948), pp. 36-37.

20,864 PRESTON, H. A. African women of Southern Rhodesia. WOMEN TODAY 6 (1963), pp. 1-4.

20,865 ROBERTS, J. G. Ancient and modern: being a contrast, with some translation, into the Chishona. NADA 23 (1946), pp. 29-30.

20,866 ROBINSON, R. Race relations in Rhodesia and Nyasaland. RHODES-LIV. J. 30 (1961), pp. 56-58.

20,867 ST. LEGER, F. Y. Crime in Southern Rhodesia. RHODES-LIV. J. 38 (1965), pp. 11-41.

20,868 "SENEX". Treatment of native servants. NADA 2 (1924), pp. 49-51.

20,869 SEPTIMA. Mrs. Mambo entertains. NADA 34 (1957), pp. 88-92.

20,870 SHAUL, J. R. H. African sample surveys in the Federation of Rhodesia and Nyasaland. ST. ANTONY'S PAPERS 10 (1961), pp. 102-119.

20,871 SHAUL, J. R. H. Population trends in Southern Rhodesia, 1941-1981. RHODES-LIV. J. 5 (1947), pp. 18-23.

20,872 STEAD, W. H. Concepts and controls in native life: elements of sociological analysis. NADA 13 (1935), pp. 6-13.

20,873 VENZO, E. La Federazione della Rhodesia e Nyasaland: Crisi di crescenza di un paese giovane. AFRICA (Rome) 13 (1958), pp. 189-192.

20,874 VENZO, E. Un paese di immigrazione: la Rhodesia offre molto ma a determinate condizioni. AFRICA (Rome) 13 (1958), pp. 145-146.

20,875 WINNINGTON-INGRAM, C. Note following a visit to some African farming areas in Southern Rhodesia. J. AFR. ADM. 7 (1955), pp. 68-74.

20,876 Bulawayo municipality. NADA 37 (1960), pp. 75-80.

20,877 Memorandum on social security in relation to the needs of the native population. NADA 22 (1945), pp. 56-60.

20,878 La question raciale en Afrique centrale britannique. ZAIRE 5 (1951), pp. 972-973.

20,879 Relations inter-africaines de la Rhodésie du Sud. ZAIRE 8 (1954), p. 198.

20,880 Report on urban conditions in Southern Rhodesia. AFR. STUD. 4 (1945), pp. 9-22.

20,881 Salisbury and its pleasures. NADA 1 (1923), pp. 81-83.

20,882 L'urbanisation en Rhodésie du Sud. ZAIRE 6 (1952), pp. 1088-1089.

See also 23105.

ZAMBIA

General

20,883 BRELSFORD, W. V. Museums and administration. RHODES-LIV. J. 4 (1945), pp. 74-79.

20,884 CLARK, J. D. The museum as a public service. RHODES-LIV. J. 4 (1945), pp. 40-54.

20,885 GLUCKMAN, M. The use of sociological research in museum display. RHODES-LIV. J. 4 (1945), pp. 66-73.

20,886 HUMPHREY, H. C. What I should like to see in the Rhodes-Livingstone Museum (a layman's view). RHODES-LIV. J. 4 (1945), pp. 80-84.

20,887 JONES, N. Symposium: the Colonial Museum. On the need for collecting and preserving objects of native material culture. RHODES-LIV. J. 4 (1945), pp. 33-39.

20,888 PLACHIN, H. Lusaka diary. AFR. SOUTH 2, no. 4 (1958), pp. 69-75.

20,889 WILSON, G. H. The Northern Rhodesia-Nyasaland Joint Publications Bureau. AFRICA 20 (1950), pp. 60-69.

Agriculture

20,890 KAY, G. Agricultural change in the Luitikila Basin Development Area, Mpika district, Northern Rhodesia. RHODES-LIV. J. 31 (1962), pp. 21-50.

20,891 WILSON, J. L. B. Co-operation and rural development. CORONA 1, no. 6 (1949), pp. 18-21.

Anthropology

20,892 AFRICANUS [pseud.] "Mulombe": a Kaonde superstition. J. AFR. SOC. 20 (1920), pp. 43-45.

20,893 ANLEY, V. R. The burial ceremony of Chief Kasempa. NADA 4 (1926), pp. 113-115.

20,894 ANLEY, V. R. Notes on burial ceremony in Kasempa district, N. Rhodesia. (Burial of chief Kasempa of the Bakaonde tribe.) J. AFR. SOC. 25 (1926), pp. 333-337.

20,895 ANLEY, V. R. Some dances (ancient and modern) of the Bakaonde tribe of Northern Rhodesia. NADA 4 (1926), pp. 83-85.

20,896 ARNAUD, M. The creation myth of the Malozi. BO 9 (1961), pp. 57-60.

20,897 ARNAUD, M. Mythologie et folklore sur le Haut-Zambèze. PRESENCE AFR. 2 (1948), pp. 244-266.

20,898 BARNES, Rev. H. B. Iron smelting among the Ba-Ushi. JRAI 56 (1926), pp. 189-194.

20,899 BARNES, J. A. Seven types of segmentation. RHODES-LIV. J. 17 (1954), pp. 1-22.

20,900 BRELSFORD, V. Babemba animal medicines. NADA 18 (1941), pp. 8-11.

20,901 BRELSFORD, V. A Bambwela purification rite. NADA 12 (1934), pp. 29-30.

20,902 BRELSFORD, V. History and custom of the Basala. JRAI 65 (1935), pp. 205-215.

20,903 BRELSFORD, V. Shimwalule: a study of a Bemba chief and priest. AFR. STUD. 1 (1942), pp. 207-223.

20,904 BRELSFORD, W. V. Insanity among the Bemba of Northern Rhodesia. AFRICA 20 (1950), pp. 46-54.

20,905 BRUWER, J. The composition of a Cewa village (Mudzi). AFR. STUD. 8 (1949), pp. 191-198.

20,906 BRUWER, J. Kinship terminology among the Cewa of the eastern province of Northern Rhodesia. AFR. STUD. 7 (1948), pp. 185-187.

20,907 BRUWER, J. Matrilineal kinship among the Kunda. AFRICA 28 (1958), pp. 207-223.

20,908 BRUWER, J. Unkhoswe: the system of guardianship in Cewa matrilineal society. AFR. STUD. 14 (1955), pp. 113-122.

20,909 CHAPLIN, J. H. A note on the brother-sister relationship in Northern Rhodesia. ETHNOS 22 (1957), pp. 15-19.

20,910 COLSON, E. Rain-shrines of the plateau Tonga of Northern Rhodesia. AFRICA 18 (1948), pp. 272-282.

20,911 COLSON, E. Residence and village stability among the plateau Tonga. RHODES-LIV. J. 12 (1951), pp. 41-67.

20,912 COLSON, E. Social control and vengeance in Plateau Tonga society. AFRICA 23 (1953), pp. 199-211.

20,913 CROWTHER, I. A. Female initiation ceremonies (sikenge) as practiced by the Subiya of Barotseland, Northern Rhodesia. NADA 9, no. 1 (1964), pp. 52-54.

20,914 CUNNISON, I. Headmanship and the ritual of Luapula villages. AFRICA 26 (1956), pp. 2-16.

20,915 CUNNISON, I. A note on the Lunda concept of custom. RHODES-LIV. J. 14 (1954), pp. 20-29.

20,916 CUNNISON, I. Perpetual kinship: a political institution of the Luapula peoples. RHODES-LIV. J. 20 (1956), pp. 28-48.

20,917 DOKE, C. M. Additional Lamba aphorisms. BANTU STUD. 4 (1930), pp. 109-135, 181-192.

20,918 DOKE, C. M. Lamba folk tales annotated. BANTU STUD. 13 (1939), pp. 85-111.

20,919 DOKE, C. M. Social control among the Lambas. BANTU STUD. 2 (1923), pp. 35-39.

20,920 DOKE, C. M. A specimen of the folk-lore of the Lamba people of Northern Rhodesia. BANTU STUD. 1, no. iii (1922), pp. 1-5.

20,921 E., T. The story of the origin of the name Makoni. NADA 14 (1936-1937), pp. 76-78.

20,922 GLUCKMAN, M. Kinship and marriage among the Lozi of Northern Rhodesia and the Zulu of Natal. AFRICAN SYSTEMS OF KINSHIP AND MARRIAGE, 1950, pp. 166-206.

20,923 GLUCKMAN, M. Succession and civil war among the Bemba—an exercise in anthropological theory. RHODES-LIV. J. 17 (1954), pp. 6-25.

20,924 GLUCKMAN, M. et al. The village headman in British Central Africa, by Max Gluckman, J. C. Mitchell, J. A. Barnes. AFRICA 19 (1949), pp. 89-106.

20,925 HARRIES-JONES, P. and CHIWALE, J. C. Kasaka: a case study in succession and dynamics of a Bemba village. RHODES-LIV. J. 33 (1963), pp. 1-67.

20,926 HUDSON, R. S. The human geography of Balovale district, Northern Rhodesia. JRAI 65 (1935), pp. 235-266.

20,927 JONES, A. M. The Kalimba of the Lala tribe, Northern Rhodesia. AFRICA 20 (1950), pp. 324-333.

20,928 KUNTZ, M. Jeux sur le Haut-Zambèze. J. SOC. AFR. 12 (1942), pp. 95-116.

20,929 KUNTZ, M. Les rites occultes et la sorcellerie sur le Haut-Zambèse. J. SOC. AFR. 2 (1932), pp. 123-138.

20,930 MacRAE, F. B. The Batwa in the Broken Hill district of Northern Rhodesia. NADA 7 (1929), pp. 63-75.

20,931 MacRAE, F. B. Some technological notes on the tribes of the Mumbwa district of Northern Rhodesia. NADA 6 (1928), pp. 56-67.

20,932 MARWICK, M. G. An experiment in public-opinion polling among preliterate people. AFRICA 26 (1956), pp. 149-158.

20,933 MARWICK, M. G. The sociology of sorcery in a Central African tribe. AFR. STUD. 22 (1963), pp. 1-21.

20,934 MARWICK, M. G. Some problems in the sociology of sorcery and witchcraft. AFRICAN SYSTEMS OF THOUGHT, 1965, pp. 171-191.

20,935 MELLAND, F. H. Some ethnographical notes on the Awemba tribe of north eastern Rhodesia (and on some portion of the Wabisa). J. AFR. SOC. 3 (1904), pp. 247-256.

20,936 MIRACLE, M. P. Aboriginal trade among the Senga and Nsenga of Northern Rhodesia. ETHNOLOGY 1 (1962), pp. 212-222.

20,937 MOLINIER, L. Croyances superstitieuses chez les Babemba. J. AFR. SOC. 3 (1903), pp. 74-82.

20,938 MOORE, R. J. B. Bwanga among the Bemba. AFRICA 13 (1940), pp.211-233.

20,939 MOORE, R. J. B. Bwanga among the Bemba. Pt. II, a linguistic consideration of the name Bwanga. BANTU STUD. 15 (1941), pp. 37-44.

20,940 MOREAU, J. Bakule menyo. NADA 27 (1950), pp. 34-38.

20,941 MUNDAY, J. T. The African child is the father to the African man. NADA 19 (1942), pp. 25-31.

20,942 MUNDAY, J. T. The creation myth amongst the Lala of Northern Rhodesia. AFR. STUD. 1 (1942), pp. 47-53.

20,943 MUNDAY, J. T. Some traditions of the Nyendwa clan of Northern Rhodesia. BANTU STUD. 14 (1940), pp. 435-454.

20,944 MUNDAY, J. T. An undistinguished African. NADA 26 (1949), pp. 59-64.

20,945 MWENYA, A. H. The burial of Chitimukulu Mubanga. AFR. AFFAIRS 46 (1947), pp. 101-104.

20,946 NELSON, J. W. Muba. CORONA 2 (1950), pp. 218-219.

20,947 NG'ANDU, L. H. A brief account of the Ndola initiation ceremony among the Nsenga of the Petauke district of Northern Rhodesia. NADA 26 (1949), pp. 70-72.

20,948 PIRIE, G. North-eastern Rhodesia. J. AFR. SOC. 5 (1905), pp. 130-147, 300-310, 432-436; 6 (1906), pp. 43-58.

20,949 POWDERMAKER, H. Social change through imagery and values of teen-age Africans in Northern Rhodesia. AMER. ANTHR. 58 (1956), pp. 783-813.

20,950 "PULA". The Barotse people and some of their customs. NADA 4 (1926), pp. 85-90.

20,951 READ, M. The moral code of the Ngoni and their former military state. AFRICA 11 (1938), pp. 1-24.

20,952 REYNOLDS, B. Kaliloze night guns. NADA 35 (1958), pp. 61-64.

20,953 RICHARDS, A. I. Anthropological problems in North-Eastern Rhodesia. AFRICA 5 (1932), pp. 121-144.

20,954 RICHARDS, A. I. A modern movement of witch-finders. AFRICA 8 (1935), pp. 448-460.

20,955 RICHARDS, A. I. Mother-right among the central Bantu. ESSAYS PRESENTED TO C. G. SELIGMAN, 1934, pp. 267-279.

20,956 RICHARDS, A. I. The political system of the Bemba tribe: North-eastern Rhodesia. AFRICAN POLITICAL SYSTEMS, 1940, pp. 83-120.

20,957 RICHARDS, A. I. Preliminary notes on the Babemba of north-east Rhodesia. BANTU STUD. 9 (1935), pp. 225-253.

20,958 RICHARDS, A. I. Tribal government in transition. The Babemba of north-eastern Rhodesia. J. AFR. SOC. 34 (1935), supplement.

20,959 RICHARDS, A. I. The village census in the study of culture contact. AFRICA 8 (1935), pp. 20-33.

20,960 SANDERSON, M. Some marriage customs of the Wahena, Nyasaland. J. AFR. SOC. 22 (1923), pp. 131-138.

20,961 SCUDDER, T. Fishermen of the Zambezi: an appraisal of fishing practice and potential of the Valley Tonga. RHODES-LIV. J. 27 (1960), pp. 41-49.

20,962 SHEANE, J. H. W. Some aspects of the Awemba religion and superstitious observances. JRAI 36 (1906), pp. 150-158.

20,963 SHEANE, J. H. W. Wemba warpaths. J. AFR. SOC. 11 (1911), pp. 21-34.

20,964 SMITH, E. W. Addendum to the "Ila-speaking peoples of Northern Rhodesia (Parts I and II)." AFR. STUD. 8 (1949), pp. 1-9, 53-61.

20,965 SMITH, E. W. The Ila-speaking people of North Rhodesia. J. AFR. SOC. 20 (1921), pp. 89-94.

20,966 SMITH, E. W. Inzuikizi. AFRICA 8 (1935), pp. 473-480.

20,967 SPEARPOINT, F. The African native and the Rhodesian copper mines. J. AFR. SOC. 36 (1937), supplement.

20,968 STEFANISZYN, B. African reincarnation re-examined. AFR. STUD. 13 (1954), pp. 131-146.

20,969 STEFANISZYN, B. Clan jest of the Ambo. NADA 28 (1951), pp. 94-107.

20,970 STEFANISZYN, B. Funeral friendship in Central Africa. AFRICA 20 (1950), pp. 290-305.

20,971 TEW, M. A further note on funeral friendship. AFRICA 21 (1951), pp. 122-124.

20,972 TUDEN, A. Ila slavery. RHODES-LIV. J. 24 (1959), pp. 68-78.

20,973 TURNER, V. W. A Lunda love story and its consequences: selected texts from traditions collected by Henrique Dias de Carvalho at the Court of Nwatianvwa in 1887. RHODES-LIV. J. 19 (1955), pp. 1-26.

20,974 TURNER, V. W. Ritual symbolism, morality and social structure among the Ndembu. RHODES-LIV. J. 30 (1961), pp. 1-10; AFRICAN SYSTEMS OF THOUGHT, 1965, pp. 79-95.

20,975 TURNER, V. W. The spatial separation of generations in Ndembu Village structure. AFRICA 25 (1955), pp. 121-136.

20,976 WATSON, W. The Kaonde village. RHODES-LIV. J. 15 (1954), pp. 1-30.

20,977 WHITE, C. M. N. Clan, chieftainship, and slavery in Luvale political organization. AFRICA 27 (1957), pp. 59-73.

20,978 WHITE, C. M. N. Conservatism and modern adaptation in Luvale female puberty ritual. AFRICA 23 (1953), pp. 15-23.

20,979 WHITE, C. M. N. Factors in the social organization of the Luvale. AFR. STUD. 14 (1955), pp. 97-112.

20,980 WHITE, C. M. N. A note on Luvale joking relations. AFR. STUD. 17 (1958), pp. 28-33.

20,981 WHITE, C. M. N. Notes on the circumcision rites of the Balovale tribes. AFR. STUD. 12 (1953), pp. 41-56.

20,982 WHITE, C. M. N. The role of hunting and fishing in Luvale society. AFR. STUD. 15 (1956), pp. 75-86.

20,983 WHITE, C. M. N. Stratification and modern changes in an ancestral cult. AFRICA 19 (1949), pp. 324-331.

20,984 WHITE, C. M. N. Witchcraft divination and magic among the Balovale tribes. AFRICA 18 (1948), pp. 81-104.

20,985 WHITE, C. M. N. et al. Comparative aspects of Luvale female puberty ritual. AFR. STUD. 17 (1958), pp. 204-220.

20,986 Exploration ethnographique de la Rhodésie du Nord. ZAIRE 5 (1951), pp. 529-530.

See also 14067, 14104, 17895, 23432, 23433.

Art. Antiquities. Archaeology

20,987 BLACKING, J. Patterns of Nsenga Kalimba music. AFR. MUSIC, 1961, pp. 26-43.

20,988 BRELSFORD, V. The Bemba tridents. NADA 13 (1935), pp. 18-21.

20,989 BRELSFORD, V. Some reflections on Bemba geometric decorative art. BANTU STUD. 11 (1937), pp. 37-45.

20,990 CLARK, J. D. Further excavations at Broken Hill, Northern Rhodesia. JRAI 89 (1959), pp. 201-231.

20,991 CLARK, J. D. A review of prehistoric research in Northern Rhodesia and Nyasaland. PROC. PAN-AFR. CONGR. PRE-HIST. 3 (1955), pp. 412-432.

20,992 CLARK, J. D. and FAGAN, B. M. Charcoals, sands, and channel decorated pottery from Northern Rhodesia. AMER. ANTHR. 67 (1965), pp. 354-371.

20,993 CLARK, J. D. et al. New studies on Rhodesian Man. JRAI 77 (1947), pp. 7-32.

20,994 DAVIDSON, M. A Lunda Kalendi. AFR. MUSIC, 1963, pp. 15-16.

20,995 DAVIDSON, M. The music of a Lunda Kalendi. AFR. MUSIC, 1964, pp. 107-108.

20,996 DENNY, S. R. Some Zambesi boat songs. NADA 14 (1936-1937), pp. 35-44.

20,997 FAGAN, B. M. A collection of nineteenth century Soli ironwork from the Lusaka area of Northern Rhodesia. JRAI 91 (1961), pp. 228-250.

20,998 FAGAN, B. M. The Iron Age sequence in the southern province of Northern Rhodesia. J. AFR. HIST. 4 (1963), pp. 157-177.

20,999 GEAR, H. S. A Boskopoid skeleton from Kalomo, Northern Rhodesia. BANTU STUD. 2 (1928), pp. 217-231.

21,000 INSKEEP, R. Recent developments in Iron Age studies in Northern Rhodesia and Nyasaland. PROC. PAN-AFR. CONGR. PRE-HIST. 4, no. iii (1962), pp. 351-356.

21,001 JONES, A. M. African music. AFR. AFFAIRS 48 (1949), pp. 290-297.

21,002 JONES, A. M. African music: the Mganda dance. AFR. STUD. 4 (1945), pp. 180-188.

21,003 JONES, A. M. The study of African musical rhythm. BANTU STUD. 11 (1937), pp. 295-319.

21,004 LUNSONGA, C. Bemba music. AFR. MUSIC, 1963, pp. 27-35.

21,005 MacCURDY, G. G. The skull from Broken Hill in Rhodesia. AMER. ANTHR. 24 (1922), pp. 97-98.

21,006 MacRAE, F. B. The stone age in Northern Rhodesia. NADA 4 (1926), pp. 67-68.

21,007 NJUNGU, A. M. The music of my people. AFR. MUSIC, 1960, pp. 48-50; 1961, pp. 77-80.

21,008 NKHATA, A. African music clubs. AFR. MUSIC, 1952, pp. 17-20.

21,009 OAKLEY, K. P. The dating of the Broken Hill, Florisbad and Saldanha skulls. PROC. PAN-AFR. CONGR. PRE-HIST. 3 (1955), pp. 76-79.

21,010 RYCROFT, D. R. Tribal style and free expression. AFR. MUSIC, 1954, pp. 16-27.

21,011 STEFANISZYN, B. The hunting songs of the Ambo. AFR. STUD. 10 (1951), pp. 1-12.

21,012 TRACEY, H. and TRACEY, P. The Lost Valley. AFR. MUSIC, 1959, pp. 44-57.

21,013 WELLS, L. H. The place of the Broken Hill skull among human types. PROC. PAN-AFR. CONGR. PRE-HIST. 3 (1955), pp. 172-174.

Biography

21,014 NORTHCOTT, C. Lion of Zambia: Kenneth Kaunda. CONTEMP. REV. 203 (1963), pp. 293-295.

21,015 C.W.B. Obituary: Peter Ian Maclaren. NIGERIAN FIELD 22 (1957), p. 143.

Economics

21,016 BALDWIN, R. E. Wage policy in a dual economy—the case of Northern Rhodesia. RACE 4, no. 1 (1962-1963), pp. 73-87.

21,017 BRELSFORD, W. V. The Bangweulu channel. RHODES-LIV. J. 1 (1944), pp. 50-54.

21,018 COLSON, E. The role of cattle among the plateau Tonga of Mazabuka district. RHODES-LIV. J. 11 (1951), pp. 10-46.

21,019 COLSON, E. The Tonga and the shortage of implements. RHODES-LIV. J. 14 (1954), pp. 37-38; rejoinder, pp. 39-40.

21,020 COLSON, E. and CHONA, M. Marketing of cattle among Plateau Tonga. RHODES-LIV. J. 17 (1965), pp. 42-50.

21,021 COOPER, G. Village crafts in Barotseland. RHODES-LIV. J. 11 (1951), pp. 47-60.

21,022 DEBENHAM, F. River development in Northern Rhodesia. CORONA 3 (1951), pp. 224-225.

21,023 G., J. A propos de la main d'oeuvre indigène en Rhodésie du Nord. ZAIRE 8 (1954), pp. 307-308.

21,024 GANN, L. H. The Northern Rhodesian copper industry and the world of copper: 1923-52. RHODES-LIV. J. 18 (1955), pp. 1-18.

21,025 GLUCKMAN, M. How the Bemba make their living: an appreciation of Richard's Land labour and diet in Northern Rhodesia. RHODES-LIV. J. 3 (1945), pp. 55-75.

21,026 GRAY, A. Africans on Copperbelt. AFR. AFFAIRS 54 (1955), pp. 8-9.

21,027 KAY, G. Sources and uses of cash in some Ushi villages, Fort Rosebery District, Northern Rhodesia. RHODES-LIV. J. 35 (1964), pp. 14-28.

21,028 LAWMAN, T. Information research: an experiment in Northern Rhodesia. CORONA 4 (1952), pp. 208-211.

21,029 MIRACLE, M. P. Ivory trade and the migration of the Northern Rhodesian Senga. CAH. ET. AFR. 3 (1963), pp. 424-434.

21,030 MIRACLE, M. P. Plateau Tonga entrepreneurs in historical inter-regional trade. RHODES-LIV. J. 26 (1959), pp. 34-50.

21,031 MITCHELL, J. C. The collection and treatment of family budgets in primitive communities as a field problem. RHODES-LIV. J. 8 (1949), pp. 50-56.

21,032 MITCHELL, J. C. The distribution of African labour by area of origin on the copper mines of Northern Rhodesia. RHODES-LIV. J. 14 (1954), pp. 30-36.

21,033 MOORE, R. J. B. Industry and trade on the shores of Lake Mweru. AFRICA 10 (1937), pp. 137-157.

21,034 MOORE, R. J. B. Labour conditions in Northern Rhodesia. J. AFR. SOC. 38 (1939), pp. 438-441.

21,035 MOORE, R. J. B. Native wages and standard of living in Northern Rhodesia. AFR. STUD. 1 (1942), pp. 142-148.

21,036 MOORE, R. J. B. The Pim report on Northern Rhodesia. J. AFR. SOC. 37 (1938), pp. 344-347.

21,037 NYIRENDA, A. A. African market vendors in Lusaka with a note on the recent boycott. RHODES-LIV. J. 22 (1957), pp. 31-63.

21,038 OSS, M. V. The North Charterland Concession Inquiry. J. AFR. SOC. 31 (1932), pp. 402-411.

21,039 PHILPOTT, R. The Mulobezi—Mongu labour route. RHODES-LIV. J. 3 (1945), pp. 50-54.

21,040 PRAIN, R. L. The stabilization of labour in the Rhodesia Copperbelt. AFR. AFFAIRS 55 (1956), pp. 305-312.

21,041 STOOKE, G. B. Memorandum on native development in Northern Rhodesia. RHODES-LIV. J. 1 (1944), pp. 15-21.

21,042 TAYLOR, W. L. Problems of economic development of the Federation of Rhodesia and Nyasaland. ECON. DEVELOPMENT FOR AFRICA, 1965, pp. 222-245.

21,043 TRENT, T. S. Colonial social accounting: an appreciation of Phyllis Deane's Colonial Social Accounting. RHODES-LIV. J. 18 (1955), pp. 38-60.

21,044 TURNER, E. L. B. and TURNER, V. W. Money economy among the Mwinilunga Ndembu: a study of some individual cash budgets. RHODES-LIV. J. 18 (1955), pp. 19-37.

21,045 VECCHI, B. V. La Rhodesia e il lavoro italiano. AFRICA (Rome) 12 (1957), pp. 68-71.

21,046 WELENSKY, Sir R. Africans and trade unions in Northern Rhodesia. AFR. AFFAIRS 45 (1946), pp. 185-191.

21,047 WHITE, C. M. N. A survey of African land tenure in Northern Rhodesia. J. AFR. ADM. 11 (1959), pp. 171-178; 12 (1960), pp. 3-10.

21,048 WHITE, C. M. N. Terminological confusion in African land tenure. J. AFR. ADM. 10 (1958), pp. 124-130.

21,049 YOUNG, T. C. The native newspaper [in Northern Rhodesia]. AFRICA 11 (1938), pp. 63-72.

21,050 Business women in Northern Rhodesia. AFR. WOMEN 3 (1960), pp. 89-90.

21,051 The economic development of Zambia. ECON. BULL. AFR. 5 (1965), pp. 84-87.

See also 20283, 20284.

Education

21,052 BRIMBLE, A. R. The construction of a non-verbal intelligence test in Northern Rhodesia. RHODES-LIV. J. 34 (1964), pp. 23-35.

21,053 HARDCASTLE, G. F. The Badge Scheme. AFR. WOMEN 3 (1960), pp. 75-82.

21,054 HAY, H. Literacy technique in Northern Rhodesia. RHODES-LIV. J. 9 (1950), pp. 1-13.

21,055 HAY, H. Mass literacy in Northern Rhodesia. INT. REV. MISSIONS 35 (1946), pp. 314-322.

21,056 HAY, H. Preparation of teaching material for literacy campaigns: Northern Rhodesia. TOWARDS A LITERATE AFRICA, 1948, pp. 30-44.

21,057 HOLMES, H. Urban schoolboys go to the country. RHODES-LIV. J. 9 (1950), pp. 31-36.

21,058 JOHNSON, E. Mindolo Women's Training Centre. AFR. WOMEN 4 (1961), pp. 63-65.

21,059 KING, E. R. G. On educating African girls in Northern Rhodesia. RHODES-LIV. J. 10 (1950), pp. 65-74.

21,060 KUNDA, A. Northern Rhodesia technical school for girls. AFR. WOMEN 4 (1961), pp. 37-38.

21,061 SCOTT, G. C. Two centres of higher learning:—I: Gordon Memorial College, Khartoum. AFR. AFFAIRS 48 (1949), pp. 226-231.

21,062 SHAW, J. R. The distribution of books in Northern Rhodesia. INT. REV. MISSIONS 47 (1958), pp. 90-95.

21,063 SHAW, M. A school village in Northern Rhodesia. INT. REV. MISSIONS 14 (1925), pp. 523-536.

21,064 TAGART, E. S. B. Northern Rhodesia: Annual report upon native affairs 1932. J. AFR. SOC. 32 (1933), pp. 376-378.

21,065 WINTERBOTTOM, J. M. An experiment in rural compulsory education. RHODES-LIV. J. 9 (1950), pp. 37-39.

21,066 Education for girls in Northern Rhodesia. AFR. WOMEN 1 (1954), pp. 9-10.

21,067 Education in Northern Rhodesia. Annual report on European education, 1932. Annual report on native education, 1932. J. AFR. SOC. 33 (1934), pp. 296-298.

21,068 Home education of the African child. AFR. WOMEN 1 (1955), pp. 31-32.

21,069 Reading habits in a part of the Mushiri Reserve. RHODES-LIV. J. 11 (1951), pp. 61-65.

21,070 Training of African nurses in Northern Rhodesia. AFR. WOMEN 1 (1956), pp. 98-99.

21,071 Women teachers in Northern Rhodesia. AFR. WOMEN 4 (1960), pp. 10-11.

See also 20348.

Geography

21,072 COCHRAN-PATRICK, C. K. Aerial reconnaissance mapping in Northern Rhodesia. GEOG. REV. 21 (1931), pp. 213-220.

21,073 DARBY, H. C. Settlement in Northern Rhodesia. GEOG. REV. 21 (1931), pp. 559-573.

21,074 DEBENHAM, F. Surveying Bangweulu. CORONA 2 (1950), pp. 215-217.

21,075 FOSBROOKE, H. A. History of Colonial Development and Welfare Scheme R.698. RHODES-LIV. J. 29 (1961), pp. 1-27.

21,076 KAY, G. Aspects of Ushi settlement: Fort Rosebery District, Northern Rhodesia. GEOGRAPHERS AND THE TROPICS, 1964, pp. 235-260.

21,077 MELLAND, F. H. Mountain and marsh in Central Africa (a short account of nature and sport in N.E. Rhodesia, B.C. Africa, between the Muchinga mountains and Bangweulu). J. AFR. SOC. 3 (1903), pp. 53-57.

Government. Politics. Administration

21,078 BARNES, J. R. Some aspects of political development among the Fort Jameson Ngoni. AFR. STUD. 7 (1948), pp. 99-100.

21,079 BILLING, M. G. Tribal rule and modern politics in Northern Rhodesia. AFR. AFFAIRS 58 (1959), pp. 135-140.

21,080 BRELSFORD, W. V. Analysis of African reaction to propaganda film. NADA 24 (1947), pp. 7-22.

21,081 BRELSFORD, W. V. Northern Rhodesia: urban councils on the Copperbelt. CORONA 3 (1951), pp. 430-432.

21,082 BURLES, R. S. The Katengo Council elections. J. AFR. ADM. 4 (1952), pp. 14-17.

21,083 C., J. Au conseil législatif de la Rhodésie du Nord. ZAIRE 6 (1952), p. 867.

21,084 CHONA, M. Northern Rhodesia's time for change. AFR. SOUTH 5, no. 2 (1961), pp. 72-76.

21,085 CLAY, G. C. R. African Urban Advisory Councils in the Northern Rhodesian Copperbelt. J. AFR. ADM. 1 (1949), pp. 33-38.

21,086 COLSON, E. Modern political organization of the plateau Tonga. AFR. STUD. 7 (1948), pp. 85-98.

21,087 CONYNGHAM, L. D. African towns in Northern Rhodesia. J. AFR. ADM. 3 (1951), pp. 113-117.

21,088 CREIGHTON, T. R. M. The future of the federation. AFR. SOUTH 5, no. 3 (1961), pp. 62-67.

21,089 GLENNIE, A. F. B. The Barotse system of government. J. AFR. ADM. 4 (1952), pp. 9-13.

21,090 GRAY, A. Accepting federation. AFR. AFFAIRS 56 (1957), pp. 106-109.

21,091 GRAY, A. N. Rhodesia constitution. AFR. AFFAIRS 57 (1958), pp. 252-254.

21,092 GRAY, A. Rhodesian uncertainty. AFR. AFFAIRS 61 (1962), pp. 107-108.

21,093 HEATH, F. M. N. The growth of African councils on the Copperbelt of Northern Rhodesia. J. AFR. ADM. 5 (1953), pp. 123-132.

21,094 HEISLER, H. Continuity and change in Zambian administration. J. LOCAL ADM. OV. 4 (1965), pp. 183-193.

21,095 HUDSON, W. J. S. Local Government reorganization in the Isoka district, Zambia. J. LOCAL ADM. OV. 4 (1965), pp. 47-50.

21,096 JONES, N. S. C. Native treasuries in Northern Rhodesia. RHODES-LIV. J. 2 (1944), pp. 40-48.

21,097 KAUNDA, K. D. Central Africa: Northern Rhodesia and federation. AFR. SOUTH 2, no. 3 (1958), pp. 61-67.

21,098 KAUNDA, K. D. Rider and horse in Northern Rhodesia. AFR. SOUTH 3, no. 4 (1959), pp. 52-56.

21,099 LOGAN, W. M. Native administration in Northern Rhodesia. RACE RELATIONS 6 (1939), pp. 50-59.

21,100 McKEE, H. K. Northern Rhodesia and Federation. AFR. AFFAIRS 51 (1952), pp. 323-335.

21,101 MAXWELL, Sir J. Some aspects of native policy in Northern Rhodesia. J. AFR. SOC. 29 (1930), pp. 471-477.

21,102 MITCHELL-HEGGS, M. Training in African local government in Northern Rhodesia. J. AFR. ADM. 5 (1953), pp. 34-38.

21,103 MOORE, R. J. The disturbances in the copperbelt. The Forster commission report. J. AFR. SOC. 41 (1942), pp. 42-45.

21,104 MURRAY, J. P. Zambia and the future. AFR. AFFAIRS 64 (1965), pp. 17-24.

21,105 NICHOLLS, E. G. L. The local authority and its African citizen. RHODES-LIV. J. 5 (1947), pp. 56-61.

21,106 NOAK, H. African leadership in Northern Rhodesia. NADA 40 (1963), pp. 86-89.

21,107 NORTH, A. C. Rural local government training in Northern Rhodesia. An account of the work of the Native Authority Development Centre, Chalimbana. J. AFR. ADM. 13 (1961), pp. 67-77.

21,108 PRIESTLEY, M. J. S. W. and GREENING, P. Ngoni Land Utilisation Survey, 1954-1955. J. AFR. ADM. 9 (1957), pp. 154-156.

21,109 ROBERTSON, D. M. Training chiefs in Northern Rhodesia. CORONA 1, no. 4 (1949), pp. 18-20.

21,110 STANLEY, H. Progress in Northern Rhodesia. J. AFR. SOC. 26 (1927), pp. 209-215.

21,111 STOOKE, G. B. Planning native development in Northern Rhodesia. AFR. STUD. 2 (1943), pp. 148-152.

21,112 WALLACE, L. The beginning of native administration in Northern Rhodesia. J. AFR. SOC. 21 (1922), pp. 165-176.

21,113 WHITE, C. M. N. Notes on the political organization of the Kabompo district and its inhabitants. AFR. STUD. 9 (1950), pp. 185-193.

21,114 WHITE, C. M. N. The place of training in the development of African local government in Northern Rhodesia. J. AFR. ADM. 2 (1950), pp. 29-31.

21,115 African Affairs Annual Report, 1956. J. AFR. ADM. 10 (1958), pp. 115-117.

21,116 Annual Report of the Northern Rhodesian Local Government and African Housing Department, 1950. J. AFR. ADM. 4 (1952), pp. 40-42.

21,117 Development in Northern Rhodesia (tables) [extracted from the Architectural Review]. AFR. AFFAIRS 50 (1951), pp. 154-159.

21,118 Elections en Rhodésie du Nord. PRESENCE AFR. N.S. 44 (1962), pp. 228-229.

21,119 The finances and functions of African local authorities. J. AFR. ADM. 2 (1950), pp. 3-9.

21,120 The Native Development Board. A useful institution in Northern Rhodesia; by a District Officer. J. AFR. SOC. 39 (1940), pp. 244-247.

21,121 Report of the Committee Appointed to Examine and Recommend Ways and Means by which Africans Resident in Municipal and Township Areas should be enabled to take an appropriate part in the administration of those areas. J. AFR. ADM. 10 (1958), p. 53.

See also 10464.

History

21,122 APTHORPE, R. Problems of African history: the Nsenga of Northern Rhodesia. RHODES-LIV. J. 28 (1961), pp. 47-67.

21,123 BARNES, J. A. History in a changing society. RHODES-LIV. J. 11 (1951), pp. 1-9.

21,124 BRELSFORD, V. The great north road: a chapter of Northern Rhodesian history. J. AFR. SOC. 36 (1937), pp. 62-66.

21,125 CUNNISON, I. Kazembe and the Portuguese, 1798-1832. J. AFR. HIST. 2 (1961), pp. 61-76.

21,126 GANN, L. H. The Northern Rhodesia Journal as an historical source book. RHODES-LIV. J. 23 (1958), pp. 47-53.

21,127 GIBBONS, A. ST. H. Marotseland and the tribes of the Upper Zambezi. ROYAL COL. INST. PR. 29 (1897-1898), pp. 260-276.

21,128 LANGLEY, M. The genesis of modern Zambia: 1890-1914. HISTORY TODAY 15 (1965), pp. 835-845.

21,129 LAWMAN, T. Kilwa Island. CORONA 4 (1952), pp. 391-393.

21,130 MARWICK, M. G. History and tradition in East Central Africa through the eyes of the Northern Cewa. J. AFR. HIST. 4 (1963), pp. 375-390.

21,131 MELLAND, F. Northern Rhodesia. J. AFR. SOC. 29 (1930), pp. 490-498.

21,132 MILLER, F. V. B. A few historical notes on Feira and Zumbo. J. AFR. SOC. 9 (1910), pp. 416-423.

21,133 PARKINSON, J. A. et al. The parliamentary visit to Northern Rhodesia, 1930. J. AFR. SOC. 30 (1931), pp. 4-26.

21,134 PIRIE, G. North-eastern Rhodesia. Its people and products. J. AFR. SOC. 5 (1906), pp. 130-147, 300-310, 432-436.

21,135 POOLE, E. H. L. An early Portuguese settlement in Northern Rhodesia. J. AFR. SOC. 30 (1931), pp. 164-168.

21,136 RANGER, T. The "Ethiopian" episode in Barotseland, 1900-1905. RHODES-LIV. J. 17 (1965), pp. 26-41.

21,137 ROBERTSON, O. H. Trade and the suppression of slavery in British Central Africa. NYASA J. 13, no. 2 (1960), pp. 16-21.

21,138 ROBERTSON, W. G. Kasembe and the Bembe (Awemba) nation. J. AFR. SOC. 3 (1904), pp. 183-193.

21,139 ROTBERG, R. I. The emergence of Northern Rhodesia; the missionary contribution 1885-1924. ST. ANTONY'S PAPERS 15 (1963), pp. 101-129.

21,140 ROTBERG, R. I. Missionaries as chiefs and entrepreneurs: Northern Rhodesia, 1882-1924. BOSTON UNIV. PAPERS IN AFR. HIST. 1 (1964), pp. 195-215.

21,141 WHITE, C. M. N. The Balovale peoples and their historical background. RHODES-LIV. J. 8 (1949), pp. 26-41.

21,142 WHITE, C. M. N. The ethno-history of the Upper Zambezi. AFR. STUD. 21 (1962), pp. 10-27.

21,143 WINTERBOTTOM, J. M. Outline histories of two Northern Rhodesian tribes. RHODES-LIV. J. 9 (1950), pp. 14-25.

21,144 YOUNG, C. Kinship among the Cewa of Rhodesia and Nyasaland. AFR. STUD. 9 (1950), pp. 29-31.

21,145 Native affairs in Northern Rhodesia [1933]. J. AFR. SOC. 34 (1935), pp. 184-189.

21,146 Three new reports [on native affairs in Northern Rhodesia, Northern Nigeria and Tanganyika for 1937]. J. AFR. SOC. 37 (1938), pp. 512-519.

See also 14791, 14871, 18246, 18330, 20536, 21457.

Language. Literature

21,147 BARNES, B. H. and DOKE, C. M. The pronunciation of the Bemba language. BANTU STUD. 3 (1927), pp. 423-456.

21,148 CARTER, H. Coding, style and the initial vowel in Northern Rhodesian Tonga: a psycho-linguistic study. AFR. LANG. STUD. 4 (1963), pp. 1-42.

21,149 CHAPLIN, J. H. A note on some Central African forenames. AFRICA 29 (1959), pp. 384-390.

21,150 DAMMANN, E. Kwangali-Texte. AFR. UND UB. 43 (1959-1960), pp. 201-227, 279-298.

21,151 DOKE, C. M. An outline of Ila phonetics. BANTU STUD. 3 (1927), pp. 127-153.

21,152 DOKE, C. M. A short Aushi vocabulary. BANTU STUD. 7 (1933), pp. 285-295.

21,153 DOKE, C. M. A study in Lamba phonetics. BANTU STUD. 3 (1927), pp. 5-47.

21,154 EEDEN, B. I. C. VAN. The phonology of Soli spoken in North-west Rhodesia. AFR. UND UB. 26 (1935-1936), pp. 241-271.

21,155 EPSTEIN, A. L. Linguistic innovation and culture on the Copperbelt, Northern Rhodesia. SOUTHWESTERN J. ANTHR. 15 (1959), pp. 235-253.

21,156 EVANS-PRITCHARD, E. E. Variations in a Zande folk-tale. J. AFR. LANGS. 3 (1964), pp. 103-134.

21,157 HAZEL, C. Some problems of double prefix distribution in Northern Rhodesian Tonga. J. AFR. LANGS. 3 (1964), pp. 241-251.

21,158 HOPGOOD, C. R. The future of Bantu languages in Northern Rhodesia. RHODES-LIV. J. 2 (1944), pp. 8-15.

21,159 HOPGOOD, C. R. Language, literature, and culture. AFRICA 18 (1948), pp. 112-119.

21,160 MADAN, A. C. Lala and the evolution of Bantu speech. J. AFR. SOC. 13 (1914), pp. 183-194.

21,161 MEEUSSEN, A. E. Morphotonology of the Tonga verb. J. AFR. LANGS. 2 (1963), pp. 72-92.

21,162 MUBITANA, M. The voice of Africa: a bit of Bunyan, by Moses Mubitana. AFRICA 16 (1946), pp. 179-182.

21,163 MUNDAY, J. T. Specimens of the Swaka and west Lala dialects. BANTU STUD. 15 (1941), pp. 157-183.

21,164 RICHARDSON, I. Examples of deviation and innovation in Bemba. AFR. LANG. STUD. 4 (1963), pp. 128-145.

21,165 RICHARDSON, I. Some observations on the status of town Bemba in Northern Rhodesia. AFR. LANG. STUD. 2 (1961), pp. 25-36.

21,166 SHARMAN, J. C. Nominal and pronominal prefixes in Bemba. AFR. LANG. STUD. 4 (1963), pp. 98-127.

21,167 SHARMAN, J. C. The tabulation of tenses in a Bantu language (Bemba: Northern Rhodesia). AFRICA 26 (1956), pp. 29-44.

21,168 SHARMAN, J. C. and MEEUSSEN, A. E. The representation of structural tones, with special reference to the tonal behaviour of the verb, in Bemba, Northern Rhodesia. AFRICA 25 (1955), pp. 393-403.

21,169 TORREND, J. Proper nouns in Rhodesian Tonga. J. AFR. SOC. 30 (1931), pp. 386-398.

21,170 WESTERMANN, D. Das Oxoriok. Eine sprachliche Skizze. AFRIKA (Berlin) 3 (1944), pp. 19-46.

21,171 WHITE, C. M. N. Modern influences upon an African language group. RHODES-LIV. J. 11 (1951), pp. 66-71.

Literature

21,172 DOKE, C. M. Lamba literature. AFRICA 7 (1934), pp. 351-370.

21,173 McDONALD, R. Sonnet: Lusaka General Hospital, 1965. TRANSITION 19 (1965), p. 25.

21,174 NKONDE, I. B. The storm [a poem]. AFR. AFFAIRS 46 (1947), pp. 104-105.

21,175 NKONDE, I. B. The voice of Africa: a Bemba poem, by I. Brains Nkonde. AFRICA 17 (1947), pp. 275-276.

21,176 SHEPPERSON, G. The literature of British Central Africa: a review article [Nyasaland: the Land of the Lake by F. Debenham, The Beginnings of Nyasaland and North-Eastern Rhodesia, by A. J. Hanna, The Birth of a Plural Society: the Development of Northern Rhodesia under the British South Africa Company, 1894-1914 by L. H. Gann]. RHODES-LIV. J. 23 (1958), pp. 12-46.

21,177 Les soirées littéraires des Babemba. Fables. J. AFR. SOC. 3 (1903), pp. 62-73.

Law

21,178 BRELSFORD, W. V. Native courts and authorities in Northern Rhodesia, by Kenneth Bradley. RHODES-LIV. J. 1 (1944), p. 72.

21,179 EPSTEIN, A. L. Divorce law and stability of marriage among the Lunda of Kazembe. RHODES-LIV. J. 14 (1954), pp. 1-19.

21,180 EPSTEIN, A. L. The role of African courts in urban communities of the Northern Rhodesia Copperbelt. RHODES-LIV. J. 13 (1953), pp. 1-17.

21,181 EPSTEIN, A. L. Some aspects of the conflict of law and urban courts in Northern Rhodesia. RHODES-LIV. J. 12 (1951), pp. 28-40.

21,182 EPSTEIN, A. L. Urban native courts on the Northern Rhodesian Copperbelt. J. AFR. ADM. 3 (1951), pp. 117-124.

21,183 FRASER, R. H. Land settlement in the eastern province of Northern Rhodesia. RHODES-LIV. J. 3 (1945), pp. 45-49.

21,184 GLUCKMAN, M. The reasonable man in Barotse law. J. AFR. ADM. 7 (1955), pp. 51-55, 127-131; 8 (1956), pp. 101-105, 151-156.

21,185 GOULDSBURY, C. Customary law of the Awemba. J. AFR. SOC. 14 (1914-1915), pp. 366-385.

21,186 GOULDSBURY, C. Notes on the customary law of the Awemba and kindred tribes. J. AFR. SOC. 15 (1915), pp. 36-53, 157-183.

21,187 LEHMANN, D. African urban marriage in Northern Rhodesia. AFR. WOMEN 5 (1962), pp. 14-16.

21,188 MITCHLEY, A. O. R. [Legal education in] Northern Rhodesia. J. AFR. LAW 7 (1963), pp. 118-120.

21,189 MOFFAT, R. L. African courts and native customary law in the urban areas of Northern Rhodesia. J. AFR. ADM. 9 (1957), pp. 71-79.

21,190 MUNDAY, J. T. The Witchcraft Ordinance of Northern Rhodesia. INT. REV. MISSIONS 37 (1948), pp. 181-187.

21,191 SCOBLE, C. N. Provocation in Northern Rhodesia. RNLJ 3 (1963), pp. 23-26.

21,192 UNSWORTH, E. G. The conflict of laws in Africa. RHODES-LIV. J. 2 (1944), pp. 49-55.

21,193 WHITE, C. M. N. The changing scope of urban native courts in Northern Rhodesia. J. AFR. LAW 8 (1964), pp. 29-33.

21,194 WHITE, C. M. N. The Supreme Being in the beliefs of the Balovale tribes. AFR. STUD. 7 (1948), pp. 29-35.

21,195 Northern Rhodesia. Report of the Legal Profession (entry and training) Committee. J. AFR. LAW 6 (1962), pp. 126-128.

21,196 A note on R. v. Chanda John and others [account of a murder which shocked Northern Rhodesia and of the subsequent trial]. RNLJ 3 (1963), pp. 15-22.

21,197 Urban land tenure in Northern Rhodesia. J. AFR. LAW 1 (1957), pp. 146-147; 2 (1958), p. 142.

Religion

21,198 CUNNISON, I. A Watchtower Assembly in Central Africa. INT. REV. MISSIONS 40 (1951), pp. 456-469.

21,199 LOURENCO, S. Como os Padres do Espírito Santo penetraram no Humbe. PORT. EM AFR. 11 (1954), pp. 205-216.

21,200 MUNDAY, J. T. A Central African question of morals. INT. REV. MISSIONS 38 (1949), pp. 443-448.

21,201 QUICK, G. Some aspects of the African Watch Tower movement in Northern Rhodesia. INT. REV. MISSIONS 29 (1940), pp. 216-226.

21,202 ROTBERG, R. The Lenshina movement of Northern Rhodesia. RHODES-LIV. J. 29 (1961), pp. 63-78.

Science

21,203 ADAMS, P. C. G. Disease concepts among Africans in the Protectorate of Northern Rhodesia. RHODES-LIV. J. 10 (1950), pp. 14-50.

21,204 CLARKE, J. H. C. Diet and health of African school boys. RHODES-LIV. J. 2 (1944), pp. 68-69.

21,205 COLSON, E. Plateau Tonga diet. RHODES-LIV. J. 24 (1959), pp. 51-67.

21,206 DAVIDSON, S. Psychiatric work among the Bemba. RHODES-LIV. J. 7 (1949), pp. 75-86.

21,207 DEANS, T. The mineral resources of Northern Rhodesia. BULL. IMP. INST. 40 (1942), pp. 295-306.

21,208 EVANS, A. J. The Ila V.D. campaign. RHODES-LIV. J. 9 (1950), pp. 40-47.

21,209 FERREIRA, G. DA V. Uma espécie nova do género Xystrocera. BSEM 84 (1954), pp. 147-149.

21,210 JEFFREYS, R. S. The true age of Africans. J. AFR. SOC. 39 (1940), pp. 170-175.

21,211 RICHARDS, A. I. and WIDDOWSON, E. M. A dietary study in North-Eastern Rhodesia. AFRICA 9 (1936), pp. 166-196.

21,212 VAUGHAN-JONES, T. G. C. A short survey of the aims and functions of the game and tsetse control department of Northern Rhodesia. RHODES-LIV. J. 6 (1948), pp. 37-47.

21,213 VAUGHAN-JONES, T. G. C. Tsetse control in Northern Rhodesia. CORONA 3 (1951), pp. 175-178.

21,214 WATT, J. M. and BREYER-BRANDWIJK, M. G. A note on phyllanthus engleri, pax. Mufweba-bachazi—a Northern Rhodesian suicide plant. BANTU STUD. 3 (1927), pp. 395-400.

21,215 WINTERBOTTOM, J. M. The ecology of man and plants in Northern Rhodesia. RHODES-LIV. J. 3 (1945), pp. 33-44.

21,216 A tenderfoot among locusts. NADA 27 (1950), pp. 50-55.

See also 16422.

Sociology

21,217 ATKINS, G. The Nyanja-speaking population of Nyasaland and Northern Rhodesia (a statistical estimate). AFR. STUD. 9 (1950), pp. 35-39.

21,218 C., J. Urbanisation et autorité en Rhodésie du Nord. ZAIRE 8 (1954), p. 949.

21,219 CHAPLIN, J. H. Suicide in Northern Rhodesia. AFR. STUD. 20 (1961), pp. 145-174.

21,220 CHAPLIN, J. H. Wiving and thriving in Northern Rhodesia. AFRICA 32 (1962), pp. 111-122.

21,221 COLSON, E. Possible repercussions of the right to make wills upon the Plateau Tonga of Northern Rhodesia. J. AFR. ADM. 2 (1950), pp. 24-34.

21,222 COLSON, E. Social change and the Gwembe Tonga. RHODES-LIV. J. 35 (1964), pp. 1-13.

21,223 COOPER, B. Race problems in Northern Rhodesia. CONTEMP. REV. 193 (1958), pp. 311-314.

21,224 DARLOW, M. The African townsman in Northern Rhodesia. AFR. WOMEN 1 (1955), pp. 57-59.

21,225 DICKSON, A. G. The African village after the war. RACE RELATIONS 11 (1944), pp. 56-60.

21,226 EPSTEIN, A. L. The network and urban social organization. RHODES-LIV. J. 29 (1961), pp. 29-62.

21,227 FISHER, W. S. Burning the bush for game. AFR. STUD. 7 (1948), pp. 36-38.

21,228 GLUCKMAN, M. Tribalism in modern British Central Africa. CAH. ET. AFR. 1, no. i (1960), pp. 55-70.

21,229 HARRIES-JONES, P. Marital disputes and the process of conciliation in a Copperbelt town. RHODES-LIV. J. 35 (1964), pp. 29-72.

21,230 HARRIS, R. The mind of the literate African on the Copperbelt as seen in letters to Luntandanya. RACE 1, no. 2 (1959-1960), pp. 59-64.

21,231 IBBOTSON, P. Federation of native welfare societies in Southern Rhodesia. RHODES-LIV. J. 2 (1944), pp. 35-39.

21,232 KAY, G. First census of the African population of Northern Rhodesia. J. LOCAL ADM. OV. 3 (1964), pp. 68-76.

21,233 KEITH, J. L. Native progress in Northern Rhodesia. J. AFR. SOC. 36 (1937), pp. 482-489.

21,234 MITCHELL, J. C. Aspects of African marriage on the Copperbelt of Northern Rhodesia. RHODES-LIV. J. 22 (1957), pp. 1-30.

21,235 MITCHELL, J. C. Differential fertility amongst urban Africans in Zambia. RHODES-LIV. J. 17 (1965), pp. 1-25.

21,236 MITCHELL, J. C. An estimate of fertility among Africans on the Copperbelt of Northern Rhodesia. RHODES-LIV. J. 13 (1953), pp. 18-29.

21,237 MITCHELL, J. C. A note on the urbanization of Africans on the Copperbelt. RHODES-LIV. J. 12 (1951), pp. 20-27.

21,238 MITCHELL, J. C. and EPSTEIN, A. L. Occupational prestige and social status among urban Africans in Northern Rhodesia. AFRICA 29 (1959), pp. 22-39.

21,239 MITCHELL, J. C. and IRVINE, S. H. Social position and the grading of occupations. RHODES-LIV. J. 38 (1965), pp. 42-54.

21,240 NORTH, A. C. et al. African land tenure developments in Kenya and Uganda and their application to Northern Rhodesia, by A. C. North, J. C. Mousley, P. Greening, and I. M. Muchangwe. J. AFR. ADM. 13 (1961), pp. 211-219.

21,241 PRAIN, R. L. The problem of African advancement on the copperbelt of Northern Rhodesia. AFR. AFFAIRS 53 (1954), pp. 91-103.

21,242 ROTBERG, R. I. Race relations and politics in colonial Zambia: the Elwell incident. RACE 7, no. 1 (1965), pp. 17-29.

21,243 THOMSON, B. and KAY, G. A note on the poverty datum line in Northern Rhodesia. RHODES-LIV. J. 30 (1961), pp. 40-49.

21,244 WHITE, C. M. N. Chieftaincy in Luvale political organization. J. AFR. ADM. 9 (1957), pp. 129-136.

21,245 WINTERBOTTOM, J. M. Africans, European culture and the English language. RHODES-LIV. J. 2 (1944), pp. 1-7.

21,246 The Rhodes-Livingstone Institute for Social Research. Director's report for the year ending 31st March 1957. J. AFR. ADM. 9 (1957), pp. 209-210.

21,247 The Rhodes-Livingstone Institute for Social Research. Director's report for the year ending March 1959. J. AFR. ADM. 12 (1960), pp. 52-53.

21,248 L'urbanisation en Rhodésie du Nord. ZAIRE 6 (1952), p. 192.

See also 16453, 16454, 16455, 16457, 16458, 16459, 16460, 16461, 16462, 20823, 20866.

MALAWI

General

21,249 The Nyasaland Society. NYASA J. 1, no. 1 (1948), pp. 4-8.

Agriculture

21,250 BADCOCK, W. J. Soil conservation in Nyasaland. CORONA 1, no. 8 (1949), pp. 15-16.

21,251 GIFKINS, A. V. Report on 1954 hatching at Nchenachena. NYASA J. 9, no. 1 (1956), pp. 51-57.

21,252 MITCHELL, J. C. Preliminary notes on land tenure and agriculture among the Machinga Yao. NYASA J. 5, no. 2 (1952), pp. 18-30.

21,253 RANGELEY, W. H. J. A brief history of the tobacco industry in Nyasaland. NYASA J. 10, no. 1 (1957), pp. 62-83; 10, no. 2 (1957), pp. 32-51.

21,254 RIMMINGTON, G. T. Agricultural development in the Dedza District of Nyasaland. NYASA J. 16, no. 1 (1963), pp. 28-48.

21,255 RIMMINGTON, G. T. The new farm in the Dedza District of Nyasaland. NYASA J. 16, no. 2 (1963), pp. 26-33.

21,256 TAWNEY, J. J. Soil conservation: an African method. CORONA 2 (1950), pp. 153-154.

21,257 TERRY, P. T. African agriculture in Nyasaland. NYASA J. 14, no. 2 (1961), pp. 27-35.

21,258 THOMSON, T. D. Soil conservation—some implications. J. AFR. ADM. 5 (1953), pp. 66-69.

Anthropology

21,259 BETTISON, D. G. and APTHORPE, R. J. Authority and residence in a peri-urban social structure—Ndirande, Nyasaland. NYASA J. 14, no. 1 (1961), pp. 7-39.

21,260 BUCHANAN, L. A. C. Notes on rain stopping in Nyasaland. J. AFR. SOC. 42 (1943), pp. 34-37.

21,261 CHAKANZA, E. T. Nyasa folk songs. AFR. AFFAIRS 49 (1950), pp. 158-161.

21,262 GARBUTT, H. W. Witchcraft in Nyasa (Manganja) Yao (Achawa), communicated by a native to H. W. Garbutt. JRAI 41 (1911), pp. 301-304.

21,263 HEMANS, T. J. Kidnapped by the Vadoma. NADA 40 (1963), pp. 4-5.

21,264 HODGSON, A. G. O. Notes on the Achewa and Angoni of the Dowa district of the Nyasaland Protectorate. JRAI 63 (1933), pp. 123-164.

21,265 LAWSON, A. An outline of the relationship system of the Nyanja and Yao tribes in South Nyasaland. AFR. STUD. 8 (1949), pp. 180-190.

21,266 MAGALHAES, M. J. DE. Em terras do Niassa. PORT. EM AFR. 7 (1950), pp. 360-364.

21,267 MAIR, L. P. Marriage and family in the Dedza district of Nyasaland. JRAI 81 (1951), pp. 103-119.

21,268 MELL, A. H. Notes on family and marriage in primitive societies. NYASA J. 4, no. 1 (1951), pp. 7-23.

21,269 METCALFE, M. Some Nyasaland folk-lore tales. NYASA J. 7, no. 2 (1954), pp. 46-49.

21,270 MITCHELL, J. C. An estimate of fertility in some Yao hamlets in Liwonde district of southern Nyasaland. AFRICA 19 (1949), pp. 293-308.

21,271 MITCHELL, J. C. Marriage, matriliny and social structure among the Yao of Southern Nyasaland. INT. J. COMP. SOC. 3 (1962), pp. 29-42.

21,272 MITCHELL, J. C. A note on the African conception of causality. NYASA J. 5, no. 2 (1952), pp. 51-58.

21,273 MITCHELL, J. C. An outline of the social structure of Malemia area. NYASA J. 4, no. 2 (1951), pp. 15-47.

21,274 MOGGRIDGE, L. T. The Nyasaland tribes, their customs and their poison ordeal. JRAI 32 (1902), pp. 467-472.

21,275 NKOJERA, A. History of the Kamanga tribe of Lake Nyasa. A native account. J. AFR. SOC. 10 (1911), pp. 331-341; 11 (1912), pp. 231-234.

21,276 PRETORIUS, J. L. The terms of relationship of the Cewa. NYASA J. 2, no. 1 (1949), pp. 44-52.

21,277 PRICE, T. The name "Anguru." NYASA J. 5, no. 1 (1952), pp. 23-25.

21,278 RANGELEY, W. H. J. The AmaCinga aYao. NYASA J. 15, no. 2 (1962), pp. 40-70.

21,279 RANGELEY, W. H. J. The aYao. NYASA J. 16, no. 1 (1963), pp. 7-27.

21,280 RANGELEY, W. H. J. Mbona—the rain maker. NYASA J. 6, no. 1 (1953), pp. 8-27.

21,281 RANGELEY, W. H. J. "Nyau" in Kotakota district. NYASA J. 2, no. 2 (1949), pp. 35-49; 3, no. 2 (1950), pp. 19-33.

21,282 RANGELEY, W. H. J. Two Nyasaland rain shrines. NYASA J. 5, no. 2 (1952), pp. 31-50.

21,283 READ, M. Native standards of living and African culture change. Illustrated by examples from the Ngoni Highlands of Nyasaland. AFRICA 11 (1938), supplement.

21,284 READ, M. Tradition and prestige among the Ngoni. AFRICA 9 (1936), pp. 453-483.

21,285 SANDERSON, G. M. Inyago. The picture-models of the Yao initiation ceremonies. NYASA J. 8, no. 2 (1955), pp. 36-57.

21,286 SANDERSON, G. M. Tumbuka proverbs. NYASA J. 5, no. 1 (1952), pp. 38-54.

21,287 SANDERSON, G. M. The use of tail-switches in magic. NYASA J. 8, no. 1 (1955), pp. 39-56.

21,288 STANNUS, H. S. Notes on some tribes of British Central Africa. JRAI 40 (1910), pp. 285-335.

21,289 STIGAND, C. H. Notes on the natives of Nyassaland, N.E. Rhodesia, and Portuguese Zambezia, their arts, customs, and modes of subsistence. JRAI 37 (1907), pp. 119-132.

21,290 STIGAND, C. H. Notes on the tribes in the neighbourhood of Fort Manning, Nyassaland. JRAI 39 (1909), pp. 35-43.

21,291 TALBOT, I. Mfumba sleeping bags. NYASA J. 9, no. 1 (1956), pp. 72-73.

21,292 TALBOT, W. D. S. A few notes on hippopotamus hunting by the Phodzo people of Port Herald District, using harpoons. NYASA J. 9, no. 2 (1956), pp. 19-20.

21,293 WILLIAMS, S. G. Lions. NYASA J. 9, no. 1 (1956), pp. 74-81.

21,294 YOUNG, C. The "Henga" people in northern Nyasaland. NYASA J. 5, no. 1 (1952), pp. 33-37.

21,295 YOUNG, C. and MALEKEBU, B. E. African playtime. NYASA J. 6, no. 1 (1953), pp. 34-44.

21,296 YOUNG, T. C. A good village. AFRICA 7 (1934), pp. 89-96.

21,297 YOUNG, T. C. Habits and customs of the olden days among the Tumbuka-Kamanga people. BANTU STUD. 10 (1936), pp. 313-357.

21,298 YOUNG, T. C. Tribal intermixture in Northern Nyasaland. JRAI 63 (1933), pp. 1-18.

21,299 YOUNG, T. C. The "Wa-henga" of Northern Nyasaland. J. AFR. SOC. 23 (1924), pp. 188-193.

21,300 Native customs in Nyasaland. NADA 16 (1939), pp. 37-47.

21,301 The religion of my fathers [by a member of a Nyasaland tribe. INT. REV. MISSIONS 19 (1930), pp. 362-376.

See also 14104, 20908, 20924, 20933, 20951.

Art. Antiquities

21,302 CARTMEL-ROBINSON, S. The Lupanda dance. NYASA J. 15, no. 2 (1962), pp. 20-23.

21,303 CHAKANZA, E. T. Nyasa folk songs. AFR. AFFAIRS 49 (1950), pp. 158-161.

21,304 CLARK, J. D. Prehistory in Nyasaland. NYASA J. 9, no. 1 (1956), pp. 92-119.

21,305 KIDNEY, E. Native songs from Nyasaland. J. AFR. SOC. 20 (1921), pp. 116-126.

21,306 L., W. D. "Machhemba"—primitive citadels. NYASA J. 3, no. 2 (1950), pp. 34-37.

21,307 LOUW, J. K. African music in Christian worship. AFR. MUSIC, 1958, pp. 51-53.

21,308 LOUW, J. K. The use of African music in the church. AFR. MUSIC, 1956, pp. 43-44.

21,309 METCALFE, M. Some rock paintings in Nyasaland. NYASA J. 9, no. 1 (1956), pp. 58-70.

21,310 NURSE, G. T. Popular songs and national identity in Malawi. AFR. MUSIC, 1964, pp. 101-106.

21,311 PIKE, J. G. Further Stone Age implements from the Karonga area. NYASA J. 12, no. 2 (1959), pp. 55-56.

21,312 PRICE, T. Mbona's water-hole. NYASA J. 6, no. 1 (1953), pp. 28-33.

21,313 RANGELEY, W. H. J. Ancient iron working on the Nyika Plateau. NYASA J. 13, no. 1 (1960), pp. 18-20.

21,314 RANGELEY, W. H. J. The earliest inhabitants of Nyasaland. NYASA J. 16, no. 2 (1963), pp. 35-42.

21,315 READ, M. Songs of the Ngoni people. BANTU STUD. 11 (1937), pp. 1-35.

21,316 STANNUS, H. S. Native paintings in Nyasaland. J. AFR. SOC. 9 (1910), pp. 184-187.

21,317 WALKER, R. A survey of early buildings in Nyasaland. NYASA J. 13, no. 1 (1960), pp. 51-61.

21,318 WERNER, A. A native painting from Nyasaland. J. AFR. SOC. 8 (1909), pp. 190-192.

21,319 WOOD, R. C. Stone Age cultures in Nyasaland. NYASA J. 4, no. 1 (1951), pp. 65-66.

21,320 Opening of the Nyasaland Museum, 2nd. July 1960. NYASA J. 14, no. 1 (1961), pp. 48-49.

21,321 Report on the I.L.A.M. Nyasaland recording tour. AFR. MUSIC, 1958, pp. 65-68.

Biography

21,322 Obituary: Patrick Hamilton Borrowman. NYASA J. 1, no. 2 (1948), p. 64.

21,323 Obituary: Sir William Tait Bowie, O.B.E. NYASA J. 2, no. 2 (1949), pp. 58-59.

21,324 Obituary: Norman Maclaren Brown. NYASA J. 7, no. 1 (1954), p. 52.

21,325 CHINGOTA, J. An autobiography. NYASA J. 14, no. 2 (1961), pp. 13-26.

21,326 Obituary: Robert Edward Clegg, M.B.E. NYASA J. 3, no. 1 (1950), p. 60.

21,327 Obituary: Elizabeth Frances Eldred. NYASA J. 6, no. 1 (1953), p. 71.

21,328 Obituary: Archdeacon A. G. B. Glossop, O.B.E. NYASA J. 3, no. 1 (1950), pp. 59-60.

21,329 Obituary: Aubrey Victor Hall, O.B.E. NYASA J. 8, no. 2 (1955), p. 73.

21,330 Obituary: Robert Stanley Harper. NYASA J. 3, no. 1 (1950), p. 59.

21,331 ARNOLD, C. W. B. Slave-boy to priest [Padre Kilekwa]. NYASA J. 2, no. 1 (1949), pp. 7-15.

21,332 Obituary: Wilfrid John Leslie. NYASA J. 5, no. 2 (1952), p. 66.

21,333 WILSON, H. F. David Livingstone. Some reminiscences. NYASA J. 12, no. 2 (1959), pp. 12-21.

21,334 CHIRGWIN, A. M. New light on Robert Livingstone. J. AFR. SOC. 33 (1934), pp. 250-252.

21,335 Obituary: Wilfrid Gray Milne. NYASA J. 3, no. 2 (1950), pp. 58-59.

21,336 Ardwell Mlenga: an autobiography. NYASA J. 17, no. 2 (1964), pp. 25-28.

21,337 Extracts from the diary and letters of Peter Moore, 1888. NYASA J. 11, no. 1 (1958), pp. 25-41; 11, no. 2 (1958), pp. 55-67.

21,338 NAMONDE, T. The story of Twaya Namonde. NYASA J. 16, no. 1 (1963), pp. 49-61.

21,339 Obituary: Gerald Patrick O'Neill. NYASA J. 4, no. 1 (1951), p. 72.

21,340 Obituary: G. Owen-Taylor. NYASA J. 7, no. 1 (1954), p. 52.

21,341 Obituary: Joseph George Parham. NYASA J. 3, no. 2 (1950), p. 58.

21,342 LESLIE, M. E. Pitgaveny, 1899-1905. NYASA J. 4, no. 1 (1951), pp. 40-53.

21,343 Obituary: Harold Robert Price, O.B.E. NYASA J. 8, no. 2 (1955), p. 73.

21,344 Obituary: W. H. J. Rangeley. NYASA J. 11, no. 2 (1958), pp. 7-8.

21,345 Obituary: John Owen Shircore, C.M.G., M.B., Ch.B., M.R.C.P. NYASA J. 6, no. 2 (1953), p. 58.

21,346 Obituary: Colin Smee. NYASA J. 1, no. 1 (1948), pp. 59-60.

21,347 Obituary: John Kirby Smith. NYASA J. 6, no. 2 (1953), p. 59.

21,348 WITHERS, F. M. A sailor who did his duty. Belated tribute to a real pioneer [Edward D. Young]. NYASA J. 4, no. 1 (1951), pp. 24-39.

21,349 Obituary: Rev. T. Cullen Young, C.A. NYASA J. 8, no. 2 (1955), pp. 73-74.

Economics

21,350 BAKER, C. A. Nyasaland, the history of its export trade. NYASA J. 15, no. 1 (1962), pp. 7-35.

21,351 DEAN, E. R. Studies in price formation in African markets. RHODES-LIV. J. 31 (1962), pp. 1-20.

21,352 FLORENCE, J. A. C. The growth of civil aviation in Nyasaland. NYASA J. 11, no. 2 (1958), pp. 14-23.

21,353 FROST, D. T. T. The economic outlook for Nyasaland. RACE 4, no. 2 (1962-1963), pp. 59-72.

21,354 HOOLE, M. C. Notes on fishing and allied industries as practised amongst the Tonga of the West Nyasa District. NYASA J. 8, no. 1 (1955), pp. 25-38.

21,355 KETTLEWELL, R. W. Nyasaland—whence and whither? AFR. AFFAIRS 63 (1964), pp. 258-265.

21,356 McDONALD, L. J. Bicycles in B. C. A. NYASA J. 15, no. 2 (1962), pp. 33-34.

21,357 MAW, A. H. Transport and travelling in British Central Africa, 1899. NYASA J. 8, no. 2 (1955), pp. 11-15.

21,358 MAXWELL, W. A. The Shire Valley Project. Criticism by W. A. Maxwell. NYASA J. 7, no. 2 (1954), pp. 39-45.

21,359 RANGELEY, W. H. J. A brief history of the tobacco industry in Nyasaland. NYASA J. 11, no. 2 (1958), pp. 24-27.

21,360 RANGELEY, W. H. J. Early postal history of the Mlanje area. Further comments. NYASA J. 11, no. 2 (1958), pp. 35-38.

21,361 REBELO, D. J. S. O chá na economia do Malawi (um estudo economico). BSEM 144-145 (1965), pp. 109-129; includes English summary.

21,362 RICHARDS, E. V. The Shire Valley Project. NYASA J. 7, no. 1 (1954), pp. 7-17.

21,363 SANDERSON, F. E. The development of labour migration from Nyasaland, 1891-1914. J. AFR. HIST. 2 (1961), pp. 259-271.

21,364 SHARPE, A. Recent progress in Nyasaland. J. AFR. SOC. 9 (1910), pp. 337-348.

21,365 TALBOT, W. D. Some notes on the dhows of Fort Johnston District. NYASA J. 15, no. 2 (1962), pp. 24-29.

21,366 TERRY, P. T. The rise of the African cotton industry in Nyasaland, 1902 to 1918. NYASA J. 15, no. 1 (1962), pp. 59-71; 15, no. 2 (1962), pp. 14-15.

21,367 TWYNAM, C. D. Early postal history of the Mlanje area. NYASA J. 9, no. 2 (1956), pp. 21-28.

21,368 TWYNAM, C. D. From concession to Ntakataka in 1927. NYASA J. 8, no. 2 (1955), pp. 16-20.

21,369 TWYNAM, C. D. Nyasaland mails and stamps. NYASA J. 1, no. 1 (1948), pp. 11-25.

21,370 WILLAN, R. G. M. The road up Zomba Mountain. NYASA J. 16, no. 1 (1963), pp. 62-70.

21,371 WILLIAMS, S. G. Some old steamships of Nyasaland. NYASA J. 11, no. 1 (1958), pp. 42-56.

21,372 W[ITHERS], F. M. Seine net fishing in Nyasa. NYASA J. 5, no. 1 (1952), pp. 26-32.

21,373 Y., N. C. Nyasaland report, 1935; by N. C. Y. J. AFR. SOC. 36 (1937), pp. 85-87.

21,374 The British Central Africa Gazette [some extracts from Nyasaland's first newspaper]. NYASA J. 8, no. 2 (1955), pp. 21-26.

21,375 Nyasaland and aluminium. J. AFR. SOC. 39 (1940), pp. 202-203; 40 (1941), pp. 295-296.

21,376 Report on the Economic Survey of Nyasaland, 1958-1959. J. AFR. ADM. 12 (1960), pp. 185-187.

See also 20283, 20284.

Education

21,377 LAWS, R. Native education in Nyasaland. J. AFR. SOC. 28 (1929), pp. 347-367.

21,378 SAUVY, J. L'Unesco à la recherche de méthodes éducatives nouvelles. PRESENCE AFR. 6 (1949), pp. 147-150.

21,379 Aims of education for girls in Nyasaland. AFR. WOMEN 4 (1962), pp. 91-92.

21,380 Girls' education in Nyasaland. AFR. WOMEN 1 (1955), pp. 61-63.

Geography

21,381 ARNOLD, C. W. B. Lake Nyasa's varying level. NYASA J. 5, no. 1 (1952), pp. 7-17.

21,382 BAKER, C. A. Blantyre District. A geographical appreciation of the growth, distribution and composition of its population. NYASA J. 12, no. 1 (1959), pp. 7-35.

21,383 BAYLISS, M. Glimpses of early Nyasaland. NYASA J. 17, no. 1 (1964), pp. 10-15.

21,384 BENSON, C. W. The Nyika Plateau. C. W. Benson's visits 1937-1953. NYASA J. 7, no. 2 (1954), pp. 28-35.

21,385 BLOOMFIELD, K. and YOUNG, A. The geology and geomorphology of Zomba Mountain. NYASA J. 14, no. 2 (1961), pp. 54-80.

21,386 BRASS, L. J. The Nyika Plateau. Varnay Expedition report 1946. NYASA J. 7, no. 2 (1954), pp. 35-38.

21,387 BRASS, L. J. The Vernay expedition. NYASA J. 2, no. 2 (1949), pp. 50-57.

21,388 CRAWSHAY, R. The Nyika Plateau. Richard Crawshay's impression in 1893. NYASA J. 7, no. 2 (1954), pp. 24-27.

21,389 DAVEY, J. B. North Nyasaland in 1907. NYASA J. 15, no. 2 (1962), pp. 16-19.

21,390 DAY, Sir A. Lake Nyasa Hydrographic Survey. Talk to the Nyasaland Society on 9th. March 1956. NYASA J. 9, no. 2 (1956), pp. 57-64.

21,391 DIXEY, F. The distribution of population in Nyasaland. GEOG. REV. 18 (1928), pp. 274-290.

21,392 DIXEY, F. The Mlanje mountains of Nyasaland. GEOG. REV. 17 (1927), pp. 611-626.

21,393 EDWARDS, A. C. T. Zomba flood, December, 1946. NYASA J. 1, no. 2 (1948), pp. 53-63.

21,394 JOHNSTON, H. C. J. The weather. NYASA J. 2, no. 2 (1949), pp. 30-34.

21,395 JOLLYMAN, W. H. Tides and seiches in Lake Nyasa. NYASA J. 8, no. 2 (1955), pp. 31-35; 9, no. 1 (1956), p. 91.

21,396 KATHAMALO. Khulubvi thicket—Port Herald. NYASA J. 18, no. 2 (1965), pp. 53-54.

21,397 LATHAM, E. W. Report on the flooding in the Chiromo/Makanga area as a result of the cyclone which crossed the territory on 5th April, 1956. NYASA J. 10, no. 1 (1957), pp. 47-61.

21,398 LATHAM, E. W. Water resources and water development in Nyasaland. NYASA J. 17, no. 2 (1964), pp. 57-69.

21,399 LIVINGSTONE, W. P. "Elephant" island on Lake Nyasa. NYASA J. 15, no. 1 (1962), pp. 36-37.

21,400 PIKE, J. G. A brief note on the upper pleistocene raised beach of the Karonga Lake shore. NYASA J. 11, no. 1 (1958), pp. 57-59.

21,401 PIKE, J. G. The movement of water in Lake Nyasa. NYASA J. 10, no. 2 (1957), pp. 58-64.

21,402 PIKE, J. G. The pre-historical climates of Nyasaland. NYASA J. 13, no. 2 (1960), pp. 79-85.

21,403 RIMMINGTON, G. T. The historical geography of population growth in the Dedza District of Nyasaland. NYASA J. 16, no. 2 (1963), pp. 43-60.

21,404 RIMMINGTON, G. T. Village types in the Kachindamoto area of the Dedza district of Nyasaland. NYASA J. 17, no. 1 (1964), pp. 7-9.

21,405 SOUSA LEITAO, A. E. DE. O levantamento hidrográfico do Lago Niassa. BSEM 130 (1962), pp. 111-124.

21,406 STARMANS, G. A. N. Note on the surface water resources of the Protectorate. NYASA J. 10, no. 1 (1957), pp. 24-44.

21,407 STARMANS, G. A. N. A preliminary note on the fluvial morphology of the rivers of Nyasaland. NYASA J. 9, no. 1 (1956), pp. 7-10.

21,408 STEELE, B. Makali. NYASA J. 10, no. 1 (1957), pp. 45-46.

21,409 STEGMAN, J. J. Nyasaland droughts. NYASA J. 4, no. 1 (1951), pp. 67-69.

21,410 STEWART, M. M. On top of Malawi—the Misuku. NYASA J. 18, no. 1 (1965), pp. 7-13.

21,411 TURNBULL, A. M. D. Extract from the diary of the late A. M. D. Turnbull. NYASA J. 15, no. 2 (1962), pp. 35-37.

21,412 WHITEHOUSE, H. E. Level of Lake Nyasa. NYASA J. 5, no. 1 (1952), pp. 18-22.

21,413 WILLAN, R. G. M. Mud-flow in the Chelinda Valley, Nyika Plateau. NYASA J. 15, no. 2 (1962), pp. 30-32.

21,414 WILLAN, R. G. Some notes on the cold spell in August 1955. NYASA J. 10, no. 1 (1957), pp. 7-10.

21,415 WILLAN, R. G. A visit to the Nyika in 1937. NYASA J. 9, no. 2 (1956), pp. 51-56.

21,416 WILLIAMS, S. G. B. Early maps of Nyasaland. NYASA J. 13, no. 2 (1960), pp. 13-15.

21,417 WOOD, C. "Elephant" island on Lake Nyasa. NYASA J. 11, no. 1 (1958), pp. 23-24.

21,418 YOUNG, C. Africa—imagined and real. NYASA J. 7, no. 1 (1954), pp. 30-35.

21,419 YOUNG, T. C. "Zovu." NYASA J. 6, no. 1 (1953), pp. 53-59.

21,420 YOUNG, W. P. Memories of the Nyika Plateau. NYASA J. 6, no. 1 (1953), pp. 45-52.

21,421 Expedition from Port Amelia to Lake Nyasa. Commanded by Major Spilsbury, delegate administrator of the Nyasaland Company August, 1900. J. AFR. SOC. 1 (1901), pp. 126-144.

21,422 Lake Nyasa in 1893. NYASA J. 15, no. 1 (1962), pp. 55-58.

Government. Politics. Administration

21,423 THE AFRICAN STUDIES BRANCH. The amalgamation of two town councils in Nyasaland. J. AFR. ADM. 7 (1955), pp. 135-138.

21,424 BANDA, T. D. T. Central Africa: Nyasaland and federation. AFR. SOUTH 2, no. 2 (1958), pp. 75-81.

21,425 CHIMWAZA, G. M. How the Colonial Fund can help Nyasaland. J. AFR. SOC. 39 (1940), pp. 320-321.

21,426 CHIUME, M. W. K. The Nyasaland crisis. AFR. SOUTH 3, no. 4 (1959), pp. 45-51.

21,427 COLBY, Sir G. Recent developments in Nyasaland. AFR. AFFAIRS 55 (1956), pp. 273-282.

21,428 GRAHAM-JOLLY, H. G. The progress of local government in Nyasaland. J. AFR. ADM. 7 (1955), pp. 188-192.

21,429 GRAY, A. Devlin report. AFR. AFFAIRS 58 (1959), pp. 276-279.

21,430 GRAY, A. Nyasaland emergency. AFR. AFFAIRS 58 (1959), pp. 102-104.

21,431 MITCHELL, J. C. The political organization of the Yao of Southern Nyasaland. AFR. STUD. 8 (1949), pp. 141-159.

21,432 ROBINS, J. W. Developments in rural local government in Nyasaland. J. AFR. ADM. 13 (1961), pp. 148-157.

21,433 ROWLAND, H. R. Nyasaland general elections, 1964. J. LOCAL ADM. OV. 3 (1964), pp. 227-240.

21,434 SMITH, G. Nyasaland. J. AFR. SOC. 24 (1924), pp. 14-24.

21,435 THOMSON, T. D. Local government training in Nyasaland. J. AFR. ADM. 8 (1956), pp. 196-202.

21,436 VELSEN, J. VAN. The missionary factor among the Lakeside Tonga of Nyasaland. RHODES-LIV. J. 26 (1959), pp. 1-22.

21,437 WISHLADE, R. L. Chiefship and politics in the Mlanje district of southern Nyasaland. AFRICA 31 (1961), pp. 36-45.

21,438 Domasi Community Development Scheme Report 1949-54 [issued on behalf of Government of Nyasaland]. J. AFR. ADM. 9 (1957), pp. 106-107.

21,439 Domasi Community Scheme, Nyasaland. Annual Report for the year 1950. J. AFR. ADM. 4 (1952), pp. 42-43.

21,440 Local Government legislation in Nyasaland. J. AFR. ADM. 6 (1954), pp. 110-114.

History

21,441 BAKER, C. A. Magomero, and the battle of Sazi Hill, Zomba 1861. NYASA J. 13, no. 2 (1960), pp. 86-95.

21,442 BAKER, C. A. A map of the Shire valley and highlands routes of Livingstone, 1859. NYASA J. 12, no. 2 (1959), pp. 22-26.

21,443 BAKER, C. A. A note on Nguru immigration to Nyasaland. NYASA J. 14, no. 1 (1961), pp. 41-42.

21,444 CARDEW, C. A. Notes re Mpimbi, Fort Sharpe and Liwonde. NYASA J. 9, no. 1 (1956), pp. 88-90.

21,445 CARDEW, C. A. Nyasaland in 1894-5. NYASA J. 1, no. 1 (1948), pp. 51-55.

21,446 CARDEW, C. A. Nyasaland in the 'nineties. NYASA J. 8, no. 1 (1955), pp. 57-63.

21,447 EMTAGE, E. How the people came. NYASA J. 13, no. 1 (1960), pp. 32-34; 13, no. 2 (1960), pp. 75-78.

21,448 EMTAGE, J. E. R. The first Mission settlement. NYASA J. 8, no. 1 (1955), pp. 16-24.

21,449 HADLOW, G. G. S. J. The history of tea in Nyasaland. An address delivered to the Nyasaland Society. NYASA J. 13, no. 1 (1960), pp. 21-31.

21,450 HASKARD, C. D. P. T. The Stevenson Stone. NYASA J. 18, no. 1 (1965), pp. 14-19.

21,451 HAYES, G. D. Lake Nyasa and the 1914-18 war. NYASA J. 17, no. 2 (1964), pp. 17-24.

21,452 HETHERWICK, A. Nyasaland to-day and to-morrow. J. AFR. SOC. 17 (1917), pp. 11-19.

21,453 JACKSON, G. Correspondence of John Kirk to Sir William Hooker, Dr. Joseph Hooker and Professor Balfour. NYASA J. 12, no. 2 (1959), pp. 40-54.

21,454 LONG, N. Bandawe Mission Station and local politics, 1878-86. RHODES-LIV. J. 32 (1962), pp. 1-22.

21,455 LUGARD, F. D. The flight against slave-traders on Nyassa. CONTEMP. REV. 56 (1889), pp. 335-345.

21,456 MacPHERSON, F. The Ncerenje memorial stone. NYASA J. 13, no. 1 (1960), pp. 62-64.

21,457 PATHAK, G. S. Malawi and Zambia. AFR. QUART. 4, no. i (1964), pp. 26-29.

21,458 PIKE, J. G. A pre-colonial history of Malawi. NYASA J. 18, no. 1 (1965), pp. 22-54.

21,459 POOLE, E. H. L. The date of the crossing of the Zambezi by the Ngoni. J. AFR. SOC. 29 (1930), pp. 290-292.

21,460 PRICE, T. More about the Maravi. AFR. STUD. 11 (1952), pp. 75-79.

21,461 PRICE, T. Yao origins. NYASA J. 17, no. 2 (1964), pp. 11-16.

21,462 RANGELEY, W. H. J. Early Blantyre. NYASA J. 7, no. 1 (1954), pp. 36-45.

21,463 RANGELEY, W. H. J. The Makalolo of Dr. Livingstone. NYASA J. 12, no. 1 (1959), pp. 59-98.

21,464 RANGELEY, W. H. J. The origins of the principal street names of Blantyre and Limbe. NYASA J. 11, no. 2 (1958), pp. 41-54.

21,465 RANGELEY, W. H. J. The Portuguese. NYASA J. 17, no. 1 (1964), pp. 42-71.

21,466 RANGELEY, W. H. J. Some old Cewa fortresses in the Kotakota district. NYASA J. 4, no. 1 (1951), pp. 54-57.

21,467 SANDERSON, G. M. Gunfire on Nyasa. NYASA J. 10, no. 2 (1957), pp. 25-31; TANGANYIKA NOTES AND RECORDS 58-59 (1962), pp. 98-102.

21,468 SHARPE, Sir A. Nyasaland. ROYAL COL. INST. PR. 39 (1907-1908), pp. 56-80.

21,469 TERRY, P. T. "The Arab war on Lake Nyasa 1887-1895" (An account of the campaign against the Slaver Mlozi). NYASA J. 18, no. 1 (1965), pp. 55-77; 18, no. 2 (1965), pp. 13-52.

21,470 TWYNAM, C. D. Incidents in the posts of Nyasaland. NYASA J. 7, no. 1 (1954), pp. 46-50.

21,471 TWYNAM, C. D. The original Blantyre-Zomba road and the half-way rest house. NYASA J. 10, no. 2 (1957), pp. 52-57.

21,472 VELSEN, J. VAN. Notes on the history of the Lakeside Tonga of Nyasaland. AFR. STUD. 18 (1959), pp. 105-117.

21,473 WATSON, J. H. E. Some historical notes on Zomba. NYASA J. 8, no. 2 (1955), pp. 58-71.

21,474 WILLIAMS, S. G. The old police posts of Nyasaland. NYASA J. 12, no. 2 (1959), pp. 31-38.

21,475 WINSPEAR, F. Some reminiscences of Nyasaland. NYASA J. 13, no. 2 (1960), pp. 35-74.

21,476 WITHERS, F. M. Nyasaland in 1895-96. NYASA J. 2, no. 1 (1949), pp. 16-34.

21,477 W[ITHERS], F. M. Nyasaland's Diamond Jubilee. NYASA J. 4, no. 2 (1951), pp. 8-14.

21,478 WOOD, R. C. An anecdote of Livingstone's first landing in Nyasaland. NYASA J. 11, no. 2 (1958), pp. 39-40.

21,479 WOOD, R. C. "Bushman occupation" at Monkey Bay. NYASA J. 2, no. 1 (1949), p. 57.

21,480 YOUNG, T. C. The Battle of Karonga. NYASA J. 8, no. 2 (1955), pp. 27-30; 9, no. 1 (1956), p. 91.

21,481 YOUNG, T. C. History of the Tumbuka-Henga people [by S. Nyirenda, tr. and ed. by T. C. Young]. BANTU STUD. 5 (1931), pp. 1-75.

21,482 A Livingstone letter. In Gubbin's collection of MSS. AFR. STUD. 6 (1947), p. 180.

21,483 North Nyasa District and the war (1914-1918). NYASA J. 17, no. 1 (1964), pp. 16-23.

21,484 The visit of Her Majesty Queen Elizabeth the Queen Mother to Nyasaland 12th-15th July, 1957. NYASA J. 11, no. 1 (1958), pp. 7-22.

See also 18246, 21144, 24028, 24040.

Language. Literature

Language

21,485 ATKINS, G. The parts of speech in Nyanja. NYASA J. 3, no. 1 (1950), pp. 7-58.

21,486 ATKINS, G. Suggestions for an amended spelling and word division of Nyanja. AFRICA 20 (1950), pp. 200-218.

21,487 GRAY, E. Some proverbs of the Nyanja people. AFR. STUD. 3 (1944), pp. 101-128.

21,488 GRAY, E. Some riddles of the Nyanja people. BANTU STUD. 13 (1939), pp. 251-291.

21,489 LEWIS, W. E. Place names. NYASA J. 9, no. 1 (1956), p. 71.

21,490 MEYER, E. Etymologische Lautlehre des Nyanja (Nyasaland). AFR. UND UB. 27 (1936-1937), pp. 1-34, 129-155, 184-211.

21,491 PRICE, T. The meaning of Mang'anja. NYASA J. 16, no. 1 (1963), pp. 74-77.

21,492 PRICE, T. Nyanja linguistic problems. AFRICA 13 (1940), pp. 125-137.

21,493 PRICE, T. The written representation of inter-vocalic glides in Nyanja. AFR. STUD. 3 (1944), pp. 89-92.

21,494 SEIDEL, A. Sprichwörter und Redensarten der Nyassa-Leute. ZAOS 1 (1895), pp. 132-137; 2 (1896), pp. 80-84.

21,495 THOMSON, T. D. Place-names in Nyasaland. NYASA J. 6, no. 1 (1953), pp. 64-66.

21,496 WERNER, A. Geschichten der Mang'anja. ZAOS 3 (1897), pp. 353-357; 4 (1898), pp. 136-145.

21,497 WERNER, A. Märchen der Mang'anja. ZAOS 2 (1896), pp. 217-219.

21,498 YOUNG, C. Place-names in Nyasaland. NYASA J. 6, no. 2 (1953), pp. 35-36.

21,499 YOUNG, T. C. Some proverbs of the Tumbuka-Nkamanga peoples of the Northern Province of Nyasaland. AFRICA 4 (1931), pp. 343-351.

Literature

21,500 MWALILINO, K. The awakening Malawi on July 6th 1964. PRESENCE AFR. N.S. 51 (1964), pp. 101-102.

21,501 SAUKILA, W. S. A Nyanja story. AFR. UND UB. 25 (1934-1935), pp. 307-315.

21,502 THEROUX, P. Two poems. TRANSITION 14 (1964), pp. 46-47.

Law

21,503 DULY, A. W. R. The Lower Shire district, notes on land tenure and individual rights. NYASA J. 1, no. 2 (1948), pp. 11-44.

21,504 DURAND, P. P. New provisions for the making of wills and inheritance by intestate succession in Malawi. J. AFR. LAW 8 (1964), pp. 109-113.

21,505 MITCHELL, J. C. Preliminary notes on land tenure and agriculture among the Machinga Yao. RHODES-LIV. J. 10 (1950), pp. 1-13.

21,506 RANGELEY, W. H. J. Notes on Cewa tribal law. NYASA J. 1, no. 3 (1948), pp. 5-68.

21,507 ROBERTS, S. A comparison of the family law and custom of two matrilineal systems in Nyasaland. NYASA J. 17, no. 1 (1964), pp. 24-41.

21,508 ROBERTS, S. The constitution of Malawi, 1964. J. AFR. LAW 8 (1964), pp. 178-184.

21,509 ROBERTS, S. Matrilineal family law and custom in Malawi: a comparison of two systems. J. AFR. LAW 8 (1964), pp. 77-90.

21,510 ROBERTS, S. A note on recent legal developments in Nyasaland. J. AFR. LAW 7 (1963), pp. 178-183.

21,511 Nyasaland [establishment of a law school]. J. AFR. LAW 6 (1962), p. 128.

See also 21440.

Religion

21,512 CARDEW, C. A. The Universities Mission. NYASA J. 2, no. 1 (1949), pp. 35-37.

21,513 GREEN, S. Blantyre Mission. NYASA J. 10, no. 2 (1957), pp. 6-17.

21,514 PRETORIUS, J. L. The story of the Dutch Reformed Church Mission in Nyasaland. NYASA J. 10, no. 1 (1957), pp. 11-22.

21,515 PRETORIUS, P. An attempt at Christian initiation in Nyasaland. INT. REV. MISSIONS 39 (1950), pp. 284-291.

21,516 YOUNG, T. C. Understanding the old. INT. REV. MISSIONS 40 (1951), pp. 450-455.

Science

21,517 ANSELL, W. F. H. et al. Notes on some mammals from Nyasaland and adjacent areas. NYASA J. 15, no. 1 (1962), pp. 38-54.

21,518 ANTHONY, H. E. Nyasaland Aloes and Crassulas. NYASA J. 4, no. 1 (1951), pp. 58-64.

21,519 ANTHONY, H. E. Rhipsalis in Nyasaland. NYASA J. 3, no. 2 (1950), pp. 38-39.

21,520 BENSON, C. W. Aquatic birds at Blantyre. NYASA J. 3, no. 2 (1950), pp. 40-45.

21,521 BENSON, C. W. The bird-life of Lake Nyasa. NYASA J. 4, no. 2 (1951), pp. 49-66.

21,522 BENSON, C. W. Evergreen forests near Blantyre. Comparative variety of bird species. NYASA J. 1, no. 2 (1948), pp. 45-52.

21,523 CHAPMAN, J. D. Some notes on the taxonomy, distribution, ecology and economic importance of Waddringtonia, with particular reference to W. Whytei. NYASA J. 13, no. 1 (1960), pp. 65-86.

21,524 GARDINER, R. Nyasaland. From primeval forest to garden landscape. AFR. AFFAIRS 57 (1958), pp. 64-69.

21,525 HARRISON, G. Aquatic birds at a dam at Chileka, Nyasaland with reference to other aquatic birds occurring in the Chileka area. NYASA J. 17, no. 2 (1964), pp. 42-50.

21,526 HAYES, G. D. The Nyala in Nyasaland. NYASA J. 1, no. 1 (1948), pp. 37-38.

21,527 HOLT, D. N. A note on the underground water resources of the Protectorate. NYASA J. 12, no. 2 (1959), pp. 60-82.

21,528 JACKSON, G. Dorstenia Walleri Hemsl. NYASA J. 12, no. 1 (1959), pp. 57-58.

21,529 JACKSON, G. Parkia Filicoidea (Welw. ex Oliv.). NYASA J. 12, no. 2 (1959), pp. 57-59.

21,530 JEFFERY, E. B. and LAYCOCK, H. T. The Grey Heron. Nesting in Nyasaland. NYASA J. 18, no. 1 (1965), pp. 20-21.

21,531 KLAMBOROWSKI, F. Our enemy the crocodile. NYASA J. 17, no. 2 (1964), pp. 51-56.

21,532 LAYCOCK, H. T. Aquatic birds at Blantyre. NYASA J. 13, no. 1 (1960), pp. 7-17.

21,533 LEMON, P. C. The Nyika wild life frontier. NYASA J. 17, no. 2 (1964), pp. 29-41.

21,534 LONG, R. C. The breeding colonies of large and marsh birds within the Port Herald District. NYASA J. 9, no. 2 (1956), pp. 29-50.

21,535 LOVERIDGE, A. Some queer adaptations of African animals. NYASA J. 2, no. 2 (1949), pp. 9-22.

21,536 LOWE, R. H. Notes on the ecology of Lake Nyasa fish. NYASA J. 1, no. 1 (1948), pp. 39-50.

21,537 MARSHAL, H. W. Observations on two purple Gallinules Porphyrio Alba (white) their single chick. NYASA J. 12, no. 2 (1959), pp. 27-30.

21,538 MITCHELL, B. L. Game preservation in Nyasaland. NYASA J. 6, no. 2 (1953), pp. 37-51.

21,539 MITCHELL, B. L. Some reptiles and amphibians of Nyasaland. NYASA J. 3, no. 2 (1950), pp. 46-57.

21,540 MORRIS, B. "Epiphytic orchids of the Limbuli stream, Mlanje." NYASA J. 18, no. 2 (1965), pp. 59-70.

21,541 MORRIS, B. Mammals of Zoa Estate, Cholo. NYASA J. 17, no. 2 (1964), pp. 71-78.

21,542 PRICE, T. Distinctive rocks on Malawe Mountain. NYASA J. 6, no. 1 (1953), pp. 60-63.

21,543 RODGER, J. A. Indigenous ornamental plants. NYASA J. 1, no. 1 (1948), pp. 26-30.

21,544 SEED, C. Trout in Nyasaland. NYASA J. 2, no. 2 (1949), pp. 23-29.

21,545 SHIRCORE, J. O. Two notes on the crowing crested cobra. AFR. AFFAIRS 43 (1944), pp. 183-186.

21,546 SWEENEY, R. C. H. The Chelonia of Nyasaland Protectorate. NYASA J. 13, no. 1 (1960), pp. 35-50.

21,547 SWEENEY, R. C. H. Notes on some birds seen in the Lake Chilwa region. NYASA J. 18, no. 2 (1965), pp. 55-58.

21,548 SWEENEY, R. C. H. Two uncommonly seen snakes in Nyasaland. NYASA J. 16, no. 1 (1963), pp. 71-73.

21,549 TOPHAM, P. Nyasaland trees and shrubs. NYASA J. 5, no. 2 (1952), pp. 11-17.

21,550 VALENTE, P. J. Conceito de doenca e cura em Caconda e Bailundo. PORT. EM AFR. 5 (1948), pp. 330-334.

21,551 WESTROP, A. R. A record "bag" at the bird bath. NYASA J. 12, no. 1 (1959), pp. 46-49.

21,552 WHITE, F. E. The birds of an African garden. NYASA J. 13, no. 2 (1960), pp. 22-34.

21,553 WILLAN, R. G. Indigenous trees of Nyasaland. NYASA J. 12, no. 1 (1959), pp. 50-56.

21,554 WILLAN, R. G. Two new records of flowering trees in Nyasaland. NYASA J. 14, no. 1 (1961), pp. 43-47.

21,555 WILLAN, R. G. Two unusual indigenous trees. NYASA J. 14, no. 2 (1961), pp. 47-53.

21,556 WILLIAMS, S. G. B. Some vipya orchids. NYASA J. 12, no. 2 (1959), p. 39.

21,557 WILLIAMSON, J. Legumes in the diet of the Nyasaland African. With notes on cooking and palatability. NYASA J. 7, no. 1 (1954), pp. 19-29.

21,558 WILLIAMSON, J. Salt and potashes in the life of the Cewa. NYASA J. 9, no. 1 (1956), pp. 82-87.

21,559 WOOD, R. C. On the contribution of the butterfly cymothoe theobene in Nyasaland. NYASA J. 11, no. 2 (1958), p. 28.

21,560 WOOD, R. C. A rare butterfly. NYASA J. 2, no. 1 (1949), p. 53.

21,561 WOOD, R. C. Small mammals of Southern Nyasaland. NYASA J. 2, no. 1 (1949), pp. 38-43.

21,562 YOUNG, W. P. A bird lover in Nyasaland. NYASA J. 1, no. 1 (1948), pp. 31-36.

Sociology

21,563 BAKER, C. A. Chigaru's: a study of its population. NYASA J. 11, no. 1 (1958), pp. 60-64.

21,564 BETTISON, D. J. The private domestic servant of Blantyre-Limbe. NYASA J. 12, no. 1 (1959), pp. 36-45.

21,565 C., J. Expérience sociale au Nyasaland. ZAIRE 6 (1952), pp. 864-865.

21,566 PRICE, T. European and African. A psychological point of view. NYASA J. 2, no. 1 (1949), pp. 53-57.

21,567 Proposed socio-economic survey by the Rhodes-Livingstone Institute in Blantyre/Limbe peri-urban area. NYASA J. 10, no. 2 (1957), p. 24.

21,568 Social research in Central Africa [work of the Rhodes-Livingstone Institute]. NYASA J. 11, no. 2 (1958), pp. 29-34.

See also 16453, 16454, 16455, 16457, 16458, 16459, 16460, 16461, 16462, 20823, 20866, 21217, 21225.

BASUTOLAND. LESOTHO (High Commission Territories in General)

Anthropology

21,569 BROWNLEE, F. Burial places of chiefs. AFR. AFFAIRS 43 (1944), pp. 23-24.

21,570 BRYCE, J. Basutoland. LIBERIA BULL. 12 (1898), pp. 67-74.

21,571 COERTZE, P. J. Huweliksgewoontes en Erfreg by die Batlokwa van Basoetoeland. BANTU STUD. 7 (1933), pp. 257-273; English summary, pp. 273-275.

21,572 ENDEMANN, C. Rätsel der Sotho. AFR. UND UB. 18 (1927-1928), pp. 55-74.

21,573 ENDEMANN, C. Sotho-Sprichwörter. AFR. UND UB. 31 (1941), pp. 51-71, 129-157, 217-237, 287-314; 32 (1942), pp. 59-78, 114-135.

21,574 GUMA, S. M. Some aspects of circumcision in Basutoland. AFR. STUD. 24 (1965), pp. 241-249.

21,575 HOFFMANN, C. Die Mannbarkeitsschule der Bassutho im Holzbuschgebirge Transvaals. AFR. UND UB. 5 (1914-1915), pp. 81-112.

21,576 JAQUES, A. A. Genealogy of male and female chiefs of a Sotho tribe. BANTU STUD. 8 (1934), pp. 377-382.

21,577 JONES, G. I. A report on the Basutoland medicine murders: a digest by the African Studies Branch. J. AFR. ADM. 3 (1951), pp. 138-141.

21,578 KRUGER, F. Märchen der Sotho. AFR. UND UB. 29 (1939), pp. 189-215.

21,579 KUHN, G. Sotho-Sprichwörter. AFR. UND UB. 20 (1929-1930), pp. 34-73, 120-148, 208-221.

21,580 LAYDEVANT, F. La coutume du Hlonepho. AFRICA 16 (1946), pp. 83-91; English summary, p. 91.

21,581 LAYDEVANT, F. The phrases of the divining bones among the Basotho. BANTU STUD. 7 (1933), pp. 341-373.

21,582 LAYDEVANT, F. Religious or sacred plants of Basutoland. BANTU STUD. 6 (1932), pp. 65-69.

21,583 LAYDEVANT, F. Le sceptre des chefs Basuto. AFRICA 18 (1948), pp. 41-44.

21,584 LAYDEVANT, R. P. J. Etude sur la famille en Basutoland. J. SOC. AFR. 1 (1931), pp. 207-257.

21,585 MacMILLAN, W. M. The Mabilles of Basutoland by E. W. Smith. J. AFR. SOC. 39 (1940), pp. 154-159.

21,586 MABILLE, A. The Basuto of Basutoland. J. AFR. SOC. 5 (1906), pp. 233-251, 351-376.

21,587 SCHAPERA, I. The political organisation of the Ngwato of Bechuanaland Protectorate. AFRICAN POLITICAL SYSTEMS, 1940, pp. 56-82.

21,588 THELEJANE, T. S. Pondo rain-making ritual: Ukukhonga. AFR. STUD. 22 (1963), pp. 33-36.

21,589 WALTON, J. The material culture of the Southern Sotho. AFR. MUSIC, 1950, pp. 28-29.

21,590 WALTON, J. Villages of the paramount chiefs of Basutoland. LESOTHO 1 (1959), pp. 15-21; 2 (1960), pp. 11-19.

21,591 WATT, J. M. and BRANDWIJK, M. G. Suto (Basuto) medicines. BANTU STUD. 3 (1927), pp. 73-100, 155-178, 329-351, 395-400.

Art. Music. Antiquities

21,592 MEIJS, L. Notes on the occurrence of petrified wood in Basutoland. LESOTHO 2 (1960), pp. 20-26.

21,593 SCULLY, N. Native tunes heard and collected in Basutoland. BANTU STUD. 5 (1931), pp. 247-251.

21,594 TRACEY, H. Folk music in Basutoland. LESOTHO 3 (1962), pp. 26-32.

21,595 TRACEY, H. The future of music in Basutoland. AFR. MUSIC, 1959, pp. 10-14.

21,596 TRACEY, H. Sotho folk music. LESOTHO 2 (1960), pp. 37-48.

21,597 WALTON, J. Early Ba-Fokeng rock shelter dwellings at Ntlo-Kholo. AFR. STUD. 10 (1951), pp. 83-86.

21,598 WALTON, J. The rock paintings of Basutoland. PROC. PAN-AFR. CONGR. PRE-HIST. 3 (1955), pp. 277-281.

21,599 WERNER, A. The ballad of Saole. J. AFR. SOC. 31 (1932), pp. 183-185.

21,600 Basutoland recording tour. November 19th to December 3rd, 1959. AFR. MUSIC, 1959, pp. 69-76.

Biography

21,601 Obituary: Thomas Mofolo. AFR. AFFAIRS 48 (1949), p. 74.

Economics

21,602 BARING, Sir E. Economic developments under the High Commission in South Africa. AFR. AFFAIRS 51 (1952), pp. 222-230.

21,603 GILBERT, G. N. The postal history of Basutoland. LESOTHO 3 (1962), pp. 16-25.

Education

21,604 Women in the educational system of Basutoland. AFR. WOMEN 1 (1954), pp. 18-19.

Geography

21,605 DRYSDALE, A. T. Notes on Basuto-land. J. AFR. SOC. 2 (1903), pp. 208-212.

21,606 MEYEROWITZ, H. V. A visit to the Bafokeng of Basutoland. J. AFR. SOC. 35 (1936), pp. 386-396.

Government. Politics. Administration

21,607 ASHTON, E. H. Democracy and indirect rule. AFRICA 17 (1947), pp. 235-251.

21,608 ASHTON, E. H. Political organisation of the southern Sotho. BANTU STUD. 12 (1938), pp. 287-320.

21,609 BARING, Sir E. Problems of the High Commission Territories. INTERNAT. AFFAIRS 28 (1952), pp. 184-189.

21,610 DUNCAN, P. Basutoland in transition. AFR. SOUTH 3, no. 3 (1959), pp. 55-59.

21,611 GRAY, A. Basutoland advances. AFR. AFFAIRS 58 (1959), pp. 108-109.

21,612 GRAY, A. Constitutional advances. AFR. AFFAIRS 59 (1960), pp. 7-9.

21,613 GRAY, A. Protectorates' report. AFR. AFFAIRS 55 (1956), pp. 6-10.

21,614 HAMNETT, I. Koena chieftainship seniority in Basutoland. AFRICA 35 (1965), pp. 241-251.

21,615 HENNESSY, J. P. I. The first Basutoland general election. J. LOCAL ADM. OV. 3 (1964), pp. 145-155.

21,616 HUGHES, P. The introduction of local government to Basutoland. J. LOCAL ADM. OV. 2 (1963), pp. 154-159.

21,617 KHAMA, T. The principles of African tribal administration. INTERNAT. AFFAIRS 27 (1951), pp. 451-456.

21,618 KOTZE, D. A. Local government in Basutoland. AFR. STUD. 24 (1965), pp. 55-61.

21,619 MARQUAND, H. The High Commission Territories. AFR. SOUTH 4, no. 4 (1960), pp. 64-68.

21,620 MAUD, Sir J. The challenge of the High Commission Territories. AFR. AFFAIRS 63 (1964), pp. 94-103.

21,621 PIM, Sir A. The question of the South African Protectorates. INTERNAT. AFFAIRS 13 (1934), pp. 668-688.

21,622 SLOLEY, H. C. Recent developments in Basutoland. J. AFR. SOC. 16 (1917), pp. 111-124.

21,623 SPENCE, J. E. British policy towards the High Commission Territories. JMAS 2 (1964), pp. 221-246.

21,624 TRACEY, H. Basutoland and its new paramount chief. J. AFR. SOC. 39 (1940), pp. 306-315.

21,625 WHITE, E. Last step towards independence. The three African Protectorates. AFR. AFFAIRS 64 (1965), pp. 261-270.

21,626 A propos des protectorats d'Afrique-du-Sud. ZAIRE 5 (1951), pp. 300-301.

See also 22465.

History

21,627 DOVE, R. The history of Basutoland camps. LESOTHO 1 (1959), pp. 22-37.

21,628 FAIRCLOUGH, T. L. Notes on the Basuto, their history, country, etc. J. AFR. SOC. 4 (1905), pp. 194-205.

21,629 HOW, M. An alibi for Mantatisi. AFR. STUD. 13 (1954), pp. 65-76.

21,630 KENNAN, T. P. Discovery and exploration of Basutoland. Notes on a journey round Basutoland. LESOTHO 1 (1959), pp. 38-48.

21,631 LANGDEN, Sir G. Basutoland and the Basutos. ROYAL COL. INST. PR. 32 (1900-1901), pp. 255-284.

21,632 OMER-COOPER, J. D. Moshesh and the creation of the Basuto nation: the first phase. TARIKH 1, no. 1 (1965), pp. 42-52.

21,633 RAWSON, H. E. The Basuto. J. AFR. SOC. 9 (1910), pp. 153-160.

21,634 SMITH, E. W. The South African protectorates. J. AFR. SOC. 37 (1938), pp. 199-205.

21,635 SOUTH AFRICAN INSTITUTE OF RACE RELATIONS. Basutoland. RACE RELATIONS J. 17 (1950), pp. 79-120.

21,636 TRACEY, H. Basutoland's gift to Britain. J. AFR. SOC. 40 (1941), pp. 132-139.

21,637 WALTON, C. E. Discovery and exploration of Basutoland. Tracing the source of the Caledon River. LESOTHO 2 (1960), pp. 27-36.

21,638 WALTON, J. Old Maseru. LESOTHO 4 (1963-1964), pp. 7-23.

21,639 The South African Protectorates [war efforts]. J. AFR. SOC. 40 (1941), pp. 293-294.

Language. Literature

Language

21,640 BOURQUIN, W. Die Sprache der Phuthi. FESTSCHRIFT MEINHOF, 1927, pp. 279-287.

21,641 HOFFMAN, C. Sotho-Texte aud dem Holzbusch—Gebirge in Transvaal. AFR. UND UB. 19 (1928-1929), pp. 268-308; 21 (1930-1931), pp. 98-122.

21,642 KUNENE, D. P. The ideophone in southern Sotho. J. AFR. LANGS. 4 (1965), pp. 19-39.

21,643 KUNENE, D. P. Notes on hlonepha among the southern Sotho. AFR. STUD. 17 (1958), pp. 159-182.

21,644 LEKGOTHOANE, S. K. Praises of animals in northern Sotho. BANTU STUD. 12 (1938), pp. 189-213.

21,645 LESTRADE, G. P. Locative-class nouns and formatives in Sotho. BANTU STUD. 12 (1938), pp. 35-62.

21,646 LESTRADE, G. P. Some recent publications concerning languages of the Sotho group. AFR. STUD. 3 (1944), pp. 22-27.

21,647 LETELE, G. L. Some recent literary publications in languages of the Sotho group. AFR. STUD. 3 (1944), pp. 161-171.

21,648 MEEUSSEN, A. E. Morfotonologie van de vervoeging in het Suthu. ZAIRE 12 (1958), pp. 383-392.

21,649 TUCKER, A. N. Sotho-Nguni orthography and tone-marking. BULL. SOAS 13 (1949-1951), pp. 200-224.

Literature

21,650 BERENG, D. T. La voix de l'Afrique: a Sotho poem by David Theko Bereng. AFRICA 17 (1947), pp. 206-207.

21,651 DAMANE, M. The structure and philosophy of Sotho indigenous poetry. LESOTHO 4 (1963-1964), pp. 41-49.

21,652 FRANZ, G. H. The literature of Lesotho (Basutoland). BANTU STUD. 4 (1930), pp. 145-180.

21,653 LEYDEVANT, F. La poésie chez les Basuto. AFRICA 3 (1930), pp. 523-535.

21,654 VEEL, G. R. The Voice of Africa: Intsomi [native stories]. AFRICA 3 (1930), pp. 103-112.

Law

21,655 MOROJOLE, L. C. Legal status of women in Basutoland. WOMEN TODAY 6 (1964), pp. 54-55.

21,656 Basutoland [Basuto Courts Proclamation, No. 23 of 1958]. J. AFR. LAW 2 (1958), p. 185.

21,657 Chieftainship in Basutoland. AFR. STUD. 4 (1945), pp. 157-179.

21,658 Constitutional progress in Basutoland. Basutoland Council: Report on Constitutional Reform and Chieftainship Affairs. J. AFR. LAW 2 (1958), pp. 142-145.

21,659 The laws of Lerotholi in Basutoland. AFR. STUD. 11 (1952), pp. 145-164.

Religion

21,660 JACOTTET, E. The French mission in Basutoland. INT. REV. MISSIONS 2 (1913), pp. 486-500.

21,661 PERROT, C. H. Premières années de l'implantation du christianisme au Lesotho (1833-1847). CAH. ET. AFR. 4 (1963), pp. 97-124.

21,662 PLYMEN, J. An introductory study of the French Protestant [Paris Evangelical Missionary Society] and Wesleyan Mission stations in the conquered territory. LESOTHO 4 (1963-1964), pp. 50-59.

21,663 Contemporary history [visit of Archbishop of Canterbury to Nyasaland and inauguration of the Province of Central Africa]. NYASA J. 8, no. 1 (1955), pp. 7-15.

Science

21,664 GROUND, K. E. A. U. The diet of the rural Basuto. MALNUTRITION IN AFR. WOMEN..., 1952, pp. 265-269.

21,665 GROUND, K. E. A. U. Dietary factors in Kwashiorkor in Basutoland. MALNUTRITION IN AFR. WOMEN..., 1952, pp. 241-242.

21,666 GROUND, K. E. A. U. Kwashiorkor in Basutoland. MALNUTRITION IN AFR. MOTHERS..., 1952, pp. 52-61.

21,667 JACOT-GUILLARMOD, A. The flora of Basutoland. LESOTHO 1 (1959), pp. 5-14; 2 (1960), pp. 5-10; 3 (1962), pp. 7-15.

21,668 THELEJANE, T. S. Some observations on the activities of Brant's or the Basuto Gerbile tatera brantsi brantsi (A. Smith)—Sotho: Letsoete—in the Roma Valley, Basutoland. LESOTHO 4 (1963-1964), pp. 24-26.

Sociology

21,669 DOUGLAS, A. J. A. The use of tax registers to determine the population distribution for sampling purposes. AFRICA 22 (1952), pp. 148-153.

BECHUANALAND

Anthropology

21,670 BLEEK, D. F. !Kun mythology. AFR. UND UB. 25 (1934-1935), pp. 261-285.

21,671 BREUTZ, P. L. Tswana tribal governments today. SOCIOLOGUS 8 (1958), pp. 140-154.

21,672 BROWN, J. T. Circumcision rites of the Becwana tribes. JRAI 51 (1921), pp. 419-427.

21,673 CAMPBELL, A. C. A few notes on the Gowi Bushmen of the central Kalahari desert, Bechuanaland. NADA 9, no. 1 (1964), pp. 39-47.

21,674 DORNAN, S. S. The Tati Bushmen (Masarwas) and their language. JRAI 47 (1917), pp. 37-112.

21,675 GARNER, R. L. Native institutions of the Ogowe tribes of west Central Africa. An appreciation of their meaning as viewed from the standpoint of the native philosopher. J. AFR. SOC. 1 (1902), pp. 369-380.

21,676 GIBSON, G. D. Herero marriage. RHODES-LIV. J. 24 (1959), pp. 1-37.

21,677 GUSINDE, M. Das Rassenbild der Buschmänner. CONG. INT. SC. ANTH. ET ETHN. 4, no. i (1952), pp. 257-277.

21,678 JAGER, E. J. DE and SEBONI, M. O. M. Bone-divination amongst the Kwena of the Molepolole District, Bechuanaland Protectorate. AFR. UND UB. 48 (1964-1965), pp. 2-16.

21,679 KIERNBERGER, A. Morphologische Boebachtungen an den Zähnen der Khoisaniden. CONG. INT. SC. ANTH. ET ETHN. 4, no. i (1952), pp. 278-279.

21,680 LANGUAGE, F. J. Die verkryging en verlies van lidmaatskap tot die stam by die Tlhaping. AFR. STUD. 2 (1943), pp. 77-92.

21,681 MARR, M. The chief comes home. NADA 26 (1949), p. 74.

21,682 REYNEKE, J. A remarkable tribe. NADA 2 (1924), pp. 91-94.

21,683 ROOS, T. Burial customs of the !kaû Bushmen. BANTU STUD. 5 (1931), pp. 81-83.

21,684 SCHAPERA, I. The Bakxatla Baxakxafêla: preliminary report of field investigations. AFRICA 6 (1933), pp. 402-414.

21,685 SCHAPERA, I. Field methods in the study of modern culture contacts. AFRICA 8 (1935), pp. 315-327.

21,686 SCHAPERA, I. Herding rites of the Bechuanaland Bakxatla. AMER. ANTHR. 36 (1934), pp. 561-584.

21,687 SCHAPERA, I. Kinship and marriage among the Tswana. AFRICAN SYSTEMS OF KINSHIP AND MARRIAGE, 1950, pp. 140-165.

21,688 SCHAPERA, I. The "little rain" (pulanyana) ceremony of the Bechuanaland Bakxatla. BANTU STUD. 4 (1930), pp. 211-216.

21,689 SCHAPERA, I. Marriage of near kin among the Tswana. AFRICA 27 (1957), pp. 139-159.

21,690 SCHAPERA, I. Oral sorcery among the natives of Bechuanaland. ESSAYS PRESENTED TO C. G. SELIGMAN, 1934, pp. 293-305.

21,691 SCHAPERA, I. The social structure of the Tswana ward. BANTU STUD. 9 (1935), pp. 203-224.

21,692 SCHAPERA, I. Sorcery and witchcraft in Bechuanaland. AFR. AFFAIRS 51 (1952), pp. 41-52.

21,693 SCHOTT, R. Die Buschmänner in Südafrika eine Studie über Schwierigkeiten des Akkulturation. SOCIOLOGUS 5 (1955), pp. 132-149.

21,694 SILBERBAUER, G. B. Marriage and the girl's puberty ceremony of the G/wi Bushmen. AFRICA 33 (1963), pp. 12-24.

21,695 WEDGWOOD, C. H. and SCHAPERA, I. String figures from Bechuanaland protectorate. BANTU STUD. 4 (1930), pp. 251-268.

21,696 WILLOUGHBY, W. C. Notes on the initiation ceremonies of the Becwana. JRAI 39 (1909), pp. 228-245.

21,697 WILLOUGHBY, W. C. Notes on the totemism of the Becwana. JRAI 35 (1905), pp. 295-314.

21,698 WILSON, M. Nyakyusa kinship. AFRICAN SYSTEMS OF KINSHIP AND MARRIAGE, 1950, pp. 111-139.

See also

Art

21,699 BALSAN, F. Découverte d'une oeuvre très ancienne dans l'art bushman à l'intérieur du Mont Tsodillo-Femelle au désert du Kalahari. J. SOC. AFR. 23 (1953), pp. 139-143.

See also 21970.

Biography

21,700 W. C. Willoughby. J. AFR. SOC. 37 (1938), p. 511.

Economics

21,701 SCHAPERA, I. Labour migration from a Bechuanaland native reserve. J. AFR. SOC. 32 (1933), pp. 386-397; 33 (1934), pp. 49-58.

See also 155, 21602.

Geography

21,702 DEBENHAM, F. Journey in thirstland: in search of water in Bechuanaland. GEOG. REV. 41 (1951), pp. 464-469.

Government. Politics. Administration

21,703 ASHTON, E. H. Notes on the political and judical organisation of the Tswana. BANTU STUD. 11 (1937), pp. 67-83.

21,704 GRAY, A. Seretse goes home. AFR. AFFAIRS 56 (1957), pp. 11-12.

21,705 MITCHISON, N. Open letter to an African chief. JMAS 2 (1964), pp. 64-72.

21,706 Déposition du chef Seretse Khama. ZAIRE 6 (1952), pp. 632-633.

See also 21607.

History

21,707 BARNES, L. The crisis in Bechuanaland. J. AFR. SOC. 32 (1933), pp. 342-349.

21,708 COUPETHWAITE, B. The Bechuanaland Protectorate. RACE RELATIONS J. 18 (1951), pp. 28-71.

21,709 ELLENBERGER, J. The Bechuanaland Protectorate and the Boer War, 1899-1902. RHODESIANA 11 (1964), pp. 1-21.

21,710 ELLENBERGER, V. History of the Batlokwa of Gaberones (Bechuanaland Protectorate). BANTU STUD. 13 (1939), pp. 165-197.

21,711 LANGUAGE, F. J. Herkoms en geskiedenis van die Tlhaping. AFR. STUD. 1 (1942), pp. 115-132; English summary, p. 133.

21,712 MacKENZIE, J. Bechuanaland. CONTEMP. REV. 73 (1898), pp. 282-297.

21,713 NETTLETON, G. E. History of the Ngamiland tribes up to 1926. BANTU STUD. 8 (1934), pp. 343-360.

21,714 SCHAPERA, I. Kinship and politics in Tswana history. JRAI 93 (1963), pp. 159-173.

21,715 SCHAPERA, I. Notes on the history of the Kaa. AFR. STUD. 4 (1945), pp. 109-121.

21,716 SCHAPERA, I. A short history of the Bangwaketse. AFR. STUD. 1 (1942), pp. 1-26.

21,717 WARREN, C. Our portion in South Africa (Bechuanaland). PRCI 17 (1885-1886), pp. 5-45.

21,718 The emancipation of the Masarwa. J. AFR. SOC. 34 (1935), pp. 446-449.

21,719 Note on the Bahurutshe. AFR. STUD. 6 (1947), pp. 176-179.

Language

21,720 JONES, D. Words distinguished by tone in Sechuana. FESTSCHRIFT MEINHOF, 1927, pp. 88-98.

21,721 KUHN, G. Tschuana-Texte. AFR. UND UB. 26 (1935-1936), pp. 301-317.

21,722 MAINGARD, L. F. The central group of the click languages of the Kalahari. AFR. STUD. 20 (1961), pp. 114-122.

21,723 MAINGARD, L. F. Three Bushman languages. AFR. STUD. 16 (1957), pp. 37-71.

21,724 MAINGARD, L. F. Three Bushman languages. Part II: the third Bushman language. AFR. STUD. 17 (1958), pp. 100-115.

21,725 SCHAPERA, I. Ethnographical texts in the Boloongwe dialect of Sekgalagadi. BANTU STUD. 12 (1938), pp. 157-187.

21,726 SCHAPERA, I. Kxatla riddles and their significance. BANTU STUD. 6 (1932), pp. 215-231.

21,727 SCHAPERA, I. Some ethnographical texts in Sekgatla. BANTU STUD. 4 (1930), pp. 73-93.

21,728 VEDDER, H. Grundriss einer Grammatik der Buschmannsprache vom Stamm der Kū-Buschmänner. AFR. UND UB. 1 (1910), pp. 5-24, 106-117.

21,729 A practical orthography for Tswana [Recommendations of a conference held at Johannesburg in 1937]. BANTU STUD. 11 (1937), pp. 137-148.

Law

21,730 SCHAPERA, I. Contract in Tswana case law. J. AFR. LAW 9 (1965), pp. 142-153.

21,731 SCHAPERA, I. The development of customary law in the Bechuanaland Protectorate. THE FUTURE OF CUSTOMARY LAW IN AFRICA, 1956, pp. 102-116.

21,732 SCHAPERA, I. The sources of law in Tswana tribal courts: legislation and precedent. J. AFR. LAW 1 (1957), pp. 150-162.

21,733 SCHAPERA, I. The work of tribal courts in the Bechuanaland Protectorate. AFR. STUD. 2 (1943), pp. 27-40.

Religion

21,734 SCHAPERA, I. Christianity and the Tswana. JRAI 89 (1958), pp. 1-9.

Science

21,735 SILLERY, A. and DAVIES, H. V. Water in Bechuanaland. CORONA 3 (1951), pp. 24-26.

21,736 SQUIRES, B. T. Malnutrition amongst Tswana children. AFR. STUD. 2 (1943), pp. 210-214.

21,737 SQUIRES, B. T. Malnutrition in the Bechuanaland Protectorate. MALNUTRITION IN AFR. MOTHERS..., 1952, pp. 62-69.

Sociology

21,738 SCHAPERA, I. Changing life in the Native Reserves. RACE RELATIONS 1 (1933-1934), pp. 3-5.

S W A Z I L A N D

Anthropology

21,739 BEEMER, H. The Swazi rain ceremony. Critical comments on P. J. Schoeman's article. BANTU STUD. 9 (1935), pp. 273-280.

21,740 BLOHM, W. Die christliche Familien-Gemeinschaft im Xosa-Volkstum. Beobachtungen in Ost-Südafrika. AFRICA 6 (1933), pp. 431-455.

21,741 COOK, P. A. W. The Inqwala ceremony of the Swazis. BANTU STUD. 4 (1930), pp. 205-210.

21,742 DUMBRELL, H. J. E. Pyre burning in Swaziland. AFR. STUD. 11 (1952), pp. 1 -191.

21,743 EISELEN, W. Uber die Hauptlingswürde bei den Bapedi. AFRICA 5 (1932), pp. 297-306.

21,744 HUNTER, M. The effects of contact with Europeans on the status of Pondo women. AFRICA 6 (1933), pp. 259-276.

21,745 HUSS, B. The evolution of the South African native mind. AFRICA 4 (1931), pp. 445-454.

21,746 KRIGE, E. J. Changing conditions in marital relations and parental duties among urbanized natives. AFRICA 9 (1936), pp. 1-22.

21,747 KUPER, H. Kinship among the Swazi. AFRICAN SYSTEMS OF KINSHIP AND MARRIAGE, 1950), pp. 86-110.

21,748 KUPER, H. The marriage of a Swazi princess. AFRICA 15 (1945), pp. 145-155.

21,749 KUPER, H. A ritual of kinship among the Swazi. AFRICA 14 (1943), pp. 230-256.

21,750 LECOSTE, B. Le système de parenté des Ngwana. ZAIRE 9 (1955), pp. 293-297.

21,751 MEEUSSEN, A. E. and LECOSTE, B. Systématique des termes de parenté Ngwana. ZAIRE 9 (1955), pp. 403-405.

21,752 SCHAPERA, I. Premarital pregnancy and native opinion: a note on social change. AFRICA 6 (1933), pp. 59-89.

21,753 SCHOEMAN, P. J. The Swazi rain ceremony. BANTU STUD. 9 (1935), pp. 169-175.

21,754 STUHARDT, J. G. A collection of Zulu proverbs. NADA 8 (1930), pp. 62-70; 9 (1931), pp. 60-67.

21,755 TWALA, R. G. Beads as regulating the social life of the Zulu and Swazi. AFR. STUD. 10 (1951), pp. 113-123.

21,756 TWALA, R. G. Umhlanga (reed) ceremony of the Swazi maidens. AFR. STUD. 11 (1952), pp. 93-104.

Art

21,757 JONES, T. R. Exhibition of stone implements from Swaziland, South Africa. JRAI 28 (1899), pp. 48-54.

21,758 KIRBY, P. R. Old-time chants of the Mpumuza chiefs. BANTU STUD. 2 (1923), pp. 23-34.

21,759 The music of the Swazis. AFR. MUSIC, 1952, p. 14.

Economics

21,760 GORDON, W. R. Swaziland. CONTEMP. REV. 177 (1950), pp. 91-94.

21,761 HUGHES, A. J. B. Reflections on traditional and individual land tenure in Swaziland. J. LOCAL ADM. OV. 3 (1964), pp. 3-13.

21,762 HUGHES, A. J. B. Some Swazi views on land tenure. AFRICA 32 (1962), pp. 253-278.

21,763 ROMANO, M. P. Aproveitamento internacional dos rios que entram em Moçambique pelos Limbobos. BSEM 118 (1959), pp. 7-11.

See also 21602.

Government. Politics. Administration

21,764 BEEMER, H. The development of the military organization in Swaziland. AFRICA 10 (1937), pp. 55-74, 176-204.

21,765 CORYNDON, R. T. Swaziland. J. AFR. SOC. 14 (1914-1915), pp. 250-265.

21,766 GRAY, A. Swaziland question. AFR. AFFAIRS 61 (1962), pp. 187-190.

21,767 STEVENS, R. P. Swaziland political development. JMAS 1 (1963), pp. 327-350.

History

21,768 COOK, P. A. W. History and Izibongo of the Swazi chiefs. BANTU STUD. 5 (1931), pp. 181-201.

21,769 KUPER, H. The development of a primitive nation. BANTU STUD. 15 (1941), pp. 339-368.

21,770 MILLER, A. M. Swaziland. ROYAL COL. INST. PR. 31 (1899-1900), pp. 274-304.

21,771 POTT, D. Swaziland: a general survey. RACE RELATIONS J. 18 (1951), pp. 126-165.

Language

21,772 ZIERVOGEL, D. Notes on the noun classes of Swati and Nrebele. AFR. STUD. 7 (1948), pp. 59-70.

21,773 ZIERVOGEL, D. A Swazi translation of 1846. AFR. STUD. 9 (1950), pp. 167-184.

Law

21,774 RUBIN, N. N. The Swazi law of succession: a restatement. J. AFR. LAW 9 (1965), pp. 90-113.

21,775 RUBIN, N. N. Swaziland. The Marriage Proclamation, 1964. J. AFR. LAW 9 (1965), pp. 60-64.

Religion

21,776 KUPER, H. The Swazi reaction to missions. AFR. STUD. 5 (1946), pp. 177-188.

21,777 SUNDKLER, B. G. M. The concept of Christianity in the African independent churches. AFR. STUD. 20 (1961), pp. 203-213.

Science

21,778 BEEMER, H. Notes on the diet of the Swazi in the protectorate. BANTU STUD. 13 (1939), pp. 199-236.

Sociology

21,779 KEEN, P. Infantile mortality in Swaziland. RACE RELATIONS 9 (1942), pp. 77-82.

21,780 KUPER, H. The uniform of colour in Swaziland. AFR. STUD. 2 (1943), pp. 97-107.

REPUBLIC OF SOUTH AFRICA

General

21,781 BAXTER, W. T. Lady Anne Barnard's Cape Town. QBSAL 1 (1946), pp. 33-39.

21,782 BOSMAN, D. B. Die eerste boekveiling aan die Kaap—en nog wat. QBSAL 1 (1947), pp. 96-97.

21,783 BRADLOW, F. R. The sources of Africana research: how to find and use them. QBSAL 14 (1960), pp. 114-125.

21,784 CASSON, L. F. The mediaeval manuscripts of the Grey Collection in salesroom and bookshop. QBSAL 14 (1959), pp. 3-33.

21,785 CASSON, L. F. Ms. Grey 3 a 11, a composite office book, 13th-16th century. QBSAL 16 (1962), pp. 164-172.

21,786 CASSON, L. F. The "Sutton" Bible: Grey Ms. 4 c 16. QBSAL 14 (1959), pp. 55-65, 86-96.

21,787 CORINTA FERREIRA, M. Algumas considerações àcerca do "Transvaal Museum." BSEM 69 (1951), pp. 99-111.

21,788 DENFIELD, J. Notes on some lost border newspapers. QBSAL 19 (1965), pp. 72-79.

21,789 EVANS, D. S. Two items of astronomical Africana. QBSAL 7 (1952), pp. 3-9.

21,790 FORBES, V.·S. Africana in the Sloane Collection, British Museum. QBSAL 6 (1951), pp. 9-17.

21,791 HERRMAN, L. Charles Darwin's first publication: a Cape discovery. QBSAL 13 (1958), pp. 11-12.

21,792 HOERNLE, R. F. A. Aspects of race relations in South Africa: the origin, purpose and task of the South African Institute of Race Relations. RACE RELATIONS 1 (1933-1934), pp. 42-44.

21,793 HOLDSWORTH, H. Bibliography in South Africa. THE JOURNAL OF DOCUMENTATION 3 (1947-1948), pp. 151-159.

21,794 JANSEN, the Hon. Dr. E. G., Governor-General of South Africa. Dr. E. G. Jansen [obituary]. QBSAL 14 (1959), p. 47.

21,795 JANSEN, the Hon. Dr. E. G., Governor-General of South Africa. The new wing of the South African Library; opening speech by H. E. the Governor-General. QBSAL 13 (1959), pp. 103-107.

21,796 JEFFREYS, M. K. Anthony Trollope on the South African Library. QBSAL 4 (1950), pp. 125-126.

21,797 LLOYD, A. C. G. Adventures in book buying. QBSAL 1 (1947), pp. 65-70.

21,798 LUNN, B. Libraries for non-whites in the Republic of South Africa. LIBRI 13 (1963-1964), pp. 127-136, 297-298.

21,799 MANDELBROTE, J. C. Joseph Suasso de Lima, 1791-1856; a bibliography. QBSAL 3 (1948), pp. 2-22.

21,800 PAMA, C. The Dutch book in the world. QBSAL 12 (1957), pp. 7-12.

21,801 RHEINALLT JONES, J. D. Conference on the welfare of the Cape coloured people. RACE RELATIONS 9 (1942), pp. 63-70.

21,802 ROBINSON, A. M. L. Charles Aken Fairbridge and his library. QBSAL 9 (1954-1955), pp. 32-49, 74-93, 116.

21,803 ROBINSON, A. M. L. A contribution to the bibliography of Spaarman's voyage to the Cape of Good Hope. QBSAL 1 (1946-1947), pp. 42-48, 124.

21,804 ROBINSON, A. M. L. A dim flash in the pan: The New Organ, 1826. QBSAL 14 (1959), pp. 50-54.

21,805 ROCHLIN, S. A. The earliest use of Greek printing type at the Cape. QBSAL 4 (1950), pp. 88-89.

21,806 SIMPSON, D. H. A note on the bibliography of George McCall Theal. QBSAL 4 (1950), pp. 126-132.

21,807 SMIT, D. E. Die Mendelssohn-Hersieningsprojek. QBSAL 16 (1961), pp. 21-23.

21,808 SPOHR, O. H. Miscellaneous notes on some libraries, book sales and early authors in Cape Town in the early 19th century. QBSAL 19 (1964), pp. 36-48.

21,809 SPOHR, O. H. More light on the Grey Collection 1860-61: Dr. Bleek at Pau. QBSAL 20 (1965), pp. 5-10.

21,810 SWART, the Hon. C. R., Governor-General of South Africa, [later] the State President. Our Hon. President. [Announcement of the Hon. C. R. Swart's acceptance of an invitation to become Hon. President of the Friends of the South African Library.] QBSAL 14 (1960), p. 107.

21,811 SWART, the Hon. C. R., Governor-General of South Africa, [later] the State President. The State President. [Announcement of the Hon. C. R. Swart's relinquishment of the honorary Presidency of the Friends of the South African Library.] QBSAL 15 (1961), p. 129.

21,812 TYRRELL-GLYNN, W. Handleiding vir siekeroosters. QBSAL 19 (1964), pp. 48-56.

21,813 VARLEY, D. H. A. C. G. Lloyd, librarian of the South African Library, 1909-38. QBSAL 11 (1957), pp. 117-121.

21,814 VARLEY, D. H. Adventures in Africana. QBSAL 4 (1949), pp. 40-84.

21,815 VARLEY, D. H. Baden-Powell and an early Swaziland postal cover. QBSAL 15 (1960), pp. 45-47.

21,816 VARLEY, D. H. An early Cape printing discovery. QBSAL 1 (1946), pp. 7-12.

21,817 VARLEY, D. H. E. F. Steeb and Colonel Graham's Savage Tribes. QBSAL 13 (1959), pp. 116-118.

21,818 VARLEY, D. H. The Grey Collection: mirror of Western culture. QBSAL 8 (1953), pp. 11-17.

21,819 VARLEY, D. H. Joachim von Dessin and his book collection. QBSAL 16 (1961), pp. 8-21.

21,820 VARLEY, D. H. The lighter reading of our English South African ancestors. QBSAL 13 (1958), pp. 22-29, 52-58.

21,821 VARLEY, D. H. A note on the South African Christian Recorder. QBSAL 13 (1958), pp. 12-15.

21,822 VARLEY, D. H. The place of the South African Library in the life of the nation. QBSAL 13 (1958), pp. 37-44.

21,823 VARLEY, D. H. Publications of the Van Riebeeck Society, 1918-48. QBSAL 4 (1949), pp. 19-24.

21,824 VARLEY, D. H. The revision of Mendelssohn's South African Bibliography. QBSAL 14 (1960), pp. 110-114.

21,825 WEBB, M. The Institute in council. RACE RELATIONS 8 (1941), pp. 22-24.

21,826 WEBB, M. The Institute in council (a personal impression). RACE RELATIONS 7 (1940), pp. 14-16.

21,827 Indian women's associations. RACE RELATIONS 1 (1933-1934), p. 18.

21,828 The Springbok Library [presented by the people of Britain as a tribute to South African hospitality to British troops]. QBSAL 1 (1946), pp. 39-41.

See also 22690.

Agriculture

21,829 BERG, D. G. VAN DEN. Soil conservation and land utilization in the native areas of South Africa. CIVILISATIONS 4 (1954), pp. 375-382; French summary, pp. 382-383.

21,830 DUERDEN, J. E. Ostrich farming in South Africa. J. AFR. SOC. 20 (1920), pp. 19-24.

21,831 FLEMMING, L. The romance of a new South African farm. J. AFR. SOC. 21 (1922), pp. 115-128.

21,832 HALL, T. D. Food for the people. RACE RELATIONS 12 (1945), pp. 17-22.

21,833 HANNON, P. J. The new agricultural movement in Cape Colony. ROYAL COL. INST. PR. 37 (1905-1906), pp. 214-226.

21,834 HUSS, B. Agriculture amonst the natives of South Africa. INT. REV. MISSIONS 11 (1922), pp. 260-269.

21,835 KARK, S. L. Cattle and milk in a native Reserve. RACE RELATIONS 11 (1944), pp. 30-34.

21,836 MASCARENHAS, J. F. A cooperativa agrícola do Limpopo. BSEM 144-145 (1965), pp. 153-160.

21,837 PEREIRA MARTINHO, J. Contribuição para o estudo da origem do Bovino Africânder. BSEM 91 (1955), pp. 31-78.

21,838 ROUX, E. Collective farming in the Reserves. RACE RELATIONS 11 (1944), pp. 10-14.

21,839 SCOTT, P. Otter-trawl fisheries of South Africa. GEOG. REV. 39 (1949), pp. 529-551.

21,840 SOUTH AFRICA, DEPT. OF AGRICULTURE. Agricultural education in South Africa. J. AFR. SOC. 13 (1914), pp. 288-295.

21,841 THWAITES, G. G. A day in the life of a low-veld farmer. J. AFR. SOC. 36 (1937), pp. 260-269.

21,842 WALLACE, R. Agriculture in South Africa. ROYAL COL. INST. PR. 32 (1900-1901), pp. 139-175.

Anthropology

21,843 AS, B. S. VAN. Die Proses van naamgewing aan die Suid-Afrikaanse inboorling. KONGO-OVERZEE 23 (1957), pp. 316-347.

21,844 BERTHOUD, H. Thonga-Märchen aus Transvaal. AFR. UND UB. 20 (1929-1930), pp. 241-256.

21,845 BEYER, G. Arzneipflanzen der Sotho-Neger; Ein Beitrag zur Südafrikanishen Materia Medica. FESTSCHRIFT MEINHOF, 1927, pp. 275-278.

21,846 BEYER, G. Sitten und Gebräuche der Basotho in Nordwest-Transvaal. AFR. UND UB. 5 (1914-1915), pp. 299-305.

21,847 BLACKING, J. The social value of Venda riddles. AFR. STUD. 20 (1961), pp. 1-32.

21,848 BOAS, F. The avunculate among the Vandau. AMER. ANTHR. 24 (1922), pp. 95-97.

21,849 BROOM, R. A contribution to the craniology of the yellow-skinned races of South Africa. JRAI 53 (1923), pp. 132-147.

21,850 BROOM, R. The genera and species of the South African fossil ape-men. AMER. J. PHY. ANTHR. 8 (1950), pp. 1-14.

21,851 BROWNLEE, C. A fragment of Xhosa religious beliefs. AFR. STUD. 14 (1955), pp. 37-41.

21,852 BROWNLEE, F. The circumcision ceremony in Fingoland. BANTU STUD. 3 (1927), pp. 179-183.

21,853 BROWNLEE, F. The in-Tonjane ceremony as observed in Fingoland. BANTU STUD. 3 (1927), pp. 401-403.

21,854 BROWNLEE, F. Some experiences of native superstition and witchcraft. J. AFR. SOC. 39 (1940), pp. 54-60.

21,855 BRYANT, A. T. The Zulu family and state organization. BANTU STUD. 2 (1923), pp. 47-51.

21,856 CALLAWAY, H. On divination and analogous phenomena among the natives of Natal. JRAI 1 (1871), pp. 163-185.

21,857 CAMPBELL, A. C. Ubukwetha amongst the Ama Xhosa. NADA 9, no. 2 (1965), pp. 52-58.

21,858 COLE-BEUCHAT, P. D. Notes on some folklore forms in Tsonga and Ronga. AFR. STUD. 17 (1958), pp. 185-191.

21,859 CUMMINS, H. Dermatoglyphics of Bushmen (South Africa). AMER. J. PHY. ANTHR. 13 (1955), pp. 699-709.

21,860 DU PLESSIS, H. Die territoriale organisasie van die Venda. AFR. STUD. 4 (1945), pp. 122-127.

21,861 EBERHARDT, J. Quelques aspects du mariage chez les Venda. J. SOC. AFR. 25 (1955), pp. 77-88.

21,862 EISELEN, W. M. The art of divination as practised by the Bamasemola. BANTU STUD. 6 (1932), pp. 1-29, 251-263.

21,863 EISELEN, W. M. Die posisie van die weduwee by die heidense en by die kristelike Batau. BANTU STUD. 9 (1935), pp. 281-284.

21,864 ESTERMANN, C. O Problema do Homicídio Ritual no Sul da Africa. PORT. EM AFR. 15 (1958), pp. 69-82.

21,865 FOX, F. W. Some Bantu recipes from the eastern Cape Province. BANTU STUD. 13 (1939), pp. 65-74.

21,866 FRANZ, G. H. Some customs of the Transvaal Basotho. BANTU STUD. 5 (1931), pp. 241-246.

21,867 FRERE, H. B. On systems of land tenure among aboriginal tribes in South Africa. JRAI 12 (1883), pp. 258-276.

21,868 GARBUTT, H. W. [comp.] Native witchcraft and superstition in South Africa. JRAI 39 (1909), pp. 530-558.

21,869 GIESEKKE, E. Wahrsagerei bei den Venda. AFR. UND UB. 21 (1930-1931), pp. 257-310.

21,870 GLUCKMAN, M. The kingdom of the Zulu of South Africa. AFRICAN POLITICAL SYSTEMS, 1940, pp. 25-55.

21,871 GLUCKMAN, M. Social aspects of first fruits ceremonies among the South-Eastern Bantu. AFRICA 11 (1938), pp. 25-41.

21,872 GLUCKMAN, M. Some processes of social change illustrated from Zululand. AFR. STUD. 1 (1942), pp. 243-260.

21,873 GLUCKMAN, M. Zulu women in hoecultural ritual. BANTU STUD. 9 (1935), pp. 255-271.

21,874 GOTTSCHLING, E. The Bawenda: a sketch of their history and customs. JRAI 35 (1905), pp. 365-386.

21,875 GRANT, E. W. The Izibongo of the Zulu chiefs. BANTU STUD. 3 (1927), pp. 205-244.

21,876 GRIESBACH, C. L. On the weapons and implements used by the Kaffir tribes and bushmen of South Africa. JRAI 1 (1871), pp. cliv-clv.

21,877 GUSINDE, M. Anthropological investigations of the Bushmen of South Africa. ANTHR. QUART. 26 (1953), pp. 20-28.

21,878 HADDON, A. C. String figures from South Africa. JRAI 36 (1906), pp. 142-149.

21,879 HAMILTON, E. The man who walked alone. AFR. AFFAIRS 46 (1947), pp. 226-233.

21,880 HAMMOND-TOOKE, W. D. The attainment of adult status among the Mount Frere Bhaea. AFR. STUD. 17 (1958), pp. 16-20.

21,881 HAMMOND-TOOKE, W. D. The Bhaea first fruit festival. AFR. STUD. 16 (1957), p. 236.

21,882 HAMMOND-TOOKE, W. D. The function of annual first fruit ceremonies in Baca social structure. AFR. STUD. 12 (1953), pp. 75-78.

21,883 HAMMOND-TOOKE, W. D. The initiation of a Baca isangoma diviner. AFR. STUD. 14 (1955), pp. 16-22.

21,884 HELLBUSCH, S. Der Totemismus der Buschmänner. AFRIKA (Berlin) 3 (1944), pp. 105-116.

21,885 HELLMANN, E. Native life in a Johannesburg slum yard. AFRICA 8 (1935), pp. 34-61.

21,886 HERSKOVITS, M. J. Some property concepts and marriage customs of the Vandau. AMER. ANTHR. 25 (1923), pp. 376-386.

21,887 HOERNLE, A. W. A Hottentot rain ceremony. BANTU STUD. 1, no. ii (1922), pp. 3-4.

21,888 HOERNLE, A. W. The social organization of the Nama Hottentots of Southwest Africa. AMER. ANTHR. 27 (1925), pp. 1-24.

21,889 HOFFMANN, C. Märchen und Erzählungen der Eingeborenen in Nord-Transvaal. AFR. UND UB. 6 (1915-1916), pp. 28-54, 124-153, 206-243, 285-326.

21,890 HOFFMANN, C. Sitten und Brauchtum der Basotho in Nord-Transvaal. Mekwa le Botlwaêlô bja Basotho ba Transvaal-Lebowa. AFR. UND UB. 40 (1956), pp. 117-124, 175-190; 41 (1957), pp. 73-86, 197-210; 42 (1958), pp. 81-93, 145-158.

21,891 HOFFMANN, C. Verlöbnis und Heirat bei den Bassutho im Holzbuschgebirge Transvaals. AFR. UND UB. 3 (1912-1913), pp. 125-139.

21,892 HOLUB, E. On the central South African tribes from the South Coast to the Zambesi. JRAI 10 (1881), pp. 2-20.

21,893 HUTCHINSON, B. Some social consequences of nineteenth century missionary activity among the South African Bantu. AFRICA 27 (1957), pp. 160-175.

21,894 JAGER, E. J. DE and GITYWA, V. Z. A Xhosa Umhwayelelo ceremony in the Ciskei. AFR. STUD. 22 (1963), pp. 109-116.

21,895 JORDAN, A. C. Towards an African literature: riddles and proverbs. AFR. SOUTH 2, no. 2 (1958), pp. 101-104.

21,896 KRIGE, E. J. Agricultural ceremonies and practices of the Balobedu. BANTU STUD. 5 (1931), pp. 207-239.

21,897 KRIGE, E. J. Note on the Phalaborwa and their morula complex. BANTU STUD. 11 (1937), pp. 357-366.

21,898 KRIGE, E. J. The place of the North-Eastern Transvaal Sotho in the South Bantu complex. AFRICA 11 (1938), pp. 265-293.

21,899 KRIGE, E. J. The social significance of beer among the Balobedu. BANTU STUD. 6 (1932), pp. 343-357.

21,900 KRIGE, J. D. Bride-wealth in Balobedu marriage ceremonies. BANTU STUD. 8 (1934), pp. 135-149.

21,901 KRIGE, J. D. The significance of cattle exchanges in Lovedu social structure. AFRICA 12 (1939), pp. 393-424.

21,902 KRIGE, J. D. Traditional origins and tribal relationships of the Sotho of the northern Transvaal. BANTU STUD. 11 (1937), pp. 321-356.

21,903 KRUGER, F. Bräuche der Lovelu. AFR. UND UB. 28 (1937-1938), pp. 241-255.

21,904 KRUGER, F. The Lovedu. BANTU STUD. 10 (1936), pp. 89-105.

21,905 KRUGER, F. Märchen der Lovelu. AFR. UND UB. 26 (1935-1936), pp. 57-74.

21,906 KRUGER, F. Tlôkwa traditions. BANTU STUD. 11 (1937), pp. 85-115.

21,907 KRUGER, F. Venda-Märchen. AFR. UND UB. 24 (1933-1934), pp. 1-14.

21,908 KRUGER, F. Venda-Sagen. AFR. UND UB. 25 (1934-1935), pp. 147-155.

21,909 LESTRADE, G. P. The Mala system of the Venda-speaking tribes. BANTU STUD. 4 (1930), pp. 193-204.

21,910 LONGMORE, L. Death and burial customs of the Bapedi of Sekukuniland. AFR. STUD. 11 (1952), pp. 83-84.

21,911 LUGG, H. C. Agricultural ceremonies in Natal and Zululand. BANTU STUD. 3 (1927), pp. 357-383.

21,912 LUGG, H. C. The practice of Lobolo in Natal. AFR. STUD. 4 (1945), pp. 23-27.

21,913 MacALISTER, A. Notes on some South African skeletons. JRAI 16 (1887), pp. 149-151.

21,914 MABONA, M. Sur l'avenir des concepts religieux chez les Nguni. PRESENCE AFR. N.S. 54 (1965), pp. 173-180.

21,915 MAES, J. Kantteekeningen bij een Studie van I. Schapera. KONGO-OVERZEE 1 (1934), pp. 228-234.

21,916 MAHLOBO, G. W. K. and KRIGE, E. J. Transition from childhood to adulthood amongst the Zulus. BANTU STUD. 8 (1934), pp. 157-191.

21,917 MAINGARD, J. F. Physical characteristics of the Korana. BANTU STUD. 6 (1932), pp. 163-182.

21,918 MAINGARD, L. F. Studies in Korana history, customs and language. BANTU STUD. 6 (1932), pp. 103-162.

21,919 MATTHEWS, Z. K. Marriage customs among the Barolong. AFRICA 13 (1940), pp. 1-23.

21,920 MDIYA, W. W. Isibongo in Xosa language. AFR. UND UB. 20 (1929-1930), pp. 148-150.

21,921 MEADE, H. M. T. The origin and universality of taboo and totemism. NADA 1 (1923), pp. 73-79.

21,922 MEINHOF, C. Korana-Erzählungen. Aufgezeichnet und übersetzt. AFR. UND UB. 26 (1935-1936), pp. 161-174.

21,923 MENDELSSOHN, S. Judaic or Semitic legends and customs amongst South African natives. J. AFR. SOC. 14 (1914-1915), pp. 24-34.

21,924 MONNIG, H. O. Lobedu kinship terminology. AFR. STUD. 20 (1961), pp. 226-236.

21,925 MONNIG, H. O. The structure of Lobedu social and political organisation. AFR. STUD. 22 (1963), pp. 49-64.

21,926 NORTON, W. A. A secwana—"House that Jack built." BANTU STUD. 1, no. ii (1922), pp. 4-5.

21,927 PAUW, B. A. Some changes in the social structure of the Tlhaping of the Taung Reserve. AFR. STUD. 19 (1960), pp. 49-76.

21,928 PITJE, G. M. Traditional systems of male education among Pedi and cognate tribes. AFR. STUD. 9 (1950), pp. 53-76, 105-124, 194-201.

21,929 PYCRAFT, W. P. On the calvana found at Boskop, Transvaal in 1913, and its relationship to cromagnard and negroid skulls. JRAI 55 (1925), pp. 179-198.

21,930 RAUM, O. F. Wandel in Kultur und Sozialstruktur der Südafrikanischen Xhosa. SOCIOLOGUS 15 (1965), pp. 111-127.

21,931 READER, D. H. Models in social change, with special reference to Southern Africa. AFR. STUD. 23 (1964), pp. 11-33.

21,932 ROUMEGUERE-EBERHARDT, J. La notion de vie: base de la structure sociale Venda. J. SOC. AFR. 27 (1957), pp. 183-196.

21,933 SAAKSE, J. The visit to Mujaji the rain-queen. NADA 29 (1952), pp. 83-86.

21,934 SANDERSON, J. Polygamous marriage among Kafirs of Natal and countries around. JRAI 8 (1878), pp. 254-260.

21,935 SCHAAR, W. Nama-Fabeln. AFR. UND UB. 8 (1917-1918), pp. 81-109.

21,936 SCHAPERA, I. Some recent South African publications. AFRICA 4 (1931), pp. 263-272.

21,937 SCHAPERA, I. South African publications relating to native life and languages, 1930-2, 1933-1934. AFRICA 5 (1932), pp. 233-241; 6 (1933), pp. 352-361; 8 (1935), pp. 244-249.

21,938 SCHAPERA, I. A survey of the Bushman question. RACE RELATIONS 6 (1939), pp. 68-83.

21,939 SCHREYER, J. Johan Schreyer's description of the Hottentots, 1679. [With introduction and notes by R. Rowen-Hart.] QBSAL 19 (1964), pp. 56-69; 19 (1965), pp. 88-101.

21,940 SICARD, H. VON. The Lemba ancestor Baramina. AFR. STUD. 12 (1953), pp. 57-61.

21,941 SIMONS, H. J. Tribal worship. AFR. SOUTH 1, no. 4 (1957), pp. 49-54.

21,942 SINGER, R. The Saldanha skull from Hopefield, South Africa. AMER. J. PHY. ANTHR. 12 (1954), pp. 345-362.

21,943 SOGA, J. H. Aba-mbo genealogical tables. BANTU STUD. 3 (1927), pp. 49-56.

21,944 STOW, G. W. Account of an interview with a tribe of bushmans in South Africa. JRAI 3 (1873), pp. 244-247.

21,945 TOBIAS, P. V. Physical anthropology and Somatic origins of the Hottentots. AFR. STUD. 14 (1955), pp. 1-15.

21,946 VELSEN, J. VAN. History or nostalgia? A study of the Bhaca [Bhaca Society, by W. D. Hammond-Tooke]. AFR. STUD. 24 (1965), pp. 63-66.

21,947 WARMELO, N. J. VAN. Multi-mouthed pots from the Northern Transvaal. NADA 21 (1944), pp. 45-47.

21,948 WATT, J. M. and WARMELO, N. J. VAN. The medicines and practice of a Sotho doctor. BANTU STUD. 4 (1930), pp. 47-63.

21,949 WERNER, A. The aborigines of South Africa. J. AFR. SOC. 5 (1906), pp. 381-386.

21,950 WERNER, A. The Matabele head-ring. NADA 4 (1926), pp. 128-129.

21,951 WERNER, A. Native affairs in South Africa. J. AFR. SOC. 8 (1908), pp. 49-61.

21,952 WRIGHT, E. B. Native races in South Africa. J. AFR. SOC. 2 (1903), pp. 261-275.

21,953 ZOUTENDYK, A. et al. The blood groups of the Bushmen. AMER. J. PHY. ANTHR. 11 (1953), pp. 361-368.

21,954 ZYL, H. J. VAN. Some of the commonest games played by the Sotho people of Northern Transvaal. BANTU STUD. 13 (1939), pp. 293-305.

See also 19892, 20922, 21755.

Art

21,955 BAKKER, E. M. VAN Z. A pollen analytical investigation of the Florisbad deposits (South Africa). PROC. PAN-AFR. CONGR. PRE-HIST. 3 (1955), pp. 56-67.

21,956 BARBER, H. M. The perforated stones of South Africa. JRAI 21 (1892), pp. 302-304.

21,957 BEIT, A. Louis Michel Thibault, Cape architect. QBSAL 1 (1947), pp. 98-103.

21,958 BLACKING, J. Musical expeditions of the Venda. AFR. MUSIC, 1962, pp. 54-78.

21,959 BLACKING, J. Problems of pitch, pattern and harmony in the ocarina music of the Venda. AFR. MUSIC, 1959, pp. 15-23.

21,960 BOCKHORST, M. Arte sudafricana alla Biennale di Venezia. AFRICA (Rome) 11 (1956), p. 114.

21,961 BONE, E. L. Les fouilles 1955 au terril de Makapansgat (N. Transvaal). PROC. PAN-AFR. CONGR. PRE-HIST. 3 (1955), pp. 149-154.

21,962 BOUWS, J. Die Musiekbeoefening aan die Kaap in die Hollandse Kompanjiestyd. QBSAL 16 (1962), pp. 104-118.

21,963 BOWLER-KELLEY, A. Sur une pointe provenant de Healdtown (Province du Cap). J. SOC. AFR. 5 (1935), pp. 113-116.

21,964 BRADLOW, F. R. The four bowler pictures of the opening of the Cape Town to Wellington railway. QBSAL 19 (1965), pp. 104-109.

21,965 BRADLOW, F. R. Illustrated notepapers and envelopes at the Cape. QBSAL 11 (1956), pp. 13-17.

21,966 BRADLOW, F. R. Nineteen originals of the Bowles lithograph. QBSAL 10 (1955), pp. 9-11.

21,967 BRAIN, C. K. New evidence for the correlation of the Transvaal ape-man bearing cave deposits. PROC. PAN-AFR. CONGR. PRE-HIST. 3 (1955), pp. 143-148.

21,968 BREUIL, A. H. Rock paintings of South Africa. ANTHR. QUART. 27 (1954), pp. 31-42.

21,969 BREUIL, H. E. P. The influence of classical civilizations on the cave paintings of South Africa. PROC. PAN-AFR. CONGR. PRE-HIST. 1 (1947), pp. 234-237.

21,970 BREUTZ, P. L. Stone kraal settlements in South Africa. AFR. STUD. 15 (1956), pp. 157-175.

21,971 BROOM, R. The fossil ape-men of South Africa. PROC. PAN-AFR. CONGR. PRE-HIST. 1 (1947), pp. 107-115.

21,972 BULL, M. and DENFIELD, J. The coming of the carte-de-visite and the cabinet photograph. QBSAL 19 (1965), pp. 109-119.

21,973 BULL, M. and DENFIELD, J. The history of early Cape photography. QBSAL 19 (1964), pp. 6-22.

21,974 BULL, M. and DENFIELD, J. Two famous South African photographs. QBSAL 20 (1965), pp. 43-48.

21,975 BURROWS, E. H. Lichtenstein and the Alberto plates. QBSAL 8 (1953), pp. 49-50.

21,976 BURROWS, E. H. The Swellendam Bowlers. QBSAL 9 (1954), p. 9.

21,977 CLAIR, A. "Come back Africa" (Reviens Afrique), film de Lionel Rogosin. PRESENCE AFR. N.S. 30 (1960), pp. 123-124.

21,978 DART, R. A. The bone tool-manufacturing ability of Australopithecus Prometheus. AMER. ANTHR. 62 (1960), pp. 134-143.

21,979 DART, R. A. The continuity and originality of Australopithecine Osteodontokeratic culture. PROC. PAN-AFR. CONGR. PRE-HIST. 4, no. iii (1962), pp. 27-40.

21,980 DART, R. A. Faunal and climatic fluctuations in Makapaansgat valley: their relation to the geological age and Promethean status of Australopithecus. PROC. PAN-AFR. CONGR. PRE-HIST. 1 (1947), pp. 96-106.

21,981 DART, R. A. The most complete Australopithecus skull from the pink breccia at Makapansgat. PROC. PAN-AFR. CONGR. PRE-HIST. 4 (1962), pp. 337-340.

21,982 DART, R. A. Recent discoveries bearing on human history in Southern Africa. JRAI 70 (1940), pp. 13-27.

21,983 DAVIES, O. The Sangoan culture in little Namaqualand. PROC. PAN-AFR. CONGR. PRE-HIST. 3 (1955), pp. 219-222.

21,984 DRENNAN, M. R. A cultural and racial parallel in two Kalk Bay rock-shelters. PROC. PAN-AFR. CONGR. PRE-HIST. 1 (1947), pp. 119-125.

21,985 DRONSFIELD, J. Mother and baby [drawing]. AFR. SOUTH 1, no. 3 (1957), p. 106.

21,986 DRONSFIELD, J. Street scene [drawing]. AFR. SOUTH 1, no. 3 (1957), p. 98.

21,987 EISELEN, W. Preferential marriage: correlation of the various modes among the Bantu tribes of the Union of South Africa. AFRICA 1 (1928), pp. 413-428.

21,988 ENGELS, L. Lithographs by Poortermans in the Mendelssohn Library. QBSAL 5 (1951), pp. 112-116.

21,989 FAGAN, B. The Greefswald sequence: Bambandyanalo and Mapungubwe. J. AFR. HIST. 5 (1964), pp. 337-361.

21,990 FAVEAUX, A. A. DE. Les brèches ossifères de Kakontwe. PROC. PAN-AFR. CONGR. PRE-HIST. 3 (1955), pp. 98-101.

21,991 FEILDEN, H. W. Notes on stone implements from South Africa. JRAI 13 (1884), pp. 162-174.

21,992 FRAMES, M. E. On some stone implements found in a cave in Griqualand-East, Cape Colony. JRAI 28 (1899), pp. 251-257.

21,993 GILLMAN, J. A note on the mummified tissue found at Cathkin Park. BANTU STUD. 7 (1933), pp. 217-219.

21,994 GOOCH, W. D. The stone age of South Africa. JRAI 11 (1882), pp. 124-183.

21,995 GOODWIN, A. J. H. [ed.] A commentary on the history and present position of South African pre-history with full bibliography, August, 1935. BANTU STUD. 9 (1935), pp. 291-417.

21,996 GROBBELAAR, C. S. The origin and distribution of the living Korana collected for a somatological study. PROC. PAN-AFR. CONGR. PRE-HIST. 3 (1955), pp. 200-206.

21,997 HOERNLE, A. W. A note on bored stones among the Bantu. BANTU STUD. 5 (1931), pp. 253-255.

21,998 HOERNLE, R. F. A. The stone-hut settlement on Tafelkop, near Bethal. BANTU STUD. 4 (1930), pp. 33-46.

21,999 HOLZ, P. Cave paintings in South Africa. CONTEMP. REV. 192 (1957), pp. 162-165.

22,000 HUTCHINSON, M. Notes on a collection of facsimile Bushman Bushman drawings. JRAI 12 (1883), pp. 464-465.

22,001 JEFFREYS, M. K. The elusive lithographer: J. C. Poortermans. QBSAL 5 (1950), pp. 1-10.

22,002 JONES, A. M. Venda note-names. AFR. MUSIC, 1962, pp. 49-53.

22,003 JONES, N. On the implement-bearing deposits of Taungs and Tiger Kloof in the Cape Province of South Africa. JRAI 50 (1920), pp. 412-424.

22,004 JONES, W. F. Religious patronage: Cyrene. AFR. SOUTH 2, no. 4 (1958), pp. 106-108.

22,005 KENNEDY, R. F. The plates in Godlonton and Irving's "Narrative of the Kaffir War." QBSAL 8 (1954), pp. 94-103.

22,006 KINGSTON, H. D. R. Notes on some caves in the T'zitzikama or Outeniqua district, near Knysna, South Africa, and the objects found therein. JRAI 30 (1900), pp. 45-49.

22,007 KIRBY, P. R. Charles Dibdin and the Cape. QBSAL 14 (1960), pp. 76-81.

22,008 KIRBY, P. R. An early Cape musical society. QBSAL 13 (1959), pp. 67-73.

22,009 KIRBY, P. R. The music and musical instruments of the Korana. BANTU STUD. 6 (1932), pp. 183-204.

22,010 KIRBY, P. R. The recognition and practical use of the harmonics of stretched strings by the Bantu of South Africa. BANTU STUD. 6 (1932), pp. 31-46.

22,011 KIRBY, P. R. The reed-flute ensembles of South Africa: a study in South African native music. JRAI 63 (1933), pp. 313-388.

22,012 LANGHAM-CARTER, R. R. Some sketches by Bishop Robert Gray and his daughter. QBSAL 19 (1965), pp. 84-87.

22,013 LANGHAM-CARTER, R. R. Sophia Gray's Cape sketches, 1849-1867. QBSAL 20 (1965), pp. 39-43.

22,014 LAYARD, E. L. Note on the stone implements of South Africa. JRAI 1 (1871), pp. xcvii-c.

22,015 LONGMORE, L. The A. A. Jaques Collection of native headrests. AFR. MUSIC, 1951, pp. 26-28.

22,016 LONGMORE, L. Music and song among the Bantu people in urban areas on the Witwatersrand. AFR. MUSIC, 1953, pp. 15-27.

22,017 MABBUTT, J. A. The physical background to the Hopefield discoveries. PROC. PAN-AFR. CONGR. PRE-HIST. 3 (1955), pp. 68-75.

22,018 MABBUTT, J. A. Some Quaternary events in the winter rainfall area of the Cape Province. PROC. PAN-AFR. CONGR. PRE-HIST. 3 (1955), pp. 6-13.

22,019 MALAN, B. D. The final phase of the Middle Stone Age in South Africa. PROC. PAN-AFR. CONGR. PRE-HIST. 1 (1947), pp. 188-194.

22,020 MALAN, B. D. The stone industry of the site at Elandsfontein, Hopefield, South Africa. PROC. PAN-AFR. CONGR. PRE-HIST. 4, no. iii (1962), pp. 225-231.

22,021 MASON, A. Y. Rock paintings in the Cathkin Peak area, Natal. BANTU STUD. 7 (1933), pp. 131-158.

22,022 MILLAR, A. K. Portraits of Lord Charles Somerset. QBSAL 13 (1959), pp. 107-110.

22,023 MURRAY, N. L. Skeletal remains from rock shelters in Cathkin Park, Natal. BANTU STUD. 7 (1933), pp. 201-215.

22,024 NGUBANE, S. S. An art exhibition by Johannesburg Africans. AFR. MUSIC, 1950, pp. 30-32.

22,025 P., J. African drama in the Transvaal, by J. P. AFR. MUSIC, 1952, pp. 8-10.

22,026 PEET, M. L'Opera italiana con voci ed orchestra di Coloureds del Capo. AFRICA (Rome) 11 (1956), pp. 76-77.

22,027 PENNING, W. H. Notes upon a few stone implements found in South Africa. JRAI 16 (1887), pp. 68-70.

22,028 RIET LOWE, C. VAN. Beads of the water. BANTU STUD. 11 (1937), pp. 367-372.

22,029 RIET LOWE, C. VAN. The development of the Hand-axe Culture in South Africa. PROC. PAN-AFR. CONGR. PRE-HIST. 1 (1947), pp. 167-177.

22,030 RIET LOWE, C. VAN. Fresh light on the prehistoric archaeology of South Africa. BANTU STUD. 3 (1927), pp. 385-393.

22,031 RIET LOWE, C. VAN. A preliminary report on the stone huts of Vechtkop. JRAI 57 (1927), pp. 217-233.

22,032 RIET LOWE, C. VAN. The rock engravings of Driekops Eiland. PROC. PAN-AFR. CONGR. PRE-HIST. 2 (1952), pp. 769-775.

22,033 RICHINGS, F. G. St. Paul's Church, Rondebosch, a century ago. QBSAL 19 (1965), pp. 79-84.

22,034 RYCROFT, D. Zulu and Xhosa praise-poetry and song. AFR. MUSIC, 1962, pp. 79-85.

22,035 RYCROFT, D. Zulu male traditional singing. AFR. MUSIC, 1957, pp. 33-35.

22,036 SANDERSON, J. Notes in connection with stone implements from Natal. JRAI 8 (1878), pp. 15-21.

22,037 SEKOTO, G. A South African artist. PRESENCE AFR. N.S. 14-15 (1957), pp. 281-289.

22,038 SINGER, R. Investigations at the Hopefield site. PROC. PAN-AFR. CONGR. PRE-HIST. 3 (1955), pp. 175-182.

22,039 SINGER, R. and CRAWFORD, J. R. The significance of the archaeological discoveries at Hopefield, South Africa. JRAI 88 (1958), pp. 11-19.

22,040 STACEY, N. The one criterion. AFR. SOUTH 4, no. 1 (1959), p. 116.

22,041 STEIN, H. B. Stone implements from the Cathkin Peak area. BANTU STUD. 7 (1933), pp. 159-181.

22,042 SWARTZ, J. F. A. A hobbyist looks at Zulu and Xhosa songs. AFR. MUSIC, 1956, pp. 29-33.

22,043 VARLEY, D. H. Bowler, Baines and the Breakwater. QBSAL 6 (1952), pp. 85-88.

22,044 VARLEY, D. H. Caring for historic buildings. QBSAL 14 (1960), pp. 72-75.

22,045 VARLEY, D. H. George Cruickshank etchings for Edward Lascelles, Gent. QBSAL 7 (1953), pp. 83-86.

22,046 VARLEY, D. H. Thomas William Bowler: some new material. QBSAL 9 (1954), pp. 7-9.

22,047 VEENSTRA, A. J. F. The Begu Zulu vertical flute. AFR. MUSIC, 1958, pp. 40-45.

22,048 WALTON, J. Early Bafokeng settlement in South Africa. AFR. STUD. 15 (1956), pp. 37-43.

22,049 WALTON, J. South African peasant architecture. AFR. STUD. 7 (1948), pp. 139-145.

22,050 WALTON, J. South African peasant architecture: Nguni folk building. AFR. STUD. 8 (1949), pp. 70-79.

22,051 WELLS, L. H. Ancient metal working, ceramics, and beads from Cathkin Park. BANTU STUD. 7 (1933), pp. 183-193.

22,052 WELLS, L. H. The archaeology of Cathkin Park: introductory. BANTU STUD. 7 (1933), pp. 113-129.

22,053 WELLS, L. H. A find of stone implements at Estcourt, Natal; with remarks on some specimens from the Weenen district. BANTU STUD. 7 (1933), pp. 221-225.

22,054 WELLS, L. H. Human crania of the Middle Stone Age in South Africa. PROC. PAN-AFR. CONGR. PRE-HIST. 1 (1947), pp. 125-133.

22,055 WELLS, L. H. Old Bantu graves in the Cathkin Park area. BANTU STUD. 7 (1933), pp. 195-200.

22,056 African music from the point of view of the record industry. AFR. MUSIC, 1963, pp. 41-42.

22,057 Recording tour of the Tswana tribe, western Transvaal and Bechuanaland Protectorate, October-November, 1959. AFR. MUSIC, 1959, pp. 62-68.

Biography

22,058 The passing of Sir Abe Bailey. J. AFR. SOC. 39 (1940), pp. 339-347.

22,059 Sir Abe Bailey's will. J. AFR. SOC. 39 (1940), pp. 298-299.

22,060 CLARKE, J. H. Bambata. PRESENCE AFR. N.S. 45 (1963), pp. 175-181.

22,061 HAWKIN, R. C. General Botha. J. AFR. SOC. 19 (1919), pp. 15-19.

22,062 PHILLIPS, L. General Botha. J. AFR. SOC. 24 (1924), pp. 10-13.

22,063 SPENDER, H. General Botha. In memory. CONTEMP. REV. 116 (1919), pp. 369-375.

22,064 GRAY, A. Wellcome Medal 1956 [recipient: E. H. Brookes]. AFR. AFFAIRS 55 (1956), pp. 212-213.

22,065 MALCOLM, D. M. Obituary: Alfred T. Bryant. AFR. STUD. 12 (1953), pp. 131-132.

22,066 SYMONS, J. Buller in South Africa. HISTORY TODAY 11 (1961), pp. 770-778.

22,067 DAWBARN, C. Lord Buxton in South Africa. CONTEMP. REV. 118 (1920), pp. 795-800.

22,068 C., J. Abdication du roi des diamants. ZAIRE 5 (1951), pp. 411-412.

22,069 BALANDIER, G. Un chef: Chaka. PRESENCE AFR. 8 (1950), pp. 159-166.

22,070 MALCOLM, Sir D. O. Drummond Chaplin: his life and times in Africa, by B. K. Long. J. AFR. SOC. 40 (1941), pp. 262-272.

22,071 GRYLLS, R. G. Bishop Colenso of Natal. CONTEMP. REV. 184 (1953), pp. 27-32.

22,072 WERNER, A. Colenso of Natal. INT. REV. MISSIONS 22 (1933), pp. 510-521.

22,073 BERNSTEIN, H. Profile of an Afrikaner [Abram Fischer]. TRANSITION 23 (1965), pp. 22-24.

22,074 HATTERSLEY, A. F. James Long Fitzpatrick. QBSAL 15 (1961), pp. 131-134.

22,075 SUTHERLAND, J. Christopher Gell: an obituary. AFR. SOUTH 3, no. 1 (1958), pp. 44-46.

22,076 FRANKEL, S. H. Jan Hendrik Hofmeyr. AFR. AFFAIRS 48 (1949), pp. 117-119.

22,077 ROBINSON, A. M. L. Alexander Johnstone Jardine; librarian and man of letters. QBSAL 16 (1962), pp. 118-137.

22,078 YALI-MANISI, D. L. P. Umnu. J. D. Rheinallt Jones. AFR. STUD. 12 (1953), pp. 72-74.

22,079 In memory of Rheinallt Jones. AFR. STUD. 12 (1953), pp. 38-40.

22,080 Obituary: Mr. J. D. Rheinallt Jones. CIVILISATIONS 3 (1953), p. 170.

22,081 CLAY, G. Portrait of a cabinet minister [Jan de Klerk]. AFR. SOUTH 1, no. 2 (1957), pp. 47-55.

22,082 Albert John Lutuli. Prix Nobel de la paix. PRESENCE AFR. N.S. 39 (1961), pp. 225-229.

22,083 LEWIN, J. Professor W. M. Macmillan—80. AFR. STUD. 24 (1965), pp. 251-252.

22,084 FREER, P. Obituary: Mrs. H. M. McKay. AFR. STUD. 11 (1952), pp. 189-190.

22,085 DOKE, C. M. Obituary: Dr. D. McK. Malcolm. AFR. STUD. 22 (1963), p. 37.

22,086 Death of Sir Ernest Oppenheimer. AFR. AFFAIRS 57 (1958), p. 59.

22,087 Portrait of a millionaire: "I Harry Oppenheimer." AFR. SOUTH 4, no. 3 (1960), pp. 7-16.

22,088 CURREY, R. N. Thomas Phipson, 1849 Natal settler. QBSAL 16 (1961), pp. 24-31.

22,089 BRADLOW, F. R. and SPOHR, O. H. King of the landlords. Johann Georg Rathfelder, 1812-1873. QBSAL 20 (1965), pp. 28-38.

22,090 Colonel Reitz in London. J. AFR. SOC. 42 (1943), p. 54.

22,091 MALAN, B. D. Obituary: Professor C. van Riet Lowe. AFR. STUD. 15 (1956), p. 145.

22,092 HART, R. R. Johan Jacob Saar's fifteen years military service, 1662. QBSAL 20 (1965), pp. 10-19.

22,093 GRAY, A. The troubled mirror: some notes on Olive Schreiner. AFR. AFFAIRS 54 (1955), pp. 300-305.

22,094 Shaka's grave at Stanger. AFR. STUD. 2 (1943), pp. 108-112.

22,095 GRAY, A. Smuts statue in London. AFR. AFFAIRS 56 (1957), pp. 14-15.

22,096 MILLIN, S. G. Smuts at eighty. FOREIGN AFFAIRS 29 (1950-1951), pp. 130-142.

22,097 RAWSON, H. E. A soldier and statesman [J. C. Smuts]. J. AFR. SOC. 16 (1917), pp. 314-325.

22,098 BRADLOW, F. R. Douglas Varley and the Quarterly Bulletin, the Friends of the South African Library and Africana. QBSAL 16 (1961), pp. 74-77.

22,099 REENEN, R. VAN. Douglas Varley. (Herdruk uit Die Burger, 4 Oktober, 1961.) QBSAL 16 (1961), pp. 71-74.

22,100 NEAME, L. E. Dr. Verwoerd. CONTEMP. REV. 196 (1959), pp. 81-84.

22,101 UYS, S. Dr. Hendrik Frensch Verwoerd, Prime Minister of South Africa. AFR. SOUTH 3, no. 2 (1959), pp. 1-11.

22,102 MILNE, J. Major Warden. LESOTHO 4 (1963-1964), pp. 27-40.

22,103 FFOLLIOTT, P. and LIVERSIDGE, R. Clemenz Heinrich Wehdemann, naturalist, 1762-1835. QBSAL 16 (1962), pp. 147-160.

22,104 ANDERS, H. D. Marginal notes to Wikar's journal (Van Riebeeck Society XV, 1935). BANTU STUD. 11 (1937), pp. 47-52.

22,105 MAINGARD, L. F. Hendrik Jacob Wikar: his editors, translators and commentators. BANTU STUD. 10 (1936), pp. 31-40.

22,106 Photographic biographies of early Cape photographers, 1846-1860. QBSAL 19 (1964), pp. 22-31.

Economics

22,107 ADAL, G. Il mercato sudafricano dei beni strumentali e il ritiro dell' Unione dal Commonwealth. AFRICA (Rome) 16 (1961), pp. 191-193.

22,108 ALI, Syed Sir R. The position of Indians in industry in South Africa. RACE RELATIONS 4 (1937), pp. 89-91.

22,109 BADEN-POWELL, G. English money in South Africa. CONTEMP. REV. 48 (1885), pp. 503-525.

22,110 BALLINGER, M. A scientific approach to the problem of post-war employment and the non-European in South Africa. RHODES-LIV. J. 3 (1945), pp. 21-32.

22,111 BARTOCCI, E. Capetown Algeri in 1100 TV a 55 di media. AFRICA (Rome) 11 (1956), p. 74.

22,112 BROWN, P. S. The anomalous course of South African gold mining since 1925. J. POLIT. ECON. 46 (1938), pp. 176-201.

22,113 BUITENDAG, F. W. C. The organisation of labour bureaux by local authorities. RACE RELATIONS J. 20 (1953), pp. 6-22.

22,114 BUNTING, B. The African in industry. AFR. SOUTH 4, no. 1 (1959), pp. 18-27.

22,115 BURTON, H. Railways and communications in South Africa. J. AFR. SOC. 18 (1918), pp. 1-8.

22,116 CLEGG, W. H. Central banking in South Africa. ECON. J. 39 (1929), pp. 520-535.

22,117 CURRIE, D. South Africa. PRCI 19 (1887-1888), pp. 223-259.

22,118 DAIRY CONTROL BOARD. The state-aided milk and butter scheme. RACE RELATIONS 6 (1939), pp. 128-129.

22,119 DENFIELD, J. Notes on some lost border newspapers. QBSAL 19 (1965), pp. 72-79.

22,120 DRAPER, M. Le coût de la vie et les revenus des familles africaines rurales (particulièrement à Johannesburg). CIVILISATIONS 14 (1964), pp. 246-250.

22,121 DYER, E. J. The South African labour question. CONTEMP. REV. 83 (1903), pp. 439-445.

22,122 FAIRBAIRN, J. The new serfdom. AFR. SOUTH 4, no. 1 (1959), pp. 34-40.

22,123 FIRST, R. Bethal case-book. AFR. SOUTH 2, no. 3 (1958), pp. 14-25.

22,124 FIRST, R. The gold of migrant labour. AFR. SOUTH 5, no. 3 (1961), pp. 7-31.

22,125 FONTAINAS, P. and PUTTE, M. VAN DE. Sur les procédés d'exploitation des mines de platine dans le Sud-Africain, d'après l'ouvrage de M. Percy Wagner. BULL. SEANCES IRCB 1 (1930), pp. 367-388.

22,126 FOURIE, L. L'économie sud-africaine en 1958. CIVILISATIONS 9 (1959), pp. 391-397.

22,127 FRANKEL, S. H. The [economic] situation in South Africa 1929-32. ECON. J. 43 (1933), pp. 93-107.

22,128 FRANKEL, S. H. Return to capital invested in the Witwatersrand gold-mining industry, 1887-1932. ECON. J. 45 (1935), pp. 67-76.

22,129 FURLONG, J. R. Paper-making materials of the British Empire. BULL. IMP. INST. 42 (1944), pp. 232-250.

22,130 GELL, C. An Eastern Cape postscript. AFR. SOUTH 2, no. 3 (1958), pp. 26-29.

22,131 GELLINI, G. Sud Africa a volo di...colombi. AFRICA (Rome) 10 (1955), pp. 263-264.

22,132 GILBERT, D. W. The economic effects of the gold discoveries upon South Africa: 1886-1910. QUART. J. ECON. 47 (1932-1933), pp. 553-597.

22,133 GIOVANNINI, A. Breve storia del lavoro italiano in Sud Africa. AFRICA (Rome) 15 (1960), pp. 190-192.

22,134 GRANT, N. South Africa to-day. CONTEMP. REV. 145 (1934), pp. 566-572.

22,135 GRAY, J. A. Studies in war-time organisation: the Union's supply effort. AFR. AFFAIRS 44 (1945), pp. 58-61

22,136 GUENAULT, P. R. and RANDALL, R. J. Some financial aspects of urban native segregation in South Africa. RACE RELATIONS 7 (1940), pp. 95-100.

22,137 HAMMOND, J. H. Riches of the Transvaal. LIBERIA BULL. 21 (1902), pp. 58-62.

22,138 HARRIS, J. H. General Botha's native land policy. J. AFR. SOC. 16 (1916), pp. 7-15.

22,139 HELM, B. The family budgets of the coloured people. RACE RELATIONS 17 (1950), pp. 15-21.

22,140 HENDERSON, J. The [industrial] situation in South Africa, with special reference to Lovedale. INT. REV. MISSIONS 3 (1914), pp. 336-343.

22,141 HEPPLE, A. African trade unions and the new powers. AFR. SOUTH 1, no. 4 (1957), pp. 21-24.

22,142 HEPPLE, A. The fiery cross of job reservation. AFR. SOUTH 2, no. 3 (1958), pp. 42-47.

22,143 HEPPLE, A. Job reservation: the Achilles heel. AFR. SOUTH 3, no. 1 (1958), pp. 39-43.

22,144 HEPPLE, A. Labour and labour laws in South Africa. AFR. SOUTH 1, no. 1 (1956), pp. 24-32.

22,145 HEPPLE, A. Unemployment by race. AFR. SOUTH 4, no. 2 (1960), pp. 48-54.

22,146 HOLZ, P. Diamonds in South Africa. CONTEMP. REV. 197 (1960), pp. 280-282.

22,147 HORRELL, M. Afrique du Sud. Situation économique et sociale des non-Européens. CIVILISATIONS 4 (1954), pp. 495-502.

22,148 HORST, S. T. VAN DER. Native labour and wages. RACE RELATIONS 4 (1937), pp. 66-70.

22,149 HORST, S. T. VAN DER. Notes on the occupational distribution of the coloured people. RACE RELATIONS J. 21, no. 1 (1954), pp. 18-24.

22,150 HUTT, W. H. Economics of wage fixation. RACE RELATIONS 6 (1939), pp. 151-156.

22,151 JOHNSTON, Sir H. H. The conditions of negro labour in the South African mines. J. AFR. SOC. 3 (1904), pp. 231-237.

22,152 JONES, J. D. R. Industrial relations in South Africa. INTERNAT. AFFAIRS 29 (1953), pp. 43-51.

22,153 KOCK, M. H. DE. The significance of the recent legislative amendments concerning the South African reserve bank. ECON. J. 41 (1931), pp. 67-73.

22,154 KRIGE, J. D. and KRIGE, E. The Tomlinson report and the Lovedu. RACE RELATIONS J. 23, no. 4 (1956), pp. 12-25.

22,155 LEHFELDT, R. A. The shift system of the Witwatersrand mines. ECON. J. 21 (1911), pp. 223-231.

22,156 LESLIE, R. South Africa and the gold standard. ECON. J. 43 (1933), pp. 88-92.

22,157 LEVY, L. African trade unionism in South Africa. AFR. SOUTH 5, no. 3 (1961), pp. 32-43.

22,158 LINDSAY, Sir H. A. F. The Imperial Institute's services to South Africa. BULL. IMP. INST. 35 (1937), pp. 163-174.

22,159 LONGMORE, L. African poverty and social unrest. AFR. AFFAIRS 57 (1958), pp. 291-294.

22,160 LOSEBY, P. J. A. An evaluation of South African grown pinus patula pulpwood by the sulphate (Kraft) process. BULL. IMP. INST. 33 (1935), pp. 162-171.

22,161 LUCAS, F. A. W. Who pays for services provided for Africans? RACE RELATIONS 20 (1953), pp. 1-5.

22,162 McLEAN, J. South Africa and the empire exhibition, Johannesburg. J. AFR. SOC. 36 (1937), pp. 298-310.

22,163 MAGNINO, L. Ancora sull' emigrazione intellettuale in Africa del Sud. AFRICA (Rome) 10 (1955), p. 80.

22,164 MARTIN, J. Group administration in the gold mining industry of the Witwatersrand. ECON. J. 39 (1929), pp. 536-552.

22,165 MAYLON, B. H. South African shipping. J. AFR. SOC. 36 (1937), pp. 438-446.

22,166 MILLER, D. The ethics of boycott. AFR. SOUTH 4, no. 2 (1960), pp. 55-58.

22,167 MOGG, E. H. The Oliphants' river irrigation scheme. AFRICA 18 (1948), pp. 199-204.

22,168 NAIDOO, S. R. The Indian in industry. RACE RELATIONS 1 (1933-1934), pp. 65-70.

22,169 NGCOBO, S. B. The economics of trusteeship. RACE RELATIONS 16 (1949), pp. 45-55.

22,170 NGCOBO, S. B. The response of Africans to industrial employment. RACE RELATIONS J. 21, no. 1 (1954), pp. 10-17.

22,171 NIEUWENHUYSEN, J. The Bantustan fantasia. AFR. SOUTH 4, no. 2 (1960), pp. 36-41.

22,172 O., C. A. Cronica mineira: ouro. BSEM 18 (1934), pp. 224-225.

22,173 OPPENHEIMER, Sir E. The discovery of gold in the Orange Free State and its economic effects. AFR. AFFAIRS 46 (1947), pp. 220-223.

22,174 OPPENHEIMER, H. The future of the non-European in industry. RACE RELATIONS 15 (1948), pp. 100-108.

22,175 PICKSTONE, H. E. V. The Cape fruit industry. J. AFR. SOC. 16 (1917), pp. 287-296.

22,176 POUTSMA, H. J. Labour struggles in South Africa. CONTEMP. REV. 105 (1914), pp. 500-503.

22,177 PRICE, L. L. Some economic consequences of the South African war. ECON. J. 10 (1900), pp. 323-339.

22,178 REBELO, D. J. S. A indústria da lagosta espinhosa na Africa Austral (um estudo económico). BSEM 135 (1963), pp. 65-82; includes English summary.

22,179 REBELO, D. J. S. O problema do chá na República da Africa do Sul (um estudo económico). BSEM 135 (1963), pp. 83-95; includes English summary.

22,180 RHEINALLT JONES, J. D. Economic maladjustments and the Civilised Labour Policy. RACE RELATIONS 2, no. ii (1934-1935), p. 134.

22,181 RICHARDS, C. S. Economic revival in South Africa. ECON. J. 44 (1934), pp. 616-630.

22,182 RICHARDS, C. S. The Kemmerer-Vissering report and the position of the reserve bank of the Union of South Africa. ECON. J. 35 (1925), pp. 558-567.

22,183 RICHARDS, C. S. Problems of economic development of the Republic of South Africa. ECON. DEV. FOR AFRICA, 1965, pp. 246-278.

22,184 ROBERTSON, H. M. The historical evolution of South African wage levels. RACE RELATIONS 6 (1939), pp. 134-137.

22,185 ROOYEN, T. S. VAN. The secular press and the Bantu, with special reference to the leading Bantu periodicals and newspapers. CHRISTIAN LIT. FOR THE BANTU OF S. AFR., 1957, pp. 103-120.

22,186 S., E. Potenziamento aero del Sud-Africa. AFRICA (Rome) 10 (1955), p. 126.

22,187 SAFFERY, A. L. Direct taxation of natives. RACE RELATIONS 3, no. ii (1936), pp. 53-56.

22,188 SCOTT, P. The Witwatersrand gold field. GEOG. REV. 41 (1951), pp. 561-589.

22,189 SIMONS, H. J. Death in South African mines. AFR. SOUTH 5, no. 4 (1961), pp. 41-55.

22,190 SOUTH AFRICAN INSTITUTE OF RACE RELATIONS. Short-term programme for African development. RACE RELATIONS J. 17 (1950), pp. 51-66.

22,191 STANTON, E. W. Native labour on repetition work. RACE RELATIONS 16 (1949), pp. 1-14.

22,192 STOPFORD, J. G. B. A neglected source of labour in Africa [elephants]. J. AFR. SOC. 1 (1902), pp. 444-451.

22,193 STRAKOSCH, H. The South African reserve bank. ECON. J. 31 (1921), pp. 172-178.

22,194 STRICKLAND, C. F. The co-operative movement in South Africa. J. AFR. SOC. 36 (1937), pp. 461-468.

22,195 TENNANT, Sir D. The railway system of South Africa. ROYAL COL. INST. PR. 29 (1897-1898), pp. 3-30.

22,196 TUROK, B. The African on the farm. AFR. SOUTH 4, no. 1 (1959), pp. 28-33.

22,197 UYS, S. The strike that failed. AFR. SOUTH 2, no. 4 (1958), pp. 44-50.

22,198 VALENTE, A. A República da Africa do Sul perante a O.I.T. PORT. EM AFR. 21 (1964), pp. 361-367.

22,199 VAN RHIJN, A. J. R. The importance of the South African mining industry. AFR. AFFAIRS 58 (1959), pp. 229-237.

22,200 WEBB, M. Vanishing lands and migrant labour. RACE RELATIONS 11 (1944), pp. 43-50.

22,201 WELSH, A. A tax on poverty. AFR. SOUTH 3, no. 2 (1959), pp. 54-60.

22,202 WHYTE, Q. Welfare and efficiency of industrial personnel. RACE RELATIONS 16 (1949), pp. 15-22.

22,203 WILLIAMSON, G. E. Labour and industry. RACE RELATIONS J. 18 (1951), pp. 170-186.

22,204 WILSON, M. Conditions in the Ciskei. RACE RELATIONS J. 21, no. 1 (1954), pp. 1-9.

22,205 WILSON, M. Effects on the Xhosa and Nyakyusa of scarcity of land. AFR. AGRARIAN SYSTEMS, 1963, pp. 374-391.

22,206 A propos de l'industrialisation de l'Afrique du Sud. ZAIRE 5 (1951), pp. 746-747.

22,207 Cri d'alarme en Afrique du Sud. ZAIRE 6 (1952), p. 191.

22,208 Diamond industry in wartime, 1941. Reprinted from The South African Mining and Engineering Journal. J. AFR. SOC. 42 (1943), pp. 129-134.

22,209 En Afrique du Sud: la question du travail indigène. ZAIRE 8 (1954), pp. 416-417.

22,210 Perspectives budgétaires de l'Afrique du Sud. ZAIRE 6 (1952), p. 745.

22,211 Situation économique de l'Afrique du Sud. ZAIRE 9 (1955), pp. 305-306.

22,212 South African gold mines and the war. J. AFR. SOC. 40 (1941), pp. 294-295.

See also 11391, 16654, 21763.

Education

22,213 BAER, G. F. A. The educability of the Bantu. HIST. EDUC. J. 4 (1952-1953), pp. 73-77.

22,214 BARNETT, P. A. Problems and perils of education in South Africa. ROYAL COL. INST. PR. 36 (1904-1905), pp. 130-155.

22,215 BERNSTEIN, R. An inquiry into literacy among adult Africans. RACE RELATIONS 10 (1943), pp. 74-85.

22,216 BLACKWELL, L. The higher education of race. AFR. SOUTH 5, no. 4 (1961), pp. 37-40.

22,217 BLAMIRES, N. South Africa: the Bantu Education Act, 1953. INT. REV. MISSIONS 44 (1955), pp. 99-101.

22,218 BROADHEAD, J. The nursery school in South Africa. AFR. WOMEN 4 (1961), pp. 39-41.

22,219 BROWNLEE, F. News of the war: a South African expedient. AFR. AFFAIRS 46 (1947), pp. 234-235.

22,220 C., J. L'enseignement indigène en Afrique du Sud. ZAIRE 8 (1954), pp. 859-860.

22,221 DOKE, C. M. Vernacular text-books in South African native schools. AFRICA 8 (1935), pp. 183-207.

22,222 GRAY, A. Apartheid school plan. AFR. AFFAIRS 54 (1955), pp. 16-17.

22,223 GRESWELL, W. The education of the South African tribes. PRCI 15 (1883-1884), pp. 68-104.

22,224 GRIEVESON, E. T. Educational needs of urbanised natives in South Africa. J. AFR. SOC. 36 (1937), pp. 321-336.

22,225 HATTERSLEY, A. F. The teaching of history in South African schools. HISTORY 3 (1918), pp. 151-158.

22,226 HEWITT, M. C. and WEBB, M. Non-European library service. RACE RELATIONS 2, no. i (1934-1935), pp. 118-121.

22,227 HEYNINGEN, C. VAN. Christian national education. AFR. SOUTH 4, no. 3 (1960), pp. 50-56.

22,228 HOERNLE, R. F. A. Native education at the cross-roads in South Africa. AFRICA 11 (1938), pp. 389-410.

22,229 HOFMEYER, J. H. The education of the South African native. J. AFR. SOC. 37 (1938), pp. 147-155.

22,230 HORRELL, M. L'éducation bantoue en Afrique du Sud. CIVILISATIONS 13 (1963), pp. 526-534.

22,231 HOUGHTON, K. A. H. The proposed South African native college. J. AFR. SOC. 11 (1911), pp. 35-46.

22,232 IMMELMAN, R. F. M. A mechanics' institute in Cape Town (1853-1878). QBSAL 11 (1956), pp. 17-27.

22,233 IMRAY, E. Christianity and native education. RACE RELATIONS 12 (1945), pp. 46-49.

22,234 JOHNSON, K. C. Non-European libraries in Johannesburg. RACE RELATIONS 8 (1941), pp. 38-41.

22,235 JONES, E. B. Rural education. RACE RELATIONS 2, no. 1 (1934-1935), pp. 122-124.

22,236 JONES, J. D. R. The crisis in native education in South Africa. INT. REV. MISSIONS 28 (1939), pp. 191-204.

22,237 LAWSON, G. W. Crisis in South African universities. UNIVERSITAS 3 (1957), pp. 11-13.

22,238 LEVY, G. University of Cape Town: early beginnings. QBSAL 11 (1956), pp. 59-62.

22,239 LORAM, C. T. The Phelps-Stokes Education Commission in South Africa. INT. REV. MISSIONS 10 (1921), pp. 496-508.

22,240 MacQUARRIE, J. W. The new order in Bantu education. AFR. ED. 1, no. 1 (1956), pp. 32-42.

22,241 MALHERBE, E. G. An educationist looks at race relations. RACE RELATIONS 15 (1948), pp. 47-66.

22,242 MATTHEWS, Z. K. Ethnic universities [South African policy of university apartheid]. AFR. SOUTH 1, no. 4 (1957), pp. 40-48.

22,243 M'TIMKULU, D. G. S. The African and education. RACE RELATIONS 16 (1949), pp. 56-63.

22,244 MUMFORD, W. B. The conference on native education in Johannesburg. J. AFR. SOC. 33 (1934), pp. 411-413.

22,245 NTANTALA, P. The abyss of Bantu education. AFR. SOUTH 4, no. 2 (1960), pp. 42-47.

22,246 PALMER, M. Higher education in Natal. AFR. AFFAIRS 50 (1951), pp. 134-139.

22,247 PERHAM, M. Out of the fellowship [South African policy of university apartheid]. AFR. SOUTH 1, no. 4 (1957), pp. 35-39.

22,248 POEL, J. VAN DER. Native education in South Africa. J. AFR. SOC. 34 (1935), pp. 313-331.

22,249 POEL, J. VAN DER. The present position of coloured education in the Cape Province. RACE RELATIONS 9 (1942), pp. 42-47.

22,250 POPE, M. Universities in ethnasia. AFR. SOUTH 4, no. 1 (1959), pp. 41-49.

22,251 RHEINALLT JONES, E. B. Crisis in native education II: a ten-year plan. RACE RELATIONS 10 (1943), pp. 40-45.

22,252 ROUX, E. Easy English for Africans. AFR. STUD. 1 (1942), pp. 261-269.

22,253 SHEPHERD, R. H. W. The South African Bantu Education Act. AFR. AFFAIRS 54 (1955), pp. 138-142.

22,254 SIHLALI, L. L. Bantu education and the African teacher. AFR. SOUTH 1, no. 1 (1956), pp. 42-51.

22,255 WEBB, M. Adult education in South Africa. RACE RELATIONS 8 (1941), pp. 42-43; 9 (1942), pp. 74-77.

22,256 WOLLHEIM, O. D. Crisis in native education 1: the present position. RACE RELATIONS 10 (1943), pp. 37-40.

22,257 Summary of proceedings of the first meeting of the South African inter-university committee for African studies. BANTU STUD. 6 (1932), pp. 89-92.

Geography

22,258 CRAIL, P. The Cape journal of William Harrison. QBSAL 13 (1958), pp. 15-22.

22,259 CROMPTON, A. W. and SINGER, R. Darwin's visit to the Cape. QBSAL 13 (1958), pp. 9-11.

22,260 GONCHAROV, I. A. A Russian view of the Cape in 1853. (Translated by N. W. Wilson from I. A. Goncharov's *Fregat Pallada*, with additional notes by D. H. Varley.) QBSAL 15 (1960), pp. 48-76; 15 (1961), pp. 83-111, 134-152; 16 (1961), pp. 31-48.

22,261 HERISSON, C. D. The 1837 visit to the Cape of the French poet, Leconte de Lisle. QBSAL 13 (1959), pp. 76-86.

22,262 HICKS, J. B. Some notes concerning the Marico district of the Transvaal. J. AFR. SOC. 23 (1924), pp. 218-227.

22,263 IMMELMAN, R. F. M. Hollandse matroosliedere op die Kaapvaart in die 17e en 18e eeu. QBSAL 14 (1960), pp. 81-86, 125-133; 15 (1960), pp. 12-17.

22,264 ISAAC, W. E. South African coastal waters in relation to ocean currents. GEOG. REV. 27 (1937), pp. 651-664.

22,265 JONES, T. R. The mineral wealth of South Africa. PRCI 18 (1886-1887), pp. 217-251.

22,266 KIRBY, P. R. Gold Dawns River. QBSAL 10 (1956), pp. 135-138.

22,267 LANGHANSZ, C. The New East Indian journey of Christoffel Langhansz. [With introduction and notes by R. Raven-Hart.] QBSAL 19 (1965), pp. 119-139.

22,268 LARPENT, G. DE H. Wealth and wonder in the Zambezi valley. Beira, past, present and future. J. AFR. SOC. 25 (1926), pp. 117-131.

22,269 McMASTER, E. The high plateaus of Natal, their climate and resources. ROYAL COL. INST. PR. 33 (1901-1902), pp. 85-108.

22,270 MacMILLAN, W. M. South Africa revisited. AFR. AFFAIRS 49 (1950), pp. 319-324.

22,271 MANN, Dr. On the physical and economical aspects of the colony of Natal. ROYAL COL. INST. PR. 2 (1870), pp. 93-112.

22,272 MARTIN, A. R. H. The history of Greenvlei, a South African coastal lake. PROC. PAN-AFR. CONGR. PRE-HIST. 3 (1955), pp. 93-97.

22,273 MOOLMAN, J. H. The Orange River, South Africa. GEOG. REV. 36 (1946), pp. 653-674.

22,274 ROMANO, M. P. Utilização das águas dos rios que córrem por mais de um Território. BSEM 132 (1962), pp. 139-143.

22,275 SELOUS, F. C. Incidents of a hunter's life in South Africa. ROYAL COL. INST. PR. 24 (1892-1893), pp. 347-363.

22,276 TATLOW, A. H. The Union of South Africa. J. AFR. SOC. 23 (1924), pp. 278-284.

22,277 THOMPSON, S. South Africa as a health resort. ROYAL COL. INST. PR. 20 (1888-1889), pp. 4-51.

22,278 VARLEY, D. H. C. F. Nicolai's imaginary travels. QBSAL 11 (1957), pp. 97-98.

22,279 WELLINGTON, J. H. Land utilization in South Africa. GEOG. REV. 22 (1932), pp. 205-224.

22,280 WEST, R. Impressions of my visit to South Africa. AFR. AFFAIRS 59 (1960), pp. 301-310.

22,281 YOUNG, Sir F. A winter tour in South Africa. ROYAL COL. INST. PR. 21 (1889-1890), pp. 5-46.

22,282 Note on Dr. Stanger's map of Natal, 1848. QBSAL 11 (1957), pp. 143-144.

See also 10348, 20380.

Government. Politics. Administration. Apartheid

22,283 AN AFRICAN NURSE and JARRETT-KERR, F. M. Apartheid in nursing: a challenge. AFR. SOUTH 3, no. 1 (1958), pp. 32-38.

22,284 AGAR-HAMILTON, J. A. I. The voortrekkers and the natives. RACE RELATIONS 5 (1938), pp. 72-76.

22,285 ALLISON, J. S. Some aspects of urban native administration II. RACE RELATIONS 7 (1940), p. 112.

22,286 ANDREWS, C. F. The agreement between India and South Africa. INT. REV. MISSIONS 16 (1927), pp. 339-349.

22,287 ANDREWS, Sir L. The unending struggle for the freedom of the press. AFR. SOUTH 2, no. 3 (1958), pp. 53-60.

22,288 B., G. Le dernier forfait de l'"Apartheid." PRESENCE AFR. N.S. 30 (1960), pp. 60-61.

22,289 BALLINGER, M. The outlook for the South African Republic. INTERNAT. AFFAIRS 38 (1962), pp. 295-303.

22,290 BALLINGER, M. South African native policies. AFR. AFFAIRS 49 (1950), pp. 32-40.

22,291 BARNETT, J. et al. Petition from gaol. AFR. SOUTH 4, no. 4 (1960), pp. 49-50.

22,292 BASSON, J. D. DU P. The case for apartheid. AFR. SOUTH 1, no. 1 (1956), pp. 14-18.

22,293 BEER, Z. DE and UYS, S. The Progressive Party. AFR. SOUTH 4, no. 3 (1960), pp. 17-23.

22,294 BENTWICH, N. Apartheid, the South African treason trial and human rights. CONTEMP. REV. 199 (1961), pp. 76-79.

22,295 BLAXALL, A. W. South Africa belongs to us. INT. REV. MISSIONS 38 (1949), pp. 295-305.

22,296 BLOM-COOPER, L. J. Referendum for a republic. AFR. SOUTH 5, no. 1 (1960), pp. 42-45.

22,297 BLOOM, H. The South African police. AFR. SOUTH 2, no. 1 (1957), pp. 8-20.

22,298 BOURNE, H. R. F. South Africa and the Aborigines Protection Society. CONTEMP. REV. 56 (1889), pp. 346-360.

22,299 BROOKES, E. H. Official discretion: the tendency to administrative despotism in the Union. RACE RELATIONS J. 23, no. 4 (1956), pp. 1-11.

22,300 BROOKES, E. H. The secession movement in South Africa. FOR. AFFAIRS 11 (1932-1933), pp. 347-354.

22,301 BROOKES, E. H. South Africa: the possibilities in an impossible situation. AFR. AFFAIRS 55 (1956), pp. 188-200.

22,302 BROOKES, E. H. South African swing-over. FOR. AFFAIRS 27 (1948-1949), pp. 143-152.

22,303 BROOKES, E. H. The Union of South Africa: the general election of 1958, and after. ST. ANTONY'S PAPERS 10 (1961), pp. 147-162.

22,304 BROOME, H. A. The progress of civil administration in the Orange River Colony. ROYAL COL. INST. PR. 33 (1901-1902), pp. 219-230.

22,305 BROWN, P. The Liberal Party of South Africa. CONTEMP. REV. 200 (1961), pp. 588-592.

22,306 BROWNLEE, F. The administration of the Transkeian native territories. J. AFR. SOC. 36 (1937), pp. 337-346.

22,307 BUNTING, B. Six portraits of apartheid: 6. Liquor and the colour bar. AFR. SOUTH 2, no. 4 (1958), pp. 36-43.

22,308 BUNTING, B. Towards a climax. AFR. SOUTH 5, no. 4 (1961), pp. 56-66.

22,309 BUNTING, S. The prisons of apartheid. AFR. SOUTH 4, no. 4 (1960), pp. 42-48.

22,310 C., J. L'Afrique du Sud après les élections. ZAIRE 7 (1953), p. 643.

22,311 C., J. Changement de premier ministre en Afrique du Sud. ZAIRE 9 (1955), pp. 165-166.

22,312 CACHALIA, Y. The ghetto act. AFR. SOUTH 2, no. 1 (1957), pp. 39-44.

22,313 CAMBRIDGE, A. A. F. W. A. G. [Earl of Athlone] South Africa and the Empire. J. AFR. SOC. 28 (1929), pp. 109-114.

22,314 CAMPBELL, C. South Africa before the elections. FOR. AFFAIRS 2 (1923-1924), pp. 622-629.

22,315 CAREW-SLATER, H. J. The Kruger tradition in South Africa. CONTEMP. REV. 181 (1952), pp. 330-334.

22,316 CARTER, G. M. Can apartheid succeed in South Africa? FOR. AFFAIRS 32 (1953-1954), pp. 296-309.

22,317 CLAY, G. and UYS, S. The press: Strijdom's "last barrier." AFR. SOUTH 2, no. 1 (1957), pp. 21-32.

22,318 COLE, G. D. H. The anatomy of revolution. AFR. SOUTH 3, no. 3 (1959), pp. 7-11.

22,319 CRESPIGNY, A. R. C. DE. No God. No home. AFR. SOUTH 3, no. 1 (1958), pp. 22-24.

22,320 DAVEY, H. W. The South African territories. CONTEMP. REV. 185 (1954), pp. 16-19.

22,321 DELIUS, A. Travels in tribalism. AFR. SOUTH 4, no. 2 (1960), pp. 27-35.

22,322 DELLICOUR, F. Le régime des Dominions britanniques. BULL. SEANCES IRCB 3 (1932), pp. 336-350.

22,323 DIDCOTT, J. Durban diary. AFR. SOUTH 1, no. 2 (1957), pp. 32-40.

22,324 DOXEY, G. V. and DOXEY, M. P. The prospects for change in South Africa. THE YEAR BOOK OF WORLD AFFAIRS 19 (1965), pp. 69-88.

22,325 DUNCAN, P. Is apartheid an insoluble problem? RACE 6, no. 1 (1964-1965), pp. 263-266.

22,326 DUNCAN, P. Passive resistance. AFR. SOUTH 1, no. 1 (1956), pp. 78-84.

22,327 EISELEN, W. W. M. The meaning of apartheid. RACE RELATIONS 15 (1948), pp. 69-86.

22,328 ERASMUS, B. P. The policy of apartheid. AFR. AFFAIRS 60 (1961), pp. 56-65.

22,329 EVANS, M. S. Present position of native affairs in the Union of South Africa. J. AFR. SOC. 12 (1913), pp. 343-353.

22,330 FAIRBAIRN, J. Zeerust: a profile of resistance. AFR. SOUTH 2, no. 3 (1958), pp. 30-38.

22,331 FIELDING, S. South Africa and world opinion. RACE RELATIONS 15 (1948), pp. 109-117.

22,332 FIRST, R. The bus boycott. AFR. SOUTH 1, no. 4 (1957), pp. 55-64.

22,333 FORMAN, L. The birth of African nationalism. AFR. SOUTH 5, no. 2 (1961), pp. 48-55.

22,334 FRANKLIN, N. N. Industrial expansion and native policy in South Africa. AFR. STUD. 1 (1942), pp. 201-206.

22,335 FREMANTLE, H. E. S. South Africa and the Commonwealth. CONTEMP. REV. 138 (1930), pp. 486-493.

22,336 FRERE, H. B. E. The union of the various portions of British South Africa. PRCI 12 (1880-1881), pp. 134-174.

22,337 GELL, C. W. M. The South African elections. CONTEMP. REV. 184 (1953), pp. 72-76.

22,338 GELL, C. W. M. South Africa's crisis. CONTEMP. REV. 182 (1952), pp. 12-16.

22,339 GOOLD-ADAMS, R. Black and white Africa—is there a frontier on the Limpopo or Zambesi? AFR. AFFAIRS 59 (1960), pp. 112-121.

22,340 GRAY, A. Anglo-S. African defence. AFR. AFFAIRS 57 (1958), pp. 5-6.

22,341 GRAY, A. Bantu areas. AFR. AFFAIRS 55 (1956), pp. 165-166.

22,342 GRAY, A. Bantu self-rule. AFR. AFFAIRS 58 (1959), pp. 195-199.

22,343 GRAY, A. Church and state. AFR. AFFAIRS 56 (1957), pp. 258-261.

22,344 GRAY, A. Coloured vote. AFR. AFFAIRS 55 (1956), pp. 85-87.

22,345 GRAY, A. Coloureds lose vote case. AFR. AFFAIRS 56 (1957), pp. 6-8.

22,346 GRAY, A. Dr. Verwoerd takes over. AFR. AFFAIRS 58 (1959), pp. 2-3.

22,347 GRAY, A. Positive apartheid. AFR. AFFAIRS 61 (1962), pp. 97-103.

22,348 GRAY, A. Rand bus boycott. AFR. AFFAIRS 56 (1957), p. 106.

22,349 GRAY, A. Republic and Union. AFR. AFFAIRS 59 (1960), pp. 282-284.

22,350 GRAY, A. Simonstown agreement. AFR. AFFAIRS 54 (1955), pp. 251-253.

22,351 GRAY, A. South Africa. AFR. AFFAIRS 60 (1961), pp. 370-372.

22,352 GRAY, A. South African affairs. AFR. AFFAIRS 61 (1962), pp. 12-14.

22,353 GRAY, A. South African changeover. AFR. AFFAIRS 54 (1955), pp. 4-5.

22,354 GRAY, A. South African elections. AFR. AFFAIRS 57 (1958), pp. 86-88, 174-175.

22,355 GRAY, A. South African opposition. AFR. AFFAIRS 56 (1957), pp. 12-13.

22,356 GRAY, A. South African Republic. AFR. AFFAIRS 60 (1961), p. 4.

22,357 GRAY, A. South Africa's status. AFR. AFFAIRS 61 (1962), pp. 182-185.

22,358 GRAY, A. Troubled South Africa. AFR. AFFAIRS 59 (1960), pp. 185-188.

22,359 GRAY, A. U.N. move against Republic [of South Africa]. AFR. AFFAIRS 62 (1963), pp. 18-19.

22,360 GRAY, A. Union and the republic. AFR. AFFAIRS 59 (1960), pp. 101-102, 282-284; 60 (1961), p. 4.

22,361 GRAY, A. Union election preliminaries. AFR. AFFAIRS 56 (1957), pp. 263-264.

22,362 GRAY, A. Union quits UNO. AFR. AFFAIRS 55 (1956), pp. 10-12.

22,363 GRAY, A. Union Senate Bill. AFR. AFFAIRS 54 (1955), pp. 167-168.

22,364 GUTTERIDGE, W. British defence interests in Southern Africa. CONTEMP. REV. 207 (1965), pp. 74-78

22,365 HAMMOND-TOOKE, W. D. Chieftainship in Transkeian political development. JMAS 2 (1964), pp. 513-529.

22,366 HAMMOND-TOOKE, W. D. Segmentation and fission in Cape Nguni political units. AFRICA 35 (1965), pp. 143-167.

22,367 HARMEL, M. Revolutions are not abnormal. AFR. SOUTH 3, no. 2 (1959), pp. 12-17.

22,368 HARRIS, J. H. South Africa: a golden opportunity. CONTEMP. REV. 115 (1919), pp. 637-643.

22,369 HAVEMANN, E. A. E. The principles underlying urban native administration in the Union. RACE RELATIONS J. 18 (1951), pp. 2-15.

22,370 HELLMAN, E. The poison of practical apartheid. AFR. SOUTH 1, no. 1 (1956), pp. 19-24.

22,371 HELLMAN, E. Six portraits of apartheid: 1. The intellectual fraud. AFR. SOUTH 2, no. 4 (1958), pp. 5-11.

22,372 HERBST, J. F. The administration of native affairs in South Africa. J. AFR. SOC. 29 (1930), pp. 478-489.

22,373 HOERNLE, A. W. Alternatives to apartheid. RACE RELATIONS 15 (1948), pp. 87-99.

22,374 HOERNLE, R. F. A. Die Protektoraat-Kwessie en die naturel. RACE RELATIONS 2, no. iii (1934-1935), pp. 160-162.

22,375 HOLLAND, K. The emperor's clothes. AFR. SOUTH 4, no. 4 (1960), pp. 52-57.

22,376 HOLLEMAN, J. F. Die Zulu isigodi. BANTU STUD. 15 (1941), pp. 91-118, 245-275.

22,377 HOOPER, C. Six portraits of apartheid: 3. Diary of a country priest. AFR. SOUTH 2, no. 4 (1958), pp. 15-22.

22,378 HORRELL, M. Union sud-africaine. CIVILISATIONS 7 (1957), pp. 627-638; 8 (1958), pp. 622-630; 9 (1959), pp. 99-106, 251-258, 535-542: 10 (1960), pp. 110-116, 269-274, 365-372, 501-507; 11 (1961), pp. 101-107, 213-219, 312-317, 478-484, 517-521.

22,379 HORWITZ, R. Six portraits of apartheid: the economic cost. AFR. SOUTH 2, no. 4 (1958), pp. 32-35.

22,380 HOUGHTON, D. H. The significance of the Tomlinson Report. AFR. SOUTH 1, no. 2 (1957), pp. 13-21.

22,381 HOUGHTON, D. H. Union Sud Africaine. CIVILISATIONS 5 (1955), pp. 285-290; 5 (1956), pp. 483-490; 7 (1957), pp. 444-452; 8 (1958), pp. 455-462.

22,382 JABAVU, D. D. T. Native unrest in South Africa. INT. REV. MISSIONS 11 (1922), pp. 249-259.

22,383 JAMESON, H. "Apartheid et Racisme." PRESENCE AFR. N.S. 32-33 (1960), pp. 103-120.

22,384 JEAL, E. F. Can white Africa adjust itself? CONTEMP. REV. 197 (1960), pp. 187-190.

22,385 JEAL, E. F. The South Africa scene. CONTEMP. REV. 191 (1957), pp. 155-158.

22,386 JEAL, E. F. Trends in South Africa. CONTEMP. REV. 193 (1958), pp. 288-291.

22,387 JONA, W. Il dramma del Sud Africa. AFRICA (Rome) 15 (1960), pp. 127-132.

22,388 JONES, E. B. South African native land policy. BANTU STUD. 14 (1940), pp. 175-197.

22,389 JONES, J. D. R. Union Sud-Africaine. CIVILISATIONS 3 (1953), pp. 147-150.

22,390 JOOSTE, G. P. South Africa's position in the western world. AFR. AFFAIRS 54 (1955), pp. 109-120.

22,391 JOSEPH, H. Women and passes. AFR. SOUTH 2, no. 2 (1958), pp. 26-31; 3, no. 3 (1959), pp. 20-28.

22,392 JOSEPH, J. The question of your removal. AFR. SOUTH 4, no. 1 (1959), pp. 69-75.

22,393 JUNOD, V. The white liberals and the treason arrests. AFR. SOUTH 1, no. 3 (1957), pp. 21-27.

22,394 KHAMA, Chief T. Native standpoints (II: against transfer) (of Protectorates). RACE RELATIONS 2, no. iii (1934-1935), pp. 152-156.

22,395 KIRKWOOD, Sir K. The constitutional crisis in South Africa. INTERNAT. AFFAIRS 28 (1952), pp. 432-444.

22,396 KIRKWOOD, Sir K. Failure of a report [of the Riots Commission of Inquiry]. RACE RELATIONS 16 (1949), pp. 97-106.

22,397 KUPER, H. and THERON, K. The labour policy of the Rand mines. RACE RELATIONS 10 (1943), pp. 69-74.

22,398 KUPER, L. The background to passive resistance (South Africa 1952). RACE RELATIONS J. 20, no. 3 (1953), pp. 17-30.

22,399 KUPER, L. Race zoning in cloud cuckoo land. AFR. SOUTH 2, no. 1 (1957), pp. 33-38.

22,400 KUPER, L. Rights and riots in Natal. AFR. SOUTH 4, no. 2 (1960), pp. 20-26.

22,401 LA GUMA, B. V. Nursing by pigment. AFR. SOUTH 2, no. 2 (1958), pp. 32-33.

22,402 LAWRENCE, H. G. The native in industry. RACE RELATIONS 6 (1939), pp. 46-50.

22,403 LAWRIE, G. G. South Africa's world position. JMAS 2 (1964), pp. 41-54.

22,404 LEWIN, J. Afrikaners and others. AFR. SOUTH 1, no. 2 (1957), pp. 41-46.

22,405 LEWIN, J. No revolution round the corner. AFR. SOUTH 3, no. 1 (1958), pp. 50-55.

22,406 LEWIN, J. The recognition of African trade unions. RACE RELATIONS 9 (1942), pp. 111-116.

22,407 LEWIN, J. Tribal tradition and native administration in South Africa. J. AFR. SOC. 38 (1939), pp. 289-299.

22,408 LONGMORE, L. South Africa: a new constitution? AFR. AFFAIRS 58 (1959), pp. 141-144.

22,409 LONGMORE, L. The South African dilemma. THE YEAR BOOK OF WORLD AFFAIRS 8 (1954), pp. 196-219.

22,410 LUCAS, F. A. W. Six portraits of apartheid: 4. The cost to law and order. AFR. SOUTH 2, no. 4 (1958), pp. 23-31.

22,411 MacCRINDLE, A. M. South Africa's growing pain. CONTEMP. REV. 189 (1956), pp. 348-352.

22,412 MacMILLAN, W. M. South Africa revisited. AFR. AFFAIRS 49 (1950), pp. 319-324.

22,413 MALAN, D. F. and GEYER, A. L. Apartheid. KONGO-OVERZEE 20 (1954), pp. 247-264.

22,414 MALAN, F. S. South Africa in world affairs. INTERNAT. AFFAIRS 16 (1937), pp. 727-742.

22,415 MANDELA, N. Out of the strike. AFR. SOUTH 6 (1961), pp. 15-23.

22,416 MANNING, C. A. W. South Africa and the world. In defense of apartheid. FOR. AFFAIRS 43 (1964-1965), pp. 135-149.

22,417 MANSERGH, N. Britain, the Commonwealth, and Western union. INTERNAT. AFFAIRS 24 (1948), pp. 491-504.

22,418 MANSERGH, N. Postwar strains on the British Commonwealth. FOR. AFFAIRS 27 (1948-1949), pp. 129-142.

22,419 MAQUIBELA, S. The problem of African political solidarity: its sources and obstacles in South Africa. PROC. 3RD. GRAD. ACAD. UCLA, 1965, pp. 15-20.

22,420 MARAIS, D. Boklaagte goes to the polls. AFR. SOUTH 2, no. 4 (1958), pp. 58-61.

22,421 MARQUARD, L. National unity in South Africa. RACE RELATIONS 17 (1950), pp. 22-28.

22,422 MASON, P. South Africa and the world. Some maxims and axioms. FOR. AFFAIRS 43 (1964-1965), pp. 150-164.

22,423 MASSEY, V. British Commonwealth relations. INTERNAT. AFFAIRS 13 (1934), pp. 815-825.

22,424 MATTHEWS, J. Revolution: further reflections. AFR. SOUTH 3, no. 4 (1959), pp. 12-16.

22,425 MATTHEWS, Z. K. An African policy for South Africa. RACE RELATIONS 16 (1949), pp. 71-83.

22,426 MEER, F. Satyagraha in South Africa. AFR. SOUTH 3, no. 2 (1959), pp. 21-28.

22,427 MILLER, J. D. B. South Africa's departure [from the Commonwealth]. J. COMM. POL. STUD. 1 (1961-1963), pp. 56-74.

22,428 MOORE, Sir W. H. The Dominions of the British Commonwealth in the League of Nations. INTERNAT. AFFAIRS 9 (1930), pp. 372-391.

22,429 MOLEMA, S. M. The African: present and future political representation. RACE RELATIONS 17 (1950), pp. 29-42.

22,430 MPHAHLELE, E. The Evaton riots. AFR. SOUTH 1, no. 2 (1957), pp. 55-63.

22,431 MPHAHLELE, E. South African report: an analysis of developments in South Africa. TRANSITION 4 (1962), pp. 33-34; 5 (1962), pp. 31-32.

22,432 MULLER, H. E. H. Separate development in South Africa. AFR. AFFAIRS 62 (1963), pp. 53-65.

22,433 MUNGER, E. S. Self-confidence and self-criticism in South Africa. FOR. AFFAIRS 36 (1957-1958), pp. 659-668.

22,434 MURRAY, J. South Africa: a visitor's view. CONTEMP. REV. 148 (1935), pp. 173-181.

22,435 NEAME, L. E. The African National Congress. CONTEMP. REV. 194 (1958), pp. 206-210.

22,436 NEAME, L. E. The English in South Africa. CONTEMP. REV. 185 (1954), pp. 351-355.

22,437 NEL, M. D. C. DE W. Fondeamenti della politica dello sviluppo separato in Sud Africa. AFRICA (Rome) 15 (1960), pp. 223-228.

22,438 NGUBANE, J. K. African political movements. AFR. SOUTH 1, no. 1 (1956), pp. 70-78.

22,439 NICHOLLS, G. H. South African native policy. AFR. AFFAIRS 44 (1945), pp. 73-80.

22,440 NIXON, C. R. The conflict of Nationalisms in South Africa. WORLD POLITICS 11 (1958-1959), pp. 44-67.

22,441 NOKWE, D. Congress and the Africanists: Congress replies: Congress replies. AFR. SOUTH 4, no. 3 (1960), pp. 33-38.

22,442 NOKWE, D. The great smear: communism and Congress in South Africa. AFR. SOUTH 6 (1961), pp. 5-14.

22,443 NOKWE, D. The South African police: laws and powers. AFR. SOUTH 2, no. 2 (1958), pp. 17-25.

22,444 O'DOWD, T. Memoirs of a tribalist [A. J. van der Merwe]. AFR. SOUTH 1, no. 3 (1957), pp. 89-93.

22,445 OPPENHEIMER, H. F. South Africa's role in a changing Africa. AFR. AFFAIRS 60 (1961), pp. 18-25.

22,446 PATTEN, J. W. Alternatives to apartheid in South Africa. FOR. AFFAIRS 31 (1951-1952), pp. 310-326.

22,447 PHILLIPS, N. A foreign correspondent in South Africa. AFR. SOUTH 5, no. 1 (1960), pp. 25-30.

22,448 PICARDIE, M. The lion and the cockerel. AFR. SOUTH 4, no. 4 (1960), pp. 22-29.

22,449 PILANE, Chief I. Native standpoints (I: in favour of transfer) (of Protectorates). RACE RELATIONS 2, no. iii (1934-1935), pp. 149-152.

22,450 PIROW, O. How far is the Union interested in the continent of Africa. J. AFR. SOC. 36 (1937), pp. 317-320.

22,451 PLESSIS, J. DU. De arm blanke en die Kleur-vraagstuk. RACE RELATIONS 1 (1933-1934), pp. 61-65.

22,452 RABOROKO, P. N. Congress and the Africanists: the Africanist case. AFR. SOUTH 4, no. 3 (1960), pp. 24-32.

22,453 RAKE, A. The pattern of South Africa's emergency. AFR. SOUTH 5, no. 1 (1960), pp. 14-20.

22,454 REEDMAN, J. N. Economic policy of the Union and the problem of poverty. RACE RELATIONS 6 (1939), pp. 28-33.

22,455 REEVES, A. The christian witness in South Africa. CONTEMP. REV. 199 (1961), pp. 120-123.

22,456 REEVES, R. A. Six portraits of apartheid: 2. The moral cost. AFR. SOUTH 2, no. 4 (1958), pp. 12-14.

22,457 REYBURN, H. A. The Atlantic Charter and Africa 1: From an American standpoint. RACE RELATIONS 10 (1943), pp. 61-63.

22,458 RHEINALLT JONES, J. D. Some considerations which arise from the administration of the Native Trust and Land Act, 1936. RACE RELATIONS 5 (1938), pp. 51-60.

22,459 RHEINALLT JONES, J. D. and BLOOM, H. S. Natives in urban areas. RACE RELATIONS 4 (1937), pp. 75-88.

22,460 RHEINALLT JONES, J. D. and JONES, E. B. Interpretations of trusteeship. RACE RELATIONS 8 (1941), pp. 34-37.

22,461 ROBERTS, E. New hope for South Africa. CONTEMP. REV. 201 (1962), pp. 179-182.

22,462 ROBERTS, E. Race policies in South Africa. CONTEMP. REV. 178 (1950), pp. 102-105.

22,463 RODDA, P. The Africanists cut loose. AFR. SOUTH 3, no. 4 (1959), pp. 23-26.

22,464 ROUX, E. Revolution in South Africa. AFR. SOUTH 3, no. 2 (1959), pp. 18-20.

22,465 RUBIO GARCIA, L. La unión de Africa del Sur y los Protectorados. CUAD. EST. AFR. 19 (1952), pp. 19-30.

22,466 SABIKHI, V. The United Nations and the racial discrimination in South Africa. AFRO-ASIAN AND W. AFF. 1 (1964), pp. 135-144.

22,467 SABIKHI, V. The United Nations report on apartheid. AFRO-ASIAN AND W. AFF. 2 (1965), pp. 381-384.

22,468 SAFFERY, A. L. The liquor problem in urban areas. RACE RELATIONS 7 (1940), pp. 88-94.

22,469 SAUNDERS, J. R. Natal in its relation to South Africa. PRCI 13 (1881-1882), pp. 103-145.

22,470 SAUNDERSON, G. Johannesburg diary. AFR. SOUTH 1, no. 3 (1957), pp. 17-20.

22,471 SCOTT, M. Elections generales en Afrique du Sud. PRESENCE AFR. N.S. 18-19 (1958), pp. 221-224.

22,472 SCOTT, M. L'essentielle mauvaise foi de l'"apartheid." PRESENCE AFR. N.S. 30 (1960), pp. 62-71.

22,473 SEGAL, R. La derrière bataille. PRESENCE AFR. N.S. 36 (1961), pp. 18-33.

22,474 SHAH, K. K. British democracy and economic sanctions against South Africa. AFR. QUART. 4, no. i (1964), pp. 4-8.

22,475 SIMONS, H. J. An addendum [to No revolution round the corner]. AFR. SOUTH 3, no. 1 (1958), pp. 56-60.

22,476 SIMONS, H. J. Disabilities of the native in the Union of South Africa. RACE RELATIONS 6 (1939), pp. 59-67.

22,477 SIMONS, H. J. Passes and police. AFR. SOUTH 1, no. 1 (1956), pp. 51-63.

22,478 SIMONS, H. J. Some aspects of urban native administration. RACE RELATIONS 7 (1940), pp. 101-111.

22,479 SISSULU, W. M. Congress and the Africanists. AFR. SOUTH 3, no. 4 (1959), pp. 27-34.

22,480 SISSULU, W. M. South Africa's struggle for democracy. AFR. SOUTH 1, no. 2 (1957), pp. 27-31.

22,481 SLOLEY, H. C. The African native labour contingent and the welfare committee. J. AFR. SOC. 17 (1918), pp. 199-211.

22,482 SMITH, R. H. Native labour and native policy. RACE RELATIONS 9 (1942), pp. 85-93.

22,483 SMUTS, J. C. Problems in South Africa. J. AFR. SOC. 16 (1917), pp. 273-282.

22,484 SNITCHER, F. The Eiselen scheme. AFR. SOUTH 1, no. 3 (1957), pp. 40-45.

22,485 SOWARD, F. H. The Commonwealth countries and world affairs. INTERNAT. AFFAIRS 27 (1951), pp. 192-203.

22,486 SPENCE, J. E. Recent trends in South Africa. AFR. AFFAIRS 59 (1960), pp. 136-143.

22,487 STANTON, H. Pretoria central gaol, 1960. AFR. SOUTH 5, no. 1 (1960), pp. 21-24.

22,488 SWANZY, H. Indians in Africa. AFR. AFFAIRS 45 (1946), pp. 111-112.

22,489 TABATA, I. B. et al. Analyse de la situation politique en Afrique du Sud, par un groupe de réfugiés. PRESENCE AFR. N.S. 50 (1964), pp. 89-95.

22,490 TANDI. Diary of a detainee. AFR. SOUTH 5, no. 2 (1961), pp. 25-47.

22,491 THOMAS, J. H. The parliamentary tour in South Africa. J. AFR. SOC. 24 (1925), pp. 77-82.

22,492 THOMPSON, D. V. The South Africa of today. AFR. AFFAIRS 56 (1957), pp. 128-136.

22,493 THORNTON, A. P. The argument about South Africa [review article on Report on Southern Africa by Basil Davidson, The dilemma of South Africa by John Hatch]. CORONA 4 (1952), pp. 427-429.

22,494 TRAPIDO, S. Natal's non-racial franchise, 1856. AFR. STUD. 22 (1963), pp. 22-32.

22,495 TRAPIDO, S. The origins of the Cape franchise qualifications of 1853. J. AFR. HIST. 5 (1964), pp. 37-54.

22,496 TRAPIDO, S. The place of boycott. AFR. SOUTH 3, no. 4 (1959), pp. 17-22.

22,497 UYS, S. Apartheid: opium of the Afrikaner. TRANSITION 19 (1965), pp. 13-16.

22,498 UYS, S. The referendum and after. AFR. SOUTH 5, no. 2 (1961), pp. 6-13.

22,499 UYS, S. The Senate farce. AFR. SOUTH 3, no. 4 (1959), pp. 5-11.

22,500 UYS, S. The white opposition in South Africa. AFR. SOUTH 1, no. 1 (1956), pp. 63-69.

22,501 UYS, S. The white opposition splits. AFR. SOUTH 4, no. 2 (1960), pp. 12-19.

22,502 VALENTE, A. Aspectos políticos do Apartheid. PORT. EM AFR. 22 (1965), pp. 103-117, 157-177.

22,503 VAN DEN BERGHE, P. L. Apartheid, fascism and the Golden Age. CAH. ET. AFR. 2 (1962), pp. 598-608.

22,504 WEBB, M. The Atlantic Charter and Africa II: in relation to the Union. RACE RELATIONS 10 (1943), pp. 63-68.

22,505 WEBB, M. The riots and after. RACE RELATIONS 16 (1949), pp. 85-96.

22,506 WERNER, A. Native affairs in Natal. J. AFR. SOC. 5 (1905), pp. 72-86.

22,507 WERNER, A. Native affairs in South Africa. J. AFR. SOC. 6 (1907), pp. 163-176; 7 (1908), pp. 175-189; 9 (1909), pp. 73-86.

22,508 WHYTE, Q. Afrique du Sud. CIVILISATIONS 5 (1955), pp. 137-142, 440-446; 6 (1956), pp. 293-300; 7 (1957), pp. 269-280; 8 (1958), pp. 369-376.

22,509 WHYTE, Q. Union Sud-Africaine. CIVILISATIONS 4 (1954), pp. 133-134.

22,510 WHYTE, Q. and HORRELL, M. Afrique du Sud. Chronique culturelle et scientifique envisagée sous l'angle des relations de race. CIVILISATIONS 4 (1954), pp. 625-631; 5 (1955), pp. 623-629.

22,511 WILLIAMS, F. The embattled press. AFR. SOUTH 4, no. 3 (1960), pp. 86-90.

22,512 WILLIAMS, O. The village and the castle. AFR. SOUTH 3, no. 1 (1958), pp. 25-31.

22,513 WYNDHAM, H. A. Union of South Africa: Report of the native affairs commission for the year 1936. J. AFR. SOC. 37 (1938), pp. 174-179.

22,514 Afrique du Sud. PRESENCE AFR. N.S. 44 (1962), pp. 229-232.

22,515 L'Afrique du Sud avant les élections. ZAIRE 7 (1953), pp. 283-284.

22,516 The Bloemfontein Charter. AFR. SOUTH 1, no. 2 (1957), pp. 22-26.

22,517 Crise constitutionnelle en Afrique du Sud. ZAIRE 6 (1952), pp. 526-527.

22,518 Diary from refuge. AFR. SOUTH 5, no. 1 (1960), pp. 31-40.

22,519 Dissolution volontaire du Conseil Représentatif indigène d'Afrique-du-Sud. ZAIRE 5 (1951), pp. 299-300.

22,520 Les élections au Bantoustan. PRESENCE AFR. N.S. 50 (1964), pp. 246-250.

22,521 Enquête américaine sur la crise d'Afrique du Sud. ZAIRE 6 (1952), pp. 634-636.

22,522 The Freedom Charter [in the Treason Inquiry]. AFR. SOUTH 1, no. 3 (1957), pp. 13-16.

22,523 The Native Bills described and analysed. RACE RELATIONS 2, no. iv (1934-1935), pp. 3-39.

22,524 The nineteen days. AFR. SOUTH 4, no. 4 (1960), pp. 6-21.

22,525 Political parties and problems of South Africa. CONTEMP. REV. 117 (1920), pp. 197-203.

22,526 Rapport sur l'Apartheid. PRESENCE AFR. N.S. 50 (1964), pp. 38-59.

22,527 Le Révérend Malan devant l'opinion anglo-saxonne. ZAIRE 6 (1952), pp. 527-529.

22,528 The Rivonia trial. AFR. QUART. 4, no. ii (1964), pp. 124-142.

22,529 The same boat. AFR. SOUTH 5, no. 2 (1961), pp. 14-24.

22,530 Situation générale de l'Afrique du Sud. ZAIRE 5 (1951), pp. 410-411.

22,531 South African affairs. J. AFR. SOC. 33 (1934), pp. 169-172.

22,532 Techniques of revolt. AFR. SOUTH 6 (1961), pp. 24-30.

22,533 Torture in South Africa: allegations of ill-treatment and torture of prisoners [United Nations Special Committee report]. TRANSITION 19 (1965), pp. 17-22.

22,534 Union Sud-Africaine. CIVILISATIONS 3 (1953), pp. 605-606.

See also 10401, 23323, 23998.

History

22,535 AFRIKANDER. Our position in South Africa. CONTEMP. REV. 72 (1897), pp. 899-908.

22,536 AMERY, L. S. The constitutional development of South Africa. TRHS, 4th series, 1 (1918), pp. 218-235.

22,537 BARNARD, K. H. Pierre-Antoine Delande, naturalist, and his Cape visit, 1818-1820. QBSAL 11 (1956), pp. 6-13.

22,538 BARNARD, K. H. Sir John Herschel and the S.A. Literary and Scientific Institution. QBSAL 9 (1954), pp. 10-11.

22,539 BAYLEN, J. O. W. T. Stead and the Boer War: the irony of idealism. CANADIAN HIST. REV. 40 (1959), pp. 304-314.

22,540 BERG, J. VAN DEN. Jan van Riebeeck en die Verre Ooste. QBSAL 6 (1952), pp. 70-76.

22,541 BIELSCHOWSKI, L. A German gardener at the Cape, 1677. QBSAL 5 (1951), pp. 118-121.

22,542 BISSET, Lieut.-Gen. South Africa and her colonies. ROYAL COL. INST. PR. 7 (1875-1876), pp. 86-121, 125-148.

22,543 BLOCH, J. DE. Some lessons of the Transvaal war. CONTEMP. REV. 77 (1900), pp. 456-471.

22,544 BLUMBERG, M. The Mafekeng Affair. AFR. SOUTH 4, no. 3 (1960), pp. 39-46.

22,545 BONDURANT, J. V. New sources for countervailing a legend: personal and political history in South Africa and India. J. MOD. HIST. 36 (1964), pp. 318-323.

22,546 BRADLOW, E. A South African year of crisis: 1899. HISTORY TODAY 11 (1961), pp. 712-719.

22,547 BRADLOW, F. R. The four Bowler pictures of the opening of the Cape Town to Wellington Railway. QBSAL 19 (1965), pp. 104-109.

22,548 BRADLOW, F. R. The 120 diagrams of Sir Andries Stockenström. QBSAL 13 (1959), pp. 111-115.

22,549 BRADLOW, F. and BRADLOW, E. Fifty years of union: South Africa, 1910-1960. HISTORY TODAY 10 (1960), pp. 406-413.

22,550 BROWNLEE, F. The clash of colour in South Africa. J. AFR. SOC. 37 (1938), pp. 227-240.

22,551 BURROWS, E. H. The first anaesthetic at the Cape. QBSAL 9 (1955), pp. 72-74.

22,552 BURSSENS, A. Bij een feestboekje over Jan van Riebeeck en een jonge natie. KONGO-OVERZEE 18 (1952), pp. 263-265.

22,553 BURT-DAVY, J. The agricultural and pastoral possibilities of the Transvaal. ROYAL COL. INST. PR. 38 (1906-1907), pp. 315-335.

22,554 BUTLER, J. Sir Alfred Milner on British policy in South Africa in 1897. BOSTON UNIV. PAPERS ON AFR. HIST. 1 (1964), pp. 243-270.

22,555 BUTLER, W. T. The Boers and the Transvaal. CONTEMP. REV. 39 (1881), pp. 220-231.

22,556 BUXTON, E. The Jameson raid [by H. M. Hole]. J. AFR. SOC. 30 (1931), pp. 113-118.

22,557 CALPIN, G. H. South Africa at war. FOR. AFFAIRS 19 (1940-1941), pp. 458-461.

22,558 CALPIN, G. H. South Africa in Afrikaner hands. FOR. AFFAIRS 29 (1950-1951), pp. 417-423.

22,559 CAMPBELL, C. The election campaign in South Africa. FOR. AFFAIRS 7 (1928-1929), pp. 658-660.

22,560 CANA, F. R. Dr. Theal's history of South Africa. J. AFR. SOC. 15 (1916), pp. 335-342.

22,561 COLENSO, F. E. Zululand after the war. CONTEMP. REV. 41 (1882), pp. 54-71.

22,562 DAVENPORT, T. R. H. Nationalism and conciliation: the Bourassa-Hertzog posture. CANADIAN HIST. REV. 44 (1963), pp. 193-212.

22,563 DAVENPORT, T. R. H. The South African rebellion, 1914. ENG. HIST. REV. 78 (1963), pp. 73-94.

22,564 DRUS, E. The question of imperial complicity in the Jameson raid. ENG. HIST. REV. 68 (1953), pp. 582-593.

22,565 DULY, L. C. The failure of British land policy at the Cape, 1812-28. J. AFR. HIST. 6 (1965), pp. 357-371.

22,566 DUNCAN, P. Toward a world policy for South Africa. FOR. AFFAIRS 42 (1963-1964), pp. 38-48.

22,567 DU TOIT, S. F. Swedish contacts with South Africa. QBSAL 2 (1947), pp. 33-35.

22,568 F.A.O. The [British] government and the South African war. CONTEMP. REV. 84 (1903), pp. 552-564.

22,569 FAIRBAIRN, J. The Sekhukhuneland terror. AFR. SOUTH 3, no. 1 (1958), pp. 16-21.

22,570 FAWCETT, M. G. Impressions of South Africa in 1901 and in 1903. CONTEMP. REV. 84 (1903), pp. 635-655.

22,571 FLETCHER-VANE, F. P. The fruits of the war in South Africa. CONTEMP. REV. 84 (1903), pp. 122-130.

22,572 FORBES, V. S. John Elliott's visit to Cape Town, 1778-1779. QBSAL 7 (1952), pp. 13-19.

22,573 FORBES, V. S. Some visits of English ships to the Cape, 1679-1703. QBSAL 7 (1952), pp. 41-48.

22,574 FOUCHE, L. The historical setting of the Great Trek. RACE RELATIONS 5 (1938), pp. 71-72.

22,575 FRERE, Sir B. Historical sketch of South Africa. TRHS N.S. 2 (1885), pp. 1-60; N.S. 4 (1889), pp. 221-284.

22,576 GAILEY, H. A., Jr. John Philip's role in Hottentot emancipation. J. AFR. HIST. 3 (1962), pp. 419-433.

22,577 GANN, L. H. Liberal interpretations of South African history: a review article [on The Story of South Africa by Leo Marquard; and The Last Trek, a study of the Boer people and the Afrikaner Nation by Sheila Patterson]. RHODES-LIV. J. 25 (1959), pp. 40-58.

22,578 GARRETT, F. E. The inevitable in South Africa. CONTEMP. REV. 76 (1899), pp. 457-481.

22,579 GARSON, N. G. The Boer rebellion of 1914. HISTORY TODAY 12 (1962), pp. 132-139.

22,580 GILLMORE, P. South Africa: the territories adjacent to the Kalahari Desert. PRCI 14 (1882-1883), pp. 125-158.

22,581 GLANVILLE, P. B. South Africa. ROYAL COL. INST. PR. 6 (1874-1875), pp. 155-188.

22,582 HAARHOOF, T. J. South Africa and the traditions of civilized life. CONTEMP. REV. 158 (1940), pp. 653-662.

22,583 HARNETTY, P. Canada, South Africa, and the Commonwealth, 1960-61. J. COMM. POL. STUD. 2 (1963-1964), pp. 33-44.

22,584 HARRISON, C. South Africa and the Chartered Company. CONTEMP. REV. 69 (1896), pp. 339-346.

22,585 HATTERSLEY, A. F. The annexation of the Transvaal, 1877. HISTORY 21 (1936), pp. 41-47.

22,586 HATTERSLEY, A. F. Byways of South African journalism in early Victorian days. QBSAL 11 (1956), pp. 48-56.

22,587 HATTERSLEY, A. F. Christopher Chapman Bird, Colonial Secretary, 1814-1824. QBSAL 10 (1956), pp. 117-128.

22,588 HATTERSLEY, A. F. The emancipation of slaves at the Cape. HISTORY 8 (1923), pp. 180-186.

22,589 HATTERSLEY, A. F. Forgotten worthies from the Little Rose. QBSAL 13 (1958), pp. 6-9.

22,590 HATTERSLEY, A. F. George Hough, senior colonial chaplain, 1817-47. QBSAL 12 (1957), pp. 143-159.

22,591 HATTERSLEY, A. F. The Great Trek, 1835-7. HISTORY 16 (1931), pp. 50-54.

22,592 HATTERSLEY, A. F. The Natal Society, 1851-1951. QBSAL 5 (1951), pp. 73-78.

22,593 HATTERSLEY, A. F. South Africa's first daily newspaper. QBSAL 11 (1957), pp. 124-129.

22,594 HATTERSLEY, A. F. The Zulu problem of 1878-9. HISTORY 2 (1917), pp. 25-32.

22,595 HAWKIN, R. C. Germany and South Africa. CONTEMP. REV. 108 (1915), pp. 491-500.

22,596 HOBSON, J. A. Capitalism and imperialism in South Africa. CONTEMP. REV. 77 (1900), pp. 1-17.

22,597 HOBSON, J. A. The proconsulate of Milner. CONTEMP. REV. 78 (1900), pp. 540-554.

22,598 HOLT, B. The journal and letters of Captain Sidney Turner. QBSAL 9 (1954), pp. 1-7.

22,599 HOLT, B. Sidney Turner and the Zulu War. QBSAL 10 (1955), pp. 13-16.

22,600 HULME, J. J. The journal of John Scott. QBSAL 11 (1956), pp. 56-58.

22,601 HUNT, D. R. An account of the Bapedi. BANTU STUD. 5 (1931), pp. 275-326.

22,602 HYAM, R. Smuts and the decision of the Liberal government to grant responsible government to the Transvaal, January and February 1906. HIST. J. 8 (1965), pp. 380-398.

22,603 JAGER, E. J. DE. Distribution of the Free State stone hut-and-kraal ruins. AFR. UND UB. 48 (1964-1965), pp. 294-302.

22,604 KANNEMEYER, M. and ROBINSON, A. M. L. The Lady Anne Barnard letters in the South African Library. QBSAL 4 (1949), pp. 1-19.

22,605 KERR, W. B. A survey of the literature on Canada's participation in the South African War. CANADIAN HIST. REV. 18 (1937), pp. 419-427.

22,606 KEY, B. On the management of the native tribes of South Africa. CONTEMP. REV. 39 (1881), pp. 516-528.

22,607 KIEWIET, C. W. DE. Loneliness in the beloved country. FOR. AFFAIRS 42 (1963-1964), pp. 413-427.

22,608 KILEY, D. The Pondoland massacre. AFR. SOUTH 5, no. 1 (1960), pp. 7-12.

22,609 KILPIN, R. Secrets of the National Convention. QBSAL 6 (1951), pp. 39-42.

22,610 KING, N. The siege of Mafeking. HISTORY TODAY 6 (1956), pp. 21-27.

22,611 KIRBY, P. R. A forgotten translation of a "Grosvenor" manuscript. QBSAL 9 (1955), pp. 117-122.

22,612 KIRBY, P. R. Gquma, Mdepa and the Amatshomane clan: a by-way of miscegenation in South Africa. AFR. STUD. 13 (1954), pp. 1-24.

22,613 KOCK, W. J. DE. The genesis of the Van Riebeeck Society: an early letter. QBSAL 11 (1957), pp. 122-124.

22,614 LLOYD, A. C. G. Duelling at the Cape. QBSAL 5 (1950), pp. 39-45.

22,615 LLOYD, A. C. G. Some memories of a private secretary. QBSAL 6 (1951), pp. 43-49.

22,616 LOVELL, C. R. Afrikaner nationalism and apartheid. AMER. HIST. REV. 61 (1955-1956), pp. 308-330.

22,617 MACDERMOT, T. W. L. Canada and South Africa. QBSAL 5 (1951), pp. 107-112.

22,618 MCINTYRE, D. An astronomical bi-centenary: the Abbé de Lacaille's visit to the Cape, 1751-1753. QBSAL 5 (1951), pp. 79-90.

22,619 MCINTYRE, D. The Herschel obelisk. QBSAL 8 (1954), pp. 87-92.

22,620 MACKARNESS, F. The causes of the Cape rebellion and its cure. CONTEMP. REV. 78 (1900), pp. 397-414.

22,621 MACKENZIE, J. The Chartered Company in South Africa. CONTEMP. REV. 71 (1897), pp. 305-328.

22,622 MACKENZIE, J. The expansion of South Africa. CONTEMP. REV. 56 (1889), pp. 753-776.

22,623 MACKENZIE, J. England and South Africa. CONTEMP. REV. 45 (1884), pp. 111-138.

22,624 MACKENZIE, N. H. Captain Cross and the first English settlement at the Cape. QBSAL 2 (1947), pp. 3-14, 49-54.

22,625 MARKS, S. Harriette Colenso and the Zulus, 1874-1913. J. AFR. HIST. 4 (1963), pp. 403-411.

22,626 MAYDON, J. G. Natal. ROYAL COL. INST. PR. 27 (1895-1896), pp. 183-216.

22,627 MILLER, A. E. The proposed suspension of the Cape constitution. CONTEMP. REV. 82 (1902), pp. 341-352.

22,628 MOLTENO, P. A. The cause of the [South African] war. CONTEMP. REV. 76 (1899), pp. 637-647.

22,629 MONNIG, H. O. The Baroka Ba Nkwana. AFR. STUD. 22 (1963), pp. 170-175.

22,630 MORGAN, B. H. The trade and industry of South Africa. ROYAL COL. INST. PR. 34 (1902-1903), pp. 131-161.

22,631 MURRAY, A. H. The trek and its legacy. RACE RELATIONS 5 (1938), pp. 76-79.

22,632 MUSKETT, J. J. The Boers at home. CONTEMP. REV. 39 (1881), pp. 506-515.

22,633 NEAME, L. E. Fifty years of the Union. CONTEMP. REV. 198 (1960), pp. 487-489.

22,634 NEGRIER, Gen. DE. Lessons of the South African war. CONTEMP. REV. 82 (1902), pp. 305-340.

22,635 NHLAPO, J. M. The story of AmaNhlapo. AFR. STUD. 4 (1945), pp. 97-101.

22,636 NOBLE, J. British South Africa and the Zulu war. ROYAL COL. INST. PR. 10 (1878-1879), pp. 105-168.

22,637 O., C. A. O nome português está ligado á descoberta das minas de ouro de Witwatersrand. BSEM 18 (1934), pp. 221-223.

22,638 O'BRIEN, W. Ireland and the Transvaal. CONTEMP. REV. 92 (1907), pp. 536-547.

22,639 OMER-COOPER, J. D. Shaka and the rise of the Zulu. TARIKH 1, no. 1 (1965), pp. 30-41.

22,640 PACHAI, B. South African Indians and citizenship: a historical survey—1855-1934. AFR. QUART. 4, no. iii (1964), pp. 167-178.

22,641 PAMA, C. Genealogy in South Africa. QBSAL 10 (1956), pp. 128-132.

22,642 PEASE, A. E. The native question in the Transvaal. CONTEMP. REV. 90 (1906), pp. 16-36.

22,643 PENNER, C. D. Germany and the Transvaal before 1896. J. MOD. HIST. 12 (1940), pp. 31-58.

22,644 PHILLIPS, L. The outlook in South Africa. ROYAL COL. INST. PR. 31 (1899-1900), pp. 305-336.

22,645 PHILLIPS, L. Some observations on South Africa. CONTEMP. REV. 77 (1900), pp. 761-776.

22,646 PIENAR, P. With De Wet. CONTEMP. REV. 79 (1901), pp. 326-334.

22,647 PINE, C. C. B. The Boers and the Zulus. CONTEMP. REV. 35 (1879), pp. 541-570.

22,648 POLLARD, A. F. The Dominions and foreign affairs. HISTORY 6 (1921), pp. 84-98.

22,649 QUAESITOR. The South African bubble. CONTEMP. REV. 72 (1897), pp. 133-152.

22,650 RAINERO, R. Gli olandesi nell' Africa del sud. AFRICA (Rome) 17 (1962), pp. 133-136.

22,651 RAINIER, M. The Barnards without Lady Anne. QBSAL 12 (1957), pp. 12-17.

22,652 RAVEN-HART, R. Johan Schreyer's description of the Hottentots, 1679. QBSAL 19 (1964), pp. 56-69; 19 (1965), pp. 88-101.

22,653 RAWSON, H. E. Some experiences with native tribes in South Africa. J. AFR. SOC. 8 (1909), pp. 357-371.

22,654 RIDGEWAY, Sir W. The future of the Transvaal. J. AFR. SOC. 6 (1907), pp. 154-162.

22,655 ROBINSON, A. M. L. A chart of Eastern Province newspapers in the South African Library. QBSAL 5 (1951), p. 121.

22,656 ROBINSON, A. M. L. Diary of the missionaries at Baviaans Kloof, Cape of Good Hope, of the year 1795. QBSAL 8 (1954), pp. 51-57, 79-87.

22,657 ROBINSON, A. M. L. Emigration to the Cape a hundred years ago. QBSAL 2 (1948), pp. 112-116.

22,658 ROBINSON, A. M. L. The Great Fire of Cape Town, 23 November, 1798. Extracts from the diary of Samuel Eusebius Hudson, Chief Clerk in the Customs in Cape Town. Memorandum & occurrences from the 17th Novr. 1798. QBSAL 8 (1953), pp. 6-11.

22,659 ROBINSON, A. M. L. The journal of Robert Warden, seaman, at the Cape, 1796-7. QBSAL 7 (1952), pp. 68-79.

22,660 ROBINSON, A. M. L. A voyage to the Cape in 1687. QBSAL 4 (1950), pp. 113-124.

22,661 ROBINSON, J. B. Glimpses of Natal. ROYAL COL. INST. PR. 9 (1877-1878), pp. 280-325.

22,662 ROBINSON, J. B. The South African settlement. CONTEMP. REV. 78 (1900), pp. 457-467.

22,663 ROCHLIN, S. A. Aspects of Islam in nineteenth-century South Africa. BULL. SOAS 10 (1940-1942), pp. 213-221.

22,664 ROCHLIN, S. A. Early Arabic printing at the Cape of Good Hope. BULL. SOAS 7 (1933-1935), pp. 49-54.

22,665 ROCKLEY, Lady [Evelyn Cecil]. Women settlers in South Africa. J. AFR. SOC. 33 (1934), pp. 123-129.

22,666 ROSE, J. H. The French East-Indian expedition at the Cape in 1803. ENG. HIST. REV. 15 (1900), pp. 129-132.

22,667 ROUTH, C. R. N. The great South African trek. HISTORY TODAY 1 (1951), pp. 7-13.

22,668 SAFFORD, F. The voice of the uitlanders. CONTEMP. REV. 76 (1899), pp. 14-21.

22,669 SALOMON, L. The economic background to the revival of Afrikaner nationalism. BOSTON UNIV. PAPERS IN AFR. HIST. 1 (1964), pp. 217-242.

22,670 SCARISBRICK, J. J. The first Englishman round the Cape of Good Hope? BULL. INST. HIST. RES. 34 (1961), pp. 165-177.

22,671 SCHREINER, W. P. South Africa and the war. J. AFR. SOC. 14 (1914-1915), pp. 117-122.

22,672 SICARD, H. VON. Shaka and the North. AFR. STUD. 14 (1955), pp. 145-153.

22,673 SMIT, D. E. Emigrasie na Suid-Afrika in die 19 de eeu. QBSAL 16 (1962), pp. 161-164.

22,674 SMIT, D. E. Het Afrikaansch Familieblad. QBSAL 15 (1961), pp. 112-114.

22,675 SMUTS, J. C. General Smuts on the war. J. AFR. SOC. 42 (1943), pp. 59-68.

22,676 SPENCE, J. E. Tradition and change in South African foreign policy. J. COMM. POL. STUD. 1 (1961-1963), pp. 136-152.

22,677 THOMPSON, L. M. Afrikaner nationalist historiography and the policy of apartheid. J. AFR. HIST. 3 (1962), pp. 125-141.

22,678 TRAPIDO, S. Developments in South Africa from the end of the 18th century to the early 20th century. J. WORLD HIST. 7 (1962-1963), pp. 911-929.

22,679 VARLEY, D. H. The Cape adventures of Joshua Penny. QBSAL 12 (1957), pp. 17-22.

22,680 VARLEY, D. H. The French diary of Augusta de Mist. QBSAL 10 (1955), pp. 11-13.

22,681 VARLEY, D. H. The Haughton letters: an Indian visitor to the Cape, 1849-50. QBSAL 10 (1955), pp. 77-89.

22,682 VARLEY, D. H. Henry Dempster and the Cape of Good Hope pamphlet, 1841. QBSAL 11 (1956), pp. 58-59.

22,683 VARLEY, D. H. Henry Willey Reveley—first colonial civil engineer at the Cape. QBSAL 12 (1957), pp. 118-121.

22,684 VARLEY, D. H. A housewife at the Cape in 1818, being extracts from the journals of Sarah Norman Eaton. QBSAL 8 (1953), pp. 45-49.

22,685 VARLEY, D. H. Jan Huygen van Linschoten and his Itinerario. QBSAL 10 (1955), pp. 52-56.

22,686 VARLEY, D. H. Letters of Joseph Holland, 1820 settler and Indian corn-grower. QBSAL 8 (1954), pp. 92-94.

22,687 VARLEY, D. H. The note-books of Arthur Barker, 1820 settler. QBSAL 13 (1959), pp. 73-76.

22,688 VARLEY, D. H. A note on Coree the Saldanian. QBSAL 1 (1947), pp. 78-81.

22,689 VARLEY, D. H. Two scrap-books of Robert Baden-Powell. QBSAL 9 (1954), pp. 11-14.

22,690 VARLEY, D. H. The Van Riebeeck Society. QBSAL 3 (1949), pp. 112-120.

22,691 VARLEY, D. H. William Leske and his Cape sermon, 1617. QBSAL 10 (1956), pp. 74-77.

22,692 WALKER, E. A. The Jameson Raid. CAMB. HIST. J. 6 (1938-1940), pp. 283-306.

22,693 WALLENBERG, J. The travels of a busybody at the Cape. Being extracts from Jacob Wallenberg's "Min son pa Galejan" (M. K. Jeffreys). QBSAL 2 (1947), pp. 36-49, 69-75.

22,694 WARREN, C. Cecil Rhodes' early days in South Africa. CONTEMP. REV. 81 (1902), pp. 643-654.

22,695 WEDDERBURN, D. South Africa. CONTEMP. REV. 42 (1882), pp. 111-129.

22,696 WILSON, M. The early history of the Transkei and Ciskei. AFR. STUD. 18 (1959), pp. 167-179.

22,697 WOOD, C. T. An experiment that failed (Rev. J. W. Saunders of the Children's Friend Society and his efforts to place children "in teen years" as domestic or farm servants in 1838). QBSAL 6 (1952), pp. 118-120.

22,698 WOODHOUSE, C. M. The missing telegrams and the Jameson raid. HISTORY TODAY 12 (1962), pp. 395-404, 506-514.

22,699 WYBERGH, W. The Transvaal and the new government. CONTEMP. REV. 89 (1906), pp. 313-323.

22,700 WYNDHAM, H. A. A history of South Africa, by C. W. de Kiewet. J. AFR. SOC. 41 (1942), pp. 129-131.

22,701 The accessibility of [South African] archives. BULL. INST. HIST. RES. 4 (1926-1927), pp. 159-160.

22,702 British rule in Transvaal. CONTEMP. REV. 85 (1904), pp. 329-351.

22,703 A chart of Cape Town newspapers. QBSAL 1 (1947), pp. 70-71.

22,704 A chart of Western Province newspapers in the South African Library (excluding Cape Town). QBSAL 3 (1949), pp. 79-80.

22,705 General Smuts [on the war effort]. J. AFR. SOC. 41 (1942), pp. 4-6.

22,706 Glencoe, Elandslaagte, Mafeking. CONTEMP. REV. 76 (1899), pp. 628-636.

22,707 The literature of the South African war, 1899-1902. AMER. HIST. REV. 12 (1906-1907), pp. 299-321.

22,708 Notes on some recent historical studies in Southern Africa. QBSAL 7 (1953), pp. 65-68.

22,709 The origin and incidence of miscegenation at the Cape during the Dutch East India Company's regime 1652-1795. RACE RELATIONS J. 20, no. 2 (1953), pp. 23-27.

22,710 Our methods in South Africa. CONTEMP. REV. 80 (1901), pp. 55-57.

22,711 Recollections of the rebellion, 1896. NADA 14 (1936-1937), pp. 49-61.

22,712 The situation in South Africa. CONTEMP. REV. 79 (1901), pp. 305-317.

22,713 South African affairs. J. AFR. SOC. 32 (1933), pp. 424-427.

22,714 South African armorial devices. QBSAL 10 (1956), pp. 132-135.

22,715 South African native movements [summary of Time Longer than Rope by E. Roux]. AFR. AFFAIRS 48 (1949), pp. 129-132.

22,716 Trois siècles d'Afrique du Sud. ZAIRE 6 (1952), pp. 525-526.

22,717 A view of the Bay of Souldania near the Cape of Good Hope on the Coast of Africa. [From R. Burton's View of the English acquisitions in Guinea and The East Indies, 1686.] QBSAL 1 (1947), pp. 71-78.

22,718 War policy of South Africa. J. AFR. SOC. 39 (1940), pp. 109-111.

See also 2703, 14750, 20596, 20606.

Language. Literature

Language

22,719 ANDERS, H. A note on a South Eastern Bushman dialect. AFR. UND UB. 25 (1934-1935), pp. 81-89.

22,720 BAUMANN, C. Nama-texte. AFR. UND UB. 6 (1915-1916), pp. 55-78.

22,721 BLEEK, D. F. Bushman grammar. A grammatical sketch of the language of the /xam-ka-/k'e. AFR. UND UB. 19 (1928-1929), pp. 81-98; 20 (1929-1930), pp. 161-174.

22,722 BLEEK, D. F. A short survey of Bushman languages. AFR. UND UB. 30 (1940), pp. 52-72.

22,723 BLERK, N. VAN. South Africanisms in the Oxford English dictionary. QBSAL 16 (1961), pp. 77-86.

22,724 BOUMAN, A. C. Some remarks on the language of a book of verse in Afrikaans: Krokos. LINGUA 11 (1962), pp. 59-66.

22,725 BOURQUIN, W. Adverb und adverbiale Umschreibung in Kafir. AFR. UND UB. 3 (1912-1913), pp. 230-243, 279-326; 4 (1913-1914), pp. 68-74, 118-155, 231-248.

22,726 BOURQUIN, W. Notes on the concords in Xhosa and Zulu, their differences and general aspect. AFR. STUD. 11 (1952), pp. 16-28.

22,727 BOURQUIN, W. The so-called article in Xhosa. AFR. STUD. 5 (1946), pp. 21-43.

22,728 BOURQUIN, W. The use of the demonstrative pronoun in Xhosa. AFR. STUD. 8 (1949), pp. 10-19.

22,729 BULCK, G. VAN. Herkomst en groei van het Afrikaans [discussion of book by G. G. Kloeke]. ZAIRE 5 (1951), pp. 1055-1058.

22,730 COLE, D. T. The grammatical structure of Zulu. AFR. STUD. 18 (1959), pp. 213-214.

22,731 COLE, D. T. Notes on the phonological relationships of Tswana vowels. AFR. STUD. 8 (1949), pp. 109-131.

22,732 COLE-BEUCHAT, P. D. The qualificative and the pronoun in Tsonga. AFR. STUD. 20 (1961), pp. 175-193.

22,733 COLE-BEUCHAT, P. D. A restatement of the Zulu verb conjugation: Part 2. AFR. STUD. 23 (1964), pp. 35-49.

22,734 COLE-BEUCHAT, P. D. Tonomorphology of the Tsonga noun. AFR. STUD. 18 (1959), pp. 133-145.

22,735 COLE-BEUCHAT, P. D. Additional notes on the tonomorphology of the Tsonga noun. AFR. STUD. 21 (1962), pp. 105-122.

22,736 COPE, A. T. The grammatical structure of Zulu. AFR. STUD. 16 (1957), pp. 210-220; 18 (1959), pp. 35-37.

22,737 COPE, A. T. Nomino-verbal constructions in Zulu. AFR. LANG. STUD. 4 (1963), pp. 69-97.

22,738 COPE, A. T. Zulu tonology. AFR. UND UB. 43 (1959-1960), pp. 190-200.

22,739 CRABTREE, W. A. Zulu origins. BANTU STUD. 1, no. ii (1922), pp. 5-7.

22,740 DAHLE, P. B. Eine Siegeshymne der Ama-Zulu. Entstehung, Text und Töne des Sandlwana-Liedes. FESTSCHRIFT MEINHOF, 1927, pp. 174-195.

22,741 DEMPWOLFF, O. Einführung in die Sprache der Nama-Hottentotten. AFR. UND UB. 25 (1934-1935), pp. 30-66, 89-134, 188-229.

22,742 DOKE, C. M. Etudes relatives aux langues Bantoues en Afrique du Sud. AEQUATORIA 7 (1944), pp. 152-154.

22,743 DOKE, C. M. European and Bantu languages in South Africa. AFRICA 12 (1939), pp. 308-318.

22,744 DOKE, C. M. Notes on a problem in the mechanism of the Zulu clicks. BANTU STUD. 2 (1923), pp. 43-45.

22,745 EISELEN, W. Zur Erforschung des Lovelu-Dialektes. AFR. UND UB. 19 (1928-1929), pp. 98-116.

22,746 ENDEMANN, P. Texte von Gesängen der Sotho. ZAS 1 (1887-1888), pp. 64-71.

22,747 ENGELBRECHT, J. A. Notes on the imperative in Zulu. AFR. STUD. 16 (1957), pp. 102-107.

22,748 FORTUNE, G. The conjugation of inchoative verbs in Shona. AFR. STUD. 8 (1949), pp. 132-140.

22,749 GERSTNER, J. A preliminary check list of Zulu names of plants. BANTU STUD. 12 (1938), pp. 215-236, 321-342; 13 (1939), pp. 49-64, 131-149, 307-326; 15 (1941), pp. 277-301, 369-383.

22,750 HOF, J. J. P. Die ontwikkeling van Afrikaans as skryftaal. QBSAL 19 (1964), pp. 4-6.

22,751 HOFFMANN, C. Sotho-Texte aus dem Holzbuschgebirge in Transvaal. AFR. UND UB. 18 (1927-1928), pp. 241-272; 22 (1931-1932), pp. 161-179; 23 (1932-1933), pp. 59-75; 24 (1933-1934), pp. 58-76, 122-150, 201-230, 282-303; 28 (1937), pp. 29-66, 123-138, 174-198.

22,752 JEANJAQUET, J. M. The relative clause in Xhosa. AFR. STUD. 4 (1945), pp. 28-36.

22,753 JEANJAQUET, J. M. The relative-locative clause or adverbial clause of place in Xhosa. AFR. STUD. 4 (1945), pp. 193-198.

22,754 KAHLER-MEYER, E. Eine Studienreise nach Südafrika. AFR. UND UB. 42 (1958), pp. 143-144.

22,755 KINGON, J. R. L. Language research—a forward movement. J. AFR. SOC. 19 (1920), pp. 214-220.

22,756 KUHN, G. Pedi-Texte. AFR. UND UB. 27 (1936-1937), pp. 161-184, 288-319.

22,757 KUNENE, D. P. Southern Sotho words of English and Afrikaans origin. WORD 19 (1963), pp. 347-375.

22,758 LA GRASSERIE, R. DE. De quelques particularités de la langue des Namas Kleine Mittheilungen. ZAOS 2 (1896), pp. 88-89, 288-289.

22,759 LANHAM, L. W. The grammatical structure of Zulu. AFR. STUD. 17 (1958), pp. 221-222.

22,760 LANHAM, L. W. The tonemes of Xhosa. AFR. STUD. 17 (1958), pp. 65-81.

22,761 LANHAM, L. W. and HALLOWES, D. P. An outline of the structure of eastern Bushman. AFR. STUD. 15 (1956), pp. 97-118.

22,762 LESTRADE, G. P. Some remarks on the practical orthography of the South African Bantu languages. BANTU STUD. 3 (1927), pp. 261-273.

22,763 LOUW, J. A. The consonant phonemes of the lexical root in Zulu. AFR. UND UB. 48 (1964-1965), pp. 127-152.

22,764 LOUW, J. A. Emphasis as expressed by the word order of the sentence in Xhosa. AFR. UND UB. 42 (1958), pp. 111-118.

22,765 LOUW, J. A. The syntactical nature of the deficient verb and its complement in Zulu. AFR. STUD. 13 (1954), pp. 147-152.

22,766 LOUW, J. A. and NGIDI, J. On the segmental phonemes of Zulu. AFR. UND UB. 46 (1962-1963), pp. 43-93.

22,767 LUGG, H. C. A method of reproducing Zulu words. AFR. STUD. 11 (1952), pp. 35-37.

22,768 MacCULLAH, A. A. What is to be the language of South Africa? CONTEMP. REV. 82 (1902), pp. 375-381.

22,769 MAINGARD, L. F. The Korana dialects. AFR. STUD. 23 (1964), pp. 57-66.

22,770 MAINGARD, L. F. [ed.] Korana names of animals and plants [collected by L. Lloyd]. BANTU STUD. 6 (1932), pp. 309-321.

22,771 MAINGARD, L. F. The origin of the word "Hottentot." BANTU STUD. 9 (1935), pp. 63-67.

22,772 MAINGARD, L. F. A revised manuscript version of the Korana catechism of C. F. Wuras. BANTU STUD. 5 (1931), pp. 111-165.

22,773 MEINHOF, C. Die Kürzung des Mittelgliedes in Zusammensetzungen. AFR. UND UB. 31 (1941), pp. 241-248.

22,774 MEINHOF, C. Versuch einer grammatischen Skizze einer Buschmannsprache. AFR. UND UB. 19 (1928-1929), pp. 161-188.

22,775 MEINHOF, C. Zur Lautlehre des Zulu. AFR. UND UB. 14 (1923-1924), pp. 241-287.

22,776 MERIGGI, P. Versuch einer Grammatik des /xam-Buschmännischen. AFR. UND UB. 19 (1928-1929), pp. 117-153, 188-205.

22,777 MULLER, P. J. Afrikaanse geskrifte in Arabiese karakters. QBSAL 15 (1960), pp. 36-45.

22,778 NAKENE, G. Tlokwa riddles. AFR. STUD. 2 (1943), pp. 125-138.

22,779 NGANI, A. Z. Utyelelo Lokumkani Nokumkanikazi Kumzantsi Weafrika. The visit of the King and Queen to South Africa. AFR. STUD. 6 (1947), pp. 121-123.

22,780 NIENABER, G. S. 'N lysie Hottentotse woorde uit 1626. AFR. STUD. 21 (1962), pp. 28-39.

22,781 NIENABER, G. S. 'N ou ongepubliseerde lys Hottentoten Xhosawoorde. AFR. STUD. 19 (1960), pp. 157-169.

22,782 NIENABER, G. S. The origin of the name "Hottentot." AFR. STUD. 22 (1963), pp. 65-90.

22,783 NIENABER, G. S. Die vroegste verslae aangaande Hottentots. AFR. STUD. 15 (1956), pp. 29-35.

22,784 NORTON, W. A. African life and language. AFR. STUD. 9 (1950), pp. 20-28.

22,785 NYEMBEZI, C. L. S. The historical background to the Izibongo of the Zulu military age. AFR. STUD. 7 (1948), pp. 110-125, 157-174.

22,786 ODENDAL, F. F. The structure of the Afrikaans root morpheme. LINGUA 10 (1961), pp. 38-56.

22,787 PANCONCELLI-CALZIA, G. Objektive Untersuchungen über die Stimmhaftigkeit der Explosivae im Zulu. AFR. UND UB. 14 (1923-1924), pp. 287-290.

22,788 POTGIETER, E. F. The Ndzundza dialect of southern Transvaal Nguni-Ndebele. AFR. STUD. 12 (1953), pp. 189-190.

22,789 RIORDAN, J. The wrath of the ancestral spirits. AFR. STUD. 20 (1961), pp. 53-60.

22,790 SANDILANDS, A. The ancestor of Tswana grammars. AFR. STUD. 17 (1958), pp. 192-197.

22,791 SILINGA, J. Dankreden für die religiösen Zusammenkünfte in Baziya und Umgegend 1934. AFR. UND UB. 29 (1939), pp. 287-293.

22,792 STEVICK, E. W. The implosive-explosive contrast in Manyika. AFR. STUD. 19 (1960), pp. 88-95.

22,793 TAYEDZERHWA, L. G. N. Umbengo—a Xhosa poem on the death of S. E. K. Mqhayi. AFR. STUD. 10 (1951), pp. 125-129.

22,794 VAN WYK, E. B. An augmentative noun class in Tsonga. AFR. STUD. 16 (1957), pp. 25-36.

22,795 VAN WYK, E. B. Potential and progressive constructions in Northern Sotho. AFR. STUD. 16 (1957), pp. 162-176.

22,796 VILJOEN, W. J. How we solved the language problem in South Africa. J. AFR. SOC. 23 (1923), pp. 1-5.

22,797 VILLIERS, M. DE. Absolute and relative tenses; empathy in Afrikaans (South African Dutch). LINGUA 4 (1954-1955), pp. 407-412.

22,798 WANDRES, C. Alte Wortlisten der Hottentottensprache. AFR. UND UB. 9 (1918-1919), pp. 26-42.

22,799 WANDRES, C. Nama-Wörter. AFR. UND UB. 16 (1925-1926), pp. 275-297.

22,800 WANGER, W. Die drei Formen des Zulusubstantivs. Prädikative Präfixe versus Pronominale Kopula etc. BIBLIOTHECA AFR. 1 (1925), pp. 114-126.

22,801 WANGER, W. Linguistics and dogma. BIBLIOTHECA AFR. 4, no. 2 (1930-1931), pp. 54-66.

22,802 WARMELO, N. J. V. European and other influences in Sotho. BANTU STUD. 3 (1927), pp. 405-421.

22,803 WARMELO, N. J. V. Die Gliederung der südafrikanischen Bantusprachen. AFR. UND UB. 18 (1927-1928), pp. 1-54, 81-127.

22,804 WESTPHAL, E. The tone of verb stems in Xhosa. AFR. STUD. 10 (1951), pp. 107-112.

22,805 WESTPHAL, E. O. J. Venda: tonal structure and intonation. AFR. STUD. 21 (1962), pp. 49-69, 123-173.

22,806 WILHELM, J. H. Aus dem Wortschatz der !Kun- und der Hukwe-Buschmannsprache. AFR. UND UB. 12 (1921-1922), pp. 291-304.

22,807 WURAS, C. F. An account of the Korana. BANTU STUD. 3 (1927), pp. 287-296.

22,808 WURAS, C. F. An outline of the Bushman language. AFR. UND UB. 10 (1919-1920), pp. 81-87.

22,809 WYK, E. B. VAN. Die kopulatiewe van Noord-Sotho. KONGO-OVERZEE 21 (1955), pp. 71-94, 241-261.

22,810 ZYL, H. J. VAN. Praises in northern Sotho. BANTU STUD. 15 (1941), pp. 119-156.

22,811 The practical orthography of Transvaal Sotho. Recommendations of the Transvaal Sotho District Committee. BANTU STUD. 4 (1930), pp. 1-9.

See also 20652, 20673.

Literature

22,812 ABASIEKONG, D. Poetry pure and applied: Rabearivelo and Brutus. TRANSITION 23 (1965), pp. 45-48.

22,813 BLOOM, H. Nice time [fiction]. AFR. SOUTH 1, no. 1 (1956), pp. 115-124.

22,814 BRUTUS, D. Poèmes. PRESENCE AFR. N.S. 50 (1964), pp. 208-213.

22,815 BRUTUS, D. Un poète de la tragédie Sud-Africaine. PRESENCE AFR. N.S. 50 (1964), p. 207.

22,816 BRUTUS, D. Two poems [Kneeling before you, A troubadour]. BO 12 (1962), p. 17.

22,817 BUCHANAN, R. The Battle of Isandula [a poem]. CONTEMP. REV. 35 (1879), pp. 153-156.

22,818 BUTLER, G. Home thoughts [a poem]. AFR. SOUTH 1, no. 1 (1956), pp. 124-128.

22,819 CALDECOTT, M. Christmas eve [a poem]. AFR. SOUTH 2, no. 3 (1958), pp. 124-125.

22,820 DAVISON, D. South African newsboy [a poem]. AFR. SOUTH 5, no. 4 (1961), pp. 117-118.

22,821 DELIUS, A. Along the line. The final canto of a South African fantasy [a poem]. AFR. SOUTH 1, no. 4 (1957), pp. 108-128.

22,822 DELIUS, A. Judgment day. The second canto of a South African fantasy [a poem]. AFR. SOUTH 1, no. 3 (1957), pp. 107-127.

22,823 FISHER, M. High fence [fiction]. AFR. SOUTH 2, no. 1 (1957), pp. 107-117.

22,824 FRIESLICH, N. South-easter [fiction]. AFR. SOUTH 2, no. 4 (1958), pp. 119-123.

22,825 GILL, D. For Dennis Brutus [a poem]. TRANSITION 11 (1963), p. 50.

22,826 GREEN, M. Thomas Pringle's "Afar in the desert." QBSAL 2 (1948), pp. 110-112.

22,827 GRIGGS, E. L. Samuel Taylor Coleridge and Thomas Pringle. QBSAL 6 (1951), pp. 1-6.

22,828 HATTERSLEY, A. F. Sam Sly (William Layton Sammons). QBSAL 9 (1955), pp. 109-116.

22,829 HATTINGH, I. Car-boy [fiction]. AFR. SOUTH 4, no. 2 (1960), pp. 120-122.

22,830 HERRMAN, L. Olive Schreiner, March 24th 1855-December 11th, 1920. QBSAL 9 (1955), pp. 69-72.

22,831 HUGHES, L. In explanation of our times [a poem]. AFR. SOUTH 1, no. 3 (1957), pp. 100-101.

22,832 HUGHES, L. Memo to the non-white peoples [a poem]. AFR. SOUTH 1, no. 3 (1957), p. 99.

22,833 JORDAN, A. C. Towards an African literature. AFR. SOUTH 1, no. 4 (1957), pp. 90-98.

22,834 JORDAN, A. C. Towards an African literature: conflicts and loyalties. AFR. SOUTH 3, no. 3 (1959), pp. 114-117.

22,835 JORDAN, A. C. Towards an African literature: the dawn of literature among the Xhosa. AFR. SOUTH 2, no. 3 (1958), pp. 112-115.

22,836 JORDAN, A. C. Towards an African literature: the early writers. AFR. SOUTH 2, no. 4 (1958), pp. 113-118.

22,837 JORDAN, A. C. Towards an African literature: the harp of the nation. AFR. SOUTH 4, no. 2 (1960), pp. 110-113.

22,838 JORDAN, A. C. Towards an African literature: land, labour, literature. AFR. SOUTH 4, no. 1 (1959), pp. 117-121.

22,839 JORDAN, A. C. Towards an African literature: literary stabilization. AFR. SOUTH 3, no. 1 (1958), pp. 114-117.

22,840 JORDAN, A. C. Towards an African literature: the mounting anguish. AFR. SOUTH 4, no. 3 (1960), pp. 112-116.

22,841 JORDAN, A. C. Towards an African literature: poetry and the new order. AFR. SOUTH 3, no. 2 (1959), pp. 74-79.

22,842 JORDAN, A. C. Towards an African literature: the tale of Nongqawuse. AFR. SOUTH 3, no. 4 (1959), pp. 111-115.

22,843 JORDAN, A. C. Towards an African literature: traditional poetry. AFR. SOUTH 2, no. 1 (1957), pp. 97-105.

22,844 JUNOD, H. A. L'Epopée de la Rainette. ZAOS 3 (1897), pp. 225-249.

22,845 KAHLER, H. Ein rezentes Werk der arabisch-afrikaansen Literatur der Kap-Malaien. AFR. UND UB. 44 (1960), pp. 110-131.

22,846 KRIGE, U. South African poetry. BLACK ORPHEUS 17 (1965), pp. 33-38.

22,847 KUMALO, A. Vengeance [a poem]. TRANSITION 19 (1965), p. 23.

22,848 KUPER, H. The amazement of Namahasha [fiction]. AFR. SOUTH 1, no. 4 (1957), pp. 102-107.

22,849 LA GUMA, A. At the portagees [fiction]. BO 11 (1962), pp. 18-21.

22,850 LA GUMA, A. Blankets [fiction]. BO 15 (1964), pp. 57-58.

22,851 LA GUMA, A. Out of the darkness [fiction]. AFR. SOUTH 2, no. 1 (1957), pp. 118-122.

22,852 LA GUMA, A. Slipper satin [fiction]. BO 8 (1960), pp. 32-35.

22,853 LA GUMA, A. Tattoo marks and nails [fiction]. BO 14 (1964), pp. 48-53.

22,854 LEONARD, D. A. The wedding party [fiction]. AFR. SOUTH 1, no. 2 (1957), pp. 120-128.

22,855 LINDFORS, B. Postwar literature in English by African writers from South Africa: a study of the effects of environment upon literature. PROC. 3RD. GRAD. ACAD. UCLA, 1965, pp. 149-162.

22,856 LIPKIN, J. Orlando, a wintertime [a poem]. AFR. SOUTH 1, no. 4 (1957), pp. 99-101.

22,857 MABONA, M. The sea [a poem]. PRESENCE AFR. N.S. 56 (1965), p. 98.

22,858 MADE, E. H. A. and DHLOMO, H. I. E. Ubambatha Kamakhwatha (Benedict W. Vilakazi, M.A., D.Litt.). AFR. STUD. 8 (1949), pp. 165-179.

22,859 MAIMANE, J. A. Just a Tsotsi [fiction]. AFR. SOUTH 2, no. 3 (1958), pp. 116-123.

22,860 MAIMANE, J. A. A manner of speaking [fiction]. AFR. SOUTH 4, no. 4 (1960), pp. 113-118.

22,861 MAIMANE, S. A. Kaffer woman [fiction]. BO 12 (1962), pp. 37-42.

22,862 MALCOLM, D. McK. Zulu literature. AFRICA 19 (1949), pp. 33-39.

22,863 MATTHEWS, J. Azikwelwa! [fiction]. AFR. SOUTH 3, no. 1 (1958), pp. 118-123.

22,864 MATTHEWS, J. Le Parc. PRESENCE AFR. N.S. 44 (1962), pp. 175-182.

22,865 MILLER, G. M. A calendar of South African English velde publications to 1859. QBSAL 5 (1950), pp. 45-54.

22,866 MODISANE, B. The situation [fiction]. BO 12 (1962), pp. 10-16.

22,867 MPHAHLELE, E. The living and dead [fiction]. AFR. SOUTH 2, no. 2 (1958), pp. 105-115.

22,868 MPHAHLELE, E. Il padrone di Doornvlei. AFRICA (Rome) 13 (1958), pp. 129-131.

22,869 MPHAHLELE, E. The suitcase [fiction]. BO 4 (1958), pp. 24-29.

22,870 MPHAHLELE, E. What the South African Negro reads and writes. PRESENCE AFR. N.S. 16 (1957), pp. 171-176.

22,871 MVUSI, S. Nightwatchman from Zululand [a poem]. AFR. SOUTH 5, no. 3 (1961), pp. 123-126.

22,872 NORDFORS, M. Bella [fiction]. AFR. SOUTH 3, no. 4 (1959), pp. 116-120.

22,873 O'DOWD, T. The potato harvest. AFR. SOUTH 4, no. 1 (1959), pp. 50-52.

22,874 PATON, A. Debbie go home [fiction]. AFR. SOUTH 3, no. 3 (1959), pp. 118-127.

22,875 PATON, A. A drink in the passage [fiction]. AFR. SOUTH 4, no. 3 (1960), pp. 117-123.

22,876 PATON, A. My great discovery [a poem]. AFR. SOUTH 1, no. 3 (1957), pp. 94-97.

22,877 REYNOLDS, R. Lebensraum in Limbo [a poem]. AFR. SOUTH 3, no. 3 (1959), p. 6.

22,878 REYNOLDS, R. Partnership [a poem]. AFR. SOUTH 2, no. 4 (1958), p. 68.

22,879 RIVE, R. Résurrection. PRESENCE AFR. N.S. 48 (1963), pp. 171-179.

22,880 ROBINSON, A. M. L. The contents of the South African Journal, 1824. I. Verse. QBSAL 12 (1957), pp. 159-167.

22,881 ROBINSON, A. M. L. The contents of the South African Journal, 1824. II. Prose. QBSAL 13 (1958), pp. 45-52.

22,882 ROBINSON, A. M. L. A letter from Thomas Pringle to Sir George Mackenzie. QBSAL 7 (1952), pp. 48-51.

22,883 ROBINSON, A. M. L. The life and death of the South African Journal. QBSAL 12 (1957), pp. 101-113.

22,884 ROBINSON, A. M. L. Thomas Pringle and Sir Walter Scott. QBSAL 6 (1951), pp. 50-56, 109-118.

22,885 ROCHLIN, S. A. A. W. Cole's "Lorimer Littlegood." QBSAL 10 (1955), pp. 16-18.

22,886 ROCHLIN, S. A. Charles Dickens and the nineteenth century Cape. QBSAL 11 (1957), pp. 87-96.

22,887 ROCHLIN, S. A. George Gordon Fletcher. QBSAL 7 (1952), pp. 9-13.

22,888 SEATH, G. Country hotel [fiction]. AFR. SOUTH 2, no. 2 (1958), pp. 116-120.

22,889 STONE, E. V. Grim fairy tales. AFR. SOUTH 2, no. 2 (1958), pp. 40-43.

22,890 STONE, E. V. Legendary literature. AFR. SOUTH 5, no. 4 (1961), pp. 67-71.

22,891 STONE, E. V. More grim fairy tales. AFR. SOUTH 3, no. 1 (1958), pp. 47-49.

22,892 STONE, E. V. Other grim fairy tales. AFR. SOUTH 4, no. 1 (1959), pp. 64-68.

22,893 TANN, J. The headmaster's books [fiction]. AFR. SOUTH 1, no. 3 (1957), pp. 102-105.

22,894 TANN, J. Jurie Taaiman's revolution [fiction]. AFR. SOUTH 4, no. 1 (1959), pp. 122-125.

22,895 TEMBA, C. Requiem for Sophiatown. AFR. SOUTH 3, no. 3 (1959), pp. 49-54.

22,896 THEROUX, P. Fists [poem] for Nelson Mandela. TRANSITION 19 (1965), p. 25.

22,897 VARLEY, D. H. Further notes on George Gordon Fletcher. QBSAL 10 (1955), pp. 3-9.

22,898 VARLEY, D. H. An original letter from William Cooper to Rev. John Newton. QBSAL 7 (1953), pp. 80-83.

22,899 VILAKAZI, B. W. In the gold mines [a Zulu poem tr. by A. C. Jordan]. AFR. SOUTH 1, no. 2 (1957), pp. 115-119.

22,900 VILAKAZI, B. W. Some aspects of Zulu literature. AFR. STUD. 1 (1942), pp. 270-274.

22,901 VILAKAZI, B. W. The voice of Africa: a Zulu poem. AFRICA 16 (1946), pp. 110-112.

22,902 WALKER, O. The Baas comes home [fiction]. AFR. SOUTH 1, no. 2 (1957), pp. 107-114.

22,903 WANNENBURGH, A. Almost home [fiction]. BO 11 (1962), pp. 172-176.

22,904 WANNENBURGH, A. Echos. PRESENCE AFR. N.S. 52 (1964), pp. 172-176.

22,905 WILKINSON, D. Of many mansions [a poem]. AFR. SOUTH 2, no. 2 (1958), pp. 121-122.

22,906 A propos de la littérature sud-africaine. ZAIRE 5 (1951), pp. 632-633.

22,907 South African English poetry then and now. QBSAL 5 (1950), pp. 37-39.

Law. Trials

22,908 ALLISON, J. S. Urban native legislation. RACE RELATIONS 7 (1940), pp. 54-62.

22,909 BALLINGER, M. African land and property rights. AFR. SOUTH 1, no. 3 (1957), pp. 52-58.

22,910 BENJAMIN, A. Kings of Alexandra. AFR. SOUTH 3, no. 3 (1959), pp. 29-34.

22,911 BERRANGE, V. C. [Opening address for the defence at the Treason Trial.] AFR. SOUTH 1, no. 3 (1957), pp. 7-11.

22,912 BLOOM, H. The trial takes shape. AFR. SOUTH 2, no. 4 (1958), pp. 51-57.

22,913 BRITTEN, H. Twala. The need for the registration of customary unions. BANTU STUD. 4 (1930), pp. 269-277.

22,914 BROOKES, E. H. The South African native bills. J. AFR. SOC. 35 (1936), pp. 65-70.

22,915 BROWNLEE, W. T. The Transkeian territories of South Africa. Notes on native law and customs. J. AFR. SOC. 24 (1925), pp. 110-116, 213-218; 25 (1925), pp. 27-46.

22,916 COETZEE, J. H. Potchefstroom University. J. AFR. LAW 6 (1962), pp. 141-142.

22,917 FAIRBAIRN, J. Mass trials. AFR. SOUTH 3, no. 3 (1959), pp. 12-19.

22,918 FAZAN, S. H. Land tenure in the Transkei. AFR. STUD. 3 (1944), pp. 45-64.

22,919 GARDINER, G. The South African treason trial. J. INT. COMM. JURISTS 1 (1957-1958), pp. 43-58.

22,920 GARTHORNE, E. R. Applications of native law. BANTU STUD. 3 (1927), pp. 245-259.

22,921 GRAY, A. Treason trial. AFR. AFFAIRS 56 (1957), pp. 109-110, 187-188; 58 (1959), pp. 269-271.

22,922 HAYMAN, R. Kaffir beer and the law. RACE RELATIONS 8 (1941), pp. 55-57.

22,923 HAYMAN, R. Legal aid for South Africa. RACE RELATIONS 8 (1941), pp. 26-28.

22,924 HOAL, W. G. The problem of the trivial offender. RACE RELATIONS 12 (1945), pp. 65-69.

22,925 HOLLEMAN, F. D. The recognition of Bantu customary law in South Africa: a case study. THE FUTURE OF CUSTOMARY LAW IN AFRICA, 1956, pp. 232-256.

22,926 HORRELL, M. La législation Sud-Africaine en 1962. CIVILISATIONS 12 (1962), pp. 422-428.

22,927 HUNT, P. M. A. The Faculty of Law, University of the Witwatersrand, Johannesburg. J. AFR. LAW 7 (1963), pp. 120-125.

22,928 JANKOVIC, B. M. International legal aspect of the problem of South-West Africa. AFR. QUART. 4, no. iii (1964), pp. 179-191.

22,929 JOSEPH, H. The living dead. AFR. SOUTH 5, no. 4 (1961), pp. 17-27.

22,930 JUNOD, H. P. Penal reform in South Africa. AFR. AFFAIRS 50 (1951), pp. 34-41.

22,931 JUNOD, H. P. The question of capital punishment. RACE RELATIONS 12 (1945), pp. 94-103.

22,932 KRIGE, E. J. Property, cross-cousin marriage, and the family cycle among the Lobedu. THE FAMILY ESTATE IN AFRICA, 1964, pp. 155-195.

22,933 KRIGE, J. D. Some aspects of Lovhedu judicial arrangements. BANTU STUD. 13 (1939), pp. 113-129.

22,934 LANDIS, E. S. La législation de l'apartheid en Afrique du Sud. PRESENCE AFR. N.S. 46 (1963), pp. 108-125.

22,935 LEONARD, D. A. The trial begins [The "treason" trials]. AFR. SOUTH 3, no. 2 (1959), pp. 39-47.

22,936 LEWIN, J. Crime in relation to native policy. RACE RELATIONS 12 (1945), pp. 59-65.

22,937 LEWIN, J. Native law and its background. RACE RELATIONS 7 (1940), pp. 42-48.

22,938 LEWIN, J. Sex, colour and the law. AFR. SOUTH 4, no. 3 (1960), pp. 63-70.

22,939 LEWIN, J. Some cases of inheritance in native law. AFR. STUD. 4 (1945), pp. 70-87.

22,940 LEWIN, J. Some legal aspects of marriage by natives in South Africa. BANTU STUD. 15 (1941), pp. 13-23.

22,941 LEWIN, J. Some Lobolo cases in native law. AFR. STUD. 3 (1944), pp. 129-139.

22,942 LONGMORE, L. Reconstituting the senate in South Africa. AFR. AFFAIRS 59 (1960), pp. 328-332.

22,943 MACLEAN. Maclean on native law and custom. AFR. STUD. 12 (1953), pp. 181-188.

22,944 MARAIS, D. A question of norm. AFR. SOUTH 2, no. 2 (1958), pp. 9-12.

22,945 O'DOWD, T. The trial takes shape. AFR. SOUTH 2, no. 1 (1957), pp. 51-56; 2, no. 2 (1958), pp. 34-36.

22,946 PALLEY, C. Rectification of written contracts in English and Roman-Dutch law. RNLJ 2 (1962), pp. 16-27.

22,947 PATON, A. Association by permission. AFR. SOUTH 1, no. 4 (1957), pp. 11-20.

22,948 PATON, A. The prevention of crime. RACE RELATIONS 12 (1945), pp. 69-77.

22,949 PONT, D. The Faculty of Law of the University College of Fort Hare. J. AFR. LAW 6 (1962), pp. 134-140.

22,950 RAMSAY, T. D. Tsonga law in the Transvaal. AFR. STUD. 5 (1946), pp. 143-156.

22,951 RHEINALLT JONES, J. D. Findings of the penal reform conference. RACE RELATIONS 12 (1945), pp. 103-110.

22,952 RHEINALLT JONES, J. D. The position of the worker under the Labour Laws of the Union. RACE RELATIONS 6 (1939), pp. 137-150.

22,953 RUBIN, L. The adaptation of customary family law in South Africa. AFR. LAW: ADAPTATION AND DEVELOPMENT, 1965, pp. 196-215.

22,954 RUBIN, L. Nationalist contempt of court. AFR. SOUTH 4, no. 2 (1960), pp. 5-11.

22,955 RUBIN, L. Transkei Constitution Act. J. AFR. LAW 7 (1963), pp. 183-187.

22,956 SCHREINER, O. D. The prisoner in court. RACE RELATIONS 12 (1945), pp. 51-59.

22,957 SCOBLE, C. N. Restraint of trade on employees. RNLJ 3 (1963), pp. 191-200.

22,958 SHIPPARD, Sir S. The administration of justice in South Africa. ROYAL COL. INST. PR. 28 (1896-1897), pp. 82-112.

22,959 SIMONS, H. J. The study of native law in South Africa. BANTU STUD. 12 (1938), pp. 237-242.

22,960 SWEENEY, G. M. J. University of Natal, Department of Law, Durban. J. AFR. LAW 6 (1962), p. 141.

22,961 TROUP, F. Four years of treason. AFR. SOUTH 5, no. 2 (1961), pp. 56-62.

22,962 TROUP, F. The height of treason. AFR. SOUTH 5, no. 4 (1961), pp. 13-16.

22,963 TROUP, F. The treason trial—forever? AFR. SOUTH 4, no. 1 (1959), pp. 57-63.

22,964 WELSH, A. S. Native customary law in the Union of South Africa. J. AFR. ADM. 10 (1958), pp. 83-94.

22,965 WELSH, T. Contrasts in African legislation. J. AFR. SOC. 2 (1903), pp. 195-207.

22,966 WENTZEL, D. The legal plight of the African woman. RACE RELATIONS 11 (1944), pp. 66-69.

22,967 African customary law, 1858-1958. J. AFR. LAW 2 (1958), pp. 139-140.

22,968 Discours de Mandela à la Cour avant le jugement. PRESENCE AFR. N.S. 46 (1963), pp. 148-162.

22,969 L'Etat sud-africain contre Nelson Mandela. PRESENCE AFR. N.S. 46 (1963), pp. 126-147.

22,970 Land tenure by Asiatics and South African coloured people in the Transvaal. RACE RELATIONS 2, no. 5 (1934-1935), pp. 42-54.

22,971 The legal status of African women in South Africa. AFR. WOMEN 3 (1958-1960), pp. 37-38.

22,972 Natal code of native law. AFR. STUD. 2 (1943), pp. 1-26.

See also 22144.

Religion

22,973 BERTHOUD, A. L. The missionary situation in South Africa. INT. REV. MISSIONS 49 (1960), pp. 83-90.

22,974 BEYERHAUS, P. Walter Freytags Begriff des Gewissens in der Sicht südafrikanischer Missionsarbeit. BASILEIA: FESTSCHRIFT FUR WALTER FREYTAG, 1959, pp. 146-157.

22,975 BUSH, T. N. W. Anglicans and apartheid. AFR. SOUTH 5, no. 4 (1961), pp. 28-36.

22,976 C., J. L'Afrique du Sud et les Missions. ZAIRE 6 (1952), p. 868.

22,977 CARSTENS, W. P. The Dutch Reformed Church militant. AFR. SOUTH 3, no. 2 (1959), pp. 48-53.

22,978 CHOATE, C. D. A tribute to Mackenzie Cobban. J. METHODIST HIST. SOC. OF S. AFR. 1, no. 2 (1953), pp. 12-14.

22,979 DU PLESSIS, J. The missionary situation in South Africa. INT. REV. MISSIONS 1 (1912), pp. 573-586.

22,980 GELL, C. W. M. Colour and the South African Church. AFR. SOUTH 1, no. 2 (1957), pp. 64-76.

22,981 GERDENER, G. B. A. The Dutch Reformed Church and the racial situation in South Africa. RACE RELATIONS 17 (1950), pp. 1-9.

22,982 GONIN, H. T. Missions of the Dutch Reformed Church in South Africa. INT. REV. MISSIONS 42 (1953), pp. 172-177.

22,983 GRAY, A. Apartheid and christianity. AFR. AFFAIRS 57 (1958), pp. 261-263.

22,984 HAMMOND-TOOKE, W. D. Some Bhaca religious categories. AFR. STUD. 19 (1960), pp. 1-13.

22,985 HELLY, D. O. The American Board for Foreign Missions in South Africa. QBSAL 11 (1957), pp. 129-143.

22,986 HEWSON, L. A. Barnabas Shaw, founder of Methodism in South Africa. J. METHODIST HIST. SOC. OF S. AFR. 2, no. 5 (1956), pp. 119-128; 2, no. 6 (1956), pp. 133-139.

22,987 HEWSON, L. A. John Kendrick and Methodism at the Cape. J. METHODIST HIST. SOC. OF S. AFR. 2, no. 1 (1953), pp. 2-15.

22,988 HEWSON, L. A. Methodist origins at the Cape. J. METHODIST HIST. SOC. OF S. AFR. 1, no. 2 (1953), pp. 2-4.

22,989 HEWSON, L. A. Rev. George Morley. J. METHODIST HIST. SOC. OF S. AFR. 2, no. 4 (1955), pp. 66-67.

22,990 HEWSON, L. A. William B. Boyce and the Euphonic Concord. J. METHODIST HIST. SOC. OF S. AFR. 2, no. 3 (1955), pp. 37-43; 2, no. 7 (1957), pp. 155-161.

22,991 HLATSWAYO, E. T. Laywomen in Church and society (South Africa). THE CHURCH IN CHANGING AFRICA, 1958, pp. 86-87.

22,992 HOLT, B. The autobiography of Dr. van der Kemp. QBSAL 5 (1951), pp. 116-118.

22,993 HURLEY, D. E. Roman Catholic bishops on the blasphemy of apartheid. AFR. SOUTH 2, no. 2 (1958), pp. 13-16.

22,994 JONES, J. D. R. Missionary work among the Bantu in South Africa. INT. REV. MISSIONS 17 (1928), pp. 175-185.

22,995 MacVICAR, N. The Christian Council of South Africa and the National Health Services Commission. INT. REV. MISSIONS 33 (1944), pp. 407-414.

22,996 MABILLE, G. A. The distribution of Christian literature among the Bantu of Southern Africa. CHRISTIAN LIT. FOR THE BANTU OF S. AFR., 1957, pp. 71-85.

22,997 MAILE, M. L. The secular press and the Bantu, with special reference to the kind and effects of, and the necessity for, non-Christian and Christian literature. CHRISTIAN LIT. FOR THE BANTU OF S. AFR., 1957, pp. 121-126.

22,998 MARKS, S. Christian African participation in the 1906 Zulu rebellion. BULL. SOC. AFR. CHURCH HIST. 2 (1965), pp. 55-72.

22,999 MARTINDALE, C. C. Are missions a menace? AFR. AFFAIRS 48 (1949), pp. 119-129.

23,000 MQOTSI, L. and MKELE, N. A separatist church: Ibandla lika-Krestu. AFR. STUD. 5 (1946), pp. 106-125.

23,001 NORTON, G. R. The emergence of new religious organisations in South Africa. A discussion of causes. J. AFR. SOC. 39 (1940), pp. 348-353; 40 (1941), pp. 48-67.

23,002 OGLETHORPE, J. The crisis in the Dutch Reformed Churches. AFR. SOUTH 5, no. 3 (1961), pp. 44-48.

23,003 OOSTHUIZEN, C. J. The production of Christian literature for the Bantu. CHRISTIAN LIT. FOR THE BANTU OF S. AFR., 1957, pp. 60-70.

23,004 OOSTHUIZEN, G. C. Theological education in South Africa. The findings of a theological institute. INT. REV. MISSIONS 52 (1963), pp. 279-289.

23,005 ORCHARD, F. H. Diary of William Todd, Byrne Settler to Verulam, 1849 to 1851. J. METHODIST HIST. SOC. OF S. AFR. 1, no. 2 (1953), pp. 7-8.

23,006 REEVES, R. A. Church and state in South Africa. AFR. SOUTH 1, no. 1 (1956), pp. 5-13.

23,007 RICHINGS, F. G. St. Paul's Church Rondebosch, a century ago. QBSAL 19 (1965), pp. 79-84.

23,008 SHEPHERD, R. H. W. Christian liberty at stake. AFR. SOUTH 1, no. 4 (1957), pp. 5-10.

23,009 SHEPHERD, R. H. W. Christian literature for the Bantu of Southern Africa: the present situation. CHRISTIAN LIT. FOR THE BANTU OF S. AFR., 1957, pp. 27-32.

23,010 SHEPHERD, R. H. W. The separatist Churches of South Africa. INT. REV. MISSIONS 26 (1937), pp. 453-463.

23,011 SHEPHERD, R. H. W. and GRANT, E. W. The Christian Council of South Africa. INT. REV. MISSIONS 23 (1944), pp. 258-266.

23,012 SUNDKLER, B. Response and resistance to the Gospel in a Zulu congregation. BASILEIA: FESTSCHRIFT FUR WALTER FREYTAG, 1959, pp. 128-145.

23,013 WHITE, J. F. Study and conference in South Africa. INT. REV. MISSIONS 49 (1960), pp. 301-309.

23,014 WHYTE, M. The bearing of literacy upon the distribution of Christian literature. CHRISTIAN LIT. FOR THE BANTU OF S. AFR., 1957, pp. 86-102.

23,015 WOOD, C. T. The building of old St. George's Church, Cape Town, 1827-1834. QBSAL 16 (1961), pp. 87-93.

23,016 WOOD, C. T. Notes on the building of the new cathedral. QBSAL 16 (1961), p. 93.

23,017 WOOLF, J. Early days [of Methodism] at Potchefstroom. J. METHODIST HIST. SOC. OF S. AFR. 1, no. 2 (1953), pp. 4-6.

23,018 ZULU, A. H. The South African Church in the light of 'Ibadan, 1958.' INT. REV. MISSIONS 47 (1958), pp. 377-385.

23,019 ZWEMMER, S. M. A survey of Islam in South Africa. INT. REV. MISSIONS 14 (1925), pp. 560-571.

23,020 Correspondence between Barnabas Shaw and the Governor at the Cape. J. METHODIST HIST. SOC. OF S. AFR. 2, no. 6 (1956), pp. 140-151.

23,021 John Ayliff of Albany. J. METHODIST HIST. SOC. OF S. AFR. 2, no. 7 (1957), pp. 182-205.

23,022 John M'Kenny, forerunner of Barnabas Shaw. J. METHODIST HIST. SOC. OF S. AFR. 2, no. 5 (1956), pp. 108-118.

23,023 The journal of John Kendrick. J. METHODIST HIST. SOC. OF S. AFR. 2, no. 4 (1955), pp. 76-93.

23,024 The Kendrik papers. J. METHODIST HIST. SOC. OF S. AFR. 2, no. 4 (1955), pp. 68-75.

23,025 The letters of John Kendrick. J. METHODIST HIST. SOC. OF S. AFR. 2, no. 4 (1955), pp. 94-104.

23,026 The Watkins papers. J. METHODIST HIST. SOC. OF S. AFR. 2, no. 7 (1957), pp. 162-179.

See also 21777.

Science

23,027 BRIDGES, A. F. B. The Kruger National Park. NIGERIAN FIELD 6 (1937), pp. 53-57.

23,028 BRODERICK, M. Fighting tuberculosis in South Africa. AFR. AFFAIRS 54 (1955), pp. 226-229.

23,029 BURROWS, E. H. The early history of the Cape hospitals. QBSAL 11 (1957), pp. 98-101.

23,030 CORINTA FERREIRA, M. Contribuição para o conhecimento dos Escarabídeos do Kalahari. BSEM 103 (1957), pp. 185-189.

23,031 CORINTA FERREIRA, M. Monografia dos Escarabaeídeos da Africa do Sul; tribo Oniticellini. BSEM 91 (1955), pp. 80-123.

23,032 CORINTA FERREIRA, M. Sobre uma oferta valiosa de coleópteros tenebrionídeos feita pelo Transvaal Museum ao Museu Dr. Alvaro de Castro. BSEM 72 (1951), pp. 27-50.

23,033 CORINTA FERREIRA, M. and FERREIRA, G. DA V. Catálogo dos Bostrichídeos existentes no Durban Museum and Art Gallery. BSEM 97 (1956), pp. 149-159.

23,034 CORINTA FERREIRA, M. and FERREIRA, G. DA V. Catálogo dos cerambicíneos existentes no South African Museum: supertribos parandrina e prionina. BSEM 93 (1955), pp. 177-197.

23,035 CORINTA FERREIRA, M. and FERREIRA, G. DA V. Catálogo dos Cerambicíneos existentes no Transvaal Museum. BSEM 98 (1956), pp. 49-70.

23,036 CORINTA FERREIRA, M. and FERREIRA, G. DA V. Da necessidade do intercâmbio científico com a União da Africa do Sul. BSEM 80 (1953), pp. 47-50.

23,037 FERREIRA, F. H. Setlhapiñ nomenclature and uses of the indigenous trees of Griqualand West. BANTU STUD. 3 (1927), pp. 349-356.

23,038 FOX, F. W. Note on the relative food value of whole milk, cheese and butter. RACE RELATIONS 6 (1939), pp. 116-117.

23,039 HAYLETT, D. G. Food resources of the Union in relation to the nutritional requirements of the population. RACE RELATIONS 6 (1939), pp. 17-24.

23,040 HELLMAN, E. Urban native food in Johannesburg. AFRICA 9 (1936), pp. 277-290.

23,041 HOERNLE, A. W. The dietetics of natives employed on the Witwatersrand gold mines: supplementary note. AFRICA 9 (1936), pp. 224-226.

23,042 HOLTZ, P. South Africa's Garden of Eden [Kruger National Park]. CONTEMP. REV. 186 (1954), pp. 301-304.

23,043 JURITZ, C. F. Science and progress in South Africa. J. AFR. SOC. 18 (1919), pp. 88-100.

23,044 KRIGE, J. D. The magical thought-pattern of the Bantu in relation to health services. AFR. STUD. 3 (1944), pp. 1-13.

23,045 LATSKY, J. M. Fish meal in South African bread. MALNUTRITION IN AFR. WOMEN..., 1952, p. 277.

23,046 McCALLIEN, W. J. The geology of South Africa: its bearing on some Gold Coast problems. UNIVERSITAS 1, no. 5 (1955), pp. 6-9.

23,047 MONOD, Th. La conférence scientifique africaine régionale de Johannesburg (17-28 octobre 1949). BULL. IFAN 12 (1950), pp. 247-249.

23,048 NKOMO, W. F. Health and Africans. RACE RELATIONS 16 (1949), pp. 64-70.

23,049 ORENSTEIN, A. J. The dietetics of natives employed on the Witwatersrand gold mines. AFRICA 9 (1936), pp. 218-224.

23,050 PINTO, A. A. DA R. Alguns novos "Records" de aves para o Sul do Save e Moçambique, incluindo o de um género novo para a sub-região da Africa do Sul, com a descrição de novas subespécies. BSEM 118 (1959), pp. 15-28.

23,051 SOUSA DIAS, A. H. G. DE et al. O problema do aproveitamento racional dos nossos recursos faunísticos naturais como forma de se obviar a uma pecuária convencional deficitária. Reflexões sobre uma visita de estudo à Africa do Sul e à Rodésia do Sul. BSEM 135 (1963), pp. 129-153.

23,052 STEVENSON-HAMILTON, J. The Transvaal game reserve. An animal sanctuary for the Union. J. AFR. SOC. 25 (1926), pp. 211-228.

23,053 UNSWORTH, W. South African flora. CONTEMP. REV. 184 (1953), pp. 299-302.

23,054 WIX, E. Industrial feeding. RACE RELATIONS J. 20, no. 2 (1953), pp. 1-22.

23,055 Preliminary estimate of the main national nutritional requirements of the total population of the Union of South Africa and of the available food for human consumption. RACE RELATIONS 6 (1939), pp. 125-127.

23,056 Sir John Herschel at the Cape (Series of articles by several authors). QBSAL 12 (1957), pp. 39-82.

Sociology

23,057 ADAMS, N. J. Co-operative societies among Africans: 1. RACE RELATIONS 7 (1940), pp. 8-10.

23,058 ANNING, C. C. P. Health policy in relation to nutrition needs. RACE RELATIONS 6 (1939), pp. 33-37.

23,059 ARCHBISHOP OF CAPE TOWN. The position of the African in South Africa. INT. REV. MISSIONS 37 (1948), pp. 273-284.

23,060 ATLEE, M. The coloured people of South Africa. AFR. AFFAIRS 46 (1947), pp. 148-151.

23,061 BADEN-POWELL, Lord. A new development in the scout movement in South Africa. J. AFR. SOC. 35 (1936), pp. 368-371.

23,062 BALLINGER, M. Native life in South African towns. J. AFR. SOC. 37 (1938), pp. 326-338.

23,063 BARRETT, H. J. Social and domestic life of the Dutch Boers of South Africa. ROYAL COL. INST. PR. 1 (1869), pp. 175-207.

23,064 BATSON, E. Contribution to the study of urban coloured poverty. RACE RELATIONS 9 (1942), pp. 1-11.

23,065 BATSON, E. The social services and the poverty of the unskilled worker. RACE RELATIONS 6 (1939), pp. 139, 156-160.

23,066 BATSON, E. The social services: discrimination and counteraction. RACE RELATIONS 7 (1940), pp. 18-23.

23,067 BEEMER, H. Living conditions among poor Indians in Johannesburg. RACE RELATIONS 1 (1933-1934), pp. 5-8.

23,068 BEGG, G. Port Elizabeth's five-year plan of sub-economic housing. RACE RELATIONS 9 (1942), pp. 36-42.

23,069 BENJAMIN, A. Jacobus and the barricades. AFR. SOUTH 4, no. 2 (1960), pp. 59-66.

23,070 BENJAMIN, A. Portrait of a suburb: Hillbrow. AFR. SOUTH 2, no. 1 (1957), pp. 57-62.

23,071 BENNUN, R. The African as industrial worker. RACE RELATIONS 12 (1945), pp. 28-32.

23,072 BETTISON, D. G. Child maintenance in a small South African town. AFR. STUD. 15 (1956), pp. 132-138.

23,073 BETTISON, D. G. Self-development in native housing in East London, Cape Province. AFRICA 23 (1953), pp. 324-330.

23,074 BLANK, J. DE. The fight is on. AFR. SOUTH 2, no. 3 (1958), pp. 6-8.

23,075 BLAXALL, A. W. Physically handicapped Africans. RACE RELATIONS 5 (1938), pp. 38-44.

23,076 BLUMBERG, M. Durban explodes. AFR. SOUTH 4, no. 1 (1959), pp. 9-17.

23,077 BOWKER, S. The native problem in South Africa: a scheme for segregation areas. CONTEMP. REV. 117 (1920), pp. 546-553.

23,078 BRANDEL, M. The African career woman in South Africa. AFR. WOMEN 2 (1956-1958), pp. 36-38.

23,079 BRANDEL, M. Urban lobolo attitudes: a preliminary report. AFR. STUD. 17 (1958), pp. 34-51.

23,080 BRANDEL, M. Urban lobolo attitudes: rejoinder. AFR. STUD. 18 (1959), pp. 83-84.

23,081 BREMER, K. Nutrition of Europeans in rural areas. RACE RELATIONS 6 (1939), pp. 3-5.

23,082 BRETT, A. C. African attitudes to South African society: the reactions of some middle-class Africans to their position in South Africa. RACE 6, no. 1 (1964-1965), pp. 52-62.

23,083 BRIDGMAN, F. B. Social conditions in Johannesburg. INT. REV. MISSIONS 15 (1926), pp. 569-583.

23,084 BROOKES, E. H. Race relations in 1947. RACE RELATIONS 15 (1948), pp. 2-11.

23,085 BROOKES, E. H. Race relations of the future in the light of the past. RACE RELATIONS 5 (1938), pp. 86-88.

23,086 BROOKES, E. H. Some municipal problems and how the Institute can help. RACE RELATIONS 1 (1933-1934), pp. 14-16.

23,087 BROOKES, E. H. The South African race problem in the light of General Hertzog's proposed legislation. INT. REV. MISSIONS 16 (1927), pp. 182-191.

23,088 BROOKFIELD, H. C. and TATHAM, M. A. The distribution of racial groups in Durban. GEOG. REV. 47 (1957), pp. 44-65.

23,089 BROWN, W. O. Race consciousness among South African natives. AMER. J. SOCIOL. 40 (1934-1935), pp. 569-581.

23,090 BRUTUS, D. A. Sports test for South Africa. AFR. SOUTH 3, no. 4 (1959), pp. 35-39.

23,091 BRYCE, J. How the Boers treat the Negroes. LIBERIA BULL. 16 (1900), pp. 57-59.

23,092 BUCHANAN, D. M. Programme for coloured progress. RACE RELATIONS 9 (1942), pp. 51-55.

23,093 BUCHANAN, K. and HURWITZ, N. The Asiatic immigrant community in the Union of South Africa. GEOG. REV. 39 (1949), pp. 440-449.

23,094 BUCHANAN, K. and HURWITZ, N. The coloured community in the Union of South Africa. GEOG. REV. 40 (1950), pp. 397-414.

23,095 BUITENDAG, F. W. C. The emergence of the urban African. RACE RELATIONS J. 18 (1951), pp. 205-211.

23,096 BURROWS, H. R. Indian life and labour in Natal. RACE RELATIONS 10 (1943), pp. 1-36.

23,097 BURROWS, R. Durban's growing pains: a racial problem. RACE RELATIONS 7 (1940), pp. 28-31.

23,098 BUXTON, Sir T. F. South Africa and its native problem. J. AFR. SOC. 20 (1921), pp. 161-173.

23,099 C., J. L'habitat indigène à Johannesburg. ZAIRE 8 (1954), pp. 952-953.

23,100 CARLIN, M. M. England, South Africa and that Encounter article. TRANSITION 14 (1964), pp. 23-27.

23,101 CELLIERS, A. C. et al. "South African Native Policy and the liberal spirit." Reviews of Professor R. F. A. Hoernlé's Phelps-Stokes Lectures. RACE RELATIONS 7 (1940), pp. 31-39.

23,102 CENTRAL HOUSING BOARD: SPECIAL COMMITTEE. Housing in urban native areas. RACE RELATIONS 7 (1940), pp. 63-70.

23,103 COOPER, L. The multi-racial conference. AFR. SOUTH 2, no. 3 (1958), pp. 39-41.

23,104 COTTON, W. A. The race problem in South Africa. INT. REV. MISSIONS 17 (1928), pp. 327-341.

23,105 CRIPPS, A. S. An Africa of the Africans. INT. REV. MISSIONS 10 (1921), pp. 99-109.

23,106 CUTTEN, A. J. The planning of a native township. RACE RELATIONS J. 18 (1951), pp. 74-95.

23,107 CUTTEN, T. E. G. The Bantu press and race relations. RACE RELATIONS 2, no. i (1934-1935), pp. 129-131.

23,108 DARRAGH, J. T. The native problem in South Africa. CONTEMP. REV. 81 (1902), pp. 87-102.

23,109 DATTA, A. K. Urbanization and apartheid in the Republic of South Africa. AFR. QUART. 3, no. ii (1963), pp. 82-91.

23,110 DAWSON, W. H. South African race problems. CONTEMP. REV. 125 (1924), pp. 726-734.

23,111 DEAN, E. A. The inter-relationship of races in the trade union movement. RACE RELATIONS 15 (1948), pp. 43-46.

23,112 DELUC, J. Quelques aspects des problèmes raciaux dans l'Union Sud-Africaine. AFR. ET ASIE 31 (1955), pp. 41-48.

23,113 DESMORE, A. The Cape coloured people to-day. An address delivered to the League of Coloured Peoples, London. J. AFR. SOC. 36 (1937), pp. 347-356.

23,114 DESSARRE, E. Douloureux Eldorado. PRESENCE AFR. N.S. 26 (1959), pp. 94-101.

23,115 DREYER, T. F. n Bioloog gee'n Kykie op Suid-Afrikaanse Sake. RACE RELATIONS 5 (1938), pp. 8-12.

23,116 DUNCAN, P. Race questions in South Africa. FOR. AFFAIRS 5 (1926-1927), pp. 293-306.

23,117 DU PLESSIS, J. The South African problem. INT. REV. MISSIONS 15 (1926), pp. 363-375.

23,118 EISELEN, W. W. M. The meaning of apartheid. RACE RELATIONS 15 (1948), pp. 69-86.

23,119 EVANS, M. S. Black and white in South Africa. INT. REV. MISSIONS 4 (1915), pp. 177-199.

23,120 FOX, F. W. Nutritional problems amongst the rural Bantu. RACE RELATIONS 6 (1939), pp. 5-7.

23,121 GELL, C. W. M. Hard choices in South Africa. FOR. AFFAIRS 31 (1952-1953), pp. 287-300.

23,122 GELL, C. W. M. Port Elizabeth diary. AFR. SOUTH 1, no. 4 (1957), pp. 65-72.

23,123 GERDENER, G. B. A. The crux of the racial situation in South Africa. INT. REV. MISSIONS 38 (1949), pp. 280-294.

23,124 GLUCKMAN, M. Analysis of a social situation in modern Zululand. BANTU STUD. 14 (1940), pp. 1-30, 147-174.

23,125 GOLDING, G. Race and opportunity in South Africa today. AFR. AFFAIRS 61 (1962), pp. 308-315.

23,126 GOODLATTE, C. R. South Africa: glimpses and comments. CONTEMP. REV. 133 (1928), pp. 347-353.

23,127 GORDIN, E. Shopping problems in the Pretoria location. RACE RELATIONS 12 (1945), pp. 32-37.

23,128 GRAAFF, Sir DE W. South African prospect: thoughts on an alternative race policy. FOR. AFFAIRS 39 (1960-1961), pp. 670-682.

23,129 GRAY, A. South Africa's Indians. AFR. AFFAIRS 56 (1957), pp. 100-103.

23,130 GRAY, J. L. Food and politics. RACE RELATIONS 6 (1939), pp. 24-28.

23,131 GRAY, J. L. High rents as a contributary cause of malnutrition among urban Europeans. RACE RELATIONS 6 (1939), pp. 118-119.

23,132 GRIMSTON, B. Native affairs in Southern Rhodesia during 1936. RACE RELATIONS 4 (1937), pp. 17-26.

23,133 GUENAULT, P. H. and RANDALL, R. J. Urban native housing in South Africa. RACE RELATIONS 7 (1940), pp. 74-82.

23,134 HALL, E. The Shiela. TRANSITION 16 (1964), pp. 38-40.

23,135 HATTERSLEY, A. F. Rathfelder's Inn, Diep Rivier. QBSAL 16 (1962), pp. 143-147.

23,136 HAWARDEN, E. Municipal policy and native welfare. RACE RELATIONS 8 (1941), pp. 46-50.

23,137 HAWARDEN, E. The social and economic cost of migrant labour. RACE RELATIONS 12 (1945), pp. 23-28.

23,138 HELLMAN, E. The application of the concept of separate development to urban areas in the Union of South Africa. ST. ANTONY'S PAPERS 10 (1961), pp. 120-146.

23,139 HELLMAN, E. Culture contacts and social change. RACE RELATIONS 15 (1948), pp. 30-42.

23,140 HELLMAN, E. The diet of Africans in Johannesburg. RACE RELATIONS 6 (1939), pp. 8-9.

23,141 HELLMAN, E. The importance of beer-brewing in an urban native yard. BANTU STUD. 8 (1934), pp. 39-60.

23,142 HELLMAN, E. Non-Europeans in the army. RACE RELATIONS 10 (1943), pp. 45-53.

23,143 HELLMAN, E. Social services for urban Africans. RACE RELATIONS 8 (1941), pp. 50-54.

23,144 HIGGINS, T. S. Social and economic influences in non-European public health. RACE RELATIONS 6 (1939), pp. 12-13.

23,145 HIGGINS, T. S. Social conditions among the coloured community of Capetown. RACE RELATIONS 1 (1933-1934), pp. 8-10.

23,146 HILLS, W. Record of a joint council. RACE RELATIONS 11 (1944), pp. 39-42.

23,147 HOERNLE, A. W. Alternatives to apartheid. RACE RELATIONS 15 (1948), pp. 87-99.

23,148 HOERNLE, R. F. A. Anatomy of segregation. RACE RELATIONS 3, no. i (1936), pp. 14-21.

23,149 HOERNLE, R. F. A. The Bantu in the city. RACE RELATIONS 5 (1938), pp. 64-66.

23,150 HOERNLE, R. F. A. On the future of the native peoples in South Africa. RACE RELATIONS 4 (1937), pp. 55-60.

23,151 HOERNLE, R. F. A. Present-day trends in S. A. race relations. RACE RELATIONS 8 (1941), pp. 13-21.

23,152 HOERNLE, R. F. A. Race attitudes in South Africa. RACE RELATIONS 4 (1937), pp. 92-94.

23,153 HOFMEYR, J. H. The approach to the native problem. RACE RELATIONS 3, no. ii (1936), pp. 27-37; J. AFR. SOC. 36 (1937), pp. 270-297.

23,154 HOLLAND, E. M. An experiment in slum clearance. RACE RELATIONS 7 (1940), pp. 70-73.

23,155 HOLLEMAN, J. F. Die twee-eenheidsbeginsel in die sosiale en politieke samelewing van die Zulu. BANTU STUD. 14 (1940), pp. 31-75.

23,156 HOLLOWAY, J. E. Booker Washington's philosophy of race relations and its application to South Africa. RACE RELATIONS 1 (1933-1934), pp. 44-48.

23,157 HORE-RUTHVEN, C. M. The South African Institute of Race Relations. J. AFR. SOC. 36 (1937), pp. 311-316.

23,158 HORRELL, M. Evolution de la conception du "Bantoustan" en Afrique du Sud. CIVILISATIONS 13 (1963), pp. 203-211.

23,159 HORRELL, M. La politique raciale en Afrique du Sud. La résistance et les réactions de la population. CIVILISATIONS 13 (1963), pp. 362-377.

23,160 HORRELL, M. The population of the Union of South Africa. RACE RELATIONS J. 20, no. 3 (1953), pp. 1-16.

23,161 HORRELL, M. Les sports inter-raciaux en Afrique du Sud. CIVILISATIONS 12 (1962), pp. 133-140.

23,162 HUNTER, M. Methods of study of culture contact. AFRICA 7 (1934), pp. 335-350.

23,163 HUTT, W. H. Distributive justice and colour antagonism. RACE RELATIONS 9 (1942), pp. 93-99.

23,164 HUTT, W. H. Wage-fixation and the coloured people. RACE RELATIONS 9 (1942), pp. 12-18.

23,165 JABAVU, D. D. T. How non-Europeans can contribute towards a better South Africa. RACE RELATIONS 1 (1933-1934), pp. 50-53.

23,166 JABAVU, D. D. T. The South African problem. INT. REV. MISSIONS 15 (1926), pp. 376-389.

23,167 JAMESON, F. W. The housing of natives by public bodies. RACE RELATIONS 4 (1937), pp. 27-34.

23,168 JANISCH, M. Health and social welfare services for natives in urban areas. RACE RELATIONS 7 (1940), pp. 83-87.

23,169 JANISCH, M. Some administrative aspects of native marriage problems in an urban area. BANTU STUD. 15 (1941), pp. 1-11.

23,170 JONES, J. D. R. Native housing in urban areas with special consideration of its social aspects. RACE RELATIONS J. 18 (1951), pp. 96-124.

23,171 JONES, J. D. R. and SAFFERY, A. L. Social and economic conditions of native life in the Union of South Africa. BANTU STUD. 7 (1933), pp. 235-255, 317-340; 8 (1934), pp. 61-94, 193-211.

23,172 JURITZ, C. F. Science and progress in South Africa. J. AFR. SOC. 15 (1915), pp. 17-23, 184-186, 256-258.

23,173 KAHLER, H. Die Kap-Malaien in der Südafrikanischen Union. AFR. UND UB. 43 (1959-1960), pp. 1-36.

23,174 KAHN, E. Immigration and the future of the non-European. RACE RELATIONS 10 (1943), pp. 53-60.

23,175 KEPPEL-JONES, A. M. The trek tradition and modern problems. RACE RELATIONS 5 (1938), pp. 79-81.

23,176 KIRKWOOD, K. Race riots in Durban: Failure of a report. RACE RELATIONS 16 (1949), pp. 97-106.

23,177 KRAUSE, F. E. T. Inside our prisons. RACE RELATIONS 11 (1944), pp. 34-39.

23,178 KRIGE, E. J. Social and economic facts revealed in native family budgets. RACE RELATIONS 1 (1933-1934), pp. 94-108.

23,179 KUPER, H. An ethnographic description of a Tamil-Hindu marriage in Durban. AFR. STUD. 15 (1956), pp. 1-14, 207-216.

23,180 KUPER, H. An ethnographic description of Kavady, a Hindu ceremony in South Africa. AFR. STUD. 18 (1959), pp. 118-132.

23,181 KUPER, H. An interpretation of Hindu marriages in Durban. AFR. STUD. 16 (1957), pp. 221-235.

23,182 KUPER, H. and KAPLAN, S. Voluntary associations in an urban township. AFR. STUD. 3 (1944), pp. 178-186.

23,183 KUPER, L. The heightening of racial tension. RACE 2, no. 1 (1960-1961), pp. 24-32.

23,184 KUPER, L. Racialism and integration in South African society. RACE 4, no. 2 (1962-1963), pp. 26-31.

23,185 LEE-WARDEN, L. B. The crime of Langa. AFR. SOUTH 1, no. 3 (1957), pp. 46-51.

23,186 LEWIN, J. Tribalism coming to town. AFR. SOUTH 3, no. 3 (1959), pp. 42-48.

23,187 LEYBURN, J. G. Urban natives in South Africa. AMER. SOCIOL. REV. 9 (1944), pp. 495-502.

23,188 LORAM, C. T. Native progress and improvement in race relations in South Africa. J. AFR. SOC. 32 (1933), pp. 74-86.

23,189 LUNN, W. S. Rehousing the non-European. RACE RELATIONS 9 (1942), pp. 33-36.

23,190 MacCRONE, I. D. The great trek and its centenary celebration in the light of group psychology. RACE RELATIONS 5 (1938), pp. 81-84.

23,191 MacCULLAH, A. A. The South African natives. CONTEMP. REV. 83 (1903), pp. 201-211.

23,192 McGREGOR, F. Wage regulation in South Africa. RACE RELATIONS 7 (1940), pp. 2-7.

23,193 MacGRINDLE, A. M. Black and white in South Africa. CONTEMP. REV. 188 (1955), pp. 36-40.

23,194 MacGRINDLE, A. M. The Indians of Natal. CONTEMP. REV. 193 (1958), pp. 45-48.

23,195 MacKENZIE, K. The Beecher story. AFR. SOUTH 4, no. 3 (1960), pp. 47-49.

23,196 MacMILLAN, W. M. South African growing pains: a second assessment. AFR. AFFAIRS 59 (1960), pp. 12-19.

23,197 MacVICAR, N. The health of Africans in rural areas. RACE RELATIONS 9 (1942), pp. 116-121.

23,198 MAFEJE, A. A chief visits town. J. LOCAL ADM. OV. 2 (1963), pp. 88-99.

23,199 MAITLAND, W. A Chinaman in California and in South Africa. CONTEMP. REV. 88 (1905), pp. 818-828.

23,200 MALHERBE, E. G. An educationist looks at race relations. RACE RELATIONS 15 (1948), pp. 47-67.

23,201 MARAIS, W. D. Reformatories and other alternatives. RACE RELATIONS 12 (1945), pp. 84-94.

23,202 MARQUARD, L. Enquiry and consultation. RACE RELATIONS 2, no. iii (1934-1935), pp. 156-160.

23,203 MARQUARD, L. The Native Farm Labour Committee Report. RACE RELATIONS 7 (1940), pp. 23-28.

23,204 MARVIN, F. S. The native question in South Africa. CONTEMP. REV. 141 (1932), pp. 476-486.

23,205 MATTHEWS, Z. K. The African response to racial laws. FOR. AFFAIRS 30 (1951-1952), pp. 91-102.

23,206 MATTHEWS, Z. K. Future race relations in South Africa. RACE RELATIONS 5 (1938), pp. 84-86.

23,207 MAUD, D. The daughters of the golden city. J. AFR. SOC. 32 (1933), pp. 379-385.

23,208 MAYER, P. The cultural prospects for the Bantu in South Africa. AFR. AFFAIRS 54 (1955), pp. 214-225.

23,209 MEER, F. African and Indian in Durban. AFR. SOUTH 4, no. 4 (1960), pp. 30-41.

23,210 MILLER, W. Sportsman boss. AFR. SOUTH 2, no. 3 (1958), pp. 48-52.

23,211 MOFFAT, J. S. The South African natives. CONTEMP. REV. 79 (1901), pp. 318-325.

23,212 MONTEVECCHI, A. L'emigrazione italiana in Sud-africa. AFRICA (Rome) 11 (1956), p. 218.

23,213 MOORE, G. If you aint white you' considered black [review article on Blame me on history by Bloke Modisane]. TRANSITION 12 (1964), pp. 49-51.

23,214 MULLER, S. Juvenile delinquency and the colour bar. AFR. SOUTH 3, no. 3 (1959), pp. 35-41.

23,215 NATIVE AFFAIRS DEPARTMENT. Minimum conditions for farm labour. RACE RELATIONS 12 (1945), pp. 14-16.

23,216 NTANTALA, P. African tragedy [native life in South African cities]. AFR. SOUTH 1, no. 3 (1957), pp. 59-67.

23,217 NTANTALA, P. The widows of the reserves. AFR. SOUTH 2, no. 3 (1958), pp. 9-13.

23,218 OLIVIER. The five fears of South Africa. CONTEMP. REV. 131 (1927), pp. 144-151.

23,219 OLIVIER. Native poverty in South Africa. CONTEMP. REV. 143 (1933), pp. 281-288.

23,220 OPPENHEIMER, H. The future of the non-European in industry. RACE RELATIONS 15 (1948), pp. 100-108.

23,221 ORENSTEIN, A. J. Diet of natives on the Witwatersrand gold mines. RACE RELATIONS 6 (1939), pp. 16-17.

23,222 PHILLIPS, R. E. The African and the cinema. RACE RELATIONS 5 (1938), pp. 61-64.

23,223 PICARDIE, M. I had a black man. AFR. SOUTH 6 (1961), pp. 111-123.

23,224 PONSONBY, E. Feeding thirteen thousand children a day on the Rand. AFR. AFFAIRS 56 (1957), pp. 123-127.

23,225 PYE, F. Aspects of the psychology of South African women. RACE 7, no. 1 (1965), pp. 123-130.

23,226 RAMBIRITCH, B. and VAN DEN BERGHE, P. L. Caste in a Natal Hindu community. AFR. STUD. 20 (1961), pp. 217-225.

23,227 READ, E. S. After-care and rehabilitation of ex-convicts. RACE RELATIONS 12 (1945), pp. 80-84.

23,228 REEDMAN, J. N. Agricultural surpluses and social policy. RACE RELATIONS 8 (1941), pp. 58-59.

23,229 REYBURN, H. A. Some factors in the South African racial situation. RACE RELATIONS 1 (1933-1934), pp. 48-50.

23,230 REYNEKE, J. Race relations of the future in the light of the past. RACE RELATIONS 5 (1938), pp. 88-90.

23,231 RHEINALLT JONES, E. B. Farm labour in the Transvaal. RACE RELATIONS 12 (1945), pp. 5-14.

23,232 RHEINALLT JONES, J. D. Conclusion. RACE RELATIONS 9 (1942), pp. 55-61.

23,233 RHEINALLT JONES, J. D. Co-operative societies among Africans: 2. RACE RELATIONS 7 (1940), pp. 10-14.

23,234 RHEINALLT JONES, J. D. Education and race attitudes. RACE RELATIONS 3, no. ii (1936), pp. 38-45.

23,235 RHEINALLT JONES, J. D. Non-European nursing services. RACE RELATIONS 1 (1933-1934), pp. 110-114.

23,236 RHEINALLT JONES, J. D. The nutrition problem. RACE RELATIONS 6 (1939), pp. 37-41.

23,237 RHEINALLT JONES, J. D. Race relations in 1935: a South African survey. RACE RELATIONS 3, no. i (1936), pp. 2-13.

23,238 RHEINALLT JONES, J. D. Race relations in 1936: a South African survey. RACE RELATIONS 4 (1937), pp. 3-16.

23,239 RHEINALLT JONES, J. D. Race relations in 1937: a South African survey. RACE RELATIONS 5 (1938), pp. 13-29.

23,240 RHEINALLT JONES, J. D. Social security and non-Europeans. RACE RELATIONS 11 (1944), pp. 14-20.

23,241 RHEINALLT JONES, J. D. Social work and the non-European. RACE RELATIONS 3, no. iv (1936), pp. 84-86.

23,242 ROBERTS, H. V. Race relations in South Africa as an international problem. INTERNAT. AFFAIRS 34 (1958), pp. 164-173.

23,243 ROCHLIN, S. A. A forgotten name for the Cape Malays. BANTU STUD. 8 (1934), pp. 95-97.

23,244 ROOYEN, P. VAN. Pushy. AFR. SOUTH 5, no. 4 (1961), pp. 119-123.

23,245 RUBIN, L. Afrikaner nationalism and the Jews. AFR. SOUTH 1, no. 3 (1957), pp. 28-34.

23,246 RUBIO GARCIA, L. Síntomas de disgregación en Africa del Sur? CUAD. EST. AFR. 20 (1952), pp. 31-42.

23,247 SAAYMAN, R. B. Naturelle opvoeding. RACE RELATIONS 1 (1933-1934), pp. 19-25.

23,248 SABIKHI, V. Indian minorities in South Africa. AFRO-ASIAN AND W. AFF. 2 (1965), pp. 57-60.

23,249 SAFFERY, A. L. African trade unions and the Institute. RACE RELATIONS 8 (1941), pp. 28-32.

23,250 SAFFERY, A. L. A colour bar question: native bus and taxi drivers. RACE RELATIONS 1 (1933-1934), pp. 17-18.

23,251 SAMPSON, A. Orlando revisited. AFR. SOUTH 3, no. 4 (1958), pp. 40-44.

23,252 SCOTT, M. Afrique du sud, société anonyme. PRESENCE AFR. N.S. 50 (1964), pp. 60-75.

23,253 SIANN, G. Bulawayo diary. AFR. SOUTH 3, no. 3 (1959), pp. 67-71.

23,254 SILVEY, J. South Africans: invalids or invalidated? TRANSITION 23 (1965), pp. 28-30.

23,255 SIMONS, H. J. The coloured worker and trade unionism. RACE RELATIONS 9 (1942), pp. 19-33.

23,256 SIMONS, H. J. Tribal medicine: diviners and herbalists. AFR. STUD. 16 (1957), pp. 85-92.

23,257 SMITH, R. H. Some economic aspects of changing native policy. RACE RELATIONS 11 (1944), pp. 51-55.

23,258 SMUTS, J. C. Africans in the Union of South Africa. J. AFR. SOC. 41 (1942), p. 87.

23,259 SMUTS, J. C. South Africa's Social and Economic Planning Council. J. AFR. SOC. 41 (1942), pp. 231-233.

23,260 SMUTS, J. C. "Trusteeship" in the Union of South Africa. J. AFR. SOC. 41 (1942), pp. 154-160.

23,261 SOFER, C. Some aspects of inter-racial marriages in South Africa, 1925-46. AFRICA 19 (1949), pp. 187-203.

23,262 STEEL, A. Sports leads the way. AFR. SOUTH 4, no. 1 (1959), pp. 114-115.

23,263 STENT, G. E. Colour problems of South Africa. YEARBOOK OF WORLD AFFAIRS 2 (1948), pp. 70-93.

23,264 STENT, G. E. Migrancy and urbanization in the Union of South Africa. AFRICA 18 (1948), pp. 161-183.

23,265 STRETFORD, W. Black, brown, and white in South Africa. CONTEMP. REV. 103 (1913), pp. 404-413.

23,266 TEMBA, C. The bottom of the bottle. AFR. SOUTH 5, no. 3 (1961), pp. 49-55.

23,267 UNGAR, A. The abdication of a community. AFR. SOUTH 3, no. 2 (1959), pp. 29-38.

23,268 VALENTE, A. A Africa do Sul e a sua situação. PORT. EM AFR. 22 (1965), pp. 76-84.

23,269 VAN DEN BERGHE, P. L. Indians in Natal and Fiji: a "controlled experiment" in culture contact. CIVILISATIONS 12 (1962), pp. 75-84; French summary, pp. 85-87.

23,270 VAN DEN BERGHE, P. L. Miscegenation in South Africa. CAH. ET. AFR. 1 (1960), pp. 68-84.

23,271 VAN DEN BERGHE, P. L. Some trends in unpublished social science research in South Africa. INT. SOC. SC. BULL. 14 (1962), pp. 723-732.

23,272 VERSTER, J. The trend and pattern of fertility in Soweto: an urban Bantu community. A report on the fertility sample survey of the Bantu population in Soweto. AFR. STUD. 24 (1965), pp. 131-198.

23,273 VILAKAZI, A. A Reserve from within. AFR. STUD. 16 (1957), pp. 93-101.

23,274 VILAKAZI, A. Urban lobolo attitudes. AFR. STUD. 18 (1959), pp. 80-82; 19 (1960), p. 44.

23,275 VILLIERS, J. P. DE. Malnutrition amongst the coloured people. RACE RELATIONS 6 (1939), pp. 9-11.

23,276 WATSON, S. P. Prison conditions. RACE RELATIONS 12 (1945), pp. 78-80.

23,277 WEBB, M. The Indian in South Africa: towards a solution of conflict. RACE RELATIONS 11 (1944), pp. 1-10.

23,278 WEBB, M. The Natal menace. AFR. SOUTH 1, no. 3 (1957), pp. 34-39.

23,279 WEBB, M. Race riots in Durban: The riots and after. RACE RELATIONS 16 (1949), pp. 85-96.

23,280 WEBB, M. Some inter-racial aspects of poverty and poor relief in Durban. RACE RELATIONS 5 (1938), pp. 3-8.

23,281 WERNER, A. The native question in South Africa. J. AFR. SOC. 4 (1905), pp. 441-454.

23,282 WHYTE, Q. Welfare and efficiency of industrial personnel. RACE RELATIONS 16 (1949), pp. 15-22.

23,283 WILLIAMSON, G. E. Multi-racial problems and the development of manufacturing industry in South Africa. RACE RELATIONS 15 (1948), pp. 12-29.

23,284 WILSON, M. South Africa. INT. SOC. SC. J. 13 (1961), pp. 225-244.

23,285 WOLLHEIM, O. D. The Cape skolly. RACE RELATIONS J. 17 (1950), pp. 46-50.

23,286 WOLLHEIM, O. D. The coloured people of South Africa. RACE 5, no. 2 (1963-1964), pp. 25-41.

23,287 WOLLHEIM, O. D. The schizophrenic heart. AFR. SOUTH 2, no. 1 (1957), pp. 45-50.

23,288 WOLLHEIM, O. D. The suicide of group areas. AFR. SOUTH 4, no. 3 (1960), pp. 57-62.

23,289 Afrique du Sud. CIVILISATIONS 3 (1953), pp. 405-410.

23,290 C.P.S. for non-European townships. RACE RELATIONS 9 (1942), pp. 100-109.

23,291 Diet scales in use at various non-European institutions. RACE RELATIONS 6 (1939), pp. 14-15.

23,292 Johannesburg en 1951. ZAIRE 5 (1951), pp. 745-746.

23,293 Juvenile crime in South Africa. J. AFR. SOC. 38 (1939), p. 482.

23,294 The nutrition survey of the Union department of public health. RACE RELATIONS 6 (1939), pp. 120-124.

23,295 Réorganisation des centres extra-coutumiers d'Afrique du Sud. ZAIRE 6 (1952), p. 529.

23,296 The South African Indians: a plea for a comprehensive programme of research. RACE RELATIONS 7 (1940), pp. 49-51.

23,297 South African mines and their native miners [culled from The South African Mining and Engineering Journal]. J. AFR. SOC. 41 (1942), pp. 152-153.

23,298 Zulu. PRESENCE AFR. N.S. 53 (1965), pp. 235-237.

SOUTH WEST AFRICA

Anthropology

23,299 CROSBY, O. T. Notes on Bushmen and Ovambo in South West Africa. J. AFR. SOC. 30 (1931), pp. 344-359.

23,300 GIBSON, G. D. Double descent and its correlates among the Herero of Ngamiland. AMER. ANTHR. 58 (1956), pp. 109-139.

23,301 HOOGENHOUT, P. J. The Strandlopers of South-west Africa. RACE RELATIONS 16 (1949), pp. 38-41.

23,302 IRLE, J. Herero-Sprichwörter. AFR. UND UB. 4 (1913-1914), pp. 1-19.

23,303 KOHLER, O. The stage of acculturation in South West Africa. SOCIOLOGUS 6 (1956), pp. 138-153.

23,304 LEBZELTER, V. Die Buschmänner Sudwestafrikas. AFRICA 7 (1934), pp. 70-81.

23,305 LEHMANN, F. R. Das Häuptlingtum der Herero in Südwest-Afrika: eine kurze übersicht über die Entwicklung der politischen Organisation und des heutigen Nationalbewubtseins der Herero. SOCIOLOGUS 5 (1955), pp. 28-43.

23,306 LOEB, E. M. The political and social structure of the Bantu tribes of Southwest Africa. CONG. INT. SC. ANTH. ET ETHN. 4, no. iii (1952), pp. 51-56.

23,307 LOEB, E. M. Transition rites of the Kuanyama Ambo. AFR. STUD. 7 (1948), pp. 16-28, 71-84.

23,308 MARSHALL, L. !Kung Bushman bands. AFRICA 30 (1960), pp. 325-354.

23,309 MARSHALL, L. !Kung Bushman religious beliefs. AFRICA 32 (1962), pp. 221-252.

23,310 MARSHALL, L. N!ow. AFRICA 27 (1957), pp. 232-240.

23,311 SANTESSON, C. G. Pfeilgift aus Südwest-Afrika (Damaraland). ETHNOS 4 (1939), pp. 29-34.

23,312 VEDDER, H. Die Bergdama in Südwest-Afrika. AFRICA 3 (1930), pp. 178-190.

23,313 WAGNER, G. Some economic aspects of Herero life. AFR. STUD. 13 (1954), pp. 117-130.

23,314 WANGLER, H. H. Uber südwestafrikanische Bogenlieder. AFR. UND UB. 39 (1954-1955), pp. 49-63; 40 (1956), pp. 163-174.

Art. Antiquities

23,315 FOCK, G. J. Beitrag zur Vorgeschichte von Südwestafrika. PROC. PAN-AFR. CONGR. PRE-HIST. 3 (1955), pp. 387-390.

23,316 GRUET and ZELLE. Découverte de sphères a Windhoeck (South West Africa). PROC. PAN-AFR. CONGR. PRE-HIST. 2 (1952), pp. 457-460.

23,317 KORN, H. and MARTIN, H. The Pleistocene in South-West Africa. PROC. PAN-AFR. CONGR. PRE-HIST. 3 (1955), pp. 14-22.

Biography

23,318 Obituary: C. H. L. Hahn. AFR. AFFAIRS 48 (1949), p. 74.

Geography

23,319 GARDINER, R. A "European" colony. AFR. AFFAIRS 54 (1955), pp. 205-208.

23,320 JAEGER, F. Das Winhuker Hochland. KOLONIALE STUDIEN: HANS MEYER FESTSCHRIFT, 1928, pp. 109-131.

23,321 SCHWARZ, E. H. L. The Kalahari and its possibilities. J. AFR. SOC. 20 (1920), pp. 1-12.

23,322 WATSON, A. C. The Guano Islands of southwestern Africa. GEOG. REV. 20 (1930), pp. 631-641.

Government. Politics. Administration

23,323 ARDEN-CLARKE, Sir C. South-west Africa, the Union and the United Nations. AFR. AFFAIRS 59 (1960), pp. 26-35.

23,324 BILSEN, J. VAN. L'affaire du Sud-ouest africain. ZAIRE 4 (1950), pp. 774-778.

23,325 BILSEN, J. VAN. Le Sud-Ouest africain. ZAIRE 4 (1950), pp. 1011-1014.

23,326 BUNTING, B. Windhoek diary. AFR. SOUTH 4, no. 3 (1960), pp. 76-83.

23,327 C., J. Nouveau parti en Afrique du Sud-Ouest. ZAIRE 8 (1954), pp. 950-951.

23,328 DATTA, A. K. South-West Africa at the world forum. AFRO-ASIAN AND W. AFF. 2 (1965), pp. 120-128.

23,329 DATTA, A. K. South-west Africa under the mandatory system. AFR. QUART. 2, no. iii (1962), pp. 155-172.

23,330 GRAY, A. South West Africa affair. AFR. AFFAIRS 61 (1962), pp. 276-279.

23,331 HORRELL, M. L'administration du Sud-Ouest Africain. CIVILISATIONS 14 (1964), pp. 134-142.

23,332 KERINA, M. A. A petitioner speaks. AFR. SOUTH 4, no. 3 (1960), pp. 84-85.

23,333 KERINA, M. A. South West Africa and the United Nations. AFR. SOUTH 3, no. 1 (1958), pp. 8-15.

23,334 KOZONGUIZI, J. Background to violence. AFR. SOUTH 4, no. 3 (1960), pp. 71-75.

23,335 LAWRIE, G. New light of South West Africa. Some extracts from and comments on the Odendaal Report. AFR. STUD. 23 (1964), pp. 105-119.

23,336 NAYAK, S. The situation in South-west Africa. AFR. QUART. 2 (1962-1963), pp. 251-262.

23,337 NAYAK, S. South-west Africa in United Nations. AFR. QUART. 3, no. iv (1964), pp. 225-241.

23,338 NAYAK, S. South West Africa: law and the mandate. AFR. QUART. 3, no. i (1963), pp. 30-41.

23,339 PARAMOUNT CHIEF OF THE HERERO PEOPLE. An open letter to the United Nations. AFR. SOUTH 3, no. 1 (1958), p. 7.

23,340 PITTIUS, E. F. W. G. VAN. Wither South-West Africa? INTERNAT. AFFAIRS 23 (1947), pp. 202-212.

23,341 PRITCHARD, S. M. Experiences in German South-west Africa. J. AFR. SOC. 16 (1916), pp. 1-6.

23,342 RUBIO GARCIA, L. Hipernacionalismo y diplomacia: el caso del Sudoeste africano. CUAD. EST. AFR. 22 (1953), pp. 19-31.

23,343 SCOTT, M. The international status of South West Africa. INTERNAT. AFFAIRS 34 (1958), pp. 318-329.

23,344 SCOTT, M. The sacred trust of South West Africa. AFR. SOUTH 5, no. 1 (1960), pp. 46-49.

History

23,345 AYDELOTTE, W. O. The first German colony and its diplomatic consequences. CAMB. HIST. J. 5 (1937), pp. 291-313.

23,346 HAILEY, Lord. South-west Africa. AFR. AFFAIRS 46 (1947), pp. 77-86.

23,347 KOMAMBO, K. Le développement du nationalisme africain en Afrique du Sud-Ouest. PRESENCE AFR. N.S. 49 (1964), pp. 88-103.

23,348 KOZONGUIZI, J. South West Africa. AFR. SOUTH 2, no. 1 (1957), pp. 64-72.

23,349 PARK, M. H. German South-West African campaign. J. AFR. SOC. 15 (1916), pp. 113-132.

23,350 SCHOLFIELD, A. German South-West Africa and the Union. CONTEMP. REV. 108 (1915), pp. 58-65.

23,351 SMUTS, J. Veldmaarschalk Smuts in het Strijdperk voor Zuidwest-Afrika. KONGO-OVERZEE 12-13 (1946-1947), pp. 107-112.

See also 18304.

Language. Races

23,352 ATKINS, G. The one-word tenses in Cokwe. AFRICA 25 (1955), pp. 261-273.

23,353 BUTTNER, C. G. Mährchen der Ova-herero. ZAS 1 (1887-1888), pp. 189-216, 295-307.

23,354 BUTTNER, C. G. Sprachführer für Reisende in Damaraland. ZAS 1 (1887-1888), pp. 252-294.

23,355 DAMMANN, E. Stimmlose Nasale im Kwangali. AFR. UND UB. 41 (1957), pp. 165-170.

23,356 DAMMANN, E. Zür Kenntnis des Kwambi. AFR. UND UB. 46 (1962-1963), pp. 200-203.

23,357 IRLE, J. Herero-Texte. AFR. UND UB. 8 (1917-1918), pp. 36-45.

23,358 KOHLER, O. Tongestalt und Tonmuster in der Infinitivform des Verbum im Herero. AFR. UND UB. 42 (1958), pp. 97-110, 159-172.

23,359 KRAPF, L. Chuo cha utenzi. ZAS 1 (1887-1888), pp. 1-42, 124-137.

23,360 LEVY-BRUHL, L. La numeration chez les Bergdama. AFRICA 2 (1929), pp. 162-173.

23,361 WANDRES, C. Tiernamen in der Nama- und Bergdama-Sprache etymologisch erläutert. FESTSCHRIFT MEINHOF, 1927, pp. 125-133.

See also 21724.

Law

23,362 COLLIARD, C. A. Le statut international du Sud-Ouest africain. RJPUF 5 (1951), pp. 94-112.

Sociology

23,363 MARR, M. Gentleman Jim. NADA 27 (1950), pp. 74-76.

23,364 MASON, P. Separate development and South West Africa: some aspects of the Odendaal report. RACE 5, no. 4 (1963-1964), pp. 83-97.

23,365 The Rehoboth community of South West Africa. AFR. STUD. 14 (1955), pp. 175-200.

ANGOLA

General

23,366 CARDOSO, C. L. Contribuição para a bibliografia dos Bochimanes de Angola. BOL. INST. ANGOLA 14 (1960), pp. 5-19.

23,367 COMHAIRE, J. Aspects divers de l'Angola. ZAIRE 6 (1952), pp. 491-497.

23,368 Essai de bibliographie angolaise. PRESENCE AFR. N.S. 42 (1962), pp. 219-220.

Agriculture

See 13784.

Anthropology

23,369 ALMEIDA, A. DE. Sobre as mutilações étnicas dos Cazamas (Angola). BOL. INST. ANGOLA 7 (1955), pp. 43-55.

23,370 ALMEIDA, A. DE and ALMEIDA, M. E. DE C. E. Sobre mutilações étnicas dos Cassequéles (Angola). BOL. INST. ANGOLA 4 (1954), pp. 13-28.

23,371 BLEEK, D. F. Bushmen of central Angola. BANTU STUD. 3 (1927), pp. 105-125.

23,372 CARDOSO, C. L. Algumas observações sobre o termo e costume osando. BOL. INST. ANGOLA 21-23 (1965), pp. 115-131.

23,373 CARDOSO, C. L. Nótulas de etnografia Angola. BOL. INST. ANGOLA 15 (1961), pp. 101-110.

23,374 CARDOSO, C. L. Novos elementos para o problema das fechadura de madeira em Angola. BOL. INST. ANGOLA 19 (1964), pp. 23-31.

23,375 CARDOSO, C. L. Trabalhos de campo da Divisão de Etnografia do Instituto de Investigação Científica de Angola. PORT. EM AFR. 20 (1963), pp. 279-282.

23,376 COELHO, M. A. T. Contribuição para o estudo da habitação indígena de Silva Porto. BOL. INST. ANGOLA 15 (1961), pp. 125-133.

23,377 CUNHA, A. X. DA. Contribuição para o estudo sociológico da tribo To. BOL. INST. ANGOLA 14 (1960), pp. 23-31.

23,378 DRENNAN, M. R. Two witch-doctor's outfits from Angola. BANTU STUD. 8 (1934), pp. 383-387.

23,379 DUFF, P. F. A circuncisão dos Vankhumbi. PORT. EM AFR. 2 (1945), pp. 82-91.

23,380 DUFF, P. F. Conceitos sôbre Deus entre os Vankhumbi. PORT. EM AFR. 1 (1944), pp. 301-309.

23,381 DUFF, P. F. A Nubilidade dos Vankhumbi. PORT. EM AFR. 2 (1945), pp. 293-297.

23,382 ENRIQUES, V. Bosquimanos de Angola. ARCH. INST. EST. AFR. 6, no. 22 (1952), pp. 7-13.

23,383 ESTERMANN, P. C. Coutumes des Mbali du Sud d'Angola. AFRICA 12 (1939), pp. 74-86.

23,384 ESTERMANN, P. C. Deficiências miúdas numa obra Monumental. PORT. EM AFR. 3 (1946), pp. 20-27.

23,385 ESTERMANN, P. C. A Etnologia angolana em três livros recentes [Le Noir d'Afrique by G. Lefrou, Racas do Império by M. Corrêa, Les Peuples et les Civilisations de l'Afrique by H. Baumann]. PORT. EM AFR. 6 (1949), pp. 65-74.

23,386 ESTERMANN, P. C. A Festa da Puberdade em algumas tribos de Angola Meridional. PORT. EM AFR. 1 (1944), pp. 340-351; 2 (1945), pp. 45-51.

23,387 ESTERMANN, P. C. Os habitantes do Namibe. PORT. EM AFR. 16 (1959), pp. 322-330.

23,388 ESTERMANN, P. C. A Investigação Etnográfica em Angola no passado, no presente e vantagem da sua intensiticação. PORT. EM AFR. 15 (1958), pp. 261-272.

23,389 ESTERMANN, P. C. Mais uma monografia sobre os Bundos de Angola. PORT. EM AFR. 20 (1963), pp. 78-88.

23,390 ESTERMANN, P. C. O Sul de Angola na Enciclopedia Portuguesa e Brasileira. PORT. EM AFR. 7 (1950), pp. 129-135.

23,391 ESTERMANN, P. C. La tribu Kwanyama en face de la civilisation Européenne. AFRICA 7 (1934), pp. 431-443.

23,392 EVAMBI, R. K. The marriage customs of the Ovimbundu translated by M. W. Ennis. AFRICA 11 (1938), pp. 342-348.

23,393 FRAZAO, S. Os Ambundos. PORT. EM AFR. 5 (1948), pp. 77-82.

23,394 FRAZAO, S. Indígenas e Gentílicos. PORT. EM AFR. 4 (1947), pp. 201-204.

23,395 GUERREIRO, M. V. Caçada aos elefantes. PORT. EM AFR. 7 (1950), pp. 154-160.

23,396 HAMBLY, W. D. Hunting customs of the Ovimbundu. BANTU STUD. 8 (1934), pp. 151-156.

23,397 HAMBLY, W. D. Occupational ritual, belief, and custom among the Ovimbundu. AMER. ANTHR. 36 (1934), pp. 157-167.

23,398 HAMBLY, W. D. Tribal initiation of boys in Angola. AMER. ANTHR. 37 (1935), pp. 36-40.

23,399 HAUENSTEIN, A. Proverbios, fábulas e contos das tribus dos Vimbundus e dos Quiocos de Angola. BOL. INST. ANGOLA 21-23 (1965), pp. 5-56.

23,400 HAUENSTEIN, A. Le serpent dans les croyances de quelques tribus de l'est et du sud de l'Angola. CONGR. INT. SC. ANTHR. ET ETHN. 6, no. ii (1960), pp. 399-400.

23,401 KAMBWA. Conteúdo filosófico dum provérbio africano. PORT. EM AFR. 21 (1964), pp. 197-201.

23,402 KOOLWIJK, M. VAN. Entre os Ganguelas: Circuncisão dos rapazes. PORT. EM AFR. 20 (1963), pp. 156-172.

23,403 KOOLWIJK, M. VAN. Entre os Ganguelas: Festa da iniciação das raparigas. PORT. EM AFR. 20 (1963), pp. 260-278.

23,404 LARCIER, H. The Union of the Angolese populations. PRESENCE AFR. N.S. 42-43 (1962), pp. 37-43.

23,405 LENK-CHEVITCH, P. Vestiges d'anciennes constructions en Angola. ZAIRE 2 (1948), pp. 675-677.

23,406 LIMA, M. Alguns aspectos da cultura Quioca. PORT. EM AFR. 21 (1964), pp. 49-60.

23,407 LOURENCO, S. O Culto dos Espíritos do Nano no Humbe. PORT. EM AFR. 12 (1955), pp. 156-162.

23,408 MARGARIDO, A. Processus de domination fondant un empire: Cas des Lunda. PRESENCE AFR. N.S. 55 (1965), pp. 100-118.

23,409 MARTINHO, A. Origem tradicional dos povos Vanhaneka. PORT. EM AFR. 18 (1961), pp. 217-224.

23,410 MITTELBERGER, C. Entre os Cuanhamas: O que precede a chuva (estudo etnografico). PORT. EM AFR. 19 (1962), pp. 220-234.

23,411 MONTEIRO, J. J. On the Quissama tribe of Angola. JRAI 5 (1875), pp. 198-201.

23,412 OLIVEIRA, M. DE. Etnografia Angolana. PORT. EM AFR. 11 (1954), pp. 217-220.

23,413 PRICE, F. G. H. A description of the Quissama tribe. JRAI 1 (1871), pp. 185-193.

23,414 READ, F. W. Iron-smelting and native black-smithing in Ondulu country, south-east Angola. J. AFR. SOC. 2 (1902), pp. 44-49.

23,415 SANTOS, E. DOS. A religião dos Quiocos. BR. INST. ANGOLA 11 (1958), pp. 27-52.

23,416 SCOTT, C. W. A note on the Luimbi of Central Angola. AFRICA 25 (1955), pp. 427-429.

23,417 SILVA, P. A. DA. Sabedoria popular do Nhaneca. PORT. EM AFR. 5 (1948), pp. 33-43; 6 (1949), pp. 87-92, 264-266; 7 (1950), pp. 203-212.

23,418 SILVA, P. A. DA. Sabedoria Popular do Nhaneca (Comparações tiradas da chuva). PORT. EM AFR. 4 (1947), pp. 47-49, 214-218, 266-273.

23,419 SILVA, P. A. DA. Sabedoria popular dos Vanyaneka. PORT. EM AFR. 2 (1945), pp. 238-244, 349-353.

23,420 SOUSA, A. N. E. Angola e o tempo. BOL. INST. ANGOLA 2 (1953), pp. 25-26.

23,421 STETSON, G. R. African folk-tales. LIBERIA BULL. 5 (1894), pp. 63-70.

23,422 TASTEVIN, C. L'oiseau sacré des Vakwa n yama: l'E-pumumu, le grand calao. BULL. IFAN 2 (1940), pp. 334-341.

23,423 THISSEN, L. A proposito de Ethnosociologia do Nordeste de Angola. PORT. EM AFR. 16 (1959), pp. 352-357.

23,424 TROESCH, J. Ideias e crenças do enclave. PORT. EM AFR. 20 (1963), pp. 305-309.

23,425 TUCKER, J. T. Initiation ceremonies for Luimbi boys. AFRICA 19 (1949), pp. 53-59.

23,426 TUCKER, L. S. The divining basket of the Ovimbundu. JRAI 70 (1940), pp. 171-201.

23,427 VALENTE, P. J. F. A Família indígena no Planalto de Nova Lisboa. PORT. EM AFR. 6 (1949), pp. 347-353.

23,428 VERLY, R. Le "Roi divin" chez les Ovimbundu et Kimbundu de l'Angola. ZAIRE 9 (1955), pp. 675-703.

23,429 VILHENA, J. DE. Folklore activities of the Museo do Dundo. AFR. MUSIC, 1959, pp. 42-43.

23,430 VISSERS, J. Alambamento e amor conjugal. PORT. EM AFR. 21 (1964), pp. 134-147.

23,431 VISSERS, J. Manifestacão moderna da sabedoria antiga. PORT. EM AFR. 10 (1953), pp. 261-274.

23,432 WHITE, C. M. N. Notes on some metaphysical concepts of the Balovale tribes. AFR. STUD. 7 (1948), pp. 146-156.

23,433 WHITE, C. M. N. Notes on the Mungongi ritual of the Balovale tribes. AFR. STUD. 13 (1954), pp. 108-116.

23,434 O Seminário Indígena de Nova Lisboa. PORT. EM AFR. 7 (1950), pp. 161-165.

See also 23307, 23308.

Art

23,435 ALMEIDA, A. DE and FRANCA, J. C. Le Magosien du Sud de l'Angola. PROC. PAN-AFR. CONGR. PRE-HIST. 5 (1965), pp. 117-126.

23,436 ANTUNES, M. T. Sur la faune de vertébrés du Pléistocéne de Leba, Humpata (Angola). PROC. PAN-AFR. CONGR. PRE-HIST. 5 (1965), pp. 127-128.

23,437 ARAMBOURG, C. and MOUTA, F. Les grottes et fentes à ossements du Sud de l'Angola. PROC. PAN-AFR. CONGR. PRE-HIST. 2 (1952), pp. 301-304.

23,438 BATALHA, F. O palácio velho de Benguela. BOL. INST. ANGOLA 19 (1964), pp. 41-44.

23,439 BREUIL, H. and ALMEIDA, A. DE. Introduction à la préhistoire de l'Angola. PROC. PAN-AFR. CONGR. PRE-HIST. 4, no. iii (1962), pp. 203-205.

23,440 BREUIL, H. and ALMEIDA, A. DE. Sur les gravures et les peintures rupestres du désert de Mozamedes (Angola). PROC. PAN-AFR. CONGR. PRE-HIST. 4, no. iii (1962), pp. 451-456.

23,441 CLARK, J. D. The distribution of prehistoric culture in Angola. PROC. PAN-AFR. CONGR. PRE-HIST. 5 (1965), pp. 225-309.

23,442 ESQUIVEL, A. As ruínas de negola na outracosta. BSEM 46, no. i (1943-1944), pp. 27-29.

23,443 FRANCA, J. C. Breve nota sobre uma jazidas pré-histórica descoberta nos arredores de Luanda. BOL. INST. ANGOLA 1 (1953), pp. 21-28.

23,444 FRANCA, J. C. Notas sobre uma estação pré-histórica de Angola. BOL. INST. ANGOLA 2 (1953), pp. 13-18.

23,445 FULLER, C. E. Can the living in Angola explain the past in Rhodesia? AFR. STUD. 11 (1952), pp. 182-188.

23,446 FURTADO, S. Apontamentos para estudo das artes decorativas Portuguesas. BOL. INST. ANGOLA 8 (1956), pp. 107-113.

23,447 FURTADO, S. Uma imagem de Santo António em Angola (Santo António da Muxima). BOL. INST. ANGOLA 14 (1960), pp. 41-51.

23,448 JENMART, J. The occurrence of Clacto-Abbevillian (Stellenbosch) artefacts in north eastern Angola. PROC. PAN-AFR. CONGR. PRE-HIST. 1 (1947), pp. 224-227.

23,449 JUNIOR, A. C. S. C. Aspectos da arte Negra nos Luchazes. BOL. INST. ANGOLA 11 (1958), pp. 149-173.

23,450 MOUTA, F. New discoveries of Stone Age sites in Angola. PROC. PAN-AFR. CONGR. PRE-HIST. 1 (1947), pp. 206-208.

23,451 MOUTA, F. Sur le Paléolithique du district de Malango (Angola). PROC. PAN-AFR. CONGR. PRE-HIST. 2 (1952), pp. 373-374.

23,452 PAMPLONA, F. DE. Pintores portugueses de aquém e de alemmar. Pinturas angolanas de Pedro Cruz. BOL. INST. ANGOLA 6 (1955), pp. 21-23.

23,453 VICTOR, G. B. Cântico a Angola. PORT. EM AFR. 18 (1961), pp. 225-226.

See also 12908.

Biography

23,454 Capitão José Agapito da Silva Carvalho, Governador Geral de Angola. BOL. INST. ANGOLA 9 (1957), pp. 11-13.

23,455 SOUSA, A. G. DE. Duas figuras notáveis de Angola: Dr. Manuel Alves da Cunha. BOL. INST. ANGOLA 6 (1955), pp. 5-12.

23,456 Ministro do Ultramar [Vasco Lopes Alves]. PORT. EM AFR. 15 (1958), pp. 260.

23,457 RIBEIRO DE SANTANA, A. Homenagem ao Padre Antunes! PORT. EM AFR. 14 (1957), pp. 33-37.

23,458 MELLA, J. Herói e mártir [Infante D Duarte de Bragança]. BOL. INST. ANGOLA 20 (1964), pp. 85-93.

23,459 Obituary: Mr. A. Vicente Ferreira. CIVILISATIONS 3 (1953), p. 171.

23,460 Vicente Ferreira. PORT. EM AFR. 10 (1953), pp. 86-87.

23,461 Dr. Mariano de Sant'Ana Godinho. BOL. INST. ANGOLA 8 (1956), pp. 5-6.

23,462 SOUSA, A. G. DE. Duas figuras notáveis de Angola: John Gossweiler. BOL. INST. ANGOLA 6 (1955), pp. 13-20.

23,463 MERWIN, U. S. To name the wrong [Agostinho Neto]. BO 15 (1964), pp. 34-37.

23,464 Dr. Clemente Pereira da Silva. PORT. EM AFR. 3 (1946), pp. 12-13.

Economics

23,465 ALVES, H. O Caminho de Ferro de Benguela. PORT. EM AFR. 9 (1952), pp. 394-403.

23,466 AMARAL, I. M. P. DO. Aspectos económicos da cidade de Luanda. BOL. INST. ANGOLA 9 (1957), pp. 51-60.

23,467 C., J. Budget de l'Angola. ZAIRE 7 (1953), p. 527.

23,468 C., J. Commerce extérieur de l'Angola. ZAIRE 8 (1954), pp. 520-521.

23,469 C., J. Situation économique de l'Angola. ZAIRE 7 (1953), pp. 526-527.

23,470 CANTO, B. DO. A pesca na Logoa Panguila e defumação de peixe. BOL. INST. ANGOLA 15 (1961), pp. 81-86.

23,471 CARVALHAL, A. V. E E. Acção social no trabalho em Angóla. Ano de 1963. PORT. EM AFR. 21 (1964), pp. 275-292.

23,472 COMHAIRE, J. L'Angola d'aujourd'hui. ZAIRE 9 (1955), pp. 143-151.

23,473 CORREIA MARQUES. Petróleo em Angola. PORT. EM AFR. 12 (1955), pp. 217-222.

23,474 COSTA, J. M. DA. Primórdios da ocupação do sul de Angola. BOL. INST. ANGOLA 1 (1953), pp. 29-36.

23,475 CUNHA, J. A. DA. Centro de Actividades Económicas Angolanas. PORT. EM AFR. 7 (1950), pp. 13-18.

23,476 DAVIDSON, B. Angola. Economie du colonialisme. PRESENCE AFR. N.S. 3 (1955), pp. 5-19.

23,477 FONSECA, D. DA. Prosperidade e futuro de Angola. PORT. EM AFR. 12 (1955), pp. 405-411.

23,478 HANCE, W. A. and DONGEN, I. S. V. The port of Lobito and the Benguela railway. GEOG. REV. 46 (1956), pp. 460-487.

23,479 JANNETTONE, G. Il regime fondiario in Angola. AFRICA (Rome) 19 (1964), pp. 133-140.

23,480 LOBO, L. Horizontes novos em Angola. BSEM 130 (1962), pp. 131-151.

23,481 NUNES, P. and FONSECA, D. DA. A pesca em Angola. BOL. INST. ANGOLA 12 (1959), pp. 103-115.

23,482 PINTO, L. M. T. and SANTOS, R. M. DOS. Problems of economic development of Angola: poles and prospects. ECON. DEV. FOR AFRICA, 1965, pp. 198-221.

23,483 SAROT, E. E. The contribution of the Italians to the knowledge of Angola. ZAIRE 9 (1955), pp. 825-847.

23,484 STONE, P. An ambitious Portuguese plan. AFR. AFFAIRS 55 (1956), pp. 320-325.

23,485 VALENTE, A. Nótula sobre o plano de acção social no trabalho em Angola. PORT. EM AFR. 20 (1963), pp. 349-356.

23,486 Grands travaux en Angola. ZAIRE 5 (1951), pp. 863-864.

See also 12714.

Education

23,487 AZEVEDO, A. DE. O ensino agrícola em angola. PORT. EM AFR. 4 (1947), pp. 339-343.

23,488 AZEVEDO, A. DE. Novos subsídios para a história do ensino em Angola (Século XIX). BOL. INST. ANGOLA 19 (1964), pp. 33-39.

23,489 AZEVEDO, A. DE. A Universidade Portuguesa em Africa. BOL. INST. ANGOLA 17 (1963), pp. 49-58.

23,490 MENDES, J. M. O ensino indígena em Angola. PORT. EM AFR. 12 (1955), pp. 432-436.

23,491 PAIXAO, B. Situação embaracosa do ensino em Angola. PORT. EM AFR. 3 (1946), pp. 161-167.

23,492 PIMENTEL, M. I. Instituto de Educação e serviço social Pio XII. PORT. EM AFR. 20 (1963), pp. 15-18.

23,493 SIMEAO VITORIA. O Problema da educação em Angola. PORT. EM AFR. 14 (1957), pp. 5-26, 75-106, 167-180, 219-246.

23,494 STRANGWAY, A. K. The advance of African women in Angola. AFR. WOMEN 1 (1956), pp. 79-84.

Geography

23,495 BARNS, T. A. Through Portuguese West Africa. J. AFR. SOC. 28 (1929), pp. 224-234.

23,496 BATALHA, F. Angola turística. BOL. INST. ANGOLA 2 (1953), pp. 45-48.

23,497 BATALHA, F. Angola turistica. Circuito regional de Benguela, Huambo e Cuanza-Sul. BOL. INST. ANGOLA 7 (1955), pp. 33-42.

23,498 BOUVEIGNES, O. DE. De Grandpré à la côte d'Angola, en 1786-1787. ZAIRE 3 (1949), pp. 1109-1117.

23,499 CLARK, J. D. Vegetation patterns, climate and sands in North East Angola. PROC. PAN-AFR. CONGR. PRE-HIST. 4 (1962), pp. 151-165.

23,500 CRUZ, F. Marés de Angola. BOL. INST. ANGOLA 3 (1954), pp. 9-26.

23,501 DAVIES, O. The raised beaches of Angola and South-West Africa. PROC. PAN-AFR. CONGR. PRE-HIST. 4 (1962), pp. 289-294.

23,502 HOUK, R. J. Recent developments in the Portuguese Congo. GEOG. REV. 48 (1958), pp. 201-221.

23,503 PERESTRELO, E. A. C. O Pôrto de Luanda. PORT. EM AFR. 2 (1945), pp. 193-202.

23,504 QUEIROS, D. X. Os climas das regiões de Luanda, Vila Salazar, Nova Lisboa e Sá da Bandeira. BOL. INST. ANGOLA 3 (1954), pp. 57-64.

23,505 WELLS, L. Angolan safari. GEOG. REV. 30 (1940), pp. 553-573.

23,506 WHITTLESSEY, D. S. Geographic provinces of Angola: an outline based on recent sources. GEOG. REV. 14 (1924), pp. 113-126.

Government. Politics. Administration

23,507 ANDRADE, M. DE. Angolese nationalism. PRESENCE AFR. N.S. 42-43 (1962), pp. 7-23.

23,508 ANDRADE, M. DE. Le nationalisme angolais. PRESENCE AFR. N.S. 42 (1962), pp. 5-24.

23,509 BILSEN, J. VAN. De reis naar Angola. ZAIRE 4 (1950), pp. 659-665.

23,510 BRASIO, P. A. A Política do Padre Duparquet no sul de Angola. PORT. EM AFR. 3 (1946), pp. 168-176.

23,511 GEORGES, G. A. Coup d'oeil sur l'Angola. AFR. ET ASIE 53 (1961), pp. 5-15.

23,512 GRAY, A. Angola policy. AFR. AFFAIRS 60 (1961), pp. 478-481.

23,513 GRAY, A. Angola unrest. AFR. AFFAIRS 60 (1961), pp. 372-374.

23,514 LARCIER, H. Présentation de l'Union des Populations de l'Angola (U.P.A.). PRESENCE AFR. N.S. 42 (1962), pp. 40-46.

23,515 M., G. Le problème angolais. ET. CONG. 3, no. 9 (1962), pp. 1-10.

23,516 McVEIGH, M. Deux témoignages du Révérend Malcolm McVeigh, de la mission d l'Eglise Méthodiste Americaine. PRESENCE AFR. N.S. 42 (1962), pp. 186-198.

23,517 MAHALA, C. Le Portugal et les colonies d'Angola et de Guinée. PRESENCE AFR. N.S. 30 (1960), pp. 25-39.

23,518 MARTELLI, G. The future in Angola. AFR. AFFAIRS 61 (1962), pp. 300-307.

23,519 MARTINS, J. De Makongos a Kapitas. BOL. INST. ANGOLA 18 (1964), pp. 51-75.

23,520 NKRUMAH, K. Angola. PRESENCE AFR. N.S. 42 (1962), pp. 25-39.

23,521 PARSONS, C. J. The torment of Angola. AFR. SOUTH 5, no. 4 (1961), pp. 72-80.

23,522 PEREIRA, F. J. Natureza e problemas da guerra psicológica. PORT. EM AFR. 18 (1961), pp. 196-208.

23,523 PEREIRA NETO, J. B. N. Política de integración en Angola y Mozambique. ARCH. INST. EST. AFR. 17, no. 65 (1963), pp. 19-48.

23,524 REDINHA, J. O caso de Angola. PORT. EM AFR. 18 (1961), pp. 271-280.

23,525 SAVIMBI, J. Declaration. ET. CONG. 7, no. vii (1964), pp. 77-79.

23,526 Aide-mémoire sur la situation en Angola. PRESENCE AFR. N.S. 42 (1962), pp. 199-205.

23,527 L'Angola et l'O.N.U. Interventions des délégués africains à la XVIe session. PRESENCE AFR. N.S. 42 (1962), pp. 92-185.

23,528 Angola toujours Portugaise. PRESENCE AFR. N.S. 45 (1963), pp. 223-224.

23,529 Bela Obra de Colonização de uma Empresa Capitalista. PORT. EM AFR. 6 (1949), pp. 257-263.

23,530 Le cas dramatique de Mgr. Pinto de Andrade. PRESENCE AFR. N.S. 45 (1963), pp. 228-229.

23,531 Connaissance du Front de l'Unité pour l'Angola (F.U.A.). PRESENCE AFR. N.S. 45 (1963), pp. 127-135.

23,532 Le corps volontaire angolais d'assistance aux réfugiés (C.V.A.A.R.). PRESENCE AFR. N.S. 42 (1962), pp. 212-213.

23,533 Déclarations du Gouverneur-général de l'Angola. ZAIRE 5 (1951), pp. 630-632.

23,534 Divisão administrativa de Angola e Mocambique. PORT. EM AFR. 11 (1954), pp. 373-378.

23,535 Images d'Angola. PRESENCE AFR. N.S. 40 (1962), pp. 160-161.

See also 12741, 12744, 14616.

History

23,536 ALMEIDA, J. L. DE. Os brazões de salão do Liceu Salvador Corrêa em Luanda. BOL. INST. ANGOLA 20 (1964), pp. 51-61; 21-23 (1965), pp. 77-80.

23,537 ALVES, V. L. Notes on Angola. AFR. AFFAIRS 55 (1956), pp. 17-26.

23,538 AZEVEDO, R. A. DE. Un aperçu de l'Angola. Province Portugaise en Afrique. BOL. INST. ANGOLA 12 (1959), pp. 53-65.

23,539 AZEVEDO, R. A. DE. Frei Alexandre da Sagrada Família, tio de Garrett ou um episodio da história de Angola. BOL. INST. ANGOLA 10 (1957), pp. 21-33.

23,540 BOXER, C. R. Background to Angola: Cadornega's chronicle. HISTORY TODAY 11 (1961), pp. 665-672.

23,541 BRASIO, A. Monumenta Missionalia Angolana. PORT. EM AFR. 9 (1952), pp. 114-119, 200-209, 270-275, 337-344, 404-409; 10 (1953), pp. 51-57, 120-124, 206-212, 275-281, 343-348; 11 (1954), pp. 52-60, 93-106, 126-130, 187-194, 258-268, 321-331, 405-413.

23,542 CABRAL, J. Portuguese colonial policy: Angola and Mozambique. AFR. QUART. 5 (1965), pp. 153-173.

23,543 CHILDS, G. M. The kingdom of Wambu (Huambo): a tentative chronology. J. AFR. HIST. 5 (1964), pp. 367-379.

23,544 CHILDS, G. M. The peoples of Angola in the seventeenth century according to Cadornega. J. AFR. HIST. 1 (1960), pp. 271-279.

23,545 DAVIDSON, B. Angola 1961. Le dossier des faits. PRESENCE AFR. N.S. 38 (1961), pp. 20-44.

23,546 DRECHSLER, H. L'Allemagne et l'Angola du Sud (1898-1903). PRESENCE AFR. N.S. 42 (1962), pp. 54-75.

23,547 DRECHSLER, H. Germany and South Angola, 1898-1903. PRESENCE AFR. N.S. 42-43 (1962), pp. 51-69.

23,548 DUFFY, J. La présence portugaise en Angola (1483-1960). PRESENCE AFR. N.S. 41 (1962), pp. 75-90.

23,549 FARIA, F. L. DE. A situação de Angola e Congo apreciada em Madrid em 1643. PORT. EM AFR. 9 (1952), pp. 235-248.

23,550 FERREIRA, E. A. V. Angola e a experiência do Brasil. PORT. EM AFR. 5 (1948), pp. 257-270.

23,551 FERREIRA, V. Numismática. BOL. INST. ANGOLA 21-23 (1965), pp. 103-114.

23,552 FUENTES, A. D. Francisco Inocêncio de Sousa Coutinho. Esboço de uma obra que se perdeu. BOL. INST. ANGOLA 4 (1954), pp. 35-40.

23,553 FUENTES, A. Suporte econômico da colónia durante a primeira fase do seu desenvolvimento. BOL. INST. ANGOLA 3 (1954), pp. 29-44.

23,554 LEITE, D. B. No terceiro centenário da reconquista de Angola. PORT. EM AFR. 5 (1948), pp. 237-241, 307-309.

23,555 NOGUEIRA, J. A. A Misericórdia de Luanda através dos séculos. BOL. INST. ANGOLA 3 (1954), pp. 49-56.

23,556 SILVA, A. J. DA. Chronologia Nhaneca. PORT. EM AFR. 10 (1953), pp. 154-166.

23,557 SILVA REGO, A. DA. Acção missionária em Angola na occupação holandesa—1641-48. PORT. EM AFR. 5 (1948), pp. 283-291.

23,558 SOROMENHO, C. Jinga, reine de Ngola et de Matamba. PRESENCE AFR. N.S. 42 (1962), pp. 47-53.

23,559 SOROMENHO, C. Portrait of Queen Jinga. PRESENCE AFR. 42-43 (1962), pp. 44-50.

23,560 TUCKER, J. T. Fifty years in Angola, Portuguese West Africa. INT. REV. MISSIONS 19 (1930), pp. 256-265.

23,561 WHEELER, D. Livingstone and Angola: some new letters, 1854-6. RHODES-LIV. J. 32 (1962), pp. 23-45.

23,562 La Révolution Angolaise. PRESENCE AFR. N.S. 45 (1963), pp. 105-126.

23,563 U.N. debate on Angola. PRESENCE AFR. 42-43 (1962), pp. 85-164.

See also 14791, 18273.

Language. Literature

Language

23,564 ENNIS, E. L. Women's names among the Ovimbundu of Angola. AFR. STUD. 4 (1945), pp. 1-8.

23,565 ESTERMANN, C. Aculturação linguistica no sul de Angola. PORT. EM AFR. 20 (1963), pp. 8-14.

23,566 LEITE, S. Padre Pedro Dias, Autor da Arte da Língua de Angola Apóstolo dos Negros no Brasil. PORT. EM AFR. 4 (1947), pp. 9-12.

23,567 PANCONCELLI-CALZIA, G. Objektive Untersuchungen über die stimmlosen Nasale im Ndonga. AFR. UND UB. 6 (1915-1916), pp. 257-263.

23,568 SILVA, A. J. DA. A fome nos provérbios da língua nhaneca. PORT. EM AFR. 15 (1958), pp. 334-343.

23,569 WESTPHAL, E. O. J. Olunkumbi vocabulary (a pre-lexicographical study). AFR. LANG. STUD. 2 (1961), pp. 49-63.

23,570 Luena. J. AFR. SOC. 11 (1912), pp. 394-400.

See also 14978.

Literature

23,571 ANDRADE, C. L'"Angolanite" de Agostinho Neto et Antonio Jacinto. PRESENCE AFR. N.S. 42 (1962), pp. 76-91.

23,572 ANDRADE, M. DE. Littérature et nationalisme en Angola. PRESENCE AFR. N.S. 41 (1962), pp. 91-99.

23,573 ESTERMANN, C. A mulher e dois filhos. Conto com diversos elementos aculturados. PORT. EM AFR. 21 (1964), pp. 325-337; also in BOL. INST. ANGOLA 17 (1963), pp. 59-73.

23,574 ESTERMANN, C. O sentido da justiça como reflexo de alguns contos colhidos entre os bantos do Sudoeste de Angola. PORT. EM AFR. 19 (1962), pp. 275-286.

23,575 MARTINHO, A. A Cobra protectora e a garantia do poder real sobre a chuva. PORT. EM AFR. 18 (1961), pp. 281-284.

23,576 MITTELBERGER, C. Entre os Cuanhamas: A Fome e a chuva. PORT. EM AFR. 19 (1962), pp. 295-309.

23,577 MORAIS, E. Duas lendas duas civilizações [fiction]. BOL. INST. ANGOLA 2 (1953), pp. 35-36.

23,578 NETO, A. Aspiration. PRESENCE AFR. N.S. 41 (1962), pp. 100-101.

23,579 NETO, A. Three poems [African poem, Friend Mussunda, Kinaxixi]. BO 15 (1964), pp. 38-40.

23,580 OLIVEIRA, M. A. F. DE. L'amour et l'avenir. PRESENCE AFR. N.S. 41 (1962), pp. 101-102.

23,581 SHORE, H. L. Angola wedding [fiction]. BO 11 (1962), pp. 28-35.

23,582 SILVA, P. A. DA. Literatura Africana (conto Nhaneca). PORT. EM AFR. 5 (1948), pp. 271-274.

23,583 TORREND, J. Contes en Chwabo ou Langue de Quelimane avec traduction. ZAOS 2 (1896), pp. 46-50, 244-248.

Law

23,584 ESTERMANN, C. O sentido da justiça como reflexo de alguns contos colhidos entre os Bantos do Sudoeste de Angola. BOL. INST. ANGOLA 15 (1961), pp. 5-18.

23,585 FURTADO, J. P. Breves notas para a história da administração da justiça de Angola. BOL. INST. ANGOLA 17 (1963), pp. 7-36.

Religion

23,586 ALEIXO, M. A. Cristo Redentor em Africa. PORT. EM AFR. 21 (1964), pp. 70-76.

23,587 BAPTISTA, P. A. N. Bodas de Diamente da Missão de Lândana (1873-1948). PORT. EM AFR. 6 (1949), pp. 141-153.

23,588 BATAHLA, F. A Igreja e o Convento dos Carmelitas de Luanda. BOL. INST. ANGOLA 1 (1953), pp. 37-40.

23,589 BRASIO, A. Criação da diocese de Angola e Congo. PORT. EM AFR. 8 (1951), pp. 133-145, 247-253.

23,590 BRASIO, A. A Igreja da Conceição de Luanda. PORT. EM AFR. 4 (1947), pp. 35-46.

23,591 BRASIO, A. As misericórdias de Angola. PORT. EM AFR. 16 (1959), pp. 193-215, 286-299.

23,592 BRASIO, A. Mons. Alves da Cunha. PORT. EM AFR. 4 (1947), pp. 321-331.

23,593 BRASIO, A. Os Padres de Libermann em Angola e Cabo Verde. PORT. EM AFR. 9 (1952), pp. 34-44.

23,594 BRASIO, A. A Padroeira do Império. PORT. EM AFR. 3 (1946), pp. 352-357.

23,595 BRASIO, A. O Patriotismo do Padre Pacheco Monte. PORT. EM AFR. 9 (1952), pp. 287-291.

23,596 CERQUEIRA, I. DE. Missões Católicas em Angola. PORT. EM AFR. 12 (1955), pp. 107-110.

23,597 CHILDS, G. M. The Church in Angola. INT. REV. MISSIONS 47 (1958), pp. 186-192.

23,598 ESTERMANN, C. O cortejo anual do boi sagrado; na terra dos Nhanecas. PORT. EM AFR. 14 (1957), pp. 212-218.

23,599 ESTERMANN, C. O que é um feiticeiro. PORT. EM AFR. 19 (1962), pp. 324-334.

23,600 ESTERMANN, C. A terminologia cristã na Diocese de Nova Lisboa. PORT. EM AFR. 8 (1951), pp. 358-364.

23,601 ESTERMANN, C. Vida e Aventuras de Um Soldado. PORT. EM AFR. 11 (1954), pp. 249-255.

23,602 FRAZAO, S. O velho missionário. PORT. EM AFR. 3 (1946), pp. 155-160.

23,603 GONCAVES, A. L. Pelos frutos conhecereis a árvore... PORT. EM AFR. 19 (1962), pp. 114-117.

23,604 HAMELBERGER, E. A escrita na areia. PORT. EM AFR. 9 (1952), pp. 323-330.

23,605 JACYNTO, F. Trapistas em Angola. PORT. EM AFR. 16 (1959), pp. 300-304.

23,606 LOURENCO, S. Retirada temporária e estabelecimento definitivo dos Padres do Espírito Santo no Humbe. PORT. EM AFR. 12 (1955), pp. 87-92.

23,607 MAIO, P. A. T. Um Ano de Apostolado dos Padres do Espírito Santo. PORT. EM AFR. 7 (1950), pp. 92-98.

23,608 NEIVA, A. T. Angola, sob o signo do protestantismo. PORT. EM AFR. 19 (1962), pp. 133-142.

23,609 NEVES, P. C. As Bodas de Prata do Maiombe. PORT. EM AFR. 4 (1947), pp. 210-213.

23,610 OLIVEIRA, H. DE. Religiões acatólicas em Angola. PORT. EM AFR. 13 (1956), pp. 36-50.

23,611 PIUS XII, Pope. Carta de S. Santidade Pio XII sobre o Apostolado Missionário de Portugal. PORT. EM AFR. 15 (1958), pp. 171-173.

23,612 SILVA, C. P. DA. Missionários para Angola. PORT. EM AFR. 3 (1946), pp. 257-260.

23,613 SILVA, P. A. J. DA. Para a História da Missão da Quiita. PORT. EM AFR. 1 (1944), pp. 169-177, 238-245.

23,614 SILVA REGO, A. DA. Missões e Política. PORT. EM AFR. 13 (1956), pp. 325-335.

23,615 SIMEAO VITORIA. Pioneiros de Angola. PORT. EM AFR. 12 (1955), pp. 229-234, 397-404; 13 (1956), pp. 23-35, 87-100.

23,616 SOUSA, P. A. DE. O Comunismo entre os Pretos de Angola. PORT. EM AFR. 6 (1949), pp. 169-180.

23,617 SOUSA DIAS, G. O Padre Duparquet e os Boeres da Huíla. PORT. EM AFR. 3 (1946), pp. 28-38.

23,618 THISSEN, L. Da vida espiritual e religiosa dos indígenas—Mussuco. PORT. EM AFR. 17 (1960), pp. 169-175.

23,619 THISSEN, L. Uma missão sobre as margens do Médio-Cuango. Mussuco. PORT. EM AFR. 17 (1960), pp. 145-155.

23,620 THISSEN, L. Os povos em contacto com a missão de Mussuco. PORT. EM AFR. 17 (1960), pp. 156-168.

23,621 TROESCHE, J. A Família Indígena no Paganismo e na Conversão. PORT. EM AFR. 11 (1954), pp. 294-302.

23,622 ZORRO, A. M. O Cruzeiro Gago Coutinho e as Missões Católicas. PORT. EM. AFR. 16 (1959), pp. 343-351.

23,623 Um Ano de Apostolado dos Missionários do Espírito Santo. PORT. EM AFR. 3 (1946), pp. 321-335.

23,624 Antologia de Libermann. PORT. EM AFR. 11 (1954), pp. 21-22.

23,625 Um Cónego Indígena. PORT. EM AFR. 4 (1947), pp. 32-34.

23,626 Exortação pastoral do Episcopado de Angola. PORT. EM AFR. 18 (1961), pp. 245-250.

23,627 O P. José Maria Antunes. PORT. EM AFR. 14 (1957), pp. 28-32.

23,628 P. António Nunes Costa. PORT. EM AFR. 5 (1948), pp. 235-236.

23,629 Seminários de Angola. PORT. EM AFR. 8 (1951), pp. 334-347.

23,630 O Sínodo de Luanda. PORT. EM AFR. 7 (1950), pp. 166-170.

See also 15325, 15343, 15654.

Science

23,631 ADRIAN, J. et al. Comparaison entre les poissons séchés de l'Angola et les farines industrielles de poissons: composition globale, acides aminés et vitamines du groupe B, by J. Adrian, R. Jacquot and C. Bertin. BOL. INST. ANGOLA 8 (1956), pp. 115-125.

23,632 ARAUJO, V. DE P. Colmeias para abelhas sem ferrão Meliponini. BOL. INST. ANGOLA 7 (1955), pp. 9-31.

23,633 BRITO TEIXEIRA, J. A accão do Padre Antunes como naturalista botânico. PORT. EM AFR. 14 (1957), pp. 38-47.

23,634 CARDOSO, J. G. A. Acerca da cor da madeira do diospyros mespiliformis: ébano Africano. Estudo histológico. BSEM 132 (1962), pp. 121-135.

23,635 CRAWFORD, J. Consideracões em torno de equus quagga intermedia Taborda Morais. BOL. INST. ANGOLA 15 (1961), pp. 77-79.

23,636 CRUZ, F. Estrelas céu de Angola. BOL. INST. ANGOLA 1 (1953), pp. 5-12.

23,637 FOX, F. D. Some notes on big game in Portuguese Angola, S. W. Africa. J. AFR. SOC. 11 (1912), pp. 430-437.

23,638 FONSECA, F. D. DA and XABREGAS, J. Problemas de nutrição de Angola. Aspectos de Luanda. BOL. INST. ANGOLA 8 (1956), pp. 85-106.

23,639 FRANCA, P. G. DA. Contribuição para o conhecimento do gén. Merllucius no Atlântico Oriental ao sul do Equador. BOL. INST. ANGOLA 11 (1958), pp. 67-104.

23,640 MARTINS, J. A. Prospecção de rochas fos fatadas na região do Lucunga, Norte de Angola. BOL. INST. ANGOLA 16 (1962), pp. 55-67.

23,641 MONTEIRO, A. J. P. Agua de Luanda. BOL. INST. ANGOLA 20 (1964), pp. 63-83.

23,642 MONTENEGRO, M. DA S. Uma Escola Médica em Luanda. BOL. INST. ANGOLA 12 (1959), pp. 5-11.

23,643 MORAIS, A. T. DE. As espécies de Lavandula cultiváveis em Angola. BOL. INST. ANGOLA 8 (1956), pp. 63-64.

23,644 MORAIS, A. T. DE. Uma nova raça nas zebras de Angola. BOL. INST. ANGOLA 9 (1957), pp. 61-71.

23,645 MORAIS, A. T. DE. Porque é notável a Welwitschia mirabilis. BOL. INST. ANGOLA 11 (1958), pp. 53-66.

23,646 MOURA, J. D. DE. Uma história entre Lendas. BOL. INST. ANGOLA 10 (1957), pp. 55-90.

23,647 NUNES, J. A. P. A farinha de peixe na alimentação humana. BOL. INST. ANGOLA 12 (1959), pp. 75-86; 15 (1961), pp. 87-95.

23,648 NUNES, J. A. P. Fome periódica e armazenamento de alimentos. BOL. INST. ANGOLA 16 (1962), pp. 69-86.

23,649 PENA, A. J. Alimentação e diabetes. BOL. INST. ANGOLA 14 (1960), pp. 33-39.

23,650 PENA, A. J. Rações de tribalho. Alimentação africana. Caso de Angola. BOL. INST. ANGOLA 17 (1963), pp. 73-88.

23,651 PIRELLI, M. A fauna de Angola. BOL. INST. ANGOLA 20 (1964), pp. 5-43.

23,652 VALE, A. J. M. DO. As campanhas do navio oceanográfico Baldaque da Silva nos mares de Angola. BOL. INST. ANGOLA 2 (1953), pp. 5-12.

23,653 VIEIRA, A. DA G. Aproveitamento da radiação solar em Angola. BOL. INST. ANGOLA 11 (1958), pp. 127-133.

23,654 XABREGAS, J. As oleaginosas na alimentação. BOL. INST. ANGOLA 2 (1953), pp. 27-34.

23,655 XABREGAS, J. Situação alimentar. BOL. INST. ANGOLA 16 (1962), pp. 35-43.

23,656 Contribuição de Angola para a Relatório da O.M.S. (1961-2) sobre a situação sanitária do Mundo. PORT. EM AFR. 21 (1964), pp. 115-124.

Sociology

23,657 AMARAL, I. DO. Subsídios para o estudo da evolução da população de Luanda. PORT. EM AFR. 19 (1962), pp. 168-184.

23,658 ANDRADE, C. Two expressions of Angolanity. PRESENCE AFR. N.S. 42-43 (1962), pp. 70-84.

23,659 C., J. L'assistance sociale en Angola. ZAIRE 7 (1953), p. 528.

23,660 C., J. L'habitat urbain à Luanda. ZAIRE 8 (1954), p. 644.

23,661 C., J. Situation démographique de l'Angola. ZAIRE 8 (1954), p. 858.

23,662 C., J. L'urbanisation en Angola. ZAIRE 8 (1954), pp. 308-309.

23,663 GONCALVEZ MARQUES, J. M. Poblando los Trópicos. Los colonatos de Angola y Mozambique. ARCH. INST. EST. AFR. 16, no. 60 (1961), pp. 131-145.

23,664 MARQUES, C. A população de Angola. PORT. EM AFR. 1 (1944), pp. 210-214.

23,665 OLIVIERA, M. A. F. DE. Aspectos sociais de Luanda inferidos dos anúncios publicados na sua Imprensa [1851, 1861, 1871]. BOL. INST. ANGOLA 17 (1963), pp. 99-110; 18 (1964), pp. 5-12; 19 (1964), pp. 45-53.

23,666 VALENTA, A. and OLIVIERA, C. Enquadramento profissional dos habitantes da Ilha do Cabo (Luanda). BOL. INST. ANGOLA 21-23 (1965), pp. 69-75.

23,667 Recensement de la ville de Luanda. ZAIRE 5 (1951), pp. 1078-1079.

See also 21227.

MOZAMBIQUE

General

23,668 ALBERTO, M. S. Notas para os anais da Sociedade de Estudos de Moçambique. BSEM 127 (1961), L 3.

23,669 COSTA, S. M. Bibliografia do território de Manica e Sofala (algumas indicações). BSEM 42, no. 1 (1940), pp. 39-46.

23,670 FERREIRA, F. A Sociedade de Estudos e o progresso de Moçambique. BSEM 127 (1961), L 1.

23,671 MOREIRA RATO, J. A estação de biologia marítima da Inhaca. BSEM 112 (1958), pp. 7-18.

23,672 ROMANO, M. P. Proposta acerca de Congressos a realizar em várias localidades de Moçambique. BSEM 127 (1961), L 2.

Agriculture. Fisheries. Forestry. Soil

23,673 ALFARO CARDOSO, J. G. Acerca da desarborização e da arborização em Moçambique. BSEM 127 (1961), I 5.

23,674 ALFARO CARDOSO, J. G. Agricultura e Florestas do Ultramar Português: Economia Agrícola e Florestal Moçambicana. BSEM 102 (1957), pp. 3-42.

23,675 ALFARO CARDOSO, J. G. Agricultura e florestas do ultramar Português. Vol. 1: Noções gerais sobre a agricultura e a indústria florestal Moçambicana. BSEM 70 (1951), pp. 1-109.

23,676 ALFARO CARDOSO, J. G. Considerações sobre a piscicultura. BSEM 127 (1961), I 2.

23,677 ALFARO CARDOSO, J. G. Da necessidade de regulamentar a queimada e estudar cientificamente os seus efeitos. BSEM 126 (1961), H 1.

23,678 ALFARO CARDOSO, J. G. Silvicultura. BSEM 99 (1956), pp. 55-60.

23,679 ALFARO CARDOSO, J. G. and VIEIRA PINTO, H. Da experimentação florestal em Moçambique. BSEM 127 (1961), I 4.

23,680 ALMEIDA, A. A. et al. Aspectos da utilização e conservação do solo nas zonas algodoeiras de Moçambique. BSEM 126 (1961), H 4.

23,681 BARRADAS, L. A. O problema Hidro agrícola do Infulene. BSEM 60 (1949), pp. 41-45.

23,682 BARRADAS, L. A. Precocidade do arroz. BSEM 49, no. i (1946), pp. 107-112.

23,683 BENTO RIPADO, M. F. B. Da necessidade da educação na conservação em Moçambique. BSEM 126 (1961), H 2.

23,684 CARVALHO, M. DE. Possibilidade de cultivo de algodões do tipo egípcio em Moçambique. BSEM 111 (1958), pp. 103-107.

23,685 CARVALHO, M. DE. Resultados dos ensaios comparativos de Variedades (1949/50 a 1951/52). BSEM 85 (Supplement) (1954), pp. 1-87.

23,686 CARVALHO, M. DE and SILVA BARBOSA, A. J. DA. Resultados dos ensaios de insecticidas realizados pelo C.I.C.A. durante as campanhas 1949/50, 1950/51, 1951/52, e 1952/53. BSEM 82 (1953), pp. 217-254; includes English summary.

23,687 CASTRO, S. DE. O funcionamento de uma Escola Agrícola no Larde de carácter particular. BSEM 80 (1953), pp. 59-75.

23,688 COSTA, J. J. Native agriculture in Mozambique after the Second World War. CIVILISATIONS 6 (1956), pp. 619-624.

23,689 COSTA, S. M. O fomento da piscicultura em Moçambique. BSEM 127 (1961), I 3.

23,690 ESTEVES, J. D. Necessidade e urgência da simplificação e actualização da Estatística Agrícola. BSEM 124 (1960), pp. 1-4.

23,691 ESTEVES, J. D. Uma solução para o ensino Médio-Agricola em Moçambique. BSEM 124 (1960), pp. 1-5.

23,692 ESTEVES, J. M. Sementes de qualidade. BSEM 124 (1960), pp. 1-4.

23,693 FALCAO DE CAMPOS, A. C. G. Algumas notas sobre a Bacteriose dos Algodoeiros em Moçambique. BSEM 124 (1960), pp. 1-18.

23,694 FALCAO DE CAMPOS, A. C. G. Nota preliminar sobre alguns solos de Mazua (Memba). BSEM 124 (1960), pp. 1-7.

23,695 FERINHO, H. Cooperativismo: a mais sólida base da promoção rural Africana. BSEM 144-145 (1965), pp. 5-87.

23,696 FERRINHO, H. M. Algumas constantes físicas dos solos das estações e campos experimentais do CICA. BSEM 124 (1960), pp. 1-8.

23,697 FIGUEIREDO GOMES E SOUSA, A. DE. Elementos para a organização dos Serviços Agrícolas de Moçambique. BSEM 6 (1932), pp. 3-25.

23,698 FIGUEIREDO GOMES E SOUSA, A. DE. Elementos para uma Organização Florestal de Mozambique. Serviço de Aguas e Florestas. BSEM 110 (1958), pp. 43-95.

23,699 FIGUEIREDO GOMES E SOUSA, A. DE. A propósito da criação do ensino agrícola em Moçambique. BSEM 78 (1953), pp. 89-123.

23,700 FIGUEIREDO GOMES E SOUSA, A. DE. A silvicultura como forma de previdência social. BSEM 73 (1952), pp. 25-34.

23,701 FIGUEIREDO GOMES E SOUSA, A. DE. Silvicultura e previdência social. BSEM 87 (1954), pp. 125-158.

23,702 GOUVEIA, D. H. G. Nota preliminar sobre os solos ferralíticos húmicos do Gurúe (Vila Junqueiro). BSEM 124 (1960), pp. 1-10.

23,703 GOUVEIA, D. H. G. and AZEVEDO, A. L. DE. Carta Provisória dos Solos de Moçambique (Nova interpretação). BSEM 124 (1960), pp. 1-5.

23,704 GOUVEIA, D. H. G. and GOUVEIA, J. Mais algumas considerações sobre os solos citizentos do Guijá. BSEM 124 (1960), pp. 1-5.

23,705 GOUVEIA, D. H. G. and GOUVEIA, J. Notas sobre alguns solos do Sul do Save. BSEM 124 (1960), pp. 1-12.

23,706 GOUVEIA, D. H. G. et al. Influência de adubações no algodoeiro (ensaios em vasos). BSEM 124 (1960), pp. 1-36.

23,707 GOUVEIA, D. H. G. et al. O método de Jenny para apreciação da fertilidade do solo. Alguns dados concretos. BSEM 124 (1960), pp. 1-35.

23,708 GOUVEIA, D. H. G. et al. O método microbiológico do Aspergillus Niger de apreciação do teor de potássio assimilável nos solos. Alguns casos concretos. BSEM 124 (1960), pp. 1-13.

23,709 GRILO, F. M. Do estabelecimento de um pôsto de experimentação agrícola do coqueiro em Moçambique. BSEM 20 (1934), pp. 279-304.

23,710 LYNE, R. N. The agriculture of Mozambique Province, Portuguese East Africa. BULL. IMP. INST. 11 (1913), pp. 102-110.

23,711 MATOS, C. DE. Parecer sôbre o aproveitamento agropecuário dos terrenos irrigáveis dos vales dos rios Limpopo e Umbeluzi. BSEM 25 (1935), pp. 47-59.

23,712 MORAIS, E. T. DE. Moçambique e o seu problema de irrigação. BSEM 5 (1932), pp. 59-72.

23,713 MOREIRA RATO, J. M. O problema das pescas marítimas na Província de Moçambique. BSEM 128 (1961), pp. 99-126.

23,714 OSORIO, C. DO A. Pontos de vista sôbre colonização—a propósito da irrigação do Vale do Limpopo. BSEM 18 (1934), pp. 193-204.

23,715 PAISANA, F. C. Algumas considerações sobre o búfalo doméstico, com vista à sua futura introdução em Moçambique. BSEM 127 (1961), J 6.

23,716 PEREIRA DOS SANTOS, M. P. Correlação entre o equivante de humanide de campo e a granulometria dos solos. BSEM 75 (1952), pp. 85-100; includes English summary.

23,717 ROSINHA, A. J. Inquérito à evolução sofrida durante um período de 10 anos, pelos núcleos de gado bovino a sul do rio Limpopo. BSEM 121 (1960), pp. 141-194.

23,718 SALVADOR, A. R. N. Contribuição para o estudo da qualidade das mandiocas em ensaio no posto agrícola da Mahalamba. BSEM 137 (1963), pp. 135-149.

23,719 SANTARENO PIGNATELLI, M. J. S. DE. Solos expansivos. BSEM 115 (1959), pp. 113-177; includes Engish summary.

23,720 SANTOS, J. G. M. A agricultura indígena e o comércio dos seus produtos. BSEM 11 (1933), pp. 15-30.

23,721 SANTOS DIAS, J. A. T. Breve sugestão para o incremento da suinicultura nas zonas glossinadas de Moçambique. BSEM 143 (1965), pp. 183-189.

23,722 SANTOS DIAS, J. A. T. O fomento pecuário de Moçambique perante o problema dos transportes. BSEM 127 (1961), J 5.

23,723 SANTOS DIAS, J. A. T. De necessidade e urgência em se definirem em Moçambique novas áreas pecuárias com vista à intensificação da criação animal. BSEM 127 (1961), J 4.

23,724 SILVA, A. M. DA. Evolução agrícola em Moçambique (subsídio para o conhecimento das culturas introduzidas). BSEM 133 (1962), pp. 75-117.

23,725 SILVA, A. M. DA. Formação profissional agrícola. BSEM 124 (1960), pp. 1-15.

23,726 SILVA, A. M. DA. Panorâmicas agrarias de Moçambique. BSEM 124 (1960), pp. 1-15.

23,727 SILVA, J. M. DA. Panorâmica da nossa pecuária. Os grandes núcleos de bovinos. BSEM 142 (1965), pp. 33-115.

23,728 SILVA, M. DA. A Africa e o desenvolvimento da agricultura em Moçambique. BSEM 99 (1956), pp. 17-50.

23,729 SILVA, R. L. DA. O chá e o povoamento de Moçambique. BSEM 124 (1960), pp. 1-6.

23,730 SILVEIRA DA COSTA, C. M. O papel da silvicultura e da piscicultura nas zonas algodoeiras [de Moçambique]. BSEM 127 (1961), I 1.

23,731 SIMAO, J. Um problema de correlação simples. BSEM 50, no. i (1946), pp. 201-212.

23,732 SOUSA MELO, J. M. Ainda a propósito das datas de sementeira na cultura do algodão. BSEM 124 (1960), pp. 1-12.

23,733 SOUSA MELO, J. M. Contribuição para o estudo das chuvas de algumas estações experimentais do C.I.C.A. BSEM 124 (1960), pp. 1-4.

23,734 TORRES, J. A agricultura no distrito de Moçambique. BSEM 5 (1932), pp. 73-77.

23,735 VIANA, P. A. F. Sobre a ocupação agrícola e florestal da Colónia de Moçambique. BSEM 25 (1935), pp. 1-12.

Anthropology

23,736 ALBERTO, M. S. Contribuição para o estudo antropológico dos Tongas do Sul. BSEM 92 (1955), pp. 165-171.

23,737 ALBERTO, M. S. A Ilha da Inhaca. BSEM 112 (1958), pp. 21-26.

23,738 ALBERTO, M. S. A Ilha da Inhaca e o seu povoamento humano. BSEM 112 (1958), pp. 145-155.

23,739 ALBERTO, M. S. A mulher indígena moçambicana perante a estrutura familiar da tribo. BSEM 83 (1954), pp. 91-104.

23,740 ALBERTO, M. S. Mutilações étnicas entre os negros de Moçambique. BSEM 90 (1955), pp. 35-44.

23,741 ALBERTO, M. S. and DIONISIO BARRETO, A. Contribuição para o estudo sobre as variações dos índices de robustez, vitalidade e corpulência dos soldados negros de Moçambique. BSEM 74 (1952), pp. 1-49.

23,742 BERTHOUD, H. Ein Thonga-Märchen. AFR. UND UB. 22 (1931-1932), pp. 114-120.

23,743 BERTHOUD, H. Weitere Thonga-Märchen. AFR. UND UB. 21 (1920-1921), pp. 54-74, 122-158, 310-319.

23,744 CAMARA REIS, D. DA. Os macuas de Mogovolas. BSEM 131 (1962), pp. 9-37.

23,745 CASTRO, S. DE. Os Lómuès do Larde. Elementos para uma monografia histórico-etnográfica. BSEM 76 (1952), pp. 41-82.

23,746 DUFF, P. F. Notas sôbre a Religião dos Vankhumbi. PORT. EM AFR. 1 (1944), pp. 162-168.

23,747 EARTHY, E. D. An African tribe in transition from paganism to Christianity. INT. REV. MISSIONS 22 (1933), pp. 367-376.

23,748 EARTHY, E. D. An analysis of folktales of the Lenge, Portuguese East Africa. ETHNOS 18 (1953), pp. 73-85.

23,749 EARTHY, E. D. The customs of Gazaland women in relation to the African Church. INT. REV. MISSIONS 15 (1926), pp. 662-674.

23,750 EARTHY, E. D. Note on the "Totemism" of the Vandau. BANTU STUD. 5 (1931), pp. 77-79.

23,751 EARTHY, E. D. Notes on some agricultural rites practised by the Valenge and Vachopi (Portuguese East Africa). BANTU STUD. 2 (1923), pp. 193-197, 265-267.

23,752 EARTHY, E. D. A probable creation—and flood—myth in Portuguese East Africa. NUMEN 4 (1957), pp. 232-234.

23,753 EARTHY, E. D. A specimen of the folklore of Gazaland. BANTU STUD. 6 (1932), pp. 255-266.

23,754 EARTHY, E. D. Sundry notes on the Vandau of Sofala, P.E.A. BANTU STUD. 4 (1930), pp. 95-107.

23,755 EARTHY, E. D. The Vandau of Sofala. AFRICA 4 (1931), pp. 222-229.

23,756 EARTHY, E. D. A Vandau ordeal of olden times. BANTU STUD. 9 (1935), pp. 159-161.

23,757 FATTON, A. L'étiquette chez les Rongas. GENEVE-AFR. 1 (1962), pp. 53-77; English summary, p. 78.

23,758 FERREIRA, A. J. DE. Some notes on the Thonga culture. ZAIRE 9 (1955), pp. 3-23.

23,759 GLUCKMANN, M. Mortuary customs and the belief in survival after death among the south-eastern Bantu. BANTU STUD. 11 (1937), pp. 117-136.

23,760 GRILO, V. H. V. Etnologia da Inhaca. BSEM 112 (1958), pp. 161-164.

23,761 GRILO, V. H. V. Os "Zimbawes," "Mipashelo" e a civilização Hindu. BSEM 111 (1958), pp. 185-190.

23,762 JUNOD, H. P. Les cas de possession et l'exorcisme chez les Vandau. AFRICA 7 (1934), pp. 270-299.

23,763 JUNOD, H. P. Coutumes diverses des Vandau de l'Afrique Orientale Portugaise. Mariage. Divination. Coutumes et tabous de chasse. AFRICA 10 (1937), pp. 159-175.

23,764 JUNOD, H. P. Notes on the ethnological situation in Portuguese East Africa on the south of the Zambesi. BANTU STUD. 10 (1936), pp. 293-311.

23,765 JUNOD, H. P. Spécimens du folklore de la tribu des Batchopi. AFRICA 6 (1933), pp. 90-95.

23,766 LOBATO, A. S. Monografia etnográfica original sobre o Povo Ajaua. BSEM 63, no. i (1949), pp. 7-17.

23,767 LOPES, M. M. Usages and customs of the natives of Sena. J. AFR. SOC. 6 (1907), pp. 350-366.

23,768 MacALPINE, A. G. Tonga religious beliefs and customs. J. AFR. SOC. 6 (1907), pp. 375-384.

23,769 MACHADO, P. Notas de Etnografia de Moçambique. PORT. EM AFR. 16 (1959), pp. 246-248.

23,770 MARTINS, A. R. Monografia sobre os usos e costumes dos Senas. BSEM 123 (1960), pp. 13-33.

23,771 MARWICK, M. G. An ethnographic classic brought to light. AFRICA 34 (1964), pp. 46-56.

23,772 NUNES, J. Apontamentos sôbre a tribu dos ba-thonga. BSEM 3 (1932), pp. 25-36.

23,773 NUNES, J. Apontamentos sôbre os usos e costumes indígenas. BSEM 27 (1935), pp. 145-155.

23,774 OLIVEIRA, O. R. DE. A fundição de ferro nativo na Africa Austral. Algumas jazidas em Manica e Sofala. BSEM 138 (1964), pp. 173-191.

23,775 RAWSON, H. E. The life of a South African tribe. J. AFR. SOC. 13 (1913), pp. 1-13.

23,776 REIS, C. M. S. A iniciação Maconde. BSEM 94-95, no. i (1955), pp. 169-204.

23,777 RITA-FERREIRA, A. Caracterização e agrupamento étnico dos indígenas de Moçambique. BSEM 111 (1958), pp. 173-183.

23,778 RITA-FERREIRA, A. Documentação etnológica de Moçambique. BSEM 117 (1959), pp. 117-132.

23,779 RITA-FERREIRA, A. Mais algumas notas sobre os Zimbas (Azimba). BSEM 98 (1956), pp. 37-48.

23,780 RITA-FERREIRA, A. Nota sobre o conceito de "Tribo" em Moçambique. BSEM 108 (1958), pp. 49-68.

23,781 RITA-FERREIRA, A. Notas adicionais sobre os Zimbas (Azimba). BSEM 93 (1955), pp. 53-72; 97 (1956), pp. 87-106.

23,782 RITA-FERREIRA, A. Os "Azimba" (Monografia Etnográfica). BSEM 84 (1954), pp. 45-140; 85 (1954), pp. 5-26.

23,783 ROCHA BRITO, A. DE. O rito da circuncisão entre os indígenas. BSEM 4 (1932), pp. 23-30.

23,784 SANTOS PEIXE, J. DOS. Ligeiros apontamentos sobre a curandice espírita entre o povo Ba-tswa. BSEM 130 (1962), pp. 5-24.

23,785 SEQUEIRA, A. DE MELO. O totemismo nas tribus do distrito de Inhambane. BSEM 23 (1934), pp. 427-439; 24 (1934), pp. 459-472.

23,786 WIESCHHOFF, H. A. Consecration of the grain among the Barwe of Moçambique. ETHNOS 3 (1938), pp. 81-83.

23,787 L'Afrique folklorique: Nouachigamba, la jolie fille (un conte du folklore tsonga). GENEVE-AFR. 1 (1962), pp. 112-114.

23,788 L'Afrique folklorique: proverbes Tsonga. GENEVE-AFR. 1 (1962), pp. 206-214; 3 (1964), pp. 90-93.

See also 17785, 19987, 20908, 20924, 20933, 21858.

Art

23,789 ALBERTO, M. S. A pré-história de Moçambique. BSEM 68 (1951), pp. 115-152.

23,790 ALBERTO, M. S. Sequência da evolução da indústria da Pedra em Moçambique a Sul do Save. BSEM 111 (1958), pp. 149-158.

23,791 BARRADAS, L. A. Age of the last transgression on the South of Mozambique coast. PROC. PAN-AFR. CONGR. PRE-HIST. 5 (1965), pp. 147-148.

23,792 BARRADAS, L. A. As formações quaternárias do sul do save e as suas relações com a pré-história. BSEM 47 (1945), pp. 1-33.

23,793 BARRADAS, L. A. Cronologia das formações quaternárias do sul de Moçambique. BSEM 60 (1949), pp. 47-63.

23,794 BARRADAS, L. A. A chronology of the Quaternary in Southern Moçambique. PROC. PAN-AFR. CONGR. PRE-HIST. 1 (1947), pp. 177-187.

23,795 BARRADAS, L. A. Contribution a l'étude de la chronologie quaternaire dans le Sud du Mozambique. PROC. PAN-AFR. CONGR. PRE-HIST. 2 (1952), pp. 247-249.

23,796 BARRADAS, L. A. Uma estação paleolítica em Magude. BSEM 45 (1942), pp. 83-101.

23,797 BARRADAS, L. A. Panorama da pré-história de Moçambique. BSEM 57-58 (1948), pp. 77-96.

23,798 BARRADAS, L. A. Quaternary formations in southern Mozambique. PROC. PAN-AFR. CONGR. PRE-HIST. 1 (1947), pp. 70-73.

23,799 BLANC DE PORTUGAL, J. Nota sobre a simbólica dum tipo de escultura indígena dos arredores de Lourenço Marques. BSEM 125 (1960), E 3.

23,800 BORGES, A. Estação pre-histórica de Mangulane. BSEM 46, no. i (1943-1944), pp. 39-43.

23,801 CARVALHA, P. DA. Rock paintings at Mount Chinhamapere, Serra Vumba, Macequece. PROC. PAN-AFR. CONGR. PRE-HIST. 1 (1947), pp. 229-232.

23,802 CASTRO, S. DE. Pinturas rupestres do Niassa. BSEM 98 (1956), pp. 29-36.

23,803 FERREIRINHA, F. A estatuária dos Macondes. BSEM 63, no. 1 (1949), pp. 19-33.

23,804 FIGUEIREDO GOMES E SOUSA, A. DE. Esbôço de uma vila-parque para Maniamba. BSEM 25 (1935), pp. 61-69.

23,805 FREITAS, A. J. DE. Notas sôbre a construção de Taipa. BSEM 8 (1933), pp. 23-25.

23,806 GRANGER, J. Construções de Taipa. BSEM 7 (1933), pp. 39-44.

23,807 JORGE, JR., T. As aptidões musicais dos indígenas de Moçambique. BSEM 17 (1934), pp. 163-184.

23,808 JUNOD, H. P. The mbila or native piano of the Tshopi tribe. BANTU STUD. 3 (1927), pp. 275-285.

23,809 KUBIK, G. Discovery of a trough xylophone in northern Mozambique. AFR. MUSIC, 1963, pp. 11-14.

23,810 KUBIK, G. Recording and studying music in northern Mozambique. AFR. MUSIC, 1964, pp. 77-100.

23,811 M., E. A. Cantos guerreiros indígenas. BSEM 6 (1932), pp. 43-46.

23,812 MOUTINHO, A. DE S. Colonização indígena—a provaçãogranja modêlo do Nhangau. BSEM 42, no. i (1940), pp. 47-68.

23,813 NUNES, J. Observações sôbre a construção de Taipa. BSEM 12 (1933), pp. 11-14.

23,814 OLIVIERA, O. R. DE. Breve notícia sobre a arqueologia de Manica e Sofala. BSEM 135 (1963), pp. 53-57.

23,815 OLIVIERA, O. R. DE. A cerâmica changa. BSEM 134 (1963), pp. 31-35.

23,816 OLIVIERA, O. R. DE. Notice sommaire sur l'archéologie du Manica et du Sofala (Mozambique). ACTA GEOGRAPHICA 48 (1963), pp. 2-3.

23,817 OLIVIERA, O. R. DE. Pinturas rupestres do contraforte da serra Vumba: Monte chinhamapere (Vila de Manica). BSEM 136 (1963), pp. 21-37.

23,818 RODRIGUES DE CAMPOS, O. A Arte Negra de Moçambique. PORT. EM AFR. 13 (1956), pp. 337-356.

23,819 SANTOS, J. G. M. Fortaleza de S. Sebastião de Moçambique. Extraído duma monografia feita pelo Tenente do D.S.M., Sr. Francisco Maria Branco. BSEM 6 (1932), pp. 39-42.

23,820 SANTOS-JUNIOR. Les peintures rupestres du Mozambique. PROC. PAN-AFR. CONGR. PRE-HIST. 2 (1952), pp. 747-758.

23,821 TRACEY, H. Bachopi ballets. NADA 21 (1944), pp. 6-18.

See also 12908, 20198.

Biography

23,822

23,823 MOREIRA RATO, J. In memoriam: Almirante Carlos Viegas Gago Coutinho. BSEM 114 (1959), pp. v-viii.

See also 14344.

Economics

23,824 ALFARO CARDOSO, J. G. Considerações sôbre o comércio e a produção de madeira na Colónia de Moçambique. BSEM 5 (1932), pp. 91-109.

23,825 ALFARO CARDOSO, J. G. Piscicultura. BSEM 99 (1956), pp. 51-54.

23,826 BARRADAS, L. A. A cultura do arroz na economia de Moçambique. BSEM 51, no. i (1946), pp. 269-288.

23,827 BORGES, A. Minerais úteis da Colónia de Moçambique. BSEM 31 (1936), pp. 141-146.

23,828 BOSAZZA, V. L. O problema das sondagems em Moçambique. BSEM 97 (1956), pp. 31-46.

23,829 CARDOSO, J. A crise da agricultura na Colónia de Moçambique. BSEM 5 (1932), pp. 9-36.

23,830 CARDOSO, J. Memória da Associação do Fomento Agricola da Provincia de Moçambique apresentada na Conferência Comercial de Lourenço Marques de 24 de Agosto de 1932. BSEM 5 (1932), pp. 37-48.

23,831 CARDOSO, J. Moeda, intercâmbio e colonização. BSEM 5 (1932), pp. 49-57.

23,832 COOPER, L. O. Pioneering on the Beira railway. CONTEMP. REV. 78 (1900), pp. 509-517.

23,833 CORREIA, R. Notas para o estudo da embalagem. BSEM 99 (1956), pp. 115-124.

23,834 FALCAO, A. F. A. Vale do Zambeze em Moçambique: cálculo do produto Interno Bruto. BSEM 137 (1963), pp. 67-111.

23,835 FALCAO, A. M. J. F. DE S. A criança e o problema do interesse. BSEM 130 (1962), pp. 69-82.

23,836 FERREIRA, A. L. and FERREIRA, V. D. Navegação entre Moçambique e os portos da Europa via Suez. BSEM 125 (1960), C 1.

23,837 FERREIRA DA SILVA, J. A crise da habitação Colonia de Moçambique. BSEM 65 (1950), pp. 33-55.

23,838 FERREIRA MENDES, M. J. Estradas económicas. BSEM 104-105 (1957), pp. 3-278; 107 (1957), pp. 3-181; 113 (1958), pp. 3-289.

23,839 FERREIRA MENDES, M. J. Para uma política de transportes em Moçambique. BSEM 126 (1961), F 8.

23,840 FIGUEIREDO GOMES E SOUSA, A. DE. Elementos para uma organização florestal em Moçambique. BSEM 94-95, no. i (1955), pp. 117-167.

23,841 FIGUEIREDO GOMES E SOUSA, A. DE. Elementos para uma organização florestal de Moçambique: fundo de silvicultura. BSEM 97 (1956), pp. 3-30.

23,842 FIGUEIREDO GOMES E SOUSA, A. DE. Elementos para uma Organização Florestal de Moçambique: rejime florestal. BSEM 108 (1958), pp. 23-47.

23,843 FIGUEIREDO GOMES E SOUSA, A. DE. Os métodos de colonização e a crise de trabalho. BSEM 14 (1934), pp. 37-52.

23,844 FIGUEIREDO GOMES E SOUSA, A. DE. Recolonização do distrito de Inhambane. BSEM 31 (1936), pp. 171-191; 32 (1936), pp. 237-292.

23,845 FONSECA, V. F. DA. Cooperativas locais de agricultores. BSEM 125 (1960), C 5.

23,846 FREITAS, A. J. DE. Algumas notas sobre jazigos minerais e trabalhos mineiros nos Territórios de Manica e Sofala e no Distrito de Tete. BSEM 2 (1932), pp. 27-41; 3 (1932), pp. 57-72.

23,847 FREITAS, A. J. DE. Desenvolvimento eoonómico de Moçambique. BSEM 27 (1935), pp. 189-193.

23,848 FREITAS, A. J. DE. A indústria do alcool na colónia. BSEM 1 (1931), pp. 13-29.

23,849 FREITAS, A. J. DE. Perspectivas de desenvolvimento de Moçambique. BSEM 125 (1960), C 4.

23,850 FREITAS, A. J. DE. Sôbre o desenvolvimento industrial da Colónia promovido pelos próprios colonos. BSEM 17 (1934), pp. 147-161.

23,851 GRANGER, J. A crise de Moçambique. BSEM 2 (1932), pp. 11-21.

23,852 GUSMAO, J. DE M. F. DE. Pelos tabacos de Moçambique. BSEM 5 (1932), pp. 141-147.

23,853 HARRIS, M. Labour emigration among the Moçambique Thonga: a reply to Sr. Rita-Ferreira. AFRICA 30 (1960), pp. 243-245.

23,854 HARRIS, M. Labour emigration among the Moçambique Thonga: cultural and political factors. AFRICA 29 (1959), pp. 50-65.

23,855 LEMOS E BRITO, J. E. DE and ALMEIDA VALENT, C. A. DE. Intervenção do Laboratório Movel n.º 2 na Construção de Estradas no distrito de Manica e Sofala. Estabilização Mecânica. BSEM 114 (1959), pp. 29-44.

23,856 LISBOA, P. O futuro profissional do natural de Moçambique. BSEM 91 (1955), pp. 175-211.

23,857 MARTINHO, J. P. A pecuária de Moçambique: necessidade de fomentar a sua produção. BSEM 99 (1956), pp. 61-93.

23,858 MOREIRA RATO, J. M. Sistemas de querenagem de embarcações: o problema em Moçambique. BSEM 132 (1962), pp. 145-161.

23,859 NEVES, A. As possibilidades da indústria pecuária na Colónia. BSEM 5 (1932), pp. 111-117.

23,860 NUNES, J. Soluções económicas. BSEM 4 (1932), pp. 9-17; 6 (1932), pp. 27-34.

23,861 OSORIO, C. DO A. Economia corporativa e colonização. BSEM 31 (1936), pp. 147-154.

23,862 PEREIRA DOS SANTOS, M. P. Alguns aspectos técnicos do problema de estradas de Moçambique. BSEM 75 (1952), pp. 25-41; includes English summary.

23,863 PEREIRA DOS SANTOS, M. P. Moçambique: síntese económica. BSEM 100 (1956), pp. 101-116.

23,864 PEREIRA DOS SANTOS, M. P. Progressos no projecto e construção de estradas em solo-cimento. BSEM 130 (1962), pp. 153-167.

23,865 PEREIRA DOS SANTOS, M. P. Tendências actuais da economia de Moçambique. BSEM 78 (1953), pp. 125-165.

23,866 PEREIRA DOS SANTOS, M. P. et al. Estradas de baixo custo. BSEM 120 (1960), pp. 5-43.

23,867 PINTO, A. DA S. Questões gerais sôbre o problema mineiro. BSEM 31 (1936), pp. 193-202; 32 (1936), pp. 331-338.

23,868 REBELO, D. J. S. O chá na economia de Mocambique (um estudo económico). BSEM 137 (1963), pp. 43-64; includes English summary.

23,869 REBELO, D. J. S. Moçambique e a exploração mundial da pesca e do comércio da lagosta (um estudo económico). BSEM 136 (1963), pp. 41-162.

23,870 REBELO, D. J. S. Subsídios para o estudo da exploração commercial de camarão na Província de Moçambique. BSEM 125 (1960), C 3.

23,871 REIS, J. P. DOS. Problemas da economia da estrada em Moçambique. BSEM 119 (1959), pp. 7-14.

23,872 RIBEIRO, C. Coqueiros. BSEM 5 (1932), pp. 127-133.

23,873 RIBEIRO, C. Sisal. BSEM 5 (1932), pp. 119-125.

23,874 RITA-FERREIRA, A. Labour emigration among the Moçambique Thonga: comments on a study by Marvin Harris. AFRICA 30 (1960), pp. 141-151.

23,875 RITA-FERREIRA, A. Labour emigration among the Moçambique Thonga: comments on Marvin Harris's reply. AFRICA 31 (1961), pp. 75-77.

23,876 ROMANO, E. P. Contribuição para o estudo do papel da economia dos caminhos de ferro na economia de Moçambique. BSEM 136 (1963), pp. 163-195.

23,877 ROMANO, M. P. Aproveitamento da energia do Rio dos Elefantes. BSEM 94-95, no. i (1955), pp. 45-48.

23,878 ROMANO, M. P. Bacias experimentais. BSEM 131 (1962), pp. 173-174.

23,879 ROMANO, M. P. Breves considerações acerca das possibilidades da Inhaca. BSEM 144-145 (1965), pp. 161-171.

23,880 ROMANO, M. P. Considerações a propósito da cultura do algodão, em Moçambique, relacionada com a hidrologia. BSEM 103 (1957), pp. 3-21.

23,881 ROMANO, M. P. Economia humanínistica: caso de Moçambique. BSEM 134 (1963), pp. 5-29.

23,882 ROMANO, M. P. Plano de estradas ou plano de transportes? BSEM 116 (1959), pp. 99-120.

23,883 ROMANO, M. P. Problemas do desenvolvimento do Niassa. BSEM 137 (1963), pp. 5-41.

23,884 ROQUE, F. C. O custo da produção do milho nas circunscrições de Chimoio de Manica. BSEM 69 (1951), pp. 19-35.

23,885 SANTARENO PIGNATELLI, M. J. S. DE. Il plano de fomento Português (Moçambique). BSEM 130 (1962), pp. 35-53.

23,886 SANTARENO PIGNATELLI, M. J. S. DE. Problemas de estradas em Moçambique. BSEM 100 (1956), pp. 3-21.

23,887 SEQUEIRA, A. DE MELO. Da instrução ao indígena e da política do imposto nas suas relações com a presente erise. BSEM 14 (1934), pp. 61-69.

23,888 SHEPHERD, W. C. A. Recruiting in Portuguese East Africa of natives for the mines. J. AFR. SOC. 33 (1934), pp. 253-260.

23,889 SHIRLEY, G. Colónias: sua colonização e exploração económica. BSEM 30 (1936), pp. 99-104.

23,890 SILVA, M. D. DA. Alguns aspectos do panorama económicosocial da cultura de trigo em Moçambique. BSEM 131 (1962), pp. 41-46.

23,891 SILVA PAES, A. R. C. O transporte aéreo em Moçambique. BSEM 138 (1964), pp. 17-48.

23,892 TORRES, J. O comercio no distrito de Moçambique. BSEM 5 (1932), pp. 79-82.

23,893 VASSE, G. The Mozambique Company's territory. J. AFR. SOC. 6 (1907), pp. 259-268, 385-389.

23,894 VIEIRA, C. DE M. As matérias primas de Moçambique no mercado da Metrópole: legislação algodoeira e sua influência sôbre a cultura. BSEM 5 (1932), pp. 83-90.

See also 12714, 21763.

Education

23,895 ALVES, C. O ensino da lingua portuguesa aos indígenas nas unidades militares da Colónia. BSEM 6 (1932), pp. 35-38.

23,896 AUGUSTO, A. Instrução. BSEM 4 (1932), pp. 19-21.

23,897 CABRAL, A. Sobre instrução aos indígenas. BSEM 22 (1934), pp. 395-402.

23,898 FIGUEIREDO, C. Educação fisica na criança. BSEM 7 (1933), pp. 33-37.

23,899 GRANGER, J. Valorização do capital humano da Colónia pelo ensino técnico. BSEM 1 (1931), pp. 31-33.

23,900 ROMANO, M. P. O ensino médio em Moçambique. BSEM 106 (1957), pp. 191-194.

23,901 SOUSA SOBRINHO, J. L. DE. Da escola à Oficina (subsídio para o estabelecimento dum servico de orientação profissional em Moçambique). BSEM 100 (1956), pp. 31-44.

23,902 TENENTE, B. Uma escola de recrutas indígenas no distrito do Niassa. BSEM 2 (1932), pp. 23-25.

Geography

23,903 ALBUQUERQUE, M. DE. Mais preciosa que as coisas paras. BSEM 120 (1960), pp. 129-154.

23,904 ALFARO CARDOSO, J. G. A barra do Limpopo. BSEM 7 (1933), pp. 21-31.

23,905 ALFARO CARDOSO, J. G. Fixação de dunas em Moçambique. BSEM 57-58 (1948), pp. 137-155.

23,906 ALFARO CARDOSO, J. G. Fixação de dunas na Ilha da Inhaca. BSEM 112 (1958), pp. 155-157.

23,907 ALFARO CARDOSO, J. G. Madeiras de Moçambique. BSEM 67, no. i (1950), pp. 43-58.

23,908 AXELSON, E. Descrição da costa de Moçambique por João de Lisboa. BSEM 57-58 (1948), pp. 31-41.

23,909 AZEVEDO, A. L. and GOUVEIA, D. H. G. Directrizes adoptadas na cartografia dos solos da provincia do Niassa. Um caso concreto. BSEM 57-58 (1948), pp. 129-135.

23,910 AZEVEDO, A. L. and GOUVEIA, D. H. G. Estudo preliminar dos solos da Península de Ferrão Veloso. BSEM 60 (1949), pp. 1-28.

23,911 BALSAN, F. La route de l'or du Matabeleland. BSEM 135 (1963), pp. 99-109.

23,912 BARAHONA FERNANDES, J. A. A hidrografia em Moçambique. BSEM 120 (1960), pp. 157-171.

23,913 BARRADAS, L. A. Ciclos transgressivos na Africa Meridional durante o Quaternário. BSEM 111 (1958), pp. 35-47.

23,914 BARRADAS, L. A. Comentário ao colóquio do Sr. Eng. Manuel Romano, sobre o aproveitamento integral dos recursos hidráulicos do Sul de Moçambique. BSEM 87 (1954), pp. 173-183; 90 (1955), pp. 137-143.

23,915 BARRADAS, L. A. Complexos geológico-arqueológicos do Quaternário no Sul de Moçambique. BSEM 90 (1955), pp. 5-22.

23,916 BARRADAS, L. A. Flutuações climáticas e eustáticas no Sul de Moçambique durante o Quaternário. BSEM 90 (1955), pp. 69-79.

23,917 BARRADAS, L. A. O aproveitamento do Limpopo. BSEM 126 (1961), F 2.

23,918 BARRADAS, L. A. O Quaternário do Antigo Lago Lunho e da Margem Portuguesa do Lago Niassa. BSEM 131 (1962), pp. 73-121.

23,919 BARRADAS, L. A. Origem dos solos quaternários do sul de Moçambique. BSEM 55, no. i (1947), pp. 197-216.

23,920 BETTENCOURT, R. J. J. "Curvas das chuvas de Lourenço Marques": aplicação au cáculo de colectores. BSEM 83 (1954), pp. 19-38.

23,921 BOLEO, J. DE O. Nótula sôbre a nomenclatura das falhas. BSEM 46, no. i (1943-1944), pp. 17-25.

23,922 BORGES, A. Notas de uma exploração na península de Ferrão Veloso, em Nacala, Moçambique. BSEM 47 (1945), pp. 51-69.

23,923 BOSAZZA, V. L. The geology and the development of the bays and coastline of the Sul do Save of Moçambique. BSEM 98 (1956), pp. 19-28.

23,924 BOSAZZA, V. L. The Kalahari system with particular reference to its occurrence on the Macondes Plateau, Northern Mozambique. PROC. PAN-AFR. CONGR. PRE-HIST. 4 (1962), pp. 167-175.

23,925 BOURBON, E. DE A. E. Vias de comunicação no Território de Manica e Sofala. BSEM 45 (1942), pp. 1-38.

23,926 CARVALHO, A. P. DE. As minas de Manica. BSEM 41, no. i (1940), pp. 1-23.

23,927 CASTRO, L. DA C. E and MAGALHAES, M. J. DE. Reconhecimento glossínico da Circunscrição de Ribáuè. BSEM 122 (1960), pp. 7-76.

23,928 CASTRO CABRITA, V. DE N. Contribuição para o estudo do resgate dos campos da Manhiça. BSEM 126 (1961), F 3.

23,929 CASTRO CABRITA, V. DE N. Possibilidades energéticas do rio Elefantes/Limpopo na Albufeira de Massinguir. BSEM 126 (1961), F 1.

23,930 CORREIA DE AGUIAR, E. DA P. A hidrologia na Direcção dos Serviços de Obras Públicas e Transportes de Moçambique. BSEM 114 (1959), pp. 3-21; includes English summary.

23,931 COSTA, I. A. DA. Pebane: porto e praia perante o interior. BSEM 85 (1954), pp. 187-190.

23,932 DIAS, M. B. Nomenclatura das formações precâmbricas da Zambézia. BSEM 126 (1961), F 5.

23,933 DIAS RAFAEL, S. Relação dos cursos de água existentes na Circunscrição de Cheringoma do Distrito de Manica e Sofala. Esboço de um dicionário hidrográfico. BSEM 129 (1961), pp. 103-154.

23,934 ESQUIVEL, A. Lições de topografia. BSEM 56 (1948), pp. 1-47.

23,935 ESQUIVEL, A. Provas meleorológicas das marés atmosféricas. BSEM 67, no. i (1950), pp. 23-25.

23,936 FERREIRA, G. DA V. Indice da carta geográfica da Província de Moçambique na escala de 1/2.000.000. BSEM 106 (1957), pp. 31-50.

23,937 FIGUEIREDO GOMES E SOUSA, A. DE. Elementos para uma Organização Florestal de Moçambique. BSEM 117 (1959), pp. 77-85.

23,938 FIGUEIREDO GOMES E SOUSA, A. DE. Elementos para uma Organização Florestal de Moçambique: reservas florestais. BSEM 103 (1957), pp. 53-94.

23,939 FIGUEIREDO GOMES E SOUSA, A. DE. Um esboco fito-geográfico de Moçambique. BSEM 57-58 (1948), pp. 97-111.

23,940 FIGUEIREDO GOMES E SOUSA, A. DE. A floresta climática de Inhaminga. BSEM 111 (1958), pp. 91-97.

23,941 FIGUEIREDO GOMES E SOUSA, A. DE. As ilhas de Angoche. BSEM 144-145 (1965), pp. 131-144.

23,942 FIGUEIREDO GOMES E SOUSA, A. DE. As ilhas Quirimbas. BSEM 121 (1960), pp. 127-148.

23,943 FIGUEIREDO GOMES E SOUSA, A. DE. O Jardim Municipal Vasco da Gama de Lourenço Marques. Notícia comemorativa do seu cinquentenário. BSEM 68 (1951), pp. 59-74.

23,944 FIGUEIREDO GOMES E SOUSA, A. DE. A protecção da natureza em Moçambique. BSEM 98 (1956), pp. 3-11.

23,945 FIGUEIREDO GOMES E SOUSA, A. DE. A protecção da natureza no Ultramar Português especialmente em Moçambique. BSEM 94-95, no. i (1955), pp. 3-25.

23,946 FIGUEIREDO GOMES E SOUSA, A. DE. A silvicultura como elemento de colonização do distrito do Niassa. BSEM 9 (1933), pp. 3-35.

23,947 FREITAS, F. Condições hidrogeológicas de abastecimento de águas subterrâneas a Lourenço Marques e arredores. BSEM 133 (1962), pp. 119-138.

23,948 GOMES GUERREIRO, M. Viagem através das Ilhas da Macaronésia. BSEM 128 (1961), pp. 127-135.

23,949 GOUVEIA, D. H. G. Método usado na cartografia geral dos solos de Moçambique. BSEM 111 (1958), pp. 53-63.

23,950 GRANGER, J. Irrigação do Vale do Limpopo. BSEM 19 (1934), pp. 227-261.

23,951 GRANGER, J. et al. Irrigação e colonização do vale do Limpopo: apreciação de cinco projectos de decreto. BSEM 25 (1935), pp. 13-45.

23,952 GREGORY, S. Annual, seasonal and monthly rainfall over Moçambique. GEOGRAPHERS AND THE TROPICS, 1964, pp. 81-109.

23,953 GUEDES CAMPOS, T. Elementos de topografia para uso dos concorrentes a lugares de Chefe de Posto, Secretário e Administrador de Circunscrição. BSEM 102 (1957), pp. 43-161.

23,954 LOBO, L. Ponte sobre o rio Mazoe em Moçambique na E. N. 103. BSEM 128 (1961), pp. 75-82.

23,955 MATA, L. P. DA. Análise das condições climáticas de Moçambique, segundo um critério de conforto humano dentro da habitação. BSEM 141 (1964), pp. 75-106.

23,956 MENDES, M. F. Vias de comunicação na Colónia. BSEM 29 (1936), pp. 1-8.

23,957 MONTEIRO, A. A. V. Principios gerais de climatização sistema de arrefecimento do ar. Aspectos económicos da climatização em Moçambique. BSEM 141 (1964), pp. 125-143.

23,958 OSORIO, C. DO A. Impressões de uma viagem ao norte da Colónia. BSEM 28 (1935), pp. 261-270.

23,959 PEREIRA, A. S. C. et al. Irrigação e colonização do vale do Limpopo: appreciação de cinco projectos de decreto. BSEM 24 (1934).

23,960 PINTO, A. DA S. Algumas considerações sôbre o problema mineiro da Colónia. BSEM 26 (1935), pp. 131-136.

23,961 PIRES DE CARVALHO, F. A. Cálculo da Secção de Vazão das Obras de Arte. Estudo de uma fórmula aplicavel aos rios de Moçambique. BSEM 114 (1959), pp. 63-70.

23,962 RAFAEL, S. D. Relação dos cursos de água existentes na circunscrição de cheringoma no Distrito de Manica e Sofala. Esboço de um dicionário hidrográfico. BSEM 134 (1963), pp. 83-135.

23,963 ROCHA FARIA, J. M. DA. Condições climáticas de Moçambique. BSEM 141 (1964), pp. 49-74.

23,964 ROMANO, E. Rios de Moçambique: O Messalo. BSEM 134 (1963), pp. 137-143.

23,965 ROMANO, M. P. Acção da vegetação na regularização dos rios. BSEM 87 (1954), pp. 101-112.

23,966 ROMANO, M. P. Acerca da crítica ao trabalho "A carta de fomento de Moçambique e a fotogrametria." BSEM 118 (1959), pp. 185-192.

23,967 ROMANO, M. P. A carta de Fomento de Moçambique e a Fotogrametria. BSEM 114 (1959), pp. 93-167.

23,968 ROMANO, M. P. Aproveitamento integral dos recursos hidráulicos do Sul de Moçambique. BSEM 87 (1954), pp. 159-172.

23,969 ROMANO, M. P. Chuva média. BSEM 92 (1955), pp. 147-155.

23,970 ROMANO, M. P. Contribuição para o estudo hidrológico da bacia hidrográfica do rio Revuè. BSEM 106 (1957), pp. 63-74.

23,971 ROMANO, M. P. Contribuição para o estudo hidrológico da bacia hidrográfica do incomáti Rios Comáti e Crocodilo (Africa do Sul e Suazilândia). BSEM 143 (1965), pp. 5-32; includes English summary.

23,972 ROMANO, M. P. Elementos para a história da cartografia de Moçambique. BSEM 106 (1957), pp. 5-27.

23,973 ROMANO, M. P. A hidraulica fluvial no desenvolvimento de Moçambique. BSEM 130 (1962), pp. 169-185.

23,974 ROMANO, M. P. Hidrologia das regiões de Moçambique situadas junto da fronteira com a Africa do Sul. BSEM 128 (1961), pp. 197-203.

23,975 ROMANO, M. P. Hidrologia do Alto Limpopo (Colóquio pronunciado no Instituto de Investigação Cientifica de Moçambique. BSEM 123 (1960), pp. 37-60.

23,976 ROMANO, M. P. Hidrologia do Rio dos Elefantes. BSEM 128 (1961), pp. 37-54.

23,977 ROMANO, M. P. Hidrologia do Sabie. BSEM 132 (1962), pp. 187-211; includes English summary.

23,978 ROMANO, M. P. Inventário dos recursos hidráulicos do distrito de Lourenço Marques. BSEM 103 (1957), pp. 137-156.

23,979 ROMANO, M. P. A localização das capitais de Província e de Distrito em Moçambique. BSEM 121 (1960), pp. 191-233.

23,980 ROMANO, M. P. O controle das cheias do rio Incomáti. BSEM 101 (1956), pp. 111-120.

23,981 ROMANO, M. P. O problema da água na Região do Maputo (Sul de Moçambique). BSEM 135 (1963), pp. 111-125; includes English summary.

23,982 ROMANO, M. P. Relações entre as velocidades das águas para vários rios. BSEM 106 (1957), pp. 209-211.

23,983 ROMANO, M. P. Relações entre velocidades de água. BSEM 108 (1958), pp. 71-73.

23,984 ROMANO, M. P. Rios de Moçambique: O Licungo. BSEM 137 (1963), pp. 229-236.

23,985 ROMANO, M. P. Secas e cheias: seus problemas em Moçambique. BSEM 137 (1963), pp. 237-270.

23,986 ROMANO, M. P. Turismo e economia humana em Moçambique. BSEM 116 (1959), pp. 173-195.

23,987 SILVA, J. C. V. DA. Tentativa de resolução do problema das curvas de vazão em rios de leito instável. BSEM 108 (1958), pp. 77-93.

23,988 TREPA, M. and ROMANO, M. P. A importancia do conhecimento da regularidade da precipitação. BSEM 92 (1955), pp. 143-146.

23,989 VIEIRA, M. C. Rio Zambeze: esquema para a organização de um sistema de aviso de cheias, em Moçambique. BSEM 126 (1961), F 4.

23,990 Caminho de Ferro e Porto da Beira. PORT. EM AFR. 6 (1949), pp. 13-19.

See also 22274.

Government. Politics. Administration

23,991 ALBERTO, M. S. Controle fisiológico da mão-de-obra indígena Moçambicana. BSEM 64 (1950), pp. 5-13.

23,992 ALBERTO, M. S. Mouzinho e a evolução das normas de Administração Ultramarina. BSEM 94-95 (1955), pp. 375-393.

23,993 CARVALHO, C. N. DE. O estado actual de abastecimento de água a povoações. Dados para a resolução do problema. BSEM 65 (1950), pp. 151-158.

23,994 CRUZ, C. S. Técnicos e colonização. BSEM 15-16 (1934), pp. 139-140.

23,995 DIAS, A. DE S. Boane. BSEM 64 (1950), pp. 15-48.

23,996 FIGUEIREDO GOMES E SOUSA, A. DE. Ensaio sôbre a colonização do distrito do Niassa. BSEM 22 (1934), pp. 369-394.

23,997 GALANTE, J. P. Estatutos da cooperativa de construções urbanas. BSEM 63, no. i (1949), pp. 36-77.

23,998 GRANGER, J. A convenção. BSEM 10 (1933), pp. 3-64.

23,999 LEMOS, V. DE. Journal de prison. Expériences d'un prisonnier politique au Mozambique. PRESENCE AFR. N.S. 54 (1965), pp. 203-220.

24,000 M., E. A. Os soldados indígenas de Moçambique. BSEM 1 (1931), pp. 39-40.

24,001 MADURO, C. A farolagem da Costa de Moçambique. BSEM 7 (1933), pp. 3-10.

24,002 MARTINS, A. A. Construção e conservação de estradas em Moçambique. BSEM 119 (1959), pp. 17-28.

24,003 MENDES, M. J. F. Os Serviços de Obras Públicas no fomento de Moçambique. BSEM 65 (1950), pp. 1-31.

24,004 MONDLANE, E. C. La lutte pour l'indépendance au Mozambique. PRESENCE AFR. N.S. 48 (1963), pp. 8-31.

24,005 MONDLANE, E. C. Le mouvement de libération au Mozambique. PRESENCE AFR. N.S. 53 (1965), pp. 9-35.

24,006 MOUTINHO, T. A. DE S. Colonização indígena. BSEM 15-16 (1934), pp. 75-95.

24,007 NUNES, J. Questões indígenas. BSEM 7 (1933), pp. 11-19.

24,008 PEREIRA, A. A. Apontamentos para a colonização europeia da região do Báruè. BSEM 27 (1935), pp. 169-177.

24,009 PEREIRA, A. J. DE A. Mecanização dos trabalhos de construção e conservação em Moçambique. BSEM 119 (1959), pp. 59-69.

24,010 SANTOS, J. G. M. A propósito dos princípios de Administração seguidos na Colónia. BSEM 4 (1932), pp. 49-54.

24,011 SANTOS, M. P. P. DOS. Alguns problemas do Município de Lourenço Marques. BSEM 64 (1950), pp. 49-117.

24,012 SANTOS, M. P. P. DOS. Missão do Laboratório de Ensaios na técnica colonial. BSEM 65 (1950), pp. 131-149.

24,013 WILLIAMS, O. Fish on fridays: a portrait of Mozambique. AFR. SOUTH 3, no. 3 (1959), pp. 60-66.

24,014 La politique portugaise au Mozambique. ZAIRE 7 (1953), p. 197.

24,015 Portuguese East Africa: the re-incorporation of the territories of the Mozambique Company into direct state administration [a statement by the Portuguese Government]. J. AFR. SOC. 41 (1942), pp. 238-239.

See also 12741, 12744, 23523, 23534.

History

24,016 ALBERTO, M. S. A carta de Sofala: ensaio histórico. BSEM 116 (1959), pp. 123-136.

24,017 BARRADAS, A. História de Moçambique. BSEM 41, no. iii (1940), pp. 3-27.

24,018 BIXLER, R. W. Anglo-Portuguese rivalry for Delagoa Bay. J. MOD. HIST. 6 (1934), pp. 425-440.

24,019 BOXER, C. R. A Dominican account of Zambezia in 1744. BSEM 125 (1960), E 5.

24,020 BOXER, C. R. Mozambique: vicissitudes of an East African colony, 1505-1955. HISTORY TODAY 6 (1956), pp. 128-135.

24,021 BRASIO, P. A. O quarto centenário de Lourenço-Marques. PORT. EM AFR. 2 (1945), pp. 257-273.

24,022 BRASIO, P. A. O regimento de Sofala. PORT. EM AFR. 5 (1948), pp. 5-9.

24,023 CASTRO, S. DE. Resenha histórica do Larde. BSEM 86 (1954), pp. 153-174.

24,024 COSTA, T. M. O ensino da história colonial na Metrópole; o ensino da história de Moçambique em Moçambique. BSEM 9 (1933), pp. 37-38.

24,025 GARLANDA, U. Mozambico rocca di conquistatori, galera dei tropici. AFRICA (Rome) 10 (1955), pp. 179-181.

24,026 GUERREIRO, J. DE A. Episódios inéditos das lutas contra os macuas no reinado de D. Maria I. BSEM 53, no. i (1947), pp. 79-109.

24,027 GUERREIRO, J. DE A. Os primeiros exploradores de Moçambique. BSEM 47 (1945), pp. 123-142.

24,028 HAMILTON, R. A. The route of Gaspar Bocarro from Tete to Kilwa in 1616. NYASA J. 7, no. 2 (1954), pp. 7-14.

24,029 IRIA, J. A. Regimento do Capitão e Escrivão da Fragata Nossa Senhora da Ajuda, na sua viagem de Moçambique para o porto de Quelimane, na monção de Março de 1686. BSEM 125 (1960), E 2.

24,030 JARDIM BARRETO, V. M. António Ennes e a Guerra de Africa em 1895. BSEM 110 (1958), pp. 101-108.

24,031 LOBATO, A. A ditadura do primeiro Governador Geral em 1753. BSEM 125 (1960), E 4.

24,032 LOBATO, A. Como se fundou o presídio de Lourenço Marques. BSEM 47 (1945), pp. 71-94.

24,033 M., E. A. As expedições de Moçambique para outras colónias. BSEM 3 (1932), pp. 73-74.

24,034 MAHAMA, C. The horror of Mozambique. AFR. SOUTH 5, no. 1 (1960), pp. 50-59.

24,035 MORAIS, E. Aspectos etnográficos africanos...Vistos pelos Portugueses do Século XIX. BOL. INST. ANGOLA 3 (1954), pp. 65-69.

24,036 MOTA, A. T. DA. Novos elementos sobre o piloto Lourenço Marques. BSEM 133 (1962), pp. 59-71.

24,037 OIDTMAN, C. VON. O porto de Sofala eo problema de Zimbauè. BSEM 108 (1958), pp. 5-19.

24,038 OLIVEIRA, O. R. DE. Breve notícia sobre a história da fortaleza de Nossa Senhora da Conceição, de Lourenço Marques, onde se encontra instalado o Museu Histórico Militar de Moçambique. BSEM 144-145 (1965), pp. 189-234.

24,039 PACHECO, A. Lourenço Marques na última década do século XIX. BSEM 133 (1962), pp. 7-58.

24,040 RANGELEY, W. H. J. Bocarro's journey. NYASA J. 7, no. 2 (1954), pp. 15-23.

24,041 RANGER, T. O. Revolt in Portuguese East Africa: the Makombe rising of 1917. ST. ANTONY'S PAPERS 15 (1963), pp. 54-80.

24,042 SEQUEIRA, A. DE M. Vilanculos. BSEM 8 (1933), pp. 37-64.

24,043 SICARD, H. DE. Quiticui. BSEM 103 (1957), pp. 95-106.

24,044 VIEIRA, T. S. Notas para a história da expansão do domínio português na Colónia de Moçambique. BSEM 15-16 (1934), pp. 97-137.

See also 20615, 23542.

Language. Literature

Language

24,045 BARRADAS, A. A toponímia Moçambicana perante a convenção ortográfica Luso-Brasileira. BSEM 48, no. i (1946), pp. 43-51.

24,046 EISELEN, W. Nasalverbindungen im Thonga. FESTSCHRIFT MEINHOF, 1927, pp. 256-262.

24,047 HARRIES, L. Maŵiha texts. BANTU STUD. 14 (1940), pp. 410-433.

24,048 HARRIES, L. An outline of Mawiha grammar. BANTU STUD. 14 (1940), pp. 91-146.

24,049 SANTOS PEIXE, J. DOS. A expressão adverbial da língua Ronga. BSEM 138 (1964), pp. 117-171.

24,050 SANTOS PEIXE, J. DOS. Línguas indígenas de Moçambique. BSEM 87 (1954), pp. 115-124.

24,051 WARMELO, N. J. V. Das Gitonga. AFR. UND UB. 22 (1931-1932), pp. 16-46.

24,052 WERNER, A. A vocabulary of the Lomwe dialect of Makua (Mozambique). J. AFR. SOC. 1 (1902), pp. 236-251.

See also 17788.

Literature

24,053 BEINART, J. Malangatana [fiction]. BO 10 (1961), pp. 22-27.

24,054 FERREIRA, M. DO N. Quenquêlêquêze. Páginas de Moçambique [poetry]. PORT. EM AFR. 17 (1960), pp. 8-16.

24,055 GONCALVES, A. DA S. Eugénio de Castro, poeta esquecido e prosador ignorado. BSEM 116 (1959), pp. 3-24.

24,056 GONCALVES, L. P. Ilse Losa e a sua actividade literária. BSEM 120 (1960), pp. 175-196.

24,057 GUERREIRO, M. V. Conto Maconde. BSEM 136 (1963), pp. 15-19.

24,058 MALANGATANA, V. Two poems [Woman, To the anxious mother]. BO 10 (1961), pp. 28-29.

24,059 MONTALVAO MARQUES, M. I. T. Contos nativos. BSEM 123 (1960), pp. 151-182.

24,060 RICARDO, C. A mensagem da "Presença"—Régio e Torga. BSEM 116 (1959), pp. 65-84.

24,061 SARAIVA BARRETO, M. Da autoria dum poema épico seiscentista relativo a Moçambique. BSEM 82 (1953), pp. 195-208.

24,062 VITORIA, A. DE M. Três poetas maiores: Pessanha, Sá-Carneiro e Pessoa. BSEM 116 (1959), pp. 27-61.

Law

24,063 CLERC, A. The marriage laws of the Ronga tribe. BANTU STUD. 12 (1938), pp. 75-104.

24,064 OLESA MUNIDO, F. F. La orientación etnológica en el proyecto definitivo de Código Penal para los indígenas de Mozambique. CUAD. EST. AFR. 6 (1949), pp. 9-34.

Religion

24,065 AFRIKANUS. A morte de Sua Eminência o Sr. Cardeal Gouveia. PORT. EM AFR. 19 (1962), pp. 118-121.

24,066 ALBERTO, M. S. O problema religioso nas populações rurais nativas de Moçambique. BSEM 84 (1954), pp. 35-43.

24,067 ANDRADE, P. Há dois anos. PORT. EM AFR. 16 (1959), pp. 65-70.

24,068 BRASIO, P. A. A lgreja em Mocambique. PORT. EM AFR. 1 (1944), pp. 285-300.

24,069 FIGUEIREDO GOMES E SOUSA, A. DE. A última carta do Padre Ladislau Menyharth, S.J. BSEM 131 (1962), pp. 177-183.

24,070 GOUVEIA, T. DE. Missões Católicas de Lourenco Marques. PORT. EM AFR. 10 (1953), pp. 138-152.

24,071 GOUVEIA, T. DE. As missões católicas portuguesas em Moçambique. PORT. EM AFR. 17 (1960), pp. 132-144.

24,072 GUERREIRO, J. DE A. Do martirológio de Moçambique. BSEM 99 (1956), pp. XIII-XXIII.

24,073 MACHADO, P. Diocese de Nampula. PORT. EM AFR. 15 (1958), pp. 233-237.

24,074 MAZULA, A. J. Sentimento patriótico. PORT. EM AFR. 19 (1962), pp. 98-113.

24,075 MIRANDA, M. DOS R. As Missões católicas em Moçambique. PORT. EM AFR. 20 (1963), pp. 341-348.

24,076 PEREIRA, G. Missão de S. João de Deus em Mocambique. PORT. EM AFR. 3 (1946), pp. 368-370.

24,077 SOUSA PREGO, I. As filhas da Caridade de S. Vicente de Paulo. PORT. EM AFR. 13 (1956), pp. 290-298.

24,078 Comunicado da Conferência episcopal de Moçambique. PORT. EM AFR. 20 (1963), pp. 107-109.

24,079 Interpretação do Estatuto Missionário. PORT. EM AFR. 8 (1951), pp. 296-305.

See also 15654, 23648.

Science

24,080 ALBERTO, M. S. Contribuição para o estudo da relação entre os grupos sanguíneos e os caracteres físicos dos negros de Moçambique (tribo Tonga-Changane). BSEM 85 (1954), pp. 137-152.

24,081 ALBERTO, M. S. Homogeneidade haematológica dos povos negros de Moçambique. Sua correlação com os povos negros dos territórios vizinhos. BSEM 132 (1962), pp. 83-89.

24,082 ALBERTO, M. S. Nota sobre a frequência dos partos Gemelares entre as Negras de Lourenço Marques. BSEM 96 (1956), pp. 59-64.

24,083 ALBERTO, M. S. and BARRETO, A. D. Contribuição para o estudo dos grupos sanguíneos dos indígenas Moçambicanos. BSEM 81 (1953), pp. 105-137.

24,084 ALBERTO, M. S. and BARRETO, A. D. Estudos antropológicos dos pavos Bantos. Melhoria constitucional observada nos soldados negros Moçambicanos e determinada pela variação do Coeficiente de Pignet-Mayet. BSEM 73 (1952), pp. 37-42.

24,085 ALBERTO, M. S. and BARRETO, A. D. Incidência da Mancha Azul Congénita ou Mongólica nos recem-nascidos negros de Moçambique. BSEM 80 (1953), pp. 11-19.

24,086 ALFARO CARDOSO, J. G. Doenças das citrinas em Moçambique. BSEM 27 (1935), pp. 179-188; 28 (1935), pp. 251-259; 30 (1936), pp. 125-135.

24,087 ALFARO CARDOSO, J. G. Do empobrecimento florestal da colónia. BSEM 3 (1932), pp. 37-40.

24,088 ALFARO CARDOSO, J. G. Experimentação florestal a plantação de essências indígenas. BSEM 67, no. i (1950), pp. 31-38.

24,089 ALFARO CARDOSO, J. G. A ferrugem do trigo. BSEM 50, no. i (1946), pp. 185-187.

24,090 ALFARO CARDOSO, J. G. Fomento florestal. BSEM 4 (1932), pp. 41-47.

24,091 ALFARO CARDOSO, J. G. O problema florestal de Moçambique. BSEM 49, no. i (1946), pp. 79-105.

24,092 ALFARO CARDOSO, J. G. Sôbre a arborização da cidade. BSEM 46, no. i (1943-1944), pp. 45-51.

24,093 ALFARO CARDOSO, J. G. Sobre arborização. BSEM 130 (1962), pp. 57-66.

24,094 ALMEIDA, A. A. DE. Influência da temperatura sensivel no desenvolvimento do Earias biplaga Wlk. BSEM 125 (1960), D 6.

24,095 ALMEIDA E CUNHA, A. D'. Criação de asilos rudimentares para indígenas velhos e inválidos. BSEM 66, no. i (1950), pp. 27-30.

24,096 AVELAR, H. DE. Medição da capacidade mental de algumas crianças de Lourenço Marques. BSEM 18 (1934), pp. 205-210.

24,097 BANHA DE ANDRADE. O Hospital de Mocambique durante a administração dos Almoxarifes. PORT. EM AFR. 13 (1956), pp. 357-370.

24,098 BANHA DE ANDRADE. O Hospital de Mocambique durante a administração dos Religiosos de S. João de Deus. PORT. EM AFR. 13 (1956), pp. 261-289.

24,099 BAPTISTA, J. E. Pragas do algodoeiro em Moçambique. BSEM 48, no. i (1946), pp. 15-42.

24,100 BARBOSA, L. A. G. Contribuição para a fitosociologia do novo "Pterocarpus Brenani." BSEM 111 (1958), pp. 69-87.

24,101 BARRADAS, L. A. As possibilidades agrícolas dos terrenos de machongo. BSEM 46, no. i (1943-1944), pp. 1-16.

24,102 BARRETO, A. D. Contribuição para o estudo da pelve das mulheres indígenas de Moçambique. BSEM 85 (1954), pp. 177-185.

24,103 BARRETO, A. D. Contribuição para o estudo dos indices cefálico e nasal dos indigenas Moçambicanos. BSEM 85 (1954), pp. 165-176.

24,104 BARRETO, A. D. Subsídios para o estudo antropológico dos indígenas Moçambicanos. Indices e coeficientes de robustez sobre 538 indígenas, adultos, do sexo masculino, da Província do Sul do Save. BSEM 68 (1951), pp. 39-56.

24,105 BEUCHAT, A. Estudo das helmintíasses e das bilharzioses no concelho de Gaza, Baixo-Limpopo. BSEM 91 (1955), pp. 137-141.

24,106 BEUCHAT, A. Mil raspagens uterinas contra a esterilidade das mulheres indígenas, na Província do Sul do Save. BSEM 66, no. i (1950), pp. 49-53.

24,107 BOSAZZA, V. L. Da eliminação de sal das areias e misturas areno-argilosas. BSEM 101 (1956), pp. 61-79.

24,108 BOSAZZA, V. L. and RODRIGUES, J. A. Comparação entre a geoquímica das águas subterrâneas dos riolitos do Sul do Save e das águas subterrâneas dos complexos granéticos do Niassa Oriental. BSEM 94-95, no. i (1955), pp. 25-43.

24,109 BORGES, A. Algumas notas sôbre minerais úteis na Colônia de Moçambique. BSEM 29 (1936), pp. 9-14.

24,110 CANAS, J. M. and VALADAO, F. G. Estudos sobre a conservação do leite pela água oxigenada, no seu transporte para Lourenço Marques. BSEM 127 (1961), J 3.

24,111 CARDOSO PAISANA, F. Reconhecimentos Glossínicos effectuados no distrito da Zambézia pelo 5º Sector Veterinário da M.C.T. BSEM 109 (1958), pp. 1-157.

24,112 CARVALHO CAMPOS, J. DE. O ácido para-amino salicílio no tratamento da tuberculose pulmonar. BSEM 62 (1949), pp. 75-80.

24,113 CAVACO, A. Contribuição para o conhecimento da flora de Moçambique—euforbiaceae. BSEM 55, no. i (1947), pp. 229-290.

24,114 COELHO, D. P. Enxertos cutâneos: possibilidades e vantagens da sua execução nos pequenos hospitais. BSEM 66, no. i (1950), pp. 15-23.

24,115 CORINTA FERREIRA, M. Algumas considerações àcerca da importância do gênero "Oryctes" ill. para as palmeiras. BSEM 73 (1952), pp. 5-21.

24,116 CORINTA FERREIRA, M. Algumas considerações àcerca dos insectos xilófagos em Moçambique. BSEM 90 (1955), pp. 87-90.

24,117 CORINTA FERREIRA, M. Algumas variedades novas de gymnopleurineos e notas sinonimicas. BSEM 85 (1954), pp. 203-206.

24,118 CORINTA FERREIRA, M. Cerambicínios colhidos na Província de Moçambique por G. da Veiga Ferreira. BSEM 103 (1957), pp. 35-51.

24,119 CORINTA FERREIRA, M. Contribuição da morfologia para a sistemática. BSEM 85 (1954), pp. 153-157.

24,120 CORINTA FERREIRA, M. Contribuição para o conhecimento de naturalistas e exploradores da fauna Africana. BSEM 101 (1956), pp. 153-178.

24,121 CORINTA FERREIRA, M. Contribuição para o estudo dos cerambicínios da Africa do Sul. BSEM 85 (1954), pp. 207-209.

24,122 CORINTA FERREIRA, M. Contribuição para o estudo dos escarabaeídeos da Africa do Sul. BSEM 84 (1954), pp. 27-31.

24,123 CORINTA FERREIRA, M. Contribuição para o Estudo dos Escarabaeídeos da Africa do Sul. Aditamento à 1 parte da Monografia dos Escarabeídeos da Africa do Sul. BSEM 80 (1953), pp. 93-102.

24,124 CORINTA FERREIRA, M. Importância da Ilha da Inhaca no levantamento biológica de Moçambique. BSEM 73 (1952), pp. 55-84.

24,125 CORINTA FERREIRA, M. Lista de tabanídeos de Moçambique. BSEM 63, no. i (1949), pp. 87-89.

24,126 CORINTA FERREIRA, M. Museus Africanos de História Natural—"O South African Museum." BSEM 94-95, no. i (1955), pp. 259-309.

24,127 CORINTA FERREIRA, M. Reconhecimento biológica dos territorios à volta do Oceano Indico. BSEM 90 (1955), pp. 91-96.

24,128 CORINTA FERREIRA, M. Reserva de caça do Maputo contribuição para o conhecimento da sua fauna entomológica. BSEM 75 (1952), pp. 9-17.

24,129 CORINTA FERREIRA, M. and FERREIRA, G. DA V. Observations on the entomological fauna of the Inhaca Island. BSEM 112 (1958), pp. 103-108.

24,130 CORINTA FERREIRA, M. and FERREIRA, G. DA V. Uma especie nova de Hovatoma lameere colhida em Moçambique. BSEM 76 (1952), pp. 29-33.

24,131 CORINTA FERREIRA, M. and FERREIRA, G. DA V. Um novo genero da sub-familia prioninae. BSEM 76 (1952), pp. 35-39.

24,132 COUTINHO, L. P. Problemas relacionados com a Panificação em Mocambique. Medidas necessárias para a sua resolução. BSEM 124 (1960), pp. 1-8.

24,133 CRUZ, C. S. Melhoramento pecuário—o problema da produção leiteira. BSEM 21 (1934), pp. 327-350.

24,134 CRUZ, J. H. M. E. Considerações sobre bilharziose vesical. A propósito do ensaio clínico do Nilodin estudo cistoscópico. BSEM 75 (1952), pp. 43-85; includes English summary.

24,135 ESQUIVEL, A. Algumas notas sobre a mortalidade dos Segurados Portugueses. BSEM 132 (1962), pp. 163-186.

24,136 ESQUIVEL, A. Determinação da intensidade da gravidade em Lourenço Marques. BSEM 49, no. i (1946), pp. 53-77.

24,137 FEIO, F. B. and DIAS, M. G. Localizações atípicas e alguns aspectos cerúrgicos das bilharzioses: schistosomiasis hematobica. BSEM 66, no. i (1950), pp. 67-81.

24,138 FENYI, J. Plantas Menyharthianas: condições climatológicas de Boroma. BSEM 30 (1936), pp. 105-123.

24,139 FERENC, H. Notícia àcêrca do Padre Ladislau Menyharth, S.J., missionário na Africa (22 de Maio de 1890 a 16 de Novembro de 1897). BSEM 44, no. iii (1941), pp. 25-50; 45, no. iii (1942), pp. 51-81.

24,140 FERNANDES, A. Como proteger a fauna da colónia. BSEM 3 (1932), pp. 17-23.

24,141 FERREIRA, A. J. DE L. Algumas observações sôbre os indígenas da Angónia. BSEM 44 (1941), pp. 1-16.

24,142 FERREIRA, A. J. DE L. Alterações do dermopapilograma em negros leprosos da Colônia de Moçambique. BSEM 45 (1942), pp. 75-81.

24,143 FERREIRA, A. J. DE L. Observações sôbre o tipo morfológico constitucional dos indígenas da Angónia. BSEM 42, no. i (1940), pp. 25-38.

24,144 FERREIRA, A. J. DE L. Primeiros subsídios para o estudo da micologia médica em Moçambique. BSEM 45 (1942), pp. 39 seq.

24,145 FERREIRA, A. J. DE L. Problemas de micologia médica em Moçambique. BSEM 44 (1941), pp. 33-64.

24,146 FERREIRA, A. J. DE L. Subsídios para o estudo dos roedores e carnivoros da Colônia de Moçambique possíveis propagadores da peste. BSEM 44 (1941), pp. 17-22.

24,147 FERREIRA, G. DA V. Considerações àcerca da acção de algumas entidades no reconhecimento biológico da Província de Moçambique. BSEM 85 (1954), pp. 197-202.

24,148 FERREIRA, G. DA V. Reconhecimento biológico dum território. Da sua necessidade. BSEM 90 (1955), pp. 53-59.

24,149 FERREIRA, J. N. and VIANA, R. L. Abcessos hepáticos amebianos. BSEM 140 (1964), pp. 169-195.

24,150 FERREIRA, J. S. Considerações sobre um caso de canero bronquico. BSEM 54 (1947), pp. 145-149.

24,151 FERREIRA DA SILVA, J. O magno problema das estradas da Colônia de Moçambique. BSEM 65 (1950), pp. 57-100.

24,152 FERREIRA DA SILVA, J. Problemas de Saúde e Higiene. BSEM 100 (1956), pp. 65-83.

24,153 FIGUEIREDO, Com. J. DE. Sôbre alguns moluscos existentes na costa do distrito de Moçambique. BSEM 14 (1934), pp. 53-60.

24,154 FIGUEIREDO GOMES E SOUSA, A. DE. Contribuição para o estudo da flora de Moçambique. BSEM 1 (1931), pp. 7-11.

24,155 FIGUEIREDO GOMES E SOUSA, A. DE. Contribuição para o estudo do fauno do distrito do Niassa. BSEM 27 (1935), pp. 195-199.

24,156 FIGUEIREDO GOMES E SOUSA, A. DE. Elementos para o estudo da flora lenhosa de Moçambique. BSEM 2 (1932), pp. 43-59.

24,156a FIGUEIREDO GOMES E SOUSA, A. DE. Plantas Menyharthianas: refacio. BSEM 29 (1936), pp. 31-38.

24,157 FIGUEIREDO GOMES E SOUSA, A. DE. The protection of nature in Mozambique. CIVILISATIONS 6 (1956), pp. 96-102.

24,158 FIGUEIREDO GOMES E SOUSA, A. DE. O reconhecimento botanico de Moçambique. BSEM 4 (1932), pp. 31-39.

24,159 FIGUEIREDO GOMES E SOUSA, A. DE. Subsídios para o estudo da flora do Niassa português. BSEM 26 (1935), pp. 71-130.

24,160 FRADE, F. Actividade do Centro de Zoologia (J.I.U.) respeitante à fauna de Moçambique. BSEM 125 (1960), D 2.

24,161 FRAGA DE AZEVEDO, J. O problema da bilharziose humana. BSEM 82 (1953), pp. 5-39.

24,162 FREITAS, A. J. DE. O estudo da geologia de Moçambique. BSEM 100 (1956), pp. 23-30.

24,163 GOMES PEDRO, J. Contribuições para o inventário Floristico de Moçambique: Dicotiledóneas (Casuarinaceae-Connaraceae), leguminosae. BSEM 91 (1955), pp. 3-30; 92 (1955), pp. 3-35.

24,164 GOUVEIA, D. H. G. A razão C/N de alguns solos do Sul do Save. BSEM 60 (1949), pp. 29-39.

24,165 GUTTERRES, J. DE B. A tuberculose nas espécies domésticas. BSEM 45 (1942), pp. 69-74.

24,166 JARA, A. B. Algumas considerações sobre o problema da bilharziose. BSEM 66, no. i (1950), pp. 57-63.

24,167 JORGE, S. C. M. Hérnia, hidrocele e elefantíase, factores de incapacidade de homens válidos. BSEM 66, no. i (1950), pp. 41-46.

24,168 KOCH, C. The tenebrionidae of Southern Africa. BSEM 94-95, no. i (1955), pp. 355-370.

24,169 MADEIRA LEITAO, M. I. Contribuição para o estudo do Xanthomonas malvacearum em Moçambique. BSEM 125 (1960), D 8.

24,170 MARTINS, A. J. A compactação de solos em Moçambique. BSEM 83 (1954), pp. 39-52.

24,171 MARTINS, J. B. Sobre a travessia de baixas pantanosas. BSEM 126 (1961), F 7.

24,172 MARTINS NUNES, D. A. Sobre a Neurosifilis entre os nativos de Moçambique. BSEM 126 (1961), G 1.

24,173 MARTINS NUNES, D. A. Sobre as psicoses entre os nativos de Moçambique. BSEM 126 (1961), G 3.

24,174 MEIRA E CRUZ, J. H. Um doente com síndromes múltiplos. BSEM 66, no. i (1950), pp. 85-101.

24,175 MORAIS, T. DE. Alguns aspectos do contrôle da Bilharziose. BSEM 118 (1959), pp. 45-49.

24,176 MORAIS, T. DE. A Bilharziose em Moçambique. BSEM 116 (1959), pp. 87-94.

24,177 MORAIS, T. DE. Considerações sobre os problemas da medicina preventiva. BSEM 117 (1959), pp. 53-64.

24,178 MORAIS, T. DE. Memória descritiva e plano de trabalhos do Projecto experimental de combate à bilharziose na ilha da inhaca— Moçambique. BSEM 126 (1961), G 2.

24,179 MORAIS, T. DE. Nota sobre a prevalência de parasitoses intestinais humanas entre os africanos da Ilha da Inhaca. BSEM 112 (1958), pp. 125-128.

24,180 MORAIS, T. DE. Nota sobre as Bilharzioses humanas e sua prevalência na Inhaca. BSEM 112 (1958), pp. 117-121.

24,181 MORAIS, T. DE. Subsídios para o estudo da endemia de bilharziose na área do Posto Administrativo de Macuze-Zambézia. BSEM 93 (1955), pp. 23-32.

24,182 MORGADO, R. Problemas de Lepra. BSEM 100 (1956), pp. 85-99.

24,183 NAVARRO SOEIRO, A. Aspectos clinicos da febre biliosa hemoglobinúrica (F.B.H.), com sugestões para o tratamento. BSEM 82 (1953), pp. 149-178.

24,184 NAVARRO SOEIRO, A. O sezonismo em Moçambique: uma contribuição para o estudo epidemiológico. BSEM 82 (1953), pp. 79-142.

24,185 NORONHA, C. Alguns aspectos da higiene dos olhos. BSEM 62 (1949), pp. 39-46.

24,186 NUNES, A. DE F. Minerais úteis de Moçambique. BSEM 74 (1952), pp. 101-105.

24,187 OLDROYD, H. Asilidae (Diptera) from Inhaca Island, Moçambique. BSEM 114 (1959), pp. 47-49.

24,188 OMER-COOPER, J. Some records of Dytiscidae (Col.) from Mozambique. BSEM 101 (1956), pp. 19-32.

24,189 PACHECO, A. O tratamento do Enfarte do Miocárdio (Revisão Geral). BSEM 118 (1959), pp. 75-101.

24,190 PALMEIRIM, V. Os fins das reuniões médicas. BSEM 20 (1934), pp. 305-308.

24,191 PALMEIRIM, V. Sôbre a etiologia da febre biliosa hemoglobinúrica, pelo Dr. Luiz Sormenho: parecer. BSEM 18 (1934), pp. 188-190.

24,192 PEDRO, J. G. Contribuições para o inventário florístico de Moçambique. BSEM 87 (1954), pp. 3-53.

24,193 PEREIRA, A. S. C. Recursos do exame físico-químico: um exemplo da prática. BSEM 19 (1934), pp. 263-277.

24,194 PEREIRA, M. DE C. Culicídeos de Moçambique. BSEM 112 (1958), pp. 65-72.

24,195 PEREIRA COUTINHO, L. Determinação das deficiências mais prováveis em amino-ácidos num grupo da população local. BSEM 124 (1960), pp. 1-6.

24,196 PEREIRA DOS SANTOS, M. P. Panorama da investigação científica em Moçambique. BSEM 76 (1952), pp. 1-16.

24,197 PINTO, A. A. DA R. A contribution towards the study of the avifauna of the Island of Inhaca. BSEM 112 (1958), pp. 29-62.

24,198 PINTO, A. DA S. Algumas considerações sôbre a Geofísica Aplicada: seu estado actual—sua intervenção no estudo de alguns problemas geológico-mineiros na Colónia. BSEM 30 (1936), pp. 65-98.

24,199 PIRES, F. A. and SANTOS DIAS, J. A. Algumas considerações sobre as helmintíases veterinárias em Moçambique. BSEM 117 (1959), pp. 135-144.

24,200 PIRES, V. Considerações sobre melhoramento de plantas. BSEM 54 (1947), pp. 125-137.

24,201 PRATAS, M. J. Estudo de cimentos de Moçambique. BSEM 132 (1962), pp. 213-251.

24,202 PRATES, M. D. Os tumores malignos na província de Moçambique. BSEM 126 (1961), G 4.

24,203 RAFAEL, A. A. G. Ensaios com o Prothidium. BSEM 117 (1959), pp. 35-50.

24,204 REBELO, A. A classificação morfológica das anemias e a sua utilidade para o diagnóstico e para o tratamento. BSEM 50, no. i (1946), pp. 213-240.

24,205 REIS, C. M. S. Alguns aspectos da Filaríase Perstans em Mocímboa da Praia. BSEM 94-95, no. i (1955), pp. 223-257.

24,206 REIS, C. M. S. Contribuição para o estudo da robustez da raça Maconde. BSEM 86 (1954), pp. 3-137.

24,207 REIS, C. M. S. Os grupos sanguíneos na determinação da origem etnológica dos Ma-Konde. BSEM 96 (1956), pp. 91-106.

24,208 REIS, C. M. S. Variações da robustez dos trabalhadores Macondes. BSEM 93 (1955), pp. 73-176.

24,209 ROMANO, M. P. Considerações acerca de medições de caudias pelo método das soluções. BSEM 96 (1956), pp. 127-131.

24,210 ROMANO, M. P. A extracção do cloreto de sódio em Mocambique. BSEM 125 (1960), C 2.

24,211 ROMANO, M. P. O problema da energia em Moçambique. BSEM 99 (1956), pp. 95-114.

24,212 ROMANO, M. P. Torrencialidade de rios. BSEM 96 (1956), pp. 65-76.

24,213 ROSA PINTO, A. A. DA. Uma lista sistemática das aves da região extremo sul da provincia de Moçambique. BSEM 77 (1953), pp. 1-72.

24,214 ROSINHA, A. J. Algumas considerações sobre a pecuária da Ilha da Inhaca. BSEM 112 (1958), pp. 131-142.

24,215 ROSINHA, A. J. O problema do leite e lacticínios. Sens aspectos na circunscrição do Maputo. BSEM 127 (1961), J 1.

24,216 ROSINHA, A. J. Valerá a pena recuperar o caça no Maputo? BSEM 125 (1960), D 1.

24,217 SALVADOR, A. R. N. Características químico-analíticas dos chás de Moçambique. BSEM 137 (1963), pp. 115-127.

24,218 SAMPAIO, M. J. F. DE. Método rápido para a determinação do limite líquido: aplicação aos solos de Moçambique. BSEM 97 (1956), pp. 47-61.

24,219 SANTARENO PIGNATELLI, M. J. DE. Microscopia electrónica. BSEM 92 (1955), pp. 119-134; includes English summary.

24,220 SANTOS, M. P. P. DOS. Um caso curioso de deslizamento circular. BSEM 69 (1951), pp. 91-96.

24,221 SANTOS, M. P. P. DOS. Ensaios normais de solo-cimento. BSEM 69 (1951), pp. 5-18.

24,222 SANTOS, M. P. P. DOS. Estabilização de solos. BSEM 81 (1953), pp. 185-221.

24,223 SANTOS, M. P. P. DOS. Posição de Lourenço Marques num futuro esquema de electrificação do Sul do Dave. BSEM 65 (1950), pp. 101-130.

24,224 SANTOS, M. P. P. DOS. Previsão dos limites de consistência de solos e mistura de solos. BSEM 96 (1956), pp. 107-125.

24,225 SANTOS DIAS, J. A. T. Contribuição ao estudo da fauna entomológica da Ilha da Inhaca. BSEM 112 (1958), pp. 77-83, 87-99.

24,226 SANTOS DIAS, J. A. T. Descoberta de uma nova espécie do género Adersia Austen, 1912 (Diptera: Tabanidae) presente na região costeira de Moçambique. BSEM 118 (1959), pp. 31-41.

24,227 SANTOS DIAS, J. A. T. Em Defesa do património naturalístico de Moçambique. BSEM 92 (1955), pp. 157-163.

24,228 SANTOS DIAS, J. A. T. Estudos sobre os hematozoários das aves de Moçambique. BSEM 87 (1954), pp. 55-68.

24,229 SANTOS DIAS, J. A. T. Haematopota vilhenai n. sp. (Diptera-Tabanidae). BSEM 106 (1957), pp. 183-187.

24,230 SANTOS DIAS, J. A. T. Notas sobre a Ixodofauna Angolana. BSEM 103 (1957), pp. 157-169.

24,231 SANTOS DIAS, J. A. T. Notas sobre alguns Tabanídeos do distrito de Cabo Delgado. BSEM 103 (1957), pp. 23-33.

24,232 SANTOS DIAS, J. A. T. Notícia sobre os viveiros temporários da Glossina austeni austeni Newstead, 1912. BSEM 121 (1960), pp. 129-132; includes English summary.

24,233 SANTOS DIAS, J. A. T. Um novo género para a Tribu Bouvieromyiini (Enderlein, 1922). BSEM 98 (1956), pp. 75-79.

24,234 SANTOS DIAS, J. A. T. Um novo género para a Tribu Haematopotini (Diptera-Tabanidae). BSEM 98 (1956), pp. 13-18.

24,235 SANTOS DIAS, J. A. T. Um novo ixodídeo do género Haemaphysalis C. L. Koch para a fauna de Moçambique. BSEM 86 (1954), pp. 139-152.

24,236 SANTOS DIAS, J. A. T. Qual seria o Status Glossínico no Território de Moçambique ao Sul do Rio Limpopo anteriormente à grande Panzootia de Peste Bovina, de 1896? BSEM 128 (1961), pp. 55-65.

24,237 SANTOS DIAS, J. A. T. Sobre alguns ixodideos (Acarina-Ixodoidea) de Angola no Museu de Hamburgo. BSEM 121 (1960), pp. 151-156.

24,238 SANTOS DIAS, J. A. T. Sobre uma pequena colecção de carraças (Acarina-Ixodoidea) colhidas pelo Dr. F. Zumpt em Moçambique. BSEM 83 (1954), pp. 106-112.

24,239 SANTOS DIAS, J. A. T. Subsídios para o estudo dos hematozoários dos répteis de Moçambique. BSEM 76 (1952), pp. 17-27; 82 (1953), pp. 43-73; 87 (1954), pp. 69-81.

24,240 SANTOS DIAS, J. A. T. Tripanosomas encontrados nos antílopes duma região de Moçambique infestada pela Glossina austeni Newstead, 1912. BSEM 123 (1960), pp. 5-9.

24,241 SANTOS DIAS, J. A. T. and SOUSA JUNIOR, J. DE. Descoberta de uma segunda espécie de tabanídeo pertencente ao género Braunsiomyia Bequaert, 1924. BSEM 106 (1957), pp. 197-206.

24,242 SCHINZ, H. Plantas Menyharthianas: Contribuição para o estudo da flora do Zambeze inferior. BSEM 29 (1936), pp. 39-55.

24,243 SILVA, J. M. DA. Aspectos das tripanosomíases animais em Moçambique. BSEM 115 (1959), pp. 5-80.

24,244 SILVA, J. M. DA. Experimentação dum novo Tripanocida no Govuro—O Berenil. BSEM 103 (1957), pp. 107-116.

24,245 SILVA BARBOSA, A. J. DA. O complexo de capsídeos do algodoeiro em Moçambique. BSEM 111 (1958), pp. 113-127.

24,246 SILVA BARBOSA, A. J. DA et al. Contribuição para o Estudo da Entomofauna de Moçambique. BSEM 125 (1960), C 5.

24,247 SOEIRO, A. A. Considerações acerca das diarreias na criança. BSEM 129 (1961), pp. 35-98.

24,248 SOEIRO, A. N. Um caso de endocardite maligna (endocardite sub-aguda bacteriana) tratado pela penicilina. BSEM 52, no. i (1947), pp. 43-47.

24,249 SOEIRO, A. N. Glomérulo-nefrites de origem sezonática (comentários acerca de um caso). BSEM 54 (1947), pp. 139-143.

24,250 SOEIRO, A. N. and MORAIS, T. DE. Nota sobre a prevalência da malária na Ilha da Inhaca. BSEM 112 (1958), pp. 111-113.

24,251 SOROMENHO, L. Sôbre a etiologia da febre biliosa hemoglobinúrica. BSEM 13 (1934), pp. 3-18.

24,252 SOUSA, A. E. DE. The use of phytocides to control stump and other secondary plant growth in areas cleared against *Glossina austeni*. BSEM 115 (1959), pp. 83-109; includes Portuguese summary.

24,253 SOUSA, J. DE. Apontamentos para o estudo do parasitismo intestinal nos indígenas de Moçambique. BSEM 1 (1931), pp. 37-38.

24,254 SOUSA SOBRINHO, J. L. DE S. A volta da higiene e saúde mental. BSEM 110 (1958), pp. 5-39.

24,255 SOUSA SOBRINHO, L. Um surto epidémico de poliomielite na Maxixe. BSEM 66, no. i (1950), pp. 31-40.

24,256 TENDEIRO, J. Sur quelques ixodidés du Mozambique et de la Guinée Portugaise. BCGP 14 (1959), pp. 21-95, 407-457; 18 (1963), pp. 223-299.

24,257 VILHENA, J. P. Algumas considerações sobre estodos para projecto e exécução de barragens. BSEM 131 (1962), pp. 125-158.

24,258 Plantas Menyharthianas: relação das plantas. BSEM 31 (1936), pp. 203-212; 32 (1936), pp. 293-330.

24,259 Relatório dos Delegados da Sociedade de Estudos de Moçambique ao 50º Congresso Anual da South African Association for the Advancement of Science. BSEM 80 (1953), pp. 53-58.

See also 23050, 23566.

Sociology

24,260 ALBERTO, M. S. Características da mestiçagem moçambicana. BSEM 90 (1955), pp. 23-34.

24,261 ALBERTO, M. S. Contribuição para o estudo da interpenetração racial em Moçambique, provocada pelo mestiçamento humano. BSEM 106 (1957), pp. 53-60.

24,262 AMBERTO, M. S. Elementos de estudo sobre a elaboração da carta demográfica de Moçambique, e sua correlação com a etnografia. BSEM 125 (1960), B 2.

24,263 ALBERTO, M. S. Ensaio de demografia etnográfica. Populações nativas do Sul do Save destrito de Lourenço Marques. 1—Os "Ronga" do Maputo. BSEM 101 (1956), pp. 81-108.

24,264 ALBERTO, M. S. O Hindú na formação da população mestiça de Lourenço Marques. BSEM 118 (1959), pp. 63-70.

24,265 ALBERTO, M. S. O mestiçamento humano em Moçambique e a sua influência na aculturação dos povos negros. BSEM 97 (1956), pp. 107-126.

24,266 ALBERTO, M. S. O problema da alimentação entre as populações rurais nativas de Moçambique. BSEM 83 (1954), pp. 113-125.

24,267 ALBERTO, M. S. Os mistos de Moçambique. BSEM 94-95, no. i (1955), pp. 49-116.

24,268 ALBERTO, M. S. Os problemas populacionais de Moçambique. BSEM 99 (1956), pp. 3-15.

24,269 ALBERTO, M. S. Perspectivas demográficas dos negros de Moçambique. BSEM 67, no. i (1950), pp. 63-94.

24,270 ALBERTO, M. S. Problemas sociais da mocidade escolar moçambicana. BSEM 125 (1960), B 4.

24,271 ALBERTO, M. S. Problemas sociais dos pavos Bantos. Elementos para a determinação das taxas de criminalidade e suas variações nos negros de Moçambique. BSEM 73 (1952), pp. 45-53.

24,272 ALBERTO, M. S. Tendências profissionais dos mestiços de Moçambique. BSEM 125 (1960), B 3.

24,273 ALFARO CARDOSO, J. G. Os censos da população indígena, pelo Ten. Mário Costa: parecer. BSEM 18 (1934), pp. 190-192.

24,274 BARROS, L. B. DE. Problemas demográficos da população não indígena de Moçambique. BSEM 81 (1953), pp. 3-98.

24,275 BOSSE CASQUEIRO, M. VON. A mulher indígena. BSEM 68 (1951), pp. 5-25.

24,276 BOSSE CASQUEIRO, M. VON. Jardins de infância. BSEM 68 (1951), pp. 29-35.

24,277 C., J. Mulâtres de Mozambique. ZAIRE 9 (1955), p. 169.

24,278 C., J. Les noirs occidentalisés au Mozambique. ZAIRE 9 (1955), p. 168.

24,279 CASTRO, L. DE. A nefasta influência da immigração asiática na Colónia de Moçambique. BSEM 5 (1932), pp. 135-139.

24,280 COSTA, T. M. Os censos da população indígena. BSEM 13 (1934), pp. 27-32.

24,281 FERREIRA, C. Indice da natalidade na subdelegação de saúde do Lago. BSEM 44 (1941), pp. 23-32.

24,282 FIGUEIREDO GOMES E SOUSA, A. DE. Elementos para uma Organização Florestal em Moçambique: a festa da árvore. BSEM 101 (1956), pp. 121-152.

24,283 FLEGG, H. O sociologista e a investigação médica. BSEM 126 (1961), G 5.

24,284 FREITAS, G. DE. Mozambique. Native cultural policy. CIVILISATIONS 6 (1956), pp. 122-124.

24,285 GAIVAO, P. Problemas citadinos. BSEM 23 (1934), pp. 403-426.

24,286 GIL, I. A mulher em Moçambique. BSEM 100 (1956), pp. 53-63.

24,287 MORGADO, R. Portuguese East Africa. CIVILISATIONS 5 (1955), pp. 453-456.

24,288 MENDES, V. M. DA C. and CASTRO, R. A. DE A. E. Nutrição: "curva de crescimento normal dos alunos e alunas do Liceu Salazar." BSEM 103 (1957), pp. 193-201.

24,289 PEIRONE, F. J. Geografia humana e missões. Inquérito à cerca da Missão de Mitucué—distrito de Niassa. PORT. EM AFR. 14 (1957), pp. 321-342.

24,290 REBELO, D. J. S. Breves apontamentos sobre um grupo de Indianos em Moçambique (a comunidade Ismaília maometana). BSEM 128 (1961), pp. 83-89; includes English summary.

24,291 RITA FERREIRA, A. Esboço sociológico do Grupo de Povoações. Meu (Homoine, Moçambique). BSEM 106 (1957), pp. 75-180.

24,292 SANTOS E SILVA, A. L. DOS. O problema do desemprêgo e o da colonização de Moçambique. BSEM 3 (1932), pp. 5-15.

24,293 SEQUEIRA, A. DE M. A emigração para o Transvaal sob o ponto de vista demográfico. BSEM 13 (1934), pp. 19-25.

24,294 SEQUEIRA, A. DE M. Vilanculos. BSEM 11 (1933), pp. 33-63; 12 (1933), pp. 15-59.

24,295 SOEIRO, A. N. Estações de cura e repouso na Província do Sul do Save. BSEM 44 (1941), pp. 149-158.

24,296 SOUSA, J. A. S. E. Factores da delinquência infantil. BSEM 129 (1961), pp. 157-182.

24,297 SOUSA SOBRINHO, J. L. DE. Apontamento psicopedagógico: aplicação da bateria factorial de aptidões mentais primárias (Thurstone) a uma parcela da população escolar do Liceu Salazar. BSEM 103 (1957), pp. 171-183.

24,298 La population asiatique au Mozambique. ZAIRE 9 (1955), pp. 306-307.

See also 23598.

MAURITIUS

General

24,299 TOUSSAINT, A. Early printing in Mauritius. QBSAL 2 (1948), pp. 75-83.

Biography

24,300 BARNWELL, P. J. Matthew Flinders. BULL. SOC. HIST. ILE MAURICE 2 (1939-1944), pp. 56-57.

24,301 LINCOLN, R. Notes biographiques sur le Baron Grant. BULL. SOC. HIST. ILE MAURICE 1 (1938-1939), pp. 24-28.

24,302 SEGRAIS, R. LE J. DE. Portrait d'un ancêtre. François-Etienne Le Juge (1710-1766), BULL. SOC. HIST. ILE MAURICE 3 (1945-1947), pp. 20-34.

See also 17992, 20226.

Economics

24,303 ANDERSON, J. F. The sugar industry of Mauritius. ROYAL COL. INST. PR. 30 (1898-1899), pp. 68-72.

24,304 ARDILL, R. H. Public relations in Mauritius. CORONA 1, no. 9 (1949), pp. 14-16.

24,305 COOMBES, A. N. The first hundred years of the Mauritian sugar industry (1650-1750). BULL. SOC. HIST. ILE MAURICE 1 (1938-1939), pp. 48-54.

Education

24,306 OPPER, C. J. Welding a people: the educational problem in Mauritius. CORONA 1, no. 5 (1949), pp. 10-12.

24,307 Girls' education in Mauritius. AFR. WOMEN 2 (1956-1958), pp. 42-43.

Geography

24,308 BROOKFIELD, H. C. Population distribution in Mauritius. An enquiry into the determinants of distribution in a tropical sugar island. J. TROP. GEOG. 13 (1959), pp. 1-22.

24,309 ONDE, H. La Réunion et l'Ile Maurice, terres de contrastes et de beauté. ACTA GEOGRAPHICA 27 (1958), pp. 9-16.

24,310 WALKER, H. J. Coral and the lime industry in Mauritius. GEOG. REV. 52 (1962), pp. 325-336.

24,311 WALKER, H. J. Overpopulation in Mauritius: a survey. GEOG. REV. 54 (1964), pp. 243-248.

Government

24,312 BOULOUX, L. G. The role of the civil commissioners in Mauritius. J. AFR. ADM. 11 (1959), pp. 118-121.

History

24,313 BARNWELL, P. J. Flinders and Mauritius, 1803-1810. BULL. SOC. HIST. ILE MAURICE 2 (1939-1944), pp. 32-43.

24,314 BERNOT, A. La Piastre Espagnole. BULL. SOC. HIST. ILE MAURICE 3 (1945-1947), pp. 92-98.

24,315 CHAPUS, G. S. La mission de félicitations du Lieutenant Colonel Middleton à Tananarive (Septembre-Novembre 1861). BULL. SOC. HIST. ILE MAURICE 3 (1945-1947), pp. 35-64.

24,316 CHAPUS, M. and AUJAS, M. Journal de James Hastie, d'après son manuscrit conservé aux Archives Coloniales de Maurice. BULL. ACAD. MALG. 4 (1918-1919), pp. 143-195.

24,317 HART, R. E. Autour du naufrage du Saint Géran. BULL. SOC. HIST. ILE MAURICE 2 (1939-1944), pp. 44-47.

24,318 JOURDAIN, H. J. Mauritius. PRCI 13 (1881-1882), pp. 263-299.

24,319 McINTYRE, D. An astronomical bi-centenary. The Abbé de Lacaille's visit to the Cape, 1751-1753. BULL. SOC. HIST. ILE MAURICE 4 (1948-1953), pp. 77-79.

24,320 O., G. C. A brief sketch of the present state of the Isle of France. BULL. SOC. HIST. ILE MAURICE 2 (1939-1944), pp. 48-50.

24,321 PELTE, S. Notes sur la triangulation de l'Isle de France par l'Abbé de la Caille. BULL. SOC. HIST. ILE MAURICE 4 (1948-1953), pp. 71-76.

24,322 RASSOOL, S. H. A. L'Ile Maurice face à son destin. AFR. ET ASIE 71 (1965), pp. 29-33.

24,323 TOUSSAINT, A. Bibliographie critique des ouvrages sur l'histoire de Maurice. BULL. SOC. HIST. ILE MAURICE 1 (1938-1939), pp. 29-47.

24,324 TOUSSAINT, A. Early almanacs of Mauritius. BULL. SOC. HIST. ILE MAURICE 3 (1945-1947), pp. 65-91.

24,325 VALETTE, J. Note sur la série HB des Archives de l'Ile Maurice. ANN. UNIV. MADAG. 4 (1965), pp. 57-62.

24,326 Bibliography of recent works on the history of Mauritius. BULL. SOC. HIST. ILE MAURICE 2 (1939-1944), pp. 64-67.

24,327 Essai sur l'Ile de France. BULL. SOC. HIST. ILE MAURICE 1 (1938-1939), pp. 55-68.

24,328 Three letters of General John Abercromby. BULL. SOC. HIST. ILE MAURICE 1 (1938-1939), pp. 69-77.

Language. Literature

24,329 MAUNICK, E. J. Deux poèmes. PRESENCE AFR. N.S. 44 (1962), pp. 173-174.

24,330 MAUNICK, E. J. L'essentiel d'un exil. PRESENCE AFR. N.S. 49 (1964), pp. 192-194.

Religion

24,331 APPOLIS, E. Les paroisses catholiques de l'Ile Maurice. ANN. UNIV. MADAG. 2 (1964), pp. 37-40.

24,332 MAMET, J. Les débuts religieux de l'Ile de France. BULL. SOC. HIST. ILE MAURICE 1 (1938-1939), pp. 14-23.

Science

24,333 DOWLING, M. A. C. Mauritius: the malaria eradication scheme. CORONA 2 (1950), pp. 452-456.

Sociology

24,334 BENEDICT, B. The plural society in Mauritius. RACE 3, no. 2 (1961-1962), pp. 65-78.

24,335 BISSOONDOYAL, B. Indians in Mauritius. CONTEMP. REV. 187 (1955), pp. 402-405.

24,336 HAZAREESINGH, K. Helping the poor in Mauritius. CORONA 2 (1950), pp. 151-152.

24,337 HAZAREESINGH, K. Women's welfare in Mauritius. AFR. WOMEN 1 (1956), pp. 89-91.

24,338 RICHARDSON, I. Evolutionary factors in Mauritian Creole. J. AFR. LANGS. 2 (1963), pp. 2-14.

24,339 SILBERMAN, L. The problem of housing in Mauritius. RHODES-LIV. J. 21 (1957), pp. 64-74.

MALAGASSY

General

24,340 CAMERON, J. The first printing-press in Madagascar. (Extract from James Cameron's Recollections of mission life in Madagascar, Antananarivo, 1874.) QBSAL 2 (1948), pp. 83-84.

24,341 PLATT, E. T. Madagascar: great isle, red isle: a bibliographical survey. GEOG. REV. 27 (1937), pp. 301-308.

24,342 Arrêté nommant les membres de l'Académie Malgache. BULL. ACAD. MALG. 10 (1927), pp. 6-11.

24,343 Arrêté relatif à l'organisation et au fonctionnement de l'Academie Malgache. BULL. ACAD. MALG. 10 (1927), pp. 4-6.

24,344 Décret reconnaissant l'Académie Malgache comme établissement public et lui conférant la personnalité civile. BULL. ACAD. MALG. 10 (1927), pp. 1-3.

Agriculture

24,345 BATTISTINI, R. Note sur l'agriculture autochtone et les déplacements agricoles saissonniers dans le delta du Mangoky. MISM 5 (1959), pp. 215-231.

24,346 DECARY, R. La protection des plantations et la conservation des récoltes a Madagascar. J. SOC. AFR. 29 (1959), pp. 193-215.

24,347 FAUBLEE, J. L'élevage chez les Bara du Sud de Madagascar. J. SOC. AFR. 11 (1941), pp. 115-123.

Anthropology

24,348 BIRKELI, E. The Bantu in Madagascar. The Malagasy race affinity (with notes by Sir Henry Johnston). J. AFR. SOC. 19 (1920), pp. 305-316.

24,349 BIRKELI, E. Folklore Sakalava recueilli dans la région de Morondava. BULL. ACAD. MALG. 6 (1922-1923), pp. 185-423.

24,350 BUETTNER-JANUSCH, J. and BUETTNER-JANUSCH, V. Hemoglobins, haptoglobins, and transferrins in the peoples of Madagascar. AMER. J. PHY. ANTHR. 22 (1964), pp. 163-169.

24,351 CALLET, P. Un chapitre du Tantara [traduction du P. Soury-Lavergne] du P. Callet. BULL. ACAD. MALG. 4 (1918-1919), pp. 71-130.

24,352 DAVID, R. La problème anthropobiologique malgache. Nouvelles observations chez les Māhafāli du Sud-Ouest de Madagascar. J. SOC. AFR. 9 (1939), pp. 119-152.

24,353 DECARY, R. Les anciennes coiffures masculines à Madagascar. J. SOC. AFR. 35 (1965), pp. 283-316.

24,354 DECARY, R. La chasse et le piégeage chez les indigènes de Madagascar. J. SOC. AFR. 9 (1939), pp. 3-41.

24,355 DECARY, R. Le crocodile malgache. Ses moeurs, son rôle dans la vie indigène. J. SOC. AFR. 19 (1949), pp. 195-207.

24,356 DECARY, R. Les eaux douces et leurs habitants dans les traditions et les industries malgaches. MISM 5 (1959), pp. 233-266.

24,357 DECARY, R. L'habitation chez quelques tribus malgaches. MISM 4 (1957), pp. 1-34.

24,358 DECARY, R. Les mortiers malgaches. MISM 1 (1952), pp. 167-179.

24,359 DECARY, R. Les tatouages chez les indigènes de Madagascar. J. SOC. AFR. 5 (1935), pp. 1-39.

24,360 DEZ, J. Chez les Betsimisaraka de la région de Nosy Varika: les Tangalamena. J. SOC. AFR. 29 (1959), pp. 229-238.

24,361 DUBOIS, H. Populations et peuplement à Madagascar: simple essai de mise au point. AFRICA 6 (1933), pp. 206-219.

24,362 DUBOIS, H. M. Etude sur les Fady (Tabous Malgaches). BIBLIOTHECA AFR. 3 (1929), pp. 117-134; 3 (1929-1930), pp. 327-341.

24,363 DUCKWORTH, W. L. H. An account of skulls from Madagascar in the Anatomical Museum of Cambridge. JRAI 24 (1895), pp. 285-293.

24,364 FALCK, K. Notes sur la possession de la terre en Vakinankaratra, Madagascar. CONG. INT. SC. ANTHR. ET ETHN. 4, no. iii (1952), pp. 57-61.

24,365 FAUBLEE, J. Techniques divinatoires et magiques chez les Bara de Madagascar. J. SOC. AFR. 21 (1951), pp. 127-138.

24,366 GAUDEBOUT, P. and MOLET, L. Coutumes et textes tanala. MISM 4 (1957), pp. 35-96.

24,367 GRANDIDIER, M. G. A Madagascar, anciennes croyances et coutumes. J. SOC. AFR. 2 (1932), pp. 153-207.

24,368 HEBERT, J. C. La cosmographie malgache suivie de l'énumeration des points cardinaux et l'importance du Nord-Est. ANN. UNIV. MADAG., Hors série (1965), pp. 83-195.

24,369 HEBERT, J. C. Filan 'ampela, ou propos galants des Sakalava. J. SOC. AFR. 34 (1964), pp. 227-253.

24,370 LEIB, A. Mystical significance of colours among the natives of Madagascar. AFR. STUD. 6 (1947), pp. 77-81.

24,371 LINTON, R. Culture areas in Madagascar. AMER. ANTHR. 30 (1928), pp. 363-390.

24,372 LINTON, R. Report on work of field museum expedition in Madagascar from January to September 9, 1926. AMER. ANTHR. 29 (1927), pp. 292X-307X.

24,373 LINTON, R. Rice, a Malagasy tradition. AMER. ANTHR. 29 (1927), pp. 654-660.

24,374 MATTEI, M. Etude ethnographique sur les Zafimaniry. BULL. ACAD. MALG. 12 (1929), pp. 1-6.

24,375 MILLOT, J. and PASCAL, A. Notes sur la sorcellerie chez les Vezo de la région de Morombe. MISM 1 (1952), pp. 13-28.

24,376 MOLET, L. La culture idigène du riz et certains de ses problèmes à Madagascar. MISM 5 (1959), pp. 197-213.

24,377 MOLET, L. Métiers à tisser betsimisaraka. MISM 1 (1952), pp. 197-208.

24,378 MONDAIN, G. Courte note sur un voyage parmi les Sakalava du Sambirano. BULL. ACAD. MALG. 12 (1929), pp. 27-30.

24,379 MULLENS, J. On the origin and progress of the people of Madagascar. JRAI 5 (1875), pp. 181-198.

24,380 OLSEN, M. Le Famadihana et ce qui l'accompagne (dans le Vakinankaratra). BULL. ACAD. MALG. 12 (1929), pp. 61-65.

24,381 PARKER, G. W. On systems of land tenure in Madagascar. JRAI 12 (1883), pp. 277-280.

24,382 PARKER, G. W. On the people and language of Madagascar. JRAI 12 (1883), pp. 478-495.

24,383 POIRIER, J. Les rites de la naissance chez les Bezanozano. ANN. UNIV. MADAG. 3 (1964), pp. 7-18.

24,384 PONT, M. Note sur les sépultures des Zafirabay d'Andranofotsy province de Maroantsetra. BULL. ACAD. MALG. 13 (1930), pp. 187-188.

24,385 RAKOTO. Un Ala-fady chez les Antevondro. BULL. ACAD. MALG. 12 (1929), pp. 21-24.

24,386 RAKOTO. Un couteau de sacrifice. BULL. ACAD. MALG. 12 (1929), pp. 25-26.

24,387 RALISON, R. Les responsabilités des Malgaches diplômés des Universités Européennes. CIVILISATIONS 2 (1952), pp. 349-355; English summary, pp. 355-357.

24,388 RAMAMONJY, G. De quelques attitudes et coutumes merina. MISM 1 (1952), pp. 181-196.

24,389 RANAIVO, F. Le folklore malgache. PRESENCE AFR. N.S. 14-15 (1957), pp. 155-164.

24,390 RASAMIMANANA. Des Bibin' Andriana ou Bêtes Royales. BULL. ACAD. MALG. 12 (1929), pp. 31-32.

24,391 RASAMUEL, M. Coutumes malgaches: Kabary am-panambadiana (discours relatifs à la cérémonie du mariage). BULL. ACAD. MALG. 11 (1928), pp. 1-52.

24,392 RAVOAJANAHARY, C. Ralambo et ses legendes. ANN. UNIV. MADAG. 4 (1965), pp. 19-31.

24,393 RENEL, . [Anciennes religions de Madagascar] Ancêtres et dieux. BULL. ACAD. MALG. 5 (1920-1921), pp. 1-171.

24,394 SAVARON, C. Les Amants de Tritriva. BULL. ACAD. MALG. 13 (1930), pp. 39-56.

24,395 SIBREE, J. Decorative carving on wood, especially on their burial memorials, by the Bètsilèo Malagasy. JRAI 21 (1892), pp. 230-244.

24,396 SIBREE, J. Notes on relics of the sign and gesture language among the Malagasy. JRAI 13 (1884), pp. 174-183.

24,397 SIBREE, J. Relationships and the names used for them among the peoples of Madagascar, chiefly the Hovas; together with observations upon marriage customs and morals among the Malagasy. JRAI 9 (1880), pp. 35-50.

24,398 WAKE, C. S. Notes on the origin of the Malagasy. JRAI 11 (1882), pp. 21-33.

Art

24,399 ARCHDEACON, S. Erotic grave sculpture of the Sakalava and Vezo. TRANSITION 12 (1964), pp. 43-47.

24,400 BATTISTINI, R. L'importance de l'action de l'homme dans les transformations protohistoriques du milieu naturel à Madagascar. ANN. UNIV. MADAG., Hors série (1965), pp. 215-223.

24,401 BATTISTINI, R. et al. Le site archéologique de Talaky, par René Battistini, Pierre Verin et René Rason. ANN. UNIV. MADAG. 1 (1963), pp. 111-153.

24,402 BERNARD-THIERRY, S. Perles magiques a Madagascar. J. SOC. AFR. 29 (1959), pp. 33-90.

24,403 CHIPPAUX, C. et al. Etude des sépultures de la grotte de Bekopaka et de l'abri sous roche du Manambolo par C. Chippaux avec la collaboration de G. Babin et J.-P. Karche. ANN. UNIV. MADAG., Hors série (1965), pp. 227-247.

24,404 DESCHAMPS, H. Les taches de l'archéologie à Madagascar. ANN. UNIV. MADAG., Hors série (1965), pp. 11-14.

24,405 DESCHAMPS, M. H. Les danses autaisaka. BULL. ACAD. MALG. 17 (1934), pp. 31-47.

24,406 DEZ, J. Quelques hypothèses formulées par la linguistique comparée à l'usage de l'archéologie. ANN. UNIV. MADAG., Hors série (1965), pp. 197-213.

24,407 FONTOYNONT. De quelques manifestations artistiques malgaches anciennes. BULL. ACAD. MALG. 14 (1931), pp. 33-38.

24,408 FONTOYNONT, G. Notice sur une pierre sculptée trouvée à Sainte-Marie. BULL. ACAD. MALG. 3 (1916-1917), pp. 259-264.

24,409 LEUZINGER, E. Zwei Aloalos aus Madagascar im Museum Rietberg, Zürich. FESTSCHRIFT ALFRED BUHLER, 1965, pp. 263-269.

24,410 LEWIS, A. L. The Menhirs of Madagascar. JRAI 47 (1917), pp. 448-454.

24,411 MATTEI, M. Note sur les Sculptures de la région d'Antalaha. BULL. ACAD. MALG. 12 (1929), p. 13.

24,412 POIRIER, J. Données écologiques et démographiques de la mise en place des Proto-malgaches. ANN. UNIV. MADAG., Hors série (1965), pp. 61-82.

24,413 RAVELONANOSY, V. De la céramique à Madagascar. PRESENCE AFR. N.S. 31 (1960), pp. 90-95.

24,414 SOLHEIM, W. Indonesian culture and Malagasy origins. ANN. UNIV. MALAG., Hors série (1965), pp. 33-42.

24,415 VALETTE, J. De l'origine des Malgaches. ANN. UNIV. MADAG., Hors série (1965), pp. 15-32.

24,416 VERIN, P. Observations sur les monuments funéraires des Antanosy Avaratra et les poteaux commémoratifs du village d'Antsary. ANN. UNIV. MADAG. 3 (1964), pp. 47-57.

24,417 VERIN, P. et al. L'ancienne civilisation de l'Isandra, par P. Verin avec la collaboration de R. Battistini et de D. Chabouis. ANN. UNIV. MADAG., Hors série (1965), pp. 249-285.

24,418 VERNIER, E. Etude sur la fabrication des lambamena. J. SOC. AFR. 34 (1964), pp. 7-34.

See also 15841.

Biography

24,419 VILLIERS, A. In memoriam: Fernand Angel. BULL. IFAN 13 (1951), p. 893.

24,420 FONTOYNONT, G. Le Rev. P. Soury-Lavergne. BULL. ACAD. MALG. 4 (1918-1919), p. 73.

Economics

24,421 BALLERINI, E. Missione nel Madagascar. AFRICA (Rome) 19 (1964), pp. 81-90.

24,422 FOURNIER, H. Tananarive, étude d'économie urbaine. MISM 1 (1952), pp. 29-157.

24,423 FROIDEVAUX, H. Une enquête scientifique et économique sur Madagascar au XVIIe siècle. RHCF 2 (1914), pp. 259-290.

24,424 HANCE, W. A. Transportation in Madagascar. GEOG. REV. 48 (1958), pp. 45-68.

See also 15888, 17182.

Geography

24,425 BATHIE, H. P. DE LA. Au sujet de la capture du Mahajamba par la Betsiboka. BULL. ACAD. MALG. 6 (1922-1923), pp. 69-71.

24,426 COLIN, R. P. E. La pression atmosphérique sur le mont Tsiafajavona (2.630 mètres). BULL. ACAD. MALG. 3 (1916-1917), pp. 199-207.

24,427 COLIN, R. P. E. La température sur le Tsiafajavona. BULL. ACAD. MALG. 3 (1916-1917), pp. 191-198.

24,428 COOMBS, G. M. Madagascar. CONTEMP. REV. 162 (1942), pp. 90-93.

24,429 DECARY, R. Les formations littorales dans la région de Mananara. BULL. ACAD. MALG. 6 (1922-1923), pp. 63-65.

24,430 DECARY, R. Sur la morphogenie de la baie de Diego-Suarez. BULL. ACAD. MALG. 4 (1918-1919), pp. 197-204.

24,431 GRANDIDIER, G. Madagascar. GEOG. REV. 10 (1920), pp. 197-222.

24,432 MUTHUON, R. P. J. L'ancien lac de Belanitra. BULL. ACAD. MALG. 9 (1926), pp. 21-22.

24,433 MUTHUON, R. P. J. L'ancien volcan d'Ambatolampy (ankaratra). BULL. ACAD. MALG. 3 (1916-1917), pp. 163-164.

24,434 MUTHUON, R. P. J. Le bassin de Mahabo et les chutes d'Andrianambo. BULL. ACAD. MALG. 14 (1931), pp. 31-32.

24,435 MUTHUON, R. P. J. Sur une ancienne porte d'entrée de l'Ikopa dans le Bassin de Tananarive. BULL. ACAD. MALG. 6 (1922-1923), p. 75.

24,436 POISSON, P. H. Activité seismique en 1928. BULL. ACAD. MALG. 11 (1928), pp. 57-59.

24,437 POISSON, R. P. Note sur une détermination de longitude faite à Tananarive en 1925. BULL. ACAD. MALG. 10 (1927), pp. 61-94.

24,438 POISSON, R. P. Sur le cyclone de Mahanoro du 21 Février 1906. BULL. ACAD. MALG. 17 (1934), pp. 50-53.

24,439 POISSON, R. P. Sur l'étude des cyclones de l'Océan Indien. BULL. ACAD. MALG. 17 (1934), pp. 1-6.

24,440 POISSON, R. P. Les tremblements de terre de 1929. BULL. ACAD. MALG. 12 (1929), pp. 15-19.

24,441 POISSON, R. P. Tremblements de terre à Madagascar 1930-1931-1932. BULL. ACAD. MALG. 15 (1932), pp. 1-6.

24,442 RAWLINS, R. E. D. Schooner to Providence. CORONA 1, no. 5 (1949), pp. 31-33.

Government. Politics. Administration

24,443 APPOLIS, E. Les Fokon'Olona, municipes ruraux de Madagascar. ANN. UNIV. MADAG. 1 (1963), pp. 39-43.

24,444 ARBOUSSET, F. Le fokon'olona a Madagascar. RJPUF 4 (1950), pp. 472-533.

24,445 BASTIAN, G. Contribution a l'étude des cadres régionaux de développement a Madagascar. ANN. UNIV. MADAG. 1 (1963), pp. 95-109.

24,446 HARDYMAN, J. T. Madagascar faces the future. CONTEMP. REV. 195 (1959), pp. 156-158.

24,447 HARDYMAN, J. T. Madagascar problems. CONTEMP. REV. 172 (1947), pp. 359-362.

24,448 HARDYMAN, J. T. Progress in Madagascar. CONTEMP. REV. 182 (1952), pp. 49-51.

24,449 JOHNSTON, A. French policy in Madagascar. J. AFR. SOC. 4 (1904), pp. 78-81.

24,450 JUMEAUX, R. Essai d'analyse du nationalisme malgache. AFR. ET ASIE 40 (1957), pp. 31-42.

24,451 K., P. Les collectivités autochtones rurales à Madagascar. CIVILISATIONS 1, no. ii (1951), pp. 19-24; English summary, p. 24.

24,452 RABEMANANJARA, J. Les fondements culturels du nationalisme malgache. PRESENCE AFR. N.S. 18-19 (1958), pp. 125-142.

24,453 RASETA, J. et al. Notre position en face du referendum. PRESENCE AFR. N.S. 20 (1958), pp. 141-142.

24,454 SIBREE, J. General Gallieni's "Neuf aus à Madagascar": an example of French colonization. J. AFR. SOC. 8 (1909), pp. 259-273.

History

24,455 ANDRIANTSILANIARIVO, E. Le Malgache du XXe siècle. PRESENCE AFR. N.S. 8-10 (1956), pp. 98-107.

24,456 APPOLIS, E. Une épidemie de ramanenjana à Madagascar (1863-1864). ANN. UNIV. MADAG. 3 (1964), pp. 59-63.

24,457 AUJUS, M. Un point d'histoire malgache. BULL. ACAD. MALG. 3 (1916-1917), pp. 213-221.

24,458 AYACHE, S. Pour un enseignement de l'histoire de Madagascar. ANN. UNIV. MADAG. 4 (1965), pp. 7-17.

24,459 AYACHE, S. Travaux d'histoire culturelle à l'Ecole Normale de Tananarive. ANN. UNIV. MADAG., Hors série (1965), pp. 287-301.

24,460 BARBIER, C. LE. Notes sur le pays des Bara-Imamono (Région d'Ankazoabo). BULL. ACAD. MALG. 3 (1916-1917), pp. 61-119.

24,461 BLIND, K. The fictitious French claim to Madagascar. CONTEMP. REV. 66 (1894), pp. 883-889.

24,462 BOUDOU, R. P. A. La Côte Ouest de Madagascar en 1852. Notes d'Edmond Samat. BULL. ACAD. MALG. 15 (1932), pp. 53-78.

24,463 BOUDOU, R. P. A. Journal de route d'une expédition de Rainimaharo en 1838. BULL. ACAD. MALG. 15 (1932), pp. 88-112.

24,464 BOUDOU, R. P. A. Une lettre du Prince Rakoto (Radama II) 1859. BULL. ACAD. MALG. 15 (1932), pp. 79-87.

24,465 BOUDOU, R. P. A. Le Prince Rakoto (Radama II) et ses premières relations avec les missionnaires catholiques 1854-1857. BULL. ACAD. MALG. 14 (1931), pp. 75-106.

24,466 BYSLMA, M. Inscriptions relevées par M. E. Drouhard sur les rochers de l'Ile de Nossi Mangabe, Baie d'Antongil. BULL. ACAD. MALG. 9 (1926), pp. 91-96.

24,467 CHAPUS, S. Quatre-vingts années d'influences européennes en Imerina. BULL. ACAD. MALG. 8 (1925), pp. 1-350.

24,468 COLBY, R. Madagascar: the great island. HISTORY TODAY 12 (1962), pp. 33-41.

24,469 DECARY, R. Documents historiques relatifs à l'établissement français de Sainte-Marie sous la Restauration. BULL. ACAD. MALG. 13 (1930), pp. 57-89.

24,470 DECARY, R. Les études historiques sur Madagascar. REV. HIST. COL. 34 (1947), pp. 9-21.

24,471 DECARY, R. Madagascar (1956-1960). REV. FRANC. HIST. OUTRE-MER 49 (1962), pp. 438-472.

24,472 DECARY, R. La reddition de Tamatave à l'Angleterre en 1811. BULL. ACAD. MALG. 15 (1932), pp. 48-52.

24,473 DECARY, R. Sur l'époque de l'introduction de l'Opuntia Dillenii Haw. ou Raiketa de Madagascar. BULL. ACAD. MALG. 17 (1934), pp. 48-49.

24,474 DECARY, R. Sylvain Roux et le serment des peuples de Tanibé a Madagascar en 1822. RHCF 29 (1936), pp. 267-290.

24,475 DESCHAMPS, H. Conceptions, problèmes et sources de l'histoire de Madagascar. J. AFR. HIST. 1 (1960), pp. 249-256.

24,476 FAUBLEE, J. Madagascar au XIXe siècle: esquisse d'histoire économique et sociale. J. WORLD HIST. 5 (1959-1960), pp. 463-491.

24,477 FOSTER, W. An English settlement in Madagascar in 1645-6. ENG. HIST. REV. 27 (1912), pp. 239-250.

24,478 FROIDEVAUX, H. Les derniers projets du duc de La Meilleraye sur Madagascar (1663). RHCF 3 (1915), pp. 401-430.

24,479 GORDGE, J. T. The outlook in Madagascar. AFR. AFFAIRS 48 (1949), pp. 133-141.

24,480 HOWE, S. E. Le role de Sir Robert Farquhar Gouveneur de l'Ile Maurice dans l'histoire de Madagascar. RHCF 28 (1935), pp 157-204.

24,481 HOWE, S. E. Un rêve anglais: Madagascar colonie britannique. RHCF 27 (1934), pp. 1-32.

24,482 JACOB, G. Léon Suberbie et les relations franco-malgaches de 1882 à 1887. REV. FRANC. HIST. OUTRE-MER 52 (1965), pp. 315-351.

24,483 JULIEN, M. G. Notes d'histoire Malgache. BULL. ACAD. MALG. 9 (1926), pp. 3-13.

24,484 MATTEI, M. Contribution à l'histoire de Benyowsky dans la baie de Ngotsy (1785-1786). BULL. ACAD. MALG. 12 (1929), pp. 7-11.

24,485 MEYZONNADE et al. Sur la capture de la Mahajamba par le Kamoro [accounts by Meyzonnade, M. F. Fraud, M. H. Perrier de la Bathie, M. Longuefosse]. BULL. ACAD. MALG. 13 (1930), pp. 91-103.

24,486 MILLOT, J. Considérations sur le commerce dans l'Océan Indien au Moyen Age et au pré-Moyen Age, à propos des perles de Zanaga. MISM 1 (1952), pp. 159-165.

24,487 MOLET, L. L'expansion tsimihety. Modalités et motivations des migrations intérieures d'un groupe ethnique du Nord de Madagascar. MISM 5 (1959), pp. 1-196.

24,488 MONDAIN, M. G. Un registre officiel du temps de Rasoherina et de Ranavalona II. BULL. ACAD. MALG. 9 (1926), pp. 63-77.

24,489 OLSEN, M. Histoire des Zafindiamanana (Tribu tanala du nord d'Ambohimanga-du-sud). BULL. ACAD. MALG. 12 (1929), pp. 37-60.

24,490 PETIT, M. and JACOB, G. Un essai de colonisation dans la baie d'Antongil (1895-vers 1926). ANN. UNIV. MADAG. 4 (1965), pp. 33-56.

24,491 RABEMANANJARA, J. L'indépendance de Madagascar. PRESENCE AFR. N.S. 20 (1958), pp. 120-122.

24,492 RABEMANANJARA, J. Madagascar 1947-1957. PRESENCE AFR. N.S. 12 (1957), pp. 73-77.

24,493 RABEMANANJARA, J. Présence de Madagascar. PRESENCE AFR. N.S. 12 (1957), pp. 89-108.

24,494 RAHARIJAONA. Au résidences royales. Essai de monographies sur Ambohimanga et Ambositra. BULL. ACAD. MALG. 14 (1931), pp. 107-136.

24,495 RAOMBANA. Manuscrit écrit à Tananarive (1853-1854). BULL. ACAD. MALG. 13 (1930), pp. 1-26.

24,496 RUSILLON, H. Notes explicatives a propos de la généalogie Maroseranana Zafimbolamena. BULL. ACAD. MALG. 6 (1922-1923), pp. 169-184.

24,497 SAVARON, C. Contribution a l'histoire de l'Imerina. BULL. ACAD. MALG. 11 (1928), pp. 61-81.

24,498 SAVARON, C. Notes d'histoire malgache. BULL. ACAD. MALG. 14 (1931), pp. 55-73.

24,499 SAVARON, C. Mes souvenirs de la descente à Majunga avec l'escorte 27 Octobre-20 Novembre 1894. BULL. ACAD. MALG. 13 (1930), pp. 27-38.

24,500 SEYRIG, A. Un Malgache, officier de Louis XIV. BULL. ACAD. MALG. 14 (1931), pp. 39-40.

24,501 SHAW, G. A. The future prospects of Madagascar. CONTEMP. REV. 44 (1883), pp. 749-758.

24,502 SIBREE, J. England, France and Madagascar. CONTEMP. REV. 43 (1883), pp. 85-99.

24,503 VALETTE, J. Travaux en cours à partir des Archives de la République Malgache. CAH. ET. AFR. 5 (1965), pp. 155-156.

Language. Literature

Language

24,504 CHAZEL, A. A propos des noms de lieux à Madagascar. BULL. ACAD. MALG. 8 (1925), pp. 353-358.

24,505 COLANCON, M. A propos d'une note sur l'emploi de l'écriture arabe a Madagascar. BULL. ACAD. MALG. 6 (1922-1923), pp. 77-84.

24,506 DANDOUAU, A. [tr.] Dialogues Francais-Sakalava (Dialecte de Nossi-Bé et du Sambirano). BULL. ACAD. MALG. 6 (1922-1923), pp. 91-157.

24,507 DEZ, J. Lexique des mots européens malgachisés. ANN. UNIV. MADAG. 4 (1965), pp. 63-86.

24,508 DEZ, J. La malgachisation des emprunts aux langues européennes. ANN. UNIV. MADAG. 3 (1964), pp. 19-46.

24,509 FAGERENG, M. E. L'orthographe de l'article défini malgache et l'emploi de l'n euphonique. BULL. ACAD. MALG. 15 (1932), pp. 27-37.

24,510 FLUTRE, L. F. De l'apport de Madagascar au vocabulaire du français d'outre-mer aux XVIIe et XVIIIe siècles. ANN. UNIV. MADAG. 1 (1963), pp. 3-21.

24,511 FLUTRE, L. F. Sur un texte du XVIe siècle en patois de Valenciennes (moyen rouchi). ANN. UNIV. MADAG. 2 (1964), pp. 3-36.

24,512 LAST, J. T. Notes on the languages spoken in Madagascar. JRAI 25 (1896), pp. 46-71.

24,513 MONDAIN, G. De l'origine de certains mots malgaches. BULL. ACAD. MALG. 15 (1932), pp. 15-26.

24,514 MONDAIN, G. Malagasy and Maanjan: a linguistic comparison [a review article on Malgache et Maanjan: Une Comparaison Linguistique by Otto Chr. Dahl]. INT. REV. MISSIONS 42 (1953), pp. 452-458.

24,515 MONDAIN, M. Complément a la note sur l'emploi de l'écriture aribico-malgache. BULL. ACAD. MALG. 6 (1922-1923), pp. 85-89.

24,516 RANDZAVOLA, M. Etude sur l'orthographe de l'article défini malgache et sur l'emploi de l'n dite euphonique ou abrégée de ny. BULL. ACAD. MALG. 15 (1932), pp. 38-47.

24,517 RASAMIMANANA. Voyage de Radama I à la côte Est: analyse du manuscrit de Ratsiambakaina suivie de quelques conclusions sur l'orthographie malgache. BULL. ACAD. MALG. 10 (1927), pp. 45-59.

24,518 RUSILLON, H. Des modifications que subit le Z placé au commencement des mots ou entre les voyelles: Z=H=K=N et de quelques observations au sujet des dialectes malgaches. BULL. ACAD. MALG. 4 (1918-1919), pp. 223-230.

24,519 RUSILLON, H. De quelques differences entre la langue hova et le dialecte sakalava. BULL. ACAD. MALG. 4 (1918-1919), pp. 231-246.

24,520 VERGUIN, J. Deux systèmes de vocabulaire parallèle a Madagascar. WORD 13 (1957), pp. 153-156.

Literature

24,521 ANDRIANARAHINJAKA, L. X. M. Ile aux vents. PRESENCE AFR. N.S. 11 (1957), p. 109.

24,522 ANDRIANARAHINJAKA, L. X. M. Ramananato, poète betsileo du début du 19e siècle. PRESENCE AFR. N.S. 55 (1965), pp. 42-72.

24,523 BEIER, U. [Jean-Joseph] Rabearivelo. BO 11 (1962), pp. 10-11.

24,524 KOSHLAND, M. The poetry of Madagascar. AFR. SOUTH 4, no. 2 (1960), pp. 114-117.

24,525 RABEARIVELO, J. J. Here she stands [a poem]. AFR. SOUTH 4, no. 2 (1960), p. 118.

24,526 RABEMANANJARA, J. Automne austral. PRESENCE AFR. N.S. 7 (1956), pp. 96-97.

24,527 RABEMANANDJARA, J. Chant XXII. PRESENCE AFR. 2 (1948), pp. 242-243.

24,528 RABEMANANJARA, J. Reveillon 47. PRESENCE AFR. N.S. 20 (1958), pp. 66-68.

24,529 RANAIVO, F. Poèmes [Chanson de jeune femme, Epithalame]. PRESENCE AFR. 3 (1948), pp. 460-465.

24,530 RANAIVO, F. Two poems translated by Miriam Koshland [My home is space, Love song]. BO 9 (1961), p. 61.

24,531 RANAIVO, F. Love song [a poem]. AFR. SOUTH 4, no. 2 (1960), p. 119.

24,532 RANDZAVOLA, H. Spécimen de poésie betsileo. BULL. ACAD. MALG. 8 (1925), pp. 359-369.

24,533 RATSIMAMANGA, A. R. and LORIN, C. M. Poètes malgaches de langue française. PRESENCE AFR. N.S. 7 (1956), pp. 26-50.

24,534 RAZAFINTSAMBAINA, G. Hommage à Rabearivelo. PRESENCE AFR. 36 (1961), pp. 120-126.

See also 22812.

Law

24,535 DECARY, R. Les contacts de civilisations et les problèmes fonciers à Madagascar. CIVILISATIONS 2 (1952), pp. 189-193; English summary, pp. 193-194.

24,536 HOLLEAUX, A. Les élections aux Assemblées des Territoires d'outre-mer. RJPUF 10 (1956), pp. 1-54.

24,537 PARKER, G. W. On the new code of laws for the Hova Kingdom of Madagascar, promulgated at Antananarivo on March 29th, 1881. JRAI 12 (1883), pp. 306-318.

24,538 RAHARIJAONA, B. La réputation et le divorce chez les Hova sous Ranavanola II et Ranavalona III. BULL. ACAD. MALG. 17 (1934), pp. 54-58.

24,539 SICARD, F. Les récentes réformes de la justice à Madagascar. REV. JURIDIQUE MADAG. 1 (1951), pp. 9-12.

Religion

24,540 ARNOLD, R. W. The ministry of missionaries in Madagascar. INT. REV. MISSIONS 51 (1962), pp. 185-188.

24,541 BIRKELI, F. The Church in Madagascar. INT. REV. MISSIONS 46 (1957), pp. 155-163.

24,542 CHIRGWIN, A. M. The growth of the Church in Madagascar. INT. REV. MISSIONS 22 (1933), pp. 94-104.

24,543 COUVE, D. Co-operation in Madagascar. INT. REV. MISSIONS 3 (1914), pp. 313-322.

24,544 DUBOIS, R. P. Sur la divinisation Malgache. BULL. ACAD. MALG. 9 (1926), pp. 97-99.

24,545 FAUBLEE, M. and FAUBLEE, J. Les religions malgaches et le mysticisme. PRESENCE AFR. N.S. 18-19 (1958), pp. 37-42.

24,546 FOURY, B. Maudave et la colonisation de Madagascar. REV. HIST. COL. 42 (1955), pp. 343-404; 43 (1956), pp. 14-81.

24,547 HARDYMAN, J. T. Church, politics and nationalism in Madagascar. INT. REV. MISSIONS 37 (1948), pp. 194-197.

24,548 HAWKINS, F. H. The centenary of missions in Madagascar. INT. REV. MISSIONS 9 (1920), pp. 570-580.

24,549 MASON, K. The Christian share in Malagasy literature. INT. REV. MISSIONS 42 (1953), pp. 178-183.

24,550 MERLO, M. Perspectives chrétiennes en Afrique Francaise et à Madagascar. CIVILISATIONS 6 (1956), pp. 91-95.

24,551 MEYER, O. B. The Norwegian mission in Madagascar. INT. REV. MISSIONS 26 (1937), pp. 372-377.

24,552 RUSILLON, H. The effect of the Gospel on the natives of Madagascar. INT. REV. MISSIONS 23 (1935), pp. 530-538.

24,553 WHITFIELD, J. N. B. Christian education in South Madagascar. INT. REV. MISSIONS 32 (1943), pp. 172-178.

Science

24,554 ANGEL, M. F. Sur l'habitat d'un certain nombre de lezards de Madagascar. BULL. ACAD. MALG. 13 (1930), pp. 109-116.

24,555 ANGEL, M. F. Sur Uroplatus phantasticus Boulgr. et Uroplatus Schneideri Lamberton. BULL. ACAD. MALG. 13 (1930), pp. 105-108.

24,556 BASSE, E. Etude géologique de la région de Tongobory. BULL. ACAD. MALG. 13 (1930), pp. 175-186.

24,557 CAMBOUE, R. P. Moustiques, mouches, araignées. Note sur une prophylaxie biologique du paludisme, des affections intestinales et de la trypanosomiase. BULL. ACAD. MALG. 4 (1918-1919), pp. 133-142.

24,558 CAMBOUE, R. P. Note biologique sur des Lépidoptères de Madagascar. BULL. ACAD. MALG. 3 (1916-1917), pp. 247-257.

24,559 CAMBOUE, R. P. Note sur le comportement de l'araignée sociale communiste de Madagascar (Stegodyphus Gregarius, var. simplicifrons). BULL. ACAD. MALG. 10 (1927), pp. 29-31.

24,560 CAMBOUE, R. P. Notes biologiques sur quelques aranéides de Madagascar. BULL. ACAD. MALG. 3 (1916-1917), pp. 173-189.

24,561 CARLE, G. Notes sur les coulées basaltiques de l'Antsifitra et du Iavoko et sur vallées de comblement qu'elles ont provoquées. BULL. ACAD. MALG. 3 (1916-1917), pp. 223-224.

24,562 CHAMPION, P. La tache pigmentaire congénitale a Madagascar et aux Comores. J. SOC. AFR. 7 (1937), pp. 79-92.

24,563 DECARY, R. La bouche et les dents dans les coutumes malgaches. J. SOC. AFR. 23 (1953), pp. 35-42.

24,564 DECARY, R. Contribution a la botanique et la géologie de la région Fort-Dauphin-Andrahomana. BULL. ACAD. MALG. 10 (1927), pp. 13-18.

24,565 DECARY, R. Contribution à l'étude de la végétation de Madagascar. La flore de la ville de Tananarive. BULL. ACAD. MALG. 13 (1930), pp. 127-149.

24,566 DECARY, R. Les dernières éruptions du massif d'Ambre. BULL. ACAD. MALG. 6 (1922-1923), pp. 67-68.

24,567 DECARY, R. Deux intéressantes fructifications de plantes malgaches. BULL. ACAD. MALG. 11 (1928), pp. 53-55.

24,568 DECARY, R. La famille des Phalloidacés et ses représentants a Madagascar. BULL. ACAD. MALG. 10 (1927), pp. 35-39.

24,569 DECARY, R. Liste d'échinodermes recueillis a Madagascar. BULL. ACAD. MALG. 6 (1922-1923), pp. 37-41.

24,570 DECARY, R. Un Mission Scientifique dans le Sud-Est de Madagascar. BULL. ACAD. MALG. 9 (1926), pp. 79-86.

24,571 DECARY, R. Notes géologiques sur l'Extrême-Sud de Madagascar. BULL. ACAD. MALG. 14 (1931), pp. 41-54.

24,572 DECARY, R. Notes géologiques sur la région de Diego-Suarez. BULL. ACAD. MALG. 6 (1922-1923), pp. 43-62.

24,573 DECARY, R. Sur quelques Stellérides d'Anjouan. BULL. ACAD. MALG. 9 (1926), pp. 15-16.

24,574 DECARY, R. and RAJAONARIVO, J. La médication antirabique chez les Antandroy. BULL. ACAD. MALG. 9 (1926), pp. 17-19.

24,575 DUFOUR, M. L. and POISSON, M. H. Notes sur quelques champignons de Madagascar. BULL. ACAD. MALG. 9 (1926), pp. 29-32.

24,576 ERHART, H. Sur les possibilités d'amélioration des terrains lateriques. BULL. ACAD. MALG. 10 (1927), pp. 26-28.

24,577 FAUBLEE, J. L'alimentation des Bara (Sud de Madagascar). J. SOC. AFR. 12 (1942), pp. 157-201.

24,578 FRANCOIS, E. Les jardins Hovas au temps de la souveraineté malgache. BULL. ACAD. MALG. 8 (1925), pp. 351-352.

24,579 FRAPPA, C. La mouche des fruits à Madagascar Drosophila repleta Woll. BULL. ACAD. MALG. 13 (1930), pp. 117-124.

24,580 FRAPPA, C. Note sur deux insectes nuisibles au caféir à Madagascar. BULL. ACAD. MALG. 13 (1930), pp. 125-126.

24,581 GRANDIDIER, G. Description d'une nouvelle espèce de Nesomys. BULL. ACAD. MALG. 11 (1928), pp. 95-99.

24,582 GRANDIDIER, G. Un nouveau type de Mammifère insectivore de Madagascar. BULL. ACAD. MALG. 11 (1928), pp. 85-90.

24,583 GRANDIDIER, G. Nouvelle espèce de Chauve-Souris frugivore. BULL. ACAD. MALG. 11 (1928), pp. 91-93.

24,584 GRANDIDIER, G. Une variété Cheiromys madagascariensis actuel et un nouveau Cheiromys subfossile. BULL. ACAD. MALG. 11 (1928), pp. 101-107.

24,585 GRANDIDIER, G. and BERLIOZ, J. Description d'une espèce nouvelle d'Oiseau de Madagascar de la famille des Rallidés. BULL. ACAD. MALG. 11 (1928), pp. 83-84.

24,586 GUILLANTON, M. Note au sujet de la carte géologique de reconnaissance du Service des mines. BULL. ACAD. MALG. 17 (1934), pp. 7-12.

24,587 HEBERT, J. C. Analyse structurale des géomancies comoriennes, malgaches et africaines. J. SOC. AFR. 31 (1961), pp. 115-208.

24,588 JUMELLE, H. Les Dypsis, palmiers de Madagascar. BULL. ACAD. MALG. 6 (1922-1923), pp. 1-20.

24,589 LA BATHIE, M. H. P. DE. Au sujet des couches les plus anciennes de la série sédimentaire du versant occidental. BULL. ACAD. MALG. 4 (1918-1919), pp. 214-221.

24,590 LA BATHIE, M. H. P. DE. Au sujet des notes de MM. Joleaud et Bertrand sur l'existence d'un grand bassin lacustre d'âge néogène à Antsirabe et des dépôts de cette region. BULL. ACAD. MALG. 9 (1926), pp. 53-62.

24,591 LA BATHIE, M. H. P. DE. Les Crassulacées Malgaches. BULL. ACAD. MALG. 6 (1922-1923), pp. 21-36.

24,592 LA BATHIE, M. H. P. DE. Fossiles du quaternaire de Majunga (Déterminations de M. Dautzenberg). BULL. ACAD. MALG. 9 (1926), pp. 87-89.

24,593 LA BATHIE, M. H. P. DE. Fruits et graines du gisements de subfossiles d'Ampasaambazimba. BULL. ACAD. MALG. 10 (1927), pp. 24-25.

24,594 LA BATHIE, M. H. P. DE. Le Manjakabetany de Tuléar. BULL. ACAD. MALG. 15 (1932), pp. 7-8.

24,595 LA BATHIE, M. H. P. DE. Note sur un nouveau Gastrorchis. BULL. ACAD. MALG. 12 (1929), pp. 33-35.

24,596 LA BATHIE, M. H. P. DE. Un nouveau genre de balsaminées. BULL. ACAD. MALG. 10 (1927), pp. 22-23.

24,597 LA BATHIE, M. H. P. DE. Nouvelles observations sur les Aloe de Madagascar. BULL. ACAD. MALG. 10 (1927), pp. 19-21.

24,598 LA BATHIE, M. H. P. DE. Les Polygala de Madagascar. BULL. ACAD. MALG. 14 (1931), pp. 1-30.

24,599 LA BATHIE, M. H. P. DE. Les terrains postérieurs au crétacé moyen de la région de Majunga. BULL. ACAD. MALG. 4 (1918-1919), pp. 205-212.

24,600 LAMBERTON, C. Contribution à l'étude anatomique des AEpyornis. BULL. ACAD. MALG. 13 (1930), pp. 151-174.

24,601 LAMBERTON, C. Notes d'ornithologie Malgache. BULL. ACAD. MALG. 10 (1927), pp. 40-42.

24,602 LAMBERTON, C. Le Pseudaelurus à Madagascar. BULL. ACAD. MALG. 3 (1916-1917), pp. 209-210.

24,603 LEANDRI, J. Sur la présence du genre Uroplatus dans la région occidentale de Madagascar. BULL. ACAD. MALG. 15 (1932), p. 14.

24,604 LEON. Notules sur la Flore de Nossi-be. BULL. ACAD. MALG. 15 (1932), pp. 9-13.

24,605 MONNIER, L. Note sur un gisement fossilifère. BULL. ACAD. MALG. 9 (1926), pp. 23-24.

24,606 MONNIER, L. and LAMBERTON, C. Note sur des ossements subfossiles de la Région de Mananjary. BULL. ACAD. MALG. 3 (1916-1917), pp. 212-213.

24,607 MUTHUON, R. P. J. Compte-rendu d'un voyage géologique dans les régions en bordure Sud et Ouest. BULL. ACAD. MALG. 3 (1916-1917), pp. 167-172.

24,608 MUTHUON, R. P. J. Le quartzite a magnétite de Bealoka. BULL. ACAD. MALG. 9 (1926), p. 20.

24,609 MUTHUON, R. P. J. La Ruisseau des tufs multicolores. BULL. ACAD. MALG. 6 (1922-1923), pp. 73-74.

24,610 MUTHUON, R. P. J. Sur de nombreux affleurements de diabase dans la région d'Antanamalaza. BULL. ACAD. MALG. 3 (1916-1917), pp. 165-166.

24,611 OLSOUFIEFF, G. La chasse nocturne des insectes à Madagascar. BULL. ACAD. MALG. 15 (1932), pp. 113-120.

24,612 OLSOUFIEFF, G. Contribution à l'étude des Cétonides malgaches. BULL. ACAD. MALG. 15 (1932), pp. 121-126.

24,613 POISSON, M. H. Note anatomo-pathologique sur le cryptoprocta ferox. BULL. ACAD. MALG. 9 (1926), pp. 33-37.

24,614 POISSON, M. H. Note complémentaire à l'étude des poissons fossiles de Bobatomendry. BULL. ACAD. MALG. 3 (1916-1917), p. 225.

24,615 POISSON, M. H. Note sur un ver rond des eaux de Madagascar. BULL. ACAD. MALG. 9 (1926), pp. 25-28.

24,616 POISSON, M. H. Notes sur un Pachypodium nouveau de la région de Diégo-Suarez. BULL. ACAD. MALG. 3 (1916-1917), pp. 235-236.

24,617 POISSON, M. H. Notes sur un Pachypodium nouveau du nord de Madagascar. BULL. ACAD. MALG. 3 (1916-1917), pp. 237-239.

24,618 POISSON, M. H. Nouvelle contribution a l'étude des pachypodium malgaches. BULL. ACAD. MALG. 6 (1922-1923), pp. 159-168.

24,619 POISSON, M. H. Principaux facies biologiques de Diégo-Suarez. BULL. ACAD. MALG. 3 (1916-1917), pp. 227-234.

24,620 POISSON, M. H. and DECARY, R. Nouvelles observations biologiques sur les Pachypodium malgaches. BULL. ACAD. MALG. 3 (1916-1917), pp. 241-246.

24,621 POISSON, R. P. Sur le concours nécessaire de la géologie pour l'étude des tremblements de terre et du magnétisme à Madagascar. BULL. ACAD. MALG. 17 (1934), pp. 25-30.

24,622 RASAMOEL, J. B. Sur la transformation en bleu de toutes les différentes colorations du béryl autres que le blanc et le rose. BULL. ACAD. MALG. 10 (1927), pp. 32-34.

24,623 RIBARD, M. E. Le vol de boeufs dans le Sud-Ouest de Madagascar. BULL. ACAD. MALG. 9 (1926), pp. 39-51.

See also 17625.

Sociology

24,624 ANDRIAMANJATO, R. La culture malgache. PRESENCE AFR. N.S. 22 (1958), pp. 58-62.

24,625 C., J. Dénombrement de Madagascar. ZAIRE 8 (1954), pp. 642-643.

24,626 COLIN, P. Aperçu de psychologie malgache. AFR. ET ASIE 18 (1952), pp. 45-54.

24,627 DECARY, R. Les conditions physiques du peuplement humain de Madagascar. MISM 1 (1952), pp. 1-12.

24,628 DESCHAMPS, H. La notion de peuples; l'exemple malgache. CONG. INT. SC. ANTHR. ET ETHN. 6, no. 1 (1960), pp. 39-42.

24,629 FAUBLEE, J. Les coutumes ancestrales et leur adaptation a l'évolution. GENEVE-AFR. 4 (1965), pp. 52-64.

24,630 GAYET, G. Immigrations asiatiques à Madagascar. CIVILISATIONS 5 (1955), pp. 54-64; English summary, pp. 65-66.

24,631 GONDOMINAS, G. La situation coloniale à Madagascar (La Société Merina). CAH. INT. SOCIOL. 30 (1961), pp. 67-74.

24,632 ISNARD, H. Disparités régionales et unité nationale à Madagascar. CAH. INT. SOCIOL. 32 (1962), pp. 25-42.

24,633 LAPIERRE, J. W. A quoi bon les sociologues? ANN. UNIV. MADAG. 2 (1964), pp. 41-56.

24,634 MOLET, L. Le boeuf dans l'Ankaizinana; son importance sociale et économique. MISM 2 (1953), pp. 1-218.

24,635 MOLET, L. La cérémonie d'intronisation à Madagascar et ses implications économiques. CAH. INT. SOCIOL. 24 (1958), pp. 80-87.

24,636 MOLET, L. Démographie de l'Ankaizinana. MISM 3 (1956), pp. 1-230.

24,637 NOOTEBOOM, C. De betrekkingen tussen Madagascar en Indonesie. ZAIRE 3 (1949), pp. 881-894.

24,638 POIRIER, J. Le relation de l'homme au sol à Madagascar. A propos de l'inventaire ethno-topographique d'un terrior malgache. ANN. UNIV. MADAG. 2 (1964), pp. 57-71.

24,639 RAHARIJAONA, S. and VERIN, P. Le système de parenté mérina: essai d'analyse. ANN. UNIV. MADAG. 2 (1964), pp. 101-113.

24,640 RAJAONA, S. Aspects de la psychologie malgache vus à travers certains traits des Kabary et quelques faits de langue. ANN. UNIV. MADAG. 1 (1963), pp. 23-37.

24,641 RAZAFY-ANDRIAMIHAINGO, S. R. La femme à Madagascar. AFRICA (Rome) 16 (1961), pp. 29-32.

24,642 RAZAFY-ANDRIAMIHAINGO, S. R. The position of women in Madagascar. AFR. WOMEN 3 (1958-1960), pp. 29-33.

24,643 RETIF, A. Problèmes démographiques et humains à Madagascar. AFR. ET ASIE 26 (1964), pp. 4-10.

24,644 TSIEN TCHE-HAO. La vie sociale des Chinois à Madagascar. COMP. STUD. SOC. HIST. 3 (1960-1961), pp. 170-181.

COMORO ARCHIPELAGO

24,645 BOURDE, A. The Comoro Islands: problems of a microcosm. JMAS 3 (1965), pp. 91-102.

24,646 GUY, P. La justice aux Iles Comores. REV. JURIDIQUE DE MADAGASCAR 1 (1951), pp. 86-89.

24,647 GUY, P. Le mariage en droit comorien. RJPUF 9 (1955), pp. 799-830; 10 (1956), pp. 307-346.

24,648 HEBERT, J. C. Fêtes agraires dans l'ile d'Anjouan (archipel des Comores). J. SOC. AFR. 30 (1960), pp. 101-116.

24,649 LUCHAIRE, F. The political and administrative system of the Territories of the Comores. J. LOCAL ADM. OV. 4 (1965), pp. 88-98.

24,650 MONDAIN, M. J. Note sur une exploration du volcan Karthala (Grande Comore). BULL. ACAD. MALG. 17 (1934), pp. 13-24.

24,651 STRUCK, B. An unpublished vocabulary of the Comoro language. J. AFR. SOC. 8 (1909), pp. 412-421.

See also 17182, 24562, 24587.

RÉUNION

24,652 LEBLOND, M. A. L'histoire à la Réunion. RHCF 25 (1932), pp. 153-158.

See also 17182.

SEYCHELLES

24,653 BAILEY, R. The birds of the western Indian Ocean. J. SEYCHELLES SOC. 3 (1963), pp. 41-49.

24,654 BARNACLE, G. A. S. The land and freshwater shells of the Seychelles group of islands (including the Amirantes, Coetivy, Farquhar, Cosmoledo and Aldabra). J. SEYCHELLES SOC. 2 (1962), pp. 53-57.

24,655 BOWIN, C. O. Geophysical studies in the Indian Ocean by R/V chain of the Woods Hole Oceanographic Institution. J. SEYCHELLES SOC. 4 (1965), pp. 60-65.

24,656 BROWNE, B. C. The British contribution to the international Indian Ocean expedition. J. SEYCHELLES SOC. 3 (1963), pp. 11-16.

24,657 CASEY, M. A centenary (1861-1961) [Sisters of St. Joseph of Cluny in the Seychelles]. J. SEYCHELLES SOC. 1 (1961), pp. 54-60.

24,658 DAVIDSON, G. B. D. American trade in the Indian Ocean 1795-1815. J. SEYCHELLES SOC. 3 (1963), pp. 1-10.

24,659 DAYER, L. M. de Malavois: l'histoire des concessions. J. SEYCHELLES SOC. 2 (1962), pp. 6-13.

24,660 ELLGOOD, C. L. Medicine in the Seychelles. J. SEYCHELLES SOC. 1 (1961), pp. 61-72.

24,661 HAINES, W. H. The essential oil industry of Seychelles. BULL. IMP. INST. 32 (1934), pp. 545-559.

24,662 JEFFREY, C. Botanical excursions in the Seychelles. J. SEYCHELLES SOC. 2 (1962), pp. 2-5.

24,663 JEFFREY, C. Cucurbits of the Seychelles. J. SEYCHELLES SOC. 3 (1963), pp. 50-63.

24,664 JONES, S. The French Patois of the Seychelles. AFR. AFFAIRS 51 (1952), pp. 237-245.

24,665 LASCH, E. E. Satellite tracking in Seychelles. J. SEYCHELLES SOC. 3 (1963), pp. 28-31.

24,666 LEWIS, M. S. Geological investigations on the reefs of Mahe. J. SEYCHELLES SOC. 3 (1963), pp. 17-23.

24,667 LIONNET, J. F. G. Agriculture in the Seychelles, a retrospect. J. SEYCHELLES SOC. 2 (1962), pp. 14-32.

24,668 LIONNET, J. F. G. Bibliographical notes. J. SEYCHELLES SOC. 3 (1963), pp. 68-69; 4 (1965), pp. 73-76.

24,669 LOUIS, P. Brayer du Barre. Les Echecs de la première colonisation des Iles Seychelles. J. SEYCHELLES SOC. 1 (1961), pp. 42-53.

24,670 LOUSTAU-LALANNE, P. Land birds endemic to the granitic group of the Seychelles Islands. J. SEYCHELLES SOC. 1 (1961), pp. 22-31.

24,671 LOUSTAU-LALANNE, P. Note sur la nidification du Cateau ou Perroquet Noir de Praslin. J. SEYCHELLES SOC. 3 (1963), p. 64.

24,672 LOUSTAU-LALANNE, P. The Seychelles white eye (Zosterops modestus) rediscovered. J. SEYCHELLES SOC. 2 (1962), p. 51.

24,673 McEWEN, A. C. Fragments of early Seychelles history. J. SEYCHELLES SOC. 1 (1961), pp. 7-21.

24,674 MACKAY, W. Soundings of the upper air over the Seychelles. J. SEYCHELLES SOC. 4 (1965), pp. 8-19.

24,675 MATTHEWS, D. H. Geological history of the Seychelles. J. SEYCHELLES SOC. 4 (1965), pp. 1-7.

24,676 MICHAEL, G. I. Education in Seychelles: the early days. J. SEYCHELLES SOC. 1 (1961), pp. 32-41.

24,677 MOINE, J. Histoire de crocodiles. J. SEYCHELLES SOC. 3 (1963), pp. 65-67.

24,678 MOINE, J. Les Seychelles à l'époque de la Révolution française. J. SEYCHELLES SOC. 4 (1965), pp. 66-72.

24,679 PIGGOTT, C. J. The outlying islands of Seychelles. J. SEYCHELLES SOC. 2 (1962), pp. 44-48.

24,680 TAYLOR, J. D. A preliminary account of the ecology of the reefs of Mahe. J. SEYCHELLES SOC. 3 (1963), pp. 23-27.

24,681 TOUSSAINT, A. Le trafic commercial des Seychelles de 1773 à 1810. J. SEYCHELLES SOC. 4 (1965), pp. 20-61.

24,682 WEBB, A. W. T. An early literary society in Seychelles. J. SEYCHELLES SOC. 2 (1962), pp. 49-50.

24,683 WEBB, A. W. T. Some aspects of Seychelles history. J. SEYCHELLES SOC. 2 (1962), pp. 33-43.

24,684 Bibliographies of Seychelles. J. SEYCHELLES SOC. 2 (1962), pp. 58-64.

24,685 Obituary: Sir John Thorp. J. SEYCHELLES SOC. 1 (1961), pp. 5-6.

ST. HELENA

24,686 GALWAY, Sir H. L. A sojourn in St. Helena. J. AFR. SOC. 40 (1941), pp. 223-237.

24,687 KITCHING, G. C. Napoleon's second funeral: an unusual item in the Fairbridge Collection. QBSAL 1 (1947), pp. 106-110.

24,688 MELLISS, J. C. St. Helena. ROYAL COL. INST. PR. 38 (1906-1907), pp. 36-53.

24,689 BLOW, N. J. A new chaplain [Alec Edward Hanley, to Tristan da Cunha]. TRISTAN DA CUNHA NEWSLETTER, no. 13, 1945.

24,690 FRANCE, W. F. Appointment of new chaplain [Harold Wilde, to Tristan da Cunha]. TRISTAN DA CUNHA NEWSLETTER, no. 6, 1933.

24,691 HATTERSLEY, A. F. Visit of the barque *Sovereign* to Tristan da Cunha (1850). QBSAL 4 (1950), pp. 85-87.

24,692 PARTRIDGE, A. G. Tristan da Cunha. TRISTAN DA CUNHA NEWSLETTER, no. 6, 1933.

24,693 SULSTON, A. E. A. News from the island [of Tristan da Cunha]. TRISTAN DA CUNHA NEWSLETTER, nos. 14-25, 1947-1960.

24,694 WILDE, H. Islands of opportunity: Tristan da Cunha. TRISTAN DA CUNHA NEWSLETTER, no. 10, 1937.

Index

A., A.J. 722, 5475-6, 6154
A., C. 410
A., E.J. 11363
A., G. 722, 5970
A., H. 19870
A., P. 1964, 4089
A., Y.B.Y. 7449
Aba, N. 7048, 7144
Abadia, R.E. See Ezquerra Abadia, R.
Abasiekong, D. 22812
Abbaba, B. 16532
Abbai, B. 1307
Abbayes, H.des 9144-50
Abbe, C. 12560
Abbo, H. 13049
Abboud, F.I. See Ferik Ibrahim Abboud
Abd el-Farag Ali 6411
'Abd al-Nāṣir, J. See Nasser, G.A.
Abdallah bin Hemedi bin Ali Liajjemi 16246, 18229
Abdallah, L. 7778
Abdel-Aziz, A. 5427
Abdel Halim, A. 6412
Abdel-Malek, A. 4372
Abdel Nabi, A. 6413
Abdelrahman, A. 5930
Abderrahim Bouabid 4941
Abdi Hirad, M. See Mohamoud Abdi Hirad
'Abdin, 'A.al-M. 6155
Abdoulaye, N. 9188
Abdulwahab, H.H. 4959, 6779
Abdurahman, M. 17689
Abdy, D.M. 17690
A'Beckett, A.W. 1514
Abedi, K.A. 16247
Abel, A. 1093
Abel, D. 6124
Abel, H. 6309, 9189-90, 9232
Abessolo, S. 6395
Abi-Saab, R. 8484, 11755
Abimbola, W. 11208, 12024-5
Abir, M. 16706-7
Abou-Siril 4373
Aboyade, O. 1094, 11364-5
Abraham, D.D. 20504
Abraham, D.P. 20505-6
Abraham, E. 16808
Abraham, W. 10466
Abrahams, C.A. 10772
Abrahams, P. 1965, 3389, 4374-5
Abrahams, R.G. 17691-2, 18484
Abreu, M.M.M.de A. 12804-6
Abu Rannat, S.M. 6372
Abun-Nasr, J. 7779
Acanfora, M.O. See Ornella Acanfora, M.
Achebe, C. 3267, 3390-2, 12026

Achille, L.T.   780, 888, 1966, 4376
Achten, L.   14602
Achufusi, M.   2678
Ackah, C.A.   10467
Ackroyd, R.   19037
Acland, P.B.E.   6414
Acock, A.M.   411
Acogny, T.   9596
Acquah, I.   10363
Adal, G.   22107
Adalbert   13791, 14886-8
Adali-Mortti, G.   10664
Adam, A.   4878, 7241
Adam, J.G.   8563
Adam, J.S.   19871
Adam, M.A.   20728
Adam, M.J.   13729
Adam, V.   17693-4, 18011
Adam, W.   8025
Adams, C.C.   2679
Adams, C.D.   8026-7, 10468, 10773-7
Adams, G.   20678
Adams, J.B.   5126
Adams, N.J.   23057
Adams, P.C.G.   21203
Adams, R.F.G.   11919-22, 12227
Adams, R.G.   See Goold-Adams, R.
Adams, W.   1841-2
Adande, A.   781-2, 7508, 9469, 9523, 9606
Adawi, I.A.   6156
Addison, F.   5857-63, 5938
Addo, N.O.   10835
Adedeji, A.   11366, 11594
Adedeji, G.O.   10941
Adegoriola I, Ogoga of Ikere.   See Oba Alaiyeluwa Adegoriola I, Ogoga of Ikere
Adekambi, S.   12027
Ademola, F.   12028
Aderibigbe, A.B.   7627, 11756
Adésànyà, A.   12029
Adesina, S.   7780, 11757-8,
Adewale, T.J.   11367
Adibe, M.L.   13748
Adie, W.A.C.   2361
Adigun, B.A.   11487
Adimola, A.B.   19102, 19166
Adjanonhoun, E.   9244
Adjaye, E.O.A.   See Asafu-Adjaye, E.O.
Adjei, A.   10015
Adjetey, P.A.   10691
Adjmia, M.B.   6728
Adler, A.   13533
Admassou Shiferaou   16533, 16629
Adotevi, S.   2362
Adriaens, E.L.   4223, 13758, 15344-7, 15403
Adriamihaingo, S.R.R.   See Razafy-Adriamihaingo, S.R.

Adrian, J. 23631
Adu, S.A. 11368
Aescoly, A.Z. 16483
Aeth, R.d'. See D'aeth, R.
Afer 4910
Afigbo, A.E. 11759
Afreh, D.K. 10692
African nurse 22283
African Society 3011
African Studies Branch 1652, 1967-9, 3621, 9814, 10364-5, 11595-9, 15865, 17584, 18450, 21423
Africanus 1970, 4118, 15990, 17015, 19689, 19707-8, 20892
Africanus, P. 1971, 2363, 9341-2, 10366
Afrikander 19726, 22535
Afrikanus 2364, 3841, 4377, 13408, 24065
Agar-Hamilton, J.A.I. 19552, 19727, 22284
Agblemagnon, F.N. 4378-81, 9396-8, 10016
Agbodeka, F. 10469
Agboola, S.A. 11527
Aglen, E.F. 5477, 5980, 6157
Agostini, E.de 6704
Agricola 7030
Aguesse, P. 6952
Aguessy, C. 9402, 9553
Aguiar, E.da P.C.de. See Correia de Aguiar, E.da P.
Aguilera, C.R. See Rodríguez Aguilera, C.
Aguirre de Cárcer, M. 7302, 7371
Aguirre de Cárcer, N. 5288
Agyemang-Duah, J. 10017, 10470-1
Ahmed Ali 17161
Ahmed Dahir Hassan 17064
Ahmed Mohamed 17016
Ahmed, Y. 16484
Aidin, R. 8028
Aidoo, C.A. 10665-6
Aimé, J. 13586, 13669
Ainslie, R. 17390
Aitken, W.G. 18057
Ajao, D.O. 12030
Ajayi, F.A. 12120-1
Ajayi, J.F.A. 11760, 11761-2, 11923, 12437
Ajayi, W.O. 12206-7
Ajose, O.A. 10942
Akala, E. See Ekondy-Akala
Akanji 466
Akar, J. 9766
Akena, N. 18653
Akesson, S.K. 10018-9
Akiga, B. See Sai, B.A.
Akindélé, A. 9402, 9510
Akingbade, P.I. 11775
Akinjogbin, I.A. 11763-4
Akinola, R.A. 11369
Akita, J.M. 10224, 10472-3
Akiwumi, A. 7741
Akpala, A. 11765
Akpan, E.E. 11600

Akpan, N.U. 1972, 11601
Akpofure, R.E.O. 11488
Al-. *For authors whose names begin with the Arabic article Al-, see the following element of the name*
Alagoa, E.J. 10943
Alao, J.A. 11447
Alaqâ Walda Maryam 16708
Alban, A.H.A. 5478
Alberich, J.C. See Cola Alberich, J.
Albert, A. 2365, 3483-4, 4382
Albert, E.M. 15563, 15658
Albertini, J.M. 1095
Alberto, M.S. See Simões Alberto, M.
Albrecht-Carrié, R. 2680
Albuquerque 23903
Alcobe, S. 4820, 15672, 15707, 15742
Aldén, K. 13792
Alderton, E.C. 11602
Alegria, M.de 412
Aleixo, M.A. 23586
Aleo, G.M. See Macaluso-Aleo, G.
Alexander, A.S., Jr. 9262
Alexander, B. 13534
Alexander, C.S. 18012
Alexander, J.T. 10238, 10300
Alexandre, P. 2366, 3012-6, 4384, 9349-50, 9355, 12928, 13050, 13290-2, 13360
Alexis, J.S. 3268, 3485, 4385
Alfaro Cardoso, J.G. 4238, 23634, 23673-9, 23824-5, 23904-7, 24086-93, 24273
Alfaro Cardoso, J.J. 19570
Ali, A. See Ahmed Ali
Ali, A.el-F. See Abd el-Farag Ali
Ali, J. See Jaafar Ali
Ali, M. 16248-9
Ali, M.W. 17065-7, 17167
Ali, N. el-H. 6027
Ali, Syed Sir R. 22108
Ali Ahmed Jahadhmy. See Jahadhmy, A.A.
Ali Ahmed Suliman 5981
Ali Gulla 6158
Ali Sheikh Mohamed 17101
Alía Medina, M. 7442, 7143, 7409, 7457-8, 15756
Aliel, M.al-. See Mustafa' al-Aliel
Aligwekwe, E. 12438
Alima, E. 3486, 13361-2
Alimen, H. 4821-2
Alimen, M.H. 4823-4
Allain, C. 7187
Allainment, Y. 9085
Allan, W. 19681
Alland, A., Jr. 9191
Allard, E. 1543, 14357-8
Allbrook, D. 19412
Allbrook, D.B. 16485

Alldridge, T.J. 9785, 9834
Allégret, E. 4386
Allen, B. 2681, 16709
Allen, B.M. 1047, 2685, 5289, 6159
Allen, C.J. 20729
Allen, G. 4960
Allen, J.G.C. 11209
Allen, J.W.T. 16123-5, 16250-3, 17919, 18441-2
Allen, K. 10239
Allen, P.M. 19413
Allen, R. 7996, 16254
Allen, R.W. 5420, 5452, 5982
Allen, S.W. 3269, 3393-7, 4387
Alliata di Montereale 4388
Alliot, M. 1843
Allison, A.C. 469, 15786-7
Allison, J.S. 22285, 22908
Allison, P.A. 7706, 11766-7, 12228-30
Allott, A.N. 3622-40, 10693-7, 12122, 16374
Allnutt, R.B. 18595
Allpress, P.L. 1515
Almásy, L.E.d'. See D'Almásy, L.E.
Almeida, A.de 470, 12668-9, 23369-70, 23435, 23439-40
Almeida, A.A. 23680, 24094
Almeida, C.L.de 12807-8, 12829, 12846
Almeida, F.da N. 12809
Almeida, F.F.M.de 8029
Almeida, J.L.de 2682, 23536
Almeida, J.M.da N. 12809
Almeida, M.E.de C.E. 23370
Almeida e Cunha, A.d'. 24095
Almeida Valent, C.A.de 23855
Alonso, J.F. See Francés Alonso, J.
Alpers, E.A. 19167
Alpha, D. 8974
Alport, Lord 17391, 20392
Alport, E.A. 6981, 7163
Alston, A.H.G. 9150
Alstyne, R.W.van 2683
Althabe, G. 13051
Altman, P. 19841
Alton, E.B.S. 10367
Altorfer, A. 17392
Altozano, H. 15719
Altrincham, Lord 1973
Aluko, S.A. 7628, 10896, 10944, 11370-2
Alvarez, H.R. 15703-5, 15767
Alvarez, J.F. See Fueyo Alvarez, J.
Alvarez, M.de T. 4389
Alvarez Corugedo, J. 15691
Alvarez Sanchez, J. 15708
Álvaro, E. 12780-1
Alverny, F.d' 4825
Alves, C. 23895
Alves, H. 3842, 4961, 23465
Alves, M.L.G. 12815, 12916

Alves, P.H. 12893
Alves, V.L. 23537
Alvord, E.D. 19860, 20507, 20679
Amadéo, G. 3641
Amamkpa, E.W. 11528
Amamoo, A.G. 1974
Amamoo, J.G. 10368-9
Amankwe, N. 10867
Amara, I.B. 9713
Amaral, I.do 23657
Amaral, I.M.P.do 23466
Amare, G. 16667
Amaro, J.P.P. 12843
Amarteifio, E. 10836
Amato, F. 13052
Amawi, J.al 7202
Amblard-Rambert, A. 8888
Ambrosini, G. 1096
Ambrosio, V. 16975
Ambrosius, P. 14889
Amedekey, E.Y. 9987
Amer Bey, M. 5149-51
Américo Ferreira 3017
Amery, L.S. 1975-8, 2684, 19663, 22536
Ames, D.W. 8497-8, 8538, 9663
Ameyaw, K. 10193
Ameye, L. 14359
Amin, A. 17017
Amirante, S. 6641
Amissah, A.N.E. 10698-9
Ammar, A. 5127-8
Amogu, O.O. 11373
Amonoo, R.F. 10629
Amoo, J.W.A. 10020
Amoo-Gottfried, K. 1653
Amorim, F.P.de. See Pacheco de Amorim, F.
Amorim, S. See Silva Amorim
Amos, R.L. 12231
Amos, S. 5290-2
Amoussouga, P. 4119, 9604
Ampomah, J.K.O. See Opoku-Ampomah, J.K.
Amsel, H.G. 5071
Amu, E. 3844
Anang, M.F.D. See Dei Anang, M.F.
Anastasio, E. 1979
Ancel, R. 7031
Ancian, G. 1980
Anciaux de Faveaux, A. 14232-4, 14260-1, 21990
Anders, H. 22104, 22719
Anderson, A.B. 6415-6
Anderson, C. 10837
Anderson, C.A. 15922, 20356
Anderson, J.F. 24303
Anderson, J.N.D. 3642-8, 6373, 7372, 12123, 16375-6
Anderson, L.S. 5864
Anderson, M.G. 10945
Anderson, M.M. 10339

Anderson, M.S. 4962
Andoh, A.S.Y. 10021
Andrada, E.de C. 4239
Andrade, B.de. See Banha de Andrade
Andrade, C. 23571, 23658
Andrade, F.da C. See Andrade, C.
Andrade, M.de 23507-8, 23572
Andrade, P. 24067
Andrés, A.F. See Fornes Andrés, A.
Andres, C.A. 7440
Andres, D.S. See Sevilla Andres, D.
Andrew, G. 1884, 4873, 5865, 6417
Andrews, A.W. 1885
Andrews, C.F. 22286
Andrews, L. 22287
Andriamanjato, R. 24624
Andrianarahinjaka, L.X.M. 24521-2
Andriantsilaniarivo, E. 1981, 24455
Andries, A. 15194
Andrzejewski, B.W. 3018, 16827-8, 17123-7
Anene, J.C. 11768
Anet, H. 14603, 15293
Anfray, F. 16534-9
Angel, M.F. 24554-5
Angell, N. 1982
Angiolino, G. 783
Angladette, A. 413
Anglin, D.G. 11603
Angulo, F.N. See Nájera y Angulo, F.
Angus, J.A. 3845
Aniebo, I.N.C. 12031
Animageddi 7977, 10946
Animashawun, G.K. 1654
Ankrah, E.M. 10838
Anley, V.R. 20893-5
Annan, K. 10667
Annequin, G. 16539
Annett, H.E. 4120
Anning, C.C.P. 23058
Anozie, I.O. 3649
Anquandah, H. 10136
Anquandah, J.R. 10137
Ansell, W.F.H. 21517
Anselme-Rabinovitch, L. 1098
Ansre, G. 10630
Anstey, D. 18058
Anstey, R.T. 12957, 19812
Anta, D.C. 8639-40
Anta Ka, A. 8662
Antangana, S. 13053
Anthony, H.E. 21518-9
Anti-Taylor, W. 2367
Antoine, M.P. 13397
Anton, F.G. See Gomez Anton, F.
António, M. pseud.of M.A.F.Oliveira. See Oliveira, M.A.F.de
Antonio de Vega, L. 5084

Antonio Valverde, J. See Valverde, J.A.
Antubam, K. 784
Antunes, M.T. 23436
Anvers, C.d'. See D'Anvers, C.
Anwyl, T.C. 9714, 11924
Anya-Noa, L. 13053-4
Anywar, R.S. 18919
Aouani, M.el- 6763
Ap Griffith, G. 19038
Aparisi, J.S.V. See San Valero Aparisi, J.
Appia, B. 7509, 8198, 8499, 9022-3, 9118
Appia-Dabit, B. 8518-20
Appiah, L.H.O. See Ofosu-Appiah, L.H.
Appolis, E. 24331, 24443, 24456
Appronti, J. 10668
Apter, D.E. 1983, 2368-9, 10370, 19103
Apthorpe, R. 2370-1, 12439, 21122, 21259
Aquina, M. 19872-5, 20819
Aragbabalu, O. 11210
Arambourg, C. 723-4, 4826-8, 6999, 23437
Aranzadi, I.de 13055
Araújo, J.S. 4121
Araújo, V.de P. 23632
Araújo Ferreira, J. 12810
Arbaumont, J.d' 13535, 13539
Arber, H.B. 6571
Arbousset, F. 24444
Arcais, G.F.d' 2372-3, 3650-2
Archbishop of Cape Town, 1948. See Darbyshire, J.R., Archbishop of Cape Town
Archdeacon, S. 24399
Archer, G.T.L. 8030
Archer, R. 5403
Ardant, P. 1099, 1858
Arden-Clarke, C. 10371-2, 23323
Ardener, E.W. 10947-8, 13462-3
Ardener, S.G. 12440, 13205
Ardill, R.H. 24304
Ardoise, P. 15148
Areal, J.A. 12712
Areje, R.A. 10868
Arenes, J. 8031, 8456
Arhin, K. 10022, 10475, 10516, 10700, 10839
Arian, A.d' 15657
Arianoff, A.d' 15564
Arié, R. 6160
Aries 6125
Arikpo, O. 10897, 11604
Arkadie, B.V. 15866-8, 17313
Arkell, A.J. 725, 4793, 4829-30, 5438, 5479-86, 6161-6, 5867-80, 6418, 6619, 7510, 12939, 13502
Arlabosse, Gen. 9086
Armas, A.R.de. See Rumeu de Armas, A.
Armattoe, R.E.G. 10023-5
Armbruster, C.H. 3224
Armstrong, A.L. 20119-20

Armstrong, C.P. 414
Armstrong, R.G. 3019-20, 4390, 10149, 11336, 11489-90, 11925-7, 12124
Arnaud, M. 1984, 5881, 20896-7
Arnett, E.J. 2685, 4391, 7742, 7782, 8220, 8270-1, 8290, 11374, 11771, 12441, 13241-2
Arnold, C.W.B. 21331, 21381
Arnold, R.W. 24540
Arnot, A.S. 11211
Arnott, D.W. 7900-2, 11928-32, 12125
Arnould, M. 9287
Arques, E. 7242
Arrabal, J.M. See Molina Arrabal, J.
Arribas Palau, M. 7303-4, 15724
Arrighi, G. 8684
Arthur, Prince 2686
Arthur, A.J.V. 6572
Arundell, R.D.H. 12531
As, B.S.van. 21843
Asaad, R.W. 5428-9
Asabia, S.O. 10950
Asad, T. 5487
Asafu-Adjaye, E.O. 7743, 10373
Asalache, K. 3398
Asamoa, E.A. 10301
Asante, D. 10669
Asante, K.B. 10374
Asante, S.K.B. 10701
Asfour, E.Y. 1100
Ashanin, C.B. 3846, 10758
Ashby, E. 1844, 7681
Ashley Montagu, M.F. 4794
Ashton, E.H. 21607-8, 21703
Ashton, E.O. 3021-2, 16126-7, 16218
Ashton, K.G. 1845
Askari, E.K. 10951
Askwith, T.G. 17368, 17393, 17633-6, 18596
Asmis, W. 10702
Assane, S. 8592-3
Assirelli, O. 16829
Assouan, R. 3487
Astrachan, A. 12032
Atangana, G.T. See Towo-Atangana, G.
Atangana, N. 3653, 4392-3
Atger, P. 9265
Atiman, A. 17988
Atiya, S.B. 6167
Atiyah, P.S. 6374
Atkins, G. 3023, 21217, 21485-6, 23352
Atkins, H.J.B. 4879, 5061, 5085-6
Atkins, P.M. 8594
Atkinson, G.A. 785, 4394, 16428
Atlee, M. 23060
Attafua, A.B. 10476
Attal, R. 6938
Attarrah, C. 3399

Attia (Attya), H. 6711-2
Attoungbré, G. 9298
Aubert, G. 8777
Auchinleck, G.G. 10340
Audas, R.S. 6573
Audax 10302
Auger, G.A. 1656-7, 1750
Augustiny, J. 16255, 17199, 17539, 18363
Augusto, A. 23896
Aujas, M. 24316
Aujoulat, L. 13445
Aujus, M. 24457
Aurigemma, S. 262, 4963
Aurillac, M. 8685
Aussel, J.M. 6893
Austen, R.A. 18144-5
Austin, D.G. 10375-9, 10477
Austin, H.H. 16673
Austin, W.G.C. 10341
Autra, R. (M.T.R.Autra), pseud. See Traoré, Mamadou, also
   called Ray Autra
Autret, M. 15348
Auzoux, A. 7305
Avelar, H. de 24096
Aventur, J. 6713
Avermaet, E.van 14890
Avermaet, G.van 13793, 14891
Awa, E. 11605-6
Awad, M. 5430
Awani, M.el-. See Aouani, M.el-
Awe, B. 11772-3
Awolowo, O. 7744
Awona, S. 13056
Awoonor, K. See Awoonor-Williams, G.
Awoonor-Williams, G. 3482, 10670, 10688
Awouma, J. 13464
Axelson, E. 23908
Ayache, S. 24458-9
Ayandele, E.A. 7090, 11774, 12208
Ayari, C. 1101
Ayats, H. 8500, 8750
Aydelotte, W.O. 23345
Ayida, A.A. 11375
Ayissi, L.M. 13363
Aymat-Mareca, J.M. 1102
Aymé, A. 7000
Ayorinde, O.J.A. 11337
Aza, M.S. See Solano y Aza, M.
Azam, P. 2687, 7210
Azed, M. 15294
Azevedo, A.de 1103, 23487-9
Azevedo, A.L.de 23703, 23909-10
Azevedo, F.A.de 14746
Azevedo, J.F. See Fraga de Azevedo, J.
Azevedo, R.A.de 23538-9
Azevedo, W.d' 3488

Azevedo, W.L.d' 9835, 12604
Azikiwe, B.N. 1659, 2375-6, 11607-8
Azu, A.A. 10478

B. 6419, 6574
B., A. 3489, 4395, 9119, 19338
B., C.W. 21015
B., D. 7243
B., E. 13794
B., E.F.N. 5488
B., E.H. 20508
B., F. 11212
B., F. 15349
B., G. 22288
B., H.J. 19876
B., J.L. 2377, 13482
B., J.P. 18654
B., L. 17314
B., P. 7989
B., R. 4671
B., R.de la B. 17200, 18485-6, 18487-91
B., R.G. 1985
B., R.M. 19039
Ba, A.H. 471, 7511, 8183, 8779, 8932-4, 8962
Ba, M.A. 8595
Ba, O. 8674
Bâ Tamsir Ousmane 8596
Babalola, A. 12033-8
Babet, V. 13503
Babiiha, J.K. 18655
Babin, G. 24403
Babo, F.de 3847
Bachelard, G. 4396
Bachelier, G. 13228
Bachmann, T. 17695
Backer, E.de 14360, 15437
Bacon, C.R.K. 5489-91, 6048-9, 6420
Bacon, L.W. 998
Bacquié 13516-7, 13543
Badcock, W.J. 21250
Baden-Powell, G. 1104, 2688, 22109, 23061
Badenoch, A.C. 19104
Badian, E. 5152
Badian, S.K. (S.Kouyaté). Cp.Kouyaté, S.B.
Badie, B.B. 9299
Badouin, R. 415, 7629
Baeck, L. 1305, 15438-9, 15659
Baer, G. 5410
Baer, G.F.A. 22213
Baer, W. 5209
Baeta, C.G. 10237
Baffour, R.P. 4099
Bagchi, G. 19369
Bagenal, C.J. 17696
Bagge, S. 17201

Bagnold, R.A. 6650
Bagshawe, F.J. 17697
Bagyire VI, O. Abiriwhene 10479
Bâhna, S. 786
Bahoken, J.C. 13057
Bailey, G. 2378
Bailey, R. 24653
Baillaud, E. 4240, 7494, 7630, 8180, 8975
Bailleul, H. 14604
Bainbridge, D.R. 5769
Baines, T. 19735
Baird, D.A. 18492
Bakari, Modibbo 13257
Bakari, K. 8139
Baker, C.A. 21350, 21382, 21441-3, 21563
Baker, E.C. 15788, 17698, 18230
Baker, G. 1516, 1986, 17699
Baker, H.G. 7495, 10803
Baker, J.N.L. 19168
Baker, J.R. 19169
Baker, P. 4122
Baker, R.H. 19877-8, 20509, 20645
Baker, S.W. 6168
Baker, S.J.K. 15959, 19040-2
Baker, T.M. 10952
Bakker, E.M.van Z. 21955
Bakole, M.M. 1846
Bal, W. 14747
Balachowsky, A.S. 8705, 9151
Balafrej, A. 7244
Balandier, G. 176, 472, 787-8, 1105-6, 1987, 3490, 4403-5,
    4397-4402, 8539, 8973, 8976, 9045, 9105, 9403, 12543,
    13644, 13687-8, 13696, 13719, 22069
Balch, E.S. 1886
Baldazzi, G. 1107, 17060
Baldé, S. 8977-8, 9024
Baldry, D.A. 12232
Baldwin, K.D.S. 7631, 10898, 11376
Baldwin, R.E. 1108, 21016
Balen, F. 1887
Balewa, A.T. 2379, 11609
Balfet, H. 6729
Balfour, H. 7512-3, 10138, 1123, 19621, 20121
Balfour, M. 9692
Balfour-Browne, J. 8457, 9377
Balil, A. 6740
Ball, J.H. 10899, 12233-4
Ball, R.S. 17184
Ballard, C.M. 13713
Ballard, J. 9555, 8272, 9554
Ballegeer, L. 14510, 14605, 14748
Ballerini, E. 24421
Balletto, G.M. 18059
Ballico, P. 416
Ballinger, M. 19682, 22110, 22909, 22289-90, 23062
Balme, D.M. 9988, 10303-5

Balmer, P.H. 11610
Balmer, W.T. 7682
Balodis, F. 5153
Balogh, T. 1109
Balout, L. 4828, 4831, 7001
Balsan, F. 19695, 21699, 23911
Bambote, M. 13600-1
Bamgboye, A. 11775, 11933-4
Bamunoba, Y.K. 18656-7, 19170
Banage, W.B. 16395, 18992
Banda, T.D.T. 21424
Banfield, J. 15827
Banha de Andrade 24097-8
Banham, M. 11214
Banow, H. 17202
Bansisa, Y. 889
Banton, M. 3848, 4406-7, 9715, 9786, 9815-6, 9970
Banwell, G.H. 1988
Baptista, J.E. 24099
Baptista, M. 3849
Baptista, M.M. See Martins Ba(p)tista, M.
Baptista, P.A.N. 23587
Baquero, M.G. See Garcia-Baquero, M.
Barahona Fernandes, J.A. 23912
Barakana, G. 15631
Barat-Pepper, E. 13585
Barata, O.S. See Soares Barata, O.
Baratz, M.S. 11377, 11611
Barback, R.H. 11378
Barbara 10240
Barber, F. 14749
Barber, H.M. 21956
Barber, J.P. 18658, 19171-4
Barber, W.J. 20282
Barbier, C.le 24460
Barbosa, A. 12782
Barbosa, A.A.M. 12783
Barbosa, A.J.da S. See Silva Barbosa, A.J.da
Barbosa, H.J. 12791-2
Barbosa, L.A.G. 24100
Barbosa, O.C.G. See Gomes Barbosa, O.C.
Barbour, G. 1004
Barbour, K.M. 5210, 6050-1
Barbour, N. 5154, 7054, 7091, 7245
Barbudo Duarte, E. 7205
Barclay, H.H. See Hay-Barclay, H.
Bardin, P. 6714-5
Bardon, P.C.M. 7164-5
Baregu, M. 15773
Barel, Y. 1110
Barford, M.F. 20820
Bargery, G.P. 11972
Baring, E. 21602, 21609
Barkan, J.D. 13206
Barker, R.D. 17700, 18060-2
Barker, T.H. 7803

467

Barlet, P. 9442
Barlow, A.R. 17540-1
Barltrop, E.W. 7632
Barnacle, G.A.S. 24654
Barnard, K.H. 22537-8
Barned, J.F.de S.L. See Lewis Barned, J.F.de S.
Barnes, B.H. 20646-7, 21147
Barnes, H.B. 20898
Barnes, J.A. 473, 19813, 20899, 20924, 21123
Barnes, J.R. 21078
Barnes, L. 21707
Barnett, A. 17637
Barnett, J. 22291
Barnett, P.A. 22214
Barnicot, N.A. 7514
Barnley, G.R. 19414
Barnor, M.A. 10778
Barns, T.A. 14551, 18063, 23495
Barnwell, P.J. 18231, 24300, 24313
Baroja, J.C. See Caro Baroja, J.
Baron, L.S. 20730
Baron, R. 7246
Barr, Fr. 20790, 20821
Barradas, L.A. 1888, 19622, 23681-2, 23791-8, 23826, 23913-9, 24017, 24045, 24101
Barragão, F.R. 12784-6
Barral, B. 9436
Barrat, R. 7055
Barre, R. 6764
Barreto, A.D. See Dionisio Barreto, A.
Barreto, M.S. See Saraiva Barreto, M.
Barreto, V.M.J. See Jardim Barreto, V.M.
Barrett, H.J. 23063
Barrett, W.E.H. 17203
Barril, M.C. See Castillo Barril, M.
Barriuso, P.G. See Garcia Barriuso, P.
Barriviera, L.B. 16540
Barros, A.de 12670
Barros, L.B.de 24274
Barry, S. 8984
Bartel, M. 9586
Bartels, F.L. 10228, 10235, 10306
Bartlett, F.C. 474-5
Bartlett, V. 2380
Bartocci, E. 1111-2, 1517-9, 4408, 5155, 22111
Barton, F. 20276, 20393
Barton, J. 17204-6, 19339
Barton, P. 11379, 12442
Barwell, C.W. 17315
Baschera, R. 1113
Bascom, W. 789-90, 1520, 3850-1, 4409-10, 7515, 10953-6, 11215, 11776-7, 12443-6
Bascoulergue, P. 4221
Bashir, M.O. 6169
Basikoro 20357
Basil, Dr. 891, 5882, 19623

Basile, K. 2689, 8273
Basilewsky, P. 8032-3, 8458, 8706, 8944, 9378, 15743
Basinski, J.J. 5453
Baslini, F. 16830
Basse, E. 24556
Basset, A. 330, 5033-4
Basset, H. 6698, 18493
Bassir, O. 9716, 12235
Basso Marques, J. 12767-8
Basson, J.D.du P. 22292
Bassori, T. 892
Bassoro, M.H. 13258
Bastian, G. 24445
Bastid, S. 2381, 15195
Bastide, H.de la 7247
Bastide, R. 478, 2690, 3270, 3491, 4411, 9540, 9601
Bastin, R. 15350
Bataille 893
Batalha, F. 23438, 23588, 23496-7
Bate, D.M.A. 15828
Bate, T.W. 20122
Bateman, H.R. 19415
Bates, J.D. 17207
Bates, M.S. 3852
Bathie, H.P.de la. See Perrier de la Bathie, H.
Batista, M.M. See Martins Ba(p)tista, M.
Batley, S.K. 12447
Batrawi, A. 5129-30
Batson, E. 23064-6
Batten, T.R. 4412-4
Battifol, H. 6894
Battistella, R. 1114
Battistini, R. 24345, 24400-1, 24417
Batty, R.B. 10957
Battye, R.K.M. 18064
Batwell, B.L. 5471
Baudelaire, H. 13293
Baudens 7092
Baudert, S. 1660
Baudissin, G.G.von 16950
Baudry, R. 13229
Bauer, G. 1083
Bauer, I. 5431, 7306
Bauer, P.T. 1115-6, 7633-4
Baumann, C. 22720
Baumann, H. 476-7
Baumann, O. 15733, 18232
Baumer, M. 5454, 6052
Baville, M.R. See Rougevin-Baville, M.
Bax, S.N. 17989, 18233, 18477
Baxendale, A.S. 19175
Baxter, G.H. 20394
Baxter, H.C. 17701-2, 17920
Baxter, P.T.W. 16486, 21781, 20510-1
Bayaka, J. 13795
Bayard, Lt. 8416

Baye, A.M. 3492
Baylen, J.O. 22539
Bayliss, M. 1117, 21383
Baza, P. 13759
Bazeley, W.S. 19879-80, 20395, 20731, 20822
Bazin, H. 1118
Beach, D.M. 3024
Beachey, R.W. 16034, 17503
Beadle, L.C. 16396, 19043
Beal, W.P.B. 12236
Beaman, A.H. 5256
Beart, C. 3271, 8365, 8749, 9474
Beaton, A.C. 5492-8, 5519, 5610, 5941-4, 6170, 6310
Beaton, W.G. 10958
Beattie, J.H.M. 1989, 15790, 18659-74, 19105, 19381-3
Beatty, M.C. 20123
Beauchamp, R.S.A. 16397
Beauchêne, G.de 372-9
Beaudet, M. 9586
Beaudoin, A. 15991
Beaumont, J.de 8459
Beaune, R.J.de 14606
Beaurepaire, C.de 7373
Beazley, C.R. 2691-3
Bebey, F. 13364
Beccaria, G.A.C. See Costanzo-Beccaria, G.A.
Beccaro, F.del 298
Becker, A. 18234-6
Beckers, H. 14607
Beckett, A.W.A'. See A'Beckett, A.W.
Beckingham, C.F. 8899, 16674-5
Beckley, V.A. 17185
Beddoes, H.R. 10959
Bedri, I. 5499-5500
Beech, M.W.H. 15791, 17208, 17585
Beecher, A.L.J. 15992, 17542
Beek, J.L.R.W. 20124
Beemer, H. 21739, 21764, 21778, 23067
Beer, C.W. 5432, 5455, 5501
Beer, Z.de 22293
Beerst, G.de 14892
Beesley, J.S.S. 18587
Beetham, T.A. 9775
Begg, A.H. See Henderson-Begg, A.
Begg, G. 23068
Beguinot, F. 4832
Behanzin, L. 1119, 2694, 4100, 10380, 10480
Behr, E. 7056
Beidelman, T.O. 15792, 17703-13, 18237, 18364-7, 18443-4,
    18451, 18597
Beier, U. 479, 790, 3272, 5945, 7978, 9524, 10139, 10960-6,
    11216-7, 11218-24, 11778-9, 12039-41, 12063, 13365, 24523
Beinart, J. 24053
Beit, A. 1661, 4123, 4415, 19690, 20396, 21957
Bekajaha 1120
Bekale, P. 12933

Bekombo, M.   417, 13058
Bekrin, A.O.A.   8663
Belcher, A.   17369
Belchior, M.D.   7783, 12894
Belgium. Ministry of Colonies   14608
Beling, W.A.   6787
Belkhodja, B.   5087
Bell, C.R.V.   17051
Bell, G.W.   5456, 5502-3, 6163-4, 6311, 6421
Bell, H.H.   11612
Bell, J.   18993
Bell, K.   5293
Bell, P.W.   18994
Bell, R.M.   18238
Bella, L.de S.   See Sousa Bella, L.de
Bellido, A.G.   See Garcia Bellido, A.
Bellin, P.   7145
Bello, A.   2379
Bello, M.   See Muhammad Bello, Emir of Sokoto
Bello, M., Minister for Community Development, Northern Region
    (Nigeria) 12448
Beloff, M.   1990
Belshaw, D.G.R.   15916, 18645, 18954
Belshaw, H.   10759-60
Beltrame, G.   5504
Beltrami, S.   3853
Bemba, S.   3400, 15137
Bembe, L.   14609
Ben-Amor, A.   2382
Ben Barka, el-M.   6788
Ben-Horin, E.   1991
Benamu, L.J.   See Jimenez Benamu, L.
Bénard, J.   1121
Bendor-Samuel, J.T.   10631
Bendor-Samuel, P.M.   7903
Bénédic, A.   1889
Benedict, B.   24334
Beneitez Cantero, V.   See Cantero, V.B.
Bengala, A.   13796
Benge, R.C.   9989, 10869
Benham, F.   1662
Beniparrell, C.de   418, 791, 4222, 4785, 16689
Benítez Cantero, V.   See Cantero, V.B.
Benjamin, A.   22910, 23069-70
Benjamin, E.   9971
Benn, A.W.   7093
Bennabi, M.   4416
Bennetez Cantero, V.   See Cantero, V.B.
Bennett, A.L.   9479
Bennett, F.J.   19416, 18675
Bennett, G.   1064, 17504-5, 18146, 19176
Bennett, N.R.   331, 4964, 16035, 17506, 17990, 18094, 18239-42
Bennion, M.J.   11613
Bennun, R.   23071
Benoist, J.   4124, 8460, 8707
Bénoit, F.P.   3654

Benoit, P.L.G. 8035
Bensabat, S.J. 7415
Benson, C.W. 21520, 21384, 21521-2
Benson, T.G. 3025, 15923
Benson, W. 1122, 1521-2, 1992
Bensusan, S.L. 7307
Bent, J.T. 19881
Bento Ripado, M.F.B. 23683
Bentsi-Enchill, K. 1523
Bentwich, N. 16710-11, 22294
Bentzmann, P.de 7784
Benumeya, R.G. See Gil Benumeya, R.
Benzies, W.R. 19728, 19882
Bequaert, M. 14235-7
Bere, R.M. 18676-8, 18846-7, 18920, 19044-6, 19177-9
Bereng, D.T. 21650
Berenguer y Elizalde, D. 1890
Berenguier, H. 7211
Beresford-Stooke, G. 9787, 10219, 21041, 21111
Berg, D.G.van den 21829
Berg, E. 8221
Berg, E.J. 1123-4
Berg, J.van den 22540
Bergé, G. 419
Berge, J.L. 6173
Bergeaud, G. 15591
Berger, J. 4417
Berger, P. 3026, 13797-9
Berger, R. 18243
Bergeret, B. 13439
Berghe, P.L.van den. See Van den Berghe, P.L.
Berghegge, F. 20358
Berghold, K. 17128
Bergna, P.C. 6674, 6699
Berland, L. 992, 1043
Berlioz, J. 24585
Berlyn, P. 19883, 20279
Bernal, J.D. 1124
Bernard, A. 1993
Bernard, E.A. 4348
Bernard, J. 480
Bernard, M. 9470, 17177
Bernard-Thierry, S. 24402
Bernardi, B. 15793, 17316
Bernardi, G. 9379, 15744
Bernardin 14511
Bernhard, F.O. 20125-6
Bernis, G.D.de 6716, 6765-6
Bernolles, J. 4418, 9480-3
Bernot, A. 24314
Bernstein, E.M. 1125
Bernstein, H. 22073
Bernstein, R. 22215
Bernus, E. 9192-3, 9245, 9266, 9306
Berque, J. 5054, 5088-91, 6953, 7028
Berrangé, V.C. 22911

Berrie, A. 8036
Berrie, G.K. 8036
Berrit, G.R. 8564, 13670, 13721
Berry, J. 9882-6, 10026, 10632-4
Berry, L. 6053
Berry, P. 13940
Berry, Q.P. See Possy-Berry, Q.
Bertaut, M. 13059
Berte, M. 4125
Berthélemy, A. 7166, 7181
Bertho, J. 7785, 8366, 8919, 9268-9, 9356, 9484, 9587-8, 11935
Berthoud, A.L. 22973
Berthoud, H. 23742-4
Bertieaux, R. 14361, 14610
Bertin, C. 23631
Bertola, A. 1, 17068
Bertrand, A. 13760, 14611
Bertrand, L. 4241
Bérubé, L. 2383
Bervoets, S. 14893
Besant, W.H. 5294
Beshir, M.O. 5983, 6028, 6174
Bessa Victor, G. 23453
Bessac, H. 4833, 8391
Bessell, M.J. 18679
Besson, M. 5295
Betham, T.A. 3854
Bethell, A.D. 16645
Bethune, E.de 2384, 3655
Beti, M. (E.Boto) 3493-4, 13366, 17574
Bette, R. 14362-3
Bettelheim, C. 1126-7
Bettencourt, R.J.J. 23920
Bettison, D.G. 20283-4, 20823, 21259, 21564, 23072-3
Betts, V.O. 9972
Beuchat, A. 24105-6
Beuchat, P.D. See Cole-Beuchat, P.D.
Beuchelt, E. 7516
Bevan, C.W.L. 7683
Bevan, L.E.W. 20323
Béville, A. 1128
Bevin, E. 1994
Bevin, H.J. 10241
Bewes, T.F.C. 17209, 17615
Beyer, G. 4349, 21845-6
Beyerhaus, P. 22974
Bezy, F. 5211, 14364-76, 14612
Bhalo, A.N.J. 16256
Bhambri, R.S. 11380
Bharati, A. 16429
Bhely-Quenum, O. 3656, 9597
Biancacci, F. 4880, 7249-50, 7158
Biberson, P. 7182, 8392
Bidwell, B. 9693
Biebuyck, D. 420, 13798-13804, 14377-8, 14894, 15196-7, 14238-9

Biek, R. 10831
Bielschowski, L. 22541
Bienen, H. 18013, 18147-8
Biesheuvel, S. 1663
Bigelow, K.W. 1847
Bigi, F. 17035-6
Bigilimana, R.B.K. 16257
Bigourdan, J. 8037
Bigwood, E.J. 4126, 4223
Bilainkin, G. 5296-7, 6758, 7250
Bilen, M. 3273
Bille, E. 1664
Billing, M.G. 21079
Bilsen, A.A.J.van 14613
Bilsen, J.van 177, 900, 1995, 13750, 14379-86, 14614-8, 14895, 15198, 15295, 15351, 15440-3, 15610-2, 15653, 19674, 23324-5, 23509
Bin Abdullah, H. See Hemedi bin Abdullah
Bin Fulani, F. See Fulani bin Fulani
Bin Hamadi Imutafi, M.b.K. See Mustafa bin Kisi bin Hamadi Imutafi
Bin Omar, S.S. See Saada Salim bin Omar
Bin Said, H.b.M. See Hamoud bin Mahomed bin Said
Bin Stamboul, O. See Omari bin Stamboul, O.
Binet, J. 9046, 13060-1, 13207, 13243, 13465-6
Binns, A.L. 1996
Biobaku, S.O. 481, 2695, 4419, 7677, 11780-5
Biraben, J.H.P. See Probst-Biraben, J.H.
Birame, S. 8521
Birch, J.P. 18680-1, 19417
Birchenough, H. 1129, 2696
Bird, B. 12042
Bird, C.H. 19180
Bird, O.M. 1997
Birdwood, Lord 5297
Birkeli, E. 24348-9
Birkeli, F. 24541
Birket-Smith, J.S.R. 12237
Birmingham, D. 14750-1
Birmingham, W.B. 7745, 10242
Birtwistle, C.A. 11786
Bishop, E.F.F. 6939
Bishop, H.L. 19748
Bishop, W.W. 18848-51, 19047, 19092
Bishop of Lagos (1923). See Melville Jones, F.
Bismuth, H. 8367
Bispham, W.M.L. 11381
Bissainthe, R.P.G. 4420
Bisset, Lt.-Gen. 22542
Bisset, C.B. 18852, 19048, 19418
Bissett, C.J. 19884
Bissoondoyal, B. 24335
Bissot, L. 14240
Bitek, J.P.O.p' See P'Bitek, O.

Bittremieux, L. 13805-11, 14241, 14752-6, 14896-9, 15138-9
Bivar, A.D.H. 11225, 11787-8, 12043
Bixler, R.W. 24018
Biyi, E. 9717-8, 9927
Biyidi, A. See Beti, M.
Bjerke, S. 5156
Blache, J. 7230
Black, L.D. 1130
Blacking, J. 894, 14242, 20987, 21847, 21958-9
Blacklock, M. 1665
Blackmore, J.T.C. 7047
Blackwell, L. 22216
Blair, D. 3274
Blair, T. 1013, 1131, 2385
Blake-Thompson, J.B. 19885-6, 20088, 20814
Blakeley, J. 12044
Blamires, N. 22217
Blanc, A.C. 4795
Blanc, P. 4221
Blanc de Portugal, J. 23799
Blanchflower, T.C. 13062
Blanco, F.L.F. See Fernandez Blanco, F.L.
Blanco, J.G. See Gelpí Blanco, J.
Blanco del Valle, J. 4881
Blanco Izaga, E. 1998
Blanco Soler, C. 1058
Blancou, L. 13012
Blank, J.de 23074
Blankenheimer, B. 1132
Blankoff, B. 13709
Blaxall, A.W. 22295, 23075
Blaxall, F.M. 19624
Blay, R.S. 10027
Bleackley, R. 17921
Bleek, D.F. 17714, 19749-53, 19558-60, 20127, 21670, 22721-2, 23371
Bleek, W.H.I. 19754
Bleeker, C.J. 5157-9
Blelloch, D. 1133
Blerk, N.van 22723
Blind, K. 24461
Bloch, J.de 22543
Blohm, W. 21740
Blok, H.P. 3027-9, 12605, 14900, 19340
Blom-Cooper, L.J. 22296
Blondel, A. 3657
Blondel, F. 13424
Blooah, C.G. 12622
Bloom, H. 22297, 22459, 22813, 22912
Bloom, L. 4422
Bloomfield, K. 21385
Bloss, J.F.E. 5505, 6175, 6422-5, 6575
Blot, M.L.T. See Tardieu-Blot, M.L.
Blount, B.G. 17394
Blow, N.J. 24689
Blowers, G.A. 6642

Bloxam, G.W. 7519
Blumberg, B.S. 10967
Blumberg, M. 22544, 23076
Blundell, M. 17395, 17507
Blunt, H.S. 6426
Blunt, M.E. 11614
Blyden, E.W. 2697, 4090, 4423, 7786, 7997, 9836, 12574-5
Boadi, L. 10635-6
Boadu, J.A. 1666
Boahen, A.A. 1070, 2698, 7787-8, 10481-4
Boak, A.E.R. 5244
Boas, F. 21848
Boateng, C.Y. 10517
Boateng, E.A. 10342-4
Bobo, J. 4834
Boccara, M.B. 6903
Boccassino, R. 18682-3
Bochet, G. 792, 9194
Bockari, J. 9887
Bockhorst, M. 21960
Böcking 17543
Bodestein, W. 19561
Bodin, V. 13562
Bodley, E.F. 6975
Boeck, E.de 3030, 14903
Boeck, J.de 14904
Boeck, L.B.de 3031-2, 14901-10
Boeg, P. 2386
Boelaert, E. 482, 1999, 4424-5, 12978, 13812-31, 14340,
    14387-8, 14552-3, 14620, 14757, 14911-4, 15199-15202,
    15296, 15140-2, 15444-6
Boelaert, P. 15297
Boesch, F. 18370
Boeta, J.R. 7433
Bogaerts, H. 13832-6, 14915, 15352
Bognini, J.M. 9276-8
Bogomas, E.V.M. 20128
Bohannan, L. 9485, 10028, 10968
Bohannan, P. 1525, 10969-71, 11382
Böhme, R. 17178
Boigny, F.H. See Houphouët-Boigny, F.
Boireau, A. 7032, 7146
Bois, C.G.B.du. See Du Bois, C.G.B.
Bois, W.E.B.du. See Du Bois, W.E.B.
Boisdon, D. 3658
Bojarski, E.A. 18244
Bolamba, A.R. 15143
Bolanjei, B. 13795
Boléo, J.de O. See Oliveira Boléo, J.de
Bollengier, I.K. 18065
Bolton, A.R.C. 5506, 6168
Bombaci, A. 16712
Bonan, J. 7374
Bonanni, C. 17061, 17145
Bonchaud, J. 3855
Bond, E. 13259

Bond, G. 19625, 20129
Bond, H.M. 7746
Bond, W.R.G. 5457-8, 6427-30, 6576
Bondurant, J.V. 22545
Bone, E. 726-7, 21961
Boned, J.R. See Ramos Boned, J.
Bonelli Rubio, J.M. 7607, 7614, 15692
Bonfiglio, E. 6662
Bonham-Carter, E. 5507
Bonn, M.J. 2387
Bonneau, R.P.J. 13730
Bonnefond 13618-9
Bonnefoy, C. 9246
Bonnet, A. 5884
Bono, F. 6620-1
Bono, S. 4965, 6675-7, 6801, 7094, 9343, 9784
Bonomi, E. 1135
Booker, H.S. 10840
Boone, O. 13837
Boorman, J. 8038-9, 12238
Booth, A.J. 19517
Booth, G.A. 6054
Booth, J.D.L. 11615, 12126
Booth, N.S. 3856
Booven, H.van 14758
Borden, R. 2000
Borello, M. 16487
Borges, A. 23800, 23827, 23922, 24109
Borgne, Capt. See Le Borgne, Capt.
Bork, F. 6312
Borneman, E. 895
Borricand, P. 8417
Bosazza, V.L. 19626, 23828, 23923-4, 24107-8
Bosch-Gimpera, P. 728, 793
Bosi, R. 483, 16713
Bosman, D.B. 21782
Bossche, J.V. See Vanden Bossche, J.
Bosschère, G.de 2388-9
Bosse Casqueiro, M.von 24275-6
Bostock, D.H. 12239
Boston, H.J.L. 2699
Boston, J.S. 926, 10972, 11226-7
Bôt Ba Njok, H.M. 13063, 13341
Boto, E., also called M.Beti. See Beti, M.
Botzaris, A. 2001
Bouabid, A. See Abderrahim Bouabid
Bouaert, J.C. 1848, 3857
Bouah, G.N. See Niangoran-Bouah, G.
Boubakar, D.T. 8985
Bouccin 13838
Bouchart, P. 13208
Bouchaud, J. 7789, 13260
Bouche, D. 8291

Boucquey, E. 3495
Boudou, A. 24462-5
Bouesnard, L. 9624
Bouet, K. 16088
Bouffil, P. 4350
Bouge, L.G. 7790
Bouhdiba, A. 5062, 6940
Bouillon, A. 13839-40
Boulègue, M. 8485
Boulnois, J. 484, 13541
Bouloux, L.G. 24312
Bouman, A.C. 22724
Bouquet, M.R. 2700
Bouquiaux, L. 11936, 13589
Bourbon, E.de A. 23925
Bourde, A. 24645
Bourdet, C. 7057-8
Bourdiec, P.le 9288
Bourdillon, B.H. 2002, 11616-8, 11789, 12240
Bourdonnec, D.P. 14554
Bourdonnec, P.M. 14916
Bourgeois-Pichat, J. 4426
Bourguiba, H. 2390
Bouritius, G. 14014
Bourjol, M. 3659
Bourke, D.O'D. 4242, 12241, 17625
Bourlon, A. 8584, 8700
Bourne, H.R.F. 22298
Bourquin, W. 3033-5, 19755-6, 21640, 22725-8
Bouscayrol, R. 9195
Bousquet, G.H. 5055
Boustead, J.E.H. 6177
Boutet, R. 2003
Boutillier, J.L. 9047, 9211, 9438
Bouvaert, A.C. 15447
Bouveignes, O.de 7700, 14243, 14555-7, 15144-5, 15592, 23498
Bouws, J. 21962
Bovet, P. 1667
Bovill, E.W. 998, 2701, 4911, 4966-8, 7623, 7791-3, 11383, 15869, 15993
Bovy, L. 1526, 4882
Bowden, B.N. 1891
Bowen, W.W. 4243, 6431-4
Bower, J.E. 5508
Bowers, J.B. 6435
Bowin, C.O. 24655
Bowker, S. 23077
Bowler-Kelley, A. 21963
Bowles, P. 7251
Bowman, A.I. 8040
Bowman, I. 7308
Bowring, W.J.W. See Warrell-Bowring, W.J.
Boxer, C.R. 2702-3, 17508, 23540, 24019-20
Boyce, A.A.R. 6055-6
Boyce, R. 7747
Boyd, A. 2391

Boyer, J. 4427
Boyle, A.K. 4127
Boyle, A.M. 10973, 10974
Boyle, C.V. 7520, 10973-5
Bowie, D.F. 17715
Braasem, W.A. 320, 3275, 15146
Brachi, R.M. 18853
Brachott 10779
Brackenbury, E.A. 10976, 11937
Brackett, D.G. 1668-9, 1816-7
Bradbury, R.E. 10977, 11790, 12045
Bradford, J.E.S. 20397
Bradley, K. 2006
Bradlow, E. 22546, 22549
Bradlow, F. 22549
Bradlow, F.R. 21783, 21964-6, 22089, 22098, 22547-8
Bradshaw, A.T.von S. 9888
Brailsford, H.N. 6789
Brain, C.K. 21967
Brain, J.L. 485, 16128, 17716-7, 18371
Braine, B. 15994, 17069
Brambilla, C. 272, 289, 3276-7, 8664
Bramly, W.E.J. See Jennings-Bramly, W.E.
Branco, A.C. See Castel-Branco, A.
Branco, A.M. 3858
Brande, P.V. 15353
Brandel, M. 23078-80
Branden, F.Van den 13761, 15354-6
Brandt, L.de 13841
Brandt, W. 3608
Brandwijk, M.G. See Breyer-Brandwijk, M.G.
Branney, L. 390, 6128, 11619, 17317, 20398
Brantenaar, A.D.J. 2004
Brásio, P.A. 2, 794, 2704-7, 3859-74, 7479, 7481, 12895, 12917-21, 14759-66, 23510, 23541, 23589-95, 24021-2, 24068
Brasnett, J. 19181
Brasnett, N.V. 421, 19049, 19419
Brass, L.J. 21386-7
Brasseur, G. 8565, 8889, 9607
Braucourt, J.de H.de 14389
Brauner, H.P. See Plazikowsky-Brauner, H.
Brausch, G. 4428, 6577, 12929, 13842, 14619, 15448-9
Brausch, G.E.J.B. 3660, 5984
Bravo, T. 7471
Brazão, A. 12740
Bredin, G.R.F. 5959
Breese, G. 5433
Brelsford, V. 4429, 5509, 19850, 19887, 20883, 20900-4, 20988-9, 21017, 21080-1, 21124, 21178
Bremard, F. 7375
Bremer, K. 23081
Brenard, R. 15960
Brendon, N.J. 19888, 20512
Brennecke, G. 3875
Brenner, Y. 7635

Bresciani-Turroni, C. 5212
Bressan, E. 1136
Bresson, Y. 9439
Breton, A.le 9373
Brett, A.C. 23082
Brett, E.A. 17318
Brett, P.M. 13843
Brettell, N.H. 20280
Breuil, H. 178, 729-30, 4835, 6622, 7002, 13630, 16543, 21968-9, 23439-40
Breuning, S. 13418, 15751
Breutz, P.L. 19562, 21671, 21970
Brewer, J.H. 10761
Brewin, D.R. 17670
Brewster, P.G. 12449
Breyer-Brandwijk, M.G. 19618, 19823, 21214, 21591
Brice-Smith, H.M. 12242
Bridges, A.F.B. 7496, 11344, 12243, 23027
Bridges, R.C. 16036, 19182
Bridgman, F.B. 23083
Brière, D. 9087
Brière, J.F. 15147
Briey, P.de 1527, 2392, 6802
Briey, R.de 14558
Brigaud, F. 8540, 8566-7, 8597, 8708
Briggs, J.H. 18245
Briggs, L.C. 4796, 6982, 13483
Briggs, W.H. 12085, 12086
Bright, G. 7636
Bright, R.G.T. 18684
Brijbhushan, J. 795
Brimble, A.R. 21052
Brincker, P.H. 3036-9
Brisley, T. 9196
Brissac, P.de C. See Cossé-Brissac, P.de
Bristow, C.M. 17381
Bristow, W.M. 10978, 11938
Britannicus 1137
Brito, A.da R. See Rocha Brito, A.da
Brito, E. 7904, 7998-9, 8140, 12792-3, 12811, 12879
Brito Teixeira, J. 23633
Britten, H. 22913
Britton, J. 17616
Broadbent, P.B. 6129, 6178
Broadhead, J 22218
Brochado, C. 3876, 5298-9
Brock, R.G.C. 5510
Brockway, F. 2005, 2393, 17396, 19106
Broden 4128
Broderick, G.E.P. 19563, 19889-90, 20399, 20513
Broderick, M. 23028
Brokensha, D. 10029-30, 10485
Brooke, C. 16676
Brooke, N.J. 3661
Brooke, N.T. 12128
Brookes, E. 1670

Brookes, E.H. 22299-22303, 22914, 23084-7
Brookfield, H.C. 23088, 24308
Brooks, D. 796
Brooks, G. 3401
Brooks, G.E. 9837, 10486, 11791
Brooks, G.S. 9838
Broom, R. 21849-50, 21971
Broome, H.A. 22304
Broomfield, G.W. 16129-34
Brosnahan, L.F. 3040-1, 10637, 11939
Brossel, C. 3662, 14767
Brosset, D. 4912
Brotto, E. 16926
Brounger, S.G. 11530
Brown, A. 12244, 12450
Brown, A.A.A. 10031, 10487
Brown, A.J. 1138-9
Brown, A.P. 8041
Brown, A.R.R. See Radcliffe-Brown, A.R.
Brown, C.H. 5300, 7309
Brown, C.V. 11384
Brown, E.J.P. 10032
Brown, G. 12544
Brown, G.G. 17718-9
Brown, G.N. 1671, 7794, 10671
Brown, H. 12245-6
Brown, H.D. 13620, 15298
Brown, J. 8042
Brown, J.A.C. 1140
Brown, J.T. 21672
Brown, L.C. 5063
Brown, L.F. See Farrer-Brown, L.
Brown, P. 7521, 22305
Brown, P.H. 17397
Brown, P. 22112
Brown, R.E. 11620-1
Brown, R.T. 17398
Brown, S. 9718
Brown, W. 19384
Brown, W.O. 280, 4430, 23089
Browne, A.J.J. 5160
Browne, B.C. 24656
Browne, G. 10900
Browne, G.B.O. See Orde-Browne, G.B.
Browne, G.St.J.O. See Orde-Browne, G.St.J.
Browne, J.B. See Balfour-Browne, J.
Browne, S.G. 15299
Browne, S.G. See Gore-Browne, S.
Brownlee, C. 21851
Brownlee, F. 19555, 19564-7, 21569, 21852-4, 22219, 22306, 22550
Brownlee, W.T. 19568, 22915
Brubaker, H.H. 19891
Bruce, C. 2008
Bruce, D. 4129
Bruce-Myers, J.M. 10033, 10095

Bruchhausen, P. 2708
Bruckner, W.D. 10339
Bruel, G. 13004, 13590
Bruel, J.van den 15450
Bruens, A. 13294
Brugière, J.M. 13671
Brugnes-Romieu, M.P. 6767
Bruhl, L.L. See Lévy-Bruhl, L.
Brunot, L. 7167
Brunschwig, H. 2394, 7795-6, 13005, 13655, 13722
Brunskill, G.S. 2709
Brunyate, W.E. 5301
Bruton, C.L. 18685
Brutsch, J.R. 13064, 13261, 13295, 13409-10, 15726
Brutus, D. 22814-6, 23090
Bruwer, J. 18246, 19569, 20905-8
Bruyas, J. 1141, 2395, 8314
Bruyne, E.de 4432
Bruyns, L. 13762, 13780, 13844, 15451-3
Bryan, M.A. 6313, 16109, 16135-6, 17567
Bryant, A.T. 21855
Bryce, J. 21570, 23091
Bryce, M.D. 1529
Brygoo, E.R.R. 13065, 13419
Bu Raqibah, H. See Bourguiba, H.
Buch, V. 3402
Buchanan, D.M. 23092
Buchanan, K. 11531-2, 23093-4
Buchanan, L.A.C. 21260
Buchanan, L.M. 6130, 19107
Buchanan, R. 22817
Buchmann, J. 2396-8
Büchner, H. 11940
Buck, A.de 14390, 15565
Buckle, D. 11792
Budd, M.S. 18924
Budhraj, V.S. 2399
Budker, P. 13694
Buelens, K. 14391
Buell, R.L. 2710, 16037
Buerkle, H. 3877
Buettner-Janusch, J.and V. 24350
Bufe, E. 13296, 14917
Buffon, J. 2711
Bugeat, L. 6717
Bugeaud, M. 7095
Buhagiar, W. 16951
Bühlmann, W. 15300, 16137
Buisseret, A. 1142
Buisson, E.M. 13066, 13163
Buitendag, F.W.C. 22113, 23095
Bulck, G.van 3, 179, 306, 486-94, 1672, 2712, 3043-6, 3664,
    3878, 12962, 13751, 13845-9, 14768, 14918-20, 14942,
    15454, 15566, 15632, 15870, 22729
Bulck, V.van 495-6, 3047-50, 13850-3, 14512, 14921-2
Bulkeley, G.V.O. 2009-10

Bull, A.F.   16138-9, 17544
Bull, M.   7252, 21972-4
Bullock, C.   19892-4, 20130-1, 20648, 20732
Bumpus, B.S.G.   10140
Bunbury, I.   1530, 1673, 4433
Bundu   19895, 20680-1, 20800
Bungener, P.   78, 2400
Bunning, P.S.C.   7522
Bunsen, B.de   15928, 18995
Bunsuru   12247
Bunting, B.   22114, 22307-8, 23326
Bunting, S.   22309
Bunting, S.A.   17721
Burbridge, A.   19896-9, 20791
Burchall, H.   1531
Burden, E.N.   1532
Burdon, J.A.   11793
Bureau, R.   13067
Burgeon, L.   15357
Burgess, R.C.   15348
Burije, J.   15607
Burk, E.I.   13854, 15148
Burke, E.E.   20235
Burke, F.   18149, 19108-9
Burke, L.J.   9957
Burkitt, M.C.   18913
Burles, R.S.   21082
Burn, H.P.   See Pelham-Burn, H.
Burness, H.M.   11491
Burnet, A.M.   18996
Burnet, E.   6943
Burnley, G.E.   13467
Burns, C.   5425
Burns, R.   332
Burqibah, H.   See Bourguiba, H.
Burrows, D.   9719
Burrows, E.H.   21975-6, 22551, 23029
Burrows, G.   13855
Burrows, H.R.   23096
Burrows, R.   23097
Burssens, A.   3609, 11941, 13591, 13660, 13856, 13869,
    14769-70, 14923-42, 14958, 14962, 14978, 15072, 15149-50,
    22552
Burssens, H.   13857, 14244-5
Burt-Davy, J.   22553
Burton, E.M.   10307
Burton, G.J.   10780
Burton, H.   22115
Burton, R.   18066
Burton, R.F.   5161, 9486, 10141
Burton, W.F.P.   13858-9, 14943
Burtt, E.   18494
Burtt, J.   12958
Buselli, G.   6889
Bush, T.N.W.   22975

Bushe, H.G. 16377
Busia, K.A. 3879-80, 7637, 7685, 7797, 8141
Busin, S. 1143
Busquet, R. 6895
Busse, J. 17545-6, 18372-6
Busse, W. 17671
Busson, F. 8735
Bustin, E. 2401, 11794, 19110
Butcher, H.L.M. 10979, 11622, 11942
Buthaud, E. 6718
Butler, B. 19518
Butler, G. 22818
Butler, J. 18997, 22554
Butler, R.A. 19709
Butler, W. 1144
Butler, W.F. 22555
Butt, J. 19729
Buttgenbach, H. 14392-3, 15358
Büttikofer, J. 12524
Buttin, P. 7253
Büttner, C.G. 16089, 16258, 23353-4
Butzer, K.W. 4836
Buxton, C.R. 16388
Buxton, E.N. 4245
Buxton, E.R. 17617
Buxton, J. 5511-2
Buxton, L.H.D. 10109
Buxton, N., Lord. See Noel-Buxton, Lord
Buxton, S.C. 2011, 22556
Buxton, T.F. 23098
Buxton, T.F.V. 1674, 9720, 15871, 16430
Buxton, V. See Buxton, T.F.V.
Buyst, J.de 14268
Bwindi, J. 13068
Byakilema, D. 15148
Byatt, H. 18247
Byng-Hall, F.F.W. 10980, 11031
Byrne, J. 9789
Byslma, M. 24466

C., A.J. 2402, 12248, 20400
C., C.C. 20369
C., E. 11227, 13860
C., E.A. 20324
C., E.G. 5513
C., E.N. 6131
C., F. 12249-53
C., H.L. 11533
C., J. 79, 180, 253, 1145, 1533, 1675, 2012, 2713-4, 3881,
    4434, 4883, 6132, 7708, 8181, 8222-5, 8261, 8343, 8368-9,
    8412, 9048, 9176, 9233, 9440, 9531, 9547, 9708, 9817,
    9973, 10308, 10381-2, 10901, 11385, 11623-5, 11795,
    12451-2, 14246, 16398, 16646, 17168, 17319, 17399-17401,
    17638-9, 18248-9, 20285, 20325, 20401, 20824, 21083,
    21218, 21565, 22068, 22220, 22310-1, 22976, 23099, 23327,
    23467-9, 23659-61, 24277-8, 24625

C., J.W.   5989, 6171
C., M.S.   7616, 15204
C., R.V.   3882
C.W.B.   See B., C.W.
Cabanas, R.   7168
Cabannes, R.J.   4797
Cabot, J.   13531
Cabral, A.   1534, 23897
Cabral, A.L.   12658-61, 12726
Cabral, J.   2013-4, 23542
Cabrera, C.G.   See Garcia Cabrera, C.
Cabrita, V.de N.C.   See Castro Cabrita, V.de N.
Cabu, F.   14247
Cacciapuoti, R.   16488
Cachalia, Y.   22312
Cadenat, J.   8043, 8709-16
Cadenat, P.   7003
Caeneghem, E.van   15455
Caeneghem, R.van   1676, 3883, 13861-9, 14248, 14949, 15151,
    15301, 14944-8
Caetano, M.   1017, 2015, 2715
Caffarelli, E.V.   See Vergara-Caffarelli, E.
Cagigas, I.de las   7376
Cagnolo, C.   17210
Cahan, T.   1146
Caillé, J.   7310, 7377-8
Caillens, J.   798-9, 4435
Cailleux, A.   4932, 5079, 12254
Caine, S.   7638
Cairene   5302, 5414
Calame-Griaule, G.   3051, 6358, 8780, 8920-1, 8935, 8948
Caldecott, M.   22819
Callaghan, J.   20402
Callaway, A.   4436, 11386, 11492
Callaway, H.   21856
Callens, M.   6954
Callet, P.   24351
Callow, J.C.   10638
Calpin, G.H.   22557-8
Calthrop, E.R.   1535
Calton, W.E.   17673, 18495
Caluwaert, R.   15359
Calvet, M.   8641
Calvocoressi, P.   2403
Calzavarini, E.   1147-8
Calzia, G.P.   See Panconcelli-Calzia, G.
Camain, P.   4165
Camain, R.   4130
Camara, C.N.   See Nénékhaly-Camara, C.
Camara, T.   4131
Camara Laye.   See Laye, C.
Câmara Reis, D.da   23744
Cambier, R.   5303
Camboué, R.P.   24557-60
Cambourne, F.J.C.   1677
Cambridge, A.A.F.W.A.G. [Earl of Athlone]   22313

Cambridge, A.W.P. See Pickard-Cambridge, A.W.
Camerlynck, G.M. 1678
Cameron, Lt. 497, 12947
Cameron, D. 18150, 18250
Cameron, J. 2404-5, 24340
Cameron, M. 8044-5, 8344, 8461, 9380
Cameron, V.L. 6180
Camille, R. 3403
Camilleri, C. 6777, 6955
Camino, S.W. 9790
Camões, L.de 3610
Campbell, A.C. 19900, 20132, 20682, 21673, 21857
Campbell, C. 22314, 22559
Campbell, D.D. 19901
Campbell, E. 19696
Campbell, E.R. 20403
Camphor, A.P. 12558
Campos, E.de 14771
Campos, F.S.de 12880
Campos, J.de C. See Carvalho Campos, J.de
Campos, O.R.de. See Rodrigues de Campos, O.
Campos, T.G. See Guedes Campos, T.
Camps, G. 7004
Camus, A. 4395
Cana, F.R. 2716, 5304, 18251, 22560
Canale, J.S. See Suret-Canale, J.
Canas, J.M. 24110
Canazzi, A. 6896-8
Candelária, M.M. See Moreira Candelária, M.
Canham, P.H. 4, 7741, 10383-4, 10781, 20404
Canie, A. 3496
Cann, G.P. 5514
Cannon, D.A. 10870
Canosa, J.M.C.R. See Castro-Rial Canosa, J.M.
Cansdale, G.S. 10782-6
Cantero, V.B. 4798, 7248, 7414
Canto, B.do 23470
Cantor, D.J. 10243
Cantrelle, P. 8184
Canu, G. 8642
Capart, A. 8717
Cape Town, John. See Darbyshire, J.R., Archbishop of Cape
   Town
Capell, A. 3052
Capell, A.E. 19902, 20359
Capelle, E. 13870, 15205
Capelle, M. 14394
Capelle, M.G. 7686
Capéran, C.D.L. 3884
Capet, M. 8226
Capot-Rey, R. 4837, 4913, 8847
Capponi, A. 13420
Capron, J. 373, 8781, 9404-5
Capus, A. 18377-8
Caputo, G. 6678
Caquot, A. 16542-4, 16714-21, 16928-31, 16976-8

Caquot, J. 16832
Carbon, L.B.de 1149
Carbutt, C.L. 20286-7, 20360-1, 20514, 20825
Cárcer, M.A.de. See Aguirre de Cárcer, M.
Cardaire, M. 4438
Cardew, C.A. 21444-6, 21512
Cardew, M. 7574
Cardi, C.N.de 10981
Cardinall, A.W. 9351, 10034-6, 10142, 10385, 10489
Cardoso, C.L. 23366, 23372-5
Cardoso, F. See Firmino Cardoso
Cardoso, J. 23829-31
Cardoso, J.G.A. See Alfaro Cardoso, J.G.
Cardoso, J.J.A. See Alfaro Cardoso, J.J.
Cardoso, L. 23374
Cardoso Paisana, F. 23715, 24111
Carew-Slater, H.J. 22315
Cariou, M. 8635
Carle, G. 24561
Carlier, J. 8315, 8684
Carlin, M.M. 15924-5, 18629, 18998, 23100
Carlp, R. 4914
Carmichael, J. 18686
Carmignani, R. 13871
Carnegie, W.A. 20515
Carnell, W.J. 17722-3
Carney, D. 9974-5
Carnochan, J. 7905, 11943-8
Caro Baroja, J. 4969, 7430
Caroe, O. 17640
Carpenter, A.J. 12255
Carpenter, G.D.H. 4246, 19420
Carpenter, G.W. 3885, 14621, 15302
Carpenter, P. 10143-4
Carr, D.E.B. 18999-19001
Carr, R.C. 7254
Carreira, A. 7523, 8142, 12671-6, 12713, 12769, 12794-5
Carret, J. 7096, 7123, 7137
Carret, J.M. 13204
Carrié, R.A. See Albrecht-Carrié, R.
Carrington, C.E. 1150, 1679, 2016-7, 2406, 4439
Carrington, J.F. 502, 13872, 14249-52, 14950-3
Carrique, Capt. 13504
Carrocera, P.B.de 14954, 15303
Carrol, K. 11228-30
Carson, J. 15829, 17586, 17626
Carstairs, C.Y. 1151, 2018-9
Carstens, W.P. 22977
Carter, E.B. See Bonham-Carter, E.
Carter, F. 19002
Carter, G. 11796
Carter, G.E. 4440
Carter, G.L. 10902
Carter, G.M. 268, 4441, 22316
Carter, H. 20649, 21148
Carter, J. 11534, 15926

Carter, M. 9976
Carter, P.J. 10145
Carter, P.L. 7878, 10145
Carter, R.R.L. See Langham-Carter, R.R.
Cartey, W.G.O. 3497
Cartland, G.B. 10488
Cartmel-Robinson, S. 21302
Cartry, M. 9406
Carvajal Ferrer, F.J. 7472
Carvalha, P.da 23801
Carvalhal, A.V.e E. 23471
Carvalho, A.de 1680
Carvalho, A.P.de. See Pires de Carvalho, A.
Carvalho, C.N.de 23993
Carvalho, J.V.de 2407
Carvalho, M.de 23684-6, 24112
Carvalho Guerra, A. 12812-3
Carvalho Viegas, L.A.de 12751
Casadio, F.A. 80, 1681, 2020
Casariego, J.E. 2717
Casas, J.M.F. See Fúster Casas, J.M.
Cascio, A. 6899
Casely-Hayford, J.E. 7757, 10419
Casey, M. 24657
Cash, W.C. 1682-3
Cashmore, T.H.R. 17509
Casimiro, A. 3611
Casqueiro, M.v.B. See Bosse Casqueiro, M.v.
Casson, L.F. 21784-6
Castagne, E. 15360, 15403
Castagno, A.A. 17402
Castel Branco, A. 4244, 12814-5
Castellani 7008
Castillo, J.de V.y F.del. See Fernandez del Castillo, J.de V.
Castillo Barril, M. 15673
Castillo-Fiel, Conde 15709
Castinel, J. 9617
Castle, B. 20405
Castle, E.B. 1684
Castro, A. 12727
Castro, A.H.de 15747
Castro, A.O.de 3612
Castro, F. 16463
Castro, L.da C. 23927
Castro, L.de 24279
Castro, L.F.de O. See Oliviera e Castro, L.F.de
Castro, M.L.P.de 3886
Castro, R.A.de A.E. 24288
Castro, S.de 23687, 23745, 23802, 24023
Castro Cabrita, V.de N. 23928-9
Castro-Rial Canosa, J.M. 7311
Catala, R. 9677
Catford, J.R. 5985, 6578
Catlin, G. 10386
Catoire, P. 15456
Caton-Thompson, G. 731, 20133

Catrice, P. 2021, 3665, 5050, 5404
Catroux, Gen. 1060
Caulker, O.K. See Kelfa-Caulker, O.
Cauneille, Capt. 4859
Cauneille, A. 4799
Causard, M. 3887
Cauwenbergh, A.van 14395
Cavaco, A. 24113
Cavalan, P. 13676
Cave, B.S. 18598
Cave, F.O. 6436-9
Cawston, F.G. 4132
Cayton, H. 10387, 10490
Cazalas, A. 9224
Cazanove, J.L.F. 8345
Cazeneuve, J. 5162
Cebe-Habersky, J.J. 81
Ceccaldi, J. 13013, 13682
Cecchella, A. 442, 1152, 4442, 12943
Cecil, Lady A., later Lady Rockley. See Rockley, Lady
Cedant, J. 8718
Celen, V. 15152
Celis, M.J. 13873-4
Celliers, A.C. 23101
Cencillo de Pineda, M. 15725, 16722
Central Housing Board: Special Committee 23102
Cepollaro, A. 2017, 4443, 7033, 7379, 16140
Cerbella, G. 264, 4444, 5163, 6623, 6651, 6679-80, 6692, 6705-6, 16545-6
Cerdá, F.J. See Jordá Cerdá, F.
Černý, J. 5164
Cerqueira, I.de 23596
Cerulli, E. 1153, 16464, 16547, 16640, 16690, 16723-5, 16833-5, 16932, 16979, 17129-30
Césaire, A. 3498-3510, 4445-6, 7027, 9075, 9120
Ceulemans, P. 14772-3, 18252
Chabas, J. 3666-7, 8253, 8316-22, 8491, 8686-9
Chabouis, D. 24417
Chabrelie, L. 13569, 13592
Chacobo, H.T. See Tabernero Chacobo, H.
Chadoro 14955
Chadwick, C.M. 2408
Chadwick, E.R. 8263, 10982-3, 11231-5, 11493-5
Chadwick, H. 3888
Chailley, Comm. 8900, 9642, 17179
Chailley, M. 8890
Chakanza, E.T. 21261, 21363
Challot, J.P. 7159
Chaloner, W.H. 5305
Chamberlain, J. 2718, 4133
Chambers, P.C. 17186
Chambers, R. 17416
Chambers, R.J.H. 17403
Champault, D. 6983-4
Champion, A.M. 17187
Champion, P. 732, 1044, 8346, 24562

Chanakira, B. 20225
Chancellor, J. 20516, 20826
Chancellor, R.J. 19058
Chanderli, A.K. 7059
Chandler, D.G. 5306
Chandler, S.E. 1536
Chantry, C. 20288
Chaouache, H. 4970
Chaparadza, W. 19903
Chapin, J.P. 4247
Chaplin, J.H. 498, 10221, 20909, 21149, 21219-20
Chapman, J.D. 21523
Chapman, P.R. 10903
Chapus, G.S. 24315
Chapus, M. 24316
Chapus, S. 24467
Charadrius 4248, 12256
Charbonnier, J. 8523
Chard, L.W. See La Chard, L.W.
Charle, E.G. 11387
Charles, P. 3889, 4447, 15206
Charles, V. 181-2, 1537, 1849, 8883, 14396-14407, 14513, 14622-31, 15207-13, 15361-2, 15457-75
Charles-Roux, F. 4971, 5307
Charlewood, C.J. 18253
Charpentier, C. 2719
Charpin, M. 13490-1
Charreau, C. 8719
Chasseloup Laubat, F.de 4838
Chataignier, A. 8305, 8643
Chataway, J.D.P. 5515-6, 5885
Chatelain, H. 14956-7
Chatterjee, S. 19710
Chaudhuri, S.P. See Chowdhry, S.P.
Chaulet, C. 6956
Chauleur, P. 1154, 6719, 8323
Chaves, L. 800, 2720
Chazel, A. 24504
Cheeseman, J.J. 12576
Chelhod, J. 394-5, 8782
Chènebaux, A. 7255, 7380
Chenet, G. 2721
Chérel, J. 4786
Cheron, G. 8185-6, 8986
Chesham, Lord 18067
Chesnau, J. 1155
Chevalier, A. 5114, 8046, 9625, 13014-5, 13697
Chevignard, A.L. See Lechevallier-Chevignard, A.
Chevitch, P.L. See Lenk-Chevitch, P.
Chew, C.W. 8047, 13421-2
Chhabra, H.S. 17510, 18254
Chidzero, B.T.G. 1156, 12953, 15995
Chidziwa, J. 20517
Chieza, G.P. 20705
Chigumi 19904

Child, G.S.   18496
Child, H.F.   19905-6, 20406, 20733
Childs, G.M.   23543-4, 23597
Childs, S.H.   12453
Chilkovsky, N.   896
Chillemi, A.   6696
Chilver, E.   82
Chilver, E.M.   7798, 10984, 11797, 13069, 13209, 13250, 13262, 13272
Chimanga, E.   20684
Chimwaza, G.M.   21425
Chinebuah, I.K.   10639
Chingota, J.   21325
Chinyandura   19571, 19908-12, 20134, 20326, 20734
Chiomìo, G.   16489
Chippaux, C.   24403
Chiraghdin, S.   16259
Chirgwin, A.M.   3890, 21334, 24542
Chirol, V.   5308
Chisholm, J.A.   17724
Chisiza, D.K.   1157, 2409, 2722, 4448
Chitepo, H.W.   3668
Chitewhe, S.S.M.   19913, 20685
Chittick, H.N.   183, 16038, 17512, 17922-4, 18255
Chiume, M.W.K.   21426
Chiva, A.D.   See Deluz-Chiva, A.
Chiwale, J.C.   20925
Chmielewski, W.   5886
Choate, C.D.   22978
Chodak, S.   2410
Chojnacki, S.   16548, 16677-8, 16726
Chombart de Lauwe, P.H.   4449, 13190
Chona, M.   21020, 21084
Chopard, L.   8462
Chorley, C.W.   19050-2, 19423-5
Chorley, T.W.   19421-2
Choto, E.   20686
Choubert, G.   4351
Chowdhry, S.P.   17641
Christaller, J.G.   6314, 7906, 9357-8, 10640-1
Christensen, J.B.   10037-8
Christian, A.   10841
Christy, C.   1892, 4134, 4249-50, 4450, 12525, 15872
Chubb, L.T.   12257
Chudson, W.A.   1158
Chukwukere, B.I.   1686
Chum, H.   16141, 16260-2
Church, R.J.H.   See Harrison-Church, R.J.
Churchill, W.S.C.   2023
Ciasca, R.   6640
Cidade, H.   3891
Cintas, P.   6741
Cipriani, L.   16490
Ciroma, M.A.L.   10985
Cissé, D.   3511

Cissé, Y. 8783
Cissokho, B. 8784
Cissoko, S.M. 8292, 8901
Ciucci, C. 1159
Civera Simón, G. 7049, 7060
Clair, A. 801, 21977
Clair, M.H. 2024-5, 14408
Clairmonte, F. 2382, 2411
Clamens, G. 9270
Clark, D. 18687-90
Clark, E. 4915
Clark, H.M. 10871
Clark, J.D. 423, 733-8, 4451, 17032, 18854, 19627, 20884, 20990-3, 21304, 23441, 23499
Clark, J.P. 3278, 3404-5, 12046-7, 19370
Clark, P.G. 15873-5, 18015
Clark, R. 1160
Clark, R.T. 16691
Clark, W. 15876
Clark, W.T. 5517
Clarke, A.F. 11496
Clarke, C.A. See Arden-Clarke, C.
Clarke, D. 7575
Clarke, E. 10039
Clarke, E.E.S. See Sabben-Clarke, E.E.
Clarke, F. 1687
Clarke, J.C. 17725
Clarke, J.D. 10986, 11236, 12258, 12521
Clarke, J.H. 8902, 10040, 22060
Clarke, J.H.C. 21204
Clarke, J.I. 6644, 6957, 9977
Clarke, P.H.C. 18379
Clarke, R.T. 13875
Clarke, W.R.E. 9839
Clarkson, M.L. 10008
Clausen, G. 17925
Clauson, G. 1161
Clauzel, J. 4884, 8922
Claveria, M.M. 7256
Clavier, J.L. 9137
Clay, G. 2208, 22317
Clay, G.C.R. 21085
Clayton, E. 1162
Clayton, E.S. 17320
Clayton, H.R. 4452
Clayton, W.D. 11535
Cleene, N.de 13876-9, 14253, 14347, 14409, 14632, 15214, 15304-5
Clegg, W.H. 22116
Cleire, R. 14958-9
Clement, N. 13297
Clément, P. 14349
Clendinning, J. 10345-6
Clerc, A. 3892, 24063
Clercq, A.de 13880-1, 14960-2, 15476

Clère, J.J. 5165
Clerq, L.de 14963
Cleve, G.L. 18380
Cliff, L. 18151
Clifford, H. 10491, 10842, 11626
Clifford, M. 10987
Clifford, W. 1688
Clignet, R. 9300-1
Clignet, R.P. 10388
Climenhaga, A.M. 20250
Clinton, J.V. 12454
Close, A.G.L. 19914
Close, J. 15396
Cloudsley-Thompson, J.L. 6440
Clough, R.H. 17321
Clozel, F.J. 9284
Clutton, S.G. 6359
Cobham, H. 10988-9
Cocatre-Zilgien, A. 1689, 2723, 5309, 8557
Cochran-Patrick, C.K. 21072
Cockcroft, I.G. 19804, 20135, 20827
Cocker, M.de 13882-4, 15306
Cocker, P.de 13885-6
Cockin, G. 11497
Cockin, M.S. 11237
Cocquyt, A. 13887
Codjo, R. 3893
Coelho, D.P. 24114
Coelho, M.A.T. 23376
Coeman, P.F. 13888
Coertze, P.J. 19757, 21571
Coetzee, J.H. 22916
Coeur, C.L. See Le Coeur, C.
Coeur, M.L. See Le Coeur, M.
Cofie, J. 10347
Coghlan, C. 20826
Cohen, A. 2026, 11388, 19111
Cohen, C.K. See Karila-Cohen, C.
Cohen, M. 16836-7
Cohen, R. 5, 499, 10990, 11389
Cohen, V. 4885
Coillie, G.van 14964
Coissy, A. 9556-7
Cola Alberich, J. 500, 1163-4, 1690, 1893, 2027, 4251-2,
    4352, 4453-7, 4787, 4800, 7169, 10474, 15996
Colançon, M. 24505
Colard, R.J.H. 13889
Colby, G. 21427
Colby, R. 24468
Colchester, G.V. 6057
Colchester, T.C. 16399, 17404
Cole, C.O.E. 9929
Cole, C.W. 11627
Cole, D.T. 3053-4, 19341, 19758, 22730-1
Cole, G.D.H. 22318
Cole, G.F. 18016, 18497

Cole, G.H. 18855
Cole, H. 17726
Cole, J.O. See Ojo-Cole, J.
Cole, J.S.R. 18152
Cole, R.L. 20289
Cole, T. 6
Cole-Beuchat, P.D. 3055, 19747, 21858, 22732-5
Coleman, J.S. 7, 802, 2028, 2369, 2412
Colenso, F. 22561
Coleson, E. 7687
Coley, D.M. 20518
Colin, M. 14514
Colin, P. 24626
Colin, P.E. 24426-7
Colin, R. 803
Colinet, G. 13298
Coll, F. 4942, 7061
Collery, M. 9558
Collet, C. 2029
Colley, W.M. 6441
Colliard, C.A. 5056, 23362
Collier, F.S. 9655, 12049, 12259-62
Collignon, J. 13016, 13023, 13648, 13672-4, 13694
Collingwood, F.W.N. 18068
Collins, E. 10492
Collins, O.R. 14774
Collins, R. 6133
Collins, R.O. 6174, 6181, 13890, 19183-5
Collins, S. 1691
Collins, W.B. 4253, 8048
Collomb, H. 8500, 8750, 8770
Colombe, L. 5258
Colombe, M. 5259-60, 5310-2
Colquhoun, A.R. 83, 2030, 16039, 20362
Colson, E. 4458, 19572, 20290, 20910-12, 21018-20, 21086,
    21205, 21221-2
Coltart, J.M. 1538
Colvin, I. 10389
Comba Ezquerra, J.A. 7451-2
Combe, E.T. 6183
Coméliau, J. 15153
Comhaire, J. 1165, 2724, 3894-5, 4459-60, 8259, 11390-1,
    11498, 12209, 12988, 13000, 13030, 13891-2, 13923,
    14775-8, 15307, 15477-8, 15596-7, 15613-4, 23367, 23472
Comhaire-Sylvain, J. 9589, 13893, 13895, 14254
Comhaire-Sylvain, S. 9589, 11392, 13894-5, 14967, 15154,
    15479-80, 16668
Comité Permanent du Congrès Colonial National 14633, 15481
Comte, P. 2413
Conan-Davies, E. 17727
Conant, F.P. 10991, 11238, 17211, 17218
Conceição Tavares da Silva, M. 4461
Conciliator 10244
Condamin, M. 9381, 12646, 13423
Condie, R.H.B. 5213, 5986
Conduto, J.E. 12787
Confalonieri, V.B. 10390, 17070

Conillera, J.S. See Solsona Conillera, J.
Coninck, A.de 2031
Connor, R.M.B. 17728
Conover, H.F. 333
Conroy, F.D. 5987
Consiglio, G. 8, 1166-9, 1539, 4886, 4943, 16692-3, 16727, 17037, 17071
Contenson, H.de 16549-56
Conti Rossini, C. 15981, 16465-6, 16491-3, 16557-9, 16679-80, 16728-30, 16838-40, 16933-5, 16980
Contini, F. 6616
Contini, P. 17153
Conton, W.F. 1692
Conyngham, L.D. 21087
Cook, A.R. 18922, 19186-9
Cook, D. 12050, 15927, 16431
Cook, M. 4462
Cook, O.F. 12561, 12577-9
Cook, P.A.W. 21741, 21768
Cook, R.C. 5518
Cooke, B.K. 6058
Cooke, C.K. 20136-7
Cooke, H.B.S. 16400, 19628
Cooke, H.J. 18069
Cooke, J.F. See Fletcher-Cooke, J.
Cooke, R.C. 5519
Cooke, S.V. 17642
Cookey, S.J.S. 14779
Cookson, C.E. 7524
Coolidge, A.C. 4972
Coombes, A.N. 24305
Coombs, D. 10493
Coombs, G.M. 8568, 20291, 24428
Cooper, A.F. 5313
Cooper, B. 17729, 21223
Cooper, B.K. 12455
Cooper, G. 20138, 21021
Cooper, H. 2414
Cooper, J.O. See Omer-Cooper, J.
Cooper, L. 23103
Cooper, L.G. 12263-4
Cooper, L.J.B. See Blom-Cooper, L.J.
Cooper, L.O. 23832
Cooper, W.G.G. 10787
Cooper, W.H. 18498
Coornaert, F. 1693
Coote, J.M. 19190
Cope, A.T. 22736-8
Cope, T. 897
Copland, B.D. 16142, 17212, 17547
Coppens, P. 13752, 14634, 15482
Coppens, Y. 13505-7
Coquery-Vidrovitch, C. 9559, 13656, 13723, 15727
Cora, G. 84, 16694
Corbeil, R. 8522-3

Corby, C. 8274
Corbyn, E. 4973, 6143, 6184, 6442
Cordero Torres, J.M. 2032-5, 2725, 7257-61, 7290-7, 7312-3, 7358, 15720
Corella, D.L.B. 15674
Coret, A. 6900
Corfec, J.le 9062
Corfield, F.D. 5520, 17405
Coriat, P. 6185
Corinta Ferreira, M. 4149, 4264-5, 19824-30, 20800, 21787, 23030-6, 24115-31
Corkill, N.L. 5521-5, 6443-6, 6579-80
Cornelis, H. 2036, 14410, 14559-60
Cornelius, D. 9990
Cornell, A. 3512
Cornet, H. 6730, 7183
Cornevin, R. 381, 1540, 2726-9, 9307-15, 9352, 9359, 9399, 9560-2, 14780
Corò, F. 4916, 5035, 6624-6, 6790, 6803, 7231, 7401, 12944
Correa, A.A.M. See Mendes Correa, A.A.
Correia, B. 12703
Correia, J.A. 11949
Correia, P. 8000, 9563, 9602
Correia, P.J.A. 3896-9, 4135, 16981
Correia, R. 23833
Correia de Aguiar, E.da P. 23930
Correia Marques. See Marques, C.
Corso, R. 6627
Corugedo, J.A. See Alvarez Corugedo, J.
Cory, A. 17732
Cory, H. 4463, 15961, 17730-40, 18070, 18153
Coryndon, R.T. 15997, 21765
Coryton, E.G. 6447-8
Cosio, R.de C. See Cossio y de Cosio, R.de
Cossé-Brissac, P.de 7314
Cossery, A. 5405
Cossio y de Cosio, R.de 15693
Costa, C.M.S.da. See Silveira da Costa, C.M.
Costa, E.C.E. 12677
Costa, F.C.da. See Costa, F.M.C.da
Costa, F.M.C.da 4136-7, 12678, 12816-21, 12834, 12845, 12847
Costa, I.A.da 23931
Costa, J.J. 23688
Costa, J.M.da 23474
Costa, M.G.da 2730-1
Costa, Mário, Lt. 24024, 24280
Costa, S.Mário 23669, 23689
Costa Andrade, F.da. See Andrade, C.
Costanzo, G.A. 185, 1170, 17052, 17072
Costanzo-Beccaria, G.A. 9
Costermans, B. 490, 6315, 13896-13912, 14255-7, 14966, 15483
Cotay, A.B. 9840
Cotran, E. 3669, 16378, 17587-8, 18452, 19385
Cott, H.B. 19426

Cottam, L. 5526
Cottam, R. 5526, 6449-50
Cotterell, F.P. 16841-2
Cotterell, G.C.B. 12265
Cotton, C.P. See Powell-Cotton, C.
Cotton, J.C. 10992-4
Cotton, P.H.G.P. See Powell-Cotton, P.H.G.
Cotton, S.A. 10041
Cotton, W.A. 23104
Couceiro, H.de P. 3613
Couchman, N.R.F. See Fuggles-Couchman, N.R.
Coulter, C.W. 12979
Counsell, E.H.M. 1894
Counil, J. 6976
Coupethwaite, B. 21708
Coupez, A. 3056, 14967-8, 15608, 15633-7, 15642
Coupland, R. 10
Cournarie, P. 13070
Coursey, D.G. 10788
Court, B. 15877, 19112
Courtney, W.F. 2415
Courtois, C. 2732
Cousins, W.M. 6804
Coussée, P. 14635
Cousteix, P.J. 13071
Coustillac, L. 6742
Couteller, I.H.le 4138
Coutinho, G. 12728
Coutinho, L.P. See Pereira Coutinho, L.
Couto, H.S. See Sá Couto, H.
Coutouly, F.de 8987
Coutrez, G. 15363
Coutts, P.G. 18071, 18856
Couve, D. 24543
Couzens, A.H. 1541
Cowan, A.A. 7799
Cowan, L.G. 85
Cowan, W. 6316
Cowen, D.V. 2416
Cowgill, J.I.W. 19915
Cowley, K. 17406
Cox, A.H. 19191
Cox, F.J. 6059
Cox, P.G. 10904
Cox, T.R.F. 18691-2, 19113, 19519
Cox-George, N.A. 1171, 7639, 9818, 9841
Coxill, H.W. 15308
Coyne, A.E. 898
Coyssi, A. 9598
Cozens, A.B. 10905, 10995-6, 12051, 12266-9, 13072
Crabb, D.W. 11950, 12456
Crabbé, J. 14411, 14636-7
Crabbe, J.R. 19427
Crabitès, P. 5314-5
Crabtree, W.A. 1172, 2733, 3057-62, 9353-4, 11798, 12930,
    15998, 16090, 19342-4, 22739

Craemer, W.de 14788-9
Crahay, F. 4464
Crail, P. 22258
Cranborne, Lord 2734
Crane, W.H. 3900
Cransac, G.P. See Poux-Cransac, G.
Crary, D.D. 5245
Craven, W.F. 2735
Crawford, D. 3063
Crawford, J. 23635
Crawford, J.R. 19916, 22039
Crawford, O.G.S. 6186-7, 6581, 15962, 16731
Crawley, A. 2417-8
Crawshay, R. 21388
Crazzolara, P. 5527-9, 18693, 19192
Creech Jones, A. 2037-40, 2138-9, 20407
Creighton, T.R.M. 3279-80, 21088
Crespigny, A.R.C.de 22319
Crespo, M.P. 12729-33, 12822-3
Crine, F. 15484
Cripps, A.S. 20280, 20408-11, 20519, 20687, 23105
Cripps, H. 19917-8, 20363, 20520, 20688
Cripps, L. 20139, 20521
Cripps, M. 20522
Cripwell, H.A. 18256, 20650
Crispi, F.P. See Palamenghi-Crispi, F.
Crocker, H.E. 7709, 11239, 13913, 14561, 20292
Crompton, A.W. 22259
Crookenden, H. 4465
Crooker, W.R. 1173
Crosby, K.H. 9721
Crosby, O.T. 23299
Cross, L. 12052
Crosse-Upcott, A.R.W. 17741-2, 17926, 18499
Crossland, C. 6451-5
Crosthwait, H.L. 15963
Crouzet, E. 1174-5
Crow, A.T. 10789
Crowder, M. 2419, 7749, 8541
Crowfoot, G.M. 5530-2
Crowfoot, J.W. 5533-6, 5887, 6396, 6582-4
Crowley, D.J. 501, 4466
Crowther, F.G. 10494-5
Crowther, I.A. 20913
Croxton, A.H. 20364
Crozier, B. 2420, 7062
Crozon, H. 9471
Cruickshank, A. 6439, 6456
Crummey, D.E. 16982
Cruz, C.S. 4139, 9525-6, 9590-1, 9608, 19831, 23994, 24133
Cruz, F. 4974, 15364, 23500, 23636
Cruz, J.H.M. See Meira e Cruz, J.H.
Cruz, V.da 1694
Cruz Ferreira, F.S.da 12824-8
Cruz Herrera, J. 7184
Cudjoe, R. 11348

Cuenot, R.P.J. 9452-3
Cuille, J. 9152
Cuisenier, J. 6731, 6768
Culwick, A.T. 4467, 17743-5, 17927-8, 18154-5, 18599-18600, 18694
Culwick, G.M. 503, 4224, 5988, 6457, 6577, 16401, 17744-6, 17928, 18155, 18500-1, 18694
Cumming, D. 1542, 16734
Cumming, D.C. 6183, 6663
Cummins, H. 21859
Cummins, S.L. 5537
Cunctator, F. 7124
Cunha, A. 12679
Cunha, A.d'A. See Almeida e Cunha, A.d'
Cunha, A.X.da. See Xavier da Cunha, A.
Cunha, C.A.do C.L. 4140
Cunha, J.A.da 23475
Cunha, J.M.da S. See Silva Cunha, J.M.da
Cunha, S. 2421, 7750
Cunha Taborda, A. 12680, 12681
Cunliffe-Lister, P. 2041
Cunningham, M.M. 4468
Cunnington, W.A. 12931
Cunnison, I. 5538-9, 20914-6, 21125, 21198
Curis, M. 13228
Currey, R.N. 22088
Currie, D. 2042, 22117
Currie, J. 2043, 6029
Curtin, P.D. 804, 2736-7, 2995, 7800
Curtis, G.E. 17162
Cuthbert, D. 3901
Cutten, A.J. 23106
Cutten, T.E.G. 23107
Cuvelier, J., Mgr. 14341, 14781, 15309
Cuyvers, J.B. 1177, 13914
Cyan 3406
Cyfer-Diderich, G. 15215
Czermak, W. 3064

D., A. 19919
D., F. 15216
D., G. 8213
D., H. 5214
D., N. 14638, 15217
D., R. 5540, 6317, 6360, 6586
D., W.A. 5989
Daaku, K.Y. 10146, 10496
Dabin, P. 14639-40
Dabit, B.A. See Appia-Dabit, B.
Dabrowska-Smektala, E. 5166
Dadie, B. 505, 3276-7, 3513-6, 4469, 8255, 8306, 8665, 9279-82
Dadzie, K.E.W. 334-5
Daeleman, I. 14969-71

D'aeth, R. 1695
Dafalla, H. 6189
Dagan, T. 8524
Dagba, E. 9472
Daget, J. 8049-50, 8347, 8720, 8779, 8785, 8884, 8945, 8963
Dagnac, Capt. 13542
Dahl, E. 17747
Dahlberg, R.E. 1895-6
Dahle, P.B. 22740
Dahya, B.W. 15794, 19520-1
Dain, F.R. 17618
Dainelli, G. 6653, 17012
Dairy Control Board 22118
Dalby, D. 7907-8, 9889-92, 12606
Daldry, L.C. 11628
Dale, I.R. 2738, 19365
Dalloni, M. 7005-6
D'Almásy, L.E. 6060-1
Dalton, G. 1178-80, 12545
Dalton, J.H. 10245
Dalziel, J.M. 8051
Dam, T.van. See Van Dam, T.
Damane, M. 21651
Damas, L.G. 1056, 3407-10
Damman, E. 1071, 3065-72, 12607-8, 16091, 16143-5, 16263-72,
  17213-4, 17548-50, 17748-50, 18381-2, 19345, 21150,
  23355-6
Dammers, A.H. 3902
Dampierre, E.de 13570
Danby, P.M. 17215
Dandouau, A. 24506
Dandy, A.J. 4353
Dane, P. 3411
Danford, J.A. 11240
Dangel-Wien, R. 11951
Daniel, F.de F. 10906, 10997, 11241, 11352
Daniel, J. 7063
Daniell, J.P.S. 5541
Daniélou, J. 3903
Daniels, W.C.E. 7990, 10703-7
Danielson, E.R. 17751, 18314
Danon, V. 6958
Danquah, J.B. 2739, 10042, 10391, 10497-8, 10672
Dantzig, A.van. See Van Dantzig, A.
D'Anvers, C. 7473
Darby, H.C. 21073
Darbyshire, J.R., Archbishop of Cape Town 23059
Dardel, J.B. 6959
Dark, P. 7576, 11242, 12457
Darker, G.F. 4141, 10998
Darling, H.S. 5459, 6458
Darling, R.C.M. See Maxwell-Darling, R.C.
Darlow, M. 21224
Darmon, J.P. 7097
Darragh, J.T. 23108

Dart, R.A.   506, 4839, 19573-5, 20140, 20523, 21978-82
Darton, G.C.   1696
Darwin, L.   11629
Dathorne, O.R.   3283, 3412-5, 12053
Datta, A.K.   10843, 23109, 23328-9
Dauzats, A.   13299
Daveau, S.   9647, 9800
Davenport, T.R.H.   22562-3
Davey, A.C.   18478
Davey, D.G.   4142
Davey, H.W.   22320
Davey, J.B.   18799, 21389
Davico, A.   16560
David, J.B.   10790
David, P.   4254, 8492
David, R.   3670, 16952, 24352
David de Sousa, M.   3904
Davidson, A.M.   11799
Davidson, B.   739, 1181, 2740-2, 8275-6, 8293, 9088, 14412, 17407, 19691, 23476, 23545
Davidson, G.B.D.   24658
Davidson, H.W.   9819
Davidson, J.   3905, 13915-6, 14972, 15485
Davidson, M.   20994-5
Davidson, N.   3416
Davidson, S.   21206
Davies, A.M.M.   See Morgan-Davies, A.M.
Davies, C.   20524
Davies, C.S.   19923
Davies, E.C.   See Conan-Davies, E.
Davies, G.   6805
Davies, H.O.   2422
Davies, H.R.J.   5542
Davies, H.V.   21735
Davies, I.   1182
Davies, J.N.P.   4143, 19428
Davies, K.A.   18955, 19053, 19193
Davies, O.   741, 4470, 7525, 7577-9, 9025, 9527, 10147-54, 10344, 10499, 21983, 23501
Davies, R.   5543-7, 6190, 6461
Davies, S.G.   10708
Davies, W.N.G.   19920
Davis, A.J.   16733
Davis, C.S.   19921-2
Davis, J.   4471
Davis, J.M.   3906
Davis, M.B.   18695
Davis, O.J.   14515
Davison, D.   22820
Davison, R.B.   7640
Davon, R.   16695, 16734
Davy, J.B.   See Burt-Davy, J.
Dawbarn, C.   22067
Dawe, M.T.   19054-5
Dawkins, H.C.   19056

Daws, H.H. 12270
Dawson, J.L. 9893, 9978
Dawson, W.H. 23110
Day, A. 21390
Day, P. 12458
Dayer, L. 24659
De Freitas, G. 10246, 24284
De Graft-Johnson, J.C. 740, 1697, 10083-4
De Graft-Johnson, J.W. 10715
De Graft-Johnson, K.E. 10851
De Graft-Johnson, S.B.G. 10808
De Heer, N.A. 10420
Dean, D. 7801
Dean, E.A. 23111
Dean, E.R. 21351
Dean, J. 296, 336
Dean, R.F.A. 4225, 19429-30
Deane, L.A. 5548
Deane, P. 20293-5
Deans, T. 21207
Deasy, G.F. 4917
Debbasch, Y. 2743
Debenham, F. 1897-8, 12948, 21022, 21074, 21702
Debernardi, L. 6769
Debien, G. 2744-6, 2749, 2823, 2912, 8208, 8216
Deboudaud, J. 13231
Deboutteville, C.D. See Delamare-Deboutteville, C.
Debrah, E.M. 2423
Debrunner, H.W. 9360, 10500, 10762
Decapmaker, I. 13917
Decapmaker, J. 13918-21, 14973, 15218
Decary, R. 24346, 24353-9, 24429-30, 24469-74, 24535,
   24563-74, 24620, 24627
Decaudin, M. 805
Dechambre, E. 2747
Déchezelles 6903
Decker, T. 9791, 9894
Decle, L. 2748
Declercq, A. 3073, 14974-6
Decloitre, L. 8348, 8721, 16402
Decottignies, R. 3671-4, 8324-6, 8690-2, 9375
Decraene, P. 2424-5, 8903
Decroux, P. 7381-2
Dedave, A. 13922
Defert, S. 7232
Deglin, C. 6944
Deguent, R. 1543
Dehalu, M. 14562-3
Dehasse, J. 14516
Dehérain, H. 7098, 7367
Deheyn, J.J. 14517
Dei Anang, M.F. 3284
Deininger-Englhart, L. 16576
Deis, E. 6643, 11393, 16647-8
Dekeyser, P.L. 1698, 4255-8, 8052-3, 8349, 8463, 8722-3,
   9153

Dekker, G. 1899
Del Valle, R. See Valle Fernández, R.del
Delacauw, A. 15219
Delacour, A. 8983, 9138
Delafosse, M. 2749, 3074, 4091, 7315, 8227, 8644
Delais, M. 8054, 8724-5
Delamare-Deboutteville, C. 9289
Delanaye, P. 14518, 14977
Delange, J. 1544, 7580
Delanghe, A. 13923
Delano, I.O. 12459
Delany, F. 5866, 5888
Delarozière, R. 13073
Delarozière, S. 13179
Delauney, C. 4472
Delavignette, R. 321, 2044, 13244
Delcourt, A. 8726
Delcroix, G. 13074
Delève, J. 8350
Delevoy, G. 424, 13763, 14413, 15365-6
Delf, B.H. 12271
Delhaye, F. 12941, 15367
Delille, A. 14978
Delisle, G. 3521
Delius, A. 22321, 22821-2
Dellicour, F. 15220, 15627, 22322
Delmé-Radcliffe, C. 19194
Delmond, P. 8143, 8277
Delobbe 13924
Deloncle, P. 2045
Delrieu, S. 9183
Deluc, J. 23112
Deluz-Chiva, A. 9197-8
Delval, J. 1183, 8893
Dema, I.S. 12272
Demaison, D. 8327-9
Demontès, V. 6806, 7092, 7099
Demonts, R. 1184
Demoz, A. 16843
Dempster, J.B. 86
Dempster, R.T. 2426, 3280, 3417
Dempwolff, O. 18383, 22741
Denaeyer, M.A. 13424
Dendrophilus 4259, 12273
Denfield, J. 21788, 22119, 21972-4
Denis, J. 13698, 14564-5
Denis, L. 13925-9, 14258
Denis, P. 13930
Denis, P.A. 8542
Denis, P.J. 13931
Denizet, J. 6807
Dennett, R.E. 8001, 10907, 10999-11001, 11952-4, 12129, 12980, 13661, 13932, 14782-4
Dennis, G.L. 12580
Dennis, P.C.W. 10392
Denny, N. 3075
Denny, S.R. 20996

Denolf, F. 13933
Denolf, P. 13934-5, 14566, 14979-80, 15486
Dent, M.J. 11630
Denton, G.C. 11349
Deny, J. 7100
Depasse, C. 13753
Depestre, R. 2046, 3286, 3522-6
Depoorter, K. 15155
Déprez, J. 8330
Derbi, M.D. 10155
Dérendinger, Gen. 13508, 13551
Derine, R. 14519
Dermenghem, E. 3527
Dernburg, B. 2047
Deroover, M. 15368
Deroure, F. 8598
Derrett, J.D.M. 3675, 12130
Desai, R.H. 15878, 16432
Desanges, J. 4975-7
Descampe, E. 14785
Descarpentries, A. 8946, 9382
Deschamps, H. 2427, 13724, 24404-5, 24475, 24628
Descloitres, C. 7147
Descloitres, R. 7147-8
Desfeuilles, P. 4978
Deshler, W. 1900, 19057
Désiré-Vuillemin, G.M. 7316, 8428
Desmarescaux, J. 2428
Desmore, A. 23113
Desmouliez, G. 4473
Desplagnes, L. 8848
Despois, J. 4788, 4887, 4918, 6654, 6761, 6808
Desportes, G. 3287-8
Dessarre, E. 276, 4474, 23114
Dessertine, A. 8599
Dessy, G.B. 17408
Detourbet, A.M. See Masson-Detourbet, A.
Deuren, P.van 14414
Devallon, C.M. See Maitre-Devallon, C.
Devaux, V. 13936, 15221, 15487
Devernois, G. 2048-9, 4475, 9344, 13245
Devine, W.A. 20735-6
Devois, J.C. 8569
Dew, R.E. See Elsdon-Dew, R.
Deyo, M. 20525
Dez, J. 24360, 24406, 24507-8
Dhanis, E. 14415
Dhlomo, H.I.E. 3076, 22858
Dia, M. 1185, 4475
Diagne, P. 4476, 7909, 8501
Diague, P. 3077
Diaka, B.M. See Mungul-Diaka, B.
Diakhaté, L. 3288, 3529, 4478, 8666-7
Diakité, L. 4144
Diallo, A.A. 9139

Diallo, B. 8668
Dianoux, H.J.de 8923
Dias, A.de S. See Sousa Dias, A.de
Dias, A.H.G.de S. See Sousa Dias, A.H.G.de
Dias, D.A.S. See Sobral Dias, D.A.
Dias, G.S. See Sousa Dias, G.
Dias, J.A.T.S. See Santos Dias, J.A.T.
Dias, M.B. 23932
Dias, M.G. 12829, 24137
Dias Dinis, P.A.J. 12682-3, 12723, 12752, 12896
Dias Nogueira, E. 3908
Dias Rafael, S. 23933, 23962
Díaz, S.M. See Montero Díaz, S.
Diaz de Villegas, J. 806, 2750-1, 4979, 7233, 7710, 7802, 15694, 15711
Diaz Marin, J. 7405
Dib, M. See Mohammed Dib
Dickens, K.J. 10642
Dickinson, R.W. 20526
Dickson, A. 19195
Dickson, A.G. 9333, 11499, 15929, 21225
Dickson, K.B. 10247, 10349, 10501
Didcott, J. 22323
Diderich, G.C. See Cyfer-Diderich, G.
Diego, A.G.G.de. See Garcia-Gallo de Diego, A.
Diène, A.L. 8751
Dieng, D. 2429
Dieterlen, G. 7526-7, 7581, 8187, 8786-92, 8810-11, 8947-9, 9407, 9410
Diffie, B.W. 2909
Diggs, I. 899
Dijkman, B. 14786, 14981
Dike, K.O. 11, 281, 2752, 11342, 11800
Diko, S. 8843
Dikshit, R.D. 9667
Dikum, L. 13367
Dillen, K. 13937-8, 14982-3
Dillon, W.S. 1850
Dilthey, R. 2050
Din, S.el- 5238
Dinis, P.A.J.D. See Dias Dinis, P.A.J.
Dionísio Barreto, A. 4145, 23741, 24083-5, 24102-4
Diop, A. 187, 807-9, 1699, 2051, 2430, 2753, 3289, 3909, 4479-82, 8600, 9063
Diop, B. 3530-1, 8307, 8669-70
Diop, C.A. 742, 1186, 4101, 4483-6
Diop, D. 3290, 3530-46, 4487, 9059, 9548
Diop, M. 2052, 8446, 8750
Diop, T. 2053-4, 2431
Dipoko, M.S. 3418, 13368-70
Dipumba, B. 15156
Dischamps, J.C. 1187
Disney, A.W.M. 5549, 6375
Dixey, F. 1901, 21391-2
Dixon, J.R. 19697
Dixon, P.A. 8055, 10791

Diza 20527
Dizian, R. 13468
Dobbs, K.A. 12274-5
Dobosiewics, Z. 87
Dobson, E.B. 17752, 18453-4
Docherty, A.J. 18696
Dodwell, H. 8601
Dogbeh, R. 1700-1
Doggett, W.G. 19432
Doig, A.B. 3910
Doize, R.L. 14259, 14279
Djan, O.S. 10156
Djibril, D. 2754
Doke, C.M. 508, 993, 6361, 3078-90, 16092, 16146, 19759-76, 20651, 20917-20, 21147, 21151-3, 21172, 22085, 22221, 22742-4
Dollman, G. 4261, 12974
Dollfus, O. 9064
Dollfus, R.P. 8727
Domenech Lafuente, A. 7212, 7431, 7453-5
Dominus 508, 19924, 20365, 20689, 20828
Donald, R.G. 8057
Donche, L.le 13743
Donckerwolcke, A. 13939
Dongen, I.S.V. 23478
Dongmo, J.L. 13371-2
Donisthorpe, J. 19433
Donohugh, A.C.L. 4488, 13940
Donohugh, T.S. 12642
Donque, G. 15964
Doob, L.W. 11002
Dor 901
Dorato, M. 88, 2055, 17053
Dori, L. 5215, 5316
Doring, P. 17246
Dorjahn, V.R. 9722-5, 9842-3
Dorman, M.H. 17929
Dornan, S.S. 19577-8, 21674
Dorsch, H. 13300-1
Doss, M. 20327
Dotson, F. 509, 20829
Dotson, L. 20829
Doublier, R. 7125
Doucet, J. 8056
Doucouré, A. 8904
Doucouré, M.B. 8905
Dougall, J.W.C. 510, 1702-3, 3911-3, 15930, 17370
Doughty, L.R. 18502
Douglas, A.B. 10309
Douglas, A.J.A. 21669
Douglass, M. 3676, 12932, 13621, 13941-7, 14416
Douib, A. 6780
Doutreloux, A. 188, 2755, 13948-9, 14417
Doutressoulle, G. 8949
Dover, C. 1031, 4489, 21627

Dowling, M.A.C. 24333
Dowsett, F.D. 16273
Dowsett, J.M. See Morewood-Dowsett, J.
Dowuona, M. 7688
Doxey, G.V. 22324
Doxey, M.P. 22324
Drago, R. 6901-2
Drague, G. 7317
Drake, S.C. 4801, 8144, 9991
Draper, M. 22120
Drayton, A.D. 3291
Drechsler, H. 23546-7
Drees, F. 6007
Drennan, M.R. 19579, 21984, 23378
Dresch, J. 1188, 2056, 9638, 14567
Drewes, A.J. 16544, 16735-6, 16844
Drexel, A. 3091-3, 6318, 7910-1, 9361, 18384
Dreyer, T.F. 23115
Dreyfus, J. 810
Driberg, J.H. 511, 3677, 5550-2, 6376, 15795, 16379, 18697
Dronsfield, J. 21985-6
Droogmans, H. 15369
Dror, Y. 2432
Drost, D. 811
Drouet, P. 8331-2
Droux, G. 13631
Drummond-Hay, E.W.H. See Hay-Drummond-Hay, E.W.
Drus, E. 22564
Dry, P. 11631
Drysdale, A.T. 21605
Drysdale, J.G.S. 10426
Du, R. See Le Du, R.
Du Bois, W.E.B. 512, 1134, 2058, 2756, 4490, 10673, 12581, 14568, 16737
Du Plessis, H. 21885, 22451, 22979, 23117
Du Sautoy, P. 4491-2, 10310
Du Toit, B.M. 678
Du Toit, P.J. 18257
Du Toit, S.F. 22567
Duah, J.A. See Agyemang-Duah, J.
Duarte, E.B. See Barbudo Duarte, E.
Duarte, F. 12742, 12753, 12796
Dubié, P. 8447, 13411
Dubief, J. 4799
Dubois, A. 15370-4
Dubois, H.M. 1704, 2057, 24361-2
Dubois, J. 6681
Dubois, R.P. 24544
Duboscq, G. 2996
Dubreuil, P. 13232
Duchac, R. 6770
Duchemin, J.G. 513, 8393, 8418, 8481, 8752
Duchêne, M.L. See Lassudrie-Duchêne, M.
Duckham, A.N. 425
Duckworth, W.L.H. 24363

Ducos, G.E. 7912
Ducret, O. 377
Dudbridge, B.J. 18156, 18503
Dudgeon, G.C. 5115-21
Dudley, B.J. 2757, 11632-5
Due, J.F. 15879
Duerden, J.E. 21830
Duff, P.C. 18157
Duff, P.F. 23746, 23379-81
Duffy, J. 2054, 23548
Dufour 1190
Dufour, J. 15197
Dufour, J.P. 15222
Dufour, M.L. 24575
Dufrénoy, P. 15223
Dugast, R. 13040, 13075-8, 13263, 13302-4, 13425, 13469
Duggan, E.de C. 11394-5, 11801
Duignan, P. 337, 2433
Dujardin 14418
Duke, H.L. 19434-5
Duly, A.W.R. 21503
Duly, L.C. 22565
Dumaine, A.L. 1189
Dumbrell, H.J.E. 21742
Dumbutshena, E. 20412
Dumont, A. 14641
Dumont, G. 15310
Dumont, R. 427-8
Dumort, J.C. 13426
Dunayevskaya, R. 2434
Dunbar, A.R. 18630, 19196-8
Dunbar, J.H. 5889
Dunbar, R. 902
Duncan, J.M. 18857
Duncan, J.R. 19925-6, 20528-30
Duncan, P. 22325-6, 22566, 23116
Duncan-Johnstone, A. 7711, 8212
Duncanson, D.J. 16953
Dunckley, H. 5317
Dundas, C. 15796, 16380
Dundas, K.R. 17216, 17753
Dunger, G.T. 12276
Dunglas, E. 9564, 11802-3
Dunham, D. 5863, 5890, 6191
Dunn, J.S. 10043
Dunn, P.W.D. 2060
Dunn, S.C. 5553-4
Dunne, J.H. See Heyworth-Dunne, J.
Dunstan, E. 13264, 13305-6
Dunwell, H. 9767
Duong-Huu-Thoi 8058
Duorin, E.P. 12960
Dupaigre, J.P.F. See Faivre-Dupaigre, J.P.
Dupin, H. 8502
Dupire, M. 8184, 9618, 9648, 9656, 9186

Dupont, R.   13602
Dupriez, G.   15224
Dupriez, L.   14642
Dupriez, L.H.   1191
Dupuis, C.E.   16681
Dupuis, J.   8793
Durand, E.   7383-4
Durand, J.   1192, 4840, 5072, 6062
Durand, P.P.   21504
Duret, J.   1193
Durieux, A.   2061-2, 12724, 14643-4, 15225-6
Duru, R.C.   7712
Dusogi, M.M.el-   5406
Duval, N.   6809
Duval, O.R.   See Rubens-Duval, O.
Duvignaud, J.   6960
Duyos, R.   3614
Dworkin, M.S.   13950
Dyer, E.J.   22121
Dyke, F.M.   12582
Dyke Neuk   19927
Dyson, P.   11636
Dyson-Hudson, N.   18698
Dyson-Hudson, V.R.   19436-7

E., B.M.   20531
E., T.   20921
E.C.A.   See Economic Commission for Africa
Eaglesome, J.   1053
Earthy, E.D.   12643, 19580, 23747-56
Easmon, C.O.   10792
Easmon, M.C.F.   9774, 9777, 9784, 9801, 9844-5, 9958
East, R.   3292, 11955-6, 12054
East African Marine Fisheries Research Organization   16147
Eban, A.S.   5407
Ebding, F.   13079, 13412
Eberhardt, J.   21861
Eberl-Elber, R.   9726-7, 9924
Eberlie, R.F.   16040
Ebers, G.   5318
Ebong, I.J.   11637
Eca, V.A.d'   2758
Échard, N.   9626
Echegaray, C.G.   See Gonzalez Echegaray, C.
Echeruo, M.J.C.   12055
Eckendorff, J.   13699
Economic Commission for Africa   1194-5
Economist   10248
Edel, M.   514
Edel, M.M.   18699
Eden, A.   2759
Edet, E.M.   11243
Edgerton, R.B.   16433, 17907, 17217-8
Edington, G.M.   10793-4

509

Edmonds, J.M. 5891-3
Edokpayi, S.I. 7641, 11396-7
Edozien, J.C. 4493
Edwardes, P.M.J. 10872
Edwards, A.C.T. 21393
Edwards, C.A. 18258
Edwards, E. 7803
Edwards, E.W. 7318
Edwards, F.A. 6192
Edwards, F.M. 5216
Edwards, J.A. 20532-3
Edwards, P. 7979
Edwards, W. 19698, 19928-30, 20534-5, 20690
Eeden, B.I.C.van 19766, 21154
Eekelaar, J.M. 20737
Efrat, E.S. 2435
Egbe, E.T. 13398
Egbunu, A. 11536
Egerton, H.E. 2760
Egerton, W. 1042
Eggeling, W.J. 18504, 18940, 19199, 19438-46
Eggins, E.C. 15660
Egwuonwu, A.N. 7804
Ehrenfels, U.R. 4494
Ehrhard, M.J. 8228
Ehrhard, S. 4165
Ehrlich, C. 2761, 18017, 18700, 18956-8
Ehsanullah, L. 10157
Eickstedt, Baron von 515
Eidarus, S.M. 17158
Eiselen, W. 3094, 21743, 21862-3, 21987, 22327, 22745, 23118, 24046
Eiseley, L.C. 19629
Eisen, A. 18018
Eisenberg, D. 2436
Eisenstadt, S.N. 516, 2437-8, 4495
Ékallé, S. 13080
Ekandem, M.J. 11003-4
Ekineh, A. 12131
Ekodo-Nkoulou-Essama, F. 4146
Ekollo, T. 4496
Ekondy-Akala 4382, 4497
Ekonyo, P. 13951-2
Ekpo, L.U. 2063
Ekundare, R.O. 11398
Ekwa, M. 1705, 14520
Ekwensi, C. 10844, 11804, 12056-7
Ekwerekwu, O. 12058
El- *For authors whose names begin with the Arabic article El-, see the following element of the name*
Elber, R.E. See Eberl-Elber, R.
Elder, E.E. 5415
Elgee, C.H. 11005, 11244
Elgood, J.H. 8057, 12277
Elgood, P.G. 5261, 5319-20

Elias, T.O. 3678-81, 7805, 12132-3, 19711
Eliet, E. 3293
Eliot, C. 16041
Elizalde, D.B. See Berenguer y Elizalde, D.
Elkan, W. 1545, 15880, 16434, 17322, 18959
Elkindy, A.M. 16274
Ellenberger, J. 21709
Ellenberger, V. 21710
Ellero, G. 16494-5, 16738
Elles, R.J. 6193
Ellgood, C.L. 24660
Ellingworth, P. 9565
Elliot, G.F.S. 18960
Elliot, J.A.G. 16042
Elliot, W. 11805
Elliott, A.V.P. 3095
Elliott, H. 2064
Elliott, H.F.I. 18072, 18137
Elliott, W.Y. 2065
Ellis, G.W. 12566
Ellis, I.P. 5064
Ellis, P.J.C. 18259
Ellison, R.E. 11006, 11245, 11806
Elsbemd, A.J. 10158
Elsdon-Dew, R. 19581
Elwell-Sutton, A.S. 2762
Emenge, A. 13795
Emerit, M. 4980, 6810-2, 17180
Emerson, R. 2439
Emile, P. 13953
Emilia, A.d' 16954
Emily, C. 6194
Emley, E.D. 17219, 18701
Emsheimer, E. 15830
Emtage, E. 21447
Emtage, J.E.R. 21448
Enchill, K.B. See Bentsi-Enchill, K.
Endemann, C. 21572-3
Endemann, K. 3096
Endemann, P. 22746
Ene, A. 11291
Enemo, E.O. 12460
Engberg, H.L. 15881
Engel, J. 89
Engelbrecht, J.A. 22747
Engels, A. 14419, 15488
Engels, L. 21988
Engeström, T. 7582, 8503, 8794, 8850
Engholm, G. 2763, 19114-5
England, D. 2764
England, J.O. 17409
England, P.J.M. 8059
Englhart, L.D. See Deininger-Englhart, L.
English, M.C. 11500
Engmann, E.A.W. 10311

Engo, P.B. 13399-13401
Enke, S. 1196
Ennis, E.L. 23564
Enonchong, H.N.A. 13402
Enright, D.J. 3419
Enriques, V. 23382
Ensor, M. 10393
Entrevan, C. 3682
Enwonwu, B. 812
Epanya, E. 813
Epelle, K. 12059
Epelle, S. 3420
Epp. R.von 2066
Epstein, A.L. 21155, 21179-82, 21226, 21238
Epton, N. 4944
Erasmus, B.P. 22328
Erekosima, T.V. 4498
Erhart, H. 24576
Erickson, E. 13338
Eriksson, O. 16669
Ermens, P. 14787
Ermont, L. 6664
Erroll, F.J. 1546
Erygoo, E. 13081
Erygoo, J. 13081
Erzuah, J.B. 10394
Escalera, C.M.de la. See Martín de la Escalera, C.
Escott, T.H.S. 5206
Esenwa, F.E. 11007
Esike, S.O. 11807
Esperandieu, G. 4841
Espírito Santo, J.do 12770, 12830-2
Esquivel, A. 23442, 23934-5, 24135-6
Essama, F.E.N. See Ekodo-Nkoulou-Essama, F.
Essen, O.von 7913, 12609
Esser, J. 12, 13954, 14346, 15375, 15489
Esteban Ibáñez. See Ibáñez, E.
Estermann, P.C. 517, 3097, 3914-5, 21864, 23383-91, 23565,
    23573-4, 23584, 23598-23601
Esteves, J.D. 23690-1
Esteves, J.M. 23692
Etherington, D.M. 17323, 17643
Étiemble, M. 4499
Euringer, S. 16561, 16983
Evambi, R.K. 23392
Evans, A. 4842, 21208
Evans, C. 17410, 15882
Evans, D.S. 21789
Evans, E.J.A. 338, 9992
Evans, F. 13041
Evans, H. 7751
Evans, M.N. 17411
Evans, M.S. 4500, 22329, 23119
Evans, P.C.C. 1706
Evans, S. 1197

Evans-Anfom, E. 8060
Evans-Pritchard, E.E. 518-9, 2440, 5555-5611, 6195,
    6319-20, 6362, 6617, 6682-3, 6700-6701, 12959, 17220,
    18702, 21156
Even, A. 13622
Everaert, J. 2765
Everwyn, G. 14420
Evrard, G.di V. See Vita-Evrard, G.di
Ewer, R.F. 743
Ewing, A.F. 1198-9
Eyidi, B. 13427
Eyken, A.G.M.van 520
Ezeani, A.O.N. 12134
Ezera, K. 11808
Ezquerra, C.M. See Medrano Ezquerra, C.
Ezquerra, J.A.C. See Comba Ezquerra, J.A.
Ezquerra Abadia, R. 7234

F., A.B.   3294
F., C.   2144
F., H.   8602, 19935-6
F., H.A.   189
F., J.   7149
F., J.C.   2441
F., J.H.   20253
F., R.   7064
F., T.   2442, 2766, 17511
F., W.A.   4262, 5073
F.A.O.   See O., F.A.
F.B.   See B., F.
Fabelurin, N.O.   11809
Faber, M.   20830
Fabia, C.   13265
Fabiyi, T.F.   11008
Fabre, J.   8226
Fabre-Luce, A.   19712
Fabro, C.   521
Fabunmi, L.A.   7642, 11638
Fagan, B.M.   744, 19630, 20992, 20997-8, 21989
Fage, J.D.   90, 2767, 7806-7, 10502-7
Fagereng, M.E.   24509
Fagg, B.   11249
Fagg, B.E.B.   7583, 11246-50
Fagg, W.   11251-4, 11810
Fagunwa, D.O.   12060
Faheil, I.   See Ibrahim Faheil
Fahm, L.A.   10249
Faillace, C.   17062
Fairbairn, J.   22122, 22330, 22569, 22917
Fairbairn, W.A.   4263, 8061-3, 12278-82
Fairbridge, K.   20280
Fairclough, T.L.   21628
Fairholm, G.W.   11639-40
Fairman, H.W.   5167
Faivre, C.   7126
Faivre-Dupaigre, J.P.   6720
Faladé, S.   4147
Falcão, A.F.A.   23834
Falcão, A.M.J.F.de S.   23835
Falcão de Campos, A.C.G.   23693-4
Falck, K.   24364
Faleti, A.   12061
Falkner, F.R.   1902
Fall, K.   4501
Fallers, L.A.   2067, 4502, 8145, 17412, 18703, 19116, 19386, 19522
Fane, R.   6462, 16435, 17188, 17415
Fanon, F.   4503-4
Fàntoli, A.   6655
Fares, B.   5408
Fargues, G.   2068
Faria, D.   3916
Faria, F.L.de   8603, 23549
Faria, J.M.da R.   See Rocha Faria, J.M.da
Faria, R.   4505

Farmer, J. 2443
Farnsworth, E.A. 8693-4
Faro, J. 7808, 10508-9, 12754-60, 12922
Farquhar, J.H. 522, 2069, 19843, 19931, 20328, 20691
Farquhar, M.A. 20329
Farrag, R. 5321
Farran, C.d'O. 6377
Farrar, F.W. 1547
Farrell, H.B.McD. 6587
Farrer-Brown, L. 4506
Farrington, J.L. 11641
Fashole-Luke, E.W. 7528
Fatton, A. 23757
Faublée, J. 1033, 6980, 6987, 6996, 24347, 24365, 24476, 24545, 24577, 24629
Faublée, M. 24545
Faublée-Urbain, M. 6985-7, 7170
Faulkner, M.S. See Shooter-Faulkner, M.
Fauque, L.P. 7138
Fauquenot, E. 7228
Faure, C. 8429, 8604-6
Faure, H.M. 13623
Faurel, L. 7141
Fauvel, L. 1200
Fauvel, P. 8728-9
Fauzi, S.el-D. See Fawzi, S.el-D.
Faveaux, A.A.de. See Anciaux de Faveaux, A.
Fawcett, D. 1548, 2070-1, 14645
Fawcett, M.G. 22570
Fawzi, S.el-D. 5990-1, 6378, 6588-9
Fazan, S.H. 22918
Fearn, H. 1201, 17513
Fearson, D. 17102
Fegan, E.S. 11009
Feilden, H.W. 21991
Feio, F.B. 24137
Feis, H. 1202
Feki, A.H. el- 5262
Fele, B. 255, 1707, 4507, 10510, 12923, 14646
Felix, J. See Jacques-Felix
Félix-Tchicaya, G. (pseud.: T.U Tam'si). See U Tam'si, T.
Fell, G. 11399
Fellows, P.A. 17003
Fendri, M. 6813-4
Fenicio 1549
Fenniche, N. 6961
Fenton, J.S. 9781
Fenyi, J. 24138
Féral, G. 8448
Ferenc, H. 24139
Ferenczi, V. 4508
Ferguson, H. 6063
Ferguson, I. 9225
Ferguson, J. 12461
Fergusson, V. 5612-5

Ferik Ibrahim Abboud 6135
Fernandes, A. 24140
Fernandes, J.A.B. See Barahona Fernandes, J.A.
Fernandes de Sá, A. 3917
Fernandez, J.W. 523, 3918, 12933, 13700-1
Fernández, R.del V. See Valle Fernández, R.del
Fernandez, T.G. See Gudin Fernandez, T.
Fernandez Blanco, F.L. 15712
Fernandez del Castillo, J.de U. See Urzaiz y Fernandez del Castillo, J.de
Fernea, R.A. 5616
Ferrandis Torres, M. 2768-70, 4729, 7319
Ferrão, J.E.M. 4226
Ferrari, E.L. See Lafuente Ferrari, E.
Ferreira, A. See Américo Ferreira
Ferreira, A.J.de L. 23758, 23836, 24141-6
Ferreira, A.R. See Rita-Ferreira, A.
Ferreira, C. 24281
Ferreira, D.J. 12684
Ferreira, E.A.V. 23550
Ferreira, F. 3683, 23670
Ferreira, F.H. 23037
Ferreira, F.S.C. 4148, 12833-4
Ferreira, G.da V. 20802, 21209, 23033-6, 23936, 24129-31, 24147-8
Ferreira, H.H. 4509
Ferreira, J. 4510, 12897
Ferreira, J.A. See Araújo Ferreira, J.
Ferreira, J.N. 24149
Ferreira, J.S. 24150
Ferreira, M.C. See Corinta Ferreira, M.
Ferreira, M.do N. 24054
Ferreira, V. 19932, 23551, 23836
Ferreira da Silva, J. 23837, 24151-2
Ferreira Mendes, M.J. 1327, 2072, 4105, 23838-9, 23956, 24003
Ferreira Paulo, Z. 382
Ferreirinha, F. 23803
Ferrer, F.J.C. See Carvajal Ferrer, F.J.
Ferrinho, H. 4511, 23695-6
Ferron, J.L. 4981-2
Ferry, R. 16739
Ferryman, A.F.M. See Mockler-Ferryman, A.F.
Fervel, J. 7034, 7142, 7150
Festa, G. 9330
Fetherstonhaugh, A.M., later Lady Cecil and Lady Rockley. See Rockley, Lady
Février, P.A. 4843
Few, H.S.S. 18704
ffolliott, P. 22103
ffoulkes, A. 10044-8
Fickendey, E. 428, 1203, 15668, 15695-6
Fiddes, E.S. 6064
Fiel, C., Conde. See Castillo-Fiel, Conde
Field, H. 5131, 5617
Field, M.J. 10009, 10049-50, 10159

Fielding, S. 22331
Fiennes, R.N.-W. 18647
Fierens, P. 1204
Figueiredo, C. 23898
Figueiredo, J.de 24153
Figueiredo, J.P.de. See Pires de Figueiredo, J.
Figueiredo, P.Á.R.de 1022
Figueiredo Gomes e Sousa, A.de 4266, 23697-23701, 23804,
    23822, 23840-4, 23937-46, 23996, 24069, 24154-9, 24282
Figueras, T.G. See Garcia Figueras, T.
Figueras, V.G. See Garcia Figueras, V.
Filesi, T. 190, 903, 1205-6, 1851, 2068-77, 2444-9, 2771-4,
    3919, 4512, 6636, 8002, 9846, 10511, 11642, 12583-4,
    13246, 15859, 15861, 17413, 18260, 20831
Fileteo 17414
Finch, F.G. 17754
Finch, F.J. 5618-9
Findlay, G.M. 8064-8
Finelle, P. 13686
Finn, D.E. 20229
Finnegan, R. 9728-9, 9895
Finzi, C.V. See Vita-Finzi, C.
Firmino Cardoso 12743
First, R. 22123-4, 22332
Firth, R. 4513, 8146
Fischer, G. 2073, 9076, 9089
Fischer, H.T. 524
Fish, G.R. 16403
Fisher, A.G.B. 1207
Fisher, H.J. 8003, 9934, 12210
Fisher, H.M. 4267
Fisher, M. 22823
Fisher, W.S. 13955, 21227
Fitzgerald, D.F.V. See Vesey-Fitzgerald, D.F.
Fitzgerald, R.T.D. 11255
Fitzgerald, W. 1903
Fitzgerald, W.W.A. 6196
Fitzjohn, W.H. 9802
Fitzpatrick, J.F.J. 11010-1
Flament, E.B. 13956
Flandrau, G. 2775
Fleay, M. 18722
Flegg, H. 24283
Fleischer, A.C. 19582
Fleischer, C. 10051
Fleming, G.J. 5620, 6065-6
Fleming, H.C. 16845
Flemming, L. 21831
Fletcher, B.A. 20330
Fletcher, J. 17382
Fletcher, J.L. 13
Fletcher, T.B. 19200
Fletcher-Cooke, J. 2450, 18158

Fletcher-Vane, F.P. 22571
Fleure, H.J. 745
Fliedner, H. 17589
Flint, J.E. 1035, 7619
Florence, J.A.C. 21352
Flory, M. 5057
Flottum, S. 13373
Flower, W.H. 6463, 13957
Floyd, B.N. 20296, 20366
Flutre, L.F. 7809, 24510-11
Fock, G.J. 23315
Fodé, F. 9140
Fodeba, K. 904, 8188, 9026, 9121
Foderaro, S. 14-15, 1208-11, 2451-2, 9234, 19683
Fofana, A. 8886
Fogg, C.D. 10908
Fogg, W. 7171-2, 7213-5, 7235
Foggin, B.J.M. 19933
Fokken, H.A. 11012
Foletier, F.de V.de. See Vaux de Foletier, F.de
Folleville, A.de 383
Folorunso, F.O. 11811
Fondeville, P.M. 905
Fonlon, B. 191, 1014, 3290-1, 12062, 13307-8, 13374, 13470-1
Fonseca, A.X.da 12898
Fonseca, D.da 23477, 23481
Fonseca, F.D.da 23638
Fonseca, J.P.C.da 12835-7, 12843
Fonseca, V.F.da 23845
Fontainas, P. 14569-70, 15376-7, 22125
Fontaine, S.H.L. See La Fontaine, S.H.
Fontaine, W.T. 4514
Fontana, M. 16644
Fontoynont 24407-8, 24420
Foon, M. 9669
Foot, H.M. 11643
Foran, W.R. 525, 13587, 17223, 19447
Forbes, A. 5322, 6464
Forbes, J.G. 8069-70
Forbes, R.H. 1904, 5246, 7713
Forbes, V.S. 21790, 22572-3
Ford, J. 18705
Ford, S.H. 10250
Ford, W.H. 15311
Forde, D. 16-17, 91, 526, 8147, 11013-9, 11644, 12135
Fordham, P. 17644, 19387
Forest, J. 8071
Forget, N. 7418
Forman, L. 22333
Fornes Andrés, A. 7419
Forster, E.B. 10795
Forster, N. 17930
Fortes, M. 527-8, 7529, 10052-62, 10845, 11812
Fortes, S.L. 10062
Fortier, J. 13484

Fortt, J.M. 16436
Fortuna, J.T. 12838
Fortuna, V.N.P. 12744
Fortune, G. 3098-9, 19934, 20652-3, 22748
Fosbrooke, H.A. 1550, 17383, 17755-61, 17931-42, 17997, 18073-4, 18261-4, 18601, 19852, 21075
Fosbrooke, J. 17943
Foster, P. 10388
Foster, P.J. 15922
Foster, W. 24477
Foté, H.M. See Memel-Foté, H.
Foti, C. 16740
Fouché, L. 22574
Foucher, L. 814, 4983-4, 6815
Foulkes, J. 17324
Fouquet, J. 8543
Fourche, J.A.T. 13958
Fourie, L. 22126
Fourmarier, P. 92, 15378-80, 18075
Fourneau, J. 12985, 13082, 13180, 13632-3
Fournier, H. 24422
Fournier, M.F. 8942
Foury, B. 24546
Foury, P. 13233
Fowler, H.W. 6465
Fowler, W. 12136
Fox, D.S. 17224
Fox, F.D. 23637
Fox, F.W. 21865, 23038, 23120
Fox, H.W. 20536
Fox, R.C. 14788-9
Fox-Pitt-Rivers, A.H.L., later A.H.L.Pitt-Rivers. See Pitt Rivers, A.H.L.
Foyle, A.M. 7584
Fozzard, P.M.H. 17944
Frade, F. 12662, 24160
Fraentel, M. 12625
Fraga de Azevedo, J. 24161
Frames, M.E. 21992
Framwell, C. 18019
França, J.C. 23435, 23443-4
França, P.G.da 23639
France, H. 10063-4
France, P.M. See Mendès-France, P.
France, W.F. 24690
Franceries, G. 20297
Francés, J. 815-6, 15686
Francés, J.M. See María-Francés, J.
Francés Alonso, J. 7469
Franceschi, F. 17038, 17073-5
Franchini, V. 16562-8
Francis, E.C. 17645
Franck, L. 14421
Franco, E.de V. See Viguera Franco, E.de
Franco, L.T.A. 12870

François, E. 24578
Francolini, B. 3920
Frank, B. 529
Frank, C.N. 18007, 18479
Frank, C.R. 15883-4
Frank, I. 1212
Frankel, S.H. 1213-5, 22076, 22127-8
Franklin, A. 4515, 3297-8, 10395
Franklin, A.de S. 2079
Franklin, C.B. 6466
Franklin, H. 19937-41, 20141, 20537-8
Franklin, N.N. 22334
Frantz, C. 4516, 20832-5
Franz, G.H. 21652, 21866
Frappa, C. 24579-80
Fraser, A. 3921
Fraser, A.G. 1708, 10065, 10312-3
Fraser, D. 817, 3922-3
Fraser, F.C. 8464, 8730, 8950, 9383, 12647, 12839
Fraser, H. 18505
Fraser, R.H. 21183
Fraud, M.F. 24485
Frazão, S. 3100, 13959, 14337, 14571, 23393-4, 23602
Frazier, E.F. 1852, 4517
Frédéric, B. 14790
Fredericks, W. 18
Freeman-Grenville, G.S.P. 2997-8, 15831-2, 15965, 16043-8,
    17103, 17514-6, 17945-7, 18265, 18351
Freemantle, J.M. 11813
Freer, P. 22084
Freitas, A.J.de 23805, 23846-50, 24162
Freitas, F. 23947
Freitas, G.de. See De Freitas, G.
Fremantle, H.E.S. 22335
French, C.N. 429
French, M.H. 18638
French-Sheldon 15797
Frend, W.H.C. 4985
Frenkiel, J. 1853
Frere, H.B. 21867, 22336, 22575
Frèrejean, L. 8430
Frey, R. 12990, 13634
Freymond, J. 2080
Freyria, C. 4518
Freyvogel, T. 17948, 18506
Frezouls, E. 4986, 6759
Friberg, D. 3924
Friedland, W.H. 18020
Fries, F.T. 16741
Frieslich, N. 22824
Frimodt-Möller, C. 3925
Frimpong, K. 10512
Fripp, C.E. 2776, 19699, 20142
Fripp, P.J. 19413
Frison, R. 7127
Froelich, J.C. 2081, 2453, 7530, 8570, 9316-9, 9355, 13083-5,
    13210

Froidevaux, H. 93, 2777-8, 7185, 8607-8, 24423, 24478
Froomkin, J. 2082
Frossart, M. 4227
Frost, D.T.T. 21353
Fry, C.H. 15713
Fry, E. 15931
Fry, E.M. 7752
Fuchs, P. 5621, 13485
Fuchs, P.L. 3926
Fuchs, V.E. 15857
Fuente, S.G. See Garcia Fuente, S.
Fuentes, Â. 23552-3
Fuertes, J.V. See Velarde Fuertes, J.
Fueter, P.D. 3927-30, 17619
Fueyo Alvarez, J. 7448
Fuggles-Couchman, N.R. 17673, 18507-8
Fulani bin Fulani 3931, 16389
Fullani bin Fullani. See Fulani bin Fulani
Fullas, H. 16846
Fuller, C. 17416
Fuller, C.C. 20413
Fuller, C.E. 19730, 23445
Fuller, H.W. 3299
Fumagalli, S. 5132
Fundikira, A.S. 18455
Funke, E. 9320-1, 9362, 9592, 11957
Furlani, G. 16847
Furley, J.T. 7810, 10513
Furley, O.W. 18706, 18961, 19201-2
Furlong, J.R. 818-9, 1551, 16404, 22129
Furtado, J.P. 23585
Furtado, S. 23446-7
Furter, P. 2454
Fusella, G. 16955
Fusella, L. 16467, 16496, 16742-4, 16936-8
Fúster Casas, J.M. 4355, 7446, 9247, 15714, 15745-6
Fyfe, C. 8004, 9725, 9776, 9782, 9803, 9820-1, 9847-52,
   9935-6, 9950
Fyfe, C.H. 9776, 9782
Fynn, J.K. 10514
Fynn, J.W.L. 20738, 20836

G., A. 16649-50
G., A.S. 2083
G., B.D. 317
G., C. 17039, 18509
G., E. 7320
G., H.L. 7811
G., H.W. 6197
G., J. 2084, 3932, 9979, 10396, 21023, 23662
G., J.L. 7065
G., M. 1055, 17181
G., N. 20539
G., P. 6816

G., P.J. 16405-6
Gabre-Medhin, T. 3442, 16939-40
Gabriel, G. 16569
Gadallah, F.F. 6397
Gaddi, S. 6136, 11814
Gage, M.F. 6198
Gailey, H.A., Jr. 22576
Gaillard, C. 4789
Gairdner, W.H.T. 4092
Gaitskell, A. 5992
Gaivão, P. 24285
Gajere 11020-2
Galaal, M.H.I. 17127
Galadanci, S.A.S. 5065
Galante, J.P. 23997
Gale, H.P. 18707
Gallagher, C.F. 7066
Gallagher, J. 2779-80
Gallay, A. 8851
Gallent, G.G. 7403
Gallissot, R. 7321
Gallo de Diego, A.G. See Garcia-Gallo de Diego, A.
Galvao, D. (pseud.). See Lemos, V.de
Galway, Lady 994
Galway, H.L. 7714, 11815-6, 24686
Gambelli, E. 1216-7
Gamble, D.P. 7715, 9730, 9805, 9980
Gambles, R.M. 12283
Gambo, F. 20540
Ganay, S.de 8795-8, 8852, 8880, 13536, 13581
Gandhi, M.K. 19713
Gani, O. 9483-4
Ganiage, J. 6817, 6962
Ganier, G. 7812, 8609, 9566
Gann, L.H. 2999, 14791, 21024, 21126, 22577
Gant, I.A. 12654
Ganzin, M.J. 4150
Gappert, G. 3300, 16407
Garbett, G.K. 20739
Garbutt, H.W. 21262, 21868
Garcia 13486
Garcia, L.P. See Pericot Garcia, L.
García, L.R. See Rubio García, L.
Garcia, M.O. See Ocaña Garcia, M.
Garcia, N.M. See Menendez Garcia, N.
Garcia-Baquero, M. 1905
Garcia Barriuso, P. 7385-6
Garcia Bellido, A. 7322
Garcia Cabrera, C. 7470
Garcia Figueras, T. 2781, 7203, 7206-7, 7323, 7417
Garcia Figueras, V. 16682
Garcia-Fuente, S. 4888
Garcia-Gallo de Diego, A. 15740
Garde, A. 375
Gardener, G. 20331

Gardi, R. 13086
Gardin, J.C. 530
Gardiner, G. 22919
Gardiner, N. 10801
Gardiner, R. 21524, 23319
Gardiner, R.K.A. 1218, 7753, 11501
Gardini, D. 1552
Gardner, Fr.T. 20143-5
Gares, V.A. 2085
Garigue, P. 1854, 7747, 8148
Garine, I.de 8731, 13087
Gariou, J. 13441
Garlake, M. 17949
Garlake, P. 17949, 20541
Garlanda, U. 820, 11023, 12934, 14572, 24025
Garle, H.E. 5411
Garlick, J.P. 531
Garlick, P.C. 10251
Garmandi, S. 6890
Garner, R.L. 21675
Garnett, C.B. 17762
Garnier, B.J. 11537
Garnier, J.B. 11538
Garnier, P. 8262
Garratt, G.T. 16745
Garrett, F.E. 19665, 22578
Garrone, D.G.M. 3933
Garroni, Z. 11400
Garrorena, R.C. 15748
Garson, N.G. 22579
Garthorne, E.R. 22920
Gartlan, J.S. 16408
Gasim, A.al-S. 6321
Gaskin, E.A.L. 11958
Gaskin, M. 15885
Gaspar, J.M. 3934
Gasparini, A. 16848
Gass, M.D.I. 10796-8
Gasse, V. 3684
Gasson, J.G.H. 20740
Gast, M. 6988
Gatacre, W. 6199
Gathorne-Hardy, G.M. 2086
Gau, A. 3093
Gaudebout, P. 24366
Gaudiche, Capt. 9649
Gaudio, A. 5069, 6628, 7432, 7524, 16570-1
Gauld, D.T. 10225, 10252-3
Gaussen, J. 8888
Gaussen, M. 8888
Gaussin, P.R. 2782
Gautherot, G. 7101
Gautier, E.F. 4889, 4920-3, 7813, 9065, 9639
Gauthier, H. 13563
Gauthier, J.G. 13088, 13375
Gavin, R.J. 192, 18266-7

Gavinet, M. 8989
Gavira, J. 7324-5
Gay, Capt. 4802
Gay, J.H. 1855
Gayer, J.H. 1553
Gayet, G. 24, 1554, 8229, 24630
Gazel, J. 13428
Gazier, F. 2455
Gazzini, M. 1555, 5323-4, 6200, 16572
Gbadamosi, B. 12063
Gbaguidi, B. 9586
Gbedemah, K.A. 10314
Gbeho, P. 10160-1
Gear, H.S. 20999
Geary, W.N.M. 7991
Gee, T.W. 19117, 19203
Geffen, D.H. 4151
Gehr, C. 13089
Geilinger, W. 18077
Geiss, I. 1556
Gelders, V. 193-4, 2082, 4519-20, 13960, 14422-3, 14647, 14689, 15227, 15615
Gelfand, M. 19942-52, 20803
Gelissen, G. 15381
Gell, C.W.M. 13715, 22130, 22337-8, 22980, 23121-2
Gellini, G. 22131
Gelpí Blanco, J. 1557
Geneviève, J. 8885
Genevo, E.di S. See Savoia-Genevo, E.di
Gengenbach, K. 13309
Genies, M.S.de 1709
Gensichen, H.W. 3935
George, L. 5993, 6467-8
George, N.A.C. See Cox-George, N.A.
George, P. 6945
George, Z. 906
Georges, G.A. 23511
Georges, P. 3685, 8695
Georges-Picot, G. 1219
Gerais, C. 12797
Gerard, J. 3686, 13961
Gerard, R.E. 19204
Gerard-Libois, J. 14424, 14648-9, 14792
Gerdener, G.B.A. 3936, 22981, 23123
Gerlach, L.P. 17225, 17325
Germain, J. 8990, 9049
Gers, J. 5075
Gerstner, J. 22749
Gertzel, C. 17417, 11817
Gervais, J. 9302
Géry, R. 9635
Gessain, M. 8504, 8991, 9122
Geurts, L. 13962
Gevaerts, T.F. 15312
Geyer, A.L. 22413
Gezau Hailemariam, A. 16573

Ggomotoka, J.T.K. 18858
Ghai, D.P. 15886, 16048, 16437, 18970
Ghai, Y. 16437, 17418
Ghalloussi, B. 6818
Ghartey, D.E.B. 3548
Ghazali, A.K. 9925, 9937
Ghenea, R. 14650
Ghirelli, A. 4987, 7451
Giama, M.O. 17076
Giampietro, M. 6743
Giannini, C. 16746
Gianturco, V. 6697
Giasti, M.H. 17077
Gibb, H.A.R. 5263-4
Gibbins, E.G. 19448
Gibbons, A.St.H. 4890, 21127
Gibbons, P.C. 10315
Gibbons, R.M. 4521
Gibbs, J.L. 9141, 12626
Gibbs, P. 4152
Gibson, A.E.M. 7532
Gibson, D. 12521
Gibson, G.D. 21676, 23300
Gidley, C.G.B. 11024
Giesekke, E. 21869
Giffard, G.G. 18077
Giffen, R. 2783
Gifford, G. 6201
Gifkins, A.V. 21251
Giglio, C. 19, 2456, 2784, 16747
Gil, I. 24286
Gil Benumeya, R. 2088, 5247, 5265-7, 6126-7, 6137, 6791
Gilbert, D.R. 14262
Gilbert, D.W. 22132
Gilbert, G.N. 21603
Gilchrist, R.D. 20837
Gilg, J.P. 1906, 13480
Gilks, J.L. 4153
Gill, D. 22825
Gill, H.C. 12284
Gill, R.W. 17419
Gillan, A. 6202
Gillan, J.A. 6067, 6203
Gillard, D.R. 16049
Gille, A. 95, 15490
Gillet, J. 13963
Gilliland, H.B. 1907
Gillman, C. 1908, 15966-7, 18078-81, 18268-9, 18510
Gillman, J. 21993
Gillmore, P. 22580
Gilmer, J.H. 1220-1, 2089-90, 6792-3
Gilmour, T.L. 11645
Gimpera, P.B. See Bosch-Gimpera, P.
Ginestous, L. 6732
Ginestous, P. 6732
Ginner, P. 17950

Ginsburg, N.S. 5412
Giorgetti, F. 5946, 13964
Giorghis, H.W. See Wolde-Giorghis, H.
Giorgi, L.de 5788
Giorio, C. 17013
Giovannini, A. 22133
Girace, A. 17063
Girão, A.de A. 4521
Girard, A. 7151
Girard, J. 8610, 8748-9
Giraud, P. 8735
Girault, R.P.L. 9408, 9454
Girgis, M. See Guirguis, M.
Girgis, S. 6469
Girola, U. 1222
Girolami, M. 4154
Girouard, P. 11818
Gisborne, W. 2091
Gitywa, V.Z. 21894
Giudice, B.L. See Lo Giudice, B.
Giulianelli, A. 6644
Giulio, F. 821
Giwa, M.Y. See Yesufu-Giwa, M.
Glanville, P.B. 22581
Glanville, R.R. 9959
Glasgow, G. 5217
Glass, J.M. 18602
Glauning, Von 16093
Gleason, J. 3301
Gleave, M.B. 12462
Gledhill, A. 3687
Gleeson, W. 19449
Gleichen, E. 4874, 5325-6, 7326
Glendale, H. 1223
Glenn, E. 13310
Glennie, A.F.B. 21089
Glennie, J.F. 6068
Glenny, H.Q. 11819
Glickman, H. 2457, 14651
Glinne, E. 14652
Glissant, E. 3302, 3549
Glories, J. 7067
Glory, A. 7186-8
Glover, L.S. 20542
Gluckman, M. 532-3, 1025, 1048, 1558, 3688, 4523-5, 5622,
    6322, 19572, 19679, 19805, 19853-4, 19953, 20885,
    20922-4, 21025, 21184, 21228, 21870-3, 23124, 23759
Glynn, F.J. 18159
Glynn, W.T. See Tyrrell-Glynn, W.
Gnawi, J.B. 6379
Gobal, M.A. See Mohammed Abdullah Gobal
Gobert, E.G. 6733, 6744-6, 6946
Godard, C. 6721
Goddard, S. 7716, 11025
Godding, R. 14425

Godfrey, J.L. 10397
Godfrey, R. 19797
Godivier, R. 13743
Goethem, E.van 13965-6
Goethem, F.van 14653
Gohr, A. 14573, 15228
Göhring, M. 13311
Gold, R.L. 15932-3
Goldenberg, G. 16849
Goldie, G.T. 1077
Goldin, B. 20741
Golding, F.D. 12285-9
Golding, G. 23125
Goldman, M.I. 1224
Golds, J.M. 17646
Goldschmidt, W. 534
Goldsmith, H.S. 7814
Goldsmith, J.H. 5623
Goldsmith, R.C.H. See Howard-Goldsmith, R.C.
Goldthorpe, J.E. 4526, 16438, 19003-4
Golemansky, V. 9154-5
Gollmer, C.A. 11026
Gollock, G.A. 16390
Gomes Barbosa, O.C. 12685
Gomes dos Santos, P.A. 3937
Gomes e Sousa, A.de F. See Figueiredo Gomes e Sousa, A.de
Gomes Guerreiro, M. 23948
Gomes Pedro, J. 24163, 24192
Gomes Pereira, A. 12686
Gomez Anton, F. 1856
Gomez Tello, J.L. 2092, 2458, 2785
Gonçalves, J.J. 882, 12802, 23603, 23663, 24055-6
Goncharov, I.A. 22260
Goncharov, L. 2459
Gondominas, G. 24631
Gonidec, P.F. 1559, 2093, 3684-8, 10709, 13247
Gonin, H.T. 22982
González de Pablo, A. 13967
Gonzalez Echegaray, C. 3101, 15734-8, 15770
Gonzalez Ramos, M. 15728
Gooch, W.D. 21994
Good, A.I. 13429
Goodall, E. 20146-52
Goode, P.M. 19005
Goodenough, K.M. 20414-5
Goodhart, A.L. 3694
Goodlatte, C.R. 23126
Goodman, C. 5327
Goodwin, A.J.H. 823, 8149, 11256-7, 19631, 21995
Goody, E. 10066
Goody, J. 2786, 4527-8, 7533, 10067-9, 10515-7, 10857
Goody, J.R. 10643
Goold-Adams, R. 22339
Gopfert, H. 13181
Gorce, J. 3695
Gordge, J.T. 24479
Gordimer, N. 3421

Gordin, E.   23127
Gordon, H.L.   15798
Gordon, J.   10518
Gordon, W.R.   21760
Gore, J.L.   3303
Gore, (W.) D.O., Lord Harlech.   See Ormsby-Gore, (W.) D.,
    Lord Harlech
Gore, W.G.A.O.   See Ormsby-Gore, W.G.A., Lord Harlech
Gore-Browne, S.   4529, 20416-7
Gori, F.   17040
Gorini, E.P.   319
Gorodiski, A.   8571
Gorvers, J.H.   11401
Gorvine, A.   2460
Gorwala, A.D.   2461
Gosselin, G.   535, 9409
Gosselin, M.   1225, 8891
Gottfried, K.A.   See Amoo-Gottfried, K.
Gottmann, J.   4891, 4924
Gottschling, E.   21874
Gouaux, A.   6903
Gouffé, C.   7914, 11959
Goulding, E.   430, 16409
Gouldsbury, C.   21185-6
Goulven, J.   4988
Goumaz, M.L.   See Liniger-Goumaz, M.
Goundiam, O.   8773
Gouron, A.   3696
Gourou, P.   1226-7, 1909
Goussault, Y.   431
Gouveia, D.H.G.   23702-8, 23909-10, 23949, 24164
Gouveia, D.T.de   3938
Gouveia, J.   23704-5
Gouveia, T.de   3939, 24070-1
Gover, M.B.   16850
Gow, J.J.   6380
Gower, L.C.B.   12137
Gower, R.H.   2095, 16149-50, 18160, 18270, 18385
Gowers, W.   2787, 4268, 19205-6, 19450
Graaff, de V.   23128
Grabham, C.W.   5624, 6069-70
Grabham, G.W.   5894, 16993
Graeve, F.de   3102
Graff, R.   6941
Graft-Johnson, J.C.   See De Graft-Johnson, J.C.
Graft-Johnson, J.W.de.   See De Graft-Johnson, J.W.
Graft-Johnson, K.E.de.   See De Graft-Johnson, K.E.
Graft-Johnson, S.B.G.de.   See De Graft-Johnson, S.B.G.
Graham, C.   11027
Graham, J.D.   11820
Graham, P. (pseud.).   See Abrahams, P.
Graham-Jolly, H.G.   21428
Graïri, A.   6747
Grall, Lt.   9619
Grand, L.L.   See Le Grand, L.
Grandão, F.   12704

Grandidier, G.   24367, 24431, 24581-5
Grandin, Capt.   9636
Grangeon, G.   13571
Granger, J.   23806, 23851, 23899, 23950-1, 23998
Grant, C.H.B.   17763, 18082
Grant, D.K.S.   18083
Grant, E.W.   21875, 23011
Grant, J.A.P.   11539
Grant, M.   6030
Grant, M.W.   9694, 9698-9
Grant, N.   22134
Grantham, D.R.   18084
Granville, R.K.   11028
Grasserie, R.de la. See La Grasserie, R.de
Gratiant, G.   3304, 3550-1
Grau, E.   10763
Gravel, P.B.   15567
Graven, J.   16956
Graven, P.   16957-8
Gravière, E.la.   4530-1
Gray, A.   1228-35, 1857, 2096-2106, 2462-6, 2783, 4093,
    4945, 4989, 5218-9, 5268, 5328-30, 5994, 6138-41, 6204,
    6794, 7050, 7102-7, 7262-3, 7755, 8230, 8894, 9263, 9670,
    9822-4, 10398-10410, 10254-6, 10519, 11402-5, 11646-54,
    11821, 13248, 14654-8, 15616, 15887, 15934, 15999,
    16000-2, 17078-82, 17104, 17326-7, 17420-43, 18161-7,
    19118-19133, 19388, 20298-20302, 20418-38, 20742, 21026,
    21090-2, 21429-30, 21611-3, 22093-5, 22135, 22222,
    22340-63, 22921, 22983, 23129, 23330, 23512-3
Gray, C.S.   11406
Gray, E.   21487-8
Gray, J.   1910, 16050, 17992, 18005, 18273-90
Gray, Sir J.   3697, 6205, 9678, 15854, 15856, 15858, 15860,
    15968, 16381, 17517, 17764-6, 17992, 18005-6, 18271-89,
    18386, 18456, 18631, 18708, 18859-62, 18935-6, 18941,
    18950, 19207-33, 19288
Gray, J.A.   195, 6513
Gray, J.D.   8072
Gray, J.L.   23130-1
Gray, R.   1911, 2467-8, 16439, 17767-70, 17951, 18291,
    18457, 20838
Gray, T.   5895
Graziosi, P.   16574, 17033
Great Britain. Colonial Office   432
Great Britain. Colonial Office. Information Department   11822
Great Britain. House of Lords   16003
Great Britain. League of Nations Union   1560
Greaves, I.C.   2789
Greaves, L.B.   1710, 2107, 3940, 15935
Grebaut, S.   16851
Grébert, F.   12935-6, 13710
Green, E.C.   17771
Green, M.   22826
Green, M.M.   11960-4
Green, R.H.   1236-8
Green, S.   21513

Green, W.S.B. 2790
Greenberg, J.H. 282, 1028, 2791, 3103-11, 5396, 7617, 7815, 7915, 11964, 16094, 17551-2
Greene, A.K. See Kirk-Greene, A.
Greenfield, R. 16670
Greening, P. 21108, 21240
Greenland, D.J. 19058
Greenstone, J.D. 19134
Greenway, P.J. 18085, 18108, 18511
Greenwood, Capt. 6071
Greenwood, A.F. 10411
Greenwood, O. 9679
Greenwood, P.H. 19451
Greg, R.P. 5168
Gregorius 15313
Gregorius, P. 13968
Gregory, H. 12290
Gregory, M.E. 10799
Gregory, S. 23952
Greig, R.C.H. 17952
Grelier, S. 8558
Grenville, G.S.P.F. See Freeman-Grenville, G.S.P.
Greschat, H.J. 3941
Greswell, W. 22223
Grevisse, F. 15490-1
Grey, R.F.A. 12291
Griaule, G.C. See Calame-Griaule, G.
Griaule, M. 20, 824, 4532, 8340, 8585, 8778, 8799, 8800-12, 8853, 8887, 8964, 8951, 9410, 9620, 9657, 13312, 13481, 13509, 13536, 16497-9, 16500-3, 16748, 16984, 16994-5
Gridelli, E. 8465
Grier, S. 1053
Grierson, P.F.H. See Hamilton-Grierson, P.F.
Griesbach, C.L. 21876
Grieveson, E.T. 22224
Griffith, A.W.M. 18044
Griffith, F.L. 5169, 5896
Griffith, T.R. 9731, 9853
Griffith, W.B. 10070, 10710
Griffith, W.J. 907, 11029
Griffiths, J. 2108
Griffiths, J.B. 17226
Griffiths, J.E.S. 17772-3, 18086, 18156, 18458
Griffiths, J.G. 5625
Grigg, E. 17328, 17444
Grigg, J.E.P. 2469
Griggs, E.L. 22827
Grigorieva, T.N. 16151
Grilo, F.M. 23709
Grilo, V.H.V. 536, 2792, 4533, 23760-1, 19583-4
Grimes, L.G. 10800-1
Grimme, H. 5036
Grimston, B. 23132
Grip, A.L. See Le Grip, A.
Grisman, C.S. 17004
Grivot, R. 9184, 9248, 9337, 9609

Grjebine, A. 13603, 13675
Grobbelaar, C.S. 21996
Grogan, V. 10412
Groom, A.H. 11030
Groot, E.de 5331, 18292
Grootaert, J.E.A. 13969, 14659, 14984
Groshens, J.C. 1858
Gross, E.A. 2470
Grottanelli, V.L. 825, 10071-2, 10162, 15799, 16642, 16852-3, 17018
Ground, K.E.A.U. 21664-6
Grove, D.L. 12138
Grove, E.T.N. 5626
Groves, A.W. 19059
Grube, W. 14985
Gruet, M. 6947, 23316
Grundy, D. 20439-42
Grundy, K. 4534
Grylls, R.G. 22071
Gualco, G. 1912
Guberina, P. 3305, 7682, 1778
Gudger, E.W. 19452
Gudin Fernandez, T. 7216
Guebels, L. 14263
Guedes, A.M. 2793
Guedes Campos, T. 23953
Guémard 6206
Guénault, P.H. 23133
Guénault, P.R. 22136
Guerin, D. 826, 2794, 4535, 10413
Guerpillon, M. 13313
Guerra, A.C. See Carvalho Guerra, A.
Guerra, F.M. 12714
Guerreiro, J.de A. 24026-7, 24072
Guerreiro, M.G. See Gomes Guerreiro, M.
Guerreiro, M.V. 23395, 24057
Guest, N.J. 18087, 18512
Guèye, M. 8559, 8611
Guèye, Y. 8493
Guèye, Y.A. 13376
Guggisberg, F.G. 10414
Gugler, J. 4536
Guglielmi, G. 4990, 15492
Guglielmi, J.L. 1239
Guglielmone, T. 1240
Guignot, F. 8466, 9384, 15749
Guilbert, D.J.C. 14986
Guilbot, J. 12991, 13090-1
Guilcher, A. 9543
Guillanton, M. 24586
Guillard, J. 8231
Guillarmod, A.J. See Jacot-Guillarmod, A.
Guillaume, M. 13211
Guillebaud, R. 15638
Guillemé, M. 4537

Guillemin 13092
Guillemin, L. 13182
Guillen, N. 3547-8, 17575
Guillou 13093
Guilmin, M. 13970-1
Guimarães, C. 12734-6
Guirguis, M. 5133, 5269
Guirguis, S. See Girgis, S.
Guiscafré, J. 4356
Gulilat, T. 16479, 16651
Gulla, A. See: Ali Gulla
Gulliver, P.H. 17227-9, 17774-6, 18021, 18293, 18459,
    18603, 18639, 18709-12, 19523
Guma, A.La. See La Guma, A.
Guma, B.V.La. See La Guma, B.V.
Guma, S.M. 21574
Gumba, E. 18713
Gumprich, D. 19954
Gunn, B. 18088, 18513
Gunn, D.L. 18514
Gunter, H. 3306
Gupta, P.S. 1241
Gupta, V.P. 17445
Gusinde, M. 5627, 13972, 21677, 21877
Gusmão, J.de M.F.de 23852
Gussman, B. 5248, 5270, 20839-40
Guth, W. 17230-1
Guthrie, M. 3112-9, 12963, 13662, 14987-8
Gutkind, P.C.W. 4538-40, 19234, 19524-6
Gutmann, B. 4541, 6381, 16440, 17777-80, 18387, 18445
Gutteridge, W.F. 2109, 4542, 22364
Gutterres, J.de B. 24165
Guy, P. 24646-7
Gwati, C. 20543
Gwellem, J.F. 13183
Gwilliam, F.H. 1711
Gwynn, C. 16749
Gwynne-Jones, D.R.G. 9806, 11540
Gyasi-Twum, K. 9798
Gysin, M. 15382

H. 5628, 7327
H., A.J.C. 6207
H., E. 9680
H., E.G. 19960
H., E.G.S. See S.-H., E.G.
H., F. 1242, 14426
H., G. 3942, 14264, 15493, 18515
H., J.A.de C. 5629
H., J.O. 7816
H., L.A. 22989
H., N.B. 5630
H., N.H.V. See V.-H., N.H.
H., P.P. 5964
H., R.S. 17446

H., S. 5631, 6360
Haarer, A.E. 4357, 13001, 18294
Haarhoof, T.J. 22582
Haastrup, A.A. 11655
al-Habbabi, M.A. See Lahbabi, M.A.
Haberland, E. 16504-5
Habersky, J.J.C. See Cebe-Habersky, J.J.
Habsburgo, O.de. See Otto de Habsburgo
Habte, A. 16671
Hackwill, G.R.J. 20743
Haddon, A.C. 307, 21878
Haddon, E.B. 537, 3120, 16095-6, 16152-3, 18714, 19235
Haddow, A.J. 18715
Hadlow, G.G.S.J. 21449
Hadow, A.L. 5632
Haene, J.de 14265
Haffenden, J.R.W. See Wilson-Haffenden, J.R.
Hager, L.M. 12546
Hagopian, E.C. 7404
Hahn, E. 1243
Hahn, L. 4946
Haig, E.F.G. 11407, 12292-6, 12317, 13234
Haile Selassie I 2619
Hailemariam, A.G. See Gezau Hailemariam, A.
Hailey, W.M. 96, 995-6, 1561, 1913, 2110-7, 2471, 2796-9, 23346
Hailù, G.Y. 16652, 16696
Hailu, S.L. 2472
Haines, W.H. 24661
Hair, P.E.H. 259, 2800, 5066, 7916, 8005, 9705-6, 9771, 9896-9904, 9938-40, 9771, 9799, 9854, 11823, 12463, 12585, 12606, 12610, 12761
Hajj, M.al- 11846, 12205
Hake, A. 17620
Halane, M.O. 17054
Halcrow, W. 12945
Haldane, J.B.S. 4269
Haldane, L.A. 18446, 18516-9
Haldane, R.H. 18519
Haldemann, E.G. 18090, 18520-1
Hale, S. 6590
Haliburton, G. 9855, 10764-5
Hall, B.E.F. 17518
Hall, D. 17081
Hall, E. 5633, 23134
Hall, F.F.W.B. See Byng-Hall, F.F.W.
Hall, J. 18963
Hall, N. 7756
Hall, R. 9856-7
Hall, R.de Z. 17781-4, 18295, 18460, 18604-5
Hall, R.N. 20153-4
Hall, T.D. 19556, 21832
Hallaire, A. 13042
Hallam, W.K.R. 11541

Halle, C. 9027
Hallemans, J. 8404
Hallett, R. 2801
Hallouin, C. 9249
Hallowes, D.P. 19771, 22761
Halpern, J. 4892
Halpern, M. 4784
Halstead, J.P. 7264
Hama, B. 8813
Hambler, D.J. 12237
Hambly, W.D. 538, 23396-8
Hamdan, G. 1914, 6072
Hamel, H. 1562
Hamelberger, E. 23604
Hamer, A.B. 8073, 10802
Hamidoun, M.O. 8437, 8573
Hamidullah, M. 2802
Hamilton, E. 21879
Hamilton, H. 10010
Hamilton, J.A.de C. 5665
Hamilton, J.A.I.A. See Agar-Hamilton, J.A.I.
Hamilton, J.S. See Stevenson-Hamilton, J.
Hamilton, P. 19861, 20841
Hamilton, R. 10163-4, 10350
Hamilton, Sir R. 97, 16382
Hamilton, R.A. 24028
Hamilton, R.W. 18461
Hamilton-Grierson, P.F. 6208
Hammerschmidt, E. 16468-9, 16985
Hammond, J. 20332
Hammond, J.H. 22137
Hammond, N.J.D. 10257
Hammond, P.B. 10073
Hammond, S.A. 1712
Hammond-Tooke, W.D. 21880-3, 22365-6, 22984
Hamnett, I. 21614
Hamon, L. 2473-5
Hamoud bin Mahomed bin Said 18296
Hamp, E.P. 6693, 18462
Hamshere, C.E. 18297
Hance, W.A. 1244, 1915, 5995, 23478, 24424
Hancock, G.L.R. 19453
Handover, D.H. 7717
Handy, E.S.C. 539
Hangartner, R. 17382
Hannan, M. 19955, 20155, 20654-5, 20804
Hannigan, A.St.J.J. 10415-7, 10711-3, 17447, 17590-1
Hannon, P.J. 21833
Hansen, B. 5220
Hanson, E.P. 12547
Haquim, M.ibn A. See Mohammad ibn Azuzz Haquim
Harbison, F. 1859
Harbron, J.D. 7328
Hardcastle, G.F. 21053
Hardie, A.D.K. 12297

Harding, J.R. 827
Hardy, G. 1713, 2795, 4991, 7108, 7329, 7817
Hardy, G.M.G. See Gathorne-Hardy, G.M.
Hardy, J. 12298
Hardyman, J.T. 24446-8, 24547
Hare, W.F. [Earl of Listowel] 2118
Hares, B. 3943
Hargreaves, J.D. 2803-5, 7818, 8612, 9778, 9825-7, 9858-9, 12586
Harkin, D.A. 18089
Harlech, Lord [(W.)D.Ormsby-Gore]. See Ormsby-Gore, (W.) D. [Lord Harlech]
Harlech, Lord [W.G.A.Ormsby-Gore]. See Ormsby-Gore, W.G.A. [Lord Harlech]
Harley, G.W. 12526, 12562
Harlow, V. 4543
Harman, H.A. 10846
Harmel, M. 22367
Harmon, R.J. 20333
Harmsworth, J. 18640, 18964-5
Harnetty, P. 22583
Harper, C.H. 10074
Harper, F.J. 12299-12303
Harper, P. 11258
Harpum, J.R. 18091
Harries, J. 14989
Harries, L. 3944-5, 14990-5, 15800, 16051, 16154-5, 16275-84, 16391-2, 17232, 17553, 17785-8, 24047-8
Harries-Jones, P. 20925, 21229
Harrigan, W.N. 9905-6
Harrington, E.M. 12139
Harris, A. 17592
Harris, B.J. 10803, 12401-2
Harris, C.C. 18168-9
Harris, C.M. 18716
Harris, G. 17233, 17448, 17592
Harris, J. 540, 1245, 16750, 19714-5
Harris, John 21, 10873-5
Harris, J.H. 2806-7, 12567, 14793, 17449, 17519, 18092, 22138, 22368
Harris, J.S. 11032-3
Harris, K.M. 12271
Harris, L. 16156
Harris, M. 23853-4
Harris, P. 7236
Harris, P.G. 7625, 11034-6, 11259, 11965, 19862
Harris, R. 541, 11037, 12140, 21230
Harris, R.G. 3946, 15936
Harris, W. 3422
Harris, W.B. 7173, 7265, 7330
Harris, W.T. 9732-3, 9907, 9930
Harris, W.V. 17789, 18522, 19454
Harrison, C. 22584
Harrison, G. 21525
Harrison-Church, R.J. 15710

Harrop, J.F. 18885
Harroy, J.P. 15598-9
Hart, J.de 2808
Hart, N.de V. 2119
Hart, R.E. 24317
Hart, R.R. See Raven-Hart, R.
Harter, P. 13094
Hartland, E.S. 11038
Hartley, B.J. 18463
Hartley, G.H. 20692-3
Hartnoll, A.V. 17672, 17790
Hartnoll, M.M. 17815, 18298, 18606
Hartog, P.J. 22
Hartweg, R. 372, 13184, 13510
Hartzell, J.C. 12587
Harvey, E. 18134
Harvey, R.J. 18000
Harvey, W.B. 10714
Harvie, C.H. 6591
Harwood, A. 17791
Harwood, F.L. 5634
Hasan ---. See also Hassan ---
Hasan, K.N. 2809
Hasan, Y.F. 6209
Haseeb, M.A. 6470-1
Haselberger, H. 7534
Haselberger-Blaha, H. 828
Hashim, I.F. 6210
Haskard, C.D.P.T. 21450
Hassan ---. See also Hasan ---
Hassan, A.D. See Ahmed Dahir Hassan
Hassan, A.M. 5221, 17014
Hassan, S. 5416
Hassan, S.M.A. 17146
Hassan, Y.F. 6398
Hassan Mohamed Hassan 1246
Hassan, T. 5897
Hassforther, E.E. 18093
Hassing, P. 18094
Hassoun, I.A. 6073
Hasta 12464
Hastie, C. 19527
Hastings, L. 2120, 20280
Hastings, S. 14660
Hatch, J. 7690, 10418
Hatch, W.R. 12304
Hatchell, C.W. 18523
Hatchell, G.W. 17520, 17792, 17953, 18022-4, 18095, 18299-18302, 18524
Hathorn, M. 10804
Hattersley, A.F. 23, 22074, 22225, 22585-94, 22828, 23135, 24691
Hattingh, I. 22829
Hau, K. 11260, 11966-7
Haugou, P. 13430, 13537

Hauenstein, A. 23399, 23400
Hauser, A. 1563, 5996, 7483-4, 8544-5, 8755-6, 9050, 9235, 13593, 13645, 13702, 13973
Havemann, E.A.E. 22369
Haviland, L.A.W.V. See Vickers-Haviland, L.A.W.
Haw, R.C. 4544, 20303, 20843
Haward, L.R.C. 542, 829
Hawarden, E. 23136-7
Hawe, A.J. 10805-6
Hawes, C.G. 18966
Hawkes, C.P. 4893
Hawkesworth, D. 5635-6
Hawkey, J.E. 20694, 20844
Hawkin, R.C. 2810, 20544, 20744, 22061, 22595
Hawking, F. 4155
Hawkins, E.K. 1247, 11408-9
Hawkins, F.H. 24548
Hawley, D.F. 5637
Hay, H. 21054-6
Hay-Barclay, H. 11261
Hay-Drummond-Hay, E.W. 5638, 11039
Haycock, B.G. 6592
Haydon, E.S. 19389
Hayes, G.D. 21451, 21526
Hayes, M.E. 19956
Hayford, J.E.C. See Casely-Hayford, J.E.
Haylett, D.G. 23039
Hayley, T.T.S. See Steiger-Hayley, T.T.
Haylù, G.Y. See Hailù, G.Y.
Hayman, R. 22922-3
Hayter, T. 1248
Hayward, V.E.W. 3947
Hazard, J.N. 2476
Hazareesingh, K. 24336-7
Hazel, C. 21157
Hazoumé, P. 4545, 9489, 9603
Head, B. 3423
Head, M.E. 19236
Heads, J. 11410
Hearn, J.M.N. 20745
Heath, F.M.N. 21093
Heaton, J. 3424
Hebbert, G.K.C. 5639
Hebbert, H.E. 6074, 6472
Hébert, J.C. 24368-9, 24587, 24648
Hébert, P. 9445
Hébert, R.P. 9199, 9446-7, 10099
Hebga, M. 4546
Hechter-Schulz, K. 19585, 19632
Hecklinger, P. 13095
Hedges, D.M. 9828
Hedges, R.Y. 12141
Hée, R.P. 13703
Heepe, M. 13314-5, 16157
Heer, N.A.de. See De Heer, N.A.
Heese, D. 18388
Hefel, A.S. See Schweeger-Hefel, A.

Hegazy, A.M. 1564
Heggs, M.M. See Mitchell-Heggs, M.
Heigham, J.B. 11542
Heijboer, B.M. 13974-6, 14794, 14996-7, 15494
Heinitz, W. 16575
Heintzen, H. 2811
Heinz, G. 15888
Heinzelin, J.de 15383
Heisler, H. 1714, 4576, 21094
Hellberg, C.J. 18303
Hellbusch, S. 21884
Helleiner, G.K. 11411-3
Heller, E. 1916
Hellier, A.B. 16158-62, 16285
Hellman, E. 19586, 21885, 22370, 23040, 23138-43
Helly, D.O. 22985
Helm, B. 22139
Helm, E. 7643
Hemans, T.J. 19957, 21263
Hemedi bin Abdullah 2812
Hemelberg, E. 9941
Hemerijckx, Fr. 15384
Henderson, G.J. 19455
Henderson, J. 22140
Henderson, J.P. 19060
Henderson, K.D.D. 5640-1, 5898, 6142, 6211
Henderson, W.O. 2813
Henderson-Begg, A. 8034, 8074
Hendrickse, B. 12465
Hendrickse, R.G. 8075
Hendry, W. 18045
Henin, R.A. 5997, 6593-4
Henne, H. 5332
Hennessy, J.P.I. 21615
Hennings, R.O. 17329, 17450, 17593
Henry, A.J. 6473
Henry, E. 14427
Henry, P.M. 1249, 2121, 2477
Hepper, F.N. 8076, 12305
Hepple, A. 22141-5
Herbert, M. 6771
Herbert, R.L.D. 20443
Herbigny, M.M.d' 3948
Herbinière, E. 8701
Herbots, J.H. 14428, 15229
Herbst, J.F. 22372
Herculano de Oliveira. See Oliveira, H.de
Herero Paramount Chief. See Paramount Chief of the Herero
   People
Herford, G.V.B. 433
Herisson, C.D. 22261
Herkovits, M.J. 546
Herman, F. 14429-31
Herman, J.M. 11824
Herment, G. 1086
Hernández Pacheco, E. 2814, 7237

Hernandez-Pacheco, F. 7443-4, 7452
Heron, D.B. 19006
Herrera, J.C. See Cruz Herrera, J.
Herrero Muñoz, L. 7406-7
Herrero Tejedor, F. 2478
Herrick, M.D. 339-40
Herrman, L. 21791, 22830
Herrmann, F. 4548
Herroelen, P. 14998-9
Herse, I.L. 15401-8
Herskovits, M.J. 24-6, 543-7, 1250, 1565, 2479, 2815, 4549-51, 7535, 9490-1, 10075, 15801, 21886
Hertefelt, M.d' 15568, 15617
Hertron, R. 16854
Hertsens, L. 13977, 15000
Hervouet, L. 1715
Herzfeld, R.F. 548
Herzog, G. 12611
Herzog, R. 5642, 6133, 6212
Hess, J.J. 6323
Hess, R.L. 2816, 4992, 17105
Hesse, P.R. 16410
Hessel, S. 1716
Hetherwick, A. 15969, 19958, 21452
Hetzron, R. 17131
Heureux, L.L' 15385
Heusch, L.de 549, 830, 4552, 13978-80, 15495
Heuzey, J.A. 8814
Hewetson, C. 19237
Hewit, M.G. 16671
Hewitt, M.C. 22226
Hewson, L.A. 22986-90
Hey, M.H. 8475
Heydorn, R. 12612-3
Heydrich, M. 550
Heyer, J. 17189
Heyer, S.S. 15774, 17647
Heymans, P. 7718
Heyningen, C.van 22227
Heyse, T. 2817, 13754, 14432-3, 14795, 15230-4
Heyworth-Dunne, J. 5397
Hibbert, G.K.C. 5846
Hichens, W. 16163, 17521
Hick, E. 20545, 20695-8, 20746
Hickman, A.S. 3425, 20219, 20233, 20546-9
Hicks, J.B. 22262
Hicks, P.H. 18967, 19046
Hicks, U.K. 2123, 11414
Hide, R.H. 11040, 11543
Hiernaux, C.R. 9303
Hiernaux, J. 551, 14266-8, 15386, 15569, 15593, 15833
Higgins, G.M. 11544
Higgins, T.S. 23144-5
Higo, A. 3426
Hilaire, J. 2480
Hildebrand, P. 14345, 14796-8, 15314

Hill, B.G. 16996
Hill, J.E. 18525, 19456
Hill, J.N. 831
Hill, M.F. 17330
Hill, P. 1253, 7529, 9640, 10011, 10258-64, 16164
Hill, R. 4925, 5439, 5956, 6075-6, 6213-6
Hillard, R.J. 6595
Hillelson, S. 5643-4, 5947, 5957, 6077, 6217, 6363-6, 6407
Hilliard, F.H. 7691, 10316
Hillier, A.P. 19587
Hills, W. 23146
Hills-Young, E. 5645
Hilton, T.E. 9443, 10351-4, 10520, 10847
Hilton-Simpson, M.W. 6989
Hilzheimer, M. 2818, 5122
Himbury, W.H. 1566
Himmelheber, H. 7537, 9226, 12655
Hinawiy, M.A. 17234
Hinde, C.A. 20699
Hinderling, P. 13096-7
Hindmarsh, R. 3307-8, 3427, 15158, 16393
Hippel, E.V. 19061, 19238, 19457
Hippodamus 10317
Hirad, M.A. See Mohamoud Abdi Hirad
Hirschberg, H.Z. (J.W.) 5092
Hirschberg, W. 552, 10076, 13098
Hirschland, H. 19633
Hirst, D. 7238
Hirst, E. 9860
Hirst, T. 10807
Hiskett, M. 7538, 7819, 7917, 11825, 12043
Hitchcock, E. 15889
Hitchen, C.S. 18025
Hlatswayo, E.T. 22991
Hlazo, T.J. 19959, 20444
Hoal, W.G. 22924
Hobbs, H.J. 10521
Hobbs, W.H. 5249
Hobhouse, C.E. 7266, 7331
Hobley, C.W. 553, 1042, 4270-1, 4553, 11415, 17235-7
Hobley, J. 9908, 12614
Hobson, J.A. 22596-7
Hockey, S.W. 15775-6
Hodent 7052
Hodgens, P.W. 20394
Hodgkin, R.A. 5899, 6031, 6078
Hodgkin, T. (fl.1899) 5333
Hodgkin, T. (fl.1958-) 2124, 2481, 2819, 7758, 7820, 8006, 9993
Hodgson, A.G.O. 17793-4, 21264
Hodgson, P.C. 3698
Hodson, A. 6079
Hodson, A.R. 10522-3
Hodson, H.V. 2125, 4554
Hoehnel, L.von. See Höhnel, L.von
Hoernlé, A.W. 1713, 21887-8, 21997, 22373, 23041, 23147

Hoernlé, R.F.A. 554, 19588, 21792, 21998, 22228, 22374, 23148-52
Hof, J.J.P.Op't. See Op't Hof, J.J.P.
Hoffman, A.C. 277
Hoffman, H.J. 20747
Hoffman, P.C. 1253
Hoffmann, C. 3121, 11968-9, 21575, 21641, 21889-91, 22751
Hoffmann, H. 16506
Hoffmann, L.F. 3309
Hoffmann, M. 7485
Hoffmann, W.H. 4156
Hoffmans, J. 14661
Hofmann, I. 11970
Hofmeister, J. 13316
Hofmeyr, I.H. 18304, 22229, 23153
Hofner, M. 16855
Hofstede, A.E. 5998
Hofstra, S. 9734
Hogarth, R. 7051
Hogarth, R.F. 11262
Hogg, V.W. 11416
Hoh, I.K. 3428
Hohenberger, J. 16097, 17554-5
Höhnel, L.von 15970
Hokororo, A.M. 17795
Holas, B. 555-6, 1063, 3949, 7486, 7539, 8992-5, 9028-31, 9200-6, 9227-8, 9304, 11041
Holden, J.J. 10524
Holden, M.J. 10909
Holderness, R. 20700
Holding, E.M. 3950
Holding, M. 17371
Holdredge, C.P. 13981
Holdsworth, H. 341, 21793
Holdsworth, M. 27
Hole, H.M. 20550
Holiday, G. 4844
Holland, E.M. 23154
Holland, F.C. 20445
Holland, J.H. 8077
Holland, K. 22375
Holland, S.W.C. 11656
Holleaux, A. 24536
Holleman, F.D. 22925
Holleman, J.F. 20748-50, 22376, 23155
Hollins, F.R. 18526
Hollis, A.C. 16052, 17239-40, 17556, 18389-90
Hollis, C. 17241, 17522, 17995, 18305
Hollis, R. 11042, 11263, 12306
Holloway, J.E. 1254, 23156
Holmes, E.G. 19458
Holmes, F. 1255
Holmes, H. 21057

Holmes, W.F. 10525
Holness, J. 1256
Hologoudou, E. See Ologoudou, E.
Holt, B. 22598-9, 22992
Holt, C. 11826
Holt, D.N. 21527
Holt, E. 2820
Holt, P.M. 5334, 6218-21
Holtsbaum, F.P. 10526
Holub, E. 1257, 21892
Holz, P. 20156, 21999, 22146, 23042
Homan, F.D. 17242, 17331-2, 17594
Hombarume 20446
Hombert, M. 5335
Homburg, L. 8645
Homburger, L. 3122-7, 5037, 7918
Homont, A. 3699
Hone, E.D. 18306
Hone, H.R. 19239, 19390
Honeyman, A.M. 16098
Honwana, L.B. 3429
Honyera 20551
Hoogenhout, P.J. 23301
Hoogstraal, H. 6474
Hooker, J.R. 557, 16751, 20792, 20845
Hoole, M.C. 21354
Hooper, C. 22377
Hooper, H.D. 3951
Hooton, E.A. 7466
Hope, A.C. 5974
Hope, J. 12065
Hope, W.A. 20751-2
Hopen, C.E. 11043
Hopgood, C.R. 21158-9
Hopkins, A.G. 11827
Hopkins, B. 12307
Hopkins, E. 19391
Hopkins, G.H.E. 16411-2, 19459-63
Hopkins, N.S. 8855
Hopkins, P.G.H. 1718
Hopkins, T.K. 19135
Hopkins, W. 9709
Hopkinson, E. 9695-6
Hopkinson, T. 1567-8
Hore, E.C. 17796
Hore-Ruthven, C.M. 23157
Horgan, E.S. 5170
Horn, A.E. 4157
Horn, J.W. 20753-4
Hornbostel, E.M.von 908-9
Hornby, H.E. 18096
Hornby, R.M. 18096
Hornell, J. 5134, 5646-7, 9735, 15802, 17293, 18719
Horner, G.R. 13099
Horner, N.A. 13100
Hornsby, G. 18046-7

Horrell, M.   22147, 22230, 22378, 22510, 22926, 23158-61, 23331
Horrocks, S.H.   342, 10876
Horst, S.T.van der 22148-9
Horsted, J.L.C.   3952
Horta, C.A.P.   12715
Horton, R.   3953, 10077, 11044-6, 11264, 12466
Horton, W.R.G.   11047-8
Horwitz, R.   2482, 22370
Hoselitz, B.F.   1258
Hoselitz, B.H.   1259
Hoskins, H.L.   2821, 5250, 5336-7
Hoskyns, C.   2483-5, 14799-14800
Hoste, H.F.   20552
Hottot, R.   13624
Houdaille, J.   2746, 2822-3
Houghton, D.H.   1569, 22380-1
Houghton, K.A.H.   22231
Houis, M.   3128, 7919-22, 8302, 8924, 9106-10, 9123, 9177
Houk, R.J.   23502
Houphouêt-Boigny, F.   2486-7
Hove, J.van   15496
How, M.   21629
Howard, A.   4272
Howard, C.   7618
Howard, F.H.   11502
Howard, L.C.   2488
Howard-Goldsmith, R.C.   1570
Howe, B.   6746
Howe, C.   17335
Howe, C.H.W.   2126, 17333
Howe, G.N.   9994
Howe, S.   16053, 24480-1
Howell, F.C.   746, 4803, 17954, 19589
Howell, P.P.   5648-59
Howes, A.M.D.   18307
Howes, F.N.   7821
Howes, R.J.C.   17451
Howie, J.W.   8078
Howitz, R.   1252
Howland, R.C.   20367, 20553-4
Howlett, J.   558, 832, 3310-1, 4555-6
Howman, E.G.   19871, 19901, 19961-3, 20555, 20755
Howman, R.   1715, 2127, 19964, 19996, 20447-9, 20556, 20756-9, 20805, 20846-7
Hoyle, B.S.   18968
Hoyle, W.E.   19240
Hoyt, E.E.   1260, 15890-1
Hrbek, I.   2824
Huard, P.   4845-6, 5076, 8854, 9627-8, 9630, 13489-91, 13511-7, 13543
Hubbard, J.W.   4557
Hubbard, P.C.   12142
Hubble, G.   3954
Huber, H.   9322, 10078-80, 11049
Hubert, H.   98
Hucks, G.W.Y.   17797, 18026, 18170

Huddle, J.G. 18918
Huddleston, C. 5660
Hudson, A. 8007
Hudson, G.F. 2128
Hudson, N.D. See Dyson-Hudson, N.
Hudson, R.S. 20926
Hudson, V.R.D. See Dyson-Hudson, V.R.
Hudson, W. 4558
Hudson, W.J.S. 21095
Huggins, G. 20450
Huggins, P.M. 17798
Hughes, A.J.B. 19965, 21761-2
Hughes, H.G.A. 384-5
Hughes, J.C.S. 12308
Hughes, L. 3430-3, 3549, 22831-2
Hughes, O.E.B. 17648
Hughes, P. 21616
Hughes, T. 18308-9
Hugo, H.C. 19966-7
Hugodot, M. 6222
Hugon, H. 6819
Hugon, M. 377-9
Hugot, H.J. 4804, 7007
Hugot, P. 13540
Huisman, M. 2825
Huizinga, J.H. 2129-30
Hulley, F. 20451
Hulme, J.J. 22600
Hulstaert, G. 196, 3129, 4559-60, 13663, 13982-99, 14269-73, 14521, 14662-3, 15001-25, 15159, 15235-8, 15387, 15497-15501
Humphrey, H.C. 20886
Humphrey-Smith, G. 19062
Humphreys, K. 7692
Hunt, D.R. 22601
Hunt, N.A. 19968-70, 20304, 20656-8
Hunt, P.M.A. 22927
Hunt, W.E. 11657
Hunter, F.P.G. 11503
Hunter, G. 28, 1720, 2490, 16004, 17799, 17955-6
Hunter, J.M. 10848
Hunter, M. 18480, 21744, 23162
Huntingford, G.W.B. 15803, 16754, 16856, 17243-4, 17557-8, 19346
Hunwick, J.O. 7487, 7923
Hurault, J. 13101
Hurley, D.E. 22993
Hurwitz, N. 23093-4
Huss, B. 21745, 21834
Hussein, A.H. 2491
Hussey, E.R.J. 1020, 1721-4, 3130, 5661-2, 7693, 15937, 16697
Hustache, A. 8351
Hutchins, D.E. 19863
Hutchinson, B. 21893
Hutchinson, J.A. 18391
Hutchinson, J.B. 434, 6475

Hutchinson, J.T. 10081
Hutchinson, M. 22000
Hutchison, W.F. 2826, 7822
Hutson, J.B. 343
Hutt, W.H. 22150, 23163-4
Huttel 9513
Hutton, E.T.H. 2827
Hutton, J.A. 7644-5
Hutton, J.H. 7540
Huxley, E. 435, 1261, 2131, 2489, 15971, 16054
Huxley, H. 15972
Huxley, J. 15973
Huybrechts, A. 14434-9
Huzzayin, S.A. 5151, 5171, 16997
Hyam, R. 22602
Hyde, H.P.T. 13564
Hyde, R.H. 10910
Hyslop, G. 910, 17294-8
Hyslop, J.R. 5271, 6143-4, 6223

I., D. 6224
I.F.A.N. See IFAN
Iannettone, G. 1262-3, 23479
Ibáñez, E. 4805-6, 7332, 7402, 7416
Ibarrola, R. 1725, 15675, 15687
Ibbotson, P. 20848-51, 21231
Ibingira, G. 16005
Ibn ---. See Bin ---
Ibrahim, A. 5440
Ibrahim, S. 9473, 9536
Ibrahim Faheil 5663
Ibrahim Mohamed 17147
Idenburg, P.J. 99, 1860, 7128
Idohou, Abbé 14263
IFAN 8996
Ige, O. 11341
Igun, A.A. 12467
Igwi, M.A.O. 11358
Ihle, A. 14801
Ijalaye, D.A. 12143
Ijere, M.O. 11372, 11417
Ijewere, G.O. 11418
Ikime, O. 11828-9
Ikombe, N. 18720
Iliffe, J. 2828
Illingworth, S. 18969, 19528
Iloeje, N.P. 11545
Ilogu, E. 12211-2, 12468
Ilori, I.O.O. See Ojo-Ilori, I.O.
Ilunga, A.R. 14664
Imam, A. 11658
Imegwu, C. 11050
Immelman, R.F.M. 22232, 22263
Imohiosen, A. 12469
Imokhuede, F.A. 3434
Imoukhude, M. See Jolaoso, M.I.
Imray, E. 22233

Imutafi, M.b.K.b.H. See Mustafa bin Kisi bin Hamadi Imutafi
Incera, L.T. See Trujeda Incera, L.
Indian Council for Africa 4561
Ingham, K. 15862, 15864, 16056, 18171, 18310, 19136-8,
    19241-4
Ingram, C.W. See Winnington-Ingram, C.
Ingrams, H. 2132
Ingrams, W.H. 18392
Ingutia, A.K. 16441
Inkomoyahlaba 20368
Innes, G. 9736, 9909-10, 12615-6
Innes, N.M. 6080
Inskeep, R. 17957, 21000
Institut Fondamental de l'Afrique Noire [Institut Français
    de l'Afrique Noire]. See IFAN
Institute of Race Relations [South Africa]. See South African
    Institute of Race Relations
Introna, S. 1264-73, 5222, 6772, 7217, 16653
Iongh, P.de 11830
Ionides, C.J.P. 18447, 18527-8
Ireland, A.W. 5664, 6476
Irele, A. 3131, 3312-5
Iria, J.A. 7823, 24029
Irle, J. 23302, 23357
Irvine, F.R. 1726, 4158, 8079-81
Irvine, S.H. 1727, 20334-5, 21239
Irwin, G.W. 252, 3000, 10527-8
Isaac, W.E. 22264
Isaacs, H.R. 1015
Isaak, B.F.A. 17132
Isekolongo, M. 14802
Isnard, H. 24632
Isong, C.N. 11419
Italiaander, R. 833-4, 12986
Itotia, J. 17559
Ittameier, E. 15026
Ittmann, J. 11051-2, 13102-7, 13185, 13317-20, 13412,
    13492, 13731-2, 14000-2, 15027
Ivy, J.W. 3316, 4562
Izaga, E.B. See Blanco Izaga, E.
Izard, M. 9411
Izzett, A. 12470

J., H.M.G. See Jackson, H.M.G.
J., L.V. 20369
Jaafar Ali 5665
Jabavu, D.D.T. 22382, 23165, 23166
Jack, D.T. 9792
Jack, J.D.M. 6477
Jackson, A.C. 19971
Jackson, A.P. 19864, 19972-3
Jackson, B.W. 1274-5, 2133
Jackson, C.H.N. 17800
Jackson, F.J. 17523, 19464
Jackson, G. 21453, 21528-9

Jackson, H.C. 5666-9, 6081-2, 6367
Jackson, H.M.G. 3700, 19806, 19882, 19974-6, 20452, 20557-9, 20701, 20760-2
Jackson, H.V. See Vernon-Jackson, H.
Jackson, H.W. 6083, 6225
Jackson, J.K. 5460, 6084-5
Jackson, J.R. 7646
Jackson, R. 1755
Jackson, S.K. 20659
Jackson, S.N.G. 19977-8, 20560-1
Jackson, T.H.E. 19465
Jackson, W.D. 7465
Jacob, E.G. 2134
Jacob, G. 24482, 24490
Jacobs, B. 19139
Jacobs, B.L. 18721-2, 18863, 19063, 19140
Jacobs, J. 559, 14003-6, 14274, 14803, 15028-32, 15160-2
Jacobsohn, H. 5172
Jacot-Guillarmod, A. 21667
Jacottet, E. 21660
Jacques-Félix, H. 4273, 13431, 13457
Jacques-Meunié, D. 7160, 7174, 8394-5
Jacquot, A. 13321, 13594-5, 13664-6
Jacquot, R. 23631
Jacynto, F. 23605
Jadin, J. 560, 14804
Jadot, J.M. 14275-7, 14522, 14665-8, 15163-5
Jaeger, A.de 15239
Jaeger, O.A. See Jäger, O.A.
Jaeger, P. 8572, 8732, 8952
Jaenen, C.J. 16753, 17082
Jaer, E.de 14441
Jäger, O.A. 16576, 21678, 21894, 22603, 23320
Jahadhmy, A.A. 15938, 16120-22
Jahn, J. 835, 3317-20, 8308
Jahoda, G. 10082, 10849-50
Jak, J. 14007-8
Jakande, L.K. 11659
Jambein, S.M. 561
Jambu-Merlin, A. 6904
Jambu-Merlin, R. 6905-10
James, A.L. 3132-3, 11971-2
James, C.L.R. 2829
James, E.T. 18723-4
James, L. 4947, 17245
James, M. 3955-6
James, R.W. 12144
Jameson, F.W. 23167
Jameson, H. 2492, 3321, 3435, 22383
Jammes, R. 7109
Jamot, E. 13432
Janbon, M.H. 6990
Janeiro, M. 3957
Janin, J. 8702
Janisch, M. 23168-9
Jankovic, B.M. 22928

Jannettone, G. See Iannettone, G.
Jannuccelli, I. 1276
Jans, P. 14278
Jansen, E.G. 21794-5
Janson-Smith, G. 6354
Janssen, E. 5670
Janssen, F. 14805
Janssens, A. 8953, 14353
Janssens, G.B.de 6977, 7129
Janusch, J.B. See Buettner-Janusch, J.
Janvier, J. 7824
Jaques, A.A. 1728, 19590, 19767, 19798, 21576
Jaquinod, R.P.F. 9412, 9455
Jara, A.B. 24166
Jardim Barreto, V.M. 24030
Jardine, D. 17106
Jardine, J. 19064
Jarovoy, M. 8952
Jarrett, H.R. 7719, 9662, 9668, 9793-4, 9807-8, 11546
Jarrett-Kerr, F.M. 22283
Jarvis, K. 3701
Jaspan, M.A. 19591
Jauffret, A. 3702
Jaugeon, R. 14806
Jaulin, R. 13493-4, 13572
Jausserand, M. 7130
Jauze, J.B. 13186-7
Jawara, A. 9702
Jeal, E.F. 4563, 22384-6
Jean, S. 372
Jean Bernard, Soeur. See Pégard, O. [Soeur Jean Bernard]
Jean-Marie 7068-9
Jeanjaquet, J.M. 22752-3
Jeanpierre, W. 3322-3
Jeanson, F. 3324
Jearey, J.H. 3703
Jebb, R. 2830
Jefferson, J.H.K. 5461-2, 5900
Jeffery, A. 5417
Jeffery, E.B. 21530
Jeffrey, C. 24662-3
Jeffreys, M.D.W. 562-571, 747, 836-8, 1084, 1571, 1917,
    3134-6, 4159, 4274-80, 6382, 7585, 7720, 7825-8, 7924,
    8906, 10165, 10911, 11053-67, 11265-72, 11357, 11359,
    11420, 11831-6, 11973, 12309-17, 12471, 13108-16, 13188,
    13266-9, 13322, 14009, 16055, 19347, 19592, 19979-81
Jeffreys, M.K. 21796, 22001
Jeffreys, R.S. 21210
Jeffries, C. 4564
Jelenski, K.A. 839
Jellicoe, M.R. 8082, 9960-1, 9981, 17801
Jellife, D.B. 12318
Jenkins, A.O. 18725
Jenkinson, H. 3001

Jenkinson, J.N. 19982
Jenks, A.E. 13117
Jenmart, J. 23448
Jennings, A.C. 20370-1, 20763-4
Jennings, I. 2493
Jennings, J.H. 11547
Jennings-Bramly, W.E. 5671, 6226, 6368
Jensen, A.E. 6399, 16507
Jensen, H. 16165-6
Jentgen, P. 15240
Jérémine, E. 9142
Jerningham, H.E.H. 2135
Jerrard, R.C. 16286, 17802, 18529, 18607
Jervis, T.S. 18311
Jesel 9474
Jesman, C. 1066, 2494, 5338-9, 14669, 16754
Jiddawi, A.M. 18312
Jimenez, R.de R. See Roda y Jimenez, R.de
Jimenez Benamu, L. 4926
Joachim, K.P. 1861
Joachim, P. 840, 3550-2, 4565, 9599
Job, H.S. 6227
Joelson, F.S. 18313
Joergens, W. 4281
Joffre, J. 9111
Johanssen, E. 15804, 17246
Johns, D.H. 16006
Johnson, C. 2136
Johnson, D. 7110, 10190, 19175
Johnson, E. 21058
Johnson, F. 16167-70, 17803, 18393-4, 20562
Johnson, G.B. 572
Johnson, H.H. 19657
Johnson, H.R.W. 12522
Johnson, J.A. 1089
Johnson, J.C.de G. See De Graft-Johnson, J.C.
Johnson, J.R., pseud. See James, C.L.R.
Johnson, J.W.de G. See De Graft-Johnson, J.W.
Johnson, K.C. 22234
Johnson, K.E.de G. See Graft-Johnson, K.E.
Johnson, M. 7586, 10529-30
Johnson, P. 1572
Johnson, R.P. 3958
Johnson, R.W.M. 20305
Johnson, S.B.G.de G. See De Graft-Johnson, S.B.G.
Johnson, V.E. 17804
Johnson, W.R. 2495
Johnsrud, R.O. 11421
Johnston, A. 1032, 1277, 1573, 2137, 4282, 6820, 7475-6,
    7647, 17524, 24449
Johnston, A.D. 10355
Johnston, H.B. 6478
Johnston, H.C.J. 21394
Johnston, H.H. 29, 100, 573-4, 1077-8, 1278, 1574, 2831,
    3137-9, 4160, 4283, 4565, 5340, 7829-31, 7925, 11974,
    12563, 12588, 15805, 15974-5, 17805, 18097, 18395,
    19657, 19732, 19832, 22151

Johnston, P.H. 17806, 18172
Johnston, R.T. 5672
Johnstone, A.D. See Duncan-Johnstone, A.
Johnstone, H.B. 17247
Johnstone, M. 7333
Johnstone, S.J. 4358
Joire, J. 8525, 8733
Jokl, E. 4567
Jolaoso, M.I. 12066
Joleaud, L. 4807, 4847, 4875, 5173, 7008-9
Jolivet, P. 8954
Jollie, E.T. See Tawse-Jollie, E.
Jolly, A. 16413
Jolly, A.R. 16659
Jolly, D. 344, 841
Jolly, H. 10809
Jolly, H.G.G. See Graham-Jolly, H.G.
Jolly, R. 19007-8
Jollyman, W.H. 21395
Jona, W. 22387
Jonckheere, F. 15388
Jones, A.C. See Creech Jones, A.
Jones, A.D. 10852
Jones, A.L. 2140
Jones, A.M. 911-24, 20927, 21001-3, 22002
Jones, A.M.K. See Keppel-Jones, A.M.
Jones, D. 3182, 19768, 21720
Jones, D.H. 10531
Jones, D.R.G.G. See Gwynne-Jones, D.R.G.
Jones, D.W.R.H. 16480
Jones, E.B. 4228, 20806-7, 22235, 22388
Jones, E.B.R. See Rheinallt Jones, E.B.
Jones, E.D. 3325, 9911-4
Jones, F.M., Bishop of Lagos. See Melville Jones, F.
Jones, G.H. 10012
Jones, G.I. 8263, 11068-78, 11273-4, 11422-3, 11660,
   11837-8, 12145, 12319, 21577
Jones, G.S. 12644
Jones, H.E.B. 12067
Jones, H.J.E. 2141
Jones, I.G. 1575
Jones, J.D.R. See Rheinallt Jones, J.D.
Jones, K. 4161
Jones, L.P. See Powys-Jones, L.
Jones, L.R. 3436
Jones, N. 19983-5, 20157-9, 20852, 20887, 22003
Jones, N.S.C. 18027, 21096
Jones, P.H. See Harries-Jones, P.
Jones, R. 386
Jones, R.L. 17169
Jones, R.T. See Trevor-Jones, R.
Jones, S. 24664
Jones, T. 9962
Jones, T.G.C.V. See Vaughan-Jones, T.G.C.
Jones, T.J. 14523
Jones, T.R. 21757, 22265

Jones, W.F.   22004
Jones, W.O.   1279
Jones, W.W.   17807
Jones-Quartey, K.A.B.   2142, 2496, 7832, 4568, 9861-2, 10236, 10532-3, 10674, 11340, 12068
Jonghe, E.de   101, 14010-3, 14524, 14574, 15033-4, 15315, 15502
Jonk, J.   14014
Joos, C.D.   13006
Joos, L.C.D.   13270-1
Jooste, G.P.   22390
Jordá Cerdá, F.   7436-7
Jordan, A.C.   21895, 22833-43
Jordan, J.D.   20306
Jordan, P.P.   See Ntantala, P.P.
Jore, L.   8613-4
Jorge, S.C.M.   24167
Jorge Júnior, T.   23807
Joseph, A.F.   6479-80
Joseph, A.T.M.   16755
Joseph, H.   22391, 22929
Joseph, J.   22392
Joseph, S.B.   13560-1
Josey, P.E.   14015
Joubert, Lt.   9621
Jouin, J.   7175, 7420
Jourdain, H.J.   24318
Jovy, R.   7152
Jowett, L.V.   19986
Jowett, P.   11275
Joyce, T.A.   14182-5, 15807
Judd, A.S.   11079, 11504, 11975
Judd, H.   4569, 10853
Juergensmeyer, J.C.   7759
Juge, P.E.   10265
Juin, H.   3321, 3553
Julien, C.   2497
Julien, C.A.   2832, 7267
Julien, M.G.   24483
July, R.W.   2143, 3327
Juma, S.K.   16287-8
Juma, W.   17808
Jumeaux, R.   24450
Jumelle, H.   24588
Jung, R.   13635-6
Jungfleisch, M.   6228
Jungraithmayr, H.   5901-2, 7926, 11080, 11976-9, 13552
Júnior, A.C.S.C.   23449
Junior, A.D.   1280
Junior, J.de S.   See Sousa Junior, J.de
Junior, S.   See Santos-Junior
Júnior, T.J.   See Jorge Júnior, T.
Junod, H.A.   575, 19593, 19692, 19814-5, 22844
Junod, H.P.   197, 576, 3140, 3704, 4570-3, 19553, 19733, 19987, 22930-1, 23762-5, 23808
Junod, V.   22393

Juritz, C.F.   23043, 23172
Jussiant, A.   14442

K., C.M.   2498
K., P.   164, 1729, 2144-5, 24451
Ka, A.A.   See Anta Ka, A.
Kabbada Mikaël.   See Kebbédé Mikaël
Kaberry, P.M.   10984, 13118, 13209, 13249-50, 13272, 13403-4
Kabore, G.V.   9413
Kabuga, C.E.S.   19245
Kabvuta   20702
Kachama-Nkoy, S.   2499
Kafuho, E.   18713
Kagame, A.   15570-2, 15628, 15643-7, 15650
Kaggwa, L.B.   18726
Kagolo, B.M.   18727
Kähler, H.   22845, 23173
Kähler-Meyer, E.   286, 1026, 3141, 13119, 13323, 13352-3, 16171, 18396, 22754
Kahn, E.   23174
Kahnweiler, D.H.   842
Kaikini, P.R.   3437
Kajubi, W.S.   18970
Kake, B.I.   8294, 19734
Kake, I.   2833
Kala-Lobe, I.   4574, 13472
Kalala, K.   14016
Kalanda, A.   14017, 14670, 15166
Kalanda, P.   19392
Kaldor, N.   1281, 1576-8
Kalonji, B.   2500, 14443
Kalu, E.   11081
Kalungano, pseud.   See Santos, M.dos
Kaumi, B.K.   19529
Kamainda, T.   14018
Kamanzi, T.   15608
Kamarck, A.M.   1579
Kamau, J.   17334
Kamau wa Ngengi (Kamaua Ngengi), later J.Kenyatta.   See Kenyatta, J.
Kambona, O.   2501
Kambwa   23401
Kamen-Kaye, M.   7035
Kamian, B.   1918
Kamil, M.   16470, 16941
Kamitin, F.R.   5948
Kamoga, F.K.   19009-10
Kamtedza, J.de D.G.   19594
Kandamakumbo   19988-91, 20256
Kane, J.J.M.   See Mensah-Kane, J.J.
Kanie, A.   3560
Kannemeyer, M.   22604
Kannenberg, H.   17809
Kanoute, P.   8895
Kantedza, J.de D.G.   See Kamtedza, J.de D.G.

Kanyamunyu, P.K. 18728
Kaplan, M. 20563
Kaplan, S. 23182
Kapuscza, A. 2502
Karani, H. 17333, 17335
Karche, J.P. 24403
Karefa-Smart, J. 2503
Kariara, J. 17958
Karila-Cohen, C. 6911
Kariuki, O. 3959
Kark, S.L. 21835
Karl, E. 9528
Karmiloff, C. 15892
Karmiloff, G. 18028
Karp, M. 1282
Karr, H.W.S. See Seton-Karr, H.W.
Karstedt, O. 2146
Kasa-Vubu, J. 2549
Kashif, H. 6032
Kasunmu, A.B. 12146
Kathamalo 21396
Katumba, A. 19246
Katz, S.I. 10266
Kauczor, D. 5673-5, 6318, 6324
Kauffman, R.A. 925, 20160
Kaunda, K. 2504, 21097-8
Kautedza, J.de D.G. See Kamtedza, J.de D.G.
Kawawa, R.M. 18173
Kay, G. 20890, 21027, 21076, 21232, 21243
Kay, H.C. 5223
Kay, R.W.W. 10810
Kayamba, H.M.T. 16442
Kaye, B. 10811, 10854
Kaye, I. 2505
Kaye, M.K. See Kamen-Kaye, M.
Kayo, P. 13377-8
Kayper-Mensah, A.W. 3438
Keable, R. 3960
Keane, A.H. 5676
Keane, G.J. 19247
Keane, G.K. 19248
Keane, G.T. 19249
Keatley, P. 20453-4
Keay, J.S. 5341
Keay, R.W.J. 8083, 12320
Keay, R.W.K. 4102
Keays, G.A.V., Bey 6229
Kebbédé Mikaël 16472, 16577
Keen, P. 21779
Kehoe, M. 16671
Keigwin, H.S. 20336, 20853
Keita, M.M. 2506, 8896-8, 9004
Keita, O. 9124
Keita Fodeba. See Fodeba, K.
Keith, A. 14019
Keith, A.B. 2147, 12147

Keith, J.L. 1862, 21233
Keith-Lucas, B. 2148, 9671
Kelfa-Caulker, O. 4575
Kelinguen, Y. 13544
Keller, I. 13120
Keller, J. 12936
Kelley, A.B. See Bowler-Kelley, A.
Kelley, H. 748, 8862, 9629, 13518, 13631, 14279, 16541
Kelly, L. 14525
Keltie, J.S. 2834
Kenadid, Y.O. 2507
Kenchington, F.E. 6481-2
Kendal, J. 19992, 20236, 20564-5
Kendall, E.M. 6483
Kennan, T.P. 21630
Kennedy, A.M. 8646
Kennedy, F.R. 19530
Kennedy, R.A. 4872, 7541, 11276
Kennedy, R.F. 22005
Kennedy, T.A. 15893, 17336
Kennedy, T.J. 15780
Kennett, B.L.A. 11082
Kenrick, J.W. 6230, 6596
Kent, R.K. 2835
Kenworthy, J.M. 15976
Kenya 17452
Kenya. Ministry of Agriculture 17453
Kenyatta, J. 2508, 17248
Keppel-Jones, A.M. 23175
Kerfoot, O. 18530
Kerick, J.W. 5677
Kerina, M.A. 23332-3
Keris, G.le B. 2149
Kerken, G.van der 14020-2, 14671-2
Kerr, A.J. 3705, 19807-8
Kerr, F.M.J. See Jarrett-Kerr, F.M.
Kerr, P. 2836
Kerr, W.B. 22605
Kersten, O. 18098
Kesby, J.D. 17674
Kesteloot, L.L. See Lagneau-Kesteloot, L.
Ketley, H.C. 11083, 12321
Kettlewell, R.W. 21355
Key, B. 22606
Khali, B. 3439
Khalil, I.M. 5999
Khalil, M.I. 6383
Khalil, O. 5342
Khaly, B. See Nénékhaly-Camara, C.
Khaly, N. See Nénékhaly-Camara, C.
Khama, T. 2151, 21617, 22395
Khamisi, F.J. 16007
Khan, R. See Ras Khan
Khane, S.A. 8671
Khonde, G. 13764
Khuri, F.I. 8150

Ki-Zerbo, J. 1731, 2512, 2839, 2970-2, 4578-9, 4756, 10534, 10614
Kiano, G. 17454
Kiano, J.G. 16008
Kiba, S. 8278
Kibaki, M. 17337
Kibwana, S. 16289
Kidamala, D. 18314
Kidd, R. 4576
Kidney, E. 21305
Kiernberger, A. 21679
Kiewiet, C.W. de 2837, 22607
Kiimbila, J.K. 16290
Kiley, D. 22608
Kilger, P.L. 15316
Killam, D. 30
Killens, J.O. 843
Killian, C. 9156-60
Killian, M. 7052
Kilner, P. 6145
Kilolo, B. 14673
Kilpin, R. 22609
Kilson, M. 2509
Kilson, M.D. de B. 9737
Kilson, M.L., Jr. 2152
Kimble, G.H.T. 1919
Kimble, H. 10318
Kimwani, E.G. 17959
King, A. 11277-8
King, A.B. 12523, 12589
King, A.V. 926, 11279
King, E.R.G. 21059
King, H.H. 6484-7
King, N. 22610
King, N.Q. 10766
King, P. 2510
King, P.V. 7927
King, V.E. 7694
King, W.S. 10912
Kingdom, Z.E. 18174
Kingdon, F.D. 6231
Kingdon, J. 844, 17299
Kingon, J.R.L. 22755
Kingslake, B. 11280-1
Kingsley, M.H. 4577
Kingston, H.D.R. 22006
Kingue, M.D. 927, 1726
Kini, N. 13764
Kinloch, B.G. 18921
Kinross, J. 2838
Kipkorir, B.E. 18820
Kipling, R. 1036
Kirby, A. 18175
Kirby, D. 9829
Kirby, P.R. 5174, 19634-8, 21758, 22007-11, 22611-2, 22266
Kirby, R.H. 436

Kirchhoff, P. 577
Kirk, J.W.C. 17019
Kirk, R. 4162, 5977, 6232, 6488-9
Kirk, W. 1920
Kirk-Greene, A. 31, 7928, 9863, 11347, 11841
Kirk-Greene, A.H.M. 2511, 10913, 11084, 11424, 11661-3, 11840-3, 11980, 12073, 12148
Kirk-Greene, A.N.M. 11839
Kirkbride, A. 6665
Kirkman, J. 17300-1, 17960
Kirkpatrick, R.T. 19073
Kirkwood, K. 23176, 22395-6
Kiro, S. 18315
Kironde, E. 19141, 19250
Kirsch, B. 8333
Kirschstein, E. 17810-2
Kirwan, L.P. 749, 6233-5
Kisob, J.A. 13212-3, 13324, 13473
Kisseih, D.A.N. 10812
Kisubi, P. 15148
Kitching, G.C. 24687
Kittermaster, H.B. 17107-8
Kitumboy, L.W.H. 15035-6
Klamborowski, F. 21531
Klamroth, M. 13168, 17813
Klaveren, J.J.van. See Van Klaveren, J.J.
Klein, W.C. 1284
Kleindienst, M.R. 15835
Kleist, A.M. 7833
Klibi, S.C. 6959
Klima, G. 17814
Klineberg, O. 4580
Klingberg, F.J. 387
Klingenheben, A. 265, 285, 294, 1010, 3142-4, 5038, 7929-32, 8647, 11844, 12617-8, 12771, 16857-60, 16942
Klingenheben - Von Tiling, M. 16357-8, 16172, 16861, 17133-7
Knak, D.S. 578
Knapen, M.T. 1732
Knapp, A.W. 7497-8, 7648
Knappert, J. 561, 2513, 3145-7, 4581, 15037, 16173-8, 16190, 16291-16308, 19348, 20660
Knight, M.M. 2514, 4894-5
Knops, P. 9207
Knowles, E.J.F. 17455
Knowles, O.S. 17595
Knox-Mawer, R. 3706
Köbben, A.J.F. 9208-10, 9285
Kobishchanow, Y.M. 15977
Koch, C. 19833, 24168
Koch, H. 13043, 13325
Kochnitzky, L. 14280
Kock, G. 5135
Kock, M.H.de 22153
Kock, W.J.de 22613
Koechlin, J. 13565, 13652, 13676-9
Koenig, O. 18316

Kohler, O. 1088, 1091, 1733, 3148, 4582, 5678, 11981, 16508, 19595, 19769, 23303, 23358
Kokot, D.F. 19834
Kolarz, W. 7760
Kole, A.M. 10535
Koller, R.P.A. 6991
Kollewijn, R.D. 3707, 7131
Kollmann 19349
Komambo, K. 23347
Komey, E.A. 10676
Konka, R. 13011
Konvitz, M.R. 12627-8
Koolwijk, M.van 23402-3
Kootz-Kretschmer, E. 18397-9
Kopoka, O.B. 16179-80, 17560
Kopytoff, I. 579, 15241
Koranteng, E.K. 9995
Kordt, E. 1285
Koritschoner, H. 15834, 17815, 18531, 18729
Korn, H. 23317
Koroma, M.S. 9738
Korostovetz, V.de 6656
Korostovtsev, M.A. 5272
Korsah, A. 7761, 10223
Koshland, M. 14281, 24524
Koti, A. 16309
Kotschar, V. 1915
Kotto, S.L. See Lafia Kotto, S.
Kotzé, D.A. 21618
Kouroubari, A. 8295
Kourouma, K. 9051
Kouyaté, S.B. 2515
Kozonguizi, J. 23334, 23348
Kpaka, J.K.M. See Mannah-Kpaka, J.K.
Kraft, C. 7933-4
Kraft, J. 7070
Kraft, L. 2153, 4896
Krapf, L. 23359
Krause, F. 580, 23177
Krause, G.A. 1039, 12772
Kravetz, L. 12985
Kréa, H. 5051, 6748, 7121
Krenkel, E. 19700
Kretschmer, E.K. See Kootz-Kretschmer, E.
Krieger, K. 12472
Krige, E. 21896, 22154
Krige, E.J. 21746, 21897-9, 21916, 22932, 23178
Krige, J.D. 21900-2, 22154, 22933, 23044
Krige, U. 22846
Krishna, K.G.V. 17338
Kronenberg, A. 5093, 5679-80
Kropp, M.E. 10644-5
Krótki, K.J. 6597
Kruger, F. 21578, 21903-8
Krumm, B. 17816
Krzeczunowicz, G. 16959-64

Kubiena, W.L. 15750
Kubik, G. 13582, 15836, 18864-6, 19639, 23809-10
Kuczynski, R.R. 4583, 8151
Kuder, G.G. 10810
Kufour, F.A. 7695
Kuhn, G. 21579, 21721, 22756
Kuhn, M. 6000
Kuiper, F. 1286
Kulick, G.D. 10267
Kulubya, S.W. 18730
Kumalo, A. 22847
Kumar, M. 2516-7
Kumar, S. 2518
Kunda, A. 21060
Kunene, D.P. 21642-3, 22757
Kuntz, M. 374, 20928-9
Kuo, F.S. See Sengat-Kuo, F.
Kuoh, F.S. See Sengat-Kuo, F.
Kup, A.P. 9864-7, 9942
Kuper, B. 19809
Kuper, H. 19716, 21747-9, 21769, 21776, 21780, 22397,
    22848, 23179-82
Kuper, L. 22398-22400, 23183-4
Kusambiza, N.F.M. 19251
Kwaku, W.A. 10222
Kwapong, A.A. 750
Kyesimira, Y. 15781
Kyiamah, A.Q. See Quamie-Kyiamah, A.

L., J.G. 14674-5, 14683
L., M. 13230
L., R.P. 7609
L., W.D. 21306
La Bathie, H.P.de. See Perrier de la Bathie, H.
La Chard, L.W. 11085, 12322
La Fontaine, S.H. 17249
La Grasserie, R.de 22758
La Guma, A. 22849-53
La Guma, B.V. 22401
La Rosa, C. 1288, 7649
La Varde, R.P.de. See Varde, R.P.de la
La Vergne de Tressan, Marquis de 7936-7, 7960, 8648, 9648
La Viña Villa, J. 5077
Labouret, H. 273, 845, 2154, 4229, 4584, 7542-6, 8189,
    8232, 8256, 8303-4, 8856, 11664, 16009
Labrecque 14023
Lacharrière, J.L.de. See Ladreit de Lacharrière, J.
Lacharrière, R.de 5058
Lacheraf, M. 7071, 7334
Lacops, B. 13765, 14526
Lacops, M. 13766-7
Lacoste, C. 7010
Lacouture, J. 7072, 7268
Lacroix, P.F. 3149, 13273, 13326
Lacy, G. 19701

Laddersous, A.M.de. See Moeller de Laddersous, A.
Ladefoged, P. 11982
Ladikpo, R. 1287, 4885
Ladipo, D. 12069
Ladkin, R.G. 18787, 19466
Ladkin, R.S. 4163
Ladreit de Lacharrière, J. 4897
Ladurie, M.le R. 10767
Laffitte, R. 7009
Lafiw Kobbo, O. 9473
Laforcade, R.de 3708
Laforgue, P. 7208, 7587, 8396-7
Lafuente, A.D. See Domenech Lafuente, A.
Lafuente, T.C.D. 5052
Lafuente Ferrari, E. 846
Lagae, C.R. 5681-2
Lagae, R. 15317
Lagercrantz, S. 581-9, 15806
Lagneau-Kestellot, L. 3328-9, 8672, 13222
Lagrave, R. 1734, 13189
Lahbabi, M.A. 4586, 7421
Lahiri, H.S. 10792, 10813
Lahlou, A. 7422
Laight 18844
Laing, E. 10772
Lakhdar, T. 6912
Lal, P. See Pyarelal, pseud.
Lala 20703
Lalanne, P.L. See Loustau-Lalanne, P.
Lallemand, A. 8084
Lallemand, V. 8085, 9385
Lalouel 13583
Laloum, C. 11282
Lamal, F. 15503-5
Laman, K.E. 12964, 13667, 15038
Lamase, M.de P.de. See Pradel de Lamase, M.de
Lamb, P.H. 10914-6, 18641
Lambdin, T.O. 5398
Lambert, H.E. 15837, 16141, 16181-7, 16261-2, 16310-26,
    17596, 17649
Lambert, N. 8398-8400
Lambert, W. 12323
Lamberton, C. 24600-2, 24606
Lambin, R. 8999
Lambo, T.A. 4587
Lambrecht, F.L. 4164
Lamburn (Lambourn), R. 17817, 18317
Lamden, S.C. 16057
Lamerton, J.F. 18532
Lami, P. 13545
Lamine, T.M. 9066
Lamming, G. 3330
Lamotte, M. 9161-2, 7721
Lampen, E. 5683
Lampen, G.D. 5684, 6236
Lamplugh, G.W. 20161

Lamprey, H.F. 18533-5
Lampué, P. 3709-10, 7132
Lamy, P. 13121
Lancaster, D.G. 17818
Lancel, S. 4993
Lanczkowski, G. 5175
Landau, J.M. 5343
Landau, R. 7269
Lander, J.R. 10536
Landes, R. 4588
Landis, E.S. 22934
Lane, L.P. 18099, 18318, 18536-7, 18608
Lane, M. 11283-5
Lang, K. 3150, 7935, 17138
Lang-Wien, K. 9915
Langden, G. 21631
Langenhove, F.van 2155, 2840
Langer, W.L. 2519, 5344
Langford-Smith, N. 1735, 17621
Langham-Carter, R.R. 22012-3
Langhansz, C. 22267
Langlands, B. 15939
Langlands, B.W. 4927, 18632, 19066, 19252
Langley, E.R. 9739
Langley, M. 9681, 21128
Lango, T.A. 4589
Langton, A.V. 2841-2, 19666
Languagc, F.J. 21680, 21711
Lanham, L.W. 3151, 19770-1, 22759-61
Lanning, E.C. 751, 18731-3, 18867-73, 18927, 19067,
    19253, 19531
Lantis, M. 10085
Laoye I, Timi of Ede 11286
Lapiccirella, V. 17163
Lapie, P.O. 2156
Lapierre, J.W. 24633
Laplante, A. 9250
Laplayne, J.R. 3561-2
Laqueur, W.Z. 2520
Lara, D.K. 2521
Larcier, H. 23404, 23514
Largie, S.A. 3563-4
Larguier, J. 3711
Larken, P.M. 5685-7
Larochette, J. 5039, 15039-40, 15506, 19772
Larpent, G.de H. 22268
Larrea, A.de 7438
Larsen, K. 18633
Larson, T.J. 19596
Lasch, E.E. 24665
Lasebikan, E.L. 310, 7948, 11983
Lassort 9112, 12527
Lassudrie-Duchêne, M. 1289
Last, D.M. 11845-6
Last, G.C. 1921
Last, J.T. 24512

Latham, E.W. 21397-8
Latham, G.C. 15940
Latham, J.D. 6821
Latham, N. 11847
Latil, M. 1580
Latsky, J.M. 23045
Laubadère, A.de 7387-9
Laubat, F.de C. See Chasseloup Laubat, F.de
Laude, T.C.N. See Norbet Laude, T.C.
Laughton, W.H. 17561
Laurentin-Retel, A. 13573
Lauwe, P.H.C.de. See Chombart de Lauwe, P.H.
Lavachery, H. 847
Lavau, G.de 9067
Lavauden, L. 12949
Laveleye, E.de 14807
Laver, J.D.M. 11984
Lavergne, G. 13122
Lavin, C.E. 1290
Lavroff, D.G. 32, 2522, 3707
Law, J.R.S. 9916
Lawler, S.D. 7514
Lawman, T. 21028, 21129
Lawrance, J.C.D. 18176, 18734, 18874-5, 19142-3, 19254
Lawrence, A.W. 7834, 9996, 10166
Lawrence, H.G. 22402
Lawrenson, T.E. 10167
Lawrie, G. 23335
Lawrie, G.G. 22403
Lawrie, J.J. 17041
Laws, R. 21377
Lawson, A. 21265
Lawson, G. 10086
Lawson, G.W. 8086, 22237
Lawson, J.B. 10814
Lawson, R. 10268-9
Lay, Y. 9131
Layard, E.L. 22014
Laycock, H.T. 21530, 21532
Laydevant, F. 21580-3
Laydevant, R.P.J. 21584
Laye, C. 3565-7, 9125
Lazzarini, P.D. 3961
Le Borgne, Capt. 8449
Le Coeur, C. 4808, 7722, 9658, 13496
Le Coeur, M. 9658
Le Du, R. 7011
Le Grand, L. 15508
Le Grip, A. 5067-8, 8342
Le Mailloux, M. 928
Le Mire, P. 8615
Le Quesne, C.M. 8296
Le Roy, A. 18100
Le Roy, J. 8486
Le Sourd, M. 9643
Le Tourneau, R. 5096, 6816, 6978

Leach, T.A. 5463, 6086
Leakey, L.S.B. 590-1, 752-3, 15838-40, 16414, 17250-2, 17302-4, 17961-2, 18876-7
Leal, E.F. 19835
Leandri, J. 24603
Leaver, K.D. 20661-2, 19993-4
Lebar, P. 3331
Lebeuf, A. 13123, 13191
Lebeuf, J.P. 3332, 8182, 8815, 13027, 13049, 13124-8, 13191, 13235, 13275, 13327, 13495, 13509, 13519-24, 13546, 13549, 13553, 13637, 14024
Lebeuf, M.D. 13525
Leblanc, M. 3152, 15507
Leblond, M.A. 24652
Lebon, J.H.G. 6087-8
Lebret, L.J. 1291
Lebzelter, V. 23304
Lecaillon, J. 1292
Lechevallier-Chevignard, A. 373-4
Leclant, J. 5176, 16472, 16509, 16577-81, 16720-1
Leclercq, H. 1293, 14445
Lecoste, B. 15041-3, 21750-1
Lecuona, M.de O. 12840
Lederbogen, W. 13129
Ledger, D.C. 11548
Ledo Pontes, L. 12788
Ledoux, P. 15389
Leduc, G. 1294-6, 7650, 8233
Leduc, M. 1297-9
Leduc, Y. 4165
Lee, H.W. 345
Lee, J.B. 1922
Lee, J.M. 19144
Lee, M. 102
Lee-Warden, L.B. 23185
Leechmann, B. 18448
Leedal, G.P. 18512
Leeming, A.J. 13276
Leenhardt, M. 8341
Lees, E.C.L. 17819
Leese, F.E. 9997
Leeson, F. 12324
Lefaivre, H. 9567
Lefebvre, J. 1300-1, 14446
Lefebvre, M.M. 3962
Lefèvre, R. 16756-9
Lefroy, H.M. See Maxwell-Lefroy, H.
Legassick, M. 10421
Legendre, M. 6822
Léger, A. 11086, 13328
Léger, J.M. 1736
Leger, R.G.T. 12325
Legesse, A. 5688
Leggett, H. 16058
Legier, H.J. 13009
Leglay, M. 6823

Legoux, P. 3713
Legrand, F. 5224
Legros, C. 8955
Legters, L.H. 33
Legum, C. 2523-7, 10422, 14676-7, 14808, 17083, 19255
Lehfeldt, R.A. 22155
Lehmann, D. 21187
Lehmann, F.R. 17820-1, 23305
Lehmann, H. 19467
Lehr, J. 6325
Leib, A. 24370
Leiris, M. 592, 8816, 8925, 13130
Leitão, A.E.de S. See Sousa Leitão, A.E.de
Leitão, M.I.M. See Madeira Leitão, M.I.
Leite, D.B. 23554
Leite, S. 23566
Leite de Faria, F. 12924, 15318-9
Leith-Ross, S. 11087, 11848, 12473-4
Lekens, B. 15044
Lekgothoane, S.K. 21644
Lelong 12527
Lem, F.H. 848, 8857, 8965
Lemaignen, R. 1302
Lemaire, Lt. 4590
Lemaire, R. 4165
Lemarchand, R. 14678
Lembezat, B. 13131
Lemee, G. 4928
Lemkin, J. 20455
Lemma, M. 16943
Lemon, P.C. 21533
Lemos, V.de 2528, 23999
Lemos e Brito, J.E.de 23855
Lenherr, J. 20162
Lenk-Chevitch, P. 23405
Lenoir, G. 4948, 6795
Léon 24604
Leonard, D.A. 19816, 22854, 22935
Léonard, H. 14447, 14809
Leone, E.de 1303, 2157, 7139
Leone, G. 6657
Leonessa, M.da 16986, 16998
Lepagnot, L. 7012
Lepesme, P. 8056, 12648, 15751
Leplae, E. 13768-74, 14448-9, 14575-6, 15390-2, 15509-10
Leportier, J. 8431
Lèques, R. 8757
Leria, M. 7477
Leriche, A. 7423, 8384-5, 8415, 8432-7, 8450-1, 8454-5, 8468, 8526-7, 8573, 9178
Leroux, C.T. See Traoré-Leroux, C.
Leroux, H. 9653
Leroy, F.M. See Morisseau-Leroy, F.
Leroy, I. 16583
Leroy, J. 16584-7
Leroy, J.F. 4284

Lerrigo, P.H.J. 3963-4, 14025, 15320
Lerugar, L. 3714
Lesage, M.C. 10815-6
Leschi, J. 8858
Leshoai, B. 929
Leslau, W. 5399, 16099, 16471, 16510-1, 16862-88
Leslie, J.A.K. 16188, 18609
Leslie, M.E. 21342
Leslie, R. 22156
Lesourd, M. 4876, 5094-5, 7176, 9328, 17170
Lester, P. 389, 7209, 8219
Lestrade, G.P. 3153-4, 19773, 21645-6, 21909, 22762
Lestrange, M.de 8648, 9000-2, 9126, 9179
Letele, G.L. 21647
Letnev, A. 8152, 8966
Letocha, T. 3715
Letourneau, R. See Le Tourneau, R.
Letouzey, R. 437
Letouzey, Y. 13192
Leubuscher, C. 1307, 1581
Leurquin, P. 1305, 15561-2
Leuzinger, E. 24409
Leva, A.E. 1012, 1923, 2843, 5177, 17109, 18610
Leverett, C.W. 18319
Lévi, C. 8734
Levine, B.B. 17650
Levine, R.A. 17253-4, 17597, 17650
Levtzion, N. 7835, 10537
Lévy, D. 3716, 7696
Levy, G. 22238
Levy, L. 22157
Levy-Bruhl, L. 23360
Lewanika, G. 20456
Lewicki, T. 2844, 4994, 6658
Lewin, E. 2845
Lewin, J. 390, 3712-3, 19810, 22083, 22404-7, 22936-41, 23186
Lewis, A.L. 24410
Lewis, B.A. 5658, 5689-90, 5993
Lewis, B.W. 1306
Lewis, D.G. 19995, 20566-9, 20704
Lewis, D.J. 6490-6
Lewis, F.A. 12326
Lewis, H.R.J. 2158
Lewis, H.S. 16760
Lewis, I.M. 594, 17020-5, 17084-6, 17110, 17139-40, 17159, 17171-3, 17651
Lewis, M.B. 20570
Lewis, M.D. 2529
Lewis, M.S. 24666
Lewis, R. 2159
Lewis, R.A. 10810, 10817
Lewis, V.A. 20705, 20765
Lewis, W.E. 21489
Lewis, W.H. 198, 2530
Lewis-Barned, J.F.de S. 18464

Leyburn, J.G. 23187
Leyden, J.L. 17111
Leydevant, F. 21653
Leynaud, E. 13574, 13625
Leys, C. 2531-2, 19145, 20457
Leys, N.M. 15807
Lézine, A. 6749, 6817-8
L'Heureux, L. 14450
Lhote, H. 4848-54, 7013-5, 7445, 7588, 8859-62, 8199,
    8907-8, 9003, 9630
Liajjemi, A.b.H.b.A. See Abdallah bin Hemedi bin Ali Liajjemi
Libois, J.G. See Gerard-Libois, J.
Libra 16059
Liebenow, J.G. 18177-80
Liell, J. 12475
Lienhardt, G. 5691-95
Lienhardt, P. 17372, 18465
Lierde, J.van. See Van Lierde, J.
Liesenborghs, O. 14026-9, 14527-30, 15045-7
Lievre, P.D. 10538
Lifchitz, D. See Lifszyc, D.
Lifszyc, D. 8817-8, 8927
Liger, P. 7036
Ligers, Z. 8818-20, 8785, 8792, 8812, 8849
Light, R. 1924
Lightheim, M. 5178
Ligthart, G.J. 1307
Lilley, C.C. 10539
Lima, A.J.S. See Santos Lima, A.J.
Lima, M. 23406
Lincoln, R. 24301
Lind, E.M. 19043, 19068
Lindan, O. 4166
Lindblom, G. 595-7, 4809, 13625, 13744, 15841
Lindblom, K.G. 849
Lindeman, H.A. 18538
Linden, T.van den 14030
Lindfors, B. 22855
Lindroth, S. 9770
Lindsay, H.A.F. 22158
Lindsell, R.F.J. 19090, 19069
Linhard, J. 8735
Liniger-Goumaz, M. 1925
Linné, S. 11287
Linton, R. 24371-3
Lionnet, J.F.G. 24667-8
Lipkin, J. 22856
Lippins, Count 14810
Lipscomb, J.F. 2533
Lironi, H.E. 10270
Lisboa, P. 23856
Lishman, J.F. 6002
Lishman, M. 12327
Lisle, M.de 13433-7
Lisowski, F.P. 5696

Lister, P.C. See Cunliffe-Lister, P.
Lister, U.G. 4285
Listowel, Earl of. See Hare, W.F. [Earl of Listowel]
Lisulo, B.J.W. 20337, 20571
Little, K. 7762, 8153-8, 9703, 9710, 9740-4, 9982-4
Little, M. See Malcolm X
Littlejohn, J. 9745-6, 9768
Littlejohn, K.G. 10917
Littlewood, S. 3719
Littmann, E. 16588-9, 16889-90
Littner, M.L. 20706
Livchitz, I.G. 5179
Liversage, V. 3720
Liversidge, R. 22103
Livie-Noble, F.S. 2160
Livingstone, A.S. 2534
Livingstone, D. 20372
Livingstone, F.B. 7547
Livingstone, I. 18971
Livingstone, W.P. 21399
Llewellin, Lord 20458
Lloyd, A.C.G. 21797, 22614-5
Lloyd, B.W. 20338
Lloyd, E.M. 20572, 20584-5
Lloyd, P. 11288
Lloyd, P.C. 11088-90, 11425, 11665-8, 11849-52, 12149-53, 12476
Lo Giudice, B. 16761
Lobato, A.S. 23766, 24031-2
Lobe, I.K. See Kala-Lobe, I.
Lobo, L. 23480, 23954
Lochner, N. 10218
Lockhart, J.G. 2161
Lockwood, J. 11505
Lodewijckx, C. 14031, 15511
Lodge, G.C. 1582
Lods, P. 14282
Loeb, E.M. 23306-7
Loewenthal, L.J.A. 19468
Lofchie, M.F. 18181-2
Logan, D.W. 1844, 1863
Logan, M.H. 5697
Logan, R.W. 2535-6
Logan, W.M. 21099
Lokke, C.L. 2846
Lollini, C. 6707
Lombard, J. 754, 4591-2, 8370, 8574, 9529, 9537, 9544, 9549-50, 9610-2, 13438, 13618-9, 13638
Lombardero, M. 1926, 7239, 15715
Lombardi, G. 4929
Lomholt, A. 5251
Lomoro, G.M. 15894
Lonergon, M.B. 7499
Long, K.R. 930
Long, N. 21454
Long, R.C. 21534

Longden, J. 11426
Longland, F. 18320
Longmore, L. 3155, 21910, 22015-6, 22159, 22408-9, 22942
Longonda, F. 13795
Longrigg, S.H. 2162, 16698
Longuefosse, M. 24485
Lonsdale, J.M. 17525
Loogman, A. 16189
Lootens, P. 15048
Lopes, E.C. 3965, 9568, 10540-1
Lopes, L.dos 12663
Lopes, M.M. 23767
López, A.O.de Z. See Ortiz de Zárate López, A.
López-Monís, C. 15752
Loram, C.T. 3966, 4167, 22239, 23188
Lord, W.B. 19735
Loreto, R. 4593, 7836
Lorimer, F.C.S. 5698, 6237
Lorin, C.M. 24533
Loseby, P.J.A. 22160
Losse, G.F. 15782
Lotar, L. 14811
Lotar, P. 14812, 15512
Lotte, Lt. 8386
Lotte, A.J. 4168, 13749
Louis, P. 24669
Louis, W.R. 2847-8, 14813-5, 19256-7
Loung, M. 931
Lourenço, S. 21199, 23407, 23606
Loussouarn, Y. 3721
Loustau-Lalanne, P. 24670-2
Loutskaia, N.S. 7335
Louw, A.A. 598
Louw, J.A. 22763-6
Louw, J.K. 21307-8
Louwers, M. 14679
Louwers, O. 4104, 14451, 15242
Lovell, C.R. 22616
Lovens, M. 14680
Loveridge, A. 6497, 9386, 18539-42, 21535
Loveridge, A.J. 3722, 4594, 9747, 10716-7
Low, A. 19146-7, 19258
Low, D.A. 18937, 19148, 19532
Lowe, C.van R. See Riet Lowe, C.van
Lowe, R.H. 21536
Lowenstein, S. 16965
Lowth, N.L.C. 18735
Loyewski, d'O. 8438
Lozano, L.P. See Perez Lozano, L.
Lozza, L. 16762
Lubamba, G. 13775
Lubambula, Y.B. 19371
Lubbock, J. 5180, 6238

Lubin, M.A. 3333
Luc, G. 13179
Lucas, A.J. 8387
Lucas, B.K. See Keith-Lucas, B.
Lucas, C.P. 2849
Lucas, F.A.W. 22161, 22410
Lucas, J.O. 11091
Lucas, L. 5699
Lucas, M. 17024
Luce, A.F. See Fabre-Luce, A.
Luce, R. 17087
Lucentini, M. 15513
Luchaire, F. 3723, 9376, 24649
Ludger, K. 18736, 19533
Ludwig, H.D. 18642
Lugard, F.D. [Lord Lugard] 103-4, 1737, 2163-4, 2850-3,
    7622, 11427, 11669-70, 11853, 16010, 21455
Lugard, Lady 7837
Lugg, H.C. 21911-2, 22767
Luís Lupi 3967
Lukas, J. 258, 290, 311, 316, 1010, 2166, 5040, 6326-9,
    7938, 11092-4, 11549, 11985-8, 12070
Luke, E.W.F. See Fashole-Luke, E.W.
Lumumba, P. 14681
Luna, I.R.de 19702
Lundman, B. 599-600
Lunet, P. 6963
Luning, H.A. 12154
Lunn, B. 21798
Lunn, W.S. 23189
Lunsonga, C. 21004
Lupi, L. See Luís Lupi
Lury, D.A. 1308
Lury, E.E. 15842
Lush, A.J. 18878
Lussy, K. 17822
Luthera, V.P. 14682, 20459
Luthuli, A. See Lutuli, A.
Lüthy, H. 2854
Lutuli, A. 2537
Lutwama, J.S.W. 19416
Lux, A. 14452, 15514
Luxembourg, R. 7153
Luxmoore, H.B. 5700
Ly, A. 2855, 7838, 8616-7, 9682
Lyall, C.E. 6598
Lyautey, L.H.G. 2856
Lynch, H.R. 7613, 7839, 9868
Lynden, B.H.de 12590
Lyne, R.N. 1927, 2167, 2857, 17562, 18101, 23710
Lynes, H. 6089
Lynn, C.W. 199
Lyon, E. 12564, 12629
Lyons, C.P. 17823

Lystad, M.H. 10168, 10855
Lystad, R.A. 4595
Lyth, R.E. 6498

M., A. 3968
M., A.F. 18543
M., E.A. 23811, 24000, 24033
M., G. 1309, 2538, 14453, 15243, 23515
M., H.B. 20164-5
M., J.P. 18544
M., L. 14683, 14716
M., L.C. 200
M., M. 4596
M., Q. 1310, 1583, 2168, 6666, 9492, 16654, 17042
M., V. 14032, 15393, 15515, 17456
M., Z. 14531
Maas, A. 18611
Maass, M. 18400
Mabbutt, J.A. 19640, 22017-8
Mabille, A. 21586
Mabille, G. 4597
Mabille, G.A. 22996
Mabogunje, A.L. 11550-3, 11671, 12155, 12477-9
Mabona, A. 4103, 4598-9
Mabona, M. 3969, 21914, 22857
McAdam, J. 20275, 20373
McAdam, K.J. 19011
McAdams, D. 201
McAdams, L.J. 19996
Macalister, A. 5181, 21913
MacAlpine, A.G. 19997, 23768
Macaluso-Aleo, G. 2858
McArdle, T.D. 8087
Macaulay, B. 3724, 10718
McAuslan, J.P.W.B. 16383
McAuslan, P. 2539
Macbeath, A. 601, 14033
MacBride, D.F.H. 11554
McCall, A.G. 6003
McCall, D.F. 7840
McCallien, W.J. 8419, 23046
McCallum, D. 18545
McClellan, F.C. 17675
McConnell, R.E. 18737
MacCrindle, A.M. 22411, 23193-4
Maccrone, I.D. 19597, 23190
MacCullah, A.A. 22768, 23191
McCulloch, M. 19851
MacCurdy, G.G. 21005
MacDermot, T.W.L. 22617
MacDiarmid, D.N. 5701-3, 6330
MacDiarmid, P.A. 6330
Macdona, B.F. 34, 2540, 15895
Macdonald, D. 19774
Macdonald, G. 4169, 7651
Macdonald, J. 19598-9

Macdonald, J.D. 6499
Macdonald, J.R.L. 15808
McDonald, L.J. 20249, 21356
McDonald, R. 21173
Macdonald, R.K. 12213
Macdonald, W.W. 19469
MacDonnell, R.G. 7841
McDougall, R.S. 9830
McDowell, C.M. 12157
McEntee, P.D. 17190
McEwan, P.J.M. 20854-6
McEwen, A.C. 24673
McEwen, W. 12482
McFarlane, J. 5225
McFarquhar, A.M.M. 1584
McFie, J. 19012
Macfie, J.W.S. 11428
MacGaffey, W. 6599
McGlade, C. 10264
McGlashan, N. 17255
Macgregor, A.M. 20808
Macgregor, B.D. 11095
McGregor, F. 23192
McGregor, I.A. 9697
Macgregor, J.J. 1311
Macgregor, J.K. 3970, 12226
MacGregor, W. 11555
Machado, P. 23769, 24073
Machado, R.de S. 7842
Macharangwada 19998
McHardy, C. 10169
McHarg, J. 932, 20166
McHugh, R. 2541
McIlwraith, M. 5273
Macinnes, C. 4600
Macintosh, E.H. 5704, 6500
McIntyre, D. 22618-9, 24319
McIntyre, W.D. 10542, 11854
Maciver, D. 5136
MacIver, D.R. See Randall-MacIver, D.
Macjajah, N.O.M. 12071
Mackarness, F. 22620
McKay, D.V. 6827
Mackay, H.D. 11989
Mackay, J.H. 10918, 12328
Mackay, M. 5274, 11289-91, 12568
McKay, V. 2169
Mackay, W. 24674
McKee, H.K. 21100
McKenna, J.C. 1738
Mackenzie, G.S. 18321
Mackenzie, J. 21712, 22621-3
Mackenzie, J.K. 13742
Mackenzie, K. 23195
Mackenzie, M.D. 12591
Mackenzie, N.H. 22624

Mackenzie, P.Z. 6239-40, 6501
Mackenzie, R.F. 12329
Mackenzie, W.F. 20707
Mackenzie, W.J.M. 2170, 18183
Mackintosh, J.P. 11672-3, 11855
Mackrell, J.E.C. 6384
McLaren, C.A. 10423
Maclaren, J.F.P. 5705, 6388, 6502
Maclaren, P.I.R. 7500, 11556, 10919-20, 12330-4
Maclatchy, A. 13704
Maclean 22943
McLean, J. 22162
Maclean, U. 12072
McLean, W.H. 1312
MacLeay, K.N.G. 6503-6
McLeod, A.N. 6642
MacLeod, J.M. 933, 7336
Macleod, M.N. 1928
McLoughlin, P.F.M. 1585-6, 6004-6, 6600-1
MacLure, H.L. 9917, 9943
McMaster, D.N. 18102, 18643, 19070, 19259
McMaster, E. 22269
MacMichael, H.A. 5904, 5706-12, 6090, 6241, 6331, 6602-3
Macmillan, H. 2542
Macmillan, W.M. 1739, 4601, 20857, 21585, 22270, 22412, 23196
McPetrie, J.C. 3725
Macphail, J.G.S. 5713
MacPherson, F. 21456
MacPherson, M. 19004
Macpherson, R. 17622
Macquarie, C. 17824
Macquarrie, J.W. 22240
MacRae, D.G. 4602
Macrae, F.B. 20930-1, 21006
Macrae, T.M. 10780
McVeigh, M. 23516
Macvicar, N. 22995, 23197
McWilliam, M.D. 17339, 17340, 20460
Madaki, P.R. 12073
Madan, A.C. 3156-9, 21160
Madden, J.F. 5714, 6507-12
Maddick, H. 6146
Made, E.H.A. 22858
Madeira Keita, M. See Keita, M.M.
Madeira Leitão, M.I. 24169
Madge, D.S. 8088
Madigan, C.T. 5905
Madumere, A. 11292
Maduro, C. 24001
Maegraith, B.G. 4170-1
Maenardus, O.F.A. 5418
Maes 14034
Maes, F. 14532-5, 15049
Maes, J. 14035-8, 14283, 14816, 15050, 21915
Maes, T. 14284

Maes, V. 14039-40, 15051
Maeyens, L. 14041-2, 14817, 15052-3
Maeyer, F.de 15054
Mafeje, A. 23198
Maffi, Q. 202, 322, 1313, 2171
Mafiamba, P.C. 13277
Mafohla 19600, 19999, 20000-2, 20766
Maga, H. 4603
Magalhães, M.J.de 21266, 23927
Magdalen, M.C. 11506
Maglitto, N. 2543
Magnino, L. 1740-1, 1864, 17055-6, 22163
Maguire, P. 7652
Maguire, R.A.J. 17825, 18466, 20461
Mahala, C. 23517, 24034
Maher, C. 17191
Mahhouk, A. 6007
Mahieu, W.de 15055
Mahjoubi, A. 6828-9
Mahlobo, G.W.K. 21916
Mahoney, F. 9683
Mai, E. 2172
Maignien, R. 9068
Maigret, J. 9090
Maile, M.L. 22997
Maillot, L. 13017, 13680-2
Mailloux, M.L. See Le Mailloux, M.
Maimane, J.A. 22859-60
Maimane, S.A. 22861
Maimo, 'S. 12074-6, 13214
Mainberger, G. 1018
Maingard, J.F. 19836, 21917
Maino, M. 17141, 19775, 21722-4, 21918, 22105, 22769-72
Maio, A.T. See Teixeira Maio, A.
Mair, L.P. 602-3, 1587, 2173-5, 4604-5, 10719, 12480,
    16384, 18738-9, 18972, 19350, 19393, 21267
Maire, L. 438
Maiter, B. 14516
Maitland, W. 23199
Maitre-Devallon, C. 7037
Majasan, J.A. 10877
Makanguile, A. 8967
Makembe, P. 13329
Makone, M. 20462
Makonnen, T. See Haile Selassie I
Maksoud, C. 2176
Makulu, H. 20793
Makumete 20809
Malala, S.N. 20663
Malan, B.D. 755, 22019, 22091
Malan, D.F. 22413
Malan, F.S. 22414
Malandra, A. 18740
Malangatana, V. 24058
Malara, A. 8234-5, 17182
Malavia, H.D. 1314

Malcolm, D.L. 22070
Malcolm, D.McK. 22065, 22862
Malcolm, D.O. 22070
Malcolm, L.W.G. 4606, 11096, 13132-3, 13278, 13330, 13413
Malcolm X 2544
Maldonado Vázquez, E. 7482
Maleche, A.J. 19013-4
Malekebu, B.E. 21295
Malengreau, G. 14347, 14454-5, 14684-7, 15244-7, 15618
Malgras, R.P.D. 8821
Malherbe, E.G. 22241, 23200
Malhomme, J. 7189
Malik, H. 850, 2177, 11293
Malinda, M., pseud. See Bemba, S.
Maling, R.W. 18741, 19470
Malinowski, B. 604-6, 2178
Maliwa, S. 20708
Malmsten, K. 11294
Malonda, M. 13776
Malonga, J. 15167
Malortie 5345
Malowist, M. 2859
Malvezzi, A. 2179
Malvezzi de' Medici, Marquis de 4104
Malzy, P. 8968, 13134-5
Mamadou, S. 9127
Mamet, J. 24332
Mammeri, M. 3440
Man, M.de 15516
Mancini, G. 1315
Mandela, N. 22415
Mandelbrote, J.C. 21799
Mandouze, A. 7073
Manera, G. 934
Manessy, G. 7939-45, 9456
Manga, F.B. 13474
Mangenot, G. 9290
Mangin, G. 3726, 13010
Mangin, T.R.O. 10087
Mangonès, A. 851
Mangwela, B.M. 16327
Manier, J.F. 9174, 9295
Manisi, D.L.P.Y. See Yali-Manisi, D.L.P.
Mann, Dr. 22271
Mann, M.A. 12335-6
Mannah-Kpaka, J.K. 9869
Manning, C.A.W. 22416
Mano, M.M. See Marques Mano, M.
Mansell, G. 7062
Mansergh, N. 2180, 22417-8
Mansfield, E.T. 10543
Manson, P. 4172-4
Mansur 5413, 5434
Mante, K.S. See Saakwa-Mante, K.
Mantran, R. 6830-3, 7111
Many, G. 13054

Manyampala, M.E. 16190
Manyuchi 20858
Maquet, E. 203-4, 15594
Maquet, J. 607
Maquet, J.J. 2545-6, 4607-9, 15517, 15573-4, 15651, 15661, 15777
Maquet, J.N. 14285
Maquet, M. 1742, 14043, 15518
Maquibela, S. 22419
Marais, D. 22420, 22944
Marais, W.D. 23201
Maral, P. 15629
Maran, R. 1049, 3568
Marapara, M. 20003
Marçais, G. 4995
Marçais, P. 4810, 7074
Marcella 7653-4, 10271-5
Marchal, M. 15394
Marchal, P.G. 14044-6, 15321
Marchand, J. 2181
Marchant, S. 4247, 8089, 12269, 12337-46
Marchat, H. 7133, 7390
Marchesseau, G. 13136
Marchovelette, E.d'O.de 14047
Marco, E. 5969
Marconnes, F. 20004, 20573-4
Marcum, J. 2547-8
Marcus, E. 7655
Marcus, H.G. 16763-6
Marcy, G. 7467
Mareca, J.A. 1588
Marealle, P.I. 17826-7
Marealle, T.L.M. 17828
Margach, T.P. 19471
Margai, M. 2549
Margai, M.A.S. 9769, 9985
Margarido, A. 23408
María Francés, J. 15697
María Fúster, J. See Fúster Casas, J.M.
Maria Rosa 12711
Maria Torroja, J. 7408
Mariam, M.W. 16699
Marie, J. See Jean-Marie
Marin, G. 17025
Marin, J. 9493
Marin, J.D. See Diaz Marin, J.
Marinelli, L.A. 12548
Marinov, V. 608
Marinucci, C. 7548
Marke, M.C. 9870
Markov, W. 2860
Marks, S. 22625, 22998
Markwei, M. 9773
Marling, P. 6091, 6242
Marmo, V. 8090
Marnham, J.E. 1317

Marodzi 19736
Marquand, H. 21619
Marquard, L. 22421, 23202-3
Marquer, P. 13584
Marques, B. 12716
Marques, C. 1010, 2182, 23473, 23664
Marques, F. 3972
Marques, J.B. See Basso Marques, J.
Marques, J.E.A.da S. 12889
Marques, M.A.da C. 3973
Marques, M.I.T.M. See Montalvão Marques, M.I.T.
Marques Mano, M. 12737
Marr, F. 20005
Marr, M. 20374, 20859, 21681, 23363
Marriott, H.P. 7549
Marriott, J.W.F. 18879
Marris, P. 12481
Marro, E. 16655, 16891
Mars, J. 4610
Mars, J.P. See Price-Mars, J.
Marsan, E. 7337
Marsden, A. 6834
Marshal, H.W. 21537
Marshall, A.H. 2183
Marshall, C.P. 11557
Marshall, G.A.K. 9163
Marshall, H. 8091-3, 12347
Marshall, J. 10088
Marshall, J.R.N. 11674
Marshall, K. 18880
Marshall, L. 19601-3, 23308-10
Marshall, O.R. 12156
Marshalldavis, F. 3569
Marsland, H. 17676
Marteau, P. 3334-5
Martel, A. 6760, 6781, 6835-8
Martelli, G. 2184, 23518
Marthelot, P. 4790, 6782-3
Marti, M.P. See Palau-Marti, M.
Martin, A.M. See Massia Martin, A.
Martin, A.R.H. 22272
Martin, B.G. 7843, 10544, 11856, 18322
Martin, B.S. See Saez-Martin, B.
Martin, C. 20142, 20167
Martin, D. 13228, 13450
Martin, E.C. 10319, 10545
Martin, F.J. 5464, 6513
Martin, F.M. See Moreno Martin, F.
Martin, H. 8388, 8482, 13137, 23317
Martin, J. 22164
Martin, P. 2550
Martin, R. 13497
Martin, R.P. 9211
Martin de la Escalera, C. 2185, 4949-50, 5097-99, 6796-7, 6839, 7038, 7338, 7270-2
Martindale, C.C. 22999
Martineau, A. 105, 6194, 8206

Martínez, J.S. See Saenz Martínez, J.
Martinez, N. 7190
Martinez Val, J.M. 15729
Martinez y Sanz, J. 15739
Martinho, A. 23409, 23575
Martinho, J. 4286, 23857
Martinho, J.P.P. See Pereira Martinho, J.P.
Martini, G. 5715
Martins, A. 2861
Martins, A.A. 24002
Martins, A.J. 24170
Martins, A.R. 23770
Martins, D. 35
Martins, I. 14818
Martins, J. 14286, 23519
Martins, J.A. 23640
Martins, J.B. 24171
Martins, J.L.R.R. See Rodrigues Martins, J.L.R.
Martins, P.J. 15322
Martins Ba(p)tista, M. 12664, 12841
Martins Meireles, A. 12687, 12887-8
Martins Nunes, D.A. 24172-3
Martins Vaz, J. 4049, 14048
Martonne, E.de 3160, 8209
Martrou 13733
Martucci, G. 1316
Marty, P. 7339, 8439, 8618-23, 9684
Marvin, D.K. 18323
Marvin, F.S. 5329, 23204
Marwick, M.G. 699, 4611-2, 5716, 15809, 20932-4, 21130, 23771
Maryam, A.W. See Alaqâ Walda Maryam
Marzorati, A. 13755, 14688-9, 15248, 15519
Masalu, M.M. 15961
Mascarenhas, J.F. 21836
Masefield, G.B. 439, 2186, 4613-4, 18324, 19260
Mason, A.Y. 22021
Mason, H. 18612
Mason, I. 10320
Mason, K. 24549
Mason, P. 4615, 20238, 20307, 20463-4, 20767, 22422, 23364
Mason, P.F. 11429, 12348-9
Massa, C.A. 8236
Massabie, G. 6734
Massaquoi, M. 12619
Massé, L. 8502, 8758-61
Massei, E. 1318, 7039, 15978, 17341
Masser, F.I. 20308
Massey, R.E. 4855, 5465, 6514-6
Massey, V. 22423
Masseyeff, R. 13427, 13439
Massia Martin, A. 7075
Massigli, R. 2187
Massio, R. 2823
Masson, A. 2862
Masson, H. 4287, 7723, 8576

Masson, P. 8535, 14287
Masson-Detourbet, A. 13251, 13639
Masson-Oursel, P. 2188
Masuka, A.A. 14049
Mata, L.P.da 23955
Matandidwala 20375
Mateene, K. 15168
Matekole, Nene A. 10276
Mateos, J.P. 7461
Mateu, J. 15753
Mateus, A. 12705
Mather, K.G. 18184
Matheson, H. 1589
Mathew, G. 16060, 17964
Mathews, A.B. 11857
Mathews, A.T. 6033
Mathews, H.F. 11098
Mathewson, R.W. 10170
Mathijsen, H. 14050
Mathot, R.E. 15395
Matilla, V. 4175-6, 15754-5
Matip, B. 2863, 8237, 13379
Matos, C.de 23711
Matson, A.T. 18325, 18742, 19261-4, 19534
Matson, J.N. 10089, 10546-7
Mattei, M. 24374, 24411, 24484
Matteis, V.de 7218
Matteotti, C. 1319
Matthew, J.G. 6604
Matthews, D.H. 24675
Matthews, J. 3441, 22424, 22863-4
Matthews, J.B. 20006-7
Matthews, J.H. 10646
Matthews, Z.K. 2189, 3974, 21919, 22242, 22425, 23205-6
Matz, D.E. 12630
Mauch, K. 20008
Maud, D. 23207
Maud, J. 21620
Maugham, R.C.F. 9652
Maund, E.A. 20575
Maunick, E. 12077, 24329-30
Mauny, R. 36, 205-6, 610, 756-8, 2864-6, 4616, 4856-7,
   4996, 5078, 7589-93, 7597, 7844-8, 8009, 8094, 8200-2,
   8297, 8397, 8401-5, 8408, 8420, 8440, 8523, 8528-30,
   8863-5, 8872-3, 9031, 9329, 9624, 9631, 10171, 10548,
   11858, 13526
Maupoil, B. 9041, 9494, 9569
Maurice, A. 14288, 14819
Maurice, G.K. 6517-8
Maurice, M. 17829-33
Maury, J. 14456, 14577-81, 18029
Maus, A. 14536
Mavungu, A. 13759
Maw, A.H. 21357
Maw, J. 16191
Mawer, R.K. See Knox-Mawer, R.

Mawhood, P.N.   18185
Maxwell, H.G.W.   See Wedderburn-Maxwell, H.G.
Maxwell, I.C.M.   7697
Maxwell, J.   10549, 21101
Maxwell, W.A.   21358
Maxwell-Darling, R.C.   6459-60, 6519
Maxwell-Lefroy, H.   1590
May, S.   1320
Mayanja, A.M.K.   19265
Maydon, J.G.   22626
Mayer, I.   17256, 17598
Mayer, J.   3161, 3336
Mayer, P.   4617, 17257-9, 17598, 23208
Mayhew, A.   1743
Maylon, B.H.   22165
Mayr, J.   3162
Mayssal, H.   13380
Mazen, L.   8264
Mazère, J.   13616
Mazery, A.des   14820
Mazrui, A.   37, 1321, 2551, 5275, 6147, 14821, 17526, 18186
Mazula, A.J.   14822, 24074
Mazza, C.   852
Mbabazane   20576
Mbaga, K.   18401
Mbambalwa, A.   15148
Mbee, G.   17834
Mbida, D.E.   13381
M'biti, J.S.   3570, 17148, 17563, 17576, 17577, 17623
Mbiye, B.   14051, 14289
Mbizo   20009-10, 20577
Mbizwo   20672
Mbofana, P.W.G.   20578
Mboya, T.   1591, 2552, 17342, 17457-9
Mc...See Mac...
Mdee, A.M.   17835
Mdiya, W.W.   21920
Mead, M.   1322-3, 10090
Meade, H.M.T.   611, 20794, 21921
Meade-Fetherstonhaugh, A., later Lady Cecil and Lady Rockley.
   See Rockley, Lady
Meakin, J.E.B.   7177
Mededji, C.   3571-2
Medhin, T.G.   See Gabre-Medhin, T.
Medici, Marquis de M.de'.   See Malvezzi de' Medici, Marquis de
Medina, M.A.   See Alía Medina, M.
Medrano Ezquerra, C.   7340
Meek, C.I.   18187-8
Meek, C.K.   1592-3, 3727, 7849, 11099, 11100-3, 11859, 11990, [12158-9
Meeo, J.F.de   4359
Meer, F.   22426, 23209
Meerhaeghe, M.van   14457-9
Meeussen, A.E.   106, 3163-9, 7946, 14052, 14894, 15056-65,
   15169, 15639, 16100, 19351-2, 19776, 21161, 21168, 21648,
   21751
Meier, G.M.   1324

Meijs, L. 21592
Meillassoux, C. 1325, 8866, 9092, 9236, 9660
Meillon, B.de 4177
Meinardus, O.F.A. 16767-8
Meinhof, C. 274-5, 279, 302, 314, 318, 996, 3170-83, 3728, 6332-5, 12967, 13331, 16101, 16328, 18402, 19777-8, 21922, 22773-5
Meinhof, H. 5041
Meinhof, K. 3729
Meira, L.V.de 12818
Meira e Cruz, J.H. 186, 24134, 24174
Meireles, A.M.(de). See Martins Meireles, A.
Mekeel, H.S. 12528, 12569
Melady, T.P. 3975
Meldon, J.A. 4811, 16102, 18743-5
Mell, A.H. 21268
Mella, J. 23458
Mellado, I.R. See Rodríguez Mellado, I.
Melland, F. 1326, 2867, 4618, 16443, 17836, 20376, 20935, 21077, 21131
Melliss, J.C. 24688
Mellor, J.E.M. 6520-3
Melly, J.M. 16769
Melo, J.M.de S. See Sousa Melo, J.M.de
Melon, A. 2863, 2868
Melone, T. 3337
Melville, A.R. 15783
Melville Jones, F. (Bishop of Lagos) 7517, 8008
Melzian, H.J. 12968
Memel-Foté, H. 4619
Memerty, W.von 20771
Memmi, A. 4620
Menage, C. 8367
Mendelssohn, S. 19604, 21923
Mendes, F.A. 12688
Mendes, F.F. 2870
Mendes, J.M. 23490
Mendes, M.J.F. See Ferreira Mendes, M.J.
Mendes, V.M.da C. 24288
Mendes Correa, A.A. 184, 612
Mendès-France, P. 1328
Mendiaux, E. 14460, 14823
Mendonca, P.C.de 12717, 12890
Menendez Garcia, N. 7724
Menendez Pidal, R. 2871
Mengrelis, T. 8822, 9005-7, 9113, 9128-9
Ménier, M.A. 13547, 13657
Menjaud, H. 9414
Mennesson-Rigaud, O. 613
Menor, J.G. 15757-8
Mensah, A.A. 10172, 10768
Mensah, A.W.K. See Kayper-Mensah, A.W.
Mensah, M. 9476
Mensah-Kane, J.J. 9998
Menyharth, L. 20795
Menzies, I.R. 18746, 19071

Mercator 1329, 7656, 10277-8, 12549, 16656
Mercer, T.M.K. 10425
Mercier, P. 1041, 1744, 2872, 4621-3, 8190, 8371, 8539, 8762-4, 9323, 9495-7, 9530, 9593, 9613-5
Meredith, L.C. 20011
Méric, E. 8425
Meriggi, P. 22776
Merino, A.S. See Santos Merino, A.
Merino, M.M. 2873
Merlin, A.J. See Jambu-Merlin, A.
Merlo, C. 9499-9500
Merlo, M. 24550
Mernier, P. 15520
Merrett, W.E.S. 12350
Merriam, A.P. 935-7, 14053, 14290-2, 15595
Merrick, G. 7947, 11104, 11991
Merrill, W. 5717
Mersadier, Y. 8546-7
Mertens, J. 14054-5, 15249
Mertens, V. 14056-7
Merton, A. 5276-8
Merwe, D.F.v.d. 19799, 20579
Merwe, W.J. 20012
Merwin, U.S. 23463
Messenger, J.C. 11295, 12160, 12214
Messia, J.Y. See Yanguas Messia, J.
Messing, S.D. 16657
Messud, G. 7040, 7076
Mestral, C.de 3976-7, 14824
Metcalfe, F. 11675
Metcalfe, G.E. 10550, 11860
Metcalfe, M. 21269, 21309
Mettam, R.W.M. 4178, 19472
Meunié, D.J. See Jacques-Meunié, D.
Meyer, E. 291, 3184, 13138, 13332-4, 15112, 21490
Meyer, E.de 15396
Meyer, E.K. See Kähler-Meyer, E.
Meyer, H. 18103
Meyer, L.M. 8191
Meyer, O.B. 24551
Meyerhof, M. 5421
Meyerowitz, E.L.R. 6148, 10091-3, 10173, 10551-4, 11296
Meyerowitz, H.V. 8159, 21606
Meyers, B.D. 2553
Meylemans, M. 14293
Meyler, H.M. 19605
Meyzonnade 24485
Mezza, E. 4624, 16011
Mfomo, G. 13054
Mhina, J.E.F. 18546
Mhlahlo 20580
Mhlanga, W. 20581
Micaia, M., pseud. See Santos, M.dos
Michael, G.I. 24676
Michalowski, K. 5346
Michel, A. 7154

Michel, C. 6194
Michel, J.C. 3978
Michell, G.B. 4812, 5042
Michell, L. 19737
Michelman, F. 3338
Michelmore, A.P.G. 6400
Michie, C.W. 8266
Mickleburgh, R. 938
Middleton, J. 18326, 18747-52, 19149-50, 19405, 19535
Middleton, R. 5182
Middleton, W.L. 4997, 6840, 7077-9
Miege, J. 9271
Miette, R. 6979, 7041-3
Migeod, F.W.H. 614-5, 7850-1, 9809, 10094, 10356, 10555, 11105, 12620, 12950, 13236, 15066, 17965
Mikaël, K. See Kebbédé Mikaël
Mikesell, M.W. 7219
Milbourne, A.H. 7657
Milburn, S. 11106
Mildenberger, K.W. 38
Miles, A.C. 10556
Miletto 13705
Milford, T.R. 12972
Milhaud, M. 1330
Mill Hill Fathers 19353
Millar, A.K. 22022
Mille, P. 8586
Miller, A. 3443
Miller, A.E. 22627
Miller, A.M. 21770
Miller, C.B. 13734
Miller, D. 19845, 22165
Miller, E.H. 20582
Miller, F.V.B. 21132
Miller, G.M. 22865
Miller, J.D.B. 22427
Miller, K. 1745, 4625
Miller, N.N. 18189
Miller, N.S. 11430, 11861
Miller, R. 2190, 5466
Miller, R.G. 18753
Miller, T.B. 5347
Miller, W. 23210
Miller, W.J. 11507
Miller, W.R. 4094
Milleron, J. 7220
Milliken, M. 11431
Millin, S.G. 4626, 22096
Milliot, L. 7080
Millman, W. 1746, 14058
Millot, J. 24375, 24486
Millous, P. 8095, 13440
Mills, M.G. 20583
Mills, W.G. 8096-7
Mills, W.L. 5718
Millward, G.R. 5719, 6524

Milne, G. 15810
Milne, J. 22102
Milner, Lord 2874
Milner, A. 12161-2
Milverton, Lord 2191, 11862
Minchin, E.A. 4179, 8098
Minervo, O.M. See Mueller-Minervo, O.
Mingoni, G. 4180-1, 4627
Minne, J. 3573
Miquel, A. 16582, 16590
Miracle, M.P. 1331, 2875, 4628, 7851, 12926, 20936, 21029-30
Miralai el-Magboul el-Amin el-Hag. See Hag, M.el-M.el-A.el-
Miranda, M.dos R. 24075
Miranda Santos, A. 2192, 2554, 3979-82, 4629-31, 15654
Mire, P.L. See Le Mire, P.
Mirot, L. 5348
Mischel, F. 616
Mischlich, A. 6401, 7852
Misipo, D. 2876
Miskin, A.B. 6149, 6385
Miskin, I. 17192
Mitchell, A.J. 18547
Mitchell, B.L. 21538-9
Mitchell, J.C. 1594, 4632-3, 20013, 20924, 21031-2, 21234-9, 21252, 21270-3, 21431, 21505
Mitchell, P. 618, 2193
Mitchell, P.E. 617, 19151
Mitchell, P.K. 9810-1, 9871
Mitchell, T.F. 6694
Mitchell-Heggs, M. 21102
Mitchison, N. 21705
Mitchley, A.O.R. 21188
Mitford, B.R. 6243
Mitra, A. 2555
Mittelberger, C. 23410, 23576
Mittwoch, E. 16892
Mjele 20810
Mkapa, B.W. 3339, 18048
Mkele, N. 23000
Mkwawa, S.N. 16329
Mntambo, P.C. 4634, 17666
Mnyampala, M.E. 15851, 15853, 16330-4
Moal, G.le 8372, 9415, 9466, 10856
Mockler-Ferryman, A.F. 11676, 19406
Modisane, B. 3340, 22866
Modisane, W. See Modisane, B.
Moeller, A. 12592, 14690, 15521-3, 15250
Moeller de Laddersous, A. 2194, 14444
Moerman, J. 1657, 1747-53
Moffat, A.L. 1332
Moffat, J.S. 23211
Moffat, R.L. 21189
Moffett, J.P. 18104-5, 18467, 18548-9, 18613
Moffitt, F.W. 4998
Mogg, E.H. 22167

Moggridge, L.T. 21274
Mohamadou, E. 13031, 13139, 13279-80, 13335
Mohamed, etc. See also Muhammad
Mohamed, A. See Ahmed Mohamed
Mohamed, A.R. 18190
Mohamed, A.S. See Ali Shcikh Mohamed
Mohamed, I. See Ibrahim Mohamed
Mohamed Farah Siad 17043, 17088
Mohamed Hassan el Zayyat 17089
Mohammad ibn Azzuz Haquim 7161, 7178, 7191, 7221, 7273-5, 7341, 7368, 7410, 7424-7
Mohammed Abdullah Gobal 6525
Mohammed Dib 7122
Mohammedi, A.A. 16335
Mohamoud Abdi Hirad 17174
Mohamud, M.Y. 17175
Mohamud, S.M. 17090
Mohamud Yusuf Aden Muro 17044
Moid, S.A. 10878
Moine, J. 24677-8
Moir, T.R.G. 5467
Moissenet, P. 6913
Moity, M. 9008
Mokeba, M.P.M. See Mukoko-Mokeba, M.P.
Mokhtar O.Hamidoun. See Hamidoun, M.O.
Mokwile, J. 20860
Mol, P.D.van 14059
Molard, J.R. See Richard-Molard, J.
Molema, S.M. 22429
Molet, L. 14060-1, 24366, 24376-7, 24487, 24634-6
Molignoni, G. 16770
Molina Arrabal, J. 15698-9
Moliner, R.R. See Romero Moliner, R.
Molinier, L. 20937
Möller, C.F. See Frimodt-Möller, C.
Möller, M. 14062
Moller, M.S.G. 17837
Molohan, M.J.B. 18191
Molteno, P.A. 22628
Momah, C.C. 10879
Momo, F. 9131
Monard, A. 8736
Monceaux, R.H. 8099
Monchicourt, C. 6841-3
Monckton, J.C. 11107
Mondain, G. 24378, 24488, 24513-5
Mondain, J. 24650
Mondjannagni, A. 9570
Mondlane, E.C. 24004-5
Mongo Beti. See Beti, M.
Moniot, H. 2877-8
Monís, C.L. See López-Monís, C.
Monneret de Villard, U. 16512, 16591-2, 17034
Monnier, L. 24605-6
Mönnig, H.O. 21924-5, 22629

Monod, T. 39, 1068-9, 1333, 1929-30, 2879, 4106-7, 4288-9,
    4360-1, 4858-9, 4930-2, 5079, 5110, 7594-7, 7621, 7853-4,
    8100-3, 8177, 8203, 8210, 8352, 8421, 8469-71, 8624, 8635,
    8737-41, 8752, 8882, 8936, 9041, 9164, 9272, 9291, 12254,
    23047
Monsabert, de 4999
Monson, C.J. 17193
Montagne, R. 2195, 3983, 4951-2, 5000, 7044, 7112, 7222,
    7276-7, 7342, 7428, 11677
Montagu, M.F.A. See Ashley Montagu, M.F.
Montague, F.A. 18192-3
Montague-Stuart-Wortley, E.J. 6244
Montaigu, G. 1334
Montalvão Marques, M.I.T. 24059
Monteil, C. 7552-3, 8160, 8909
Monteil, J. 1335
Monteil, V. 293, 1931, 3002, 3185-6, 4091, 5001, 8161, 8192,
    8389, 11508
Monteilhet, J. 8625
Monteiro, A. 2880
Monteiro, A.A.V. 23957
Monteiro, A.J.P. 23641
Monteiro, J.J. 23411
Monteith, W.N. 5720
Montenegro, J.P. 3187
Montenegro, M.da S. 23642
Montereale, A.di. See Alliata di Montereale
Montero Díaz, S. 2881
Montéty, H.de 6778
Montevecchi, A. 23212
Monteyne, L. 3610, 14294, 15170-3
Monteyne, R. 14301, 15323
Montez, C. 853
Moody, R. 854, 2196, 17343, 18973, 19394
Moolman, J.H. 22273
Moore, C.H. 8426
Moore, F.J. 11678
Moore, G. 323, 619, 3341-7, 7980, 8309, 10677, 12078,
    13382, 19266, 23213
Moore, H.F. 440
Moore, R., pseud. See Rive, R.
Moore, R.J.B. 20938-9, 21033-6, 21103
Moore, W.H. 22428
Moorsel, H.van 14295
Moraes, F. 2556
Moraini, O. 6629
Morais, A.T.de 23643-5
Morais, E. 4636, 23577, 24035
Morais, Tito de 4182, 24175-81, 24250
Morais, Trigo de. See Trigo de Morais
Morais Trigo, A.B. 12762
Moral, D. 2882
Morales, R.R. See Reyes Morales, R.
Morales Oliver, L. 2883, 3354, 3984, 5002
Moran, W.E. 1336
Morant, A. 13414

Mordini, A. 4860, 16593-16604
Moreau, J. 20940
Moreau, P. 6964
Moreau, R.E. 17838
Moreira, A. 2197-8, 3730, 4637, 12745-6
Moreira, E. 2199, 19800
Moreira, J.M. 7554, 12891
Moreira Candelária, M. 3985
Moreira da Silva, M. 2200
Moreira Rato, J. 23671, 23713, 23823, 23858
Morel, E.D. 2201, 2884, 8279, 14691, 14825-6
Morel, J. 7016
Moreno, J.A.M. 15676, 15730-1
Moreno, M.M. 16771, 16893-7, 17142
Moreno Martin, F. 4183
Morenz, S. 5419
Morere, M. 7391
Morewood-Dowsett, J. 4290, 4354, 5003
Morgado, R. 24182, 24287
Morgan, A.E. 1932
Morgan, A.R. 18974
Morgan, B.H. 2885, 22630
Morgan, D. 1865
Morgan, G.D. 2557, 15941
Morgan, J.C. 17966-7
Morgan, J.T. 1337
Morgan, L. 12631
Morgan, P.R. 18109
Morgan, R.W. 12483
Morgan, W.B. 7501, 11432, 11558-62
Morgan-Davies, A.M. 18557
Morgantini, A.M. 17091
Mori, F. 4861
Morin, J.V. 4638
Morison, C.G.T. 5812
Morison, T. 17841
Morisseau-Leroy, F. 939
Morizot, J. 7081
Morkel, E.R. 20014-6, 20465
Morlighem, H. 13958
Mormino, G. 5183
Moro, N.B. 5004
Morojole, L.C. 21655
Morrice, H.A. 6008-9
Morrill, J.L. 1863
Morris, B. 21540-1
Morris, H.F. 18754-5, 18881, 19267-8, 19354-5, 19372, 19395-7
Morris, H.S. 15811
Morris, R.M. 20811
Morris, S.E. 19693, 20664
Morris, T.D.H. 18756
Morrison, A.F. 18558
Morrison, C.M. 10818-9
Morrow, J.J. 346
Mors, P.O. 18644, 18757-8
Morse, D.A. 1338

Mortelmans, G.   287, 14201, 14296-9, 14300, 15323
Morten, I.H.   19865, 20309
Mortier, R.   14063-5, 14827, 15067-8
Mortimer, M.   2558, 11679
Morton, M.A.   11433
Morton-Williams, P.   7855, 10110, 11108-10, 11195, 11680, 12484-5, 12512
Mortti, G.A.   See Adali-Mortti, G.
Moser, E.   10831
Moser, G.M.   3348
Moses, M.   19269
Mosher, N.W.   1339
Mosley, J.S.   10678
Moss, R.P.   1933, 11562
Mostaza, B.   2202, 2559, 13777
Mostyn, J.P.   5721
Mota, A.T.da.   See Teixeira da Mota, A.
Mota, M.   5005
Mottoule   15397
Mottram, B.H.   19072
Motyka, J.   9149
Mouasso-Priso, F.   13383
Moubray, J.M.   441
Mouchet, J.   5043, 13140-5, 13336-8, 13415, 13441-2, 13557-8
Moulaert, G.   14461, 14537, 14692, 14828-30
Moulaert, J.   14462
Mouleres, G.   9586
Moulero, T.   9501, 9571-2
Moulinard   13498
Moumouni, A.   4362
Mounier, E.   4639
Mountmorres, Viscount   7856
Moura, J.D.de   23646
Mouradian, J.   9918
Mourant, A.E.   620
Mousley, E.   2197
Mousley, J.C.   21240
Moussi, E.E.   621
Mouta, F.   759, 23437, 23450-1
Moutinho, A.de S.   23812, 24006
Moyal, M.   4898
Moyo, P.H.   20861
Moys, E.M.   10880
Mphahlele, E.   3349-52, 3444, 4640-1, 11509, 12486, 22430-1, 22867-70
Mpologoma, F.   16444
Mpongo, D.S.   20466
Mpuzarima   20017
Mqotsi, L.   23000
Msiteli   19846
Mtandika, A.J.   16336
Mtawa, A.B.M.   17842
Mtekteka, J.   17843
Mtepuka, E.M.   20467
Mtila, M.M.   16337
M'timkulu, D.G.S.   3986, 22243

Mubitana, M. 21162
Muchangwe, I.M. 21240
Mueller, E.W. See Müller, E.W.
Mueller-Minervo, O. 6645, 6773
Mugalula-Mukiibi, A.A. 19416
Muhammad. See also Mohamed, Mohammad, Mohammed, Mohamoud, Mohamud
Muhammad, H.N.A.N. See Noor Muhammad, H.N.A.
Muhammad, I. See Ibrahim Mohamed
Muhammad Bello, Emir of Sokoto 7857
Mühl, J. 6735
Muhlanga, S. 20584-5
Muir, E. 4184
Mukarovsky, H. 8649
Mukasa, D.K. 3987
Mukasa, E.W.S. 19270-1
Mukasa, H. 19152-3, 19274
Mukasa, S.K.B. 18759
Mukherjee, S.N. 40
Mukhtar O.Hamidoun. See Hamidoun, M.O.
Mukiibi, A.A.M. See Mugalula-Mukiibi, A.A.
Mukoko-Mokeba, M.P. 13146, 13215, 13252
Mukwereza, E. 20709
Mulago, V. 3988
Mulhacen, Marqués del 4363, 5349
Mulhall, H. 11078
Mulhall, M.G. 2886, 5226
Mulira, E.M.K. 19015
Müllendorff, P. 13216
Mullens, J. 24379
Müller, E.W. 14066, 15524
Muller, H.E.H. 22432
Muller, P.J. 22777
Muller, S. 3616, 23214
Müller-Minervo, O. See Mueller-Minervo, O.
Mumford, W.B. 622, 1754-5, 4642, 15896, 15942, 17844, 18049-50, 22244
Munanairi, C. 1756
Munday, J.T. 14067, 20941-4, 21163, 21190, 21200
Munday, M.C. 20812
Mungati, J. 20710
Munger, E.S. 10279, 17384, 22433
Mungonya, Z.C.K. 19275
Mungul-Diaka, B. 15525
Muñido, F.F.O. See Olesa Muñido, F.F.
Muñiz, A. 7456
Muñoz, L.H. See Herrero Muñoz, L.
Munro, P. 5722
Munyai 20768
Murabet, M. 6695
Murashiki, A.M. 2887
Muratori, C. 5723, 6245-6, 6336, 19356
Muraz, G. 12981, 13018
Murcier, J.P. 3731
Murdock, G.P. 1934
Murè, G. 1340

Muro, M.Y.A. See Mohamud Yusuf Aden Muro
Murombo 20377
Murray, A.H. 10426, 22631
Murray, A.V. 1757, 12215, 19662
Murray, G.S. 20018
Murray, G.W. 5137, 6337-8
Murray, H.D. 7598
Murray, J. 22434
Murray, J.P. 21104
Murray, K.C. 885, 7599, 11111-2, 11297-9, 11300-3, 11863-4
Murray, N.L. 22023
Murray, R.N. 1866
Murray, S.S. 1341
Murray, W.A. 6339
Murumbi, J. 15897
Musad, M.M. 6247
Musgrove, F. 1758, 15943, 19016-8, 19073
Mushanga, M. 19373
Mushoma 20019
Muskett, J. 22632
Mussett, A.E. 4364
Mussio, G. 1935, 2888
Mustafa, B.M. 6150
Mustafa al-Aliel 4123
Mustafa bin Kisi bin Hamadi Imutafi 16338
Mustapha, T.M. 10857
Mustoe, K.W.L. 17460
Mustoe, N.E. 16772
Muthuon, R.P.J. 24607-10, 24432-5
Mutiga, J.G. 3445, 19374
Mutwakil, H. 6526
Mva, J.L.D. See Dongmo-Mva, J.L.
Mveng, E. 260, 856-7, 3003, 13193
Mvusi, S. 22871
Mwalilino, K. 21500
Mwenda, E.A. 16339
Mwene Karolo Ilonga II bin Sasawata
Mwenya, A.H. 20945
Mwindadi, J. 16340
Myburgh, C.A.L. 20268
Myers, C.S. 5138-40, 5828
Myers, J.M.B. See Bruce-Myers, J.M.
Myers, O.H. 5906-7, 11113, 11304
Mynors, T.H.B. 5611, 5724-5, 5960, 6034
Myrdal, G. 1342-3
Myres, J.L. 7017

N. 7278
N., J. 2204
N., P. 1595
N., W.H.H. 20022
Nade, A.M. 7981
Nadel, S.F. 623, 3732, 5726-8, 6402-3, 11114-9, 16966
Naemen, L.van 14831
Naessens, H. 14068

Naga, P. 2889
Nagenda, J. 19375-6
Nager, O.A.el- 11865
Naidoo, H.A. 4643
Naidoo, S.R. 22168
Naigiziki, S. 15651
Nair, P. See Pyarelal, pseud.
Naish, M.E. 12163
Nájera y Angulo, F. 1596
Nakene, G. 22778
Nalder, L.F. 5729-31, 6158, 6404
Naldoni, N. 2205, 4953
Namonde, T. 21338
Nana, S.J. 11563
Nansubaga, G. 19416
Napolitano, G. 1344-5
Nardin, J.C. 12593
Nasi, G. 14582
Nāsir, J.'A.al-. See Nasser, G.A.
Nason, C.S. 18760
Nasri, A.R.el- 5440
Nassau, R.H. 624
Nasser, G.A. 5350
Nassir, A., also called A.N.b.J.Bhalo. See Bhalo, A.N.J.
Nataf, A. 5100
Nathan, M. 1037, 10557-8, 10612
Native Affairs Department (Economic Development) 20310, 23247
Nauwelaert, P. 14069
Nava, J.N. See Nosti Nava, J.
Navarro Soeiro, A. 24183-4, 24248-50, 24295
Naville, E. 5184-5
Naville, P. 1597, 2206, 2560, 2890, 4644-5
Nawar, A. 5240-1
Nawar, G. 5422-3
Nayak, S. 11681, 23336-8
Nazareth, J.M. 17461
Nchami, V.C. 12079
Ncube, R.M.M. 20586
Ndanema, I. 9748, 9944
Ndau 20020
Ndegwa, P. 1346-7, 15868, 15898-9
Ndembe, D. 15065
Ndhlovu, S. See Sikobole Ndhlovu
N'dintsouna, F. See Sengat-Kuo, F.
Nditsouna, F. See Sengat-Kuo, F.
Ndongmo, A. 13223
Ndu, P.N. 12080-2
Ndumbu, J.M.G. 17564
Neal, E.E. 7698
Neame, L.E. 22100, 22435-6, 22633
Needham, R. 17260
Neesen, V. 4646, 15662-3
Négrier, Gen.de 22634
Neher, G. 11120, 11305
Nehru, J. 2207, 2561
Neill, S. 3989
Neisser, C.S. 11510

Neiva, A.T. 3990
Nekes, P.H. 13339
Nel, M.D.C.de W. 22437
Nelson, F.B. 15933, 15944, 16445
Nelson, J.W. 20946
Nenekhaly-Camara, C. 1283, 2150, 2891, 4642, 9024, 9130, 13527
Nenquin, J. 760-1, 858, 14202-3
Neogy, R. 3446-7, 17299
Nerfin, M. 4648
Nesham, W.T. 20311
Ness, P. 11564, 15900
Neto, A. 23578-9
Neto, J.B.N.P. See Pereira Neto, J.B.N.
Nettelton, G.E. 21713
Netting, R.M. 11434
Nettl, B. 9324
Neuk, D. 20021, 20587
Neumann, H. 2208
Neves, A. 23859
Neves, A.de S. See Sousa Neves, A.de
Neves, C.M.B. 12842-3
Neves, J.B. 12665
Neves, M.J.G.V. See Ventim Neves, M.J.G.
Neves, P.C. 23609
Neveu, C.A.le 5006
Neville, G.W. 7658, 11356
Newberry, R.J. 11121-2
Newbold, D. 4877, 5908-9, 6092-4, 6151, 6248, 6340, 6527-9, 6605
Newbury, C.C. 9574
Newbury, C.W. 7858-9, 8280-1, 9575
Newlands, H.S. 10174, 10233
Newlyn, W.T. 1348-9
Newman, E.W.P. 2892, 5007, 5227, 5279, 5351-4, 16012, 16773, 17005
Newman, P. 11992-3, 15901
Newman, P.K. 15902
Newns, F. 9963
Newton, A.P. 2893
Newton, R. 12351, 13443
Newton, T.C. 12352
Nfoulou, J. 3991
Ngande, C. 13384-7
Ng'andu, L.H. 20947
Ngango, G. 4649-50
Ngani, A.Z. 22779
Ngare, N. 16341
Ngatho, Z. 17652
Ngcobo, S.B. 22169-70
Ngengi, K., later: J.Kenyatta. See Kenyatta, J.
Ngidi, J. 22766
Ngoi, P. 14070, 15398
N'gom-N'goudi, P. 1350-1
N'goma, A. 4096
Ngonyama, S. 20339

N'goudi, P.N. See N'gom-N'goudi, P.
Ngubane, J.K. 22438
Ngubane, S.S. 20168, 22024
Ngugi, J.T. 3353, 17578
Nhlapo, J.M. 22635
Niane, D.T. 8310, 8910, 9043, 9093
Niang, L. 8673
Niangoran-Bouah, G. 9212-4
Niani, D.T. See Niane, D.T.
Nicaise, J. 14463-70, 14693-5, 15251-4, 15526-8, 15600
Nichol, E.P. 9964
Nicholas, W.B. 11682
Nicholls, E.G.L. 21105
Nicholls, G.H. 1352, 19685, 22439
Nicholls, L. 20711
Nicholls, W. 5468, 5732
Nicholson, H.A. 6341
Nicholson, H.B. 6249
Nicholson, M. 1759, 11683
Nicholson, R. 1050
Nicholson, W.E. 11123
Nickels, A. 8010
Nicklès, M. 13444, 13457
Nicol, A. See Nicol, D.
Nicol, D. (A.Nicol) 2562, 4651, 7699, 7725, 7860, 7982-3,
    9926, 11505, 12083, 12353-4
Nicol, J.M. 7502
Nicolas, A. 9242
Nicolas, F. 6992, 9661
Nicolas, F.J. 940, 8441, 9416-7, 9457-8
Nicolas, J.P. 1936, 4185, 8575, 13147, 13237, 13370
Nicolle, W.H.H. 20023, 20588
Nicolson, H. 2209
Nicolson, T.R. 2210
Niculescu, B.M. 2563, 10280
Nida, E.A. 15069
Niddrie, D. 20312
Nielson, J. 3992
Nielson, M.S. 12355
Nienaber, G.S. 19779, 22780-3
Nieuwenhuysen, J. 22171
Niger, F. 2564
Niger, P. 3574-6
Nigeria. Northern Region. Ministry for Local Government 11684
Nigeria. Northern Region. Public Relations Office 11685
Nile, L.U. 18761
Niles, D.T. 3993
Nilsson, E. 16415
Nitsche, G. 5756
Niven, C.R. 11435, 11565, 11686, 11866-7, 12997
Nixon, C.R. 22440
Njau, E. 859-860, 17968
Njau, R. 17579-80
Njok (Njock), H.M.B.B. See Bôt Ba Njok, H.M.
Njoya, I.M. 13281
Njungu, A.M. 21007

Nketia, J.H.   941-2, 3994, 7948, 10175-80, 10321, 10679, 11306
Nkhata, A.   21008
Nkojera, A.   21275
Nkomo, J.   20468-9
Nkomo, W.F.   23048
Nkonde, I.B.   21174-5
Nkosi, L.   3448-9
Nkoudou, J.R.O.   13148
Nkoulou-Essama, F.E.   See Ekodo-Nkoulou-Essama, F.
Nkoy, S.K.   See Kachama-Nkoy, S.
Nkrumah, K.   2565-6, 2894, 10427, 10559, 10720, 23520
Nkwain, F.   12084-6
Nkwenga, J.   13282, 13388
Nnunduma, B.E.   15070
Noa, L.A.   See Anya-Noa, L.
Noak, H.   21106
Noamesi, G.K.   10780, 10820
Nobbs, K.J.   5733
Noble, B.P.   8696
Noble, F.S.L.   See Livie-Noble, F.S.
Noble, G.W.   20862
Noble, J.   22636
Nobre, A.   3617
Noel-Buxton, Lord   16774-5, 17006
Nogara, A.   108
Nogueira, A.   12689-94, 12763, 12899
Nogueira, A.R.   12870
Nogueira, E.D.   See Dias Nogueira, E.
Nogueira, J.A.   23555
Noguer, S.A.   See Alcobé Noguer, S.
Nokwe, D.   22441-3
Nolde, E.   2211
Nollevaux, P.J.   14071
Noon, J.A.   1598, 11124
Noor Muhammad, H.N.A.   17154
Noordman, H.   14072
Nooteboom, C.   2212, 24637
Norbeck, E.   625
Norbet Laude, T.C.   14471
Nordfors, M.   22872
Norman, H.   5355
Noronha, C.   24185
Norris, A.W.   7726, 10560-1
Norris, H.T.   4813, 8442, 8483
Norris, R.   9576
North, A.C.   21107, 21240
Northcote, G.A.S.   18762
Northcote, R.C.   17845
Northcott, C.   21014
Northey, E.   16061
Nortje, K.A.   3450
Norton, E.A.   20169
Norton, G.R.   23001
Norton, I.H.   18194
Norton, W.A.   626, 3188, 19641, 21926, 22784

Nosti Nava, J. 1353, 7496, 15669, 15700, 15760
Nottingham, J.C. 17261, 17473
Nouacer, K. 7223, 7429
Nougier, L.R. 4862
Noumouke, D. 8978
Nouschi, A. 7113-4
Nove, A. 2567
Nowell, C.E. 2895
Noyes, I.P. 12594
Nsimbi, M.B. 18764-5
Nsimbi, N.B. 18763
Ntahokaja, J.B. 3189
Ntantala, P. 22245, 23216-7
Ntare School History Society 19276
Ntemo, F.D. 18328
Ntiro, S. 15843
Ntundu, Y. 17846
Nunes, A.de F. 24186
Nunes, D.A.M. See Martins Nunes, D.A.
Nunes, F.J.S.de F.P. 12844
Nunes, J. 23772-3, 23813, 23860, 24007
Nunes, J.A.P. 23647-8
Nunes, P. 23481
Nunn, N. 5734, 6530
Nur, M.A. 17164
Nur, M.I.el 6386
Nur Muhammad, H.N.A. See Noor Muhammad, H.N.A.
Nurse, G.T. 21310
Nutman, F.J. 15903
Nwabara, S.N. 11868-9
Nwankwo, N. 3451, 12087
Nwanodi, G.O. 12088
Nwedo, A. 4186
Nwoga, D.I. 12089
Nwogu, E.D. 11436
Nwogugu, E.I. 12164
Nwokwu, M.E. 11307
Nwosu, B.E. 7861, 11870
Nwoye, S.C. 10881
Nyamweya, J. 17462
Nyanzi, S. 15904-5
Nyasuru, M.B.K. 16342
Nye, G.W. 18766-7
Nye, J. 18030
Nye, J.S., Jr. 15906, 16013
Nye, P. 9444
Nyembezi, C.L.S. 22785
Nyendwoha, S. 18768
Nyerere, J. 2379, 2568-74, 16014, 16385, 18195-6, 18468
Nyirenda, A.A. 21037
Nyssen, R. 15410
Nyunaï 3577, 3733, 8937-8
Nzau, T. 15255
Nzimiro, F.I. 11687
Nzimiro, I. 12487
Nzouankeu, J.M. 13389

O., A.V. 18769
O., C.A. 22172, 22637
O., E. 261
O., F.A. 22568
O., G. 5978
O., G.C. 24320
O., R.K. 3995
O.A.U. See Organization of African Unity
Oakes, F. 17847
Oakley, K.P. 762, 21009
Oates, F. 18559-60
Oba Alaiyeluwa Adegoriola I, Ogoga of Ikere 11871
Obama, J.B. 861-2, 943-6
Obayan, E.O. 11437
Oberg, K. 18770-2
Oberholser, H.C. 12649
Obi, D.S. 3452, 10882
Obi, S.N.C. 12165
Oboli, H.O.N. 11566
Obote, M. 19153
O'Brien, C.C. 10562, 14832
O'Brien, P.K. 5228
O'Brien, T.P. 18882
O'Brien, W. 22638
Ocaña Garcia, M. 15716
Ocheng, D. 18975, 19154, 19398
Ochoa, A.S. See Sierra Ochoa, A.
O'Connell, J. 7763-4, 11688, 12216
O'Connor, A.M. 15979
O'Connor, J. 16015
Odeku, E.L. 12356
Odendal, F.F. 22786
Odendall, P.J. 20024
Odhiambo, T.R. 19473
Odin, K. 19377
Odone, A. 17045
Odongo, T.O. See Okelo-Odongo, T.
Odonkor, S.S. 10769
O'Donovan, P. 10428, 14696
O'Dowd, T. 22444, 22873, 22945
Odukoya, M.A. 11125
Odutola, S.O. 12217
O'Ferrall, R. 15174
Offor, R. 347
Ofori, G.T. 9999
Ofosu-Amaah, G.K.A. 10721
Ofosu-Appiah, L.H. 1867, 10429, 10647
Ogan, O. 8104
Ogbomo 11308
Ogden, G.W. 6010, 6531
Ogilvie, A.G. 1937-8, 4108
Oglethorpe, J. 23002
Ogot, A. 17527
Ogot, B. 2575, 5735, 17528
Ogot, G. 3453, 15812
Ogundana, B. 11567

Ogunkoya, T.O. 11872
Ogunremi, 'D. 11131
Ogunsheye, A. 2576, 4652, 7765, 11438
Ogunsheye, F.A. 12488
Ogwurike, C. 12166
O'Hagan, C.C. 18110
O'Hagan, D. 17463
Ohly, R. 16192
Ohonbalu, O. 12167
Oidtman, C.von 20170-1, 24037
Ojo-Cole, J. 11873, 12090-1
Ojo-Ilori, I.O. 11126
Okafor, M. 12092
Okara, G. 3190, 3454-5, 11127, 12093-5
Okediji, F.O. 4653-4, 11439
O'Keeffe, S.M.L. 20589
Okello, Y.K. 18773
O'Kelly, E. 13217, 13253
Okelo-Odongo, T. 1354
Okigbo, C. 3456-60, 12096
Okigbo, P. 7862
Okoli, J. 11874-5
Okonga, S. 17112
Okonjo, C. 11440-1, 12489
Okonkwo, C.O. 12168-9
Okorie, K. 10883-4
Okot (p'Bitek). See p'Bitek (O.)
Okoye, M. 2577, 11442
Okoye, N. 11689
Oku, E.E. 10885
Olaaiye, N. 12097
Olajubu, O. 11876
Olakanpo, O. 11443-4
Olamijulo, J. 11877
Olangua, A. 15741
Olbrechts, M. 41, 9215-6, 14073, 14304
Oldaker, A.A. 18197
Oldfield, G.A. 11445
Oldham, J.H. 1760-1, 2896, 3996-8, 4187, 16016
Oldroyd, H. 24187
Olesa Muñido, F.F. 3734, 24064
Oliensis, D. 15945
Oliphant, J.N. 442
Olisa, M. 3461, 12098
Oliva, E.T. See Toda Oliva, E.
Oliveira, A.G.d'. 3999
Oliveira, C.P.de 15175
Oliveira, F.R.de 1762
Oliveira, H.de 2122, 4000, 23610
Oliveira, J.P.de. See Pereira de Oliveira, J.
Oliveira, M.A.F.de 23580, 23665
Oliveira, M.de 23412
Oliveira, O.R.de 19817, 23815-7, 23774, 24038
Oliveira, P.H.L.de 14833
Oliveira Boléo, J.de 12738, 23921
Oliver, B. 12357

Oliver, H.F. 20378
Oliver, J. 6095
Oliver, L.M. See Morales Oliver, L.
Oliver, R. 16062, 18774-5, 18883, 19277-9
Oliver, R.A.C. 1763, 17373
Oliver, S. 2213, 2897
Oliver, S.C. 17262
Olivier, Gouv.gén. 8218
Olivier, G. 13149-51, 13445
Olivier, H. 18976
Olivier, L. 7648
Olivier, Lord S. 2214, 2899, 16017, 23218-9
Oliviera, C. 23666
Oliviera, O.R.de 23814, 23816
Oliviera e Castro, L.F.de 1685, 2898
Ollennu, N. 7992, 10722
Ollier, C.D. 18884-5
Olmsted, D.L. 11994
Ologoudou, E. 9600
Oloko, O. 12490
Olory-Togbe, G. 9605
Olsen, F. 14583
Olsen, M. 24380, 24489
Olson, H.S. 18404
Olsoufieff, G. 24611-2
Olumide, A.O. 11568
Olusanya, G.O. 11690
Oluwasanmi, H.A. 10921, 11446-7
Olyech, E. 18775
Olympio, S.E. 2578
Omaboe, F.N. 10281
O'Mahoney, K.E. 20531
Omari, A. 14074
Omari bin Stamboul 17529
Ombredane, A. 14472, 15529
Omer-Cooper, J. 24188
Omer-Cooper, J.D. 2900, 12491, 21632, 22639
Ominde, S.H. 17653-4
Onaeko, E.A. 11569
Onde, H. 1939, 24309
Oni of Ife 11448
Onitiri, H.M.A. 1355, 11449-52
Onori, E. 10821
Onslow, Earl of 4291
Onwuteaka, V.C. 11691
Onyenacho, B.N. 11511
Onyido, U. 11309
Oosthuizen, C.J. 23003
Oosthuizen, G.C. 23004
Op't Hof, J.J.P. 22750
Opoku-Ampomah, J.K. 10096-7
Oppenheimer, E. 22173
Oppenheimer, H.F. 19847, 22174, 22445, 23220
Opper, C.J. 17848, 24306
Optimist 1764
Orchard, F.H. 23005

Orchardson, I.Q. 17263
Ord, H.W. 1356
Orde, M.H. 9672
Orde Browne, G.B. 4431
Orde Browne, G.St.J. 797, 1042, 1528, 1599, 2007, 3042, 3663, 17264, 17720, 18014
Orekyeh, R.O. 10922-4
Orenstein, A.J. 23049, 23221
Orewa, G. 11453, 11692
Orfond, P.S.d'. 9872
Organization of African Unity 2578
O'Riordan, M.C.M. 1765
Orme, U.M. 12492
Orme-Smith, R. 11454
Ormiston, W. 11310
Ormsby, G. 10648
Ormsby-Gore, (W.) D. [Lord Harlech] 2094, 19731
Ormsby-Gore, W.G.A. 443, 1766, 2215, 2684, 15907
Ornelas, M.C.de J.C.de O. 4001
Ornella, G.B.de P.d' 6096
Ornella Acanfora, M. 16605
O'Rourke, V.A. 5356
Orr, C. 11878
Orr, C.W. 11128, 12946
Orr, G.B. 9779
Orr, J.R. 1767
Orsini, d'A. 207, 14473
Ortiz de Rivero, M. 7462, 15721, 15761-2
Ortiz de Zárate López, A. 15670
Ortoli, H. 8823-4, 8969
Orts, M.P. 2216
Oryem, P. 18776
Osadebay, D.C. 7948
Osadeby. See Osadebay, D.C.
Osafo, F.O. 10181
Osborn, R.D. 5357
Osborne, J.F. 15908
Osborne, J.M. 18329
Osman, O.M. 6011
Osmaston, H.A. 18777, 18886, 19074-5
Osório, C.do A. 23714, 23861, 23958
Oss, M.V. 21038
Ostini, F. 16606, 16967-8
O'Sullevan, J.J. 18330
Osuna, M.G. 7478
Othieno, T.M. 18645
Othman, G. 16343
Otieno, N.C. 1868, 16416-7
Ottenberg, S. 11129-30, 11693, 12170
Otto, B. 3191
Otto de Habsburgo 2580
Oudenrijn, M.C.van den 16776
Ouedraogo, J. 9418
Ouegin, M. 3578
Oulton, A.D.M. 17599
Ouologuem, Y., also called Yambo 2656, 8940-1

Oursel, P.M.   See Masson-Oursel, P.
Ousmane, B.T.   See Bâ Tamsir Ousmane
Ousmane, D.   9094
Ousmane, S.   See Sembene, O.
Ovazza   13019
Ovejero, A.   863, 7115
Ovir, E.   16193, 18405
Owen, Prof.   5141
Owen, A.W.E.   17305
Owen, G.   10322
Owen, J.F.   2901
Owen, J.S.   6532-4
Owen, R.   6667
Owen, T.R.H.   5736-8, 5920, 6387, 6535-7
Owen, W.E.   16018
Owiredu, P.A.   10098, 10649-50
Owoade, A.   11131, 11455, 14834
Owuor, H.   17306
Owusu, C.A.P.   10323
Oyawoye, M.O.   11553, 11570
Oyelese, J.O.   11456
Oyler, D.S.   5739-44, 6250
Ozanne, P.   9664, 10182-90, 10199
Ozenda, P.   7141
Ozor, C.N.   7863

P., C.   14697
P., D.   1600
P., E.T.   20340
P., H.P.   5964
P., J.   22025
P., L.van   14538
Pablo, A.G.de.   See González de Pablo, A.
Pachai, B.   10563, 22640
Pacheco, A.   24039, 24189
Pacheco, E.H.   See Hernández Pacheco, E.
Pacheco, F.H.   See Hernández Pacheco, F.
Pacheco de Amorim, F.   1357
Packham, E.S.   10430
Paden, J.N.   12099
Padmore, G.   2581, 10234, 10564
Padwick, C.E.   5069, 7140
Paes, A.R.C.S.   See Silva Paes, A.R.C.
Page, A.   1768, 7392
Page, C.H.   6097-8
Page, L.R.   16418
Page, R.E.   10565
Pageard, R.   3355-6, 5358, 7864, 8774, 8825-7, 8911-2, 8943,
   9419-20, 9424, 9448
Pagès, A.   14075, 15575-7, 15619, 15648
Paget, E.F.   20470
Paias, J.D.   14835
Pairault, C.A.   13499-13500
Paisana, F.C.   See Cardoso Paisana, F.
Paix, H.   4292

Paixão, B. 4002, 23491
Pakenham, R.H.W. 16194, 17849
Pakenham, T. 16777
Palacin, A.de L. 4863, 7192, 15677, 15688, 15770
Palacios, A. 3580
Palamenghi-Crispi, F. 1358
Palau, M.A. See Arribas Palau, M.
Palau Marti, M. 391-5, 7550, 9502, 9577, 11097
Palès, L. 266, 627-8, 13020, 13528, 13548, 19642
Palley, C. 20769-70, 22946
Pallister, J.W. 19076
Pallottino, M. 6844
Palmeirim, V. 24190-91
Palmer, F.R. 16898-9, 16900
Palmer, H.R. 4814, 4864, 5008-9, 5745, 6251-3, 6405, 7555,
    7766, 7865, 7949, 8011, 9685, 11132, 11311, 11571, 11618,
    11879-82, 12218
Palmer, M. 22246
Palmer, R. See Palmer, H.R.
Palmer, R.C. See Selborne, Lord [R.C.Palmer]
Pama, C. 21800, 22641
Pamplona, F.de 23452
Panassie, H. 947
Panconcelli-Calzia, G. 3192, 13342, 16195, 22787, 23567
Pandombiri 20863
Pane, H.T. 2582
Panetta, E. 6703
Paniagua y Santos, J.M. 7393
Pankhurst, R. 16658, 16778-90
Panofsky, H.E. 1601, 2583
Pant, A.B. 2902
Panyella, A. 12982, 13152-3, 15678-80, 15689-90, 15771
Papafio, A.B.Q. See Quartey-Papafio, A.B.
Papi, M.R. 16987
Papp, C.S. 8105
Papy, L. 8494
Pâques, V. 4815-6, 5101, 6622, 6630, 8828-30
Paquet, J. 20590
Paradis, J. 14076
Paradisi, U. 6631
Paramount Chief of the Herero People 23339
Parant, R. 7082
Parasassi, M. 1359-61
Paré, I. 13154, 13194-5, 13343
Parenko, P. 10099
Parent, J. 1362
Parenti, R. 17026
Paret, R. 16344
Paris, E. 8390
Paris-Teynac, E.J. 4865
Park, A.E.W. 12171-2
Park, E. 11353
Park, G.K. 17850-1
Park, M.H. 23349
Parker, B.N. 1754
Parker, F. 20341

Parker, G.W.   24381-2, 24537
Parker, H.   9665
Parker, J.S.F.   5280
Parker, M.   17464, 17655
Parker, S.C.   20591, 20708
Parkes, A.S.   4605
Parkes, R.   1869
Parkhurst, D.C.H.   20025, 20813
Parkin, D.J.   19536
Parkin, G.R.   1870
Parkinson, F.   2217
Parkinson, J.   7727, 10100, 11133-6, 12595, 17027, 17385, 19703, 21133
Parnis, R.O.   12219
Parnwell, E.C.   3193
Parr, M.   4655
Parr, M.W.   5746
Parrinder, G.   4003, 8012-4, 7556, 7600, 8373, 9503, 11137
Parry, E.   1602
Parry, J.   12100
Parry, R.E.   18887, 19077
Parry, S.B.   1769
Parsons, C.J.   23521
Parsons, F.V.   7343-4, 7866
Parsons, F.W.   7950-3, 11995
Parsons, R.T.   4004, 9749-53
Partridge, A.G.   24692
Partridge, C.   11138, 12173
Pascal, A.   24375
Pasqual, J.H.   12358-9
Pasquier, R.   396, 8487, 8626, 8697
Passau, G.   15399
Passemard, E.   13529
Passeron, R.   7134
Passmore, F.R.   7504
Patel, K.H.   397
Patel, R.B.   16196
Patel, S.J.   1199, 1363-4, 15909
Paterfamilias   6035
Paterson, E.   864-5, 20172
Paterson, R.L.   17677
Pathak, G.S.   21457
Patiko, J.   18746
Paton, A.S.   4005, 22874-6, 22947-8
Patri, A.   3581-2, 4656
Patriarca, G.   6684
Patrick, C.K.C.   See Cochran-Patrick, C.K.
Patricolo, M.   444
Patten, J.W.   22446
Patterson, C.J.   4657
Patterson, T.T.   20471
Patteson, J.E.   10384
Patz, M.J.   18888
Paul, A.   5359, 5747-50, 5910, 6254-6
Paul, E.C.   629, 4658
Paul, H.G.B.   5911-2, 5949-50, 6406

Paul, J.C.N.   16969
Paulha   3194
Paulian, R.   9273, 13446
Paulinus, B.   16197
Paulme, D.   398, 630-2, 2903, 4659-60, 8817, 8831-3, 9009-12, 9217-8, 10191
Paulo, Z.F.   See Ferreira Paulo, Z.
Paulus, J.M.   3735
Pauphilet, D.   6722, 6948, 6951, 13475
Pautrat, R.   3736
Pauvert, C.   399, 866, 1770, 9400, 10431, 13028-9
Pauw, B.A.   19818, 21927
Pauwels, J.L.   15071
Pauwels, J.M.   15256
Pauwels, M.   14077-81, 15578-80, 15583, 18889
Pauwels, P.H.   15581
Pauwels, P.M.   15582
Paver, F.R.   19643
Paya, J.E.   15681
Paye, L.   1771
Payne, E.G.S.   11694
Payne, P.   11883
Payre, G.   7155
P'Bitek, O.   4006-7, 18774, 18778-80, 19378, 19537
Peacock, A.T.   1365
Peake, F.G.G.   6538
Peal, J.   11572
Peal, W.J.   18977
Pearce, S.   18890
Pearsall, A.W.H.   9873
Pearsall, M.   15813
Pearson, D.S.   1366, 20289
Pearson, E.O.   445
Pearson, P.   18781
Pearson, V.   12360
Pease, A.E.   2904, 22642
Pecci, D.   16513
Pedler, F.J.   1603, 7661, 11457
Pedrals, H.de   13155
Pedraza, G.J.W.   17344
Pedrazzi, O.   4899
Pedro, J.G.   See Gomes Pedro, J.
Pedro Romano, M.   See Romano, M.P.
Peele, C.R.de   20026
Peeler, E.H.   348
Peeraer, S.   14082-7, 15072, 15176
Peéson, Y. (?). See Person, Y.
Peet, G.A.   18111
Peet, M.   22026
Peeters, G.   13778-9, 14474
Peeters, R.P.   14263
Pégard, O. [Soeur Jean Bernard]   9421
Peiffer, E.   8193, 13156
Peillon, P.   1772
Peirone, F.   4008, 24289
Peiser, G.   1367, 8698, 13711

Peixe, J.dos S. See Santos Peixe, J.dos
Pekkola, W. 6539-40
Pélage 633
Pélage, Mme. 13156
Pélage, S. 13156
Pelham-Burn, H. 17465
Pélichy, A.G.de 4009
Pélissier, P. 8495, 8742, 9069
Pélissier, R. 400, 15732
Pelt, A. 109
Pelte, S. 24321
Peltier 8743
Pelzer, K.J. 1369
Pena, A.J. 23649-50
Pendered, A. 20027-9, 20771
Pendleton, R.L. 14584
Penfield, F.C. 4900
Penn, A.E.D. 5751, 5913
Penner, C.D. 22643
Penney, J.C. 18198
Penning, W.H. 22027
Pennington, A.L. 18331
Penreath, R. 18782
Penwill, D.J. 17466-7, 17656
Pepper, E.B. See Barat-Pepper, E.
Pepper, H. 11312, 12987, 13585, 13640
Pepper, J.L.W. 8106
Perbal, A. 110
Percy, R.C. 19474
Pereira, A.A. 24008
Pereira, A.G. See Gomes Pereira, A.
Pereira, A.J.de A. 24009
Pereira, A.S.C. 23959, 24193
Pereira, B. 1001
Pereira, F.J. 23522
Pereira, G. 24076
Pereira, M.de C. 24194
Pereira Coutinho, L. 24132, 24195
Pereira de Oliveira, J. 12900-1
Pereira dos Santos, M.P. 23716, 23862-6, 24196
Pereira Martinho, J.P. 446, 21837
Pereira Neto, J.B.N. 23523
Pérès, J.M. 8107, 8472, 8744
Perestrelo, E.A.C. 23503
Pérez, V.T. 7224
Perez Lozano, L. 7229
Perham, M. 42, 1051-2, 2218-2222, 12493, 18199, 22247
Pericot Garcia, L. 763-7, 2905, 7434-5
Périé, J. 9644-5
Perier, G.D. 14305
Perin, F. 14698
Peris, S.V. 15717
Peristiany, J.G. 17265-6
Perkins, E.A.T. 19475-8
Perlman, E.H. 19479

Perlman, M.L. 18783, 19399
Perlstein, M. 12995
Perono, J. 13157
Perpiñá 15701
Perraudin, J. 14836
Perregaux, W. 10566
Perret, J.L. 13447
Perret, R. 4866, 4933-4, 7018
Perrett, M. 5124
Perrier de la Bathie, H. 24425, 24485, 24589-98
Perrot, C.H. 21661
Perrott, R. 2584
Perroux, F. 1184, 2223
Perry, J.S. 19480
Perry, R. 11884
Perryman, P.W. 18784, 19538
Person, Y. 634, 7867-8, 8913, 9032, 9042, 9095, 9504-8, 9578
Persse, E.M. 18785-6
Perth, Lord 2224
Peshkin, A. 1773
Petch, G.A. 9795
Peterec, R.J. 1915
Petermann, A. 6257
Peters, C. 19644
Peters, L. 9687-9
Peters, W. 10432
Peterson, V.C. 1368
Pétillon, Gov.Gen. 14700
Petit, M. 24490
Petot, F. 8775
Petráček, K. 16607, 16901
Petrie, W.F. 5186-8, 5360
Petterson, O. 635
Pettinen, A. 5752-6
Pettit, E.R. 10925
Pfeffer, G. 7984
Pfeffer, K.H. 2585
Phadnis, U.N. 17468
Phanzu, F. 13775
Phatak, D.M. 2906, 18332-4
Philby, H.St.J.B. 5010, 5281
Philip, A. 1370
Philip, D. 7083, 7279
Philippe, R. 14088-91, 14475-6, 14539, 14837, 15073, 15257, 15264, 15722
Philipps, J.E.T. 2225, 5757-8
Philipps, T. 208-9, 4663, 6685, 15400
Philippson, M. 14477
Phillips, A. 3737-9, 4662, 8334, 15530, 16386, 17600
Phillips, A.S. 1774
Phillips, G. 20342
Phillips, J. 10013
Phillips, J.H. 1775
Phillips, L. 22062, 22644-5
Phillips, N. 22447

Phillips, R.C. 14092
Phillips, R.E. 23222
Philombe, R. 3583, 13390-2
Philopher 12494
Philpot, W.T.A. 11996
Philpott, R. 21039
Phipps, B.A. 19019
Phipps, P.E. 19020
Pic, M. 4293, 8108-11, 8473, 8956, 9387-8, 15763
Picard, G.C. 5011, 6845
Picard, J. 8745, 12650
Picardie, M. 3462, 22448, 23223
Picavet, R. 15074
Piccinni, F.G. 1021
Pich, V.M. 17469
Pichat, J.B. See Bourgeois-Pichat, J.
Pichl, W. 8650-2, 8675
Pick, F.W. 2907
Pick, H. 2586
Pickard-Cambridge, A.W. 10324
Picks, M. 16198
Pickstone, H.E.V. 22175
Picot, G.G. See Georges-Picot, G.
Picot, J. 9070
Pidal, R.M. See Menendez Pidal, R.
Pienaar, P.de V. 3195
Pienar, P. 22646
Pieraerts, J. 15401-3, 15435
Pierchon, M. 4130
Piermé, M.L. 13427, 13439
Pierrard, G.A. 14093
Pierre, F. 1059
Pierre, J.A.A. 12632
Pierre, N. 13344
Pierret, F. 13007
Piganiol, A. 5102
Piggott, C.J. 24679
Piggott, D.W.I. 18031, 18112, 18335, 18614
Pignatelli, M.J.S.de S. See Santareno Pignatelli, M.J.S.de
Pignon, J. 6708, 6762, 6846-9
Pike, A.G. 18113
Pike, A.H. 5252, 17678
Pike, J.G. 21311, 21400-2, 21458
Pike, V.F. 17149
Pilane, I. 22449
Pilkington, F. 7767, 11139, 11695-6, 12220-1, 12495-6
Pillay, V. 1371, 14478
Pilszczikowa, N. 10651
Pim, A. 1372, 21621
Pimentel, M.I. 23492
Pina, J.R.de 349
Piñar Lopez, B. 1006
Pincus, J.A. 1373
Pine, C.C.B. 22647
Pineda, M.C.de. See Cencillo de Pineda, M.

Pinho, D.M.A.de 4010
Pintassilgo, A.R. 14094
Pinto, A.A.da R. See Rosa Pinto, A.A.da
Pinto, A.da S. 23867, 23960, 24198
Pinto, A.R. 12845
Pinto, H.V. See Vieira Pinto, H.
Pinto, L.I. 2587
Pinto, L.M.T. 23482
Pinxten, K. 13780, 15453, 15601
Piovani, P.G. 16902
Pira, G.L. 3357
Pirelli, M. 23651
Pirenne, J. 16608
Pires, F.A. 4294-5, 24199
Pires, V. 24200
Pires de Carvalho, A. 23926, 23961
Pires de Figueiredo, J. 12707
Pirie, G. 20948, 21134
Pirone, M. 17092-3, 17113
Pirow, O. 22450
Pissaloux, R. 6784, 6949
Pissard, R. 9477
Pitje, G.M. 21928
Pitman, C.R.S. 18930, 18946, 19078, 19280, 19481-9
Pitot, A. 4296-8, 8265, 8576, 9165
Pitout, J.A. 20592-3
Pitt, J. 17679
Pitt, W.J. 10101, 10567
Pitt Rivers, Maj.-Gen. 5189-90
Pitt-Schenkel, C.J.W. 17680
Pittius, E.F.W.G.van 23340
Pius XII, Pope 4011, 23611
Plachin, H. 20888
Plae, E.le. See Leplae, E.
Plancquaert, M. 14585
Planert, W. 19780
Plant, A. 1374
Plantey, A. 7394
Plas, V.H.van den. See Van den Plas, V.H.
Plass, M.W. 10192
Platt, B.S. 4230-1, 9698-9
Platt, E.T. 24341
Platt, W. 16063
Platzer, H. 13476
Playne, B. 16609
Plazikowsky-Brauner, H. 16831, 16903-7
Plessis, J.du. See Du Plessis, J.
Plotnicou, L. 12497
Plowman, C.H.F. 16514
Plumb, J.H. 5361, 7869
Plumbe, W.J. 350
Plymen, J. 21662
Poblete, O. 1375
Pocock, D.F. 15814
Podlewski, A.M. 13158, 13477
Poel, J.v.d. 22248-9

Pognon, A. 9509
Pogucki, P.J.H. 10723-4
Poirier, J. 3740-4, 8335, 24383, 24412, 24638
Poisson, M.H. 24575, 24613-20
Poisson, R. 9389, 24436-41, 24621
Poitrineau, A. 6944
Polanyi, K. 7660
Poldervaart, A. 19704
Polinard, E. 15404
Polk, W.R. 4901
Pollard, A.F. 22648
Pollard, W.G. 12361
Pollet, G. 8834
Pollett, H. 20594
Pollett, J.D. 9965
Pollins, H. 4664
Pomeroy, A.W.J. 12362
Pomorska, I. 5201
Pompei, S. 6965
Poncet, J. 5012, 6723, 6850-1, 6966
Ponoukoun, K.B.G. 9538
Pons, J. 15682
Pons, R. 2226-7
Ponsonby, A. 5282
Ponsonby, C.E. 2228, 16019, 19705
Ponsonby, E. 23224
Pont, D. 22949
Pont, M. 24384
Pontes, L.L. See Ledo Pontes, L.
Poole, E.H.L. 21135, 21459
Poole, E.J. 11275
Poole, R.S. 5191-2
Pooley, R.P. 12550
Pope, M. 22250
Pope-Simmonds, E.W. 20772
Popplewell, G.D. 17852
Poréko, D.O. 9013, 9114
Porter, A. 7700
Porter, A.T. 9831, 9945
Porter, D.B. 351, 3358
Porter, J.A. 867
Porter, P.W. 17386
Portères, R. 447, 4299, 7557, 8298, 8979, 9115, 9292
Portugal, J.B.de. See Blanc de Portugal, J.
Posnansky, M. 868, 15844-5, 18851, 18890-5
Posnett, R.N. 19079
Posselt, F. 3745, 20343, 20379
Posselt, F.W.T. 20030-5, 20595-6, 20712, 20773
Posselt, H. 20597
Posselt, W. 20380, 20598
Possoz, E. 636, 2229, 3746-9, 4665, 14095-9, 15075-6, 15258-64
Possy-Berry, Q. 2588
Post, K.W.J. 11668, 11697-9, 14699
Post, L.van der. See Van der Post, L.

Postel, R. 4165
Postioma, A.de 4012, 15324-5
Potekhin, I.I. 210, 1376, 3750, 4666
Potgieter, E.F. 22788
Pott, D. 21771
Pouillon, J. 13567
Poujade, J. 9096, 9166
Poulton, J. 19407
Pourquie, A. 8421
Poussibet, F. 8776, 8928-30
Poussin, J.de la V. 14586
Poutsma, H.J. 22176
Poux-Cransac, G. 5951
Povey, J.F. 3359
Powdermaker, H. 20949
Powell, E.C. 12498
Powell, G.B. See Baden-Powell, G.
Powell, J. 5759
Powell, R.J. 20036-41
Powell-Cotton, C. 18896
Powell-Cotton, P.H.G. 14587, 15980
Power, A.D. 4188-9, 12363
Power, M.G. 17470
Powys-Jones, L. 20042, 20472
Poynton, H. 1377
Pradel de Lamase, M.de 6852
Pradhan, R.C. 2230, 2589, 14701-2
Prain, R. 20313, 21040, 21241
Pralus, M. 7135
Prasad, A. 10433, 16446, 19539
Prasse, K.G. 5044
Pratas, M.J. 24201
Prates, M.D. 24202
Pratt, C. 18615
Pratt, R.C. 15946
Pré, R. 1378
Preaux, C. 5335
Prego, I.S. See Sousa Prego, I.
Preiswerk, R. 7768
Prentice, A.N. 19490
Prescott, J.R.V. 11573-5, 11589, 11700, 20381
Pressat, R. 4667
Preston, H.A. 20864
Pretorius, J.L. 21276, 21514
Pretorius, P. 21515
Preuss, K.T. 637
Price, E.W. 15077
Price, F.G.H. 5142, 23413
Price, J.H. 9673-4, 10434-6, 10725, 12499
Price, L.L. 22177
Price, M.P. 5362
Price, O.J. 20774
Price, T. 4013, 21277, 21312, 21460-1, 21491-3, 21542, 21566
Price-Mars, J. 768, 2908, 3360, 4668
Price-Williams, D.R. 11140

Priesner, H. 13021
Priestley, M.A. 211, 10226, 10568-72
Priestley, M.J.S.W. 21108
Priestley, N. 4300, 12364
Prietze, R. 7601, 7954-5, 8112, 9363, 11997
Prince, R.H. 12500
Pring, R.W. 12365
Prins, A.H.J. 638, 16199, 16345, 17028, 17267, 18336
Prior, K.H. 12222
Priso, F.M. See Mouasso-Priso, F.
Pritchard, E.E.E. See Evans-Pritchard, E.E.
Pritchard, S.M. 23341
Probst-Biraben, J.H. 5070, 6993
Probyn, E.H. 12101
Probyn, L. 9874
Probyn, L.C. 1379
Probyn, M. 18561
Procter, J. 17853, 18114
Proctor, R.A. 5193
Prorok, B.K.de 5013
Prosser, R.C. 17471
Prost, A. 4669, 8831, 8931, 9364-5, 9449-50, 9455, 9459
Prost, G. 6724, 6736-7
Prothero, M. 17530
Prothero, R.M. 1940, 4670, 8162, 11141, 11576, 12501-3
Proudfoot, L. 9738, 9875, 9946-8
Proudfoot, S.L. 9765
Prouteaux, M. 8194, 9219
Prusso, P. 7193
Puchol, R.T. See Tatay Puchol, R.
Pugh, J.C. 11577-8
Pugh, K.T. 18115
Puglisi, G. 16999
Puigaudeau, O.du 7019, 7194-5, 7198-9, 8406-7, 8409, 8443, 16610
Pula 20950
Pumphrey, M.E.C. 5760-1
Puplampu, D.A. 10102
Purcell, J.F.H. 2590
Puri, G.S. 1380
Purseglove, J.W. 19540-1
Purvis, J.T. 18032
Putte, M.van de 14479, 22125
Pyarelal, pseud. [P.Nair]. 19717
Pycraft, W.P. 1076, 21929
Pye, F. 23225
Pynaert, L. 15405-6

Qasim, A.al-S. See Gasim, A.al-S.
Quaesitor 22649
Quaison-Sackey, A. 2591-2
Quali 17657
Quamie-Kyiamah, A. 10726
Quarcoo, A.K. 10190, 10193
Quartey, K.A.B.J. See Jones-Quartey, K.A.B.

Quartey-Papafio, A.B.   10103-5, 10727-8
Queirós, D.X.   23504
Queiroz, M.I.P.de   4014
Quenum, O.B.   See Bhely-Quenum, O.
Quenum, S.   4301
Quermonne, J.L.   2593, 5059
Quesne, C.M.L.   See Le Quesne, C.M.
Quick, G.   21201
Quilliam, A.   9876
Quinche, C.   19920
Quinquad, J.   9097
Quintano Ripollés, A.   5363, 6668
Quintavalle, B.A.   1381
Quintino, F.R.   See Rogado Quintino, F.
Quiring, D.P.   18116
Quirini, P.de   14100
Quirion, J.M.   1382
Quirós, C.   5014-5, 7395
Quix, J.P.   19281
Quoniam, P.   5016
Qureshi, M.A.   12551

R., A.   3751
R., A.E.   5952
R., C.F.   20713-5
R., J.   7280-1, 7345
R., P.   6669-70
Raaflaub, F.   13416
Rabéarivelo, J.J. (J.C.)   24525
Rabemananjara, J.   2231, 3361, 3584-5, 4672, 9077, 24452,
    24491-3, 24526-8
Rabinovitch, L.A.   See Anselme-Rabinovitch, L.
Raboroko, P.N.   22452
Racine, J.   7396-7
Radcliffe, C.D.   See Delmé-Radcliffe, C.
Radcliffe-Brown, A.R.   639-640, 14101, 19842
Rado, E.R.   10282, 15947, 16659, 18978, 19008
Rafael, A.A.G.   24203
Rafael, S.D.   See Dias Rafael, S.
Rageau, J.   13442
Ragir, S.   769
Raglan, Lord   5762, 19357
Raguin, E.   8113
Raharijaona, Dr.et Mme.   24494
Raharijaona, B.   24538
Raharijaona, S.   24639
Rahmani, H.S.   4817
Rahmani, S.   6994
Rai, K.B.   2594-5
Rainero, R.   2596, 4673, 22650
Rainier, M.   22651
Rains, A.B.   12366
Raj, K.N.   1383
Rajaona, S.   24640
Rajaonarivo, J.   24574

Rake, A. 2597, 17601, 22453
Rakoto 24385-6
Rakowski, R.F. 14306
Ralibera, P.R. 4015
Ralison, R. 24387
Ramamonjy, G. 24388
Ramanoelina, M. 1384, 2598
Rambert, A.A. See Amblard-Rambert, A.
Rambiritch, B. 23226
Ramchandani, R.R. 18979
Ramm, A. 16064
Ramos, M.G. See Gonzalez Ramos, M.
Ramos Boned, J. 4183
Ramsaran, J.A. 8311
Ramsay, J.C. 18117
Ramsay, T.D. 22950
Ranaivo, F. 3586, 24389, 24529-31
Randall, R.J. 22136, 23133
Randall-MacIver, D. 5194, 7020
Randell, J.R. 6099-6100
Randier, R. 1385
Randzavola, M. 24516, 24532
Rangeley, W.H.J. 16065, 21253, 21278-82, 21313-4, 21359-60, 21462-4, 21506, 24040
Ranger, T. 15948, 19667, 20473, 20599, 21136, 24041
Ranson, H. 9812
Rao, U.R. 2599
Raombana 24495
Raoult, A. 8353
Raper, A.B. 18787, 19467
Rapp, E.L. 9366, 10652
Rappard, W.E. 2232
Ras Khan 10675, 10680
Rasamimanana 24390, 24517
Rasamoel, J.B. 24622
Rasamuel, M. 24391
Raschi, R. 1604, 16660
Raseta, J. 24453
Rashad, I. 5229
Rasilly, R.P.B.de 9422
Rason, R. 24401
Rassool, S.H.A. 24322
Ratcliffe, B.J. 16200-3
Rath, U.C.W. 6101
Ratnesar, V.C. 10822
Rato, J.M. See Moreira Rato, J.
Ratsimamanga, A.R. 24533
Ratton, C. 7602
Rattray, R.S. 641, 1038, 2233, 7559, 7769, 7985, 10106-9, 10190, 10283
Rau, E. 3752-4, 8627, 8699
Rau, V. 2909
Raulin, H. 9654
Raum, J. 4016, 16203, 17565, 18051
Raum, O.F. 642, 3196, 17854-6, 18406-7, 19561, 21930
Ravelonanosy, V. 24413

Raven-Hart, R. 22092, 22652
Ravenstein, E.G. 19080
Ravisse, P. 13683
Ravndal, G.B. 1605
Ravoajanahary, C. 24392
Rawlins, R.E.D. 24442
Rawson, H.D. 20382
Rawson, H.E. 1941, 2228, 19718, 21633, 22097, 22653, 23775
Raymakers, P. 15326
Raymond, A. 6853-4
Raymond, J. 5364
Raymond, R. 6855
Raymond, W.D. 15815, 18616
Raynal, P. 7116
Rayne, H. 17155, 17268
Razafintsambaina, G. 24534
Razafy-Adriamihaingo, S.R. 24641-2
Rea, C.J. 10858
Rea, F.B. 20796-7
Rea, W.F. 20600-1
Read, E.S. 23227
Read, F.W. 23414
Read, J.S. 2235, 3649, 3755-6, 10729-30, 17602, 18469
Read, M. 11512, 20951, 21283-4, 21315
Reade, H. 1776
Reader, D.H. 1386, 21931
Rebelo, A. 24204
Rebelo, D.J.S. 1606, 16447, 17345, 18033, 18980, 21361,
    22178-9, 23868-70, 24290
Rece, G. 17114
Recoules, J. 7282-3, 7346-7
Reder, D.G. 5195
Redinha, J. 23524
Redmayne, A. 17857
Reed, J. 3362, 20255, 20474
Reed, L.N. 7560
Reed, P. 1777
Reed, W. 5469, 6012
Reedman, J.N. 22454, 23228
Reenen, R.van 22099
Rees, A.F. 18562-3
Rees, J.G. 9704
Rees, P.M. 10926
Reese, T.R. 2600
Reeve, H. 8703
Reeve, W.H. 17969
Reeves, A. 22455
Reeves, R.A. 22456, 23006
Rego, A.da S. See Silva Rego, A.da
Rego, C.A.de F.S. 12718
Rego, F.A.do 12902-7
Regulus 20220, 20344
Rehfisch, F. 6013, 6258-9, 6606, 13159-60
Rehse, H. 18408-10
Reichman, S. 9796

Reid, J.A. 5763, 6260-3, 6388
Reid, R.E. 20602
Reid, R.T. 5365
Reining, C.C. 352, 401, 6014
Reining, P. 18200
Reis, C.S. 12846-7, 23776, 24205-8
Reis, D.da C. See Câmara Reis, D.da
Reis, J.A. 13448
Reis, J.P.dos 23871
Reisdorf, G. 17658
Reisner, A. 6264
Reisner, G.A. 5914-8
Relly, H. 13161
Remondon, R. 8204
Remy, G. 1906
Renard, M. 6750
Renaud, Ct. 9510
Renaut, F.P. 2910
Rendinger, de 12969
Renel 24393
Renier, M. 14102
Renison, P. 17531
Rennell, Lord [Rodd, F.J.R.] 2236, 4863, 5017
Renner, G.T. 7728
Renner, W. 8114
Rennie, G. 2601, 20475
Repin 9545
Resende, D.S.de 4018
Retel, A.L. See Laurentin-Retel, A.
Rétif, A. 1061, 4019, 5053, 13254, 24643
Reusch, R. 17858, 18118, 18337-8
Reut, C. 1387
Revault, J. 6751-3
Reverdy, J.C. 7147, 7148
Revington, T.M. 17859-60, 18119-20
Rewane, O.N. 12174
Rex, F.J. 111
Rey, C.F. 16515, 16791
Rey, P.A. 4020
Rey, R.C. See Capot-Rey, R.
Reyburn, H.A. 22457, 23229
Reyes Morales, R. 15531
Reygasse, M. 729, 7021
Reymond, F. 2911
Reynard, R. 13725-8
Reynardson, H.B. 19675
Reyneke, J. 21682, 23230
Reyner, A.S. 7284
Reynier, E. 8444
Reynolds, B. 20952
Reynolds, F.A. 18411
Reynolds, H. 14103
Reynolds, R. 3463, 19801, 20603, 20716, 22877-8
Reynolds, V. 4302-3
Rgwatinyanya, A. 20717
Rheinallt Jones, E.B. 22251, 23263

Rheinallt Jones, J.D. 19684, 19844, 21801, 22152, 22180,
    22236, 22389, 22458-60, 22951-2, 22994, 23170-1, 23232-41
Rhijn, A.J.R.van. See Van Rhijn, A.J.R.
Rhodes, W. 43, 948-9, 20173
Rhodius, G. 14540
Rhotert, H. 6632
Riad, M. 5143, 5253, 11885
Rial Canosa, J.M.C. See Castro-Rial Canosa, J.M.
Ribard, M.E. 24623
Ribas, T. 12908
Ribeaucourt, J.M. 14788, 14789
Ribeiro, C. 23872-3
Ribeiro de Santana, A. 23457
Ricardo, C. 24060
Riccardi, T. 16700
Ricci, L. 269, 16611-9, 16641, 16908, 16944-5, 16988, 17007,
    17143
Ricci, M. 16516-8
Richard, J. 16792
Richard, R. 2912, 8531-2
Richard-Molard, J. 112, 1388, 1942, 4232, 4674-6, 8207,
    8352, 8374, 8408, 8577, 9071, 12748
Richards, A. 10110
Richards, A.I. 643-5, 4677, 5764, 14104, 16020, 18981,
    20953-9, 21211
Richards, C.S. 22181-3
Richards, C.G. 353, 17581
Richards, E.V. 21362
Richards, G.E. 6036
Richards, J.B. 20043
Richards, M.G. 5765-7
Richards, T.H.H. 10573
Richardson, B. 2602
Richardson, C.B. 20476
Richardson, C.H. 13345
Richardson, I. 3197, 21164-5, 24338
Richardson, J.N. 5768
Richardson, R.B. 12596, 18339
Richardson, S.S. 11701-2, 12175
Richings, F.G. 22033, 23007
Richter, J. 4021
Ricketts, E. 15949
Riddell, J. 1607
Ridgeway, W. 22654
Ridley, M.W. 19474, 19491
Rieger, M. 3004-5
Riehl, P.A. 14105, 15327
Riel, J.van 4190, 12975
Rieser, H.F. 869
Riet Lowe, C.van 17963, 20163, 22028-32
Rigaud, O.M. See Mennesson-Rigaud, O.
Rigby, P.J.A. 17861-3
Riley, N.D. 8115
Riley, W.T.C. 10357
Rimmer, D. 212, 1389
Rimmington, G.T. 21254-5, 21403-4

Riordan, J. 22789
Riou, G. 9251
Ripado, M.F.B.B. See Bento Ripado, M.F.B.
Ripollés, A.Q. See Quintano Ripollés, A.
Rippen, B.van 646
Risbec, J. 8354-7
Risley, R.C.H. 15852, 15854
Rist, L. 1390
Ristorcelli, M. 9167
Rita-Ferreira, A. 23777-82, 23874-5, 24291
Ritchie, J.F. 647
Ritsert, K.E. 11513-4
Ritzenthaler, R.E. 13162, 13255
Rive, R. 3464, 22879
Rivenc, P. 1778, 7689
Rivero, M.O.de. See Ortiz de Rivero, M.
Rivers, A.H.L.P. See Pitt Rivers, A.H.L.
Rivers, W.H.R. 5144
Riverson, I.D. 10195
Rivière, C. 9060
Rivière, T. 6980, 6995-6
Rivierez, H. 213
Rivkin, A. 1391, 2237, 2603-4, 2913, 11458, 14838
Riza, S. 6967
Rizkana, I. 5145
Roach, H. 10574
Robbie, J. 6541-2
Robert, A. 3757
Robert, A.P. 3758, 8336-7
Robert, D. 7468
Robert, M. 1775, 14588-9, 15407
Robert, S. 16204, 16346-51
Roberts, A.D. 16473, 19282-3, 19358
Roberts, C.C. 17603
Roberts, D.F. 5769, 15816
Roberts, E. 22461-2
Roberts, H.M. 20345
Roberts, H.V. 23242
Roberts, J. 17307
Roberts, J.G. 20044-7, 20665-6, 20865
Roberts, M. 2605
Roberts, R.O. 19492-3
Roberts, S. 21507-10
Roberts-Wray, K. 3759-63
Robertson, D.M. 21109
Robertson, H.M. 22184
Robertson, J. 1392, 6265, 11703-4
Robertson, J.M. 5366
Robertson, J.W. 5770-1
Robertson, O.H. 21137
Robertson, W.G. 21138
Robertson, W.S. 10859
Roberty, G. 7729, 8116, 8358, 8578, 8959
Robin, J. 8548, 8628, 8765, 9641
Robin, M. 9646
Robins, J.W. 21432

Robins, R.E. 15910
Robinson, A. 1393
Robinson, A.E. 870, 4678, 4867, 5103, 5772-3, 6102, 6266-74, 15846, 16066-9, 16620, 16793, 17970
Robinson, A.E.P. 20477
Robinson, A.M.L. 21802-4, 22077, 22604, 22655-60, 22880-4
Robinson, C.H. 7871-2
Robinson, D.A. 19866
Robinson, E.A. 6272
Robinson, J. 2914
Robinson, J.B. 22661-2
Robinson, K. 2238, 2606, 8283, 8375, 12570
Robinson, K.E. 8282
Robinson, K.R. 20174, 20604
Robinson, L.K. 20048
Robinson, M.S. 11459
Robinson, P. 5367
Robinson, R. 20866
Robinson, R.E. 2239-41, 3764
Robinson, S. 7662
Robinson, S.C. See Cartmel-Robinson, S.
Robson, E. 2915
Robson, J.R.K. 18564
Robson, P. 1394, 8587
Robyns, W. 15401, 15408
Roch, R. 18565
Rocha, F.N.da 4022
Rocha Brito, A.da 23783
Rocha Faria, J.M.da 23963
Rochard-Molard, J. See Richard-Molard, J.
Roche, J. 2242, 7196, 8238-9
Roche, J.C. 1395
Roche, P. 12365, 12367-9
Rocher, L. 4954-5
Rochlin, S.A. 19781, 21805, 22663-4, 22885-7, 23243
Rockley, Lady; formerly the Hon.Lady Evelyn Cecil 22665
Roda y Jiménez, R.de 7610
Rodan, P.N.R. See Rosenstein-Rodan, P.N.
Rodd, F.J.R. See Rennell, Lord [Rodd, F.J.R.]
Rodd, P.R. 5045
Rodd, R. 5368
Rodda, P. 22463
Rode, P. 8359
Rode, P.de 15177
Rodger, F.C. 10823
Rodger, J.A. 21543
Rodger, J.P. 10358
Rodhain, A. 4191, 15409-10
Rodinson, M. 13049, 13283, 13524, 13549
Rodney, W. 7873
Rodolph, U., pseud. See Ouologuem, Y.
Rodrigues, A.D. 3198
Rodrigues, J.A. 24108
Rodrigues, J.F. 12749
Rodrigues, J.H. 2916

Rodrigues, M.S. See Sarmento Rodrigues, M.
Rodrigues de Campos, O. 4023, 23818
Rodrigues Martins, J.L.R. 4192
Rodriguez, C.Q. 5018-9
Rodríguez Aguilera, C. 7398
Rodríguez Mellado, I. 5435
Roehl, K. 15640-1, 16103
Roelandt, R. 4024
Roewer, C.F. 8360
Roeykens, A. 308, 2917, 4025, 14839-41, 15328-9
Roffo, P. 729
Rogado Quintino, F. 7558, 7870, 12695-9, 12708-9, 12719, 12773
Roger, A. 8284
Rogers, C.A. 12504, 20478, 20835
Rogers, F.H. 18982
Rogin, M. 2607
Rogozinski, S. 13346
Rohdie, S. 10437
Roldan, J.de L 7411
Rolleston, I.H.O. 17864
Rollings, P.J. 8163
Rollinson, D.H.L. 19494
Rollnick, J. 390, 648
Romanelli, P. 6856
Romaniuk, A. 15532
Romano, E.P. 23876, 23964
Romano, M.P. 4661, 19706, 21763, 22274, 23672, 23877-9, 23881-3, 23900, 23965-86, 23988, 24209-12
Rombauts, H. 14106-7, 15078-81
Romer, J.D. 4304, 12370
Romero Moliner, R. 2243, 2918, 15759, 15768-9
Romieu, M.P.B. See Brugnes-Romieu, M.P.
Rommes, M. 15082
Romulo, C.P. 2919
Ronaivoarivony, G.de P. 4679
Rondeau, A. 6785
Rondelez, V. 14343
Rondot, P. 2244, 6857, 6738, 6942, 6968
Rood, N. 14108-9, 14842, 15083, 15178
Roome, J.W. 12951
Roos, T. 21683
Roosevelt, E. 2608
Root, J.W. 7663
Rooth, A.R. 2920
Rooyen, P.van 23244
Rooyen, T.S.van 22185
Rop, A.de 14110-1, 14307, 15084-91, 15179, 15330
Roper, E.M. 6369
Roque, F.C. 23884
Rosa, C.L. See La Rosa, C.
Rosa, M. See Maria Rosa
Rosa Pinto, A.A.da 4305, 23050, 24197, 24213
Rosberg, C.G., Jr. 2609
Roscoe, J. 17269, 18788-9, 19155

Rose, Sister 18121
Rose, B.W. 649
Rose, J.H. 22666
Rose, J.R. 9966-8
Rosemond, C.C.de 17971
Rosenstein-Rodan, P.N. 1396
Rosenzweig, M. 12628
Rosevear, D.R. 12371-82
Roseveare, R. 4680
Rosinha, A.J. 23717, 24214-6
Rosner, M.S. 4681
Ross, A.S.C. 7956
Ross, D.A. 11886
Ross, E. 2245, 12565, 13716
Ross, E.D. 7348, 16683, 16794-5
Ross, R. 4193-4
Ross, S.L. See Leith-Ross, S.
Rossi, E. 6686-7, 16621-2
Rossignol, M. 13218
Rossini, C.C. See Conti Rossini, C.
Rostow, W.W. 2610
Rotberg, R.I. 2921, 14843, 16021, 19738, 21139-40, 21202,
   21242
Roth, N.R. 19542
Rothchild, D. 2611-2, 16023
Rouamba, T. 9423
Rouanel, J. 7022
Rouanet, R. 9168
Roubet, F.E. 7023-4
Roucek, J.S. 2246
Rouch, J. 3363, 8195, 8836, 9220, 9305-6, 9437, 9622-3, 9632,
   10860, 11142
Rougeot, P.C. 13449, 13745-6
Rougerie, G. 7721, 9069, 9072, 9237, 9350, 9252-5, 9293
Rouget, G. 950-1, 9033, 9511, 9531, 9594, 11313
Rougevin-Baville, M. 2247
Rouleau, E. 14703
Roumain, J. 3465-6, 3587
Roumeguère, P. 19645
Roumeguère-Eberhardt, J. 650, 19645, 21932
Rounce, N.V. 17684
Rouse, R. 4026
Rousse, J.P. 6914-5
Rousseau, J.A. 13347
Rousseau, R. 8629, 8746-7
Rousselot, R. 8958, 9659
Roussier, J. 5060, 6916
Roussier, P. 16070
Routh, C.R.N. 22667
Routh, E. 7349
Roux, A. 9231
Roux, C. 13022-3
Roux, E. 21838, 22252, 22464
Roux, F.C. See Charles-Roux, F.
Roux, R. 1397

Rovere, P.F. 6702
Rowe, J.A. 18947, 19284-6
Rowe, J.W.F. 15911
Rowe, R.H. 7730
Rowe, S. 9949
Rowell, T.E. 19495
Rowland, H.R. 21433
Rowland, J.H. 20775
Rowlands, E.C. 11998-12001
Rowlands, J.S.S. 17604
Rowlatt, M. 5283-4, 5369, 10284
Rowley, J.V. 5774
Rowling, C.W. 1608, 12176
Rowling, F. 3199, 19408
Rowse, E.A.A. 16661
Roy, A.L. See Le Roy, A.
Roy, C. 3467
Roy, F.J. 3588
Roy, H.van 14112-3
Roy, J.L. See Le Roy, J.
Roy, R. 9161
Royal African Society 448
Royer, P. 13163
Rózsa, G. 354
Ruas, A. 4195, 12848
Rubadiri, D. 3364
Rubbens, A. 1398, 4682, 14114, 14704-7, 15265, 15533-4, 15602
Rubens-Duval, O. 376
Rubenson, S. 16796-7
Rubin, L. 22953-5
Rubin, N.N. 21774-5, 22955
Rubio García, L. 2246, 6671, 17346, 22465, 23246, 23342
Rudigoz, C. 8653
Ruel, M. 11143, 17270-3, 13164-5
Ruete, T. 7664
Ruffer, A. 5424
Ruhlmann, A. 7179, 7197
Rumann, W.B. 11144
Rumberger, J.P. 17984
Rumeu de Armas, A. 2922-4
Ruocco, D. 1399
Ruoff, T.B.F. 1609
Ruoro, P. 17582
Rushby, G.G. 4306, 17865-7
Rusike, I. 20692-3
Rusillon, H. 24496, 24518-9, 24552
Rusmini, E. 15982
Russel, B. 4027
Russell, A. 18340-1, 19543
Russell, A.C. 10438, 10824-5
Russell, C.E.B. 12383
Russell, F.F. 16970
Russell, H.B.L. 4196-7
Russell, P. 214

Russell, T.A. 12384
Russell, W.H. 5370
Russinger, A. 7136, 7156
Ruthven, C.M.H. See Hore-Ruthven, C.M.
Rutten, A. 15535
Ruxton, F.H. 11145-6
Rwiza, K.J. 17866
Ryckbost, J. 15266-7
Ryckmans, A. 14115, 14308, 15536
Ryckmans, G. 16623
Ryckmans, P. 2249, 15411, 15537-8
Rycroft, D. 14309, 19782-3, 21010, 22034-5
Ryder, A.F.C. 7603, 10575, 11350, 11887-9
Rydings, H.H. 9780
Ryelandt, D. 13756

S., C.H. 6543
S., C.T. 20776
S., E. 1400, 12993, 22186
S., F. 12385
S., G. 8217
S., G.H. 18568
S., J. 14481
S., N.H.D. 14116, 20175-6, 20667
S., W.H. 20074
S., W.J.S. 11579
S.H. See H., S.
S.-H., E.G. 5775, 5922-3
Sá, A.F.de. See Fernandes de Sá, A.
Sâ, C.de 12720
Sá, F.V.de 449
Sá Couto, H. 4028
Saada Salim bin Omar 18617
Saadi, K.A.O. 18342
Saakse, J. 21933
Saakwa-Mante, K. 4198
Saayman, R.B. 23247
Sabater, J. 12982, 15679
Sabater Pi, J. 15764
Sabbadini, E. 1401, 1610-1, 4935, 5080, 5196-7, 5400, 5919,
   14482, 19359
Sabben-Clarke, E.E. 2925
Saberwal, S.C. 17274
Sabet, A.A. 5111
Sabikhi, V. 22466-7, 23248
Sacchetti, A. 16519
Sachs, I. 1402
Sackey, A.Q. See Quaison-Sackey, A.
Sackville (de la Warr), H.E.D.B. 2250
Sacré-Coeur, M.A.du 3765, 4683
Sadji, A. 3365, 8312, 8676
Sadler, E.H. 17387
Sadler, J.H. 19156
Sadler, W. 12559
Sadlier, T.R. 17972

Sādwā, P. 16946
Sady, E.J. 2251
Sadza, D. 20049
Saenen, J. 14117, 15180
Saenz Martínez, J. 15683
Saez-Martin, B. 4869
Saffery, A.L. 22187, 22468, 23171, 23249-50
Safford, F. 22668
Sagar, J.W. 6275
Sagaye, G.M. See Gabre-Medhin, T.
Sai, B.A. 11147
Sai, F.T. 10826
Saidu, C. 8117
Sailer, T.H.P. 5242
Saint-Floris, H.de 13529
Saint-Jacques 1612
Saint-Joseph, L.M.de 8677
St.Leger, F.Y. 20867
Saint-Martin, Y. 7874, 8299, 8630-1
Saint-Pereuse, T.de 19642
Sainte-Marie, J.F. 4902
Sainville, L. 3366, 9061
Sakah, B.T. 13166
Sakiliba, D.F. 3200
Salacuse, J.W. 12177
Salama, P. 5020
Salasc 13238
Salazar, A.de O. 2252
Saleh, I. 18343
Salerno, N. 1403
Salih, M.M. 6015
Salmon, C.S. 7875-6
Salmon, J. 14708
Salmon, R. 6276
Salome, F. 17094
Salomon, L. 22669
Salomonson, J.W. 4870, 6754
Saloway, R. 10439
Salt, G. 18123
Salubi, A. 11890
Salvador, A.R.N. 23718, 24217
Salvador, P. 2253
Salvadori, M. 16448, 17472
Salvadori, R. 7877, 9052-3
Salvo, C.S. 12976
Salvy, G. 4956, 5081
Samain, A. 14118
Samantar, M.S. 17095
Samantar, Y.O. 2614, 17096-7
Samaran, C. 6917-9
Samarin, W.J. 3201-2, 13575, 13596-9, 13668
Sampaio, M.J.F.de 24218
Sampedro, J.L. 1404
Sampil, M. 8982, 9014
Sampson, A. 10440, 23251

Sampson, D.N.   18122, 18569
Sampson, M.J.   10231
Samuel, F.   18034
Samuel, H.   14844
Samuel, J.T.B.   See Bendor-Samuel, J.T.
Samuel, P.M.B.   See Bendor-Samuel, P.M.
Samuels, L.H.   1405
Samuelson, L.M.   19606
San-Bento, O.   3618
San Valero Aparisi, J.   2929
Sanceau, E.   651, 17160
Sanches, G.   4029
Sanchez, J.A.   See Alvarez Sanchez, J.
Sánchiz, J.C.   5230
Sancho de Sopranis, H.   2926, 5021, 5026
Sandars, G.E.R.   5776, 5920, 6277
Sander, E.   2254
Sander, F.   12386-7
Sanderson, F.E.   21363
Sanderson, G.M.   21285-7, 21467
Sanderson, G.N.   2927, 5371, 5441, 6278-9, 16798
Sanderson, J.   21934, 22036
Sanderson, L.   6037-41
Sanderson, M.   18790, 20960
Sanderson, R.W.   10576
Sandes, S.D.   20177
Sandford, D.A.   16799
Sandford, K.S.   4936
Sandilands, A.   3292, 22790
Sandison, P.J.   6607
Sandon, H.   6016, 6544
Sanger, C.   2615, 17473, 20479
Sankale, M.   8766
Sano, M.   9034
Sanogo, M.   9424
Sansumwa, M.   1406
Santa Rita, J.G.   2928
Santagata, F.   1407-8
Santana, A.R.de.   See Ribeiro de Santana, A.
Santandrea, S.   5777-88, 6280-2, 6342-3, 18412
Santareno, J.A.L.M.   12666, 12721, 12849-50
Santareno Pignatelli, M.J.S.de   23719, 23885-6, 24219
Santesson, C.G.   15412, 16520, 23311
Santo, J.do E.   See Espírito Santo, J.do
Santos, A.G.dos   4030
Santos, A.M.   See Miranda Santos, A.
Santos, E.dos   15584, 23415
Santos, J.G.M.   23720, 23819, 24010
Santos, J.M.P.   See Paniagua y Santos, J.M.
Santos, L.F.dos   3203
Santos, M.dos (pseud.: Kalungano)   2255, 3559
Santos, M.P.dos   4109, 24011-2, 24220-4
Santos, M.P.P.dos.   See Pereira dos Santos, M.P.
Santos, P.A.G.   See Gomes dos Santos, P.A.
Santos, R.M.dos   23482

Santos Dias, J.A.T. 4199, 4260, 4307-9, 6547, 15413,
    15765, 17165, 19431, 23721-3, 24199, 24225-41
Santos e Silva, A.L.dos 24292
Santos-Junior 23820
Santos Lima, A.J. 12700-1
Santos Merino, A. 4183
Santos Peixe, J.dos 23784, 24049-50
Sanz, J.M. See Martinez y Sanz, J.
Sap, S. 11460
Sapir, E. 12621-2
Saprassasson, B. 3468
Sar, A. 1780
Saraiva Barreto, M. 24061
Sarbah, J.M. 7505, 10577, 10731
Sardinha, R.M.de A. 1409, 12722
Sarel, B.S. See Sternberg-Sarel, B.
Šarevskaja, B.I. 652
Sargent, D. 17388
Sarmento Rodrigues, M. 1410, 4031, 12803
Sarolea, C. 2930
Sarot, E.E. 23483
Sartre, J.P. 3367, 4684-5, 14709
Sassoon, H. 17667, 17942
Sassoon, M. 11148
Sastre, R. 4032, 4686, 10578
Satti, S.A. 6017
Saukila, W.S. 21501
Sauldie, M.M. 19158
Saulnier, E. 8632
Saulnier, M. 8633
Saumagne, C. 3766, 5022-4, 6858-69, 6920
Saunders, G.F.T. 10827
Saunders, J.R. 22469
Saunders, L.H. 4233, 4310, 7506, 10927-34, 12388
Saunders, M.M. 19021-2
Saunderson, G. 22470
Sauter, R. 16624-5
Sautoy, P.du. See Du Sautoy, P.
Sautter, G. 9403, 11149, 13617, 13649-51, 13689,
    13695, 15539
Sauvaget, J. 8914
Sauvy, A. 1411
Sauvy, J. 21378
Savage, D.C. 19157
Savani, M. 13284
Savard, G.C. 16521
Savaron, C. 24394, 24497-9
Saville, R.V. 5789
Savimbi, J. 23525
Savoia-Genevo, E.di 16522
Savonnet, G. 8579, 8767, 9425-7, 9467
Savory, B. 16419
Savory, D. 5285
Sawanhu, J. 20605
Sawe, J.A. 18124

Sawyer, C.R. 355
Sawyerr, A.W. 9758
Sawyerr, H. 4033, 7561, 8015, 9754-7, 9919, 9931, 11008
Saxton, S.W. 10579
Sayce, A.H. 5372
Sayous, A. 6870
Scaetta, H. 16800
Scaff, A.H. 18983
Scaglione, F.A. 2256, 6646
Scalais, F. 14541
Scalapino, R.A. 2616
Scarbrough, E.M. 12656
Scarisbrick, J.J. 7878, 22670
Scarpa, A. 12851
Scek, M.A. 17115
Schaar, W. 21935
Schaeffer, E. 3767-8
Schaeffner, A. 952-3, 8816, 9015, 9035, 13196
Schaetzen, A.de 14119
Schapera, I. 653, 1025, 19607-8, 19739, 19837, 19848,
    21587, 21684-92, 21695, 21701, 21714-6, 21725-7,
    21730-4, 21738, 21752, 21936-8
Scharf, J.W. 450
Schatz, S.P. 11461-4
Schebesta, P. 654, 14120-7, 14590, 15092, 15331, 15540,
    20050-1
Schedl, K.E. 9390
Schefer, C. 7117
Scheibler, P. 10111-2
Scheibling 13517
Schenkel, C.J.W.P. See Pitt-Schenkel, C.J.W.
Schiller, A.A. 3769, 3770
Schingen, S.J.van 14128, 24242
Schlippe, P.de 5470-1
Schlunk, M. 7957
Schmid, S. 15093
Schmidt, A. 13167, 13219
Schmidt, W. 488, 1781, 19609
Schmiedel, H. 18003
Schmitz, L. 1613
Schnapper, B. 2931
Schneider, G. 11150-1, 11314
Schneider, H.K. 17275, 17867, 18618
Schneider, R. 16626-8, 16836-7, 16947
Schneider, W. 14542
Schnell, R. 7562, 7731, 8118-20, 9036, 9073, 9169-71,
    9229, 9256, 9294
Schober, R. 9331
Schoelcher, V. 2953
Schoell, F.L. 215, 2617
Schoeman, P.J. 21753
Schoentjes, R. 15541
Schofield, A.T. 18897
Schofield, J.F. 20178, 20606
Scholfield, A. 23350

Schols, J.P. 4687
Scholten, H. 18481
Schott, R. 21693
Schotter, G. 7141
Schouteden, H. 15414-6
Schreiner, O.D. 22956
Schreiner, W.P. 22671
Schreyer, J. 21939
Schubart, O. 8121
Schuler, E. 13348
Schulz, K.H. See Hechter-Schulz, K.
Schulz-Weidner, W. 16523
Schulze, W. 7701
Schumacher, P.J. 490, 3204, 14129-32, 15417, 15585-7, 15655
Schumann, C. 18413
Schürle, G. 13168
Schuster, C. 5790
Schwab, W.B. 11152-5
Schwartz, J. 16909, 16524
Schweeger-Hefel, A. 9428, 13714, 15542, 23321
Schwetz, J. 4200, 14591, 15418-9
Sciascia, G. 1782, 19671
Scoble, C.N. 21191, 22957
Scotland, D.W. 9772, 9813, 9877, 9969
Scott, A. 3469, 5025, 10828, 23416
Scott, D.J.R. 2251, 7770
Scott, G.C. 6042, 21061
Scott, H.S. 1783-4, 15950, 17532
Scott, J.G. 8122
Scott, J.R. 6546
Scott, M. 22471-2, 23252, 23343-4
Scott, M.N.O.C. 4034
Scott, P. 20314, 21839, 22188
Scott, R. 19081
Scott, R.D. 15912, 19023
Scott, R.R. 16205, 18125, 18898
Scott, W.R. 2932
Scotton, C.M.M. 16206
Scrivenor, T.V. 17868
Scudder, T. 20961
Scully, N. 21593
Seabrook, A.T.P. 18035
Seager, C.E. 20052
Seath, G. 22888
Seaton, S.W. 12597
Sebag, P. 6774, 6871-3, 6969-70
Sebiva, G. 15620, 18939, 20053, 21678
Seck, A. 2933, 7665, 8240
Sedki, L.K. 5436
Sedler, R.A. 16971-3
Seed, C. 21544
Seed, J.H. 20607
Seely, H.C. 17474
Seers, D. 1412-4
Segal, A. 2618, 16022
Segal, B. 19838

Segal, D. 18126
Segal, R. 22473
Ségalen, P. 13044, 13450
Segalerva, E.Z. See Zarco Segalerva, E.
Segonzac, R.de 1054, 7350
Segrais, R.le J.de 24302
Segun, M. See Jolaoso, M.I.
Séguy, E. 8474
Segy, L. 871, 4688, 13712, 14310
Seheme, L. 3470
Seidel, A. 6891, 9367, 10229, 16207-9, 18400, 18414-20, 19360, 19784, 21494
Seidel, H. 9368
Seidenberg, A. 3205
Seidman, R.B. 3771, 10732, 12178
Seitz, T. 655, 6971, 18895
Sekoto, G. 872, 22037
Sékou Touré, A. See Touré, A.S.
Sekyi, K.A. 10733-4
Selassie, H. See Haile Selassie I
Selborne, Lord [R.C.Palmer] 11705, 19719
Seligman, B.Z. 656, 5791, 5797-8, 6344-5
Seligman, C.G. 5198, 5792-8, 5921, 6547, 17276
Sellers, W. 4201, 9645, 10000, 13530
Selous, F.C. 19839, 20608, 22275
Sembene, O. [Sembene Ousmane] 3579
Seme, P.K.I. 2934
Semonin, P. 7879
Sempebwa, E.K.K. 18899
Semple, T. 8123
Senex 20868
Sengat-Kuo, F. 2258-62, 10441, 10580, 13221
Senghor, B. 954
Senghor, L.S. 2263-4, 2620-1, 3368-9, 3589-93, 4689-91, 7771, 8654-6, 8678-80, 9374, 15181
Senior, H.S. 17869, 18036
Senior, M.M. 4035, 9920
Senkatuka, M.E. 19544
Sénones, M. 7019, 7194-5, 7198-9, 8409, 16610
Seppo, P. 13417
Septima 20869
Sequaris, M. 1785
Sequeira, A.de M. 23785, 23887, 24042, 24293-4
Sequeira, J.H. 16801
Serjac, J. 8427
Serle, W. 4311, 8124-5, 12389-97, 13451
Sertorio, G. 11706
Service, M.W. 12398
Servier, J.H. 5104, 6997
Servoise, R. 1415
Sethom, H. 6739, 7162
Seton, R.S. 11156
Seton-Karr, H.W. 5924
Seumois, A. 4036-7
Seurin, J.L. 8376

Sevenet, Lt. 8422
Sevilla, D. 2265, 2935, 7351-2
Sevy, G.V. 12937, 13576
Seweje, M.A. 216
Sewell, P.H. 5442
Sewell, W.G. 10325
Sey, K.A. 10681
Seymour, L.F. 20055, 20777
Seyrig, A. 24500
Shack, W.A. 16525-6
Shackell, R.S. 18791, 19545-6
Shadbolt, K.E. 18201
Shafer, R. 8657
Shaffer, J. 14311-2
Shah, K.K. 22474
Shamuyarira, N.M. 20480
Shann, G.N. 18052, 18344, 18421
Shannon, M. 17659-60
Shantz, H.L. 1943, 15609
Sharland, R.E. 8126-8, 12399-12402
Sharman, J.C. 21166-8
Sharp, A.E. 17566, 18422
Sharpe, A. 4312, 21364, 21468
Sharr, F.A. 10886-7
Sharwood-Smith, J. 11891
Shaul, J.R.H. 20870-1
Shaw, A. 5799
Shaw, C.T. 10196-7
Shaw, E.M. 19610
Shaw, F.L. 2936
Shaw, G.A. 24501
Shaw, J.R. 19672, 21062
Shaw, J.V. 10581, 18202
Shaw, M. 21063
Shaw, S. 20481
Shaw, T. 873, 11315
Shaw, W.B.K. 5925, 6094, 6103
Shawki, M.K. 5460
Sheane, J.H.W. 20962-3
Shebeika, Mekki Eff. 5443
Sheffield, A.F.W. 11892
Sheldon, F. See French-Sheldon
Shelford, F. 113, 1614-5, 7615, 7666, 7732-3, 9878, 10582,
    10735, 17277
Shelton, A.J. 44, 2937, 3370, 4692-3, 7986, 11157-8,
    12002, 12102
Shepherd, G.W. 2260, 2622, 19099
Shepherd, R.H.W. 22253, 23008-11
Shepherd, W.C.A. 23888
Shepperson, G. 2938-9, 14845, 16071, 19819-20, 21176
Sherbini, A.A.el- 6608
Sheridan, L.A. 2267
Sherwood, E.G.P. 770
Shiferaou, A. See Admassou Shiferaou
Shillito, J.F. 18792
Shils, E. 2268, 7702, 8164

Shinar, P. 5105, 5199, 18619
Shinnie, P.L. 771, 5199, 5926-9, 5967, 10198-9, 11225, 18900, 18943
Shippard, S. 22958
Shircore, J.O. 21545
Shirley, G. 23889
Shock, M. 5373
Shooter-Faulkner, M. 7612
Shore, H.L. 955, 18449, 23581
Shorthose, W.T. 12103-5, 12403-5
Shoup, H. 9921
Shoush, M.I.el- 6370
Shriver, S. 1786
Shropshire, D. 657-8, 20056-60, 20383, 20609
Shrubsall, F. 659-660, 5146, 10113
Shrubsole, A.C. 17374
Siad, M.F. See Mohamed Farah Siad
Siann, G. 23253
Sibree, J. 24395-7, 24454, 24502
Sicard, F. 24539
Sicard, H.von 4038, 4903, 19611-3, 20061-7, 20179-81, 20610-5, 20668, 21940, 22672, 24043
Sicé, A. 12977, 12983
Sidibé, M. 8837, 9221
Sieber, D. 11159
Sieber, J. 11159, 13169
Sieber, R. 874-6
Sieffermann, G. 13450, 13452
Siegel, M. 2623, 14846
Siegfried, A. 5231
Sierra Ochoa, A. 877
Siertsema, B. 12003-4
Sigola, S. 20616, 22254
Sikes, S.K. 4313, 12406-8
Sikobole Ndhlovu 20271, 21694
Silberman, L. 4694-5, 13002, 16024, 16802, 17661, 18620, 24339
Silinga, J. 22791
Silkin, J. 13717
Sillans, R. 376, 4314, 12927, 12994
Sillaret, M. 9283
Sillery, A. 6672, 17870, 17998, 18423-5, 18570, 21735
Sillitoe, K.K. 17347-8, 17475
Silone, I. 878
Silva, A.A.da 7880, 9037, 12798-12800
Silva, A.de N.W.da 4202
Silva, A.J.da 23556, 23568
Silva, A.L.dos S. See Santos e Silva, A.L.dos
Silva, A.M.da 451, 23724-6
Silva, C.da 4039, 23612
Silva, F.da 4040
Silva, G.da 9512
Silva, J.C.V.da 23987
Silva, J.D. 2940
Silva, J.F.da. See Ferreira Da Silva, J.

Silva, J.M.da 4295, 23727, 24243-4
Silva, M.C.T.da. See Conceição Tavares da Silva, M.
Silva, M.da 23728, 23890
Silva, M.M.da. See Moreira da Silva, M.
Silva, P.A.da 3619, 23417-9, 23582, 23613
Silva, R.L.da 23729
Silva Amorim 114, 3839
Silva Barbosa, A.J.da 23686, 24245-6
Silva Cunha, J.M.da 1176, 2624, 12741
Silva e Sousa, J.A. 24296
Silva Paes, A.R.C. 23891
Silva Rego, A.da 2941, 2269, 12747, 23557, 23614
Silva Teixeira, A.J.da 4315
Silva Teixeira, R.de C.S.da 4315
Silveira da Costa, C.M. 23730
Silvera, V. 6921-36
Silvera, W.D. 4203
Silverstov, Y. 9172
Silvestre, F. See Andrade, C.
Silvey, J. 1787-8, 14600, 15951, 23254
Simão, J. 23731
Simar, T. 2942
Simeão Vitória 4041, 23493, 23615
Simenauer, E. 17871
Simey, P.A.T. 2270, 20068
Simmance, A.J.F. 17476, 17605-6
Simmonds, E.W.P. See Pope-Simmonds, E.W.
Simmonds, R.G.S. 20069
Simmons, D.C. 11160-3, 11893, 12005-7, 12106-8
Simmons, F.J. 4316
Simmons, J. 15853, 15855
Simmons, W.C. 19496-7
Simões Alberto, M. 467-8, 536, 4145, 4204, 19557, 23668,
    23736-41, 23789-90, 23991-2, 24016, 24066, 24080-5,
    24260-72
Simon, E. 4696
Simon, H. 7285
Simoni, M. 1416-7, 2625
Simonini, G. 16522
Simons, H.J. 21941, 22189, 22475-8, 22959, 23255-6
Simoons, F.J. 661, 879, 16527, 16630, 16684
Simpson, D.H. 18634, 21806
Simpson, G.E. 11164-5
Simpson, M.W.H. See Hilton-Simpson, M.W.
Simpson, S.R. 1617, 3772, 4697, 6389-90
Sinclair, W. 2943
Singer, H.W. 1418
Singer, R. 662, 4205, 21942, 22038-9, 22259
Singh, D. 2265, 2625, 7118, 16449
Singh, K.H. See Hazareesingh, K.
Singh, K.R. 7286
Singh, P. 8241
Sircar, P.K. 10285
Sirry Bey, H. 5232
Sissoko, F.D. 4698, 9116

Sissulu, W.M.   22479-80
Sithole, E.F.C.   2627
Sithole, N.   663
Six, E.P.   14133
Skalnikova, O.   4699
Skeel, C.A.J.   7480
Skeens, S.R.   19287
Skeet, T.H.H.   4904
Skene, R.   15817
Skilleter, M.   12409
Skinner, A.N.   1944
Skinner, E.P.   8016, 8165, 9429, 9465, 9468
Sklar, R.L.   11707-8
Skorov, G.   299
Skotnicki, M.   9257
Skurnik, W.A.E.   8588
Skutil, J.   19614
Slade, R.   14847
Slama, B.   6874
Slater, M.   17607
Slater, M.K.   18470
Slater, R.   10359, 10583-4
Slawecki, L.M.S.   2628
Slim, H.   6875-6
Slim, T.   6877
Sloan, A.   20070
Sloan, R.   1871
Sloley, H.C.   21622, 22481
Sluys, M.   14848, 15367
Sluysmans   14483
Smal   14484
Small, W.   18646
Smart, H.W.   20617
Smart, J.K.   See Karefa-Smart, J.
Smektala, E.D.   See Dabrowska-Smektala, E.
Smit, D.E.   21807, 22673-4
Smith, A.   2266, 16025, 17872, 18127
Smith, C.E.   622
Smith, D.A.   6548, 16420
Smith, D.N.   3773
Smith, E.A.   7604
Smith, E.L.   8017
Smith, E.M.   7605
Smith, E.W.   115, 664-6, 1419-20, 1789, 2944, 4700, 10114,
   10217, 11709, 15094, 16072, 17349, 17662, 18128, 19740,
   20964-6, 21634
Smith, G.   21434
Smith, G.H.   See Humphrey-Smith, G.
Smith, G.J.   See Janson-Smith, G.
Smith, H.   880, 4206
Smith, H.B.W.   See Wenban-Smith, H.B.
Smith, H.F.C.   5930, 7881-2, 11515, 11894
Smith, H.L.   956
Smith, H.M.   18482
Smith, H.M.B.   See Brice-Smith, H.M.

Smith, H.S. 20618
Smith, I.D. 20482
Smith, J. 452, 6549
Smith, J.H. 2511
Smith, J.R. 18621
Smith, J.S. 7883
Smith, J.Sharwood. See Sharwood-Smith, J.
Smith, J.S.R.B. See Birket-Smith, J.S.R.
Smith, K.G. 12410
Smith, M.G. 667, 3774, 8166, 11465-8, 11895, 12179, 12505
Smith, N.L. See Langford-Smith, N.
Smith, R. 1790-1, 2273, 5243, 11316, 11896-9, 23257
Smith, R.B. 4701
Smith, R.H. 22482
Smith, R.O. See Orme-Smith, R.
Smith, R.W. 18203
Smith, T.E. 2629
Smith, V.W. 12411-2
Smith, W.C. 8475
Smith, W.W. See Wenban-Smith, W.
Smithies, F. 12413
Smolla, G. 17973
Smuts, J. 2274-5, 19720, 19741, 22483, 22675, 23258-60, 23351
Snitcher, F. 22484
Snow, O.W. 5472
Snow-White, A. 15850, 15852, 16352-3
Snowden, A.E. 20071, 20182-3
Snowden, F.M. 772, 16803
Snoxall, R.A. 15860, 15862, 16104, 16210-4, 17999, 18793, 19288, 19361-3, 19379, 19498
Soares, A.C. 12725
Soares Barata, O. 2276
Sobral Dias, D.A. 116
Sobrinho, J.L.de S. See Sousa Sobrinho, J.L.de
Söderberg, B. 13641
Soeiro, A.A. 24247
Soeiro, A.N. See Navarro Soeiro, A.
Sofer, C. 19547, 23261
Sofer, R. 19547
Sofoluwe, G.O. 12180
Soga, J.H. 21943
Sohier, A. 14134, 15238, 15268-9, 15270-8, 15543-6
Sohler, J. 13453-4
Sokunbi, D.O.B. 11466
Solanke, L. 2945, 7884, 11169-70
Solano y Aza, M. 7353
Soler, B. 7447
Soler, C.B. See Blanco Soler, C.
Solheim, W. 24414
Solignac, M.J. 6950
Solsona Conillera, J. 7412
Solus, H. 3775
Someren, V.G.L.van 17627
Somerset, F.R.R. 5800

Somerset, H.C.A. 19024-5
Somerville, A.A. 18129
Somerville, J.J.B. 20483
Sommerfelt, K. 19499
Song, M. 11710
Sonubi, O. 11467
Soors, M. 14135, 14313, 14849, 15547
Soper, R.C. 11317
Soper, T. 1421, 1617, 2630-1
Soper, T.P. 1458
Sopranis, H.S.de. See Sancho de Sopranis, H.
Soret, M. 12984, 13606, 13658, 14136-7
Soromenho, C. 23558-9
Soromenho, L. 24251
Sorrensen, M.P.K. 17350, 17533
Sory, A. 9131
Sory, B. 8980
Sosa, L.de 5027
Sossouhounto, F. 9579
Souce, O. 8681
Soupart, H. 15279
Sourd, M. See Le Sourd, M.
Sournies, J. 9238
Sousa, A.de F.G. See Figueiredo Gomes e Sousa, A.de
Sousa, A.E.de 24252
Sousa, A.G.de 23455, 23462, 23842
Sousa, A.N.de 12909-10, 23420
Sousa, J.A.S. See Silva e Sousa, J.A.
Sousa, J.de 24253
Sousa, M.D.de. See David de Sousa, M.
Sousa, P.A.de 23616
Sousa, P.A.N. 12911
Sousa Bella, L.de 12774
Sousa Dias, A.de 23995
Sousa Dias, A.H.G.de 23051
Sousa Dias, G. 3907, 23617
Sousa Junior, J.de 24241
Sousa Leitão, A.E.de 21405
Sousa Melo, J.M.de 453, 23732-3
Sousa Neves, A.de 20384
Sousa Prego, I. 24077
Sousa Sobrinho, J.L.de 23901, 24254-5, 24297
Sousberghe, L.de 4702, 14138-40, 14314-5, 15280, 15588
Soustelle, J. 4905
South Africa. Central Housing Board. See Central Housing
   Board
South Africa. Dept.of Agriculture 21840
South Africa. Native Affairs Department. See Native Affairs
   Department
South African Institute of Race Relations 21635, 22190
Southall, A.W. 4703, 14710, 18794-5, 19159, 19289
Southon, H.A.W. 16421
Southorn, T. 9686
Southwold, M. 19400, 19500
Souto, A.M.do 20315

Souza, N.F.de 9580
Sow, A.I. 9117
Sowa, R.von 18426-7
Sowah, E.N.P. 10736
Sowande, F. 957, 11318
Soward, F.H. 22485
Sowerby, T.W. 11711
Soyer, L. 13024
Soyinka, W. 3466, 12109, 17583, 18901
Spaandonck, M.van 14316, 15095
Spadaro, S. 1422, 3776
Spalding, J. 18037
Spanolo, L.M. 5801
Spanton, E.F. 4042
Speares, J. 20072, 20619
Spearpoint, F. 20967
Speeckaert, G.P. 117
Speed, F. 11171
Speke, J.H. 19290
Speller, C. 17351
Spence, B. 5802, 6550
Spence, J.E. 21623, 22486, 22676
Spencer, H.A. 4317
Spencer, J. 3206
Spencer, P. 17278
Spender, H. 14850, 22063
Spengler, J.J. 4704-5
Spens, T. 1792
Speyer, H. 14711
Spicer, C. 20281
Spicer, N.H.D. 20712
Spies, E. 17873
Spillmann, G. 1423, 7354
Spilsbury, A.G. 12954
Spire, F. 5803, 18796
Spiro, J.M. 1424
Spitaleri, O. 1618
Spitz, M. 4043
Spohr, O.H. 21808-9, 22089
Spottiswoode, H.E. 11580-1, 12414-5
Spray, E.G. 8266
Spry, J.F. 18204, 18571-2
Spurling, A.C. 3777
Spyer, G. 356
Squires, B.T. 21736-7
Squires, H.G. 20778
Sram, J. 13239, 13455
Stacey, C.P. 5374
Stacey, N. 22040
Stadelmann, E. 4937
Stafford, D.N. 18797-8, 18933
Stahl, F. 12416
Stahl, K.M. 18345
Stainer, M. 9016
Staley, E. 1425, 7225
Stamberg, F. 17874-5

Stammers, F.A.R.   4207, 8129
Stamp, L.D.   7734, 11582
Stampa, L.   3655
Standing, P.C.   5028, 16701
Stanfield, D.P.   12506
Stanier, M.W.   19501
Staniforth, G.R.   6018
Stanislas, P.   14141-2
Stanley, C.V.B.   6659
Stanley, H.   2277, 21110
Stanley, J.H.   20555
Stanley, M.   18053
Stanley, W.R.   12552
Stanner, W.E.H.   16026
Stannus, H.S.   18799, 21288, 21316
Stanovnik, J.   1426
Stansgate, Viscount, 1925-.   See Benn, A.W.
Stanton, E.A.E.   5804, 5953, 6019, 6043, 6104-6, 16073
Stanton, E.W.   22191
Stanton, H.   22487
Stanton, W.R.   10935
Stapleton, G.B.   10861
Stapleton, J.H.   8838
Stapleton, W.H.   3207, 15096
Stappers, L.   14143-55, 14317, 15097-9, 15100-8, 15182-3
Starmans, G.A.N.   21406-7
Stas, J.B.   14156
Staude, W.   373, 8839, 16631-2
Staveley, R.O.   7703
Stayt, E.   19870
Stayt, H.A.   14157
Stazyk, K.   1427
Stead, C.   1793
Stead, W.H.   20073-7, 20184, 20316, 20872
Stebbing, E.P.   454, 1945-6, 5805
Stechman, S.   6660
Steel, A.   23262
Steel, R.W.   455, 1947-9, 4706, 10286
Steele, B.   21408
Steemers, J.C.S.   10115-6
Steere, E.   15818
Stefaniszyn, B.   20968-70, 21011
Stegman, J.J.   21409
Steiger-Hayley, T.T.   18717-8, 18800
Stein, H.B.   22041
Steiner, F.B.   17876
Steinmann, A.   16528
Stempffer, H.   9391, 12651
Stengers, J.   2946-7, 14348, 14851
Stenmans, A.   14485
Stenning, D.J.   4707, 11172, 18801, 19401
Stent, G.E.   23263-4
Stephens, J.E.M.   19364
Stern, A.   5375
Stern, H.   6755

Stern, R.M. 7667
Sternberg-Sarel, B. 5106
Sterry, W. 6407
Stetson, G.R. 1428, 4044, 4208, 4708, 14592, 23421
Steudel, Prof. 4209
Stevens, C.G. 20185
Stevens, G.A. 10200
Stevens, J.C. 12598
Stevens, R.A. 2278, 11712
Stevens, R.P. 21767
Stevens, T.E. 18130
Stevenson, M.S. 17279
Stevenson, R.A. 13559
Stevenson, R.C. 5806, 6346-8
Stevenson-Hamilton, J. 23052
Stevick, E.W. 3208, 12008, 20669, 22792
Stewart, D. 5376
Stewart, J.L. 10201
Stewart, J.M. 9274, 10653
Stewart, K.M. 10682
Stewart, M. 10683
Stewart, M.L. 1794, 7704
Stewart, M.M. 21410
Stierling, Dr. 17877
Stigand, C.H. 4318, 5807-9, 6107, 6551, 21289-90
Stinson, L. 16529
Stirling, D. 16027
Stocker, J. 11319
Stockley, G.M. 18131-2
Stokes, E. 2948
Stokes, R.R. 2279
Stolper, W. 1429-30, 11468-9
Stolz, A. 18428
Stone, E.V. 22889-92
Stone, P. 23484
Stonehouse, J. 20484
Stonelake, A. 15332
Stones, P.B. 12417
Stones, R.Y. 19082
Stooke, G.B. See Beresford-Stooke, G.
Stopford, J.G.B. 7993-4, 15983, 22192
Stopford, R.W. 2280, 7488, 7668
Storbeck, F. 13349-50
Storch, R.F. 10684-5
Storelli, L. 2632
Storme, M. 4938, 14593, 14852-3
Storms, A. 14158, 15548
Storrar, A. 17352
Story, T.H.S. 12418
Stoufflet, J. 3778
Stow, G.W. 21944
Stowell, R.F. 17974
Strakosch, H. 22193
Strange, B.F. 17194
Strange, S. 1431, 5286

Strangway, A.K. 23494
Strelcyn, S. 45, 16474, 16837, 16910, 16989, 17000-2
Stretford, W. 23265
Strevens, P.D. 10654
Strickland, C.F. 1432-3, 22194
Strickland, P. 1619
Strovy, B. 2633
Strube, H. 668
Struck, B. 669, 3204, 5444, 5810, 12009, 16105, 18802, 24651
Strümpell, F. 13351
Struyf, I. 14594
Struyf, V. 14159
Struyfs, Y. 14160
Stuart, D. 3347, 15952
Stuart, G.H. 7355
Stuart, P.A. 20385
Stuart, V. 5200
Stuart-Wortley, E.J.M. See Montague-Stuart-Wortley, E.J.
Stubbs, J.M. 5811-2, 6552
Stubbs, J.N. 5813
Stuhardt, J.G. 20346, 21754
Stuhlmann, F. 12970
Stumme, H. 6892
Sturdy, D. 17681
Styler, W.E. 6044
Sudan. Intelligence Department 6108
Sudi, A.A. 16354-5
Suliman, A.A. See Ali Ahmed Suliman
Sulston, A.E.A. 24693
Sulzmann, E. 14318
Summer, C. 16990
Summers, R. 19886, 20186-90, 20620
Summers, R.F.H. 19985
Summerscales, J. 2949
Sunderland, B. 12599
Sundkler, B.G.M. 16394, 19615, 21777, 23012
Suret-Canale, J. 1620, 2281, 4365, 4437, 8300, 8915, 9024,
    9054-5, 9098-9, 9534, 13008
Surin, R. 6725
Surridge, F.H. 20621
Susini, J. 13452, 13456
Sutherland, A.C. 10862
Sutherland, E.T. 10686
Sutherland, J. 22075
Sutton, A.S.E. See Elwell-Sutton, A.S.
Sutton, F.X. 1434, 1795
Sutton, J.E.G. 18820, 19264
Swanzy, F. 7735
Swanzy, H. 1435-6, 1621-3, 1796, 2282-4, 5377, 10585-6,
    11713-4, 14712, 17308, 18984, 20485, 22488
Swart, C.R. 21810-1
Swart, Y. 19952
Swartenbroeckx, P. 13627, 14161
Swartz, J.F.A. 22042
Swartz, M.J. 18205

Swayne, A.C.C. 12110
Swayne, H.G.C. 2950
Sweeney, G.M.J. 22960
Sweeney, R.C.H. 21546-8
Swift, P. 20078
Swindell, K. 9811
Swithenbank, M. 10117
Switzer, C.W. 18803
Swynnerton, B. 18573
Swynnerton, C.F.M. 18574
Swynnerton, J.R.M. 17195
Swynnerton, R.J.M. 15784
Sy, L. 3594
Syad, W. 17116, 17150-1
Sydow, E.von 881-2, 11320
Sykes, J. 19380, 19502
Sylvain, J.C. See Comhaire-Sylvain, J.
Sylvain, P.G. 16481
Sylvain, S.C. See Comhaire-Sylvain, S.
Symes, S. 2285, 16450
Symons, J. 22066
Synge, P.M. 19083
Sytek, W.L. 17353
Szczudlowska, A. 5201
Szereszewski, R. 10287
Szumowski, G. 8533, 8867-71, 9038
Szymański, E. 7287

T., A.D.F. 18985, 19503
T., A.J. 5814
T., E. 12419
T., F.S. 5814
T., G.W. 5815-7, 5931
T., H.B. 18010
T., H.R. 17534
T., J. 9056
T., J.E.S. 20079, 20242
T., J.M.C. 7288
T., L.R. 303
Tabata, I.B. 22489
Taberer, W.S. 20080
Tabernero Chacobo, H. 7441, 15723
Tabler, E.C. 20622, 19855
Tabmen, W.T. See Tame-Tabmen, W.
Taborda, A.C. See Cunha Taborda, A.
Tacconi, S. 6688
Tafari Makonnen. See Haile Selassie I
Tagart, E.S.B. 2285, 19686, 21064
Tagwireyi, J.H. 20624
Tahir, I. 12111-2
Taïeb, J. 6786
Tait, D. 8840-1, 9325-6, 9369, 10118-22, 10242, 10288-9, 10737, 10863
Takizala, H.D. 14543, 14713

Talbi, M. 6878
Talbot, I. 21291
Talbot, P.A. 7563, 7736, 11173-5
Talbot, W.D.S. 21292, 21365
Tallon, D. 6937
Tamayi 20386
Tame, G.B. 6283
Tame-Tabmen, W. 12655
Tam'si, T.U. See U Tam'si, T.
Tamuno, T.N. 11900
Tanburn, E. 4709
Tandi 22490
Tanganyika. See also Tanzania
Tanganyika. Ministry of Local Government and Administration.
   18206
Tanghe, B. 12010, 13577, 14162-7, 14854, 15109
Tanghe, J. 14168-70, 14319, 15184-6
Tanghe, M.B. 13588
Tann, J. 22893-4
Tanner, R. 16451
Tanner, R.E.S. 15621, 17280, 17354, 17682, 17878-87,
   17975-7, 18207, 18471, 18575-6, 18622-4
Tanret, M.G. 15402
Tanzania. See also Tanganyika
Tanzania 18208
Tanzania Episcopal Conference 16215
Tappen, N.C. 9759
Tapson, R.R. 3472, 20625, 20779
Tarantino, A. 18804-6, 19291
Taraoré, D. 9222
Taraoré, Moussa. See Travelé, M.
Tarde, A.de 7356
Tardieu-Blot, M.L. 9150, 13457
Tardits, C. 9539, 9542
Tarn, P. 7289
Tarradell, M. 773, 7200-1
Tastevin, C. 670, 3210, 8658, 23422
Tatay Puchol, R. 14486, 15684
Tate, E.R. 17608
Tate, G.H.H. 9258, 12998
Tate, H.R. 1053, 1950, 2287, 2951, 4045, 4710, 10587,
   16028, 16074, 17281-3
Tatham, M.A. 23088
Tatlow, A.H. 22276
Taufflieb, R. 13019, 13684-6
Taute, M. 18346
Tauxier, L. 8842, 9223, 9430-1
Tavares, A. 12801
Tavares da Silva, M.C. See Conceição Tavares da Silva, M.
Tawa, A.A. 12420
Tawney, J.J. 17683, 17888-9, 18209, 21256
Tawse-Jollie, E. 20387
Tay, J. 10326
Tayedzerhwa, L.G.N. 22793
Tayib, A.al- 5818-9, 6544, 8505

Tayib, G.el- 6045
Tayire 9132-3
Taylor, A. 4711
Taylor, A.J.P. 5378, 7357
Taylor, A.R. 12960
Taylor, B. 883, 3473-4
Taylor, C.J. 10655
Taylor, C.T.C. 20626
Taylor, F.W. 7958-9, 11901, 12011
Taylor, G. 7053, 20081-4, 20627, 20670
Taylor, J.D. 19785, 24680
Taylor, J.H. 3371
Taylor, J.V. 19409
Taylor, M. 5425
Taylor, M.E. 20085, 20718-9
Taylor, O.W. 11902
Taylor, R.E. 6464
Taylor, W.A. See Anti-Taylor, W.
Taylor, W.E. 16356
Taylor, W.H. 19092
Taylor, W.L. 21042
Tchernonog 13405
Tchicaya, F.G. (pseud.: T.U Tam'si). See U Tam'si, T.
Tchidimbo, R. 4712
Teague, M. 12764
Teale, E. 17890, 18133-4, 18577-8
Tedeschi, S. 16991
Tegethoff, W. 958
Teixeira, A.J.da S. See Silva Teixeira, A.J.da
Teixeira, J.B. See Brito Teixeira, J.
Teixeira, R.de C.S.da S. See Silva Teixeira, R.de C.S.da
Teixeira da Mota, A. 7489, 7737, 12657, 12667, 12706, 12710, 12739, 12765-6, 24036
Teixeira Maio, A. 3971, 15333, 23607
Tejedor, F.H. See Herrero Tejedor, F.
Telli, D. 2634, 9017
Tello, J.L.G. See Gomez Tello, J.L.
Tema, S.S. 4713
Temba, C. 22895, 23266
Tempany, H. 456
Tempels, P. 3211, 4714-5, 14171-2, 15110-1, 15281
Temperley, H.W.V. 2952
Temple, P.H. 15984, 18986, 19084-5
Temple, R. 5379, 6284
Tendeiro, J. 4319-31, 8130-1, 12852-68, 12925, 24256
Tendenguwo 20628
Tenente, B. 23902
Tennant, D. 22195
Tennent, J.R.M. 17609
Tenraa, W.F.E.R. 17978
Tepowa, A. 11176, 11903, 12012
Tercafs, J. 15112
Tereau 9513
Terlinden, C. 18347
Terry, P.T. 21257, 21366, 21469

Tersen 2953
Tessa, A. 13748
Tevoedjre, A. 2635
Tew, M. 14173, 15113, 20971
Teynac, E.J.P. See Paris-Teynac, E.J.
Thabit, T.H. 6285
Thackeray, R.H. 19658
Thambipillai, V. 7570
Theis, E. 1092
Thelejane, T.S. 21588, 21668
Theobald, A.B. 6286-7
Theron, K. 22397
Theroux, P. 3475, 12113, 21502, 22896
Thesiger, W.P. 6553
Theuws, T. 4716, 14174-6
Thiam 3372, 4717
Thiel, E.P. 18807, 18949
Thiel, H.van 14177-80, 15114-6
Thieme, D.L. 959
Thierry, S.B. See Bernard-Thierry, S.
Thiriet, A. 8768
Thissen, L. 15187, 23423, 23618-20
Thoi, D.H. See Duong-Huu-Thoi
Thoiré, G. 9275
Thokozane, J. 20629
Tholley, A.S. 9843
Thomas, Fr. 18135
Thomas, A.R. 2288
Thomas, A.S. 18808, 19548
Thomas, B.E. 46, 1896, 4906
Thomas, D.K. 17284, 18579-82
Thomas, E.S. 671, 5202
Thomas, H.B. 1091, 6288, 15850, 15857, 15859, 15863, 15985,
    16075-80, 17389, 17535, 18348, 18902, 18928, 18931-4,
    18944, 18948, 18951-3, 18987, 19086-90, 19292-19310,
    19365, 19504
Thomas, I. 18809, 19091
Thomas, I.B. 2289-95, 2636, 4718, 10290
Thomas, I.F. 19311
Thomas, J.H. 22491
Thomas, J.M.C. 12937, 13604-5
Thomas, L.V. 672, 3373, 4046, 4234, 4719-21, 7564-5, 7885,
    8018, 8506-17, 8549, 8634
Thomas, M. 4722
Thomas, Sir M. 20317
Thomas, M.A. 11177
Thomas, M.E. 14855
Thomas, N.W. 3212-3, 7566, 9760, 10202, 11178-80, 12013,
    14856
Thomas, T.H. 16685
Thomas, T.M. 20086
Thomas, T.S. 10588
Thomas, W.E. 20087
Thomassey, P. 8872-3, 8892
Thompson, A. 20780-1

Thompson, A.B.   4366
Thompson, C.H.   3006
Thompson, D.V.   22492
Thompson, E.W.   1797
Thompson, F.   19026
Thompson, G.C.   See Caton-Thompson, G.
Thompson, H.N.   11583
Thompson, J.B.   See Blake-Thompson, J.
Thompson, J.L.C.   See Cloudsley-Thompson, J.L.
Thompson, L.C.   20089, 20815-6
Thompson, L.M.   22677
Thompson, M.D.   19505
Thompson, P.E.S.   673
Thompson, S.   22277
Thompson, W.L.   20671
Thomson, B.   21243
Thomson, C.   18349
Thomson, G.   2637, 11904
Thomson, J.   674, 16081, 19312, 20486
Thomson, T.D.   21258, 21435, 21495
Thomson, W.P.G.   5659, 5820
Thorburn, D.H.   5954
Thorburn, J.W.A.   11905-6
Thoré, L.   8769-70
Thornton, A.P.   22493
Thornton, D.   17684
Thornton, I.W.B.   6554
Thoyer, J.R.   10730
Threlfall, H.R.   18136
Thurnwald, R.C.   675, 4047, 4723-4, 15819
Thwaites, G.G.   21841
Tiano, M.   7226
Tichelen, H.E.van   15603
Tidiany, C.S.   3595-7, 4725-6
Tidjani, A.S.   4727, 9514-6, 9581, 12507
Tiendrebeogo, Y.   9451
Tiger, L.   10442
Tignor, R.L.   5125, 5380
Tiling, M.von.   See Klingenheben-Von Tiling, M.
Tillion, G.   6998
Timothy, E.B.   9761
Tindall, H.D.   9711
Tinker, H.   2638-40, 4728
Tirolien, G.   3476, 3598, 9650
Tischhauser, G.   13352-3
Tisserant, C.   13568, 13578-9
Titherington, G.W.   5821-2, 5932, 6555
Titus   12508
Tixier, G.   7669, 9286
Tixier, J.   7025
Tizirai, P.   20630
Tobias, P.V.   676-7, 11321, 19616, 21945
Toda Oliva, E.   884
Todd, C.   18903
Todd, J.A.   457

Todd, R.S.G. 20487
Todd, T.W. 5426
Todhunter, J.H. 3477
Togbe, G.O. See Olory-Togbe, G.
Toit, B.M.du. See Du Toit, B.M.
Toit, P.J.du. See Du Toit, P.J.
Toit, S.F.du. See Du Toit, S.F.
Tolémée, P. 5029
Tolen, A. 2641-2, 16029
Tomlinson, G. 1034
Tomy, M.el- 5220
Tong, R. 3478, 11907-8, 12114
Toniolo, E.V. 5823, 6289
Tonkin, T.J. 8019
Tooke, W.D.H. See Hammond-Tooke, W.D.
Top, W. 8377
Topham, P. 21549
Torday, E. 679, 12955, 14181-5
Tordeur, J. 13781
Tordo, G.C. 12869
Tordoff, W. 2643, 10589-92, 18210-1
Torrend, J. 21169, 23583
Torres, J. 23734, 23892
Torres, J.M.C. See Cordero Torres, J.M.
Torres, M.F. See Ferrandis Torres, M.
Torroja, J.M. See Maria Torroja, J.
Toscano, F. 680
Toso, V. 10656
Tothill, B.H. 5254, 6109-10
Tothill, J.D. 6556-9
Toulmond, L. 15117
Toupet, C. 1951, 8383, 8413-4, 8423-4, 8580, 9651
Touré, A.S. 217, 2645-6, 4730, 9078
Toure, L. 9173
Touré, M. 1437-9, 2296
Touré, S. See Touré, A.S.
Tourneau, R.L. See Le Tourneau, R.
Toussaint, A. 24299, 24323-4, 24681
Toussaint, C.E. 2297
Tovar, A. 5046
Towa, M. 1798, 4731, 13224
Towell, M. 19313
Towet, T. 3374
Towo-Atangana, G. 13170
Tracey, A. 17309, 20191-2
Tracey, C.B. 5824, 6290, 6609
Tracey, H. 960-73, 1027, 1078, 1090, 15847-8, 17979, 17993,
    19646-50, 20090-4, 20193-20200, 21012, 21594-6, 21624,
    21636, 23821
Tracey, L.T. 20095
Tracey, P. 21012
Tramond, J. 2954
Tranakides, G. 10593
Trancart, A. 8452, 8959
Tranquilli, I. See Silone, I.

Traoré, B. 4732-3
Traoré, Mamadou, also called Ray Autra 1658, 7567, 8972, 8982, 9044
Traoré, Moussa. See Travélé, M.
Traoré-Leroux, C. 3599
Trapido, S. 22494-6, 22678
Trasselli, C. 16686
Travélé, M. 8856
Travers, R. 16122
Tredgold, C. 19721-2
Tredgold, R. 20631
Tregear, P.S. 1799
Tremearne, A.J.N. 11181
Tremearne, B.A. 11182
Trenchard, Visc. 2298
Trent, R.D. 10829
Trent, T.S. 21043
Trento, P.G.da 16911
Trepa, M. 23988
Tressan, de la V.de. See La Vergne de Tressan, de
Trevelyan, M. 1872, 4734
Treves, P. 16662
Trevor, J.C. 17891
Trevor, T.G. 19694, 20201
Trevor-Jones, R. 20202
Trezenem, E. 13628, 13706, 13735
Tricart, J. 9187, 9259, 12553
Tricker, B.J.K. 19092
Trigo de Morais 23712
Trimingham, J.S. 9950
Trincão, C. 12870
Tringali, G. 16633
Tripe, W.B. 17892-3
Trochain, J.L. 1952, 4332-3, 13025-6, 13607-14, 13652
Troesch, J. 13782, 14186-7, 14857-8, 15118-9, 15334, 23424, 23621
Trolli, G. 15420-1, 15549
Trombetti, A. 3214
Troup, F. 22961-3
Troup, R.S. 4110
Troupeau, G. 16837
Trouwborst, A. 15589, 15664
Trowell, H.C. 4210-1, 4235, 17628, 19506-7
Trowell, M. 885, 2955, 7886, 18810, 18904-5
Trujeda Incera, L. 2299, 4735, 15706, 15772
Tsala, T. 13171, 13197
Tschoffen, P. 14859
Tschudi, J. 4871
Tsegaye, G.M. See Gabre-Medhin, T.
Tshakalisa 20672
Tshaparadza, W. 20720
Tsien Tche-hao 24644
Tual 9546
Tubiana, J. 13538, 15820, 16475, 16530, 16687, 16804-6
Tubiana, M.J. 13501, 13532, 13550

Tucker, A.N. 47, 312, 3215-9, 5825-7, 6348-51, 16106-9, 16216-8, 17567, 19366-7, 21649
Tucker, A.W. 5828
Tucker, C.B. 20096
Tucker, J.T. 23425, 23560
Tucker, L.S. 23426
Tuden, A. 20972
Tudhope, W.T.D. 10291
Tugarinov, A. 12421
Tugbiyele, E.A. 11715-6
Tuley, P. 11183-4
Tun Wai, U 1624, 9332
Tuninetti, D.M. 4939
Turaiev, B. 16476
Turnbull, A.M.D. 21411
Turnbull, C.M. 14188-90, 15335
Turnbull, R.W. 17152
Turner, D.C. 12422
Turner, E.L.B. 21044
Turner, G.C. 15953
Turner, H.W. 8020-2, 12223-4
Turner, L.E. 6020
Turner, R.W.S. 20234
Turner, V.W. 681, 15821, 20973-5, 21044
Turok, B. 22196
Turpin, C.A. 19314
Turroni, C.B. See Bresciani-Turroni, C.
Turyagyenda, J.D. 19549
Tutschek, K. 6335, 6352
Tutuola, A. 12115
Tuzet, O. 9174, 9295-6
Twala, R.G. 21755-6
Twining, E.F. 18212, 18350, 19315
Twining, W.L. 3779, 6391-2
Twum, K.G. See Gyasi-Twum, K.
Twynam, C.D. 16082, 19687, 21367-8, 21470-1
Tyler, J.W. 18213
Tyrrell-Glynn, W. 21812

U Tam'si, T. 3220, 3479, 3547, 3600-1, 15188-9
U Tun Wai. See Tun Wai, U
U.N.E.S.C.O. See UNESCO
U.N.O. See United Nations Organization
Uchendu, V.C. 11185-6, 12181
Ucin, F. 5829
Ucko, P.J. 4830, 5147
Udo, B.U. 11187
Udo, R.K. 10936, 11584-5
Uganda 19160
Uganda, J.J., Bishop of. See Willis, J.J., Bishop of Uganda
Ugeux, W. 14714
Ugoh, S.U. 11470-1
Ukeni, L.O. 12116
Uldall, H.J. 7961

Ullendorff, E. 16807, 16912-5, 16949
UNESCO 4111, 4736, 6649
Ungar, A. 23267
United Africa Company 11472
United Nations Organisation. Economic Commission for Africa. See Economic Commission for Africa
Unsworth, E.G. 21192
Unsworth, W. 23053
Unwin, A.H. 10937
Unyerekupi 20782
Unzueta y Yuste, A.de 15718
Upcott, A.R.W.C. See Crosse-Upcott, A.R.W.
Upton, M. 11473
Upward, A. 11188, 12182
Urbain, Y. 14487
Urvoy, Y. 7887, 8874-5, 9647
Urzaiz y Fernandez del Castillo, J.de 7474
Usborne, C.V. 2300
Usborne, M. 20488
Usher, A.A. 1440
Usher-Wilson, L.C. 18811-2
Usoro, E.J. 12509
Utton, A.E. 12183
Uvarov, B.P. 4791
Uwechue, R.C. 1800
Uys, S. 22101, 22197, 22293, 22317, 22497-9, 22500-1
Uzan, M. 6951
Uzel, B. 17183
Uzoaga, W.O. 11474

V., B. 2646, 14715-6
V., F. 6757
V., I. 14860
V., J. 2301
V.-H., N.H. 18583
Vaccaro, F. 16634
Vachon, M. 8476
Vadala, R. 6689
Vaillant, A. 13045, 13458
Vaizey, J. 1801
Vajda, G. 6879, 7987
Val, J.M.M. See Martinez Val, J.M.
Valadao, F.G. 24110
Valantin, S. 8771
Valantin, X. 1441
Valdeyron, G. 4792, 6726
Valdez, V. 4331, 8130-1, 12868
Vale, A.J.M.do 23652
Valensi, L. 6880-1
Valent, C.A.de A. See Almeida Valent, C.A.de
Valente, A. 22198, 22502, 23268, 23485, 23666
Valente, M.G. See Malangatana, V.
Valente, P.J. 21550, 23427
Valentine, M. 19145

Valette, J. 24325, 24415, 24503
Valin, R. 7084-5
Valle, C.della 6647
Valle, J.B.del. See Blanco del Valle, J.
Valle, R.del. See Valle Fernández, R.del
Valle Fernández, R.del 1442, 4907, 12989, 20318
Valoura, F. 12789
Valverde, J.A. 7463-4
Vambe, L.C. 20489
Van Dam, T. 7606
Van Dantzig, A. 10594
Van den Berghe, P.L. 682-3, 4737, 22503, 23226, 23269-71
Van den Bossche, J. See Vanden Bossche, J.
Van den Plas, V.H. 5830, 6560
Van der Post, L. 2302
Van Klaveren, J.J. 12510
Van Lierde, J. 14350
Van Rhijn, A.J.R. 22199
Van Wyk, E.B. See Wyk, E.B.van
Vancoillie, G. 14191-2
Vanden Bossche, J. 14320
Vandenhoudt, N. 14321
Vandenhoute, P.J. 7568
Vandeplas, A. 118, 14595, 14861-3
Vanderlinden, J. 3780, 13783, 15282
Vandervelde, E. 14717, 14864
Vanderyst, H. 13784-5, 14322-3, 14596-7, 15422
Vandewalle, F.A. 14865-6
Vanhouteghem, A. 15120
Vanhove, J. 15652
Vanmaele, G. 2303
Vanneste, M. 3221, 4048, 15121-4, 19316
Vannini, V. 14867
Vansina, I. 14598, 15283, 15604
Vansina, J. 774, 2647, 7800, 14193-8, 14488, 14868-73, 15125, 15190, 15550, 15630
Varde, R.P.de 8467, 15766
Varebeke, F.J.de 14489
Vargues, H. 4940
Varlet, F. 9260-1
Varley, D.H. 357-8, 21813-24, 22044-6, 22278, 22679-91, 22897-8
Varley, E.R. 17629
Varley, W.J. 10327, 10595
Varma, S.N. 18214. Cp.also Verma, S.N.
Vasey, E.A. 17355
Vassal, G. 12999
Vassal, P.A. 4818
Vasse, G. 23893
Vaufrey, R. 775
Vaughan, J.H. 11189, 13285
Vaughan, J.K. 974
Vaughan-Jones, T.G.C. 21212-3
Vautherin, R. 13647

Vaux de Foletier, F.de 3007-8
Vaz, J.M. See Martins Vaz, J.
Vaz, M. 684, 4050-1, 14199
Vázquez, E.M. See Maldonado Vázquez, E.
Vecchi, B.V. 119, 16663, 16702, 21045
Veciana, A.de 14200, 15685
Vedder, H. 19786, 21728, 23312
Vedovato, G. 1443-5
Védy, J. 9633-4
Veel, G.R. 21654
Veenstra, A.J.F. 22047
Vega, L.A.de. See Antonio de Vega, L.
Veiga, J. 685, 3620, 4052
Velarde Fuertes, J. 15702
Velat, B. 16837, 16948
Velsen, J.van 18813, 21436, 21472, 21946
Vendeix, J. 5107
Venkataraman, K. 2648
Venner, W. 9797
Vennetier, P. 13690
Venning, J.H. 20203
Ventim Neves, M.J.G. 12871
Ventura, R. 1446, 5030
Venzo, E. 19867, 20319, 20873-4
Verbeeck, A. 15423, 14201-2, 14324
Verbeken, A. 14203, 14325
Vercoutter, J. 5933, 6291
Verdat, M. 6690, 8635, 9100
Verdcourt, B. 18584-5
Verdier, E.T. 1802-3
Verdier, R. 686, 3781, 4738
Vergara-Caffarelli, E. 6633-5
Verger, P. 687, 4739, 7888, 9517-9, 9540, 9582,
   11190, 11322, 11909-11
Vergne de Tressan, Marquis de la. See La Vergne de
   Tressan, Marquis de
Verguin, J. 24520
Verhaegen, B. 1804, 1873, 14490, 14544, 14718-20,
   14874, 15551
Verhaegen, P. 1805, 4212, 14204
Verin, P. 24401, 24416-7, 24639
Verlinden, C. 2956
Verly, R. 14326, 23428
Verma, S.N. 48. Cp.also Varma, S.N.
Vermeulen, V. 14721
Vermoesen, F.M.C. 13786
Verner, S.P. 688
Vernier, E. 24418
Vernon-Jackson, H. 11323, 13286
Veronese, V. 120
Verplaetse, J. 12571
Versluys, J.D.N. 6021
Versteijnen, F. 16359
Verster, J. 23272
Verstraete, M. 15284-5

Vertenten, P. 15191
Verwilghen, A. 14327
Verwilghen, J.P. 15286
Verwilghen, P. 14205, 15126
Vesey-Fitzgerald, D.F. 18586-7
Vető, M. 15822-3
Viaene, L. 14206-8, 14722, 15192
Vialle, J. 4740
Viana, P.A.F. 23735
Viana, R.L. 24149
Vicari, E. 6022
Viccars, J.D. 14209
Vicente, M.L. See Lombardero Vicente, M.
Vickers-Haviland, L.A.W. 17980
Victor, G.B. See Bessa Victor, G.
Vidrovitch, C.C. See Coquery-Vidrovitch, C.
Vieillard, G. 7569, 8876, 8939, 9018, 9101
Vieira, A.da G. 23653
Vieira, C.de M. 23894
Vieira, M.C. 23989
Vieira, R.A. 12702, 12872-3, 12892
Vieira, S. 24044
Vieira Pinto, H. 23679
Vielhauer, A. 13353
Vielrose, E. 6610
Vierstraete, G. 15336
Vieyra, P.S. 975-980
Vigneron, B. 9074
Vignes, K. 2957-8
Vignols, L. 3009, 11912
Vignon, R. 9616
Viguera Franco, E.de 7399
Vilakazi, A. 4053, 4741, 23273-4
Vilakazi, B.W. 19802, 22899, 22900-1
Vilhena, J.de 23429
Vilhena, J.P. 24257
Viljoen, D.J. 1447
Viljoen, W.J. 22796
Villa, J.la V. See La Viña Villa, J.
Villar, E.H.del 7413
Villard, U.M.de. See Monneret de Villard, U.
Villari, L. 16808
Villegas, J.D.de. See Diaz de Villegas, J.
Villeneuve, A.de 17029
Villiers, A. 4258, 4334-6, 5082, 8132-3, 8361, 8405, 8463,
   8477-8, 8722-3, 8741, 8748, 9297, 9338, 9392-5, 12652,
   12874-5, 24419
Villiers, J.P.de 23275
Villiers, M.de 22797
Villiers, S. 12876
Villoresi, M. 2649
Viña Villa, J.L. See La Viña Villa, J.
Vinay, J.P. 3222
Vincent, A. 16030
Vincent, F. 4742
Vincent, H. 2959

Vincent, J. 4743
Vincent, J.F. 13659, 13691
Vincke, J.L. 689
Vindeb 2304
Vindevoghel, J. 15287
Vine, R.A.L. See Levine, R.A.
Viré, M.M. 8916-7
Virmani, K.K. 16219
Vischer, H. 1806-7, 7962
Vissers, J. 23431-2
Vita-Evrard, G.di 5031
Vita-Finzi, C. 4872
Vítor, G.B. See Bessa Victor, G.
Vitória, A.de M. 24062
Vitoria, J.L. 11913
Vitória, S. See Simeão Vitória
Vitta, G. 14599
Vivian, H. 6882
Vleeschauwer, M.A.de 15337
Voelckel, J. 13459
Vogeli-Zuber, M. 9162, 9174, 9295, 9296
Voghel, R.de 1808
Vohsen, E. 7963
Volckers, O.G. 6329
Vonderheyden, M. 5083
Voorhoeve, J. 13172, 13354-5
Vorbichler, A. 14210-1, 15127
Vorst, G.van der 16220
Vossart, J. 13287
Vouilloux 13225
Voussure, G. 14491
Voute, C. 11586
Vowles, P.F. 19027
Vriese, G.de 14212
Vrydagh, J.M. 8960
Vubu, J.K. See Kasa-Vubu, J.
Vuillemin, G. 8411
Vuillemin, G.M.D. See Désiré-Vuillemin, G.M.
Vuillemont, G. 7026
Vycichl, W. 3223, 5032, 5381, 8453, 16809-11, 16916-21

W. 458
W., A. 20632
W., A.A. 1448
W., A.F. 9951
W., A.R. 19680
W., C.A. 6611-2
W., E.M.B. 20240
W., F.L. 18925
W., J.C. 14492, 14723
W., K. 18814, 19317
W., M.J. 5831
W., R.C. 21560
W., R.S. 6613

Wachs, O. 5382
Wachsmann, K.P. 981-2, 18906-7
Wachuku, J.A. 2650
Waddy, B.B. 10596
Wade, A. 690, 1449-50, 1809, 2305-6, 3375, 3602-4, 3782-3, 8636, 8682-3, 17610, 17630
Wade, E.K. 1953
Wade, F.B. 17996
Wadiyar, J.C. 2960
Wadlow, R. 4744
Wagner, G. 5832, 17285-8, 17894, 23313
Wahlen, F.T. 1451
Wai, U T. See Tun Wai, U
Wainwright, G.A. 5934-5, 16110, 19318
Wake, C.S. 24398
Wakefield, A.J. 17685
Wakkad, M.el- 10001, 10597
Waldecker, B. 14213
Waldman, M.R. 7889
Waldow, A.von 17895
Waley, A. 3224
Walford, A.S. 16221
Wali, O. 3376-7
Waligórski, A. 1452
Walker, A. 13707, 13728, 13736-41, 13747
Walker, A.J. 10598
Walker, D. 1453, 1625, 15913, 18988
Walker, E.A. 2307, 19742-3, 22692
Walker, H.J. 24310-1
Walker, J. 6292, 18351
Walker, O. 22902
Walker, R. 21317
Walker, R.H. 19028
Walkley, C.E.J. 6293
Wall, P. 1954
Wallace, J.G. 11191
Wallace, J.M. 18815
Wallace, L. 21112
Wallace, R. 19868, 21842
Wallbank, T.W. 17536
Walle, E.van de 15605-6
Wallenberg, J. 22693
Wallerstein, E. 8167
Wallerstein, I. 8168, 8286, 8378, 9079, 10443
Wallis, B. 9763
Wallis, C.A.G. 2308-9, 2651, 6152, 10444-5, 14724
Wallis, C.B. 9762
Wallis, J.P.R. 20633
Wallis, J.R. 10599
Wallis, L.G.C. 11717-9
Walls, A.F. 7890, 9952-4
Walmsley, L. 1626
Walschap, A. 14328
Walsh, M.J. 11192
Walsh, R.H. 5833
Walshe, C.I. 18816

Walston, Lord   19723
Walter, A.   15986
Walter, C.   8479
Walter, J.   12877
Walters, J.H.   9700
Walther, D.   13718
Walther, K.   18429, 19368
Walton, C.E.   21637
Walton, G.   4745
Walton, J.   886, 19617, 19651, 20204, 21589-90, 21597-8, 21638, 22048-50
Wamuyu, C.D.   17375
Wandres, C.   22798-9, 23361
Wane, F.J.   20097
Wane, Y.   9019
Wanger, W.   691, 3225-8, 22800-1
Wängler, H.H.   7964, 23314
Wannenburgh, A.   22903-4
Wannijn, R.   14329
Wantman, M.J.   1810
Ward, A.H.   10328
Ward, B.   9401, 10864
Ward, B.E.   10123, 16452
Ward, C.   2310
Ward, E.H.   17196
Ward, H.   14214
Ward, I.   3229-32, 7965-7, 8304, 9690, 11919, 12014-5
Ward, R.E.K.   16031
Ward, W.E.   1811, 10124, 10203, 10600
Warden, L.B.L.   See Lee-Warden, L.B.
Wardman, L.K.   9583
Wardrop, T.N.   12328
Warhurst, P.R.   20634
Warmelo, N.J.van   3233, 15128, 21947-8, 22802-3, 24051
Warmington, W.A.   13173
Warner, W.L.   692
Warrell-Bowring, W.J.   18215
Warren, C.   21717, 22694
Warren, J.H.   2311
Warren, M.A.C.   4054
Warriner, D.   5233, 5287
Warthin, M.   12952
Washington, B.T.   4055
Wason, C.   16083
Wason, J.C.   2312, 7891-2
Wasserman, B.   10601
Wasserman, M.J.   16664
Waterfield, G.   16084, 17098
Waterlow, J.C.   4213, 9700
Watermeyer, A.M.   18137
Waters, M.W.   20098
Watherston, A.E.G.   10602
Watkins, M.H.   8169
Watkins, O.F.   17356
Watney, N.B.   19093

Watson, A.C. 23322
Watson, C.M. 6294
Watson, D.N. 11587
Watson, G.C. 20490
Watson, G.D. 11588
Watson, J. 2313
Watson, J.H.A. 8285
Watson, J.H.E. 21473
Watson, J.M. 17117, 18817, 18648, 18651, 19508-9, 19514
Watson, M. 4214
Watson, S.P. 23276
Watson, W. 20976
Watt, I. 4527
Watt, J.M. 19618, 19840, 21214, 21591, 21948
Watt, K.S. 17357
Watteau, M. 4746
Waughray, V. 5108
Wauters, G. 14215
Wayland, E.J. 1955, 18908-13, 19094-8, 19510, 19550
Weatherby, J.M. 18818-20, 18914, 19319
Weatherhead, A. 2652
Weatherhead, H.W. 19029
Webb, A.W.T. 24682-3
Webb, E.J. 2961
Webb, M. 21825-6, 22200, 22255, 22504-5, 22226, 23277-80
Webster, E.J. 16922
Webster, J.B. 11361, 18352
Webster, S. 1874
Wedderburn, D. 22695
Wedderburn-Maxwell, H.G. 5834
Wedgwood, C.H. 21695
Wedgwood, J.C. 5383, 15914
Wedgwood Benn, A. See Benn, A.W.
Weekes, J.T. 19511
Weeks, J.H. 13629, 14216
Weeks, S.G. 1875, 17376, 19030
Weekx, G. 14217
Weghsteen, J. 14218-9
Weidenreich, F. 20099
Weidner, W.S. See Schulz-Weidner, W.
Weigt, E. 15915
Weill, G. 7119
Weiller, J. 1454
Weinberg, L. 7772
Weinberg, S. 20783
Weiner, J.S. 662, 7570
Weinstein, B. 9080, 13708
Weiss, H.F. 8379
Weiss, P.H. 6353
Weissenborn, J. 693
Weissleder, W. 16812
Welbourn, F. 218, 694-5, 4056, 18657, 18726, 18821-2, 19161, 19246, 19320-2, 19410
Welbourn, H. 3480
Welch, J.R. 18138

Welch, J.W. 4057, 11193-4
Weld, H. 5234
Welensky, R. 20491, 21046
Welle, J. 14330
Wellington, J.H. 20320, 22279
Wells, A. 20100
Wells, F.A. 11475
Wells, J. 6111
Wells, J.C. 7670, 11476-7
Wells, L. 23505
Wells, L.H. 19652, 21013, 22051-5
Welman, C.W. 10125
Welman, J. 4337, 7738, 10938, 12423, 12511
Welmers, W.E. 49, 4058, 7968, 12529, 12623-4, 16923
Welsh, A. 22201
Welsh, A.S. 22964
Welsh, T. 22965
Wembi, A. 2384
Wenban-Smith, H.B. 18038
Wenban-Smith, W. 17896, 18353
Wenchi, Omanhene of 10603
Wendel, H.C.M. 7298
Wentzel, D. 22966
Werbner, R.P. 20101
Werder, P.von 696, 7571
Werlin, H. 17477-8
Werner, A. 121, 697-9, 1455, 3234-41, 7969, 14220, 15824-5,
    16111-2, 16360-8, 17289-91, 17537, 17568, 17897-9,
    18823, 19619-20, 19653, 19787, 19803, 19821, 21318,
    21496-7, 21599, 21949-51, 22072, 22506-7, 23281, 24052
Wertheimer, M. 7045
Wescott, J. 11195, 11324
Wescott, R.W. 3242, 7970, 11914, 12016, 12225
West, H.W. 19402
West, I.G. 4059
West, L.C. 6112
West, R. 22280
West, R.L. 17358
Westermann, A. 7974
Westermann, D. 122, 271, 313, 700, 1085, 2962-3, 3243-50,
    7572, 7971-3, 8023-4, 8170, 9370-1, 9520, 10126, 10657-9,
    12017, 12971, 21170
Westermarck, E. 7180, 8410
Westlake, J. 5384, 7893
Weston, A.B. 16222, 18472
Westphal, E. 19654, 19788-93, 20673, 22804-5, 23569
Westrop, A.R. 21551
Whalley, R.C.R. 5835, 6561
Wheeler, D. 23561
Wheeler, M. 17981
Wheeler, N.F. 5936
Wheeler, S.H. 17359
Wheeler, W.R. 13460
Wheelwright, C.A. 19724
Whisson, M.G. 18824, 19323
Whitaker, P. 2653, 11720, 14600, 14725-6

White, C.M. 10888
White, C.M.N. 3784, 6023, 19794-6, 20977-85, 21047-8, 21113-4, 21141-2, 21171, 21193-4, 21244, 23432-3
White, E. 21625
White, F. 16813, 20205-6
White, F.E. 21552
White, H.P. 7739, 9339, 10014, 10292, 11589, 18989
White, J. 1456, 19856
White, J.F. 23013
White, K. 10329
White, K.K. 4367
White, R. 19744
White, R.F. 17292
White, S. 13046
Whitehead, E. 20492
Whitehead, E.F. 19324
Whitehead, G.O. 5473, 5836-8, 5937-8, 6113, 6295-7, 6371
Whitehouse, A.A. 11196-7
Whitehouse, C. 5385
Whitehouse, G.C. 17360
Whitehouse, H.E. 21412
Whiteley, W.H. 16113-8, 16223-30, 17479, 17564, 17569, 17982, 18216, 18401, 18430-3
Whitfield, J.N.B. 24553
Whitley, O.J. 1627
Whitney, E.C.P. 20580
Whitting, C.E.J. 11915
Whittlesey, D. 2344, 4957, 8581-2, 11590, 17480, 23506
Whittow, J.B. 19099
Whitty, A. 20207
Whybrow, C. 18588-9
Whyte, H. 11325
Whyte, M. 23014
Whyte, Q. 22202, 22508-10, 23282
Whyte, W.H. 11478
Wian, G. 6798
Wickens, G.M. 5386
Wickers, S. 8338
Wickert, F.R. 50
Widdowson, E.M. 21211
Wiegräbe, P. 9372, 10204, 10687
Wiehr, E. 7648
Wien, K.L. See Lang-Wien, K.
Wien, R.D. See Dangel-Wien, R.
Wieschhoff, H.A. 701, 20102, 23786
Wiet, G. 5387
Wigglesworth, A. 1457, 2964, 17361
Wignaraja, P. 1458
Wigny, P. 14727-30
Wijeyewardene, G.E.T. 15826, 17663
Wilcher, L.C. 1459, 6046
Wilcox, D. 11916
Wild, R.P. 10127, 10205-14
Wilde, H. 24694
Wilde, L.O.J.de 13787-8, 15288-9, 15424, 15590

Wildeman, E.de 4338, 1956, 13789-90, 14355, 15425-35
Wilder, H.H. 12653
Wilhelm, J.H. 22806
Wilkie, A.W. 12226
Wilkie, M.B. 10051
Wilkinson, D. 22905
Wilkinson, F.O.G. 20798
Wilks, I. 359, 7894, 10002, 10128-9, 10572, 10597, 10604-11, 10660
Willaert, M. 14493
Willan, R.G.M. 12424, 21370, 21413-5, 21553-5
Willans, R.H.K. 9764
Willems, M. 2315-6, 15552
Willett, F. 7507, 11254, 11326-9, 11810
Willett, K.C. 18590
Williams, A.G.M. 20347
Williams, A.W. 19512
Williams, B. 11721
Williams, C.B. 4339, 12425
Williams, D. 702, 3481, 5955, 7773, 11330-1, 11722, 12542
Williams, D.M. 7671
Williams, D.R.P. See Price-Williams, D.R.
Williams, E. 4747
Williams, F. 22511
Williams, F.L. 18649, 18825-33, 18938, 19325-7
Williams, F.R.J. 18834
Williams, G.A. See Awoonor-Williams, G.
Williams, G.M. 2654-5
Williams, G.W. See Awoonor-Williams, G.
Williams, J.G. 1628, 19513
Williams, J.W. 7672, 10293-4
Williams, L.A.J. 17631
Williams, O. 22512, 24013
Williams, P.M. See Morton-Williams, P.
Williams, R. 1629
Williams, R.J. 5203
Williams, R.O. 18039
Williams, R.W. 1630
Williams, S. 1631
Williams, S.G. 21293, 21371, 21416, 21474, 21556
Williams, W.H. 19328
Williamson, B. 7895
Williamson, G.E. 22203, 23283
Williamson, J. 1957, 16119, 16231-3, 17570, 21557-8
Williamson, K. 11198, 12018
Williamson, L. 20208
Williamson, S.G. 10770-1
Willimott, S.G. 6114-5
Willis, C. 5388
Willis, C.A. 5839, 6409
Willis, J.J., Bishop of Uganda 17624, 19411
Willis, R.G. 17900, 18354, 18625
Willmer, J.E. 10360
Willms, A. 7369, 11988
Willoughby, P.G. 12184

Willoughby, R.W.H. 12426
Willoughby, W.C. 3251, 4060, 19660, 21696-7
Wills, J.T. 1632
Willson, B. 7359
Wils, J. 3252
Wilson, A. 5235-6, 10661, 20103-5, 20721-3
Wilson, A.F. 8134
Wilson, B.J. 20230
Wilson, C.E. 3253, 4061, 6562-5
Wilson, C.W. 5148
Wilson, D. 1460
Wilson, E.M. 5255
Wilson, F. 459, 17197
Wilson, G. 703, 17901-3, 18473, 19329
Wilson, G.H. 20889
Wilson, G.McL. 17904
Wilson, H.F. 1023, 21333
Wilson, H.S. 4062, 9765, 9879
Wilson, J. 10330
Wilson, J.A. 5204
Wilson, J.F. 4215
Wilson, J.G. 18914
Wilson, J.L.B. 20891
Wilson, J.O. 123, 12535, 12538, 12572, 12600
Wilson, L.C.U. See Usher-Wilson, L.C.
Wilson, M. 17905-6, 19100, 21698, 22204-5, 22696, 23284
Wilson, N.H. 20106, 20493-4
Wilson, P.N. 18650-1, 19514
Wilson, R.G. 17362
Wilson, T. 11516
Wilson, W.A.A. 7975, 9922-3, 10662, 12775-8
Wilson-Haffenden, J.R. 11199, 11200-1
Wiltshire, H.C. 17644
Winans, E.V. 17907, 18040, 18474
Windels, A. 14221-3
Winder, R.B. 8171
Wing, J.V. 14224-8, 14331-2, 15129-30
Wingard, P. 19031
Wingate, F.R. 6298
Wingate, R. 124, 1002, 1090, 2965, 5971, 5979, 6691, 19678
Winid, B. 1958
Winnington-Ingram, C. 4748, 18217, 20875
Winspear, C.F. 19745
Winspear, F. 21475
Winston, F.D.D. 7976, 12019-21
Winter, E.H. 19162, 18835
Winterbottom, J.M. 1812-3, 4749, 10830, 16422, 20674, 21065, 21143, 21215, 21245
Wioland, F. 8659-60
Wipper, A. 8242
Wirth, A. 3254
Wirth, F. 2966
Wischnegradsky, D. 983
Wise, M. 15773
Wise, R. 17908-9, 17983

Wiseman, H.V. 7774
Wishlade, R.L. 21437
Wisse, J. 704
Wiste, M. 4750, 14731
Witherell, J.W. 402
Withers, F.M. 21348, 21372, 21476-7
Witte, P.de 14229, 15131-3
Wix, E. 23054
Wohlgemuth, N. 10130
Wolde-Giorghis, H. 4751
Wolf, J. 219-222, 8589, 9327
Wolfe, A.W. 4752, 13174
Wolfe, M.S. 10831
Wölfel, D.J. 705
Wolff, H. 3255, 11332, 12022
Wollacott, R.C. 20107
Wollheim, O.D. 22256, 23285-8
Wondji, C. 9267
Wonodi, O. See Nwanodi, G.O.
Wood, A.S. 9955
Wood, C. 21417
Wood, C.T. 9956, 22697, 23015-6
Wood, H.H. 19551
Wood, M. 16032
Wood, M.G. 12427
Wood, N.P. 10331
Wood, P.J. 17686-7
Wood, R.C. 21478-9, 21319, 21559-61
Woodall, J.P. 4216, 16423
Woodburn, J. 17910-2
Woodhouse, C.A. 11202
Woodhouse, C.M. 22698
Woodman, G.R. 10739-40
Woodman, H.M. 6566-7
Woodroffe, I. 2317
Woods, F.J. 12428
Woods, G.G.B. 20108, 20635
Woods, O. 2318
Woods, W.W. 10612
Woodward, H.W. 18434-6
Woodward, S.F. 12429
Woolbert, R.G. 403, 2319, 7299, 16814-7, 17008
Woolf, J. 23017
Worker, J.C. 19330
Worms, A. 18437-8
Worrall, G.A. 6116-7
Worsley, P.M. 10131, 17984, 20799
Worsley, R.R.le G. 15785, 18591
Worthington, E.B. 4112, 4340, 15987, 16424-5
Wortley, E.J.M.S. See Montague-Stuart-Wortley, E.J.
Wouters, J. 15134
Wraith, R.E. 2320, 7775-6, 10446, 11723, 12513
Wray, K.R. See Roberts-Wray, K.
Wrench, W. 1959, 7240
Wright, A.C.A. 16085, 17118, 17913, 18836-9, 19331, 19515

Wright, C.A. 18139
Wright, E.B. 21952
Wright, E.J. 9783, 9880
Wright, J. 10689
Wright, J.W. 2321, 6118-9, 6354
Wright, M. 16235
Wright, M.J. 18777, 18840-2, 18942
Wright, R. 3605, 4753
Wright, S. 16477, 16635, 16924
Wright, V. 10132
Wright, W.D.C. 7673
Wrigley, C. 770, 2967, 11479, 18843, 19332
Wrigley, G.M. 2968
Wrong, M. 1814-7, 4063, 10447, 1668-9
Wuras, C.F. 22807-8
Wurie, A. 9881
Würtz, F. 16236, 17571-3
Wuta, S.K. 13393
Wyatt, A.W. 17914-5, 18140
Wyatt, B. 125
Wyatt, E.G. 17481
Wybergh, W. 2969, 22699
Wyk, E.B.van 22794-5, 22809
Wyld, J.W.G. 5840, 6614
Wyndham, H.A. 2322-3, 4754, 7674, 19668, 19688, 19746, 22513, 22700

X. 4755
X, M. See Malcolm X
Xabregras, J. 460, 4236, 23638, 23654-5
Xavier da Cunha, A. 504, 706, 23377

Y., N.C. 21373
Yagi, M.A. 6299
Yahya, G.el-D. 5389
Yakemtchouk, R. 1633
Yaker, L. 7086
Yali-Manisi, D.L.P. 22078
Yambo, O. See Ouologuem, Y.
Yanguas Messia, J. 2657
Yannay, Y. 2658
Yaro, J. 8843
Yeld, E.R. 11517
Yeld, R. 18626
Yemitan, E.O. 12117
Yeo, P.H. 18355
Yesufu, T.M. 11480
Yesufu-Giwa, M. 12058
Yonge, D.D. 18356-7
Yonke, J.P. 13047
York, R.N. 10215
Yorke, W. 20817
Yoshida, M. 15916

Younes, Y. 6775
Young, A. 21385
Young, C. 21144, 21294-5, 21418, 21498
Young, C.G. 12397
Young, E.H. See Hills-Young, E.
Young, F. 9675, 22281
Young, F.W. 707
Young, J. 11333
Young, K. 13981
Young, R.R. 10332
Young, T.C. 2324, 4064, 19822, 21049, 21296-9, 21419,
    21480-1, 21499, 21516
Young, T.L. 15917
Young, W.P. 21420, 21562
Younn, S.S. 10832-3
Yudelman, M. 461
Yunia, E. 13394
Yunis, N. 5841
Yunis, Y. See Younes, Y.
Yunis, Y.N. See Yuzbashi Negib Eff.Yunis
Yuste, A.de U. See Unzueta y Yuste, A.de
Yusuf, A.A. 17046
Yusuf, K.A. 17119
Yuzbashi, pseud. 5842
Yuzbashi Negib Eff.Yunis 5843

Z., E. 15918
Z., X.Y. 18915
Zaal, C. 12938, 14230
Zache, R. 16369
Zahan, D. 7740, 8844-6, 8877-80, 9432-3
Zajaczkowski, A. 2659, 8257, 10133, 10613
Zakwany, A.S. 16370
Zancanella, A. 15988, 17176
Zandee, J. 5205
Zandijcke, A.van 14875-6
Zani, Z.M.S. 16237
Zanna, E.L. 14494, 18041
Zaragoza, J.de M. 7400
Zárate López, A.O.de. See Ortiz de Zárate López, A.
Zarco Segalerva, E. 15671
Zaremba, P. 1461
Zarr, G.H. 12633
Zartman, I.W. 7777
Zavatti, S. 5390
Zayyat, M.H.el-. See Mohamed Hassan el Zayyat
Zecca, G. 6883
Zech, Von 9340
Zelle 23316
Zeltner, Fr.de 4819, 8205, 8881
Zeltner, J.C. 13288
Zemp, H. 9230
Zengeni, S. 20109
Zenkovsky, S. 5844-5

Zerbo, J.K. See Ki Zerbo, J.
Zerkovitz, P. 7046
Zghal, A. 6727, 6731, 6972
Ziadeh, N.A. 5109
Zibondo, E. 18844
Ziccardi, F. 4341-3, 17047-8
Ziegert, H. 6661
Ziegler, J. 4757, 10112, 15553
Zielinski, J.G. 11481
Ziervogel, D. 21772-3
Zilgien, A.C. See Cocatre-Zilgien, A.
Ziliotto, G. 270, 6024, 16703
Zimmerman, A. 1462, 2325, 16818
Zinevrakis, E. 984, 6618, 6638-9
Zintgraff, E. 13356
Ziyadah, N.A. See Ziadeh, N.A.
Zohoncon, C. 9584
Zolberg, A.R. 9264
Zorro, A.M. 23622
Zousmanovitch, A.Z. 14877
Zoutendyk, A. 21953
Zuber, M.V. See Vogeli-Zuber, M.
Zuccarelli, F. 8590, 8637-8
Zuccari, P.L. 16086
Zugnoni, J. 5846
Zulu, A.H. 23018
Zuure, B. 15649
Zwemmer, S.M. 4097, 23019
Zwernemann, J. 9434-5, 9460-4, 12530
Zyhlarz, E. 3256-7, 5047-9, 5401-2, 5939, 5355-7, 16925
Zyl, H.J.van 21954, 22810

Ref
Z
3501
A73

DEC 2 1975